ASPEN PUBLISHERS

Lawyer's Desk Book
2009 Edition

By Dana Shilling

The **Lawyer's Desk Book, 2009 Edition** incorporates recent court decisions, legislation, and administrative rulings. Chapters are in sections on areas including: business planning and litigation, contract and property law, financial and credit law, personal planning, tax issues, civil litigation, criminal law, and law office issues.

Highlights of the 2009 edition include:

- Discussion of Congress's initial attempts to cope with the financial crisis, the form of the Housing and Economic Recovery Act of 2008 (P.L. 110-289, aka HERA) and the Emergency Economic Stabilization Act of 2008 (EESA, P.L. 110-343). HERA grants a tax credit for first-time home buyers, imposes reforms on the regulation of lending, and permits refinancing of certain mortgages that have become unaffordable. EESA includes tax benefits for adoption of energy efficient technology and for disaster recovery; extends the state and local sales tax deduction as an alternative to deduction of state income tax; adopts a further one-year AMT patch; and makes permanent the requirement of parity between mental and physical illnesses in employment-related health plans. EESA created a Financial Stability Oversight Board and a program for purchasing troubled assets from financial institutions [§§ 3.07[G], 10.12[C], 14.01[A], 20.02].

- The FICA base rose from $102,000 per year to $106,800 [§ 3.04[B][1]].

- Secondary actors cannot be sued under Rule 10b-5 for "scheme liability" in securities fraud cases; the Supreme Court rejected a suit against third-party suppliers who were accused of participating in sham transactions to inflate another company's share prices [§ 6.01[A]].

- P.L. 110-322 enacts new Federal Rule of Evidence 502, to reduce the extent of waiver of attorney-client and work-product privilege caused by inadvertent disclosure of protected information [§ 23.03[A]].

- The Supreme Court ruled that the Second Amendment protects individual rights to own weapons, not just collective or militia rights — but does not preclude the imposition of certain limitations on gun ownership [§§ 18.10[F], 26.02[H][6]].

 Wolters Kluwer
Law & Business

- The Supreme Court decided a number of ADEA cases, ruling that the Reasonable Factors Other than Age (RFOA) defense is an affirmative defense — i.e., it is up to the defendant to prove it; that it is up to the District Court to determine on a case-by-case basis if testimony from employees who did not have the same supervisor as the plaintiff should be admitted; and that age discrimination retaliation causes of action can be asserted by federal employees under 42 USC § 1981. The combination of an EEOC intake questionnaire and a detailed affidavit can operate as an ADEA "charge" even if the official charge form is not filed until after the complaint. However, not all of this year's Supreme Court ADEA decisions were pro-plaintiff: the Supreme Court also held that it does not violate the ADEA for a disability pension system to add years of service to enhance pensions of employees disabled before Normal Retirement Age but not to those disabled after Normal Retirement Age. Nor can a federal employee assert equal protection claims against the government employer using a "class of one" theory [§§ 3.11[A][2], 3.13[B]].

- A plan administrator's dual role in both determining eligibility and paying benefits is a factor in determining whether the decision will be reviewed de novo or merely for abuse of discretion [§ 3.07[F]].

- Participants in a defined contribution plan can bring suit for fiduciary misconduct even after they cash out their plan accounts; the Supreme Court ruled that there can be actionable fiduciary misconduct if the participant's benefits are reduced, even if the plan as a whole remains solvent [§ 3.05[E]].

- The ADA was amended by P.L. 110-325, the ADA Amendments Act of 2008, which overrules several Supreme Court decisions in order to make it easier to satisfy the definition of "disability" [§ 3.14[A]].

- The Supreme Court ruled that the National Labor Relations Act preempts a California law forbidding grantees of state funds to use the grant money to assist, promote, or deter Union organizing [§ 3.02[B][1]].

- With respect to the death penalty, the Supreme Court ruled that the three-drug protocol in most executions is not unconstitutionally cruel, and that the death penalty for rape of a child (where there was no intent to cause death) is disproportionate [§ 26.04[M]]. A capital sentence was reversed because of the prosecutor's improperly racially motivated challenges to black potential jurors [§ 26.04[H][1][a]].

- On other criminal law issues, the Supreme Court ruled that the right to counsel attaches at the first appearance before a magistrate, whether or not the prosecutor is present [§ 26.02[D][3]], and that it is legitimate for states to limit pro se representation by defendants who are competent to stand trial, but whose mental illness prevents them from being able to represent themselves adequately [§ 26.03[D][2]], and that a sentencing court's discretion to depart from the Sentencing Guidelines means that sentencing judges are not required to apply the Guidelines ratio between sentences for crack and powder cocaine offenses [§ 26.04[L][5][a]], and that the mere advisory status of the Guidelines means that judges are not required to notify either prosecution or defense if they intend to sentence outside the Guidelines range [§ 26.04[L][1]].

- The doctrine of "patent exhaustion" (sale of a patent item terminates patent rights in the item, so the patent holder cannot restrict the purchaser's use of the item) was reaffirmed by the Supreme Court [§ 12.06[G]].

- The Supreme Court ruled that the Federal Arbitration Act (FAA) supersedes state laws that give jurisdiction over a dispute subject to an arbitration clause to any agency other than the arbitrator [§ 25.03], and ruled that the parties to an arbitration agreement do not have the power to consent to judicial review of the arbitrator's award broader than the limited review provided under the FAA [§§ 24.03, 25.08].

- Connecticut joined Massachusetts in permitting same-sex marriage. A California court decision required the state to recognize same-sex marriages, but was quickly overturned by the voters under Proposition 8 [§ 16.03[D][2]].

4/09

For questions concerning this shipment, billing, missing pages, or other customer service matters, call our Customer Service Department at 1-800-234-1660.

For toll-free ordering, please call 1-800-638-8437.

ASPEN PUBLISHERS

LAWYER'S DESK BOOK

2009 EDITION

Dana Shilling

Wolters Kluwer

Law & Business

AUSTIN   BOSTON   CHICAGO   NEW YORK   THE NETHERLANDS

This publication is designed to provide accurate and authoritative information in regard to the subject matter covered. It is sold with the understanding that the publisher is not engaged in rendering legal, accounting, or other professional services. If legal advice or other professional assistance is required, the services of a competent professional person should be sought.

—From a *Declaration of Principles* jointly adopted by
a Committee of the American Bar Association and
a Committee of Publishers and Associations

Printed in the United States of America

ISBN 978-0-7355-8120-3

1 2 3 4 5 6 7 8 9 0

About Wolters Kluwer Law & Business

Wolters Kluwer Law & Business is a leading provider of research information and workflow solutions in key specialty areas. The strengths of the individual brands of Aspen Publishers, CCH, Kluwer Law International and Loislaw are aligned within Wolters Kluwer Law & Business to provide comprehensive, in-depth solutions and expert-authored content for the legal, professional and education markets.

CCH was founded in 1913 and has served more than four generations of business professionals and their clients. The CCH products in the Wolters Kluwer Law & Business group are highly regarded electronic and print resources for legal, securities, antitrust and trade regulation, government contracting, banking, pension, payroll, employment and labor, and healthcare reimbursement and compliance professionals.

Aspen Publishers is a leading information provider for attorneys, business professionals and law students. Written by preeminent authorities, Aspen products offer analytical and practical information in a range of specialty practice areas from securities law and intellectual property to mergers and acquisitions and pension/benefits. Aspen's trusted legal education resources provide professors and students with high-quality, up-to-date and effective resources for successful instruction and study in all areas of the law.

Kluwer Law International supplies the global business community with comprehensive English-language international legal information. Legal practitioners, corporate counsel and business executives around the world rely on the Kluwer Law International journals, loose-leafs, books and electronic products for authoritative information in many areas of international legal practice.

Loislaw is a premier provider of digitized legal content to small law firm practitioners of various specializations. Loislaw provides attorneys with the ability to quickly and efficiently find the necessary legal information they need, when and where they need it, by facilitating access to primary law as well as state-specific law, records, forms and treatises.

Wolters Kluwer Law & Business, a unit of Wolters Kluwer, is headquartered in New York and Riverwoods, Illinois. Wolters Kluwer is a leading multinational publisher and information services company.

ASPEN PUBLISHERS SUBSCRIPTION NOTICE

This Aspen Publishers product is updated on a periodic basis with supplements to reflect important changes in the subject matter. If you purchased this product directly from Aspen Publishers, we have already recorded your subscription for the update service.

If, however, you purchased this product from a bookstore and wish to receive future updates and revised or related volumes billed separately with a 30-day examination review, please contact our Customer Service Department at 1-800-234-1660 or send your name, company name (if applicable), address, and the title of the product to:

ASPEN PUBLISHERS
7201 McKinney Circle
Frederick, MD 21704

Important Aspen Publishers Contact Information

- To order any Aspen Publishers title, go to *www.aspenpublishers.com* or call 1-800-638-8437.
- To reinstate your manual update service, call 1-800-638-8437.
- To contact Customer Care, e-mail *customer.care@aspenpublishers.com,* call 1-800-234-1660, fax 1-800-901-9075, or mail correspondence to Order Department, Aspen Publishers, PO Box 990, Frederick, MD 21705.
- To review your account history or pay an invoice online, visit *www.aspenpublishers.com/payinvoices.*

Wolters Kluwer
Law & Business

CONTENTS

Note: A detailed synopsis appears at the front of each chapter.

Introduction

Part I: Business Planning and Litigation

Chapter 1 Organization of the Business Enterprise

Chapter 2 Commercial Transactions Under the UCC

Chapter 3 Employer—Employee Relations

Chapter 4 Business Taxes

Chapter 5 Mergers and Acquisitions

Chapter 6 Securities Regulation

Chapter 7 Business Dealings with Consumers

Chapter 8 Antitrust

Part II: Contract and Property Law

Chapter 9 Contracts

Chapter 10 Property

Chapter 11 Environmental Law

Chapter 12 Intellectual Property

Chapter 13 Insurance Law

Part III: Financial and Criminal Law

Chapter 14 Credit, Collections, and Disclosure

Chapter 15 Bankruptcy

Part IV: Personal Planning

Chapter 16 Family Law

Chapter 17 Estate Planning

Chapter 18 Torts

Chapter 19 Immigration

Part V: Tax Issues

Chapter 20 Personal Income Tax and Tax Planning

Chapter 21 Tax Enforcement

Part VI: Civil Litigation

Chapter 22 Federal Civil Procedure

Chapter 23 Evidence

Chapter 24 Appeals

Chapter 25 Arbitration and Alternative Dispute Resolution (ADR)

Part VII: Criminal Law

Chapter 26 Criminal Law

Part VIII: Law Office Issues

Chapter 27 Regulation of the Practice of Law

Chapter 28 Computers and the Law

Index

INTRODUCTION

In 2008, the two most dramatic events were not, strictly speaking, legal matters, but they will have major impact on the legal system: the election of Barack Obama as President, and the system-wide impact of the collapse of the housing, securities, and other financial markets.

One of the earliest congressional responses to the crisis was P.L. 110–289, the Housing and Economic Recovery Act of 2008 (HERA), including housing finance reform; FHA reforms; a tax credit for first-time home buyers; and a mortgage licensing act. HERA includes a short-term (until September 30, 2011) HOPE for Homeowners program permitting refinancing of some mortgages that have become affordable into 30-year fixed rate mortgages.

The Emergency Economic Stabilization Act of 2008 (EESA; P.L. 110–343)'s central provisions give the Treasury authority to restore financial stability by maintaining a Troubled Assets Relief Program (TARP) to buy up assets such as mortgages and related securities; the Treasury will then guarantee principal and interest on the troubled assets, subject to administration by a Financial Stability Oversight Board. Financial institutions that participate in the TARP will be subject to limitations on executive compensation, although these limitations do not extend throughout the economy at large.

Other EESA provisions include an increase in the amount of FDIC insurance per account from $100,000 to $250,000, another one-year AMT patch, a permanent requirement of parity between mental health and physical health care in employment-related health plans, and revival of some expired tax deductions. In December 2008, however, in response to the financial crisis, certain Pension Protection Act provisions were modified by the Worker, Retiree, and Employer Recovery Act of 2008, P.L. 110–458 (WRERA). For calendar 2009 only, the rules mandating Required Minimum Distributions from defined contribution and IRA plans are suspended. As relief for hard-pressed sponsors of defined benefit plans, some of the more onerous requirements of the PPA are relaxed, and sponsors are not required to reach full funding levels as quickly as PPA originally provided.

A one-time federal economic stimulus payment of up to $600 per person, $1,200 per couple, plus $300 per eligible child, was issued in mid-2008.

In the criminal law realm, the Supreme Court held:

- The three-drug protocol used by nearly all the states and by the federal government does not impose such objectively intolerable risk of harm to constitute cruel and unusual punishment: Baze v. Rees, 128 S. Ct. 1520.
- The Constitutional requirement of proportionality forbids imposing the death penalty for rape of a child, when the crime was not intended to cause the victim's death, and the victim survived: Kennedy v. Louisiana, 128 S. Ct. 2641.

- Disqualification of all five black potential jurors on pretextual grounds led to reversal of a black defendant's murder conviction and death sentence: Snyder v. Louisiana, 128 S. Ct. 1203.
- Although the right to possess weapons is not absolute (e.g., guns can be banned in government buildings; felons can be forbidden to possess weapons), the Supreme Court ruled that the Second Amendment protects individual rather than collective or militia rights to "keep and bear arms": District of Columbia v. Heller, 128 S. Ct. 2783.
- Judges are not required to notify either prosecutors or defendants of their intention to impose a sentence outside the Guidelines range; notification was required only when the Guidelines were mandatory: Irizarry v. United States, 128 S. Ct. 2198.
- Spears v. United States, No. 08-5721 (1/21/09), reiterates that the sentencing ratio between crack and powder cocaine is purely advisory. It is permissible for District Court judges to refuse to apply the ratio for policy reasons, as well as when the lower sentence is based on a determination that apply the ratio is too severe in the case of an individual defendant.
- Under Hedgpeth v. Pullido, No. 07-544 (12/2/08), a conviction under a general verdict can be challenged if the jury was instructed on alternative theories of guilt, and may have relied on the wrong one to convict. The Supreme Court ruled that the test is whether the instructions had a substantial and injurious effect or influence on the jury verdict.
- If a state allows untimely appeals of state convictions, the one-year AEDPA "clock" does not start until after the appeal has been completed, because the conviction is not ultimately final until then: Jimenez v. Quarterman, No. 07-6984 (1/13/09).
- A habeas claim based on allegedly erroneous jury instructions should be granted only if the state court's decision was objectively unreasonable (not merely an incorrect application of the law), and the instruction must have tainted the whole trial: Waddington v. Sarausad, No. 07-772 (1/21/09).
- Guns and drugs found when a person was arrested (pursuant to an arrest warrant that actually had been withdrawn) were held admissible. The majority applied a sliding-scale analysis of whether there was deliberate police abuse so culpable that the justice system should exclude the evidence. In this case, the Supreme Court concluded that the failure to update the record was an isolated act of negligence unrelated to the arrest. Herring v. U.S., No. 07-513 (1/14/09).
- Prosecutors are absolutely immune from 42 USC § 1983 suits for actions intimately connected to the judicial phase of the criminal process, but immunity is not absolute for investigations or administration (i.e., where the prosecutor is not acting as an officer of the court). Hence, supervisory prosecutors were immune when a prisoner alleged that the prosecution failed to disclose evidence that could have been used to impeach the prosecution's main witness. Decisions about the extent of disclosure are basic matters of

trial advocacy, and it would be irrational to immunize the prosecutor who made the decision while making his or her supervisor liable for negligent training or supervision. Van de Kamp v. Goldstein, No. 07-854 (1/26/09).

- A traffic stop for an infraction punishable by citation is analogous to a *Terry* stop, so the police can take command of the situation and question passengers in the car and pat them down. Inquiries about unrelated matters (in this case, gang affiliation) during a traffic stop do not render the stop unlawful as long as they do not extend the duration of the stop significantly. Arizona v. Johnson, No. 07-1122 (1/26/09).
- When there has been no prosecution appeal or cross-appeal, a Court of Appeals does not have the power to increase the sentence on its own motion. In a "sentencing package" case where there was a multi-count indictment, where some but not all counts of the conviction are challenged, it is permissible for the Court of Appeals to vacate the entire sentence and send it back to the trial court, which can reform the sentence plan, increasing the sentence on certain counts but not the aggregate initial sentence: Greenlaw v. United States, 128 S. Ct. 2559.
- *Apprendi* does not apply to decisions as to whether concurrent or consecutive sentences will be imposed for multiple crimes. Consecutive sentences can be imposed by a judge based on facts not found by the jury, e.g., the judge's conclusion that the defendant is likely to re-offend after release: Oregon v. Ice, No. 07-901 (1/14/09).
- A conviction for failure to report to prison is not a "violent felony conviction" triggering the 15-year mandatory sentence under the Armed Career Criminal Act: Chambers v. United States, No. 06-11206 (1/13/09). The salient quality of a violent felony is action, and failure to report is a crime of omission.

In the tax arena:

- The Supreme Court upheld the "unitary business" test under which a state can tax an apportioned share of a multistate's business activities taking place both inside and outside the state, holding that "unitary business" rather than "operational purpose" is the correct test: MeadWestvaco Corp. v. Illinois Dept of Revenue, 128 S. Ct. 1498.
- The Supreme Court held that a tax deficiency is an element of the offense of tax evasion (Code § 7201) so the president of a close corporation was not guilty of criminal tax evasion for not paying taxes on a distribution from the corporation — the corporation did not have Earnings & Profits at that point, so he received a distribution of capital that was tax-free up to his basis in the stock: Boulware v. United States, 128 S. Ct. 1168.
- For state income tax purposes, most of the states make interest on the state's own bonds tax-exempt for residents, but impose tax on interest on out-of-state bonds — a practice that was upheld by the Supreme Court as consonant with the Commerce Clause: Kentucky v. Davis, No. 06-666 (5/19/08).

In terms of business law developments:

- The Supreme Court held that parties to private contracts cannot draft their contracts to expand the (very limited) scope of judicial review of arbitration awards allowed under the FAA: Hall Street Associates, LLC v. Mattel, 128 S. Ct. 1396. In another arbitration case, the Supreme Court held that when parties agree to arbitrate all disputes arising under a contract, the FAA supersedes any state law that awards jurisdiction to any other entity. (This case involved a California statute giving the Labor Commissioner exclusive jurisdiction over fee disputes between talent agents and clients.) Preston v. Ferrer, 128 S. Ct. 978.

- The doctrine of patent exhaustion (the sale of a patented item terminates patent rights in the item, and therefore the patent holder cannot restrict what the purchaser does with the item) was upheld by the Supreme Court, as long as the only reasonable and intended use of a device is to practice the patent: Quanta Computer v. LG Electronics, 128 S. Ct. 2109.

- The Supreme Court did not allow private securities fraud suits against secondary actors for "scheme liability." (In this case shareholders wanted to sue corporate suppliers who they accused of engaging in sham transactions to inflate the company's revenue figures and therefore boost its stock price.) Stoneridge Inv. Partners, LLC v. Scientific-Atlanta, Inc., 128 S. Ct. 761.

- After many years of a trend toward deregulation, the Consumer Product Safety Improvement Act of 2008, P.L. 110–314, was signed August 14, 2008, imposing safety standards for children's products, and placing some products under a requirement for third-party safety testing. The statute requires the Consumer Product Safety Commission to set up a product safety database that is accessible to the public. The statute enhances the agency's powers to recall products and impose corrective action plans.

- The Supreme Court allowed state-law fraud claims to be made about the marketing of "light" cigarettes. The court ruled that the Federal Cigarette Labeling and Advertising Act does not preempt such claims, because the purpose of the Labeling Act is to inform the public about smoking risks, and a fraud charge is not based on the health dangers of smoking: Altria Group, Inc. v. Good, No. 07-562 (12/15/08).

Major employment law changes include:

- The ADA Amendments Act of 2008, P.L. 110–325, passed unanimously and was signed September 25, 2008, make it clear that remedial measures (other than eyeglasses or contact lenses) are not considered in determining whether an impairment substantially limits a major life activity. ADA plaintiffs do not have to prove that their impairment prevents or severely restricts their ability to carry out normal activities. The statute includes a non-exclusive list of tasks (e.g., manual work, walking, working, caring for one's self) that are considered normal daily activities. An impairment that substantially limits any major life activity can constitute a disability even if other major life activities are not affected.

- The Supreme Court's holding that if the decision-maker had a conflict of interest about whether to grant or deny health plan benefits is a factor determining whether the decision will be reviewed de novo or only for abuse of discretion. This is true whether the plan is self-insured or funded by insurance: Metropolitan Life Insurance Co. v. Glenn, 128 S. Ct. 2343 (2008).
- The EEOC's extensive revision of its guidelines on religious discrimination: [EEOC, *Compliance Manual*, <http://www.eeoc.gov/policy/docs/religion.html>.
- Former participants of a defined contribution plan can sue the plan's fiduciaries for misconduct even after the ex-participants have cashed out their interest. Although ERISA § 502(a)(2) does not offer remedies for individual (as distinct from plan) injuries, suit can be brought if a fiduciary's breach has the effect of impairing the value of the plan assets in the individual plaintiff's account, because fiduciary misconduct can reduce the individual benefits even if the solvency of the plan as a whole is not threatened: LaRue v. DeWolff, Boberg & Associates Inc., 128 S. Ct. 1020 (2008).
- The Supreme Court's ADEA caseload was unusually heavy in 2008. The Supreme Court ruled that the Reasonable Factors Other Than Age (RFOA) defense is an affirmative defense — i.e., the employer must meet both the burden of production and the burden of proof on the defense; employee plaintiffs do not have to rule it out: Meacham v. Knolls Atomic Power Labs, 128 S. Ct. 2395. Sprint/United Management Co. v. Mendelsohn, 128 S. Ct. 1140 also deals with proof issues in ADEA cases. The Supreme Court allowed retaliation claims under 42 USC § 1981 (CBOCS West, Inc. v. Humphries, 128 S. Ct. 1951 and under the specific ADEA provision applicable to federal employees (Gomez-Perez v. Potter, 128 S. Ct. 1931). The Supreme Court also upheld the calculations of the Kentucky retirement system (years of service were added to enhance disability pensions only for persons disabled before rather than after normal retirement age) against an ADEA challenge, finding that it is appropriate to take age and service into account when computing disability retirement benefits: Kentucky Retirement Systems v. EEOC, 128 S. Ct. 2361.
- The Genetic Information Nondiscrimination Act (GINA; P.L. 110–233) forbids discrimination in employment or health insurance based on any genetic traits or tendencies that can be discovered by genetic testing (analysis of chromosomes, DNA, or RNA).

NOTE: In a development too late to be fully reflected in the text of this book, Congress passed the Lilly Ledbetter Fair Pay Act, P.L. 111–2, to reverse the decision in Ledbetter v. Goodyear Tire & Rubber Co., 550 U.S. 618 (2007). The statute amends Title VII, the ADEA, the ADA, and the Rehab Act. The law provides that an unlawful employment practice occurs not only when a discriminatory practice (such as paying women less than men for the same job) is adopted, but also when an individual becomes subject to that decision or practice, and when the decision or practice is applied. Each payment of compensation is another unlawful employment practice that can give rise to a discrimination charge.

Court cases in California (*In re* Marriage Cases, 43 Cal. 4th 757) and Connecticut (Kerrigan v. Comm'r of Public Health, 289 Conn. 135) authorized same-sex marriage, but the California decision was almost immediately voted down by a referendum.

The first Connecticut same-sex marriages took place in October, 2008.

To reduce the cost of privilege review and document production (especially for electronic discovery), Congress passed P.L. 110–322, enacting a new Federal Rule of Evidence 502. As long as disclosure was inadvertent and the holder of the privilege acted reasonably, disclosure of protected information will not result in waiver of attorney-client or work-product privilege.

Part I

BUSINESS PLANNING AND LITIGATION

Chapter 1

Organization of the Business Enterprise

§ 1.01 INTRODUCTION

For-profit businesses can be organized in many forms. (See § 1.15 for not-for-profit organizations, and § 4.12[C] for taxation of not-for-profit organizations.) The choice of a form of organization will determine many things about what the business and its participants can and cannot do; who will be subject to liability; how the entity must handle its profits; and how it will be taxed.

The main choices for organizing a business entity are:

- General partnership
- Limited partnership
- Limited liability partnership (LLP) (see § 1.03 for a discussion of partnership law and taxation)
- Limited liability company (LLC)
- Subchapter S corporation
- Subchapter C corporation.

The basic corporate form is the C Corporation, but certain small non-public corporations can make a Subchapter S election, which permits them to become pass-through entities that are taxed more like partnerships than like corporations. (See Chapter 4 for a discussion of partnership and corporate taxation.)

There is no central repository of corporate law, although there is a Model Business Corporations Law (MBCL) that state legislators can consult. Many states have adopted the Uniform Partnership Act (UPA), first published in 1914, and the Uniform Limited Partnership Act (ULPA; 1916) or Revised Limited Partnership Act (RULPA). RULPA was broadly adopted in the 1980s and 1990s.

Federal corporate tax was first imposed (albeit at low rates) in 1909; corporate rates did not reach high levels until World War II. Subchapter S was added to the Internal Revenue Code (IRC) in 1958. The first LLC statute was Wyoming's 1977 law, but the form remained obscure until 1988, when the IRS conceded that LLCs could be taxed as partnerships. All the states allow LLCs, but there is no Uniform Act. Forty-eight states permit LLPs (limited liability partnerships), a hybrid between general and limited partnership.

The Supreme Court reversed a jury verdict against Arthur Andersen's auditor who handled the Enron account. The auditor was found guilty of violating 18 USC § 1512(b) [corrupt persuasion to induce another to alter documents for an official proceeding], but the Supreme Court reversed because the jury instructions incorrectly stated the elements of the corrupt persuasion offense.[1]

§ 1.02 CHOOSING THE ENTITY

The choice of entity depends on practical[2] and tax factors. It should be noted that the states do not always follow federal tax concepts: not all states have their own version of Subchapter S, for instance, so a corporation that is not federally taxed at the entity level may nevertheless be subject to state taxation.

The state and/or municipality may impose property taxes, sales taxes, taxes on income earned inside and/or outside the state, intangible property, stock transfers, etc. State or local taxes on unincorporated business are another possibility. Some areas make an effort to attract and retain businesses (and create jobs) by offering tax incentives.

A business entity that does business in more than one jurisdiction will be obligated to register in the foreign jurisdictions, which will not necessarily have rules as generous as the home state's.

Delaware incorporation is a popular choice, because of that state's historic role in creating innovative corporate law. However, for a small or relatively small or new business, the disadvantages of having to register as a "foreign" corporation in the state in which business is actually being done are likely to outweigh the benefits obtained by any difference between local and Delaware corporation law.

It is possible to change the form of a business' organization, as its needs change; as the ownership group changes due to expulsion, withdrawal, death, or retirement; or to correct mistakes. However, the tax consequences of a change in form can be quite negative, so the best move is to make the correct selection at the outset.

The U.S. Troop Readiness, Veterans' Care, Katrina Recovery, and Iraq Accountability Appropriations Act, P.L. 110-28, at § 8215, enacts a new Code § 761(f). Under this provision, for tax years beginning on or after December 31,

---

[1] Arthur Andersen LLP v. U.S., 544 U.S. 696 (2005).

[2] For instance, depending on the entity selection, an individual who also has some ownership interest in the entity may be either a "partner" who is not entitled to protection of anti-discrimination laws, or an "employee," who is protected.

2006, a qualified husband-wife joint venture by spouses who file a joint tax return is not treated as a partnership. Instead, all items of income, gain, loss, deduction, and credit are divided between the spouses in proportion to their interests in the venture. Each spouse treats the items as if they derived from a sole proprietorship. A qualified joint venture is a venture between husband and wife only; both materially participate; and both elect to treat the venture as a qualified husband-wife joint venture.

[A] Franchising

A franchise is a compromise between working as an employee store manager and setting up an entirely independent business. A franchisee is an entrepreneur who invests in one unit of a multi-unit marketing system, and in return for agreeing to abide by the franchise's methods of doing business, is entitled to use the franchise's name, trademark, and business methods in an exclusive territory.

The typical franchise relationship provides training for the franchisee. During the term of the franchise agreement (typically, a term of years, with automatic renewal or options to renew, but with provisions permitting the franchisor to terminate the agreement of franchisees whose performance is deemed substandard), the franchisee makes continuing payments to the franchisor, typically based on sales volume. The franchisor usually imposes quality standards, and may require purchase of essential items from the franchisor itself or acceptable suppliers; the franchise agreement sets out the respective rights and obligations of the franchisor and franchisee.

Although many franchises are quite successful, both for the central operation and most of the franchisees, there is significant potential for economic loss and also exploitation of the franchisee. The Federal Trade Commission (FTC) has an extensive disclosure rule, found at 16 CFR Part 436, setting out the disclosure obligations that franchisors have to potential franchisees. The required disclosures must be provided in a single prospectus, including the franchisor's balance sheet and income statement, current as of the close of the franchisor's most recent fiscal year.

In early 2007, the FTC announced the first major overhaul of its franchising regulations in three decades, with the revisions to take effect in 2008. The FTC called for greater disclosure, to avoid harm to potential franchisees. Another FTC objective is reconciling the federal and state requirements for the Uniform Franchise Offering Circular, and clarifying the procedure for reporting "churn" (turnover among franchisees). The proposal requires disclosure if confidentiality agreements are required. The franchisor must provide information about any franchisee organizations, so prospective franchisees can research the background of the franchise. The previous rule required disclosure of suits by franchisees against the franchisor; the proposal also requires disclosure of suits brought by the franchisor against franchisees. Disclosure of the type and cost of computer equipment franchisees must maintain is also required. Although franchisors do not have to disclose their financial performance, any financial representations made must be accurate. Unlike the previous rule, business opportunities are not covered; franchises are more heavily regulated because they require a greater initial investment, are a longer-term commitment, and place the franchisee into a dependent relationship with the franchisor.[3]

In March 2007, the FTC amended the Franchise Rule (originally published in 1978). One of the FTC's goals was to achieve conformity with state franchise disclosure laws; another was to incorporate new technology into the regulation of franchises (e.g., e-commerce was not a factor in 1978 when the original rule was published; the new rule permits franchisors to file disclosure documents online rather than meeting with franchisees in person to turn over printed documents). Franchisors were given the option of applying the new rule as of July 1, 2007, or continuing to comply with the original rule or state disclosure laws until July 1, 2008, when compliance with the new rule became mandatory. The FTC now requires disclosure of 23 specific items, such as the franchise's litigation history, a list of past and present franchisees with contact information, the extent of any exclusive territory offered for the franchise, what the franchisor does for its franchisees, and the cost of buying a franchise and starting up the franchised business. Franchisors who make representations about the financial performance of the franchise must disclose the basis of those representations. However, the FTC did not adopt comments calling for mandatory disclosure of the profitability of an average unit. The 1978 Rule covered both franchises and business opportunity ventures in the same CFR Part, but the FTC now treats them as distinct (e.g., business opportunities typically do not involve the right to use a trademark).

§ 1.03 PARTNERSHIP

A partnership is a business association of two or more co-owners who:

- Carry on a business for profit
- Share profits and losses
- Jointly own and control the firm's capital or property
- Have joint control and management over its business.

Usually, a partnership can consist of any combination of natural persons; other partnerships; corporations; estates and trusts. (See § 27.06[A] for special issues affecting law firm partnerships.) A partnership is not a taxpayer; instead, the partnership files an information return (Form 1065), and the partners pay taxes based on rules summarized in § 4.02.

There are several kinds of partnership: general, limited, and limited liability. In a general partnership, all partners have equal liability. Every partner is the agent

---

[3] Richard Gibson, *FTC Looks to Aid Franchisees*, Wall St. J. 3/7/07 at B3G. The business opportunity rule has been moved to 16 CFR Part 437; the amended Franchise Rule is Part 436. *See* Richard Gibson, *FTC'S Revised Disclosure Rules Make More Information Readily Available*, Wall St. J. 7/29/09 at B7.

of every other partner, and has a fiduciary duty to the other partners. Partnerships are obligated to indemnify their partners who make payments, or are subjected to personal liability, for actions in the ordinary and necessary course of partnership business.

Limited partnerships have at least one fully liable general partner, plus one or more limited partners. The limited partners' liability is limited to the amount they have invested in the partnership. Limited partners do not have the power to control management of the partnership, and they are not liable for its debts over and above their investment.

In 2004, the Supreme Court ruled that a proper tax assessment against a partnership extends the statute of limitations for collection of tax in a judicial proceeding against the general partners. Once the tax has been properly assessed, the IRS is not required to make separate assessments of the same tax against individuals who are not the actual taxpayers—even though, under state law, they are responsible for the taxpayer's debts.[4]

[A] Organization of a Partnership

A partnership is permitted to use any name that is not deceptive and does not violate trademark or licensing rights of any other business. Many states require registration of partnership names with the Secretary of State, county clerk, or other filing officer. Some states do not permit the name of a deceased person to be included in a partnership name.

Partners can make their contribution to the organization of a partnership in cash, property, or services. In addition to making capital contributions, partners can also lend or rent property to the partnership, and receive loan repayment or rent payments. Loaned or rented property does not become part of the partnership's capital, and is not available to satisfy partnership debts. But property acquired with partnership funds becomes partnership property.

The general rule is that partnerships do not pay interest to partners on their capital contributions. However, the partnership agreement can provide for interest, and might be especially likely to do so if the partnership is subject to regulatory requirements that require large amounts of liquid capital.

In late 2007, the IRS proposed regulations and held a public hearing on recognition of gain and loss on partners' contributions to the partnership when the partnership merges with another partnership.[5]

---

[4] United States v. Galletti, 541 U.S. 114 (2004). The Ninth Circuit, discussing the interface between TEFRA's requirement of determining the tax treatment of partnership items at the partnership level and Bankruptcy Code § 505(a)'s authorization for bankruptcy courts to re-determine debtors' tax liability, held that the district courts have subject matter jurisdiction to review the tax treatment of partnership items. The IRS filed a $13.1 million tax claim in a debtor's Chapter 11 case. The district court ruled that it lacked subject matter jurisdiction over any partnership item administratively determined by the IRS, but the Ninth Circuit found jurisdiction under 11 USC § 505(a)(1): Central Valley Ag Enterprises v. United States, 531 F.3d 750 (9th Cir. 2008).

[5] REG-143397-05, 2007-41 IRB 790.

[1] Partnership Agreement

The partnership agreement resolves matters such as:

- Initial contributions by partners
- Subsequent capital contributions
- Loans by partners to the partnership
- Duties and responsibilities of each partner
- Percentage share of profits and losses of each partner
- Partnership "draws" (regularly paid amounts)
- Admission of new partners; limitations on transfer of partnership interests
- Withdrawal and expulsion of partners
- Right of partners to withdraw capital
- Payments to estate of deceased partner[6]
- Survival of the partnership after an event that could result in dissolution
- Methods for resolving partnership disputes
- Methods for amending the partnership agreement
- Designation of the Tax Management Partner, who is the partnership's liaison with the IRS.

If the partnership intends to engage in a business requiring a license or permit, the agreement should provide that it does not become effective until the license or permit has been secured.

Unless the agreement is to the contrary, all partners have equal rights in the management and conduct of partnership business. Any limits on the assignability of partnership interests, and the rights and duties of the assignee, also belong in the agreement.

Usually partners are compensated for their work by receiving a share of partnership profits rather than a salary. However, the partnership agreement can provide for salary or other reasonable compensation for services actually performed.

[B] Dissolution of a Partnership

Dissolution can either be voluntary or mandated by events. A partnership that is created for a specific term dissolves at the end of that term. A partnership at will has no specified duration, and can be terminated at the wish of any partner.

Other dissolution events include:

- Death of any partner
- Bankruptcy of the partnership itself, or any partner

---

[6] Such payments could represent the withdrawing partner's capital interest; his or her pro rata interest in unrealized receivables and fees; share of potential gain or loss on partnership inventory; or insurance secured by the other partners to make payments to the estate. The partnership agreement should clarify the nature as well as the amount of the payments, especially for tax purposes.

- Any event that interferes with a partner's, or the partnership's, carrying on of business (e.g., loss of license)
- Expulsion of a partner under the terms of the partnership agreement.

UPA § 31 provides for automatic dissolution of a partnership whenever any partner dies or withdraws, unless the agreement provides for continuation. It is common to provide for continuation, and also to require withdrawing partners to give the partnership or the other partners a right of first refusal on the partnership interest.

The agreement should specify whether the price will be paid in a lump sum (usually preferred by the recipient) or in a series of payments (usually preferred by the partnership). See Code § 2703 for criteria the buyout price must satisfy to be accepted by the IRS as the estate tax valuation of the decedent's interest. Broadly speaking, the price must be equivalent to the fair market price that would be received in an arm's-length transaction.

The partnership agreement can also provide for the interest of a deceased partner to pass to spouse, children, or other pre-approved successor. In a professional partnership, of course, the successor must also be licensed to practice the profession.

Partnerships are subject to judicial dissolution, if a partner has breached the partnership agreement severely, or is mentally incapacitated or otherwise unable to continue as partner, with the result that maintaining the partnership business is impractical. Judicial dissolution is also available if it becomes impossible to maintain the partnership business at a profit.

When a partnership is dissolved, it can continue doing business until winding-up is completed. The process of winding-up consists of terminating the partnership's business, paying its debts and distributing any remaining assets. Debts owed to non-partner creditors get first priority, followed by loans made by partners to the partnership, then capital contributions made by the partners, and finally distribution of profits to the partners. If the partnership's liabilities exceed its assets, the partners are obligated to make up the shortfall, in proportion to their share of the partnership profits. See UPA §§ 38 and 40.

[C] Agency Issues in Partnership

Generally, any partner is an agent of the partnership for the purpose of its business. A partner who acts in the course of the usual business of the partnership will bind the partnership, unless the partner lacks authority to do so, and the other party to the transaction is aware of this fact.

For acts outside the ordinary course of partnership business, a partner can bind the partnership only with authorization from all the other partners. Some very significant transactions (e.g., disposal of partnership goodwill; confession of judgment; submitting a partnership claim to arbitration; assigning partnership property in trust for creditors; any act that would make it impossible to carry out the partnership's business) also require unanimous consent of all partners.

Partners are always entitled to access to the partnership's books and records. They have a duty to account to the partnership for any benefit derived without consent of the other partners. Any partner wrongfully excluded from partnership business has a right to demand a formal accounting.

[D] Limited Partnership

As noted above, a limited partnership has two tiers of membership: general and limited partners. The general partner(s) are in the same position as partners within a general partnership. The limited partners exchange loss of active management control for limitation of their liability: their maximum liability is the amount invested, plus any mandatory further contributions required by the partnership agreement. Generally speaking, limited partnership interests are assignable. Assignment of a limited partnership interest does not dissolve the partnership, or even make the assignee a partner; it merely gives the assignee a right to receive whatever distributions the partnership would have made to the assignor.

Under the Uniform Limited Partnership Act (ULPA) and Revised Uniform Limited Partnership Act (RULPA), creation of a limited partnership requires both an agreement among the partners, and state registration resulting in issuance of a certificate of limited partnership status. The certificate must be amended whenever new limited partners are admitted.

Limited partnerships can be attractive if the business includes a participant who could not qualify as an S Corporation shareholder; if there are more shareholders than Subchapter S will permit; if the entity wants to make distributions that are not proportionate to ownership shares (S Corporations are not allowed to make disproportionate distributions); or if the business has losses that can best be used to reduce participants' personal income taxes in limited partnership form.

RULPA provides for dissolution and winding up of a limited partnership according to its certificate; on written consent of all partners; or based on a judicial decree of dissolution. Dissolution also occurs on the withdrawal of a general partner (by death, retirement, or incapacity) unless the certificate gives the remaining general partners the right to continue the business, or unless all partners consent in writing within 90 days of the withdrawal.

[1] Limited Liability Partnerships

The Limited Liability Partnership (LLP) form of organization is usually used by professional firms. It is essentially a type of general partnership, but with some limitations on the personal liability of partners. For example, one LLP partner will not be liable for negligent torts committed by another partner, unless the tortfeasor was under the other partner's direct supervision. Personal liability other than for negligent torts remains unlimited. Formation of an LLP requires filing a certificate with the state.

In 1995, the National Conference of Commissioners on Uniform State Laws (NCCUSL) amended the Revised Uniform Partnership Act to include full-shield

LLP provisions. Since that time, all the states have adopted LLP provisions, either by adopting the Revised Uniform Partnership Act (RUPA) or adding full-shield provisions to an existing UPA-based statute. In states with full-shield laws, LLPs and member-managed LLCs are very similar. Professional service organizations are more likely to use LLP than LLC form.[7]

§ 1.04 PROFESSIONAL CORPORATIONS

At one time, very few pension and benefit options were available outside large C Corporations. That created a dilemma for doctors, lawyers, accountants, and other professionals. They wanted to be able to create generous benefit plans for their professional firms; they also wanted limitation of liability, but they wanted to practice in a state-authorized form with some of the simplicity and collegiality of partnership.

The solution was the Professional Corporation, or PC. All member-shareholders must be licensed to practice the profession at issue. State law treats the PC as a limited-liability form (although PC shareholders are still fully liable for their own professional negligence and the negligence of those they supervise). Members of a PC are not liable to the PC's trade creditors.

Code § 269A says that a PC will be taxed as a corporation, and will give its members and their employees full access to the range of corporate employee benefits, as long as the corporation acts as a separate entity; performs meaningful business functions; and its principal purpose is some legitimate objective other than avoiding federal income taxation.

An entity that is a PC for state purposes is a "corporation" for federal diversity suit purposes, no matter the citizenship of its members. The PC's citizenship is its state of incorporation and principal place of business. The Seventh Circuit deemed adoption of a mechanical rule the best way to reduce uncertainty.[8]

§ 1.05 SUBCHAPTER S CORPORATIONS

An S Corporation, although it is a corporation (and therefore its stockholders are entitled to limited liability protection), is taxed by and large as a corporation. It is a pass-through entity, and in most instances, there will be no tax at the corporate level (see § 4.12[A] for the exceptions). See Code §§ 311 and 1366–1368, and § 4.12[A] of this volume, for S Corporation taxation.

As originally drafted, Subchapter S permitted only 75 shareholders, and one class of stock.

For tax years beginning after 2004, the American Jobs Creation Act of 2004, P.L. 108-357, increases the number of permitted shareholders from 75 to 100. In certain circumstances, several members of a family can be treated as one shareholder. All shareholders must be natural persons, estates, some trusts, or tax-exempt entities. Non-resident aliens are not allowed to be S Corporation shareholders.

---

[7] NCCUSL press release, http://www.nccusl.org/nccusl/DesktopModules/NewsDisplay.aspx?ItemID=160 (7/13/07).

[8] Hoagland v. Sandberg, Phoenix & von Gontard PC, 385 F.3d 737 (7th Cir. 2004).

An S Corporation that merges into an LLC (discussed in the next paragraph) is subject to capital gains tax on all appreciation in its assets.

§ 1.06   LIMITED LIABILITY COMPANIES

The LLC is another hybrid entity. It is governed by state law. Its stockholder-members can elect to have the entity taxed as either a corporation or a partnership; usually they elect partnership treatment. Unlike a partnership, however, LLC stockholder-members are entitled to limited liability. Unlike the stockholders of a C Corporation, they are not subject to double taxation (once at the corporate level, once when dividends are paid).

An LLC's managing member, or any member who participates in operation of the LLC's business for more than 500 hours a year, is subject to self-employment tax on compensation received from the LLC.

The first Uniform Limited Liability Company Act (ULLCA) was adopted in 1994. At that time, most of the states had LLC statutes, but there was little uniformity among them. The ULLCA relied heavily on RUPA, especially for member-managed LLCs. The statute reflected the federal tax classifications then extant. Since that time, all the states have adopted LLC statutes, and many states have revised their statutes significantly, to deal with issues such as mergers of LLCs and conversions of unincorporated entities.

In 1997, there was a major change in federal tax treatment; the "check the box" regulations, making it clear that an entity can be taxed like a corporation based on an election. Clarifying this situation made single-member LLCs much more popular.

At its July 14, 2006 meeting, NCCUSL approved a Revised Uniform Limited Liability Company Act (RULLCA). The revision expands the freedom of business founders to use the operating agreement to set out governance rules. The revised Act clarifies the duty of loyalty and the extent to which it can be limited. NCCUSL decided to retain the distinction between manager-managed and member-managed LLCs. LLCs can have perpetual duration, like ordinary corporations.

The RULLCA, like a typical corporate statute, explains how to reserve a name, create an operating agreement for the business, file a certificate of organization, and deal with company members and outsiders. The foundation document for the LLC is the operating agreement. Within limits, the operating agreement can be drafted to immunize LLC members from liability for breach of fiduciary duty. The Act explains authorization of foreign LLCs and direct and derivative actions by LLC members. A "shelf LLC" is one for which a Certificate of Organization is formed before there are any initial members. RULLCA provides that the LLC is not formed until there is at least one member, and the organizer makes a filing stating this fact.

Partnership law (e.g., the original 1914 version of the Uniform Partnership Act) granted statutory apparent authority to partners who appear to act in furtherance of partnership business. This concept has been applied in various subsequent partnership and LLC statutes. However, NCCUSL's position is that this concept works for general and limited partnerships, where third parties expect a partner to be able to bind the entity, but not for LLCs, where it is difficult or impossible to tell if the entity is member- or manager-managed. ULLCA § 301(a) states that a member is not necessarily an agent of the LLC, and questions about power to bind are determined by agency law. The ULLCA permits an LLC to file a public statement of authority covering a position, rather than designating an individual, so authority to transact can be conveyed without revealing the entire operating agreement to third parties.[9]

The Fifth Circuit joined the First and Seventh Circuits in holding that, for diversity jurisdiction purposes, the citizenship of an LLC is determined by the citizenship of each of its members rather than the state where the LLC is organized. If a member of the LLC is a corporation, it will be a citizen of the state where it was incorporated and of the state where it has its principal place of business, if that is different.[10]

§ 1.07 BUSINESS CAPITALIZATION

Every business will have some initial group of owners and investors, no matter how the members of this group are characterized for legal purposes. Furthermore, the capital can come in the form of cash, property, and/or services. The contributions can be treated as either a capital investment in the enterprise (equity) or a loan (debt). Equity entitles the contributor to some share of the corporation's profits, but need not be repaid if there are no profits. Debt does have to be repaid.

In some situations, contributions are made by unsophisticated parties who do not insist on a clear statement of the business entity's intentions. Or, there may be documents (even well-drafted ones) that do not conform to IRC principles and will not be effective for tax purposes.

The American Jobs Creation Act, P.L. 108-357, requires the costs of organizing a business and business start-up costs to be amortized over 15 years rather than over a period of at least 60 months (as prescribed by earlier law).

[A] Debt: Equity Ratios

An entity organized as a corporation has tax incentives to claim that much of its capital comes in the form of debt. A corporation can deduct interest it pays on loans, but cannot deduct the dividends it pays to its shareholders. Someone who lends money to a business entity is not taxed on return of the principal (although the interest is taxable income); a corporate stockholder who redeems shares is likely to be taxed on capital gains or dividends.

---

[9] NCCUSL press release, http://www.nccusl.org/nccusl/DesktopModules/'NewsDisplay.aspx ?ItemID=160 (7/13/07).

[10] Harvey v. Grey Wolf Drilling Co., No. 07-31106 (5th Cir. 9/15/08); following Pramco, LLC *ex rel.* CFSC Consortium, LLC v. San Juan Bay Marina Inc., 435 F.3d 51 (1st Cir. 2006) and Wise v. Wachovia Securities, LLC, 450 F.3d 265 (7th Cir. 2006). Carden v. Arkoma Associates, 494 U.S. 185 (1990) makes an unincorporated entity a citizen based on the citizenship of each of its members.

Code § 385(b) prescribes rules to distinguish between business debt and partnership equity or stock ownership. Factors in distinguishing between debt and equity include:

- Presence of a written, unconditional promise to pay
- Due date for the payment (or promise to pay on demand)
- Agreement to pay a determined amount
- Fixed rate of interest
- Question of whether this obligation is preferred or subordinated to other business obligations
- Ratio of debt to equity in capitalization of the corporation
- Whether or not the obligation can be converted to stock
- Whether the so-called debt is proportionate to the so-called lender's stock ownership.

The IRS has the power to re-characterize alleged debt as equity, if this reflects corporate realities. S Corporations are particularly at risk if re-characterization occurs, because the so-called debt might be treated as a second class of stock, thus destroying the S Corporation status.

Code § 1361(c)(5)(A) permits a safe harbor for "straight debt": i.e., an unconditional promise to pay a sum certain, payable in money (not property), either on a date certain or on demand. The interest rate of S Corporation straight debt must not be contingent on the corporation's discretion, on its profits, payment of dividends on its common stock, or similar factors that point to equity rather than debt status.

Straight debt must not be convertible (directly or indirectly) into stock or other equity interest in the corporation. Furthermore, the creditor must be an individual who is a U.S. citizen or resident alien, or an estate or trust that is a permissible S Corporation shareholder.

Also see Code § 279, which restricts the corporate interest deduction on some subordinated debt that is convertible or issued with warrants, and that is used to finance corporate acquisitions.

[B] § 351 Transactions

Code § 351 says that neither the corporation (C or S) nor a shareholder has gain or loss if: either appreciated or depreciated property is contributed to the corporation, in exchange for shares and nothing else; if the shareholder(s) making the contribution is in control of the corporation right after the contribution.

Control, as defined by § 368(c), means ownership of at least 80% of the total combined voting power of all the corporation's voting stock, plus at least 80% of all non-voting shares (measured by number of shares).

If the transaction involves "boot" (something other than shares in the donee corporation), the recipient of the boot has taxable gain: §§ 351(b), 1001.

If a corporation issues its stock in exchange for services rather than money or property, § 351(d) provides that gain or loss can be recognized. The corporation gets to deduct the compensation; the recipient has ordinary income. Also see § 83, which says that the recipient is taxable when the stock can be sold or otherwise transferred to someone else, or is no longer subject to a substantial risk of forfeiture.

In a § 351 transaction, § 358 sets the shareholder's basis for the stock at the basis of the transferred property. A corporation that receives a contribution of securities has the same basis as the transferor had.

§ 1.08   ORGANIZING A CORPORATION

The most common business form is the corporation, because it is both a powerful and a flexible form. It provides the advantages of limited liability for shareholders, indefinite existence, centralized management, and free transferability of its stock and other business interests.

Apart from federal corporate taxation, bankruptcy, and securities law, most corporate law issues are governed by state law. The corporation must be validly created under the law of one state (usually either Delaware or the corporation's home state). Corporations doing business in additional states will be required to register as foreign corporations.

Delaware adopted several amendments to its General Corporation Law, taking effect August 1, 2004. Many of the terms of the Certificate of Incorporation can be made dependent upon facts that are extrinsic to the document—for example, formula provisions. Certificates of Incorporation are public documents, but this provision permits incorporation by reference of non-public documents (although the underlying facts must be ascertainable by shareholders). However, the corporation's name, registered agent in Delaware, the names and addresses of the incorporators and initial board of directors and the classes, and number and par value of shares authorized must be stipulated in the Certificate of Incorporation and not made dependent on outside documents.

The amended Delaware statute allows a board of directors to delegate the nomination or removal of directors to a committee. Corporations can now accept cash or any tangible or intangible property or benefits to the corporation as consideration for issuance of stock, as long as the aggregate benefit to the corporation at least equals the par value of the stock.[11]

[A] Mechanics of Corporate Formation

State law imposes some fairly minimal requirements for creating a corporation:

- Selecting a corporate name that neither duplicates an existing name nor is deceptively similar

---

[11] DGCL §§ 102, 141, 152; *see* Frederick H. Alexander and Steven L. Lobb, *Delaware Corporation Law Amendments Now in Effect*, 72 LW 2136 (9/14/04).

- Naming one or more incorporators (depending on state practice, they may have to be natural persons rather than organizations, and may have to be state residents)
- Filing a Certificate of Incorporation
- Holding an organization meeting
- Electing an initial slate of directors
- Holding the first meeting of the board of directors
- Adopting by-laws
- Getting a taxpayer ID number
- Setting up accounts for tax withholding and payment of FICA, FUTA (unemployment), Workers' Compensation, and other amounts relating to employee compensation.

[1] Reservation of Corporate Name

State laws provide for reserving a corporate name with the Department of State for future use. Typically, the reservation lasts for a short period of time, with one or two extensions permitted; after the last extension, the reservation lapses unless a corporation has been created under that name.

Selection of the corporate name is a difficult problem (and, in fact, there are expensive consulting firms that do nothing but advise on this question). Clearly, the businesses cannot register a name that infringes upon an existing and active corporate name; but a company that wants to do business in many states, or internationally, may discover that its name is valid in the jurisdiction of registration but unavailable elsewhere. (The name may also be innocuous in English but insulting or obscene in other languages!) Names should be chosen that do not create a risk of confusion with another party's trademark, especially a "famous" trademark (see § 12.09[A][1]). The availability of the corporate name as an Internet domain name is another important issue, which is related but not identical to the trademark question: see § 28.06.

The corporation must designate an office within the state. The Secretary of State is the default agent for service of process on the corporation; most corporations will wish to designate their own agent.

[B] Certificate/Articles of Incorporation

The Certificate of Incorporation (called the Articles of Incorporation in some jurisdictions), filed by the incorporator(s) with the Secretary of State, discloses basic information about the corporation. It can also be an important corporate governance document, if the entrepreneurs include optional provisions that determine the way the corporation will be run, e.g.:

- Grant of preemptive rights (the right to prevent dilution of one's stock ownership by acquiring newly issued shares in the same proportion as one's original ownership)

- Supermajority requirements (requirement of a unanimous, or more than 50%, vote for certain significant corporate actions)
- Limited term for the corporation
- Making stockholders personally liable for corporate debts
- Indemnification of directors and officers for liability to the corporation or its stockholders for fiduciary breaches. (However, indemnification is not available for breaches of the duty of loyalty to the corporation; bad faith; intentional misconduct; knowing violations of the law; improper payment of dividends; or improper receipt of personal benefits.) Indemnification provisions are often handled in the Certificate of Incorporation, rather than by contract or insurance, precisely because it is hard to amend
- Permitting the board of directors (in addition to, or instead of the shareholders) to adopt, amend, and repeal bylaws
- Changing the meeting requirements — e.g., Delaware gives stockholders a statutory right to take action on written consent, without a meeting. This right can only be limited or removed in the corporation's Certificate of Incorporation. In states that do not have a statutory provision allowing shareholder or board meetings by written consent, telephone, or electronically, such powers can probably be created via the Certificate of Incorporation.

[C] Bylaws

Matters of corporate governance that are not provided by state law, or included in the Certificate of Incorporation, can be enacted in the corporation's bylaws. Usually, bylaws are adopted by either the incorporators or the shareholders at the organization meeting.

However, either state law or the Certificate of Incorporation may provide for adoption of bylaws by the board of directors. In general, bylaws can be amended by shareholder vote (perhaps a supermajority will be required for amendment). Many states allow the directors to amend the bylaws, as long as this is authorized by other bylaws adopted in the Certificate of Incorporation or by the stockholders.

Typical bylaw subjects include:

- Location of the corporate headquarters
- Date of the annual meeting
- How to call a special meeting of stockholders
- How to provide notice to stockholders of annual and special meetings
- Quorum and other factors in the conduct of the meeting
- Record date for the meeting — i.e., the date on which stock ownership entitles a person to vote
- Rules for proxy voting
- Vote required to elect directors and take other measures (e.g., simple majority vs. supermajority)
- Ability of stockholders to act on written consent, without a meeting

- Number and term of directors
- Qualifications for serving as a director
- Rules for holding directors' meetings; whether they must be held in person, or whether the board can take unanimous, supermajority, or majority action in writing, by telephone, or online
- Compensation of directors
- How to remove and replace directors
- Board duties and actions that can be delegated to a committee, such as an investment committee, compensation committee, or due diligence committee to examine possible mergers and acquisitions (Check state law — delegation of certain crucial functions may be barred.)
- Indemnification of directors, officers, and managers; advancement of litigation expenses
- Selection, qualifications, duties, and liabilities of corporate officers
- Removal and replacement of officers
- Regulation of corporate stock, including issuance of certificates; transfer restrictions; record date for determining stock ownership before a meeting; how to replace lost, stolen, or destroyed certificates
- Maintenance of the corporate books and records, such as stock and stock transfer records, and minutes of meetings.

[D] Registration of Foreign Corporation

A corporation that begins to do business in an additional state, or that has incorporated in Delaware despite having headquarters elsewhere, will be required to file a certificate with the Secretary of State of each state in which it does business as a foreign corporation. The typical certificate discloses:

- Corporate name
- Corporate purposes
- Capitalization (number of authorized shares; classes or series of shares; par value)
- Structure of the board of directors (size; qualification of directors; classification of directors; power to adopt and amend bylaws; power to remove directors, fill vacancies, and create new directorships)
- Powers reserved to the shareholders.

An agent for service of process within the state should be designated.

§ 1.09 SPECIAL PROBLEMS OF CLOSE CORPORATIONS

Although most of the largest businesses are publicly owned (i.e., their securities are freely traded on exchanges), most businesses are close corporations, whose shares have no public market. A typical pattern is for a company to start up, then "go public": make an Initial Public Offering of its shares.

However, before the IPO, or in the case of companies that have no potential for a public market, a typical set of problems often occurs. In these companies (many of them family-owned), there is a small group of shareholders. Generally speaking, few or no outsiders would be interested in buying corporate shares. However, sometimes competitors of the business are quite interested in purchasing a controlling interest, or enough stock to be a nuisance (by finding out about corporate technological developments or marketing plans, for instance).

A typical pattern develops in small companies: once some of the original founders have retired or died, their families receive gifts of corporate stock, or inherit it from the founders. Soon, there are two groups: an insider group that actually manages the business, and outsiders who are not actively involved in the business. The interests of the two groups are naturally opposed.

Members of the insider group frequently argue that the best use of corporate funds is increasing their own salaries and benefits (which are deductible), and that the corporation should limit its dividend payments and retain capital for future expansion, at least up to the point that the retention is subject to tax penalties (see § 4.07). The outsiders, however, have limited or no dividend income, and no ready market for their shares — other than to the insider group, or perhaps to a competitor.

Many states have passed statutes to prevent oppression of minority share-holders in close corporations. For instance, they can be given the right to petition for dissolution of the corporation if the control group is guilty of illegal, fraudulent, or oppressive actions, or if the control group wastes or loots corporate assets or diverts them for non-corporate purposes.

The corporation and its majority shareholders can avoid the dissolution pro-ceeding by buying out the plaintiff(s) at a price and on terms set by the court. The court will set the price based on what a bona fide purchaser would pay for the business as a going concern (not its liquidating value). The value is not necessarily limited by the shareholder agreement.

As a supplement, or in states where there are no statutes, shareholder agree-ments can be used to cope in advance with governance problems.

§ 1.10 SHAREHOLDER AGREEMENTS

Shareholders in close corporations frequently enter into agreements to settle issues of corporate governance, prevent dissension and oppression of minority shareholders, and provide a mechanism for buying out dissidents without involving the courts or dissolving the corporation.

Shareholder agreements are often classified as pooling agreements, proxy agreements, or voting trusts. They are arrangements under which shareholders agree to vote together, or to give their proxies to someone else, who will vote them in a way designed to minimize dissension.

A pooling agreement, also known as a voting agreement, is allowed in most states as long as there is no fraud, vote selling, or oppression of the other shareholders. It obligates the signers to vote in a pre-determined manner in electing directors, amending the corporation's charter and bylaws, etc. A well-drafted agreement will include an enforcement mechanism (such as giving the signer the right to sue non-complying signers for equitable remedies, on the grounds that the signers are at risk of irreparable harm that cannot be redressed by money damages if the agreement is breached). Even absent an enforcement mechanism, it is likely that the state court will grant specific performance of the agreement.

A voting trust is an arrangement under which several shareholders place their shares into trust, and the trustee votes the entire block in accordance with the terms of the agreement. A voting trust might be preferred to a voting agreement if, for instance, some of the shareholders are minors or incapacitated persons. A voting trust is more complex than a simple voting agreement, because the trust becomes the legal owner of the shares.

Under a proxy agreement, the parties give another shareholder or a neutral third party the right to vote their shares — either under all circumstances, or only when necessary to prevent deadlock. Corporate proxies are governed by agency law, and the general agency rule is that proxies can always be revoked unless they are coupled with an interest in the corporation or its stock. Some states provide that proxies can become irrevocable if the designated proxy-holder is a party to the voting agreement or voting trust, and the text of the actual proxy says that it is irrevocable.

[A] Checklist for Shareholder Agreements

Typical shareholder agreement provisions include:

❑ Size of the board of directors
❑ Quorum for the board
❑ How officers and directors will be elected
❑ How successors will be appointed if a director or officer dies, withdraws, retires, or is removed
❑ How often board meetings will be held; who can call one; what can be on the agenda
❑ Limitations on the powers and duties of corporate directors and officers
❑ Compensation of directors
❑ Designation of the corporation's attorneys and accountants
❑ Provisions that will require a "supermajority" (i.e., more than the normal majority vote for corporate decisions), e.g.,
  ❑ Amendments to the charter and bylaws
  ❑ Corporate investments, loans, mortgages, or pledges of assets greater than a stated amount
  ❑ Buying or leasing property from, or employing (e.g., as consultants) corporate insiders

- Changes in the corporation's business purpose
- Mergers and acquisitions
- The corporation's repurchase or redemption of its own securities
- Issuing or offering stock or additional classes or issues of stock
- Declaration of dividends Arbitration clause

❑ Provisions for specific performance of agreement provisions
❑ The corporation's undertaking not to reflect transfers on its books if they violate the agreement
❑ Covenant of active shareholders not to compete with the corporation
❑ Rights of shareholders to inspect books and records
❑ Circumstances justifying termination of the agreement
- Written consent of all the shareholders
- Sale of all of the corporation's shares to one stockholder
- Sale of all or substantially all of the corporate assets
- Liquidation, dissolution, or bankruptcy of the corporation
- Initial public offering.

Although the general rule of corporate law is that a corporation is managed by its board of directors, some states let the shareholders of a close corporation control the directors' decision-making. However, if this is done, the shareholders and not the directors become liable for errors and omissions.

Check local law. Some shareholder agreement provisions (such as those permitting direct election of officers by shareholders; control of directors' decisions; supermajority requirements) may have to be endorsed on the stock certificate to be fully enforceable.

§ 1.11 CORPORATE STOCK

The number of shares that the corporation issues at startup has some minor consequences. The filing fee for a Certificate of Incorporation depends on the number and value of shares; franchise tax also is usually calculated based on the number of shares.

Shares can be issued with a par value; their initial purchasers must pay at least that amount. No-par shares can also be issued.

Unless the relevant state statute or the corporation's charter provides to the contrary, all shares of stock have equal voting, dividend, and other rights. Corporations can issue one or more classes of preferred stock, which have greater rights to receive dividends or liquidating distributions than common stock or junior preferred stock.

As long as the corporation is solvent, it can declare and pay dividends. (Dividend payments by insolvent corporations constitute fraudulent conveyances.) Generally, dividends come out of corporate surplus: the corporation's net assets minus its stated capital. Stated capital, in turn, equals the number of shares issued times their par value (or, for no-par shares, the amount allocated to stated capital).

Dividends paid out of capital rather than earned surplus must be accompanied by a notice of effect on the corporation's stated capital and surplus.

A corporation can mandate declaration of dividends, but generally one of the most important functions of the board of directors is to decide whether a quarterly dividend will be declared, and how large it will be. As long as the decision is legitimate and not fraudulent, it will be entitled to the protection of the business judgment rule, and courts will not challenge the rationale for the decision.

If the charter permits, the corporation can have classes or series of shares that can be redeemed by the corporation itself: the company buys back its shares out of surplus at any time that it is solvent. The reacquired shares are either canceled by the corporation, becoming authorized but unissued shares that can be re-issued at a later date; or, the corporation itself holds them as treasury shares.

[A] Transfer Restrictions

Another method for controlling the management of a non-public corporation is to impose transfer restrictions on sales, gifts, pledges, and other transfers of the shares. For instance, transfers to competitors can be forbidden, as can unregistered sales of securities that must be registered to be sold legally, or sales that destroy an S Corporation's eligibility for that status.

The typical form of transfer agreement defines the permitted class of trans-ferees, such as shareholders, their families, and trusts they have established. It is against public policy to impose restrictions that eliminate all possibility of transfer, but reasonable restrictions that serve a valid business purpose are permissible.

The corporation or its shareholders can be given a right of first refusal before a transfer to an outsider will be permitted. A provision calling for repurchase by the corporation when a shareholder dies not only serves the corporation's purposes, but serves the estate planning needs of the shareholders. Another possibility is for the other shareholders to have a right of first refusal, with a right of second refusal for the corporation, on the occurrence of events such as a shareholder's death, insolvency, or permanent disability.

A "drag along" clause, used where an entire company has to be sold at once to make a deal work, allows the minority shareholders to compel the majority shareholders to join in the sale. The corresponding "tag along" structure gives minority shareholders the right to participate in a sale.

The main pricing mechanisms are book value (in which case, the date of calculation is crucial); dollar value mutually agreed by the parties; market price or highest price a bona fide purchaser would offer; and the price set by appraisal.

Be sure to consult local law, because some states provide that a corporation can repurchase its own shares only out of surplus, and cannot buy back shares when it is insolvent or when the repurchase would lead to insolvency. The corporation has to be recapitalized, or raise additional funds, if it has a contractual obligation to repurchase shares.

[B] Buy-Sell Agreements

Corporate buy-sell agreements overlap with shareholder agreements and voting restrictions, but can serve somewhat different purposes. The agreements safeguard corporate continuity by providing a mechanism for keeping the shares of a retiring, disabled, or deceased member of the management group within the corporation or within the same management group.

There are many ways to structure these agreements. The corporation or the surviving shareholders might be obligated to purchase the shares, and the estate of a deceased shareholder might be obligated to sell. Or, the corporation, and then the surviving shareholders, could be given an option to buy the decedent's shares; the estate is obligated to sell if the option is exercised. Still another variation gives the estate of a deceased stockholder the right to put the stock to either the surviving stockholders or the corporation. Or, there could be no obligation on either side, but if a stockholder or estate wanted to sell, the corporation or survivors might be given a right of first refusal before the stock could be offered to outsiders.

Valuing the shares that will be purchased is a crucial function of the buy-sell agreement. Usually, the agreement sets an initial price, with a schedule for revising the price. Or, the signatories could agree to accept the price set by an outside appraiser. The agreement can also include a valuation formula, based on factors such as the corporate net worth, book value, capitalization of profits, or a hybrid method.

It is also crucial for the agreement to set a funding method for the purchase. If the triggering event is a shareholder's death, life insurance is the normal funding mechanism.

If the insurance is owned by the corporation (corporations have a clear insurable interest in the lives of their management, so this is not a problem), the agreement is known as an "entity purchase" agreement. If the other stockholders own the insurance, it is known as a "cross purchase" agreement. Insurance can also be used to fund purchases that are triggered by the disability of a shareholder. However, an agreement used to provide retirement funds and a smooth corporate transition does not involve an insurable event — so either the corporation must have funds available for the purchase, or the other stockholders must use their private funds.

Agreements for purchase of a decedent's shares can also be used to set the estate tax value of the shares. However, for the IRS to accept such valuation, the price must be fixed in the agreement; it must be a fair price that would be acceptable in an arm's-length transaction; and the parties to the agreement, not just their survivors or estates, must be obligated to sell at the fixed price.

§ 1.12 EMPLOYMENT AGREEMENTS

Although, as § 3.16[A] discusses, most employees who do not work under a Collective Bargaining Agreement (CBA) are "at-will" employees who do not have a formal contract, it is often a good idea for a business to enter into employment agreements with at least some of its employees. Employment agreements are more likely to be useful for top management or employees with specialized skills who have to be specially recruited, and who are likely to be actively solicited to change jobs.

The employment agreement could be negotiated at the behest of the corporation, which is eager to protect itself and its intellectual property in case the employee wants to leave. Or, the impetus could come from an employee who wants to make sure he or she will be paid for the full contract term even if the contract ends prematurely, or who wants matters such as stock options and bonuses to be promised rather than left to future discretion.

Typical subjects include:

- Duration of the agreement; grounds for termination of employment
- "Golden parachutes" — compensation paid if the employee loses his or her job because of a change in corporate ownership
- Advance consent to resolution of claims (including discrimination claims) by means of arbitration rather than litigation
- Covenants not to compete (which must be reasonable in terms of both duration and geographic scope, and which must not have the effect of preventing the signer from earning a living; protection of the employer's intellectual property is considered a valid motivation)
- Bonuses
- Ownership of patents and other intellectual property developed by the employee
- Renewal of the agreement; usually, such agreements are renewed automatically unless notice is given in time. Renewal is either on the original terms, or on terms to be negotiated in good faith at the time of renewal.

If an employment contract is breached by the employer's unjust firing of the employee, then monetary damages will be awarded, but the court will not order reinstatement. Damages are likely to include back pay (including benefits, raises, fringe benefits, and promotions whose likelihood can be established with reasonable certainty), front pay for the balance of the contract term, minus mitigating amounts earned by the plaintiff by exercising reasonable diligence in finding a new job.

Naturally, no court will order an employee who quits during the term of a contract to go back to work, but the employer will be entitled to consequential damages arising from the breach of contract, such as lost profits and the cost of hiring a replacement. In the alternative, the employer will be entitled to liquidated damages or forfeiture of bonuses the employee would otherwise have received.

§1.13 CORPORATE GOVERNANCE

Once a corporation is in operation, it must satisfy certain formal requirements. The board of directors must meet as necessary. Shareholders must meet at least once a year. Important business decisions must be memorialized in resolutions, adopted by the directors and/or shareholders (depending on the subject matter and the structure of the corporation's authorizing documents). Minutes must be taken at meetings, and those minutes must be kept on file for examination by stockholders and regulators. If the company is a "reporting company" under the Securities Exchange Act of 34 (see § 6.05), then periodic and annual reports must be submitted to the SEC. Some reports must also be sent to shareholders.

The financial crisis of 2008 cast a (often unflattering) light on corporate governance, and the extent to which corporations properly scrutinized complex transactions. Shearman & Sterling's sixth annual Corporate Governance Survey (based on the proxy statements of the 100 largest U.S. corporations) showed that public companies, in response to shareholder pressure, are adopting better governance practices. Out of that sample, 71 now elect directors by majority vote even in an uncontested race (only 11 companies did this in 2006), and 76 companies (36 in 2006) require directors to resign if they do not get a majority. Electronic proxy delivery was permitted starting in 2007; 35 of the respondents use the "notice and access" model, where shareholders receive a notice explaining where to find the materials online. Corporations are adding additional committees (such as executive, finance, and public policy) to supplement the existing categories such as compensation, audit, and governance committees.[12]

[A] Annual Meeting

One of the most vital functions of the annual meeting of stockholders is to elect the board of directors. Most stockholders, of course, do not know who the candidates are (and probably do not really care, as long as the stock price holds up and dividends are steady). Therefore, management, and sometimes dissident groups, solicit proxies: they ask shareholders for the right to determine how the shareholders' votes will be applied in the board election. See § 6.06 for SEC rules for proxy solicitation in reporting companies, and § 6.10 for Sarbanes-Oxley Act effects on corporate governance.

Ordinarily, each share of stock represents one vote for each director. However, cumulative voting gives the stockholder a total quantum of voting power based on the number of shares times the number of directors to be elected, and stockholders can allocate any part or all of the total to the election of a particular director: for example, a stockholder who owns 500 shares might distribute votes for five directors to several candidates, or only one.

The Delaware Supreme Court struck down a shareholder bylaw that would have required the company to reimburse challengers who succeeded in being elected to the Board of Directors. A pension fund sought reimbursement if they elected at least one independent candidate to the board. The Delaware Supreme Court found the bylaw invalid because it denied the company's Board of Directors

---

[12] Sheri Qualters, *Corporations Responding to Shareholder Pressure on Governance Practices, Survey Finds*, Nat'l L.J. 10/2/08 (law.com).

the discretion to exercise their judgment about the appropriateness of reimbursement. In this view, boards should not be compelled to reimburse challengers if a proxy contest is motivated by petty concerns or seeks to promote interests contrary to those of the corporation.[13]

[B] Resolutions

Resolutions are the corporate equivalent of the bills passed by a state legislature. In most corporations, both the board and the stockholders vote on and pass resolutions on matters of importance to the operation of the corporation. Typical subjects include hiring major executives; setting up bank accounts; taking loans, lines of credit, and other financing mechanisms; entering into major leases; issuing stock options; creating or modifying employee benefit plans; and declaring dividends.

[C] Corporate Stock and Dividends

All corporations have to have one class of common stock; they can adopt additional classes of stock as well, with different voting rights and entitlements to dividends. However, Subchapter S Corporations are only allowed to have one class of stock (although some differences within the class are permissible). Ordinary common stock has voting rights, but non-voting common stock can be issued.

Preferred stock is preferred in the sense that its holders have a right to receive dividends or liquidating distributions superior to the rights of common stock holders, or the holders of junior classes of preferred stock. The holders of cumulative preferred stock are entitled to make-up payments for quarters in which no dividends were declared, before other stockholders are entitled to receive current dividends.

The corporation's directors decide whether a dividend will be issued (unless the organizing documents require mandatory dividends), and how large it will be. Usually, this is done on a quarterly basis. (The dividend is "passed" in quarters in which no dividend is declared.) Dividend declaration is subject to the business judgment rule (§ 1.14[C]), and if the decision is made legitimately and without fraud, it will not be changed by a court. Dividends can be paid in either cash or stock.

A corporation has the right to declare and pay dividends at any time it is not insolvent — but issuance of dividends by an insolvent corporation is a fraudulent conveyance. It is also generally true that dividends must come out of corporate surplus, defined as the corporation's net assets minus its stated capital. Stated capital, in turn, consists of the number of shares issued times the par value of each; a no-par share is valued at its amount allocated to stated capital. If dividends are paid out of anything other than earned surplus, the corporation must disclose

---

[13] C.A. v. AFSCME Employees Pension Plan, No. 329 (Del. 2008); *see* Kara Scannell and Judith Burns, *Delaware Court Rules for CA in Suit*, Wall St. J. 7/18/08 at C6.

the effect of the declaration on its stated capital and surplus. The resolution declaring a dividend should indicate a record date (a date for determining who is the official owner entitled to receive the dividend) and a date for payment.

In a case of first impression, the Delaware Court of Chancery ruled that 8 Del. Code § 151(c) does not require preferred shares to pay dividends. The statute says that stockholders are entitled to dividends on the conditions stated in the certificate of incorporation.[14]

[1] Redemption

The corporation's charter can be drafted or amended to authorize classes or series of shares that can be redeemed by the corporation. A corporation authorized to do so can buy or redeem its shares out of surplus at any time it is not insolvent (or does not become insolvent as a direct result of the purchase or redemption). The corporation either cancels the reacquired shares or holds them as treasury shares. Unless the charter forbids it, the shares can be re-issued at a later time.

The effect of redemption is to return more shares and more value to the corporation itself, increasing its ability to borrow. Also, shares that are not held outside the corporation cannot be voted contrary to corporate policy, and cannot be acquired by a party contemplating a hostile takeover.

[2] Preemptive and Appraisal Rights

The corporate balance of power changes if the board of directors issues a large number of new shares. The effect is to dilute the voting power of the existing shareholders. Preemptive rights give existing shareholders the right to preserve their percentage ownership by purchasing enough of the newly issued shares to retain the same proportion of the total. States differ in the way they treat preemptive rights. In Delaware, for example, these rights exist only if adopted in the corporate charter; in New York, they exist unless they are excluded by the charter.

Appraisal rights are entitlement to get paid in cash for shares in case the corporation undertakes major actions (e.g., merger, consolidation, sale of assets, charter amendments) that the stockholder disapproves of. Before exercising appraisal rights, the stockholder must file a written objection to the action no later than the shareholder meeting at which the action will be voted on, in which he or she demands appraisal rights.

The stockholders surrender their shares, and have no further shareholder rights other than the right to be paid for the shares. The corporation must offer its good faith estimate of the fair market price of the shares. If the surrendering shareholders are unwilling to accept this amount, a court proceeding is required to set the price of the shares.

---

[14] Shintom Co. v. Audiovox Corp., No. 693-N (Del. Ch. 5/4/05) *aff'd* 888 A.2d 225 (Del. 2005).

[D] Sarbanes-Oxley Act Effects

In addition to increased criminal penalties for corporate financial misfeasance (see § 26.02[H][8][d]) the Sarbanes-Oxley Act of 2002, P.L. 107-204, has many provisions dealing with the governance of public corporations (i.e., those that have one or more issues of registered securities). These provisions are scattered throughout the lengthy Act, but are concentrated in Title III, Corporate Responsibility, Title IV, Enhanced Financial Disclosures, and Title X, Corporate Tax Returns.

Corporations subject to the Sarbanes-Oxley Act are required to:

- Maintain an audit committee consisting of outside directors (people who serve on the corporation's Board of Directors, but are not otherwise employed or retained by the corporation) to review the work of the accounting firms that audit the corporation's books
- Have the corporation's CEO and CFO review all reports filed with the SEC; the corporate officers must certify that the figures in the reports are accurate and that the corporation maintains adequate internal financial controls
- Make the CEO and CFO reimburse the corporation for any bonuses received in the 12 months prior to the issuance of a financial report that later has to be restated because of misconduct in connection with financial reporting requirements
- Increase the depth of financial disclosure in SEC reports, including all material "off-balance sheet" transactions; pro forma figures must not be misleading, and must be reconciled with the company's financial condition and results of operations under GAAP[15]
- Furnish the SEC with an annual internal control report describing the company's financial control structure and an assessment of how well it is operating
- Adopt a Code of Ethics for the corporation's CFO and other senior financial officers.

§ 1.14   CORPORATE DIRECTORS

Remember, the formal responsibility for management of a corporation rests with its board of directors, so directors have substantial responsibility under corporate law. Failure to meet appropriate standards often results in suit by the corporation, by its stockholders, or by third parties affected by corporate actions. However, as discussed below, it is common for directors to have liability insurance (also see § 13.07[D]) and for them to be entitled to be indemnified by the corporation.

---

[15] In January 2003, the SEC adopted rules about disclosure of pro forma financial information: Regulation G. *See* SEC Release 2003-6, http://www.sec.gov/news/press/2003-6.htm.

The Sarbanes-Oxley Act, P.L. 107-204, allows the SEC to seek equitable relief against corporate officers and directors, on behalf of a public corporation's stockholders. Under this Act, directors and officers are forbidden to buy, sell, or otherwise acquire or transfer the corporation's stock while the company's stock is subject to a "blackout period" that prevents rank-and-file employees from trading employer stock held in their pension accounts.[16] Public corporations are forbidden to make personal loans to directors and officers (with exceptions for, e.g., home improvement loans and issuance of credit cards).

In mid-2006, the SEC adopted disclosure rules for providing information about the compensation of directors and senior executives. In general, plain English principles must be applied to increase the usefulness of the information. The rule calls for both tabular and narrative disclosure about the CEO, CFO, directors, and three highest-paid executives of public corporations. The Compensation Discussion and Analysis (CD&A) is filed, and therefore must be certified by the corporation's CEO and CFO. The compensation committee must report on whether it has reviewed and discussed the CD&A with management. For individuals covered by disclosure requirements, the corporation must disclose their salary, bonuses, perquisites, and equity-based awards for the previous three years, with extensive disclosure related to grants, valuation, and exercise of stock options. Detailed disclosure is also required as to retirement plans and post-employment benefits, with a narrative description of any arrangement for making payments on termination, change in responsibilities, or change in the control of the company. Transactions between the corporation and a related person must still be disclosed, but the safe harbor for small transactions rises from $60,000 to $120,000. A new Item 407 has been added to Regulations S-K and S-B, to consolidate information about the independence of directors and nominees for directors.[17]

[A] Duties of Directors

The corporation's directors must carry out their duties in good faith, using the degree of care that an ordinary prudent person would use in the same situation. There is a duty of reasonable inquiry; instead of rubber-stamping all proposals from corporate management, they must investigate (although they can place reasonable reliance on data from the corporation's officers, employees, and retained professional experts).

Directors also have a duty of loyalty. They must not put their own private benefit above the needs of the corporation or its stockholders. They cannot compete with the corporation, unless the non-interested directors have been notified and have given their approval.

---

[16] In January 2003, the SEC adopted Regulation BTR governing insider trading during blackout periods. *See* SEC Release 2003-6, http://www.sec.gov/news/press/2003-6.htm.

[17] SEC Release 2006-123, "SEC Votes to Adopt Changes to Disclosure Requirements Concerning Executive Compensation and Related Matters," http://www.sec.gov/news/press/2006/2006-123.htm (7/26/06).

Directors cannot favor one group of stockholders over another; they must abide by the corporate governance instruments (e.g., setting out the rights of preferred stockholders). In some situations, they may have the option of considering the interests of non-stockholder constituencies, such as employees, retirees, suppliers, and the local community.

Outside directors (those not employed by the corporation) must maintain the confidentiality of information they learn about the corporation, its operations, and its intellectual property. Outside directors must be careful to avoid even apparent, and of course actual, conflicts of interest between serving on this board and their other business, government, or outside director responsibilities.

An interested director is one who is involved in a potential corporate transaction: for example, the corporation wishes to buy equipment from a company owned by one of its outside directors, or wishes to retain the law firm of an attorney-director. Transactions between a corporation and its interested directors are not necessarily void or improper, although the interested director is not allowed to vote on the transaction, and there should be full disclosure and the approval of the other directors. Interested director transactions are permissible only if they are fair to the corporation. Ratification by shareholders may be required: e.g., if the corporation makes a loan to a director.

A corporation's directors who willfully issue improper dividends or violate restrictions on the repurchase or redemption of corporate stock are jointly and severally liable for the wrongdoing. The liable directors are entitled to contribution from the other directors who voted for the improper action.

In 2006, Delaware rejected "deepening insolvency" (i.e., poor business decisions that exacerbate the corporation's financial problems) as an independent cause of action under state law.[18] In 2007, the state's supreme court agreed that a "putative creditor" could not bring a direct suit for breach of fiduciary duty against the board of directors of a corporation that is insolvent or in the zone of insolvency. However, a derivative suit maintained by a creditor's committee, bankruptcy trustee, or receiver might be sustainable. In the Third Circuit's view, Pennsylvania law requires fraud (and not mere negligence) to support a "deepening insolvency" claim involving deterioration in corporate finances.[19]

---

[18] Trenwick America Litigation Trust v. Ernst & Young LLP, 906 A.2d 168 (Del. Ch. 2006).

[19] North American Catholic Educational Programming Foundation Inc. v. Gheewalla, 90 A.2d 92 (Del. 2007). Sheri Qualters, *Ruling Makes Bankruptcy Suits Harder*, Nat'l L.J. 6/12/07 (law.com); *see also* Charles R. Goldstein, Chapter 7, Trustee for Just For Feet Inc. v. Ruttenberg, No. 01-06833 (Jefferson Co., Ala., Cir. Ct. March 2007), a bankruptcy trustee's suit in Alabama against directors, officers, and accountants for their actions in the zone of insolvency, alleging that the defendants' failed to restructure the corporation in Chapter 11 in timely fashion. The Third Circuit case is *In re CitX Corp. Inc., Gary Seitz, Chapter 7, Trustee v. Detweiler Hersey & Associates P.C.*, 448 F.3d 672 (3d Cir. 2006).

[B] Derivative Suits

Theoretically, corporations not only can but should sue directors who have violated their duties. But in many cases, the errant director controls the board, or acted with the connivance of other directors, so a suit by the corporation is not a real possibility.

In response, corporation law gives stockholders the right to bring derivative suits: the stockholder sues on behalf of the corporation, to redress wrongs committed against the corporate entity. Derivative suit judgments or settlements, if any, are paid to the corporation itself, not the derivative plaintiff.

Some improprieties that could justify a derivative suit include:

- Improper loans to shareholders
- Negligence about attending or participating in board meetings that permits wrongdoing to flourish
- Improper use of corporate funds in proxy contests
- Failure to detect and prevent antitrust violations
- Improper or imprudent investment of corporate funds
- Failure to detect and prevent embezzlement
- Improper conduct in connection with takeover defense
- Wasting corporate assets.

Before bringing a derivative action, the stockholder must demand that the board itself take action, and the demand must be wrongfully refused. The demand need not be made if there is reasonable doubt that the board is disinterested and independent.

Under California law, a plaintiff who no longer owned stock in a corporation because he received shares in the acquiring corporation in a merger cannot pursue a derivative action against the company for securities fraud. The corporation was incorporated in Delaware, and Delaware law requires a derivative suit plaintiff to have continuous stock ownership as long as the action is pending. Delaware allows two limited exceptions to this requirement: a cashed-out plaintiff can maintain a suit if the merger itself is alleged to be a fraud entered into solely to deprive shareholders of standing, or the merger is actually a reorganization that does not affect the plaintiff's ownership interest. California requires the plaintiff to be a shareholder at the time of the transaction, with exceptions for circumstances in which the plaintiff became a shareholder before wrongdoing was disclosed, and not granting the plaintiff standing would permit the defendant to retain the proceeds of willful breach of fiduciary duty. Because corporations are managed by their directors and not their stockholders, the objective of a derivative action is to enforce the corporation's rights when the board refuses to do so. The claim does not belong to the stockholder, so it cannot survive the termination of stockholder status.[20]

---

[20] Grosset v. Wenaas, 42 Cal. 4th 1100 (Cal. 2008).

In 2008, the New York Court of Appeals permitted members of LLCs to bring derivative suits on behalf of the LLC, even though state law does not explicitly provide for this option. According to the majority opinion, members of an LLC have the same entitlements as corporate shareholders, and it is always improper for corporate fiduciaries to enrich themselves with company assets.[21] Subsequently, however, a New York lower court limited standing in derivative actions to current rather than former members of an LLC; the plaintiff lost his right to sue his former associates when he withdrew from the LLC and sued the company and its remaining principals.[22]

[C] The Business Judgment Rule

The business judgment rule insulates a corporation's directors against liability if they behave reasonably and exercise appropriate judgment. The business judgment defense is not available if the director has breached the duty of loyalty or due care (e.g., by self-dealing), but it is available and useful in situations where directors acted sensibly and honestly, but made decisions that had bad financial consequences.

The other side of the coin is the doctrine of ultra vires: a corporation follows objectives or enters into transactions that are improper because they are not authorized by state law or the corporation's charter or bylaws. Ultra vires actions can be challenged by stockholders, and the state's Attorney General can seek dissolution of the corporation to prevent further unauthorized actions. However, it is a defense if the stockholders ratify an ultra vires action.

[D] Indemnification

Given the potential for significant personal liability, many talented individuals might refuse to accept a new corporate job or refuse to serve as outside director. Corporation law allows a corporation to indemnify its directors, officers, and employees against the consequences of their conduct, as long as the individuals were not guilty of deliberate wrongdoing.

The corporate charter can be drafted or amended to rule out monetary liability of directors and officers to the corporation for breaches of fiduciary duty (even those stemming from gross negligence), but not intentional misconduct, self-dealing, breach of the duty of loyalty, or wrongful payment of dividends or repurchase of corporate stock.

An initial distinction must be drawn between conduct undertaken in the scope of employment and that allegedly harmed someone other than the corporation, and

---

[21] Tzolis v. Wolff, 10 N.Y.3d 100 (N.Y. 2008); *see* Joel Stashenko, *N.Y. High Court Approves Derivative Lawsuits for LLCs*, N.Y.L.J. 2/15/08 (law.com).

[22] Billings v. Bridgeport Partners, LLC, No. 7898/07. 2008 N.Y. Slip Op. 28351 (N.Y. Supreme Erie County 2008); *see* Joel Stashenko, *Standing to Sue LLC Ruled Limited to Current Owners*, N.Y.L.J. 10/2/08 (law.com).

conduct alleged to harm the corporation itself. It is much more likely that indemnification will be available in the former situation than in the latter.

Authority for the corporation to indemnify can come from several sources: state corporation law; provisions of the corporate charter and bylaws; private agreements such as employment contracts; and resolutions passed by the board or shareholders.

State laws can furnish either mandatory or permissive indemnification in shareholder or non-shareholder suits or criminal actions. Directors, officers, employees, or agents who prevail in a suit are likely to be entitled to indemnification for their defense costs. Indemnification may also be available for settlements and judgments against the individual. Depending on state law, a corporation may be allowed to indemnify persons who acted in good faith and in a way reasonably believed to be in the best interests of the corporation. State law may also permit the board to advance defense or other expenses to the indemnified person.

"D&O liability insurance" (see § 13.07[D]) covers two types of expenses that might occur: liability incurred by an individual director or officer, and expenses that the corporation incurs when indemnifying such persons. The policy usually covers whatever a party pays for damages, judgments, settlements, costs, charges, or expenses incurred in connection with any proceeding, suit, or action — whether or not indemnification is available under state law.

In this context, a wrongful act is negligence, breach of duty, error, misstatement, omission, etc., charged against a person solely by reason of his or her actions or status as director or officer.

Individuals cannot insure themselves against their own deliberate wrongdoing, and the same principle would probably apply to extreme (but not ordinary) negligence. D&O policies typically exclude acts undertaken for personal profit, such as "short-swing" stock trading; liability arising out of takeover activity; and pollution. It is also typical to exclude indemnification of fines or penalties imposed by law. The corporation's authority to buy D&O insurance stems from state law and/or the corporate charter and bylaws.

In 2008, the Delaware Chancery Court issued three decisions about advancement of legal fees to corporate officers and directors; some corporations may have to change their bylaws to conform. The court held that a company's litigation counsel was entitled to advance legal fees when it was sued by a shareholder who gained control of the corporation in a shareholder dispute; the law firm was acting as the company's agent when it was sued, and there was no bylaw protecting the company. In the second case, former directors of a corporation were held to be entitled to advancement of legal fees for a securities fraud case, once the directors were close to the policy limits for their D&O policy, so they could have continuous coverage of legal fees. However, in a third case, it was held that the former managing partner and chairman of a venture capital firm was not entitled to advancement of legal fees because the LLC's charter and bylaws permitted advancement of legal fees only for defense of suits relating to corporate duties; in this case, the suit did not occur until after the person seeking advancement of legal fees had been removed from office.[23]

§1.15 NOT-FOR-PROFIT ORGANIZATIONS

A not-for-profit organization is created and run for purposes other than pecuniary gain to its founders. Some states allow incorporation of not-for-profit organizations, but they cannot issue stock, and they are not allowed to distribute assets, income, or profits to an ownership group. If there is any incidental profit from operations, it must be devoted to the organization's exempt purpose and not distributed to shareholder equivalents.

Not-for-profit organizations usually (but not always) qualify for federal tax exemption. That is, they are not subject to federal taxation on income that stems from their exempt purpose, although they are subject to tax on any unrelated business income they earn. Further qualifications are required before donors can deduct contributions they make to a charitable organization.

Not-for-profit organizations can operate as either charities (which make grants or provide services directly) or membership organizations. Membership organizations derive their revenue from membership dues, user fees, perhaps commercial revenue, and investment income; charities also get contributions and grants.

[A] Federal Tax Exemption

The main IRC section governing tax-exempt organizations is § 501(c), which allows a federal tax exemption to a charity or membership organization that is organized and operated for a not-for-profit purpose, and both intends and ensures that no benefits inure to private individuals related to the entity. That is, the organization is allowed to pay reasonable salaries, but cannot distribute the equivalent of profits.

No tax is imposed on "exempt function income" such as dues and contributions or funds deriving from activities related to the exempt purpose.

Tax is imposed at corporate rates on Unrelated Business Taxable Income (UBTI) — income from a regularly maintained trade or business that is carried on by the organization, and that does not further the exempt purpose (other than by generating income). Not only is UBTI taxed, but excessive business activities can lead to loss of exempt status. However, the IRS can be fairly generous in interpreting this rule, for example, allowing museums to operate shops with a wide range of merchandise. Passive income, such as rents, royalties, and interest is not considered UBTI.

---

[23] Jackson Walker LLP v. Spira Footwear Inc., No. 3150-VCP (New Castle County, Del. Ch. 2008); Barrett v. American Country Holdings Inc., No. 3071-VCS (New Castle County, Del. Ch. 2008); Donohue v. Corning, No. 3733-VCS (New Castle County, Del. Ch. 2008); see Sheri Qualters, *Legal Fee Bylaws May Need Change*, Nat'l L.J. 7/28/08 (law.com).

Usually (although not always) federal tax-exemption will trigger similar treatment at the state and local level. The organization may also qualify for exemption from the franchise tax on unincorporated business. Charities may also be exempt from sales tax and property tax on both their purchases and sales. In fact, exemption from property tax may be the leading factor in the viability of an organization, or the decision to operate a borderline organization in not-for-profit rather than profit form. See § 4.12[C] for further tax information.

The Pension Protection Act, at § 1211, mandates the creation of an official report on the acquisition of insurance contracts, so the Treasury can decide whether charitable split dollar insurance is consistent with the exempt mission of not-for-profits. Section 1212 doubles the taxes when a charity commits misconduct such as failing to distribute income, maintaining excess business holdings, or holding investments that jeopardize the organization's charitable purpose.

[B] Organization of a Not-for-Profit Corporation

A not-for-profit organization can be an unincorporated association, an inter vivos trust, or a testamentary trust, but most are organized and operated in corporate form. As a general rule, state laws permit not-for-profit corporations to be organized either as membership organizations, with boards of directors elected by the membership, or as non-membership organizations with a self-perpetuating board of directors. Differing classes of membership are usually permitted. Votes can be cast in person or by proxy, and class and cumulative voting are often permitted.

Like a profit-making corporation, a not-for-profit must be formally organized, with one or more incorporators and filing of the Certificate of Incorporation with the Secretary of the state. An organization meeting is held for the initial members or directors to ratify the incorporation and adopt bylaws and elect the slate of officers for the first year. Resolutions are passed dealing with matters such as the corporate seal, its fiscal year, and authority for the initial slate of officers to seek tax-exempt status for the organization. Depending on the organization's exempt mission, it may be necessary to obtain authorization from state regulatory agencies (e.g., for a health care or educational organization).

Not-for-profits that operate in other states will probably have to register as "foreign" not-for-profit organizations, and will be subject to the jurisdiction of the state Attorney General with respect to solicitation of funds.

Many states allow not-for-profits to raise "subventions," which are long-term capital contributions to the organization that pay below-market rates of return. When the organization dissolves, subvention holders have a preference over other members, but are subordinate to the organization's creditors. Ordinary loans from organization members to the organization are also permitted.

[C] Reporting and Management of the Not-for-Profit

States generally require registered not-for-profit organizations to submit annual financial reports. Organizations that solicit financial contributions must report in greater detail. If a donor earmarks a contribution for a specific purpose, it must be accounted for separately and either used for the designated purpose or for related administrative expenses.

The Financial Accounting Standards Board (FASB)'s SFAS 116 covers reporting of contributions, and SFAS 117 requires financial reporting more or less on the same terms as a for-profit business organization.

Managers of a not-for-profit are subject to the business judgment rule, including their investment decisions. The Uniform Management of Institutional Funds Act authorizes significant discretion, subject to the standard of acting like an ordinary prudent person. Day-to-day operations can be delegated to officers and staff, and financial decisions can be delegated to expert advisers. Not-for-profit managers are entitled to rely on information received from advisers, officers, employees, or specialized committees of the organization, as long as the advisers are chosen with due care; their performance is monitored; and reliance occurs in good faith.

Not-for-profit managers can be sued on behalf of the organization by the state Attorney General; by the organization itself; or derivatively by a director, officer, or member for negligent or self-interested breaches of fiduciary duty. Not-for-profit managers owe an additional duty, to the public, over and above general fiduciary responsibility. A self-interested transaction could have the effect of terminating the organization's not-for-profit status, if it is deemed to constitute inurement for private advantage.

Not-for-profits can indemnify their directors and officers in the Certificate of Incorporation or bylaws, or by subsequent resolution or agreement. State law often provides additional protection (such as a broader scope of indemnification for directors and officers who are volunteers rather than paid professionals). A common pattern is for a non-profit to pay its officers, but for its directors to receive expense reimbursement but no compensation.

[D] Federal Classification of Tax-Exempt Organizations

Code § 501 divides tax-exempt organizations into two main categories ("group entities" and "charitable entities") and many sub-categories.

Group entities, as defined by § 501(c)(4)–(8), (10), and (19), are:

- Civic leagues and organizations
- Labor, agricultural, and horticultural organizations
- Business leagues, chambers of commerce, real estate boards, and boards of trade
- Social clubs
- Fraternal organizations
- Veterans' organizations.

Group entities receive tax exemption by applying on IRS Form 1024 and paying a user fee with Form 8718. If the IRS approves the application, it issues a letter granting tax-exempt status. Once exempt, the organization must file Form 990 (the equivalent of a tax return) within 4½ months of the close of its tax year.

Charitable entities, as defined by § 501(c)(3), are organizations organized for charitable, educational, religious, scientific, literary, or cultural purposes, or for the prevention of cruelty to children or animals. The application for exemption is made on Form 1023, with the user fee paid with Form 8718, and a Form 990 information return must be filed each year. (Private foundations file Form 990 PF.)

Section 501 provides that paying reasonable compensation does not constitute forbidden private inurement, and fund-raisers can be paid a reasonable percentage of the funds they raise.

Limitations are imposed on the political activities of charities, and excessive lobbying or political activity can result in loss of exemption. See §§ 501(h) and 527.

One of the subtitles of the Pension Protection Act (PPA; P.L. 109-280) is called "Reforming Exempt Organizations," and this 2006 legislation deals with, for example, whether charitable split dollar arrangements are compatible with tax-exempt missions. The PPA doubles the taxes that would otherwise be due if a charity fails to distribute its income, maintains excess business holdings, or continues to hold investments that jeopardize the charitable purpose. Organizations that fail to provide the required notices of excess income can lose their exempt status.

In mid-2007, the IRS proposed an overhaul of Form 990 to make it easier for both the IRS and the public to obtain information about the salaries of charities' top managers, and the percentage of revenue used for fundraising. This was the first major redesign in 25 years. The IRS' goal was to finalize the form for use in 2008 reporting. Although the number of schedules for the Form 990 would rise from three to 15, most organizations would only be obligated to complete a few schedules. However, see IR-2007-129 (7/12/07) for the new annual e-filing requirement, using the "electronic postcard" Form 990-N. Certain small non-profits must use this online-only form for annual reporting, even though they are not required for file Form 990 or Form 990-EZ. Temporary Regulations at 72 FR 64147 (11/15/07) point out that the Pension Protection Act requires revocation of tax-exempt status is a non-profit fails to file a required form for three consecutive years.[24]

[E] Private Foundations and Public Charities

If an exempt organization is a "private foundation" (usually created by a wealthy family to make grants to public charities) rather than a "public charity," it will be subject to additional financial and disclosure regulation.

---

[24] Stephanie Strom, *I.R.S. Seeks More Charity Transparency*, N.Y. Times 6/15/07 at A21; the draft form is available at http://www.irs.gov/charities/article/0,,id=171216.00 html. IR-2007-129 is available at http://www.irs.gov/newsroom/article/0,,id=172440,00.html (7/12/07).

Under § 509(a), a tax-exempt organization is presumed to be a private foundation unless it proves that it is actually a public charity. A public charity can be one which gets its support from the general public (not a single family); serves public functions such as education or health care; is a "supporting organization" for a particular public charity; or gets at least one third of its support from grants, user fees, sales, and charitable activities, and less than one third of its support from investments or UBTI.

The Pension Protection Act (P.L. 109-280) has extensive provisions about "donor-advised funds," a type of tax-exempt organization that is owned and controlled by a private foundation sponsoring organization and is identified by reference to the contributions of one or more donors who maintain the power of advising the fund about investments or distributions. (There are exemptions for, e.g., funds that make distributions only to a single organization, or that use a committee to make travel, study, or similar grants.) The legislation mandates that the Treasury study donor-advised funds and supporting organizations and report on whether contributions to these organizations should remain tax-deductible. A 20% penalty tax is imposed on donor-advised funds' taxable distributions (i.e., distributions not subject to expenditure responsibility of the sponsoring organization). The PPA also covers the tax return obligations of sponsoring organizations, penalties for excess benefit transactions and excess business holdings.[25]

[F] Deductibility of Contributions

Many organizations are tax-exempt, in the sense that they are not liable for income tax, but their donors are not entitled to a tax deduction for contributions. Contributions to a public charity are generally deductible, although a limit is imposed on the income tax (but not estate tax) deductibility of very large charitable contributions.

Section 6115 requires that charities disclose the extent to which contributions over $75, for which the donor receives something (e.g., the right to attend a benefit; concert tickets), are deductible. All contributions over $250 must be documented.

The Pension Protection Act (PPA, P.L. 109-280) contains several provisions tightening up the rules for charitable deductions. Section 1217 requires donees to give a written statement giving the organization's name and the date and amount of the donation, for the donor to be able to deduct a contribution of money. Section 1215 requires donors to recapture and include in income their donations of tangible property, where the donee organization used the property for purposes unrelated to its exempt function, or if the donee disposes of the property within three years without certifying that the original intended use has ceased to be practical.

---

[25] *See, e.g.*, PPA §§ 1221–1242.

Chapter 2

Commercial Transactions Under the UCC

§ 2.01   INTRODUCTION

Although "Uniform" is something of a misnomer, because of state-to-state differences in text, the Uniform Commercial Code (UCC) is designed to provide uniform rules for transactions, especially transactions between "merchants" (i.e., professional sellers of goods or services).

In its present form, the UCC includes:

- Article 1: general principles and definitions
- Article 2: sales of goods
- Article 2A: leasing
- Article 3: commercial paper
- Article 4: bank deposits and collections
- Article 4A: funds transfers
- Article 5: letters of credit
- Article 6: bulk sales
- Article 7: documents of title
- Article 8: ownership and transfer of securities
- Article 9: secured transactions.

The law of commercial transactions cannot be considered in the abstract. Many questions of transactional law will involve contract law: see Chapter 9. Business torts may be alleged (§ 18.08[D]). Products liability questions (§ 18.10) may arise.

In 2002, many changes were made in Articles 3, 4, and 4A, especially to adapt to electronic transactions and electronic signatures. Various provisions (e.g., §§ 3-106, 3-312, 4-212) now call for "record providing notice" rather than "written notice," taking into account the possibility of electronic records and signatures. (See § 2.13 for discussion of UETA and eSIGN.)

§ 2.02 SALES OF GOODS

A sale means that the title to goods passes from the seller to the buyer, in exchange for a price. The conceptual and legal problems of an immediate sale, for cash, of goods to a purchaser who takes the goods away then and there are fairly minimal (although if the purchaser is a consumer, there may be warranty and products liability problems to worry about). But this pattern is not very common in "merchant" transactions (i.e., those involving two businesses, not a retailer and a consumer). Both parties tend to have a great deal of paperwork: requests for quotes, bid forms, order forms, contracts of sale, invoices, and the like.

Commercial law has done a fairly good job of sorting out the complexities of paper-based documents exchanged between merchants, especially the "battle of the forms" (§ 2.02[D][1]) where each side signs a form purporting to contain the terms of the deal, but the two are inconsistent. An entirely new series of issues is emerging, as "e-commerce" (commerce transacted electronically, especially over the Internet) becomes more common. Now, it is often necessary to decide what a "signature" is in the electronic world; how to determine if parties are who they purport to be; and to make new rules for electronic payments.

The law of sales has to deal with many problems involving risk: who takes the risk if goods are not delivered, are stolen or destroyed, or are damaged in shipping? What happens if the seller's position is that the goods conform to the order, while the buyer alleges defect or non-conformity?

On or off the Internet, the complexities of commercial law multiply as more parties get involved: there may be suppliers involved at various parts of the supply chain; shippers of goods; and, because few merchant transactions are cash-only, various lenders may be involved. Even in a cash transaction, the goods may serve as collateral for loans obtained by the buyer and/or seller.

[A] Credit Sales

Under the UCC, any agreement for delay in payment (even if no interest is charged) makes the deal a credit transaction.

A retail installment sales contract (which is typically subject to state Retail Installment Sales Acts, or RISAs, and/or the UCC and the Uniform Consumer Credit Code, or UCCC) involves a down payment plus deferred payments. These payments constitute the cash price which, in conjunction with the finance charge, adds up to the total price. "Commercial paper" means the loan agreements, security agreements, and financing statements generated by retail installment sales. Some dealers (e.g., car and furniture dealers) have their own charge account plans or act as intermediaries to match up buyers with banks that want to make loans that will enable the consumers to buy big-ticket items.

The transaction often becomes an indirect loan, because the seller assigns the retail installment sales agreement to its bank or finance company as security for the money it has borrowed from the bank. Or, the bank or a third party might "discount" the commercial paper: that is, the dealer assigns the sales contracts to the buyer, who pays less than their full face value because of the delay in collection and the risk that not all buyers will pay in full. The bank can aggregate chattel paper from many transactions and use it as security for bonds. If the ultimate obligor is a consumer, the holder of the chattel paper will probably be subject to the same claims and defenses as the seller.

[B] Sales on Open Account

Sales on open account involve only two parties, both merchants: a buyer and a seller. The buyer issues a purchase order for the goods. The seller investigates the buyer's credit-worthiness (usually by getting a credit report) and, if the result is satisfactory, the seller will send the goods and an invoice. Payment is usually due at the end of that month, or 30 or 60 days after the invoice date or the end of the month in which the invoice was issued. It is common for sellers to offer a discount (e.g., 2% for payment within 10 days) for prompt payment.

The invoice letter of credit is a slightly more elaborate, three-party variation used when the seller requires additional proof of the buyer's credit status. The buyer arranges a line of credit, gives security to its own bank, or arranges for guarantees by credit-worthy individuals or businesses. Given these assurances, the buyer's bank is able to issue a standby letter of credit in favor of the seller. Therefore, when the buyer has issued an order and goods have been shipped, the seller will bill the buyer directly. If the buyer fails to pay, the buyer's bank is willing to pay the seller under the standby letter of credit, because the buyer will either pay the bank or the bank can use the collateral or guarantees.

[C] Auctions

An auction is a particular kind of sale, where the price of goods is determined by competitive bidding instead of being set in advance. The UCC provision governing auctions is § 2-328. A reserve is a minimum price that the buyer must pay; if no bidder offers the reserve or a higher price, the item is withdrawn from the auction. Unless stated to the contrary, all auctions are conducted subject to a reserve, so the owner of the item can terminate the auction even after bidding begins, or can "bid in" (buy the item itself). However, if the original owner manipulates the bidding, § 2-328(4) gives the buyer a choice between avoiding the sale and buying the item at the last legitimate bid.

In an auction with a reserve, the bids are offers, and acceptance occurs when the hammer falls. Until the hammer falls, any bid or offer can be revoked. Every higher bid operates as a rejection of the prior bid.

In an auction without a reserve, articles or lots cannot be withdrawn once the auctioneer calls for bids, unless no bid at all is received within a reasonable time: § 2-328(3).

[D] Formation of a Contract

UCC § 2-201 holds that contracts for the sale of goods costing $500 or more are enforceable only if they are in writing (the "Statute of Frauds" requirement). However, the contract can be enforced even if material terms are omitted, imprecisely stated, or incorrectly stated as long as the parties sign the contract and specify the quantity of goods involved. The price, time, place of payment or delivery, or even particular warranties can be left out. But if the quantity of goods is incorrectly stated, then the contract is only enforceable up to the quantity stated in the contract. Once there has been partial performance of the contract, the part already performed is not subject to the Statute of Frauds.

Also see § 1-206. A contract for the sale of personal property (rather than goods, securities, or property covered by a security agreement) can only be enforced by lawsuit (or a defense asserted) up to $5,000 unless there is a written contract of sale, signed by the party against whom enforcement is sought, giving the price of the property.

Section 2-201(2) says that an oral contract between two merchants is binding as long as a written confirmation is given after the oral agreement is reached — and if the party who receives the written confirmation lets 10 days elapse after receiving the confirmation without objecting to its contents. Furthermore, an oral agreement can be binding with respect to specially manufactured goods that cannot be re-sold in the normal course of the seller's business, as long as the seller made a substantial beginning on the manufacture or committed to buy the supplies needed to manufacture the special goods: § 2-201(3)(a).

The "parol evidence" rule applies under UCC § 2-202: the written terms cannot be contradicted by evidence of earlier agreements or contemporary oral communications. But a written contract can be explained or supplemented (as distinct from contradicted) by evidence of additional terms consistent with the contract, or by the usual course of dealing or usage of the relevant trade.

When a merchant makes a firm offer to buy or sell goods via a signed agreement, but provides no date for either purchase or sale, UCC § 2-205 requires that the offer remain open for a "reasonable" time, not to exceed three months. Offers made by merchants can be accepted by other merchants in any medium and manner reasonable under the circumstances: § 2-206. It is no longer required that the acceptance be made in the same medium as the offer.

The "battle of the forms" arises when an offer is made on the offeror's form, and the offeree uses its own form to accept, possibly adding terms or changing the terms of the offer. Under Article 2, a contract is accepted when the recipient accepts it or makes a written confirmation, even if the acceptance includes additional or different terms from the offer (unless the acceptance is conditional on explicit approval of the new terms). If both of the contracting parties are merchants, additional terms are treated as proposed additions to the contract, which become part of the contract unless:

- The addition is a material alteration
- The offer expressly says that additional terms are forbidden, or
- The offeror objects to the additional terms within a reasonable time (§ 2-207).

These UCC provisions for the "battle of the forms" change pre-UCC laws, which basically required offers either to be rejected, or accepted on their original terms. Current law is based on revisions submitted by the American Law Institute to the NCCUSL in 1999.

Revised § 2-204(b) allows a prompt, definite indication of acceptance to become effective, even if it includes additional or different terms. However, revised § 2-203(d) says that if the offer is expressly and conspicuously limited to the proposed terms, there will be no contract if the offeree attempts to modify the terms — unless the parties agree on the modified terms, or their actions show that they both believe a contract has been formed.

The revised version of § 2-207(b) governs the terms of a contract that has been formed by a § 2-204(b) acceptance. The contract includes all the terms that appear in the documentation of both parties, plus nonstandard terms that both parties agree to (even if they are not recorded), plus standard terms supplied by the one party and assented to by the other, plus "gap-filler" terms and other terms supplied by the UCC.

The revised provision does not distinguish between terms suggested by the offeror and those counter-suggested by the offeree. Nor does it matter whether the parties are consumers or merchants.

[E] Checklist for Drafting a Contract of Sale

Issues to be covered in the contract include:

- ❑ Parties
- ❑ Date
- ❑ Seller's agreement to deliver goods; buyer's agreement to pay
- ❑ Indication of how the offer is to be accepted
- ❑ Description of the goods
- ❑ Quantity of goods (including output terms, reflecting the seller's entire production, and requirements terms, reflecting the buyer's entire needs)
- ❑ Price or mechanism for setting the price
- ❑ Payment terms
- ❑ How, when, and where delivery will be made
- ❑ Buyer's right to inspect the goods

❑ Express warranties; disclaimers
❑ Remedies for breach
❑ Modification and cancellation of contract
❑ Assignability[1]
❑ Renewal terms
❑ Exclusive dealing; scope of territory
❑ Liquidated damages clauses

[F] Warranties

The UCC has extensive warranty provisions. A warranty is a statement that goods conform to certain properties: for instance, that they conform to a sample item or to a particular description (§§ 2-313, -317).[2]

Additional statements of fact (not expressions of opinion) or promises made by the seller about the goods become express warranties binding on the seller (§ 2-313). In addition to express warranties stated by a seller, there may be implied warranties that arise out of the relationship between seller and buyer. If representations made during a sale constitute an express warranty, any inconsistency between the express warranty and a written disclaimer are resolved in favor of the express warranty.[3]

Sellers warrant that they are conveying good title, free of security interests or liens that the buyer does not know about: § 2-312. Sellers who are merchants of the particular type of goods being sold warrant that their goods are "merchantable" (§ 2-314), i.e., suitable for ordinary purposes; of fair average quality; fitting the trade's definition of similar goods; adequately packaged and labeled; and in conformity with any representations made on the label.

When the buyer relies on the seller's expertise, and the seller knows the purpose for which the buyer wants the goods, then the seller warrants not only that the goods are merchantable in general, but that they are fit for the buyer's intended use (§ 2-315).

Items can be sold "as is," free of warranties. (But see below for implied warranties that cannot be disclaimed in consumer transactions.) A buyer who is permitted to inspect the goods but chooses not to do so will not be entitled to any warranty as to defects that could have been detected by inspection (§ 2-316). Contracts can be drafted to limit remedies for breach of warranty.

---

[1] Under UCC § 2-210(1), unless the agreement is to the contrary, either party can delegate its duties, unless the other party has a substantial interest in performance by the original party. § 2-210(2) says that (unless the parties agree to the contrary) rights in a contract for the sale of goods can be assigned unless the non-assigning party's duties change materially, its risks increase materially, or its chance of getting return performance diminishes materially. Even if the contract limits assignability, rights that are no longer executory (such as the right to receive payment; damages for breach) can still be assigned.

[2] Warranting the performance of goods for five years is a warranty of future performance, so the cause of action did not accrue when the goods were delivered, but when the breach was or should have been discovered: Wyandanch Volunteer Fire Co. Inc. v. Radon Constr. Corp., 19 A.D.3d 590 (2d Dept. 2005), *mod. on other grounds* 29 A.D.3d 685 (2d Dept. 2006).

[3] Liimatta v. V&H Truck Inc., 2005 WL 2105497 (D. Minn. 8/30/05).

Section 2-317 says that, if possible, all express and implied warranties will be construed together and operate cumulatively. If this is not reasonable, the parties' intention governs, interpreted according to the principle that express warranties prevail over inconsistent implied warranties (other than the warranty of fitness); exact or technical specifications prevail over samples, models, or general descriptions; and samples prevail over general descriptions of the merchandise.

[1] Consumer Warranties

UCC § 2-318 deals with warranties in the case where a product causes personal injury or property damage. States can choose among three versions of this section. One of them extends the warranty to anyone in the buyer's family, household, or guests who are physically harmed. Another one covers personal injuries to any reasonably foreseeable user of items purchased by an individual. The third alternative also extends the warranty to cover property damage.

The Ninth Circuit dismissed all claims in a class action alleging breach of warranty and fraud in connection with defective head gaskets in Dodge Neon cars. The express warranty claim was dismissed because the gasket did not fail until after expiration of the express warranty, and the implied warranty claim failed for lack of privity between the plaintiff and DaimlerChrysler. The statute of limitations had run on state fraud claims before the case was initiated, and Magnuson-Moss claims stand or fall with the accompanying warranty claims.[4]

If the buyer is a consumer rather than a merchant, federal law requires additional warranty coverage. (See § 7.06 for a discussion of the Magnuson-Moss Act, and § 18.10[B] for warranty implications in products liability litigation.)

[G] Gap Filler Terms

Under the UCC, there are many circumstances in which a seemingly incomplete document becomes a valid and enforceable contract, because the UCC provides methods for "filling the gaps."

[1] Price Terms

If the contract does not specify a price, UCC § 2-305(1) sets the price as a reasonable price at the time of delivery. The methods for setting price in commercial transactions include:

- Cost plus (e.g., overhead and profit)
- Market price: the selling price on an organized exchange
- Price in a trade journal

---

[4] Clemens v. DaimlerChrysler Corp., 530 F.3d 852 (9th Cir. 2008). *See also* Daugherty v. American Honda Motor Co., 144 Cal. App. 4th (2006) [express warranty does not cover repairs made after the specified time/mileage period has elapsed]; Anunziato v. eMachines, Inc., 402 F. Supp. 2d 1133 (C.D. Cal. 2005) states the California requirement of vertical contractual privity with the defendant for breach of warranty claims.

- Price by leading suppliers
- Price as set by an expert appraiser
- Price to be agreed on later; if the parties fail to agree, § 2-305 requires a reasonable price unless the agreement indicates that the parties intended the contract to fail if they do not reach an agreement
- Price set by seller or buyer; § 2-305(2) imposes a requirement of good faith
- Escalator clauses: regular adjustments (usually increases) to reflect a standard price index (e.g., Consumer Price Index or Wholesale Price Index promulgated by a government agency or other trusted source).

Under § 2-305(4), if the parties do not intend to be bound unless the open price term is supplied, then there is no contract if it is not supplied. In that situation, the buyer must return the goods, or pay the reasonable value of the goods if return is impossible, and the seller has to return any proceeds received. A breach of the 2-305 requirement that a party that can set open price terms unilaterally must do so in good faith can constitute 2-714 nonconformity. In this case, franchisees alleging abusive gasoline prices lost, because they failed to give proper notice of the alleged breached.[5]

[2] Quantity Terms

A contract can provide for the sale of a seller's entire output, or a buyer's entire requirement; good faith must be exercised in specifying the size of output or requirement (§ 2-306(1)). In a § 2-306 "exclusive dealings" contract, under which a retailer agrees not to carry competing merchandise, the seller must use its best efforts to supply the quantity that the buyer needs, and the buyer must use its best efforts to sell the merchandise.

[3] Delivery Terms

If the contract does not specify a place of delivery, § 2-208 sets the place of delivery as the location of the goods where they were identified to the agreement (i.e., allocated to the particular buyer). If the goods are not identified to the agreement when the contract is made, then delivery will be made from the seller's place of business (or home, if he has no place of business) unless otherwise agreed.

Standard commercial abbreviations are often used for delivery terms. The UCC includes these definitions (see, especially, § 2-319). FOB stands for Free on Board; FAS stands for Free Along Side (i.e., of a ship or other vessel):

- FOB (Place of Shipment): Unless otherwise agreed, the seller is responsible for shipping the goods and paying for putting the goods in the hands of the shipper. The seller has to notify the buyer of the shipment and deliver

---

[5] Dixie Gas & Food v. Shell Oil Co., 2005 WL 1273273 (N.D. Ill. 5/25/05).

the documents of title that will permit the buyer to obtain possession. The buyer has a duty to give the seller proper shipping instructions.

- FOB (Place of Destination): Unless otherwise agreed, the seller has the obligation of paying to transport the goods to the place of destination. The seller is obligated to give the buyer reasonable notification so it can take delivery. The seller must tender delivery at a reasonable time, and keep the goods available for a reasonable time to permit the buyer to take possession.
- FOB (Car or Other Vehicle): In addition to putting the goods in the carrier's possession, the seller has an additional obligation to load them on board the carrier's vehicle.
- FOB (Vessel): The seller must place the goods on board the vessel designated by the buyer. If necessary, the seller must furnish a proper form bill of lading.
- FAS (Vessel): The seller is responsible for delivery (and the cost of delivery) of the goods alongside the vessel designated by the buyer (or on the dock designated in the usual manner for that port). The seller has an obligation to get a receipt, in exchange for which the carrier is obligated to issue a bill of lading.
- CIF (§ 2-320): The price of the goods includes the cost of the goods plus insurance and freight to the designated destination. The seller is obligated to load the goods, get a receipt showing that freight has been paid or provided for, get a negotiable bill of lading, insure the goods for the buyer's account, and forward all necessary documents to the buyer promptly. If delivery is to be made to the buyer, the buyer has to furnish facilities reasonably suited for accepting the delivery. If the agreement calls for delivery to the buyer without moving goods that are in a warehouse or otherwise in the possession of a bailee, the seller has to provide a negotiable document of title or get the bailee to acknowledge the buyer's right to possession of the goods.
- C&F or CF: These terms are equivalent to CIF, except that the price includes only the goods themselves plus freight to the named destination. Insurance is not included.

If the agreement does not give a time for delivery, § 2-309 uses the standard of commercial reasonableness to require delivery within a reasonable time. A contract of indefinite duration covering successive performances can be terminated at any time by either party on reasonable notice.

Unless the agreement is to the contrary, § 2-307 provides that all goods will be shipped in a single delivery, with payment due when the goods are tendered to the buyer. If the agreement or circumstances dictate delivery in lots, the seller can apportion the price and demand payment for each lot as it is delivered. Generally, payment is due under § 2-310(a) at the time and place where the buyer is to receive the goods.

Late delivery can be excused if it is due to a contingency whose nonoccurrence was a basic assumption underlying the contract. Good-faith compliance with applicable government regulations also excuses late delivery: § 2-615.

Delivery delays are excused under §§ 2-311 and 2-610(a) if performance is suspended because of the buyer's repudiation or the buyer's failure to cooperate as required by the agreement.

When one party is given the right to specify the terms of performance, § 2-311, Official Comment (1) says that commercially reasonable specifications made in good faith will be upheld. Agreements that say the buyer will receive an assortment of goods will be interpreted to permit the buyer to determine the assortment, unless the agreement is to the contrary.

[H] Buyer's Rights

If the buyer has the right to return goods purchased for personal use, the contract is considered a sale on approval. But if the buyer is acquiring goods for resale, the contract is a sale or return (§ 2-326(1)). The difference is that in a sale on approval, the seller has the obligation of return and the risk of loss. In a sale or return, the obligation of return is on the buyer unless otherwise agreed: § 2-327. A "consignment" or "on memorandum" sale is considered a sale or return.

A manufacturer of t-shirts showing monkeys drinking hot sauce, with the caption "Smile Now, Cry Later" was sued in Hawaii for trademark infringement by the holder of the Smile Now, Cry Later registered trademark. A preliminary injunction was denied on the grounds that there was no likelihood of confusion. At that point, the parties settled. A purchaser of the shirts then sued in California for breach of the § 2-312(3) statutory warranty that the t-shirts were free of "the rightful claim of any third person by way of infringement or the like." The trial court granted summary judgment for the manufacturer, treating the claims of infringement as not "rightful" because the court found that there was no likelihood of confusion. The California Court of Appeals, noting decisions in other states, found that a "rightful" claim merely has to be nonfrivolous; it does not have to be meritorious. The Court of Appeals held that extending the warranty to all claims of infringement that could affect the buyer's ability to use the goods is beneficial, because it provides certainty to the parties to a commercial transaction.[6]

[1] Inspection

The buyer has the right to inspect the goods that are being purchased, when tender of delivery has been made or the goods have been identified to the agreement (§ 2-513). If payment is required before inspection, then nonconformity of goods does not excuse the buyer unless the nonconformity is so obvious that it can be determined without inspection (§ 2-512). An agreement to pay against documents may waive the buyer's right to inspection, as does a C.O.D. delivery term (§ 2-513(3)).

The right of inspection extends to inspection by any reasonable manner, including reasonable testing of the goods. Unreasonable testing (using up an

---

[6] Pacific Sunwear of California, Inc. v. Olaes Enterprises, Inc., 167 Cal. App. 4th 466 (Cal. App. 2008).

extraordinary quantity of goods in testing; performing unnecessary tests) may be construed as an acceptance. The buyer is responsible for costs of inspection and testing, but if the goods are rejected because they have been found not to conform to the agreement, § 2-513(2) allows the buyer to recover the reasonable cost of inspection and testing from the seller.

[2] Rejection

Section 2-602 makes it easier to reject goods than to revoke acceptance. The nonconforming goods must be rejected within a reasonable time. The seller must be notified of rejection. The buyer cannot exercise any ownership rights over rejected goods. A buyer who has physical possession but no security interest in the goods has a duty of reasonable care to hold the goods long enough for the seller to remove them.

The definition of "acceptance" under § 2-606 is that the buyer does not reject the goods, after a reasonable opportunity to inspect them; tells the seller that the goods are conforming or will accept them notwithstanding nonconformity; or acts in a manner inconsistent with the seller's ownership of the goods.[7]

The buyer has the right to reject nonconforming goods: see §§ 2-508(1) and 2-601. If the seller tenders delivery or delivers the goods before the contract deadline, and the buyer rejects the goods as nonconforming, the seller can always cure by giving the buyer timely notice and making a conforming delivery within the deadline. The right to cure exists even if the contract says it does not.

The "perfect tender" rule of § 2-601 covers situations in which the goods or tender of delivery fail to conform to the contract in any way (not necessarily a serious, harmful, or material way). The buyer can either accept all the goods; reject all the goods; or accept any number of commercial units (e.g., crates or cartons) and reject the rest. The perfect tender rule does not apply to installment contracts, and is modified by the seller's right to cure.

After goods have been accepted, § 2-608 allows revocation of acceptance within a reasonable time of the discovery of nonconformity. However, the nonconformity must substantially impair the value. Revocation is permitted if the nonconformity was hard to detect before acceptance; the buyer relied on the seller's assurances; or the buyer reasonably believed the nonconformity would be cured, but it was not.

[I] Seller's Rights

Unless the contract says otherwise, the buyer's tender of payment is a condition to the seller's duty to tender and complete delivery (§ 2-511(1)). The buyer's check is a conditional payment, which is defeated if the check bounces (§ 2-511(3)). If this occurs, the seller has a right to recover the goods, unless the buyer has transferred

---

[7] In an installment contract, which requires or permits delivery of separate lots, each lot can be separately accepted: § 2-612.

them to a good-faith purchaser. The seller can also sue for the price of the goods based either on the dishonored check or on the underlying agreement.

The seller has the right to re-sell goods that were wrongfully rejected by the buyer (§§ 2-703(d), -706). The seller is also allowed by § 2-703 to withhold delivery, cancel the contract, and sue for the price of the goods or damages for their non-acceptance.

[J] Passage of Title

Before the UCC, title to goods was the crucial determinant of issues of risk and control; the UCC separates questions of risk (see below) from title, but it is still often important to identify when title has passed from seller to buyer. Note that, under § 2-401(4), title revests in the seller by operation of law if the buyer refuses to accept the goods, or withdraws acceptance.

In general, § 2-401 provides that title passes to the buyer once the seller has completed its performance by delivering the goods. So if the contract calls for delivery FOB cars at the seller's warehouse, title passes as soon as the goods are placed on the cars at the seller's warehouse. If the agreement calls for the seller to send the goods to the buyer, but does not require delivery at the place of destination, title passes to the buyer at the time and place of shipment. If the seller is obligated to deliver the goods to the buyer at the place of destination, title passes to the buyer on delivery.

Title passes at the time and place of delivery of the title document, if delivery is to be made without moving the goods and the seller is required to deliver a document of title (e.g., warehouse receipt). For delivery without moving goods that have already been identified to the agreement and where no document of title is required, title passes to the buyer as soon as the agreement is made.

[K] Risk of Loss

If possible, the intention of the parties concerning risk of loss will be respected. Also note that if trade custom or usage requires owners to insure work in progress against fire loss, the owner bears the risk of loss unless the agreement is to the contrary. The UCC's general risk rule is that the party best able to bear the loss, or the party who should be expected to bear it, will be at risk for the loss.

Several UCC sections provide risk rules for situations in which the contract does not specify:

- If the seller is required to deliver the goods to the carrier, risk of loss shifts to the buyer as soon as the seller delivers the goods to the carrier (§ 2-509).
- For goods sold FOB place of shipment, the buyer is at risk of loss as soon as the goods are placed in the hands of the shipper; if sold FOB destination, risk of loss shifts to the buyer at the time and place of delivery or the time and place of tender of delivery to the buyer (§ 2-319).

- § 2-509 provides that, if the seller is obligated to deliver goods to the destination, the risk of loss shifts to the buyer when delivery is tendered to the buyer, who is then able to take possession. The same section provides that, when a merchant seller agrees to deliver goods at the seller's place of business or the present location of the goods, the buyer has risk of loss upon receipt of the goods. But if a nonmerchant seller is required to deliver goods to the seller's place of business or the present location of the goods, and the buyer is not a merchant, the buyer does not have risk of loss until tender of delivery.
- For conditional sales, § 2-327 provides that goods sold for resale (on sale or return) place the risk of loss during the return on the buyer. But for a sale on approval (goods sold primarily for use of the purchaser), the buyer has the risk of loss as soon as the goods are accepted. The seller is at risk of loss during return of nonaccepted goods.
- For nonconforming goods, the risk of loss remains on the seller until the buyer accepts the goods despite their nonconformity, or until the nonconformity is cured: § 2-510.
- § 2-510 also provides that if the buyer justifiably revokes acceptance, the buyer can treat the risk of loss as having been with the seller to the extent of any deficiency in the seller's insurance coverage.
- If, instead, the buyer repudiates the agreement while title to the goods still rests with the seller, the seller can treat the risk of loss as having rested on the buyer for a commercially reasonable time. If the seller's effective insurance coverage is defective, however, the insurance "gap" limits the buyer's liability.
- The risk of loss is generally on the seller if goods identified to the agreement are destroyed, by no fault of the buyer or seller, before risk has shifted to the buyer. But if the goods are totally destroyed, the seller has the right to avoid the agreement. See UCC § 2-613. If the destruction is only partial, the buyer has a choice between letting the seller avoid the agreement, and taking the goods at a correspondingly reduced price.
- If the loss was caused by a third party and occurred before the goods were identified to the agreement, § 2-722 lets the seller sue the third party. The same section provides that both buyer and seller can sue a third party who is responsible for loss of goods identified to the contract. Any damages recovered go to whomever had the risk of loss at the time it occurred.

Section 2-501 gives the buyer an insurable interest in goods identified to the contract even if they are nonconforming, and even if the buyer has to option to return or reject them. The seller's insurable interest continues as long as it has title or a security interest in the goods.

[L] Excuse of Performance

UCC §§ 2-613, -615, -616, and -718 give rules for circumstances under which the seller will be excused from performance under the agreement. This occurs, e.g., when goods identified to the contract that are destroyed before the risk of loss shifts to the buyer, as long as neither party was at fault in the destruction. If there is a total loss, the contract is avoided, and the buyer can get back any down-payment it has made. (In this situation, the seller should have maintained insurance that would compensate.) As noted above, partial destruction or deterioration of the goods gives the buyer a choice between a voided contract or goods accepted at a reduced price.

If performance is rendered commercially impracticable because of a contingency that the buyer and seller relied on not occurring, the seller is excused by § 2-615. This is also true if foreign or domestic government regulations prevent performance. If only part of the seller's productive capacity is affected, the UCC requires the seller to allocate the remaining productive capacity among buyers, and to notify each customer of its share of the limited capacity.

The notice triggers the buyer's right to terminate the agreement or accept the allocation of merchandise offered by the seller (if the shortage substantially impairs the value of the contract). Sellers can allocate part of the limited production to regular customers, even if the regular customers do not have explicit contracts.

There is no statutory definition of unconscionability, but § 2-302(1) permits a court to decide, as a matter of law, whether an entire contract or any part of it is unconscionable. The court can deny enforcement to the entire contract, strike out the unconscionable portions, or limit application of a clause to prevent an unconscionable result.

[M] Article 2 Remedies

The general objective of UCC remedies is to put the aggrieved party in the same position as if the breaching party had performed (§ 1-106(1)).

Liquidated damages clauses are enforceable only on the basis of the anticipated or actual harm from the breach; the difficulty of proving loss; and impracticality of other remedies (§ 2-718(1)). A clause that sets the liquidated damages too low is unconscionable under § 2-302, but one that imposes excessively heavy damages is also void, as a penalty, under § 2-718(1).

[1] Sellers' Remedies

The seller's damages for wrongful rejection, repudiation of the contract or revocation of acceptance equal the difference between the market price at the time and place for tender and the unpaid contract price plus incidental damages, reduced by any expenses saved because of the buyer's breach (§ 2-708). An alternative measure of damages is what the seller would have received from performance: the profits, including reasonable overhead, to be expected from the deal, plus incidental damages and costs incurred because of the breach, reduced by the proceeds of resale.

The seller can recover incidental damages but not consequential ones (§ 2-710). Incidental damages are direct results of the buyer's breach, such as the cost of stopping delivery, holding the goods after the breach, resale expenses, but not attorneys' fees.

Also see §§ 2-702, -705 (remedies if the buyer is insolvent). The seller can stop delivery of goods not yet received by the insolvent buyer. The seller can withhold the delivery of goods not yet shipped, and can demand payment in advance even though the contract calls for a credit sale. The seller can also give notice within 10 days of receipt to reclaim the goods. The 10-day limitation is not imposed when the buyer made false representations of solvency within three months of delivery.

[2] Buyers' Remedies

Naturally, Article 2 also provides remedies for buyers. If the seller fails to deliver or repudiates the contract, or if the buyer rightfully rejects the goods or revokes acceptance, then § 2-711(1) allows the buyer to cancel the contract and receive a refund of money paid to the seller, subject to the seller's right to cure, which extends until the time for performance has expired (§ 2-508). Furthermore, the buyer has a security interest in the goods to the extent of payments made and expenses of inspection, care, and transportation (§ 2-711(3)), so the buyer can hold and resell the goods to satisfy this interest.

"Cover" is the buyer's right under § 2-712 to purchase goods elsewhere while receiving damages for the goods affected. It is a form of mitigation of damages. Damages for nondelivery or repudiation by the seller are governed by § 2-713. To the extent the buyer has not covered, the damages equal the difference between the market and contract prices, plus incidental and consequential damages (note that sellers are not entitled to consequential damages), minus expenses saved as a result of the breach. In this context, incidental damages involve things done to the goods.

Consequential damages result from the known needs of the buyer that could not have been prevented (by cover or otherwise) and include personal injury and property damage proximately caused by the breach of warranty. Consequential damages can include lost profits, loss of goodwill, and interruption of production.

If the buyer fails to notify the seller that goods are nonconforming, § 2-607(3)(a) denies damages to the buyer. The remedy allowed by § 2-714 when the buyer does notify equals the value of the goods as warranted minus the value of the nonconforming goods, plus incidental and consequential damages in appropriate cases. The buyer may be able to obtain specific performance, under § 2-716(1), if the goods are unique or there are other justifying circumstances. Section 2-717 lets the buyer deduct damages for breach from any amount still due under the contract, but the buyer must notify the seller before doing so (Official Comment (2)).

§ 2.03 ARTICLE 2A: LEASES

UCC Article 2A covers leases (arrangements under which the owner receives regular payments in exchange for letting someone else use vehicles, equipment, or other property). Goods leased to consumers are also covered by Chapter 5 of the

Truth in Lending Act and the FTC's Regulation M, as long as the lease lasts four months or longer. Leased property worth over $25,000 is immune from these two requirements.

[A] Consumer Lease Disclosures

The required Article 2A disclosures for consumer leases include:

- Description of the leased property
- The amount to be paid when the lease is signed; status of the payment as refundable security deposit, advance lease payment, credit for trade-in allowance, etc.
- The number of lease payments to be made
- The amount and due date for each payment
- The total of all the scheduled lease payments
- Taxes and official fees for the full term of the lease
- Mandatory charges that are not part of the periodic payments (e.g., delivery, pick-up)
- Extent to which the lessee is required to maintain insurance coverage
- Any express warranties made by the manufacturer and lessor
- Who is responsible for maintenance and servicing of the property. Usually the lessee is responsible, and the lessor is permitted to impose a charge for excess wear and tear, as long as its standards are reasonable
- Any security interest that the lessor obtains in the property of the lessee
- Late payment and default charges
- Whether the lessee has an option to purchase the leased property; if so, when it can be exercised (e.g., only at the end of the lease term; throughout the lease term) and how much the lessee must pay or how the purchase price will be calculated
- Amount of (or method of calculating) charges for default or early termination of the lease; the lessor is forbidden to exact unreasonable charges
- Whether, at the end of the lease, the lessee is required to pay the difference between the estimated value of the property and its actual value.

Disclosures are also required in advertisements for consumer leases. The advertisement must disclose that the transaction is a lease; how large a downpayment is required; and the number and size of the lease payments. The lessee's responsibilities at the end of the lease term must also be disclosed.

§ 2.04 ARTICLE 2B

Legal rules that make sense for shipping a boxcar full of industrial chemicals do not help very much in drafting or interpreting contracts that deal with software or the licensing of information. For one thing, once Company A sells the chemicals to Company B, Company A is no longer able to sell the same chemicals to

Company C. Yet a programmer who develops a software program, or a publisher who creates a database or other electronic document, may be able to sell or license the same intangible to dozens, hundreds, or thousands of satisfied customers.

Proposed Article 2B was an attempt by the National Conference of Commissioners on Uniform State Laws to codify the law of software and information leasing.[8] The leading court case on the subject, *ProCD v. Zeidenberg*[9] holds that "shrink-wrap" licenses — printed license terms distributed with commercial software — are enforceable. "Click-wrap" licenses are their Web counterparts: access to some Web sites is limited to people who click "I agree" to a recitation of the site's terms of service. The issue is whether these licenses, which users have no opportunity to negotiate individually, should be enforced or rejected as contracts of adhesion.

The NCCUSL drafting committee decided in November 1998 to limit the scope of Article 2B to computer-related industries (software and database), specifically excluding entertainment and broadcast media, based on opposition from these industries.

[A] Uniform Computer Information Transactions Act

In April 1999, however, the NCCUSL and the American Law Institute announced that they had abandoned attempts to pass Article 2B. Instead, they would shift their attention to developing a uniform law, the Uniform Computer Information Transactions Act (UCITA), for consideration by the states in the fall of 1999.[10] NCCUSL gave its official approval to the UCITA on July 29, 1999.

UCITA covers licensing of information that is communicated electronically (e.g., software and databases), but is not a general licensing statute or a general intellectual property statute. (In fact, the draft has been criticized for creating inconsistent approaches to communications, depending on the medium in which they are made.)

UCITA gives statutory recognition to shrink-wrap and click-wrap (Internet) licenses. Consumer rights are promoted by explicit warranty rules and the right to a refund if the consumer does not find the terms of service for the software acceptable. However, the sellers of software would have the right to disable the software after a license is canceled. The UCITA allows licensors to impose controls on the usage of software; the FTC's position is that the UCITA does not require such controls to be disclosed conspicuously enough.

Only two states adopted UCITA (Maryland and Virginia), and in fact Iowa, West Virginia, and North Carolina actually passed statutes making

---

[8] Drafts of Article 2B are available at http://www.law.upenn.edu/library/ulc/ulc/htm. Also *see* various expert practitioners' comments at http://www.2BGuide.com.

[9] 86 F.3d 1447 (7th Cir. 1996).

[10] *See* 67 L.W. 2615 and 68 L.W. 2069; Brenda Sandburg, "UCC2B is Dead — Long Live UCITA," http://www.lawnewsnet.com/stories/A1807-1999May26.html; and Carlyle C. Ring, H. Lane Kneedler and Gail D. Jaspen, *Uniform Law for Computer Info Transactions is Offered*, National Law Journal 8/30/99 p. B7.

UCITA-governed contracts unenforceable in the state. In 2003, the NCCUSL ceased its legislative efforts to get additional legislative adoptions of the statute.[11]

§ 2.05 COMMERCIAL PAPER

Medieval and Renaissance merchants faced some formidable problems: not only shipping goods under very difficult conditions, but somehow getting paid when currencies were far from standardized, banking was primitive, and even bookkeeping was an exotic novelty. Some of the devices they created still influence the law of "commercial paper" — the devices used to transfer funds from one party to another.

Articles 3, 4, 5, and 7 deal with commercial paper: Article 3 with negotiable instruments, Article 4 with bank deposits and collections, Article 5 with letters of credit, and Article 7 with warehouse receipts.

[A] Bankers' Acceptances

A banker's acceptance is a "facility": a service offered by a commercial bank. It is a hybrid negotiable instrument, often used in import-export transactions. First, a drawer "utters" (i.e., creates) a draft. The drawee bank accepts the draft (indicates willingness to pay it). In this instance, the bank is really just an intermediary. It creates the acceptance, so the borrower gets credit. The bank generally re-sells the acceptance right away.

[B] Negotiable Instruments

There are many instances in commercial operation when it is more convenient to satisfy an obligation to other businesses by transferring obligations owed to one's own business. A negotiable instrument is a contract for the payment of money, involving transferable intangible rights in the instrument. An important feature of negotiable instruments is that, in some circumstances, a good faith transferee can actually have greater rights than the transferor.

There are three common types of negotiable instrument: the draft, the check, and the promissory note. Notes have gained prominence because of their role in consumer credit (e.g., car loans). In order to protect consumers, some limits are imposed on the negotiability of consumer notes, and the holder is subject to defenses that could be asserted against the seller (e.g., poor quality or dangerous nature of goods purchased with proceeds of the notes). Even commercial debtors may have causes of action. Since the 1980s, for instance, a "lender liability" cause of action has gained recognition, e.g., when a bank calls demand notes under unfair circumstances.

In order to understand negotiable instruments, it is necessary to understand that "money" is any medium that a seller or service provider is willing to accept,

---

[11] *See* 72 L.W. 2080.

and "payment" is any transfer of "money," usually but not always to pay for goods or services.

Bank deposits are actually debts that the bank owes to its depositors, because the depositors are lending their funds to the bank. When a bank pays a check, it transfers some of its debt from the drawer of the check to the payee. The drawer is the party writing the check; the drawee is the bank or other party expected to pay the check.

A negotiable instrument is an unconditional order or promise to pay a fixed amount of money, with or without interest: § 3-104. There are many kinds of negotiable instruments; and a negotiable instrument can be payable either on demand or at a specific time, and either to order (a specified payee) or to bearer (whoever has it).

Section 3-104 further defines a check as a draft that is payable on demand and drawn on a bank. (A money order is considered a check.) A cashier's check is a special check drawn on the payor's own bank; a teller's check is a special check issued by a bank itself (usually in exchange for a cash payment). A traveler's check requires a second signature by its drawer, as a condition of payment. A Certificate of Deposit is a bank's acknowledgment that money has been deposited and will be repaid to the depositor with interest. In effect, it is a note with the bank as maker.

An instrument is negotiated (i.e., transferred or made available for transfer) either by delivery (for bearer paper) or indorsement plus delivery (for order paper). Usually, the indorsement is made on the back of the instrument. Unless the instrument clearly indicates that it is made in some other capacity, any signature will be considered an indorsement (§ 3-402).

[C] Promissory Notes

A promissory note (e.g., an installment note or mortgage note) is a written promise to pay a certain sum, either on demand or at a specified future time. In a promissory note, the issuer promises to pay; in contrast, in a bill of exchange (a check or draft), the maker or drawer of the instrument orders a drawee (e.g., a bank) or acceptor to pay.

The note is conditional, and therefore not negotiable, if, for instance, it is expressly conditioned on the carrying out of an executory (future) promise; if the note is subject to or governed by another instrument; or if the note can be paid only from a particular fund. Section 3-109 explains what makes a note payable to order or bearer; § 3-110 gives rules for identifying the payee when this is not clear. There is no interest payable on an instrument unless the instrument calls for interest, which can be either fixed or variable (see § 3-112), and either antedated or post-dated instruments are permitted by § 3-113. Even an incomplete but signed instrument can be given effect (see § 3-115), but it has been "altered," and remedies are available under § 3-407, if words or numbers are added to an incomplete instrument without the maker's authority.

A negotiable instrument must contain the "words of negotiability": it must say that it is payable to order or bearer. Under § 3-109, a note payable to order is payable to the order of a named person; the assigns of a named person; or to his or her order.

An instrument is payable to bearer if it is payable to "cash"; if it says it is payable to "bearer"; or if no payee is indicated. An instrument is an order instrument, payable to an identified person, if it is payable, e.g., "to John Smith" or "to John Smith or order." Under § 3-401, a negotiable instrument (e.g., a promissory note) is binding only on someone who signs it. Thus, a joint tenant who signed a deed of trust to secure a loan, but did not sign the promissory note for the loan, was not liable on the note.[12]

A bearer instrument becomes an order instrument if the bearer indorses it to a specified person. An order instrument becomes a bearer instrument if the identified payee indorses it but does not name a specific payee. The indorsement rules appear at §§ 3-204–206.

A bearer instrument is payable to anyone who has it and wants to negotiate it. Therefore, if a bearer instrument is lost or stolen, and ends up in the hands of a bona fide purchaser for value, that purchaser is entitled to negotiate it.

[D] Checks

Both Articles 3 and 4 have to be considered, because a check is a negotiable instrument, but it is also an item which is deposited in a bank and which goes through the collection process.

The UCC permits orders to stop payment of a check that has been issued. Payment can be stopped (via an oral or written stop payment order) at any time before acceptance, certification, or actual payment. An oral order is good for only two weeks, while a written one is valid for six months (§ 4-403(b)). In practice, even 30-day-old checks are viewed with suspicion, so it is unlikely that a written order would have to be renewed. Payments made contrary to an effective stop order are improper. The bank is liable for damages suffered, although the customer has the burden of proving the amount of loss: § 4-403(c).

The effect of certification, as described in § 3-411, is to make the bank directly liable on the instrument once it is properly indorsed. The "obligated bank" has to compensate the person entitled to enforce the check, if the bank wrongfully refuses to pay a cashier's or certified check, or stops payment on its teller's check. Damages include expenses and loss of interest stemming from nonpayment. In fact, the obligated bank becomes liable for consequential damages if it still refuses to pay after being notified of circumstances mandating payment.

The drawer can no longer stop payment on the check, no matter who requested the certification. Even if the drawer's signature is forged, the certifying bank will be liable to a holder in due course, on the theory that it knows the drawer's signature and, by certifying, warrants its genuineness.

The states have "bad check laws," making it an offense to issue or negotiate a check that the drawer knows will bounce. Usually, the offense is a misdemeanor, although if the amount involved is large enough, it might be a felony. Intent to defraud is rebuttably presumed from the mere issuance of the check and its subsequent dishonor for lack of funds.

---

[12] Dobbins v. Cunningham, 618 S.E.2d 589 (W. Va. 2005).

UCC § 4-401(a) permits a bank to charge a customer whenever the customer writes a check that creates an overdraft but is otherwise properly payable. The customer remains liable, and the check is good. The bank usually imposes a service charge or treats it as a loan. (This rule does not apply if the customer did not sign the check and did not benefit from it.)

[E] Holders in Due Course

Negotiability is valuable because the owner of commercial paper can gain financial benefit without waiting until the due date of the paper, by exchanging it or selling it to someone else. The new owner of the paper is known as the "holder." The holder of a negotiable instrument takes it subject to all valid claims against it; all contract defenses; and various other defenses.

A holder who qualifies as a "holder in due course" is in a more favorable legal position, because he or she takes the instrument free of claims and defenses (e.g., assignment of a claim) that would be available against another holder. To be a holder in due course, § 3-302 provides that the holder must have:

- Taken an instrument that did not appear forged or altered; has no notice of alteration or unauthorized signature of an instrument that looks valid
- Taken the instrument for value
- Taken it in good faith
- Had no notice that it is overdue
- Had no notice of dishonor
- Been unaware of any default, defense or claim against the instrument.

Personal defenses (e.g., failure of consideration; mistake; breach of warranty) cannot be asserted against a holder in due course, but "real" defenses (e.g., forgery; fraud in the inducement; fraud in execution; infancy) remain available. But if the underlying contract has been partially performed, the holder in due course has rights only as against the unperformed part.

Nevertheless, when a negotiable instrument is sold or assigned, consumers may retain certain claims and defenses as a result of the Federal Trade Commission's Trade Regulation Rule (16 CFR Part 433). Under the rule, it is an unfair and deceptive trade practice for a seller who finances or arranges the financing of consumer goods or services to make the consumer's duty to pay independent of the seller's duty to fulfill its obligations.

The FTC requires notice when a seller of goods refers consumers to a creditor. When a seller and lender work together to arrange financing for consumer goods, the loan contract must include the required FTC notice, even if the lender does not pay referral fees to the seller.

Consumer credit contracts must include a clause (in 10-point boldface type) notifying consumers that claims or defenses that could be raised against the seller can also be raised against the holder. UCC § 3-106(d) provides that no one can become holder in due course of an instrument subject to such consumer defenses.

§ 2.06 ARTICLE 4: BANK DEPOSITS AND COLLECTIONS

Article 4 covers the relationship between a customer who has a bank account and the bank itself (which is the payor bank for the customer's checks). This relationship is contractual. The customer deposits funds into the bank; the bank agrees to pay the checks written by the customer, and "properly payable" (as defined by § 4-401) but not those that are forged.

The bank has the right to pay valid items and charge them to the customer's account in any order — even if the result is to create an overdraft, leading to "bounced" checks and fees charged to the customer: § 4-303(b).

Checks (other than certified checks) become formally stale after six months (§ 4-404); usually, the bank will ask the customer for permission to pay a check presented after that time.

North Dakota held that Article 4 was not applicable when the state's Department of Financial Institutions sought to prevent a debt collection agency from electronically collecting fees for bounced checks. An electronic debit is not an "item" as defined by Article 4, nor does Article 4 apply to any funds transfer that is governed by the Electronic Funds Transfer Act.[13]

[A] The Collection Process

The payee (person to whom the check is payable) indorses the check (adds a signature indicating desire to get value for the check) and brings it to the bank with a deposit ticket. When the deposit is made, the payee's account is credited with the amount of the check, but only provisionally; if the check bounces, the credit will be reversed.

Sometimes a bank's customer will deposit checks in a bank that, coincidentally, is the bank where the drawer of the check has an account. In that case, the depositary bank is also the payor bank, and the check is an "on us" item. See § 4-105. Otherwise, the check goes through "clearing," the process under which the various banks receive all the checks written on them and deposited with other banks. The purpose of clearing is to settle accounts among the banks as well as to update the accounts of drawers of checks.

Federal laws, including the Expedited Funds Availability Act, 12 USC § 4000, and Regulation CC, 12 CFR Part 229, set limits on the maximum time a bank can take before finally (rather than provisionally) crediting the account. The federal rules preempt inconsistent UCC and state-law rules.

"Check 21," the Check Clearing for the 21st Century Act, P.L. 108-100, took effect October 28, 2004. The statute's purpose is to speed up check clearing. To that end, banks are permitted to engage in "truncation" and use "substitute checks." That is, instead of returning paper checks to bank customers after the checks have been cashed, banks are permitted to send the customer electronic data

---

[13] CybrCollect, Inc. v. North Dakota Dep't of Financial Institutions, 703 N.W.2d 285 (N.D. 2005).

or a complete image of the check, and then destroy the paper item. As long as the substitute check contains all the necessary information, it is legally equivalent to the paper check.

A bank that transfers, presents, or returns a substitute check and receives consideration for it warrants to the transferee, the drawer, the payee, and the banks in the chain of title that the substitute check meets the legal requirements, and that no duplicate payments will ever be required based on the substitute check or its paper original. Customers, in turn, are entitled to expedited recredit when their bank improperly charges them for a substitute check, or the customers have a warranty claim for the substituted check.

When a check is returned to the payor bank, the payor bank must either "finally pay" the check or dishonor (bounce) it (§ 4-215). The determination depends on whether the check appears to be legitimate, not forged or altered; whether there is a stop-payment order on record; and whether the drawer's account contains sufficient funds to pay the check. UCC § 4-214 governs reversing the provisional settlement and charging back the provisional credit if the check is dishonored.

It was not a violation of the duty of good faith and fair dealing for a bank to post a method for dealing with checks that overdrew an account in a way that maximized rather than minimized the fees customers would have to pay for overdrafts. The posted method was one of the methods authorized by the UCC, and the bank had no duty to adopt the authorized method that was least expensive for customers.[14]

[B] Properly Payable Items; Forgery; Fraud

Traditionally, banks returned canceled checks to their customers, or provided a monthly or other periodic accounting of items. (The current trend is to make images of the checks available on request, or available online, but not to return the actual checks.) The customer then has a duty to examine the record of statement, and to give the bank prompt notification of any improper items;[15] failure to do so can deprive the customer of remedies against the bank for improper payment of the items: § 4-406. But if the customer was negligent and the bank also failed to use ordinary care in paying the item, then the loss is apportioned between the bank and customer: § 4-406(e).

It makes a difference when the check was actually written by the customer, but the amount of the check was raised by a dishonest person. In that case, the bank has a right to charge the customer's account for the original amount (§ 4-401(d)(l)), whereas if either the signature on the check or the indorsement is forged, the check

---

[14] Hill v. St. Paul Fed. Bank, 263 Ill. Dec. 562, 329 Ill. App. 3d 705, 768 N.E.2d 322 (2002).

[15] The customer cannot make claims against the bank based on unauthorized signatures or alterations of checks more than one year after the statement was issued or the checks were returned to the customer: § 4-406(a) and (f). The statute of limitations for having the account re-credited based on an unauthorized indorsement is three years: § 4-111.

is not properly payable (§ 4-401(a)), and the bank should not charge the customer's account. The theory is that the bank has the drawer's signature on file, so it can check to see if it appears to be forged (even though it would be grossly impractical to review all signatures).

If it does charge the customer's account, and the customer promptly reviews the canceled checks and notifies the bank of the forgery, the bank must re-credit the customer's account (§ 4-401).

The customer may become partially liable if its negligence made it easier for the malefactor to forge or alter the check: see § 3-406, showing the interrelation between the UCC provisions for commercial paper and those for bank deposits and collections. Furthermore, a check is considered properly payable (as long as the bank acts in good faith and exercises ordinary care) even if the payee is an impostor, or a fictitious party (e.g., a nonexistent company whose existence is asserted under a fraudulent scheme): see § 3-404.

Companies are also stuck with the loss if their own employees divert corporate checks for their own benefit, on the theory that corporations have a greater ability to hire honest employees and supervise them than banks have to detect check scams: see § 3-405 Official Comment 1.

Revised § 3-403(b) treats a check lacking a required signature as an "unauthorized signature" because a missing endorsement is an unauthorized endorsement. The UCC supplants the common law in this situation, so a co-payee on the check could not recover on a common-law negligence theory.[16]

In mid-2006, the Seventh Circuit ruled that, under the law of check presentment (which it criticized as being out of line with modern banking practice), a drawee bank is entitled to indemnification from the presenting bank even if the original check is no longer available for examination to see if it is forged or altered. (The drawee bank made an electronic copy and destroyed the original.) The UCC allocates the burden according to who can police which issues at lowest cost, so the drawee bank warrants to the presenting bank that the check is not forged, whereas the presenting bank warrants that it has not been altered.[17]

The California Court of Appeals ruled in 2008 that a bank was not liable to investors when checks written to one entity were deposited in a related entity's bank account. The investors wanted to buy investment units in "Third Eye Systems, LLC." Nine checks were made payable to "Third Eye Systems, LLC," one to "Third Eye" and one to "Third Eye Systems." The checks were cashed by Third Eye Systems Holdings, Inc. The investors sought reimbursement from U.S. Bank, which cashed the checks, because Third Eye Systems, LLC was worth much less without their investments, and they could not access Third Eye Systems Holdings, Inc's assets to make up for their investment losses. The Court of Appeals ruled for the bank on the UCC §§ 4-207 and 4-208 claims. Neither the transfer nor the

---

[16] Gil v. Bank of America NA 136 Cal. App. 4th 1371, *aff'd* 138 Cal. App. 4th 1371 (Cal. App. 2006).

[17] Wachovia Bank N.A. v. Foster Bancshares Inc., 457 F.3d 619 (7th Cir. 2006).

presentment warranty under Article 4 inures to the benefit of the drawer of a check: the warranty goes to the transferee of the check, not its drawer. The § 4-208 warranty inures to the benefit of the drawer's bank and not the drawer. The investors were also unsuccessful in using § 4-205, because it only warrants that the depositary bank made a deposit into the customer's account or paid the customer, and does not warrant that the payment was made to the payee identified on the check. The investors also charged U.S. Bank with statutory negligence under UCC Article 3, but there were no fraudulent or forged endorsements or impersonation of the payee, so Article 3 was also inapplicable. The management of Third Eye Systems, LLC was entitled to endorse checks for deposit in the account of Third Eye Systems Holdings, Inc.[18]

[C] Stopping Payment

A check is really the customer's direction to the bank to pay on behalf of the party designated by the customer. The customer (but not the payee or the indorsee) has the right to stop payment on a check by giving the bank reasonable notice (oral or written) of his or her intention: § 4-403. The stop payment order lasts for six months, but oral stop-payment orders lose effectiveness after 14 days if they are not reduced to writing in the interim. Of course, the bank must get the order in time to act on it; it is too late once the check has been either paid or certified (§§ 4-303, 401(c)).

[D] Wrongful Dishonor

Not only must the bank take steps to pay only checks that are proper, it must take steps to pay *all* checks that are proper, without "wrongfully dishonoring" a properly payable check. See §§ 4-401(a) and -402(a). Section 4-402(a) gives the bank the right to dishonor an item that creates an overdraft, unless overdraft protection has been arranged.

Under § 4-402(b), a customer who suffers wrongful dishonor of an item is entitled to actual damages, including consequential damages (which could include damages for being arrested or prosecution for check fraud). It is a fact question whether wrongful dishonor of the item was the proximate cause of the customer's damages.

Revised § 4-402 permits the "customers" of a payor bank to collect damages for wrongful dishonor of checks. However, persons charged a $10 fee for cashing a check drawn on a bank, when they did not have accounts at that bank, were not customers and could not assert § 4-402.[19]

---

[18] Mills v. U.S. Bank, No. D049805 (Cal. App. 9/10/08).

[19] Kronemeyer v. U.S. Bank NA, 368 Ill. App. 3d 224 (Ill. App. 2006).

§ 2.07 ARTICLE 4A: FUNDS TRANSFERS

The adoption of Article 4A required the creation of a completely new system for commercial funds transfers, also known as wholesale wire transfers. However, some important classes of transfers are excluded from the scope of Article 4A, including the consumer funds transfers governed by the Electronic Funds Transfers Act, P.L. 95-630, 15 USC § 1693 *et seq.*, and Regulation E, 12 CFR Part 205. Any funds transfer sent by Fedwire is subject to Article 4A, even in states that have not adopted it. Also note that funds a bank receives via funds transfer must be made available for withdrawal not later than the banking day after the banking day on which the funds were received, because of the Expedited Funds Availability Act, 12 USC § 4002(a).

UCC Article 4A does not preempt state law claims against a bank that received wire transfer funds that it knew or should have known were fraudulently obtained. According to the Eleventh Circuit, preemption does not apply because mandating disgorgement of illegally obtained funds is not inconsistent with the goals of Article 4A, and the UCC itself provides many references to common law remedies.[20]

[A] Payment Orders

Article 4A transfers are made via "payment orders." See §§ 4A-103, -104. A payment order is a written, oral, or electronic order to a receiving bank directing it to pay a fixed or determinable amount of money to a beneficiary, if:

- The sender pays the receiving bank
- The sender transmits instructions directly to the receiving bank, or to an agent, funds transfer system, or communication system for transmission to the receiving bank
- There are no conditions on the order other than the time of payment.

The payment order is issued when it is sent to the receiving bank. The beneficiary is the person to be paid by the beneficiary's bank, which in turn is the bank identified in a payment order by which the beneficiary's account is to be credited. The sender is the person who gives instructions to the receiving bank.

Usually the payment order is sent to the receiving bank through a communications system such as CHIPS or SWIFT. Such a communications system is the sender's agent for the purpose of transmitting the payment order to the bank. Under § 4A-206(a), the information sent by the communications system operates as the terms of the sender's payment order. However, this rule does not apply to amounts sent via Federal Reserve System funds transfer systems, and any erroneous processing by the FRB is treated as a § 4A-303 erroneous execution of the originating bank's payment order.

---

[20] Regions Bank v. The Provident Bank Inc., 345 F.3d 1267 (11th Cir. 2003).

Section 4A-104 defines the originator as the sender of the first payment order in a funds transfer. The originator's bank is the receiving bank to which the originator's payment order is issued. An intermediary bank is a receiving bank other than the originator's or beneficiary's bank. A funds transfer is a series of transactions, beginning with the originator's payment order, engaged in to make payment to a beneficiary, and completed when the beneficiary's bank accepts the payment order for the benefit of the beneficiary.

A receiving bank can encounter obligations, and perhaps liabilities, in several contexts:

- Accepting, amending, or rejecting payment orders (§ 4A-211)
- Executing payment orders (§ 4A-210)
- Making payments.

See § 4A-212 for the receiving bank's liability on an unaccepted payment order; §§ 4A-301–305 for its obligations and liabilities with respect to execution of the order, and §§ 4A-402 and -403 for the concerns of the receiving bank.

[B] Payment Problems

Article 4A deals intensively with the question of what happens if payments are made in the wrong amount or to the wrong person. Under § 4A-201, allocation of liability depends on whether a security procedure was in place and was used.

Security procedures are agreed on by customers and receiving banks to verify orders or find errors in transmission. Algorithms and other codes, encryption, and callback procedures are accepted security procedures.

Even unauthorized orders are binding on the customer if the security procedure was commercially reasonable; the bank accepted the order in good faith and pursuant to the procedure; and the bank followed any limitations that the customer imposed on payment orders in the customer's name.

A payment order received by a receiving bank is treated as an authorized order of any identified sender who either authorized it or is responsible for it under agency law (§ 4A-202).

However, if a receiving bank accepts a payment order for which the customer is not liable, the receiving bank may have to refund the amount of the order, plus interest, to the customer. The customer has an obligation to exercise ordinary care to report unauthorized payments to the bank.

The rule of § 4A-205 is that if the order is transmitted in accordance with a commercially reasonable security procedure, but nonetheless is sent to the wrong beneficiary, as a duplicate of a legitimate order, or in excess of the amount ordered, the sender is not obligated if the error would have been detected by proper use of the security procedure.

In a Sixth Circuit case, a bank sent a wire transfer on behalf of a debtor in ten times the amount that the debtor ordered. The Sixth Circuit ruled that the bank was entitled to restitution from the creditor that received the payment. The creditor could not assert a discharge for value defense under UCC § 4A-303(1), because it was on notice of the mistake before crediting the debtor's account with payment (although it was not aware of the mistake before receiving the funds).[21]

California held in mid-2007 that the UCC cause of action displaces all other common law actions in allocating an embezzlement loss between the embezzler, the bank that honored fraudulent payment orders, and the company that employed the embezzler. Therefore, the victim had to recover, if at all, from the bank that honored the orders.[22]

The Sixth Circuit ruled against an investor who sued her bank under Article 4A when the bank followed her instructions and those of her investment advisor and disbursed funds to a company that went bankrupt. A payment order is not unauthorized if the sender authorizes it, or is otherwise chargeable under agency law, and in this case the investment advisor had both apparent and actual authority to move funds out of the investor's accounts, and the investor ratified the advisor's actions.[23]

[C] Acceptance of the Payment Order

A bank that is not the beneficiary's bank "accepts" a payment order when it executes the order (§ 4A-209). This is done by paying the beneficiary; notifying the beneficiary that his or her account will be credited; or that the order is rejected. A payment order is rejected by the receiving bank when it gives oral, electronic, or written notice of rejection to the sender: § 4A-210. (It is impossible to prevent acceptance of a payment made by Fedwire.)

Section 4A-405 defines payment as the beneficiary's bank crediting the beneficiary's account; the beneficiary is notified of the right to withdraw the credit (or the bank applies the credit to a debt of the beneficiary or otherwise makes the funds available to the beneficiary). When the receiving bank accepts and executes the payment order, the sender becomes obligated to pay the amount of the payment order to the receiving bank (§ 4A-402(c)).

The sender can amend or cancel a payment order by giving the receiving bank oral, written, or electronic notice: § 4A-211. A payment order is deemed canceled by operation of law if it is not accepted by the end of the fifth business day after its execution date or the payment date of the order. This section also provides that even the sender's death or incapacity will not revoke the payment order, unless the receiving bank is aware of the fact and has a reasonable opportunity to act on it before accepting the order.

The Arizona Court of Appeals held that a customer's letter, instructing the bank to transfer funds automatically whenever the balance reached a certain level, did not constitute a payment order under Article 4A, because it placed a condition

---

[21] First Nat'l Bank v. Brant, 398 F.3d 555 (6th Cir. 2005).

[22] Zengen v. Comerica Bank, 41 Cal. 4th 239 (2007).

[23] Pavlovich v. National City Bank, 435 F.3d 560 (6th Cir. 2006).

on the bank over and above the time of payment. The customer sought to be reimbursed for interest that was not accrued because the transfer was not made, but was unsuccessful because the court refused to apply Article 4A remedies.[24]

Federal Reserve regulations have the force of federal law, and preempt inconsistent 4A provisions; so do Federal Reserve Bank operating circulars, even though they do not have the force of law. See § 4A-107.[25]

In the Second Circuit view, the one-year statute of limitations for objections to unauthorized funds transfers (§ 4A-505) is a jurisdictional bar. That is, it is mandatory and cannot be altered by agreement between the bank and its customer.[26]

§ 2.08   ARTICLE 5: LETTERS OF CREDIT

A letter of credit is part of a multi-party transaction, usually where the parties are too far apart from each other to be able to make an accurate assessment of the risk that the seller will not deliver or will deliver defective goods, or that the buyer will pay late or not at all. The customer (usually the buyer of merchandise, who will need a way to pay once delivery is made) gets its bank to agree to honor drafts on the bank as long as the conditions set out in the letter of credit are met. Letters of credit are irrevocable. (The buyer pays its bank a fee for the service.)

The seller of the merchandise is the beneficiary of the letter of credit. It will be able to draw a draft on the issuer bank by producing a bill of lading and any other required documentation (e.g., import documents; inspection certificates) called for by the letter of credit. In effect, the bank is a mutually trusted third party intermediary. Because both buyer and seller trust the bank, neither has to trust the other.

In Article 5 parlance (as defined by § 5-102), an "applicant" gets a letter of credit issued. The "beneficiary" is entitled to have its "documentary presentation" honored by the "issuer" bank. The letter of credit is the issuer bank's undertaking to honor a proper documentary presentation (i.e., the appropriate documents are delivered to prove that payment is due).

Under § 5-108, the issuer has a reasonable time, not to exceed seven business days, to review the presentation and honor it if it appears to satisfy the terms and conditions of the letter of credit. If the documents do not appear proper, and unless the applicant made other arrangements, the issuer must dishonor the presentation. The issuer is not responsible for performance of the underlying contract. The rules for identifying and coping with fraudulent or forged documents appear in § 5-109; § 5-111 provides remedies for wrongful dishonor or repudiation of a letter of credit, subject to the one-year statute of limitations found in § 5-115.

---

[24] Trustmark Ins. Co. v. BankOne, Arizona, 202 Ariz. 535, 48 P.3d 485 (Az. App. 2002).

[25] The FRB returned the complement: on November 30, 1990, it adopted Article 4A as Appendix B, Subpart B of 12 CFR Part 210.

[26] Mendes-Regatos v. North Fork Bank, 431 F.3d 394 (2d Cir. 2005).

The Ninth Circuit ruled in mid-2008 that under UCC § 5-106(d), a letter of credit was not "perpetual" because it was not described as perpetual. Therefore, it did not expire five years after the stated date of issuance. The irrevocable letter of credit, securing performance of a hold harmless agreement in connection with two leases, expired one year after its date of issue, with automatic additional one-year periods unless the transferor of the leases agreed not to require renewal. The acquirer of the leases sued the transferor in California state court for improper failure to terminate the letter of credit. The state court eventually ruled that the letter of credit should remain in effect. Eventually, the transferor drew on the letter of credit. The bank that was the successor of the bank that originally issued the letter of credit dishonored it, taking the position that it was perpetual and therefore had expired. The Ninth Circuit ruled that the plain meaning of § 5-106 said that the letter of credit stated that it would expire, and therefore it was not perpetual.[27]

When a presentation is honored, the beneficiary warrants, under § 5-110, that no forged documents were involved, and drawing on the letter of credit does not violate any agreement between the applicant and the beneficiary, who are typically the buyer and seller, respectively, in a business transaction.

Generally speaking, as a result of § 5-112 letters of credit are not transferable, but § 5-114 permits the beneficiary to assign the cash, check, or other proceeds paid when the letter of credit is honored.

The various articles of the UCC complement one another; they do not exist in a vacuum. So Article 2 rules must be consulted about the underlying sale. Also see Article 9 for "trust receipts" used by buyers for secured financing of transactions that will be implemented through letters of credit. Letters of credit can also be security when a seller wants to acquire goods from a manufacturer for re-sale to customers.

Note that letters of credit are often used in the international context, so rules and practices of international trade are quite important.[28] Many letter of credit transactions are governed by the International Chamber of Commerce Publication No. 500, "Uniform Customs and Practice for Documentary Credits," and not by Article 5. But if a Letter of Credit says that it is subject to the Uniform Customs and Practices for Documentary Credits, the UCP terms replace the UCC only where there is a direct conflict. Where the UCP is silent, the UCC applies.[29]

§ 2.09 ARTICLE 6: BULK SALES

Traditionally, Article 6 dealt with "bulk transfers," but the 1989 revision gave states two options. One was repealing the article altogether; the other was to adopt a revised and renamed article. Nearly all the states chose to repeal the old Article 6 but did not adopt the Revised Article 6.

---

[27] Golden West Refining Co. v. SunTrust Bank, 538 F.3d 1233 (9th Cir. 2008).

[28] The Article 5 choice of law rules appear at § 5-116.

[29] Mid-America Tire, Inc. v. PTZ Trading Ltd., 95 Oh. St. 3d 367, 768 N.E.2d 619 (Ohio 2002).

The problem of bulk sales is one of debtor-creditor relations. Without controls imposed by state law, a desperate creditor might be tempted to sell all of its property and inventory (even those subject to security interests), take the money, and confront creditors with a situation on which there were no remaining goods to seize.

Hence, under the current version of Article 6, the debtor must provide notice in advance to its creditors, at least 45 days before the sale of all or virtually all property. If the creditor group is small, individualized notice is required; if it is large, notice can be made by filing (§ 6-105).

Even the buyer has obligations under §§ 6-104 and 6-106(4), which may include distributing the purchase price for the bulk sale merchandise among the claimants named by the seller.

Article 6 applies only to property whose value otherwise available to creditors is at least $10,000; minor transactions are not covered. But neither are very major transactions, exceeding $25 million (§ 6-103(1)).

If a debtor carries out what is in effect a bulk sale without giving the appropriate notice, the sale is not void, and the buyer gets good title to the goods — but § 6-107 makes the seller liable to its creditors for any damages that result from failure to comply.

§ 2.10 ARTICLE 7: DOCUMENTS OF TITLE

This part of the UCC deals with bills of lading, warehouse receipts, delivery orders, and other documents that are used in the process of transporting goods. They prove that the carrier has received the goods and subsequently shipped them, and identify the goods stored in a warehouse. Documents of title are used in bailment relationships — that is, situations in which someone such as a warehouseman has lawful possession of goods that actually are owned by someone else.

The concept of negotiability is important in this context as well as in the context of commercial paper, since deliveries can be made either to order (a designated recipient) or to bearer (whoever presents the appropriate documents). See § 7-501.

It is also possible to buy or sell the document and thereby gain rights in the underlying goods. Just as a check or other draft tells a bank or other drawee to give money to a payee, a delivery order instructs a bailee to deliver goods to a purchaser or other deliveree. A negotiable document of title can only be negotiated to a holder, who acquires the document for value, in good faith, and without knowing about any claims or defenses affecting the documents: § 7-501. Section 7-502 governs the rights acquired through due negotiation of a document of title.

If the document is not negotiable, naturally it cannot be negotiated, but it can be transferred (§ 7-504), although the transferee gains only the rights that the transferor had or had actual authority to convey, and the transferor's creditors may have rights superior to those of the transferee.

The warehouseman has an obligation to keep goods covered by a particular warehouse receipt separate from all other goods, except for fungible goods (commodities) that can legitimately be commingled: § 7-207.

Although generally a carrier or warehouseman must deliver the goods to the party stipulated in the documents, there are situations under § 7-403 in which such delivery is excused. For instance, the seller can direct that delivery be stopped.

If someone else has better title to the goods, delivery can be made to that party (for instance, the goods have been sold in the interim; there is a lien on the goods which gets enforced). If the goods are lost, destroyed, delayed, or damaged under circumstances for which the bailee is not liable, then the bailee is not required to make delivery. This does not, however, relieve the bailee of the duty of ordinary care toward the merchandise, as set out in § 7-309. If there are competing claimants for the goods, the bailee does not have to deliver them before a reasonable time to determine who has the best claim — or to bring suit for interpleader: § 7-603. A court can order delivery of goods, or issuance of a replacement document, on proof of the loss, theft, or destruction of the original document: § 7-601.

Sections 7-208 and 7-306 deal with forged and altered documents of title, much as there are rules for forged or altered checks.

Article 7 must be read in conjunction with Article 2's rules on risk of loss and with Article 9's rules for secured transactions.

§ 2.11 ARTICLE 8: OWNERSHIP AND TRANSFER OF SECURITIES

The original version of Article 8 was created in the 1940s and 1950s, at a time when ownership of securities was usually evidenced by stock certificates, and physical possession of stock certificates was the most relevant measure of ownership.

Article 8 was amended in 1978 to cover situations in which a security is sold without a certificate. But further changes were needed, culminating in a 1994 revision that is the current version of Article 8.

Under current practice, most mutual fund shares are "uncertificated." Stock certificates are still issued for most corporate shares, although it is far more typical for the certificates to be held by clearing corporations.[30] Article 8 covers corporate stock, even if it is not publicly traded: §§ 8-102(a)(15), 8-103(a).

It also covers certain "financial instruments," such as commercial paper and Certificates of Deposit, that are not securities. Part 5 of Article 8, but not the other Parts, applies to stock options that are issued and cleared through the Options Clearing Corporation. But commodity contracts, such as futures contracts and commodity options, do not come under Article 8 because § 8-103(f) treats them as neither securities nor financial assets.

---

[30] The Depository Trust Company is a trust that acts as a depository for about 600 broker-dealers and banks; its nominee name is the familiar Cede & Company. When trades have been cleared, and accounts have been "netted," (i.e., amounts owned by broker-dealers to other broker-dealers are established), the National Securities Clearing Corporation instructs DTC how to adjust its participants' accounts.

Trades are typically made through broker-dealers, and the most significant records are the computer entries in the records of the clearing corporations.

[A] Transfer of Certificated Securities

The current version of Article 8 copes with the dual system by maintaining rules for transfer of certificated securities. But Part 5 of Article 8 has another set of rules for indirect holdings (the common situation in which an individual owns securities, but a securities intermediary holds the certificates). The central concept of Part 5 is the "security entitlement," defined by § 8-102(a)(17) as the rights and property interest of the stockholder in a financial asset.

A security entitlement is acquired, under § 8-501, when a securities intermediary credits financial assets to that person's account. The intermediary is required by § 8-504 to maintain enough financial assets to satisfy the claims of all entitlement holders. Such assets are held for the entitlement holders, and are not the property of the securities intermediary or subject to the claims of the intermediary's general creditors (§ 8-503).

The Second Circuit certified the question to the New York Court of Appeals as to whether a particular group of promissory notes constituted "securities" under UCC 8-102(15). The court of appeals said that they were, because they met the tests of transferability, divisibility, and functionality. The notes were not in bearer form, but their form contemplated potential future transfers; note holders could demand registration of transfers. Therefore, as provided by § 8-102(12)(I), they were transferable, because they constituted obligations represented by a security certificate in registered form. The court of appeals required the functionality test to evolve to conform to commercial practice — and the securities industry treated the notes as securities.[31]

Under Article 8, the issuing corporation is vicariously liable for diminution in the value of stock when the transfer agent misplaced packages of stock certificates for over 40 days. The duty to register the transfer of the securities falls on the issuer, who is liable for damages resulting from unreasonable delay in registration, or the failure or refusal to register a transfer.[32]

In an action arising out of mistaken issuance of stock, a broker who redeemed stock for a customer was not liable to the transfer agent. The certificate was not stolen; the broker did not collude with the customer to violate the transfer agent's rights; and the broker acted as a passive conduit and was not responsible for policing the appropriateness of the transactions. Section 8-115 protects brokers in their dealings with financial assets at the direction of customers.[33]

The Eastern District of Pennsylvania applied a catch-all six-year statute of limitations to Rev. §§ 8-401 and 8-407 claims about delays in the ability to sell stock issued in a merger. Allegedly, the loss of value was caused by the issuer's negligence or other culpability. The catch-all timing was adopted because the 8-401

---

[31] Highland Capital v. Schneider, 485 F.3d 690 (2d Cir. 2007).
[32] Bahn v. Compuware Corp., 2006 WL 572697 (Mich. App. 3/9/06).
[33] H&R Block Fin. Advisors Inc. v. Express Scripts Inc., 2006 WL 897440 (E.D. Mich. 4/6/06).

cause of action is a creature of statute, so neither the tort nor the contract statute of limitations would be appropriate.[34]

[B] Security Interests in Securities

A security interest in securities is created in the same way as any other security interest: i.e., by agreement of a debtor and a secured party (see § 9-203). There is no requirement of transfer of the securities or delivery of certificates.

Although a security interest in securities can be perfected in the ordinary way, by filing a financing statement (see § 2.12[C]), a secured party who has control has priority over a secured party who does not. See § 9-116 for automatic perfection of the intermediary's security interest in the financial asset, even if there is no security instrument.

§2.12 SECURED TRANSACTIONS

Article 9 sets out the rights of both debtor and creditor when an extension of credit is made on a secured basis (when personal property is used as collateral).

Security interests include pledges, conditional sales contracts, liens, chattel mortgages, and trust receipts. Article 9 applies to both merchant-to-merchant and consumer transactions, so in addition to Article 9, federal consumer credit laws and/or state consumer protection laws may come into play in a particular transaction.

It is quite common for the same collateral to be subject to more than one security interest, so an important function of Article 9 is to determine priority issues among creditors.

According to NCCUSL, the two key concepts in Article 9 are "attachment" and "perfection," the former being the point at which a security interest is created, and the second being the point at which the creditor establishes primary rights over other creditors who have an interest in the same collateral. There are three basic requirements for attachment of a security interest, as defined by § 9-203: giving value; the debtor's rights in the collateral; and a security agreement that provides an adequate description of the collateral and is signed or otherwise authenticated by the debtor.

Under the current version of § 9-108(c), a description reasonably identifies collateral if the identity of the collateral is objectively determinable. However, an excessively generic description such as "all assets of the debtor, now owned or hereafter acquired" will not be considered an adequate description in a security agreement, although it will be permitted in a financing statement. Describing collateral by type is generally acceptable, but greater detail is required for certain consumer transactions.

---

[34] Jodek Charitable Trust RA v. VerticalNet Inc., 2006 WL 213665 (E.D. Pa. 1/26/06).

In general, perfection is achieved by being the first to file a financing statement evidencing the security interest. However, in some fact situations, perfection is achieved by taking control over the collateral.

Article 9 has always had a broad scope, and Revised Article 9 added more categories of property and transactions to the range of Article 9 (e.g., sales of promissory notes; government debtors' security interests; consignments; and commercial tort claims).[35]

[A] Article 9 Definitions

Within Article 9, the term "consumer goods" applies to those purchased or used primarily for personal, family, or household purposes. "Equipment" refers to goods used or bought primarily for use in business, as well as goods that do not constitute consumer goods, farm products, or inventory. "Inventory" means goods held for sale or lease, or that will be furnished under a service contract. Raw materials and work in progress for eventual business use are also inventory. See § 9-106. A snowmobile counts as a "consumer good," not a "motor vehicle," so it is not necessary to file a financing statement to perfect a security interest in a snowmobile.[36]

Financial instruments may also be covered by Article 9. An "account" is the right to be paid for goods or services rendered—including payment obligations arising out of leases and licenses, and credit card receivables (§ 9-102(a)(2)). "Chattel paper" is the documentation of a monetary interest that gives rise to a security interest in specific goods (§ 9-105).

All personal property that does not satisfy the definition of goods, contract rights, negotiable instruments, or accounts falls into the § 9-106 definition of "general intangibles."

A "purchase money security interest" (PMSI), which is accorded special priority, is an interest retained by the seller of the collateral; or by a financing agency that advanced money to the seller, and to which chattel paper covering the collateral has been assigned; or benefiting someone who advanced money to the buyer for the purpose of buying the collateral itself. (In other words, if someone puts up collateral to secure credit for another purpose, the creditor is entitled to a lower priority than if the collateral secures the advance of credit used to buy the collateral itself.)

Article 9 is not necessarily the whole story when it comes to the secured transactions of consumer-debtors. Creditors may find that federal or state consumer

---

[35] *See* Summary: Uniform Commercial Code Revised Article 9—Secured Transactions, http://www.nccusl.org/Update/uniformact_summaries/uniformacts-s-uccra9st1999.asp; Steven O. Weise, *An Introduction to the Revised UCC Article 9*, http://www.hellerhrman.com/docs/en/revised _UCC_article9_Jan12005.pdf (1/1/05).

[36] *In re* Lance, 2006 WL 1586745 (Bank. W.D. Mo. 3/7/06).

protection laws limit their options. For instance, Article 9 might permit seizure of collateral — but consumer protection laws might limit the creditor's ability to seize without notice and hearing.

Under the earlier version, the financing statement was supposed to be filed where the collateral was located; the revised version requires filing where the debtor is located. (Of course, they are often the same!) See §§ 9-301, 9-307 for the place to file the financing statement. Generally speaking, if the debtor is an entity (e.g., a corporation) created by making an official state filing, the debtor is "located" in the state of filing (e.g., a New Jersey corporation). For other types of entities, the location is the executive office; an individual's location is his or her principal residence.

The financing statement must include the debtor's name (§ 9-502(a)(1)) — and the name must be accurate enough so that a standard computer search would disclose the existence of the debt: § 9-506(c). A party doing a search is entitled to rely on the correctness of the name as filed, so financing statements have been held to be seriously misleading under Revised 9-506 where the secured party's name was given as "Roger" rather than the correct "Rodger," or where initials without periods were used in the name of the debtor corporation.[37]

See § 9-109(d) for categories excluded from Article 9, including landlord's liens, statutory liens (except agricultural ones), wage assignments, sales of intangibles that occur in connection with the sale of a business, assignments of receivables for purposes of collection only, and real property liens. However, although Article 9 does not apply to real estate liens, § 9-109(b) provides that it applies to a security interest in a note secured by real estate. Software that is embedded in goods to the part of becoming part of the goods is considered "goods" for Article 9 purposes; otherwise, it is considered a "general intangible." See § 9-102(44) and 9-102(75). "Supporting obligations" are items such as guarantees that are treated similarly to the debt that they accompany (§§ 9-102(a)(77), 9-203(f), 9-308(d)). That is, when a security interest is created in a payment obligation, the supporting obligations are subject to the same security interest, and perfection of a security interest in the underlying obligation automatically perfects the security interest in the supporting obligation.

[B] Security Agreement Checklist

Issues to be considered when drafting a security agreement include:

❑ Whether the language reflects the UCC's basic requirements for a security agreement
❑ Nature of the collateral

---

[37] Pankratz Implement Co. v. Citizens Nat'l Bank, 281 Kan. 209 (Kan. 2006); *see also* Host America Corp. v. Coastline Fin. Inc., 2006 WL 1579614 (D. Utah 5/30/06).

❑ Whether the collateral is already encumbered by any other security interests (this can be determined by searching the UCC filings under the debtor's name)

❑ Whether the collateral is in the debtor's possession, or elsewhere

❑ Whether the debtor's other assets are already subject to liens

❑ Whether the debtor has been notified of a federal tax lien

❑ (For corporate debtors) whether appropriate corporate resolutions have been passed to make the agreement effective and enforceable

❑ If the agreement extends to after-acquired collateral (i.e., collateral acquired after the agreement is in place)

❑ Whether the collateral consists of consumer goods, inventory, accounts, or general intangibles

❑ If the goods are likely to be attached to real estate, thus becoming "fixtures"

❑ If the debtor's spouse or ex-spouse has protectable rights in the collateral

❑ (In the consumer context) whether Truth in Lending requirements, including disclosure, have been satisfied

Before Article 9 was revised, it required that the security agreement be "signed" by the debtor; the creditor's signature was not required. To facilitate electronic filing, § 9-502 Comment 3 says that the debtor's hand-written signature is no longer required.

It is also permissible for the secured party to file a financing statement that has not been signed by the debtor — but only if the debtor authorized the filing: § 9-509, either in the security agreement or (if the security agreement has not been signed yet) by express authorization or by ratification of a filing that already occurred.

Debtors have certain basic rights, which they may not waive (e.g., the right to receive an accounting after a default; the right to have the collateral handled lawfully; and remedies against the secured party for failure to satisfy statutory requirements) nor can a guarantor waive the debtor's access to these basic rights. There is a safe harbor under §§ 9-312 to -316 if the secured party provides a plain-English notification, a reasonable time in advance, to the debtor of:

• Its intention to sell the collateral
• A description of the collateral involved
• Where and when the sale or other disposition will take place
• Disclosure that the debtor may still owe money after the disposition
• A telephone number the debtor can call to find out how much is owed; contact information to find out how that amount was calculated.

Notice to a commercial debtor is considered reasonable if it is given after default and at least 10 days before the sale: § 9-613. A consumer debtor can claim that even 10 days' notice is unreasonable under the facts of the case: § 9-614.

[C] Perfecting a Security Interest

UCC § 9-203 provides that a security interest attaches when the parties agree that it will attach; value has been given (satisfying a pre-existing debt counts as value); the debtor acquires rights in the collateral; and a written security agreement has been created. The security interest is perfected, as described by § 9-303, when it has attached and the steps for perfection given in § 9-302 (agricultural liens) and §§ 9-304–306 (deposit accounts, investment property, and letters of credit in that order) have been completed.

Some security interests are automatically perfected, including a PMSI in consumer goods (other than motor vehicles that have to be registered: § 9-311(a)(2); see § 9-310 for other interests that can be perfected without filing). Otherwise, there are two ways in which a creditor can perfect a security interest. The first is to take possession of the collateral (§ 9-313). The second, and far more common, method is to file a "financing statement." The transition from paper to electronic filing and record-keeping is almost complete, aided by the UCC's shift from requiring "signatures" on documents to requiring "authentication of records."

If the goods are covered by a negotiable document, § 9-312(c) holds that while the goods are in the possession of the issuer of the document, the security interest in the goods is perfected by perfecting a security interest in the document.

Originally, § 9-306 provided that a security interest in the proceeds of the sale of inventory would remain perfected for only 10 days after the debtor's receipt of the collateral, unless the filed financing statement also covered proceeds, or the secured party got possession within the 10-day period. The current text, however (the provisions have been moved to § 9-315), says that a security interest loses perfection 21 days after the security interest attached to the proceeds, unless the filed financing statement covered the original collateral or the proceeds are collateral for which a security interest can be perfected by filing in the same office as the financing statement.

Adoption of Revised Article 9 required creation of a set of transition rules. If a security interest was perfected under the prior Article 9, Revised § 9-703 provides that the interest remains perfected, and the creditor need not do anything additional. However, for security interests that were perfected under the old law but would not be perfected under the revision, and if the lapse in perfection is not related to filing, the secured creditor gets a one-year grace period to perfect the security interest in conformity with the new rules. Revised § 9-705(c) provides that security interests perfected under the old law by financing statements that satisfied Revised Article 9 continue to perfect the security interest until the earlier of their date of lapse under the revision and June 30, 2006. Continuation requires either a continuation statement or initial filing of an "in lieu" financing statement as described in § 9-706. A debtor who signs a security agreement thereby authorizes the lender to file as many initial financing statements as are required to perfect the security interest.

When a debtor transfers collateral (e.g., selling inventory; licensing property; investment distributions), §§ 9-203(f) and 9-315(a)(2) automatically attach the security interest that covered the collateral to the proceeds of the collateral.

If someone other than the debtor or the secured party actually possesses the collateral (e.g., it is stored in a warehouse), then the security interest is only perfected by possession if the bailee makes an authenticated record admitting that it holds the collateral for the benefit of the secured party. See § 9-313(c). For investment property (which is not tangible and in a sense cannot be "possessed"), Article 8 and § 9-314(a) prescribe "control" rather than "possession" as a means of perfecting the security interest.

Section 9-406(d) holds that restrictions in accounts, promissory notes, payment intangibles, or chattel paper are completely invalid if they interfere with the creation or perfection of a security interest in the right to payment, or prevent the secured party from enforcing its security interest.

[D] After-Acquired Property and Floating Liens

Generally speaking, the UCC treats after-acquired property clauses as valid. See § 9-204. Revised 9-204(c) authorizes a dragnet clause that makes the security interest also secure any other loans — including credit card loans — the borrower has obtained from the lender. The lender can secure the credit card debt even though the lender's proof of claim described that debt as unsecured. For bankruptcy purposes, a claim is secured if the collateral is in the bankruptcy estate, unsecured if the collateral is not.[38]

An underlying obligation and/or future advances of credit can be secured by collateral that the debtor acquires after the security agreement is signed. However, after-acquired property clauses can be used in consumer goods security agreements only if the debtor gets rights in the goods within 10 days after the secured party gives value. Consumer "accessions" (§ 9-335), items that are installed or affixed to other consumer goods, can also be the subject of an after-acquired property clause.

A floating lien secures a creditor's interest in collateral that constantly changes: e.g., a store's inventory. The UCC permits floating liens, but does not guarantee that the secured creditor will have priority over all liens that subsequently attach to or are perfected in the same collateral. The floating lien may lose out to a federal tax lien or to a PMSI.

Section 9-204(c) states that there can be a valid security interest in collateral securing amounts that will be advanced in the future, whether or not the advances are made pursuant to prior commitments.

---

[38] *In re* Nagata, 2006 WL 2131318 (Bankr. D. Haw. 7/20/06).

[E] Priorities Under the UCC

Unless the authorizing statute is to the contrary, § 9-333 gives priority to common law or statutory liens for services or materials: for instance, "mechanic's" and "materialmen's" liens.

Section 9-317 holds that an unperfected security interest is subordinate to:

- Persons entitled to priority under UCC § 9-322 or the special rules discussed below
- Lien creditors who gain that status before the security interest is perfected, or before a financing statement is filed and one of the § 9203(b)(3) conditions is met
- Buyers who give value and receive delivery without knowledge of a security interest, and before the security interest is perfected, if the collateral consists of tangible chattel paper, documents, goods, or instruments
- Lessees who give value and receive delivery of collateral without knowledge of the unperfected security interest
- Licensees of general intangibles, or buyers (who are not secured parties) of accounts, electronic chattel paper, most investment property, or general intangibles

Filing a financing statement with respect to a PMSI either before the debtor acquires the collateral or within 20 days after delivery ensures that the security interest has priority over the interests of buyers, lessees, and lien creditors that arise during the period between attachment of the security interest and the time of filing.[39]

[Note: See Chapter 15 for a discussion of the effect of BAPCPA on PMSIs on "910 vehicles": vehicles purchased within 910 days of the bankruptcy filing.]

Not all PMSIs go to the seller of the collateral. Anyone who gives value to enable the debtor to get the collateral can get a PMSI: see § 9-103. The best way for the lender to be protected is to pay the seller directly.

In general, a buyer in the ordinary course of business takes the merchandise free of the security interest, even if it has been perfected or the purchaser has actual knowledge of the security interest. A bona fide purchaser for value of consumer goods, who buys the goods primarily for personal, family, or household use, and who has no knowledge of the security interest, takes the goods free of an unfiled security interest: § 9-320.

Under § 9-331, a holder in due course of a negotiable instrument; a holder to whom a negotiable document of title has been negotiated; or a bona fide purchaser of a security takes priority over an earlier perfected security interest. However, an

---

[39] § 9-317(e); *but see* §§ 9-320 and -321 for exceptions to this general rule, e.g., the § 9-320(e) exception for security interests in goods that are in the possession of the secured party pursuant to § 9-313.

Article 9 filing does not constitute notice of the security interest to holders or purchasers.

The California Court of Appeals, in a case of first impression, held that an unsecured judgment creditor that satisfies its judgments from a deposit account containing proceeds of the debtor's accounts receivable and inventory is a "transferee" under § 9-332(b). Therefore, it takes the funds free of security interests. Therefore, another creditor could not sue the judgment creditor for unjust enrichment and could not impose a constructive trust on the funds collected by the judgment creditor. Although the secured creditor would normally have higher priority than the unsecured judgment creditor, in this case the question was whether it was improper to satisfy the judgment from the deposit account, and it was not improper.[40]

Security interests in fixtures (and crops) are now covered by § 9-334, although ordinary building materials incorporated into land improvements are not considered fixtures. The UCC does not preempt real estate law encumbrances on fixtures. In general, a perfected security interest in fixtures has priority over a conflicting interest that is a PMSI, the interest arose before the goods became fixtures, and a fixture filing no later than 20 days after the goods become fixtures perfects the security interest. A perfected security interest in fixtures is superior to certain conflicting interests in the real property where the fixtures are attached — for example, if the security interest was perfected before the goods became fixtures, and the fixtures consist of factory or office machinery. A security interest in fixtures — whether or not it is perfected — takes priority over conflicting interests of persons who own or encumber the real property, if the encumbrancer or owner has consented in an authenticated record to subordination, or the debtor has a right to remove the goods. In general, a security interest in fixtures is subordinate to a construction mortgage that was recorded before the goods became fixtures.

Section 9-335 deals with "accessions": attachments to other goods. A security interest created in an accession continues in collateral that becomes an accession. A security interest that was perfected when the collateral becomes an accession remains perfected after the collateral is re-characterized as accessions.

Section 9-336 is concerned with commingled or processed goods. A perfected interest in the goods survives their becoming part of a product or mass, if processing destroys the identity of the goods, or the financing statement covers the product too. If there is more than one interest in the mass or product, their rank is proportionate to their status as perfected or unperfected at the time the collateral became commingled goods. If there is more than one perfected security interest in the commingled goods, priority is granted in proportion to their value within the collateral when the materials became commingled.

---

[40] Orix Financial Services, Inc. v. Kovacs, 167 Cal. App. 4th 242 (Cal. App. 2008).

[F] Default

Part 6 (Part 5, before the revision) of Article 9 deals with default by the debtor. The UCC allows the secured party to reduce a claim to judgment, foreclose, or enforce the security interest through judicial proceedings. UCC § 9-609, taken by itself, lets the secured party take possession of the collateral on default, without judicial process, as long as this can be done without a breach of the peace. Or, the creditor can take steps to make equipment unusable if the debtor defaults.

However, if the debtor is a consumer, there will probably be consumer-protection law limits on "self-help repossession" and other creditors' remedies that do not permit the debtor to get a hearing and assert defenses.

Although it was proposed that self-help repossession be outlawed by Revised Article 9, this proposal was not adopted, and Revised § 9-609 continues to permit self-help repossession as long as there is no breach of the peace. The creditor is given fairly wide latitude to repossess the automobile before a breach of the peace will be held to have occurred.

Under Revised § 9-604(d), a secured party that removes collateral must reimburse the owner of the real property where the collateral was located, for damages caused by the removal. However, in 2006, the New York Court of Appeals said that when the secured creditor got a court order under which the marshal repossessed the property, the secured creditor was immune from claims by the landlord, because the marshal was independent from the secured party and acted under court authorization.[41]

After default, the secured party can sell, lease, or otherwise dispose of the collateral. Section 9-608 requires the proceeds to be applied in this order:

- Reasonable expenses of retaking, holding, and selling the collateral, including reasonable attorneys' fees
- Satisfying the indebtedness secured by the collateral
- Satisfaction of any indebtedness to junior debtors.

If there is any surplus left over, the secured party must account to the debtor for the difference between the amount obtained and the amount secured by the agreement. The debtor remains indebted for any deficiency. The rules are somewhat different if the underlying secured transaction is a sale of chattel paper or contract rights. Unless the agreement provides to the contrary, the debtor is neither entitled to surplus nor liable for deficiencies.

The secured party can dispose of the collateral either publicly or privately, in a commercially reasonable fashion. Notice to the debtor is required unless a perishable commodity, or a commodity for which there is a recognized market, is involved. Those who purchase collateral from a secured party after default take it free and clear of all rights and interests that the debtor may have had — even if the secured party fails to satisfy the UCC requirements or requirements imposed by a judicial proceeding.

---

[41] Cla-Mil East Holding Corp. v. Medallion Funding Corp., 6 N.Y.3d 375 (2006).

Revised § 9-626 adopts a "rebuttable presumption" rule with regard to creditor misbehavior in foreclosure. The value of the collateral is deemed to equal the unpaid balance of the debt unless the creditor proves otherwise, by introducing evidence of value independent of the foreclosure price. However, this rule applies only to commercial, not to consumer, transactions.

The former § 9-507(l) has been replaced by Revised § 9-625(c)(2), imposing a minimum civil penalty for creditor misbehavior in consumer foreclosures equal to the entire finance charge plus 10% of the original principal.

§ 2.13 ESIGN

The Electronic Records and Signatures in Global and National Commerce Act, nicknamed eSign, P.L. 106-229, was passed on June 30, 2000 and enacted at 15 USC § 7001 *et seq.* The basic rule under this statute is that, in all transactions in interstate and foreign commerce, contract signatures made in electronic form must be given the same legal effect and be just as enforceable as if they were made in conventional written form. (However, wholly intrastate transactions are not subject to this federal statute.)

An electronic signature is defined as any electronic sound, symbol or process attached to or associated with a document if it is used with the intention of signing the record. Notarization, authorization, and the like can also be performed with electronic signatures. However, eSign does not apply to court orders, notices, briefs, pleadings, or other writings executed in connection with litigation. ESign does not apply to the execution of wills, codicils, or testamentary trusts or to state family law statutes.

ESign does not alter basic contract principles. Private parties (as distinct from government agencies) cannot be forced to agree to, use, or accept electronic records. The 2002 revision to Article 3 provides (at § 3-604(c)) that for a non-written record, "signed" means "attachment to or logical association with the record of an electronic symbol, sound or process with the present intent to adopt or accept the record."

Disclosure and other requirements of writings for consumer contracts can be satisfied by electronic documents, but only if the consumer gives informed consent in advance to receiving the disclosure or other information in electronic form. Consumers have the right to receive a hard copy of electronic documents and also to withdraw their consent to receiving their information digitally. Timing requirements for disclosures are the same whether the disclosures are made in writing or electronically.

When a law imposes a record retention requirement, eSign provides that electronic records will comply with the requirement if they accurately reflect the underlying information and if, for at least as long as the record must be retained, the electronic records remain accessible in a format that can be consulted for later reference. Requirements for retaining checks can be satisfied by retaining an electronic record of the information on the front and back of the check.

Chapter 3

Employer—Employee Relations

PART 3: EMPLOYMENT DISCRIMINATION

§ 3.01   INTRODUCTION

For most people in the United States, paid employment is a feature of most or all of their adult lives. For most businesses, it will be necessary to have at least some employees during at least part of the business cycle. The relationship between the two covers many areas.

The discussion of employment issues is divided into three parts: Part 1, on labor law; Part 2 beginning at § 3.05, dealing with pension and benefit issues; and Part 3 beginning at § 3.10, dealing with questions of employment discrimination.

PART 1:   LABOR LAW

§ 3.02   BASIC CONCEPTS OF LABOR LAW

A body of federal labor law developed in the wake of the Depression and World War II. Today, those laws are still in force, although only about one-seventh of workers are unionized. Labor unions are most powerful in manufacturing, and play a less significant role in service industries. Today's economy is service-based, and manufacturing plays a much smaller role than it did in earlier years.

Most labor law is federal law. The Wagner Act (1935), also known as the National Labor Relations Act (NLRA), established the National Labor Relations Board (NLRB) and cemented the status of labor unions as legitimate bargaining agents.

NLRA § 7 gives employees the right to engage in "protected concerted activity": that is, they can act together to form or join a union, present grievances, bargain collectively (negotiate a contract for the whole union), go on strike, and picket.

According to the NLRB, it was not a violation of the NLRA to fire a worker for soliciting a coworker to testify in support of the first worker's sexual harassment claim. The activity was not protected concerted activity because it was not for mutual aid and protection of workers.[1]

Federal labor law determines the tactics that can legitimately be used by both management and labor during the certification process (campaign to unionize a workplace). A union can be decertified if it is guilty of misconduct, or if it ceases to represent employee interests. Labor law also determines the process of bargaining

---

[1] Holling Press Inc., 343 NLRB 45 (10/15/04).

for a Collective Bargaining Agreement (CBA) and settling disputes over the inter-pretation of a CBA.[2]

It also determines when a lawful strike can be called, what tactics are lawful during the strike, the extent to which the employer can hire replacements for strikers, and the extent to which strikers have to be reinstated after a strike ends. The NLRA, at 29 USC § 152, says that the statute governs the rights of "employees," and that "supervisors" are not included in this classification, so individuals who are classified as supervisors (i.e., need to make independent, individual judgments at work; able to reward or discipline employees; able to resolve employee grievances) or managers (able to set corporate policy) are not entitled to unionize.

Reversing the NLRB, in 2001 the Supreme Court determined that registered nurses who direct the work of non-R.N. health care employees are supervisors who exercise independent judgment. Therefore, the R.N. supervisors cannot be organized in the same bargaining unit as the non-R.N.s.[3]

In August 2000, the NLRB reversed its longstanding policy that temporary workers could only be organized in a bargaining unit with permanent workers if both the "supplier employer" (such as a temporary placement agency) and the "user employer" (workplace where the services were provided) agreed. The 2000 decision gave unions the right to show that supplier and user employers are actually joint employers, both of whom control the terms and conditions of employment.[4]

The rule changed yet again in late 2004, when the NLRB overruled its earlier *M.B. Sturgis* decision. Under current law, the NLRB now requires the consent of both the staffing firm and the user employer before it will allow a representation election for a unit consisting of both permanent workers who work only for the user employer and temporary workers who are jointly employed by the staffing firm and user employer.[5]

The NLRB is empowered to enter a situation if it is a labor dispute (e.g., strike, walkout, picketing, employer refusal to bargain) affecting interstate commerce. When the NLRB issues a complaint or files an unfair labor practices charge, it can petition the District Court to issue a temporary injunction. Permanent injunctions are quite rare in labor law, because most permanent injunctions are forbidden by the Norris-LaGuardia Anti-Injunction Act.

---

[2] In the Seventh Circuit's reading, LMRA § 302(5) merely requires CBAs to be written — not signed. Therefore, a contractor that demonstrated, by performance, intent to be bound by the CBA had to contribute to the union pension fund even though the contract was never actually signed: Bricklayers Local 21 v. Banner Restoration, 384 F.3d 911 (7th Cir. 2004).

[3] NLRB v. Kentucky River Community Care Inc., 532 U.S. 706 (2001). The Eighth Circuit applied this decision to hold that television producers were supervisors because they exercised independent judgment at work. Multimedia KDSK Inc. v. NLRB, 303 F.3d 896 (8th Cir. 2002).

[4] M.B. Sturgis Inc., 331 NLRB No. 173 (8/25/00).

[5] HS Care LLC, 343 NLRB 76 (11/9/04).

The Labor-Management Relations Act (LMRA) § 301(a) gives the District Court jurisdiction over suits for violations of a collective bargaining agreement. The LMRA preempts most state law claims. State laws are preempted in any case in which it is necessary to interpret a collective bargaining agreement, although mere reference to a CBA is not sufficient to invoke preemption.[6] If the CBA includes the common provision for arbitration or a contractual grievance procedure, potential plaintiffs must exhaust their remedies before bringing suit under LMRA § 301.

Certain situations have been found not to involve CBA interpretation, and therefore not to trigger LMRA § 301 preemption: for instance, retaliatory discharge; discharge of an employee in violation of public policy; claims on implied contracts, such as alleged promises of lifetime employment.

Because of a 1999 Supreme Court decision, states cannot be sued against their will by public employees who allege violations of federal labor law such as the overtime pay requirements. The analysis of *Alden v. Maine*[7] is that the Constitution protects states that have not waived sovereign immunity against either suit in federal court or suit in state court to enforce federal rights.

Bankruptcy labor law is becoming a sub-specialty of its own, particularly for airlines. The Bankruptcy Abuse Prevention and Consumer Protection Act of 2005, P.L. 109-8 (BAPCPA) provides that the bankruptcy estate of an employer does not include funds that the employer withheld, or funds that the employer received from employee wages for contribution to ERISA pension and benefit plans.[8]

BAPCPA § 1403 amends § 1114 of the Bankruptcy Code, giving the bankruptcy court the power to reverse changes to retiree health plans imposed by the employer within the 180-day period before the bankruptcy filing, unless the balance of equities clearly favors the changes. BAPCPA also raises (from $4,925 to $10,000 per employee) unpaid wages and benefits that are priority claims, and from 90 to 180 days pre-filing for the period when the claims can be recognized. BAPCPA also limits severance and retention bonuses that can be paid to top management and other insiders.

The Labor-Management Reporting and Disclosure Act (LMRDA) requires employers to file the LM-10 form each year to disclose payments (other than de minimis payments of up to $250) to unions and union officials. Filing is due within 90 days of the end of the employer's fiscal year.[9]

---

[6] Lividas v. Bradshaw, 512 U.S. 107 (1994). Textron v. UAAIW, 523 U.S. 653 (1998) holds that an allegation that an employer violated a collective bargaining agreement presents a federal question, but allegations that the employer defrauded the union into signing a contract and promising not to strike by promising not to subcontract out work, were not governed by LMRA § 301 and did not present federal questions.

[7] 527 U.S. 706 (1999).

[8] BAPCPA § 323.

[9] DOL, *Form LM-10—Employer Reports—Frequently Asked Questions*, http://www.dol.gov/esa/regs/compliance/olms/LM10_FAQ.htm.

[A] Unfair Labor Practices

An unfair labor practice is a violation of federal labor law by either employer or union. The NLRB has the power to issue "cease and desist" orders when it finds an unfair labor practice. The Board can also extend mandatory orders, e.g., ordering an employer to bargain with a union.

NLRA § 8 defines unfair labor practices to include:

- An employer's or union's refusal to engage in collective bargaining
- Employer domination of a union
- Retaliation against employees who file charges with, or testify before, the NLRB
- Discrimination against employees based on union activities or refusal to join a union; discrimination includes refusal to hire, firing, refusal to reinstate, demotion, discrimination in compensation, or in work assignments. (However, if a union security clause (§ 3.02[B][1]) is in place, employees can be required to pay union dues, but cannot be forced to join the union.)
- Featherbedding — deliberately inefficient work practices that require an unreasonably large number of workers to be employed
- Some practices in relation to strikes and picketing.

The Labor-Management Relations Act of 1947 (LMRA; also known as the Taft-Hartley Act) extends the NLRB's powers and outlaws certain strikes, including jurisdictional strikes, strikes that serve to maintain unfair labor practices, and secondary boycotts (actions taken against a neutral company to discourage it from dealing with another company with which the union has a dispute). The following union actions are unfair labor practices under the LMRA:

- Restraining or coercing employees who exercise their right to vote against unionization, to choose a representative, or to bargain collectively
- Causing an employer to discriminate against an employee
- Refusing to participate in collective bargaining
- Striking or any other concerted activity undertaken as a boycott or for another improper purpose
- Imposing excessive initiation fees or dues on a union shop
- Featherbedding

It was an Unfair Labor Practice for the employer to announce possible increases in pensions to discourage the employees from supporting the union — even though the announcement occurred during the organization drive, but before the representation petition was filed.[10]

To the D.C. Circuit, the employees' personal interest in being able to gain access to the employer's property for union organizing activity outweighed the

---

[10] NLRB v. Curwood Inc., 397 F.3d 548 (7th Cir. 2005).

employer's property and security concerns (based on past acts of vandalism by others). Therefore, the employer had to permit off-duty employees to give out handbills in the parking lot.[11] An employee's after-hours distribution of flyers criticizing a layoff was protected concerted activity. Therefore, coercive interrogation of the employee was an Unfair Labor Practice even though the employer asserted that it had a policy against distribution of any material not produced by the employer. The policy was overbroad and unenforceable, so the employee did not lose protection by violating it.[12]

The D.C. Circuit ruled in 2005 that workplace surveillance is a mandatory bargaining subject: it is plainly germane to the work environment, and is not within the core of entrepreneurial control. However, the employer's duty to bargain extends to the use of cameras and general reasons why surveillance is necessary, but the employer is not obligated to inform the union where the cameras will be placed or when they will be used.[13] An off-duty employee's actions of wearing a pro-union t-shirt in the store and inviting employees to a union meeting did not violate the company's anti-solicitation policy, so it was an Unfair Labor Practice to discipline the employee.[14]

The Third Circuit ruled that the LMRA precludes a malpractice suit by a union member against the lawyer that the union hired to represent the worker at arbitration. The First, Second, Ninth, and Tenth Circuits also have granted LMRA immunity to lawyers, on the theory that the union rather than the lawyer actually represents the worker. (LMRA § 301(b) makes a money judgment against a union enforceable only against the union as an entity, not its individual members or their assets.) In the Third Circuit case, the plaintiff charged her lawyer with deceiving her into withdrawing her grievance, and therefore was guilty of inaction rather than action; but the court treated not arbitrating a claim as an activity performed in relation to a Collective Bargaining Agreement.[15]

[B] Union Elections

A union that gains "certification" by winning a representation election under the supervision of the NLRB becomes the authorized bargaining agent for the employees in the bargaining unit. The employer is obligated to bargain in good faith with the union.

The campaign begins with a petition for certification, filed by a union or an employee who favors unionization. To be valid, at least 30% of the employees in the bargaining unit must indicate interest in joining a union. If the employer does not oppose holding an election, an election is held on consent. Otherwise, the NLRB is responsible for determining if the representation petition is valid.

---

[11] ITT Indus. Inc. v. NLRB, 413 F.3d 64 (D.C. Cir. 2005).

[12] United Services Auto. Ass'n v. NLRB, 387 F.3d 908 (D.C. Cir. 2004).

[13] Brewers and Malsters v. NLRB, 414 F.3d 36 (D.C. Cir. 2005).

[14] Wal-mart Stores v. NLRB, 400 F.3d 1093 (8th Cir. 2005).

[15] Carino v. Stefan, 376 F.3d 156 (3d Cir. 2004).

The period between filing of a representation petition and an election is known as the "critical period." The NLRB can invalidate the election if either side committed unfair labor practices (e.g., violence; threats; employer's announcement of new benefits to discourage pro-union votes) or otherwise interfered with the conduct of a fair election.

To win, the union needs a majority of the voters, rather than a majority of those eligible to vote. But the election is invalid unless a "representative number" of eligible voters actually voted.

For a period of one year after the election, rival unions are not allowed to seek certification to replace the incumbent union.

Late in 2004, the NLRB reversed an earlier decision, and now will no longer presume that an employer's threat to close the plant if the workers vote to unionize will be disseminated throughout the bargaining unit.[16]

[1] Union Security

Closed shops, where no one can be hired without already belonging to the union, are illegal. The NLRA also forbids preferential hiring, where the employer has to hire only union members as long as the union can supply enough qualified applicants.

However, union shops are allowed by the LMRA. In this arrangement, all current employees must be union members. New hires can be required to join the union once they are hired. Agency shops are also allowed: workers must pay initiation fees and union dues, but do not actually have to join the union.

It is not a violation of the union's duty of fair representation for the union to sign a Collective Bargaining Agreement that contains a union security provision that merely echoes the statutory wording.[17]

About a quarter of the states (primarily in the South and West) have adopted "right to work" laws, under which unwilling employees cannot be compelled to join a union or pay dues.

When a union operates an exclusive hiring hall, any breach (even a negligent breach) of its established procedures that results in loss of hiring opportunities for an applicant is a breach of the duty of fair representation.[18]

In mid-2007, the Supreme Court held that a state can require public employee unions to get affirmative consent from nonmembers before using their agency fees (amounts paid by nonmembers in lieu of dues) for political purposes. The Court concluded that it violates the First Amendment for public employee unions to use nonmembers' agency fees for ideological purposes that are distinct from the union's collective bargaining duties.[19]

---

[16] Crown Bolt Inc., 343 NLRB 86 (11/29/04).

[17] Marquez v. Screen Actors Guild, 525 U.S. 33 (1998).

[18] Jacoby v. NLRB, 233 F.3d 611 (D.C. Cir. 2000).

[19] Davenport v. Washington Educational Ass'n, 127 S. Ct. 2372 (U.S. 6/14/07); *see* Fred Schneyer, *U.S. Supreme Court Deems WA Union Fee Law Constitutional*, Plansponsor.com (6/19/07).

The Supreme Court struck down California Gov't Code §§ 16645–16649, a law forbidding companies that receive state grants over $10,000 to use the grant money to assist, promote, or deter union organizing. The Supreme Court found the statute to be preempted by the NLRA: federal policy favors preemption of state laws whenever Congress wanted a type of conduct to be governed by market forces and not by state regulation, with union organization reserved as a free-market zone for open debate (as long as employers do not attempt to coerce employees).[20]

It can be an unfair labor practice for an employer to refuse to hire union organizers — if the company was hiring, or had concrete plans to hire, at the time of the alleged unlawful conduct; the applicants either were qualified for the job or the employer failed to adhere to its own nominal standards; and anti-union animus was at least a factor in the decision. The employer can defend against such a prima facie case by showing that the applicants would not have been hired even if they had not been union "salts." Some courts also require proof that there were enough job openings for all the rejected applicants.[21]

It is a defense for the employer that the union organizers had a disabling conflict with the employer's interests. The D.C. Circuit, however, has held that this defense can only be asserted if the organizer applies for a job while engaging in an economic strike against the employer, or if the alleged protected union organizing activity really disguises unlawful attempts to sabotage the employer or drive it out of business.[22]

Executive Order 13202 says that when federal agencies award contracts, they can neither require nor prohibit the contractors from entering into or adhering to agreements with unions. The D.C. Circuit upheld the order as legitimate proprietary action, not regulation, and therefore within the President's powers and not preempted by the NLRA.[23]

[C] Collective Bargaining

A collective bargaining agreement (union contract) sets out most of the important work-related issues, including compensation and benefits. Even when a contract is in place, it may be necessary to bargain on the "mandatory" issues described by 29 USC § 158(a)(5), and allowable to bargain on "permissible" issues. Mandatory issues are those that materially or significantly affect the terms and conditions of employment, whereas permissible bargaining subjects have a remote or incidental effect.

---

[20] Chamber of Commerce of the USA v. Brown, 128 S. Ct. 2408 (2008). Florida, Illinois, Maine, Massachusetts, Minnesota, New York, North Dakota, Ohio, and Rhode Island passed similar laws, and bills of this type were introduced in Michigan and New Jersey.

[21] Starcon, Inc. v. NLRB, 176 F.3d 948 (7th Cir. 1999).

[22] Casino Ready Mix v. NLRB, 321 F.3d 1190 (D.C. Cir. 2003).

[23] Building & Constr. Trades v. Allbaugh, 295 F.3d 28 (D.C. Cir. 2002).

If bargaining reaches an impasse, when neither side is willing to concede, and neither has any new proposals to submit, the employer can lawfully cease negotiating and implement its own proposals.

A union's failure to act with due diligence can relieve the employer of the duty to bargain.[24]

When a collective bargaining agreement expires, there is no contract left to be enforced. However, labor law (NLRA § 8(a)(5)) requires the employer to maintain the status quo, at least until an impasse is reached.

In a unionized company, the employer is allowed to make unilateral decisions about subjects that are deemed to be management prerogatives, but has to bargain in good faith about other issues. Managerial prerogatives include terminating operations completely; selling an entire business; relocating unit work to a new location; or a partial closing that has business rather than anti-union motivation.

It is an unfair labor practice for an employer to enter into a contract, then disavow it based on doubts about the union's majority status, if the employer already had information justifying the doubts when it entered the contract. In that situation, the employer should have refused to enter into a CBA with a non-representative union, rather than entering into and then seeking to repudiate the contract.[25]

An employer violated the NLRA's § 8(a)(1) and (5) requirement that employees must be permitted to bargain through representatives of their choosing by holding bargaining sessions during regular business hours, and insisting that employees on the bargaining committee use paid leave to attend the sessions. (The union asked for unpaid leave for the committee, but the company permitted unpaid leave only for long-term absences.)[26]

A 1999 NLRB holding[27] created a "successor bar" rule. Under this rule, the incumbent union would be given a reasonable amount of time after a corporate takeover to bargain with the successor employer. During this time, challenges to the union's majority status would not be allowed. However, the NLRB overruled its own earlier decision in 2002. The current rule is that the incumbent union is entitled to a rebuttable presumption of its continued majority status. However, that presumption will not prevent an otherwise valid challenge to majority status.[28]

[D] Labor Arbitration

Arbitration, and other forms of alternative dispute resolution, are becoming more and more common in our society, which is highly litigious but has a court

---

[24] AT&T Corp., 337 NLRB No. 105 (5/24/02).

[25] Auciello Iron Works Inc. v. NLRB, 517 U.S. 781 (1996). *See also* Chelsea Industries v. NLRB, 285 F.3d 1073 (D.C. Cir. 2002), upholding the NLRA's policy that it is an unfair labor practice for an employer to use information obtained during the certification year to withdraw recognition of the union for non-majority status after the certification year.

[26] Ceridian Corp. v. NLRB, 435 F.3d 352 (D.C. Cir. 2006).

[27] St. Elizabeth's Manor, 329 NLRB 341 (1999).

[28] MV Transp., 337 NLRB No. 129 (7/19/02).

system far too small to meet all demands for dispute resolution. The LMRA is drafted to encourage arbitration. When a union agrees to arbitrate an issue, it more or less agrees not to strike over the issue, and the employer also agrees to avoid unilateral action.

Labor arbitration is divided into two main categories: grievance arbitration or rights arbitration, used to resolve disagreement about interpreting an existing contract; and contract or interest arbitration, used to determine which provisions should be included in a new, renewed, or reopened CBA.

The three 1960 Supreme Court cases known collectively as the *Steelworkers' Trilogy*[29] have determined that if it is not clear whether a company has agreed to arbitrate a particular issue, the issue is deemed arbitrable.

If a CBA contains both an arbitration clause and a no-strike clause, any dispute about the application and interpretation of the CBA is arbitrable unless the contract terms specifically reject arbitration. Arbitrators begin by considering the CBA language, but they can also use the "law of the shop" — practices that have evolved in that particular company. Arbitrators can consider factors such as the effect of a decision on productivity, morale, and workplace atmosphere.

Arbitration begins with a "demand"; usually either the American Arbitration Association or the Federal Mediation and Conciliation Service will be involved in the process. Even if there is no arbitration clause in the CBA, the employer and union can sign a one-time "submission agreement" agreeing to be bound by the arbitration decision in a particular instance.

Once an arbitration award is rendered, it is usually final, binding, and not subject to judicial review by any court.

The Supreme Court decided in March 2001 that the Federal Arbitration Act is generally applicable to employment contracts. Although the language of the FAA exempts "contracts of employment of seamen, railroad employees, or any other class of workers engaged in foreign or interstate commerce," the exemption is limited to transportation workers. It does not extend to all workers engaged in interstate commerce. Therefore, predispute arbitration clauses are not necessarily unenforceable merely because they involve workers in interstate commerce.[30]

A number of recent cases permit enforcement of predispute arbitration agreements.[31]

See §§ 25.06 and 25.07 for further discussion of arbitration of employee claims.

---

[29] Reported beginning at 363 U.S. 564.

[30] Circuit City Stores v. Adams, 532 U.S. 105 (2001).

[31] *See, e.g.*, Chanchani v. Salomon/Smith Barney Inc., 2001 WL 204214 (S.D.N.Y. 3/0/01) (arbitration policy expressed in employee handbook); Wright v. SFX Entertainment Inc., 2001 WL 103433 (S.D.N.Y. 2/7/01) (arbitration clause in written employment agreement); Marcus v. Masucci, 118 F. Supp. 2d 453 (S.D.N.Y. 2000) (securities industry arbitration agreement).

[1] Arbitrable Issues

The issues that can be arbitrated are quite similar to those that are mandatory bargaining subjects, because arbitration and CBA negotiation are complementary processes. Potentially arbitrable issues include:

- Sale of a business
- Relocation of operations
- Contracting out bargaining unit work
- Temporary shutdowns
- Layoffs
- Choosing employees for reinstatement after a layoff
- Discharge of single employees
- Work schedules and assignments
- Compensation, including overtime pay, incentive pay, bonuses, and severance pay
- Employer's contributions to pension and welfare benefit plans.

Courts show a strong partiality for directing arbitration of disputes, and if one clause is invalid, in many cases the court will sever it but enforce the rest of the contract.[32]

[E] Strikes

The NLRA makes it legal for employees to engage in "protected concerted activities," including organizing, protesting, and going on strike (although without threats, violence, or sabotage). Where a threatened strike imperils national health or safety, the President of the United States has the power to order the U.S. Attorney General to petition the appropriate federal court to enjoin the strike during an 80-day cooling-off period when negotiations can continue.

NLRA § 8(g) requires ten days' written notice before a strike against a health-care institution. Although the notice can be extended by written consent from both sides, unilateral deviations are not permitted. Therefore, the Eighth Circuit held that it was an illegal strike for nurses to start a strike four hours after the time designated on the notice, and the hospital was justified in firing them.[33]

NLRA § 8(b)(4) bans secondary strikes and secondary boycotts — actions taken against one employer to put pressure on a different employer that is engaged in a dispute with the union. Companies subjected to secondary strikes or boycotts can sue for damages under LMRA § 303.

---

[32] *See, e.g.,* Booker v. Robert Half Int'l Inc., 413 F.3d 77 (D.C. Cir. 2005).
[33] Minnesota Licensed Practical Nurses Ass'n v. NLRB, 406 F.3d 1020 (8th Cir. 2005).

Strikes are lawful in three situations:

- Economic disputes with the employer
- Unfair labor practices
- Unreasonably dangerous workplace conditions.

If a strike begins as an economic strike, it can be converted to an unfair labor practices strike if the employer acts unfairly or refuses to accept legitimate offers to return to work. The main difference between an economic strike and an unfair labor practices strike is the extent of employees' right to reinstatement after the strike ends.

A sitdown strike (illegal takeover of part or all of the employer's premises) or wildcat strike (called by the rank-and-file without authorization from the union) is illegal, because it is not protected concerted activity as defined by federal labor law.

If the CBA includes a no-strike clause, then an unfair labor practices strike can be lawful, but an economic strike is not protected concerted activity. Therefore, the employer can legitimately fire strikers and deny them reinstatement.

[1] Lockouts

The lockout is the employer's counterpart of a strike; it consists of refusing to let employees come to work. Labor law allows an employer that undertakes a lockout for business reasons to hire replacement workers, but not to use the lockout to permanently contract out work formerly performed by unionized employees. If employees violate a CBA no-strike clause and go on strike, the employer is justified in locking them out.

Lockouts are not permitted if the employer uses them to prevent unionization, or as a means to avoid bargaining with an incumbent union. A lockout is an unfair labor practice if it is inherently destructive of the rights of employees, or if it is undertaken without legitimate economic business justification.

[2] Striker Replacements

During a strike, it is lawful for the employer to hire temporary replacement workers. Under some circumstances, the employer will be able to hire permanent replacements, denying reinstatement to strikers. It may also be permissible to outsource functions previously performed by employees.

Certain circumstances deprive strikers of their employee status, and therefore they are no longer protected under the NLRA and it is not an unfair labor practice to discharge them. People who engage in unlawful strikes (i.e., strikes that are not called by an organized bargaining representative; sitdown strikes; strikes that are not called after a CBA expires, and that are not economic or unfair labor practices strikes) or engage in severe violence lose employee status.

In an economic strike, the employer can hire permanent replacements and keep them on the payroll after the strike ends. However, strikers who have not been replaced are entitled to reinstatement, and it is an unfair labor practice to delay their reinstatement.

If the replacement worker quits or is terminated, the employer must reinstate any former economic striker who makes an unconditional application for reinstatement. The reinstated striker must be treated on a par with nonstrikers and permanent replacements (e.g., benefits and seniority), unless there is valid business justification for treating that worker differently.

If there are no job openings at the time of the application, the employer must reinstate the ex-striker as soon as a job becomes available — unless the ex-striker gets regular and substantially equivalent employment somewhere else, or unless the ex-striker has committed violence or sabotage, or the employer has another good business reason to refuse reinstatement.

A "Laidlaw vacancy," also known as a "genuine job vacancy," occurs if replacement workers cannot reasonably expect to be recalled after being laid off by the employer. In this situation, strikers are entitled to reinstatement.

[F] The WARN Act

A federal statute, the Worker Adjustment Retraining and Notice Act ("WARN Act," 29 USC § 2101), requires large employers to notify employees of events that will result in large-scale job loss. Employers are subject to the law if they have 100 or more full-time employees, or a combination of full-time and part-time employees adding up to the equivalent of 100 people and 4,000 weekly work hours.

Before any plant closing (termination, prolonged layoff, serious cutback in work hours) or mass layoff, the employer must give at least 60 days' notice to employees, union, and the federal government.

If the employer fails to give the required notice, each affected employee is entitled to receive up to 60 work days' back pay and benefits. A federal civil penalty of up to $500 per day can also be imposed. Unions can sue for damages on behalf of their employees.

The WARN Act requires 60-day notice whenever there is a plant closing, even though the employees lose their jobs more than 30 days before the actual closing. As long as there is a plant closing, the 30-day aggregation period is irrelevant to determine who must be notified. The employer in this case (which closed down an unsafe mine) said that it had to give notice only to employees whose actual layoff came within the 30-day aggregation period that defines plant closing. But in the Fourth Circuit view, everyone affected by the closing is entitled to notice. The 30-day period relates to whether or not 50 people are involved, triggering the numerical threshold.[34]

The WARN Act and the Labor-Management Relations Act (LMRA) preempt state-law liens that relate to sanctions for WARN Act noncompliance (as well as unpaid wages and amounts claimed under a CBA). LMRA § 301 preempts CBA claims, so employee claims to bankruptcy priority liens arising out of vacation pay,

---

[34] United Mine Workers v. Martinka Coal Co., 202 F.3d 717 (4th Cir. 2000).

wages, pension contributions, or health claims under a CBA are necessarily preempted.[35]

The Tenth Circuit ruled in mid-2004 that back pay awards are not proper under ERISA § 510 in plant closing cases, because back pay and damages stemming from plant closings are not the kind of equitable relief available to plan participants under ERISA § 502(a)(3).[36]

§ 3.03 OTHER STATUTES AFFECTING THE EMPLOYMENT RELATIONSHIP

Various other statutes that do not come under the rubric of labor law nevertheless affect the employer-employee relationship, including unemployment insurance programs, workers' compensation, and occupational safety and health laws. See § 3.10 below, for antidiscrimination statutes.

The Workers Economic Opportunity Act, P.L. 106-202, amends the Fair Labor Standards Act, so that stock options are not included in the regular rate of pay when FLSA calculations are made.

The Intelligence Reform and Terrorism Prevention Act of 2004, signed December 17, 2004, permits private employers to access information from the FBI's criminal database about people working as, or applying for jobs as, private security officers.[37]

[A] Unemployment Insurance

The states administer an insurance system to provide payments to unemployed workers. Employers pay into the fund. Ex-employees may qualify for benefits depending on various factors, including whether they were involuntarily terminated or quit voluntarily. Employees can qualify for benefits if the employer had good cause to fire them (e.g., tardiness or poor work performance), but not if they were guilty of serious misconduct such as theft. Employees who quit their jobs are not entitled to benefits, unless some wrongful situation operated as a constructive termination.

The employee must have worked at least as long as the "base period" in order to qualify for benefits. The usual base period is the first four of the preceding five calendar quarters. The person seeking unemployment insurance benefits must make a good-faith effort to find another job that is suitable for someone of similar education, training, and experience. Eligibility is terminated by refusal of an offer of suitable work. Benefits are also unavailable in any week in which the claimant receives a pension, annuity, retirement pay, or other payment based on past work history, but not profit-sharing distributions (because those are not compensation for work).

---

[35] *In re* Bluffton Casting Corp., 186 F.3d 857 (7th Cir. 1999).

[36] Millsap v. McDonnell Douglas Corp., 162 F. Supp. 2d 12 (N.D. Ok. 2003), *rev'd*, 368 F.3d 1246 (10th Cir. 2004).

[37] *See* 73 L.W. 2391.

The amount of the benefit is based on the claimant's wages, either the average or the highest wage earned in any calendar quarter of the base period. Calculations are usually based on a 52-week benefit year specific to each claimant, beginning when the claim is filed. Most states provide a maximum benefit period of 26 weeks for the basic benefit. Extensions may be available for weeks 27–39 under the Federal-State Extended Benefits program created by the Employment Security Amendments of 1970.[38] Some states have extended-benefit funds that are completely funded by the state, without federal involvement.

When a person applies for unemployment compensation, his or her last employer is contacted and asked for an explanation of the termination. The employer has a period of time to contest the award of unemployment benefits; after that time passes, the employer has waived the right to protest. The state department that handles unemployment benefits determines whether or not benefits are available. The decision can be appealed to an Administrative Law Judge, an administrative board, and finally in the court system.

Employers are allowed to challenge unemployment insurance claims because the unemployment insurance rate they pay is partially based on the "experience" (the number of claims filed against them). The Pension Protection Act, P.L. 109-280 § 1105, forbids states to reduce unemployment compensation because pension distributions were rolled over and thereby escaped federal tax.

Title IV of H.R. 2642, the Supplemental Appropriations Act of 2008, signed June 30, 2008, provides for the Emergency Unemployment Compensation program, which makes certain persons who have exhausted their regular state benefits eligible for up to 13 weeks more benefits. States can elect to enter into an agreement with the Secretary of Labor to receive federal grant money to provide the benefits to eligible individuals. Eligible persons are those who had 20 weeks of full-time insured employment during the base period in which they received unemployment benefits and have exhausted all their state and federal unemployment benefits. The weekly benefit amount equals the unemployment benefits the person was entitled to under state law. The state sets up an emergency unemployment compensation account for each eligible person, and the federal government reimburses the state for the EUC paid out to eligible persons. This is a temporary program, and benefits are payable only for weeks of unemployment occurring after the state signs an agreement with the Department of Labor and before March 31, 2009. No compensation can be paid for any week beginning after June 1, 2009.[39]

---

[38] For extensions to the unemployment program, *see* P.L. 108-1 and P.L. 108-26; the latter lasting until December 31, 2003.

[39] *See* http://workforcesecurity.doleta.gov/unemploy/supp_act/asp; *see also* http://www.servicelocator.org/OWSLinks.asp for links to state unemployment offices.

[1] FUTA Tax

In addition to insurance under the state system, employers must pay a Federal Unemployment Tax Act (FUTA) tax of 6.2% of the first $7,000 of each employee's wages. Any employer who had at least one common-law employee on one day in 20 different weeks, or paid $1,500 or more in wages in any calendar quarter, is subject to FUTA tax.

Unlike FICA (Social Security) tax, FUTA is imposed only on the employer, not both employer and employee. However, most employers qualify for a credit under Code § 3302, for state unemployment taxes, so the usual effective rate is only 0.8% of the first $7,000 of wages. Employers whose FUTA liability exceeds $500 for any of the first three quarters of the year must make quarterly deposits. If the FUTA liability for the fourth quarter, plus undeposited amounts from earlier quarters, exceeds $500, a deposit must be made by January 31 of the following year. If it does not, then the employer has the option of either making the deposit with the Federal Tax Deposit Coupon, Form 8109, or through the Electronic Federal Tax Payment System (EFTPS), or paying the amount by January 31 with Form 940 or Form 940-EZ.[40] The FUTA tax rate includes a 0.2% surtax. Although it was scheduled to expire at the end of 2007, P.L. 110-140 amends Code § 3301 to extend the surtax for one more year.

[B] Workers' Compensation

As a general rule, employees who are injured at work or who suffer work-related illness are not entitled to bring tort suits against their employers. The doctrine of "Workers' Compensation exclusivity" means that their sole means of redress is to receive benefits under the state-run Workers' Compensation system.

The Workers' Compensation (WC) system is funded by employer payments. Depending on state requirements and the employer's option, the funding may take the form of setting aside reserves (self-insurance), purchasing insurance, or making payments into a state fund. Insurance rates depend on the "manual rate" charged for the relevant industry classification, adjusted by the employer's own experience of WC claims. In the context of bankruptcy, the premiums owed to a Worker's Compensation carrier do not receive priority under Bankruptcy Code § 507(a)(5) as unpaid contributions to an employee benefit plan.[41]

When an employee claims job-related injury or illness, the claim is heard by a WC tribunal (usually called either a board or a commission) which determines the validity of the claim. If the claim is adjudged valid, the worker is awarded reimbursement of medical expenses, plus weekly income, usually limited to half or two-thirds of the previous wage. Compensation benefits do not begin until a three-to seven-day waiting period has elapsed, to distinguish between minor and serious incidents. However, most states provide retroactive payments back to the original injury or onset date, if the disability continues for a period of time (e.g., over seven weeks).

---

[40] *See* IRS Tax Topics Topic 759, http://www.irs.gov/taxtopics/tc759.html.
[41] Howard Delivery Serv. Inc. v. Zurich Am. Ins. Co., 547 U.S. 651 (2006).

Most states follow the "agreement system," under which uncontested claims lead to a settlement negotiated by the parties, or by the employee and the employer's WC insurer. Contested cases are decided by the agency administering the system, and appeals rights are granted to both employer and employee.

Benefits are awarded in four categories: permanent total disability; permanent partial disability; temporary total disability (the most common category); and temporary partial disability. There is also a schedule of reimbursement for the so-called "schedule injuries," loss of a finger, toe, arm, eye, or leg. Death benefits are also available to the survivors of persons killed in work-related incidents.

In general, WC is a no-fault system, and negligence by any party is irrelevant. However, in some states, a worker's failure to use safety equipment can reduce (but not eliminate) the benefit.

Most states have statutes penalizing employer retaliation against employees who file WC claims.

Pennsylvania's Workers' Compensation Act requires that, once liability is no longer contested, the employer or its insurer must pay for all reasonable or necessary treatment. However, it is permissible to withhold payment for disputed treatment until an independent third party has performed utilization review. This statute was construed by the Supreme Court in *American Manufacturer Mutual Insurance Co. v. Sullivan*.[42] The *Sullivan* plaintiffs sued state officials, Workers' Compensation insurers, and a self-insured school district, charging that benefits had been withheld without notice, depriving them of a property right.

Their arguments were unsuccessful. The Supreme Court decided that private insurers are not state actors, and therefore their utilization review activities do not raise Due Process issues. Employees do not have a property right until the treatment they seek has been determined to be reasonable and necessary, and therefore there is no right to notice and hearing until that point.

On a related issue, in its January 10, 2007 decision in *Norfolk Southern Railway Co. v. Sorrell*, 549 U.S. 158 (2007), the Supreme Court did not define the standard of causation to be used when a railroad employee is injured and brings suit under the Federal Employers' Liability Act — but the same standard must be used to determine the railroad's liability and the employee's contributory negligence. The case arose in Missouri, where stricter standards were applied to employers than to employees.

[C] Occupational Safety and Health

The federal Occupational Safety and Health Act (OSH Act) is enforced by the Occupational Safety and Health Administration (OSHA). OSHA's mandate is to protect employees against unreasonably hazardous workplaces.

All employers must satisfy the "general duty standard" of providing a workplace that is reasonably free of recognized dangers. Other OSHA standards apply to specific situations, especially within the construction industry. OSHA's General

---

[42] 526 U.S. 46 (1999).

Industry Standards cover, e.g., condition of floors in the workplace; number and design of entrances and exits; personal protective equipment; fire prevention and safety; guards on machinery; cutting and welding; proper tool use; and control of electrical and chemical hazards.

The OSH Act gives OSHA the authority to inspect workplaces, order correction of violations, and impose penalties if correction does not occur or is too slow.

The Act also requires employers to record all meaningful workplace injuries and illnesses on the official OSHA-301 Supplementary Record of Occupational Injury and Illnesses, and to use this information to create annual reports (Forms OSHA-300 and 300A, Log and Summary of Work-Related Injuries and Illnesses) which must be forwarded to OSHA and disclosed to the workers. The OSH Act covers all employers whose operations affect commerce among the states. There is no minimum number of employees triggering coverage, although certain small-scale or low risk operations are entitled to take advantage of reduced reporting requirements.

The OSH Act imposes requirements for personal protective equipment, lockout/tagout (preventing moving parts of machinery from causing injury), and exposure to hazardous materials. The OSH Act sets Permissible Exposure Limits (PELs) for materials such as asbestos and lead. The PEL is the level of contact that is safe for an employee. The employer must monitor the plant environment to make sure that PELs are not exceeded, to provide appropriate safety equipment, and to train employees in safety. Hazardous materials must be stored properly, and employees must be informed about their presence and trained in the appropriate precautions. The OSH Act also treats excessive noise as a hazardous phenomenon that must be monitored and reported.

Occupational safety enforcement is coordinated between the federal government and the states. States are permitted to draft their own regulatory plans; the plan becomes an "approved state plan" if the federal Department of Labor deems the plan adequately protective of workers' safety. About half the states have approved state plans. In the other states, OSHA has primary responsibility for safety enforcement, but states can regulate issues not covered by the OSH Act, such as furnace and boiler safety.

Inspections of premises are made, either routinely or based on complaints. OSHA can issue citations if hazardous conditions are found during an inspection. In general, employers are given 30 days to abate the violation by correcting the hazardous conditions. There are schedules of monetary penalties, based on factors such as the current number of violations, number found in the past and not corrected, and the actual danger of the violation. In egregious cases, criminal penalties can be imposed. Also see 29 USC § 666(e), penalties for willful violations of OSHA standards that result in the death of an employee. Employers are given the right to challenge citations and proposed penalties.[43]

---

[43] It is not double jeopardy to impose administrative penalties on an employer that has already been convicted of criminal OSHA violations, because the administrative penalties are purely civil and do not carry the possibility of imprisonment: S.A. Healy Co. v. OSHRC, 138 F.3d 686 (7th Cir. 1998).

§ 3.04 FAIR LABOR STANDARDS ACT

The Fair Labor Standards Act (FLSA; 29 USC §§ 201–219, 251–262) governs wage and hour issues in both the public and private sectors, including the minimum wage (remaining steady at $5.15 per hour for many years) and time-and-a-half overtime payments for non-exempt workers. The minimum wage was raised at last by 2007 legislation.[44] The minimum wage rose to $5.85 per hour 60 days after enactment, to $6.55 per hour 12 months later, and to $7.25 per hour 24 months after the second increase.

The FLSA provides a private right of action for employees for unpaid minimum wages and/or overtime,[45] plus liquidated damages, attorneys' fees, and court costs. The Secretary of Labor can also sue for unpaid minimum wages and overtime, which are paid to the employees. Further violations can be enjoined. Willful FLSA violations can be criminal, subject to prosecution by the federal Attorney General's office. Legal and equitable relief can be ordered against employers who retaliate against workers who make FLSA complaints.

In November 2005, the Supreme Court decided *IBP, Inc. v. Alvarez*, 546 U.S. 21(2005). Under the Portal-to-Portal Act, working hours subject to the FLSA do not include walking to and from the employee's principle work location once the employee has entered the employer's workplace. Activities that are "preliminary" or "postliminary" to the principal work task are also not part of the FLSA-covered workweek. *Alvarez* concerns the pay status of time spent putting on and removing safety gear, when wearing the gear is a mandatory part of the employee's job. The Supreme Court ruled that time spent walking from the changing area to the production line is compensable, and so is time spent leaving the production floor to take off the protective gear. But the time employees spend waiting to put on the first piece of protective gear is a preliminary activity, so it is not covered by the FLSA.

[A] Employee Status

Various benefits are available to, or must be provided to, a company's "employees," so it is often important to distinguish employees from independent contractors, or to determine which company actually employs an individual and therefore is responsible for wage-and-hour compliance.

For instance, a company must pay its share of FICA taxes for its "employees," but independent contractors must pay 100% of their own FICA tax. Whether a benefit plan is discriminatory depends in large part on the percentage of "employees" it covers, and how their benefits compare to those of highly compensated

---

[44] U.S. Troop Readiness, Veterans' Care, Katrina Recovery, and Iraq Accountability Appropriations Act. P.L. 110-28 Title VIII, amending 29 USC § 206(a)(1).

[45] *See* http://www.dol.gov/elaws/otcalculator.htm, the DOL Wage & Hour Division's Web tool for calculating overtime pay, based on various scenarios including bonuses, commissions, and shift differentials, discussed in Adrien Martin, *DoL Unveils Web-based Overtime Pay Calculator*, Plansponsor.com (5/9/07).

employees (HCEs). Eligibility for participation in pension and welfare benefit plans is usually restricted to employees.

Leased employees — who are formally employed by a company that then leases their services to other companies — may have to be treated as employees of the company where their services are actually performed, if the lease arrangement is long-term rather than limited in duration. See Code § 414(n) and cases interpreting it.[46] It is also possible that both leasing company and recipient will be treated as co-employers.

The higher the degree of control the potential employer exercises over a person's working environment and tasks, the more likely that person is to be an employee; the lower the degree of control, the more likely the relationship is to be one between independent contractor and client.

Under the Internal Revenue Code, licensed real estate agents working under written contracts describing them as independent contractors are not employees[47], but full-time life insurance salespersons, corporate officers, full-time traveling salespersons, and certain delivery drivers are statutory employees.

IRS' IR-96-44, "Independent Contractor or Employee?" sets out a 20-factor test for assessing status, for example:

- If the worker is given instructions that must be followed
- If training is provided
- If the services are integrated into the employer's ordinary work or separate
- If the worker works for others at the same time
- If work is performed on the employer's premises or at another location
- If the employer provides tools and materials
- If the worker holds him- or herself out as providing services to the public.

Similar tests are used by states, e.g., for unemployment insurance purposes.

---

[46] The EEOC's guidance on leased employees is published at http://www.eeoc.gov/press/12 -8-97.html. Bronk v. Mountain States Telephone & Telegraph Inc., 98-1 USTC ¶50,316 (10th Cir. 1998) finds it lawful to draft a plan to exclude leased employees, even those who are common-law employees, on the grounds that the Code and ERISA merely require leased employees to be treated as employees, not necessarily that they be offered plan participation. In contrast, the Ninth Circuit's decisions in Vizcaino v. Microsoft, 97 F.3d 1187 (9th Cir. 1995), aff'd, 120 F.3d 1006 (9th Cir. 1997) and #98-71388, 99-35013 entitle individuals who had long-term assignments at Microsoft through temporary agencies, who Microsoft claimed were independent contractors, to participate in Microsoft stock purchase plans.

[47] Flanagan v. Allstate Insurance Co., No. 01 C 1541 (N.D. Ill. 5/23/08); see Fred Schneyer, *Allstate Agents Dealt Legal Setback in Employment Status Case*, Plansponsor.com (5/29/08).

[A dispute lasting more than seven years ended in the conclusion by the Northern District of Illinois that changing the status of insurance salespersons from "employee-agent" to independent contractor did not illegally deprive them of benefits. The agents' ERISA § 510 claims (that they were constructively terminated to keep them from receiving benefits) were dismissed. The judge found valid business reasons for the change, such as providing more convenient evening and weekend hours for customers to deal with agents. Even though the effect was that a number of agents quit, the court refused to treat this as proof of intent to violate ERISA § 510.]

Section 530 of the Revenue Act of 1978 permits a safe harbor if the employer, acting reasonably and in good faith, characterized the worker as an independent contractor, based on industry practice or published authority from the IRS itself or the court system. The employer must have treated the individual consistently as an independent contractor (e.g., by filing Form 1099 recording each year's compensation) and must never have treated the individual as an employee. If the safe harbor applies, the IRS will not be able to re-classify the worker as an employee, assess back taxes or penalties, or require payment of back FICA/Medicare taxes.

The Community Renewal Tax Relief Act of 2000, P.L. 106-554, expanded the Tax Court's jurisdiction in employment status determination proceedings, retroactive to assessments made on or after August 5, 1997. See Notice 2002-5, 2002-3 I.R.B. 320, for the IRS' procedure for issuing a Notice of Determination of Worker Classification. A taxpayer dissatisfied with the classification can petition the Tax Court under Code § 7436 for a re-determination. The IRS will issue a Notice only if it determines that persons who are performing services for the employer are wrongly classified and the safe harbor does not apply. The employer is the sole party that can petition the Tax Court (the employees cannot, and neither can third parties), and the petition is proper only after the notice has been issued.

As a result of the Pension Protection Act of 2005 (P.L. 109-280), the Tax Court's special trial judges can issue decisions in employment status cases that are small case proceedings under § 7436(c).

[B] Employment Tax Compliance

The employer is required to withhold income taxes from the compensation of common-law employees, based on the amount of wages paid, the worker's marital status, and the number of exemptions claimed on the W-4 (the IRS form used to claim withholding exemptions).

Withholding is done either by the percentage method or the wage bracket method. The percentage method uses tables of withholding allowances and wage rates; the wage bracket method uses tables to compute the withholding per pay period based on wage level, marital status, and the number of exemptions claimed. The official withholding tables are usually found in IRS Publication 15. In many instances, withholding is also required from pension payments. (In certain circumstances, the retiring employee is entitled to elect exemption from withholding.) Pension payments in annuity form can follow ordinary withholding procedures, using the number of withholding exemptions claimed by the retiree on Form W-4P.

A lump sum or other non-periodic payment that is eligible for rollover, and that is rolled over (see § 3.05[C][1]) does not require withholding. Ineligible amounts are subject to withholding; see the instructions for IRS Form 1099-R.

[1] Trust Fund Taxes

FICA (Social Security/Medicare) taxes have two equal components: one paid by the employer, one by the employee. The rate is 7.65% of compensation for each, consisting of OASDI (Social Security) tax of 6.2% and Medicare tax of 1.45%. OASDI tax is charged only on the first $94,200 (2006), $97,500 (2007), $102,000 (2008), and $106,800 (2009) of compensation (the "wage base"); Medicare tax is charged on all compensation. If a person has more than one employer during a calendar year, the wage base is applied to compensation from each employer. If this results in over-withholding, the employee must claim a credit for the excess payments.

FICA (and income) taxes withheld from employees are "trust fund taxes"; the employer's share of FICA tax and Federal Unemployment Tax Act (FUTA) taxes are a responsibility of the employer, but are not deemed trust fund taxes.

Under Code § 6672, a "responsible person" (i.e., responsible for remitting the taxes) is subject to a 100% penalty for willful failure to submit withheld trust fund taxes to the government. Corporate officers, shareholders, and directors can be responsible persons, depending on their level of responsibility within the corporation; even lower-level managers, or bankers or accountants, can become responsible persons if they have actual responsibility for tax remittance.

The penalty cannot be discharged in bankruptcy, and all of the personal assets of the responsible person are subject to this penalty. Under the Taxpayer Bill of Rights 2 (see § 21.08[D]) the IRS must give 60 days' advance written notice of intent to impose the penalty (unless collection is in jeopardy).

[2] Routine Tax Compliance

When a new qualified plan is created, it must apply to the IRS for a determination letter, using Form 5300. Form 5310 redetermines qualification when a plan is terminated; Form 5310A is notice to the IRS of plan merger, consolidation, or transfer of assets.

The annual report of a pension plan is filed on the Form 5500 series. The electronic Form 5500 filing system is known as EFAST. The IRS, DOL, and the PBGC collaborated on the system, which can accept machine-printed and hand-printed forms. Participating plans must apply for a PIN number, and only approved software can be used for electronic filings. A Final Rule for EFAST, for plan years beginning on or after 1/1/08, was published in 2006, and supplemented by a Proposed Rule.[48]

The Pension Protection Act, at § 1103, exempts one-person plans with assets under $250,000 from the requirement of filing Form 5500. ERISA § 502(c)(2) imposes civil penalties for failure to file the 5500-series form if it is required.

---

[48] *See* 71 FR 31077 (6/1/06), 71 FR 41392 and 41359 (7/21/06); EBSA's FAQ is posted at http://www.dol/gov/ebsa/faqs/faq_efast.html, and the DOL's 2/2/06 draft of *User's Guide for Electronic/Magnetic Media Filing of Forms 5500 and 5500-EZ* is available at http://www.dol .gov/ebsa/pdf/efast-a.pdf. Effective for 2005 and later plan years, the IRS determined that Schedule P (Annual Return of Fiduciary Benefit Trust) is no longer required in connection with filing of Form 5500-EZ; for all other forms in the 5500 series, Schedule P is eliminated for 2006 and later years. The elimination of this form is part of the transition to electronic filing. [Announcement 2007-63, 2007-30 IRB 236 "Elimination of Schedule P of Form 5500 Series."]

Various forms must be submitted in connection with employee compensation:

- W-2: compensation paid for each employee
- W-3: transmittal form for all W-2 forms for the employer company
- W-4P: employee's election to opt out of withholding, or increase withholding, on pension and annuity payments
- 1096: omnibus transmittal form summing up other transmittal forms submitted by the employer
- 1099-R: reporting of lump sums and periodic distributions
- 941/941E: quarterly returns of federal income tax. Form 941 is used by employers who withheld or paid FICA taxes, 941E by those who did not
- 5300: excise tax form for failure to meet the minimum funding standard.

The IRS' objective is to eliminate business tax filing on paper and move to an entirely electronic system. For tax years ending on or after 12/31/05, Form 1120 and 1120-S must be filed electronically by corporations whose assets exceed $50 million if they file at least 250 returns a year (including income tax, employment tax, and information returns). For tax years ending on or after 12/31/06, the same requirement applies to corporations with assets over $10 million, filing 250 returns a year. W-2 forms can also be filed electronically, but they are sent to the Social Security Administration rather than the IRS.

Withholding on pension payments is reported once a year on Form 945, Annual Return of Withheld Federal Income Tax.

Employee compensation for the year is reported on Form W-2. The transition from filing on paper forms to a fully electronic system is almost complete.[49] Code § 6662 imposes an accuracy-related tax penalty for substantial overstatement of pension liability resulting in underpayment of tax.

[C] Routine PBGC Compliance

The Pension Benefit Guaranty Corporation (PBGC) insures part or all of the benefit that employees and retirees would otherwise lose when a defined benefit plan terminates. (The PBGC does not insure defined contribution benefits, because each participant can get his or her individual account balance when the plan terminates.)

Employers must pay a basic premium for PBGC coverage. For many years, the premium remained level at $19 per participant per year. Underfunded plans (those lacking the funding to meet anticipated obligations) were subject to an additional premium of $9/$1,000 of unfunded vested benefits. The Deficit Reduction Act of 2005, P.L. 109-171 § 8201, increases the basic premium to $30/participant/year, and calls for an annual premium rate adjustment based on

---

[49] For medium-sized and large businesses, *see* http://www.irs.gov/businesses/corporations/article/0,,id=146959,00.html; for self-employed individuals and small businesses (the test is assets below $10 million), *see* http://www.irs.gov/efile/article/0,,id=118520,00.html.

changes in the national average wage index.[50] For 2008, the variable-rate premium remains $9 per $1,000 of unfunded vested benefits, and the flat-rate premium rises to $33 and $9 per participant in single-employer and multi-employer plans respectively. For 2009, the premium is $34 per participant for single-employer, remaining $9 per participant for multi-employer plans. Final Regulations published in December, 2007 state that the flat rate premium can never go down because of an inflation adjustment, only up; and the premium must always be rounded to the nearest whole dollar, which the PBGC interprets to mean must be rounded up to the nearest whole dollar.

All PBGC-insured plans are required to file Form PBGC-1 each year as a combined annual report and declaration of premium payments. Form 200 must be filed with the PBGC within 10 days of any time at which the company has failed to meet the minimum funding standard by $1 million or more, and no waiver of minimum funding has been granted.

Plan administrators are obligated to report certain unusual events to the PBGC if the events might eventually lead to payment of insurance benefits. The events include the plan's bankruptcy, insolvency, merger, consolidation, or transfer of assets; the sponsoring company's bankruptcy or insolvency; or determination of the plan's noncompliance by a regulatory agency (PBGC, IRS, DOL).

[D] Compensation Deductions

Code § 162 permits a corporation to deduct its ordinary and necessary business expenses, including "reasonable" compensation for services actually rendered.

For tax years beginning after 1993, Code § 162(m) precludes a public company from deducting any portion of employee compensation (including both salary and benefits) that exceeds $1 million. Qualified retirement benefits are not counted for this purpose. Sales commissions, payments pursuant to a contract in effect on 2/17/93, and performance-based compensation measured by objective goals and approved by a compensation committee of the board of directors, are also excluded.

The Emergency Economic Stabilization Act of 2008 (EESA; P.L. 110-334) imposes certain limits on executive compensation, such as restrictions on the compensation tax deduction, ruling out certain golden parachutes, recapture of some compensation already paid, and a ban on incentives that could induce executives to take "unnecessary and excessive risks." However, the compensation limits apply only to senior executive officers of financial institutions that received federal bailouts under the Troubled Asset Relief Program (TARP). TARP is scheduled to end December 31, 2009, although the Secretary of the Treasury has the power to extend it until October 3, 2010.[51]

---

[50] PBGC, *What's New for Practitioners*, http://www.pbgc.gov/practitioners/Whats-New/whatsnew/page15560.html; see also Proposed Regulations 72 FR 30308 (5/31/07); see also Final Regulations, 72 FR 71222 (12/17/07).

[51] Frederick W. Cook & Co., Inc., *Congress Curbs Compensation of Executives Under Financial Rescue Plan*, 10/6/08 (benefitslink.com).

[E] Severance Pay

An employer's one-time decision to offer severance benefits to a single individual does not involve ERISA, but a severance pay "plan" (even an informal or unwritten arrangement) is subject to ERISA. A severance pay plan could be either a pension or a welfare benefit plan. Under DOL Reg. § 3510.3-2(b) and 29 CFR § 2510.3-1(a), the arrangement will not be a pension plan (and will therefore be analyzed under the more liberal requirements for welfare benefit plans) if:

- The recipient is able to seek another job without forfeiting any benefits
- Overall payments are not greater than twice the recipient's compensation for the year immediately preceding the termination
- Payments end within 24 months of termination — or, for a "limited program of terminations," end within 24 months of the time the employee reaches normal retirement age, if that is later.

[1] Parachute Payments

"Parachute" payments are special severance benefits triggered by a hostile takeover or takeover attempt. Usually these are "golden parachutes" that protect the target corporation's top executives, but a few states mandate "tin parachutes" for rank-and-file workers who lose their jobs due to corporate transitions. The theory is that an obligation to make large payments to workers disadvantaged by the transaction will discourage unwanted takeover attempts. A "single-trigger" parachute agreement gives an executive a right to additional compensation whenever the employer company merges or is acquired; a "double-trigger" imposes the additional requirement that the executive be terminated or demoted or otherwise suffer real economic injury.

If a parachute payment is so large that it depletes the corporate treasury, it might be vulnerable to a suit by stockholders charging corporate waste. However, the corporation, and the directors who authorized the arrangement, would probably be able to interpose a business judgment defense (see § 1.14[C]) on the grounds that the parachute plan defends the corporation against unwanted takeovers, and makes executives more productive by relieving them of economic anxiety.

The Internal Revenue Code (§§ 280G(b), 4999) imposes a 20% excise tax on "excess" parachute payments. Payments from qualified pension plans; payments made by S Corporations; and payments by non-public corporations that are approved by 75% of the company's stockholders, are exempt from the excise tax.

An excess payment (an amount that does not represent reasonable compensation, and that is more than three times the employee's "base amount") cannot be deducted as an ordinary and necessary business expense. The base amount is the executive's average annual compensation (including bonuses, fringe and pension benefits, and severance pay) for the five years just before the change in corporate control. As noted above, financial institutions that accept federal assistance must limit golden parachute payments that they make to their top management.

[F] Overtime and Exemption

Under the FLSA, each worker is either salaried and exempt, or an hourly worker entitled to receive time-and-a-half for overtime (more than 40 hours worked in a workweek). Hourly workers are paid for the number of hours actually worked, and are subject to having their wages docked based on variations in quality and quantity of work.[52] Workers are exempt if their primary duties are executive, administrative, or professional, or if they are outside salespersons. Overtime pay is not required for retail or service workers whose pay derives 50% or more from commissions, as long as the regular pay rate is at least 150% of the minimum wage.

If an individual is entitled to overtime pay, he or she must receive 150% of the normal pay rate (including commissions) for every hour over 40 worked during a workweek. The workweek is not necessarily Monday–Friday, 9–5: it can be any period of 168 consecutive hours. It is not necessary to pay overtime merely because weekend work is required, or if a particular work day lasts over 8 hours: 29 CFR § 778.602(a) requires overtime only if the entire workweek exceeds 40 hours. Overtime must either be paid in cash, on the regular payday for the pay period in which the overtime was worked, or in the form of "comp time" (an hour and a half off for every overtime hour).

On April 23, 2004, the Department of Labor published a lengthy Final Rule amending 29 CFR Part 541 to explain the FLSA § 13(a) overtime exemption for executives, administrative, professional, outside sales, and computer workers, raising the minimum salary test for white-collar workers from $155 to $455 a week. Anyone who earns less than $23,660 a year is automatically entitled to overtime for work over 40 hours a week, including blue-collar workers. Overtime entitlement depends on actual duties, not the job title, so employers cannot use "promotions" or inflated titles to avoid overtime payment.[53]

The Supreme Court ruled in 2007 that home care workers who provide companionship services to the elderly and infirm are not covered by minimum wage or overtime, whether they are officially employed by the family or by an agency.[54]

PART 2: PENSION AND BENEFIT ISSUES

§ 3.05 PENSION AND BENEFIT ISSUES IN THE
EMPLOYMENT RELATIONSHIP

The Department of Labor's site intended to provide guidance on compliance matters can be found at http://www.dol.gov/.compliance.

---

[52] However, the mere possibility of salary reductions for disciplinary infractions does not make an otherwise salaried worker a non-exempt hourly worker: Auer v. Robbins, 519 U.S. 452 (1997).

[53] 69 FR 22122 (4/23/04); *see* Wage and Hour Division's Fair Pay Fact Sheets at http://www.dol.gov/esa/regs/compliance/whd/fairpay/.

[54] Long Island Care at Home v. Coke, 127 S. Ct. 2339 (U.S. 6/11/07).

[A] Basic Concepts

There are several reasons for dividing employee compensation into current compensation (paid each week, every other week, every month, etc.) and deferred compensation (usually not paid until after the employee has retired, although there may be other ways to access such funds).

For one thing, employees may not save for retirement, so the deferred compensation plan protects them in their later years. For another thing, current compensation is generally taxed in the year it is paid, and high-income persons can face a heavy tax burden. The deferred compensation might be paid in a post-retirement year in which the recipient is in a lower tax bracket, thus saving taxes.

Pension law is considered an area of federal preemption, so nearly all pension issues are federal issues. The rules are quite complex, in part because there are both tax rules contained in the Internal Revenue Code, and rules of substantive law found in the Employee Retirement Income Security Act (ERISA). The rules also change frequently.

Major legislation, the Pension Protection Act, P.L. 109-280, was passed to cope with the problems of underfunded plans and to improve the smooth operation of 401(k) plans. In December 2008, however, in response to the financial crisis, certain Pension Protection Act provisions were modified by the Worker, Retiree, and Employer Recovery Act of 2008, P.L. 110-458 (WRERA).

Late in 2008, the House Committee on Education and Labor held hearings to investigate the causes behind the financial crisis. According to the CBO, assets in defined benefit plans lost 15% of their value over the preceding year; the situation was probably worse for defined contribution plans, which are more stock-oriented. The CBO estimated that overall, retirement plans declined in value by $2 trillion. For 60% of workers, 401(k) plans are their primary savings vehicle, and current conditions are leading to reassessment of whether the system's reliance on 401(k) plans was prudent.[55]

[1] Basic ERISA Concepts

ERISA establishes detailed rules for "qualified" plans — that is, plans for whose costs employers are entitled to take a tax deduction. It is also lawful for employers to maintain nonqualified plans, whose costs probably will not be currently deductible.

ERISA also governs welfare benefit plans: plans provided by employers on behalf of employees, but providing fringe benefits rather than post-retirement income.

Certain basic concepts are applicable to both pension and welfare benefit plans. All plans must be operated for the exclusive benefit of plan participants and their beneficiaries, not for the financial benefit of the employer or any private

---

[55] Nevin E. Adams, *Congress Considers Market Impact on Retirement Security*, Plansponsor .com (10/7/08); Jennifer Levitz, *Workplace Retirement Plans Suffer $2 Trillion in Losses*, Wall St. J. 10/8/08 at D2.

person. This requirement is interpreted to mean that plans cannot cover independent contractors, only common-law employees.

Each type of plan may be subject to a participation requirement (explaining the criteria employees must meet to be eligible for coverage under the plan) and a coverage requirement (at least a certain percentage both of all eligible employees and of employees overall must be covered).

To a certain extent, qualified plans can be more favorable to executives and managers than to rank-and-file employees, but such plans are subject to nondiscrimination rules that limit the extent to which highly compensated employees (HCEs) can be favored. Employers can establish nonqualified plans (§ 3.05[B][6]) instead of, or in addition to, qualified plans, but nonqualified plans limit the extent to which the employer can take current deductions for plan costs.

ERISA governs the way that qualified plans are set up, the form in which they are administered, which employees are entitled to participate, and how much must be and can be contributed on behalf of each employee. In most instances, ERISA requires plans to be in writing. Plan participants and beneficiaries are entitled to disclosure of the plan's terms and explanations of how it operates, including receiving a Summary Plan Description (SPD), annual reports, and explanation of material changes in the plan.

The management, investment, and distribution of plan assets and plan benefits come under ERISA, and so does the conduct of fiduciaries (trustees and others with responsibility for plan assets). ERISA's tax provisions are administered by the IRS; the labor law provisions come under the control of the Department of Labor. Title I of ERISA covers labor-law issues such as plan structure, fiduciary conduct, and prohibited transactions. Title I, Subtitle B contains many of the most important provisions, including reporting and disclosure; funding standards; fiduciary requirements; and continuation coverage for health insurance. Title II is the tax title.

[2] Defined Benefit Plan Concepts

The traditional pension plan is a defined benefit plan, where the employer's responsibility is to contribute enough each year so that, at retirement, employees will be able to receive a retirement benefit set at a particular number of dollars or defined by a formula (e.g., $x a month for every year worked for the employer). Such plans can be difficult and expensive to administer, and the employer has the investment risk: if the value of the plan's investment declines, the employer will have to contribute more to compensate.

They are also subject to the minimum funding requirement of Code § 412; the employer's failure to put enough money into the plan is penalized by excise taxes. Quarterly payments must be made; see § 412(m)(1). Underfunding also has to be reported to the PBGC. An employer that fails to fund its plan properly is subject to a lien on all its assets, and the PBGC may become involved in enforcing the lien. However, § 4972 also imposes excise taxes on overfunding of qualified plans, so the employer needs skillful actuarial advice on how much to contribute.

Before EGTRRA, the full funding limitation (the amount that the employer had to contribute to keep the plan economically sound in the long run) was defined as the amount by which the smaller of the plan's accrued liability or 160% of its current liability exceeded its assets. EGTRRA increases the current liability full funding limit from 160% to 165% of current liability for plan years that begin in 2002, and to 170% for plan years that begin in 2003. However, EGTRRA repeals the full funding limit for plan years that begin between 2004 and 2010. (Remember that all EGTRRA provisions sunset at the end of 2010.) Therefore, for plan years between 2004 and 2010, the full funding limit is simply the difference between the plan's accrued liability and the value of its assets. The Pension Protection Act adds complex new funding rules that increase the amount that must be contributed for the plan to remain fully funded, and imposes operational limits on many discretionary actions by underfunded plans. See § 3.05[H]. WRERA relaxed these rules somewhat, for the years 2008–2010.

In September 2008, the IRS finalized its 2007 Proposed Regulations, in response to the Pension Protection Act of 2006, governing mortality assumptions that set present values for minimum funding of defined benefit plans. If permission is obtained to use substitute tables, they must be gender-specific, generational, and based on a significant amount of experience (at least 1,000 deaths over a study period of two to five years). Notice 2008-85, 2008-42 IRB 905 provides the static mortality tables to calculate items such as the funding target level for valuation dates in calendar years 2009–2013. The Notice also contains a modified unisex mortality table to be used to determine minimum present value under Code § 417(e)(3)/ERISA § 205(g)(3) for distributions with annuity starting dates in periods beginning in calendar years 2009–2013. See Rev. Proc. 2008-62, 2008-42 IRB 935, updating Rev. Proc. 2007-37, 2007-25 IRB 1433, to explain how sponsors of single-employer defined benefit plans can get approval to use plan-specific substitute mortality tables.

[3] Defined Contribution Plan Concepts

Defined contribution plans, that set the employer's responsibility at contributing a certain amount per employee per year, are becoming the dominant form of pension. There are also variants and hybrid plans. Some employers are discontinuing pension plans entirely in favor of 401(k) plans (see § 3.05[B][1][a]), funded by elective deferrals of the employees' salaries.

Before the Small Business Job Protection Act of 1996 (SBJPA), employees could be compelled to start receiving their pension payments at the plan's normal retirement age (NRA),[56] even if they continued to work. Current law, however, allows them to defer payment until actual retirement. Furthermore, the plan must continue to make contributions or accrue benefits for the older employee.

---

[56] Most plans have an NRA of 65, but the plan can set the NRA below 65 if this is customary for the company or its industry. If the NRA is below 55, § 415(b) requires reduction of the maximum pension payable under the plan. In a plan with an NRA over 65, or one which does not specify the NRA, each participant's NRA is the later of his or her 65th birthday or fifth anniversary of plan participation.

[B] Requirements for Qualified Plans

Any qualified plan (defined benefit, defined contribution, cash balance, or other) must meet many requirements; depending on the type of plan, some or all of these must be satisfied:

- The plan must be in writing.
- The formal structure of the plan must be a trust, except for certain plans funded with insurance.
- Participants must be informed about the existence of the plan and how it works.
- The plan must be funded by employer contributions, with or without employee contributions; employee contributions can be either voluntary or mandatory.
- The plan benefits must vest (become nonforfeitable) according to a schedule that is acceptable under Code § 411(b).
- Employees must be eligible for plan participation as long as they are 21 years old or older, and have worked for the employer for a year. Part-time employees must be covered if they put in 1000 hours of work for the employer within a 12-month period.
- Defined benefit plans must meet "minimum participation" requirements. On each day of the plan year, the plan must benefit either 50 people, or 40% of the workforce, whichever is less. (Before the Small Business Job Protection Act of 1996, defined contribution plans also had minimum participation requirements, but this is no longer the case.)
- Either a defined benefit or a defined contribution plan must satisfy "minimum coverage" rules found in Code § 410(b). Either the plan must cover a reasonable, nondiscriminatory classification of employees, or the percentage of rank-and-file employees covered must be at least 70% of the percentage of HCEs covered. The contributions made on behalf of rank-and-file employees (defined contribution plan) or the benefits provided to them (defined benefit plans) must be at least 70% of the ratio for HCEs.
- The employer is not required to consider pre-break service when determining the person's eligibility to participate in the plan if there is a one-year "break in service" (12-month period in which the individual works less than 501 hours for the employer). If the person works between 501 and 1000 hours for the employer in a year, the employee does not have to be given "service credit" for the year, but cannot be penalized for a "break in service." Furthermore, due to the Retirement Equity Act of 1984, breaks in service caused by parenting obligations usually cannot be penalized.
- Plan amendments generally cannot reduce accrued benefits, even with consent of the employees, although plan sponsors can reserve the right to amend the plan in the future: § 411(d)(6). Exceptions are allowed in certain cases of business hardship and for some retroactive amendments adopted shortly after the end of a plan year.

[1] Plan Types

A defined benefit plan is structured to provide a particular level of benefit when the employee retires. The employer relies on actuarial assumptions to fund the plan each year, so that sufficient funds will have been set aside to provide the necessary level of benefits for each covered employee.

The formula uses factors such as age at retirement, number of years of service for the employer, and compensation. Compensation is usually defined as compensation earned in the year of retirement; average compensation over the entire career with the employer; or for several years in which earnings were highest.

Most defined benefit plans are noncontributory (i.e., employees do not contribute to their own accounts). However, it is not unlawful for a plan to accept employee contributions, or even to mandate them as a condition of participation. The early 1999 Supreme Court case, *Hughes Aircraft Co. v. Jacobson*,[57] deals with a contributory defined benefit plan. A large part of the plan could be traced to employee contributions. The employer suspended its contributions at a time when the plan was operating at a surplus. Hughes also amended the plan to include early retirement benefits and a new benefit structure for new participants, funded by the plan surplus.

The employees sought a share of the plan surplus, but lost. The Supreme Court's reading is that the employer accepts investment risk in a defined benefit plan; if the plan runs at a surplus, it is legitimate for the employer to use that surplus to satisfy other plan obligations, as long as vested benefits are provided according to the plan.

A defined contribution plan (including pension plans, profit-sharing, money purchase, and 401(k) plans) involves a separate account for each employee. The employer's responsibility is to make contributions to each account each year, usually set at a percentage of that year's compensation.

A money purchase plan provides definitely determinable benefits, funded by fixed contributions from the employer. The plan has an allocation formula that sets the amount the employer must contribute, and the amount allocated to each participant's account.

In contrast, a profit-sharing plan has separate formulas for the employer contribution and the allocation to each account. The formula for making the contribution can be set each year, and contributions can be omitted in certain years. Before 1986, contributions to a profit-sharing plan could only be made in years in which the corporation had a profit, but that limitation has been removed.

[a] 401(k) Plans

A 401(k) plan, also known as a CODA (Cash or Deferred Arrangement) takes its basic funding from the employee's own compensation. The employee is allowed to decide how much compensation will be deferred instead of being paid currently

---

[57] 525 U.S. 432 (1999).

in cash, up to a statutory limit: $15,000 for 2006, $15,500 for 2007-2008, $16,500 for 2009. The advantage to the employee is not only forced savings, but the fact that increase in the value of the account is not taxed until retirement. Many 401(k) plans call for the employer to match part of the employee's deferral. These plans are subject to nondiscrimination requirements.

EGTRRA made significant changes in the 401(k) plan rules, and later so did the PPA.

Employees aged 50 and over are allowed to make additional catch-up contributions to their 401(k) plans. That is, they can agree to have especially large amounts deferred from their salary and placed into the plan instead of being paid currently in cash. This provision is effective for tax years beginning after December 31, 2001. The maximum catch-up contribution allowed for 2002 is $1,000, rising to $2,000 in 2003 and up to $5,000 in 2006, at which time the amounts will be indexed in increments of $500 (The 2009 amount is $5,500). Another EGTRRA provision says that if all employees who have reached age 50 are allowed to make catch-up contributions, the amount of the catch-up contributions will not be considered in calculating limits on contributions. Nor will the catch-up amounts be used in nondiscrimination testing.

Low-income 401(k) participants of any age can get a tax credit for 401(k) plan deferrals. This "Saver's Credit" was originally enacted as a temporary one, for tax years beginning between 1/1/02 and 12/31/06, but was made permanent by the PPA.

The "same desk rule" provided that distributions could not be made to a terminated employee who has been rehired and continues to perform the same job functions for a successor employer. But, for distributions made after December 31, 2001, EGTRRA repeals this rule for 401(k), 403(b), and 457 plans, but not for conventional employer-sponsored qualified plans. Repeal refers to the date that the distribution was made and not to the date when the individual stopped working for the initial employer.

Starting in 2006, under new Code § 402A, participants in 401(k) plans will be able to treat the plans like Roth IRAs, with deferrals being taxable income when they are made, but not taxed when they are withdrawn after age 59½ (or when the participant dies or becomes disabled).[58]

An "orphan" plan is one whose sponsor has gone out of business without terminating the plan. It was often difficult for plan participants to access their account balances, because financial institutions would refuse to release funds unless either the sponsoring company authorized it, or the Department of Labor appointed an independent fiduciary. Under DOL rules released in the spring of 2006, account holders in orphan plans no longer require court approval to roll over their 401(k) balances. The rules also explain how to file a simple terminal report to close down an orphan plan.[59]

---

[58] Final Regulations governing Roth 401(k) plans can be found in T.D. 9237, 2006-6 IRB 394, and Proposed Regulations for Roth 401(k) distributions were published at 71 FR. 4320 (1/26/06).
[59] 71 FR 20820 (4/21/06).

[b] Cash Balance Plans

In the late 1990s, many major employers converted their pension plans to cash balance form. A cash balance plan is a hybrid plan that is subject to regulation as a defined benefit plan, despite its adoption of certain defined contribution features. The corporation's books carry an individual account for each participant, funded with contributions from the employer, based on a percentage of pay. Because there are individual accounts, the cash balance plan offers more portability than a conventional defined benefit plan. A participant who changes jobs can get a lump sum reflecting the balance in the plan at the time of termination.

Each participant's account accrues interest at a rate specified by the plan; the employer can reduce its contributions if the actual rate of return exceeds the plan rate. The eventual pension that the employee receives reflects two components: the annual benefit credit (a percentage of pay) and the annual interest credit at the specified plan rate.

ERISA and the Code allow employees to be given control over investment of their individual accounts — but this also means that they bear the investment risk, whereas the employer bears the investment risk in a defined benefit plan, and may have to make significant additional contributions to make up for declining investment values.

The IRS took the view that converting a defined benefit plan to a cash balance plan does not violate ERISA's ban on age discrimination in benefit accruals and does not constitute age discrimination. See 67 FR 76123 (12/11/02) for IRS Proposed Regulations on cash balance plans. These proposals were later modified in response to public comments. The IRS withdrew the part of the proposal that would have added more methodologies that employers could have used to satisfy the nondiscrimination testing requirements.[60]

Before the enactment of the Pension Protection Act of 2005, P.L. 109-280, courts differed in their assessments of cash balance plans.[61] The PPA endorses cash balance plans and specifies that a properly-drafted cash balance plan will not be considered discriminatory — but such treatment applies only to plans adopted after the PPA takes effect; earlier plans remain in limbo.

[2] Nondiscrimination

A qualified plan must not discriminate in favor of HCEs, although a non-qualified plan is permitted to do so. The general rule is that the percentage of compensation allocated to funding pensions for rank-and-file employees must

---

[60] Announcement 2003-22, 2003-17 IRB 846.

[61] *Cf.* Campbell v. BankBoston N.A., 327 F.3d 1 (1st Cir. 2003) *with* Esden v. Bank of Boston, 229 F.3d 154 (2d Cir. 2000). Many cases follow the analysis of Cooper v. IBM Personal Pension Plan, 457 F.3d 636 (7th Cir. 2006), that cash balance plans do not discriminate against older workers; any differences in benefits represent the effects of the time value of money. *See, e.g.*, Hirt v. The Equitable Bryerton v. Verizon, 533 F.3d 102 (2d Cir. 2008); *see* Fred Schneyer, *Federal Appellate Panel Clears Two More Cash Balance Plans*, Plansponsor.com (7/10/08).

be at least as great as the percentage of HCE's compensation that is allocated toward their pensions.

Like most legal rules, however, this one is subject to certain exceptions. "Permitted disparity," also known as "integration" (with Social Security) allows the employer to reduce the allocation to take FICA taxes and future Social Security benefits into account. Typically, HCEs will have some or a great deal of compensation that is above the Social Security maximum, whereas most or all of the compensation of rank-and-file employees will be subject to FICA taxes, so the practical effect is to allow greater allocation for HCEs without losing plan qualification.

The Code contains special, strict rules for "top-heavy" plans — those that provide 60% or more of benefits to HCEs.

[3] Plan Maximums

Limits are imposed on the greatest amount that a qualified plan can add to a defined contribution account, or contribute toward a defined benefit. As the table below shows, EGTRRA significantly increases the plan limits. The plan limits are the maximum amount that an employer can contribute to the plan or provide as a benefit and still qualify for a full tax deduction; there is no obligation to meet the maximum amounts, or indeed to maintain a pension plan at all. Many EGTRRA provisions call for phased increases up to a particular year, at which point the figure will be indexed for inflation. Bear in mind that, unless extended by Congress, all EGTRRA provisions end on January 1, 2011.

For plan years that end after December 31, 2001, the Code § 415(b) limit on the annual benefits that can be provided under a defined benefit plan goes up to $160,000, which will be indexed in increments of $500. Pre-EGTRRA law required an actuarial reduction in the size of the maximum benefit provided at early retirement (after age 62, before age 65) to take into account the larger number of payments that would be made. EGTRRA allows payment of an unreduced benefit at early retirement, as long as the retiree has reached age 62.

Description	EGTRRA Limit	2004 Limit	2005 Limit	2006 Limit	2007 Limit	2008 Limit	2009 Limit
Defined benefit annual benefit	$160,000 (indexed for inflation)	$165,000	$170,000	$175,000	$180,000	$185,000	$185,000
Annual contribution to defined contribution plan	$40,000; 100% of compensation	$41,000; 100% of compensation	$42,000; 100% of compensation	$44,000; 100% of compensation	$45,000; 100% of compensation	$46,000; 100% of compensation	$49,000 100% of compensation
Maximum 401(k) deferral	$11,000 (2002), phasing up to $15,000 (2006), then indexed	$13,000	$14,000	$15,000	$15,500	$15,500	$16,500

The concept of Highly Compensated Employee (HCE) occurs in several pension-related contexts, especially testing a plant to see whether it provides a high enough proportion of benefits to rank-and-file employees rather than the top-paid group. The definition of HCE is now a person who earns $110,000 or more per year (2009).[62]

Starting in 2002, the amount of compensation that can be taken into account in calculating plan benefits under Code § 401(a)(17) is $200,000. In later years, it will be indexed for inflation in increments of $5,000. (Before EGTRRA, the limit was $170,000.) This rises to $210,000 for 2005, $220,000 for 2006, $225,000 for 2007, $230,000 for 2008, and $245,000 (2009).

[4] Benefit Accrual

Benefit accrual is the extent to which funds are contributed toward an employee's eventual defined retirement benefit. Vesting (see below) is the extent to which the funds belong absolutely to the employee and cannot be forfeited.

The Code includes three permitted systems of benefit accrual. The objectives are that benefits must accrue in a more or less level fashion, in order to provide the scheduled benefit at normal retirement age. Some plans, especially hybrid plans such as cash balance plans, have more than one formula for accruing benefits. From the participants' point of view, the best outcome is for their benefit to equal the greatest benefit produced by any of the plan formulas, but this can create technical problems related to anti-discrimination testing. In mid-2008, the IRS issued Proposed Regulations creating a safe harbor for these "greatest of" formulas. Otherwise, the plan might be disqualified based on the interactions among the formulas.[63]

[5] Vesting

There are two basic vesting schedules for defined benefit plans: five-year cliff vesting, and three-to-seven graded vesting. Vesting is not an issue for defined contribution plans, because each participant has an individual account, which will be available at retirement, as long as the employer makes the appropriate contributions.

In a plan with cliff vesting, participants are not vested at all for five years — but after five years of plan participation, they are 100% vested as to employer contributions.[64] In a graded plan, there is no vesting for the first three years, then vesting is phased in until it is complete after seven years.

---

[62] *See* the EGTRRA statute for the fundamental computations. Each year the IRS publishes an IR news release with the updated figures; 2009 figures are found in IR-2008-118 (10/16/08).

[63] Notice of Proposed Rulemaking, RIN 1545-BH50, 73 Fed. Reg. 34665 (6/18/08); *see* Buck Research FYI, *IRS Proposed Regulations Would Encourage Generosity in Cash Balance Conversions*, 7/7/08 (benefitslink.com).

[64] In a plan that requires, or even accepts, employee contributions, employees must always be 100% vested in their own contributions.

If employees are kept out of plan participation for two years (rather than the normal one year), they must be 100% vested after two years. This combination of deferred participation and faster vesting might be suitable for a company with high employee turnover.

Top-heavy plans (plans that include a high proportion of HCEs) must vest even faster (three-year cliff or six-year graded). The Code vesting requirements are minimums; employers are always allowed to permit faster vesting. The rule has always been that employees are 100% vested in their own elective contributions to a pension plan. EGTRRA changes the vesting schedule for an employer's matching contributions that respond to an employee's elective contribution. Vesting is required either on a three-year cliff schedule, or a six-year graded schedule, beginning with 20% vesting in the second year of the employee's service.

Years of service earned before the enactment of ERISA, and also before the participant reached age 22, can be excluded when applying ERISA's vesting rules.[65]

[6] Nonqualified Plans

The employer can establish and maintain nonqualified plans that do discriminate in favor of top executives or highly compensated employees (HCEs), instead of or as supplements to qualified plans. However, the employer is not entitled to deduct plan costs until the favored employee receives distributions from the plan and includes them in income. See § 404.

Code § 83 taxes the employee when benefits under the plan are either actually or constructively received. Constructive receipt means that the employee is entitled to receive income, but has deliberately chosen to reject it.

ERISA includes elaborate management requirements for keeping qualified plan funding in trust; these requirements do not apply to nonqualified plans. In fact, some employers do not fund their nonqualified plans in advance. Instead, they use current income to pay plan benefits. If the corporation does reserve funds for paying claims under nonqualified plans, the corporation's general creditors are entitled to make claims against those funds, but not against qualified plan trusts.

There are many forms of nonqualified plans currently in use, such as:

- Supplemental Executive Retirement Plan (SERP), also called an excess-benefit plan, defers amounts greater than those allowed for qualified plans.
- A rabbi trust sets aside assets to pay nonqualified benefits in an irrevocable trust. The employer cannot take back the trust assets until all of its deferred compensation obligations are satisfied. However, the funds are subject to the claims of the employer corporation's creditors.
- A secular trust is an irrevocable trust that secures the executive's right to receive the compensation. The assets cannot be reached by the employer

---

[65] Silvernail v. Ameritech Pension Plan, 439 F.3d 355 (7th Cir. 2006).

corporation's creditors. However, the employee is taxed on the employer contributions to the trust, and sometimes on the income the contributions earn within the trust.

* A top hat plan is an unfunded plan of deferred compensation.

Note that the American Jobs Creation Act of 2004 (AJCA, P.L. 108-357) imposes strict limitations on deferred compensation plans to prevent identified abuses in failing corporations or corporations with improper accounting practices. The AJCA enacted a new Code § 409A.

By and large, AJCA provided business-friendly provisions. However, AJCA reduces the amount of flexibility available under deferred compensation plans, with heavy penalties (interest plus 20% excise tax) for premature withdrawals and fewer options for altering the payments under the plan. The changes respond to charges that executives in failing corporations or those with improper accounting practices abused deferred compensation, often at the expense of rank and file employees.

Final Rules were issued in April 2007, reflecting legislative changes wrought by the Pension Protection Act. (T.D. 9312, 73 FR 19234 (4/10/07)). The Final Regulations define the types of plans exempt from § 409A: e.g., Stock Appreciation Rights, short-term deferral of compensation. The plan documents for a § 409A plan must reflect limitations on amounts that can be deferred in the plan, or distributed out of it. The plan must be in writing, and must disclose the payment schedule, events that will trigger payments, amounts that will be paid, amounts that can be deferred, and when payments of deferred amounts will be paid. The Final Regulations add far more categories of plan subject to § 409A to previous law: e.g., separation pay arrangements and split-dollar insurance arrangements. The non-qualified plans of public companies must be amended to make it explicit that key employees cannot receive benefits for at least six months after separation from service. Amounts are completely exempt from § 409A "separation pay" as long as they do not exceed $450,000 and are completed by the end of the second calendar year post-separation. Larger amounts are subject to § 409A only to the extent of the excess. When a non-qualified plan is terminated and its benefits distributed, there will generally be taxation under § 409A, unless all plans of the same type are terminated, distributions occur over a period of 12–24 months, and the sponsor does not create replacement plans of the same type for three years.

[C] Distributions from the Plan

The basic method of distributing pension plan benefits is the annuity — a stream of regular payments beginning at retirement. For unmarried employees, the basic payment method is an annuity for the post-retirement lifetime of the employee.

For married employees, the basic payment method is the QJSA (qualified joint and survivor annuity). Payments continue for the lifetime of both spouses, although it is typical for the annuity payment to be reduced when one spouse dies. (The employer can choose to subsidize an unreduced annuity for the survivor.)

The plan must also offer a QPSA (qualified pre-retirement survivor annuity) if a married plan participant dies before the annuity begins.

Qualified plans have to offer such annuities; they can choose to offer additional payment choices, such as lump sums. However, a married plan participant needs the written consent of his or her spouse to elect an alternate payment form. (The theory is that employee spouses should not be allowed to deprive their spouses of retirement income without their knowledge and consent.) The consent requirement stems from the Retirement Equity Act of 1984.

Although usually a spouse, ex-spouse, child, sibling, or other individual will be named as beneficiary for plan benefits after the death of the employee, a person with a sophisticated plan might direct payment of the benefits into a trust.

The plan cannot force a participant to "cash out" (accept a lump sum if he or she prefers an annuity payment) unless the balance is very small: $5,000 or less. See T.D. 8794, 63 FR 70335 (12/21/98).

Pension payments cannot be assigned in advance, and creditors cannot reach pension payments until each payment has actually been made to a retiree: ERISA § 206 and Code §§ 401(a)(13), 404(a)(2).

There is one significant exception to this rule. A divorce court can order a Qualified Domestic Relations Order (QDRO), Qualified Medical Child Support Order (QMCSO), or both, calling for payments to the nonemployee divorcing spouse and/or maintenance of health insurance for the couple's children. Under appropriate circumstances, QDRO payments can even begin before the employee's retirement. The administrator's duty, when receiving an order that purports to be a QDRO, is to see if it satisfies the definition of a QDRO; if it does, the administrator must comply with it.[66]

Under the Katrina Emergency Tax Relief Act (KETRA), P.L. 109-73, persons within the disaster zones for Hurricanes Katrina, Rita, and Wilma who suffered hurricane-related economic losses could take "qualified hurricane distributions" of up to $100,000 from IRAs, 401(k)s, and other retirement plans before January 1, 2007 without incurring the excise tax on premature distributions, and rules on plan loans were also relaxed. EGTRRA modifies the anti-cutback rule formerly found in ERISA § 204(h). The result is that employers are permitted to eliminate certain forms of plan distribution when benefits are transferred to a new plan, as long as employees retain the right to elect a lump-sum payout. EGTRRA also streamlines plan administration by permitting elimination of certain optional benefit forms, as long as lump sums are still available, and the rights of participants are not adversely affected. Employers that modify their plans in this way must be sure to comply with the new Code § 4980F, added by EGTRRA, imposing a penalty of $100 a day for

---

[66] If the employee/ex-spouse objects to the terms of the order, he or she must litigate with the non-employee/ex-spouse in state court, but the plan administrator has no liability for complying with the QDRO: Blue v. UAL Corp., 160 F.3d 383 (7th Cir. 1998).

failure to provide adequate notice to participants of significant reductions in the rate of future benefit accruals.[67]

The Supreme Court struck down a Washington State law that made all beneficiary designations (in employee benefits plans and life insurance) invalid when a couple divorced. The Supreme Court view is that ERISA preempts such a statute, because it relates to an ERISA plan, and states are precluded from making rules in the ERISA plan area.[68]

[1] Withholding and Rollovers

The purpose of the various ERISA and Code provisions is to preserve retirement plan funds until the employee retires. Therefore, a tax penalty is imposed on premature withdrawals (other than those related to disability or significant financial needs that are recognized as requiring special treatment). However, in the current economic environment, employees frequently change jobs, and benefit by pension portability (ability to transfer balances between various qualified plans and IRAs). A rollover is a transfer from one plan to another; it has no income tax consequences if the Code criteria are satisfied. EGTRRA makes it easier to roll over distributions between employer-sponsored qualified plans, IRAs, 401(k) plans, and 403(b) and 457 plans [non-profit and government plans].

To allow capital gains and income averaging, distributions from a qualified plan must be rolled over to a conduit IRA before being rolled over into a qualified plan, rather than simply rolled over to the second qualified plan. Employees' after-tax contributions to 401(k) plans can be rolled over to a qualified plan or to an IRA.

Plan administrators are required to impose mandatory income tax withholding on "designated distributions." This requirement stems from Code §§ 401(a)(31) and 3405(c). A designated distribution is an amount eligible for a rollover, but not in fact rolled over. All or part of the employee's balance in a qualified retirement plan is rollover-eligible, except:

- Substantially equal periodic payments over the life of the employee or joint lives of employee and spouse
- Annuities for a term of years lasting at least 10 years
- Mandatory distribution of pension payments beginning at age 70½ for officers, directors, and 5% stockholders. (Rank-and-file employees are allowed to defer their first pension payment until they have actually retired, if they choose to work past 70½).

---

[67] In April 2003, the IRS issued a major document about disclosures to plan participants when there are significant reductions in the rate of future benefit accruals or reductions in early retirement benefits and subsidies. T.D. 9052, 2003-19 IRB 879. *See also* T.D. 9219, 2005-38 IRB 538, for further developments of the anti-cutback rule.

[68] Egelhoff v. Egelhoff, 532 U.S. 141 (2001).

Individuals who are entitled to receive a plan distribution, but who do not want a large sum of taxable cash at that particular time, are allowed to roll over the distribution into an eligible retirement plan: an IRA or another qualified plan.

[2] Required Minimum Distributions

At one time, it was an important part of tax policy to encourage people to use up their retirement accounts during their lifetimes, rather than accumulating funds to leave to their survivors. Therefore, a penalty was imposed on a person who failed to take a required minimum distribution from either a qualified plan account or an IRA. This rule remains in place for IRAs. For qualified plans, the requirement of minimum distributions applies only after a person actually retires. The excise taxes once imposed both on persons who took excess distributions from their plans during life, and those who accumulated excessive pension funds within their estates, have been repealed.

For either qualified plans or IRAs, IRS regulations proposed at 66 FR 3928 (1/17/01) and finalized at 67 FR 18988 (4/17/02) make the calculation process much simpler. There is a single, easy-to-use table for calculating the minimum distribution, whether the named beneficiary is a spouse, another natural person, or a charitable organization. (Earlier rules made the calculation much more complicated if the beneficiary was not a spouse.) The Final Regulations include new mortality tables, reflecting increasing life expectancies. Retirees are subject to income tax on whatever they actually receive from their pension plans, in addition to an excise tax if they fail to make at least the minimum withdrawal. There is no penalty for taking more than the minimum, although that will generate more taxable income, and there will be a risk of outliving the funds in the account.

Additional Final Regulations about required minimum distributions (from defined benefit plans and defined contribution plans that make distributions by purchasing annuities) were published at 69 FR 33288 (6/15/04). The rule explains the types of benefit increases (e.g., cost-of-living adjustments (COLAs), increases under a plan amendment, refunds of contributions made by deceased employees) that will be permitted. The form of distribution can be changed prospectively when a plan terminates or when an employee retires, even if another form of payment was used before the termination of the plan or pre-retirement.

The rule includes a table for determining whether a joint and survivor annuity with someone other than the participant's spouse satisfies the rule that pension plans cannot provide non-pension benefits unless they are merely incidental. To prevent abusive estate planning devices (e.g., payments extending over decades because a grandchild is chosen as a joint annuitant), the Final Rule forbids a joint and survivor annuity with a 100% survivor benefit if the beneficiary is more than 10 years younger than the employee. Additional adjustments are required if the employee starts to receive benefits before age 70 (because the earlier start means that more payments will be made).

As a result of the Worker, Retiree, and Employer Recovery Act of 2008 (P.L. 110-458; WRERA), for the calendar year of 2009 only, defined contribution plans and IRAs will not be required to make Required Minimum Distributions to participants. At first, there was hope that relief would also be available for 2008, but WRERA does not include such a provision, and the Department of the Treasury declined to provide administrative relief.

[3] Plan Loans

Although heavy tax penalties are imposed on premature withdrawal of funds from a qualified plan (except when a person becomes disabled, encounters a major financial challenge, or dies and his or her estate makes the withdrawal), many plans are drafted to permit an employee to borrow against the balance in the plan.

Loans that must be repaid in not more than five years, in substantially level installments, generally will not be treated as deemed distributions as defined by § 72.

The Sarbanes-Oxley Act, P.L. 107-204, also includes provisions (effective July 30, 2002) forbidding public companies (i.e., those with stock traded on an exchange) from making personal loans to their corporate officers and directors, so these provisions may rule out plan loans (as well as benefit programs such as split-dollar insurance). However, most corporations in the United States are not publicly traded, so this ban will not apply.

[4] Divorce-Related Issues

As noted above, plan administrators must divide pensions based on valid QDROs, but that principle does not solve all problems that arise in the divorce area. If there is an unusual fact pattern, or where valuation issues arise, the courts often become involved.

Pension benefits earned by the husband during his first marriage are not marital property with respect to dissolution of his second marriage — even though this case had the unusual fact pattern that both marriages and both divorces involved the same woman! In the analysis of the Pennsylvania Superior Court, the pension rights were acquired prior to the current marriage and therefore are separate property.[69]

[D] Disclosure to Plan Participants

One of ERISA's most important functions is to specify the amount and form of disclosure documents that plans must routinely give their participants and beneficiaries of those participants. Certain documents must be provided routinely; other information must be kept available for inspection by any participant, beneficiary, or representative who requests it.

The DOL published Final Rules Relating to Use of Electronic Communication and Recordkeeping Technologies by Employee Pension and Welfare Benefit

---

[69] Smith v. Smith, 26 FLR 1260 (Pa. Super. 3/17/00).

Plans, updating 29 CFR Part 2520.[70] The rules permit electronic media to be used to maintain and retain records as long as the electronic records are reasonably reliable, are securely stored and backed up, and can be converted into legible hard copy. The employer must retain paper copies of all data that could not be converted to an acceptable electronic format. The PBGC has a Proposed Rule under 29 CFR Part 4000, covering the use of digital media for filings and record retention.[71]

[1] Summary Plan Description

The central disclosure document is the Summary Plan Description (SPD).[72] It must specify what type of plan it is, circumstances under which benefits can be denied or lost, and the effect of termination of the plan and the disposal of its assets. Plan participants get an SPD when they begin to participate in the plan; plan beneficiaries get an SPD when they start to receive benefits.

The SPD must disclose a "reasonable" procedure for handling claims: i.e., one which describes all claims procedures and their time limits, including how denied claims will be reviewed, and the right of dissatisfied claimants to bring suit under ERISA § 502(a).

If the plan is ever amended, an updated SPD, showing changes in the past five years, must be issued every five years (starting from the time the plan first becomes subject to ERISA). An update must be issued every 10 years even if there have been no amendments.

A named fiduciary who did not make the initial determination must perform the review, and the review must take into account all information submitted by the claimant (even if it was not submitted as of the time of the initial claim). Adverse determinations must cite the section of the plan (or its internal rules, guidelines, and protocols) that justifies the denial.

[2] Summary Annual Report

When the plan files its 5500-series form each year, participants must be given a Summary Annual Report (SAR). The SAR gives the plan's basic financial statement, including its expenses; the net value of plan assets; whether the assets increased or decreased in value over the year; and whether the minimum funding standards were satisfied (for defined-benefit plans only).

---

[70] 67 FR 17264 (4/9/02). *See also* IRS proposed regulations, 70 FR 40675 (7/14/05), giving guidance on the use of electronic media to communicate with employees (giving notices to plan participants; registering consents to employee benefit plan actions), finalized as T.D. 9294, 2006-48 IRB 980.

[71] 68 FR 7544 (2/14/03).

[72] *See* ERISA § 104(a), Labor Reg. § 2520.104a and 104b, and 67 FR 17264 (4/19/02).

[3] Disclosure of Changes

The Summary of Material Modifications (SMM) must be given to plan participants, and submitted to the Department of Labor, whenever the plan is modified significantly.

In addition to notices that must be given to all participants and beneficiaries, the plan is obligated to provide certain individual notices, such as notices to employees leaving the company's employ when they are entitled to vested benefits; when a claim is denied; before a person receives a plan distribution that could be rolled over into an IRA or another qualified plan to save taxes; and an explanation of QJSA and QPSA benefits and Qualified Domestic Relations Orders (QDROs).

[4] Blackout Notices

Under the Sarbanes-Oxley Act, P.L. 107-204, if there will be a "blackout period" (a time when plan participants' ability to trade their 401(k) or other individual plan accounts is impaired), advance notice is required. A blackout period is a period of more than three consecutive business days, during which 50% or more of the plan's participants or beneficiaries are impaired in their ability to trade the employer's stock. However, only temporary events are considered blackout periods; permanent amendment or termination of rights does not fit into this category. Regularly scheduled blackouts (e.g., imposed every quarter when earnings figures are released) are not subject to the notice requirement if they are disclosed in the Summary Plan Description or other plan communications.

Generally speaking, notice must be given at least 30, but not more than 60, days before the start of the blackout period, although exceptions can be recognized based on the facts and circumstances of the case. The notice must explain, in plain English, the start and end dates of the blackout period, the reason why it was imposed, and its effect on participants' ability to trade or get plan loans.[73]

[E] Fiduciary Duty

The trustees of an ERISA plan, as well as their investment advisors and others to whom they delegate responsibilities, are fiduciaries as to the plan, its participants, and their beneficiaries. Fiduciaries have an obligation to administer the plan for the sole benefit of participants and beneficiaries. They also have a common-law duty of loyalty that impels them to provide complete, accurate information rather than partial or fragmentary information to beneficiaries. If silence could be harmful, fiduciaries have a duty to disclose even information that was not specifically requested.[74]

Plan fiduciaries have an obligation to disclose proposals for improvements in the plan (e.g., early retirement incentives) as soon as the proposals are under serious consideration.[75]

---

[73] Notice requirements: 68 FR 3715 (1/24/03); Civil Money Penalties, 68 FR 3729 (1/24/03).

[74] Krohn v. Huron Mem'l Hosp., 173 F.3d 542 (6th Cir. 1999).

[75] Fischer v. Philadelphia Elect. Co., 96 F.3d 1533 (3d Cir. 1996); McAuley v. IBM Corp., 165 F.3d 1038 (6th Cir. 1999).

In many cases, plan participants have experienced declines in the value of their pension accounts when the value of the employer corporation's stock declined, and some of them have tried to sue the plan's fiduciaries for imprudently maintaining the employer's stock as an investment for the plan. In almost all cases, stock-drop suits have been unsuccessful. Many plaintiff classes fall afoul of federal securities law rules about class actions. Other individual or group plaintiffs have had problems establishing their standing to sue. In many cases, the courts have held that the plaintiffs had standing to sue — but the plan's trustees were held not guilty of any misconduct by maintaining the employer stock as an investment for the plan.[76]

If there is more than one plan fiduciary, they are jointly and severally liable.

The ability of former participants to sue for fiduciary misconduct after they cashed out their plan accounts was problematic until early 2008. At that point, the Supreme Court held that although ERISA § 502(a)(2) does not provide a remedy for individual injuries as distinct from plan injuries, this provision authorizes recovery for fiduciary breaches that impair the value of the plan assets in the individual plaintiff's account. The plaintiff in this case alleged misconduct that falls within ERISA § 409, the duty to administer the plan on behalf of participants and beneficiaries. He charged that his plan lost $150,000 because of the plan administrator's failure to follow his investment directions. In a defined contribution plan, fiduciary misconduct can reduce the benefits a participant receives even without threatening the solvency of the plan as a whole.[77]

In the wake of *LaRue*, both the First and Fourth Circuits ruled that individual claims can be pursued after a participant cashes out his or her plan balance. In the Fourth Circuit case, the plaintiffs alleged that it was a violation of ERISA fiduciary duty for their plan to invest in mutual funds that engaged in market timing (a potentially risky practice). The court said that the plaintiffs were seeking additional benefits (in the form of money that would have been in their accounts if the fiduciaries had been more cautious) rather than money damages.[78]

The First Circuit made a similar ruling when two cashed-out participants sued charging that their lump sum distributions were smaller than they should have been because the plan imprudently continued to invest in the employer's stock after its value fell. The court's rationale for permitting the suit was that participants in a defined contribution plan are entitled to the value their accounts would have if there had never been any fiduciary misconduct.[79]

---

[76] *See, e.g.*, Kirschbaum v. Reliant Energy Inc., 526 F.3d 243 (5th Cir. 2008), discussed in Fred Schneyer, *Reliant Wins 2nd Stock Drop Case Ruling*, Plansponsor.com (4/29/08): the Fifth Circuit affirmed dismissal of a stock-drop case because, even if the defendants had a fiduciary duty to liquidate the stock fund and stop buying the employer's stock (the express requirements of the plan did not only forbid but mandated the purchases), the plaintiffs failed to meet their burden of rebutting the presumption that the defendants satisfied their legal obligations.

[77] LaRue v. DeWolff, Boberg & Associates Inc., 128 S. Ct. 1020 (2008).

[78] Wangberger v. Janus Capital Group Inc. (*In re* Mutual Funds Investment Litigation), 529 F.3d 207 (4th Cir. 2008); *see* Fred Schneyer, *Cashed-Out Participants Keep Legal Standing in ERISA*, Plansponsor.com (6/17/08).

[79] Evans v. Akers, 534 F.3d 65 (1st Cir. 2008); *see* Rebecca Moore, *Another Circuit Says Cashed-Out Participants Have Right to Sue*, Plansponsor.com (7/22/08).

However, the Southern District of Iowa ruled that participants who charged that they were induced to roll over their plan balances to a proprietary IRA with excessively high fees had standing to pursue their claims despite being cashed out, but they failed to allege any fiduciary breach for which classic equitable remedies (such as disgorgement of profits or having funds returned to the 401(k) account) would be available.[80]

[F] Termination of a Pension Plan

Although pension plans are supposed to have an indefinite duration, sometimes the sponsoring company goes out of business or merges with another company. The plan itself might be terminated, even though the sponsor company is still operational. Sometimes the PBGC has authority to get a court order terminating a badly managed plan.

Generally speaking, when a plan is terminated or partially terminated, all accrued benefits must vest immediately, even benefits that would not be vested yet under normal circumstances. This rule is imposed to reduce employers' incentive to terminate pension plans for financial reasons.

Plans can be terminated either voluntarily, at the option of the plan sponsor, or involuntarily, if the plan is shut down for improper operations.

The case of *Hughes Aircraft v. Jacobson*, 525 U.S. 432 (1999), involves plan termination as well as plan surplus issues. The company suspended its plan contributions at a time when the plan had a surplus, and created a new, noncontributory plan for new participants. The participants in the existing plan alleged that the plan had been terminated or, in the alternative, that they were entitled to demand involuntary termination of the plan.

The Supreme Court refused to treat the changes as the equivalent of termination, and refused to recognize either a standard or a distress termination in a situation in which the plan continued to provide benefits and to accumulate funds to make payments in the future.

The Supreme Court ruled in June 2007 that a bankrupt company does not have a fiduciary duty to consider a labor union's offer to take over the company's pension plans and merge them into the union's multi-employer plan. Putting the plan through a standard termination and buying annuities to cover payment obligations did not violate ERISA; in fact, terminating the plan this way ended the applicability of ERISA to the plan's assets and the employer's obligations.[81]

See 63 FR 48376 (9/9/98) for amendments to 29 CFR § 2520-102-3(1), the SPD requirements for disclosure of plan termination options. If the plan includes any provisions that allow the sponsor or other party to terminate the plan or

---

[80] Young v. Principal Financial Group, No. 4:07-cv-386 (S.D. Iowa 4/21/08); *see* Sutherland Asbill Legal Alert, *Former Participants Have Standing to Pursue Equitable, But Not Legal Remedies With Respect to IRA Rollovers*, 5/5/08 (benefitslink.com).

[81] Beck v. PACE Int'l Union, 127 S. Ct. 2310 (2007); *see* Adrien Martin, *Supreme Court: Plan Mergers Considered an Alternative to Termination*, Plansponsor.com 6/12/07, and (AP) *High Court Goes Against Labor in Pension Case*, 6/12/07 (law.com).

eliminate some or all plan benefits, participants must be informed of the circumstances under which benefits can be altered or terminated.

In the bankruptcy context, the decision whether an employer must terminate a pension plan in order to remain in business and pay its debts, all of the employer's plans must be considered in the aggregate. The Third Circuit ruled in mid-2006 that the "reorganization test" is not applied to each plan individually.[82]

In order to reduce the size of its liability exposure, the PBGC issued a Proposed Rule in 2008. When an underfunded single-employer pension plan insured by the PBGC terminates when the employer is in bankruptcy, the PBGC will treat the filing date of the bankruptcy petition as the termination date of the plan, even if actual termination occurs later. This proposal helps the PBGC because it usually reduces the amount of guaranteed benefits. For example, amounts earned by participants after the bankruptcy filing date are not guaranteed.[83]

[1] Standard, Distress, and Involuntary Terminations

A standard termination, as described by ERISA § 4041, is used by plans that have enough assets to pay the level of benefits guaranteed by PBGC insurance (see below). A standard termination requires prior notice (60–90 days before termination) to participants, beneficiaries, and alternate payees under QDROs (see § 3.05[C][4]) that the plan will be terminated. A contact person must be identified so questions about termination can be answered.

The plan files Form 500 (Standard Termination Notice) with the PBGC, and participants and beneficiaries must be notified again, this time of what their benefits will be, factors used to calculate the benefits, and how payment will be made. The plan administrator gets a certificate from an actuary and submits the certificate to the PBGC.

The PBGC has the right to review the plan and can object to improper terminations. If the PBGC does not object, the plan will be terminated and its assets will be distributed.

Plans that do not have the assets to satisfy their liabilities can apply to the PBGC for permission to do a "distress" termination. The plan must prove financial hardship — e.g., bankruptcy or insolvency, or the sponsor corporation's need to terminate the plan in order to pay its debts and stay in operation. PBGC Form 601 is the request for a distress termination. Participants and beneficiaries must also be notified.[84]

ERISA § 4042 gives the PBGC the right to force an involuntary termination, supervised by a trustee appointed by the District Court, if the plan cannot pay

---

[82] *In re* Kaiser Aluminum Corp., 456 F.3d 328 (3d Cir. 2006).

[83] 73 Fed. Reg. 37390 (7/1/08); *see* Fred Schneyer, *PBGC Releases Bankruptcy Plan Termination Rule*, Plansponsor.com (7/1/08).

[84] For 2008 valuation dates, tables have been published under ERISA § 4044 for determining the present value of annuities issued when there is an involuntary or distress termination of a single-employer plan: http://www.pbgc.gov/practitioners/Mortality-Table/content/page16254.html. 2009 figures are at http://www.pbgc.gov/practitioners/Mortality-Table/content/page16629.html.

benefits when they are due; the plan has not satisfied its minimum funding requirements; inappropriate distributions have been made to major stockholders of the corporation; or termination is needed to keep the plan's liabilities from increasing unreasonably.

The PBGC has an obligation to seek involuntary termination if the plan does not have enough assets to pay current benefits that are already due (as opposed to being able to continue paying benefits as they fall due), or the plan has applied for a distress termination but is too short of funds to pay the guaranteed benefits. Although the automatic stay (§ 15.09) halts most forms of litigation, the PBGC has the power to apply for involuntary termination even against a company that has filed for bankruptcy protection or is the subject of an involuntary petition.

IRS Form 5310 is used to seek an IRS determination letter about the status of the trust associated with the pension plan.

The PPA (P.L. 109-280) imposes stricter controls on terminating plans and plans of bankrupt employers — in particular, such plans will not be permitted to increase benefits to highly compensated employees while rank-and-file employees are at risk or lose benefits.

[2] PBGC's Role

The Pension Benefit Guaranty Corporation (PBGC) supervises termination of defined benefit plans and, if necessary, takes over payment of the insured portion of employees' pensions. (The termination of a defined contribution plan is much simpler — each employee just gets his or her own account balance, so federal supervision is not required.) When the PBGC has to pay benefits, it looks to the employer for reimbursement if the plan terminates when the company's assets are insufficient to pay benefits. Liability is capped at 70% of the employer's net worth, or 75% of the unfunded guaranteed benefit.

The PBGC covers "basic benefits": a monthly annuity for the life of the participant of the terminated pension plan, starting at age 65. ERISA § 4022(a) sets the maximum guaranteed benefit; the 2009 level is $54,000 a year (at age 65).[85]

[G] Early Retirement

Although in most cases it is unlawful to discharge employees or force them to resign merely on account of age (as long as they are capable of adequate job performance), in fact there are many reasons why employees leave the work force well before normal retirement age. Sometimes early retirement is motivated by poor health; sometimes it is a personal choice; and sometimes the employer offers incentives to leave the workforce early.

The Older Workers Benefit Protection Act (OWBPA) governs early retirement incentives. Voluntary incentives are permissible. Employers can

---

[85] Press Release, *PBGC Announces Maximum Insurance Benefit for 2009*, http://benefitslink. com/pr/detail.php?id=42424 (11/3/08).

provide subsidies in the form of dollar amounts, extra benefits, or percentage increases. Early retirees can be treated as if they retired at a later age, if this will increase their pension benefits.

The Supreme Court decided in mid-2004 that the ERISA § 204(g) "anti-cutback" rule forbids plan amendments that suspend payments of early retirement benefits the retiree has already accrued. The plaintiffs in this case took early retirement at a time when the plan suspended pension payments to anyone who took another job as a construction worker. The plaintiffs were re-employed as construction supervisors; the plan was later amended to suspend pension payments to anyone who worked in the construction industry in any capacity. The Supreme Court struck down the amendment because workers are entitled to rely on the terms of the plan when they make their choices as to when to retire and what to do then.[86]

[1] Retiree Health Benefits

Some employers permit their employees to retain coverage under the EGHP, even after they have retired; others provide health benefits as a separate retirement benefit, perhaps as an incentive for early retirement.

However, it should be noted that retiree health benefits (like all welfare benefits) do not vest.[87] Therefore, it is lawful for an employer that retains the right to amend, modify, or terminate health benefits to cut back on retiree health benefits (e.g., by requiring an employee contribution to a previously noncontributory plan) or eliminate the benefits entirely. However, in some circumstances, an employer's promise to retain benefits at a particular level will create promissory estoppel, and the employer will not be able to change the benefit.

Employer group health plans are required to cover over-65 active employees on equal terms with younger employees: either the cost per employee must be the same no matter what the employee's age, or equal benefits must be offered to all. Age Discrimination in Employment Act § 3(f)(2) creates a safe harbor under the ADEA and the Older Workers Benefit Protection Act if the employer abides by the terms of a bona fide employee benefit plan.

The Medicare Prescription Drug, Improvement and Modernization Act (MPDIMA; P.L. 108-173), passed in late 2003, offers a prescription drug benefit under Medicare, starting in 2006. The prescription drug benefit is optional; older people can purchase coverage by paying a monthly premium. MPDIMA also includes

---

[86] Central Laborers' Pension Fund v. Heinz, 541 U.S. 739 (2004).

[87] Because the benefits were not vested, it did not violate ERISA for an employer to end its practice of reimbursing retirees' Medicare Part B premiums or its dental benefits for retirees. Non-vested benefits can be terminated at the employer's will: Senior v. NSTAR Elec. & Gas Corp., 372 F. Supp. 2d 159 (D. Mass. 2005). The Third Circuit ruled that a retiree and the widow of a plan participant did not have standing to sue the plan administrator after retiree benefits were modified, because they were neither participants nor beneficiaries with standing. In this reading, a retiree has standing only if he or she can prove that he or she would still be a plan participant if misrepresentations had not been made: Leuthner v. Blue Cross/Shield of Northeastern Pa., 454 F.3d 120 (3d Cir. 2006).

provisions for giving subsidies to employers who provide their retirees with prescription drug coverage that is actuarially equivalent to the Medicare coverage. See also Rev. Rul. 2004-65, 2004-27 IRB 1: if an employer offers to enhance pension benefits in exchange for an employee's waiver of coverage for retiree health benefits, and the employee accepts the offer, there has been an employer-initiated reduction in coverage (see § 420(c)(3)(E)) that must be taken into account in determining whether the employer has significantly reduced retiree health coverage.

[H] Pension Protection Act of 2006 and WRERA

The Pension Protection Act (PPA; P.L. 109-280) was adopted to stem the tide of companies terminating their pension plans, freezing their plans, or seeking bankruptcy protection in large part to relieve themselves of pension obligations. This very lengthy statute, as its name suggests, concentrates on pensions, but also includes miscellaneous provisions affecting other areas, especially estate planning.

The PPA contains extensive provisions altering the obligations of sponsors toward plans that are insufficiently funded. A new statutory category of "at-risk" plans has been created. (However, plans with under 500 participants are exempt from the "at-risk" category irrespective of their funding status.) The plan's liabilities are compared to a yield curve based on high-grade corporate bonds. The plan's "target liability" is the liability for benefits already earned by participants. The plan's "normal cost" is the liability for benefit accruals in the current year. The minimum contribution for the year is the normal cost plus any amount required to amortize any shortfall over seven years. By 2011, rules will be phased in under which a plan is at risk if it is less than 80% funded.

A plan's status "at risk" has many consequences. Corporations are penalized if they directly or indirectly set money aside to fund non-qualified benefits during a "restricted period" — when the sponsor is a debtor in bankruptcy; when any qualified defined benefit plan within the controlled group is at risk; and during the 12-month period beginning six months before termination of a qualified defined benefit plan unless its assets are sufficient to satisfy its liabilities. Tax penalties are also imposed on the corporation's top executives if a nonqualified deferred compensation plan that covers them sets aside assets while the rank-and-file plan is at risk — or if any qualified plan within the controlled group is at risk. The § 409A penalties are imposed: 20% tax plus interest for the period that the compensation was deferred. The penalty is imposed even if the reserved assets can be reached by the corporation's creditors.

Pre-PPA law forbade bankrupt employers to increase benefits until reorganization took place. PPA § 116, however, holds that if the plan's current funding limitation percentage is below 60%, the increase cannot take effect until the percentage reaches 60%, with other limitations based on the ratio of assets to liabilities. If the adjusted funding target attainment percentage for a plan year falls below 60%, the plan will not be allowed to pay shutdown benefits or make accelerated payments (including lump-sum payments) during the year, and all benefit accruals will be frozen. If the percentage falls in the range of 60–80%, lump sum distributions are restricted, and the balance of the benefit must be paid in annuity form. For collectively bargained plans, effectiveness of § 116 is delayed until the 2010 plan year or the expiration of the CBA, whichever comes first.

The PPA provides legislative support for cash balance and other hybrid plans, clarifying that there is no violation of the ADEA or of ERISA § 204(b)(1)(H) as long as the accrued benefit of each participant is equal to or greater than the accrued benefit of any similarly situated younger individual. It is permissible to express the accrued benefit under a plan as the balance of a hypothetical account. Wearaway is forbidden in conversions after December 29, 2005. Participants must be permitted to access any subsidized early retirement benefits they qualify for. To eliminate whipsaw, interest must be credited at rates that do not exceed market rates. Variable interest rates cannot be used to reduce the account below the value of the contributions. However, this relief is prospective only, and the PPA expresses no opinion as to the legality of plans adopted before the PPA gave its approval to hybrid plans. See PPA § 701.

The PPA also contains many important provisions governing 401(k) plans, which are now the dominant form of retirement saving. Section 902 expands the availability of automatic enrollment in 401(k) plans, and creates special safe harbors for nondiscrimination testing.

To avoid loss of value in accounts that are heavily invested in employer stock, § 901 requires defined contribution plans to permit participants to diversify immediately out of employee contributions or elective contributions invested in publicly traded securities of the employer. Once an employee has participated in the plan for three years or more, he or she must be allowed to diversify out of employer stock at any time. The PPA expands employers' ability to maintain 401(k) plans that have automatic enrollment, so employees who do not want to participate have to opt out, rather than employees who do wish to participate having to enroll.

Under pre-PPA law, combined defined benefit/401(k) plans were not allowed, but PPA § 903 permits a company with 500 or fewer employees to create a combined plan (for plan years after 2009 maintained under a single plan document, although each part must follow the appropriate accounting rules for that plan type).

Probably in response to both demographic trends (an aging population) and business trends (fears of shortages of skilled workers as baby boomers retire) § 905 expands the extent to which businesses can make in-service distributions to persons who are already partially retired, so that they can reduce their work schedule in a phased retirement program. In mid-2007, the IRS released final regulations under Code § 401(a)(36) (phased retirement), permitting a pension trust to make in-service distributions at age 62. If the plan sets Normal Retirement Age at 62 or later, this will get safe harbor protection because it will be deemed not to be earlier than the typical retirement age for the relevant industry.[88]

Effective on enactment, states are not allowed to reduce unemployment compensation for pension distributions that escaped federal tax by being rolled

---

[88] Adrien Martin, *IRS Solidifies Phased Retirement Rules*, Plansponsor.com (5/22/07).

over: § 1105. There is a safe harbor, under § 1107, for the anti-cutback rules as long as the plan is amended to satisfy the PPA before the end of the first plan year that begins on or after January 1, 2009.

One factor that placed many plans at risk of failure was the use of overly optimistic interest rate assumptions, resulting in unrealistically small employer contributions and funds unequal to the task of paying future benefits. PPA § 301 deals with interest rates in various situations for plan years 2006–2007. Broadly speaking, plan funding (and PBGC premiums) are calculated based on the rates earned by long-term corporate bonds.

PPA § 401 maintains the PBGC variable-rate premium at $9 per $1,000 of unfunded vested benefits.[89] For 2006 and 2007, unfunded vested benefits are valued with an interest rate based on corporate bonds. For 2008 and later years, valuation will depend on a yield curve based on a monthly corporate bond rate. The PPA also makes the special $1,250 per participant distress termination premium, originally enacted as a temporary measure, permanent. Section 405 enacts a special reduced variable-rate premium for very small employers (those with 25 or fewer employees). The reduced premium is $5 times the square of the number of participants — i.e., $500 for a plan with 10 participants (10 × 10).

PPA § 403 provides that if a plan is amended to increase benefits, the PBGC will only guarantee the extra benefits on a schedule phasing in over five years. (Shutdown benefits will be guaranteed, because they are usually based on pre-existing provisions of the plan, not new amendments.) If a plan terminates when the employer is in bankruptcy, § 404 provides that the date of bankruptcy is treated as the termination date with respect to the applicable maximum guarantee and the five-year phase-in of enhanced benefits. Under § 406, the PBGC is authorized to pay interest on overpaid premiums.

With respect to distributions from qualified plans, PPA § 1001 mandates that DOL issue regulations within one year, providing that a court order can qualify as a QDRO no matter when it is issued — even if it is later than, or revises, another order.

For plans that are required to offer the QJSA option (a requirement that applies to most plans), for plan years beginning after 2007 (or 2008 for collectively bargained plans), a joint and 75% survivor annuity option must be offered in addition to the conventional joint and 50% survivor annuity (§ 1004). Section 1102 extends the time (for plan years beginning after 2006) during which plan participants can elect benefits in non-QJSA form, from 90 to 180 days.

Plans are subject to detailed requirements for communication with participants, and PPA § 501 requires plan administrators to furnish a summary of the Summary Annual Report 60 days after it is filed. Section 501 is effective for filings beginning in 2008. Participants in underfunded single-employer defined benefit

---

[89] The fixed-rate premium was raised from $19 to $30 per participant by the Deficit Reduction Act of 2005, P.L. 109-171; this premium will be indexed annually for inflation. The 2007 level is $31: rising to $33 in 2008 and $34 in 2009.

plans are entitled to receive the ERISA § 4011 funding notice at the same time as the SAR. The PPA requires a new funding notice for defined benefit plans, due 120 days after the plan year (or with the filing of the annual report of a plan with 100 or fewer participants). The notice must explicate the plan's funding in detail, including whether the plan is endangered or its funding status is critical. If the plan's funding target attainment percentage is below 80%, the plan must file actuarial information, financials for the sponsoring company, and information about termination liabilities. Section 801 increases the size of the deduction available to the employer for contributing to the plan.

For plans that undergo distress terminations, or that become the subject of an involuntary termination instituted by the PBGC, § 506 requires the plan sponsor or administrator to pass along to participants the termination-related information submitted to the PBGC. The PBGC must disclose the administrative record supporting the decision to seek involuntary termination.

The PPA limits the tax advantage of corporate-owned life insurance (COLI), § 863. For such policies purchased after the PPA's effective date, the corporation can receive life insurance proceeds tax-free only up to the total of premiums paid by the employer. There is a safe harbor under which pre-PPA rules apply if, during the 12 months immediately prior to death, the insured was employed as an officer, director, Highly Compensated Employee, or among the 35% highest paid employees, and notice and consent requirements are satisfied. The company must inform the potential insureds of the intent to insure their lives and the maximum face amount of insurance desired. Written notice to the insured that the death benefit will be paid to the corporation, and the insured's written consent to the arrangement, are required to qualify for the safe harbor. Policies acquired post-PPA through a § 1035 exchange of a pre-PPA policy are exempt from the new rules.

Before the PPA, it was questionable whether plans could provide investment advice to participants without getting into trouble. Under PPA § 601, however, a Prohibited Transaction Exemption is available under § 601 when a plan provides investment advice by means of a computer model certified by an independent party, or when participants can contact an adviser whose compensation is not affected by the participant's choice of investments.

The PPA improves the tax situation of plan beneficiaries who are not the spouses of the deceased plan participant. PPA § 826 permits an event to be treated as a hardship, giving rise to withdrawals from the plan without penalty, based on a hardship event involving a plan beneficiary, even if he or she is not the spouse or dependent of the participant. Section 829 amends IRC § 402(c) to permit a beneficiary to roll over inherited plan benefits to an IRA or to a qualified plan that accepts such benefits, whether or not the heir is the deceased participant's spouse. However, non-spouse beneficiaries must begin minimum distributions from the inherited IRA starting at age 70½; spouse beneficiaries can continue to keep the funds in the IRA even after 70½ without penalty. Section 830 mandates that the IRS develop a form that taxpayers can use to deposit their tax refunds directly into their IRAs.

An employer can transfer plan assets to a § 401(h) account if the assets are at least 120% of the current liability or funding target, with the transfer constituting two or more years of estimated retiree medical costs, up to a maximum of 10 years' estimated retiree costs or 120% of current liability. During years in which such transfers are made, the employer must either make contributions that maintain the 120% funding level, or re-transfer assets back from the 401(h) plan to the pension plan (PPA § 841, effective for transfers in tax years beginning after 2006).

For plan years after 2005, PPA § 832 provides that, for the § 415 compensation limits, compensation is counted depending on when the person works for the employer, not merely when he or she is a plan participant.

Filing of Form 5500 will no longer be required for a one-person plan that has assets under $250,000; PPA § 1103 also requires the Departments of Labor and Treasury to devise simplified reporting for plans with fewer than 25 participants, for plan years beginning after 2006.

Full implementation of the PPA became problematic in light of the financial crisis that was recognized in 2008. Congress responded to demands for relief by passing P.L. 110-458, the Worker, Retiree, and Employer Recovery Act of 2008 (WRERA). Transition relief is provided for single-employer plans that achieve at least 92% of their funding target in 2008, 94% in 2009, and 96% in 2010.

Some plans can reduce their deficit reduction contributions, and amortize the shortfall over seven years. The rules for determining if a plan is "at risk" and therefore must reduce distributions have been relaxed somewhat. Defined benefit plans can use "asset smoothing" over a 24-month period to reduce the impact of fluctuations in asset values, although the smoothed values must fall within the range of 90–110% of the fair market value of the assets.

Plans can still cash out balances under $5,000, even if the plan is less than 80% funded. For the 2009 calendar year only, required minimum distributions do not have to be made from IRAs or from 401(k) and other defined contribution plans.[89A]

§ 3.06 INDIVIDUAL RETIREMENT ACCOUNTS (IRAS)

An IRA is a personal account, established by a person or couple in their own behalf, funded with their contributions. Anyone with earned income, or whose spouse has earned income, can establish an IRA.[90]

[89A] Transamerica Center, TCRS 2008-12, *The Worker, Retiree, and Employer Recovery Act of 2008 — Defined Contribution-Related Provisions*, http://www.transamericacenter.org/resources/TCRS%202008-12_WRERA.pdf (12/24/08); Milliman Employee Benefits Client Action Bulletin CAB 08-24R (12/18/08) (benefitslink.com); Groom Law Group, *Key Provisions of the "Worker, Retiree, and Employer Recovery Act of 2008" — a Bit More Than PPA Technical Corrections*, (12/19/08) (benefitslink.com).

[90] 2006 legislation, the Heroes Earned Retirement Opportunities Act (P.L. 109-227) allows military servicemembers receiving combat pay to make conventional and Roth IRA contributions, despite Code § 112's exclusion of combat pay from gross income. The law is effective for tax years beginning after December 31, 2003.

Once an IRA is established, it is not necessary to make contributions in any year, and the owner has discretion to contribute less than the maximum permitted contribution, although amounts in excess of the permitted contribution will be subject to an excise tax penalty if they are not removed from the account. It is also permissible for an individual to have several IRA accounts, as long as the contribution to all accounts in any year does not exceed the maximum.

Since 1997, IRAs have been divided into two main categories: back-loaded (Roth) and conventional. The theory is that taxpayers can accumulate funds within an IRA, without paying tax on the appreciation in the value of the account while the account remains intact in accumulation status. However, even though appreciation is not taxable, it should not be reported as tax-exempt interest on the tax return.

Taxpayers are also allowed to contribute up to $2,000 per year per child, until the child reaches age 18, to an "education IRA," aka a "Coverdell Education Savings Account."

EGTRRA revolutionizes IRAs by providing much larger contribution limits. Before EGTRRA, the largest permitted contribution was $2,000 a year. Under EGTRRA, for the years 2002–2004, contributions to either conventional or Roth IRAs can be as high as $3,000 per taxpayer, rising to $4,000 a year for 2005–2007 and $5,000 in 2008. After 2008, the $5,000 limit will be indexed.

Taxpayers who have reached age 50 are allowed to make larger contributions, on the theory that they need to catch up by the time they reach retirement age. For 2008, the maximum catch-up contribution for persons over 50 is $2,500 if the employer's plan falls under § 401(K)(11) or § 408(p), or $5,000 for plans governed by other Code sections. For 2009, the contribution remains $2,500 for §§ 401(k)(11) and 408(p) plans but rises to $5,500 for other plans.[91]

Low-income taxpayers are entitled to a tax credit for their conventional and Roth IRA contributions. This is known as the "Qualified Retirement Savings Contributions Credit," under Code § 25B. The credit phases down as AGI increases. A tax credit provides more benefit than a tax deduction because it has a more powerful effect on reducing tax liability. The Saver's Credit was scheduled to expire January 1, 2007, but it was made permanent by the Pension Protection Act of 2005: see § 3.06[H]. Because the IRA is supposed to be a retirement account, taxpayers will be subject to an excise tax penalty if they make withdrawals before they reach age 59½, unless the withdrawals fall into a permitted hardship category.

A conventional IRA is not supposed to be a primary estate planning tool either, so in most years, Minimum Distribution Requirement (MDR) rules apply. That is, another excise tax penalty is imposed if the taxpayer fails to begin withdrawals from the IRA by April 1 of the year following the year in which he or she reaches age 70½.

The tax is imposed on the difference between the required minimum withdrawal, calculated based on the account owner's life expectancy, or adjusted joint expectancies of owner and beneficiary, and the actual withdrawal. There is no

[91] IR-2007-171 (10/18/07), http://benefitslink.com/pr/detail.php?id=4127, IR-2008-118 (10/16/08).

penalty for excessive withdrawals: a taxpayer can withdraw up to the entire balance in any year. However, amounts withdrawn from a conventional IRA constitute taxable ordinary income. For calendar year 2009 only (not for 2008), The Worker, Retiree, and Employer Recovery Act of 2008 (P.L. 110-458) waives the requirement of taking the MDR from conventional IRAs.

In contrast, contributions to a Roth IRA (which are subject to the same dollar limit as conventional IRA contributions) are never tax-deductible. Thus, this form of retirement investing may be attractive to a high-income person who would not be entitled to a conventional IRA deduction.

In 2005 and later years, amounts that have remained within a Roth IRA for five years or more will be able to be withdrawn tax-free. Nor are Roth IRAs subject to MDRs, so a person who has adequate retirement income may choose to retain funds within the Roth IRA so that they can be transmitted to heirs. Effective for tax years after 2009, the Tax Increase Prevention and Reconciliation Act of 2005 (TIPRA; P.L. 109-222) permits taxpayers whose AGI exceeds $100,000 in the year of the conversion, to convert conventional to Roth IRAs; prior law forbade high-income taxpayers to do this.[92]

[A] IRA Deductibility

A married couple filing jointly can each contribute the maximum to their IRAs, even if one is a homemaker who does not work outside the home. (The deduction is reduced for certain very low-income couples.)

If neither spouse is covered by an employer's qualified pension plan, then the full amount can be deducted.

A person who is covered by a qualified plan may be entitled to a partial IRA deduction, although the deduction phases down depending on modified AGI and phases out based on a complex schedule.

[B] Employment-Related IRAs

In small companies, or companies where the management is unwilling to offer conventional pension plans, Simplified Employee Pension (SEP) and Savings Incentive Match Plan for Employees (SIMPLE) are IRA-type plans that are initiated by the employer, not the individual employees.

In a SEP plan, the employer makes contributions to employees' IRAs, pursuant to a nondiscriminatory written plan. The employee can make the maximum IRA contribution to his or her account, and the employer makes additional contributions (which do not disqualify the employee contributions). The employer can contribute up to the defined-contribution plan limit. A SEP plan can operate much like a 401(k) plan, by salary reduction, and EGTRRA raises the limits on salary reduction SEPs to equal those of 401(k) plans.

---

[92] *See* 72 Fed. Reg. 21103 (4/30/07) for Final Regulations on distributions from Roth 401(k) accounts.

In a SIMPLE plan (available only in companies with 100 or fewer employees), see Code § 408(q), the employer uses the employees' IRAs as a funding vehicle. The employer can either base its contribution on a percentage of the employee's compensation, or match a portion of the employee's elective deferral. EGTRRA created the concept of the "deemed IRA," where contributions are made by the employer but treated as if they had been made by the employee. Each deemed IRA must be held in a separate account or annuity, not commingled with others or with other retirement funds. Deemed IRAs are regulated as IRAs rather than under the far more onerous rules for qualified plans, so the employer need not satisfy ERISA's coverage and nondiscrimination requirements.

§ 3.07 HEALTH BENEFIT PLANS

Employee group health plans (EGHPs) and fringe benefit plans are another important element in employee compensation. To an increasing extent, health benefits are being offered in the form of managed care, discussed in § 14.08[B]; see § 13.08 for a discussion of health insurance in general.

Employers are not required to offer any health or fringe benefits at all, but if benefits are offered, certain requirements (e.g., nondiscrimination) are imposed. ERISA considers health and other fringe benefits to be "welfare benefits," not pension benefits. Therefore, the detailed rules governing pension plans are not applicable, and the benefits are not subject to vesting.

Most EGHPs are insured — that is, the employer purchases policies from an insurance company, and care is rendered under those policies. At one time, employers usually paid the entire premium; over time, a trend has emerged to require employees to pay an ever-increasing share of the premium. Employees also have copayment responsibilities, including deductibles (an amount they must pay before there is any coverage under the plan) and coinsurance (a percentage of the cost of each covered service that the employee is responsible for).

Some plans are self-insured. Instead of paying premiums for an insurance policy, the employer sets aside an equivalent sum of money that is invested and used to pay employee health claims. See § 13.08[A] for a discussion of indemnity health insurance, and § 13.08[B] for managed care.

The Supreme Court decided two cases about HMOs in the spring of 2003. The Court upheld state "any willing provider" statutes (laws requiring managed care organizations to enter into contracts with any licensed health care providers who apply to participate). The managed care organizations argued that the ability to exclude health care providers controlled costs by reducing fees, but the Supreme Court ruled that it was more important to allow health care professionals a wider scope of practice and to give patients a wider choice of health care providers.[93] In the other case, RICO allegations that managed care organizations engaged in a pattern of refusing to reimburse health care providers for services they had provided were held to be subject to a mandatory arbitration under the contract

---

[93] Kentucky Ass'n of Health Plans v. Miller, 538 U.S. 329 (2003).

between the organizations and the health care providers. The Supreme Court rejected the providers' argument that the clause was unenforceable because it ruled out punitive damages, which are an important part of the RICO enforcement regime. The Supreme Court held that RICO treble damages are not punitive damages.[94]

[A] ERISA Preemption

For the past decade or so, most cases involving EGHPs had to be tried in federal court because ERISA preempts state laws that "relate to" employee benefit plans covered by ERISA Title I, including health insurance welfare benefit plans. However, state laws are not preempted if the case involves insurance rather than plan benefits.

The traditional analysis is that ERISA preempts state laws if the employee seeks benefits or protests a benefit denial under the plan, because construction of the plan language is required. In contrast, ERISA does not preempt state law in medical malpractice cases or cases challenging the quality of care, although in many such cases, the plaintiff would be able to proceed against the allegedly negligent doctor or hospital, but not against the managed care plan, on the theory that the managed care plan has not provided the care and is not responsible for its quality.

The Supreme Court decided the crucial case of *Pegram v. Herdrich*[95] in June 2000. The petitioner in this case was an insured employee who suffered a ruptured appendix and peritonitis after the managed care physician delayed approval of a diagnostic test for eight days. The petitioner sued her HMO in state court. The basic claim was one of fraud (denying access to care without disclosing the financial incentives given to participating physicians to limit the number of diagnostic procedures ordered). The case was removed to the federal system on ERISA preemption grounds.

According to the Supreme Court, in effect the petitioner had no forum in which to bring her complaint against the HMO (although a state-law malpractice claim against the physician remains a possibility). ERISA preempts state litigation, but the Supreme Court held that the petitioner did not assert a valid ERISA claim against the HMO. The rationale was that an HMO does not serve as a fiduciary when, acting through its physicians, it makes decisions about treatment and subscriber eligibility for the medical interventions that they seek.

In the Supreme Court view, courts are not able to distinguish between good and bad HMOs as they exercise their function of rationing care. Although the petitioner's contention was that it is inherently wrong for HMOs to give their physicians incentives to restrict care, the Supreme Court treats rationing of care as an essential part of managed care.

---

[94] Pacificare Health Sys. v. Book, 538 U.S. 401 (2003).
[95] 530 U.S. 211 (2000).

Furthermore, in the Court's analysis, HMOs are not fiduciaries of the employer-sponsored health care plans, because they do not administer the plan, and decisions about eligibility for care do not fit into the traditional fiduciary framework, which has evolved from the role of the trustee relative to a trust.

In mid-2002, the Supreme Court ruled that ERISA does not preempt Illinois' law (which is similar to provisions enacted by at least 40 states) providing for independent medical review when an HMO subscriber seeks a procedure that is denied by the HMO as not medically necessary.[96] In the Supreme Court view, although an employee benefit plan was at stake, ERISA preemption could not be applied because the savings clause, 29 USC § 1144(a), exempts from preemption laws that "regulate insurance," and the Illinois HMO Act in question was directed toward the insurance industry. The Supreme Court refused to set up a distinction between health care and insurance; HMOs must be treated as insurers. The Supreme Court noted that the Illinois statute was consistent with the ERISA scheme, which requires employee benefit plans to provide a review mechanism for beneficiaries when benefits are denied. Nor did the state law create new remedies over and above those available under ERISA; in fact, it strongly resembled the accepted rule of seeking a second opinion in disputed cases.

In mid-2004, the Supreme Court ruled that ERISA § 502(a) completely preempts state-law claims that a managed care plan improperly denied care. The plaintiffs in these two consolidated cases charged the plan with requiring one to take a lower-cost drug rather than a safer, more expensive drug that was not covered, and premature discharge from a hospital.[97]

Another significant issue is the extent to which a plan will be able to get reimbursement for funds advanced for treatment of a plan participant who is injured in an accident or otherwise becomes entitled to a tort recovery. A 2002 Supreme Court case[98] prevents plan fiduciaries from suing participants under ERISA § 502(a)(3) when participants fail to reimburse the plan out of their tort recoveries. The Supreme Court's rationale is that this ERISA provision allows fiduciaries to sue for equitable relief, but not for relief that would traditionally have been obtained through an action at law.

The Supreme Court returned to the question of "subrogation" (rights to recoup treatment expenses from an injured plan participant's tort judgment) in 2006. The Supreme Court ruled that an insurer was entitled to recover its expenditures on the injured person's medical care out of a tort settlement; the insurer acted as a fiduciary seeking "appropriate equitable relief" under ERISA § 502(a)(3) because, in this case, unlike *Knudson*, the disputed funds were in the possession of the plan participants, and the money had been set aside in an identifiable separate account. The claim was equitable not because it was a subrogation claim, but

---

[96] Rush Prudential HMO v. Moran, 536 U.S. 355 (2002).

[97] Aetna Health Inc. v. Davila & Cigna Healthcare of Texas, Inc. v. Calad, 542 U.S. 200 (2004).

[98] Great-West Life & Annuity Ins. Co. v. Knudson, 534 U.S. 204 (2002).

because it was an action to enforce an equitable lien created by agreement.[99] Insurers must go to state, not federal, court to recover payments on behalf of injured federal employees. Even though the federal health plan provides that the terms of the plan's insurance preempt state or local law, the Supreme Court held that the insurer's quest for reimbursement does not arise under federal law, and therefore the federal courts do not have jurisdiction.[100]

[B] EGHP Tax Issues

The main tax sections covering EGHPs are §§ 104–106, explaining plans of "Accident and Health Insurance" (A&H). A properly structured A&H plan permits the employer to deduct the costs of the plan, and does not create taxable income for the participating employee.

If the employee pays for the A&H plan, or if benefits paid by the plan can be traced back to employer contributions that were already taxed to the employee, § 104 provides that payments from the plan are not gross income for employees who receive them.

Code § 105 makes amounts received from an A&H plan taxable if they are paid directly by the employer, or come from employer contributions that were not already taxed. But the employee might be eligible for an offsetting medical expense deduction under § 213.

Section 106 states that employees do not have gross income if their employers provide A&H insurance.

[C] Medical Expense Reimbursement Plans

A medical expense reimbursement plan is a plan that covers employees (although not necessarily all employees). If the plan is a welfare benefit plan for ERISA purposes, it must be in writing; otherwise, the plan can be an informal arrangement, as long as the employees receive reasonable notice of the plan's existence and how it operates.

The typical plan is self-insured and provides direct reimbursement to employees of medical expenses up to a certain amount per year. For tax purposes, the critical question is whether the plan shifts risk to a third party (an insurer, or anyone other than the employer or employee). A plan can get administrative services from an insurance company and still be considered self-insured if the employer retains the risk.

Code § 105(h) requires self-insured medical expense reimbursement plans to satisfy coverage and nondiscrimination tests. At least 70% of employees must be eligible for coverage, and at least 80% of the eligible employees, and 70% of all employees, must actually be covered by the plan. The plan is not required to cover employees under 25 years old, part-time or seasonal employees, employees of under three years' tenure, or those covered by a collective bargaining agreement.

---

[99] Sereboff v. Mid Atlantic Med. Servs. Inc., 547 U.S. 356 (2006).
[100] Empire Healthchoice Assurance Inc. v. McVeigh, 574 U.S. 677 (2006).

The nondiscrimination requirement demands that benefits for HCEs and their dependents must also be provided for rank-and-file employees. The plan can impose a dollar maximum on benefits, but the maximum cannot be defined as a percentage of compensation, because that would provide an unfair advantage to HCEs.

[D] Archer Medical Savings Accounts (MSAs), FSAs, HRAs, and HSAs

Internal Revenue Code § 220 deals with Medical Savings Accounts (MSAs). The MSA is somewhat similar to an IRA. Qualified individuals can take a tax deduction for their contributions, and amounts remain tax-free as long as they stay in the account. MSA accounts are coordinated with "high-deductible" health plans. Funds withdrawn from an MSA are not tax-deductible when used to pay medical expenses (because a deduction has already been taken). Funds withdrawn for other purposes are taxable income and also subject to a 15% excise tax. See also § 20.06[E][1].

Authorization for Archer MSAs has expired and been renewed several times, most recently by the Tax Relief and Health Care Act of 2006, P.L. 109-432.

High-deductible plans are also crucial to the structure of the Health Savings Account (HSA), a new form of employee benefit enacted by the Medicare Prescription Drug, Improvement and Modernization Act (P.L. 108-173, abbreviated MPDIMA).

Contributions to the HSA can be made on behalf of any person under age 65 whose only health plan is a high-deductible plan (a deductible of at least $1,100 (2008 figures) or $1,150 (2009), with a cap on out-of-pocket expenses of $5,600 for single coverage ($5,800 for 2008), or $2,200 and $11,200 respectively for family coverage in 2008, $2,300 and $11,600 for 2009). The general rule is that the maximum contribution is $2,900 a year for individual health policies, $5,800 a year for family coverage for 2008, and $3,000 and $5,950 respectively for 2009. Catch-up contributions of $800 a year (rising to $1,000 a year starting in 2009) can be made on behalf of persons over 55 and under 65. [Rev. Proc. 2007-36, 2007-22 IRB 1335; Rev. Proc. 2008-29, 2008-22 IRB 1039; Rev. Proc. 2008-66, 2008-45 IRB 1107] Employers and/or employees can contribute to HSAs. Employee contributions are tax-deductible — even if the contributor takes the standard deduction rather than itemizing — and contributions made by the employer are not taxable income for the employee on whose behalf they are made. HSAs can be included in cafeteria plans.

As a result of the Tax Relief and Health Care Act, P.L. 109-432, the limit on HSA contributions is an indexed dollar amount — even if that is higher than the annual HDHP deductible. Employers can make contributions to HSAs for employees who are not Highly Compensated Employees (HCEs) that are larger, or a higher percentage of compensation, than the employer's contributions on behalf of HCEs, without violating the comparability rules. TRHCA also permits employees to make a one-time distribution of up to the HSA contribution limit to transfer IRA funds to an HSA.[101]

While amounts remain within the HSA, investment appreciation is not taxable income for the account owner. Funds can be withdrawn from the HSA on a tax-free basis to pay medical expenses, but money withdrawn for other purposes is taxable income and is also subject to a 10% penalty. The penalty is not imposed on withdrawals occasioned by death, disability, or after the account owner reaches age 65. Spouses (but not other beneficiaries) can inherit HSAs tax-free.

Other health benefit alternatives include Flexible Spending Accounts (FSAs) and Health-Related Arrangements (HRAs). An FSA, as defined by Code § 106(c)(2) and Prop. Reg. § 1.125-2, Q&A-7(c), is a benefit program provided by an employer to reimburse specified expenses incurred by plan participants. The plan must impose reasonable conditions, such as limitations on reimbursement. The maximum reimbursement for a period of coverage must not exceed 500% of the value of the coverage. FSAs are subject to IRS rules about cafeteria plans, and they are also subject to the COBRA and HIPAA requirements for health plans. They are also regulated as ERISA welfare benefit plans and must satisfy Code § 105(h) nondiscrimination rules for self-insured medical expense reimbursement plans. Unused FSA benefits cannot be carried over to future years.

An HRA, however, is a plan that is 100% funded by employer contributions in order to reimburse medical expenses that were incurred during the 12-month plan year. HRAs not only allow carryovers of unused benefits; they must be drafted to carry over the unused amounts. HRAs are subject to the § 105(h) nondiscrimination requirements. If there is a COBRA event, the balance in the HRA must be used to cover the employee's medical expenses. In addition, HRAs can reimburse any amount that qualifies as a medical expense under Code § 213(d) — including health insurance premiums.

However, it is forbidden for HRA funds to be used to pay long-term care insurance premiums. Amounts can be distributed from the HRA to employees, former employees, spouses and dependents of employees, and qualified beneficiaries under COBRA. However, HRA distributions made as bonuses, severance pay, or payments to the estate of a deceased participant are taxable income (as are all distributions from the account in that year), even if they were used to pay medical expenses. HRAs can be coordinated with cafeteria plans by offering the HRA account with a major medical plan whose premiums are paid through salary deduction.[102] Several technical changes to the rules affecting HSAs, and permitting better coordination with FSAs and HRAs, were added by the Tax Relief and Health Care Act of 2006, P.L. 109-432. For example, employees make a one-time rollover of funds from an FSA or HRA into an HSA.

---

[101] *See* Gary Lesser, *State Conformity to the Federal Tax Treatment of HSAs*, Benefits Link Message Boards 6/5/07.

[102] The IRS issued several rulings about the differences among MSAs, FSAs, and HRAs: *see, e.g.*, Rev. Rul. 2002-41, 2002-28 IRB 75 and Notice 2002-45, 2002-28 IRB 93.

[E] 401(h) Plans

A 401(h) plan is a pension or annuity plan that also provides incidental health benefits (for sickness, accident, hospitalization, medical expenses) for retirees. The health-related benefits must be subordinated to the retirement benefits. All incidental benefits (health plus insurance) must not cost more than 25% of the employer's total contributions to a defined benefit plan.

401(h) plans must maintain separate accounts for retiree health benefits and pension benefits. The employer must make separate, reasonable, and ascertainable contributions to fund the health plans.

Pension Protection Act § 841 provides that for transfers in tax years after 2007, an employer can transfer plan assets from a fully funded plan to a § 401(h) account if the transfer constitutes between two and ten years' worth of estimated retiree medical costs.

[F] Claims Procedures

ERISA § 503 requires all employee benefit plans to give adequate written notice of claims denial. Participants whose claims have been denied must be given a reasonable opportunity to have a plan fiduciary review the denial.

See 65 FR 70246 (11/21/00) for the Final Rule on claims procedures for ERISA health and disability benefits. Under this rule, plans must expedite decision-making about health claims and must also render faster decisions when employees appeal denied claims. The timetables are shorter for preservice claims (i.e., when approval of treatment is sought — and the employee might have to do without treatment if approval is not granted) than for postservice claims where the employee has already received treatment and the issue is merely one of payment.

Under prior rules, disability claims had to be resolved within 60 days, or 120 days if an extension was granted. The current rules require resolution within 45 days, although one 45-day extension can be granted.

The DOL Regulations, 29 CFR § 2560.503-1, require plans to provide full and fair review of adverse benefit determinations, and claimants must be given at least 180 days to appeal once a claim has been turned down. Plans can impose a second level of appeal before claimants will be able to use the court system to challenge a denial.

Whether a plan is self-insured or insurance-funded, the decision-maker's conflict of interest is one of the factors in determining whether de novo review is appropriate. In this case, an employee with heart disease received 24 months of disability benefits. The insurer administering and funding the plan directed her to apply for Social Security Disability Income benefits, which were granted based on the Social Security Administration's determination that she was totally and permanently disabled. Then the insurer terminated disability benefits on the grounds that the claimant was capable of sedentary work. The Supreme Court held that a plan administrator's dual role of both determining eligibility and paying benefits is a conflict of interest that is relevant to the standard of review. Making benefit determinations is a fiduciary act, so ERISA obligates the decision-maker to act in the best interests of plan participants.[103]

[G] Mandates

Certain federal and state laws impose mandates on health plans. The Veterans' Affairs, Housing and Urban Development and Independent Agencies Appropriation Act, P.L. 104-204, requires EGHPs with 50 or more employees to grant parity between benefits for physical and mental illness.

That is, if the plan does not impose lifetime or annual benefits on medical/surgical benefits, limits cannot be imposed on mental health benefits. Most plans do have limits; in this case, the statute requires the same limit to be applied to both kinds of benefits.

The Mental Health Parity Act was a temporary measure requiring EGHPs to require equal treatment of costs of physical and mental illnesses. The mental health parity requirement does not mandate addition of mental health benefits to a plan that does not provide them. Substance abuse treatment is not covered. The plan can have different deductibles, coinsurance amounts, or number of days or visits of coverage for physical and mental ailments, as long as the overall plan limit is the same. Plans are exempt from the statute if parity would raise the cost of the plan by 1% or more. After a number of one-year extensions, the mental health parity requirement was made permanent by the "bailout bill," P.L. 110-334. For most plans, effective January 1, 2010, copayments and deductibles must not be greater for mental or behavioral health claims than for physical health claims. For the first time, substance abuse treatment is covered rather than excluded. Employers with fewer than 50 employees are exempt. The Congressional Budget Office estimated that the requirement would increase premiums by about 2/10 of 1%.[104]

The Newborns' and Mothers' Health Protection Act of 1996, P.L. 104-204, and the Taxpayer Relief Act of 1997, P.L. 105-35, generally require group health plans to cover a hospital stay after childbirth of at least 48 hours (at least 96 hours for a Cesarean section). This requirement applies to both self-insured and insured EGHPs, whatever their number of employees; state laws that require a longer hospital stay are not preempted. *See* 73 FR 62410 (10/20/08) for Final Rules, applying to plan years beginning on or after January 1, 2009.

The Women's Health and Cancer Rights Act of 1998, P.L. 105-277 (10/21/98) requires EGHPs that cover mastectomy to cover reconstructive breast surgery that the mastectomy patient wants and that has been prescribed by the attending physician. The statute is effective for plan years beginning on or after October 21, 1998.

---

[103] Metropolitan Life Insurance Co. v. Glenn, 128 S. Ct. 2343 (2008).

[104] Robert Pear, *Equal Coverage for Mental and Physical Ailments Is Required in Bailout Law*, N.Y. Times 10/6/08 at A13.

[H] Dental Plans

Dental plans provide coverage of tooth and gum treatment. Most of them are fee-for-service plans, although managed care forms such as HMOs and PPOs are becoming more common. Most dental plans have a schedule of covered procedures and the payments for each procedure, defined either as a dollar amount or a percentage. Usually, the lower the cost of the procedure, the higher the percentage of coverage, so employees generally have a high copayment responsibility for the more expensive procedures.

Dental plans are subject to the COBRA continuation coverage requirements § 3.07[K].

[I] Family Benefits

Some employers choose to offer coverage under their plans for the spouses and dependent children of the covered employees. It is common to require employees to pay for dependent coverage, or to pay more for dependent coverage than for their own.

As § 16.05[D] discusses, Qualified Domestic Relations Orders (QDROs) are used to direct distribution of pension benefits to an ex-spouse. QDROs have a counterpart, the Qualified Medical Child Support Order (QMCSO), issued to EGHPs to prevent children from losing health coverage when their parents divorce. QMCSOs identify children entitled to coverage. In many instances, the employee-parent has an obligation to make payments to the plan to maintain coverage for the children.

Some companies choose to provide coverage for the "domestic partners" — unmarried cohabitants — of employees. An interesting twist: in mid-1999, the Southern District of New York ruled[105] that it is not discriminatory to offer domestic partner coverage to same-sex couples but deny it to heterosexual couples. The employer's rationale, as upheld by the court, was that heterosexual couples have the option of getting married if they wish to secure benefits, whereas same-sex couples do not.[106]

[J] The Family and Medical Leave Act

The Family and Medical Leave Act (FMLA), 29 USC § 2601, requires employers to provide up to 12 weeks' unpaid leave in each "leave year." FMLA leave is available to employees who are sick, or who need to care for a newly born or adopted child or for a sick family member (spouse, child, parent, or step-parent, but not sibling or parent-in-law). To qualify for leave, the employee

---

[105] Foray v. Bell Atlantic, 56 F. Supp. 2d 327 (S.D.N.Y. 1999).

[106] The unavailability of marriage for same-sex couples was also cited in Tanner v. Oregon Health Sciences Univ., 971 P.2d 435 (Ore. App. 1998), justifying class treatment for unmarried same-sex couples. The Oregon Constitution forbids discrimination on the basis of sexual orientation, so discrimination against the class violated the state Constitution and was not a permissible distinction on the basis of marital status. Note that, as of 2008, same-sex marriage was available in some states, but not including Oregon.

must have worked at least 1,250 hours for the same employer in the previous year (e.g., new hires are not eligible). A leave year is a 12-month period; it can be a calendar year, plan year, or year since the employee's last exercise of FMLA rights. The 12-week limitation is applied per year, not per illness. Employers are subject to the FMLA if they have 50 or more employees in each working day in each of 20 or more workweeks in a leave year. Early in 2008, the National Defense Authorization Act of 2008, P.L. 110-181, added a new category of FMLA entitlement. An employee can take up to 12 weeks of FMLA leave made necessary by a spouse, child or parent's active duty service or callup for active military service. Up to 26 weeks of FMLA leave can be taken in order to care for a spouse, parent, child, or next of kin who is unable to continue military service because of a serious service-related injury or illness.

Although the leave is unpaid, and seniority and additional benefits do not accrue during FMLA leave, the employee cannot be deprived of benefits that accrued prior to leave. Health care coverage must be maintained. When the employee returns from leave, he or she must either be reinstated in the former job, or offered another job with equivalent conditions, benefits, and pension rights.[107]

FMLA leave does not have to be taken in a block: employees can take intermittent leave (e.g., every Tuesday afternoon to receive chemotherapy) as long as it does not add up to more than 12 weeks per leave year.

If the leave is taken for non-emergency purposes (e.g., to care for a person after a scheduled operation) the employer can require 30 days' advance notice of the time the leave is expected to begin.

29 USC § 2612 defines damages for violations of the FMLA as lost compensation or the cost of providing health care for the person requiring care, if no compensation was lost. Jury trials are permitted in FMLA cases.[108] The *McDonnell-Douglas* analysis does not apply to FMLA cases. Instead, the plaintiff must prove, by a preponderance of the evidence, that he or she was discharged in violation of FMLA rights.[109] The statute of limitations is two years, or three years for a willful violation.

In March 2002, the Supreme Court struck down a DOL FMLA Regulation (29 CFR § 825.700(a)). Under the Regulation, employers who did not notify the employee that their leave was designated as family leave would not be able to use that leave to reduce the employee's 12-week entitlement to leave for that year. The Supreme Court found the Regulation invalid because it categorically penalizes employer behavior, contrary to the legislative intention behind the FMLA. The Supreme Court interprets Congress' intention as requiring a showing of prejudice to employee rights as a precondition to imposing penalties on employers.[110]

---

[107] *But see* Tardie v. Rehabilitation Hosp. of R.I., 168 F.3d 538 (1st Cir. 1999): reinstatement is not required if the employee is no longer able to perform the essential functions of the job, and the FMLA (unlike the ADA) does not impose a requirement of reasonable accommodation on employers.

[108] Frizzell v. Southwest Motor Freight, 154 F.3d 641 (6th Cir. 1998).

[109] Diaz v. Fort Wayne Foundry Corp., 131 F.3d 711 (7th Cir. 1997).

[110] Ragsdale v. Wolverine World Wide Inc., 535 U.S. 81 (2002).

[K] COBRA Continuation Coverage

The loss of employment-related coverage can be financially quite severe for an individual or family. Therefore, the Comprehensive Omnibus Budget Reconciliation Act, Code § 4980B, gives a "qualified beneficiary" the right to a certain number of months of "continuation coverage"; the number of months depends on the "qualifying event." COBRA regulations first proposed in 1987 were at last finalized in 1999: see 64 FR 5160 (2/3/99).

Employers are subject to COBRA if they maintain an EGHP (either an insured or self-insured plan), and if they have 20 or more employees on the average working day.

For qualifying events that occur on or after January 1, 2002, T.D. 8928, 2001-8 IRB 685, 66 FR 1843 (1/10/01) provides that all benefits offered by a business are treated as a single plan, unless the governing instruments make it clear that the benefits come from separate plans.

[1] Qualifying Events

A former employee or the ex-employee's spouse and dependents have the right to take over payment of the group policy premium (plus an administrative fee that is not permitted to exceed 2% of the premium)[111] and continue coverage under the EGHP. Qualifying events include termination (other than for gross misconduct), resignation, layoff, retirement, or the employer corporation's filing for Chapter 11 bankruptcy.

After a divorce, after an ex-employee dies, or when an ex-employee becomes eligible for Medicare, the ex-employee's spouse and dependents have their own rights to continuation coverage. Ex-employee's children also have continuation coverage rights once they lose their coverage as "dependents" under the EGHP; this usually occurs at age 19, if they are not full-time students.

The right to continuation coverage is not limited to common-law employees; partners, self-employed people who are plan participants, and eligible independent contractors covered by an EGHP also have COBRA rights.

The basic duration of COBRA coverage is 18 months. However, if the employee is totally disabled at the time of termination, the ex-employee and family members are entitled to 29 months' coverage but for the 11 months that follow the regular 18-month period, the employer is allowed to charge 150% rather than 102% of the basic premium. Spouse and dependents of an ex-employee who has become Medicare-eligible are entitled to 36 months of continuation coverage.

An additional type of COBRA eligibility was added by the Trade Act of 2002, P.L. 107-210: Trade Adjustment Assistance or TAA, covering persons aged 55–64

---

[111] For a self-insured plan, the ex-employee is charged a "premium" that represents a reasonable estimate, based on reasonable actuarial assumptions, of the cost of providing health coverage for a similarly-situated person.

who receive monthly payments from the PBGC and unemployed persons who are entitled to benefits under the Trade Act.

Furthermore, the Trade Act adds a tax credit under Code § 35 equal to 65% of the premiums that displaced workers pay for COBRA coverage. The credit is refundable (i.e., can create a tax refund for a person who has no tax liability), and can be used for state-law continuation coverage that is broader than COBRA, or state risk-sharing pools that insure high-risk individuals. The credit amount can be forwarded to the health plan, so eligible persons will have to pay only 35% of their COBRA premiums out-of-pocket.

[2] COBRA Notice

Employees are entitled to a written notice, as defined by Code § 4980B(f)(6)(A) and ERISA § 606, as soon as they become eligible for continuation coverage. The notice must explain COBRA rights, including duration of continuation coverage, how to make the election, and events that permit termination of continuation coverage (e.g., the employee gets another job and becomes entitled to coverage under another EGHP). Qualified beneficiaries must be given a period of at least 60 days to elect continuation coverage.

In mid-2004, Final Rules were published: 69 FR 30083 (5/26/04), with a subsequent set of model notices. Compliance is required as of January 1, 2005 for calendar-year plans. Covered employees and covered spouses must get COBRA notice on the earlier of 90 days from the first date of coverage (or the date on which the plan first becomes subject to COBRA, if that is later) or the date on which the plan administrator has to provide a COBRA election notice. This initial notice, informing new employees of their COBRA rights, can be combined with the Summary Plan Description (SPD). The election notice must be furnished within 44 days of the qualifying event — or, if the plan dates the start of COBRA coverage at the loss of plan coverage, within 44 days of the date the qualified beneficiary ceases to be covered under the plan.

Unlike the proposal, the Final Rules say that the COBRA election notice does not have to inform qualified beneficiaries about alternative coverage available to them instead of COBRA. Nor must they be informed of options to convert their coverage after COBRA eligibility ends. Nevertheless, if the plan allows conversion to individual coverage, conversion must be made available for 180 days after qualified beneficiaries exhaust their COBRA eligibility.

The Final Rules require plan administrators to provide notice of termination of COBRA coverage, and notice when coverage is unavailable, although there is no official model notice; plans have to draft their own.

Failure to abide by COBRA requirements can subject an employer to a penalty of up to $110 per day per beneficiary (with a family maximum of $220/ day), with an aggregate maximum of $500,000 or 10% of the costs paid or incurred for the EGHP in the previous year (whichever is less). The employer also loses the tax deduction for the health plan, because a non-COBRA-compliant plan does not give rise to "ordinary and necessary business expenses" deductible under § 162.

There is also a private right of action on behalf of anyone wrongfully deprived of COBRA continuation coverage rights.

[L] Health Insurance Portability Under HIPAA

The Health Insurance Portability and Accessibility Act of 1996 (HIPAA), also known as the Kennedy-Kassebaum Act, adds a new Chapter 100, §§ 9801–9806, to the Internal Revenue Code, providing health insurance portability when workers change jobs.

Work done after 7/1/96 can give rise to "creditable coverage" that can be transferred between EGHPs. However, creditable coverage terminates if the individual has gone for 63 or more days without some form of coverage (from an EGHP, individually purchased policies, Medicare, or Medicaid) — an incentive to maintain COBRA continuation coverage to prevent a lapse in coverage.

It is unlawful under HIPAA for a plan to condition eligibility or ongoing coverage on an employee's or dependents' health status, claims experience, medical history, insurability, or disability. Nor can employees be charged higher premiums or copayments based on their health status.

HIPAA also limits the use of preexisting condition limitations (i.e., denials of illnesses beginning prior to plan coverage). The second plan cannot use a more stringent definition of preexisting condition than the mental or physical condition for which medical advice, diagnosis, care, or treatment was sought during the six months before enrollment in the second plan. The maximum duration of preexisting condition limitations is 12 months from initial plan eligibility.

Preexisting condition limitations cannot be imposed on pregnancy, and usually are barred with respect to employees' newly born or adopted children.

Health plans that fail to comply with HIPAA are subject to penalties: $110 per person per day of noncompliance, up to a maximum of the lesser of $500,000 or 10% of the EGHP's costs for the preceding year. Small employers (2–50 employees) are exempt from penalties that are traceable to insurer error or misconduct. But if a plan is found to be out of compliance with HIPAA after it has received notice of income tax examination, a mandatory tax of $2,500 or the tax that would otherwise be imposed, whichever is less, is imposed and cannot be waived.

HIPAA also makes it harder for insurers to turn down applications for coverage, especially applications for small (2–50 person) group plans.

[M] Disability Plans

Inability to work due to injury or illness is addressed by both the private and public sectors: the private sector, by disability insurance and self-insured plans offered by employers; the public sector, by providing Social Security disability benefits for persons who are permanently and totally disabled.

Private-sector plans can cover either short- or long-term disability; the usual dividing line is to call a disability "short-term" if it lasts either less than six months or less than a year. Long-term disability coverage begins when short-term coverage is exhausted, and lasts either for a period of years (e.g., five years) or until the individual reaches 65 and presumably would be eligible for pension and/or Social Security benefits even without a disability. Typically, the plan replaces only part of income, such as 70% of pre-disability income, and the benefits are reduced by government benefits and tort damages.

An "own occupation" plan defines a person as disabled if he or she can no longer perform the work tasks of the pre-disability occupation. An "any occupation" definition makes benefits available only if the employee is unable to work at all, or unable to do any work suitable for his or her education and training.

For ERISA purposes, most disability plans are welfare benefit plans, subject to disclosure, filing, and fiduciary requirements: see § 3.09. However, some are top-hat plans limited to executives, so they have more limited disclosure obligations.

Code § 106 excludes from income coverage received under an employment-related accident and health insurance plan. Either premiums paid by the employer for disability insurance or the value of coverage under a self-insured disability plan will satisfy this requirement. If and when the employee receives disability benefits, they are included in gross income to the extent that they come from previously-excluded employer contributions. Direct payments by the employer are also included in gross income. But payments made for permanent loss of a body part, or loss of use of a body part, or for disfigurement are not included in gross income, if they are computed without regard to absence from work.

In deciding whether an applicant is eligible for disability benefits, the Social Security Administration follows the "treating physician rule." That is, the opinion of a physician who has actually treated the patient is given more weight than the opinion of one who has merely reviewed the documents in the patient's file. In May 2003, the Supreme Court resolved a Circuit split as to whether the treating physician rule applies to ERISA-covered plans, holding that it does not. The Supreme Court ruled that neither ERISA nor DOL regulations mandate any special consideration for the treating physician's opinion.[112]

When denial of long-term disability benefits was based on an independent medical examiner's report that was not shown to the participant until after the administrator made his final decision, the plan administrator failed to conduct the required full and fair review.[113]

The Third Circuit granted a victory for patients in mid-2004, ruling that a woman with multiple sclerosis was entitled to long-term disability benefits because her disease was not a pre-existing condition when her symptoms were being treated but she had not been diagnosed. She was treated for numbness in her arm in February, and was referred to two neurologists before the policy became effective in April — but her condition was not diagnosed until August. The Third Circuit ruled that the District Court erred by "reading back" the diagnosis to exclude coverage before the diagnosis. The policy did not define "treated for" or

[112] Black & Decker Disability Plan v. Nord, 538 U.S. 822 (2003).
[113] Abram v. Cargill Inc., 395 F.3d 882 (8th Cir. 2005).

"symptom," so the Third Circuit construed the ambiguity against the insurance company, which served as both the funder and administrator of the plan, and was therefore subject to a heightened standard of review.[114]

§ 3.08 NON-HEALTH FRINGE BENEFITS

Especially for small, start-up, or otherwise cash-poor companies, fringe benefits can be an important element in compensation. They can also be used as a motivational device to improve employee performance.

Code § 6039D sets out the reporting requirements for fringe benefit plans. The employer must provide information about, e.g., its total number of employees; number of employees eligible to participate; number actually participating; percentage of HCEs participating; total cost of the plan for the year. If the plan includes any taxable fringe benefits, the employer can either add their value to the regular wages for a payroll period, or withhold federal income tax at the 28% flat rate used for supplemental wages.

The treatment of the employer's contributions to welfare benefit plans is almost opposite to that of contributions to pension plans. In the pension context, the Code and ERISA make sure that the employer's contributions are adequate. But for fringe benefits, §§ 419 and 419A specify a maximum funding level for welfare benefit trusts, and excessively large trusts lose their tax-exempt status. The employer's tax deduction for maintaining a welfare benefit trust is limited to the "qualified cost" of the plan for the year: the direct cost of funding benefits, plus additional amounts permitted by § 419A.

ERISA defines a welfare benefit plan as a plan created by a corporation and administered to provide participants who are common-law employees and their beneficiaries with benefits such as:

- Health care and medical benefits
- Accident insurance
- Disability benefits
- Supplemental unemployment benefits
- Vacation pay
- Day care centers
- Prepaid legal services.

[A] Stock Options

Stock options permit employees to buy shares of the employer company's stock, on terms set out in the agreement. Naturally, the expectation is that the value of the stock will increase significantly, so employees will gain a windfall by exercising stock options, purchasing stock, and eventually re-selling it on the open market. Stock option plans can be structured in many ways; the choice of

---

[114] McLeod v. Hartford Life & Accident Ins. Co., 372 F.3d 618 (3d Cir. 2004).

form, and the facts at the time of grant, exercise, and re-sale, will determine the tax consequences of the transaction.

It is very common for the employee to have a put obligation: i.e., to be required to sell the stock back to the corporation when employment terminates, at book value, a set price/earnings ratio, or other price defined by the contract.

A stock bonus plan is similar to a profit sharing plan for tax and ERISA purposes, but the distributions are made in the employer's common stock rather than in cash. In this instance, if the stock is not readily traded on an established market, the put option serves to protect employees by entitling them to have shares repurchased by the corporation.

An Employee Stock Ownership Plan (ESOP) is a stock bonus plan or a hybrid stock bonus/money purchase plan. Such plans invest primarily in the employer's common stock. A KSOP is a 401(k) plan structured as a stock bonus plan investing in employer stock. An HSOP is an ESOP combined with a 401(h) retiree health plan (see above): the plan borrows funds to buy employer securities. As the securities are allocated to employees' benefit plan accounts, they fund retiree health benefits for the participants.

[1] ISOs and NQSOs

See Code § 422 for the tax-favored category of Incentive Stock Options (ISOs). An ISO plan does not have to be nondiscriminatory, but favorable tax consequences are available to the employee only if the shares are retained for at least one year from the exercise of the option (i.e., actual purchase of the shares) or two years from the grant of the option (i.e., the first date at which shares could be purchased). ISOs cannot be granted to persons who own more than 10% of the issuing corporation's stock.

Section 422 requires ISO plans to state the aggregate number of shares that can be optioned, and which employees are qualified to buy them. ISO plans must be approved by the corporation's shareholders. Options can be granted only during a period of 10 years after adoption of the plan (although further plans can be adopted later).

ISOs must have an option price equal to or greater than the fair market value of the stock at the time the option is granted; they cannot be issued at a bargain price. No employee can have an aggregate fair market value of stock greater than $100,000 (measured as of the grant of the option) in the first calendar year for which the options are exercisable. Any amount over $100,000 is denied ISO treatment.

The employee has no taxable income when ISOs are granted or exercised, but does have taxable capital gain or loss on disposition of stock acquired under an ISO. Nor can the employer deduct the cost of providing the plan. If the employee disposes of ISO shares within two years of the grant of the option, or one year of its exercise, the gain or loss is ordinary, not capital.

Nonqualified Stock Options (NQSOs) are stock options that fail to satisfy the § 422 tests for ISOs. There is no tax effect when an NQSO is issued, as long as the option itself is not actively traded and does not have a readily ascertainable market value. When the option is exercised, the employee has taxable income equal to the FMV of the stock less the consideration paid for the option.

But if the stock is not transferable and subject to a substantial risk of forfeiture, then the income is not taxed until the condition lapses, at which time the gain is calculated based on the FMV as of that time. The FMV at the time of exercise, minus the price of the option, is a preference item for Alternative Minimum Tax purposes. For more recent rules about taxation of stock options, see P.L. 109-433, The Tax Relief and Health Act of 2006. FR 34344 (6/9/03).

However, with the collapse of financial markets and general economic slowdown in 2008, stock options became much less attractive, and the salient question was often how to treat "underwater" stock options (i.e., options to purchase at prices above the actual market value of the stock).

[2] Tax Issues Under § 83

Code § 83 governs stock options, and also other transfers of property in exchange for performance of services. The person who performs the services has ordinary income when rights in the property become transferable or are no longer subject to a substantial risk of forfeiture. (A substantial risk of forfeiture includes the right to the stock being conditioned on the continuing employment of the worker in the same company.) The income equals the FMV of the property minus any payments made by the employee.

Options are taxed as soon as they are granted if they are freely tradable with an independent market value. Otherwise, there is no taxable event until the option is exercised. The employee is taxed once again (probably at capital gains rates) when he or she sells the stock received under the option plan.

The employer can deduct the amount of compensation that the employee includes in income under § 83, as long as the compensation is reasonable. The deduction is taken in the employer's taxable year that includes the year in which the employee includes the sum in income.

The Emergency Economic Stabilization Act, P.L. 110-343, provides AMT relief for certain liabilities generated by underwater stock options, and some taxpayers will be able to reclaim AMT previously paid in connection with such options.

[B] Life Insurance Fringe Benefits

There are several Code provisions dealing with life insurance in the employment context. If the employer pays the premiums and the proceeds go to the employee's designated beneficiary (as opposed to "key-person" insurance payable to the corporation itself), the employee has taxable income, and the employer can deduct the cost of providing the insurance, as long as it is an ordinary and necessary business expense. See Reg. § 1.1035-1.

Code § 101 prevents the proceeds from being taxed to the beneficiary. The employee benefits, despite the taxable status, because of the ability to get significant insurance coverage at low cost.

Such insurance plans are not required to be nondiscriminatory, so they can legitimately be limited to higher-paid employees, or employees whom the employer particularly wishes to motivate.

The employee does not have taxable income on account of receiving group-term life insurance coverage, as defined by § 79, up to $50,000 in coverage. If a particular employee's coverage is greater, he or she does have taxable income, measured by the Uniform Premium Table found in the IRS Regulations.

Group-term life plans (unlike other plans under which the employer pays for insurance) generally must cover at least 10 employees, and must either be available to all full-time employees with at least three years' tenure, or be available to groups of employees defined in a way that does not allow selection, exclusion, or amount of coverage to be set on the basis of personal characteristics.

The Regulations prescribe nondiscrimination tests for § 79 plans. If the plan is discriminatory, then key employees must include the full cost of coverage in taxable income.

A split-dollar plan is a method of financing insurance. Employer and employee enter into an agreement. Usually, the employer contributes an amount each year equivalent to the increase in the policy's cash value over the year. When the employee dies, the employer either is reimbursed for the premiums paid or receives a portion of the proceeds equivalent to cash value. The employee's beneficiary gets the balance of the proceeds.

The Pension Protection Act, P.L. 109-280, enacts a new Code § 101(j), creating a general rule covering Company Owned Life Insurance (COLI), which benefits the corporation when the insured employee dies. Insurance proceeds on the life of an employee are income for the payee corporation (minus costs, such as premiums paid by the corporation), unless the corporation gave the employee notice of intent to insure him or her, and the employee consented after receiving disclosure that the employer would receive the proceeds.

[C] Cafeteria Plans

A cafeteria plan, as governed by § 125, is a "menu" of benefits from which employees can select the ones they prefer; to a certain extent, they can substitute cash for benefits. The plan itself must be in writing, and must provide at least a choice between cash and one taxable and one nontaxable benefit. The cafeteria plan can include a 401(k) (Cash or Deferred Arrangement) component, but no other deferred compensation.

Cafeteria plans can include (* means a nontaxable benefit):

- *Accident and health plans
- *Group-term life insurance, not limited by the $50,000 that can be received tax-free
- *Disability coverage
- *Dependent care assistance

- *Vacation days
- Benefits that are not otherwise qualified because they discriminate in favor of the highly compensated
- Group automobile insurance or other benefits paid for with the employee's after-tax dollars
- *Medical expense reimbursement.

Cafeteria plans must be nondiscriminatory. Benefits for HCEs must not be greater than 25% of the total benefits for the year. The election between cash and benefits must be made before the plan year begins, and can be changed only based on changes in family status, not employee preference.

[D] Education Assistance

Code § 127 governs the tax treatment of educational assistance supplied by employers to employees and received tax-free. Qualified employer education assistance includes up to $5,250 a year for tuition, fees, and related expenses (but not room and board or transportation). This provision was scheduled to expire in 2001, but it was made permanent by EGTRRA, which also extended it to cover graduate-level as well as undergraduate courses.

Tax-qualified educational assistance plans must be written plans, disclosed to employees. Education benefits cannot be included in a cafeteria plan. The plan must be nondiscriminatory, and at least 95% of the benefits must go to rank-and-file employees. The employer must submit an information return to the IRS each year, explaining the provisions of the plan.

[E] Dependent-Related Plans

Dependent care assistance plans, under § 129, can either be structured as direct payments by the employer for care of employees' dependents, or payments by employees that are reimbursed by the employer. The employer must explain to employees that the plan exists and how it works. It is not required that the employer fund the plan in advance.

Dependent care expenses that can be covered under § 129 are household services and other costs that permit a person to accept paid employment. Eligible dependents are children under 13 or spouses or other dependent relatives who are physically or mentally incapable of caring for themselves.

Dependent care assistance is not taxable, subject to somewhat restrictive conditions. The plan's dependent care payment cannot exceed the employee's compensation. The employee has taxable income if the § 129 benefits exceed the income of the employee's spouse, unless that spouse is a full-time student or disabled. The employer contribution that can be excluded from income pursuant to § 129 is also subject to dollar limitations.

Dependent care assistance plans are required to be nondiscriminatory: i.e., not more than 25% of contributions to the plan or benefits received under the plan can go to shareholders, owners of 5% or more of the company's stock, or their families. The average benefits for rank-and-file employees must be at least 55% of the average benefits to HCEs. If the plan fails the nondiscrimination tests, HCEs (but not rank-and-file employees) will have taxable income as a result of the plan.

[1] Adoption Assistance

For years after 2002, employers can establish a written adoption assistance program, pursuant to § 137, providing benefits of up to $10,000. Like so many figures used for tax purposes, this amount is adjusted for inflation; the 2007 amount is $11,390; the 2008 amount is $11,650, and the 2009 amount is $12,150.

EGTRRA changed the prior law, under which a greater degree of employer assistance could be excluded from the employee's income if the adoptee had special needs. Under current law, the $10,000 figure is the same for all adoptees. However, only certain qualified adoption expenses qualify for exclusion from income if the adoptee does not have special needs. The $10,000 figure is the maximum exclusion from taxable income; it is reduced for persons whose modified Adjusted Gross Income (AGI) is above $150,000 (2007 figure: $170,820; 2008 figure: $174,730, 2009 figure: $182,120).

[F] Miscellaneous Fringe Benefits

Code § 132 provides that employees do not have taxable income from certain minor fringe benefits that the employer provides to all employees in a nondiscriminatory fashion. This category includes employee discounts; subsidized cafeterias that benefit the employer by shortening employees' meal breaks; some moving expense reimbursement; and transportation fringe benefits such as parking spaces and van pools.

Also see § 119, excluding from gross income meals and lodging that are furnished on the business premises for the convenience of the employer.

If employers provide qualified transportation fringe benefits to their employees, up to $215 a month (2007) can be received for qualified parking expenses without the recipient employee having taxable income. Up to $110 a month for the combined value of transit passes and van pool transportation can be excluded from the recipient employee's income. The respective 2008 values are $220 a month for qualified parking and $115 a month for transit passes versus $230 and $120 for 2009.

§ 3.09   ERISA ENFORCEMENT

ERISA imposes numerous and detailed requirements on plan sponsors and plan fiduciaries and administrators. The overriding objective is operating the plan only for the benefit of its participants and their beneficiaries, and making sure that benefits are provided in accordance with the terms of the plan. ERISA compliance requires regular reporting, plus reporting of unusual events as they occur. It also requires notification to plan participants and beneficiaries.

Civil money penalties (CMPs) are imposed under ERISA §§ 209(b), 502(c), and 503(c) for deficiencies such as failure to furnish or maintain records; failure to inform plan participants of their rights; and failure to file required reports and documents. The penalties are usually defined as a maximum amount per day; courts can reduce or abate the penalty after considering factors such as the employer's degree of good or bad faith and its ability to pay. Most penalties are subject to a maximum of $100 or $110, or $1000 or $1100 a day. Penalty levels are supposed to be adjusted for inflation at least once every four years. The Sarbanes-Oxley Act, P.L. 107-204, increased penalty levels for certain ERISA violations, even if they do not involve corporate governance malfeasance.

Various types of ERISA violations can be corrected voluntarily by employers in order to avoid imposition of penalties. The Department of Labor's Employee Benefits Security Administration (EBSA), formerly known as Pension and Welfare Benefits Administration (PWBA) maintains the VFC (Voluntary Fiduciary Correction) program for this purpose. Violations suitable for voluntary correction include buying or selling assets to and from parties in interest or making below-market loans. A plan that engages in voluntary correction must restore any losses or lost profits with interest, and must notify participants and beneficiaries of the changes and file an application with the PWBA regional office.

If the plan carries out the correction, the PWBA will issue a no-action letter, will not take any further enforcement action about the corrected problem, and will not impose civil money penalties. However, IRS excise taxes will still apply, because the PWBA has no jurisdiction over the IRS.[115]

The IRS has its own program, the Employee Plans Compliance Resolution System (EPCRS), under which employers can return to compliance. EPCRS offers three levels of complexity: the Self-Correction Program (SCP) allows 403(b) plans, SEPs, and SIMPLE IRAs to correct minor operational failures. The Voluntary Correction Program (VCP) allows a plan sponsor who detects mistakes before an audit to correct the mistakes. It is not available for deliberate violations of the rules, such as use of abusive tax shelters. The Correction on Audit Program (Audit CAP) allows corrections once an audit has already occurred; the penalties imposed on audit are higher than those where the employer voluntarily comes forward to correct the problems.

[A] Fiduciary Duty Under ERISA

Naturally, a plan's trustees are fiduciaries and thus have fiduciary duty to the plan and the people covered by it. Other classes of people are also ERISA fiduciaries, including those who are paid by the plan to give investment advice; those with any authority (even if not discretionary) over management and disposition of plan

---

[115] The VFC program began as an interim pilot project in March 2000 (*see* 65 FR 14164, 3/15/00) and was finalized two years later: 67 FR 15016 (3/28/02). *See* 71 Fed. Reg. 20136 and 20261 (4/19/06) and Fact Sheet, *Delinquent Filer Voluntary Compliance Program*, http://www.dol.gov/ebsa/newsroom/0302fact_sheet.html (April, 2005). For IRS rules on voluntary correction, *see, e.g.*, Rev. Proc. 2006-27, 2006-22 IRB 945.

assets;[116] those with any discretionary authority or control over plan management; and those with discretion or authority over day-to-day administration of the plan.

One of the most active litigation areas today is the "stock-drop" suit, in which qualified plan participants charge the plan's fiduciaries with retaining the employer's stock as a plan investment at a time when it was imprudent to do so, resulting in loss in value of the employees' accounts. However, by and large these suits have been unsuccessful — not least because courts have often concluded that the plaintiffs were seeking legal relief for themselves as individuals, not the type of equitable relief afforded by ERISA.

ERISA fiduciaries have four basic duties:

(1) Loyalty
(2) Prudence (behaving with the care, skill, and diligence that a hypothetical prudent person familiar with the plan would use)
(3) Compliance with the plan's governing instrument and other relevant legal documents. There is also a clear fiduciary duty to provide copies of mandated plan documents, such as the Summary Plan Description and Summary of Material Modifications
(4) Keeping informed of the performance of the other fiduciaries.

In general, fiduciaries have a duty to diversify the plan's investment portfolio unless it is prudent *not* to diversify.

A fiduciary who is guilty of a breach of duty is personally liable to the plan and must make reimbursement for any loss in value of the plan assets caused by the violation. See ERISA § 409 for the fiduciary's obligation to disgorge any improper personal profits deriving from breach of fiduciary duty. The plan can get a court order removing a fiduciary who has breached his or her duty. See ERISA § 409 for suit by the plan against the fiduciary, and § 502(a)(3) for suits by participants and beneficiaries. ERISA § 502(i) governs civil penalties imposed by the Department of Labor on fiduciaries — or non-fiduciaries who knowingly participate in a fiduciary violation.

A plan cannot contain language that limits the fiduciary's liability for breach of fiduciary duty: ERISA § 410. The employer (as distinct from the plan) is allowed to indemnify the fiduciary or buy insurance covering the fiduciary. The fiduciary can also buy liability insurance personally.

At the end of its 2000 term, the Supreme Court decided the case of *Harris Trust & Savings Bank v. Salomon Smith Barney Inc.*, 530 U.S. 238 (2000), interpreting ERISA § 406 (the ban on prohibited transactions with a party in interest). The Supreme Court resolved a circuit split by determining that even an individual

---

[116] Note that, under John Hancock Mut. Life Ins. v. Harris Trust, 510 U.S. 86 (1993), assets held in an insurer's general account, not guaranteed by the insurer, are plan assets subject to the fiduciary requirements of ERISA.

or business that is not a fiduciary as to the plan can be sued for appropriate equitable relief by any participant, beneficiary, or fiduciary of the plan.

[B] Prohibited Transactions

Because interested parties cannot be expected to be objective, ERISA bans certain types of transactions between plans and "parties in interest"[117] and "disqualified persons" — even if in fact the transaction is fair.

Prohibited transactions include buying, selling, or leasing property to or from a plan insider; extending credit; performing services; making payments to a fiduciary; conflicts of interest by a fiduciary. The IRS imposes an excise tax on prohibited transactions (Code § 4975), and the Department of Labor also imposes similar penalties on nonqualified plans (see ERISA § 502(i)). A disqualified person who engages in a prohibited transaction is subject to the excise tax even if he, she, or it did not know that the transaction was prohibited.

ERISA § 408 exempts certain classes of prohibited transactions from sanction;[118] the DOL and the IRS have the right to exempt particular transactions on request of the intended parties to the transaction. An exemption will be granted only if the proposed exemption serves the best interests of plan participants and beneficiaries and protects their rights.

[C] ERISA Lawsuits

Plan participants and beneficiaries, the DOL, and other fiduciaries have a broad range of causes of action under ERISA § 502. Section 502(a)(1)(B) lets participants and beneficiaries (but no one else) sue to recover benefits due under the terms of the plan, to enforce rights under the terms of the plan, or to clarify rights to future benefits under the plan.

The sponsor corporation acts as a plan fiduciary when it gives out information about benefit security, and therefore a deliberate falsehood can be punished as a breach of fiduciary duty.[119]

This principle has been extended by various cases requiring the employer to disclose not only the terms of existing plans, but possible changes in the plan that are under serious consideration by decision-makers who can implement them (as distinct from mere research into plan alternatives, or purely hypothetical scenarios).[120]

---

[117] ERISA § 3(14) defines a party in interest as fiduciaries, plan employees, plan service providers, their relatives, employers, unions whose members are covered by the plan, employees, officers, and directors of the plan, and other groups.

[118] For instance, loans to parties in interest where the plan gives all participants and beneficiaries approximately equal access to loans; paying reasonable compensation to a party in interest for services actually rendered to the plan; buying insurance from an insurance company related to the plan sponsor; investing more than 10% of plan assets in the securities of the employer.

[119] Varity Corp. v. Howe, 516 U.S. 489 (1996).

[120] See, e.g., Fischer v. Philadelphia Elec. Co., 96 F.3d 1533 (3d Cir. 1996); Bins v. Exxon Co., 189 F.3d 939 (9th Cir. 1999); Wayne v. Pacific Bell, 189 F.3d 982 (9th Cir. 1999).

Any participant, beneficiary, or the DOL can sue under § 502(a)(2) based on an allegation of breach of fiduciary duty under ERISA § 409. Injunctions or equitable relief ordering specific performance of the terms of the plan are available to the DOL, participants, beneficiaries, or other fiduciaries under ERISA §§ 502(a)(3) and (a)(5).[121]

The Fourth Circuit permitted an early retiree whose employer misled him about the tax consequences of making a lump-sum election to rescind the election, deeming rescission to constitute an appropriate equitable remedy under ERISA § 502(a)(3).[122]

Monetary penalties are imposed for each day of failure to supply mandated information: see § 502(a)(1)(A).

The Department of Labor is empowered to bring suit under § 502(a)(6) to collect the excise tax on prohibited transactions, and the DOL is not only allowed to, but obligated to, impose civil penalties under § 502(1) for certain fiduciary violations (including non-fiduciaries who participate in the violation).

Both civil and criminal penalties are imposed under ERISA § 510 for interference with ERISA rights. The typical example is firing an employee to prevent benefits from accruing,[123] but all forms of adverse job action (suspension, discipline, discrimination) are forbidden. Force, fraud, or violence to restrain, coerce, or intimidate a participant or beneficiary to prevent exercise of ERISA rights is a crime: ERISA § 511.

Because § 510 does not include an explicit statute of limitations, the First Circuit held that the **state** statute of limitation for the most similar type of case should be applied in § 510 cases. Furthermore, the First Circuit used the state's three-year statute of limitations for personal injury cases, not the six-year statute of limitations for contract cases — so the plaintiff's suit was dismissed as time-barred.[124]

An employer that is delinquent in making contributions to fund its plans can be sued under ERISA § 515.

PART 3: EMPLOYMENT DISCRIMINATION

§3.10 BASIC CONCEPTS OF EMPLOYMENT DISCRIMINATION

In a perfect world, all employers would focus only on each applicant or employee as an individual, and would never be influenced by prejudices. In our

---

[121] *But see* Mertens v. Hewitt Assoc's, 508 U.S. 248 (1993): § 502(a)(3) remedies are not available against a non-fiduciary who allegedly knowingly assisted a fiduciary to breach fiduciary duty.

[122] Griggs v. DuPont, 385 F.3d 440 (4th Cir. 2004).

[123] The benefits need not be vested, or even of a type subject to vesting, so improprieties relating to welfare benefit rather than pension plans are covered: Inter-Modal Rail Employees v. Atchison, Topeka & Santa Fe R.R., 520 U.S. 510 (1997). However, in this context, ERISA preempts state-court suits for wrongful termination, and all claims of benefit-related firing or retaliation must be brought in federal court: Ingersoll-Rand v. McClendon, 498 U.S. 133 (1990).

[124] Muldoon v. C.J. Muldoon & Sons Inc., 278 F.3d 31 (1st Cir. 2002).

own very imperfect world, federal and state laws forbid discrimination on the basis of suspect classifications such as age, sex, race, nationality, and disability, in all of the "terms and conditions of employment," including hiring; compensation; working conditions; and discipline and dismissal.

Major federal statutes in this regard are Title VII of the Civil Rights Act of 1964 (as amended), and the Equal Pay Act. (Sexual harassment is covered under Title VII as a form of sex discrimination.)

The Americans with Disabilities Act (ADA) requires employers to make "reasonable accommodation" to the needs of applicants and employees who are "qualified individuals with disabilities." Both of the phrases in quotation marks have been quite controversial, and have given rise to significant litigation.

Employees are entitled to a working environment free of sexual or racial harassment, and this has been an important area of regulation and litigation in recent years. It is also unlawful for employers to retaliate against employees who make charges under anti-discrimination laws.

[A] Employment Discrimination Charges and Litigation

Depending on the type of claim and the circumstances, charges of employment discrimination can be based on "disparate treatment" (unfair treatment of a suspect classification) and/or "disparate impact" (facially neutral practices that have a disproportionately negative effect on a suspect classification). The selection of a theory affects issues such as statute of limitations, burden of proof, and potential remedies.

Under *St. Mary's Honor Center v. Hicks*, 509 U.S. 502 (1993), the discrimination case plaintiff always has the "ultimate burden of persuasion." Thus, a plaintiff who fails to offer enough evidence can lose a discrimination case, even if the judge or jury (whichever is the trier of facts for the case) does not believe the employer's explanation of its conduct.

If an employee is fired or quits, and subsequently brings a discrimination charge, the employer can investigate the employee's conduct during work. Evidence of conduct during employment that is acquired after employment ended is admissible at trial of the discrimination charge.[125] Such "after-acquired evidence" will not give rise to summary judgment, but can be used to limit the remedies available to the plaintiff.

Under the ADEA, a suit cannot be brought until 60 days after the filing of a charge with the EEOC, but the statute does not define "charge." Early in 2008, the Supreme Court held that the combination of EEOC's Form 283 intake questionnaire and a detailed affidavit operated as a charge, because it provided the necessary information (it was in writing; named the respondent; and gave a general description of the allegedly discriminatory actions). The Supreme Court conceded that it was unfortunate that the case went to court without the EEOC having an opportunity to attempt conciliation, but did not feel that the deficiency was severe

---

[125] McKennon v. Nashville Banner Pub. Co., 513 U.S. 352 (1995).

enough to oust the EEOC's discretion over the matter. The case was remanded, and the Supreme Court said that the court hearing the case on the merits could stay the proceedings to permit conciliation.[126]

[B] Discrimination in Hiring Practices

To avoid discrimination, employers should review their recruitment practices. If recruitment is limited to a particular neighborhood, or to the family and friends of current workers, it is likely that any past patterns of discrimination will be repeated. Recruitment among the general population, including outreach efforts to find qualified applicants from groups not part of the traditional workforce, is more likely to survive a challenge.

Pre-employment inquiries should be made uniformly of all applicants — e.g., it is improper to ask female applicants with children if they are able to undertake a significant amount of business travel, if male applicants with children are not asked the same question. In fact, information about marital and family status is not relevant until and unless a person has been hired and is about to be enrolled in a health plan, so such questions should not be asked until the company is ready to extend a job offer.

For companies (e.g., manufacturers) that are federal contractors, EEOC regulations at 41 CFR Part 60 require job applications to invite Vietnam veterans, disabled veterans, and persons with disabilities to identify themselves, because federal contractors have affirmative action responsibilities in these regards.

[1] Pre-Employment Testing

It is legitimate for employers to assess the relevant job-related skills of job applicants. However, written tests can have a disparate impact on some groups whose members have suffered educational disadvantage. It is discriminatory to give pre-employment tests **only** to members of minority groups, but the Civil Rights Act of 1991 makes it equally unacceptable to have a lower passing grade for minority-group members, or to grade their test scores on a curve.

Pre-employment testing should measure the applicant's ability to perform specific tasks that will be used in the job, not to categorize applicants in the abstract.[127] *Albemarle v. Moody*[128] permits a test that has a disproportionate impact on a minority group, as long as the test has been validated by testing professionals and the test actually predicts important elements of work behavior.

[2] Disability

If a qualified person with a disability is hired, or a current employee becomes disabled, the ADA requires the employer to provide reasonable accommodation

---

[126] Federal Express Corp. v. Holowecki, 128 S. Ct. 1147 (2/27/08).
[127] Griggs v. Duke Power Co., 401 U.S. 424 (1971).
[128] 422 U.S. 407 (1975).

to the disability (see § 3.14). However, current interpretations of the ADA forbid certain pre-employment inquiries about health status as discriminatory: e.g., whether the applicant has been treated for certain diseases; whether he or she has ever been hospitalized; prescription drug history. It is improper to ask if there are any health reasons that prevent the applicant from doing the job applied for, but permissible to restrict the inquiry to specific job functions (lift 25 pounds; work rotating shifts; drive a tractor-trailer) and ability to perform them with or without accommodation.

Other questions can legitimately be asked — but only after the employer has extended a conditional job offer (i.e., may be willing to employ the applicant).

It is not permissible to ask a job applicant about past receipt of Workers' Compensation benefits, but if a conditional job offer is made, the employer can ask about past injuries that may require reasonable accommodation.

[3] Immigration Issues

See Chapter 19 for a discussion of U.S. immigration law in general. The Immigration Reform and Control Act of 1986 (IRCA), 8 U.S.C. § 1324a, requires employers to verify the employment status of all newly hired persons. The employer must employ only a U.S. citizen or a non-citizen holding a visa that permits him or her to work in the United States (i.e., not a tourist). The labor certification process requires the employer to petition the DOL's Employment and Training Administration (ETA), using Form 9089, Alien Employment Certification. The employer explains the job duties and the qualifications required to hold it. In appropriate cases, the ETA certifies that hiring a foreigner is appropriate because there is no U.S. worker available to take the job. Once labor certification is obtained, the employer files USCIS Form I-I40, Immigrant Petition for an Alien Worker.[129] See P.L.105-277, the American Competitiveness and Workforce Improvement Act, increasing the number of H1-B non-immigrant visas that can be issued for temporary employment of foreign professionals, but also requiring measures to prevent replacement of U.S. workers with H1-B visa holders.

The newly hired person must submit a Form I-9 within three days of being hired, documenting his or her immigration employment status. Civil and criminal penalties can be imposed on employers who hire persons who are not eligible to work in the United States. Penalties are also imposed for document fraud on the part of either employer or job applicant.

The H-1B Visa Reform Act of 2004, part of the appropriations legislation P.L. 108-447, exempts up to 20,000 H-1B visa applicants from the annual cap of 65,000 visas per year if they have a Master's or higher degree from an American educational institution. An Interim Final Rule on H-1B applications grants 20,000 additional visas, with filing fees of $2,300 per visa (for companies employing

---

[129] *See* DOL, *Hiring Foreign Workers*, http://www.workforcesecurity.doleta.gov/foreign/ hirng.asp; USCIS, *The Form I-9 Process in a Nutshell*, http://uscis.gov/graphics/servicds/employer info/EIB102.pdf.

25 persons or fewer) or $3,000 for larger companies. Visas can be processed in 15 days in exchange for a "premium processing" fee of $1,000.[130]

In August 2007, a package of rules was announced raising the fines for hiring illegal immigrants by 25%. The federal government announced enhanced immigration enforcement, a stronger program of uncovering document fraud, and "E-Verify" a better electronic system for verifying employment eligibility. The new rules, scheduled to take effect in September of 2007, were enjoined by the Northern District of California, and the injunction was upheld by the Ninth Circuit. Critics of the rules said that the Social Security Administration database is flawed, and is unprepared to handle hyphenated names (e.g., Ruiz-Garcia) that are common among immigrants, including lawful workers.[131]

A 2002 Supreme Court decision precludes the NLRB from ordering back pay for a wrongfully laid-off illegal alien, because he was not legally authorized to work in the United States.[132]

[4] Credit Reporting in the Hiring Process

Section 14.04 discusses fair credit reporting in the context of granting or denying credit. Credit reports are also sought by potential employers checking up on job applicants. The Fair Credit Reporting Act, 15 USC § 1681a *et seq.*, as amended (effective 9/30/97) by the Consumer Credit Reporting Reform Act of 1996, P.L. 104-208, governs the use of credit reports and investigative credit reports.

An FCRA provision, 15 USC § 1681b(3)(B), specifically permits requesting a credit report for employment purposes ("evaluating a consumer for employment, promotion, reassignment or retention as an employee"). If the report results in an adverse action, the employer is required to give the consumer oral, written, or electronic notice of the adverse action, including information about how to review the file and correct errors. The employer must also furnish any credit reporting agency it uses with a statement that the employer complies with federal law about the use of credit reports by employers.

A credit report is a written or oral communication from a consumer reporting agency dealing with a consumer's creditworthiness, character, reputation, lifestyle, or personal characteristics.

An investigative credit report is based on personal interviews with persons who claim to have information about the consumer. Employers must give job applicants a written disclosure statement, and obtain their written consent, before requesting either kind of report about the job applicant. Further written disclosure

---

[130] P.L. 108-447; *see* 73 L.W. 2636; *see also* 70 FR 23,775 (5/5/05).

[131] Aramark Facility Services v. SEIU Local 1877, 530 F.3d 817 (9th Cir. 2008). *See*, e.g., Pamela A. MacLean, *Workplace Security Rules Stalling,* National L.J. 10/24/07 (law.com); Adrien Martin, *Court Grants Temporary Restraining Order Against 'No-Match' Letters,* Plansponsor.com 9/11/07. Robert Block, *Bush May Raise Fine for Hiring Illegals*, Wall St. J. 8/11-12/07 at A2.

[132] Hoffman Plastic Compounds Inc. v. NLRB, 535 U.S. 137 (2002).

mailed no later than three days after requesting an investigative report is mandatory, informing the applicant that the report covers matters such as character and conduct.

[5] USERRA

The Uniformed Services Employment and Reemployment Rights Act[133] (USERRA) is a broad anti-discrimination statute that provides rights for members of the uniformed services (including the Coast Guard), the military reserves, and the National Guard if they are called to active service then return to work after their discharge. The employer has a legal duty to re-employ the former service member in the job he or she would have held but for the period of military service, including status and compensation that would have accrued as a result of increased seniority. However, the employer does not have to offer reemployment at the same location, and the employer is excused from reemploying the ex-service member if circumstances have changed so much that it would be impossible or an unreasonable burden to do so.

Employers are not required to pay their employees, or contribute to their 401(k) plans, while they are on military leave. Being called for active service is also a COBRA event, allowing the service member and family to continue coverage for up to 18 months, so notice must be given (see § 3.07[K][2]). When active duty lasted 181 days or more, the reemployed person is entitled to be fired only for cause during the first year back at work (or the first six months back at work after active duty lasting 30 to 180 days). Creditors, including the pension plan with respect to outstanding plan loans, are required to reduce their interest rates to 6% or less on debts owed by persons entering military service.

Late-2003 legislation (the Servicemembers Civil Relief Act, P.L. 108-189) limits the 6% interest rate ceiling to obligations and liabilities the servicemember incurred prior to military service. For example, a qualified plan can charge its usual interest rate to a servicemember who takes out a plan loan while he or she is on active service. However, if the rate ceiling applies, any excess interest must be forgiven, and not just postponed until after the end of military service.

The Veterans Benefits Improvement Act of 2004, P.L. 108-454, allows servicemembers to continue health coverage for up to 18 months at their own expense — up to 24 months, for elections made after December 10, 2004. All employers (no matter how many employees they have) must give all their employees (not just those known to have military obligations) a notice of USERRA rights, benefits, and obligations. The notice can be hand-delivered, mailed, e-mailed, or posted in the workplace.[134] Final Regulations, 70 FR 75313 (December 19, 2005), effective January 18, 2006, require employers to catch up with any pension plan

---

[133] 38 USC § 4301 *et seq.; Notice of Rights and Duties Under the Uniformed Services Employment and Reemployment Rights Act*, RIN 1293-AA14, 70 Fed. Reg. 75313 (12/19/05).

[134] *See* http://www.dol.gov/vets/programs/userra/userra_Private.pdf for the official text of the notice.

contributions that were not made while an employee was on active military duty. The Final Regulations give the employer 90 days or until the normal date for making the contributions, although the Department of Labor wanted employers to be required to catch up within 30 days of the employee's return from active duty. Normally, employees who are called up for military duty must give their employers notice if the employees want to retain employment-related health coverage, but the Final Rule requires employers to reinstate health coverage retroactively for employees who could not reasonably give notice (e.g., for reasons of military necessity). Reinstatement is required regardless of health plan waiting periods or preexisting condition limitations.

The Heroes Earnings Assistance and Relief Tax (HEART) Act, P.L. 110-245, was signed by the President on June 17, 2008. The legislation permits a full survivor pension to be paid to survivors of reservists and National Guard personnel killed in action. Employers must deem the decedent to have returned to work the day before his or her death, thus triggering entitlement to death benefits under the employer's qualified plans. In general, the new rules apply retroactively to July 1, 2007, but plans do not have to make a formal amendment until the last day of the 2010 plan year.

The HEART Act solves a problem in earlier law and permits a full survivor pension to be paid to the survivors of reservists and National Guard personnel killed in action. As a result of the amendment, to comply with USERRA, the employer must act as if the decedent had returned to work the day before his or her death, thus triggering payments of death benefits from the qualified plan. The employer can also make contributions to a qualified plan on behalf of an employee killed or disabled in combat. If a plan offers survivor benefits to the survivors of participants who die during combat, the employer must offer the same benefits to the survivors of employees who die on active service.

Employers have the option to amend their FSA plans to provide that reservists who are called up for at least six months of active duty can withdraw their FSA balances as a taxable cash distribution; otherwise, they might lose the money because mobilization prevents them from using the money for health care. The HEART Act also revives (and makes permanent) an expired tax code provision allowing reservists serving at least six months of active duty to make withdrawals from a defined contribution plan (including a 401(k) plan) without having to pay the 10% penalty.

If the employer provides differential pay (a supplement equaling the difference between military pay and the employee's salary), the HEART Act requires the employer to recognize that compensation in calculating pension benefits. Differential payments are also subject to wage withholding. Small businesses can get a $4,000 tax credit for making differential payments.[135]

---

[135] McDermott Newsletters, *HEART Act Provides Benefits for Employees on Active Military Duty*, 7/3/08 (benefitslink.com); Rick Maze, *Bush Signs New Military Tax Breaks Into Law*, http://www.armytimes.com/news/2008/06/military_taxbill_061808w/ (6/30/08); Rebecca Moore,

§ 3.11   TITLE VII

Title VII of the Civil Rights Act of 1964, 42 USC § 2000e, forbids discrimination in the terms and conditions of employment. Job applications; interviews; hiring; retention; promotion; compensation; benefits; and dismissal are all treated as terms and conditions of employment. Retaliation against employees who exercise their Title VII rights, or participate in an investigation or proceeding, is also unlawful.[136]

A mid-2006 Supreme Court decision clarifies that Title VII's substantive and anti-retaliation provisions have different definitions. Thus, protection against retaliation is not limited to adverse employment action in the sense of employment-related actions occurring at the workplace. The purpose of the anti-retaliation provision is to prevent the employer from interfering with employees' efforts to enforce the guarantees of the law. However, to support a suit, an employer's action must be severe enough that a reasonable worker might well have been dissuaded from going forward with a discrimination charge. Even if both past and current duties are within the same job description, the Supreme Court ruled that reassignment can constitute retaliation. A 37-day unpaid suspension constituted a hardship, even though the plaintiff eventually received a back pay award. The Supreme Court concluded that it was reasonable for the jury to find that assigning the plaintiff to harder, dirtier tasks, and depriving her of more than a month's pay (even temporarily) constituted materially adverse acts of retaliation.[137]

Only employers[138] with 15 or more employees are covered by Title VII.[139] However, the Ninth Circuit ruled that a U.S.-based parent company could be sued, despite having only six employees, because its wholly owned Mexican subsidiary had more than 50 employees.[140]

Reservist Benefits Bill Signed Into Law, Plansponsor.com (6/19/08). *See also* P.L. 109-227, the Heroes Earned Retirement Opportunity Act, allowing combat pay to be considered compensation, thus allowing servicemembers whose only income is combat pay to make IRA contributions.

[136] A former employee is an "employee" entitled to bring a retaliation action: Robinson v. Shell Oil Co., 519 U.S. 337 (1997). In the Fifth and Eighth Circuits, a viable retaliation claim requires an ultimate employment decision (e.g., termination), whereas the Third, like several other Circuits, permits retaliation claims based on severe or pervasive harassment in a hostile work environment: Jensen v. Potter, 435 F.3d 444 (3d Cir. 2006). Someone named as a voluntary witness in a Title VII case is entitled to protection against retaliation, even if he or she is not called to testify: Jute v. Hamilton Sundstrand Corp., 420 F.3d 166 (2d Cir. 2005).

[137] Burlington Northern & Santa Fe Ry. Co v. White, 548 U.S. 53 (2006).

[138] Most of the Circuits have already ruled that Title VII liability is limited to employer companies, not individuals. *See* the cases cited in Lissau v. Southern Food Serv., 159 F.3d 177 (4th Cir. 1998).

[139] The calculation includes everyone on the payroll — including part-time employees: Walters v. Metropolitan Educ. Enters., 519 U.S. 202 (1997). The Supreme Court's February 2006 decision in Arbaugh v. Y&H Corp., 546 U.S. 500 (2006), holds that although an FRCP 12(b)(1) claim that a federal court lacks subject-matter jurisdiction can be raised at any stage of the trial, the issue of whether the employer has at least 15 employees is not jurisdictional. It goes to the adequacy of the Title VII claim, and to the plaintiff's potential remedies, but it is waived if it is not raised early enough.

[140] Kang v. U Lim America Inc., 296 F.3d 810 (9th Cir. 2002).

The forbidden grounds of discrimination are race, color, religion, sex, pregnancy, and national origin.[141] Sexual orientation discrimination is not forbidden by federal law, although a number of state and local anti-discrimination laws do forbid it.

In April 2006, the EEOC issued new guidance about discrimination on the basis of race or color, including a Question & Answer fact sheet. Equal employment opportunity must not be limited on account of racial group or perceived racial group, including race-linked characteristics such as facial features or hair texture. Discrimination on the basis of association with persons in certain racial groups is also forbidden. Discrimination is forbidden on the basis of any race, color, or ethnicity (e.g., white, black, Asian, Latino, Arab, multi-racial). Racial harassment and racially hostile work environments are forbidden, although conduct is unlawful only if it is unwanted, severe, and pervasive.[142]

The "reasonable accommodation" concept, central to the Americans with Disabilities Act, also applies to making reasonable accommodations to employees' religious practices, such as allowing them to use vacation or personal days for religious observance and accommodating religious dress in the workplace. On July 22, 2008, the EEOC published a 97-page revision of its guidelines on religious discrimination. The EEOC reported that in FY 2007, 2,880 charges of religious discrimination were filed with the agency — the largest number for any year to date. The EEOC's position is that Title VII forbids differential treatment of employees or job applicants because of their religious beliefs or practices including atheism. Religious harassment, including harassment of employees because of their associates (e.g., attending a place of worship with a radical cleric) and retaliation also violate Title VII. Employers must provide reasonable accommodation when an employee requests accommodation based on sincerely held religious beliefs. The definition of religion is very broad, encompassing individualized beliefs and moral and ethical convictions as well as traditional organized religion. Religious accommodation includes, for example, time off to attend services or permitting Muslim employees to wear headscarves. The EEOC does not require accommodations that impose more than a minimal cost or burden, and violating established CBAs or seniority systems to provide accommodation is not required. An employer can avoid liability by using reasonable care to prevent religious harassment — or by correcting it promptly if it occurs.[143]

---

[141] The Tenth Circuit permitted a case to go to trial on the basis that a city's English-only policy for its employees caused Hispanic workers to be taunted — and that the managers expected this result. There was no substantial job-related justification for the policy. The court held that a disparate impact claim predicated on a hostile work environment is cognizable. Maldonado v. Altus, Okla., 433 F.3d 1294 (10th Cir. 2006).

[142] Guidelines at http://www.eeoc/gov/types/race.html (4/19/06); press release at http://www.eeoc.gov/press/4-19-06.html.

[143] EEOC, *Compliance Manual,* http://www.eeoc.gov/policy/docs/religion.html; *Questions and Answers: Religious Discrimination in the Workplace,* http://www.eeoc.gov/policy/docs/qanda_religion.html and *Best Practices for Eradicating Religious Discrimination in the Workplace,* http://www.eeoc.gov/policy/docs/best_practices_religion.html; *see* Rebecca Moore, *EEOC Updates Compliance Manual Section on Religious Discrimination,* Plansponsor.com (7/23/08).

Federal legislation banning discrimination on the basis of genetic characteristics was passed in mid-2008: the Genetic Information Nondiscrimination Act (GINA), P.L. 110-233. The statute forbids discrimination in employment and health insurance on the basis of genetic traits or tendencies that can be uncovered by genetic testing. "Genetic testing" is defined as the analysis of chromosomes, DNA, or RNA. Insurers and health plans can only require genetic testing or use the test results in limited circumstances. Health plans cannot require employees or their families to have genetic tests, although it is permissible for health care providers to request genetic tests for treatment purposes.

GINA tracks Title VII by forbidding refusal to hire, firing, discrimination in employment conditions, or retaliation on the basis of genetic information — and makes Title VII penalties applicable to violations. In addition to Title VII penalties, the Department of Labor can impose fines of up to $100 a day, with a minimum penalty of $2,500 and a maximum penalty of $15,000 for serious violations, if a health plan violates the statute.[144]

Title VII bars both disparate treatment discrimination (overt intentional classifications that advantage certain groups and disadvantage others) and disparate impact discrimination (facially neutral practices that have a disproportionately unfavorable impact on certain groups, e.g., minimum height requirements that limit the employment of women and certain non-Caucasian groups). Usually, disparate treatment cases are proved with direct or indirect evidence of explicit discrimination. Disparate impact cases usually involve introduction of statistics, but statistics are not necessarily persuasive, especially in the case of a small, unrepresentative sample.

The basic Title VII case is a three-step process. The plaintiff establishes a prima facie case by introducing facts suggestive of discrimination. Next, the employer is permitted to rebut the charge, by proving legitimate nondiscriminatory reasons or business necessity for the conduct. Finally, the plaintiff is permitted to show pretextuality — that the employer's stated explanation is merely a pretext for discrimination.

In a disparate impact case in which the employer asserts a business necessity defense, the plaintiff can prevail by showing that the employer refused to adopt a nondiscriminatory alternative practice that would have satisfied its business needs.

Where there are many factors behind a workplace decision and the plaintiff challenges more than one criterion, the plaintiff must be able to prove disparate impact of each criterion.

A "mixed-motive" case is somewhat different: in such cases, the employer has several motivations behind a decision, some lawful and some discriminatory. The plaintiff can win by showing the influence of the discriminatory motive; it is not necessary to show that there were no legitimate motivations for the decision.

---

[144] Sheppard Mullin, Labor Employment Law Blog: *The Genetic Information Nondiscrimination Act Of 2008: Civil Rights Or Science Fiction?* http://www.laboremploymentlawblog.com (5/22/08).

But if the employer would have acted in the same way even without the discriminatory motive, the plaintiff's remedies will be reduced: § 107(b) of the Civil Rights Act of 1991 limits relief in mixed-motive cases to injunctive and declaratory relief, but not damages.

In mid-2003, the Supreme Court ruled that a Title VII plaintiff is entitled to get a jury instruction on mixed motive even without a showing of direct evidence of discrimination. The rationale is that the statute does not mandate direct evidence so proof by either direct or circumstantial evidence, is acceptable.[145]

In April 2008, the Seventh Circuit refused to rule whether it violates Title VII to discriminate on the basis of interracial relationships, because it held that the plaintiff, a black UPS manager who said he was fired because black co-workers objected to his dating and then marrying a white woman, did not have enough evidence. (According to UPS, he was fired for violating the non-fraternization policy that forbids supervisors to date any rank-and-file workers, even those they do not directly supervise.) Plaintiff Ellis stated that about 20 other couples violated the non-fraternization policy but were treated more favorably than he was. The Seventh Circuit held that those couples were not similarly situated, because the disciplinary decisions were not made by the same decision-maker as the district manager who fired Ellis.[146]

In many instances, employees seek to bring their cases in state court, believing that they will get a faster resolution, more sympathetic juries, and access to additional remedies (e.g., emotional distress damages and punitive damages). It is often possible for the employer to get the case removed to federal court, for instance if the issue is preempted by a federal law such as ERISA.

[A] Title VII Remedies

Some discrimination claims are breach of contract claims, but most of them are tort claims. In contract cases, the remedy is to put the plaintiff in the position that would have been obtained if the contract had been fulfilled, probably lost earnings and fringe benefits, perhaps out-of-pocket expenses of mitigating damages by finding another job.

Title VII tort damages are drawn from reinstatement, back pay (including fringe benefits; limited to two years), front pay from the end of the trial, lost earnings, medical expenses, pain and anguish, attorneys' fees, and emotional distress. Further discrimination can be enjoined: see 42 USC § 2000e-5(g).

The District of Columbia Circuit ruled that punitive damages are never available in Title VII cases absent egregious conduct by the employer. The Supreme Court relaxed that standard somewhat in *Kolstad v. American Dental Ass'n*, 527 U.S. 526 (1999), finding that punitive damages can be ordered even if the employer's conduct

---

[145] Desert Palace Inc. v. Costa, 539 U.S. 90 (2003).
[146] Ellis v. UPS, 523 F.3d 823 (7th Cir. 2008).

is not egregious. However, the employer will not be liable for punitive damages on the basis of conduct by a manager that violates the employer's good-faith effort to provide a workplace that is compliant with the requirements of federal law.

The Civil Rights Act of 1991 (CRA '91), P.L. 102-166, caps the total damages that can be received by any successful Title VII plaintiff, including punitive damages and most compensatory damages (but not medical bills and other monetary losses incurred before the trial as a result of discrimination). The cap depends on the employer corporation's size, not the seriousness of the discrimination charges.

Companies with fewer than 15 employees are exempt from Title VII, so the smallest unit for CRA '91 purposes is the company with 15–100 employees; the damage cap is $50,000. It is $100,000 for companies with 101–200 employees, $200,000 for 201–500 employees, and $300,000 if the company has more than 500 workers.

Front pay ordered as a discrimination suit remedy is not considered "compensatory damages," and therefore is not subject to the CRA '91 cap.[147]

28 USC § 1658(a) provides a four-year statute of limitations for statutes enacted after December 1, 1990. In a suit for wrongful discharge, wrongful refusal to transfer and hostile work environment, the District Court held that the claims arose under CRA '91, and therefore were governed by § 1658 and not by the state two-year statute of limitations. The Seventh Circuit reversed, stating that § 1658 does not apply to a cause of action based on a post-1990 amendment to an existing statute. The Supreme Court reversed yet again, on the grounds that § 1658's purpose of eliminating uncertainty and mandating uniform rules could not be carried out if it applied only to new sections of the U.S. Code. The claims arose under CRA '91 because they were made possible by it; racial harassment was not cognizable prior to CRA '91.[148]

Clearly, breach of contract damages are taxable income for the plaintiff, because they replace earned income that would have been taxable. Tort damages received for "personal injury" are tax-free. However, a 1992 Supreme Court decision[149] characterizes Title VII damages as taxable income, because they are not sufficiently similar to bodily injury damages in traditional tort cases.

The Small Business Job Protection Act of 1996 amended Code § 104(a)(2) to provide that, effective August 21, 1996, damages received for physical illness and other "personal [i.e., bodily] physical injuries" will be tax-free. Damages for emotional distress are taxable except to the extent of medical expenses for treatment of emotional distress.

---

[147] Pollard v. duPont, 532 U.S. 843 (2001).

[148] Jones v. R.R. Donnelley & Sons, 541 U.S. 369 (2004).

[149] United States v. Burke, 504 U.S. 229 (1992). This is also true of Age Discrimination in Employment Act damages: Comm'r of Internal Revenue v. Schleier, 515 U.S. 323 (1995).

2004's American Jobs Creation Act § 703 amended Internal Revenue Code § 62 to provide that attorneys' fees and court costs incurred in order to obtain recovery in an employment discrimination or "whistleblower" suit will be treated as an adjustment to gross income and not as an itemized deduction, with the result that the fees and costs will not increase the successful litigant's Alternative Minimum Tax liability.

In its January 25, 2005, decision, *Commissioner v. Banks*, 543 U.S. 426, the Supreme Court resolved a longstanding Circuit split by ruling that a judgment or settlement paid to a winning plaintiff's attorney under a contingent fee arrangement is nevertheless included in the plaintiff's gross income. One respondent in this case settled a Title VII suit for $464,000, $150,000 of which was paid to his attorney. The other settled a suit for wrongful interference with his employment contract, receiving almost $5 million; the defendants paid close to $4 million directly to the plaintiff's attorney pursuant to the contingent fee contract. *Banks* was decided after the enactment of the ACJA, but, as the opinion notes, the ACJA is not retroactive, so the Supreme Court decision will have an impact on a good many pre-ACJA cases.

[1] Exemptions from Discrimination Laws

A neutral, bona fide seniority system that does not manifest discriminatory intent is permissible, even if it provides different terms or conditions of employment for employees with differing seniority — and even if the effect of the system is to maintain past discrimination. See 42 USC § 2000e-2(h).

Employers are not guilty of discrimination if their conduct is justified by a Bona Fide Occupational Qualification (BFOQ). For instance, authenticity might dictate hiring a male rather than a female for a role in a film. Privacy might dictate hiring a female rather than a male as a dressing room attendant. Public safety might require a pilot or police officer to be young enough to have youthful reflexes. However, the BFOQ defense is not accepted in cases of alleged racial discrimination.

A business necessity defense is also possible if alleged discriminatory conduct is needed to maintain safety and efficiency.

[2] The Civil War Acts

The Civil Rights Act of 1866, 42 USC § 1981, gives all citizens the same employment and contractual rights as "white citizens." It covers employers of all sizes; the 15-employee limit of Title VII is not applicable, and at-will employees can sue under § 1981. It is not necessary to exhaust administrative remedies before bringing a § 1981 suit, and there is no limitation on the amount of compensatory and punitive damages that can be awarded.

The Civil Rights Act of 1991 generally requires race discrimination claimants to proceed under § 1981 before accessing Title VII. Title VII compensatory and punitive damages are not available to persons who can receive such damages under § 1981.

Four Circuits permit suits by at-will employees under 42 USC § 1981 when they allege termination of the at-will employment for racially discriminatory reasons.[150]

In 2008, the Supreme Court allowed an African-American restaurant manager, who charged that he was fired for protesting the racially motivated firing of another employee, to use § 1981 to pursue his retaliation charges even though his Title VII claim was dismissed for failure to pay filing fees on time. The defendant argued that retaliation claims should not be allowed under § 1981, not only because the statute itself does not provide for retaliation claims (although the related § 1982 does) but because allowing retaliation actions under § 1981 would make it possible for some plaintiffs to pursue Title VII claims that were ruled out by Title VII procedural rules. The Supreme Court rejected this argument, holding that Congress intended for Title VII and § 1981 remedies to overlap.[151]

[B] Sex Discrimination

Discrimination on account of sex is unlawful under Title VII. In addition, Executive Order 11246 forbids sex discrimination by government contractors and subcontractors; violators can be barred from doing business with the federal government.

Under a 1983 Supreme Court decision,[152] it constitutes sex discrimination for an employer to provide more benefits for male employees and their spouses than for female employees and their spouses.

The Pregnancy Discrimination Act (PDA; 42 USC § 2000e(k)) bars discrimination on the basis of pregnancy or related conditions. A common misunderstanding is that the PDA requires employers to treat pregnancy as a disability. What the act really does is to require any pregnancy-related disability to be covered by employer plans to the same extent as other non-work-related disability.

---

[150] Lauture v. IBM, 216 F.3d 258 (2d Cir. 2000); Perry v. Woodward, 199 F.3d 1126 (10th Cir. 1999); Spriggs v. Diamond Auto Glass, 165 F.3d 1015 (4th Cir. 1999); Fadeyi v. Planned Parenthood, 160 F.3d 10 (5th Cir. 1998). On a related issue, Domino's Pizza, Inc. v. McDonald, 546 U.S. 470 (2006) — no relation to the hamburgers — holds that a black sole shareholder of a corporation could not sue under § 1981 based on allegations that Domino's Pizza broke construction contracts out of racial animus toward the plaintiff. The Supreme Court said that a corporate shareholder is not liable under the corporation's contracts and therefore has no rights under them, so an individual in this situation could not be deprived of the right to make and enforce contracts.

[151] CBOCS West, Inc. v. Humphries, 128 S. Ct. 1951 (2008).

[152] Newport News Shipbuilding v. EEOC, 462 U.S. 669 (1983). In late 2008, the Supreme Court heard arguments in a case brought by four women who lost seniority credit for maternity leaves taken before the PDA became effective. The defendant, AT&T, argued that the PDA is not retroactive, and the claims should have been brought when the seniority determinations were first made. The plaintiffs argued that if a plan is facially discriminatory, every reduced pension payment is an additional act of discrimination: AT&T v. Hulteen, No. 07-543 (pending); see Sam Hananel (AP), *Supreme Court Weighs How Maternity Leaves Affect Pensions*, 12/11/08 (law.com).

The PDA does not require an employer to add health care coverage if it would not otherwise provide it. However, if health care coverage is provided, pregnancy-related conditions must be covered on terms of equality with non-pregnancy-related conditions.

The Seventh Circuit ruled in 2008 that PDA coverage can be triggered even before pregnancy has occurred; terminating an employee for taking time off to have fertility treatment can violate the PDA.[153]

The Equal Pay Act, 29 USC § 206 (EPA) is a statute outside Title VII that forbids sex discrimination in compensation. It covers employers of two or more (versus 15 or more for Title VII coverage). Discrimination is forbidden in salary or other compensation on the basis of sex, if the jobs require equal skill, effort, and responsibility and are performed under similar working conditions. Therefore, the EPA does not cover "comparable worth" allegations that women are being under-paid as compared to men who perform different jobs of allegedly lesser value.

[C] Title VII Pleadings

In 2002, the Supreme Court simplified the requirements for pleading employ-ment discrimination cases. The complaint in a discrimination suit is adequate if it satisfies the FRCP 8(a)(2) requirement of a short and plain statement of a claim showing the pleader's entitlement to relief, even if the pleading does not assert specific facts establishing the prima facie case.[154]

The following month, the Supreme Court upheld an EEOC Regulation that permits amending the complaint to correct failure to verify. The amendment relates back to the date of the original charge. The Supreme Court held that the rule was a valid interpretation of Title VII's mandate that charges be written and subscribed under oath or affirmation.[155]

§3.12 SEXUAL HARASSMENT

Sexual harassment is the subjection of an employee to unwanted sexual con-tact, solicitation, or innuendoes. It is considered a form of sex discrimination that violates Title VII. Both quid pro quo harassment (employee is either threatened with detrimental consequences for not providing sexual access, or offered job benefits for providing it) and hostile environment harassment[156] are actionable.

Harassment of an individual is actionable whether the harasser is of the opposite sex or the same sex, and either males or females can bring sexual harass-ment claims.[157] In the view of the EEOC, conduct is unwanted if the employee did not solicit or initiate it, and he or she finds the conduct undesirable or offensive.

---

[153] Hall v. Nalco Co., 534 F.3d 644 (7th Cir. 2008).

[154] Swierkiewicz v. Sorema NA, 534 U.S. 506 (2002).

[155] Edelman v. Lynchburg Coll., 535 U.S. 106 (2002).

[156] This cause of action was first recognized by the Supreme Court in Meritor Savings Bank v. Vinson, 477 U.S. 57 (1986).

[157] Same-sex harassment cognizable: Oncale v. Sundown Offshore Servs. Inc., 523 U.S. 45 (1998).

Most sexual harassment cases involve harassment allegedly committed by a supervisor, although in some cases, conduct by a co-employee or a customer (e.g., a bar patron who harasses a cocktail waitress) is actionable. In virtually all instances, the proper defendant is the employer corporation; the individual harasser generally cannot be sued.

The Eleventh Circuit recognized a sexual harassment hostile work environment cause of action in a case where the plaintiff was constantly subjected to sexual and misogynistic invective, although most of it was directed at women in general rather than specifically to her. The court considered the harassment extensive enough to meet the "severe and pervasive" element of the cause of action, and accepted that sex-specific profanity can be more offensive to women than to men. Although the plaintiff continued to receive acceptable performance evaluations throughout her tenure, the Eleventh Circuit ruled that conduct can be actionable even if it does not prevent the plaintiff from doing her job.[158]

In 1999,[159] the Supreme Court resolved questions of what the employer can do to free itself of liability in harassment cases. If the employment action had adverse effect on the harassment victim, the employer is absolutely liable. If there was no adverse employment effect, the employer is liable unless it maintained proper anti-harassment and grievance policies.

Obviously, employers must create, promulgate, and enforce an anti-harassment policy, and must have a complaint mechanism that allows employees to assert harassment claims (and to someone other than the direct supervisor, if he or she is the alleged harasser).

If the investigation reveals that the claim is well-founded, some action must be taken that is not punitive to the victim of harassment. Depending on circumstances, it could include firing the harasser; subjecting the harasser to a lesser degree of discipline; transferring either the harasser or victim to prevent further contact; or other appropriate response.

In October 2008, one of the first arguments heard by the Supreme Court was *Crawford v. Nashville & Davidson County*, No 05-1595, on the issue of whether it violates Title VII to retaliate against employees for sexual harassment complaints made during an internal investigation (prior to filing of formal charges). The Sixth Circuit dismissed the case on the grounds that the plaintiff did not engage in the type of "active opposition" to the employer's policies required by Title VII.[160]

For the EEOC's interpretation of an employer's duties in the post-Faragher/Ellerth environment, see "Enforcement Guidance: Vicarious Employer Liability for Unlawful Harassment by Supervisors," http://www.eeoc.gov/docs/harassment.html. In 2004, the Supreme Court ruled that where there has been constructive discharge (i.e., using objective standards, a reasonable person would have felt

---

[158] Reeves v. C.H. Robinson Worldwide Inc., 525 F.3d 1139 (11th Cir. 2008).

[159] Burlington Indus. Inc. v. Ellerth, 524 U.S. 742 (1998); Faragher v. City of Boca Raton, 524 U.S. 775 (1998).

[160] Tony Mauro, *Supreme Court Hears Environmental, Employment Discrimination Cases*, Legal Times 10/9/08 (law.com).

compelled to resign), there has been adverse employment action. However, although firing an employee is always an official act that will make the *Ellerth/ Faragher* affirmative defense unavailable to the employer, in constructive discharge cases, the employer is entitled to assert and prove an affirmative defense if the events leading up to the constructive discharge were not official acts chargeable to the employer.[161]

§ 3.13 ADEA

The Age Discrimination in Employment Act, 29 USC § 621 *et seq.*, generally protects individuals over 40 from age-based job discrimination. Employers are subject to the ADEA if they have 20 or more employees.[162]

The Fourth Circuit upheld the EEOC regulation extending the ADEA to apprenticeship programs, finding it to be a permissible interpretation of the statute.[163]

The ADEA covers discrimination in hiring, firing, and terms and conditions of employment, including benefits. A 1989 Supreme Court case, *Public Employees Retirement System of Ohio v. Betts*[164] held that the ADEA does not cover employee benefits, but in 1990, Congress passed the Older Workers Benefit Protection Act (OWBPA) to make it clear that benefit discrimination does indeed come under the ambit of the ADEA. The OWBPA allows employers to reduce severance benefits by sums such as retiree health benefits; supplemental unemployment insurance benefits; and additional pension benefits provided as early retirement incentives.

In 2004, the Supreme Court refused to permit one group of over-40 workers to use the ADEA to challenge giving better retiree health benefits to another, even older, group of over-40 workers, on the grounds that the ADEA permits favoring older workers — even at the expense of other workers in the protected group.[165]

The EEOC proposed amendments to 27 CFR Part 1616, affect the procedure for bringing an age discrimination suit.[166] Under the proposal, the EEOC would issue a Notice of Dismissal or Termination (NDT) when it disposes of an age discrimination charge, by dismissal or otherwise. The notice tells the charging party that he or she has a right to sue the alleged discriminator — but the right

---

[161] Pennsylvania State Police v. Suders, 542 U.S. 129 (2004).

[162] The shareholders in a PC are not counted in determining whether there are 20 "employees"; the test is whether the economic realities of a person's work are closer to employment or to, e.g., being a partner: EEOC v. Sidley Austin Brown & Wood, 315 F.3d 696 (7th Cir. 2002).

[163] EEOC v. Seafarers Int'l Union, 394 F.3d 197 (4th Cir. 2005).

[164] 492 U.S. 158 (1989).

[165] General Dynamics Land Sys. Inc. v. Cline, 540 U.S. 581 (2004); *see also* Lawrence v. Town of Irondequoit, 246 F. Supp. 2d 150 (W.D.N.Y. 2002), allowing enhancement of retiree health benefits for retirees who had attained age 80. The EEOC proposed Regulations conforming to *Cline* in 2006: 71 F.R. 46177 (8/11/06) and finalized them in mid-2007: 72 F.R. 36873 (7/6/07). The Final Rule permits favoring an older over a younger individual even if both are within the protected group, but employers are not required to prefer older individuals, and applicable state or local laws forbidding preferences for older individuals remain valid.

[166] 67 FR 52431 (8/12/02).

expires 90 days after the NDT's issue date. This is similar but not identical to the way a Right to Sue Letter works. The ADEA plaintiff can file suit at any time once 60 days have passed since the charge was filed with the appropriate anti-discrimination agency; it is not necessary to wait for an NDT.

In 2008, the Supreme Court decided an unusually large number of ADEA cases, including:

- The combination of an EEOC intake questionnaire and an affidavit can operate as a "charge" because it provides the statutory minimum information required for a charge.[167]
- An individual employee of a government agency cannot use the "class of one" theory to bring equal protection claims against the government employer.[168]
- However, the specific ADEA provisions covering federal employees can be used to bring a retaliation claim.[169]

In mid-2003, the EEOC reversed its earlier position and proposed regulations under which employers can legitimately change or even eliminate retiree health benefits once the retiree becomes eligible for Medicare. Benefits for spouses and dependents could also be eliminated under the same provisions.[170]

The AARP brought suit to challenge the EEOC's new position. Judge Brody of the Eastern District of Pennsylvania ruled that the EEOC regulation was invalid because it conflicted with a Third Circuit decision dating back to 2000, forbidding employers to reduce benefits on the basis of Medicare eligibility. Then, in September 2005, Brody vacated her own earlier decision, because in the interim, the Supreme Court had decided *National Cable and Telecommunications Association v. Brand X Internet Services*. In Brody's view, this decision requires greater deference to be given to administrative regulations, because regulations that conflict with a judicial decision are entitled to deference unless the litigation precedent unambiguously eliminates the interpretation chosen by the agency. That is, a judicial decision precludes administrative interpretation of the underlying statute only if the decision sets out a single permissible reading of the statute — not merely identifies the best among the alternative interpretations.[171] In 2007, the Third Circuit upheld the EEOC regulations, finding them to fall within the agency's authority under ADEA § 9. The Third Circuit found that the regulation was also valid under the APA, because it was in the public interest, and narrowly

---

[167] Federal Express Corp. v. Holowecki, 128 S. Ct. 1147 (2008).

[168] Engquist v. Oregon Dep't of Agriculture, 128 S. Ct. 2146 (2008).

[169] Gomez-Perez v. Potter, 128 S. Ct. 1931 (2008).

[170] Proposed 29 CFR § 1625.32, added by 68 Fed. Reg. 41542 (7/12/03).

[171] AARP v. EEOC, No. 05-cv-509, Memorandum and Order E.D. Pa. 9/27/05; *see* Shannon P. Duffy, *Federal Judge Affirms EEOC Proposed Regulation in Wake of High Court Decision*, The Legal Intelligencer 9/29/05 (law.com). *Brand X*, 125 S. Ct. 2688 (2005). The earlier E.D. Pa. decision is available at 2005 WL 723991.

drawn to meet the goals of the ADEA. Although the regulation represented a change in agency policy, it was not arbitrary or capricious because it was a reasoned change.[172]

[A] ADEA Exclusions

A Supreme Court ADEA case from early 2000 strikes down 1974 amendments to the ADEA that abrogated the states' sovereign immunity against age discrimination suits brought by state employees. In this view, Congress exceeded its powers, because abrogation is so disproportionate to the documented history of state conduct that the amendments did not constitute "appropriate legislation" such as Congress is empowered to enact by Section 5 of the Fourteenth Amendment.[173]

The Supreme Court refused to rule out the possibility of disparate impact ADEA claims, although the court did note that, because of differences in the statutory language between Title VII and the ADEA, the possible scope of disparate impact claims under the ADEA is narrower.[174]

To a limited extent, a Bona Fide Occupational Qualification (BFOQ) defense can be raised to an ADEA charge: if, for instance, a police officer or firefighter has to be under 40 to have the physical fitness needed for the job.

Reasonable Factors Other than Age (RFOAs) can also provide an ADEA defense, if the employer can prove that it used objective, uniformly applied, job-related criteria to make the decision that is being attacked as age-based.

A related business necessity defense is available: for instance, if older employees were being discharged or laid off because their salaries were higher than those of potential younger replacements. 29 USC § 623(f)(2) creates an ADEA exception for actions taken in compliance with a bona fide seniority system or employee benefit plan. However, this defense cannot be used to justify failure to hire or involuntary retirement.

Mandatory retirement is permissible in the case of persons who have reached age 70, and who were bona fide executives or held a high policy-making position at least two years before the forced retirement, as long as they were entitled to immediate nonforfeitable annual retirement benefits of $44,000 a year or more. EEOC Guidelines at 29 CFR § 1625.12(d) define executives and policy-makers.

---

[172] AARP v. EEOC, 489 F.3d 558 (3d Cir. 2007); on August 21, 2007, the Third Circuit refused to re-hear the case. *See* Shannon P. Duffy, *3rd Circuit: Employers May Modify Medicare-Eligible Retirees' Health Benefits*, The Legal Intelligencer 6/6/07 (law.com).

[173] Kimel v. Florida Bd. of Regents, 528 U.S. 52 (2000). Indiana held that a state government unit with 20 or more employees is subject to the ADEA and not the state Age Discrimination Act, because the state law's definition of "employer" specifically excludes government agencies covered by the ADEA: Montgomery v. Board of Trustees of Purdue Univ., 75 LW 1072 (Ind. 6/29/06).

[174] Smith v. Jackson, Miss., 544 U.S. 228 (U.S. 2005). Accordingly, the EEOC proposed regulations in early 2008, at 73 Fed. Reg. 16807 (3/31/08), that would amend 29 CFR § 1625.7 to state that an employment practice that adversely affects persons over 40 because of their older age is discriminatory, unless the practice is justified by a Reasonable Factor Other than Age.

Tenured university professors can also be required to retire on the basis of age, under the Higher Education Amendments of 1998, H.R. 6 (10/7/98).

[B] Proof of the ADEA Case

Although most discrimination charges involve immutable characteristics, such as race and sex, age discrimination cases present some philosophical questions because of the inevitability of human aging.

The basic prima facie ADEA case is:

- The plaintiff belongs to the protected group (persons over 40)
- The plaintiff was qualified for the job he or she held or applied for
- Adverse action was taken on account of age
- (In appropriate cases) the plaintiff was replaced by one or more other employees.

A 1993 Supreme Court case[175] makes it possible to win an ADEA case based on proof of improper age-related motives for discharge, even if the replacement employee is over 40.

It is up to employers who assert a Reasonable Factors Other than Age defense about a challenged employment practice to meet both the burden of production and the burden of proof on this affirmative defense. ADEA plaintiffs do not have to make the lack of RFOAs part of their prima facie case. The effect was to make it easier for plaintiffs to prevail.[176] Testimony of former co-workers with a different supervisor should not necessarily have been excluded from an ADEA case; the District Court should decide whether such testimony is more likely to be probative than prejudicial.[177]

A number of ADEA cases really allege "age-plus" rather than simple age discrimination. That is, the plaintiff charges that he or she has been fired because lengthy employment and a good track record have made the employee's salary high enough so that the company can save money by replacing the employee with a lower-paid neophyte. *Hazen Paper Co. v. Biggins*, 507 U.S. 604 (1993), requires the plaintiff to prove that age itself, not just age-related factors such as long tenure, influenced the employer's conduct.

In *Kentucky Retirement Systems v. EEOC*,[178] the Supreme Court held that a disability pension system that added years of service to enhance the pension of persons disabled before Normal Retirement Age, but not those disabled later, did not violate the ADEA. The court's rationale was that workers were treated differently based on their pension status, not on age. Furthermore, although the

---

[175] O'Connor v. Consolidated Coin Caterers Corp., 517 U.S. 308 (1997).

[176] Meacham v. Knolls Atomic Power Laboratory, 128 S. Ct. 2395 (2008); *see, e.g.*, (AP) *Supreme Court Rules for Workers in Age Bias Suit*, 6/19/08 (law.com).

[177] Sprint/United Management Co. v. Mendelsohn, 128 S. Ct. 1140 (2008).

[178] 128 S. Ct. 2361 (2008).

individual plaintiff (who continued to work past NRA and became disabled when he was already eligible for a pension) fared worse under this system, some older workers with different fact patterns could benefit from it. The Supreme Court found that the system did not discriminate against older workers: taking age and service into account is reasonable when computing disability retirement benefits.

In June 2000, the Supreme Court eased the burden facing age discrimination plaintiffs. The issue in this case is whether an ADEA defendant can obtain a judgment as a matter of law (JMOL; see FRCP 50) after the plaintiff presents a case limited to a prima facie case of discrimination, and then offers rebuttal evidence to the employer's defense that it had a legitimate nondiscriminatory rationale for the challenged conduct. The 57-year-old petitioner was one of three supervisors in a department that allegedly suffered from poor management and impaired productivity. He was fired after an audit of the department. The employer contended that he was fired for poor performance. He claimed that the employer's response was pretextual.

The Supreme Court permitted the trier of fact to conclude that discrimination occurred on the basis of a prima facie case plus evidence justifying the trier in fact in treating the employer's explanation as pretextual. However, the Supreme Court merely allowed the trier of fact to find for the plaintiff in such a situation; it did not compel it. The employer would be able to get a JMOL based on a record making it conclusive that the asserted nondiscriminatory reason for the action was valid. Consideration of the JMOL motion should include consideration of evidence favorable to both the moving and nonmoving parties.[179]

[C] ADEA Releases

The Older Workers Benefit Protection Act permits exiting employees to release their ADEA claims, as long as the waiver is knowing and voluntary. A valid release must:

- Refer specifically to ADEA claims
- Give the employee at least 21 days to consider (at least 45 days, if a group of employees is being terminated at one time)
- Give the employee at least seven days after signing to withdraw the release
- Inform employees that the release is a legal document, and that they can get legal counsel before signing it.

See 29 CFR Part 1625 for the EEOC policy on waivers under the OWBPA. A Final Rule on ADEA waivers was published at 63 FR 30624 on June 5, 1998. The employee who signs a valid waiver must receive additional valuable consideration for signing that would not be available without waiving ADEA claims.

An employee who wishes to bring suit notwithstanding having signed a release is not required to "tender back" (return) the consideration received for

---

[179] Reeves v. Sanderson Plumbing Prods., 530 U.S. 133 (2000).

the release as a precondition of bringing suit: *Oubre v. Entergy Operations, Inc.*, 522 U.S. 422 (1998).[180] According to the Tenth Circuit, the OWBPA requires an employer who seeks releases to provide personalized information about why that particular employee was chosen for layoff — with the result that a release that was defective in this regard would not prevent the former employee from suing under the ADEA.[181]

§ 3.14 ADA

The Americans with Disabilities Act of 1990 (42 USC § 12101) covers public accommodations discrimination, but this discussion deals with disability discrimination in employment, employment-related practices, and terms and conditions of employment (including benefits). Employers (but not individuals)[182] are liable under the ADA if they discriminate against a qualified individual with a disability.

Disability is a physical or mental impairment that substantially limits at least one life activity;[183] the ADA is triggered by a person's being perceived as disabled even if in fact no disability exists. Determination of disability is made after mitigating factors (e.g., medication, assistive devices, eyeglasses or contact lenses) are applied.[184]

Reasonable accommodation can include making the workplace accessible, changing work schedules, modifying or purchasing new equipment, or reassigning the disabled individual to a vacant position. It is not necessary to create a new job, fire or demote another employee, or provide any accommodation that is an undue

---

[180] The EEOC's proposed regulations to implement *Oubre* are found at 64 FR 19952 (4/23/99) and http://www.eeoc.gov/regs/tender.html. A Question and Answer sheet about the proposal appears at http://www.eeoc.gov/regs/quanda.html.

[181] Kruchowski v. Weyerhaeuser, 423 F.3d 1139 (10th Cir. 2005).

[182] Mason v. Stallings, 82 F.3d 1007 (11th Cir. 1996).

[183] Being HIV-positive is a disability because it limits the major life activity of reproduction: Bragdon v. Abbott, 524 U.S. 624 (1998). Having sight in only one eye is not a disability, because this impairment does not substantially limit the major life activity of seeing, because the plaintiffs could drive, use tools, read, etc., and were not restricted in their activities: EEOC v. United Parcel Serv., 02 CDOS 9672, 71 L.W. 1206 (9th Cir. 2002). It was not a violation of state privacy laws for a doctor treating a workplace injury to disclose the worker's HIV-positive status to the employee's employer. The employee signed a hospital consent form that authorized the release of medical information, including HIV test results, in the event of an injury at work. By signing the release and applying for Worker's Compensation, the employee put his medical condition at issue: Melo v. Barnett, 157 S.W.3d 596 (Ky. 2005). In mid-2008, the D.C. Circuit ruled, in a case of first impression, that sleeping is a major life activity for ADA purposes. An ADA plaintiff need not prove that the sleep disability affected daytime activities to pursue a discrimination claim. (The plaintiff was a candidate at the FBI Academy who had insomnia secondary to PTSD resulting from being held hostage.) The D.C. Circuit accepted his argument that the FBI's stated reasons for dismissing him from the Academy (lack of maturity and cooperation) were really a pretext for discriminating against him for suffering from PTSD: Desmond v. Mukasey, 530 F.3d 944 (D.C. Cir. 2008); *see* Marcia Coyle, *D.C. Circuit: Sleeping Is 'Major Life Activity*, Nat'l L.J. 7/18/08 (law.com).

[184] Sutton v. UAL, 527 U.S. 471; Murphy v. UPS, 527 U.S. 516 (1999); Albertsons v. Kirkingburg, 527 U.S. 555 (1999).

hardship to the employer. Employer and employee are directed to engage in an interactive process to find suitable accommodations.[185]

A qualified individual with a disability is one who has the experience and education, and is otherwise able to perform the essential functions of the job, either with or without reasonable accommodations made by the employer. It is unlawful to discriminate against now-sober persons who used to abuse alcohol or drugs, but current substance abuse is not a disability for ADA purposes.

Mixed-motive ADA cases (i.e., disability discrimination was one factor among others leading to termination) and hostile environment ADA cases can be brought.[186]

Employers are not permitted to ask job applicants about their disability or health status. However, once the employer is willing to extend a conditional job offer, it can lawfully ask applicants about their ability to perform the essential job functions, and ask about accommodations that may be required.

After hiring, the employer is permitted to make inquiries and require a medical examination based on objective evidence of a medical condition that limits the employee's ability to perform essential job functions, or that makes him or her a safety threat.

The ADA envisions an interactive process of accommodation, where the employee requests accommodation, the employer offers what it believes to be practical and achievable accommodations, and they arrive at a mutually acceptable accommodation. In the case of Wal-Mart's demotion of a pharmacy technician who had cerebral palsy (he was assigned to collect shopping carts in the parking lot instead of the pharmacy job he was hired for), the Second Circuit ruled that where an employee's disability is obvious, the employer has an obligation to accommodate even if the employee does not request accommodation. The jury awarded $2.5 million in compensatory and $5 million in punitive damages — an amount reduced by the Second Circuit to $900,000 in compensatory and punitive damages and $644,000 in attorneys' fees.[187]

The ADA is jointly enforced by the EEOC and the Department of Labor. ADA procedures, timing requirements, and remedies are similar to those for Title VII.

Employers are permitted to make benefit plan determinations consistent with sound underwriting principles, unless the determinations are a subterfuge to avoid ADA compliance. It is not lawful to refuse to hire, or to fire, a person because of the effect his or her disability will have on the cost of the group health plan.[188] Preexisting condition limitations are permissible.

---

[185] After the interactive process, failure to implement accommodations with reasonable promptness can give rise to liability, e.g., Battle v. United Parcel Serv., 438 F.3d 856 (8th Cir. 2006).

[186] Mixed motive: McNely v. Ocala Star-Banner Corp., 99 F.3d 1068 (11th Cir. 1996); hostile environment: Hendler v. Intellicom U.S.A. Inc., 963 F. Supp. 2000 (1997).

[187] Brady v. Wal-Mart Stores, Inc., 531 F.3d 127 (2d Cir. 2008); *see* Mark Hamblett, *2nd Circuit Affirms Award Against Wal-Mart in Disability Bias Case*, N.Y.L.J. 7/8/08 (law.com).

[188] In 2008, the Tenth Circuit permitted a couple to pursue claims under the ADA (and ERISA); they alleged that they were fired because of the high cost of their son's terminal illness to the EGHP. The parents were fired two weeks after their son suffered a relapse of his brain tumor that proved to be fatal. Trujillo v. Pacifica Corp., 524 F.3d 1149 (10th Cir. 2008).

Applying for SSDI benefits is not necessarily inconsistent with making an ADA claim, given that SSDI focuses on inability to work, and the ADA permits consideration of ability to work with reasonable accommodation. The plaintiff is entitled to explain the discrepancy between claiming disability and claiming to be able to work with reasonable accommodation.[189]

In the spring of 2001, both the Fourth and Fifth Circuits held that a qualified person with a disability can bring suit for disability-related harassment that arises to the level of a hostile work environment.[190] And in late 2004, the Tenth Circuit joined the Fourth, Fifth, and Eighth Circuits in ruling that ADA hostile work environment claims can be maintained, because of the similarity in language between that statute and Title VII.[191]

The ADA has two anti-retaliation provisions. According to the Third Circuit, the broader of the two provisions can be used by third parties who claim that they were retaliated against because another person exercised rights under the statute. But the second, narrower provision can only be used by the person who exercised the statutory rights. (The Third Circuit says that only the victim of discrimination can claim retaliation under the ADEA.)[192]

[A] Recent Supreme Court Rulings; Congressional Response

Since 2001, the Supreme Court has made a number of significant ADA rulings.

Once again finding that Congress had exceeded its powers, the Supreme Court decided in February 2001 that Congress improperly abrogated Eleventh Amendment immunity when it permitted ADA suits against state government employers. The Court's rationale was that Congress acted without adequate evidence that handicap discrimination in state employment was a serious problem.[193]

An assembly line worker's inability to perform the manual tasks associated with her job (the plaintiff suffered from carpal tunnel syndrome) was held not to constitute an ADA disability, because she did not experience a permanent or long-term limitation in her ability to perform self-care tasks of central importance to daily life.[194]

In January 2002, the Court permitted the EEOC to pursue an ADA case, even one that seeks specific relief for particular individuals who are alleged to be the victims of disability discrimination, even if the employee was covered by a mandatory pre-dispute arbitration agreement. Although the agreement would

---

[189] Cleveland v. Policy Management Ass'n, 526 U.S. 795 (1999).

[190] Flowers v. Southern Reg'l Physician Services, 247 F.3d 229 (5th Cir. 2001); Fox v. General Motors, 247 F.3d 169 (4th Cir. 2001).

[191] Lanman v. Johnson Co., Kansas, 393 F.3d 1151 (10th Cir. 2004).

[192] Fogleman v. Mercy Hosp. Inc., 283 F.3d 561 (3d Cir. 2002). The broader anti-retaliation provision is 42 USC § 12203(b); the narrower one is § 12203(a).

[193] Board of Trustees of the Univ. of Ala. v. Garrett, 531 U.S. 356 (2001).

[194] Toyota Motor Mfg., Kentucky, Inc. v. Williams, 534 U.S. 184 (2002); this is one of the cases reversed by the 2008 federal legislation.

permit the employee filing an individual suit, it would not prevent the EEOC from seeking relief on his or her behalf.[195]

Reassigning an employee to accommodate his or her disability has been held not to be reasonable if it violates an established seniority system.[196]

The holding of *Chevron USA Inc. v. Echazabal*, 536 U.S. 73 (2002), is that the ADA language about "direct threat" (42 USC § 12113(a)) can permissibly be used by an employer to avoid employing a person whose own health would be threatened by workplace conditions, as well as a person who constitutes a threat to the safety of others.

The case, brought by an oil refinery worker whose liver condition was likely to be exacerbated by workplace chemicals, upholds the validity of the EEOC Regulation, 29 CFR § 1630.15(b)(2), giving the employer an affirmative defense for failure to hire a person who poses a direct threat to his or her own health or safety.

In the Supreme Court's view, this regulation is legitimate because it permits employers to harmonize their obligations under the ADA with their obligations under the OSH Act.

Another ADA case from the same term does not deal with private employers: it rules out punitive damages in cases against government agencies that fail to provide reasonable accommodation to the needs of the disabled in public accommodations and programs that receive federal funding.[197]

In April 2003, the Supreme Court ruled that the appropriate test of employee status was the economic reality of the situation, so four physicians who were shareholders and directors of a medical PC were not employees. Therefore, the corporation had fewer than 15 employees, thus ruling out an ADA suit by the corporation's bookkeeper.[198]

On a related issue, the Supreme Court ruled that, in a suit under the Federal Employers Liability Act, damages for mental anguish (fear of developing cancer as a result of asbestos exposure) can be recovered if the plaintiff has already suffered

---

[195] EEOC v. Waffle House Inc., 534 U.S. 279 (2002). The Northern District of Illinois extended *Waffle House* beyond the arbitration context and permitted the EEOC to pursue individual monetary relief on behalf of law firm partners with time-barred ADEA claims, because the EEOC has been granted the statutory right to enforce the anti-discrimination laws in the public interest. EEOC v. Sidley Austin Brown & Wood LLP, 406 F. Supp. 2d 991 (N.D. Ill. 12/20/05); *aff'd* 437 F.3d 695.

[196] U.S. Airways v. Barnett, 535 U.S. 391 (2002).

[197] Barnes v. Gorman, 536 U.S. 181 (2002).

[198] Clackamas Gastroenterology Associates, PC v. Wells, 538 U.S. 440 (2003). However, an employer with fewer than 15 employees, although ADA-exempt, can be sued under the Rehabilitation Act: Schrader v. Fred A. Ray, M.D., PC, 296 F.3d 968 (10th Cir. 2002). The Seventh Circuit permitted the managers of a diner to be counted toward the 15-employee limit in a sexual harassment case, because they did not have an ownership interest in the business. The court refused to apply *Clackamas*, treating the source of authority as the key: any power the managers had was delegated from the employer: Smith v. Castaways Family Diner, 453 F.3d 971 (7th Cir. 2006).

another actionable injury, such as development of asbestosis. The plaintiff must prove that the fear is genuine and serious.[199]

The ADA Amendments Act of 2008, P.L. 110-325, was signed into law on September 25, 2008, after unanimous passage by both the Senate and the House of Representatives. The statute takes effect January 1, 2009. The statute specifically states that it is intended to reverse certain recent Supreme Court decisions (1999's *Sutton v. UAL* and 2002's *Toyota Motor Manufacturing v. Williams*).

Under the amendments, remedial measures (other than ordinary eyeglasses or contact lenses) are not taken into account in determining whether an impairment substantially limits a major life activity. ADA plaintiffs will no longer be required to prove that their impairment prevents or severely restricts the plaintiff's ability to carry out activities of central importance to most people's daily lives. The amendments give self-care, doing manual tasks, seeing, hearing, eating, sleeping, walking, standing, lifting, bending, speaking, breathing, learning, reading, concentrating, thinking, communicating, and working as examples of major life activities; this list is not exclusive. The operation of a major bodily function (e.g., immune system function, digestion, respiration) is also defined as a major life activity. An impairment that substantially limits one major life activity can be considered a disability even if other major life activities are unaffected. An episodic impairment, or one that is in remission, can still be considered a disability if, when it is active, it substantially limits a major life activity. Under the Amendments, a plaintiff will be "regarded as having" an impairment if an ADA violation results from an actual or perceived physical or mental impairment — whether or not the impairment limits or is perceived to limit a major life activity. However, this protection does not extend to transitory and minor impairments (actual or expected duration of six months or less).

[B] FMLA

The Family and Medical Leave Act of 1993 (FMLA; 29 USC § 2601 *et seq.*) entitles employees who have worked for the company for at least a year to take up to 12 weeks unpaid leave per year to deal with their own medical problems ("serious health condition") or medical and caregiving needs of their immediate family (e.g., parenthood leave for those who have just had or adopted a baby). The 12-week limit applies per year, not per illness. Certain family members of active-duty military servicepersons can take up to 12 weeks (or 26 weeks, if the servicemember has suffered a serious service-related illness or injury) of FMLA leave. See the National Defense Authorization Act of 2008, P.L. 110-181.

The Employee Benefits Security Administration (EBSA) rendered an advisory opinion in 2005 that the legislative history of the FMLA makes it clear that Congress intended state laws that grant extra protection to workers to survive preemption by federal laws such as ERISA and the FMLA.[200]

---

[199] Norfolk & Western Ry. Co. v. Ayers, 538 U.S. 135 (2003).

[200] EBSA Advisory Opinion 2005-13A at http://www.dol.gov/ebsa/pdf/ao2005-13a.pdf; *see* 73 L.W. 2777.

With limited exceptions, the employee is entitled to be reinstated in the original or a fully comparable job when returning from leave. Persons on FMLA leave do not accrue additional seniority or benefits, but it is illegal for employers to deprive employees of seniority or benefits already accrued to punish employees for exercising their legal rights to family leave. Wherever possible, employees must give advance notice that they will require leave; and employers must disclose to employees what their FMLA rights are and how to exercise them.

In March 2002, the Supreme Court struck down a Department of Labor FMLA Regulation (29 CFR § 825.700(a)) saying that if the employer fails to notify the employee that leave is designated as FMLA leave, the employer will not be permitted to use such leave to reduce the employee's 12-week-a-year allotment of FMLA leave. The Supreme Court held that the Regulation is not valid because it categorically penalizes employer behavior, whereas the intent of the FMLA is to limit the guarantee of leave to 12 weeks a year and to require a showing that employee rights were prejudiced before an employer can be penalized.[201]

In 2008, the Ninth Circuit upheld an award of $1,100 in lost wages for time that the plaintiff (a bus driver) missed at work because of emotional stress caused by wrongful denial of FMLA leave. The plaintiff had multiple health problems, including diabetes, pulmonary disease, eczema, depression, anxiety, and adjustment disorder. His employer conceded that FMLA requests were wrongfully denied, but took the position that Congress did not intend to make consequential or emotional distress damages available under the FMLA. The Ninth Circuit held that the damages were not for emotional distress, but compensation for days the plaintiff was unable to work because of the harm inflicted by wrongful denial of his requests for leave.[202]

The Eighth Circuit refused to impose strict liability under the FMLA on a hospital that fired a nurse, because whether or not she took protected leave, her disruptive behavior would have led to her termination.[203]

The Fifth Circuit applied mixed motive analysis to an FMLA retaliation claim: employer liability if retaliation was one factor in the adverse employment decision. However, the plaintiff still lost the case, because the court concluded that her attendance record was so poor that a reasonable jury would have to conclude that she would have been fired even absent retaliation.[204]

In FMLA litigation, the employee retains the burden of proving the right to reinstatement, even if the employer asserts that the employee would have been dismissed even if no FMLA leave had been taken. Therefore, a jury instruction that

---

[201] Ragsdale v. Wolverine World Wide Inc., 535 U.S. 81 (2002).

[202] Farrell v. Tri-County Metropolitan Transportation District of Oregon, 530 F.3d 1023 (9th Cir. 2008). The Fifth, Sixth, Seventh, Tenth, and Eleventh Districts have already rejected the possibility of emotional distress damages in FMLA cases: see Rodgers v. City of Des Moines, 435 F.3d 904 (8th Cir. 2006) and the cases it cites.

[203] Throneberry v. McGehee Desha County Hosp., 403 F.3d 972 (8th Cir. 2005).

[204] Richardson v. Monitronics Int'l Inc., 434 F.3d 327 (5th Cir. 2005).

requires the employer to prove a nondiscriminatory reason for the dismissal is incorrect.[205]

The FMLA cause of action is not limited to current employees. Ex-employees can bring a suit alleging that they were terminated in retaliation for exercising their FMLA rights.[206] Although it ruled that Congress went too far and exceeded its powers when it made state employers subject to the ADA and ADEA, the Supreme Court took the opposite tack with respect to the FMLA, ruling in 2003 that the Congressional abrogation of state sovereign immunity was valid and legitimate.[207]

§3.15 LITIGATION ISSUES IN DISCRIMINATION SUITS

An individual who believes that he or she has suffered workplace discrimination must exhaust administrative remedies. The employee who charges employment discrimination must file a charge either with the EEOC or with the state or local anti-discrimination agency. If the employee starts with an EEOC filing, the federal agency generally "defers" to the state or local agency (see 29 CFR § 1601.74)—i.e., it forwards the paperwork to the other agency, giving it 60 days to resolve the complaint.

The EEOC has a dual role. Not only does it investigate allegations and seek to conciliate (bring employer and employee to a compromise that satisfies both), it has independent power to investigate and bring suits as a plaintiff. Furthermore, there is no statute of limitations for EEOC suits.

If the EEOC cannot settle a charge informally, it determines whether or not there is reasonable cause to believe that the employee's charge is well-founded. See 29 CFR § 1601.24(a) for criteria for this "reasonable cause" determination. Although EEOC probable cause determinations are per se admissible in a discrimination trial, the Ninth Circuit ruled that excluding such a decision and order was not an abuse of the District Court's discretion. The decision was conclusory that a violation had occurred, which might have been prejudicial to the jury.[208] If the EEOC determines that reasonable cause is not present, the agency informs the charging party of its decision. If the employee still intends to sue, he or she must get a "right to sue" letter in a Title VII or ADA case (but this is not required in an Equal Pay Act or ADEA case). The potential plaintiff is then required to file suit within 90 days of receiving the right to sue letter, or the claim will be waived.

Title VII and ADA charges must be filed with the EEOC within 180 days of the alleged act of discrimination (or the last in a series of alleged discriminatory acts) if there is no "deferral" agency involved, or within 300 days of the alleged

---

[205] Rice v. Sunrise Express Inc., 209 F.3d 1008 (7th Cir. 2000).

[206] Smith v. Bellsouth Telecomm. Inc., 273 F.3d 1303 (11th Cir. 2001).

[207] Nevada Dep't of Human Resources v. Hibbs, 538 U.S. 721 (2003).

[208] Amantea-Cabrera v. Potter, 279 F.3d 746 (9th Cir. 2002). The EEOC's determination (after an investigation) that there is reasonable cause to sue the employer is not judicially reviewable: EEOC v. Caterpillar Inc., 409 F.3d 831 (7th Cir. 2005).

discrimination and 30 days of the time the deferral agency terminates processing of the charge.

In mid-2002, the Supreme Court clarified the timing requirements for Title VII cases. If the claim is for discrete acts of discrimination or retaliation, the claim must be filed within 180 days (or 300 days in a deferral state). But if the claim is of a hostile work environment, alleging acts that are part of the same practice, the cause of action is timely as long as at least one act occurred during the relevant 180- or 300-day period. In either event, the Supreme Court made it clear that the court can either toll or limit the period to whatever extent equitable doctrines permit.[209]

The Supreme Court's May 2007 *Ledbetter* decision made it much harder to sue for pay discrimination. The plaintiff charged that, as a result of sex discrimination, she received poor evaluations, which had a ripple effect in denying her pay increases throughout her career. By the time she retired, she earned much less than male colleagues. The Supreme Court held that her claim was untimely because the clock does not re-start when past discrimination has ongoing effects. Thus, employees who allege disparate treatment on account of race or gender must bring the charge within 180 days of the initial discriminatory action — and not within 180 days of any subsequent nondiscriminatory act, even if it reflects past discrimination. However, the clock does re-start when there is a separately actionable instance of intentional discrimination.[210]

ADEA charges follow a similar trajectory, however, ADEA suits can be brought as soon as administrative proceedings are completed, and there is no requirement of a "right to sue" letter. The would-be ADEA plaintiff must bring suit within 90 days of the time the EEOC either makes a ruling or dismisses the charge.

Generally, the various time limits are strictly enforced. However, tolling of the statute of limitations is permitted in a narrow class of cases, including deception by the employer that prevented timely filing; timely filing in the wrong court; timely filing of a defective pleading; and the employer's failure to post the required EEOC notices that explain employees' rights.

According to the Third Circuit, the requirement of filing discrimination charges with the EEOC under oath is not jurisdictional. Therefore, it can be waived; an employer that responds to an unverified charge cannot seek dismissal on the basis that the charge was not sworn.[211]

In many instances, defendant employers will take the position that litigation of discrimination claims is inappropriate, because the claimant is covered by a Collective Bargaining Agreement or an individual employment contract that contains an arbitration clause. Under *Wright v. Universal Maritime Service Corp.*,[212]

---

[209] National R.R. Passenger Corp. v. Morgan, 536 U.S. 101 (2002).

[210] Ledbetter v. Goodyear Tire & Rubber Co., 127 S. Ct. 2162 (5/29/07); *see, e.g.*, Tony Mauro, *Supreme Court Limits Time Frame for Filing EEOC Claims*, Legal Times 5/30/07 (law.com), Fred Schneyer, *U.S. Supreme Court Hears Historical Pay Complaint Case*, Plansponsor.com (11/27/06).

[211] Buck v. Hampton Township Sch. Dist., 452 F.3d 256 (3d Cir. 2006).

[212] 525 U.S. 70 (1998).

a CBA must be specific as to which statutory discrimination claims must be arbitrated. A general requirement of arbitration rather than litigation is not enforceable.[213]

In a sexual harassment case, New Jersey ruled in 2008 that punitive damages must be ordered to punish the actual defendant's wrongdoing, not to "send a message," but the jury should consider the defendant's financial condition at the time of the wrongdoing, even if by the time of the trial it was out of business and insolvent.[214]

[A] EEO Records

Companies with 100 or more employees are required to file an annual report, the Employer Information Report (EEO-1) with the EEOC by September 30 of each year. This report is a simple two-page form tracking the composition of the workforce. The most current report must be filed at headquarters or at every company unit required to file.

The EEOC revised the EEO-1 form in late 2005. Filing must be done on-line unless the employer is unable to obtain Internet access. The form lists seven racial/ethnic categories, including "two or more races," and the former "Officials and Managers" job category has been divided into the Executive/Senior Level and First-Mid-Level Officials and Managers group. Instead of making their own visual determinations of ethnicity, employers are directed to ask employees to make their own identifications.[215]

Records of application forms, requests for accommodation, and other employment-related data must be retained for one year (running from the later of collecting the data or taking personnel action). 29 CFR § 1602.14 requires that all records of a personnel action that becomes the subject of a discrimination charge must be retained until the case is over, or the statute of limitations has run on the charge.

---

[213] *See also* Albertson's v. United Food & Commercial Workers, 157 F.3d 758 (9th Cir. 1998): an employment contract between a company and a single worker can require arbitration of FMLA claims, but a CBA covering an entire bargaining unit cannot. The Third Circuit upheld the enforceability of the arbitration clause in an employment contract, and mandated arbitration of a wrongful termination case, even though the employee did not understand English. The court adopted an objective theory of contract formation, holding that it was the employee's obligation to be sure he understood the agreement before signing it. (The employer asked a bilingual employee to translate the contract, but that employee testified that he omitted the arbitration clause.) [Morales v. Sun Constructors, Inc., 541 F.3d 218 (3d Cir. 2008)].

[214] Tarr v. Bob Ciasulli's Mack Auto Mall, 194 N.J. 202 (2008); *see* Mary Pat Gallagher, *N.J. Supreme Court: Punitives for Wrongdoer Only, Not for General Deterrence*, N.J. L.J. 3/28/08 (law. com). At an earlier stage, Tarr v. Bob Ciasulli's Mack Auto Mall, Inc., 181 N.J. 70 (2004), New Jersey ruled that sexual harassment plaintiffs can recover for mental anguish even without proof of severe emotional or physical injury, and also held that business owners are not individually liable for sexual harassment unless they aided the harassment or creation of the hostile environment.

[215] *See* 70 FR 72194 (11/28/05); the format for the report to be filed by September 30, 2007 is available at http://www.eeoc.gov/eeo1/index.html, with guidance at http://www.eeoc.gov/eeo1/qanda.html.

§3.16 WRONGFUL TERMINATION

Some employees work under union contracts that contain disciplinary and grievance procedures outlining steps that must be followed to discipline or fire an employee for cause. Other employees have negotiated individualized contracts specifying their tenure, circumstances under which they can be fired, and circumstances under which their compensation must be continued even if their services are dispensed with.

Most workers, however, are "at-will" employees. Their employment is conceptualized as continuing at the will of the employer, and they can be fired with or without cause if the employer wants to cut the payroll or is dissatisfied in some way with the employee. An at-will employee can be fired for good cause, or for no cause at all — but not for an unlawful cause.

As the preceding discussion shows, various groups are entitled to civil rights protection, and refusing to hire a person, firing that person, discriminating in working conditions, or otherwise disfavoring a person in employment because of membership in such a group is illegal.

As a general rule, "statutory" claims (claims arising out of a civil rights suit; Family and Medical Leave Act claims) must be brought under those statutes, which will usually mean following the EEOC procedure and perhaps eventually suing in federal court.

However, if the allegation does not involve job action in violation of federal law, or if the employer is too small to be covered by the federal law, then the employee, would-be employee, or ex-employee may be able to sue in state court, under a state anti-discrimination law, for breach of express or implied contract, or under a tort theory.

The advantage of suing in state court is that cumbersome EEOC procedures need not be followed (although the state law may have its own cumbersome requirements). The time to get to trial may be much shorter in the state system, and additional remedies such as punitive damages and damages for emotional distress may be available in state courts when they would not be available under federal civil rights law.

The Fourth Circuit would not permit removal of state wrongful discharge claims to federal court. The Fourth Circuit did not accept the argument that the claims were preempted by NLRA §§ 7 and 8 (the right to bargain collectively and the ban on Unfair Labor Practices). It was not a diversity case, and no federal questions were raised, so the District Court would not have had original jurisdiction. Under this analysis, complete preemption occurs only if there is a preexisting federal cause of action.[216]

---

[216] Lontz v. Tharp, 413 F.3d 435 (4th Cir. 2005). *See also* Eastman v. Marine Mechanical Corp., 438 F.3d 544 (6th Cir. 2006): a state whistleblower suit cannot be removed to federal court merely because the whistleblower charged the employer with violating the False Claims Act — a federal statute that has no private cause of action, so there is no substantial federal question giving rise to federal jurisdiction.

An employee who can be terminated only for cause can assert a tort cause of action for wrongful discharge, and can bring the tort suit even without exhausting administrative or contractual remedies. Some earlier Washington decisions suggested that only at-will employees (or only private rather than government employees) can bring a common-law wrongful discharge claim. However, according to a 2000 Washington decision, that analysis blurs the fundamental distinction between tort and contract claims. The tort wrongful discharge claim is not based on contract terms. Rather, it stems from the employer's duty to conform to public policy. Public employers are not exempt from this duty.[217]

The NLRB ruled that it was lawful to terminate a group of employees, most of whom were pro-union, for failure to disclose their criminal records on their job applications, because the company policy mandating disclosure was well-publicized.[218]

There are two broad categories under which wrongful termination suits are usually brought:

- Implied contract theories
- Public policy theories.

[A] Implied Contract Theories

Implied contract theories take the position that the employer's words or actions, or those of its agents, create a contract under which the employee cannot be fired without good cause and without due process.

One stream of cases involves employee handbooks. These handbooks often contain language about "lifetime employment" or "no one will be fired without good cause." However, the handbooks also usually contain a conspicuous express statement that the employee handbooks are not contractual in nature, and do not constitute an employment contract; the employees continue to work at will. Although there are some cases treating employee handbooks as contracts, and thus requiring employers to go through the full grievance and discipline procedure stated in the handbook before firing an employee, handbook provisions will usually not be treated as contracts of employment.

Another stream of cases uses a promissory estoppel theory.[219] A person who is induced to leave an existing job, and perhaps move to a new city, sell one home and buy another, etc., may be treated as entitled to a promise of indefinite or at least several years' tenure, if he or she acts in reliance on the offer of the new job.

In some cases, the Statute of Frauds acts as a bar, on the theory that a contract lasting more than a year must be in writing to be enforceable; yet courts determined

---

[217] Smith v. Bates Technical Coll., 991 P.2d 1135 (Wash. 2000).

[218] Overnite Transp. Inc., 343 NLRB 1234 (12/16/04).

[219] See, e.g., Kidder v. American South Bank, 639 So. 2d 1361 (Ala. 1994); National Sec. Ins. Co. v. Donaldson, 664 So. 2d 871 (Ala. 1995); Choate v. TRW, Inc., 14 F.3d 74 (D.C. Cir. 1994); Pickell v. Arizona Components Co., 1997 WL 27173 (Colo. 1/27/97).

to find for the plaintiff will also find that the Statute of Frauds problem is solved by treating the contract as one that could be ended in less than a year by the employee's death or disability.

[B] Public Policy Theories

These theories state that it is improper to terminate an employee for lawful or even laudable behavior. For example, it is unlawful to fire an employee for serving jury duty or carrying out a military reserve or National Guard commitment, or with the motive of preventing the employee from qualifying for ERISA-protected benefits. Retaliation for filing a Workers' Compensation claim may also be treated as contrary to public policy.

A very significant public policy theory involves "whistleblowers": individuals who report corporate wrongdoing, or participate in investigations. Many states have whistleblower statutes protecting the employment rights of such persons. However, recent cases tend to treat whistleblower protection quite narrowly, and local case law should always be consulted before bringing suit. The Sarbanes-Oxley Act of 2002 (P.L. 107-204), whose major purpose is deterring corporate financial wrongdoing, includes protection for whistleblowers. Companies that issue registered securities are forbidden to take adverse employment action (including threats and harassment) against any employee who provides information or cooperates with an investigation of securities fraud. A whistleblower seeking relief is given 90 days to file a complaint with the Secretary of Labor. If the Secretary of Labor does not issue a final decision within 180 days, the employee can go to the appropriate federal District Court seeking review. There is no dollar limit on such actions. Prevailing whistleblowers are entitled to all forms of make-whole relief, including reinstatement with the seniority they would have had absent discrimination, back pay with interest, and litigation costs (including expert witness fees as well as attorneys' fees). Note, however, that protection under Sarbanes-Oxley § 806 (whistleblowers who work for publicly traded companies) does not apply to persons who are employed outside the United States by foreign subsidiaries of U.S. companies.[220]

The 1998 Supreme Court case of *Haddle v. Garrison*[221] holds that an allegation that an at-will employee was fired for cooperating with a criminal investigation of the employer (here, for Medicare fraud) states a cause of action under 42 USC § 1985(2), because an injury to person or property has occurred.

---

[220] Carnero v. Boston Scientific Co., 433 F.3d 1 (1st Cir. 2006).
[221] 525 U.S. 121 (1998).

Chapter 4

Business Taxes

§ 4.01   INTRODUCTION

Business taxation is divided into two broad categories: taxation of the partnership and its partners (because the partnership is a pass-through[1] entity, the salient issue becomes how much tax the partners will have to pay on account of partnership items), and taxation of the corporation. Both the corporation and its stockholders are subject to taxation.

Although having two sets of books is often a sign of dishonesty, it is quite legitimate to maintain tax records that use different accounting conventions than other business records. To reduce taxes, corporations will probably want to take the largest permissible deductions, as early as possible — yet they will also want to

---

[1] The Internal Revenue Code uses the barbaric spelling "pass-thru."

report large and increasing earnings, which suggests taking as few deductions as possible and taking them over a longer period of time.

Also see the discussion of at-risk rules and passive activities at § 4.02[I]. Although these concepts primarily arise in personal income tax, personal service corporations and some closely held C Corporations are also subject to these rules.

Like many other entities within our legal system, the IRS is interested in expanding the use of Alternative Dispute Resolution in appropriate situations. The IRS' Large and Mid-Size Business Division has a permanent fast-track settlement procedure. There is also a permanent fast-track mediation procedure for taxpayers who fall under the jurisdiction of the Small Business/Self-Employed Division. Fast-tracking is not permitted for cases that have been set down for litigation, or in situations where resolving the issue with one party could create inconsistent adjudication when the issue arises with a different party. Mediation is not allowed in cases that are potential subjects of litigation; where there is no binding legal precedent on the issue; or the Circuits are split on treatment of the issue.[2]

Internal Revenue Code § 7422(a) requires a taxpayer who seeks a refund of unlawfully assessed taxes to file an administrative claim with the IRS. Under § 6511(a), the claim must be filed within three years of the filing of the tax return, or two years of payment of the tax, whichever is later. However, the Tucker Act permits claims against the government to be brought within six years of the challenged conduct. Coal companies paid export taxes under a Code section that was later found unconstitutional (as a violation of the Export Clause). They filed administrative claims and received refunds for 1997–1999, but also sued in the Court of Federal Claims for refunds without following the Code's procedure. The Supreme Court held that the violation of the Export Clause was irrelevant; a timely administrative refund claim is an absolute prerequisite to obtaining the refund. The Tucker Act cannot be used to do an end run around the Code requirements.[3]

The Ninth Circuit ruled that wrongful levies are treated like overpayments of tax — so the 1 1/2 point reduction in the interest rate for amounts in excess of $10,000 (Code § 6621) applied to a case where the IRS, incorrectly concluding that a corporation was the nominee of its founder, issued a jeopardy levy on the corporation and collected $353,000 from the corporate checking account. Code § 7426(h) provides statutory damages when an IRS employee intentionally, recklessly, or negligently disregards any Code provision. The District Court ordered the government to pay $1.4 million to the corporation for the wrongful levy, plus interest. The Ninth Circuit allowed the government to reduce the interest rate because the wrongful levy exceeded $10,000.[4]

---

[2] Rev. Proc. 2003-40, 2003-25 IRB 1044; Rev. Proc. 2003-41, 2003-25 IRB 1047.

[3] United States v. Clintwood Elkhorn Mining Co., 128 S. Ct. 1511 (2008).

[4] Cheung v. United States, No. 07-35161 (9th Cir. 9/23/08).

[A] 2004–8 Legislation

Two 2004 statutes had significant effects on business taxation: the Working Families Tax Relief Act of 2004 (WFTRA), P.L. 108-311; and the American Jobs Creation Act (AJCA), P.L. 108-357.

WFTRA provides an estimated $14 billion in business tax breaks for 2005, including extensions to business credits such as the Research & Development credit and the Welfare to Work Credit.

The AJCA increased the amount of spending on "listed property" that could be expensed rather than depreciated for 2006 and 2007, but imposed heavy penalties for premature withdrawals from deferred compensation plans and limited the options for altering payments under the plan.

P.L. 109-58, the Energy Tax Incentives Act of 2005, enacts a new credit under Code § 25C, given to homebuilders who construct energy-efficient homes. A deduction for energy-efficient improvements to commercial buildings was enacted for 2006 and 2007, which permits homebuilders to get a credit of up to $2,000 for each highly energy effective dwelling unit.

TIPRA (Tax Increase Prevention and Reconciliation Act of 2005; P.L.109-222)'s major business tax provisions include:

- Extension of first-year expensing under § 179 until the end of 2009.
- The "active business" test for tax-free spin-offs under § 355 is simplified by considering all corporations in the affiliated groups of the distributing corporation and the spun-off subsidiary (for distributions after the enactment of TIPRA and before January 1, 2011).
- Increased estimated tax requirements for corporations whose assets exceed $1 billion, but the due date for certain corporate estimated tax payments has been extended.
- As an incentive for taxpayers to settle with the EPA for site cleanup funds for long-running cases, TIPRA grants relief from federal income tax on some settlement funds received under consent decrees set up after TIPRA's enactment but before January 1, 2011, to resolve pre-CERCLA claims.

The 2007 legislation, the U.S. Troop Readiness, Veterans' Care, Katrina Recovery, and Iraq Accountability Appropriations Act, P.L. 110-28, at § 8215, enacts a new Code § 761(f). Under this provision, for tax years beginning on or after December 31, 2006, a qualified husband-wife joint venture by spouses who file a joint tax return is not treated as a partnership. Instead, all items of income, gain, loss, deduction, and credit are divided between the spouses in proportion to their interests in the venture. Each spouse treats the items as if they derived from a sole proprietorship. A qualified joint venture is a venture between husband and wife only; both materially participate; and both elect to treat the venture as a qualified husband-wife joint venture.

Subtitle B of P.L. 110-28, designated as the Small Business and Work Opportunity Tax Act of 2007, extends and modifies work opportunity tax credit; allows greater expensing by small business; clarifies the credit for certain taxes paid with respect to employees' cash tips; and modifies the collection due process procedures for employment tax liabilities.

The Tax Technical Corrections Bill of 2007, P.L. 110-172, allows some real estate and venture capital partnerships to get forbearance under the Code § 470 "sale in-lease out" rules. This legislation also makes it easier to use certain long-term credits for Alternative Minimum Tax purposes, and revises the time to assess a penalty if an incorrect appraisal results in substantial and gross misstatement of valuation (Code § 6692A).

The Mortgage Forgiveness Debt Relief Act, P.L. 110-142 increases the penalty for late filing of a partnership return (Code § 6698) from $50 per month per partner, for a period of up to five months, to $85/month/partner for up to 12 months, effective for Form 1065 flings after December 20, 2007. The Virginia Tech Victims Tax Bill, P.L. 110-141, increases this to $86 per partner per month for tax years beginning in 2008. P.L. 110-142 also amends Code § 6699 to impose a penalty of $85 per shareholder per month when S Corporations fail to file Form 1120S on time.[4A]

The Worker, Retiree, and Employer Recovery Act of 2008 (P.L. 110-458), although primarily concerned with relaxing pension plan requirements in light of the financial crisis, also increases (by $4 per partner or shareholder) the penalty for failure to file a partnership or S Corporation tax return.

[B] Disaster Relief Legislation

In response to the devastating 2005 hurricane season, two major pieces of relief legislation were passed: the Katrina Emergency Tax Relief Act of 2005 (KETRA), P.L. 109-73, and the Gulf Opportunity Zone Act of 2005 (GO Zone Act), P.L. 109-35. (KETRA was also significant in terms of personal income taxes and employee benefit plans.)

The entire states of Alabama, Florida, Louisiana, and Mississippi are considered the Hurricane Katrina Disaster Area, and part of that area is also a covered disaster area for tax relief purposes; the hardest-hit part of the area has been designated as the Gulf Opportunity (GO) Zone. In addition to a tax extension until February 28, 2006, for tax filings due between August and October of 2005, KETRA and the GO Zone Act contain a number of business tax provisions:

- Additional charitable deductions for food or textbooks contributed between 8/27/05 and 1/1/06 to charitable organizations;
- For property involuntarily converted (i.e., destroyed and replaced by an insurance or condemnation award) as a result of Hurricane Katrina, the

---

[4A] See Sharon Kreider, *Last Minute 2007 Tax Legislation*, http://www.westerncpe.com/forms/LastMinute2007TaxLegislation.pdf for discussion.

replacement period is five years rather than the normal two years for non-recognition of gain on involuntarily converted property, provided that substantially all of the use of the replacement property is in the Katrina Disaster area;

- NOLs that are qualified GO Zone losses can be carried back to the five tax years before the year of the NOL, rather than the two tax years otherwise permitted;
- Qualified GO Zone Property (generally, tangible property depreciated under MACRS with a recovery period of 20 years or less, rental real property, and certain computer software) placed in service after 8/27/05 qualifies for a special first-year depreciation allowance if purchased after the hurricane and before 2008 — before 2009, for real property;
- Property within the GO Zone qualifies for an increased § 179 deduction;
- 50% of qualified GO Zone clean-up costs (removing debris from, or demolishing structures on, GO Zone property) incurred between 8/27/05 and 1/1/08 can be deducted in the year paid or incurred, rather than being capitalized.

The Emergency Economic Stabilization Act of 2008 (EESA; the financial "bailout" bill) permits immediate write-off of demolition, clean-up, and environmental remediation expenses resulting from disasters during the period 12/31/07–1/1/10. Businesses in a presidentially declared disaster area are entitled to claim an additional first-year depreciation deduction equal to 50% of the cost of new investment in real and personal property.[5]

§ 4.02 PARTNERSHIP TAXATION

Partnership taxation is governed by Subchapter K of the Code. For tax purposes, a partnership is a business entity involving two or more members that chose, or defaulted to, partnership status under the "check-the-box" regulations, and is not compulsorily taxed as a corporation. The election is made on Form 8832, Entity Classification Election.

Effective January 1, 2000, a foreign partnership with under $20,000 in U.S. source income and no income that is effectively connected to business in the United States does not have to file a return unless 1% or more of any item of gain, loss, deduction, or credit is allocable to direct U.S. partners. A partnership return is not required if there are no U.S. partners or income effectively connected to business in the United States, even if there is some U.S. source income.

Business entities are given broad discretion to determine how they will be taxed (as long as they conform to the minimum requirements for the form they have chosen). Reg. § 301.7701-3 allows a newly formed general partnership that has at least two partners to elect to be taxed as either a partnership or a corporation. If no election is made, the entity will be taxed as a partnership. In effect, an entity that is

---

[5] Seyfarth Shaw LLP, *Detailed Summary: The Emergency Economic Stabilization Act of 2008*, http://www.seyfarth.com/index.cfm/fuseaction/publications.publications_detail/object_id/faea 1910-e1bc-42b7-9869-6f767357151d/DetailedSummaryoftheEmergencyEconomicStabilizationActof 2008.cfm.

a partnership as defined by state law can elect to be taxed as either a C or an S corporation, but an entity that is a corporation under state law cannot elect to be taxed as a partnership.

A limited liability company (LLC) is a state-regulated business entity that, if not required to be taxed as a corporation under those "check the box" regulations, can elect either partnership or corporate taxation. Once again, if there is no election, the LLC will be taxed as a partnership. Whichever tax structure it chooses, its participants will still have limited liability.

The 100% owner of a single-member Limited Liability Company (LLC) elected to have it treated as a "sole proprietorship" rather than as an "association" that is taxed like a corporation. Therefore, the Second Circuit found the owner personally liable for the company's employment tax liabilities (close to $65,000 in payroll taxes for a two-year period) after the IRS assessed the amount against the owner personally and put a lien on his property. The owner objected, citing a Connecticut corporation law that says that the members of an LLC are not personally liable for its debts. The Second Circuit agreed with the IRS: the Internal Revenue Code does not have a category for LLCs, so the IRS adopted Regulations to govern LLCs. The Second Circuit found that the Regulations are not arbitrary, capricious, or unreasonable; they give LLCs a trade-off between taxation as a corporation (double taxation, but immunity from personal liability) or a non-corporate entity (personal liability, but freedom from double taxation).[6]

See § 1.03[D] for the distinction between general and limited partners. Prop. Reg. § 1.1402(a)-2(h) says a person is a limited partner and not a general partner unless:

- He or she is personally liable for partnership debts or claims against the partnership by reason of being a partner
- State law gives him/her the authority to contract on behalf of the partnership
- He or she spends more than 500 hours per year on the partnership's trade or business.

Prop. Reg. § 1.1402(a)-2(h) also governs LLCs. P.L. 105-34 § 935 (8/5/97), imposed a moratorium on further Regulations defining "limited partner" under § 1402(a)(13). (Section 1402 deals with net earnings from self-employment, a category where allocation of partnership items has obvious relevance.)

A partnership is a pass-through entity for tax purposes: income is taxed at the partner rather than the entity level. Because an S Corporation is also a pass-through entity, many businesses will have to decide which form to operate in. A partnership, unlike an S Corporation, can have any number of partners, with no limitation

---

[6] McNamee v. IRS, 488 F.3d 100 (2d Cir. 2007); *see also* Proposed Regulations at 70 FR 60475 (10/18/05), which would treat the LLC as the employer for employment tax purposes — but the Second Circuit noted that the proposal has not been finalized, so it does not replace the Regulations already in existence. Littriello v. United States, 484 F.3d 372 (6th Cir. 2007) holds that the "check-the-box" regulations are valid.

on their identity. A partnership can make special allocations of profit, loss, and credits among the partners. A partner's basis in his or her partnership interest includes his or her share of partnership liabilities.

Section 6031 requires partnerships to file Form 1065 as an information return reporting gross income and deductions for the tax year. (Filing is not required for any period before the partnership received its first taxable income or had deductible expenses, or any year in which the partnership does not carry on business within the United States and has no U.S.-source income.)

The due date of Form 1065 is the fifteenth day of the fourth month after the close of the partnership's tax year: § 6072(a). Each partner (or nominee for a partnership) must receive a copy of Schedule K-1, Form 1065, disclosing that partner's share of partnership items.

Under §§ 771–777, an "electing large partnership" having at least 100 members can adopt a simplified reporting system, reducing the number of items that must be reported to partners. Most items of income, deduction, credit, and loss can be calculated at the partnership level if this election is made; net amounts are passed through to the partners. Audit requirements for electing large partnerships are also streamlined by §§ 6240–6255.

For purposes of the Social Security self-employment tax, a general partner is taxed on his or her distributive share of the partnership's income and losses (even if not distributed), plus his or her entitlement to guaranteed payments (i.e., payments for services, or for use of capital, that are not based on partnership income). See Reg. § 1.1402(a)-1(a)(2). A limited partner is taxed only on guaranteed payments for services rendered: Prop Reg. § 1.1402(a)-2(d)(g).

A partnership can receive an automatic three-month extension of the time to file the partnership return via Form 8736; the IRS can respond to a request on Form 8800 for a longer, discretionary extension. The fact that a partnership gets an extension does not extend the individual partners' time to file their individual tax returns.

However, to prevent abuse of the partnership form, the § 701 "anti-abuse" Regulations give the IRS power for income tax (but not for other taxes) to recast transactions to achieve an "appropriate" result when partnerships are formed or availed of to reduce partners' tax liability in a manner inconsistent with Subchapter K.

[A] Partnership Tax Year

Unless it makes an election or can satisfy the IRS that there is a business purpose for a different year, § 706(b) sets the partnership's tax year as:

- The majority interest tax year (the tax year of one or more of the partners holding an aggregate interest of 50% or more)
- If there is none, the tax year of all of its 5% or more partners (i.e., calendar year if they are natural persons)

- If they do not have the same tax year, the tax year that results in the smallest amount of deferral
- If all else fails, calendar year.

Section 444 permits a partnership to elect a different tax year, as long as it is not abusive. The deferral period of the year elected (i.e., the number of months from the beginning of the elected tax year to the following December 31) cannot exceed three months. The election is made on Form 8716.

In 2004, the Supreme Court ruled that a proper tax assessment against a partnership extends the statute of limitations for collection of tax in a judicial proceeding against the general partners. Once the tax has been properly assessed, the IRS is not required to make separate assessments of the same tax against individuals who are not the actual taxpayers — even though, under state law, they are responsible for the taxpayer's debts.[7]

[B] Tax Issues in Creation of a Partnership

A partner's contributions to the partnership are generally tax-free under § 721 (no gain or loss recognized to either the partner or the partnership), unless, e.g., the transaction was entered into in an individual capacity, not when acting as a partner; or if the partnership assumes the partner's indebtedness. There is no taxable gain or loss to either the partnership or the partner if appreciated or depreciated property is transferred to a partnership solely in exchange for a partnership interest.

Furthermore, if a partner receives a capital interest in the partnership in exchange for services, the partner has taxable compensation income. If a partner receives an interest in partnership profits in exchange for services, he or she has compensation income only if the stream of income from the partnership assets is substantially certain and predictable (or if the partner disposes of the interest within two years of acquiring it).

Regulations were proposed on the tax treatment of transferring a partnership interest for services; the transfer is taxed to the provider of the services under § 83, whether the transferred interest is a profits interest or a capital interest. Both interests are personal property and both give access to the partnership's future earnings, so they are taxed similarly. Taxation under § 83 is triggered when the interest becomes substantially vested and is no longer subject to a substantial risk of forfeiture. The compensation that the service provider must include in income — and that the partnership can deduct — is the fair market value (FMV) of the partnership interest. The capital account of the person providing the services is increased by money paid for the interest and the amount included in income. There is no gain or loss to the partnership on the partnership interest. The Notice provides a valuation safe harbor: the FMV of the interest is its liquidation value.[8]

---

[7] United States v. Galletti, 541 U.S. 114 (Sup. Ct. 2004).
[8] Notice 2005-43, 2005-24 IRB 1221.

The partnership has the same basis in the contributed assets as the contributing partner had, plus any gain the contributing partner had to recognize under § 721(b): § 723. The partnership's holding period (used to distinguish short-term from long-term items) includes the partner's holding period (§ 1223(2)).[9] Although the American Jobs Creation Act, P.L. 108-357, is by and large a strongly pro-business statute, it limits the ability of partners and partnerships to use contributions of property with built-in losses to the partnership as a means of tax saving for the partnership and the other partners.

The basis of a partnership interest acquired by a tax-free contribution of money and/or property is defined by § 722 as the total of contributed cash plus the adjusted basis of contributed property. The partner's basis in encumbered property is reduced by the amount of indebtedness that the other partners assume. The basis of a capital interest acquired for services is the value of the capital interest.

Once the partnership is under way, the partner's basis must be adjusted in various ways as prescribed by §§ 705 and 732(c). Basis is increased, e.g., by further contributions; by an increase in the partner's share of partnership liabilities; and by his or her distributive share of partnership income. See T.D. 8847, 1999-52 IRB 701, finalizing Regulations under Code §§ 734, 743, 751, and 755 dealing with optional adjustment to the basis of partnership property, after partnership interests have been transferred to harmonize the transferee's economic and tax consequences.

The AJCA requires partnerships to perform basis adjustments when certain kinds of distributions are made, if the basis of partnership assets would be reduced by over $250,000 — even if an election has not been made under § 754. Partnerships that have a substantial built-in loss ($250,000 or more) at the time of the transfer must also adjust the basis of partnership property once the interest has been transferred. These rules apply to transfers on or after October 22, 2004. Partnerships that are required to reduce basis must attach a statement to their tax returns explaining the changes.[10]

Under § 733, the partner's basis is reduced (but not below zero) by any part of the interest that has been sold; by money and property distributed to the partner in a non-liquidating distribution from the partnership;[11] by the partner's distributive share of partnership losses; and by any decrease in his or her share of partnership liabilities.

Within the partnership, entitlement to income (or responsibility for liabilities) may be quite different for different partners. The basic rule of § 704 is that the

---

[9] Regulations have been proposed, at § 1.1223-3 (8/9/99) as to the partner's holding period in his, her, or its partnership interest.

[10] Notice 2005-32, 2005-16 IRB 895.

[11] A partner who receives a liquidating distribution has capital gain only to the extent that cash received exceeds the partner's adjusted basis in the partnership interest. Loss is recognized on liquidation of the partner's entire interest if the distribution is limited to cash, inventory, and unrealized receivables.

partnership agreement determines the allocation of items among the partners. If there is no partnership agreement, or if a purported agreement lacks substantial economic effect, allocation for tax purposes will follow the comparative size of the partners' interests in the partnership.

[C] Partnership Tax Management

Unlike an S Corporation, which is taxed on some limited items of income (see § 4.12[A]), a partnership is a pure conduit. Under § 701, only the partners are liable for taxes on partnership income. Partners receive their share of the partnership's income and deductions. The partnership files Form 1065, an information return, disclosing each partner's distributive share of the tax items.

The partners are required to include their distributive shares (including guaranteed payments of salary and interest) of partnership items on their own tax returns. The items are included in the partner's return for his or her tax year in which the partnership's tax year ends (§ 706; this provision is required because most partners are individuals, who have a calendar tax year, whereas partnerships often have fiscal years). They must treat the tax items consistently with the partnership's treatment of the items. Section 6222(a) obligates them to file Form 8082 to disclose and explain any inconsistent treatment.

Also see § 6621, providing that the treatment of partnership items on a partner's individual return can be changed only by unified proceedings at the partnership level. Additions to tax and penalties are also determined at the partnership level.

The Ninth Circuit, discussing the interface between TEFRA's requirement of determining the tax treatment of partnership items at the partnership level and Bankruptcy Code § 505(a)'s authorization for bankruptcy courts to re-determine debtors' tax liability, held that the District Courts have subject matter jurisdiction to review the tax treatment of partnership items. The IRS filed a $13.1 million tax claim in a debtor's Chapter 11 case. The District Court ruled that it lacked subject matter jurisdiction over any partnership item administratively determined by the IRS, but the Ninth Circuit found jurisdiction under 11 USC § 505(a)(1).[12]

"Guaranteed payments" (see § 707(c)) are made to partners who have contributed services or capital. The payments are made without regard to partnership income — for instance, a payment defined as 10% of profits does not satisfy the definition of guaranteed payment. Guaranteed payments are taxed to the partner as salary or interest payments, not as partnership distributions. The partnership can deduct the payments (in arriving at partners' distributive shares) only if the payment would be deductible if made to a non-partner employee or lender.

When the partnership is operating at a loss, a partner's deduction for partnership losses cannot exceed his or her basis in the partnership interest: § 704(d). Depending on the nature of the partnership's business and the individual partner's role within it, a partner's loss may also be limited by the at-risk and passive activity rules (see § 4.02[I]).

---

[12] Central Valley Ag Enterprises v. United States, 531 F.3d 750 (9th Cir. 2008).

Section 707(b)(1) disallows a loss deduction on sales or exchanges involving a partnership and the owner of a 50% or greater interest in its capital or profits, and between two partnerships in which the same persons own 50% or more of the capital or profit interests. However, if the transferee of the partnership property later re-sells the same property at a gain, the gain is taxed only to the extent that it exceeds the previously disallowed loss.

Under § 731(b), the partnership (subject to certain exceptions under §§ 736 and 751) has neither gain nor loss on either ordinary or liquidating distributions to partners. Section 731(a)(1) requires the partner to recognize gain only if the distribution exceeds the partner's adjusted basis in the partnership interest. The partner recognizes loss under § 731(a)(2) if his or her adjusted basis exceeds the money, receivables, and inventory received in a liquidation of the partner's interest in the partnership.

[D] Tax Matters Partner

Every partnership must have a Tax Matters Partner (TMP): see Code § 6231(a)(7). The partnership can designate any of its general partners to act as TMP. If the partnership fails to make a designation, the general partner with the largest profits interest automatically becomes the TMP; if two general partners hold equal interests, the one whose name comes first in alphabetical order becomes the TMP.

If, for some reason, that selection procedure is impractical, the IRS has statutory authority to designate any partner (even one who does not become a general partner until after the designation) for this role. Before the IRS makes a designation, however, it will notify the partnership, giving it 30 days to make its own selection of TMP.

Instead of dealing with all of the partners, the IRS deals primarily with the TMP, who represents the other partners and the partnership. IRS notices and orders are sent to the TMP, and the TMP represents the partnership at audits and in litigation. The TMP has the power to petition the Tax Court to readjust partnership items determined by the IRS: § 6226.

[E] Taxation of Disposition of Partnership Interests

The partner's basis computation is also affected by § 732, which sets the basis of property received in liquidation of a partnership interest at the partner's adjusted basis for the interest minus funds distributed in the same transaction, with adjustments prescribed in § 732(a) and (c)–(e). Section 733 provides that a partner's adjusted basis in the partnership interest is reduced by the value of distributed money and property, but not below $0.

For property that is not received in a liquidation, the basis is carried over from the partnership's basis in the same property, but cannot exceed the partner's adjusted basis in the interest minus cash received in the transaction. TRA '97 sets the rules for allocating basis adjustment in assets distributed to the partner.

When a partner sells a partnership interest, or the interest is liquidated, the partner's gain or loss is usually capital, because § 741 treats the transaction as a capital transaction rather than a sale of a proportionate interest in each of the partnership assets. Reference should be made, however, to § 751, which may require some of the gain or loss to be treated as ordinary in nature (if, for instance, it derives from the partnership's unrealized receivables or inventory).

In general, sale of the partnership interest has no effect on the partnership's tax position, but it can elect under § 754 to step up its basis in the relevant assets to reflect the gain recognized by the selling partner.

If all the partners sell their shares, the status of the transaction as either a sale of assets or a sale of partnership interests depends on whether mere assets were sold, or whether the partnership itself was sold as a going business.

[1] Payments to Retiring Partners

The first question is how much of the payment received represents payment for capital assets, and how much represents the retiring partner's share of partnership income.

Payments received on liquidation of an interest (e.g., when a partner retires, or payments to the estate of a deceased partner) are treated as guaranteed payments or income distributions to the extent that they exceed the value of the partner's interest in the partnership property.

When payments are made to a retiring partner, or to the estate of a deceased partner, each element of the payment must be analyzed to determine whether it is capital gain or ordinary income. The characterization depends on whether it can be traced to a share of the fair market value of partnership assets; an interest in unrealized receivables; or under an agreement with the other partners that has the same effect as an insurance policy.

Under § 736, distributions for interests in partnership property are taxed as if they had been made by an ongoing partnership, and therefore will be capital gains unless they are disproportionate distributions or distributions deriving from substantially appreciated inventory. Distributions not made for interests in partnership property are taxed either as distributive shares of partnership income, or as guaranteed payments.

[F] Tax Consequences of Termination

For partnership tax years beginning after 1997, § 706(c)(2) provides that the partnership's tax year is closed with respect to any partner when the partner's entire interest in the partnership terminates: e.g., he or she dies, retires, or transfers his or her entire partnership interest. Partnership items for that short tax year go into the partner's final income tax return.

For tax purposes, a partnership generally will not terminate until its operations discontinue (i.e., no part of its operation is carried on by any partner), or until 50% or more of the total interests in the partnership are sold or exchanged within a

12-month period. As § 1.03[B] shows, local law may force the termination of a partnership whenever any partner departs (the partnership or this life), so once again tax treatment differs from substantive regulation of business.

[G] Family Partnerships

The family partnership is sometimes used as a financial management and estate planning device, to coordinate lifetime and post-death shifts in asset ownership within the family.

Code § 704(e) provides that if capital is not a material income-producing factor for the partnership, a family member will be recognized as a partner only if he or she contributes substantial services to the partnership. However, if capital is a material income-producing factor, then intrafamily gifts of capital interests are permissible. A minor can be a partner in a family partnership on two conditions: if the child has a guardian; or if the child, although legally a minor, is in fact competent to manage property.

Also note that § 8215 of the U.S. Troop Readiness, Veterans' Care, Katrina Recovery, and Iraq Accountability Appropriations Act, P.L. 110-28, creates Code § 761(f), under which married couples who engage in qualified joint ventures can elect not to have the business taxed as a partnership; instead, the venture is treated as if each spouse were a sole proprietor.

[H] Publicly Traded Partnerships

As a general rule, partnership interests are not very liquid, because of the risk of unlimited liability and the lack of perpetual continuity. However, there are some instances in which partnership interests, especially limited partnership interests, are offered to the public. Code § 7704 provides that a publicly traded partnership (including one described as a master limited partnership) will be taxed as a corporation, notwithstanding its description as a partnership, unless at least 90% of its gross income derives from qualifying passive-type income. Qualifying income includes, e.g., interest; dividends; rent; and gain from the disposition of real property: § 7704(d).

[I] Special Rules for Real Estate Partnerships

It is common for real estate to be owned and operated by multi-level partnerships, with a few general partners and a larger number of investor limited partners. Under prior law, real estate investment often operated as a tax shelter. However, current law combines a small number of comparatively low tax brackets with crack-down efforts on perceived abusive tax shelters.

Under the § 465 "at-risk" rules, a taxpayer's loss deduction in connection with an investment is limited to the amount at risk in the transaction. Therefore, for instance, it is no longer possible to claim losses on property purchased with non-recourse obligations. The at-risk rules apply to most business activities that are not carried on by widely-held corporations, so obviously they are of concern in calculating partners' taxes, and especially those of limited partners. (Losses that cannot be currently deducted because of the at-risk rules can be carried over to other tax years, so the deduction is not necessarily entirely lost.)

The maximum loss that a partner can deduct is either the partner's basis or the amount the partner has at risk in partnership activities, whichever is lower. However, certain nonrecourse financing in real estate transactions will not be subject to the at-risk rule.

Individuals (including partners), personal service corporations, and closely-held C Corporations are subject to the "passive loss" limitations of § 469. Taxpayers who do not "materially participate" in the business activity can only use net losses and credits from passive activities to offset income from other passive activities. The losses and credits cannot be claimed against salary or portfolio income.

An exception is made for individuals who actively participate in real estate activities and whose gross income does not exceed $150,000. Certain rental real estate losses can be used to reduce nonpassive income, notwithstanding the basic § 469 rule. When the individual's entire interest in the passive activity is disposed of in a fully taxable transaction, any unused passive losses can be used to offset either passive or nonpassive income.

In this context, material participation means regular, continuous and substantial involvement in the activity, so limited partners do not qualify.

§ 4.03 CORPORATE TAX

[A] Tax Rates

Certain businesses operated in forms similar to corporations, and even certain corporations, are not subject to corporate tax at all. Limited liability companies (§ 1.06) are taxed as partnerships (see above for issues of partnership taxation). Subchapter S Corporations are also "pass-through" entities that are not taxed at the corporate level. Subchapter C Corporations ("C Corporations"), however, are subject to corporate tax.

"Qualified personal service corporations" as defined by § 448(d)(2) are required by § 11(b)(2) to pay a flat rate of 35% of their taxable income. A personal service corporation (PSC) is a C Corporation whose principal activity is the rendition of personal services (such as performing arts, law, health care, and consulting) which are substantially performed by one or more employee-owners. Such personal services are the corporation's principal activity if more than 50% of the company's payroll is allocable to the personal services. The services are substantially performed by stockholder-employees if 20% or more of the compensation cost for personal services is attributable to them.[13]

---

[13] Note that, under § 269A(a), the IRS can reallocate income, deductions, credits, and other tax items between the corporation and its owner-employee or -employees, if the PSC is "availed of principally" for tax avoidance in that it gives a 10% owner-employee significant tax benefits that would otherwise be unavailable.

Other domestic corporations are taxed at graduated rates. Theoretically, there are only four corporate brackets, but the effect of "surtax" is to create additional brackets for practical purposes.

As a result of the Jobs and Growth Tax Reform and Reconciliation Act of 2002 (JGTRRA; P.L. 108-27), for 2003 the effective corporate tax rate is 15% on the first $50,000 of taxable income; 34% for taxable income between $75,000 and $100,000; 39% for taxable income between $100,000 and $335,000; and 35% for income up to $1 million.

Because JGTRRA built on tax cuts already made by EGTRRA, the net effect is that corporate rates are no longer lower than individual rates on the same income. Therefore, operating in proprietorship, partnership, or Subchapter S form (i.e., as a pass-through entity) may be more attractive from the strictly tax viewpoint than operating as a C Corporation, although the C Corporation continues to offer advantages such as limitation of liability and the potential to make a public offering of stock.

Corporate capital gains, unlike the capital gains of individuals, are not taxed at preferential rates. However, the capital/ordinary asset distinction remains meaningful to corporations, because corporate capital losses are deductible only to the extent of capital gains, and §§ 1211(a) and 1212(a) allow some carry-forwards and carry-backs.

Foreign corporations are taxed at U.S. rates on income that is effectively connected with doing business in the United States. U.S.-source income of other kinds (e.g., investment income) is taxed at a 30% flat rate.

In mid-2006, the Supreme Court ruled that a group of plaintiffs who alleged that their local and state tax burdens were increased because of tax breaks (franchise and property tax) provided to an automobile manufacturer did not have standing to challenge the state franchise tax credit. Thus, the Supreme Court vacated the judgment below that the state tax credit violated the Commerce Clause.[14]

[B] Corporate Tax Compliance

The basic corporate income tax return is Form 1120. The short-form 1120A can be filed by a corporation whose ownership is concentrated and whose gross receipts, total income, and total assets are all under $500,000. Personal holding companies must file Schedule PH with their returns, and Subchapter S Corporations file an information return (because they are not generally separate taxpayers) on Form 1120S. The Sub S Corporation must show actual and constructive distributions to the shareholder on the 1120S, and must disclose this information to the shareholders on or before the filing date of the 1120S. Corporate returns must be signed by an authorized officer, such as President, treasurer, or controller. The due date for a Form 1120 or 1120A is March 15 for calendar-year corporations, or the fifteenth day of the third month after the end of a fiscal-year corporation's tax year.

---

[14] DaimlerChrysler Co. v. Cuno, 548 U.S. 920 (2006).

The tax must be paid in full by the original due date for the return: § 6151(a). A corporation that expects a net operating loss (NOL) in the current year can file Form 1138 (see § 6164) to get an extension on filing the preceding year's tax return, so that the current-year NOL can be carried back without needing to file a return followed by an amended return.

Form 7004 provides an automatic extension of six months of any corporation's[15] time to file its income tax return, but this form does not extend the time to pay. An extension of time to pay the tax of up to six months can be granted to corporations that file Form 1127 and demonstrate undue hardship if forced to pay the tax on time. See § 6161(a). Form 1127 must be filed no later than the due date of the return. Unlike income taxes, employment taxes must be filed on time. The IRS will not grant an extension: Reg. § 31.6162(a)(1)-1.

Reg. § 31.6302-1(h)(2)(B)(ii) provides that whenever a corporation has to deposit more than $200,000, it must make an electronic transfer to the IRS' general account.

Corporations must file tax returns even in years in which they have no taxable income (§ 6012(a)(2)), and § 6020 empowers the IRS to file a required return for a corporation that was required to, but failed to do so. However, a shell corporation that has a charter but no business activity can be excused from filing, under Reg. § 1.6012-2(a)(2), if it submits a statement to the local District Director to the effect that it has not yet perfected its organization; does not transact business; and has received no income from any source.

Even after a corporation terminates its business and dissolves, retaining no assets, it must make a return for the part of the year it was still in existence. This return is due on the fifteenth day of the third month after the dissolution and liquidation. If any cash at all is retained, returns are due until all the cash has been distributed.

[1] Corporate Estimated Tax

The general rule is that the corporation must pay 100% of the current year's tax (ordinary income tax plus AMT, minus allowable credits) in its four estimated tax installments. Section 6655 provides that the minimum amount that must be paid to avoid penalty is 25% of the smaller of either 100% of the current year's tax liability or 100% of the previous year's tax liability (if the tax liability was more than zero and the previous year was a full 12-month year). Furthermore, under § 6655(d)(2) and (g)(2), a large corporation (one with over $1 million in taxable income in any of the three immediately preceding years) can use the past year's tax liability to determine only the first installment of estimated tax. After that, the figures for the current year must be projected. Of course, in many cases, to avoid

---

[15] The IRS will permit a partnership or other noncorporate business to use this Form to get the six-month extension as well: IR-2006-29, http://www.irs.gov/newsroom/article/00, id= 154554,00.html.

underpayment and consequent penalties, the corporation will end up overpaying, thus accelerating the point at which the Treasury receives the payments.

TIPRA, the Tax Increase Prevention and Reconciliation Act, P.L. 109-222, imposes some special requirements on corporations with assets over $1 billion. Such corporations must make estimated tax payments of 105% of the tax otherwise due in July, August, or September of 2006 (depending on the fiscal year); the next payment will be reduced accordingly. Adjustments continue until 2013. However, the due date for certain corporate estimated tax payments has been extended. P.L. 110-289, the Housing and Economic Recovery Act, § 3094 repeals the TIPRA adjustment for payment of corporate estimated tax for 2012, changing the percentage to "100%" and stating that no other provision of law can change that percentage. The percentage under TIPRA § 401(1) in effect on the date of enactment of the HERA is increased by 16.75 percentage points for 2013.

Form 8109 is used for corporate estimated tax payments. Installments are due on the fifteenth day of the fourth, sixth, ninth, and twelfth month of the corporation's fiscal year. The general rule is that each installment must be accompanied by at least 25% of the income tax liability for the year. However, § 6655 allows the corporation to take advantage of rules for "annualized income installments" or "adjusted seasonal installments," which permit eligible taxpayers to lower their estimated tax payments somewhat. P.L. 110-28 § 8248 requires certain corporations to make estimated tax payments of at least 114.25% of liability to avoid having to pay an underpayment penalty.

Corporate as well as individual taxpayers use Form 2220 to calculate and remit the underpayment penalty. The § 6655 penalty is waived if a corporate taxpayer owes less than $500, or if the failure to pay one or more required installments was the result of a Chapter 11 filing.

If the estimated tax payments exceed the actual tax liability for the year, the corporation can file on Form 4466 for an expedited (not over 45 days) refund, as long as the overpayment is not only at least $500 but also at least 10% of the tax for the year. The appropriate time to file the form, as prescribed by § 6425, is after the tax year has ended but before the 16th day of the third month after the end of the year; in any case, before the tax return for the year has been filed. Obtaining an automatic extension of the time to file does not extend the time to claim the expedited refund. However, if the corporation claims an excessive refund, interest (at the rate the IRS charges for underpayments) on the excessive refund is treated as an addition to tax.

[2] AMT

The Alternative Minimum Tax is imposed by § 55 to prevent taxpayers entitled to significant deductions and credits from escaping federal taxation altogether. Taxable corporations, individuals, and complex trusts are subject to AMT, but partnerships, S Corporations, and grantor trusts are not. The corporate AMT rate set by § 55(b)(1)(B) is 20% of a tax base including various adjustments and preference items excluded from the calculation of ordinary corporate taxes. The calculation involves Adjusted Current Earnings, a concept related to the accounting concept of Earnings & Profits (E&P).

The Taxpayer Relief Act of 1997 and technical corrections added by the Internal Revenue Service Restructuring & Reform Act of 1998 amend § 55(e): small corporations are exempt from AMT for tax years beginning after 1997. For this purpose, a small corporation is one that has gross receipts under $5 million for each of three years beginning after 12/31/93, and ending before tax year for which AMT exemption is sought.

Once small corporation status is established, the corporation remains AMT-exempt as long as its average gross receipts for the three years prior to the current tax year do not exceed $7.5 million ($5 million for a corporation with only one prior tax year). Furthermore, all corporations are generally treated as AMT-exempt for their first year of existence, no matter what their receipts are.

A non-exempt corporation may nevertheless be free from AMT, based on the § 55(d)(2) exemption of $40,000.

Although individuals pay either the regular tax or the AMT, whichever is greater, corporations that are subject to the AMT must pay both the regular tax and any AMT they are subject to. Form 4626 is the corporate AMT form. However, in the tax year after a year in which AMT was payable, the corporate taxpayer is entitled to a "minimum tax credit" (§ 53) against regular tax. Form 8827 is used to claim the credit.

[3] Tax Year

The general rule of § 441 is that a taxpayer's tax year is the year (calendar or fiscal) on which it keeps its books. Taxpayers that do not keep books, or that do not have an annual accounting period, or whose annual accounting period does not qualify as a fiscal year, must have a calendar tax year. (A fiscal year is a 12-month period that ends on the last day of any month other than December.) Other taxpayers can choose between a calendar and a fiscal year; IRS permission is not needed to adopt any year that is permissible. The taxpayer must adopt its first tax year on or before the date for filing the return for that year, including any extensions obtained.

Unless it makes an election (e.g., to retain the business year in effect before the corporation became an S Corporation), an S Corporation must have a "permitted year." The permitted year is defined by § 1378 as either a calendar year or an accounting year adopted for business purposes acceptable to the IRS.

Section 441 provides that a personal service corporation also must have a calendar year unless it makes a fiscal year election[16] or proves the business purpose of the fiscal year to the IRS. Under § 444, the election cannot result in a deferral of more than three months.

---

[16] Form 1128, "Application for Change in Accounting Period."

Once an accounting period has been adopted, § 442 and its Regulations allow certain changes to be made automatically, without approval by the IRS. All other changes do require advance approval from the IRS, which is solicited by filing Form 1128. The IRS will grant the request only if the taxpayer not only shows a substantial business purpose for the change, but agrees to meet any terms and conditions mandated by the IRS to prevent substantial distortion of the taxpayer's income. Furthermore, under § 442, once a change in accounting period is approved, the IRS will not approve another request for a change until ten years have elapsed.

[4] Taxpayer's Accounting Method

The accounting method that the taxpayer adopts determines, for instance, the amount of income, gain, loss, deduction, or credit that the taxpayer claims, and when it realizes or recognizes income and other items. Various methods and hybrids are permissible, in various circumstances, but the principle of the Code is that whatever method is chosen must clearly reflect the taxpayer's income and must be used consistently. The major Code sections governing accounting methods are §§ 446 and 448.

The two major accounting methods are cash and accrual. A taxpayer that does not have inventory (e.g., a PSC) must always use the cash method. However, businesses for which the production, purchase, and/or sale of merchandise is an income-producing factor (obviously, a category that includes most businesses) must use the accrual method unless the IRS permits a change in accounting method or unless the taxpayer's average annual gross receipts are under $1 million and the taxpayer uses the cash method in its books. The IRS estimated the half a million businesses would qualify for this relief. These businesses get three choices: either the old rule, applying § 417 inventory accounting; keeping books on the accrual basis, but accounting for inventory items as supplies; and keeping books on the cash basis, with inventory items treated as supplies.

Eligible companies can change to cash basis by filing Form 3115, Application for Change in Accounting Method. Businesses that make this election do not have to use the § 263A uniform capitalization rules to account for their inventory. Instead, they can simply treat the inventory as materials and supplies, using Reg. § 1.162-3.

Furthermore, a C Corporation that is not a PSC, or a partnership that has a C Corporation as a partner, is not permitted to use the cash method (even if it would otherwise be allowed) if its annual gross receipts for the past three years averaged more than $5 million. (For entities that have not yet been in existence for three years, the entire period of existence is the measuring factor.)[17] See § 448(b)(3), (c)(1).

Cash-method taxpayers include in gross income all cash or property actually or constructively received during the tax year. (Most cash-method taxpayers will

---

[17] To the extent that a tax-exempt trust has unrelated business taxable income (UBTI), § 448(d)(6) requires it to be treated as a C Corporation.

also have a calendar year, although it is not absolutely impossible for a cash-method taxpayer to have a fiscal year.)

An item of income is constructively received if receiving or deferring the item is wholly within the taxpayer's control, and is subject to the taxpayer's unconditional demand for payment. Cash-method taxpayers take deductions in the year money and/or property is paid or transferred. Under the cash method, it is irrelevant when income is actually earned or expenses are actually incurred.

In contrast, under the accrual method, income is reported in the year the **right** to receive the income becomes fixed: all the events entitling the taxpayer to receive the income have occurred, and the amount of the income can be determined with reasonable accuracy. By the same token, a deduction is permitted when all events creating the taxpayer's obligation to pay a reasonably determinable amount have occurred.

If the taxpayer knows from experience that payment will not be received for certain services, § 448(d)(5) permits the taxpayer not to accrue such income, unless the taxpayer imposes a late payment penalty or interest in conjunction with those services. An accrual-method taxpayer can deduct all properly accrued expenses, whether or not the expense has actually been paid.

When the right to receive income is contingent, the taxpayer does not have to accrue the income until the event occurs. Income must be recognized when the taxpayer is the plaintiff in a suit; the defendant concedes liability; and the taxpayer can accurately estimate the recovery. On the other hand, if the defendant does not concede liability, income accrues when the litigation concludes or is settled.

[5] Inventory Valuation

Inventory is usually valued by one of two methods: either its cost, or the cost or the market value of the item, whichever is lower (§ 471). Section 471 requires taxpayers to use the method prescribed by the Secretary of the Treasury as the clearest reflection of income, and which satisfies the best accounting practices of the relevant trade or business. The "lower of cost or market" calculation is performed for each item; the taxpayer is not permitted to compare the total cost of all inventory items to their aggregate value. Once an inventory method is adopted, the taxpayer must maintain consistency.

The cost of goods on hand at the start of the accounting period must be equal to their value in the closing inventory for the previous accounting period. The cost of purchased goods is their invoice price, minus any trade or other discounts, but plus shipping and other charges necessary for the buyer to take possession of the goods.

For a taxpayer who produces goods, cost equals the opening inventory plus the cost of supplies and raw materials used in the manufacturing process; direct labor costs (both regular and overtime); and certain indirect costs.

If inventory is actually unsaleable, as a result of, e.g., damage, imperfection, or changes in style (and is not merely slow-moving), the taxpayer can "write it down" for tax purposes: value it at its selling price minus the direct costs of disposition.

The basic method for tracking inventory is FIFO (First In, First Out): the assumption is that items are disposed of in the order they were purchased. In many instances, that means that lower-priced items are deemed to have been used first, with more potential taxable income for the taxpayer.

Certain taxpayers can elect the § 472 LIFO (Last In, First Out)[18] method by filing Form 970 with the return for the tax year in which this method is initially adopted. Once made, the LIFO election applies to all subsequent years unless the IRS authorizes a change back (§ 472(e)).

LIFO taxpayers assume that their most recently purchased or produced items are the first to be sold. The general rule of § 472(b) is that the LIFO election is available only to taxpayers who value their inventory at cost (not the lower of cost or market). Under § 472(c), taxpayers who use LIFO for tax purposes are also obligated to use the system for credit purposes and in reports issued to partners and stockholders. (In other words, if the business insists on using a system that depresses its taxable income, it must equally depress the results reported to stockholders and analysts.)

The Sixth Circuit held that an automobile dealership's correction of its accountant's failure to index inventory values as required by the LIFO method was a "change in method of accounting" for § 481 purposes. Therefore, the IRS could correct accounts for years that would otherwise be time-barred.[19]

In 2003, the IRS at last updated guidelines dating back to 1977 and issued new rules for determining the fair market value of inventories acquired in the course of purchasing a company's assets, or for stock purchases where the acquiring company elects under § 338.[20]

[C] Employment Tax Withholding

Companies must withhold income taxes from the "wages" paid to "employees" (§§ 3401, 3402). In many instances, companies will wish to avoid the compliance burden — and the individuals performing services will prefer to be treated as independent contractors whose compensation is not subject to withholding.

The issue is even more salient when it comes to FICA (Social Security) taxes because employer and employee are each required to pay 7.2% of employee compensation up to the wage base, plus a Medicare tax of 1.45% each on all compensation. Independent contractors are responsible for 100% of the FICA tax. The wage base has risen sharply, from $87,000 in 2003 to $106,800 in 2009.

---

[18] Additional refinements such as "simplified dollar value LIFO" are explicated at § 474(a). Section 474(c) defines an eligible small business as one with average annual gross receipts under $5 million for the preceding three years.

[19] Huffman v. CIR, 518 F.3d 357 (6th Cir. 2008); the Sixth Circuit cites the Tax Court's opinion in this case, 126 T.C. 322 (2006), as a good explanation of dollar-value link-chain LIFO accounting, one of three acceptable LIFO methods.

[20] Rev. Proc. 2003-51, 2003-29 IRB 121.

To make small business tax compliance easier, the IRS announced at the end of 2004 that quarterly Federal Unemployment Tax Act (FUTA) deposits would be required only if the accumulated tax was $500 or more. (The previous level of $100 had not been changed since 1970.) Because the maximum FUTA payment is $56 per employee per year, only employers with eight or more employees must make quarterly deposits.[21]

In June 2002, the Supreme Court held that the IRS was justified in using the "aggregate estimation method" to determine the FICA tax that should have been withheld on the tips given to a restaurant's employees. The "aggregate estimation method" was based on projecting the percentage listed as tips on credit card slips to cover customers who paid cash. The restaurant had paid FICA taxes based on tip amounts reported by the employees. IRS assessments are legally presumed to be correct, and this implies the power to use reasonable methods to estimate tax liability. However, taxpayers are free to present evidence that a particular IRS estimate is inaccurate.[22]

The basic test of whether a person performing services is an employee or an independent contractor is whether the payor for the services controls both what is done and how the work is to be done. The IRS rules include a "20-factor test" (see § 3.04[A]). Some of these factors imply that the person performing the services is an employee (whether the payor sets working hours; whether the payor trains the person providing the services); others imply that the person performing the services is an independent contractor (e.g., his or her services are made available to the public; his or her investment in office space, equipment, advertising).

Employee status also has other implications: see, e.g., § 3.05 for the determination of who is entitled to coverage under a company's pension and fringe benefit plans. Whether a pension or welfare benefit plan is discriminatory depends on the number and percentage of "employees" it covers. Coverage under various antidiscrimination laws (§ 3.10) is also pegged to the number of "employees," so mischaracterization of employees as independent contractors can have unintended consequences outside the tax arena.

For individuals who are, indeed, employees, the employer performs income tax withholding on the gross wage, before FICA, pensions, union dues, and other items are deducted. The Code, at § 3402(b) and (c), authorizes two methods of calculating the amount to be withheld: the wage bracket method, under which the employer refers to officially published tables; and the percentage method, involving separate computations.

Code § 3405(c) imposes a requirement of 20% withholding on distributions from pension plans that are eligible to be rolled over (to another qualified plan or to an IRA) but which are not, in fact, rolled over. Required distributions under § 401(a)(9) (generally, distributions to owner-employees who have reached age 701/2 but have not yet retired) are exempt from this requirement. So are annuity

---

[21] 69 F.R. 68,819 (12/1/04); *see* 73 LW 2336.
[22] United States v. Fior D'Italia, Inc., 536 U.S. 238 (2002).

payments and other periodic payments made for life; for the joint life of the employee and designated beneficiary; or for a term of years lasting at least 10 years. Even if the employee is theoretically subject to the 20% withholding requirement, he or she can opt out by filing Form W-4P.

Section 3405(a) also requires withholding on periodic payments, based on the number of withholding exemptions claimed on Form W-4. If there is no W-4 on file, withholding is done as if the employee were married with three exemptions. 10% withholding is required on non-periodic distributions (e.g., lump sums) unless the employee files a W-4P to prevent withholding. Form 945 is used by the employer to report the total of its withholding on all nonpayroll amounts. Form 945 is due on January 31 of the year after the year of the payments, or on February 10 if all amounts were deposited in a timely fashion: § 31.6071(a)-1(a)(1).

At the time of hiring, new employees are supposed to fill out a W-4 withholding analysis certificate, indicating the number of withholding exemptions (reflecting the number of the employee's dependents and other factors, such as holding another job, that affect withholding): § 3402.

Employees are exempt from withholding if they had no income tax liability in the previous tax year, and certify on the W-4 that they do not expect any tax liability this year (e.g., low-wage casual workers; workers entitled to Earned Income, child tax, and other credits that wipe out tax liability).

The employer is required to file Form 941, a quarterly statement reflecting withholding performed in the quarter just ended. Due dates for the 941 are April 30, July 31, October 31, and January 31. It is permissible for the employer to file the 941 up to 10 days later, as long as the taxes were deposited on a timely basis. Depending on the amount of employment taxes incurred in the previous year, Reg. § 31.6032-1(a) requires the employer to make either monthly or semi-weekly tax deposits. Furthermore, if the employer fails to collect, account for, or deposit income or employment taxes, § 7512 gives the IRS the power to order the employer to make its deposits to a special trust account.

In addition to its reporting obligations to the IRS, the employer has obligations to its employees. It must furnish the employees with the appropriate number of copies of the W-2 form (depending on whether the employees are subject to local as well as federal and state income tax) no later than January 31 following the year in which the wages were paid.

§ 4.04   INCOME ITEMS

The corporation's potentially taxable income is made up of a number of items, each of which can generate its own problems of interpretation.

The main categories of income items are:

- Gross sales receipts
- Dividends and interest received
- Rent and royalty income
- Capital gains from disposition of capital assets.

In February 2000, the Supreme Court struck down California's scheme for allocating the interest expenses of foreign corporations between California and non-California income. The system was invalid because it had the effect of imposing tax on non-California income, rather than reasonably allocating the expense deduction to the income generated.[23]

If a multi-state corporation engages in a "unitary business," then a state can tax an apportioned share of that multi-state's business activities both inside and outside the state. Mead, an Ohio corporation wholly owned by MeadWestvaco, sold its Lexis business division. Illinois taxed Mead's capital gains. The Supreme Court ruled in 2008 that this was the correct test, and the state courts erred in imposing tax because Lexis served an "operational purpose" in Mead's business. The Supreme Court remanded for a determination of whether Mead was a unitary business (based on hallmarks such as functional integration, centralized management, and economies of scale).[24]

The Supreme Court refused to hear an appeal sought by a Lehman Brothers subsidiary disputing a $10 million tax bill from Delaware. The subsidiary challenged the state's tax rules as unconstitutional, because all of the earnings of the subsidiary were subject to tax even though the bank earned only about 2% of its income in Delaware. Delaware's position is that banks with Delaware headquarters can exclude only income generated by branches or subsidiaries outside the state — and this subsidiary did not have any branches. The Supreme Court refused to hear the appeal.[25]

Code § 1341(b)(2) provides that the credit for tax paid on income is not available for items that were included in gross income on account of sale of inventory. The Ninth Circuit denied a refund to Texaco, which sought a $101 million tax refund after a settlement with the Department of Energy required payment of $1.25 billion already included in gross income, (Texaco sold products between 1973 and 1981 at prices above the federal petroleum price ceilings then in effect), accepting the government's argument that the items were included in gross income because of "sale or other disposition of stock in trade of the taxpayer."[26]

[A] Corporate E&P and Dividends

A corporation must calculate its earnings and profits (E&P) both for rendering accounting reports and in preparing its tax returns. However, the E&P calculation will not necessarily be the same for both purposes.

The general rule of § 316 is that a distribution made by a corporation to its shareholders is a dividend, and will be taxable to the shareholders. However, this is

---

[23] Hunt-Wesson Inc. v. Franchise Tax Bd. of Cal., 528 U.S. 458 (2000).

[24] MeadWestvaco Corp. v. Illinois Dept of Revenue, 128 S. Ct. 1498 (2008).

[25] Lehman Brothers Bank v. State Bank Commr, 128 S. Ct. 2081 (2008); AP, *High Court Rejects Lehman Brothers Appeal in Tax Case* 4/28/08 (law.com).

[26] Texaco Inc. v. United States, 528 F.3d 703 (9th Cir. 2008). *See also* Alcoa, Inc. v. United States, 509 F.3d 173 (3d Cir. 2007), denying application of § 1341 to expenses incurred by Alcoa in its 1993 tax year for pollution occurring earlier.

true only if the distribution comes from current or accumulated E&P. Taxpayers include amounts they receive as dividends (as defined by § 316) in their gross income. Other distributions are applied to reduce the taxpayer's adjusted basis in the stock, and any non-dividend distributions over and above the taxpayer's basis are taxed as capital gains. See § 312 for the effect of distributions of various kinds of property (e.g., appreciated; encumbered) on the corporation's E&P.[27]

The Supreme Court ruled that the existence of a tax deficiency is an element of the offense of tax evasion under Code § 7201. Therefore, when the founder/president/controlling shareholder of a close corporation received a distribution from the corporation at a time when it did not have E&P (earnings and profits), the distribution was held to have constituted a distribution of capital and was tax-free up to his basis in the stock, and he was not guilty of criminal tax evasion.[28]

[B] Installment Sales and Long-Term Contracts

A taxpayer who is not actually a dealer in the type of property involved, who sells property under an agreement calling for at least one payment in a year after the year of sale, generally reports gain (but not loss) from the transaction under § 453's installment sale rules. (Installment sale characterization applies unless the taxpayer opts out (§ 453(d)); but this method cannot be used for sales of securities traded on an established market.)

Under the installment method, the taxpayer reports the gain element of each payment as it is received, rather than "bunching up" all the gain on the transaction in the year of the sale. The gain for each year, as reported on Form 6252, consists of the installment payments received in that year, times the gross profit ratio. The gross profit ratio equals the gross profit already or to be realized, divided by the total contract price.

A related concept, the long-term contract, is governed by § 460. The basic rule for a contract for manufacture, building, installation or construction of property that is not completed in the tax year in which the contract was entered into is that the "percentage of completion" method is used to report income. (The actual time to completion, not whether the taxpayer reasonably expected completion within one tax year, is determinative.)

In practice, the percentage of completion method is used most often for construction contracts, because § 460(f)(2) provides that the method is used for manufacturing contracts only if the item to be manufactured is unique (not of a type normally included in the taxpayer's inventory) or fabrication normally takes more than 12 months.

The taxpayer can also elect a modified percentage of completion method. The taxpayer can elect not to recognize income under the contract, and not to take into

---

[27] The amount of depreciation used to calculate E&P is lower than the amount allowable in computing taxable income in general.

[28] Boulware v. United States, 128 S. Ct. 1168 (2008).

account any costs allocable to the contract in any tax year in which less than 10% of the estimated total costs are incurred.

[C] Damages

The general rule (also applicable to individual tax returns) is that punitive damages are taxable income for the recipient. A business has ordinary income from damages or settlements for claims of injury to the business that causes lost profits. Amounts received from business interruption insurance also constitute taxable income.

§4.05 BUSINESS DEDUCTIONS

Once a corporation's income is computed, it becomes necessary to determine what deductions are permissible, and in what tax year.

The key section here is § 162, which permits a deduction of a business' "ordinary and necessary" expenses. This category includes reasonable compensation paid to employees, but not bribes or other illegal payments, costs of influencing legislation, or excessive remuneration to employees.

The most typical classes of business deductions include:

- Payroll
- Repairs and maintenance
- Taxes
- Licenses
- Interest paid
- Depreciation and depletion
- Advertising
- Deductible contributions to qualified pension and welfare benefit plans.

[A] Start-Up Expenses

As a general rule, a newly organized corporation cannot deduct its costs of organization, such as legal fees and state-imposed registration charges. Prior to the American Jobs Creation Act (AJCA), P.L. 108-357, § 248 permitted organization expenses (the costs of creating the corporation itself) to be deducted over a period of at least 60 months from the start of operations, as a deferred expense. Code § 195 allowed the corporation to elect to amortize start-up expenses (i.e., the costs of making it possible to produce goods or services) over a period of at least 60 months. AJCA, however, requires organization and start-up costs to be amortized over a 15-year period.

[B] Compensation Deductions

The basic rule is that a corporation can deduct reasonable compensation (including pensions and benefits and severance pay) for personal services actually rendered to the business. However, a public corporation is not permitted to deduct more than $1 million a year for its CEO and its four other highest-paid officers: § 162(m). It is not illegal to make higher payments; the excess merely becomes non-deductible by the corporation.

Nor are "excess parachute payments" deductible. A parachute payment is a guarantee to top executives (defined as the business owner, officer, shareholders, and highly compensated employees) that they will not suffer financially if they lose their jobs in a corporate takeover. An excess parachute payment is defined as a payment, contingent on change in corporate ownership, that is more than three times the "base amount." The base amount is roughly equivalent to the parachute recipient's average gross income for the preceding five years. Again, deductibility, not legality, is at issue. See § 280G.

An employer can deduct contributions made to a welfare benefit fund (a plan providing non-pension employee benefits such as a health plan), but not in excess of the qualified cost of the welfare benefit plan: § 419. Reg. § 1.162-10(a) defines some of the deductible welfare benefit costs.

The general rule is that the employer is not entitled to a compensation deduction for stock transferred under a statutory stock option or ESOP plan, unless the employee disposes of the stock prematurely and recognizes income: § 421.

Under Reg. § 1.162-7(b)(1), amounts claimed as compensation might be recharacterized by the IRS as dividends (i.e., taxable to the recipient, but not deductible by the corporation) if they are proportionate to the recipient's stockholdings, and appear suspicious because they do not reflect the reasonable value of the services performed by the recipient.

In September 2008, the IRS finalized its 2007 Proposed Regulations, in response to the Pension Protection Act of 2006, governing mortality assumptions that set present values for minimum funding of defined benefit plans. They provide that if permission is obtained to use substitute tables, they must be gender-specific, generational, and based on a significant amount of experience (at least 1,000 deaths over a study period of two to five years).[29]

[C] Rentals and Related Expenses

Rent on property used in trade, business, professionals, or production of income is deductible under § 162(a)(3), but personal-use rent is not deductible. However, renting property from related parties (e.g., family members or stockholders) will be scrutinized. Any excessive portion of the rent will not be deductible, and may be treated as a dividend.

---

[29] Notice 2008-85, 2008-42 IRB 905 provides the static mortality tables to calculate items such as the funding target level for valuation dates in calendar years 2009–2013. The Notice also contains a modified unisex mortality table to be used to determine minimum present value under Code § 417(e)(3)/ERISA § 205(g)(3) for distributions with annuity starting dates in periods beginning in calendar years 2009–2013. *See* Rev. Proc. 2008-62, 2008-42 IRB 935, updating Rev. Proc. 2007-37, 2007-25 IRB 1433, to explain how sponsors of single-employer defined benefit plans can get approval to use plan-specific substitute mortality tables.

The cost of acquiring a lease is not deductible; Reg. § 1.162-11(a) requires it to be amortized over the unexpired period of the lease. The lessor's costs of leasing property (as well as a lessee's costs of subleasing property) are also amortized, ratably over the term of the lease.

It is often important to distinguish between rent (of property that the renter does NOT intend to buy) and a conditional sales contract. Payments under the conditional sales contract are not deductible as rent (although it may be possible to capitalize them based on the useful life of the property). Whether a lease with option to buy is a sale depends on factors such as the amount required to purchase the property after the lease term; and whether "rent" payments are applied to create equity. Problems of characterization may also arise under a sale-leaseback arrangement (A sells a property to B, but A continues to occupy the property, paying rent to B).

[D] Net Operating Loss (NOL) Deductions

If a corporation's deductions (calculated for this purpose with certain modifications from ordinary tax principles) exceed its gross income for the year, the corporation has a net operating loss (NOL) as governed by § 172. The corporation has a choice of how to treat this loss for tax purposes. It can be carried back to past years (thus resulting in a tax refund) or forward (to reduce the tax for future years).

The general rule of § 172(b)(1), instituted by TRA '97, is that NOLs can be carried back for two years, forward for 20. (The pre-TRA rules, effective for tax years beginning before 8/6/97, called for carrying NOLs back three years, forward for 15.) However, a fanning corporation, or a small business with average gross receipts under $5 million a year, can carry its casualty, theft, and disaster losses back for three years even post-TRA '97: § 172(b)(1)(F). Under special § 172(f) provisions, product liability losses can be carried back ten years or forward 20 years.

The taxpayer can also make an irrevocable election, under § 172(b)(3), to carry all NOLs forward and waive all carrybacks.

The JCWAA also extends the carryback period on many NOLs from two years to five years for losses arising in 2001 or 2002. See Rev. Proc. 2002-40, 2002-23 IRB 1096, for details about how to either use or opt out of the new provision. NOLs can be used to offset up to 100% of the corporation's Alternative Minimum Tax (AMT) liability. Corporate taxpayers that filed their returns before JCWAA became effective can either amend their corporate tax return (Form 1120X) or file Form 1139 (Application for Tentative Refund). Also see the Working Families Tax Relief Act of 2004, P.L. 108-311, for technical corrections to the Net Operating Loss rules.

NOLs were also addressed by the Supreme Court in mid-2001. Under Code § 172(b), the carryback period for a Product Liability Loss (PLL) is 10 years. A PLL equals the company's product liability losses that do not exceed its NOL, so a company that has positive income rather than NOLs cannot claim a

PLL. The PLL for an affiliated group of corporations must be computed on a consolidated single-entity basis, and not by aggregating PLLs determined separately for each company.[30]

Taxpayers affected by Hurricanes Katrina, Wilma, and/or Rita may be entitled to carry back NOLs within the Gulf Opportunity (GO) Zone for five years rather than the normal two years, as a result of P.L. 109-73 and P.L. 109-135.

[E] Meals and Entertainment

Code § 274 provides that corporations are not entitled to deduct the cost of entertainment, amusement, or recreation unless such costs are directly related to the active conduct of their trade or business, or unless the entertainment is provided directly before or after a substantial bona fide business discussion. Furthermore, the deduction is limited to the portion of the cost related to business. In general, only 50% of the cost of business meals is deductible. Rev. Proc. 2006-41, 2006-43 IRB 777 updates Rev. Proc. 2005-67, 2005-42 IRB 729, giving rules for substantiating employee business expenses for meals and lodging, and meals and incidental expenses incurred while traveling.

[F] Corporate Charitable Deduction

Section 170(b)(2) allows a corporation to deduct up to 10% of its taxable income (measured without regard to charitable contributions, dividends received, and carrybacks for net operating losses and capital losses) each year for contributions made to one or more charitable organizations recognized by the IRS as qualified to receive deductible contributions. Contributions are not necessarily deductible just because they are made to an organization that is tax-exempt as to its own income. Contributions in excess of the limit can be carried forward for five years under § 170(d)(2). An accrual corporation will be permitted to treat a contribution as being made during its tax year if the contribution was authorized by the Board of Directors in that year and paid no later than 2½ months after the close of the tax year (§ 170(a)(2)).

The basic rule of valuation is that donated property is valued at its fair market value at the time of the contribution, minus any amount that would have been ordinary income in a hypothetical sale.

Code § 170(e) contains special, more generous rules for C Corporation donations of materials used for the ill, needy, or for infants (e.g., a drug company contributes inventory) or scientific property donated to an institution of higher education or a tax-exempt organization.

[G] Other Corporate Deductions

The American Jobs Creation Act adds new Code § 177, permitting a deduction for income from "domestic production activities" (including construction,

---

[30] United Dominion Indus. Inc. v. United States, 532 U.S. 822 (2001).

manufacture of tangible personal property, software, sound recordings, electricity, or natural gas). The deduction begins at 3% in 2005 and 2006, rises to 6% in 2007–2009, and reaches its maximum of 9% for 2010 and later years. TD 9263, 2006-25 IRB 1063 and Rev. Proc. 2006-22, 2006-23 IRB 1033 contain lengthy Final Regulations about the domestic production activities deduction.

The treatment of business bad debts under § 166 is somewhat different from the treatment of non-business bad debts. A business can deduct debts that are partially or wholly worthless, and it is an ordinary rather than a capital loss. The deduction is taken in the year the debt becomes worthless. To be deductible, a partially worthless debt must be only partially recoverable; it must not be evidenced by a security; and it must be charged off on the corporate books during the tax year.

A corporation's legal expenses are currently deductible unless they are capital expenditures, or expenses of acquiring, perfecting, or defending title to property: Reg. § 1.212-1(k).

Insurance premiums that constitute business expenses are probably deductible. Insuring business property is a deductible expense. However, if a corporation chooses to self-insure (i.e., maintain reserves for possible future payments) instead of buying insurance, the reserves are not deductible.

Life insurance on the lives of employees that is an employee benefit (see § 3.08[B]) is generally deductible. However, if the corporate taxpayer itself is the beneficiary (e.g., key-man insurance on the corporation's top officers), the premiums are not deductible.

Penalties or fines imposed for violating a law (including the tax laws) are nondeductible: § 162(f). But in the case of civil litigation rather than criminal charges, judgments or settlements that the taxpayer has to pay that are directly connected with the taxpayer's business are deductible.

For dividends received from other corporations, the taxpayer corporation is entitled to deduct 100% if the payor corporation is in the same affiliated group as the taxpayer, 80% if the taxpayer corporation owns between 20% and 80% of the payor corporation's stock, and 70% if it owns less than 20% of the payor corporation's stock.

Naturally, federal income taxes are not deductible in determining corporate taxable income, but do affect the calculation of income subject to accumulated earnings tax and personal holding company tax. A corporation (or a partnership) can deduct state and local income taxes as a business expense (§ 275).

§4.06 TREATMENT OF CAPITAL EXPENDITURES

Unlike a current expense, which relates only to the current year of corporate operations, a capital expenditure has anticipated benefits that last more than one year. Capital expenses can be expenses of building, buying, improving, adding value, or extending the useful life of corporate property.

In some instances an entire capital expenditure can be "expensed" (deducted in a single year as permitted by § 179); the basic rule of § 263 is that capital expenditures will have to be "recovered" over time (i.e., amortized, depreciated, or depleted over a period of years)—even if in fact the corporation spent all the money in a single year.

Under prior law, corporations could "expense" (take a current-year deduction for) up to $25,000 worth of equipment. JGTRRA raises this amount to $100,000 a year. The $100,000 figure will be indexed for inflation in 2004 and 2005. Qualifying property for § 179 purposes means tangible personal property that would otherwise be depreciable (i.e., has a useful life of more than one year), purchased for use in a trade or business.

The § 179 limit was scheduled to drop to $25,000 at the end of 2005 but was kept at the same level (adjusted for inflation) by the American Jobs Creation Act of 2004 (AJCA), P.L. 108-357. Further relief was provided by TIPRA.

JGTRRA provided 50% bonus depreciation for property acquired between May 5, 2003 and January 1, 2005.

A corporation's depreciation deductions are reported on Form 4562. Land is not depreciable, because it is not subject to wear and tear or obsolescence. Other real and personal property is defined as depreciable by § 167 if it is:

- Used in the corporation's trade or business, or held for the production of income
- Has an exhaustible useful life that can be determined
- Is not inventory, stock in trade, or held as an investment.

Section 263 provides that capital expenditures are not deductible. This category includes amounts paid for new buildings, restoring property, or permanent improvements that increase the value of property. Amounts that qualify as R&E spending or § 179 costs are not treated as capital expenditures.

If the property that is acquired or constructed will serve as inventory, then its cost is included in the corporate cost of inventory. Non-inventory property, however, generally has to be capitalized or amortized. Code § 263A's uniform capitalization system mandates corporations[31] to include the "allocable costs" of inventory property in the calculation of the value of the inventory. The rules of § 263A apply to real or tangible personal property produced by the taxpayer for use in business, produced by the taxpayer for resale to customers, or acquired by the taxpayer for resale to customers. The allocable cost of all other property must be capitalized. Allocable costs are direct costs of property, and certain indirect costs (e.g., taxes). However, sales and marketing expenses and research and experimentation expenses are excluded from the category of "allocable costs." Section 263A includes methods for allocating labor costs and capitalizing interest. The rules under §§ 263 and 263A were not altered by JGTRRA.

---

[31] Corporations are exempt if their annual gross receipts for the preceding three years averaged less than $10 million, with respect to personal property acquired for resale: § 263A(b)(2)(B).

The Taxpayer Relief Act of 1997 created a new 15-year amortization provision (enacted as § 197) for certain intangibles acquired by the taxpayer (e.g., goodwill; patents, copyrights, and designs; customer- and supplier-based intangibles; franchises, trademarks, and trade names).

The treatment of computer software is extremely complex, and depends on factors such as whether the taxpayer created or merely acquired the software, and whether it is an off-the-shelf, generally available product or customized by or for the corporation's individual needs.

Some taxes and carrying charges that could otherwise be deducted currently or amortized can, if the corporation so elects, be capitalized under § 266. The effect is that, if the property is depreciable, the deduction is deferred until the later years in the depreciation schedule; otherwise (e.g., for unimproved real estate), the effect of capitalization is to increase the basis and therefore reduce the eventual capital gain when the property is sold.

Natural resources, such as timber, oil, gas, and minerals in the ground, are treated under "depletion" rather than depreciation rules (§§ 612–614). Most depletion is measured using the "cost depletion" method, but the more generous "percentage depletion" (a percentage of the gross income of the corporation taking the deduction) is permitted for mining and some oil and gas well interests.

Rev. Proc. 2008-66, 2008-45 IRB 1107, states that the § 179 limit for taxable years beginning in 2009 is $133,000, an amount that will be reduced, but not below zero, to the extent that § 179 property placed in service during the year costs over $530,000.

[A] MACRS System

Congress has taken many approaches to capitalization of business-related costs. Before 1987, the Accelerated Cost Recovery System (ACRS) was in force, and indeed certain businesses still have assets in use that were placed into service between 1980 and 1986 and continue to be subject to ACRS rules.

Depreciation begins when property is placed in service — a determination that is governed by Tax Code conventions, not the actual date of first use. These conventions may reduce the amount of deductible depreciation if, for instance, a piece of machinery is treated as if it had been in use for only half a year, so only a half measure of depreciation is allowable in that year. Depreciation ends when the property is retired from service; when it is sold; or when the cost or other basis has been fully recovered — whichever comes first.

Under the Modified Accelerated Cost Recovery System (MACRS), recovery property (depreciable tangible property used in a trade or business, or for the production of income) is depreciated by a prescribed method over its recovery period, which in turn depends on the kind of asset it is. MACRS classes call for depreciation over 3, 5, 7, 10, 15, or 20 years. A longer depreciation period, 27.5 years, is called for residential real estate, and an even longer 39-year period applies to non-residential real estate placed in service after May 12, 1993. The American

Jobs Creation Act of 2004 enacts a temporary (until 2006) 15-year depreciation period for certain improvements made by owners to commercial real estate.

The taxpayer can elect to use straight-line depreciation (i.e., the same percentage is used to calculate depreciation throughout the whole recovery period). The Alternative Depreciation System (ADS), more or less a straight-line depreciation method with a longer recovery period, is optional for some assets and mandated for others. Real property must be depreciated on a straight-line basis in any case. Depreciation elections are made in the year the property is placed in service (§ 168(b)(5)) and are irrevocable.

If the business use of property drops below 50% level, depreciation must be recaptured. In other words, the taxpayer must give back tax benefits that were obtained on the basis of a business use of the property that is no longer applicable. Form 4797 is used to report the recapture amount, which equals the expense deduction taken minus the MACRS depreciation that would have been allowed.

Recapture of depreciation is governed by §§ 1245 and 1250. If business policy calls for getting rid of an asset that has not yet reached the end of its depreciation schedule (so recapture would be necessary on sale), recapture can be avoided by making a tax-free exchange for other property; keeping the property in use until the end of the depreciation schedule; or retaining the property but borrowing against its value (a tactic that is especially practical in the case of buildings).

[B] Amortization

Intangible assets, movies, videos, and master sound recordings are not depreciable under MACRS; instead, they are subject to amortization.

Section 197 governs the amortization of goodwill; going concern value; market share; customer lists; franchises, trademarks, and trade names; and patent, copyrights, formulas, processes, and designs. But § 197(c) says that interests in a partnership or corporation; computer software available to the general public; or patents and copyrights acquired in any transaction other than acquisition of the assets of a business are not § 197 intangibles.

In addition, § 167 provides that non-MACRS property that is not subject to § 197 is to be depreciated on a straight-line basis over its "useful life." With certain exceptions, computer software is to be depreciated on a straight-line basis over 36 months.

[C] Basis of Corporate Property

Under § 1012, the determination of basis of corporate property begins with the cost of the property, deemed to include liabilities the property is subject to, even if the corporation did not assume them in purchasing the property. A cash basis corporation's basis in accounts receivable is zero. The basis of intangibles such as patents, copyrights, goodwill, and covenants not to compete is what was paid for them.

Basis is then adjusted by adding capital expenditures relating to the property, but basis is not increased by items that can be deducted as expenses (e.g., carrying charges) unless they were capitalized rather than deducted. Basis is reduced by depreciation, cost recovery, and amortization deductions taken with respect to the property (§ 1016). A corporation's basis in property acquired from its shareholders as contributions to capital equals the shareholder's basis, plus any gain the shareholder recognized on the transfer: § 362(a)(2).

If corporations merge or are acquired, basis considerations come into play both for the acquiror and for the target. If the transaction is structured as a tax-free reorganization (see § 4.11[C]), the acquiror's basis in property received in the transaction equals the target company's basis in that property plus gain to the target. The exception is a transfer of securities in the target corporation: this basis rule obtains only if the securities were acquired in exchange for securities of the acquiring company (§ 362(b)).

[D] Gain and Loss on Dispositions of Property

A taxpayer has gain on property if the cash received for the property, plus the fair market value of non-cash property received, exceeds the property's adjusted basis (its cost plus improvements, but minus depreciation: § 1011). If the buyer pays or assumes any of the seller's indebtedness on the property, then this amount is added to the amount received. The amount of the mortgage on encumbered property is considered part of the sales price, even if the seller is not personally liable for the mortgage debt, and whether or not the buyer assumes the mortgage. See § 1001.

A cash basis seller reports the gain of a profitable transaction in the year of actual or constructive receipt of the sale proceeds; cash basis losses are reported in the year the transaction is completed by a fixed, identifiable event. An accrual basis seller reports either gain or loss in the year of the completion of the sale, when there is an unqualified right to receive the purchase price. In any transaction involving stock, the trade date (the date the sale was entered into) and not the settlement date is what counts.

Under § 1032, a corporation has neither gain nor loss when it sells or exchanges its own stock for cash or property, or when a warrant or option to buy or sell its stock lapses.

The computation of tax on corporate capital gains is significantly simpler than the routine individual taxpayers must follow (§ 20.05). The general rule is that the corporation must include all of its capital gains, net of all capital losses, in taxable income. A corporation can deduct capital losses, but only to the extent of its capital gains. Losses can be carried back three years and forward five years; but a carried-over capital loss is treated as short- rather than long-term. See § 1211.

Gain must be recognized, but losses cannot be, in sales and exchanges between "related taxpayers" as defined by § 267. See § 267(b). Related taxpayers include a corporation and a taxpayer owning 50% or more of the corporation's stock; a corporation controlled by a trust or the trust's grantor and a fiduciary; two or more corporations within a controlled group of corporations; a corporation and a partnership, if the same persons own 50% or more of the value of each; two S Corporations meeting that criterion; or an S Corporation and a C Corporation each controlled by the same persons.

§ 4.07 ACCUMULATED EARNINGS TAX

A corporation cannot deduct the dividends that it pays to its shareholders, even though the dividends are taxed to the shareholders who receive them. Therefore, corporations (especially closely held corporations) have some incentive to retain money within the corporation instead of paying it out as dividends.

Code §§ 531–537 are designed to reduce this incentive, by imposing an "accumulated earnings tax" on accumulated taxable income, imposed over and above all other taxes due for the year. To determine whether this tax is due, the corporation is entitled to a deduction for any income reasonably accumulated for current or projected business needs, such as working capital, business expansion, debt retirement, reserves against product liability claims, and acquisitions. The taxpayer has the burden of proof on the issue of whether retention was reasonable. JGTRRA (P.L. 108-27 § 302(e)(5)) reduced the § 531 rate from the highest tax bracket that could be imposed on an individual's income to 15% of the corporation's total income.

[A] Personal Holding Companies

A tax at the highest individual rate, also in addition to other taxes due, is imposed on undistributed Personal Holding Company (PHC) income that is not subject to the accumulated earnings tax. A PHC, as governed by §§ 541–547, is a company at least 60% of whose AGI for the year consists of PHC income, and at least 50% of whose outstanding stock (at any time during the second half of the taxable year) is held by one to five stockholders. PHC income, in turn, consists of AGI from sources such as personal service income, interest, dividends, rent, and royalties, rather than manufacturing or wholesale or retail sales of goods and services. If the principal purpose of such a corporation is tax avoidance, the IRS has the power to reallocate tax items between the corporation and the individual service provider(s), so that the reported tax will more accurately reflect financial reality.

§ 4.08 BUSINESS TAX CREDITS

The general business credit allowed under § 38 is the total of various incentive credits, including the investment credit, the disabled access credit (limited to small businesses that make their premises accessible), and the low-income housing credit.

The § 38 credit allowed in any particular year equals the current year's credit, plus carryforwards and carrybacks to that year, subject to limitations based on the corporation's "net income tax." Net income tax is the regular tax, plus Alternative Minimum Tax, minus certain credits.

In general, for years after 1997, the general business credit can be carried back one year and forward 20 years. For tax years beginning in 2002 and later years, EGTRRA adds credits for the start-up costs of a small employer adding a pension plan, and for employer costs of providing child care to employees.

Corporations that are subject to foreign taxes can claim a dollar-for-dollar tax credit under § 901. However, it is not mandatory that the credit be used: §§ 27 and 164 give the taxpayer a choice each year between deducting the taxes and claiming them as a credit.

§4.09 EFFECT OF THIN CAPITALIZATION

In general, as § 1.07[A] shows, the organizers of a corporation have broad latitude in determining whether to issue common stock, preferred stock, or debt securities, as well as broad latitude in deciding the proportion of each in the corporation's capital structure.

However, the Code in some ways favors debt capitalization over equity, because a corporation is entitled to deduct the cost of its debt service but is not entitled to deduct the dividends it pays to its stockholders. The way a corporation characterizes its securities when they are issued is binding on the corporation and the holders of the securities — but not necessary on the IRS (§ 385(c)).

If a corporation is capitalized too "thinly" (i.e., too much debt to equity), the IRS has the power to treat certain securities as equity rather than as debt, and correspondingly deny "interest" deductions. The factors include the debt:equity ratio, the business purpose or economic reality behind the transaction, whether securities are convertible, presence or absence of a fixed maturity date, subordination of the securities, and holders' rights.

§4.10 CONTROLLED AND AFFILIATED GROUPS

Groups of related corporations may be treated as controlled groups under § 1561, with the result that even if they file separate tax returns, the brackets will be applied to the aggregated taxable income of the entire group (in other words, the benefit of the lower tax brackets will apply only once, not once per corporation). Furthermore, the entire group is entitled to only one accumulated earnings tax credit and one AMT exemption. Section 1563 defines two kinds of controlled group: the parent-subsidiary and the brother-sister.

In a parent-subsidiary controlled group, the parent corporation owns at least 80% of the voting power in at least one corporation in the ownership chain. Each corporation within the chain (other than the parent) has at least 80% of its voting power owned by one or more corporations in the chain.

In a brother-sister group, at least 80% of the voting power of each corporation is owned by one to five individuals, estates, or trusts; and these persons own 50% or more of the voting power of each corporation within the group.

Treatment as a controlled group is somewhat undesirable (in that it tends to increase taxes), but Code §§ 1501–1505 allow the creation of an "affiliated group," a move that can have positive tax consequences. The corporations can make an election (generally irrevocable) to file a consolidated return, based on connection of their stock ownership through a common parent corporation.

A group, for instance, might choose to do this if taxes can be saved if there are significant intragroup payments of dividends (which are 100% deductible when issued within a group), or if one group member has operating losses that would serve to offset operating profits elsewhere in the group. See the Regulations for § 1502 for allocation of tax items within the group.

The parent corporation must own 80% of the voting power and 80% of the total value of the stock of at least one corporation within the group. One or more corporations within the group must own at least 80% of the stock in the other corporations in the group (not the parent).

The consolidated return for the group is filed by the parent corporation, on Form 1120. For the first year of the election, it must be accompanied by Form 851 (affiliation schedule) and Form 1122 (consent from each corporation within the group).

§ 4.11 REORGANIZATIONS AND RELATED TRANSACTIONS

The Code provides for many tax-free or partially tax-free transactions between corporations, or between a corporation and its shareholders. This category includes A-G reorganizations; incorporation; transfers of property to a controlled corporation; and redemption of a corporation's own stock.

The concept of "boot" — consideration other than corporate stock — is significant in such transactions. Sometimes the receipt of boot will disqualify the transaction from tax-free status; sometimes the boot itself will bear unfavorable tax consequences, but the underlying transaction will be tax-free.

[A] § 351 Transfers and Distributions

When a business incorporates, or when a transfer of property is made by a party to a corporation it controls, the transfer is generally tax-free, and no gain or loss is recognized. (This section cannot be used for transfers in bankruptcy, receivership, or foreclosure.) The transferred property can be cash; tangible property; or intangible personal property (but not the transferor's services to the transferee corporation, or indebtedness of the transferee corporation that is not evidenced by a security).

To qualify for § 351 treatment, the transfer must be made to a corporation, solely in exchange for that corporation's stock (but not rights, warrants, or options or certain preferred stock). Immediately after the transfer, the transferor(s) must control the transferee corporation. Control means owning at least 80% of the transferee corporation's voting stock and at least 80% of all other classes of stock. A transaction can satisfy § 351 if certain transferors receive voting stock while others get non-voting preferred shares, as long as the 80% requirements are met overall.

In transactions that would qualify under § 351 except that boot is received, no transferor can recognize loss as a result of the transaction. However, gain is recognized, up to the amount of the boot (defined as the amount of cash plus the FMV of boot property). The transferred property retains its characterization as ordinary income property (e.g., inventory) or capital assets, so this determines whether the transferor's gain is capital or ordinary.

Section 357 provides that a transfer remains tax-free if the transferred property was encumbered (subject to liabilities), but the liabilities constitute boot if the transferor had a tax avoidance motivation, or if there was no business purpose for having the transferee assume the liabilities. If the assumed liabilities exceed the transferor's adjusted basis, the excess constitutes gain.

Under Section 311, a corporation can recognize gain but not loss when it distributes property to shareholders other than in the course of liquidation. A corporation never has either gain or loss on distribution of its own stock or stock rights. If a non-liquidating distribution of appreciated property is made, the corporation has gain to the same extent as if it had sold the property to the stockholders receiving it, at its fair market value as of the time of the distribution: § 311(b).

[B] Redemptions

Transfer of stock from a stockholder to the issuing corporation is often treated as the corporation's "redemption" of those shares (whether the corporation cancels the stock, retires it, retains it as treasury stock, or does anything else with it: § 317(b)).

If the transaction falls under the § 302 redemption provisions, the distribution from the corporation is treated as payment for the stock in a sale or exchange, so the stockholder is likely to have capital gain because the stock will probably be a capital asset in the hands of the taxpayer. See § 318 for attribution rules, under which one taxpayer will be deemed to own shares belonging to another, related taxpayer such as a family member or a trust, S Corporation, partnership, or C Corporation that the taxpayer controls.

Four kinds of transactions are treated as redemptions, and therefore as payment for stock, under § 302(b):

- A redemption that is "substantially disproportionate" as to the shareholder
- Complete redemption of all of the shareholder's shares (if he or she owns both common and preferred shares, all shares of both types must be redeemed)
- A redemption that is not essentially equivalent to a dividend
- Redemption of the stock of a non-corporate shareholder, as part of a partial liquidation of the corporation whose shares are involved.

Similar rules apply under § 303 to redemption of the shares of a decedent, with the proceeds used to pay death taxes.

As you would expect, each type of redemption has its own rules, which are laid out in § 302(b). For the redemption to be substantially disproportionate, two tests must be met. After the redemption, the stockholder must own less than half of the corporation's voting stock. Furthermore, the percentage of the voting stock and common stock now held must be less than 80% of the level held before the redemption.

A redemption does not have the effect of a dividend as long as it causes a meaningful reduction in the stockholder's proportionate interest in the corporation. If the shareholder owned over 50% of the voting power before the redemption, reduction to a minority level will probably be treated as meaningful. For someone who held a substantial minority interest prior to the redemption, the reduction will be meaningful if it increases the number of other shareholders' collaboration needed in order to control the corporation. Any redemption in a low percentage minority interest will probably be considered meaningful.

A redemption in conjunction with a partial liquidation must go to a non-corporate shareholder; must not be dividend-equivalent (from the corporation's viewpoint, not the stockholder's); and must be made pursuant to a plan, in the year the plan was adopted or the following year. See § 302(e).

Estate-tax-oriented redemptions of a decedent's shares that are included in his or her gross estate are permitted up to the total federal and state death taxes imposed on the estate (including interest), plus deductible funeral and administration expenses. Section 303(a) imposes three tests. The redeemed stock must constitute at least 35% of the adjusted gross estate,[32] and the redemption distribution must occur after the decedent's death, but no later than three years and 90 days after the filing of the estate tax return. Furthermore, the shareholder must have the burden of taxes or expenses, and payment of death taxes, funeral and administration expenses, reduces his interest.

Also see § 304, which deals with the situation in which a shareholder owns stock in two related controlled corporations, and sells stock in the issuer corporation to the acquirer corporation for cash or property. If the corporations are part of a brother-sister controlled group, the transaction is a redemption by the acquirer corporation. If the issuer corporation is the parent corporation of the acquirer corporation, then the transaction is treated as a redemption by the issuer corporation.

[C] Corporate Reorganizations

The underlying theory under the Internal Revenue Code's treatment of reorganizations is that a qualifying reorganization will have no tax consequences, because the same underlying investment is merely being transmuted in form.

---

[32] The stock of two or more corporations can be aggregated, if at least 20% of the stock of each corporation is included in the decedent's estate.

All qualified reorganizations share several characteristics, as laid out in §§ 356 and 368:

- The transaction must have a business purpose; it must not be solely tax-motivated[33]
- There must be a "plan" of reorganization (and copies of the plan have to be filed with the returns of the corporations participating in the plan)
- The stock to be exchanged must come from a corporation that is a party to the reorganization or, in certain circumstances, the parent corporation of a party
- There must be continuity of interest: i.e., after the reorganization, the target shareholders must still have a significant proprietary stake in the reorganized corporation(s). In most instances, this requires that much of the consideration for the transaction must be in the form of the stock of the acquiring corporation (or, perhaps, its parent corporation)
- There must be continuity of enterprise: the acquiring corporation must continue to carry out the acquired corporation's historic business, or use a significant portion of the acquired corporation's historic business assets in business.

[1] Classification of Tax-Free Reorganizations

Tax-free reorganizations are described as types A through G. The letters are subsections of § 368(a)(l). A "triangular" transaction, permitted in types A, B, and G, involves the stock of the acquiring corporation's parent corporation rather than that of the acquiring corporation itself.

A type A reorganization is a merger or consolidation carried out under federal law or the laws of a state.[34] But taxation is not inevitable, because some divisive transactions qualify for tax-free status under § 355.[35]

---

[33] IRS has the power, under § 269, to disallow deductions and credits if control of a corporation, or that corporation's assets, is acquired principally to avoid tax by making use of the deductions and credits. Also *see* §§ 382 and 384, limiting the extent to which an acquired corporation's built-in gains can be used to offset the acquiring corporation's losses, and to which the acquired corporation's excess credits and net capital losses can be used. "Trafficking" in NOLs is forbidden.

[34] Notice 2005-6, 2005-5 IRB 448 (*see also* REG-125628-01, 70 F.R. 749, 1/5/05) sets out rules for § 354 tax-free treatment of cross-border mergers organized under foreign law (exchanges of securities for stock or securities). This represents a change from prior law, under which only mergers organized under U.S. law (federal or state) could be tax-free. Rules have been promulgated under § 368(a)(1)(A) for cross-border mergers, covering topics such as basis and holding periods, triangular reorganizations, asset transfers, and the application of § 367.

[35] *See* T.D.s 9242 and 9243, 2006-7 IRB 422, 475 for comprehensive Final Regulations on the definition of statutory merger and consolidation, to determine if the transaction is an A reorganization. Certain transactions under the laws of foreign jurisdictions can now qualify. The basis of stock and securities received in a reorganization is calculated with the § 358 rules, subject to special basis and holding requirements for triangular reorganizations. Treatment as a statutory merger or consolidation is denied if the deal is structured as acquisition of the stock of a target corporation which is then converted to an LLC.

In a B reorganization, the acquiring corporation gets stock in the target corporation in exchange for nothing but voting stock in the acquiring corporation, and the acquiror is in control of the target following the reorganization.

In a C reorganization, substantially all the properties of the target corporation are acquired for voting stock of the acquiring corporation. The statute and regulations do not explicitly define "substantially all," but there is case law to the effect that 68% is not sufficient. The IRS will only issue a favorable advance ruling if the target transfers at least 90% of the fair market value of its net assets and 70% of its gross assets. The target corporation must liquidate (distribute everything received, and all its other properties, to its shareholders) unless the IRS waives the distribution requirement. A C reorganization can involve "boot" (consideration other than voting stock of the acquiring corporation), but at least 80% of the value of all of the target's properties must be exchanged for voting stock of the acquiring corporation.

Unlike a "stock for stock" C reorganization, a D reorganization involves the transfer of some or all of the target company's assets to another corporation, with the result that right after the transfer, the transferor and/or its shareholders control the transferee corporation. Furthermore, the transferor either distributes all of its assets (including the stock of the transferee corporation) to its shareholders in a liquidation that is part of a plan of reorganization, or distributes the transferee corporation's stock in a tax-free spin-off, split-off, or split-up under §§ 354–356. If a complex transaction fits the rules for both a C and a D reorganization, § 368(a)(2) says that it will be treated as a D reorganization.

A type E reorganization involves only one corporation, which undergoes a change in capital structure, such as exchanging old bonds for new ones, making changes in stock to conform to charter amendments, or exchanging one class of common stock for another. A type F reorganization is a change in identity, form, or place of organization of just one corporation. A type G reorganization is a corporation's transfer of part or all of its assets to another corporation under a court-approved plan of bankruptcy, receivership, or foreclosure, with the securities of the transferred corporation distributed in a transaction that satisfies §§ 354, 355, or 356.

[2] Corporate-Level Effects

For most reorganization transactions, "control" is defined as 80% of combined voting power plus 80% of the total shares of each class of non-voting stock, but different rules, involving 50% ownership, apply to D reorganizations.

As a result of § 354, no gain or loss is recognized when the holder of stock or securities receives stock and nothing else under a plan of reorganization. Nonrecognition also applies when stock in a company that is a party to the reorganization is exchanged for other securities whose face amount does not exceed the face amount of surrendered securities. For D and G reorganizations to operate as nonrecognition transactions, the transferee corporation must get substantially all of the transferor corporation's assets, and the transferor must make a full distribution.

Section 356(a)(1) provides that if any boot is received, then all of the recipient's gain on the exchange is recognized, and is taxed up to the amount of the boot. It will be taxed as an ordinary dividend to the extent that the exchange has the same effect as the declaration of a dividend; any balance will be taxed as gain from the exchange of property.

At the corporate level, § 361 says that a corporation involved in a reorganization has no gain or loss on the exchange of its property solely for stock and/or securities of another corporation involved in the reorganization. If the corporation (rather than the stockholders) receives boot, then gain is recognized on the exchange, but only up to the extent of boot that is not distributed to stockholders. Distribution of appreciated property to stockholders may require recognition of gain.

The acquiring corporation can make an irrevocable election, under § 338, to treat the purchase of a target corporation's stock as if it were a purchase of assets, if it is possible and desirable to step up the basis of the target's assets. This might occur where the target has significant losses that can offset the acquiror's gains; if the target owns a great deal of depreciated property; or if major depreciation and amortization deductions are available. (If this is done, the target and the selling shareholders may have to recognize gain, because the target is taxed as if it had sold all its assets at fair market value.) The election is made by the acquiring corporation, on Form 8023-A, which is due the fifteenth day of the ninth month after the month of the acquisition.

Note that owning § 306 stock, which is issued in connection with a reorganization (or as a stock dividend) will usually give rise to ordinary income rather than capital gains when the holder sells it or it is redeemed. Also see § 355, which governs spin-offs, split-offs, and split-ups, which are tax-free methods of dividing a corporation into two or more corporations so that the stockholders of the former corporation continue to own the new corporations, although not necessarily in the same proportions.

[D] Corporate Liquidations

Liquidation, as governed by §§ 331–336, is a corporation's process of dissolving completely and distributing all assets to its shareholders. The corporation can have taxable gain or loss when the property is sold or distributed in connection with the liquidation. Usually, the shareholders will have capital gain or loss on the distribution, on the theory that they receive full payment in exchange for their stock, measured by comparing the cash and fair market value of property received to their basis in the stock.

However, if the corporation is a "collapsible" corporation as defined by § 341 (i.e., one created specifically to be liquidated to take advantage of tax benefits stemming from ordinary income assets such as inventory), anyone who owns 5% or more of the shares will be denied capital gains treatment on liquidation to the extent that the gains are attributable to ordinary income assets.

§ 4.12 SPECIAL CORPORATIONS

The discussion above involves the conventional, C Corporation. The Internal Revenue Code includes rules for taxation of various other kinds of corporations.

[A] Subchapter S Corporations

The ordinary, or C Corporation, is a taxpayer separate and apart from its stockholders. The corporation itself must calculate its income, deductions, credits, and other items, and must prepare a tax return and make corresponding payments. The dividends paid to stockholders then become taxable income for the stockholders.

This double taxation is resented by most taxpayers, and the Code has responded by permitting certain small corporations to operate under Subchapter S of the Code, §§ 1361–1379. These "S Corporations," somewhat like partnerships, are "pass-through" entities. That is, there is little or no taxation at the entity level.[36] Instead, tax items are passed through to partners and S Corporation shareholders, and are taxed at that level.

All corporations are C Corporations unless a valid Subchapter S election is in place.

Under the circumstances laid out in T.D. 8869 (65 FR 3843, 1/25/00), a Subchapter S Corporation can liquidate and reabsorb its corporate subsidiary by making an election. The process will not be treated as a step transaction.

[1] Criteria for S Corporation Election

To make the election, a corporation (or unincorporated entity taxed as a corporation) § 1361 requires that it must:

- Be a U.S. entity
- Be eligible to make the election (e.g., insurance companies are not allowed to elect Sub S)
- Not have more than 100 shareholders (but certain family members are counted as a single shareholder)[37]
- All shareholders must be individuals, decedents' estates, bankruptcy estates, trusts permitted to own S Corp. stock, 501(c)(3) tax-exempt organizations, or 401(a) qualified plan trusts

---

[36] However, S Corporations are subject to tax on their built-in gains; their net capital gains, their excess passive income; and on investment credit that must be recaptured from the time after the creation of the corporation but prior to its Sub S election. *See* §§ 1363(d)(l), 1374, and 1375(a).

[37] Notice 2005-91, 2005-15 IRB 1164 provides preliminary guidance on how a family can elect to be treated as a single shareholder when the 100-shareholder limitation on an S Corporation is calculated. The election is made by notifying the corporation; notice to the IRS is not required. The notice must state who is making the election, the common ancestor the family claims, and the first tax year for which the election is effective.

- Not have any non-resident alien shareholders
- Have only one class of stock.

The American Jobs Creation Act of 2004 revises S Corporation governance, increasing the number of eligible businesses. The changes make it easier for C Corporations to convert to S Corporations, and for new businesses to make an S election, which has gained attractiveness because of the cuts in individual tax rates. The IRS has expanded powers to grant relief to a corporation that inadvertently makes an election that could cost it its S Corporation status.

As a result of the changes, shareholders within six generations of one family are considered a single shareholder. Powers of Appointment that are not exercised are not counted in determining the potential beneficiaries of an electing small business trust, and beneficiaries of an eligible small business trust who cease to be eligible to be S Corporation stockholders are given a year rather than the prior-law 60 days to dispose of the shares. Transfers of stock to a spouse or ex-spouse incident to a divorce can include transfers of suspended losses. When the trust disposes of S Corporation stock, its beneficiary can deduct suspended losses under the at-risk and passive-loss rules.

Initially, the eligibility of trusts to own Sub S shares was quite limited, but it has been expanded over time, and now many classes of trusts are permitted by § 1361(c)(2) to own Sub S shares. Grantor trusts, § 678 trusts (in which someone other than the grantor is treated as substantial owner of the Sub S stock), testamentary trusts (for two years after they are funded after the testator's demise), Electing Small Business Trusts (§ 1361(e)), and Qualified Subchapter S Trusts (§ 1361(d)) are all permissible shareholders. A voting trust (see § 1.10) is also a permissible shareholder, but each trust beneficiary counts toward the limit.

[2] Single Class of Stock

Although an S Corporation can have only one class of stock, this is not necessarily a severe limitation. As defined by § 1361(c)(4), a corporation has only one class of stock when no shares have been issued as a second class (e.g., an S Corporation cannot issue both preferred and common shares), and all stockholders have equal rights on the dissolution or liquidation of the corporation. Differential voting rights (including voting and non-voting common) are permissible.

Agreements that affect the transferability of the corporation's shares (such as buy-sells, redemption agreements, and transfer restrictions) do not create a second class of stock as long as they set a stock price reasonably close to FMV, and they are not intended to evade § 1361.

An option, warrant, or similar security, however, might constitute a second class of stock if it is issued at a price significantly below the fair market value of the shares and is therefore substantially certain to be exercised. Because of § 1361(c)(5), straight debt is not a second class of stock unless it is actually treated as equity under general tax principles, and is used to evade the reach of § 1361.

[3] Procedure for S Corporation Election

The rule of § 1362 is that the S election is made on Form 2553, which must be signed by an authorized corporate officer, and must evidence consent of all the shareholders.

The election can be made in one tax year for the following tax year, or until the 15th day of the third month of the year for which the election is supposed to take effect.

The IRS has the power, under § 1362(a)(5) to waive invalidity in an election, or to treat a late election as if it had been timely made (or even to treat a corporation as an S Corporation when no election was filed at all).

T.D. 9203, 2005-25 IRB 1285 contains Final Regulations for a simplified procedure for making the S Corporation election. A timely and valid S Corporation election will automatically be treated as an election to be classified as an association taxed as a corporation. So it is no longer necessary to file Form 8832 (Entity Classification Election) before the Sub S election; the Form 2553 Election by a Small Business Corporation serves both functions. This rule applies to elections filed on or after July 20, 2004, although taxpayers who filed earlier timely elections can also rely on it.

[4] Tax Treatment of S Corporation Stockholders

Once the election is effective, § 1366 provides that the S Corporation allocates items of income, loss, deduction, and credit for each day in the tax year on a pro rata basis among the individuals and entities who were shareholders on that day. A separate allocation to each shareholder is required whenever such treatment could affect the shareholder's own tax liability. The S Corporation files a tax return each year on Form 1120S, although this is a reporting return; the S Corporation itself is not a taxpayer. P.L. 110-142, the Mortgage Forgiveness Debt Relief Act, imposes a penalty of $85 per shareholder per month for failure to file a timely Form 1120S.

The shareholder takes the items into account in the shareholder's tax year that includes the last day of the S Corporation's tax year. (This provision is necessary because most S Corporation shareholders are individuals with calendar years, whereas fiscal years are very common for S Corporations.)

The amount of a distribution from an S Corporation to its shareholder is defined by §§ 301(c) and 1368(a) as the sum of cash and the fair market value (as of the time of the distribution) of any property distributed.

If the S Corporation did not have earnings and profits (E&P) as of the time of the distribution, the amount of the distribution reduces the shareholder's basis. If the distribution exceeds the shareholder's basis, then it is deemed payment for the stock and therefore will probably constitute capital gain for the shareholder.

If the corporation did have E&P as of the time of distribution, then § 1368 prescribes a complex series of calculations based on the corporation's Accumulated Adjustment Account.

Deductions, capital losses, and net operating losses are passed through and deducted by the shareholders, but § 1366(d)(1) limits the deduction to the shareholder's adjusted basis in the stock, adjusted for increases (attributable to the stockholder's share of S Corporation income) and decreases (for non-dividend distributions and debts of the corporation to the shareholder). The shareholder's basis cannot be reduced below zero (§ 1367), but carryovers are permitted for items that cannot be currently deducted. For contributions made in taxable years beginning after December 31, 2005, and before December 31, 2007, Pension Protection Act (P.L. 109-280) § 1203 amends Code § 1367(a) to provide that Sub S shareholders' reduction in basis by reason of the corporation's contributions of property to charity equals the shareholder's pro rata share of the adjusted basis of the property.

Notice 2008-1 provides rules under which 2% shareholder employees in an S Corporation can take a deduction under § 162(l) for accident and health premiums paid or reimbursed by the S Corporation and included in the shareholder's gross income. A&H premiums paid by an S Corporation for services rendered are considered partnership guaranteed payments under § 707(c), and are wages for withholding purposes but are not subject to FICA or Medicare taxes if the exclusion requirements of § 3121(a)(2)(B) are satisfied. The shareholder must include the premiums in gross income; although § 106 excludes employer-provided A&H coverage, it specifies that 2% shareholders are not considered employees. Code § 162(l)(1)(A) allows the shareholder to take a deduction against reported gross income if the S Corporation reports the premiums as wages on the W-2 form for the relevant year.[38]

Early in 2001, the Supreme Court ruled that discharge of the indebtedness of an insolvent S Corporation is not gross income for the corporation. However, it is an item of income that passes through to the shareholders under § 1366(a)(1), thus increasing their basis in the stock.[39]

Code § 6037(c) requires S Corporation shareholders to treat tax items consistently with the way they were reported by the S Corporation on its 1120S information return. Taxpayers who treat items inconsistently are obligated to file Form 6037 to notify the IRS of the discrepancy.

Because JGTRRA reduced tax rates for individual taxpayers but not corporations (although corporations did receive significant tax relief with respect to depreciation and expensing of equipment), this legislation complicated the traditional analysis for choosing between C and S Corporation form. The pass-through entity may gain attractiveness if the stockholders can expect to be taxed at lower rates than a C Corporation would incur.

---

[38] Notice 2008-1, 2008-2 IRB 251.
[39] Gitlitz v. CIR, 531 U.S. 206 (2001).

[5] Termination of S Corporation Status

The S Corporation election can be revoked on consent of the holders of a majority of the corporation's issued and outstanding stock (including any non-voting stock). Yet another possibility is involuntary termination of the election by the IRS, if and when the company ceases to qualify as an S Corporation (e.g., it has too many stockholders, or any ineligible stockholders) or if the corporation began as a C Corporation, accumulated E&P as a C Corporation, converted to Subchapter S status, and derived 25% or more of its income from passive sources for three consecutive years. See § 1362(d)(2).

For revocations and terminations occurring in 1997 and later years, § 1362(g) provides that five years must elapse before the corporation again elects Sub S status, unless the IRS permits an earlier election.

[B] Other Special Corporations

Two sections of the Code provide favorable treatment for the shareholders of small businesses. Under § 1202, a shareholder who received stock in the original issue of stock by a "qualified small business," and who received the stock in exchange for money, services to the corporation, or property other than corporate stock, and who holds the stock for at least five years before selling it, can exclude 50% of gain from taxable income.

A shareholder who sells certain small business stock covered by § 1244 can treat any gain as capital gain, but is entitled to treat any loss as an ordinary loss.

[C] Tax-Exempt Organizations

Although the bulk of business activities are conducted by for-profit corporations (or at least corporations intended to earn a profit, whatever actually happens), hundreds of thousands of organizations, ranging from small groups with limited activities to quasi-businesses with thousands of employees and millions of dollars in annual turnover, are operated as not-for-profit organizations.

There are two aspects of not-for-profit organization operation under the Internal Revenue Code. The first is whether the organization is an "exempt" organization in the sense that it is exempt from corporate tax on its own activities (other than income-earning business activities that are not related to the organization's exempt purpose).

The other is whether it is a "donative" non-profit: that is, whether contributors are entitled to donate contributions they make to the organization. (Note that, as discussed at § 20.06[H], an individual's donations to all charities are limited by the individual's "contribution base," but estates are entitled to an unlimited charitable deduction.)

Application for non-profit status is made on Form 1023 for 501(c)(3) organizations, Form 1024 for other kinds of tax-exempt organization. In mid-2007, the IRS proposed an overhaul of Form 990 (the not-for-profit tax return) to make it easier for the public — and the IRS! — to learn about the salaries of top management at charities and how much the organizations spend on fundraising. It was the first major redesign in more than two decades. The new form, with more schedules (15 rather than three, but most organizations would have to use only a few), is intended for use in reporting on the 2008 tax year.[40]

[1] Categories of Tax-Exempt Organizations

Once an organization is established as a tax-exempt organization, the next level of inquiry is whether it renders its services broadly and is under public or widely disseminated management. If so, it will be considered a "public charity." But an exempt organization whose aims are narrower, and/or which is dominated by a single family or company, may be treated as a "private foundation" and subjected to stricter tax requirements.

The Code recognizes many types of exempt organizations, including:

- § 501(c)(3) organizations, the best-known type; organizations with religious, charitable, scientific, literary, educational, or similar purposes
- § 501(c)(4) non-profit civic organizations for social welfare
- § 501(c)(5) labor, agricultural, and horticultural organizations
- § 501(c)(6) chambers of commerce, business leagues, boards of trade
- § 501(c)(7) social clubs.

In order to qualify as a § 501(c)(3) organization, an applicant must be organized and operated for its stated exempt purpose. No part of its net earnings can inure to private individuals. (This requirement prohibits profit-sharing, but not payment of reasonable salaries.) The organization can have members, but cannot have shareholders.

"Action organizations" devoted to propaganda, lobbying, and influencing legislation are not entitled to § 501(c)(3) characterization. (Charitable organizations that want to do substantial lobbying generally create a related organization that is not qualified under § 501(c)(3), and which solicits contributions that are not tax-deductible.)

A 501(c)(3) organization can lose its non-profit status if it engages in excessive lobbying, unless it qualifies under § 501(h) to make a revocable election on Form 5768 to spend permissible amounts on lobbying without sacrificing not-for-profit status. A two-tier excise tax is imposed on excessive political expenditures by § 4955. Code § 7409 gives the IRS power to apply for an injunction against flagrant political activity by a tax-exempt organization.

If an organization is, in effect, an ordinary profit-making business, it will be taxed on all its income — even if the income goes directly to an exempt organization, unless it qualifies as a § 502 "feeder" organization. A feeder

---

[40] The form is available at http://www.irs.gov/charities/article/0,,id=171216.00 html. *See* IR-2007-2004.

organization is exempt if it is controlled by, and provides services solely for, a single exempt organization or group of related exempt organizations.

The D.C. Circuit struck down IRS Regulations that insulated the IRS from disclosing written determinations about the denial or revocation of an organization's tax-exempt status. The court found that the regulations were contrary to the plain language of Code §§ 6104 and 6110's provisions about disclosure of tax-related information. Therefore, the IRS must comply with a proper disclosure request.[41]

[2] UBTI

The annual tax return for non-profits is Form 990. If the organization has Unrelated Business Taxable Income (UBTI) as defined by §§ 511–512, that income must be reported on Form 990-T.

UBTI is income deriving from a trade or business that the organization regularly carries out (even if it does so on a seasonal basis) that provides funding for the organization but is not otherwise related to the exempt purpose. However, if an activity is entirely carried out by volunteers, it will not generate UBTI.

UBTI is business income, not investment income: dividends, interest, rent, and royalties received by a not-for-profit organization are not taxed as UBTI.

Rev. Rul. 2004-51, 2004-22 IRB 974 deals with a university's joint venture with for-profit training firms to offer skills seminars for teachers. Because the seminars are substantially related to the university's exempt purpose, the university retains its § 501(c)(3) status if it contributes part of its assets and conducts part of its activities through a Limited Liability Company (LLC) formed with a for-profit corporation. The university's distributive share of the LLC's income does not constitute UBTI.

[3] Private Foundations

All 501(c)(3) organizations are presumed to be private foundations, unless they notify the IRS of their public charity status on Form 1023 within 15 months of the end of the first month in which the charity has been organized. (Churches and organizations with annual gross receipts under $5,000 are exempt.)

A private foundation is a non-profit that is not a "50% charity" (one eligible to receive contributions of a large part of a donor's income), is not publicly supported, or is controlled by "disqualified persons" who have too close a relationship to the organization.

Private foundations are subject to a number of excise taxes, imposed by §§ 4940–4945, that do not apply to other charitable organizations:

- Tax on net investment income
- Tax on self-dealing with closely related persons such as family members of the person who set up the foundation or major contributors

---

[41] Tax Analysts v. IRS, 350 F.3d 100 (D.C. Cir. 2003).

- Tax on a non-operating foundation's failure to distribute its net income
- Tax on investments that place the charitable purpose in jeopardy
- Tax on propaganda and political activities.

The private foundation income tax return is the Form 990-PF, an information return due on the fifteenth day of the fifth month after the close of the foundation's tax year. See the Pension Protection Act, P.L. 109-280, for limitations on the activities of "donor-advised funds" — private foundations that give donors a high degree of control over operations. In general, reform of non-profit organizations and charitable giving is an objective of the PPA.

Chapter 5

Mergers and Acquisitions

§ 5.01 INTRODUCTION

In the 1980s, the law governing mergers and acquisitions, especially hostile takeovers, was one of the most volatile and eagerly followed areas of the law. It became quiescent in the 1990s, until the emergence of commercial activity on the Internet lead to a rash of initial public offerings — and a high degree of concentration as failing companies merged or stronger companies acquired their weaker competitors. Thus, at the end of the 1990s, M&A law once again became a hot topic, a situation that was only exacerbated by the dot.com collapse of 2001, although eventually the IPO and merger markets recovered somewhat.

In 2008, turmoil in the credit markets made it difficult to raise capital for deals, leading to a significant reduction in deal volume. For example, in the first nine months of 2007, $3.3 trillion in deal volume was announced — versus only $2.5 trillion (a 25.5% decline) in the first three quarters of 2008. As of the third quarter of 2008, there were 20,368 completed deals worth a total of $2 trillion — versus 23,307 completed deals and $2.8 trillion total value for the year before; deal value therefore declined more than 25%.

However, some deals continued to be consummated with innovative capital structures. For example, two companies financed a strategic merger by having the buyer issue cash and stock to the target's shareholders. The buyer could also use secured notes for some of the cash obligations under the deal, if no third-party financing is available. Although previously, leveraged buyouts usually were done with cash, some recent deals have made part of the compensation to the target's shareholders in the form of notes and equity in the merged entity. A common British tactic, the "certain funds provision," is gaining popularity in the United States: private equity funders are required to consummate the deal unless there is a breach of the representations made by the seller in the acquisition agreement. Other transactions are being structured with a fall-back option in case the most desirable option falls through (e.g., preferred structure of cash and stock versus alternative of cash, stock, and senior secured notes if the purchaser cannot secure bank financing).[1]

The financial crisis actually promoted certain types of transactions — for example, mergers or takeovers of financial services firms that were overwhelmed by bad debt. The Emergency Economic Stabilization Act (EESA; P.L. 110-334) § 126(c) makes agreements unenforceable if they attempt to restrict the sale of any lending institution after the FDIC has taken a role in confronting "systemic risk" in the mortgage market. This provision came into play during litigation over Citigroup's unsuccessful attempt to purchase Wachovia Corp. Wachovia's argument was that Citigroup's letter agreement to purchase Wachovia violated this section and therefore was unenforceable on public policy grounds.[2]

As soon as a corporation becomes public, and its shares can be freely purchased by anyone, the corporation becomes a potential target for a hostile takeover or "greenmail" (i.e., a person who does not actually want to take over the corporation to run it threatens a takeover, hoping to be paid to go away). See § 5.03 for a discussion of "poison pills" and other measures that a company can take to protect itself against hostile takeovers.

If one or both corporations involved is very large, or if the market in which they operate is so small that eliminating a competitor could have a major effect on competition, antitrust issues may arise. See § 8.05 for a discussion of approval under the Hart-Scott-Rodino Act, and other antitrust implications.

---

[1] Sheri Qualters, *Creative Financing Closes Deals in Tight Credit Market*, Nat'l L.J. 10/10/08 (law.com).

[2] *See, e.g.*, Mark Hamblett, *Citigroup Drops Bid to Block Wachovia Sale, Presses Ahead With $60 Billion Suit for Damages*, N.Y.L.J. 10/14/08 (law.com).

Section 702 of the Pension Protection Act, P.L. 109-280 (see § 3.05[H]), gives the Treasury 12 months to issue regulations covering M&A issues when a pension plan is converted to cash balance form.

Note that the Small Business Administration's rule, effective June 30, 2007, covering new federal contracts lasting five years or more also covers contracts where a novation, merger, or acquisition has occurred. Federal contracting officers must request companies that obtained contracts as small businesses to recertify their small business status within 30 days of a merger or novation. Contracting officers have the discretion to terminate the contract if recertification is not made, but termination is not mandatory.[3]

In 2008, the Delaware Court of Chancery ordered a private equity firm and a chemical manufacturer to make their best effort to close the acquisition of another chemical company, and to comply with the merger agreement. The next day, Texas' Montgomery County District Court issued a TRO against two banks forbidding them to take any action that would impair the consummation of financing for that transaction. After the deal had been negotiated, but before regulatory approval had been secured, the target company reported poor quarterly figures. The planned acquirer made a declaratory judgment motion for permission to cancel the deal, on the grounds that the target company had suffered a material adverse effect on its business, and the combined company would be insolvent. The now-unwilling potential acquirer also asked the court to cap its termination fee for exiting the deal. However, the Delaware Court of Chancery denied the motions, finding that the company intentionally breached its contract and also violated an implied covenant of good faith and fair dealing in connection with the merger. The court found that both companies are solvent and profitable.[4]

§ 5.02 TYPES OF TRANSACTIONS

Various kinds of transactions involving either aggregation or disaggregation of companies can be carried out. The particular structure that is chosen determines what kind of agreements can be made; who has to approve them (e.g., the Boards of Directors of all corporations involved; all the shareholders; a plurality or majority of shareholders); whether tax will be due for the year of the transaction; and the future tax status of the surviving corporation(s).

Seven kinds of transactions can be engaged in tax-free: Types A, B, and C reorganizations; spin-off, split-off, or split-up; recapitalization; change in identity or form; or transfer of assets from a bankrupt corporation to another corporation. As a general rule, tax-free reorganizations are governed by Internal Revenue Code

---

[3] 71 FR 66434 (11/15/06); *see* Manik K. Rath and Tamara Jack, *Practical Implications of New Small Business Rule on M&A Activities*, Special to law.com (7/18/07).

[4] Hexion Specialty Chemicals Inc. v. Huntsman Corp., No. 3841-VCL (Del. Ch. 2008); Huntsman Corp. v. Credit Suisse Securities (USA) LLC, No. 08-09-09258 (Tex. Dist. Ct. 2008); *see* Sheri Qualters, *Banks Feel the Texas Heat Over Chemical Companies' Merger Deal*, 10/2/08 (law.com).

§ 368. In addition to the requirements of the Code, courts have imposed various conditions on tax-free reorganizations: e.g., that there be a continuity of business enterprise and business purpose as well as continuity of interest in the shareholder group before and after the transactions. The target company's shareholders will be considered to have an ongoing proprietary interest if they receive approximately 40–50% of the acquiring company's stock, although there is no requirement that they retain it for any particular length of time. If the transaction fails to fit into one of these categories, it will be taxable, and all realized gain or loss must be recognized. See § 4.11[C] for taxation of reorganizations.

One of the most significant issues is whether the merged or acquired corporation will sell its assets, or will sell its stock. It is also very significant what consideration the surviving/acquiring corporation will furnish: all cash, all shares of its own stock, or somewhere in between. The buyer has a natural interest in deriving as much of the consideration as possible from shares of its own stock rather than cash, but a rise in stock prices can make an acquisition more expensive than originally planned.

The price of the transaction can be fixed and determined in advance; or it might be contingent on various things; or it may be subject to an obligation to make continuing payments, which in turn may be contingent on earnings, profits, or other factors.

For tax purposes, a statutory merger (one that satisfies state law) is known as a Type A reorganization. Type B is a stock-for-stock transaction; Type C involves exchange of one corporation's stock for another corporation's assets.

[A] Sale of Assets

A corporation can sell all or part of its assets to another corporation; and a potential buyer can acquire certain assets while rejecting others. The buyer is entitled to step up the basis in the acquired assets to reflect fair market value as of the acquisition.

The stockholders of the seller corporation must approve the transaction, but the buyer corporation does not have to obtain approval from its own shareholders. In many cases, the seller will need permission from lenders and other major creditors, because loan and sale contracts often require permission before the buyer/debtor sells its assets or otherwise engages in transactions out of the ordinary course of business.

However, a sale of assets is more expensive (because schedules of assets have to be prepared, and each asset has to be valued) and takes longer to consummate than a sale of stock. It may also be disfavored by the seller, because it is subject to double taxation. Dissenting stockholders in the selling corporation may have appraisal rights: i.e., the right to have their shares bought back by the selling corporation.

The Second Circuit identified continuity of ownership as the essence of a merger; unless this is present, the New York doctrine of de facto merger will not make the purchaser of assets liable to the trade creditors of the asset seller for contract debts.[5] The Delaware Supreme Court ruled that stockholders could not block the sale of a subsidiary — the parent corporation continued to retain other assets, so it was not selling substantially all of its assets.[6]

Under California law, a plaintiff who ceases to be a stockholder in a corporation because of the corporation's merger loses standing to continue litigating a derivative action. The business in question was incorporated in Delaware, and Delaware law requires a derivative suit plaintiff to have continuous stock ownership as long as the suit is pending. (Some limited exceptions are recognized — e.g., when it is alleged that the merger itself is a fraud entered into solely to deprive shareholders of their standing, or the merger is actually a reorganization and the plaintiff's ownership interest is not affected.) The California statute requires the plaintiff to be a shareholder at the time of the allegedly improper transaction giving rise to the suit, unless the plaintiff became a shareholder before the wrongdoing was disclosed, and denying the plaintiff standing to sue would permit the defendant to retain profits from willful breach of fiduciary duty. But, in general, California requires continuous ownership, because corporations are managed by their Boards of Directors and not their shareholders. A derivative action is brought for stockholders to enforce the corporation's rights when the board refuses to do so. The claim belongs to the corporation, not the stockholders, so the stockholder relationship is a prerequisite to standing to sue.[7]

Effective May 30, 2006, Rev. Proc. 2006-21 (2006-24 IRB 1050) and T.D. 9264 (2006-26 IRB 1150) reduce the reporting requirements for tax-free transfers to corporations in connection with mergers, spin-offs, and liquidations. Only significant shareholders (owning 5% of a public corporation or 1% of a private one) and holders of securities with a basis of $1 million or more must file information statements for § 351 transfers.

Although most of this discussion deals with corporate mergers, IRS's REG-143397-05[8] proposes regulations for treatment of property distributions in connection with an asset-over merger between two partnerships, because Code § 704(c)(1)(B) generally requires partners to recognize gain or loss on the distribution of property they contributed to the partnership if it is distributed to another partner within seven years of the initial contribution. But this general rule does not apply to an arrangement to transfer all of the assets of one partnership to another partnership, liquidating the transferor partnership.

---

[5] Cargo Partner AG v. Albatross Inc., 352 F.3d 41 (2d Cir. 2003).

[6] Black v. Hollinger Int'l Inc., 872 A.2d 559 (Del. 2005). Delaware H.B. 150 (2005) permits sales of corporate assets to a wholly-owned and controlled subsidiary without approval of the shareholders of the parent corporation.

[7] Grosset v. Wenaas, 42 Cal. 4th 1100 (Cal. 2008).

[8] 2007-41 IRB 790.

[B] Sale of Stock

Most transactions are carried out as either a merger or consolidation (in which both constituent companies dissolve and are replaced by a surviving company); a stock-for-stock sale, in which the selling company surrenders its own stock in return for stock of the buying company; or a deal in which the acquiring company buys the selling company's stock. It should be noted that, in a stock deal, the buyer company assumes all of the liabilities of the seller company — a result that is not necessarily obtained in an asset sale.

The selling company's stockholders must consent to the transaction; in many situations, the buyer company's stockholders must also consent. Appraisal rights may be available to dissenting stockholders.

Although a sale of stock can be structured to be tax-free, the selling corporation does not get a step up in basis for the assets that come along with the stock, unless the deal satisfies Code § 338.[9]

[C] The Due Diligence Process

Before entering into a major transaction, a corporation must engage in "due diligence" — a complete examination of all facets of the potential deal. Failure to engage in due diligence can subject the corporation, and perhaps its officers, to liability to its own stockholders.

If due diligence is not performed, the acquiring corporation may find that it is a successor that has assumed some of the acquired corporation's obligations (such as its union contracts) or liabilities (such as environmental liability; products liability; unpaid taxes and penalties).

The due diligence process requires asking the other corporation for detailed information about its customers, work force, products, hard assets, intellectual property and other intangible assets, and financial condition. Moreover, all such contentions must be verified, not merely accepted on trust.

Financial due diligence issues include:

- Are the figures audited, and has the company received a clean opinion from its auditor?
- What are the profit margins on the various product lines?
- Are each operation's sales and general expenses modest or oversized?
- Are each operation's accounting assumptions conservative or aggressive, and what can be done to harmonize discrepancies?
- What is the capital structure (debt vs. equity) of each, and how much working capital does each have?
- What are the business and strategic plans for each?
- What are the sales forecasts and budgets for each?

---

[9] *See* T.D. 9271, 2006-33 IRB 224, permitting certain multi-step transactions to qualify under § 338 without receiving unfavorable treatment as abusive "step transactions."

- What deferred compensation and employee benefit plans does each maintain, and will the new entity adopt the more or the less generous plan structure?
- How reliable are the internal controls within each organization?

Corporate due diligence must also be performed, determining what provisions appear in the corporation's charter and bylaws; what resolutions have been passed; whether the corporation is a subsidiary or has subsidiaries; and how the securities are held.

It must be determined whether the deal could involve antitrust or other regulatory problems. The tax implications of various potential deal structures must be considered, and an important part of the negotiation will be choosing structures favorable to the negotiating entity.

[D] Documents and Drafting

The due diligence process (see § 5.02[C]) requires each corporation to learn a great deal about the other. To prevent misuse of confidential and proprietary information, negotiating parties generally begin by signing a non-disclosure agreement (NDA). In some transactions, the agreement is precedent by a Letter of Intent (LOI). Furthermore, if the acquiring company is a public company, securities law may require it to disclose to the public when negotiations are under way.

[1] Letter of Intent

The Letter of Intent includes full disclosure of:

- Non-disclosure provisions (unless an NDA is already in place)
- Preliminary pricing data
- A "no-shop" provision, also known as a "lock-up," which prevents the potential seller from seeking a higher offer elsewhere
- The seller's covenant to continue doing business normally during the negotiations, and not to divest assets or otherwise decrease its value
- Allocation of expenses of the transaction between the parties
- Provision for a breakup fee — an amount to be paid in case the transaction is not consummated.

[2] Contract of Sale

The contract of sale includes:

- Conditions for closing the deal (e.g., approval by lenders and stockholders)
- Final pricing structure, e.g., $X in cash and Y shares of stock in the buyer corporation, to be paid pursuant to a particular schedule; or exchange of X shares of the seller corporation's stock for every Y shares of the buyer corporation's

- Representations and warranties by the party; most of these relate to the seller rather than the buyer
- Agreements about how the business will be maintained until the closing
- Reciprocal indemnification of the parties
- Other documents attached as schedules or appendices (e.g., financial statements; union contracts; long-term business contracts).

[E] Effect of Accounting Issues

For accounting purposes, in an asset-purchase deal, the buyer values the acquired assets and liabilities at their fair market value. When assets are written up to reflect the increase in market value since their acquisition, the amount of the write-up must be depreciated. Goodwill (the difference between the actual purchase price and the aggregate FMV of the assets) must be amortized over a period of years.

This is one of the areas in which tax accounting diverges from general accounting. For tax purposes, the taxpayer usually wants as many deductions as possible, and wants to take those deductions in a single year or over a short period of time. But for general accounting purposes, the corporation usually wants to show high earnings, and does not want depreciation and amortization to continue to depress earnings for many years at a time.

The current standard for accounting for mergers and acquisitions is FAS 141, Business Combinations, which replaces APB 16. Previously, "pooling" (combining results for acquired and acquiring companies) offered favorable results in many deals, but it was forbidden for business combinations initiated after June 30, 2001. Current accounting treatment does not permit amortization of goodwill or intangible assets with indefinite lives. Otherwise, intangible assets must be amortized over their useful life; the former limitation of the theoretical useful life to 40 years has been removed.

[F] State and Local Tax Issues

The treatment of a transaction under state and local tax regimes is not necessarily the same as its treatment under the Internal Revenue Code. It is important to determine ahead of time what state and local tax consequences will ensue; in which jurisdiction(s) nexus is present so that the transaction can be subjected to tax; where sales and transfer taxes will be imposed; and what filings and other compliance measures will be required. In some instances, acquiring assets within a state will create nexus, so that the acquiror will be subject to local tax for the first time.

According to a 1977 Supreme Court case, the Commerce Clause requires fair apportionment of tax, on the basis of services provided by the state, without discrimination against interstate commerce.[10]

---

[10] Complete Auto Transit Inc. v. Brady, 430 U.S. 274 (1977).

§ 5.03   DEFENSIVE MEASURES

Incumbent management, understandably, often opposes unsolicited takeover attempts. In some instances, a corporation can attempt to protect itself against hostile takeovers by adopting Articles of Incorporation provisions or bylaws that discourage takeover attempts.

Depending on the nature of the corporation, how its stock is held, the terms of the proposed takeover, and the success of the current management, the stockholders may be grateful for these protective measures — or may deem them to be an abusive attempt by incompetent managers to protect their own jobs at the expense of stockholder interests.

Given the role of Delaware as the home of so many major corporations, the leading case law on hostile takeovers comes from the Delaware courts, especially its Court of Chancery.

[A] The Business Judgment Rule

Although the business judgment rule applies to all corporate actions, it is perhaps most often evoked in the M&A context. Corporate directors are not personally liable for their business decisions if they act in good faith, on sufficient information, and as they reasonably believe is in the best interests of the corporation's shareholders. Business decisions are presumed to satisfy this rule if all three tests are satisfied, and if there has been no fraud, bad faith, or self-dealing. However, if the presumption is unavailable, then the directors must prove that their actions were fair.[11] In the tender offer context, the business judgment rule will apply, subject to additional scrutiny. (Heightened scrutiny is applied because of the potential conflict of interest between directors who want to retain their power, and stockholders the valuation of whose shares might increase under another regime.)

Delaware ruled in late 2003 that if the price paid to acquire a company is fair, the bad faith of its independent directors or the unfairness of the procedure for approving mergers is irrelevant. Although it was procedurally improper to allow the target's CFO to participant in the board's deliberations, the shareholders were not awarded any damages because the price was fair.[12]

The basic test of *Unocal v. Mesa Petroleum*[13] is that directors who adopt defensive measures against a takeover must have acted on a reasonable belief that the takeover threatened corporate policy and effectiveness. The defensive measures must have been reasonable in the context of the actual threat. Furthermore, all decisions by directors must have been made based on complete information about the situation; hasty and ill-informed decisions are likely to result in personal liability for the directors.[14]

---

[11] *See* Aronson v. Lewis, 473 A.2d 805 (Del. 1984); Cede & Co. v. Technicolor, 634 A.2d 345 (Del. 1993).

[12] Emerald Partners v. Berlin, 840 A.2d 641 (Del. 2003).

[13] 493 A.2d 946 (Del. Sup. 1985).

[14] *See, e.g.*, Smith v. Van Gorkom, 488 A.2d 858 (Del. 1985).

The board must get complete information about all available offers. Once it becomes inevitable that the corporation's control will shift (whether the corporation itself initiated the sale process or the takeover attempt was unsolicited), or that it will be broken up, the board of directors have a fiduciary obligation to "auction" the company in a way resulting in the greatest possible value to shareholders.[15] However, a "just say no" strategy is permissible if an unsolicited takeover bid is deemed by the board to violate the corporate culture or otherwise harm the shareholders.[16] The board must provide enough information so stockholders can make an informed decision, including enough financial information to determine if a proposed transaction is in their best interests.[17] Dealing with only one bidder, taken by itself, is not a breach of fiduciary duty, because expediting the sale process can be advantageous to the corporation that is sold.[18] Under Delaware law, a corporation's Certificate of Incorporation can limit or eliminate the personal financial liability of directors when shareholders sue for breach of fiduciary duty, as long as the director did not breach the duty of loyalty.[19] A provision of this type will justify dismissal of a suit against directors brought by shareholders for breach of the duty of care, but not a suit for breach of the duty of care brought by creditors of an insolvent company.[20]

Judicial review of a transaction will use the "entire fairness to stockholders" standard only as a last resort for protecting shareholders against self-dealing by the board of directors. The standard is not used if the transaction provided procedural protections such as approval by independent directors or ratification by shareholder vote.[21] However, if the standard does apply, directors will be held liable for violations of the duty of loyalty even if they did not receive direct personal benefit from the transaction.[22] In 2003, the Delaware Court of Chancery applied the "entire fairness" standard to a merger with the company's majority shareholder on the grounds that such transactions are inherently coercive. Therefore, even minority shareholders who voted for the transaction can sue based on a claim that the price was unfair.[23]

[B] Poison Pills and Other Devices

Various provisions can be adopted by a corporation to make itself a less attractive target for a hostile takeover. However, the obligation of the corporation's board of directors is to act in the best interest of stockholders, which can include

---

[15] Revlon, Inc. v. MacAndrews & Forbes Holdings, Inc., 506 A.2d 173 (Del. 1986).
[16] Paramount Communications, Inc. v. Time, Inc., 571 A.2d 1140 (Del. Sup. 1989).
[17] Turner v. Bernstein, 776 A.2d 530 (Del. Ch. 2000).
[18] In re Pennaco Energy, Inc., 787 A.2d 691 (Del. Ch. 2001).
[19] Lu v. Malpiede, 780 A.2d 1075 (Del. 2001).
[20] Pereira v. Cogan, 275 B.R. 472 (S.D.N.Y. 2001); Steinberg v. Kendig, 2000 WL 28266 (N.D. Ill. 2000).
[21] In re Staples Inc. Shareholder Litigation, 792 A.2d 934 (Del. Ch. 2001).
[22] Strassburger v. Earley, 752 A.2d 557 (Del. Ch. 2000).
[23] In re JCC Holding Co. Shareholders Litig., 72 LW 1311 (Del. Ch. 9/30/03).

auctioning off the company to the highest bidder once the company is "in play" (a potential takeover target). Defensive measures must not be "draconian," "coercive," or "preclusive": i.e., they may operate to make the eventual transaction more beneficial to stockholders, but may not operate to prevent any transaction at all under any circumstances.[24]

In a decision that assumed additional significance because so many public corporations are incorporated in Delaware, the Delaware Supreme Court decided in early 2003 that even though a "board-packing" plan (the incumbent management voted to add two new, and presumably sympathetic, directors to the five-member board) was permitted by the company's bylaws, it was still invalid. Because the change in corporate governance occurred during a contested election (the entrenched board expected that two dissidents would be elected to the five-member board), the defensive move violated the shareholders' rights to corporate democracy. The business judgment rule did not shelter the directors' action, because their primary purpose was the improper one of interfering with a shareholder vote.[25]

[1] Lock-Ups

A "lock-up" is an arrangement under which a potential acquiror (typically, a "white knight" favored by the current management) takes an option or has the right to acquire major corporate assets or blocks of the target corporation's stock. Lock-ups are not illegal, but they are invalid if adopted to favor one potential bidder and prevent other potential bidders from engaging in the auction required by *Revlon*. Granting a lock-up can breach the directors' duty of loyalty if it is adopted for a self-interested or other improper purpose.

The target corporation can lawfully offer break-up or engagement fees to compensate a white knight for its expenses of a contest for control, as long as the effect is to increase the competitiveness of the auction, rather than precluding a vigorous bidding contest.[26]

[2] Shareholder Rights Plans

A shareholder rights plan, often known as a "poison pill," is a plan to discourage hostile takeovers while encouraging friendly offers. A legitimate shareholder rights plan must not have the purpose or effect of discouraging proxy contests or fair offers for acquisition of the entire company.

The poison pill works by giving the pre-takeover shareholders the right to buy stock in the target (or, sometimes, the potential acquiror) at a deep discount, if

---

[24] For instance, *see* Unitrin, Inc. v. American General Corp., 651 A.2d 1361 (Del. 1995); Moore Corp. Ltd. v. Wallace Computer Services, 907 F. Supp. 1545 (D. Del. 1995).

[25] MM Cos. Inc. v. Liquid Audio Inc., 813 A.2d 1118 (Del. 2003).

[26] Samjens Partners I v. Burlington Indus. Inc., 663 F. Supp. 614 (S.D.N.Y. 1987); CRTF Corp. v. Federated Department Stores, Inc., 683 F. Supp. 422 (S.D.N.Y. 1988); Brazen v. Bell Atlantic Corp., 695 A.2d 43 (Del. 1997).

certain business combinations occur or if a specified percentage of the target's stock is acquired. The effect is to dilute the interest already acquired by the acquiror.

Under appropriate circumstances[27] adoption of a poison pill can be a permissible defensive measure that satisfies the business judgment rule. However, a plan that makes it impossible to undertake any hostile takeover is invalid, because it entrenches existing management even if this is not in the best interests of the shareholders.[28]

§ 5.04 SECURITIES LAW IMPLICATIONS

In some instances, it will be possible to do a "street sweep": acquire enough securities on the open market to gain control. Generally, however, a hostile takeover will be structured either as a proxy contest or a tender offer. The proxy contest is a method of gaining voting control over a corporation by getting existing stockholders to give the contestant the right to vote their shares. A tender offer solicits stockholders to sell their shares. Federal securities law requires adequate disclosure of the proposed transaction.

[A] Tender Offers

If a target's board of directors is hostile to the possibility of merger or acquisition, the buyer often responds by making a tender offer directly to the shareholders: i.e., offering to purchase shares that they "tender," or make available.

The Williams Act, '34 Act §§ 13–14, is designed to protect target shareholders from raiders. Like most securities statutes, it is disclosure-oriented. Notification must be filed with the SEC of the buyer's background, identity, residence, and citizenship; the purpose of the stock purchase; source and amount of funds used to buy the shares; the number acquired; and disclosure of any contracts, arrangements, or understandings about the target company's securities. The SEC's Tender Offer Statement is Schedule 14D-1.

Tender offers must be kept open for at least 20 business days, plus at least 10 business days after a change in the amount of securities sought or the price offered for them, so target stockholders will have a chance to review the disclosure materials provided to them.

[B] The Regulation M&A Release

The SEC's Regulation M&A Release, Release 33-7760, 17 CFR §§ 229.1000–1016, was one of the biggest changes in the regulation of mergers and acquisitions in a generation. Under previous rules, a quiet period was imposed from the time a merger was announced until the approval of the registration or

---

[27] Moran v. Household Int'l, Inc., 490 A.2d 1059 (Del. Ch.), *aff'd*, 500 A.2d 1346 (Del. 1985).

[28] City Capital Associates Ltd. Partnership v. Interco Inc., 551 A.2d 787 (Del. Ch. 1988); Grand Metro. PLC v. Pillsbury Co., 1988–1989 CCH Fed. Sec. L. Rep. § 94,104 (Del. Ch. 12/16/88).

proxy statement. However, Regulation M&A gave merging companies greater freedom to communicate with the investing public. As long as written communications are filed with EDGAR, the merging companies can make public statements before the effective date. Oral communications (e.g., speeches, conference calls, slide shows) can be made without filing.

Before this Release, the SEC treated a stock offer as a sale of securities for which a registration statement must be filed. Regulation M&A changed this rule in order to facilitate non-cash takeovers in situations where the acquiror prefers to use stock.

An offeror can use "early commencement" by filing a registration statement and starting the exchange offer immediately. However, the purchase of the tendered securities has to wait until effectiveness, the 20-business-day-tender offer period has expired, and the holders of the securities get disclosure of all material changes to the offering documents in time to review and act on the changes.

The M&A Release calls for consolidation of all schedules for issuer and third-party tender offers into a single Schedule TO. A summary term sheet in plain English must be furnished for all tender offers, mergers, and going-private transactions; as it streamlines the requirements for disclosing financial statements for business combinations.

§ 5.05 M&A ANTITRUST ISSUES

Gun-jumping by coordinating activities between now-competitors that plan to merge, or combining distribution networks before the transaction, can have negative (even criminal) antitrust consequences. Gun-jumping comes from the Sherman Act prohibition on conduct that unreasonably restrains trade. Acquiring firms can get into trouble if pre-merger conduct (before the two enterprises become a single one) involves, e.g., shared distribution channels or rationalization of production facilities. Pre-closing integration is forbidden even if the actual merger does not raise antitrust concerns.

The FTC and DOJ admit that merging firms can legitimately coordinate in the context of due diligence and transition planning, but a legal team can help by putting firewalls around the integration team so information is shared only on a need-to-know basis. Sometimes the best strategy is for competitively sensitive data to be transmitted to a third-party consultant who prepares summaries for the integration team. It is permissible for the merged entity to launch a new Web page right after closing, with input from the IT team before the closing, as long as the site does not give access to sensitive competitive information such as customer names or price lists.

To avoid accessing too much sensitive information, the integration team can start by accessing only the information needed for the broadest decisions (e.g., about plant closings), and then move into a narrower focus. However, some cost information may still be so sensitive that the detailed information should be in the possession of a third party, with the integration team receiving only a summary version. If the deal falls through, less information will have been disclosed.

Antitrust specialist James T. McKeown counsels continuing to compete vigorously until actual consummation of the transaction. Designate a small team to communicate about the pending transactions, and make sure everybody else refers queries to them. Existing agreements with suppliers, dealers, and franchisees should be reviewed for existing confidentiality provisions that could limit information exchange. Current or future pricing strategies (e.g., dealer discounts) should not be discussed with current customers. Neither of the potential merged organizations should be given veto power over transactions by the other. Sales personnel should not be shared or exchanged. Current customers should not be advised to direct business to the future merger partner but current competitor. Each company's fall-back plans (in case the deal does not close) should not be shared with the potential merger partner.[29]

Clayton Act § 7 allows the federal government to block any acquisition that has the effect of lessening competition substantially or creating a monopoly. The determination depends on factors such as the market share of buyer and seller and the market dominance that would be gained by a proposed merger. The FTC can issue a preliminary injunction against a proposed merger, under FTC Act § 13(b), pending the resolution of Clayton Act § 7 charges.

In practice, however, the unsuccessful 2004 attempt by the Department of Justice's Antitrust Division to block the merger between Oracle Corporation and PeopleSoft was the last time the DOJ went to trial to block a merger.[30]

Note that *Cargill v. Monfort*[31] holds that a business cannot bring a Clayton Act case challenging a merger of two competitors on the basis of an alleged "cost-price squeeze" from the merged companies. In the Supreme Court's analysis, any such price reductions would be laudable price competition, not violative anticompetitive conduct.

Since 1976, the Clayton Act has also contained § 7A, added by the Hart-Scott-Rodino Antitrust Improvements Act of 1976 as amended by the Twenty-First Century Acquisition Reform and Improvement Act of 2000, effective February 1, 2001. Companies that desire a merger must give the government specified information about the transaction, and must abide by a waiting period that gives the FTC time to assess potential antitrust impact. The waiting period is 30 days, reduced to 15 days for a cash tender offer.

Both the acquiring and acquired companies must file pre-merger notification if three conditions are all present:

(1)   Either one is engaged in interstate commerce or in any activity affecting interstate commerce. (If either company is listed on a stock exchange, stock exchange requirements may also have to be satisfied.)

---

[29] James T. McKeown, *Don't Jump the Gun: Antitrust Limits on M&A Pre-Closing Conduct,* The Corporate Counselor 10/21/08 (law.com).

[30] Jason McLure, *Has the Antitrust Division Lost Its Nerve?* Legal Times 1/11/07 (law.com).

[31] 479 U.S. 104 (1986).

(2) The acquiring company has $100 million in annual net sales or total assets and the acquired company has $10 million in total assets or net sales, or vice versa. (HSR figures are subject to inflation adjustment.)

(3) The acquiror would have at least 15% of the acquired company's stock, or would own over $15 million of combined stock and assets of the acquired company.

The FTC revised the Hart-Scott-Rodino thresholds under the Clayton Act § 7A, raising the $10 million figure to $12 million, and $100 million to $119.6 million. The revisions take effect 30 days after publication of the notice in the Federal Register.[32]

The Department of Justice's October 2004 guidelines allow the government to order remedies that are less drastic than stopping a merger: for example, negotiated settlements and "fix it first" remedies to protect competition itself, rather than competitors in the market.

"Structural" merger remedies generally require the merging firms to sell physical assets or create new competitors, such as through the licensing of intellectual property assets. "Conduct" remedies are usually injunctions that regulate the post-merger conduct of the regulated firm. The DOJ prefers structural remedies to avoid the necessity of ongoing supervision that conduct remedies bring with them. Full divestiture, including tangible and intangible assets, is preferred to partial divestiture.

However, conduct relief is justified in limited situations, for example, where the merged firm's conduct would have to be modified for structural relief to be effective, or where prohibiting the merger would reduce the efficiency of the industry. To be acceptable, "fix-it-first" remedies are judged by the same standard as consent decrees, and must be designed to eliminate the competitive harm that the proposed merger could do.[33]

§ 5.06 TRANSACTION TAX ISSUES

The Tax Court required[34] a bank to capitalize costs, such as investigative costs and legal fees, incurred before deciding to implement a merger. The costs had to be capitalized, and could not be deducted currently as costs related to expanding an ongoing business. Capitalization is required because of the connection to a transaction with significant long-term benefits. However, if the merger had been abandoned rather than consummated, the costs would have been deductible.

The Tax Court also required legal fees to be deducted when they arose in connection with anti-trust litigation and an FTC consent decree connected to one store chain's acquisition of another store chain.[35] The basic principle is that fees

---

[32] FTC Notice Billing Code 6750-02P; FTC File No. P859910 (1/16/07); http://www.ftc.gov.

[33] Antitrust Policy Division Guide to Merger Remedies, http://www.usdoj.gov/atr/public/guidelines/205108/htm (10/21/04); see 73 L.W. 2243.

[34] Norwest Corp., 112 T.C. No. 8 (1999).

[35] American Stores Co. v. Comm'r, 114 T.C. No. 27 (5/26/00).

paid to lawyers and investment bankers in connection with a friendly takeover are capital expenses if they result in a long-term benefit to the organization that emerges from the transaction. The expenses of resisting a hostile takeover are deductible if the resistance effort succeeds in preventing the takeover.

The American Jobs Creation Act of 2004, P.L. 108-357, added a new Code § 6034A. If the shareholders of a target corporation recognize any gain from the transaction, the acquiring corporation has additional reporting requirements to the IRS and the target company's shareholder. This provision applies whether the target's stock or assets were acquired.

Mergers or consolidations of pension plans, or spinoffs or a single plan into multiple plans, as well as transfer of assets or liabilities between pension plans, must be reported on IRS Form 5310-A.

In early 2005, rules were published for tax-free treatment under § 354 for cross-border mergers organized under foreign law. This is a departure from prior law that only granted tax-free status to mergers organized under federal or state U.S. law. The rules also cover the application of § 367 and basis, holding periods, asset transfers, and triangular reorganizations under § 368(a)(1)(A).[36]

Comprehensive Final Regulations were issued on the definition of a statutory merger or consolidation, to determine if a transaction is an A Reorganization. T.D. 9242 allows some transactions under foreign jurisdictions, including U.S. possessions, to qualify as an A Reorganization. Nonrecognition treatment is available pursuant to T.D. 9242 if the corporation continues as a consolidated or amalgamated corporation and the separate legal existence of the target is terminated. The rules of § 358 are used to test the basis of stock or securities received in the reorganization, with special basis and holding requirements for triangular reorganizations. Treatment as a statutory merger or consolidation is not available if the transaction is structured as acquisition of the stock of the target corporation, and conversion of the target into an LLC. In general, U.S. taxpayers must recognize gain on transfers of property to foreign corporations, but, unless there is an indirect stock transfer, this rule does not apply to §§ 354 or 356 exchanges of stock or securities under an asset reorganization. Form 926, which must be filed by U.S. taxpayers who transfer property to a foreign corporation (see Code § 6038B), no longer requires a manual signature and therefore can be e-filed.[37]

---

[36] Notice 2005-6, 2005-5 IRB 448; REG-125628-01, 70 F.R. 749 (1/5/05).

[37] T.D.s 9242, 9243, 2006-7 IRB 422, 475. T.D. 9259, 2006-19, IRB 874, provides transitional relief for certain statutory mergers and consolidations occurring before the January 23, 2006 effective date of T.S. 9242.

```
┌─────────────────────────────────────────────┐
│              ╭─────────────╮                  │
│              │  Chapter 6  │                  │
│              ╰─────────────╯                  │
│                                               │
│          Securities Regulation                │
│                                               │
└─────────────────────────────────────────────┘
```

Chapter 6

Securities Regulation

§ 6.01   INTRODUCTION

Securities such as stocks and bonds are a vital part of the U.S. economy, and therefore, disturbances in the financial services industry in 2008 had severe repercussions throughout the economy. Corporations that have been operating privately can raise capital by making an initial public offering of securities (IPO). Once it is public, a corporation can make further (secondary) offerings of stock,[1] and can offer its bonds to investors. However, the vast majority of securities trading occurs on secondary markets: persons and institutions who own securities sell them to someone else, with no direct involvement by the company that issued the securities. In recent years, securities trading on-line (using the Internet) has undergone explosive growth, creating both practical and regulatory problems (see § 6.15).

Securities are regulated both by the federal government and by the states (Blue Sky Laws). The federal government allows states to supplement, but not contradict, federal law-making in this area. Most securities laws focus on disclosure, not quality. That is, the law forbids deception and manipulation, and specifies the amount and form of information that must be disclosed to potential buyers and to stockholders.

However, the fact that a security is registered does not constitute a government endorsement of the current or potential future value of the security. The objective of securities regulation is to provide a continuous flow of information about the business entity whose securities are being traded, with extra disclosure when a decision is required (e.g., proxy voting).

Because of the risk of manipulative and deceptive practices, all securities laws have general antifraud provisions, covering manipulation of stock prices, misstatements by corporate management, and trading by insiders based on non-public information.

---

[1] A "double-barreled" offering involves both primary elements (the issuer sells stock to the public) and secondary elements (shareholders sell stock).

"The two major federal securities regulation statutes are the Securities Act ("'33 Act"; 15 USC § 77a; the regulations appear in 17 CFR Part 230) and the Securities and Exchange Act ('34 Act; 15 USC § 78, regulations at 17 CFR Part 240), but they have been supplemented by many other statutes. In recent years, the focus has been on limiting securities fraud suits that are perceived by Congress as invalid and as limiting the development of the economy: see §§ 6.13, 6.14.

The '33 Act (§ 6.03, below) regulates public offerings of securities. It prohibits offers and sales of securities that are not registered with SEC unless they qualify for an exemption from registration. This statute also prohibits fraudulent or deceptive practices in the offering or sale of securities. The secondary (post-IPO) market is regulated by the '34 Act (§ 6.05 below). It imposes disclosure requirements for public corporations, bans manipulative or deceptive devices; and sets limits on margin transactions. It gives the SEC authority to supervise exchanges and clearing-houses. Broker-dealers have to be registered with, and regulated by, the SEC.

In 1933, the Glass-Steagall Act was enacted, forbidding banks to deal in securities other than government bonds, based on the then-current belief that unwise securities dealings by banks led to bank failures and losses to depositors. Glass-Steagall was repealed in 1999 by the Gramm-Leach-Bliley Act,[2] which adopted a regulatory system giving various government agencies regulatory power over the activities of financial institutions offering multiple services. Therefore, financial institutions' securities activities will be regulated by the SEC, their banking activities by federal or state bank regulators, and their insurance activities by state insurance regulators. Some types of financial activities, such as credit default swaps, were not regulated at all, and therefore lead to catastrophic losses.

From the 1980s to early in the 21st century, securities regulation activity slowed down. Statutes such as the Private Securities Litigation Reform Act (PSLR; see § 6.13[A]) and Securities Litigation Uniform Standards Act (SLUSA; § 6.13[B]) were passed to limit what was perceived to be excessive and abusive litigation about securities.

In 2001 and 2002, however, scandals involving, e.g., insider trading and accounting fraud in companies such as Enron and WorldCom were highly publicized, and the pendulum swung in favor of greater regulation and enforcement, typified by the Sarbanes-Oxley Act of 2002 (P.L. 107-204).

As of mid-2006, the trend in "stock-drop" suits (brought by employees whose retirement plans declined in value because the price of the employer's stock declined) was generally pro-defendant, although there were a number of large settlements paid to plaintiffs. The issue is when a trustee has a fiduciary duty to remove the employer's stock from the plan's investment options.[3]

---

[2] 15 USC §§ 6801–6809.

[3] Amanda Bronstad, *Defense Scores in Pension Plan Stock-Drop Suits*, Nat'l L.J. 8/9/06 (law.com), discussing DiFelice v. U.S. Airways, 2006 WL 763657 (E.D. Va. 2006); WorldCom Inc. ERISA Litigation, 354 F. Supp. 2d 423 (S.D.N.Y. 2005); Summers v. State Street Bank & Trust Co., 453 F.3d 404 (7th Cir. 2006).

A full discussion is beyond the scope of this book, but it should be noted that as of May 2006, securities regulators had launched about two dozen investigations of corporate backdating of options — i.e., changing documents and records to alter the effective date of a grant to improve the financial consequences for the grantee. The issue attracted attention because it was noted that some executives received large option grants shortly before upturns in the value of their company's stock. One enforcement problem is the statute of limitations: the Sarbanes-Oxley statute of limitations is five years from the event or two years from discovery, so many allegations would be untenable unless they came under the discovery rule. A number of shareholders suits were also filed to challenge backdating.

The first fine agreed upon in a backdating case was $7 million paid by Brocade Communications Systems Inc. in connection with improper issuance of options. The SEC's commissioners differ on the value of penalties; Republicans tend to oppose penalties, finding it unfair to, in effect, penalize shareholders again after they have already suffered by being defrauded. William McGuire, the former CEO of UnitedHealth, settled backdating charges with the SEC, in what the SEC described as the largest backdating settlement arranged up to that point. At one time, his unexercised options were worth more than $1.75 billion. In 2006, he agreed to return and re-price $200 million in options. McGuire was permitted to manipulate the process by choosing his own dates for option awards. His 2007 settlement with the SEC had a value of $468 million, including surrender of $320 million in stock options and a $7 million civil penalty, but without admission of guilt. Those actions resolved the SEC civil complaint and shareholder derivative suit. UnitedHealth paid $895 million to settle its own part of the suit.[4]

However, some commentators say that although backdating impairs the efficiency of the market, it is not really fraudulent or larcenous; there is no harm to the stockholders, for example, and no intent to achieve wrongful gains.[5]

Federal law also regulates the activities of brokerage and investment advisory firms. A dealer is a firm that buys and sells securities for its own account, hoping to resell them at a profit. A broker transacts on behalf of a customer. Securities firms typically operate as broker-dealers, carrying out both functions. A market maker is a firm that buys and sells a particular security in order to maintain a liquid market.

The Investment Company Act of 1940 (§ 6.08) gives the SEC regulatory authority over public companies (e.g., mutual funds) investing and trading in securities. The SEC has the power to regulate the management of investment

---

[4] Tom Murphy (AP) *Former UnitedHealth Group CEO to Pay $30 Million to Settle Options Lawsuit*, 9/11/08 (law.com); Kara Scannell, *Backdating Fine May Set Model*, Wall St. J. 5/31/07 at A3; previously, Analog Devices Inc. and Mercury Interactive Corp. announced preliminary agreements with the SEC that included penalties, and, as of mid-2007, over 140 backdating investigations were still in progress.

[5] Peter J. Henning, *Are Backdating Cases Really Securities Fraud?* special to Law.com 7/27/06; no byline, *What Backdating of Stock Options Means*, Wall St. J. 5/24/06 at p. C1; Amanda Bronstad, Next Step in Stock Option Probes: "Backdate" Lawsuits, Nat'l L.J. 6/9/06 (law.com).

companies; their capital structure; and their transactions with related parties such as directors, officers, and affiliates.

The Investment Advisers Act of 1940 (§ 6.09) imposes requirements for the registration and regulation of investment advisors similar to, but looser than, regulation of broker-dealers.

Although speculation is inherently risky, investors are entitled to be protected against fraud (as distinct from inevitable market risk). The Securities Investor Protection Act of 1970 established the Securities Investor Protection Corporation (SIPC), which supervises the liquidation of securities firms and pays off claims from their investors.

[A] Responses to the Crisis of 2008

The Emergency Economic Stabilization Act of 2008 (EESA; P.L. 110-334) set up a basic framework for the federal government's bailout of the financial sector of the economy, but it made few substantive changes in securities laws. As the crisis deepened, the SEC imposed a series of temporary limits on short selling of a small number of stocks, but the effect of the limitations was unclear.[6]

A significant factor in the financial crisis was the existence of a $43 trillion market in unregulated credit default swaps. (A credit default swap is a credit derivative contract whose buyer is supposed to make regular payments to the seller for the right to be paid if there is a default or credit event. They were used to hedge declines in the market for complex securities.) The banks that lost money would probably attempt to sue the sellers, although picking a law firm can be difficult when so many major firms have conflicts from representing other banks.[7]

Although many securities fraud and breach of fiduciary duty suits were contemplated, Lehman's bankruptcy and the bailout of Fannie Mae and Freddie Mac put those suits on hold. The defense bar argued that companies (and their directors and officers) should not be held to blame for uncontrollable economic forces. The *Stoneridge* decision could also limit the ability to sue third parties who approved dubious investments, although it would not protect directors and officers. Securities lawyers suggested that the litigation climate would be more difficult than the wake of the Enron and WorldCom disasters, because those debacles involved more explicit fraud and other illegalities.[8]

As could be expected in a litigious society, attempts were made to locate potentially liable persons and institutions with deep pockets. The number of securities class action filings rose from 116 in 2006 to 166 in 2007; at least 32 of the

---

[6] Floyd Norris, *Did It Help to Curb Short Sales?* N.Y. Times 8/13/08 at C1.

[7] Robin Sparkman, *Is Credit Default Swap Litigation the Next Big Thing?* The American Lawyer 10/3/08 (law.com).

[8] Amanda Bronstad, *Shareholder Suits Face Uncertainty, Higher Hurdles*, Nat'l L.J. 9/29/08 (law.com).

2007 cases involved subprime mortgages. However, recent Supreme Court hold-ings preclude suit in many situations.[9]

In January 2008 (i.e., before the crisis was recognized), the Supreme Court ruled that shareholders cannot maintain a securities fraud case against third-party suppliers who entered into sham transactions that helped a public company to inflate its reported revenue figures. This decision is highly significant for people who lost money during the crisis, because it precludes suits under 10(b) or Rule 10b-5 against secondary actors for "scheme liability," although it left open pos-sible SEC suits. However, depending on the circuit, the SEC may be unable to prove the necessary degree of scienter to maintain a successful aiding and abetting claim. The Supreme Court dismissed the claims against the third-party suppliers for lack of reliance, and therefore lack of causal connection between the misrep-resentation and injury to the plaintiffs. The Supreme Court also held that there was no duty to disclose the transactions to investors, and the scheme was never com-municated to the public, so there could not be fraud on the market (which requires misrepresentations to be reflected in the market price). The Supreme Court rejected the scheme liability theory, finding it a tactic for imposing the kind of "aiding and abetting" liability that Congress sought to rule out by passing the PSLRA.[10]

§ 6.02   WHAT IS A SECURITY?

To be subject to securities regulation, a financial instrument must first be defined as a security. Stock issued for investment purposes is clearly a security. In *Landreth Timber Co. v. Landreth*,[11] the Supreme Court rejected the argument that the sale of a business, by transfer of all of its outstanding stock, should not be considered a sale of securities. Some of the characteristics of stock identified in this case are:

- The right to receive dividends out of corporate profits
- Negotiability

---

[9] Relevant trends in legal thinking are discussed in Scott Balber, *Recent Pro-Defendant Trends in Securities Class Action Litigation*, special to Law.com 5/16/08.

[10] Stoneridge Inv. Partners, LLC v. Scientific-Atlanta, Inc.,128 S. Ct. 761 (2008); *see* Harold Gordon and Tracy V. Schaffer, *The SEC's Role in Pursuing Secondary Actors Following 'Stone-ridge'* special to Law.com 5/27/08. The article notes that in an SEC administrative action, liability can be imposed for aiding and abetting on the grounds of recklessness. The Ninth and Tenth Circuits allow imposition of liability for recklessness, but the D.C. Circuit requires the SEC to prove ignoring "red flags" or other extreme or severe recklessness, and at least two District Courts within the Second Circuit have held that the SEC must prove knowing misconduct; even for fiduciaries, recklessness is not enough to create liability. *See also* Lattanzio v. Deloitte & Touche LLP, 476 F.3d 147 (2d Cir. 2007), holding that auditors who did not issue a report in connection with a quarterly filing are not subject to primary securities fraud liability and Overton v. Todman & Co., 478 F.3d 479 (2d Cir. 2007) [unless an auditor's opinion is communicated to the investing public, the auditor is not pri-marily liable under securities laws, but can be liable if the auditor does not try to withdraw or correct an opinion after learning that the materially misstated financial statements were issued].

[11] 471 U.S. 681 (1985).

- Ability to be pledged or hypothecated
- Voting rights
- Potential for appreciation in value.

Although they are securities, bonds are covered by the Trust Indentures Act rather than by the '33 and '34 Acts. As for notes, they're securities unless they bear a "strong family resemblance" to an accepted exception such as home mortgages and commercial lending. The analysis[12] requires a look at:

- The motivation of lenders and borrowers
- Whether the notes are traded for investment
- Whether a reasonable member of the public would consider the instrument an investment
- If it is already regulated in a way that makes it unnecessary to apply securities laws.

The Supreme Court's January 13, 2004 decision in *SEC v. Edwards*, 540 U.S. 389, makes it clear that an investment contract offering a fixed rate of return can nevertheless be a "security" subject to SEC regulation, thus allowing the agency to proceed against an alleged Ponzi scheme involving purchase and lease-back of payphones with a promised 14% return.

Life insurance policies, annuities, and CDs are exempt from the '33 Act registration provisions, but not from the anti-fraud provisions. However, variable annuities are securities, and are "covered securities" under the Securities Litigation Uniform Standards Act (SLUSA); see § 6.13[B].[13]

Puts, calls, and options are definitely securities, but contracts for future delivery of commodities are regulated by the Commodity Futures Trading Commission (CFTC), not the SEC. The Eleventh Circuit has held that trading of Treasury bond futures is subject to commodities rather than securities regulation.[14]

The factors in characterizing an unusual or hybrid investment include whether there is an investment in a common enterprise and expectation of profits from the efforts of a promoter or third party. For instance, limited partnership interests generally are securities, but general partnership interests are not, because

---

[12] Under Reves v. Ernst & Young, 494 U.S. 56 (1990).

[13] SEC v. Variable Annuity Life, 359 U.S. 65 (1959); SEC v. United Benefit, 387 U.S. 202 (1967). On SLUSA issues, *see* Herndon v. Equitable Variable Life Ins. Co., 325 F.3d 1252 (11th Cir. 2003). *See also* SEC Release No. 34-52046A, available at both http://www.nasd.gov and http://www.sec.gov for regulation of sales of variable annuities, especially vis-a-vis suitability issues. In mid-2008, the SEC proposed to place equity-indexed annuities under the supervision of the Financial Industry Regulatory Authority, a non-governmental supervisor of financial firms, by defining the annuities as securities rather than as insurance products to be regulated by the states. The financial services industry opposed the proposal, stating that it would reduce sales and force many agents out of business: Daisy Maxey, *Battle Looms on Indexed Annuities*, Wall St. J. 8/7/08 at D6.

[14] Messer v. E.F. Hutton Co., 847 F.2d 673 (11th Cir. 1988).

general partners' profit expectations come from their own participation in the enterprise.

According to the Fourth Circuit, a 25% investor in a limited liability company in the telecommunications industry, who took an active executive role and possessed shared managerial control over the enterprise did not own "stock" or an "investment contract," even though his co-participants were more technologically sophisticated than he was.[15]

Certain securities are subject to general anti-fraud and civil liability provisions, but are not subject to registration and disclosure requirements:

- Obligations issued, guaranteed by U.S., state, or local government ('33 Act § 3(a)(2))
- ('33 Act only) Securities issued by banks and savings & loan institutions; bankruptcy certificates; insurance policies and annuity contracts (§ 3(a)(2)); notes arising out of current transactions with maturity under 9 months (§ 3(a)(3)) (Exchange Act § 3(a)(10) excludes *all* notes with maturities under 9 months)
- ('33 Act) § 3(a)(9), (10) securities issued in exchange for other securities
- § 3(a)(11) intrastate offerings
- § 3(b) small (not exceeding $5 million) offerings.

§ 6.03   THE '33 ACT AND ITS REGISTRATION PROCESS

The '33 Act provides that (unless an exemption is available), unregistered securities cannot be sold in interstate commerce. Once registration has occurred, the security can only be sold if it is accompanied by a prospectus that discloses the mandated information about the security. '33 Act § 2(a)(10) defines a prospectus as any communication that offers a security for sale or confirms a sale, but a communication is not a prospectus if it is delivered with a prospectus or merely identifies the price of the security and where orders can be executed.[16]

---

[15] Robinson v. Glynn, 349 F.3d 166 (4th Cir. 2003). A 2008 Second Circuit securities fraud case revolved around whether investors in two film companies were passive or actively involved in management. The court decided that investors who spend $10,000 for shares in movies were victims under § 10(b), because they had no meaningful management role. The Second Circuit said that the *Howey* factors are not merely assessed in formal terms, but on the basis of whether or not the investors have significant control. In this case, there were many investors, but only a few served on committees, so there was no real potential for investor control: United States v. Leonard, 529 F.3d 83 (2d Cir. 2008); discussed in Mark Hamblett, *2nd Circuit Clarifies Investor Role in Establishing Fraud*, N.Y.L.J. 6/18/08 (law.com).

[16] Section 2 has provisions dealing with the full statutory prospectus (§ 10(a)); the preliminary prospectus, also known as the "red herring" and summary prospectus (§ 10(b)); the "tombstone ad" (§ 2(10)(b) and Rule 134); the ad is called a tombstone because it merely states bare facts about the transaction and does not include copy to motivate sales; and supplemental sales literature (§ 2(10)(a)).

There is a private right of action if materially false statements are made (or material facts are omitted) in a registration statement or in connection with the sale of a security (§ 11).

Remedies under the '33 Act are available only to purchasers. The '34 Act has remedies for sellers as well. In addition, the SEC can sue in federal court if the '33 Act or its rules are violated.

As noted above, the focus of the '33 Act is disclosure, not regulation of the quality of proposed IPOs. (The theory is that the investment banking firms that underwrite the issues will distinguish between high- and low-quality proposals, and will refuse to participate in the latter.)

Major provisions of the '33 Act include:

- §§ 3,4: types of securities and transactions exempt from registration requirement
- § 5: forbidding the offer or sale of an unregistered security unless it is entitled to an exemption ("jumping the gun")
- §§ 6, 8: procedure for registration
- § 7: information to be disclosed in the registration process; Schedule A is a disclosure checklist
- § 8A: SEC cease and desist proceedings
- § 10: information required in the prospectus
- § 11: civil liability for misstatement or omission in a registration statement
- § 12(1): civil liability for offers or sales that violate § 5
- § 12(2): liability for misstatements or omissions in any offer or sale of registered, unregistered, or exempt securities
- § 16: limitations on class actions; see § 6.13[B]
- § 17: fraudulent or deceitful practices in connection with any interstate offer or sale of securities (registered or not)
- § 18: limits on state regulation; see § 6.04
- § 19: SEC powers
- § 20: prosecution of, and injunctions against, securities offenders.

In October 2004, the SEC proposed major changes in the offering process in order to harmonize the '33 and '34 Act regulatory processes and to take advantage of modern technology and communications (e.g., e-mail and Web sites replacing telephone calls and printed paper). The disclosure requirements would be lower for "well-known seasoned issuers" (with a high volume of recent offerings) than for "seasoned issuers" (those eligible to use Forms S-3 or F-3), "unseasoned issuers" (reporting companies that cannot use those short forms), and "nonreporting issuers."

In July 2007, the SEC proposed a new and optional disclosure and reporting regime for small companies, defined as those with a public float under $75 million. The existing categories of small business issuer and non-accelerated filer would, in effect, be combined into a new category of smaller reporting companies, with the

Regulation S-B disclosure requirements for smaller reporting companies integrated into Regulation S-K.[17]

Although current rules require a "quiet period" before a stock issue, when issuers are not permitted to accept or solicit offers, the proposal would change the ban on "jumping the gun" (promoting a stock offering before the registration statement has been filed) so that well-known seasoned issuers would be allowed additional communications, including a new type of prospectus ("free-writing prospectus"). Less experienced issuers would be allowed some pre-filing communications, but to a lesser extent. The process of "shelf registration" (filing documents in advance to ease the path of an issue that might be made in the future) would be expanded under the proposal.

The proposal also would allow final prospectuses to be "distributed" by being made available electronically, rather than through physical distribution of printed materials.[18]

More specifically, '33 Act § 11 provides that, if at the time a registration statement became effective, it contained an untrue statement of material fact, or omitted a material fact needed to prevent the statement from being misleading, the acquiror of the security can sue for the difference between the price paid for the security and the sale price or value at the time of the suit. (However, the calculation of the price paid is limited to the public offering price, not any higher price the purchaser may have paid.)

The purchaser does not have to show reliance unless he or she purchased the securities at a time after the issuer had published an earning statement covering a period of at least 12 months after the effective date of the registration statement. (In that case, the purchaser should reasonably have consulted the earnings statement and used it as part of the decision to purchase.)

Under § 12, a purchaser who did not know of the untruth or omission can either tender the securities and recover what he or she paid for them, or can sue for damages if he or she no longer owns the securities. According to a 1995 Supreme Court decision,[19] § 12 does not apply to secondary trading or to IPOs other than public offerings made by statutory prospectus, and the purchaser can only sue the seller of the securities.

Where there is a bankruptcy as a complicating factor, the Second Circuit ruled that individual investors' '33 Act claims must be heard in federal rather than state court. '33 Act § 22(a) generally bars removal of state cases to federal court. But 28 USC § 1452(a) allows removal of any civil action related to bankruptcy. This provision, unlike the general removal statute, 28 USC § 1441(a), does not make an exception for suits under a statute that includes an anti-removal provision.

---

[17] SEC Release Nos. 33-8819, 34-56013, 39-2447, http://sec.gov/rules/proposed/2007/33-8819.pdf (7/5/07).

[18] Proposed Rule, Securities Offering Reform, Release Nos. 33-8501, 34-50624 (10/26/04), http://www.sec.gov/rules/proposed/33-8501.html.

[19] Gustafson v. Alloyd, 513 U.S. 561 (1995).

The Second Circuit concluded that Congress' intention was to centralize all bankruptcy-related litigation in federal court.[20]

The three-year period for § 12(a)(1) liability set by '33 Act § 13 is a statute of repose, triggered by the first bona fide public offering of the security, not the last offering.[21]

[A] Registration Statement

If registration is required, it is performed by filing a registration statement. A '33 Act registration statement covers only the particular securities that are offered, for the purposes of the offering described in the statement (§ 6(a)). (In contrast, the '34 Act covers entire classes of securities.) The registration statement consists of a prospectus, which must be furnished to every purchaser, and information and exhibits that are filed with the SEC and made available to the public at the SEC office, but do not have to be given to every purchaser.

Section 6(a) requires the issuer to sign the registration statement; everyone who signs the registration statement is subject to liability under § 11(a)(1) for false or misleading statements.

The basic, long-form registration form is Form S-1, although in some circumstances, the SB-1 or SB-2, a briefer, less detailed form can be used. Form S-2, limited to companies that have been reporting under the '34 Act for at least three years, lets the issuer meet its burden of disclosure by including its latest annual report in the registration statement and prospectus, and incorporating its latest SEC annual report (Form 10-K) by reference.

Form S-3 also incorporates by reference information that is already circulating in the public markets. A company that has been a '34 Act reporting company for at least 12 months can use this form to register secondary offerings of senior securities, or new offerings of equity securities if the market value of publicly-held voting stock is at least $75 million.

Form S-4 is used in conjunction with mergers and acquisition transactions, Form S-8 for Employee Stock Ownership Plans (ESOPs), and Form S-11 for real estate companies.

Regulation S-B provides forms that small business issuers can use for disclosure and reporting under both Acts. (See § 6.03[B] for small offering exemptions that can be used to raise limited amounts of capital bypassing the laborious and expensive registration process.)

Form SB-1 is a streamlined disclosure document that gives the registrant a choice between traditional "narrative" disclosure and the question-and-answer format of Regulation A (see § 6.03[B][4]). It can be used by a company qualifying under Rule 405 to issue up to $10 million in securities sold for cash in any 12-month period. The full-scale S-1 filing requires compliance with financial reporting

---

[20] CALPERS v. WorldCom Inc., 368 F.3d 86 (2d Cir. 2004).
[21] P. Stoltz Family Partnership LP v. Daum, 355 F.3d 92 (2d Cir. 2004).

requirements set out in Regulation S-X, whereas the SB-1 financial statements merely have to conform to Generally Accepted Accounting Principles.

The SB-2 can be used for an offering of any size made by a small business issuer qualifying under Rule 405. Form S-4 is used for mergers and acquisitions; S-8 by Employee Stock Ownership Plans (ESOPs); and S-11 by real estate companies.

In August 2000, the Tenth Circuit joined the First, Second, and Ninth Circuits in holding that fraud in the initial registration statement will support a '33 Act § 11 action against the issuer, by investors who bought on the secondary market rather than in the initial issue, because the wording of § 11 does not limit the cause of action to the initial issue.[22]

[1] The Registration Process

Regulation C, Rules 400–498 under the '33 Act, details how to register an issue of securities, and gives the general form for registration statements and prospectuses. It should be read in conjunction with Regulation S-T, 17 CFR Part 232, the rules for electronic filings. Most registrants will be required to file documents (e.g., registration statements, proxy materials) in electronic rather than paper form, unless a hardship exemption is available or unless confidential data is involved.

Securities Act § 8(a) provides that registered securities can be sold to the public as soon as the registration statement becomes "effective." (Earlier sales are considered "gun-jumping" and are banned by § 5(c).) Unless the SEC delays or suspends effectiveness, this occurs 20 days after filing. The effective date can be accelerated by the SEC to a period of less than 20 days; see Rule 461. Each time the prospectus is amended, another 20-day period starts to run. Even if the SEC does not require any amendments, at least one amendment will usually be required: the actual price at which the securities will first be issued.

However, Rule 430A permits information about the price of the offering and terms of underwriting to be left out of the registration statement at the time it becomes effective, as long as the information is provided in a final prospectus filed under Rule 424 or Rule 497. If, however, the final prospectus is not filed within 15 days of the effective date, a post-effective amendment will be required. Rule 434 permits supplementing the preliminary prospectus with a "term sheet" containing additional information about the offering.

In theory, § 8(b) permits the SEC to issue a "refusal order" denying effectiveness to any statement that, on its face, is "incomplete or inaccurate in any material respect." A § 8(d) "stop order" suspends the effectiveness of a registration statement that is found to omit or misstate a material fact. In practice, however, the SEC never issues refusal orders, and few stop orders are issued. Instead, "deficiency letters," also known as "letters of comment," are issued, refusing acceleration. Given that the issuer and underwriter usually want to sell the stock as soon

---

[22] Joseph v. Wiles, 223 F.3d 1155 (10th Cir. 2000) and the cases cited therein.

as the price of the offering has been determined, denial of acceleration is a powerful sanction.

The traditional underwriting process (which is being altered to some extent by the Internet; see § 6.15) involves one or more investment banks as underwriter. The underwriter buys securities from the issuer and distributes them to investors.

In firm commitment underwriting, the underwriters are principals in the deal. They buy the securities from the issuer and/or stockholders of the issuer, resell the securities to dealers, who sell them to the public. Usually, the offering is made at a fixed price, and the dealers agree to offer the securities at the price stated in the prospectus.

Underwriters who are more dubious about an issue's prospects may insist on a best-efforts underwriting, in which they sell as many shares as they can, in exchange for a commission, but are not required to pay the issuer for the entire offering.

Underwriters are liable under § 11 for false or misleading statements in the registration statement, unless their sole interest in the deal consists of distributing the securities in exchange for a commission.

SEC Release No. 33-7943 creates a safe harbor for integrated offerings under Rule 155. An issuer that initiates either a private or public offering, but does not sell any securities, can abandon the private offering and go public instead. The prior, unsuccessful offering must be disclosed. In general, the issuer must wait 30 days between terminating one form of offering and adopting the other.

An earlier release, 33-4552, provides tests for determining whether offerings are integrated:

- Are they part of a single plan of financing?
- Do they involve the same class of securities?
- Were they made at about the same time?
- Do they serve the same general purpose?
- Is the same type of consideration received for each?

[2] Timing Requirements

The timing requirements of '33 Act § 5 divide the process into five parts: the pre-filing stage; the filing date; the waiting period, until the SEC permits the offer to become effective; the effective date; and the post-effective period. No offers to sell the securities can be made before the registration statement is filed. No actual sales can be made before the effective date. Once effectiveness occurs, securities cannot be sold without delivery of a prospectus, and the prospectus must conform to the statutory requirements.

During the waiting period (which begins when the registration statement is filed, and ends when it becomes effective), offers to buy are permitted, but the securities cannot be sold. During this time, only two kinds of written materials (and their electronic counterparts) are allowed: "red herrings" (preliminary prospectuses,[23] so-called because of the warning statement in red type on the cover) and tombstone ads (simple statements that securities can be purchased subsequent to review of the prospectus).

Unusual publicity about the issuer's business, or even its industry, may be deemed an offer. On the other hand, reporting companies have an obligation of continuing disclosure, so '33 Act Rule 135 lets the issuer put out a press release or notice of offering in bare-bones terms, balancing the obligation to communicate with the investing public against the duty to refrain from providing incomplete or inaccurate information.

Although companies "going public" for the first time must use the cumbersome IPO process, a company that is already public can use the Rule 415 "shelf registration" procedure. An offering of securities can be registered and distributed at a later time, or can be registered and distributed in several installments, with pricing based on current market conditions.

Effective in 1997, the SEC requires prospectuses to be in plain English: *see* Securities Act Release No. 7497 (1/22/98) for guidelines. On and after 10/1/98, registration statements must also be in plain English.

Rule 421 defines "plain English" to mean:

- Understandable language
- Use of tables or bullet lists to make information easier to access
- Use of common words instead of technical jargon
- Organizing the material with headings and subheadings.

[B] Exemptions from Registration

The full registration process is cumbersome, expensive, and not really appropriate in certain circumstances — as Congress recognizes by enacting registration exemptions. Securities can be offered without registration based on the characteristics of the securities themselves; the nature of the issue or issuer; or because the securities are marketed in a way that does not create a risk that naïve purchasers will acquire the securities without adequate disclosure. The exemptions overlap, and often the potential issuer will be able to structure the offering to fit one of several exemptions. In most instances, the anti-fraud rules will continue to apply, even though registration is not required.

Short-term commercial paper (with a term under nine months) can be issued without registration, under '33 Act § 3(a)(3), 15 USC § 77c(a)(3). Section 3(a)(8)

---

[23] Governed by Rule 430. *See also* Rule 431 for the summary prospectus, which can be used post-effectiveness in some cases. After the registration statement becomes effective, §§ 5(a)(2) and 5(b)(2) require delivery of securities to buyers to be preceded by or accompanied by a copy of the final prospectus. Dealers are subject to prospectus requirements if they sell any securities registered during the previous 90 days (40 days for issuers who have already registered an issue of securities): § 4(3), no matter how often the shares have changed hands since the IPO. If the securities are listed on a stock exchange or on NASDAQ, the additional prospectus requirement is reduced to 25 days.

exempts the sale of insurance policies and annuity contracts by sellers subject to state insurance or banking regulation.

The Gramm-Leach-Bliley Act repealed a broad exemption and instead adopted specific exemptions from registration for certain activities conducted by banks. Otherwise, to avoid the need to register, other securities activities must be performed by a registered broker acting for the bank. The SEC and the Federal Reserve Board issued Final Rules on this exemption in October 2007. Activities subject to the rule include third-party brokerage arrangements, sweep accounts, private securities offerings, and custody of securities. Banks can engage in certain transactions with non-U.S. persons, involving securities that are exempt from registration under Regulation S where the bank acts as a "riskless principal." Banks can lawfully engage in "conduit lending" of securities without being regarded as dealers, provided that the lending activity involves either a large pension plan or a qualified investor under '34 Act § 3(a)(54)(A).[24]

[1] Sale-Based Exemptions

Because the purpose of the '33 Act is to regulate issuers and underwriters, § 4(4) exempts brokerage transactions on customers' orders that do not involve an issuer, underwriter, or dealer. This exemption removes the huge "secondary" market (sales by one investor to another) from the '33 Act.

Section 4(2) makes "nonpublic" offerings exempt. In a typical § 4(2) "private placement," all the offerees are either institutional investors or sophisticated private individuals, so there is no need to protect the public via the registration process.[25] A private placement may not be advertised to the public, but a brokerage firm handling a private placement is permitted to communicate to its customers who are sophisticated investors. It is permissible to qualify an offering under both § 4(2) and Regulation D (Securities Act Rules 501–508); it is not necessary to decide before the offering which exemption it will satisfy.

[2] Intrastate Offerings

Federal law does not apply to strictly intrastate offerings, so they are exempt from registration under § 3(a)(11). (See below for a discussion of state Blue Sky Laws, which do govern intrastate offerings.) It should be noted that many companies doing business in other states prefer to incorporate in Delaware, but doing so prevents use of the intrastate offering exemption. The intrastate-offering exemption is lost entirely (not reduced proportionately) if any of the offerees or purchasers of the securities reside outside the state.

---

[24] Release No. 34-56501, 72 FR 56514 (10/3/07); Release No. 34-56502, 72 FR 56562 (10/3/07). Joint rulemaking by the two agencies was mandated by the Financial Services Regulatory Relief Act of 2006, P.L. 109-351.

[25] The classical test under SEC v. Ralston Purina, 346 U.S. 119 (1953) is the ability of offerees to "fend for themselves."

Rule 147 provides a safe harbor for intrastate offerings,[26] but does not permit resales outside the state for at least nine months after the completion of the intrastate offering.

[3] Issue-Based Exemptions

Under § 3(b) of the '33 Act, the SEC can exempt issues of up to $5 million. Under § 4(6), issues of up to $5 million can be sold to accredited investors, as long as there is no public solicitation or advertising, and as long as the issuer notifies the SEC that it is relying on this exemption. An accredited investor is a person or institution who is able to assess the value of an offering, and does not need the protection of the normal disclosure rules, based on "such factors as financial sophistication, net worth, knowledge, and experience in financial matters, or amount of assets under management."

[4] Regulation A

Regulation A, 17 CFR § 230.251–263, is the most widely used of the § 3(b) exemptions. The issuer can issue a total of $5 million a year, and does not have to aggregate Regulation A offerings with Rule 504 or 505 offerings. Of that $5 million, up to $1.5 million can come from sales of the securities by affiliates of the issuer.

Although Regulation A securities can lawfully be sold without full-scale registration, the issuer has to go through a "mini-registration" process including disclosure and a prospectus-like "preliminary offering circular" that must be given to offerees and purchasers. See Rule 255 for the disclosure requirements.

If the issuer is in a state whose Blue Sky law requires registration, but permits "registration by coordination" between state and federal regulators, Regulation A will be a poor choice. Regulation A is denied to "bad boys": if either the corporation or an officer, director, or major stockholder has ever been found culpable of disclosure violations, Regulation A will be unavailable.

[5] Rule 701

Rule 701 allows up to $1 million in securities to be issued in a 12-month period (possibly higher, depending on the corporation's assets and prior stock issues; disclosure requirements are higher if the issuer sells over $5 million in securities under Rule 701), in connection with employment contracts or written compensation plans. There can be any number of offerees and any number of purchasers among the issuer's employees, management, and their family members who get the securities as gifts from insiders or pursuant to divorce-related court

---

[26] The issuer is a state resident, is headquartered in the state, and does business within the state; it is organized under the laws of that state and gets 80% of its gross revenues and assets from that state. Furthermore, 80% of the net proceeds of the offering are applied to in-state operations. All offerees live or have their principal office within the state.

orders. Rule 701 securities are restricted securities, but their restricted status terminates 90 days after the issuer becomes a '34 Act reporting company.

[6] Regulation D

Regulation D is another method of issuing securities without registration. It authorizes three registration exemptions:

(1) Rule 504 exempts "small offerings." It can be used to offer up to $1 million in securities a year, by "small issuers" — companies that are not "reporting companies" under the '34 Act (see below) and are not investment companies. There is no restriction on the number of purchasers, and purchasers do not have to meet suitability tests.

General advertising or solicitation for Rule 504 securities is not permitted, unless the activities are limited to (a) state(s) whose Blue Sky Laws require pre-sale delivery of a disclosure document (and the document is provided as required); if disclosure documents from one state are provided in all states; or if the securities satisfy a state-law requirement allowing advertising as long as all sales are limited to accredited investors. In states that do not require disclosure documents, Rule 504 sales may not exceed $500,000.

(2) Rule 505 exempts offerings of up to $5 million per year.[27] The offering can be made to any number of accredited investors, and up to 35 "other purchasers." A corporation counts as a single purchaser. So does each client of an investment advisor or broker, so this exemption cannot be used to distribute securities widely among a broker's clients. What counts is the number of offerees, not the number of purchasers, so it is quite possible that the maximum permissible number of offerees will be solicited, but few or none will choose to acquire the securities.

(3) Rule 506 permits offering and sale of any amount of securities to a group of any number of accredited investors, plus not more than 35 investors qualified by "knowledge and experience in financial matters," provided either by the investors themselves or their purchaser representatives. The issuer must check the credentials of all purchasers, though not necessarily of all offerees. If all offerees are accredited investors, then it is not necessary to provide a disclosure document in a Rule 506 offering.

An "accredited investor," as defined by Rule 501, is an institutional investor; private business development company; tax-exempt organization with more than $5 million in assets; corporation or partnership with assets over $5 million (but not an entity formed specifically to acquire the security); trusts with assets over

---

[27] The $5 million limit is applied to the 12-month period prior to the current Rule 505 offering, and covers the aggregate of all securities sold under Rules 504 and 505, plus any Regulation A securities and any securities that should have been but were not registered.

$5 million and a sophisticated adviser; and entities wholly owned by accredited investors.

Natural persons count as accredited investors if they are officers, directors, or general partners of the issuer, or if their net worth is high enough. The net-worth standard is $1 million (for a person, or a married couple). A person can also become an accredited investor by satisfying an income test: earning at least $200,000 a year ($300,000 for a married couple) for the past two years, with the income level expected to continue.

A company that is already a "reporting company" under the '34 Act cannot use Rule 504 for later offerings of securities, although it can use Rule 505 or 506, and in fact can use its '34 Act reports to satisfy the disclosure requirements under these rules.

There is no specific information disclosure requirement for Rule 504 offerings, although compliance with the antifraud rules may make it necessary to disclose the issue's financial background. Rule 505 and 506 offerings are covered by Rule 502, which mandates financial and non-financial disclosure, in amounts depending on the size of the offering and the issuer's status as a reporting or non-reporting company.

Form D itself is filed with the SEC, within 15 days after the exempt securities have begun to be sold. It informs the agency of the issuer's identity and management; describes the exempt securities and their offering price; explains how the proceeds will be used. If the issue is otherwise complying, failure to file the form with the SEC will not remove the exemption from the securities, but could preclude the issuer from using Regulation D for later offerings.

[C] Steps in a Registered Offering

Usually, the company and its managing underwriter begin the process by signing a letter of intent. The issuer's securities counsel begin to draft the registration statement. The attorney(s) for the managing underwriter and other members of the managing syndicate start to draft the full-scale underwriting agreements, covering the relationship among the underwriters, designating a lead underwriter, and also covering the relationship between underwriters and issuer.

The underwriters agree on the number of shares to be purchased and the price to the syndicate. The syndicate also enters into agreements with dealers, governing the discount at which the dealers can purchase securities. Although underwriting agreements between underwriter and issuer are negotiated and drafted early in the process, they are not actually signed until the effective date of the prospectus.

In the early stages, the issuer undertakes any necessary corporate steps, such as passing resolutions and getting authorizations.

A draft registration statement is filed with the SEC. The agency has 30 days to comment on the statement, and usually takes full advantage of this option.

The underwriters and dealers use preliminary prospectuses to build interest in the impending issue.

The draft registration statement is amended to prepare for effectiveness, based on the SEC comments, and to fill in previously unavailable terms.

The underwriters make the final decision to defer or pursue the offering and set the offering price. However, a price amendment is often filed with the SEC on the effective date of the prospectus. Rule 424 requires a final prospectus to be filed after effectiveness.

When trading opens, the securities are priced by the underwriter, but the expectation is that the price of the stock will rise much higher, creating opportunities for quick profits for those who received shares of stock that they could re-sell on the first day or first few days of trading. The issuer receives only the initial price and does not benefit directly by the price run-up (although it can benefit indirectly by being perceived as issuing a "hot" stock). From the issuer's point of view, the difference between the trading price and the issue price is thought of as "leaving money on the table."

[D] Resale of Securities

Once a security is registered, any holder can easily find a buyer on the open market. As a worst-case scenario, the broker-dealer that is the "market maker" will purchase the security and hold it until another buyer is found. But the picture is more complex for securities that have been issued in a private placement and are exempt from registration.

Section 4(1) of the '33 Act covers transactions by persons other than the issuer of the securities, underwriters, or dealers—typically, corporate insiders or purchasers under a private placement or Rule 506. For § 4(1) purposes, an affiliate has the direct or indirect power to control the policies and direction of the corporation's management, even if the power is never actually exercised.

Restricted securities are acquired either directly or indirectly from the issuer without a public offering, via Rules 144A, 504, 505, or 506. Resales are forbidden for a period of time, unless the securities are registered or unless the conditions for one of the exemptions are present. However, Rule 504 securities are not restricted if the issue was registered under a state law that calls for disclosure, or if the issue comes under a state law allowing general solicitation and offering to accredited investors and no one else. Effective February 15, 2008, the SEC amended Rules 144 and 145, reducing the minimum holding period before restricted securities of reporting companies could be resold to six months. (The minimum holding period remains one year for non-reporting companies.) Once the holding period ends, stock owners who are not treated as affiliates of the seller can re-sell their securities more or less without limitations, and they are not required to file Form 144. Affiliates still must file Form 144 reports, if they intend to sell more than 5,000 shares or more than $50,000 worth of restricted securities within any three-month period.[28]

---

[28] Release No. 33-8869 (12/6/07), published as SEC Final Rule, *Revisions to Rules 144 and 145*, 72 F.R. 71546 (12/17/07).

§ 6.04   BLUE SKY LAWS: STATE SECURITIES
         REGULATION

Even before the '33 Act, states had laws to prevent securities fraud and induce disclosure in connection with securities sales. The states regulate the issue of securities, and may require a registration process even for securities that do not require federal regulation. Typically, however, the "Blue Sky" process is less difficult and expensive than federal registration.

In contrast to SEC regulation, which centers around disclosure, some states do practice "merit regulation," and can deny approval to an issue that is believed to be financially unsound (or whose issuer is believed to be financially unsound). But most states follow the federal model, limiting the registration process to disclosure. About three-quarters of the states permit "registration by coordination," in which federal registration is also operative at the state level. The Uniform Securities Act, adopted by most states, permits registration by coordination, qualification (full-scale disclosure) or notification (a simplified procedure for established companies that already have publicly traded securities).

The states also license broker-dealers and investment advisers, and offer remedies to investors injured by the conduct of issuers or brokers. When Blue Sky laws are violated, the buyer may be entitled to rescission of the transaction; the issuer may be able to rescind all purchases of a violative issue, with adequate disclosure of the nature of the violations.

The National Securities Markets Improvement Act of 1996 limited the state role in securities regulation, by preempting state regulation of mutual funds as well as state registration of securities listed on the American or New York Stock Exchanges or participating in the NASDAQ system: '33 Act § 18.

§ 6.05   THE SECURITIES EXCHANGE ACT

The Securities Exchange Act of '34 (the '34 Act), unlike the '33 Act, deals with securities after they have been released onto the market. The '34 Act penalizes manipulation, especially fraud, in the market for post-IPO securities, and limits trading by insiders (e.g., corporate officers). The '34 Act includes criminal penalties for violations; the '33 Act does not.

The '34 Act controls the activities of "reporting companies": those that must report to the SEC because they have issued securities that are registered on an exchange, or registered for over-the-counter (OTC) trading under Exchange Act § 12.

The '33 Act requires registration of securities sold in a particular offering or transaction. The '34 Act works differently; it requires registration of classes of securities. The basic registration forms are Form 10, 10 S-B (for small business), and 8-A for companies already reporting under '34 Act § 13 or 15(d). See '34 Act § 13, requiring quarterly reports (Form 10-Q) and annual reports (10-K) to the SEC, plus Form 8-K disclosure of material transactions and events such as acquiring or divesting major assets or changing auditors.

Regulation S-K (17 CFR Part 339) contains the general disclosure rules; small businesses may be entitled to the less cumbersome Regulation S-B disclosure format.[29] In addition to disclosures that must be made to the SEC, stockholders are entitled to annual reports and proxy statements in appropriate statutory form.

An important feature of the 10-K and 10-Q reports is the "MD&A" (management discussion and analysis) of the corporation's financial condition, for instance trends and events likely to influence the company's financial affairs and results.

The general rule is that all filings must be made electronically, becoming part of the SEC's EDGAR (Electronic Data Gathering, Analysis & Retrieval) database, although hardship exceptions can be granted for companies unable to file electronically. See Regulation S-T, especially the EDGAR Filer Manual (17 CFR § 232.301) for instructions.

Under '34 Act § 13(d) and (g), any individual who is beneficial owner of 5% or more of a reporting company's securities must file a statement with the SEC disclosing the size of his or her holdings.

Section 16 of the '34 Act places limitations on the reporting company's directors, officers, and 10% shareholders. They are not allowed to sell the corporation's stock short. They must file reports with the SEC disclosing their holdings and transactions in the issuer's securities. Section 16(b) permits the issuer itself, or any shareholder suing on the issuer's behalf (but not the SEC), to force the insider to disgorge the "short-swing" profits earned by buying and then selling, or selling and then buying, the issuer's stock without the mandatory six-month holding period. In general, short-swing profits are forbidden even if no inside information was used, but SEC Rule 16b-3 exempts many employee benefit plan transactions from the short-swing rule.

[A] Anti-Fraud Rules

An important function of the Exchange Act is to penalize securities fraud and manipulation, and offer remedies to those injured. Exchange Act § 9 forbids manipulative practices in trading the securities of any reporting company that is listed on a national exchange. Victims can recover the difference between the security's actual value and the price as affected by manipulation. Recovery can also include costs and attorneys' fees.

Perhaps the central section of the Exchange Act is § 10(b), which forbids any deception or omission of material fact in securities transactions. This section applies even if the issuer is not a reporting company and its shares are not listed on an exchange. It prohibits "any manipulative or deceptive device or contrivance in contravention of such rules and regulations as the commission [i.e., the SEC] may prescribe as necessary or appropriate in the public interest or for the protection of investors."

---

[29] It is not necessary to disclose, in Item 402(g), the value of stock options awarded to non-employee directors measured as of the date of grant: Seinfeld v. Bartz, 322 F.3d 693 (9th Cir. 2003).

Materiality is a mixed question of fact and law. For instance, it is not possible to give a simple answer as to whether misstating an item representing only 1.7% of corporate revenues is material. At least at the pleading stage, a bright-line test cannot be used to assess materiality: all factors must be considered.[30]

The traditional "fraud on the market theory," espoused by *Basic, Inc. v. Levinson*, 485 U.S. 224 (1988) is that there is a presumption that securities in which plaintiffs invested were based on the integrity of the stock price set by the market, and therefore they indirectly relied on any misstatement that affected the stock price.

Late in 2008, the Second Circuit put research analysts in the same category as stock issuers vis-a-vis liability for misrepresentation under the fraud on the market theory. However, the court vacated class certification in a case charging an analyst with issuing false research reports. Individual investors can be presumed to rely in an efficient market where the defendant made public material misrepresentations about a stock. *Basic v. Levinson* says that plaintiffs do not have to prove that the misrepresentations had a measurable effect on the stock price because the market readily incorporates all of the information (whatever its source) into the price. But the Second Circuit's 2006 decision requires the District Court to make a definitive assessment before a class is certified that the predominance requirement of Rule 23(b)(3) has been met; at this point, the defense can rebut the *Basic* presumption.[31]

An important question about the anti-fraud rules was resolved in 2005, when the Supreme Court adopted the majority view and rejected the Ninth Circuit's minority view of loss causation. The Supreme Court ruled that a plaintiff cannot prevail by alleging that the defendant's fraud inflated the price of a publicly traded security when she bought it, because that fails to plead the defendant's fraud as the proximate cause of the loss. An allegation of inflated purchase price does not establish economic loss, because a share of stock is worth what the buyer pays for it at the time of purchase, and even an inflated price could still yield a profit for the buyer if someone else is willing to purchase the share at a yet higher price.[32]

The Supreme Court returned to the issue of scienter in its 2007 *Tellabs* decision, increasing the burden of proof that plaintiffs must meet in their initial pleadings with respect to the defendant's intention to deceive or defraud. The plaintiff's inferences about the defendant's knowledge of wrongdoing must be cogent, and must be at least as compelling as the inference that the defendant did not have fraudulent intent. That is, the Supreme Court rejected the standard that the plaintiff is merely required to allege facts from which a reasonable person could infer fraudulent intent. In the Supreme Court view, personal financial gain is a factor weighing in favor of scienter, but allegations are not viewed in isolation,

---

[30] Ganino v. Citizens Utils. Co., 228 F.3d 154 (2d Cir. 2000).

[31] *In re*: Salomon Analyst Metromedia Litigation, 06-3225-cv (2d Cir. 2008), *see* Mark Hamblett, *2nd Circuit: Analysts Bound by Same Liability Presumption as Issuers for 'Fraud on Market,'* N.Y.L.J. 10/2/08 (law.com); the 2006 decision is *In re* IPO Securities Litigation, 471 F.3d 24 (2006).

[32] Dura Pharm. Inc. v. Broudo, 541 U.S. 901 (2005).

so it might be possible to plead a proper complaint without alleging personal financial gain by the defendants.

Early in 2008, the Supreme Court ruled that customers and suppliers of a corporation, who allegedly engaged in a scheme under which a corporation over-stated its income, were not liable under 10(b) or 10b-5. The third-party defendants in this case were not involved in preparing or disseminating the financial statements, so the Supreme Court ruled that investors did not rely on the third-party defendants. The decision was viewed as favorable to other potential third-party defendants in "scheme liability" securities cases, such as law firms, accountants, and bankers, but the Supreme Court pointed out that even though there is no private cause of action, such third parties are vulnerable to SEC enforcement.[33]

In June 2002, the Supreme Court (reversing the Fourth Circuit) held that a broker who sold securities from a discretionary account without the client's knowledge or consent and kept the sales proceeds himself committed fraud "in connection with the sale of securities" and therefore violated § 10(b) and Rule 10b-5. In this reading, the fraud coincided with a security sale and therefore fell under the anti-fraud rules, even though there was no manipulation of an individual security, and even though the integrity of the market as a whole was not threatened.[34]

[1] 10(b) Rules

The SEC has promulgated many rules under 10(b). Exchange Act rules are found in 17 CFR and are numbered, e.g., Reg. § 240.10b-1, etc.

- Rule 10b-1 forbids market manipulation, even if the securities are exempt from registration
- Rule 10b-3 forbids broker-dealers to manipulate or deceive with regard to municipal securities or securities not listed on an exchange
- Rule 10b-5 forbids material misstatements and omissions; it has been the focus of a great deal of litigation as to its scope
- Rule 10b-10 imposes requirements for confirmation of transactions
- Rule 10b-17 requires announcement of events such as dividends and stock split either to be made pursuant to the rules of an exchange, or to be disclosed to the National Association of Securities Dealers (NASD) at least ten days before the record date.
- Rule 10b-18 is a safe harbor under which an issuer is not liable for misrepresentation if it repurchases its own common stock on the open market. The SEC sets requirements for the price, volume, manner, and time of such purchases. A late-2003 amendment extends the safe harbor to certain after-hours repurchases, imposes a uniform price limit on all issuers, and increases the

---

[33] Stoneridge Investment Partners v. Scientific-Atlanta Inc. and Motorola Inc., 128 S. Ct. 761 (2008). *See, e.g.*, Tony Mauro, *High Court's 'Stoneridge' Ruling a Win for Business Defendants*, Legal Times 1/16/08 (law.com).

[34] SEC v. Zandford, 535 U.S. 813 (2002).

volume that can be repurchased to 100% of the average daily trading volume following a market-wide suspension.[35]

There is no private right of action for aiding and abetting a § 10(b) violation: *Central Bank of Denver v. First Interstate Bank of Denver.*[36] The duty to disclose is not necessarily a duty to update, so it was not fraud under 10b-5 for a company to fail to update its 10-K to reflect disciplinary action imposed by the FDA (leading to a $168 million charge on the company's books). The Seventh Circuit ruled that as long as annual reports are filed as required, continuous disclosure is not mandated. Nor does the quarterly 10-Q report require disclosure of regulatory problems.[37]

[2] Other Anti-Fraud Rules

Section 12(2) of the '33 Act bars material misrepresentation or omission of material fact in a prospectus or oral communication. The Supreme Court limits this to public offerings made by an issuer or controlling shareholder.[38]

Section 18(a) of the '34 Act imposes liability on anyone responsible for material misstatements or omissions in any document filed with the SEC under the '34 Act. Investors who read and rely on such documents have a private right of action. Officers and directors of the reporting company are personally liable, unless they acted in good faith and without knowledge that the statements were false and misleading.

Exchange Act § 14(a) makes a knowingly false statement of reasons, opinions, or beliefs in a proxy statement actionable. Mere proof of disbelief or undisclosed belief or motivation is not a source of liability unless the statement also expressly or impliedly stated something false or misleading about its subject matter. There is no implied private right of action under § 14(a) for a shareholder whose vote is not required to authorize a transaction, because the shareholder has no damages.

[3] Safe Harbor

There are safe harbor rules under Securities Act Rule 175 and Exchange Act Rule 3b-6 for "forward-looking statements" (projections made in registration statements). Forward-looking statements are not fraudulent if they were accurate at the time they were made, even if they were no longer accurate at the time that the document became effective. Under Securities Act § 27A and Exchange Act § 21E, there is no liability in connection with forward-looking statements that are accompanied by meaningful cautionary statements.

---

[35] *See* 72 L.W. 2284.
[36] 511 U.S. 164 (1994).
[37] Gallagher v. Abbott Labs. Inc., 269 F.3d 806 (7th Cir. 2001).
[38] Gustafson v. Alloyd Co., 513 U.S. 561 (1995).

[4] Litigation Issues

Successful securities fraud plaintiffs can recover their "actual damages," which are defined as the market-adjusted value of their losses due to fraud.

The question of statute of limitations is a complex one. Traditionally, securities fraud statutes of limitations were borrowed from state law. The 1991 Supreme Court case *Lampf Pleva Lipkind Prupis & Pettigrow v. Gilbertson*,[39] sets the statute of limitations at one year from discovery of the fraud, and three years from its occurrence, which had the effect of barring a significant number of potential suits.

Congress enacted § 27A of the '34 Act to overturn *Lampf Pleva*, but the Supreme Court found this statute unconstitutional, in that it violates the separation of powers doctrine by requiring the federal courts to re-open final judgments entered before the enactment of § 27A.[40]

The Third Circuit revived an investor suit against Merck & Co., holding that the District Court misconstrued the plaintiffs' claims by ignoring allegations that Merck supported its stock prices with reassuring but untrue statements. The Third Circuit said that security analysts' continuing to issue growth ratings for Merck while the safety of Vioxx was being questioned is relevant to whether there were "storm warnings" about the stock, resulting in untruthful reassurances.[41]

[B] Insider Trading

Corporate insiders get early access to information about the corporation's future plans (e.g., mergers; acquisitions; earnings; new products). This information would permit them to speculate unfairly and manipulate the market, to the injury of public investors, so insider trading is illegal. Although there is no statutory definition of "insider trading," there is legislation and case law on the subject. Insider trading can be summed up as the purchase or sale of securities by insiders who gain access to material information that is not available to the public.

The misappropriation theory[42] holds that merely having information creates a duty to respect the confidentiality of that information, even if the securities being traded are not issued by the client or employer of the person possessing the information.[43]

Material information[44] is information that a reasonable shareholder would consider important in making a decision about a stock: for instance, earnings,

---

[39] 501 U.S. 350 (1991). *See also In re* NAHC Securities Litigation, 306 F.3d 1314 (3d Cir. 2002).

[40] *See* Plaut v. Spendthrift Farm, 514 U.S. 211 (1995).

[41] *In re* Merck & Co. Inc. Securities, 543 F.3d 150 (3d Cir. 2008); *see* Shannon P. Duffy, *3rd Circuit Revives Investors' Claims Against Merck*, The Legal Intelligencer 9/10/08 (law.com).

[42] Set out in United States v. O'Hagan, 521 U.S. 642 (1997).

[43] SEC v. Adler, 137 F.3d 1325 (11th Cir. 1998) says that the defendant has to use, not merely possess, material non-public information to be guilty of insider trading, but possession of information at the time of a trade gives rise to a rebuttable inference that the information was "used."

[44] As defined by TSC Indus. Inc. v. Northway, 426 U.S. 438 (1976).

dividends, new products or contracts, major litigation developments, major changes in the corporation's financial condition.

Insider fiduciaries, such as corporate officers and directors, are clearly barred from insider trading.[45] Outsiders, such as underwriters, lawyers working on a securities transaction, printers, or others who get non-public information in the course of a confidential business relationship are also barred from trading.[46] An insider who gives investment tips to a non-insider, and the "tippee," can also be liable, but tipping liability requires an intent to get direct or indirect personal gain from disclosing the information.

Insider traders can be liable under '34 Act § 21(d)(3) for a civil penalty, payable to the U.S. Treasury of up to $500,000. (There are three tiers of penalties, graded by level of culpability.) Administrative sanctions are also available against anyone who fails to submit a report required by either the '34 Act or the Williams Act (see § 6.07), which governs mergers and acquisitions. "Controlling persons" (employers of individuals who engage in illegal insider trading) who knew of the violation, or who recklessly disregarded the likelihood of insider trading and failed to prevent it, are liable. '34 Act § 15(f), and a parallel provision in § 204A of the Investment Advisers Act, require corporations to maintain written policies to prevent misuse of material non-public information.

"Contemporaneous traders" who trade at the same time as insiders, but without access to the material information have a private right of action under '34 Act § 20A.

The Second Circuit affirmed the acquittal of a floor trader who was accused of "interpositioning" (trading for the firm's account at a price between the buy and sell orders he handled). At worst, the defendant tried to cover up a violation of an NYSE rule; there was no evidence that he misled investors, whether or not they relied on statements he made.[47]

A director of a financial services company traded on confidential information about a pending acquisition. The Ninth Circuit reversed the District Court's grant of summary judgment for the director in the SEC's civil suit, finding that he could be held liable but there was a genuine issue of fact on materiality. According to the District Court, he did not owe a fiduciary duty of confidentiality to the company whose shares he bought, knowing it would be acquired. Because he was not an insider in that corporation, liability could be imposed only under the misappropriation theory, which requires knowing misappropriation of confidential, material, nonpublic information in a breach of duty owed to the source of the information under a relationship of trust and confidence. The Ninth Circuit agreed with the SEC that the director had a duty to keep the impending transaction confidential.

---

[45] Chiarella v. United States, 445 U.S. 222 (1980).

[46] Dirks v. SEC, 463 U.S. 646 (1983).

[47] United States v. Finnerty, 533 F.3d 143 (2d Cir. 2008); *see* Mark Hamblett, *2nd Circuit Upholds Acquittal of Trader*, N.Y.L.J. 7/22/08 (law.com).

The Ninth Circuit does not require a continuous chain of duties for misappropriation liability, and the duty must be owed to the "source" of the information but not necessarily the "originating source."[48]

Rule 14e-3 bars insider trading during an existing or planned tender offer, even in the absence of fiduciary duty to stockholders.

On August 10, 2000, the SEC announced two insider trading rules under 10b-5.[49] Under Rule 10b5-1, trading "on the basis" of inside information occurs if the individual is "aware" of the inside information at the time of the purchase or sale. However, affirmative defenses are available if the information, although known, was not a factor in the decision to enter into the transaction.

Rule 10b5-2 imposes a duty of trust and confidence (and therefore potential liability for misrepresentation) when:

- The potentially liable person agreed to keep the information confidential
- The person who communicated the non-public information had a reasonable expectation of confidentiality based on, e.g., a history or pattern of shared confidences
- The alleged tippee got the information from a close family member.

See § 6.10[A], below, for reporting requirements under the Sarbanes-Oxley Act.

[C] Regulation FD

Regulation FD ("Fair Disclosure"), 17 CFR Part 243, was promulgated by the SEC on August 10, 2000. Its purpose is to require companies that disclose material information at all to do so broadly to the entire market of investors and potential investors, rather than limiting information access to institutional investors and Wall Street analysts.

In general, Regulation FD applies to securities that are already on the market. Communications in connection with most registered offerings are exempt. But once the senior officials of an issuing company know (or are reckless in not knowing) that material non-public information will be selectively disclosed, the company must release the information to the public. Furthermore, if improper selective disclosure is made (e.g., important information given only to analysts in a conference call), the issuer has an obligation to make a public disclosure within 24 hours.

Because Regulation FD is a disclosure regulation, violations are not subject to anti-fraud enforcement. The SEC has the power to file an administrative proceeding to secure a cease-and-desist order against a violator.

---

[48] SEC v. Talbot, 530 F.3d 1085 (9th Cir. 2008).
[49] *See* 69 L.W. 2094.

[D] Regulation of Broker-Dealers

Exchange Act § 15(a) requires broker-dealers to register with the SEC unless their activities are purely intrastate and do not involve any facility of a national securities exchange. Section 15(b)(7) gives the SEC power to impose standards for broker-dealers' operational and financial competence. Rule 15c1–7 forbids "churning" (recommendations to buy or sell motivated by the broker's desire to enhance commissions rather than increase the value of the customer's account). Rule 10b-6 requires disclosure of the cost of margin transactions (those in which securities are purchased on credit).

The federal securities laws are interpreted based on the "shingle theory": that, by hanging out a shingle, the broker holds himself or herself out as an expert either in investment in general or in the securities of a particular issuer. Therefore, a high standard of care will be required when the broker makes representations and recommends investments. The recommendation implies that the broker has enough information to form an opinion about the merits of the security.

Broker-dealers are organized into self-regulatory organizations (SROs). The SROs have their own rules about suitability and knowing the customer. It is unethical for brokers to recommend investments that do not meet known needs of the client.

Transactions in foreign currency options that occur over the counter, rather than on a regulated exchange or board of trade, are exempt from the Commodity Exchange Act, and are not subject to regulation by the CFTC.[50]

A number of SEC rules have been promulgated under '34 Act § 15(c), which prohibits manipulative, deceptive, or fraudulent acts or practices by broker-dealers:

- Rule 15c1–2 (§ 240.15c1–2) is another ban on fraud and misrepresentation
- 15c2–5 requires broker-dealers who control or are controlled by an issuer to disclose the relationship before entering into a customer's transaction. Rule 15c1–6 requires disclosure of their extent of participation or interest in a distribution
- 15c1–8 forbids sales "at the market" unless the broker-dealer has a reasonable belief that a general market exists
- 15c2–7 forbids fictitious market quotations, and impels disclosure of the identity of the broker-dealer placing each quote
- 15c2–8 makes it a deceptive act or practice to fail to deliver a prospectus that is required by the '33 Act.

Brokerage agreements typically include arbitration clauses, so most broker-client disputes are arbitrated rather than litigated. *Shearson-American Express v. McMahon*,[51] compels enforcement of the arbitration clause when the client asserts

---

[50] Dunn v. CFTC, 519 U.S. 465 (1997).
[51] 482 U.S. 220 (1987).

a § 10(b) claim. The Securities Investors Protection Act applies to customers who try to invest even if the broker (here, using a Ponzi scheme) diverts the funds before they can be invested in securities.[52]

The Supreme Court ruled in mid-2007 that the securities laws preclude the application of antitrust laws to conduct of investment banks in connection with IPO syndicates. Thus, the antitrust laws do not apply to "laddering" (refusal to sell shares in an IPO unless the potential purchaser agrees to buy more shares later at a higher price), unusually high commissions on subsequent purchases from the same underwriter, and tying (having to buy into other issues to secure shares in a desired issue). In the Supreme Court's view, the SEC has the expertise to regulate the securities industry.[53]

In mid-2002, the Treasury Department issued a Final Rule[54] requiring broker-dealers to file suspicious activity reports (SARs) covering customer activity that suggests violation of U.S. laws or regulations (e.g., evidence of money laundering). Any questionable transaction or series of transactions involving more than $5,000 must be reported to the Treasury's Financial Crimes Enforcement Network (FinCEN) within 30 days of the broker's discovery that the transaction is suspicious. Red flags include customers who cannot describe their own so-called business or industry; those who have multiple accounts or use multiple names without an apparent justification; and customers who are willing to accept any level of fees on their transactions.

§ 6.06 PROXY REGULATION

In many instances, corporate decision-making (e.g., election of the board of directors; approval of mergers or other extraordinary transactions) will require a vote by stockholders. Very few stockholders are willing to turn up at corporate annual meetings, so the actual voting process is conducted by getting stockholders to sign proxies allowing someone else to cast their votes. The June 2003 SEC Release 34-48108[55] gives shareholders the right to approve or disapprove stock option plans and other equity compensation plans.

In addition to the proxy regulation imposed by federal securities laws, the proxy process is also subject to state corporate law and to the principles set out in the corporation's own articles of incorporation and bylaws (see § 1.08).

[A] Form and Content of Proxies

The Exchange Act governs disclosure and other aspects of the proxy process: e.g., Exchange Act Regulation 14A (17 CFR § 240.14a-1 *et seq.*), Rules 14a-3 and

---

[52] *In re* Primeline Sec. Corp., 295 F.3d 1100 (10th Cir. 2002).

[53] Credit Suisse Securities (USA) v. Billing, 127 S. Ct. 2383 (U.S. 6/18/07); *see, e.g.,* Tony Mauro, *Supreme Court Grants Banks Broad Implied Immunity From Antitrust Lawsuits*, Legal Times 6/19/07 (law.com).

[54] 67 FR 44048 (7/1/02); related SEC rules appear at SEC Release No. 34-47752, IC-266031.

[55] http://www.sec.gov/rules/sro/34-48108.htm.

14a-4, and Schedule 14A set out the content and form of the proxy statement. Proxy materials have to be filed with the SEC (Rule 14a-6). The purpose of Schedule 14A is to ensure that the proxy materials as a whole will provide enough information for a reasonably prudent shareholder to make intelligent decisions about candidates and proposals.

Rule 14a-3 requires all stockholders to get an annual report, and prescribes the form for the report. Rule 14a-4 sets the form of the proxy, and requires that it indicate whether it is being solicited on behalf of management or someone else. Rule 14a-5 requires additional information to be disclosed. Rule 14a-7 sets out the circumstances under which a shareholder is entitled to get a complete shareholder list, for use in soliciting proxies for a dissent slate or in support of a stockholder proposal. Rule 14a-9 forbids false and misleading statements in proxy statements.

Under SEC Release 33-7912, an issuer can satisfy the proxy delivery requirement by sending a single proxy statement to two or more investors in the same household — although a separate proxy card must be issued for each shareholder account.

[B] Shareholder Proposals

Rule 14a-8 gives stockholders a limited right to insist that their own proposals be included in the proxy statement so that other shareholders can vote on the proposal. The right is limited because, under corporate law, many issues (including the conduct of ordinary business operations) are under the control of the Board of Directors and corporate management, and therefore are not appropriate for a shareholder vote. The corporation can omit a stockholder proposal that deals with a personal grievance and does not offer benefits to the shareholders in general.

Exchange Act Release No. 39093 (9/18/97) makes it easier for shareholders to get proposals into the proxy statement, but also makes it easier for companies to reject repeat proposals that have already been submitted to, and rejected by, the stockholders.

Also see Exchange Act Release No. 40018, (5/21/98), holding that employment-related shareholder proposals dealing with social policy issues are not automatically excludable as within the discretion of management. Release 40018 also requires an "override" procedure for including proposals that have attracted significant shareholder interest.

If a shareholder proposal is included in the proxy materials, the company has the right to make a statement in opposition, but the proponent of the proposal must then be given 30 days' notice before the mailing of the proxy statement, to reply. If the company deems the proposal to be inappropriate for inclusion in a proxy statement, it must notify the SEC and give the proponent 80 days' notice before the definitive proxy statement is filed with the SEC. It is often wise, in controversial cases, for the company to get a "no action" letter from the SEC if it wants to omit a proposal.

In 2006, the Second Circuit held that Rule 14a-8 does not permit corporations to exclude shareholder proposals from the proxy if the proposal calls for amending the bylaws to create a procedure for including shareholder nominees for director in the proxy materials. According to the Second Circuit, exclusion is permitted only for proposals that oppose solicitations about an identified board seat in an upcoming election—not the election procedure itself.[56]

The SEC disagrees with this ruling, taking the position that any proposal that could result in a contested election can legitimately be rejected, because it is not expected that opposing nominees would be listed in the same proxy materials. Furthermore, the SEC is opposed to election contests undertaken without engaging in proxy solicitation—and the accompanying disclosures.

In July 2007, the SEC proposed changes in the rules about shareholder proposals, electronic communications with shareholders, and the disclosure requirements of Schedules 14A and 13G. Under the proposal, certain qualified shareholders (e.g., those holding enough shares to be subject to Schedule 13G) would be permitted to propose bylaw amendments. The SEC finalized the Rule 14a-8 amendments, effective January 1, 2008. The SEC specifically sought to overrule *AFSCME v. AIG*. The Final Rule covers shareholder proposals submitted during the 2008 proxy season. Under the Final Rule, a proposal can be excluded from management proxy materials if it creates an immediate election contest or would create a process under which shareholders could conduct a future election contest. Management can exclude proposals that have the effect of disqualifying board nominees who are standing for election, removing directors from office during their term, questioning the competence or business judgment of directors, or requiring management to solicit proxies on behalf of shareholder nominees. However, proposals cannot be excluded if they relate to the qualifications of directors or the structure of the corporation's board, certain voting procedures (e.g., cumulative voting); or nominating procedures that do not place shareholder nominations in management proxies.[57]

In November 2003, the SEC adopted rules requiring public companies to disclose their processes for nominating directors, as well as their communications mechanisms between shareholders and directors. Disclosures are now required on the proxy statement as to whether the board has a process for shareholders to communicate with the board (or why the company has chosen not to have one); the policy about board members attending annual meetings; the number of board

---

[56] AFSCME v. AIG, 462 F.3d 121 (2d Cir 2006).

[57] Proposed Rules, Release No. 34-56160, IC-27913, http://www.sec.gov/rules/proposed/2007/34-56160.pdf (7/27/07), and Release No. 34-56161, IC-27914, http://www.sec.gov/ruls/proposed/2007/34-56161.pdf (7/27/07); Final Rule, Release No. 34-46914, IC-28075, http://www.sec.gov/rules/final/2007/34-56914.pdf (12/6/07). The SEC reversed its earlier position and held that shareholders must be allowed to vote on a proposal for universal health coverage. The shareholder proposal does not force companies to provide health insurance for their employees, only to have executives view the issue as one of social policy. The SEC said that it was appropriate for shareholders to express views about significant social policy issues—but they are debarred from commenting on the day-to-day operations of the business. *See* Rebecca Moore, *SEC Says Companies Must Let Shareholders Vote on Health Care*, www.plansponsor.com (6/2/08).

members at the previous year's annual meeting; and how the company decides which messages from shareholders should be passed along to the board.[58]

§ 6.07 TENDER OFFER DISCLOSURE (WILLIAMS ACT)

In addition to proxy solicitation by management (to elect its chosen slate to the board of directors), proxy solicitation is also used in attempts to take over the corporation. If enough shareholders give their proxies, the party seeking the take-over can elect a majority, or at least a substantial plurality, of the board of directors, and thus control or at least influence board decisions.

An alternative takeover method is the acquisition of enough shares to dominate the board of directors. Parties seeking control make a "tender offer": i.e., they invite stockholders to tender (turn over) their shares.

There is no statutory definition of "tender offer," so whether a transaction constitutes a tender offer is gauged based on factors such as whether there was widespread, active solicitation of public shareholders; if the purchase of a substantial portion of the target's stock was contemplated; if the potential purchaser made a firm offer that was not negotiable; if the offer was made at a premium over the market price; and whether rapid accumulation of shares took place in a publicly announced program of acquisition.

Each takeover method has its advantages and disadvantages. A proxy contest is much less expensive, because there is no need to actually purchase shares. On the other hand, a tender offer leaves the offeror in the position of owning securities, which can appreciate in value.

The Williams Act requires that a tender offer made by a third party (rather than an issuer seeking to re-acquire its own stock)[59] must be kept open for at least 20 business days from the time the offering materials are filed with the SEC and given to shareholders (Rule 14e-1). The bidder must either pay promptly for the tendered shares, or return them after withdrawing the tender offer. Furthermore, because of Rule 10b-13, as long as the offer is open, the bidder can only buy shares pursuant to the tender offer, not on the open market.

Schedule 14D-1, the tender offer statement, must be filed with the SEC, the exchanges, and the target company: see Rule 14d-3(a). Communications to the target shareholders are controlled by Rules 14d-2, -3 and -4. Rule 14e-4 forbids "short tenders" (tendering of stock not currently owned, unless the tenderer has an option on the stock).

If the percentage of the company's securities sought in the tender offer goes up or down, or if the offering price changes, the offer must be kept open for an additional 10 business days. While the offer is open, Rule 14d-7 mandates that stockholders must have the right to withdraw shares that they have tendered.

---

[58] Release No. 33-8340.

[59] If the offeror tries to repurchase securities to frustrate a tender offer, Rule 13e-1 requires the issuer to disclose the purchases to the SEC.

The target company is given 10 days, by Rule 14e-2, to inform its stockholders of its position with regard to the tender offer (including "none"). A "stop, look and listen" letter is permitted — i.e., the target company can suggest that stockholders refrain from tendering until the target company's board of directors makes a recommendation.

Perhaps the most significant section of the Williams Act is Exchange Act § 13(d), which imposes the requirement of filing Schedule 13D to disclose purchases of the target company's stock in a tender offer. The acquiror must disclose its identity and background; its relationship to the issuer of the stock; how much was paid; the source of funds for the payment; and the reason for the acquisition, as soon as it reaches 5% ownership of the target's stock. (Other Williams Act forms include the Schedules 13E and G, 14D, 14D-1 disclosure by bidders as to the bidder's purpose in making a tender offer, and the 14D-9 filed by targets informing the SEC of their recommendations as to tender offers.) "Beneficial owners" of tendered stock must file, but parties with purely ministerial responsibilities do not have to.

In the view of the Southern District of New York, the purpose of the '34 Act § 13(d) obligation is to protect the target shareholders. Therefore, shareholders of the potential acquiror do not have standing to sue. In fact, the statutory scheme does not even entitle them to receive Schedule 13D.[60]

Exchange Act § 14(e) forbids material misstatements and omissions and fraudulent, deceptive, or manipulative acts or practices in connection with a tender offer. However, under *Schreiber v. Burlington Northern, Inc.*,[61] a § 14(e) action cannot be maintained unless the defendant committed misrepresentation or nondisclosure.

At one time, bidders attempting a hostile takeover of a corporation could put pressure on target shareholders by making discretionary tender offers that favored those who surrendered their securities earliest. However, the "all-holders" rule now requires equal access to the tender offer for all holders of the target securities (Rule 14d-10), and everyone who tenders must get the same price.

§ 6.08 THE INVESTMENT COMPANY ACT OF 1940

This statute, 15 USC § 80a-1 through 80a-52, protects investors who entrust their funds to mutual funds and other investment companies in order to obtain expert management and portfolio diversification. It regulates the capital structure of investment companies and determines who can serve on an investment company Board of Directors. Convicted criminals and persons who have been detected in prior securities law violations are barred from responsible positions in investment companies.

All investment companies that do not qualify for an exemption must register with the SEC on Form N-8A. Investment companies must file their sales literature

---

[60] *In re* Dow Chemical Securities Bhopal Litigation, 2000 WL 1886612 (S.D.N.Y. 2000).
[61] 472 U.S. 1 (1985).

with the SEC within 10 days of issuance. Fees paid to the company's own investment advisers must be disclosed. The Investment Company Act protects investors against conflicts of interest on the part of investment companies and strengthens the anti-fraud and private remedies provisions of the '33 and '34 Acts. One powerful sanction is that contracts of non-registered, non-exempt investment companies are unenforceable.

Companies subject to the Act are classified into three groups: unit investment trusts; companies that issue face-amount certificates; and management companies. Management companies, e.g., mutual funds, are the largest category, subdivided into open-end or closed-end, diversified or non-diversified.

The Investment Company Act does not apply to broker-dealers, banks, insurance companies, savings and loan institutions or small loan companies, because they are already regulated. Pension plans and not-for-profit voting trusts are also exempt.

In April 2004, the SEC adopted the first of a number of rules intended to prevent further mutual fund abuses by leveling the playing field between favored and ordinary customers. Effective December 5, 2004, additional disclosure was required about the fund's procedures for market timing, the risks of market timing, and the extent to which a fund uses "fair value" pricing for lightly traded issues. Insurance companies that sell variable annuities must provide the same disclosures to annuity purchasers. The SEC has also required all funds to have chief compliance officers, and to disclose the fund's complete portfolio every quarter.[62]

In 2004, the SEC adopted a rule requiring mutual fund boards to include 75% independent directors, as well as a chairman independent of the fund's management. The rule was supposed to take effect early in 2006. However, on June 21, 2005, the D.C. Circuit, accepting arguments raised by the securities industry, held that the rule violated the Administrative Procedure Act because the SEC failed to consider either the cost of implementation or alternative approaches suggested by two of the SEC's commissioners. Notwithstanding the decision, on June 29, the SEC voted 3-2 to re-adopt the rule.[63]

Late 2007's Investment Company Act Release No. 28064 (November 12, 2007) proposes fundamental changes in Form N-A, governing the format and delivery of prospectuses. The proposal calls for a new summary section at the beginning of the prospectus, providing key information (e.g., the fund's investment objectives, top 10 portfolio holdings, costs, performance, risks, and principal investment strategies) in plain English in a standardized format. Funds would be allowed to sell shares with only a summary prospectus, if the entire prospectus is made available online. (The SEC has therefore revised Rule 498 to provide that Securities Act § 5(b)(2) is satisfied by providing the new form of summary

---

[62] Release No. 33-8408; *see* Tom Lauricella and Karen Damato, *Mutual Funds' Scandal Spawns New SEC Rules*, Wall St. J., 4/14/04 at p. C1; Karen Damato and Judith Burns, *Cleaning up the Fund Industry*, Wall St. J., 4/5/04 at p. R1.

[63] Chamber of Commerce v. SEC, 412 F.3d 133 (D.C. Cir. 2005).

prospectus.) The SEC described the new approach as "layered disclosure," with the most vital information furnished in a format that invites comparison, with the rest of the information on the Internet. The proposal also requires the prospectus for a mutual fund to provide a risk/return summary and some new information. In a multiple-fund prospectus, each fund or series of funds must have a separate summary, because combined summaries make it difficult to compare performance.[64]

In mid-2008, the Seventh Circuit rejected the test that "reasonableness" is the standard for excessive fee claims under the Investment Company Act § 36(b), instead adopting the Third Circuit test of whether fees are fully disclosed. (Investors sued a fund adviser for deceiving them and taking excessive compensation.) The Seventh Circuit held that judges cannot effectively regulate rates; the market should set the fees, and the test is whether the client made a voluntary choice based on adequate information. Thus, the Seventh Circuit rejected the District Court's requirement that the fees must be related to the worth of the services.[65]

§ 6.09 INVESTMENT ADVISERS ACT OF 1940

"Investment advisers" — persons who receive compensation for advising others "as to the value of securities or as to the advisability of investing in, purchasing or selling securities" — are regulated by 15 USC § 80b-1 *et seq*. However, a number of professional groups are excluded from the definition: advisers who work solely for insurance companies; banks; lawyers, accountants, engineers, and teachers rendering incidental advice to their clients; broker-dealers providing incidental advisory service; and bona fide news media including general-circulation financial publications.

The question of investment newsletters is a difficult one. The public must be protected, but so must First Amendment rights of commercial speech. The Supreme Court's view of the proper balance[66] is that an investment newsletter providing investment advice that is not tailored to the specific needs of individual clients is not an investment adviser.

Persons falling within the definition of investment adviser are required to register with the SEC on Form ADV. They must provide periodic disclosure to the SEC on ADV-5 reports. Much of that information must be given to clients and prospective clients. They are subject to minimum fair dealing requirements and can

---

[64] Paul Hastings, *SEC Proposes New "Layered" Prospectus Disclosure and Delivery Regime* (12/07) www.paulhastings.com.

[65] Jones v. Harris Associates, 537 F.3d 728 (7th Cir. 2008); *see* Sutherland Legal Alert, *Seventh Circuit Rejects "Reasonableness" as the Standard for Excessive Fee Claims Under Section 36(b) of the 1940 Act*, 5/30/08 (benefitslink.com); Zach Lowe, *7th Circuit Ruling a Big Win for Mutual Fund Advisers*, The American Lawyer 5/22/08 (law.com). The reasonableness test comes from Gartenberg v. Merrill Lynch Asset Management Inc., 694 F.2d 923 (2d Cir. 1982) and was adopted by the Fourth Circuit: Migdal v. Rowe Price-Fleming Int'l, 248 F.3d 321 (4th Cir. 2001); the Third Circuit focused on disclosure rather than reasonableness: Green v. Fund Asset Mgm't LP, 286 F.3d 682 (3d Cir. 2002).

[66] Lowe v. SEC, 472 U.S. 181 (1985).

be penalized for fraudulent or deceptive practices. However, the SEC has the power to prescribe standards of qualifications and competence for broker-dealers, but not for investment advisers. Investment advisers are subject to SEC monetary penalties, imposed through administrative proceedings or civil suits, and even criminal penalties.

Under the anti-fraud provision of the Investment Advisers Act (§ 206(l)), reckless or knowing conduct can constitute scienter. Willful intent to defraud is not required.[67]

The Investment Advisers Act (IAA) was amended in 1990 to give the federal district courts jurisdiction over actions at law to enforce any duty or liability created by the statute. However, there is no private right of action for damages: private plaintiffs remain limited to their pre-existing implied rights of action for rescission and restitution.[68]

In mid-2004, the SEC adopted rules mandating that investment advisory firms adopt a code of ethics including elements specified by the SEC. The code of ethics must provide standards for business conduct and require supervised persons to comply with federal securities laws. Certain supervised persons must report their personal securities dealings. Employees of investment advisory firms must report violations of the code of ethics to the firm's chief compliance officer.[69]

Brokers and dealers are exempt from the IAA when their advice is solely incidental to conducting business as a broker or dealer, and they are not specially compensated for the advice. Then, in 2005, the SEC promulgated a final rule exempting brokers and dealers from the IAA even if they do get special compensation. The D.C. Circuit found that fee-based brokerage accounts (accounts that compensate brokers with a fixed annual fee rather than commissions per trade) violated securities laws, and required termination of such accounts as of October 1, 2007. The SEC, however, adopted temporary rules to be in effect until 2009, giving the SEC time to adopt permanent regulations.[70]

§ 6.10   THE SARBANES-OXLEY ACT OF 2002

In mid-2002, in response to widespread financial scandals involving many major corporations, Congress passed the Sarbanes-Oxley Act of 2002, P.L. 107-204. Sarbanes-Oxley is made up of 11 titles. Title I establishes a Public Company Accounting Oversight Board. Title II enhances the independence of auditors. Title III on corporate responsibility requires public companies to have audit committees.

---

[67] Vernazza v. SEC, 327 F.3d 851 (9th Cir. 2003).

[68] Filson v. Langman, 2002 WL 31528616 (D. Mass. 2002).

[69] New Rule 204A-1; amended Rule 204-2 under the Investment Advisers Act.

[70] Financial Planning Associates v. SEC, 482 F.3d 481 (D.C. Cir. 2007), holding that Rule 202(a)(11)-1, 70 FR 20,424 (4/19/05), is invalid.

[A] Reporting of Blackout Periods

One of the most resented aspects of the financial scandals was the perception that corporate insiders enriched themselves by selling their own shares of stock before the company's stock price collapsed, whereas rank-and-file workers lost a great deal of the value of their retirement savings because they were trapped by "blackouts" and unable to sell employer stock in their pension and especially in their 401(k) accounts.

Sarbanes-Oxley amends ERISA to give participants in a 401(k) or other individual account plan at least 30 days notice before there will be a blackout period affecting the plan. For this purpose, a blackout period is a period of more than three business days during which the rights of plan participants to change the investments in their accounts, and/or to get plan loans or distributions, are suspended, limited, or restricted (however, limits imposed by securities law, regularly scheduled limits disclosed in plan documents, and actions in compliance with a QDRO — see § 3.05[6] — are not considered blackout periods).

The blackout notice must be in plain English; must explain why the blackout is imposed, which investments are affected, and how long the period is expected to last; and must warn participants to consider the validity of their investment choices.

The notice can be provided less than 30 days in advance in connection with a merger, acquisition, or divestiture, or if the plan administrator is unable to provide the full 30-day notice. However, notice must be given as far in advance as is reasonably practicable.

During a blackout period that affects 50% or more of the company's individual plan participants, the company's directors and executive officers are forbidden to trade or transfer any employer securities that they own and that they acquired in connection with employment. (Securities bought on the open market for investment are not covered by this provision.) The insider-trading provisions are also effective as of January 26, 2003.

In January 2003, the SEC adopted Regulation BTR (Blackout Trading Restrictions) forbidding trades by directors and officers when at least 50% of the individuals covered by the plan are subject to a trading blackout of more than three consecutive business days. See 17 CFR Part 245.

[B] Corporate Responsibility and Enhanced Disclosures

Insiders, also known as reporting persons (officers and directors of a reporting company; persons who are beneficial owners of more than 10% of any class of a reporting company's securities) must report to the SEC whenever they become insiders, when they change their securities holdings, or when they engage in swap transactions affecting their holdings in the subject company. Form 4 is the relevant SEC form for transaction reporting.

Before Sarbanes-Oxley, the transactions had to be reported no later than 10 days after the close of the calendar month in which a transaction took place. Sarbanes-Oxley speeds this up, requiring the report to be made by the end of the second business day after the day of execution of the transaction. SEC Release Nos. 34-46421, 35-27563 (http://www.sec.gov/rules/final/34-46421.htm), effective August 29, 2002, provides rules for complying with the Sarbanes-Oxley Act's amendments to Exchange Act § 16(a).

In addition to the disclosures already required by Exchange Act § 13, reporting companies must make real-time disclosures, in plain English, of any information about material changes in the company's financial condition or operations that the SEC finds necessary to protect investors. The SEC can require disclosure of trend and qualitative information and graphics.

Sarbanes-Oxley also requires that, for companies filing periodic reports under Exchange Act § 13(a) or 15(d), each annual and quarterly report must be certified by the corporation's principal executive officer(s) and principal financial officer(s). The corporate officers must certify that they have reviewed the report and, to the officer's knowledge, the report does not contain any untrue statement of material fact, and nothing is omitted to prevent statements of material fact from being misleading. The officers must also certify that, to their knowledge, the financial information in the report (including the financial statements) fairly states the company's financial conditions and results of operations.

When a company is required to restate its accounting data because of misconduct involving financial reporting, the company's CEO and CFO are required to repay to the company not only any bonus or incentive compensation they received during the 12 months after the filing of the improper document, but any profit they earned selling the company's securities during that 12-month period.

Sarbanes-Oxley amends Exchange Act § 13 to require any SEC filing that contains financial statements and that is required to conform to Generally Accepted Accounting Principles (GAAP) to reflect whatever material corrections are identified by the firm's accountants consonant with GAAP and SEC rules. All material off-balance sheet transactions that may have a material effect on the corporation's financial condition must be disclosed. Pro forma financial information must be reported completely and with true statements of all material facts.

Limitations are imposed on direct or indirect personal loans to executives, although home loans and loans constituting consumer credit are still permitted.

Reporting companies must disclose to the SEC whether or not they have adopted a code of ethics governing senior financial officers (CFO, comptroller, and/or principal accounting officer), and amendments to the code must be reported to the SEC on Form 8-K.[71] Reporting companies must also disclose to the SEC whether their audit committees include at least one member who is a financial expert.

An SEC rule issued March 16, 2004 adds eight new items to the "triggering events" that require a corporation to issue a Form 8-K. For most items, the deadline is four days after the triggering event. The items include entering into, or materially amending, a material definitive agreement that is outside the ordinary course of

---

[71] See SEC Release No. 33-8177A, http://www.sec.gov/rules/final/33-8177A.htm.

business; some executive compensation agreements fall into this category. The SEC has the power, under Sarbanes-Oxley § 409, to determine which changes must be reported on a current basis by public companies.

The other new items are: termination of an agreement that is not in the ordinary course of business; creating a material obligation by use of an off-balance-sheet arrangement; incurring material costs of exit or disposal activities; material impairment of corporate assets; the corporation's stock being de-listed or failing to satisfy the requirements for continued listing; and a previously issued document (e.g., financial statement, audit report, or interim review) that can no longer be relied on. Under the Regulation, a material definitive agreement is an agreement dealing with obligations that are material to and enforceable against the registrant or involving rights that are material to the registrant and enforceable by it against someone else. Filing of Form 8-K is required for management contracts, and for compensation plans, including those that award more than trivial amounts of options or other equity. Disclosure is not required if the plan is available to officers, directors, or employees generally, with the same method of benefit allocation applied to both management and non-management participants.[72]

The Sarbanes-Oxley legislation obligates the SEC to step up its review of reporting companies' periodic disclosures, including 10-K forms and financial statements, in order to protect investors. Each reporting company must be reviewed at least once every three years.

A new § 15D has been added to the Exchange Act, giving the SEC one year to adopt rules about research reports and recommendations made by securities analysts, to prevent conflicts of interest and enhance the objectivity of the reports and recommendations. The SEC's rules on the issue of independence of research are found at Release No. 34-48252, http://www.sec.gov/rules/final/34-48252.htm.

The SEC gains the authority, under new Exchange Act § 21C(f), to issue an order barring anyone who is the subject of a cease-and-desist order for violating § 10(b) from acting as an officer or director of a company that has registered any securities or is a reporting company, if that person's conduct demonstrates unfitness to serve. The order can be conditional or unconditional and can be made either permanent or for a period of time. A similar order can be issued under Securities Act § 8A(f) in connection with cease-and-desist proceedings under Securities Act § 17(a)(1).

Sarbanes-Oxley also contains various criminal provisions relating to fraud and other white-collar crimes: see § 26.02[H][8][d].

In late 2002, the SEC proposed broad rule changes greatly expanding the extent to which corporate lawyers would be required to report evidence of fiduciary breaches or securities law violations by their clients, through adopting a new Part 205, Standards of Professional Conduct for Attorneys Appearing and Practicing Before the SEC, in the SEC Rules of Practice. The rules apply to both house counsel and retained attorneys. Under the proposal, attorneys would have an

---

[72] Release No. 33-8400, 69 FR 15594 (3/25/04).

obligation to contact the company's CEO and/or Chief Legal Officer (CLO) to report suspected irregularities. If that did not lead to correction of the problem, the attorney would be permitted (and, in some instances, required) to make a "noisy withdrawal." Reporting wrongdoing to the SEC would not be considered a breach of attorney-client confidentiality. The proposal would subject an attorney who violates these rules to the full range of the remedies under the '34 Act, including injunction, cease-and-desist order, and exclusion from the securities industry. In response to negative comments, the SEC modified the proposal so that "noisy withdrawal" would not be required; instead, the client company, and not the attorney, must notify the SEC of the withdrawal.[73]

The SEC issued the first guidance in mid-2007 about how to evaluate corporate internal controls in light of the size of the corporation. On the same day, the SEC approved another rule under which an auditor can issue a single opinion covering both corporate internal controls on financial reporting and management assessment of the controls. (Previously, two separate reports were required.) The objective is to streamline public companies' audit process so they can concentrate on the areas where fraud risk is greatest.[74]

§ 6.11   SEC ENFORCEMENT

In addition to formally promulgated regulations, the SEC makes its policies known in various forms. SEC Releases are statements distributed to interested parties. No-action letters are responses to private inquiries, so called because SEC says it will "take no action" with regard to proposals that do not violate any laws.

If the SEC does believe that laws have been violated, its actions will depend on the nature of the perceived violation and who has committed it:

- Against a broker-dealer or registered investment advisor, the SEC can bring a proceeding to revoke/suspend registration or take intermediate disciplinary action. Initial findings are made by an ALJ, with the final decision coming from the SEC
- Against issuers registering under '33 Act, the SEC can seek to suspend the effectiveness of the registration statement
- Against anyone: a cease-and-desist order forbidding further violations
- Administrative proceedings seeking disgorgement orders and/or fines
- Suits in District Court for injunction against future violations
- Referral to the Department of Justice for prosecution of egregious criminal violation of securities laws.

---

[73] 17 CFR §§ 205–205.7; *see* Tamara Loomis and Otis Bilodeau, *SEC Eases Off on Provisions for Attorneys*, N.Y.L.J. 1/24/03 (law.com).

[74] Siobhan Hughes, *Sarbanes-Oxley Is Eased*, Wall St. J. 5/24/07 at C1; Eric Dash, *S.E.C. Revises Its Standards for Corporate Audits*, N.Y. Times 5/24/07 at C3.

In fiscal 2008, the SEC brought 671 enforcement actions—the second-highest annual total it had ever brought. The rise in enforcement actions include an increase of over 25% in insider trading cases and 45% more market manipulation cases than 2007. The SEC announced that there were more than 50 investigations going on in the subprime mortgage market. Recoveries distributed to injured investors were over $1 billion in each of fiscal 2007 and 2008.[75]

In mid-2006, the SEC adopted disclosure rules for providing information (in plain English, and in both narrative and tabular form) about the compensation of executives and directors of public corporations. The Compensation Discussion and Analysis (CD&A) is filed, and therefore must be certified by the corporation's CEO and CFO. For individuals covered by disclosure requirements (the CEO, CFO, directors, and three highest-paid executives), the corporation must disclose their salary, bonuses, perquisites, and equity-based awards for the previous three years, with extensive disclosure related to grants, valuation, and exercise of stock options and retirement benefits. Transactions between the corporation and a related person must still be disclosed, but the safe harbor for small transactions rises from $60,000 to $120,000. A new Item 407 has been added to Regulations S-K and S-B, to consolidate information about the independence of directors and nominees for directors.[76] The financial crisis of 2008 created controversy over the role that very high executive compensation played in the economy's difficulties. The "bailout bill," P.L. 110-334, included some limitations on compensation of top management of financial institutions accepting federal assistance, but did not cover executive compensation in general.

The SEC proposed to develop strategies for phasing in International Financial Reporting Standards (IFRS) as of 2014. The plan calls for an initial phase of large U.S. multinational corporations voluntarily adopting international standards until 2010. In 2011, the SEC plans to decide if investors would be better off if IFRS were adopted and, if so, take a vote on making IFRS mandatory. If IFRS is mandated, large corporations would have to adopt the system by 2014, mid-sized companies in 2015, and small companies in 2016. The plan calls for FASB and the International Accounting Standards Board to collaborate on the change.[77]

According to the Second Circuit, it does not constitute double jeopardy to require a securities offender to disgorge profits and pay a civil fine for a securities fraud for which he had already been convicted and ordered to pay restitution, because the disgorgement and fine were not criminal in nature and were not ordered for punitive purposes.[78]

---

[75] Sheri Qualters, *SEC Brings Second-Highest Number of Enforcement Actions in Its History*, Nat'l L.J. 10/27/08 (law.com).

[76] SEC Release 2006-123, SEC Votes to Adopt Changes to Disclosure Requirements Concerning Executive Compensation and Related Matters, http://www.sec.gov/news/press/2006/2006 -123.htm (7/26/06).

[77] Rebecca Moore, *SEC Proposes Move to International Financial Reporting Standards*, Plansponsor.com (8/27/08).

[78] SEC v. Palmisano, 135 F.3d 860 (2d Cir. 1998).

SEC disciplinary orders can be enforced via summary proceedings in District Court. Due Process requires notice to the disciplined parties and an opportunity to respond before the order is enforced, but a full-scale civil action is not required.[79]

[A] Commodities Enforcement

Commodity Exchange Act § 4m(1) requires registration with the Commodity Futures Trading Commission of all persons who are paid to advise others (whether the advice is given in a print or electronic medium) about the value or advisability of trading commodities futures. But, for First Amendment reasons, it does not apply to a publisher of investment advice, because imposing the requirement on a publisher of impersonal trading advice would be an impermissible prior restraint on speech.[80]

Although in general private fraud actions under the Commodity Exchange Act are subject to a two-year statute of limitations, it is permissible for contracting parties to draft the contract to shorten the statute of limitations.[81]

§ 6.12 SECURITIES ARBITRATION

The Supreme Court has established parameters for resolution of securities claims through arbitration rather than litigation, starting with a 1987 ruling holding that the pro-arbitration policy of the Federal Arbitration Act favors enforcement of an arbitration agreement covering a 10b-5 suit against a broker.[82]

The Supreme Court went on to rule, in 1989, that an arbitration agreement with a broker precludes a dissatisfied customer from suing the broker under Securities Act § 12.[83] At the end of 2002, the Supreme Court returned to the topic of securities arbitration by holding that the NASD's Code of Arbitration Procedure 10304, which provides that no dispute is arbitrable more than six years from the event, is a procedural rule. Because it is procedural and not a question of substantial arbitrability, issues arising under the rule are determined by the arbitrator and not by the court system.[84]

§ 6.13 LIMITS ON SECURITIES LITIGATION

In the 1980s and 1990s, many fraud cases were filed by disgruntled investors. Concerns were raised that "professional plaintiffs" would file what were essentially strike suits in order to collect judgments or force parties with little or no

---

[79] SEC v. McCarthy, 322 F.3d 650 (9th Cir. 2003).

[80] Commodity Trend Serv. v. Commodity Futures Trading Comm'n, 1999 WL 965962 (N.D. Ill. 1999). The principle that publishers of non-personalized advice about stock trading need not register was established by Lowe v. SEC, 472 U.S. 181 (1985).

[81] Stephan v. Goldinger, 325 F.3d 874 (7th Cir. 2003).

[82] Shearson v. McMahon, 482 U.S. 220 (1987).

[83] Rodriguez v. Shearson, 490 U.S. 477 (1989).

[84] Howsam v. Dean Witter Reynolds Inc., 537 U.S. 79 (2002).

culpability to settle. Congress passed legislation, in 1995 and 1998, to deter improper securities litigation.

[A] Private Securities Litigation Reform Act (PSLR)

The Private Securities Litigation Reform Act of 1995, P.L. 104-67, was vetoed by President Clinton on December 19, 1995, but was re-passed over his veto on December 22, 1995. The PSLR adds a new § 27, "private securities litigation," to the '33 Act and also amends § 21 of the '34 Act.

The objective of the PSLR is to discourage frivolous securities litigation. However, Congress acknowledges that securities fraud does in fact occur, and the PSLR strengthens the audit requirements by requiring accountants to examine corporate books for signs of fraud. Suspicious phenomena must be reported to corporate management; if management refuses to take action, whistle-blowing is required.

Under SLUSA (see [B], below), most class actions involving publicly-traded securities must be brought in federal court (although this requirement is not imposed on individual or derivative suits). Federal preemption applies to fraud-related claims, but not state law causes of action for conversion, breach of contract, or breach of fiduciary duty.

Many pre-PSLR cases arose when stockholders claimed that they lost money by relying on corporate predictions. The PSLR includes safe harbor provisions for oral or written forward-looking statements, such as earnings projections that do not pan out. To qualify for the safe harbor, the statement must be issued in conjunction with "meaningful cautionary statements," specific discussion of factors that could prevent the predictions from coming true. This safe harbor is a statutory exemption of the "bespeaks caution" doctrine adopted by at least five Circuits: i.e., that alleged omissions or misrepresentations become immaterial, as a matter of law, if they are accompanied by adequate cautionary language.

There is no duty to update forward-looking statements, so there would be no liability if a corporate officer truthfully announced that a new pharmaceutical had performed well in lab tests — but did not issue a later statement after side effects were discovered.

The safe harbor is not available in IPO registration statements or sales of penny stock; in financial statements prepared in accordance with GAAP; in connection with tender offers; in § 13(d) statements disclosing beneficial ownership; or in connection with an offering of a partnership, limited liability company, or direct participation program.

Yet another Sarbanes-Oxley Act provision amends 28 USC § 1658 to provide that the statute of limitations for a claim of fraud, deceit, manipulation, or contrivance that violates the securities laws is the earlier of five years after the violation or two years after discovery of the facts constituting the violation. This statute of limitations applies to proceedings commenced on or after the enactment of Sarbanes-Oxley. However, Sarbanes-Oxley merely explicates and strengthens existing securities laws; it does not create any additional private rights of action. This provision (Sarbanes-Oxley § 804) is not retroactive. The Second and Eighth Circuits have held that neither the statutory language nor the legislative history show congressional intent to revive expired claims.[85]

[1] Class Actions

The selection of lead plaintiff (and hence of the attorneys who may be able to bill large fees) is critical to the PSLR case, and rivalry among candidates is often intense. According to the Northern District of California, a group of unrelated investors with nothing in common other than sharing an attorney were not suitable lead plaintiffs for a class action. In this reading, institutional investors are presumptive lead plaintiffs because of their greater capacity for managing the case.[86]

Most of the PSLR deals with class actions rather than individual actions.[87] Congress was worried about the prevalence of "professional plaintiffs," who purchased a few shares of stock merely to be able to sue the issuer, and were not representative of long-range investors. Under the PSLR, the party with the greatest financial interest in the proposed relief is rebuttably presumed to be the "most adequate plaintiff" who must lead the class action.[88]

No one can act as lead plaintiff more often than five times in a three-year period. The lead plaintiff is entitled only to a pro rata share of the judgment, not a "bounty" for bringing the case. The most adequate plaintiff's selection of counsel for the class requires approval of the court hearing the class action.

If there are multiple defendants, their liability is proportionate, not joint and several, because Congress was concerned about the possibility of deep-pocket defendants being forced to settle cases in which they had little or no culpability, simply to avert joint and several liability on a massive judgment. In 2008, the Eleventh Circuit ruled on an issue of first impression: the extent to which the proportionate liability scheme under PSLRA amends Exchange Act § 20(a), which makes a person who controls a violator of the Exchange Act jointly and severally liable with the violator. The Eleventh Circuit ruled that § 21(D)(f) does not enlarge the class of liable parties; it merely governs the allocation of liability among defendants who are liable. The PSLRA does not increase the range of the

---

[85] Kinermon v. Cadogan, 409 F.3d 974 (8th Cir. 2005); Aetna Life Ins. v. Enterprise Mort. Acceptance Co., 391 F.3d 401 (2d Cir. 2004).

[86] *In re* Network Assoc's Inc. Sec. Litigation, 76 F. Supp. 2d 1017 (N.D. Cal. 1999).

[87] *Also see* Matsushita Elec. Industrial Co. v. Epstein, 516 U.S. 367 (1996), requiring the federal courts to give full faith and credit to a Delaware court's release of '34 Act class action claims, with respect to parties who failed to either object or opt out.

[88] There can be more than one lead: *see* Cephalon Sec. Litigation, CCH Fed. Sec. L. Rep. ¶99,313 (E.D. Pa. 8/27/96). A presumptive lead plaintiff cannot be disqualified because of the inadequacy of the lawyers chosen to represent the plaintiff, or the fee arrangements with those lawyers—unless the arrangement is so irrational or tainted by self-dealing or conflict of interest that it casts doubt on the plaintiff's ability to represent the class: *In re* Cavanaugh, 316 F.3d 726 (9th Cir. 2002).

controlling person's liability, but it changes the rules for allocating damages by imposing proportionate rather than joint and several liability once liability has been imposed. The controlling person is liable to the same extent as the controlled person unless the controlling person can affirmatively establish that it acted in good faith and did not induce the controlled person to violate securities law.[89]

Oral or written "forward-looking statements" may qualify for safe-harbor protection under the PSLR. Such statements are not actionable unless they are material. Statements are not actionable if they are accompanied by "meaningful cautionary statements" about the factors that could prevent the predictions from being met.

To prevail, the plaintiff must be able to prove that the maker of the statement had actual knowledge that it was false or misleading, not merely foolishly optimistic or inaccurate.

For statements made by a corporation or other entity, the standard is whether the statement was made by or with the approval of an executive officer of the entity who knew it was false or misleading.[90] The safe harbor is not available to issuers who were convicted or subjected to a decree involving a securities law violation in the three years before the statement was made.

The Fifth Circuit, taking the position that defendants should not be coerced into settlements by erroneous class certification, refused to permit Enron Corporation shareholders to maintain a class action against investment banks that failed to detect securities fraud. The attorneys general of 30 states, including Connecticut, Illinois, Texas, New Jersey, and Pennsylvania, favored class certification, and the SEC has already obtained large settlements from firms such as Merrill Lynch, JP Morgan Chase, and Citigroup for failing to discover the fraud.[91]

The Second Circuit held in 2007 that WorldCom bondholders were members of a class designated in a class-action complaint, so the statute of limitations was tolled during the time a class action on their behalf was pending.[92]

The Eleventh Circuit held that non-intervening objectors to the settlement of a securities fraud class action do not have standing to appeal the court's approval of

---

[89] LaPerriere v. Vesta Insurance Group Inc., 526 F.3d 715 (11th Cir. 2008).

[90] A statement is not material, and therefore cannot give rise to liability, if investors have access to other documents that suggest caution. For instance, warnings in a registration statement can immunize a press release: Grossman v. Novell Inc., 120 F.3d 1112 (10th Cir. 1997).

[91] Michael Kunzelman (AP), *5th Circuit Rules Out Class Action in Enron Shareholders' Suit*, 3/20/07 (law.com). Early in 2008, the Supreme Court declined to review *Regents of the University of California v. Merrill Lynch*, a case involving alleged participation of banks in deceptive deals that helped Enron to report fictitious profits. The court's decision was not surprising in light of *Stoneridge*. The petitioners in the Enron case charged that financial professionals deliberately misled investors; the Supreme Court's rejection of the case suggests an intent to apply *Stoneridge* to all categories of third parties. *See* Tony Mauro, *Supreme Court Denies Review of Enron Case*, Legal Times 1/23/08 (law.com).

[92] *In re* WorldCom Securities Litig., 496 F.3d 245 (2d Cir. 2007). The court held that American Pipe & Construction Co. v. Utah, 414 U.S. 538 (1974), does not restrict tolling to actions filed after certification.

the settlement. *Devlin v. Scardeletti*, 536 U.S. 1 (2002), doesn't apply, because that case involved class members who were bound by the judgment, rather than non-members of the class who were not bound.[93]

[2] Scienter and Other Pleading Requirements

PSLR litigation often turns on the question of whether the plaintiff has adequately pleaded scienter (the defendant's knowledge and state of mind). The PSLR increases the pleading obligation of the plaintiff. For each statement made by the defendant that the plaintiff alleges to be misleading, the plaintiff must give the reason(s) why the statement is misleading. For allegations made on information and belief, the information on which the belief is based must be pleaded. Facts giving rise to a strong inference that the defendant acted with the requisite state of mind must be specifically alleged.

The one-year/three-year statute of limitations deriving from *Lampf Pleva* is retained under the PSLR.[94]

The PSLR clarifies that there is no express private right of action against aiders or abettors of a securities law violation. (As noted above, *Central Bank of Denver* holds that there is no private right of action under 10b-5 for aiding and abetting.) The PSLR rules out securities fraud as a predicate offense for civil RICO claims.[95]

Within 20 days of filing the complaint, the filing plaintiff must notify class members using a wire service or "widely circulated business publication." According to the legislative history, e-mail or other electronic notice methods are acceptable.

If the court deems a securities suit to be abusive, Rule 11 sanctions can be imposed (see § 27.05) and the plaintiff class can be ordered to pay the defendant's attorneys' fees. The plaintiff class (or their attorneys) can be required to provide undertakings for payment of the attorneys' fees. If the plaintiff class prevails, its attorneys' fee award is limited to a reasonable percentage of the damages and prejudgment interest actually paid to the plaintiffs. Funds disgorged under an

---

[93] AAL High Yield Bond Fund v. Banc of America Sec. LLC, 361 F.3d 1305 (11th Cir. 2004).

[94] The one-year statute of limitations begins when the plaintiff knew, or would have known with reasonable diligence, that the defendant knowingly made a false representation: Law v. Medco Research, 113 F.3d 781 (7th Cir. 1997). The Eastern District of New York held that a class action over misrepresentations about a drug was time-barred because it was not brought within two years of the time the plaintiffs reasonably should have known that the alleged fraud caused them damages. Although the plaintiffs said that statute started to run when the New York Times published articles about the dangers of the drug, the Eastern District pointed to earlier "storm warnings" — information available to the stock market that puts well-informed investors on notice of the need for additional investigation: *In re* Zyprexa Products Liability Litigation, No. 07-cv-1310 (E.D.N.Y. 2008); *see* Mark Fass, *Judge Finds Securities Lawsuit Over Zyprexa Is Time-Barred*, N.Y.L.J. 5/1/08 (law.com).

[95] The bar on securities fraud as a civil RICO predicate is not retroactive, so a plaintiff who had pending claims when the PSLR was enacted can pursue the claims: Mathews v. Kidder Peabody & Co., 161 F.3d 156 (3d Cir. 1998).

SEC administrative action or suit do not affect attorneys' fees, because they are not considered part of the fund created under the securities class action.

[B] Securities Litigation Uniform Standards Act

The PSLR has been supplemented by further legislation, the Securities Litigation Uniform Standards Act of 1998 (11/3/98). The 1998 law enacts a new '33 Act § 16, and a new '34 Act § 28(f) with identical language: "No covered class action based upon the statutory or common law of any state or subdivision thereof may be maintained in any State or Federal Court by any private party alleging" misstatement or omission of material fact, or certain manipulative or deceptive conduct.

In other words, this does not just bar class actions in state court, but eliminates state-law causes of action as pendent claims in a federal case. It is not yet clear if contractual causes of action (e.g., borrowing or merger transactions) are preempted; Congress probably wanted to be comprehensive.

A covered class action involves 50 or more claimants and relates to the purchase or sale of a covered security — i.e., one that is listed or authorized for listing on the NYSE, American Stock Exchange, or NASDAQ.

Thus, IPOs are covered only if they were authorized for listing at the time of the alleged unlawful act. However, if a company issues any covered securities, any of its other securities that are of equal or senior status to those securities (e.g., preferred stock of a company whose common stock is listed) are also considered covered, even if they are not publicly traded.

The Supreme Court held early in 2006 that the SLUSA provision that preempts state class actions that allege fraud in connection with the purchase or sale of a covered security (15 USC § 78bb(f)(1)) has the same scope as the "in connection with" requirement of Section 10(b) and Rule 10b-5. Therefore, SLUSA preempted state class actions based on charges that class members were defrauded into holding or delaying sales of covered securities; preemption is not limited to cases in which there were purchases or sales.[96] The practical effect of the Supreme Court's decision is that more actions will remain in state court — and corporate defendants will be less able to wear out plaintiffs through years of litigation about the propriety of remand. However, after remand to state court, the *Kircher* plaintiffs will have to show that their claims are not "holder" claims of the type that *Dabit* holds are precluded by SLUSA.[97] Although in some respects tax-deferred annuities are insurance products, both the Second and the Eighth Circuits have held that claims about these annuities are subject to SLUSA's preemption and removal provisions.[98]

---

[96] Merrill Lynch, Pierce Fenner & Smith v. Dabit, 547 U.S. 71 (2006).

[97] Kircher v. Putnam Funds Trust, 547 U.S. 633 (2006).

[98] Dudek v. Prudential Sec. Inc., 295 F.3d 875 (8th Cir. 2002); Patenaude v. Equitable Life Assurance Soc., 290 F.3d 1020 (9th Cir. 2002), Lander v. Hartford Life & Annuity Ins. Co., 251 F.3d 101 (2d Cir. 2001).

Individual claims are not preempted unless they can be aggregated and analyzed as a constructive class action involving more than 50 persons seeking damages. This provision can be used strategically by a defendant who is sued by an individual, but then seeks consolidation of claims for discovery purposes, or who attempts to prevent "stock drop" cases (allegations that the fall in price of a security can be blamed on corporate misrepresentations) from being brought in state court.

SLUSA includes a provision known as the "Delaware carve-out" (15 USC § 77p(d)(1)) allowing certain class actions for breach of fiduciary duty of disclosure to the shareholders, to be brought in state courts. (The provision is not limited to Delaware state courts.)

§ 6.14   OTHER RECENT LEGISLATION

The Securities Enforcement Remedies and Penny Stock Reform Act, P.L. 101-249; the Market Reform Act P.L. 101-432, and the Securities Act Amendments (P.L. 101-550) expand SEC enforcement powers and add new remedies.

P.L. 101-249 adds remedies such as cease and desist orders against securities violation; disgorgement and civil penalties; and the SEC's ability to petition the federal courts for civil money penalties over and above disgorgement. The agency can also seek an injunction preventing a person found guilty of fraud offenses from service as an officer or director of a reporting company. The SEC's enforcement powers with respect to penny stocks (low-priced issues) are also strengthened.

P.L. 101-432 amends the Exchange Act to extend the SEC's powers to prevent market crashes by extending emergency powers and adding tools to combat market volatility. P.L. 101-550 gives the SEC greater power to work with foreign governments against international securities fraud. It also increases mutual fund shareholders' access to information and speeds up the schedule for delivering proxy materials.

P.L. 104-290, the National Securities Markets Improvement Act of 1996 (as amended by P.L. 105-8) adds a new category of private investment companies exempt from registration. The objective is to give venture capital firms better access to money that can be used to fund start-ups. This statute also authorizes the SEC to set standards for a single nationwide marketplace for the mutual fund industry. In a suit brought by the State of California about "shelf space agreements" (extra payments by a mutual fund to a broker-dealer for preferential marketing of the fund's shares), the California Court of Appeals held that the suit was not preempted by the National Securities Markets Improvement Act, and the California action was explicitly permitted by that statute and does not conflict with Rule 10b-10. Although the statute forbids states to prohibit, limit, or impose conditions of use on offering documents, it also permits state securities regulators to bring actions for fraud or deceit, or charging unlawful broker/dealer conduct. The text of Rule 10b-10 says that compliance with the rule does not prevent brokers from facing charges under 10b-5, or under state regulation.[99]

§6.15 SECURITIES ACTIVITIES ON THE INTERNET

The widespread availability of connections to the Internet has changed almost every aspect of the securities market. The number of individual investors has grown hugely; trading is available worldwide 24 hours a day, and there is extensive price competition now that commissions have been deregulated. The Eastern District of Pennsylvania has held that Esign (see § 2.13) does not obligate a mutual fund broker to accept transfer requests in electronic form. The court interpreted the purpose of the statute as protecting e-contracts against challenges based solely on their electronic form. The statute says that use or acceptance of electronic signatures is not mandatory, so unwilling parties cannot be forced to contract in electronic form.[100]

Traditionally, securities disclosure revolved around personal or mail delivery of printed materials (prospectuses, proxy statements, etc.). Before an IPO, selected institutional and qualified investors might be invited to a "road show," or could have telephone "conference calls," at which the new issue was discussed or analysts discussed the business prospects of an issuing company.

Under current regulatory policy, much of this information can be placed on the Internet.[101] Starting in April 2003, '34 Act § 16(a) ownership reports (Forms 3, 4, and 5) could be created and submitted electronically, using a new Web site posted by the SEC: http://www.onlineforms.edgarfiling.sec.gov. Later in 2003, electronic submission would become mandatory rather than optional.

Effective March 16, 2009, Form D must be filed electronically; voluntary electronic filing began in September 2008, when the electronic system was implemented. One practical effect of electronic filing is that Form D is readily available online; it is no longer necessary to travel to the SEC's Washington office to view the filings. However, the SEC eliminated the requirement of disclosing investors owning more than 10% of a class of securities; nor is disclosure of the identity of limited partners in venture capital or private equity partnerships required.[102]

---

[99] People v. Edward D. Jones & Co., 154 Cal. App. 627 (Cal. App. 2007).

[100] Prudential Ins. Co. of Am. v. Prusky, 2005 WL 1715659 (E.D. Pa. 2005).

[101] *See* Securities Act Release No. 7233/Exchange Act Release No. 36345 (10/6/95). *See* also Securities Act Release No. 7299/Exchange Act Release No. 37182 (5/9/96) for online activities of broker-dealers and investment advisers and Sec. Act Release No. 7289 (also 5/9/96) allowing electronic media to use any reasonable means of stressing information that must be printed in red ink or boldface type in its paper version. Exchange Act Release 7516 (3/23/98) explains the SEC's approach to materials that are online and offshore (originate outside the U.S.): an issue has not been made in the U.S., for registration purposes, if the offeror takes adequate measures to prevent participation by U.S. persons.

[102] Brian Gormley, *Start-Ups, Venture Firms to File SEC Form Electronically*, Wall St. J. 3/4/08 at B5.

As of late 2008, the SEC began phasing in a system called Interactive Data Electronic Applications (IDEA) as a replacement for EDGAR. The new system will be online, fully searchable, and will give access to searchable data on public companies' and mutual funds' financials.[103]

---

[103] Judith Burns, *SEC Unveils a Filing System Intended to Replace Edgar*, Wall St. J. 8/20/08 at C4.

Chapter 7

Business Dealings with Consumers

§ 7.01　INTRODUCTION

Although it is no longer the hot topic that it was in the 1970s, consumer protection nevertheless remains the subject of numerous federal and state laws. See Chapter 14 for protection of consumer debtors against unfair credit practices, including failure to disclose credit terms, improper use of credit information about consumers, and inappropriate practices when collecting consumer debts.

The Consumer Product Safety Improvement Act of 2008, P.L. 110-314, was signed August 14, 2008. It reauthorizes the Consumer Product Safety Commission (CPSC) and sets funding levels through fiscal 2014. The statute imposes safety standards for children's products (e.g., mandatory toy safety standards, prohibition on using certain phthalates in children's products, severely reducing the maximum permitted lead paint levels, and requiring third-party testing for some products). The CPSC is required to set up a consumer product safety database that is accessible to the public. The CPSC's recall powers and powers to impose corrective action plans have been enhanced.

A putative class action brought in Illinois against McDonald's was dismissed. It alleged that McDonald's violated federal nutrition labeling requirements for food served to children, and therefore was liable under Illinois consumer fraud and deceptive practices law. The Illinois Court of Appeals found the claims to be preempted by federal law: the National Labeling and Education Act of 1990 and the FDA regulations.[1]

The litigation achieved more success elsewhere. The class action charging McDonald's with contributing to obesity and other health damage was partially reinstated in early 2005. The Second Circuit ruled that New York's General Business Law § 349 (deceptive business practices) does not require proof of actual reliance. Information about the plaintiffs' heredity and eating habits is the type of information that the discovery process is designed to elicit; it is not part of the pleading requirements.[2] The Southern District of New York held in 2008 that New York City had the power to require fast food chains with 15 or more outlets nationwide to include calorie information on their menus (Health Code § 81.50). The regulation replaced the one that was struck down last year as preempted by the Nutrition Labeling and Education Act of 1990. In the Southern District's view, the current rule is not preempted because the NLEA gives state and local governments the power to mandate restaurant nutrition labeling, and the required disclosures are reasonably related to the government interest in informing consumers. Nor were the First Amendment rights of restaurants unduly infringed.[3]

According to the Fourth Circuit, consumers do not have standing under Lanham Act § 43(a) to sue for false advertising, under the rationale that Congress intended to protect businesses against unfair competition, and so a consumer group, which is not engaged in commercial activity, is not a proper plaintiff.[4]

According to the Third Circuit, federal law preempts state law false advertising claims, because the FDA has exclusive regulatory authority over prescription drug advertisements. (The dissent said this was an invalid argument because the FDA does not have pre-approval jurisdiction over drug advertisements, and lacks the practical power to police the ads once the drugs are approved.) Thus, a proposed class action, charging Zeneca, Inc. with misleading doctors and consumers that Nexium was better than Prilosec was filed shortly before generic Prilosec became available. According to the suit, the advertisements compared Nexium to a smaller dose of Prilosec. The district court dismissed the suit, holding that the advertisements complied with the FDA-approved labeling. The plaintiffs' argument on appeal was that FDA approval merely made it lawful to sell Nexium, not to make false claims about it in advertisements. The Third Circuit rejected the argument: FDA regulation of drug advertising preempted state consumer protection laws.[5]

---

[1] Cohen v. McDonald's Corp., 347 Ill. App. 633 (Ill. App. 2004).

[2] Pelman v. McDonald's Corp., 396 F.3d 508 (2d Cir. 2005).

[3] N.Y.S. Restaurant Ass'n v. N.Y.C. Board of Health, 08 Civ. 1000 (S.D.N.Y. 2008); *see* Mark Hamblett, *New York City Wins Bid to Force Fast-Food Chains to List Calorie Count on Menus*, N.Y.L.J. 4/17/08 (law.com).

[4] Made in the USA Found. v. Phillips Foods Inc., 365 F.3d 278 (4th Cir. 2004).

[5] Pennsylvania Employees Benefit Trust Fund, et al. v. Zeneca Inc. 499 F.3d 239 (3d Cir. 2007); *see* Shannon P. Duffy, *In Win for Drug Manufacturers, 3rd Circuit Rules Only FDA Can Regulate Ads*, The Legal Intelligencer 8/22/07 (law.com).

"Check 21" (the Check Clearing for the 21st Century Act, P.L. 108-100) took effect in October 2004. It provides for "substitute checks" — that is, instead of returning canceled checks to its customers, a bank is justified in providing customers with copies of the front and back of the check and destroying the original paper check. The substitute check operates as the legal equivalent of the original. (This is known as "truncation.")

Each unit placed in commerce is a separate offense under the Consumer Product Safety Act requirement of reporting of product hazards (15 USC § 2064(b)). Therefore, it was permissible to impose a $300,000 penalty on the manufacturer of 30,000 to 40,000 potentially hazardous juicers. The company said that it committed only 23 violations — the units that consumers complained about exploding — and that "consumer product" means a product model rather than individual units. The Ninth Circuit, however, held that the statute is drafted with a small fine per unit and a cap indicating intention to apply the penalty on a per unit basis. The statute does not trigger the obligation to report only when there are customer complaints. The size of the penalty was upheld as reasonable vis-à-vis the $1.5 million that could have been ordered.[6]

Although 1994 legislation required promulgation of regulations on dietary supplements, the FDA did not actually issue them until mid-2007, effective August 24, 2007 (although applicability phases in over three years in order to give small manufacturers time to comply). All U.S. or foreign manufacturers that manufacture, package, or label supplements for sale in the United States must monitor suppliers and strengthen quality control and record-keeping procedures. The FDA has power to ask for removal of an ingredient or revision of a label if an ingredient is adulterated or misbranded, and can bring suit and seize such products. Prior to issuance of these regulations, dietary supplements, including vitamins, minerals, herbs, and sports nutrition supplements, were regulated as foods, subject only to nonbinding guidelines and voluntary recalls.[7]

Commentators have identified a trend of consumer class action litigation focusing on advertising and foregoing older liability theories like design defect or failure to warn. It is also more likely that a class action seeking economic damages will be certified if the allegations involve misleading advertising rather than personal injuries caused by defective products. However, misrepresentation must involve facts, not a mere expression of opinion or subjective description of product qualities.[8] For example, the Northern District of New York ruled[9] that statements about the quality of a bar review course were mere puffery and would not mislead a reasonable third-year law student. Illinois held that puffery means a statement whose truth or falsity cannot be determined, and calling a

---

[6] United States v. Mirama Enter., 387 F.3d 983 (9th Cir. 2004).

[7] Jane Zhang, *Diet-Supplement Rules Tighten*, Wall St. J. 6/23-6/24 at A3.

[8] Barbara's Sales, Inc. v. Intel Corp., 879 N.E.2d 910 (Ill. 2007), discussed in Thomas E. Riley and Ellen A. Black, *Case Law Highlights Puffery as a Defense to Consumer Fraud Class Actions*, Special to Law.com 2/21/08.

[9] Provenzano v. Thomson Corp., No. 1:07-CV_00746 (N.D.N.Y. 12/3/07).

microprocessor "4" does not state that it is better than a microprocessor called "III."[10] In case alleging that a window company misrepresented that its windows were durable, high quality, and maintenance-free, the Northern District of Illinois dismissed claims of deceptive trade practices (because the claims were subjective), but would not dismiss claims for statutory and common-law fraud.[11] In a case challenging Kentucky Fried Chicken's use of trans fats, the Southern District of California held that statements like "the best food," "highest quality ingredients," and "all foods can fit into a balanced eating plan," were not actionable because there were no definite assertions of fact, and no reasonable consumer could consider them specific representations.[12]

§ 7.02 THE FTC ACT

Federal Trade Commission Act § 5, 15 USC § 41 *et seq.*, bars all unfair and deceptive acts and practices in commerce. The current standard, set by the FTC Act Amendments of 1994, P.L. 103-312, 15 USC § 45(n), is that an act or practice is unfair if it is likely to cause substantial injury to consumers, if the injury could not have been avoided by the consumers (e.g., by making more careful inquiries), and if the potential harm stemming from the practice is not outweighed by benefits to consumers or to competition. Consumer injury is substantial if a large number of consumers suffer minor injury, or a smaller number sustain major injury.

Representations are deceptive if necessary qualifications are not made, material facts are not disclosed, or disclosures and qualifications are not presented conspicuously enough.

[A] FTC Credit-Related Rules

The Federal Trade Commission has promulgated rules (Trade Regulation Rule on Credit Practices, 16 CFR Part 444) making it an unfair act or practice, violating FTC Act § 5, for a lender or installment seller "in commerce" to directly or indirectly take or receive from a consumer:

- Cognovit notes[13] (contracts that contain a confession of judgment at the time they are signed, allowing the creditor to win a default judgment based on the consumer's admission of liability and waiver of notice)
- Security interests in the debtor's household goods, except for Purchase Money Security Interests (PMSIs) obtained by advancing the funds used to buy the household goods

---

[10] Barbara's Sales, Inc. v. Intel Corp., 879 N.E.2d 910 (Ill. 2007).

[11] Saltzman v. Pella Corp., No. 06C4481, 2007 WL 844883 (N.D. Ill. 3/20/07); similarly, Heath v. Palmer, 915 A.2d 1290 (Vt. 2006) dismissed a consumer fraud claim because "we take pride in quality construction with exceptional value" was subjective and not amenable to objective verification.

[12] Fraker v. KFC Corp., No. 06-CV-01284-JM, 2007 WL 1296571 (S.D. Cal. 4/30/07).

[13] Consumer debtors have a general right to notice and hearing before their goods are repossessed: *see, e.g.,* Fuentes v. Shevin, 407 U.S. 67 (1972) and Sniadach v. Family Fin. Corp., 395 U.S. 337 (1969).

- Late charges imposed on other late charges rather than on the unpaid balance
- Most assignments[14] of the debtor's wages, especially those imposed by a creditor after default has occurred.

However, wage assignments are permissible if they are voluntary and the debtor has the right to cancel them at any time; if only wages already earned, not future wages, are assigned; or if the assignment is part of a payroll deduction plan authorized by the debtor at the time of the credit transaction.

The TILA Regulations provide (see 12 CFR § 226.4(d)(1)(i)) that the premiums for credit insurance need not be disclosed as part of the finance charge if consumers are informed that they do not have to purchase credit insurance, so loan packing can be a violation of this provision. Coercion to purchase the insurance might also violate the state's insurance laws or its UDAP.

Remember that debtors who prepay part of the loan balance are entitled to a proportionate refund of the unearned premium for credit insurance, because it is no longer necessary to secure repayment.

Also note that a "cooling off" period is required for home improvement contracts and other contracts secured by the debtor's principal residence (and that therefore could result in its foreclosure). The FTC requires that consumers must be given a period of at least three days during which they have an absolute right to cancel the contract. If state law requires a longer period, the creditor must abide by it.

The FTC's rule on Preservation of Consumers' Claims and Defenses is found at 16 CFR § 433.1. All consumer credit contracts must include a provision, in 10-point bold type, informing the consumer that any holder of the contract (see § 2.05[E] for rights of holders in due course) is subject to any claims and defenses that the consumer could assert against the seller of the merchandise.

This provision was drafted to prevent the once-common situation of sales of overpriced, low-quality merchandise to vulnerable consumers. When consumers attempted to return the merchandise, or refused to pay for defective merchandise, they were deprived of remedies because the merchants had negotiated the consumers' contracts to someone else (often a related party) who escaped responsibility because of the holder-in-due-course doctrine.

[B] Regulation of Telemarketing

There has been more than a decade of legislation aimed at preventing abuses of marketing via telephone and other communications devices. The Telephone Consumer Protection Act of 1991 (TCPA), P.L. 102-243 (enacted at 47 USC § 227), made it illegal to make prerecorded telephone calls to a home unless the

---

[14] *See also* 29 CFR Part 870, Department of Labor rules limiting garnishments. The Fair Labor Standards Act, at 29 USC § 206(a)(1) includes a general exemption from garnishment equal to 30 times the minimum wage or 75% of the debtor's disposable earnings, whichever is greater. Disposable earnings means gross pay minus taxes and other deductions mandated by law.

recipient agreed to receive such calls, or unless there is an emergency. Autodialed calls to emergency lines, pagers, and cell phones are forbidden. Any autodialed call that is permitted must begin with an identification of the business placing the call, including an address or telephone number. The autodialed call must disconnect within five seconds of the time that the system becomes aware that the recipient of the call has hung up (i.e., the autodialer must not be permitted to tie up the phone line). The statute also forbids unauthorized use or sale of identification obtained from using an autodial system.

This federal statute does not preempt stricter state laws. Consumers can sue in state court for violations of the TCPA, but only for repeat telephone solicitations, not the initial one. State Attorneys General can sue in federal court for injunctive and monetary relief if there has been a pattern or practice of violative calls within the state.

In 1994, the Telemarketing and Consumer Fraud and Abuse Prevention Act, P.L. 103-297, was enacted (15 USC § 6101). It gives the FTC rule-making power to control telemarketing acts or practices that are deceptive or otherwise abusive. It extends to calls made by live solicitors, not just autodialed calls. Unsolicited calls may not be made in a pattern that is coercive or violates the privacy of the persons called. The caller must disclose the fact that it is a sales call. Unsolicited calls are not permitted during very early or very late hours. The Act allows state Attorneys General to sue in federal District Court to enjoin or obtain damages for abusive telemarketing.

Another statute from the same year, the Senior Citizens Against Marketing Scams Act of 1994, 18 USC § 2325, enhances the criminal penalties for certain telemarketing frauds perpetrated against older people.

In response to numerous consumer complaints, the FTC forbade telemarketers from making pre-recorded sales calls unless the consumer specifically agrees to receive them, rejecting industry suggestions that calls should be permitted whenever there is an established business relationship. (FCC rules allow pre-recorded calls premised on an existing relationship.) All pre-recorded sales calls must also have an opt-out feature so the customer can put him- or herself on the Do Not Call list immediately. The rule exempts automated information calls (e.g., flight cancellations or reminders about a doctor's appointment). Charities are exempt, but must offer opt-out. Banks, telephone companies, and insurers are not subject to FTC jurisdiction if they make the calls themselves, but might be if they use outside telemarketers.[15]

For years, many of the states maintained "do not call" registries, permitting consumers to indicate that they did not wish to receive telemarketing calls.[16] However, the various state provisions were inconsistent.

The FTC initiated a nationwide registry by Proposed Rule (published at 68 FR 4491 (1/30/02). In March 2003, a federal law, the Do-Not-Call Implementation

---

[15] Brent Kendall, *FTC Limits Prerecorded Calls*, Wall St. J. 8/20/08 at D3.
[16] For an updated list, *see* http://www.the-dma.org/government/donotcalllists.shtml.

Act (P.L. 108-10) was signed. The statute appropriated about $18 million for the first fiscal year of the program; after that, the FTC was authorized to collect fees from telemarketers for five years to fund the program.

Under the statute, making calls to a blocked number was punishable by fines of up to $11,000 per call.[17] However — and thereby hangs a tale — there were various statutory exceptions to the rule. The law allowed companies to place unsolicited calls to consumers who have made a purchase from them, or tendered a payment, within the preceding 18 months. Political and charitable solicitations were permitted even to people on the registry.

The FCC issued an order on February 10, 2005 reaffirming that the Do Not Call registry is the appropriate means of stemming unwanted commercial contact. The agency's order says that company-specific Do Not Call requests are good for five years from the date of the request (whether that was before or after the implementation of the registry). A telephone company can use a bill insert or message to satisfy the requirement of giving its customers annual notice about the registry. Pre-recorded debt collection calls need not provide the company's state-registered name if doing so would conflict with the Fair Debt Collection Practices Act (FDCPA). The order clarifies that a company can call with respect to financial contracts such as loans or mortgages provided that the customer has not ordered that calls not be made.[18]

A mid-2005 FTC ruling clarifies that phone solicitors can lawfully call people who are on the Do Not Call list for the limited purpose of informing them of a product safety recall. The announcement noted that there were 88 million phone numbers on the registry.[19]

In early 2004, the FTC adopted a final amendment to the Telemarketing Sales Rule. Effective January 1, 2005, marketers subject to the Do Not Call rule are required to examine the registry every 31 days to purge their call lists of numbers on the registry. Initially, lists were required to be scrubbed once a year, but the Consolidated Appropriations Act of 2004 ordered the FTC to adopt an amendment calling for monthly examinations.[20] The FTC proposed amendments to the Telemarketing Sales Rule, increasing the fees that industry must pay to access the Do Not Call registry. Not-for-profit organizations get access to the data without charge, in case they want to make a voluntary effort to avoid annoying potential donors. Almost 123 million home landlines and personal cell phones have been registered

---

[17] Under Regulations 69 FR 45580 (7/30/04), as of September 1, 2004, telemarketers are required to pay $40 per area code (an increase from the previous level of $25) to access registry numbers to remove people who do not want to be called from their calling lists. The maximum fee for searching all area codes rose from $7,375 to $11,000. As of January 1, 2005, telemarketers are obligated to "scrub" their calling lists every 31 days to remove individuals who are on the Do Not Call list.

[18] *See* 73 L.W. 2493.

[19] *In the Matter of* Rules and Implementing the Telephone Consumer Protection Act of 1991, FTC CG Docket No. 02-278 (ruling 6/14/05); *see* 73 L.W. 2763.

[20] 69 FR 16367 (3/29/04).

with the Do Not Call registry. A Final Rule was published July 31, 2006, raising the fee to $62 per area code ($31 during the second six months of the annual subscription period), capped at $71,050. The FTC returned to the subject in October 2006, rejecting a request for a new safe harbor that would allow pre-recorded messages in calls to a business' existing customers. In fact, the FTC proposed to forbid pre-recorded messages unless the consumer consented in writing in advance.[21]

An FTC proposal, effective January 2, 2007, forbids "robo calls" (recorded sales calls) without the customer's written permission. However, recorded calls are permitted to customers with whom the company already has an established business relationship. The FCC has forbidden recorded telephone solicitations since 1991, and the FTC since 2003, but the FTC did not really enforce the ban. The FCC regulations create a loophole: a company can make telemarketing calls to a consumer for up to 18 months after a single purchase, even if the consumer is on the Do Not Call list.[22]

On a related issue, the FCC took actions against junk faxes. In conjunction with the general telemarketing/Do Not Call rules, the FCC was going to require senders of unauthorized fax ads to get written consent and signatures from recipients. However, the effective date of the rule was postponed until January 1, 2005. Despite the extension, senders of advertising faxes are required to get the prior consent of recipients who do not have an established business relationship with them, but the requirements that the consent be written and signed and include a fax number will not be applied.[23]

Although the Telephone Consumer Protection Act, 42 USC § 227(b)(3), creates a private cause of action in state court for angry recipients of unwelcome unsolicited fax advertisements, the Second Circuit held in 2006 that there is no implied repeal of federal diversity jurisdiction, and therefore federal suits remain sustainable. Many of the Circuits have found preemption of federal question jurisdiction, but the Second Circuit deemed diversity jurisdiction to be available.[24]

The District Court for the District of Maryland ruled in early 2004 that under the USA PATRIOT Act, the FTC retains jurisdiction to regulate the activities of professional telemarketers soliciting contributions on behalf of not-for-profit organizations, whereas the organizations themselves are not subject to FTC jurisdiction. The court also upheld various provisions of the Telemarketing Rule against First Amendment and Equal Protection challenges, including the ban on calling people who asked not to be called, the requirement that Caller ID information be transmitted and not blocked, and the time frame during which calls are permitted.[25]

---

[21] Proposed Rule: 71 FR 25,512 (5/1/06); *see* 74 LW 2672; Final Rule 71 FR 43048 (7/31/06); Proposed Rule 71 FR 58716 (10/4/06).

[22] Erika Lovley, *FTC Readies Stricter Rules for "Robo Calls,"* Wall St. J. 11/28/06 at A4.

[23] FCC GG Docket No. 02-278, Order on Reconsideration 8/18/03; *see* 72 L.W. 2127.

[24] Gottlieb v. Carnival Corp., 436 F.3d 335 (2d Cir. 2006); *see, e.g.*, Brill v. Countrywide Home Loans Inc., 427 F.3d 446 (7th Cir. 2006) on preemption of federal question jurisdiction.

[25] National Fed'n of the Blind v. FTC, JFM-03-963, 72 L.W. 1552 (D. Md. 2/24/04), *aff'd* 420 F.3d 331 (4th Cir. 2005). The Eighth Circuit upheld North Dakota's similar statute, finding it

The Controlling the Assault of Unsolicited Pornography and Marketing (CAN SPAM) Act, P.L. 108-87, requires all commercial e-mails to include a valid (not counterfeit) return address, a postal address, and a usable method of opting out of receiving any more mailings. The FTC's Proposed Rule says that whether the primary purpose of an e-mail is commercial is determined based on factors such as whether it has content other than advertising or promotion, or whether the recipient would reasonably conclude that commercial content predominates over other content.[26]

Although there was a good deal of support for a federal Do Not Spam list as a counterpart to the Do Not Call list, both the FTC and the FCC decided not to create such a registry on the grounds that it could not be enforced effectively and would raise privacy concerns. As an alternative, the FTC encouraged industry to develop methods such as e-mail authentication and accreditation.[27] However, the FCC issued a rule in August 2004 which forbids sending commercial messages to wireless phones without express prior permission.[28] The Maryland Court of Special Appeals upheld the state's anti-spam law, which forbids deceptive subject lines and transmission paths in any commercial e-mail sent to Maryland residents or from a computer in Maryland. The court found it to be acceptable under the dormant commerce clause, because it protects state residents without unduly burdening commerce.[29]

The constitutionality of the federal ban on unsolicited faxes has been upheld in that advertisers have access to many permitted methods of disseminating commercial speech.[30] Note, however, that the Junk Fax Prevention Act of 2005, P.L. 109-21, was enacted amending 47 USC § 227(a) to permit businesses to send unsolicited faxes to persons with whom they have an established business relationship, or to numbers obtained from recipients who voluntarily made their numbers available to a directory or Web site. Even permissible unsolicited faxes must include a clear, conspicuous disclosure of the procedure for opting out of future advertisements.[31]

---

acceptable because it is narrowly tailored and content-neutral: Fraternal Order of Police v. Stenehjem, 431 F.3d 591 (8th Cir. 2005); *semble*, National Coalition of Prayer Inc. v. Carter, 455 F.3d 783 (7th Cir. 2006).

[26] FTC proposed rule, 69 FR 50091 (8/13/04); *see* 73 L.W. 2091.

[27] http://www.ftc.gov/reports/canspam05/050616canspamrpt.pdf; *see* 73 L.W. 2780.

[28] The August 3, 2004 order is on the FCC Web site: http://hraunfoss.fcc.gov/edocs_public/attachmatch/FCC-04-194A.1.doc (no www). *See* 72 L.W. 2776, 73 L.W. 2090.

[29] MaryCLE LLC v. First Choice Internet Inc., 166 Md. App. 481 (Md. Spec. App. 2006).

[30] Rudgayzer & Gratt v. Enine, No. 2002-1700, consolidated with Bonime v. Johnson, No. 2002-1740 (N.Y. Appellate Term 2004); Missouri *ex rel.* Nixon v. American Blast Fax Inc., 323 F.3d 649 (8th Cir. 2003), discussed in Cerisse Anderson, *N.Y. Appellate Court Holds Law Against Unwanted Faxes Constitutional*, N.Y.L.J. 4/21/04 (law.com).

[31] *See* 74 L.W. 2015, 2607. The FCC adopted a Final Rule about the Junk Fax Prevention Act on April 5, 2006. Commercial faxes must include an opt-out notice, and requests to opt out must be honored with reasonable promptness, and in any case within 30 days. There is no exemption for small

[C] Other FTC Rules

Detailed enforcement guidance is provided by numerous other Rules drafted by the FTC and published in 16 CFR, such as:

- Credit practices, 16 CFR § 444
- Used cars § 455
- Funerals § 453
- Cooling-off period for door-to-door sales § 429
- Mail order merchandise § 435[32]
- Deceptive pricing § 233.5 (e.g., permanent "going out of business" sales; advertising that prices are "below cost" or "wholesale")
- Negative-option plans (where once the consumer signs up, merchandise is sent unless it is specifically refused) § 425
- Home insulation § 460
- Retail food store advertising and marketing § 424 (requiring stores to have adequate supplies of the "specials" they advertise; compliance can be achieved by providing rain checks or offering substitute merchandise).

The FTC proposed its first new rule in many years, regulating business opportunities, e.g., work at home opportunities. The agency saw the need to cope with the risk of frauds and scams in business opportunities other than franchises. The proposed rule requires a simple one-page disclosure statement: whether or not the parties offering the opportunity make earnings claims; if they are the subject of criminal or civil enforcement actions; the terms of any cancellation and refund policy; the total number of purchasers over the past two years, and the number of those who sought to cancel; and a list of references. Opportunity offerors who make earnings claims must substantiate the claims. The proposal forbids unfair or deceptive practices such as the use of shills and failure to abide by

---

businesses or nonprofit organizations, but it is permissible to send unsolicited faxes to a consumer on the basis of an existing business relationship. Report and Order, http://www.fcc.gov/omd/pra/docs/3060-1088/3060-1088-05.doc; FAQ at http://www.fcc.gov.cyb/consumerfacts/unwantedfaxes.html.

[32] If the seller is unable to ship the merchandise within 30 days, the buyer must be given the choice between canceling the order and continuing to wait. The seller is not in compliance by shipping only part of the order without giving the buyer a chance to cancel: e.g., shipping a computer without software. *See* the consent decree, FTC v. Dell Computer, 5 CCH Trade Regulation Reporter § 24,411 (W.D. Tex. 1998). Although federal law permits the recipient of unordered merchandise in the mail to treat the merchandise as a gift, the Third Circuit has held that there is no private right of action for individuals to sue if they claim they were duped into paying for unordered goods; the statute is enforced by the FTC. Current interpretation centers around the question as to whether Congress intended a statute to be enforced by private plaintiffs as well as agency enforcement; in this case, the Third Circuit deemed Congress to have intended only agency enforcement. Wisniewski v. Rodale Inc., 510 F.3d 294 (3d Cir. 2007); *see* Shannon P. Duffy, *3rd Circuit Finds No Private Right to Sue Over Unwanted Mail*, The Legal Intelligencer 12/17/07 (law.com). The statute in question is § 3009 of the Postal Reorganization Act.

territorial guarantees and refund provisions.[33] The FTC announced updated franchising regulations, taking effect in 2008 — the first major change in three decades. The FTC required additional disclosure (e.g., suits brought either by franchisor against franchisees, or vice versa; types of computer equipment franchisees will be required to maintain), and sought to reconcile the federal and state requirements for the Uniform Franchise Offering Circular.[34]

The FTC's position is that the same principles of full, fair disclosure and truth in advertising apply to Internet advertising and Web sites as to print and broadcast ads. For standards on "Dot-com Disclosures," see http://www.ftc.gov/bcp/rulemaking/elecmedia/index.htm.

The D.C. Circuit dismissed a petition for review of the FTC's 2005 letter about its funeral rule. The D.C. Circuit held that, under the Federal Trade Commission Act, the court only has jurisdiction over trade regulation rules and their substantive amendments, and the challenged letter was neither.[35]

§ 7.03 GRAMM-LEACH-BLILEY

Financial institutions have an obligation, under the federal Gramm-Leach-Bliley Act (GLB; 15 USC §§ 6801–6809) to protect the privacy of their customers' financial information. The statute defines financial institutions so broadly that many businesses that deal with consumers (for example, car dealerships, home repair contractors, real estate agents) have GLB obligations.[36] Consumers who claim that their GLB rights were violated do not have a direct federal right of action, but it may be possible to combine GLB claims with state UDAP claims (see below).

Under the statute, nonpublic personal information means any financial information that is associated with a person who can be identified and that a consumer gives the financial institution in connection with a transaction or service. The financial institution must not only provide the right to opt out of disclosure of this information to third parties, but must inform the consumer of the right to opt out. GLB bans obtaining consumer financial information by fraudulent means, and the financial institution's security and privacy policies must be disclosed.

---

[33] MaryCLE LLC v. First Choice Internet Inc., 166 Md. App. 481 (Md. Spec. App. 2006). 16 CFR Part 437; *see* press release, http://www.ftc.gov/opa/2006/04/newbizopprule.htm (4/5/06).

[34] Richard Gibson, *FTC'S Revised Disclosure Rules Make More Information Readily Available*, Wall St. J. 7/29/09 at B7 and Richard Gibson, *FTC Looks to Aid Franchisees*, Wall St. J. 3/7/07 at B3G. The 1978 Rule covered both franchises and business opportunity ventures in the same CFR Part, but the FTC now treats them as distinct (e.g., business opportunities typically do not involve the right to use a trademark).

[35] Funeral Consumer Alliance, Inc. et al. v. FTC, 481 F.3d 860 (D.C. Cir. 2007); the letter is at http://www.ftc.gov/os/2005/07/050707funeralruleadvoopin.pdf.

[36] *See* 65 FR 33646 (5/24/00), also available at http://www.ftc.gov/privacy/glbact/index.html, for regulations on this issue.

Consumers are entitled to an initial disclosure statement when the relation-ship with the financial institution begins, with annual reminders. It is permissible to combine the privacy notice with Regulation Z or Regulation DD disclosure as long as all the requirements of both rules are satisfied (e.g., with respect to which disclosure items must be conspicuous).

§ 7.04 STATE UDAPs

A UDAP law is a law barring unfair and deceptive acts and practices. These are typically broad-based statutes,[37] creating causes of action for everyone injured by commercial deception (even persons other than the actual buyer of the product). Post-sale activities, such as warranties, can also be covered.

If there is a statutory or regulatory duty to disclose, UDAPs usually treat failure to disclose as a violation, even if the defendant does not actually know the information.

As a threshold issue, UDAPs often refer to "goods" or "merchandise" and perhaps to consumer goods or services, so that consumer credit is probably covered but business transactions might not be. FTC regulation of the industry does not prevent UDAPs from regulating banks,[38] but some UDAPs exempt transactions covered by Truth In Lending, Equal Credit Opportunities Act, and other federal consumer credit laws.

Whether real estate transactions are subject to a state's UDAP depends on the terms of the statute, and whether real estate sales are deemed to fall within the category of trade or commerce,[39] or sale of merchandise[40] although an isolated sale of real estate by a nonmerchant (e.g., sale of a home by the owner) probably will not be subject to the UDAP.[41] Real estate leases have been held to come under the UDAP,[42] and tenants of a mobile home park have been permitted to bring UDAP actions even though there is a state statute regulating the operation of the park.[43] However, states differ on whether or not landlord-tenant law preempts the UDAP.[44]

Federal securities laws preempt state laws that conflict with them, or when it would be impossible to comply with both sets of laws.[45] The California Unfair

---

[37] Although attempts have been made to apply UDAPs to medical malpractice cases, they are usually unsuccessful, although medical billing practices might be covered. Legal services are not immune from UDAPs, but liability probably runs only to the client, or perhaps foreseeable benefi-ciaries such as the heirs of a testator.

[38] Normand Josef Enters. v. Connecticut Bank, 230 Conn. 486 (1994).

[39] Forton v. Laszar, 239 Mich. App. 711, 609 N.W.2d 850 (2000).

[40] Cornerstone Realty Inc. v. Dresser Rand Co., 994 F. Supp. 107 (D. Conn. 1998).

[41] Provenzale v. Forster, 318 Ill. App. 3d 869 (Ill. App. Ct. 2d Dist. 2001); Snierson v. Scruton, 761 A.2d 1046 (N.H. 2000).

[42] Benik v. Hatcher, 358 Md. 507, 750 A.2d 10 (2000).

[43] Ethridge v. Hwang, 105 Wash. App. 447, 20 P.3d 958 (2001).

[44] *Cf.* Carlie v. Morgan, 922 P.2d 1 (Utah 1996) (yes) with Weiner v. People *ex rel.* Abrams, 464 N.Y.S.2d 919 (Sup. Ct. 1983) (no preemption).

[45] Dahl v. Charles Schwab & Co., 545 N.W.2d 918 (Minn. 1996) (claims about securities order flow preempted by federal laws).

Competition Law has been held to apply to securities transactions, and not pre-empted by federal law.[46]

Although, as noted above, the FTC has narrowed the class of practices that it will consider unfair and deceptive, many state UDAPs maintain the older *Sperry-Hutchinson* standard[47] that a practice is unfair (whether or not it is deceptive) if it offends public policy; inflicts or threatens substantial injury to consumers; or is immoral, unethical, oppressive, or unscrupulous.

Some states consider charging an unconscionable price to be a UDAP violation, based on factors such as:

- Knowingly taking advantage of vulnerable consumers (e.g., illiterate, non-English-speaking, ignorant, infirm)
- Knowingly setting prices much higher than prices for comparable items
- Entering into a sale knowing that the consumer will not be able to pay the full price
- Making a knowing misstatement of opinion, when it is likely that the consumer will rely detrimentally on the statement
- Refusing to make refunds in cash (unless the refund policy was conspicuously posted); however, cash refunds may be required by warranty.

Other conduct that may trigger UDAP coverage:

- Bait and switch — i.e., enticing customers with a low price; when they come to the store, only inferior and higher-priced merchandise is available for actual sale
- Selling used or reconditioned merchandise as new
- Selling damaged goods
- Substituting inferior goods for the floor sample
- "Slack filling": i.e., using a large package to make it appear that the consumer is getting a lot of merchandise
- Passing off an inferior product as a better-quality or more desirable product
- Taking layaway deposits, and commingling them with other business funds, without disclosing that the seller is about to go out of business
- Sewer service, inconvenient forum, or other litigation abuse.
- Some states have separate laws about unfair insurance practices, and the state insurance department may have to be notified before a consumer files suit. The consumer has the burden of proof on the bad faith issue: i.e., that the insurer knew or should have known that there was no reasonable basis for denying the claim.

---

[46] Roskind v. Morgan Stanley Dean Witter & Co., 80 Cal. App. 4th 345, 95 Cal. Rptr. 2d 258 (2000).

[47] Deriving from FTC v. Sperry & Hutchinson Co., 405 U.S. 233 (1972).

Unless the state statute is to the contrary, a practice can be held deceptive even without proof of intent to deceive. Proof of scienter (knowledge of the falsity of the statements) is generally not required either.

[A] UDAP Practice

States vary in the extent to which private causes of action are recognized under the UDAP; they may be purely administrative statutes, permitting enforcement by consumer protection authorities but not by consumers.

UDAPs may also be triggered when a consumer wins a judgment against a merchant, which the merchant tactically refuses to pay (on the assumption that enforcement is not cost-effective). The consumer may do better by bringing a UDAP case for statutory, treble, or punitive damages than by enforcing the original judgment.

Personal jurisdiction is available against out-of-state defendants who intentionally enter the market in the state, and jurisdiction can be exercised over an out-of-state parent company that exercises control over its in-state subsidiary.[48]

In some states, a UDAP case must be proved by clear and convincing evidence, but the majority rule is proof that it was more likely than not that the plaintiff suffered an ascertainable loss from the deceptive practice.[49] The general rule is that it is not necessary to prove reliance, although it may be an element of damages. It has been held that reliance is not required where the omission of disclosure was knowing[50] or where the misrepresentations are material.[51] In jurisdictions that do require proof of reliance, purchase of the product subsequent to the misrepresentations may be considered adequate to show reliance.[52] However, it has also been held that if the consumer actually knew the facts that were not disclosed, then failure to disclose cannot be the proximate cause of damages to the consumer.[53] The consumer's contributory negligence is not a defense to a UDAP action. Nor do other tort defenses such as estoppel or statute of frauds apply. A UDAP case is a statutory cause of action. Because it is not a contract claim, privity is not required.

Although the FTC standard of deceptiveness is whether a reasonable consumer would be fooled, some states extend additional protection to the more vulnerable. The Texas UDAP, for instance, defined an act or statement as false, misleading, or deceptive if it has the potential for deceiving an ignorant, unthinking, or credulous consumer.[54]

---

[48] Logan Prods., Inc. v. Optibase, Inc., 652 N.Y.S.2d 749 (A.D. 1997) (personal jurisdiction); N.C. Steel Inc. v. National Council on Compensation Ins., 496 S.E.2d 69 (N.C. 1998) (control of subsidiary).

[49] Service Road Corp. v. Quinn, 241 Conn. 630, 698 A.2d 258 (1997).

[50] Cannon v. Cherry Hill Toyota Inc., 161 F. Supp. 2d 362 (D.N.J. 2001).

[51] Pyles v. Johnson, 143 Ohio App. 3d 720, 758 N.E.2d 1182 (2001).

[52] Siemer v. Associates First Capital Corp., 2001 U.S. Dist. LEXIS 12810 (D. Ariz. 3/29/01).

[53] Gill v. Boyd Distribution Ctr., 64 S.W.3d 601 (Tex. App. 2001).

[54] Top Rank Inc. v. Gutierrez, 2001 WL 1018371 (W.D. Tex. 3/2/01).

A statement can be deceptive for UDAP purposes even if it is literally true.[55] It is deceptive to promote a free trial period without disclosing that monthly charges will be imposed unless the consumer cancels the account.[56]

Failure to disclose necessary information can also be a forbidden practice. Disclosure might be required of, for instance, a dangerous or defective condition; the history of the goods; the fact that a transaction is illegal (e.g., illegal multi-family houses or loft conversions); risk of future price increases; kickbacks and referral fees involving other parties to a complex transaction; or the consumer's right to rescind.

The falsity need not refer to events that have already happened: a false statement about a future event can violate a false advertising statute and constitute an unfair or deceptive practice.[57] An oral misrepresentation can be a UDAP even if the written contract was accurate. Furthermore, disclosures made after signing of the contract are not considered in analyzing deceptiveness.[58]

Home Depot charged 10% of the regular rental fee for a waiver of damages when tools were rented. In exchange for the fee, Home Depot waived its right to hold the renter liable for damage to the rented product (other than damage caused by abuse or misuse of the tools). A class action was brought, charging that the damage waiver violates the Illinois Consumer Fraud and Deceptive Business Practices Act because it does not provide any additional protection over and above the basic rental agreement. The Seventh Circuit held that the damage waiver was not valueless, although it covered a limited range of occurrences; the plaintiff confused "damage" with the "normal wear and tear" for which customers are not held liable.[59]

The New Jersey Appellate Division held in mid-2008 that a bank is liable under the Consumer Fraud Act if its employee does not carry out a promise to invest the client's money in a mutual fund, because the employee failed to perform an advertised service. The court rejected the defendant's argument that the statute does not apply to securities. The complaint was not that the money was invested poorly, but that it was not invested at all; it was not clear what did happen to the $2,000 the plaintiff gave the bank employee to buy shares in a particular mutual fund. The plaintiff alleged that the bank employee offered her $1,500 not to mention the transaction. The plaintiff then brought suit under the consumer fraud law; the New Jersey Appellate Division held that the two-year statute of limitations under the state securities law did not apply, because the plaintiff did not allege a securities violation.[60]

---

[55] DeBondt v. Carlton Motorcars, Inc., 536 S.E.2d 399 (S.C. Ct. App. 2000).

[56] Minnesota *ex rel.* Hatch v. Fleet Mort. Corp., 158 F. Supp. 2d 962 (D. Minn. 2001).

[57] Parker-Smith v. STO Corp., 262 Va. 432, 551 S.E.2d 615 (2001).

[58] Miller v. William Chevrolet/Geo Inc., 326 Ill. App. 3d 642 (2001).

[59] Rickher v. Home Depot, Inc., 535 F.3d 661 (7th Cir. 2008); the waiver has also been found to provide value by Pacholec v. Home Depot USA Inc., No. 06-827 (D.N.J. 7/31/07).

[60] Lee v. First Union Bank, No. A-1517-06 (N.J. App. Div. 2008); *see* Michael Booth, *N.J. Court: Consumer Fraud Act Applies if Bank Fails to Make Investment as Promised*, N.J.L.J. 8/28/08 (law.com).

Where UDAP punitive damages are available, the injured consumer can recover the punitive component from each defendant contributing to the consumer's damages.[61]

[B] Automobile-Related Claims

The status of the automobile as an expensive, necessary, dangerous item, containing many hard-to-understand and even harder-to-fix components, opens the way for many areas of potential consumer abuse.

The sale of an automobile often involves multiple fees, and less-scrupulous dealers may reduce the type size and list their fees near the government-imposed fees and taxes to deceive consumers into believing that the amounts are government-mandated. It is deceptive to fail to disclose fees that are not optional; all fees that are part of the Truth in Lending finance charge must be disclosed as such.

Excessive fees can be unconscionable. It is also improper to add more fees after a price has been agreed on, because that's a unilateral modification of the contract.

Collusion by unscrupulous dealers to charge the same excessive fees could be a treble-damage antitrust violation. Also note that it violates the Fair Credit Reporting Act for an automobile dealer to get a credit report about a person who is shopping for a car, but has not actually applied for credit.

Other areas in which abuses have been identified:

- Kickbacks to dealers from lenders to whom auto loans are steered
- "Spot delivery" violations, in which the seller offers a price for "delivery on the spot," then subsequently tells the buyer that the deal was not approved, and the buyer must either surrender the car or pay a higher price, higher fees, or higher rates. The buyer is often rendered more vulnerable by a false representation that the traded-in vehicle has already been sold (a practice nicknamed "unhorsing")
- Odometer fraud
- Inflation of the trade-in price offered for the buyer's current vehicle, paired with even greater inflation of the price of the vehicle the dealer wants to sell.

Under the relevant UDAP, auto repair shops may be required to disclose their method for calculating labor costs, and the major provisions of the warranties they offer. The consumer is entitled to receive either a written warranty or a statement that work is done on a no-warranty basis.

A car owner objected to the state's sale of vehicle registration information to a law firm that was researching litigation against automobile dealerships. He brought suit for violation of the federal Driver's Privacy Protection Act, which is intended to reduce access to private information. The Eleventh Circuit upheld the District Court's grant of summary judgment for the defense: the sale of the information

---

[61] Mohamed v. Fast Forward, Inc., 682 N.E.2d 1363 (Mass. App. 1997).

came within one of the 14 statutory exceptions. The exceptions include police usage and use in background checks, but there is also an exception for "research activities" and one for "investigations in anticipation of litigation."[62]

§7.05 OTHER STATE CONSUMER PROTECTION LAWS

All of the states have at least some consumer protection laws, and some have numerous enactments and an active enforcement program. In recent years, many states have passed or amended laws dealing with issues such as collection agency operations; identity theft (misappropriation of personal identification information, usually for fraudulent purposes), regulation of loan brokerage, and limitations on charges that can be imposed on returned checks.

Retail Installment Sale Acts (RISAs) regulate credit transactions, setting maximum and minimum finance charges and delinquency charges. Some states have general RISAs, others limit coverage to motor vehicles; a third group of RISAs covers all merchandise except motor vehicles. New Jersey held that a rent-to-own contract is similar enough to a retail installment sales contract to apply the state's RISA — and the state criminal usury law's 30% interest cap — to rent-to-own contracts.[63]

States also deal with weights and measures; unit pricing and disclosure of prices; consumer product safety; financial supervision of health clubs (e.g., escrow requirements); and set plain English requirements for consumer contracts.

State interest and usury laws set maximum legal rates of interest: the legal rate, the contract rate (agreed on by the parties), the corporate rate, and the judgment rate (imposed on court judgments between the date they were handed down and the date of actual payment). As a general rule, state regulation of interest rates on first mortgages on residences is preempted by federal law, the Depository Institutions Deregulation and Monetary Control Act, P.L. 96-221. However, about a quarter of the states exercised their right to override federal preemption.[64]

States set limits on wage assignments (made voluntarily by a debtor) and garnishments (court-ordered anticipation of future wages), although the Fair Labor Standards Act at 29 USC § 206(a)(1), preserving at least a minimum amount of salary from garnishment, supersedes state laws that are less protective of the worker. But if the debt comes from taxes, alimony, or child support, larger garnishments are permitted.

Some regulation of credit insurance (insurance purchased by a consumer to satisfy the consumer's obligations if he or she dies or becomes disabled before the obligation is fully paid) is also universal among the states. Some states simply permit credit insurance to be sold within the state; others regulate who can issue it,

---

[62] Thomas v. George, 525 F.3d 1107 (11th Cir. 2008), discussed in John Pacenti, *11th Circuit Puts the Brakes on Privacy Suit Against Law Firm*, Daily Business Review 5/13/08 (law.com).

[63] Perez v. Rent-a-Center Inc., 186 N.J. 188 (2006).

[64] The states are Colorado, Georgia, Hawaii, Idaho, Iowa, Kansas, Mississippi, Minnesota, Nebraska, Nevada, North Carolina, South Carolina, and South Dakota.

the amount that can be issued, premiums that can be charged, the debtors' rights, and state-imposed penalties for violations.

The Pennsylvania practice of forbidding anyone except a licensed funeral director from discussing pre-need funeral contracts or giving price information is an improper restraint on First Amendment speech. The Middle District of Pennsylvania held that unlicensed persons can give the information, as long as the actual services are rendered and contracts negotiated by a licensed funeral director.[65]

The Second Circuit (reversing the Northern District of New York) found that New York's General Business Law § 251-f–j, requiring airlines to provide air circulation, clean toilets, food, and water to passengers on planes grounded for more than three hours, is preempted by the federal Airline Deregulation Act of 1978. According to the Second Circuit, the matters covered by the New York statute constitute "service," and the Airline Deregulation Act preempts state regulation of matters of price, route, or service.[66]

[A] The U3C

The Uniform Consumer Credit Code (U3C) is the state-law counterpart to the federal Truth in Lending laws. The U3C's subject matter includes retail installment sales, consumer credit, small loans, and bans on usury, if the purchase was made primarily for personal, family, household, or agricultural purposes, where the amount of consumer credit is $25,000 or less.

Only 10 states have adopted the U3C: Colorado, Idaho, Indiana, Iowa, Kansas, Maine, Oklahoma, South Carolina, Utah, and Wyoming.

The U3C is a comprehensive statute designed to replace other state statutes dealing with retail installment sales, revolving credit, home solicitation sales, home improvement sales and loans, and truth in lending. The purpose of the U3C is to restrict creditor abuses and further debtors' rights, especially through administrative enforcement by the state.

Creditors are permitted to repossess collateral when a debtor defaults. States impose statutory requirements on repossession, such as filing an affidavit of entitlement to the merchandise; bonding requirements; and rights of third parties to assert their own rights in the repossessed collateral.

Unlike the federal consumer credit laws, which are oriented toward disclosure, the U3C imposes rate ceilings; the general interest rate ceiling is 18%, and non-bank lenders who charge higher rates are subject to licensing and supervision requirements.

---

[65] Walker v. Flitton, 364 F. Supp. 2d 503 (M.D. Pa. 2005).

[66] Air Transport Ass'n of America v. Cuomo, 520 F.3d 218 (2d Cir.2008); *see* Daniel Wise, *2nd Circuit Strikes Down N.Y. 'Passenger Bill of Rights*,' N.Y.L.J. 3/26/08 (law.com), reversing No. 1:07-cv-1103 (N.D.N.Y. 2007). Rowe v. New Hampshire Motor Transport Ass'n, 128 S. Ct. 989 (2008) found preemption of a Maine law under another, but similarly worded, federal statute; neither law has a public safety exception.

§ 7.06   WARRANTIES UNDER THE MAGNUSON-MOSS ACT

The Magnuson-Moss Act, 15 USC §§ 2301–2312 creates new federal law covering consumer warranties, but does not entirely preempt Uniform Commercial Code or state requirements. The Magnuson-Moss Act covers consumer products costing $15 or more. A consumer product is tangible personal property normally used for personal, family, or household purposes. Property that is intended to be attached or installed in real property is also covered. However, products purchased solely for commercial or industrial use are excluded.

Manufacturers of consumer products are not required to provide warranties. But if written warranties are offered, they must satisfy the federal disclosure standard. Consumers must be informed:

- Who is entitled to warranty protection
- Which parts of the product are warranted
- What will be done to correct defects or failures (including allocation of expenses between warrantor and consumer)
- If the warranty does not become effective on the date of purchase, when it does become effective
- How the consumer can obtain performance under the warranty (e.g., name and address of the warrantor, and of a department responsible for warranty obligations, or a toll-free telephone information number).

Additional warranty requirements are imposed on the sale of used cars. The seller must either display the warranty conspicuously as part of the merchandise display, or maintain a binder in each department where consumer goods are sold, so that customers can view the warranty before buying the product: 16 CFR Part 702.3.

Consequential damages (e.g., damage to the consumer's other property; consequences of loss of use of the product) can be disclaimed in a full warranty only if the face of the warranty states the disclaimer conspicuously. Furthermore, if federal or state law forbid disclaimers of consequential damages, so does the Magnuson-Moss Act.

In 2002, the Fifth Circuit struck down 16 CFR § 703.5(j), an FTC regulation forbidding binding arbitration of Magnuson-Moss claims. The court found that the Magnuson-Moss text and legislative history do not show any Congressional intent to overcome the normal presumption of arbitrability. The statute (at 15 USC § 2310(a)) gives warrantors the right to require that consumers use their informal dispute settlement procedures before going to court, but the Fifth Circuit used the analogy of Title VII to hold that the availability of a conciliation program does not preclude the use of binding arbitration.[67]

---

[67] Borowiec v. Gateway 2000, 209 Ill. 2d 376 (Ill. 2004); Walton v. Rose Mobile Homes LLC, 298 F.3d 470 (5th Cir. 2002); *see also* Davis v. Southern Energy Homes Inc., 305 F.2d 1268 (11th Cir. 2002).

The Central District of California dismissed all claims in a class action charging breach of warranty and fraud because of defective head gaskets in Dodge Neon automobiles. The express warranty claim failed because the head gaskets did not fail until after expiration of the express warranty. Lack of privity between the plaintiffs and DaimlerChrysler ruled out implied warranty claims. The case was not filed until after the three-year statute of limitations for California state fraud claims had run. Neither tolling of the statute of limitations nor the discovery rule was available to allow a similar action in Illinois. Magnuson-Moss claims are dependent on the underlying warranty claims.[68]

According to the Seventh Circuit, an angry automobile buyer cannot satisfy the Magnuson-Moss $50,000 minimum jurisdictional requirement by citing the $69,000 purchase price of his allegedly defective Jaguar. The appropriate formula is the purchase price minus the current value and the value of the beneficial use of the item obtained prior to the suit.[69]

The Illinois Court of Appeals decided that the court's retention of jurisdiction to enforce the terms of a settlement between a consumer and refrigerator manufacturer provided a strong enough judicial imprimatur to make the consumer a prevailing party entitled to an attorneys' fee award under Magnuson-Moss.[70]

The Fifth Circuit vacated certification of a nationwide class of Cadillac DeVille owners who alleged that defects in the sensing modules for the air bags breached express and implied warranties. The law of the forum state (Louisiana) applied the laws of all of the states because that was where the owners used the vehicles. According to the Fifth Circuit, variations among state laws can defeat predominance of common claims, thus ruling out a class action. The would-be plaintiffs must provide an analysis of the variations among state laws or face decertification. In this case, although the plaintiffs asserted that state laws were fairly uniform nationwide, the Fifth Circuit found meaningful variations in, e.g., whether a buyer must show reliance for a statement or representation to be the basis of the bargain for express warranty purposes (see UCC § 2-313). The privity requirement is more strictly enforced in implied warranty than in express warranty cases. Many jurisdictions deny economic loss recovery when defects are purely latent and have not yet manifested. There are state-to-state differences as to whether implied

---

[68] Clemens v. DaimlerChrysler Corp., 530 F.3d 852 (9th Cir. 2008). Daughtery v. Am. Honda Motor Co., 144 Cal. App. 4th 824 (2006) holds that express warranties do not cover repairs made after the expiration of the mileage or time period of the warranty. California law provides (although some states disagree) that a consumer who buys from a retail dealer is not in privity with the manufacturer: Anunziato v. eMachines, Inc., 402 F. Supp. 2d 1133 (C.D. Cal. 2005).

[69] Schimmer v. Jaguar Cars Inc., 384 F.3d 402 (7th Cir. 2004), *followed*, Golden v. Gorno Bros. Inc., 410 F.3d 879 (6th Cir. 2005), holding that the measure of damages is the difference between the price of a replacement item and the value of the allegedly defective product, as reduced by the value of the plaintiff's beneficial use of the product. There was no standing to sue in a case where the would-be plaintiff revoked acceptance. Therefore, the plaintiff lacked standing with respect to the revocation of acceptance of a $43,000 vehicle worth $25,000 at the time of revocation, despite his contention that the contract price, including finance charges, was approximately $62,000.

[70] Melton v. Frigidaire, 346 Ill. App. 3d 331 (Ill. App. 2004).

warranties extend to purchasers of used goods, and whether a vehicle will be presumed merchantable if it is used without problems for a certain period of time.[71]

In the New Jersey view, a lessee of a motor vehicle who is an assignee of the dealer's warranty has the right to enforce the warranty, and therefore, under one of the three Magnuson-Moss definitions of "consumer," is a consumer (ability to enforce the warranty). However, Arizona held in 2006 that a person who leases a car from a car dealership is not a consumer for Magnuson-Moss purposes, because the lessee has not purchased the vehicle, and in effect the dealer purchased the vehicle for resale.[72]

§ 7.07 ARBITRATION OF CONSUMER CLAIMS

Many consumer contracts include an arbitration clause, limiting the consumer's right to litigate. Generally, these clauses will be given effect despite the nature of the contract as a contract of adhesion, although enforcement may be denied in an especially unfair or exploitative situation. A related question is whether consumer contracts can preclude class arbitration of complaints.

The recent trend has been to uphold mandatory arbitration requirements under consumer contracts. The Third Circuit held in 2007 that an arbitration agreement is not unconscionable merely because it requires consumers to sign a class action waiver, striking down local court rulings that the Third Circuit said were preempted by the FAA. The plaintiff contracted for services to monitor and improve her credit, and argued that the service provider violated its obligations under the federal Credit Repair Organizations Act and Pennsylvania's Credit Services Act. The defendant moved to compel individual arbitration. The plaintiff alleged that the state and federal laws provided her with the right to a judicial forum, and federal law explicitly permits class arbitration. The Third Circuit, however, said that the agreement was to be interpreted under Virginia law, which did not treat the class action waiver as unconscionable.[73]

---

[71] Cole v. General Motors, 484 F.3d 717 (5th Cir. 2007).

[72] *Cf.* Ryan v. American Honda Motor Co., 186 N.J. 431 (N.J. 2006) *with* Parrot v. Daimler-Chrysler Co., 130 P.3d 530 (Ariz. 2006) and the similar New York ruling in Di Cintro v. Daimler-Chrysler Corp., 768 N.E.2d 1121 (N.Y. 2002). An insurer sued the manufacturer of a fire sprinkler for breach of warranty in connection with an allegedly defective sprinkler that damaged a building owned by one of the insurer's customers. The Seventh Circuit affirmed the grant of summary judgment for the manufacturer. There was no agreement between the insured bank and the manufacturer when the sprinkler was purchased, so there was no privity of contract. The sprinkler had a one-year warranty for replacement of sprinkler heads, but it was limited to the original purchaser, the subcontractor who handled the installation of the sprinkler system. In Wisconsin, the breach of warranty claim ran only to the original purchaser of the sprinkler system, not to the bank where it was installed or to the insurer as subrogee of the bank. The subcontractor was not the bank's agent; and even if the prime contractor was the bank's agent there was no intent to have the contractor act on behalf of the bank, and the bank did not retain control over the work. Merely paying for the sprinklers did not create an agency relationship between the property owner and the subcontractor: St. Paul Mercury Insurance Co. v. Viking Corp., 539 F.3d 623 (7th Cir. 2008).

[73] Gay v. CreditInform, 511 F.3d 369 (3d Cir. 2007); *see* Shannon P. Duffy, *3rd Circuit Rejects Superior Court Precedents in Arbitration Case*, The Legal Intelligencer 9/21/07 (law.com).

The Eighth Circuit compelled individual arbitration in a Truth in Lending Act (TILA) case where the plaintiff alleged that the contract's waiver of class arbitration was unconscionable. The Eighth Circuit upheld the District Court's findings that the class action waiver was conspicuous, and the plaintiff was not economically debarred from arbitrating her small claim without a class action, because the TILA remedial provision, 15 USC § 1640(a)(3), permits recovery of fees and costs.[74]

The Federal Arbitration Act (FAA) requires enforcement of arbitration agreements that have been agreed to by the parties, so the FAA's policies supporting enforcement of arbitration clauses do not come into play to determine whether an agreement to arbitrate exists.

When the FAA governs a transaction, it preempts any state law that prohibits enforcement of all arbitration clauses. It also preempts any state law that applies only to arbitration clauses. In 1996, the Supreme Court ruled that the FAA preempts state laws (e.g., conspicuousness requirements) that purport to regulate the format of binding arbitration clauses.[75]

However, the FAA probably does not preempt a state procedural law as to which cases can be appealed.[76]

The FAA applies only to interstate commerce, but this is not a severe limitation because a number of transactions that might seem intuitively to be intrastate in nature have been held to constitute interstate commerce.[77]

The California Court of Appeals ruled that a consumer contract containing a mandatory arbitration provision cannot require a consumer plaintiff to pay fees beyond his or her ability to pay — that is, contracts that debar litigation while imposing prohibitively high fees for the use of the arbitral forum are substantively unconscionable. In this case, the plaintiff alleged that given the size of the damages sought in a class action charging automobile dealership bait-and-switch practices, he would have had to put up about $8,000 to initiate arbitration. The defendant said that this sum could be recovered at the end of a successful case, but the Court of Appeals found that this was inadequate because consumers must not be unreasonably discouraged from pursuing claims. The Court of Appeals remanded to the Superior Court for a determination of whether the unreasonable fees were adopted in bad faith — an issue that would determine whether the provision would be

---

[74] Pleasants v. American Express Co., 541 F.3d 853 (8th Cir. 2008).

[75] Doctor's Assoc's Inc. v. Casarotto, 517 U.S. 681 (1996).

[76] Simmons Co. v. Deutsche Fin. Servs. Corp., 243 Ga. App. 85, 532 S.E.2d 436 (2000); Wells v. Chevy Chase Bank, 363 Md. 232, 768 A.2d 620 (2001); *but contra* Dakota Wesleyan Univ. v. HPG Int'l Inc., 1997 S.D. 30, 560 N.W.2d 921 (1997).

[77] *See, e.g.*, Thompson v. Skipper Real Estate Co., 729 So. 2d 287 (Ala. 1999) (sale of real estate); Warren-Guthrie v. HealthNet, 84 Cal. App. 4th 804, 101 Cal. Rptr. 2d 260 (2000) (health insurance contract); *In re* FirstMerit Bank, 52 S.W.3d 749 (Tex. 2001) (mobile home lending contract). However, a payday loan from an Alabama bank to an Alabama resident has been held to be an intrastate transaction and thus not subject to the FAA: Alternative Fin. Solutions v. Colburn LLC, 821 So. 2d 981 (Ala. 2001).

severed and the rest of the contract enforced, or whether the contract as a whole would be invalidated.[78]

The Fifth Circuit enforced the arbitration clause in a nursing home agreement signed by the demented resident's mother. Under state law, the mother was a surrogate who had the power to bind the daughter vis-à-vis health care. Under federal law, the daughter was an intended third-party beneficiary and thus bound by the arbitration requirement.[79]

The Ninth Circuit found arbitration clauses in cell phone service agreements to be substantively unconscionable and unenforceable under Washington State Law because of a ban on class relief and limitations on punitive damages. The plaintiffs sued for improper charges for services (e.g., roaming) that should have been free.[80]

See Chapter 25 for further discussion of arbitration.

---

[78] Gutierrez v. Autowest, 114 Cal. App. 4th 77 (Cal. App. 2003, *modified* 1/8/04).

[79] J.P. Morgan Chase & Co. v. Conegie, 492 F.3d 596 (5th Cir. 2007);. Covenant Health Rehab. of Picayune, LP v. Brown, 949 So. 2d 732 (Miss. 2007) also upholds the arbitration clause in a convalescent center resident agreement signed by a health care surrogate to bind a resident of a convalescent center, and did not treat the agreement as a void contract of adhesion.

[80] Lowden v. T-Mobile USA, Inc., 512 F.3d 1213 (9th Cir. 2008); Shroyer v. New Cingular Wireless Servs., Inc., 498 F.3d 976 (9th Cir. 2007), involving the same contract language, already held that a class action waiver is unconscionable under California law if it occurs in a contract of adhesion, and consumers allege that they were unfairly deprived of small amounts of money. The Ninth Circuit held that the FAA does not preempt the California law, because unconscionable clauses are unenforceable whether they occur inside or outside the contract of an arbitration agreement. The Fifth Circuit found a mobile phone service agreement arbitration clause to be unconscionable, because the service provider had a choice between litigation and arbitration, but consumers could only arbitrate their disputes: Iberia Credit Bureau Inc. v. Cingular Wireless LLC, 379 F.3d 159 (4th Cir. 2004).

Chapter 8

Antitrust

§ 8.01 INTRODUCTION

Business competition is one of the most important tenets of the American legal system. As distinct from the trusts that are used in estate planning, a "trust" or business combination was often used in the nineteenth century to centralize business operations and prevent competitors from entering the marketplace. Antitrust laws were therefore passed to preserve competition for the benefit of consumers.

It is important to note that the federal antitrust laws are not interpreted to protect individual competitors, only competition within the market itself: *Brooke Group, Ltd. v. Brown & Williamson Tobacco Co.*, 509 U.S. 209 (1993).

RICO, at 18 USC § 1962, forbids patterns of racketeering activity, and creates a private cause of action for anyone injured in business or property by a violation of the substantive provisions of RICO, as long as the alleged violation was the proximate cause of the injury. The Supreme Court ruled that one competitor could not bring a RICO suit against another competitor, charging that the second competitor unfairly cut its prices by failing to charge sales tax to customers. Proximate cause requires a direct relation between the alleged injurious conduct and the asserted injury, and here, the victim of the wrongdoing was the State of New York, not the RICO plaintiff.[1]

---

[1] *Anza v. Ideal Steel Supply Corp.*, 547 U.S. 451 (2006).

U.S. Postal Service is part of the federal government, not a separate "person." Therefore, it cannot be sued by a mail sack manufacturer alleging that the Postal Service attempted to monopolize the production of mail sacks.[2]

The most important federal antitrust laws are the Sherman, Clayton, and Robinson-Patman Acts. Federal Trade Commission (FTC) Act § 5 forbids unfair methods of competition and unfair or deceptive acts or practices in commerce.

States also have a part in antitrust enforcement, especially in the context of unfair trade practices and mergers and acquisitions. A takeover, or even a voluntary merger, might be enjoined, or might become the subject of a government or private suit, if it has an anticompetitive effect by unduly concentrating an industry or reducing the number of participants within the relevant market.

Certain activities are exempt from the antitrust laws, including the "business of insurance" that is subject to state regulation[3] and collective bargaining.[4]

Visa announced an agreement to pay as much as $1.89 billion, and Master-Card to pay up to $862.5 million, to Discover Financial Services LLC to settle a 2004 antitrust suit charging Visa and MasterCard with interfering with Discover's business by preventing banks from issuing Discover cards. Earlier in 2008, similar allegations from American Express were settled through Visa's agreement to pay up to $2.25 billion, and MasterCard to pay up to $1.8 billion.[5]

The *Noerr-Pennington* doctrine[6] creates antitrust immunity for concerted activity engaged in to influence any kind of antigovernmental action, even if the desired action (such as legislation or amendments) is anticompetitive.

In effect, intellectual property laws create sanctioned, legitimate monopolies, although licensing of patents, trademarks, and copyrights can create some troublesome issues.

Pricing of products is one of the most significant antitrust issues, because it is so crucial to competition and to consumers' preferences and ability to purchase. Yet almost any kind of pricing behavior could, by a *reductio ad absurdum*, be challenged. Excessively high prices are evidence of monopolization; excessive low prices are predatory — and identical prices might be viewed as evidence of conspiracy!

An antitrust class action by IPO investors was dismissed, granting broad implied antitrust immunity to the syndication and marketing techniques used in IPOs. The plaintiffs charged that the defendants, more than a dozen investment banks and underwriters, manipulated the dot-com IPO market in the period 1997–2000, using tactics such as tying (requiring investors to buy less desirable issues in order to get an allotment of more desirable ones) and imposing higher commissions

---

[2] United States Postal Serv. v. Flamingo Indus. Inc., 540 U.S. 736 (2004).

[3] The McCarran-Ferguson Act, 15 USC § 1011-15.

[4] Clayton Act § 6, 15 USC § 17, and the Norris-LaGuardia Act, 29 USC § 101.

[5] (AP), *Visa, MasterCard to Pay up to $2.75 Billion in Antitrust Settlement*, 10/29/08 Law.com.

[6] So-called because it derives from Eastern Railroad Presidents' Association v. Noerr Motor Freight, 365 U.S. 127 (1961) and United Mine Workers v. Pennington, 381 U.S. 657 (1965). *See, e.g.,* Freeman v. Lasky, Haas & Cohler, 410 F.3d 1180 (9th Cir. 2005) [*Noerr-Pennington* immunity is available in connection with Sherman Act claims that are not objectively baseless.].

on later offerings to inflate stock prices. The Supreme Court concluded that the SEC has better qualifications than judges or juries to assess the legality of IPO conduct — a line of argument that is sure to be raised in the context of other forms of regulation in the future.[7]

In the term ending in June 2007, the Supreme Court heard four antitrust cases (an unusually large number), and ruled for the defendants in each instance.

§ 8.02 THE SHERMAN ACT

Under Sherman Act §§ 1 and 2, the plaintiff faces factual issues such as:

- Proving the existence of an agreement among defendants
- Defining the relevant market
- Proving that "market power" exists in a rule of reason case
- Demonstrating monopoly power or substantial threat of monopoly power in a § 2 case
- Showing anticompetitive effects
- (Private suits) Demonstrating antitrust injury.

Note that the Antitrust Technical Corrections Act of 2002, P.L. 107-273, adds a new § 3(b) to the Sherman Act. Under this provision, monopolization, attempt to monopolize, or combination or conspiracy to monopolize is a felony punishable by a fine of up to $350,000 for an individual defendant, $10 million for a corporation, and/or up to three years' imprisonment.

[A] Section 1

Sherman Act § 1 penalizes "combinations" (trusts or otherwise) or conspiracies in restraint of trade. There must be an express or at least tacit agreement, including conscious commitment to a common scheme that is designed to achieve an unlawful objective: *Monsanto Co. v. Spray-Rite Service Corp.*, 465 U.S. 752 (1984). Given that malefactors are usually somewhat secretive about their wrongdoing, proof of such an agreement is usually circumstantial rather than direct. However, the evidence must tend to exclude the possibility of independent conduct, and conduct that is just as consistent with competition as with antitrust conspiracy is not adequate.

Under *Matsushita Electric Industries Co. v. Zenith Radio Corp.*, 475 U.S. 574 (1986), "consciously parallel" conduct (i.e., following industry practices without actually entering into an agreement to do so) is not a conspiracy unless "plus factors" are present, for example:

- Conduct that is contrary to the actor's independent economic self-interest
- Pretexts are asserted for actions

---

[7] Credit Suisse Securities v. Billing, No. 127 S. Ct. 2383 (6/18/2007); *see* Tony Mauro, *Supreme Court Grants Banks Broad Implied Immunity From Antitrust Lawsuits*, Legal Times 6/19/07 (law.com).

- Several companies engage in identical actions when they have had motive and opportunity to conspire.

Unilateral actions by one company cannot violate § 1, because a company cannot conspire with itself, with its wholly owned subsidiary, or with another corporation under common ownership and control.[8]

The Supreme Court's *Twombly* decision of May 2007 holds that more than a bare assertion of conspiracy is required to survive summary judgment in a Sherman Act § 1 action, and corporations should not have to settle worthless claims merely to avoid becoming embroiled in abusive discovery. Successful pleading of a § 1 claim requires enough factual allegations to make the right to relief more than speculative, with enough facts to make it reasonable to believe that discovery will reveal illegal agreements. The case was brought by a class of local telephone and Internet subscribers who charged that regional telephone companies engaged in parallel conduct not only to avoid competition with each other but to keep new entrants out of the market. The Supreme Court found that the plaintiffs did not show the plausibility of their claims. Parallel conduct is admissible evidence from which an agreement can be inferred, but it is not an offense in and of itself, and is not conclusive proof of agreement.[9] Soon afterwards, the Third Circuit used *Twombly*'s analysis to hold that a beauty supplies company failed to show that it suffered a group boycott by distributors of salon-only hair care products. The evidence was consistent with independent action by the distributors. Conscious parallelism was not enough when market realities suggested that each defendant had individual reasons to prevent diversion of products away from salons, when the industry's marketing strategy depended on exclusivity.[10]

Also see *Nynex Corp. v. Discon Inc.*, 525 U.S. 128 (1998): one buyer's choice of seller, resulting in termination of a purchasing relationship with another seller, cannot violate the rule that group boycotts are per se illegal, because there was no horizontal agreement between direct competitors, even if the motivation for the change was an improper one. Corporations probably cannot conspire with their employees, officers, or agents except to the extent that such individuals have independent interests.

If an agreement is proved, it is either horizontal (involving competitors or parties at the same level of distribution of a product) or vertical (involving businesses at different levels of distribution). Horizontal agreements are deemed to present a greater threat to competition than vertical ones.

---

[8] Copperweld Corp. v. Independence Tube Corp., 467 U.S. 752 (1984). *See, e.g.*, Health Am. Penn. Inc. v. Susquehanna Health Sys., 72 L.W. 1068 (M.D. Pa. 7/21/03), holding that doctors and hospitals participating in a health care alliance administered by a joint board of directors are part of a single entity that cannot conspire with itself to fix fees for § 1 purposes.

[9] Bell Atlantic v. Twombly, 127 S. Ct. 1955 (2007); *see* Tony Mauro, *Supreme Court Makes It Harder for Private Plaintiffs to Sue Companies for Antitrust Violations*, Legal Times 5/22/07 (law.com), and Marcia Coyle, *A Tough High Court Term for Antitrust Plaintiffs*, Nat'l L.J. 7/6/07 (law.com).

[10] Cosmetic Gallery Inc. v. Schoeneman Corp., 495 F.3d 46 (3d Cir. 2007); Shannon P. Duffy, *3rd Circuit Tosses Out Cosmetic Antitrust Suit*, The Legal Intelligencer 7/23/07 (law.com).

Restraint of trade occurs when an agreement has anticompetitive effects that outweigh its pro-competitive benefits. Depending on the circumstances, analysis involves either a presumption of per se illegality or the "rule of reason" (see below); the inquiry is essentially the same in either case, according to *National Society of Professional Engineers v. U.S.*, 435 U.S. 679 (1978).

Per se illegality is a conclusive presumption that manifestly anticompetitive conduct (such as "naked" anticompetitive agreements for which no plausible efficiency arguments can be made) has the effect of restraining trade. Horizontal price-fixing, horizontal divisions of the market, and horizontal group boycotts or concerted refusals to deal are all per se illegal.

In traditional antitrust analysis (now somewhat modified by more recent Supreme Court rulings), two kinds of vertical agreements were illegal per se: resale price maintenance and some "tying" agreements. Resale price maintenance is setting a minimum price at which the buyer can re-sell an item. Suggested retail prices have long been deemed permissible, as long as there is no attempt to enforce them against unwilling purchasers. According to *Sylvania*,[11] vertical assignments of territories are considered fundamentally pro-competitive, and therefore are analyzed under the rule of reason rather than being considered per se illegal.

As a result of *State Oil Co. v. Khan*, 522 U.S. 3 (1997), agreements that set a **maximum** resale price are not per se illegal. *USA Petroleum, Inc. v. ARCO*, 495 U.S. 328 (1990) holds that a competitor does not have standing to sue to challenge vertical maximum price fixing. When ex-competitors entered into an economically integrated joint venture to refine and sell gasoline, the Supreme Court held that the companies did not commit a per se antitrust violation when they set prices for the products. Although horizontal price fixing by competitors is per se illegal, the two companies were ex- and not current competitors. It would have been acceptable to sell gasoline under a newly created joint brand; it was also acceptable to sell gasoline at the same price under the existing brands through the new joint venture.[12]

The Supreme Court ruled, in mid-2007, that the per se rule — dating back to the 1911 *Dr. Miles* case — no longer has relevance and is invalid, so minimum retail price maintenance by manufacturers will no longer be considered a per se violation of the Sherman Act. Minimum retail price maintenance by manufacturers is no longer a per se violation of the Sherman Act; the majority held that the per se rule no longer has relevance and is invalid. Vertical price restraints are analyzed under the rule of reason. Thus, resale price maintenance is analyzed in the same way as other restraints, and is still wrongful if it is not reasonable and is not supported by pro-competitive justification.[13]

---

[11] Continental TV Inc. v. GTE Sylvania, 433 U.S. 36 (1977).

[12] Texaco Inc. v. Dagher, 547 U.S. 1 (2006).

[13] Leegin Creative Leather Prods v. PSKS Inc., 127 S. Ct. 2705 (2007); discussed in Tony Mauro, *Supreme Court Overturns "Dr. Miles" Antitrust Precedent*, Legal Times 6/28/07 (law.com) and Joseph Pereira, *Price-Fixing Makes Comeback After Supreme Court Ruling*, Wall St. J. 8/18/08 at p. A1.

A tying agreement involves the sale of two distinct products. The customer cannot purchase the "tying" product it wants without also buying the "tied" product. Whether a tying agreement is per se illegal depends on factors such as how substantial an amount of commerce is involved, and whether the seller has enough market power to create an anticompetitive effect in the market for the tied product.

Early in 2005, the Federal Circuit upheld the traditional Sherman Act § 1 rule: when purchase of a patented product is tied to purchase of an unpatented one, the defendant is rebuttably presumed to have market power in the patented product However, in 2006, the Supreme Court reversed, holding that a patent does not necessarily convey market power, so tying case plaintiffs must prove that the defendant had market power over the tying product.[14]

An additional layer of complexity was added in mid-1999 by *California Dental Association v. FTC*.[15] The Supreme Court disapproved the use of "quick look" analysis (a truncated application of the rule of reason). According to the Supreme Court, the reasonableness of a restraint (in this case, advertising restrictions imposed on members of a non-profit dental association) should be analyzed on a continuum, not restricted to three categories (per se illegal; quick look; rule of reason).

If the plaintiff proves market power, the defendant can rebut with evidence of the pro-competitive benefits of the agreement, such as providing operating efficiencies; making more products available to consumers; or increasing output. The plaintiff can show that the asserted benefits are mere pretexts and do not really exist, or that they could be achieved in a less restrictive fashion.

The Seventh Circuit ruled that football franchises did not violate the Sherman Act by joining together to license NFL apparel. A clothing manufacturer that lost its license when the NFL awarded most of the licenses to Reebok alleged conspiracy in restraint of trade (on the grounds that licensing all team-logo hats to Reebok excluded others from getting licenses from the individual teams). Because the teams have a common interest in the popularity of football, it is not unlawful for them to cooperate so NFL football can compete more effectively against other kinds of entertainment. Claims under both Sherman Act § 1 and 2 were dismissed.[16]

Similar considerations applied in a case where Major League Baseball Properties Inc. (MLBP), which controls licensing of baseball collectibles, sued a licensee for selling collectibles for a team logo, for which he was not licensed. The defendant counterclaimed by characterizing the exclusive licensing system as a per se Sherman Act violation. The Second Circuit accepted MLBP's argument that it does not have market power, because it is only one aspect of a broad market

---

[14] Independent Ink Inc. v. IL Tool Works, 396 F.3d 1342 (Fed. Cir. 2005), *rev'd sub. nom.* Illinois Tool Works Inc. v. Independent Ink Inc., 547 U.S. 28 (2006).

[15] 526 U.S. 756 (1999).

[16] American Needle Inc. v. NFL, 538 F.3d 736 (7th Cir. 2008).

for sports and other leisure options. Per se analysis is not applied to sports leagues because cooperation among teams can have legitimate purposes such as scheduling. In this reading, quick look analysis is not appropriate when it is not obvious that an agreement is anticompetitive, and it could be neutral or even have a pro-competitive effect.[17]

The rule that indirect purchasers lack antitrust standing does not prevent purchasers of physical copper from pursuing Sherman Act claims that hoarding manipulated the copper futures market. However, the injury of such hoarding to scrap dealers is too indirect and speculative to give them standing in a case about the physical copper market.[18]

[1] The Microsoft Case

Perhaps the most famous antitrust case of recent years, litigation against Microsoft, was filed on May 18, 1998. The federal government and the Attorneys General of 20 states alleged Sherman Act §§ 1 and 2 violations involving monopoly power in the personal computer operating systems market, including unlawful tying of the browser to other products. In April 2000, the District Court for the District of Columbia issued conclusions of law, finding that Microsoft had maintained monopoly power in the relevant market (Intel-compatible operating systems for personal computers) by anticompetitive means. The D.D.C. ordered the draconian remedy of splitting up Microsoft into two companies — one selling the Windows operating system, the other selling other products. Needless to say, this remedy was never implemented. In June 2001, the D.C. Circuit upheld the finding that Microsoft engaged in monopolistic conduct, but vacated the order to break up the company, on the grounds that the harsh divestiture remedy was not supported by sufficient evidence.[19]

Litigation with many of the states, and with the Department of Justice, resulted in settlements. Out of 206 class actions filed against Microsoft, 108 were consolidated in federal court and 96 in state courts. One of the last remaining cases settled in September 2007.[20]

The Fourth Circuit ruled that plaintiffs who bought computers from Original Equipment Manufacturers or retailers are indirect purchasers of the Microsoft operating system that they leased. Therefore, the *Illinois Brick* doctrine prevents them from suing Microsoft under Sherman Act § 2 for taking advantage of a monopoly to overcharge the indirect purchasers, and they cannot seek damages under Microsoft's settlement with the DoJ. Although the end-user license agreement gave the buyers some financial rights against Microsoft, they were still

---

[17] MLB Properties v. Salvino, 542 F.3d 290 (2d Cir. 2008).

[18] Loeb Indus. Inc. v. Sumitomo Corp., 306 F.3d 469 (7th Cir. 2002). *Also see* Bunker's Glass Co. v. Pilkington plc, 72 L.W. 1139 (Ariz. 8/25/03), holding that the state's antitrust statute permits indirect purchasers to sue.

[19] United States v. Microsoft, 253 F.3d 34 (D.C. Cir. 2001).

[20] (AP) *Judge Approves Final Settlement in Iowa Microsoft Lawsuit*, 9/4/07 (law.com).

indirect purchasers because the price of the licenses was set by the intermediaries.[21]

[B] Sherman Act § 2

Sherman Act § 2 forbids monopolization, defined as possession of monopoly power, plus willful acquisition or maintenance of monopoly power by predatory tactics. Having a better product (or good luck) is not considered predation.

Predatory tactics include refusals to deal with competitors without legitimate business justification (or citing a pretextual explanation); denying competitors access to an essential facility that cannot be duplicated; or predatory pricing (below reasonable cost measures).

Monopoly power is roughly equivalent to market power — the ability to control prices — with the additional element of being able to exclude competition.

Section 2 also forbids attempted monopolization and conspiracy to monopolize. The elements of attempted monopolization are:

- Predatory conduct
- Specific intent to monopolize, shown either by direct evidence or inferred from anticompetitive conduct
- Dangerous probability of success of the attempt, shown by a market share above 50%.[22]

The elements of conspiracy to monopolize are:

- Existence of a combination or conspiracy
- Overt acts (not necessarily illegal) in furtherance of the conspiracy
- Specific intent to monopolize.

The Eleventh Circuit said that claims of refusal to deal and denial of essential facilities, brought by an ISP against a telephone carrier whose lines were used to provide DSL service to the ISP's customers, were barred by a 2004 Supreme Court case. The Supreme Court ruled out refusal to deal claims because the parties did not voluntarily enter into an intercommunication agreement; they were compelled to do so by the Telecommunications Act of 1996. Furthermore, access to the defendant's lines was available, precluding the essential services claim. However, a claim based on a price squeeze could proceed, using traditional analysis under *Brooke Group v. Brown & Williamson*.[23]

---

[21] Kloth v. Microsoft, 444 F.3d 312 (4th Cir. 2006); the "indirect purchaser" doctrine stems from Illinois Brick v. Illinois, 431 U.S. 720 (1977). See Michael Felberbaum (AP), *Microsoft Cleared in Federal Class Action Suit*, 4/20/06 (law.com).

[22] *See* Spectrum Sports, Inc. v. McQuillan, 506 U.S. 447 (1993).

[23] Covad Communications Co. v. BellSouth Corp., 374 F.3d 1044 (11th Cir. 2004); the Supreme Court case is Verizon Communications Inc. v. Law Offices of Curtis v. Trinko LLP, 540 U.S. 398 (2004).

[1] Predatory Pricing

Predatory pricing is a somewhat nebulous concept; one good formulation is deliberate sacrifice of current revenues with the objective of driving rivals out of business, followed by raising prices to monopoly levels once competition is eliminated. However, the Circuits differ as to how costs should be calculated, and even which costs should be considered fixed and which are variable.

To be predatory, prices must be maintained long enough to drive rivals out of the market; an introductory low price for a product is not considered predatory. Also see Robinson-Patman Act § 2(b), 15 USC § 15(b), which permits good-faith price reductions to meet competition, even if the reduced price is below cost.

Furthermore, recent Supreme Court cases seem to indicate that injury to competition occurs only if the defendant is in a position to recoup the losses it sustains through predatory pricing, and recoupment is not very plausible in a market that is highly diffuse and competitive, where entry barriers are low, or both. In October 2006, the Supreme Court refused to consider Spirit Airlines' suit against Northwest Airlines Corp., charging Northwest with using predatory pricing to push Spirit out of the Detroit-Boston and Detroit-Philadelphia markets. Although the case involves important antitrust issues such as the quantum of proof of predatory pricing, the case was rejected because Northwest was five days late in filing its appeal of the Sixth Circuit's ruling in favor of Spirit Airlines. The Supreme Court refused to ignore the untimeliness of the filing.[24]

The two-part test for recovering on a predatory pricing claim was held by the Supreme Court to apply to predatory buying claims as well, because the two causes of action are similar. The end result is that few plaintiffs in predatory buying cases will be able to satisfy the test.[25]

§ 8.03   THE CLAYTON ACT

The Sherman Act is generalized, condemning any practice that has certain forbidden effects on commerce. The Clayton Act is more particularized, forbidding specific acts and practices engaged in by parties engaged in interstate commerce.

Clayton Act § 2 bans discriminatory pricing by a seller, if the effect is anti-competitive; forbids price discrimination that is induced, or even knowingly received, by a buyer; bans discrimination in allowances for services or facilities; and also forbids certain brokerage payments and discounts.

Section 3 makes it illegal to have an agreement, arrangement, or condition whose effect is to keep a product's buyer or lessee from using or dealing in products that compete with that product. Tying agreements and exclusive dealing agreements are covered. Section 3 applies only if the limitations on dealing tend to create a monopoly or have the effect of substantially limiting competition.

---

[24] AP, *Supreme Court Denies Northwest Airlines Appeal in Key Antitrust Case*, 10/3/06 (law.com).

[25] Weyerhaeuser Co. v. Ross-Simmons Hardwood Lumber Co., 549 U.S. 312 (U.S. 2007).

A putative class action by lessees of new cars, seeking damages under Sherman Act § 1 and Clayton Act § 4, was dismissed by the First Circuit in mid-2008. The plaintiffs charged auto manufacturers with conspiring to restrict the entry of cheaper Canadian cars into the U.S. market when the U.S. dollar was high vis-a-vis the Canadian dollar, resulting in higher lease prices for cars. The First Circuit ruled that the plaintiffs were indirect purchasers as defined by *Illinois Brick* and therefore did not have standing under Clayton Act § 4; in this view, there would be a risk of multiple recoveries if both direct and indirect purchasers could sue.[26]

A hospital that purchased Johnson & Johnson products from a third-party distributor did not have standing under Clayton Act § 4 in a case charging Johnson & Johnson with leveraging monopoly power in one product to create a monopoly in a related product through market share purchase agreements that granted discounts and rebates conditioned on the buyer purchasing most of its requirements from Johnson & Johnson. The Ninth Circuit refused to create an exception to the "indirect buyer" rule for hospitals. However, the hospital's case was consolidated with cases of two direct purchasers, so the suit, involving a bundled market for sutures and endomechanical products, could continue.[27]

Section 7, discussed in § 8.05, below, forbids certain mergers and certain acquisitions of stock or assets. Section 8 places stringent limits on "interlocking directorates": i.e., corporate boards that share directors or officers.

A private Clayton Act § 7 suit challenging the merger of two airlines is subject to a two-year statute of limitations. The continuing violation theory of tolling that is applied to Sherman Act conspiracies is not applicable, because the merger is a discrete act. Holding and use of assets without change in utilization does not impose liability for an indefinite period.[28]

Clayton Act § 12 provides that a company can be sued in any district in which it is an inhabitant, transacts business, or can be found. The Third Circuit ruled that therefore foreign corporations are subject to worldwide service of process and personal jurisdiction in federal antitrust suits, on the basis of the foreign corporation's contacts with the entire United States, not merely the forum state. This case also holds that even if personal jurisdiction is contested, discovery of documents held by the foreign defendant can be obtained using the Federal Rules of Civil Procedure rather than under Hague Convention procedures.[29]

The automatic stay does not apply when a state attorney general brings a Clayton Act § 16 suit for injunctive relief in the form of divestiture and the defendant is a bankruptcy debtor. Such a suit is a Bankruptcy Code § 362(b)(4)

---

[26] *In re* New Motor Vehicles Canadian Export Antitrust Litigation, 533 F.3d 1 (1st Cir. 2008).

[27] Bamberg County Memorial Hosp v. Johnson & Johnson, 523 F.3d 1116 (9th Cir. 2008).

[28] Midwestern Mach. Co. v. Northwest Airlines Inc., 392 F.3d 265 (8th Cir. 2004).

[29] *In re* Automotive Refinishing Paint Antitrust Litig., 358 F.3d 288 (3d Cir. 2004). It has also been held that personal jurisdiction over a corporate defendant is based on minimum contacts with the United States as a whole: Action Embroidery Corp. v. Atlantic Embroidery Inc., 368 F.3d 1174 (9th Cir. 2004).

suit by a governmental unit to enforce police or regulatory powers. The District Court does not have discretion to stay the case until a relevant rule of law is settled, because the Ninth Circuit deemed it likely that state electricity consumers would be harmed if the antitrust case were not permitted to proceed.[30]

§ 8.04 THE ROBINSON-PATMAN ACT

The Robinson-Patman Act, which includes provisions amending the Clayton Act, concentrates on price discrimination by the seller (15 USC § 13(a); "primary-line injury") and its counterpart, solicitation or acceptance of price discrimination by the favored buyer (15 USC § 13(f); "secondary-line injury"[31]). The Act is violated only if the effect of price discrimination is to substantially lessen competition; tend to create a monopoly in any line of commerce; or injure, destroy, or prevent competition with any person.

The FTC used to bring a fairly large number of Robinson-Patman Act cases, but these are now quite rare. Twenty-two states have laws forbidding price discrimination, so in these states, the Attorney General may take a role in enforcement of price fairness. There is also a private right of action under §§ 4 and 16 of the Robinson-Patman Act (15 USC §§ 15, 26).

Certain Robinson-Patman Act violations are criminal: for instance, territorial price discrimination implemented in order to destroy competition or eliminate a competitor; charging unreasonably low prices for the same reasons; or discrimination in granting discounts, rebates, or allowances (15 USC § 13a, which is not the same as 13(a)). The criminal provisions are not considered an "antitrust law" as defined by the Clayton Act, so there is no private right of action for damages or injunctive relief.

Under Robinson-Patman Act § 2(a), the seller has an affirmative defense to a prima facie price discrimination case: that the lower price made available to only some customers was offered in good faith to match a competitor's price.

[A] Price Discrimination

The prima facie case for price discrimination by a seller, with respect to purchase of commodities[32] of like grade and quality, is:

- A seller engaged in interstate commerce
- Discriminates in the course of commerce
- Actual sales are made; offers do not count

---

[30] Lockyer v. Mirant Corp., 398 F.3d 1098 (9th Cir. 2005). The principle of staying cases until the rule of law is resolved dates all the way back to Landis v. North Am. Co., 299 U.S. 248 (1936).

[31] Liability for secondary-line injury is derivative — there must have been a preceding primary line injury — and defenses such as meeting competition and cost justification apply to both primary and secondary line injury.

[32] The Robinson-Patman Act covers only sales and purchases of tangible commodities, not real estate or intangibles.

- At least one transaction crosses a state line; interstate "effect" is insufficient
- Differentiation in price or related terms of sale (such as credit and freight allowances).

Goods having physical differences that affect marketability are not of "like grade and quality," so they can legitimately have different prices. But labeling, or factors that affect consumer acceptability, are irrelevant under the Robinson-Patman Act.

Competitive bidding situations are excluded from the Robinson-Patman Act; it is not a violation to beat a competitor's price: *Great Atlantic & Pacific Tea Co. v. FTC.*[33]

The Robinson-Patman Act does not require suppliers to offer discounts based on their customers' functions as wholesalers or retailers within the supply chain. However, any discounts that are offered must have a reasonable relationship to the value of those services to the supplier, or the customer's actual cost of performing the function: *Texaco, Inc. v. Hasbrouck.*[34]

A price differential is legitimated by 15 USC § 13(a) if it reflects an allowance for differences in the cost of manufacture, sale, or delivery resulting from different quantities or methods of delivery. A good-faith defense is also available if prices were changed to equal (but not to undercut) what the seller believed was a competitor's price: see *A&P v. FTC*, above. Vending machine retailers were customers who had standing to raise Robinson-Patman Act § 2(d) and (e) claims that their competitors at convenience stores got a better deal on promotional rebates. The Sixth Circuit ruled that those sections protect purchasers who buy for resale.[35]

Under the Robinson-Patman Act, a secondary-line case (involving competition among customers of a seller) requires the favored customer to benefit by the diversion of sales or profits from customers who were discriminated against. A truck dealer who did not bid on special orders from retail customers was not in competition with dealers who did bid, so the non-bidder did not have an antitrust case when it did not receive the discounts made available to bidders.[36]

§ 8.05 ANTITRUST ASPECTS OF MERGERS

The Federal Trade Commission and/or Department of Justice may have to be notified, and may exercise or attempt to exercise the power to enjoin a large-scale merger that could have a significant effect on competition (e.g., creating a very large, affluent entity that knocks out competitors and creates barriers to entry of new firms).

Clayton Act § 7 forbids any "person" (not necessarily a corporation) from acquiring the stock or assets of another person if the acquisition may have the effect of substantially lessening competition, or may tend to create a monopoly in any line

---

[33] 440 U.S. 69 (1979).

[34] 496 U.S. 543 (1990).

[35] Lewis v. Philip Morris Inc., 355 F.3d 515 (6th Cir. 2004).

[36] Volvo Trucks North America v. Reeder-Simco GMC Inc., 546 U.S. 164 (2006).

of commerce, in any section of the country. Clayton Act § 7 applies to horizontal (among competitors), vertical (among members of the supply chain), and conglomerate (among unrelated companies) mergers. However, being acquired by another person (even on consent) is not penalized by § 7.

The FTC challenged the merger between Whole Foods Market and Wild Oats Markets, Inc. The FTC applied for a preliminary injunction to block the merger, which was denied, and the merger took place in August, 2007. However, the Seventh Circuit concluded in a July 29, 2008 opinion, which was amended and reissued November 21, 2008, that the District Court should have granted the injunction. The FTC's position was that Whole Foods and Wild Oats were competitors in the "premium, natural, and organic supermarket" market, and in many states, they were the only entrants in this market, so the merger would cause a monopoly. The District Court treated the two stores as part of a broader supermarket/grocery market. The D.C. Circuit agreed with the FTC's definition of the market, and held that the court system could grant relief to the FTC even though the merger had already occurred.[36A]

Clayton Act § 7A[37] imposes a requirement that parties planning a large-scale merger must notify the Department of Justice or the FTC at least 30 days in advance. The notice, of course, gives the agencies a chance to assess the competitive effect of the transaction and, if necessary, seek an injunction. If the agencies need more information, the waiting period can be extended by an additional 20 days, running from the time the additional information is received (plus, of course, any time the potential merger parties take to compile and submit the information). FTC regulations may impose additional advance notification requirements based on the industry involved (e.g., food distribution).

Transactions involving small companies are exempt. So are transactions in which the acquiror ends up with less than 15% or less than $15 million worth of the target's voting securities or assets. Also exempt are, e.g., acquiring real or personal property in the ordinary course of business; additional acquisitions of control by a party that already owns at least 50% of the target's outstanding voting securities; pure investment transactions of less than 10% of a company's outstanding voting securities; and acquisitions that do not increase the acquiror's percentage ownership of the target. The DOJ and FTC have the power to exempt any party or transaction that is not deemed likely to violate the antitrust laws.

However, if a manufacturing acquiror or target that has total net sales or total assets over $10 million as adjusted for inflation (or any other acquiror or target has total assets over $10 million, irrespective of sales) intends a transaction with annual net sales or total assets over $100 million, notification is required. Both parties in a non-exempt transaction must file a report form. The FTC revised the Hart-Scott-Rodino thresholds under the Clayton Act § 7A, raising the $10 million figure to

---

[36A] FTC v. Whole Foods Market, Inc., No. 07-5276 (D.C. Cir. 11/21/08).

[37] Enacted by the Hart/Scott/Rodino Antitrust Improvements Act of 1976, so this procedure is sometimes described as Hart/Scott/Rodino or HSR.

$12 million, and $100 million to $119.6 million. The revisions take effect 30 days after publication of the notice in the Federal Register.[38]

For large-scale tender offers, the would-be acquiror is required to file pre-merger notification; the target is not obligated. The standard waiting period for a tender offer is only 15 days, which can be extended 10 days if more information is sought by the federal enforcement agencies.

The Department of Justice and the Federal Trade Commission's relationship, and their oversight of mergers and acquisitions, have resulted in an evolving series of guidelines. Guidelines were released April 7, 2000, for antitrust analysis of broad horizontal agreements (e.g., joint ventures and strategic partnerships) among competitors. Agreements will not be challenged if they do not harm competition, and where market power is not present. Arrangements probably will not be challenged where the aggregate market shares of all collaborators are below 20%, or the agreement tends to promote research and innovation.[39] In April 2003, the FTC issued a policy statement on negotiating remedies in merger cases: in most horizontal merger cases, divestiture will be required to protect competition, but mergers will probably be allowed to proceed if the FTC believes the merger will reduce anticompetitive effects in the relevant market.[40] In October 2004, the DOJ Antitrust Division released new guidelines containing new merger remedies that stop short of actually forbidding the merger, e.g., negotiated settlements and "fix it first" remedies. Negotiated settlements and "fix it first" remedies fall into this category. The Antitrust Division accepts early-stage remedies only if there is reason to believe that the merger will violate Clayton Act § 7. Nexus is required between the alleged violation and the proposed remedies. To avoid obligations of ongoing enforcement, the DOJ generally prefers "structural" remedies (e.g., sales of physical assets or licensing of intellectual property assets) to "conduct" remedies (e.g., injunctions governing the firm's post-merger conduct). For the same reason, full divestiture is preferred to partial divestiture that requires supervision.[41]

In March 2006, the FTC and DOJ released a joint commentary on the horizontal merger guidelines, explaining how the agencies analyze whether a proposed merger creates, enhances, or facilitates market power. These guidelines are organized into five sections, dealing with market definition and concentration; adverse effects on competition; entry analysis; efficiencies; and ventures that fail

---

[38] FTC Notice Billing Code 6750-02P; FTC File No. P859910 (1/16/07); http://www.ftc.gov. The agency also authorized publication of higher thresholds for interlocking directorates pursuant to Clayton Act § 8, with the figure for § 8(a)(1) set at $24,001,000 and $2,400,100 for § 8(a)(2), the mandated annual adjustment reflecting changes in the GNP.

[39] http://www.ftc.gov/os/2000/04/ftcdojguidelines.pdf.

[40] See 71 L.W. 2629; see also http://www.ftc.gov/opa/2002/10/mergerbestpractices.htm for DOJ/European Commission best practices for multinational merger review.

[41] Antitrust Policy Division Guide to Merger Remedies, http://www.usdoj.gov/atr/public/guidelines/205108/htm (10/21/04); see 73 L.W. 2243.

or leave the market. The factors are applied in all cases; they do not constitute a sequential five-step test.[42]

§8.06 STANDING AND ANTITRUST INJURY

According to *Associate General Contractors v. California State Council of Carpenters*, 459 U.S. 519 (1983), factors in antitrust standing include:

- Whether the plaintiff was an intended victim of the harm
- Causal connection between an antitrust violation and harm to the plaintiff
- Whether the plaintiff is a consumer or a competitor of the alleged miscreant
- Whether the plaintiff's damage is provable or speculative
- Directness of the injury
- Presence or absence of other, more appropriate plaintiffs.

The Foreign Trade Antitrust Improvements Act of 1982 (FTAIA), 15 USC § 6a, states that the Sherman Act does not apply to trade or commerce with foreign nations. There is, however, an FTAIA exception for conduct that imposes significant harm on domestic commerce, imports, or U.S. exporters. A class action by vitamin purchasers, alleged a price-fixing conspiracy by vitamin manufacturers and distributors. The defendants, who became the petitioners before the Supreme Court, sought to dismiss the suit as to foreign companies that purchased vitamins only outside U.S. commerce. The Supreme Court held that the Sherman Act does not apply to a claim based solely on an adverse foreign effect, even if the alleged price-fixing conspiracy also has effects with the United States, if the foreign and domestic adverse effects are independent of one another.[43]

The Ninth Circuit held that the FTAIA's requirement (15 USC § 6a) that foreign conduct subject to Sherman Act regulation must have "direct, substantial and reasonably foreseeable effect" on U.S. commerce is a modification of the common law requirements preceding the enactment. Therefore, conduct that has only a substantial, but indirect, effect on commerce in the United States is not covered.[44]

In the wake of *Empagran*, the Second Circuit reversed itself and affirmed the dismissal of the class action charging European banks with antitrust violations for setting currency exchange rates higher than the competitive level. This time, the claim was deemed not to be proper for the U.S. courts, because the plaintiffs failed to show that the alleged injury in Europe depended on the effects of the alleged conspiracy on the United States.[45]

---

[42] http://ftc.gov/opa/2006/03/mergercom.htm (3/27/06); *see* 74 LW 2581.
[43] Hoffman-LaRoche Ltd. v. Empagran S.A., 542 U.S. 155 (2004).
[44] United States v. LSL Biotechnologies, 379 F.3d 672 (9th Cir. 2004).
[45] Sniado v. Bank Austria AG, 378 F.3d 210 (2d Cir. 2004).

Furthermore, to succeed, an antitrust plaintiff[46] must demonstrate both injury to competition and personal antitrust injury. Under *Brunswick Corp. v. Pueblo Bowl-o-Mat*,[47] treble damages are unavailable without proof of antitrust injury, and *Cargill, Inc. v. Monfort of Colorado, Inc.*[48] requires antitrust injury for a private party to get injunctive relief.

Antitrust injury is the kind of injury the antitrust laws were enacted to prevent and punish. The injury must flow from the anticompetitive implications of the challenged process.[49] The Ninth Circuit held that an antitrust action, challenging the marketing agreement between the online company Amazon.com and the brick-and-mortar bookstore Borders Group, was properly dismissed for lack of standing. The plaintiff did not have standing because he lacked injury in fact: he could not show that he ever paid more for any item as a result of the marketing agreement. During the term of the agreement, Borders agreed to refrain from online sales, which the plaintiff characterized as per se market allocation in violation of Sherman Act § 1. The plaintiff conceded that book prices on Amazon.com declined after the agreement, but alleged that they would have fallen even further absent the agreement.[50]

The Second Circuit vacated the dismissal of a suit for lack of standing, holding that mandatory arbitration clauses in credit card contracts give rise to a Constitution Article III injury in fact if the clauses result from illegal collusion among providers of credit. The suit was filed by cardholders who alleged that banks and card issuers conspired to force their cardholders to accept mandatory arbitration clauses. In the Second Circuit view, coercion that prevents free choices among market alternatives can constitute antitrust injury. Conspiracy to preclude class actions can subject cardholders to additional effort and legal fees to police their agreements, making the card less valuable. A card that imposes a mandatory arbitration requirement is also less valuable than one that offers a choice between arbitration and litigation.[51]

In a Clayton Act § 4 private suit, antitrust injury is present only if the disfavored customer's ability to compete is impaired.[52] A favored buyer's ability to attract customers away from disfavored buyers can constitute injury to competition.[53]

Also note that the "disaggregation rule" is often applied in antitrust cases. That is, if the plaintiff charges several, discrete unlawful acts or practices, the damages cannot be proved in the aggregate. The plaintiff must prove the damages

---

[46] Either a private plaintiff or the government, suing in its proprietary capacity, for Clayton Act § 4 monetary relief or Clayton Act § 16 equitable relief.

[47] 429 U.S. 477 (1977).

[48] 479 U.S. 104 (1986).

[49] Atlantic Richfield Co. v. USA Petroleum Co., 495 U.S. 328 (1990).

[50] Gerlinger v. Amazon.com Inc., 526 F.3d 1253 (9th Cir. 2008).

[51] Ross v. Bank of America N.A. (USA), 524 F.3d 217 (2d Cir. 2008).

[52] J. Truett Payne Inc. v. Chrysler, 451 U.S. 557 (1981).

[53] Falls City Indus. Inc. v. Vanco Beverage, Inc., 460 U.S. 428 (1983).

flowing from each separate area of anticompetitive conduct. This rule is applied by courts that feel that aggregate damages might be too speculative.

§ 8.07 ANTITRUST REMEDIES

According to the District Court for the District of Columbia, the FTC has the power to order disgorgement of illegal profits stemming from large price increases in the prices of two generic drugs.[54]

The FTC exercised its power to demand disgorgement in another context: Hearst Corporation was forced to surrender $19 million in merger profits (the money went to customers who paid higher prices as a result of the merger) as a penalty for violating the Hart-Scott-Rodino Act through an improper acquisition of an information vendor and through failure to disclose all relevant documents.[55]

New York held in early 2007 that treble damages under the state's General Business Law § 340 are a penalty, as defined by the state's Civil Practice Law & Rules § 901(b). Therefore they cannot be recovered in a class action. The action was brought on behalf of consumers who purchased tires that used the defendant's rubber-processing chemicals, and who allegedly were injured by overcharges caused by price fixing. The case also alleged unjust enrichment, but while strict privity is not required, the state's court of appeals held that the connection between chemicals used to make rubber and tire buyers was too remote to support a claim.[56]

---

[54] FTC v. Mylan Labs Inc., 62 F. Supp. 2d 25 (D.D.C. 1999).

[55] *See* Jaret Seiberg, *FTC Brandishes "Disgorgement" As Enforcement Tool*, The Deal 12/18/01 (law.com).

[56] Sperry v. Crompton Corp., 8 N.Y.3d 204 (N.Y. 2/22/07).

Part II

CONTRACT AND PROPERTY LAW

Chapter 9

Contracts

§ 9.11   **Defenses**
   [A]   **Incapacity**
   [B]   **Duress and Related Concepts**
   [C]   **Undue Influence**
   [D]   **Misrepresentation**
   [E]   **Mistake of Fact**

§ 9.01   INTRODUCTION

A contract is simply a legally enforceable promise, either made by one side (a unilateral contract) or, much more commonly, reciprocal promises made by two sides in exchange for one another (a bilateral contract). All parties to all contracts have a duty of good faith and fair dealing in the performance and enforcement of contracts: see Restatement (2nd) of Contracts § 205.

In most circumstances, an oral contract will theoretically be valid, although it will be difficult to prove the terms of the contract unless there is a document to consult. (Certain types of transactions, such as real estate transactions and contracts that, by their nature, take more than one year to perform, fall under the Statute of Frauds — see § 9.04 — and therefore are invalid unless the contract is expressed in writing.)

Contract law usually deals with express contracts (intended by both sides to be contracts), although sometimes a contract will be implied in the interests of justice. The legal system makes a promise enforceable if valid consideration was received for it: if the person receiving the promise relied on the promise in a financially disadvantageous way ("detrimental reliance"), or if the promise is made enforceable by a statute.

In many instances, particularly if both parties are merchants, the Uniform Commercial Code (especially Article 2, on the sale of goods) will apply to a contract. See Chapter 2.

In 2006, the Supreme Court refused to permit a black owner of a corporation to use the civil rights statute, 42 USC § 1981 to raise claims that contracts with his corporation were breached as a result of racial discrimination against him. The Supreme Court's view was that § 1981 gives citizens of all races the same right to make contracts as white citizens — on their own behalf, not as agents for a corporation; one major corporate characteristic is precisely the separation between the corporation and its stockholders.[1]

The Supreme Court, presuming that unless there is serious harm to the public interest, contracts will be treated as just and reasonable, made it difficult for utility companies to challenge costly long-term supply contracts negotiated during an energy crisis seven years earlier. However, the Supreme Court did hold for the

---

[1] Domino's Pizza v. McDonald, 546 U.S. 470 (2006).

utilities on one issue, requiring the FERC to give a more detailed explanation of why it upheld the contracts because it deemed the contracts not to be contrary to the public interest.[2]

In mid-2008, the Supreme Court refused to expand False Claims Act (FCA) liability broadly, but it also applied the FCA for the first time to subcontractors on government projects. Traditionally, FCA cases involved knowing presenting of false or fraudulent claims to the U.S. government. Recently, there have been many suits seeking to impose liability for using a false record or statement to get a government claim paid, or a conspiracy to defraud the government by getting a false claim paid. Plaintiffs in these suits seek to impose liability for false claims rendered to a private entity that will use government funds to pay them. The Supreme Court ruled that FCA liability requires that a defendant make a false statement for the purpose of causing the government to pay a claim; private entities using government funds are not covered. But if a false statement is made for the purpose of causing the government to pay a claim, then liability is possible — for example, where the government pays a prime contractor based on false statements made by a subcontractor. Subcontractors can also be liable if they make false statements in connection with fixed price contracts, where they falsely certify the amount of progress made.[3]

§9.02 CONTRACT REQUISITES

To create a contract, the parties must bargain to set the terms; there must be an offer; and there must be acceptance of the offer.

[A] Required Terms

In a bargained-for contract, both parties must manifest their intention to be bound, and they must arrive at an agreement that is specific and definite enough for the court system to enforce. It is not necessary that every term be spelled out — only that a court can determine what the parties intended and hold them to it. The requirement of definiteness applies to the contract itself, not to the offer.

The degree of definiteness required depends on the type of contract, with the highest level reached, e.g., in the case of a real estate contract for which specific performance (a court requirement that a party conform to the contract) is requested. Specific performance will be granted only if the contract outlines all of its material terms with certainty and definiteness.

The material terms are the parties; the price; and the subject matter. Although the time for performance is important, the court is likely to read in a requirement of

---

[2] Morgan Stanley Capital Group v. Public Utility District 1, American Electrical Power Service Corp. v. PUD 1, 128 S. Ct. 2733 (2008); *see* (AP), *High Court Makes Electric Rate Challenge Difficult*, 6/26/08 (law.com).

[3] Allison Engine Co. v. United States *ex rel.* Sanders, 128 S. Ct. 2123 (2008); *see* Linda L. Listrom, *U.S. Supreme Court Monitor—Winners and Losers After Supreme Court's Decision in 'Allison Engine,'* Special to Law.com 6/16/08.

performance within a reasonable time, thus satisfying the requirement. Whether a contract term is material also depends on the circumstances. For instance, interest rates are likely to be material—but only if the contract calls for a series of payments over time.

The Uniform Commercial Code (UCC) makes provisions for "gap-fillers": information added to an incomplete contract to make it enforceable. See § 2.02[G].

[B] Consideration

To create an enforceable contract, there must also be consideration—i.e., each side must receive something of value, as in the situation where one party sells goods that are purchased by the other party.[4] The return promise or performance can come from someone other than the original promisee, or go to a third party other than the original promisor. However, there is no consideration if only an illusory promise is made. Contracts require especially close scrutiny if they are conditional on an event within the control of the promisor.

Legally adequate consideration can be quite disproportionate to the benefits received or expected under the contract. The adequacy of the consideration may be relevant to the availability of some remedies or defenses, but not to whether there was a contract in the first place.

An oral contract can serve as consideration if the obligor of a promise that is unenforceable under the Statute of Frauds signs a written memorandum.

A promise to perform a legal duty that already exists under a binding contract is not consideration to support the other party's promise to undertake additional duties. However, if one party is already in breach, an additional promise to carry out the contract and not sue might be binding.

The law of contracts is, in large measure, state law. There are few federal statutes that affect contract law. However, in many situations, the determination of a contract question will require reference to the Uniform Commercial Code (UCC; see the Commercial Transactions chapter), especially if one or both parties is a merchant (dealer in the kind of property covered by the contract).

[C] Unilateral and Bilateral Contracts

Most business contracts are bilateral: each party promises to act or refrain in a particular way, in return for the other party's promise to act or refrain in a particular way. If a promise is made solely in return for the offeree's act or forbearance from action, the contract is unilateral, because the offeror is the only side to be bound. The offeree has not promised anything, and therefore cannot be sued for non-performance.

---

[4] *But see* UCC § 2-209(1), allowing a good faith modification of a contract without new consideration.

Under both the Uniform Commercial Code and the Restatement (2nd) of Contracts, an offer that reasonably expresses a desire for a return promise is an offer to create a bilateral contract, and a contract results when the offeree accepts. However, an offer that expresses a desire for performance, but does not request a return promise, is an offer for a unilateral contract. The contract is created (and the offeror becomes bound) when the offeree performs as requested. If it is not clear whether the offer is bilateral or unilateral, the offeree can accept in any way it chooses.

[D] Severable Obligations

A contract might provide for several items of performance and return performance that can be analyzed as separate and severable: for instance, a landlord might contract with a tree surgeon to remove a tree from one location for $300 and another, more obstinate, tree somewhere else for $500. The obligations can be treated as severable if:

- The same number of actions must be taken by each party
- Each party's performance can be divided into parts, and the value of the parts is not inter-dependent
- Performance of each task by each party is done in exchange for the corresponding task from the other party (e.g., x number of tasks versus x number of payments).

The significance of severability is that the breaching party is liable for damages for any part(s) of the contract that is or are breached. Nevertheless, the breaching party retains the right to perform (or sue under) severable parts of the contract that are not breached.

[E] Third Party Beneficiaries

A contract can be enforced by someone other than the original parties. A third party beneficiary can enforce the contract, but only if the original principal parties intended the third party to have enforceable legal rights. (A third party who is not intended to have enforceable rights is known as an incidental beneficiary; an example might be a homeowner whose home becomes more valuable when a golf course is constructed nearby, although this was not the intention of the golf course architect or the owner of the property.)

A third party beneficiary is subject to any defenses that the promisor is entitled to assert, other than defenses arising out of a transaction between the third party beneficiary and the promisee under the original contract.

§9.03 OFFER AND ACCEPTANCE

Rules have evolved to determine when a valid offer has been made, and when it has been accepted (or only made the subject of further negotiations) by the offeree.

[A] The Offer

An offer is proof of willingness to be bound, definite enough so that a reasonable person would think that making a promise or carrying out a requested act would result in a contract. The element of definiteness is what distinguishes an offer from preliminary negotiations that have not resulted in a contract. The objective actions that a party communicates have more significance than the party's subjective intent.

The general rule is that offers are made to a specific party, and are not assignable. One exception is the "option contract," under which the offeree has provided consideration so that the offer will not be revoked, and therefore is allowed to assign the promise. Offers do not become effective until they are communicated to the offeree.

If an offer contains a time limit, the offer terminates at that time, and any attempt to accept after the time limit is considered a counter-offer, not an acceptance, and a counter-offer is treated as an implied rejection that terminates the offer.

Silence or failure to respond is generally not considered acceptance of an offer, although it might act as such as part of a continued series of dealings between two parties. The common-law rule is that a person who receives goods knowing that they are for sale accepts the goods, and becomes obligated to pay for them, by keeping the goods. However, there are statutes that alter this rule: state consumer protection statutes, for instance, may treat unsolicited merchandise sent by merchants to consumers as gifts to the consumers.

Similarly, when services are offered in the expectation of compensation, the accepting party will be liable for the stated value of the services, or their reasonable value if none is stated, if the circumstances provided a reasonable opportunity to reject them.

Furthermore, if the offeree unconditionally rejects the offer, it is considered terminated for contract-law purposes, and cannot be revived by the offeree's decision that it should have been accepted after all. Once again, the rejection becomes effective when it is received by the offeror. (In practice, the offeror will probably be glad to renew the offer, as long as no one else has purchased the offered item(s) in the interim.)

The offeror generally has the power to revoke an offer at any time until someone accepts it. The exceptions are option contracts (the offeree has paid for the privilege of non-revocability); situations in which the offeree detrimentally relied on the offer staying open; the UCC or another statute makes the offer irrevocable; or the contract is unilateral, and the offeree has already begun its performance. In all other circumstances, the offeror can revoke the offer, even if the offeror represented that it would remain open for a particular period of time. Circumstances that would induce a reasonable offeree to believe that the offer was revoked will result in revocation; but if the offeree accepts the offer before learning of those circumstances, then a contract is created.

Under contract law, the offeror is treated as master of the offer, and therefore is able to specify not only the terms of the future deal but the means for acceptance, which is effective as soon as it is sent if the offeree uses the means specified by the offeror; it does not become effective until it is received if the offeree does not use the specified method.[5] An advertisement is probably not an offer, because the advertiser does not know who sees the advertisement, and steps (beyond merely seeing the advertisement) must be taken to create a contract.

[B] Acceptance and Counter-Offer

Under contract law, an acceptance must be unconditional and must conform completely to the terms of the offer. A so-called acceptance that contains additional or different terms really is not an acceptance at all; it is a counter-offer. The party that made the original offer can create a contract by accepting the counter-offer. If the offeree agrees to be bound by the offeror's terms, but merely suggests (and does not insist on) a change, that is an acceptance. (See § 2.02[D][1] for the UCC rule, found at § 2-207(1).)

[C] Conditions

Frequently, one party's contract performance is conditional on performance by the other party. In fact, both performances might be conditional — in which case, as a practical matter, someone will have to break the deadlock! Restatement (2nd) of Contracts defines a condition as an event that is not certain to occur, and which either must occur or an excuse must be granted, before return performance under the contract is due.

Conditions can be used either offensively (suit for breach of promise) or defensively (against a charge of nonperformance). Conditions can be expressed in the contract, implied under the contract (for instance, someone will have to let the plumbers onto the premises before the plumbing system can be upgraded), or constructive (imposed by the court to achieve a fair result).

The traditional rule of law is that an express condition must be fully and literally satisfied before the other party's duty arises, but this often provides results that are so harsh that courts look for escape clauses, because forfeitures are disfavored.

Modern contract doctrine, as expressed in Restatement (2nd) of Contracts § 241, is that failure to meet conditions should be analyzed according to:

- The extent to which the injured party is deprived of reasonably expected benefits
- The extent to which those lost benefits can be compensated

---

[5] The UCC rule is a little different: § 2-206 says that, unless the language of the offer or the circumstances are to the contrary, an offer invites acceptance by any reasonable medium or manner.

- The extent to which the breaching party would be forced to forfeit by strict enforcement
- Breaching party's ability to cure
- Whether the breaching party acted in good faith and dealt fairly; there can never be substantial performance if the breaching party knowingly and willfully departed from the contract requirements.

However, if the express condition for payment is the approval of a third person (for instance, certification by an inspector), the condition probably will be literally enforced if this can be done without imposing a forfeiture. The court probably will not look behind the honest judgment of a third party who was designated by the contracting parties.

The Fifth Circuit held that a widow was not entitled to proceeds under her husband's life insurance policy: the application imposed a condition precedent of the applicant's good health for the policy to take effect. The decedent applied for $1 million in whole-life insurance in April of 2002; at that point, he had been treated for sore throats for two years, and had sought care for the lump on his neck that eventually proved to be a fatal cancer, so the Fifth Circuit held that the requirement of initial premium payment made when the applicant was in good health was never met, so the decedent was never covered by the policy.[6]

[1] Excuse of Conditions

A condition can be legally excused if:

- A party attempts to tender payment or other performance in a way that complies with the contract, but the tender is refused by the other party
- A prior condition fails
- The other party engages in anticipatory repudiation: i.e., announces that it will not go through with the contract
- Compliance is impossible (e.g., the subject matter of the contract has been destroyed)
- It is evident that it is extremely unlikely that the other party will be able to perform, especially if the unlikelihood is the result of that other party's own actions
- The other party agrees not to insist on the occurrence of a condition that is not material to the contract. (If the condition is material, then a contract modification is necessary to waive it.) Waiver of a condition becomes irrevocable if the beneficiary of the waiver reasonably relied on it to the point that it is no longer reasonable to reinstate the waived term.

Although a technical distinction can be drawn between a condition precedent (precedent, that is, to the other party's performance) and a condition subsequent

---

[6] Assurity Life Ins. Co. v. Grogan, 480 F.3d 743 (5th Cir. 2007).

(which removes an existing duty of performance instead of giving rise to a duty), they are enforced similarly. In fact, a condition subsequent can be considered a way of breaking up a contract into a series of payments, with the condition precedent for each being that the condition subsequent has **not** occurred.

§ 9.04 STATUTE OF FRAUDS

The Statute of Frauds, a traditional English principle adopted in U.S. law, bars enforceability of long-term oral contracts. As a general rule, a contract that cannot be fully performed within one year will be enforceable only if it is in writing. The criterion is whether the terms of the contract actually preclude performance within one year (for instance, a requirement of delivering a summary of the news of the past month, for 15 months). So many contracts that appear to come within the Statute of Frauds, such as a three-year fire insurance policy, are actually exempt (because, in this example, the house could burn down in the first year).

The Statute of Frauds also applies to sale of real property and real estate interests; leases and brokerage agreements with a duration of one year or more; suretyship and guaranty; and promises to pay time-barred debts or debts that have been discharged in bankruptcy.

The Uniform Commercial Code has its own Statute of Frauds requirements, such as § 2-201 (requiring a writing for a sale of goods worth $500 or more); § 8-319 (contracts for the sale of securities); and § 9-203(1)(a) (agreements about security interests in personal property or fixtures).

The Statute of Frauds is satisfied by a signed[7] writing that reasonably identifies the subject matter of the contract; indicates that a contract has been made; and defines the unperformed portion of the contract with reasonable certainty: Restatement (2nd) of Contracts § 131. For this purpose, the necessary writing can consist of several documents, including unsigned documents that are clearly related to the transaction. Testimony can also be used to establish the contents of a lost writing.

[A] Reliance

Detrimental reliance on a promise can create a contract by promissory estoppel: i.e., the party that did not rely detrimentally is estopped from denying the existence of enforceable obligations.

Detriment, for legal purposes, is broader than the concept of harm. It constitutes doing something one was not previously obligated to do, or refraining from something legally permissible. Therefore, there is no detriment in performing a duty that was already in existence.

The Restatement (2nd) of Contracts § 87(2) provides that if an offeror makes an offer that is reasonably expected to induce substantial action or forbearance, and

---

[7] Although it is preferable for both parties to sign, it is only mandatory for the party to be charged to sign the document.

if the offeree does act or forbear, then the offer becomes a binding option contract to the extent needed to prevent injustice.

§ 9.05 CONTRACT INTERPRETATION

If there have been two or more inconsistent expressions of intent, the latest one controls the earlier ones (because it shows the most contemporary intention of the party). If the offer is made on a printed form, but the parties add hand-written terms, the hand-written terms will control because they express later and more personal intention.

The prior course of dealing between the parties, and usages prevailing in the relevant trade or community will also be consulted. (For instance, trade custom may determine the standard quantity of a commodity to be packaged and sold as a unit.) What emerges in performance may be enough to make a contract enforceable even though, without the course of performance, it would have been too vague to enforce.

According to the Restatement (2nd) of Contracts § 203, an interpretation that makes the contract's terms reasonable, lawful, and effective will be preferred to an interpretation that will result in invalidation. The express terms of the contract will be given more weight than the usages of the trade or prior course of dealing; specific terms are more influential in interpretation than general language.

Section 202 provides that words and conduct will be interpreted in light of all relevant circumstances. If the parties' principal objective in entering into the contract is known, it will be given great weight. Any writing is interpreted as a whole, and all of the writings relevant to a particular transaction are interpreted together.

The legal system understands that, in the interests of saving time, many transactions will involve standardized "contracts of adhesion" such as forms, where there is little or no opportunity for individual negotiation. Although contracts of adhesion are not per se unconscionable, they will be interpreted against the party that drafted the form.

The California Supreme Court created a potential conflict with the U.S. Supreme Court by expanding the power of trial court judges to review arbitration awards for legal error if the arbitration agreement provides for review. The decision came five months after the U.S. Supreme Court ruled that parties cannot expand the scope of judicial review by agreement. The California case was filed by retailers who had a contract with DirecTV Inc. to provide customers with equipment to receive satellite broadcasts. According to the retailers, DirecTV withheld their commissions and imposed improper charges. When the matter was arbitrated, the panel of arbitrators ruled that class arbitration was available. The L.A. County Superior Court reversed, holding that the arbitrators exceeded their authority by substituting their judgment for the intent of the parties. The California Court of Appeals reversed again, holding that the judge should not have reviewed the arbitration award on the merits. The California Supreme Court reversed yet again, on the grounds that contracting parties can limit the arbitrator's authority and permit review of the award for legal error. The California Supreme Court justified its decision by citing a line in the Supreme Court's *Hall Street Associates* opinion permitting more searching review of arbitration awards based on authority such as state statutory or common law.[8]

California's Talent Agencies Act forbids unlicensed talent managers to get jobs for their clients. If an unlicensed manager does so anyway, the state labor commissioner determines whether any portion of the artist's contract will be nullified. A manager sued an actor client for failure to pay commissions; she asserted that he was not a licensed manager. The Labor Commissioner nullified the contract, but the California Supreme Court ruled that the legislature failed to impose a clear penalty for violation of the licensing law. The Court held that voiding the contract, or severing improper provisions, are available but not mandatory remedies.[9]

[A] The Parol Evidence Rule

The parol evidence rule, which is actually a substantive principle of contract law, not just an evidentiary rule, says that if the parties have expressed their agreement in a completely integrated writing, neither can introduce evidence of extrinsic agreements that were prior to or contemporaneous with the contract for the purpose of adding new terms or modifying the existing terms. However, evidence can be offered of subsequent agreements, such as contract modifications. Although "parol" implies spoken words, parol evidence is anything (including other writings) that is extrinsic to the contract that is being construed.

A partial integration is a writing that is final but is not complete. Extrinsic evidence of prior or contemporaneous intentions can be introduced either for terms that are consistent with the writing and are supported by separate consideration, or terms that might "naturally" have been omitted from the contract by parties who are similarly situated to the actual parties. A document that appears to constitute a complete contract will probably be treated as one, especially if it has a "zipper" (integration) clause identifying the document as the complete agreement between the parties.

The parol evidence rule only applies to evidence that is being introduced in order to modify the contract. Extrinsic evidence is perfectly proper to prove contract defenses, such as misrepresentation, mistake, duress, and unconscionability.

Although evidence of trade usage or the course of dealings between the parties cannot be introduced to contradict a written contract, such evidence can be used to supply consistent additional terms or interpret the language of the underlying contract. The performance history of the contract can be used to prove waiver or modification of the contract.

---

[8] Cable Connection Inc. v. DIRECTV Inc., 82 Cal. Rptr. 3d 229 (Cal. 2008); *see* Mike McKee, *Calif. High Court Surprises by Expanding Arbitration Review*, The Recorder 8/26/08 (law.com). The Supreme Court decision is Hall Street Associates LLC v. Mattel Inc., 128 S. Ct. 1396 (2008).

[9] Marathon Entertainment Inc. v. Blasi. 42 Cal. 4th 474 (Cal. 2008); *see* Cheryl Miller, *Actors, Managers Win Some, Lose Some in Closely Watched Case*, The Recorder 1/30/08 (law.com).

Testimony can be introduced about specific statements and agreements as to the parties' intention about the meaning of terms in the contract only if the contract is ambiguous (i.e., even by applying the usual interpretive methods, the court is unable to construe the contract language).

§ 9.06 CONTRACT DRAFTING CHECKLIST

Certain basic elements must be found in most, if not all, contracts:

❑ Identification of the document as a contract of a particular type
❑ Identification of the parties. If there are multiple parties on one or both sides of the contract, whether their responsibilities are individual or joint and several
❑ Subject matter of the contract, including definitions of terms
❑ Consideration, including issues such as fees, late charges, points, and currency risk (if the consideration is not entirely payable in U.S. dollars)
❑ Representations and warranties. Typically, in a business contract both buyer and seller represent and warrant that they are corporations in good standing, and that the corporation is authorized to enter into the transaction and has obtained any necessary resolutions. The seller represents and warrants that it has title to goods, that there are no pending lawsuits or intellectual property issues to prevent the transaction, that its financial statements are accurate and in proper form, and either that there is no finder's or brokerage fee due on the transaction, or that arrangements have been made for paying it
❑ Allocation of risk of loss, including when risk shifts to the buyer, and any requirements for maintaining insurance
❑ Conditions on the transaction, e.g., regulatory approval; availability of imported merchandise in adequate amount and quality
❑ What constitutes adequate performance under the contract
❑ Term of the contract; dates for performance
❑ Boilerplate provisions, such as choice of law (which state's law will govern interpretation of the contract); severability of invalid provisions and enforceability of the rest of the contract; and integration (the "zipper clause" stating that the contract represents the entire agreement of the parties and cannot be altered by parol evidence)
❑ Signatures.

[A] Merchant Contracts

If the contract covers a sale of goods between merchants, typical terms will include:

❑ Description of the goods
❑ Price and method of payment
❑ Warranties and limitations of warranties

❑ Risk allocation
❑ Conditions that will excuse sale or alterations of the terms (for instance, increases in the costs of materials or labor)
❑ When, where, and by what method the goods will be delivered
❑ Installation and maintenance provisions
❑ Assignability of the contract.

See Chapter 7 for a discussion of consumer protection, and § 14.02 for disclosure and other requirements in consumer credit contracts.

[B] Employment Contracts

Typical provisions in employment contracts:

❑ When employment will begin
❑ Nature of duties; who the newly hired person will report to; title the newly hired person will hold
❑ Signing bonus
❑ Regular pay
❑ Conditions for paying other bonuses
❑ Stock options and limitation on sale of the issuer company's stock
❑ Fringe benefits
❑ Ownership of intellectual property developed by the employee during employment
❑ Conditions under which employment can be terminated, possibly including continuing payment of compensation after premature termination
❑ Agreement not to compete with the employer after leaving the employment covered by the contract; agreement not to solicit the employer's customers or employees after employment ends.

A television producer complained that the show she was producing did not satisfy the network's own internal ethical standards. She refused to continue acting as producer. She was fired and brought a federal diversity suit for breach of contract. The Seventh Circuit upheld the dismissal of her complaint for failure to state a claim. According to her former employer, her contract was terminated as part of an economic program of layoffs. The plaintiff's position was that her contract contained an implied restriction against firing her for refusing to participate in an unethical program (a sting operation targeting Internet sexual predators). The Seventh Circuit did not find any such implication: although lawyers are subject to formal ethical standards, and cannot be fired for observing those standards; ethical duties are not implied for other professions such as journalism.[10]

---

[10] Bartel v. NBC Universal, Inc., 543 F.3d 901 (7th Cir. 2008).

[C] Contract Formalities

Traditional language, such as "recitals" ("Whereas, East Wind Realty owns a property located at 2209 Elm Plaza, an offer to purchase said property having been made by Kludgeonics Electronic Corp. and having been accepted . . .") and "testimonium clauses" (e.g., "In witness hereof, the parties have executed this agreement on the 29th day of March 2000") are not really necessary, as long as the contract fully expresses all necessary elements of the agreement between the parties.

The best case, of course, is either for the parties to draft a contract specifically for their relationship, or for a form contract to be used and all the blank spaces to be completed in accordance with the agreement between the parties. (Where it is intended that a portion of the preprinted form be inoperative, the best practice is to strike it out or draw a line through the blanks, indicating that the parties were aware of the provision but did not find it applicable to their agreement.)

If blank spaces are left when the contract is signed, the question then becomes whether the contract is valid as it stands (probably yes, if all material terms are completed) and whether one party can fill in the blanks (yes, if the party has express authority to do so, or if authority can be implied on the basis of the agreement).

Under current law, "signature" usually means a handwritten signature, although digital signatures can be legally enforceable. A corporation does business through its human staff, so the proper signature is the typed corporate name, "by" a named person who signs the contract personally. The person's corporate status should be given: for instance, "Bigcorp by Steven Anderson, President." If any other documents are incorporated by reference, it makes sense to attach a copy of the document to the contract into which they are incorporated.

Deeds and other documents affecting real property (e.g., tax deeds and mortgages) may have to be recorded; check the local requirements. UCC filings (see Chapter 2) may be advisable to protect the rights of the secured party under a security agreement.

§ 9.07 ASSIGNMENT AND DELEGATION

Although the phrase "assignment of a contract" is often used, in fact what is assigned is a right under a contract — for instance, one party does work under a contract, but payment goes to a creditor of that party. If rights are embodied in a tangible object (e.g., a season ticket for sporting events), the object itself must be transferred before the assignee can enforce the right.

The obligor under a contract has a valid objection to an assignment only if the duty is materially changed; if the risk of not getting return performance is materially increased; or the value of performance under the contract is significantly reduced.

Contract law recognizes that assigning rights under a contract is an accepted financing device.[11] Therefore, a contract clause that limits assignments will be strictly construed. An outright ban on assignment is often construed to mean that rights can be assigned but duties cannot be delegated. "Rights shall not be assigned" is considered a promise not to assign, with the result that the assignment is effective, but the obligor can sue the assignor for breach of the promise. A provision that "attempted assignment is null and void" is usually applied only for the benefit of the obligor, who can refuse to deal with the assignee. The assignment remains valid as between the assignor and the assignee, and between the assignor and its creditors or subsequent assignees.

[A] Revocable and Irrevocable Assignments

Ordinarily, assignments are revocable at the will of the assignor. Assignments are also deemed revoked by:

- Subsequent assignment of the same right
- The assignor's demand for performance from the obligor
- The assignor's death, bankruptcy, or loss of capacity.

However, certain circumstances will render an assignment irrevocable:

- The assignee provides consideration for the assignment. An assignor who receives value for an assignment warrants that the underlying right exists, and that it is not subject to any defenses other than those disclosed by the assignor. The assignor also warrants that he, she, or it is not aware of any factor impairing the value of the right, and will not do anything in the future to impair its value
- The underlying rights are represented by an object or document which has been delivered to the assignee
- The assignee has changed position in reasonable reliance on the assignment
- The assignee has either been paid by the obligor or has obtained a judgment against the obligor, or has a contract with the obligor that modifies the underlying obligation.

[B] Delegation of Duties

Duties of performance under a contract cannot really be transferred. Duties can be delegated, but the original party is still responsible for the performance. When the promisee party agrees to release the original promisor and accept the delegate instead, a novation has occurred, not just a delegation. Novation requires

---

[11] *See* UCC § 9-318, which prohibits restrictions on assignability of the right to be paid for goods which have been sold or leased; for services rendered. It also forbids restrictions on assignment for security of other rights to receive money.

consent of the original parties and the new substitute party. There must have been an existing previous obligation, intent to waive the duties under the old agreement, and creation of a new, valid, enforceable contract.

Duties can be delegated (to someone with the appropriate skills and experience) unless they are inherently personal. Painting a portrait is personal, because the purchaser wants it to be done by a particular artist, but painting a barn is not, as long as the barn is adequately weatherproofed. A duty to pay money or supply fungible goods or ordinary services is not personal.

§ 9.08 QUASI-CONTRACT

Quasi-contract is the obligation to prevent unjust enrichment by making restitution in exchange for benefits that were obtained without a contract. For example, a seller who is overpaid would be required to return the excess. When goods or services are supplied with the expectation of compensation, and it is reasonable to assume that the recipient would have expected to pay for them, the court may recognize a quasi-contractual right of recovery for the reasonable value of the goods, or the reasonable rate that would be included in a contract for services.

Quasi-contract is invoked in situations such as:

- Benefits conferred by mistake
- Necessaries
- Aid rendered in an emergency
- Work done under an oral or other contract that is unenforceable because of the Statute of Frauds
- Discharge of another party's duty (e.g., a tenant pays the real estate taxes on a property to prevent foreclosure).

§ 9.09 CONTRACT REMEDIES

When one party has breached the contract, and the non-breaching party sues and proves its case, the question for the court becomes what remedies should be awarded. Depending on the circumstances, the proper remedy might be to put the innocent party in the position it would have been in if the contract had been fully performed — or the status quo if the contract had never been signed in the first place. There are several major approaches to contract remedies: rescission (cancellation of the contract) and money damages to reflect expectation, reliance, and restitution interests.

Damages awarded in a contract action must be reasonable, foreseeable, and quantifiable with a reasonable degree of certainty. General damages are the type of damages that are the natural and probable result of breaching a particular type of contract. The defendant is deemed to have anticipated such damages to occur, so the plaintiff will not be required to prove foreseeability. Special (also known as consequential) damages arise out of the facts of the case, and can be recovered only if the defendant could have anticipated them at the outset of the contract. The New York

Court of Appeals permitted commercial property owners to seek consequential damages from insurers who breach their policies. Therefore, damages can exceed the stated value of the policy if the damages are natural and probable consequences of the breach of contract. (The dissenting judges said that the majority permitted a prohibited punitive damage claim by re-labeling it a consequential damage claim.) The plaintiff, a meat market, charged that it was driven out of business after a fire because its insurer paid only $163,000 (far less than the $407,000 awarded under ADR), and the insurer paid for only seven months of lost income although the policy covered a year. According to the majority, many businesses are unable to operate after a covered loss without insurance proceeds, so limiting the damages to the policy amount (which should have been paid in the first place) would not put the insured in the position it would have been in if the contract had been performed. The majority treated consequential damages as a means of compensating parties for reasonably foreseeable damages, and saw them as distinct from punitive damages, which are intended to punish wrongdoing. In a related case, the majority awarded consequential damages such as lost rent and interest on loans for repairs the insurer refused to cover in a case involving damage during repair work to the structure.[12]

Emotional distress is usually not considered foreseeable in the contract context,[13] and therefore such damages are seldom awarded in contract cases.

Non-breaching parties are subject to a duty to mitigate; they cannot recover whatever damages could have been avoided by reasonable effort and without undertaking unreasonable risks. For instance, consequential damages will not be awarded for nondelivery of merchandise that could readily have been purchased from other sources.

On a question certified by the Second Circuit, the New York Court of Appeals ruled in 2007 that there is a tort of interference with either current or prospective contracts (e.g., inducing away customers from a competitor), but more protection is given for current contracts. In a contract interference case, the plaintiff must show the existence of a valid contract with a third party; the defendant's knowledge of that contract; and the defendant's intentional, improper procurement of a breach of that contract, leading to damages. A defense of protecting the defendant's own legal or financial stake in the breaching party's business is available, but not to competitors of the plaintiff who knowingly solicit the plaintiff's customers.[14]

The Ninth Circuit ruled that intentional breach of contract is non-dischargeable under Bankruptcy Code § 523(a)(6) if and only if it involves conduct that constitutes a tort under state law. After a malpractice suit, an attorney settled with the former client-plaintiff, assigning 50% of attorneys' fees from the attorney's personal injury case load. Then the lawyer refused to abide by the agreement,

---

[12] Bi-Economy Market, Inc. v. Harleysville Insurance Co. of NY, 10 N.Y.3d 187 (N.Y. 2008); *see* Joel Stashenko, *N.Y. High Court Approves Consequential Damages Claims Against Insurers,* N.Y.L.J. 2/20/08 (law.com).

[13] With some exceptions, such as a funeral home's mishandling a dead body.

[14] USCOA v. Cintas Corp., 8 N.Y.3d 422 (N.Y. 2007); the issue was certified by White Plains Coat & Apron Co., Inc. v. Cintas Corp., 460 F.3d 281 (2d Cir. 2006).

taking the position that his ex-client did not have a valid claim, and filed a Chapter 7 bankruptcy petition. The ex-client sought a declaration that the breach of contract was non-dischargeable. The Ninth Circuit ruled that willful failure to pay contract debts is not tortious, and that there was no fiduciary relationship between the two, because the settlement agreement was not part of the attorney-client relationship.[15]

The Uniform Commercial Code has its own remedy rules, involving concepts such as rightful rejection of goods and having defective goods repaired or replaced; see Chapter 2.

[A] Expectation

Analysts think of the "expectation interest" as a basic part of entering into a contract. A person who has not received the benefit of the bargain as expected is entitled to money damages for breach of contract. The calculation of damages begins with the expected profits that would have accrued if the contract had been performed. The initial sum is reduced by sums saved by not having to perform under the contract. In other words, the non-breaching party receives the benefits that would have come from full performance of the contract as expected. Where the performance is incomplete rather than defective, the measure of expectation damages is the cost of completing the contract, not the reduction in value attributable to incomplete performance.

[B] Reliance

In certain situations, it is clear that the defendant has breached the contract, causing damage to the plaintiff, but the amount of expectation damages cannot be established.

The damages for the non-breaching party are the expenses or losses incurred in reasonable reliance on the contract (e.g., a homeowner contracts to have his home remodeled, and buys tiles, wallpaper, and roofing material to be used by the contractor). The purpose of the remedy is to return the non-breaching party to his or her pre-contract status quo.

Reliance damages will not be awarded if they exceed expectation damages.

[C] Restitution

The purpose of a restitution remedy is to make the defendant give up the benefits obtained by entering into and breaching a contract. Unlike expectation and reliance remedies, the restitution remedy looks at what the breaching party gained and not what the non-breaching party lost or failed to receive.

Restitution damages do not even require proof of the existence of a contract. They can be recovered in quasi-contract (§ 9.08) cases and some tort cases (for instance, intellectual property licensing cases). Constructive trust, equitable lien, accounting for profits, subrogation, indemnity, and contribution are all restitutionary remedies.

---

[15] Lockerby v. Sierra, No. 06-15928 (9th Cir. 8/7/08).

[D] Rescission

Rescission can be voluntary — both parties agree to rescind the old contract and substitute a similar new contract, such as one with lower prices reflecting a change in market conditions, or ordered as a remedy.

[E] Quantum Meruit

This phrase, which is Latin for "what he deserves," is a remedy involving recovery of benefits conferred on someone else. Traditionally, a party who breached a contract after part performance would not be entitled to receive quantum meruit damages for the part of the contract actually performed. Current practice does not entirely rule out quantum meruit damages for a breaching party: see, e.g., UCC § 2-718(2). Quantum meruit damages are often an issue when a lawyer has been dismissed by a client prior to conclusion of a legal matter: see § 27.07[G].

[F] Liquidated Damages

Liquidated damages are either a sum of money agreed on in advance, or other remedies (such as a commitment to make repairs) also agreed on in advance.

They are most appropriate if, based on the facts available at the time of contracting, the parties agree that it would be difficult or impossible to quantify damages in case of breach. In fact, a minority of jurisdictions will not enforce a liquidated damages clause without proof that damages could not be reliably ascertained after the breach. On the other hand, a party's attempt to restrict its exposure by negotiating an unreasonably small amount of liquidated damages will probably be enforceable unless the clause is unconscionable.

Liquidated damages are unenforceable if they constitute a penalty.[16] Damages for delay are more likely to be upheld if the amount increases as the delay continues, rather than a single flat sum irrespective of the duration of the delay.

Liquidated damages are especially appropriate in personal service contracts, because specific performance is not available. An employer's legitimate interest in contract enforcement could be frustrated if specific performance clauses are forbidden as in terrorem provisions.[17]

Although the contract ruled out incidental, special and consequential damages the Western District of Wisconsin ruled that the winner of a breach of contract action could recover prejudgment interest, because it does not fall into any of those categories.[18]

---

[16] Even though the phrase "penalty provision" is accepted terminology in the construction industry for a liquidated damages clause, the word "penalty" should be avoided in contract drafting for this reason.

[17] Arrowhead School Dist. v. Klyap, 2003 Mt. 294 (Mont. 2003).

[18] CERAbio and Phillips Plastics Corp. v. Wright Med. Technology Inc., 2006 WL 1666308 (W.D. Wis. 6/13/06).

[G] Punitive Damages

A defendant who engages in fraudulent, malicious, oppressive or otherwise reprehensible conduct in connection with a contract might be required to pay punitive damages, measured by the defendant's capacity to pay rather than by quantifiable damage to the plaintiff. However, punitive damages are quite rare in the contractual context, although the defendant's conduct might be tortious as well as constituting a breach. Although punitive damages are usually unavailable in contract cases, there may be an exception when public policy issues are involved. A New Jersey Superior Court found public policy issues of patient care involved, and awarded $2.5 million ($1 million compensatory damages and interest, $1.5 million punitive damages) to a doctor who was fired from a hospital cardiology department. The appellate panel ruled that there was no evidence of harm to the patients, so dismissed the finding of breach of contract and the $570,000 in compensatory damages, remanding only on breach of contract. The appellate court said that there was no special relationship; it was simply an employment case, and thus punitive damages were unavailable.[19]

The California Supreme Court upheld $300 million in damages against Genentech for cheating the City of Hope out of royalties on City of Hope's genetic engineering process. However, the Supreme Court reversed awards of punitive damages and post-judgment interest, on the grounds that punitive damages can be awarded for breach of contract only if the parties had a fiduciary relationship. It held that the fact that one party lets another develop valuable intellectual property does not necessarily create a fiduciary relationship, although the secrecy of the information disclosed for commercial purposes is a factor in the determination.[20]

[H] Specific Performance

It is unusual for specific performance (forcing a breaching or unwilling party to perform a contract) to be granted, because in most instances money damages will adequately compensate the plaintiff, and will not involve the court in the need to supervise continuing compliance. However, specific performance might be ordered in the case of a unique item of property (e.g., a work of art), and each parcel of property is considered unique. Because specific performance is a remedy that derives from equity, it will be granted only if the court determines that, as of the time of the making of the contract, it was fair and equitable. Furthermore, it will be granted only if the material terms of the contract are certain (e.g., if the property in question is adequately described).[21]

---

[19] Kurnik v. Cooper Health System, No. A-4686 (N.J. App. Div. 2008); *see* Henry Gottlieb, *Punitive Damages Not Recoverable in Doctor's Suit Over Dismissal*, N.J.L.J. 7/31/08 (law.com).

[20] City of Hope National Medical Center v. Genentech Inc., 43 Cal. 4th 375 (Cal. 2008); *see* Mike McKee, *$300 Million Award Stands Against Genentech, but $200 Million in Punitives Get Tossed*, The Recorder 4/25/08 (law.com).

[21] Whitney v. G. Harvey Kennington Revocable Trust, 62 Fed. Appx. 794 (9th Cir. 2003); Makowski v. Waldrop, 584 S.E.2d 714 (Ga. App. 2003).

The availability of money damages does not necessarily rule out the availability of specific performance.[22]

Specific performance will not be ordered if performance depends on the approval of a third party who is not a party to the contract.[23]

§9.10 EXCUSE OF PERFORMANCE

Under most circumstances, a party who guessed wrong or made an incorrect prediction will be required to abide by its contract obligations — or face penalties for breach — even if performance turns out to be more difficult or more expensive than anticipated. However, performance will certainly be excused if performance becomes impossible: an art dealer will not be required to deliver a Rembrandt painting that was destroyed in a fire after being sold but before delivery, for instance.

The more difficult question is when performance will be excused when it is merely impracticable, not absolutely impossible. The defense of impracticability requires four elements:

- An event (such as a natural disaster) has occurred to make performance impracticable, at least as contemplated; related higher costs are not enough to excuse performance, but hugely higher costs might be
- The event is not the fault of the party seeking to be excused
- The event is one whose non-occurrence was a basic assumption underlying the contract. In contrast, a party who enters into a futures contract can be presumed to know that prices will fluctuate, since that's the rationale for futures contracts
- The party seeking excuse did not agree to assume the risk of what actually occurred, either in express contract language, or by assenting to a list of conditions other than the one that actually occurred.

The doctrine of economic frustration covers the situation in which post-contract events make performance, even though it is perfectly possible, useless to one party. Just after Prohibition was declared, for instance, breweries had plenty of beer, but their tavern customers could not use it (well, not legally, anyway).

Restatement (2nd) of Contracts § 265 permits discharge of future duties under a contract if the party is not at fault and the principal purpose motivating the contract is frustrated by an event whose non-occurrence was a basic assumption underlying the contract. (Discharge is not permitted if the contract contains language to the contrary.) However, even if discharge is granted, the other party may be entitled to restitution of benefits already provided under the contract, or reliance damages to compensate for having changed position in reliance on the contract.

---

[22] Aerovox, Inc. v. Parallax Power Components LLC, 281 B.R. 419 (B.D. Mass. 2002).
[23] Kaiser v. Bowlen, 181 F. Supp. 2d 1200 (D. Colo. 2002).

§ 9.11 DEFENSES

A party accused of breach of contract may be able to stave off the accusations by proving that no valid contract was ever formed; that the defendant's conduct did not in fact breach the contract; or that a defense is available.

A 2008 Third Circuit opinion holds that a Spanish-speaking worker was bound by the mandatory arbitration clause in his employment agreement, written in English, although he said he did not understand it. The court applied an objective theory of contract formation, where outward expressions of assent and not subjective intent counts. When there is no fraud, the offeree's inability to read English is irrelevant to the enforceability of the contract. A bilingual worker was assigned to translate the contract, but he testified that he did not interpret the arbitration clause. The Third Circuit majority opinion noted that the plaintiff had paid translators in the past to translate English documents for him, and that he should have done it in this instance as well.[24]

All claims in a class action charging breach of warranty and fraud in connection with defective head gaskets in Dodge Neon cars were dismissed. The express warranty claim was dismissed because the head gasket did not fail until after the express warranty expired. The implied warranty claim failed because there was no privity between the plaintiff and DaimlerChrysler. The statute of limitations had run on state fraud claims before the case was initiated, and Magnuson-Moss claims stand or fall with the accompanying warranty claims. The plaintiff missed the three-year California statute of limitations for fraud claims, and he could not use the discovery rule or tolling to file a similar action in Illinois.[25]

An insurer sued the manufacturer of a fire sprinkler for breach of warranty in connection with an allegedly defective sprinkler that damaged a building owned by one of the insurer's customers. The Seventh Circuit affirmed the grant of summary judgment for the manufacturer. There was no agreement between the insured bank and the manufacturer when the sprinkler was purchased, so there was no privity of contract. The sprinkler had a one-year warranty for replacement of sprinkler heads, but it was limited to the original purchaser, the subcontractor who handled the installation of the sprinkler system. In Wisconsin, the breach of warranty claim ran only to the original purchaser of the sprinkler system, not to the bank where it was installed or to the insurer as subrogee of the bank. In this case, the court found that the subcontractor was not the bank's agent, and even if the prime contractor was the bank's agent there was no intent to have the contractor act on behalf of the bank,

---

[24] Morales v. Sun Constructors Inc., 541 F.3d 218 (3d Cir. 2008); *see* (No by-line) *3rd Circuit: Agreement Can Be Enforced Despite Language Barrier*, The Legal Intelligencer 9/2/08 (law.com).

[25] Clemens v. DaimlerChrysler Corp., 530 F.3d 852 (9th Cir. 2008). Daughtery v. Am. Honda Motor Co., 144 Cal. App. 4th 824 (2006) holds that express warranties do not cover repairs made after the expiration of the mileage or time period of the warranty. California law provides (although some states disagree) that a consumer who buys from a retail dealer is not in privity with the manufacturer: Anunziato v. eMachines, Inc., 402 F. Supp. 2d 1133 (C.D. Cal. 2005).

and the bank did not retain control over the work. Merely paying for the sprinklers did not create an agency relationship between the property owner and the subcontractor.[26]

[A] Incapacity

Contracts may become either voidable or absolutely void if entered into by parties lacking contractual capacity. However, the promise of incapacitated persons still constitutes consideration, so they can enforce contracts that cannot be enforced against them. Contracts are voidable rather than void if the incapacity is only partial.

Minors' contracts, except for contracts for necessities (such as food and medical care) are voidable (by themselves or their guardians), once the minor reaches adult age, unless the minor chooses to reaffirm them after becoming an adult. If the contract is disaffirmed, the legal effect is to revest the contract property in its original owner. In many instances, this is a practical impossibility, because the property has been consumed, destroyed, or transferred to someone else. Some jurisdictions require the minor to reimburse the other party for such losses.

For adults, where the question is impairment by reason of developmental disability, mental illness, or aging-related deterioration, the standard of contractual capacity is fairly low: the ability to understand the nature of the transaction and its implications. A distinction may be drawn between impaired persons who lack cognitive capacity (such contracts could be treated as voidable whether or not the other party knew or could have known about the impairment) and those who suffer mental illness that impairs their motivational control (contracts probably voidable only if the other party knew or should have known of the illness).

Another approach some jurisdictions take is to allow contracts to be avoided on the grounds of incapacity if the status quo can be restored, even if there was no reason for the other party to know of the condition.

The burden of proof is on the party seeking to avoid the contract. Rescission will be available if the contract is still executory, but unless the other party took advantage of an impaired person, the right of avoidance may be limited to the part of the contract that has not already been performed.

In addition to the potential for avoidance of the contract, mental impairment might be relevant to claims of undue influence.

[B] Duress and Related Concepts

A contract is obtained by duress if a significant threat of unlawful harm or economic loss is applied to motivate the contract. A threat to act in a legal manner (e.g., to bring suit or publicize someone else's conduct), even if the consequences of doing so would be very serious, does not constitute duress.

---

[26] St. Paul Mercury Insurance Co. v. Viking Corp., 539 F.3d 623 (7th Cir. 2008).

Contracts can also be avoided if they have illegal subject matter (e.g., assassinations; drug deals); if they violate public policy (e.g., racially restrictive covenants in property deeds); and if they are unconscionable (so unfair that the legal system will not become involved in their enforcement).

Furthermore, an exculpatory contract term is not enforceable if it has the effect of relieving a party from liability for harm that is intentionally inflicted on others, or that results from reckless conduct.

[C] Undue Influence

Duress is severe enough to overbear the will. Undue influence is related but less severe. Undue influence consists of taking advantage of someone else's mental state or personal characteristics to prevent free choice and induce that person to enter into an unfair contract. The person's immaturity, illness, bereavement, lack of sophistication, etc., has the effect of limiting the ability to make valid decisions.

Undue influence can also be asserted in the context of a fiduciary relationship, where the non-fiduciary naturally relies on the fiduciary's judgment. In such situations, unfair contracts can be set aside, even if there was no conscious abuse of the relationship on the fiduciary's part.

[D] Misrepresentation

Misrepresentation is an assertion that is not in accordance with the true state of facts. Concealment of negative facts also constitutes misrepresentation; so does failure to disclose but only if there is a duty to disclose (e.g., imposed by a statute; implied as part of a fiduciary relationship; needed to correct a previous assertion that was accurate when made but has been rendered inaccurate by subsequent events). There may also be a duty to disclose in situations where the potential discloser is aware that the other party is operating under a mistake.

The doctrine of "fraud in the factum" says that there is no contract if alleged consent is obtained by misrepresentation—e.g., the individual did not think that the document he or she signed was a contract. The difference between no contract, in the case of fraud in the factum, and a voidable contract, in the case of misrepresentation where the innocent party knew that a contract was created, becomes significant if a bona fide purchaser for value enters the situation.

Contracts can be avoided for misrepresentation only if the misrepresentation was material, fraudulent, or both. A misrepresentation is material in general if it would be likely to induce a reasonable person to enter into the contract. In a particular situation, a misrepresentation can be material if it was known to operate as an inducement to a particular person (a fanatical electric train collector or fervent Greek patriot, for instance). Even an innocent or negligent material misrepresentation can justify avoidance of a contract.

A representation is fraudulent if it is made with the intention of inducing reliance, and it was either known to be false or the maker of the representation lacked sufficient facts to be aware of whether it was true or false. An opinion can be a misrepresentation, but only if the speaker believes the assertion to be false.

The party seeking to avoid the contract must have relied on it (it must have contributed significantly to the decision to enter into the contract). Either that party must have had pecuniary detriment, or must not have received the expected bargain. Furthermore, reliance must have been reasonable, as judged from the viewpoint of a person in that party's situation. Reliance on a pure statement of opinion is not justified. In general, statements of future intentions cannot be relied upon, because people can change their minds.

[E] Mistake of Fact

Mistake of law usually does not offer a contract defense, because everyone is presumed to know the law (however distant that assumption is from real life).

On the other hand, a significant enough mistake of fact operates as a defense, because it prevents a contract from being formed at all (e.g., mistake about the identity of the parties). An offer that is the product of a mistake is not an effective offer and cannot create a contract. Nor is there a contract if communications are exchanged that include materially different meanings, and neither side has reason to know what the other party meant. The classic case involves two ships named "Peerless" that were shipping cargo at the same time.

A fundamental unilateral error that the other party knows about could operate as a defense; so could a misunderstanding about the contract terms that cannot be resolved by a court's interpretation of the contract.

A mistake of fact involves present factual matters in existence at the time the contract was created. A mistaken prediction of what will happen (e.g., the price of wheat six months in the future) does not qualify as a mistake of fact. Furthermore, since the principle is that contracts are made to be performed rather than avoided, relief on the basis of mistake of fact is the exception, not the rule.

Under Restatement (2nd) of Contracts § 152, a mutual mistake that is material to the agreed-on exchange of performance allows avoidance of the contract by the adversely affected party, unless that party bore the risk of mistake on such issues. (A unilateral mistake actually induced by representations of the other party might give rise to a defense of misrepresentation.) The facts must have existed when the contract was signed.

A party who assumes the risk of mistake with regard to the accuracy of facts has no defense if the facts are wrong. This might occur in a futures contract, which reflects assumptions about future price trends, or if the contract itself reflects the assumption, such as a construction contract reciting that the contractor has tested the soil conditions.

Chapter 10

Property

§ 10.01 INTRODUCTION

In many ways, property law is one of the most archaic areas of the law, the one in which concepts that predate the American Revolution, and even many medieval concepts, are still influential. The very concept of a "landlord" goes back to the time when those who owned land were, indeed, lords.

Title is a central concept for property law. Title is lawful ownership. Sometimes property is in the possession of someone who does not have title, such as a thief or embezzler. In other instances, several people acting lawfully may have competing claims to some or all of the property. Examination of the chain of title is essential to determine who was the true owner at any alleged point of transfer, as well as to determine the respective rights of those asserting conflicting claims. No one can convey better title than he or she actually has. See § 2.05[E] for a discussion of the related concept of "holder in due course."

There are two basic forms of outright transfer: the inter vivos "conveyance," and the testamentary "devise" or "bequest." (Technically speaking, real property is devised and personal property is bequeathed; so it is possible to "bequeath and devise" one's entire estate, but each individual item must be either bequeathed or devised, not both.)

The traditionally staid subject of takings jurisprudence took center stage in 2004–2005, with several Supreme Court decisions and potential for legislative action to limit their applicability.

In 2005, the Supreme Court held that there is no constitutionally protected property right in having a state-law restraining order enforced by the police.[1]

Under New York law, property owned by a foreign government is tax-exempt when it is used exclusively for diplomatic offices or as housing for ambassadors. The City of New York levied property taxes against foreign governments for the portion of diplomatic office buildings used to house employees below ambassadorial rank and their families. India refused to pay the tax, and the city sued in

---

[1] Town of Castle Rock v. Gonzales, 545 U.S. 748 (2005).

New York State court to establish the validity of its tax liens. India claimed immunity under the Foreign Sovereign Immunities Act of 1976, and the case was removed to federal court. In mid-2007, the Supreme Court ruled that 28 USC § 1605(a)(4) abrogates immunity with respect to rights in "immovable property situated in the United States" — an exception broad enough to cover all rights in property, not just title, ownership, or possession. Thus, a suit about the validity of a tax lien clearly would implicate rights in immovable property. The Supreme Court held that owning property is not an inherently sovereign function, and at the time of the enactment of the Foreign Sovereign Immunities Act, international practice recognized a real property exception.[2]

§ 10.02 ADVERSE POSSESSION

In many instances, if the owner of real property neither sells it, uses it, nor rents it to someone else, squatters will move in. The owner can then sue the squatters for ejectment, in order to have them removed from the property.

But if the owner fails or neglects to do so before the statute of limitations runs (there is no single statute of limitations; each state sets its own), then the squatters can acquire good title under the doctrine of adverse possession. They can file an action to quiet title to establish their ownership as soon as the statute of limitations elapses. Furthermore, they are considered to be the owners as of the time the owner who abandoned the property initially acquired it.

There are five elements in establishing adverse possession. In essence, the squatter must act like an ordinary owner of property, and must use the property in the same way (payment of real estate taxes on the property may be required). The elements are:

- Actually inhabiting the land
- Open and notorious, not covert, possession
- Exclusive
- Continuous throughout the entire limitations period (although use by a tenant of the squatter is deemed use by the squatter)
- "Hostile" — i.e., the squatter intends to be recognized as the true owner; in some states a subjective test of belief in one's true ownership of the property is imposed. Some states also shorten the statute of limitations (making adverse possession possible at an earlier time) if the squatter uses the property based on a document granting possession, but the document is invalid or defective.

§ 10.03 PRESENT AND FUTURE INTERESTS

Modern property law recognizes several kinds of interests in property, reflecting centuries of modification of medieval concepts of property ownership. Even the names of interests reflect medieval French and Latin terms.

---

[2] Permanent Mission of India to the United Nations v. City of N.Y., 127 S. Ct. 2352 (U.S. 6/14/07).

Not only are several varieties of present ownership recognized, there are several categories relating to rights to acquire ownership of property in the future. Property interests can change based on conditions stated in the deed or other instrument creating the property interest: based on facts; or by operation of law. A seller or donor of property interests is the grantor; the recipient is the grantee.

[A] Present Possessory Interests

The fullest possible present ownership interest is the fee simple absolute, full ownership with no termination date and with no restrictions on future transfers. (Even a fee simple absolute can be subject to some restrictions on land use, such as zoning laws.) The signal in a deed of a fee simple absolute is language such as "To Grantee and his/her heirs."

There are also four lesser forms of present possession:

- Fee simple determinable, which ends automatically based on the occurrence or non-occurrence of an event specified in the governing instrument; in this case, title to the property reverts to the grantor (or the successors of a deceased grantor)—although legal action may be necessary to make the grantee surrender possession! The signal deed language is something like "so long as" or "until."
- Fee simple on condition subsequent, which ends based on the occurrence or non-occurrence of a specified event, but only if the grantor or grantor's successor decides to take back the property. The signal is something like "provided that," "on condition that," or "but if," plus an explanation of the right of the grantor or grantor's successor to take back the property.
- Fee simple conditional, preventing the grantee from making further grants of the property; this is the U.S. successor of the British "entail," preventing conveyance of the estate away from the grantee's heirs (or his or her male heirs). Many states forbid fee simple conditional grants limited to biological heirs.
- Life estate, which is a full possessory estate, but limited in time either to the life of the grantee or the life of another specified person, signalled by "To X for life, and then to Y" or "To X for the life of Y, and then to Z." The holder of the life estate can transfer his or her rights to someone else, but the transferee's rights end when the transferor (or the named life) dies.

[B] Future Interests

Future interests are divided into three main categories, each of which has subcategories, depending on criteria such as whether they belong to the grantor or another party; whether they are vested or contingent (i.e., certain to happen, or may possibly happen, respectively); and what event is necessary to trigger them.

- Reversionary interests are vested interests retained by the grantor, e.g., the right to re-possess the property after a fee simple determinable has ended, or the right to take steps to terminate a fee simple on condition subsequent when the specified event has occurred. A reversion is what the grantor retains after transferring only part of his or her interest in the property. The reversion itself is a property right that can be given away, sold, or devised in a will.
- Remainder interests are future interests given, sold, or left by the grantor to someone else. Remainder interests are created at the same time as a present interest: i.e., the property goes to Alice Ames for 25 years, with a remainder to Bob Blake. A remainder can be contingent (e.g., a remainder to all of the grantor's grandchildren who are alive in 2013), and can terminate when a specified event occurs.
- Executory interests are future interests transferred by the grantor to someone else, and which have the effect of eliminating the grantor's retained interest in the property or dispossessing someone else.

Note that, for gift tax purposes, a gift of a present interest can qualify for the annual exclusion, but a gift of a future interest cannot: see § 17.13.

[C] Rule Against Perpetuities

This rule exists to frustrate attempts to tie up property forever, without its ever becoming freely transferable. The rule provides that property interests must vest (if they ever do) no later than 21 years (plus nine months for gestation of a conceived but unborn heir) after the life of a person who was already alive when the interest was created.

In other words, it is not possible to set up a non-charitable trust that will last forever, or to tie up land ownership forever. (The Rule Against Perpetuities does not apply to charitable trusts.)

Some states have adopted the Uniform Statutory Rule Against Perpetuities, which says that a non-vested interest that actually does either vest or fail within 90 years of creation is valid. In the other states, the common-law "wait and see" doctrine applies: instead of declaring an interest invalid at the outset, the decision is deferred until actual events make it possible to determine if vesting has occurred. The doctrine of *cy pres* (as close as possible) permits reformation of documents so that it becomes clear whether or not the interest will vest in time.

§ 10.04 SHARED OWNERSHIP

There are various situations in which property has more than one owner concurrently. The most common forms of shared ownership are joint tenancy with right of survivorship (JWROS) and tenancy in common. There are also forms of tenancy limited to married couples: community property, and a special JWROS form, tenancy by the entireties.

Tenancy in common can be created by deed, by will, or when there is no will and property is inherited by intestate succession.

Tenants in common are equally entitled to possess the property, although they may own different shares in it. Tenants in common can sell, give away, or devise their ownership shares without consent of the other tenant(s) in common. The cotenants can agree to partition the property, or partition can be ordered by a court.

In contrast, when one joint tenant with right of survivorship dies, his or her ownership share passes automatically, by operation of law, to the surviving joint tenant(s), each of whom now has a larger percentage ownership. (If there is only one, he or she has 100% ownership.) A JWROS tenancy cannot be created by intestate succession, only by deed or by will. JWROS requires four conditions:

- Cotenants must acquire their interests in the property at the same time
- They must have acquired their interests under the same deed or other instrument, or because of the same act of adverse possession
- They must have the same interest in the property
- Each must be entitled to possess the whole property

Although any joint tenant can sever the joint tenancy, thus eliminating the right of survivorship, and although any joint tenant can compel partition, an attempt to sell or give away a JWROS interest makes the buyer or donee a tenant in common with the other joint tenants. (The acquiror does not become a joint tenant because the interests were created at different times; if the intention is to create a new joint tenancy, the old one must be severed and a new one created respecting the "four unities.")

Tenancy by the entireties is a marital joint tenancy that offers additional protection from claims of creditors.

Community property is a legal fiction that a married couple's property is held not by the spouses as individuals, but the marital "community." As § 16.05[C] shows, it may be necessary to distinguish between the separate property of the spouses, and community property. Generally speaking, anything acquired prior to the marriage is separate; anything acquired during the marriage is community; and the community property states have taken various approaches to, for instance, income earned during marriage on separate property. Spouses may also be able to alter the state community property rules by pre- or post-nuptial agreement, and make interspousal gifts that turn community into separate property.

When the spouses divorce, each spouse takes back his or her separate property (if any), and the community property is divided. Spouses in community property states can devise their separate property, but community property passes automatically by operation of law.

The basic contemporary rule (which has been altered by some state statutes) is that if a conveyance does not indicate the form in which multiple owners will hold the property, it will be presumed to be a tenancy in common. (This is a change from the traditional presumption of JWROS.) Evidence can be produced to rebut the presumption. Some of the state statutes presume that a conveyance to a married couple is intended to make them joint tenants or tenants by the entireties.

§ 10.05 REAL ESTATE TRANSACTIONS

Some houses are "FISBOs" — For Sale By Owner — with no involvement of a real estate broker. However, most residential sales, and nearly all commercial sales, involve a real estate broker.

Many problems arise because of the multiplicity of documents that can be used in the course of a real estate transaction, and potential for misunderstanding of each document. A common sticking point is the use of a "binder" or pre-contract; before there is a closing or even a contract of sale, the potential buyer decides not to buy, or the potential seller gets a better offer, and it then becomes necessary to decide whether the binder is indeed an enforceable contract or merely an agreement to agree.

Generally speaking, the contract of sale will obligate the seller to convey good marketable title at the time of the closing. Therefore, the seller must use the pre-closing period to remove any encumbrances from the chain of title, and cure any defects (e.g., unrecorded conveyances) in the chain of title. Failure to do so permits the buyer to sue for breach of contract. Most buyers will also have title insurance which will compensate them if good title is not delivered.

If the seller breaches the contract, the buyer may be entitled to specific performance; because real property is unique, a damage award would not necessarily fully compensate the buyer. The buyer can, however, sue for damages, especially if specific performance is unavailable (e.g., the house has burned down). The buyer can also obtain rescission of the contract and return of the deposit. State law usually requires that the deposit be placed in escrow until the closing.

Few courts would order specific performance by a breaching buyer; it is more likely that the buyer would be ordered to pay damages that compensate the seller for the loss of the bargain. If rescission is obtained in this situation, the seller would be entitled to keep the down payment. A common-sense rule is to make sure that the deposit is large enough to cover the broker's commission, expense of title search, and to compensate for the additional time needed to find another buyer if the first buyer defaults.

Contracts of sale are often drafted subject to "contingencies," the most common being the potential buyer's ability to obtain mortgage financing on satisfactory terms before the closing. A purchase money mortgage (PMM) is provided by the seller rather than by a lending institution: i.e., instead of the buyer paying the full price at closing, the buyer pays part of the price, then makes continuing payments to the seller. It is common for the PMM to be a second mortgage, with the first mortgage conventionally financed by a lender.

The lender may also be willing to have the buyer "assume" the seller's mortgage — i.e., instead of the seller paying off the mortgage balance at closing, the lender merely transfers the mortgage obligation to the buyer. Loans that are backed by the Federal Housing Administration (FHA) or Veterans' Administration (VA) can always be assumed by the buyer at the rate of interest paid by the seller.

Another issue is the interpretation of the "listing agreement" between the seller and the broker. In agency terms, the broker is the agent of the seller; it is also possible for buyers to hire a broker to act as their agent. A state license is required to act as broker, and brokers are considered fiduciaries.

Disputes often arise as to whether or not a particular broker is actually the procuring cause of a sale, and therefore entitled to a commission — a problem that will become more acute as listing properties for sale on the Internet becomes more common. If the buyer is willing to consummate the transaction and the seller is not, the seller may be liable for the broker's fee, because the broker produced a suitable willing buyer.

Local practice determines the respective roles of attorneys, brokers, and title insurance agents; often, the transaction is handled and the closing held with very little attorney involvement. However, non-lawyers should be careful to avoid over-stepping the bounds and engaging in unauthorized practice of law.

The Department of Justice announced a settlement in mid-2008 with the National Association of Realtors in an antitrust case about control of online home listings. The realtors agreed not to adopt rules that could impair discount brokerage operations online. The settlement did not require any payment or acknowledgment of wrongdoing by the realtors. The industry newsletter RealTrends said that the average commission on home sales in 2007 was 5.2%, about the same as 2006 and slightly higher than the 5% average from 2005. Discount brokers had only about 10% of the market.[3]

[A] Elements of Contract of Sale for Residential Property

Apart from the practical value of stipulating every feature of a deal involving large amounts of money, contracts for the sale of real estate are subject to the Statute of Frauds, and are not enforceable without a writing.

- Parties and their addresses
- If seller is married, spouse joins in the conveyance
- Description of property
  — buildings
  — structures
  — improvements

---

[3] James R. Hagerty and John R. Wilke, *Realtors Agree to Open Listings to Online Discounters*, Wall St. J. 5/28/08 at B1; Eric Lichtblau, *Settlement In Lawsuit Vs. Realtors*, N.Y. Times 5/28/08 at C1. *Cf.* Reifert v. South Central Wis. MLS Corp., 450 F.3d 312 (7th Cir. 2006) [tying access to MLS with membership in the Realtors' Association was not an antitrust violation because MLS had no competition in the tied market] *with* Freeman v. San Diego Ass'n of Realtors, 322 F.3d 1133 (9th Cir. 2003) [the Realtors' Association violated the Sherman Act by setting support fees for the MLS database above the competitive price].

- —personal property included with the sale—e.g., appliances that are not fixtures; custom-made draperies
  - —fixtures
- Type of deed granted
  - —encumbrances, e.g., zoning laws, existing party walls, taxes, lines, easements, restrictions
- Plans of the property
- If the seller must provide a survey at his/her own expense; when the survey must be delivered; how long the buyer has to raise survey-based objections. As an alternative, the contract can provide that the property is delivered subject to local zoning and setback ordinances (and that the seller is not aware of any violation of those ordinances); that the contract is subject to the state of facts that would be shown by an accurate survey; and subject to any recorded covenants or restrictions that do not render title unmarketable
- Representations and warranties; warranties are usually implied that the seller will deliver marketable title, and that the property will be habitable. An express warranty that the buyer's intended use does not violate the zoning ordinance is common.
  - —Environmental, related problems—radon, brownfields, lead paint, LUSTs (leaking underground storage tanks), smoke detectors, termites
- Seller agrees to deliver any necessary instruments so the buyer can get Certificate of Title
- Purchase price
  - —Deposit already in escrow; conditions of escrow
  - —Payable at closing
  - —Adjustments to be made at closing—e.g., taxes, water bills, oil in tank
- Time for performance and delivery of deed; conditions excusing performance
- Condition of premises warranted when Buyer takes title; or extension to perfect title and get premises in shape; refund in case of failure—unless Buyer elects to proceed with title as-is
- Seller has fully performed when Buyer accepts title
- Buyer who defaults has to forfeit deposit
- Insurance (e.g., fire) Seller has to maintain until delivery of title
- Seller's obligation to pay broker's fee.

For multi-family residential properties, it is important to determine whether the property will be delivered vacant (with no tenants residing there) or subject to existing leases. The buyer should ascertain rather than assume that all of the rental apartments are lawful and have a Certificate of Occupancy.

The buyer must ascertain if there are any pending landlord-tenant actions; if the tenants' apartments are habitable; if any repairs are required; what the rent roll is; and if there are any rent control or rent stabilization laws in effect and if the sitting tenants are entitled to any special protection against eviction (e.g., if they are aged or handicapped).

[B] The Closing Process

Local custom varies widely as to what formalities occur in order to "close" the real estate deal. The fundamental transaction is the exchange of the purchase price for the deed to the property. Unless the buyer is in a position to pay all cash, mortgage or other financing has to be obtained. At the closing, the buyer signs the mortgage documents and the seller signs and transfers the deed — or these steps have already been taken, and only representatives rather than the principals themselves appear at the closing. Both the mortgage and the deed should be recorded as soon as possible post-closing.

Prior to the closing, the buyer's down payment is held in escrow. Depending on local practice, the escrow agent might be the seller's lawyer, a title company representative, or a loan officer at the institution issuing the mortgage.

To satisfy the Statute of Frauds, and to be eligible for official recordation, a property deed must:

- Be written;
- Be signed by the grantor;
- Indicate a present (not future) transfer of ownership;
- Describe the property accurately.

A "general warranty deed" promises that the grantor has never impaired the title, and neither has any prior owner. A "specialty warranty deed" promises that the grantor has never impaired the title, but makes no warranties as to anyone else. A quitclaim deed simply transfers the grantor's title, whatever that may be worth and whatever claims may exist against it.

A seller who agrees to deliver "marketable title" promises that the title is not encumbered by mortgages or anything else affecting the value or use of the property. This is the most common contract requirement. If the seller promises to deliver marketable record title, then the state of title and the chain of ownership must be provable by deed records. Where the contract is silent, a promise to convey marketable title will probably be implied.

The appropriate division of labor between lawyers and non-lawyers in the closing process is controversial. According to late 2003 Georgia decisions, only a licensed attorney can be permitted to select, prepare, and execute deeds for real estate transactions, on the theory that the client will thereby have recourse in malpractice if the preparer is negligent. However, only the state bar, and not a private bar association, has standing to sue a title company for engaging in unauthorized practice of law by performing real estate closings.[4]

Traditionally, property deeds are recorded in large books that are summarized in an index of grantors and grantees, and title is searched in order to trace a chain (and also to see if any co-owners have granted interests in the property inconsistent

---

[4] *In re* UPL, Advisory Op. 2003-2 (Ga. 11/10/03); GUECAA, Inc. v. Omni Title Servs. Inc., (Ga. 11/10/03), both 72 L.W. 2324.

with the potential purchaser's ownership rights). The immense task of transferring these records to computer is being undertaken — naturally, it is much easier to click the mouse a few times than to look through huge, dusty volumes. In a state with a "marketable title" act, it is only necessary to establish the chain of title for a certain period of time (e.g., 20 years), not back to the time of the earliest records.

If competing claims of title are asserted, the states have various approaches to settling the priority. A "race" statute (referring to the "race to the courthouse") means that the first person who records the deed wins. A "race-notice" statute means that the first person to record the deed wins, unless he or she actually is aware of someone else who has been granted the same property. A "notice" statute makes an unrecorded deed invalid against a bona fide purchaser who has done a title search but does not have notice of the competing claim.

Sellers who take back a purchase-money mortgage should also record this mortgage.

The National Conference of Commissioners on Uniform State Laws (NCCUSL) finalized its draft of a proposed Uniform Real Property E-Recording Act, designed to phase in computerized title recording systems to replace the paper records.[5] As of October 2007, it had been adopted in Arizona, Arkansas, Delaware, the District of Columbia, Florida, Idaho, Illinois, Kansas, Nevada, New Mexico, North Carolina, Tennessee, Texas, Virginia, and Wisconsin. In mid-2004, the Texas Attorney General issued an opinion stating that county clerks are not required to record land records that contain a printed copy of an electronic signature. The Attorney General held that neither E-SIGN (the Electronic Signatures in Global and National Commerce Act; P.L. 106-229; see § 28.03[A]) nor the Uniform Electronic Transactions Act requires recognition of printed memoranda of electronic signatures. California and New York also have issued similar Attorney Generals' opinions.[6]

[1] Title Insurance

Cautious buyers protect themselves by purchasing title insurance. The buyer pays the premium (usually as part of the closing costs). The policy is delivered at closing, after title company attorneys have had a chance to search the title (consult records that demonstrate ownership). If the title proves to be defective, the buyer can collect insurance proceeds as well as carry out the underlying remedy of suing the buyer for breach of the warranty that marketable title will be delivered.

Buyers sometimes protect themselves by hiring an attorney who drafts an opinion letter as to the state of title, including any defects or encumbrances. If anything goes wrong, the buyer may have the additional remedy of suing the lawyer if the letter of opinion was inaccurate.

---

[5] http://www.law.upenn.edu/bll/ulc/urpera/Approvedfinal2004.htm; *see* 73 L.W. 2088.

[6] Texas Op. AG No. GA-0228, http://www.oag.state.tx.us/opinions/ga/ga0228.pdf; *see* 73 L.W. 2126.

Also see P.L. 107-326, the FHA Downpayment Simplification Act of 2002, which deals with mortgage insurance for single-family homes.

[C] RESPA

The lending institutions involved in real estate purchases can impose quite a few fees, which in the aggregate can become substantial. A federal law, the Real Estate Settlement Procedure Act of 1974 (RESPA 12 USC §§ 2601–2617) requires advance disclosure of the nature and extent of these fees in connection with "federally related" first mortgages on one- to four-family properties.

Under the USA PATRIOT Act, the anti-terrorism act passed after the 9/11 attack, "persons involved in real estate closings and settlements" have a legal obligation to maintain programs to prevent property purchases from being used for money laundering. On April 10, 2003, the Treasury Department published an Advance Notice of Proposed Rulemaking, defining, e.g., real estate brokers, attorneys for buyers and sellers, title insurance companies, escrow agents, appraisers, and inspectors as parties subject to the rule.[7]

A federally related mortgage is made, insured, guaranteed, or supplemented by the federal Department of Housing and Urban Development (HUD); is made in connection with a federal housing program; or will be re-sold by the lender to the Federal National Mortgage Association (FNMA, nicknamed "Fannie Mae"), Government National Mortgage Association (GNMA, "Ginnie Mae"), Federal Home Loan Mortgage Corporation (FHMLC, "Freddie Mac"), or to a financial institution that will sell the mortgage in turn to FHMLC.

Certain transactions are exempt from RESPA, e.g., refinancing, home improvement loans, construction loans, loans to construct a building on land the builder already owns, and loans to purchase more than 25 acres.

If the transaction is subject to RESPA, the lender must mail a copy of the official HUD guide to settlement costs to every loan applicant not later than three days after receipt of the application. The official guide explains the services involved in the settlement process and the fee structure for them.

Also within three days of receipt of the application, the lender must disclose the lender's good faith estimate of the settlement costs. HUD requires the estimates to "bear a reasonable relationship to the charge a borrower is likely to be required to pay at settlement, and must be based upon experience in the locality or area in which the mortgaged property is located."

Revised RESPA rules were released in November 2008, and use of the new official form will be mandatory as of January 1, 2010, although HUD stated that it lacked authority to impose penalties for violation of the rules. Under the revised rules, which HUD estimated would reduce loan closing costs by an average of about $700 per transaction, borrowers must receive a three-page good faith estimate explaining subjects such as rates, fees, prepayment penalties, and potential

---

[7] 68 FR 17569 (4/10/03).

increases in monthly payments. For certain fees, increases will be limited to 10% above the initial estimate.[7A]

Lenders who require borrowers to use (and pay for) the services of a particular title company, insurer, or attorney must disclose whether or not these service providers have a business relationship with the lender, and their fees must be included in the estimate. It is unlawful (and buyers can recover three times the charge for title insurance) for a seller of real estate that will be financed by a federally related mortgage to directly or indirectly condition the sale on the buyer's purchase of title insurance from a particular company. RESPA forbids kickbacks and fee splitting (payments to persons who did not earn a portion of the fee). However, payments under multiple listing services, or agreements between real estate agents and brokers, are exempt from this provision.

Even if a payment is legitimate, it must be disclosed to the person being referred for the services. If the referral is made face-to-face, in writing, or by electronic media, disclosure must occur at or before the time of the referral. If the referral is made by telephone, written disclosure must be provided within three days.

RESPA does not control the price of settlement services, so some courts have ruled that it is not a violation of RESPA § 8(b) for lenders and closing agents to pass along increases in the price of settlement services to homeowners, as long as the increased prices are not rebated to service providers.[8] RESPA § 8(b) forbids giving or accepting any portion, split, or percentage of any charge for a real estate settlement service, other than services actually performed. The Fourth, Seventh, and Eighth Circuits have ruled that § 8(b) does not provide a cause of action for mark-ups or overcharges. The Second Circuit position is that it does not apply to overcharges (although there is a HUD policy statement that unreasonably high prices violate RESPA) but does apply to mark-ups. The other circuits say there is a violation if and only if there is someone who gives and someone else who receives the improper fee, but the Eleventh Circuit says that there can be a violation even absent a culpable acceptor and giver. The Second Circuit took an intermediate position: because the statute is ambiguous, the HUD policy statement has enough gravity to be entitled to deference.[9]

[7A] HUD Press Release No. 08-175, http://www.hud.gov/news/release.cfm?content=pr08-175.cfm (11/12/08); the Good Faith Estimate Form was posted to http://www.hud.gov/content/releases/goodfaithestimate.pdf.

[8] Krzalic v. Republic Title Co., 314 F.3d 875 (7th Cir. 2002); Boulware v. Crossland Mort. Corp., 291 F.3d 261 (4th Cir. 2002). In another case, the Eleventh Circuit rejected RESPA claims by a class of borrowers who alleged that charging buyers who get mortgages $35 for a credit report violates the anti-kickback provisions. The plaintiffs' contention was that the defendant received free credit reports for applicants who did not get loans, but the Eleventh Circuit said that the credit reporting agency received the same amount in all cases, and the lender continued to get its credit reports from the same source before and after it charged $25 to all applicants and then charged $35 only to applicants who actually got a mortgage. There was no kickback, which would have required additional business secured by making an improper payment: Krupa v. Landsafe, Inc. 514 F.3d 1153 (11th Cir. 2008).

[9] Kruse v. Wells Fargo Home Mort. Inc., 383 F.3d 49 (2d Cir. 2004); Sosa v. Chase Manhattan Mort. Corp., 348 F.3d 979 (11th Cir. 2003).

In addition to its disclosure requirements, RESPA limits the amount that buyers can be required to place in escrow accounts toward their real estate taxes and insurance. The maximum deposit that lenders can require is the amount due and payable at the time of the settlement, plus one-twelfth of the estimated total real estate taxes and insurance for the first post-closing year.

If the mortgage is an adjustable-rate mortgage with a term of a year or more, Regulation Z (the Truth in Lending implementing regulation) requires the creditor to provide the buyer with the official *Consumer Handbook on Adjustable-Rate Mortgages*, or another publication with comparable content.

At the closing, the person conducting the closing of a federally related mortgage loan must complete HUD Form 1, the Uniform Settlement Statement, itemizing all charges paid by either buyer or seller at the closing. (Charges that are paid "outside the closing" by agreement need not be included.) Neither the lender nor the borrower can lawfully be charged a fee for preparing the RESPA statement.

If there is no formal closing, or neither the borrower nor the borrower's agent attends the closing, the lender's obligation is to deliver a completed settlement statement to the buyer as soon as possible after the transaction closes.

Where the seller assumes all the settlement-related expenses, or the total the buyer must pay at settlement is a fixed amount that was disclosed at the time of the loan application, it is not necessary to provide HUD Form 1.

At the time of consummation of the loan, the lender must provide a Truth in Lending statement disclosing the annual percentage rate (effective interest rate) for the mortgage. The borrower can also request this information at the time the loan application is made.

§ 10.06   PROPERTY TAXES

Taxes on commercial and residential property are an important source of income for states and municipalities, used to finance projects such as public works and schools. Although rebates and exemptions are often available (e.g., to induce a large employer to either settle there or refrain from moving away), the basic rule is that property taxes are imposed at a rate multiplied by the assessed value of the property.

Taxpayers who believe the assessment on their property is excessive can petition for reduction of the assessment. The process generally begins with a formal protest and application for correction addressed to the taxing authority. A denial can be reviewed in court. The three main grounds for reducing an assessment are:

- Overvaluation (higher than the full and fair market value of the property)
- Inequality (disproportionate to the valuation of comparable properties in the same area)
- Illegality (irregular manner of imposing the tax, or including exempt realty in the assessment)

Review of the assessor's report may disclose factual errors that can be corrected to the advantage of the property owner. For income-producing property, the history of recent past income and expenses is highly relevant to market value. Expert testimony (about what constitutes a comparable property, and the market value and assessments of "comps"; about the condition of the building or its reproduction cost) is critical to the assessment appeal.

A trend dating from late 2007 is the conflict between taxpayers protesting increases in property taxes and jurisdictions suffering revenue reductions because of the housing market slump. Tax assessments lag behind the market, so tax rates are often based on price levels that became unrealistic. In 1978, California adopted Proposition 13, which capped taxes at 1% of assessed value and prevented a home's base assessment from rising more than 2% a year before it was sold. The state's Proposition 8 also allows homeowners to have their assessments reduced temporarily during a weak housing market, until the prices rebound.[10]

Under Georgia law, most commercial and industrial properties are valued locally by county boards of taxation. A late-2007 Supreme Court case was brought by a railroad whose property was initially valued by the state. In 2002, the Georgia state board changed its methodologies, resulting in a 47% increase in the valuation of the railroad's properties within the state, and much higher taxes. The railroad sued under the Railroad Revitalization and Regulatory Reform Act of 1976, which forbids states to assess railroad property at a higher ratio to the property's market value than the ratio used for commercial and industrial property in the same jurisdiction. The Supreme Court allowed railroads to show that the methodology yields a discriminatory determination of market value. In this reading, forbidding states to tax railroad property at a higher ratio than other property does not destroy state discretion: states can choose any method that is not discriminatory.[11]

In the case of a property that was put up for sale after taxes became delinquent, the Supreme Court mandated that states take further reasonable and feasible steps when a notice of tax sale is returned unclaimed. Notice is constitutionally sufficient when it is reasonably calculated to reach the intended recipient; and the obligation is on the state to give notice, not on the homeowner to provide a current address, because of the irreversible consequences of forfeiture of property. The Supreme Court did not mandate a particular form of notice, but pointed out that states have used a variety of methods, such as re-sending the notice by ordinary mail and posting a notice on the front door of the property. The Supreme Court held that it would be unduly burdensome to require state tax authorities to search government records or phone books.[12]

---

[10] Amy Merrick, *Property-Tax Frustration Builds*, Wall St. J. 12/18/07 at A6.

[11] CSX Transportation, Inc. v. Georgia State Board of Equalization, 128 S. Ct. 467 (2007); the relevant Railroad Revitalization and Regulatory Reform Act provisions are 49 USC § 11501(b)(1), (c).

[12] Jones v. Flowers, 547 U.S. 220 (2006).

§ 10.07 LANDLORD-TENANT LAW

A residential or commercial lease is a contract governing the tenant's occupancy of the premises for a certain period of time. At the end of the lease, the landlord re-takes occupancy. The lease itself is subject to the Statute of Frauds — i.e., if the term is a year or more, it will not be enforceable without a writing.

A tenancy for a term of years begins and ends on specified dates, at which time the lease terminates. Notice is not required to terminate the lease in accordance with its terms. In contrast, a tenancy at will continues as long as both parties want it to. It can be terminated by either without prior notice.

A periodic tenancy (year-to-year, month-to-month, etc.) lasts the specified period of time, and is automatically renewed when each cycle ends, unless either landlord or tenant gives timely written notice of termination. Notice is timely if it arrives by the last day of the month or other period before the period when the tenancy is supposed to end.

Although there are some exceptions, leases for more than a year are subject to the Statute of Frauds, and therefore must be written to be enforceable. However, state laws to protect tenants often provide that a landlord who fails to sign and deliver a lease that has been signed by the tenant will be bound by the lease as if it had been properly executed.

It is not uncommon for tenants to "hold over" — i.e., simply fail to vacate the premises at the end of the lease term. The landlord can either attempt to evict the tenant (which can be very difficult, especially in cities with low vacancy rates where the landlord-tenant judge or hearing officer is likely to feel sympathetic toward the tenant) or accept the tenant as a periodic "tenant at sufferance."

The Uniform Residential Landlord and Tenant Act allows the landlord either to accept the holdover tenant as a month-to-month tenant, or to sue for eviction. The landlord can obtain damages of up to three months' rent or three times the actual damages (whichever is greater), plus attorneys' fees, if the tenant willfully held over the property in bad faith.

The basic rule is that either landlord or tenant can assign or transfer his or her interest. However, if the lease limits the tenant's ability to transfer, such restrictions will be enforceable and strictly construed. An "assignment" covers all of the tenant's interest in the remaining term of the lease; a "sublease" is for less than the entire term. A lease that forbids "subleases" will not prevent the tenant from making an enforceable assignment. It is common for lease provisions to be drafted so that the landlord must not unreasonably refuse consent to assignment or sublease.

It is typical in both residential and commercial leases for the tenant to make a deposit which the landlord can use if the tenant ceases to pay rent, damages the premises, or otherwise defaults on the lease. For tax purposes, the deposit remains the property of the tenant until and unless the landlord is entitled to take the funds on the tenant's default.

Many states have laws limiting the size of security deposits that can be charged on residential leases. The landlord may also have an obligation to pay interest to the tenant when the security deposit is returned at the end of the lease, and/or keep the security deposits in special accounts that are not subject to the claims of the landlord's creditors.

A few cities impose some degree of control over residential rents, by limiting the rent that can be charged to a new tenant and rent increases when tenants renew their leases. However, apartments may become "decontrolled" when a new tenant moves in, or newly constructed buildings may be exempt from rent control. Rent control ordinances, if properly promulgated, are not unconstitutional "takings,"[13] but rent control ordinances are inconsistent with the current legal climate, and are likely to be restricted or repealed in the future.

[A] Commercial Leases

The commercial lease contains certain features absent from the residential lease — and lacks certain other features (such as pro-tenant protections intended to prevent homelessness, that are not relevant in the commercial context).

Commercial leases frequently give the tenant the option to renew the lease, either indefinitely or a certain number of times, as well as an option to purchase the building on stated terms.

The square footage of a residential apartment is usually not very controversial, but highly varying methods are used to calculate the size of a commercial property, possibly including storage areas, common areas, and staircases and elevators. It is common for commercial leases to require payment of taxes and/or utility charges by the tenant, or for the stated rent to increase automatically based on these factors or reflecting actual increases. Tenants may be obligated to pay maintenance and service charges (cleaning, snow removal, etc.), or else either to pay the landlord for the items or subcontract out their performance.

Commercial leases often last for many years, or even for decades, so it is critical to include a mechanism for adjusting the rent (from the landlord's perspective) and controlling rent increases (from the tenant's). A "step-up" lease gradually increases the rent at stated intervals. An "escalator" lease is the most common long-term office lease form. The tenant's basic rent is fixed, but the tenant is also obligated to pay a stated percentage of real estate taxes, insurance, and non-structural repairs. The rent could be adjusted based on changes in the cost of living or other objective index.

A net lease requires the tenant to pay not only a fixed base rental but all property-related costs, including taxes and assessments, heating and air conditioning, routine maintenance, and repairs. (Such a lease is "net" because the landlord receives a net figure with no need to pay related costs.)

A percentage rental, often used in shopping center leases or long-term (over three year) store leases, starts with a fixed base amount for rent but is adjusted by a percentage of sales the store makes. Of course, the definition of "sales" or "net sales" subject to the percentage is crucial, and handling of factors such as phone,

---

[13] Pennell v. City of San Jose, 485 U.S. 1 (1988).

mail, and on-line orders, returns, and shipping and handling charges must be built into the definition. The tenant should be required to maintain books and records showing the sales and any permissible deduction from sales, and the landlord should be given the right to audit the books.

A commercial tenant's needs frequently change over time, resulting in a need for more or less space. The adjustments are often handled by options within the lease. A cancellation option gives the tenant the right to give notice at designated times to reduce the amount of rented space (usually with a penalty payable to the landlord). The additional space option gives the tenant the right to give notice to rent additional space in the same building, or another building owned by the landlord. Advance permission to sublease is another possibility.

Other issues that may arise in the commercial lease: environmental premises liability (see § 11.07) and compliance with the public accommodations require- ments of the Americans With Disabilities Act § 3.14.[14]

Bankruptcy issues also arise in connection with leases; see, e.g., Bankruptcy Act § 365, allowing assignment of leases irrespective of lease restrictions. If the lease involves space in a building that is under construction or under renovation, the lease must resolve issues of liability if the premises are not ready for occupation on time, if changes are made from the blueprints and specifications included with the lease, or if changes are made to suit the tenant's requirements. In the latter case it must be determined who is liable for expense and damages, and whether the changes must be left in place after the tenancy terminates, or whether the tenant is permitted or required to remove them and restore the premises to their original condition.

The commercial lease also governs the availability of storage space, parking spaces, loading facilities, and the availability of elevators, heating, water, and air conditioning outside normal business hours. To an increasing extent, provision of phone lines and Internet connections will become a critical part of the lease obligation.

[B] Lease Interpretation

Ambiguous terms in a lease — like ambiguous insurance policy provisions — are usually construed against the party who drafted the document. Another principle is that leases are interpreted in the way that is least restrictive to the tenant's lawful use of the property.

---

[14] Corporations operating resorts with pools with narrow decks and ramps that are too narrow for wheelchairs were sued by disability advocates. 42 USC § 12182 requires disability access to the maximum extent feasible, and 28 CFR § 36.402(a) requires accessibility to altered portions of a building. The Second Circuit ruled in 2008 that alterations to the resort complexes were enough to trigger the accessibility requirement. It held that once a plaintiff identifies a way for the alteration to be made readily accessible to wheelchair users, a defendant has the burden of proving that this is not possible. It is up to the plaintiff to suggest a plausible, cost-effective proposal for removing barriers: Roberts v. Royal Atlantic Corp., 542 F.3d 363 (2d Cir. 2008); *see* Mark Hamblett, *2nd Circuit Finds Alterations May Open Resort to Disabilities Act*, N.Y.L.J. 9/19/08 (law.com).

In case of "superseding illegality" (i.e., the tenant takes the property for a use that was legal when the lease was signed, but which later becomes illegal, and the lease restricts the use to the one illegal one) the tenant will generally have the right to terminate the lease. However, if the tenant's use of the premises is not restricted, the tenant probably will not have the right to terminate the lease even if, in practical terms, the tenant does not obtain the intended results. A tenant who could have, but did not get, a zoning variance that would permit the use is not entitled to remedies because of the zoning law. The tenant has the risk of failing to get the zoning variance.

The doctrine of "commercial frustration" covers the situation in which a government act makes the premises less valuable for a commercial purpose, but does not out-and-out ban the intended use. If the government act was not reasonably foreseeable when the lease was signed; the landlord knew how the tenant intended to use the premises; and the commercial value of the premises is eliminated or catastrophically reduced, the tenant may be able to terminate the lease. However, some jurisdictions require the tenant to continue to pay rent despite commercial frustration.

At common law, any changes to the premises made by the tenant constituted "waste," so the tenant was obligated to remove them and surrender the property in its original condition when the lease terminated. This was true even of changes that enhanced the value of the property. Current law usually does not treat changes as waste unless the property's value is seriously impaired.

[C] Landlord's Remedies

The tenant's obligation to pay rent is an important part of the lease relationship. If the tenant fails to pay rent, the landlord can sue to recover the unpaid amount (although the tenant may be able to assert a defense that poor conditions justify such a withholding).

Usually, the lease gives the landlord the right to sue for possession of the premises if the rent is unpaid — i.e., to evict the tenant. Evictions of "holdover" tenants — those who do not leave at the expiration of the lease term — are also permitted. Most states forbid self-help eviction (i.e., the landlord removes the tenant's property — or the tenant — by force and locks up the premises). Instead, the landlord must bring eviction proceedings, usually known as "summary proceedings" because they are handled in a relatively expedited fashion. The landlord must give the tenant "notice to quit" explaining why eviction is justified. Then the landlord and tenant get a hearing shortly after the notice is issued, generally in a special landlord-tenant court or court part.

An "acceleration" clause makes all rent for the balance of the term due immediately as soon as the tenant stops paying rent, or otherwise seriously breaches the lease.

It is much easier for the landlord to sue for the entire balance of the rent than to have to bring multiple suits based on multiple non-payments. However, the landlord has to choose: either accelerate the rent obligation or terminate the lease and re-take the premises, but not both.

The tenant must be given notice and a reasonable amount of time to cure before acceleration is imposed. Furthermore, for a long-term lease, the court may award the landlord only the present value of the future rent obligation, not the sum itself.

If the tenant stops paying rent and moves out, the landlord cannot — but does not need to — bring an eviction proceeding, because the premises are already vacant. The landlord can terminate the lease and find another tenant; keep the premises vacant and sue the tenant as unpaid rent falls due; or find another tenant, and apply that tenant's rent to the abandoning tenant's liability.

The landlord is only entitled to rent arrears if it accepts the surrender of the premises and terminates the lease.

The Restatement (2nd) of Property § 12.1 does not obligate the landlord to mitigate damages by finding another tenant, so the landlord can keep the premises vacant and sue for future rent as each payment falls due. However, several states (and the Uniform Residential Landlord-Tenant Act) reject this position, and do require the landlord to mitigate damages if possible.

[1] Fixtures

When personal property is permanently attached to a structure, it becomes a fixture: for instance, cabinets or appliances built into a kitchen wall. The common-law rule was that any fixtures added by tenants to the premises automatically became the landlord's property. Most American states consider the fixtures to be the property of the tenant unless the tenant gave objective indication of intention (e.g., difficulty of removing fixtures without severe damage to premises) to make the fixtures part of the property that would remain at the termination of the lease.

Trade fixtures (used in business) are analyzed somewhat differently. According to the Restatement (2nd) of Property § 12.2(4), tenants are allowed to remove trade fixtures on or before the termination date of the lease, but they are responsible for repairing any damage caused by removal (e.g., holes in the wall). Trade fixtures that remain in place when the lease ends become property of the landlord.

[D] Tenant's Remedies

Although a tenant has no duty to take possession of the leased premises, the landlord has a duty to deliver actual possession of the premises on the first day of the lease term. The tenant's remedies, if the landlord fails to do so, are either to rescind the lease and sue for actual damages, or confirm the lease, move in as soon as possible, and sue for actual damages for the time when possession was denied.

Leases imply a covenant of quiet enjoyment: that the tenant can maintain use and enjoyment of the premises without disturbance from the landlord or anyone who claims title from the landlord or title superior to the landlord's.

Actual eviction occurs when the tenant is physically expelled from the premises or excluded from possession of the premises. Wrongful eviction by the landlord or someone with title superior to the landlord's allows the tenant to terminate the lease, sue for damages, or remain in possession but without paying rent. If the landlord's breach of the covenant of quiet enjoyment prevents the tenant from using part of the premises, this will be considered a partial actual eviction.

Constructive eviction is action or failure to act by the landlord that results in the tenant being deprived of use and enjoyment of the leased premises to a substantial extent. This argument is often raised by tenants who claim that the landlord failed to make repairs or provide essential services. The tenant must notify the landlord of the condition, and give the landlord a reasonable opportunity to repair, before asserting constructive eviction. Some statutes and case law require the tenant to vacate the premises, but the Restatement (2nd), bearing in mind the difficulty of finding affordable housing, does not impose this requirement.

A tenant subjected to wrongful eviction has the options of staying on the premises and withholding rent; terminating the lease; and suing for damages. (The Restatement (2nd) of Property does not allow tenants to remain and withhold rent after a partial eviction.)

The traditional common law rule was that tenants took the property as is, with whatever patent or latent defects were present. Current law usually implies a warranty of habitability in residential leases (less commonly in commercial leases, which can and sometimes do place the duty to repair on the tenant). Commercial leases may be interpreted under an implied warranty of "suitability" for the intended commercial purpose.

This implied warranty obligates the landlord to deliver premises in a habitable condition at the beginning of the term, and to maintain habitability throughout the lease (e.g., by performing necessary repairs). The general rule is that the warranty of habitability cannot be waived. The landlord must be given notice of the defect and reasonable opportunity to repair it before breach of warranty is asserted.

Depending on local law, the warranty might be breached if the local housing code is violated; if the premises are unsafe; if there are latent defects that would not be detected by reasonable inspection prior to signing the lease; or if a reasonable person would not deem the premises to be habitable. The tenant's remedies for breach of warranty of habitability can be:

- Damages (including punitive damages and damages for infliction of emotional distress)
- Specific performance (ordering the landlord to provide a habitable apartment)
- Rescission of the lease (requiring the tenant to move out)
- Reformation of the lease (e.g., a period of free or reduced rent).

It is a defense against eviction if the tenant can prove that the landlord's motivation is retaliation against the tenant for the tenant's assertion of a breach of the warranty of habitability.

At common law, landlords were not liable for personal injuries suffered on the leased premises. Today, a significant amount of statutory and case law alters that result, especially if the common areas (rather than individual leased premises that tenants might be expected to repair) contain defects; if the injury is due to a latent defect; or if the landlord did make repairs but did so negligently, leading to injury. Under the law of premises liability, the landlord's liability for criminal acts on the premises is limited, but the landlord may be liable if security on premises is inadequate and/or the landlord is on notice of foreseeable risk of criminal activity.

[E] Fair Housing Laws

Some degree of protection against housing discrimination has been in place since 1866, when 42 USC § 1982 was enacted, giving all citizens the same rights as "white citizens" to "inherit, purchase, lease, sell, hold, and convey real and personal property." More than a century later, housing discrimination was still rampant, leading to the passage of the Fair Housing Act, which is part of Title VII (42 USC § 3601 *et seq.*).

The Fair Housing Act makes it illegal to discriminate on the basis of race, color, religion, sex, having children in the family (but not marital status), national origin, or handicap, either by disparate treatment or disparate impact. FHA violations include:

- Refusal to sell or rent a dwelling
- Discriminating in the terms or conditions of housing sale or rental; refusing to permit a handicapped person to make reasonable modifications to a housing unit
- Discriminatory advertising
- False representations: i.e., telling a black applicant that the apartment is rented, while subsequently showing it to a white applicant
- "Blockbusting": inducing sales or rentals by claiming that members of a disfavored group are about to move in to the area.

Single-family dwellings, owner-occupied dwellings of up to four units, private clubs, and housing projects for the elderly are exempt from the Fair Housing Act.

In addition to the federal law, most states and many localities have their own fair housing laws.

Constitutional arguments often fail in the fair housing context, because the Equal Protection Clause requires state action — at least state action in letting the courts enforce private restrictive covenants such as those barring persons of a particular race or religion from purchasing property[15] and that involve intentional discrimination, not just disparate impact.[16]

---

[15] Shelley v. Kraemer, 334 U.S. 1 (1948); Barrows v. Jackson, 346 U.S. 249 (1953).

[16] Arlington Heights v. Metropolitan Housing Dev. Corp., 429 U.S. 252 (1977).

Furthermore, an early 2003 ruling by the Supreme Court says that the principles of vicarious liability do not justify making the owners or officers of a corporation personally liable for Fair Housing Act violations committed by the employees and agents of the corporation — although, of course, the corporation itself is vicariously liable for the violations.[17]

[F] Regulation of Expressive Activity

Property rights need to be balanced with rights of other kinds, including First Amendment rights. The Ninth Circuit struck down a local ordinance requiring a permit for any meeting or parade that could impede the free use of a sidewalk. The court found the ordinance contrary to the First Amendment because it was not narrowly tailored to balancing the interest in traffic control with the actual size and possible implications of the event.[18] The Second Circuit held that the city of Ithaca violated the First Amendment by using an ordinance forbidding noise that could be heard 25 feet away to silence a street evangelist. Because most human activity does result in noise, the court found that the statute is not narrowly tailored to furthering the city's interest in preventing noise pollution.[19]

The New Jersey Supreme Court ruled that it is permissible for a private residential community to regulate expressive activity. Thus a homeowner's association can set rules for political signs, impose an editorial policy on the community newsletter, and charge rent for use of the community room. The court held that the restrictions on the time, place, and manner of speech were reasonable. The court was not persuaded by cases about shopping malls, because the residents of a private residential community have agreed to abide by its rules. Furthermore, New Jersey provides other protections against infringement of free speech. The business judgment rule obligates the governing association to behave reasonably, and the Planned Real Estate Development Full Disclosure Act requires homeowners' associations to act in the best interests of unit owners.[20]

The Eighth Circuit held that the University of Arkansas' limits of five days per semester imposed on street preaching was not narrowly tailored enough to pass muster. However, rules requiring a permit, three days' advance notice, and not preaching during final exams or at commencement were upheld as reasonable restrictions of time, place, and manner of speech.[21]

A San Diego shopping mall required a permit for expressive activities onsite, and imposed a condition on issuing a permit that the applicant had to promise not to urge consumers to boycott tenants of the mall. The NLRB treated this as an Unfair Labor Practice because it violated the California Constitution's right of free

---

[17] Meyer v. Holley, 537 U.S. 280 (2003).

[18] Santa Monica Food Not Bombs v. Santa Monica, Cal., 450 F.3d 1022 (9th Cir. 2006).

[19] Deegan v. Ithaca, New York, 444 F.3d 135 (2d Cir. 2006).

[20] Committee for a Better Twin Rivers v. Twin Rivers Homeowners Association, 192 N.J. 344 (N.J. 2007).

[21] Bowman v. White, 444 F.3d 967 (8th Cir. 2006).

speech. The D.C. Circuit certified the case to the Supreme Court of California, which ruled that the practice violated the state Constitution. When the case returned to the D.C. Circuit, the mall argued that its Fifth and Fourteenth Amendment rights were violated. The D.C. Circuit ruled that the constitutional argument was forfeited by not being raised in the petition for review by the D.C. Circuit.[22]

In general, rights of unions to engage in expressive activities in public places are governed by state law. Violation of a state law that grants access also violates the National Labor Relations Act. Rules that regulate speech are considered content-neutral if they are not related to the subject of the speech; but rules generally are content-based if the regulator must examine the speech for acceptability.

Courts are usually critical of restrictions based on hostility or favoritism toward particular messages. The Ninth Circuit rejected shopping mall rules that restricted speech critical of the mall's tenants (because it impaired discussion of issues). Speech aimed at peacefully persuading customers to shop elsewhere is acceptable, because it does not interfere with normal commercial operations. The ban on signage was not narrowly tailored to address valid considerations such as safety. With respect to picketing, the employer's business is often the only effective place for labor picketing. Although the NLRB permitted bans on expressive conduct on exterior sidewalks, the Ninth Circuit found the bans contrary to California precedents.[23]

§ 10.08 CONDOMINIUMS AND COOPERATIVES

The major distinction between the two ownership forms (condominium and cooperative) is that the purchaser acquires ownership of the unit itself in a condominium, plus the right to use the common areas (also known as common elements) such as lobby and any recreational facilities. A condominium is real property, on which real estate taxes are separately assessed, and which can be separately financed by an individual mortgage. Unit owners will be assessed charges for maintenance of the common areas. The condominium operates under a "declaration" or "master deed" and is managed by a homeowner's association (sometimes referred to as the unit owners' association or property owners' association).

A co-op "purchaser" actually acquires personal property in the form of shares in a cooperative corporation. The corporation exercises a significant degree of control over operations, including who will be allowed to purchase the shares. The entire project has a single mortgage (buyers get personal loans to finance their share purchases) and a single real estate tax bill. Maintenance charges cover mortgage financing and real estate taxes as well as the upkeep of shared areas.

Creation of a condominium requires the owner or developer of the property to record the declaration, including a description of the physical layout of the project and the Articles of Incorporation and bylaws that will govern its operation.

---

[22] Fashion Valley Mall LLC v. NLRB, 524 F.3d 1378 (D.C. Cir. 2008); the California decision is at 172 P.3d 742 (Cal. 2007).

[23] Carpenters & Joiners of America v. NLRB, 540 F.3d 957 (9th Cir. 2008).

Many states require a registration process similar to that required for a "Blue Sky" stock issue. The offering plan for the condominium may have to be submitted to the city or state Attorney General for review. A preliminary "red herring" prospectus for the sale of condominium interests or co-op shares may have to be prepared and submitted for approval.

Conversion of an existing project to condominium or co-op form may require an agreement by a certain percentage (e.g., 15%) of the tenants that they will buy their apartments or shares before the regulatory authorities will approve the conversion. Usually tenants who agree to buy their apartments during a short time frame, such as 90 days, are entitled to a lower, insider's price; other people who buy later, or after the conversion, have to pay a higher outsider's price for the unit or shares.

State and local law determine whether a developer who engages in a conversion has the right to evict non-purchasing tenants. Tenants may be given the option of remaining as rent-paying tenants after the conversion; or the landlord may be able to sell the occupied apartments to an investor who hopes to be able to re-sell the apartment when the current tenant moves out or dies. There may be a special provision protecting low-income, senior citizen, or disabled tenants from eviction during a conversion, or requiring the developer to provide relocation assistance.

§ 10.09 REAL ESTATE INVESTMENT TRUSTS (REITs)

A REIT, a form that has been in existence since 1960 (and has had several peaks and troughs of popularity since then), is a structure for real estate investment and for raising funds for real estate development. In essence, it is a mutual fund that invests in real property rather than securities. Tax treatment is governed by IRC §§ 856 and 857.

REITs can be pass-through entities (i.e., items are passed through to participants, with no tax at the entity level)[24] if all of these criteria are met:

- There are at least 100 shareholders
- Most of the entity's income derives from qualifying rents and interest. That is, at least 75% of income must come from real estate activities, and at least an additional 20% must come either from real estate activities or other passive sources; active trade or business income outside the real estate context must be 5% or less
- The majority of the entity's assets must be real estate and/or mortgages secured by real estate
- At least 95% of annual income must be distributed to shareholders
- Certain services performed for tenants of property owned by the entity must be performed by independent third-party professionals.

---

[24] *But see* § 857(b), imposing entity-level taxes on, e.g., violation of the income tests or receipt of income from prohibited transactions.

REIT distributions are either ordinary income or capital gains to the shareholders, in the year of receipt. They are ordinary income up to the extent of REIT earnings and profits. Shareholders are taxed only on actual distributions, but REITs are not permitted to pass through losses.

A REIT is treated as a domestic corporation for federal income tax purposes, although there is generally no tax at the entity level. It files an annual return on Form 1120-REIT.

REITs can be organized as C Corporations, in which case investors' equity interests are in the form of shares of stock, or as a trust, in which case investors receive common shares of beneficial interests. REIT ownership interests are "securities" for purposes of the '33 Act (see § 6.03), and are usually registered on Form S-11.

§ 10.10 EASEMENTS AND COVENANTS

Under some circumstances, someone other than the owner may be permitted to exercise certain rights over the owner's property, without affecting the ownership of the land. For instance, a person whose property is surrounded by someone else's property may be granted an easement to use a driveway to leave his own property and connect with the public road. The presumption is that easements are attached to the land and automatically belong to a person acquiring the land; some easements are personal, however, and are not transferred unless there is an express transfer.

Easements can either be positive (such as right to do something) or negative (forbidding the property owner to do something that would work to the disadvantage of the person holding the easement). They usually require a writing signed by the owner of the land affected by the easement. However, easements may be implied in cases of strict necessity, or where usage has continued for a long period of time without protest.

A real covenant is a similar device, but it is contractual, usually expressed in a deed. It, too, can be either positive (affirmative covenants) or negative (restrictive covenants). The covenant "runs with the land," so it stays in place when ownership changes. A suit for specific performance can be brought with respect to either an easement or a real covenant; the practical difference is that money damages can be awarded for breach of a covenant but not of an easement.

§ 10.11 LAND USE PLANNING

At common law, ownership of land implied the right to use the land in any way the owner desired. Present-day law, however, makes the owner's unfettered use of land subject to the police power to protect public health and safety, including the power to determine how many and what kinds of structures can be built and operated in a particular area.

Most zoning laws are state laws that delegate the actual power to prescribe land use to cities or other units of local government. They are so-called because the area is divided into zones, some of which are purely residential, others commercial, agricultural, industrial, or mixed-use. The theory of use zoning is that single-family residential use is the highest and best use, followed by two-family, then multi-family, commercial, and industrial uses. Higher uses are allowed in lower zones, but not vice versa. Exceptions for lower uses can be granted by a zoning board, but only on a showing of justification, not as of right. Under appropriate circumstances, the locality can even condemn land (take it over, with compensation to the owner).

The U.S. Supreme Court ruled in 2008 that Delaware has the right to forbid British Petroleum from opening a natural gas terminal, pursuant to a 1972 statute forbidding heavy industry in the coastal zone. Although most of the terminal would be on New Jersey soil, a 2,000-foot pier would extend into Delaware River waters belonging to the state of Delaware, and the state of New Jersey did not have exclusive authority over the entire project. (The case was heard by the Supreme Court under its original jurisdiction, as the sole court that can hear disputes between states.) The Supreme Court decided that New Jersey historically accepted Delaware jurisdiction over the area until this project came up. Although Delaware would not be entitled to impede ordinary and usual exercises of riparian rights in coastal lands, this was an extraordinary project that Delaware could regulate, pursuant to its ban on heavy industry in the coastal zone.[25]

[A] Zoning

The locality develops a master land-use plan which is embodied in zoning ordinances. A zoning ordinance can be challenged, and invalidated, if it fails to comply with the plan, and if the required notice procedures are not observed. Zoning ordinances are also vulnerable to challenges based on due process, equal protection, takings, or if they have the effect (even if not the purpose) of excluding members of a suspect classification (generally a race or nationality group) from the area.

A variance is an administrative grant (usually issued by a Board of Adjustment) that allows a use contrary to the zoning ordinance. If it is anticipated that non-authorized uses will have some justification, the zoning ordinance may provide for special permits allowing such uses. Non-conforming uses that predate the zoning ordinance are likely to be grandfathered in.

Zoning can impose content-neutral regulation even if a First Amendment defense is raised, if the zoning ordinance serves a substantial governmental interest (e.g., requiring adult entertainment enterprises to be located at least 1,000 feet away from residential zones, dwellings, schools, and churches).[26] Commercial speech regulation in billboards and other outdoor advertising is acceptable if these rules are narrowly tailored and do not restrict the content of the advertiser's proposed commercial speech.[27]

---

[25] New Jersey v. Delaware, No. 134 Orig.; *see* Tony Mauro, *Supreme Court Upholds Delaware's Veto Power Over British Petroleum Project*, Legal Times 4/1/08 (law.com).

[26] City of Renton v. Playtime Theatres, Inc., 475 U.S. 41 (1986).

[27] City of Ladue v. Gilleo, 512 U.S. 43 (1994).

In 2001, the Supreme Court struck down the Massachusetts Attorney General's regulations limiting outdoor advertising of tobacco products (e.g., a ban on such advertisements within 1000 feet of schools and playgrounds). The regulations were preempted by the Federal Cigarette Labeling and Advertising Act, which forbids the states to regulate cigarettes that are labeled in conformity with the federal requirements. The Massachusetts regulations were unacceptable because there was no reasonable fit between the ends and the means of the regulatory scheme. Although protecting children is a reasonable state objective, the Supreme Court deemed the statute, in conjunction with the local zoning regulations, to do too much to interfere with communications between advertisers and adults.[28]

It is improper to have a zoning ordinance that explicitly discriminates on the basis of race or nationality. However, in general a zoning ordinance can impose restrictions (such as minimum lot size) that have a disproportionately negative effect on low-income minority groups,[29] although disparate impact of this type may be covered by Fair Housing laws. In 2005, the Supreme Court ruled that an individual cannot use 42 U.S.C. § 1983 to enforce the limitations on local zoning authority imposed by Communications Act § 332(c)(7).[30]

Property owners who allege that granting a zoning variance will reduce their property values have standing to challenge the variance (in this case, a storage facility in a residential area) because they have stated a sufficiently concrete injury. However, the Third Circuit dismissed 42 USC §§ 1981 and 1983 civil rights claims as too speculative. (The plaintiffs charged that residential housing was blocked to keep the majority of the neighborhood white and to reduce the political impact of black homeowners.)[31]

Several states (e.g., New Jersey, California, Oregon, Florida, and Washington) require zoning ordinances to take into account the need for affordable housing.

According to the Supreme Court, the right of a family to live together is a fundamental right that cannot be impaired by zoning ordinances; no such fundamental right exists for unrelated persons to live together. Thus, a zoning ordinance that bans communes or even roommate relationships can be Constitutional. But a home for the mentally disabled cannot be zoned based on neighbors' fears or prejudices about the mentally ill.[32] Members of a county council who enact an ordinance denying a conditional use permit are merely enforcing the existing zoning ordinance with respect to a particular property owner. They are not making law in general. Therefore, according to the Ninth Circuit, the council members are not entitled to absolute immunity under 42 USC

---

[28] Lorillard Tobacco Co. v. Reilly, 533 U.S. 525 (2001).

[29] Village of Arlington Heights. v. Metropolitan Housing Dev. Corp., 429 U.S. 252 (1977).

[30] City of Rancho Palos Verdes v. Abrams, 544 U.S. 113 (2005).

[31] Taliaferro v. Darby Township Bd. of Zoning, 458 F.3d 181 (3d Cir. 2006).

[32] Moore v. City of E. Cleveland, 431 U.S. 494 (1977) (grandmother and grandsons are a "single family"); Belle Terre v. Boraas, 416 U.S. 1 (1974) (unrelated persons); Cleburne v. Cleburne Living Ctr., 473 U.S. 432 (1985) (mentally disabled persons).

§ 1983 if they are sued by the property owner who was denied the desired permit.[33]

[1] "Takings"

Except as discussed below, about condemnation, governments are not allowed to seize or "take" privately owned land. The Fifth Amendment requires just compensation if private property is taken by the federal or a state government for public purposes. A court that must decide whether restrictions on property use or reductions in property value violate Constitutional rights must consider factors such as:

- Does the regulation impose physical confiscation?
- Does the owner still have access to an economically viable use of the property?
- Was the regulation enacted to prevent a noxious use?
- Were some parties unfairly singled out to bear what should be a generalized public burden?
- Does the regulation provide public benefits that outweigh the detriment to the property owner?
- Is the regulation necessary to carry out a substantial public purpose?

A valid zoning ordinance is not considered a "taking,"[34] but a zoning ordinance that removes all viable uses for the property will constitute a taking,[35] which can lead to invalidation of the ordinance. The owner who has suffered damages as a result of an inappropriate zoning ordinance may be able to recover those damages from the municipality.[36]

In recent years, the Supreme Court has considered "takings" issues many times.

In a 2001 Supreme Court case, a landowner was denied permission to fill 18 acres of coastal wetlands. His litigating position was that he wanted to develop the land as a 74-acre subdivision, although he never applied for approval of a subdivision. The state (Rhode Island) court held that his takings claim was not ripe for review, in that the lack of an application meant that he had never received a final decision as to the applicability of the challenged regulations to his property. However, the Supreme Court held that the claim was indeed ripe. It was clear what position the agency took and the extent to which development was permitted.

The Supreme Court refused to rule outright that a purchaser is barred from claiming that regulations already in place at the time of the purchase constitute a taking. A challenge might be permitted if the incoming landowner's reasonable investment-based expectations are frustrated.[37]

---

[33] Kaahumanu v. Maui Co., 315 F.3d 1215 (9th Cir. 2003).

[34] Euclid v. Ambler Realty Co., 272 U.S. 365 (1926).

[35] Lucas v. South Carolina Coastal Council, 505 U.S. 1003 (1992).

[36] First English Evangelical Lutheran Church v. County of Los Angeles, 482 U.S. 304 (1987).

[37] Palazzolo v. Rhode Island, 533 U.S. 606 (2001).

In the same year, the Supreme Court held that the Clean Water Act does not give the Army Corps of Engineers the power to regulate the dredging and filling of isolated intrastate wetlands, as distinct from navigable waters.[38]

Perhaps the most significant of this series of "takings" cases was 2005's *Kelo*, holding that it can be a permissible public use to take private property (with proper compensation) under a comprehensive plan that provides benefits such as new jobs and increased tax revenue to a distressed community. Eminent domain was exercised even though the development benefited private parties, with the result that homeowners lost out when the plan called for seizure of their homes to build an industrial park.[39] After *Kelo*, 34 of the states enacted laws or adopted ballot measures increasing requirements for negotiation and disclosure prior to property takings.[40]

Yet another Supreme Court takings case decided, in mid-2005, that the "substantially advances" formula (from *Agins v. City of Tiburon*, 447 U.S. 255 (1980)) cannot be used to see if a government regulation has resulted in a taking, because that analysis is limited to due process issues. The Supreme Court held that a regulation that deprives the owner of all economically beneficial usage of the property is a categorical taking. But if all that happens is that the owner's reasonable investment-based expectations are interfered with, a more flexible analysis is applied.[41]

There is no exception to the "full faith and credit" requirement of 28 U.S.C. § 1738 for Takings Clause claims.[42]

The Supreme Court has ruled[43] that a takings claim is ripe when the relevant regulatory agency has made a final decision about how the regulations apply to the property (e.g., the extent of permitted development).

[2] Regulation of Adult Uses

One common exercise of the zoning power is to place limits on establishments offering adult entertainment (pornography; nude or scantily clad "dancers"). There are two basic approaches that zoning boards tend to take toward

---

[38] Solid Waste Agency of Northern Cook County v. United States Army Corps of Eng'rs, 531 U.S. 159 (2001).

[39] Kelo v. New London, Conn., 545 U.S. 469 (2005). In mid-2006, city officials voted to evict the last two Kelo plaintiffs (the other five plaintiffs settled their claims and moved away). After the vote, the last two plaintiffs finally settled, although no details of the settlement were released: Stephen Singer (AP), *Conn. Officials Vote to Evict Homeowners in Landmark Eminent Domain Dispute* 6/7/06 (law.com); Susan Haigh (AP), *Last Holdouts in Eminent Domain Battle Reach Tentative Deal With Conn. City*, 6/27/06 (law.com). Ohio has ruled that its state constitution forbids appropriation of private property premised on the potential for economic benefit of development to the community. The municipal code's definition of "deteriorating area" was also found to be void for vagueness: Norwood, Ohio v. Horney, 110 Ohio St. 3d 353 (Ohio 2006).

[40] Terry Pristin, *Voters Back Limits on Eminent Domain*, N.Y. Times 11/15/06 at C6.

[41] Lingle v. Chevron, 544 U.S. 528 (2005).

[42] San Remo Hotel v. City and County of San Francisco, 545 U.S. 323 (2005).

[43] Palazzolo v. Rhode Island, 533 U.S. 606 (2001).

adult establishments: the cluster method and the dispersal method. The cluster method segregates adult uses into a "combat zone," whereas the dispersal method imposes minimum-distance rules to limit the number of adult establishments in a residential or family area.

In 2000, the Supreme Court permitted bans on nude dancing in part of a content-neutral regulation intended to fight negative secondary effects (e.g., drug dealing and other crimes connected with adult establishments).[44] A valid ordinance must further a substantial governmental interest, be content neutral, be aimed only at preventing negative secondary effects, and must allow alternative means of communication.

In 2004, the Tenth Circuit ruled that if the zoning ordinance does not explicitly permit decisions on the basis of expression, a nude dancing club cannot bring a facial challenge to the ordinance by alleging that there is an unconstitutional prior restraint on speech in the form of unbridled discretion to deny a permit. (The ordinance allowed "wholesome entertainment" in the industrial park.) According to the Tenth Circuit, zoning ordinances are usually laws of general applicability and are not the kind of expression-based regulations that pose a threat of censorship.[45]

The Supreme Court returned to the subject of adult zoning in mid-2004, holding that a city's decision to deny a license under the "adult business license" ordinance can be appealed to the state District Court. The Supreme Court overruled the Tenth Circuit, which had ruled that the statute failed to provide the constitutionally required prompt judicial decision; the Supreme Court found that adequate review was available via ordinary judicial review. The licensing scheme did not seek to censor material, and provided reasonably objective, fair, non-content-related criteria for adult businesses. The simplicity of the review process meant that it would probably be expeditious, and the simplicity of implementation made it unlikely that any specific item of adult material would be totally suppressed.[46]

According to the Second Circuit, before passing a zoning ordinance that excludes strip clubs, a city must provide evidence of negative secondary effects (e.g., increased crime, reduced property values). The test is whether the ordinance furthers a substantial or important government interest. There must be a connection between the regulated speech and the secondary effects, although the Second Circuit did not require the city to either prove the link or prove that the ordinance will effectively suppress the secondary effects. The Supreme Court has upheld ordinances because they were enacted after hearings and review of reports on other cities, where the city relied on its own findings plus evidentiary foundation deriving from earlier cases, or relied on studies, even those done many years before the enactment of the ordinance. However, an ordinance is not acceptable merely

---

[44] City of Erie v. Pap's A.M., 529 U.S. 277 (2000); Barnes v. Glen Theatre, Inc., 501 U.S. 560 (1991) permits restrictions on nudity to protect public order and morality.

[45] Tool Box, Inc. v. Ogden City, Utah, 316 F.3d 1167 (10th Cir. 2004).

[46] City of Littleton, Co. v. Z.J. Gifts D-4, 541 U.S. 774 (2004).

because it is based on some evidence; there must have been pre-enactment evidence.[47]

In 2001, the Eleventh Circuit struck down a county ordinance forbidding the sale of alcohol in adult-entertainment establishments. Many similar ordinances have been upheld, but this one was not, because local research showed that crime rates did not increase when adult businesses were allowed to serve liquor.[48]

On the grounds that the First Amendment rights of a topless bar would not be violated by requiring the bar to relocate, the Eastern District of New York refused to enjoin enforcement of a town adult use ordinance. The former owner of the bar settled a challenge to the ordinance (which required adult businesses to move out of neighborhood business zones by 1998) by promising to make a good-faith effort to relocate by September, 2003. However, instead of relocating, the club owner sold it to its current owner. The new owner challenged the constitutionality of the ordinance when the town tried to shut down the club. The Eastern District of New York held that objections about price, availability of space, and future use of the space do not make the locations that were acceptable to the town for adult businesses unavailable under a *Renton* analysis.[49]

[3] Regulation of Religious Uses

Ironically, not only are adult entertainment establishments frequently the target of hostile zoning treatment — so are churches. Because churches and other religious buildings are usually exempt from real estate taxes, they do not provide revenue for localities, whereas a commercial establishment doing business in the same location presumably would pay real estate taxes. (For convenience, the term church will be used to include synagogues, mosques, temples, and other religious uses.) Churches are sometimes unwelcome in residential areas because of actual or perceived noise and parking problems.

The majority of states follow the so-called New York Rule, which states that churches cannot be absolutely excluded from residential areas. The minority, or California, rule is that there are at least some circumstances that will justify a municipality's exclusion of churches from a residential area.

The Supreme Court's classic statement on religious uses comes from 1993. The Free Exercise of Religion clause applies to protect religious activity if a law discriminates against some or all religious beliefs or regulates or prohibits conduct because it is undertaken for religious reasons. Therefore, forbidding religious assembly under conditions when other forms of assembly would be permitted

---

[47] White River Amusement Pub Inc. v. Town of Hartford, 481 F.3d 163 (2d Cir. 2007); *see* Mark Hamblett, *2nd Circuit: To Ban Strip Clubs, Towns Must Show Evidence of "Negative Secondary Effects,"* N.Y.L.J. 4/2/07 (law.com).

[48] Flanigan's Enters. Inc. of Ga. v. Fulton County, Ga., 242 F.3d 976 (11th Cir. 2001).

[49] TJS of New York Inc. v. Town of Smithtown, 03-cv-4407 (E.D.N.Y. 2008); *see* Vesselin Mitev, *Ordinance Requiring Relocation of Topless Bar Survives First Amendment Challenge,* N.Y.L.J. 6/4/08 (law.com).

violates the Free Exercise clause. Any law burdening religious practice must be of general applicability, or it will be invalid.[50]

The Religious Land Use and Institutionalized Persons Act (RLUIPA) of 2000, 42 USC §§ 2000cc–2000cc-5, was enacted to protect religious land use from discrimination and undue burdens. The RLUIPA forbids the government from imposing or implementing land use regulations in any manner that imposes a substantial burden on religious exercise. The permissible exception is a regulation that is the least restrictive means of furthering a compelling governmental interest.

RLUIPA forbids implementation of land use regulations in any manner that disfavors religious institutions as compared to nonreligious ones.

In 2005, the Supreme Court upheld the validity of RLUIPA § 3, ruling that it is not barred by the Establishment Clause.[51]

Federal approval of an airport rebuilding plan calling for moving a church cemetery was not a federal "action" subject to the Religious Freedom Restoration Act, so there was no violation of the RFRA (42 USC §§ 2000bb–2000bb-4).[52]

[4] Regulation of Home-Based Businesses

Given the concept that residential use is higher than commercial use, it is common for zoning codes to limit or even forbid commercial use of homes. A statutory exception for professional offices (e.g., doctors' offices) is sometimes interpreted to forbid other types of home-based business.

Zoning codes that allow home-based business nearly always impose limitations on the size and scope of business use (e.g., not more than 25% of the floor space of the home; within the home only, not in outbuildings; using the original floor plan only, without alterations; refraining from installing or using equipment not normally found in homes). Other common restrictions include bans on advertising visible from the outside of the premises, manufacturing or storing inventory on premises, making sales or having customers visit, and employing persons other than family members in the business.

[B] Condemnation and Eminent Domain

The police power of the state government includes acquiring land by eminent domain, if the acquisition is necessary for the public good and the land is used for public purposes.

The acquisition requires appropriate notice and compensation at a fair rate (a rate that leaves the former owner in no worse position than if condemnation had never occurred). Generally speaking, this will be fair market value, reflecting the

---

[50] Church of the Lukumi Babalu Ayo v. City of Hialeah, 508 U.S. 520 (1993). *See also* Schad v. Borough of Mount Ephraim, 452 U.S. 1 (1981) (the First Amendment demands strong justification for excluding an entire broad category of protected expression).

[51] Cutter v. Wilkinson, 544 U.S. 709 (U.S. 2005).

[52] Bensenville, Ill. v. Federal Aviation Admin., 457 F.3d 52 (D.C. Cir. 2006).

highest and best use for the property rather than its actual use. Objective standards, rather than any additional personal value the property has to the owner, will govern.[53] Just compensation is required whether the vehicle for the taking is eminent domain, adverse possession, or prescription.[54] See above for discussion of *Kelo*.

When business property is condemned, in general the government only has to pay for the land, not lost business goodwill—unless there is some reason why it is impossible for the business to relocate. In a condemnation proceeding, property is valued as if environmental problems had been remediated. The assigned value of the property is escrowed with the court handling the proceeding. The condemnor has the right to seek an order to set aside some of the funds in escrow to cover the property owner's costs of remediation and transfer of the property.[55]

The Second Circuit ruled that a condemnor must give as much notice to the property owner as is practicable, so a property owner could go to trial on the issue of whether he received actual notice of proceedings to condemn his property for a mixed-use waterfront development. The Second Circuit used a bright line test: if the names and addresses of a person affected by a proceeding are available, then notice must be mailed unless so many people are affected that notice by mail would be impracticable—notice by publication is not adequate.[56]

New Jersey held in mid-2004 that a municipality cannot condemn property by declaring it not fully productive and thus in need of development; government cannot redevelop private property merely because it is not optimally used. Thus, the state could not take 63 acres of undeveloped wetlands property for use as a deepwater port. New Jersey's Supreme Court said that the statutory definition of "blight" evolved to prevent a domino effect as one slum reduced the value of nearby properties, but there was no evidence of damage offered.[57]

A city violates the Establishment Clause by exercising eminent domain over a blighted area in order to turn it over to a religious organization for construction of a parochial school. That is, although eliminating blight is a valid public purpose, designating an area as blighted does not render the character and status of the developer irrelevant.[58]

A lessee who has a long-term lease at below fair market rental may be entitled to part of the condemnation proceeds, since the lessee loses economic benefits because of the condemnation. Some states call for payment of the full proceeds to the lessor, making it up to the lessee to recover a fair share.

---

[53] *See, e.g.*, United States v. 564.54 Acres of Land, 441 U.S. 506 (1979).

[54] Pascoag Reservoir & Dam Inc. v. Rhode Island, 217 F. Supp. 2d 206 (D.R.I. 2002).

[55] Housing Auth. of New Brunswick v. Suydam Investors LLC, 826 A.2d 673 (N.J. 2003).

[56] Brody v. Village of Port Chester, 434 F.3d 121 (2d Cir. 2005); *see* Mark Hamblett, *2nd Circuit Clarifies Notice Provision of New York's Eminent Domain Law*, N.Y.L.J. 12/9/05 (law.com).

[57] Gallenthin Realty Dev. Inc. v. Paulsboro, 191 N.J. 344 (N.J. 2007); *see* Michael Booth, *N.J. Court Sets a Tougher Test of "Blight" for Using Eminent Domain*, N.J.L.J. 6/18/07 (law.com). The statute is the Local Redevelopment and Housing Law, N.J.S.A. § 40A:12A-5(e).

[58] *In re* Condemnation of 1839 N. Eighth Street, 74 LW 1486 (Pa. Comm. 2/6/06).

Inverse condemnation, also known as regulatory taking, occurs when there has been no physical seizure of the property, but government actions impair the use of the property. The property has been "taken" if the state regulation does not advance a legitimate state interest or, even if the objective is legitimate, the effect is to deprive the owner of all economically viable uses.

Reduction in value of the property is a factor, but by itself does not constitute a taking. The more that the government action interferes with the reasonable expectation of investors in the property, the more likely it is that a taking will be found.[59]

Any physical invasion of property, even a trivial one, will be considered a taking: e.g., a state law requiring building owners to provide physical access to cable companies to install cables and boxes.[60]

More recent cases deal with the question of trade-offs (individual applies for permit or variance, and is told that it will be issued conditional on the applicant doing something for the public benefit). At least rough proportionality is required between the cost or other inconvenience to the applicant and the public benefit supposedly obtained.[61]

[C] Nuisance

The way that a property owner behaves with respect to the property can have unreasonably negative consequences for others, constituting a private and/or public nuisance. (See § 11.03[C] for discussion of nuisance and trespass in the environmental context.)

At times, the same conduct may constitute both trespass and nuisance, but the traditional distinction drawn between the two torts is that trespass is an interference with a property owner's possessory interest in the property.

Nuisance, in contrast, interferes substantially and unreasonably with the right to use and quiet enjoyment of the property (although rights to view, or light and air unobstructed by other buildings, are not protectable by suit for nuisance). Trespass generally requires a physical entrance onto the property, so intangible entrances such as pollution and noise are more likely to constitute nuisance. By and large, either trespass or nuisance liability requires intentional rather than negligent acts.

If nuisance is proved, injunction is the traditional remedy, although modem practice allows damages to be awarded if the use that constitutes the nuisance has enough social utility to make an injunction inappropriate.

---

[59] Penn Central Transp. Co. v. New York City, 438 U.S. 104 (1978) (*re* landmark restrictions on alteration of appearance of property); Agins v. Tiburon, 447 U.S. 255 (1980); Keystone Bituminous Coal Ass'n v. DeBenedictis, 480 U.S. 470 (1987); Yee v. City of Escondido, 503 U.S. 519 (1992).

[60] Loretto v. Teleprompter Manhattan CATV Corp., 458 U.S. 419 (1982).

[61] Nollan v. California Coastal Comm'n, 483 U.S. 825 (1987); Dolan v. City of Tigard, 512 U.S. 374 (1994).

[D] Brownfields

Early in 2004, the EPA released interim guidance on what landowners can do to avoid having CERCLA liability imposed under the 2002 statute, the Brownfields Act. (See § 11.03[D].) The Brownfields Act and the EPA's Common Elements Guidance (March 2003) describe the requirements for relief from landowner liability (e.g., research into past uses, prevention of continuing releases, reducing harm from contamination, and compliance with land use requirements). The 2004 document adds specific advice for owners of contiguous properties. Prospective purchasers can buy a site they know is contaminated, but contiguous property owners can only avoid liability if they buy without knowledge of the contamination or reason to know about it. Furthermore, contiguous owners must: prove they are not Potentially Reliable Parties; prove they did not cause, contribute to, or consent to the release; take steps to prevent future releases or contamination; comply with applicable land use rules; and if issued with a CERCLA subpoena or a request for information they must comply. They must not block access to the property by anyone authorized to conduct response actions, and they must have carried out appropriate research into past uses of the property. The 2004 guidance states that a case-by-case analysis will be made as to whether the site has been affected by a distant property in the same way it would have been by an adjacent property.[62]

§ 10.12 MORTGAGES AND FORECLOSURE

A mortgage is a written document proving a security interest in real property. The mortgagor is an owner or potential owner of property who needs financing for the property. The mortgagee is a bank or other lender (e.g., the seller of the property; a private investor) who advances the financing, receiving in turn a security interest in the property. On default, the mortgagee is entitled to foreclose, and if there is a balance still outstanding after the foreclosure, the mortgagee can get a deficiency judgment enforceable against the borrower's other assets.

A deed of trust is a variant used in some localities. The mortgagor conveys the property to a trustee, in trust for the mortgagee; the property is conveyed back to the property owner when the balance is paid in full. If the property owner/borrower defaults, the lender exercises its power of sale rather than foreclosing on the mortgage.

Most mortgages are "amortizing mortgages": the borrower agrees to make a series of payments, each consisting of interest and principal, until the entire amount has been paid off. There may be a larger "balloon payment" due at the end of the term.

---

[62] Interim Enforcement Discretion Guidance Regarding Contiguous Property Owners, http://www.epa.gov/compliance/resources/policies/cleanup/superfund/contig-prop.pdf (1/22/04), discussed in (no by-line), *EPA Guidance Issued on Avoiding Liability for Properties Tainted by Contiguous Sites*, 72 L.W. 2448 (2/3/04).

Some states conceptualize mortgages under the "title theory": that is, the mortgagee has the title to the property, but allows the mortgagor to use the property until the mortgage is satisfied, at which point title returns to the mortgagor. But this is the minority view. Most states follow the "lien theory," which gives the mortgagee a lien on the property until the loan is paid off.

There can be more than one mortgage on a property. The first mortgage is known as the senior or primary mortgage; subsequent mortgages are junior or secondary mortgages. Mortgage priority depends on the date of recordation, not the size of the debt or even the intentions of the parties.

[A] Construction Financing

The lender on a conventional residential or commercial mortgage is at least able to inspect the property, estimate its value, and determine the creditworthiness of the mortgagor. Construction financing is riskier, because the funds are needed to build the project in the first place — and a variety of factors can delay completion of the project (and its potential to earn income that can be used to repay the financing) or even prevent completion indefinitely. It is also quite common for projects, even those finished on time, to go over budget.

The general rule is that construction financing is short-term (often running 12–18 months; almost always lasting less than five years). Some lenders are legally barred from writing construction loans, and others simply prefer not to. The most usual construction lenders are commercial banks, savings institutions, private mortgage companies, and some wealthy private individuals.

A "take-out" commitment is a commitment to provide permanent mortgage financing once construction is completed. A stand-by commitment is the lender's agreement to make a permanent mortgage loan in a specified amount, if called upon by the borrower within a specified time. In contrast, under an open-end loan, the borrower does not have a commitment for permanent financing, so the construction lender is at risk that it will be impossible to get a mortgage on the completed building.

The construction lender reviews the potential borrower's plans and specifications, gets a "desk opinion" from its appraisal division as to the soundness of the application, then inspects the site, does a formal appraisal, and reviews the credit rating of the potential borrower and the contractor for the project.

The loan amount is set at a percentage of the improved value of the property, subject to guidelines (such as 70% of value for an office building or apartment project, 50% for specialized commercial properties). Lenders often limit the construction loan to 90% of the "take-out" (permanent mortgage commitment).

The interest rate for construction financing is typically a few points above the prime rate, i.e., the rate charged to a bank's best customers.

The process of securing permanent financing is similar, involving disclosure to the lender and commitments and warranties on both sides.

[B] Home Equity Loans and Reverse Mortgages

The conventional mortgage is used to purchase a property and thereby gain at least some degree of home equity. The owner's equity in the property increases as the mortgage balance is paid off, and also increases based on general inflation and specific increases in the value of the property.

A home equity loan is a means of tapping into the equity. The homeowner is permitted to borrow up to a specified percentage of the equity (i.e., fair market value minus mortgages and other encumbrances).

A reverse mortgage is an arrangement under which a homeowner (usually an elderly or disabled person who needs funds for medical or long-term care) gets a loan representing a percentage of home equity. Either a single payment is made, continuing payments are made (this is known as a reverse annuity mortgage), or a line of credit is set up that can be accessed as needed.

The elderly mortgagor does not make repayment while he or she continues to live and reside in the home. Instead, the repayment (loan amount plus interest) is taken when the mortgagor (and spouse, if any) no longer resides there (i.e., has died, becomes a permanent resident of a nursing home, or sells the property). Some reverse mortgage arrangements have an "equity kicker" entitling the mortgagee to part of any appreciation in the value of the property.

The advantage of reverse mortgages to the elderly is that they can get money for medical or other needs, or a continuing income stream to supplement their pensions and Social Security. Furthermore, the payments are considered a debt rather than income, and therefore do not affect eligibility for public benefits.

[C] Foreclosure

What happens if the mortgagor falls behind on mortgage payments? In the real world, it is often possible for the mortgagor to restructure the arrangement (although at a cost of additional fees and probably additional interest), or get a deferral — because the foreclosure process is cumbersome and expensive for the mortgagee.

Generally speaking, the mortgage instrument will require the lender to give notice of default, and provide a period (e.g., 30 days) to cure the default, before instituting foreclosure proceedings.

Jurisdictions vary in how they treat mortgages: whether as an absolute conveyance of property that becomes void as soon as the mortgagor complies with all the conditions, including all payments (title theory); or merely as a lien on the property, or security for performance of the mortgage obligations (lien theory).

Under either theory, the mortgagee has a choice between initiating a judicial proceeding or placing the property up for public sale. Thus, the mortgagor will have an opportunity to redeem his or her interest by paying the debt, or be entitled to any realized value that exceeds the mortgage.

The general rule is that even after default on the underlying mortgage obligation, the mortgagor has the right to cure the default by paying the debt ("equitable redemption"). This right continues until the property is sold under a decree or judgment of foreclosure. Some states provide a statutory right of redemption, usually lasting one year, during which time the mortgagor can reclaim the property even after a sale. When this period ends without a redemption, the property is deeded to the purchaser. The purchaser receives whatever title the mortgagor had at the time the mortgage was created.

Sometimes the simplest alternative for a mortgagor who has no defense and is unable to redeem the property is simply to turn over the deed to the property and convey it to the mortgagee, in exchange for cancellation of the mortgage debt, thus avoiding the inconvenience and expense of a foreclosure proceeding.

U.S. jurisdictions have adopted four different types of foreclosure:

- Strict foreclosure: the mortgagee must maintain an action for foreclosure. Once the court issues a decree of foreclosure, the mortgagor is given a short period of time, such as six months, to redeem the property by paying the mortgage debt plus the mortgagee's litigation expenses.
- Judicial foreclosure, then sale: unlike strict foreclosure, once the redemption period has expired, a public sale of the property is required. Although theoretically any proceeds in excess of the debt will belong to the mortgagor, the most likely scenario is that the sale will occur during a time of depressed markets, so the mortgagee will be the only bidder. The court has the power to set an upset price (lowest acceptable bid), and can refuse to confirm the sale, for instance if the mortgagee is the sole bidder and places an unreasonably low valuation on the property. This is the most common form of foreclosure.
- Nonjudicial foreclosure, then sale: The mortgage or deed or trust explicitly awards a power of sale to the mortgagee, on specified incidents of default, without need for a judicial proceeding. The sale must be public and properly advertised. The mortgagor may or may not be given a right of redemption following the sale.
- Judicial foreclosure by entry and possession: A judicial proceeding is held, resulting in a decree of foreclosure. After the redemption period, the mortgagee can enter and take possession of the property. A second redemption period is available after repossession. No judicial proceeding is required if repossession can be made without force.

The unpaid debt that the mortgagee can recover includes the costs of foreclosure. Most mortgages provide for post-default interest. The foreclosure court may or may not approve an attorneys' fee award that is not specifically provided for in the mortgage. Some jurisdictions also allow the addition of insurance premiums to the unpaid debt, as long as the mortgage instrument provides for this.

In August 2002, the NCUSSL approved the Uniform Nonjudicial Foreclosure Act, allowing three types of foreclosure to be carried out without judicial intervention: either a conventional foreclosure by auction sale, or foreclosure by either negotiated sale or appraisal. The secured lender chooses which form of foreclosure it will exercise. First, the lender must give the debtor notice of default with a 30-day period to pay the overdue debt. The next step is notice of foreclosure, which must be deferred for at least 90 days after this notice. The Uniform Nonjudicial Foreclosure Act provides protective measures for residential debtors. For example, deficiency judgments cannot be entered against them if they act in good faith with respect to the foreclosure and the underlying property.[63]

The collapse of the sub-prime lending market, beginning in 2007 and continuing throughout 2008, had serious effects on the housing market, which were expected to continue for several years. In June 2008, RealtyTrac reported that there were about 250,000 foreclosure filings in June — actually 3% lower than the previous month. However, the decline could be the result of state and local moratoria on foreclosures. For example, California law requires lenders to wait 30 days after a homeowner misses the first payment before filing a default notice, and efforts to modify the loan are required. Massachusetts gives homeowners a three-month grace period after default before the lender can file for foreclosure — a rule that reduced petitions by 84%; this period is supposed to be used to restructure the loan to prevent foreclosure.[64]

In response, Congress passed the Mortgage Forgiveness Debt Relief Act of 2007, P.L. 110-142. This statute amends Code § 108 [cancellation of debt income] to provide that taxpayers who lose their houses to foreclosure will not sustain the additional blow of incurring additional tax obligations. For discharges of indebtedness that take place between January 1, 2007 and December 31, 2009, discharge in whole or in part of qualified principal residence indebtedness is not included in the taxpayer's gross income. Qualified principal residence indebtedness is acquisition indebtedness (i.e., not home equity loans) on a principal residence (not vacation homes, investment, or rental property), with a limit of $2 million (or $1 million on a married person's separate return).[65]

P.L. 110-289, the Housing and Economic Recovery Act of 2008, signed July 30, 2008, includes a Division A on Housing Finance Reform. This legislation includes reform of the regulation of lending, including a Federal Housing Finance Agency and Federal Housing Finance Oversight Board. The bill imposes limitations on golden parachutes and capital requirements for housing lenders, revises the standards for FHA appraisals and other reforms to the FHA, including

---

[63] http://www.law.upenn.edu/bll/ulclufbposa/2002act.htm (8/5/02).

[64] Michael Corkery, *Slowing Foreclosures May Mask Breadth of Woes*, Wall St. J. 8/11/08 at A2. In response to a 150% increase in foreclosures between 2005 and 2008, New York implemented a Residential Foreclosure Program, to educate homeowners and speed up settlement of foreclosure matters. (The default rate in foreclosure cases is about 90%, so in some cases homeowners may not even be aware of the foreclosure.) Parties will be notified of community resources, and hearing officers will be involved in developing settlement or case management plans. *See* Mark Fass, *N.Y. Chief Judge Unveils Program to Deal With Dramatic Rise in Foreclosures*, N.Y.L.J. 6/19/08 (law.com).

[65] See Sharon Kreider, "Last Minute 2007 Tax Legislation," www.westerncpe.com/forms/LastMinute2007TaxLegislation.pdf. The "bailout bill," the Emergency Economic Stabilization Act, P.L. 110-343, extends this provision until 2012.

a prohibition on sellers furnishing assistance with down payments. P.L. 110-289 includes the S.A.F.E. Mortgage Licensing Act. The legislation also includes mortgage foreclosure protection for service members, and housing matters for veterans. Tax provisions (a tax credit for first-time home buyers; extension of deductibility of real estate taxes by non-itemizers) are also included.

The HOPE for Homeowners program permits some homeowners to refinance mortgages that are no longer affordable. Up to $550,440 can be refinanced as a 30-year, fixed-rate mortgage, with a maximum 90% loan to value ratio. To participate, owners must negotiate with the first lien holder to extinguish subordinate liens. The intention is to prevent foreclosures and deterioration in value of foreclosed properties and areas where there are many foreclosed properties. Participation by lenders is voluntary. Borrowers pay an initial premium of 3% of the original mortgage and another 1.5% of the outstanding mortgage each year, and agree to share appreciation in value of the property with the federal government. The HOPE for Homeowners program runs from October 1, 2008–September 30, 2011 (unless extended). Participation is limited to owner-occupiers who own only one home.

The Federal Housing Administration attempted to raise its upfront premiums from 1.5% of principal to 1.75%, effective October 1, 2008. However, P.L. 110-289 reinstated the 1.5% premium rate until October 1, 2009. Annual premiums for FHA insurance remain in the range of 0.5–0.55% of loan balance. In 2006, only 1.8% of mortgages were FHA-insured, but that percentage rose to 23% in July 2008, because non-federally-backed mortgage securities became extremely undesirable as a result of the collapse of the subprime lending market, and Fannie Mae and Freddie Mac suffered severe losses in this market.[66]

[D] Deductibility of Mortgage Interest

In the business context, this is seldom a problem, because mortgage interest will normally be an ordinary and necessary business expense deductible under § 162.

For individuals, the deduction provided by § 163(h) is limited to "qualified residence interest." There are two permissible categories of qualified residence interest: acquisition indebtedness (used to purchase, construct, or substantially improve a qualified residence), and home equity indebtedness secured by a qualified residence of the taxpayer. As long as the loan is secured by a qualified residence, the loan proceeds can be used for non-housing-related purposes without destroying deductibility.

Qualified acquisition indebtedness[67] is limited to $1 million ($500,000 for a married taxpayer filing a separate return). Home equity indebtedness is limited to $100,000 ($50,000 for married persons filing separately), or to the FMV of the

---

[66] James R. Hagerty, *FHA Raises Its Premiums to Insure Repayment of Mortgages*, Wall St. J. 8/27/08 at A11.

[67] Qualified acquisition indebtedness incurred prior to October 13, 1987 is grandfathered in; its interest is deductible even if the indebtedness exceeds $1 million.

qualified residence minus the acquisition indebtedness, whichever is lower. The $1 million and $100,000 limits are applied separately.

[1] Points

Points are charges such as loan origination fees imposed at the outset of a mortgage transaction. The general rule is that they are considered prepaid interest and thus must be deducted over the term of the mortgage. However, under certain circumstances, points paid on a principal residence, that are defined as a percentage of the loan, that are normally charged in the area and that do not exceed the locally prevailing amount, may qualify for a current deduction. See IRS Publications 535 and 936 for details.

Some points are paid by the seller, such as loan placement fees that the seller pays to induce a lender to lend to the purchaser, thus facilitating the transaction. These are not treated as interest at all, but are considered selling expenses that reduce the potentially taxable amount that the seller realizes on the sale.

§ 10.13 PERSONAL PROPERTY

Some very old rules of law still survive to govern personal property (i.e., property other than real estate and interests in real estate). The UCC, in particular, often protects bona fide purchasers for value, even if the person selling them the property did not have good title.

Sovereign immunity does not apply to unconstitutional, ultra vires actions, so the Ninth Circuit permitted claims that personal property and financial assets were improperly taken under an escheat scheme that was invalid. Eleventh Amendment immunity might have been available if the plaintiffs were trying to get funds out of state coffers, but not if they were trying to get back their own property that had been wrongfully seized after their property was liquidated and ownership documents were destroyed.[68]

[A] Gifts

A lawful transfer of title to property can be either a sale — i.e., in exchange for some degree of consideration (although not necessarily fair market value) or gratuitous — a gift. Creation of a valid gift involves three elements:

(1) Intent to make a present rather than a future gift
(2) Delivery of the gift (or something representing the gift, such as a title deed) to the donee or a representative of the donee (e.g., a parent who becomes custodian of a gift or transfer to a minor donee)
(3) Acceptance of the gift

---

[68] Suever v. Connell, 439 F.3d 1142 (9th Cir. 2006).

Unless the potential donee has provided consideration, a promise to make a gift in the future is not enforceable.

A gift "causa mortis" is made in contemplation of imminent death; but if the potential donor survives the immediate hazard that inspired the gift (e.g., survives an operation; returns home from a war zone), the gift is automatically revoked.

[B] Bailments

A bailment is an arrangement under which the owner of personal property permits someone else to have temporary possession of the goods, even though the underlying ownership is not altered, and even though the bailee (party receiving temporary possession) has an obligation to return the goods to the bailor. Failure to return the goods would make the bailee liable; the bailee could be ordered to return the goods or compensate the bailor for their value.

At common law, the standard of care was higher for commercial bailments (e.g., leaving a damaged item for repair) than for gratuitous bailments (e.g., lending an item to a friend). Many states, however, have statutes or case law requiring ordinary prudence of all bailees, whether paid or gratuitous.

Bailment contracts are permitted to limit the bailee's liability for losses, as long as the bailor accepts the conditions, and as long as the bailee does not try to limits its liability for willful actions or gross negligence.

[C] Accessions

Work done on property, or other goods added, can increase the value of property. "Accessions" are the additional goods and/or services. The general rule is that the owner of the underlying goods is entitled to the accessions if someone else's work results in only a slight increase in the value of the property. However, the worker may be entitled to ownership if the accessions significantly increase its value.

If underlying property is significantly changed by adding goods of several owners, the finished "third good" probably becomes the property of the owner of the underlying goods that were altered.

[D] Joint Accounts

Joint bank and brokerage accounts create some difficult problems, especially for divorce and estate planning. A "true" joint account is intended to belong to both (or all, if there are more than two) depositors, whereas a "convenience" joint account is often used by a disabled person who wants someone else to be able to perform banking transactions, but who remains the owner of the funds in the account at all times.

Generally, a true joint account will be a JWROS account, so it will pass by operation of law to the surviving joint tenant(s) on the death of the first joint tenant to die. Thus it should not be possible for the first joint tenant to dispose of the account balance by will. A convenience joint account will be the property of the owner, and therefore can be bequeathed. However, state law may impose different rules. The most important factor is usually the signature card signed when the account was created, indicating whether or not survivorship is present.

The POD (payable on death) and Totten trust accounts are related forms, similar but not identical to the convenience joint account. Ownership remains at all times in the depositor, but the signature card indicates who should receive the account proceeds at the time of the depositor's death.

A bank is always justified in paying account proceeds (up to and including 100% of the balance) to any joint tenant, even a non-depositing one. However, a joint tenant who withdraws more than a proportionate share can be required to account to the other joint tenant.

Chapter 11

Environmental Law

§ 11.01   INTRODUCTION

The regulation of the environment is primarily a federal function, for various reasons. Interstate commerce is obviously heavily involved, and contaminated air and water as well as escaped toxic substances can end up quite far from the place of contamination or release. The implications for public safety and health are immense, and there is value in nationwide uniformity. However, this is not an area of complete federal preemption, and the states are permitted to play a role—particularly if they choose to adopt standards more protective than the federal requirements.

The various federal statutes give the Environmental Protection Agency (EPA) broad powers to detect and punish violations of environmental statutes. In flagrant instances, criminal as well as civil penalties can be imposed on polluting corporations — and on individuals responsible for pollution. In addition, most of the statutes authorize citizen suits. However, environmental litigation in 2008 was marked by a number of suits pitting state Attorneys General against the EPA — with the state goal of requiring the EPA to take enforcement steps that the EPA did not wish to take.

During arguments heard at the beginning of the term in October 2008, the U.S. Supreme Court appeared receptive to Bush administration's argument that a coalition of environmental groups did not have standing to challenge U.S. Forest Service regulations because the claims did not apply to a particular site or project. The coalition challenged the regulations under the Forest Service's Appeals Act, which exempts some projects from the requirements of notice, comment, and appeals. The District Court enjoined implementation of a project in the Sequoia National Forest. The administration's argument was that environmental groups could only establish standing to challenge the regulations by showing imminent injury in the form of harm to a site-specific activity. The environmental groups' position was that they could have posed a facial challenge to the regulations outside the context of the Burnt Ridge Project as long as they showed that the regulations were applied to a project and affected the plaintiffs on an ongoing basis.[1] On November 12, 2008, the Supreme Court removed restrictions on the Navy's use of sonar during training exercises, ruling that the need for training outweighed the asserted public interest based on alleged risks to marine mammals in the area where the sonar was used.[2]

Note: for coverage of environmental liability under liability and other insurance policies, see § 14.07[B][2].

The U.S. Supreme Court refused, without comment, to hear Exxon's appeal of a punitive damage award of $112 million in an environmental suit brought by a former Louisiana judge who alleged that a contractor that cleaned pipes for Exxon left radioactive waste on his land. The trial jury awarded $56 million in compensatory and $1 billion in punitive damages, but the Louisiana Court of Appeals reduced the punitive damages to $112 million.[3]

---

[1] Summers v. Earth Island Institute, No. 07-463 (pending) discussed in Laurel Newby, *Supreme Court Argument Report: Environmental Groups Out on a Limb?* Special to Law.com (10/9/08). On a similar issue, the Second Circuit held that a confederation of towns in the Catskill and Delaware watershed region did not have standing to obtain review of two EPA Safe Drinking Water Act actions; the Second Circuit held that they had not suffered injury in fact from the steps taken by the EPA: The Coalition of Watershed Towns v. EPA, Nos. 07-2449-ag, 07-3912-ag (2d Cir. 12/29/08).

[2] Winter v. Natural Resources Defense Council, No. 07-1239 (11/12/08); *see* (AP), *Supreme Court Rules for Navy in Use of Sonar*, 11/12/08 (law.com).

[3] Exxon Mobil v. Grefer, 128 S. Ct. 2054 (2008); *see* Christopher S. Rugaber (AP), *Supreme Court Turns Down Exxon's Appeal of $112 Million Verdict*, 4/22/08 (law.com).

§ 11.02 FEDERAL ENVIRONMENTAL LAWS

Since the issue came to public note in the 1970s, Congress has passed numerous federal environmental laws dealing with various forms of pollution and the proper disposition of potentially hazardous wastes:

- The Clean Air Act, 42 USC § 7404, as amended by P.L. 101-549
- The Clean Water Act (formally known as the Federal Water Pollution Control Act), 33 USC § 1365
- The Comprehensive Environmental Response, Compensation and Liability Act (CERCLA, or "Superfund"), 42 USC § 9659
- Emergency Planning and Community Right to Know Act, 42 USC § 11046
- Resource Conservation and Recovery Act (RCRA), 42 USC § 6901
- Safe Drinking Water Act, 42 USC § 300j-8, reauthorized in 1996 by P.L. 104-182
- Toxic Substances Control Act, 14 USC § 2619
- Asbestos Hazard Emergency Response Act of 1986, TSCA Title III, P.L. 99-579, 20 USC § 4011
- Oil Pollution Act of 1990, 33 USC § 2701[4]
- Hazardous Materials Transportation Authorization Act, 49 USC § 5101, including rules for safe packaging of hazardous materials
- Land Disposal Flexibility Act of 1996, P.L. 104-119.
- Small Business Liability Relief and Brownfields Revitalization Act of 2002, P.L. 107-118 (see § 11.03[D])

See 40 CFR § 19.4 in the current year's edition for a table of environmental civil penalties as adjusted for inflation.

In addition to federal and state public enforcement, most environmental statutes permit citizen suits by private plaintiffs. (Unlike a toxic tort suit seeking compensation for personal injuries or property damage, a citizen suit seeks correction of pollution and the payment of fines into the public treasury.)

Most of the federal environmental statutes carry the potential for criminal charges against polluting corporations and/or individuals within the corporation responsible for environmental harm. Note that the federal sentencing guidelines for corporations do not apply to environmental offenses.

§ 11.03 CERCLA

CERCLA, enacted in 1980, provides funds and enforcement power to clean up "brownfields" (contaminated sites) and respond to spills of dangerous

---

[4] The Oil Pollution Act covers an oil spill into a drainage ditch that is not navigable in itself, but is adjacent to a navigable body of water. Thus, the company that pumped the oil is liable to the federal government for cleanup costs: United States v. Needham, 354 F.3d 340 (5th Cir. 2003).

substances.[5] See § 11.06 below for a discussion of RCRA, which regulates active hazardous waste sites; CERCLA deals with cleanups of sites already contaminated, as well as current reporting of releases of potentially hazardous materials. CERCLA has been a very active area of litigation, because a very wide range of potential defendants can be involved, and because CERCLA deals with conditions that may have been created many years before the enforcement efforts.

One reason CERCLA has been controversial is the number of enforcement avenues (i.e., potential ways in which a property owner or company involved with a site can become liable). CERCLA § 106(a), 42 USC § 9606, gives the Environmental Protection Agency (EPA) power to obtain a court order to abate a condition of imminent and substantial danger to the public because of an actual or threatened release of a hazardous substance from a facility. CERCLA § 106(a) orders can compel investigation and remediation by private parties at waste disposal sites.[6]

Another possibility is for the EPA to perform a response action, then sue the responsible parties for cost recovery. The EPA is the arm of the federal government empowered to "respond" to the presence of forbidden substances at a site, giving rise to "response costs." The definition of response costs is broad enough to encompass the federal government's costs of overseeing a cleanup performed by a private party.[7]

Under CERCLA § 104(e), the EPA has the power to enter facilities[8] and take samples, as well as to secure information and documents from site owners. The EPA does a preliminary assessment of the site, based on all available information. The next step is a field assessment of the conditions. The Hazard Ranking System of 40 CFR Part 300, Appendix A gives each site a score; high-scoring sites are placed on the National Priorities List (NPL) of sites for which federal CERCLA funds can be appropriated for cleanup. Putting a site on the National Priorities List is rulemaking that is subject to judicial review under CERCLA § 113(a). However, a challenge to the expansion of a Superfund site is treated as a challenge to putting

---

[5] The Northern District of California ruled that the plain statutory language of CERCLA says that the law applies only to land within the states, territories, and possessions of the United States. Therefore, contaminated property at former military bases in the Philippines is not covered: Arc Ecology v. Department of the Air Force, CO2-05651JW, 72 L.W. 1376 (N.D. Cal. 12/3/03).

[6] Merely issuing a CERCLA § 106 cleanup order is not an unconstitutional deprivation of property. However, the District Court for the District of Columbia held that General Electric could pursue its claims that the EPA engaged in a pattern or practice of using § 106 in non-emergency situations without providing the prompt hearings required by due process, and that the agency administered fines and penalties coercively: General Elec. v. Johnson, 754 F.2d 1475 (D.D.C. 3/30/05). *See also* Memo Op. No. 00-2855 (JDB) (D.D.C. 9/12/06).

[7] United States v. Lowe, 118 F.3d 399 (5th Cir. 1997).

[8] A farm with 24 chicken houses is a single "facility" for CERCLA purposes, even if there are multiple sources of ammonia emissions: Sierra Club v. Tyson Foods Inc., 299 F. Supp. 2d 693 (W.D. Ky. 2003).

the site on the List in the first place. Therefore, § 113(a) confers exclusive jurisdiction on the District Court.[9]

EPA performs an RI/FS (Remediation Investigation/Feasibility Study) at the site to determine the best way of cleaning it up. The agency notifies potentially responsible parties (PRPs) that it believes them to be liable. The RI/FS is published for comment. After the comment period, the EPA publishes a plan for remediation. The PRPs could enter into a consent decree to carry out the plan. If they disagree, the EPA can sue for an injunction ordering the PRPs to carry out the plan. Alternatively, the EPA can perform the cleanup and sue the PRPs for cost recovery.

Release, or threatened release, of any hazardous substance, pollutant, or contaminant into air, surface water, groundwater, or soil comes under CERCLA. So does a release or threatened release that causes anyone to incur "response costs," even if no actual contamination occurred.[10]

A government or private plaintiff who encounters "response costs" and seeks to recover them from the responsible party has to prove three elements:

- Plaintiff's actions taken in response to a release or a threatened release of a hazardous substance
- Defendant's status as a potentially responsible party (PRP)
- Expenditure by the plaintiff as part of its response.

40 CFR Part 302 is the EPA's list of hazardous substances. More than 700 substances have been named, including everything that is a "hazardous waste" for RCRA purposes, or anything targeted under the Clean Air, Clean Water, or Toxic Substances Control Acts. However, asbestos in a building structure does not fall within the definition of "waste site" or "release," so response costs are not recoverable.

A release is any way in which a substance can enter the environment, except for the following, which are excepted by CERCLA § 101:

- Releases permitted under another federal statute (e.g., Clean Water Act NPDES permits; see § 11.04 below)
- Workplace exposures (these fall under OSHA jurisdiction)
- Vehicle exhaust

---

[9] United States v. ASARCO Inc., 214 F.3d 1104 (9th Cir. 2000). The D.C. Circuit ruled that when the EPA lists a site on the Superfund National Priorities List, it is not obligated to discuss potential response actions at that stage. The court said that even if the plaintiff is correct that the agency's real goal is to dredge the river, the plaintiff can raise its concerns at the point at which the dredging plan is proposed: Honeywell Int'l Inc. v. EPA, 374 F.3d 1363 (D.C. Cir. 2004).

[10] Dedham Water Co. v. Cumberland Farms Dairy Inc., 889 F.2d 1146 (1st Cir. 1989). Connecticut ruled that workplace toxins carried to workers' homes and cars on their clothing are not released into the environment for CERCLA purposes. Therefore, the CERCLA statute of limitations does not preempt the state statute of limitations for wrongful deaths of exposed workers: Greco v. United Technologies Corp., 277 Conn. 337 (2006).

- Certain radioactive contamination already within the jurisdiction of other federal statutes
- Normal use of fertilizer.

When a release occurs, the person in charge of the facility must report to the Coast Guard National Response Center. See 42 USC § 9603 for CERCLA penalties for failure to notify. 42 USC § 9607 provides that an owner/operator or person in charge of a transportation, treatment, storage, or disposal facility can be liable for remedial costs, treble punitive damages (for failure to implement a Presidentially ordered remedial action), and up to $50 million for injury or loss of natural resources.

As a result of the Superfund Amendments and Reauthorization Act of 1986 (SARA), P.L. 99-499, the EPA has an obligation to select remedies that are cost-effective, and also protect human health and the environment; to make the maximum practicable use of permanent solutions; and to attain the "applicable, relevant and appropriate requirements" (ARARs) for environmental cleanliness. All responsible parties are jointly and severally liable. The potentially liable parties select a contractor to do the cleanup work, but the EPA has the power to disapprove this choice.

Environmental consent decrees are required to serve the public interest. They must be legal, fair, and reasonable in terms of the site's previous and current condition; other alternatives for cleaning up the site; the technical adequacy of the proposal; and whether the consent decree serves the public interest and furthers the goals of CERCLA. Once entered, a consent decree serves as a final judgment.

The Constitutionality of CERCLA has been challenged several times, but has always been upheld, on the grounds that the Commerce Clause empowers Congress to handle multi-state issues such as proper waste disposal and site cleanup. According to the Eleventh Circuit, CERCLA § 113(h) bars any pre-enforcement review of hazardous waste cleanup decisions, whether the challenge is premised on the Constitution or the CERCLA statute itself.[11] In contrast, the D.C. Circuit ruled in 2004 that § 113(h) does not apply to a constitutional challenge to the statute itself.[12]

As initially enacted, CERCLA did not have a statute of limitations. The SARA amendments specify that a cost recovery suit in a removal action must be brought within three years of the removal of the toxic substance. In a remedial action, the initial action must be brought within six years of the start of physical construction on the site. The EPA can institute further actions for follow-up costs, but all actions must be brought within three years of the end of the cleanup.

Under CERCLA § 309, in private tort suits alleging injury to persons or property, the state statute of limitations begins to run when the plaintiff knew or should have known that the hazardous substance, pollutant or contaminant "caused

---

[11] Broward Gardens Tenants Ass'n v. EPA, 311 F.3d 1066 (11th Cir. 2002).
[12] General Elec. v. EPA, 360 F.3d 188 (D.C. Cir. 2004).

or contributed to" the injury or damages. Although CERCLA permits affirmative defenses, laches is not one of them.

The six-year statute of limitations under CERCLA § 113(g)(2)(B) runs from the start of the cleanup, provided that the § 113 contribution actions take place at the same time as the initial § 107 recovery action. Otherwise, contribution claims are subject to a three-year statute of limitations.[13] In late 2000, the Fifth Circuit joined the Tenth Circuit in holding that the statute of limitations for a contribution action applies unless a statutory event occurs to trigger the statute of limitations.[14]

Not all courts permit a private right of action under CERCLA § 107(a), but it is clear that attorneys' fees awards are not available in cost recovery actions: *Key Tronic Corp. v. U.S.*, 511 U.S. 89 (1994). A suit in state court, seeking damages because a federal superfund cleanup allegedly contaminated the plaintiff's property, does not require the court to construe CERCLA. Therefore, the suit can be maintained in state court, and cannot be removed to federal court as a suit "arising under" federal law.[15]

Medical monitoring costs can be recovered under CERCLA for the limited purpose of studying the environmental impact of a release of hazardous substances.

Although citizen suits under CERCLA are not permitted until the remedial action is complete, a citizen group can bring suit to challenge a cleanup decision after the remedial measures have been taken, but while effectiveness of the action is still being monitored by enforcement agencies.[16]

[A] Potentially Responsible Parties

CERCLA § 107 defines three classes of "potentially responsible parties" (PRPs) who can be held liable for CERCLA response costs:

- Present or past "owners or operators" of the contaminated site
- Those who transported waste to the site
- "Generators" of the waste who arranged with the owner/operator or transporter to have the wastes either disposed of or treated.[17]

---

[13] Sun Co. (R&M) v. Browning-Ferris Inc., 124 F.3d 1187 (10th Cir. 1997). The Ninth Circuit says that the six-year statute of limitations for an initial action to recover remedial costs runs from the final adoption of the plan of remediation: California v. Neville Chem. Co., 358 F.3d 661 (9th Cir. 2004).

[14] Geraghty v. Miller, 234 F.3d 917 (5th Cir. 2000), *following* Sim Co. v. Browning-Ferris Inc., 124 F.3d 1187 (10th Cir. 1997).

[15] MSOF Corp. v. Exxon Corp., 295 F.3d 485 (5th Cir. 2002).

[16] Frey v. EPA, 270 F.3d 1129 (7th Cir. 2001).

[17] This category includes someone who approved of previous dumping and ordered that a truckload of waste be "handled," because it can be inferred that dumping was intended: United States v. Greer, 850 F.2d 1447 (11th Cir. 1988). A pesticide manufacturer is a "generator," because it arranged for and contributed to handling and disposal of the waste, even though it hired a formulation facility to process the pesticides: United States v. Aceto Agric. Chems. Corp., 872 F.2d 1373 (9th Cir. 1989).

PRPs are subject to strict liability: any PRP is responsible for cleanup costs attributable to waste it has generated or otherwise handled within the ambit of CERCLA, whether or not that particular PRP is at fault. However, innocent land-owners are entitled to a defense if they acquire land when they have no reason to know (despite adequate inquiry) that hazardous substances have ever been present on the property.

The Ninth Circuit held the federal government itself 100% responsible for cleanup costs at a California site that was used to manufacture synthetic rubber during World War II. In the Ninth Circuit's view, it was equitable to allocate the full amount to the government, because the federal government not merely owned and operated the property and supervised the manufacturing process, but agreed to indemnify the corporate operator of the site.[18]

The Third Circuit ruled in 2006 that a polluter that voluntarily cleans up a site cannot receive contribution from the federal government, even if the government was also a polluter. Then, in 2007, the Third Circuit reversed its earlier holding, and decided that three polluters could maintain a suit to get the U.S. government to contribute to the cost of voluntary cleanup of 15 sites that were owned or operated by the United States, holding that changes in environmental law allow PRPs to obtain relief under § 107.[19]

All PRPs will be jointly and severally liable (see below for the availability of contribution among them), unless there is a reasonable basis for allocating certain portions of the overall environmental harm to particular PRPs.

CERCLA continues to apply to a corporation after its dissolution, even if, under state law, there is no longer any entity with capacity to be sued, so the dissolved corporation still has to defend against a suit for response costs.[20] Whether or not a limited partner is an "owner" for CERCLA purposes depends on state partnership law.[21]

---

[18] Cadillac Fairview/California Inc. v. Dow Chem. Co., 299 F.3d 1019 (9th Cir. 2002). The Federal Circuit required the federal government to reimburse a World War II defense contractor for cleanup costs at a bomber plant, based on a contract agreeing to indemnify the contractor for claims "not now known." Even though the contamination occurred long before the passage of CERCLA, the indemnification clause was broad enough to cover CERCLA claims: Ford Motor Co. v. United States, 378 F.3d 1314 (Fed. Cir. 2004). *See also* Fireman's Fund Ins. Co. v. Lodi, Cal., 72 L.W. 1424 (E.D. Cal. 12/22/03) (if a city itself is a PRP (here, a leaky sewer system contributed to ground water pollution), the city's ordinance insulating itself from Superfund liability, and making the other PRPs jointly and severally liable for remediation costs, is invalid because it is preempted by CERCLA). Although the U.S. Supreme Court decided Hall Street Associates v. Mattel, 128 S. Ct. 1396 (2008), involving a landlord's right to indemnification from the tenants for clean-up costs, the Court addressed only the arbitration aspects of the case, not the underlying indemnifcation issue.

[19] DuPont v. United States, 508 F.3d 126 (3d Cir. 2007), *reversing* 460 F.3d 515 (3d Cir. 2006); *see* Shannon P. Duffy, *3rd Circuit Changes Direction in "DuPont" Environmental Cleanup Case*, The Legal Intelligencer 11/28/07 (law.com).

[20] New York v. Panex Indus. Inc., 860 F. Supp. 977 (W.D.N.Y. 1996).

[21] Redwing Carriers Inc. v. Saraland Apartments, 94 F.3d 1489 (11th Cir. 1996).

A parent corporation can be deemed the operator of a facility owned by a subsidiary of the corporation only if the corporate veil can be pierced; but if it can be pierced, the parent corporation can have both "owner" and "operator" liability for the subsidiary's facility.[22] The Sixth Circuit permits a corporation's sole shareholder to be held liable as an operator, but again only if state law permits the corporate veil to be pierced.[23]

There is a split in authority as to whether the liability of successor corporations is determined by state law, or whether there is a federal common law of CERCLA successor liability. State law is applied by the First, Sixth, Ninth, and Eleventh Circuits, whereas the Second, Third, Fourth, and Eighth apply federal common law.[24]

The substantial continuity test of whether a company is a successor relies on the extent to which the predecessor's business is continued. The Second Circuit said that this test is not sufficiently established as part of federal common law to impose CERCLA liability. Because the test has been accepted only by a handful of states, the Second Circuit found that it cannot govern CERCLA liability subsequent to an asset purchase, and New York State could not recover the $10.8 million it spent to clean up a landfill.[25]

A corporate officer's or director's personal liability under CERCLA is broader than ordinary corporate tort liability, but they are not subjected to strict liability merely because they hold corporate office. The test is whether the individual's power, title, and percentage of ownership provided the power to prevent or significantly abate the release of hazardous substances into the environment; absent such power, there is no liability.

The individual is not an "owner" as defined by CERCLA, but may become an "operator" based on job functions and activities. To the Eighth Circuit, an employee is liable only if authority to control hazardous waste disposal is actually exercised; mere presence of authority will not support liability.[26]

In the Third Circuit view, to be a CERCLA arranger, a party must possess a hazardous substance and either control the production process or have knowledge that processing could lead to release of the substance. Intent to treat or dispose of the substance is not required.[27] To be liable as an "arranger," an officer or director of a company is subject to the same standard as liability of the parent company: presence or absence of authority to exercise direct or indirect control over disposal

---

[22] United States v. Cordova Chem. Co., 59 F.3d 584 (6th Cir. 1995) and 113 F.3d 572 (6th Cir. 1997); Schiavone v. Pierce, 79 F.3d 2603 (2d Cir. 1996).

[23] Donahey v. Bogle, 129 F.3d 838 (6th Cir. 1997).

[24] The case law is summarized in Atchison, Topeka & Santa Fe R.R. v. Brown & Bryant Inc., 132 F.3d 1295 (9th Cir. 1997).

[25] New York v. National Servs. Indus. Inc., 352 F.3d 682 (2d Cir. 2003). United States v. Bestfoods, 524 U.S. 51 (1998) requires the application of common-law rules rather than idiosyncratic CERCLA rules to determine successor liability.

[26] United States v. Gurley, 43 F.3d 1188 (8th Cir. 1994).

[27] Morton Int'l Inc. v. A.E. Staley Mfg. Co., 345 F.3d 669 (3d Cir. 2003).

practices, plus actual exercise of that authority. To be liable as a "transporter," the individual must actually participate in the conduct leading to liability, and must be aware of the company's substantial participation in choosing disposal facilities and accepting material for transport.[28]

An excavator that moves contaminated soil on a site can be liable for cleanup costs as an "operator" and/or "transporter," but a manufacturer that gives technical advice about the safe disposal of a chemical after a spill or leak has not "arranged for disposal" and thus is not liable.

Under the Superfund Recycling Equity Act of 1999, a recycler is not treated as arranger or transporter of the recycled materials. SREA has been held to apply retroactively to state cost recovery actions that were pending on its enactment date.[29]

At the end of 2004, the Supreme Court ruled that contribution under § 113(f) is not available unless the party seeking contribution has been sued under § 106 or § 107(a). In this case, Cooper owned four properties and sold them to Aviall. Aviall concluded that both it and Cooper had contaminated the properties. Aviall notified the state (Texas) of the contamination, but neither the state nor the EPA required cleanup. Aviall performed cleanup actions under state supervision, and then sold the properties again to a third party. After the sale, Aviall still had contractual obligations for more than $5 million in cleanup costs and tried — but failed — to get contribution from Cooper.[30]

A lessee, whose full extent of control over the contaminated property is to sub-lease it to someone else, is not an owner subject to CERCLA liability. According to the Second Circuit, if this were sufficient to subject the lessee to liability, the statute would not be drafted with separate categories of "owner" and "operator" liability.[31]

In a suit against PRPs for response costs, a consent decree with the federal government involving the same site and owner is an "initial action," for which the case against the PRPs can be a "subsequent action" for statute of limitations purposes — even if the consent decree includes neither a finding nor an admission of liability.[32]

CERCLA § 113(f) gives courts the power to immunize from liability parties who are only de minimis contributors to the hazardous conditions of a site. In this reading, imposing joint and several liability is not fair to companies that did not create serious environmental harm. Those who did not dispose of a meaningful amount of waste did not cause the plaintiffs to incur measurable response costs to cope with those wastes. The First Circuit held that the discretion to allocate liability based on equitable factors is extensive enough to provide forgiveness for

---

[28] Arranger liability: United States v. TIC Investment Corp., 68 F.3d 1082 (9th Cir. 1995); transporter liability: United States v. USX Corp., 68 F.3d 811 (3d Cir. 1995).

[29] Department of Toxic Substances Control v. Interstate Non-Ferrous Corp., 99 F. Supp. 2d 1123 (E.D. Cal. 2000).

[30] Cooper Indus. v. Aviall Servs. Inc., 540 U.S. 1099 (2004).

[31] Commander Oil Corp. v. Barlo Equip. Corp., 215 F.3d 321 (2d Cir. 2000).

[32] United States v. Findett Corp., 220 F.3d 842 (8th Cir. 2000).

contributing trace amounts.[33] The Fifth Circuit held that a party in a CERCLA § 113(f) contribution action is liable only for its own proportionate share of cleanup costs, not jointly and severally liable with other PRPs; joint and several liability is an option only in a § 107(a) cost recovery action in which one PRP sues another.[34]

The Supreme Court's 1998 decision[35] that it is an unconstitutional "taking" to apply the 1992 Coal Industry Retiree Health Benefits Act retroactively has been interpreted to mean that this statute cannot be extended to CERCLA or used to avoid cleanup liability.[36]

[B] Contribution

Contribution is the process under which one PRP, which has already been ordered to pay cleanup costs, looks to other PRPs for their fair share of the cost.

The Supreme Court returned to the issue of contribution in June 2007, in a case where the defendant cleaned up a government site that the defendant contaminated in the course of retrofitting rocket motors for the federal government, then sued the government to obtain § 107(a) cost recovery. The Supreme Court read § 107(a)(4)(B) to allow one PRP to recover costs from another PRP. Section 113(f)(1) permits a contribution action when PRPs have common liability as a result of an action instituted under § 106 or 107(a). Section 107(a) allows cost recovery — as distinct from contribution — when a private party has incurred cleanup costs. The Supreme Court treated the two remedies as complementary. At least in the context of reimbursement, a PRP cannot opt for the longer § 107(a) statute of limitations or avoid equitable distribution of reimbursement costs among PRPs under § 113(f) by opting to impose joint and several liability under § 107(a). Even if such a choice of remedies was available, the PRP defendant in a § 107(a) suit would be able to defeat the maneuver by filing a counterclaim under § 113(f). The Supreme Court noted that § 113(f)(2) prohibits contribution claims against a party that has resolved its liability to the United States or to a state via settlement, but a District Court applying equity rules would consider prior settlements when making decisions about liability.[37]

Under California law, a liability insurer's obligation to indemnify the insured under a policy provision referring to "all sums that the insured becomes legally obligated to pay" is limited to payments made pursuant to a court order. Therefore, the insurer need not cover the cost of compliance with an administrative cleanup order.[38]

---

[33] Acushnet Co. v. Mohasco Corp., 191 F.3d 69 (1st Cir. 1999).

[34] Elementis Chromium LP v. Coastal States Petro. Co., 450 F.3d 607 (5th Cir. 2006).

[35] Eastern Enterprises v. Apfel, 524 U.S. 498 (1998).

[36] Combined Properties/Greenbriar Ltd. Partnership v. Morrow, 58 F. Supp. 2d 675 (E.D. Va. 1999); United States v. Alcan Alum. Co., 49 F. Supp. 2d 96 (N.D.N.Y. 1999).

[37] United States v. Atlantic Research Corp., No. 06-562 (U.S. 6/11/07); see, e.g., Pete Yost (AP), *Justices Allow Companies to Seek Recovery of Costs in Voluntary Superfund Cleanups*, 6/12/07 (law.com).

[38] Certain Underwriters at Lloyds' London v. Superior Ct. of Los Angeles County, 16 P.3d 94 (Cal. 2001).

Costs to determine the extent of contamination are not "response costs" where there was not only no actual cleanup but no intent to clean up. Site investigation and other preliminary costs incurred purely in anticipation of litigation are not response costs.[39]

A final, signed administrative agreement is a prerequisite to a contribution action: it is not enough that the state gives written assurances that it has worked out the basic terms of a settling party's CERCLA liability.[40]

The apportionment of response costs is one of the ultimate issues to be decided by the District Court in a contribution action; it is improper for the magistrate judge to allocate cleanup costs without the approval of the parties.[41]

[C] Property Issues

According to *Lucas v. South Carolina Coastal Commission*, 505 U.S. 1003 (1992), a state cannot deny all or substantially all of the benefits of land ownership by imposing environmental rules that do not provide compensation, but the Supreme Court did not provide guidance as to what would constitute adequate compensation in this situation.

Under a mid-2001 Supreme Court decision,[42] a "takings" claim about land use regulations is ripe when the agency implementing the regulations has reached a final decision on the applicability of the regulations to the property at issue — that is, when the agency determines the extent of development that will be permitted on the land. Because the petitioner was barred from doing any filling or development in wetlands, there was no need for him to apply for permission to build houses on land that he was not even permitted to fill. The Supreme Court did not consider his challenge to the regulations to be barred by the fact that he acquired the land after the effective date of the regulations, presumably with notice of them, because a contrary ruling would insulate states from challenges to invalid regulations posed by transferees of property.

Although certiorari was granted in a case holding that it was not a "taking" to forbid a sand and gravel company to dig in a contaminated landfill area, the Supreme Court did not reach the merits of the case because of a determination that the District Court had the right to raise the issue of timeliness on its own motion, even if the parties did not raise it.[43]

In April 2002, the Supreme Court permitted the use of environmental concerns to impose temporary limitations on land development. In this case, a 32-month moratorium was imposed on building of retirement homes in the Lake Tahoe area in order to prepare an environmental growth strategy. The majority held that the moratorium did not work an unconstitutional taking on

[39] Young v. United States, 394 F.3d 858 (10th Cir. 2005).
[40] Waukesha, Wis. v. Viacom Int'l Inc., 362 F. Supp. 2d 1025 (E.D. Wis. 2005).
[41] Beazer East Inc. v. Mead Corp., 412 F.3d 429 (3d Cir. 2005).
[42] Palazzolo v. Rhode Island, 533 U.S. 606 (2001).
[43] John R. Sand & Gravel Co. v. United States, 128 S. Ct. 750 (2008).

the property. The majority opinion also held that if development agencies were required to compensate property owners for loss of value, the agencies might feel constrained to rush through the evaluation process.[44]

In a case seeking declaratory and injunctive relief from the Bureau of Land Management's (part of the Department of the Interior) alleged failure to protect public lands from environmental damage claimed to be caused by off-road vehicles, the Supreme Court ruled in mid-2004 that the alleged failure to act cannot be remedied under the Administrative Procedures Act. The relevant statute, 5 USC § 701(1), applies only to failure to take a discrete agency action that is legally binding on the agency. It does not apply to broad program decisions that carry out statutory objectives, because a contrary decision would obligate the court system to enforce broad mandates. Land use plans are not enforceable, legally-binding commitments.[45]

One formulation is that a court setting value in condemnation proceedings must consider the degree of environmental contamination of the property, and the cost of remediation.[46] Another approach is to value the property as if it were remediated. The valuation amount is escrowed with the court, and the condemnor can apply for an order to set aside some of the escrowed funds to cover remediation and transfer costs.[47]

[1] Passive Migration

The Circuits are split on the issue of whether a site owner can be liable under CERCLA for disposal of hazardous substances on the basis of passive spread of contaminants. The Fourth circuit says yes, but the Second, Third, and Sixth require active human conduct before disposal will be deemed to have occurred. The Ninth Circuit decided in September 2000 that passive migration could constitute disposal, but the court reversed itself in late 2001.[48]

The Fourth Circuit deems passive disposal of hazardous waste to be a lesser included offense of active disposal. Therefore, a plaintiff can allege them in the alternative. If it is found that the defendant did not actively dispose of waste, then the trial court can consider if waste leaked into the soil or groundwater during the defendant's term of ownership.[49]

---

[44] Tahoe-Sierra Preservation Council, Inc. v. Tahoe Regional Planning Agency, 535 U.S. 302 (2002).

[45] Norton v. Southern Utah Wilderness Alliance, 542 U.S. 55 (2004).

[46] Northeast Connecticut Econ. Alliance Inc. v. ATC Partnership, 776 A.2d 1068 (Conn. 2001); later proceedings require consideration of offsetting funds such as development grants and CERCLA contribution recoveries: 861 A.2d 473 (Conn. 2004).

[47] Housing Auth. of New Brunswick v. Suydam Investors LLC, 826 A.2d 673 (N.J. 2003).

[48] Carson Harbor Village v. Unocal Corp., 227 F.3d 1196 (2000), rev'd, 270 F.3d 863 (9th Cir. 2001). A mid-2003 decision of the Central District of California holds that passive migration of a substance counts as a "release," even though under Ninth Circuit law it is not a "disposal": Castaic Lake Water Agency v. Whittaker Corp., 272 F. Supp. 2d 1053 (C.D. Cal. 2003).

[49] Crofton Ventures Ltd. Partnership v. G&H Partnership, 258 F.3d 292 (4th Cir. 2001).

[D] Brownfields Act

The Small Business Liability Relief and Brownfields Revitalization Act, P.L. 107-118, deals with a number of CERCLA issues. This "Brownfields Act" creates a new CERLCA § 107(o), a "de micromis" exemption (i.e., one that is even smaller than a "de minimis" exemption) under which no one is liable for response costs of a CERCLA facility based on very small amounts (under 110 gallons of liquids; under 200 pounds of solids) disposed or, treated, transported, or accepted for transport before April 1, 2001. The de micromis rules do not apply if the President determines that:

- the materials significantly contributed (or could significantly contribute) to the response costs or the costs of restoring the facility
- the person has failed to comply with an administrative subpoena or information request
- the person is impeding the cleanup (by action or failure to act)
- the de micromis conduct has led to a criminal conviction that has not been overturned on appeal.

These Presidential determinations are not subject to judicial review. In a contribution action brought by a private (non-governmental) party, the burden of proof is on the party seeking contribution to prove that the de micromis exemption does not apply.

The Brownfields Act also creates a new CERCLA § 107(p), an exemption for municipal solid waste (basically, ordinary household garbage) disposed at a facility by the owner, operator, or lessee of the residential property that generated the waste, or by a small business that had fewer than 100 full-time employees. Here again, relief is not available if the impact of the action is severe, or if there has been non-compliance or impeding conduct. Contribution actions by private parties are not permitted under § 107(p). Furthermore, defendants in private contribution actions who qualify for the de micromis or municipal solid waste exemptions are entitled to recover costs and attorneys' fees from the plaintiff if the defendants are not liable for CERCLA contribution because of these exemptions.

The Brownfields Act amends CERCLA § 122(g), adding § 122(g)(7), an expedited settlement procedure under which a PRP who is unable to pay response costs, or has a limited ability to pay such costs and still maintain normal business operations, can receive relief, including alternate payment methods. A party making a settlement of this type must waive all claims (e.g., for contribution) against other PRPs for response costs in connection with the facility. Settlements of this type are divulged to the other PRPs of the facility.

Title II of the Brownfields Act provides funding, via federal grants and loans to local government and appropriate nonprofit organizations, for revitalization of "brownfields sites," defined as property whose expansion, redevelopment or reuse "may be complicated by the presence or potential presence of a hazardous substance, pollutant, or contaminant." Sites that are the subject of an ongoing or planned removal action and facilities already on the National Priorities List or are proposed for listing do not qualify as brownfields.

Subtitle B of Title II, "Brownfields Liability Clarifications" adds yet another subsection, § 107(q), to CERCLA. Under this provision, owners of property located near contaminated property, and therefore vulnerable to contamination by a release of hazardous substances from the contiguous property, are not liable under CERCLA because of releases from that other property that they did not cause, contribute, or consent to. Such innocent owners are not required to conduct groundwater investigations or install groundwater remediation systems. The new CERCLA § 211(a)(40) defines a "bona fide prospective purchaser" or BFPP (who will not have CERCLA liability merely because of the purchase) as a purchaser, or tenant of a purchaser, who acquires ownership after the Brownfields Act takes effect; where all disposals of hazardous substances occurred before the acquisition; and the acquiror made commercially reasonable inquiries about the history of the property before acquiring it.

The BFPP must exercise due care to stop continuing release of hazardous materials, prevent threatened future releases, and prevent or limit harm from past releases. However, if there are unrecovered costs of a response action regarding the property, and the response action increases the property's fair market value, the United States has a lien on the facility for the unrecovered response costs.

The Brownfields Act also clarifies CERCLA's definition of "innocent landowner," as one who has no reason to know of the contamination despite having performed all appropriate inquiry. Under an EPA Direct Final Rule,[50] for property purchased on or after May 31, 1997, observation of ASTM Standard E1527-2000 ("Standard Practice for Environmental Site Assessment") will be deemed adequate.

The EPA published a Final Rule at 68 FR 3430 (1/24/03), amending 40 CFR Part 312 Subpart A, explaining how owners of contaminated sites should conduct assessments to avoid CERCLA liability, and how prior uses of brownfields can be traced so prospective purchasers will not be held liable. The NCCUSL also adopted a model uniform state law in August 2003, explaining when land use and other restrictions on brownfields would be enforceable when property is transferred. Under the uniform act, property owners and state and federal agencies would be able to enforce existing institutional controls even after the land changes ownership.[51]

The EPA issued further rulemaking in January and August of 2004. The January guidance deals with criteria for qualifying for immunity as a "contiguous property owner" who did not cause, contribute to, or consent to the release of hazardous materials. It also covers the effect of § 107(q) on current and former owners and sets up a discretionary mechanism for the EPA to resolve questions

---

[50] 68 FR 3430 (1/24/03).

[51] *See* http://www.environmentalcovenants.org and 72 L.W. 2079.

about contiguous property owners. Liability relief is available only if the landowner is not a PRP, complies with land use rules, cooperates with CERCLA
subpoenas, and takes steps to prevent future releases.[52]

The EPA published further guidance in August 2004, implementing the
Brownfields Act by setting standards that must be met by owners or potential
buyers for "all appropriate inquiries" assessments of potentially contaminated
properties. Owners and potential buyers have a duty to hire an environmental
professional to review the history of the site (including interviews with past and
present owners and occupants), check official records, investigate any evidence
of past cleanups, and perform a visual inspection of the site and surrounding
properties.[53]

§ 11.04   THE CLEAN WATER ACT

In 1972, one of the first federal anti-pollution laws, the Federal Water Pollution Control Act, was passed. In 1977, it was renamed the Clean Water Act. It
consists of five elements:

(1)   Water quality standards
(2)   A program for issuing discharge permits
(3)   Industry standards for maximum permissible levels of effluent discharge
(4)   Provisions about chemical and oil spills
(5)   Grants and loans for building public water treatment facilities.

The CWA gives states broad authority to protect not only water quality, but
also the quantity of water flowing into streams and rivers. A state can mandate a
minimum water flow needed to protect fish in a river, and supervision of hydroelectric projects can extend to wildlife protection as well as water quality.

Under CWA § 311 (33 USC § 1321), it is unlawful to discharge RQs (reportable quantities) of hazardous substances into or upon surface waters or shorelines.
RQs are set in 40 CFR Part 117, and the EPA's list of which substances are deemed
hazardous for this purpose appears at 40 CFR § 116.4.

The National Pollutant Discharge Elimination System (NPDES) requires
permits before discharging any pollutant into water. Permits can be issued for
ocean discharges only if the issuing authority determines that the planned discharge will not degrade the environment unreasonably. At first, the CWA called
for the EPA to issue the permits, but states have been given the option to take over
the process, and nearly all of them have done so.

---

[52] Interim Enforcement Discretion Guidance Regarding Contiguous Property Owners, http://
www.epa.gov/compliance/resources/policies/cleanup/superfund/contig-prop.pdf (1/13/04), discussed
in (no by-line), *EPA Guidance Issued on Avoiding Liability for Properties Tainted by Contiguous
Sites*, 72 L.W. 2448 (2/3/04).

[53] EPA Proposed Rule 69 FR 52541 (8/26/04); *see* 73 L.W. 2121.

The NPDES permit establishes "performance levels" that the discharger is expected to meet. If the standards are not met, the discharger is required to make a prompt report. The D.C. Circuit held in 2006 that CWA § 303(d)(1)(C) requires states to set total maximum daily loads for various pollutants; it is not acceptable for the EPA to set seasonal or annual limits instead.[54]

The CWA initially places each state's NPDES permit program under EPA administration. Then, however, CWA § 402(b) says the EPA "shall approve" transfer of permit authority to any state that applies and shows that it meets nine criteria. Section 7(a)(2) of the Endangered Species Act requires federal agencies to consult with agencies designated by the Department of Commerce and the Department of the Interior to ensure that the proposed agency action does not jeopardize any endangered or threatened species. When Arizona applied for control of the permit program, the EPA, after consulting with the Fish and Wildlife Service, transferred CWA enforcement, although the Fish & Wildlife Service wanted to consider potential impact on species but was told not to do so.

The Ninth Circuit held that the EPA acted arbitrarily and capriciously because it took irreconcilable positions on its responsibilities under § 7(a)(2), but in June 2007, the Supreme Court reversed the Ninth Circuit, finding that its decision was not supported by the record. To be vacated as arbitrary and capricious, an agency decision must rely on factors that Congress did not want the agency to consider; entirely omit a important aspect of the problem that the legislation was designed to solve, give an explanation that is counter to the evidence, or is so implausible that it could not reflect the agency's expertise or give a different view of the problem. In this case, the Supreme Court noted that EPA's final approval notice for the transfer indicated that the § 7(a)(2) process had been concluded, whereas the EPA's litigating position was that a § 402 transfer application does not trigger the § 7(a)(2) consultation requirement — but the Supreme Court did not deem this to be an error requiring a remand. The Supreme Court held that the statute includes only nine criteria, and the Ninth Circuit was wrong to attempt to add a further condition of not jeopardizing listed species.[55]

In a Clean Water Act suit to compel the EPA to promulgate guidance on effluent limitations and new source performance standards for storm water pollution discharges caused by the construction industry, the Ninth Circuit upheld a permanent injunction ordering the EPA to act. CWA § 304(m) obligates the EPA to publish a plan in the Federal Register every two years to identify sources that discharge pollutants for which guidelines and performance standards have not been issued. The EPA is required to promulgate guidelines within three years of publication of the plan. According to the plaintiffs, the EPA violated its duty to issue standards. A rule on storm water discharge from construction sites was proposed in mid-2002, then withdrawn in April 2004. The EPA announced that it had decided not to promulgate standards, choosing instead to rely on existing programs

---

[54] Friends of the Earth Inc. v. EPA, 446 F.3d 140 (D.C. Cir. 2006).

[55] National Ass'n of Home Builders v. Defenders of Wildlife, 127 S. Ct. 2518 (2007).

for control of storm water runoff. The EPA characterized the existing programs as adequate and the cost of new regulation as disproportionately high. The EPA removed the construction industry from its published plans. In 2008, the Ninth Circuit ruled that once the EPA listed the construction industry as a point source category in a plan, promulgating guidelines and standards was mandatory, holding that the CWA does not give the EPA authority to remove a point source category from a § 304(m) plan.[56]

The Bush Administration sought to overturn the Court of Appeals' decision in *South Florida Water Management District v. Miccosukee Tribe*, a case in which certiorari was granted. The tribe brought suit under the CWA, claiming that a federal permit was necessary because a high volume of polluted runoff from suburban residences and manufacturing was dumped into the Everglades. The water management district conceded that the water was polluted, but it did not have an alternative disposition plan. The case is of great interest to Western states concerned about whether their regional water diversion efforts would fall afoul of federal anti-pollution rules. On March 23, 2004, the *Miccosukee* decision was remanded for further proceedings to determine whether the canal and the wetland can meaningfully be treated as distinct bodies of water.[57] In mid-2006, the Supreme Court held that a hydroelectric dam had the potential to discharge into navigable waters of the United States, affecting river flow and movements. Therefore, CWA § 401 required state certification that the dam would not violate water protection laws.[58]

The Ninth Circuit held, in late 2007, that the EPA improperly issued NPDES permit under CWA permitting mining-related discharges of copper into a creek that already had more copper than water quality standards permit. The creek is included on the list of impaired waters. Compliance schedules must include all discharges, not just those allowed under a permit. To obtain a permit, a discharger must show how the water quality standard will be met if the discharger is allowed to continue discharging permits into impaired waters.[59] The effect of mining waste on water continued to be an important issue in late 2008. The EPA approved a proposal allowing mining companies to dump waste near streams. The rule, proposed by the Department of the Interior's Office of Surface Mining, but opposed by the governors of Tennessee and Kentucky, creates a 100-foot buffer zone around streams. In the buffer zone, mining companies would be required to avoid dumping — or, if avoidance is impossible, they must minimize environmental

---

[56] Natural Resources Defense Council v. EPA, No. 07-55183 (9th Cir. 9/18/08).

[57] South Florida Water Mgmt. Dist. v. Miccosukee Tribe, 541 U.S. 95 (2004).

[58] S.D. Warren Co. v. Maine Bd. of Envtl. Protection, 547 U.S. 370 (2006).

[59] Friends of Pinto Creek v. EPA, No. 504 F.3d 1007 (9th Cir. 2007); the impaired waters list is drafted pursuant to 33 USC § 1313(d). *See* Ian Talley and Stephen Power, *EPA Backs Rule Easing Mining-Waste Disposal*, Wall St. J. 12/2/2008 and 73 Fed. Reg. 75813 (12/12/08). The Supreme Court case is Coeur Alaska, Inc. v. Southeast Alaska Conservation Council et. al., No. 07-984/State of Alaska v. SACC, No. 07-990 (2008). *See* Matthew Daly (AP), *High Court to Hear Dispute Over Alaska Gold Mine*, 1/12/09 (law.com).

harm to the extent possible. In January 2009, the Supreme Court heard arguments on whether the Clean Water Act forbids dumping of metal waste in a lake; the mine secured a permit from the U.S. Army Corps of Engineers. This was the first permit issued that would allow discharge of mining wastewater into a navigable waterway.

The mere fact that a substance is natural does not remove it from the CWA's jurisdiction. Storage and spreading facilities for manure are point sources subject to the CWA's permit requirements.[60] Ground water that is discharged into a river after methane gas is extracted from underground seams of coal is considered a pollutant for which a permit is required. Even though the methane extraction operation does not intentionally do anything to the water, the result of the process is to increase salt levels, add contaminants, and preclude the water from being used for irrigation.[61] Replacing the turbine generators at a dam requires state water quality certification, because the increased flow of water into the river below the dam is an activity that may result in discharge, as governed by CWA § 401(a)(1).[62]

The Tenth Circuit held a negligent discharge occurring without an NPDES can violate the CWA even if the discharger does not know that the pollutant ends up in protected waters. The Tenth Circuit reinstated convictions for two discharges, which was enough to enhance the sentence under Guideline 2Q1.3(b)(1)(A) for ongoing, continuous, or repetitive discharge; the Guideline does not limit the enhancement to knowing discharges.[63]

There is no reasonable expectation of privacy in wastewater flowing through a private pipe to the public sewer system, so EPA inspectors were entitled to qualified immunity when they lifted the manhole cover on private property to take samples from the pipe.[64]

Farmers have standing to challenge water diversions under a federal reclamation project, because of the credible threat of harm to their crops if the salt content of their irrigation water increases. Whether or not there has been a violation of a statute, standing is present under Article III of the Constitution because the threat of harm is deemed to constitute actual injury.[65]

The Safe Drinking Water Act, initially passed in 1974 and amended in 1986 and 1988, is designed to protect water quality. The EPA sets national standards for contaminants in drinking water. The EPA also advises states on the protection of single-source aquifers (underground sources of drinking water). Lead-free

[60] Community Ass'n for Restoration of the Environment v. Bosma Dairy, 305 F.3d 943 (9th Cir. 2002).

[61] Northern Plains Resource Council v. Fidelity Exp. & Dev. Co., 325 F.3d 1155 (9th Cir. 2003).

[62] Alabama Rivers Alliance v. Federal Energy Reg. Comm'n, 325 F.3d 290 (D.C. Cir. 2003).

[63] United States v. Ortiz, 427 F.3d 1278 (10th Cir. 2005).

[64] Riverdale Mills Corp. v. Pimpare, 392 F.3d 55 (1st Cir. 2004).

[65] Central Delta Water Agency v. United States, 306 F.3d 1938 (9th Cir. 2002); Friends of the Earth v. Laidlaw treats possible future injury as injury in fact.

materials must be used in all water systems and water coolers. The SDWA attempts to control use of underground injection as a means of waste disposal. In states where underground well injection could endanger drinking water, 40 CFR Parts 124 and 144–148 require the state to have an EPA-approved injection control program.

Forty-eight states have adopted standards "no less stringent" than the federal standards and have "adequate" enforcement procedures. Therefore, they have been granted primary enforcement authority for their public water systems.

A January 2000 Supreme Court decision holds that a decrease in the aesthetic and recreational value of a waterway is adequate to prove injury, even without proof of actual harm to the water. Both injury and traceability can be proved with circumstantial evidence, e.g., closeness to polluting sources, past pollution, or predictions of influence the discharge will have.[66]

Although the Army Corps of Engineers has regulatory jurisdiction over navigable waters, that phrase cannot properly be interpreted to include non-navigable, intrastate, isolated waters merely because they provide a habitat for migratory birds.[67]

The First Circuit ruled that the CWA final rule, calling for an informal adjudicatory hearing before a discharge permit or thermal variance is issued is a reasonable interpretation of the "public hearing" requirement, thus overruling its own previous ruling that an evidentiary hearing is required.[68]

[A] Penalties

If an RQ discharge occurs (unauthorized discharge of an impermissibly large — and hence reportable — quantity of a hazardous substance), the person in charge of the facility where the discharge occurred must telephone the Coast Guard National Response Center immediately. Failure to report is penalized by a fine of up to $12,000 and/or a year's imprisonment.

Willful failure to report can be penalized by up to $250,000. An additional penalty of up to $6,200 a day can be imposed on the owner/operator or person in charge of the facility for each day the discharge continues (even if it is reported), and they can be made to pay the government's cleanup costs resulting from the discharge.

In a CWA civil penalty action, jury trial is available.[69]

The CWA contains criminal sanctions, § 309(c)(2). To convict a corporate officer, the prosecution must show that the officer knew the nature of his or her acts and performed them intentionally, but it is not necessary to prove knowledge that

---

[66] Friends of the Earth v. Laidlaw, 528 U.S. 1674 (2000).

[67] Solid Waste Agency of Northern Cook County v. Army Corps of Eng'rs, 531 U.S. 159 (2001).

[68] Dominion Energy Brayton Point LLC v. Johnson, 443 F.3d 12 (1st Cir. 2006); the prior case is Seacoast Anti-Pollution League v. Costle, 572 F.2d 872 (1st Cir. 1978).

[69] United States v. Tull, 481 U.S. 412 (1987).

the conduct was illegal. Conviction of a CWA felony requires proof that the defendant acted knowingly with respect to each element of the offense.[70]

[B] Citizen Suits

CWA § 505 authorizes a "citizen" (a person or persons having an interest which is or may be adversely affected) to bring suit. Citizen suits can be brought against the discharger, or against the EPA for failure to enforce the law. However, at least one continuing violation must exist to support a citizen suit for violation of the NPDES permit system. The suit cannot be premised merely on past violations, although the plaintiff need only show a reasonable likelihood of continuing violations at the time the suit is filed. The suit does not become moot if there are no further violations after the filing.[71]

CWA § 309(a)(6) rules out federal citizen suits when a state is diligently prosecuting an environmental action under a comparable state enforcement scheme. According to the Sixth Circuit, Tennessee law does not provide adequate scope for citizen participation. Therefore, citizens can bring their own federal suit in an effort to expedite enforcement of a CWA discharge permit.[72]

The "60-day letter" is the notice of intent to sue given by citizen suit plaintiffs to potential defendants. According to the Ninth Circuit, a notice letter is adequate if it includes specific dates for some violations, if the other violations alleged come from the same source, and are similar in nature. The notice letter need not give the exact date of every alleged violation, but must be specific enough for the defendant to identify the violations and take corrective action.[73] The Eleventh Circuit held that Federal Rules of Civil Procedure 6(a), the procedural rule for computing statutorily prescribed time periods, applies to the calculation of the CWA 60-day notice period. The legislative intent was to give the government and alleged violators at least the full 60 days to consider and take action. Therefore, a suit on the 61st day was premature, because the 60th day, a Sunday, did not count.[74]

FIFRA, the law governing insecticides, does not have a citizen suit provision, but the Second Circuit held that it is independent of the CWA, which does have a citizen suit provision and does not rule out a CWA citizen suit alleging that New York City's mosquito spraying program discharged pollutants into navigable waters without permits.[75]

---

[70] United States v. Hopkins, 53 F.3d 533 (2d Cir. 1995); United States v. Weitzenhoff, 35 F.3d 1275 (9th Cir. 1994); United States v. Ahmad, 101 F.3d 386 (5th Cir. 1996).

[71] Gwaltney v. Smithfield Ltd. v. Chesapeake Bay Found. Inc., 484 U.S. 49 (1987), *remanded*, Chesapeake Bay Found. Inc. v. Gwaltney, 890 F.2d 690 (4th Cir. 1989).

[72] Jones v. Lakeland, Tenn., 224 F.3d 518 (6th Cir. 2000).

[73] San Francisco Bay Keeper v. Tosco Corp., 309 F.3d 1153 (9th Cir. 2002); Community Ass'n v. Bosma Dairy, 305 F.3d 943 (9th Cir. 2002).

[74] American Canoe Ass'n v. Atalla, Ala., 363 F.3d 1085 (11th Cir. 2004). *See also* Lockett v. EPA, 319 F.3d 678 (5th Cir. 2003): the CWA notice period is mandatory, but not jurisdictional.

[75] No-Spray Coalition Inc. v. New York City, 351 F.3d 602 (2d Cir. 2003).

§ 11.05 THE CLEAN AIR ACT

The Clean Air Act covers stationary sources of pollution; mobile sources of pollution (e.g., vehicles); the definitions and standards used in judicial review; and acid deposition control (reduction of the emission of nitrogen and sulfur oxides; control of truck emissions). The EPA and the states share responsibility for defining and preserving air quality.

In 2004, the Supreme Court ruled that a regional air quality management district's rules, requiring Los Angeles vehicle fleet operators to deploy low-emission or alternative fuel vehicles, were likely to be preempted by CAA § 209. The rules are not preempted as vehicle emission "standards" because they do not apply to vehicle manufacturers at the point of sale, but they nevertheless relate to vehicle emission characteristics. Rather than invalidating the rules entirely, the Supreme Court remanded the case for determination of whether they were completely preempted by § 209.[76]

Also in 2004, the Supreme Court ruled that the CAA gives the EPA the right to halt construction of a facility that emits pollution, even if the facility has a state permit, if the state authority's determination that the facility used the best available control technology was not reasonable under the guidelines provided by 42 USC § 7479(3).[77]

The EPA has a duty, under CAA § 108, to issue a list of pollutants emitted from numerous or diverse sources, and which can reasonably be expected to endanger public health or welfare. The EPA must set a National Ambient Air Quality Standard (NAAQS) for each (CAA § 109). All substances that endanger the public health must be placed on the list. Neither cost nor technical feasibility of eliminating the hazard can be considered in compiling the list. Early in 2001, the Supreme Court upheld CAA § 109(b), finding that it does not improperly designate legislative powers to the EPA. The Supreme Court also held that the EPA is not allowed to consider how much implementation will cost when the agency sets NAAQS. However, the Court of Appeals has jurisdiction to review the EPA's interpretation of particular NAAQS (for ozone, in this case). The Supreme Court found that the EPA's ozone implementation policy was unlawful because the agency's interpretation was unreasonable for going beyond the text of the statute.[78]

The D.C. Circuit vacated two EPA final rules under the CAA dealing with air pollution caused by processing plywood, because the EPA failed to follow the statutory requirement of setting emission standards for a list of hazardous air pollution. The D.C. Circuit agreed with the plaintiff, National Resources Defense Counsel, that the EPA did not have the authority to create a subcategory of low-risk processes, or to extend the compliance deadline.[79]

---

[76] Engine Mfrs. Ass'n v. South Coast Air Quality Mgmt. Dist., 541 U.S. 246 (2004).

[77] Alaska Dep't of Envtl. Conservation v. EPA, 540 U.S. 461 (2004).

[78] Whitman v. American Trucking Ass'ns Inc., 531 U.S. 457 (2001).

[79] Natural Resources Defense Council v. EPA, 489 F.3d 1364 (D.C. Cir. 2007).

The Federal Motor Carrier Safety Administration (FMCSA) did not violate the National Environmental Policy Act or the Council of Environmental Quality rules when it decided not to prepare a CAA Environmental Impact Statement after the President exercised his authority to lift the congressionally imposed moratorium on Mexican motor carriers operating in the United States. The FMCSA did not have the power to prevent the Mexican carriers from doing business in the United States. An agency's decision to avoid preparing an Environmental Impact Statement can be set aside only for being arbitrary and capricious. The Supreme Court found that any increased pollution from the entry of the Mexican vehicles would be a consequence of the President's action, not the FMCSA's, and therefore the agency did not err in refraining from drafting the EIS.[80]

Early in 2003, the D.C. Circuit ruled that a utility industry group does not have standing to challenge the EPA's interpretation of CAA's rules for operating programs (including the power of agencies that issue permits to enhance the permit conditions on a case-by-case basis). The court held that the would-be plaintiffs failed to allege actual or imminent concrete or particularized injury they suffered, and also failed to show negative effects of the policy on any group member's permits.[81]

The Eleventh Circuit held that environment protection organizations did not have standing to petition for review of the EPA's decision not to move against the states of Alabama and Florida's permit programs for major stationary sources of air pollution. The court reached this conclusion because the organizations did not show injury in fact to their members.[82]

28 USC § 2462 provides that fines, penalties, and forfeitures are available for a period of four years back if the defendant can be served within the United States. According to the Southern District of Indiana, the federal government is therefore barred from seeking civil penalties for air pollution violations more than five years old. Nevertheless, the government can obtain a court's judgment stating that the violations occurred.[83]

A "PSD area" is one whose air quality is better than the national standards require. A "nonattainment area" fails to comply with the standards. In nonattainment areas, new or modified sources of pollution are required to meet additional anti-pollution requirements, based on technological feasibility. (See 42 USC §§ 7470–7479.) Owners of "major emitting facilities" in PSD areas must get a permit before building a new facility or substantially modifying an existing facility.

In April 2007, the Supreme Court held that, although it is acceptable for a word to be defined differently in different regulations, Duke Energy Corporation's changes to a coal-fired plant required a permit, because the work constituted a

---

[80] Department of Transp. v. Public Citizen, 541 U.S. 752 (Sup. Ct. 2004).

[81] Utility Air Regulatory Group v. EPA, 320 F.3d 272 (D.C. Cir. 2003).

[82] Legal Environmental Assistance Found. v. EPA, 400 F.3d 1278 (11th Cir. 2005).

[83] United States v. Southern Ind. Gas & Elec. Co., 245 F. Supp. 2d 994 (S.D. Ind. 2002).

"major modification" requiring a permit even though the work did not increase the plants' hourly emission rates. Therefore, the work had to conform to the New Source Performance Standards, which require a stationary source to use the best available technology to limit pollution.[84]

CAA § 110 requires each state to have a State Implementation Plan (SIP). Either the state drafts an SIP that is adequate to meet the NAAQS, or the EPA imposes one. SIPs can include provisions more stringent than the federal standards, if this is necessary to attain the national standards for air quality. The Federal Highway Administration has a duty to promulgate guidelines so that federal highways will satisfy approved SIPs for ambient air quality: see 23 USC § 109(j).

The Clean Air Act Amendments of 1990, P.L. 101-549, broaden EPA enforcement powers. Title III of the statute embodies a comprehensive plan for reducing the amount of nearly 200 toxic air pollutants emitted into the atmosphere, especially those resulting from the combustion of solid waste. Title IV adds regulatory powers to limit "acid deposition." Title V creates a system of operating permits similar to the NPDES program. The enforcement title, VII, adds more criminal violations and increases the number of felony violations (e.g., emission of hazardous air pollutants creating an imminent risk of death or serious injury).

The 1990 CAA amendments require certain stationary sources of air pollution to obtain permits from state and local authorities setting out emission limits for the source. The permits must also include monitoring requirements to ensure compliance with the terms and conditions of the permit: see 42 USC § 76610(c). The EPA issued a rule preventing state and local authorities from supplementing monitoring requirements that they considered inadequate. The D.C. Circuit vacated the EPA rule for violating the statutory requirement of including adequate monitoring requirements in all rules. The 1990 amendments (Title V of the CAA) brought together requirements previously scattered throughout the statute to create a national permit program jointly administered by the EPA and state and local permitting authorities. The statute defines the EPA's role as supervising the program, including identifying minimum elements that must be included in each permit. The EPA has the power to add new compliance procedures and object to permits that do not satisfy the CAA's requirements. State and local authorities can only issue permits if the EPA has approved the authorities' proposals for implementing the permitting process; if an agency does not propose an acceptable program, responsibility for issuing permits shifts to the EPA.

The EPA issued rules in 1992, which the D.C. Circuit vacated for failure to provide for notice and comment. The EPA proposed another rule in 2002, with a notice and comment period. This rule was unpopular with industry groups, so the EPA settled a suit by offering to adopt a final rule that would forbid state and local authorities to supplement monitoring requirements. The rule was issued in 2004, giving the EPA sole power to respond to inadequate periodic monitoring requirements. The rule was re-issued in 2006 and adopted late in 2006. Environmental

---

[84] Environmental Defense v. Duke Energy Corp., 127 S. Ct. 1423 (2007).

groups challenged the monitoring provisions as arbitrary, capricious, and contrary to the CAA. The D.C. Circuit vacated the rule in mid-2008, finding that it was not entitled to deference because it violates the underlying legislation on which the agency operates. According to the D.C. Circuit, Title V gave the EPA two options: to use its rulemaking process to fix inadequate monitoring requirements before permits are issued, or allow the issuers of permits to supplement inadequate monitoring requirements on a case-by-case basis. The EPA refused to take the first choice, so some permit programs ceased to comply with Title V because the EPA neither fixed inadequate monitoring requirements in the applications nor allowed states and localities to fix them. The D.C. Circuit ruled that Congress did not intend permits to be issued without adequate monitoring from some authority.[85]

In 2002, the District of Columbia Circuit ruled that the EPA's compliance testing program, allowing vehicle manufactures to devise tests to be submitted for EPA approval, is void, because CAA § 206(a) requires the EPA to devise the tests.[86] The Circuit ruled that it was reasonable for the EPA to use particulate matter as a surrogate for a range of other substances, and therefore upheld the agency's emission limits for primary copper smelters.[87]

Violations of the CAA are subject to administrative, civil, and criminal enforcement. Under 42 USC § 7413, when the CAA is violated, the EPA can:

- Obtain an administrative compliance order[88]
- Impose penalties of up to $31,500 per day of violation
- Bring a federal civil suit for temporary and/or permanent injunctive relief, with or without civil penalties of up to $31,500 a day
- Seek criminal penalties of 1 to 15 years' imprisonment. Criminal penalties are imposed, e.g., for knowing violation of a SIP permit; knowingly making a false material statement or omitting material facts in CAA reports; or knowing or even negligent release of hazardous pollutants.

In August 2003, the EPA issued a Final Rule under which equipment replacement activities at facilities such as electric power plants will not trigger a requirement of new source review, so pollution controls will not have to be installed when equipment is replaced. The EPA also defined an activity costing less than 20% of the current replacement value of a unit as routine maintenance and repair. The D.C.

---

[85] Sierra Club v. EPA, 536 F.3d 673 (D.C. Cir. 2008); *see* Mark Scarcella, *D.C. Circuit Bolsters State Monitoring of Air Pollution*, Legal Times 8/20/08 (law.com). The rules are found at 40 CFR Part 70.

[86] Ethyl Corp. v. EPA, 306 F.3d 1144 (D.C. Cir. 2002).

[87] Sierra Club v. EPA, 353 F.3d 976 (D.C. Cir. 2004).

[88] In mid-2003, the Eleventh Circuit ruled that 42 USC § 7413 violates due process in that it allows the EPA to issue an Administrative Compliance Order, violation of which can trigger civil and/or criminal penalties, based merely on information in the EPA Administrator's possession. The Eleventh Circuit's rationale was that it is unfair to place an administrative respondent at risk of penalties without a formal adjudication: TVA v. Whitman, 336 F.3d 1236 (11th Cir. 2003).

Circuit vacated a 2003 EPA rule exempting stationary sources from New Source Review, permitting them to use the routine maintenance/repair/replacement exception as long as the cost of the project was less than 20% of the replacement value of the unit. The D.C. Circuit found this regulation conflicted with the statute, which requires New Source Review of any physical change that increases the amount of emissions. The D.C. Circuit did not examine the reasonableness of the agency action, because Congress had already regulated the issue. In May 2007, the Supreme Court refused to review the standards after state and local regulators blocked their implementation — and upheld the D.C. Circuit's ruling that the regulations were so lenient that they violated the CAA.[89]

A suit was filed in the D.C. Circuit by 12 states challenging the EPA's failure to regulate global warming gas emissions from refineries. The plaintiffs called the EPA refinery regulations inadequate because they failed to provide standards for greenhouse gas emissions from new or updated equipment.[90]

A building owner's criminal conviction for violating the CAA's asbestos rule has been held[91] not to violate the Commerce Clause, because the CAA's standards are directly related to asbestos removal and commercial real estate operation. These are activities that have substantial relation to interstate commerce.

The Ninth Circuit view is that it does not constitute double jeopardy to prosecute someone in federal court for violating the CAA asbestos removal standards after that person has incurred a county civil penalty for violating county regulations that track the federal statutory language. In this reading, conduct that violates the laws of separate sovereigns can be punished by each of them, and enforcement of the state air quality plan constitutes state rather than federal enforcement.[92]

In a case of first impression on the scope of jurisdiction over CAA citizen suits under 42 USC § 7604(a), plaintiff-appellants sought an injunction to bar construction of a coal-fired power plant. The Fifth Circuit upheld dismissal of the case, holding that there is no jurisdiction over citizen suits for pre-permit, pre-construction, pre-operation violations of the CAA under § 7604(a)(1). Section 7604(a)(3) does not authorize pre-construction suits against any entity that has a permit or is in the process of obtaining one. The Fifth Circuit noted that even if the District Court had subject matter jurisdiction, it could abstain under *Burford*

---

[89] New York v. EPA, 443 F.3d 880 (D.C. Cir. 2006) *aff'd sub nom* EPA v. New York, No. 06-736, and Utility Air Regulatory Group v. New York, No. 06-750 (2007); *see* Pete Yost (AP), *High Court Deals Setback to Utility Industry in Clean Air Case*, 5/1/07 (law.com). Industry standards are relevant in the determination of whether a project is routine maintenance and thus exempt from Clean Air Act new source review, but they cannot be the sole factor in the decision: United States v. Cinergy, 74 LW 1560 (S.D. Ind. 2/16/06).

[90] The plaintiff states were California, Connecticut, Delaware, Massachusetts, Maine, New Hampshire, New Mexico, New York, Oregon, Rhode Island, Vermont, and Washington; the District of Columbia and New York City also sued. *See* Ana Campoy, *States Sue EPA Over Refinery Emissions*, Wall St. J. 8/26/08 at A3.

[91] United States v. Ho, 311 F.3d 589 (9th Cir. 2002).

[92] United States v. Price, 314 F.3d 417 (9th Cir. 2002).

because timely, adequate state court review was available, and federal review would interfere with state efforts to set policy on a matter of public concern.[93]

The District Court for the District of New Jersey allowed a citizens' group to sue (under Title VI of the Civil Rights Act of 1964) claiming that the state's environmental agency committed intentional discrimination against black and Hispanic persons by allowing a polluting facility to be built in an area largely populated by minority-group members.[94]

In the Spring of 2002, the Northern District of New York struck down the New York State Air Pollution Mitigation Law, which imposes a 100% financial penalty on the sale of pollution credits to polluters in other states. The state law, aimed at controlling acid rain, was held to violate the Supremacy and Commerce clauses of the Constitution by interfering with the federal CAA's regulatory scheme. Federal law preempted this state law because the state law interferes with the CAA's methodology for controlling pollution, and permits one state to control emissions in other states,[95] and the Second Circuit affirmed in 2003.

A citizen suit under the CAA is permitted when the EPA has failed to act, but the Sixth Circuit ruled that the federal court involved in a government CAA settlement can only impose stricter injunctive remedies if there has been an evident failure of enforcement.[96]

Because 40 CFR § 80.1045 [requirement that the EPA administrator propose requirements to control automobile emissions] imposes a non-discretionary duty, a citizen suit can be brought to enforce it.[97]

[A] Greenhouse Gases

It is now accepted that the Earth is undergoing climate changes, often referred to as "global warming," as a result of the emission of "greenhouse gases" that raise temperatures and cause other phenomena. By early 2007, over a dozen

---

[93] Clean Coalition v. TXU Power, 536 F.3d 469 (5th Cir. 2008). Coal-fired plants continued to be in the news in late 2008. EPA administrator Stephen L. Johnson ruled that permitting authorities cannot consider greenhouse gas outputs when utilities apply for permits for new coal-fired power plants. Johnson stated that there are sound policy reasons for not considering carbon dioxide a pollutant to be regulated in the permit process. *See* Matthew L. Wald and Felicity Barringer, *E.P.A. Ruling Could Speed Up Approval of Coal Plants*, N.Y. Times 12/19/08.

The D.C. Circuit reversed its earlier decision, and temporarily reinstated the Clean Air Interstate Rule, the administration's plan for reducing emissions from coal-fired power plants. The D.C. Circuit, holding that a temporary, flawed rule was better than no regulation at all, ordered the EPA to revise the rule but did not set a specific deadline. As a result of this decision, levels of nitrogen oxides must be reduced in 28 states starting January 2009, and sulfur dioxide must be reduced as of January 2010. *See* Felicity Barringer, *In Reversal, Court Allows a Bush Plan on Pollution*, N.Y. Times 12/24/08.

[94] South Camden Citizens in Action v. New Jersey Dep't of Envtl. Protection, 254 F. Supp. 2d 486 (D.N.J. 4/16/03).

[95] Clean Air Markets v. Pataki, 194 F. Supp. 2d 147 (N.D.N.Y. 2002), *aff'd*, 338 F.3d 82 (2d Cir. 2003).

[96] Ellis v. Gallatin Steel Co., 390 F.3d 461 (6th Cir. 2004).

[97] Sierra Club v. Leavitt, 355 F. Supp. 2d 544 (D.D.C. 2005).

lawsuits about global warming had been filed against public and private defendants, using various liability theories:

- Clean Air Act liability (*Massachusetts v. EPA*, 549 U.S. 497 (2007); see
  below
- Tort suits for nuisance, against power companies and automobile manufac-
  turers charged with contributing to global warming, e.g., California ex rel.
  Lockyer v. General Motors Corp., No. 3:2006 Civ. 05755-MJJ (9/20/06).
- NEPA's (42 USC 4321–4325) requirement that the federal government must
  assess the environmental impact of its decisions (*Friends of the Earth, Inc. v.
  Watson*, 2005 U.S. Dist. LEXIS 42335 (N.D. Cal. 2005), or state statutes
  imposing similar duties on state government
- Class actions: e.g., *Comer v. Nationwide Mutual Ins. Co.*, 2006 U.S. Dist.
  LEXIS 33123 (S.D. Miss. 2006), although federal preemption of state require-
  ments (e.g., emission standards) is a strong possibility (see, e.g., *Central Valley
  Chrysler-Jeep v. Witherspoon*, 456 F. Supp. 2d 1160 (E.D. Cal. 2006).

Arguments for the defense can include:

- characterizing climate change issues as nonjusticiable political issues; *Connecticut v. American Electric Power Co.*[98] was dismissed under this rationale
- denying that the plaintiffs have suffered particularized personal harm that can
  give rise to standing[99]
- challenging whether the defendant's actions are the proximate cause of the
  injuries asserted by plaintiffs — e.g., whether the defendant's small contribution to overall greenhouse gases can legitimately be blamed for damage.[100]

A suit brought in 2006 by the California Attorney General, charging
automobile companies with environmental harm caused by their vehicles, was
dismissed in 2007 by the Central District of California on the grounds that such
issues were properly resolved by the legislature. The state of California continued
to litigate global warming issues, arguing that its proximity to the Pacific put it at
greater risk from global warming than other states, and that its program has better
technical credentials than the federal one. A group of other states adopted the
California standards and sought to intervene on California's behalf. In November
of 2007, the Ninth Circuit held that the administration's fuel economy standards for
SUVs, minivans, and pickups were inadequate, because the standards failed to
explain why light trucks should be given more leeway than cars, when so many
light trucks are passenger rather than commercial vehicles. In December of 2007,

---

[98] 406 F. Supp. 2d 265 (S.D.N.Y. 2005).

[99] Korsinsky v. EPA, 2006 WL 2255110 (2d Cir. 2006).

[100] Stuart M. Feinblatt and Monique Cofer, *Is Global Warming a Hot New Litigation Frontier?*
N.J.L.J. 3/13/07 (law.com).

the Central District of California rejected auto industry arguments that only the EPA has the power to regulate carbon dioxide and other greenhouse gas emissions from cars. This decision cleared the way for California to impose tighter emissions standards for cars, SUVs, and pickup trucks for 2009 and later models, provided that a waiver is obtained from the EPA. However, the EPA denied the waiver on December 19, 2007, and California brought suit against the federal government to force the EPA to review its decision.[101]

The Attorneys General of Arizona, California, Connecticut, Delaware, Illinois, Iowa, Maine, Maryland, Minnesota, New Jersey, New Mexico, New York, Oregon, Rhode Island, Vermont, Washington, and officials from Pennsylvania, New York City, Baltimore, and the District of Columbia sued the EPA to force compliance with the Supreme Court ruling requiring action on global warming. The petition sought to have the D.C. Circuit order the EPA to act within 60 days. The EPA's argument was that it has done a thorough job of regulating all greenhouse gas emissions in a holistic manner, and it would be premature to make determinations about vehicle emissions.[102]

CAA § 202(a)(1) requires the EPA to issue emissions standards for any class of new motor vehicles which the EPA deems to contribute to air pollution in a manner reasonably anticipated to endanger public health. An "air pollutant" is defined as a physical or chemical air pollution agent emitted into ambient air. The EPA denied a petition by a group of private organizations who wanted the EPA to regulate emissions of carbon dioxide and three other greenhouse gases. The EPA refused, stating that it does not have authority under the CAA to issue mandatory regulations to address climate change. The agency did not believe that there is unequivocal proof that such gases created global warming, and opposed a piecemeal approach as contrary to the administration's comprehensive nonregulatory policy of seeking voluntary reductions.

In April 2007, the Supreme Court ruled that the petitioners had standing to challenge the EPA's denial of their rulemaking petition. The proper construction of a federal statute is an appropriate question for a federal court to resolve, and 42 USC § 7607(b)(1) authorizes such challenges. As long as there is one petitioner with standing, review is available of right without meeting standards for redressability and immediacy. Massachusetts, as a sovereign state owning territory that

---

[101] [No by-line], *EPA Justifies Its Decision to Deny California's Waiver*, Wall St. J. 3/1-2/08 at A2; Samantha Young (AP), *California Sues EPA Over Tailpipe Rules*, 1/3/08 (law.com); Central Valley Chrysler Jeep v. Goldstone, No. 04-6663 (E.D. Cal 2007), Cheryl Miller, *Federal Ruling Boosts California's Ability to Curb Auto Emissions*, The Recorder 12/13/07 (law.com); Paul Elias (AP), *9th Circuit Tosses Out New Federal Fuel Economy Standards*, 11/16/07 (law.com). Other states seeking to adopt the California rules include Connecticut, Maine, Maryland, New Jersey, New Mexico, New York, Oregon, Pennsylvania, Rhode Island, Vermont, and Washington. Cheryl Miller, *Federal Judge Tosses California's Global Warming Suit*, The Recorder 9/18/07 (law.com); Adam Liptak, *Suit Blaming Automakers Over Gases Is Dismissed*, N.Y. Times 9/18/07 at A18.

[102] Jay Lindsay (AP), *18 States Going to Court to Force EPA to Respond to Supreme Court Ruling on Global Warming*, 4/3/08 (law.com); *see* Ian Talley, *EPA to Further Push Back Action on CO2*, Wall St. J. 3/28/08 at A6 for background.

could be affected by rulemaking, had standing to challenge EPA actions. In general, an agency's refusal to start enforcement proceedings is not subject to judicial review — but there is a difference between refraining from enforcement and denying a rulemaking petition that was explicitly authorized by Congress.[103]

§ 11.06 RESOURCE CONSERVATION AND RECOVERY ACT

RCRA, as amended by the Hazardous and Solid Waste Amendments of 1984, imposes complete control over generation, transport, and disposal of "active" waste. "Solid waste" means all discarded material other than household refuse and industrial discharges that are otherwise subject to permit requirements; see RCRA Subtitle D, 42 USC §§ 6941–6949a and 40 CFR Parts 240–257. RCRA forbids states to permit the creation of additional open waste dumps and requires states to schedule closing or upgrades to existing open dumps.

"Hazardous waste" is solid waste which is a health risk because of its quantity, concentration, or nature (physical, chemical or infectious). (See 40 CFR Parts 264 and 266.) Also see § 11.03[D] for the Brownfields Act's exemption for household solid waste.

Generators and transporters are required to handle waste properly, and to report to the EPA on what they have done. RCRA also regulates "TSD" (treatment, storage, and disposal) facilities, which operate subject to permits issued by the EPA: 40 CFR Parts 264 and 265. The statute gives the EPA broad authority to inspect operations that generate hazardous waste.

A RCRA permit is not required if a facility accepts and burns only non-hazardous waste, but a Clean Air Act permit will be required for the emissions of such a facility, and the permit will have more stringent provisions if it is issued in a non-attainment area (one in which air quality standards are not met).

RCRA's "cradle to grave" tracking system requires everyone who transports hazardous waste to have an EPA registration number. Waste generators are obligated to package and label waste properly. Before shipment, they must confirm that the TSD facility is willing to accept the waste, and has the capacity to handle it properly. The generator has to fill out a four-part "manifest" that can be used to track the progress and eventual disposition of the waste.

Under 42 USC § 6973(a), the EPA can sue to enjoin the disposal of any waste (even if it is not hazardous) that may present an imminent and substantial danger to health or the environment. Anyone who contributed to the threat can be ordered to take any action necessary to abate the hazard, and fines can be imposed for non-compliance.

There is no RCRA statutory requirement for reporting spills, but EPA regulations at 40 CFR § 264.51 do require TSD facilities that handle hazardous waste to create a contingency plan and designate an emergency coordinator to

---

[103] Massachusetts v. EPA, 549 U.S. 497 (2007); *see, e.g.*, Tony Mauro, *High Court Orders EPA to Review Greenhouse-Gas Emissions*, Legal Times 4/3/07 (law.com).

notify the community if a spill, fire, or explosion at the facility endangers the community.

A 1988 RCRA amendment, the Medical Waste Tracking Act (P.L. 100-582), enacted at 42 USC §§ 6903 and 6992, covers New York, New Jersey, Connecticut, the area contiguous to the Great Lakes, and any other state or geographic region that opts in to coverage. The EPA Administrator has a duty to create programs to track the movements of medical waste from generators to disposal facilities. Shipments of medical waste must be appropriately labeled, handled, and stored. The EPA has the right to demand information about medical waste from any handler.

The EPA can revoke the operating permit of a facility that fails to comply with the terms of the permit (42 USC § 6928). The EPA can also issue a compliance order, or seek civil penalties (criminal penalties, for knowing failure to get a required permit, or knowing violation of permit requirements; the penalty increases if a knowing violation endangers the life of any person). The EPA can get a court order restraining disposition of hazardous or solid waste that may present an imminent and substantial danger to human health or to the environment. Violation of, or noncompliance with, such an order is punishable by a fine. 42 USC § 6972 permits citizen suits for violation of any RCRA permit, standard, regulation, or requirement.

According to the Tenth Circuit, the EPA can initiate a RCRA enforcement action even though a state with an approved RCRA program has initiated action on the same violation.[104]

[A] Citizen Suits

Under a 1996 Supreme Court decision,[105] the current owner of property cannot bring a RCRA citizen suit against a former owner to recover money spent to clean up a site that once was but no longer is imminently hazardous. The Court's rationale is that RCRA's citizen suit provision refers to "restraining" contamination posing "imminent and substantial endangerment," and the cleanup removed the risk.

In a RCRA suit by residential neighbors of a former Honeywell chemical plant site, the Third Circuit upheld the order to clean up, holding that the District Court was correct that the most recent remedial measures were inadequate, and that a permanent remedy should be implemented.[106]

The Seventh Circuit permitted a property owner to bring a RCRA suit prior to the investigation to require cleanup of contamination caused by a leaking underground storage tank on the adjacent property.[107] The court analyzed this as a conventional attempt to settle a claim.

---

[104] United States v. Power Eng'g Co., 125 F. Supp. 2d 1050 (D. Colo. 2000), aff'd, 303 F.3d 1232 (10th Cir. 2002).

[105] Meghrig v. KFC Western Inc., 516 U.S. 479 (1996).

[106] Interfaith Community Org. v. Honeywell Int'l, 399 F.3d 248 (3d Cir. 2005).

[107] Albany Bank & Trust Co. v. Exxon Mobil Co., 310 F.3d 969 (7th Cir. 2002).

On a related issue, the Eighth Circuit has decided that RCRA § 7002, the citizen suit provision, does not contain an implied private right of action for recovery of cleanup costs, and the District Court for the District of Oregon held that companies can't use RCRA to recover any costs for remedies that were in place, or substantially in place, before the citizen suit was filed.[108] A labor group made up of several unions had standing to apply for a RCRA injunction to have solid and hazardous waste cleaned up from sites where the group's members worked. The Second Circuit ruled that the group, if successful, would promote workplace safety, which is germane to the group's purpose. "Germaneness" merely requires that an organization's litigation goals be related to the group's nature and the reason for its members to associate.[109]

States can adopt solid-waste management standards that are more stringent than RCRA's minimum federal standards. But, once adopted, the standard becomes state law, and cannot be used as the premise for a RCRA citizen suit.[110]

[B] State Regulation of Solid Waste Disposal

A state's interest in solid waste within the state — especially solid waste coming from other states — is easy to understand. However, statutory distinctions drawn by the state between in-state and out-of-state wastes are likely to be challenged under the Commerce Clause.

To survive, a statute must address legitimate local concerns, and must have only a minor impact on interstate commerce. Regulating waste shipments (e.g., by requiring a certificate of public convenience and necessity) is probably permissible; forbidding waste shipments probably is not. Out-of-state waste handlers must be given a chance to compete for disposal business.[111] A 1994 Supreme Court decision[112] says that it is per se invalid to discriminate in favor of local business or investment, and against interstate commerce, unless that is the only way to advance the legitimate local interest. This decision builds on an earlier one[113] which holds that an ordinance can violate

---

[108] Furrer v. Brown, 62 F.3d 1092 (8th Cir. 1995); Express Car Wash Corp. v. Irinaga Brothers Inc., 967 F. Supp. 1188 (D. Ore. 1997).

[109] Building and Constr. Trades Council v. Downtown Dev. Inc., 448 F.3d 138 (2d Cir. 2006).

[110] Ashoff v. Ukiah, Cal., 130 F.3d 409 (9th Cir. 1997).

[111] National Solid Waste Management Ass'n v. Alabama Dep't of Envtl. Mgmt., 924 F.2d 1001 (11th Cir. 1990); Hunt v. Chemical Waste Management Inc., 584 So. 2d 1367 (Ala. Sup. 1991); National Solid Waste Management Ass'n v. Voinovich, 959 F.2d 590 (6th Cir. 1992); Waste Treatment Council v. State of S. Car., 945 F.2d 781 (4th Cir. 1991); Hazardous Waste Treatment Council v. Reilly, 938 F.2d 1390 (D.C. Cir. 1991); Government Suppliers Consolidating Servs. Inc. v. Bayh, 975 F.2d 1267 (7th Cir. 1992), Kleenwell Biohazard Waste v. Nelson, 48 F.3d 391 (9th Cir. 1995); Harvey & Harvey Inc. v. Chester County, Pa., 68 F.3d 788 (3d Cir. 1995); Gary D. Peake Excavating Inc. v. Town Bd. of Hancock, N.Y., 93 F.3d 68 (2d Cir. 1996).

[112] C & A Carbone v. Clarkstown, N.Y., 511 U.S. 383 (1994).

[113] Pike v. Bruce Church Inc., 397 U.S. 137 (1970); *see also* United Haulers Ass'n v. Oneida-Herkimer Solid Waste Mgmt. Auth., 261 F.3d 245 (2d Cir. 2001), applying the Pike balancing test to a flow control ordinance that requires delivery of all solid waste to a publicly owned facility.

the Commerce Clause even without overtly discriminating against interstate commerce, if the actual burden on interstate commerce clearly outweighs the local benefits.

The Tenth Circuit said that CERCLA preempts municipal zoning ordinances that prohibit maintenance of hazardous waste concentrations in areas zoned for industrial use.[114]

There have been several Supreme Court decisions on this subject. The Commerce Clause is violated by a state statute that forbids private landfill operators to accept refuse generated outside the county in which the disposal facility is located.[115]

In 2006, the Sixth Circuit ruled that a county ordinance, requiring haulers to deposit waste only at the county landfill or transfer station, violates the commerce clause by discriminating against out-of-state disposal sites, whereas the Second Circuit ruled that requirement of delivery to a publicly owned facility within the county was acceptable under the commerce clause, because the local benefits outweighed the modest burden on interstate commerce.[116]

The EPA did not exceed its authority by deciding that discharging Arkansas sewage would not cause a violation of the downstream water quality standards imposed in Oklahoma.[117] The Court has also ruled that higher processing charges for out-of-state wastes violate the Commerce Clause.[118]

§ 11.07   OTHER FEDERAL ENVIRONMENTAL LAWS

The first federal environmental law was the National Environmental Policy Act, 42 USC §§ 4321–4347. It declared that environmental protection was a national policy and that federal legislation and decisions about grants and permits must reflect concern for the environment. Title I of NEPA sets out general federal policy. Title II creates the Council on Environmental Quality, whose regulations appear at 40 CFR Part 1500 *et seq.*

NEPA requires all legislation and major federal actions "significantly affecting the quality of the human environment" to be preceded by an Environmental Impact Statement. Federal agencies must consider environmental impact throughout their processes of decision-making, although they need not prepare a final Environmental Impact Statement until they make a recommendation or report on a proposal.

The Toxic Substances Control Act of 1986, 15 USC §§ 2601–2629, gives the EPA the power to regulate all phases of chemical manufacture, processing, use and

---

[114] United States v. Denver, Colo., 100 F.3d 1509 (10th Cir. 1996).

[115] Fort Gratiot Sanitary Landfill v. Michigan Dep't of Natural Resources, 504 U.S. 970 (1992).

[116] *Cf.* National Solid Wastes Mgmt. Ass'n v. Daviess County, Ky., 434 F.3d 898 (6th Cir. 2006) with United Haulers Ass'n v. Oneida-Herkimer Solid Waste Mgmt. Auth., 438 F.3d 150 (2d Cir. 2006).

[117] Arkansas v. Oklahoma, 503 U.S. 91 (1992).

[118] Oregon Waste Sys. v. Department of Envtl. Quality of Ore., 511 U.S. 93 (1994).

disposal. The EPA can require testing of substances (even substances already in use) such as carcinogens or teratogens that present an unreasonable risk to health or the environment.

Manufacturers must give the EPA 90 days' notice before the introduction of a new chemical. If testing of the new substance discloses a risk, the EPA must take action proportionate to the risk, e.g., by mandating disclosure of the risk on the label, or limiting or even forbidding manufacture. The analysis is a risk-benefit analysis of both exposure (probability of harm) and effect (severity of harm). TSCA requires the "responsible party" to give notification to the EPA of PCB spills that contaminate water.

The Emergency Planning and Community Right to Know Act (EPCRA) is designed to cope with the situation in which extremely hazardous materials are spilled into water or air: see 42 USC § 11004 *et seq.* and 40 CFR Part 355. The owner or operator of the facility is obligated to notify the state and/or local emergency planning committee when an unexpected release, not covered by a permit, occurs. Immediate notice by telephone, backed up by written notice, is required, disclosing the substance identified, how much was released, when the release occurred and how long it lasted, what the health risks are, and suggested emergency measures the community can undertake.

The D.C. Circuit held that methyl ethyl ketone is not a "toxic" chemical under the EPCRA because, although it contributes to the formation of another harmful chemical, in low doses it is not harmful in itself. Therefore, the EPA's decision to keep the chemical on the Toxic Release Inventory List was not entitled to deference.[119]

A coalition of 12 states sued the EPA for cutting back on regulations about reporting of the use, storage, and release of toxic chemicals. A suit was filed in late 2007 in the Southern District of New York to restore the reporting requirements formerly imposed under the Toxics Release Inventory program created in 1986 after the Bhopal chemical disaster. The EPA rules allow a company to file the less detailed short form for a storage or release of less than 5,000 pounds of toxic chemicals. The prior rules required filing of the long form at the 500-pound level.[120]

The Federal Insecticide, Fungicide and Rodenticide Act (FIFRA), 7 USC § 136, preempts state regulation of these substances (including state regulation of packaging and labeling).[121] FIFRA creates a uniform federal procedure for clearing new substances before they can be marketed, and for surveillance of substances already on the market to prevent unreasonable risks to human health or the environment. The EPA published a Final Rule forbidding pesticide testing

---

[119] American Chemistry Council v. Johnson, 406 F.3d 738 (D.C. Cir. 2005).

[120] Anthony DePalma, *E.P.A. Is Sued By 12 States Over Reports on Chemicals,* N.Y. Times 11/29/07 at A25. The 12 states are Arizona, California, Connecticut, Illinois, Maine, Massachusetts, Minnesota, New Hampshire, New Jersey, New York, Pennsylvania, and Vermont.

[121] *But see* Wisconsin Public Intervenor v. Mortier, 501 U.S. 597 (1991) holding that FIFRA does not preempt regulation of pesticides by local government.

that intentionally exposes children or pregnant women to pesticides. Under the ethical standards for testing of other human subjects in studies prepared for submission to the EPA, the subjects must be fully aware of test risks. Pesticide researchers must submit the design for EPA review before the testing begins.[122]

The Ninth Circuit mandated that the Nuclear Regulatory Commission consider the potential danger of terrorist activity before approving a spent fuel storage facility at a nuclear power plant. The NRC's environmental analysis omitted this factor on the grounds that it is a sensitive national security issue, and the risk could not be accurately calculated in any event. The Ninth Circuit, noting that there is a federal Office of Nuclear Security and Incident Response, required consideration of terrorism risk.[123]

The Endangered Species Act, 16 USC §§ 1531–1544 protects plants, animals, and habitats. Plaintiffs who bring citizen suits against the government for violation of the procedures of the Endangered Species Act must assert an interest in preserving the species. Therefore, ranchers and irrigation districts do not have standing.[124]

The District Court issued an injunction forbidding further planting of genetically engineered alfalfa pending the preparation of an environmental impact statement by the Department of Agriculture Animal and Plant Health Inspection Service. The injunction was sought by conventional alfalfa-seed farms and environmental groups concerned that conventional alfalfa would be cross-pollinated by the genetically modified crop. Some customers (e.g., organic farmers and non-U.S. customers opposed to genetic engineering) would not be willing to buy alfalfa that cannot be guaranteed free of genetic modification. The Ninth Circuit upheld the District Court, using an abuse of discretion standard. The District Court held a hearing on the nature of the violation and two hearings on the scope of injunctive relief. The injunction was limited to the time needed to prepare the environmental impact statement, and farmers who had already invested in the seed were allowed to plant, grow, and harvest it.[125]

The Fourth Circuit refused to grant a tobacco industry petition for judicial review of the EPA study classifying second-hand smoke as a known carcinogen. The Fourth Circuit's rationale was that the study is not a "final agency action" subject to review under the Administrative Procedures Act. The study was ordered under federal legislation, the Radon Gas and Indoor Air Quality Research Act, but the statute provides that the report has no regulatory effect or direct legal impact on third parties.[126]

---

[122] Final Rule, http://www.epa.gov/oppfead1/guidance/human-test.htm 1/26; *see* 74 LW 2439.

[123] San Luis Obispo Mothers for Peace v. Nuclear Regulatory Comm'n, 449 F.3d 1016 (9th Cir. 2006).

[124] Bennett v. Plenert, 63 F.3d 915 (9th Cir. 1995).

[125] Geertson Seed Farms v. Monsanto, No. 07-16458 (9th Cir. 9/2/08).

[126] Flue-Cured Tobacco Coop. Stabilization Corp. v. EPA, 313 F.3d 852 (4th Cir. 2002).

[A] Asbestos Control

Asbestos is regulated under several federal statutes, including OSHA. The Asbestos Hazard Emergency Response Act of 1986 (AHERA), P.L. 99-579, 20 USC § 4011 *et seq.*, is Title III of the Toxic Substances Control Act (see above). AHERA's application is limited to schools, where the EPA must inspect and set up abatement programs to control asbestos.

Nearly all the states have their own, broader asbestos programs, usually calling for inspection of all types of buildings to detect asbestos, and regulating operations for removal and disposal. Regulations have been adopted under TSCA (40 CFR Part 763, Subpart I) to phase out the manufacture, importation, processing, distribution, and other commercial use of asbestos.

Given the recognized dangers of asbestos, it is understandable that many building owners seek to remove asbestos that is in place — but also understandable that improper removal actions generate further hazards. See 40 CFR Part 763 and OSHA regulations at 29 CFR § 1926.58 for standards for proper abatement.

The National Emission Standards for Hazardous Air Pollutants (NESHAP) require completion of Waste Shipment Records whenever asbestos waste is transported or disposed of. The asbestos materials must be wet during shipment (to prevent dispersion of fibers). The material must be sealed in leak-proof containers labeled with the name of the waste generator and the location where the waste was generated.

Transportation of asbestos is also governed by 49 USC §§ 1801–1819 and Department of Transportation regulations (49 CFR Parts 172, 173) dealing with transportation of hazardous materials. Containers must be transported in a way that keeps them intact and prevents asbestos fibers from escaping.

The owner or operator of an active waste disposal site that receives asbestos-containing waste either must ensure that no visible asbestos fibers appear, or must have an acceptable procedure for suppressing the dust each day.

Building owners must give the EPA at least 10 days' written notice of intent to demolish a structure that contains RACM (regulated asbestos-containing materials).

§ 11.08   ENVIRONMENTAL CLASS ACTIONS

[NOTE: See § 22.09[E][5] for discussion of the Class Action Fairness Act (CAFA) and the extent to which it permits defendants to remove state class actions to federal court.] For example, an environmental exposure suit could not be remanded to state court under the Class Action Fairness Act's "local controversy" exception to the rule of federal jurisdiction. The plaintiffs failed to prove that more than two-thirds of the plaintiffs were Alabama citizens, and also failed to prove that the defendant they singled out really was significant.[127]

---

[127] Evans v. Walter Indus. Inc., 449 F.3d 1159 (11th Cir. 2006).

The Supreme Court found class action certification inappropriate for settlement of current and future asbestos claims. Absentees were not properly represented. Potential class members were not similar enough in their exposure to asbestos. The interests of already injured individuals (seeking current compensation) conflict with those of individuals who have been exposed to asbestos but who have not manifested injury (and who want funds retained for later claims).[128] The Supreme Court deemed the "sprawling" putative class to be unworkable, but did not rule on whether the exposure-only claimants have standing to sue.

In 1999, the Supreme Court returned to the subject of asbestos class actions,[129] striking down a global settlement of asbestos-related claims against a vinyl siding manufacturer. To the Court, if the amount of money available for a settlement is limited, the proponents of the settlement must prove the practical or other extra-contractual limitations. The process for allocating proceeds among the claimants must address any conflicting interests within the plaintiff class.

§ 11.09 ENVIRONMENTAL TAX ISSUES

The Taxpayer Relief Act of 1997 enacted a rule, permitting qualified brownfields cleanup costs paid or incurred before December 31, 2000 to be deducted currently if the taxpayer elects to expense them. (The costs must be capitalized if the taxpayer does not make this election.) Only the costs of cleaning up hazardous substances, as defined by CERCLA, at qualified contaminated sites, are deductible. When the property is sold, any gain attributable to the cleanup cost deduction is treated as ordinary income.

The Fourth Circuit ruled in 2000 that environmental remediation costs of the taxpayer's real property were "permanent improvements," in that they make the land safe for a broader range of uses. Therefore, the costs had to be capitalized and not deducted as ordinary and necessary business expenses.[130]

According to a late 2001 Sixth Circuit decision, cleaning up soil contamination caused by the prior owner of a property must also be capitalized, in that the taxpayer did not contaminate the property in the ordinary course of business, and the clean-up permits new uses of the property rather than merely restoring its former condition.[131]

A 2005 Revenue Ruling says that the cleanup costs of an employer that contaminated its own land must be capitalized, not deducted. Like repair costs, they must be allocated to inventory produced during the tax year in which the costs were incurred.[132]

---

[128] Amchem Prods. Inc. v. Windsor, 521 U.S. 591 (1997).

[129] Ortiz v. Fibreboard, 527 U.S. 815 (1999).

[130] Dominion Resources, Inc. v. United States, 219 F.3d 359 (4th Cir. 2000).

[131] United Dairy Farmers Inc. v. United States, 267 F.3d 510 (6th Cir. 2001).

[132] Rev. Rul. 2005-42, 2005-28 IRB 67.

Also note that the Working Families Tax Relief Act of 2004, P.L. 108-311, allows environmental remediation costs paid or incurred after 2003 and before 2006 to be expensed.

As an incentive for taxpayers to settle with the EPA for site cleanup funds in long-running cases, the Tax Increase Prevention and Reconciliation Act (TIPRA; P.L. 109-222) grants relief from federal income tax on certain settlement funds received under consent decrees reached after TIPRA's enactment but before January 1, 2011.

Chapter 12

Intellectual Property

§ 12.01 INTRODUCTION

Whether our society is viewed as an industrial one, or a post-industrial one, intellectual property law plays a vital role in furthering creativity by ensuring that inventors, artists, and other creators will be able to profit from developing their work, free of infringement.

Intellectual property includes copyright, trademark, trade secret, and patent law, although in an individual case overlapping claims may be raised. Many of the most critical intellectual property issues currently under review and development involve computers and the Internet; see § 28.06.

§ 12.02 SHRINK-WRAP AND CLICKWRAP LICENSES

A shrink-wrap license, containing terms imposed by the seller of software, is so-called because it appears inside a software package, or on the package itself. A clickwrap license functions similarly for a Web site.

Although both shrink-wrap and clickwrap agreements have been found to be valid and enforceable,[1] such agreements have often been challenged as contracts of adhesion, or as insufficiently conspicuous.

---

[1] Zeidenberg v. ProCD, 86 F.3d 1447 (7th Cir. 1996); followed in, *e.g.*, M.A. Mortenson Co. v. Timberline Software Co., 998 P.2d 305 (Wash. 2000).

The Eastern District of New York ruled that the forum selection clause in an ISP's Terms of Service was not unconscionable merely because it appeared some 300 lines into the document. (Only about 10 lines were visible on screen at any one time.) The clause passed muster because: its language was not unconscionable; the typeface was readable; and no steps were taken to prevent users from reading the entire seven-and-a-half page document.[2]

§ 12.03 COPYRIGHT

The current law, 17 USC § 101 *et seq.*, derives from revisions and amendments to the 1978 Copyright Act, P.L. 94-553. Since 1988, the United States has been one of the signatories to the Berne Convention, dealing with international copyright protection. See below for 1998 copyright legislation; see § 12.03[K] for a discussion of copyright issues in the Internet world.

The Family Entertainment and Copyright Act of 2005, P.L. 109-9, provides that it is not illegal to use filtering technology without the consent of the copyright owner of the underlying property to produce family-friendly versions of a film, nor are licensing fees charged for this function. However, the edited version is not granted copyrighted protection. The statute also imposes a penalty for bootleg filming of theatrical films and for distributing movies or music before the official release date.

The first conviction under the Family and Entertainment Copyright Act was handed down by the Central District of California in 2006.[3]

In mid-2006, the District Court for the District of Colorado ruled that it is not fair use to sell or rent censored DVDs, thus granting the injunction sought by Hollywood studios and directors. In this interpretation, editing out content that the editor finds offensive does not constitute transformative fair use, because that would require adding something rather than merely deleting part of the original content. Although the Family Entertainment and Copyright Act amends 17 USC § 110 to permit editing of movies by private households as long as no fixed copy is made, the defendant in this case did make and sell fixed copies.[4]

Rules were proposed in mid-2005 for pre-registering works that are at risk of infringement even before their public release, using the electronic Form PRE. The intent is to protect them immediately as published works. The rules implement the Artists' Rights and Theft Prevention Act (ART Act). New penalties were imposed for infringement that occurs before authorized commercial distribution — for

---

[2] Novak v. Overture Servs. Inc., 309 F. Supp. 2d 446 (E.D.N.Y. 2004).

[3] United States v. Sandoval, No. 06cr00054 (C.D. Cal. 2006), discussed in Amanda Bronstad, *Anti-Piracy Law Gets First Tryout*, Nat'l L.J. 5/4/06 (law.com); *see also* United States v. Salisbury, No. 05cr00505 (N.D. Cal), United States v. Thomas, No. 06cr00033 (M.D. Tenn.). United States v. Hoaglin, No. 05cr01001 (C.D. Cal.) was resolved via a guilty plea.

[4] Clean Flicks of Colo. LLC v. Soderbergh, 75 LW 1053 (D. Colo. 7/6/06).

example, when movies are made available on the Internet before their release. Pre-registration is effective as long as the copyright owner completes the registration within three months after publication, or one month of discovering the infringement. The rules apply to unpublished works in the process of being prepared for commercial distribution, where there is a distribution agreement in place with an established distributor. Works are covered if they fall into a class identified by the Register of Copyrights as vulnerable to pre-release infringement. Sound recordings, music works embodied in sound recordings, and motion pictures have been identified as vulnerable classes. (However, films that are supposed to be limited to online or direct-to-video distribution are not covered.)[5]

Copyright is often and productively described as a "bundle of rights." Creation of a copyrightable work generates several legal rights. The rights can be donated, sold, or assigned independently. The end result is that someone who wants to use or adapt a copyright work (especially one that has been in existence for some time, or has been exploited in several media) may have to deal with several owners of various rights — and the threshold determination of who owns which right can be quite difficult.

The bundle of rights comes into being when a work of authorship is completed. Registration is valuable evidence of copyright, but all unpublished works are automatically entitled to copyright protection. If a work is published without copyright notice, the copyright proprietor's remedies in case of infringement will be limited, but the work will not be deprived of copyright protection. (Copyright notice does, however, preclude a defense of innocent infringement.)

[A] Scope of Copyright Law

Copyright applies to the expression of ideas in written, musical, visual, filmed, or similar form. Ideas are not copyrightable; neither are phrases or the titles of songs, films, books, etc. (However, deliberately deceptive use of an existing title may constitute unfair competition.) To be entitled to copyright, there must be a "work of authorship" that is fixed in tangible form.

17 USC § 102 gives a non-exclusive list of works of authorship that can be copyrighted:

- Literary works
- Musical works
- Dramatic works
- Pantomimes and choreographic works
- Pictorial, graphic, and sculptural works
- Audiovisual works (this is the category that includes motion pictures)
- Sound recordings
- Architectural works

---

[5] 37 CFR § 202.16.

[1] The Bundle of Rights

The copyright holder is entitled, under 17 USC § 106, to exclusive use of the copyrighted material, including reproduction of the works in any manner; preparation of derivative works;[6] transfer of ownership;[7] and public performance or display. These powers are sometimes called the "bundle of rights" controlled by the copyright holder; they can be transferred together or separately.

Therefore, it is a copyright violation to create new works of authorship using the characters of copyrighted works without permission, even if new plots are devised, or different media (e.g., making a video based on a comic strip) are used.

The copyright holder has the right to sell, rent, or lease copies of the work to the public. However, this is modified by § 109(a), the "first sale" doctrine, which allows the owner of a lawfully acquired copy, manufactured in the United States, of a copyrighted work, to use it as he or she pleases. In *Quality King Distributors, Inc. v. L'Anza Research Int'l Inc.*,[8] the Supreme Court extended the first sale doctrine to imported copies (gray market goods).

The first sale doctrine is what makes it possible for a library to lend copyrighted books, or a video store to rent copyrighted videocassettes without violating the Copyright Act — or, indeed, paying royalties. However, the Computer Software Rental Amendments Act of 1990, P.L. 101-650, enacted at 17 USC § 109(b), creates an exception. Nonprofit libraries and educational institutions can lend and lease copies of software and phonorecords, but for-profit businesses are not permitted to do so.

In a case of first impression, the Sixth Circuit held that the record-rental exception to the first-sale doctrine (17 USC § 109(b)(1)(A)) applies only to sound recordings and not to audiobooks. Thus, copyright infringement claims, but not trademark infringement claims, should have been dismissed when a competitor

---

[6] A derivative work is a separate work, that can itself be copyrighted, that recasts, transforms, or adapts an underlying work.

[7] Note that copyright registration, rather than filing of a UCC-1 statement, is the only manner in which a security interest in the copyright of a film can be registered: National Peregrine Inc. v. Capitol Federal S&L Ass'n of Denver, 116 B.R. 194 (C.D. Cal. 1990).

[8] 523 U.S. 135 (1998). The U.S. International Trade Commission forbade the importation of the European version of the John Deere forage harvester on the grounds of trademark infringement. (19 USC § 1337 gives the ITC the power to prevent importation of goods that would violate the Lanham Act if sold in the United States.) The test of gray market goods is not whether the mark was validly affixed, but whether the foreign and domestic products are materially different — even if both are manufactured in the U.S. In this context, material difference merely means that consumers would be likely to consider the differences significant to the purchase decision, with the result that the goodwill of the domestic product could be eroded. Bourdeau Bros. Inc. v. Int'l Trade Comm'n and Deere & Co., 444 F.3d 1317 (Fed. Cir. 2006). The Ninth Circuit ruled that the first sale doctrine is not available as a defense when legitimate products are purchased on the gray market and imported into the United States without consent of the trademark holder. (Costco sold authentic imported Omega watches whose design was copyrighted, without Omega's consent.) According to the Ninth Circuit, this did not conflict with *L'Anza*, because L'Anza deals with domestically manufactured copies: Omega S.A. v. Costco Wholesale Corp., 541 F.3d 982 (9th Cir. 2008).

re-packaged and re-labeled licensed audiobooks and rented them out under the authorized publisher's trademark. Under trademark law, the first sale exception says there is no confusion when a genuine article is sold under its true mark. There are two exceptions for resale items: when there is inadequate notice of repackaging, and when the alleged infringer sells goods that are materially different from those sold under the same trademark by the trademark owner.[9]

European law provides for a generalized "droit morale" (right of a creator to prevent distortion of his or her work, and to share in appreciation in its value). This concept has not been adopted in full form in U.S. law, but the Visual Artists Rights Act extends limited protection to works for visual art (other than works made for hire). The artist's "right of attribution" allows the artist either to claim authorship or have his or her name removed from work he or she did not create or that has been mutilated or distorted. The "right of integrity" permits the artist to prevent intentional distortions of original works in a manner prejudicial to the artist. The Visual Artists Rights Act does not give the creator of a site-specific work the right to prevent the work from being moved, although the statute does refer to the "placement" of the work. The First Circuit affirmed summary judgment for a real estate company that was sued under VARA by the artist when the artwork was removed, because by its terms, VARA does not apply to site-specific artworks.[10]

The Supreme Court refused to accept publishers' contention that articles that are part of a collective work (such as a newspaper or magazine) can be placed in an online database without either the consent of the author or prior grant of electronic rights. The court did not agree with the theory that inclusion in the database is a mere revision of the collective work that can be performed unilaterally by the publisher.[11]

National Geographic's publication of a CD edition, containing articles and photographs originally published in magazine form, was challenged by photographers in both the Second and Eleventh Circuits. In *Greenberg I*, the Eleventh Circuit held that the digital compilation was not privileged under Copyright Act § 201(c): considering the replica issues plus the computer program and an introductory sequence, the compilation was a new product in a new medium, not a mere reproduction. *Tasini* held that 201(c) does not apply when works are removed from their original context.

In light of *Tasini*, the Second Circuit affirmed the Southern District of New York's grant of summary judgment for National Geographic in a copyright case about the CD edition brought by a freelance photographer. In *Greenberg II*, the Eleventh Circuit said that *Tasini* created a new framework for analyzing the § 201(c) privilege: whether the revision preserves the original context of the collective work. In this case, the articles were presented in their original context, albeit with a few seconds of added video material. The Eleventh Circuit said that

---

[9] Brilliance Audio Inc. v. Haights Cross Communications, Inc., 474 F.3d 365 (6th Cir. 2007).
[10] Phillips v. Pembroke Real Estate Inc., 459 F.3d 128 (1st Cir. 2006).
[11] New York Times Co. v. Tasini, 533 U.S. 483 (2001).

the minimal amount of video clips did not outweigh the 1,200 issues of the magazine. Hence, National Geographic was not liable for infringement of the cover photograph of the 1962 issue as photographed by Greenberg.[12] The case returned to the Eleventh Circuit in 2008, once again resulting in victory for National Geographic, on the grounds that a freelancer's work can legitimately be reproduced in a reprint of the original collective work the freelancer contributed to; a revision of the collective work; or a later collective work in the same series. However, reproduction in a new work would be infringing. The Eleventh Circuit said that in this case, unlike *Tasini*, the complete magazine was reproduced in its original form. Adding operating software and search capability did not add enough new material to turn the Complete National Geographic into a new copyrightable collective work.[13]

The Southern District of New York certified a class of freelance writers, and approved a settlement of their copyright infringement claims stemming from unauthorized use of their works in online databases. Three ongoing class actions were suspended pending resolution of *Tasini*; after it was decided, the three actions were revived and consolidated with a fourth similar action. However, in late 2007, the Second Circuit vacated class certification and approval of the settlement — § 411(a) of the Copyright Act makes registration of copyright jurisdictional, and most of the works in question were unregistered.[14]

Under Copyright Act § 204(a), transfer of the exclusive rights to reproduce, publish, display, etc., must be in writing. However, a non-exclusive license can be granted orally or even by implication. The Ninth Circuit view is that the existence of an implied grant is a state-law question; state law is used to fill gaps in the federal law.[15]

The exclusive licensee of a copyright must have the consent of the licensor to assign license rights, unless the license itself explicitly authorizes assignment.[16] According to the Third Circuit, a Chapter 11 debtor was entitled to royalties under an intellectual property licensing agreement even after having sold the underlying intellectual property. (The new owner obtained the debtor's assets but rejected the

---

[12] Greenberg v. National Geographic Society, 488 F.3d 1331 (11th Cir. 2007).

[13] Greenberg v. National Geographic Society, 488 F.3d 1331 (11th Cir. 2008); *see* R. Robin McDonald, *11th Circuit Sides With National Geographic in Copyright Case*, Fulton County Daily Report 7/2/08 (law.com) and *1976 Copyright Law Meets 21st Century in Case Before 11th Circuit*, Fulton County Daily Report 2/27/08 (law.com). Certiorari was denied in December, 2008: No. 08-428.

[14] *In re* Literary Works in Electronic Databases Litigation, 509 F.3d 116 (2d Cir. 2007). *See also* Well-Made Toy Mfg. Corp. v. Goffa Int'l Corp., 354 F.3d 112 (2d Cir. 2003) on the jurisdictional status of copyright registration.

[15] Foad Consulting Group Inc. v. Musil Govan Azzalino, 270 F.3d 821 (9th Cir. 2001). *See also* 68 FR 16958 (4/8/03) for the Copyright Office's Final Rule on termination of authors' grants of licenses or transfers, effective January 1, 2003. Under the amended version of 17 CFR § 201.10(b)(1)(i), the notice of termination must specify whether termination occurs under 17 USC § 304(c) or 304(d).

[16] Gardner v. Nike Inc., 279 F.3d 774 (9th Cir. 2002).

licensing agreement). The rejection severed the right to royalties from ownership of the intellectual property.[17]

The developer of computer code that he made available for free public download subject to an open source license sued commercial software developers for putting his code into one of their software packages without obeying the license terms. The Federal Circuit held that merely because no money is charged for an open source license does not mean that there is no economic consideration. Consideration is present in the form of, e.g., enhanced market share and reputation. The question in this case was whether the license terms were conditions of, or merely covenants to, the license. In general, a copyright owner who grants a nonexclusive license waives the right to sue for infringement, and can sue only for breach of contract, but suit for infringement is possible when the licensee acts outside the scope of a limited license. In this case, the Federal Circuit noted that the license stated on its face that it imposed conditions on the right to modify and distribute the software (decoder chips for controlling model trains). The limitations furthered goals such as increasing traffic at the open source Web page and informing users about new developments. The Ninth Circuit remanded the case for determination of the propriety of an injunction against usage contrary to the license.[18]

The Tax Increase Prevention and Reconciliation Act (TIPRA; P.L. 109-222) permits writers of music to treat the sale or exchange of compositions or copyrights in musical works as the sale or exchange of capital assets. This provision is effective in tax years beginning after TIPRA's enactment and before January 1, 2011. A qualified financial sponsor of a songwriter can amortize certain expenses incurred on a music composition over five years, if the composition is placed into service after December 1, 2005 and before January 1, 2011. This is an exception to the general rule of IRC § 1221(3)(C) that copyrights, artistic compositions, and literary and musical properties owned by their creator are ordinary, not capital, assets.

In Louisiana, the economic benefit of a copyrighted work is community property that can be divided in a divorce proceeding. The Copyright Act does not preempt state law because this is a matter of family law — a traditional state purview — not intellectual property law where federal law must prevail.[19]

[2] Preemption

Certain subjects are deemed to be so inherently federal in their nature that state regulation is preempted, and some aspects of copyright law fall within this category.

---

[17] Schlumberger Resource Mgmt. Servs. Inc. v. Cell Net Data Sys. Inc., 327 F.3d 242 (3d Cir. 2003).

[18] Jacobsen v. Katzer and Kamind Assocs, 535 F.3d 1373 (Fed. Cir. 2008). For the principle that nonexclusive license waives infringement, *see* Sun Microsystems Inc. v. Microsoft Corp., 188 F.3d 1115 (9th Cir. 1999).

[19] Rodrigue v. Rodrigue, 218 F.3d 432 (5th Cir. 2000).

The California Court of Appeals decided in February 2000 that state law claims can be maintained for misappropriation of a person's likeness and image, when photographs are used on the Internet without consent of the subjects, despite the defendants' argument that federal copyright law preempts such state court claims. But the decision[20] said that the likeness itself is not subject to copyright, even if it is embodied in a copyrighted photograph. The tort here is misappropriation of the image (by placing it on a Web site). The cause of action can be maintained whether or not the individual whose image is used is a celebrity.

Copyright Act § 106 does not preempt an Illinois state-law right of publicity claim (arising out of the continued use of a model's photograph on product packaging after the contract expired). The state-law cause of action does not deal with a particular photographic or other image, but with the plaintiff's identity, which cannot be fixed in a tangible medium of expression. The validity of the copyright on the packaging was irrelevant to the right of publicity claim.[21]

State-court claims by musicians, alleging that a music producer and the distributor of audio recordings violated their right of publicity are not preempted by the Copyright Act. An individual's name and likeness cannot be copyrighted, and the state misappropriation tort does not conflict with federal copyright law. The state tort deals with the persona of the artist, which is outside copyright law. Preemption exists only when the content of the protected right falls within the subject matter of copyright, and the state law right purports to cover any of the exclusive rights under the federal copyright statute.[22]

About a dozen states have Truth In Music Advertising Acts, forbidding the use of a band name by performers who were not in the original band. Tribute bands are exempt, as are valid licensees of band trademarks, and groups with at least one original member of the band who retains the legal right to use the band name.[23]

According to the Ninth Circuit, perfection of, and priority in, security interests in unregistered copyrights are governed by state, not federal law. In this area, the Copyright Act does not preempt the UCC.[24]

[3] URAA

The Uruguay Round Amendments Act (URAA) P.L. 103-465 § 514 (enacted at 17 USC §§ 104A and 109), which implements Berne Convention Article 18, copyrights various kinds of work that have fallen into the public domain. The D.C. Circuit upheld the constitutionality of the statute against a challenge that it violated the Copyright and Patent Clause.[25]

---

[20] KNB Enters. v. Matthews, 78 Cal. App. 4th 362 (Cal. App. 2000).

[21] Toney v. L'Oreal, 400 F.3d 964 (7th Cir. 2005).

[22] Brown v. Ames, 201 F.3d 654 (5th Cir. 2000).

[23] Cheryl Miller, *California Considering Legislation to Ban 'Imposter Bands,'* The Recorder 6/18/07 (law.com).

[24] Aerocon Eng'g Inc. v. Silicon Valley Bank, 303 F.3d 1120 (9th Cir. 2002).

[25] Lucks Music Library, Inc. and Moviecraft, Inc. v. Gonzalez, 407 F.3d 1262 (D.C. Cir. 2005); *semble* Golan v. Gonzalez, 2005 Westlaw 914754 (D. Colo. 4/20/05).

In 2007, the Second Circuit affirmed the grant of a preliminary injunction to prevent infringement of a copyright restored under § 104A for "troll dolls" that fell into the public domain because of some sales without copyright notice.[26]

[B] Copyrightable Subject Matter

To be entitled to a patent, an invention must be unique and non-obvious in light of existing technology. This standard is much higher than the copyright standard, which requires originality, but only a small amount of it.

Under U.S. law, the "sweat of the brow" theory does not apply. That is, even if a good deal of effort or expense is needed to compile a database or other collection of factual information, a mere compilation of facts is probably entitled to minimal, if any, copyright protection. For instance, a telephone book is not copyrightable, so a competitor's use of the listings to prepare its own directory was held not to constitute infringement.[27] The "merger doctrine" says that form and expression merge if there is only one way to say something. But the Northern District of Illinois refused to apply this doctrine to model building code provisions. The guidelines were not a mere recipe lacking in expressive elements; a competitor could not justify copying of language and tables via the merger doctrine.[28]

It should be noted that the European Union affords significantly greater protection to information compilations, including computer databases, and that this legal disparity is likely to create significant difficulties with respect to databases that can be accessed over the Internet.

When a work of authorship is copyrighted, only the expression is protected, not the idea, procedure, process, etc. that is embodied in the work.

Government publications may not be copyrighted, but the government can hold and receive copyrights transferred by assignments.

Clearly, reports of jury verdicts are in the public domain. The Eleventh Circuit ruled that the Copyright Act preempts state law claims by a legal publisher alleging unfair competition and deceptive trade practices relating to the use of information from the jury verdict reports. The federal law preempts the state law because compilations of fact fall within the subject matter of copyright, and the plaintiff sought to protect copyright rights.[29]

Building blueprints have always been copyrightable. The Architectural Works Protection Act, effective 12/1/90, also permits copyrighting the actual building. The New York Mercantile Exchange (NYMEX) could not enforce a copyright in the settlement prices it produces to value customers' open stock

---

[26] Troll Company v. Uneeda Doll Co., 483 F.3d 150 (2d Cir. 2007). *See, e.g.*, Alameda Films v. AARC, 331 F.3d 472 (5th Cir. 2003) (decision favorable to a group of Mexican copyright holders who sued over the copyright of 88 Mexican films distributed in the United States).

[27] Feist Publ'rs Inc. v. Rural Tel. Serv. Co., 499 U.S. 340 (1991). *See also* Bell South Advertising & Publ'g Corp. v. Donnelley Info. Publ'g Inc., 977 F.2d 1435 (11th Cir. 1993).

[28] International Code Council Inc. v. National Fire Protection Ass'n, 74 LW 1617 (N.D. Ill. 3/27/06).

[29] Lipscher v. LRP Publ'ns Inc., 266 F.3d 1305 (11th Cir. 2001).

positions to determine if they must meet margin calls. The Second Circuit did not resolve the question of whether the prices are created by NYMEX, but held that enforcing a copyright would protect the idea itself rather than expression: facts are discovered, not created, so they cannot be copyrighted. Furthermore, the merger doctrine precludes a copyright where there are so few ways to express an idea that allowing a copyright would, in effect, protect the underlying idea itself.[30]

[C] Music Recording Rights

P.L. 104-39, the Digital Performance Right in Sound Recordings Act of 1995, amends 17 USC §§ 106 and 114. Creators and performers of music do not have a comprehensive right to control public performance, but they do have a narrow performance right dealing with certain digital transmissions of sound recordings.

One of the most contentious issues is how to control music copyrights when it is so easy to download music files from the Internet.

In 2004, the Ninth Circuit ruled in favor of a peer-to-peer file sharing service, on the grounds that there was no central location at which files could be policed, and that the software was amendable to substantial non-infringing use. Then, in mid-2005, the Supreme Court reversed, holding that the distributor of a device — even one for which lawful use is possible — is liable for third-party infringement if there are clear expressions of intent or affirmative steps to foster infringement. Mere distribution with knowledge of third-party actions is insufficient to create liability. In this case, the defendant announced its intention to provide service to former users of Napster. No filters or other means were used to limit infringement. The service's profitability depended on achieving a heavy volume of traffic to view the advertisements on the site. Grokster took an active role, encouraging use of its software to download copyrighted files.[31]

Using file sharing software to download copyrighted music to a personal computer is not fair use. The Seventh Circuit rejected the defendant's argument that she was engaging in permissible time-shifting or sampling music to decide what to purchase. She retained copies of the music, so she was not shifting a single listening to a more convenient time. Nor did she use any of the many sites where legal downloads were available. The Seventh Circuit upheld the District Court's award of $22,500 ($750 for each of the 30 works that were copied), rejecting her argument that the statutory minimum damages of $200 for innocent infringement should apply — the copies that she had access to carried a copyright notice.[32]

After four years of litigation over music downloads, the RIAA won a jury case of willful copyright infringement. The jury ordered downloader Jammie Thomas to pay $220,000 ($9,250 for each of 24 works placed on a file-sharing network). Over 26,000 suits have been filed since 2003; this was the first one to get

---

[30] NYMEX v. ICE, 497 F.3d 109 (2d Cir. 2007).

[31] MGM v. Grokster Ltd., 545 U.S. 913 (2005).

[32] BMG Music v. Gonzalez, 430 F.3d 888 (7th Cir. 2005).

a full trial, although many cases have been settled, typically for a payment of about $4,000-5,000. However, the District Court for the District of Minnesota granted her a new trial in 2008, based on an erroneous jury instruction; the court ruled that the law requires proof of actual distribution, not merely making music available for copying. The damages were also far in excess of the potential lost income from songs that were the equivalent of three CDs.[33]

A negotiated license to make and distribute "phonorecords" of a licensed song is not a license to upload the song to a server for streaming over the Internet. Even a § 115 compulsory license does not authorize streaming, because the compulsory license applies to manufacture of records for sale to private individuals.[34]

The Second Circuit upheld the validity of 18 USC 2319A(a)(1), (3) [criminalizing bootlegging of live performance], finding it a valid exercise of Congressional power under the Commerce Clause. Because of the differences between the anti-bootlegging and copyright laws, the Second Circuit traced Congress' power to the Commerce rather than the Copyright Clause, and rejected the defendant's argument that the statute created a conflict between the two clauses because performers' rights under the anti-bootlegging law were unlimited in time and did not require fixation of the performances.[35]

A late 2003 Ninth Circuit case involves the sampling of a six-second, three-note musical sequence from a jazz piece for flute recorded by its composer. The Beastie Boys, who included the sample over 40 times in their recording, had a license from the record company holding the copyright on the sound recording, but did not secure a license from the composer (holder of the copyright on the composition). The Ninth Circuit found that the composer's copyright was not infringed, because the use was de minimis. The sequence appeared only once in the four-and-a-half minute composition, and was not a significant part of the whole work either in terms of quantity or quality. The sequence was also a common element frequently used in contemporary music.[36]

Also in connection with sampling, the Sixth Circuit ruled that the owner of the copyright in the sound recording — and not the underlying composition — has the exclusive right to control sampling. If the actual recording is copied to any extent, the court ruled that no de minimis defense is available. The copyright holder for the recording is not obligated to show substantial similarity.[37]

---

[33] Sarah McBride, *Music Industry Wins Digital Piracy Case*, Wall St. J. 10/5/07 at B4; Jeff Leeds, *Labels Win Suit Against Song Shares*, N.Y. Times 10/5/07 at C1; Steve Karnowski (AP) *Judge Grants New Trial in Landmark File-Sharing Case*, 9/25/08 (law.com).

[34] Rodgers & Hammerstein Org. v. UMG Recordings Inc., 2001 U.S. Dist. LEXIS 16111 (S.D.N.Y. 2001).

[35] United States v. Martignon, 492 F.3d 140 (2d Cir. 2007); *see* Mark Hamblett, *2nd Circuit Upholds Congress' Power to Pass Anti-Bootlegging Law*, N.Y.L.J. 6/14/07 (law.com).

[36] Newton v. Diamond, 349 F.3d 591 (9th Cir. 2003), *cert. denied*, 545 U.S. 1114 (2005).

[37] Bridgeport Music v. Dimension Films, 383 F.3d 390 (6th Cir. 2005).

The New York Court of Appeals ruled in 2005 that state common law protects interests in sound recordings that are not covered by the federal Copyright Act (which does not cover recordings made before 1972).[38]

The Ninth Circuit ruled that, although earlier cases involving singers Bette Midler and Tom Waits permit relief from unauthorized vocal imitation for advertising purposes, a record company was within its rights in permitting another company to sample a song for which it held the copyright and controlled the use of the singer-songwriter's name and likeness. The licensee record company was not imitating the plaintiff's voice. Although California law recognizes a right of publicity in the person's voice, copyright law preempts the misappropriation-of-voice claim where the entire performance is contained in a copyrighted medium. The right of publicity does not constrain the copyright holder's right to license the copyrighted work.[39]

The Third Circuit held that a copyright registration was invalid because a work that should have been described as a song was incorrectly described as an audiovisual work. Given the invalidity of the registration, there was no subject matter jurisdiction over the infringement suit. The error was material, because the Copyright Office's decision to issue the registration would reflect the registrant's lack of authorship of the audiovisual work. Furthermore, the error could not have been inadvertent, because songs and audiovisual works are different enough to prevent mix-ups.[40]

The Ninth Circuit ordered karaoke publishers to obtain a license for lyrics as well as music, holding that displaying lyrics in conjunction with music for commercial gain is not fair use. The court rejected the defendant's arguments that the words were included for educational purposes, or that there was no market for song lyrics isolated from a musical performance. The Ninth Circuit rejected the contention that karaoke products are "phonorecords," so complying with the compulsory license would be adequate. The Ninth Circuit held that karaoke songs are "audiovisual works" subject to additional licensing requirements.[41]

Distributors of karaoke records insist on sellers having full copyright clearance. A 2008 Ninth Circuit case involved a karaoke record producer who charged that its competitors lie about having full clearance in order to avoid paying fees. The Ninth Circuit held that a party without standing to bring a copyright infringement suit also lacks standing under the Lanham Act, RICO, or state unfair competition law for competitive injury from alleged infringement, if such a case would require litigating the underlying claim of infringement. An interest in a divisible copyright transferred by one co-owner of the copyright, without participation of the other co-owners, is not an assignment or exclusive license that gives the transferee

---

[38] Capitol Records, Inc. v. Naxos of Am. Inc., 4 N.Y.3d 540 (2005).

[39] Laws v. Sony Music Entertainment Inc., 448 F.3d 1134 (9th Cir. 2006).

[40] Raquel v. Education Mgmt. Corp., 196 F.3d 171 (3d Cir. 1999).

[41] Leadsinger v. BMG Music Publ'g, 512 F.3d 522 (9th Cir. 2008); *see* Zusha Elinson, *9th Circuit Harmonizes With IP Holders in Karaoke Case*, The Recorder 1/3/08 (law.com).

a co-ownership interest. In short, a non-exclusive licensee cannot sue to enforce a copyright, even if the infringement operates to the detriment of the licensee.[42]

[D] Works for Hire

The copyright of a work made "for hire" belongs to the employer, not the employee who actually created the work. The Supreme Court defined "work for hire" in *Community for Creative Non-Violence v. Reid*.[43] The test is whether the work was done by an employee or independent contractor, using traditional tests such as ownership of the tools and studio; hiring of assistants; availability or absence of employee benefits; and the creator's ability to set his or her own working hours. Control over the final product is not determinative. There is a strong presumption that works created by freelancers will not be "works for hire."

P.L. 106-379, the Work Made for Hire and Copyright Corrections Act of 2000, removes 1999 amendments that added sound records to the list of creations that could be works for hire. The purpose of the 2000 legislation is to return to the status quo, where courts and the Copyright Office were responsible for deciding which musical compositions are works for hire.

According to the Second Circuit, dances created by pioneering modern-dance choreographer Martha Graham when she served as artistic director of the Martha Graham Center were works for hire. Creating dances was an important part of her job. The Second Circuit did not accept the argument that Graham's estate owned the works because she was a major artist and therefore exempt from the work-for-hire rules. However, the suit was permitted to continue with respect to seven dances created between 1956 and 1966, when Graham's primary role at the Center did not involve choreography.[44]

[E] Term of Protection

Prior to the 1978 Copyright Act, the initial copyright term was 28 years, with one 28-year extension available.[45] Thus, under prior law, "renewal copyright" was

---

[42] Sybersound Records, Inc v. UAV Corp., 517 F.3d 1137 (9th Cir. 2008).

[43] 490 U.S. 730 (1989).

[44] Martha Graham Sch. and Dance Found. v. Martha Graham Ctr., 380 F.3d 624 (2d Cir. 2004).

[45] The Copyright Renewal Act of 1992, P.L. 102-307, granted an automatic 47-year renewal of copyrights that came into existence between 1/1/63 and 12/31/77. Prior to the '78 Act, when the first 28-year copyright term was completed, the renewal copyright reverted to the author or a specified beneficiary. This renewal feature was dropped other than for works that were in their first term of copyright protection on 1/1/78. Instead, the author or certain specified heirs were given the ability to terminate transferred rights "at any time during a period of five years beginning at the end of 56 years from the date the copyright was originally secured," or 1/1/78, whichever was later. The Second Circuit permitted the creator of Captain America to terminate Marvel's copyright in the character, despite a settlement agreement with the comic publisher under which Joseph H. Simon conceded that the Captain America series was a work for hire. The Second Circuit ruled that grants in a work for hire cannot be terminated, but the status of the work as work for hire was in doubt. Marvel Characters Inc. v. Simon, 310 F.3d 280 (2d Cir. 2002).

an important concept (one which still has some validity for older works that have not yet reverted to the public domain).[46] The '78 Act provides that, for works created after January 1, 1978, the statutory term of protection is the life of the author plus 50 years. (This is also the term provided by the Berne Convention.)

For works done for hire, or for anonymous or pseudonymous works, the '78 Act term is 75 years from the time of publication, or 100 years from creation, whichever is shorter. For works already under copyright when the '78 Act took effect, the initial term would be 28 years from first publication, plus a renewal term of 47 years; renewal was required prior to expiration of the 28-year initial term. However, the '78 Act did not restore copyright protection to works that had fallen into the public domain.

As a result of 1998's Sonny Bono Copyright Term Extension Act, P.L.105-298, both initial and renewal term of copyright have been extended by 20 years, to conform to the greater scope of protection permitted under European Union law. The basic term of copyright protection is now the life of the author plus 70 years, and an additional 20 years is added to the term of unpublished, anonymous or pseudonymous works, and works for hire. (There is an academic fair use exception for reproduction, display, and performance of works in the last 20 years of their copyright term — i.e., the newly-added extension — if it is impossible to obtain the works commercially at a reasonable price.)

The Supreme Court upheld the validity of the Copyright Term Extension Act,[47] on the grounds that the extension was a rational use of Congressional power to conform U.S. to EU copyright law; that the copyright grant does not violate the Copyright Clause language of protection for a limited time; and that it is not inconsistent with the First Amendment.

A challenge to the Sonny Bono Act and URAA § 514 [see § 1203[A][3]] brought by a group of orchestra conductors, performers, film archivists, teachers, and other people in the arts, involving works that fell into the public domain in the United States for failure to comply with U.S. formalities, was heard by the Tenth Circuit in 2007. The plaintiffs charged that § 514 interferes with free expression by removing works from the public domain and making their performance subject to prohibitive licensing fees and royalties. The court held that bringing the United States into conformity with the Berne Convention was a rational action related to the objectives of the Commerce Clause, but remanded to determine if § 514's restrictions are content-based (and hence subject to additional scrutiny) or content-neutral.[48]

---

[46] PC Films Corp. v. MGM/UA Home Video Inc., 138 F.3d 453 (2d Cir. 1998) holds that a grant of perpetual distribution rights under the 1909 Copyright Act grants a license that applies to the renewal term as well as the initial term.

[47] Eldred v. Ashcroft, 537 U.S. 186 (2003). The Northern District of California denied claims by archivists (who said their ability to make copyrighted works available after a reasonable time was burdened) and upheld the constitutionality of the Copyright Renewal Act of 1992, the Sonny Bono Copyright Term Extension Act, and the Berne Convention Implementation Act: Kahle v. Ashcroft, 73 L.W. 1352 (N.D. Cal. 11/19/04).

[48] Golan v. Gonzales, 501 F.3d 1179 (10th Cir. 2007).

The Ninth Circuit rejected claims that changing the focus of the copyright system from opt-in to opt-out violated First Amendment rights, and also found the current copyright term requirements consistent with the Constitutional grant of copyrights "for a limited time." The plaintiff wanted to create an Internet archive, including orphan works for which it is difficult or impossible to determine who holds the rights. Before 1978, there were few orphan works, because failure to renew a copyright meant that the work lapsed into the public domain.[49]

The 1976 Copyright Act endowed artists, songwriters, and authors with a new right to recapture control of works that they sold early in their careers, presumably when they were at a disadvantage vis-à-vis publishers and studios. The provision permits termination of transfers, after 35 to 40 years, of interests assigned to publishers for works created after 1978. However, there are complex notification requirements. The creator must notify the publisher two to ten years in advance, and file a notice with the Copyright Office; the publishers have a right to protest termination. In 2003, the notice window opened for works to be reclaimed in 2013. Although there are no termination rights for works for hire, it is often controversial whether a work was for hire. Under California law, for example, songwriters who create works for hire are employees, so their employers are obligated to make payments and withhold accordingly.

A Sixth Circuit reclamation case awarded half of the royalties to the composer's surviving spouse, and half to his children. However, A.A. Milne's granddaughter was unable to recapture rights, on the grounds that a 1983 renegotiation of a transfer by Milne's son Christopher Robin satisfied the statutory purpose.[50]

When the 1976 Act took effect, "Lassie Come Home" was in its renewal copyright term. The Ninth Circuit ruled that assignment of rights did not extinguish the author's daughter's termination rights. The author died in 1943, before renewal rights had vested. Under the law then prevailing, the interest in renewal copyright vested in his wife and their three children. Each of them filed a timely renewal. One of the daughters assigned her 25% share of movie, TV, and radio rights in 1976, for the full period of the renewal copyright and any further renewals or extensions. In 1996, the daughter (Mewborn) filed a timely notice of termination to recapture movie, TV, and radio rights. In 1998, the successor in interest of the transferee

---

[49] Kahle v. Gonzales, 474 F.3d 665 (2006), *reh'g denied, amended* 487 F.3d 697 (9th Cir. 2007). In another case, Google agreed to pay $125 million to settle a copyright suit about Google's project for putting books online. Google agreed to pay 63% of the revenue from its electronic book database (stemming from advertising and sales of book downloads) to publishers and authors. The Book Rights Registry (which remits funds to copyright owners) is to be funded with $34.5 million. Authors and publishers whose books were uploaded without permission are to receive $45 million, and another $30 million is to go to attorneys' fees. *See* Zusha Elinson, *Google to Pay $125 Million in Settlement Over Book Digitization*, The Recorder 10/29/08 (law.com).

[50] Pamela A. MacLean, *Copyright Bomb Quietly Ticking*, Nat'l L.J. 4/12/06 (law.com). *See, e.g.*, Milne v. Stephen Slesinger, Inc., 430 F.3d 1036 (2005).

rejected the notice. In 2004, Mewborn found out that a new Lassie movie was being considered, and sought a share of rights. The Ninth Circuit found her termination of the 1976 assignment to be valid and enforceable, because it occurred during the "window" for recapturing rights to both the short story and the novel "Lassie Come Home."[51]

The Second Circuit ruled that a 1938 agreement under which John Steinbeck gave sole and exclusive rights in several works (including "Of Mice and Men") to Viking Press was terminated and extinguished by a 1994 agreement between Steinbeck's widow and Penguin Books. Therefore, the 17 USC § 304(c), (d) notice of termination filed by Steinbeck's son and grandson was invalid. Steinbeck died in 1968, leaving money to his children and the copyrights to his wife. A 1994 contract between the widow and Penguin terminated and superseded the 1938 agreement, leaving no pre-1978 grant to which § 304(d) could apply.[52]

A composer who granted a nonexclusive license to use a jingle she wrote doesn't have to wait for the 35-year period under Copyright Act § 203 (allowing termination of a nonexclusive license during the five-year period that begins 35 years after the grant of the license) to expire before bringing suit for infringement.[53]

There is a Circuit split[54] as to whether the license can be canceled while the 35-year period is running, if state contract law permits this. The Eleventh Circuit's reading is that Copyright Act § 203 permits termination of any license that is still in effect after 35 years, but does not prevent parties from contracting for a shorter license term. In the Eleventh Circuit view, a statutory provision permitting license termination under certain circumstances does not necessarily preclude termination under all other circumstances. The Eleventh Circuit copes with the language in § 203(b)(6), "unless and until termination is effected under this section, the grant, if it does not provide otherwise, continues in effect for the term of copyright provided by this title" by saying that any state law governing contracts of indefinite duration does provide otherwise.

[F] Digital Millennium Copyright Act/TEACH Act

The Digital Millennium Copyright Act (DMCA; P.L. 105-304 (10/28/98)) is another late-1998 copyright statute. It implements two copyright treaties

---

[51] Classic Media, Inc. v. Mewborn, 532 F.3d 978 (9th Cir. 2008).

[52] Penguin Group (USA) Inc. v. Steinbeck, 06-3226-cv (2d Cir. 2008), discussed in Mark Hamblett, *Steinbeck Descendants Lose Bid to Renegotiate Publishing Rights*, N.Y.L.J. 8/14/08 (law. com). The Sixth Circuit has held that Congress intended for § 304(a) to give a 50% interest to the surviving spouse, with the other 50% divided equally among the children — and not to give the spouse and each child equal shares. Broadcast Music Inc. v. Roger Miller Music Inc., 396 F.3d 762 (6th Cir. 2005).

[53] Korman v. HBC Fla. Inc., 182 F.3d 1291 (11th Cir. 1999).

[54] Rano v. Sipa Press Inc., 987 F.2d 580 (9th Cir. 1993) interprets § 203 to mean that a license of indefinite duration has a minimum term of 35 years. Walthal v. Rusk, 172 F.3d 481 (9th Cir. 1999) doesn't deem there to be any minimum term; the Eleventh Circuit adopted this position.

("the World Intellectual Property Organization (WIPO) Copyright Treaty and the Performances and Phonograms Treaty") and updates the Berne Convention (international law of copyright protection) for new technology. A phonogram is a sound recording, and the corresponding treaty deals with protection of sound recordings distributed over computer networks in digital form. According to the Northern District of California, statutory damages under the DMCA are ordered based on the same factors as statutory damages for copyright violations: e.g., the profits derived from improper conduct; the plaintiff's revenue loss; willfulness of the infringement; and the policy need to deter future violations.[55]

Because of DMCA, new Chapter 12 of the Copyright Act provides for digital "watermarking" of copyrighted material, by affixing electronic files containing information about the proprietorship of the material. It is a crime to remove or alter the watermarking information without permission, or to sell technology for circumventing the watermarking process. Certain exceptions are allowed, such as security testing and reverse engineering; broadcasters can make short-term copies (for instance, creating a CD with multiple music selections, for convenience in on-line broadcasting).

The DMCA also absolves Internet Service Providers and other on-line "broadcasters" of liability for direct contributory, or vicarious copyright infringement in situations in which they serve as a conduit for infringement by routing, caching, storing, or linking copyrighted material without consent of the proprietor, but have no editorial involvement with the material. To qualify under this safe harbor, service providers must create, publicize, and enforce a policy of removing material from the service as soon as they become aware of infringement, and must designate an agent to whom infringements can be reported.[56]

Content owners are demanding that the operators of video-sharing sites take a more active role in controlling infringement; the site owners claim entitlement to the DMCA safe harbor; and each side treats the other as responsible for policing sites to find infringing content. In 2008, the Northern District of California held that a video sharing site qualifies for the safe harbor against monetary claims for copyright infringement if it actively enforces a user policy, promptly removes infringing material, and attempts to prevent re-posting after takedowns.[57]

---

[55] Sony Computer Entertainment Am. Inc. v. Filipiak, 74 LW 1415 (N.D. Cal. 12/27/05).

[56] The Copyright Office published, 37 CFR § 201.38, for designation of agents; see 63 FR 59233 (11/3/98). According to Marjorie Heins and Tricia Beckles, http://www.fepproject.org/policy reports; see 74 LW 2356, artists need to become better informed about fair use and how to respond to take-down orders; in many instances, claims are weak or the artist has a valid First Amendment claim to use and adapt the copyrighted work.

[57] Io Group Inc. v. Veoh Networks Inc., 2008 U.S. Dist. Lexis 65915 (N.D. Cal. 8/27/08), discussed in Richard Raysman and Peter Brown, *DMCA: A Safe Harbor for Video Sharing?* N.Y.L.J. 10/17/08 (law.com). *See also* Perfect10 v. CCBill LLC, 488 F.3d 1102 (9th Cir. 2007): a service provider acts reasonably if its notification system works, it maintains a procedure for dealing with notifications that comply with the DMCA, and it does not actively deter copyright owners from acquiring the information needed to issue notices. In 2008, the Southern District of New York ordered

Other DMCA provisions deal with compulsory licensing of music for Internet transmission of music,[58] with accompanying royalty provisions, and distance education and academic fair use.

The DMCA also permits the owner of a copyright to serve a subpoena on an ISP to get the names of customers alleged to infringe the owner's copyrights. This provision has been upheld by the District Court for the District of Columbia, which found that it does not violate the First Amendment rights of ISP subscribers, or the Article III powers of the federal courts.[59] The D.D.C. applied this DMCA provision (17 USC § 512(h)) to allow enforcement of a subpoena even though the allegedly infringing material was stored on the user's computer rather than on the ISP's network[60] but at the end of the same year, the D.C. Circuit reversed[61] finding that subpoenas can validly be issued only to an ISP whose own servers store the infringing materials.

The 21st Century Department of Justice Appropriations Authorization Act, P.L. 107-273 (signed 11/2/02) includes the Technology, Education and Copyright Harmonization Act (TEACH Act). This legislation is designed to increase the flexibility of Internet use by clarifying the educational fair use exception when copyrighted materials are used in distance learning programs maintained by accredited nonprofit educational institutions.

Educational use of a nondramatic literary or musical work is considered fair use if it is made by or under the direction of an instructor as part of instruction at an accredited nonprofit educational institution. The transmission must be limited to students officially enrolled in the class; the students must be notified of the copyright status of the work; and digital transmissions must use reasonable technological measures to prevent improper use. However, in late 2003, the Seventh Circuit ruled that the defense of academic fair use could not be raised when unauthorized copies of software were made available on the Internet, merely because the site was operated by a professor and site members did not pay for downloads.[62]

Even if, as asserted, a teacher's intent was to criticize standard testing, it was not fair use for him to copy and publish the entire text of standardized tests created

---

three major online services to pay ASCAP royalties of 2.5% of music-related revenues from music streamed over the Internet between 2002 and 2009. The order, which covers music that was heard at the time of download rather than being stored on a hard drive for later listening, could yield as much as $100 million. The online services had already reached a deal with BMI. *See* Ethan Smith, *Songwriters to Get Online Royalties*, Wall St. J. 5/1/08 at p. B5.

[58] *See* 69 Fed. Reg. 11566 (3/11/04) for proposed amendments to the rules for service of notices on copyright holders for purposes of the § 115 compulsory license.

[59] *In re* Verizon Internet Serv. Inc., 71 L.W. 1685 (D.D.C. 4/24/03). Therefore, peer-to-peer file sharing sites are not subject to § 512(h): RIAA v. Charter Communications Inc., 393 F.3d 771 (8th Cir. 2005).

[60] *In re* Verizon Internet Services Inc. Subpoena Enforcement Matter, 240 F. Supp. 2d 24 (D.D.C. 2003).

[61] 351 F.3d 1229 (D.C. Cir. 2003).

[62] United States v. Slater, 348 F.3d 666 (7th Cir. 2003).

and copyrighted by a school district. The Seventh Circuit held that fair use permits copying of only enough of the text to critique it. Academics are not entitled to destroy the value of tests, even if their motive is other than commercial competition.[63]

[G] Fair Use

There are various situations in which undoubted use of copyrighted materials, without the consent of the copyright proprietor, will be permitted. The "fair use" exception is set out in 17 USC § 107. For instance, a limited amount of material can be quoted, e.g., in a scholarly article or book review, in order to further the argument of the article or give review readers a chance to form their own opinion of the work. Reproduction for criticism, comment, news reporting, teaching, scholarship, or research is deemed to be permissible fair use.

However, the amount of "taking" of the copyrighted work must not be excessive relative to the purpose of the alleged fair-use work and the market for the original product and authorized derivative works.

The factors involved in distinguishing fair use from infringement include:

- Purpose and character of the use
- Nature of the copyrighted work
- Amount used in relation to the copyrighted work as a whole
- Effect of the use on the potential market for the product.[64]

The Southern District of New York ruled that a reference work, "The Harry Potter Lexicon," infringed on J.K. Rowling's work, because it appropriated too much of the underlying original works. The Southern District permanently blocked publication and awarded $6,750 in statutory damages. The publisher's contention was that even though copying occurred, there was no infringement either because there was no substantial similarity between a reference book and a series of novels, or it was fair use as a work of reference and commentary. The Southern District ruled that, although the use was transformative, it was nonetheless infringing because of extensive verbatim copying, in excess of what was needed to produce a non-fiction work, and ruled that "The Harry Potter Lexicon" could diminish the market for Rowling's own planned non-fiction guide to the Potter books. Rowling said that she sued because the Lexicon copied large amounts of text and, unlike other works of criticism that were not challenged, did not offer original insights.[65]

---

[63] Chicago Bd. of Educ. v. Substance Inc., 354 F.3d 624 (7th Cir. 2003).

[64] This is the most important element; *see, e.g.*, Basic Books, Inc. v. Kinko's Graphics Corp., 758 F. Supp. 1522 (S.D.N.Y. 1991), where the court held that copying large portions of textbooks adversely affected sales of the textbooks, as well as permission fees that constitute a significant income source for textbook authors.

[65] Warner Bros. Entertainment Inc. v. RDR Books, No. 07 Civ. 9667 (S.D.N.Y. 2008); *see* Mark Hamblett, *Judge Blocks Book That Takes 'Too Much' From 'Harry Potter*, N.Y.L.J. 9/9/08 (law.com).

The Ninth Circuit deemed Court TV's use of video clips of Reginald Denny being beaten by Los Angeles police officers to be fair use, even though the clips were used to promote Court TV's coverage of a related trial. The Ninth Circuit's rationale was that transformative fair use was made of the material and the copyright holder's market for the film was not impaired.[66]

Parody is a sub-type of fair use. Of course, at least some elements of the parodied work must be duplicated for the audience to recognize that a parody is involved; see *Campbell v. Acuff-Rose Music, Inc.*, 510 U.S. 569 (1993).

Initially, the copyright proprietors of "Gone With the Wind" succeeded in securing a preliminary injunction against distribution of Alice Randall's "The Wind Done Gone," a novel depicting the same story from the slaves' point of view. However, late in 2001, the Eleventh Circuit reversed the grant of preliminary injunction, finding it unlikely that the plaintiff would prevail. In this reading, "The Wind Done Gone" was entitled to a parody defense and made fair use of plot elements of "Gone With the Wind" to critique racism. A parody must resemble the underlying copyrighted work to be recognizable. In May 2002, the Mitchell estate agreed to settle the case on undisclosed terms, but the book would continue to be labeled "The Unauthorized Parody."[67]

[H] Other Defenses to Infringement Charges

Remember, only specific expressions of ideas and not the ideas themselves can be copyrighted. It is a defense to infringement that the defendant, rather than infringing on a copyrighted work, made use of a common body of materials on which both expressions drew. This is sometimes referred to as the "scene a faire" (obligatory scene) doctrine. That is, the mere fact that two detective stories each involve a scene in which the detective calls the suspects together and explains which one is guilty does not mean that the second to be published or filmed plagiarizes the earlier one. This is a fundamental element (or cliché) of the genre, which can be used by many authors.

In any infringement case (here, charges that a film about a father trying to buy a popular Christmas toy infringed on the plaintiff's film treatment) the issues are access and similarity. Access is proved by showing the defendant's opportunity to observe the plaintiff's work. A mere possibility of access is not enough. In the Second Circuit, there are two essential elements in a "substantial similarity" suit (i.e., one which asserts infringement based on the substantial similarities between the two works). The elements are copying by the defendant, and that the copying constituted improper appropriation. The determination of whether copying was improper is done from the point of view of the ordinary observer, and therefore expert testimony is used for the issue of whether copying occurred, but not on the issue of impropriety. The Ninth Circuit uses a different two-part test: extrinsic

---

[66] Los Angeles News Serv. v. CBS Broad. Inc., 305 F.3d 924 (9th Cir. 2002).

[67] SunTrust Bank v. Houghton Mifflin Co., 252 F.3d 1165 (11th Cir. 2001); David D. Kirkpatrick, *Mitchell Estate Settles "Gone With the Wind" Suit*, N.Y. Times, May 10, 2002 at C6.

(whether expression has been copied, as well as ideas) and intrinsic. Here, too, the second test depends on the standards of the ordinary reasonable person, so expert testimony is not admitted. In the Sixth Circuit, however, the analysis is to identify any elements of the plaintiff's work that are protectable, then determine if the alleged infringing work is substantially similar to the protectable elements. An element that appears in both the plaintiff's work and work completed by the defendant before access to the plaintiff's work cannot be used as proof of infringement.[68]

There is a split in authority as to the availability of laches as a copyright defense. The Sixth Circuit finds that it is theoretically available, yet rarely appropriate.[69]

[I] Registration and Notice

Copyrights are registered by filing a form with the Copyright Office, and depositing copies of the work with the Copyright Office and the Library of Congress.[70]

For works published after March 1, 1989, according to the Berne Convention Implementation Act, P.L. 100-568, copyright protection does not require that published copies carry a copyright notice. Nevertheless, copyright notice is useful, to identify the owner and show date of publication, and it eliminates the possible defense of innocent infringement.

Early in 2005, a pilot project for electronic registration certificates was launched, beginning with certificates registering audiovisual works such as movies. Although applicants continue to use the Form PA paper application, the certificate of copyright is generated from information scanned in from the paper form.[71]

In yet another victory for state immunity from lawsuit, the Fifth Circuit decided early in 2000 that the Copyright Remedy Clarification Act (which makes the states subject to suit for copyright infringement) is invalid, because Congress lacked the authority to abrogate Eleventh Amendment immunity in a situation where there had been no documented pattern of abuses requiring redress.[72]

For another of a line of recent decisions expanding the rights and immunities of state agencies, see also the Fifth Circuit's earlier decision on the issues.[73] The Patent and Plant Variety Protection Remedy Clarification Act was struck down by

---

[68] Murray Hill Publ'ns, Inc. v. Twentieth Century Fox Film Corp., 361 F.3d 312 (6th Cir. 2004).

[69] Chirco et al. v. Crosswinds Communities, Inc., 474 F.3d 227 (6th Cir. 2007).

[70] An interim rule under 17 USC § 408 was published at 63 FR 59235 (11/3/98). It permits the use of supplementary registration to add the name of a co-owner or other copyright claimant who should have been but was not named on the original registration.

[71] 70 FR 3231 (1/21/05), http://www.copyright.gov/docs/certificate_sample.pdf.

[72] Chavez v. Arte Publico Press, 204 F.3d 601 (5th Cir. 2000).

[73] Rodriguez v. Texas Comm'n on the Arts, 199 F.3d 279 (5th Cir. 2000).

the Supreme Court in 1999.[74] Both statutes aimed at protecting the same interest, and the abrogation provisions in both were more or less identically phrased, so both statutes should stand or fall together.

[J] Remedies and Copyright Litigation

17 USC § 501(b) gives the legal or beneficial owner of an exclusive right the ability to sue for infringement of that particular right, occurring during ownership of that right. There are two elements in an infringement case: proof of ownership of a right in a valid copyright; and direct or circumstantial proof of copying. Circumstantial proof can exist through proof of access and substantial similarity of expression. (Similarity of ideas is not enough, because the ideas are not copyrightable.)

The assignee of an accrued claim for copyright infringement who holds only that claim but does not have a legal or beneficial interest in the underlying copyright does not have standing to sue for infringement of the copyright. (In this case, the assignee wrote a screenplay as a work for hire, explaining her lack of interest in the underlying copyright; the movie studio assigned the right to sue a film that allegedly infringed on the copyright of her screenplay.)[75]

The owner-operator of a flea market that rents space to vendors is vicariously and contributorily liable for infringement when counterfeit CDs and cassette tapes were sold. The owner-operator received direct financial benefit from the infringement and supervised and controlled the premises (including a daily walk-through to police the commercial activities going on there). The owner also maintained detailed records of the types of merchandise sold there. The District Court for the District of New Jersey held that constructive knowledge of infringement is sufficient to support contributory liability.[76]

[1] Injunction

The availability of preliminary injunction in an infringement case depends on the normal factors: the likelihood that the plaintiff will succeed on the merits; the risk of irreparable harm; the presence or absence of serious questions on the merits of the case; and the balance of hardships between the parties. See 17 USC § 502(a). Irreparable injury will be presumed on proof of reasonable likelihood of success on the merits, or presentation of a prima facie case of infringement.

[2] Money Damages

The plaintiff in an infringement case can recover either actual damages (e.g., lost profits) or statutory damages as prescribed by 17 USC § 504. Statutory damages can range from $500 to $20,000 "as the Court considers just."

---

[74] Prepaid Postsecondary Educ. Exp. Bd. v. College Sav. Bank, 527 U.S. 666 (1999).

[75] Silvers v. Sony Pictures Entertainment, 402 F.3d 881 (9th Cir. 2005).

[76] Arista Records Inc. v. Flea World Inc., 74 LW 1616 (D.N.J. 3/31/06).

In March 1998, the Supreme Court held that there is no statutory right to a jury trial in a Copyright Act § 504(c) case, in which the copyright owner seeks statutory damages,[77] because the statute refers to what the "Court" will do. Nevertheless, a jury trial is available under the Seventh Amendment on all of the issues pertinent to the § 504(c) award, including the amount of damages, because historical precedents support the jury's role in setting damages. Punitive damages are not available in infringement cases.[78]

Also note that statutory damages are not available unless the copyright in the allegedly infringed work was registered before the alleged infringement occurred; § 412 also denies an award of attorneys' fees against an infringer of an unregistered copyright.[79] A published work is entitled to a three-month grace period, even if the infringement had occurred pre-registration, as long as the copyright was registered within three months of first publication.

The *Gore v. BMW* guidelines on punitive damages (see § 18.13) do not apply to awards of Copyright Act statutory damages because they are a substitute for actual damages.[80]

The author him- or herself must register the copyright in an individual article to be able to bring an infringement suit (Copyright Act § 411(a)). The author cannot rely on the publisher's copyright registration in the entire magazine. In this case,[81] the author retained the copyright; the publisher had a 90-day exclusive license in the article; and the Second Circuit position is that a licensee is not a copyright holder.

A federal jury awarded Mattel $100 million in damages against the manufacturer of Bratz dolls: $90 million on three causes of action related to the designer Carter Bryant's employment contract with Mattel, plus $10 million for infringement. Bryant came up with the idea for Bratz dolls while he was still employed by Mattel. The $90 million represented $20 million against MGA and $10 million against its chief executive on each of three counts (intentional interference with contractual relations; aiding and abetting breach of fiduciary duty; aiding and abetting breach of the duty of loyalty). Bryant settled with Mattel just before the trial, on undisclosed terms.[82]

---

[77] Feltner v. Columbia Pictures Television Inc., 523 U.S. 340 (1998).

[78] Oboler v. Goldin, 714 F.2d 211 (2d Cir. 1983); Cormack v. Sunshine Food Stores, Inc., 675 F. Supp. 374 (E.D. Mich. 1987).

[79] As a general rule, the standard for attorneys' fee awards is the same against the defendant as against the plaintiff — i.e., inappropriate or abusive litigation: *see* Fogerty v. Fantasy, Inc., 510 U.S. 517 (1994).

[80] Lowry's Reports Inc. v. Legg Mason Inc., 302 F. Supp. 2d 455 (D. Md. 2004).

[81] Morris v. Business Concepts Inc., 259 F.3d 65 (2d Cir. 2001).

[82] Gillian Flaccus (AP), *Jury Awards Mattel $100 Million in Bratz Suit*, 8/27/08 (law.com). In October, Mattel applied to the District Court for an injunction against the manufacture or sale of Bratz dolls; a hearing on the injunction was scheduled for November 10, 2008. (AP) *Mattel Asks Judge to Halt Production of Bratz Dolls*, 10/1/08 (law.com).

[3] Willful Infringement

Criminal penalties can also be imposed, under 17 USC § 506(a) and 18 USC § 2319. Criminal infringement is willful infringement undertaken for purposes of commercial advantage or private financial gain. It can be penalized by up to a year's imprisonment and/or a $25,000 fine; higher penalties are imposed for certain motion picture and sound recording infringements.

These provisions are supplemented by The No Electronic Theft Act of 1997, P.L. 105-147, which imposes penalties for willful copyright infringement, especially in the electronic arena. This statute clarifies that it is not necessary that a defendant receive commercial gain from infringement for the infringement to be punishable. This Act imposes criminal penalties of up to six years, depending on the number of works improperly reproduced, their value, and whether it is a first or repeat offense.

[K] Technology and Copyright

The Digital Theft Deterrence and Copyright Damages Improvement Act, P.L. 106-160 (12/9/99), increases some penalties for copyright infringement by 50%, so that the range of damages is from $750 to $30,000, or $150,000 in the case of willful violation. In large part, the statute implements the digital piracy provisions of the No Electronic Theft Act, on the theory that prosecutors might be deterred from bringing meritorious cases if the appropriate penalty is in doubt.

The Intellectual Property Protection and Courts Amendments Act, P.L.108-482 (signed December 23, 2004), increases the criminal penalties for trafficking in genuine labels that are applied to counterfeit or bootleg copies of records, movies, computer programs, or other copyrighted works. Under 18 USC § 2318 as amended, it is illegal for the seller of a pirated work to package it with a genuine certificate of authenticity. Violative articles can be impounded. The injured party can be awarded fees and costs, actual damages, and either statutory damages or disgorgement of the violator's profits. A copyright (or trademark) violation is deemed willful if the violator knowingly provided false contact information to register or renew a domain name. The statute also enacts new 18 USC § 3559, either doubling or adding seven years to a sentence for a felony involving false registration of an Internet domain name.

Although the holders of copyrights in films claimed that the sale of video-cassette recorders to the public constituted contributory infringement, the Supreme Court squelched that argument in 1984.[83] To the Supreme Court, VCRs were used primarily for "time-shifting" (recording a broadcast program for viewing at a more convenient time), thus increasing the viewing audience. The Court did not believe that viewing rented videocassettes impaired the commercial value of film copyrights or created likelihood of future harm.

---

[83] Sony v. Universal City Studios, 464 U.S. 417 (1984).

The Second Circuit ruled that Cablevision's proposal for remote storage digital video recording did not violate the Copyright Act, so movie and TV producers should not have been granted an injunction. The system, RS-DVR, would allow customers to record programs to Cablevision's hard drives without a set-top box or separate digital video recorder such as TiVO. The Second Circuit held that the data was not in the buffers long enough to constitute copying. In effect, Cable-Vision was in the same position as a shop that makes photocopy machine available to the public — the copying is done by the members of the public, not the shop owner. The Second Circuit also rejected the argument that the system would infringe the 17 USC § 106(4) rules about public performance, because Cablevision proposed to make transmissions to individual subscribers using copies made by that subscriber. The Second Circuit did not, however, rule on issues of a network operator's liability for unauthorized reproduction or contributory infringement.[84]

Computer source code can be copyrighted, and the terms "idea" and "expression" are not unconstitutionally vague when used in this context. (The issue was whether a search tool could determine if new software violated copyrights or patents — by comparing the software to copyrighted code.)[85]

§ 12.04 TRADEMARKS AND TRADE NAMES

Although a patent is an authorized monopoly, with the result that the patented product will have limited sources (only the patent holder and its assignees and licensees), most goods and services are available from many sources.

Trademarks and trade names identify the source of goods (and service marks perform the same function for services), permitting sellers to develop a brand name and image that will encourage purchasers to select their products rather than competing products. A trademark is usually associated with a specific product. A trade name is representative of the business' established reputation and goodwill. The symbol^{TM} can be used to indicate that trademark rights are being asserted in a name, phrase, symbol, etc. The symbol® is restricted to trademarks that are registered with the federal Patent and Trademark Office (PTO), whether the trademark is registered on the principal or supplemental register (see § 12.04[B] below).

The federal government has preempted patent and copyright regulation, but the states have a major role in trademark regulation. Furthermore, the regulation of trademarks overlaps with prohibitions on unfair competition and other business improprieties.

Given the growing internationalization of trade, other countries also have a role to play. P.L. 105-330, enacted 10/30/98, implements the 1994 Trademark Law

---

[84] Cartoon Network LP, LLLP v. CSC Holdings, Inc., 536 F.3d 121 (2d Cir. 2008); *see* Mark Hamblett, *2nd Circuit Backs Cablevision's Remote Recorder Against Programmers' Lawsuit*, N.Y.L.J. 8/5/08 (law.com).
[85] Aharonian v. Gonzales, 2006 WL 13067 (N.D. Cal. 2006).

Treaty and makes small changes needed to harmonize the Lanham Act (the U.S. trademark statute) with world practice.[86]

On international issues also see the Madrid Protocol Implementation Act, P.L. 107-273 (11/2/02), bringing the United States into closer harmony with international trademark practice. Under this statute, a "basic registration" is granted after a "basic application" has been submitted. Trademark users can register their marks based on a declaration of bona fide intention to use the mark in commerce. The International Bureau of the World Intellectual Property Organization can issue international trademark registrations to real and artificial persons.

[A] The Lanham Act

The federal trademark statute is the Lanham Act, 15 USC Chapter 22, which has been amended many times.

The Lanham Act definition of a trademark is "any word, name, symbol, or device, or any combination thereof, adopted and used by a manufacturer or merchant to identify his goods and distinguish them from those manufactured or sold by others." Service marks (for services rather than products) and collective marks (for membership in an organization) can also be federally registered.

Color alone can be registered as a trademark (e.g., a green-gold color used in dry cleaners' pressing pads), as long as it is nonfunctional and has secondary meaning.[87]

The duration of a trademark registration is 10 years, with further 10-year extensions permitted. Lanham Act § 8 requires filing of an affidavit six years after registration to demonstrate continuing use in commerce.

Although trademarks are usually registered after they have been placed into use, a trademark can be registered based on intent to use in the future.

The two primary enforcement sections of the Lanham Act are §§ 32(1) and 43(a). A trademark registrant has a private right of action against an infringer who uses in commerce a "reproduction, counterfeit, copy or colorable imitation" of the registered mark in a way that is likely to deceive or cause confusion. Furthermore, if a counterfeit mark is applied to labels or packaging that is used in trade, the trademark holder has a cause of action — but only if the infringer acted with knowledge that the imitation was intended to be confusing or deceptive.

---

[86] The Lanham Act applies to activities of a United States company in Scandinavia if the defendant company is a U.S. citizen; the defendant's foreign trademark rights conflict with the plaintiff's U.S. trademark rights; and the defendant's conduct has a substantial effect on U.S. commerce: Piccoli A/S v. Calvin Klein Jeanswear Co., 19 F. Supp. 2d 157 (S.D.N.Y. 1998). An unregistered, but distinctive, service mark of a foreign owner, whose services (a casino in Monaco that welcomes U.S. gamblers) are advertised in the United States and furnished to U.S. citizens outside the U.S., is used in commerce for Lanham Act purposes. Foreign trade with U.S. citizens is deemed to be "commerce": International Bancorp LLC v. Societe des Bains de Mer, 329 F.3d 359 (4th Cir. 2003).

[87] Qualitex Co. v. Jacobsen Prods. Co., 514 U.S. 159 (1995).

Section 43(a) covers a broad range of confusing conduct, whether or not a registered trademark is involved. Any person who believes that he or she is likely to be damaged by a forbidden act can bring suit under § 43(a). The forbidden acts are use of words, symbols, devices, false designations of origin, or false or misleading descriptions of fact, as long as the wrongful act occurs in commerce. Section 43(a) makes all activities illegal that are likely to cause confusion or mistake about the affiliation, connection, or association between people, or the origin or sponsorship of goods and services.

Various types of confusion are actionable: source confusion (consumers think that a product is made by someone other than its actual manufacturer); confusion about sponsorship or approval (e.g., whether goods are endorsed by the NBA); reverse confusion (the public believes that an established product is actually made by a newcomer); subliminal or associational confusion (consumers think they have seen the trademark or something resembling it before).

The doctrine of "initial interest confusion" is often cited in Internet cases about domain names and metatags, and the doctrine can permit a trademark owner to recover even if there is no likelihood of confusion at the point of sale. But there must be commercial competition; merely diverting Web users from one site to another is not enough to be actionable.[88]

The Lanham Act does not have a statute of limitations, so laches is a significant issue in trademark enforcement. In 2004, the Fourth Circuit ruled that a 30-year delay did not constitute laches that would preclude enforcement of the trademark, because during that lengthy period of time there was no likelihood of consumer confusion and therefore no infringement. In this reading, the right to sue does not ripen until there is a likelihood of the junior user's entry into the senior user's geographic territory and thus the likelihood of confusion becomes meaningful.[89]

In mid-2003, the Supreme Court explored the junction between copyright and trademark law. The Court held that Lanham Act § 43(a) does not prevent unaccredited copying of public domain works. For § 43(a) purposes, the "origin" of goods is the producer of tangible goods rather than the author of the communications embodied in the tangible goods. In this case, the copyright on a television series expired and was not renewed. The series fell into the public domain. The defendant sold videotapes of the series without crediting the original copyright proprietor. The Supreme Court ruled that the defendant was not guilty of reverse passing off, because the defendant made its own tapes and packaging for the public

---

[88] *Initial Interest Confusion Doctrine Finding Its Way in Different Ways into Online Cases,* 72 L.W. 2186 (10/7/03) (no by-line). The Southern District of Ohio applied the doctrine to metatags in 2006, holding that inducing customers to visit a site by using someone else's trademark in metatags constitutes initial interest confusion infringement of the mark, even though the users eventually discover the difference between the two sites. Initial interest confusion substitutes for the "actual confusion" factor in the analysis of alleged infringement: Tdata Inc. v. Aircraft Technical Publ'rs, 411 F. Supp. 2d 901 (S.D. Ohio 2006).

[89] What-a-Burger of Va., Inc. v. Whataburger, Inc., 357 F.3d 441 (4th Cir. 2004).

domain work, and did not repackage tapes made by the original holder of the expired copyright.[90]

The Eighth Circuit affirmed summary judgment for the defendant in a case charging trademark infringement for the use of "Brick Oven" for frozen pizzas. The PTO has concluded three times that "Brick Oven" is generic for pizza (frozen or otherwise) for pizzas that appear to have been baked in a brick oven, producing a crust that is crisp on the outside and soft inside. A term can be generic if it began as a coined term, or if it was commonly used before association with a particular item. The Eighth Circuit concluded that the term was in common use before either the plaintiff or the defendant made frozen pizzas.[91]

An award of "profits" for a § 43(a) violation cannot be increased by aggregating it with the treble damages, because § 35(a) allows adjustment of the profits award only in the interests of justice.

Fee awards, available under Lanham Act § 35(a) in exceptional cases, are not limited to willful infringement. They can be granted against a party guilty of vexatious litigation conduct, by analogy with patent cases where the statutory language about attorneys' fees is similar.[92]

Under 15 USC § 1117(b), attorneys' fees can be awarded in exceptional cases — but if and only if there were actual damages. Section 1117(c), the statutory damage provision, allows statutory damages in lieu of actual damages and profits, but does not mention attorneys' fees. The Ninth Circuit held that, where the plaintiffs opted for statutory damages for trademark counterfeiting (only 89 sets of infringing decals were sold on eBay, for a total of $267), the District Court abused its discretion by awarding $100,000 in attorneys' fees.[93]

[1] Dilution of Famous Trademark

The Federal Trademark Dilution Act of 1995 (FTDA), P.L. 104-98, adds a new subsection to Lanham Act § 43, 15 USC § 1125. Once a mark becomes "famous," owners of the mark can get an injunction against subsequent commercial use of a mark or trade name that dilutes the famous mark.

Factors in determining which marks are "famous" include:

- Inherent or acquired distinctiveness of the mark
- Duration and extent to which the owner has used and publicized it

---

[90] Dastar Corp. v. Twentieth Century Fox Film Corp., 539 U.S. 23 (2003).

[91] Schwan's IP, LLC v. Kraft Pizza Co., 460 F.3d 971 (8th Cir. 2006). According to the Ninth Circuit, "disinfectable" is a generic mark and cannot be trademarked for manicure tools; various state laws require disinfection of multiple-use tools, and historically "disinfectable" has been used generically not only in nail care but in other fields such as dentistry: Rudolph Int'l Inc. v. Realys Inc., 482 F.3d 1195 (9th Cir. 2007).

[92] Secura Comm Consulting Inc. v. Secura-Com Inc., 224 F.3d 273 (3d Cir. 2000).

[93] K and N Engineering, Inc. v. Bulat, 510 F.3d 1079 (9th Cir. 2007).

- Channels of trade in which it is used
- Degree of recognition
- Extent of use of similar marks by third parties (i.e., not involved in the current dispute over dilution).

In 2003, the Supreme Court made it more difficult for trademark owners to maintain dilution actions, ruling that the FTDA requires proof of actual dilution and not the mere likelihood of harm to the trademark. Consumers' mental association between trademarks is not dilution. However, it is not necessary to prove actual loss of sales or profits.[94]

The Northern District of Ohio defined noncommercial use as First-Amendment-protected speech. Therefore, a political candidate's reference to a famous trademark was held to be core political speech likely to qualify for the noncommercial use exception.[95]

Rebuilt surgical instruments retained a piece of the original instrument carrying the name of the original manufacturer. In the Ninth Circuit view, repairing or rebuilding a trademarked product, resulting in a different product, can constitute a use in commerce likely to cause confusion as defined by the Lanham Act. The defendant did not prevail on its argument that customers would not be confused because they ordered a reconditioned instrument. However, the court refused to stipulate a bright-line test for whether all rebuilt goods use trademarks in commerce; the result depends on the nature and degree of alterations to the original equipment, the presence or absence of markets for service and spare parts, and the likelihood of confusion to end users.[96]

In 2002, the Ninth Circuit adopted the Second Circuit's test of whether the use of another party's trademark in a title infringes that trademark. In this analysis, the title of a literary work does not identify its publisher or producer. It thus fails to satisfy the major function of a trademark: identifying origin. A song called "Barbie Girl" was held not to infringe Mattel's trademark, because the title related to and was an accurate description of the song's content. The song was also a parody qualifying as noncommercial use under the FTDA, even though the records were intended to be sold at a profit, because parody, satire, and editorialization were treated as constitutionally protected.[97]

The Fourth Circuit ruled that product parodies do not automatically give rise to trademark dilution (in this case, "Chewy Vuitton" dog toys that were part of a

---

[94] Moseley v. V Secret Catalog Inc., 537 U.S. 418 (2003).

[95] American Family Life Ins. Co. v. Hagan, 266 F. Supp. 2d 682 (N.D. Ohio 2002).

[96] Karl Storz Endoscopy-America Inc. v. Surgical Technologies Inc., 285 F.3d 848 (9th Cir. 2002).

[97] Mattel Inc. v. MCA Records Inc., 296 F.3d 894 (9th Cir. 2002). The Ninth Circuit granted summary judgment for the defendant in another Barbie case, finding that the use of a nude Barbie doll in photographs was transformative parody use of the symbolism of Barbie as the "ideal woman" of American culture, thus ruling out trademark, trade dress, and copyright claims: Mattel Inc. v. Walking Mountain Products, 353 F.3d 792 (9th Cir. 2003).

line satirizing various luxury trademarks). A defendant's use of a parody mark can be considered as to whether the parody is likely to impair the distinctiveness of the famous mark, but in this case the imitation was not close enough to diminish the capacity of the real Louis Vuitton trademark to identify the source of the goods. The Fourth Circuit did not believe there could be confusion between the parody and the original. The Fourth Circuit imposed the same standards on a trade dress as on a trademark infringement claim, and held that parodying altered elements of a Louis Vuitton design did not infringe Vuitton copyrights.[98]

A trademark holder cannot assert a dilution claim on the basis that a licensee Web site links to a pornography site. A link to another, potentially offensive, site does not tarnish the underlying trademark.[99]

[2] Trademarks on the Internet

The Anticybersquatting Consumer Protection Act (ACPA), P.L. 106–113, was passed to prevent a predictable form of abuse of the system of registering Web addresses (Uniform Resource Locators, or URLs). It is a violation of the ACPA to register a domain name with the intent of hindering the use of the name by a party with legitimate rights in it. The ACPA permits an action to recover a domain name that was registered before the enactment of the ACPA but re-registered somewhere else after the effective date of the ACPA. The Third Circuit deemed the term "registration" to include a change of registrar.[100]

According to the Northern District of New York, the ACPA does not authorize in rem jurisdiction over domain names in any forum other than where the registrar is located.[101]

The Third Circuit view is that "typosquatting" — intentional misspelling of a trademark used in a domain name — is actionable under the ACPA.[102]

The federal antidilution statute does not necessarily give the owner of a famous trademark the right to use its trademark as a domain name (in this case, "Clue Computing" versus Hasbro's "Clue" trademark for a board game). Even the fact that consumers will discover that they've gone to the wrong site, and must do a search to find the right one, is not deemed substantial enough to constitute confusion for legal purposes.[103]

---

[98] Louis Vuitton Malletier S.A. v. Haute Diggity Dog, LLC, 507 F.3d 252 (4th Cir. 2007).

[99] Voice-Tel Enterprises Inc. v. Joba Inc., 71 L.W. 1648 (N.D. Ga. 3/31/03).

[100] Schmidheiny v. Weber, 319 F.3d 581 (3d Cir. 2003).

[101] Standing Stone Media Inc. v. Indiancountrytoday.com, 193 F. Supp. 2d 528 (N.D.N.Y. 2002). Nor can a plaintiff file a complaint in a different district, then deposit documentation about the domain name with the court to trigger in rem jurisdiction, because nexus is with the district of registration. The Second Circuit held that Congress did not intend to create nationwide in rem jurisdiction, only jurisdiction in the judicial district in which the registrar or other domain name authority is located: Mattel Inc. v. Barbie-club.com, 310 F.3d 293 (2d Cir. 2002).

[102] Shields v. Zuccarini, 254 F.3d 576 (3d Cir. 2001).

[103] Hasbro Inc. v. Clue Computing Inc., 232 F.3d 1 (1st Cir. 2000).

Various phrases including "Playboy" were fair use for a one-time Playmate of the Year to describe herself on her personal Web site. According to the Ninth Circuit, the terms were used in a nontrademark manner, as an accurate description of her past connection with the magazine. Despite Playboy's evidence of initial confusion, the former Playmate's inclusion of Playboy in the metatags (indexing information) for her site also constituted fair use.

However, the Ninth Circuit remanded on the issue of potential infringement or dilution in connection with the use of PMOY '81 as wallpaper on the Web site, because that is not nominative use, and the trademark implications of Web site design elements have not been resolved.[104]

The Sixth Circuit's position is that a domain name is a designation of origin and is vital for identifying the source of the Web site. Unauthorized use of someone else's trademark in a domain name constitutes infringement.[105] Even a disclaimer on the site is viewed too late to prevent initial interest confusion; Web surfers are more likely to be confused about origin than customers in a bricks-and-mortar store.[106] However, using someone else's trademark in the part of the URL after the domain name (e.g., http://www.fredsbeverages.com/pepsicola) is not trademark infringement — even if the site is for a product that competes with the trademarked product — unless there is evidence that consumers are likely to be confused about the source, because the post-domain-name portion of the URL merely identifies the way files are organized on a computer server.[107]

In 2004, the Sixth Circuit held that, by itself, use of another party's mark in the domain name of a "gripe site" (a site containing complaints about a product or service) does not constitute bad faith intent to profit. There was no evidence that the dissatisfied customer of Lucas Nursery traded on the company's goodwill in the site he created to publicize his views about the company's poor service.[108]

---

[104] Playboy Enterprises v. Welles, 279 F.3d 796 (9th Cir. 2002). *See also* Bihari v. Gross, 119 F. Supp. 2d 309 (S.D.N.Y. 2000) (use of another party's trademark in the metatags for a Web site, but not in the part of the site visible to casual Web users, does not violate the Anticybersquatting Consumer Protection Act because it falls within the ambit of fair use. Because of the low probability of confusion, there was no Lanham Act § 43(a) violation either); Promatek Indus. Ltd. v. Equitrac Corp., 300 F.3d 808 (7th Cir. 2002) (it is permissible to use another party's trademark in metatags in a legitimate and nondeceptive fashion, as long as the trademark is not used to deceive consumers about origin of trademarked merchandise). In contrast, however, Horphag Research Ltd. v. Pellegrini, 328 F.3d 1108 (9th Cir. 2003), finds infringement because a site (including its metatags) used a trademarked term so pervasively — and in excess of nominative fair use for identifying the product — so that a connection would probably be falsely inferred between the site and the unaffiliated holder of the trademark.

[105] According to the District Court for the District of Delaware, the use of a trademark in a domain name is "use in commerce" that will confer standing to sue under the ACPA. The plaintiff is not required to prove that there was an attempt to sell the domain name back to the plaintiff, because that is not the only way to prove a bad-faith intent to profit from the mark: Argos v. Orthotek LLC, 03-0757-SLR, 72 L.W. 1456 (D. Del. 1/8/04).

[106] PACCAR Inc. v. TeleScan Tech. LLC, 319 F.3d 243 (6th Cir. 2003).

[107] Interactive Products Corp. v. a2z Mobile Office Solutions Inc., 326 F.3d 687 (6th Cir. 2003).

[108] Lucas Nursery & Landscaping Inc. v. Grosse, 357 F.3d 811, 359 F.3d 806 (6th Cir. 2004); *see also* TMI Inc. v. Maxwell, 368 F.3d 433 (5th Cir. 2004).

The Ninth Circuit also ruled that expressing an opinion about goods or services is not using the trademark in connection with those goods and services, so the use of a trademark in a gripe site domain name does not constitute infringement or dilution.[109] The Northern District of Georgia ruled that the Wal-Mart name and marks are strong enough so that no one would be confused by parody t-shirts or other items making fun of Wal-Mart (e.g., slogans like "Wal-Ocaust" and "Wal-Qaeda.") The parody items were treated as protected noncommercial speech because the goal was criticism of Wal-Mart's merchandise quality and customer service, not profit. Only 62 t-shirts were sold, 15 of them to Wal-Mart's law firm. The court said that parody protected by the First Amendment does not tarnish a trademark. Speech that consists primarily of noncommercial elements such as religious or political commentary can constitute noncommercial speech even if it benefits the speaker economically.[110]

The Ninth Circuit's position is that registration and use of a domain name that is identical to a trademark is not enough to establish initial interest confusion. This is especially true of a weak trademark. The Ninth Circuit looks at three factors: the similarity of the marks; relation between the goods and services involved; and the extent to which both parties use the Web as a marketing channel. Where products are very different and confusion on the part of targeted consumers very unlikely, the Ninth Circuit will not find trademark infringement.[111]

If the phrase "you have mail" is merely used to alert e-mail users to the presence of messages, the phrase is generic and cannot be protected as a trademark. Therefore, the Fourth Circuit ruled in favor of AT&T rather than AOL, in that AOL did not use the phrase consistently to describe a service. Furthermore, even if AOL could establish de facto secondary meaning, in that the public associated the phrase with AOL, it could not prevent functional use of common English words by others.[112]

Using "lawoffices" in a domain name for an attorney is descriptive, and therefore unprotectable, as to legal information and attorney referrals. The Sixth Circuit held that West's use of "lawoffice.com" for an online directory of legal information therefore did not infringe.[113]

Distributing software over the Internet is "use in commerce" that is sufficient to establish trademark rights (in this case, in the term "Coolmail") given the public's association between the mark and the software.[114]

---

[109] Bosley Med. Inst. Inc. v. Kremer, 403 F.3d 672 (9th Cir. 2005). *See* Lamparello v. Falwell, 420 F.3d 309 (4th Cir. 2005) and Coca-Cola Co. et al. v. Purdy, 382 F.3d 774 (8th Cir. 2004) for partisan political use of URLs that sound similar to a political opponent's name or site.

[110] Smith v. Wal-Mart, No. 1:06-cv-526 (N.D. Ga. 2008). *See* Janet L. Conley, *Parody of Wal-Mart Trumps Its Trademark*, Fulton County Daily Report 3/26/08 (law.com).

[111] Interstellar Starship Servs. Ltd. v. Epix Inc., 304 F.3d 936 (9th Cir. 2002).

[112] AOL v. AT&T, 243 F.3d 812 (4th Cir. 2001).

[113] DeGidio v. WestGroup Corp., 355 F.3d 506 (6th Cir. 2004).

[114] Planetary Motion Inc. v. Techsplosion Inc., 261 F.3d 1188 (11th Cir. 2001).

The Southern District of New York ruled in mid-2008 that Tiffany cannot hold eBay liable for contributory infringement when counterfeit Tiffany jewelry is sold there. The test of contributory infringement is not whether eBay could anticipate that infringement would occur, but whether it continued to provide services to particular sellers that it knew or had reason to know were infringing Tiffany trademarks. The Southern District ruled that eBay acted promptly once it was on notice that specific infringing items were offered. The S.D.N.Y. refused to order eBay to monitor its site to remove infringing listings before they became public. The Southern District also characterized eBay's use of Tiffany trademarks on its advertisements, home pages, and sponsored links on Yahoo and Google as protected nominative fair use. Allegations of unfair competition, false advertising, and dilution were dismissed, and the SDNY rejected a presumption that any seller offering five or more pieces of Tiffany jewelry was selling counterfeits. The question was not whether counterfeits were sold on eBay — obviously they were — but whether eBay had direct control over the means of infringement. eBay did not have physical control over the items and could not physically inspect them. However, a French court ordered eBay to pay more than $61 million to LVMH Moet Hennessy Louis Vuitton SA for sales of knock-off merchandise.[115] A trademark licensor can be held responsible (in its role as "apparent manufacturer") for defective products that are negligently placed in the stream of commerce and that bear the licensor's logo, because consumers expect licensors to oversee production. However, the licensor's liability is limited based on its actual role in design, manufacturing, and distribution.[116]

[B] Federal Trademark Registration

The Lanham Act calls for maintenance of a "principal" and a "supplemental" register of trademarks. The principal register is for "true" or "technical" marks: i.e., coined, arbitrary, fanciful, or suggestive names or combinations of name and image. Federally registered marks must be used in connection with goods sold in interstate commerce.

Marks do not qualify for registration in the principal register if they are merely descriptive of the goods ("Green Spinach"; "Moldable Plastic"). Trademarks that give an inaccurate description are equally unsuitable for registration. Pure geographical descriptions, whether accurate or deceptive, cannot be registered. Last names cannot be registered as trademarks, unless it can be shown that they have "secondary meaning" (i.e., that the trademark is recognized as associated with a specific source of goods). Proof of continuous use of a last name as a trademark for five years makes out a prima facie case of secondary meaning.

---

[115] Tiffany (N.J.) Inc v. eBay, Inc., No. 04 civ. 4607 (S.D.N.Y. 2008); *see* Mark Hamblett, *Tiffany Fails to Prove eBay Contributed to Mark Violation*, N.Y.L.J. 7/15/08 (law.com).

[116] Kennedy v. Guess Inc., 802 N.E.2d 776 (Ind. 2004).

With respect to trademark priority, "use in commerce" means lawful use, which, in turn, means use that complies with federal labeling requirements.[117]

Although the defendant "Yellow Cab" company obtained summary judgment at the District Court level, the Ninth Circuit reversed because there are issues of material fact as to whether "Yellow Cab" is generic, and if it is descriptive, whether it has secondary meaning. "Yellow Cab" is not a federally registered trademark. The burden of proof on the validity and protectability of an unregistered trademark falls on the party claiming protection. A plaintiff alleging infringement of a federally registered mark is entitled to a presumption that the mark is not generic.[118]

[1] Unavailable Trademarks

Certain trademarks will not be granted:

- Anything involving the name, portrait, or signature of a living person who has not given consent
- Name, portrait, or signature of a deceased U.S. President as long as the President is survived by a widow who has not given consent
- Material that is "immoral, deceptive or scandalous"
- False suggestion of anyone (living or dead), or with institutions, beliefs, or national symbols
- Disparagement of people, institutions, beliefs, or symbols; bringing them into disrepute or contempt
- Anything similar to a trademark already registered or used and not abandoned, if its use is likely to deceive purchasers, or cause confusion or mistake.

Marks that do not qualify for registration in the principal register can still be registered on the supplemental register, as long as they have been used in commerce for at least a year, and provide distinctive identification of the applicant's merchandise.

The TTAB canceled the mark "Washington Redskins," but the D.C. Circuit overturned the decision, finding a lack of proof that at the time six marks were registered (starting in 1967), a substantial percentage of the Native American population considered them to be demeaning. The D.C. Circuit also found that laches barred action against the mark at this late date. The trademark owner would also suffer substantial economic prejudice if it were canceled, because of investment in advertising and merchandise.[119]

---

[117] Creagri, Inc. v. Usana Health Sciences Inc., 474 F.3d 626 (9th Cir. 2007).

[118] Yellow Cab of Sacramento v. Yellow Cab of Elk Grove Inc., 419 F.3d 925 (9th Cir. 2005).

[119] Although 15 USC § 1064(3) says that a trademark can be cancelled "at any time" if it is disparaging, the D.C. Circuit ruled in mid-2005 that laches is a defense that can bar a suit by Native Americans seeking to cancel the "Redskins" trademark. In this reading, although there is no statute of limitations for the action, equitable doctrines such as laches are applicable. The D.C. Circuit would not, however, apply the defense to a plaintiff who was only a year old in 1967, when the mark was first

Although § 6 of the Paris Convention (dealing with international protection of intellectual property) requires acceptance of trademarks that are duly registered in their country of origin, the Federal Circuit ruled in early 2005 that the Principal Register is not obligated to register a foreign mark that is unacceptable under Lanham Act § 44(e) because it is primarily a surname.[120]

In 2004, the TTAB ruled that "Realtor" and "Realtors" are protectable trademarks, not generic terms for real estate agents, and therefore denied a petition to cancel those marks. The TTAB deemed the relevant population (for determining if consumers perceive the mark to be generic) to be brokers as well as consumers. The marks had not been abandoned, and generic use was not permitted to continue unopposed.[121]

A trademark using XXXX as a placeholder for missing elements cannot be registered (e.g., a group of shampoos called Rich XXXX, where XXXX is the name of a fruit or flower) because the Lanham Act limits each application to only one mark. The court's rationale is that allowing registration of such a phantom mark would impair trademark searching, and would not put other potential users on notice of what had been claimed.[122]

[2] Effect of Registration

Registration in either register gives the registrant:

- Statutory remedies
- The right to sue in federal court
- Protection against registration in either register of the same mark or any confusingly similar mark.

In addition, registration on the principal register constitutes constructive notice of the claim of ownership of the trademark. The registrant can prevent importation of goods carrying an infringing mark. Registration in the principal register is prima facie evidence of the registrant's ownership of the mark; the validity of the registration; and the registrant's exclusive right to use the mark, subject to any conditions and limitations stated in the registration itself.

A trademark registration becomes incontestable, under 15 USC § 1065, if there has been five years of continuous post-registration use without challenges posed to the validity of the trademark. The trademark user must submit an affidavit, within one year after the end of the five-year period, that the mark is still in use. Even after a trademark has become incontestable, functionality can still be raised

---

registered: Pro-Football Inc. v. Harjo, 415 F.3d 44 (D.C. Cir. 2005). *Semble* Bridgestone/Firestone Research Inc. v. Automobile Club de L'Ouest de la France, 245 F.3d 1359 (Fed. Cir. 2001), *but contra* Marshak v. Treadwell, 240 F.3d 184 (3d Cir. 2001).

[120] *In re* Rath, 402 F.3d 1207 (Fed. Cir. 2005).

[121] Zimmerman v. National Ass'n of Realtors, TTAB No. 9302360 (3/31/04); *see* 72 L.W. 2657.

[122] *In re* International Flavors & Fragrances Inc., 183 F.3d 1361 (Fed. Cir. 1999).

as a defense against infringement. Even after the five years have elapsed, a trademark can be challenged if it was obtained fraudulently, if the trademark holder has abandoned it (no longer uses it in commerce; a trademark is presumed abandoned after three years elapse without use in commerce), or if the mark has stopped functioning as a trademark and has become generic (now identifies an entire class of goods without limitation to a single source).

At the end of 2004, the Supreme Court ruled that even if a trademark is incontestable, the party alleging infringement still has to prove infringement under § 1114, which requires proof of the likelihood of consumer confusion.[123]

According to the Eleventh Circuit, the defense of functionality (that no trademark can be granted in the functional features or shapes of a product) is a judicially created doctrine that predates the Lanham Act.

The Eleventh Circuit notes that the concept of functionality is not mentioned in the Lanham Act at all, so its omission from the list of Lanham Act defenses is not dispositive. The court also noted that the functionality defense was applied long before the 1998 amendments, and found it unlikely that Congress would enact only part of the doctrine and not all of it.[124]

[3] Form of the Application

The registration application must be filed in the name of the owner of the trademark or servicemark. The application calls for information such as:

- Date of first use of the mark on or in connection with the goods listed on the application
- Date of first use in interstate commerce
- How the mark is used in connection with goods
- What class(es) of merchandise is/are involved
- Statement of ownership
- Statement of right to use the mark
- Signature and verification
- A drawing of the mark
- Five specimens or facsimiles.

The drawing must be a substantially exact representation of the mark as it is actually used. The specimens should duplicate actual labels, tags, containers, or displays.

If it appears that the application is acceptable for registration in the principal register, the PTO will publish the application in the *Official Gazette*. If there is no opposition, a certification of registration is issued.

Anyone who opposes the registration of a trademark on the principal register can use 15 USC § 1063 to file a verified opposition during the 30-day period

---

[123] KP Permanent Make-Up Inc. v. Lasting Impression I Inc., 543 U.S. 111 (2004).

[124] Wilhelm Pudenz GMBH v. Littlefuse Inc., 177 F.3d 1204 (11th Cir. 1999).

beginning with publication in the *Official Gazette*. The Trademark Trial and Appeal Board handles the dispute.

The PTO determines who is entitled to register, if the agency detects a conflict between two applications pending at the same time. In mid-2004, the PTO finalized rules (under 37 CFR § 2.172) for amending or correcting trademark registrations. Under the Final Rule, 69 FR 51362 (8/19/04; effective 9/20/04), it is not necessary to request the correction within one year of registration; the PTO proposed a time limit in December 2003 Proposed Regulations but in light of comments decided not to adopt it as a requirement. Nor must the registrant submit the original certificate or a copy of it.

Note, however, that the PTO position is that the prefixes "e" and "i" and the suffix ".com" are purely descriptive and therefore not entitled to trademark protection when coupled with other purely descriptive terms.[125]

[C] Trademark Infringement

The Stop Counterfeiting in Manufactured Goods Act, P.L. 109-181, was signed on March 16, 2006. The objective was to make it illegal to traffic in counterfeit labels and packaging, even if they are separate from goods; see 18 USC § 2320 as amended. Unless a federal enforcement agency requests otherwise, a court hearing a forfeiture proceeding must direct that articles consisting of or bearing counterfeit marks be destroyed. Under prior law, only counterfeit goods could be ordered destroyed; this legislation also permits destruction of equipment used in counterfeiting. Convicted persons must forfeit all property within the U.S. that was used in the crime, and must pay restitution to the owner of the mark and any other victims of counterfeiting. The forfeiture proceedings follow the procedures of the Comprehensive Drug Abuse Prevention and Control Act, 21 USC § 853.[126]

In the Fourth Circuit's view, when it comes to coverage under the advertising injury provision of a business liability insurance policy, trade dress infringement claims and trademark dilution claims are virtually indistinguishable from trademark infringement claims. Thus, if the policy excludes trademark infringement, the insurer is not obligated to defend trade dress or dilution claims either.[127]

The Eleventh Circuit joined other Circuits in holding that the standard of good faith is whether the alleged infringer sought to trade on the good will of the actual owner of the trademark by creating confusion about the source of the goods.[128]

---

[125] Sabra Chartrand, *The Rush to Ask for Trademarks Slows*, N.Y. Times, April 1, 2002 at C2.

[126] *See* 74 LW 2571. Congress perceived a need to close up a loophole created by United States v. Giles, 213 F.3d 1246 (10th Cir 2000), holding that there was no criminal offense unless the labels or packaging were affixed to goods.

[127] Superperformance Int'l Inc. v. Hartford Cas. Ins. Co., 71 L.W. 1808 (4th Cir. 2003).

[128] International Stamp Art Inc. v. United States Postal Serv., 456 F.3d 1270 (11th Cir. 2006).

[1] Attorneys' Fee Awards for Trademark Infringement

In 2002 the First Circuit joined the Third, Eighth, and Tenth Circuits in holding that exceptional, willful conduct can justify an attorneys' fee award under Lanham Act § 35 even in the absence of fraud or bad faith.[129] The Second, Fourth, and Fifth Circuits disagree. However, the First Circuit listed factors that would militate against a fee award, such as the plaintiff's failure to register the mark, the defendant's reasonable belief that its conduct was noninfringing, the defendant's lack of intent to deceive or confuse, absence of actual damages to the plaintiff, and whether there was a close legal question as to whether infringement had occurred.

[D] Trademark Searches

It makes sense to search the federal registers before applying for a trademark registration, to make sure that the one desired is not identical or confusingly similar to an existing trademark. Failure to search could result in an expensive product launch that has to be withdrawn because the new product duplicates an existing trademark.

There are two main collections to be searched: one covering current and expired registrations, the other the published and pending registrations. Trademarks that consist of words are indexed alphabetically. There is a system for classifying symbols and other nonverbal marks.

The search process has some flaws. Prior unregistered marks are not indexed. There's no way to check phonetically similar trademarks that are not alphabetically similar, and no provision is made for synonyms or foreign equivalents. The Patent and Trademark Office (PTO) maintains records of assignments of registered trademarks. Its *Official Gazette* lists registered trademarks, so it should be consulted frequently to stay current. The PTO is engaged in an ongoing process of making the entire current and historical record available on-line, although the project is not yet complete.

[E] Protection of Trade Names

The name of a corporation or of a product may have commercial value. Corporate names can be protected by incorporating — even without an active business — in the states within the market area. Product names can be protected by incorporating them into a trademark that is registered and actively used.

Nearly all the states have some form of "fictitious name statute" requiring registration of fictitious or assumed names used in business. These statutes offer only limited protection of trade names. They insure that the same name will not be adopted as a corporate name by another entity within the same state, or by a foreign corporation seeking authorization to do business within the state. However, the

---

[129] *See* Tamko Roofing Prods. Inc. v. Ideal Roofing Co., 282 F.3d 23 (1st Cir. 2002) and the cases cited therein.

typical statute will not impede the adoption of a company's trademark as a corporate name by another business.

U.S. Magistrate Judge Theodore Katz issued a permanent injunction forbidding designer Joseph Abboud to put his name on a new line of men's clothing; he sold the marketing rights to his name in 2000, so continued use violated the trademark rights of the purchaser.[130]

[F] Trade Dress

Trade dress consists of nonfunctional features of product design and packaging. In 1992, the Supreme Court held trade dress to be protectable if it is inherently distinctive, even if it does not have secondary meaning. The Eighth Circuit went further: trade dress is protectable if it is fanciful or arbitrary (not dictated by the nature of the product), even if it is not "striking in appearance" or "memorable." But secondary meaning must be proved to protect trade dress that is dictated by the nature of the product.[131]

A March 2000 Supreme Court case says that in a § 43(a) Lanham Act trade dress infringement case dealing with product design, the product design is distinctive and hence protectable only if it has secondary meaning. Product design is not inherently distinctive. Like product color, consumers have no predisposition to use it to identify the source of the goods.[132]

In 1995, the Supreme Court found that color, although not inherently distinctive, can acquire protectable secondary meaning to identify the source of goods.[133]

The Supreme Court returned to trade dress issues in 2001, ruling that the fact that a product feature was disclosed in an expired utility patent is strong evidence that the feature is functional, and therefore cannot be protected as trade dress. (The burden of proving non-functionality is on the party asserting that the trade dress is protectable.)[134]

Lanham Act trade dress protection is not available for the overall appearance, design, and configuration of an unpatented multi-use tool. A patent is the only available form of protection for utilitarian features that are the essence of a product. In this reading, a functional feature is the actual benefit that the consumer buys the product for, whereas a trademark is an identification of the source or endorsement of a product. Only a completely nonfunctional configuration can constitute a

---

[130] Zach Lowe, *The Designer Formerly Known as Joseph Abboud*, The American Lawyer 6/6/08 (law.com).

[131] Two Pesos Inc. v. Taco Cabana Inc., 503 U.S. 957 (1992); Stuart Hall Co. v. Ampad Corp., 51 F.3d 780 (8th Cir. 1995).

[132] Wal-Mart Stores Inc. v. Samara Bros. Inc., 529 U.S. 205 (2000).

[133] Qualitex v. Jacobson Prods. Co., 514 U.S. 159 (1995). Elements that serve to identify source but have not yet developed secondary meaning might qualify for a copyright or a design patent: *see* Robert S. Kate and Helen Hill Minsker, *Design Patent + Trademark=Better Protection*, Nat'l L.J. 5/1/00 p. C19).

[134] TrafFix Devices Inc. v. Marketing Display Inc., 532 U.S. 23 (2001).

trademark or trade dress. Adding nonfunctional arbitrary features cannot be used to extend protection.[135]

Late in 2000, the Third Circuit ruled that Lanham Act § 43(a) protection of trade dress extends to non-identical items within a product line, as long as there is a consistent overall look that conveys a single continuing commercial impression. Protection is not available if the trade dress varies so widely that consumers would not perceive a single source for the goods.[136]

A plaintiff trying to protect the trade dress of an entire product line (in this case, items of jewelry) must be able to articulate the design elements making up the trade dress. Inability to do so suggests that the manufacturer seeks to protect an unprotectable style, theme, or idea.[137]

In a case in which the circular shape of a thermostat was claimed as trade dress, the Seventh Circuit ruled that even after a trademark has become incontestable, its validity can still be challenged on the basis of functionality.[138]

The manufacturer of the artificial sweetener Splenda secured an injunction against distribution of store-brand artificial sweetener in similar packages. The District Court rejected the argument that Splenda's package uses generic trade dress elements and thus cannot be distinctive. The court said that the package is distinctive, and in the non-caloric sweetener market, yellow is distinctive because Equal uses blue and Sweet'n'Low uses pink. Initially, the District Court refused to grant the injunction, but the Third Circuit remanded the case for determination of whether the store-brand packaging should be enjoined. On remand, Judge John R. Padova found that the plaintiff's trade dress was fanciful, and therefore distinctive, and had secondary meaning.[139]

[G] State Trademark Laws

As a general rule, federal registration is more protective than state registration. A broader class of marks can be registered under federal law. State trademark law does impose higher penalties than federal law, but there are more avenues of relief under federal law.

A federal trademark registration provides notice of the trademark nationwide, and federal (but not state) registration also opens up the possibility of trademark registration in other countries. The holder of a federal trademark can prevent importation of goods that carry infringing marks. Perhaps most important, any case involving a federal trademark can be heard in federal court; a case involving a state-registered trademark requires other jurisdictional elements.

---

[135] Leatherman Tool Group Inc. v. Cooper Indus., 199 F.3d 1009 (9th Cir. 1999).

[136] Rose Art Indus. Inc. v. Swanson, 235 F.3d 165 (3d Cir. 2000).

[137] Yurman Design Inc. v. PAJ Inc., 262 F.3d 101 (2d Cir. 2001).

[138] Eco Mfg. LLC v. Honeywell Int'l Inc., 357 F.3d 649 (7th Cir. 2003).

[139] McNeil Nutritionals v. Heartland Sweeteners, No. 07-2644 (E.D. Pa. 6/26/08), on remand from 511 F.3d 390 (3d Cir. 2007); *see* Shannon P. Duffy, *Splenda Awarded Injunction Against Generic Sweetener*, The Legal Intelligencer 7/9/08 (law.com).

[H] Preserving Trademark Rights

It is important to be able to document and substantiate when the trademark was first used in commerce. For instance, an invoice showing the trademark followed by a generic description of the product, a bill of lading, or a letter from a buyer mentioning the trademark and acknowledging receipt of the product, all indicate use in commerce on a particular date.

Once the first use has been documented, the owner of the trademark should be careful to preserve the trademark, and prevent it from becoming an unprotectable generic term. (At one time, for instance, "aspirin" was a trademark, but it became generic because of failure of protection.) Under common law, failure to use a trademark or trade name can result in its abandonment. 15 USC § 1127 provides that nonuse of a registered mark for two consecutive years is prima facie abandonment.

The trademark should be used frequently in advertising and promotional copy, but it should be distinguished typographically from body copy (by using boldface, a different typeface, a different color, a larger size, etc.). The symbols^{TM} (for trademark),^{SM} (for service mark), and® (for registered trademark) should be used where appropriate.

Once a mark is adopted, it should be used consistently, including pictorial elements such as color, use of symbols, type face used for the name, and relationship between the name and the pictorial elements. Protests should be made whenever the brand name is used as a generic description for a kind of product: e.g., "Snorple® brand furnish-sifters are a product of the Vreeble Corporation; please respect the trademark and do not use Snorple as a term for all furnish-sifters." (One advantage of the World Wide Web is that it is easy to find sites that refer to a particular product, and see who is using the name in what context.)

§ 12.05   TRADE SECRETS

Many businesses have processes, products, or combinations of the two that are not patentable (or that the company deems would not be beneficial to patent). Although there is no specific federal statute extending trade secret protection in line with copyright, trademark, and patent protection, various state laws extend the common-law protection of trade secrets. Forty-one states (but not including New York, a major commercial center) have adopted the Uniform Trade Secrets Act (UTSA).

A trade secret is a formula, pattern, program, device, method, technique, or collection of information used in business in order to obtain competitive advantage. A corporation's strategic or marketing plans; its customer lists (if not generally known or easily derived from public sources; its databases and computer programs, product specifications, recipes, and employee manuals, might all constitute trade secrets.

The subject matter of the trade secret must be kept secret, not disclosed, and the owner must take reasonable steps to maintain secrecy. Matters of public knowledge, or that are well-known within an industry, do not qualify for trade secret status. The Uniform Trade Secrets Act requires that keeping the information secret must have actual or potential independent economic value.

However, unlike patent or copyright protection, there is no requirement of novelty, creativity, non-obviousness, or originality for trade secret protection. In some ways, trade secret protection is broader than other forms of intellectual property rights. Patents are available only for processes, machinery, manufactures, or compositions of matter. There are no corresponding limitations on trade secrets. Trade secret protection is simple and inexpensive: no searches have to be made, and registration is not required.

The UTSA imposes liability only if misappropriation has occurred — that is, either acquisition of someone else's trade secret by improper means, or use or disclosure of trade secrets acquired improperly or in violation of a duty of confidentiality. Improper means include theft, bribery, and industrial espionage. However, independent invention, reverse engineering, licensing, and discovery from observing public domain processes are legitimate means that do not create UTSA liability.

The Restatement (3rd) of Unfair Competition gives a trade secret owner a claim for mere improper acquisition of a trade secret, even if the acquiror does not use it.

Suit can be brought (especially for an injunction rather than damages) as soon as disclosure of the trade secret is threatened, because trade secret protection is lost as soon as the information becomes generally known.[140] The grant of injunction would probably be limited to the time before the material would become known anyway.

The statute of limitations for a UTSA action is three years from the time the owner of the trade secret discovers, or reasonably should have discovered, the misappropriation of the trade secret.

The California Court of Appeals held that the three-year statute of limitations for a trade secret holder to sue third parties begins to run when the plaintiff has any reason to suspect that a third party knew it received goods that violated a trade secret. Both sides claimed victory. Trade secret holders said it was beneficial because they would not lose rights before becoming aware of them, but third parties said the decision protected them, because it put the burden of action on the owner of the trade secret.[141]

Monetary damages (instead of or in addition to injunction) might be measured by the loss to the owner of the trade secrets (such as lost profits or the cost of developing the trade secret); the misappropriator's gain (including savings due to increased efficiency); or a reasonable royalty that might have been charged if the trade secret had been licensed instead of appropriated. In very serious cases, punitive damages might be allowed.

---

[140] This is the rationale for Federal Rules of Civil Procedure 26(c), permitting a motion to protect trade secrets from disclosure via litigation.

[141] Semiconductor v. Superior Court (Silvaco Data Systems), 163 Cal. App. 4th 575 (2008); see Zusha Elinson, *Calif. Court Resets Trade Secrets Clock*, The Recorder 6/3/08 (law.com).

[A] Protecting Secrecy

There are no exceptions to the UTSA rule that trade secret protection requires the owner to safeguard the confidentiality of the material. Appropriate security steps include:

- Drafting a written security manual
- Making sure that employees know what material is confidential
- Having employees sign an agreement indicating that they will keep trade secret material to which they have access secure and confidential
- Holding exit interviews with departing employees, stressing the inappropriateness of disclosing trade secrets, especially to a new employer
- Sending a follow-up letter to ex-employees reminding them of the confidentiality obligation
- Keeping trade secret documents apart from other documents in a locked and fireproof location
- Making employees sign out files containing trade secret materials
- Labeling trade secret materials as such; consider reproducing them on paper that defeats further copying
- Shredding or otherwise destroying extra copies of materials relating to trade secrets
- Having a sign-out process to trace who uses trade secret files
- Consulting computer and network security professionals to make sure that access to trade secret material in digital form is properly restricted (e.g., with passwords and encryption) — and that materials that are supposed to be deleted from the computer are indeed deleted and cannot be recovered!
- Informing customers and licensees of their obligation to maintain confidentiality of trade secrets that they are entitled to use
- Reviewing press releases, trade show speeches, technical articles published by employees, etc., to make sure that trade secrets are not disclosed.

§ 12.06 PATENTS

In a way, the patent is the most absolute form of intellectual property. It is quite possible for two similar works both to qualify for copyright (as long as one does not plagiarize the other), or for two similar trademarks to be granted (as long as they are not confusingly similar). But the grant of a patent requires a patent examiner's determination that the same invention has not already been patented, and that the current invention is not an obvious development of existing public domain or patented inventions.[142]

---

[142] A mid-1999 Supreme Court decision, Dickinson v. Zurko, 527 U.S. 150 (1999), holds that when the Federal Circuit reviews PTO findings of fact, the standard of review is whether the agency's decision was supported by substantial evidence, not whether the determination was clearly erroneous.

Although in general monopolies are disapproved of, a patent is a "statutory monopoly," permitting the patentee exclusive use (within the United States) of the invention for a 20-year term, running from the date of filing (35 USC § 154).[143] The holder of the patent can prevent unauthorized persons from manufacturing, using, offering to sell, or selling the invention. When a patent expires, the item or process goes into the public domain.

The status of patents as lawful monopolies creates some tension between patent and antitrust law. The Supreme Court ruled early in 2006 that a patent does not necessarily give the patentee market power. Therefore, in tying cases, the plaintiff must prove the defendant's market power over the tying product.[144]

The Third Circuit permitted a patent holder to be sued under antitrust law for deceptive conduct toward an organization that promulgates uniform standards for telecommunications. Standard-setting organizations require patent-holders to agree to license their technology on fair, reasonable, and non-discriminatory (FRAND) terms. The Third Circuit held that the FRAND principle is a control on monopolies, and the standard-setting group was lured into adopting the patented technology as a standard rather than an unpatented one. To the Third Circuit, a patentee's intentionally false promise to grant FRAND licenses, in conjunction with reliance by a standard-setting organization and breach of promise, is actionable as anticompetitive conduct.[145]

In January 2007, the Supreme Court made it easier to challenge a licensed patent by holding that a licensee can file a declaratory judgment action to challenge the validity of the underlying patent while remaining in compliance with the licensing agreement.[146]

[A] Patentable Subject Matter

Any "new and useful process, machine, manufacture or composition of matter, or any new and useful improvement thereof" can be granted a utility patent: 35 USC § 101. The invention must be new; useful; and non-obvious to a person who has ordinary skill in "the art" (i.e., the type of technology for which the patent has been issued).

A design patent covers an object's non-functional visual and tactile characteristics (e.g., the shape and decoration of a table lamp, but not the way its wiring or bulb works). The design patent term (35 USC § 171) is 14 years.

---

[143] Prior to the United States' adoption of GATT, the General Agreement on Tariffs and Trade, the duration of a patent was 17 years from its date of issue. For patents issued based on a filing made before 6/8/95, the term is either 17 years from issue or 20 years from filing, whichever is longer.

[144] Illinois Tool Works Inc. v. Independent Ink Inc., 547 U.S. 28 (2006).

[145] Broadcom Corp. v. Qualcomm Inc., 501 F.3d 297 (3d Cir. 2007), discussed in Mary Pat Gallagher, *3rd Circuit Rules on Patent Holders' Antitrust Liability in Qualcomm Case*, N.J.L.J. 9/6/07 (law.com).

[146] MedImmune v. Genentech, 549 U.S. 118 (2007), discussed in Charles S. Barquist and Jason A. Crotty, *"MedImmune v. Genentech": The Supreme Court Upends the Federal Circuit's Declaratory Judgment Jurisprudence*, Special to law.com (1/29/07).

In 2008, the Federal Circuit fundamentally changed design patent law by setting aside the decades-old "point of novelty" test. Instead, the Federal Circuit adopted the point of view of an ordinary observer. The issue is whether the allegedly infringing design embodies the appearance of the allegedly infringed patented design, leading deceived consumers to buy the wrong product. Previously, the Federal Circuit held that similarity is not enough; to infringe, the accused design must incorporate the novelty of the patented design. But that test was hard to apply when there were many design features that could be considered points of novelty. The case involved nail buffers, and the Federal Circuit held that it would be impossible to mistake a buffer with padding on three sides for one padded on four sides.[147]

Making one product imitate another is considered utility within the 35 USC § 101 definition, and the imitation product is not rendered unpatentable on the grounds that it is deceptive.[148] The Patent Act does not involve moral considerations, and many imitation products, such as artificial fibers and cubic zirconia, have been patented.

Certain subject matter is not entitled to patents, such as laws of nature, natural phenomena or principles, or mathematical algorithms.[149] Although traditionally patents were denied for systems or methods of doing business, several Internet-related patents have been issued for business methods, e.g., "reverse auctions" conducted online. It was not clear that business methods were patentable until the Supreme Court's 1998 *State Street* decision.[150]

The PTO has granted a number of business methods patents for computer and commercial techniques (e.g., AT&T's patent for call message recording, which was upheld by the Federal Circuit.[151] Some of these patents, especially those for e-business techniques, have been challenged by competitors and have attracted criticism.

Reversing the trend of giving greater patent protection to business methods, the Federal Circuit ruled in late 2008 that a method or process is patentable only if it involves physical transformation or is associated with a machine. In this case, the Patent Office and Board of Patent Appeals and Interferences refused to grant a patent for a method of hedging commodities trading risks.[152]

---

[147] Egyptian Goddess v. Swisa, 498 F.3d 1354 (Fed. Cir. 2008); *see* Mike Scarcella, *Federal Circuit Ruling Sets Legal Standard for Design Patent Infringement*, Legal Times 9/24/08 (law.com).

[148] Juicy Whip v. Orange Bang Inc., 185 F.3d 1364 (Fed. Cir. 1999).

[149] *But see* State Street Bank v. Signature Fin. Corp., 149 F.3d 1368 (Fed. Cir. 1998), *cert. denied*, 119 S. Ct. 851, permitting patenting of business algorithms that produce a "useful, concrete and tangible result." The Supreme Court granted certiorari to determine the patentability of basic scientific relationships (in the context of a lab test for vitamin deficiencies), but in mid-2006, certiorari was dismissed as improvidently granted. Lab Corp. of Am. Holdings v. Metabolite Labs Inc., 548 U.S. 124 (2006).

[150] State Street Bank & Trust Co. v. Signature Fin. Group, 149 F.3d 1368 (Fed. Cir. 1998).

[151] AT&T Corp. v. Excel Communications Inc., 173 F.3d 973 (Fed. Cir. 2000).

[152] *In re* Bilski No. 2007-1130 (Fed. Cir. 10/30/08); *see* Mike Scarcella, *Federal Circuit Restricts Patent Protection of Business Methods*, 10/31/08 (law.com).

A so-called "plant patent," under 35 USC § 161 *et seq.*, is issued on a method of asexually reproducing a plant. P.L. 103-349, the Plant Variety Protection Act Amendments of 1994, conforms U.S. law to the International Convention for the Protection of New Varieties of Plants.[153] Also see P.L. 105-289, the Plant Patent Amendments of 1998, protecting the owner of a plant patent against unauthorized sale of parts taken from an illegally reproduced plant.

Seeds and seed-grown plants are patentable under 37 USC § 101 even though protection is also available under the Plant Patent Act and Plant Variety Protection Act, and even though the same subject matter could have different rights and obligations depending on the patentee's choice of statute. A legal or property interest can be governed by more than one statute, e.g., ornamental design can come under either design patent or copyright.[154]

Invention, for patent purposes, has two phases: conception and reduction to practice. Reduction to practice can be either actual (making a tangible exemplar or embodiment of the invention) or constructive (by setting out a detailed description in the patent application).

[1] Novelty; Non-Obviousness

In order to be patented, an invention must be novel. 35 USC § 102(a) denies patentability to inventions "patented or described in a printed publication in this or a foreign country, before the invention thereof by the application for patent."

35 USC § 103 imposes a further requirement of non-obviousness. *Graham v. John Deere Co.*[155] sets out a three-part test for non-obviousness:

- Scope and content of prior art
- Differences between the patent claims and prior art
- Level of ordinary skill in the art found among other potential inventors and practitioners.

In a case involving mechanisms for automobile pedals, the Supreme Court made it easier to challenge or deny patents on obviousness grounds by holding that obviousness is assessed under the "TSM Test" (teaching, suggestion, or motivation) under which a patent is obvious only if the prior art, the nature of the problem, or the knowledge of a person with ordinary skill in the art would reveal a motivation or suggestion to combine prior art teachings. To the Supreme Court, a technique used to improve a device is obvious if a person of ordinary skill in the art would want to use it to improve similar devices. Any problem known in

---

[153] Infringement of a plant patent means asexual reproduction of the actual patented plant, not just creating a plant with the same essential characteristics: Imazio Nursery Inc v. Dania Greenhouses, 69 F.3d 1560 (Fed. Cir. 1995).

[154] J.E.M. Ag. Supply Inc. v. Pioneer Hi-Bred Int'l Inc., 534 U.S. 124 (2001).

[155] 383 U.S. 1 (1966).

the field and addressed by the patent can be a reason for combining the elements as claimed — making the disputed claim obvious.[156]

"Double patenting" — the issuance of multiple patents on the same invention — is barred. An inventor who has patented an invention cannot also patent the means of producing the patented invention. If the inventor later improves on the invention, additional patents can be granted on the improvements.

The late 2004 enactment the Cooperative Research and Technology Enhancement Act (CREATE Act; P.L. 108-453) amends 35 USC § 103(c) to redefine certain secret information as not operating as prior art that will invalidate a patent. To qualify, the claimed invention must be made within the scope of a joint research agreement, and the application must either disclose or be amended to disclose the names of the parties to the research agreement.

Although there are no state patent laws, federal preemption of this area is not complete. According to the Federal Circuit[157] a state-law claim of unfair competition against the holder of a patent is not preempted by federal patent law, as long as the defendant could be found liable under state law without actually conflicting with the federal law. Nor does patent law preempt the state law of trade secrets,[158] because the two forms of protection serve different purposes, and patent law revolves around complete disclosure, whereas trade secret law requires complete secrecy.

[B] The Patent Application

Substantive legal requirements for patent applications are found in 35 USC § 111; the required disclosures are set out in § 112. The application is made to the Commissioner of Patents and Trademarks. Requirements appear at 37 CFR § 1.51, 1.52, and 1.58. The application must contain:

- The specification, including at least one patentable claim
- The inventor's oath or declaration
- Drawings showing each feature of the invention, if needed to understand the subject matter. (Most applications do require drawings.)

More specifically, the application must include:

- A descriptive title
- Cross-references to any related patent applications

---

[156] KSR Int'l Co. v. Teleflex Inc., 127 S. Ct. 1727 (2007); *see* Tony Mauro, *Supreme Court Adopts New Standard on Patent Litigation*, Legal Times 5/1/07 (law.com). According to Peter Lattman, *How a Patent Ruling Is Changing Court Cases*, Wall St. J. 7/31/07 at B1; this case has been cited to dismiss or grant review of infringement suits on the grounds that the allegedly infringed patents are obvious — a power shift in favor of defendants, and some commentators believe PTO examiners are rejecting more applications on obviousness grounds.

[157] Hunter Douglas Inc. v. Harmonic Design Inc., 153 F.3d 1318 (Fed. Cir. 1998).

[158] Kewanee Oil Co. v. Bicron Corp., 416 U.S. 470 (1974).

- A brief summary of the invention
- A brief description of the drawings, if any
- A detailed description of the inventor's "preferred embodiments" of the invention
- The actual patent claims
- A brief abstract of the invention.

The patent application should be filed by the inventor — i.e., the person who took the inventive step. If there is more than one inventor, each one should apply as a co-owner. When the patent is granted, each co-owner obtains an undivided interest in the entire patent. However, there are special rules applicable to assignment or licensing of co-owned patents, so a patent attorney should be consulted prior to the transaction.

In order to cope with a backlog of 700,000 applications and an average review time of 31 months, the PTO proposed rules in June 2007 that would increase public review of applications and require inventors to disclose more information.[159] The proposals would reduce the number of claims defining a patent to 25 and allow only three continuations. (Prior law did not limit either.) GlaxoSmithKline obtained a preliminary injunction against implementation by arguing that it has many pending patent applications and would suffer permanent injury from implementation of the rules.[160]

Effective October 2, 2008, certain PTO fees went up by 4–5%.[161]

As long as a PTO request under 35 CFR § 1.105 (information needed for proper examination of the patent) is not arbitrary and capricious, the applicant must comply with it, even if the applicant believes the information is irrelevant to patentability. The Federal Circuit granted deference to the agency's interpretation of its own regulations.[162]

For a biological invention that cannot be practically described in writing, the 35 USC § 112(l) requirement can be satisfied by depositing the material publicly and referencing the deposit in the patent specification.[163]

An employee-inventor who has assigned ownership of the invention to his or her employer nevertheless has standing under 35 USC § 256 to seek correction of the inventor listed on the patent. The employee has standing based on a financial interest in royalties and licensing fees, as well as enhancement of professional reputation from being listed as an inventor, even though the employee's expectation of ownership has been extinguished by the assignment.[164]

---

[159] Phyllis Korkki, *Note to Inventors: Please Curb Your Enthusiasm*, N.Y. Times 6/10/07 at B2.

[160] Tafas v. Dudas, No. 1: 67cv 846 (JCC) (E.D. Va. 10/31/07), discussed in Zusha Elinson, *Patent Rules Put on Hold by Va. Judge*, The Recorder 11/1/07 (law.com).

[161] Jeff Jeffrey, *Patent Office Raises Fees*, Legal Times 10/6/08 (law.com).

[162] Star Fruits SNC v. United States, 393 F.3d 1277 (Fed. Cir. 2005).

[163] Enzo Biochem Inc. v. Gen-Probe Inc., 296 F.3d 1316 (Fed. Cir. 2002).

[164] Chou v. University of Chi., 254 F.3d 1347 (Fed. Cir. 2001).

Starting on February 12, 2004, WIPO can be used as the receiving office for multinational electronic patent filing, providing patent protection in 123 countries. The PCT-SAFE system under the WIPO Patent Cooperation Treaty offers the advantages of lower fees, lower costs for printing, copying and mailing, searchable documents, and immediate notification of receipt and processing of applications.[165]

35 USC § 112 requires the application to make full disclosure of the invention, to the extent that any person with ordinary skill in the art can manufacture or otherwise practice the invention. The patent application must disclose the "best mode" that the inventor knows for practicing the invention.

However, according to a 2002 ruling, the inventor's subjective preferences for practicing the invention must be disclosed only if they have a material effect on the properties of the invention. Therefore, failure to disclose the inventor's preferred starting material for synthesizing the antibiotic Cipro did not invalidate the drug's patent.[166]

In order to establish the priority date, the inventor can file a provisional application (35 USC § 111(b); 37 CFR § 1.53(2)). Later on, when a full formal application is filed, its filing date will be deemed to be that of the first provisional application to properly disclose the subject matter. However, if the formal application is not filed within 12 months, the patent application is deemed abandoned.

The American Inventors Protection Act of 1999 requires publication 18 months after the filing date for which a priority or benefit is sought. Final Rules were published for applications filed on or after November 29, 2000 for determining the date from which the 18-month requirement runs.[167]

Once filed, the application is sent to an examining group within the Patent and Trademark Office that is familiar with the subject matter. If the examiner is satisfied, the patent is issued. Otherwise, the examiner can issue an "examiner's action" giving specific reasons why the claims in the application are formally defective or are not patentable in light of the prior art.

An "objection" relates to formal defects in the application, whereas a "rejection" goes to the merits. The applicant can either abandon the application, disagree with the decision, or amend the claims in light of the comments.

If an applicant fails to advance its prosecution of a patent within a reasonable time, the PTO can reject the application for laches (in this case, multiple continuations without substantial amendments dragged the process out for a dozen years).[168]

---

[165] *WIPO Begins Online Patent Filing to Cover Inventions Internationally*, 72 L.W. 2504 (2/24/04) (No by-line). The Trilateral Offices (the U.S. Patent Office, Japanese, and European Patent Offices) signed a Memorandum of Understanding at the end of 2004 for work sharing and development of electronic techniques, search strategies, and tools to make it easier for the offices to work together and share data with less duplication of efforts: (no by-line), *Three World Patent Chiefs Agree to Share Efforts in Patent Searches, Filing,* 73 L.W. 2349 (12/14/04).

[166] Bayer AG v. Schein Pharm. Inc., 301 F.3d 1306 (Fed. Cir. 2002).

[167] *See* 70 L.W. 2419.

[168] *In re* Bogese, 303 F.3d 1362 (Fed. Cir. 2002).

[1] Appeal of Rejection

If a claim is rejected twice, or gets a final rejection, the claimant can appeal to the Board of Patent Appeals and Interferences, 35 USC § 134, 37 CFR § 1.191. The appellant files a notice of appeal and supporting brief. The patent examiner has the right to answer. The appellant is entitled to file a reply brief, but it is limited to new points raised by the answer. The appellant can request oral argument before an administrative panel of senior examiners.

A losing appellant can request reconsideration of the senior examiners' decision (see 37 CFR § 1.197(b)). If the reconsideration is also negative, the appellant can either get review in the Federal Circuit or can sue the Commissioner of Patents and Trademarks in the District Court for the District of Columbia.

Amending a patent claim after final rejection of the application supports the argument to broaden the scope of the patent only if it contains supporting information from the applicant and the patent examiner, explaining not only the need to broaden the claim but why the change was delayed.[169]

35 USC § 302 and 37 CFR § 1.510 provide that, once a patent is in force, anyone (including the patentee, or the Commissioner of Patents and Trademarks acting on his own motion) can get the patent re-examined via a PTO administrative proceeding. The PTO issues a certificate giving the results of the re-examination and the content of the patent after re-examination.

The PTO published new rules for appeals to the Board of Patent Appeals and Interferences, taking effect six months after their June 10, 2008 publication date. The agency streamlined the process for requiring faster information exchange and refining the issues of the dispute at an earlier stage. Examiners must give their reasons for rejecting a patent more quickly, and an outlining requirement has been mandated for appeal briefs, making them more like federal court briefs.[170]

The Administrative Procedures Act calls for review using a substantial evidence standard when PTO findings of fact are appealed to the Federal Circuit.[171] *Dickinson v. Zurko*, 527 U.S. 150 (1999) calls for application of the APA rather than review to see if the PTO was clearly erroneous. However, the APA includes two tests, one of the presence of substantial evidence, the other of arbitrary and capricious agency action. The Federal Circuit opted for the former (whether a reasonable finder of fact could have reached the same decision). This standard is less deferential than the arbitrary and capricious test, which requires a clear error of judgment for reversal.

The PTO has an obligation to issue a detailed opinion that explains its factual conclusions. Federal Circuit review is confined to that record.

However, the Constitutional validity of the entire process has been cast into doubt. George Washington University law professor John F. Duffy reported a

---

[169] Genzyme Corp. v. Transkaryotic Therapies, Inc., 346 F.3d 1094 (Fed. Cir. 2003).

[170] Sheri Qualters, U.S. Patent Office Rolls Out New Rules for Appeals, Nat'l L.J. 6/11/08 (law.com).

[171] *In re* Gartside, 203 F.3d 1305 (Fed. Cir. 2000).

constitutional flaw in the process that had been used for eight years to appoint patent judges. Forty-six judges (out of a total of 74) were appointed by the director of the PTO under the process, which transferred authority to appoint from the Secretary of Commerce to the PTO director. Duffy pointed out that the Constitution requires appointments to be made by the President, the courts, or a department head (such as a Cabinet secretary). It's possible that the procedure will pass muster under an argument that patent judges are not "inferior officers" as described by this provision of the Constitution, but in 1991, the Supreme Court described Tax Court judges as inferior officers, and the Board of Patent Appeals has even more power than the Tax Court. The argument could also be made that the head of the PTO is a department head with power to appoint, but that Supreme Court case defines "department head" as a Cabinet-level officer.[172]

[2] Reissue of Patents

To the District Court for the District of Massachusetts, *Dickinson v. Zurko* doesn't change the standard that District Courts use to assess the validity of reissue patents; the test is whether there was substantial evidence supporting the PTO determination. Review of an original patent under 36 USC § 251 to see if there has been an impermissible recapture in a reissue patent does not have to consider all the applications related to the patent that is corrected by the reissue.[173]

[3] Corrections to Patents

The Patent Act, at 35 USC §§ 255, 256 permits correction of minor and/or clerical mistakes in an application. However, if a so-called correction broadens the scope of the claim and is not clearly evident from the specification drawing or claim history, then the change is too drastic to be made under these sections. An attack on the validity of a certificate of correction is an attack on the validity of the underlying claim, so the standard of proof is the same: clear and convincing evidence.[174]

The correction process does not authorize a District Court to issue an order to the Director of the PTO to correct the order of inventors listed on a patent.[175]

Because of immunity under the Eleventh Amendment, a state university cannot be sued for correction of the inventorship listed in a patent.[176]

---

[172] Adam Liptak, *In One Flaw, Questions on Validity of 46 Judges*, N.Y. Times 5/6/08 at A18; Marcia Coyle, *Could Constitutional Flaw Unravel Eight Years of Patent Board Rulings?* Nat'l L.J. 4/28/08 (law.com). *See* Freytag v. Comm'r, 501 U.S. 868 (1991).

[173] United States Filter Corp. v. Ionics Inc., 68 F. Supp. 2d 48 (D. Mass. 1999).

[174] Superior Fireplace Co. v. Majestic Prods. Co., 270 F.3d 1358 (Fed. Cir. 2001).

[175] Fina Technology Inc. v. Ewen, 265 F.3d 1325 (Fed. Cir. 2001).

[176] Xechem Int'l Inc. v. University of Texas M.D. Anderson Cancer Ctr., 382 F.3d 1324 (Fed. Cir. 2004).

[C] Patent Bars

There are various factors that can prevent the issuance of a patent, or can result in the invalidation of an already issued patent.

If it is proved that a patent is issued in the name of anyone who is not the true inventor(s), the patent can be invalidated, unless the patent proponents can show that the wrong party was included erroneously, without deceptive intent.

35 USC § 102(c) provides that an inventor who has "abandoned the invention" is not entitled to a patent. Abandonment can be either express or implied by the inventor's conduct. An inventor who conceals an invention and refrains from patenting it (because the patent process involves disclosure of the invention) is not entitled to claim prior right against a subsequent inventor who applies for a patent on that independent invention in good faith and without knowledge of the first. What constitutes unreasonable delay, concealment, or abandonment is a fact issue that must be decided on a case-by-case basis.

Under § 102(d), the U.S. patent application must be filed within 12 months of an application in another country; failure to do so bars the issuance of a U.S. patent.

A U.S. patent issued to someone else, describing each element of the claimed invention, is a prior-art reference, so if another application is filed before the claimant's application, and a patent is issued after the claimant's application filing date, § 102(e) bars issuance of a patent to the claimant. An invention derived from someone else's work innocently, intentionally, or from prior art is denied a patent under § 102(g), because the claimant is not considered the "inventor" of the invention.

[1] On-Sale Bar

The patent application must be made within one year of the time the invention was first described in a publication, used publicly, or placed on sale by the inventor. This is referred to as the "on-sale bar" (35 USC § 102(b)). The "on-sale" bar can begin to run even before the invention is reduced to practice.[177] The Supreme Court held that the bar period starts only when the invention is ready for patenting, i.e., the drawings and descriptions are advanced enough for a person skilled in the art to reproduce the invention.[178]

If a patent application was filed in another country, application for the U.S. patent should be made within one year of the foreign filing. The filing date is important because, if two or more parties compete for a patent on the same invention, the first to file generally prevails, unless the second to file manages to sustain a very heavy burden of proving to be the first inventor.

---

[177] Pfaff v. Wells Electronics Inc., 525 U.S. 55 (1998).

[178] According to the Federal Circuit, the on-sale bar doesn't apply to design patents at all, because design patents are reduced to practice as soon as the embodiment is built: Continental Plastic Containers Inc. v. Owens-Brockway Plastic Products Inc., 141 F.3d 1073 (Fed. Cir. 1998).

Factors in priority of invention include:

- Reduction of the invention to practice (i.e., getting it into usable form that can be produced outside the laboratory environment)
- Diligence in adapting and perfecting the invention
- Disclosing it to others
- Making the first written description and the first drawing.

With respect to the on-sale bar, an invention is not "ready for patenting" if it is a bare idea and its inventor is unable to produce a 35 USC § 112 enabling disclosure. Therefore, offering for sale an engineering proposal that might not even work will not subject the eventual invention to the on-sale bar.[179]

Nor was the on-sale bar triggered by marketing activity designed to create interest in the invention, but not tantamount to a commercial offer for sale. Potential distributors could not have entered into a contract by simple acceptance of the offer. Taking purchase orders on a "will-advise" basis is not an offer for sale.[180]

In determining whether the on-sale bar applies, the customs of the relevant industry, as well as the contract principles reflected in the UCC, must be considered; however, UCC § 1-205 was drafted to reflect industry practice as a factor.[181]

[2] Shop-Right and Employee Inventors

Many inventors are employees of research organizations, and develop inventions in the course of employment.[182]

"Shop-right" is a concept that gives the employer an implied entitlement to assignment of ownership of such inventions. It applies if the employee was specifically hired to invent on behalf of the employer, or if the job gives rise to the expectation that inventions would be assigned to the employer. Furthermore, if the employee is able to patent an invention developed during working hours, on the company's time, and with its material, shop-right permits the employer to use the invention in its own business.

Scientists and other potential inventors and their employers should have express contracts resolving the extent of the employer's rights in inventions

---

[179] Space Systems/Loral Inc. v. Lockheed Martin Corp., 271 F.3d 107 (Fed. Cir. 2001).

[180] Group One Ltd. v. Hallmark Cards Inc., 254 F.3d 1041 (Fed. Cir. 2001); Linear Tech. Corp. v. Micrel Inc., 273 F.3d 1040 (Fed. Cir. 2001).

[181] Lacks Indus. Inc. v. McKechnie Vehicle Components USA Inc., 322 F.3d 1335 (Fed. Cir. 2003).

[182] The Bayh-Dole Act, 35 USC § 202(c)(7)(B) requires universities and other not-for-profit organizations that receive federal funding to share patent royalties with employee inventors. However, the statute was enacted to regulate the commercial exploitation of federally funded inventions, and only incidentally to benefit the inventors themselves, so it does not provide an implied private right of action for employee-inventors who seek a specific profit percentage: Platzer v. Sloan-Kettering Inst., 983 F.2d 1086 (2d Cir. 1992), cert. denied, 507 U.S. 1006.

developed by or with contributions from the employee. From the employer's perspective, an obligation to assign patent rights is not enough to protect the employer fully: the employee should also agree not to disclose secret or confidential information obtained during employment. A reasonable non-compete clause can be a good idea. An employee can be obligated to assign improvements made to an invention after employment has terminated, as long as the improvements relate to an invention created during employment.

[D] Patent Search

A preliminary patent search, also known as a patentability search, is done to make sure that there are no existing patented inventions that prevent the current invention from being considered novel and therefore patentable. The search also assists the patent attorney in preparing the application.

Searches are also performed if the searcher already has a patent that someone else is contesting, with the objective of invalidating the interfering patent. An infringement search is done to see if a proposed invention or improvement infringes on current valid patents. An index search ascertains what patents have been issued to a particular inventor or patent holder, and an assignment search determines the current recorded owner of a particular patent. (A patent is an item of property, which can be sold, gifted, or assigned, so the inventor is not always the owner of the patent at a particular point in time.)

The Patent and Trademark Office (PTO) is engaged in an ongoing process of making all patent information available on-line, at no charge, so that eventually the entire search will be able to be performed electronically.

[E] Patent Transfers

A patent is assigned when all the rights to an invention are granted exclusively to another party. A license is a grant of an exclusive right under the patent which does not include the right to make, the right to use, and the right to sell the invention. A territorial grant (transfer of full rights, but only within a particular geographic area) is considered an assignment.

Patent licenses do not have to be recorded, but assignments should be. If an infringement suit is brought, all owners of title must join in the suit; generally speaking, a licensee does not have to join the suit.

A patent license that requires royalty payments to continue after the expiration of the patent term is illegal and unenforceable. The Seventh Circuit felt constrained to follow a 1964 Supreme Court decision, suggesting that the Supreme Court should overturn its own precedent.[183]

Note that IRC § 1235(a), as amended by the IRS Restructuring and Reform Act of 1998, provides that "unless the transfer is made by gift, inheritance, or devise, when an inventor or certain investors transfer a patent before it is reduced to practice,

---

[183] Scheiber v. Dolby Labs. Inc., 293 F.3d 1014 (7th Cir. 2002).

it will be treated as if the inventor or investor held the patent for more than 18 months [i.e., the capital gain is long-term] regardless of the actual holding period."

[F] Interference Proceedings

It is easy to imagine two applications, or an application and a patent, claiming the same invention. This situation is subject to 35 USC § 102(g), permitting either an applicant or a patent examiner to initiate an "interference," an administrative proceeding before the Patent and Trademark Office. See 37 CFR §§ 1.601–1.690. (If two already issued patents claim the same subject matter, an interference is inappropriate; the correct action is a civil suit: 35 USC § 291.)

The parties to the interference are designed "junior" and "senior," based on their filing dates. The junior party has the burden of proving priority of invention. If one party was the first to conceive of the invention and also the first to reduce it to practice, he or she will prevail. The first to conceive wins even if not the first to reduce it to practice, as long as the first to conceive exercised due diligence in maintaining a reasonable, continuous attempt to reduce the invention to practice.

In an interference proceeding, the burden of proving priority is always on the junior party and never shifts. The burden of proving priority is on the party seeking to rebut the presumption that inventions were made in the order of the filing dates of the patent applications (37 CFR § 1.657).[184]

A plaintiff seeking to use 37 USC § 102(d) to defeat patentability by proof of prior invention must show due diligence throughout the critical period, although it is permissible to have gaps in activity that can reasonably be explained by evidence.[185]

If a District Court, reviewing a Board of Patent Appeals and Interferences interference ruling, takes live testimony on all the matters that the Board considered, the Board's factual findings are reviewed de novo. The District Court has a considerable advantage, because the Board cannot hear live testimony. Review of interference decisions is governed by 31 USC § 146.

Dickinson v. Zurko (§ 12.06[B][1] above) dealt with direct appeals from the PTO to the Federal Circuit, so it didn't resolve the interference issue. Nor does this decision prescribe how District Courts should review factual findings in a case where the testimony relates only to some, not all, of the facts or issues that were before the Board.[186]

The inter partes procedure began in 1999 as a way for alleged infringers to challenge a patent at far less cost than litigation. According to the USPTO, the procedure is gaining in popularity, with 70 requests in 2006 and 90 in the first half of 2007. Of inter partes re-examinations completed, 88% resulted in invalidation of the patent. Judges usually stay litigation once the PTO agrees to re-examine a patent (60 stays out of 83 requests), which adds pressure to settle the case. However, if the

---

[184] Brown v. Barbacid, 276 F.3d 1327 (Fed. Cir. 2002).
[185] Monsanto Co. v. Mycogen Plant Science Inc., 261 F.3d 1356 (Fed. Cir. 2001).
[186] Winner Int'l Royalty Corp. v. Wang, 202 F.3d 1340 (Fed. Cir. 2000).

PTO upholds the patent, the trade-off is that the challenger can no longer dispute the validity of the patent in any other forum, including the court system.[187]

[G] Patent Infringement

Because the holder of the patent has sole control over the technology for a period of time, anyone who reproduces the same technology without having an assignment or license may be guilty of infringement. See 37 USC § 271. Infringing any claim is considered to infringe the entire patent.

It should be noted, however, that in June 1999, the Supreme Court ruled, in the case of *Florida Prepaid Postsecondary Education Expense Board v. College Savings Bank*,[188] that the doctrine of sovereign immunity insulates states against suit for patent infringement. According to the District Court for the District of Delaware, however, even if the state cannot be sued for direct infringement, the Eleventh Amendment does not rule out a suit against a private actor alleging that the private actor induced a state university to infringe a patent.[189]

A 1992 federal statute, the Patent and Plant Variety Protection Remedy Clarification Act, grants the right to sue states for patent infringement, but the Supreme Court found that Congress lacked substantiation of the assertion that patent infringement by states was a significant problem; hence, it lacked authority to enact the statute.

The patent owner also has a cause of action against a party who induces someone else to infringe on the patent, or who contributes to patent infringement. 27 USC § 1338(a) gives the federal courts exclusive jurisdiction over patent infringement, and 35 USC § 281 grants civil remedies to the patent owner.

In mid-2008, the Supreme Court affirmed the 150-year-old doctrine of patent exhaustion, under which the sale of a patented item terminates patent rights in the item and the patent holder cannot restrict what the purchaser does with the item. (In this case, the question was what buyers of Intel components did with the parts, such as combining them with non-Intel parts in a way that exercised another company's patents.) The Supreme Court, reversing the Federal Circuit, applied the patent exhaustion doctrine to method patents (describing the operations to make or use a product), thereby reducing the protection available to patent holders. The Supreme Court ruled that the contrary holding would have undermined the exhaustion doctrine, because applicants would have an incentive to draft their claims in terms of methods rather than apparatus. The Supreme Court held that patent exhaustion is triggered when the only reasonable and intended use of a device is to practice the patent.[190]

---

[187] Jessie Seyfer, *High-Stakes Patent Battle Banks on New Litigation Tool*, The Recorder 9/12/07 (law.com).

[188] 527 U.S. 627 (1999).

[189] Syrrx Inc. v. Oculus Pharm. Inc., 71 L.W. 1152 (D. Del. 8/9/02).

[190] Quanta Computer v. LG Electronics, 128 S. Ct. 2109 (2008); *see* Tony Mauro, *Supreme Court Limits Companies' Ability to Collect Multiple Royalties on Their Patents*, Legal Times 6/10/08 (law.com).

In general, U.S. patent law does not treat activity as infringement if a patented product is made and sold in another country, but there is infringement if components of a patented invention are supplied from the United States for combination elsewhere: 35 USC § 271(f). In April 2007, the Supreme Court ruled on the applicability of § 271(f) to computer software that is sent out of the United States electronically, or on a master disk, to be copied in another country and installed on computers manufactured and used outside the United States. AT&T sued Microsoft, alleging that Windows installed on computers outside the United States infringes on AT&T's patent for digital compression of speech. Microsoft denied that software can be treated as a component of an invention. The Supreme Court agreed with Microsoft, ruling that the copies of Windows installed on the foreign computers are not exported from the United States, so Microsoft is not liable under § 271(f). (The court hinted that this is a weakness in the drafting of the legislation that Congress might address.) The potential component would be a copy of Windows, not the Windows operating system in the abstract. The Patent Act does not deal with the issue of copying; the Supreme Court concluded that copying a software master outside the United States is not "supplying" components from the United States. Foreign law, not U.S. law, governs the manufacture and distribution of patented inventions outside the United States, so AT&T should have used foreign patents to protect itself.[191]

[1] Proof of Infringement

There are two steps in determining whether a patent claim has been infringed:

- Construct the claim and determine its scope and meaning
- Compare the claim to the device or process accused of infringing the patent.

The Federal Circuit ruled that a patent infringement case should not have been dismissed for lack of personal jurisdiction without considering the impact of Internet contacts with the forum — e.g., use (if any) of interactive features of the site; degree to which forum residents used the site; sales of infringing products within the forum; and extent of the defendant's control over third-party sites linking to its allegedly infringing products.[192]

Markman v. Westview Instruments Inc.[193] makes claim construction a matter of law, for the court (so when it is appealed, a de novo standard of review is applied).[194]

---

[191] Microsoft v. AT&T, 550 U.S. 437 (2007).
[192] Trintec Indus. Inc. v. Pedre Promotional Prods. Inc., 395 F.3d 1275 (Fed. Cir. 2005).
[193] 517 U.S. 370 (1996).
[194] Cybor Corp. v. FAS Technologies Inc., 138 F.3d 1448 (Fed. Cir. 1998). When claim terms have to be interpreted, the Federal Circuit ruled that credible evidence about the meaning of a term of art (in this case "glide" in a claim for a sorting machine) cannot be contradicted by the ordinary dictionary definition of the term: Vanderlande Indus. Nederland BV v. International Trade Comm'n, 366 F.3d 1311 (Fed. Cir. 2004).

In practice, a *Markman* hearing takes place early in the case to determine the scope of the claims. Claims construction requires consideration of the claims; the specification; and the patent's prosecution history. Prosecution history is an especially important factor where there is a great deal of prior art, or the applicant wants to distinguish his or her claim from particular prior art. Wherever possible, claims are construed to be valid over prior art, and to cover at least one embodiment disclosed in the specification.

Under 35 USC § 271(a), the occurrence of direct infringement (which, unlike claims construction, is a fact question for the trier of fact) can be literal or under the doctrine of equivalents. The patentee always has the burden of proving infringement. For the mere fact of infringement, the standard is preponderance of the evidence; clear and convincing evidence is required to prove that the infringement was willful (and, perhaps, additional damages are warranted).

Where patent and trade secret claims have the same set of facts, they should not be bifurcated, but should be tried together for damage determination, and review by the Federal Circuit.[195]

A 2007 Federal Circuit case made it much harder to find willful patent infringement (for which treble damages can be assessed), holding that the test of willful infringement is whether the patentee shows by clear and convincing evidence that the infringer acted despite an objectively high likelihood that its actions were infringing — with more emphasis on what a hypothetical reasonable business would have done, and less emphasis on whether a favorable opinion of counsel was secured; failure to secure an opinion letter would not be proof of willful infringement. This case also involved an important issue of attorney-client privilege. Accused infringers usually get a letter from a lawyer known as "opinion counsel" as to whether the defendant infringed the patent in question; at trial, privilege is waived to introduce favorable letters. Introducing such a letter was often enough for the court to rule out willful infringement. The Federal Circuit ruled that waiving privilege for opinion counsel does not also waive privilege for the defendant's communications with its trial lawyer, because trial and opinion counsel serve different functions so waiver of privilege as to one is not necessarily waiver as to the other.[196] This decision reduced the number of companies obtaining such letters. In 2008, however, opinion letters regained popularity based on another Federal Circuit decision, this time holding that the jury should consider the absence of an opinion letter, because the presence or absence of an opinion letter can reflect on whether an alleged infringer knew or should have known that its actions would induce patent infringement.[197]

---

[195] Nilssen v. Motorola Inc., 255 F.3d 410 (7th Cir. 2001).

[196] *In re* Seagate Technologies, 497 F.3d 1360 (Fed. Cir. 2007), discussed in Jessie Seyfer, *Patent Defendants Score Big at Federal Circuit*, The Recorder 8/21/07 (law.com); semble, Knorr-Bremse Systeme fuer Nutzfahrzeuge GmBH v. Dana Corp., 383 F.3d 1337 (Fed. Cir. 2004).

[197] Qualcomm v. Broadcom, 543 F.3d 683 (Fed. Cir. 2008), discussed in Zusha Elinson, *Ruling in Qualcomm-Broadcom Fight Brings Back Opinion Letters for Patent Cases*, The Recorder 9/25/08 (law.com).

[2] Doctrine of Equivalents

A finding of literal infringement is made after the court has defined the claims that have allegedly been infringed. The finder of fact compares these claims with the allegedly infringing device and determines if they are the same. The "doctrine of equivalents" holds that making a trivial change or slight improvement does not prevent a finding of patent infringement, as long as the invention has been misappropriated from its true owner.

This doctrine was upheld in 1997 by the Supreme Court, which applied the doctrine to each element or limitation, not to the patent as a whole. But in practice, "file wrapper estoppel" (also known as prosecution history estoppel) will prevent application of the doctrine in many cases.

A claimant who narrows or abandons part of a claim to meet the examiner's objection, or to get around prior art, can't revive the abandoned claims in an infringement suit. If there is no explanation for a change in claims during the application process, there is a rebuttable presumption that the change is based on reasons related to patentability.[198]

A "pioneer invention" — one which is a major advance in its field — will be given the protection of many equivalents, whereas a narrower scope of protection will be given to more modest inventions.

Infringement can be proved without proof of copying (after all, practitioners of an art are supposed to be familiar with prior art, including the information disclosed in patent applications). The infringer's knowledge of the patent, or even its intent to infringe, is not very relevant to a direct infringement case. However, these are important elements in proving willful infringement that will support additional or treble damages under 35 USC § 284.

Direct infringement must be proved before a case of contributory infringement can be made. To prove contributory infringement[199] the patent owner must show:

- The alleged infringer sold, offered for sale, or imported articles for use in the patented invention
- Those articles are a material part of the patented invention
- The infringer knew the articles were especially designed or adapted for use in infringing the patented invention
- Those articles are not a staple of commerce suitable for noninfringing use.

The contributory infringement case requires mere knowledge, not intent.[200]

---

[198] Hilton Davis Chem. Co. v. Warner-Jenkinson Co. Inc., 520 U.S. 17 (1997). *Also see* Roton Barrier Inc. v. Stanley Works, 79 F.3d 1112 (Fed. Cir. 1996): to prove infringement under the doctrine of equivalents, the plaintiff must prove not only traditional infringement elements, but also that any difference between the products is insubstantial.

[199] Aro Mfg. Co. v. Convertible Top Replacement Co., 377 U.S. 476 (1964).

[200] Hewlett-Packard v. Bausch & Lomb, 909 F.2d 1464 (Fed. Cir. 1990).

The cause of action for inducement of infringement also depends on proof of direct infringement. Most courts will not impose liability unless the inducement was knowing and intentional.

The doctrine of equivalents protects patent owners not only against literal infringement by an identical product or process, but against infringement by one that serves the same function in the same way as the patented device or method. In May 2002, the Supreme Court made it clear that the doctrine of equivalents continues to be valid, reversing a Fourth Circuit case that imposed an absolute bar based on the prosecution history of the patent. That is, if a patent claim was amended, this interpretation would not permit extension of the claim beyond the actual words used in the application.

Instead of this absolute bar, the Supreme Court required a "flexible bar," so that a claim element (even one that has to be amended during the prosecution of the patent for reasons related to patentability) can still cover equivalent subject matter that is not literally stated in the claim. The extent to which the bar will be applied depends on the relationship of the claim amendment to the patentability questions.

Under the Supreme Court's ruling, prosecution history estoppel occurs only when claims are amended for a limited set of reasons:

- The amendment is in response to one of the statute's requirements for patentability
- The effect of the amendment is to narrow the claim, or an element of the claim
- Estoppel extends only to the particular element that was amended or added to the claim, and the extent of estoppel depends on the nature of the amendment and its relation to the patentability issues.[201]

When it decided the remand of this case in 2003, the Federal Circuit ruled that it is up to the judge, rather than the jury, to determine the applicability of the doctrine of equivalents to a particular case.[202]

[3] Defenses to Allegations of Infringement

Alleged infringers are entitled to defenses, such as denying that infringement occurred; asserting that their use is non-infringing; and asserting invalidity of the patent.[203] However, under 35 USC § 282, an issued patent is presumed to be valid, so the challenger must offer clear and convincing evidence of invalidity.

---

[201] Festo v. Shoketsu Kinzoku Kogyo Kabushiki Co., 535 U.S. 722 (2002).

[202] Festo Corp. v. Shoketsu Kinzoku Kogyo Kabushiki Co., 304 F.3d 1289 (Fed. Cir. 2003).

[203] The patent owner is estopped from asserting the validity of the patent if the patent was earlier declared invalid in a proceeding where the owner had a full and fair opportunity to litigate: Blonder-Tongue Lab, Inc. v. University of Ill. Found., 402 U.S. 313 (1971). A patent licensee is allowed to assert invalidity as a defense against a claim of infringement, but an assignee is estopped from challenging the validity of the patent.

A patent that is obtained by fraud or inequitable conduct is unenforceable.[204] Patent misuse — extending the patent monopoly past the claims asserted in the patent application as it was granted — does not invalidate the patent, but may prevent a patent owner who has "unclean hands" from obtaining remedies for infringement as long as misuse continues. (In 1988, 35 USC § 271(d) was amended to make it clear that mere refusal to use or license any rights to a patent does not constitute patent misuse).

As a result of 1984's Drug Price Competition and Patent Term Restoration Act, 35 USC § 271(e)(1), there is a safe harbor for use of a patented invention solely for development and submission of information to the FDA for drug approval.

The Supreme Court ruled in mid-2005 that 37 USC § 273(3)(1) permits the use of patented compounds in pre-clinical studies, if there is reasonable basis to believe that the tested compound could be the subject of an FDA submission, and the testing will provide information of the type used in new drug applications.[205]

Patentees are allowed to fix the price at which a licensed manufacturer can sell the patented article; the patentee may not fix the resale price of the patented item once it has been sold. The owner of a license may not combine with another patentee under a cross-license to fix prices under their respective patents. A patent owner is not allowed to condition the grant of one license on the prospective licensee's acceptance of a license on unwanted patents.

Alleged infringers are entitled to assert the affirmative defense of laches. Laches is rebuttably presumed to be present given a six-year delay in filing the infringement suit if the delay materially injured or prejudiced the defendant. However, the defense of laches bars relief only for infringement before the filing of the suit; it is no defense to infringement occurring post-filing. If the patent owner's statements or conduct led the infringer to believe that the owner would not sue, leading to detrimental reliance on the part of the infringer, the owner will be estopped from suing.

[4] Infringement Remedies

It is unusual for a preliminary injunction to be granted in an infringement action. For one thing, if it is later determined that there was no infringement, the enjoined party would have a good cause of action against the party who obtained the injunction. The case for preliminary injunction (see 35 USC § 283) requires proof of irreparable harm if infringement continues; proof beyond a reasonable doubt that the defendant is indeed an infringer; and proof that the patent is clearly valid.

---

[204] A patent for synthesizing a cancer drug was found to be unenforceable because the inventors failed to disclose to the examiner an article they themselves had written, casting doubt on two of the chemical components recommended in the patent. If disclosed, the article would have raised an issue to the reasonable examiner as to whether the invention had been enabled within the definition of Patent Act § 112: Bristol-Myers Squibb Co. v. Rhone-Poulenc Rorer Inc., 326 F.3d 1126 (Fed. Cir. 2003).

[205] Merck v. Integra Lifesciences, 545 U.S. 193 (Sup. Ct. 2005).

However, traditionally, once infringement was found, an injunction generally issued. The Supreme Court altered this tradition through its mid-2006 eBay decision. The Supreme Court applied the conventional equity four-factor test determining whether a prevailing plaintiff can secure permanent injunctive relief in a Patent Act case. The factors supporting the issuance of an injunction are irreparable injury; inadequacy of remedies at law; a balance of hardships favoring an equity remedy; and a permanent injunction promotes or at least does not disserve the public interest. It will no longer be presumed that an injunction should issue whenever infringement is found. The Supreme Court's target was the "patent troll": a patent holding company that acquires patents not to profit from manufacturing the product, but to demand licensing revenues from actual manufacturers who prefer to pay off the trolls and avert litigation. But the Supreme Court refused to impose a bright-line denying injunction to any party that solely licenses patents and does not manufacture; an academic researcher or garage inventor might have legitimate reasons for licensing rather than practicing the patent.[206]

A mid-2000 Supreme Court case arose when the petitioner went to federal court, seeking a declaratory judgment that its products did not infringe on the respondent's trade dress. The respondent asserted a compulsory counterclaim of patent infringement against the petitioner. The Supreme Court's ruling was that the Federal Circuit does not have jurisdiction of a case of this type — where, although there is a patent counterclaim in the answer, the complaint itself does not assert patent claims.[207]

Where the plaintiff in a patent infringement case merely seeks an injunction, and the defendant only asserts affirmative defenses and no counterclaims, there is no right to jury trial, because the case is purely equitable.[208]

The 35 USC § 271(e)(2) cause of action for technical infringement is also purely equitable; the statute expressly prohibits damage claims. Therefore, a defendant sued under this section cannot get a jury trial on a counterclaim alleging invalidity of the patent.[209]

With respect to another equity concept, litigation misconduct on the part of the patentee can constitute unclean hands that can justify dismissal of the patentee's suit to enforce the patent. However, the patent itself becomes unenforceable only if the patentee committed fraud on the PTO, not on the court. Where the inequitable conduct involved the PTO, no one can enforce the patent; otherwise, the doctrine of unclean hands bars only the offender.[210]

---

[206] eBay Inc. v. MercExchange LLC, 547 U.S. 388 (2006); *see* Eric Wesenberg and Peter O'Rourke, *The Toll on the Troll: The Implications of eBay v. MercExchange.* Special to Law.com (5/22/06).

[207] Holmes Group Inc. v. Vornado Air Circulation Sys. Inc., 535 U.S. 826 (2002).

[208] Tegal Corp. v. Tokyo Electron Am. Inc., 257 F.3d 1331 (Fed. Cir. 2001) (distinguishing *Markman* because damages were sought in that case).

[209] Glaxo Group Ltd. v. Apotex Inc., 130 F. Supp. 2d 1006 (N.D. Ill. 2001).

[210] Aptix Corp. v. Quickturn Design Sys. Inc., 269 F.3d 1369 (Fed. Cir. 2001).

The damage standard of 35 USC § 284 is damages adequate to compensate for the infringement, but not less than a reasonable royalty for the use made by the infringer. A standard for a reasonable royalty would be set by industry standards or, if there are none, by the price a willing licensor and licensee would agree on.

35 USC § 394 permits arbitration of infringement claims. The arbitrator's award is final and binding on parties to the arbitration, but not to others. *Aro Manufacturing Co.*, above, defines infringement damages as the owner's pecuniary loss, without regard to whether the infringer actually profited by the infringement. Lost profits, including lost sales, can be recovered.

Where the owner gives the trier of fact clear and convincing evidence of willful infringement, the court can increase the damages (up to treble). To avoid being held liable for willful infringement, product users have an affirmative duty of care to ascertain whether or not their proposed products infringe on any patents; the duty includes securing competent legal advice.

The prevailing party (plaintiff or defendant) can get an award of attorneys' fees in an "exceptional" case. Pre-judgment interest and costs can be awarded in a willful infringement case.[211] The Southern District of New York awarded $16.8 million plus interest as legal and expert fees in a patent case in which the defendants, generic drug companies, showed exceptional bad faith by attempting to infringe on a drug patent, raised a baseless challenge to the validity of the patent (the Southern District found the patent to be non-obvious), and engaged in burdensome delay and other reprehensible litigation conduct. It was the largest fee award in a patent case under the Hatch-Waxman Act, 21 USC § 355.[212]

When a fee award is sought in the patent context, a prevailing party is one who gets at least some relief on the merits, altering the legal relationship between the parties (e.g., a defendant who asserts collateral estoppel to get the patent invalidated, or when the case is stayed pending a reissue examination that results in the cancellation of the patent). In this case, the District Court's judgment for the defendant on the infringement issue constituted relief, so the case was remanded to determine if the circumstances were exceptional enough to justify a fee award.[213]

[211] Pre-judgment interest can be awarded in any case of willful infringement; there is no exceptionality requirement: General Motors Corp. v. Devex Corp., 461 U.S. 648 (1983).

[212] Takeda Chemical Industries v. Mylan Laboratories, 03 Civ 8253 (S.D.N.Y. 2007), discussed in Beth Bar, *Federal Judge Awards $16.8M in Pharmaceutical Patent Case*, N.Y.L.J. 3/23/07 (law.com).

[213] Inland Steel Co. v. LTV Steel Co., 364 F.3d 1318 (Fed. Cir. 2004).

§ 13.01 INTRODUCTION

As a result of natural disaster, illness, accident, or the negligence or misconduct of human beings or organizations, people, property, and businesses can suffer various kinds of accident or damage with financial implications. Public policy supports legitimate activities such as operating a business or supporting a family, so insurance is recognized by law and even given favorable tax status (e.g., in many situations, insurance proceeds are not taxable income for income tax purposes; and, as § 17.11 shows, under appropriate circumstances life insurance proceeds can be excluded from the estate of the insured decedent).

Insurance exists to transmute the risk of a large, unpredictable loss into a smaller, more predictable obligation to pay insurance premiums. If and when an insured event occurs, insurance proceeds are available to cushion the financial implications of the event.

However, for various reasons, the insurance is unlikely to remove all financial impact. Most policies do not start paying until a deductible has been satisfied. In many, if not most, situations, the insured will have coinsurance responsibilities: the insurance will pay only a percentage of the loss. Even if there are two or more policies that might potentially provide coverage, they will be "coordinated" so that coverage will not exceed 100% of the loss.

There are many kinds of insurance, and many variations of policy design within each kind. It can be categorized as coverage for individuals or businesses; or coverage of the person (e.g., life and health insurance) versus property insurance. Another division is that between first-party coverage (the insured is reimbursed for his, her, or its own losses) and third-party coverage (the injured person is reimbursed by the insurer of the party responsible for the losses. Liability insurance includes two important components: reimbursement of the individual's obligations to other people (such as persons injured in automobile accidents caused by the insured) and the insurance company's duty to defend by supplying an attorney or paying the costs of the attorney selected by the defendant-insured.

There are also some important differences between individual and group policies. Technically, the entity buying the group policy is the policyholder; the individuals covered under the plan are "certificate holders." Furthermore, the entity selects the policy and the carrier, and pays part or all of the premium — with the result that it might select provisions that save money for the entity but are not the ones the individual members might have chosen.

Despite the variety of provisions, many insurance policies are organized similarly. The insured person is entitled to the "coverages" specified in the policy, up to policy limits, but is not entitled to coverage under the circumstances specifically excluded by the policy. Coverage does not begin until any deductible is satisfied, and is subject to the insured's copayment responsibilities. It is very common for the exclusions, deductibles, coinsurance, and policy limits to be different for the different coverages.

Insurance law draws a distinction between cancellation and nonrenewal of a policy. The insurer's ability to cancel a policy that has an indefinite duration is quite limited, and usually requires some form of wrongdoing by the insured (such as misrepresentation on the application). But if a policy has a designated term (e.g., five-year term life insurance), the insurer often has the option to deny renewal, even if the insured has complied with all obligations under the policy.

The concept of subrogation applies in most insurance situations. That is, an insurer that pays benefits is likely to be entitled to a share of any contract or tort recovery that compensates the party receiving the benefits for the events causing the injury or damage. For instance, a health insurer that pays hospital bills may be entitled to part of the injured person's recovery against the negligent driver. However, insurers are also subject to any defenses that the defendant can assert against the recipient of the benefits.

Insured parties must notify their insurers whenever an event occurs that affects the policy — usually because the insured claims that policy benefits are due, but sometimes so that the insurer can stay up to date on the insured's financial condition. In addition to prompt notice of claim, the insured must file "proof of claim" (a signed, sworn statement giving details of the incident) within a specified time, such as 60 days.

Although the Supreme Court seldom decides insurance law cases, a mid-2003 ruling strikes down California's Holocaust Victim Insurance Relief Act, which required insurers to provide information about policies issued in Europe between 1920 and 1945 (i.e., which might have been payable to victims of Nazism). The Supreme Court found the law to be invalid because it interfered with the President's Constitutional power to manage the nation's foreign policy.[1]

Some states have enacted "notice-prejudice" statutes, under which an insurer can reject a claim on the basis of late filing if, and only if, the delay actually prejudiced the insurance company financially. A 1999 Supreme Court decision[2] holds that ERISA does not preempt these state laws.

---

[1] American Ins. Ass'n v. Garamendi, 539 U.S. 396 (2003).

[2] UNUM Life Ins. Co. of Am. v. Ward, 526 U.S. 358 (1999). As of mid-January 2009, New York will no longer allow personal injury or wrongful death insurers to disclaim coverage on grounds of late notice of claim, unless they were materially prejudiced by the delay. (The new rules do not apply to property or health policies.) If the claim was filed within two years of the

By and large, insurance law is state law. However, the federal McCarran-Ferguson Act, 15 USC §§ 1011–1015 exempts "the business of insurance" from antitrust scrutiny[3] and, in some cases, preempts state regulation of insurance. For instance, McCarran-Ferguson protects insurers against state charges that they conspired with foreign insurers to keep foreign coverage off the market.[4]

However, Humana Inc. v. Forsyth[5] holds that the Racketeer Influenced and Corrupt Organizations Act (RICO) does not invalidate or supersede state insurance laws, so a RICO suit (creating the possibility of treble damages) could be maintained by employee-participants in an employee group health plan (EGHP) claiming overbilling and excessive copayments as part of an insurance fraud conspiracy. Like most federal laws, other than antitrust laws, RICO applies to insurance unless it invalidates, impairs, or supersedes a state insurance law.

The City of New York has already received almost 10,000 claims from police officers, firefighters, construction workers, and others alleging respiratory illnesses related to the 911 attack. Congress set up a $1 billion captive insurance fund for these claims. According to the Southern District of New York, the excess insurers have an ongoing duty to defend New York City and its contractors in personal injury cases relating to the World Trade Center site cleanup, stemming from the exhaustion of the underlying Liberty Mutual insurance policy. The City was heavily criticized for using the fund to pay legal bills instead of compensating injured first responders.[6]

§ 13.02 LIFE INSURANCE

It might seem that life insurance is not really insurance, because everybody is certain to die sooner or later. But a legitimate element of risk shifting is present, because it is not certain that the individual will die while insured by a life insurance policy.

---

accident, the insurer has the burden of proving it was prejudiced; if later, the insured has to prove that the insurer was not prejudiced by the delay. Typically, the policies last for a year, so for practical purposes, policies written until January 18, 2010, follow the old rules. The statute also allows injured parties whose claims are denied for late notice to apply for a declaratory judgment in a personal injury or wrongful death case to find out if the defendant has enough insurance coverage for a suit to be worth pursuing (so that cases that are not worth pursuing will not clog the calendars). *See* Joel Stashenko, *New Late-Notice Rule in N.Y. Shifts Burden to Insurer to Prove Harm*, N.Y.L.J. 7/30/08 (law.com). The New York statute is A11541/S8610; Arkansas, Colorado, Idaho, Illinois, Georgia, Mississippi, and Nevada also have "no prejudice" rules for late claims.

[3] Approval of insurance rates by state officials does not insulate a title company from federal liability for price fixing, because the state approval does not oust federal antitrust law: FTC v. Ticor Ins. Co., 504 U.S. 621 (1992).

[4] Hartford Fire Ins. Co. v. California, 509 U.S. 764 (1993).

[5] 525 U.S. 299 (1999).

[6] WTS Captive Ins. Co. Inc. v. Liberty Mutual Fire Ins. Co., 07 Civ. 1209 (S.D.N.Y. 2008); *see* Mark Hamblett, *Insurers Told to Cover NYC's Defense Costs Over Sept. 11 Health Claims*, N.Y.L.J. 3/27/08 (law.com).

Life insurance companies do business either as "stock" companies which, like conventional corporations, are owned by stockholders, or as "mutual" companies owned by the owners of policies. Mutual companies pay dividends to their policyholders, which can be received in cash, accumulated to earn interest, applied against future premiums, or used to purchase paid-up insurance (i.e., insurance for which no further premiums will be charged).

Congress has granted life insurance extremely favorable tax status. As long as the insured person had no "incidents of ownership" (rights to control the policy) at the time of death, and did not have such incidents during the three years prior to death, and as long as the insurance is payable to a named insured rather than the insured person's estate, the insurance proceeds will not be included in the decedent's estate, no matter how large they are.

Combined with the unlimited marital deduction (see § 17.12[C]), this treatment makes it possible for a married person to provide generously for a surviving spouse without estate tax liability in the first estate. (The estate of the surviving spouse, however, may be quite large and generate significant estate tax.)

Life insurance is also significant in corporate planning. Insurance is frequently used to fund buy-sell agreements (see § 1.11[B]) under which owners of a partnership or closely-held corporation buy out the interest of a deceased owner.

Company-Owned Life Insurance (COLI) has also been used simply for tax planning, with the company taking a tax deduction for premiums on the life of employees and then collecting benefits on the employee's death. Such arrangements have been criticized when the employees in question were rank-and-file employees, not major executives of the corporation, and when the employees in question did not consent to or even know about the arrangement. The Pension Protection Act of 2006 (PPA; P.L. 109-280) reduces the tax advantages of Company-Owned Life Insurance purchased after the PPA's effective date. See PPA § 863. (Post-PPA acquisitions of policies by § 1035 exchanges of pre-PPA policies are also exempt from the PPA requirements.)

The new general rule is that employers can receive COLI proceeds tax-free after the death of an employee only up to the total premiums paid by the employer. Any COLI proceeds paid to the insured's beneficiary rather than to the corporation must be used to buy back the insured's equity in the corporation measured as of the time of death. However, the pre-PPA rules continue to apply under a safe harbor for policies on the lives of corporate directors or highly compensated employees if they were employed by the corporation within the 12 months immediately prior to their deaths. The safe harbor requires notice to the insured about the corporation's intent to purchase COLI; that the insurance will benefit the corporation; and the maximum amount desired. The insured must consent in writing to the corporation insuring his or her life.

Another potential area of abuse is addressed by the Military Personnel Financial Services Protection Act,[7] which forbids insurers to offer or sell any life

---

[7] P.L. 109-290 (passed July 19, 2006).

insurance product to a service member or to a service member's dependent on a military installation unless the mandatory standard disclosures have been provided. The sale of noncomplying life insurance products is voidable by the service member or dependent. Anyone who intentionally violates the rules is barred from engaging in the business of insurance (except for servicing existing policies) to federal employees on federal land. The Secretary of Defense must maintain a list of barred insurers (and financial advisors who have fallen afoul of similar rules) covering broker/dealers and investment advisors who operate at military bases.

[A] Whole Life, Term, and Investment-Oriented Insurance

"Whole life" insurance can be maintained for an indefinite number of years, as long as the insured or other policy owner continues to pay the premiums. Whole life insurance also has cash value.[8] The general rule is that the premium for a whole life policy remains level as long as the policy is maintained; it does not increase as the insured gets older (and, presumably, is more likely to die). That means that the premium charged is higher than the pure cost of insurance in the early years of the policy, creating cash value that can be borrowed against or used as security for other loans.

A single-premium policy exchanges a sum of money for immediate protection and cash value; the policy remains in force without additional premium payments.

In a conventional whole-life policy, the insurance company controls investment of the premiums paid by insureds. Investment-oriented policies such as variable life, universal life, and the hybrid variable-universal life policy allow the insured to select investment alternatives, similar to mutual funds, for the premium, and sometimes for additional sums deposited by the insured.

The death benefit in a variable life policy is always at least equal to the minimum guaranteed by the contract. If the policyholder's investment decisions work out well, the death benefit can increase. The cash value of the policy also fluctuates, and is not protected by any minimum guarantee.

The death benefit of a universal life policy is guaranteed only for the first month of the contract. Subsequently, a minimum interest rate is guaranteed, but the death benefit fluctuates. The policyholder also has control over the premium payments, and can increase or decrease them, changing the amount of insurance.

[B] Term Insurance

In contrast to whole-life insurance, term insurance lasts only for a certain number of years (typically, five). At that point, the coverage expires. If desired, the owner can renew the policy, but most term insurance policies cannot be renewed more than a certain number of times, or after a certain age (e.g., 75). Furthermore,

---

[8] Technically, the cash value is cash surrender value, the amount that will be paid if the policy is surrendered to the insurance company at a point after it has become incontestable.

term insurers usually refuse to sell new policies to older individuals. Sometimes the premium remains level during the term; some policies call for annual increases. It is almost certain that the premium for a renewal policy will be higher, based on the insured's increased age.

In addition to term policies whose amount of coverage remains the same, "increasing" and "decreasing" term policies adjust coverage during the term, to cope with anticipated increases or decreases in financial responsibilities.

[C] Policy Ownership

The simplest case is for a person to purchase coverage on his or her own life, designating one or more beneficiaries (and preferably designating one or more contingent beneficiaries, in case the original beneficiary predeceases the insured person).

However, anyone who has an "insurable interest" in someone else's life can purchase insurance on that person, or can become the owner by transfer of the insurance. Insurable interest means a reasonable expectation of financial benefit from the policy, or from the person's estate. Thus, a spouse, close relative, or business partner would have an insurable interest, but a stranger would not.

The owner of a policy can name anyone as beneficiary — the beneficiary does not have to have an insurable interest in the life of the insured.

As noted above, good estate planning frequently calls for individuals to avoid owning policies on their own lives, or to transfer the policies and hope to survive the transfer by at least three years. Another possibility is for spouses each to purchase coverage on the spouse's life, rather than on their own.

The "incidents of ownership" of a policy (relevant not only between the insurer and its customers, but in determining whether proceeds should be included in the estate of the insured) include the ability to surrender the policy and receive its cash value (in the form of cash or paid-up insurance), the right to take policy loans, and the right to designate the beneficiary. The owner can also assign the policy, with the result that the assignee and not the original owner can now exercise the incidents of ownership. The general rule is that policies can be assigned to anyone, although some jurisdictions do limit assignment to persons with an insurable interest in the owner's life.

[D] Standard Provisions of Life Insurance Policies

Most of these provisions are required by state law, although some of them are choices adopted by insurers seeking to increase the attractiveness of their products:

- Death benefit (or face value): the amount that will be paid to the benefi- ciary(ies) if the insured person dies when the policy is in force.
- Cash value: value built up within a whole life policy; if the policyholder surrenders the policy, he or she will receive the cash value.

- Loan value: most whole-life policies set a guaranteed interest rate for loans against the cash value. (Any unpaid loans at the time of the insured's death will be subtracted from the death benefit paid to the beneficiary(ies).)
- Designation of beneficiaries and contingent beneficiaries.
- Incontestability: Once the policy has been in force for a period (generally two years; sometimes one year), the insurer cannot contest the payability of the death benefit, even if the insured committed suicide or if the original application for the policy was not accurate. An exception is that misrepresentations as to an insurance applicant's age will reduce the death benefit. Suicide while the policy is still contestable will result in return of the premiums paid, but not payment of the full death benefit.
- Misrepresentations: if an applicant misrepresents a material fact (e.g., state of health), the policy is voidable if disclosure of the actual facts would have prevented issuance of the contract at that premium level (e.g., standard rather than the more costly "rated up"). The insurer can rescind the policy based on deliberate concealment by the applicant of a material fact, but minor misrepresentations will not justify rescission. Jurisdictions differ as to whether an insurer can rescind a policy on the basis of material but innocent misrepresentations (if so, the insured is entitled to a refund of the premiums paid). Another factor is that in some jurisdictions, insurers will not be allowed to avoid policies on the basis of obvious misrepresentations, or misrepresentations that would have been discovered pursuant to an adequate investigation.
- Nonforfeiture: Amount of insurance that can be taken in lieu of cash when a policy is surrendered; naturally, this is lower than the amount of insurance that would be available if premium payments continued. States require nonforfeiture provisions because otherwise policy owners could pay premiums for many years and have nothing to show for it if they let the policy lapse during the lifetime of the insured.

An insurance company approved an application for life insurance. The policy was mailed March 3, 2004. The policy stated that the policy year began March 3, but there would be no coverage until the applicant paid the first premium while in good health. The applicant received the policy on March 10 — the day he died of a heart attack. His wife mailed the first premium the next day and then applied for benefits. The Third Circuit held that the policy never took effect: the applicant was unable to satisfy the unambiguous requirement of the contract — paying the first premium while in good health. Although the backdating would have resulted in less than a full year of coverage, the court did not view this as mandating coverage.[9]

---

[9] Wise v. American Gen. Life Ins. Co., 459 F.3d 443 (3d Cir. 2006). *See also* Assurity Life Ins. Co. v. Grogan, 480 F.3d 743 (5th Cir. 2007): a policy was mailed August 30th; the insured signed a certification that his health had not changed, and paid the first premium on September 6th. On October 7th, a lump on his neck, which he had been aware of for at least a year, was diagnosed as cancerous, and he died the following February. The insurer declined payment on the grounds that he was not in

A life insurer refused to pay when the insured died in a car accident with blood alcohol levels three times the legal limit. The insurer treated the death as a non-accidental, self-inflicted injury. The Eastern District of Michigan ruled that this characterization was arbitrary and capricious: although drunk driving is reprehensible behavior, it is not reasonably foreseeable that it will result in death.[10]

[E] Riders

In addition to the basic coverage available under the policy chosen, additional benefits can be obtained by supplementing the basic contract with "riders." Some riders are free; others carry a surcharge. Appropriate selection of riders depends on the purchaser's objectives for the insurance.

- Waiver of premium: this rider continues the insurance in full force, without additional premium payments, if the policyholder becomes totally and permanently disabled, and the disability lasts a stipulated period of time (usually six months). The cash value continues to grow while the premium is waived.
- Disability payout: the face amount of the policy is parceled out in a series of continuing payments starting when the policyholder becomes totally disabled.
- Disability income: a certain amount of income (typically, 1% of the policy's face value) is paid after a waiting period (e.g., six months) to a totally and permanently disabled insured. Generally speaking, payments continue until age 65, at which point the death benefit is paid out in cash.
- Accidental death benefit: a multiple of the face value of the policy (e.g., "double indemnity") is paid if the policyholder dies as a result of an accident. (Usually, the death must follow the accident by no more than 90 days.) Some policies, especially in the group insurance market, provide additional benefits for accidental death and dismemberment (loss of a body part, or function of a body part).

---

good health. The Fifth Circuit concluded that the policy never took effect: he must have had cancer when he made the initial premium payment. A widow could not collect life insurance benefits, because her late husband's policy had lapsed for nonpayment and had not been reinstated at the time of his death. The Third Circuit pointed out that the policy clearly stated that paying the overdue premium was not enough to restore coverage; underwriting requirements had to be satisfied. A mere assertion that a person expected coverage is not enough to overrule an unambiguous exclusion in the policy: West v. Lincoln Benefit Life Co., 509 F.3d 160 (3d Cir. 2007).

[10] Lennon v. Metropolitan Life Ins. Co., No. 05-73450 (E.D. Mich. 2006). *But see* Eckelberry v. ReliaStar Life Ins. Co., 469 F.3d 340 (4th Cir. 2006). The Fourth Circuit reversed an award of benefits under an employment-related AD&D policy to the widow of a drunk driver, because of the well-known hazards of drunk driving. Thus, the death was not an "accident," which is defined as something the insured did not foresee: Rebecca Moore, *Court Overturns Benefits Ruling for Widow of Drunk Driver*, Plansponsor.com (11/21/06).

- Guaranteed insurability: the rider specifies "option dates" at which the insured can purchase additional insurance at standard rates, without proof of continued insurability.
- Automatic premium loan: the insurer is given authorization to borrow from the cash value to pay a forgotten premium (or a premium the insured cannot afford), to keep the policy in force so that it does not lapse. State law, or company policy, may call for older insureds to designate an agent who will be notified of possible lapse, and who can pay the premium to keep the policy in force.
- Retirement option: the policy's cash value and accumulated dividends can be paid out as an annuity (for life, joint lives of the insured and spouse, or for a term of years) when the insured person retires.
- Long-term care: responding to the needs of an aging populace, more and more policies are allowing access to policy benefits during life, to satisfy the cost of nursing homes or long-term home care at home.

[F] Settlement Options

When an insured person dies and the policy is incontestable, the death benefit must be paid to the beneficiary, or to the contingent beneficiary if the beneficiary predeceased the insured. The basic form of payment is a lump sum, but in some instances the beneficiary does not want the lump sum, or is not capable of administering it.

A settlement option is an arrangement under which the insurance company retains control over the death benefit, making payments of interest and/or principal to the beneficiary, for life or for a term of years. That way, the beneficiary has regular income but is not saddled with a large sum of money that might be wasted or invested improvidently.

It should be noted that lump-sum life insurance proceeds are not taxable income for the recipient. However, the part of a settlement option check that represents interest earned on the funds after the insured's death constitutes taxable income.

[G] Viatication, Accelerated Death Benefits, and Life Settlements

Policy loans are one way to get value out of a life insurance policy prior to the death of the insured. Viatication and accelerated death benefits are other methods.

Viatication is the irrevocable assignment of a policy, usually by a terminally ill person, to a third party who pays a discounted portion of the death benefit to the "viator" (insured). The longer the insured is predicted to live, the deeper the discount, because the investor expects to have to wait longer to collect. Viatication has the same effect as selling the policy to a third party. The life settlement is a similar transaction in which a person over 62 (not necessarily terminally ill) makes a third-party irrevocable assignment.

Accelerated Death Benefits (ADB), in contrast, are offered by the insurer. The insurer offers ADB as a rider (often without additional premium); the rider contains a schedule of the amount that can be accessed under various conditions. ADB does not have to be repaid, but advances will, of course, reduce the death benefit that is eventually paid to the beneficiary.

Viatication, life settlements and ADB offer an additional source of cash for elderly or ill persons who need money (to pay for medical treatment or otherwise). Under Code §§ 101(g)(1)(A) and 7702B, ADB and viatical settlement funds can sometimes be received tax-free. Terminally ill persons can receive the funds (within dollar limits) tax-free no matter how they apply them; chronically ill persons get the tax advantage only if they use the funds for medical care.

After a terminally ill resident of Virginia sold her life insurance policy to a Texas viatical settlement company at a deep discount, she attempted to invoke the minimum pricing provision of the Virginia Viatical Settlements Act (Code Ann. § 38.2-600 et. seq.). The Fourth Circuit ruled that McCarran-Ferguson applies because the sale of life insurance policies directly and substantially affects the business of insurance.[11]

[H] Insurance Sales by Banks

The National Bank Act, a federal statute, authorizes a national bank doing business in a community with a population of 5,000 or less to act as agent for any insurance company. The Comptroller of the Currency interprets this to mean that insurance can be sold in any town where the population does not exceed 5,000, even if the bank's central office is in a larger city.[12]

§ 13.03 CASUALTY INSURANCE

The broad rubric of casualty insurance includes many of the types of insurance other than life and health insurance. Liability insurance; burglary and theft insurance; property damage; collision; glass; boiler and machinery; Worker's Compensation policies maintained by employers; credit insurance; and fidelity and surety bonds are all considered casualty insurance. A Comprehensive policy (e.g., for an automobile) combines fire and casualty insurance.

An "all risk" (also called "open perils") policy covers any kind of damage to the covered property that results from any cause that is not specifically excluded by the policy. In contrast, a "specified risk" policy is limited to damage caused by something specifically included in the policy. Fire and collision insurance are issued as specified risk policies.

---

[11] Life Partners Inc. v. Morrison, 484 F.3d 284 (4th Cir. 2007).
[12] U.S. National Bank of Oregon v. Independent Ins. Agents of Am., 508 U.S. 439 (1993).

A "valued" policy stipulates the value of the insured property at the outset, and any insurance payment made during the policy term will be calculated on the basis of this value. This provides the security of knowing in advance how the value will be set, and eliminates disputes, but will not necessarily reflect the actual market value of the property. In contrast, an "open" policy does not set the value in advance; it must be determined if and when loss occurs.

If more than one policy covering the same insured property, interest in the property, and risk is in force at the time the property is damaged or destroyed, the coverage must be coordinated. Some policies have an "other insurance" clause that excludes coverage altogether if other insurance is in force; others declare that they are excess insurance, triggered only if the other policy is exhausted. (If both policies say this, the insured can have problems.) The most common "other insurance" provision is pro rata: that is, the insurer who has issued 2/3 of the insurance has 2/3 of the risk.

Although it usually is purchased and benefits the owner of the covered property, casualty insurance can be assigned to someone who has an economic interest in the property, such as a mortgagee or major creditor.

[A] Terrorism Risk Insurance Program

A November 2002 federal statute, the Terrorism Risk Insurance Act of 2002, P.L. 107-297, created a temporary program, the Terrorism Risk Insurance Program, designed to sunset on December 31, 2005.[13] Under this program, when there is an act of terrorism as certified by the Secretary of the Treasury, the Secretary of State, and the Attorney General, the government will join with private industry in compensating those who suffer property/casualty losses.

All insurers are required to participate in the program. Because of the potential for federal involvement, insurers are obligated to insure terrorism risk in commercial property/casualty policies on the same terms as non-terrorism risks. They must also make clear and conspicuous disclosure of the premium for losses covered by the program.

The federal payment for a covered terrorism loss depends on a system of deductibles and sharing of the excess loss between the insurer and the government, with the government role phasing out gradually. The Department of the Treasury has the power to impose surcharges on policyholders to recoup the cost of payments under the program. In effect, the federal government acts as a reinsurer. Insurers make claims against the fund, subject to deductibles calculated based on their direct earned premiums. When the deductible is satisfied, the insurer receives federal payments of 90% of its insured losses above the deductible. However, the

---

[13] *Also see* the Interim Final Rule at 68 FR 19302 (4/18/03). *See also* the Department of the Treasury's Press Release at http://www.treas.gov/press/releases/js897.htm 10/10/03 and a Final Rule on disclosures to policyholders and a Proposed Rule on litigation management issues, 69 FR 25341 (5/6/04).

federal government's responsibility is limited to an overall $100 billion a year limitation and federal payments will not be made in respect of punitive damages.

When the extension to the end of 2007 expired, Congress voted a further seven-year extension of the Terrorism Insurance program under the Terrorism Risk Insurance Program Reauthorization Act of 2007, PL 110-160. This was a compromise: the House version of the bill provided a 15-year extension, with special assistance to New York City and other areas that have already suffered terrorist attacks. The Senate version, and the White House, preferred to phase out TRIA in favor of a more market-oriented solution.[13A]

The New York Court of Appeals ruled in mid-2008 that a tenant of a commercial building violated its lease by getting insurance that covered damage caused by many typical acts of terrorism, but had a binder excluding terrorism. The lease required the tenant to be fully insured against damage caused by windstorm, hail, smoke, riot, civil commotion, and contact of an airplane with the building. The landlord informed the tenant that it was in default on the lease because the insurance was inadequate; the tenant sued. The Court of Appeals held that the policy violated the minimum coverage of New York's Insurance Law § 3404 by excluding coverage for terrorism. (After the policy was purchased, the New York Department of Insurance circulated a letter to insurers stating that terrorism exclusions are forbidden in a standard fire insurance policy because they violate public policy.) As damages, the court granted the landlord's request for the cost of the extra insurance purchased based on the belief that the tenant was under-insured, plus attorneys' fees.[14]

§ 13.04   PROPERTY INSURANCE

Property insurance covers direct loss to tangible property, such as buildings and their contents, suffered as the result of a covered "peril." It usually covers loss of use of damaged property. Consequential loss coverage (loss of use, or reduced value of property that is not actually damaged) can often be added for an additional premium. "Multiple-peril coverage" includes several separate coverages.

Some significant questions arise as to whether there has been an "occurrence" that is covered by the policy; sometimes it is not doubted that damage has taken place, but there is a lively contest as to whether there was any "occurrence" within the meaning of the policy.

Timing is also important. In an "occurrence" policy, coverage is provided when the insured event occurs while insurance is still in force, even if the claim is not made until much later (e.g., ceiling collapses because of undetected slow, persistent water leak). A "claims-made" policy, in contrast, allows the insurer much greater

---

[13A] David Rogers, *Congress Extends Terrorism Insurance Program*, Wall St.J. 12/19/07 A10. Because the Treasury Department implements the program, see http://www.ustreas.gov for updates on the terrorism insurance program, including regulations and interpretive guidance.

[14] TAG 380 LLC v. ComM, 10 N.Y.3d 507 (N.Y. 2008); *see* Joel Stashenko, *N.Y. High Court: Insurance Excluding 'Terrorism' Violates Lease*, N.Y.L.J. 6/5/08 (law.com).

certainty because it covers only claims actually made during the time when the insurance is in force. Claims-made policies are also usually subject to a "retroactive date": even if claims are made while the policy is in force, they will be excluded if they relate to events occurring before the policy became effective.

See § 13.03[A] above, for the Terrorism Risk Insurance Act of 2002, P.L. 107-297, with implications for property as well as casualty insurance.

[A] Floater Policies

Floater policies are so-called because they cover property that is not always used or kept in the same place. Floaters are all-risk policies. A personal property floater covers items such as expensive jewelry and camera equipment.

A business floater policy covers all of the company's equipment or inventory, even if it is located off business premises (e.g., at a trade show; in transit). "Block" policies are adapted to all the requirements of a particular business or industry. Block policies have been developed for jewelers, furriers, dealers in cameras and musical instruments, and heavy equipment retailers, for instance.

[B] Fire Insurance

Fire insurance covers the perils of direct loss by fire and lightning, plus certain types of smoke damage. However, certain types of smoke damage (e.g., caused by a defective heating apparatus) are excluded. Fire insurance often draws a distinction between "friendly" and "hostile" fire, excluding or limiting claims relating to "friendly" fire such as furnaces and fireplaces, as distinguished from "hostile" fires that start outside the premises or accidentally within the premises.

Fire insurance can be combined with other perils in an "extended coverage" endorsement to the policy. This endorsement insures against windstorm, hail, explosion, riot, civil commotion, aircraft damage, smoke, explosion, and vehicle damage. The "additional extended coverage" endorsement adds coverage for building collapse, explosion of steam or hot water systems, fallen trees, glass breakage, vandalism and malicious mischief, vehicles owned or operated by the insured or insured's tenants, water damage, ice and snow, and freezing.

"Allied lines" coverage is either an endorsement to fire insurance, or written as a separate policy. It covers destruction caused by natural disasters and events such as fire sprinkler leakage.

It is a typical requirement of home mortgages that the mortgagor must carry fire insurance representing at least a certain percentage (e.g., 80%) of the current value of the home. A "co-insurance clause" provides that, if the building is under-insured when a loss incurs, the owner's insurance recovery will be reduced in proportion to the underinsurance.

Assume that a home is worth $250,000 and is subject to an 80% insurance requirement, and that the owner maintains $200,000 worth of insurance. That is deemed adequate, so the owner will be entitled to receive covered losses (subject to the deductible) up to the policy limit.

However, if only $150,000 in insurance had been maintained, then only three-quarters of the loss otherwise recoverable could be recovered, because the insured had only three-quarters of the required amount of insurance.

In 1997, State Farm changed the coverages offered to their customers, discontinuing guaranteed replacement cost coverage (which had provided that the insurer would pay the full cost of repairing a damaged or destroyed dwelling with like or equivalent construction, even if that exceeded the policy limits). A homeowner was notified of the change, and got yearly reminders that she was responsible for increasing coverage if the value of her house increased. Her house burned down, and State Farm paid $138,000 for structural loss and $76,000 for personal property. She brought suit for breach of contract, breach of duty of good faith, reformation, and misrepresentation, claiming that she was entitled to guaranteed replacement coverage, because the policy was unclear. The California Court of Appeals held in 2008 that the policy clearly limited payments to the amounts on the declaration page, and the plaintiff was not justified in assuming that the policy's inflation adjustment constituted a promise that the policy would always pay 100% of the replacement cost of the property.[15]

[C] Katrina and Related Claims

The catastrophic 2005 hurricane season highlighted a problem that attracted little attention previously: the near-universal casualty insurance provision, the "anti-concurrent causation" clause. The clause, which provides that wind damage coverage is not triggered if the property is damaged both by wind and by flood, has become the subject of a great deal of Katrina-related litigation. The federal government-backed flood and earthquake policies are not a complete solution, because the maximum flood coverage is only $250,000, far less than the cost of most homes, and earthquake policies in areas where earthquakes are a meaningful risk are sold subject to high deductibles.[16]

"Windstorm deductibles" require insured to assume a deductible, e.g., 1–5% of value — or as much as 25% of value in hurricane-prone coastal areas — before windstorm damage is covered. The deductibles were introduced in 1992, after Hurricane Andrew caused immense damage in Florida and Texas, and are now used in 18 states and the District of Columbia.[17]

Early in 2007, the litigation climate looked bad for insurers. State Farm was ordered to pay $1 million for just one home, and agreed to pay $79.5 million to settle Katrina-related claims for 640 families. Other insurers settled with homeowners. However, the Fifth Circuit has ruled that provisions in homeowners' policies excluding flood damage are enforceable.[18] The Fifth Circuit held, in a

---

[15] Everett v. State Farm Gen. Ins. Co., 162 Cal. App. 4th 649 (2008).

[16] Joseph B. Treaster, *Small Clause, Big Problem*, N.Y. Times 8/14/06 at p. C7.

[17] Alina Tugend, *Another Way for Wind to Put Holes in Homeowners' Pockets*, N.Y. Times 9/15/07 at C5; *see* the Insurance Information Institute, http://www.iii.org site.

[18] Liam Pleven and Peter Lattman, *Rulings Bolster Insurers*, Wall St. J. 12/7/07 at C1.

Katrina "slab" case, that under Mississippi law, "storm surge" merely means tidal wave or wind-driven flood—which is an excluded peril. The policy explicitly excluded damage from flood, waves, tidal waves, and overflow from a body of water (whether or not wind-driven). The Fifth Circuit agreed that the ACC clause was valid and enforceable. In the Fifth Circuit view, the hurricane deductible endorsement does not make the ACC clause ambiguous; it applies the higher deductible percentage to losses attributable to hurricane occurrences, but does not change the rest of the policy at all. Mississippi courts had not decided whether a homeowner's insurance policy can preclude recovery for damages from the concurrent action of wind and water in a hurricane, but the Fifth Circuit's projection was that ACC clauses are enforceable.[19]

Early in 2008, the United States Supreme Court rejected appeals from Xavier University and other Louisiana policyholders who sued for refusal to cover water damage caused by the breach of New Orleans' levees. The Fifth Circuit held, in August 2007, that water damage from levee failures was not covered. The Fifth Circuit refused to certify the issue as a question for the Louisiana Supreme Court; the United States Supreme Court refused to review the denial. In 2008, the Louisiana Supreme Court also held that water damage from the post-Katrina failure of the levees was not covered—reversing the state appellate decision holding the policy language ambiguous and therefore unable to exclude all forms of flooding. The Louisiana Supreme Court permitted insurers to limit liability to cover wind damage but exclude flooding.[20]

Homeowners whose house was destroyed by Katrina sued State Farm. The District Court granted them JMOL (judgment as a matter of law). The jury awarded $2.5 million in punitive damages, which the District Court remitted to $1 million. The Fifth Circuit reversed the JMOL, vacated the punitive damage award, and remanded for a new trial. The homeowners did not have flood insurance; they claimed under their homeowner's policy. The adjuster decided that the damage was attributable more to flood than to wind, and State Farm denied the entire claim. The homeowner's litigation theory was that Katrina was a windstorm, and they were covered because wind was a named peril; they said they should be able to recover for any losses that State Farm could not show were caused by the excluded peril of water. The Fifth Circuit held that the grant of JMOL was erroneous, so it reversed and remanded and vacated the punitive damage award. Although the District Court permitted punitive damages to be imposed for negligent claim

---

[19] Tuepker v. State Farm Fire & Casualty Co., 507 F.3d 346 (5th Cir. 2007). On the ACC clause, *see* Leonard v. Nationwide Mut., 499 F.3d 419 (5th Cir. 2007); *In re* Katrina, 495 F.3d 221 (5th Cir. 2007) [Louisiana law] and Bilbe v. Belsom, 530 F.3d 314 (5th Cir. 2008).

[20] Xavier Univ. of Louisiana v. Travelers Casualty Property Co. of America, 128 S. Ct. 1230/ Chehardy v. Allstate Indemnity Co., 128 S. Ct. 1231 (2008); Sher v. Lafayette Ins. Co., 2008 WL 928486 (La. 4/8/08) *aff'd in part, rev'd in part* 988 S. 2d 186 (La. 7/7/08); *see* Michael Kunzelman (AP), *Supreme Court Rejects Katrina Victims' Flood Insurance Case, but La. Court Is Set to Tackle the Issue*, 2/21/08 (law.com) and *La. Supreme Court Sides With Insurers in Suit Over Katrina Levee Failures*, 4/8/08 (law.com).

investigation, the Fifth Circuit said that additional investigation could not yield any more evidence from a concrete slab.[21]

Louisiana's Valued Policy Law (VPL) provides that a fire insurance policy must cover loss if there is a valuation on wind and rain but excludes flood. The Fifth Circuit held that the VPL did not apply to homes totally destroyed by Hurricanes Katrina and/or Rita when the total loss does not come from a covered peril. (A number of other states have enacted VPLs to protect insured homeowners by requiring insurers to pay the policy amount rather than actual cash value when they claim the property is over-insured.) The Fifth Circuit concluded that it would contravene the statutory purpose to make insurers pay when damage results from a non-covered peril.[22]

The National Flood Insurance Program (NFIP) was set up by Congress to provide coverage at or below actuarial rates. NFIP is supported by the U.S. Treasury and administered by FEMA. FEMA sets the terms of Standard Flood Insurance Policies (SFIPs). Some SFIPs are issued directly by FEMA, others by private insurers who act as fiscal agents of the United States (see 42 USC § 4071(a)(1)). A condominium association insured under a $12 million NFIP policy received almost $1 million after Katrina, but submitted a claim for $462,000 in additional damages, which was denied. The Fifth Circuit affirmed the grant of summary judgment for the insurer in the subsequent lawsuit: failure to submit proof of loss meant that the claim was properly rejected.

The condominium association argued that proof of claim had been waived in other cases, but 44 CFR § 61, appendix A(2) forbids waiver of any SFIP provision without express written consent of the federal insurance administrator. The regulations also forbid an insured to sue for additional federal benefits unless he or she can show full compliance with all policy requirements. In general, the deadline for filing sworn proof of loss is 60 days, although the federal insurance administrator extended it to one year post-Katrina. The Fifth Circuit applied the proof of loss requirement strictly. The extension from 60 days to one year extended the time, but did not remove the requirement of submitting proof of loss. In any event, the second claim was not denied for failure to file, but because the insurer thought the second claim was excluded.[23]

In a case where there was layered blanket insurance (a primary layer of All Risk Including Earthquake, Flood, Boiler & Machinery, and an All-Risk excess layer excluding earthquake and flood), the insurer denied coverage for Katrina water damage because of the flooding exclusion. Although the District Court granted summary judgment for the insured, finding the flood exclusion

---

[21] Broussard v. State Farm Fire and Casualty Co., 523 F.3d 618 (5th Cir. 2008). The ACC clause was upheld in Leonard v. Nationwide Mutual Ins. Co., 499 F.3d 419 (5th Cir. 2007).

[22] Chauvin v. State Farm Fire & Casualty Co., 495 F.3d 232 (5th Cir. 2007).

[23] Marseilles Homeowners Condominium Assn. Inc. v. Fidelity Nat'l Ins. Co., No. 07-31005 (5th Cir. 9/10/08). Shuford v. Fidelity Nat'l Prop. & Cas. Ins. Co., 508 F.3d 1137 (11th Cir. 2007) requires strict compliance with the proof of loss rule.

ambiguous, the Ninth Circuit reversed and remanded for determination of whether the California doctrine of "efficient proximate cause" required coverage. The Ninth Circuit held that the flood exclusion was not ambiguous; a "flood" is rising and overflowing of a body of water, especially onto what would otherwise be dry land. It was not an ambiguity that the basic and excess policies had different definitions; the two types of policy are intended to operate differently.[24]

§ 13.05 AUTOMOBILE INSURANCE

The no-fault system (see § 18.09[A]), although it limits the number and complexity of automobile-related tort suits, certainly does not eliminate the need for automobile insurance, because availability of liability insurance is central to no-fault.

It is a requirement of obtaining or renewing a driver's license that the driver demonstrates "financial responsibility" by having an adequate amount of liability insurance. This is a legal requirement, not a personal decision. Many motorists also choose to protect themselves with first-party coverage. Comprehensive insurance combines liability insurance with first-party property insurance. Collision insurance covers damage to the insured's vehicle. The decision to maintain collision or comprehensive insurance often depends on the age and value of the vehicle; the cost of insuring an older or modest vehicle is often heavy in comparison to the amount of benefits that can be paid after damage.

§ 13.06 BUSINESS INSURANCE

In addition to the CGL and EPLI liability policies discussed in §§ 13.07[B] and 13.07[E] respectively, there are many kinds of property insurance that are typically owned by businesses rather than by private individuals.

[A] Burglary and Theft Insurance

Burglary and theft insurance is written in many variations:

- Open stock burglary policies cover loss by burglary of merchandise, furniture, fixtures and equipment, and damage to the premises during a burglary, but not loss of money, securities, records, or accounts
- Mercantile safe burglary policies cover loss of money, securities, and other property, as well as damage resulting from burglary of a safe
- Mercantile robbery policy covers robbery hazards inside and outside business premises
- Paymaster robbery policies cover the risk of robbery of payroll funds
- Storekeeper's burglary and robbery policies are small-scale package policies

---

[24] Northrop Grumman Corp. v. Factory Mutual Ins. Co., 538 F.3d 1090 (9th Cir. 2008).

- Office burglary and robbery policies are their counterparts for service businesses and professional offices
- Money and securities broad form policies offer comprehensive coverage for most losses of money and securities, including but not limited to burglary and robbery.

In a Fifth Circuit case losses incurred as a result of a pattern of embezzlement lasting 10 years constituted a single "occurrence," so even though $1.5 million was embezzled, the insurer was only required to pay the policy limit of $350,000. The Fifth Circuit rejected the plaintiff's argument that there was an occurrence in each of the ten years in which the policy was renewed.[25]

[B] Surety and Fidelity Bonds

Suretyship is the relationship between one individual, corporation, or partnership and another to whose obligations it lends its name or credit. For instance, a founder of a start-up corporation might provide a personal guarantee of corporate debts.

Bonding is an important aspect of suretyship. Many transactions are dependent on a bonding company or insurance company issuing a bond that can be used to pay a defaulter's obligations.

- Contract bonds secure satisfactory completion or performance of a major long-term contract; the bond cannot be canceled during the term of the contract.
- Performance bonds cover various kinds of contractual performance. A construction contract bond guarantees the contractor's performance when it constructs a building. A completion bond is a variation that runs to the lender who finances the construction project. A labor and material performance bond ensures that, if the contractor fails to pay for labor and materials, the bond will take over. (This could be either a separate policy or a component of a construction contract bond.) A maintenance bond (which, again, can be discrete or part of a construction contract bond) provides coverage if the contractor's product is defective as to workmanship or materials. A supply contract bond guarantees a contract to supply goods or materials.
- Bid bonds are usually required when contractors bid on public works projects, and are sometimes required by private companies letting a contract. The bond guarantees that if the bidder is awarded the contract, it will enter into the contract and provide a performance bond and, if required, a payment bond.

The fidelity bond covers the employer against employee dishonesty that results in loss of money, securities, or other business property. Some bonds insure

---

[25] Madison Materials Co. Inc. v. St. Paul Fire & Marine Ins. Co., 523 F.3d 541 (5th Cir. 2008).

only named individuals; some cover whoever holds named positions, and some cover all of the firm's employees. (Partners are not considered employees of their partnerships.) Corporate officers are considered employees, and thus are covered by the fidelity bond, but corporate directors are covered only if they are inside directors or officers.

[C] Package Policies

A multiple-peril, or package, policy includes many coverages in a single policy. The policy could be written on either an all-risk or a specified basis.

- Manufacturer's output policy: covers the merchandise and other personal property of the manufacturer, such as large stocks of goods in dispersed locations, when the materials are off the manufacturer's premises
- Industrial property policy: all of the personal property of a manufacturer (and perhaps its buildings), plus property of other parties that is on the premises
- Commercial property policy: covers personal property of retailers and wholesalers, on or off the premises. However, this coverage is not sold to jewelers, furriers, or others who can buy block policies
- Office contents policy: covers the personal property located in an office; the building owner and the tenants are eligible to be insured. The building owner's policy is designated as the office package policy.

[D] Credit Insurance

In the consumer credit arena, credit insurance is purchased by a mortgagor or person with a large loan. The insurance provides funds to pay the debt in case of the death or disability of the debtor.

In the business arena, credit insurance indemnifies a manufacturer, wholesaler, or jobber for unusual losses caused by customers' failure to pay. Usually, this coverage is not available to retailers, because it is too difficult to assess the creditworthiness of their customers.

A general policy covers all accounts of the insured described in the policy, usually restricted to those of a specified credit rating so that it will not be necessary for the insurer to undertake individual investigation. A specific policy relates only to particular, investigated accounts.

[E] Consequential Loss Coverage

Often, a peril will not only cause direct damage (for instance, burning or smoke damage to merchandise) but indirect damage (for instance, water damage caused by firefighters). In fact, a business can suffer economic loss even as a result of perils to others: a retail store that does not receive merchandise it ordered because of a fire at the factory, for example. Many commercial contracts disclaim responsibility for buyers' consequential damages, so first-party coverage for such losses can be especially valuable.

Consequential loss coverage reimburses businesses for the loss of use of damaged or destroyed property, and property loss that is indirectly connected with a hazard.

Business interruption insurance is the best-known form of consequential loss coverage. Coverage could also be available for contingent business interruption (interruption of business of a channel partner, such as a supplier, which has a ripple effect on the insured's business); extra expense coverage (costs of responding to an emergency); rent insurance (issued to a landlord who loses rent revenue because of damage to a building); delayed profits insurance (compensating for profits lost because a project is completed late); leasehold insurance (compensating a tenant for losses attributable to nonrenewal of the lease); and profits and commission insurance (used for seasonal goods and individualized manufactures, where finished goods are destroyed and consequently profits are lost)

The New York Court of Appeals permitted commercial property owners to seek consequential damages from insurers who breach their policies. Therefore, when the damages are the natural and probable consequences of breach of contract, damages can be recovered in excess of the stated value of the policy. The plaintiff was a meat market that said it had to go out of business after a fire because the insurer paid only $163,000, much less than the $407,000 awarded by the arbitrator, and the business lost a year of income but recouped only seven months' worth from the insurer. The Court of Appeals said that many businesses will be unable to operate without the insurance proceeds, so limiting the damages to the amount of the policy (the amount that should have been paid in the first place) would not put the insured in the place it would have been if the contract had been performed. The majority in this 5-2 decision said that consequential damages, which compensate parties for reasonably foreseeable damages, are distinct from punitive damages; consequential damages serve to make the insurer live up to its bargain, not to punish it. A similar split decision was reached in a case awarding consequential damages such as lost rent and interest on loans for repairs the insurer refused to cover when premises were damaged during repair work.[26]

§ 13.07 LIABILITY INSURANCE

Remember, in a first-party coverage, the insured person (or the insured person's beneficiary) looks to his, her, or its own insurer for coverage of covered perils. But in third-party coverage, the insured has harmed the person or property of someone else in some way covered by the policy. Therefore, the insurer's duty to defend is triggered, and if the insured is found liable to someone else, some or all of

---

[26] Bi-Economy Market, Inc. v. Harleysville Ins. Co. of N.Y.,10 NY 3d 187 (N.Y. 2008); Panasia Estates, Inc. v. Hudson Insurance Co., 10 N.Y.3d 200 (N.Y. 2008); *see* Joel Stashenko, *N.Y. High Court Approves Consequential Damages Claims Against Insurers*, N.Y.L.J. 2/20/08 (law.com).

that liability will be satisfied or reimbursed by the insurer. Many cases have found the duty to defend broader than the duty to indemnify — all it takes is the assertion of claims that could be covered under the policy, even if the defendant eventually prevails.

The duty to defend is extremely significant, but not without its problems. The insured may feel that the insurer does not provide top-quality counsel, or that the attorney is more cognizant of the insurer's interests than those of the insured. The insurer could press for a quick settlement, when the insured is more interested in continuing the fight to vindicate its reputation. The insurer may also take the position that a "claim," creating a duty to defend, does not arise until litigation has actually been commenced, while the insured may feel that legal counsel is acutely required during time-consuming, expensive administrative phases (such as investigations by OSHA, the EEOC, or the EPA).

The usual pattern for liability insurance is a division into Coverage A (bodily injury) and Coverage B (damage to property); some policies add Coverage C (advertising injury), if this is suitable for the objectives of the policy.

Certain types of liability may be excluded from liability insurance, or coverage limited, on public policy grounds. For instance, insurance coverage of punitive damages is problematic, because the intended deterrent function would be unavailable if the insurer bore the burden. Coverage of intentional wrongdoing is also likely to be barred for public policy reasons.

However, neither exclusion is absolute, especially since corporations are chargeable with misconduct of individual employees (such as those who commit sexual harassment), and an argument could be made that the corporation itself is a victim of the wrongdoing.

The Eastern District of Pennsylvania ruled that when a policy was created in Pennsylvania, but the reason for indemnification arose in California, Pennsylvania law applied. Therefore, the insurer had to indemnify PhotoMedex Inc. and pay its attorneys' fees. California law does not require indemnification of malicious prosecution claims, so Pennsylvania and California laws differ enough to create a true conflict requiring a choice of law. Pennsylvania had the stronger interest in application of its laws. Pennsylvania law favors the contacts related to the insurance contract rather than those related to the underlying tort. Although some states disagree, Pennsylvania public policy does not rule out insurers' defense of malicious prosecution claims.[27]

[A] Basic Liability Coverage

The Owners' Landlords' and Tenants' Liability policy is a "scheduled" policy (setting out the properties insured and the risks against which they are

---

[27] PhotoMedex Inc. v. St. Paul Fire & Marine Ins. Co. No. 07-0025 (E.D. Pa. 2008); Gina Passarella, *Pa. Law Controls in Insurance Case Involving Calif. Tort Action*, The Legal Intelligencer 2/22/08 (law.com). The "true conflict" standard comes from Hammersmith v. TIG Ins. Co., 480 F.3d 220 (3rd Cir. 2007).

insured) covering premises such as office buildings, retail stores, theaters, and hotels. The Manufacturers' and Contractors' Liability policy performs a similar function in those industries.

Products liability coverage deals with the goods or products that the insured manufactures, sells, handles, or distributes, if they are defective or unsafe. Service businesses and contractors who install equipment also use this coverage to cope with claims of defect in the equipment or its installation.

Contract liability insurance protects businesses that are required to indemnify another business and hold it harmless as a result of a contract between the two. It is also used by lessees who are required to indemnify the lessor for consequences of the condition of the leased property.

The Owners' and Contractors' Protective Liability policy covers owners or contractors who become liable in tort or for warranty claims because of the actions of subcontractors and independent contractors.

[B] CGL

The Comprehensive General Liability (CGL) policy is the standard business liability insurance policy. The CGL insurer promises to pay "all sums which the insured shall become legally obligated to pay as damages because of bodily injury or property damage to which this insurance applies caused by an occurrence."

That seemingly bland statement includes at least three potential time bombs: defining "bodily injury," "property damage," and "occurrence." The CGL defines bodily injury as injury, sickness, or disease sustained by any person during the policy period; death that results from such an injury or illness is covered even if it occurs after coverage ends.

Property damage means destruction or injury to tangible property during the policy period, or loss of use of such property at any time resulting from property damage, plus loss of use of tangible property that was not destroyed or injured, if the loss of use stems from an occurrence during the policy period.

An occurrence is an accident which results, during the policy period, in bodily injury or property damage which the insured neither intended nor expected.

Different jurisdictions take different approaches to "long-tail" claims (such as products liability or environmental claims) where it takes a long time for harmful effects to manifest themselves or be discovered. The issue is trivial if the insured person has had adequate coverage at all of the relevant times from the same insurer, but can have significant implications if there was a gap in coverage or one or more changes of insurer.

Under the "manifestation" approach, the insurer who issued the coverage in effect when the damage became manifest is liable. The "exposure" approach triggers the policy that was in effect when the claimant was exposed to the instrumentality that caused the harm. A "continuous" trigger makes all policies that were in effect during exposure times liable. The injury in fact trigger involves only the policy that was in force when the actual injury occurred, even if it did not manifest itself until later.

An attorney defending a corporate client charged with intellectual property infringement has no duty to investigate whether the client's CGL policy might provide indemnification or defense costs. There might be an obligation for the lawyer to raise the insurance issue in some contexts, such as automotive personal injury. In a business case, however, there is no duty to inquire into the availability of insurance for the client.[28]

[1] CGL Exclusions

The CGL includes many exclusions. One of the most important is the "business risk" exclusion. There is no coverage for delay or lack of performance under a contract. Also not covered are breach of warranty or consequential damages attributable to poor quality of the insured's products. The theory is that a business that wants such coverage should obtain a performance bond. Nor does the CGL cover intentional wrongdoing by the insured.

The CGL is designed to provide third-party liability coverage, so property owned, rented, or occupied by the insured is not covered by the CGL; first-party insurance is supposed to deal with those situations. Damage caused by escape of harmful materials from the insured's property to nearby properties might be covered — although, as the next paragraph shows, efforts have been made to remove environmental liability from the ambit of the CGL.

The plain meaning of insurance policy language can be established by considering the language in the context of the policy, even if it has other meanings in different contexts. The California Court of Appeals construed the "wrongful eviction" coverage under the personal injury heading of the CGL. The court accepted the insurer's argument that, elsewhere in the policy, "person" always referred to a natural person. Therefore, there was no coverage for alleged wrongful eviction of a corporation.[29]

Insurance for advertising injury that covers infringement of copyright, title, and slogan does not cover patent infringement, because the insurer did not include this type of injury in the list of covered incidents. In this context, title means the name of a copyright work, not title to an invention.[30]

[2] Environmental Claims and the CGL

In 1973, the standard CGL policy was amended to provide a qualified pollution exclusion. Pollution damage (bodily injury or property damage caused by

---

[28] Darby & Darby PC v. VSI Int'l Inc., 701 N.Y.S.2d 50 (N.Y. App. Div. 2000).

[29] Mirpad v. California Ins. Guarantee Org., 132 Cal. App. 4th 1058 (Cal. App. 2005).

[30] U.S. Test Inc. v. NDE Envtl. Corp., 196 F.3d 1376 (Fed. Cir. 1999). *Also see* Superperformance Int'l Inc. v. Hartford Cas. Ins. Co., 332 F.3d 215 (4th Cir. 2003): the Fourth Circuit deemed trade dress infringement and trademark dilution claims to be virtually indistinguishable from trademark infringement claims, so they are not covered under any CGL policy that excludes trademark infringement claims, and the insurer has no duty to defend.

the discharge, dispersal, release, or escape of pollutants) was excluded from CGL coverage. However, the exclusion was subject to an exception for "sudden and accidental" releases. Many cases were decided, reaching varying and sometimes opposing conclusions as to what sorts of movement of what sorts of substances would be considered sudden and accidental. There were also important issues as to what stage an environmental complaint would have to reach to trigger the liability insurer's duty to defend: outright litigation, private-party litigation only,[31] EPA notification of potential liability, attempt by another party in the chain to make the insured jointly and severally liable, consent decree, etc.

The standard policy was amended again, in 1986, to absolutely exclude any coverage of any pollution-related claim. Nevertheless, the exclusion is not entirely absolute. Some courts have found the new version to be ambiguous, and therefore have construed against the insurer. Disputes have arisen about the characterization of particular substances as "pollutants," whether there was a discharge, release, dispersal, or escape, and whether the insured was "performing operations" at the source of the discharge.

In a case of first impression in California, the state's Court of Appeals said that in a CGL policy, "occurrence" means injurious exposure to asbestos, not the manufacture and distribution of products containing asbestos. (The insurer unsuccessfully sought a declaratory judgment that the per-occurrence limits on liability had already been paid out; the California Court of Appeals refused, because there were many occurrences so it was impossible to tell if the policies were fully exhausted.)[32]

A 2005 Washington case held that the environmental exclusion in an apartment building's CGL ruled out claims relating to personal injuries allegedly caused by toxic fumes from the waterproofing sealant applied to the building's deck.[33] However, just a few weeks earlier, New Jersey ruled that personal injuries caused by floor sealant are not the traditional types of environmental pollution excluded by the CGL.[34]

Later in 2003, New York did not apply the pollution exclusion to personal injury claims about inhalation of paint fumes, because even if the fumes were pollutants, they were not discharged and did not disperse, seep, or otherwise behave according to the language of the exclusion.[35]

According to the California Court of Appeals, California law does not require a CGL insurer to indemnify its insured for cleanup costs incurred under state orders. Such costs are not "damages" that the insured is obligated to pay because of property damage resulting from acts covered by the CGL, so the insurer is not responsible.

---

[31] For instance, the holding of Cincinnati Ins. Co. v. Miliken & Co., 857 F.2d 979 (4th Cir. 1988) is that the objective of the United States in bringing suit is to obtain equitable relief, not legal damages that could be covered by a liability insurance policy.

[32] London Market Insurers v. Superior Court (Truck Ins. Exchange), 146 Cal. App. 4th 648 (2007).

[33] Quadrant Corp. v. American States Ins. Co., 110 P.2d 733 (Wash. 2005).

[34] Nav-Its Inc. v. Selective Ins. Co. of Am., 869 A.2d 1192 (N.J. 2005).

[35] Belt Painting Corp. v. TIG, 100 N.Y.2d 377 (N.Y. 2003).

Here, the insured complied with the administrative orders, so no attempts were made at judicial enforcement. The insured's contention was that it would have been in serious legal jeopardy if it had failed to comply, so it was legally obligated to pay sums for which it should have been indemnified. But the court held that administrative proceedings, even if coercive, are merely the equivalent of claims or demands, and not lawsuits triggering the duty to defend.[36]

[3] Extending the CGL

"Follow-form" excess liability insurance increases the total coverage under the CGL (and Worker's Compensation and Business Automobile Liability coverage), but only the amount increases. The terms and exclusions of the original coverage continue in effect.

Umbrella policies are more broadly defined and sometimes cover situations excluded by the underlying policy, because the definition of "personal injury" for an umbrella policy is quite extensive. It typically includes bodily injury, mental injury, mental anguish, shock, sickness, disease, discrimination, humiliation, libel, slander, defamation of character, and invasion of property. Thus, it could cover some of the same employment-related claims as Employment Practices Liability Insurance (EPLI; see § 13.07[E]).

[4] The Duty to Defend

The First Circuit required two insurers to defend a business insured against a third-party complaint for contribution to environmental clean-up costs. Summary judgment in favor of the third insurer was affirmed. Citizens Communications Company was sued for discharging pollutants into the Penobscot River; it sought contribution and/or indemnification from Barrett Paving Materials (among other businesses). Barrett applied for defense from its insurers, who refused, on the grounds that the policy had a pollution exclusion (other than for sudden and accidental discharges). The First Circuit held that the insurers had a duty to defend because the allegations in the complaint were not inconsistent with the possibility that a sudden and accidental discharge had occurred. The insured's denial that any such discharge had occurred went to the obligation to indemnify, not the obligation to defend.[37]

The owner of an auto repair business bought a property in 1964; it contained an underground storage tank for the heating oil used in the business. In 1982, he retired, and leased the property to a lessee who continued to store oil there until 1997. In 1979, the property next door was sold; when the purchasers applied for a mortgage, they found that the tank had leaked, causing substantial contamination.

---

[36] Certain Underwriters at Lloyds v. Superior Ct. of Cal., 16 P.3d 94 (Cal. 2001); San Diego County, Cal. v. Ace Prop. & Cas. Ins. Co., 127 Cal. Rptr. 2d 672 (Cal. App. 2002). *See also* Foster-Gardner v. National Union Fire Ins. Co., 959 P.2d 265 (Cal. 1998) (a CGL carrier has no duty to defend in a state administrative enforcement action that seeks site cleanup).

[37] Barrett Paving Materials, Inc. v. Continental Ins. Co., 488 F.3d 59 (1st Cir. 2007).

The Massachusetts environmental regulators ordered them to clean up the spilled oil. They asked the lessor of the property next door to take responsibility. When he refused, they cleaned up the property and sued him for trespass, nuisance, negligence, response costs, and damage to their real property. He filed a claim for defense and indemnification under the CGL. His insurer rejected coverage, citing the environmental exclusion. The District Court said that heating oil is a pollutant, so this was not a covered loss, and there was no duty to defend. The First Circuit upheld, finding that the CGL section excluding liability for property damage arising from actual discharge, dispersal, release, or escape of pollutants excluded coverage for damages caused by the insured's occupation of the premises.[38]

According to an insurer, the pollution exclusion meant that it did not have to defend a suit against an engineering company for negligently failing to find construction debris and fuel tanks during an environmental site assessment. The engineering company issued an opinion that there were no recognized environmental conditions found, so its client purchased the property and later discovered debris, drums, and half of an underground storage tank. The Eleventh Circuit agreed that the pollution exclusion (which excluded damages, claims, and suits from actual or threatened discharge of pollutants) applied. The Eleventh Circuit held that negligent hiring, retention, and supervision were excluded, and therefore so was negligent performance of an environmental site assessment.[39]

[C] E&O Coverage

Errors and Omissions (E&O) coverage pays, on behalf of the insured, any loss the person has to pay because of a wrongful act he or she committed or attempted, that is not indemnified by the insured organization. Many companies use this coverage as a complement to Directors and Officers liability coverage (see below), which covers the company for its losses from indemnifying its directors and officers for their acts undertaken in their official capacities.

[D] D&O Liability

The conduct of a corporation's Directors and Officers (D&O) is vulnerable to litigation on many fronts. In order to attract and retain directors and officers, corporations frequently offer some degree of indemnification (see § 1.14[D]), and insurance is an important factor in the indemnification process.

D&O liability insurance contains two separate insuring agreements. One of them protects the individual director or officer against losses arising from claims made against the director, to the extent that the corporation has not indemnified the director or officer, or is not legally required to or permitted to indemnify.

---

[38] Nascimento v. Preferred Mutual Ins. Co., 513 F.3d 273 (1st Cir. 2008).
[39] James River Ins. Co. v. Ground Down Eng'g, Inc. 540 F.3d 1270 (11th Cir. 2008).

The other insuring agreement protects the corporation when it has indemnified the director or officer, or when it is subject to loss at the corporate level because of claims against the director or officer. Depending on the way the policy is written, the insurer could be responsible for the full amount of indemnification that the corporation could provide, or could only be required to reimburse the corporation for indemnification actually provided. Policies written for not-for-profit organizations might cover committee members, trustees, and volunteers as well as directors and officers.

Strictly speaking, D&O coverage is indemnity rather than liability insurance. That is, a person or corporation will be reimbursed for loss, but the insurer does not have a duty to defend. Loss is defined as settlements, damages, costs, and expenses, but fines, treble damages, and criminal fines and restitution are excluded. In this context, a wrongful act means breach of duty, neglect, error, misstatement, misleading statement, or omission, where it is alleged that the wrongful act occurred solely by reason of the person's role as director or officer.

D&O coverage is "claims-made": that is, coverage is provided for claims first made against the director or officer during the policy period. "Long-tail" claims based on conduct during the policy period, but asserted later, are not covered.

Depending on the policy, a claim could mean any demand for payment or threat of litigation, or might be limited to actual filing of a suit. Because many of the potential claims are employment-related, D&O coverage is more valuable if it covers administrative proceedings (e.g., local human rights agencies; the EEOC) as well as litigation.

Securities-law charges involving backdating of stock options may raise issues of D&O policy coverage. D&O policies usually cover defense and liabilities resulting from the "wrongful acts" of directors and officers; generally both the individuals and the company's obligation to indemnify are covered. Many D&O policies extend to corporation's liability resulting from wrongful acts of the D&O.

Coverage under these policies can depend on whether the allegation of backdating is charged as a single course of action or as various unconnected acts. D&O policies are frequently drafted so that the insurer's spending on defense reduces the potential liability coverage, so the insured must decide how much of the policy benefits to devote to investigation or defense.

It is also very likely that coverage will depend on the company giving prompt notice to its insurer that charges of backdating have been raised. If it is a "claims-made" policy, coverage will also depend on notice being given while the policy is in force, not after it has expired. However, when D&O policies do pay claims, all claims within a corporation are typically paid from a single pool — so defense or indemnification of any one person reduces the amount of funds available to colleagues. In some cases this will lead to conflicts of interest among the directors and officers, so it may be better for some of them to obtain separate insurance coverage.[40]

---

[40] Jonathan M. Cohen and John P. Sheahan *Backdating Issues? Remember Your Company's Insurance Coverage*, Legal Times 9/15/06 (law.com).

In a breach of contract action brought by former bank directors against an insurer, the Eighth Circuit held that the insurer cannot avoid its duty to indemnify under a D&O policy for wrongful conduct merely by stating that the director was also an owner or shareholder. The insurer was obligated to explain how the dual capacity facilitated or at least related to the allegation of wrongful conduct for which indemnification was sought.[41]

[1] D&O Exclusions

Some D&O policies specifically exclude employment practices liability, such as claims that an antidiscrimination statute was violated; retaliation; wrongful termination; or breach of employment contract. (See the next section for discussion of specialized EPLI coverage.)

Other typical exclusions from D&O policies:

- Breach of written contract
- Bodily injury,[42] personal injury, and property damage
- Libel, slander and defamation
- Dishonest, fraudulent or criminal acts
- Environmental liability
- Liability stemming from FDIC or other federal financial regulator's activity
- Activities yielding improper personal profit to the director or officer
- ERISA claims
- "Insured vs. insured": i.e., a claim by the corporation or another director or officer against the insured director or officer.

Some policies also exclude merger and acquisition-related liability, mutual fund activities, and joint ventures or limited partnership activities.

D&O coverage is usually excess insurance, so there is no coverage until the limit of the other policy has been exhausted. The "self-insured retention" amount (the counterpart of the deductible) is usually higher for the corporate than the individual part of the coverage.

[E] Employment Practices Liability Insurance (EPLI)

Although most employment-related claims wash out before reaching the courts, or are usually decided in favor of employers, nevertheless employers can be required to pay multimillion-dollar judgments if they lose a major employment-related case.

The ISO EPLI form modifies the basic claims-made structure in a way that helps employers. A claims-made policy is one that provides coverage when claims are made while the insured still has coverage. But the ISO EPLI form also covers

---

[41] McAninch v. Wintermute, 491 F.3d 759 (8th Cir. 2007).

[42] Emotional distress claims are not excluded by a bodily injury exclusion, unless the emotional distress has physical manifestations.

claims made during the 30 days right after the policy expired, unless another insurer is already in the picture. If the same employee makes multiple claims, they are all considered to have arisen on the date of the first claim, so there will be no gap in coverage and it will not be necessary to figure out whether the initial or the later insurer is responsible.

§ 13.08 HEALTH INSURANCE

The first form of health insurance to emerge was indemnity coverage, permitting the patients to select their own health care providers. Since the 1970s, managed care has become the dominant form of health insurance. There are many kinds of managed care plans; they all involve some degree of "gate-keeper" mechanisms (limitations on which doctors the patient can see) and incentives or requirements that the insured person use health care providers who are part of the plan. See §§ 3.07–3.07[M] for discussion of health insurance as an employee benefit.

Health insurance covers "reasonable and medically necessary" services only, and nearly always excludes "experimental" treatment. Therefore, a major litigation issue is determining when a particular treatment has achieved acceptance in the medical profession and can no longer be excluded as experimental.

Pennsylvania's Workers' Compensation Act requires that, once liability is no longer contested, the employer or its insurer must pay for all reasonable or necessary treatment. However, it is permissible to withhold payment for disputed treatment until an independent third party has performed utilization review.

This statute was construed by the Supreme Court in *American Manufacturer Mutual Insurance Co. v. Sullivan.*[43] The *Sullivan* plaintiffs sued state officials, Workers' Compensation insurers, and a self-insured school district, charging that benefits had been withheld without notice, depriving them of a property right.

Their arguments were unsuccessful. The Supreme Court decided that private insurers are not state actors, and therefore their utilization review activities do not raise Due Process issues. Employees do not have a property right until the treatment they seek has been determined to be reasonable and necessary, and therefore there is no right to notice and hearing until that point.

See § 3.07[A] for discussion of ERISA issues in employment-related health insurance policies. The Supreme Court struck a further blow against managed care patients' quest for redress in its June 2004 decision that ERISA § 502(a) completely preempts state-law claims that a managed care plan denied care improperly.[44]

---

[43] 526 U.S. 46 (1999).

[44] Aetna Health Inc. v. Davila, and Cigna Healthcare of Texas, Inc. v. Calad, 542 U.S. 200 (2004).

[A] Indemnity Insurance

Indemnity[45] plans are often divided into "basic" and "major medical" models. Basic coverage includes payments for surgery, hospitalization, and care rendered by doctors during hospitalization. A major medical plan covers costs excluded by other policies. A comprehensive major medical plan includes both basic and major medical aspects, whereas a supplemental major medical plan is pure excess insurance.

The typical indemnity plan imposes deductibles (either by the year or by family member) and coinsurance. Payment under indemnity plans is often based on a fee schedule of "usual, customary and reasonable" charges for each service, so the insured person will have additional payment responsibilities if the doctor's actual charge is higher than the schedule charge. The plan sets overall limits on yearly coverage or lifetime coverage.

In compensation, most indemnity plans provide a "stop-loss" limit (a maximum out-of-pocket payment any employee will have to make in any year).

Indemnity insurance plans allow insured persons to choose their own health care providers, and do not impose limits on the number of doctor visits or the number or identity of specialists consulted. For these reasons, indemnity insurance premiums can be quite high, and can increase unpredictably from year to year. Understandably, indemnity plans are not very popular with employers who have to pay all or most of the premium for the policies in their Employee Group Health Plans (EGHPs).

[B] Managed Care

The objective of managed care is to reduce the cost of health are by reducing unneeded care. There are two major mechanisms for doing so: gatekeeper mechanisms and provider networks. A gatekeeper mechanism, e.g., utilization review, requires permission before accessing specialist care, hospitalization, or other expensive intervention.

Nearly all managed care plans cover care only if it is provided by a "network provider": i.e., a doctor, hospital, nursing home, testing laboratory, etc., that has a contract with the managed care organization and agrees to accept its rate schedule or capitation rates.

Capitated plans pay the health care provider a flat amount per month or year for each person enrolled, regardless of how much or how little care the person actually uses; this is supposed to discourage the doctor from prescribing unneeded tests or repeat visits.

There are many kinds of managed care entities, but the leading form is the Health Maintenance Organization (HMO). Patients covered by an HMO are expected

---

[45] Some policies operate on a reimbursement rather than an indemnity basis. Reimbursement pays back the insured person for incurred expenses, whereas indemnity provides funds that can, but need not, be used for medical care.

to get all or most of their care from providers who participate in the HMO. In exchange for this limitation, they are relieved of most out-of-pocket medical expenses (although they may be responsible for small deductibles for prescriptions and visits to the doctor). The HMO concept has variations, such as the "staff model HMO," "group model HMO," and Individual Practice Association (IPA).

A Preferred Provider Organization (PPO) is a company set up by insurers, health care providers, or a coalition. The preferred providers agree to accept the managed care organization's rate schedule, although they are not employees of the managed care organization.

A Point of Service (POS) plan has some features of the HMO, some of the PPO. Patients have a wider choice of health care provider, but their copayment responsibility increases if they choose a non-network health care provider.

[C] Health Insurance Renewals

Health insurance policies may fall into five categories of renewability:

- Cancelable policy (least protective for the insured): the insurer can increase premiums whenever and to whatever extent is permitted by state regulators; the insurer can terminate the policy at any time by notifying the insured and returning any premiums paid in advance
- Optionally renewable policy: the premium can be raised for an entire class of insureds, but not for an individual who has made large claims. The policy can be terminated on the date set by the contract (typically, the policy anniversary)
- Conditionally renewable policy: the insurer can terminate this type of policy because of a condition named in the contract (e.g., reaching a particular age), but not because of deterioration in health. Premium increases must be class-wide, not individual
- Guaranteed renewable policies: must be renewed at the insured's option until a specific age (usually 60 or 65), and premium increases must be classwide
- Noncancelable health policies: quite rare, they continue until the insured reaches age 65 (the age of Medicare eligibility), and the insurer can neither terminate the coverage nor increase its premium.

[D] Medigap

Medicare Supplementary (Medigap) insurance supplements the coverage that senior citizens and disabled persons receive under the federal Medicare system. Although Medicare offers fairly extensive benefits for hospitalization and doctor bills, coverage is subject to deductibles and coinsurance. Medigap insurance reimburses policy owners for those deductibles and coinsurance. When Part D (prescription drug coverage) was added to the Medicare system, new Medigap policy forms were drafted.

Medigap insurance is subject to an unusual degree of federal regulation. Except in a few states that have opted to maintain their own system of regulation, Medigap insurance is subject to federal laws that impose uniformity.

As a general rule, Medicare beneficiaries who get their care from a Medicare managed care organization don't need and should not pay for a Medigap policy, because they should not have gaps in coverage or out-of-pocket expenses high enough to justify purchase of a policy. However, a person who leaves the Medicare managed care system and returns to conventional fee-for-service Medicare may need to purchase or reinstate Medigap coverage.

[E] Long-Term Care Insurance

Although Medicare covers many of the acute health interventions required by senior citizens, the Medicare system excludes custodial care, such as long-term nursing home care or extensive care at home. Many senior citizens suffer from cognitive disabilities, such as Alzheimer's Disease, or from overall frailty, but not from specific diseases that are Medicare-covered.

Long-term care insurance (LTCI) is a specialized health coverage designed to address senior citizen health needs. The basic LTCI policy covers skilled or custodial care in a nursing home; most LTCI policies also cover home care, either as part of the policy or by addition of riders. Some LTCI policies also cover additional innovative benefits such as adult day care and specialized housing for the elderly.

Unlike most policies, LTCI policies do not have a deductible, although many policies have a waiting period (10–100 days) before coverage begins, which serves a similar function. LTCI policies usually pay a certain amount per day (e.g., $100–$250) for nursing home care. The basic amount of home care coverage is half the nursing home amount, but additional home care coverage can be added by rider. LTCI policies are usually written for either two years, three years, four years, five years, or lifetime of the insured.

The Health Insurance Portability and Accountability Act of 1996, P.L. 104-191 (HIPAA), added tax incentives for "qualified" LTCI policies. (Qualification depends on the policy satisfying various administrative and consumer protection standards.) Part of the premium for a qualified policy may be deductible,[46] and policy benefits can be received tax-free (within limits). Nonqualified policies can lawfully be sold, but they do not get the favorable tax treatment. HIPAA makes it clear that LTCI policies are treated like accident and health insurance policies if they are offered by an employer as an employee fringe benefit. However, they cannot be included in either a cafeteria plan or a flexible spending account.

For 2009, benefits of up to $280 a day (or the actual cost of care, if this is higher) can be received tax-free. The portion of the premium that is potentially

---

[46] The Internal Revenue Code contains a schedule of potential deductions based on the policy owner's age. The deduction is "potential" in that the amount is considered a medical deduction, and as such is deductible only to the extent that all allowable medical deductions exceed 7.5% of Adjusted Gross Income.

deductible for 2009 ranges from $320 a year for persons who have not reached age 40 to $3,980 a year for those over 70.

The Pension Protection Act of 2006 (PPA; P.L. 109-280), at § 844, permits annuity contracts to have long-term care (LTC) riders, with special tax treatment for the LTC portion of the life insurance or annuity contract. Cash value of the contract can be used to pay the LTC benefit. Amounts paid out for care of the insured person reduce the basis in the policy. The rules of § 844 are effective for contracts issued after 1996, but only with respect to taxable years after 2009. For exchanges occurring after 2009, one annuity contract can be exchanged tax-free for another annuity contract under § 1035, even if one of the annuity contracts has an LTC rider.

§ 13.09 BAD FAITH

Although insurance policies are contractual in nature, they involve issues and funds that can be crucial to a business or a family. Therefore, a body of insurance "bad faith" law has evolved explaining the duty that insurers owe to insureds when they deny claims. The insured is entitled to prompt consideration of all claims, as well as notice of claims denial and an honest and comprehensible explanation of the reasons supporting the denial.

Some of the states treat health insurance bad faith as a separate tort, not just a breach of the insurance contract. In such cases, the insurance company's conduct must be worse than mere negligence. Intentional bad faith is required: actual knowledge that there was no reason to deny the claim, or intentional failure to make an adequate investigation. However, unlawful or malicious conduct need not be proved. Remedies for health insurance bad faith can include the benefits that should have been paid; direct and foreseeable economic harm resulting from the nonpayment of benefits; emotional distress; attorneys' fees; and perhaps punitive damages (depending on state law and the facts of the case).

Federal law preempts state-law claims of negligence and bad faith against the insurer of a policy issued under the National Flood Insurance Act. The Third Circuit ruled in late 2004 (even before Hurricanes Katrina and Rita put flood insurance in the spotlight) that permitting state court suits would undermine the efficiency of the National Flood Insurance Act program.[47]

The insurer also has an incentive to delay or refuse to settle tort cases where the potential settlement is at or near the policy limit. To the insurer, the best-case scenario is that the case will go to trial, with a defense verdict. The worst-case scenario is that the plaintiff will win; but whether the case is settled or decided at trial, the insurer's maximum liability is the policy limit. Furthermore, if the case is tried to a plaintiff's verdict, a period of time (perhaps several years) will have elapsed between the settlement negotiations and the verdict.

To the defendant, however, the situation is very different. If the case is settled below the policy limits, the defendant doesn't have to pay anything personally. If it

---

[47] C.E.R. 1988 Inc. v. Aetna Cas. and Sur. Co., 386 F.3d 263 (3d Cir. 2004).

goes to trial, and the verdict is greater than the policy limit, the defendant is personally responsible for the difference.

If bad faith can be proved, the insurer may be required to pay claims even in excess of the policy limit, or that would otherwise be excludable for some reason, and may also be liable for damages or even punitive or treble damages.

The result of the "double insurance" doctrine is that a person cannot collect the full amount under separate policies covering the same loss. The standard fire insurance forms used in California include an "other insurance" clause making each insurer liable only for the part of the loss equivalent to the fraction of all the insurance covering the same peril that its policy represents — whether the other insurance is collectable or not.[48]

The insured is not the only potential plaintiff who could bring a bad-faith case. The case might be brought by an accident victim or other person who is disadvantaged by the lack of a prompt, reasonable settlement. It might also be brought by a reinsurer who is forced to shoulder an unfairly high burden because the primary insurer did not act in good faith.

In mid-2004, the California Supreme Court said that insurers could be held liable for attorneys' fees in bad faith suits about contractual benefits. In this case, involving a house fire that the insurer called suspicious, the jury found that the plaintiffs were not at fault and the insurer acted in bad faith. The jury awarded close to $3.6 million in compensatory damages, $5 million in punitive damages, and almost $1.2 million in "Brandt fees" — bad faith damages including the cost of hiring an attorney on a contingent fee basis to seek benefits under the contract. The insurer's position was that the Brandt fees should be limited to 40% of the disputed benefits (which were only about $40,000) rather than 40% of the total compensatory damages. However, the court said that the plaintiff's obligation was to pay the attorney 40% of the total recovery, whatever that turned out to be, and required the trial judge to set the fee based on the number of hours worked to recover benefits under the contract (to which the 40% contingency applies) rather than hours worked both on that issue and the suit against the insurer. Apportioning the hours is the responsibility of the plaintiff.[49]

An insurer accused of breach of the covenant of good faith and fair dealing because it failed to settle a case cannot charge the insured with "comparative bad faith" on the basis of the insured's conduct in the underlying personal injury case. (In this case the insured, a manufacturer of water slides, did not mention earlier injuries in its response to interrogatories.) In this analysis, breach of the covenant of good faith is usually analyzed as a breach of contract. However, tort theories are applied to breaching insurers (but only to them, and not to the insureds). In this case, the insurer should have settled the case, irrespective of the insured's improper conduct.[50]

---

[48] Burns v. California Fair Plan, 152 Cal. App. 4th 646 (Cal. Ct. App. 2007).

[49] Cassim v. Allstate Ins., 33 Cal. 4th 780 (Cal. 2004).

[50] Kransco v. American Empire Surplus Lines Ins. Co., 97 Cal. Rptr. 2d 151 (Cal. 2000).

Part III

FINANCIAL AND CRIMINAL LAW

Chapter 14

Credit, Collections, and Disclosure

§ 14.01   INTRODUCTION

In most editions of this book, Credit and Collections was a fairly inactive subject area. However, by mid-2008, with disturbances in the economy caused by subprime lending and the collapse of the housing bubble, it had achieved central importance.

The Uniform Commercial Code deals largely (although not exclusively) with transactions between merchants. An extensive body of (primarily federal) statutory law, and a surprisingly robust group of current cases, deals with credit and collections, especially in the consumer context.

Federal Truth in Lending law (15 USC § 1601 *et seq.*; the implementing regulation is Regulation Z, 12 CFR Part 226)[1] requires a significant amount of disclosure to be given of the terms of consumer credit transactions, using standard disclosure formats. Finance charges — interest and related costs of credit — are an important part of the mandatory disclosure.

The subject of creditors' rights usually involves state law. However, debt collection is a highly regulated area. Debtors are protected against abusive collection efforts by the federal Fair Debt Collection Practices Act (FDCPA). There is also an intimate connection between creditor's rights and bankruptcy; the debtor's right to a fresh start limits the creditor's right to receive the promised amounts.

In our information society, data about a person's credit history is easily transmitted, and false or incorrect data can have a significant negative impact. Therefore, the federal Fair Credit Reporting Act (FCRA) contains limitations on

---

[1] *See* 62 FR 10193 (3/6/97), 63 FR 16669 (4/6/98), 64 FR 16614 (3/31/99), 65 FR 58908 (10/3/00), 66 FR 17338 (3/30/02) and 66 FR 65617 (12/20/01) for Regulation Z amendments and updates. The 1999 update prohibits issuance of unsolicited credit cards and gives guidance for calculation of payment schedules for transactions involving private mortgage insurance and transactions involving a down payment that combines cash and a trade-in. In December 2004, the FRB issued an Advance Notice of Proposed Rulemaking, announcing its intention to review Regulation Z over a period of years to settle questions such as whether the current credit card disclosure statements provide consumers the information needed to make informed decisions. The Board expects to make revisions on revolving credit, predatory mortgage lending, closed-end mortgage loans, home equity credit lines, and adjustable-rate mortgages. 69 Fed. Reg. 70,925 (12/8/04); *see* 73 L.W. 2342.

how data can be collected, who has access to it in what context, and also provides a right of reply for consumers who believe that their credit file contains incorrect information.

There are two circumstances in which consumers are given a three-day "cooling off" period, during which they can give written notice of rescission of a transaction for any reason or no reason, without penalty. One of them is the door-to-door sale; the other is a transaction that is not a home mortgage but that grants a security interest in the consumer's personal residence (e.g., a home repair contract). Rescission of the contract voids any lien on the consumer's home.

Section 1220 of the Pension Protection Act (P.L. 109-280) imposes additional standards for credit counseling organizations that seek to operate in tax-exempt non-profit form. The organization must provide credit counseling and debt management services to the general public. It is forbidden to make loans (other than no-fee, no-interest loans) or negotiate loans, or to accept fees for improving any consumer's credit record or rating. Counseling services must not be conditioned on ability to pay, or on eligibility for enrollment in a debt management plan or willingness to enroll in such a plan. The organization must keep its fees reasonable, make provisions for waivers for clients who are unable to pay, and must not set fees as a percentage of the debt, the payments under a debt management plan, or the amount the consumer is expected to save by signing up for a debt management plan. Not more than half of the organization's revenues can come from debt management plan fees.

In mid-2007, the Department of Education issued a proposal to restrict payments from lenders to college financial aid officers, on the grounds that such inducements endanger the rights of borrowers. The rules, expected to be finalized in late 2007 and to take effect in 2008, would forbid lenders to pay for equipment for school administrators or to provide staffing or other assistance to college financial aid offices. Limits would also be imposed on listing preferred lenders. Schools would not be permitted to recommend only one preferred lender; at least three must be designated, with disclosure of what makes them preferred. Students must be informed of the right to select their own lenders. To make it more difficult for lenders to exploit loopholes (such as making donations to alumni groups rather than to the school itself), lenders would be forbidden to provide scholarships, services, or equipment to colleges in return for preferred status.[2]

Many states have adopted the Uniform Consumer Credit Code (U3C), so it should be consulted in the debtor-creditor context; see § 7.05[A], in the consumer protection chapter.

Businesses also have creditors; see § 14.07 for a discussion of creditor's remedies largely (though not entirely) in the business context.

---

[2] Anne Marie Chaker, *U.S. Tackles Student Lending*, Wall St. J. 6/2-3/07 at A6.

[A] Legislation in Response to the Financial Crisis

In mid-2007, after financial markets were rocked by problems in the subprime lending sector, the Federal Reserve, Comptroller of the Currency, FDIC, Office of Thrift Supervision, and the National Credit Union Administration announced stronger guidelines for subprime mortgage loans. In 2006, about three-quarters of subprime adjustable rate mortgages had a low flat teaser rate for the first two or three years followed by a higher floating rate for the rest of a 30-year term. More than 8,000 federally regulated lenders are subject to the guidelines, which require loan underwriting to be based on the borrower's ability to pay adjusted rates, not just an artificially low initial rate. However, the agencies rejected a proposal from consumer groups that borrowers be required to qualify at the highest rate allowed under the loan. The regulations increase the amount of information lenders must collect to demonstrate ability to pay. The new rules require lenders to allow borrowers to refinance out of an ARM at least 60 days before the interest rate rises, without penalty.[3]

Collapse of the housing bubble in mid-2008 led to problems in many other financial sectors, and to federal legislation intended to support the U.S. economy by stabilizing financial markets.

P.L. 110-289, the Housing and Economic Recovery Act of 2008, signed July 30, 2008, includes a Division A on Housing Finance Reform. This legislation includes reform of the regulation of lending, including a Federal Housing Finance Agency and Federal Housing Finance Oversight Board. The bill imposes limitations on golden parachutes and capital requirements for housing lenders, revises the standards for FHA appraisals and other reforms to the FHA, including a prohibition on sellers furnishing assistance with downpayments. P.L. 110-289 includes the S.A.F.E. Mortgage Licensing Act. The legislation also includes mortgage foreclosure protection for servicemembers, and housing matters for veterans. Tax provisions (a tax credit for first-time home buyers; extension of deductibility of real estate taxes by non-itemizers) are also included.

The HOPE for Homeowners program permits some homeowners to refinance mortgages that are no longer affordable. Up to $550,440 can be refinanced as a 30-year, fixed-rate mortgage, with a maximum 90% loan to value ratio. To participate, owners must negotiate with the first lien holder to extinguish subordinate liens. The intention is to prevent foreclosures and deterioration in value of foreclosed properties and areas where there are many foreclosed properties. Participation by lenders is voluntary. Borrowers pay an initial premium of 3% of the original mortgage and another 1.5% of the outstanding mortgage each year, and agree to share appreciation in value of the property with the federal government. The HOPE for Homeowners program runs from October 1, 2008-September 30, 2011 (unless extended). Participation is limited to owner-occupiers who own only one home.

---

[3] Damien Paletta, *Regulators Tighten Subprime-Lending Rules*, Wall St. J. 6/30-7/1/07 at B1; Floyd Norris, *Regulators Set Rules to Limit Subprime Mortgage Lending*, N.Y. Times 6/30/07 at C2.

By September, it became clear that federal action to bail out failed financial institutions was necessary, although the first legislative package that was introduced did not secure passage. Legislation was finally adopted on October 3, 2008, in the form of the Emergency Economic Stabilization Act of 2008 (EESA), P.L. 110-343, comprising subtitles such as the Troubled Assets Relief Program, Energy Improvement and Extension Act of 2008, Tax Extenders and Alternative Minimum Tax Relief Act of 2008, etc.

EESA defines its purpose as providing authority for the Treasury to restore liquidity and stability in the U.S. financial system and protect savings, investment, and homeownership. EESA authorizes the Treasury to establish a Troubled Assets Relief Program to buy assets such as mortgages and related securities issued on or before March 14, 2008. The Secretary of the Treasury is mandated to publish guidelines for selecting and pricing assets and selecting asset managers. Once the program is in operation, the Treasury has to guarantee up to 100% of principal and interest on these troubled assets. Participating financial institutions pay premiums for the guarantee.

EESA establishes a Financial Stability Oversight Board to review the administration of the program. For purchased assets that are secured by residential real estate, the Treasury is required to maximize assistance for homeowners and encourage the use of HOPE for Homeowners and other programs to reduce foreclosures. Federal entities that hold mortgages and mortgage-backed securities are required to maximize their assistance to homeowners. Financial institutions that sell troubled assets and give the Treasury a meaningful equity position must accept standards for executive compensation and corporate governance. Golden parachute payments are forbidden as long as the Treasury holds an equity position; managers must not be given financial incentives to take inappropriate risks; and "clawback" of excessive incentive payments are required.

The intention of the program is that the Treasury will hold the troubled assets until they can be re-sold to maximize investor returns. EESA gives the Secretary of the Treasury an immediate appropriation of $250 billion for asset purchases. Another $100 billion is available based on Presidential certification to Congress that more money is needed; a further $350 billion can be released based on the President's written report to Congress if Congress does not pass a joint resolution disapproving the request. There is no statutory limit on the amount of troubled assets that the Treasury can purchase from a single institution. After five years, the President will submit a legislative proposal for recouping amounts lost by the federal government from the financial services industry.

Although some mortgage relief is included, the EESA does not permit bankruptcy judges to modify the mortgages on debtors' primary residences. It is still unclear how many mortgages the Treasury will end up owning after purchasing "toxic mortgage assets" from financial institutions. Tenants in foreclosed properties are protected from eviction as long as they live up to the terms of their leases.

Although the first rescue program that was proposed did not have any provisions for supervision or oversight of Treasury performance, the EESA includes a number of checks and balances. The President must appoint a special Inspector

General for the program. A congressional oversight panel (five members appointed by congressional leaders) must report to Congress every month on how the Secretary of the Treasury is using his authority.

To increase confidence in bank deposits, the EESA raises the per-account amount insured by the FDIC from $100,000 to $250,000; this provision is scheduled to expire December 31, 2009.

EESA also contains some tax and miscellaneous provisions, such as technical corrections to TILA, a requirement of parity between treatment of mental and physical health in employers' health plans, broader disaster relief, another one-year AMT patch, revival of some expired tax deductions, and alternative energy tax credits.[4]

Another financial crisis-based law, the Worker, Retiree, and Employer Recovery Act of 2008 (P.L. 110-458) concentrated on relief from pension provisions that had become onerous because of changed financial conditions. One of the lenders with the worst records, Countrywide Financial Corp., was acquired by Bank of America. Bank of America entered into a settlement with the Illinois Attorney General to avert foreclosures and modify deceptive mortgage loans covering almost 400,000 customers in 11 states (Illinois, California, Arizona, Connecticut, Florida, Iowa, Michigan, North Carolina, Ohio, Texas, Washington), for a total of $8 billion. Payments will be revised so that borrowers will not have to pay more than one-third of their income; in some cases, interest rates and principal will be adjusted to prevent loss of equity. Bank of America waived imposing loan modification fees or prepayment penalties.[5]

§ 14.02   TRUTH IN LENDING

The Truth in Lending Act (TILA; 15 USC § 1601 *et seq.*), implemented by Regulation Z (12 CFR Part 226), is a disclosure-based statute. That is, quite stringent limits are placed on how lenders and other credit extenders communicate with their customers. But if the appropriate disclosures are made, the credit extender has significant discretion in shaping the transaction.

For TILA purposes, credit means the right to defer payment of a debt. Any person or business that extends or arranges for the extension of credit, in the ordinary course of business, is a creditor. All consumer-related installment sales that involve four or more payments are subject to TILA.

TILA is exclusively a consumer statute, governing lenders and companies that sell goods on credit (i.e., installment sales; providing store credit cards or credit lines). TILA applies if a consumer credit arrangement calls for payment

---

[4] Seyfarth Shaw LLP, *Detailed Summary: The Emergency Economic Stabilization Act of 2008*, http://www.seyfarth.com/index.cfm/fuseaction/publications.publications_detail/object_id/faea1910-e1bc-42b7-9869-6f767357151d/DetailedSummaryoftheEmergencyEconomicStabilizationActof2008.cfm; Tara Siegel Bernard and Kate Galbraith, *Bailout Brings With It Diverse Perks*, N.Y. Times 10/4/08 at C6; Fred Schneyer, *Treasury Details Executive Comp Standards*, Plansponsor.com (10/14/08).

[5] Christopher Wills (AP), *Bank of America Settles Suits Over Bad Mortgages*, 10/6/08 (law.com); Cheryl Miller, *Countrywide Deal Includes Reworked Mortgages*, The Recorder 10/7/08 (law.com).

in more than four installments, or if charges (such as a finance charge) apply to the transaction. As a general rule, extensions of credit over $25,000 are exempt from TILA, but TILA applies to mortgages and other extensions of credit secured by the debtor's personal residence. Responsibility for making all Truth in Lending disclosures falls on the lender. An automobile lender cannot rely on the fact that the consumer eventually learned about the fees on the transaction from the dealer that sold the motor vehicle.[6]

Although, when first drafted, TILA contemplated that disclosures would be made in writing, the eSIGN provision that authorizes electronic signatures on documents also allows disclosures to be made in electronic form provided that the consumer consents in advance to this form: 15 USC § 7001(c)(i).

[A] Structure of TILA

Part A of TILA, 15 USC §§ 1601–1615, covers general definitions and enforcement provisions. Part B, §§ 1631–1648, sets out the disclosures to be made in open-and closed-end credit.[7] Part C, §§ 1661–1665b, governs the information that must be included in advertisements for credit plans. The Fair Credit Billing Act, Part D, §§ 1666–1666j, requires creditors to have a reasonable procedure for resolving credit disputes, and to notify consumers of how to use the procedure. Part E is the Consumer Leasing Act, §§ 1667–1667e.

The underlying purpose of TILA is to make sure that consumers have enough information to determine the true cost of credit, and compare the true cost of credit alternatives. The required disclosures must be made clearly and conspicuously, not in obscure fine print.

[B] Finance Charge

The central disclosure is the "finance charge," the dollar cost of consumer credit. Finance charge is a somewhat broader concept than "interest," in that it includes all direct and indirect charges imposed for credit. Late charges are not included in the finance charge, because they are not imposed routinely, but only if a consumer debtor is late in making a required payment. A national bank is permitted to impose a late charge that is permitted by the state in which the bank is located, even if the actual consumer lives in a state that forbids the fee. The Supreme Court upheld a Commissioner of the Currency interpretation that late fees are a component of interest. The National Bank Act, 12 USC § 85, allows banks to impose charges allowed in their home states and preempts inconsistent state laws.[8]

---

[6] Vallies v. Sky Bank, 432 F.3d 493 (3d Cir. 2006).

[7] The Regulation Z provisions for open-end disclosures begin at 12 CFR § 226.5; closed-end credit disclosures start at 12 CFR § 226.17. Regulation Z Subpart E was added in 1996 (see 61 FR 14952), governing disclosure for home mortgages, including post-consummation disclosures when terms change; see § 226.56 for home equity plans. Section 226.32 covers closed-end home mortgages, including APR calculations for adjustable rate mortgages; § 226.33 deals with reverse mortgages.

[8] Smiley v. Citibank, 517 U.S. 735 (1996).

In April 2007, the Supreme Court held that National Banking Act preemption extends to bank subsidiaries, which are treated as equivalents of the parent bank, because the federal role in regulating bank mortgage business predominates over the state regulatory role, even if the business is carried out through subsidiaries. The Supreme Court precluded states from interfering with the business of banking by subjecting operating subsidiaries that are licensed by the Office of the Comptroller of the Currency to multiple audits and multiple oversight regimes. The decision pleased the banking industry, which did not want to face tougher state enforcement.[9]

Nor does the finance charge include taxes, registration fees, or other costs that are imposed equally on cash and credit customers. See Regulation Z § 226.4(a).

The finance charge must be expressed in the standard form of the Annual Percentage Rate (APR), so that consumers can make meaningful comparisons of the cost of credit from different sources.

[C] TILA Forms

The lender must provide a clear, plain English disclosure statement before the consumer enters into a credit transaction. The consumer must be permitted to retain a copy of the document. Periodic notices must be given, explaining credit activity in any billing period in which the customer's account is either debited or credited. All dollar amounts and percentages must be in boldface type. Annual percentage rates and finance charges must not only be bold, they must be in larger type than other terms.

Lenders who use the "model forms" given in an Appendix to Regulation Z are automatically deemed to comply with truth-in-lending requirements. Regulation Z also includes "sample forms." Use of the sample forms — or individually drafted forms that include all of the mandatory disclosures and other mandatory language — is not illegal, but does not carry this degree of protection.

[D] TILA Remedies

There is a private right of action for TILA violations, including compensatory and punitive damages, attorneys' fees, and costs. See 15 U.S.C. § 1640. The creditor is liable to the consumer for twice the finance charge. For closed-end transactions secured by a dwelling or real property, there is a statutory minimum damage award of $200, but damages cannot exceed $2000. Damages in consumer lease transactions range from $100–$1,000; there is no minimum or maximum in other individual TILA cases. Damages in a class action are capped at the lesser of $500,000 or 1% of the credit grantor's net worth. At the end of 2004, the Supreme Court ruled (in *Koons Buick Pontiac GMC Inc. v. Nigh*, 543 U.S. 50) that the $100 floor and $1,000 ceiling on damages for disclosure violations in consumer loans

---

[9] Watters v. Wachovia Bank, 550 U.S. 1 (2007), discussed in *Tony Mauro, Supreme Court Says Federal Government Is Sole Regulator of Bank Subsidiaries*, Legal Times 4/18/07 (law.com).

was not affected by a 1995 amendment that raised the penalties with respect to closed-end lending (e.g., mortgages). Because the statutory caps remain in place, the aggrieved consumer was not permitted to recover twice the finance charge.

TILA does not specifically mention injunctive or declaratory relief, but some courts have granted such relief.[10]

Courts have held that actual damages cannot be awarded if the customer failed to read the disclosure statement,[11] or had no intention of shopping for better terms.[12]

Personal jurisdiction is available over a creditor in a TILA case where the cause of action arose, or where the creditor engaged in continuous or systematic conduct. There will usually be jurisdiction over the creditor in the debtor's home state because the loan was probably made there, and because of the continuing lender-borrower relationship.[13]

Truth in Lending violations do permit rescission of a mortgage (see 15 USC § 1635), but the right of rescission expires three years after the loan closing. *Beach v. Ocwen Federal Bank*, 522 U.S. 912 (1998) holds that the three-year period is not a statute of limitations, but a limitation on the use of the rescission defense. Although the Ninth Circuit disagrees, the Sixth Circuit decided in 2006 that the right under TILA to rescind a loan transaction within three years if the lender failed to comply with the disclosure requirements extends to loans that have been refinanced, even if the original lender no longer holds security on the loan. The Sixth Circuit noted that 12 CFR § 226.23(a)(3), which defines the right to rescind, does not make an exception for refinancing.[14]

For closed-end credit secured by real estate, the court has discretion to set the statutory TILA damages anywhere between $200 and $2,000.[15]

The Truth in Lending Act statute of limitations is subject to equitable tolling — for instance, if the creditor concealed misrepresentations that were made on a disclosure statement.[16]

[E] TILA Exemptions

States can seek exemption from the Federal Reserve Board from certain TILA requirements, if they have consumer credit laws "substantially similar" to TILA, e.g., the Uniform Consumer Credit Code (U3C).

---

[10] *See, e.g., In re* Consolidated "Non-Filing Insurance" Fee Litigation, 195 F.R.D. 684 (M.D. Ala. 2000).

[11] Parra v. Borgman Ford Sales Inc., 2001 WL 1836190 (W.D. Mich. 2001).

[12] Mayberry v. Ememessay, Inc., 201 F. Supp. 2d 687 (W.D. Va. 2002).

[13] Rose v. Rusnak Automotive Group, 2002 WL 741290 (S.D. Ohio 4/11/02).

[14] Barrett v. J.P. Morgan Chase Bank, 445 F.3d 874 (6th Cir. 2006); *contra*, King v. California, 784 F.2d 910 (9th Cir. 1986).

[15] *In re* Rodrigues, 278 B.R. 683 (Bank. D.R.I. 2002).

[16] Ellis v. GMAC, 160 F.3d 703 (11th Cir. 1998).

Certain types of transactions are exempt:

- Extensions of credit for business purposes (even small ones)
- Transactions over $25,000 that do not grant a security interest in the borrower's principal residence
- Agricultural transactions over $25,000
- Budget plans for paying for home heating fuel
- Student loans issued or guaranteed by federal agencies
- Some personal property leases that are incident to leases of real property
- Purchase-money second mortgages (i.e., financed by the seller of the home), because the seller is not considered a "creditor" because this is a one-time transaction rather than part of an ongoing business.

TILA amendments passed as part of the Omnibus Consolidated Appropriations Act of 1996, P.L. 104-208, permit TIL coverage to be waived by the Federal Reserve Board, by regulation, for wealthy consumers (annual income over $200,000, or net assets over $1 million), as long as the opulent consumer signs a handwritten assent to the waiver.

[F] Closed-End Credit

Closed-end credit is a single extension of credit, such as a loan or purchase of an item of property "on time." The rules for closed-end credit are somewhat more stringent than the regulation of open-end credit, such as credit cards (see below).

[1] Loan Disclosures

The mandated disclosures for a loan are:

- Date of the transaction, or other date on which the finance charge begins to accrue
- Annual percentage rate (APR) of the finance charge[17]
- The number of scheduled payments
- The dollar amount of scheduled payments
- When the payments are due
- The total dollar value of all scheduled payments
- Whether a "balloon" payment (single large payment at the end of the term) is due; if so, its amount
- How late payment charges will be computed
- Identification of any security interest retained by the lender
- Identification of the collateral
- The amount financed (the credit extended: i.e., the amount of credit other than prepaid finance charges)

---

[17] Disclosure is not required of certain very small amounts.

- Amount of any prepaid finance charges
- Amount of any deposit
- Sum total of prepaid finance charges and deposits
- Total finance charge
- Disclosure of any right of rescission (e.g., loans secured by principal residence).

Chase Bank extended credit to its cardholders by mailing them preprinted "convenience checks" which, when used, were charged against the customer's credit account, with associated finance charges and transaction fees. The plaintiffs in a Ninth Circuit case decided in early 2008 used the checks and incurred the fees. California Civil Code § 1748.9 mandates a disclosure for a preprinted check or draft that it will be charged to the user's credit account; the APR and finance charges; and whether finance charges are triggered as soon as the check is used. The plaintiffs also alleged a violation of California Business & Professional Code § 17200, committing an unlawful business practice by failing to make required disclosures. Chase removed the case to federal court, and took the litigating position that the California laws were preempted by the National Bank Act and the regulations of the Comptroller of the Currency. The Ninth Circuit agreed, stating that states cannot impose regulations that limit the power of federally chartered banks to lend money on personal security.[18]

[2] Credit Sale Disclosures

The mandatory disclosures for closed-end credit sales are quite similar, other than differences reflecting the variation between an extension of credit from the seller of a big-ticket item and extension of credit by a lender who advances a sum of money. Phrases in quotation marks are statutory terms that must be used in the disclosure statement. The credit sale disclosures are:

- Date of transaction, or other date on which the finance charge begins to accrue
- Finance charge expressed as an APR (this requirement is excused for very small sums)
- For a variable-rate APR, circumstances under which it can change; effect of a rate increase; any limit on rate increases
- Amount of finance charge; description of each of its components (this is not required in most sales of dwellings)
- Number, amount, and due dates of scheduled payments
- "Total of payments": i.e., the number of payments times the amount of each
- Any balloon payment required
- "Cash price": i.e., the cost of buying the property or services if no credit were extended

---

[18] Rose v. Chase Bank USA, 513 F.3d 1032 (9th Cir. 2008).

- "Cash down payment": itemized account of down payment made by the buyer, including "trade-ins"; disclosure of the "total down payment" (cash plus trade-ins)
- "Unpaid balance of cash price": i.e., cash price minus total down payment
- Individual itemization of charges (over and above the cash price) that are included in the amount financed but are not part of the finance charge; they are referred to as the "unpaid balance"
- Amount of the unpaid balance
- Amounts that will be deducted for "prepaid finance charge." If there is a "required deposit balance," it must be disclosed, and so must the "total prepaid finance charge and required deposit balance."
- The "amount financed" is the unpaid balance plus the prepaid finance charge or required deposit balance or total prepaid finance charge, minus the required deposit balance
- The "deferred payment price" is the cash price plus all other charges that are part of the amount financed but are not finance charges, plus the finance charge. (This disclosure is not required in sales of dwellings.)
- Method of computing late payment charges
- Property to which the security interest relates
- Disclosure of the security interest held or to be acquired by the creditor, including security interests in after-acquired property or to secure future extensions of credit
- Explanation of any prepayment penalty
- Refund provisions for unearned finance charges when prepayment is made[19]
- Disclosure of any right of rescission available to the buyer.

[G] Open-End Credit

In closed-end credit, a loan is made, or an item is purchased. Usually what happens is that the balance declines steadily, as the borrower/buyer makes the scheduled payments (although there may be complications if the consumer misses a payment and late charges are imposed).

Open-end credit, such as credit cards and lines of credit, creates more complicated problems. The debtor has the right to get new advances of credit, for instance by buying further items with a credit card, when there is still a balance from prior extensions of credit. Finance charges are not imposed if the debtor pays the entire balance by the due date for the billing. But if there is a continuing balance, finance charges are imposed. The typical customer makes the required minimum payment or a higher payment, but maintains an ongoing balance, so the balance is in a constant state of flux as new charges are made but earlier balances are reduced.

---

[19] Debtors who prepay are also entitled to refund of the unearned portion of any credit insurance premium already paid.

The Fair Credit Disclosure Act, (FCDA) P.L. 100-583, entitles consumers to information about credit and charge cards before they apply for a new card. Four key terms must be disclosed in mail and phone solicitations for credit card applications: APR; the annual fee for the card; the grace period during which payments can be made before interest becomes due; and the method used to calculate the balance subject to the finance charge.

A credit card still fits under the 15 USC § 1602(i) definition of open-end credit even if it is a specialized credit card than can be used only for the purchase of a particular big-ticket item (e.g., a satellite dish) and related items, and even if the credit limit is not much more than the cost of the big-ticket item itself.[20]

Several courts have ruled that banks do not have a duty to non-customers whose personal information is used by an identity thief to secure a credit card from the bank by impersonating someone else. In other words, there is no tort of negligent facilitation of consumer fraud.[21]

[1] Disclosures for New Accounts

A set of disclosures is required when a person who has been solicited for open-end credit decides to accept the credit card or other account:

- Conditions under which a finance charge may be imposed
- Grace period — i.e., period of time during which payments can be made in order to avoid a finance charge
- How the balance subject to finance charge will be determined
- Method of determining the finance charge, and components of the charge
- The periodic rate(s) that will be used to compute the finance charge; how those rates are applied (e.g., an APR of X% for the first $Y of balance, Z% for the rest of the balance)
- Conditions for imposing other charges, such as late charges; calculation method for other charges.

An FRB Final Rule published at 65 FR 58903 (10/3/00) adds to the disclosures required on credit card solicitations and applications. The APR for purchases must be disclosed in 18-point type, under a separate heading from the rates charged as penalties. The disclosures must be readily noticeable, made in 12-point or larger type, and in reasonably understandable language. The APRs for cash advances and balance transfers must be disclosed in the same table as the APR for purchases.

The Federal Reserve proposed rules for additional and more consumer-friendly disclosure of credit card terms in May 2007, the first major review of disclosure requirements since the early 1980s. Under the proposals, credit solicitations must conspicuously display information about penalties and how payments

---

[20] Benion v. Bank One, 144 F.3d 1056 (7th Cir. 1998).

[21] *See, e.g.,* Huggins v. Citibank NA, 355 S.C. 329 (S.C. 2003); Smith v. Citibank, 2001 WL 34079057 (W.D. Mo. 2001); Polzer v. TRW Inc., 682 N.Y.S.2d 194 (N.Y.A.D. 1998).

will be allocated (to new balance and past balance). Periodic statements will have to warn consumers about the risks of making only the minimum payment. Issuers would be required to give 45 days' notice before increasing the interest rate on account of default or delinquency.[22]

[2] Disclosures on Periodic Statements

Each periodic statement issued[23] to a cardholder must, under 15 USC § 1637(b) and Regulation Z § 226.7, give the following information about the cardholder's account:

- Beginning balance
- Identification of the amount and date of each extension of credit
- Total amount credited to the cardholder's account during the billing period
- Itemized finance charge
- Total finance charge, and the range of balances it applies to
- The periodic rate or rates, and the APR(s), and the range of balances each applies to
- The balance subject to finance charge, and how it was determined
- The outstanding balance at the end of the period
- The date by which the balance must be paid to avoid further finance charges
- Creditor's address for reporting billing errors.

TILA, at 15 USC § 1640, grants a civil remedy for creditors' failure to comply with the disclosure requirements, including the amount of the "finance charge."

The $1,000 cap on statutory damages for disclosure violations in consumer credit transactions secured by personal property (15 USC § 1640(a)(2)(A)) remains in effect. The Supreme Court held in late 2004 that the 1995 Truth in Lending amendments did not limit the applicability of the cap to lease transactions. The cap applies to statutory damages ($100–$1,000) in cases where there are no actual damages; otherwise, TILA allows recovery of twice the actual damages.[24]

Regulation Z does not categorize over-limit fees (charges for exceeding the cardholder's credit limit) as finance charges. A cardholder who was allowed to exceed her $2,000 credit limit in exchange for a $29 over-limit fee for each month in which her balance exceeded $2,000 sued because the monthly statement disclosed the fee but did not include it in the finance charge. In 2004, the Supreme Court upheld the Regulation Z categorization, finding it a reasonable interpretation of the statute made by an agency that holds regulatory authority. To the Supreme

---

[22] Christopher Conkey, *Fed Plans Credit-Card Changes*, Wall St. J. 5/24/07 at D6.

[23] It is not necessary to send a statement during any billing cycle unless a finance charge was imposed during that cycle, or there was an outstanding credit or debit balance greater than $1 at the end of the cycle.

[24] Koons Buick Pontiac GMC Inc. v. Nigh, 543 U.S. 37 (2004).

Court, over-limit charges are not obviously related to finance charges, which are automatic rather than being imposed as penalties for default.[25]

A fee for expediting payments so a credit card user can avoid a late fee is not considered an "other charge," and therefore need not be disclosed as such.[26] The Final Rule also permits an issuer to replace an accepted credit card with more than one replacement card, as long as all the cards have the same terms and conditions, and the consumer's liability for unauthorized use does not increase due to the additional cards.

[3] Billing Errors

The Fair Credit Billing Act (FCBA), 15 USC §§ 1666–1666j requires card issuers and other providers of open-end credit to maintain reasonable dispute resolution procedures, and to disclose them to cardholders. A billing error is a cardholder's request for clarification of a billed item, or the customer's complaint that the statement reflects an extension of credit that was not made to the cardholder, was made without his or her authorization, does not properly credit payments made by the cardholder, or reflects merchandise that was ordered but not delivered.

The FCBA gives the cardholders 60 days (dating from the creditor's transmission of the first billing statement containing the error) to make a written complaint about the error. (If the statement gives a telephone number for complaints, it must also disclose that telephoned complaints do not preserve the customer's FCBA rights.) When the complaint is received, the creditor has a duty to either correct the error or give the cardholder a detailed, comprehensible explanation of why the bill was correct.

Federal Reserve Board Official Staff Commentary § 226.12(c)(2)-2 says that a card issuer must do a reasonable investigation, including independent assessment of information provided by both merchant and cardholder, before concluding that a dispute is settled. Nor is a matter resolved merely because the cardholder does not provide a requested document or piece of information; the cardholder might not have access to the information.

Even if the error correction procedure is not invoked, a billing error can be raised as a defense in a collection action.[27]

A cardholder's liability for unauthorized use of his or her credit card is generally limited to $50: see 15 USC § 643. Unauthorized use is use by someone other than the cardholder, without actual, implied or apparent authorization for the use, and providing no benefit to the cardholder. Unauthorized use is considered a billing error, subject to the same notification and investigation requirements.

A cardholder's failure to review monthly billing statements does not grant apparent authority to an employee who misuses a corporate card to the extent that

---

[25] Household Credit Serv. Inc. v. Pfennig, 541 U.S. 232 (Sup. Ct. 2004).

[26] 68 FR 16185 (4/3/03).

[27] Peoples Bank v. Scarpetti, 1998 WL 61925 (Conn. Super. 1998).

the limitation on liability for unauthorized use becomes inoperative. However, because the corporate cardholder paid over $100,000 in improper charges over a period of about a year without protest, at some point the credit card issuer would have been justified in assuming authority. The corporation's lack of benefit from the use of the card is irrelevant, because the defense to the liability limitation involves both lack of benefit and lack of apparent authority.[28]

[H] 1998 FRB Final Rule

On April 6, 1998, the Federal Reserve Board published a Final Rule revising the Official Staff Commentary on Regulation Z, effective 3/31/98. See 63 FR 2616 (4/6/98).

The Final Rule provides guidance for open-end credit plans whose rates increase when a payment is late or the consumer exceeds credit limits, and explains how to calculate the APR for "multi-feature" plans such as cash advances and overdraft checking. It also requires disclosure of the costs of any related annuity provided in connection with a reverse mortgage, whether issued by the creditor or by a third party.

[I] Home Equity Lending

A home equity loan or line of credit, which is secured by the borrower's equity in his or her personal residence, is considered open-end credit. P.L. 100-709, the Home Equity Loan Consumer Protection Act of 1988, enacted at 15 USC § 1637A, mandates disclosures for open-end consumer credit secured by the borrower's principal residence:

- Limited period of availability, or other condition on availability of the terms
- Repayment options
- Minimum periodic payments, including the length of time to repay a hypothetical $10,000 credit advance by making only the minimum payment
- Fixed APR or method of calculating a variable APR,[29] including disclosure of a "worst case scenario"; the fact that a home equity loan APR includes only interest, not other charges
- Tax implications of the transaction
- If there is a possibility of negative amortization (i.e., the debt grows more quickly than it is reduced by the borrower's payments)
- Points or other fees charged
- Warning that default can lead to loss of the home.

---

[28] DBI Architects PC v. American Express Travel-Related Serv. Co., 388 F.3d 886 (D.C. Cir. 2004).

[29] Rate adjustments must be made according to a publicly available index that is not controlled by the creditor: 15 USC § 1647.

Section 1665b regulates advertisements for home equity loans. It should be noted that, although creditors are not subject to liability if they violate TILA's other advertising rules, actual damages, attorneys' fees, and possibly statutory damages are available for improper advertising of HELCs.

Also see § 1638(b)(2), requiring good-faith estimates of disclosure amounts in closed-end residential mortgage transactions to be given to the borrower within three days after receipt of the borrower's written loan application, or before consummation of the transaction (whichever is earlier).

A 1994 enactment, the Home Ownership and Equity Protection Act (HOEPA) P.L. 103-325, 15 USC § 1602(aa), prohibits abusive loan terms and predatory lending practices imposed on low-income, high-equity home owners who are pressured to take on excessively large, high-fee home equity loans that carry an above-market rate of interest. Loans are covered if their APR is 8 (as amended; originally 10) percentage points or more above the yield of Treasury bills. However, the statute does not cap rates on home equity loans. The HOEPA disclosures required by 15 USC § 1639 supplement, rather than replace, the ordinary TILA disclosures called for by 15 USC § 1638.

Violation of the Home Ownership and Equity Protection Act is punishable by civil liability for statutory damages, actual damages, fees, and costs. The homeowner is given additional rights to rescind the transaction, and state Attorneys General have the power to bring their own proceedings. See 15 USC § 1640(a). Purchase money mortgages, reverse equity mortgages, and construction loans are exempt.

Late in 2001, the Federal Reserve Board approved a rule broadening the scope of loans subject to HOEPA. As of the rule's October 1, 2002 effective date, HOEPA is triggered if the APR of a refinancing transaction for a first-line mortgage is more than eight points above the Treasury rate for instruments of comparable maturity.

When HOEPA is triggered, certain loan terms are forbidden, such as balloon payments for short-term loans. Additional disclosures are also required. The December 2001 rule also bans "flipping," the resale of a refinancing loan within the loan's initial 12 months, unless this is in the best interests of the homeowner. The anticipated result of the change was that the percentage of "sub-prime" first mortgages subject to HOEPA would rise from 12.4% to 38%.[30]

The Homeowners Protection Act of 1998, P.L. 105-216 (7/29/98), 12 USC § 4901, requires automatic cancellation (and notice of cancellation rights) in transactions where private mortgage insurance is a prerequisite (e.g., the home buyer is permitted to make a smaller down payment on condition of maintaining private insurance that will make good if he or she defaults). It also limits the amount of private mortgage insurance that home buyers can be required to purchase.

---

[30] See Law on Mortgages is Expanded (no by-line), N.Y. Times, 12/14/01, p. C12. Additional HOEPA rules are found at 66 FR 65604 (12/20/01) and 68 FR 16185 (4/3/03).

[J] Payday Loans

A borrower of two-week "payday loans" stated a TILA claim that can survive a 12(b)(6) motion to dismiss by alleging that the lender made a practice of stapling cash register receipts to the loan agreement in a way that blocked the disclosure statement, and that the receipts failed to describe the costs as finance charges.[31] Disclosures cannot be "clear and conspicuous" if something blocks them. However, in the Seventh Circuit view, the statement "Your post-dated check is security for this loan" was an acceptable TILA disclosure when measured from the viewpoint of the ordinary consumer.

The Ninth Circuit has held that statutory damages are not available for violation of 15 USC § 1632(a) or § 1638(b)(1), and also rejected an award of actual damages in a case involving a bankruptcy debtor who got a payday loan with a stated APR of 782.143%, with disclosures in the same font and size as the rest of the note. The bankruptcy trustee alleged that the debtor failed to receive the required notice. The trustee filed a creditor's proof of claim on behalf of the payday lender, and also filed an adversary proceeding seeking disallowance of the claim for failure to provide conspicuous disclosures. The Ninth Circuit held that statutory damages were not warranted, because § 1640(a) rules out statutory damages for violations of § 1638(b)(1) [timing of disclosures]. The Ninth Circuit held that statutory damages are not available for failure to make disclosures more conspicuous than the rest of the text. Actual damages for a TILA violation require a showing of detrimental reliance (that the borrower would not have taken the loan, or would have gotten a better rate somewhere else if the appropriate disclosure had been made).[32]

Payday lending is legal in nearly all of the states (37 states plus the District of Columbia), but a great deal of reform legislation has been introduced: at least 52 payday loan bills introduced in state legislatures in 2007, according to the National Conference of State Legislators. The 2006 federal legislation forbids interest over 36% on loans to servicemembers — a demographic often targeted by payday lenders. Some states (e.g., New Mexico; Oregon) impose a cap on fees and a maximum interest rate.[33] Several states moved against payday lenders by adopting "fair lending" laws that impose interest rate caps (e.g., 28%). New Hampshire capped interest rates on payday and car-title loans at 36%. In 2004, Georgia made payday lending a felony, and the law survived appellate challenge. In 2005, North Carolina made payday lending illegal. In 2005, many payday lenders ceased doing business in New Hampshire, Oregon, and Ohio in response to rate caps.[34]

The Federal Deposit Insurance Corporation (FDIC) revised its Guidelines for Payday Lending in March 2005. Although only 12 of its 5,200 supervised

---

[31] Smith v. Cash Store Mgmt. Inc., 195 F.3d 325 (7th Cir. 1999).

[32] *In re* Ferrell, 539 F.3d 1186 (9th Cir. 2008).

[33] Christopher Conkey, *Payday Lenders Strike a Defensive Pose*, Wall St. J. 2/21/07 at A8.

[34] Conor Dougherty, *States Imposing Interest-Rate Caps to Rein in Payday Lenders*, Wall St. J. 8/9–10/08 at A3.

institutions do payday lending, the FDIC holds institutions responsible even for programs administered by a third-party contractor.[35]

The FDIC requested public comments on its compliance guidelines for examiners. Under these guidelines[36] payday loans are considered inimical to the standards of safety and soundness required of federally-insured institutions, although these strictures are not applied if an institution makes occasional small short-term loans to customers.

Payday loans are part of a broader phenomenon of subprime lending — a field that is open to abuses, especially when the borrowers are elderly or have limited English proficiency. As of March 2003, four states (California, Georgia, New York, and North Carolina) had legislation forbidding predatory lending, and similar legislation has been introduced in 25 other states. Household Finance settled predatory lending charges made by 20 state Attorneys General by agreeing to pay $484 million.[37]

§ 14.03 EQUAL CREDIT OPPORTUNITY: REGULATION B

The Equal Credit Opportunity Act, 15 USC § 1691 *et seq.*, and its implementing Regulation B (12 CFR Part 202), are designed to protect credit-worthy members of traditionally disfavored groups against credit discrimination on the basis of race, national origin, sex, marital status, or age (although positive discrimination in favor of senior citizen borrowers is permissible). Credit discrimination against public assistance recipients is also forbidden.

Although business judgments about creditworthiness do not violate the ECOA, the judgment must be based on objective factors about the applicant, not conclusions about the affluence or reliability of an entire group of people.

A married credit applicant must be allowed to secure credit based only on his or her own income, resources, and credit history, without the necessity of having the other spouse join in or even approve the extension of credit. Creditors are prohibited from asking certain questions (e.g., except in community property states or states in which spouses are responsible for necessaries purchased by their spouses, marital status is not a permissible inquiry on an application filed by only one obligor).

It is forbidden to make an oral or written statement that might have the effect of discouraging a potential borrower from applying for credit. Unless the application states conspicuously that disclosure of such information is optional, the creditor may not inquire about alimony or child support payments unless the applicant lists these as a potential source of income that could support repayment.

---

[35] http://www.fdic.gov/news/news/financial/2005/fil1405a.html (3/2/05); *see* 73 L.W. 2520.

[36] http://www.fdic.gov/regulations/laws/PublicComments/Payday1.html.

[37] *See* Tamara Loomis, *Predatory Lending Law Upsets Investment Firms*, N.Y.L.J. 3/28/03 (law.com).

Regulation B includes model application forms. Their use is not mandatory (and in fact the ECOA does not require the use of written application forms at all), but using the model forms does provide a safe harbor.

ECOA or Regulation B violations can be punished by civil liability of actual damages (without limit) plus punitive damages of up to $10,000. Class-action damages are limited to 1% of the creditor's net worth or $500,000 (whichever is less), plus costs and attorneys' fees.

§ 14.04   FAIR CREDIT REPORTING ACT (FCRA AND FACTA)

The Fair Credit Reporting Act, Title VII of TILA, 15 USC §§ 1581–1681T, governs the activities of consumer reporting agencies in collecting, processing, and especially in disseminating information about consumers. The FCRA preempts state laws on credit reporting only to the extent that they are inconsistent with the federal law.

In addition to the consumer and the consumer reporting agency, the FCRA affects the activities of users of consumer reports (e.g., lenders who decide whether or not to grant credit; landlords who decide whether or not to rent an apartment; employers who decide whether or not to extend a job offer). Users of consumer reports must inform consumers when any such denial is made based on a consumer report. The user of the report must identify the reporting agency that is the source of the report.

Any information (oral or written; positive or negative) that bears on a consumer's creditworthiness, credit standing, credit capacity, character, personal characteristics, mode of living, or reputation is treated as a consumer report, if it is collected, used, or expected to be used for a business purpose such as establishing the consumer's eligibility for consumer credit, insurance, or employment.

If credit is denied because of information from any source other than a consumer report, the creditor must inform the consumer of the right to request the nature of the negative information within a 60-day period.

An insurance company is entitled to get a consumer credit report on a prospect, if the company intends to use the information to make a firm offer of insurance — even if the potential customer has not applied for the policy, because 15 USC § 1681b(a)(C) permits furnishing of credit reports for insurance underwriting.[38] 2003 amendments to 15 USC § 1681b(c)(1)(B)(i) permit a credit reporting agency to furnish a credit report that is not authorized by the consumer when a "firm offer of credit" has been made. Several cases involve the legality under the FCRA of sending unsolicited offers of credit based on a list of "pre-screened"

---

[38] Scharpf v. AIG Mktg. Inc., 242 F. Supp. 2d 455 (W.D. Ky. 2003). The FCRA's requirement that insurers disclose adverse actions when rates are raised in response to credit information (15 USC § 1681a(k)(1)(B)(i)) applies to the first rate charged in an initial policy, not just to rate increases when a policy is extended or renewed.

individuals purchased from a credit reporting agency. FCRA limits the use of credit information without the consumer's consent. One acceptable use is extending a "firm offer of credit." Violation is punishable by actual damages or statutory penalties of $100–$1,000 per person. According to the First Circuit, a letter to homeowners with at least $10,000 in revolving debt and a credit score over 500 was a firm offer of credit even though it did not include an interest rate or the duration of the loan available to qualifying customers.[39]

The First Circuit held that under the FCRA, a firm offer of credit means an offer that will be accepted if the customer satisfies the criteria and further conditions established before the offer. The First Circuit rejected the plaintiff's argument that it violated the FCRA to send him a solicitation flyer based on information in his credit report, and to fail to include material terms in the flyer. According to the First Circuit, all that is required is that the potential lender discloses the existence of pre-selection criteria. Disclosure of loan terms is governed by TILA, not FCRA. Although it could be argued that the mailing violated the plaintiff's privacy, the First Circuit said the plaintiff should have used the FCRA opt-out procedure instead of bringing suit.[40]

Under FCRA, insurance companies are required to send adverse action notices to consumers when insurance rates are increased based on information from consumer credit reports: see 15 USC § 1681a(k)(1)(B)(i) and 1681m(a). The Supreme Court ruled in mid-2007 that willful failure includes reckless disregard of the obligation to give notice. There is a private right of action under the FCRA, comprising actual damages for negligent violations and actual, statutory and punitive damages. The initial rate charged for a new policy can be an adverse action (if it is higher than the rate available to other consumers), but a rate increase is based on a credit report only if the report is a necessary condition of the increase. To determine if a first-time rate places the customer at a disadvantage, it is compared to the rate that would have been charged if the company had not considered credit scores. Thus, one of the plaintiffs was not entitled to notice, because his initial policy rate was the same as if his credit score had not been considered; the other defendant might have violated the FCRA but was not reckless because it was not aware of an unjustifiably high risk of harm from its rate-setting practices.[41]

A mid-2005 Ninth Circuit decision holds that the FCRA preempts California laws that require consumers to consent to financial institutions' sharing of information about the consumers with business affiliates. However, the federal law does

---

[39] Sullivan v. Greenwood Credit Union, 520 F.3d 70 (1st Cir. 2008).

[40] Dixon v. Shamrock Fin. Corp., 522 F.3d 76 (1st Cir. 2008); *see also* Perry v. First Nat'l Bank, 459 F.3d 817 (7th Cir. 2006).

[41] Safeco Ins. Co. of America v. Burr, 127 S. Ct. 2201; consolidated with Geico v. Edo (U.S. 2007). *See also* State Farm Mut. Auto Ins. Co. v. Willes, 127 S. Ct. 2933 (2007), granting certiorari and remanding the case to the Ninth Circuit for reconsideration in light of *Burr*. On remand, Willes v. State Farm Fire and Casualty Co., 512 F.3d 565 (9th Cir. 2008), applying the principle that notice is required only when the credit report is a necessary condition for the higher rate, the Ninth Circuit held that the insurer was not liable; its rate quote was not influenced by the credit report.

not preempt state law's similar consent requirement for data-sharing with non-affiliated third parties.[42]

Effective June 1, 2005, an FTC rule requires businesses and individuals to take appropriate steps to dispose properly of sensitive information obtained from consumer reports. The rule covers everyone who uses consumer reports for business purposes. Entities that dispose of records containing consumer personal or financial information must take protective steps even if they are exempt from the rule. Protective steps (e.g., shredding, burning, or pulverizing papers; destroying or erasing computer files in a way that prevents their reconstruction) must be taken to prevent unauthorized access to the information. A business that hires a document construction contractor must apply due diligence in selecting it and monitoring its performance.[43]

The Credit Repair Organizations Act, 15 USC § 1679 *et seq.*, provides a cause of action for consumers harmed by credit repair organizations' unscrupulous business or advertising practices. However, there is a statutory exemption (15 USC § 1679a(3)(B)(i)) for nonprofit organizations that are exempt under Code § 501(c)(3). The First Circuit held that to qualify for the exemption, mere 501(c)(3) status (which depends on information provided by the applicant to the IRS) is not enough. The organization must demonstrate that it operates in fact as a nonprofit organization.[44]

[A] 1997 Amendments

Major FCRA amendments, enacted as part of the Omnibus Consolidated Appropriations Act of 1996 (P.L. 104-208), took effect on September 30, 1997:

- Credit bureaus are obligated to resolve consumer complaints about disputed information faster, and must offer more options.
- Employers are limited in their ability to obtain and use credit reports in the hiring process.
- Each credit offer must include toll-free credit bureau numbers, so consumers can have their names removed from the lists used to solicit credit cards and insurance. Credit bureaus must also provide written forms so consumers can have their names permanently removed from solicitation lists.
- When a consumer complains about information in the file, the credit bureau has an obligation to investigate, review all relevant information, and report inaccuracies and omissions to all other national credit bureaus.

The states have the power to take enforcement action on behalf of consumers in federal or state court, up to $1,000 per violation; the FTC is empowered to seek up to $2,500 per violation.

---

[42] American Bankers Ass'n v. Gould, 412 F.3d 1081 (9th Cir. 2005).

[43] http://www.ftc.gov/bcp/conline/pubs/alerts/disposalalart.pdf.

[44] Zimmerman v. Cambridge Credit Counseling Corp., 409 F.3d 473 (1st Cir. 2005).

Several decisions hold that consumers have an implied private right of action under the FCRA to sue companies that make initial negative reports to credit reporting agencies and then fail to make a proper investigation after a consumer challenge to the accuracy of the information.[45]

Under 15 USC § 1691p, the FCRA statute of limitations is two years from the date liability arose. In case of willful misconduct by the defendant, the statute of limitations is two years from the date of discovery.

A company cannot gain access under the FCRA to consumers' credit reports merely by offering them a $300 credit that can only be used to buy a car. The Seventh Circuit found that such an offer is so small, so limited, and so lacking in disclosure of key terms such as interest and repayment terms that it could not justify access to valuable consumer credit information.[46]

[B] GLB Privacy Requirements

Under the Gramm-Leach-Bliley Act (GLB; P.L. 106-102), effective July 1, 2001, the credit services industry is severely limited in its ability to market consumer data (e.g., by matching up names with addresses and Social Security and phone numbers). Resale of data without consumer consent is forbidden.

The FTC promulgated a rule defining the entire credit report including the "credit header" (address and related data) as subject to the GLB privacy restrictions. The rule has been upheld in federal court in litigation brought by federal agencies (including the Federal Reserve Board and the FTC) against Trans Union LLC, Equifax, and other generators of consumer credit data.[47]

The D.C. Circuit found the FTC's interpretation (that credit reporting agencies are financial institutions subject to the Gramm-Leach-Bliley privacy rules about nonpublic personal information) to be reasonable and therefore entitled to deference.[48]

Rules published in April 2004 expanded the reach of medical privacy rights by forbidding banks to consider a person's health condition (including possible terminal illness) when granting credit. The consumer's physical, mental, or behavioral health condition and history cannot be taken into account. Under the rules, a borrower's existing medical debt can be taken into consideration in granting credit, but only to the same extent as other debts.[49] A Final Interim Rule (effective March 7, 2006) was issued under FACTA § 411 in June 2005. Creditors are forbidden to use medical information in eligibility decisions, subject to certain exceptions.

---

[45] Dornhecker v. Ameritech Corp., 99 F. Supp. 2d 918 (N.D. Ill. 2000); Campbell v. Baldwin, 90 F. Supp. 2d 754 (E.D. Tex. 2000); Nelson v. Chase Manhattan Mort. Corp., 282 F.3d 1057 (9th Cir. 2002); *but contra* Carney v. Experian Info. Solutions, 57 F. Supp. 2d 496 (W.D. Tenn. 1999).

[46] Cole v. United States Capital Inc., 389 F.3d 719 (7th Cir. 2004).

[47] *See* Glenn R. Simpson, *Judge Upholds Tough New Restrictions on Sales of Certain Personal-Credit Data*, Wall Street Journal, 5/8/01, p. A28.

[48] TransUnion LLC v. FTC, 295 F.3d 42 (D.C. Cir. 2002).

[49] Robert Pear, *Proposal Bars Banks from Using Medical Data to Decide Loans*, N.Y. Times, 4/28/04 at p.A16.

The rule explains how creditors can share medical information with their affiliate companies without being considered consumer reporting agencies.[50]

The GLB privacy provision does not prevent an insurance company from disclosing to private litigants, under a discovery order, records of insured persons who were not litigants; GLB, at 15 USC § 6802(e)(8), exempts disclosures in response to judicial process.[51]

[C] Fair and Accurate Credit Transactions Act (FACTA)

FACTA, P.L. 108-396, makes nationwide standards for credit reporting permanent, and increases the responsibilities of consumer reporting agencies and federal regulators to improve reporting of consumer credit information and combat identity theft. The statute requires the FTC to work with banks to draft guidelines for recognizing when identity theft has occurred. Merchants must take steps to avoid facilitating identity theft (i.e., by using only a few digits of credit or debit cards on receipts, so identity thieves cannot use discarded receipts to reconstruct the numbers). FACTA also gives consumers new rights, including the right to receive one free consumer report per year and the right to block out credit report information that stems from fraudulent transactions rather than the consumer's own actions.

On February 2, 2004, the FTC and the FRB approved joint final rules governing FACTA's effective dates. Provisions not requiring major changes in business operations, such as the statute of limitations, became effective March 31, 2004. The effective date for more effortful requirements such as notifying consumers and implementing procedures to detect identity theft was set at December 1, 2004.[52]

A Final Rule, effective December 1, 2004, was published to define "identity theft" and "identity theft report" under FACTA. Identity theft is fraud either attempted or committed via unauthorized use of another person's identity information. Attempts are penalized because even if a new account is not opened, the attempt to open the account could affect the victim's credit score. Identifying information is any information that could be used to identify a specific person. Consumers who file an identity theft report are required to allege identity theft with as much particularity as possible. The Final Rule gives creditors and credit bureaus the right to make reasonable requests for further information from consumers reporting identity theft to help them determine whether identity theft occurred. The rule requires credit reporting agencies to develop reasonable tactics for correctly matching customers and files. The recommended data set for a file match is the consumer's full name; current or recent address; Social Security Number; and date of birth. The rule suggests that as additional proof of identity, the credit

---

[50] Final Interim Rule, 70 FR 33,958 (6/10/05); see 73 L.W. 2761.

[51] American States Ins. Co. v. Capital Assoc. of Jackson Co. Inc., 392 F.3d 939 (7th Cir. 2004).

[52] See 72 L.W. 2462; the final rule adopts in large part the Interim Final Rule at http://www.ftc.gov/opa/2003/12/fyi0372.htm, discussed at 72 L.W. 2359.

reporting agency should request copies of government-issued IDs, utility bills, or the answers to questions only the consumer would know.[53]

Also note that the Identity Theft Penalty Act of 2004, P.L. 108-275, adds two years to the prison sentence when the defendant is convicted of stealing personal identity information in the course of a crime such as mail or wire fraud.

On June 8, 2004, the FRB released model notices under FACTA § 217 and Regulation V (12 CFR § 222) that financial institutions can use to inform consumers that unfavorable information about them has been sent to a credit bureau. The rule applies to a wide range of financial institutions, not merely those subject to the FRB's jurisdiction. For example, merchants and debt collectors are covered. The FRB promulgated one notice to be used before the information is disclosed to the credit bureau, another to be used for notification after disclosure but within the 30-day limit permitted by FACTA.[54]

In order to make identity theft more difficult, FACTA forbids electronic receipts to list more than five digits of the consumer's credit or debit card. It is also forbidden to include the expiration date of the card on the receipt. Damages of up to $1,000 per violation are available. Putative class actions have been filed in New Jersey and several other states against major corporations alleging violations of this provision.[55]

FACTA § 213 directed the FTC to enact a rule dictating the form of simple, plain English notices informing consumers of their right to opt out of receiving any more "pre-screened solicitations" (e.g., offers of pre-approved credit cards) by calling a toll-free number. The notice must be prominent and conspicuous (in at least 12-point type) and must be found on the front of the first page of a paper solicitation or on the first screen of an electronic one.[56]

In late 2007, the Seventh Circuit decided a group of consolidated cases on the issue of whether the FCRA amendments taking effect August 20, 2004, eliminating private causes of action for certain FCRA claims, had an impermissible retroactive effect on claims accruing before the amendment's effective date. One of the plaintiffs received a pre-screened credit offer before August 20, 2004, and alleged that

---

[53] 69 Fed. Reg. 63,922 (11/3/04); *see* 73 L.W. 2263.

[54] http://www.federalreserve.gov/BoardDocs/Press/bcreg/2004/200406082/default.htm; *see* 72 L.W. 2752. The model notices reflect proposals published at 69 FR 19,123 (4/12/04), requiring the model notice to be brief, written, clear and conspicuous, and separate from the initial Truth in Lending disclosures.

[55] Charles Toutant, *Litigation Mounts Over Retail Chains' Data-Rich Sales Receipts*, N.J.L.J. 5/17/07 (law.com); the relevant FACTA provision is 15 USC § 1681c(g)(1).

[56] Early in 2005, the FTC issued Final Regulations requiring marketers to improve the notices informing consumers of their right to opt out of prescreened solicitations for credit or insurance. Pre-approved credit card offers and the like are required to inform consumers that they can opt out of future offers by calling a toll-free number. All prescreened solicitations must include a prominent notice of the right to opt out and the number for doing so, with additional disclosure in the body of the mailing piece. The FTC gave sample language in English and Spanish that could be used but did not mandate any particular form of words. http://www.ftc.gov/os/2005/01/050124factafrn.pdf (1/24/05); *see* 73 L.W. 2437.

the FCRA disclosures were not clear and conspicuous. The second plaintiff applied for automobile insurance, and charged that the insurer violated FCRA by raising his rate because of negative information in his credit report and did not give him the required notice of the adverse action. Both complaints were dismissed under FACTA § 311, which amended the FCRA to eliminate certain private causes of action. In one case, the Seventh Circuit held that the retroactivity question could not be decided at the summary judgment stage, because there might have been an FCRA violation that occurred before FACTA's effective date, and Congress did not make it clear whether § 1681m(h)(8) applies to FCRA claims arising between FACTA's enactment and its effective date. If the amendments would impair existing rights, then the presumption of "prospective application only" would apply. In the automobile insurance case, however, it was not clear when the FCRA violation was supposed to have happened, and the renewals were after the amendment's effective date, so the conduct was not actionable.[57]

FACTA reduces the amount of identifying information (e.g., full credit card numbers or expiration dates) that can be included on a receipt. Statutory damages are $100–$1,000 per violation. More than 300 class actions have been filed against retailers like IKEA and Toys'r'Us, charging that they have facilitated identity theft by putting too much information on receipts. The Southern District of Florida held that FACTA covers store receipts on the Internet. The Ninth Circuit is considering whether classes should be certified, in light of defendants' argument that they would be "annihilated" by having to pay large statutory damages, and a number of applications for class certification are on hold until the Ninth Circuit resolves this issue. The Seventh Circuit has rejected the argument and certified several classes.[58]

§ 14.05   FAIR DEBT COLLECTION PRACTICES ACT (FDCPA)

Although all may be fair in love and war, federal law limits the extent to which threats (even threats of lawsuit), harassment, pressure, and humiliation can be used to collect debts from consumers who obtained extensions of credit for personal, family, or household needs.

Applicability of the FDCPA, 15 USC § 1692 *et seq.*, depends on the existence of a covered debt, and actions of a debt collector (i.e., a party who regularly rather than casually makes efforts to collect debts).

The creditor itself is not a debt collector subject to the FDCPA, as long as it uses its own name; but FDCPA coverage can occur if the creditor uses an assumed name that suggests the intervention of a third party: according to the Second

---

[57] Killingsworth v. HSBC Bank Nevada, 507 F.3d 614 (7th Cir. 2007).

[58] Tresa Baldas, *Landslide of Suits Over Data on Receipts*, Nat'l L.J. 4/7/08 (law.com); *see* Grabein v. 1-800-Flowers.com Inc., No. 07-22235-CIV (S.D. Fla. 2008); Soualian v. Int'l Coffee and Teas, No. 07-56377 (9th Cir. pending); Murrah v. GMAC Mortgage Corp., 434 F.3d 948 (7th Cir. 2006); Cicilline v. Jewll Food Stores, No. 07CV2222 (N.D. Ill. pending).

Circuit, dunning letters sent by the creditor's in-house collection unit, under a different name, could be deceptive to unsophisticated consumers. Therefore, the FDCPA is triggered.[59]

The FDCPA requires debt collectors who collect debts from consumers to provide them with disclosure as to their right to dispute the debt.

Consumer debtors are protected against unfair or unconscionable debt collection methods, harassing, oppressive, or abusive conduct, and false, deceptive, and misleading statements in connection with debt collection.[60]

The FDCPA (at 15 USC § 1692k(d)) gives state and federal courts concurrent jurisdiction over claims of unfair collection practices. If the FDCPA is violated, consumers are entitled to statutory damages even without proof of actual damages.[61] They can also receive compensatory damages (including damages for emotional distress), costs, and attorneys' fees. The statute of limitations is one year from mailing of the collection letter or filing of an improper legal action. FDCPA class actions are permitted.

[A] What Is a "Debt"?

According to the Eleventh Circuit, Congress did not necessarily intend complete preemption when it passed the National Bank Act. Therefore, a state-law usury case against a national bank associated with H&R Block in making tax refund anticipation loans could remain in state court, and could not be removed to federal court by exercising the complete preemption doctrine.[62]

The Seventh, Eighth, and Ninth Circuits have ruled that a dishonored check creates a payment obligation, so third-party attempts at collecting bounced checks are subject to the FDCPA.[63]

Companies that enforce the subrogation rights of insurance companies (for instance, on tort recoveries) are subject to the FDCPA. The Fifth Circuit reached

---

[59] Maguire v. Citicorp Retail Servs. Inc., 147 F.3d 232 (2d Cir. 1998). Much later, the Third Circuit remanded an FDCPA class action involving a collection letter signed "Unifund Legal Department" for a determination whether Unifund, which purchases overdue consumer debt from credit card companies and generates automated collection letters, actually has a legal department. This is a factual question, not a question of law: Rosenau v. Unifund Group Corp., 539 F.3d 218 (3d Cir. 2008).

[60] Although in general FDCPA liability is strict, § 1692k(c) permits a safe harbor if the debt collector shows, by a preponderance of the evidence, that the violation was not intentional and resulted from a bona fide error by a company that generally maintains reasonable procedures to prevent errors.

[61] Factors in the statutory damage award include the frequency and persistence of non-compliance by the collector; the nature of the non-compliance; and whether it was intentional: § 1692k. Statutory damages are limited to the smaller of $500,000 or 1% of the collector's net worth. (Compensatory damages are not capped.)

[62] Anderson v. H&R Block Inc., 287 F.3d 1038 (11th Cir. 2002).

[63] Bass v. Stolper Koritzinsky, Brewer & Neider, 111 F.3d 1322 (7th Cir. 1997); Duffy v. Landberg, 133 F.3d 1120 (8th Cir. 1998); Charles v. Lundgren & Assocs. PC, 119 F.3d 739 (9th Cir. 1997).

this conclusion because the insurance claim is a debt that arises out of the purchase of insurance, which is a transaction for personal, family or household purposes.[64]

A debt collector's attempt to enforce a lien for an unpaid municipal water service bill is subject to the FDCPA even though the lien itself operates in rem. The debt collectors in this instance were a law firm hired by a city to collect overdue bills. The collection letters sent were defective in that they failed to include the required debt verification language, didn't state that they were issued by a debt collector seeking to collect a debt, and didn't say that information obtained from the letter would be used to collect the debt.[65]

[B] Who Is a "Debt Collector"?

A 1995 Supreme Court decision says that attorneys who regularly engage in litigation to collect consumer debts are FDCPA-covered debt collectors: *Heintz v. Jenkins.*[66]

Whether a law firm regularly engages in debt collection is not exclusively dependent on the number of times it assists in collection or the amount of the revenue involved; the salient factors are having specialized personnel, an organized system, and the number of collection notices sent out for a particular client.[67]

In the Sixth Circuit view, an attorney or law firm regularly collects debts if it does it as a matter of course for its clients; for certain clients; or if debt collect is a substantial (whether or not it is the principal) part of the practice. The firm involved in this case[68] did between 50 and 75 collections a year, representing about two percent of its practice, and it did not have any dedicated staff or software for collections. It was deemed not to be a debt collector.

A law firm's filing of a summons and complaint in a state collection suit is an initial communication with the debtor that triggers FDCPA notification requirements — whereas a mere collection letter does not. The summons and complaint becomes a communication because it conveys information about the debtor's debt.[69]

---

[64] Hamilton v. United Healthcare of L.A. Inc., 310 F.3d 385 (5th Cir. 2002).

[65] Piper v. Portnoff Law Assoc. Ltd., 396 F.3d 227 (3d Cir. 2005).

[66] 514 U.S. 291 (1995).

[67] Goldstein v. Hutton, Ingram, Yuzek, Gainen, Carroll & Bertolotti, 374 F.3d 56 (2d Cir. 2004).

[68] Schroyer v. Frankel, 197 F.3d 1170 (6th Cir. 1999).

[69] Thomas v. Simpson & Cybak, 354 F.3d 696 (7th Cir. 2004). The Second Circuit held that a lawyer's filing of a state court suit to collect back rent is an initial communication with the debtor that triggers the § 1692g obligation to give FDCPA notice of, e.g., the creditor's identity, the amount of the debt, and the 30-day period that the debtor has to dispute the validity of the debt. The Second Circuit acknowledged that consumers could be confused if the validation notice arrived with or shortly after the summons and complaint, but the law firm making the notification could handle this issue by making it clear that the FDCPA does not affect the defendant's rights or duties with respect to the suit, and that the court filing deadlines are different from the FDCPA timing requirements: Goldman v. Cohen, 445 F.3d 152 (2d Cir. 2006).

As of mid-2007, at least 19 FDCPA suits against debt collection lawyers had been filed in states including New York, Florida, Illinois, Michigan, and Massachusetts. There were various reasons for such suits, including BAPCPA effects (debtors who are unable to file for bankruptcy seek other ways to deal with debt) and purchases of debt by parties who do not have enough information to file valid pleadings, with the result that they make invalid attempts to collect debts.

The Fourth Circuit ruled that law firms are not immune for claims based on statements made during judicial proceedings — in fact, even general immunity in state court would not be a defense in a federal FDCPA case. The Sixth Circuit held in 2006 that a law firm that tried to garnish a debt holder's account was not entitled to witness immunity when it acted as a complaining witness. Debt collection attorneys can raise the defense of bona fide error (a mistake that occurred despite efforts to maintain accuracy), but the Circuits are split as to whether that applies to mistakes of law, misjudgments by attorneys, or is limited to simple clerical errors.[70]

Credit counseling organizations are not debt collectors, and therefore their clients cannot sue them under the FDCPA.[71]

[C] Verification Requirement

Within five days after its initial communication with the debtor, the debt collector must provide a disclosure statement that has been described as a "civil Miranda warning." See 15 USC § 1692g. (The disclosure is not necessary if the information already appeared in the initial communication, or if the debtor has paid the debt before the five days elapse.) The required disclosures are:

- The amount of the debt
- The identity of the creditor
- Warning that the debt is presumed valid unless the consumer disputes[72] all or part of the debt within 30 days of receipt of the notice
- Statement that, if the debt collector receives a written protest within 30 days, it will send the debtor verification of the debt or a copy of the judgment against the debtor
- Disclosure that the debtor has 30 days to make a written request for the name and address of the current creditor, if different from the original creditor with whom the debtor did business.

---

[70] Sheri Qualters, *Debt Firms Slammed by Consumer Lawsuits*, Nat'l L.J. 6/12/07 (law.com); the Fourth Circuit case is Sayyed v. Wolpoff & Abramson, 485 F.3d 226 (4th Cir. 2007); the Sixth Circuit case is Todd v. Weltman, Weinberg & Reis Co., 434 F.3d 432 (6th Cir. 2006).

[71] Limpert v. Cambridge Credit Counseling Corp., 328 F. Supp. 2d 360 (E.D.N.Y. 2004).

[72] The debtor must be told to contact the debt collector, not the creditor, because contacting the creditor will not preserve the debtor's rights: Blair v. Collectech Sys. Inc., 1998 U.S. Dist LEXIS 6173 (N.D. Ill. 4/17/98); Macarz v. Transworld Sys., 26 F. Supp. 2d 368 (D. Conn. 1998).

This disclosure statement must be conspicuous, and must not be overshadowed by conflicting statements, e.g., orders to the consumer to pay before the 30 days elapse.[73] A debt collector that threatens to sue within the 30-day period must explain the relation between the creditor's right to sue and the debtor's right to validation of the debt.

The Third Circuit reversed the District Court and held that a plaintiff asserted a valid FDCPA claim because she received a letter from a collection agency that said that unless she arranged to pay within five days, the matter "could" result in referral to an attorney and "could" result in filing of a lawsuit. The plaintiff's position was that the use of "could" was deceptive because the agency had no intention of actually pursuing the claim in the court system. The Third Circuit agreed that an unsophisticated consumer might feel at risk of suit unless payment were made within the five days.[74]

[D] Forbidden Conduct

The general test of whether a communication violates the FDCPA is whether the least sophisticated consumer would be deceived or would feel threatened.[75]

15 USC § 1692e(11) requires disclosure that communications are for debt collection purposes. It is not, for instance, permissible to tell debtors that their work address is needed as part of a survey. Section 1692e(5) makes it unlawful to threaten any illegal action; any action that is not intended to be taken (typically, a lawsuit) or to misstate the debtor's liability for civil damages or multiple penalties. It is also unlawful under this section to collect any amount (including interest) that is not specifically authorized by law or by the underlying contract.

No one who is not an attorney can claim to be one (§ 1692e(3)) and if an attorney's name or letterhead is used, the attorney must have real involvement in the case. Debt collectors are not allowed to use names or statements that falsely suggest that they are credit reporting agencies or government agencies (§ 1692e; this section also lists 16 other forms of false, deceptive, or misleading representations that are forbidden).

Collectors are forbidden to use harassment (repeated or anonymous phone calls; obscene or profane language; threats of violence). They are not permitted to communicate with debtors at inconvenient times (times before 8 a.m. and after 9 p.m. are presumed to be inconvenient); at work, if personal communications are forbidden; or at all, if the debtor is represented by counsel. Third parties (persons other than the debtor's spouse) can only be contacted once and then only to get information about the debtor's location. See §§ 1692b-d and f.

---

[73] Chauncey v. JDR Recovery Corp., 118 F.3d 516 (7th Cir. 1997).
[74] Brown v. Card Serv. Ctr., 464 F.3d 450 (3d Cir. 2006).
[75] Taylor v. Perrin, Landry, deLaunay & Durand, 103 F.3d 1232 (5th Cir. 1997); Clomon v. Jackson, 988 F.2d 1314 (2d Cir. 1993).

For creditors who undertake their own collection efforts, § 1692j bars furnishing forms that are used to deceive the consumer into believing that someone other than the creditor is undertaking the collection.

The Seventh Circuit ruled in mid-2004 that the remedies of the FDCPA and those of the Bankruptcy Code are intended to overlap — the Bankruptcy Code does not preempt the FDCPA. Therefore, the FDCPA can be used against a debt collector who wrongfully attempts to collect from a debtor who has filed for bankruptcy protection.[76]

Under 15 USC § 1692e(2)(A), debt collectors are forbidden to make a false representation of the character, amount, or legal status of any debt. The representation merely has to be false; there is no intent requirement, but the debt collector has a defense if it proves by a preponderance of the evidence that the violation was not intentional, and was a bona fide mistake that slipped through a reasonable procedure designed to avoid errors. The Seventh Circuit ruled that a bankrupt debtor could not complain about an attempt to collect a debt that actually was discharged in bankruptcy. The debt collector did a bankruptcy search for "Lisa Ross" when the plaintiff filed as "Delisa Ross." However, the plaintiff had an obligation to list debts contracted under other names on the bankruptcy petition, and she failed to do so.[77]

It was a violation of the FDCPA for a government contractor collecting student loans to use Official Business envelopes with a Department of Education return address, because the misrepresentation created a false sense of urgency about the repayment; § 1692e(14) and f(8) forbid the use of false return addresses.[78]

The FDCPA requires a collections letter to state the amount of the debt. The Seventh Circuit found that a letter was inadequate because it gave both a credit card "balance" and a phone number that could be called for "the most current balance information." The Seventh Circuit found that this was inappropriate because of the risk that a significant fraction of the recipients would be confused.[79]

§ 14.06 PERSONAL PROPERTY LEASING

Federal statutory rules about personal property leases lasting four months or more appear beginning at 15 USC §§ 1667–1667e, the Consumer Leasing Act as amended by the Omnibus Consolidated Appropriations Act of 1996, P.L. 104-208. The one-year statute of limitations for civil actions under the Consumer Leasing Act begins once the lessee no longer has possession of a vehicle — whether the loss of possession was due to voluntary surrender or repossession.[80]

---

[76] Randolph v. IMBS Inc., 368 F.3d 726 (7th Cir. 2004).

[77] Ross v. RJM Acquisitions Funding LLC, 480 F.3d 493 (7th Cir. 2007).

[78] Peter v. G.C. Servs. L.P., 310 F.3d 344 (5th Cir. 2002).

[79] Cherway v. National Action Fin. Servs. Inc., 362 F.3d 944 (7th Cir. 2004).

[80] Carmichael v. Nissan Motor Acceptance Corp., 291 F.3d 1278 (11th Cir. 2002).

The implementing regulations found in the Federal Reserve Board's Regulation M, 12 CFR Part 213,[81] deal with consumer leasing. UCC Article 2A should also be consulted; it regulates lease transactions, without limitation to consumer leases.

Like most consumer credit regulation, Regulation M is highly disclosure-oriented; it also contains substantive limitations on "balloon payments" (disproportionately large payments at the end of the lease term).

Regulation M applies to leases of personal property for personal, family, or household purposes, as long as the lease lasts at least four months and has a total contractual obligation of $25,000 or less. It does not apply — although general Truth in Lending principles do apply — if the transaction is actually a credit sale (an arrangement where the lease payments are at least as great as the price of the property, and the lessee has an option to purchase the property at a nominal payment).

Regulation M deals with several issues:

- Mandatory disclosure of all material lease terms before the lease agreement is signed
- Limitation on the consumer's liability at the expiration or termination of a lease
- Mandatory, permitted and forbidden expressions in advertisements for consumer leases
- Cause of action for consumers injured by Reg. M violations[82]
- Survival of state laws and regulations that are not inconsistent with Reg. M. The FRB can exempt any class of lease transactions from Reg. M coverage if the transactions are subject to substantially similar state-law regulation.

Credit grantors and their counsel should also consult the Uniform Consumer Sales Practices Act, which identifies factors states can use in determining if a consumer contract is unconscionable (i.e., so unfair that the state will not participate in enforcing it):

- Transaction is unfairly one-sided in the seller's favor
- Unusually vulnerable consumer (aged, ill, illiterate, not fluent in English, etc.)
- Grossly unfair price, as compared to similar goods obtained from other sources
- As of the time of the transaction, it was obvious that the merchandise would be repossessed, because of the impossibility of payment in full

---

[81] See 61 FR 52246 (10/7/96), 62 FR 15364 (4/1/97), 63 FR 52107 (9/29/98) and 64 FR 16612 (3/31/99) for the evolution of Regulation M.

[82] TILA § 183(a) requires the lessor to pay the consumer's attorneys' fees in a leasing case, unless the lessor can prove that the excess liability resulted from major physical damage or unreasonable wear and tear to the leased property.

- As of the time of the transaction (with no consideration of later developments) it was impossible for the consumer to receive significant benefits from the transaction
- The seller made a misleading statement of opinion that consumers were likely to rely on to their detriment.

[A] Regulation M Disclosure

The mandatory disclosures must be readable — either written or in permissible electronic form,[83] and the document must be given to the consumer before consummation of the lease transaction. If any figures are estimated rather than precise, this fact must be disclosed.

12 CFR §§ 213.3 and 213.4 set out the required disclosures, e.g.:

- A brief description of the leased property
- Total amount the lessee pays when the lease is consummated (e.g., advance payment; refundable security deposit)
- Number, amount, and due dates of the periodic payments; total of all periodic payments; method for calculating the periodic payments on a motor-vehicle lease
- Itemization and total of taxes, fees, and other charges
- Disclosure of the amount of insurance provided by or through the lessor; mandatory types and amounts of coverage the lessee is required to obtain through a third party
- (For motor vehicle leases): Gross capitalized cost (defined as the agreed upon value of the vehicle plus items such as service contracts and insurance paid over the term of the lease) and capitalized cost reduction (net trade-in allowance or rebate); adjusted capitalized cost (amount used to calculate periodic payments)
- "Rent charge": the difference between all base periodic payments minus depreciation and amortized amounts
- Who is responsible for maintaining or servicing the leased property
- Amount and method of calculating penalty or delinquency charges
- Express warranties and guarantees offered by the manufacturer or lessor on the leased property
- When (if ever) the lessee has an option to purchase the property; what the purchase price will be
- Conditions under which either party can terminate the lease; calculation of any penalty or other charge, including a warning that a motor-vehicle lease can include a charge up "up to several thousand dollars"

---

[83] *See* the Interim Rule for Regulation M electronic disclosures at 66 FR 17322 (3/20/01); generally, electronic disclosures will be permissible if the consumer gave advance permission to receiving electronic rather than conventional written disclosures.

- If the lessee's liability at the end of the term is based on the estimated value of the property, a statement of the value of the property when the lease is consummated, the itemized total lease obligation at the end of the lease, and the difference between the two
- If the lessee will be responsible for the difference between the estimated value of the leased property and its actual value when the lease is terminated, this fact must be disclosed
- (Open-end leases): informing the lessee of the right to get an independent third-party professional appraisal of the value of the leased property when the lease is terminated, and that this appraisal will be binding.

Regulation M limits the extent to which the consumer can be held liable for diminution in the value of the property when the lease terminates. The creditor can legitimately impose a penalty charge equal to actual harm caused by the consumer's delinquency, default, or early termination, but only to an extent that is reasonable in light of the anticipated or actual harm caused by the consumer. There is a rebuttable presumption that the creditor's estimate is unreasonable if it exceeds three monthly payments. To recover a larger sum, the creditor must sue the consumer — the obligation cannot be imposed in the leasing agreement.

Section 213.5 covers the rights of lessees when the lease is renegotiated or replaced. New disclosures are not required when someone else assumes a consumer's lease, even if the lessor charges a fee for the assumption.

[B] Regulation M Advertising Requirements

Lessors must either refrain from including details about the lease in their ads, or must make complete disclosure as prescribed by § 213.7. That is, if the advertisement states the number of required payments or the amount of any payment, or mentions the down payment required (or that the property can be leased with no money down) then all material lease terms must be disclosed, e.g.:

- That the advertised transaction is a lease
- Amount of any required down payment
- Total number of payments
- Number, amounts, due dates, or periods of scheduled payments
- Total amount of payments
- Whether or not a security deposit is required
- Potential for liability based on diminution in the value of the property.

Television or radio advertisements can comply by giving a toll-free number or referring to a printed ad where complete disclosure information is available.

Creditors should also be aware that, although Regulation M does not apply to certain rent-to-own (RTO) leases of appliances if the consumer retains the right to terminate the lease at any time without penalty, several states have passed laws to control RTO abuses.

[C] State Automobile Leasing Statutes

Regulation M preempts inconsistent state laws (see § 213.9(a)), but not those that are more protective of the consumer, and many states have taken up the subject of automobile leasing. States can apply to the Federal Reserve Board for exemptions from Regulation M. Some state laws can and do require additional disclosures or cover leases over $25,000 that are excluded from the Consumer Leasing Act, or provide treble damages and other non-CLA remedies.

New York ruled in 2002 that, because there is no "sale" in an automobile lease, the Magnuson-Moss Act does not apply, and Arizona reached the same conclusion in 2006, whereas New Jersey construed the lessee of a motor vehicle/ assignee of the dealer's warranty to satisfy one of the three Magnuson-Moss definitions of "consumer" by reason of having the right to enforce the warranty.[84]

§ 14.07 CREDITORS' REMEDIES

High-priority secured creditors are in the best position, because they can seize the collateral (as long as this has not already been done by a higher-priority creditor). Of course, the proceeds of the collateral, after expenses, may be quite a bit lower than the debt.

Although consumers may have additional protection (as described above), debtor/creditor law prescribes a range of remedies for creditors, including provisional remedies; assignment for the benefit of creditors; and composition. Creditors have rights against fraudulent conveyances as well. However, creditors' remedies, even in the business realm, must be assessed in light of the possibility of future bankruptcy filing, either voluntary by the debtor or involuntary at the impetus of another creditor.

Lockhart v. United States, 546 U.S. 142 (2005), says that the time limit under the Debt Collection Act, 31 USC § 3716(e)(1), does not prevent the government from offsetting Social Security benefits to repay a federally reinsured student loan, even though Social Security benefits could not be reached under the version of 20 USC § 1091a(a)(2)(D) originally passed and later amended. The Eighth Circuit ruled in mid-2006 that 20 USC §§ 1081a(a)(2)(D), 1087aa, and 1087cc eliminate the time limits on collecting payments on "Perkins Loans," so there is no time limit that prevents offsetting Perkins debts against Social Security benefits. The plaintiff said that it was inequitable for the government to collect after an extreme delay, and the long lapse of time made it harder for her to find documentation of the loan. The Eighth Circuit ruled that the government did not engage in extreme delay. Defaulted loans were assigned to the government in 1987 and 1989; the

---

[84] *Compare* Parrot v. Daimler Chrysler Co., 130 P.3d 530 (Ariz. 2006) and DiCintio v. Daimler Chrysler Corp., 768 N.E.2d 1121 (N.Y. 2002) *with* Ryan v. American Honda Motor Co., 186 N.J. 431 (2006).

government began sending letters in 1989 and assigned the case to collection agencies between 1989 and 2002. The six-year and ten-year time limits were eliminated only four years after the first loan was assigned to the Department, so the time limits never expired and no claims against the plaintiff were "revived." The Eighth Circuit did not treat the defense of laches as available against the federal government, and in any event did not believe that laches was present, because there had not been an inexcusable delay in collection.[85]

The Bankruptcy Reform and Consumer Protection Act of 2005 (BAPCA) in general will make it more difficult for consumers to file for bankruptcy protection; if they do file, they will probably have to repay a greater portion of the debt than under prior law.

The Third Circuit rejected a class action by uninsured hospital patients who alleged violation of consumer protection laws and discrimination when they were charged more than insured patients or patients whose care was paid for by Medicare or Medicaid. In the Third Circuit view, health care costs are a political problem, and courts are not in a position to decide what constitutes a fair rate. The plaintiff alleged unjust enrichment, but admitted he did not pay his bill, so no one was enriched. The Third Circuit ruled that a hospital does not have a fiduciary duty with respect to its billing practices, and in general, fiduciary duty is not applied from creditor to debtor.[86]

[A] Provisional Remedies

Creditors can apply to the appropriate civil court for discretionary provisional remedies that prevent the debtor from conveying property or otherwise impairing the rights of creditors. Provisional remedies are granted or rejected at the court's discretion.

Depending on the jurisdiction and the facts, provisional remedies might include attachment (seizure of a debtor's property before trial); garnishment (seizure of a debtor's property that is in the hands of a third party); injunction (e.g., against conveyance of property); receivership; and notice of pendency (informing potential purchasers that property is the subject of litigation, thus deterring them from buying it).

Usually, attachment is granted in connection with a suit for a money judgment, where the plaintiff shows some reason for feeling insecure: for instance, the defendant is a nondomiciliary residing outside the state; the defendant is foreign corporation not qualified to do business in the state; or the defendant may have secreted property or disposed of it with fraudulent intent. A "levy" is a collection action based on an attachment order. Other parties who have interests in levied property can bring a proceeding to determine their respective rights. The defendant can get the attachment discharged by substituting adequate security (or, of course, by paying the underlying debt).

---

[85] Lee v. Spellings, 447 F.3d 1087 (8th Cir. 2006).

[86] DiCarlo v. St. Mary Hosp., 530 F.3d 255 (3d Cir. 2008); see Shannon P. Duffy, *3rd Circuit: Class Action No Cure for Uninsured Patient's Bill*, The Legal Intelligencer 6/27/08 (law.com).

[B] Assignment for the Benefit of Creditors

A debtor who acknowledges inability to satisfy creditors' claims might make a voluntary assignment for the benefit of creditors; or liquidation or receivership might be imposed by operation of law.

In a voluntary general assignment for the benefit of creditors, all of the debtor's property is placed into an express trust designed to liquidate the property and distribute the proceeds to the creditors. Technically, a debtor can do this without consent of the creditors, but in practice notice to creditors is required and a nonconsenting creditor can force an involuntary bankruptcy filing in lieu of the assignment. After the assignment, there is no discharge of the debtor; fraudulent conveyance concepts (§ 14.07[D]) apply; and creditors still have a legal right to pursue their remedies other than levying on the assets of the assigned estate.

The assignment results in the secured creditors receiving "dividends" equal to the balance due on the claims of each, minus the value of all security that is not exempt from the claims of unsecured creditors and not released or secured to the liquidator.

[C] Composition with Creditors

In a composition, an insolvent or financially embarrassed debtor agrees with two or more creditors that they will discharge their claims for less than the full amount. The creditors agree among themselves on the percentage they will settle for. However, if the composition is a fraudulent conveyance, it can be set aside by creditors who did not agree to the composition.

[D] Fraudulent Conveyances

As long as individuals and businesses continue to pay their debts, they can arrange their financial affairs as they like. But an insolvent debtor (the present fair market value of whose saleable assets that are not exempt from liability for debts is less than the total debts) may be guilty of "fraudulent conveyance" in transferring assets in a way that impairs the ability of other creditors to collect the full amount of the debt to them.

A conveyance can be fraudulent (even if the debtor is not insolvent) if it is made with an actual intent to defraud creditors, or if the conveying party is a defendant in a lawsuit or against whom judgment has been entered.

The Uniform Fraudulent Conveyance Act and state fraudulent conveyance statutes also cover "constructive fraud": situations where there may be no intent to defraud, but creditors are placed at a disadvantage (e.g., the conveyance has the effect of making a solvent person insolvent;[87] the conveyance is made by an undercapitalized business). "Badges of fraud" include:

---

[87] But if a conveyance is made by a solvent person, it cannot be rendered fraudulent retrospectively by later insolvency.

- Transfers made in contemplation of a pending suit
- Transfer of substantially all the debtor's assets[88]
- Failure to record transfers that should have been recorded
- Transfers to family members
- Continued use or occupation of allegedly transferred property.

Given actual fraudulent intent, the consideration for the conveyance is irrelevant. But in other situations, a conveyance is not fraudulent if it is made for adequate and fair consideration. A conveyance is not fraudulent if it does not diminish the assets remaining available to creditors. A voluntary conveyance with no or only nominal conveyance is presumed fraudulent. Unless there is proof to the contrary, the debtor is presumed insolvent, and the debtor must rebut the presumption.

A fraudulent conveyance is not absolutely void, but it can be voided by creditors who are placed at a disadvantage by the conveyance. A preferential transfer (which gives favored creditors a higher percentage of their claim than non-favored creditors who have the same degree of legal priority) can be attacked by the nonfavored creditors, but only if it had been made with actual intent to defraud, delay, or hinder the other creditors.

[E] Arbitration

One of the most actively litigated issues in credit/collections is the extent to which arbitration clauses in consumer credit contracts can be enforced. Clearly, these are contracts of adhesion; the question is whether this, or other aspects of the clauses themselves, will prevent enforcement. Note that, since the Supreme Court's February 2006 decision,[89] the authority of courts to invalidate arbitration clauses has been limited — because it is up to the arbitrator, not the courts, to hear challenges to the validity of the entire contract rather than just the arbitration clause.

Late in 2000, the Supreme Court answered some — but not all — questions about arbitration of consumer finance agreements. According to the Supreme Court, a District Court's final order compelling arbitration and dismissing underlying claims is a final decision affecting arbitration and therefore can be appealed under FAA § 16(a)(3).

However, the Supreme Court did not permit the consumer-borrower to invalidate the arbitration agreement using the argument that its silence on allocation of costs put her at risk of encountering prohibitive costs. The party seeking invalidation has the burden of proving the likelihood of costs, a subject on which the consumer introduced little evidence.[90]

---

[88] To transferees of the debtor's choice, as distinct from an assignment for the benefit of creditors, where the property is transferred to a trust benefiting the creditors.

[89] Buckeye Check Cashing v. Cardegna, 546 U.S. 440 (2006).

[90] Green Tree Fin. Corp.-Ala. v. Randolph, 531 U.S. 79 (2000), *on remand*, Randolph v. Green Tree Fin. Corp., 244 F.3d 814 (11th Cir. 2001), holding that a TILA arbitration clause is enforceable even if it prevents plaintiffs from bringing class claims.

The Eighth Circuit has compelled individual arbitration in a class action suit brought by a consumer who charged American Express and American Express Incentive Services with violating TILA by issuing pre-loaded stored value cards without making TILA disclosures. The plaintiff was given three prepaid cards for participating in online surveys; the cards could be used for purchases at stores that accepted American Express, and used a card to pay a restaurant bill. The restaurant processed the card for $45 more than its value, and American Express Incentive Services billed the plaintiff and imposed a late fee, a transaction fee, and a shortage fee. The plaintiff sued on her own behalf and on behalf of similarly situated consumers, charging that there was an extension of credit but the cards were not described as debit or credit cards. The District Court dismissed the case on the grounds that American Express was not a TILA creditor. American Express Incentive Services moved to compel individual arbitration as required by the contract. The Eighth Circuit agreed that the class action waiver was conspicuous and enforceable. It was not unconscionable, because the plaintiff could arbitrate her small claim without bringing a class action; the TILA remedial provision, 15 USC § 1640(a)(3), allows recovery of fees and costs, so small claims can be pursued without undue expenditure.[91]

Unconscionability can be procedural (based on the way the contract was obtained) or substantive (contract terms were imposed without choice, and/or unduly favor one party). The *Harris* plaintiffs claimed procedural unconscionability based on the consignment of the arbitration clause to obscure small print. The Third Circuit found this to be a sustainable argument under state law, but not one supported by FAA precedents. The agreement was enforceable even though consumers were compelled to arbitrate, but the lender could litigate certain claims.

The California Court of Appeals permitted a credit card issuer to enforce a ban on cardholders bringing class and representative action about disputes. The cardholders failed to show that it was procedurally unconscionable to require arbitration to be conducted under South Dakota law — and South Dakota law does not forbid class action waivers. The California court found the requirement permissible because there was a procedure for cardholders to opt out of arbitration, use their cards until they expired, and pay off the balance under the terms of the existing agreement.[92]

A number of federal courts have taken the position that arbitration of an entire class of claims can occur only if the agreement specifically provides for this option; entitlement to class arbitration will not be implied.[93]

---

[91] Pleasants v. American Express Co., 541 F.3d 853 (8th Cir. 2008).

[92] Jones v. Citigroup Inc., 135 Cal. App. 4th 1491 (Cal. App. 2006).

[93] *See, e.g.*, Johnson v. West Suburban Bank, 225 F.3d 366 (3d Cir. 2000); Deiulemar Compagnia di Navigazione S.p.A. v. M/V Allegra, 198 F.3d 473 (4th Cir. 1999); Champ v. Siegel Trading Co. Inc., 55 F.3d 269 (7th Cir. 1995).

[F] Class Actions

The Fifth Circuit held that the claims of more than a million debtors alleging that Sears, Roebuck coerced bankrupt customers into paying pre-petition debt that had actually been discharged could not be maintained as a class action. The rationale is that the predominant interest in the litigation was individual damages, not injunctive relief.[94]

A few weeks later, the same court held that a class of automobile lessees seeking actual damages under TILA could not be certified. The would-be class members alleged that the lessor wrongfully failed to itemize the $400 acquisition fee charged to dealers at the beginning of the leases. But the Fifth Circuit required proof of reliance as a prerequisite to awarding actual damages. A failure to disclose causes actual damages only if the customer can prove that a different, less expensive transaction would have resulted if proper disclosures had been made.[95]

In 2008, the Seventh Circuit joined the First and Fifth Circuits in holding that TILA does not permit class action rescission of mortgages (noting, however, that as the economy deteriorates, district courts are more inclined to permit class rescissions). According to the Seventh Circuit, rescission is a personal remedy, unsuited to class actions. The plaintiffs in this case fell into a "trap for the unwary," signing up for adjustable-rate loans that allowed them to change their payments based on their monthly cash flow; they encountered negative amortization, and found the mortgage term getting longer and longer.[96]

The Sixth Circuit refused to certify a Rule 23(b)(2) class action in a case in which ECOA plaintiffs sought both compensatory damages and injunctive relief. The plaintiffs alleged that black automobile buyers had to pay a higher mark-up than white buyers. The court found that individual determinations of damages would have to be made, so the proposed class would be inefficient. The court did not accept the argument that individual lawsuits would not be feasible, because prevailing ECOA plaintiffs are entitled by statute to attorneys' fee awards.[97]

§ 14.08 HANDLING COLLECTION CLAIMS

In addition to complying with all applicable laws, handling collection claims creates various practical problems. Not every claim can economically be recovered by litigation, even in small claims court.

In addition to FDCPA liability, the collector might also be liable for defamation, invasion of privacy, bankruptcy misconduct, or negligent or intentional infliction of mental anguish, and the creditor might have derivative liability. Therefore, it is important to work with collectors who are ethical and aware of their legal

---

[94] Bolin v. Sears, Roebuck & Co., 231 F.3d 970 (5th Cir. 2000).

[95] Perrone v. GMAC, 232 F.3d 433 (5th Cir. 2000).

[96] Andrews v. Chevy Chase Bank, No. 07-1326 (7th Cir. 2008); *see* Pamela A. MacLean, *Mortgage Lenders Fight Off Rescission Class Action in 7th Circuit*, Nat'l L.J. 9/30/08 (law.com).

[97] Coleman v. GMAC, 296 F.3d 443 (6th Cir. 2002).

responsibilities (and to supervise them to make sure that they maintain good practices).

[A] Claims Checklist

- ❑ Debtor's name
- ❑ Debtor's address
- ❑ Was the debtor a minor when the debt was contracted? If so, was the debt reaffirmed post-majority, or for necessities?
- ❑ Debtor's marital status
- ❑ Is the spouse also obligated?
- ❑ Are there any other co-signers or guarantors?
- ❑ Nature of the claim (i.e., for goods, services, installment contract, money lent)
- ❑ Evidence of the claim
- ❑ Security for the claim
- ❑ Evidence of bills sent to the debtor and accepted without protest
- ❑ Past payment history on the claim
- ❑ Defenses (if any) to the claim
- ❑ Lowest settlement the creditor will accept
- ❑ Witness list and other evidence for litigating the claim
- ❑ Is the debtor judgment-proof?
- ❑ Has the debtor filed for bankruptcy protection? If not, is an attempt to enforce the claim likely to trigger a filing?

Chapter 15

Bankruptcy

§ 15.01   INTRODUCTION

The bankruptcy system is designed to give individuals and businesses a fresh start when they are overwhelmed by debt. However, it is necessary to balance this objective against the needs of creditors and the prevention of fraud. After many years of attempts to institute major changes in the bankruptcy law, Congress finally passed reform legislation in 2005 — the Bankruptcy Abuse Prevention and Consumer Protection Act (BAPCPA), P.L. 109-8: see Part 2 of this Chapter. Part 1 covers the basic statute as it existed pre-2005, because this is the framework from which the reform legislation takes off.

At press time in early 2009, the implications of the final crisis were still emerging, with numerous businesses and individuals considering the option of bankruptcy protection. It was not clear whether BAPCPA would be amended, for example, to assist homeowners facing foreclosure or ease business reorganization. According to the Administrative Office of the U.S. Courts, in 2006 there were 19,695 business bankruptcies; and 28,322 in 2007. In the first quarter of 2008, there were over 8,700 business bankruptcy filings, almost 39% higher than in the first quarter of 2007. In the 12 months ended June 30, 2008, there were 967,831 personal and business filings, almost 30% higher than the previous 12 months. Nearly all of the bankruptcy filings were personal; between 6/30/07–6/30/08, there were 592,376 individual Chapter 7 filings, 340,852 Chapter 13 filings, and 780 Chapter 7 filings by individuals who had more debt than Chapter 13 permits. Of the 33,822 business cases between 6/30/07–6/30/08, 23,372 were Chapter 7 filings, 6,513 were Chapter 11, 314 were Chapter 12, and 3,569 were Chapter 13. University of Texas law professor Jay Westbrook pointed out some difficulties caused by BAPCPA's business reorganization provisions. BAPCPA gives retailers only 210 days after filing to either assume or terminate store leases — yet retailers need to see holiday season results to decide which stores to keep open. The deadline is also problematic for lenders, because it often takes 150 days to obtain permission for a store-closing sale and arrange the sale, leaving only 60 days for a back-up plan. When banks demand that a company either be sold within 60 days or liquidated, sale is often impossible to arrange, leading to more liquidations. BAPCPA also requires companies entering Chapter 11 to give adequate assurance of future payment of utility bills. Bankruptcy courts have often interpreted this to mean that a cash deposit must be posted for each location at the beginning of the case, further reducing the debtor's liquidity. BAPCPA excludes derivatives, including the credit default swaps that are so heavily involved in the economic crisis, from the automatic stay, so troubled financial institutions often lost many of their assets to creditors at the start of the bankruptcy process.[1]

Modern bankruptcy law dates back to 1978, with the adoption of the Bankruptcy Code, Title 11 of the U.S. Code, enacted by the Bankruptcy Reform Act of 1978, P.L. 95-598. (The prior statute was referred to as the Bankruptcy Act.) In addition to the substantive provisions found in Title 11, the jurisdictional provisions for bankruptcy actions are found in Title 28, and some important tax issues are tackled in Title 26.

In the form originally passed by Congress, the 1978 Act provided for a significant shift in power from District Court judges, who serve for life, to bankruptcy judges, who were to be presidentially appointed for a 14-year term. In its 1982 decision in *Northern Pipeline Construction v. Marathon Pipeline Co.*,[2] the Supreme Court ruled that this shift violated the Constitutional guarantee of separation of powers.

In response, Congress enacted 28 USC § 157(b)(1), creating a new system under which the Court of Appeals names bankruptcy judges. Furthermore, bankruptcy judges can handle only core proceedings (e.g., administration of the estate;

---

[1] Jacqueline Palank, *Bankruptcies Rise Sharply on Credit Woes*, Wall St. J. 6/4/08 at B6B; Pamela A. Maclean, *Bankruptcy Filings Up 30 Percent in Last 12 Months*, Nat'l L.J. 6/4/08 (law.com); Kristina Doss, *A Kinder Bankruptcy Law is Sought as Filings Soar*, Wall St. J. 1/21/09, http://www.online.wsj.com/article/SB123250034296300681.html.

[2] 458 U.S. 50.

proceedings involving preferences, discharge, plan confirmation, or the automatic stay). District Court judges handle all other aspects of bankruptcy cases. See 28 USC § 157(b)(2). A core proceeding is an inherent, fundamental part of a case arising under the Bankruptcy Code.

The evolution of modern bankruptcy law continued with the Bankruptcy Amendments and Federal Judgeship Act of 1984, P.L. 98-353; the Bankruptcy Judges, U.S. Trustees and Family Farmer Bankruptcy Act of 1986, P.L. 99-554; and the Bankruptcy Reform Act of 1994, P.L. 103-394, which appointed the Bankruptcy Reform Commission that filed recommendations on October 20, 1997, and most recently, with BAPCPA. In most of this volume, "Code" refers to the Internal Revenue Code. In this chapter, however, "BCode" refers to the Bankruptcy Code, and reference will be made to Internal Revenue Code or IRC.

This chapter is structured first to discuss the basic concepts of bankruptcy law, as they existed before BAPCPA, then to consider the changes made by BAPCPA, which made vast changes but retained the basic structure of, for example, liquidating or non-liquidating bankruptcy, wage earner plans, marshalling of the bankruptcy estate, reaffirmation or repudiation of debts, discharge, and discharge exceptions.

[A] Amendments to the FRBP

In addition to the U.S. Code provisions, bankruptcy practitioners should consult the Federal Rules of Bankruptcy Procedure (FRBP, aka the Bankruptcy Rules), which were initially promulgated by the Supreme Court in 1983 and have been extensively amended since then.[3] Local bankruptcy rules are usually numbered to correspond to the FRBP provisions they supplement. BAPCPA made enormous changes in the rules and the forms carrying them out.

Here is a list of the many new rules and amendments that took effect in 2008:

- Rule 1005: debtors must disclose all names and aliases used in eight rather than six years before filing. The title of the bankruptcy case must include the last four digits on an individual taxpayer's EIN.
- Rule 1006: Chapter 7 debtors must use the appropriate Official Form to apply for a waiver of the filing fee.
- Rule 1007: debtors must file the documents required by BAPCPA, the rule reduces extensions of time to file schedules and statements in small business cases, and requires Chapter 15 (foreign) petitions to include a list of US entities with whom the filer is engaged in litigation.
- Rule 1009, Rule 1015: technical corrections of cross-references.
- Rule 1010: foreign representative has to serve a summons and petition on the debtor and entities from whom provisional relief is sought. Corporate

---

[3] A cumulative list of amendments is maintained at: http://www.uscourts.gov/rules/newrules6 .html. [Proposed Rules amendments approved by Supreme Court, eff. 12/1/08; see http://www .uscourts.gov/rules/supct0108/summary_of-rules_for_Supreme_court_2007.pdf].

ownership disclosure statements are also required from corporate petitioners in involuntary cases.

- Rule 1011 also requires corporate disclosure statements in involuntary cases, to conform to BAPCPA's Chapter 15.
- Rule 1017 gives parties in interest the right to move to dismiss abusive consumer Chapter 7 cases; motions under BCode § 707(b)(1) or (b)(3) must state with particularity the abuse.
- Rule 1019: when a Chapter 13 is converted to Chapter 7, the deadline for motions to dismiss under § 707(b) is preserved.
- Rule 1020: procedures for determining if the debtor qualifies as a small business; time limit on objections to small business status.
- Rule 1021: procedures for designating or objecting to debtor as a health care business.
- Rule 2002: the court must give all creditors a copy of the trustee's statement about whether the debtor's case is presumed to be abusive. The court must also notify debtors and entities against whom provisional relief is sought of hearings on petition for recognition of a foreign proceeding.
- Rule 2003: if the debtor has solicited acceptance of a plan before commencing the case, the court can waive the creditors' meeting.
- Rule 2007.1: elected trustees must file an affidavit disclosing any connection with anyone (e.g., creditors) having an interest in the case.
- Rule 2007.2: procedures for appointing, waiving, objecting to, or terminating appointment of a patient care ombudsman where the debtor is a health care business.
- Rule 2015: a small business Chapter 11 debtor must file periodic reports (finances and operations); foreign representative must file notice of changes of status.
- Rule 2015.1, 2015.2 health care provisions (reporting requirements for health care ombudsmen; patients' rights when a trustee attempts to relocate patients when a facility closes). See also Rule 6011 re destruction of medical records.
- Rule 2015.3: financial reporting requirements for entities controlled by a Chapter 11 trustee or Debtor in Possession.
- Rule 3002: Additional time to file proof of claim for government units and foreign creditors; Rule 3003 also permits an extension for foreign creditors.
- Rule 3016: exempts small business debtors from disclosure statement requirements if the plan has enough information to make the statement unnecessary.
- As long as a plan is intended to provide adequate information, Rule 3017.1 would permit a small business Chapter 11 plan to be approved conditionally.
- Rule 3019: procedure for filing objections to proposed modification of a confirmed individual Chapter 11 plan.
- Rule 4002: documentation (including tax information) the debtor must bring to the creditors' meeting.
- Rule 4003 would give the trustee up to a year after the closing of a case to object to a fraudulent exemption; the state homestead exemption could

be limited based on the debtor's felony conviction, or certain types of debt.

- Rule 4006: when no discharge is entered, the clerk must notify the debtor and all other parties in interest.
- Rule 4007: time limits for filing a complaint to determine whether a particular debt is dischargeable in a Chapter 13 case.
- Rule 4008: documentation requirements and filing deadline for reaffirmation agreement.
- Rule 5001: in an emergency, bankruptcy judges can hold hearings outside the district where the case is pending.
- Rule 5003: taxing authorities can designate addresses for service of BCode § 505(b)(1) notices.
- Rule 5008: clerk must notify all creditors within 10 days of filing of an individual consumer debt case filing, when the filing triggers the presumption of abuse.
- Rule 6004: in some instances, a consumer privacy ombudsman will have to be appointed if the trustee proposes to sell personal identification information.
- Rule 8001: Implementation of the BAPCPA procedure for direct appeal to the Court of Appeals; Rule 8003 allows certification by a lower court, or leave to appeal granted by the Circuit Court, to operate as the equivalent of a motion for leave to appeal.
- Rule 9006: A small business debtor cannot receive extensions of time for filing schedules and the statement of financial affairs beyond the time limits of BCode § 1116(3).
- Rule 9009: It is not necessary to use an Official Form for a small business Chapter 11 plan of reorganization/disclosure statement.

§ 15.02 BANKRUPTCY PROS AND CONS

In the best case scenario, a person or business overburdened with debt will seek bankruptcy protection. A plan will be structured for repayment of certain debts; other debts will be discharged.[4] After the bankruptcy process is completed, the debtor gets a fresh start. In many business bankruptcies, the debtor remains a "debtor in possession," able to maintain control of its assets and able to continue doing business (and to keep its employees working). The company may be able to return to profitability thanks to the relief offered by bankruptcy.

However, bankruptcy is not always a superior option. The advisability of bankruptcy filing, and the best time to file the petition, depends on the amount and

---

[4] There are some differences among the Chapters as to discharge practices. Only an individual, not a corporation, can receive a Chapter 7 discharge. A Chapter 11 debtor, whether individual or corporate, receives a discharge when the Chapter 11 plan is confirmed, but BCode § 523 describes certain important categories of debts that are not dischargeable (*see* § 15.14[A]). The Chapter 13 debtor is discharged when the scheduled payments are completed. The effect of discharge is to void judgments relating to the debtor's liability on the debt, and prevents filing or continuation of suits to collect dischargeable debts. Nondischargeable debts, however, remain collectable.

type of debts burdening the debtor. Debtors who select a particular Chapter of the Bankruptcy Code must be sure that they can satisfy its requirements.

In the wake of the financial crisis of 2008, restructuring attorneys wondered how many businesses would actually seek bankruptcy protection: debt-burdened companies had more secured debt than in previous downturns, reducing the amount of potential restructuring. Some businesses also had loans with more generous terms, such as "covenant-lite" agreements providing more leeway to avoid default. Some troubled companies are involved with hedge funds and private equity investors that want to avoid lengthy Chapter 11 proceedings, and that have experience in restructuring deals without court intervention. Prepackaged, out-of-court reorganizations have become more common, and are completed in less time than the 18 months required under BAPCPA.[5] Furthermore, more companies conceded that restructuring would be impossible, because of the unavailability of credit, and simply sold their assets. In 2007, there were about 18,750 business liquidations — about 50% higher than the 2006 level.[6]

But a debtor who is at risk of property execution by unsecured creditors is likely to benefit greatly from bankruptcy. Liens and garnishments will be suspended during the automatic stay. Creditors whose claims are dischargeable will not be able to get a lien, and many liens already in existence can be eliminated. If there is a genuine controversy about the validity of a debt (for instance, if it is alleged that consumer protection laws have been violated), the bankruptcy court may offer a forum that is both more knowledgeable and more sympathetic than state lower courts.

Bankruptcy does carry a stigma; one which creditors are at pains to emphasize. Bankruptcies become part of the debtor's credit history, and the Fair Credit Reporting Act (FCRA) permits reporting of bankruptcies for ten years.[7] Ironically, some creditors seek out Chapter 7 debtors to offer them credit, knowing that the debtor will not be able to obtain another Chapter 7 discharge for six years as a result of § 727(a)(8). If the debtor is especially interested in satisfying a particular debt, see § 524(c) for voluntary post-bankruptcy payments and reaffirmation of a debt.

Once the decision to file for bankruptcy protection has been made, the question arises as to the appropriate form of bankruptcy; and whether, now that BAPCPA has taken effect (see Part 2 of this chapter), the desired form is available to the debtor. To a certain extent, BAPCPA permits debtors to control whether, e.g., the means test will apply, by selecting the optimum time for the petition. For business debtors, Chapter 11 is usually preferable, because the debtor will be able to retain control over its assets. (Note that Bankruptcy Code § 727 limits the use of the term "discharge" to individual, rather than corporate, debtors.)

For individual debtors, Chapter 13 is probably the best form if there are pressing secured creditors. A common situation is the impending repossession of a car that the debtor needs to remain employed; the filing staves off the

---

[5] Lynne Marek, *Corporate Bankruptcy Filings Lag, for Now*, Nat'l L.J. 6/18/08 (law.com).

[6] Kristina Doss and Peg Brickley, *More Companies Sell Off Assets*, Wall St. J. 5/14/08 at B5A.

[7] *See* FCRA § 605(a)(1).

repossession and allows the debtor to keep earning an income. The discipline of making regular Chapter 13 payments can be helpful to persons with poor financial planning skills.

[A] Pre-Bankruptcy Checklist

Questions that an attorney might ask a client contemplating bankruptcy include:

- Which debts are most troublesome?
- Are the debts secured?
- How were they incurred?
- What is the balance between business and consumer indebtedness?
- (Individual debtors) Does the debtor have enough discretionary income to support a Chapter 13 plan?
- (Individual debtors) If the debtor is married, should the bankruptcy filing be joint? In most cases, it will be preferable to file jointly.
- Are creditors about to take action (e.g., repossessing collateral) that could limit the debtor's options?
- Has the debtor made any payments or transfers that operate as fraudulent conveyances or preferential transfers?

Attorneys for individual debtors should ascertain whether the debtor has a claim or potential employment discrimination claim, because such a claim against the employer is an estate asset that must be disclosed on the petition. The claim will be administered by the trustee. The schedules are signed under penalty of perjury, and failure to disclose can result in denial of damages in the employment case on the grounds of judicial estoppel (but an inadvertent failure probably will not lead to estoppel).

There is no uniform federal standard for judicial estoppel, but factors in the analysis include: fairness to the opposing party; whether another tribunal has clearly accepted the employee's position; and whether the employee takes a clearly inconsistent position before the bankruptcy court as to the existence or merits of the employment discrimination claim.[8]

The client should also be informed about the operation of the automatic stay, so that creditors who attempt improper debt collection can be told to back off. The bankruptcy attorney should inform the client not to pay old debts during the stay, other than those paid outside a Chapter 13 plan or those that will survive the bankruptcy. Clients should also be told not to acquire new debts without the permission of the trustee. They should be instructed to report after-acquired property (such as inheritances) and changes of address to the bankruptcy court.

---

[8] *See, e.g.*, Barger v. City of Cartersville, 348 F.3d 1289 (11th Cir. 2003); De Leon v. Comcar Indus. Inc., 321 F.3d 1289 (11th Cir. 2003); Casey v. Peco Foods Inc., 297 B.R. 73 (S.D. Miss. 2003).

[B] Timing of Filing

Another important question, once it has been decided to file at all and once a chapter has been selected, is the appropriate timing for the petition. In some cases, the client's financial affairs are in a crisis, and the sooner the petition can be filed, the better. In others, significant advantages can be achieved by delay.

Because it may be possible to keep property acquired after filing out of the bankruptcy estate, it may be advisable for filings to be accelerated so they can be completed before a large amount of anticipated property is received. In contrast, a debtor who has already made transfers will want to defer filing until the transfers are no longer preferential or objectionable (see § 15.13).

PART 1: BASIC AND PRE-BAPCPA CONCEPTS

§ 15.03 FORMS OF BANKRUPTCY

Under pre-BAPCPA law, filing was permitted under appropriate circumstances under Chapter 7 (liquidation or straight bankruptcy); Chapter 11 (reorganization), Chapter 12 (family farmers), and Chapter 13 (wage earner plans where installments payments from future earnings would be made to liquidate some or all debts). Bankruptcy could be initiated either by a voluntary filing by the debtor or an involuntary filing, although involuntary Chapter 13 filings were forbidden by Bankruptcy Code (BCode) § 303(b).

Involuntary Chapter 7 or Chapter 11 proceedings could be brought by three or more creditors, holding at least a minimum amount of noncontingent, undisputed claims over and above their liens on the debtor's property. The amounts are governed by BCode § 303(b) and are increased every three years by notice of the Judicial Conference of the United States. The Eleventh Circuit (although calling for re-examination of the precedents) said that its precedents make 11 USC § 303(b)'s requirements for filing an involuntary bankruptcy petition a matter of subject matter jurisdiction, and therefore cannot be waived. (The Second Circuit also finds the § 303(b) requirements jurisdictional; the Ninth Circuit disagrees.)[9]

In any bankruptcy, it is very unlikely that all creditors will be paid in full, so an important function of the bankruptcy system is allocating the limited funds to the various creditor claims.

[A] Chapter 7

Pre-BAPCPA law allowed any individual residing, domiciled, or having a place of business in the United States to file under Chapter 7. It was not required that the debtor be insolvent, but courts had limited power, pursuant to BCode § 707(b), to dismiss Chapter 7 petitions for substantial abuse of the bankruptcy system by an individual owing consumer debts.

---

[9] Trusted Net Media Holdings, LLC v. The Morrison Agency, Inc., 530 F.3d 1363 (11th Cir. 2008).

The Chapter 7 case was commenced by filing a simple two-page petition, Official Form 1, including either a schedule of liabilities or a list of creditors. Most consumer Chapter 7 filings were "no asset" cases, where no assets were available for liquidation because all the property was either exempt (homesteads and furnishings) or the full value of the property was subject to liens.

Filing of the petition was followed by appointment of an interim trustee from the judicial district's panel of trustees, and the automatic stay (see § 15.09) took effect. The interim trustee continued to serve as trustee unless someone else was elected at the initial meeting of creditors.

Former BCode § 341(a) governed the initial meeting of creditors, usually held 20–40 days after filing. There was a deadline of 60 days after the first date set for the meeting, for creditor claims and objections to discharge in general or with regard to a specific debt. The creditors are permitted to create a creditors' committee of three to eleven members to advise the trustee. The creditors' committee has standing to appear in court.

Unless an objection has been filed, the Chapter 7 debtor is permitted to retain all exempt property (see § 15.06). If the debtor is an individual who has property securing a consumer debt, and has filed a § 521(2) statement of intention to redeem the property under § 722, or intends to surrender it or reaffirm the debt under § 524(c), the debtor has 45 days to do so. The 45-day deadline can be extended by the bankruptcy court.

If there are meaningful non-exempt assets (which is not always the case, especially in consumer Chapter 7 cases), § 521(4) requires the debtor to turn them over to the trustee. Claims, even contingent claims, must be disclosed.

The trustee collects and liquidates (i.e., converts to cash) all other property of the estate. The trustee can sell estate assets by public auction or private sale, but must give 20 days' notice of the intention to sell. A Chapter 7 trustee can be given authorization to operate the debtor's business, but only for a limited time and for the purpose of liquidating the estate; Chapter 11 is the appropriate filing if long-term continuance of the business is desired.

The trustee evaluates the claims of creditors, and objects to any improper claims. Any proof of claim made in proper form is deemed (by § 502(a)) to be allowed if no objection is filed. If an objection is filed, the Bankruptcy Court rules on it as a contested matter (FRBP 9014).

Under the Bankruptcy Abuse Prevention and Consumer Protection Act of 2005, P.L. 109-8 the bankruptcy court, on its own motion or motion of the trustee or any person in interest, can dismiss a Chapter 7 filing, and can dismiss a Chapter 7 case or convert it to another Chapter, if the debtor seeks to abuse the bankruptcy process. (Prior law required "substantial abuse" for the court to do this.) Furthermore, a Chapter 7 filing is presumed abusive if the debtor's current monthly income is above the state's median monthly income. To rebut the presumption, the debtor must document special circumstances justifying the Chapter 7 relief.

The Supreme Court held that the debtor could not convert his Chapter 7 case and proceed in Chapter 13, because BCode § 706(a) bars conversions in bad faith. The Supreme Court did not define bad faith, other than stating it is worse than usual bankruptcy conduct. The petitioner misrepresented the value of property and concealed the fact of a transfer, so the trustee and the principal creditor (a bank) objected. The Supreme Court said that he forfeited the right to convert (although Senate and House Committee Reports describe the right to convert as absolute) because § 706(d) limits conversion to those who could be debtors under that chapter; Chapter 13s are routinely dismissed for cause, so the Supreme Court deemed that to be the equivalent of not qualifying to be a debtor.[10]

After the deadline for filing claims has passed, the trustee distributes "dividends" to creditors (i.e., repayment of their claims), in the order prescribed by § 726:

1) Claims that have status as priority claims, in the same order set out in § 507 (e.g., administrative expenses, wages owed by the debtor, employee benefits for which the debtor is responsible, child support and alimony)
2) Allowed unsecured claims that were either filed on time, or tardily filed for good reason
3) Other allowed unsecured claims
4) Certain fines and punitive damages
5) Interest on claims
6) The debtor.

If there is not enough money to pay all the claims of a particular class in full, claims within the class are paid pro rata. See § 726(b). See §§ 101(7), 541(a)(2), and 726(c) for modifications that are made in community property states.

Finally, after the estate has been distributed, the trustee files a final report with the court explaining how the estate was liquidated and disbursed.

BCode § 507(a) gives priority, among unsecured creditors' claims, to unpaid wages, salaries, or commissions, and to unpaid contributions to an employee benefit plan. After a Chapter 11 filing, the bankrupt company's Worker's Compensation insurer filed an unsecured creditor's claim for premiums, calling them contributions to an employee benefit plan. The Supreme Court ruled in mid-2006 that, although it is a close question, the premiums are not entitled to § 507(a)(5) priority, because they are more akin to automobile liability insurance than contributions to fringe benefits that are part of a pay package. In this reading, Worker's Compensation is not the equivalent of bargained-for compensation that benefits the employee; it benefits both workers and their employers by offering benefits to one and exemption from liability for the other. Finally, the court also determined that granting priority to Worker's Compensation claims would defeat the objective of making sure that at least part of a bankrupt employer's pensions and benefits would be paid.[11]

There is a limited right of redemption, pursuant to Bankruptcy Code § 722, available only in Chapter 7 cases filed by consumer debtors. For certain dischargeable secured consumer debts, the debtor can pay the creditor the amount of

---

[10] Marrama v. Citizens Bank of Mass., 549 U.S. 365 (2007).
[11] Howard Delivery Serv. Inc. v. Zurich American Ins. Co., 547 U.S. 651 (2006).

the allowed secured claim and thereby eliminate the security interest. This provision applies only to debts secured by tangible personal property which is either exempt or abandoned by the trustee. One problem with § 722 is that the total amount must be paid in cash at once, unless the creditor is willing to agree to accept payment in installments.

An individual's discharge in Chapter 7 is effective as to all debts except some taxes; debts not listed in the schedule; certain fines and penalties payable to government entities; alimony and support debts; certain student loans; and other items specifically exempted from discharge (see § 15.14[A]). However, § 727(a)(2) permits a creditor to object to a Chapter 7 discharge of a debtor who transferred, removed, concealed, or destroyed property with the intention to hinder, delay, or defraud creditors.[12]

Unlike Chapter 13 cases, which will be dismissed if the debtor decides that the filing was a bad move, § 707(a) permits dismissal of Chapter 7 cases only for cause, after notice and hearing. On its own motion, or the motion of the U.S. Trustee, the court can dismiss an individual debtor's case in which granting relief would be a substantial abuse of Chapter 7: § 707(b).

Debtors are not permitted to make Chapter 7 filings within 180 days of having another bankruptcy case dismissed for willful failure to appear or to abide by orders of the court. Chapter 7 is also unavailable to debtors who voluntarily discontinued a bankruptcy case less than 180 days earlier after filing of a § 362 request for relief from the automatic stay. A Chapter 7 discharge cannot be granted within six years of any other Chapter 7 case, or some Chapter 13 cases resulting in discharge: § 727(a)(8). There is no comparable provision under Chapter 13.

[B] Chapter 11

Chapter 11 of the Bankruptcy Code governs the method for drafting a reorganization plan, getting it confirmed, having a trustee appointed if the bankruptcy court deems it necessary,[13] and paying at least part of the appropriate debts to the creditors. Generally, this is all done with the debtor remaining in possession — i.e., continuing to operate its business.

The DIP (Debtor in Possession) has most of the powers and duties of a trustee. The DIP does not have to file schedules with the court, or investigate the debtor's (i.e., its own) assets, liabilities and financial condition, although a trustee would have to do so.

Generally speaking, there will be a period of 120 days during which the debtor and no one else has the right to file a voluntary Chapter 11 plan. This period is allotted to allow negotiations with creditors. The reorganization plan designates classes of claims and interests and indicates whether or not their right to receive payment is impaired by the plan.

---

[12] This section covers transfers of the debtor's property within one year before the bankruptcy filing, or transfers of property of the bankruptcy estate post-filing.

[13] Bankruptcy Code § 1104(a)(1) gives the court the power to appoint a trustee "for cause," and according to *In re* Marvel Entertainment Group Inc., 140 F.3d 563 (3d Cir. 1998), acrimony between the debtor-in-possession and a creditor is sufficient cause supporting the appointment.

In a Chapter 11 plan that provides for full payment of all claims, claims brought by nonconsenting creditors against parties other than the debtor can be enjoined using Bankruptcy Code § 1123(b)(6), if the injunction serves the purpose of facilitating the plan of reorganization.[14]

There are three ways to purchase assets from Chapter 11 estates:

- A BCode § 363 sale
- Purchase under the Chapter 11 reorganization plan
- From a post-confirmation liquidating trust.

[1] Trustee and/or Committees

Under Bankruptcy Code § 1102(a)(1), the U.S. Trustee appoints an unsecured creditors' committee as soon as possible after the order of relief has been entered. Section 1102(a)(2) permits any party in interest (i.e., anyone with a direct financial stake in the outcome of the case) to request the appointment of additional committees of creditors or holders of equity securities, to ensure their adequate representation. Section 1103 authorizes the committee to retain and pay professionals such as attorneys and accountants. The function of the committee is to consult with the DIP or trustee; investigate the debtor's financial condition and business operations; and participate in the creation of the plan.

A trustee can be appointed at any time after the commencement of a Chapter 11 case and before the confirmation of the plan, at the request of any party in interest or the U.S. Trustee. The court makes the appointment, after a hearing on notice, either for cause or in the interest of the estate, the creditors, or the company's stockholders: BCode § 1104. But if there is no trustee, the court must appoint an examiner to investigate the debtor (e.g., allegations of fraud, dishonesty, incompetence, misconduct, or mismanagement of the business), if either the appointment is in the best interests of the creditors, or the fixed, liquidated, unsecured debts of the debtor exceed $5 million (§ 1104(c)). The trustee's duties include investigation, reporting, and taking care of the property of the estate.

Just as the trustee can be appointed after notice and hearing, BCode § 1105 provides for termination of the trustee appointment, on request of a party in interest or the U.S. Trustee. The effect is to make the debtor a DIP.

[2] The Chapter 11 Plan

Bankruptcy Codes §§ 1121–1129 set out the requirements for the plan. The plan must be "feasible": i.e., the court must believe that the plan can be carried out without the debtor having to liquidate or make further bankruptcy filings.

All claims or interests in a class must be treated on a parity, unless the claimant accepts less favorable treatment. The debtor must give the creditors notice of the plan, disclosure of its terms, and an opportunity to be heard. All

---

[14] *In re* Dow Corning Corp., 280 F.3d 648 (6th Cir. 2002).

administrative and priority claims, and all case administration fees prescribed by 28 USC § 1930, must be paid in full as soon as the plan becomes effective: Bankruptcy Code § 1129(a)(12).

It is not necessary for all creditors or security holders to file proof of claim or proof of interest, because the claims disclosed on the debtor's schedules are deemed filed. However, the creditor must file proof of claim if the claim is listed incorrectly on the schedule, or is described as disputed, contingent, or unliquidated.

Section 1122 says that claims can only be put in the same class if they are similar, but fails to decide whether similar claims can be assigned to different classes.

If 120 days from the order of relief expire without the debtor's filing a plan, or if the debtor files a plan but each class of impaired claims did not accept the plan within 180 days of the order for relief, then § 1121(c) lets the other parties in interest file their own plans.

Section 1123 provides that the plan contain, for example:

- The classes of claims
- Information about which claims are not impaired
- Treatment of the impaired classes of claims
- Material showing that all claims in a class will be treated equally, unless the holder of a claim accepts less favorable treatment
- Explanation of how the plan will be implemented.

[3] Disclosures to Creditors

Bankruptcy Code § 1125 requires the debtor to draft a written disclosure statement, which must be approved by the court, informing creditors of whatever information a hypothetical reasonable investor, who holds claims within the relevant class, would require to make a decision about voting for or against the proposed plan. All creditors in a given class must receive the same disclosure statement, but § 1125(c) allows the debtor to prepare different disclosure statements for different classes of creditors.

Information subject to disclosure includes, for example:

- The circumstances behind the filing of the bankruptcy petition
- A description and valuation for the available assets
- The debtor's future plans
- Sources of the information in the disclosure statement
- The debtor's financial condition and its performance in Chapter 11 to date
- The financial and accounting assumptions used to prepare the statement
- Information about the claims pending against the bankruptcy estate
- Disclosure of any pending non-bankruptcy litigation, including predicted outcome
- What the creditors would receive in Chapter 7 (an important figure, because a valid Chapter 11 plan must give creditors at least as much as they would receive in Chapter 7, unless they consent to take less)

- Information about the debtor's future management, including executive compensation
- Collectibility of the debtor's accounts receivable
- Summary of the proposed plan
- Estimated administration expenses for completing the plan
- Estimated value of avoidable transfers
- Tax consequences of the proposal
- Any other financial information needed to make an informed decision about accepting the plan.

All creditors whose claims are **not** impaired by the plan are deemed by Bankruptcy Code § 1126 to approve the plan, so only impaired[15] creditors with approved claims get to vote. A class of claims approves the plan if more than half the number of creditors in the class, and the holders of more than two-thirds of the aggregate amount of claims in the class, vote in favor of the plan: BCode § 1126(c).

In a small business bankruptcy case (defined by BCode § 101(51C) as one involving aggregate noncontingent, liquidated debts [whether secured or unsecured] under $2 million at the time of the petition), BCode § 1125(f) provides for an expedited solicitation of consent procedure, combining the disclosure statement and the confirmation hearing.

[4] Confirmation of the Plan

The effect of confirmation of a Chapter 11 plan is to re-vest all the property in the debtor. This is not an unalloyed benefit to the debtor: it also means that the automatic stay is lifted, and actions against the debtor can proceed.

Whether the court will confirm the debtor's plan depends on fairness issues such as full disclosure and the best interests of the creditors. Either the plan must give each creditor at least as much as it would receive in liquidation, or the creditor must agree to a less favorable provision (BCode § 1129(a)(7)). If the plan fails to satisfy the statutory requirements, the court can deny confirmation, even if none of the creditors object.

If confirmation of the plan is inappropriate, the court can either dismiss the Chapter 11 case or convert it to Chapter 7, whichever is in the best interests of the creditors and the estate: § 1112(b).

When there are competing plans before the court, BCode § 1129(c) provides that only one can be confirmed, even if more than one plan satisfies the standards for confirmation.

---

[15] A claim is impaired if the holder's legal, equitable, and/or contractual rights are altered, and the plan would not result in cure of all prior defaults.

[5] Cramdown

The "cramdown" concept may come into play even if not all creditors agree, if the plan is fair and equitable and does not discriminate against impaired classes of claimants who do not accept the plan. BCode § 1129(b) allows the proponent of a plan that has not secured the consent of the necessary proportion of the creditors to petition the court to confirm the plan anyway. In other words, the plan is crammed down the throats of the objecting creditors. "Cramdown" is only available in plans that are free of unfair discrimination, and that are fair to the classes of creditors that rejected the plan.

Either the plan must pay all unsecured claims in full, or holders of interests with lower priority than the unsecured claims do not get anything from the plan because of interest. This is known as the "absolute priority" rule. Bankruptcy Code § 1129(b)(2)(A)(i) requires the plan to preserve secured creditors' liens, up to the allowed amount of the secured claim, whether the subject property is transferred or kept by the debtor.

There is a recognized exception to the absolute priority rule called the "new value" exception. It allows creditors to assist the debtor's successful reorganization by contributing significant amounts of new capital. Since this furthers the aims of the Bankruptcy Code, some courts treat it as an exception to the absolute priority rule.

In May 1999, the Supreme Court decided a case on this topic,[16] but did not resolve the Circuit split and did not decide whether or not the Bankruptcy Code makes an exception for new value that enhances reorganization. (It did decide that the particular plan in controversy was not fair.)

BAPCPA added an unnumbered hanging paragraph to § 1325(a); stating that BCode § 506(a) (which allocates loans between secured and unsecured portions) does not apply to certain secured loans. The issue what happens in a cramdown when the new paragraph takes § 506 out of the equation. The majority view is that § 1325(a)(5)(C) permits surrender of the collateral to the lender, resulting in full satisfaction of the borrower's obligation; in effect, the secured loan becomes non-recourse, no matter what the original contract said. The minority view is that Article 9 and contract law permit the creditor to receive an unsecured deficiency judgment after surrender of the collateral, unless the contract says the loan is without recourse. In this scenario, the unsecured balance is merely one more unsecured Chapter 13 debt. In this case, the hanging paragraph applies, because the debtors owed more on a purchase money car loan than the value of the car which they bought within 910 days of commencement of bankruptcy. The Seventh Circuit concluded that the hanging paragraph returns the parties to their rights under the contract; UCC rights remain in place, and the local version of UCC § 9-615(d)(2) requires obligors to satisfy the deficiency if the collateral is insufficient.[17]

---

[16] Bank of America v. 203 North LaSalle St. Partnership, 526 U.S. 434 (1999).

[17] *In re* Wright, 492 F.3d 829 (7th Cir. 2007).

[C] Chapter 12

Chapter 12, dealing with family farm bankruptcies, was originally enacted in 1986, with a sunset date in 1993. Several extensions were granted, and BAPCPA § 100 made Chapter 12 permanent (as well as extending it to cover fishermen).

[D] Chapter 13

The Bankruptcy Abuse Prevention and Consumer Protection Act of 2005, P.L. 109-8, makes many modifications in Chapter 13, as to, e.g., conversion between chapters, discharge, priorities, dismissal, and attorney's responsibilities.

Chapter 13 provides for "wage earner" plans for natural persons who have regular income and who reside, are domiciled, or have a place of business in the United States (§ 109(e)). The definition of "regular income" is broad enough to encompass items such as alimony and Social Security benefits, not just salary. The debtor, under § 1303, has the same rights as a bankruptcy trustee. There is no requirement that the debtor be insolvent as of the time of filing.

Eligibility for Chapter 13 is also subject to financial limits: no debtor or joint-debtor couple can have more than $336,900 in non-contingent, liquidated, unsecured debt, or over $1,010,650 in non-contingent, liquidated, secured debt.[18]

[1] Chapter 13 Procedure

Commencement of a Chapter 13 case is done by filing Official Form 1, a simple petition. The petition can be accompanied by schedules, a statement of financial affairs, disclosure of attorneys' fees, and documentation of the Chapter 13 plan; or the document can be filed not later than 15 days after filing of the petition.

The intent of the Bankruptcy Code is to allow Chapter 13 debtors maximal flexibility in devising their repayment plans, although certain requirements must be met under § 1322:

- All § 507 priority claims (e.g., attorney and trustee fees) must be paid in full, unless the creditor agrees to smaller payments — even if the claims could be discharged in Chapter 7.
- The present value of payments to unsecured creditors must be at least as great as if the debtor had filed under Chapter 7.
- For each allowed secured claim, either the claimholder accepts the plan; or the plan provides for payments whose present value is at least equal to the amount of the claim, with the lien continuing; or the debtor surrenders the property to the creditor. If the plan proposes to cure a default on a secured claim, the debtor must make regular payments on the obligation as they come due. Unless local practice forbids, the payments can be made directly to the

---

[18] 11 USC § 104(b) ; 72 FR 7082 (2/13/07).This amount applies to cases filed on or after 4/1/07; the amounts are adjusted every three years.

creditor, thus saving the trustee's fee (which is typically 9–10% of the amount paid out).

- If any party in interest objects, the plan must either call for full payment of all unsecured claims, or the debtor must agree to devote all disposable income for three years to accomplishment of the plan.

Unless the court orders to the contrary, § 1326(a)(1) obligates the debtor to begin plan payments within 30 days of the filing of the plan.

A § 341(a) hearing is held in Chapter 13 cases, usually 20–50 days after the filings. It resembles the Chapter 7 meeting, but may allow a greater degree of negotiation between creditors and debtor (who is obligated to attend the meeting in person). Note that, at least until the plan has been confirmed, a creditor who does not get "adequate protection" is entitled to relief from the automatic stay.

The Chapter 13 plan is the debtor's statement of how payments and distributions should be made. There is no standard form, although some local rules allow or require the trustee to draw up a formal plan.

The plan must indicate the portion of future disposable income that the debtor will devote to creditor repayment (§ 1322(a)(1)). If the plan classifies claims, all claims within a class must be treated alike; otherwise, the debtor is given total flexibility.

A Chapter 13 plan can call for payments over as much as five years, but § 1322(d) requires court approval, based on a showing of good cause, if payments are to extend longer than three years. Claims can be paid outside the plan — which has the effect of saving trustee fees which can add up on large claims.

The plan can call for either assumption or rejection of unexpired leases and executory contracts (i.e., contracts where some continued performance is required of each side): § 1322(b)(7). Bankruptcy Court approval is required for assumption of leases or executory contracts. The decision usually can be made at any time until confirmation of the plan; see § 365(d)(2).

Like Chapter 11, Chapter 13 provides for cramdown: BCode § 1322. It is permissible for the debtor's plan to modify the rights of holders of most secured claims. For instance, the debtor could pay less than the original agreement called for; could make lower payments; stretch out the payment schedule; defer payment of a particular debt until other debts are cleared; or even not pay a claim at all.

Various theories were applied to determine the rate of interest applicable in Chapter 13 cramdown situations. Finally, the Supreme Court resolved the issue in mid-2004, requiring a prime-plus or formula rate to be used rather than the original contract rate, a rate based on the cost of funds, or one that assumed a coerced loan had been made. The Supreme Court upheld the proposed rate of 9.6% because it was higher than the risk-free rate. Therefore, it satisfied the 11 USC § 1325(a)(5)(B)(ii) requirement of accounting for the time value of money — although it was lower than the 21% contract rate of interest on the debtors' used truck. According to the Supreme Court's majority opinion, the appropriate rate was high enough to compensate the creditor for its financial risk, while reasonable enough to make it possible for the debtor to return to financial balance, and was equitable and easy to administer.[19]

The Chapter 13 plan can also provide for curing a default over a reasonable period of time. *Rake v. Wade*[20] permits creditors to demand interest on arrears that are cured under a Chapter 13 plan, because the arrears are treated as a separate allowed secured claim.

[2] Confirmation of the Chapter 13 Plan

Chapter 13 cases also require a § 1324 confirmation hearing. Depending on local practice and the facts of the case, the confirmation hearing could be held on the same day as the § 341(a) hearing, or several months later. The meeting must be held on at least 25 days' notice to creditors, who can object on the grounds that the plan fails to conform to the objectives of Chapter 13. If confirmation is denied, the debtor will usually be given an opportunity to amend the plan in light of creditor objections. In any event, § 1323 allows modification of Chapter 13 plans at any time prior to confirmation.

The court has the power under § 1325 to refuse to confirm any proposed Chapter 13 plan that fails to satisfy two tests. The first, the "best interests of creditors" criterion, demands that the plan place unsecured creditors in no worse a position than they would have had under Chapter 7. The second requires either that unsecured creditors be paid in full, or that the debtor commit all disposable income for at least three years to complying with the plan.

Disposable income is defined by § 1325(b)(2) as income not reasonably necessary for the maintenance and support of the debtor and dependents. In practice, many debtors have little or no disposable income, so this test is of little comfort to creditors. The plan must be "feasible" (§ 1325(a)(6)): i.e., the debtor must be able to comply with the plan and make all the plan payments. A plan mandating payments disproportionate to income, or calling for a large balloon payment with no indication of how it can be made, will be denied confirmation.

After the plan is confirmed and until it is completed, § 1329(a) allows the debtor, an unsecured creditor, or trustee to seek upward or downward modification of the payment schedule based on a substantial change in the debtor's circumstances. In practical terms, this provision is usually used by debtors

---

[19] Till v. SCS Credit Corp., 541 U.S. 465 (2004). A post-BAPCPA Chapter 13 case provided for interest on the secured claim on the debtors' pickup truck at a "prime-plus" rate rather than the 17.95% interest rate in the purchase contract. The plan called for keeping the truck and paying the secured claim in installments with 6% interest. The concept of property includes the time value of money, so a Chapter 13 plan must provide for interest rates, but the Bankruptcy Code does not have detailed interest-rate rules. The Fifth Circuit held that BAPCPA did not change the definition of value or remove Bankruptcy Courts' power to change the contract terms for secured claims, *Till* so remained valid: Drive Fin. Servs., LP v. Jordan, 521 F.3d 343 (5th Cir. 2008).

[20] 508 U.S. 424 (1993).

seeking lower payments; creditors probably wouldn't be aware of increases the debtor's income.

In most cases, confirmation is granted, and the debtor and all creditors will be bound by the terms of the plan. Title to property re-vests in the debtor, and the trustee makes the payments in accordance with the plan. The debtor still has the ability to modify the plan, but only after a hearing on notice to creditors.

Chapter 7 filings can be converted to Chapter 13 if the debtor prefers; see § 706(a).

[3] Discharge of the Chapter 13 Debtor

As soon as possible after the plan has been completed, a discharge hearing can be held at the discretion of the court (see BCode § 524) and discharge is granted under § 1328.

The discharge covers all debts provided for in the plan, other than:

* Long-term debts with final payment due after completion of the plan
* Certain student loan debts
* Most alimony and support debt
* Some fines, etc. related to crimes or restitution.

Even after discharge, § 350(b) gives the debtor the right to reopen the case for additional relief. The confirmation order binds the debtor and all creditors, even those who raised objections to or rejected the plan (see § 1327(a)). Once the appeal period passes, the order becomes res judicata as to all objections to confirmation that could have been, but were not, raised.

[4] Alternatives to Completion of the Chapter 13 Plan

Sometimes the debtor is unable to complete the Chapter 13 plan: for instance, if he or she gets fired and no longer has salary from which to make the payments. The Bankruptcy Code provides for four options in this situation:

* Hardship discharge under § 1328(b), if there have been circumstances beyond the debtor's control, and modification of the plan is not feasible. A hardship discharge does not require full payment of priority claims, but it does require the unsecured creditors to get as much as they would have gotten in Chapter 7.
* Modification of the plan (including reduction or even termination of the payments under the plan), as provided by § 1329. Priority claims and allowed secured claims must be paid.
* Conversion to Chapter 7. Section 1307(a) makes conversion the debtor's right, and hardship need not be shown.
* Dismissal as of right (as long as the Chapter 13 filing was not already converted from another chapter) under § 1307(b). Dismissal has the effect of returning the parties to their status quo before the filing of the petition.

As is true of Chapter 7, a new Chapter 13 filing is barred within 180 days of dismissal for cause of a previous petition. However, a Chapter 13 discharge can be granted to a debtor who received a Chapter 7 discharge within the previous six years.

§ 15.04 BANKRUPTCY COURT PROCEDURES

Under 28 USC § 157(b)(2), "core proceedings" are matters such as the administration of the estate; preference proceedings; motions to modify the automatic stay; and confirmation of the plan. Any case within the bankruptcy jurisdiction and involving the debtor can be filed, pursuant to 28 USC § 1409(a), in the bankruptcy court in which the bankruptcy case is pending, even if long-arm jurisdiction would otherwise be lacking. Process can be served nationwide, usually by first-class mail. The significance of the concept of "core proceedings" is that the bankruptcy judge can both hear the matter and issue a final order in a core proceeding. In a non-core proceeding related to a Title 11 case, the bankruptcy judge has the power to hear the matter. But unless the parties have consented to the issuance of a final order, the bankruptcy judge submits findings of fact and conclusions of law to the District Court. If a party objects to them, the findings and conclusions are reviewed by the District Court de novo.

A 1989 Supreme Court case[21] holds that a defendant in a preference or fraudulent conveyance action who has not filed a claim against the estate has a Seventh Amendment right to trial by jury. 28 USC § 157(e) empowers the bankruptcy judge to conduct the jury trial in any proceeding he or she is authorized to hear, provided that the District Court designates the bankruptcy judge for this purpose, and all parties consent. Also see FRBP 9015.

A Bankruptcy Court's order allowing an uncontested proof of claim is a final judgment on the merits and hence is res judicata. The Second Circuit rejected the argument that only a litigated judgment can be res judicata. A judgment is final even if a Rule 60(b) motion can be filed, and even that was unavailable in this case because the debtor had been discharged and the bankruptcy proceeding closed.[22]

In 2007, the amounts in 11 USC § 104(b) were adjusted for inflation:

- A trustee can commence a proceeding to recover a money judgment of $1,100 (was $1,000), or property worth less than $16,425 (was $15,000) for consumer debt or $10,950 (was $10,000) of non-consumer debt against a non-insider (28 USC § 1409(b).
- Under 11 USC § 101(d), the $150,000 amount rises to $164,250; the § 101(18) definition of "assisted person" uses a figure of $3,237,000 rather

---

[21] Granfinanciera, SA v. Nordberg, 492 U.S. 33 (1989).

[22] EDP Medical Computer Systems Inc. v. United States, 480 F.3d 621 (2d Cir. 2007). Orsini Santos v. Mender, 349 BR 762 (1st Cir BAP 2006) says an order allowing or disallowing a claim is final and appealable, but here the Second Circuit said that doesn't really matter because finality for appellate review purposes is not dispositive of finality for res judicata purposes.

than $3,644,525 or Update of 11 USC 104(b) amounts, rounded to nearest $25. These increases apply to cases filed on and after the April 1, 2007 effective date, with corresponding amendments to Official Forms 6E and 10.[23]

[A] Bankruptcy Forms

The bankruptcy petition for all Chapters is filed on Official Form 1, a short form that summarizes the relief sought and asserts the court's jurisdiction and venue. It is supplemented by Official Form 6, Schedules A through J that promulgate a standard format for collecting information about the debtor's assets, liabilities, and disposable income, so that the bankruptcy estate can be administered:

- Schedule A: real property
- Schedule B: personal property
- Schedule C: property for which exemption is claimed
- Schedule D: secured creditors
- Schedule E: priority unsecured creditors
- Schedule F: non-priority unsecured creditors.

Debts cannot be discharged unless they are noted on the schedule. It is especially important to verify the addresses of all creditors, because no discharge can be obtained against a creditor who did not receive proper notice of the bankruptcy filing (because such a creditor will be unable to assert its claims and object to the discharge). It should also be noted if any debt is contingent, unliquidated, or disputed.

- Schedule G: unexpired leases that are not terminated by their own terms, and executory contracts (contracts on which both sides still owe substantial performance). The trustee may have power to reject such leases and contracts.
- Schedule H: individuals (other than spouses in a joint bankruptcy case) who are codebtors with the debtor filing the petition.
- Schedule I: the debtor's income. If the debtor is a married person, the income of both spouses must be included, even if only one spouse files, unless the spouses are separated.
- Schedule J: expenses of the debtor and family. In a Chapter 13 filing, Schedules I and J must prove the availability of enough disposable income to support the plan.

Usually a summary will be prepared of all debts, property, income, and expenses; local rules dictate whether the summary should be placed before or after the schedules.

---

[23] 72 F.R. 7082 (2/13/07).

Form 2 is a corporation's or partnership's declaration under penalty of perjury. Form 3A is the application to pay the filing fee in installments; Form 3B is the application for waiver of the Chapter 7 filing fee. Form 4 is a listing of the 20 creditors with the largest unsecured claims. Form 5 is the involuntary petition form.

Form 7 is a statement of financial affairs. Form 8, used in Chapter 7, is a statement of intention as to property that secures consumer debts. The debtor can retain the property; claim it as exempt; surrender it; or announce an intention to redeem the collateral (i.e., pay the lienholder the value of the property) or reaffirm the debt for payment in the future. In many jurisdictions, the debtor can simply continue payments on an auto loan, without either redeeming the automobile or reaffirming the debt.

Form 9 is the notice of commencement, broken down into sub-forms for various types of filing (e.g., corporate/partnership no asset; individual/joint case with assets). Form 10 is proof of claim. Form 11A and B are general and special powers of attorney, respectively. Form 12 is the notice and order for a hearing on the disclosure statement; Form 13 is the court order approving the disclosure statement. Form 14 is the ballot for acceptance or rejection of a plan of reorganization. Form 15 is the order confirming the plan, and Form 16 is the caption. Objections to a claim are filed on Form 20B, and Form 20A is notice of a motion or objection. Form 17 is the notice of appeal in a bankruptcy situation. The debtor's discharge is memorialized on Form 18. Form 19 is used by non-attorney bankruptcy preparers to identify themselves and make disclosures. Form 21 is the statement of Social Security Number. Form 22 contains the Chapter 7 calculations of the means test and monthly income and disposable income. Form 23 is the debtor's certificate of having completed the financial education required by BAPCPA. Form 24 is the certification to the Court of Appeals.

FRBP 2016(b) requires disclosure of fees paid to the debtor's attorney; commercially printed sets of bankruptcy forms include this form.

[B] Case Law on Bankruptcy Procedure

In its January 23, 2006, decision in *Central Virginia Community College v. Katz*, the Supreme Court ruled that Congress has the power under the Bankruptcy Clause to decide whether states should be treated like other creditors or should be permitted to assert sovereign immunity. Therefore, a bankruptcy trustee could attack preferential transfers to a state agency, and the agencies could not assert sovereign immunity.[24]

The Third Circuit held in mid-2008 that a Chapter 13 debtor could not invalidate a lien on her property (in this case, the mortgage on her primary residence) by providing for it as an unsecured claim in the plan without initiating an adversary proceeding under Rule 7001(2), which requires an adversary proceeding to resolve matters such as the validity, priority, or extent of a lien. The debtor claimed that she owed only $1,000 in unsecured debt for the "alleged mortgage," rather than the

---

[24] 546 U.S. 356 (2006).

$40,000 balance the lender asserted. According to the debtor, the lien was invalidated by listing the claim as unsecured, and by the creditor's failure to object. However, the Third Circuit ruled that lien stripping relates to the valuation of collateral, not the validity of a lien. The lender's failure to object did not oust all of the procedural protections granted by the FRBP.[25]

§ 15.05   THE BANKRUPTCY ESTATE

The bankruptcy estate consists of all of the debtor's property rights that can be administered by the court (acting through the trustee). The bankruptcy estate can include interests in property that creditors could not otherwise attach (e.g., interests in community property). See BCode § 363(h) for protection of a joint owner of property who does not file for bankruptcy when another joint owner does file.

An important part of the bankruptcy process is compiling schedules of property. Neglect or refusal to list property in the schedules can result in denial or even revocation of discharge. The trustee and/or creditors may also be able to assert claims against such property, even if claims would be untenable with respect to property that was properly included on the schedules.

The Fifth Circuit held in 2008 that a reorganized Chapter 11 debtor does not have standing to pursue claims based on the way a bank or other financial institution managed the assets of the estate before confirmation. (The debtor, an oil and gas company, alleged that better management would have produced higher well yields and therefore a higher buy-out price.) Confirmation of the plan meant that the bankruptcy estate no longer existed, so the debtor's ability to pursue claims as if it were a trustee also expired. Although 11 USC § 1123(b)(3) sometimes gives the reorganized debtor standing to bring post-confirmation actions, that power is limited to plans of reorganization that expressly provide for the debtor's retention and enforcement of the claim. Bankruptcy's objective of starting over again with a clean slate also applies to claims the estate had before its dissolution, unless there has been a reservation of rights.[26]

§ 15.06   EXEMPTIONS

Theoretically, all of the debtor's property is required to be used for satisfaction of debts. However, debtors are permitted to retain the items they need for daily life — if only to prevent them from becoming public charges. Most household goods of consumers are exempt under § 522. As a practical matter, the trustee is likely to abandon or allow the debtor to purchase personal property that has limited value and has so little encumbered value that it does not repay the cost and trouble of liquidating it.

In general, exemptions do not affect valid security interests or other liens on the property of the debtor. Usually, the debtor eliminates the lien by paying the creditor the amount of the secured claim, so the exempt amount is the total debt minus the lien.

---

[25] *In re* Mansaray-Ruffin, 530 F.3d 230 (3d Cir. 2008).
[26] *In re* Dynasty Oil & Gas, 540 F.3d 351 (5th Cir. 2008).

[A] Opt-Out States

Although bankruptcy is essentially governed by federal law, state laws have some place in bankruptcy. A few states give debtors the choice between the exemptions defined by the Bankruptcy Code and those defined by state law, but most states have "opted out" of the federal exemptions, so debtors in those states (Alabama, Alaska, Arizona, California, Colorado, Delaware, Florida, Georgia, Idaho, Illinois, Indiana, Iowa, Kansas, Kentucky, Louisiana, Maine, Maryland, Mississippi, Missouri, Montana, Nebraska, Nevada, New Hampshire, New York, North Carolina, North Dakota, Ohio, Oklahoma, Oregon, South Carolina, South Dakota, Tennessee, Utah, Virginia, West Virginia, Wyoming) are only permitted to claim the state exemptions, plus federal exemptions deriving from non-bankruptcy law (e.g., protection of pension plans and other trusts).

In opt-out states, or in the other states where the debtor so elects, the state exemptions are used. Bankruptcy Code § 522(b)(2)(B) allows a debtor who claims the state exemptions to claim as exempt interests in property held as a joint tenant or tenant by the entireties immediately before commencement of the bankruptcy proceeding, to the extent that such an interest would be exempt from process under applicable non-bankruptcy laws. This provision protects property that someone who is a creditor only of the bankruptcy filer, and not of the other joint tenant, could not have levied on as of the date the petition was filed. There is no limit on the amount of real or personal property that can be sheltered under this provision.

There are also some exemptions that do not arise under § 522(d), for example, federal benefits such as Social Security benefits (42 USC § 407), veterans' benefits (38 USC § 5301(a)), and civil service retirement benefits (5 USC § 8346).

[B] Effect on Exempt Property

With only a few exceptions (support/alimony debt; nondischargeable taxes; liens that were not avoided during bankruptcy) BCode § 522(c) provides that no creditor with a pre-bankruptcy claim can ever execute against exempt property. In other words, even if a particular claim has not been discharged, exempt property is permanently shielded from execution. Some debtors are wholly or partially denied a discharge (e.g., on debts that were not listed, or because the debtor has committed bankruptcy fraud), but are still protected in practical terms because they have very little property, and most or all of what they do have is exempt.

[1] List of Federal Exemptions

The federal exemptions, as laid out in § 522(d), are quite modest. (The dollar amounts which are inflation-adjusted every three years, most recently in February, 2007,[27] are doubled in joint cases):

---

[27] *See* 72 FR 708: (2/13/07). The evolution of the exempt amounts can be traced in 11 USC § 104.

- The debtor's interest in a homestead, up to, $20,200[28]
- A motor vehicle worth up to $$3,225
- Household goods up to $/525 item, $10,775 per debtor
- Jewelry up to $1,350
- Other items up to $1,075 aggregate plus up to $10,125 of unused exemption amounts
- Tools of the debtor's trade up to $2,025
- Compensation for bodily injury or loss, up to $20,200
- Any unmatured life insurance without cash value (e.g., term insurance); up to $10,775 in life insurance cash value
- Luxury goods or cash advances obtained during the 60 days prior to filing, up to $1,350
- The right to receive future payments of Social Security, unemployment, welfare, disability and illness benefits; the right to receive future payments of alimony and child support, but only to the extent reasonably necessary for support of the debtor and debtor's dependents
- Employee contributions to qualified retirement and benefit plans; see below
- Certain funds deposited into a qualified educational funding program or qualified state tuition funding program, for the benefit of the debtor's child(ren) or grandchild(ren), if the deposit was made more than 365 days pre-filing; the exemption for deposits made more than one but less than two years pre-filing is limited to $5,475.

Under BCode § 522(b), the debtor can choose between the state and federal exemption schemes and make a list of claimed exemptions from the bankruptcy estate. FRBP 4003(b) allows the creditor and any bankruptcy trustee to file objections to the list of exemptions within 30 days of the creditors' meeting. The Second Circuit has ruled that the 30-day period does not start over again when a Chapter 11 case is converted to Chapter 7. FRBP 1019(2) is explicit in stating that the conversion does not restart the clock.[29]

A mid-2008 Third Circuit case holds that, where a Chapter 7 debtor indicates an intent to exempt her entire interest in property by claiming its full value as an exemption, and the trustee does not object in time, the debtor is entitled to keep all of the property. The trustee cannot move to sell the property if he finds out later that it is worth more than the claimed exemption. The debtor, a caterer, listed $10,718 in business equipment as exempt: $1,850 under § 522(d)(6), the balance under § 522(d)(5). The trustee's subsequent appraisal showed a value of approximately $17,200, and the trustee moved to sell the equipment to add about $7,000 to the bankruptcy estate. The Third Circuit ruled that it was obvious that the debtor

---

[28] There is also a limit on state homestead value of $125,000 for property acquired within 1,215 days prior to filing. The cap does not apply to interests transferred from the previous personal residence. The homestead cap can be limited based on various kinds of financial misconduct on the bankruptcy petitioner's part.

[29] *In re* Bell, 225 F.3d 203 (2d Cir. 2000).

planned to exempt all the kitchen equipment; if the trustee disagreed with the valuation, he should have obtained the appraisal earlier, or used Rule 4003(c) to apply for a hearing. Although acknowledging that other Circuits have disagreed, the Third Circuit held that, once 30 days passed, the property became fully exempt no matter what its market value was. The Third Circuit adopted this position to satisfy the objective of giving the debtor a fresh start.[30]

[2] Trusts and Pensions

The beneficiaries of a trust, including a trust that is part of an employee benefit plan (see § 3.05[B]) or a spendthrift trust, are in an especially favorable position when they file for bankruptcy protection. The Fifth Circuit held that although a spendthrift trust was used as part of a scheme to defraud creditors, the trust itself could not be declared a sham: under Texas law, that concept is applied only in marital litigation. (BCode § 541(c)(2) excludes the property in a spendthrift trust from the bankruptcy estate if local law protects the property from the debtor's creditors, but Texas law does not protect self-settled trusts.) The Fifth Circuit held that the trustee did not establish the applicability of the constructive trust doctrine, because proof of fraud is an essential element. Nevertheless, the court denied the debtor a discharge, because concealment of property had been proved.[31]

Any amounts that creditors could not reach absent bankruptcy cannot be reached in bankruptcy. The Supreme Court's crucial 1992 ruling[32] treats ERISA as "applicable non-bankruptcy law," with the result that a debtor's pension interests never become part of his or her bankruptcy estate, because ERISA prevents creditors from anticipating the pension payments.

In 2005, in *Rousey v. Jacoway*, the Supreme Court eliminated uncertainty about the bankruptcy treatment of IRAs by adopting the majority position (held by the Second, Fifth, Sixth, and Ninth Circuits) rather than the Eighth Circuit position, finding that early withdrawal penalties on IRAs are substantial, and the right to withdraw funds without penalty is causally connected to age; thus, IRAs should be treated in the same way as qualified plans.[33]

BAPCPA enacts a new § 541(c)(2), excluding 403(b) plans from the estate. Under prior law, the D. Vermont Bankruptcy Court permitted a bankrupt couple to exclude the wife's 403(b) plan assets from the Chapter 7 bankruptcy estate, by analogy with exclusion of qualified plans and 401(k) plans, and rejected the trustee's argument that funds could be excluded only during the time between the

---

[30] *In re* Reilly, 534 F.3d 173 (3d Cir. 2008).

[31] Bradley v. Ingalls, 501 F.3d 421 (5th Cir. 2007).

[32] Patterson v. Shumate, 504 U.S. 753 (1992).

[33] 526 U.S. 434 (U.S. 2005). Similarly, 403(b) accounts have been excluded from the estate: *In re* Gould (Bankr. W.D. Pa 4/12/05).

employer's withholding of compensation until the funds are placed in the 403(b) plan.[34]

Note that the debtor's interests in all trusts should be listed on Schedule B, whether or not the interest is properly includible in the bankruptcy estate. Any exemptions should be claimed on this schedule.

The debtor can avoid non-possessory interests in items such as clothing, household items, and professional tools, as long as the creditor does not have a purchase money security interest (PMSI) in the items.

[3] Homestead

Family homes receive special consideration in bankruptcy — so much so that sometimes high-asset individuals in risky businesses select domiciles based in part on the size of the homestead exemption. BCode § 522(q), as amended by BAPCPA, limits a state homestead exemption to $125,000 in cases in which the debtor has been convicted of a felony, or the debt arises from certain causes of action. It is unclear what provisions will be made to protect homeowners in the wake of the late 2008 housing market collapse and credit crisis.

The Third Circuit allowed exclusion (under § 522) of a home owned by an individual debtor with her husband as tenants by the entireties. One spouse's bankruptcy does not remove the immunity from the entireties estate. The Third Circuit rejected the trustee's argument that the debts were incurred for necessaries.[35]

A Florida homestead retains its exempt character even if it was acquired with the specific intent of hindering, delaying, or even defrauding creditors.[36]

The Tenth Circuit permitted Chapter 7 debtors, beneficiaries of a self-settled revocable living trust, to claim the homestead exemption on property owned by the trust, because their status as beneficiaries gave them an equitable interest sufficient to bring the property into the bankruptcy estate.[37]

[C] Avoidance of Liens

Section 522(f)(1)(A) gives the debtor an unqualified right (except for certain family-related debts) to avoid any "judicial lien" (including levies, judgment liens, and confessed judgments) that would impair an exemption. But if the lien only partially impairs an exemption, only the part that impairs it can be avoided.

---

[34] *In re* Leahy, No. 06-10574 (Bankr. D. Vt. 7/3/07); *see* Fred Schneyer, *Court Allows 403(b) Bankruptcy Exclusion* Plansponsor.com 7/11/07. See also *In re* Laher, 496 F.3d 279 (3d Cir. 2007): a TIAA-CREF retirement annuity under a 403(b) plan was excluded from the Chapter 7 estate; the Third Circuit rejected the argument that CREF is a trust but a TIAA account is not, finding no reason to distinguish between the two funding vehicles.

[35] *In re* O'Lexa, 476 F.3d 177 (3d Cir. 2007).

[36] Havoco of America Ltd. v. Hill, 790 So. 2d 1018 (Fla. 2001).

[37] *In re* Kester, 493 F.3d 1208 (10th Cir. 2007).

The First Circuit held in 2007 that § 522(f) allows a debtor to avoid a judicial lien that existed at the time of filing, but was satisfied after the bankruptcy case closed but before the debtor moved to avoid. (In this case, it was a judicial lien on the debtor's residence.) The First Circuit says there are three requirements for the debtor to avoid fixing of a lien: the lien was fixed on the debtor's interest in property; it is a judicial lien; and it impairs an exemption that the debtor would be entitled to. The measuring date is the petition date, and § 522(f) can work retrospectively to annual fastening. But the First Circuit also said that avoidance should be denied if the creditor can raise equitable defenses such as prejudice, fraud, laches, or detrimental reliance.[38]

The holding of a 1991 Supreme Court case is that § 522(f)(1) can be used[39] to avoid fixing of a lien on the debtor's interest in the property that predated the lien. The rationale is that a divorce decree ended the debtor's half interest in the marital home, giving him a new fee simple interest. The ex-wife's lien did not attach to any pre-existing interest, and therefore could not be avoided.

The WARN Act and the Labor-Management Relations Act (LMRA) preempt state-law liens with respect to sanctions imposed for WARN Act noncompliance, as well as unpaid wages and amounts claimed under a Collective Bargaining Agreement (CBA). LMRA § 301 preempts CBA claims, so employees' claims of entitlement to bankruptcy priority liens arising out of vacation pay, wages, pension contributions, or health claims under the CBA are necessarily preempted.[40]

§ 15.07 THE ROLE OF THE TRUSTEE

The U.S. Trustee appoints a trustee (chosen from the list of serving trustees for the district) in every Chapter 7 or Chapter 13 case: 28 USC § 586(a)(l). Frequently, a single trustee, known as the "standing trustee," handles all Chapter 13 cases for a district or portion of a district. (This is possible because the trustee's role in Chapter 13 is fairly minimal.)

The trustee has the power to sue or be sued with respect to claims made on behalf of, or against, the bankruptcy estate. The trustee must also:

- Marshall the property of the estate; see BCode §§ 542 and 543 for the turnover or surrender of property held by third parties and in which the debtor has an interest
- Invalidate inappropriate transfers of estate assets
- Raise any available objections to the debtor's claims to exemption, or to the discharge
- Liquidate all property that is not exempt (turn it into cash that can be used to pay debts)

---

[38] *In re* Wilding, 475 F.3d 428 (1st Cir. 2007).
[39] Farrey v. Sanderfoot, 500 U.S. 291 (1991).
[40] *In re* Bluffton Casting Corp., 186 F.3d 857 (7th Cir. 1999).

- Distribute the available funds to creditors, in accordance with the plan and the statutory priorities
- Make a final accounting to the U.S. Trustee and the bankruptcy court.

The Chapter 13 trustee must attend all the hearings about value of property in Chapter 13 estates subject to liens; must attend hearings about confirmation or modification of debtors' plans; and must make sure that the debtor abides by the plan as structured. See BCode § 1302(b).

"Concealment" from the trustee (18 U.S.C. § 152(l)) is defined broadly to cover any action that reduces the trustee's ability to account for assets and distribute them to creditors, so a debtor who interferes with the trustee's access to real property has committed concealment.[41]

According to the Eleventh Circuit, the Chapter 11 trustee's fees, which are based on disbursements (see 28 USC § 1930) should reflect all of the debtor's disbursements, including those made in the ordinary course of business, and not just those made under the confirmed Chapter 11 plan.[42]

§ 15.08   THE CREDITOR'S MEETING

Bankruptcy Code § 341(a) requires a hearing to give the parties a chance to examine the debtor as to financial affairs, information that is also needed by the trustee. Interim Rule 2003, promulgated to reflect BAPCPA, states that in general, in Chapter 7 or Chapter 11, the U.S. trustee will call the creditor's meeting to be held 20–40 days after the order for relief; in an individual Chapter 13, the meeting will generally be held 20–50 days after the order for relief.

It can be held either at the bankruptcy court or at any place convenient to the parties. In a typical Chapter 7 case, the meeting takes only a few minutes. Few creditors take advantage of their ability to attend, and the bankruptcy judge is actually forbidden to attend.

§ 15.09   THE AUTOMATIC STAY

One of the major benefits of bankruptcy is to impose a delay on pending and threatened litigation (of all types) against the debtor. Although it has no fixed duration, the BCode § 362 automatic stay usually lasts at least 30 days. The court has the power to lift the stay sooner for perishable property, but this is much more common in business than in consumer cases. The automatic stay can last as long as the entire bankruptcy case, which would be about 3–6 months in a Chapter 7, or as much as five years for a Chapter 13. In practical terms, creditors don't always spring into action as soon as the automatic stay is lifted, so debtors may have an even longer period of forbearance.

---

[41] United States v. Wagner, 382 F.3d 598 (6th Cir. 2004).

[42] Walton v. Jamko Inc., 240 F.3d 1312 (11th Cir. 2001). The Sixth Circuit bases the fee on all expenditures paid until the case is closed, converted, or dismissed: Robiner v. Danny's Markets Inc., 266 F.3d 523 (6th Cir. 2001).

During the automatic stay, creditors cannot:

- Commence or continue any judicial or administrative proceeding against the debtor (even if the proceeding is not debt-related) that arose before the commencement of the case, although the debtor retains the power to institute and continue actions. Permission of the bankruptcy court is required to take any steps in proceedings that are subject to the automatic stay.
- Create, perfect, or enforce any lien against the property of the estate.
- Engage in any other act to collect, assess, or recover a claim against the debtor arising before commencement of the case.
- Commence or continue a Tax Court proceeding against the debtor.
- Engage in collection efforts by mail, phone, in person, or by other means.
- Set off (e.g., a bank account) against a precommencement debt. However, a bank can freeze[43] a debtor's bank account while the automatic stay is in effect, on the grounds that this is not a setoff (which involves actually removing funds from the account).
- [In Chapter 11] enforce judgments against the debtor on property of the estate, if the judgments were obtained before commencement of the bankruptcy case; create, perfect, or enforce liens that secure a claim arising before commencement of the case.
- [In Chapter 13] pursue a civil suit or other action to collect all or part of a consumer debt from a codebtor rather than the principal debtor who is also the bankruptcy filer. This stay ends automatically if the Chapter 13 case is closed, dismissed or converted to Chapter 7 or 11.

Activities undertaken contrary to the automatic stay are void even if the creditor did not have actual knowledge of the stay. Pursuant to § 362(f), the court can enjoin violations of the automatic stay, and has discretion to order other statutory and administrative remedies.

Bankruptcy Code § 362(a), staying commencement or continuation of an action, not merely forbids starting new cases but imposes an affirmative duty on creditors to discontinue pending state actions.[44]

The debtor, under BCode § 362(h), can recover actual damages, costs, attorneys' fees, even punitive damages in appropriate cases, if any creditor injures the debtor by a willful violation of the automatic stay. In this context, "willful" means "knowing"; malice is not a required element. Refusal to rectify actions taken after notice of the stay is also subject to § 362(h).

Also note that BCode § 366 provides that, for a period of at least 20 days after filing of the petition, public utilities are not permitted to alter, refuse, or discontinue service or discriminate against a debtor solely because there is an unpaid prepetition debt, or on the grounds that the debtor has filed for bankruptcy protection.

---

[43] Citizens Bank of Md. v. Strumpf, 516 U.S. 16 (1995).
[44] Eskanos & Adler PC v. Leetien, 301 F.3d 1210 (9th Cir. 2002).

However, it is permissible to terminate service if, within 20 days of the filing, the debtor fails to furnish adequate assurance of future payment. This can take the form of a deposit or other security (such as lien on the debtor's property to be executed in case of further delinquency). In many states, regulations limit the size of the deposit that a utility can require in this context.

In addition to the automatic stay, the bankruptcy court has the general injunctive power (under § 105) to stay actions that are not subject to the automatic stay.

A reaffirmation agreement with a creditor is not a "prior final judgment on the merits," because it is a voluntary agreement that would not affect litigation over the dischargeability of the item (unless it was incorporated into a court order). Therefore, it is permissible for the debtor to proceed with a class action against the creditor for violation of the automatic stay and the Bankruptcy Code's discharge provisions.[45]

Although § 525(b) forbids firing an individual merely because he or she is a bankruptcy debtor, this has been held by the Ninth Circuit not to apply to someone who is fired after he says that he is going to file, but before the bankruptcy petition is actually filed.[46]

[A] Exceptions to the Automatic Stay

The automatic stay does not prohibit commencement or continuation of criminal proceedings, even those that are related to the debt: BCode § 362(b)(1). Collection of alimony, maintenance, or child support from property that is **not** within the bankruptcy estate is not stayed. Furthermore, § 362(b)(2)(A) permits litigation to establish paternity during the automatic stay; litigation to establish or modify a court order requiring payment of alimony, maintenance, or support is also permitted.

UCC filings relating back to the creation of a security interest can be made during the automatic stay (§ 362(b)(3)), and other actions can be taken to perfect or continue perfection of security interests in property within the bankruptcy estate.

Although Tax Court proceedings are barred, § 362(b)(9) allows taxing authorities to audit bankruptcy debtors, issue notices of deficiency against them, and assess taxes, but can only impose liens if the tax is a debt that will not be discharged and the property revests in the debtor. See § 362(b)(18) for the extent of the exception for post-petition statutory liens for property taxes.

Creditors can apply for relief by filing motions for termination, annulment, modification, or conditions on the automatic stay: see § 362(d) and FRBP 4001(a). At least a preliminary hearing must be held within 30 days of filing of such a

---

[45] Rein v. Providian Fin. Co., 252 F.3d 1095 (9th Cir. 2001).

[46] Leonard v. St. Rose Dominican Hosp. (*In re* Majewski), 310 F.3d 653 (9th Cir. 2002). *See also* White v. Kentuckiana Livestock Mkt. Inc., 397 F.3d 420 (6th Cir. 2005): a married couple who were fired by their employer just after publication of their notice of bankruptcy filing could not prove that they were fired solely because of it; they could not prevail on a mere showing that the filing was at least a substantial factor in their termination.

motion; the stay terminates by operation of law if there is no hearing (§ 362(e)). At the hearing, § 362(g) places the burden of proof on the party seeking relief from the stay to prove the debtor's equity in the property; on other issues, the burden is on the party opposing the relief.

Because BCode § 362(a) says that criminal proceedings are not stayed, the automatic stay does not apply to criminal proceedings, even if their purpose is debt collection.[47] *Gruntz* overrules an earlier decision which did place criminal proceedings for debt collection within the ambit of the automatic stay.

The Southern District of New York ruled that continued imprisonment of a debtor for contempt of court (in connection with very large arrears of non-dischargeable family support) does not violate the automatic stay, because the purpose of imprisonment was to collect non-dischargeable items from property falling outside the bankruptcy estate.[48]

Sanctions for frivolous litigation (here, an appeal that fell within the definition of a frivolous appeal in FRAP 38) are not subject to the automatic stay in a lawyer's Chapter 11 case. BCode § 362(b)(4) makes the stay inapplicable in actions or proceedings by governmental units to enforce police or regulatory powers, and the Ninth Circuit interprets the sanction as carrying out government policy, not protecting private rights or the government's pecuniary interest in the lawyer's property.[49]

§ 15.10 ASSUMPTION OR AVOIDANCE OF OBLIGATIONS

Various cases outline the extent to which claims are avoidable or must be assumed.

State law may grant the power to avoid transfers that are not enforceable against a bona fide purchaser of real estate, and thus may permit the debtor to avoid foreclosure sale transfers that have not been completed by the filing of a deed.

The Bankruptcy Code limits the DIP's ability to assume an unexpired lease: it must be done earlier than 120 days after the date of the order for relief, or the date of entry of the confirmation order for the plan. Rejection of the lease is treated as a breach of lease. The lessor can seek damages as a pre-petition claim, and § 502(g) permits the lessor to apply for general unsecured creditor priority. Therefore, the date of the lease rejection is key, because before that date, the landlord can get the full rental as a priority claim, but afterwards, the landlord drops down to being a general unsecured creditor who will probably receive only a fraction of the rent. The Second Circuit declined the opportunity to rule whether the Bankruptcy Court has the equitable power to make lease rejection retroactive, because none of the

---

[47] Gruntz v. Los Angeles County, 202 F.3d 1074 (9th Cir. 2000), overruling Hucke v. Oregon, 992 F.2d 950 (9th Cir. 1993).

[48] *In re* Bezoza, 271 B.R. 46 (Bankr. S.D.N.Y. 2002).

[49] Berg v. Good Samaritan Hosp., 230 F.3d 1165 (9th Cir. 2000).

parties raised the issue before the District Court, so the Second Circuit refused to disturb the retroactive rejection.[50]

Once a lease is assumed, rent under that lease is treated as a priority administrative expense, even if the debtor later decides to reject the lease.[51]

Unless the court orders otherwise, Bankruptcy Code § 365(d)(1) requires Chapter 11 trustees to perform the debtor's obligations under an unexpired personal property lease arising 60 days after the order of relief and until the lease is assumed or rejected. The Fourth Circuit held that the lessor of personal property is entitled to get all past due payments in the post-60-day period; the lessor is not required to show that the lease payments are actual and necessary expenses of preserving the estate.[52]

Bankruptcy Code § 365, dealing with rejection of executory contracts, applies to contracts the debtor entered into pre-petition. For contracts entered into by the estate post-petition, the trustee is simply one more party that can be subjected to normal remedies, including specific performance.[53]

A 2006 Ninth Circuit case permits a trustee who rejects a commercial lease to recover the remaining security deposit. In the Ninth Circuit view, rejection constitutes waiver of future benefits under the lease, but does not rescind the lease or eliminate claims or defenses that the debtor had with respect to the lease.[54]

The "strong arm clause" (BCode § 544) gives the trustee the power to avoid transfers governed by state law, such as unrecorded security interests. Also see § 1513 for the trustee's power to avoid improper transfers. The strong arm clause (Code § 544) does not give the trustee the power to defeat the exemption for property held by the entireties with a spouse. The Fourth Circuit would not permit the trustee to claim to be in the same position as the IRS, because the IRS is not a creditor that extends credit as defined by § 544.[55]

BFP v. Resolution Trust Corp.[56] holds that a regularly conducted, non-collusive foreclosure sale, or a foreclosure sale on behalf of an Article 9 secured creditor, cannot be avoided, but BFP is a narrow decision that is inapplicable to tax lien executions and other creditors' remedies that do not include auctions.

Section 545 permits avoidance of certain statutory liens, even if they have already been enforced by sale of the encumbered property: for instance, liens that became effective upon the insolvency of the debtor; liens that could be defeated by a bona fide purchaser; and liens for rent.[57]

---

[50] Adelphia Bus. Solutions, Inc. v. Abnos, 482 F.3d 602 (2d Cir. 2007). Pacific Shores Dev, LLC v at Home Corp., 392 F.3d 1064 (9th Cir. 2004) cites equitable authority and EOP-Colonnade of Dallas Ltd Pship v. Faulker, 430 F.3d 260 (5th Cir. 2005) suggests its applicability.

[51] *In re* Klein Sleep Prods., 78 F.3d 18 (2d Cir. 1994).

[52] CT Communications Corp. v. Midway Airlines Inc., 406 F.3d 229 (4th Cir. 2005).

[53] *In re* Kreger, 296 B.R. 2002 (D. Minn. 2003).

[54] First Avenue West Building LLC v. James, 439 F.3d 558 (9th Cir. 2006).

[55] Schlossberg v. Barney, 380 F.3d 174 (4th Cir. 2004).

[56] 511 U.S. 531 (1994).

[57] Also note that IRC § 6323(a) provides that an unfiled or improperly filed tax lien is not valid against a purchaser or judgment lien creditor.

For Chapter 7, but not for Chapter 13, BCode § 724(a) permits avoidance of liens imposed for penalties, fines, and punitive damages imposed on the debtor, to the extent that the amount secured by the lien does **not** represent compensation for pecuniary loss. This is broad enough to permit avoidance of a tax lien securing late-payment penalties.

Section 522(j) specifies that avoidance operates only up to the limit of the exemption permitted for the particular category of property. To the extent the debtor could exempt the property, however, § 522(i)(2) provides that property can be preserved for the benefit of the debtor after a transfer has been avoided or the trustee has recovered property.

The general rule of BCode § 550 is that property can be recovered after avoidance from either the initial or a subsequent transferee.

The statute of limitations for an avoidance action is two years after entry of the order for relief (this is usually the bankruptcy petition), one year after appointment of the trustee, or the time the case is closed or dismissed — whichever comes first: BCode § 546.

[A] Employee Benefits

The BAPCPA adds protections for employees of bankrupt companies, a trend continued by the Pension Protection Act, P.L. 109-116 (PPA). For example, PPA § 116 provides that if a pension plan maintained by a bankrupt employer is severely underfunded (the new current funding limitation percentage is under 60%), any increase in benefits must be delayed until the percentage reaches 60%, with additional limitations based on the asset:liability ratio. This is another issue that will have to be re-examined in light of post-2008 market and business conditions.

§ 15.11 IMPACT OF BANKRUPTCY ON SECURED CREDITORS

Pre-BAPCPA law could be harsh to secured creditors. The automatic stay usually prevents the creation, perfection, or enforcement of a lien once the petition has been filed. Turnover under §§ 542 and 543 often permits the debtor to get back property from a creditor who obtained possession before commencement of the bankruptcy case.

Bankruptcy Code § 506 defines an "allowed secured claim" as a claim secured by a lien or setoff, to the extent of the creditor's interest. Any difference between the claim and the creditor's interest operates as an allowed unsecured claim. Thus, the claim is bifurcated into "collateral" (what the creditor would get by enforcing its claim) and everything else.[58]

---

[58] Revised 9-204(c) of the UCC authorizes a comprehensive "dragnet" clause that makes the security interest also secure any other loans — including credit card loans — the borrower has obtained from the lender. The lender can secure the credit card debt even though the lender's proof of claim described that debt as unsecured. For bankruptcy purposes, a claim is secured if the collateral is in the bankruptcy estate, unsecured if the collateral is not. *In re* Nagata, 2006 WL 2131318 (Bankr. D. Haw. 7/20/06).

The rule of *Dewsnup v. Timm*[59] is that a Chapter 7 debtor cannot have a lien voided even though the claim did not fit the definition of "allowed secured claim." In this reading, § 506(d) can be applied only if the lien secures a claim that was disallowed under § 502, such as a claim to which the debtor has a valid defense. Bankruptcy Code § 506(a) says an allowed claim is secured only to the extent of the value of the collateral, and § 506(d) voids a lien to the extent that it is not an allowed secured claim. Reading the two sections together, the Sixth Circuit ruled in 2003 that a Chapter 7 debtor cannot strip off an unsecured junior lien on residential property if the senior lien is larger than the fair market value of the property. *Dewsnup* forbids stripping off a totally unsecured second mortgage as well as a strip-down of a partially unsecured first mortgage.[60] Sales before confirmation of the debtor's plan of reorganization do not qualify for the BCode § 1146(c) exemption from state and local transfer taxes. The exemption is available only to a "confirmed" Chapter 11 plan.[61]

The Third Circuit adopted the "gavel rule," under which the right to cure mortgage defaults ends when the property is auctioned, although some courts permit cure until delivery of the deed. The Third Circuit said the gavel rule has the better policy rationale, because the homeowner receives notice of the auction but not of delivery of the deed.[62]

Two early 2007 Chapter 13 cases from the Fourth Circuit resulted in differing results when the trustees sought to modify a confirmed plan to increase the amount payable to unsecured creditors. In the *Goralski* case, a debtor's income was cut in half, so he and his wife couldn't keep up with the plan and still meet their living expenses. They were permitted to refinance their home mortgage, and got some equity in cash in exchange for debt. The Chapter 13 trustee wanted some of this money to go to the unsecured creditors. In the *Murphy* case, court permission was granted to sell his condominium. Post-confirmation increase in value would give him $80,000 in cash; the trustee wanted $18,000 of that to pay the unsecured creditors in full. The motion to modify was granted in Murphy's case, but not the Goralskis'. A Chapter 13 plan can be structured either as a percentage plan, designating the percentage going to each unsecured creditor, without specifying the exact amount the debtor must pay, whereas a pot plan orders payment of a certain amount, with the unsecured creditors' percentages remaining open until the claims are approved. Both of these were pot plans. BCode § 1329 permits modification of a confirmed plan until payments are completed, but res judicata prevents the plan (which is contractual in nature) from being modified unless the bankruptcy court determines that the debtor experienced a post-confirmation substantial, unanticipated financial change. The Goralskis converted some of their equity to cash,

---

[59] 502 U.S. 410 (1992).

[60] Talbert v. City Mort. Servs., 344 F.3d 555 (6th Cir. 2003).

[61] Illinois v. National Steel Corp., #03 C 3932, 72 L.W. 1183 (N.D. Ill. 9/8/03).

[62] *In re* Connors, 497 F.3d 314 (3d Cir. 2007); *see* Mary Pat Gallagher, *3rd Circuit: Time to Cure Mortgage Default Ends at Auction*, N.J.L.J. 8/10/07 (law.com). Semble Cain v. Wells Fargo Bank, 423 F.3d 617 (6th Cir. 2005).

but also increased their debt, so the plan could not be modified; Murphy's plan could be modified because he received significant amounts of cash with no increase in debt.[63]

The Tenth Circuit decided, in 2007 that, after a conversion, a Chapter 7 trustee cannot bring claims that the Chapter 11 debtor-in-possession could not (in this case, a derivative claim on behalf of the creditors' committee). After conversion, a Chapter 7 trustee cannot assert rights that were waived by the DIP prior to the conversion, and DIPs often have to surrender some rights of the estate to obtain financing to continue the business. If the creditor's committee has objections, it should raise them to the financing order, or seek to defer the conversion until it can bring an avoidance action. The conversion to Chapter 7 terminates the Chapter 11 committee — and with it, the committee's right to bring an avoidance action.[64]

§ 15.12 VALUATION OF PROPERTY

The value of prior liens must be subtracted in valuing claims, with the result that the allowed secured claim will be $0 if the other liens exceed the value of the collateral.

Nobelman v. American Savings Bank, 508 U.S. 324 (1993), allows liens to be "stripped down" — reduced to the value of their collateral — in Chapter 13.

To prevent windfalls, the First Circuit requires that whenever a debtor strips down a mortgage (thus frustrating the interests of unsecured creditors), is discharged, and then sells the mortgaged property, all proceeds above the stripped value must be disgorged.[65]

§ 15.13 IMPROPER TRANSFERS

The Bankruptcy Code includes provisions for dealing with two types of transfers made by a debtor that have undue negative impact on the ability of creditors to receive repayment: preferential transfers and fraudulent conveyances. A secured creditor can object, under § 523(a)(2)(A), to the discharge of a particular claim, based on proof that the debtor willfully and maliciously converted the collateral.

[A] Preferential Transfers

A preferential transfer is not necessarily wrongful per se, but it is unfair when the interests of other creditors are considered. A transaction by the debtor constitutes an avoidable preference that can be reversed by the trustee if:

- It was made at a time when the debtor was insolvent
- It is made to a creditor for a pre-existing debt (i.e., is not the purchase of new items)

---

[63] *In re* Murphy, 474 F.3d 143, *In re* Goralski, 474 F.3d 173 (both 4th Cir. 2007).
[64] *In re* MS55, Inc. (MS55 Inc. v. Akamai Technologies, Inc.), 477 F.3d 1131 (10th Cir. 2007).
[65] Barbosa v. Soloman, 235 F.3d 312 (1st Cir. 2000).

- It gives the creditor a higher percentage of repayment than Chapter 7 would allow
- It is made less than 90 days before the bankruptcy filing—or less than one year, if the receiving creditor is an "insider" (related to the debtor by blood or business relationship).

Bankruptcy Code § 547(c) provides that substantially contemporaneous exchanges for new value are not preferences; nor are payments of debts in the debtor's ordinary course of business or financial operations. Secured creditors who provided funds to keep a corporation afloat can be considered the BCode § 550 estate for whose benefit preferential transfers can be recouped, because indirect benefit to the estate is sufficient to permit recoupment.

The Supreme Court held that the states' ratification of the bankruptcy clause of the Constitution constituted waiver of sovereign immunity. Therefore, the defense could not be raised when bankruptcy trustees asserted that Virginia state colleges received preferential transfers from an insolvent bookstore.[66]

The Supreme Court has held that the determination (under BCode § 547(c)(3)(B)) as to whether a security interest was perfected within 20 days of a transfer (i.e., is not preferential) is not affected by a state relation-back statute that makes the preference period longer than 20 days.[67]

The Bankruptcy Code § 547(c)(2)(C) "ordinary course of business" defense to preferential transfers extends to the full, broad range of practices that are not deemed unusual within an industry. The defense is not limited to transactions that are average for the industry.[68]

[B] Fraudulent Conveyances

Bankruptcy Code § 523(a)(6) gives the trustee the power to recover fraudulent conveyances (i.e., bring the transferred assets back into the bankruptcy estate). The trustee can avoid fraudulent conveyances under § 544 (also see § 548).

Under § 548, the trustee can set aside fraudulent conveyances, which are defined as transfers or obligations:

- Entered into within the year before filing of the bankruptcy petition
- Whose purpose is hindering, defrauding, or delaying creditors;

Or,

- The debtor did not receive fair value for an obligation incurred at a time when the debtor was insolvent or was about to incur debts the debtor was unable to repay

---

[66] Central Va. Community Coll. v. Katz, 546 U.S. 356 (2006).
[67] Fidelity Fin. Servs. Inc. v. Fink, 522 U.S. 211 (1998).
[68] Ganis Credit Corp. v. Anderson, 315 F.3d 1192 (9th Cir. 2003).

- A business debtor was about to engage in business or transactions while having unreasonably small capital
- The debtor intended to incur or believed he, she, or it would incur debts beyond the ability to pay.[69]

There is a rebuttable presumption that cash advances and luxury goods and services were acquired fraudulently if the debtor acquired a debt of $1,150 or more owed to a single creditor during the 60 days before filing of the petition: § 523(a)(2)(C). The solution is to defer filing of the petition until 60 days have passed since the last such transaction.

Also note that the debtor (not the trustee) can set aside a transfer made involuntarily (e.g., property was repossessed); the property could have been exempt (see § 15.06); and the debtor did not conceal the property: BCode § 522(h).

The Bankruptcy Code was amended in 2000 to prevent exemption of any student loan debt relating to fraud.

§ 15.14 DISCHARGE

Discharge is barred under BCode § 523 for debts arising out of various kinds of wrongful or inappropriate behavior, e.g.,

- Property obtained by fraud (§ 523(a)(2))[70]
- Liability arising out of fiduciary wrongdoing (§ 523(a)(4))
- Willful or malicious injury to others (§ 523(a)(6))[71]
- Debts that the debtor failed to list on the schedules filed with the bankruptcy petition (§ 523(a)(3)).

Discharge is also unavailable for certain obligations that are deemed especially important:

- Certain tax obligations (§ 523(a)(1))
- Alimony, maintenance, and support obligations (§§ 523(a)(5) and (18), as modified by (a)(15))

---

[69] According to Rembert v. AT&T Universal Card Serv., 141 F.3d 277 (6th Cir. 1998), the test is the debtor's subjective intent to avoid repayment, ascertained by the totality of the circumstances. Mere inability to repay at the time the debt is incurred is not enough.

[70] A debtor's obligation to pay treble damages to tenants because of rent overcharges cannot be discharged. The entire sum, including fees and costs, stems from "actual fraud" and thus is non-dischargeable: Cohen v. DeLaCruz, 523 U.S. 213 (1998).

[71] *But see* Kawaauhau v. Geiger, 523 U.S. 57 (1998): a medical malpractice judgment obtained based on a doctor's gross errors is nevertheless dischargeable in bankruptcy, because even egregious malpractice does not constitute willful or malicious injury, in that there was no desire to injure the patient.

- Student loans made or guaranteed by a government agency or not-for-profit organization (§ 523(a)(8)), although discharge can be granted on the basis of undue hardship to the debtor or debtor's dependents
- Court filing fees (§ 523(a)(17)).

FRBP 4004's time limit for filing objections to discharge has been held by the Supreme Court to be a claim processing rule. It is not jurisdictional. If it is not raised timely, it can be waived, and the debtor will no longer be able to challenge a creditor's amended complaint.[72]

Attempts to collect discharged debts violate FDCPA and state debt collection statutes, and also may be a tort under state law. According to the Seventh Circuit, the remedies of the Bankruptcy Code and the FDCPA (see § 14.05) are intended to overlap, and the Bankruptcy Code does not preempt FDCPA remedies. Therefore, the FDCPA can be used against a debt collector who wrongfully attempts to collect from a debtor who has filed for bankruptcy protection.[73]

The First Circuit ruled that a creditor's general awareness of bankruptcy is not enough to impose a burden to intervene in the bankruptcy proceeding; a creditor is entitled to assume that it will be notified before its claim is extinguished. Bankruptcy distinguishes between known creditors who must be notified at each stage and unknown creditors, for whom notice by publication is sufficient. In this case, a known creditor did not have actual knowledge of the bar date, confirmation hearing, or the details of the plan, so the creditor could not be held in contempt for continuing to press claims after the debtor's discharge.[74]

Nine Circuits have followed the Second Circuit test for hardship discharge: the debtor must show inability, at his or her current level of income and expenses, to maintain a minimal standard of living. The debtor must show the likelihood that this state of affairs will persist for a significant portion of the repayment period, and there must be good-faith efforts to repay. However, the Eighth Circuit uses a totality-of-circumstances test.

In mid-2003, the Third Circuit made it more difficult for debtors to assert undue hardship to obtain forgiveness of student loans.[75] The Third Circuit, like the Second, Sixth, and Ninth, requires the bankruptcy court to consider whether the debtor incurred substantial expenses beyond basic necessities, and whether the debtor attempted to restructure the loan before filing for bankruptcy protection.[76]

---

[72] Kontrick v. Ryan, 540 U.S. 443 (2004).

[73] Randolph v. IMBS Inc., 368 F.3d 726 (7th Cir. 2004).

[74] *In re* Arch Wireless, Inc., 534 F.3d 76 (1st Cir. 2008).

[75] *See* Pennsylvania Higher Educ. Assistance Agency v. Faish, 72 F.3d 298 (3d Cir. 1995). According to the Ninth Circuit, determinations about undue hardship with respect to discharge of student loans in a Chapter 13 plan are appropriate well before the plan is completed. Although some courts require waiting until the plan is complete, the Ninth Circuit said that the determination can be made much earlier, based on evidence of whether there has been a good-faith effort to repay: *In re* Coleman, No. 06-16477 (9th Cir. 8/1/08).

[76] Pelliccia v. United States Dep't of Educ., 67 Fed. Appx. 88 (3d Cir. 2003).

According to the Ninth Circuit, Bankruptcy Code § 105(a) gives the bankruptcy courts equitable authority to grant a partial discharge of student loan debt to the extent that the discharged portion creates undue hardship; the standards for partial and full discharge are the same.[77]

In mid-2004, the Supreme Court refused to deal with the Eleventh Amendment issue, but ruled that discharge of student loan debt that was guaranteed by a state agency does not involve the state's immunity. The discharge does not waive the state's ordinary immunity from suit, but, in effect, a state can be required to participate in bankruptcy proceedings against its wishes.[78]

On a related issue — dischargeability of Health Education Assistance Loans — the Fourth Circuit ruled late in 2003 that discharge is available only by satisfying the stringent 42 USC § 292f(g) requirement that it would be unconscionable not to discharge the liability, based on the totality of circumstances affecting the debtor and his or her obligations. Relevant factors include income, earning potential, assets, age, health, educational background, and family situation. In most cases, discharge is denied.[79]

[A] Exceptions to Discharge

As noted above, family-related obligations are considered quite important, and the general rule of BCode § 523(a)(5) is that a discharge in bankruptcy does not discharge any debt owed to a spouse, ex-spouse, or child that actually is for support, maintenance, or alimony provided by a separation agreement or court order. But like most rules this has an exception: § 523(a)(15) makes discharge of such debts permissible if the debtor lacks the ability to pay, or if the benefit of the discharge to the debtor outweighs the detriment to the spouse, ex-spouse, or children. The needs of a new spouse or cohabitant are considered.

The Supreme Court's March 2002 decision in *Young v. U.S.*,[80] requires tolling of the 11 USC § 507(g)(8)(A)(ii) look-back period for Chapter 7 debtors during the pendency of an earlier, dismissed Chapter 13 petition. In this case, the debt was for taxes for which a return was due three years before filing. It would not have been dischargeable if the Chapter 13 proceeding had been completed. The Chapter 13 automatic stay precluded IRS enforcement action.

Bankruptcy Code § 523(a)(1)(B), provides that tax debts are not dischargeable if no "return" was filed, but does not define "return." According to the Sixth

---

[77] Saxman v. Educational Credit Mgmt. Corp., 325 F.3d 1168 (9th Cir. 2003). The Sixth Circuit allows a Bankruptcy Court to grant a partial discharge of student loan debt, but only to the extent that the discharged portion imposes an undue hardship: Miller v. Pennsylvania Higher Educ. Auth., 377 F.3d 616 (6th Cir. 2004). *See also* Department of Educ. v. Blair, 301 B.R. 181 (D. Md. 2003) (denying a two-year moratorium on student loan obligations for failure to prove undue hardship; the court treated the moratorium as a partial discharge because of its effect on the creditor's ability to collect interest).

[78] Tennessee Student Assistance Corp. v. Hood, 541 U.S. 440 (2004).

[79] DHHS v. Smitley, 347 F.3d 109 (4th Cir. 2003).

[80] 533 U.S. 43 (2002).

and Ninth Circuits, a return is a document that: purports to be a return; is signed under penalty of perjury; provides enough data for the tax to be calculated; and is an honest and reasonable attempt to comply with the requirements of tax law. The Fourth Circuit considered delay as one element in determining if a return was filed, and rejected the argument that the IRS abated some of the taxpayer's debt proved that the document was reasonable and honest.[81]

The Supreme Court returned to the subject of exceptions to discharge in 2003. The Court held that a debt owed under a settlement agreement under which a fraud claim was released in return for promise to pay on a promissory note was not dischargeable, because the debt was obtained by fraud.[82]

The Sarbanes-Oxley Act (P.L. 107-204) amends 11 USC § 5623(a) by adding a new subsection (19): a debt resulting from a judgment, order, consent order, decree, or settlement is nondischargeable if it arose in connection with violation of state or federal securities laws, or common-law fraud, deceit, or manipulation in connection with the purchase or sale of any security.

Even outside the Sarbanes-Oxley context, discharge is also unavailable if the debt arises out of "willful and malicious injury." The Ninth Circuit ruled that intentional breach of contract is nondischargeable under BCode § 523(a)(6) if and only if it involves conduct that constitutes a tort under state law. After a malpractice suit, an attorney settled with the former client-plaintiff, assigning 50% of attorneys' fees from the attorney's personal injury case load. Then the lawyer refused to abide by the agreement, taking the position that his ex-client did not have a valid claim, and filed a Chapter 7 bankruptcy petition. The ex-client sought a declaration that the breach of contract was nondischargeable. The Ninth Circuit ruled that willful failure to pay contract debts is not tortious, and there was no fiduciary relationship between the two, because the settlement agreement was not part of the attorney-client relationship.[83]

The Bankruptcy Court found a judgment for willful copyright infringement nondischargeable under BCode § 523(a)(6), as a willful and malicious injury, because the jury found willful infringement. The BAPS (Bankruptcy Appeal Services) treated willful infringement as nondischargeable as a categorically harmful activity. However, the Ninth Circuit reversed, holding that there was a genuine issue of material fact, and precedent in that Circuit requires separate consideration of the malice requirement and the willfulness requirement.[84] The Eighth Circuit held that judgment debt from an employment case (sexual harassment, constructive discharge, and retaliation) could not be discharged; the jury that ruled for the plaintiff found that the defendant deliberately and intentionally inflicted injury on the plaintiff.[85]

---

[81] Moroney v. United States, 352 F.3d 902 (4th Cir. 2003); *see also In re* Payne, 431 F.3d 1055 (7th Cir. 2005).

[82] Archer v. Warner, 538 U.S. 314 (2003).

[83] Lockerby v. Sierra, No. 06-15928 (9th Cir. 8/7/08).

[84] *In re* Barboza, No. 06-56319 (9th Cir. 9/23/08).

[85] Porter v. Sells, 539 F.3d 889 (8th Cir. 2008).

The Tenth Circuit ruled that BCode § 523(a)(7) does not forbid discharge of a default judgment entered against the Chapter 7 debtor when he guaranteed a bail bond, and the defendant jumped bail. The debtor was a mere guarantor, not the bail-jumping defendant, so the debt could be discharged.[86]

Under extreme circumstances, a discharge can be revoked after it is granted. The Fourth Circuit considered the standard of "intransigence" for revoking a discharge in 2008. The debtor filed a Chapter 7 petition, and the Bankruptcy Court issued the standard administrative order forbidding sale or transfer of the property without the trustee's approval, and the standard warning that the discharge could be revoked for cause. The trustee accepted the figures submitted by the debtor at the initial creditors' meeting: equity of $5,000 (claimed as exempt) and FMV of $225,000. The trustee's own market analysis showed a value of $250,000 and net post-sale value of $1,264, which the trustee considered too small to be worth holding a sale. The debtor obtained a discharge in 2005.The debtor refinanced the house (without the trustee's consent or even knowledge), paying off two mortgages and receiving about $15,000 cash; a deed of trust for $231,000 was recorded. The trustee then received an offer of $227,000 and made an application to sell it. When he discovered the refinancing, he withdrew the application to sell and moved to revoke the discharge for failure to comply with the court order. The Bankruptcy Court, affirmed by the District Court, revoked the discharge, but the Fourth Circuit reversed, finding revocation to be a harsh measure applicable only in extraordinary cases where the debtor refuses rather than just fails to comply.[87]

§ 15.15 ATTORNEYS' FEES

The GAO reported in mid-2008 that attorneys' fees for individual Chapter 7 cases rose about 50% since BAPCPA took effect (from an average of $712 in 2005 to $1,078 in 2007); for Chapter 13, the median pre-BAPCPA fee was $2,000 versus $3,000 after BAPCPA, reflecting the increased amount of work created by the statute, especially in connection with the means test. Implementing the means test was also expensive for the federal government; the Department of Justice spent $72.4 million upgrading the U.S. Trustee Program to handle BAPCPA, and $42 million of that amount was spent to implement the means test. From 2007 to 2008, bankruptcy filing fees rose by $90 (to $299) for Chapter 7, and by $80, to $274, for Chapter 13.[88]

Early in 2004, the Supreme Court ruled that Bankruptcy Code § 330(a)(1) authorizes a fee award to the debtor's attorney out of the funds of the estate only if

---

[86] *In re* Sandoval, 541 F.3d 997 (10th Cir. 2008).

[87] *In re* Jordan, 521 F.3d 430 (4th Cir. 2008). *See also* White v. Nielsen, 383 F.3d 922 (9th Cir. 2004), where the court refused to revoke a discharge for failure to list the largest unsecured creditor in the Chapter 7 mailing matrix. Even though that creditor did not receive notice, the discharge could not be said to have been obtained by fraud.

[88] Jacqueline Palank, *Filing for Bankruptcy Becomes More Costly*, Wall St. J. 7/31/08 at D4.

the employment of the attorney is authorized under Bankruptcy Code § 327. Therefore, the attorney must be employed by the trustee, and the hiring must be approved by the court. The attorney in this case lost entitlement to a fee, because he was hired by a Chapter 11 Debtor in Possession, and the case was subsequently converted to Chapter 7.[89]

The Supreme Court, reversing an earlier precedent, ruled that contract-based attorneys' fee claims can be asserted in bankruptcy, because a contract that is enforceable under substantive non-bankruptcy law is also enforceable in bankruptcy unless the Bankruptcy Code rules it out. BCode § 502(b) lists nine exceptions to allowable creditors' claims, but the situation of this case (fees authorized in an indemnity agreement that became the subject of litigation) does not fall under any of them.[90]

According to the Seventh Circuit, Bankruptcy Code § 727 allows discharge of attorneys' fees, whether they were rendered for pre- or post-petition legal services. The entire agreement reached pre-petition, calling for some payments before and some after bankruptcy filing, can be discharged, even if the amount of the fee is reasonable. The Seventh Circuit overruled the Bankruptcy Court, which had cited § 329(b) as authority for the proposition that reasonable fees cannot be discharged.[91]

BCode § 328(a)'s provisions on retainers hourly rates, and contingency fees — and not the § 330(a)(1) lodestar — is the proper criterion for reviewing a special counsel's application for legal fees submitted to the trustee.[92]

Bankruptcy Code § 506 allows the holder of an oversecured claim to recover any reasonable fee provided by the agreement that created the claim. In the Eleventh Circuit view, the bankruptcy court has to determine the reasonableness of attorneys' fees, even if the fees are enforceable under state law. The reasonable part of the fee then becomes a secured claim, whereas any unreasonable balance operates as an unsecured claim.[93]

Because federal and state bar admissions are separate, an Illinois lawyer who is admitted before the District of Arizona but not in the Arizona state courts is entitled to receive fees for work before the Bankruptcy Court of the District of Arizona.[94]

---

[89] Lamie v. United States Trustee, 540 U.S. 526 (2004). *See also* Fickling v. Flower, Medabe & Markowitz, 361 F.3d 172 (2d Cir. 2004) (holding that debt for attorneys' fees earned in a Chapter 11 case before its involuntary conversion to Chapter 7 is pre-petition debt and therefore dischargeable and cannot be recovered from the Chapter 7 debtor; the fees are not a Bankruptcy Code § 503(b) administrative expense, and § 329 — the bankruptcy court's authority to review the reasonableness of fees — does not preclude the discharge).

[90] Travelers Casualty & Surety Co. of America v. Pacific Gas & Electric Co., 549 U.S. 443 (2007); the reversed precedent is In re Fobian, 951 F. 2d 1149 (9th Cir. 1991).

[91] Bethea v. Robert J. Adams & Assoc's, 352 F.3d 1125 (7th Cir. 2003).

[92] Peele v. Cunningham, 218 F.3d 443 (5th Cir. 2000). *See also* Committee of Equity Security Holders of Federal-Mogul Corp. v. Official Committee of Unsecured Creditors, 348 F.3d 390 (3d Cir. 2003).

[93] Welzel v. Advocate Realty Investments LLC, 275 F.3d 1308 (11th Cir. 2001).

[94] Brown v. Smith, 222 F.3d 618 (9th Cir. 2000).

Section 330(a) of the Bankruptcy Code has been amended to remove the phrase "or the debtor's attorney" from the list of people eligible to get fees for post-petition services. However, a 1999 case from the Ninth Circuit treats this as a scrivener's error, saying that the deleting was inadvertent and renders the statutory language ambiguous.[95]

In contrast, the Fifth and Eleventh Circuits and some Bankruptcy Courts have ruled that the language is not ambiguous and the fee award is precluded.[96] In the Ninth Circuit view, before 1994, it was clear that Chapter 7 attorneys could collect fees for post-petition services. After the amendment, the list of categories eligible for reasonable compensation is different from the classes to whom the court may award payment, and the sentence as it stands is grammatically incorrect.

The Ninth Circuit ruled that a breach of contract claim under a commercial property sublease is not entitled to administrative expense priority. Bankruptcy Code § 365(d)(3) is not applicable to debtor-lessors. Nor is the BCode § 503(b)(1)(A) priority available, because the claim does not come from a post-petition transaction, and it does not benefit the debtor's estate.[97]

§ 15.16 BANKRUPTCY APPEALS

Technically, bankruptcy courts are units of the federal District Court. Appeals of their final judgments, orders, and decrees go to the District Court as a whole, except in Circuits in which some or all districts have BAPS (Bankruptcy Appeal Services).

BAPS panels consist of three bankruptcy judges. BAPS have been created in the First, Second, Sixth, Eighth, Ninth, and Tenth Circuits. Bankruptcy court orders can be appealed to the BAPS instead of to the District Court on consent of all parties, and if the District Court judges for that district permit. Appeals from the BAPS (as well as the District Court) go to the Court of Appeals: BCode § 158(d).

BAPCPA enacted 28 USC § 158(d)(2), under which a Circuit Court can directly review a Bankruptcy Court judgment, order, or decree if:

- The Bankruptcy Court or District Court certifies there is no controlling Supreme Court or Court of Appeals ruling (or the precedents are in conflict)
- The case involves a matter of public importance
- An immediate appeal could materially advance the progress of the bankruptcy proceeding.

---

[95] U.S. Trustee v. Gainey, Schubert & Barer, 195 F.3d 1053 (9th Cir. 1999); *In re* Top Grade Sausage, 227 F.3d 123 (3d Cir. 2000) and the cases cited therein.

[96] Falligant, Horne, Covington & Nash PC v. Moore, 197 F.3d 1354 (11th Cir. 1999); Andrews & Kurtz LLP v. Family Snacks Inc., 157 F.3d 414 (5th Cir. 1998).

[97] Einstein/Noah Bagel Corp. v. Smith, 319 F.3d 1166 (9th Cir. 2003).

The 2006 proposed amendment to Rule 8001: permits direct appeal to the Court of Appeals based on certification by any of the courts involved in bankruptcy; Rule 8003 treats the certification as the equivalent of leave to appeal, even if no motion for leave to appeal has been filed.

Bankruptcy appeals are subject to the Federal Rules of Appellate Procedure; see especially Rule 6, appeal from a final judgment, order, or decree of a District Court or BAP.

An appellate court reviews District Court and Bankruptcy Court determinations of law de novo, and reviews Bankruptcy Court factual determinations for clear error.[98]

§ 15.17   TAX ISSUES IN BANKRUPTCY

Internal Revenue Code § 1398 provides that the bankruptcy estate itself is a taxpayer, with individual rules for deductions and other tax compliance issues. For instance, the bankruptcy estate is entitled to use the IRC § 121 capital gains exclusion for sale of a principal residence, just as the debtor him or herself would be, because the residence becomes part of the bankruptcy estate.

Although IRC § 6658(a) states that additions to tax are not imposed for failure to make timely payments when a bankruptcy case is "pending," there is no statutory definition of that term. Rev. Rul. 2005-9, 2005-6 IRB 470 fills the gap by stating that a case ceases to be pending when it has been closed or dismissed by the court.

In the spring of 2004, the Ninth Circuit joined the Eleventh Circuit in holding that whether or not the IRS' claim is secured, an IRS claim for unpaid trust fund taxes (e.g., Social Security taxes) cannot be discharged by a confirmed Chapter 11 plan. Confirmation of the plan is not res judicata as to the IRS' claim. Nor did the confirmation discharge the obligation to pay "gap period" interest on federal income taxes; the gap period runs from filing of the petition to the time of its confirmation.[99]

The IRS is obligated to make an immediate assessment of tax, interest, and penalties, under IRC § 6871 (even if the 90-day letter has not yet issued) if the taxpayer is declared bankrupt in a liquidation proceeding; if any other bankruptcy petition has been filed by or against the taxpayer; or if a receiver has been appointed for the taxpayer.

IRC § 108 permits an insolvent debtor to exclude discharged liabilities from income. Insolvency is defined as having liabilities in excess of the fair market value of assets. In addition, the Mortgage Forgiveness Debt Relief Act, P.L. 110-142, provides for an exclusion from gross income for tax purposes for taxpayers who lose their homes to foreclosure. However, this exclusion does not apply to taxpayers in Chapter 11; the existing IRC exclusion continues to apply. Taxpayers

---

[98] Drive Fin. Servs., LP v. Jordan, 521 F.3d 343 (5th Cir. 2008). BAPs use similar standards in reviewing Bankruptcy Court determinations: Audre, Inc. v. Casey, 219 B.R. 19 (9th Cir. 1997).

[99] Miller v. United States, 363 F.3d 999 (9th Cir. 2004).

who are insolvent, but not in bankruptcy, are entitled to the P.L. 110-142 exclusion unless they elect to apply § 108(a)(1)(A).

BCode § 505(a) authorizes bankruptcy courts to redetermine a debtor's tax liability — whereas TEFRA, the 1982 federal tax legislation, requires the tax treatment of partnership items to be determined at the partnership level. The federal government submitted a $13.1 million tax claim in a Chapter 11 case. The District Court held that it did not have subject matter jurisdiction over any partnership item administratively determined by the IRS. The Ninth Circuit disagreed, holding that 11 USC § 505(a)(1) gives District Courts subject matter jurisdiction to review the tax treatment of partnership items.[100]

Real estate taxes assessed after filing of the petition are "incurred" by the estate, and therefore take first priority as administrative expenses.[101]

In addition to income and real estate taxes, bankruptcy cases may give rise to local "stamp taxes" on transactions. After a corporation made a Chapter 11 filing, but before its plan was submitted to the Bankruptcy Court, the Bankruptcy Court allowed the corporation to sell its assets, approved a settlement agreement with its creditors, and granted a tax-stamp exemption under BCode § 1146(a) [assets transfers under a confirmed plan]. The Chapter 11 plan was filed after the sale. The Florida Department of Revenue objected to confirmation of the plan, on the grounds that the transfers were not exempt from stamp tax because the plan had not yet been confirmed. The Eleventh Circuit ruled for the corporation, but the Supreme Court reversed, limiting the exemption to transfers made pursuant to a plan that has already been conferred, not transfers necessary to carrying out the plan.[102]

PART 2: BAPCPA

§ 15.18 BAPCPA GENERALLY

The 2005 enactment of BAPCPA (P.L. 109-8; signed April 20, 2005) marks the first major revision of the Bankruptcy Code in 25 years.[103]

BAPCPA makes many changes to consumer bankruptcy, and imposes many new requirements on bankruptcy lawyers. The changes to business bankruptcy are somewhat less dramatic, but the statute concentrates on small business bankruptcy.

Although it does not eliminate individual Chapter 11 cases, BAPCPA makes them more like Chapter 13 cases. All property acquired between the

---

[100] Central Valley Ag Enters. v. United States, 531 F.3d 750 (9th Cir. 2008).

[101] White Plains v. A&S Galleria Real Estate Inc., 270 F.3d 994 (6th Cir. 2001).

[102] Fla. Dep't of Revenue v. Piccadilly Cafeterias, Inc., 128 S. Ct. 2326 (2008).

[103] Official Forms can be found at http://www.uscourts.gov/rules/BK_Official_Forms.pdf. Interim rules reflecting BAPCPA's effect on practice can be found at http://www.uscourts.gov/rules/interim.htm. The interim rules are discussed in this chapter at § 15.01[A]. *See* http://ustnet/bankruptcy/bankruptcy_reform/bci_data.htm (no www) for Census Bureau and IRS financial data. In addition to the BAPCPA changes, see the Deficit Reduction Act of 2005, P.L. 109-171 § 10002, for amendments to 28 U.S.C. § 1930(a)(1) increasing bankruptcy fees.

commencement and the closing of the case becomes property of the estate, and so do all of the debtor's earnings from services after commencement (new Bankruptcy Code § 1115). Under the newly enacted Bankruptcy Code § 365(p)(3), if a lease is not assumed in an individual Chapter 11 case, the lease is deemed rejected as of the conclusion of the confirmation hearing — and the automatic stay is terminated. Unless the court orders otherwise for cause, there can be no discharge in Chapter 11 until all of the plan payments have been made.[104] The individual Chapter 11 debtor can seek modification of the plan before completion to alter the size of the payments or the time to pay — but Bankruptcy Code § 1127(e) as amended also permits the U.S. Trustee or an unsecured creditor to apply for higher payments or shorter time to pay.

Miscellaneous BAPCPA provisions include protection for patients of healthcare facilities that file for bankruptcy protection. A new Chapter (Chapter 15) on cross-border insolvency cases, based on the U.N. Commission on International Trade Model Law, has been added to the Bankruptcy Code. Some BAPCPA provisions may be getting rather more use in 2008 and later years than Congress intended: BAPCPA Chapter 7 covers liquidation of stockbrokers, commodity brokers, and clearing banks.

For residences purchased within three years and four months of filing, the state homestead exemption is capped at $136,875. BAPCPA also reduces the extent to which trusts can be used to shelter assets in bankruptcy.

On the business side, goods purchased in the ordinary course of business and delivered within 20 days of filing now count as an administrative expense and so, like legal fees, they can be paid on the effective date of the reorganization plan.

Bankruptcy Code § 523(a) as amended expands the categories of debts that cannot be discharged in bankruptcy:

- All domestic support obligations are precluded from discharge in any chapter. Bankruptcy Code § 101(14A) now has a very broad definition of domestic support obligations, and § 1129(a)(14) requires payment in full of domestic support obligations that arise after the filing date, so it will be very difficult or perhaps impossible to use Chapter 11 to get relief from family law property settlements. However, payment of domestic support obligations (including those owed to government agencies) cannot be treated as a preference: Bankruptcy Code § 547(c)(7).
- Debts (e.g., plan loans) owed to a pension, profit sharing, or thrift plan.
- All student loans (whether the lender is governmental or private) unless repayment imposes undue hardship on the debtor and his or her dependents.
- Credit card debts are presumed nondischargeable if they are owed to one creditor for over $550 for luxury goods or services incurred on or within 90 days of filing. Luxury means items not reasonably necessary for the support of the debtor or dependents.

---

[104] Bankruptcy Code § 1141(d)(5).

- The same is true of credit card cash advances over $825 taken on or within 70 days of filing.

It is now a requirement, rather than just a possibility, that the Bankruptcy Court hold status conferences as required for the expeditious resolution of the case.[105]

§15.19 DRAs AND ATTORNEY LIABILITY

BAPCPA makes bankruptcy practice far more onerous, not only by requiring the attorney to undertake significant investigation and file numerous documents, but by imposing heavy penalties for failure. If the attorney falls down on the job, there will be no automatic stay, the case can be dismissed, and fines and/or sanctions can be imposed on the attorney.

BAPCPA introduces the concept of Debt Relief Agencies (DRAs) — individuals and organizations who assist debtors. Although creditors who restructure debts and non-profit organizations qualified as such under the Internal Revenue Code are not considered to be DRAs, bankruptcy attorneys emphatically are.[106]

Bankruptcy Code §526(a) requires DRAs to perform the services they promise and forbids them to make untrue or misleading statements when counseling debtors. Nor may they misrepresent their services or the risks and benefits of filing for bankruptcy protection, or advise clients to take on additional debt to pay for the services of the DRAs.

DRAs are obligated to provide notices in several situations: the notice required by §324(b); a notice informing debtors of their right to proceed pro se. Within three business days of the initial offer of assistance, the DRA must inform the potential client that: debtors must provide complete and accurate data, including full disclosure of assets and liabilities; figures for monthly income and disposable income must reflect reasonable injury; and all information is subject to audit. DRAs must maintain documentation of these notices for two years.[107]

The DRA must provide clients with a written contract explaining services and fees. The contract must be provided within five days of first providing assistance — and before the petition is filed. All advertisements must include the mandatory text, "We are a debt relief agency. We help people file for bankruptcy relief under the Bankruptcy Code."

Failure to comply not merely voids the contract, but can make the DRA liable to the debtor for actual damages, attorneys' fees, and costs if a hearing finds that the DRA intentionally or even negligently failed to comply, or intentionally or negligently disregarded material requirements of the Bankruptcy Code or rules.

---

[105] Bankruptcy Code § 104(d).
[106] Bankruptcy Code § 101(12A).
[107] Bankruptcy Code § 527.

DRAs are subject to the same penalties if a case is dismissed or converted because of their refusal or failure to provide a required document.[108]

Unless the court orders otherwise, the attorney must file the following:

- Certification that the client received the notice required by Bankruptcy Code § 342(b);
- Evidence of the debtor's income for 60 days prior to filing;
- The debtor's itemized statement of monthly net income; and
- The debtor's disclosure of any reasonably anticipated increases in income or expenditures over the course of the twelve months after filing.

If the debtor fails to do any of these within 45 days, Bankruptcy Code § 521(i)(1) says that the case is automatically dismissed on the 46th day; the court "shall" enter an order of dismissal within five days of a request from a party in interest. Statement of intention to surrender the property, or to retain it (and, if retained, whether it will be redeemed or the obligation will be reaffirmed):

- The debtor must file a certificate from an approved budget and credit counseling agency stating what services were provided, with a copy of any debt repayment plan that was a product of the counseling.
- At least seven days before the § 341 meeting, the debtor must give the case trustee a tax return or transcript for the most recent year. The court and creditors are entitled to ask for additional tax returns. The debtor's failure to provide the trustee with a tax return is grounds for dismissal of the case unless the debtor can demonstrate that compliance was impossible because of circumstances beyond the debtor's control.[109]

In Chapter 7 cases, if the trustee prevails on a motion to dismiss the petition or convert it to another chapter, and if the debtor's attorney violated Rule 9011 by filing the petition, the attorney can be held liable for the trustee's attorneys' fees and costs. Civil penalties (payable to the Chapter 7 trustee or the U.S. Trustee) can be assessed based on the court's finding that the attorney violated Rule 9011. The attorney's signature on a petition, pleading, or motion certifies that the attorney, after a reasonable investigation, found the document to be well-grounded in fact and supported either by existing law or a good-faith argument for extension of the law. Furthermore, the attorney's signature on the petition certifies that the attorney has inquired and has no knowledge that the information in the schedules is incorrect.

---

[108] Bankruptcy Code §§ 526–528.

[109] The statute permits submission of either a copy of the tax return itself or the IRS transcript. The transcript contains rather less information, which could be desirable strategically. Returns can be obtained from the IRS by submitting Form 4506; transcripts can be obtained by faxing Form 8821 (Tax Information Authorization) and Form 4506-T (request for transcript) to the IRS.

The Eighth Circuit invalidated the BAPCPA provision that forbids attorneys to advise their clients to take on more debt before a bankruptcy filing. The Eighth Circuit, noting that sometimes it is in the client's best interests to take on more debt, found that this provision violated attorneys' rights to free speech.[110]

§ 15.20 WHO CAN FILE?

In effect, it is now the responsibility of the debtor's attorney to prove that the would-be Chapter 7 debtor is qualified to use that chapter. There is now a "means test" (Bankruptcy Code § 707(b)), imposing a presumption of abuse if the means test applies and the debtor has excess income. If the presumption cannot be rebutted, then the case must either be dismissed or converted to Chapter 13. But if the means test applies, and the debtor can pay at least $100 per month for five years, he or she must file in Chapter 13 rather than in Chapter 7.

For this purpose, "household income" means the total income for the six months prior to filing of the petition, divided by 6 and multiplied by 12. Household income includes the income of non-debtor members of the household who contribute income. The implication of this definition is that debtors have a degree of control because they can often time the filing after a decrease in income and/or before an expected increase.[111]

Would-be debtors must complete a brief credit counseling course, lasting approximately 90 minutes, before filing the petition. This requirement is waived in emergencies or if the debtor is disabled, incapacitated, or serving on active military duty. The counseling requirement is fairly minimal; it can be satisfied by participating in an individual or group briefing that is done by phone or on the Internet.[112]

At the other end of the process, Bankruptcy Code § 727(a)(11) requires the debtor to complete a debtor education class as a condition of discharge. If the debtor fails to do so, the case will be closed without a discharge, and the debtor will have to file a motion to reopen it to prove that the course was completed at last.

[A] Rules for Repeat Filings

A person whose prior bankruptcy case was dismissed within the previous 180 days for willful failure to abide by court orders or who failed to appear to prosecute the case is precluded from re-filing. This is also true of a debtor who asked for voluntary dismissal of an earlier case after a request for relief from the automatic stay.[113]

---

[110] Brent Kendall, *Court Finds Violation in Bankruptcy Law*, Wall St. J. 9/5/08 at C4.

[111] This discussion relies on the NYCLA materials for the New York County Lawyers Association September 13, 2005 CLE program, "Consumer Bankruptcy Law Changes Under the Bankruptcy Abuse Prevention & Consumer Protection Act of 2005" and the 2008 edition of William C. Hillman and Margaret M. Crouch, "Bankruptcy Deskbook" [4th edition].

[112] Bankruptcy Code § 109.

[113] Bankruptcy Code § 109(g).

A person who has already been discharged under Chapter 7 or Chapter 11 must wait eight years from the prior filing date to be discharged in a subsequent Chapter 7 proceeding. A person who received a Chapter 7 or Chapter 11 discharge must wait four years from the prior filing to be discharged in Chapter 13. At least two years must elapse between a first and second Chapter 13 discharge. However, a person who paid 100% of the allowed unsecured claims in a prior Chapter 13 proceeding can file under Chapter 7 without a waiting period. Payment of 70% of allowed unsecured claims in a previous Chapter 7 proceeding will permit filing with no waiting period, as long as the plan is proposed in good faith as the debtor's best effort to repay debts. But if that is not the case, six years must elapse between the prior Chapter 13 discharge and discharge in a subsequent Chapter 7 case. Chapter 11 cases can be filed without time limits premised on previous discharges in Chapters 7, 11, or 13.[114]

A Chapter 13 petition filer informed the court and his creditors that he would soon receive several hundred thousand dollars under an arbitration award, and that he would use the money to fund his Chapter 13 plan. He did receive the money, but did not comply with the court order calling for it to be turned over to the Chapter 13 trustee. When the Bankruptcy Court discovered this, the court converted the Chapter 13 case to Chapter 7 on its own motion. Before the formal order of conversion was filed, the debtor sought to voluntarily dismiss the petition (11 USC § 1307(b)). The Ninth Circuit, however, held that the debtor's right of voluntary dismissal is not absolute, but is subject to an implied exception for bad faith conduct or abuse of bankruptcy process, and it was not clear error for the Bankruptcy Court to treat the debtor's conduct as bad faith.[115]

§ 15.21 CHANGES TO THE AUTOMATIC STAY

Various kinds of actions are exempt from the automatic stay (Bankruptcy Code § 362 as amended), and BAPCPA also shortens the duration of the stay in various situations.

The automatic stay does not keep domestic relations actions from going forward (e.g., paternity suits; divorce cases; litigation over support, custody and visitation; domestic violence cases). There are limits on the stay in residential eviction actions, and the stay does not apply to withholding and collection of wages to repay loans from qualified plans.

On the business side, the automatic stay does not apply if the debtor is already a debtor in a pending small business case when the new petition is filed, or if the debtor was confirmed or had a small business case dismissed within two years of the filing of the present small business case. Nor does the automatic stay apply if the debtor acquired substantially all its assets from a small business debtor in one of those categories, unless the debtor can show by a preponderance of the evidence that the assets were acquired in good faith, not to evade the Bankruptcy Code.

---

[114] Bankruptcy Code §§ 727(a)(8), (9), and 1328(f).

[115] *In re* Rosson, 545 F.3d 764 (9th Cir. 2008).

The automatic stay ends 30 days after a Chapter 7, 11, or 13 filing by an individual who had a bankruptcy case dismissed within the previous year. (This does not apply to re-filing in Chapter 11 or Chapter 13 after a dismissal under § 707(b).) However, the court can extend the stay past the 30 days after a hearing and a finding that the case was re-filed in good faith. Bad faith is presumed where there was more than one pending bankruptcy case in the previous year that was dismissed for the debtor's fault (unless there has been a substantial change of circumstances, or a creditor obtained or moved for relief from the automatic stay). A debtor who had two or more cases pending during a single year, where both were dismissed, is not entitled to the automatic stay in any chapter, other than for cases re-filed in Chapter 11 or Chapter 13 after a § 707(b) dismissal.

The bankruptcy court has the power to order in rem relief with respect to real property owned by the debtor, if the bankruptcy petition was part of a scheme to delay, hinder, or defraud creditors by use of multiple bankruptcy filings or via transfer of an interest in the property without court approval or the consent of the secured creditor. A properly recorded order for in rem relief is binding on all owners of the property for two years from the date of entry. When an in rem relief order has been entered, there is an exception to the automatic stay to enforce a lien or security interest once an in rem relief order has been entered.[116] BCode § 362(h)(1) contains a self-executing provision (no motion or hearing required) if an individual debtor fails to satisfy his or her duties within the time schedule set out in § 521, the automatic stay is terminated with respect to the personal property of the estate or of the debtor subject to a Purchase Money Security Interest, and such property ceases to be property of the estate.

Section 362(j) allows creditors to request a "comfort order" once the automatic stay has terminated, to prove that the stay has ended. This is especially useful when the debtor is a repeat filer, when clarification of status is helpful.

§ 15.22 RETIREMENT PLANS

BAPCPA § 224(a) permits individual debtors to exempt the assets within certain tax-favored retirement accounts from the bankruptcy estate. Congress wished to expand protection for assets not already covered by Bankruptcy Code § 541(c)(2) under *Patterson v. Shumate* or other state or federal law. The BAPCPA provision applies to funds or accounts exempt under IRC §§ 401, 403, 408, 408A, 414, 457 or 501(a), such as tax-sheltered annuities, government plans, church plans, and both conventional and Roth IRAs. The April 2005 Supreme Court decision in *Rousey v. Jacoway* excluded IRA funds from the bankruptcy estate, but did not indicate whether Roth or only conventional IRAs were excluded, so BAPCPA provides welcome clarification. *Rousey v. Jacoway*, 544 U.S. 320 (2005), resolved a Circuit split about whether IRAs were protected from creditor claims by BCode § 522(d)(10)(E). Then BAPCPA added more protection for IRAs. In 2008, the Third Circuit ruled that, for pre-BAPCPA cases, *Rousey* overruled an

---

[116] Bankruptcy Code §§ 362(b)(4) and 362(b)(20).

earlier Third Circuit case — with the result that whether or not an IRA was in pay status at the time of bankruptcy filing, the IRA would be exempt.[117]

A debtor's retirement plan assets are presumed to be exempt from the bankruptcy estate if the plan has a favorable determination letter in effect as of the filing date of the debtor's bankruptcy case. Even if there is no determination letter, exclusion is still possible, premised on the debtor's demonstration that the funds have not been the subject of an earlier unfavorable determination by the IRS or by a court, and the plan is in substantial compliance with the rules. Section 224(e) imposes a $1 million cap (to be adjusted periodically for inflation) on the exemption for a conventional or Roth IRA, but the cap does not apply to rollovers from qualified plans or earnings on the rollover. The cap can be lifted in the interests of justice.

Pursuant to BAPCPA § 205, funds placed within education IRAs or 529 accounts within 365 days before a bankruptcy filing are included in the bankruptcy estate, but within limits, funds deposited a year or more before the filing are excluded. For funds deposited more than one year but less than two years before the filing, the limit is $5,000. The beneficiary of the account must be the debtor's child (including an adopted or foster child), grandchild, step-child, or step-grandchild.

However, there are stringent rules to prevent bankruptcy abuse in connection with plan loans. Plan loans cannot be discharged in bankruptcy. No Chapter 13 plan will be permitted to materially alter the terms of a plan loan. Amounts required to repay plan loans are not considered "disposable income" under Chapter 13. Amounts withheld from the debtor's wages to repay a plan loan from a pension, profit-sharing or stock bonus plan, or from some thrift savings plans, are not subject to the automatic stay.

The Eighth Circuit refused to permit a debtor to average her current monthly payments over the life of a 401(k) loan to determine her disposable income (and, thus, the amount available to repay her creditors). The debtor's net monthly income was $352 (a total of $21,143 over the life of the Chapter 13 plan). She owed six monthly payments of $50 for a 401(k) loan and 13 $100 payments for another loan. The debtor wanted to deduct $9,000, for the payments on the two loans times the 60 months of the loan terms, allowing her to pay $12,143 to unsecured creditors and retain the other $7,400. The Eighth Circuit BAP ruled that § 1332(f) does not treat amounts to repay a 401(k) loan as disposable income for § 1325 purposes — but, because only $1,600 is required to repay this loan, once it has been repaid, the debtor must use that amount each month to pay her unsecured creditors.[118]

---

[117] *In re* Krebs, 527 F.3d 82 (3d Cir. 2008); *see* B. Janell Grenier, *Third Circuit Opines That Rousey Overruled Clark*, 5/25/08 (benefitslink.com).

[118] *In re* Lasowski, No. 07-6063 (8th BAP 3/31/08); *see* Fred Schneyer, *Bankruptcy Appellate Panel Limits 401(k) Loan Deduction*, Plansponsor.com (4/1/08).

[A] Retirement Plans in Corporate Bankruptcy

BAPCPA also affects corporate bankruptcies. Under § 323 of BAPCPA, funds withheld by an employer, or received by the employee from employee wages for payment to benefit plans, defined contribution plans, and tax-deferred annuities are excluded from the employer's bankruptcy estate. The exclusion applies to ERISA plans (other than SERPs or excess plans), government plans under IRC §§ 414(d) and 457, and health insurance plans regulated by state law.

Bankruptcy Code § 1114 precludes a Chapter 11 debtor from unilaterally terminating or modifying retiree welfare benefits that it is legally obligated to provide. Negotiation with retiree representatives is required. Once a Chapter 11 petition has been filed, benefits subject to § 1114 must be maintained unless the court mandates or at least permits termination or modification. BAPCPA § 1403 clears up a past area of confusion: whether § 1114 applies to situations in which the debtor reserved the right to modify or terminate the benefits. The BAPCPA provision permits the bankruptcy court to set aside modifications of retiree welfare benefits made within 180 days before filing unless the court finds that the balance of equities clearly favors the modification.

Wages, salaries, and commissions for post-petition services are administrative expenses that can properly be paid out of the bankruptcy estate, with priority over prepetition claims. Under prior law, up to $4,925 of unpaid wages and benefits per employee, earned prior to filing, constituted a priority claim. BAPCPA § 1401 increases this to $10,000, and includes unpaid vacation, severance, and sick leave. Priority is now granted to amounts earned within 180 days (rather than the 90 days under prior law) before the bankruptcy filing or the end of the debtor's business, whichever occurs first. The definition of fraudulent transfers is expanded, by BAPCPA § 1402, to include those made to or incurred for the benefit of insiders under employment contracts, and with a look-back period of two years rather than one. A transfer under an employment contract but outside the ordinary course of business can be avoided irrespective of its effect on the debtor's solvency.

Pre-BAPCPA, Chapter 11 debtors often sought approval of retention plans providing stay bonuses and severance for employees at all levels. BAPCPA § 331 amends Bankruptcy Act § 503 to forbid payment of retention bonuses or severance benefits to insiders unless the payment is reasonable. Insiders are directors, officers, general partners, persons in control of the debtor, and their relatives. A retention bonus is allowable only if it is essential to preventing a crucial executive from accepting a bona fide job offer paying at least as much as the current job. An acceptable bonus is limited to ten times the average bonus paid to non-management employees in the same calendar year. If there were no such payments, the limit is 25% of the amount paid to the insider for any purpose. This BAPCPA provision also forbids other transfers or obligations outside the ordinary course of business that are not justified by the facts of the case. For example, transfers to, or obligations incurred on behalf of, officers, managers, or consultants hired after the filing of the petition would be analyzed under this provision.

BAPCPA § 1213 provides that if a trustee uses Bankruptcy Code § 547(b) to avoid a transfer to an entity that is not an insider, but the transfer is made for the benefit of an insider creditor, the transfer is avoidable only with respect to the insider creditor.[119]

The Pension Protection Act (PPA; P.L. 109-280) greatly limits the extent to which a bankrupt company can selectively increase benefits under its pension plans. The intent of the legislation is to preserve benefits for the rank and file to the extent compatible with the needs of reorganizing the bankrupt company.

§ 15.23 REAFFIRMATION AND REDEMPTION

The requirements for reaffirmation of debts have been changed. The debtor now has 30 days from filing to give the court a statement of intention to reaffirm a debt secured by property. The debtor can retain the property only by reaffirming within 45 days after the § 321 meeting. Section 542(k) lays out the disclosures the creditor must make before the debtor signs a reaffirmation agreement. The debtor must also file a signed statement giving income, expenses, and the balance available to make payments. If the balance is too small to support the payments, undue hardship will be presumed. The presumption must be overcome for the court to approve the reaffirmation agreement. The debtor's attorney must certify that the debtor gave informed consent to the agreement, after a full explanation from the attorney — and, in the attorney's opinion, if the presumption of hardship applies, the debtor can nevertheless make the payments.[120]

Previously, some Circuits permitted "ridethrough" — that is, a debtor could retain possession of an automobile without either reaffirming or redeeming the debt, as long as current payments were made. However, BAPCPA has eliminated this, and codifies a Supreme Court decision:[121] the value of property retained in a Chapter 13 cramdown is the replacement value (i.e., what the debtor would have to pay to obtain property of like age and condition). No deduction is made for the cost of sale or marketing the property.

BAPCPA is ambiguous about certain aspects of the treatment of "910 vehicles" (personal-use vehicles purchased during the 910 days before the petition was filed, and in which the creditor has a purchase money security interest: see 11 USC § 1325(a)). BAPCPA does not explain what happens to the balance on the loan when the car is surrendered. The unnumbered "hanging paragraph" says that § 506 (the provision allowing bifurcation of a claim into secured and unsecured portions) does not apply to PMSIs on 910 vehicles.

At first, when cases on this issue were before the district courts, the trend was to treat surrender as full satisfaction of the creditor's claim — holding that

---

[119] *See* Hewitt Associates, *Employee Benefit Provisions in Bankruptcy Abuse Prevention and Consumer Protection Act of 2005*, http://was4.hewitt.com/hewitt/resource/legislative-updates/united_states/pdfs/ee_benefi_provision.pdf (no www).

[120] Bankruptcy Code §§ 521(a)(2)(A) and 521(a)(6).

[121] Associates Commercial Corp. v. Rash, 520 U.S. 953 (1997); Bankruptcy Code § 506(a)(2).

cramdown does not apply to 910 vehicles; the full claim was considered secured, and had to be paid as filed.

Then a number of cases were decided in which the debtors wanted to keep the vehicles and pay the contract balance, raising the issues of whether the creditor could continue to pursue the unpaid balance as an unsecured deficiency; whether the creditor could receive post-petition interest and what the value of the claim should be.

In 2008, the Eleventh Circuit joined the Fourth, Sixth, Seventh, Eighth, and Tenth Circuits in holding that, when a debtor surrenders a 910 vehicle, the creditor can still file an unsecured claim for the balance — although the courts did get to that result using different rationales. The Eleventh Circuit concluded that Congress wanted to assist car lenders and other lienholders, not restrict their remedies.[122]

Under Bankruptcy Code § 722 as amended, the debtor can redeem property by paying the full amount of the secured claim (measured as of the time of redemption). A statement of intention is required for redemption as well as for reaffirmation.

§ 15.24 BUSINESS PROVISIONS

Most of BAPCPA's changes affect consumer bankruptcies, but there have been some changes to business bankruptcy as well (e.g., a 210-day limit on the debtor's assumption or rejection of nonresidential leases; the period of exclusivity during which only the debtor can file a reorganization plan is cut back to 18 months; and purchases within 20 days of filing obtain administrative expense priority).

Most of the basic Chapter 11 rules remain in place, although some changes have been made to expedite case processing, and in some places the statute says relief "must" be granted, thus limiting the court's discretion. Bankruptcy Code § 1104 has been amended to expand the grounds for appointment of a trustee or examiner. It is harder for a Debtor in Possession to defeat a motion to convert or dismiss the case because of the changes in Bankruptcy Code § 1112. However, if the debtor has filed a prepackaged plan, a party in interest can move to have the U.S. Trustee ordered not to have a § 341 meeting; the bankruptcy court has the power to make such an order on notice and hearing.[123]

The prior-law limit of $4 million has been removed, so a case of any size can proceed as a single-asset real estate case.[124]

---

[122] *In re* Barrett, 543 F.3d 1239 (11th Cir. 2008); *see also In re* Wright, 492 F.3d 829 (7th Cir. 2007), Capital One Auto Finance v. Osborn, 515 F.3d 817 (8th Cir. 2008), *In re* Long, 519 F.3d 288 (6th Cir. 2008), AmericCredit Fin. Servs. Inc. v. Moore, 517 F.3d 987 (8th Cir. 2008), *In re* Ballard, 526 F.3d 634 (10th Cir. 2008), *In re* Jones, No. 07-3256 (10th Cir. 7/7/08); Tidewater Fin. Co. v. Kenney, 531 F.3d 312 (4th Cir. 2008).

[123] Bankruptcy Code § 341(e).

[124] NYCLA materials for 9/20/05 Business Bankruptcy Law Changes Under BAPCPA.

[A] Small Business

BAPCPA amends Bankruptcy Code § 101 to add a definition of "small business": a natural person, partnership, or corporation with debt below $2 million, as adjusted for inflation other than debt owed to insiders or affiliates. If the U.S. Trustee has appointed a creditor's committee, or a committee was appointed but the court decides it is not active and representative enough to oversee the reorganization, the case is not considered a small business case. The exclusive period (that is, the time during which only the debtor — and not creditors — can submit a plan) has been cut back to 180 days from the order of relief.

Small business debtors are subject to reporting requirements under Bankruptcy Code § 308. They must file periodic reports on their profitability (i.e., the money earned and lost during the current and recent past filing periods). They must also provide a reasonable approximation of the cash receipts and disbursements expected in the future — and, furthermore, must reconcile projected past reports to the actual figures. The debtor must confirm that it has filed and paid all taxes and complied with all applicable rules and document submission requirements. The incentive for doing all this is Bankruptcy Code § 1112(b)(4)(F), which mandates dismissal or conversion of the case on motion of any party in interest if all the requirements are not met, unless there is a reasonable justification for missing a deadline. As drafted, the statute apparently makes dismissal mandatory, even if the plan could be confirmed within a reasonable period of time; there is no provision for a balancing test.

Standard forms have been promulgated for the disclosure statement (although filings on non-standard forms are acceptable). There is a new streamlined procedure under which a plan can be approved conditionally, subject to final approval at the confirmation hearing.

In a small business case, § 1129(e) now provides that the court is supposed to confirm the plan within 45 days. Irrespective of who files the plan and disclosure statement, the due date is 300 days after the order for relief. The 180-day and 300-day time frames can be extended only if, before the due date, an order is entered setting a new date. To get an extension, the debtor must show by a preponderance of the evidence that it is more likely than not that the court will confirm the plan within a reasonable period of time.

[B] Preferences

Under the BAPCPA version of Bankruptcy Code § 547, it is easier for creditors to demonstrate that funds they received did not constitute preferential transfers, because now they need to show that the debtor incurred the debt in the ordinary course of its business or made the transfer in accordance with ordinary business terms; it is no longer necessary to show both.

Secured creditors now have a longer grace period to perfect their transfers — although the way BAPCPA is drafted creates potential for conflicts with the UCC, especially Article 9.

For cases commenced a year or more after BAPCPA's enactment, the trustee can look back two years (not one, as provided by earlier law) to avoid or recover fraudulent transfers: Bankruptcy Code § 548(a)(1). Corporate debtors that pay retention bonuses to keep key officers from taking other jobs must also be aware of Bankruptcy Code § 503(i), which specifies a safe harbor but at the cost of treating certain retention benefits paid to insiders as fraudulent transfers.

[C] Treatment of Taxes in Chapter 11

Bankruptcy Code § 1129(a)(9), as amended by BAPCPA, requires Chapter 11 plans to call for regular installment payments, in cash, of the allowed amount of priority tax claims (plus interest), over a period of five years or less. The interest rate on tax claims is the rate set by applicable non-bankruptcy law (new Bankruptcy Code § 511). While the bankruptcy case is pending, taxes must be paid as they come due — and tax authorities can get the case converted or dismissed if tax returns are not filed after the commencement of the bankruptcy case.[125] The priority tax claims must receive treatment at least as favorable as the non-priority unsecured claims that receive the highest level of repayment. Tax claims secured by a lien or warrant must be treated on a parity with unsecured priority claims.

BAPCPA amends Bankruptcy Code § 724: ad valorem taxes on the bankruptcy estate's real or personal property are not subject to subordination, although they can be subordinated to wage, salary, and employee benefit claims. Administrative expenses (other than administrative wages) can be paid prior to tax liens in Chapter 7, but not in Chapter 11. Amended Bankruptcy Code § 545(2) does not permit trustees to avoid unperfected statutory liens if the purchaser is described in IRC § 6323 or a comparable state or local law. Furthermore, the bankruptcy trustee must use up all of the estate's unencumbered assets before subordinating a tax lien.

Taxes assessed during the 240 days before filing, plus any period when collection of taxes was stayed, plus another 90 days, are given priority. The priority period is also extended by times when a debtor's request for appeal or hearing on a collection action is pending. Bankruptcy Code § 362(b) now provides that government units can set off tax refunds for periods ending before the bankruptcy order of relief, against pre-order of relief tax liabilities.

Even after confirmation of the plan, a corporate Chapter 11 debtor is not discharged from fraudulent debts, including taxes the debtor willfully attempted to evade or filed a fraudulent return. Unless there was a proper request for an extension, whenever a bankruptcy debtor fails to file a tax return due at any time after the bankruptcy filing, the taxing authority can use amended Bankruptcy Code § 521 to seek to have the bankruptcy case dismissed or converted to another Chapter.

---

[125] 28 USC § 960, as amended; Bankruptcy Code § 521.

Under prior law, the automatic stay applied to tax proceedings against any debtor, but now Bankruptcy Code § 362(a)(8) provides that the bankruptcy court determines the duration of the stay for corporate debtors. For individual debtors, tax proceedings are only stayed for the tax years ending before the bankruptcy case commenced.

Rev. Proc. 2006-24, 2006-22 IRB 943 explains how trustees and DIPs representing a bankruptcy estate exercise the right, created by BAPCPA, to get a prompt determination of the estate's unpaid tax liabilities for the period of estate administration.

Part IV

PERSONAL PLANNING

§ 16.01   INTRODUCTION

Family law deals with the formation and dissolution of families — usually, though not always, by marriage, birth of children, and perhaps divorce. Other family law issues (e.g., adoption and technologically assisted conception) of same-sex couples are also prominent in the court system and the legislatures.

§ 16.02   ANTENUPTIAL AGREEMENTS

Antenuptial agreements dealing with property are quite traditional. For many years, American law disfavored antenuptial agreements "in contemplation of divorce," but it is now well-accepted that persons planning to marry may legitimately enter into a contract dealing with post-marital financial and other issues, including support as well as property division.

Antenuptial agreements must meet ordinary contract requirements, and are subjected to additional scrutiny because of the close relationship between the parties, and because of public policy considerations (e.g., signatories to antenuptial agreements should not be forced into poverty — and into becoming public charges — if the marriage ends).

The general rule is that, to be enforceable, the agreement must be written. However, exceptions might be found if the parties relied on the agreement; if partial performance occurred; or if non-enforcement would promote fraud. It is also generally true that each party to the agreement must make full disclosure of financial and other facts, although perhaps this requirement can be waived by a signatory. It is better practice for each signatory to have independent legal counsel.

Duress or overreaching will vitiate an agreement. It is one thing for a couple to agree that a premarital agreement is worthwhile; it is something else entirely for one party to turn up right before the wedding ceremony and demand that it be signed or the wedding is off!

To be entitled to court enforcement, the agreement must be fair and reasonable — both as of the time it was signed, and as of the time enforcement was sought. For example, a major change in circumstances since the signing would be likely to induce the court to modify the agreement or refuse to enforce it.

It should be noted that gifts between spouses are free of gift tax, but gifts to engaged persons are not. Therefore, if very large gifts are contemplated (perhaps to equalize the two spouse's estates to save future estate tax), they should be made after rather than before the marriage.

Pennsylvania is a no-fault state in the sense that, when an engagement is terminated, the fiancee is obligated to return the ring or pay the equivalent of its value in cash, no matter which party decided to call off the engagement. In this interpretation, an engagement ring is a conditional gift, conditional on the marriage actually occurring, not just on acceptance of a marriage proposal.[1]

Similarly, the New York Supreme Court ordered a woman to return an expensive engagement ring to her former fiance, on the grounds that it was a gift in contemplation of marriage, which is recoverable irrespective of fault as to why the marriage never took place. Although there was no explicit proposal of marriage, it was clear that she accepted the ring as an engagement ring. (She returned the ring the day before the decision was rendered.)[2]

A District of Columbia case holds that a spouse who executes a valid prenuptial agreement that waives pension rights on divorce cannot use ERISA to cancel the waiver — ERISA does not preempt state matrimonial laws allowing prenuptial agreements.[3]

A Colorado case on the same issue[4] says that ERISA imposes a consent requirement for the waiver of survivor benefits, but is silent on waiver of other types of pension benefits, so waivers by an ex-spouse are certainly permissible.

Florida ruled that an express provision in a prenuptial agreement can be used by the parties to contract away the future obligation to pay attorneys' fees in a suit to enforce the prenuptial agreement itself. The Florida trend is to require pre-dissolution support, but to extend the ability to make contracts waiving post-dissolution support. The prospective waiver of attorneys' fees was permitted, even though the losing party brought a meritorious claim in good faith, because a clause of this type does not implicate the state's interest in spousal support during the marriage.[5]

---

[1] Lindh v. Surman, 742 A.2d 643 (Pa. 1999).

[2] Lucchetti v. DiGaetano, No. 109231/05 (N.Y. Sup. 2005), discussed in Mark Fass, *Ex-Fiancee Told to Give Back $53,000 Ring*, N.Y.L.J. 8/25/05 (law.com).

[3] Critchell v. Critchell, 746 A.2d 282 (D.C. 2000).

[4] Rahn v. Rahn, 914 P.2d 463 (Colo. App. 1995).

[5] Lashkajani v. Lashkajani, 923 So.2d 502 (Fla. App. 2006) and 950 So.2d 842 (Fla. App. 2007).

§ 16.03 MARRIAGE

The general rule is that, marriage is permitted only between male/female couples, not same-sex couples. The federal Defense of Marriage Act, 28 USC § 1738C (9/21/96) says that states have no obligation to give full faith and credit to same-sex marriages performed in other states.[6] However, Massachusetts, California, and Connecticut permitted same-sex marriage — although at press time, the California court decision authorizing same-sex marriage had been voted down by referendum.

There are various prerequisites to a civilly valid marriage:

- Mutual intent to marry
- Ability to understand the nature of marriage (a ward may be able to marry, with permission of his or her guardian)
- A license issued by civil authorities
- Performance of a religious or civil ceremony by a clergymember, judge, or other authorized officiant. (The marriage might be valid or valid for certain purposes, if one party enters into it in good faith, while the other knows that the ceremony is invalid.)
- Recording of the marriage license, with endorsement indicating performance of the ceremony, with the appropriate state official.

Under the Uniform Marriage and Divorce Act, a marriage license becomes effective three days after it is issued (i.e., there is a waiting period to prevent over-hasty marriages) and expires after 180 days.

Certain marriages are barred: between blood relatives or even "step" relatives, for instance. Most states permit marriage at 18, or at 16 with parental consent or an enabling court order. The underage spouse (but not the spouse of full age) can get an annulment for infancy; some states permit a parent of the underage spouse to get the marriage annulled. However, a common rule is that, if the spouses continue to cohabit after the underage spouse reached majority, the marriage has been ratified and can no longer be annulled on the basis of infancy.

The general rule is that the validity of a marriage is determined by the law of the place in which it was celebrated. The Restatement (2nd) of Conflicts says that, for each issue, the law of the state with the most significant relationship to the spouses and the marriage will govern.

---

[6] An intermediate-level New York court decided in early 2008 that the Canadian same-sex marriage of Patricia Martinez must be recognized, and her employer, Monroe Community College, must provide health benefits for her spouse, on the grounds that New York law does not forbid recognition of out-of-state same-sex marriages. See Rebecca Moore, *NY [sic] Court Rules to Recognize Same-Sex Marriages from Other States*, http://www.plansponsor.com/pi_type10_print.jsp ?RECORD_ID=40295 (2/4/08).

[A] Common-Law Marriage

About a dozen states still recognize common-law marriage: a quasi-marital state in which a couple live together and hold themselves out as husband and wife. In other words, a common-law marriage is a valid marriage even though it was not created by a marriage ceremony.[7]

It should be noted that non-residents of a state recognizing common-law marriage may be treated as common-law spouses on the basis of contact with the forum (e.g., vacationing there). Common-law marriage can be raised against a party. That party might not be allowed to benefit from the assertion of the existence of a common-law marriage, on the theory that a party desiring the benefits of the married state has the option of securing those benefits via a ceremonial marriage.

[B] Putative Marriage

A putative spouse is a person who participates, in good faith, in a legally invalid marriage: e.g., marries someone whose prior marriage, unknown to the putative spouse, has not been dissolved. A good-faith partner in a bigamous marriage may even be entitled to alimony when the relationship terminates, and children of such a union are considered legitimate. As long as the good-faith belief in the validity of the marriage continues, a putative spouse has the same rights as a legal spouse.

The Social Security Administration has elaborate rules concerning the rights of various kinds of deemed, putative, and quasi-spouses to receive OASDI benefits based on the earnings record of the other partner to the alleged marriage: see 20 CFR Part 440, especially 440.345 and .346.

[C] Cohabitation

Although some states still have never-enforced laws forbidding cohabitation, the predominant legal issue is the extent to which cohabitation gives rise to enforceable economic relationships between the partners. An increasing number of corporations make "domestic partner" benefits available to unmarried cohabitants, but this is still a minority position. An unmarried person can be named as beneficiary of an insurance policy, will provision, or pension, but will not be entitled to a share of such assets automatically, by operation of law.

A few cases do permit an economic partnership ("palimony") argument to be made by cohabitants who allegedly had an unwritten understanding that the poorer cohabitant would be supported by the richer one. But there is no body of statutory and case law giving cohabitants the kind of rights (e.g., election against the will) available to participants in a formal marriage.

---

[7] Pennsylvania abolished common-law marriage in 2003: PNC Bank Corp. v. Workers' Comp. Appeal Bd. (Stamos); *see* Asher Hawkins, *Pa. Court Abolishes Common-Law Marriage*, The Legal Intelligencer 9/19/03 (law.com).

Therefore, cohabitants who are very concerned about financial issues are often well-advised to enter into a written agreement expressing their financial understanding and the expected consequences on the death of one cohabitant, or the termination of the relationship.

The problem is that, although individuals who happen to cohabit can validly enter into contracts, a "meretricious relationship" does not furnish consideration for a contract. In other words, care must be taken to draft the agreement so that there is no suggestion that one cohabitant is paying the other for sexual services. Safer ground is to premise the support agreement on, e.g., one cohabitant's participation in the other's business, or career opportunities foregone by one cohabitant in order to accompany the other.[8]

Unlike most state courts that have ruled on the issue, the New Jersey Supreme Court decided in 2008 that cohabitation is not an absolute requirement for success in a palimony claim; it is just one of the factors for the judge to consider. Cohabitation may be impossible if, for example, one partner is a student or a military servicemember. Under this analysis, the partner seeking palimony has to prove the existence of a quasi-marital relationship. In the case at bar, the plaintiff's employer set her up in an apartment, and she said he promised to leave his wife; when they broke up, the defendant evicted the plaintiff from the apartment. The plaintiff's claim failed because she did not prove that they held themselves out as married, or that her lover promised to support her.[9]

In the tax context, see *Reynolds*, TC Memo 1999-62, (3/4/99). When a cohabitation relationship terminated, the Tax Court held that the payment made by the male to the female cohabitant was not taxable compensation for services during the relationship. Instead, it was payment for property previously given to her. There was no gain for the female cohabitant, because the property was now worth less than her basis.

Because Ohio's Defense of Marriage Act (DOMA) denies state recognition of the quasi-marital status of any relationship other than legal marriage, the Ohio Court of Appeals ruled that the domestic violence statute is invalid to the extent it grants protection to a "person living as a spouse." (In this case, a male cohabitant charged his female cohabitant with assaulting him.)[10]

---

[8] Under Wilcox v. Trautz, 693 N.E.2d 141 (Mass. Sup. Jud. Ct. 1998), palimony agreements are enforceable in Massachusetts as long as they are not made in consideration of sexual services; the mere fact of a sexual relationship between the parties does not invalidate an otherwise proper contract.

[9] Devaney v. L'Esperance, 195 N.J. 247 (N.J. 2008); *see* Michael Booth, *Cohabitation Not a Requirement for Palimony Claim, Says N.J. Supreme Court*, N.J.L.J. 6/18/08 (law.com). A bright-line cohabitation rule was also rejected in Carina v. O'Malley, 2007 WL 951953 (D.N.J. 2007), a palimony case with parties in New Jersey and Pennsylvania. New Jersey required cohabitation for palimony claims since Kozlowski v. Kozlowski, 80 N.J. 378 (1979).

[10] State v. Ward, 74 LW 1600 (Ohio App. 3/24/06).

[D] Same-Sex Unions

For a couple of centuries, it was deemed to go without saying that "marriage" in U.S. law was by its nature a relationship between one man and one woman. Hawaii was an early battleground. The state's 1995 statute refusing marriage licenses to same-sex couples was followed by a 1998 amendment to the state Constitution, empowering the legislature to reserve marriage for male/female couples. The state's Supreme Court ruled that the constitutional amendment removes the statute from the purview of the state's Equal Protection clause.[11]

Over time, the issue of legal recognition of same-sex unions has become more and more active, culminating with a tremendous amount of court, legislative, and administrative activity since 2004. The issue is highly contentious, involving deeply-held beliefs about religion and morality as well as important practical issues (e.g., what steps employers would have to take to change their benefit structures if same-sex marriage is recognized). Many states have reacted to the problem by adopting Defense of Marriage Acts or similar constitutional provisions, or by introducing such measures. Other states, however, have moved in the opposite direction, either authorizing marriage by same-sex couples or by recognizing domestic partnerships or civil unions. (Some domestic partnership laws are available to male/female couples as well as same-sex couples.) It is not uncommon for a state's legislature to move in one direction while its courts move in the other.

[1] Domestic Partnership/Civil Union

In 2000, a voter initiative amended the Nebraska State Bill of Rights to state that same-sex civil unions, domestic partnerships, and similar relationships are not valid or recognized under state law. A case was brought challenging the amendment as an unconstitutional Bill of Attainder, punishing an ascertainable population group without due process. The District Court for the District of Nebraska ruled in mid-2005 that the amendment is an unconstitutional Bill of Attainder; it violates equal protection; and deprives citizens of First Amendment associational rights.[12]

Although it did not permit same-sex marriage, on January 8, 2004, New Jersey adopted a domestic partnership law (available to both same-sex couples and male-and-female couples over 62 — an option adopted to preclude loss of pension benefits). New Jersey gives full faith and credit to partnerships from other states such as Vermont civil unions and Hawaii Reciprocal Beneficiary Relationships. To be eligible for domestic partnership, a couple must share a common residence, be willing to support each other if necessary, and already have a relationship of financial interdependence (e.g., shared mortgages or will provisions benefiting the other partner). Siblings and first cousins are not permitted to enter into a domestic partnership.

Domestic partners can file joint state tax returns. Insurance companies have to offer spousal coverage to domestic partners, but employers are not obligated to treat

---

[11] Baehr v. Miike, 950 P.2d 1234 (Haw. 1999).

[12] Citizens for Equal Protection v. Bruning, 73 L.W. 1713 (D. Neb. 5/12/05).

domestic partners as married. Discrimination on the basis of domestic partner status by employers, landlords, and lenders is forbidden. A domestic partner can visit his or her partner in the hospital, consent to organ donation, or serve as health care proxy. However, domestic partners are not entitled to support from one another.

A same-sex domestic partnership can be terminated on grounds of adultery, desertion, cruelty, habitual drunkenness or living separate and apart for 18 months, but the dissolution court does not apply equitable distribution to divide partnership property, and there are no automatic rights over children of the relationship.

Spouses and domestic partners are treated equally for inheritance tax purposes, but domestic partners do not have rights of intestate succession or right of election, although domestic partnership presumably will be a significant factor in a will contest.

New Jersey did not amend its tort laws, so domestic partners do not have statutory standing to bring injury or wrongful death suits when their partners are injured or killed.

In February, 2007, New Jersey implemented same-sex civil union, carrying with it legal rights comparable to marriage. The state also recognizes same-sex marriages and civil unions solemnized in jurisdictions where they are legal Relationships that are marriages in the jurisdiction where they are performed (e.g., Canada, Massachusetts) or civil unions (e.g., Vermont) will be treated as civil unions by New Jersey. Relationships granting a lesser degree of quasi-marital rights (e.g., Maine) will be treated as domestic partnerships in New Jersey.[13]

Maine has forbidden same-sex marriage since 1997, but the state enacted a domestic partnership bill on April 28, 2004, taking effect 90 days later. Domestic partners (who can be same-sex or male-female couples who cohabit in long-term arrangements) have the same right of intestate succession as married people.

A California state law, A.B. 205, codified at Family Code § 297.5, makes the rights and responsibilities of registered domestic partners very similar to those of married persons. The California Supreme Court has jurisdiction over proceedings for domestic partners to separate, or to nullify or dissolve a registered domestic partnership, including division of property, support, and custody of children of the partnership. To the extent that state and not federal rights are involved, employee benefits for "spouses" must also be extended to registered domestic partners (e.g., employer payment of premiums and the CalCOBRA requirement that employers of 2–19 employees provide continuation coverage). In workplaces with 20 or more employees (i.e., where federal COBRA applies), Registered Domestic Partners of employees who elect continuation coverage are entitled to continuation coverage also, as dependents. Employers are obligated to obey garnishments involving Registered Domestic Partners, and the California Family Rights Act, which requires up to 12 weeks of unpaid leave for reasons including the serious health

[13] Lewis v. Harris, 188 N.J. 415 (N.J. 2006); *see* Michael Booth, *N.J. Supreme Court Punts Same-Sex Marriage to Legislature*, N.J.L.J. 10/26/06 (law.com). *See also* Geoff Mulvihill (AP), *N.J. Says It Will Recognize Gay Unions From Other States, Nations* (2/20/07) (law.com).

condition of a "close family member," presumably also applies to Registered Domestic Partners.[14]

Under the California Domestic Partner Rights and Responsibilities Act, a person's reasonable good-faith belief that his or her domestic partnership was validly registered with the California Secretary of State entitles that person to the rights and responsibilities of a registered domestic partner, even if in fact the registration never occurred. The person is in the same position as an equitable putative spouse in an invalid marriage. Status as a putative spouse is determined by whether a reasonable person could have a good-faith belief that a marriage or domestic partnership had been contracted. (The trial court dismissed a dissolution petition because the domestic partnership was never registered; the appellant said that he believed that his partner had completed the registration process after the documents were signed and notarized.)[15]

In California, the approximately 23,000 same-sex couples registered as domestic partners are subject to divorce law if they wish to dissolve the relationship, unless they give written notice to the state. Community property principles are applied upon dissolution, irrespective of title. But, because federal tax law does not recognize same-sex marriage, the recipient of any court-ordered support or property will be taxed on the distribution. Couples who sign a contract to opt out of divorce law often use the same lawyer, which probably disqualifies the agreement from operating as a prenuptial agreement under California law, which requires separate representation and a waiver of marital rights.[16]

In April 2007, effective January 1, 2008, New Hampshire passed a civil union bill. Clergymembers are permitted, but not obligated, to perform civil unions. A marriage or civil union that is legal in another state will be recognized in New Hampshire. Thus, as of mid-2007, Massachusetts was the only state recognizing same-sex marriage (joined by Connecticut in 2008); Oregon, New Hampshire, Vermont, California, New Jersey, Maine, and Washington had civil unions.[17]

In February 2004, the Ohio legislature approved H.B. 272, one of the broadest bans on same-sex partnerships in the United States. The law forbids state agencies to give benefits to domestic partners. The statute does not forbid private companies from offering domestic partner benefits if they so choose, although it is possible that a suit could be brought under the statute to enjoin private domestic partner benefits.[18]

---

[14] *See, e.g.*, Mark Terman, *New Law Modifies Reach of Workplace Domestic Partnership Rights*, Reish Luftman Reicher & Cohen newsletter 2/05 http://reish.com/publications/article_detail.cfm?ARTICLEID=507; California has placed the Domestic Partner Registration form online at http://www.ss.sa.gov.

[15] *In re* Domestic Partnership of Ellis and Arriaga, 162 Cal. App. 4th 1000 (2008).

[16] Leigh Jones, *Gay Divorce as New Practice Area*, Nat'l L.J. 7/7/04 (law.com).

[17] CCH Benefits newsletter, *Oregon, New Hampshire, New York Extend Domestic Partner Benefits*, http://www.hr.cch.com/news/benefits/051807.asp 5/2/07; Pam Belluck, *New Hampshire Adopts Same-Sex Unions*, N.Y. Times 6/1/07 at p.A1; Katie Zezima, *Rhode Island Steps Toward Recognizing Same-Sex Marriage*, N.Y. Times 2/22/07 at p. A19.

[18] James Dao, *Ohio Legislature Votes to Ban Same-Sex Unions*, N.Y. Times, 2/4/04 at p. A12.

[2] Same-Sex Marriage

There is a federal statute, the Defense of Marriage Act (DOMA) that defines marriage as a relationship between one man and one woman.[19] Therefore, partners in same-sex unions are not entitled to the benefits provided to married persons under federal programs (e.g., Social Security), and states are not obligated to grant full faith and credit to same-sex unions even if they are lawful in other states. However, same-sex marriage was granted legal status in Massachusetts, California, and Connecticut (although there was the possibility that this would be altered by the courts or legislatively, as occurred in California).

In mid-2008, the California Supreme Court said that denial of same-sex marriage violated the California Constitution. The court did not find the contrary rulings in other states an obstacle because those states have a different statutory scheme from California, which already had a comprehensive domestic partnership scheme. The California Supreme Court held that given the significance of the fundamental constitutional right to form a family relationship, same-sex couples must be allowed to marry as well as to maintain domestic partnerships.[20] Proposition 8, a ballot initiative to reverse this decision, was placed on the ballot for November 2008, and the California Supreme Court allowed the voting. Gay rights proponents said that it should not be on the ballot because it was a constitutional revision (requiring legislative approval) and not a constitutional amendment. However, the California Supreme Court, like most courts, left the measure on the ballot for voters to accept or reject,[21] and the initiative passed on November 4, 2008.

A suit brought in 2004 by eight Connecticut couples resulted in an October 2008 ruling that the state constitution does not permit same-sex couples to be denied freedom to marry.[22]

After the referendum seeking a statewide vote on the Oregon Domestic Partnership law was kept off the ballot on the grounds that it did not have enough signatures, voters favoring Referendum 303 appealed the District Court's denial of an injunction. The Ninth Circuit affirmed the ruling that the Oregon Secretary of

---

[19] The District Court for the District of Utah upheld that state's prohibition of polygamy as constitutional; even in the post-*Lawrence* era, states retain the power to regulate marriage: Bronson v. Swensen, 73 L.W. 1576 (D. Utah 2/15/05).

[20] *In re* Marriage Cases, 43 Cal. 4th 757 (Cal. 2008).

[21] Bennett v. Bowen, S164520 (filed 6/20/08). *See* (No by-line) *Calif. Ruling on Gay Marriage Sparks Joy, Outrage*, The Recorder 5/16/08 (law.com); Mike McKee, *Challenge to Calif. Gay Unions Measure Fails*, The Recorder 7/17/08 (law.com).

[22] Kerrigan et al. v. Comm'r of Public Health, 289 Conn. 135 (Conn. 2008), http://www.plansponsor.com/uploadfiles/ctsamesex.pdf; *see* Dave Collins (AP) *Conn. high court rules gay couples can marry*, Yahoo News 10/10/08 (law.com). The decision eliminated same-sex civil union, on the grounds that it violated the state constitution to have a form of quasi-marital partnership that fell short of full-scale parity with male/female marriage. The first same-sex marriages were performed in October 2008. However, some couples did not apply right away, because the licenses expired after 65 days, and the couples wanted to plan elaborate wedding celebrations. *See* Lisa W. Foderaro, *A New Day for Marriage in Connecticut*, N.Y. Times 11/13/08 at p. A31.

State's procedures for verifying petition signatures did not deny equal protection or due process rights.[23]

The Middle District of Florida rejected the arguments of a female couple married in Massachusetts that the federal DOMA is unconstitutional based on full faith and credit, due process, or equal protection.[24]

In September 2006, a Massachusetts judge permitted a Rhode Island couple to marry because Rhode Island did not have a statute forbidding same-sex marriage, and in February, 2007 Rhode Island's Attorney General said that same-sex marriages performed in Massachusetts should be recognized in Rhode Island.[25]

Michigan was one of the 13 states to approve a Defense of Marriage Amendment in November 2004. In March 2005, the state's Attorney General held that in view of the DOMA, state employees would not be eligible for domestic partner benefits in future CBAs. The ACLU and 21 couples filed a suit to clarify the status of these benefits, taking the position that the voters did not want to take away the health benefits of non-married couples, but merely wished to limit the definition of "marriage."[26]

The New York same-sex marriage litigation ended in mid-2006 with a ruling that the state Constitution does not give same-sex couples the right to marry. No federal issues were raised, so the case could not go to the U.S. Supreme Court. The New York court adopted the now-traditional rationales that limiting marriage to male-female couples promotes the rational state interest of stable environments for raising children, and that there is no tradition of same-sex marriage as a fundamental right.[27] The Eighth Circuit upheld Nebraska's 2000 amendment to the state constitution, forbidding not only same sex marriage but also civil unions and domestic partnerships, finding it sustainable because sexual orientation is not a suspect classification, and the provision did not violate equal protection; was not a bill of attainder; and served rational state objectives.[28]

The Arizona Court of Appeals upheld the state statute limiting marriage to male-female couples claiming it was rationally related to the state's legitimate interest in encouraging childrearing within the marital relationship—an interest that is not vitiated by permitting male-female couples to marry yet refrain from procreating.[29]

The crucial Massachusetts case authorizing same-sex marriage was decided in late 2003, when the Supreme Judicial Court held that the statute denying

---

[23] Lemons v. Bradbury, 538 F.3d 1098 (9th Cir. 2008).

[24] Wilson v. Ake, 354 F. Supp. 2d 1298 (M.D. Fla. 2005).

[25] CCH Benefits newsletter, *Oregon, New Hampshire, New York Extend Domestic Partner Benefits*, http://www.hr.cch.com/news/benefits/051807.asp 5/2/07; Pam Belluck, *New Hampshire Adopts Same-Sex Unions*, N.Y. Times 6/1/07 at p. A1; Katie Zezima, *Rhode Island Steps Toward Recognizing Same-Sex Marriage*, N.Y. Times 2/22/07 at p. A19.

[26] Rick Lyman, *Gay Couples File Suit After Michigan Denies Benefits*, N.Y. Times 4/4/05 at A16.

[27] Hernandez v. Robles, 7 N.Y.3d 338 (2006).

[28] Citizens for Equal Protection v. Bruning, 455 F.3d 856 (8th Cir. 2006).

[29] Standhardt v. Superior Ct., 77 P.3d 451 (Ariz. App. 2003).

same-sex marriage licenses violates rights under the state Constitution with respect to the benefits and protections of civil marriage, and was not rationally related to legitimate state objectives.

Massachusetts did not grant everything sought by same-sex couples. On August 18, 2004, the Superior Court upheld the state's law (dating back to 1913) prohibiting marriages of non-residents that would not be legal in their home state.[30] A 2006 ruling, however, permitted Rhode Islanders Wendy Becker and Mary Norton to marry in Massachusetts, because Rhode Island state law neither authorizes nor prohibits same-sex marriage, although same-sex couples from Connecticut, Vermont, Maine, or New Hampshire cannot marry in Massachusetts because their state law forbids same-sex marriage.[31]

In 2004, the Western District of Washington upheld the constitutionality of the Defense of Marriage Act, with the result that two women who were married in British Columbia were not permitted to file a joint bankruptcy petition, because their marriage was not valid in Washington State.[32] Washington decided in 2006 (although the panel split 5-4) that the ban on same-sex marriage under the state's DOMA is constitutional; that the provision did not create privilege or immunity for a favored majority class at the expense of a minority; and that the state rationally held that limiting marriage to male/female couples favored legitimate interests such as procreation and the well-being of children.[33] The Rhode Island Supreme Court said that same-sex couples who marry in Massachusetts cannot divorce in Rhode Island. Rhode Islanders can marry in Massachusetts because Rhode Island has not definitively forbidden same-sex marriages, but that legislative silence also means that there is no procedure for dissolving a same-sex union.[34] In contrast, on the basis of political changes, including New York Governor David A. Paterson's directive requiring state agencies to recognize same-sex marriages performed outside New York, New York Supreme Court Justice Rosalyn Richter permitted a lesbian couple who married in Massachusetts to divorce in New York.[35]

---

[30] Jennifer Peter, *Gay Couples Plan to Appeal Mass. Ruling*, AP 8/19/04 (law.com). Same-sex couples whose marriage would be unlawful in their home state cannot marry in Massachusetts, and Massachusetts does not recognize marriages that are void in the state in which they were contracted. Municipal clerks have a duty to check that nonresidents applying for marriage licenses who intend to reside outside Massachusetts are not forbidden to marry in their home state: Cote-Whitacre v. Department of Public Health, 446 Mass. 350 (Mass. 2006).

[31] Katie Zezima, Rhode Island Couple Win Same-Sex Marriage Case, N.Y. Times 9/30/06 at p. A9.

[32] *In re* Kandu, 73 L.W. 1117 (B.W.D. Wash. 8/17/04).

[33] Andersen v. King County, 138 P.3d 963 (Wash. 2006).

[34] Chambers v. Ormiston, 935 A.2d 956 (R.I. 2007), Katie Zezima, *Court Rules Against Same-Sex Divorce*, N.Y. Times 12/8/07 at p. A14.

[35] Noeleen G. Walder, *N.Y. Judge Grants Divorce to Lesbians Wed in Massachusetts*, N.Y.L.J. 10/24/08 (law.com), citing Martinez v. County of Monroe, 50 A.D.3d 189 (4th Dept. 2008) granting recognition to same-sex marriages performed in Canada.

Connecticut refused to hear a divorce petition to dissolve a Vermont civil union, on the grounds that the state does not give full faith and credit to such relationships. However, this ruling also implies that the partners in the union can simply dissolve it informally without involvement from the legal system.[36] New York's Supreme Court, New York County said that two men may have been mistaken about the legal validity of their 2005 marriage in Massachusetts (because New York did not recognize same-sex marriage), but they must still live up to their separation agreement because it is a contract. Male cohabitants cannot get divorced, but can distribute their property by private agreement.[37]

Washington State denied summary judgment on the issue of whether a decedent's property was jointly acquired with his same-sex life partner, holding that this is an equitable claim that does not depend on the legality of the relationship, or the gender or sexual orientation of the persons involved.[38]

Under Kansas law, a man cannot marry a post-operative male-to-female transsexual, because they are not "of the opposite sex," even though the purported wife had an amended Wisconsin birth certificate showing her sex as female.[39] Early in 2003, the Florida Circuit Court ruled that a female-to-male transsexual was a man, and his marriage to a woman was legal; he was awarded custody of the couple's two children. However, the ruling was overturned in mid-2004 by the state's Second District Court of Appeals, which found that Michael Kantaras was legally female, and the marriage to Linda Kantaras was invalid. The decision affected an undetermined number of marriages, because although Florida forbids same-sex marriage, it does not require proof of gender when a couple claiming to consist of one man and one woman seeks to marry.[40]

A 2002 Ohio case[41] allows a name change to a hyphenated name for a same-sex couple and their children, using the rationale that a state law that allows a name change for any reasonable and proper cause.

---

[36] Rosengarten v. Downes, 802 A.2d 170 (Conn. App. 7/30/02). In early 2004, the Washington Court of Appeals applied equitable distribution principles to divide the property of a female couple when their ten-year relationship terminated. The court noted that whether or not same-sex couples are allowed to marry, equitable distribution principles have been applied even in meretricious relationships: Robertson v. Gormley, discussed in Associated Press, *Washington State Appeals Court Upholds Gay Equity Ruling*, AP 2/4/04, http://seattletimes.nwsource.com/cgi-bin/PrintStory.pl?document_id=2.

[37] Anemona Hartocollis, *Married Or Not, Gay Couple's Separation Agreement Is Held Valid*, N.Y. Times 1/9/07 at p. B4.

[38] Vasquez v. Hawthorne, 33 P.3d 735 (Wash. 2001).

[39] *In re* Estate of Gardiner, 42 P.3d 120 (Kan. 2002). Similarly, Ohio ruled that it was not a violation of equal protection to deny a marriage license to a woman and her female-to-male transsexual partner, nor was the trial court obligated to give full faith and credit to an amended Massachusetts birth certificate reflecting the gender reassignment: *In re Application of* Nash and Barr, 72 L.W. 1440 (Ohio App. 12/31/03).

[40] Kantaras v. Kantaras, 71 L.W. 1568 (Fla. Cir. Ct. 2/21/03); Vickie Chachere, *Court: Transsexual Is Legally a Woman*, AP 7/23/04 (law.com).

[41] *In re* Bicknell, 771 N.E.2d 846 (Ohio 2002); *In re* Bacharach, 780 A.2d 597 (N.J. Super. 2001) is similar.

§ 16.04 ANNULMENT

Annulment is the retroactive determination by a court that a purported marriage was never valid because it was, e.g., incestuous; bigamous; the product of fraud or duress; or contracted by parties incapable of marrying because of age or mental status. Annulment actions are now comparatively rare, although they were common when the legal barriers to divorce were sturdier and unhappy marriage partners had to prove that their marriage had never validly come into effect. (The Uniform Marriage and Divorce Act uses the term "Declaration of Invalidity" rather than "annulment.")

A distinction should be drawn between marriages that are absolutely void and those that are only voidable. Because a void marriage is contrary to public policy, there is no need for the court system to intervene to declare the marriage invalid. However, a marriage that is merely voidable remains valid until and unless one spouse raises the invalidity of the marriage. Therefore, a voidable marriage can be ratified by the conduct of the "innocent spouse," and if a voidable marriage was not annulled as of the death of the first spouse, the other spouse will have a right of election against the decedent's will.

For a marriage to be annulled on the grounds of fraud, the fraudulent representations must have been made prior to the marriage, not afterwards; must be material; must have been relied on by the innocent party; and must go to the essence of the marriage contract (e.g., a representation to a Catholic fiancee of being a widower rather than divorced).

If a marriage is only voidable, not absolutely void, the spouse who is defending against the annulment action can raise defenses such as estoppel, ratification, and unclean hands. An absolutely void marriage cannot be ratified, although a party's unclean hands will prevent him or her from deriving any benefits from a void marriage.

The Hartford Supreme Court refused to permit two women to annul their Massachusetts civil marriage, because both states considered it invalid: Massachusetts, because the spouses were out-of-state residents and the marriage was illegal in their home state; Connecticut, because it deems same sex marriage contrary to public policy. In Connecticut, marriages can be annulled if they are void or voidable under Connecticut law or the law of the state where performed, but the judge refused to take jurisdiction.[42]

Many states (Alaska, Connecticut, Delaware, Illinois, Iowa, Michigan, Minnesota, New York, Oregon, Texas, Washington, Wisconsin) allow "equitable distribution" (see § 16.05[B] below) in annulment cases, although if the purported marriage was of short duration, the annulment court may refuse to make a property distribution because of the limited economic impact of the short "marriage."

---

[42] Lane v. Albanese (Hartford Supreme Ct. 2005); *see* Thomas B. Scheffey, *Court Powerless to Annul Same-Sex Marriage*, The Connecticut Law Tribune 3/31/05. (law.com).

§ 16.05 DIVORCE

Traditional religious concepts, which were very influential in civil law, considered marriage to be essentially indissoluble. Although on appropriate proof a legal separation (including support payments for the wife) could be granted, such a decree would not permit either spouse to remarry. As the twentieth century went on, divorce became far more socially acceptable, and there was significant demand for liberalization of divorce laws. Eventually, fault-based divorce became more easily accessible to plaintiffs who could prove, e.g., adultery, desertion, or physical or mental cruelty. (In many instances, the "evidence" was collusive or entirely fabricated, on behalf of a couple who simply did not want to be married to each other any more.)

Over time, a demand arose for "no-fault" divorce, based on a declaration by one or both spouses that the marriage was irretrievably compromised. All of the states have some form of no-fault divorce, but most of them also permit fault divorces. (Divorces generally can be granted more quickly on a fault basis; no-fault divorces often require a period of separation before the decree.) It is also possible that proof of fault will influence property division and spousal support in a no-fault divorce (i.e., the party at fault may have to pay more or receive less, especially if the marital fault itself was not only distressing to the party not at fault, but directly involved family finances).

A no-fault divorce is granted (depending on state law and circumstance) based on proof of irretrievable breakdown of the marriage or incompatibility of the partners. Another approach to no-fault divorce is the "conversion" divorce, finalized after the parties have been living apart for a stated period of time. Some conversion divorce statutes require the separation to have occurred pursuant to a separation agreement or court order.

The property of the spouses can be divided pursuant to a legal separation, and support can be ordered for the poorer spouse, but the parties remain married until such time as the marriage is actually dissolved by divorce.

A guardian has standing to proceed with a dissolution action filed by the ward before the adjudication of incapacity. Illinois joined several other jurisdictions in holding that the guardian's right to proceed with the action (although a guardian cannot initiate a divorce action on the ward's behalf) is implied even though it is not explicit in the statute.[43]

New York courts decided that a divorce can be granted for cruel and inhuman treatment on the basis of the wife's extramarital liaison (with a man she married after the divorce) but not for racial insults, which were not deemed to constitute cruel and inhuman treatment, at least if they did not threaten the victim's health or safety.[44]

---

[43] *In re* Burgess, 725 N.E.2d 1266 (Ill. 2000).

[44] Gentner v. Gentner, 736 N.Y.S.2d 431 (App. Div. 2001) (adultery); Omahen v. Omahen, 735 N.Y.S.2d 236 (App. Div. 2001) (racial slurs), both discussed in John Caher, *New York Court Reviews What Is "Cruel and Inhuman" in Divorce Case*, N.Y.L.J., 1/2/02 (law.com).

New Hampshire refused to grant a husband a divorce on adultery grounds based on his wife's sexual relationship with another woman. The court cited the dictionary definition of "intercourse" to deny that a lesbian relationship could constitute adultery.[45]

In a few states (e.g., South Carolina), an attorney who represents him- or herself in a divorce case is not entitled to an award of counsel fees, because the *pro se* divorce litigant does not incur an obligation to pay fees.[46]

Traditionally, causes of action were recognized for "criminal conversation" (engaging in sexual relations with a married person) and for "alienation of affections" (in essence, improper interference with the marital relationship), but a number of states have abolished these torts.[47]

Under New York law, avoidance of marital sexual relations for a period of a year or more constitutes constructive abandonment. The Westchester Supreme Court ruled, in a wife's divorce suit for cruel and inhuman treatment and constructive abandonment, the testimony of the husband's doctor that the husband had used four sample Viagra pills and used two of the ten prescribed pills required dismissal of the divorce complaint. The judge found the husband's statement that marital relations had occurred to be more credible than the wife's statement that they had not.[48]

[A] Divorce Instruments

The separation agreement is the central document in the process of divorce. Although only a court can issue a divorce decree (thus formally terminating the marriage), in practice courts generally approve the arrangements already agreed upon by the divorcing spouses and memorialized in the separation agreement.

Under the Uniform Marriage and Divorce Act, the court is bound by the provisions of the proposed agreement that deal with the relationship between the spouses (unless the proposals are unconscionable) but is not bound by provisions dealing with the support and custody of the children of the marriage. In non-UMDA jurisdictions, a separation agreement might be rejected by the court if it is unfair; if the parties failed to make full disclosure during the negotiation of the agreement; or if one party was represented by counsel but the other was denied access to legal advice.

An important issue is whether the separation agreement is intended to survive the divorce decree, or if it is intended to merge with the decree. If it merges (is incorporated) into the decree, then the agreement itself achieves the status of a court judgment. Violations can be punished as contempt of court. But flexibility is

---

[45] *In re* Blanchflower, 150 N.H. 226 (N.H. 2003).

[46] Calhoun v. Calhoun, 529 S.E.2d 14 (S.C. 2000).

[47] *See* the analysis in Helsel v. Noellsch, 107 S.W.3d 231 (Mo. 2003), especially Thomas v. Siddiqui, 869 S.W.2d 740 (Mo. 1994).

[48] C.W. v. G.W., No. 01112/05 (Westchester Sup. 2006), discussed in Mark Fass, *Proof of Viagra Use Rebuts Wife's Claim of Abandonment*, N.Y.L.J. 5/15/06 (law.com).

sacrificed: the provisions that derive from the separation agreement can only be modified to the extent that the judgment can be modified.

If, in contrast, the separation agreement is incorporated into the decree by reference, but does not merge, then the agreement becomes res judicata between the parties but is not a court judgment. Enforcement is via suit for breach of contract, not contempt of court, and it is unclear if the court even has continuing jurisdiction to hear an application for modification.

A couple will be permitted to make a separation agreement, incorporated into the divorce decree, that divests the court of jurisdiction to modify the amount of support. The amount of support specified in this manner cannot be modified, even if circumstances change.[49]

[B] Property Distributions

Until the 1960s, property distribution worked very differently in the community-property states (Arizona, Georgia, Idaho, Louisiana, Nevada, New Mexico, Texas, Washington, and Wisconsin) than in the other ("common-law") states. The community property states deemed the "community property" to belong to both spouses, and therefore it would have to be divided between the spouses incident to a divorce, no matter who formally owned the property, or whose funds had been used to acquire it. Division could be done equally (50% of the community property to each spouse) or using other approaches and formulas.

The common-law states tended to use a title theory: that is, property would be distributed to the spouse in whose name title was held. Usually, this was the husband, so wives often emerged from divorce with little or no property. Theoretically, some of the harshness of this result was ameliorated by the assumption that the husband would be required to pay alimony or other support to the wife, although ordered amounts often proved to be uncollectible in practice.

Since the 1960s, all the states, community and common-law, have been greatly influenced by equitable distribution concepts. The theory behind equitable distribution is that marriage is an economic as well as emotional partnership, and that both spouses make a contribution to the family's economic success. The contribution could be made in non-economic terms (homemaking and child rearing) as well as by earning money or investing the family's income.

Given this postulate, it is equitable to divide the couple's marital property to reflect their respective contributions as well as their financial needs. But that creates a complex system of interrelations between property division and orders for ongoing support. Furthermore, for couples with children, the financial needs of the children are a crucial factor. Because alimony is deductible by its payor and child support is not, there may be an incentive to structure the transaction to favor alimony; naturally the Internal Revenue Code, Regs., and court cases include some disincentives to abusive structures.

---

[49] Toni v. Toni, 636 N.W.2d 396 (N.D. 2001).

Depending on circumstances, distribution of assets may direct conveyance of specific assets to one spouse; or it may be necessary to sell certain assets in order to share the value equitably. A court in one state does not have the power to directly affect title to real property located in another state, but the court's personal jurisdiction over the parties is broad enough to order the parties to perform legal acts, such as quitclaiming property to the other spouse.

Many state divorce statutes provide for division of marital liabilities as well as marital assets. Even in the other states, debts related to acquisition of marital property will probably be subtracted when the value of such property is calculated.

[1] Bankruptcy Issues

NOTE: This discussion refers to pre-Bankruptcy Abuse Prevention and Consumer Protection Act of 2005 (BAPCA) law. BAPCA adds new Bankruptcy Code § 1129(a)(14), requiring payment in full of all "domestic support obligations" (broadly defined) that arise after the filing date of the bankruptcy petition. This provision was added to prevent divorcing persons from filing Chapter 11 petitions motivated by the desire to avoid complying with spousal property settlements. See Chapter 15 for more discussion.

Under Bankruptcy Code § 523(a)(5), discharge of property settlement obligations is possible, although arrears of payments supposed to be made but not made are not dischargeable.

A family home in Louisiana — community property — was awarded to the wife by partition incident to divorce, before the husband filed for bankruptcy. Therefore, it never became part of the husband's Chapter 7 bankruptcy estate.[50]

Minnesota's bankruptcy exemption for retirement benefits does not apply to an interest in an IRA that the debtor obtained through a divorce settlement rather than through employment.[51]

An award of half the husband's pension benefit to his wife, effective when he becomes eligible to retire, is an award of future benefits that is not dischargeable in bankruptcy.[52]

The Fifth Circuit ruled in late 2003 that a divorce-related transfer that does not divide the property equally between the spouses cannot be avoided in bankruptcy under Bankruptcy Code § 548 (as a transfer for less than reasonably equivalent value). The Fifth Circuit refused to second-guess the state court, in which the issue was fully litigated. (The debtor in this case was the wife, who received a less-than-50% share based on findings that she had dissipated marital assets and engaged in unreasonable litigation conduct that increased the attorneys' fees for the case.[53])

---

[50] Anderson v. Conine, 203 F.3d 855 (5th Cir. 2000).

[51] Anderson v. Seaver, 269 B.R. 27 (8th Cir. 2001).

[52] Brown v. Grossman, 259 B.R. 708 (Bankr. D.N.D. 2001).

[53] Ingalls v. Erlewine, 349 F.3d 205 (5th Cir. 2003).

[C] Separate vs. Community or Marital Property

However, an essential part of the community property or equitable distribution process is dividing the MARITAL property that belongs to the couple. In most cases, at least some items of property will actually be separate property of one spouse, and thus not subject to equitable distribution. Predictably, the allocation between marital and separate property can become a very contentious issue.

Certain types of property are usually accepted as separate:

- Property acquired before the marriage
- Property inherited by one spouse (unless the bequest was in the form "my niece Alice and her husband Greg")
- Gifts made to one spouse by someone other than the other spouse
- Each spouse's Social Security benefits (although the respective size of each spouse's benefit could affect the spousal support obligation: see § 16.05[F])
- Property subject to an agreement, such as an antenuptial or postnuptial agreement that exempts certain items from equitable distribution; perhaps property covered by a separation agreement.

If separate property is mingled with community or marital property, "transmutation" into marital property may occur if it becomes impossible to determine the nature of certain assets.

Certain items are more problematic, and state legislatures and courts in the various states have reached widely varying conclusions:

- Income or appreciation in value accruing during the marriage, on separate property
- Property acquired during marriage, but in exchange for separate property
- Personal injury proceeds received by one spouse; the issue could be whether the injury affected only that spouse, or (to the extent that the injury occurred and/or proceeds were received during the marriage) affected the family's overall financial status.

It is also vital to establish a "cutoff date" after which time property items will clearly not be marital, because the marriage has terminated. The cutoff date might be the date of the divorce; the date on which a decree of legal separation was entered; the date of the separation agreement between the parties (which can be much earlier than a litigation-related date, because the parties control the timing of their own agreement, without being bound by court calendars), or the valuation date for the property itself.

[1] Status of Special Items

If the property is of a type that generates income (e.g., stocks that pay dividends), further issues arise, especially as to the correct relationship between property division and ongoing spousal support. If the income-producing asset is used by one spouse in his or her work, the asset will probably be distributed to him or her. Other factors include which spouse is less financially well-off after the divorce (the poorer spouse is likely to be awarded a higher share of the income-producing property) and whether the income-producing asset is more closely connected to one spouse than the other (e.g., one spouse provided the funds to purchase the asset; if stock was issued as a bonus to an employee spouse).

Most of the states (although not New York, which is certainly the situs of a great many divorces) treat an advanced degree or professional license as the separate property of the spouse who earned it. However, even in states that generally treat the degree or license as separate, a different result might be reached in a case in which there are few other assets (e.g., the divorce occurs shortly after graduation or licensure) and the non-degreed spouse would receive little or no spousal support under the state's rules. Another possibility is that, although the degree or license will be the sole property of the person earning it, the other spouse might be awarded money plus interest as compensation for the investment the non-degreed spouse put into the earning of the degree. (The classic instance is the nurse who puts her husband through medical school, or the secretary who contributes toward her husband's law school tuition.)

In contrast, the goodwill of a business, or even of a professional practice, is commonly treated as a marital asset. Recent cases often add a refinement: the goodwill of a professional practice might be deemed marital only if it could be sold separately as a business asset, and is not dependent on the personal reputation or continued presence within the firm of the divorcing spouse.

Another recent trend is to treat "celebrity status" (which might be interpreted as the goodwill of an "entertainment" or "sports" practice) as a marital asset.

At least four analyses have been applied to Workers' Compensation benefits:

(1) If the claim accrued during marriage, the benefits are marital, even if payments have not begun, and the claim has not been liquidated, as of the time of the divorce

(2) The claim is marital only to the extent that it compensates for injury to the marital estate

(3) Payments received before the cutoff date can be marital, but those received afterwards are separate

(4) Benefits are marital only to the extent that they can be traced either to wages lost during the marriage, or to medical expenses paid for with marital funds.

Another issue is that, even if the benefits are considered marital, the underlying injury is likely to affect the injured spouse's economic status and therefore his or her equitable share of marital assets and entitlement to spousal support.

A tax loss carry-forward occurring during the marriage is divisible marital property, because the nature of a marital asset is a thing of value arising out of the marital relationship.[54]

[D] Pensions and Divorce

A very common situation is for divorcing couples to have only two significant assets: a family home and pension rights belonging to one spouse, often the husband. If the pension rights are approximately equivalent in value to the home, then a simple structure that often works well is for the wife to be awarded the home, and the employee-husband to get 100% ownership of the pension rights. However, if the couple does not own a home, or if the value of the home is divided, then awarding the pension rights entirely to the employee spouse would leave the non-employee spouse with few assets and little financial security in his or her old age.

The timing of the divorce is quite significant. It is one thing if the employee spouse has already retired and is receiving pension benefits, or has elected a lump sum (see § 3.05[C] for discussion of retirement planning issues).

Therefore, division of pension rights is significant in many divorce cases. The state statute could make explicit how vested and non-vested pension rights should be distributed; or it could be a matter of case law. Pensions earned during the marriage are usually considered a marital asset, whether or not they are vested at the time of the divorce. The Fourth Circuit upheld the constitutionality of the Uniformed Services Former Spouses' Protection Act of 1982 (10 USC § 1408 *et seq.*). The Act lets states treat a servicemember's military retirement pay as property that can be divided on divorce, and allows state courts to order direct payment of part of the pension to the non-military spouse. A group of service-members and retired servicemembers brought a due process and equal protection challenge and charged that full faith and credit requires the treatment of military pay to be uniform nationwide, but the Fourth Circuit found the constitutional claims meritless.[55]

Statutes and case law are not consistent as to how post-retirement Cost of Living increases will be divided; whether the non-employee spouse can benefit from pension enhancements attributable to raises that the employee spouse earned after the divorce; and what happens to stock acquired under option plans where the exercise occurred after the divorce. IRA and 401(k) accounts raise similar issues to pension plans provided by employers.

Although state law is very important in this context, federal law, especially ERISA, cannot be ignored. For one thing, if the separation agreement or court decree calls for diversion of part of the pension benefit (currently or when payments begin in the future), the plan administrator can abide by this provision only if presented with a valid Qualified Domestic Relations Order (QDRO). QDROs are

---

[54] Finkelstein v. Finkelstein, 701 N.Y.S.2d 52 (App. Div. 2000).

[55] Adkins v. Rumsfeld, 464 F.3d 456 (4th Cir. 2006).

subject to various requirements, including one that a plan administrator cannot be ordered to make payments in any form that the plan does not otherwise provide.

Early in 2001, the Supreme Court ruled that ERISA preempts a Washington State statute that automatically revokes benefit designations (for life insurance as well as employee benefits) when the employee spouse and the named beneficiary divorce. State law regulation is preempted because this is a core ERISA area.[56]

Given the inevitability of some degree of tax liability, the Minnesota rule is that tax consequences are a factor to be considered in dividing property, and retirement benefits can be valued on an after-tax basis.[57]

[E] Equalization Payments

In some cases, it is possible simply to draw up a schedule of assets, and make an allocation of assets so that, once each spouse has received certain specified assets, the division will be accepted as equitable by both sides. In other cases, it will make sense to distribute certain assets to one spouse rather than to the other. For instance, if the husband is a truck driver and the wife operates a desktop publishing business, it makes sense to distribute the truck to him and the computer to her. Yet this allocation may result in one spouse receiving assets with an aggregate value greater than the percentage of marital assets that is considered equitable for that spouse.

Equalization payments are cash awards ordered by the divorce court, instead of or in conjunction with the property awards. Equalization payments are part of the property division; they are not alimony or maintenance payments. Instead, they are ordered to compensate a spouse who receives tangible assets lower than his or her equitable share. The usual measure of the equalization payment is the present value of the property that the payment replaces.

[F] Alimony and Spousal Support

Traditionally, when a woman entered into marriage, she surrendered the right to own property (even property that had belonged to her prior to the marriage). In some degree of compensation, traditional legal doctrine required that, on the (very rare) occasion of the termination of a marriage, the husband would be required to make alimony payments for the support of the wife for her lifetime.

Current concepts about alimony (called spousal support in many states) are very different. First of all, under the Supreme Court's 1979 decision in *Orr v. Orr*,[58] alimony must be available on a unisex basis: the richer spouse must become responsible for the support of the poorer spouse, or the spouse with greater needs. Although it is more common for the payor to be male and the payee to be female, this is by no means obligatory. Texas law does not provide for ongoing spousal support; all the other states have at least some provision.

---

[56] Egelhoff v. Egelhoff, 532 U.S. 141 (2001).
[57] Maurer v. Maurer, 623 N.W.2d 604 (Minn. 2001).
[58] 440 U.S. 268 (1979).

Because alimony is ordered in conjunction with a property division, the focus has shifted from an obligation spanning the payee spouse's life to smaller amounts and shorter periods of time. In many circumstances (e.g., the marriage was childless and of short duration; both spouses earned or are deemed capable of earning a good income), alimony will not be ordered at all. Another possibility is rehabilitative alimony: a short-term award made to put one spouse in a position where he or she will have enhanced earning potential (e.g., until he or she has finished a degree or other training).

If the parties' circumstances change — for instance, if the recipient becomes wealthier than the obligor — the court can extinguish the permanent alimony obligation, even if the obligor is still alive and the recipient has not remarried. The relevant statute does not say that alimony cannot be terminated. The word "permanent" is just used to distinguish it from other forms of alimony, and does not necessarily mean that the payments will have to continue until the recipient's death.[59]

The support award can be modified by the court based on a significant change in the circumstances of either payor or recipient. However, courts are not likely to be sympathetic where the payor alleges a need to opt out of the materialistic milieu that supplied a high income before the award was ordered.

Where the parties' income is greater than the maximum amount in the tables, state support guidelines do not determine the amount of spousal support to be ordered. Instead, the case should be treated like a high-income child support case: i.e., the obligor's ability to pay should be balanced against the recipient's needs.[60]

A divorce decree requiring the husband to provide the wife with health insurance equivalent to the coverage during marriage obligated the husband to provide a level of coverage at least as great as his employment-related coverage. When the husband provided an inferior conversion policy, that made him a self-insurer, liable for the wife's medical expenses to the extent of the shortfall.[61]

According to the Missouri Court of Appeals, it was not an abuse of discretion to order a husband to pay the wife's legal fees (including the fees for the appeal rendering this decision), given her limited assets and earning abilities. His conduct during the marriage, including spousal abuse, was also a factor. In contrast, however, North Dakota treated general fault in marriage as an inadequate reason for ordering the husband to pay the wife's legal fees where she was the higher earner. In this analysis, income and litigation conduct — not marital conduct — are the most relevant factors.[62]

The payor's bankruptcy filing does not discharge the alimony obligation (indeed the Bankruptcy Code specifically makes alimony and child support

[59] De Grazia v. De Grazia, 741 A.2d 1057 (D.C. 1999).
[60] Mascaro v. Mascaro, 764 A.2d 1085 (Pa. Super. 2000).
[61] Blair v. Blair, 527 S.E.2d 177 (Ga. 2000).
[62] *Compare* Brady v. Brady, 39 S.W.3d 557 (Mo. App. 2001) *with* Reiser v. Reiser, 621 N.W.2d 348 (N.D. 2001).

obligations nondischargeable; see § 523), but might be considered a change in circumstances justifying downward modification of the obligation. In this context, federal bankruptcy law, and not state domestic relations law, determines whether a disputed payment can be characterized as alimony or child support rather than as an ordinary, dischargeable obligation.

The general rule is that the death of either the payor or the payee terminates the obligation, but a separation agreement can validly provide for continuation of payments from the estate, after the payor's death. It makes practical sense for a separation agreement (or antenuptial agreement) calling for post-death alimony to provide for a lump sum or a present-value calculation to simplify estate administration. Another possibility is for the obligor spouse to maintain insurance on his or her own life, with the payee spouse named as irrevocable beneficiary.

The Equal Credit Opportunity Act (ECOA) and its implementing Regulation B give alimony recipients a choice: they can either cite alimony as an income item when they apply for credit, or they can omit it and have their creditworthiness assessed without consideration of alimony.

[G] Tax Issues in Divorce

Some potential tax issues for divorcing couples are eliminated by IRC § 1041, which provides that property transfers between spouses incident to divorce are not taxable. A transfer to a third party on behalf of a spouse is also tax-free (Reg. § 1.1041-1T(c)), but sale of property by one spouse to a third party is taxable, even if the proceeds of the sale are used to satisfy obligations under a divorce decree.[63] However, many other issues remain current, including the extent to which a tax return signed during marriage by an "innocent spouse" can nevertheless result in tax penalties for him or her.

Broadly speaking, an alimony payor can deduct the payments, and the recipient must treat them as taxable income (IRC § 71) — with the result that it becomes necessary to distinguish between payments made for spousal versus child support; as alimony rather than as a property distribution; and current payments vs. arrears. No alimony deduction is available for amounts paid pursuant to a written schedule of payments submitted to the payee spouse's attorney; the Tax Court treated such payments as purely voluntary, neither made subject to a court decree nor a written separation agreement.[64]

In 1998, the Supreme Court struck down a New York State law that permitted alimony deductions on resident but not on nonresident state income tax returns, finding[65] no rational support for the distinction.

---

[63] Ingham v. United States, 167 F.3d 1240 (9th Cir. 1999).

[64] Keegan v. Comm'r, TC Memo 1997-359 (1997).

[65] Lunding v. New York Tax Appeals Tribunal, 521 U.S. 1102 (1998).

[1] Innocent Spouse Relief

The Internal Revenue Service Restructuring and Reform Act of 1998 (IRSRRA '98, P.L. 105-205), added IRC § 6015, for the benefit of innocent spouses who would otherwise face tax penalties because of tax wrongdoing by the other spouse. Rev. Proc. 2000-15, 2000-5 IRB 447 explains how divorced and separated spouses can obtain equitable relief as "requesting spouses." The Form 8857 Request for Innocent Spouse Relief (and Separation of Liability, and Equitable Relief) must be filed no later than two years after the IRS' first collection activity taken against the requesting spouse. An executor is entitled to seek tax relief on behalf of a deceased innocent spouse: Rev. Rul. 2003-36, 2003-18 IRB 849.

Early in 2001, the Treasury proposed Regulations on innocent spouse relief (66 FR 3888 (1/17/01)), finalized with some changes in July 2002: 67 FR 47278 (7/18/2002). The proposals define an "erroneous item" that gives rise to potential liability as any item that causes the liability to be reduced because of improper reporting. A spouse who knows that an item exists cannot qualify as an innocent spouse, even if he or she does not know the proper tax characterization of the item.

The Tax Court has decided many innocent spouse cases, centering around issues such as the spouse's knowledge of the items and when a spouse has benefited by the other spouse's tax and other transactions.

§ 16.06 EFFECT OF DIVORCE ON CHILDREN OF THE MARRIAGE

When children have been born of a marriage, and at least one is still a minor at the time of separation or divorce, it becomes necessary to make arrangements for their custody; for visitation by the noncustodial parent; and for their financial support. Because this is an area in which uniformity is important, many states have adopted uniform laws: first the Uniform Child Custody Jurisdiction Act (UCCJA), which was adopted by all the states, then the revision, the Uniform Child Custody Jurisdiction and Enforcement Act (UCCJEA). As of mid-2007, NCCUSL announced that South Carolina had become the forty-sixth state to adopt the Uniform Child Custody Jurisdiction Enforcement Act, with Massachusetts, Missouri, New Hampshire and Vermont as the sole holdouts. The UCCJEA is designed to avoid impasses where State #1 awards custody to one parent, but the other parent takes the child to another state and seeks a change in custody. Under the UCCJEA, home-state jurisdiction has priority, and an order made by a state with continuing exclusive jurisdiction can be enforced in all the other states. Nor can other states modify the order unless the first state agrees to surrender jurisdiction. The Act also permits interstate registration and expedited enforcement of custody orders, and grants protection to victims of domestic violence.[66]

---

[66] NCCUSL press release, *Final Push for Nationwide Enactment of UCCJEA*, http://www.nccusl.org/nccusl/DesktopModules/NewsDisplay.aspx?ItemID=182. (6/11/07)

These statutes provide that the court that originally had jurisdiction over a custody case retains jurisdiction even if the children move to another state. The statutes include procedures for filing the decree with the courts of other states. Only the original court can modify the decree — unless the original state loses all ties with the case, or the original court refuses to exercise jurisdiction (e.g., the petitioner has unclean hands or has intentionally interfered with visitation).

The federal Parental Kidnapping Prevention Act of 1980 (PKPA) gives full faith and credit to custody decrees (unless the issuing court lacked jurisdiction, declines to exercise its jurisdiction, or it is necessary to take emergency measures to protect a child who is at risk). The PKPA creates remedies for interstate "child snatching" (kidnapping by the noncustodial parent).

In the international arena, most nations have signed the Hague Convention. Congress has implemented the Hague Convention in the International Child Abduction Remedies Act, 42 USC § 11601, for civil remedies,[67] and the International Parental Kidnapping Crime Act, 18 USC § 1204.

[A] Custody

While a marriage continues, both parents have custody of the children of the marriage. If one of the parents dies, the other parent automatically gains sole custody. If both parents die, the local family court will appoint a guardian. If the deceased parent(s) designated a guardian in advance, that designation will probably be given effect by the court, unless there is some reason why the designated guardian is inappropriate.

While a divorce case is pending, the divorce court has jurisdiction to enter temporary orders of custody, which can be made permanent when the divorce is granted. Usually, the parent who has physical custody will also have legal custody, and will be given decision-making powers over the way the child(ren) will be raised.

[1] Evolution of the "Best Interests" Standard

The basic common-law concept was that children were essentially property, and like other marital property belonged to the husband and father. Thus, custody was always awarded to the father. As divorce became more common, a new theory evolved: that children of "tender years" should be in the custody of their mothers.

That theory has been replaced by an inquiry into the best interests of the child, which could call for either parent to be awarded sole custody, or for the parents to be given joint legal custody. Joint legal custody gives the parents equal responsibility for making crucial decisions about the children, such as providing medical

---

[67] A finding under the Hague Convention that a wrongfully removed child is at grave risk of harm if returned to the child's country of habitual residence makes further inquiries irrelevant; the remedies of the home jurisdiction's courts need not be explored: Danaipour v. McLarey, 386 F.3d 289 (1st Cir. 2004).

care. It may or may not give the parents equal physical custody (the actual right to have the children live with them at stated times).

Although a few states disfavor joint custody, most states at least treat it as an option; many states create a rebuttable presumption that joint custody will be awarded, absent a reason to award sole custody to one parent. Split custody awards custody of some of the children to one parent, some to the other. It will usually be disfavored; in fact, it is unusual even for half- and step-siblings to be split up, unless there is some good reason for the children to have different homes.

The current presumption is that the parent who is the primary caretaker (responsible for spending time with the child, preparing meals, doing laundry, and other physical and emotional tasks) will be awarded custody, unless there is a good reason to make other arrangements. Some states seek to preserve the relationship with both parents by giving a custody preference to the "friendly parent" who is less likely to interfere with visitation. The parent who will least disrupt the child's accustomed environment (neighborhood, school, activities, etc.) may also be preferred.

At least theoretically, courts are not supposed to give preference to the more affluent parent, and economic inequality between parents that is harmful to the children is supposed to be adjusted by child support, and perhaps by spousal support and division of marital property.

If the child is mature enough to express a reasonable preference, the child's preference may be consulted, but is not likely to be determinative. UMDA § 310 permits the court to appoint an attorney specifically to represent the child(ren) on custody issues. The fee is paid by one or both parents, or by the state if the parents are indigent.

The "best interests" analysis has more or less replaced an inquiry into the "fitness" of parents. Although it was traditional to deny custody to a parent who violated conventional beliefs about morality (especially sexual morality), there is an increasing trend to disregard the parent's sexual behavior (and perhaps past or even current alcohol or substance use) in the custody determination unless the behavior has some deleterious effect on the children.

In a case of first impression, the Texas Court of Appeals ruled that the trial court's power to issue permanent injunctions to protect the best interests of the children extends to a permanent injunction against either ex-spouse having overnight visitors when the child is present. (Temporary restraining orders forbidding overnight guests are fairly common, but such orders usually are issued pendente lite only.) The court rejected the father's argument that his stable relationship provides a family atmosphere for the child. The appellate court did not find the injunction to constitute an abuse of discretion.[68]

---

[68] Peck v. Peck, 172 S.W.3d 26 (Tex. App. 2005); *see* John Council, *Court Restricts Overnight Visitors for Divorced Parents*, Texas Lawyer 8/8/05 (law.com).

However, a number of states have statutes disfavoring awarding custody to a parent who has committed any one act of serious domestic violence, or has engaged in a pattern of lesser abuse.[69]

The Mississippi Court of Appeals ruled in early 2005 that it was proper for the trial court to consider the mother's lesbian lifestyle and her failure to take the children to church in changing custody to the father. Although an unmarried parent's sexual relations cannot be the sole factor in determining custody, having a relationship was a substantial change. Although churchgoing was not required by any court order, the childrens' religious development is a factor in custody determinations.[70]

It was an error for the trial court to award custody to the father on the basis that the children might be harassed because the custodial mother's paying tenant was a lesbian (the mother did not have a sexual relationship with the tenant). There was no evidence that the children were harmed in any way by this residential situation.[71]

In a case where the mother wanted the 9-year-old child baptized into the Russian Orthodox Church and the father wanted baptism delayed until the child was 12, the trial court ordered that baptism be deferred at least until age 13, when the child herself would be asked to make the decision. However, the Pennsylvania Superior Court ruled that the mother should not have been enjoined from having the child baptized, because baptism does not create a significant risk of harm and should be permitted under the heading of the parent's right to provide religious instruction.[72]

In rare instances, non-parents will seek custody of children who have one or both living parents, but it is very unusual that a court will prefer a non-parent over a parent unless the parent has been in some way abusive or seriously unfit.

Half-siblings can be separated even without a showing of actual harm if the children were kept together. In this case, a father was awarded custody of a five-year-old boy whose half-brother remained with the mother, based on the father's more stable living situation and greater ability to provide for the child.[73]

A female couple conceived a child with sperm donated by a man who was also a partner in a same-sex relationship. When the women's relationship ended, the Minnesota Court of Appeals granted their request for joint legal custody. The biological mother's grant of physical custody was conditioned on her moving back to Minnesota where her former partner and the sperm donor lived.[74]

---

[69] A proposed statute of this type was approved as Constitutional by Opinion of the Justices to the Senate, 691 N.E.2d 911 (Mass. Sup. Jud. Ct. 1998).

[70] Davidson v. Coit, 899 So.2d 904 (Miss. App. 2005).

[71] Taylor v. Taylor, 353 Ark. 69 (Ark. 2003).

[72] Hicks v. Hicks, 868 A.2d 1245 (Pa. Super. 2005).

[73] Viamonte v. Viamonte, 748 A.2d 493 (Md. Spec. App. 2000).

[74] La Chapelle v. Mitten, 607 N.W.2d 151 (Minn. App. 2000).

California issued a number of ground-breaking decisions about the parental rights of female-female couples. Two women can be dual parents of a child — opening the way for counties to sue for child support after the termination of a relationship, at least where there was an agreement that the woman who did not give birth would provide support to the children born during the relationship. A birth mother was unsuccessful in overturning a court judgment that she and her ex-partner were both legal parents of their child; the court said she could not attack the validity of an agreement she had stipulated to.[75]

Vermont ruled that two women who had a civil union are both mothers of their daughter. After the dissolution of the relationship, Virginia granted sole custody to the birth mother, on the grounds that same-sex unions are void in all respects under Virginia law. However, in November 2006, the Virginia Court of Appeals accepted the Vermont Supreme Court ruling giving parental rights to both, holding that the PKPA required Virginia to defer to the Vermont court and give full faith and credit to the Vermont court order, irrespective of the validity of the civil union.[76]

In an Ohio case, one female partner donated an ovum and the other partner carried the pregnancy. When their relationship ended, both sought to be named as co-custodians. The trial court held that the petition could only be made in a custody dispute, but the Ohio Court of Appeals held that they should have been allowed to move for shared custody. The case was remanded for a determination of which woman should be deemed the birth mother.[77]

New Jersey's Burlington County Family Court, pursuant to the state Supreme Court's October 25, 2006 decision that same-sex couples must receive the same rights and protections as male/female couples, held that both mothers can be listed as parents on their newborn's birth certificate if they are registered as domestic partners. The Attorney General's office announced that it would no longer oppose such applications. The effect is that both mothers are full parents and the non-birth mother does not have to adopt the child. However for male couples who employ a surrogate mother, the birth mother cannot surrender parental rights until after the child's birth, at which point the non-biological father must adopt the child.[78]

---

[75] Elisa B. v. Superior Ct. (Emily B), 37 Cal. 4th 108 (El Dorado Co. 2005); K.M. v. E.G., 05 CDOS 7504; Kristine H. v. Lisa R., 37 Cal. 4th 156, discussed in Mike McKee, *Calif. Same-Sex Couples Win Parenting Rights* (8/24/05) (law.com).

[76] Adam Liptak, *Ruling Lets Women Share Rights in Fight Over Custody*, N.Y. Times 11/29/06 at p. A20 and Adam Liptak, *Parental Rights Upheld for Lesbian Ex-Partner*, N.Y. Times 8/5/06 at p. A11; for the history of the litigation, *see* Miller-Jenkins v. Miller-Jenkins, 180 Vt. 441 (Vt. 2006); Miller-Jenkins v. Miller-Jenkins, CJ04-280 (Va. Cir. Ct. 10/15/04). *See also* King v. S.B., 818 N.E.2d 126 (Ind. App. 2004) (treating both women as mothers of a child conceived by artificial insemination during their relationship; they agreed to raise the child, so both of them are legal parents, by analogy with a husband who consented to artificial insemination of his wife).

[77] *In re JDM*, 73 L.W. 1272 (Ohio App. 10/11/04).

[78] Laura Mansnerus, *Child Born to Lesbian Couple Will Have 2 Mothers Listed*, N.Y. Times 11/16/06 at p. B3.

[2] Modification and Enforcement of Custody Orders

The general rule is that the custodial parent will be allowed to move out of the city or state for bona fide reasons (e.g., remarriage; a new job; a military commitment), taking the child(ren) along, even if this makes it more difficult for the non-custodial parent to see the child.[79] But if a move is allowed, it is very likely that the non-custodial parent will be granted longer visits, e.g., weekends or part or all of school holidays.

Like all rules, this one is subject to exceptions. In 2004, California held that a number of factors, including the relationship with the non-custodial parent, must be considered before a court will permit a custodial parent to move. Other factors include: the interest of the children in stability and continuation of the same custodial arrangement; the length of the move; the children's wishes; the reason for the planned move; and the relationship of the children to both parents. The California legislature considered a bill to preserve the presumptive right of the custodial parent (who is usually the mother) to relocate.[80]

A New York trial court permitted a woman to move to Toronto with the son of her first marriage, but only on condition that she place $60,000 in escrow as security against interference with the boy's father's court-ordered visitation. The mother also had to pay travel expenses for her ex-husband to travel to visit the boy. The mother remarried and had two children in the second marriage; her husband wished to move to Toronto. The court permitted this but ordered payment of $50 per month from the escrow to a lawyer for managing the account.[81]

A court's custody order can be enforced in contempt, and the appropriate remedy for a non-custodial parent who alleges interference with visitation is to apply for a court order. Withholding alimony will probably not be considered appropriate. Withholding child support will certainly not be considered an appropriate self-help measure, because impairing the child's standard of living is hardly a rational response to denial of visitation. (By the same token, custodial parents who allege non-payment of support are supposed to seek enforcement of the support order rather than interfering with visitation.)

As court orders, custody orders are subject to modification. Usually, the standard is whether there has been a change in circumstances such that the best interests of the child would be served by modification. The Uniform Marriage and Divorce Act imposes a stricter standard, however: modification is permitted only if continuation of the original order would pose a serious danger to the child's well-being.

A parent with joint custody can be prosecuted for conspiracy and custodial interference for kidnapping a child from the other parent who has joint custody.

---

[79] *See, e.g., In re* DMG, 66 L.W. 1496 (Mont. Sup. 1/5/98).

[80] *In re* the Marriage of LaMusga, 32 Cal. 4th 1072 (Cal. 2004), discussed in Mike McKee, *Divorced Parents Must Consider Ex if Moving Away.* The Recorder 5/3/04 (law.com).

[81] Tortomas v. Andrade, No. 003519-2003 (Suffolk Sup. Ct. 2005); *see* Andrew Harris, *Court Orders $60,000 Bond to Ensure Visitation Rights*, N.Y.L.J. 8/10/05 (law.com).

The knowledge and intent elements of the custodial interference statute must be proved beyond a reasonable doubt.[82]

Before a child is seized to enforce a default judgment awarding custody to the other parent in another state, Due Process requires a pre-enforcement hearing for the custodial parent.[83]

[3] Custody Suit Procedures

In a custody case, the Guardian ad Litem is appointed primarily to serve the best interests of the child. An attorney/GAL also acts as a neutral factfinder for the judge. Where there is no conflict, an attorney/GAL also acts as the lawyer representing the child's own wishes. However, an attorney who perceives a conflict should notify the court to consider appointing an additional attorney specifically to advance the child's viewpoint. It is inappropriate for an attorney/GAL to testify as a fact witness in the case.[84] To be awarded emotional distress damages against a lawyer who allegedly mismanaged a custody suit, the malpractice plaintiff must show either physical consequences or malicious conduct on the attorney's part.[85] Another divorce-related malpractice case denies punitive damage to a malpractice plaintiff because, although the professional negligence action technically sounds in tort, it bears a stronger resemblance to a breach of contract action, for which punitive damages are not available.[86]

[B] Child Support

Divorce terminates the status of two adults as one another's spouses, but (at least unless a step-parent adoption occurs), the two adults continue their status as the parents of children born or adopted during the marriage.

Child support continues until:

- The child reaches majority
- The child becomes emancipated (e.g., by marriage, employment, or military enlistment)
- Parental rights are terminated (based on abuse, or when the child is adopted by the new spouse of the custodial parent)
- The child dies
- The payor parent dies. However, the Uniform Marriage and Divorce Act § 316(c) holds that the death of the payor parent does NOT terminate the support obligation, although the obligation may be revoked, modified, or commuted to a lump sum if the interests of justice so require.

---

[82] State v. Vakilzaden, 251 Conn. 656, 742 A.2d 767 (Conn. 1999).

[83] Morrell v. Mock, 270 F.3d 1090 (7th Cir. 2001).

[84] Meekins v. Corbett, 26 FLR 1231 (D.C. Super. 2/17/00).

[85] Long-Russell v. Hampe, 39 P.3d 1015 (Wyo. 2001).

[86] O'Connell v. Bean, 556 S.E.2d 741 (Va. 2002).

Usually the child support obligation will end when the child reaches 18, but some divorce courts will order the obligor parent to pay higher education expenses for a child over 18. (This is true even though, in an ongoing marriage, the court would not intervene to require parents to pay college expenses.)

In order to receive federal funding, states are required to have child support guidelines in place, focusing on the payor parent's income level (rather than on the needs of the child), or the combined income of both custodial and non-custodial parent. The result is that a very wealthy child support obligor may be required to make extremely high child support payments. Changes in the financial circumstances and needs of either the child or the payor can lead to modification of the child support obligation.

The Uniform Interstate Family Support Act (UIFSA) has replaced earlier legislation on this topic, the Uniform Support of Dependents Law (USDL), Uniform Reciprocal Enforcement of Support Act (URESA), and Revised Uniform Reciprocal Enforcement of Support Act (RURESA). Although in many instances so-called uniform laws are subject to significant state-to-state differences, UIFSA has been adopted by all the states in more or less the same form. Technically, UIFSA applies to spousal as well as child support, but many of its provisions are drafted with child support in mind. When the custodial parent files a support action in the jurisdiction in which the child lives, the case will then be referred and heard in the jurisdiction in which the allegedly defaulting child support obligor lives.

Long-arm jurisdiction is available under the UIFSA under eight grounds, including personal service within the state; consent; having resided with the child within the state; or even having engaged in sexual relations within the state that could have led to conception of the child requiring support.

The court issuing a UIFSA child support order retains continuing exclusive jurisdiction over the award, and it can be modified by another state (i.e., the state in which the potential payor resides) only under very limited circumstances. Other states cannot modify a UIFSA spousal support order at all, so a payor seeking modification must litigate in the courts of the state in which the payee resides.

[1] Factors in Setting the Level of Support

Although some states use the "income shares" model (i.e., the child's access to each parent's income should not be affected by divorce), Kentucky refused to apply the child support guidelines in a case where one parent had income far in excess of the guidelines (here, $57,000 a month, where the guidelines only went up to $15,000 a month).[87]

Pennsylvania ruled in 2004 that where there is a significant disparity of income, and it serves the child's best interest, the parent with primary custody can be ordered to pay child support to the parent with partial custody.[88]

---

[87] Downing v. Downing, 45 S.W.3d 449 (Ky. App. 2001).
[88] Colonna v. Colonna, 579 Pa. 704 (Pa. 2004).

The Oregon Court of Appeals upheld a state statute permitting a divorce court to order either parent, or both parents, to support a child who is in college. The court did not find the Equal Protection argument (that married parents who live together are not subject to such an obligation) compelling, because of the state's interest in a well-educated population, and because divorced people have not experienced a legacy of prejudice that would make them a suspect class. Furthermore, because child support is not ordered in intact families, there is no body of precedent to draw on.[89]

When both parents were fairly affluent, it was permissible to order the out-of-state father to pay half the expenses of the child's state college, even though the child had funds of her own from scholarships and UGMA funds from grandparents. (The court refused to accept the father's argument that the obligation should be limited to half the in-state tuition.) The parents' lifestyle also made it reasonable to expect them to pay the child's car insurance and sorority fees when she was in college.[90]

Former football player Michael Strahan was ordered to pay $18,000 a month in child support in 2006. His appeal succeeded in 2008; the New Jersey Court of Appeals found the amount too high and unfairly apportioned. The lower court did not make the findings of fact that would be necessary to sustain the decision and order support that exceeds the guidelines by $200,000 a year. The Court of Appeals held that it was unfair to assign 91% of the support obligation to Strahan, particularly since his wife has a college education and could work but chooses not to. (In 2007, Strahan earned close to $6 million.) The appellate court said that the trial court failed to distinguish between needs that are reasonable for children their age (the couple's twin girls were born in 2004) and the children's demands. Although it is acceptable for a custodial parent to receive incidental benefits from child support, in this case it appeared that some of the payments actually benefited the ex-wife, notwithstanding that the couple had a pre-nuptial agreement and no alimony was awarded. The case remanded to determine how much income should be imputed to the ex-wife. The appellate court also reversed the trial court's order that Strahan maintain a $7.5 million disability policy as security for future payments, because a divorced parent can seek modification of the support obligation if circumstances change, and Strahan retired from playing football and became a sport commentator, a job with much less risk of injury.[91]

A woman who quit a full-time job so she could work part-time and take care of the children of her current marriage was considered voluntarily unemployed with respect to her support obligations toward the children of her first marriage.

---

[89] *In re* McGinley, 19 P.3d 954 (Or. App. 2001).

[90] Saliba v. Saliba, 753 So. 2d 1095 (Miss. 2000).

[91] Strahan v. Strahan, No. A-3747-06 (N.J. App. 2008); Michael Booth, *"Three Pony Rule" Invoked to Cut Former NFL Player's Monthly $18K Child Support*, N.J.L.J. 8/27/08 (law.com); the rule that "no child needs more than three ponies" no matter how wealthy the parents are comes from *In re* Patterson, 920 P.2d 450 (Kan. App. 1996).

However, the court held[92] that after the presumptive support obligation was set, an adjustment could be made based on the support needs of the children of the second marriage.

In contrast, Wisconsin ruled that it was not a dereliction of the child support obligation for a divorced doctor who had joint custody to quit her job to stay at home with the children. The court upheld the father's (also a doctor's) obligation to pay child support under an amendment to the divorce decree. Because of the stock market decline, the mother was unable to use her own investment income to support the children.[93]

With respect to a father's obligation to support his children, a cohabitant's contribution to the mother's expenses should not be treated as imputed income that reduces the father's obligation. In this case, the cohabitant paid a share of the rent, but he made payments directly to the landlord, not to the mother of the children.[94]

Despite an agreement that the mother of a nonmarital child would not seek support from the father, the Pennsylvania Superior Court permitted a child support action to proceed. The child's right to parental support cannot be given away, even if the discussion about support occurred before conception, and even if the father of the child said he would not have continued the relationship with the child's mother if he thought that financial liability might be imposed.[95]

[2] The Child Support Recovery Act

A 1992 statute, the Child Support Recovery Act of 1992 (CSRA), 18 USC § 228, makes a federal crime of willful failure to support a child living in another state. The Deadbeat Parents Punishment Act of 1998, P.L. 105-187, amends 18 USC § 228 to make it a federal felony, punishable by up to two years' imprisonment, to fail to pay court-ordered child support for a child who lives in another state. (The obligor is rebuttably presumed able to pay.) If the obligation is more than a year overdue or exceeds $5,000, or the obligor crossed state lines or left the United States to evade the obligation, mandatory restitution is also imposed.

The CSRA was frequently challenged in court, and for a brief time the Sixth Circuit took the position that the statute was invalid because Congress exceeded its powers in passing it. In 2001, however, the Sixth Circuit reversed its position and joined ten other Circuits in upholding the validity of the statute.[96]

---

[92] Pollard v. Pollard, 991 P.2d 1201 (Wash. App. 2000).

[93] Chen v. Warner, 695 N.W.2d 758 (2005).

[94] Allred v. Allred, 744 A.2d 70 (Md. App. 2000).

[95] Kesler v. Weniger, 744 A.2d 794 (Pa. Super. 2000).

[96] *See* United States v. Faasse, 265 F.3d 475 (6th Cir. 2001) and the cases cited therein. More recently, the Third Circuit upheld the statute over a Commerce Clause challenge: failure to pay child support creates a debt, which constitutes local activity that is part of a national problem with substantial impact on interstate commerce. Inability to pay is a defense under the Deadbeat Parents Act, but ability to pay is not an element of the offense, and the defendant cannot collaterally challenge the validity of the support order: United States v. Kukafka, 478 F.3d 531 (3d Cir. 2006); there is Third Circuit precedent that the Act is constitutional: United States v. Parker, 108 F.3d 28 (3d Cir. 1997).

A group of plaintiffs, incarcerated for civil contempt for failure to make payments under New Jersey support orders, claimed that 42 USC § 1983 was violated by the judges' failure to advise them of their right to counsel and to appointed counsel. The Third Circuit invoked *Younger* abstention, holding that the Constitutional issue should have been raised in state court, in light of the states' primary role in child support enforcement. There was no proof that the Constitutional claims could not have been raised at that stage.[97]

Any person who is $5,000 or more delinquent in paying child support cannot receive a new passport or have a passport renewed (42 USC § 652(k)) — a statute that has been upheld by the Second and Ninth Circuits.[98]

The definition of "child" under the Child Support Recovery Act extends to a person over age 18 who is entitled to support — e.g., a college student whose tuition is required to be paid under the divorce decree.[99]

There is no private right of action under the CSRA by a custodial parent against a noncustodial parent who moved out of state and failed to comply with the support order.[100] Nor can custodial parents maintain a class action suit against the county child support enforcement agency for failure to provide the federally mandated child support collection services. The Sixth Circuit deemed the parents' interests too vague and amorphous to support the suit.[101]

[3] Bankruptcy Issues

Alimony payments received after a Chapter 7 filing are not property of the bankruptcy estate, even though Bankruptcy Code § 541(a)(5)(B) incorporates property from a settlement agreement or divorce decree into the estate.[102]

Postpetition interest on child support obligations that are nondischargeable is also nondischargeable. The Ninth Circuit ruled, based on an analogy with the bankruptcy treatment of nondischargeable student loan debt, that the obligation remains a personal liability of the debtor, and interest is integral to a continuing debt.[103]

The Second Circuit ruled that a family court order requiring the father to pay the mother's attorneys' fees for a custody case is nondischargeable, because it is in the nature of support for the child. However, the Tenth Circuit permitted discharge of attorneys' fees from a custody case that a mother was ordered to pay, as an "unusual circumstance" as defined by Bankruptcy Code § 523(a)(5). The court reached this conclusion not based on whether the payor was the custodial or the

---

[97] Anthony v. Council, 316 F.3d 412 (3d Cir. 2003).

[98] Weinstein v. Albright, 261 F.3d 127 (2d Cir. 2001); Eunique v. Powell, 281 F.3d 940 (9th Cir. 2002).

[99] United States v. Molak, 276 F.3d 45 (10th Cir. 2002).

[100] Salahuddin v. Alaji, 232 F.3d 305 (2d Cir. 2000).

[101] Clark v. Portage County, Ohio, 281 F.3d 602 (6th Cir. 2002).

[102] Kelly v. Jeter, 257 B.R. 907 (8th Cir. 2000).

[103] Sacramento County v. Foross, 242 B.R. 692 (9th Cir. 1999).

noncustodial parent, but because the fees equaled about five years' support and would limit the mother's ability to support the child.[104]

The Seventh Circuit held that the Bankruptcy Court was correct to deny confirmation to a Chapter 13 plan. The plan called for payment of two-thirds of the nondischargeable child support debt owed to the county, but no payments at all to other unsecured creditors (including the IRS). It was not an abuse of discretion to reject the plan, because it unfairly shifted nondischargeable debt to other creditors.[105]

The Ninth Circuit joined the majority of the Circuits, ruling that under Bankruptcy Code § 523(a)(15) only a current or former spouse or child of the bankruptcy debtor is entitled to a determination that a debt for unpaid legal fees is nondischargeable. Therefore, the attorney to whom the fees are owed cannot get such a determination.[106]

To the Eighth Circuit, nondischargeability under Bankruptcy Code § 523(a)(5) is a function of the nature of the debt, not the nature of the payee. So a court order to pay support and certain expenses for a nonmarital child is not dischargeable, even though the child's mother was not a spouse or ex-spouse, and even though the mother rather than the child was the payee.[107]

The automatic stay in bankruptcy does not apply to state criminal proceedings for nonsupport relating to arrears of child support.[108]

[C] Visitation

Unless there is some reason why it would be deleterious to the child(ren), it is almost certain that the non-custodial parent will be permitted visitation. To prevent future problems, it is better to draft separation agreement provisions to be specific ("Visitation on the first and third weekends of each month, starting Friday at 4 p.m. and ending Sunday at 4 p.m.") rather than vague ("adequate visitation"). The UCCJA and PKPA generally apply to visitation, and courts will generally be required to enforce other states' decrees respecting visitation without modifying them. Some states also make it a crime to interfere with visitation.

A non-custodial parent who has obtained a court order for visitation has a liberty interest in the care, custody, companionship, and decision-making for the children.[109]

Courts also have the power to order visitation by non-parents. If this is done at all, it is usually in the case of grandparents. Numerous cases have been brought on an "equitable parenting" theory (e.g., the former cohabitant of an unmarried

---

[104] *Compare* Falk & Siemer LLP v. Maddigan, 312 F.3d 589 (2d Cir. 2002) *with In re* Lowther, 321 F.3d 946 (10th Cir. 2002).

[105] *In re* Crawford, 324 F.3d 539 (7th Cir. 2003).

[106] Ashton v. Dollaga, 260 B.R. 493 (9th Cir. 2001).

[107] Williams v. Kemp, 232 F.3d 652 (8th Cir. 2000).

[108] Gruntz v. Los Angeles, 202 F.3d 1074 (9th Cir. 2002).

[109] Brittain v. Hansen (9th Cir. 06/22/06 — No. 03-57012) http://caselaw.lp.findlaw.com/data2/circs/9th/0357012p.pdf.

parent), although in many instances courts have declined to intervene in non-marital situations,[110] or have placed the parent's right to control access to the child above the associational right of the person seeking visitation.[111]

In mid-2000, the Supreme Court made one of its rare forays into family law, affirming the Washington State court that struck down Rev. Code § 26.10.160(3), a statute permitting the state courts to grant visitation to any party, to the extent that this is in the best interests of the child(ren).[112] The Supreme Court agreed with the state court that the statute is unconstitutional because of its overbreadth (any person can petition for visitation) and its interference with the parents' Due Process right to control association with their children.

Recent cases in New Jersey, Pennsylvania, and Maryland stand for the proposition that after termination of a lesbian relationship, the nonbiological parent who acted as "psychological parent" has standing to seek visitation with the ex-partner's children. Under the facts of the Maryland case, however, visitation was denied as contrary to the best interests of the child, because it caused behavior problems.[113]

[D] Neglect and Abuse Proceedings

It can be hard to distinguish between genuine accidents of childhood and injuries that result from poor supervision of, or deliberate attacks on, children. Physical abuse is often signaled by a discrepancy between the physical condition of the children and the parent's explanation: if there's no tree in the backyard, a broken arm could not have been caused by falling out of the tree; a sibling blamed for an injury might not be strong enough to inflict it; a baby might not have been able to roll off the changing table. A classic symptom found in battered children is multiple fractures at different stages of healing.

State laws forbidding child neglect are often rather unspecific (and some challenges have succeeded on the grounds that such laws are void for vagueness), giving judges significant latitude to decide if children are being deprived of material needs or parental guidance. Generally speaking, neglect is a parent's failure to provide a child with an appropriate home, medical care, education, supervision, and emotional nurturance.

However, it should be noted that the Supreme Court has ruled[114] that states are not under a Constitutional duty to protect children from parental abuse. *Doe v. D.C.,*[115] holds that there is no private right of action under 42 USC § 1983 to

---

[110] *E.g.,* Van v. Zahorik, 227 Mich. App. 90 (1998), 460 Mich. 320 (1999).

[111] The Iowa law allowing grandparents to seek visitation after a divorce has been held to be facially invalid, because a fit parent is presumed to act in the best interests of the children-including deciding whether they should see their grandparents: *In re* Howard, 71 L.W. 1712 (Iowa 5/7/03).

[112] Troxel v. Granville, 530 U.S. 57 (2000).

[113] TB v. LRM, 786 A.2d 913 (Pa. 2001); SF v. MD, 751 A.2d 9 (Md. App. 2000); VC v. MJB, 748 A.2d 539 (N.J. 2000).

[114] DeShaney v. Winnebago County DSS, 489 U.S. 189 (1989).

[115] 93 F.3d 861 (D.C. Cir. 1996).

enforce the state's obligation under the Child Abuse Prevention and Treatment Act to investigate and act on child abuse reports.

All the states have "mandatory reporting" legislation under which defined categories of people who work with children (e.g., teachers, doctors, nurses) are required to report suspected child abuse. (The statutes include penalties for malicious false reports, but indemnify individuals who make good-faith reports that, on investigation, are discovered to be unfounded.) One weakness of these laws is that there are no real penalties for failure to make the "mandatory" report.

According to the Seventh, Tenth, and Eleventh Circuits, a social worker who has objectively reasonable grounds for the belief that children were at risk of abuse may be able to remove them from the home without a warrant. In these jurisdictions, Due Process analysis of warrantless removals involves all the factors (including the extent of the risk and the immediacy of the danger to the children), not just whether or not a warrant could have been obtained before the removal. However, in the Second Circuit, a social worker who can obtain a court order is required to do so before removing the children.[116]

[E] Termination of Parental Rights

Usually, the legal system will do everything in its power to prevent termination of the parental relationship. However, there are some cases of outright abandonment of children, and severance of the birth relationship is necessary to permit adoption by a willing and suitable family. In other instances, the parent(s) want(s) to retain custody, but has been guilty of neglect or abuse serious enough to place the child(ren) at severe risk, so that termination is required to protect the child(ren).

The Supreme Court has addressed the question of termination of parental rights several times. *Santosky v. Kramer*,[117] provides that, to terminate parental rights, unfitness must be proved by clear and convincing evidence. Under *Lassiter v. DSS*,[118] states are not required to appoint counsel for indigent parents who are the subject of termination proceedings. However, under *M.L.B. v. S.L.J.*[119] indigent parents cannot be precluded from challenging a termination decision merely because they are unable to afford the required transcript of the proceedings. *Wyman v. James*,[120] authorizes investigative home visits by welfare workers.

California held that the Sixth Amendment right of a criminal defendant to confront his or her accusers does not apply to parents in state dependency proceedings.[121]

---

[116] *Compare* Doe v. O'Brien, 329 F.3d 1286 (11th Cir. 2003); Roska v. Peterson, 304 F.3d 982 (10th Cir. 2002); and Brokaw v. Mercer County, 235 F.3d 1000 (7th Cir. 2000), *with* Tenenbaum v. Williams, 193 F.3d 582 (2d Cir. 1999).

[117] 455 U.S. 745 (1982).

[118] 452 U.S. 18 (1981).

[119] 519 U.S. 102 (1997).

[120] 400 U.S. 309 (1971).

[121] *In re* April C, No. B178548 (Cal. 7/27/05).

§ 16.07 ISSUES OF JURISDICTION, FORUM, AND CHOICE OF LAW

[A] In General

It is very common for more than one state to be involved, or potentially involved, in divorce litigation: the state where the plaintiff spouse lives; the state where the defendant spouse lives; the state in which one spouse resides with the children; the state to which children have allegedly been unlawfully removed; the state where part or all of the marriage occurred; the state in which marital real property is located. Hence, jurisdictional issues and choice-of-law questions often arise in family law cases.

It has been held Constitutional for a state to impose a durational residency requirement: e.g., all divorce plaintiffs must have lived in-state for a period such as one year.

A plaintiff who lives within a state can be granted an ex parte divorce by that state, even if that state's courts do not have personal jurisdiction over the other spouse. The ex parte decree will be entitled to full faith and credit in other states as to the marital status of the divorce plaintiff (i.e., he or she cannot be charged with bigamy for remarrying after receiving the ex parte decree). However, an ex parte decree cannot effectually divide property or assign support, because jurisdiction over the putative obligor is required to do that.

If the court has personal jurisdiction over both spouses (e.g., both consent to appear in court), the decree is entitled to full faith and credit even if neither spouse was actually a domiciliary of the state whose courts issued the decree. This is a long-standing doctrine, dating back to *Sherrer v. Sherrer*, 334 U.S. 343 (1948), which denies collateral attack on a decree of a court where both spouses made personal appearance and had the opportunity to contest the issue of domicile.

In the divorce context, personal jurisdiction might be obtainable even over a non-resident spouse, on the basis of long-arm jurisdiction (see § 22.03[E]) premised on contacts with the forum that was at one time the marital domicile. (See *Burham v. Superior Court of California*, 495 U.S. 604 (1990)). Personal service on a non-resident spouse might be possible at a time when he or she is in the state temporarily, e.g., on a business trip or to visit the children of the marriage. It is unclear whether rights to property on divorce are governed by law of forum state or state where property is located.

Family law is almost exclusively state law (other than in federal areas such as regulation of pensions) and federal courts usually abstain in domestic relations matters.[122]

Early in 2007, the ABA approved four Uniform Acts drafted by NCCUSL, including the Uniform Child Abduction Prevention Act, setting out guidelines for courts to use in divorce and custody proceedings. The court can hear evidence about the risk of abduction based on factors such as previous abduction by a

---

[122] Under Ankenbrandt v. Richards, 504 U.S. 598 (1992).

party, threats, domestic violence history, or disobedience of existing custody orders.[123]

[B] International Issues

Hague Convention § 13(b) justifies withholding return if there is clear and convincing evidence of grave risk of physical or psychological harm, or an otherwise intolerable situation for the child. However, the court must at least consider ways to return the child to his or her home country without subjecting the child to risk of danger, based on an assumption that the courts of the home country will be able to issue any necessary protective orders. The mere fact that the country of a child's habitual residence has child protection statutes is not enough to justify sending the child back to an abusive custodial parent. The federal court has a duty, under the Hague Convention, to find out if the child really will be protected against grave risk of harm.[124]

In a Second Circuit case, the mother admitted that she wrongfully removed the children from France and forged the father's signature to obtain passports for them, but she claimed this was done to protect at-risk children. The father petitioned the U.S. court system for return of the children. The District Court cited grave risk of harm, and the Second Circuit ruled that the District Court's conclusion was supported by adequate factual evidence. The Second Circuit instructed the District Court to contact the French government to develop a method for returning the children to a safe setting in France. If there was no effective way for the District Court to carry this out, the father's petition could be dismissed.[125]

A Mexican decree giving the father visitation rights and barring the mother from removing them from Mexico without the father's consent did not give the father the right of custody under the Hague Convention. The mother moved to the United States, taking the children with her, and sought asylum on the basis of abuse. The Ninth Circuit said that, because the father did not have custodial rights, the U.S. court did not have jurisdiction to return the children to Mexico.[126]

According to the Eighth Circuit, where children were born in the United States; the family lived in Israel for 11 months; and the mother brought the children back to the United States, custody issues had to be resolved in Israel; Minnesota could not be described as their primary residence at the time of their wrongful removal. The Eighth Circuit did not accept the mother's characterization of Israel as a war zone that was too risky to allow children to remain there.[127]

---

[123] NCCUSL press release, *ABA Approves Four Uniform Acts*, http://www.nccusl.org/nccusl/ DesktopModules/NewsDisplay.aspx?ItemID=178 (2/12/07).

[124] Van de Sande v. Van de Sande, 431 F.3d 567 (7th Cir. 2005).

[125] Blondin v. Dubois, 189 F.3d 240 (2d Cir. 1999).

[126] Arce v. Gutierrez, 311 F.3d 942 (9th Cir. 2002).

[127] Silverman v. Silverman, 338 F.3d 886 (8th Cir. 2003).

The International Child Abduction Remedies Act (implementing legislation for the Hague Convention) does not give federal courts jurisdiction to hear "right of access" (i.e., visitation) claims, because that is a matter for state jurisdiction.[128]

§ 16.08   OTHER FAMILY LAW ISSUES

Although the federal Family and Medical Leave Act (FMLA; see § 3.14[B]) requires employers to grant up to 12 weeks of unpaid leave for the birth or adoption of a child or for the worker's own serious health problems or those of a close family member, California has a more expansive state statute that requires certain employers to provide *paid* leave in certain cases. The program is funded by contributions made by employees; the employer does not contribute.

California's State Employment Development Department reported in mid-2005 that in the first full year of the California Family Rights Act (CFRA) program, about 1.1% of eligible workers used paid family leave insurance, receiving an aggregate of about $300 million in benefits. The maximum benefit was 55% of weekly pay, capped at $849 a week. FMLA and CFRA leave must be taken at the same time. Almost nine-tenths of the claims were made by new parents (83% from mothers, 17% from fathers), and 70% of the employees taking leave to care for family members were female.[129]

A legal spouse (although not a cohabitant) is entitled to "elect against the will" if he or she is left out of the will, or if his or her provision falls below the statutory share (typically, 1/3 or 1/2, depending on the state and whether or not there are surviving children of the marriage).

The traditional right of election could be defeated fairly easily, by the spouse who did not intend to leave the statutory amount making lifetime gifts or placing assets into trust. For this reason, the Uniform Probate Code calls for calculation of the elective share on the basis of the "augmented" estate, including certain transferred property. Depending on state practice, the spouse may have to receive the elective share outright; or trusts, similar to the QTIP trust used in estate planning (see § 17.12[C][2]) may be a permissible form of provision.

Interspousal tort immunity has more or less been abrogated, and both spouses can probably get damages for loss of consortium, once limited to amounts husbands could receive for loss of their wives' household and sexual services. However, some states allow both spouses to recover, but some states will not allow it for either.

Under *Trammel v. United States*,[130] a spouse can testify voluntarily against the other spouse in a federal case, but cannot be compelled to disclose information privately imparted by the other spouse. The spousal privilege is inapplicable in cases involving allegations of spousal or child abuse.

---

[128] Cantor v. Cohen, 441 F.3d 196 (4th Cir. 2006).

[129] Judy Greenwald, *Calif. Paid Leave Program Draws 1% of Workers*, Business Insurance July 5, 2005 (http://benefitslink.com; no www).

[130] 445 U.S. 40 (1980).

P.L. 106-395, the Child Citizenship Act of 2000, amends Immigration and Naturalization Act § 320 to increase the number of children who qualify for automatic U.S. citizenship or certificates of naturalization based on their relationship to at least one parent who is a native or naturalized U.S. citizen.

Indiana wiretap law covers unpermitted recording of one estranged spouse's telephone conversations by the other spouse.[131]

[A] Prevention of Family Violence

Family courts (and sometimes, criminal courts) have the power to issue orders of protection or no-contact orders. This jurisdiction is broad enough to interdict conduct that is not criminal or even tortious. Violation of a court order constitutes criminal, not merely civil, contempt. The general rule is that, unless a special relationship exists, the police are not liable for failure to protect a person who is attacked by a spouse notwithstanding an order of protection.

Expert testimony on "battered woman syndrome" may be admissible, e.g., in a homicide prosecution where a person claiming repeated battering killed the allegedly abusive spouse, but at a time or under circumstances not constituting self-defense against an attack that was actually occurring at the time of the killing.

The New York Court of Appeals struck down a blanket policy of removing children because their mothers are victims of domestic violence. Removals can only be done on a case-by-case basis, and suffering abuse does not make a mother presumptively neglectful of the child; not every child is impaired by living in a violent household.[132]

Ohio would not permit the court-appointed guardian for a child rendered comatose by abuse to authorize withdrawal of life support until parental rights had been terminated, on the theory that permitting withdrawal of life support would be tantamount to termination of parental rights without due process.[133]

§ 16.09 ESTABLISHMENT OF PATERNITY

Traditionally, children born out of marriage have been treated very harshly. Even in the supposedly rational legal arena, it was common to deny inheritance from the father (and perhaps even from the mother) to non-marital children, even those whose paternity was acknowledged by the father. Over time, the rights of non-marital children vis-à-vis their parents have expanded. The rights of a father who acknowledges paternity have also expanded. No longer are non-marital children legally considered strangers to their families of blood, although the blood relationship can be legally severed by adoption (which then places the child within another family).

---

[131] State v. Lombardo, 738 N.E.2d 653 (Ind. 2000).

[132] Nicholson v. Scopetta, 3 N.Y.3d 357 (2004).

[133] *In re Guardianship of* Stein, 821 N.E.2d 1008 (Ohio 2004).

In 1971, the Supreme Court upheld[134] a Louisiana law that denied the right of an illegitimate child (even if acknowledged) to inherit from the father. This very harsh result has been modified by later Supreme Court cases. 1977's *Trimble v. Gordon*,[135] uses Equal Protection grounds to strike down a law precluding non-marital children from inheriting from their deceased intestate fathers. The distinction between marital and non-marital children was not deemed to advance a legitimate state objective. However, under *Lalli v. Lalli*,[136] it is permissible for a state to require that paternity be proved during the father's lifetime for non-marital children to take in intestacy.

During the father's lifetime, it is impermissible for state law to deprive non-marital children of the right to support from their fathers;[137] nor can a state discriminate against non-marital children when it comes to providing welfare benefits.[138]

Even if the biological father denies this role, it may be possible to determine scientifically (normally, by DNA testing) that he has fathered the child. In a 1987 case,[139] the Supreme Court ruled that it is not unconstitutional to establish paternity by preponderance of evidence rather than beyond a reasonable doubt. Once made, a judicial determination of paternity is entitled to full faith and credit in other jurisdictions.

The Supreme Court has not determined exactly how long a mother or child can wait to establish paternity, but the holding of *Clark v. Jeter*,[140] is that a six-year statute of limitations is too short for this purpose. The federal child support laws have a statute of limitations of at least 18 years (i.e., until the child reaches majority).

Under the Uniform Parentage Act, as enacted in about half the states, if both spouses consent, a child born to a married woman by artificial insemination is deemed to be a child of the marriage, and the husband becomes the child's legal father. The sperm donor has no rights or obligations vis-à-vis the child.

In fact, the presumption that a married woman's child is the child of her husband is a very strong one, and could be used by a husband to block custody of the child by the unmarried biological father.[141]

According to the California Court of Appeals, a "presumed father," as defined by California Family Code § 7611(d), has standing to prosecute a Uniform Parentage Act case.[142]

---

[134] Labine v. Vincent, 401 U.S. 532.

[135] 430 U.S. 762 (1977).

[136] 439 U.S. 259 (1978).

[137] Gomez v. Perez, 409 U.S. 535 (1973).

[138] New Jersey Welfare Rights Org. v. Cahill, 411 U.S. 619 (1973).

[139] Rivera v. Minnich, 483 U.S. 574 (1987).

[140] 486 U.S. 456 (1988).

[141] Michael H. v. Gerald D., 491 U.S. 110 (1989).

[142] Librers v. Black, 129 Cal. App. 4th 114 (Cal. App. 2005).

Indeed, in 2002, the California Court of Appeals allowed a woman to use the Uniform Parentage Act to apply a "presumption of maternity" to establish her relationship to an allegedly abandoned child that she had raised from birth, just as paternity can be presumed when a man takes a child into his home and holds it out as his.[143]

New York imposed equitable paternity (also called "paternity by estoppel") on a man who carried through on his incorrect assumption that a child was his daughter by helping to pay pregnancy expenses and admitting paternity so the child could immigrate to the United States. The consequence was that he was required to pay child support even though DNA testing showed that he could not have fathered the child. The Court of Appeals, acting on a best interests of the child rationale, ordered him to continue support and catch up on support arrears. In this reading, it would be unfair to the child to terminate support abruptly.[144]

A child, who is not a party to the paternity action, is not barred by the mother's settlement with the biological father, because the mother has no right unilaterally to terminate the child's right to a relationship with, and support from, the father.[145]

A June 2004 Los Angeles case applied the Uniform Parentage Act in a gender-neutral manner to treat a woman as a "presumed father" if she received her female partner's child into her home and openly held out the child as her own natural child. The two women had a court-approved agreement before the child's birth, stipulating that they would be co-parents. After the couple separated, the biological mother tried to eliminate her ex-partner's parental rights. The District Court found the pre-birth agreement void on the theory that parentage cannot be settled by agreement. But the court treated the second woman as a presumed father under California Family Code § 7611(d), reading this statute to contemplate two legal parents, although not necessarily one male and one female.[146]

§ 16.10   ADOPTION

Adoption is the creation of a parent-child relationship. Once adopted, a child has the same status as a child born into the family. For instance, the child becomes a distributee of relatives who die intestate.

Children become available for adoption in various ways. The parental relationship may be terminated, e.g., for severe abuse. A child who has no living or identified parents can be made available for adoption. However, the majority of adoptions are stepparent adoptions: i.e., the child legally becomes the child of one

---

[143] Department of Children & Family Serv. v. Karen C., 124 Cal. Rptr. 2d 677 (Cal. App. 2002).

[144] Matter of Shondel J. v. Mark D, 7 N.Y.3d 320 (2006).

[145] Shasta County *ex rel.* Caruthers v. Caruthers, 38 Cal. Rptr. 18 (Cal. App. 1995).

[146] Kristine Renee H. v. Lisa Ann R., 37 Cal. 4th 156, discussed in Mike McKee, *Calif. Court Breaks Precedent, Says Woman Can Be Dad*, The Recorder 7/2/04 (law.com).

biological parent and the biological parent's spouse or new spouse. If the other natural parent is still alive, the adoption requires surrender of parental rights.

Parental rights cannot be surrendered in the abstract: they must either be transferred to an adoption agency, or directly to a stepparent or other potential adoptive parent. A child generally cannot have more than two legal parents, so it is not always possible for a stepparent (or same-sex partner of a biological parent) to adopt a child without the other biological parent surrendering or being deprived of parental rights.[147]

Most adoptions are of infants or young children, but it is generally permissible for one adult to adopt another, e.g., for estate planning purposes. Adoption of an adult requires consent by adoptee, adopter, and adopter's spouse. State law may require consent of the biological parents whose rights are terminated, or proof that the adoption creates a genuine parent-child relationship rather than adding economic rights to a non-marital liaison. A posthumous adoption has even been permitted, so that potential adoptive parents could maintain a wrongful death action against a surgeon who operated on the child they wanted to adopt, although the decision was later reversed.[148]

In a 2007 New York case, adoptive parents asserted three causes of action against an adoption agency: fraud and wrongful adoption, negligence/breach of fiduciary duty, and intentional infliction of mental distress. Before the adoption, they said they wanted a healthy infant from a healthy family. Some physical illnesses within the family were disclosed, but not mental illnesses. The child suffered from mental illness (eventually being diagnosed as a paranoid schizophrenic) and was violent. In 1999, the parents saw an article about an adopted child with a history of familial mental illness, they sought the boy's health records and then brought suit. The Court of Appeals pointed out that New York law did not require disclosure of medical history to adoptive parents until 1985; prior to that time, agencies believed that a good home could overcome heredity and therefore did not disclose family history.

To establish a prima facie case of adoption fraud, plaintiffs must show that the defendant falsely represented material facts with intent to deceive, justifiable reliance on the statements operating as inducement to engage in a course of conduct, and pecuniary loss from the course of conduct. A punitive damage award requires a

---

[147] Some cases forbid a "stepparent adoption" by a non-marital partner unless the biological parent surrenders parental rights, *e.g., In re* Adams, 189 Mich. App. 540, 473 N.W.2d 712 (1991); Georgina G. v. Terry M., 184 Wis. 2d 492, 516 N.W.2d 678, *reconsideration denied*, 525 N.W.2d 736 (Wis. 1994); *In re Adoption of* TKJ, 931 P.2d 488 (Colo. App. 1996). However, other jurisdictions allow adoption by the biological parent's partner as long as this is in the best interests of the child, *e.g., In re* KM, 274 Ill. App. 3d 189, 653 N.E.2d 888 (1995); *In re* Adoption of Jacob/*In re* Adoption of Dana, 86 N.Y.2d 651, 660 N.E.2d 397, 636 N.Y.S.2d 716 (1995); *In re* Petition of DLG and MAH, 22 Family Law Rep. 1488 (Md. Cir. Ct. 1996). 15A Vermont Stat. Ann. § 1102(b) permits adoption by the parent's partner, without termination of the biological parent's rights, if this is in the best interests of the child.

[148] Adoption of Baby T., 308 N.J. Super. 344 (N.J. Super. 1997) *rev'd* 311 N.J. Super. 408 (1998).

showing of moral turpitude and wanton dishonesty. Because the agency conceded that concealment of the mental health history was intentional, the Court of Appeals found that there were enough triable facts to proceed on the compensatory damages claim for fraud, but the agency's conduct was not bad enough to justify punitive damages. It may have been foolish to think that the history of mental illness was irrelevant, but they acted on the basis of the laws then in force and sociological opinion then prevailing.

The claims of negligence and intentional infliction of emotional distress were barred by the three-year statute of limitations (negligence) and the one-year statute of limitations for infliction of emotional distress. The plaintiffs sought equitable estoppel, but they could not cite any acts justifying estoppel other than the acts underlying the claim. Mere failure to disclose wrongdoing will not trigger equitable estoppel, and the defendant did not take any action to block them from bringing suit.[149]

Adoptive parents of children with special needs, who receive adoption assistance payments from the state have standing to sue under 42 USC § 1983 when the payments are reduced.[150]

In 2004, the California Supreme Court denied a claim of intestate inheritance on the grounds of equitable adoption. A foster child lived with the decedent's family (along with other foster children) for 20 years. He was never adopted; the foster parents believed this could not be done unless he was removed from their home, and they were afraid he would be placed in an unsafe situation. At least 27 states have permitted equitable adoptees to take in intestacy, but 10 states have rejected the argument. California requires a showing of intent to adopt in the statements and conduct of the parties, which was held not to be present in this case, precluding inheritance.[151]

A couple who visited a child for over a year, in anticipation of adopting him, came to stand in loco parentis to the child, and therefore had standing to seek custody or visitation after his birth mother decided not to finalize the adoption.[152]

Late in 2000, the United States implemented another Hague Convention relating to children, this one on Protection of Children and Co-Operation in Respect of Intercountry Adoption. See P.L. 106-279, the Intercountry Adoption Act of 2000. The law is designed to control inappropriate adoption practices, such as adoption of children in the United States who have been wrongfully taken from families in other countries; excess fees paid to international adoption facilitators; and failure to disclose the medical and psychological condition of adopted children so that adoptive parents can care for them properly.

The Internal Revenue Code (§§ 23 and 137) permits taxpayers who adopt to take a tax credit for their adoption expenses, and, within limits, adoption financial

---

[149] Ross v. Louise Wise Services Inc., 8 N.Y.3d 478 (NY 2007).

[150] ASW v. State of Ore., 424 F.3d 970 (9th Cir. 2005).

[151] Bean v. Ford, 32 Cal. 4th 160 (2004).

[152] Silfies v. Webster, 713 A.2d 639 (Pa. Super. 1998).

assistance provided by an employer is excludable from gross income. For 2009, the adoption expense credit is $12,150, but the benefit phases out for higher-income taxpayers.

"Fostering Connections to Success and Increasing Adoptions Act of 2008" PL 110-351 (10/7/08) amends SSA Title VI Parts B and E to provide more support for relatives caring for kids, better outcomes for children in foster care, and more adoption incentives, especially for older and special needs children. The legislation allows states to enter into "kinship guardianship assistance agreements" to make payments to grandchildren and other relatives who are already caring for relatives as foster parents, and who wish to adopt the children. However, the payment cannot exceed the payment made for the children as foster children. The Secretary of HHS is authorized to make matching grants to state and local child welfare agencies and nonprofit organizations to help find suitable relatives that children in or at risk of entering foster care can live with. Reasonable efforts must be made to place siblings together. The legislation provides for transitional assistance for children aging out of foster care and coordinated health care for children in foster care. Potential adoptive parents of foster children must be informed of potential eligibility for a tax credit under IRC § 23. The statute also changes the definition of "qualifying child" under Internal Revenue Code 152 (tax deduction for dependents). When a child is removed from the custody of his or her parent(s), the state will notify adult relatives of the option of fostering or adopting the child, subject to licensing standards for relatives providing care.

PL 110-351 adds a requirement that, to be a "qualifying child," the individual must be younger than the taxpayer and must be unmarried. A person can be considered the qualifying child of someone who is not the child's parent if neither of the child's parents claims him or her as a qualifying child, and the nonparent's AGI is higher than either of the parent's.

[A] The Placement Process

Traditionally, the adoption process was controlled by adoption agencies. The agencies served as intermediaries and could conceal the identity of women giving birth at a time when non-marital childbirth was viewed as disgraceful. Today, there is much greater acceptance of single parenthood, and potential adopters often prefer to deal directly with biological mothers. Nearly all of the states allow "direct placement" adoptions with no involvement by an agency.

It is allowable for adopters to pay maternity expenses, legal expenses, and incidental living expenses of the biological mother, but it is illegal to make payment of expenses contingent on the mother's consent to the adoption and surrender of parental rights. If improprieties occurred (such as excessive or inappropriate payments), the adoption will probably be allowed to proceed, if it is in the best interests of the child, but other sanctions will be applied.

An adoption proceeding is a legal action. The court will only approve the proposed adoption if a home study, done by a court-appointed investigator, confirms the suitability of the applicants. (This requirement is waived for stepparent adoptions.) Adoptions are not finalized for a period such as three months, six months, or a year, and the court retains ongoing jurisdiction for the protection of the potential adoptee.

Generally, the birth mother will not be allowed to consent to adoption until after the baby's birth, although some states do allow prenatal consent that is affirmed after the child is born. A valid consent to adoption must either be written and witnessed, or made orally before a judge or court-appointed referee.

The Uniform Adoption Act § 2-406 requires the consent for direct placement or relinquishment to an adoption agency to provide plain language consent to transfer of legal and physical custody and termination of parental rights. The form must be executed in the birth mother's native language. The document must disclose that consent is final and irrevocable except under circumstances given in the document itself. Under the Uniform Act, there is a period of 192 hours after birth during which prenatal consents can be revoked.

If, as often happens, the birth mother is a minor, a guardian ad litem will be appointed for her, or the adoption court may, on its own motion, develop evidence about the validity of her surrender of parental rights.

If the biological father of the baby is known, he will generally be entitled to notice of the adoption proceeding, and to participate in it, although he will probably not be given outright veto power over the adoption. The rights of an unmarried father whose children are proposed for adoption depend on the nature and extent of the father's relationship with the children. A parent who lived with the child(ren) is entitled to notice and hearing before the adoption[153] but a father who never legitimated the child and provided support only intermittently does not have veto power over the proposed adoption.[154]

In contrast, a father who lived with the children for five years and continued to support them even though no longer living with them was permitted to block a stepparent adoption by the mother's new husband.[155] Some states maintain a Putative Father Registry; in order to contest an adoption, a man must sign the registry and admit paternity (thus rendering himself liable for child support). Florida held that an unmarried biological father's rights in a child can be terminated (pending adoption of the child) based on his failure to file a paternity claim with the state putative father registry if, and only if, the father was served with the statutory notice but failed to comply with it on a timely basis.[156]

There is an increasing trend to permit "open adoptions," in which the biological mother and the adopters are aware of each other's identity. Some laws permit the birth mother the option of visiting the child, and the child is aware

---

[153] Stanley v. Illinois, 405 U.S. 645 (1972).

[154] Quilloin v. Walcott, 434 U.S. 246 (1978).

[155] Caban v. Mohammed, 441 U.S. 380 (1979).

[156] Heart of Adoptions, Inc. v. J.A., 963 So.2d 189 (Fla. 2007).

of her biological motherhood. In most states, adoptees can get at least some health and genetic information about the birth parents, with identifying information removed. Some states maintain registries that permit birth parents and adoptees to indicate interest in contacting each other or in receiving information. The increase in open adoptions has been credited with the significant increase in the number of infants available for adoption in the United States. Several states consider "wrongful adoption" — negligent material misrepresentation of fact about an infant's origin or health history — to be a tort for which compensatory damages can be recovered.[157]

By the late 1980s, all of the states had adopted the Interstate Compact on Placement of Children, to protect children placed across state lines. The "sending agency" is required to transmit a form to the appropriate welfare department official in the receiving state, giving a social and case history of the child and a home study of the applicants for adoption.

[1] Access to Records

In some cases, adoptees want to get information about their birth parents. The birth parents may or may not want this information to be disclosed, and they may be longing for reunion or very unwilling to be contacted by children once surrendered for adoption.

The group of surrendering birth mothers claimed that they were explicitly promised continued anonymity by doctors and social workers (acting as state agents). However, there has never been a recognized state-law contract right to total anonymity for birth mothers. Disclosure of this information does not violate the constitutionally protected right to bear children. Nor is surrendering children for adoption a fundamental right, so there is no corresponding fundamental right to have the adoption handled in a manner that completely prevents disclosure of the birth parents' identity.

Pennsylvania ruled in 2000 that adoption records can be unsealed only if the adoptee (who wants medical background information for health treatment) shows, by clear and convincing evidence, a cause sufficient to justify the release of the records, balancing the adoptee's needs against the needs of biological and adoptive parents and the integrity of the adoption process.[158]

[2] Second-Parent Adoptions

It has long been accepted that when a parent remarries, the new spouse/ stepparent will be permitted to adopt the children. However, it has been held that a same-sex life partner is not a spouse under state law and thus cannot be a

---

[157] *See, e.g.*, Jackson v. Montana, 1998 MT 46 (Mont. Sup. 1998), holding that Montana law imposes a common-law duty on the state to exercise due care when giving potential adopters information that could affect the adoption decision. In this case, the state was held liable for wrongful adoption after concealing the mental health status of an adoptee's parents.

[158] *In re* Long, 745 A.2d 673 (Pa. Super. 2000).

stepparent who is entitled to adopt the other life partner's biological child without the birth parent surrendering parental rights. Such "second-parent adoptions" are illegal in Florida and subject to an effective ban in Utah and Mississippi, but are authorized by statute or case law in 22 states, including California, Illinois, New York, Pennsylvania, Vermont, Rhode Island, New Jersey, and Connecticut.[159]

On a related issue, in 2004, a New York intermediate appellate court permitted two unmarried female adults to jointly adopt a child who was not the biological child of either one of them. The lower court had rejected the application because the statute does not specifically authorize joint adoption by unmarried couples, but the Appellate Division ruled that it was in the best interests of children to be adopted by fit parents. (The petitioners have another child, whom they adopted separately.) Almost half of the states recognize same-sex co-parent adoptions, where one partner adopts the biological child of the other partner.

Florida is the only state that categorically denies gay people the ability to adopt — a position that has been upheld by the Eleventh Circuit on the grounds that it serves the legitimate state interest of promoting adoption by married couples rather than single people or same-sex couples. Because the statute says that "a resident of Indiana" can adopt, the Indiana Court of Appeals held in 2006 that an unmarried couple, irrespective of their gender or sexual orientation, can file a joint petition to adopt a minor. Indiana banned second-parent adoptions (i.e., sequential adoptions of the same child by unmarried partners) but the court permitted joint adoptions by unmarried couples. Married couples must petition jointly, to settle issues such as inheritance and child support.[160] The Tenth Circuit struck down a state statute forbidding recognition of out of state or foreign adoptions by same sex couples, on the grounds that the law violates the rights of gay citizens to be parents, and violates full faith and credit by denying enforcement to the outside adoption decrees.[161]

Both Mississippi and Utah have statutes that forbid joint adoptions by same-sex couples, and Utah will not permit unmarried male-female couples to adopt, but one-party adoptions by gay people are possible in these states.[162]

---

[159] *See* Erica Goode, *Group [the American Academy of Pediatricians] Wants Gays to Have Right to Adopt a Partner's Child,* N.Y. Times, 2/4/02, p. A17. In 2002, Pennsylvania ruled that a same-sex life partner could not adopt a partner's child without the biological parent surrendering parental rights *In re* Adoption of RBF, 762 A.2d 739 (Pa. Super. 2000), but this decision was reversed in 2002: 803 A.2d 1195 (Pa. 2002). In 2003, the California Supreme Court ruled that second-parent adoptions are valid: Sharon S. v. Superior Court (Annette F.), 31 Cal. 4th 417 (2003); in fact, this case permits a second-parent adoption to be pursued by the biological mother's former lesbian partner after the relationship ended, because the mother failed to make a timely withdrawal of her consent to the second-party adoption.

[160] RKH *ex rel.* MAH v. Morgan County Office of Family and Children, 74 LW 1666 (Ind. App. 4/13/06).

[161] Finstuen v. Crutcher, 496 F.3d 1139 (10th Cir. 2007).

[162] Matter of Adoption of Carolyn B., 6 A.D.3d 67 (A.D. 4th Dept. 2004); the Eleventh Circuit ruling is Lofton v. Sec'y of Dep't of Children and Family Servs., 358 F.3d 804 (11th Cir. 2004).

[B] Foster Parents

Foster parenthood is designed as a temporary arrangement for the protection of children who do not have a safe, appropriate, permanent home.

The Southern District of New York ruled that foster parents whose relationship with the child showed some indicia of permanence had a protected liberty interest in being able to adopt the child, and would be entitled to notice and a hearing before the child was removed from their home. However, two years later, the Second Circuit reversed, finding that New York statutes and regulations do not create a protected liberty interest under which foster parents and children have an enforceable right to remain together.[163]

Arkansas struck down the state child welfare board regulation, forbidding homosexuals and people who live with homosexuals to become foster parents. The regulation was found unconstitutional because it violates separation of powers and does not satisfy the objective of promoting the safety and welfare of children. However, the court rejected constitutional arguments based on equal protection, privacy, and the right of intimate association.[164]

A 1997 federal law, the Adoption and Safe Families Act of 1997, P.L. 105-89, strives to coordinate foster placement with termination of parental rights, with a view toward promoting adoption of children by their foster parents. Enforcement of this statute rests entirely with HHS. There is no private right of action on the part of foster children who allege that they should have gained prompt placement for adoption.[165]

Follow-up legislation, P.L. 106-324, the Strengthening Abuse and Neglect Courts Act of 2000, implements a provision of the Adoption and Safe Families Act that requires states to move to terminate parental rights with respect to children who have been in foster care for 15 of the previous 22 months, in order to facilitate adoption of the children. To reduce court backlog, the 2000 legislation calls for a computerized case tracking system, an increase in the number of family court judges; longer court hours; better training for judges; and volunteer CASA (Court Appointed Special Advocate) programs.

With respect to civil rights liability under 42 USC § 1983 [deprivation of Constitutional rights by a state actor], the Third Circuit ruled in 2005 that foster parents are not "state actors." In this case, a former foster child sued her foster parents and Social Services officials for burns sustained when she was two years old as a result of the foster parent's negligence. Although a private person can be a state actor if the private activities are so integrally related to the state that holding the state responsible is fair, state regulation of the activity is not enough. A private person who performs a function that is traditionally and exclusively public can

---

[163] Rodriguez v. McLoughlin, 20 F. Supp. 2d 597 (S.D.N.Y. 1998), *rev'd*, 214 F.3d 328 (2d Cir. 2000).

[164] Department of Human Servs. v. Howard, 367 Ark. 55 (Ark. 2006).

[165] 31 Foster Children v. Bush, 329 F.3d 1255 (11th Cir. 2003).

become a state actor, but raising children, or even placing children in foster homes, is considered private behavior and not state action.[166]

§ 16.11   REPRODUCTIVE TECHNOLOGY

Various forms of reproductive technology are used so that fertile women who have infertile male partners, or no male partners at all, can have children, or so that fertile males can have children despite their female partners' inability to conceive or carry a pregnancy to term. These arrangements can create legal problems if they go wrong, or when a relationship is terminated.

Children conceived after a man's death by his widow, using his preserved sperm, can be "issue" for intestacy purposes, if there is a paternity judgment and the surviving parent proves that the decedent consented to the use of his sperm and was willing to support the resulting children.[167]

A cancer patient deposited sperm before undergoing chemotherapy. Ten months after his death, his widow used the stored sperm to conceive twins. The District Court ruled that the children were not entitled to Social Security child's insurance benefits because they were not his dependents prior to his death (and in fact had not been conceived at that point). The Ninth Circuit reversed, holding that the twins are the decedent's legitimate children under state law, and therefore are deemed to be his dependents, rendering the benefits payable.[168]

The Pennsylvania Supreme Court ruled that a man who donated sperm for in vitro fertilization who orally waived parental rights could not be required to pay child support for the twins born of the procedure. The lower court found the contract unenforceable on the grounds that parents cannot contract away their children's right to support. The Supreme Court, however, found the doctrine outmoded, given the increased role of technically assisted reproduction, sometimes involving known donors. (The donor was the mother's ex-lover; they remained friendly after their break-up.)[169]

---

[166] Leshko v. Servis, 423 F.3d 337 (3d Cir. 2005). Rayburn v. Hogue, 241 F.3d 1341 (11th Cir. 2001) also holds that foster parents are not state actors, although they have been held to be "county employees": Patterson v. Lycoming County, 815 A.2d 659 (Pa. Comm. 2002).

[167] Woodward v. Comm'r of Social Security, 760 N.E.2d 257 (Mass. 2002). The New York Surrogate's Court ruled that the grantor's intent governs, so children conceived with frozen sperm and born several years after their father's death should be treated as "issue" and "descendents" of the deceased trust beneficiary. A recent amendment to New York's EPTL prevent post-conceived children from taking under the parent's estate, but that applies only to wills and after-born children of the testator; in this case, a trust created by the children's grandfather was at issue Matter of Martin B., (NY Surrogate's Ct 2007); *see* Mark Fass, *Sons Conceived In Vitro Ruled Covered by Trusts*, N.Y.L.J. 8/1/07 (law.com); see Matter of Fabbri, 2 N.Y.2d 236 (1957) for the proposition that the beneficiaries of a trust are determined according to the grantor's intent as determined from the trust instrument.

[168] Gillett-Netting v. Barnhart, 371 F.3d 593 (9th Cir. 2004). *See also* Woodward v. Comm'r of Social Security, 760 N.E.2d 257 (Mass. 2002) (permitting a posthumously conceived child to inherit from a decedent where the donor agreed to postmortem use of donated semen and also to support children conceived in that manner).

[169] Ferguson v. McKiernan, 581 Pa. 629 (Pa. 2007); *see* Amaris Elliott-Engel, *Sperm Donor Not Required to Pay Child Support*, The Legal Intelligencer 1/4/08 (law.com).

It is unlikely that a surrogacy contract (under which a woman is impregnated with sperm of a man who intends to gain custody of the child) will be enforced if the surrogate does not wish to surrender custody after the baby is born,[170] and courts may decline to hear such cases. The Ohio Court of Appeals held that a surrogacy contract, calling for a married woman to be impregnated with another man's sperm, was valid and not contrary to public policy. The surrogate mother and her husband could not be obligated to surrender the triplets born of this arrangement, but they did have to indemnify the man for his expenses and court-ordered child support.[171]

The Kansas Supreme Court upheld the constitutionality of a state law denying parental rights to sperm donors unless they have a written agreement. The donor, an attorney, failed to secure a written agreement, but he did not sign the sperm bank's waiver of parental rights. He said he intended to co-parent; the mother said that she intended to be a single mother. Sperm donor Daryl Hendrix petitioned for certiorari, but was denied.[172]

Arizona passed a statute, voided on Equal Protection grounds, that allowed a biological father, but not a surrogate mother, to rebut the presumption that the surrogate mother's husband was the parent of the child. A surrogate mother must be given access to a "maternity" proceeding to determine the true parenthood of the child.[173]

Where fertility technology is used by a married couple, questions may arise as to the paternity of the child. The New York case of *Kass v. Kass* has been litigated several times. The Court of Appeals, New York's highest court, decided in mid-1998[174] that fertilized "pre-zygotes" that a couple had frozen during marriage could not be used by the wife to get pregnant over the husband's objections. The consent form they signed, calling for surrender of the pre-zygotes for biological research, prevails over the ex-wife's desire for "sole custody" of the fertilized eggs.

A married couple who went to an in vitro fertilization clinic signed a series of consent forms specifying that, if they separated, the wife would be entitled to receive and implant the frozen pre-embryos stored at the clinic. Massachusetts' highest court refused to enforce the agreement because it could make one now-divorced spouse become a parent involuntarily.[175] The Massachusetts court said that the contract was intended to govern the relationship between the couple and the clinic, not to adjust rights between the spouses. The court also said that the contract includes the phrase "should we become separated," but fails to define it.

---

[170] *E.g.*, R.R. v. M.H., 426 Mass. 501 (Mass. Sup. Jud. Ct. 1998).

[171] J.F. v. D.B., 165 Oh. App. 3d 791 (2006).

[172] *In re* KMH, No. 96, 102 (Kan. 2007), http://www.kscourts.org/Cases-and-Opinions/opinions/supct/2007/20071026/96102.htm, *cert. denied* No. 07-1201 (10/6/08); *see* AP, *Sperm Donor Case Heads for U.S. Supreme Court*, 3/21/08 (law.com).

[173] Soos v. Maricopa County Superior Ct., 182 Ariz. 470 (Ariz. App. 1994).

[174] 91 N.Y.2d 554 (1998).

[175] AZ v. BZ, 725 N.E.2d 1051 (Mass. 2000).

A 2001 New Jersey decision upholds an ex-wife's right to mandate destruction of frozen pre-embryos created during the marriage, because her privacy right in not being forced to procreate outweighs the ex-husband's right to donate the pre-embryos to another couple.[176] Although the consent form for the in vitro fertilization program said that control of the pre-embryos would revert to the program in case of dissolution of marriage, it also said "unless the court specifies who takes control and direction of the tissues," so the consent form did not provide a clear manifestation of intent for disposal of pre-embryos.

Although the couple had a prior written agreement to discard the frozen embryos if they divorced, the Texas District Court nevertheless awarded three frozen embryos to the wife as part of a divorce-related property division. Then the Texas Court of Appeals reversed and remanded, entering an order for destruction of the embryos. In 2002, just before implantation was scheduled, the (However, they remained frozen until exhaustion of all appeals.) In 2002, just before the scheduled implantation, the husband withdrew his consent and filed for divorce. The wife sought to have the embryos implanted, but to relieve the husband of financial liability. The Texas Court of Appeals held that the Uniform Parentage Act does not explain what should be done with embryos for contingencies such as death and divorce, so the contract provisions — calling for the embryos to be discarded if the couple divorced — should be enforced.[177]

After a couple had two children, the husband had a vasectomy. Both spouses signed consent to artificial insemination using frozen donor semen. During the resulting pregnancy, the couple separated. Their separation agreement said the husband was not a responsible relative vis-a-vis the baby. They petitioned for an uncontested divorce and stipulated that he would not be financially liable for support of the child. However, a New York trial judge nevertheless ordered him to pay child support: The indemnification was void as against public policy. Although he did not sign the specific consent form required by the state's Domestic Relations Law § 73, he consented to the insemination and had to support the child.[178]

A woman who was erroneously implanted with another couple's embryo, and who gave birth to one of her own babies and one of the other couple's babies, was denied visitation rights after the other baby was ordered returned to his genetic parents. The New York Appellate Division treated the case as analogous to babies mixed up by a hospital.[179]

---

[176] JB v. MB, 783 A.2d 707 (N.J. 2001). *See* Davis v. Davis, 842 S.W.2d 588 (Tenn. 1992): "ordinarily the party wishing to avoid procreation should prevail."

[177] Roman v. Roman, 193 S.W.3d 40 (Tex. App. 2006), discussed in Erica Lehrer Goldman, *Contract Law Found to Govern Disposition of Frozen Embryos in Divorce*, Texas Lawyer (2/24/06) (law.com).

[178] Laura G. v. Peter G., (Sup. Ct. 2007), discussed in Mark Fass, *Judge: Paternal Duties Apply to Child Born of Artificial Insemination*, NYLJ 1/24/07 (law.com).

[179] Perry-Rogers v. Fasano, 715 N.Y.S.2d 19 (N.Y.A.D. 2000).

Chapter 17

Estate Planning

§ 17.01 INTRODUCTION

Most people have a goal of accumulating at least enough money to take care of their needs comfortably during life. It is also extremely common to want to leave funds for the surviving spouse (whether in the form of life insurance or otherwise), and many people want to make provision for their children, grandchildren, more remote relatives, friends, and favorite charities.

Estate planning involves applying both federal and state concepts, in the practical and tax arenas, to draft wills, trusts, and other documents. Tax considerations include eliminating or reducing the federally taxable estate. It also includes planning for gift and generation-skipping taxes and considering the income tax issues of trust grantors, trust beneficiaries, the trust itself, the estate, and its beneficiaries.

The estate planning process involves working with several different entities that can be described as "estates": the total estate, consisting of all tangible and intangible assets of the decedent; the probate estate, consisting of property that can be disposed of by will (see § 17.02[A] for a discussion of will substitutes and property that cannot be disposed of by will); the gross estate for federal tax purposes (which, as § 17.03 shows, often includes property that was disposed of by the decedent and no longer belongs to him or her); and the federal taxable estate, arrived at by adjusting the gross estate for deductions (as prescribed by Code §§ 2051–2056) and credits (§§ 2010–2016).

In one sense, the 2001 legislation, EGTRRA (the Economic Growth Tax Reform and Reconciliation Act of 2001, P.L. 107-16) made earth-shattering changes in estate taxation: see below. Yet, in other ways, EGTRRA preserved the basic structure of the estate tax, although phasing in lower tax rates and higher exemptions from federal estate taxation.

For the single year of 2010, estate tax is abolished — although gift tax will be in force, at the highest income tax rate. The EGTRRA legislation sunsets on January 1, 2011, so the pre-EGTRRA estate and gift tax rules will be restored as of that time, unless Congress takes steps in the meantime to abolish the estate tax permanently, or otherwise modify it.

Finally, if any taxable estate remains, estate tax rates are applied.[1] Before EGTRRA took effect, estate tax rates ranged from 37–55%. Because of EGTRRA, the top estate bracket dropped to 50% for calendar 2002, with further reductions of 1% a year until the level of 45% is reached in 2007. For certain very large inter-generational transfers (doubled for married transferors who agree to split their gifts), a generation-skipping tax at the highest estate tax rate is imposed in addition to the estate tax.

Although the rules for state death taxes may be different, federal estate tax does not apply unless the gross estate subject to tax exceeds a minimum amount. Until 1997, it was simple to say what that amount was: it had been frozen at the $600,000 level for many years.

---

[1] Current law provides that, as the higher unified credit phases in, the minimum tax rate will also increase (because amounts once subject to the lowest tax rate will be freed of estate tax).

The Taxpayer Relief Act of 1997, among other significant changes, increased the unified credit against gift and estate tax (see § 17.01[A] for a definition) so that the amount of assets that can be transmitted free of tax for 1999 is $650,000; the corresponding level for 2000 and 2001 is $675,000. Because of EGTRRA, the unified credit (and amount exempt from generation-skipping transfer taxes) for deaths occurring in calendar 2002 and 2003 is $1 million. The corresponding figure is $1.5 million for 2004 and 2005, $2 million for 2006–2008, peaking at $3.5 million for 2009.

Any estate smaller than this "unified credit amount" will therefore be entirely free of federal estate tax. Because no gift tax is imposed on transfers between spouses, married couples can "estate-split" (use interspousal gifts to create two estates of approximately equal size), so that a couple whose belongings might otherwise be subject to estate tax can create two estates, each below the threshold, and so that tax will be avoided no matter which spouse dies first.

EGTRRA also adds reporting requirements. A donor who makes a non-charitable gift of more than $25,000 must inform the IRS of the identity of the donee; the nature of the gifted property; the donor's adjusted basis for the property when the gift was made; the donor's holding period in the property; and whether selling the property would result in ordinary income or capital gain. To facilitate compliance, much of the same information must also be given to the donee.

The Conference Report for EGTRRA says that, except as provided by regulations, as of 2010, all transfers into trust will be treated as taxable gifts (i.e., taxed at the top income tax bracket) except for grantor trusts that are deemed to be wholly owned by the grantor or the grantor's spouse. For the year of estate tax repeal, EGTRRA adds rules about the basis of inherited property. Under prior law, the donee of a lifetime gift had the same basis in the gift property that the donor had. Inherited property was subject to a carryover basis (Code § 1014(b)) valued as of either the date of death or the alternate valuation date six months later.

EGTRRA, however, gives each decedent's estate a single $1.3 million "step-up" in basis that the executor can use to enhance the basis of estate assets. Property transferred to the surviving spouse qualifies for an additional step-up of as much of $3 million. However, the basis step-up is not available for certain types of securities (e.g., in some foreign companies) or property that was acquired by the decedent by gift rather than by purchase or inheritance, during the three-year period before his or her death. Interspousal gifts qualify for the basis step-up no matter when they were made.

For joint property or property held by the entireties, half is deemed to belong to the decedent and therefore qualifies for the basis step-up. In a community property state, both spouses' shares qualify for the step-up. Some losses belonging to the decedent (e.g., net operating losses) can also be used by the executor to increase the basis of inherited assets.

The unlimited marital deduction (§ 17.12[C]) can be used to defer tax in the first estate entirely. It's accurate to refer to *deferral* rather than *elimination* of tax, because (unless the surviving spouse remarries and repeats the process), whatever assets the surviving spouse inherits but does not spend will likely be included in the survivor's taxable estate.

In practice, very few estates are subject to federal tax, either because they are too small; because they are "first estates" (estates of the first spouse to die, with the major tax problem postponed until the "second estate"); or because legal and tax planning steps have been undertaken to minimize tax impact. Lifetime gifts (to individuals and charities) can be made to remove assets from the estate. Trusts, including QTIP, Irrevocable Life Insurance (ILIT) and credit-shelter ("bypass") trusts can achieve significant tax savings.

Although, as the title suggests, the Pension Protection Act, P.L. 109-280, primarily deals with pensions, it also includes some provisions affecting estate planning. Both spousal and non-spousal beneficiaries can roll over inherited plan benefits to an IRA or to a qualified plan that accepts such rollovers. If the heir is not the decedent employee's spouse, however, the beneficiary must begin minimum distributions from the inherited IRA no later than age 701/2, whereas there is no penalty if spouse beneficiaries retain funds in the IRA after that age.

The PPA also tightens up rules for charitable contributions. PPA § 1215 requires donors to recapture (that is, include in income) donations of tangible property if the donee uses the property for purposes unrelated to the donee's exempt function, or if the donee disposes of the property within three years without certifying that the intended use has become impractical. PPA § 1218 enacts a redesignated Code § 170(o), limiting deductions for contributions of fractional interests, calling for recapture if the balance of the fractional interest is not donated at the donor's death or within ten years. For years 2006–2007 only, the PPA permits a tax-free rollover from an IRA to a charity of up to $100,000. According to the National Committee on Planned Giving (which favors making the provision permanent), at least $25 million was donated under this provision.[2] The charitable IRA rollover provision was extended through 2009 by the Emergency Economic Stabilization Act, P.L. 110-334.

The 2008–2009 events in the financial sector created new challenges for estate planners, because many plans were premised on valuations for real estate and securities in the estate that declined significantly. The challenges of escaping estate taxation were reduced — but the challenges of providing for the survivors were increased.

[A] Unified Tax System

Gift and estate taxes are supposed to work hand in hand. Small gifts, and even larger gifts in forms that Congress seeks to encourage (such as interspousal gifts; annual exclusion gifts; and charitable gifts) are not subject to gift tax. Large gifts deplete the unified credit that is available against both gift and estate tax. The credit is unified to make it harder for the affluent to circumvent the transfer tax system by making lifetime gifts.

If an individual makes taxable lifetime gifts (defined at § 17.04), the unified credit is applied to insulate the donor from actually paying the tax during lifetime;

---

[2] Arden Dale, *Charities Love IRA Rollovers*, Wall St.J. 1/27-28/07 at p. B2.

no one actually has to pay gift tax until the unified credit is used up. (However, application of the unified credit is mandatory: taxpayers are not given the option of paying gift tax in an earlier year so that the unified credit can be used by their estates in a later year.)

Properly planned outright or trust gifts can be used to remove assets from the gross estate for tax purposes. However, the converse is that improperly planned gifts can have the practical effect of depriving the donor of control over the gifted property (and of the income earned by that property!), yet the so-called gifts will nevertheless be included in the donor's gross estate. Such a result can encumber the estate planner with anything from deep remorse to a ruinous malpractice suit.

[1] Generation-Skipping Tax

If wealth is transferred from the donor to persons in the same generation as the donor's grandchildren, there is also the potential for imposition of a generation-skipping tax (GST) on the transfer. The GST is set at the same rate as the top estate tax bracket, so in a worst-case scenario, the estate tax and GST imposed on a generation-skipping transfer can actually be higher than the amount transferred (estate tax plus GST).

Definitions of related concepts are not necessarily the same for the three transfer taxes (gift, estate, and GST): for instance, it is not always true that a completed gift has been removed from the estate, or that an amount removed from the estate has been the subject of a completed gift. Even if the gift is completed, it may be tax-free for one reason or another.

The Taxpayer Relief Act of 1997 mandated inflation-indexing for various amounts related to transfer taxes, e.g., the annual exclusion and the GST exemption. However, because of the way the indexing provision is defined, it is much more likely that the GST exemption will be indexed (because a 1% change in the indexing amount is required) than the annual exclusion (which requires a 10% change). See § 17.12[D][2] for a discussion of the interrelation between the unified credit and small-business estate tax relief.

Under this inflation adjustment provision, the exemption rose to $1,060,000 in 2001 and $1,100,000 for 2002, $1,120,000 (2003) and $1,500,000 (2004-5). Code § 2631 has been amended so that, starting in 2004, the GST exclusion is the same as the § 2010 exclusion.

The IRS published several rules implementing an EGTRRA provision that permits severing trusts that are designed to last more than one generation, so that each trust can be treated as a separate trust. Under the proposed rule, if a purported severance is not a "qualified severance" but the trusts are separate for state-law purposes, the GST exemption can be separately allocated to one or more trusts, which will otherwise be treated as separate for GST purposes.[3]

---

[3] *See* 72 F.R. 42291, 42340 (8/2/07), discussed in Allison Bell, *IRS Completes One Trust Rule, Proposes Another*, National Underwriter Online News Service 8/2/07; *see also* Final Regulations in T.D. 9348, 2007-37 IRB.

[2] Planning for Retirement Benefits

For many years, tax policy called for disbursement of retirement benefits during the retiree's life, so tax penalties were imposed for insufficient withdrawals and excessive accumulation of retirement benefit funds within the estate. These rules were relaxed somewhat in the 1980s, but estate planning for qualified plan benefits and IRAs was subject to a complex series of rules governing minimum distributions during life. Also see § 3.05[C]: as a matter of ERISA law, married plan participants must receive their benefits in the form of a Qualified Joint and Survivor Annuity with the spouse, unless the spouse consents to receiving the benefit in another form, or to the designation of one or more other persons as beneficiaries.

In January 2001, the IRS proposed regulations (66 FR 3928 (1/17/01)) greatly simplifying the rules for lifetime distributions — by promulgating a single, easy-to-use table, based only on the age of the employee, irrespective of whether the beneficiary of benefits remaining at the employee's death is a person (and whether the person is a spouse or someone else), a trust, or an entity such as a charitable organization. The rules for distribution of balances after the death of the original owner are also greatly simplified.

A subsequent Final Rule, T.D. 9130, provides a table for determining whether a joint and survivor annuity with a non-spouse beneficiary satisfies the "incidental benefit" rule (the rule that a pension plan must be maintained primarily to provide post-retirement income for employees, with other benefits only incidental to this main purpose). To avoid abusive arrangements deferring taxes excessively by stretching out the payments over too long a period, a joint and survivor annuity cannot provide a 100% survivor annuity if the beneficiary is more than 10 years younger than the employee.[4]

Pension Protection Act (P.L. 109-280) § 829 amends IRC § 402(c) to permit a beneficiary to roll over inherited plan benefits to an IRA or to a qualified plan that accepts such benefits, whether or not the heir is the deceased participant's spouse. However, non-spouse beneficiaries must begin minimum distributions from the inherited IRA starting at age 70½; spouse beneficiaries can continue to keep the funds in the IRA even after 70½; without penalty.

The Worker, Retiree, and Employer Recovery Act of 2008 (P.L. 110-458; also known as WRERA) modified the PPA requirements in light of the financial crisis. WRERA clarifies that, for plan years beginning after December 31, 2009, tax-qualified plans must allow non-spouse beneficiaries of plan benefits to make direct rollovers of inherited amounts to IRAs. Rollover notices must also be given. WRERA waives the requirement of taking Required Minimum Distributions (RMD) from defined contribution plans and IRAs for the calendar year 2009 only. (Relief is not available for 2008, despite the problems caused by taking

---

[4] *See* Code § 401(a)(8)(F) for the circumstances under which payments to a child will be treated as favorably as payments to a spouse (e.g., when payments are made until the child reaches majority, or dies before attaining majority); when payments are made to a disabled child; or to a student under age 26.

minimum distributions from a severely depleted account.) As a result, people who reach age 70½ in 2009 will have to take their first RMD by December 31, 2010.

§ 17.02 DEFINING THE "ESTATES"

Determining what a person owns at the time of death might seem obvious and without challenges. However, in addition to easily observed assets, individuals may have rights of which they are unaware (e.g., general powers of appointment: see § 17.10) or have forgotten (e.g., vested pension rights from long-ago employers). Rights might be contingent (e.g., on surviving someone else) and assets or liabilities might be uncertain (e.g., the decedent might have been a party in a lawsuit with issues of liability and damages unresolved at the time of death). Even if the number and nature of assets is undisputed, § 17.12[D] shows that the valuation of assets can be a difficult task.

[A] Defining the Probate Estate

State probate courts are charged with the tasks of probating wills and supervising the administration of the estate. Probating means decreeing that a document introduced as the will of a particular individual is indeed the last will and testament of that individual, who had capacity to make a will as of that time, and furthermore that it was validly created in accordance with state law, complies with the necessary formalities, and is not tainted by forgery, fraud, or undue influence.

Certain assets pass outside the probate process:

- Life insurance payable to a named beneficiary (rather than to the decedent's estate)
- Employment-related retirement plans and IRAs for which a beneficiary has been designated
- Joint tenancy with right of survivorship (the other joint owner(s) automatically get the property)

The nature and effect of bank accounts depend on local law, and can be complex. If the account is a true joint account, with each person named on the signature card having the right to withdraw up to the entire sum in the account, it will operate like a joint tenancy. But if it is a mere convenience joint account, with a second name added for the convenience of the actual depositor, it is possible that the depositor will have the right to dispose of the account balance by will, because the additional name was not given the full rights of a co-holder of the account.

A "Totten trust" or POD (Payable on Death) account (the two forms have some minor differences, but are basically similar), on the other hand, does not give the designated beneficiary the right to make withdrawals while the depositor is still alive; but at the depositor's death, the designated beneficiary is entitled to the account balance.

Another important group of will substitutes is the inter vivos revocable trust (often marketed as a "living" trust). Once again, on the death of an income beneficiary (whether or not the beneficiary is also the trust's grantor), the trust corpus is disposed of in accordance with the terms of the trust and not in accordance with the decedent's will.

§ 17.03 THE FEDERAL GROSS ESTATE

The Internal Revenue Code contains a number of overlapping sections mandating inclusion of items within the gross estate, which might in turn become the taxable estate if the size of the estate exceeds the applicable exclusions, deductions, and credits. The Code's rule is that if an item might be included under more than one section, the interpretation that yields the largest inclusion will be used.

The Internal Revenue Code is not by any means an intuitive document, and sometimes the gross estate will include items no longer in the decedent's possession, or even items that were never in the decedent's possession, based on a theory that ability to control disposition of an asset is tantamount to ownership of the asset.

[A] Assets Subject to Inclusion

The basic theory is found in Code § 2031, defining the gross estate as all property subject to §§ 2033–2045. Property is to be valued at fair market value: that is, the price that would obtain between a willing buyer and willing seller. The presumption is that valuation will be done as of the date of death, but see § 17.25[C][1] for the use of the alternate valuation date, prescribed by § 2032, which can be used to value the entire estate when the estate's assets have declined in value during the six-month period following the decedent's death.

Under § 2033, the gross estate is the value of all property to the extent of the decedent's interest in the property. This section brings into the estate rights to income that the decedent possessed at death, e.g., Income in Respect of a Decedent items such as salary and bonuses for the year of death. (IRD is primarily an income tax issue: see § 17.25[D][3].) Rent on real and personal property owned by the decedent and dividends on stock he or she owned, are also brought into the estate by this section. However, § 2040 rather than § 2033 governs inclusion of joint property where the decedent's interest ends at his or her death.

Insurance policies owned by the decedent (on his or her own life or anyone else's) might be covered by § 2033, although they might also be covered by § 2042 (§ 17.11). Section 2033 is also the section that mandates inclusion of corporate business stock owned by the decedent (whether or not as sole shareholder) and interests in proprietorships, partnerships, and other unincorporated businesses.

On a related issue (tax treatment of the principal residence), EGTRRA provides that, starting in 2010, the Code § 121 exclusion of home-sale profits from taxable income can be used not only by a living homeowner, but by the estate of a deceased homeowner; someone who inherited a decedent's principal residence; or a qualified revocable trust that received the residence on the death of the grantor of the trust. The decedent's ownership and use of the property are used in determining the ownership and use tests under § 121.

Trust assets that a trustee (and life income beneficiary) misappropriated were included in his gross estate when he died, and no deduction was allowed for claims against the trustee by the trust's beneficiaries. The income went to the trustee for life, with a remainder to his children. He breached his fiduciary duty by taking all of the trust's assets — and losing them by day trading. The District Court for the District of Virginia included the assets in his estate, because he exercised dominion and control over the assets contrary to the rights of the beneficiaries. The children did not assert any claims against his estate, so a § 2053(a) deduction was unavailable.[5]

[B] Dower and Curtesy Interests

Code § 2034 is something of a curiosity: it provides that the decedent's estate is not reduced for amounts subject to dower or curtesy. These are common-law spousal interests that have by and large been replaced by the spouse's right of election against the estate (§ 17.24[C]). See § 2056, discussed in § 17.12[C], for the estate tax marital deduction.

A so-called "transfer" that is made for full and adequate consideration is not really a transfer, so is not subject to estate inclusion. If a transfer is made for some consideration, but less than full and adequate consideration, § 2043(b) provides that the transfer is included in the estate only to the extent of the gap between consideration received and full and adequate consideration.

This section provides that relinquishing dower and curtesy rights does not constitute consideration. However, community property rights are not the equivalent of dower or curtesy, so relinquishment of community property rights (e.g., in the divorce context) might provide consideration. If a divorce agreement relinquishes marital rights covered by § 2043, and the obligor spouse dies, the claim against the estate is probably rendered nondeductible by § 2053.

[C] Other Interests

Section 2044 is the section that insures that QTIP property (see § 17.12[C][1]) will eventually be included in the estate of the surviving spouse. Property included as a result of this section qualifies for § 6166 installment payment relief.

For transactions brought into the gross estate by §§ 2034–2042, § 2045 provides that the time of the transaction is irrelevant except to the extent that the law specifically provides an applicability date.

Section 2046 is merely a cross reference to the § 2518 rule for disclaimers. It is possible to disclaim unwanted property, thus reforming the estate plan postmortem. On a subtler level, it is also possible to disclaim powers of appointment; perhaps

[5] Estate of Hester v. United States, 99 AFTR2d 2007-1288 (D.Va. 2007).

surprisingly, the consequences of disclaiming such powers are different from the consequences of letting the powers lapse by not exercising them.

§ 17.04   § 2035: GIFTS WITHIN THREE YEARS OF DEATH

The Internal Revenue Code has always contained a concept of gifts made in contemplation of death. It is perceived as a loophole if wealthy individuals can retain enjoyment of property for most of their lives, shifting ownership only when they are aware of impending death. However, the current Code version does not refer explicitly to the decedent's subjective intention in making the gift. Nor are gifts in general made within three years of death brought back into the estate. Section 2035 mandates inclusion of several kinds of transfers within the three-year period ending on the decedent's death:

- Life insurance incidents of ownership that would otherwise be included under § 2042
- Property that, without the transfer, would be included in the estate under §§ 2036–2038 (and, therefore, NOT property that would be included under §§ 2039–2041, even if the transfer was immediately before death and/or had an explicit motivation of contemplation of death)
- Gift tax on transfers made within the three-year period. See § 17.13[B] for a further discussion of the interplay between gift and estate tax.

The Taxpayer Relief Act of 1997 added a new § 2035(e), stating that transfers of any portion of a trust, made while the decedent had grantor powers as defined by § 676, will be attributed to the decedent. The result is that any gifts made out of a revocable trust during the three years preceding the decedent's death will be thrown back into his or her estate.[6]

§ 17.05   § 2036: TRANSFERS WITH RETAINED LIFE ESTATE

The § 2036 inclusion is popularly known as a transfer subject to a retained life estate. It mandates inclusion of the date-of-death (or alternate valuation date) value of the transferred property, which could be the entire corpus of a trust created by the decedent. Case law also mandates inclusion of income accumulated within the trust if inclusion of the corpus is required. If more than one transferor is involved, only transfers attributable to the decedent are included in his estate.

The most obvious example of a transfer with retained life estate is a family home, whose ownership is transferred to the owners' children, but subject to the parents' right to live in the home for the rest of their joint lives. However, § 2036 applies, sometimes in very unexpected ways, to a broader range of transfers than

---

[6] This section was enacted to reverse the result in Estate of Jalkut v. Comm'r, 96 TC 675 (1991) and the cases following it.

the classical life estate. This section includes in the gross estate interests retained by the decedent for:

- Life
- A period that is not ascertainable without reference to the decedent's death
- A period that does not actually end before the decedent's death (e.g., the decedent retained a 10-year interest in certain property, but in fact died six years after the transfer).

One surprising effect of § 2036 is that, if trustees of a trust were required to apply trust income to satisfy the decedent's obligation to support his or her dependents (as distinct from trustees other than the decedent having discretion to do so), the trust corpus could be included in the decedent's estate.

Under § 2036(a)(2), the estate includes property over which the decedent retained the right to control who would enjoy the property or its income, even if the decedent could not enjoy the property or income personally. However, as long as a trustee is not related to the transferor, or subordinate to the transferor (as defined by § 672(c)), a grantor's power to remove one trustee and substitute another will not result in estate inclusion.

[A] The Effect of Control

Ability to direct income to others is sufficient control to place the underlying property in the estate of the person holding such a power. This is so even if the power can be exercised only in conjunction with another individual (and even if that other individual's interest is adverse — e.g., a remainderman who is interested in the preservation of trust corpus rather than its dispersion).

However, estate inclusion on this ground can be avoided by drafting the trust so that the consent of all potential beneficiaries is required to direct the income stream. But if the grantor/trustee's ability to direct income is subject to an ascertainable standard, such as the health, education, welfare, and support of the income recipient, § 2036 inclusion can be averted except in cases where the distribution of income satisfies the grantor's support obligation.

Because control is the key to § 2036 (and many other estate tax provisions), direct or indirect retention of voting rights in a corporation controlled by the decedent will mandate inclusion of the stock in the decedent's estate, even though the decedent no longer holds the actual stock. In this context, control means that the decedent continues to own stock carrying at least 20% of the combined voting power of all classes of the corporation's stock (including stock whose ownership is attributed under § 318).

[B] Effect of Full Consideration

Transfers will not be subject to § 2036 if they are made for "adequate and full consideration." The theory is that there is no real diminution in the potentially taxable amount, because the consideration received by the transferor, plus its investment return between the time of the transfer and the time of death, should replace the transferred amount.

Although the IRS has litigated this issue repeatedly, it is well-accepted that in this context, adequate and full consideration is the actuarial value of the transferred remainder, with no consideration of the retained life estate.[7]

[C] Trust Issues

In the numerous cases in which the grantor of a trust also serves as trustee, the trust corpus will probably not be included in the grantor's estate merely because of the retention of typical fiduciary managerial powers (such as selling securities held by the trust and replacing them with others).

Drafters should also be alert to the doctrine of "reciprocal" or "crossed" trusts which applies to § 2038 and other transfer-oriented provisions as well as to § 2036. The IRS may seek to disregard arrangements under which, for instance, John creates a trust benefiting Mary's family while Mary creates a similar trust benefiting John's family.

If a person who makes a transfer but retains a life estate subsequently decides to transfer the life estate as well, § 2035 will bring that transfer back into the estate if it occurs within three years before the decedent's death. But if the transfer is more remote in time, it will not be included in the estate.

See T.D. 9414, 2008-35 IRB 454 for Final Regulations explaining treatment of the portion of transferred property that is included in the grantor's gross estate under § 2036 (and § 2039) if the grantor retained either the use of the property or the right to payment from the property for life; for a period not ascertainable without reference to the grantor's death; or for a period that does not end before the grantor's death. The Final Regulations took effect July 14, 2008. The general rule is that where both § 2036 and § 2039 could apply to a retained payment, then § 2036 will prevail; generally speaking, § 2039 will not apply. The IRS explained that the purpose of § 2036 is to require inclusion in the gross estate of property over which the decedent retained rights during a lifetime interest — not to require inclusion of the retained interest itself. T.D. 9414 explains that the IRS does not accept the argument raised by some taxpayers, that inclusion is not required when the present value of the remainder interest is zero. The proponents of this argument say that in that case, the full and adequate consideration exception under § 2036 is satisfied. T.D. 9414, however, says that there is a difference between selling property to a third party and receiving an annuity in exchange, and retaining an annuity interest in property transferred to a third party. If the grantor retains the interest for life, a period only ascertainable by reference to the grantor's death, or a period that in fact ends before the grantor's death, then under T.D. 9414, the property is brought into the grantor's gross estate by § 2036. The includible portion of the

---

[7] *See, e.g.*, Estate of D'Ambrosio v. Comm'r, 78 AFTR2d 96-7347 (3d Cir. 1996); Wheeler v. United States, 116 F.3d 749 (5th Cir. 1997).

property is that portion necessary to generate the annual payment without invading principal, using the applicable § 7520 interest rate for the grantor's death (or the alternate valuation date, if this is elected).

[D] FLP Issues

A Family Limited Partnership (FLP) is an estate planning and asset protection device under which the older generation makes gifts of interests in the partnership to their children or other intended beneficiaries of the estate plan; the intended benefits include discounting the value of the transferred interests for lack of liquidity. For the plan to succeed, the partnership must be created with appropriate partnership formalities, meaningful assets must actually be transferred to the partnership, and the partnership must be maintained (e.g., annual reports filed filing fees paid).[8]

The Tax Court treated a couple's transfers of stock to two FLPs as indirect gifts of stock to their children, largely because of the failure to keep books or observe other business formalities. Therefore, the gift tax was calculated based on the value of the stock rather than the value of the FLP interests that were transferred. The negative result came about in large part because the FLP failed to observe business formalities and kept no books other than its tax returns.[9]

§ 17.06   § 2037: TRANSFERS TAKING EFFECT AT DEATH

Conditional transfers that are not bona fide sales are subject to estate inclusion under § 2037, but only if possession or enjoyment of the property is contingent on surviving the transferor, and the transferor retained a meaningful reversionary interest (i.e., as of the time just before the decedent died, there was an actuarial probability equal to or greater than 5% that the transferor would get the property back).

§ 17.07   § 2038: REVOCABLE TRANSFERS

On the simplest level, § 2038 covers transfers where, as of the date of death, the decedent had the power to change enjoyment of interests in the transferred property (whether or not by taking back the once-transferred property) — e.g., by terminating a trust. The typical example is an inter vivos trust paying income to the grantor, intended as a probate avoidance measure (and perhaps as a measure for administering the property of an incapacitated person). Once again, bona fide sales for adequate and full consideration are exempt.

Estate inclusion occurs when a person who transfers property for the benefit of a minor (typically, a child or grandchild) pursuant to the Uniform Gifts to Minors or Transfers to Minors Acts (UGMA and UTMA, respectively) also serves as custodian for the property. Of course, inclusion is easily defeated by naming a custodian other than the transferor.

---

[8] *See, e.g., Family Limited Partnerships,* http://www.assetprotectionbook.com/family_limited_ partnerships.htm.

[9] M. Senida, TC § 45,206(M).

If the decedent was also a trustee of a trust which he or she created, the power to name new trust beneficiaries and redistribute beneficial interests within a class of trust beneficiaries is sufficient to bring the trust back into the estate under § 2038.

The mere power to remove one independent trustee and substitute another will not put the trust property back into the grantor's estate, but retention of an unrestricted power to discharge a trustee and assume the trustee's duties will have that effect: Reg. § 20.2038-1(a)(3). However, if there is no power to change **who** will receive funds from the trust, the grantor can retain powers to control investment of the trust without encountering § 2038 inclusion.

A power that is restricted by an objective standard, such as health and support of the beneficiary, is not a general power, and therefore will not result in estate inclusion. But the fact that the power must be exercised in conjunction with someone else is irrelevant, unless local law requires the consent of all vested and contingent beneficiaries, and unless local law gives the entire beneficiary class the right to cooperate and alter the trust (as is the case, for instance, in New York State).

Relinquishment of a § 2038 power within three years before death also subjects the property covered by the power to estate inclusion.

§ 17.08 § 2039: ANNUITIES

In broad outline, an annuity is an arrangement under which a continuing stream of payments is received. (See § 72 for the basic rules of income taxation of annuities.) The annuity could have come from a retiree's former employer, as a payment method for deferred compensation (see § 3.05 for further discussion of pensions and other deferred compensation). It might have been purchased from an insurance company as an investment.

A "private annuity" is an arrangement with a family member (or someone else who is not in the financial services business) under which a person transfers a capital sum to someone else who promises to make continuing payments. A "charitable annuity" is a similar arrangement with a charitable organization. To be actuarially sound, an annuity should represent a fair return based on the transferor's life expectancy and reasonable rates of return on the annuity amount.

In essence, an annuity is a gamble: the transferor wants to divest large amounts of funds that would otherwise end up in the estate, but hopes to live longer than his or her predicted life expectancy. The annuity payor hopes, on the contrary, that the payee will die sooner than anticipated, so that the principal amount will have been received in exchange for a smaller-than-predicted number of payments.

Annuities can be provided for a term of years, but it is more common for them to last either for one person's lifetime, or for the joint lifetime of two persons (typically a married couple). Another variation is whether the "survivor" annuity (paid after the first person has died) continues at the original level, or is reduced because only one person's living expenses have to be met.

Single-life annuities are not covered by § 2039, because the rights of the annuitant are extinguished by his or her death, and there is nothing left to be included in the estate. However, § 2039 operates in a perhaps surprising way on annuities with survivorship features or guarantees (e.g., payments will be made to the estate if the annuitant dies after receiving less than 10 years' worth of payments). Amounts receivable by the beneficiary are included in the estate of the decedent, to the extent that the decedent supplied consideration for the annuity.

For instance, if a husband purchases a survivor annuity, the anticipated payments to be received by his wife would be included in his estate; but if he paid only a portion of the purchase price, only a portion of the value of the survivorship benefit will be included in his estate. For employment-related annuities, all consideration contributed by the decedent's employer will be attributed to the decedent, so a high percentage of estate inclusion is likely.

Annuity payments deriving from insurance on the life of the decedent are excluded from this provision, although some complex and innovative hybrid products are marketed that can make it difficult to determine if life insurance is present or not. Various tests are applied under the Code and Regulations, but the essential test is whether there has been shifting of mortality risk (i.e., a risk that the insured person will die before the insurance company has recovered enough premiums to cover the death benefit).

Further issues are raised when the annuitant dies before annuity payments are scheduled to begin. (See § 3.05[C] for the related question of "qualified pre-retirement survivor annuities" paid by qualified retirement plans to the surviving spouses of employees.) Section 2039 is not triggered if the decedent's right to future payments is forfeitable. But with respect to nonforfeitable rights, § 2039 may require inclusion in the decedent's estate of the survivor's interest in the annuity.

The value of the survivor's interest is the fair market value (as of the date of death or alternate valuation date). For commercial annuities purchased from an insurer, the criterion is the cost of a comparable contract issued by the same company, purchased at the date of the decedent's death, and offering the same benefits.

[A] Applicability of Tables

Otherwise, the IRS annuity tables are used for valuation (e.g., in the case of a private annuity), based on the assumption that the item to be valued is the present value of the right to receive continuing payments. If the decedent paid more for a private annuity than the prospect of future payments would justify, the transaction also includes a gift element.

Generally, the unisex actuarial tables promulgated by the IRS and enacted at Code § 7520 will determine the valuation of a life estate, remainder, or reversion. However, the tables cannot be used where the person whose life expectancy (the "measuring life") is known to be terminally ill: to have an incurable illness or other deteriorating physical condition, with a 50% or greater probability of death within one year. If in fact the measuring life survives for 18 months, the presumption of terminal illness can be reversed, and the tables can be used instead, unless the party disputing the use of the tables (generally the IRS) provides clear and convincing evidence that the person's condition was truly terminal.

The tables could be used to value the charitable deduction portion of a bequest to a Charitable Remainder Unitrust and a life estate for the decedent's stepson. The stepson was diagnosed with cancer about five months after the decedent died, and lived for approximately a year after the diagnosis. The tables had to be used because at the relevant time — the decedent's date of death — he was not known to be terminally ill.[10]

The Fifth Circuit required a non-transferable private annuity to be valued, for estate tax purposes, by using the tables. The decedent in this case received a structured settlement after an accident in the form of three annuities issued by insurance companies. The decedent died at a time when he was scheduled to receive ten more annual payments from one annuity and ten years of monthly payments from each of the other two. The estate estimated the present value of the right to guaranteed payments as about $2.3 million, with a tax liability of approximately $468,000; the IRS audited the estate and concluded that an additional $143,000 was owed. After paying the deficiency, the estate claimed that it was entitled to a $427,000 refund because the annuities had been overvalued. Instead of applying the tables, they should have been valued at fair market value because they were non-transferable and therefore subject to a restriction (Reg. § 20.7520-3(b)(1)(ii)). The Fifth Circuit held that valuation does not depend on who owns the annuity; what is being valued is the right to receive payments. The cited Regulation refers to a situation where there is a clear risk the payee will not receive the anticipated return, a factor that was not present in this case.[11]

§ 17.09 § 2040: JOINT PROPERTY

Where ownership of an asset is shared by two or more people, the form of ownership determines how ownership can be transferred, and also determines the way the asset will be handled for estate purposes. If the property is jointly owned with right of survivorship (JWROS), further distinctions are drawn between joint tenancies between spouses and those involving non-spouses.

For married couples who acquired property by purchase, 50% of the value of the property is included in the estate of the first spouse to die, no matter which spouse provided consideration for the purchase. This current rule is a complement of the unlimited marital deduction, a tax provision that was added by 1981's ERTA.

If the joint owners are not spouses, then 100% of the value is included in the estate of the first joint owner to die, unless the surviving joint owners can prove that they contributed part of the consideration — in which case, inclusion in the first estate is proportionate to the consideration contributed by that person. Amounts that can be traced back to the decedent are not considered contributed by the survivor. This is also the rule followed when the joint tenants are married, but the surviving spouse is not a U.S. citizen.

---

[10] L. Burchell Estate, 2001-1 USTC § 60,410 (S.D.N.Y. 5/29/01).

[11] Anthony v. United States, 520 F.3d 374 (5th Cir. 2008).

However, if joint property was acquired by gift or inheritance rather than purchase, the marital status of the co-owners becomes irrelevant. At the death of one co-owner, the property is treated as if he or she had contributed a proportionate share (50% if there were two owners, 33⅓% of three, and so forth).

§ 17.10 §§ 2041, 2514: POWERS OF APPOINTMENT

Control is a very important concept in transfer taxation. The ability to control property, even without ownership, can result in the imposition of gift and/or estate taxes. A power of appointment, which can be inter vivos or testamentary, is the authority to decide who will receive property or the income from the property. A distinction must be drawn between a limited power of appointment, which will not have transfer tax consequences for the holder of the power, and a general power of appointment, which will result in the "appointive property" being included in the estate of the holder.

It should also be noted that a durable power of attorney, used to manage the property of an incapacitated person, might be a general power of appointment for transfer tax purposes. If the agent (person permitted to exercise the durable power of attorney) predeceases the principal (person whose property is under administration), property belonging to the principal and subject to the durable power of attorney/general power of appointment will be included in the estate of the agent, even though the agent never actually owned the property.

[A] General Powers of Appointment

A general power of appointment allows the holder of the power to appoint property to him- or herself, his or her estate, his or her creditors, and the creditors of his or her estate. Removing some of these powers prevents the power from being general.

An "ascertainable standard" power is not a general power: i.e., a power that can only be exercised in conformity with a standard that refers to the potential recipient's health, education, support, and/or maintenance. So, for instance, Michael's power to invade a trust created by his father Paul, on behalf of his mother Ernestine, is not a general power if Michael can only invade when Ernestine requires additional funds in circumstances related to her health or support. See § 2041(b)(1)(A).

[B] Limited Powers of Appointment

Whether the holder of the power can exercise it alone, or whether the consent of others is needed, is also a significant factor as to whether the power is general or not. Section 2041(b)(1)(C) provides that a power is not a general power if, to exercise it, the holder of the power must obtain consent from:

- The creator of the power
- Someone with a substantial adverse interest in the property

- A person to whom property could be appointed before the holder of the power can exercise it.

Oddly, the consequences of exercising a power of appointment and releasing it (permitting it to lapse) are exactly the same for the holder of the power. The theory is that the holder who exercises a power has made a gift to the new recipient of the property; the lapse is a gift to whoever would have lost the property if the power had been exercised.

However, if a "5 or 5" power (the power to demand either $5,000 or 5% of trust corpus, whichever is greater) lapses, there are no tax consequences; and if such a power is exercised, only the amount involved greater than "5 or 5" will be taxed: § 2041(b)(2). It is also possible to execute a § 2518 disclaimer (see § 17.18) to escape the tax consequences of holding an unwanted power of appointment.

[C] Gift Tax on Powers of Appointment

In the gift tax context, § 2514 governs power of appointment transactions. The definition of "general power of appointment" is the same as in the estate context, so a power is not general if it is subject to an ascertainable standard, or if the creator of the power, a person with an adverse interest, or a potential appointee must join with the holder to exercise the power. Either the exercise or release of a power (other than a 5-or-5 power) is a gift, but disclaimer of a power is not.

§ 17.11 § 2042: INSURANCE ON THE DECEDENT'S LIFE

Taxation of life insurance on the life of the decedent is subject to § 2042; if the decedent owned policies on someone else's life, those might be brought into the decedent's estate by § 2033. Included in the decedent's estate is insurance on the decedent's life that is payable to his or her executor, or is payable to a named beneficiary but the decedent had incidents of ownership in the policy at the time of death, or surrendered them within three years of death. (In the community property states, insurance purchased with community funds is only 1/2 in the estate of the decedent, even if payable to the decedent's estate, because it is a community asset.)

More to the point, insurance that is payable to a named beneficiary and is not in any of these categories is not included in the decedent's estate.

§ 17.12 CALCULATING AND PAYING THE FEDERAL ESTATE TAX

Once the gross estate has been calculated, and once the amount of gift tax paid on gifts within the three years before death has been determined (the estate is "grossed up" by adding these taxes), a tentative estate tax can be calculated. In virtually all cases, the tentative tax will be significantly higher than the actual tax, because various deductions and credits are available to reduce or eliminate the estate tax.

The estate tax is the tentative tax on the entire taxable estate and adjusted taxable gifts, reduced by gift taxes payable on gifts made after 1976. Effective January 1, 2005, the previous provision for a state death tax credit was repealed and replaced by a deduction for state death taxes.

[A] §§ 2053, 2054: Debts, Expenses, Taxes, and Losses

A deduction is available under § 2053 for funeral expenses and claims against the estate, including the decedent's debts and the actual expenses of administering the estate. Claims against the estate are limited to personal obligations of the decedent that were valid and enforceable as of the time of death, not, for instance, claims on which the statute of limitation had expired.

Administration expenses are actual necessary costs for marshalling and distributing the decedent's property, a category that includes executor's commissions, court costs, and attorneys' fees for services rendered to the estate as distinct from services to individual beneficiaries.

Expenses of the decedent's last illness that were not reimbursed by insurance or otherwise (e.g., Medicare) qualify for an estate tax deduction under § 2053(a)(3). Such expenses, if paid by the estate within one year of death, can be claimed as an income tax deduction on the decedent's final return (see § 17.25[D][3] for a discussion of IRD and other issues of the final return), but claiming the income tax deduction requires a statement that the estate tax deduction has not been allowed and has been waived. Also see § 642(g) for limits on the extent to which "overlapping" expenses (which might qualify for both estate and income tax deductions) can be claimed on both returns.

Section 2054 provides a deduction for casualty and theft losses of estate property occurring before settlement of the estate. The deduction is limited to amounts not reimbursed by insurance or otherwise, and an election must be made between claiming an income tax or estate tax deduction. Although marginal estate tax rates are much higher than marginal income tax rates, most estates are exempt from estate tax — but most individuals are subject to income tax! See *Commissioner of Internal Revenue* v. *Estate of Huber*, 520 U.S. 93 (1997), on the effects of material limitations on the surviving spouse's right to use income.

According to the Eleventh Circuit, the amount of the Code § 2053(a)(3) deduction for claims against the estate is based on valuation at the date of death, without adjustment for events occurring after the decedent's death. (In this case, the item to be valued was stock in a close corporation.) The Fifth, Ninth, and Tenth Circuits also use date-of-death valuation in this situation. However, the First, Second, and Eighth Circuits permit consideration of post-death events in the valuation, on the grounds that the claims were merely theoretical at the time of death.[12]

---

[12] *See* Estate of O'Neal v. United States, 258 F.3d 1265 (11th Cir. 2001) and the cases cited therein.

[B] § 2055: The Estate Tax Charitable Deduction

Although income tax charitable deductions are limited by the concept of a "contribution base" linked to the contributor's income, there is no limit on the estate tax charitable deduction, provided that the bequest is made for "public, charitable and religious uses." In other words, bequests to public charities are not limited, but those to private foundations are.

A trust that had equal charitable and noncharitable beneficiaries was denied an estate tax charitable deduction because there was a noncharitable distribution for less than full and adequate value, and the non-charitable portion was not a CRAT, CRUT, pooled income fund, or non-trust remainder interest in a personal residence or farm. Therefore, the trust failed to satisfy the requirements of § 2055(e)(2), and the deduction was unavailable.[13]

Until 1969, the federal estate tax deduction for a charitable remainder trust was the estimated present value of the remainder; in that year, Congress limited the deduction to charitable remainder unitrusts (CRUTs). Later, a safety valve was adopted so a CRT that was not a CRUT could qualify for the deduction by becoming a CRUT. The change might require a judicial proceeding. A late 2007 Seventh Circuit case involved a decedent who died in 2000, leaving most of the $3.4 million estate to the living trust he created. The estate tax return claimed a $1.5 million deduction for the trust remainder, which went to the Catholic Church. The IRS disallowed the deduction because the trust was not a CRUT: the instrument neither specified a fixed dollar amount or a percentage of fair market value to be paid to the income beneficiaries, a fundamental defect that could have been corrected only by a judicial proceeding within 90 days of the due date of the estate tax return. The trustee did not prepare a complaint to reform the trust for more than eight months, and never actually filed it. Three years after the decedent's death, the executor circulated a proposal to reform the trust to the income beneficiaries, but one of them refused to sign it. The trustee's position was that she substantially complied with the Code by administering the trust as if it were a qualified unitrust, but the Seventh Circuit rejected the argument. The trustee was represented by counsel, and was aware that reformation would be required to preserve the extensive tax deduction. The Code makes the federal deduction dependent on satisfying the laws of the forum state; and all the states, including Illinois, have provisions for reforming trusts on consent of all the beneficiaries.[14]

[C] § 2056: The Marital Deduction

An unlimited estate tax marital deduction, the counterpart of the unlimited gift tax marital deduction (see § 17.16) is permitted for two kinds of transfers to the surviving spouse: outright bequests, and Qualified Terminable Interests in Property (QTIPs). (In addition to transfers qualifying for the marital deduction,

---

[13] Galloway v. United States, 492 F.3d 219 (3d Cir. 2007).
[14] Estate of Tamulis v. CIR, 509 F.3d 343 (7th Cir. 2007).

many estate plans make part or all of the credit shelter trust payable to the surviving spouse.)

A marital deduction is available only if, as of the decedent's death, the couple were legally married: it is not available to cohabitants, for instance, and the federal Defense of Marriage Amendment precludes same-sex spouses from using the marital deduction. Nor is it available to an ex-spouse subsequent to an absolute divorce. However, if local law provides that a couple is married after they have secured an interlocutory but before they have secured a final divorce decree, then they are married and the marital deduction can be used.

To qualify for the marital deduction, the interest passing to the spouse must have been included in the decedent's gross estate (thus, no marital deduction is available for tenancies in common and community property, because they do not pass through the gross estate); must not be deductible under § 2053 (e.g., commissions received by the surviving spouse in his or her role as executor of the estate); and must not be a terminable interest other than a QTIP.

Although there is no gift tax imposed on any amount of gift passing from one U.S. citizen spouse to the other, gifts to non-citizen spouses are free of gift tax only up to $125,000 (2007 figure), $128,000 (2008 figure), or $133,000 (2009 figure) in present-interest gifts.

[1] QTIPs

QTIPs are often used so that a person planning an estate can make sure that his or her surviving spouse will have lifetime income, but that after the second spouse's death, the trust corpus will pass as directed by the deed or will of the first spouse to die: e.g., in a second marriage, life income to the second spouse, remainder to the children of the first marriage. QTIPs are also used if the person planning the estate does not believe the surviving spouse will be able to manage a large inheritance, but will be able to manage current income.

QTIPs can be created either inter vivos or by will; the most common form is the testamentary trust. An interest is a qualified terminable interest (qualified in the sense that it is eligible for the marital deduction) if the surviving spouse receives all the income from the subject property during his or her life. The trustee can be permitted to invade the QTIP for the benefit of the surviving spouse (but for the benefit of no one else), and the surviving spouse can be given a power of appointment over the property. Whatever property remains as of the surviving spouse's death will be included in his or her estate, notwithstanding the fact that the surviving spouse does not have the power to dispose of the property by will.

Because only 50% of joint property acquired by a married couple by purchase (as distinct from gift or inheritance) is included in the gross estate of the first spouse to die, only 50% qualifies for the marital deduction. Therefore, the surviving spouse gets a stepped-up basis in only 50% of the joint property. For certain marital joint tenancies created before 1977, however, a basis step-up is available in the entire value of the property.

If the surviving spouse is not a U.S. citizen, then QTIP treatment is not available, but a somewhat similar mechanism, the Qualified Domestic Origin Trust (QDOT) is available under § 2056A.

[D] Valuation Issues

Since the tax depends on the size of the estate, valuation of non-cash property within the estate becomes crucial. It is important for owners of valuable property to maintain current appraisals (which are also needed if, for instance, an outright or split gift of the property is made). Clearly, the financial crisis of 2008 has greatly reduced the size of many estates, but in late 2008, the legal system had no time to respond to this phenomenon.

In certain situations, usually involving securities, the property will be valued for gift and/or estate tax purposes at a discount from the fair market value that would obtain in an arm's-length transaction. For example, a minority interest in a closely-held corporation will often be valued at a discount because the owner of such an interest is unable to control corporate policy.

If the stock is subject to transfer restrictions, these restrictions affect marketability and therefore might also give rise to a discount, but see below for the IRC Chapter 14 rules on transfer restrictions. In the opposite situation, a "blockage" discount could apply if selling a large block of stock all at once would have the effect of depressing the price of the shares. It should also be noted that the IRS may seek to impose a valuation **premium** rather than a discount if a transferee or heir acquires the ability to control a corporation.

The problems of valuing an outright gift can be difficult enough; when future interests such as remainders and reversions are involved, the problems multiply. In a common arrangement, the grantor retains the right to receive income for life from a trust, with the remainder going, e.g., to a spouse or child. The gift is valued on the basis of the present interest of the remainder, calculated on the basis of the grantor's life expectancy. Similar considerations come into play for charitable remainder trusts and for more complex transactions.

The Eleventh Circuit agreed with the estate. When valuing a decedent's share in a closely held investment holding company that owned appreciated marketable securities, a 100% dollar-for-dollar discount should be applied to the $51 million contingent capital gains tax liability. This was required for a decedent's share in a closely held investment holding company that owned appreciated marketable securities. The analysis assumed that the entity would be liquidated on the valuation date, and all its assets sold. The Eleventh Circuit affirmed the Tax Court's grant of a 10% lack-of-control discount and a 15% lack-of-marketability discount.[15]

The Tax Court's position is that a valuation is an admission by the estate, and therefore the estate cannot lower the value it asserts later without cogent proof that the earlier value was wrong. In this case, the Tax Court held the estate to its original

---

[15] Estate of Jelke v. CIR, 507 F.3d 1317 (11th Cir. 2007); the 100% discount analysis follows Estate of Dunn v. Comm'r, 301 F.3d 339 (5th Cir. 2002).

appraisal of the value of the decedent's business at $2 million, rather than the $863,000 or $400,000 value asserted by the estate's expert witnesses at the trial four years later — especially because the initial appraisal was consistent with the IRS' value and the probate court valuation.[16]

[1] Valuation Under Chapter 14

Before Chapter 14 was enacted, donors tried to accomplish several objectives with complex donative transactions. Of course, they wanted to reduce the size of their taxable estates by removing valuable assets from the estate. But, at the same time, they sought to reduce the gift tax cost of making the transfer, by claiming that the remainder interest, the subject of the gift, had a low value whereas the retained interest had a high value. They also wished to assign most or all of the appreciation potential to the remainder interest, with the result that a small gift tax cost would shift an appreciating asset to its donees, with the appreciation itself escaping both gift and estate taxation.

Only intrafamily transactions are subject to Chapter 14, although the definition of *family* is quite broad and includes adoptees, relatives of the half blood, and spouses as well as blood relatives. Under Chapter 14, relatively favorable tax treatment is available for transfers of Qualified Interests (QIs) within the family, but correspondingly harsh treatment is assigned to transfers of interests that do not conform to the QI definition.

For gift tax purposes, a non-QI is assigned a value of zero, so that the entire amount of the transfer is assigned to the remainder and thus is a taxable gift. Although most Chapter 14 transactions involve trusts, the chapter applies to non-trust transactions as well.

A Qualified Personal Residence Trust (QPRT) is treated as a legitimate exception to the general § 2702(a) rule that the value of the retained interest after an intrafamily transfer is zero. A QPRT is a transfer in trust of a personal residence that will be lived in by holders of term interests in the trust. The trust must be irrevocable, and cannot contain any assets other than one residence and insurance policies on that residence, although it is permissible for additional funds to be deposited from time to time to meet expenses such as mortgage payments, property taxes, improvements, or purchase of a replacement residence subject to an existing contract of sale. At least once a year, the trustee must distribute the net income of the QPRT to the transferor, and any cash in the QPRT other than that needed for (e.g., taxes and maintenance), must also be distributed. However, all other distributions of income and principal are forbidden. The transferor is not allowed to sell or commute his or her interest in the QPRT.

It should be noted that Code § 6662, which imposes accuracy-related penalties in a number of contexts, also imposes a penalty for serious valuation errors or misconduct on gift and estate tax returns. The penalty is 20% of the tax underpayment attributable to a valuation that is 50% or less of the actual value of the asset;

---

[16] Estate of Leichter v. C.I.R., TC Memo 2003-66.

40% of the underpayment, if the valuation was 25% or less of what it should have been. The penalty is waived if the underpayment attributable to the valuation was under $5,000.

[2] Family Business Interests

In response to concerns about adverse estate taxation of small business, Congress adopted a "QFOBI exclusion" in TRA '97, enacted as new Code § 2033A. That is, certain amounts attributable to qualified family-owned business interests could be excluded from the estates of deceased business owners. The exclusion operated reciprocally with the unified credit: the amount potentially excludable was the difference between $1.3 million and the then-prevailing amount that could be sheltered by the unified credit. Thus, the QFOBI would phase down as the unified credit phased up.

As originally enacted, the QFOBI provisions contained some serious ambiguities. TRA '97 did not make it clear whether specific property could be excluded from the estate, or only the value of the property, and this ambiguity made it hard to determine how the QFOBI exclusion would work in conjunction with the marital deduction, the § 1014 calculation of basis of property acquired from a decedent, the GST rules, § 2032A special use valuation, and § 6166's provisions for installment payment of estate tax.

IRSRRA dealt with these problems by changing the QFOBI exclusion under § 2033A into an estate tax deduction enacted by a section redesignated as § 2057. (The deduction is unavailable in the gift tax and GST contexts.) Section 2057(a)(1) allows a deduction of up to $675,000 for the adjusted value of qualified family owned business interests that the decedent owned, provided that at least half of the estate consists of the adjusted value of the business, plus certain inter vivos gifts of interests in the business to family members.

EGTRRA repeals the QFOBI deduction for the estates of persons dying after December 31, 2003.

§ 17.13 GIFT TAX

One way to decrease the size of the estate is to spend money. Another way, certainly more palatable to the donees, is to give money away. Theoretically, the unified transfer tax system will capture the transaction either way, taxing the gift at one end (under IRC Chapter 12) and amounts not gifted or expended at the other. However, many gifts are exempt from tax (gifts between spouses; small gifts; certain gifts for minors) and, in any event, the gift tax is applied only to "completed" gifts, so planning advantages can be secured by allowing the donor to retain enough "strings attached" to prevent the completion of the gift.

[A] Completed Gifts

A gift is completed when the transferor relinquishes dominion and control over the property that is the subject of the gift. A simple example is giving a person an art object, or mailing a check payable to a person or a charitable organization. A gift of shares of stock becomes complete when the change of ownership is registered; a gift of real property is complete when the deed is recorded.

Conversely, a gift is not complete if the donor has the outright power to revoke it, or has lesser powers nonetheless treated by the IRC as tantamount to power to revoke. Thus, if the grantor has the power to remove a trustee and take the trustee's place, the gift is not complete; nor is it complete if the donor can change the beneficiaries of the gift, even if the donor cannot receive the money or property personally. If the donor can change the time or manner in which a beneficiary can enjoy his or her interest, but not the identity of the beneficiary, that power has estate tax consequences (under Reg. § 20.2038-1(a)) but does not make the gift incomplete. Any contingency within the donor's control is ignored in determining whether a gift is complete.

[B] Effect of Unified Rates

Until 1976, the gift tax rates were set at only 75% of the estate tax rates, as an incentive to prefer lifetime gifts over bequests. Since then, the taxes have been imposed at the same rates, but are figured differently, so that estate tax can be imposed on the amount of estate tax as well as the amount of the underlying taxable estate. Another complicating factor is that, although most gifts made within three years prior to a decedent's death are removed from his or her estate, the gift tax paid on those gifts is included in the taxable estate.

[C] Gift Tax Compliance

The gift tax return, Form 709, is due annually, covering all taxable gifts for the year (i.e., no matter how large the gifts, it is not necessary to file on a gift-by-gift basis). However, the unified credit operates so that individuals who make taxable inter vivos gifts do not have the option of either applying the unified credit to the gifts or paying the tax during life in order to retain the unified credit for use in the estate. The credit must be applied to lifetime gifts, with the result that less or none of the credit will be available subsequent to making large gifts or funding large trusts.

The gift tax statute of limitations is three years from the filing date of any return actually filed, or six years if a return was filed but omitted 25% or more of the value of the gift: see Code § 6501(e)(2). There is no statute of limitations, and tax can be assessed at any time, if a necessary return was not filed and transfers subject to §§ 2701 or 2702 (transfers of corporate or partnership interests, or of unitrust or annuity interests) were made, or if a fraudulent return is filed.

One of the many TRA '97 provisions affecting estate planning provides that, as long as a gift was adequately disclosed (on a gift tax return or other notice to the government), the IRS will not be permitted to challenge the valuation placed on the gift once the statute of limitations has expired.

T.D. 8845, 1999-51 IRB 684 prescribed what constitutes adequate disclosure of a gift that will be sufficient to prevent its revaluation with respect to gift tax on the later gift. The disclosure must include:

- Description of the transferred property
- Consideration, if any, received by the transferor
- Identity of each transferee; relationship to the transferor
- If a trust in involved, the trust's TIN and a brief description of its terms (or a copy of the trust instrument)
- Either an appraisal or a description of how the property was valued
- Disclosure of any position taken contrary to IRS positions.

The T.D. holds that any completed transfer to a family member in the ordinary course of operating a business is adequately disclosed even if it is not reported on a gift tax return, as long as all the family members involved report it properly for income tax purposes.

§ 17.14 § 2503: TAXABLE GIFTS AND THE GIFT TAX ANNUAL EXCLUSION

Theoretically, the rule is that gifts are taxable unless covered by a specific exemption, but in practical terms, the gift tax exemptions are broad enough to remove most gifting from the transfer tax ambit. Most importantly, § 2503(b) creates a per-donee annual exclusion of $10,000 which will be adjusted for inflation over and above 1998 baseline levels. However, because the exclusion must go up in increments of $1,000, the adjustment will not take place until the CPI has increased by 10%. The annual exclusion did not rise (to $11,000) until 2002.[17] The $11,000 amount did not rise in 2003–2005, but rose to $12,000 for 2006–2008 and to $13,000 for 2009.

There is no limit on the number of donees, so it is clear that a systematic gifting program involving several siblings, children, grandchildren, and friends each year can have the effect of removing a significant amount of assets from the potentially taxable estate without incurring any gift tax cost.

A married person whose spouse agrees to join in the gift can "gift split" (see § 2513), making gifts of up to twice the annual exclusion per year per donee.

[A] *Crummey* Powers

However, the annual exclusion is only available for gifts of a present interest, not of a future interest. Thus, writing a check to a nephew qualifies for the annual exclusion; naming the nephew as remainderman of a trust generally would not.

---

[17] *See* Rev. Proc. 2003-85, 2003-49 IRB 1184, Rev. Proc. 2004-71, 2004-50 IRB 970.

The exception is the *Crummey* power, named after *Crummey v. C.I.R*, 397 F.2d 82 (9th Cir. 1968). A *Crummey* power turns what would otherwise be a future interest into a present interest qualifying for the annual exclusion. The power requires that, for a period of at least 60 days a year, trust beneficiaries must be given the right to demand invasions of trust principal. This power, even if it is never exercised (and, in the real world, it never is), converts the interest to a present interest.

[B] § 2503(C) Trusts

Section 2503(c) permits a trust gift to a minor to be treated as a gift of a present interest as long as:

- Trust principal and income can be expended by or for the minor until he or she reaches age 21.
- Anything not so expended and remaining in the trust when the minor reaches 21 goes to the minor at age 21. (If the minor dies before reaching age 21, the trust corpus goes into the minor's estate or as the minor exercised a general power of appointment over the property — even if local law forbids minors to make wills or exercise GPAs.)

However, the property can remain within the trust after the minor reaches age 21, if he or she consents to continuation of the trust.

[C] Direct Payments

Under § 2503(e), no gift tax is ever assessed on direct payments made to a provider of education or medical services, on behalf of someone other than the payor. In other words, a person can devote any amount, without gift tax, to paying tuition or medical bills for a relative or friend, although giving money directly to the person who needs the services (or that person's parent) would be a taxable gift unless another exemption is available.

§ 17.15   § 2522: CHARITABLE DEDUCTION

Unlike the income tax charitable deduction the gift tax charitable deduction is unlimited, but the amount of the deduction is reduced by the annual gift tax exclusion: see § 2524.

The deduction is naturally available for outright gifts. A gift tax charitable deduction is also available for certain split-interest transfers: transfers to a Charitable Remainder Annuity Trust (CRAT), Charitable Remainder Unitrust (CRUT), or pooled fund only (see § 17.21). The deduction is the present value of the interest the charity is expected to receive in the future (calculated on the basis of the IRS actuarial tables). If the split-interest transfer is not a CRAT, CRUT, or pooled fund, the gift tax deduction will not be available, although it is possible that an estate tax deduction will be.

§ 17.16   §§ 2523, 2516: MARITAL PLANNING

Gifts from one spouse to the other are free of gift tax, regardless of amount. However, the gift must be made subsequent to the marriage (a gift from one engaged person to another is not exempt from gift tax, even if the engaged couple marries and files a joint return in the year of the gift). If a couple divorces, gifts in the year of the divorce but subsequent to the divorce are not deductible either. The gift tax marital deduction is available only when the donee spouse is a U.S. citizen. However, for non-citizen donees, § 2523(i) permits a $110,000 annual exclusion for present-interest gifts (as a compromise between the ordinary § 2503(b) $12,000 annual exclusion and the unlimited marital deduction permitted for citizen spouses). As a result of inflation adjustments, this figure went up to $120,000 for 2006, $125,000 for 2007, $128,000 for 2008, and $133,000 for 2009.

Gift tax issues also arise in conjunction with the dissolution of a marriage. There is no gift when one spouse agrees to pay a lump sum to discharge support obligations to the other spouse and the children of the marriage (§ 2516).

§ 17.17   OTHER GIFT TAX ISSUES

As a result of § 2512, gifts are valued as of the date they are completed. In other words, there is no gift tax alternate valuation date. However, control premiums, or discounts for minority interests, lack of marketability, or blockage can be applied in the valuation of gifts.

If a transfer is made for partial value (other than an unsuccessful but arm's-length business deal), § 2512(b) provides that the transfer is a part-gift, part-sale.

Transfers involving life estates, income, annuities, remainders, and reversions are valued under § 7520, using officially promulgated unisex tables of life expectancies. The tables are used for income, estate, and GST purposes as well as gift tax purposes.

However, the tables cannot be used to value transfers by a terminally ill person. For this purpose, a terminally ill person is defined as having an incurable illness or other deteriorating physical condition, whose probability of death within one year of the death of the person whose estate is being valued is at least 50%. If the "measuring life" survives the decedent by eighteen months, it is then presumed that the measuring life was not terminally ill, unless the terminal condition can be proved by clear and convincing evidence.

§ 17.18   § 2518: DISCLAIMERS

Although disclaimers appear in the Code with the gift tax provisions, they are perhaps more useful in the estate planning context. A qualified disclaimer, made in writing and no later than nine months after the creation of the interest being disclaimed, prevents an individual from receiving property that would be undesirable for tax or other reasons. Disclaimer of an inheritance must be made within nine months of the death; disclaimer of a gift must be made within nine months of the time that the gift becomes complete.

Before December 31, 1997, there was a difficulty in disclaiming spousal joint tenancies: the interest was sometimes deemed created at the time the tenancy was created, thus rendering untimely a disclaimer after one spouse's death.

T.D. 8744, published on that date, adds Final Regulations under § 25.25282-(c)(4)(i) permitting a surviving spouse to disclaim survivorship interest in a marital joint tenancy at any time within the nine months after the death of the first spouse to die, no matter when the tenancy was created, and whether or not either spouse could have severed the tenancy unilaterally. The effect of a disclaimer is that half of the property can pass under the will of the deceased spouse.

T.D. 8744 also clarifies that mere creation of a joint bank or brokerage account is not a completed gift because the creator of the account has the power to remove the contents of the account without consent of the joint tenant (and therefore disclaimers of interests in such accounts are timely within nine months of completion of the gift, not the mere creation of the account).

Supreme Court cases involving estate planning are rather rare. The December 1999 case of *Drye v. United States*,[18] holds that the taxpayer's interest as heir to his mother's estate was a right to property under Code § 6321, so merely carrying out a disclaimer under state law was not enough to defeat a federal tax lien.

§ 17.19 TRUSTS

A trust is an arrangement for dividing the ownership of assets from management of those assets, and it usually also involves a division between income and remainder interests. Trusts serve important practical purposes (continuing professional management of assets; carrying out a complex dispositive plan; managing the assets of an incapacitated person) as well as important tax planning purposes. The settlor, creator, or grantor places funds into trust, to be managed by one or more trustees (who may include the grantor). One broad analytic division is between revocable trusts, whose grantor retains the power to amend or revoke the trust, and irrevocable trusts, where this power has been surrendered. Revocable trust assets are always included in the estate of the grantor, because the retention of the power to revoke subjects the trust to taxation under § 2038.

Several factors determine whether or not an irrevocable trust will be included in the estate. Several IRC sections and Regulations, and many cases, deal with the question of which powers on the part of the grantor will be sufficient to make the trust a "grantor" trust (whose income is taxed to the grantor rather than the trust itself or its beneficiaries) and which powers will result in estate inclusion.

During the term of the trust, some or all of its income is paid out to one or more income beneficiaries. A trust is a simple trust in a year in which all trust income is paid out and none is accumulated; it is a complex trust, subject to

---

[18] 528 U.S. 49 (1999).

additional difficulties in tax computations, in a year in which some or all income is retained.

As the name suggests, a "spendthrift" trust is one whose beneficiary (traditionally, an irresponsible young rotter) cannot compel invasion of the principal, and one whose principal cannot be reached by the beneficiary's creditors. In some states, the courts will invade the principal of a spendthrift trust on public policy grounds, e.g., to cover alimony arrears and child support.

ILITs, or Irrevocable Life Insurance Trusts, are often used to plan for potentially taxable estates. Having a trust purchase a policy, or placing a policy into the trust (in the hope of outliving the three-year period during which transfer of incidents of ownership will result in estate inclusion) makes it possible to create a large fund that can be administered in accordance with the estate plan. The fund can be created by recurring small contributions (premium payments), and perhaps at a discount (if the insured person dies relatively soon after the purchase of the policy). Private annuity trusts are often used to reduce the tax impact of sales of highly appreciated real estate. Appreciated assets are exchanged for a fixed annuity stream, with the capital gains tax payable over the term. The trust (set up as an irrevocable trust, with no invasion of principal) sells the assets and uses the sale proceeds to fund a life annuity — the life annuity form is chosen so that there is no estate tax, unless there are accumulated payments. During the annuitant's lifetime, each payment is partially taxed as ordinary income, part as capital gains; annuitants who outlive their actuarial life expectancy must treat the entire annuity payment as ordinary income.

On August 3, 2000, the NCCUSL approved the Uniform Trust Code,[19] a pioneering attempt at codifying trust concepts nationwide. In the NCCUSL view, the Restatement (2nd) of Trusts fails to cope with some important practical issues. The Uniform Trust Code concentrates on the powers and duties of the trustee and incorporates the Uniform Prudent Investor Act. Article 6 of the Uniform Trust Code deals with revocable trusts, a little-explored subject in state probate codes. As of late 2007, the Uniform Trust Code had been adopted in Alabama, Arkansas, the District of Columbia, Florida, Kansas, Maine, Missouri, Nebraska, New Hampshire, New Mexico, North Carolina, North Dakota, Ohio, Oregon, Pennsylvania, South Carolina, Tennessee, Utah, Virginia, and Wyoming, The UTC supersedes Article VII of the Uniform Probate Code and the Uniform Prudent Investor Act and the Uniform Trustee Powers Act.[20]

As a countervailing trend, a number of states attempted to be hospitable to trusts, for example, by not imposing taxes on trust assets or income. Delaware and New Hampshire do not tax trusts with out-of-state beneficiaries, and New York does not tax trusts whose creator lives outside New York. New Hampshire enacted

---

[19] The text is available at http://www.law.upenn.edu/bll/alc/uta/trst00ps.htm; for adoptions, see http://www.nccusl.org/Update/uniformact_factsheets/uniformacts-fs-utc2000.asp.

[20] *See, e.g.*, Rachel Emma Silverman, *Trust Laws Get a Makeover*, Wall St. J., 7/29/04 at D1, http://www.utcproject.org.

generous rules in 2006, such as permitting perpetual duration trusts — but only for a specific purpose such as maintaining an art collection, not for benefit of individual persons. New Hampshire also insulates trustees from suits by beneficiaries who charge losses due to inadequate diversification of trust assets. Asset protection trusts that shelter assets from creditors, divorce, and litigation judgments, are permitted in Alaska, Colorado, Delaware, Missouri, Nevada, Oklahoma, Rhode Island, South Dakota, and Utah. Dynasty trusts are allowed in Alaska, Arizona, Colorado, Delaware, the District of Columbia, Florida, Idaho, Illinois, Maine, Maryland, Missouri, Nebraska, Nevada, New Hampshire, New Jersey, Ohio, Rhode Island, South Dakota, Utah, Virginia, Washington, Wisconsin, and Wyoming.[21]

[A] Duration and Termination of a Trust

When the trust's term ends, or when a determinative event happens or fails to happen (e.g., when Person A dies; if Person B fails to receive an M.D. degree from an accredited university), the corpus remaining in the trust will be distributed to remaindermen as prescribed by the terms of the trust. The income beneficiary(ies) and/or remaindermen can be people and/or charitable institutions.

The general rule is that merger will occur, and the trust will be disregarded for legal purposes, if the sole trustee, income beneficiary, and remainderman are all the same person, although some state statutes do grant validity to such "one-person" trusts.

Another general rule is that a charitable trust can be drafted to be perpetual, but that trusts for natural persons are subject to the Rule Against Perpetuities: the trust must end and its corpus be distributed not more than 21 years after the death of the last person named in the trust who was alive when it was created. However, states such as Alaska and Delaware permit perpetual trusts benefiting individuals, and also allow other favorable features (such as allowing self-settled spendthrift trusts).

In many instances, creation of a trust will include at least some element of a completed gift, and therefore at least some gift tax will theoretically be generated. (Except for very wealthy people, gift tax remains theoretical because the unified credit is drawn down first, and no actual cash payment of gift tax will be required until the unified credit is exhausted.) With revocable trusts, the completed gift element is absent, because of the grantor's retained power to revoke the trust. The ability of the grantor's creditors to reach the trust can also prevent completion of the gift.

§ 17.20 GRANTOR TRUSTS

Most trusts are grantor trusts for income tax purposes: that is, no matter who actually receives the income, the trust grantor is taxed on it. (Charitable

---

[21] Rachel Emma Silverman, *States Court Family-Trust Business*, Wall St. J. 6/22/06 at p. D1.

remainder trusts and pooled income funds are exempt from the grantor trust rules, which appear at §§ 671–678.) A trust is treated as a grantor trust because of the extent of control that the grantor exercises, or is permitted to exercise (even if he or she never actually does so) over the trust, its income, and its administration.

The Code contains a number of overlapping provisions, and avoiding grantor trust characterization can be very difficult in drafting one that escapes *all* the grantor trust provisions.

Although grantor trust treatment in one sense appears to be punitive — trusts are usually employed by wealthy individuals who are already in the highest tax bracket, so additional income from the trust will be taxed at their marginal rate — in another sense it is beneficial. Because the grantor pays the tax, the trust itself does not, so the trust need not be invaded to pay taxes, and the trust continues to appreciate tax-free. The longer the term of the trust, the more powerful this effect will be. Grantor trust treatment can apply to the entire trust, or only to the trust income.

Reg. § 1.671-3 provides that a grantor who is treated as the owner of the entire trust must take all trust income, deductions, and credits into his or her own income, as if the trust did not exist. But if the grantor is treated as an owner only because of a share of trust income, the grantor takes into account only that share of trust tax items that a current income beneficiary would report.

The grantor is the "owner" of the trust if he or she retains the power to revoke, terminate, or amend the trust, or appoint its income or principal: §§ 671, 676. This is true even if the power is never in fact exercised. But the grantor will not be treated as owner if such a power can only be exercised in conjunction with an adverse party: § 676(a).

Under § 672(e), a power held by either spouse is attributed to the other, so no tax advantages can be gained by one spouse setting up a trust rather than the other.

[A] § 674 Grantor Trust Provisions

Section 674(a) makes the grantor the owner of any part of a trust by which the grantor has power to control the beneficial enjoyment of income, corpus, or both. That is, even if the grantor doesn't actually derive financial benefit from the trust, "pulling the strings" to determine who will get the benefits is an ownership power. If the grantor can only exercise this power in conjunction with an adverse party — i.e., someone whose financial interests oppose those of the grantor — then § 674(a) will not apply.

But if the consent of someone who is a neutral (non-adverse) party is required, § 674(a) does apply. (A non-adverse party is one who has no financial interest in the trust, or whose interest is unaffected by whatever the grantor chooses to do.) If an independent trustee (one who is not subject to the control of the grantor or grantor's spouse) has a "spray" or "sprinkle" power to direct income or corpus within a specified class, this power will **not** make the grantor taxable on the trust. See § 674(c).

The grantor will not be treated as the owner of the trust purely by reason of these powers:

- Power to apply income to the support of his or her dependents
- A power exercisable only by will
- Certain powers to distribute corpus
- Power to defer the payment of income
- Power to define a particular payment as income or invasion of principal
- Power to withhold income from a minor or disabled beneficiary.

[B] Administrative Powers Under § 675

Section 675 details which administrative powers will force ownership treatment:

- Ability to dispose of trust income and/or corpus for less than its fair market value
- Power to borrow from the trust without paying adequate interest or providing adequate security
- Actual borrowing by the grantor or grantor's spouse, unless full repayment (including interest) is made by the beginning of the tax year.

Section 675 also makes the trust a grantor trust on the basis of any power of a nonfiduciary (unless supervised by a fiduciary) to vote the trust's stock holdings in a corporation controlled by the grantor; to repurchase trust assets; or control investments to the extent that the trust owns stock in a corporation controlled by the grantor.

[C] § 677 Income Paid or Payable to the Grantor

The grantor is taxed on the trust income if that income (without need for approval by an adverse party):

- Is actually or constructively distributed to the grantor or spouse
- Is held or accumulated for future distribution to the grantor or spouse
- Is used to pay premiums for insurance on the lives of the grantor or spouse (unless a charity is the irrevocable beneficiary of the policy): § 677(a)(1)-(3).

If trust income is actually used to support a dependent of the grantor (other than the grantor's spouse), such income is taxed to the grantor under § 677(b). The mere possibility that trust income could be used to satisfy the grantor's support obligations does not make the income taxable to the grantor unless he or she can collect income for this purpose in his or her individual capacity (not his or her capacity as trustee).

[D] Reversionary Interests

Another grantor trust provision, § 673(a), makes the grantor the owner of the trust based on a 5% or greater reversionary interest. The value of the reversion is calculated as of the inception of the trust, and as if the grantor exercised his or her maximum discretionary powers. Section 673(b) provides that the grantor will not be treated as owner merely because of a reversion that takes place only if the beneficiary (who is a lineal descendant of the grantor) dies before reaching age 21, and if the beneficiary held all present interests in the trust.

[E] Estate Inclusion

In addition to the income tax issues addressed in the grantor trust sections, it is important to determine whether or not a trust will be included in the grantor's gross estate for federal estate tax purposes. Clearly, § 2038 brings revocable trusts into the estate.

Even nominally irrevocable trusts may be subject to estate inclusion because of §§ 2036–2038, depending on the extent of the donor's retained control. Certain powers are permitted, and will not trigger estate inclusion; others will.

Relevant issues include:

- Who serves as trustee
- Who can change the identity of the trustee
- Who can receive income and/or corpus from the trust, and who makes the decision
- Who is permitted to change the trust.

It should also be noted that if a trustee is required to use trust funds to satisfy the grantor's obligation to support his or her children, the trust will be brought into the grantor's estate under § 2036, but this will not occur merely because the trustee has discretion to use trust funds to pay for items that fall under the grantor's support obligation.

If the trust is drafted so that a trustee other than the grantor (and even if the trustee is the grantor's spouse) has the power to amend or revoke the trust, or the right to decide who will get trust corpus and income, but the grantor does not have this power, the trust may be able to escape inclusion in the grantor's estate. The trustee's powers will not be attributed to the grantor.

The most cautious drafter would simply assure that the grantor did not retain any powers over the trust. However, it is common for planning clients to refuse to surrender complete control, and for them to seek to retain the greatest possible quantum of control that will not trigger estate inclusion or other avoidable adverse tax consequences. (As already noted, the grantor will probably have to accept the fact that the trust's income will be taxed to him or her.) Under statute, Regulations, and case law, certain grantor powers are permitted without triggering estate inclusion:

- Power to replace the trustee (as long as the grantor is not a potential replacement[22]). But retention of the right to serve as trustee in the future, even if never exercised, will place the trust in the grantor's estate.
- Power to direct the trustee's investments within a trust that the grantor cannot revoke or modify (as long as the trustee remains subject to state-law standards of fiduciary conduct).
- Power to take certain property out of the trust and replace it with other property of equal value (so that the overall value of the trust remains the same, even though the identity of its assets has changed).

[1] Implications of the Durable Power of Attorney

A Durable Power of Attorney (DPA) is a document permitting a designated agent to make financial decisions for the principal (grantor of the power). The power is durable because it survives the disability of the grantor. The basic principle is that a gift by a DPA agent is sufficient to remove the donated property from the grantor's estate only if at least one of two conditions is met. Either the transaction must be of a type specifically authorized by the document, or it must be stated as a power of the agent under the relevant state law.

A new version of the Uniform Power of Attorney Act is one of four uniform acts approved by NCCUSL in early 2007. The new law, adopted in New Mexico and introduced in the legislatures of Maine, Maryland, Michigan, and Minnesota in 2007, is largely structured as a set of default rules that drafters can alter at will. However, to clarify the authority of agents (and protect the principal from financial abuse) agents can exercise certain powers only if they have specifically been conferred by the instrument. The presumption has been reversed since the 1979 power of attorney act: now a Power of Attorney is presumed durable unless it states that it is not. The 2007 statute includes an optional statutory form Power of Attorney, intended to make it easier to create a power — and more likely that financial institutions will accept it. The new Act applies only to property powers; health care powers of attorney are subject to the Uniform Health Care Decisions Act.[23]

Gifts of real estate made by an agent were excluded from the principal's estate in *S. Pruitt Estate*[24] although the DPA lacked an express gifting power.

---

[22] Estate of Wall v. C.I.R., 101 TC 300 (1993).

[23] NCCUSL press releases, *ABA Approves Four Uniform Acts*, http://www.nccusl.org/nccusl/DesktopModules/NewsDisplay.aspx?ItemID=178 (2/12/07), and *New Act Updates the Rules on Powers of Attorney*, http://www.nccusl.org/Update/DesktopModules/NewsDisplay.aspx?ItemID=159 (7/13/06). The 2007 Act has been adopted in New Mexico and was introduced in the legislatures of Maine, Maryland, Michigan, and Minnesota in 2007.

[24] TC Memo 2000-287 (9/12/00).

The Tax Court inferred the gifting power from the general language of the instrument. Oregon state law does not forbid gifts by an agent, and the agent acted consistently with the principal's established pattern of giving. The gifts were not fraudulent, and they did not deplete the principal's estate to a detrimental extent. Therefore, the gifts were in the principal's best interests and carried out her intentions.

However, because Connecticut law requires explicit authorization for an agent to make gifts, $144,000 in gifts made by the decedent's attorneys-in-fact were included in her estate. There was no established pattern of giving to follow, and no indication that the principal intended to establish a gifting power.[25]

§ 17.21   CHARITABLE TRUSTS

Although a wide variety of trust structures can be used to benefit charity, only three qualify for favorable tax treatment under § 664, and therefore are the most prevalent: the charitable remainder trust (CRT), which has two subdivisions (Charitable Remainder Annuity Trust, or CRAT; Charitable Remainder Unitrust, or CRUT); the charitable lead trust (CLT, similarly divided into CLAT and CLUT); and the pooled fund. Sample forms for (grantor and non-grantor) charitable lead annuity trusts making payment to one or more charitable beneficiaries for the annuity period, and then distributing assets to non-charitable remaindermen, have been published: inter vivos trusts in Rev Proc 2007-45, 2007-29 IRB. . . . ; and testamentary in RP 2007-46, 2007-29 IRB. . . .

A split interest trust is so-called because it benefits both the charity and individuals (typically the grantor and/or members of the grantor's family). If the individuals get income for a period of time, and then the charity gets the corpus, the trust is a charitable remainder trust. If the charity gets income and later the individuals get the corpus, it is a charitable lead trust.

The trust is an annuity trust if the income payment is defined as a dollar amount. To qualify for tax benefits, the amount must be at least 5% of the initial fair market value of the trust (measured as of the time of its creation). The trust is a unitrust if the payment is defined as a percentage (which must be at least 5%) of the trust's value for the current year. Additions are permitted to an ongoing unitrust, but no additions can be made to an annuity trust after its initial funding. A pooled fund is a single fund administered by a charitable organization; it serves trust-like functions for sums of money too small to be administered as separate trusts.

TRA '97 tightened the requirements for qualified CRTs by mandating that the annual non-charitable annuity or unitrust interest cannot exceed 50% of the value of the trust property. Furthermore, the charity's remainder interest must be worth at least 10% of the initial value of the contribution. The interaction of the two provisions means that CRTs cannot be used to achieve very high income for the donor or other recipient of the current income, and the younger the income beneficiary, the smaller the rate of return that can be provided.

---

[25] M. Gaynor Estate, TC Memo 2001-206 (8/6/01).

Early in 2001, the IRS finalized anti-abuse regulations for both charitable lead and charitable remainder trusts, T.D. 8923 (2001-6 IRB 485). The regulations rule out "ghoul trusts" (more formally known as trusts *pur autre vie* — for another life). The abusive tactic was to choose, as measuring life, a young person who, although not terminally ill, was nevertheless seriously ill enough to have less than a normal life expectancy. Under the Treasury Decision, the only acceptable measuring lives for charitable lead trusts are the donor, the donor's spouse, or a person who is a lineal ancestor (or spouse of a lineal ancestor) of all of the noncharitable remaindermen.

§ 17.22   GENERATION-SKIPPING TRANSFERS

A wealthy family with dynastic aspirations could, theoretically, place vast sums of wealth into trusts and keep the funds tied up for generation after generation. There are two limitations on this tactic: first, the Rule Against Perpetuities, which requires the trust corpus to be distributed within lives in being plus 21 years (but which is being eroded by the "Alaska-type" trust statutes discussed in § 17.19[A]).

The other is the federal tax on generation-skipping transfers (GST), which is imposed at the highest estate tax flat rate. The GST is imposed in addition to the estate or gift tax on the transaction, so it is perfectly possible for the tax on a transfer to be larger than the transfer itself! GST is of concern only to the affluent, because such large amounts are exempted. Code § 2631 has been amended so that, starting in 2004, the GST exclusion is the same as the § 2010 exclusion.

A generation-skipping transfer (whether outright gift, in trust, or otherwise) is one made to a close relative of the grandchild's generation or any younger generation, or to a remote relative or non-relative who is 37.5 or more years younger than the transferor. A person's spouse is always deemed to belong to the same generation as that person, whatever the actual age may be, and adopted persons are treated in the same way as blood relatives.

There are three kinds of generation-skipping transfers, each bearing different tax consequences. A "direct skip" is an outright gift. A "taxable distribution" is a distribution from an ongoing trust; a "taxable termination" is a distribution in conjunction with the termination of a trust (e.g., one that calls for income for a period of years to A, then remainder to B, C, and D).

Also note that if a direct skip is a net gift (i.e., the transferor pays the GST, so the skip person receives the intended amount of the gift in full), the GST paid by the donor is considered an additional gift, which gives rise to additional GST liability.

§ 17.23   PLANNING THE ESTATE AND DRAFTING THE WILL

An estate that is below the amount that can be protected by the unified credit, or one that qualifies for the marital deduction in whole or in large part will not be subject to federal estate taxation (although it may be subject to inheritance taxation in one or more states). Nevertheless, the estate still has to be planned.

A will is an "ambulatory" document, which can theoretically be revoked and replaced at any time. Certainly, wills should be redrafted based on major changes in the law, or major changes in circumstances (such as a marriage, divorce, or significant change in the size or composition of the estate). The difficulty is that clients will not always be conscientious about such matters. They may also lose testamentary capacity before the time that a will change becomes necessary.

Testamentary capacity is a modest standard (ability to understand the nature and approximate size of one's assets, and to recognize one's "natural objects of bounty" such as family members), but nevertheless some people are unable to satisfy it. In arguable cases, some attorneys videotape the execution of the will, so that eventually the probate court will be able to observe the demeanor of the testator. Some very cautious attorneys videotape will executions routinely, so that no inference will be drawn that the capacity of a particular testator was dubious.

According to the California Court of Appeals, when a conservator seeks approval of the estate plan during the conservatee's lifetime, any challenge to the will must be raised then, not when the conservatee dies. Once the court accepts a revised estate plan, it has exercised substituted judgment, and further modifications will not be allowed after the conservatee's death.[26]

The "second estate problem" occurs at the death of a surviving spouse who has not remarried. In many instances, the size of the estate has increased because of investment returns, and it exceeds the amount that can be protected by the unified credit; or it is in one of the higher estate tax brackets. The decedent has no surviving spouse, so the marital deduction is unavailable.

In the smaller estate, use of a credit shelter trust reduces or eliminates the second estate problem. The amount that can be sheltered by the unified credit is placed into a trust, benefiting either the surviving spouse, the testator's children, or other desired beneficiary(ies). The surviving spouse then reduces his or her estate by charitable gifts, a giving program, or expenditures, so that the credit shelter trust can pass intact at his or her death. The balance of the estate, if any, will be subject to estate taxation.

Life insurance or "second to die" insurance (which is purchased when both spouses are alive, but payable only on the second death) can provide liquidity to pay estate taxes without reducing the amount available to heirs. No matter what the source of the funds, the will should clarify the apportionment of estate and other transfer taxes, that is, whether each legacy is reduced by a share (proportionate or otherwise).

The needs of the recipient, not just the testator, should be considered. It is unwise to leave sums of money outright to a person with Alzheimer's disease, or

---

[26] Murphy v. Murphy, 164 Cal. App. 4th 376 (Cal. App. 2008); Pamela A. MacLean, *In Appellate First, Attacks on Wills Barred After Estate Owner Dies*, Nat'l L.J. 7/14/08 (law.com).

who is otherwise incapable of managing it. In that situation, a disposition in trust might be better. But if the person received Medicaid or other public benefits, even an interest in a trust could impair the availability of benefits. No one should be named as executor or trustee unless he or she can be expected to be physically mobile and mentally alert throughout the entire period that a fiduciary could be expected to be required.

§ 17.24 DRAFTING STRUCTURES

It is not quite a truism to say that the function of a properly drafted will is to administer the disposition of exactly 100% of the testator's assets that can pass by will. An improperly drafted will might attempt to dispose of assets that pass by operation of law, assets that no longer form part of the estate, or might make $3 million worth of dispositions of an estate whose actual value is only $1 million!

[A] Will Formalities

A properly drafted will naturally satisfies locally-required formalities, such as the number of witnesses to the will and where signatures should appear. The general rule is that a will must be signed at the end, so anything added below the signature will have no effect. Corrections or additions placed on the document after its execution will also be void.

Most jurisdictions allow "self-proving affidavits": affidavits signed by the witnesses when the will is executed, to the effect that they observed the signing of a document that appeared to be the will of a testator competent to sign it and not under duress. The value of the affidavit is that the will can be probated on the basis of the affidavit, without the testimony of the witnesses.

The testator should sign only one document, which becomes the original will which will eventually be submitted for probate. (If multiple originals are executed, it will probably be necessary to produce all of them for probate.)

Wills, preferably accompanied by an accurate current inventory of property and related documents (e.g., deeds and mortgages), must be kept in a safe place. The testator's own safe deposit box is a poor choice, because it is generally not opened until an executor has been appointed. In fact, it may be necessary to refer to the will to determine who has been named as executor! However, the testator's safe, a fireproof will vault in a lawyer's office, or the safe deposit box of a reliable person who is not expected to predecease the testator, can be good choices. In some jurisdictions, the wills of living persons can be deposited with the probate court for safekeeping. If this is done, it is important to remove revoked wills and replace them with the new wills.

[B] Bequests

Perhaps the simplest disposition is the specific bequest ("The set of eight walnut Chippendale chairs to my niece Helen") or the pecuniary bequest ("The sum of $100,000 to my business partner Edwin Steengard"). It is of course clear what $100,000 means, but the drafter should be careful to avoid ambiguity in the description of hard assets and art works. The major risk of this type of disposition is one of ademption: that the decedent will no longer own a specific asset at the time of his or her death (in which case the legatee gets nothing; he or she does not receive a substitute item).

It is frequently a good idea to provide for "abatement" (reduction of some or all specific bequests if the value of the estate falls beneath a certain amount). Specific bequests are paid first, but the typical will leaves the residue (money and property remaining after satisfying specific bequests) to the spouse, children, or other persons the testator particularly wants to favor. Without an abatement clause, the residue could shrink significantly.

Dispositions can, of course, be quite complex. They can be conditional ("If he has completed at least two years of study at an accredited medical school, with passing grades"). They can involve discretion ("In such shares as my spouse chooses to appoint"). Funds can pass from the will to a trust (known as a "pour-over") or from a trust to the estate, to be administered in accordance with the will (a "pour-up").

Dispositions to the spouse are often made as formula pecuniary bequests, nonformula fractional shares, or formula fractional shares. A formula pecuniary bequest would give the spouse the maximum amount that can be sheltered by the marital deduction, minus any interests passing to the surviving spouse that are in the gross estate but not the probate estate (e.g., will substitutes), and minus any amount that can be used to take advantage of all available credits and deductions.

A formula fractional share gives the surviving spouse an amount calculated as the maximum marital deduction amount, minus reductions as above, divided by the entire residuary estate. A nonformula fractional share simply leaves a specified percentage of the residuary estate to the surviving spouse.

[C] Right of Election, Disinheritance, Pretermission, and Lapse

State law provides for an "elective share": a share of the estate that the surviving spouse is entitled to receive. If the deceased spouse's will provides less than the elective share, the survivor has a legal right to "elect against the will": demand to receive that statutory share. States differ in the size of the spouse's elective share and how it is computed. Factors include the size of the estate; whether there were children and how many; and the length of the marriage. In some states, the right of election applies only to the probate estate; in others, it applies to will substitutes and perhaps to inter vivos transfers as well. State law also determines whether, to avoid the right of election, provision for the spouse must be an outright bequest, or whether bequests in trust or other terminable interests count also.

Because of the right of election, it is difficult to disinherit a spouse, unless the spouse has waived the right of election or has some other reason for declining to challenge disinheritance or provision smaller than the elective share. As a general rule, testators are permitted to disinherit children or anyone else other than the spouse.

Some states make provisions for "pretermitted heirs" (children who are born after execution of a will, or who are not named in the will and are presumed to be forgotten rather than deliberately excluded). A testator who wishes to disinherit a child can usually do so by mentioning the child in the will (to reverse the presumption of pretermission) and stating an intention to disinherit. A trivial (e.g., $1) bequest can have the same effect.

The will must also cope with the possibility of lapse (predecease of the legatee). There are two main ways of doing this: by "gift over" ("I leave the sum of $10,000 to Robert O'Bannon if he survives me; if he does not survive me, I leave the sum of $10,000 to his alma mater, Columbia University") or by lapse into the residue. That is, bequests left to predeceased persons become part of the residue.

Many states have "anti-lapse" statutes that provide that lapsed bequests to close family members do not become part of the residue; instead, they go to the surviving spouse and/or children of the legatee. Many states also follow the rule of "no residue in a residue," so that any portion of the residue that lapses passes by the state's rules for intestacy, not according to the will.

The other side of the coin is that some states deal with the very common situation of couples divorcing without updating their wills by making wills invalid upon divorce — or by maintaining the will, but invalidating dispositions to "my spouse" who is now an ex-spouse.

[D] Class Gifts

Instead of dispositions to a named individual, they might be made to a class of persons ("the sum of $5,000 to each of my grandchildren who survives me"). These days, "children" could include half-and step-siblings, adopted children, children born via reproductive technology, and variations on these themes, so it may be worthwhile to draft wills and trusts to clarify who is included and who is excluded.

If a class includes both individuals of a particular generation, and descendants of a deceased individual of the same generation, a class gift could pass either per capita or per stirpes ("stirpes" is Latin for "branch," as in branch of a family tree).

If the testator whose will leaves money or property to "My brothers and sisters who survive me, or their surviving children if they predecease me" dies leaving two surviving siblings and a predeceased sibling who has four surviving children, amounts left to the class "per capita" would be divided into six parts (one each for the siblings and the four surviving children of the dead sibling).

Amounts left to the class "per stirpes" would go one-third to each of the siblings, and one-twelfth each to the four nieces and nephews, because the nieces and nephews take equal shares of the share of their predeceased parent.

The New York Surrogate's court held that children born by in vitro fertilization with a decedent's frozen sperm, three and six years after his death, were his "issue" and "descendents" of the decedent, a trust beneficiary. The surrogate held that the grantor's intent governs, and concluded that the trust's grantor (the father of the decedent) would have intended to include them. New York treats a child born of consensual artificial insemination during marriage as a legitimate child. New York's Estates Powers and Trusts Law was amended to prevent children conceived after a parent's death from taking under the parent's estate — but, in this case, the Surrogate's Court restricted applicability of the statute to wills and to children of the testator; this case involved a trust created by a grandfather.[27]

A 2007 New Jersey court holds that a trust benefiting Union Carbide heir Halsted Vander Poel, to be distributed among his "lawful issue" at his death, did not benefit his stepdaughter. Vander Poel married Jane Vander Poel's mother when the girl was four years old; Vander Poel already had two biological children at that point. Jane was given the Vander Poel name and treated as Halsted's daughter, but she was not formally adopted until she was 33 years old. The family lived in New York, but the trust was established under New Jersey law, which at the time was somewhat more favorable. The litigation involved Halsted's bequest of his share of the trust created by his mother to Jane. When the trust was established, New Jersey law provided that unless there was a declaration to the contrary, an adoptee was not included in a class gift if the donor was a "stranger to the adoption" — i.e., was not the adoptive parent. Although New Jersey law has since been changed, the court applied the law in effect when the trust was created, and declined to give the law change retrospective effect with regard to a person adopted as an adult. The holding might have been different for a child adoptee. Jane's attorney advanced an "equitable adoption" theory but it was rejected because that doctrine was applied only to correct evident injustices. In this case, Jane's father made ample provision for her, indeed favoring her over his biological children — perhaps in part because he was aware that she would be excluded from his mother's trust.[28]

---

[27] Matter of Martin B., (N.Y. Surrogate's Ct 2007), discussed in Mark Fass, *Sons Conceived In Vitro Ruled Covered By Trusts,* N.Y.L.J. 8/1/07 (law.com). Matter of Fabbri, 2 N.Y.2d 236 (1957) says that the beneficiaries of a trust are determined by the grantor's intent, as determined from the trust agreement.

[28] In the Matter of the Trust of Blanche P. Billings Vander Poel, No. A-0983-04, (N.J. App. Div. 2007); *see* Michael Booth, *Adult Adoptee of Union Carbide Heir Can't Share in Fortune, Court Rules,* N.J.L.J. 10/19/07 (law.com). The New York Court of Appeals held in 2008 that a child adopted out of a family is not entitled to share in a class gift to trusts set up in 1926 and 1963. The intervenor, an out-of-wedlock child born to a trust beneficiary, was adopted in 1955, and there was no evidence that the trustor even knew that she existed. Under New York law, the presumption is that an adopted-out nonmarital child is not "issue" entitled to an interest under a class gift. The Court of Appeals rejected the intervenor's equal protection argument, because the deciding factor was not her illegitimacy, but her being adopted out of the family. At the time the trusts were created, adopted-out children did not share in class gifts, because the policy was to assimilate the child into the adoptive family. To promote finality, trust determinations are made without considering the remote possibility

§ 17.25 ESTATE ADMINISTRATION

This discussion (except for § 17.26) assumes that a will of at least arguable validity exists and can be located. As soon as possible, the executor designated by the will should present it for probate and seek letters testamentary (official appointment as executor). The official appointment will be necessary for many practical tasks, and useful for others.

The executor must collect any amounts owing to the estate, such as amounts earned by the decedent but not paid during his or her life. The executor must find out about all valid claims against the estate (such as last illness expenses; debts owed but not paid by the decedent) and satisfy them. The executor must offer the will for probate and, once it is probated, distribute the remaining estate (after satisfaction of claims) to the beneficiaries.

[A] Probate

The probate process requires notice to named heirs, and also to the distributees who would receive part of the estate in intestacy. Generally speaking, the probate process is uncomplicated (although it can be lengthy, time-consuming, and productive of extensive professional fees). However, in some instances, disappointed distributees or legatees who did not receive as much as they expected contest the will. Possible grounds for contest include:

- The purported will is a forgery, not the actual will of the testator
- The purported will was revoked by a later will, which the will contestants can produce
- The testator did not have testamentary capacity at the time the will was signed
- The formal execution of the will was defective (e.g., it was not signed, it was improperly signed or witnessed)
- The will was a product of force or duress imposed on the testator
- The will was a product of undue influence on the testator.

An "in terrorem" clause in a will revokes any bequest made to a person who challenges the will. However, if the will contest is successful, the in terrorem clause, and indeed the entire will, becomes irrelevant.

To many clients, probate avoidance is an important goal of estate planning. Revocable trusts, and other will substitutes that pass by operation of law, do not enter the probate estate, and therefore probate is avoided as to such assets. The smaller the probate estate, the lower the official schedule of probate fees. The disadvantage is that assets in a revocable trust are also part of the potentially taxable estate for federal purposes.

---

of the subsequent appearance of a child who was adopted out of the family: In the Matter of the Accounting by Fleet Bank (*In re* Piel) 10 N.Y.3d 163 (N.Y. 2008); *see* Mark Fass, *N.Y. High Court Finds Adopted-Out Child Has No Claim to Jell-O Fortune*, N.Y.L.J. 3/14/08 (law.com).

Many people own real property in states other than their state of domicile: for instance, a "snowbird" who lives in a northern state but has a Florida or Arizona residence. Ancillary probate of the real property will be required in the state in which it is located. The need for ancillary probate can be removed by making a lifetime gift of the property, or by placing its ownership into a trust in the state of the owner's domicile.

The "probate exception" to federal jurisdiction rules makes cases about the administration of probate of wills and estates subject to state rather than federal jurisdiction. Although it is usually applied to diversity cases, in 2006 the Seventh Circuit held that it applies on the same terms to federal question jurisdiction. The plaintiff alleged improprieties in the guardianship of her now-deceased father. The district court dismissed the suit under the *Rooker-Feldman* doctrine (see § 22.03[C]), finding that it is improper for federal courts to hear state appeals. But the Seventh Circuit held that the plaintiff was not attacking the state court judgment, making abstention inappropriate. Nevertheless, the probate exception might still rule out federal jurisdiction, because in effect the plaintiff inappropriately sought to have the federal court administer her father's guardianship estate. The plaintiff also raised tort claims about breach of fiduciary duty, but the parties were non-diverse and the fiduciary duty claim was a state claim.[29]

While the Texas probate system was handling the estate of Anna Nicole Smith's 90 year old husband, Smith filed for bankruptcy in California. There was no testamentary provision for her, but she contended that her husband intended her to benefit from trusts. The decedent's son (Marshall) filed claims in the bankruptcy case, charging Smith with defamation; she alleged truth as a defense and counterclaimed, charging the son with tortious interference with the gift she expected from her husband. The counterclaim made the bankruptcy case an adversary proceeding. Eventually, the probate court upheld the decedent's estate plan. The District Court awarded Smith over $80 million in compensatory and punitive damages from Marshall, for tortious interference with her expectancy. The Ninth Circuit reversed, stating that the probate exception prevents the federal courts from exercising jurisdiction. The Supreme Court reversed yet again, holding that the District Court had jurisdiction over Smith's counterclaim, which did not involve probate or estate administration: federal courts can hear claims from creditors, legatees, and heirs, as long as probate is not interfered with.[30]

In the Second Circuit view, *Marshall* changed the scope of the probate exception, permitting some claims to remain in the federal court system. The Southern District of New York used the probate exception to dismiss claims against a bank and law firm for fiduciary misconduct. The Second Circuit, however, concluded that *Marshall* limited the exception, to the point that federal courts should decline jurisdiction only if the plaintiff wishes to probate a will or reach a res in state custody. So some claims were dismissed, but claims for breach of fiduciary duty,

---

[29] Jones v. Brennan, 465 F.3d 304 (7th Cir. 2006).
[30] Marshall v. Marshall, 547 U.S. 293 (2006).

aiding and abetting the breach, fraudulent misrepresentation and fraudulent concealment remained in federal court.[31]

Many states have "slayer statutes" under which a person will be precluded from inheriting from a person that he or she killed. The Wisconsin Court of Appeals allowed a wife and daughter who provided assistance in the suicide of a terminally ill testator (they gave him a loaded shotgun) to take under his will. The state's slayer statute precludes inheritance on the basis of intentional killing, but the Court of Appeals held that the decedent chose to deprive himself of life. No criminal charges were filed, although Wisconsin imposes a penalty of up to six years for assistance in suicide.[32]

[B] Tasks for the Executor

The estate administration process requires the executor to:

- Get multiple copies of the death certificate; they will be required in many contexts
- Make multiple copies of the will, for distribution, e.g., to heirs and distributees
- Investigate insurance coverage on the decedent's life (including employment-related coverage); file a claim
- Determine if credit insurance is available to satisfy debts of the decedent
- Find out all banks, brokerages, mutual funds, etc., where the decedent had an account; find out which accounts pass by operation of law (e.g., joint and Payable on Death accounts) and which become part of the estate
- Make sure that personal property in the estate is secure, physically safe, and properly insured at all times until it is sold or distributed in kind
- Get appraisals of property whose value could be controverted
- Find out where the decedent had a safety deposit box; make arrangements for opening the box (representatives of taxing authorities may have to be present) and inventorying its contents
- Check the disposition of the decedent's pension and IRA accounts
- Collect the information needed for the decedent's final income tax return
- Notify the Social Security Administration of the decedent's death; if necessary, assist survivors in applying for Social Security benefits (e.g., as surviving spouse, mother of deceased worker's minor child, etc.)

---

[31] Lefkowitz v. Bank of New York, 528 F.3d 102 (2d Cir 2007); *see* Mark Hamblett, *2nd Circuit Re-Examines Standard for Probate Exception*, N.Y.L.J. 7/3/07 (law.com). *See also* Moser v. Pollin, 294 F.2d 335 (2002) for the proposition that the question is whether the federal court is asked to probate a will or directly administer an estate.

[32] Estate of Lemmer v. Schunk, 2007 AP 2680 (Wis. App. 9/25/08); *see* Ryan J. Foley, (AP), *Appeals Court: Relatives Who Assist in Suicide Can Inherit Estate*, 9/26/08 (law.com).

- Find out if the decedent's estate or survivors are entitled to buy-out of business interests or stock in closely-held corporations; if required, put the stock or satisfy the business', partners', or other stockholders' right of first refusal
- Determine the amount of any transfers made within three years of death that must be included in the gross estate (e.g., life insurance transfers)
- If necessary, obtain a bond covering services as executor. (Especially if the executor is a family member or friend, the will may call for service without bond.)
- Keep track of administration expenses
- Set up accounting system for the estate, and for any trusts
- Submit the will for probate.

[C] Tax Aspects of Estate Administration

The estate itself is capable of earning income (indeed, one of the executor's duties is to make it productive without violating fiduciary principles), and therefore is capable of becoming a taxpayer. A simple estate is likely to be settled in less than a year, but more complexity takes more time to work through, and the estate may have to cope with income tax returns for several years.

[1] Relief Provisions

Even if two estates are the same size, and contain the same proportion of property subject to estate tax, the two are not necessarily equal in other respects. One estate may consist entirely of cash and marketable securities; the other, of illiquid assets such as hard-to-sell and hard-to-value interests in close corporations. Although no one enjoys paying estate taxes, the hardship on the latter type of estate is obviously much greater than on the former.

Therefore, the Code contains several provisions that can be interpreted as relief provisions for illiquid estates, including closely-held businesses and family farms. The provisions are:

- § 2032 — alternate valuation date; executor's election to value all property in the gross estate as of six months post mortem, not the date of death; anything disposed of within the six-month period is valued as of the date of disposition.
- § 2032A — covering up to $750,000, as adjusted for inflation, for farms and other real estate used in business and constituting a major part of the estate. The inflation-adjusted amount is $800,000 for the year 2001, rising to $1 million in 2009.
- § 2057 — small business interests.
- § 6166 — extension of time to pay estate tax in installments, including a preferential interest rate on the installment payments. For 2009, the amount used to compute the 2% portion of the tax payable in installments is $1,330,000.

EGTRRA modifies the § 6166 installment payment procedure by allowing it to be used with regard to a business with up to 45 partners or shareholders (triple the previous limit). The modification is effective for the estates of persons dying after December 31, 2001. EGTRRA also allows certain lending and finance businesses that were barred from this treatment under prior law to qualify, but they will only be allowed to make installment payments over five years (not 10) and they will not be allowed to defer principal payments.

The IRS issued guidance on extensions in 2006. Form 4768 can be used for a six-month extension to file or pay estate tax and generation-skipping tax, and the form no longer requires a written signature, making it easier to file electronically. Form 8892 can be used to get an automatic six-month extension for filing Form 709 even if a Form 4868 has not been filed.[33]

The § 2057 relief can be recaptured, and additional estate tax imposed, if one of four events happens within 10 years of the decedent's death, and before the death of the qualified heir:

- The qualified heir ceases material participation in the business, and no family member takes his or her place
- The qualified heir disposes of any qualified interest outside the family
- The company no longer maintains its principal place of business within the United States
- The qualified heir ceases to be a U.S. citizen.

In other words, the point of § 2057 is to provide advantages to family businesses within the United States; change in the nature of the business can make the relief retrospectively unavailable.

The additional estate tax is a declining percentage of the tax saving attributable to the qualified interest, plus interest at the rate charged on underpayments of income tax. The percentage is 100% for years 1–6 after the decedent's death, phasing down to 20% in year 10, and phasing out after 10 years.

[2] Apportionment

It is not enough just to figure out how much tax is due, or who makes the initial payment. Sooner or later, a calculation must be made of the ultimate apportionment of tax responsibility among various potential payors. Section 2205 makes the executor primarily liable for payment of the federal estate tax. But if the executor fails to make the payments, the unpaid estate tax becomes a lien on the property interests within the gross estate, and the transferees can be held liable. After that happens, beneficiaries whose interests were diminished by the executor's failure to carry out fiduciary duties may be entitled to reimbursement from the estate or from the other beneficiaries.

---

[33] IR-2006-29, http://www.irs.gov/newsroom/article/00,id=154554,00.html.

Under § 2206, the beneficiaries of the proceeds of insurance policies that are included in the gross estate can be required to contribute proportionately to their share of the proceeds, but the surviving spouse is not obligated to pay a share of estate tax based on receiving any insurance proceeds that qualify for the marital deduction.

Similarly, under § 2207, persons who receive power of appointment property that is included in the gross estate are responsible for contributing to the estate tax, unless the will provides to the contrary, or unless the marital deduction is available. See § 2207A for rules for QTIP property.

It is good drafting practice to indicate how the estate tax liability should be apportioned. The tax could be assigned to specific legatees, or could be assigned to the residue. Some state laws prorate the state estate tax based on beneficial interests in the estate. Therefore, amounts that qualify for the marital or charitable deduction pass free of estate tax.

[3] Bankruptcy Issues

NOTE: The Bankruptcy Abuse Prevention and Consumer Protection Act of 2005 (BAPCPA) increases the extent to which priority tax claims must be repaid by bankrupt persons.

The automatic stay prevents a tax lien from attaching to an asset that the debtor inherits in the course of a bankruptcy proceeding, although a tax lien that is perfected prepetition usually attaches to after-acquired assets by operation of law.

Under the principle of equitable recoupment, the Tax Court permitted two estates to offset a time-barred overpayment of estate tax against the decedent's federal income tax liabilities.[34]

A Tax Court memo decision from early 2001 permits the IRS to collect estate tax liability from a transferee of estate assets. The transferee was liable because the notice of transferee liability satisfied the § 6901(c) one-year limitations period. The IRS was not guilty of laches — there had been no inexcusable delay — and the beneficiary had unclean hands, because he was aware of the tax liability when he received the assets from the estate.[35]

[D] Income Tax Issues

Although most of the planning attention revolves around estate tax and GST (because the potential tax rates are so high), it should not be forgotten that estates and trusts often become taxpayers in their own right, with income tax issues. An estate ceases to be a separate taxpayer once the estate is settled — i.e., assets have been marshaled and claims against the estate have been paid. Reg. § 1.641(b)-3(a) gives the IRS power to "deem" an estate settled after what it considers to be a reasonable time, if administration continues to drag on.

---

[34] H. Orenstein Estate, TC Memo 2000-150 (4/26/00).

[35] E. Fridovich, TC Memo 2001-32 (2/12/01).

The beneficiaries of trusts and estates also encounter income tax issues, especially in connection with the basis of distributed property.

[1] Trust and Estate Income Tax

The income tax return for a trust, decedent's estate, or bankruptcy estate is Form 1041. For 2009, the income tax rates are 15% on taxable income up to $2,300; 25% on taxable income between $2,300 and $5,350; 28% on taxable income between $5,350 and $8,200; 33% on income between $8,200 and $11,500; and 35% on income over $11,150. (See Rev. Proc. 2008-66, 2008-45 IRB 1107) Trustees must provide each beneficiary with Schedule K-1 of the Form 1041, and copies of all the K-1s must be filed with the trust's return. Effective for tax returns due on or after January 1, 2009, the IRS shortened the extensions for filing estate, partnership, and trust returns (Form 1041, Form 1065, Schedule K-1). The new due date for extended returns is September 15 rather than the previous October 15. The purpose is to get the information to individual taxpayers faster, so they can prepare their own returns.[36]

The general rule is that if the income of a trust or estate is distributed it will be taxed to the beneficiary (unless it is a grantor trust: see § 17.20). If the income is retained, it will usually be taxed to the trust or estate itself. If a married decedent leaves community property, income from half of the community property is taxed to the estate; income from the other half is taxed to the surviving spouse.

Distributable Net Income (DNI) is a tax accounting concept that places limits on both the trust or estate's deduction for distributions made, and the amount that can be taxed to the beneficiary. DNI is the trust's or estate's taxable income (its gross income minus deductions), with various adjustments prescribed by Code §§ 651 and 661.

A trust's or estate's gross income includes the income accumulated or held for future distribution under the terms of its governing instrument, plus currently distributable income, and income that the fiduciary has discretion to either distribute or retain: § 641(a).

The trust or estate is entitled to a deduction for distributions made to beneficiaries, up to DNI. The deduction is computed differently for a complex than for a simple trust.[37] The trustee of a complex trust (or the executor of an estate) can also make an election, under § 663(b), to treat amounts paid or credited in the first 65 days of a tax year as if they had been paid or credited on the last day of the preceding tax year. The election is made by checking a box on the Form 1041.

In general, a trust or estate does not recognize gain or loss when it makes an in-kind distribution of property to a beneficiary. The exception is distribution of property to satisfy a pecuniary bequest, or to satisfy a bequest of a different item of specific property: Reg. § 1.661(a)-2(f)(1).

---

[36] Martin Vaughan, *IRS Shortens Extensions for Some*, Wall St. J. 7/1/08 at D6.

[37] A trust is simple if it must distribute all of its income currently; does not make charitable contributions; and does not make distributions from corpus. Otherwise, the trust is complex.

An estate or trust can take an unlimited charitable deduction for any amount that its governing instrument directs to be paid for a charitable purpose (§ 642(c)). An estate, but not a trust (other than a pooled income fund), can deduct any amount of gross income permanently set aside (rather than actually paid) for charitable purposes.

The trust is entitled to a deduction for administrative expenses, but only if these expenses are not used to reduce the decedent's estate for estate tax purposes: § 642(g). Section 642(b) gives an estate a $600 personal exemption. A simple trust gets a $300 personal exemption, but only $100 for a complex trust. The exemption increases to $3,500 (2008 figure) if the trust is a "qualified disability trust."[38] Personal exemptions are not allowed in a trust's or estate's final year. Neither an estate nor a trust gets a standard deduction (§ 63(c)(6)(E)), but either can claim a net operating loss deduction under § 642(c).

The Supreme Court held, in early 2008, that a trust's investment advisory fees are deductible only to the extent they exceed the 2% floor on miscellaneous itemized deductions. The trust argued that the floor was not applicable, because trusts can fully deduct amounts paid or incurred in connection with trust administration that would not have been incurred if the property had not been in trust. The Supreme Court did not accept the argument that the trustee's obligations under the Uniform Prudent Investor Act required the trust to incur investment advisory fees, because it is common for individuals to retain investment advisors. A footnote to the opinion says that, although the question was raised in the trust context, the same principle applies to the administrative expenses of estates.[39]

Code § 645 permits an election to have a revocable trust treated, and taxed, as part of the estate it relates to, and not as a separate trust. The executor and the trustee of such a "Qualified Revocable Trust" must agree to make the election. The Final Regulations explaining how to make the election, the tax treatment of the trust while the election is in force, termination of the election, and reporting rules can be found in T.D. 9032, 2003-7 IRB 471.

Code § 6034A obligates beneficiaries to treat items consistently with their treatment by the payor trust or estate. Most trusts and some estates have to make quarterly estimated tax payments, using Form 1041-ES. However, § 6654(l)(2) exempts estates and grantor trusts that receive the residue of a probate estate from having to make estimated tax payments for their first two tax years after the decedent's death.

As § 17.07 shows, revocable trusts are included in the gross estate of the deceased grantor. Code § 645 tackles a related issue by permitting the trustee and executor (both must join in the election) to elect to have the revocable trust treated as part of the estate for income tax purposes, rather than as a separate trust.

---

[38] A trust established solely for the benefit of a totally disabled person under age 65; the exemption is reduced if the trust's modified AGI exceeds $159,950 (2008). Qualified funeral trusts do not get any personal exemption.

[39] Knight, Trustee of William L. Rudkin Testamentary Trust v. CIR, No. 06-1286 (1/16/08).

Combining the two could be more convenient and less costly than separate tax compliance.

Two or more trusts can be treated for tax purposes as a single trust, pursuant to § 643(f), if the multiple trusts were created with tax avoidance as a principal motive, and all the trusts have substantially the same grantor(s) and primary beneficiary(ies). A married couple is treated as one person.

[2] Tax Issues for Beneficiaries

Section 652(a) provides that the beneficiary of a simple trust is taxed on either his or her proportionate share of the trust's DNI, or trust income required to be distributed to him or her (whether or not it is actually distributed) — whichever is lower. The rules for taxation of beneficiaries of complex trusts, found in § 662(a), are beyond the scope of this discussion.

The beneficiary is not taxed on amounts paid as a gift or bequest of a specific sum of money, or specific items of property, as long as the distribution is made in a lump sum or in only two or three installments: § 663(a).

The beneficiary's basis in property distributed from the trust or estate depends on whether the trust or estate elected to recognize gain on the distribution. See §§ 643(e), 662(a)(2). The basis computation begins with the adjusted basis that the trust or estate had in the property just before the distribution, adjusted for the gain recognized by the trust or estate on the distribution.

See also § 678, which provides that a beneficiary or trustee can be taxed as the owner of trust income based on a power (including a *Crummey* power) to vest corpus or income in him- or herself, if the power can be exercised alone. This section is broad enough to encompass individuals who have modified or released a power, but who still retain enough control over the trust so that a grantor would be taxed in the same circumstances.

[3] IRD and Related Issues

An individual's tax year ends with the death of that person. Nearly all decedents will have been cash basis taxpayers, and their final return must include income actually or constructively received prior to death. The estate, or anyone else acquiring rights and obligations related to the decedent, will be required to report such items as Income in Respect of a Decedent (IRD) or post-mortem deductions: § 691.

IRD is income (including capital gains) that the decedent had a right to receive but did not actually or constructively receive before death. It includes taxable distributions from qualified plans; a deceased partner's partnership income; and a deceased shareholder's Subchapter S income.

IRD might be reportable on the decedent's final income tax return. If not, it is reported in the tax year of receipt, by the estate (if it received the right to the item from the decedent) or by any non-estate party that received the income. The characterization of the items is the same in the hands of the recipient as it was in the hands of the decedent. The recipient of IRD is permitted, under § 691(c), to deduct estate tax and generation-skipping transfer tax attributable to the inclusion of IRD in the gross estate.

§ 17.26 INTESTATE ADMINISTRATION

In the absence of a will, or if it is so clear that a purported will is invalid that there is no proponent to seek its probate, assets will pass by intestacy (the state's dispositive scheme) to "distributees." For a married person, the typical intestacy scheme transfers all or most of the estate to the surviving spouse; if there are children, the spouse's share is often reduced correspondingly. If there is no spouse, the assets are divided among the surviving children; if none, among other relatives.

An appropriate person will receive "letters of administration" to administer the estate, much as an executor would do.

Eighteen states, including Michigan, Montana, New Jersey, North Dakota, and South Dakota, have changed their intestacy laws to provide that the spouse receives the entire intestate estate and the children do not receive distributions — a change that creates problems if the spouses were involved in divorce proceedings when one spouse died; several cases have been filed seeking posthumous divorce settlements in accordance with the distributions that would have been made if the spouse had lived long enough for divorce litigation to be completed.[40]

Initially, a North Carolina trial court permitted a personal representative to be substituted for a deceased divorce litigant in order to pursue an action for equitable distribution, on the grounds that the equitable distribution of property was separate from the personal action of divorce. However, the trial court's decision was reversed. On appeal, it was held that only a living person can be divorced. Because the equitable distribution action is inextricably connected to the divorce case, it abates at the litigant's death.[41]

---

[40] Tresa Baldas, *A New Twist: Divorce After Death*, Nat'l L.J. 7/5/06 (law.com).
[41] Brown v. Brown, 524 S.E.2d 89 (N.C. App.), *rev'd*, 539 S.E.2d 621 (N.C. 2000).

Chapter 18

Torts

§ 18.01   INTRODUCTION

A crime (see § 26.01 *et seq.*) is a wrongdoing against (a) person(s) or property that is prosecuted and punished by the state. A tort is wrongdoing outside the contractual system that can become the subject of private litigation. In many situations, the same conduct is both tortious and criminal: e.g., committing homicide also involves the tort of wrongful death; committing theft involves the tort of conversion.

Crimes are nearly always intentional (although extreme negligence can be severe enough to be punished criminally, e.g., criminally negligent homicide). The harm caused by a tort can be intentional or unintentional. See § 18.08 for a discussion of intentional torts. There are three major situations in which someone who has suffered unintended harm may be able to recover from the tortfeasor (party committing the tort): negligence, strict liability, or no-fault. (A fourth, prima facie tort, as defined by Restatement (2nd) of Torts § 870, imposes liability outside the regular tort categories for injury caused by culpable, non-justifiable conduct.)

The policy behind tort law is a balance between encouraging valuable (especially economically valuable) activities, while protecting the public against excessive risk. Where the balance will be struck depends on social and political perceptions about what constitutes a reasonable risk, and how individuals and businesses are expected to conduct themselves.

One formula that is often used to analyze tort cases is whether the foreseeable probability and gravity of harm is greater than the burden of taking action (e.g., redesigning a product) to prevent the harm. Factors in the determination include the value of the activity; the feasibility of alternatives; the cost of safer alternatives; and the relative safety of the alternatives (e.g., air bags reduce the damage caused by some automobile accidents — but the air bags themselves sometimes cause injuries).

However, in the current pro-business climate in Congress, state legislatures, and the courts, there is a possibility that the government will reduce its regulatory role, on the grounds that businesses will be deterred from marketing unsafe products by the tort system (rendering government regulation unnecessary) — while injured persons are shut out of the courthouses by tort reform measures.

Given the difficulty of certifying personal injury class actions (e.g., many rulings finding that the facts and circumstances of the individual plaintiffs are too different), plaintiffs' lawyers are turning to state consumer protection laws. Settlements have been obtained in cases involving the drug Paxil and benzene levels in soft drinks, based on assertions that the product would not have been purchased if the purchaser had been aware of the risk of physical harm.[1]

The 2002 appropriations bill for the Department of Justice (P.L. 107-273) includes the Multidistrict, Multiparty, Multiforum Trial Jurisdiction Act covering major mass disasters such as plane and train crashes. When more than 75 accidental deaths are caused in a mass accident, the case must be filed in federal district court. Discovery on all cases is consolidated before one federal judge. Then the case returns to the original district court for resolution of liability and damage issues.

§ 18.02 NEGLIGENCE

If a party has a legal duty to act or refrain from acting, but breaches that duty, with the result that someone else suffers harm, then that party has probably been negligent and is probably liable to the victim of the negligence. Whether or not the defendant was negligent is a fact issue to be determined by the jury.

There are some exceptions. The connection between negligence and harm may be too remote to support liability. The victim's recovery may be denied (contributory negligence) or limited (comparative negligence) because of the victim's own negligence or wrongdoing.

[A] Cause of Action

The basic standard for a negligence cause of action is:

- Duty (e.g., of due care) owed by the defendant to the plaintiff
- Breach of that duty

---

[1] Amanda Bronstad, *Consumer Class Actions Usurping Personal Injury Claims*, Nat'l L.J. 7/11/07 (law.com).

- Direct connection between the breach and the injury ("proximate cause")
- Actual loss or damage, not just risk of loss or damage.

The scope of legal duty is a question of law, to be decided by the court, not a fact issue for the jury.

The general rule is that there is no duty to assist a person in peril, although a duty to assist arises out of a special relationship (such as that between a lifeguard and swimmers, or between family members). Someone who does volunteer to come to the aid of others has a duty to act with due care — but many states have adopted Good Samaritan laws relieving volunteers of liability for harm accidentally caused to persons they were intending to aid.[2]

The "postal exception" to the Federal Tort Claims Act (28 USC § 2680(b)) is limited to barring suits about lost, late, or damaged mail, and does not preclude a plaintiff from suing the Postal Service based on an allegation that the mail carrier negligently left mail on her porch, causing her to slip and fall.[3]

If a statute is applicable, violation of the statute may be treated as prima facie negligence or negligence per se; or it could be considered simply evidence of negligence to be weighed by the jury.

The traditional rule was that there was no tort liability for failure to perform a gratuitous promise (i.e., one for which no consideration had been given, and no contract had been formed). More recent cases do allow a plaintiff to recover in this situation, on the basis of reasonable reliance on the promise resulting in detriment to the plaintiff. Once a person begins performance of a gratuitous promise, it is clear that a duty has been created to perform with reasonable care.

In some circumstances, the party will be partially or entirely responsible for torts committed by someone else (a concept classically known as *respondeat superior*). For instance, employers will be responsible for the torts of employees committed in the scope of employment; partners and joint venturers will be liable for one another's torts. Traditionally, the "fellow-servant" doctrine shielded employers from liability for the negligence of one employee that injured another employee (unless the employer was negligent in hiring or supervising the tortfeasor employee). Today, however, it is likely that workplace injuries will be subject to Workers' Compensation, a no-fault system.

Georgia refused to hold a pharmacist liable for failure to warn a customer of the potential for the serious, but rare, reaction that she suffered. Although the rules of the state pharmacy board impose a duty to disclose "common severe side

---

[2] Although in general there is no duty to come to the aid of another person, sometimes a duty will be implied in special situations. Tarasoff v. Regents of Univ. of Cal., 551 P.2d 334 (Cal. 1976) imposes a duty on a therapist to warn persons whom the therapist's patient has indicated an intention to harm. More recently, however, the Texas Supreme Court denied that a psychiatrist must violate confidentiality when a patient threatens to kill someone else: Tapar v. Zezulka (Tex. Sup. 6/24/99), discussed in Nathan Koppel, *Psychiatrists Have No Duty to Warn of Patients' Threats*, http://www.lawnewsnet.com/stories/A3050-1999Jul2.html.

[3] Dolan v. United States Postal Serv., 546 U.S. 481 (2006).

effects," the doctor and not the pharmacist remains the "learned intermediary" responsible for warning the patient.[4]

In Hawaii, a claim for negligent infliction of emotional distress is cognizable when a plaintiff is exposed to AIDS-contaminated blood. Damages can be awarded based entirely on emotional distress; physical injury is not required. However, the period of damages is limited, running from the time of discovery of the actual exposure to the time of the first reliable test showing the exposed person's HIV-negative status. Liability attaches only to the extent that the mental distress does not exceed what a reasonable person would feel under the same circumstances.[5]

Texas ruled in 2008 that the federal Consumer Product Safety Act preempts tort claims against the manufacturer of cigarette lighters, reversing a design defect claim in a case where more than $3.7 million was awarded to a child who suffered third-degree burns over 55% of her body when her brother set fire to her dress when playing with a lighter. In 2003, the trial court awarded $3 million in actual damages, plus another $2 million in punitive damages based on a finding that defendant Bic acted with actual malice. The $2 million was reduced to $750,000 under the state's cap on exemplary damages. The Court of Appeals ruled that federal standards did not preempt the design defect claim, and affirmed the finding of malice. The Texas Supreme Court reversed the Court of Appeals on the mother's design defect claim (on the grounds that the lighter satisfied federal standards for child resistance, and it would frustrate the federal objectives to impose tougher state standards), but remanded on other claims including defective manufacturing.[6]

[B] Standards for Plaintiff and Defendant

Negligence is failure to act in the way that an ordinary, prudent person would have acted in the same situation. A person who holds him- or herself out as having special qualifications, knowledge, or skills will be held to a corresponding standard. For instance, a surgeon will be required to behave as an ordinary reasonable surgeon. However, as a general rule, people who are less intelligent than average will be held to the average standard.

---

[4] Chamblin v. K-Mart Corp., 272 Ga. App. 240 (Ga. App. 2005).

[5] Roe v. FHP Inc., 985 P.2d 661 (Haw. 1999). Early in 2008, the New York Court of Appeals removed the six-month limitation on emotional distress damages for people waiting to discover if they have contracted HIV, finding that AIDS-phobia after a negligent exposure can last longer than six months. A nurse who was stuck by a needle in the bedding of a dying AIDS patient was awarded $330,000 for past pain and suffering and $15,000 in lost wages; she never tested positive for HIV. However, she was never informed that she would probably be safe if her HIV tests continued negative after six months; she became depressed; and had to quit nursing because she was afraid of additional exposures: Ornstein v. N.Y. City Health and Hospitals Corp., 10 N.Y.3d 1 (N.Y. 2008); *see* Joel Stashenko, *N.Y. High Court Ruling Ends 6-Month AIDS-Phobia Cutoff*, N.Y.L.J. 2/11/08 (law.com). The six-month limitation comes from Brown v. NYC Health & Hospitals Corp., 225 A.D.2d 36 (1996), which notes that if seroconversion occurs after a needle-stick, it generally happens within six months.

[6] Bic Pen Corp v. Carter, 251 S.W.3d 500 (Tex. 2008); *see* Mary Alice Robbins, *Texas High Court Finds Federal Pre-emption Trumps State Tort Claim*, Texas Lawyer 4/28/08 (law.com).

A child plaintiff or defendant will be compared to an ordinary reasonable child of comparable age, intelligence, and experience. Some states apply a conclusive presumption that children under a particular age (e.g., 7) are not capable of negligence, and make the same presumption rebuttable for older minors. But a minor who engages in an adult activity such as driving will be held to adult standards.

A child's own action for injuries will frequently be entitled to tolling for minority: i.e., the individual gets a certain amount of time after reaching adulthood to sue for injuries sustained during minority. However, a parent's derivative actions (such as loss of companionship of the child) will not be entitled to tolling.

Once a baby is born alive, recovery for prenatal injuries becomes possible. It is less clear whether such injuries are recoverable with respect to a fetus that was miscarried or stillborn. (The question of when a fetus becomes a "person" is bound up with the question of the legality and morality of abortion, as well as tort issues.) Some jurisdictions permit a wrongful death claim for the death of a fetus; others limit recovery to fetuses that were viable at the time of the injury.

On January 10, 2007, the Supreme Court ruled that the same standard must be applied to determine railroad liability and employee contributory negligence when an injured employee sues under the Federal Employers' Liability Act (FELA) — although the Supreme Court did not spell out the actual standard that must be applied equally to both.[7]

In addition to intentional infliction of emotional distress (§ 18.08[B]) negligent infliction of emotional distress may be considered tortious in certain circumstances. Initially, jurisdictions that recognized this cause of action limited it to emotional injuries derivative of physical injuries caused by impact with the plaintiff's body. That is no longer required in most jurisdictions, although many jurisdictions do require the plaintiff to have been in the zone of danger where damaging physical impact could have been caused.

A bystander to a particularly shocking incident, especially one that involves a family member, may also have a claim of this kind. Intentional infliction of emotional injury may be recognized in a case that does not involve a physical calamity: sexual harassment or defamation, for instance. However, physical manifestations of emotional harm (such as weight loss or insomnia) will probably be a prerequisite of maintenance of the cause of action.

[C] Proximate Cause, Intervening Causes, and Multiple Causation

In the simplest case, the defendant's negligence is the only factor causing the injuries. However, in more complex situations, the defendant's negligence is only one factor. The defendant is not liable unless his, her, or its conduct is the proximate (direct) cause of the injuries. Proximate cause is a difficult concept to define;

---

[7] *See* Norfolk Southern Railway Co. v. Sorrell, 549 U.S. 158 (2007).

it is often described as "but for" or "sine qua non" causation. That is, the damage would never have occurred without the defendant's negligent or wrongful conduct.

An intervening cause is subsequent to the original cause, and might prevent the defendant from being held liable (for instance, if the intervening cause is intentional or criminal conduct by a third party). However, the defendant is still liable if he, she, or it should have foreseen the intervening cause. For instance, a hit and run driver should be able to foresee that someone else might hit an unconscious person left lying in the road.

In situations of multiple causation, each defendant's conduct must be a material element and substantial factor in causing the overall harm. In situations where two or more parties had to be negligent to produce the harm, the tortfeasors will be jointly and severally liable (see § 18.13).

Where there are multiple causative agents, each is responsible for all divisible harm each has caused, unless they acted in concert or in a joint enterprise. However, if the first tortfeasor not only injures the plaintiff but renders the plaintiff vulnerable to injuries by others (e.g., incompetent doctors), the first tortfeasor will be liable for the second tortfeasor's actions.

In a case where there are two or more possible tortfeasors but only one actually caused the injury (e.g., plaintiff was shot by only one bullet, which could have been fired by either of two hunters), all possible tortfeasors will be liable unless they can prove their freedom from responsibility.

§ 18.03 STRICT LIABILITY

Strict liability, or liability without fault, is imposed in circumstances where the defendant engages in conduct (such as manufacturing a dangerous but useful product) that is useful enough to be permitted rather than outlawed, but dangerous enough to be analyzed under special rules. Using explosives in construction, and storing hazardous materials, are examples of strict-liability activities.

The plaintiff's comparative or even contributory negligence is not a defense to strict liability.

Under Oklahoma law, sellers of used products who merely resell products in the same condition they acquired them are not strictly liable to persons injured by the products, in that the defects (if any) were caused by the manufacturer and not the seller.[8]

§ 18.04 *RES IPSA LOQUITUR*

This Latin phrase means "the thing speaks for itself." The doctrine of *res ipsa* is an inference available to plaintiffs seeking to prove their cases. It is merely an inference; the jury is not obligated to find for the plaintiff.

Res ipsa can be applied in cases where the alleged negligence falls within the scope of the defendant's duty to the plaintiff; negligence is the only or most reasonable explanation for the event; the instrumentality of damage was under

---

[8] Allenberg v. Bentley Hedges Travel Serv. Inc., 22 P.3d 223 (Okla. 2001).

the defendant's sole control; and neither the plaintiff nor third parties could have been negligent. See Restatement of Torts (2nd) § 328D. Therefore, *res ipsa* is probably not available in a multi-defendant case, unless vicarious liability is present or unless they are jointly liable.

The classic products liability *res ipsa* case is a foreign object in a sealed package; the classic medical malpractice *res ipsa* case is a large surgical instrument left inside an incision.

§ 18.05 MEDICAL MALPRACTICE

One of the most commonly asserted (and most contentious) negligence causes of action is the one for medical malpractice — an assertion that a physician has failed to satisfy the requisite standard of care. It is important to note that physicians are not required to save every patient or provide a good result in every case — only to act with the necessary knowledge, skill, and care of a physician with comparable training. (Specialists are held to a higher standard than generalists.)

The cause of action requires proof that this failure to manifest due care was the proximate cause of injuries to the plaintiff. Of course, proximate cause is an issue in all tort cases, but it is especially significant in medical malpractice cases because of the need to distinguish between harm caused by negligence and the disease process itself.

Medical malpractice can manifest itself in the context of diagnosis, medical treatment, surgery, and other contacts between provider and recipient of care. At one time, the "locality rule" was extremely significant, with the standard of care measured by other practitioners in the same geographic area. In current practice, and in large part because of improved communications, the extent to which a health care practitioner has specialized is more significant than the locality in which he or she practices.

The Patient Safety and Quality Improvements Act of 2004, P.L. 109-41, sets up a system for health care professionals to make voluntary reports of health care errors. The reports are confidential and inadmissible in either civil or criminal proceedings. The statutory objective is to create a database to improve knowledge of the effectiveness and side effects of various treatments.

[A] Liable Parties

In traditional medical practice, if nothing else, it was easy to identify the defendant, because a single physician commenced and completed treatment. Today, the question is far more difficult. It is very common for a patient to consult an internist or other general physician, who then refers the patient to one or more specialists, and such arrangements create potential for liability.[9]

---

[9] But an "on-call" arrangement among doctors is not a joint venture that makes each liable for the professional negligence of the others, because there was no mutual control or sharing of profits, and they did not follow treatment plans developed by the doctors for whom they covered: Rossi v. Oxley, 495 S.E.2d 39 (Ga. Sup. 1998).

Sometimes the patient must go through a "gatekeeper" in order to have specialty care reimbursed by his or her HMO or other managed care organization (MCO). That opens up significant questions of whether referrals were properly made or improperly withheld, as well as the evolving jurisprudence about the role of MCOs. It is possible to commit malpractice by not treating, when treatment is required, as well as by mismanaging a course of treatment. Questions of denial of treatment and abandonment are especially salient in the managed care context.

Traditionally, many cases against MCOs were preempted by ERISA, because the patient received care through an employer's group health plan. ERISA preempts state-law causes of action "relating to" a pension or benefit plan.

In a watershed decision from 2004, the Supreme Court held that ERISA § 502(a) completely preempts claims brought under state law charging that a managed care plan's denial of care was improper.[10]

The relationship between patient and care provider is supposed to be a fully voluntary one, based on the patient's informed consent to treatments recommended by the care provider. There is a fiduciary element in the relationship, obligating the doctor to perform in good faith and provide fair dealing. Therefore, failure to warn (as long as the failure was material and would have affected a reasonable person's decision to accept or refrain from treatment) can be an independent ground for malpractice liability, or part of a larger malpractice case.

The patient has a reciprocal responsibility to provide accurate information and inform the doctor of changes during the course of treatment. A patient's failure to do this might be considered contributory negligence, reducing or even eliminating the potential recovery.

The principle of *res ipsa loquitur* (§ 18.04) is applicable in medical malpractice cases, e.g., when a surgical instrument is found in the abdomen of a person who underwent abdominal surgery. The *res ipsa* doctrine might also be applied if a part of the body that was not being treated is injured; if an operation is performed on the wrong patient or on the wrong part of the patient's body; or if a patient is burned during treatment. If a foreign object is discovered and removed promptly, the patient's damages would be small, based on the need to undergo a second operation, but with little or no recovery for pain and suffering.

[B] Doctor-Patient Relationship

Except in emergencies, doctors have the right to refuse to enter into a doctor-patient relationship (e.g., if the patient is uninsured and unable to pay out-of-pocket, and the doctor is in private practice). But once the relationship is created, the doctor has an obligation to continue treatment as long as it is reasonably required, until the doctor has notified the patient of intent to terminate treatment, until another doctor is substituted as treating physician or the patient withdraws from further treatment. Failing to follow up (e.g., interpreting the results of medical tests ordered by the doctor) can constitute abandonment; so can failing to give the

---

[10] Aetna Health Inc. v. Davila, and Cigna Healthcare of Texas v. Calad, 542 U.S. 200.

patient information about side effects that must be reported, or how to take medication safely.

However, the relationship is created by the patient's desire to consult the doctor, and the doctor's acceptance of the patient for treatment. Therefore, there is no doctor-patient relationship if someone other than the patient is the actual employer of the physician. (This is distinct from the question of who actually pays for the treatment or reimburses a patient who advances payment for treatment.)

For instance, a doctor who performs an employment physical or examines a Workers' Compensation claimant is working for the employer or Compensation system, not the patient, and thus can disclose medical information about the patient even if the patient does not want the information disclosed.

Depending on the facts and applicable law, more than one party may be involved and named as malpractice defendants. For instance, a hospital may be negligent in permitting certain doctors to have practice privileges. A hospital might also be negligent in supervising its house staff (doctors in training), or in permitting them to undertake procedures that are too sophisticated for their skill levels.

However, if a doctor transfers the care of a patient to a specialist or sends the patient to another health care provider for diagnostic tests or treatment, the negligence of these other providers will probably not be imputed to the first doctor (unless he or she had some reason to know that the other practitioners were not qualified). Similarly, if several doctors are treating a patient for different conditions, negligence will probably not be imputed.

Hospitals are clearly responsible for proper hiring and supervision of physicians who are hospital employees.

Florida ruled that a malpractice plaintiff can discover a hospital's list of doctors granted privileges by the credentials committee. (In this case, the plaintiff sued a doctor she claimed was not credentialed to perform an obstetric procedure on her.) Hospitals are averse to revealing doctors' privileges, on the grounds that discovery would compromise the confidentiality of peer review, but the Florida Supreme Court said that plaintiffs should be able to retrieve this information from hospital records that are not privileged rather than from peer review files.[11]

In the case of a mistake in filling a prescription, giving an injection, or transfusing blood, a nurse or technician might be directly liable for the error, but there may also be vicarious liability of the doctor or hospital that failed to supervise properly. Generally speaking, the intervening or supervening negligence of another person relieves the doctor of malpractice liability. However, if the plaintiff was treated by many doctors and it is impossible to apportion liability (e.g., in a teaching hospital), then all will be liable.

---

[11] Brandon Regional Hosp. v. Murray, 957 So.2d 590 (Florida 2007); *see* Daniel Ostrovsky, *Fla. Supreme Court: Hospital Privileges Must Be Revealed in Med-Mal Cases*, Daily Business Review 5/17/07 (law.com).

In some instances, someone other than the patient becomes the plaintiff: e.g., when wrongful death is alleged, or when the non-patient suffers emotional distress. States vary in their approach to emotional distress claims. The emotional distress must be reasonably foreseeable.

Except in very limited circumstances, strict liability in tort will not be applied to medical services. Even cases involving pharmaceuticals and, e.g., HIV-infected blood, are often dismissed on the theory that the health care provider offers services rather than products, so warranty and strict liability theories are inapplicable. Furthermore, any products liability claims that are tenable may have to be pursued against the manufacturer or distributor of the product, and not against the doctor or hospital that prescribed or used the product.

[C] Duty of Care

Except in an absolute emergency, the duty of due care requires the physician to get a complete medical history, containing elements such as these:

- Patient's chief complaints
- Present symptoms
- Past history
- Hospitalizations
- Prescriptions now being taken
- Family history.

The patient's failure or refusal to provide complete, accurate information can operate as comparative negligence, reducing the potential recovery.

New York ruled that there is no duty to non-patients. Thus, a doctor who treated an infectious meningitis sufferer did not owe a duty of care to the patient's friend to inform the friend of the risk of contracting the illness.[12]

[1] Medical Tests

After taking the patient's history, the doctor has an obligation to perform a physical examination, including recognized tests to discover the cause of the patient's symptoms. As long as the necessary equipment, and personnel qualified to interpret results, are available, it can violate the standard of care to fail to do tests such as CAT scans and MRIs.

The standard of care requires the performance of appropriate lab tests as required for diagnosis. Misinterpretation of test results also departs from the standard of care, although a non-specialist doctor is entitled to rely on conclusions drawn by a radiologist or other specialist.

"Self-regulatory" standards are an important indication of the duty of care. The malpractice attorney should consult the standards promulgated by the AMA

---

[12] McNulty v. New York City, 100 N.Y.2d 227 (2003).

(e.g., Principles of Medical Ethics) and the standards of local medical societies. The medical profession enforces these standards by removing hospital privileges of doctors who fail to meet the standards.

Hospitals have various review committees (tissue review committees that examine tumors and other tissues removed from patients); mortality review committees, and chart review committees. These committees issue reports after investigation of a negative result, or routinely. Committee reports can be important in establishing a doctor's departure from the standard of care, although these reports are often written in very discreet terms just for this reason.

Information provided by the patient is confidential, and must not be disclosed by the doctor except in appropriate circumstances (e.g., as directed by the patient; in response to a subpoena). However, in some circumstances doctors are actually required to report information that would otherwise be confidential: e.g., when they treat a gunshot or knife wound; if they have reason to believe that a domestic partner or child has been physically or sexually abused.

If the medical profession deems several alternative procedures to be acceptable, a doctor will not be culpable by choosing one acceptable procedure rather than the others.

Continuing practice of medicine implies a duty to keep up with developments in medical care (including discovery of side effects of previously accepted treatments). If a case clearly exceeds a generalist's knowledge and skills, it is malpractice not to make a referral to a specialist. A doctor can be negligent in failing to order further medical tests that are warranted based on clinical observation or the results of earlier tests. Negligence can also be present if the doctor does not test for sensitivity to prescription drugs or fails to warn of the risk of side effects.

[2] Loss of Chance

Although it is not universally recognized, many jurisdictions permit a "loss of chance" argument to be made, on the theory that incorrect diagnosis leads to incorrect treatment — and, more importantly, to treatment other than treatment that could have saved the patient's life, health, or function.

A possible problem with this theory is that a patient who suffers from a very fast-spreading disease (e.g., ovarian cancer) might not have had a chance of survival even if a correct diagnosis had been made. Loss of chance requires proof that is more likely than not that loss of chance was due to physician's negligence rather than the underlying disease.

[D] Tort Reform in Medical Malpractice Cases

States have adopted various tort reform measures to limit the amount of malpractice litigation. These measures include permissive or mandatory arbitration of claims; increases in the plaintiff's burden of proof; requirement that the plaintiff's attorney provide a certificate of merit before a case can be filed; need for an expert witness affidavit or summary of expert testimony as a prerequisite to filing; and caps on damages (typically, non-economic damages such as pain and suffering; attorneys' fee awards may also be limited).

Malpractice panels usually include a judge, an attorney, and a doctor. Some panels have jurisdiction to make awards; some make an initial determination on liability and damages; others are limited to a fact-finding role. However, sometimes the trial itself is a de novo hearing (practice varies as to whether the panel's decision is admissible) and either side might be given the right to demand a de novo hearing.

If a state has a malpractice panel, resort to the panel is probably obligatory. Failure to do so can deprive the courts of subject-matter jurisdiction. The general rule is that the statute of limitations is tolled after a timely filing with the panel; while the panel is reviewing the claim; and for a prescribed time afterwards. Even if the panel ruled for the plaintiff, its conclusion will not be enough to support a jury verdict; expert testimony will still be required.

Because the patient has little or no opportunity to negotiate the contract, due process claims against mandatory arbitration may be successful. Because the arbitration panels typically include health care providers (doctors, hospital administrators), the panels can also be attacked for bias.

California imposed a damage cap in 1975, but did not see lower insurance premiums until 1988 — when a state law was passed forbidding insurers to raise premiums without economic justification. In other words, for more than a dozen years, tort reform measures were in place, but did not result in lower malpractice insurance premiums.

Some states utilize a variation on the cap such as a state malpractice pool or Patient Compensation Fund that limits the liability of individual physicians but provides a source other than the doctor or the doctor's malpractice carrier for recovery for the injured person. The fund can come out of general state revenues or surcharges on physicians.

[E] Informed Consent

Except in rare cases (e.g., an unconscious patient is brought to a hospital Emergency Room), treatment is not imposed on patients by the medical system. Instead, patients who have the legal right to control their own bodies seek medical assistance, and the health care provider renders services based on the informed consent of the patient. Carrying out medical treatment without the patient's consent (or without the consent of a surrogate decision-maker for a minor or incompetent patient), or carrying out treatment beyond the scope of the consent, could constitute assault and battery.

Although they may seem to be contractual in nature, patients' claims revolving around informed consent are really negligence claims: the patient takes the position that the doctor failed to make a full and accurate disclosure of the material risks inherent in the treatment (such as anesthesia risks in surgery; risks of medication side effects), with the result that the patient consented to procedures that he or she would have refused if given adequate information (or that a reasonable patient would have refused with the same knowledge). Risks are material if they would influence the treatment choice of a reasonable person. In other words, then, the failure to disclose was the cause of the injuries.

Anesthesia risks are especially high, so extensive warnings are required. Patients could aspirate vomit while unconscious; could be allergic to anesthetic agents; could receive an excessively high dose, leading to respiratory suppression and death or brain damage; and could be physically injured by a needle or tube used to induce anesthesia. Explosion of anesthetic gases is also a potential risk.

In special circumstances, the duty to warn might be excused: if the risk of not treating a patient whose consent cannot be obtained in an emergency outweighs the risks of treatment. A patient's emotional state might be such that the disclosure itself would be harmful.

[1] Exceptions to Informed Consent

Sometimes the patient is unable to consent (is a child; is unconscious; is seriously mentally ill; is developmentally disabled). In such a situation (other than a severe emergency where there is no time to seek consent), informed consent must be obtained from an appropriate surrogate: a parent, court-appointed guardian, or agent serving under a durable power of attorney for health care, for instance.

If no guardian is available, it will often be necessary for the health care provider to bring an emergency guardianship proceeding so that a guardian can be appointed who can consent to the treatment. Guardianship statutes typically provide that a hospital or doctor has standing to file a guardianship petition to ensure that treatment can be provided legitimately — and that reimbursement will be available for the cost of treatment, which was not undertaken on a volunteer basis.

§ 18.06 MALPRACTICE LITIGATION

The question of what was actually done during treatment, and how it compares to what should have been done, is naturally a highly technical question, most aspects of which are beyond the scope of lay testimony. (The plaintiff can, of course, testify as to topics such as pain and limitation of function.)

Therefore, the medical malpractice case is highly dependent on expert testimony, to show what the standard of care was; that the standard was breached; that the breach was the proximate cause of the plaintiff's injuries; and the amount of the damages.

For obvious reasons, defense expert witnesses are easier to find that plaintiffs' witnesses. Many doctors are unwilling to testify against their fellow physicians. Furthermore, since malpractice defense is largely conducted by insurance companies, they have access to a group of experts willing to testify.

The plaintiff's attorney often finds it easier to get "out of town" experts to testify, but the jury may discount their testimony, especially if they are perceived as "professional witnesses" who are far more interested in earning large fees than in actually caring for patients. Some expert witnesses always testify for plaintiffs or for the defense; others can be hired by either side. The latter group of witnesses can either be seen as more credible (because they are not biased for one side or the other) or as less credible (if they are seen as "hired guns" whose testimony can be purchased by the highest bidder).

The "locality rule" is still in effect in 21 states: that is, the standard of care is based on the local community. This requires local witnesses, and doctors may be unwilling to testify against fellow-members of a small medical community. In Idaho and New York, "community" means the same town or city; Arizona, Virginia, and Washington apply a statewide standard, and eleven states (e.g., Michigan, Illinois, North Carolina) use the standard of the same or a similar community — thus allowing testimony by out-of-state doctors who work under similar standards. Some states allow out of state doctors to testify, based on the expert's familiarity with similar communities, or because an affirmation that the doctor met "the highest standard of practice anywhere" must necessarily include the locality.[13]

An expert witness must be familiar enough with the field to provide helpful testimony, of course. Generally, the witness must be someone who has published significant relevant research, although an expert's prior writings can also be used to impeach him or her or show that the expert's treatment strategies have changed over time (with the implication that the current testimony is equally subject to error).

---

[13] Tresa Baldas, *Movement Building to Abolish "Locality Rules" in Med-Mal Litigation*, Nat'l L.J. 7/23/07 (law.com). On testimony of out of state doctors, *see, e.g.*, Benefield v. Clarkston, No. 2:06 CV 2 (W.D.N.C. 2006); Travis v. Ferrariccio, No. M2003-00916-COA (Tenn App 2005); Christian v. Surgical Specialties of Richmond, 268 Va. 60 (Va 2004); Carpenter v. Klepper, 205 S.W.3d 474 (Tenn. App. 2005). The National Conference of State Legislatures' report on 2005–6 state activity on medical malpractice legislation: Medical Malpractice Tort Reform http://www.ncsl.org/standcomm/sclaw/medmaloverview.htm. (2/8/07) covers categories such as pre-trial ADR, certificates of merits, medical peer review panels, and "doctor apology" statutes. The traditional advice to doctors was to "deny and defend" in cases of bad patient outcomes, but some top medical centers (including Johns Hopkins and Stanford) are moving toward early acknowledgment of medical errors, with apologies and compensation, to improve future medical care as well as defusing patients' anger. The expected rush of lawsuits did not occur, and legal costs dropped. The University of Michigan Health System found that claims and suits dropped from 262 (in 2001) to 83 (in 2007) after adopting a policy of apologizing for negative results. The University of Illinois' malpractice filings were cut in half. Only one patient out of 37 cases where the hospital apologized for preventable errors has sued. Thirty-four states have laws making an apology for a medical error inadmissible; four states protect admissions of culpability, and seven require notification of serious unanticipated outcomes. *See* Kevin Sack, *Doctors Start to Say "I'm Sorry" Long Before "See You in Court"*, N.Y. Times 5/18/08 at A1. According to "States With Apology Laws," http://www.sorryworks.net/lawdoc.phtml, the states are Arizona, California, Connecticut, Delaware, Florida, Georgia, Hawaii, Idaho, Iowa, Illinois, Louisiana, Maine, Massachusetts, Maryland, Missouri, Montana, Nebraska, North Carolina, North Dakota, Ohio, Oklahoma, Oregon, South Carolina, South Dakota, Tennessee, Texas, Utah, Virginia, Vermont, Washington, West Virginia, and Wyoming.

Medical treatises are generally hearsay, although may be admissible under an exception within the Federal Rules of Evidence. If an expert witness characterizes a treatise or article as authoritative, he or she can be impeached with statements from that publication. But if neither side accepts it, the publication cannot be used for impeachment.

Although physical, hard-copy medical records are the property of the health care provider, the information on those records belongs to the patient. Depending on state law, plaintiffs' attorneys may have a right to access such records before suit is filed; or the patient may have the right to authorize release of the records to him- or herself or to an attorney or other designated agent.

Sometimes the most important parts of the records are those that are not present: have any records one would expect to find been removed, lost, or altered? Were entries made contemporaneously, or retrospectively (to make the health care provider look better)?

§ 18.07 MALPRACTICE DEFENSES

It is by no means certain that any person bringing a malpractice claim will prevail. Every element of the plaintiff's case can be challenged: that the health care provider was negligent at all; that the action was timely filed; that injury occurred as claimed; that the plaintiff has gone to the malpractice panel or satisfied other presuit requirements; that the defendant rather than someone else was responsible; that the defendant's conduct was the proximate cause of injury; that the plaintiff's damages are as high as asserted. There are also various defenses characteristic of malpractice cases:

- Assumption of risk by the plaintiff as shown by consent forms. However, the forms are really contracts of adhesion, and may be given little credence. However, the risk of bad results in a procedure that is performed without negligence, and subject to the patient's informed consent, falls on the patient.
- Contributory or comparative negligence by the patient. If the patient could have prevented injury by following instructions, this may reduce damages or relieve the health care provider of liability. The patient's failure to disclose facts about his or her medical condition falls into this category (although the jury may believe that the provider should have been able to discover the true facts); so does leaving a hospital against medical advice. Failure to seek medical advice about an obviously serious medical condition could also constitute negligence (although this argument may lose force in an age of medical "gatekeepers").

Although many jurisdictions have special rules for notice of claim in malpractice actions, the plaintiff's failure to file probably will not result in absolute termination of the action; he or she can re-file the suit as long as the statute of limitations has not run.

§ 18.08 INTENTIONAL TORTS

The torts discussed above involve failure to satisfy a standard of reasonable conduct. Intentional torts involve some degree of willfully wrongful conduct. The standard of intent for intentional torts is the intent to cause a consequence: e.g., breaking a window is a consequence of throwing a rock. Motives, such as revenge or self-defense can aggravate or mitigate liability for intentional torts. If the motivation is self-defense, there will be no liability; a malicious motive could lead to the imposition of punitive damages.

[A] Defamation

Defamation consists of communicating damaging factual information that is either false, or was communicated with reckless disregard as to whether or not it was true. Communications are considered damaging if they lower the reputation of the party described.

There must be communication to a third party; a communication that goes only to the subject of the communication is not defamatory no matter how unfavorable (or how untrue) it is.[14] A defendant is liable for foreseeable re-publication by third parties who repeat the statement. The plaintiff has the burden of proving the untruth of a defamatory statement.

Defamation constitutes slander if one-to-one communication occurred; libel, if publication (including electronic publication) occurred. Pure opinion statements are not defamatory, but context must be considered to determine whether a statement is factual or pure opinion.[15]

Inaccurate or fabricated quotations attributed to a person can be defamatory, if they attribute an untrue factual assertion to the speaker, or imply that the speaker holds an attitude he or she does not, in fact, hold.[16]

In July 2002, the New York Court of Appeals decided that the "single publication" rule applies to cases alleging defamation disseminated on the Internet. That is, although the site can be viewed many times, the posting itself is the single event from which the "clock" begins to run for limitations purposes. When the site is modified in ways that do not relate to the allegedly defamatory material, those changes are not "republications" that can be used to extend the statute of limitations (although reprinting a newspaper article in a book would be).[17]

The Communications Decency Act (CDA) § 230 provides a safe harbor for ISPs that, in effect, transmit content provided by others, but the ISP itself has no involvement with providing or reviewing the content.

---

[14] A limited exception is made for "compelled self-publication," when the subject of the communication is forced to repeat it — for instance, citing the reason for being fired from a job.

[15] Milkovich v. Lorain Journal, 497 U.S. 1 (1990).

[16] Masson v. New Yorker, 501 U.S. 496 (1991).

[17] Firth v. State, 98 N.Y.2d 365 (2002), the Ninth Circuit reached the same conclusion in Oja v. Army Corps of Eng'rs, 440 F.3d 1122 (9th Cir. 2006).

The New Jersey Court of Appeals ruled that alleged targeting of a New Jersey audience was enough to justify suing a California resident in New Jersey for libel in a Web forum. Other courts, e.g., in Connecticut, Pennsylvania, and Minnesota, have held that jurisdiction lies in the state where the allegedly defamatory material was posted. In this case, however, the alleged libel referred to a New Jersey community's police department, so the defendant should have foreseen the risk of being sued in New Jersey.[18]

In an unusual case of defamation by fiction, the Georgia Court of Appeals permitted an Atlanta woman to pursue claims that she was libeled as a promiscuous alcoholic in the novel "The Red Hat Club." The book contains a disclaimer stating that it is fiction and has not been endorsed by the Red Hat Society, a real-life organization for older women. The court noted that there were 25 specific similarities: for example, both the plaintiff and the fictional character lost their husbands to automobile accidents; both had problems with settling the case because of the action of a subsequent romantic partner; and both became flight attendants. The book also used local details to bolster its appearance of realism. The plaintiff and defendant knew each other for 50 years, and there was evidence that the plaintiff's friends thought the fictional character portrayed her. However, the Court of Appeals dismissed charges against secondary publishers (e.g., large-print edition), and dismissed false light, invasion of privacy, and infliction of emotional distress damages against the author and publisher.[19]

Lawyers' absolute privilege in judicial proceedings does not insulate them against defamation liability for communications with news media about a pending case. The purpose of the privilege is encouraging zealous advocacy, a value that is not served by unrestricted contact with the press. In fact, a lawyer can be sued for defamation based on communications that more or less restate the allegations of the client's pleading.[20]

The absolute privilege for defamatory statements made during litigation does not immunize a lawyer's post-trial statements to the media. Once the trial ends, there is no longer a connection to the judicial proceeding justifying the privilege.[21]

The slander exception to Federal Tort Claims Act liability (§ 2680(h)) protects a Congressman in connection with remarks to a journalist linking a non-profit group to terrorism. Although the subject of the interview was the Congressman's marital separation, the interview occurred in his office during work hours and is within the scope of employment because it was at least partially motivated by a desire to inform his constituents.[22]

---

[18] Goldhaber v. Kohlenberg, No. A-5114-05 (N.J. App. 2007), discussed in Henry Gottlieb, *Californian Can Be Sued in N.J. for Alleged Libel on Internet*, N.J.L.J. 8/6/07 (law.com).

[19] Smith v. Stewart, 291 Ga. App. 86 (Ga. App. 2008); Alyson M. Palmer, *Art Imitates Life Too Closely, Says Woman Suing Over "Red Hat Club" Book*, Fulton County Daily Report 4/1/08 (law.com).

[20] Kennedy v. Zimmerman, 601 N.W.2d 61 (Iowa 1999).

[21] Brown v. Gatti, 99 P.3d 299 (Ore. App. 2004).

[22] Council on American Islamic Relations v. Ballenger, 444 F.3d 659 (D.C. Cir. 2006).

[1] Private and Public Figures

The highest degree of protection is given to a purely private person who alleges defamation by another purely private person. If the plaintiff is an elected official or public figure, or if the defendant is a newspaper, television station, or other news medium, more leeway will be given, in light of First Amendment issues arising out of the public's interest in knowing about current news and issues.[23]

The basic formulation comes from 1964's *New York Times v. Sullivan*:[24] whether or not the defendant is a news organization, actual malice is required to find defamation if the plaintiff is a public official or a public figure.

A public figure maintains pervasive power and influence, or has purposefully "injected" him- or herself into debate or into public notice, and therefore can no longer claim to be a private person entitled to a higher degree of protection.

On December 15, 2008, the Supreme Court denied certiorari, preventing Steven J. Hatfill from reviving his libel lawsuit against the New York Times for articles that incorrectly implicated Hatfill in the 2001 anthrax attacks. The Fourth Circuit dismissed the suit on the grounds that Hatfill was a public figure and failed to prove that the columns were published maliciously.[25]

Punitive damages[26] and damages for intentional infliction of emotional distress[27] will be available only if the statements were published with actual malice. A news medium is guilty of actual malice when it publishes statements that are known to be false, or published with reckless disregard of their truth or falsity. However, mere failure to investigate is not actual malice, even if a reasonable party would have investigated.

The "neutral reporting" privilege may also protect news media that report on defamatory statements uttered by others, if the rationale is to report that the utterance occurred, rather than to promulgate it as the truth. However, it did not shield a newspaper's reckless reporting of false charges against public officials, because the statements were made with actual malice. Pennsylvania distinguished the case from the fair report doctrine that applies to reports of governmental proceedings; these statements were not made in the course of official proceedings.[28]

The Supreme Court ruled in mid-2005 that a petitioner's challenge to the permanent injunction that forbade him to picket Johnnie Cochran or make hostile

---

[23] *But see* Hawar v. Globe Int'l Inc., 79 Cal. Rptr. 2d 178 (Cal. 1998), denying a newspaper the defense that it was merely republishing a libel committed by someone else against a private person; in this reading, the "neutral reporting" principle applies only to statements about public figures.

[24] 376 U.S. 254 (1964).

[25] Hatfill v. New York Times, No. 08-483 (12/15/08).

[26] Gertz v. Robert Welch Inc., 418 U.S. 323 (1974).

[27] Hustler Magazine v. Falwell, 485 U.S. 46 (1988).

[28] Norton v. Glenn, 860 A.2d 48 (Pa. 2004).

statements about him was not rendered moot by Cochran's death, because his widow could be substituted as a party.[29]

Florida permitted a damage action for disclosure of HIV test results in violation of privacy rights, even though generally the state upholds an impact rule for emotional distress damages. A nurse's HIV test, after an occupational risk of exposure, were faxed to two unsecured office machines instead of being hand-delivered, so many unauthorized people saw the results.[30]

[2] Defamation *Per Se* and *Per Quod*

Traditionally, a distinction was drawn between defamation *per se* and *per quod*, although this distinction is being phased out. A *per se* statement involves a claim that an individual has committed a crime; suffers from a loathsome disease; is guilty of serious sexual misconduct; or has done something incompatible with his or her business, trade, profession, or public office. See Restatement (2nd) of Torts § 570.

The defamatory nature of a *per se* statement is apparent on its face, whereas extrinsic facts are needed to show the defamatory character of a *per quod* statement. Proof of special damages may be required to maintain a case of defamation *per quod*. Any defamation case requires proof of at least some damages, although they can be intangible (for instance, damage to reputation).

According to the First Circuit, after *Lawrence v. Texas* (the Supreme Court decision striking down sodomy laws), calling a person "homosexual" no longer imputes criminal conduct. Therefore, even if the statement is not in fact true, it does not constitute defamation *per se*. (The plaintiff was a former boyfriend of Madonna, who was incorrectly identified in a photo caption in a way that he said implied that he was a homosexual.)[31]

The Communications Decency Act gives Internet service providers (ISPs) immunity if defamatory statements are posted to the service by a third party (with no participation by the ISP); see § 28.05[A].

Generally speaking, defamation claims are inherently personal and non-survivable, so the death of the allegedly defamed person terminates the action.

There is an absolute privilege for statements made in judicial or quasi-judicial proceedings (e.g., administrative hearings), as long as the statements refer to the subject matter of the proceedings. Qualified privilege applies to statements made to law enforcement officials in the course of an investigation, or where there is a

---

[29] Tory v. Cochran, 544 U.S. 734 (2005).

[30] Florida Department of Corrections v. Abril (Fla. 2007); *see* Jordana Mishory, *Fla. High Court Rules Those Who Disclose HIV Results Can Be Sued for Damages*, Daily Business Review 10/22/07 (law.com).

[31] Amrak Prods. Inc. v. Morton, 410 F.3d 69 (1st Cir. 2005). On another post-*Lawrence* issue, Virginia found that its state anti-fornication law violated due process, thus permitting a cause of action for negligent transmission of herpes. The infectious party is no longer entitled to the defense that no tort cause of action will lie for injuries incurred in the course of illegal activities: Martin v. Ziherl, 607 S.E.2d 367 (Va. 2005).

statutory privilege (for instance, for making a good-faith report of suspicions of child abuse or elder abuse). The Connecticut Court of Appeals applied the privilege for fair reporting of a judicial decision that includes defamatory statements to a substantially accurate account, even if some details in the article were inaccurate. (The plaintiff was an attorney subject to sanctions, who charged that the article contained falsehoods and injured her reputation.) The court held that the publisher had no duty to interview the lawyer or reflect her side of the story.[32]

A libel suit can be brought in any forum where the defendant has minimum contacts.[33]

[B] Other Intentional Torts

The Supreme Court held that the Federal Tort Claims Act (FTCA) includes an exception for claims arising in a foreign country (28 USC § 2680(k)), precluding suit for injuries suffered in a foreign country, no matter where the tortious act or omission occurred. The Supreme Court refused to apply the "headquarters doctrine" to an arrest occurring in Mexico, because the connection between decisions made at DEA headquarters in the United States was not close enough to the ultimate injury for liability to be imposed. The Supreme Court also ruled that the Alien Tort Statute is a jurisdictional statute that does not create any new causes of action. Although the fact pattern is somewhat exotic (the target of a drug investigation was abducted in Mexico and brought to the United States to be tried for kidnapping and murder, but he was acquitted), the Supreme Court's ruling has broader implications, such as potential liability for anti-terrorist activities that span several countries, and whether or not U.S. corporations can be sued in the United States by non-citizens of the United States for human rights violations.[34]

In May 2008, the Supreme Court was unable to intervene in a case about the right of apartheid victims to bring suit in the United States against United States corporations. Four out of the nine justices had to recuse themselves because of stock-ownership-based conflicts. Therefore, the suit was permitted to continue.[35]

See below for business torts; this list covers non-business intentional torts:

- The tort of battery consists of offensive touching (offensive to a reasonable sense of dignity, performed by someone who intends harmful or offensive conduct). It includes violent attacks and sexual harassment that incorporates physical contact as well as verbal behavior.[36]

---

[32] Burton v. American Lawyer Media Inc., 847 A.2d 1115 (Conn. App. 2004).

[33] Keeton v. Hustler Magazine, 465 U.S. 770 (1984).

[34] Sosa v. Alvarez-Machain, 542 U.S. 692 (2004).

[35] American Isuzu Motors v. Mtsebeza, 128 S. Ct. 2424 (5/12/08); *see* Mark Sherman (AP), *Supreme Court Allows Apartheid Victims' Lawsuit Against U.S. Companies to Proceed*, 5/12/08 (law.com).

[36] *See* Duncan v. Scottsdale Med. Imaging, 205 Ariz. 306, 70 P.3d 435 (2003), holding that it constitutes battery for a health care provider to administer medication contrary to the patient's

- The tort of assault consists of placing the victim in apprehension of imminent unwelcome physical conduct (i.e., threat of battery or other physical injury). Therefore, the crime of assault corresponds to the tort of battery; the tort of assault corresponds to the crime of menacing or stalking. The plaintiff has to apprehend the imminent contact, but need not necessarily suffer fear.
- The tort of false imprisonment is intentional wrongful confinement of a plaintiff who is aware of the confinement. (If the plaintiff was unconscious, and actual harm resulted from the false imprisonment, damages are available despite the lack of consciousness of confinement.[37])
- Malicious prosecution is improper triggering of groundless criminal proceedings against a plaintiff. Giving information about actual crimes committed by the plaintiff, leading to prosecution, is not malicious prosecution even if the motivation was to damage the plaintiff. Once proceedings have commenced, abuse of process is the malicious use of the legal process.
- Intentional infliction of mental distress (or anguish) is extreme or outrageous conduct that can be expected to distress a person of ordinary sensibilities. The defendant's conduct must be intolerable, extreme, and outrageous, not merely annoying.

  The plaintiff must suffer severely; many jurisdictions require bodily manifestations (e.g., weight loss, aggravation of an ulcer) of the mental distress. In some circumstances, emotional distress to one person, caused by conduct toward another person may be actionable: seeing an attack on a family member, for instance.
- Individuals are given the right to control how their name and image are used, so that either violation of the right of privacy (by using name or image without permission) or right of publicity (by exploiting image value that rightfully belongs to the person) can be tortious.[38]

  These rights are broader as to living people than as to the estates of decedents, and exceptions are made for legitimate news communications about people of public interest, as distinguished from ordinary private citizens.

---

express wishes, striking down the state's Revised Statutes § 12-562(B), immunizing the health care provider in this situation. The court found that the statute was void as contrary to the state constitution because it abrogates a common-law right to damages.

[37] *See* El Al Israel Airlines Ltd. v. Tseng, 525 U.S. 155 (1999): a tort suit cannot be brought in state court, alleging that an intrusive security search was tantamount to assault and false imprisonment, but no bodily injury occurred. The Warsaw Convention's coverage is limited to "bodily injury" incurred in flight, embarking, or disembarking. *See also* Ehrlich v. American Airlines Inc., 360 F.3d 366 (2d Cir. 2004): under the Warsaw Convention, mental injuries are recoverable if and only if they are caused by physical injuries, and do not merely accompany physical injuries.

[38] Sometimes a distinction is drawn between a celebrity's right of publicity and common-law appropriation of the name or identity of an ordinary citizen: *e.g.,* PETA v. Bobby Berosini, Ltd., 867 P.2d 1121 (Nev. 1994). A model alleged that her picture continued to be used on product packaging after the contract expired; the Seventh Circuit held that her Illinois state right of publicity claim was not preempted by the federal copyright law: Toney v. L'Oreal, 406 F.3d 905 (7th Cir. 2005).

Restatement (2nd) of Torts § 652A distinguishes between four categories: intrusion; appropriation of name and likeness; giving unreasonable publicity to private facts; and putting the plaintiff in a "false light" before the public.

One analysis is that invasion of privacy consists of public disclosure of embarrassing facts, so that personal matters are publicized in a way that an ordinary person would find highly offensive, when there is no legitimate public concern over the information.

- Trespass to land. Traditionally, this tort was committed by intentional entry on property (whether or not the intent was to trespass), and actual damages did not have to be shown, and at least nominal damages were always awarded when any trespass was proved.

Today, trespass can be either an intentional or a negligent tort, and liability will probably not be imposed without actual damage, unless the trespasser was reckless or at least negligent. Contemporary trespass damages are all direct harm from the trespass, plus consequential damages (e.g., water damage caused by a faucet that the trespasser turned on but failed to turn off). Depending on the jurisdiction, environmental trespass (such as entry of airborne particles, or contamination of underground water) might be treated as either trespass or nuisance.

- Trespass to chattel and conversion are intentional torts to personal property. Trespass to chattel is intentional interference with the owner's rights, e.g., by destroying or damaging the property, using it without permission, or depriving the owner of possession or control. Trespass to chattel is solely an intentional tort, although wrongful motive is not required; liability will probably not be imposed without actual damage to the chattel.

Conversion, another purely intentional tort, is severe, aggravated trespass to chattel that permanently deprives the owner of control. In effect, the trespass is so severe that the court forces the tortfeasor to "buy" the chattel, because the measure of damages is the entire value of the chattel plus interest.

Liability in a trespass to chattel or conversion case depends on factors such as the extent and duration of control exercised by the tortfeasors; extent of assertion of rights inconsistent with the rights of others; the tortfeasor's good or bad faith; the degree of harm to the chattel; and the degree of inconvenience or expense resulting from the harm.

Some jurisdictions treat "spoliation" — intentional or negligent interference with a civil action by destruction of evidence — as a separate tort

[C] Misrepresentation and Fraud

Misrepresentation torts usually occur in a business context. See immediately below for business torts; see also § 2.02[F] for a discussion of warranties, Chapter 7 for consumer protection law, and § 6.05[A] for securities litigation premised on alleged misrepresentation by the issuer company.

Under traditional tort principles, misrepresentation damages were limited to pecuniary harm caused by the misrepresentation to the persons to whom the misrepresentations were made. However, the Restatement (2nd) of Torts § 531 position is that misrepresentation liability extends to anyone who could be foreseen to rely on the truth of the representations.

Misrepresentation liability usually requires scienter: the person making the statement must have known that it was false. A representation is not fraudulent if the person making the representation believes it, even if belief is foolish.

Negligent misrepresentation might be actionable if it caused actual physical harm, or if there was some duty (such as fiduciary duty) running from the person making the representation to the recipient of the representation. A negligent misrepresentation could also furnish a defense (if someone who relied on the misrepresentation is sued, e.g., for breach of contract) or a counterclaim.

Misrepresentation is only actionable if reliance on the representation was justifiable. The highest standard is required of factual representations apparently within the speaker's knowledge, that are material[39] to the transaction. Hearers are expected to "discount" statements based on the speaker's obvious interest (e.g., a used-car dealer's description of the cars on the lot).

There may also be a duty to disclose facts discovered after making a representation that was true or believed true, but which has now been rendered untrue or misleading by subsequent events.

Misrepresentation plaintiffs' remedies fall into two categories: keeping the transaction intact and receiving fraud remedies, or undoing part or all of the transaction. Another option is to stop performing on the contract, then raise fraud as a defense to suit for breach of contract.

[D] Business Torts

Torts committed in the course of business include:

- Unfair competition, which can be committed, e.g., by confusion of trade identity, palming off (substituting goods other than those ordered); misappropriation of a distinctive characterization; and false advertising
- Copyright infringement
- Trademark infringement
- Trademark dilution
- Patent infringement

---

[39] Restatement (2nd) of Torts § 538(1) states that even a fraudulent representation is not actionable if it is not material; the test is whether an ordinary reasonable person would have relied on the representation. Although ordinary negligence is not a defense to intentional fraud, reliance on obviously incredible statements is not considered reasonable.

- Disparagement or trade libel: i.e., non-privileged statements about the quality of a business' property or products, if the statements are, in fact, false and cause actual damage. In some jurisdictions, disparagement/trade libel causes of action will be cognizable only if the defendant acted with actual malice. Disparagement of someone else's products must be distinguished from "puffing" of one's own products, which is considered permissible as long as it is not tantamount to deception of consumers.
- Misappropriation of trade secrets
- Tortious inducement of breach of contract (e.g., inducing a supplier to renege on its contracts to supply a competitor; inducing an individual to abandon an employment contract).

If the defendant's duty arises out of a contractual relationship between the parties, there is no tort liability for any harm caused by breaching the contract by not starting performance in the first place. However, once performance begins, tort liability can be imposed for intentional, reckless, or negligent misperformance, including either misfeasance or nonfeasance.

The Southern District of New York dismissed a much-publicized class action by minors alleging that they became obese because of consumption of fast food. The plaintiffs charged McDonald's Corporation with negligence and deceptive trade practices. The case was dismissed for failure to state a cause of action, and for failure to plead with specificity that the health hazards of high-calorie foods are not common knowledge.

The plaintiffs were given leave to replead to allege that McDonald's had a duty to warn because its products are so altered (e.g., with additives) so that consumers no longer have an adequate understanding of product-related risks. However, on the second outing, the case was dismissed with prejudice because claims were time-barred, the plaintiffs failed to prove reliance on the allegedly deceptive advertising; and they failed to exclude other causes of the health problems they attributed to consumption of fast food; the case was revived in 2005.[40] D.D.C. Judge James Robertson dismissed a suit charging KFC with failure to disclose its use of trans fats; the opinion said that the plaintiff, a doctor, failed to show harm from KFC's practices. KFC's parent company announced that it had adopted soybean oil to remove trans fats from its products.[41]

---

[40] Pelman v. McDonald's Corp., 237 F. Supp. 2d 512 (S.D.N.Y. 2003); 72 L.W. 1142 (S.D.N.Y. 9/3/03); 396 F.3d 508 (2d Cir. 2005) (partially reinstating the action on the grounds that General Business Law § 349, the ban on deceptive business practices, does not require proof of actual reliance, and data about plaintiffs' heredity and eating habits are not part of the pleading, but information to be obtained in the course of discovery).

[41] (AP) *Trans Fat Lawsuit Against KFC Tossed Out*, 5/3/07 (law.com).

[1] Employment Torts

The employment relation can also give rise to tort claims:[42] for instance, that the employer wrongfully terminated an employee, that sexual harassment occurred, or that the employee suffered emotional injury (with or without physical consequences).

In many instances, state-law claims will be preempted by federal laws such as the anti-discrimination laws discussed at § 3.10 to the extent that they involve the federal statutes themselves. However, in some instances state tort claims will be permitted: for instance, if the employer company is too small to be covered by the federal statutes.

Employers have the right to dismiss at-will employees for good cause, or for no reason at all, but are not permitted to dismiss them for an improper cause, such as discrimination against a suspect classification (e.g., race, sex, or age discrimination) or retaliation for exercising a legal right (e.g., filing a legitimate Workers' Compensation claim).

In some circumstances, the discharge will be wrongful because it violates public policy. Examples include discharging an employee who serves on a jury, or a "whistleblower" who exposes the employer's unlawful conduct. Note, however, that in 2007 the Supreme Court limited the availability of whistleblower recoveries under the False Claims Act by requiring relators to show they are the original source of the information, with direct and independent knowledge of the facts underlying the allegations that the whistleblower prevails on — not information supporting publicly disclosed allegations.[43]

[E] "Life Torts"

This category includes several controversial related torts. These torts are controversial in that not all jurisdictions recognize them as causes of action, or to the same extent. These torts are easy to confuse, but the potential plaintiff or litigator must distinguish between them based on who is permitted to sue, on what grounds, and for what elements of damages:

- Wrongful pregnancy is the parent's claim that a healthy but unwanted child was born because of the defendant's negligence in prescribing birth control or performing sterilization or abortion. Depending on the jurisdiction, damages may be denied altogether (on the grounds that birth of a healthy child is not a

---

[42] Breach of contract claims in the employment context are somewhat limited, because most employees are "at-will" employees who do not have an employment contract. In some instances, the employer's communications or conduct will be deemed to have created a contract, but in general employee claims tend to be statutory or tort-based.

[43] Rockwell International Corp. v. U.S., 549 U.S. 457 (2007); *see* Marcia Coyle, *Supreme Court: More Scrutiny Required in Whistleblower Claims*, Nat'l L.J. 4/6/07 (law.com).

compensable injury); limited to the cost of rearing the child reduced by benefits of having a child; damages including the cost of rearing the child may be granted, or some damages permitted but childrearing expenses excluded.

- Wrongful birth is the parent's cause of action alleging that the pregnancy would not have been conceived or carried to term if they had been properly warned of genetic characteristics leading to the child's defect. The elements of damages include the extra expenses of rearing a disabled child and the parents' emotional distress.
- Wrongful life is the impaired individual's own cause of action based on grossly poor quality of life due to the defect.
- The tort of wrongful survival is closely related to battery: it refers to life-saving or life-sustaining treatment provided contrary to the expressed wishes of the patient.

Like most states, Maryland does not have a wrongful life cause of action (brought by a child asserting that he or she should never have been born) because it is too difficult to calculate damages for the difference between a normal and an impaired life. (By contrast, California, New Jersey, and Washington do permit wrongful life cases.) However, the majority rule, also followed in Maryland, is that a wrongful **birth** cause of action, for the additional costs of raising a disabled child, can be maintained.[44]

Oklahoma recognizes a cause of action for the wrongful death of a nonviable fetus that was nevertheless born alive, but not for the loss of a nonviable fetus that was stillborn. The rationale is that life begins at conception.[45]

In Minnesota law, doctors have a duty of care to the parents of patients who are tested for inheritable genetic disorders, because it is foreseeable that the parents might rely on the test results in deciding to have more children, who might also have the disease.[46]

Texas ruled that a hospital was not liable in battery or negligence for requiring a doctor to resuscitate a premature infant without getting the parents' consent. The infant was certain to die without resuscitation, and it would not be possible to determine the infant's condition until after birth. (The baby was born with critical multiple handicaps; both parents stated that they did not want the baby to be resuscitated.) Although the trial court awarded $60 million in actual and punitive damages, plus interest, the appellate court invalidated the entire award, finding that there is an exception to the informed consent requirement in an emergent situation where there is no time to consult the parents. Because the doctor could not be held

---

[44] Kassama v. Magat, 767 A.2d 348 (Md. App. 2001).

[45] Nealis v. Baird, 996 P.2d 438 (Okla. 1999). In Mississippi, the wrongful death of a fetus is cognizable if it occurs after quickening, a standard that the state's Supreme Court considered less arbitrary than trying to assess viability: 66 Federal Credit Union v. Tucker, 853 So. 2d 104 (Miss. 2003).

[46] Molloy v. Meier, 679 N.W.2d 711 (Minn. 2004).

liable, neither could the hospital that promulgated a policy mandating resuscitation of all infants over 500 grams.[47]

§ 18.09   AUTOMOBILE-RELATED TORTS AND NO-FAULT

The operation of automobiles can cause physical injury to the occupants of one's own car or other cars, and property damage (to other vehicles as well as other objects). The obvious defendant in an automobile-related case is the driver, but other persons may be liable instead or additionally. The owner of the car may be liable, based on agency concepts or the "family purpose" doctrine (where someone else is allowed to drive the car for the benefit of the owner's family).

A person who allows a minor, incapacitated, or drunken person to drive might be liable for "negligent entrustment." If the driver was an employee acting in the scope of employment, the employer might be liable on agency principles. "Dram-shop" liability is imposed on bars and restaurants (and sometimes on social hosts) for furnishing liquor to an obviously intoxicated person who then drove unsafely.

See § 13.05 for a discussion of automobile insurance and § 26.02[H][5] for drunk driving offenses.

[A] No-Fault

Many of the injuries that the tort system has to cope with are the result of automobile accidents. These accidents differ greatly in the conduct and liability of the drivers. Sometimes both were seriously negligent or even reckless; sometimes neither was in any way culpable — or anything in between. If every automobile case were litigated, the court system, already strained by many other kinds of cases, would be completely unworkable.

Many states have adopted some kind of "no-fault" system to relieve pressure on the court system, reduce insurance premiums, and speed up recoveries that injured persons can use to get medical care, or owners of damaged cars can use to get repairs or new cars. Massachusetts was the first state to adopt no-fault insurance, in 1971. Today, most of the states have adopted some kind of no-fault system, whether in the form of an "add-on" that leaves tort litigation intact, or a fairly comprehensive system under which only very serious injuries can be litigated.

Classic tort litigation is a third-party system. That is, when someone is injured or his or her car is damaged, the tortfeasor (or, more practically, the tortfeasor's insurance company) has to pay. Under a first-party system, the person who suffers injury or property damage looks to his or her own insurer for compensation.

A no-fault system has more first-party than third-party elements. In theory, all persons suffering automobile-related bodily injury or economic loss can get compensated, whether they had any share in causing the accident or not. The system is financed by automobile drivers, via compulsory insurance (rather than public funds or the pool of potential victims). However, the no-fault system does not compensate pain and suffering; such damages are available only if the injured

---

[47] Miller v. HCA Inc., 118 S.W.3d 758 (Tex. 2003).

person is able to bring — and win — a tort suit. In one sense, the no-fault system is broader: it covers situations such as one-car accidents in which there is no tortfeasor to be blamed.

No-fault benefits are often referred to as PIP (Personal Injury Protection).[48] PIP reimburses (up to the policy limit) medical expenses, lost wages, cost of rehabilitation, and "replacement services" (i.e., tasks the injured person is unable to do because of the injury). It also provides death benefits.

A pure no-fault system completely eliminates tort litigation in automobile injury cases, and does not provide any compensation for non-economic damages. Pure no-fault has not been adopted in any U.S. jurisdiction, but it is in force in several other countries (e.g., parts of Canada, Israel, Sweden, Finland).

In a threshold (also called combination) system, an injured person gets first-party no-fault benefits from his or her own insurer. Depending on the jurisdiction, the threshold could refer either to the extent of the injury or the cost of treating it. Once the threshold is reached, litigation against the tortfeasor is permitted.

No-fault systems differ as to:

- Whether any minimum level of injury is required for coverage
- Whether a top limit is imposed on reimbursement under the system
- The role, if any, played by traditional tort litigation
- How the pool of insurance funds is allocated.

[1] State Requirements

Forty states require all motorists to maintain liability insurance covering bodily injury claims made by persons injured by the motorist. However, in the "financial responsibility" states, motorists are only required to maintain bodily injury (BI) liability insurance if they have had accidents or been detected in automotive violations in the past.[49]

Colorado, Delaware, Hawaii, Kansas, Kentucky, Massachusetts, Michigan, Minnesota, New Jersey, New York, North Dakota, Oregon, Pennsylvania, and Utah require motorists to maintain both no-fault insurance and BI liability coverage; Florida merely requires them to maintain no-fault insurance.

The states with an "add-on" system are Arkansas, Delaware, Maryland, New Hampshire, Oregon, South Dakota, Texas, Virginia, Washington, and Wisconsin. In these states, automobile insurers are required to offer all motorists no-fault

---

[48] MP, or Medical Payments, first-party coverage is sold in states that do not have a no-fault system; it is an optional coverage that is often sold only in conjunction with the purchase of liability coverage. It covers the occupants of the insured vehicle; PIP is broader, covering uninsured pedestrians who are struck by an insured vehicle.

[49] According to Robert H. Joost, *Automobile Insurance and No-Fault Law* (2d ed.), 1998 Cumulative Supplement § 1:8 (WestGroup), Alabama, Arizona, California, Florida, Iowa, Mississippi, New Hampshire, Rhode Island, Tennessee, Virginia, and Wisconsin. The information in this section about state legislation comes from Joost.

coverage, but injured persons still have unlimited rights to sue tortfeasors. Any tort recovery is simply added to the no-fault benefit.

"Auto choice," which is now enacted in Kentucky, New Jersey, and Pennsylvania, and is the subject of several bills introduced in Congress, gives motorists a choice between PPI (Personal Protection Insurance) and TMC (Tort Maintenance Coverage). TMC is similar to conventional tort law; PPI is first-party coverage similar to no-fault. No matter which coverage a motorist chooses, he or she can sue a negligent driver for economic losses that are not compensated by the insurance.

Under the "no pay-no play" rule, which prevails in California, Louisiana, and New Jersey, injured motorists are denied damages, or limited in the damages they can receive, if they were not insured at the time of the accident.

When an out-of-state motorist is injured in a no-fault jurisdiction, he or she can probably collect no-fault benefits (as long as he or she maintained whatever insurance coverage was required by the home state). The right to sue, if any, depends on the law of the state of injury. An uninsured out-of-state motorist cannot collect no-fault benefits but may be able to sue (e.g., in a threshold state where the injury exceeds the threshold).

The preceding discussion assumes that it is possible both to determine who caused the accident, and to collect a judgment against him or her. UM (Uninsured Motorist) coverage is first-party coverage that deals with the situation in which the other driver has no insurance, or cannot be located (e.g., a hit and run accident). UIM, Underinsured Motorist, coverage is supplemental first-party coverage payable if an identified tortfeasor has BI liability insurance coverage that is lower than the amount of the injured person's damages. According to the Third Circuit, the State of Limitations on a claim for underinsured motorist benefits starts when the insured settles with the other driver for an amount lower than the damages. (In Pennsylvania, the statute of limitations is four years.) The court rejected the insurer's claim that the statute of limitations starts with the accident — and also rejected the trial court's view that the clock starts to run when the insurer rejects the underinsured motorist claim. In the Third Circuit view, the date of settlement with the other motorist is the significant date because it is the starting point at which the insured can determine his own damages and the other driver's policy limits.[50]

§ 18.10 PRODUCTS LIABILITY

A product can cause harm in many ways, even if it is properly used by the consumer (who can be, but is not always, the person who purchased the product). The product could be defectively designed. The specifications that are supposed to be valid could be appropriate, but the individual item could have been manufactured in such a way as to become unsafe. Perhaps the product could be reasonably

---

[50] State Farm Mutual Automobile Ins. v. Rosenthal, 484 F.3d 251 (3d Cir. 2007); *see* Shannon P. Duffy, *3rd Circuit: Settlement Starts the Clock in Underinsured Motorist Claims*, The Legal Intelligencer 4/27/07 (law.com); *see* Motorist Mutual Ins. Co. v. Durney, (E.D. Pa. 2005) for the proposition that contract law prevents the underinsured motorist insurance cause of action from accruing until the claim is denied.

safe in theory, but is dangerous in practice because the manufacturer failed to supply adequate instructions or warnings.

Foreseeable accidents must be accommodated: for instance, cars must be designed to be as safe as possible after a crash, even though the car is not designed to crash. If it is foreseeable that consumers will endanger themselves by misusing the product, then there may be a duty to design the product to reduce the risks of such foreseeable misuse.

Although traditionally "privity of contract" was required (i.e., only the actual buyer of the product could sue the manufacturer for injuries caused by the product), privity of contract is no longer relevant.

In many instances, strict products liability will be imposed on the manufacturer (and others in the supply chain, such as distributors and retailers); it will not be necessary to plead or prove negligence.

Trademark licensing is growing as a factor in the global economy, and close to one-third of all trademark licensing commerce is generated outside the United States. There are two theories under which trademark licensors can be subject to products liability in the United States: enterprise liability theory and the "apparent manufacturer" doctrine (Rest.3d of Torts § 400). Enterprise theory subjects a non-manufacturer to strict liability as the functional equivalent of the manufacturer if design, manufacturing, or warning defects make the product unreasonably dangerous. The "apparent manufacturer" doctrine imposes the same liability on a person who puts out a good as its own manufacturer as on the actual manufacturer; it is usually applied only if the licensor actually sells or distributes the licensed goods. The Restatement (3d) of Torts limits application of this doctrine to product sellers or distributors, not pure licensors.[51]

Early in 2008, the Second Circuit upheld the dismissal of Agent Orange-related suits by 16 Vietnam veterans and their relatives against Dow Chemical and other manufacturers, because the suits were precluded by the government contractor defense. These plaintiffs were not part of the original class that reached a $180 million global settlement in 1984. The opt-out plaintiffs lost either because they could not prove harm from Agent Orange, or because they couldn't prove which defendant manufactured the products that they alleged harmed them. Furthermore, the military contractor defense applied: the unique federal interest in completing defense-related projects sometimes requires protection of independent contractors from tort liability for defense work. The defense requires the government to exercise discretionary authority over the subject of the state litigation. In this instance, the Second Circuit ruled that the government continued to order Agent Orange, so it must have deemed its toxicity levels to be acceptable. Cases by Vietnamese nationals under the Alien Tort Statute were dismissed.[52]

---

[51] David L. Wallace and Allison M. Alcasabas, *Trademark Licensor Liability for Defective Products Under U.S. Law*, Special to law.com 5/16/07.

[52] Vietnam Ass'n for Victims of Agent Orange v. Dow, 517 F.3d 104 (2d Cir. 2008); Isaacson v. Dow, 517 F.3d 129 (2d Cir. 2008); *see* Mark Hamblett, *2nd Circuit Rejects Agent Orange Claims by*

The Consumer Product Safety Commission imposed a $1 million civil penalty (the highest to date under the Federal Hazardous Substances Act) against Reebok International Inc. for issuing charm bracelets with hazardous lead levels. Recalls of other products containing excessive lead created a demand for better testing programs and contracts imposing more responsibility on suppliers. For example, as contracts with non-U.S. manufacturers expire, more companies are adding arbitration clauses to the new contracts to handle contamination problems. (The Chinese legal system more or less precludes lawsuits either in the United States or in China.)[53]

Although the sale of lead paint was banned in 1978, there are still many older homes in which lead paint is present. In 2006, a verdict was rendered in Rhode Island against three major paint companies for creating a public nuisance by manufacturing and selling a toxic product (lead paint). Then the Rhode Island Supreme Court overturned the verdict, so the industry decided it would not be necessary to invest billions of dollars to clean up contaminated homes. A few lead paint suits remain unresolved, but New Jersey and Missouri rejected public nuisance theories in 2007, and a November 2007 Milwaukee case found for the defense in a case alleging lead poisoning.[54]

Attempts have been made to use public nuisance suits to require manufacturers to pay for removal of lead paint, but this has not been a successful cause of action. California, Maryland, New Jersey, and New York have ruled that a public nuisance claim cannot be based solely on a legal product that is later discovered to cause injury.[55] According to the Sixth Circuit, the Lead-Based Paint Poisoning Prevention Act, 42 USC §§ 4821–4846, the U.S. Housing Act, and the administrative regulations for those statutes do not create an individual federal right that can be enforced under 42 USC § 1983.[56]

In addition to lead paint, other major products liability issues are tobacco (especially punitive damages); the diet drug "fen-phen"; and the arthritis drug Vioxx, which has been widely blamed for causing cardiovascular symptoms.

U.S. Veterans, Vietnamese Nationals, N.Y.L.J. 2/25/08 (law.com). The federal contractor defense is recognized by Boyle v. United Technologies Corp., 487 U.S. 500 (1988); *see* Sosa v. Alvarez-Machain, 542 U.S. 692 (2004) for international law tort standards.

[53] Sheri Qualters, *Lead Scare Brings Prospect of More Corporate Liability*, Nat'l L.J. 4/2/08 (law.com).

[54] Eric Tucker (AP), *Rhode Island High Court Overturns Lead Paint Verdict*, 7/1/08 (law.com).

[55] City of Chi. v. American Cyanamid Co., 823 N.E.2d 126 (Ill. App. 2005). The duty to remediate was assigned to landlords, not paint manufacturers, so the suit should have been brought, if at all, much earlier and against landlords. The California Court of Appeals reinstated lead paint public nuisance strict liability claims after the trial court dismissed them, and also permitted governmental entities (as class representatives and on behalf of the people of California) to amend their complaint to add a continuing trespass cause of action: County of Santa Clara v. Atlantic Richfield Co., 137 Cal. App. 4th 292 (Cal. App. 2006).

[56] Johnson v. City of Detroit, 446 F.3d 614 (6th Cir. 2006).

Products liability is present when a plaintiff (or plaintiff's property) is physically harmed by the unsafe condition of a product. Claims may lie against the designer, manufacturer, or seller of the product, based on negligence concepts (e.g., negligent design or testing of a product; improper manufacturing; improper packaging; failure to warn of dangers); breach of warranty; or strict liability.

The manufacturer of brand-name Prozac was not liable for injuries caused by the generic equivalent of the drug. Unless they participate in a common scheme to commit torts, manufacturers are not responsible for the products of other manufacturers.[57]

The Supreme Court seldom decides tort or tort-related cases, so an early 1998[58] case was unusual. It holds that the Constitution's Full Faith and Credit Clause does not obligate a state court to enforce another court's injunction forbidding employees from testifying in a product liability case brought against a company with whom they had settled employment claims, with a "gag order" as part of the settlement.

The statute of limitations for toxic tort claims involving the fungicide Benlate did not start until the plaintiff learned about a possible link between fungicide exposure and birth defects. In other words, the discovery rule for latent injuries cases applied where the injuries were immediate but the underlying cause was not discovered until much later.[59]

District Court Judge Claire Eagan of the Northern District of Oklahoma vacated a $15 million jury verdict against Ford and ordered a new trial in a case involving the 2003 death of a teenager in a rollover crash. Eagan held that the unprecedented level of non-economic damages showed that the jury was prejudiced by the conduct of plaintiff's counsel. (The plaintiff's closing argument charged Ford Explorers with causing 10,000 deaths a year, a figure that the lawyer compared to Iraq war deaths; Judge Eagan pointed out that this statement was made at the end of the closing argument, when the defense was unable to respond.) Ford's position was that it was not responsible for the crash and that the vehicle exceeded federal standards.[60]

The Consumer Product Safety Commission's request to a manufacturer to take voluntary corrective action with respect to an alleged hazard of the product is not a formal adjudication on the record. Because it is not a final agency action, it cannot be reviewed under the Administrative Procedures Act. Nor can it be challenged in federal court.[61]

---

[57] Goldych v. Eli Lilly & Co., 2006 U.S. Dist. LEXIS 49616 (N.D.N.Y. 2006).

[58] Baker v. General Motors, 522 U.S. 222 (1998).

[59] Brown v. duPont, 820 A.2d 362 (Del. 2003).

[60] (AP), "Unprecedented" $15M Jury Award Thrown Out; New Trial Ordered for Ford 3/23/07 (law.com).

[61] Reliable Automatic Sprinkler Co. v. CPSC, 324 F.3d 726 (D.C. Cir. 2003).

Under the Indiana Products Liability Act, the manufacturer of a defective product is not liable if the product itself is damaged, but there is no other personal injury or property damage.[62]

[A] Strict Products Liability

Restatement of Torts (2nd) § 402A makes any seller liable for the sale of "any product in a defective condition unreasonably dangerous to the user or consumer or to his property." Strict liability is imposed only if:

- The seller is engaged in the business of selling such products
- The product reaches the user or consumer in substantially the same condition as it was manufactured.

Assumption of risk is a defense to strict liability, but contributory negligence is not. There may be a duty to design a product that is safe not only for its intended use, but for foreseeable misuse. Products that are likely to be involved in accidents, such as vehicles, must be made as safe as possible if such foreseeable accidents occur.

Comment *k* to § 402A copes with the situation of the "unavoidably unsafe product": those that are useful but nevertheless cannot be made safe for their intended use. The classic example is a valuable drug that has dangerous side effects. As long as the product is accompanied by the appropriate warnings, it is neither defective nor unreasonably dangerous, and therefore the manufacturer is not liable even if harm results. But the manufacturer can be liable if it negligently fails to test the product before it goes on the market, therefore failing to discover its dangers; or if there is a negligent failure to warn of known dangers.[63]

Product injuries (especially drug-related ones) may not manifest themselves for many years. It can be difficult for the injured person to remember or ascertain the manufacturer of the drug or other product, creating serious statute of limitations and joinder problems. (The problems are especially acute for generic drugs.)

Some courts cope with these by imposing "enterprise liability" or "market-share liability," permitting the plaintiff to sue all manufacturers of the relevant product and either forcing them to exculpate themselves or subjecting them to liability based on their share of the market for the product at the relevant time.

---

[62] Progressive Ins. Co. v. GM Corp., 749 N.E.2d 484 (Ind. 2001). *But see* Jimenez v. Superior Ct. of San Diego Co., 127 Cal. Rptr. 2d 614 (Cal. 2002), finding a manufacturer of windows for mass-produced houses strictly liable for harm caused to other parts of the house. The court treated the product as the window, not the whole house, so the economic recovery rule did not bar recovery against the manufacturer.

[63] Even if warnings are inadequate, a manufacturer is not liable if the plaintiff failed to heed the warnings that were given if following the instructions would have averted the injury; in that situation, the manufacturer is not to blame for the harm: General Motors Corp. v. Saenz, 62 L.W. 2384 (Tex. Sup. 11/24/93).

[B] Warranty Issues

Products liability cases are a cross between a strict-liability tort action and a warranty action, which is contractual in nature. Courts often use contract principles to assess economic damage claims in products liability cases, while using tort principles for personal injury claims in the same cases. Theoretically, warranty liability is strict, but a seller will be liable only if.

- It gets reasonably prompt notice of breach of warranty
- The plaintiff really did rely on the warranty
- The warranty could have been, but was not, limited or disclaimed. Sellers can decline to furnish any express warranties, selling goods "as is" — but it is impossible to disclaim strict liability or liability for personal injury caused by breaches of the two implied warranties (UCC § 2-719(3)).

In addition to any express warranties offered by the manufacturer or dealer (§ 2-313), products carry two implied warranties, of merchantability and fitness.

The implied warranty of merchantability promises that the goods are in adequate condition (vis-à-vis both quality and safety) to be sold: see UCC § 2-314. If the purpose for which the goods are purchased is known, and the buyer relies on the seller for advice, there is an implied warranty under § 2-315 that the goods are fit for the purchaser's purpose.

Traditionally, many potential warranty actions were barred by the doctrine of privity of contract: that is, only the actual purchaser could sue if injured by the product. Today, however, not only the purchaser but other foreseeable users (such as household members and guests of the purchaser) are covered by the warranties.

If a claim is for personal injuries only and is based entirely on tort doctrines, the tort statute of limitations governs. Generally speaking, the claim accrues and the statute of limitations begins to run at the time of the injury, not the sale of the product. Some jurisdictions will permit accrual of the claim to be delayed until the injury is either perceptible or actually perceived by the plaintiff. However, warranty cases may compute the statute of limitations from the sale of the product — so the statute of limitations may run before the discovery of a slow-to-manifest injury.

In addition to the statute of limitations, the state may impose a "statute of repose" to protect professionals such as doctors and architects against "long-tail" claims. A statute of repose sets a fairly long time (e.g., 10–25 years) from the sale of the product or rendition of service, during which the claim must be brought.

[C] Restatement (3rd)

Much of the Restatement of Torts is still in its second iteration, but Restatement (3rd) of Torts has been published for products liability.

The basic premise of the Restatement (3rd), as expressed in its § 1, is that someone who is in the business of selling or otherwise distributing products will be liable for harm to persons or property caused by defects in the product. (Section 21 deals with economic harm resulting from product defects.) Sellers and distributors are also liable for harm resulting from inadequate instructions or warnings, if the plaintiff can prove that better design, instructions, or warnings would have made the product safer.

Section 2 defines a product as defective if, at the time of sale or distribution, it had a manufacturing defect (it was different from the intended design, even if all possible care was taken in manufacturing); was defectively designed (foreseeable risks could have been reduced or avoided by adopting a reasonable alternative design); or its warnings or instructions were inadequate.

In general, warnings are not required for risks that are obvious or generally known to foreseeable users. Warnings of potential allergic reactions must be given if a substantial number of people are allergic to the product; the more severe the harm, the smaller the number of people affected before a warning will be required. Section 10 imposes liability for failure to warn if the risk of harm to foreseeable recipients of a warning is such that a reasonable person would warn. Failure to comply with a government recall will give rise to liability. In the right fact circumstances, failure to comply with a voluntary recall imposed by the manufacturer can give rise to liability.

According to California law, a manufacturer is not obligated to warn ordinary consumers of dangers that are generally known — or sophisticated users of risks generally known within the specialist's profession. Therefore, an air conditioning technician who suffered a dangerous lung disease when repairing an air conditioning system could not sue the manufacturer for negligence or failure to warn; he should have known that heating a refrigerant pipe would generate phosgene.[64]

Failure to comply with an applicable safety statute or administrative regulation makes the product defective with respect to the risks addressed by the law or rule (Restatement (3rd) § 4). However, a product that complies with the applicable rulings can still be defective.

Section 6 defines a prescription drug or medical device as unsafe if its foreseeable harm exceeds its benefits, to the point that a reasonable practitioner would not prescribe or recommend it. A medical item can become unsafe through manufacturing defect, design defect, or failure to warn. Direct warnings (such as patient package inserts) may be necessary even if the end user consults a "learned intermediary" (prescribing doctor).

Restatement (3rd) § 7 deals with defects in food products; § 8 covers used products, including those that have been re-manufactured.

Even if the product itself is not defective, § 9 makes sellers and distributors liable for damages caused by misrepresentations (even if innocent) of material

---

[64] Johnson v. American Standard Inc., 43 Cal. 4th 56 (Cal. 2008); Mike McKee, *Calif. Supreme Court Ruling Gives Manufacturers Added Protection From Lawsuits*, The Recorder 4/4/08 (law.com).

facts about the product. Section 12 covers the liability of successor corporations; §16 deals with "enhanced" harm when the product defect interacts with other factors; and §17 deals with the effect of the plaintiff's negligence, misuse, or alteration of the product on products liability.

The Restatement (3rd)'s version of the res ipsa doctrine is the "indeterminate product defect test": even without proof of a specific defect, an inference can be drawn that harm was caused by a product defect if the harm-producing incident was of a type ordinarily resulting from a product defect and not solely traceable to other causes.

[D] Preemption Issues

NOTE: As a result of The Class Action Fairness Act of 2005, P.L. 109-2 (see §18.15), most class actions seeking $5 million or more in damages must be heard in federal rather than state court if more than one-third of the plaintiffs have the same citizenship as the primary defendant.

The Food and Drug Administration (FDA) has a procedure for approving medical devices before they are placed on the market, pursuant to the Medical Device Amendments Act. Under *Medtronic Inc. v. Lohr*,[65] the fact that a medical device has received FDA approval does not preclude claims against the manufacturer for defective design of the device. The Eleventh Circuit has extended *Lohr* by permitting state products liability claims against a pacemaker manufacturer, on the theory that premarket approval deals with the minimal safety requirements for products that can be sold to the public, not the liability standards that apply to devices once they are on the market.[66]

In its February 20, 2008 decision in *Riegel v. Medtronic Inc.*, the Supreme Court held that as long as a medical device has received pre-market approval from the FDA, the Medical Device Amendment's preemption clause prevents plaintiffs from using the state courts to challenge the safety or effectiveness of a medical device. Common-law claims are preempted because they impose requirements that are in addition to, or differ from, the federal safety and effectiveness requirements. The device in this case, a catheter that ruptured during heart surgery, is a Class III medical device, which can be marketed only after the FDA's most extensive level of review.[67]

In January 2006, the FDA published rules increasing the number of prescription drug cases in which state failure-to-warn claims would be preempted. The FDA's rationale is that it is solely responsible for setting the requirements for prescription drug labels, so a label that is different, even if it provides a greater quantum of information, would have to be treated as false or misleading. The Northern District of California used this rationale to dismiss state-law claims about the labeling of arthritis drugs Bextra and Celebrex, but the District Court

---

[65] 518 U.S. 470 (1996).

[66] Goodlin v. Medtronic Inc., 167 F.3d 1367 (11th Cir. 1999).

[67] No. 06-179.

for the District of New Jersey and the Eastern District of Pennsylvania ruled that the state labeling requirements did not conflict with federal law.[68]

The courts responded in various ways to the FDA's position (in the preamble to drug labeling rules published June 30, 2006) that federal approval of a drug preempted state-law failure to warn actions.[69]

In September 2007, the Supreme Court agreed to hear a case on preemption of state law in pharmaceutical products liability. Michigan plaintiffs brought suit alleging injuries from Rezulin, a diabetes drug that was taken off the market by the FDA in March 2000. In 2005, the District Court dismissed the suit under a Michigan law forbidding liability suits against FDA-approved pharmaceuticals. The statute contains an exception if the pharmaceutical company was guilty of misrepresentation in the information submitted to the FDA. The District Court invalidated that provision on the grounds of federal preemption. The Second Circuit reinstated the suit, holding that the state law was not preempted, causing a circuit split. The Supreme Court split 4-4, affirming the lower court. Justice Roberts recused himself because of his stock ownership in the parent company of the defendant drug company. Because of the 4-4 split, the Supreme Court ruling was not precedential, but Supreme Court has agreed to hear a case dealing with a similar issue.[70]

At the end of 2002, the Supreme Court decided that the Federal Boat Safety Act does not preempt state tort actions with respect to injuries that are allegedly attributable to a boat manufacturer's failure to install propeller guides.[71]

The Supreme Court's February 2001 ruling in *Buckman Co. v. Plaintiffs' Legal Committee*[72] is that state courts are not the proper forum for claims that a manufacturer defrauded the FDA in its application for exemption from pre-market approval of a medical device. The FDA's regulatory role in policing fraud means that such cases are subject to implied preemption by the Medical Device Amendments to the FDA Act.

In late 2007, the Supreme Court ruled that the Federal Aviation Administration Authorization Act (FAAAA) preempts the Maine law against Internet sale of

---

[68] 71 FR 3921 (1/24/06); the FDA reaffirmed this position in the Preamble to drug labeling rules published June 30, 2006. *see* Stephanie A. Scharf, *New Rulings in Drug Cases Highlight Debate over Pre-Emption*, special to law.com 10/25/06.

[69] Pennsylvania Employees Benefit Trust Fund, et al. v. Zeneca Inc. 499 F.3d 239 (3d Cir. 2007); *see* Shannon P. Duffy, *In Win for Drug Manufacturers, 3rd Circuit Rules Only FDA Can Regulate Ads*, The Legal Intelligencer 8/22/07 (law.com).

[70] Warner-Lambert v. Kent, 128 S. Ct. 1168 (2008); *see* Christopher S. Rugaber (AP), *Supreme Court to Address Pharmaceutical Companies' Protection From State Suits* 9/27/07 (law.com); *Roberts' Recusal Is Poison Pill for Drug Case Before Supreme Court*, Legal Times 3/4/08 (law.com). The case to be heard in 2009 is Levine v. Wyeth, 129 S. Ct. 337, 172 L. Ed. 2d 14 (2008).

[71] Sprietsma v. Mercury Marine, 537 U.S. 51 (2002). *See also* Busch v. Ansell Perry Inc., 73 L.W. 1656 (W.D. Ky. 3/8/05) finding failure-to-warn claims about latex gloves were preempted, but design-defect claims were not, because there are no FDA design requirements and the gloves had not gone through the intensive pre-approval testing process.

[72] 531 U.S. 341 (2001).

tobacco to minors, which requires carriers to verify that packages of tobacco products were sent by licensed retailers, and that the purchasers are adults.[73]

According to the Third Circuit, the Federal Insecticide Fungicide and Rodenticide Act (FIFRA; 7 U.S.C. § 136 *et seq.*) preempts claims that a manufacturer did not provide proper labeling about the way a product should be opened and stored. However, FIFRA does not preempt claims of negligent packaging of the product. FIFRA is broad enough to cover the labeling issue, but not the packaging claim, because the EPA packaging regulations (40 CFR § 157.20) are limited to child safety. The plaintiff alleged injuries to her throat, lungs, and breathing occurring when she opened a container of chlorine tablets for swimming pools. She claimed that the manufacturer should have warned of the risk of off-gassing if the product decomposed, and should have changed the packaging to eliminate or at least limit the risk.[74]

A 2005 Supreme Court significantly limits the range of federal preemption of farmers' state-law tort claims for harm allegedly caused by pesticides and herbicides, on the grounds that defective design, defective manufacture, negligent testing, and breach of warranty are not requirements for packaging and labeling. To be preempted, a state rule must impose packaging or labeling requirements different from, or in addition to, those set out in FIFRA. Below, the Fifth Circuit adopted the defense argument that the suit was preempted because a victory by the plaintiffs would probably lead to a change in labeling. The Supreme Court, however, ruled that state suits and jury verdicts are not "requirements" as defined by FIFRA. The defective design and manufacture, negligent testing, and breach of express warranty claims were held not to be preempted. The fraud and failure to warn claims were remanded, because they are more closely related to labeling requirements.[75]

The Third Circuit ruled that federal preemption occurs only when federal law conflicts with state law, not in all instances in which a federal agency has studied or considered an issue. Hence, the FDA's decision to issue a non-binding warning to consumers about risks of mercury in tuna, but not to regulate mercury levels, did not preempt California regulation of mercury levels. The FDA's decision not to require federal warnings did not preclude states from imposing a duty to warn.[76]

[E] Tobacco Issues

The dangers of smoking have long been known, and litigation about the ill effects of cigarettes has continued for decades, involving issues such as the accuracy of cigarette labeling and the relative safety of cigarettes described as "light." The important issues in tobacco litigation include the propriety of class certification for various charges, and the availability and especially the size of punitive damage awards.

---

[73] Rowe v. New Hampshire Motor Transport Ass'n, et al., 128 S. Ct. 989 (2008).

[74] Hawkins v. Leslie's Pool Mart Inc., 184 F.3d 244 (3d Cir. 1999).

[75] Bates v. Dow Agrosciences LLC, 544 U.S. 431 (2005).

[76] Fellner v. Tri-Union Seafoods, LLC, 539 F.3d 237 (3d Cir. 2008).

In March 2000, the Supreme Court ruled that the FDA does not have authority to regulate tobacco products. The FDA's theory was that nicotine is a drug delivered in the form of cigarettes, thus supporting its right to regulate. But to the Supreme Court, Congress already has a comprehensive statutory scheme for coping with tobacco health risks, and the FDA does not fit into it. The Supreme Court noted that adopting the FDA analysis would require suppression of cigarettes, which remain legal. Furthermore, the FDA position, upheld for many years, was that the agency lacked authority to regulate tobacco unless the manufacturers made health claims in favor of tobacco.[77]

Many state cases have been filed charging that it is misleading to call a cigarette "low tar," "light," or "mild." The Federal Cigarette Labeling and Advertising Act forbids state requirements about the advertising or promotion of cigarettes, so the extent of its preclusive effect must be determined. In December 2008, the Supreme Court ruled that the Federal Cigarette Labeling and Advertising Act did not preempt state-law fraud claims. The rationale for the decision was that preemption is generally disfavored when the wording of an express preemption clause will support more than one plausible meaning. The Supreme Court deemed the purpose of Labeling Act to be informing the public about the health risks of smoking. Fraud claims are not expressly preempted, because an allegation that a duty not to deceive has been violated is not based on the health dangers of smoking.[78]

The Supreme Court ruled that a suit charging Philip Morris with deceiving consumers about the health effects of light cigarettes must be tried in Arkansas state court and cannot be removed. The plaintiffs charged that two brands of cigarettes were not as low in tar and nicotine as advertised. The Supreme Court rejected the argument that FTC regulation of cigarettes is so pervasive that removal to federal court is mandatory.[79]

The Ninth Circuit ruled in mid-2006 that a cigarette company cannot defend against a warranty of merchantability claim by asserting that the plaintiff's decision to smoke was unreasonable, because the argument that a plaintiff chose to use a product known to be dangerous or defective presumes that the product is reasonably

---

[77] FDA v. Brown & Williamson Tobacco Co., 529 U.S. 120 (2000).

[78] Altria Group v. Good, No. 07-562 (12/15/08). The nominal subject matter of Rowe v. New Hampshire Motor Transport Association, 128 S. Ct. 989, decided February 20, 2008, was cigarettes, although in essence it is a preemption case. The Supreme Court held that Maine laws, imposing conditions intended to prevent sale of tobacco to minors, are preempted by the Federal Aviation Administration Authorization Act (FAAAA), which forbids states to enact or enforce laws dealing with motor carriers' price, service, or routes. The Supreme Court found that the state laws were closely enough connected to motor carrier services to interfere with federal regulation. The Maine law imposed too heavy a burden on carriers, placing them at risk of liability unless they checked every package to make sure there was no unlicensed tobacco inside. The Supreme Court rejected Maine's argument that it passed the laws to promote public health, because there is no public health exception to federal preemption under the FAAAA.

[79] Andrew DeMillo (AP), *Supreme Court: Philip Morris Cannot Move Case to Federal Court Based on FTC Regulation*, 6/12/07 (law.com).

safe under normal circumstances — which is not true of cigarettes. However, the Ninth Circuit left open the possibility of asserting the defense if the consumer's unreasonable conduct was overwhelming — e.g., continuing to smoke after a diagnosis of lung disease.[80]

In the First Circuit's view, there was no independent duty to warn non-English-speaking residents of Puerto Rico of the health hazards of smoking, because the hazards were common knowledge. A professor of Caribbean social history testified that the hazards were well-known in the 1950s and 1960s.[81]

The Supreme Court's February 20, 2007 decision in Philip Morris USA v. Williams[82] was the court's first punitive damages case since *Campbell* in 2003. The *Williams* case invalidated a $79.5 million punitive damage award in a wrongful death smoking case where compensatory damages were $821,000; even as reduced on appeal, the punitive damages were 39 times the compensatory damages. The Oregon trial court reduced the punitive damages to $32 million for excessiveness and subjected the compensatory damages to the statutory cap on noneconomic damages. The Court of Appeals reinstated the punitive damages. There was a remand after *Campbell*, and the state Supreme Court reinstated the entire punitive damage award, comparing the tobacco industry's conduct to second-degree manslaughter. The Supreme Court said that states are not justified in basing massive punitive damage awards on injuries to persons who are not parties to the litigation, although it is proper for jurors to consider harm to non-parties in assessing whether the defendant's conduct was reprehensible. In terms of litigation implications, it is possible that FRE 403 can be used to exclude evidence about harm to others, on the grounds that its probative value is outweighed by potential prejudice. Defense attorneys can seek a motion in limine to exclude evidence of conduct that is not similar, and can preserve their objections to admission of evidence of harm to non-parties.[83]

After rejecting the $79.5 million punitive damage award twice (and Oregon reinstating it twice) the Supreme Court announced in mid-2008 that it would review the award once again. The third time around, the only remaining issues are whether the Oregon Supreme Court ignored the ruling that the award must reflect only the damages to the individual plaintiff, not other smokers with similar claims, and whether the size of the award is constitutionally permitted. The state of Oregon has a significant interest

---

[80] Haglund v. Philip Morris Inc., No. 03-56499 (9th Cir. 5/17/06).

[81] Cruz-Vargas v. R.J. Reynolds Tobacco Co., 348 F.3d 271 (1st Cir. 2003). *See also* Alvarez v. R.J. Reynolds Tobacco Co., 405 F.3d 36 (1st Cir. 2005). The First Circuit affirmed judgment for the defense in a wrongful death action, in that no reasonable jury could have found that the general public in Puerto Rico in 1960, when the decedent started smoking, could have been unaware of the dangers of smoking. The plaintiff's evidence failed to show failure to warn or design defect to be the proximate cause of the decedent's lung cancer death.

[82] 549 U.S. 346 (2007).

[83] Tony Mauro, *High Court Rejects $79.5 Million Award in Philip Morris Case*, Legal Times 2/21/06 (law.com); Tracy M. Braun and Thalia L. Myrianthopoulos, *"Philip Morris" Decision May Be Hazardous to Jurors' Comprehension*, Special to law.com (5/15/07).

in the litigation, because 60% of punitive damages go to the state crime victim fund, and the award, including interest, is close to $143 million.[84]

However, the Oregon court that imposed tremendous punitive damages on the tobacco industry rejected a class action for medical monitoring costs for smokers whose health had not yet suffered. Suit was filed on behalf of about 400,000 citizens of Oregon, charging the tobacco companies with negligence because they knew or should have known cigarettes contained harmful substances, and should pay for tests to detect small (and still treatable) lung tumors.[85]

A $580 million appellate fund was created in Engle v. Liggett, 945 So.2d 1246 (Fla. 2006) to avoid a challenge to the state law that changed the rules for appellate bonds. Smokers who registered in time were given a chance to prove four elements: that they smoked, were addicted to cigarettes, resided in Florida, and had a smoking-related illness before November 21, 1996. Prior law would have required cigarette makers to pay 115% of the verdict to appeal. As of mid-2008, there were also 8,000 "Engle progeny" cases by individual smokers seeking compensatory damages from cigarette makers.[86] Subsequently, federal judges in Miami, Tampa, and Jacksonville struck down part of a Florida Supreme Court decision and dissolved a statewide tobacco class action. However, future plaintiffs can continue to use the Miami jury's findings on industry negligence in 23-smoking related illnesses in future personal injury suits against cigarette makers. About 4,000 "Engle progeny" cases remained viable: approximately 600 cases filed in federal court, 3,400 cases filed in state court but removed by the defendants.[87]

Early in 2008, the Supreme Court denied the tobacco industry's request that the Supreme Court intervene in a suit brought by smokers in West Virginia charging the tobacco industry with secretly agreeing to keep safer cigarettes off the market, while falsely claiming that their own brands were safe. The "reverse bifurcation" trial procedure (which has also been used in asbestos and phen-fen cases) requires the jury to determine if punitive damages will be awarded to smokers as a group, before setting the compensation for any individual smoker. Another jury addresses each plaintiff's unique issues. In practice, this procedure is seldom used in full, because settlements are common.

---

[84] Philip Morris USA v. Williams, No. 07-1216, (AP), *Supreme Court Will Again Review $79.5M Punitive Damages Award Against Philip Morris*, 6/10/08 (law.com); Tim Fought (AP), *Oregon High Court Reaffirms $79.5 Million Award in Philip Morris Case*, 2/1/08 (law.com). When arguments were heard in December 2008, Chief Justice Roberts hinted that the case could be resolved by dealing with broader constitutional questions. If the other justices agree, both sides would probably be asked for additional written arguments, with another hearing scheduled in the spring of 2009. *See* Mark Sherman (AP), *High Court Hears $79.5 Million Philip Morris Punitives Case for Third Time*, 12/4/08 (law.com).

[85] *See* William McCall (AP), *Ore. Court Rejects Medical Costs Claim on Tobacco Industry*, 5/2/08 (law.com).

[86] Billy Shields, *40,000 Claims Filed for $580 Million Smokers' Trust Fund*, Daily Business Review 6/17/08 (law.com).

[87] Billy Shields, *Federal Judges: Fla. High Court Got It Wrong in Historic Tobacco Case*, Daily Business Review 9/10/08 (law.com).

The Supreme Court accepted the smokers' argument that Supreme Court involvement would prolong the case to the point that many of the plaintiffs would die before it could be resolved.[88]

Public hospital districts could not use either RICO or the antitrust laws to force tobacco manufacturers to pay the otherwise unreimbursed costs of tobacco-related illnesses. The Ninth Circuit ruled that nexus was not shown between the injury and the defendants' conduct.[89] Nor could asbestos companies look to tobacco companies to indemnify them against some of the liability of the asbestos manufacturers to asbestos-exposed persons who also smoked, finding that the connection was too remote to support a recovery.[90]

In 2008, the Second Circuit reversed certification of a class of cigarette smokers who claimed they were deceived into believing that light cigarettes were healthier than conventional ones. The Second Circuit ruled out (b)(3) certification because individual issues outweigh issues subject to common proof. Because the claims were stated as RICO fraud claims, each plaintiff would have to prove reliance, injury and damages, with the additional complication that an undetermined number of the claims would be time-barred.[91]

[F] Gun Issues

Under some circumstances, gun sales are legal, and in most instances, guns perform as they are designed to do, raising many complex tort issues that interact with questions about the proper interpretation of the Second Amendment. In mid-2008, the Supreme Court ruled definitively that the Second Amendment protects individual and not collective or militia rights to possess weapons, invalidating the District of Columbia's ban on handguns and its requirement of trigger locks on other firearms. The court held that, like any other right, the Second Amendment right is not unlimited, and is not a right to keep and carry any weapon at any time for any purpose. Prohibitions on concealed weapons are acceptable, as are bans on guns in schools or government buildings and controls on weapon ownership by felons or the mentally ill.[92]

However, most gun cases involve products liability rather than constitutional issues and principles.

---

[88] Philip Morris USA v. Accord, 128 S. Ct. 1447 (2008); *see* (AP), *Justices Side With West Virginia Smokers in Lawsuit Against Tobacco Companies*, 2/25/08 (law.com).

[89] Association of Washington Public Hosp. Districts v. Philip Morris Inc., 241 F.3d 696 (9th Cir. 2001). The Eighth Circuit would not permit an HMO to sue tobacco companies to recover the amount the HMO claimed it spent to treat its subscribers' tobacco-related illnesses; the Eighth Circuit found that the HMO's cost estimate was purely speculative: Group Health Plan Inc. v. Philip Morris USA Inc., 344 F.3d 753 (8th Cir. 2003).

[90] Owens Corning v. R.J. Reynolds Tobacco Co., 868 So. 2d 331 (Miss. 2004); Lane v. R.J. Reynolds Tobacco Co., 853 So. 2d 1144 (Miss. 2003) precludes all tobacco products liability cases, including those brought by manufacturers of other substances identified as dangerous.

[91] McLaughlin v. Philip Morris USA, Inc., 522 F.3d 215 (2d Cir. 2008).

[92] District of Columbia v. Heller, 128 S. Ct. 1695 (2008); *see* Tony Mauro, *Supreme Court Strikes Down D.C. Gun Ban*, Legal Times 6/27/08 (law.com).

The Ninth Circuit ruled in 2003 that individual victims of gun violence could sue manufacturers, using the theory that the manufacturer oversaturated the law enforcement market, making the weapon prestigious among lawbreakers.[93] On a related issue, the Sixth Circuit ruled that families of a victim of gun violence do not have a cause of action against the producers and distributors of entertainment media with violent content; there is no duty to avoid desensitizing viewers to violence.[94]

Since the beginning of the twenty-first century, many cases have been brought by various states and municipalities, with the government units attempting to impose liability on gun manufacturers for the medical and law enforcement costs of gun crimes. The theory is that manufacturers negligently permit guns to be acquired outside legitimate channels, resulting in societal costs.[95]

When the Supreme Court re-convened in October 2005, one of the actions of the first day of term was to refuse to rule out further litigation of the District of Columbia's attempt to impose liability on allegedly negligent gun manufacturers for firearms violence. This topic, however, was rendered moot by the passage, later that month, of federal legislation immunizing the gun industry against suits brought by jurisdictions seeking reimbursement for the costs of gun crime.[96]

---

[93] Ileto v. Glock Inc., 349 F.3d 1191 (9th Cir. 2003).

[94] James v. Meow Media Inc., 300 F.3d 683 (6th Cir. 2002).

[95] See, e.g., City of New York v. Beretta USA Corp., 401 F. Supp. 2d 244 (E.D.N.Y. 2004) (public nuisance suit against gun manufacturers stated a cause of action.) The Second Circuit dismissed New York City's gun suit, based on the Protection of Lawful Commerce in Arms Act, 15 USC § 7901–7903, which insulates gun makers from liability. The Second Circuit ruled that the New York public nuisance law is not an exception to the statute. New York City said that suppliers failed to monitor private sales and gun shows, resulting in second degree criminal nuisance. The Second Circuit found that the federal law was a valid exercise of Congressional power under the Commerce Clause: City of NY v. Beretta USA Corp., 524 F.3d 384 (2d Cir. 2008); see Mark Hamblett, *2nd Circuit Dismisses NYC's Suit Against Gun Manufacturers*, N.Y.L.J. 5/1/08 (law.com). The case of City of New York v. A-1 Jewelry & Pawn Inc., No. 06-cv-2233, 2238 [dealing with knowing or negligent sales to straw buyers] continued, but just before the scheduled opening arguments, the Eastern District of New York granted a motion for default judgment: see Mark Fass, *New York City Prevails in Gun Shop Nuisance Case* N.Y.L.J. 6/3/08 (law.com) The last of 27 out-of-state gun dealers reached a settlement with New York City in September 2008, agreeing to a 10-point program to reduce illegal sales, including videotaping all firearms transactions and maintaining a computerized gun tracking system: Mark Fass, *NYC Settles Last Suit With Out-of-State Gun Dealer*, N.Y.L.J. 9/25/08 (law.com).

For gun litigation in Illinois, see Chicago v. Beretta USA Corp., 213 Ill. 2d 351 (2004), rejecting a public nuisance claim based on the theory that the gun industry knew that guns would be re-sold to urban criminals. Young v. Bryco Arms, No. 93678 (Ill. 11/18/04), a suit for damages by private individuals for deaths caused by illegal weapons in Chicago, was also dismissed; Philadelphia v. Beretta USA Corp., 277 F.3d 415 (3d Cir. 2002), the city's claims dismissed for lack of proximate cause; manufacturers have no duty to protect citizens from unlawful gun use, and municipal claims are too remote, speculative, and derivative to be sustained.

[96] Beretta v. District of Col., 546 U.S. 928, discussed in Gina Holland (AP), *Supreme Court Refuses to Block Lawsuit Against Gun Manufacturers* (10/4/05); Laurie Kellman (AP) *Congress Passes Lawsuit Shield for Gun Industry* (10/21/04) (law.com).

[G] Pharmaceuticals and Medical Devices

Litigation about pharmaceuticals and medical devices is particularly difficult, not only because of preemption issues but because of difficulties in getting a class certified against objections that plaintiffs' medical condition and experience are too diverse to support a class action. Furthermore, a growing number of cases holds that once the FDA has approved a drug or medical device, various kinds of state claims will be preempted.

In recent years, cases involving the combination diet drug "fen-phen" (fenfluramine and phentermine) were common, leading to some major rulings and settlements.[97]

---

[97] *See, e.g.*, Petito v. A.H. Robins Co., 750 So. 2d 103 (Fla. Dist. App. 3d Dist. 1999). *In re* Diet Drugs Prods. Liab. Litigation, 69 L.W. 1136 (E.D. Pa. 8/28/00). In May 2001, the Third Circuit approved the fen-phen settlement; approval became final in January 2002, when the appeals deadline expired. Late in 2005, the Third Circuit ruled that three groups of appellants were bound by the settlement: *In re* Diet Drugs Prods. Liab. Litigation, 431 F.3d 141 (3d Cir. 2005) *In re* Briscoe, 448 F.3d 201 (3d Cir. 2006). In the fen-phen "super-mega-fund" class action, attorneys from over 70 firms were awarded more than $412 million in fees; interim fees of more than $156 million had already been awarded in 2002. The original settlement, for $3.75 billion, allowed individual litigation by class members even after their participation in the original settlement, if their health deteriorated. There was a matrix of benefits ranging from about $8,000 to more than $1.6 million. About 205,000 class members received echocardiograms; 386,000 got refunds of the amount they spent on diet drugs, 5,098 received matrix benefits, 47,000 got medical services, and about 60,000–70,000 plaintiffs opted out and received compensation for injuries. *See* Shannon P. Duffy, *$412 Million in Attorney Fees Awarded to Plaintiffs Lawyers in Fen-Phen Litigation*, The Legal Intelligencer 4/10/08 (law.com).

In May 2008, a Texas court reversed a $26 million verdict against Merck (originally $253 million, but reduced because of the state's cap on punitive damages), holding that there was no evidence that the decedent's heart attack was caused by a Vioxx-induced blood clot. On the same day, a New Jersey appellate court reduced a $13.9 million award to $4.9 million in John McDarby's case, holding that the New Jersey Product Liability Act was preempted by the federal Food Drug and Cosmetic Act, and upholding a verdict for Merck in the case of heart attack survivor Thomas Cona. [Jeffrey Gold (AP), *N.J. and Texas Courts Scrap Awards From Early Vioxx Cases*, 5/29/08 (law.com).] *See also* Mary Alice Robbins, *Texas Appeals Court Does About-Face in Vioxx Case*, Texas Lawyer 12/12/08 (law.com), when *Garza*, one of the early Vioxx cases, was reversed and remanded for new trial because of juror misconduct. Texas' Fourth Circuit Court of Appeals reversed the earlier holding that the plaintiff's pre-existing heart problems could not be ruled out. The Fourth Circuit found that the plaintiff presented legally sufficient evidence that his heart attack was caused by Vioxx, and could support a marketing defect claim (that doctors did not receive enough warnings about the heart risks of Vioxx) but the Fourth Circuit found for Merck on the design defect claim.

A fen-phen suit in Texas resulted in a $1 billion verdict ($900 million of that in punitive damages) in 2004. The defendant appealed; both sides settled in April, 2007 to set aside the trial court judgment and remand the case to trial court to consider a take-nothing judgment and a settlement for minor plaintiffs. The jury awarded almost $113 million in actual damages to a victim of primary pulmonary hypertension. The plaintiffs' theory was that she became ill because of Pondimin and other weight loss drugs. The settlement means that the parties will not have to determine the validity of the statutory cap (where punitives are limited to twice the compensatory damages plus an amount not to exceed $750,000). However, the jury also found knowing spoliation of evidence, so it is possible that the cap would not have applied because of the presence of a fraud cause: Coffey v.

More recently, Vioxx cases have dominated the dockets. There were about 27,000 Vioxx suits nationwide, more than 15,000 of them filed in New Jersey (headquarters of defendant Merck). By March, 2007, there had been 15 Vioxx trials, resulting in 10 defense and only five plaintiffs' verdicts. When the defense prevailed, it used arguments such as provision of adequate warnings (e.g., compliance with FDA requirements) and lack of causation (e.g., Vioxx use stopped well before the plaintiff's heart attack; the plaintiff was generally in poor health).

In mid-2008, Merck entered into a $58 million multistate settlement of claims that Vioxx advertisements deceptively failed to disclose health risks. Merck agreed to permit the FDA to review all new commercials before they air, and also agreed to end the practice of medical "ghostwriting" (where scientists put their names on articles actually written by Merck's own medical writers). Twenty-nine states are involved in the settlement; each has discretion about how to apply its share of the settlement (for example, for consumer protection funds or litigation costs).[98]

The New Jersey Supreme Court held that Merck did not have to provide medical monitoring for Vioxx users who did not claim an existing injury, leading to dismissal of a class action brought by asymptomatic users.[99]

In 2002, Pfizer began to settle suits about the painkillers Celebrex and Betra. Over 3,000 claims about heart attacks and strokes were filed. Pfizer offered $40,000–$50,000 in Bextra cases and up to $200,000 in Celebrex cases.[100]

Pfizer agreed to settle approximately 92% of the Bextra lawsuits — about 7,000 cases — for $894 million, also covering Celebrex (the only drug out of Vioxx, Bextra, Celebrex still on the market). The agreement also covers insurers' and patients' suits to recover the cost of the drugs, and state attorney generals' claims of improper promotion. Of that amount, $745 million went toward the PI settlements, $89 million for reimbursement for consumer fraud, and $60 million to the Attorneys General of 33 states and the District of Columbia.[101]

Wyeth (Tex. App. settlement 2007). See Brenda Sapino Jeffreys, *$1 Billion Fen-Phen Case Settles Before Appellate Oral Arguments*, Texas Lawyer 4/16/07 (law.com). *See*, however, Amaris Elliott-Engle, *Jury Renders Defense Verdict in Diet Drug Case*, 10/24/08 (law.com), reporting a defense verdict in Crowder v. Wyeth, one of the last 100 remaining Pondimin cases. A jury in Philadelphia found a failure to prove by a preponderance of the evidence that Pondimin caused the decedent's heart valve disease. Punitive damages were already ruled out because in Pennsylvania, punitive damages cannot be imposed for failure to warn of risks of drugs prescribed in another state.

[98] Martha Raffaele (AP), *Merck Agrees to $58 Million Settlement Over Vioxx Ad Claims*, 5/21/08 (law.com); No by-line, *Merck Settles With States on Vioxx Ads*, N.Y. Times 5/21/08 at C3; Kevin Kingsbury, *Merck Will Pay $58 Million to Settle Vioxx Ad Claims*, Wall St. J. 5/21/08 at B3. The participating states are Arkansas, California, Connecticut, Florida, Hawaii, Idaho, Illinois, Iowa, Kansas, Maine, Maryland, Massachusetts, Michigan, Nebraska, Nevada, New Jersey, North Carolina, North Dakota, Ohio, Oregon, Pennsylvania, South Carolina, South Dakota, Tennessee, Texas, Vermont, Washington, and Wisconsin.

[99] No by-line, *Merck Wins Suit on Vioxx Monitoring*, Wall St. J. 6/5/08 at D8; Jeffrey Gold (AP), *Merck Need Not Monitor Vioxx Users Not Claiming Injury*, 6/4/08 (law.com).

[100] No by-line, *Pfizer Begins Settling Painkiller Cases*, N.Y. Times 5/3/08 at C8; Nathan Koppel and Heather Won Tesoriero, *Pfizer Settles Lawsuits Over Two Painkillers*, Wall St. J. 5/3–4/08 at A3.

[101] Linda A. Johnson (AP), *$894 Million Deal Ends Pain of Pfizer's Lawsuits*, 10/20/08 (law.com).

Hormone replacement therapy (HRT) for women is another growing litigation area; estrogen formulations such as Wyeth's Prempro have been accused of
causing breast cancer. As of early 2008, there were more than 5,000 suits pending
involving the drugs Premarin and Prempro. In 1992, the FDA required breast
cancer warnings for estrogen products but not for progestin products. A Little
Rock woman who suffered breast cancer after receiving hormone replacement
therapy was awarded $27 million by a federal jury: $19.3 million from Wyeth
and $7.7 million from Upjohn. The previous month, the jury awarded her $2.75
million in compensatory damages. However, a $3 million jury award in an HRT
case was overturned by the judge. In 2007, three Nevada women were awarded
$134 million ($35 million compensatory, $99 million punitive), but in February
2008, the judge reduced this amount to approximately $58 million ($23 million
compensatory, $35 million punitive damages), finding the original award excessive
and the result of passion and prejudice.[102]

However, in mid-2008, two HRT breast cancer cases in New Jersey were
dismissed, with negative implications for the other 168 pending cases in that state.
The judge handling all the New Jersey cases ruled that the plaintiffs failed to rebut
the presumption of adequate labeling imposed by the state's Products Liability Act.
Warnings approved by the FDA are presumed adequate, and proof of intentional
misconduct is required to rebut the presumption.[103]

In a major victory for drug companies, the Third Circuit ruled in the spring of
2008 that the manufacturers of Paxil and Zoloft cannot be sued for failure to warn
of suicide risk. The FDA refused to order such a warning, so giving the warning
would conflict directly with an FDA action. However, the Third Circuit majority
limited its holding to the circumstances where the FDA has rejected a warning that
the plaintiff sought.[104]

Mississippi ruled in 2004 that the trial court abused its discretion by allowing
joinder of 56 plaintiffs in litigation over a drug for acid reflux. There was no single
transaction that connected all 56 plaintiffs and the 42 physicians named as defendants. Each doctor/patient dyad generated a unique set of facts, precluding the
satisfaction of state requirements for permissive joinder.[105]

In June, 2007, a Court of Federal Claims tribunal consisting of three Special
Masters heard arguments in the case of *Cedillo v. Sec'y of HHS*, the first judicial
proceeding dealing with the often-advanced argument that the thimerosal

---

[102] Andrew DeMillo (AP), *Jury Orders Wyeth, Upjohn to Pay Arkansas Woman $27 Million in
Hormone Suit*, 3/7/08 (law.com); Scott Sonner (AP), *Judge Slashes $134 Million Judgment Against
Wyeth*, 2/20/08 (law.com).

[103] Bailey v. Wyeth Inc., L-9999-06; *see* Mary Pat Gallagher, *N.J. Hormone Replacement Drug
Suits Dismissed Under Product Liability Act*, N.J.L.J. 7/15/08 (law.com); Andrew DeMillo (AP), *Jury
Orders Wyeth, Upjohn to Pay Arkansas Woman $27 Million in Hormone Suit*, 3/7/08 (law.com); Scott
Sonner (AP), *Judge Slashes $134 Million Judgment Against Wyeth*, 2/20/08 (law.com).

[104] Colacicco v. Apotex Inc./McNellis v. Pfizer Inc., 521 F.3d 253 (3d Cir. 2008); *see* Shannon
P. Duffy, *Suicide Warning Suits Pre-Empted; Makers of Paxil, Zoloft Win*, The Legal Intelligencer
4/9/08 (law.com).

[105] Janssen Pharmaceutica Inc. v. Armond, 866 So. 2d 1092 (Miss. 2004).

preservatives in vaccines cause autism. It was selected out of 4,800 claims as a test case to reduce the need for expert testimony and repetitive discovery. The case is a test of the vaccine compensation system created by Congress in 1986 to limit the liability of vaccine manufacturers while still compensating persons harmed by vaccines. Persons who allege injury sue the United States in the Court of Federal Claims rather than suing manufacturers, and the Special Masters have the power to award damages if a causal connection is established in an individual vaccine case. Lost earning, medical and educational expenses, and attorneys' fees can be awarded, but damages for pain and suffering are capped at $250,000. The autism-related claims are the largest group of vaccine claims: since 1999, 5100 autism claims were filed, versus 2,700 for all other vaccine claims.[106]

Plaintiffs who sued the manufacturers, distributors and others in the chain of distribution of allegedly defective bone screws did not present a cognizable conspiracy cause of action under the Food, Drug & Cosmetic Act. The plaintiffs claimed that manufacturers, distributors, doctors, and other health care professionals conspired to market and sell devices lacking the necessary FDA approval. As evidence, the plaintiffs cited intensive marketing of the devices to surgeons and incentives offered to the surgeons to use the devices.

The Eighth Circuit overturned certification of a national class of 11,000 recipients of allegedly faulty heart valves, on the grounds that each plaintiff must establish the link between reliance on claims about the value and his or her subsequent injury. Another panel of the Eighth Circuit previously rejected health monitoring for users of the Silzone heart valve, which was voluntarily recalled by its manufacturer based on claims that the valve's silver coating was defective.[107]

The Eleventh Circuit upheld summary judgment for the defendant manufacturer in a case in which a plaintiff accidentally administered an overdose of morphine to her mother with a morphine pump. The rationale was that the manufacturer has no duty to warn patients or third parties about the dangers of use by persons other than doctors or patients — in other words, the learned intermediary rule applies to medical devices as well as drugs. (The plaintiff settled her suit against the hospital where the mother was being treated for $8 million.)[108]

According to the Third Circuit, there was no Federal Tort Claims Act cause of action against the FDA for approving the allegedly defective bone screws, because ruling that a new Class III medical device is "substantially equivalent" to an approved device is a discretionary function exempt from the coverage of the FTCA.[109]

---

[106] Tony Mauro, *Test Case Linking Vaccines and Autism Reaches Federal Court*, Legal Times 6/5/07 (law.com). *See also* Moss v. Merck & Co., 381 F.3d 501 (5th Cir. 2004), because thimerosal is not a vaccine and not produced by a "vaccine manufacturer," the National Childhood Vaccine Injury Act does not prevent state court suits against thimerosal manufacturers.

[107] *In re*: St. Jude Medical, Inc., Silzone Heart Valve Products Liability Litigation, 522 F.3d 836 (8th Cir. 2008); *see* Pamela A. MacLean, *Reversal of Heart Valve Class Action Called 'Disturbing'*, Nat'l L.J. 4/15/08 (law.com).

[108] Ellis v. C.R. Bard Inc., 311 F.3d 1273 (11th Cir. 2002).

[109] *In re* Orthopedic Bone Screw Prods. Liab. Litigation, 264 F.3d 344 (3d Cir. 2001).

§ 18.11   PREMISES LIABILITY

Premises liability is liability of the owner or operator of premises — e.g., a store or office building — for injuries occurring on the property, caused by accidents or crimes. The question then becomes what the defendant's duty of care was, and whether it was satisfied.

Early in 2004, the Supreme Court decided a case involving a 1997 international flight. The wife of an asthmatic passenger asked to move him away from the smoking section of the plane. The flight attendant refused three times, and the passenger died. Under the Warsaw Convention, an airline is only liable for death or bodily injury occurring by "accident." The Supreme Court decided that this was an accident — that is, an unusual or unexpected event that was external to the passenger — rather than the passenger's idiosyncratic reaction to the expected operation of the aircraft. Where there has been a chain of events, the passenger can recover as long as any link in the chain (here, the flight attendant's repeated refusal to re-seat the passenger) is an accident. Although smoking on international flights may have been normal in 1997, repeated refusals to cooperate with a passenger's requests were not.[110]

California law does not impose a duty on the owner of premises (here, an underground parking garage) to hire security guards or otherwise prevent crimes by third parties (in this case, rape of the plaintiff) unless the owner is on notice because of a history of comparable crimes on the premises. The plaintiff introduced evidence of deteriorating conditions in the garage (dirt, broken security cameras, burned-out lights), but the court did not find this persuasive, on the grounds that better maintenance would not necessarily have deterred a rapist.[111]

California held that a landowner can be liable to an employee of an independent contractor, if the employee is injured by an unknown, hidden hazard. (In this case, it was asbestos.) Generally, a landlord has no duty to an independent contractor's employees, but failure to warn of a known hazardous condition can implicate the landlord.[112]

The Third Circuit joined the Fifth Circuit in applying the "sphere of control" test in premises liability cases, and thus dismissed a case brought by a man who became quadriplegic as a result of a bodysurfing accident in the Virgin Islands. The Third Circuit said that property owners have a duty to warn of unsafe conditions outside their premises only if the location is within the owner's sphere of control. The plaintiff therefore must either prove the property owner's legal right to control the area or that the owner intended to control the area. The plaintiff's theory was that

---

[110] Olympic Airways v. Husain, 540 U.S. 644 (2004). On another premises liability issue, the Supreme Court ruled in United States v. Olson, 546 U.S. 43 (2005) (negligence of federal mine inspectors allegedly helped cause a mining accident) that the Federal Tort Claims Act waives sovereign immunity only where local law would subject a private party to tort liability, not where local law would make a state or city liable.

[111] Sharon P. v. Arman Ltd., 91 Cal. Rptr. 2d 35 (1999).

[112] Kinsman v. Unocal Corp., 37 Cal. 4th 659 (2005).

the accident was caused by a dangerous "shorebreak" condition off the beach, where the water becomes shallow and increases the velocity of the waves, and that a warning was due because the condition would not have been apparent to a visitor. The Third Circuit ruled that the test is whether a hotel operator has enough control over adjacent property to be able to undertake protective measures to reduce risks; in this case, the National Park Service and not the hotel controlled the beach.[113]

The view of the California Supreme Court is that store owners become liable for injuries caused by spilled liquids on the premises (in this case, a puddle of milk in a KMart store) if they fail to remove the hazard with reasonable promptness. The plaintiff has the burden of proving failure to clean up in reasonable time.[114]

In December 2001, the Florida Supreme Court shifted the burden of proof, requiring the store to prove that it used reasonable care to keep floors clean, rather than requiring the plaintiff to prove that the store permitted a hazardous condition to continue when it should have been remedied. Often, a "15-minute rule" is applied — i.e., finding the store at fault for failing to detect and clean up the condition within that time.[115]

Public housing tenants do not have a private cause of action under the Lead Based Paint Poisoning Prevention Act or the U.S. Housing Act that would support a 42 USC § 1983 civil rights suit for poisoning damages to children allegedly stemming from the city's failure to abate lead paint hazards. According to the Sixth Circuit, the LBPPPA focuses on agency mandates, not individual rights, and the law does not contain the kind of rights-creating language that would be required to support a § 1983 claim.[116]

Employers are facing a new area of suit: harm allegedly caused by second-hand exposure to asbestos brought home on employee's clothes. Several cases permit suit by, e.g., homemakers who contracted mesothelioma after washing contaminated work clothes, although some cases reject liability, for example, on the grounds that the employer did not owe a duty of care to family members of employees. The defense bar suggests that these suits are being brought because the few remaining asbestos manufacturers tend to be bankrupt, so there is a desire to find viable, solvent defendants. New Jersey ruled in mid-2006 that landowners have an obligation to warn spouses of their workers of foreseeable risks of being exposed to asbestos when they wash workers' clothes. (New York and Georgia ruled to the contrary in 2005.) New Jersey held that it was negligent for an oil company to fail to warn of the known danger of bringing asbestos dust into a home; the duty of care to workers at a job site extends as needed to prevent foreseeable

---

[113] Fabend v. Rosewood Hotels & Resorts, 381 F.3d 152 (3d Cir. 2004), the Fifth Circuit precedent is Banks v. Hyatt Corp., 722 F.2d 214 (5th Cir. 1984).

[114] Ortega v. KMart Corp., 26 Cal. 4th 1200 (Cal. Sup. 2001); *but see* Saelzler v. Advanced Group, 25 Cal. 4th 763 (Cal. Sup. 2001) granting summary judgment for a building owner in a case brought by a delivery worker who suffered an assault on the premises.

[115] Susan R. Miller, *Slipping Straight to the Jury*, Miami Daily Business Review, 12/13/01 (law.com).

[116] Johnson v. Detroit, 446 F.3d 614 (6th Cir. 2006).

harm. Tennessee permitted a suit against the father's employer by the family of a woman who died at age 25 of asbestos-related mesothelioma after lifelong exposure to her father's asbestos-stained work clothes. The Tennessee Supreme Court held that the employer should have foreseen that negligent failure to prevent employees from taking home contaminated clothes would endanger non-employees. The employer failed to follow federally imposed preventive measures, and did not disclose risks.[117]

§ 18.12   TORT DEFENSES

The mere fact that the plaintiff has suffered loss or damage does not mean that the defendant is necessarily liable. The defendant's conduct must either have been intentional or must have failed to satisfy the standard of reasonableness. Furthermore, the defendant's conduct must have been the proximate cause of the injuries.

A recent Colorado decision holds that filing a personal injury suit waives physician-patient privilege in the plaintiff's medical and pharmaceutical records. However, the waiver is limited to records relevant to the injuries claimed in the suit. The party asserting privilege must submit an adequately detailed privilege log so that the opposing party can ask the court to review the challenged documents.[118]

The ten-year statute of repose under the Nebraska Products Liability Act applies notwithstanding any other statute, including tolling for infancy.[119]

[A] Contributory/Comparative Negligence

Traditionally, the concept of contributory negligence barred recovery by a plaintiff who had been negligent at all, in any degree. Because this led to harsh results in many cases, it has largely been replaced by the concept of comparative negligence (the recovery of a negligent plaintiff will be reduced in proportion to the degree of the plaintiff's negligence).

Depending on the circumstances and the jurisdiction, even a plaintiff who was almost entirely at fault may be entitled to a small recovery; or, recovery might

[117] Satterfield v. Breeding Insulation Co. (Tenn. Supp. 2008); Rebecca Moore, *Family of Child Who Died from Asbestos Exposure Since Birth Can Sue*, Plansponsor.com (9/12/08); Rochon v. SaberHagen Holdings Inc., No. 58579-I (Wash. App. 8/27/07); Chaisson v. Avondale Industries Inc., 947 So.2d 171 (La. App. 2006); Olivo v. Exxon Mobil, 377 N.J. Super. 286, 872 A.2d 814 (2005), *certification granted*, 185 N.J. 39, *contra* Holdampf v. AC&S Inc., 840 N.E.2d 115 (N.Y. 2005); CSX Transp. Inc. v. Williams 608 S.E.2d 208 (Ga. 2005). *See* Tresa Baldas, "Take-Home" *Asbestos Suits Go After Employers, Get Mixed Results*, Nat'l LJ 9/26/07 (law.com) and Michael Booth, *N.J. High Court: Companies Have Duty to Warn Workers' Spouses of Asbestos Dust*, N.J.L.J. 5/3/06 (law.com). Connecticut ruled that workplace toxins that are carried to the workers' homes and cars on their clothing are not released into the environment as defined by the federal environmental statute CERCLA (*see* § 11.03). Therefore, the CERCLA statute of limitations does not preempt the state statute of limitations for wrongful death of workers exposed to such toxins: Greco v. United Technologies Corp., 277 Conn. 337 (2006).
[118] Alcon v. Spicer, 113 P.3d 735 (Colo. 2005).
[119] Budler v. General Motors, 689 N.W.2d 847 (Neb. 2004).

be barred if the plaintiff was more than 50% responsible for the injury. Another variation is whether the plaintiff's negligence is a defense that must be pleaded and proved by the defendant, or whether the plaintiff's case includes proof of freedom from negligence. Whether or not the plaintiff was negligent is a fact issue, to be decided by the jury.

Although failure to wear a seat belt generally is not evidence of negligence under the mandatory seat belt law, the plaintiff's failure to wear a seat belt is admissible in a crashworthiness case. Even if they do not claim that a product defect caused the accident itself, plaintiffs who charge that a design defect exacerbated their injuries when they collided with the vehicles themselves are stating a crashworthiness claim.[120]

[B] Last Clear Chance

The "last clear chance" doctrine is a traditional attempt to avoid unfairness caused by strict application of contributory negligence concepts. This doctrine applies where the plaintiff was in a zone of danger because of his or her own negligence, but the defendant is nevertheless liable because the defendant had the last opportunity to avert the harm. The "discovered peril" rule is a variation that only comes into play if the defendant is aware of the risk to the plaintiff.

[C] Assumption of Risk

The affirmative defense of assumption of risk asserts that the plaintiff voluntarily chose to accept a risk caused by the defendant's known negligence. Assumption of risk can be done expressly, for instance by a release or disclaimer, or can be implied (e.g., going to a baseball game creates a risk of being hit by a fly ball). Implied assumption of risk is manifest consent to a voluntary encounter with risk, in full understanding of the danger.

This, too, is a fact question within the province of the jury. The test is subjective — the plaintiff's actual knowledge. The doctrine will not be applied in cases of obvious unfairness, or where the defendant committed an intentional tort or whose conduct was willful or wanton.

A New York intermediate-level court ruled that summary judgment was correctly granted in the case of an Olympic speed skater who suffered a spinal injury during training. The question was whether the padding on the boards complied with International Skating Union standards. There was no indication that the padding was damaged or defective, so it was held that the skater assumed the risk of an injury. On appeal, the case could raise questions of whether assumption of risk, continues to apply when facilities or equipment are defective.[121]

---

[120] Gable v. Gates Mills, 816 N.E.2d 1049 (Ohio 2004).

[121] Ziegelmayer v. United States Olympic Committee, No. 97705 (N.Y.A.D. 3d Dept. 2006); *see* John Caher, *Panel Rules Hurt Olympic Skater Assumed "Inherent Risk" of Sport*, N.Y.L.J. 5/1/06 (law.com).

According to the Hawaii Supreme Court, a golfer is not liable for accidentally hitting another golfer in the eye with a golf ball; the nature of the game is such that balls don't always go where directed. Shouting "fore" or another warning is golf etiquette but not a legal requirement. (The defendant said that he didn't see the victim's golf cart, so he did not shout "fore!")[122]

A New York lower-level court ruled that a mother injured by a bat swung in an off-field area during a Little League game assumed the risk of injury by voluntary proximity to the playing area. The improvised warm-up area was an open and obvious condition that could have been avoided by spectators with reasonable care; the risk of harm from being hit by a baseball bat was obvious.[123]

The New Jersey Supreme Court held that if a hockey arena satisfies its limited legal duty to protect spectators, it will not be liable to a person hit by a puck outside the shielded seating area — even if the injury occurred during a warm-up before the game started. The limited duty of care requires the arena to install screening in the areas where spectators are at greatest risk, with additional protected seating on request. New Jersey did not impose a separate duty to warn of the risks of objects flying off the field.[124]

[D] Consent

Consent (as long as the plaintiff had capacity to consent) is a defense against most torts. Consent can be manifested by silence and inaction in a situation in which a non-consenting person would be expected to protest. It can also be inferred from custom and usage. Consent is implied in some circumstances: for instance, to give medical treatment in an emergency to an unconscious person. Consent that stems from the plaintiff's ignorance, misunderstanding, or material mistake is nevertheless valid in the tort context, unless the defendant knew of the mistake or induced it through misrepresentation.

The defendant's mistake (even if not negligent) is not necessarily a defense to an intentional tort claim. However, mistake is often relevant to the existence of a privilege that insulates the defendant's actions from liability. Privilege could be asserted based on the defendant's reasonable belief about the state of facts, especially if the plaintiff induced the mistake.

[E] Self-Defense

Self-defense is a defense to claims of assault, battery or unlawful imprisonment, if the defendant acted to prevent a threat of unlawful confinement or even

---

[122] Yoneda v. Tom, 111 Haw. 12 (2006); *see* (AP), *Hawaii Supreme Court Rules Golfers Not Liable for Errant Balls* 5/17/06 (law.com).

[123] Roberts v. Boys and Girls Republic, Inc., No. 1860 (AD 1st Dept 2008), discussed in Noeleen G. Walder, *Spectator Hurt by Little League Batter Assumed Risk of Injury, Court Finds,* N.Y.L.J. 1/14/08 (law.com).

[124] Sciarrotta v. Global Spectrum, 194 N.J. 345 (N.J. 2008); Michael Booth, *N.J. High Court: Sport Arena Not Liable for Spectator's Pre-Game Injury,* N.J.L.J. 4/14/08 (law.com).

negligently caused harm. However, the defendant is justified in using only enough force as immediately necessary for self-protection and the protection of others. Reasonable force can be used in defense of property, but only if actual intrusion has occurred, or there is a threat of immediate interference with the defendant's possession of property.

Accidental injuries caused to third persons in the course of self-defense are analyzed on a negligence standard.

A limited self-help privilege is allowed for immediate forcible retaking of chattels that have been wrongfully taken by force, or that have been obtained by fraud or duress. This is the principle that authorizes reasonable detention of shoplifters and prevents it from constituting unlawful imprisonment.

§ 18.13 TORT DAMAGES

The basic elements of tort damages are property damage plus direct medical and surgical costs, plus past and future lost earnings, plus pain and suffering. Sometimes "hedonic" damages (for loss of quality of life) will be available. See § 18.10[E] for discussion of punitive damages in tobacco cases.

In a wrongful death case, the traditional measure of damages was pre-death pain and suffering of the victim,[125] plus income lost by the dependents of the decedent. Originally, lost income was the only recoverable element. Over time, additional elements were added.

Husbands of injured or deceased wives could recover for "consortium" (loss of households and sexual services). The loss-of-consortium action has become unisex, and has been extended to non-economic and non-sexual aspects of family relationships.

There is a trend toward permitting the children of decedents to recover for loss of emotional support and parental guidance, as well as for lost financial support, and parents may be able to recover for loss of companionship and perhaps economic loss when their children are injured or killed. (In some cases, even parents of adults will have a cause of action of this type.)

In April 2003, the Supreme Court held that, on proof that the fear is genuine and serious, railway workers who suffer from asbestosis can also recover damages for fear of developing asbestos-related cancer. The court also held that a railroad can be held fully liable for employment-related asbestos claims, even if other factors contributed to the diseases developed by the plaintiffs.[126]

The Supreme Court ruled in 2006 that state Medicaid programs violate federal law if they authorize the program to place a lien on a Medicaid recipient's

---

[125] There is a split in authority as to proper treatment of pre-death fright of a victim who dies instantly on impact. According to Beynon v. Montgomery Cablevision LP, 718 A.2d 1161 (Md. 1998), eight jurisdictions have allowed this element of damages, whereas four have denied it.

[126] Norfolk & Western Ry. Co. v. Ayers, 538 U.S. 135 (2003).

tort settlement in an amount that is greater than the part of the tort settlement that represents reimbursement for medical payments.[127]

[A] Shared Liability

In many situations involving multiple tortfeasors, liability will be joint and several. That is, the plaintiff has the option of suing any tortfeasor, all of them, or any combination of tortfeasors. Defendants can then bring in other potentially liable parties if they believe that it is unjust for them to stand trial without the others. Furthermore, if a judgment or verdict is granted, it is the plaintiff's option which defendant(s) to pursue for payment, although joint tortfeasors who pay more than their fair share are entitled to contribution from other liable parties in percentages reflecting the liability of the others.

Contribution has to be distinguished from indemnification. Contribution is sharing of the liability among defendants to reflect their relative culpability. Indemnification shifts the entire loss from one tortfeasor to another, because the relieved tortfeasor is entitled to indemnification by law or as a result of a contract. All jurisdictions allow indemnification, although some do not provide for contribution.

The basic rule is that all damages are to be recovered at once, in a single suit, to restore the plaintiff to pre-injury condition.

The "collateral source" rule permits plaintiffs to recover damages for medical expenses and time lost from work, even if the plaintiff did not pay for these out of pocket, and a "collateral source" (such as insurance or professional courtesy) made the actual payment.

The general rule is that tort plaintiffs have an obligation to mitigate damages, such as taking reasonable steps to treat injuries and prevent future harm to property. A minority of jurisdictions impose this requirement in advance of the injury, for instance by wearing a seat belt or helmet. If so, the defendant will not be liable for whatever percentage of the injury is attributable to the plaintiff's failure to take such steps.

Another general rule is that a prevailing party is entitled to receive attorneys' fees and litigation costs as an element of damages only if an applicable statute authorizes such an award. Otherwise, each party remains responsible for its own fees and costs.

[B] Structured Settlements

Tort settlements are frequently "structured," especially if the plaintiff is a child or incapacitated person. In a structured settlement, the plaintiff receives a series of annuity-type payments rather than a lump sum.[128] This is preferable for

---

[127] Arkansas Dep't of Health & Human Servs. v. Ahlborn, 547 U.S. 268 (2006).

[128] Lump sum verdicts are reduced to present value to reflect the interest to be earned in the future, but most jurisdictions do this only for the portion of the verdict related to past injuries and do not reduce damages for future non-economic harm such as pain and suffering expected to be experienced in the future, disability, and disfigurement.

the payor, of course, who can either continue managing the principal sum and make only the required payment each year, or who can purchase an annuity to make the payments. Structuring the settlement benefits a plaintiff who might otherwise do a poor job of managing a large sum, and therefore is better off with guaranteed income.

Structured settlements need to be handled carefully to assure that the correct fee is paid to the successful attorney who secured the settlement. If the plaintiff receives or has received Medicaid benefits (the health care program for the indigent), the settlement must be structured to preserve continuing benefit eligibility. It is extremely likely that at least part of the tort award will be subject to a high priority claim by the state Medicaid agency, to reimburse the agency for care provided after the injury and before the case was resolved.

[C] Measures of Damages

The recovery for harm (not tantamount to conversion) to personal property is either its pre-tort value minus its post-tort value, or the reasonable cost of repairing the property (even if this is greater than the original value), plus any residual diminution in its value, plus the cost or renting substitute property (or other damages for loss of use). However, the damages will be limited to the post-tort diminution of value in a situation in which a reasonable plaintiff would have written off the property and acquired replacement property.

For conversion, the measure of damages is the value at the time of conversion, plus interest since that time and damages proximately caused by loss of use.

For harm to real estate, the measure of damages is the loss of value of the property, or the reasonable cost of restoration plus loss of use and damages for bodily harm, harm to chattels, and mental distress attributable to invasion of the property.

A personal injury plaintiff whose medical bills are paid in full by an insurer can recover only the amount actually paid for the care by the insurer plus the plaintiff's own copayments. The nominal amount of the medical bill is not recoverable because the patient does not have to pay any amount that the health care provider writes off, and therefore should not be able to collect such amounts as windfall damages.[129]

The New Jersey Appellate Division held in mid-2008 that a $100,000 pain and suffering award to a woman who suffered multiple leg amputations was much too low, representing only $8 a day for her projected 30-year life expectancy. The court upheld the liability verdict and $800,000 in economic damages (e.g., a big contract her printing business lost because of her injuries), but ordered a new trial on damages. The plaintiff lost most of her leg to gangrene; a vascular surgeon who recommended an immediate arteriogram said that she would need to have another doctor arrange the test, because he was not in her insurance plan. The surgeon said that he only saw the plaintiff as a courtesy to a colleague, and there was no doctor-patient relationship, but

---

[129] Hull v. Jackson, 794 So. 2d 349 (Ala. 2001).

the Appellate Division said that when he examined her, he assumed a duty of care with respect to that examination and any resulting recommendations.[130]

A Philadelphia jury awarded $20.5 million to the parents of an 18-year-old college student who died after liposuction ($20,000 under the Wrongful Death Act, $5,000 for failure to obtain informed consent, $2 million for negligent infliction of emotional distress on the decedent's mother, $3.5 million under the survival act, and $15 million in punitive damages.[131]

A Tennessee court has upheld $5 million in compensatory and $13 million punitive damages awarded in a wrongful death suit; when a car was rear-ended, an 8-month-old baby in the back seat died; the front passenger seat collapsed and fractured his skull. However, the state Supreme Court reversed a lower-court award of over $6 million in punitive damages to the baby's mother for emotional distress. The initial award was $98 million in punitive damages, reduced to $13 million for wrongful death and $6 million for emotional distress. The state Supreme Court held that the evidence showed the manufacturer (who continued to market the vehicle as a safety-conscious choice) ignored warnings about the safety of the seats.[132]

Ongoing medical monitoring (to detect future manifestations of exposure to toxic substances) is frequently sought as a remedy, although it is often denied.[133]

[D] Fraud Damages

Damages must be proven with reasonable certainty; the damages must be proximately caused by the wrongful act of the defendant. Direct damages do not require proof of foreseeability, although consequential damages do. Depending on the facts of the case and the jurisdiction, damages for fraud could give the defrauded party the benefit of the bargain, including lost profits (the majority rule) or out-of-pocket loss. However, if the misrepresentation was negligent, damages will probably be limited to out-of-pocket loss. Sometimes a defrauded buyer will obtain rescission: returning the property to the seller, and receiving a refund.

[E] Punitive Damages

An award of punitive damages is always discretionary, not mandatory. Punitive damages are appropriate only if the defendant's conduct was outrageous, not

---

[130] Walsh v. Disciglio, A-0185-07 (N.J.A.D. 2008); *see* Mary Pat Gallagher, *Court Calls $8-a-Day Med-Mal Award for Amputee a 'Miscarriage of Justice'*, N.J.L.J. 8/25/08 (law.com).

[131] Amaris Elliott-Engel, *Jury Awards $20.5 Million for Fatal Liposuction*, The Legal Intelligencer 5/27/08 (law.com).

[132] Flax v. DaimlerChrysler (Tenn. 2008), discussed in Kristin M. Hall (AP), *Court Upholds $13 Million in Punitives Against DaimlerChrysler*, 7/28/08 (law.com).

[133] *See*, e.g., Hinton v. Monsanto Inc., 813 So.2d 827 (Ala. 2001);. Henry v. Dow Chem. Co., 701 N.W.2d 684 (2005). The Sixth Circuit held that medical monitoring is one of the range of possible remedies for tort, but is not a separate tort cause of action: Sutton v. St. Jude Med. S.C. Inc., 419 F.3d 568 (6th Cir. 2005).

merely negligent or an appropriate subject of strict liability.[134] In instances in which the tortious conduct also violates a criminal statute, it does not constitute double jeopardy to impose punitive damages in addition to a criminal sentence.

There must be compensatory damages to support an award of punitive damages, although in the right case, nominal damages may be adequate. Because the purpose is punitive, the defendant's financial condition is always relevant to the size of the award.

A grossly excessive punitive damage award violates Constitutional protections.[135] Excessiveness depends on three major factors:

- How reprehensible the manufacturer's conduct was (e.g., number of people potentially harmed; degree of harm; intentionality; pattern of wrongdoing)[136]
- Extent to which punitive damages exceed compensatory damages
- How comparable wrongdoing has been punished in other cases (both civil and criminal; punitive damages are more likely where criminal sanctions are also a possibility).

In April 2003, the Supreme Court not only overturned a $145 million punitive damage award as grossly disproportionate to the $1 million in compensatory damages, but also ruled that punitive damages should never be permitted to rise into double-digit multipliers of the compensatory damages, and that in many cases punitive damages should not exceed the compensatory damages at all. Neither the defendant's wealth nor its conduct in other states should be considered in making the award, because the punitive damage award is supposed to punish the defendant for harm caused to the plaintiff, not for unsavory conduct. The defendant's wealth cannot justify an award that would otherwise be unconstitutional.[137] See § 18.10[E] above for the Supreme Court's *Williams* decision ruling out punitive damages premised on harm to non-parties.

The Supreme Court ordered the California Court of Appeals to review its $82.6 million verdict for a woman paralyzed after the rollover of a Ford Explorer, to determine if the verdict was consonant with the new principle of restricting punitive damages to harm to the plaintiff. This was the first Ford Explorer rollover

---

[134] However, in an employment case, "egregious" conduct by the employer is not required, but the employer will not be liable for punitive damages in a case in which a supervisor's conduct violated the employer's good-faith attempt to provide a workplace that complies with federal and state law: Kolstad v. American Dental Ass'n, 527 U.S. 526 (1999).

[135] BMW of North America Inc., v. Gore, 499 U.S. 1 (1991). *See also* Philip Morris USA v. Williams, 549 U.S. 346 (2007), holding that it violates due process to use a punitive damage award to redress injuries to non-parties to the litigation.

[136] The Sixth Circuit reduced the ratio of punitive to compensatory damages in a motor vehicle design wrongful death case to 2:1, because few of the "reprehensibility" factors were present: Clark v. Chrysler Corp., 436 F.3d 594 (6th Cir. 2006).

[137] State Farm Mutual Auto Ins. Co. v. Campbell, 538 U.S. 408 (2003). On remand, the Utah Supreme Court reduced the punitive damages to $9 million, finding that to be the reasonable and proportionate amount: Campbell v. State Farm Mut. Auto Ins. Co., 2004 Ut. 34, 98 P.3d 409 (2004).

case, and at first the jury awarded $369 million, including $246 million in punitive damages. The verdict was reduced twice, with the California Court of Appeals finally approving a total of $82.6 million, including $55 million in punitive damages.[138]

The Exxon Valdez oil spill in Alaska gave rise to extensive punitive damage litigation. Since the oil spill, Exxon has spent $2.1 billion to clean up the spill; the company pleaded guilty and paid criminal fines and settled federal and Alaska civil actions for $900 million, and made a further $303 million in voluntary payments to private parties. Exxon and the captain who ran aground, causing the spill, were found liable for punitive damages for recklessness. Some plaintiffs settled their compensatory damage claims for $22.6 million, and the jury awarded a further $287 million in compensatory damages. Then the jury awarded $5,000 in punitive damages against Captain Hazelwood and $5 billion against Exxon. The Ninth Circuit remitted the punitive damages to $2.5 billion. Exxon appealed to the Supreme Court. The Supreme Court split 4-4 on whether maritime law permits a corporation to be held liable for punitive damages based on the acts of its managerial agents, with the result that the Ninth Circuit's opinion remains undisturbed, but the Supreme Court did not set precedent on derivative liability.

The Clean Water Act's water pollution penalties do not preempt punitive damage awards in maritime spill cases, and clearly do not preempt compensatory damages for economic losses, and the Supreme Court does not favor severing remedies from causes of action. The Supreme Court held that the punitive damages were excessive as a matter of maritime common law, and should not have exceeded the compensatory damages. Maritime cases are decided under judge-made federal common law, rather than under due process standards.

The Supreme Court refused to impose a dollar cap on maritime punitive damages, preferring to set a ratio with compensatory damages. The Supreme Court analyzed thousands of cases, finding that the median ratio of punitive to compensatory damages in cases involving very bad conduct, so the Supreme Court ruled that this is a fair upper limit for maritime cases. Commentators noted that the Federal Employers' Liability Act and 42 USC § 1981 cases are also decided under federal common law, so similar punitive damage limitations might apply to such cases.[139]

---

[138] Ford Motor Company v. Buell-Wilson, *cert. granted* No. 06-1068, 127 S. Ct. 2250 (5/14/07); (AP), *Supreme Court Orders Lower Court Review of $82.6M Award in Ford Explorer Rollover*, 5/15/07 (law.com). The Supreme Court granted certiorari and remanded the case to the California Court of Appeals, which upheld the award on the grounds that it considered the repeated nature of Ford's actions when determining reprehensibility, not reflecting harm to third parties. *See* Mike McKee, *Despite Remand, Ford Motor's Loss Stands at $82.6 Million*, The Recorder 3/11/08 (law.com); Don Thompson (AP). *Ford Agrees to Settle Explorer Rollover Suit Covering a Million Owners in Four States*, 11/29/07 (law.com).

[139] Exxon Shipping Co. v. Baker, 128 S. Ct. 2605 (2008); *see* Marcia Coyle, *Punitives Take Hit in 'Exxon' Ruling, but How Hard?* Nat'l L.J. 7/1/08 (law.com).

Later, the Supreme Court refused to decide whether Exxon must pay interest to the victims of the oil spill, leaving the interest issue up to the Ninth Circuit,[140] but Exxon negotiated a settlement under which $383 million will be released to pay some of the punitive damages, but negotiations continued over a further $70 million in damages and almost half a billion dollars in interest.[141]

The New Jersey Supreme Court ruled in 2008, in a sexual harassment suit, that punitive damages cannot be awarded as a general deterrent, only to punish a particular defendant's actual wrongdoing. In this reading, the jury should consider the defendant's financial condition not only at the time of the verdict (when it may be insolvent and out of business) but at the time of the wrongdoing.[142]

Code § 104(b)(2) excludes from taxable income damages received "on account of personal injury," but, according to *O'Gilvie v. United States*,[143] punitive damages in a personal injury case are taxable, because they are NOT received on account of personal injuries. Nevertheless, the D.C. Circuit ruled in 2006 that a $70,000 award to a whistleblower for blacklisting and bad references (in retaliation for reporting environmental hazards), consisting of $45,000 for emotional distress and mental damages, and $25,000 for injury to professional reputation, was not includible in the taxpayer's gross income. The court found that none of the award was for lost wages or earning capacity; the plaintiff suffered physical consequences of the retaliation against her; and her good reputation and emotional well-being did not constitute income, so an award to restore them should not be considered income either. In 2007, the D.C. Circuit reversed its earlier ruling, determining that the proceeds were taxable income for the payee.[144]

Under Arizona law, a claim for punitive damages is survivable and can be maintained against the estate of the tortfeasor. However, this is a minority position. Most states take the position that the estate was not involved in wrongdoing and should not be liable for punitive damages.[145]

---

[140] (AP), *High Court Declines to Rule on Exxon Valdez Interest Payments*, 8/13/08 (law.com).

[141] (AP), *Partial Settlement Reached in Exxon Valdez Case*, 8/27/08 (law.com). For background, *see, e.g.*, Tony Mauro, *Exxon Asks Supreme Court to Limit $2.5 Billion Spill Tab*, Legal Times 10/30/07 (law.com).

[142] Tarr v. Bob Ciasulli's Mack Auto Mall, 194 N.J. 212 (N.J. 2008); *see* Mary Pat Gallagher, *N.J. Supreme Court: Punitives for Wrongdoer Only, Not for General Deterrence*, N.J.L.J. 3/28/08 (law.com). Earlier, in Tarr v. Bob Ciasulli's Mack Auto Mall, Inc., 181 N.J. 70 (2004), New Jersey ruled that sexual harassment plaintiffs do not need severe emotional or physical injury to recover for mental anguish, but held that business owners are not individually liable unless they aided harassment or the creation of a hostile environment.

[143] 519 U.S. 79 (1996).

[144] Murphy v. IRS, 460 F.3d 79 (D.C. Cir. 2006), *rev'd* 493 F.3d 170 (D.C. Cir. 2007); *see* (AP), *D.C. Circuit: Damages for Emotional Distress Part of Gross Income*, 7/5/07 (law.com). Polone v. CIR took a similar path. In 2006, the Ninth Circuit ruled that payments pursuant to a settlement entered into before the effective date of the amendment could be excluded from income (449 F.3d 1041), but in 2007, the Ninth Circuit withdrew that opinion and substituted 479 F.3d 1019 (9th Cir. 2007), holding that payments received after the effective date of the amendment must be included in gross income.

[145] Haralson v. Fisher Surveying Inc., 31 P.3d 114 (Ariz. 2001).

Legislation has been introduced in California under which 75% of punitive damage awards would be payable not to the plaintiff but to the state treasury. Statutes of this type ("split-recovery laws") are in force in Georgia, Illinois, Indiana, Iowa, Oregon, Alaska, Missouri, and Utah. In some of these states, the funds go to general revenues; in others, the funds go to reparations or victim services agencies. In Illinois, the trial judge determines the amount that goes to the state; in the others, it ranges from 50–75%, although some of the states make the computation before the deduction of attorneys' fees, and some make that computation afterwards.[146]

§ 18.14   TORT REFORM

See § 18.05[D] above for tort reform in medical malpractice cases.

It is often perceived — especially by potential defendants — that the current court system permits exploitation of jurors' emotions and their hostility toward "deep pockets" so that immense awards can be ordered in cases where injury is trivial and/or liability is questionable.

The legislative response has been enactment of tort reform measures in many states, such as increased sanctions for frivolous litigation; requirements of mandatory arbitration prior to litigation; and damage caps, especially caps on non-economic damages (e.g., punitive damages and damages for pain and suffering). Some statutes make an exception in the case of exceptionally severe injuries. Many statutes have also been enacted to limit or eliminate joint and several liability, on the theory that it is unjust to penalize a defendant for having a deep pocket rather than for its true share in the plaintiff's injuries.

These tort reform statutes raise Constitutional issues — not always resolved in the same way! — such as whether the Sixth Amendment right to jury trial or entitlement to Equal Protection of the Laws or Due Process are impaired. For instance, Kansas imposes a cap of $250,000 on non-economic loss in personal injury cases. The "cap" statute has been upheld by the Tenth Circuit, against claims that it violated the Americans with Disabilities Act and the Equal Protection clause.[147]

In 1998 and 1999, however, several state courts permitted awards in excess of the cap, finding the cap offensive to the state Constitution.

The Ohio Supreme Court upheld the state law limiting damages for pain and suffering in defective product cases. The statute, which caps awards at the greater of three times economic damages or $250,000 (with exceptions for permanent disability or loss or a limb or bodily organ system), was held not to violate due process, equal protection, the right to trial by jury, or the right to remedies. Punitive damages are limited to twice compensatory damages. A similar law was struck

---

[146] Adam Liptak, *Schwarzenegger Seeks Money for State in Punitive Damages*, N.Y. Times, 5/30/04 at p. A16.

[147] Patton v. TIC United Corp., 77 F.3d 1235 (10th Cir. 1996).

down in 1999; since then, the legislature passed a revised law, and the composition of the state bench changed.[148]

In mid-1999, Oregon's Supreme Court rejected the state's statutory cap on noneconomic damages ($500,000 per plaintiff: Rev. Stat. § 18.560(1)), finding that it violated the state Constitution's guarantee of the right to trial by jury.

Federal tort reform was also an important component of President Bush's second-term strategy. The Class Action Fairness Act of 2005 (P.L. 109-2) was passed February 10, 2005. Under this statute, class actions filed subsequent to the effective date of the law would have to be filed in federal rather than state court if the claimed damages exceed $5 million and fewer than one-third of the plaintiffs are citizens of the state in which class certification would be sought. Congress' concern was that state forum-shopping resulted in dysfunctionally large awards preventing companies from doing business. (Some major drug litigation would not be affected, because it is brought in individual rather than class form — but another Bush initiative, to preclude state claims on preemption grounds — would tend to rule out such suits.) See § 22.09[E][5] for more discussion of CAFA.

---

[148] Arbino v. Johnson & Johnson, 116 Oh. St. 3d 468 (Ohio 2007); *see* Terry Kinney (AP), *Ohio Supreme Court: Law Limiting Damages for Pain and Suffering Is Constitutional*, 12/28/07 (law.com).

Immigration

§ 19.01 INTRODUCTION

NOTE: The agency formerly known as the Immigration and Naturalization Service (INS) has been divided into two bureaus, the Bureau of Immigration Services and the Bureau of Immigration Enforcement, and enforcement of the immigration laws now comes within the purview of the Department of Homeland Security.

Although the United States is proverbially a nation of immigrants, and it is still a desirable destination or would-be destination for immigrants and refugees, current U.S. immigration law is fairly restrictive. The number of visas granted is far lower than the number of people desiring them. Immigration law intersects with labor law, in that employers often claim a need to hire foreign workers, while advocates of the U.S. labor force claim that employers underpay and exploit immigrant workers to avoid paying standard wages to U.S. workers.

In addition to issues such as granting visas and asylum, immigration law must distinguish between legal immigrants permitted to work in this country and those who are not; prevent or detect immigration fraud involving marriage; determine immigrants' eligibility for government services and benefits; and deport illegal aliens, especially those who have committed crimes in the United States.

Contemporary immigration law is founded in the Immigration and Naturalization Act of 1952 (INA) and its amendments, as supplemented by the Immigration Reform and Control Act of 1986 (IRCA)[1] and the Immigration Act of 1990 (IMMACT). IMMACT technical amendments were passed in 1991.

The 911 attack had a profound impact on the treatment of immigration (see § 19.01[A] below). In November 2001, Attorney General John Ashcroft announced the division of the INS into two bureaus: the Bureau of Immigration Services and Bureau of Immigration Enforcement, as part of the initiative to protect the United States against unlawful entrance by terrorists. A later restructuring move, in April 2002, sought to improve the efficiency of the Border Patrol and prevent abuse of illegal alien minors entering the United States unaccompanied by parents.[2]

Documentation requirements were increased for U.S. citizens traveling to the Caribbean, Canada, and Mexico, and for non-U.S. citizens entering the United States from those places. Passports will be required by January 8, 2007 for entries through airports and seaports, and by January 1, 2008 for land borders. Passports will be required for all children, no matter how young. Issuance of U.S. "e-passports," containing a computer chip with encrypted identification data, began in August 2006, but holders of valid paper passports do not have to replace them immediately.[3] For immigration statistics, such as estimates of the number of foreign-born persons and illegal aliens in each state, and annual reports on refugees, asylees, and legal immigrants, see http://www.ins.usdoj.gov/graphics/aboutins.

---

[1] IRCA also included a one-time amnesty for certain illegal aliens already within the United States.

[2] Marjorie Valbrun, *INS Streamlines Border Patrol, Sets Up Office to Handle Children*, Wall St. J., April 8, 2002 at A8. The INS functions were transferred to the Department of Homeland Security by the Homeland Security Act of 2002, P.L. 107-296; *see* 68 FR 9824 (2/28/03), 68 FR 10922 (3/6/03) and 68 FR 35273 (6/13/03) for implementing regulations.

[3] Department of Homeland Security, *Privacy Impact Assessment Update for the United States Visitor and Immigrant Status Indicator Technology (US-VISIT) Program*, http://www.dhs.gov/interweb/assetlibrary/privacy_pia_usvisit_epassport.pdf (8/18/06) and 71 FR 42605 (7/27/06) and 46155 (8/11/06); Scott McCartney, *U.S. Travelers Face New Passport Rules*, N.Y. Times 9/5/06 at p. D1. On ePassports, *see* http://www.state.gov/r/pa/prs/ps/2006/61538.htm.

A Final Rule on professional conduct by attorneys and representatives appearing before the Executive Officer for Immigration Review (EOIR) was published at 65 FR 39,513 (6/27/00). The rule imposes sanctions for frivolous conduct in immigration proceedings and details the mechanism for investigating complaints against immigration practitioners. The reviewing body for disciplinary determinations has been changed: this responsibility now belongs to the Bureau of Immigration Appeals (BIA), not the Disciplinary Committee. Despite this disciplinary authority, nothing in federal law precludes a state from disbarring an attorney for misconduct committed in the course of federal immigration practice.[4]

[A] Recent Statutes

Three major statutes affecting immigration were passed in 1996: the Antiterrorism and Effective Death Penalty Act (AEDPA, P.L. 104-132; see § 26.04[N][1][a] for a discussion of its impact on criminal law), the Personal Responsibility and Work Opportunity Reconciliation Act (PRWORA, P.L. 104-193; see § 19.06), and the Illegal Immigration Reform and Immigrant Responsibility Act (IIRIRA, P.L. 104-208).

AEDPA makes it easier to deport aliens convicted of crimes (any crimes — not necessarily violent crimes) or based on moral turpitude. A final order against an alien convicted of a crime is "not subject to review by any court," and collateral attack of deportation orders is also limited.

IIRIRA imposes more border control, stricter enforcement of laws against smuggling aliens, and further limitations on public benefits for aliens. Document fraud penalties and penalties for employment of undocumented aliens are enhanced.[5]

IIRIRA makes it harder for immigrants whose visas have expired to use their continued presence in the United States to attain valid immigration status. Some earlier provisions for "adjustment of status," permitting aliens to remain within the United States instead of leaving and seeking legal immigration status from outside, have been terminated. Neither employment nor marriage to a U.S. citizen automatically permits permanent residence. Nonimmigrant visas become void as soon as they expire. Absent extraordinary circumstances, the alien will not be issued a new U.S. visa to anywhere except his or her home country.

Both AEDPA and IIRIRA expand the definition of "aggravated felonies" such as will make it impossible for the convicted felon to avoid removal from the United States. The current definition includes passport fraud, gambling offenses, and offenses subject to a sentence of a year or more (even if the sentence was

---

[4] Gadda v. Ashcroft, 363 F.3d 861 (9th Cir. 2004).

[5] *But see* Walters v. Reno, 145 F.3d 1032 (9th Cir. 1998), enjoining as constitutionally inadequate the forms and procedures INS used to notify aliens accused of document fraud of their rights. INA § 274C authorizes unappealable final orders deporting aliens accused of document fraud, unless the alien requests a hearing in writing within 60 days of receipt of notice. The Ninth Circuit deemed the notices to be incomprehensible. Aliens must be informed that waiving a hearing on the document fraud issue is tantamount to consent to deportation.

suspended). Prior law defined aggravated felonies as those punishable by a sentence of five years or more.

P.L. 105-277, the American Competitiveness and Workforce Improvement Act of 1998, increases the number of H-1B visas that can be issued to highly skilled foreign workers for temporary assignments in the United States. See § 19.04.

Under P.L. 106-313, employment-based visas that go unused in a particular calendar quarter can be carried over to subsequent quarters without regard to per-country limits. The visas that were not used in fiscal 1999 and 2000 were "banked" for use in later fiscal years where the demand for visas outpaces the cap for the year.

One of the provisions of the 21st Century Department of Justice Appropriations Authorization Act, P.L. 107-273, permits an H-1B nonimmigrant whose six years of visa eligibility are about to expire to get an extension of H-1B status based on labor certification or I-140 form filed at least 365 days before the request for exemption is made. The Bureau of Citizenship and Immigration Services is obligated to grant the extension unless there had been a final negative decision on that person's labor certification, petition to change to immigrant status, or I-485 application.

Congress passed P.L. 107-40, a joint resolution authorizing military response to the September 11 attack. Under the implementing order,[6] military commissions not subject to the usual federal rules of criminal procedure or evidence have jurisdiction over individuals (other than U.S. citizens, who are tried in regular courts) accused of terrorism. A two-thirds vote of the tribunal can impose sentence, including sentences of death or life imprisonment. Evidence is admissible if a reasonable person would deem it to be probative. Non-citizens can be tried by the tribunals if it is determined that the best interests of the United States require placing that person under military jurisdiction, and that there is reason to believe that the individual belonged to a terrorist organization or engaged in, conspired in, or aided and abetted terrorist acts within the United States.

Executive Order 13224, Blocking Property and Prohibiting Transactions With Persons Who Commit, Threaten to Commit, or Support Terrorism (9/23/01) states that, in response to the national emergency, all property and interests of property of terrorists and terrorist supporters is blocked. The economic sanctions apply to "foreign persons" who are listed in the Annex to the Executive Order (e.g., members of Al Qaeda), or who are determined by the Secretary of State, Secretary of the Treasury, and Attorney General to have committed or who pose significant risk of committing acts of terrorism that threaten the security of U.S. nationals, or the national security, foreign policy, or economy of the United States.

The USA Patriot Act, P.L. 107-56 (also discussed in § 26.04[A][2] includes several provisions with immigration impact. INA § 212(a)(3)(B) already barred non-citizens from entering the United States if there is reasonable grounds to believe they would engage in terrorist activity, and permitted the Secretary of State to create a list of terrorist organizations (INA § 237(a)(4)(B)).

---

[6] *See* 70 L.W. 2301.

The USA Patriot Act strengthens and extends these provisions by broadening the definition of a "terrorist organization" whose members cannot be admitted to the United States, or who can be deported once admitted. Spouses and children of people involved in terrorism in the previous five years are inadmissible, unless that person did not know or have reason to know of the activity, or unless terrorist activity has been renounced.

USA Patriot Act § 412 not merely permits but requires the Department of Justice to place any non-citizen suspected of terrorism in detention for up to seven days. It is not necessary to file charges. After the seven-day period elapses, the non-citizen must be released if immigration or criminal charges have not been filed. (However, immigration violations are very common, so it is quite likely that a detainee, even if not involved in terrorism in any way, would not be in compliance as to his or her immigration status.) Detention can continue for an additional six months if two conditions are met: that the individual's release threatens safety or national security, and that it is unlikely that the person can be removed in the foreseeable future. Section 412 also limits habeas in these cases.

Section 414 calls for better screening of aliens seeking admission to the United States and better tamper-proof identity documents, as well as closer monitoring of foreign students in the United States. The USA Patriot Act contains relief provisions for people whose immigration status was adversely affected by the 911 attack (e.g., relatives of victims of the attack; people whose documents were delayed because of the attack).[7]

The Enhanced Border Security and Visa Entry Reform Act of 2002, P.L. 107-173, sets up a monitoring program for foreign students and requires greater oversight of sponsorship of nonimmigrant visitors by institutions. The statute calls for a more technologically sophisticated system for issuing visas, more secure travel documents, and better data sharing among agencies concerned with immigration and law enforcement.

Effective March 8, 2005, the H-1B Visa Reform Act of 2004, part of P.L. 108-447, the appropriations act, exempts up to 20,000 H-1B from the cap of 65,000 visas per year, if the visa holders have Masters' or higher degrees from an American college or university. Interim Final Rules were published in May 2005. There is a filing fee of $2,300 per visa for companies with 25 or fewer employees or $3,000 for larger companies; the application can be processed within 15 days in exchange for a "premium processing fee" of $1,000.[8]

The REAL ID Act of 2005 is part of P.L. 109-13, the emergency supplemental appropriations bill for the fiscal year ended September 30, 2005. As the title suggests, this legislation is concerned with improving security of driver's licenses and other personal identification, and criminalizes trafficking

---

[7] *See* Stanley Mailman and Stephen Yale-Loehr, *As the World Turns: Immigration Law Before and After September 11*, and *An Overview of the USA Patriot Act's Immigration Provisions*, 6 Bender's Immigration Bulletin 1149, 1154 (11/15/01).

[8] 70 F.R. 23775 (5/5/05); *see* 73 L.W. 2636 and 2666.

in authentication features for use in making false identification documents. The prior law limitation of 10,000 asylees per fiscal year becoming lawful permanent residents has been removed. To meet the burden of proof, asylum applicants must testify credibly and persuasively to specific facts, and the trier of fact can require submission of corroborating evidence. The same standards of proof and credibility apply when non-asylees seek relief from removal.

REAL ID expands the grounds under which a person can be deported or ruled inadmissible on the grounds of terrorist or terrorist-related activity, and the definition of "terrorist organization" has been broadened. However, the Secretary of Homeland Security also has sole unreviewable discretion to determine that aliens, spouses, or their children will not be held inadmissible on terrorism-related grounds.

Section 106 of REAL ID prevents inadmissible arriving aliens from using habeas, mandamus, or other extraordinary petitions to obtain judicial review of removal orders. Similar limitations apply to discretionary relief for criminal aliens, other than petitions for review that raise questions of law or constitutional claims. Judicial review can be obtained under the INA for removal petitions or other claims arising under the U.N. Convention Against Torture, but it is the sole avenue for review of such claims.[9]

Title IV, the Save Our Small and Seasonal Businesses Act of 2005, amends the rules for counting the number of H-2B nonimmigrants granted visas as temporary nonagricultural workers. Employers are subject to a fraud prevention and detection fee for H-2B petitions, and the penalty imposed on employers for willful misrepresentation or failure to meet the conditions of the H-2B petition is increased. No more than 33,000 of the 66,000 immigrants allowed under H-2B can enter during the first six months of the fiscal year.

A number of state laws affecting immigration have been passed, and many more bills have been introduced, dealing with topics such as employment verification, penalties for employing illegal immigrants, and restrictions on public benefits (including drivers' licenses) for illegal immigrants.

§ 19.02   VISA CATEGORIES

Visas — permission to enter the United States — are issued in many categories, depending on whether or not the entrant intends to become a U.S. citizen or permanent resident, or merely intends to spend a period of time in the United States and return home. Visas are also divided into categories based on family sponsorship, employment, and diversity (redressing the effect of earlier immigration laws that discriminated against certain parts of the world).

There are numerical quotas for various categories of family-and employment-related immigration. Legal immigration is permitted outside the

---

[9] These provisions are retroactive as to all pending orders, irrespective of the date of the final administrative order: Fernandez-Ruiz v. Gonzales, 410 F.3d 585 (9th Cir. 2005).

quota system in some instances — e.g., for close family members of U.S. citizens, and for workers whose skills are needed in the United States.

The presumption is that anyone who enters the United States is an immigrant who must meet the legal requirements of immigration, unless he or she can prove nonimmigrant status, for instance by having a "B visa" for a business trip (B-1) or tourist or pleasure travel (B-2). However, H-1B visas (see § 19.04 below) are exempt from the presumption of intent to immigrate.

There are many visa categories, with a high degree of overlap among them. The practice of immigration law includes determining which categories the client can fit into; preparing the papers; and making sure that statements are not made that are detrimental to the client's visa application.[10]

The "dual intent" doctrine permits a person who enters the United States with a visa authorizing temporary residence to make a subsequent application for permanent residence, as long as he or she had the proper intent at the time each application was made.

Multiple claims are permitted, but the risk is that the INS could grant only one application, leaving the client in limbo if there are no available visas in the category of qualification.

The Secretary of Homeland Security has discretion under 8 USC § 1155 to revoke visas. The Third Circuit joined the Seventh in holding that a decision to revoke is not judicially reviewable under 8 USC § 1252(a)(2)(B)(ii). However, the Ninth Circuit disagrees. The Third Circuit distinguished its own 2004 decision on the grounds that it involved denial of a visa application, which does not have a strong enough discretionary element to preclude judicial review.[11]

[A] Family-Related Immigration Visas

Under INA § 201(c), up to 480,000 visas can be issued per year[12] for immediate relatives and persons sponsored by a family member. An immediate relative is defined by INA § 201(b) as a parent, spouse, or child of a U.S. citizen. INA § 201(b)(2)(A)(i) further provides that a surviving spouse of a deceased citizen can remain an immediate relative (and so can the alien's children) after the citizen spouse's death, provided that they had been married for at least two years and were not legally separated at the time of the citizen spouse's death. The alien surviving spouse must file a petition to retain this status within two years of the citizen spouse's death. Remarriage removes the immediate family status.

---

[10] *See* 71 FR 37494 (6/30/06) for documentation requirements for nonimmigrant visas.

[11] Jilin Pharmaceutical USA Inc. v. Chertoff, 447 F.3d 196 (3d Cir. 2006); *see also* El-Khader v. Monica, 366 F.3d 562 (7th Cir. 2004) and Ghanem v. Upchurch, 481 F.3d 222 (5th Cir. 2007), *but contra* ANA Int'l Inc. v. Way, 393 F.3d 886 (9th Cir. 2004); the 2004 case is Soltane v. DOJ, 381 F.3d 143 (3d Cir. 2004).

[12] At least 226,000, but not more than 480,000, family-related visas must be issued each year; up to 140,000 employment-related visas can be issued. If fewer than the maximum number of employment-related visas are issued, the unissued visas can be used for family-related immigration.

Without relief, the immigration system might require families to be divided. To prevent this, INA § 203(d) allows the spouse or child of an alien who has a visa to get a visa in the same preference category and principal alien as the spouse or parent, even if he or she would not otherwise be entitled to a visa. The spouse or child must accompany or "follow to join" the alien who receives the visa. This relief is not available to persons who marry aliens after they become U.S. permanent residents, or to children born after permanent resident status is secured.

Family-related immigration is divided into four preference categories by INA § 203(a):

- First preference: 23,400 visas (plus any unused visas from lower preferences) for unmarried adult sons and daughters of U.S. citizens ("children" of U.S. citizens — i.e., unmarried minors — can be admitted to the United States without quota restrictions)
- Second preference: 114,200 visas (77% for spouses and children, 23% for unmarried adult sons and daughters) of aliens who are lawful permanent residents of the United States
- Third preference: 23,400 married sons and daughters of U.S. citizens; if there are any unused visas from the first and second preference, they can be transferred to this category
- Fourth preference: adult brothers and sisters of U.S. citizens; 65,000 visas are allotted, plus any unused visas from first, second, and third preference.

The V-1, -2, and -3 visa categories apply to the spouses of lawful permanent residents of the United States.

Two statutes from 2000 affect family-related immigration. P.L. 106-279, the Intercountry Adoption Act of 2000, authorizes the United States to implement the Hague Convention on Protection of Children and Co-Operation in Respect of Intercountry Adoption. The Department of State serves as the central authority for liaison under the Hague Convention. Congress found it necessary to subscribe to this treaty to control abuses in international adoption, such as exorbitant fees to facilitators, adoption of children who are not available for adoption, failure to prepare adoptive families to carry out their responsibilities, and failure to disclose the medical conditions of potential adoptees.

The Child Citizenship Act of 2000, P.L. 106-395, amends INA § 320 to make automatic U.S. citizenship available to children under 18, when at least one of the parents is a U.S. citizen by birth or naturalization, if the children are in the United States in the legal and physical custody of the citizen parent, pursuant to lawful admission for permanent residence. A citizen parent can also get a certificate of naturalization for a child born outside the United States who normally lives outside the United States, but who is temporarily lawfully present within the U.S.

However, persons who were over 18 on February 27, 2001, the effective date of Title I of the Child Citizenship Act, do not qualify for automatic citizenship even if they satisfy the other statutory criteria.[13] The BIA held that adopted children cannot use 8 USC § 1153(a)(4) (visa preference for qualified immigrants who are siblings of U.S. citizens) to benefit their biological siblings. The District Court granted deference to the agency determination, and the Third Circuit affirmed.[14]

A piece of legislation from 2002, the Family Sponsor Immigration Act, P.L. 107-150, provides that when a petitioner dies, another close relative can be substituted as the sponsor of an alien. Most forms of family-based immigration, and some employment-related forms, require a sponsor to support an affidavit of support. USCIS published Final Rules for the affidavit of support process in mid-2006.[15] As of October 19, 2006, the two new forms, Form I-864EZ ("EZ Affidavit of Support") and I-864W ("Intending Immigrant's I-864 Exemption") must be used; the old forms will no longer be valid.[16] In mid-2001, the Supreme Court upheld 8 USC § 1409(a), which makes it easier for a child born outside the United States to unmarried parents to obtain U.S. citizenship when the U.S. citizen parent is the mother instead of the father. The Supreme Court's view is that the distinction does not violate Equal Protection, because it is easier to prove maternity than paternity.[17]

An interim rule for implementing the new K nonimmigrant classification of the spouses and children of U.S. citizens and their children, under the Legal Immigration Family Equity Act of 2000 (LIFE Act), effective August 14, 2001, was published at 66 FR 42587 (8/14/01). Such individuals are admitted to the United States initially as nonimmigrants; their status is adjusted to immigrant when they are in the United States.

On September 7, 2001, the INS implemented a new status, "V" for spouses and minor children of lawful permanent residents. V status individuals can work in the United States while they are waiting to receive an immigrant visa number.

[B] Employment-Related Immigration Visas

Before IMMACT, only 54,000 visas for immigration of employees were permitted. IMMACT raised that number to 140,000, divided into five categories set out in INA § 203(b):

- First preference: 28.6% of the number of employment-related visas, plus any unused fourth- or fifth-preference visas, for persons of extraordinary ability in

---

[13] Drakes v. Ashcroft, 323 F.3d 189 (2d Cir. 2003); Hughes v. Ashcroft, 255 F.3d 752 (9th Cir. 2001).

[14] Kosak v. Aguirre, 518 F.3d 210 (3d Cir. 2008).

[15] 71 FR 35732 (7/21/06).

[16] The forms were posted at http://www.uscis.gov/graphics/formsfee/forms.

[17] Nguyen v. INS, 533 U.S. 53 (2001).

science, art, education, business or athletics; outstanding professors and researchers; and some executives and managers of multi-national corporations. See INA § 101(a)(44).

- Second preference: 28.6% of the total, plus unused first-preference visas, for professionals with advanced degrees or persons of exceptional ability (a lower standard than "extraordinary") in science, art, or business (but not education or athletics, as allowed by the first preference). The general rule is that a person applying for a second-preference visa must be able to prove a job offer in the United States, unless the Attorney General waives this requirement.
- Third preference: 28.6% plus unused first- and second-preference visas, for skilled workers whose skills are hard to find in the United States; professionals who have a college degree but not an advanced degree, and other workers in fields that are in short supply in the United States (but only 10,000 people a year in this sub-category are allowed to immigrate).
- Fourth preference: 7.1%, with no access to unused visas. This is a category for "special" immigrants (INA § 101(a)(27)): religious workers, plus some ex-employees of the U.S. government and international organizations.
- Fifth preference: 7.1%, for "employment creation": investors who wish to immigrate to the United States and start a business that creates at least 10 jobs in the United States. The immigrant investor generally must invest at least $1 million in the enterprise; as much as $3 million, in a low-unemployment area (i.e., where job creation is less crucial).

[C] Diversity-Related Immigration Visas

IRCA and IMMACT include programs (known as DV-1) for permitting additional immigration from certain countries (particularly in Europe) that have been underrepresented in recent years. The NP-5 and AA-1 programs are lotteries under which visas are allotted randomly to applicants. The number of visas depends on a formula calculating the disparity between actual visas issued in a particular country and a number of visas that would have been representative.

DV-1 diversity visas are the first visas allowing immigration without proof of a sponsoring immediate relative or a pre-arranged U.S. job for which there is a labor shortage. However, the applicant must have either a high school education or two years of work experience in a skilled occupation.

[D] Special Immigration

INA § 101(a)(27) sets out several categories of "special" immigrants, e.g.:

- Resident aliens coming back to the United States after a temporary trip outside the U.S.
- Ex-U.S. citizens
- Ministers of religion, their spouses, and children

- Officers and employees of international organizations and their families
- Certain children eligible for foster care
- Former employees and retirees of the U.S. government with at least 15 years' tenure
- Doctors and medical students who entered the United States as nonimmigrants and continued to provide medical services
- Immigrants who served 12 years or more in the U.S. military.

Before IMMACT, an indefinite number of these visas could be issued each year. Under current law, however, a quota is imposed on the total of "special" immigrant visas other than returning resident aliens and ex-U.S. citizens, which can still be issued free of numerical limitations.

"Commuter aliens" from Mexico (and some from Canada) are allowed to enter the United States on a daily or seasonal basis to work here, e.g., in agriculture. 8 CFR § 211.5 treats them as residents returning from temporary trips abroad.

The International Patient Act of 2000, P.L. 106-406, amends the INA (at 8 USC § 1229c(a)(2)) to set up a three-year pilot project. Under this program the Attorney General has discretion for humanitarian purposes to extend the period for voluntary departure of nonimmigrants who were admitted under the INA § 217 visa waiver program, if the individuals require medical treatment (and the treatment will not be at the expense of Medicaid or other U.S. public benefit programs).

[E] Waiver Program

In 1986, a pilot program was created under which nationals of eligible countries can visit the United States for periods of up to 90 days, for purposes similar to those governed by B-1 and B-2 visas, without actually requiring a visa. The pilot program was made permanent by P.L. 106-396, the Visa Waiver Permanent Program Act, enacted at 8 USC § 1187.

§ 19.03 REFUGEES AND ASYLUM

IMMACT changed the process under which refugees can become permanent residents. The permanent residence application can be made one year after a grant of asylum.

Certain issues arise frequently: allegations that if returned, the asylum applicant will face torture and other forms of religious and political persecution; claims based on China's coercive population policies; claims involving female genital mutilation.

A refugee (INA § 101(a)(42)) is a person who seeks to stay within the United States, asserting a well-founded fear of persecution in the native land on the basis of race, religion, nationality, or membership in a social or political classification. Each year, the President and Congress are empowered by INA § 207(a)(2) to set the number of refugees that will be admitted for that year, and to allocate this number by geographic region. Each refugee must have an organizational sponsor within the

United States, or have a relative or other person willing to take responsibility for his or her support.

Asylum is invoked by a person already in the United States or seeking admission at a border; a person outside the United States can seek refugee status. As noted above, there are quotas for refugees from a particular area and overall; there is no numerical limitation on asylum applications. Before seeking review, petitioners who claim asylum on humanitarian grounds must exhaust their administrative remedies.[18]

Asylum and refugee status are not granted to persons fleeing economic hardship in the home country, but only to individuals who have a well-founded fear of persecution (i.e., the subjective state of fear must have objective justification) and must be at risk of prosecution and severe punishment for leaving the homeland without permission, if asylum is not granted. See 8 CFR § 208.13: the applicant is required to prove refugee status, which can be done by showing a pattern or practice of persecution in the country of origin. 8 CFR § 208.13(a)[19] does not require corroboration of credible testimony. However, the fact that an applicant for asylum has already established a credible fear of persecution under INA § 235(b)(1)(B) is not enough to prove eligibility for asylum.

In the Second Circuit's view, in order to establish eligibility for relief based exclusively on the petitioner's activities within the United States, an alien must make some showing that the authorities in the home country are aware, or at least likely to become aware, of those U.S.-based activities. The Second Circuit was skeptical because, although the asylum applicant said that he was at risk because of his work for the China Democratic Party, he nevertheless went to renew his passport at the Chinese consulate even though he had no specific trip planned.[20]

Temporary Protected Status (TPS) is granted, under INA § 244, to refugees who are unable to return home because of disaster or war. TPS refugees are entitled to employment certification.

Asylum applications can be either affirmative (made by a person who wishes to enter the United States) or defensive (made by a person who is at risk of being removed). If asylum is denied, the usual result is voluntary departure or removal of the alien. However, INA § 241(b)(3)(A) provides that aliens cannot be removed to a country in which their life or freedom is in jeopardy because of their race, religion, political opinion, or other asylum ground.[21]

It is easier to meet the test for the grant of asylum (well-founded fear of persecution) than to have deportation withheld (which requires proof of a clear

[18] Liti v. Gonzalez, 411 F.3d 631 (6th Cir. 2005).
[19] As amended by 64 FR 8488 (2/19/99) and 65 FR 76133 (2/6/00).
[20] Leng v. Mukasey, 528 F.3d 135 (2d Cir. 2008).
[21] This provision does not apply to persons who themselves have engaged in persecution, or to persons who committed serious crimes inside or outside the United States, have been involved in terrorism, or otherwise threaten the national security of the United States. See 8 CFR § 208.14(d). Thapa v. Gonzales, 460 F.3d 323 (2d Cir. 2006), holds that the Court of Appeals has jurisdiction under INA to stay an IJ's order of voluntary departure.

probability of persecution). Therefore, if an individual fails to qualify for asylum, it is not necessary for the court to consider the propriety of withholding deportation.[22]

INS asylum officers process affirmative applications: see 8 CFR § 208.1(b). Defensive asylum claims are raised before the immigration judge, and if denied, can be appealed to the BIA and then to the Court of Appeals. Asylum is not a right; it is granted as a matter of jurisdiction. Under INA § 208(a)(2), the Attorney General has discretion to turn down the asylum application if a third country (other than the country of origin and the U.S.) is willing to accept the individual.

Refugees who have spent a year in the United States and have not become permanent residents are required, by INA § 209(a), to report to the INS for inspection. The alien will become a lawful permanent resident if he or she is otherwise eligible, but asylum status will be terminated if the individual no longer fits the INA definition of "refugee." After a year's residence, an asylee can apply for adjustment of status to permanent resident alien: see 8 CFR § 209.1, but only 10,000 such adjustments are permitted per year.

Seekers of asylum pursuant to the U.N. Convention Against Torture ("CATS") have the burden of proof to establish that it is more likely than not that they would be tortured if removed to the proposed country of removal.[23]

In 2003, the Third Circuit (joining the First, Second, and Ninth) ruled that a federal District Court can exercise habeas corpus jurisdiction in a case where an individual claims that deportation is likely to result in his or her torture, imprisonment, or execution in the home country. The Third Circuit found that the Foreign Affairs Reform and Restructuring Act of 1998 (FARRA) implements the U.N. Convention Against Torture. Although the DOJ argued that the CAT is not a self-executing treaty, and therefore habeas review is available only if specifically granted by Congress, the Third Circuit found that the question is not whether there has been an explicit grant of habeas jurisdiction, but whether Congress took any steps to prevent habeas review, and concluded that it did not.[24]

---

[22] Aguilar-Solis v. INS, 168 F.3d 565 (1st Cir. 1999).

[23] Al-Saher v. INS, 268 F.3d 1143 (9th Cir. 2001). Probability of torture at private hands will justify withholding of removal under CATS. The asylum applicant need not show a threat of torture committed by public officials or while in public custody: Azanor v. Ashcroft, 364 F.3d 1013 (9th Cir. 2004). The converse, however, is that official maltreatment is not necessarily torture. The Third Circuit ruled that CATS does not apply to an alien subject to deportation to Haiti for criminal activity within the United States. The court defined "torture" as specific intent to cause severe physical or mental pain and suffering. The terrible prison conditions in Haiti are not considered torture because of the lack of specific intent directed at particular prisoners: Auguste v. Ridge, 395 F.3d 123 (3d Cir. 2005).

[24] Ogbudimkpa v. Ashcroft, 342 F.3d 207 (3d Cir. 2003). *See also* Lian v. Ashcroft, 379 F.3d 457 (7th Cir. 2004), in which the Seventh Circuit vacated an Immigration Judge's removal order and sent the case for re-examination by a different judge because of the first judge's failure to analyze massive evidence submitted that it was likely that the illegal entrant would be tortured on return to China.

The Ninth Circuit held in mid-2001 that the BIA's interpretation of the changed country standard is unreasonable and therefore not entitled to deference. The BIA position was that, to qualify for waiver of the requirement of fear of future persecution, the alien seeking asylum must show ongoing physical or emotional sequelae of past persecution. But according to the Ninth Circuit, severity of past persecution is adequate to justify the alien's unwillingness to return to the country where persecution occurred.[25] See also 65 FR 76121 (12/6/00) for a Final Rule on asylum procedures, prescribing the factors for exercising discretion when past persecution has been shown but fear of future persecution might not be well-grounded, or where the applicant could escape persecution by moving within the home country.

Evidence of ethnic hatred against a group, and a systematic campaign of ethnic cleansing to eliminate that group from the country or region where removed persons would have to return, can establish past persecution or well-founded fear of future persecution.

The Seventh Circuit stayed a mother's deportation, pending a petition to reopen, because the BIA probably abused its discretion by failing to consider that if the mother returns to Nigeria, her daughter, a U.S. citizen, would go with her and would be at risk of genital mutilation.[26]

Initially, in 2002 the Ninth Circuit ruled that a Chinese woman's resistance to a coerced pelvic exam (part of that country's repressive population-control program) was not sufficiently similar to forced abortion or sterilization to support an asylum claim, but the court reversed itself in a 2004 en banc decision, noting that abortion and sterilization of her partner were threatened.[27]

A husband can "stand in his wife's shoes" and bring an asylum claim based on a well-founded fear that the wife would be persecuted under China's coercive

---

[25] Lal v. INS, 255 F.3d 998 (9th Cir. 2001).

[26] Mamokolo v. INS, 71 L.W. 1434 (7th Cir. 12/27/02). The Sixth Circuit treated both an Ethiopian woman and her minor daughter as members of a social group with a well-founded fear of persecution on the grounds that 90% of Ethiopian women have been subjected to genital mutilation, therefore making both of them refugees eligible for a discretionary grant of asylum: Abay v. Ashcroft, 368 F.3d 634 (6th Cir. 2004). However, the Fourth Circuit affirmed a BIA final order of removal, finding that the petitioner did not establish clear probability of persecution if she was returned to Senegal; the claim could not be based on fear that her five-year-old daughter, a U.S. citizen, would be subjected to female genital mutilation (FGM) in Senegal, where it is illegal but commonly practiced. If the evidence supports either the petitioner's or the IJ's position, reversal is only appropriate if the reviewing court finds that the evidence compels adopting the petitioner's view. Although derivative asylum claims are possible under 8 USC § 1158(b)(3), so that the accompanying spouse or child of an asylee can also receive asylum, derivative claims are not available to parents of U.S. citizens. In this reading, persecution requires a threat to the applicant's life or freedom. The psychological harm from injury to another person is not enough, and psychological harm without accompanying physical harm does not rise to the level of persecution: Niang v. Gonzales, 492 F.3d 505 (4th Cir. 2007). The Fourth Circuit has ruled that FGM can constitute persecution of a victim or potential victim: Barry v. Gonzales, 445 F.3d 741 (4th Cir. 2006).

[27] Li v. Ashcroft, 312 F.3d 1094 (9th Cir. 2002), *overruled*, 356 F.3d 1153 (9th Cir. 2004).

population policy.[28] The Ninth Circuit reversed a denial of asylum; the applicant's attempt to prevent China's birth control officials from confiscating and destroying his family's property constituted "other resistance" as defined by 8 USC § 1101(a)(42)(B).[29]

The Ninth Circuit resolved a case of first impression by holding that the child of a parent who was forcibly sterilized in China (after having a forbidden third child) is not automatically eligible for asylum under 8 USC § 1101(a)(42)(B). The child did not suffer persecution and does not have a well-founded fear of future persecution if returned to China. Forcibly sterilized persons and their spouses are deemed eligible for asylum on the grounds that they have been persecuted for political opinions, but the statute does not explicate the status of their children. In such situations of ambiguity, the court defers to the BIA's reasonable interpretation of the statute. The case was remanded for a new determination of asylum eligibility based on questions such as whether the petitioner suffered economic deprivation tantamount to persecution, and whether her hardships should be considered cumulatively rather than singly.[30]

The Ninth Circuit has held that gay Mexican men with female sexual identities are an identifiable social group at risk of sexual assault by police in their home country. Therefore, they are entitled to asylum based on well-founded fear of persecution.[31] The First, Third, and Seventh Circuits define social groups more

---

[28] Chen v. Atty Genl, 491 F.3d 100 (3d Cir. 2007).

[29] Lin v. Gonzales, 472 F.3d 1131 (9th Cir. 2007).

[30] Zhang v. Gonzales, 408 F.3d 1239 (9th Cir. 2005). On coercive Chinese population policy, *see also* Chen v. Gonzales, 457 F.3d 670 (7th Cir. 2006). A Chinese petitioner was ordered removed in 2001, but removal did not occur. She sought to reopen the removal proceeding based on China's stricter enforcement of its one-child policy; the petitioner had one Chinese- and two American-born children. The Seventh Circuit agreed that enforcement had become stricter, and she would be at risk of forcible sterilization if returned to China. The alternative would be a fine equal to six years' income, and the BIA has ruled that an onerous fine can constitute persecution. The Seventh Circuit remanded for the BIA to determine the likely consequences if the petitioner and her son were returned to China, and whether relocation to a part of China other than her home province of Fukien (where enforcement was especially strict) would be helpful: Lin v. Mukasey, 532 F.3d 596 (7th Cir. 2008). *But cf.* with Yu v. Att'y General, 513 F.3d 346 (3d Cir. 2008) holding that fear of forced sterilization on return to China was unreasonable, because there were no proven instances of forced sterilization of emigrants who had more children outside China.

[31] Hernandez-Montiel v. INS, 225 F.3d 1084 (9th Cir. 2000) and the cases cited therein. *See also* Karouni v. Gonzalez, 399 F.3d 1163 (9th Cir. 2005), holding that a gay Lebanese person with AIDS showed a well-founded fear of persecution as a member of a particular social group by demonstrating Lebanon's religious and cultural intolerance toward homosexuality. On the issue of homosexuals as a social group, *see also* Amalfi v. Ashcroft, 328 F.3d 719 (3d Cir. 2003), Kimumwe v. Gonzales, 431 F.3d 319 (8th Cir. 2005). The First Circuit granted asylum to an Indonesian Muslim doctor who argued that persecution on the basis of his sexual orientation prevented him from working in Indonesia. 8 CFR § 1208.16(b)(1) creates a rebuttable presumption that past persecution would be likely to recur if the petitioner returned to his or her home country. The standard of economic persecution is deliberate imposition of severe economic disadvantage or deprivation of liberty, food, shelter, employment, or other essentials of life: Kadri v. Mukasey, No. 06-2599. 07-1754 (1st Cir. 9/30/08); the standard for economic persecution comes from *In re* T-Z, 24 I&N Dec. 163 (BIA 2007).

narrowly, requiring immutable common characteristics fundamental to identity. In contrast, the Ninth will allow a social group to be defined by voluntary associational relationships. The IJ held that a lesbian activist asylum seeker suffered because of her sexual orientation, but she experienced isolated instances that did not rise to the level of persecution, particularly since abuse by her family was private and not sponsored or authorized by the government.

The Eighth Circuit ruled that the IJ erred in requiring government involvement for a finding of persecution, which can be based on activities by a person or organization that the government cannot control. The BIA does not have the authority to engage in factfinding (see 8 FR § 1003.1(d)(3)(iv), so the Eighth Circuit sent the case back to the BIA for further proceedings.[32]

A Peruvian who overstayed his tourist visa and applied for asylum was turned down under the "persecutor bar" of §§ 1158(b)(2)(A)(i) and 1231(b)(3)(B)(i) [persons who persecuted others are ineligible for asylum]. He was targeted by the Shining Path guerillas for his alleged participation in a massacre of civilians. The First Circuit ruled in 2007 that the persecutor bar should not be applied if the finder of fact accepts the applicant's version of his state of mind, and remanded, giving DHS a chance to show that the applicant was not credible (specific findings, with support on the record, showing that he lied or evaded questions and should not be believed when he denied knowledge of the massacre).[33]

The Ninth Circuit held that disabled children and their parents are a protected group for asylum purposes, permitting the parents of a disabled child to seek asylum and withholding of removal secondary to the persecution the child suffered as a disabled person in the Soviet Union.[34]

An alien who is firmly resettled in a country other than the United States or his or her country of origin is not entitled to asylum in the United States. The key factor is whether any form of permanent resident status is available in that country, not the totality of circumstances in the environment in which the alien has resettled.[35]

The Ninth joined the other Circuits in holding that in a "firm resettlement" case, the DHS must show that some kind of official status was offered that would permit indefinite residence in the third country (other than the original land of citizenship and the United States). The DHS must produce direct evidence of an offer by the government, or circumstantial evidence sufficient to show that the alien's indefinite stay would be tolerated. Once that is shown, the alien must show that he or she was not firmly resettled. In this case, the record included a work

---

[32] Nabulwala v. Gonzales, 481 F.3d 1115 (8th Cir. 2007). *See* Suprun v. Gonzales, 442 F.3d 1079 (8th Cir. 2006) for the proposition that activity uncontrolled by the government can constitute persecution.

[33] Castan~eda-Castillo v. Gonzales, 488 F.3d 17 (1st Cir. 2007).

[34] Tchoukhrova v. Gonzales, 404 F.3d 1181 (9th Cir. 2005).

[35] Abdille v. Ashcroft, 242 F.3d 477 (3d Cir. 2001).

permit and a Canadian refugee application, but the record was undeveloped, and the matter was remanded for further development.[36]

In 2007, the Ninth Circuit joined the Second, Sixth, and Seventh Circuits holding that injuries to the applicant's family must be considered when the events forming the basis of a past persecution claim occurred when the petitioner was a child (and took a child's eye view of events). Failing to consider the impact of the events on children of similar age is legal error.[37]

The Second Circuit ruled that it was not an error for a BIA member to affirm an IJ's rejection of an asylum request unilaterally, without referring it to a three-member BIA panel. The single-member decision is the product of 1999's "streamlining" regulations adopted at 8 CFR § 1003.1(e) and amended in 2002; a three-member panel is convened only in special circumstances (e.g., to resolve a matter of national importance or resolve inconsistent judgments among IJs). When a BIA member affirms an IJ's decision without opinion, 8 CFR § 1003.1(e)(4) directs the BIA member not to provide an explanation of the reasoning behind the affirmance, so there is nothing that a reviewing court can review. Hence, the Second Circuit concluded that the Court of Appeals does not have jurisdiction to review a BIA member's decision to affirm the IJ without opinion.[38]

§ 19.04 NONIMMIGRANT VISAS

Whether the statement is made in good faith or not (or whether or not the individual's intentions change), many people claim that they want to travel to or live in the United States temporarily, without intending to become permanent residents or U.S. citizens. Over 90% of visas are issued to nonimmigrants, mostly tourists.

Most nonimmigrant visas are not subject to quotas; any number can be issued per year. However, limitations are imposed on H-1B visas (for professionals) and

---

[36] Maharaj v. Gonzales, 450 F.3d 961 (9th Cir. 2006). *See also* Tandia v. Gonzales, 437 F.3d 245 (2d Cir. 2006), holding that the IJ and BIA impermissibly relied on the former text of 8 CFR § 208.13(d) and denied an asylum application on the grounds that a Mauritanian found a "safe haven" in France before coming to the United States. The proper question was whether or not he had been "firmly resettled." Reliance on an off-the-record asylum interview constituted impermissible speculation and conjecture. A Mauretanian, forcibly deported because of his race and told he would be killed if he returned, was denied asylum by an IJ on the grounds of firm resettlement. The Second Circuit ruled that the IJ erred by putting the burden of proof on the asylum applicant, and by finding firm resettlement without substantial evidence. The IJ also failed to properly shift the burden to the government, on the issue of withholding of removal, after the applicant showed past persecution; the government had the burden of proving a fundamental change in Mauretania. The Second Circuit held that the applicant had not resettled in Mali, where he lived on charity and lacked official recognition or documentation — a marginal existence that could not be characterized as lengthy and peaceful residence in a third country other than the U.S. or the applicant's country of origin: Makadji v. Gonzales, 470 F.3d 450 (2d Cir. 2006).

[37] Hernandez-Ortiz v. Gonzales, 496 F.3d 1042 (9th Cir. 2007).

[38] Kambolli v. Gonzales, 449 F.3d 454 (2d Cir. 2006). Yu Sheng Zhang v. DOJ, 362 F.3d 155 (2d Cir. 2004) upholds the validity of the streamlining process over a Due Process challenge.

H-2B temporary agricultural worker visas. The numerical limitations apply only to the workers, not to spouses and children accompanying them. See INA § 101(a)(15) and 8 CFR § 214.2 for basic rules.

Visas to enter the United States lawfully are issued in U.S. consulates and embassies in the various countries. However, certain visas (those for temporary workers,[39] or immediate relatives or intended spouses of U.S. citizens) require filing of a petition in the United States with the Immigration and Naturalization Service (INS), which is an agency of the Department of State.[40]

The decision to grant or deny the visa is made by consular officers. Visa refusals are reviewed by another consular officer, and the Visa Office in Washington, D.C. can resolve disputes between consular officers.

Under most circumstances, a visa applicant can get neither administrative nor judicial review of the denial.[41]

Under IMMACT, as amended, there are many types of nonimmigrant visas, identified by letter. (TN visas can be issued to NAFTA professionals.)

- A visas: diplomats (A-1), foreign government employees and their families (A-2); servants of A-1 and A-2 visa holders (A-3). A-1 and A-2 visa holders can work within the U.S. if they get permission by submitting Form I-566
- B visas: tourists (B-1); business visitors (B-2). The visa is valid for a year and can be renewed every six months. B visa holders are not allowed to work within the United States. Persons from 25 countries are allowed to enter the United States for up to 90 days without a tourist visa, using Form I-94W, but they cannot adjust their status to become immigrants
- C visas: persons in transit
- D visas: crew members of ships and aircraft
- E visas: traders and investors (E-1 for traders and their families; E-2 for investors and their families), who are doing business under a commercial treaty[42]
- F visas: students of academic curricula in high schools or at the college level (F1) and their families (F-2). The student must be able to prove that a home is maintained in the country of origin, and intent to return there after completing

---

[39] Either the alien or the employer files the petition, using Form I-140; INA § 204(a)(1)(D) generally requires filing by the employer rather than the potential immigrant for second and third preference employment-related immigration.

[40] The U.S. sponsor files the petition, using Form I-130, or Form I-600 for a person seeking to adopt an orphan. INA § 204(f) contains special provisions for immigration of Amerasians fathered by U.S. citizens between 1950 and 10/22/82. The petition requires proof that the petitioner is a U.S. citizen or lawful permanent resident, and proof of the familial relationship.

[41] Review unavailable: *e.g.*, Li Hing of Hong Kong, Inc. v. Levin, 800 F.2d 970 (9th Cir. 1986); Ventura-Escamilla v. INS, 647 F.2d 28 (9th Cir. 1981), but judicial review of denial available under the Administrative Procedure Act held available by Abourezk v. Reagan, 785 F.2d 1043 (D.C. Cir. 1986).

[42] As a result of REAL ID, P.L. 109-13, up to 10,500 Australians per fiscal year can enter on E nonimmigrant visas for specialty occupations covered by employers' labor attestations.

the academic course. The duration of F visas is limited to the length of the course, plus 60 days to move back home.

F-1 students are permitted to work part-time, but their families are not allowed to work at all. Persons holding a tourist visa may be able to change their status to F-1 student, and after completing his or her studies, an F-1 student may be able to get an H-1B visa to work in a specialty occupation. It is possible that the student would contract a valid marriage with a U.S. citizen, and thus be able to immigrate on that basis. Immigration on the basis of a second or third employment-related preference is also a possibility. See the Regs. at 8 CFR § 214.2.

- G visas: employees of international organizations
- H visas: temporary workers who are hired to cope with an employer's immediate but temporary need for labor. H-1A visas are for registered nurses.

The EB-3 category covers immigrant workers who hold bachelor's degrees and perform professional-level work and skilled workers (immigrants who do skilled jobs that require at least two years' education, training, or experience).[43] See § 3.10[B][3] for a discussion of employers' obligations connected with hiring non-citizens, a process that requires collection of documentation of employment eligibility and verification that citizens are not available to take the job. Employers are permitted to maintain, sign, and store their I-9 forms in electronic form rather than on paper.[44]

In July 2006, a federal program was announced to discourage employers from hiring illegal immigrants, and to report illegal immigrants already hired. Employers can volunteer for the Basic Pilot Employment Verification Program by having their records audited by immigration agents, naming a compliance officer, and training their personnel to verify employment documents.[45]

H-1B covers professionals and persons of exceptional scientific or artistic ability, as well as "specialty occupations." A specialty occupation calls for both theoretical and practical exercise of a body of specialized knowledge; the typical case is a software engineer. H-1B visas require advanced degrees and/or professional experience. If the occupation requires a state license, the H-1B visa holder must also possess the license.

The American Competitiveness and Workforce Improvement Act, P.L. 105-277, strives to balance employers' needs for certain skills against the political mandate to protect American jobs.

---

[43] EB-3 petitions can get Premium Processing Services by filing Form I-907 and paying a $1,000 fee; USCIS either approves the application or gives notice of intent to deny within 15 calendar days of receiving the form. If necessary, USCIS will start a fraud investigation. *See Premium Processing Services Expanded*, 11 Bender's Immigration Bulletin 1086 (9/15/06).

[44] 71 FR 34510 (6/15/06).

[45] Julia Preston, *U.S. Seeks Employers' Aid on Immigration*, N.Y. Times 7/27/06 at p. A22.

An H1-B dependent company (defined as one with at least 15% of its workforce holding such visas) has an obligation to attest that it will not lay off any employee in the 90 days before or after filing a petition to hire an H-1B holder for the same job. Job contractors are not permitted to place an H-1B holder in a job held by a U.S. citizen who was laid off in the 90 days before or after the placement.

To protect U.S. jobs, the employer of an H1-B worker must pay the higher of the actual wage for the job or the prevailing wage for the same position. A willful violation involving a layoff or underpayment of an H-1B worker can be penalized by three years of federal contract debarment plus a $35,000 fine. H-1B visas are tied to employment, and therefore a number of H-1B workers who lost their jobs due to declines in the technology industry were also legally required to leave the United States.

As noted above, P.L. 107-273 permits extension of H-1B visas; the application for extension must be made a year before the visa would expire.

Effective March 8, 2005, the H-1B Visa Reform Act of 2004, part of P.L. 108-447, the appropriations act, exempts up to 20,000 H-1B from the cap of 65,000 visas per year, if the visa holders have Masters' or higher degrees from an American college or university. Interim Final Rules were published in May 2005. An Indian with a valid H-1B visa, allowing him to work initially until May 15, 2002, extended to January 15, 2003, began to work for a second company in March 2002, three months before his new employer filed an H-1B petition on his behalf. INS found him while executing a search warrant on his new employer. The Seventh Circuit agreed with the IJ: the petitioner could be deported for starting to work for the second employer before he had authorization. The H-1B visa is conditioned on working only for the employer who secured the visa, or for a second employer — if the alien did not perform unauthorized work before the filing: see 8 USC § 1184(n)(2). Under 8 USC § 1227(a)(1)(C)(i), an alien is deportable for failure to maintain or comply with the conditions of the nonimmigrant status under which he or she was admitted.[46]

Because of INA § 242(a)(2)(B)(ii), a Court of Appeals does not have jurisdiction to review INS' denial of an H-1B petition.[47]

The H-1C visa category is for nonimmigrant nurses working in areas of the United States that have a nursing shortage. See the Nursing Relief for Disadvantaged Areas Act of 1999, P.L. 106-95.

The Department of Labor's Assistant Secretary for Employment Standards has been designated as the person responsible for implementing the DOL's employment standards, labor standards, and labor-management policies, programs and activities.[48]

---

[46] Ali v. Mukasey, No. 07-2462 (7th Cir. 9/8/08).

[47] CDI Info. Servs. Inc. v. Reno, 278 F.3d 616 (6th Cir. 2002).

[48] 66 FR 29655 (5/31/01).

H-2A visas are for seasonal agricultural workers, H-2B for temporary assignments outside agriculture.[49] H-3 visas are for persons coming to the United States for a training course lasting up to two years. H-4 visas go to families of the holders of H-1, -2, and -3 visas; these people are only allowed to work in the United States if they are included in the employer's petition that permits the temporary worker to enter the U.S.

H-1 visas are issued for an initial period of up to three years. H-2 visas are supposed to be temporary or seasonal, and are limited to the employment period that the employer specifies in the petition

- I visas: journalists
- J visas: exchange visitors (J-1 for program participants, J-2 for their families)
- K visas: persons engaged to U.S. citizens or to children of U.S. citizens; this visa lasts only 90 days, and is for the specific purpose of coming to the United States to be married. A medical examination is required, although it is not required for other nonimmigrant categories. K-1 visas are for fiance(e)s; K-2 visas for their children; K-3 visas are for spouses of U.S. citizens; K-4 visas for the unmarried children of holders of K-3 visas
- L visas: transferees from one branch of a company to another branch of the same company
- M visas: vocational students (as distinct from F visa students of more academic curricula)[50]
- N visas: (relatives of G visa personnel)
- O visas: individuals of demonstrated great achievement or unusual ability in art, science, athletics, education, or business, in order for them to work temporarily exercising their talents. O-1 visas are for aliens seeking work in their areas of expertise, where the Attorney General has determined that such work will benefit the United States. O-2 visas are for persons accompanying and assisting an O-1 visa holder (e.g., a singer's accompanist; an athlete's trainer), and O-3 visas are for families of O-1 or O-2 holders. Usually, the duration of the visa is limited to a particular performance or event
- P visas: athletes, entertainers, or members of performing groups (P-1 for the group member; P-2 for performers or support staff for international exchange groups; P-3 for artists or entertainers in a "culturally unique" group; and P-4 for spouses and children)

---

[49] The Save Our Small and Seasonal Businesses Act of 2005, Title IV of P.L. 109-13, changes the calculation of the number of H-2B visas, increases the penalty for employer misconduct, and allows only half of the H-2B visa holders to enter during the first half of the fiscal year. *See also* proposed regulations at 70 FR 3983 (1/27/05), simplifying the two-step application process to a single form to be e-mailed by the employer to the Department of Homeland Security, certifying compliance with the requirements.

[50] *See* 67 FR 76256 (12/11/02) for a Final Rule, effective 1/1/03, for reporting and record retention requirements for the F, J, and M nonimmigrant visa categories, and procedures for the Student and Exchange Visitor Information System. Later, an Interim Rule was issued: 68 FR 28129 (5/23/03).

- Q visas: participants in international cultural exchange programs
- R visas: religious workers
- T visas: victims of trafficking in human beings, such as slavery or compelled prostitution. Up to 5,000 visas can be issued in this category per year, pursuant to P.L. 106-386, the Victims of Trafficking and Violence Protection Act of 2000. Visas can also be issued to the spouses, children and parents of such persons
- U visas: up to 10,000 visas a year (also under the Victims of Trafficking Act) for witnesses or persons cooperating in investigations of crimes against humanity, and family members of such persons.

22 CFR Part 41 contains various requirements for nonimmigrant visa applications. Depending on the desired visa, it may be necessary to show acceptance at an accredited school, a petition by an employer or prospective spouse, etc. When holders of nonimmigrant visas enter the United States, they are issued Form 1-94, which explains the length and conditions of their lawful stay within the United States. For instructions on using the I-129 (Petition for Nonimmigrant Worker) for, e.g., H-1B, P-1 (athlete or entertainer); H-1C (registered nurse); H-3 (trainee); F-2 (participant in artistic exchange); Q-1 (participant in international cultural exchange program), see the USCIS Web site. Form I-129 is not required for initial entry of E treaty traders, TN Canadian citizens entering the U.S. under NAFTA, or R-1 religious workers, although they do use the I-129 to apply for change of status, extension of their stay, or change of employment.[51]

Under INA § 248, most persons admitted to the United States under a nonimmigrant visa can apply to the INS to have their visa changed to another category. The change is discretionary with the INS. Generally, the alien will have to show that he or she does not plan to remain in the United States permanently, and did not plan to change status before arriving in this country.

[A] Adjustment of Status

Although nonimmigrant visas do not permit indefinite residence and employment within the United States, it is possible for the holder of such a visa to apply for "adjustment of status" — i.e., to seek to become an immigrant. (However, adjustment of status is not available for D visas or most B visas.)

The practical problem is that adjustment of status not only requires legal entry into the United States and satisfaction of the eligibility requirements for one of the immigration visa categories — there must also be an available immigration visa for the home country of the person seeking adjustment of status. INA § 245(c) does not permit adjustment of the status of any person who was unlawfully in the

---

[51] USCIS, *Temporary Benefits Employment Categories and Required Documentation*, http://www.uscis.gov/portal/site/uscis/menuitem.5af9bb95919f35e66f614176543f6d1a/?vgnextoid=229c6138f898d010VgnVCM10000048f3d6a1RCRD&v

United States at any time, or who worked illegally. (Exceptions are made for immediate relatives of U.S. citizens; foreign doctors licensed to practice in the U.S.; and people who engaged in technical immigration violations for which they were not at fault.)

Severe limitations are also imposed on individuals who seek adjustment of status based on a marriage contracted during removal proceedings; it may be necessary for the individual to leave the United States for two years and seek re-entry at that time (INA § 204(g)).

The adjustment of status application is Form I-485, filed with the INS district office nearest the alien's place of residence.

Under prior law, people who entered the U.S. illegally, and "overstayed" (people who remained in the United States after their visas expired, or who acted contrary to the terms of the visa) could apply for adjustment of status, but that is no longer allowed, unless a petition was filed before 1/1/98. Now, if such persons leave the United States, they will not be allowed back in for three years or ten years (if they spent a year or more in the U.S. as illegal aliens), depending on the circumstances.

INA § 212(a)(6)(G) provides that a student who fraudulently or willfully contravenes the terms of the student visa, or any alien who fraudulently or willfully misrepresents a material fact to improve his or her immigration status, cannot enter the U.S. legally and cannot be issued a visa.

The Ninth Circuit found 8 CFR § 245.1(c)(8) [forbidding arriving aliens to seek adjustment of status in removal proceedings] to be invalid, because it conflicts with the governing statute, 8 USC § 1255(a).[52]

§ 19.05 EMPLOYMENT OF IMMIGRANTS

Persons who work in the United States notwithstanding their lack of autho-rization to do so (e.g., they immigrated illegally; they overstayed a student or tourist visa that did not permit U.S. employment) may be viewed in one of two ways. They may be seen either as illegal aliens (and threats to U.S. jobs and wage scales) or as undocumented workers (at risk of exploitation by unscrupulous employers who refuse to pay them, underpay them, or subject them to dangerous working conditions and excessive hours). See INA § 247A for the ban on employ-ment of aliens not authorized to work in the United States and the requirements for documenting identity and employment authorization for those who are authorized to work in this country.

[A] DOL Certification

If an alien is offered a permanent job in the United States, and wishes to immigrate to take that job, "certification" from the Department of Labor will

---

[52] Bona v. Gonzalez, 425 F.3d 663 (9th Cir. 2005), *following* Succar v. Ashcroft, 394 F.3d 8 (1st Cir. 2005).

probably be required. The DOL must certify that the job in question will not adversely affect wages or working conditions in the United States, and there is no qualified citizen willing to accept the job. The employer must cooperate with the DOL Employment and Training Administration and the Department of Homeland Security's U.S. Citizenship and Immigration Services (USCIS). The employer certifies to the USCIS that hiring the alien is appropriate because of the unavailability of citizens. Application is made on ETA Form 9089 (Alien Employment Certification).[53] Certification is required for H-2 nonimmigrant visas, and for second preference (professionals with advanced degrees; persons of exceptional ability) and third preference (skilled workers and professionals not holding advanced degrees). However, priority workers (first preference: persons in job categories in which the U.S. has a persistent shortage, such as nurses and physical therapists) are not subject to the certification requirement. When certification has been obtained, the employer files Form I-140, Immigrant Petition for an Alien Worker, with the USCIS.[54] Although immigration is nearly exclusively a subject for federal law, state employment service offices have a significant involvement in the certification procedure, e.g., by establishing prevailing local wage rates and testing the job market.

The DOL has two schedules of occupations. Schedule A (20 CFR § 656.10), occupations where workers are needed from outside the United States, e.g., nursing and physical therapy, and Schedule B (20 CFR § 656.11), unskilled occupations with no labor shortage in the U.S. Certification is automatic for Schedule A but a hard-to-obtain special waiver is required for Schedule B occupations.

For occupations that are not "scheduled," the employer must submit Department of Labor Application for Alien Employment Certification Form to the state job service office, with documentation of failure to find a U.S. worker on comparable terms — and documentation that the employer has not discriminated against qualified U.S. applicants. See 20 CFR § 656.21 as amended by 66 FR 40590 (8/3/01).

[B] Employer Sanctions

Since IRCA, employers of immigrants who are not eligible to work in the U.S. (but not the immigrants themselves) are subject to sanctions under 8 USC § 1324a. It is illegal to knowingly hire an unauthorized alien, or to continue to employ someone who is not authorized to work in this country.

The employer is required to use Form I-9 to verify each new hire's identity and eligibility for U.S. employment. The employer is subject to a complex schedule of civil and criminal penalties, with escalating penalties for repeat violations, if I-9 forms are not obtained and retained as required.

---

[53] *See* 71 FR 7655 (2/13/06).

[54] DOL, *Hiring Foreign Workers*, http://www.workforcesecurity.doleta.gov/foreign/hiring.asp; USCIS, *The Form I-9 Process in a Nutshell*, http://uscis.gov/graphics/servicds/employerinfo/EIB102.pdf.

Employers can complete the Form I-9 either at the time of hiring, or before hiring (once a commitment to hire has been made). However, they must complete the form at the same point in the employment process for all employees.

The Proposed Rule[55] includes a new Form I-9A, for re-verification of employment eligibility that has already been established.

The Supreme Court ruled that undocumented workers are not covered by Title VII.[56]

Civil RICO cannot be used to assert a claim that an employer knowingly recruited illegal aliens as a way of forcing down wages, because such a claim would treat the employer as both the RICO person and the enterprise, and it is impossible for a single party to conspire with itself.[57]

§ 19.06 PUBLIC BENEFITS FOR IMMIGRANTS

PRWORA denies federal public assistance to immigrants other than "qualified aliens." A qualified alien is either a refugee, deportee from another country, or alien who had been in the United States for more than five years, or a lawful permanent resident with at least 40 quarters of U.S. work history.

Food stamp and Supplemental Security Income (SSI) eligibility was terminated for persons entering the United States legally before August 22, 1996. Qualified aliens in the United States on that date who became eligible for Medicaid before the PRWORA effective date would continue to be eligible. Each state can decide whether or not to provide non-emergency Medicaid benefits to legal aliens.

Persons entering the United States after 8/22/96 (even if they enter legally) will not be entitled to Medicaid or other federal means-tested program benefits during the five years after entry. Refugees, deportees from other countries, persons receiving political asylum, and military personnel from other countries are exempt. Benefit eligibility is possible after the five years elapse, but the assets of the immigrant's spouse and sponsor are taken into account, which will result in many disqualifications.

The Tenth Circuit upheld a Colorado law denying Medicaid coverage to legal aliens who are not qualified aliens as defined by PRWORA. The court used a rational basis test rather than applying strict scrutiny; under that standard, the statute did not deny equal protection.[58]

§ 19.07 NATURALIZATION

Technically speaking, "immigration" involves intent to remain in the United States permanently, or at least indefinitely (with no fixed date of departure). "Permanent residence" is intent to reside in the United States, with or without

---

[55] Published at http://www.ins.usdoj.gov.

[56] Hoffman Plastic Compounds v. NLRB, 535 U.S. 137 (2002).

[57] Baker v. IBP Inc., 357 F.3d 535 (7th Cir. 2004).

[58] Soskin v. Reinerston, 353 F.3d 1252 (10th Cir. 2004).

establishing a domicile there. A permanent resident might spend significant amounts of time outside the United States.

To become a legal permanent resident with a "green card" (actually Form I-151 has not been green for several years), an individual has to receive labor certification from the Department of Labor (i.e., that the immigrant has not taken a job away from a qualified U.S. citizen), file a preference petition, and apply for permanent residence.

Naturalization is the process of becoming a U.S. citizen. The INS determines which applicants are qualified to become citizens; they become so by taking an oath before the U.S. District Court.

A legal permanent resident can become a naturalized U.S. citizen after five years in that status — three years, if married to a U.S. citizen, as long as at least half that time has been spent within the United States (INA §§ 316(a), 319). Section 316(a) also places upon the applicant for naturalization the burden of proving that he or she has been a person of good moral character during the entire period of U.S. residency. The applicant must be able to read, write, speak, and understand simple English, and must have a basic knowledge of U.S. history and the principles of its government (§ 312). The naturalization application is Form N-400; it requires the applicant to provide background information about the details of his or her period of residency in the United States.

The first step is an appearance before a naturalization examiner, as prescribed by INA § 335(a). A denied application is reviewed by another immigration officer: § 336(a). Since IMMACT, aliens have had the right to de novo judicial review of denials of naturalization (§ 336(b)).

Also note that a person can become a U.S. citizen in four ways: naturalization, naturalization of the parent of a minor (person under 18), birth within the United States or its territories, or having a U.S. parent even if the person is born outside the U.S. See INA §§ 301(a), 322(a).

According to the Ninth Circuit, the Department of Homeland Security's regulation about assessment of good moral character of applicants for naturalization is constitutional, and is not ultra vires with respect to its governing statute.[59]

The First Circuit affirmed an award of EAJA fees to an applicant who sued to force the government to act on his naturalization application; he prevailed, and the government had taken an unreasonable position, and failed to explain why it did not follow its own procedure (for performing background checks). More than 18 months after his interview, the naturalization applicant brought suit, seeking that his application be granted, or at least remanded to USCIS's directions to adjudicate it (see 8 USC § 1447(b), permitting a District Court hearing if 120 days pass without determination of a naturalization application). After the action was filed, USCIS finished the review and approved his naturalization, and he became a citizen. The First Circuit found that an order containing an agreement can operate as a consent decree; there can even be judicial imprimatur if there is no

---

[59] United States v. Dang, 488 F.3d 1135 (9th Cir. 2007).

judgment on the merits, and the consent decree is not incorporated into a court order. A government position is substantially justified if its actions are required by a statute, but in this case the statute only required a personal investigation, not the procedure adopted by USCIS. In fact, the 18-month delay violated the statute.[60]

[A] Family Law Issues in Immigration

Issuance of a spousal visa requires the alien visa-seeker to have a "valid and subsisting marriage" with a U.S. citizen, determined by the laws of the country in which the marriage took place. However, marriages that are illegal in the United States, such as polygamous marriages, incestuous marriage, or marriages of same-sex couples, do not give rise to "spouse" status for this purpose.

There are four steps to becoming a lawful permanent resident on the basis of marriage. First, the U.S. citizen fiancé(e) files a petition for the K visa. Then, the marriage occurs; if it does not occur within 90 days of entry, the non-citizen must leave the United States. The third step is an application to adjust status; until 1986, this was automatic, but it now requires an application. For the first two years, permanent resident status is only conditional; at that point, the couple can make a joint petition for unconditional residence, based on a representation that the couple did not marry for immigration reasons, and are still married. A K visa entrant came to the United States in 1998 as the fiancée of a U.S. citizen. They were married in early 1999, and she filed an application on April 14, 1999, to adjust her status to lawful permanent resident. On April 9, 2001, while the alien was still waiting for her INS interview, she was divorced. INS denied her application for adjustment on August 27, 2001, because she was divorced, taking the position that a visaholder's status cannot be adjusted if the marriage ends before adjudication of the application. However, the Ninth Circuit granted a petition for review, taking the position that 8 USC § 1186(c)(4)(B) allows a waiver if the marriage was entered into good faith; the focus is the rationale for the marriage, not whether it ended.[61]

If a couple marries without valid intent to live as husband and wife in the United States, the marriage is not valid. A separation agreement with the U.S. citizen spouse will preclude the alien spouse from filing a visa petition premised on marital status. However, if the marriage was valid at its inception, a later separation or divorce will not alter the alien spouse's permanent resident status.

Furthermore, a person who was permitted to immigrate because of marriage to a U.S. citizen cannot make a petition on behalf of a subsequent spouse who is an alien during the five years after becoming a lawful permanent resident (unless the first U.S. citizen spouse died, or the permanent resident can prove that the first marriage was non-fraudulent): INA § 204(a)(2).

[60] Aronov v. Chertoff, 536 F.3d 30 (1st Cir. 2008); *see* Fact Sheet, USCIS Press Office, *Immigration Security Checks—How and Why the Process Works* 2 (April 25, 2006), available at http://www.uscis.gov/files/pressrelease/security_checks_42506.pdf.

[61] Choin v. Mukasey, 537 F.3d 1116 (9th Cir. 2008).

A person who knowingly enters into a fraudulent "green card" marriage can be imprisoned for up to five years and/or required to pay a fine of up to $250,000. Penalties are also imposed on lawyers who willfully misrepresent material facts, or conceal material facts, as to alien marriages.

Because of IMMACT, even marriages entered into during the pendency of deportation or exclusion proceedings can be recognized, but clear and convincing evidence is required that the marriage was entered into in good faith and not as an immigration fraud. Under IIRIRA, the determination of whether immigration-related marriage fraud has occurred is not completely discretionary with the INA, and therefore the Court of Appeals can properly review a BIA determination; the Court of Appeals' role is not limited to review of removal orders under 8 USC § 1227(a)(1)(G)(ii).[62]

Alien spouses granted conditional U.S. residence can petition for removal of the condition if the marriage ended in less than two years of the grant of residence — whether the alien or citizen spouse sought the divorce. The conditional residence requirement can be waived for the benefit of an alien spouse, or child of an alien, who is the victim of battery or domestic abuse.

A "green card" marriage is only voidable, not void, so it is bigamy to remarry without legally terminating the green card marriage.

To obtain a K-1 visa for a fiance or fiancee, the U.S. citizen must file Form I-129F with the USCIS. If the potential foreign bride or groom has children, they are eligible for K-2 visas; the children should be listed on the I-129F application, but do not require separate petitions. As a general rule, a successful I-129F application must prove that the two people had an in-person meeting within two years of filing the petition (a requirement that can be waived in appropriate circumstances, e.g., an arranged marriage in a culture where spouses are forbidden to meet before the wedding); that they have a bona fide intention to marry; and are legally permitted to marry within 90 days of the foreign person entering the U.S.

The International Marriage Broker Regulation Act of 2005 (IMBRA, P.L. 109-162) aims to protect "mail order brides" against abuses when they come to the United States for marriages facilitated by Internet sites or marriage brokers. The potential fiancees must receive background information about the U.S. potential fiance's criminal record, if any, and must be informed of U.S. laws against domestic violence. In general, the U.S. citizen is only allowed to file three petitions for admission of a fiance or fiancee, and simultaneous petitions cannot be filed for more than one prospective spouse.[63]

P.L. 104-51 amends INA § 101, to change the statutory vocabulary used to classify children. Children are now referred to as born "in wedlock" or "out of wedlock," rather than "legitimate" or "illegitimate." An out-of-wedlock child can

---

[62] Nakamoto v. Ashcroft, 363 F.3d 874 (9th Cir. 2004).

[63] *See* Jill A. Apa, *Bringing Fiances and Fiancees to the United States*, 11 Bender's Immigration Bulletin 2/15/06 at p. 159. The mid-2006 revised Form I-129F can be found at http://www.uscis.gov/graphics/formsfee/forms/i-129f.htm.

qualify for a U.S. visa based on the relationship to the natural mother, or to a natural father who has or had a bona fide parent-child relationship: INA § 101(b)(1)(D).

In an April 1998 decision, the Supreme Court construed INA § 309(a)(4), which holds that, for a child to assert U.S. citizenship, paternity must be proved by age 18 if a child's father is a U.S. citizen and the child's birth occurred outside both the United States and wedlock. The timing requirement is not imposed when the child's mother is a U.S. citizen. The Supreme Court denied Equal Protection claims premised on this gender distinction, although there are three separate opinions as to why this is so.[64]

Under IIRIRA, a person who acts as sponsor for an immigrant relative must give an affidavit agreeing to support the alien, if necessary, at a level of at least 125% of the federal poverty line. The sponsor also has an obligation to reimburse the federal government for any means-tested public benefits (e.g., Medicaid; SSI; but not Medicare, which is not means-tested) received by the alien during his or her first ten years in the United States.

§ 19.08   BORDER PATROLS AND OTHER INS SEARCHES

The powers of the INS to detain individuals, to question them about their immigration status, and to search vehicles depend on the location of the contact between the INS officer and the suspected illegal alien. INS powers are greatest at the border; intermediate within 100 miles of the border; and weakest 100 miles or more within U.S. territory.

INA § 235 gives the INS the power to stop and search any vehicle and/or question any person at any U.S. border. Boats and planes are subject to search if they could contain aliens. In June 2008, the Supreme Court rejected an application from environmental groups to restrict the Bush administration's power to construct a fence at the Mexican border. (Part of the fence had already been constructed, and a number of laws and regulations had been waived to speed up construction.)[65]

Aliens can be "inspected" at the border to see if they are entitled to enter the U.S. lawfully. "Secondary inspection" means detaining aliens who may be inadmissible to verify their status. Aliens applying for admission always have the right to withdraw their application and leave the U.S. immediately. INA § 212(d)(5) allows temporary parole of an alien until the investigation is complete; parole probably will not be granted if the alien is inadmissible as a criminal or threat to U.S. national security.

Persons on immigration parole are entitled to a short-form hearing before removal from the U.S., but are not entitled to full-scale formal removal proceedings. INS' decision to grant or deny parole is discretionary, and there is no administrative review procedure, although it may be possible to get a declaratory judgment or habeas corpus through the federal District Courts.

---

[64] Miller v. Albright, 523 U.S. 420 (1998).

[65] (AP), *High Court Rejects Environmental Groups' Challenge to Mexican Border Fence*, 6/23/08 (law.com).

The Second Circuit held that the Bureau of Customs and Border Protection did not violate the Administrative Procedures Act, the Religious Freedom Restoration Act, or the First or Fourth Amendments by searching and detaining five Muslim U.S. citizens at the Canadian border when they returned after an Islamic conference in Toronto. Customs received intelligence that people with terrorist ties would attend some Islamic conferences, so everyone who attended the conferences received additional screening. The plaintiffs had no criminal records, and were not the object of individualized suspicion of association with terrorism. They were detained, questioned, patted down, fingerprinted, and photographed. The Second Circuit held that Customs did not violate the APA because it acted under statutory authority; the searches occurred at the border, where the government has plenary authority; the searches were not invasive enough to raise Fourth Amendment problems; and the inspection policy passed muster under the First Amendment and the Religious Freedom Restoration Act, because it was narrowly tailored to achieve the government objective of excluding terrorists.[66]

The INS also maintains check-points away from the borders, as well as roving patrols. *United States v. Brignoni-Ponce*, 422 U.S. 873 (1975) requires suspicion based on specific, articulable facts in order to stop vehicles that are not at the border. Random stops for the purpose of detecting illegal aliens are inappropriate. However, brief stops at fixed immigration check-points are permissible even without suspicion, on balance between the need to enforce immigration laws and the brevity of the detention and notice to motorists that detention will occur: *United States v. Martinez-Fuerte*, 428 U.S. 523 (1976).

Early in 2002, the Supreme Court held that the totality of circumstances that suggested drug smuggling and rebutted the defendant's claim that an innocent family picnic was taking place justified the Border Patrol in making an investigative stop at the border. Therefore, the large quantity of marijuana seized during the stop was admissible.[67]

INA § 287(a)(3) authorizes warrantless immigration searches of vehicles even away from the border. The Supreme Court has read the Fourth Amendment exception for border searches to permit customs officials to remove, disassemble, and reassemble the fuel tanks of vehicles crossing a border, even absent individualized suspicion.[68]

INA § 283(a) bars roving patrols and fixed check-points more than 25 miles within U.S. borders, but aliens can be briefly detained for interrogation based on a reasonable belief of illegal aliens status. Searches of vehicles and places of employment are appropriate with a search warrant, but a warrant authorizing

---

[66] Tabbaa v. Chertoff, 509 F.3d 89 (2d Cir. 2007).

[67] United States v. Arvizu, 534 U.S. 266 (2002).

[68] United States v. Flores-Montano, 541 U.S. 149 (2004). The Ninth Circuit did not require reasonable suspicion for a federal customs inspector to cut open a traveler's spare tire in the course of a warrantless border search; this was not considered a destructive intervention that would be particularly offensive under the Fourth Amendment: United States v. Cortez-Rocha, 383 F.3d 1093 (9th Cir. 2004).

search for property does not justify searching a place of business for undocumented workers. Illegal aliens can be arrested without a warrant, based on the INS officer's reason to believe that the person is in the United States illegally and is likely to escape before a warrant could be secured.

§ 19.09 REMOVAL

Removal proceedings are instituted in two circumstances: exclusion of an individual seeking to enter the United States, but who is not eligible for entry, and deportation of a person already present in the United States, but without legal authorization. Citizens — even those whose status was obtained fraudulently — are not subject to removal. Diplomats and their families are also immune from removal.

Under prior law, the exclusion and deportation proceedings were distinct, but IIRIRA provides for a single form of removal proceeding covering both situations. Removal of an alien may also require U.S. citizen children of the alien to leave the U.S. when the alien is removed.

Under the INA, outside of circumstances in which the Attorney General can order removal of certain aliens, the Immigration Judge is the only party that can issue an order of removal. The BIA cannot order removal when the Immigration Judge has not made an initial ruling of deportability.[69]

"Expedited removal" is available when an inadmissible person seeks to enter the United States. There are no rights of hearing or appeal, unless the individual is an asylum applicant or asserts a fear of persecution in the home country.

Removal is considered a civil rather than a criminal proceeding (even though many removal proceedings in fact involve persons convicted of crimes within the U.S.), so Miranda warnings are not required.

The Supreme Court ruled that 8 USC § 1231(a)(5), which reinstates prior removal orders against aliens re-entering the United States illegally, and which does not allow judicial review, applies to aliens who re-entered before the effective date of the statute. It is not impermissibly retroactive with respect to aliens who stayed in the United States illegally after the effective date.[70]

The Third Circuit adopted the same standards as the First, Second, and Sixth Circuits. In these courts (although not in the Eleventh Circuit, which imposes stricter requirements, or the Ninth, which is less strict) an alien seeking a stay of deportation must satisfy a four-part test, similar to the test used to analyze a request for a preliminary injunction. The petitioner seeking a stay must show: likelihood of success on the merits; irreparable harm if the stay is not granted; that the stay is in the public interest; and that the potential harm to the movant if the stay is denied exceeds the potential harm to the objector if the stay is granted. In the Ninth Circuit, the stay can be granted if the alien merely shows probability of success and possibility of irreparable injury or, in the alternative, that the case

---

[69] James v. Gonzales, No. 464 F.3d 505 (5th Cir. 2006).
[70] Fernandez-Vargas v. Gonzales, 548 U.S. 30 (2006).

raises serious legal questions and the balance of hardship is sharply in the alien's favor. At the other pole, the Eleventh Circuit requires proof by clear and convincing evidence that the removal order is contrary to law. Despite the articulation of the test, the Third Circuit ruled that it had no jurisdiction to review the appeal; the petitioner had a second conviction that was unquestionably an aggravated felony.[71]

If an alien is taken into custody after an immigration arrest, INA § 236(a) says that the alien can be kept in custody; released on bond of at least $1,500; or released on conditional parole. (If the alien was admitted lawfully, but removal is sought due to a conviction for aggravated felony, release on bond requires demonstration of willingness to appear at hearings, and lack of danger to the community; see INA § 238(a)(3) for special expedited removal proceedings for convicted aggravated felons.)

Under 8 CFR § 239.1, the removal process is commenced by filing of Notice to Appear issued by an official qualified to issue warrants, based on a prima facie showing that the alien can be removed from the United States.

Removal proceedings, under INA §§ 239–240, require proper notice to the alien, who has the right to counsel (including appointed counsel) and can offer evidence and cross-examine the witnesses against him or her. Any order of removal must be based on reasonable, substantial, and probative evidence (i.e., not proof beyond a reasonable doubt; once again, this is not a criminal proceeding). If the alien has already been admitted, the INS has the burden of proof (with a clear and convincing evidence standard) of showing removability.

The alien must be given a chance to designate a country where he or she will be sent if removal is ordered (INA § 241(b)(2)).

Once removed, INA § 212(a)(6)(B) provides that special permission from the Immigration and Naturalization Service is required for the removed person to reenter the U.S. at any time within five years of the removal.

Although the INA allows detention of removable aliens after the 90-day statutory removal period has elapsed, indefinite detention is not permitted merely because the home country refuses to allow removal of the alien to the home country. Detention cannot exceed six months unless the Attorney General can rebut the alien's showing that removal is not likely within the foreseeable future.[72] Early in 2005, the Supreme Court extended *Zadvydas* to inadmissible aliens as well as those who have been admitted. In either case, detention in excess of 90 days is allowed only for as long as needed to achieve removal, and the same six-month period (after which condition release is required if there is no significant likelihood of removal in the foreseeable future) applies: *Clark v. Martinez*, 543 U.S. 371 (2005).

---

[71] Douglas v. BIA, discussed in Shannon P. Duffy, *3rd Circuit Adopts Middle Ground for Testing Deportation Challenges*, The Legal Intelligencer 7/13/04 (law.com).

[72] Zadvydas v. Davis, 533 U.S. 678 (2001).

The INS implemented the *Zadvydas* decision in an Interim Rule on Continued Detention of Aliens Subject to Final Orders of Removal.[73] The Interim Rule sets the procedures for adjudicating claims, releasing aliens who have made out a case, and for detaining "special circumstances" aliens even if they cannot be removed. Special circumstances include involvement in terrorism, contagious disease, adverse foreign policy consequences if that person is released, danger to the public from persons convicted of violent crimes, the mentally ill, and those suffering from personality disorders. The Ninth Circuit ruled in mid-2004 that *Zadvydas* does not justify indefinite detention of an alien on the grounds that he or she is mentally ill and dangerous to the community.[74]

The Supreme Court resolved a circuit split in April 2003, in its decision in *Demore v. Kim*, 538 U.S. 510 (2003). The Supreme Court allowed imprisonment pending deportation for lawful permanent residents subject to deportation because of criminal convictions. A bail hearing is not required, and detention does not depend on a prior finding of risk or harm or flight risk if the person is released. The court refused to extend its earlier *Zadvydas* decision (which limits indefinite detention after deportation has been ordered), because detention under § 236(a), pending removal proceedings, is much shorter; its typical duration is about six weeks. In this reading, detention is a constitutionally valid element of the deportation process where, as here, there is a meaningful probability that the individual will leave the United States. However, the Supreme Court held that it had jurisdiction to review the law in the context of a detainee's habeas petition.

The Fifth Circuit ruled in early 2008 that 8 USC § 1231(a)(6) does not allow indefinite detention of a removable alien based on the government's determination that the alien has a mental illness that makes him or her a risk to the community. In this case, the Vietnamese immigrant was admitted as a refugee and eventually became a lawful permanent resident. In 1984, after convictions of firearm possession and assault on his wife, he was confined to a mental institution. After his release from a halfway house, he murdered his wife and was sentenced to 18–20 years. In 1998, the Department of Homeland Security initiated deportation proceedings based on a conviction of a crime of violence. The IJ found him removable to France or Vietnam, but neither country would take him. DHS detained him because he could not be deported. In 2001, after *Zadvydas*, he sought release from custody. DHS moved under 8 CFR § 241.14(f), which allows ongoing detention of an alien whose mental condition makes future acts of violence likely. The Ninth Circuit granted habeas, holding that *Zadvydas* does not authorize a special category of indefinite detention as a result of mental illness.[75]

---

[73] 8 CFR § 241.13, 66 FR 56967 (11/14/01).
[74] Thai v. Ashcroft, 366 F.3d 790 (9th Cir. 2004).
[75] Tran v. Mukasey, 515 F.3d 478 (5th Cir. 2008).

[A] Grounds for Removal

Pre-IIRIRA law recognized several grounds for excluding potential entrants, e.g., criminal convictions; terrorism; voluntary membership in a Communist or other totalitarian party; becoming a public charge within five years of entry; and a catch-all barring entrance of a person whose entrance would be contrary to U.S. foreign policy. INA § 212(a) contains the current list of grounds for inadmissibility, e.g., ineligibility for citizenship; health reasons; criminal record; U.S. national security issues; likelihood of becoming a public charge if admitted. IIRIRA added a category of aliens who overstay a visa or otherwise are unlawfully remaining within the U.S.

The applicant for admission has the burden of proof, under INA § 240(c)(2)(A), of proving "clearly and beyond doubt" that he or she does not fall into any category of inadmissible persons. The burden then shifts to the INS to prove, by clear and convincing evidence, that removal is appropriate.

See INA § 237(a) for the numerous categories of circumstances that will justify removal of a person who has already entered the United States. Persons who are entitled to conditional permanent resident status can be removed unless they convert their status to unconditional permanent resident. Removal for marriage fraud is also provided by § 237(a)(1)(G).

Commencement of removal proceedings is by INS Notice to Appear, directing the alien to appear at immigration court to defend against a charge of inadmissibility: see INA § 239.

INA § 236(c), detention of criminal aliens pending final determination of removability, cannot be applied to a lawful permanent resident alien. According to the Tenth Circuit, such application would violate substantive Due Process because of the lack of provision for individual hearings on dangerousness or flight risk.[76]

It is inadequate for an immigration judge merely to state at a group deportation proceeding that there is a right to counsel. Group silence is not probative; the judge must ask each alien if he or she wants counsel. Although not all procedural defects will invalidate a deportation hearing, denial of counsel was held by the Ninth Circuit to be clearly prejudicial, because counsel might have informed the petitioner of the available options, including the possibility of discretionary waiver of deportation.[77]

Post-IIRIRA, judicial review of an order of expedited removal is quite limited. INA § 242(e)(2) now limits review to a habeas corpus proceeding, involving only four issues: whether the petitioner is an alien; whether his or her removal was ordered under INA § 236(b)(1); whether the alien can prove lawful permanent resident status by a preponderance of evidence; and whether asylum or refugee status is available. See also § 242(a)(2)(A), depriving all courts of jurisdiction to

---

[76] Hoang v. Comfort, 282 F.3d 1247 (10th Cir. 2002).
[77] United States v. Ahumada-Aguilar, 295 F.3d 943 (9th Cir. 2002).

review the Attorney General's decision to use expedited removal, or the expedited removal of individual aliens.

If a removable alien fails to raise a legal or constitutional challenge to the decision to place him or her in removal proceedings, the Court of Appeals does not have jurisdiction to consider a petition for relief.[78]

The Supreme Court ruled in 1995 that filing a motion to reopen or reconsider BIA proceedings does not toll the statutory time limit for filing a petition for review in the Court of Appeals. In 2008, the Ninth Circuit said that the converse is also true. Filing a petition for review in the Court of Appeals does not toll the statute's time limit for filing the motion to reopen before the BIA.[79]

Under 28 USC § 2243, a writ of habeas corpus is directed to the person having custody of the detainee. For a detained alien pending deportation the First Circuit says this would be the District Director of the INS Service Center where the alien is detained, and not the U.S. Attorney General. However, the Ninth Circuit deems the proper respondents to be the Secretary of Homeland Security and the U.S. Attorney General rather than the director of the detention facility.[80] Whereas the Southern District of New York has held that the Attorney General plays a unique role in immigration cases and therefore is the proper respondent for a habeas petition by a detainee (rather than the official with immediate physical custody).

According to the Eighth Circuit, venue for habeas proceedings under 28 USC § 2241 is the judicial district in which the alien is detained; forum choice is not expanded because the Secretary of Defense is the defendant in enemy combatant cases. However, the Eighth Circuit disagrees, and a nationwide class has been certified on this issue.[81]

An early 1999 Supreme Court decision[82] holds that the IIRIRA limitations on judicial review (INA § 242(g)) prevent federal courts from reviewing pre-IIRIRA attempts to deport resident aliens, even if it is alleged that the deportation attempts were discriminatory and premised on the individual's unpopular political views.

Aliens lacking proper documentation when they seek to enter the U.S. can be removed from the U.S. without prior hearing or opportunity for review, unless the alien seeks asylum or expresses a fear of persecution if returned to the home country.

The Second Circuit ruled that a petitioner's being 15 minutes late to a removal proceeding constituted brief, innocent lateness and was not a "failure to appear" as defined by 8 USC § 1229a(b)(5). Therefore, it was improper to issue an in absentia order of removal. The petitioner said that he went to his

---

[78] Ali v. Mukasey, 524 F.3d 145 (2d Cir. 2008).

[79] Dela Cruz v. Mukasey, 532 F.3d 946 (9th Cir. 2008); the Supreme Court ruling is Stone v. INS, 514 U.S. 386 (1995).

[80] *Compare* Vasquez v. Reno, 233 F.3d 688 (1st Cir. 2000) *with* Armentero v. INS, 340 F.3d 1058 (9th Cir. 2003). Garcia-Rivas v. Ashcroft, 2004 WL 1534156 (S.D.N.Y. 2004).

[81] *Cf.* Al-Marri v. Rumsfeld, 360 F.3d 707 (7th Cir. 2004) *with* Jama v. INS, 329 F.3d 630 (8th Cir. 2003).

[82] Reno v. American-Arab Anti-Discrimination Committee, 525 U.S. 471 (1999).

lawyer's office, waited for an hour, then went to the court house but, as a result of a delay in getting through security, he arrived at 9:15 for the hearing scheduled at 9:00; his lawyer arrived three minutes later. The Second Circuit did not believe that Congress could have intended to authorize in absentia orders of removal (which are more or less irrevocable) for lateness during normal court hours; the severe sanction must have been intended to penalize deliberately avoiding a court appearance to avoid being removed.[83]

Even if the mistake was made by a paralegal giving scheduling information, a lawyer's giving the client the wrong date for an immigration hearing and then failing to tell the client about the deportation order made in absentia can be an exceptional circumstance permitting reopening of the deportation order.[84]

[1] Criminal Law Issues

Conviction of a criminal offense in the United States is grounds for removal, if a moral turpitude felony[85] is committed within five years of admission (or two moral turpitude crimes at any time). Conviction is defined as a guilty verdict or

---

[83] Abu Hasirah v. Dept of Homeland Security, 478 F.3d 474 (2d Cir. 2007). Alarcon-Chavez v. Gonzales, 403 F.3d 343 (5th Cir. 2005) and Cabrera-Perez v. Gonzales, 456 F.3d 109 (3d Cir. 2006) excuse comparable tardiness resulting from traffic delays or getting lost. Early in 2008, the Ninth Circuit found that the BIA erred by entering an order of removal in absentia on the grounds of non-appearance, and then denying a motion to re-open when an alien was about two hours late for an appearance because his car broke down. The Ninth Circuit held that traffic and parking problems can be expected, so they do not offer an excuse, but the breakdown was unanticipated and outside the alien's control. As long as the IJ is still in the courtroom, a party should be allowed to make a tardy appearance: Perez v. Mukasey, 516 F.3d 770 (9th Cir. 2008).

[84] Aris v. Mukasey, 517 F.3d 595 (2d Cir. 2008).

[85] Construed to include violent offenses, including domestic violence; drug offenses; fraud; larceny; many sexual offenses. INA §§ 101(a)(43) and 237(a)(2)(iii) permit removal of a person convicted of any aggravated felony within the U.S. The Eighth Circuit treated the offense of uttering terroristic threats as a crime of moral turpitude, and thus a person convicted of this is not of good moral character, rendering cancellation of removal unavailable. Chanmouny v. Ashcroft, 376 F.3d 810 (8th Cir. 2004).

Because Congress has not defined "moral turpitude," the BIA gets deference as long as its interpretation of 8 USC § 1227(a)(2)(A)(i) is reasonable. The Eighth Circuit agreed with the BIA that second degree assault (causing serious physical injury by striking someone) can be a moral turpitude offense, because the reckless conduct was aggravated by the seriousness of the victim's injury: Godinez-Arroyo, 540 F.3d 848 (8th Cir. 2008).

The Ninth Circuit granted cancellation of removal, finding that the BIA erred about the moral turpitude of past offenses. The petitioner had two past convictions. One, a misdemeanor, qualified for the "petty offense" exception, but the other was for false identification to a peace officer. The IJ treated this as a moral turpitude offense, but the Ninth Circuit said it was not; the only benefit was impeding enforcement of the law. The case was remanded to see if cancellation of removal should be granted. The Ninth Circuit noted that immigration proceedings do not give rise to Sixth Amendment rights. Therefore, claims of ineffective assistance of counsel are analyzed using a Fifth Amendment due process standard — whether the ineffective counsel prejudiced the alien because proceeding was so fundamentally unfair that the alien was prevented from reasonably presenting his or her case: Blanco v. Mukasey, 518 F.3d 714 (9th Cir. 2008).

judicial decision or a guilty or nolo contendere plea, plus some form of punishment, plus a possibility of sanctions for probation violations or failure to comply with a court order.[86]

In late 2004, the Supreme Court held that a state Driving Under the Influence offense that has no malign intent element is not a crime of violence and therefore not an aggravated felony: *Leocal v. Ashcroft*, 543 U.S. 1 (2004). Other offenses can also be grounds for removal, e.g., violation of any drug law (even if not tantamount to conviction of a moral-turpitude felony) or becoming a drug addict, as well as specific immigration-related offenses such as high-speed flight from an immigration checkpoint or assisting someone else to prepare a false immigration-related document. "Undesirables," including aliens convicted of domestic violence offenses or stalking, are also removable. Because the immigration consequences of a serious conviction are so drastic, the lawyer representing an alien defendant might want to suggest an immediate plea bargain to a misdemeanor or other charge not involving moral turpitude. A person who entered the U.S. as a refugee, and whose status was adjusted to lawful permanent resident, nevertheless can be removed based on a conviction of an aggravated felony or two crimes of moral turpitude, even if refugee status was never terminated.[87]

The 2003 update of the U.S. Sentencing Guidelines (see § 26.04[L][1] for more information about the Guidelines) relies on several recent immigration cases to clarify points of law about the interface between criminal law and immigration law. Guideline 2L1.2 has been strengthened to enhance the offense level for people who illegally return to the United States after removal subsequent to a criminal conviction.

The Guidelines now provide that an alien smuggling offense includes transporting aliens brought into the United States.[88] The Ninth Circuit joined the Tenth and Eleventh in holding that Sentencing Guidelines 2L1.2 does not impose any age limit on the age of the convictions used to enhance a sentence.[89]

The Anti-Drug Abuse Act of 1988, P.L. 100-690, created the category of "aggravated felony," including murder, drug trafficking crimes, and firearms

---

[86] According to the Ninth Circuit, drunk driving is not a moral turpitude offense, but unlicensed drunk driving is; when the two offenses are combined, then deportation is appropriate. Marmolejo-Campos v. Gonzales, 503 F.3d 922 (9th Cir. 2007); see Justin Scheck, *9th Circuit Judges Define Moral Turpitude*, The Recorder 9/14/07 (law.com). In December 2006, after a split in a three-judge panel, the Ninth Circuit heard arguments en banc as to whether being an accessory to a crime constitutes moral turpitude, but at press time in 2007, the en banc panel had not rendered its decision.

[87] Romanishyn v. Attorney Gen. of the U.S., 455 F.3d 175 (3d Cir. 2006); semble Kaganovich v. Gonzales, 470 F.3d 894 (9th Cir. 2006).

[88] This adopts the holding of United States v. Solis-Campozano, 312 F.3d 164 (5th Cir. 2002). The D.C. Circuit permitted extraterritorial application of 8 USC § 1324(a) (criminal conspiracy to induce aliens to enter the United States illegally) on the grounds that it is fundamentally a statute of international application: United States v. Delgado-Garcia, 374 F.3d 1337 (D.C. Cir. 2004).

[89] United States v. Olmos-Esparza, 484 F.3d 1111 (9th Cir. 2007); semble United States v. Torres-Duenas, 461 F.3d 1178 (10th Cir. 2006); United States v. Camacho-Ibarquen, 410 F.3d 1307 (11th Cir. 2005), *cert. denied* 126 S.Ct. 457.

trading. A number of cases have ruled on precisely what constitutes an aggravated felony — leading to several Circuit splits.

In December, 2006, the Supreme Court resolved one split by holding that drug offenses (e.g., first offenses of simple possession) that are felonies under state law but are misdemeanors under the (federal) Controlled Substances Act are not "aggravated felonies" for which removal is always appropriate.[90]

A conviction for filing a false tax return (26 USC § 7206(1)) is not an aggravated felony.[91] Nor are the offenses of evading an officer or unlawfully taking and driving a vehicle under the California Vehicle Code, because the first is not categorically a crime of violence and the second is not categorically a theft offense.[92] Offenses that have been held to constitute aggravated felonies include solicitation of a minor for sexual acts,[93] smuggling aliens,[94] and second degree forgery.[95]

The REAL ID Act, P.L. 109-13, which took effect May 11, 2005, removed District Court habeas corpus jurisdiction over orders of removal — now the Courts of Appeals are the only courts with the power to review these orders. The Ninth Circuit rejected a Constitutional challenge that posited that District Courts are a superior forum to Courts of Appeals because the District Courts can hold evidentiary hearings. The Ninth Circuit, however, deemed the Court of Appeals proceeding an adequate substitute for habeas. REAL ID loosened some of the jurisdictional restraints of 8 USC § 1252(a)(2)(C) with respect to questions of law raised by aliens, to prevent aliens convicted of crimes from having an avenue of habeas relief that is not available to non-criminal aliens. Under current law, the Court of Appeals has jurisdiction over claimed legal errors in a BIA final order of removal, eliminating the need for habeas review.[96]

---

[90] Lopez v. Gonzales, 549 U.S. 47 (2006). At the same time, the Supreme Court dismissed certiorari in the companion case of Toledo-Flores v. U.S., 549 U.S. 69 (2006), as improvidently granted, because the petitioner contested a prison term that had already been served, rather than an order of removal on the basis of aggravated felony. *See also* Jeune v. Att'y Gen'l, 476 F.3d 199 (3d Cir. 2006) on the difficulties of defining "trafficking." The Ninth Circuit held in 2008 that a state felony conviction for possession of a controlled substance with intent to sell has a "trafficking" element and therefore is an aggravated felony: Rendon v. Mukasey, 520 F.3d 967 (9th Cir. 2008).

[91] Lee v. Ashcroft, 368 F.3d 218 (3d Cir. 2004).

[92] Penuliar v. Gonzales, 435 F.3d 961 (6th Cir. 2006).

[93] Gattem v. Gonzales, 412 F.3d 758 (7th Cir. 2005).

[94] Zhang v. INS, 274 F.3d 103 (2d Cir. 2001).

[95] Richards v. Ashcroft, 400 F.3d 125 (2d Cir. 2005).

[96] Puri v. Gonzales, 464 F.3d 1038 (9th Cir. 2006); Balogun v. United States Att'y Gen'l, 425 F.3d 1356 (11th Cir. 2005). *See also* Lee v. Gonzales, 410 F.3d 778 (5th Cir. 2005) (as long as there are other procedural avenues to obtain review of a BIA decision, an immigrant cannot use habeas), and Sosa-Martinez v. United States Att'y Gen'l, 420 F.3d 1338 (11th Cir. 2005) (holding that the courts do not have jurisdiction to review removal orders in cases of crimes of moral turpitude — a category that includes aggravated battery). The petition for review must be filed within 30 days after the order of removal has issued. 8 USC § 1252(a)(5) makes this the sole means of judicial review. Aliens whose orders of removal were issued before REAL ID, and who failed to petition within 30 days, argued before the Second Circuit that the REAL ID Act violates the Suspension Clause of the Constitution by removing an existing right to habeas. The Second Circuit upheld the statute, finding

However, offenses of various types have been held not to constitute aggravated felonies and/or moral turpitude crimes, e.g., third-degree aggravated assault on a police officer. The Third Circuit said that the moral turpitude decision depends on the criminal statute and the record of conviction, not the conduct. A statute that includes both turpitudinous and other acts is divisible, and the court must determine which portion the immigrant was convicted under. The test has long been the presence of evil or malicious intent, and such intent is not present in negligence offenses.[97]

In April 2001, the California Supreme Court permitted aliens to raise claims of ineffective assistance of counsel if they claim they were inadequately informed of the consequences of pleading guilty to criminal charges within the United States, even though judges are obligated to inform noncitizen defendants that a guilty plea is likely to result in deportation.[98]

[B] Discretionary Relief

NOTE: Because of the REAL ID Act's (P.L. 109-13) amendments to 8 USC § 1252(a)(2)(C), the Court of Appeals has jurisdiction over challenges to BIA final orders of removal, thus ruling out habeas review. These cases reflect earlier law.

Immigration judges have the power to grant discretionary relief at the application of the alien, postponing removal or permitting the alien to remain within the U.S. The alien must prove eligibility for discretionary relief (see INA § 240A and 8 CFR § 240.8), but it is up to the immigration judge to grant or deny any discretionary relief for which the alien is eligible. IIRIRA limits judicial review of decisions about discretionary relief.

There are seven categories of discretionary relief:

- Voluntary departure
- Cancellation of removal

---

that the Suspension Clause was not violated, but required a 30-day grace period from REAL ID's effective date for the benefit of persons whose petitions became untimely because of REAL ID. *See* Ruiz-Martinez v. Mukasey, 516 F.3d 102 (2d Cir. 2008).

[97] Partyka v. Attorney Gen'l of the U.S., 417 F.3d 408 (3d Cir. 2005). Gill v. U.S., 420 F.3d 82 (2d Cir. 2005) held that reckless offenses are not turpitudinous: Kawashima v. Gonzales, No. 04-74313 (9th Cir. 9/18/07).

[98] *In re* Resendiz, 25 Cal. 4th 230 (Cal. Sup. 2001). The Ninth Circuit noted that immigration proceedings do not give rise to Sixth Amendment rights. Therefore, claims of ineffective assistance of counsel are analyzed using a Fifth Amendment due process standard — whether the ineffective counsel prejudiced the alien because proceeding was so fundamentally unfair that the alien was prevented from reasonably presenting his or her case: Blanco v. Mukasey, 518 F.3d 714 (9th Cir. 2008). *See also* People v. McDonald, 1 N.Y.3d 109 (N.Y. 2003): an alien must show prejudice to prove that inaccurate advice about the immigration consequences of a guilty plea constitutes ineffective assistance. To the Fifth Circuit, the key question is whether the defendant's decision to plead guilty would have been affected by a proper admonition from the court. The error is harmless for a citizen, but not harmless for a non-citizen: Vannortrick v. Texas, No. 05-03-01436-CR and -01437-CR (5th Cir. 6/27/07).

- Restriction of removal
- Stay of removal
- Adjustment of status
- Asylum
- Other discretionary relief.

In rare cases, governmental misconduct will be held to estop removal of an alien (or other negative immigration action).

Voluntary departure is an alien's agreement to leave the United States, at his or her own expense: INA § 240B. An alien who elects voluntary departure can choose his or her next destination, and can attempt to re-enter the United States without being subject to the 10-year bar on re-entering the United States after removal (20 years after a second removal; the bar is permanent after conviction of an aggravated felony).

Cancellation of removal, governed by INA § 240A, means permitting certain long-term residents to remain within the United States if they have not been convicted of crimes, are persons of good moral character, and their removal would create exceptional and extremely unusual hardship to immediate family members (not the alien him- or herself). (*See INS v. Hector*, 479 U.S. 85 (1986).) If cancellation of removal is granted, the alien's status is altered to that of permanent resident, but only 4,000 adjustments to permanent resident status can be made per year on this basis. In a case of first impression, the First Circuit held in 2007 that 8 USC § 1229b(a) means that an alien who used fraud or misrepresentation to acquire lawful permanent resident status was never lawfully admitted. Therefore, the alien is ineligible for cancellation of removal.[99]

[C] Appeals

Aliens who have been found removable by an immigration judge can either take administrative or judicial appeal (subject to AEDPA and IIRIRA limitations), or apply for discretionary relief. Relief must be requested before the order of removal is executed. See 8 CFR § 3.23 for the motion to reopen or reconsider (using Form I-328).

The 90-day deadline imposed by 8 CFR § 3.23(b)(1) for reopening deportation proceedings is not jurisdictional. It is subject to equitable tolling for ineffective assistance of counsel — as long as the alien is diligent in pursuing the case throughout the tolling period.[100]

The Department of Justice changed its rules to streamline BIA proceedings. The number of board members was reduced from 23 to 11, and summary affirmance of most appeals can be performed by one member rather than requiring a

---

[99] Mejia-Orellana v. Gonzales, 502 F.3d 13 (1st Cir. 2007).

[100] Iavorski v. INS, 232 F.3d 124 (2d Cir. 2000). *See also* Rashid v. Mukasey, 533 F.3d 127 (2d Cir. 2008): the defense of ineffective prior counsel was unavailable because the alien did not exercise due diligence once he discovered the first lawyer's alleged ineffectiveness.

three-member panel. The District Court for the District of Columbia affirmed the validity of the new rules under the Administrative Procedures Act in mid-2003, finding that the changes serve valid functions and were not adopted arbitrarily or capriciously.[101]

In mid-2007, the Tenth Circuit decided a case of first impression as to what constitutes a "final order of removal" for appellate jurisdiction under 8 USC §§ 1252(a)(1) and 1101(a)(47)(A). Where the IJ does not make a finding of deportability, there is no final order of removal that can be reviewed, and no jurisdiction under 8 USC § 1252.[102]

[1] Executive Office for Immigration Review

The Executive Office for Immigration Review (EOIR) is an administrative body (not, for Constitutional purposes, a court system), comprising the immigration courts and the Board of Immigration Appeals. It is independent of the INS and provides some degree of review power for INS decisions.

The immigration judges handle the unified removal hearings prescribed by IIRIRA, as well as proceedings to rescind adjustment of status and withdraw approval of schools attended by nonimmigrant foreign students. Decisions of immigration judges become final unless appealed to the Board of Immigration Appeals (BIA). The 15-member BIA is divided into five permanent three-judge panels. See 8 CFR §§ 3.1–3.8 for the requirements for BIA appeals.

Eight circuits have upheld the validity of the BIA's streamlined review procedure (8 CFR § 3.1(a)(7)), under which a single BIA member, rather than a three-member panel, can affirm an IJ's decision. The procedure survived a due process challenge before the Eighth Circuit. The right of administrative appeal for aliens is not constitutional or statutory; it depends on regulations issued by the Attorney General. The streamlined procedure does not preclude the Circuit Courts from reviewing IJ decisions directly.[103]

[2] Judicial Review

Many Constitutional provisions are limited in their applicability to U.S. citizens, or at least to legal residents. Recent legislation has greatly limited the extent to which would-be immigrants and potential deportees can use the court system.

---

[101] Capital Area Immigrants' Rights Coalition v. DOJ, 317 F.3d 1089 (D.D.C. 2003).

[102] Sosa-Valenzuela v. Gonzales, 483 F.3d 1140 (10th Cir. 2007).

[103] Loulou v. Ashcroft, 354 F.3d 706 (8th Cir. 2003, amended 4/28/04); the procedure also has been upheld by Kambolli v. Gonzales, 449 F.3d 454 (2d Cir. 2006) and Yu Sheng Zhang v. DOJ, 362 F.3d 155 (2d Cir. 2004); Papageorgiou v. Gonzales, 413 F.3d 356 (3d Cir. 2005); Falcon Carriche v. Ashcroft, 335 F.3d 1009 (9th Cir. 2003); Georgis v. Ashcroft, 328 F.3d 962 (7th Cir. 2003); Mendoza v. United States Attorney General, 327 F.3d 1283 (11th Cir. 2003); Soadjede v. Ashcroft, 324 F.3d 830 (5th Cir. 2003); and Albathani v. INS, 318 F.3d 365 (1st Cir. 2003).

Both AEDPA and IIRIRA have restricted the judicial review of immigration decisions, stating that discretionary decisions of the Attorney General (other than asylum decisions) cannot be judicially reviewed. However, the Ninth Circuit position[104] is that all judicial review cannot be eliminated. Therefore, to the extent that INA § 242(g)'s current provisions rule out court review of a final deportation order that is premised on criminal activity, then the alien can use 28 USC § 2241, the general habeas corpus statute.

In 2003, Justice Kennedy, sitting as a single justice, held that reviewing courts are obliged to uphold administrative determinations in immigration cases absent compelling evidence for the contrary conclusion. Therefore, Justice Kennedy held that a person who overstayed his visa (and who was wanted on criminal charges in his home country) was not entitled to stay of removal from the United States because there was no reasonable likelihood that denial of his asylum application was improper.[105]

In another asylum case,[106] the Supreme Court held that when an alien petitions for review of the BIA's denial of an asylum/withholding of deportation petition, the Court of Appeals generally speaking cannot conduct a de novo inquiry. The INS has the power to make the basic decision on eligibility for asylum. The Supreme Court held that the Court of Appeals should have remanded the issue to the BIA for additional investigation (e.g., of whether the alien had a cognizable fear of persecution for his political opinions).

The Second Circuit granted a petition for review, holding that the BIA improperly applied a strong presumption that notice sent by regular (not certified) mail was received. The petitioner in this case probably would have appeared if he had been notified, because he had obtained labor certification and would be motivated to appear.[107]

An IJ's decision to establish or enforce filing deadlines for documents is reviewed for abuse of discretion. The Second Circuit held in mid-2008 that an IJ has broad discretion in managing the docket to enforce the filing deadline under local rules — and therefore can deviate from local rules based on a showing of good cause for delay, where enforcement of deadlines would cause substantial prejudice.[108]

The Third Circuit held that it was arbitrary and an abuse of discretion to deny a continuance in an I-130 case [residency based on marriage to a U.S. citizen] based on the Department of Justice completion goals for the type of case, rather than the individual facts of the case.[109]

---

[104] As articulated in Magana-Pizano v. INS, 152 F.3d 1213 (9th Cir. 1998).

[105] Kenyeres v. Ashcroft, 538 U.S. 1301 (2003).

[106] INS v. Orlando Ventura, 537 U.S. 12 (2002).

[107] Silva v. Mukasey, 517 F.3d 156 (2d Cir. 2008).

[108] Dedji v. Mukasey, 525 F.3d 187 (2d Cir. 2008).

[109] Hashmi v. AG of the United States, 531 F.3d 256 (3d Cir. 2008).

[D] Criminal Immigration Offenses

Federal criminal prosecutions of immigrants reached a record high in March 2008 (73% higher than March 2007). Nearly all immigration case referrals resulted in charges, although the median sentence for convicted persons was only one month.[110]

Under INA § 275, it is an offense, punishable by a fine and/or up to six months' imprisonment, for an alien to enter or attempt to enter the United States without authorization, by escaping inspection or making a willfully false misrepresentation of material fact. Repeat offenses can be penalized by up to two years' imprisonment. In addition, civil penalties of up to $500 can be imposed for repeat offenses of actual or attempted improper entrance.

Section 276 makes it a felony (maximum sentence: two years) for a person to re-enter or attempt to re-enter the United States after removal, except in the rare cases where the Attorney General has authorized the re-entry.[111] Pleading guilty under § 275 or 276 will render the individual vulnerable to removal. Domestic battery can be treated as a crime of violence that increases the offense level significantly when a person makes an illegal re-entry into the United States after removal subsequent to conviction of a crime of violence.[112]

Early in 2007, the Supreme Court ruled, in U.S. v. Resendiz-Ponce, 127 S. Ct. 782, that an indictment charging that a defendant "attempted" to enter the United States alleged the necessary overt act. Therefore, the indictment was not defective, and the conviction should not have been reversed. The Supreme Court did not feel obligated to rule whether omission of an element of an offense from an indictment can ever be harmless error.

A mid-2005 Ninth Circuit case held that in a case of unlawfully entering the United States after exclusion, deportation or removal, the prior deportation is the critical element of the offense. Nevertheless, *Apprendi* does not make 8 USC § 1326 unconstitutional, because the jury decides on a reasonable-doubt standard whether the deportation was ordered. In such cases, the prosecution cannot rely on the deportation hearing, but must separately prove the exclusion element. The deportation hearing is subject to judicial, including collateral, review, so all facts must be proved to the jury beyond a reasonable doubt.[113]

Separate incidents of illegal re-entry after conviction should not be grouped for sentencing purposes, because they caused separate rather than a single

---

[110] Julia Preston, *More Illegal Crossings Are Criminal Cases, Group Says*, N.Y. Times 6/18/08 at p. A14.

[111] A previously deported alien who re-enters the United States illegally has been "found in the United States" if apprehended by local police, it is not necessary that immigration enforcement officials make the capture for 8 USC § 1326 to apply, because this is a continuing offense: United States v. Jimenez-Borja, 363 F.3d 956 (9th Cir. 2004).

[112] United States v. Alvarenga-Silva, 324 F.3d 884 (7th Cir. 2003).

[113] United States v. Bahena-Cardenas, 411 F.3d 1067 (9th Cir. 2005).

composite harm, and because the defendant did not engage in them as part of a common scheme or plan.[114]

Once in the United States for 30 days or more, aliens have a duty to register and be fingerprinted; willful failure to comply carries a fine and up to six months' imprisonment (INA § 266(a)), with lesser penalties for failing to provide written notice of change of address. Non-compliance is also grounds for removal. These provisions are seldom enforced.

It is unlawful, with a penalty of a fine and/or up to five years' imprisonment, to smuggle (or attempt to smuggle) aliens into this country: see INA § 274(a)(l)(A). A fine and up to a year's imprisonment per transaction can be imposed under § 274(a)(2) for bringing or attempting to bring an unauthorized person into the U.S., knowingly or with reckless disregard of the person's immigration status. The sentence can be up to 10 years if § 274(a)(2) is violated for commercial gain; the sentence range is five to fifteen years for third or subsequent offenses. Even if the alien never manages to enter U.S. territory, conspiracy to violate § 274 is nevertheless illegal.

See also § 274(a)(1)(A)(ii) for penalties for knowing or reckless transportation of an alien within the United States, if such transportation is in furtherance of the alien's immigration offense. Harboring or sheltering an illegal alien is penalized by § 274(a)(1)(A)(iii). Inducing or encouraging illegal immigration is unlawful under § 274(a)(1)(A)(iv). Heavier penalties are imposed, under § 277, if the alien in question is a criminal or subversive. Section 278 penalizes importing aliens for prostitution or other immoral purposes.

In addition to the general federal perjury statute (18 USC § 1621) and the general ban on false statements and misrepresentations in matters under the jurisdiction of the U.S. government (18 USC § 1001), immigration-related perjury can violate several specific immigration statutes, including INA § 287(b) and 18 USC §§ 1424, 1426.

Willful false representations of U.S. citizenship can lead to fines and imprisonment under 18 USC § 911. Knowingly providing false identity information to secure a visa, after a previous application has been denied, constitutes willful misrepresentation of a material fact under 8 USC § 1182(a)(6)(C)(i).[115]

See 18 USC § 1546 for penalties in connection with visa fraud and INA § 275(c) for fraud in connection with "green card" marriages.

---

[114] United States v. Bahena-Guifarro, 324 F.3d 560 (7th Cir. 2003).
[115] Emokah v. Mukasey, 523 F.3d 110 (2d Cir. 2008).

Part V

TAX ISSUES

Chapter 20

Personal Income Tax and Tax Planning

§ 20.01   INTRODUCTION

The much-loathed and despised personal income tax is imposed by § 61 on all income other than that specifically exempted. The basic tax computation therefore consists of aggregating all income items; taking certain deductions to compute

Adjusted Gross Income (§ 62); either itemizing other deductions or claiming the standard deduction; and claiming personal and dependency deductions. Taxable income is then determined by using the tax tables (for taxable income under $100,000) or the tax rate schedules (for greater income). Finally, any applicable credits are used to reduce the amount of tax.

For most individuals, withholding during the year will represent the full amount of tax liability, and therefore the taxpayer will have a choice between receiving a refund and applying the excess to the following year's taxes.

Self-employed persons, persons with significant non-employment income (e.g., from investments), and high-income persons (whose employment income is higher than the maximum amount covered by withholding tables) will have to make quarterly estimated tax payments in addition to the annual return. If the quarterly payments are insufficient by more than 20%, they will also have to pay a penalty excise tax in addition to making up the shortfall.

U.S. citizens are subject to income tax on all their income, whether or not it derives from sources within the United States. More or less the same is true of resident aliens. Non-resident aliens are subject to taxation on U.S. source investment income and income connected with U.S. businesses, even if the actual source of the income is outside the United States.[1]

Certain concepts are sometimes needed to file personal income tax returns, but are more common in the corporate tax context. See, for instance, the discussion of depreciation at § 4.06.

In 2001, the Economic Growth Tax Reform and Reconciliation Act (EGTRRA), P.L. 107-16, made major changes in many items of estate planning, pension, and IRA taxation, although many of these changes were scheduled to sunset in 2011, making it a major issue whether Congress will make these changes permanent. See, e.g., §§ 3.05, 3.06, and 17.01. EGTRRA also cut tax brackets, provided a degree of relief from the marriage penalty, and offered tax assistance for the costs of secondary and college education. (See § 20.02 for a summary of recent tax legislation.)

The Mortgage Forgiveness Debt Relief Act, P.L. 110-142, copes with the expected two and a half million taxpayers who will lose their homes to foreclosure in the next few years as a result of the subprime lending crisis.

P.L. 110-142 also amends Code § 121(b)(4) to extend the $500,000 exclusion of gain on the sale or exchange of a principal residence to sales and exchanges occurring after December 31, 2007, if the transaction is done by a surviving spouse, within two years of the spouse's death, at a time when the surviving spouse has not remarried.

---

[1] Under § 6013(g) and (h), a U.S. citizen or resident alien and his or her nonresident alien spouse can join in an election to be taxed as U.S. residents, on all income worldwide, for the year of the election. T.D. 9194, REG-159243-03, 2005-20 IRB 1016 contains proposed, temporary, and final rules on allocation of income to prevent U.S. citizens and residents from avoiding tax on appreciated property by declaring residence in a U.S. possession.

P.L. 110-172, the Tax Technical Corrections Bill of 2007, adds a one-year AMT "patch" to reduce the number of middle-income taxpayers who become subject to AMT.

[A] Obligation to File

Persons with very low incomes are not obligated to file income tax returns; persons over 65 are allowed to have slightly more income than "junior citizens" before a tax return will be required.

IRS Tax Tip 2008-02[1A] states that in general, a joint return is not required until the income level is $17,500, but self-employed persons with net income over $400 must file a return. Filing a tax return was also necessary to receive the economic stimulus payment, to demonstrate earned income of at least $3,000 or eligibility as a result of, e.g., Social Security benefits, even if there was no tax owed.

All married persons filing separately must file a return.

Some persons with even lower incomes are obligated to file. For example, a person who can be claimed as a dependent on someone else's tax return must file a return if his or her gross income exceeds the standard deduction (see § 20.01[K]), or has unearned income over $950 (2009). However, a return does not have to be filed for a child subject to "kiddie tax" if the child's parents elect to include the child's income on their own return(s).

[B] Tax Brackets

Before EGTRRA, there were four personal income tax brackets: 15%, 28%, 31%, and a top bracket of 39.6%. EGTRRA cut taxes somewhat, but made the system more complicated by adding a new 10% bracket at the bottom of the tax structure and gradually reducing the other brackets over a six-year period.

According to Rev. Proc. 2008-66, the tax brackets for 2009 are as follows:

	10%	15%	25%	28%	33%	35%
Joint return	16,700	67,900	137,050	208,850	372,950	372,950+
Single	8,350	33,950	82,250	171,550	372,950	372,950+
Married filing separately	8,350	33,950	68,525	104,425	186,475	186,475+
Head of Household	11,950	45,500	117,450	182,400	372,950	372,950+
Trusts and estates	N/A	2,300	5,350	8,200	11,150	11,150+

The question of tax brackets is complicated for high-income individuals because the applicability of various deductions phases out when income exceeds certain levels. The phase-out of itemized deductions is referred to as "Pease" (after the lawmaker who drafted the provision), and the phase-out of the personal exemption is referred to by the acronym PEP. Children under age 18 are subject to the "kiddie tax" (§ 20.01[C][4]) imposed to limit the advantages of shifting income within the family.

[1A]http://www.irs.gov/newsroom/article/0,,id=105097,00.html

[C] Filing Status

The basic filing statuses are:

- Single
- Married, filing a joint return
- Married, filing a separate return
- Head of household.

In addition, special tax rules apply to children who have not reached age 19 and widows and widowers for the two years following the death of the spouse. (For the actual year of the spouse's death, the widow/er is permitted to file an ordinary joint return, unless he or she remarries by the end of the year, or unless an executor or administrator is appointed by the end of the year: § 6013(a)(2).)

[1] Marital Status

In most instances, a marital joint return will give the best tax consequences, marital separate returns will give the worst. However, some high-income married couples have experienced a "marriage penalty" and in fact pay more than they would if they were unmarried and cohabiting.

Reducing the "marriage penalty" is one of EGTRRA's and JGTRRA's legislative objectives. See § 20.06[K].

Marital status is determined as of the close of the tax year (or as of the date of a spouse's death). In general, two persons are married if they are married under state law, but the federal Defense of Marriage Act, P.L. 104-199 (9/21/96) restricts the definition of marriage to a relationship involving one man and one woman. Cohabitants are not married for tax purposes unless they have a locally recognized common-law marriage.

To be able to file an ordinary joint return, a couple must not be legally separated under a decree of divorce or separate maintenance on the last day of the tax year, and neither of them may be a nonresident alien. If one spouse is a U.S. citizen or U.S. resident and the other is a nonresident alien, the couple can elect to file U.S. joint returns by agreeing to be taxed on their worldwide income (not just their U.S. income). They must also supply all books and records relevant to determining their tax liability: see Code § 6013(g).

Marriage is terminated by a decree of divorce or separate maintenance, but not by mere separation or the granting of an interlocutory decree. The IRS has long ruled that a pattern of end-year divorces, followed by remarriage early in the new year, will not be given effect to avoid the marriage penalty; the divorces will simply be disregarded.[2] For tax purposes, an annulment is treated as if the couple had never been married, so they must file amended returns for pre-annulment years in which they filed joint returns.

---

[2] Rev. Rul. 76-255, 1976-2 CB 40.

[2] Head of Household Status

Head of household status, which is generally less favorable than married/ joint filing, but more favorable than filing as a single person, is available to taxpayers who are unmarried, or married but living apart from their spouses, while maintaining a household in which a qualified person (generally, a child, elderly parent, or other relative) lives for more than half the tax year. See § 2(b)(1).

A child of divorced parents is presumed to live with the parent who has legal custody. The presumption can be rebutted if the child actually lives with the parent who does not have legal custody. It is not relevant which parent can claim the dependency deduction.

Head of household status is also available if the taxpayer maintains a household where his or her dependent parents live, even if the taxpayer lives somewhere else. To claim head of household status, the taxpayer must provide at least 50% of the expenses of running the qualifying household. Taxpayers who qualify for head of household status may also qualify for other tax relief provisions, such as the Earned Income Credit and Child Care Credit.

[3] Tax Status of Surviving Spouse

Although technically a decedent's death ends his or her tax year, the surviving spouse is permitted to file a joint return by § 6013(a)(2) for the year of the decedent spouse's death unless the decedent had filed prior to dying; or unless a personal representative has been appointed before the return has been filed (and also before its due date). (Once appointed, the personal representative's duties include filing the final income tax return.)

A decedent's final tax return is still due on the same date it would have been due if he or she had survived and, although the final return is a short-period return, the decedent is entitled to claim the full standard deduction and personal exemption. These need not be prorated for the portion of the year the decedent lived.

A surviving spouse is also entitled, under § 1(a)(2), to use joint-return rates for two years following the date of the spouse's death, if he or she has not remarried and maintains (paying at least 50% of the cost) a household for a dependent child. To qualify for this relief, the surviving spouse must have been able to file a joint return in the year of the decedent spouse's death (i.e., must not have been divorced or legally separated).

[4] Kiddie Tax

Code § 1(g) imposes a tax on the unearned income of certain children. In 2008, kiddie tax applies to persons who have not reached age 19, and full-time students up to age 24 as long as they remain dependents of their parents. The standard deduction for a person subject to kiddie tax is $950 (2009), and income over $1,800 is taxed.[3] The parent can make an election, using Form 8814, to include the child's income on the parent's return (saving the trouble of filing a return for the child). The election is available if the child has income between $950 and $9,500 (2009 figure)[4] for the year.

There is also a special Alternative Minimum Tax (AMT) rule for child taxpayers. For 2009, the exemption is limited to $6,700 plus the child's earned income for the year.[5]

§ 20.02 SUMMARY OF TAX LEGISLATION

- The 2003 tax bill was designated as the Jobs and Growth Tax Relief Reconciliation Act of 2003 (JGTRRA; P.L. 108-27). It reduced income taxes, especially on dividends, and provided business tax relief, particularly with respect to depreciation.

The Working Families Tax Relief Act of 2004, P.L.108-311, the fourth tax-cut bill in four years, was signed by President Bush on October 4, 2004. (A fifth, the American Jobs Creation Act, is primarily a business-tax statute — but see below.) A number of tax breaks (e.g., the child tax credit) were either revived after expiration or extended past a scheduled expiration date.

The American Jobs Creation Act of 2004, P.L. 108-357, introduced a new concept that has been revived several times: taxpayers who itemize can elect to take an itemized deduction for state and local sales taxes rather than one for state and local income taxes — a boon for taxpayers in states with low or no income taxes. Taxpayers who make the election can either deduct the amount they can actually substantiate via receipts, or use IRS tables; taxpayers who use the tables can still deduct sales taxes on big-ticket items like cars.

The Tax Increase Prevention and Reconciliation Act (TIPRA; P.L. 109-222) preserved a number of favorable EGTRRA provisions from expiration, such as favorable capital gains rates, and permission (for 2010 only) to convert conventional to Roth IRAs irrespective of income. However, TIPRA extended the "kiddie tax" to children up to 18 years old. TIPRA also enacted one of a series of one-year AMT patches.

The Tax Relief and Health Care Act of 2006 (TRHCA; P.L. 109-432) extends a number of popular provisions that were scheduled to expire (deductibility of state and local sales taxes in lieu of state and local income taxes; AMT relief for taxpayers who exercise ISOs; the business tax credit for research costs).

In addition to enacting kiddie tax changes, and some small business tax relief provisions, the U.S. Troop Readiness, Veterans' Care, Katrina Recovery, and Iraq Accountability Appropriations Act, P.L. 110-28, provides for suspension of some

---

[3] *See* § 8241 of the U.S. Troop Readiness, Veterans' Care, Katrina Recovery, and Iraq Accountability Appropriations Act, P.L. 110-28 and Rev. Proc. 2008-66, 2008-45 IRB 1107.

[4] The 2009 figures and adjustments can be found in Rev. Proc. 2008-66.

[5] Rev. Proc. 2008-66.

penalties and interest, increases preparer penalties for unreasonable positions taken on tax returns, and makes some IRS user fees, enacted as temporary, permanent.

A one-time federal economic stimulus payment of up to $600 per person, $1,200 per couple, plus $300 per eligible child, was issued in 2008. The payments could be directly deposited into whatever account the taxpayer designated for receipt of tax refunds. Stimulus payments could be withdrawn from the account without penalty until the time for filing their 2008 return (including extensions). The funds were treated as neither contributed to nor distributed from the account.[6]

Under the HEART Act, various benefit provisions for military servicemembers are extended or modified. For tax years beginning after December 31, 2007, the election to treat combat pay excluded by § 112 as earned income for the earned income credit is made permanent. A servicemember who is on active duty for more than 30 days is considered severed from employment with respect to elective deferrals under a 401(k) plan, 403(b) salary reduction arrangement, or 457(b) plan, so they can take distributions — but cannot make elective deferrals or employee contributions to the plan in the six months after the distribution.[7]

The two major bills responding to 2008's economic crisis, the Housing and Economic Recovery Act of 2008 (HERA; P.L. 110-289) and the Emergency Economic Stabilization Act of 2008 (EESA; P.L. 110-343), the financial system bailout bill, contain tax provisions, although the impact of this legislation on personal income taxes is not great.

HERA § 3011 creates a new Code § 36, a credit for first-time buyers of a principal residence (using the same definition as Code § 121). The credit equals 10% of the purchase price, subject, however, to a limit of $7,500 ($3,750 for married persons filing separate returns). The amount is also reduced (but not below zero) for taxpayers whose modified AGI is greater than $75,000 ($150,000 on a joint return). The credit cannot exceed $7,500 in total if it is allocated among two or more joint purchasers (who are not a married couple). The credit is not available for purchases from a related person. A residence constructed by a taxpayer is treated as if it had been purchased by the taxpayer on that date of initial occupation. The credit is subject to recapture over a 15-year period (unless the taxpayer dies; there is an involuntary conversion; interspousal transfer incident to divorce; or the taxpayer acquires a new principal residence within two years of leaving the residence for which the credit was taken).

HERA also limits the ability to claim a full exclusion of home sale gains when a one-time rental or vacation home has been converted to a primary residence.

---

[6] Denise Appleby, *IRS Provides Tax Relief for Certain Recipients of Stimulus Payments*, http://www.retirementdictionary.com/Updates-Tax-Relief-Stimulus-Payments.htm; CCH Pension and Benefits, *IRS allows tax-free withdrawal of "Economic Stimulus Payments" from IRAs*, 5/13/08 (benefitslink.com).

[7] CCH Pension and Benefits, *Military bill with payroll provisions cleared for President*, 6/4/08 (benefitslink.com).

No exclusion of gain is permitted for periods allocated to non-qualified use after 2008.[8] The EESA provisions include:

- The Mortgage Forgiveness Debt Relief Act of 2007 is extended through 2012, so mortgage forgiveness does not constitute taxable income
- The 30% tax credit for rooftop solar panels is extended for eight years, and the previous law credit limit of $2,000 is removed
- A new 30% credit is available for installing geothermal heat pumps and small wind turbines
- The credit for improving energy efficiency in existing homes is extended
- Contractors can get a credit of up to $2,000 for installing highly efficient heating/cooling systems in new construction
- Another one-year AMT patch has been adopted, with an exemption of $46,200 for individuals and $69,950 for joint filers
- The 10% penalty for premature IRA withdrawals is suspended for victims of Midwest storms, and in general, more disaster victims will be allowed to claim individual casualty losses to property
- For disasters occurring in the period 12/31/07–1/1/10, demolition, cleanup, and environmental remediation expenses can be written off rather than depreciated
- The period for claiming disaster-related casualty losses rises from two to five years
- The itemized deduction for state and local sales taxes in lieu of a state income tax deduction is revived and extended through the end of 2009; this provision is especially popular in states such as Florida, Texas, and Washington that do not have a state income tax
- The ability of donors aged 70½ and older to make charitable contributions of up to $100,000 from their IRAs is extended through 2009
- The exclusion of mortgage forgiveness from taxable income has been extended through 2012.[9]

The "Fostering Connections to Success and Increasing Adoptions Act of 2008" P.L. 110-351 (10/7/08) amends Title VI, Parts B and E of the Social Security Act to provide additional support for relatives who care for children, with additional adoption incentives, especially for older and special-needs children. The legislation adds a requirement that a person described as a "qualifying child" must be unmarried, and must be younger than the taxpayer claiming the incentives. A child can be a "qualifying child" of someone who is not the child's parent, as long as neither of the child's parents claim him or her as a qualifying child, and the non-parent has AGI higher than either of the parents. In addition to pension

---

[8] Tom Herman, *House-Hoppers May Suffer Under New Tax Rules*, Wall St. J. 8/6/08 at p. D3.

[9] Tara Siegel Bernard and Kate Galbraith, *Bailout Brings With It Diverse Perks*, N.Y. Times 10/4/08 at C6; Seyfarth Shaw LLP, *Detailed Summary: The Emergency Economic Stabilization Act of 2008*, http://www.seyfarth.com/dir_das/news_item/faea1910-e1bc-42b7-9869-6f767357151d_document upload.pdf; Tom Herman, *Bailout Includes Key Tax Breaks*, Wall St. J. 10/8/08 at p. D2.

provisions intended to cushion the impact of the Pension Protection Act's provisions on financially strapped corporations, the Worker, Retiree, and Employer Recovery Act of 2008 (WRERA; P.L. 110-458) includes some personal income tax provisions. Taxpayers are not required to take required minimum distributions from 401(k) and IRA plans for 2009 (although this relief is not available for 2008).

§ 20.03 FORMS AND TAX COMPLIANCE

The basic personal income tax form is the "long-form" 1040, for which many schedules and attachments are available. A shorter form, 1040A, is intended for use by taxpayers with simpler tax situations. An even simpler "postcard" form, the 1040EZ, can be used by taxpayers who do not have multiple sources of income and who do not itemize. However, several common credits cannot be claimed on the 1040EZ, only on one of the longer forms.

Starting in 2007, taxpayers can use Form 8888, Direct Deposit of Refund, to have the refund deposited in two, or three accounts (checking, savings, IRAs, HSAs, MSAs, or Coverdell Education Savings Accounts) as directed by the taxpayer. The IRS took this step to reduce the demand for high-interest, potentially exploitive refund anticipation loans. Taxpayers who want the refund deposited into a single rather than split accounts signal this on the Form 1040; no separate form is required.[10]

[A] Electronic Filing

The IRS has permitted various forms of electronic filing for several years (from submission of supporting documentation to filing of an entire form, with a written signature supplied separately). Businesses were supposed to be compelled to file in electronic form, but difficulties with implementing the IRS computer systems have led to several delays in the mandate of electronic filing.

The IRS Restructuring and Reform Act of 1998 (IRSRRA), P.L. 105-206, reinforces Congress' commitment to moving tax compliance from an all-paper system to a predominantly electronic one. At least 80% of tax filing is supposed to be in electronic form by 2007.

In January 2007, the IRS announced the Free File program, under which taxpayers with AGI under $52,000 (approximately 70% of filers, or 95 million taxpayers) could file online through privately operated Websites. Filing is free (except for the cost of postage) but taxpayers who do their own calculations must pay for the software, which usually costs about $30.[11]

By May 16, 2008, the IRS had received over 86 million electronically filed returns (60% of returns already filed), versus fewer than 80 million in 2007. It is possible that some new e-filers were individuals who would not ordinarily have filed a return, but did so to obtain the stimulus payment. By May 29, 2008, the IRS

---

[10] IR-2006-134, http://www.irs.gov.

[11] http://www.irs.gov/efile/article/0,,id=118986,00.html; see Robert Guy Matthews, *IRS's Free File Gets a Revamp*, Wall St.J. 1/16/07 at p. D3. For information about e-filing 2008 returns, *see* http://www.irs.gov/efile/article/0,,id=118508,00.html.

had issued about 90 million refunds aggregating $214 billion. About 4.6 million returns were filed using FreeFile, a partnership with private tax software companies that provide free software for moderate-income taxpayers (AGI under $54,000); this was 21% more than FreeFile returns filed in 2007.[12]

"Telefile," telephone filing of forms such as 1040EZ, which started in 1997, was phased out in 2004. Form 941 could be telefiled for the second quarter of 2005, and 1040EZ forms could be filed up through the August 15, 2005 extended deadline for 2004 returns, but at that point the program was terminated.[13]

FS-2000-03 is the IRS' authorization of the use of a credit card to make a tax payment associated with an automatic extension of the time to file. (The automatic extension does not extend the time to pay the tax liability). Starting on March 1, 2001, the IRS has accepted credit card payments for estimated taxes as well. A preauthorized direct debit can be used to satisfy liability under a balance-due tax return.

Credit card charges can be made by phone to an American Express, Discover, or MasterCard. Provisions are made for taxpayers to file their returns as soon as they are complete, while deferring phoning in the credit card payment authorization until the due date of the return. (The IRS is willing to do this because faster submission of returns speeds up processing, even if the payment has not yet been made.)

[B] Compliance for Household Workers

The so-called "Nanny tax" imposed under § 3510 requires the employer of a "domestic service" worker such as a child care worker or housekeeper to withhold income tax and withhold and pay FICA tax on cash remuneration that exceeds $1,600 (2007–8) or $1,700 (2009). However, unlike a corporate employer (see § 3.04[B]), the household employer does not have to make regular deposits of employment-related taxes or file Form 940. Nanny tax is reported on Form 1040, Schedule H.

[C] Extensions

Starting with 2005 returns, taxpayers can now obtain an automatic six-month extension of the time to file by filing Form 4768; under prior law, there was an automatic four-month extension, and the IRS could grant a second, discretionary two-month extension. In 2006, the requirement of a manual signature was eliminated, making it easier to file the Form 4768 electronically, and the IRS encouraged e-filing of the request. The automatic extension merely extends the time to file. For most taxpayers, more than enough will have been withheld from their paychecks so that they do not owe a balance. But for those who obtain an extension of time to file and do owe taxes, they will be subject to interest on past-due tax amounts, and possibly to a late payment penalty for failure to pay the balance due by the due date. This problem can be avoided by making a payment by check, credit card, or electronic funds transfer to accompany the extension request.

---

[12] (AP), *IRS Sees a Sharp Rise in E-Filings*, N.Y. Times 5/29/08 at D2.
[13] Announcement 2005-26, 2005-17 IRB 969.

An extension of the time to **pay** the tax (§ 6161(a)) can be granted, on a showing of hardship (not merely inconvenience) by filing Form 1127. The extension will be granted for a reasonable time, but not to exceed six months unless the taxpayer is outside the United States. The request must be filed on or before the due date for the tax.

An extension of the time to pay calls for a lump sum, but delays the due date for the single payment. Form 9465 is a request pursuant to § 6159 for permission to pay a tax liability in installments. It should be filed with the return for which a balance is due. The request is subject to a user fee and a late payment penalty of 1/2 of 1% per month. If the taxpayer's unpaid balance exceeds $10,000, financial statements must be submitted with the request.

Also note that a Form 1040X (amended return) can be filed at any time until the statute of limitation has run on a return, to claim a refund.

[D] Estimated Tax

For the self-employed individuals with significant investment income, and others whose tax situation is complex and therefore not fully addressed by employment-related withholding, quarterly estimated tax filings (on Form 1040-ES) and payments are required by § 6654. Some taxpayers will be subject to four estimated tax filings each year; others will not become subject to estimated tax until part-way through the year, so one, two, or three quarterly filings will be required.

An underpayment penalty is imposed if the taxpayer fails to pay 25% (or the appropriate proportion, if fewer than four estimated filings are due) of the "required annual payment" with each quarterly estimated payment. In general, the required annual payment is either 90% of the current year's tax liability, or 100% of the previous year's tax liability. All withholding imposed on the taxpayer's income is treated by § 6654(g) as estimated tax paid. Furthermore, the underpayment penalty is waived if tax due after estimated tax and withholding is $1,000 or less, or for hardship or for reasonable cause during the period after retirement or disability. See § 6654(e)(1).

If the taxpayer files the tax return for a calendar year on or before January 31 of the following year and pays the balance of any tax due, no penalty will be imposed for not making the fourth-quarter estimated tax payment, and any underpayment penalty for the first three quarters will not be increased.

§ 20.04 INCOME ITEMS

As noted above, income is taxable unless specifically exempted. The "tree and fruit" principle holds that, once a taxpayer is entitled to income, he or she will be taxed on it, even if he or she transfers the income to someone else. (In fact, the transfer itself might be a taxable gift; see the discussion of gift tax at § 17.13.) However, if the actual income-producing item itself is transferred, then the transferee will be responsible for tax on the post-transfer income.

Principal amounts received by a life insurance beneficiary on the death of an insured are not taxable income. However, if the beneficiary elects a "settlement option" (the insurer retains the funds and pays them out in a series of payments rather than a lump sum), the portion of each payment that represents appreciation is taxable, while the portion that represents the underlying insurance payment is tax-free. Certain terminally ill and chronically ill individuals can exclude part or all of benefits received by anticipating insurance death benefits, or assigning insurance policies to a third-party payor. See § 101(g) for details.

Unemployment benefits are fully taxable (see § 85(a)); because of § 86(a)(l), Social Security benefits may be anywhere from 50–85% taxable, if the individual's AGI, adjusted for certain amounts, exceeds a base amount that ranges from $0 for married persons filing separate returns, to $32,000 for married persons filing joint returns.

Rent received by taxpayers, and royalties (both for mineral rights and for intellectual property such as patents and copyrights) are included in income under § 61, although taxpayers are allowed to deduct legitimate business expenses of producing such forms of income.

[A] Taxation of Damages

Damages for breach of contract are includible in income, because they replace taxable income that would have been received if there had been no breach. Compensatory tort damages are tax-free if they are received for physical injuries or illnesses. However, non-physical injuries (e.g., slander, employment discrimination) are generally included in income under § 104(a). Emotional distress is not deemed to be a physical injury, but if there are physical consequences of the distress calling for medical treatment, amounts attributable to that treatment can be excluded from taxable income. Punitive damages of all kinds are generally included in income. Settlements are treated in the same way as verdicts and judgments.

The Ninth Circuit held in mid-2006 that payments received after the effective date of the § 104(a)(2) amendments, pursuant to a settlement agreement in a defamation case signed before the effective date, must be included in the recipient's gross income. The taxpayer was a talent agent who sued his former employer for wrongful termination and defamation. The $4 million in defamation damages under the settlement were paid via two payments of $1 million each in 1996, one in 1997, and one in 1998. In May 1996, § 104(a)(2) exempted damages on account of personal injuries or sickness. In August, the exemption was amended effective August 20, 1996 to limit it to "personal physical injuries or physical sickness," thus excluding nonphysical injuries. The amendment excepted amounts received under an agreement or award made before September 13, 1995. The Tax Court said that the first payment was tax-exempt and the others taxable, and the Ninth Circuit affirmed. Although he settled in 1996, the other three payments were received after the effective date of the amendment. The Ninth Circuit found that the amendment was not an impermissible ex post facto law — it did not alter the legal consequences of payments already made. The Ninth Circuit refused to apply the rules of § 1001 (taxable gain on the sale or disposition of property) because that provision applies only to transferable property that has an adjusted basis. Personal injury claims cannot be transferred under California law; Civ. Code § 9543 treats defamation claims as purely personal, unlike claims such as breach of contract claims that can be transferred. Defamation damages do not give rise to gain because they place the taxpayer in the position he or she would have been in absent defamation. In 2007, however, the Ninth Circuit withdrew its opinion and held that payments received after the amendment of § 102(a)(2), pursuant to a settlement before the effective date, must be included in the payee's gross income.[14]

Early in 2005, the Supreme Court resolved a Circuit split by ruling that no matter how state law characterizes the contingent-fee attorney's interest in the legal fees, the contingent fee paid to the lawyer under a money judgment or settlement is nevertheless gross income to the client. The Supreme Court's rationale was that the litigant owns and controls the source of income and merely makes an anticipatory assignment to the lawyer.[15]

Also see § 703 of the American Jobs Creation Act of 2004, which provides that (for employment discrimination and whistleblower suits only) attorneys' fees and court costs incurred to obtain a recovery are an adjustment to gross income rather than an itemized deduction — so the fees and costs will not increase the prevailing plaintiff's liability for AMT. As *Banks* notes, this provision is not retroactive.

[B] Investment Income

Traditionally, a distinction has been drawn between ordinary income and capital gains produced by selling capital assets: i.e., investment assets, as distinguished from inventory used in business. (A business' income from the sale of its inventory is ordinary income.) For a brief period, individuals were required to pay the same or virtually the same rates on ordinary income and investment capital gains. This unpopular provision was terminated by the Taxpayer Relief Act of 1997 (IRA '97), which once again drew a significant distinction between the rates to be charged on the two types of income.

[1] Dividends

Individual investors who receive corporate dividends have ordinary income from those dividends. Under §§ 301(c) and 316(a), a distribution from a corporation to its shareholders is a dividend (and therefore creates ordinary income for the shareholders) to the extent that the corporation has earnings and profits (E&P). Distributions in excess of E&P are deemed to be tax-free returns of capital, but they

---

[14] Polone v. Comm'r of Internal Revenue, 449 F.3d 1041 (9th Cir. 2006) withdrawn; 479 F.3d 1019 (9th Cir. 2007) substituted.

[15] CIR v. Banks, 543 U.S. 426 (U.S. 2005).

reduce the taxpayer's basis in the shares. Once the basis is reduced to zero, any further distribution is treated as a payment for the stock. In most cases, the taxpayer will hold the stock as a capital asset, so the payment will be taxed as a capital gain.

In addition to explicit dividends, stockholders (especially in close corporations) may be taxed on "constructive" dividends (amounts that are equivalent to dividends even though described as something else). For instance, a corporation that overpays a shareholder for services performed or property sold to the corporation, or that sells corporate assets to a shareholder at an unreasonably low price, has actually issued a dividend to the stockholder. (Corporations are apt to do this because they can claim a deduction for compensation paid, and can often deduct or depreciate purchased property, but cannot claim a deduction for dividends paid to their stockholders.)

Retroactive for dividends received in tax years beginning after 2002, and sunsetting on December 31, 2008, JGTRRA provides a maximum tax rate of 15% on any "qualified dividends" received by most taxpayers (5% for most low-income taxpayers). For persons in the 10% and 15% brackets, capital gains are not taxed at all for years 2008–2010.[16]

Of course, dividends are generally received by high-income taxpayers, so the ultra-low rates have little practical applicability. Furthermore, dividends paid to tax-exempt entities such as 401(k) plans derive no benefit from the cut in tax rates on dividends.

[2] Interest Received

Section 61 makes interest received by a taxpayer (e.g., on bonds purchased for investment) taxable unless specifically exempted. Interest on federal government obligations, such as Treasury securities, is taxable for federal income tax purposes, but § 103 exempts interest on most state and local bonds from inclusion in gross income.

Nevertheless, such income may have an effect on federal income tax, because it is taken into account in determining the taxability of Social Security benefits, and is included in the calculation of Alternative Minimum Tax. Some municipal bonds (e.g., arbitrage bonds, private activity bonds) are not tax-free, so it is important to determine the status of a bond before investing. The general rule is that interest on U.S. savings bonds is taxable (§ 454), but individuals who are paying qualified higher education expenses as defined by § 135 can exclude income from such bonds.

The Supreme Court upheld the existing treatment, under which a state can make interest on its own bonds tax-exempt for state residents, but require them to pay state income tax on interest on bonds from other states. (Forty-two states take this position, and allege that their financial straits would be even worse if they could not use this incentive to market municipal bonds.) The petitioners argued

---

[16] Tom Herman, *Congress Set to Eliminate Loophole On Some Long-Term Capital Gains*, Wall St.J. 2/14/07 at p. D2.

unsuccessfully that it violates the Commerce Clause for states to discriminate against bonds issued by other states. The Supreme Court ruled that states are given more leeway as market participants than as market regulators.[17]

A taxpayer who makes a loan of over $10,000 at below-market rates (e.g., to a friend, family member, or corporation with which the taxpayer is associated) has taxable income, under § 7872, equal to the foregone interest — interest that would have been received if the loan had been made on arm's-length terms.

[3] Original Issue Discount (OID)

Debt securities issued at a discount, such as zero-coupon bonds, are subject to the Original Issue Discount (OID) provisions of § 1272. OID is present if the taxpayer acquires a debt instrument from its issuer (not on the secondary market) for less than the maturity value of the instrument. In effect, the taxpayer must pay tax on part of the discount each year, even though no corresponding income is received, because the discount is treated as the counterpart of taxable interest. OID is not taxable if it comes from tax-exempt securities (unless they are stripped), U.S. savings bonds, and short-term obligations with a maturity under one year.

[4] Annuities

Theoretically, annuitization is the process of trading a lump sum for a stream of benefits; the annuity can begin either immediately or in the future (deferred annuity). Most pensions are paid in annuity form; see § 20.05[H][1] for a discussion of the special rules applicable to retirement annuities.

Annuities are also a fairly common investment, especially for middle-aged and older taxpayers who are not required to pay income tax each year on the appreciation in value of their annuity accounts. However, once they begin to receive annuity payments, § 72 prescribes the tax consequences. An amount is received "as an annuity" if it is paid at regular intervals occurring at least once a year after the start date. Lump sums and other withdrawals that are not received in annuity form are taxed to the extent that they exceed the cost of the contract.

The annuitant must compute an "exclusion ratio" to determine what part of each payment is a non-taxable return of capital, and what part is taxable appreciation. The exclusion ratio is simply the cost of the contract divided by its expected return.

For a term annuity (e.g., one that will make payments for 10 years — to the designated beneficiary, if the annuitant is no longer alive), the expected return is just the number of payments times the amount of each payment. For a life or joint life annuity, the expected return equals the payments to be made in one year, times the life expectancy(ies) as measured by official IRS tables.

---

[17] Kentucky v. Davis, 127 S. Ct. 2451 (2008); *see* Pete Yost (AP), *High Court Upholds Municipal Bond Exemption*, 5/19/08 (law.com).

Once the entire "investment in the contract" (capital; the total premiums paid before the annuity starts, minus any amount received before the start date and not included in income for tax purposes) has been recovered (typically, when the taxpayer reaches his or her actuarially predicted life expectancy), each payment is fully taxable.

If there is no investment in the contract (e.g., the annuity was received as a gift, or is provided by someone else's will), then all payments are 100% taxable. In contrast, if the investment in the contract exceeds the expected return, then no tax is imposed on the payments. The investment in the contract must also be reduced if the annuity has a refund feature, because the annuitant's risk is less and therefore there is more taxable income.

A single-life annuity terminates with the death of the annuitant. If the annuitant dies before his or her predicted life expectancy, the unrecovered investment in the contract can be deducted on the deceased annuitant's final income tax return. See § 72(b)(3)(A). Because such an annuity ends when its recipient dies, there is nothing to include in his or her taxable estate: § 2039. However, if the annuity is a joint and survivor annuity (payments are made while both annuitants are alive, and continue, often in reduced form, to the survivor), then when one annuitant dies, § 2039 requires inclusion in the estate of the decedent the present value of payments that will be made to the survivor.

The tax code's annuity provisions also require annuity contracts to provide that, if the annuitant dies on or after the start date, with part of the investment in the contract still undistributed, the balance must be distributed to the designated beneficiary at least as rapidly as payments would have been made to the annuitant. Section 72(s)(1) provides that, in case of death before the annuity start date, the entire interest must be distributed within five years; or, if a beneficiary has been designated, the interest can be distributed over the beneficiary's life or a period of years that does not exceed the beneficiary's predicted life expectancy.

§ 20.05 CAPITAL GAINS TAX

A capital asset is one that is amenable to appreciation (or depreciation) in value, and that is not inventory or stock-in-trade for the taxpayer. For most tax-payers, the two commonly-found categories of capital assets are investment securities (e.g., stocks and bonds) and the family home(s). Long-term capital gains receive more favorable tax treatment than short-term gains.

[A] Capital Gain/Loss Calculation

Section 1222 provides a somewhat cumbersome set of rules for calculating an individual's capital gains or losses. First, all short-term transactions are aggregated, to determine the net short-term gain or loss. Next, the same calculation is performed for all long-term transactions. The individual taxpayer's net capital gains consist of the excess of his or her net long gains over net short losses. The taxpayer has capital gain net income, which must be included in gross income, to the extent that capital gains minus capital losses exceed $0. There is no limit on the amount of capital gain a taxpayer may have to recognize — but the capital loss current deduction is subject to strict limits.

Limitations are placed on individual taxpayers' capital loss deductions by § 1211(b). The taxpayer can deduct only the net loss (losses minus gains) or $3,000 ($1,500 for a married taxpayer filing a separate return), whichever is lower. Capital losses can be carried forward indefinitely. When items are carried forward, they retain their characterization as short- or long-term. The deductible amount of capital losses remained at the same level for many years — a cause of some bitterness among taxpayers who lost a lot of money in the financial crisis of 2008, to little effect on their tax bills.

[B] Holding Period

Under TRA '97, the rules originally enacted effective for sales after 5/6/97 defined long-term capital gain as gain deriving from the sale of an asset held at least 18 months. The maximum capital gains tax rate was set at 20%, a significant reduction from the 28% rate imposed by prior law. Furthermore, taxpayers in the minimum (15%) income tax bracket were to be taxed only 10% on their long-term capital gains.[18]

The Tax Technical Corrections Act of 1998, Title VI of the IRSRRA, P.L. 105-206, changed the rules once again, by reinstating the definition of long-term assets as those held for 12 months or more. The change is effective after December 31, 1997. Inherited property is deemed to have been held for 12 months, and thus to be eligible for long-term capital gain treatment.

TRA '97 adds a category that might be called "ultra-long-term capital gains": that is, sales occurring after 12/31/2000, of assets held for at least **five** years, are taxed by § 1(h) at 18% (or 8%, for lowest-bracket taxpayers). This category was suspended by JGTRRA until 2009. Repeal of the 8% rate is retroactive to May 6, 2003.

One of JGTRRA's major legislative objectives is reduction in capital gains tax rates (for both ordinary income tax and AMT purposes). For sales and exchanges made, and payments received, on or after May 6, 2003, the maximum capital gains tax rate is 15% (reduced from 20%). JGTRRA provided that the 20% capital gains rate (10% for low-income taxpayers) would be restored January 1, 2009. However, TIPRA, P.L. 109-222, extended the EGTRRA capital gains provisions until 2010.

[C] Small Business Stock Provisions

The maximum tax rate is also 28% on § 1202 gain: that is, 50% of the gain on qualified small business stock held for five years or more. (The other 50% is

---

[18] There was a special transition rule for sales between 5/6/97 and 7/29/97, when assets held at least 12 months were deemed long-term. For certain post-7/29/97 sales of assets held 12–18 months, an intermediate rate of 28% was imposed.

excluded from income.) A qualified small business corporation is a C corporation with aggregate gross assets under $50 million.

Section 1244 provides that the original purchaser of such stock from the corporation (but not a transferee of the original purchaser) can benefit in two ways. Gain, if any, on the stock is capital gain, but if a loss occurs, it is an ordinary loss. Section 1244 limits the ordinary loss to the lesser of the actual loss or $50,000 ($100,000 on a joint tax return); any additional loss must be treated as a capital loss. (Remember, an ordinary loss is more valuable to a high-bracket taxpayer than a capital loss, because it reduces ordinary income that would otherwise be taxed at above-capital-gains rates.)

Section 1231 covers another category of "capital gain[19] ordinary loss" property: real estate; depreciable tangible and intangible personal property used in business, if it was a long-term asset as of the time of its sale, exchange, or involuntary conversion. Inventory does not qualify as § 1231 property. Nor does property held for sale to customers in the course of business, or copyrights and artistic creations in the hands of their creators or donees of their creators.

[D] Home Sale Gains

Under prior law, the financial importance of the family home in most financial plans was addressed by two tax relief provisions. One of them, which could be used repeatedly, permitted a "rollover" of capital gain when a more expensive residence was purchased (i.e., it was not necessary to pay tax on the theoretical gain on selling one residence if another was purchased shortly before or afterward). The other was a one-time exclusion available only to persons over 55.

In effect, TRA '97 combines the characteristics of both provisions (former §§ 121 and 1041) in a single Code § 121. An unmarried taxpayer can exclude capital gains on home sales of up to $250,000; up to $500,000 can be excluded on a joint return. Furthermore, the exclusion can be repeated on subsequent sales, but not more often than once every two years.

Timing requirements (how long the residence was owned; how long it operated as the taxpayer's principal residence) must also be met. In general, the property must have been owned and used as the taxpayer's principal residence for two out of the five years preceding the sale. Some newly-married or remarried taxpayers may have to prorate or lose the exclusion. The Tax Technical Corrections Act further liberalized this provision by allowing a prorated exclusion for those unable to satisfy the "2 of 5" test.

In August 2004, the IRS published Final Regulations, somewhat modifying Final Regulations issued in 2002. There are three grounds for claiming the capital gains exclusion (i.e., change in place of employment; poor health; and unforeseen circumstances), each of which has at least one safe harbor. Taxpayers who do not qualify for a safe harbor can still claim an exclusion, although less than the maximum, if the taxpayer can show that the facts and circumstances of the case

---

[19] Treated as long-term capital gain.

prove that the primary reason for selling or exchanging the principal residence was one of the three permissible grounds.

The definition of "unforeseen circumstances" has changed from an event that the taxpayer factually did not anticipate to one that the taxpayer could not reasonably have anticipated before purchasing the residence. An improvement (rather than a deterioration) in the taxpayer's financial circumstances, or a preference for another home, will not be considered an unforeseen circumstance. However, disaster, involuntary conversion, death, unemployment, multiple births, divorce or legal separation, and change in employment resulting in inability to pay housing costs will be treated as safe harbor events, as will events determined by the Commissioner in published guidance of general applicability (as distinct from a ruling for a particular taxpayer). In line with the objectives of the Military Family Tax Relief Act of 2003, a qualified taxpayer or spouse on military duty can suspend the running of the five-year period (for calculation of the two-out-of-five test) for up to 10 years as a result of active military service.[20]

In 2007, the Mortgage Forgiveness Debt Relief Act made it easier for surviving spouses to make use of the exclusion of gain on the sale or exchange of a principal residence.[21]

[E] Basis of Capital Assets

Although the issue is more common for corporations (see § 4.06[C]), individual taxpayers sometimes encounter basis issues, e.g., when they receive a gift or inheritance including capital assets. Section 1015 states that the basis of property acquired by gift is the same as the donor's adjusted basis. However, if at the date of the gift, the fair market value of the gift property is below the donor's adjusted basis (i.e., the donor is making a gift of depreciated rather than appreciated property), the basis for determining the donee's loss is fair market value at the time of the gift. If the fair market value is greater than the donor's adjusted basis, the donee's basis is also increased by any gift tax paid that can be traced to net appreciation in the value of the gift.

See § 17.01 for a discussion of EGTRRA's effect on basis calculations for inherited assets.

[F] Fringe Benefits

Fringe benefits offered by employers to their employees are included in the recipient employee's gross income unless there is a specific reason for the exclusion (§ 61(a)). If a fringe benefit is taxable, the employee's income is the fair market value of the benefit (the price that would be paid for it in an arm's length exchange), minus any amount the employee paid for it and also minus any other exclusion permitted by the Code.

---

[20] T.D. 9152, 69 FR 50302 (8/16/04).
[21] P.L. 110-142

A vehicle provided by the employer is taxed to the employee at the value of a lease of a comparable vehicle (Reg. § 1.61-21(d)).

Section 132 is the main section dealing with fringe benefits, although various other sections may have to be consulted in a particular case. To be excluded from gross income, some fringe benefits must be provided under an employer plan that is nondiscriminatory; that is, it must not be limited to highly-compensated employees, and it must not be disproportionately favorable to HCEs.

Fringes that are excluded from income, either because they are too trivial to be worth accounting for, or because the IRC wants to permit them preferential status, include:

- Services that generate no additional cost for the employer, such as use of the employer's extra capacity: § 132(a)(1)
- Discounts employees get when they buy the employer's products: § 132(a)(2)
- "Working condition fringes" defined by § 132(a)(3) that would be deductible if the employee paid out-of-pocket, e.g., business travel, use of corporate vehicles
- De minimis fringes such as occasional meals or transportation home after working late; office parties; meals in an employer-operated facility whose revenues are at least equal to its direct operating costs: § 132(a)(4)
- Qualified transportation fringes under § 132(a)(5) and (1)(5), such as vanpooling, transit passes, and parking, subject to dollar limits
- Qualified moving expense reimbursement: § 132(a)(6)
- Benefits under a cafeteria plan, defined by § 125 as a plan that gives employees a choice between taking certain compensation in cash and making their own personal choice of benefits from a "menu." Permissible cafeteria benefits include group-term life insurance, accident and health insurance, dependent care assistance, and extra vacation days. (Dependent care assistance is made excludable under § 129, up to $5,000 per employee, or $2,500 per married employee filing a separate return; the assistance must be provided under a written, nondiscriminatory plan.)
- Meals and lodging furnished for the convenience of the employer rather than the employee: § 119
- Adoption assistance of up to $12,150: § 137(a), (b). The same employee can exclude adoption expenses and simultaneously claim the adoption-expense credit (§ 20.07[C][1]), but cannot double-dip for the same expense
- Educational assistance of up to $5,250, whether or not job-related
- Premiums for life insurance on the life of the employee (e.g., a key executive) if the insurance is payable to the corporation rather than to the employee's survivors: Reg. § 1.62-2(d)(2)
- Group-term life insurance payable to the employee's chosen beneficiary, up to $50,000: § 79. If coverage exceeds $50,000, the employee does have taxable income, equal to the cost of the extra coverage, defined by IRS tables. However, group-term life insurance in excess of $2,000, on the life of an

employee's spouse or dependent, is a taxable fringe benefit rather than a tax exempt one (Reg. § 1.61-2(d)(2)(ii)(b)); so is group-permanent life insurance on the employee's own life: Reg. § 1.79-1(d). The taxable income equals the premiums paid by the employer for the group-permanent life insurance

- The employer's reimbursement of medical expenses incurred by the employee, his or her spouse, and his or her dependents: § 105(b). The employee has income to the extent that the reimbursement exceeds the actual expense, or if a medical expense deduction has already been taken for the same expense

- Health insurance coverage provided by the employer under an Accident & Health (A&H plan; see § 20.05[J]). Premiums paid by a partnership on behalf of its partners, or by an S Corporation on behalf of its 2% shareholders, are not excludable. HCEs who benefit from a self-insured plan (i.e., the corporation sets aside sums for health reimbursement instead of buying insurance policies) have taxable income to the extent of reimbursement received for benefits not available to other participants in the plan: see § 105(b)

- Employer contributions to a Medical Savings Account (Archer MSA, § 20.06[C]) on behalf of eligible employees, subject to § 106(b)(1)'s dollar limits. MSAs cannot be included in cafeteria plans

- Worker's Compensation benefits, except to the extent they are traceable to medical expense deductions taken in a prior year (§ 104(a)(1)).

[G] Stock Options

A stock option is a form of employee compensation. A corporation offers its employees the right to buy shares of the company's stock, generally at a time in the future, with the "exercise price" (the price for the future purchase) set by the option plan. Often, the shares will be subject to restrictions that prevent the person exercising the option from selling the shares immediately. In any case, the intention is that the person will be able to buy valuable shares for far less than their market price, and will be able to profit by increases in the company's stock price. In some instances, stock options will be subject to the new Code § 409A (non-qualified deferred compensation) added by The American Jobs Creation Act of 2004 (P.L. 108-357), although Incentive Stock Options (ISOs) are exempt from § 409A.

[1] Taxable Option Events

A stock option plan therefore includes at least three potentially taxable events: the time that the option is granted; the time that the holder of the option exercises the option and acquires shares of the corporation's stock; and the time that the stockholder sells the shares to someone else, hoping to earn a profit. The actual tax consequences depend on whether the option plan conforms to the IRC requirements for an Incentive Stock Option (ISO), as laid out in §§ 421–422, or Employee Stock Ownership Plan (ESOP; see § 423). These plans are entitled to favorable tax consequences. Other options are considered NQSOs (Nonqualified Stock Options), with less positive tax results.

Taxation of stock options stems from § 83, which provides that, in general, receipt of stock or other property for services will create compensation income equal to the value of the property at the time it was received.

But if the interest in the property is restricted (there is a substantial chance of forfeiture of the right to receive the property), then it is not necessary to report the income until the risk of forfeiture is eliminated, or until the property is transferred. In turn, substantial risk of forfeiture includes a requirement that the option holder continue to work for a particular company, or continue to refrain from performing services.

Section 83 also gives taxpayers the right to accelerate taxability of such income (e.g., at the time the option is granted), a choice that might be made to incur a small tax bill at the time of grant in order to avoid a much larger tax on capital gains if the optioned stock appreciates significantly.

[2] Incentive Stock Options (ISOs)

An ISO is not taxed when the option is granted or when the employee exercises the option and acquires shares of stock — only when the employee eventually sells those shares, at which point the income is capital gain and not compensation income (and thus not subject to self-employment tax).[22]

However, the employee must refrain from selling the ISO shares until two years after the grant of the option or one year after exercising the option. The option holder must work for the company granting the option from the date of the grant until three months before its exercise (one year before the exercise, if the holder is permanently and totally disabled).

Failure to satisfy these requirements means that the employee will have income in the year the shares are sold. This income will be ordinary income, not capital gain, to the extent of the fair market value of the shares at the exercise date minus the option price, or the amount realized from disposition of the stock minus the option price, whichever is less. The Tax Relief and Health Care Act of 2006 (P.L. 108-432) provides Alternative Minimum Tax relief for qualifying taxpayers who exercise ISOs.

[3] Employee Stock Ownership Plans (ESOPs)

ESOPs give employees a chance to buy the employer's stock without taxation on the grant or the exercise, until the stock is disposed of. If the option price is greater than the FMV at the time of the grant, then the employee has a capital gain on the sale. However, the employee has ordinary income if optioned stock is sold within two years of the grant of the option or one year of its exercise.

If the option price is below the FMV at the time of the grant, but is at least 85% of the FMV, the optionee has ordinary income on the disposition after the

---

[22] Regulations on the treatment of statutory options granted after June 9, 2003 were proposed at 68 FR 34344 (6/9/03).

holding period ends. The ordinary income is the smaller of the difference between the fair market value of the option at the time of the grant, less the option price; or the fair market value as of the time of disposition or a deceased employee's death minus the amount paid to exercise the option.

[4] Non-Qualified Stock Options (NQSOs)

Options that are neither ISOs nor ESOPs are NQSOs. If an NQSO has a reasonably ascertainable value at the time of the grant (i.e., options in that company's stock are actively traded on a recognized market, so the trades furnish pricing information), § 83 provides that the employee has compensation income at the time of the grant. It works out better for employees if the option does not have an ascertainable value because then they do not have compensation until they exercise the option and acquire shares in the employer corporation. Under Reg. § 1.83-7(a), the amount of income is the fair market value of the shares at the time of the transfer, minus whatever the employee paid for them.

The Fifth Circuit joined the Tax Court, the Ninth Circuit, and the Court of Federal Claims in holding that, for non-statutory stock options, the taxable transfer occurs when the options are exercised. This is true whether or not margin debt is used to finance the purchase. Numerous taxpayers have argued unsuccessfully that exercise of an option on margin does not constitute a taxable transfer because their own capital was not at risk, but the Fifth Circuit focused on factors such as acquisition of beneficial ownership and the fact that the taxpayer could vote the shares and receive dividends; furthermore, the margin agreement put his capital at risk.[23]

[H] Other Deferred Compensation: Qualified Plans

If an employer maintains a qualified plan (§ 3.05[B]), there are two main consequences. From the employer's viewpoint, the cost of providing the program is tax-deductible. From the employee's viewpoint, there are no tax consequences until the employee retires and begins to draw a pension. Presumably, the retiree's tax bracket will be lower than the employee's was, so there has been an overall tax saving as well as a means of providing financial security after employment ends.

Taxpayers are given a certain amount of flexibility to allocate retirement funds among accounts (e.g., to deposit funds into a new employer's pension plan; to move funds from one IRA to another). However, because the purpose of tax incentives for IRAs and qualified plans is to provide for deferred, post-retirement income, taxpayers are not given complete freedom to use these funds. As a general rule, IRA or pension funds are not taxable income to the

---

[23] Cidale v. United States, 475 F.3d 685 (5th Cir. 2007); Facq v. Comm'r, 91 T.C.M. 1201 (2006), and so did many other courts: United States v. Tuff, 469 F.3d 1249 (9th Cir. 2006); Miller v. United States, No. 04-17470, 2006 WL 3487016 (9th Cir. Dec. 4, 2006); see also Palahnuk v. United States, 70 Fed. Cl. 87 (Fed. Cl. 2006) and Racine v. CIR, 493 F.3d 777 (7th Cir. 2007): under § 83, occurrence of the transfer cannot be postponed by claiming that borrowing to finance the transaction generates a new option replacing the original one.

taxpayer if they move directly from one trustee to another, with the funds never being in the taxpayer's hands; or if the funds are in the taxpayer's hands for less than 60 days before being rolled over into another qualifying account.

However, Rev. Proc. 2003-16, 2003-4 IRB 359, broadens the circumstances under which the IRS can waive strict application of the 60-day rule. Under prior law, the waiver was permitted only for persons in active military service or affected by a presidentially-recognized disaster. Rev. Proc. 2003-16 expands eligibility (for distributions made after December 31, 2001) in hardship cases and if the taxpayer is unable to comply despite good-faith efforts (e.g., the taxpayer is hospitalized; a financial institution commits an error affecting transfer of the funds; transfer instructions are lost in the mail).

The Worker, Retiree, and Employer Recovery Act of 2008, P.L. 110-458, provides that, for plan years beginning after December 31, 2009, qualified plans must permit non-spouses who inherit balances from the plan to roll over the inherited amount to an IRA, and must give rollover notices. For the 2009 calendar year only (but not for 2008), minimum required distributions do not have to be taken from 401(k) plans or IRAs; the normal penalties for failure to take out at least the minimum required amount are suspended.

[1] Pensions Paid in Annuity Form

The basic form of paying pensions is the annuity (a joint and survivor annuity, if the retiree is married). See § 3.05[C] for a discussion of other available choices. Taxation of retirement annuities is quite similar to taxation of investment annuities (§ 20.04[B][4]). However, the employee's investment in the contract includes not only contributions made by the employee to a contributory plan, but certain employer contributions that were previously taxed to the employee: see Code §§ 72(f), (m)(3), and (o)(1). (The greater the exclusion ratio, of course, the less tax the employee has to pay, so a higher ratio is desirable from the employee's viewpoint.)

1996's Small Business Job Protection Act (SBJPA) simplified annuity taxation for single-life retirement annuities beginning after 11/18/96; TRA '97 did the same for qualified joint and survivor annuities (QJSAs) beginning after 12/31/97. (A somewhat similar "safe-harbor" calculation is available for annuities with start dates before November 19, 1996; otherwise, earlier annuities required actuarial calculations, which could be complex.)

The current calculation sets the exclusion ratio as investment in the contract divided by a number of monthly payments, found in § 72(d)(1)(B)(iii) and (iv), applicable to an entire range of ages. For persons under 55, it is assumed there will be 360 payments, versus 310 payments for persons over 55 but under 60, 260 for persons over 60 but not over 65, 210 for those over 65 but under 70, and 160 for those over 70.

A similar calculation is made by adding the ages of both spouses for QJSA payments (annuity payments made to married workers). For joint ages under 110, it is assumed that 410 payments will be made. The assumption is 360 payments for joint ages of 110–120, 310 payments for joint ages of 120–130, 260 for joint ages of 130–140, and 210 payments for joint ages over 140.

[I] Other Deferred Compensation: Non-Qualified Plans

To the employer, maintaining one or more qualified plans creates various problems. The plans themselves are cumbersome, hard to set up, and hard to administer. They must be nondiscriminatory, which can frustrate the top management's intention to reserve the bulk of plan benefits for their peers. Therefore, the Tax Code makes provision, in § 83 (already discussed in § 20.05 in conjunction with stock options) for non-qualified plans of deferred compensation. These plans exist in many forms (see § 3.05[B][6] for a substantive discussion) such as top-hat plans, rabbi trusts, secular trusts, and SERPs (Supplemental Executive Retirement Plans).

The basic rule of Code § 83 is that, if the non-qualified plan is funded (i.e., the employer makes regular contributions each year, as it is required to do for a qualified plan), the employee is taxed in the first year that the employee can either transfer his or her rights in the plan, or there is no substantial risk of forfeiture. Nonqualified plans are typically drafted to be subject to the claims of the corporation's priority creditors, and thus there is a substantial risk of forfeiture and executives receiving non-qualified deferred compensation can defer tax on these amounts.

Most non-qualified deferred compensation plans are unfunded, in which case § 83 provides that the employee will not have taxable income until actually receiving the funds (i.e., after retirement), as long as:

- The employee agrees in advance to defer receipt of the income
- The employer's promise to pay is merely contractual, not secured
- The funds to pay the deferred compensation are NOT placed into an unconditional trust or escrow account; they remain part of the corporation's general assets.

After many years without tax-law changes, deferred compensation became a legislative target because of perceived abuses by executives at Enron, WorldCom, and other companies involved in financial scandals. The American Jobs Creation Act of 2004, P.L. 108-357, imposes stricter limits and tax penalties on non-qualified plans, including penalties for premature withdrawals (other than those taken in emergencies or when there has been a change in control of the corporation) and earlier deadlines for determining whether or not bonuses will be deferred rather than being paid immediately in cash. Premature distributions are subject to a 20% excise tax plus interest. However, limits are also placed on participants' ability to delay distributions.

[J] Health Insurance and Related Payments

The general rule is that amounts received under a policy of accident and health insurance (A&H) do not constitute income. However, health insurance reimbursement is included in AGI if the reimbursement can be traced to earlier medical expense deductions; if the reimbursement comes directly from the employer (§ 105(b)) or is attributable to employer contributions not already included in the employee's income. See § 104(a)(3).

Benefits received under a "qualified" long-term care insurance policy (§ 13.08[E]) are treated as accident and health insurance benefits under § 7702B(a)(1). However, there is no limitation on the amount of ordinary insurance reimbursement that can be exempted from tax. Long-term care insurance reimbursement is tax-free up to a maximum of $175 a day (as adjusted for inflation; the 2009 figure is $280). If the policy pays on the basis of actual costs, reimbursement is tax-free up to the actual cost of care, even if that exceeds the excludable amount for the year of payment.

§ 20.06 DEDUCTIONS

Ascertaining a taxpayer's gross income is only a small part of the tax computation. A wide variety of deductions is available. It is important to distinguish between AGI deductions, used to compute Adjusted Gross Income, and itemized deductions, some of which are based on or limited to a percentage of AGI.

[A] AGI Deductions

Under Code § 62, the deductions used to arrive at AGI include trade and business expenses; property losses; deductions related to the production of rent and royalties; a self-employed person's health insurance; IRA and MSA contributions; work-related moving expenses; and alimony payments. Note that most of the AGI deductions are related to business or the production of income.

[B] Classes of Itemized Deductions

Itemized deductions include:

- Unreimbursed medical expenses (deductible only to the extent that they exceed 7.5% of AGI)
- Mortgage interest
- Foreign-country, state and local taxes, including real estate taxes, income taxes, and personal property taxes (§ 164(a))[24]
- Casualty and theft losses.

---

[24] In certain years, the deduction for state and local sales taxes in lieu of a deduction for state and local income taxes is permitted, pursuant to the American Jobs Creation Act of 2004 and extenders.

Miscellaneous itemized deductions (which can be claimed only to the extent they exceed 2% of AGI) include:

- Unreimbursed business expenses of employees
- Investment expenses other than interest
- Union dues
- Work clothes not suitable for general wear
- Costs of finding a new job in the same trade or business (Expenses of finding a job in a new line of business are not deductible.)
- Fees for services in connection with determination of taxes (e.g., appraisals)
- The home office deduction for employees
- Hobby losses (§ 183(a)).

Before EGTRRA, Code § 68 reduced most types of itemized deductions (but not medical expense, gambling losses, casualty and theft losses, or investment-oriented interest) for high-income taxpayers. For 2009, deductions are reduced if AGI is greater than $166,800 (or $83,400 for married persons filing separately).

[C] Criteria for Deductibility

Moving expenses, defined by § 217(b) and reported on Form 3903, are deductible if a new job adds more than 50 miles to the commute the employee would face by remaining at his or her present home. The actual costs of moving furniture and other household goods are deductible, as are the employee's costs of moving (and taking the family) to the new home. Lodging, but not meal, costs during the transition period are also deductible.

Casualty and theft losses can be claimed on non-business property. A casualty is a discrete, identifiable event that is sudden, unexpected, and/or unusual (e.g., fire, flood, explosion), so progressive deterioration of the condition of the taxpayer's property does not qualify. Furthermore, the item must suffer physical damage — not just a loss in value.

Casualty and theft losses are subject to a "floor" for each incident; after many years of being set at $100, the floor amount rose to $500 in 2009. See IRS Publication 17. No deduction is allowed under § 165(h) unless the taxpayer's total, unreimbursed casualty and theft losses for the year exceed 10% of AGI. Section 165(i) allows taxpayers (generally by means of an amended return) to claim a casualty or theft loss for the year **before** the loss actually occurred, so that they can receive tax relief more speedily. The amount of a casualty loss is the lower of the adjusted basis just before the casualty, or the difference between the fair market values just before and just after the casualty.

For federal income tax purposes, state, local, and foreign taxes on income and real property, and state and local taxes on personal property, can be deducted under § 164(a). As an alternative, § 901 permits a dollar-for-dollar credit of foreign against U.S. taxes.

Ordinary federal income taxes are not deductible; neither is AMT (§ 20.10), estate tax (§ 275(a)(3)), nor the employee share of FICA tax. Generation-skipping tax (§ 164(a)(5); see § 17.27) imposed on income distributions is deductible; so is the estate tax imposed on Income in Respect of a Decedent (§ 17.25[D][3]), and half of the self-employment tax (§§ 164(f); 62(a)(1)).

Section 183(a), which is applicable to individuals, partnerships, estates, and S Corporations, but not C Corporations, governs losses incurred in activities that are not engaged in on a businesslike basis with a reasonable history or expectation of profit. Such losses may be deductible, but only to the extent of the larger of items that are deductible for another reason (e.g., real estate taxes on property used for horse breeding) or deductions that would be permitted to a business, but only to the extent that gross income exceeds the non-business deductions. An activity is presumed to be carried on for profit if it produces income in excess of the deductions in three of the five years prior to the current tax year. For horse breeding, the presumption requires profits in five years out of the preceding seven.

Gambling losses can be deductible, but only to the extent that they offset reported gambling wins: § 165(d).

Non-business bad debts can be deducted, but only if they are wholly worthless. The deduction is taken in the year the debt becomes worthless (unrecoverable). However, non-business bad debts give rise to short-term capital losses (see § 20.05[A]). They are not ordinary losses that simply reduce ordinary income: § 166.

[D] Employment-Related Expenses

Employees can deduct ordinary and necessary expenses of business travel when they are away from home on an overnight trip: costs such as air fares, meals, and lodging. See § 274. Transportation costs can only be deducted if the trip is made primarily for business, but if the trip also has an element of pleasure travel, then the entire transportation cost can be deducted, but only the hotel and meal costs allocable to the business part of the trip can be deducted. If the employee brings a spouse or other companion on the trip, and that person is not a business associate, none of the expenses of the spouse's travel can be deducted.

As for travel when the employee is not away from home, ordinary commuting expenses are not deductible, but if a person has two jobs, the expense of traveling from the first to the second job is deductible. (Reg. § 1.162-2.)

Expenses associated with an automobile used for business are deductible, but an allocation must be made between personal and business use of the vehicle. Furthermore, the deduction for automobile costs is a miscellaneous deduction, subject to the 2% floor. Instead of keeping track of actual expenses, either an employee or a self-employed person who uses a car for business purposes can claim a mileage allowance; the allowance for 2009 is 55 cents a mile. Employees claim their vehicle expenses on Form 2106; for the self-employed, it is a Schedule C line item, with Form 4562 used to claim depreciation on a business vehicle.

Entertainment expenses are deductible, within limits, if they are ordinary and necessary, such as meeting with an established or potential business associate (a supplier or customer; an employee or potential employee; a professional advisor). No deduction is available for "lavish or extravagant" food and beverage expenses. As a general rule, the § 274 deduction is limited to 50% of the cost of the meal or entertainment. The deduction is clearly available if entertainment occurs in a business setting, such as a convention hospitality suite. Otherwise, if the entertainment is preceded or followed by active, bona fide business discussion, the deduction should be available.

The expenses (e.g., legal and accounting fees) that are "ordinary and necessary" for the determination, collection, or refund of any tax (not just a federal tax) are deductible under § 212(3).

The tax treatment of an employee's expense account is more favorable if the plan is "accountable," as defined by Reg. § 1.162-2(c) — that is, if the employee is required to provide a current accounting for the funds, must be able to substantiate how much was actually spent (especially in the case of entertainment expenses) and is required to return any part of an expense account advance exceeding the actual business expense. Employees are not taxed on advances or reimbursement from accountable plans. However, advances under the laxer non-accountable plans are treated as taxable income subject to FICA tax and withholding.

[1] Home Office Deduction

The perpetually contentious home office deduction rules can be found at § 280A. A home office must be a part of the taxpayer's residence used exclusively for business. (A portion of a room can qualify under this test.)

Furthermore, it must be used on a regular basis as the taxpayer's principal place of business for a trade or business. This business use renders the applicable part of the residence depreciable (although the depreciation will have to be recaptured when the residence is sold). Whether the home office is the principal place of business depends on the time spent at each business location, and the relative importance of activities at each location.

For tax years beginning after 12/31/98, a home office deduction can be claimed for administrative and management activities carried on there, as long as the taxpayer has no other fixed location for performing such activities (e.g., a surgeon who operates at the hospital, but requires an office to keep records and prepare bills).

The home office deduction can always be claimed for a separate structure used regularly and exclusively for business (e.g., the archetypal garage from which software companies emerge) and for a part of a residence used exclusively and regularly to meet clients (e.g., a CPA's or therapist's in-home office) even if the taxpayer usually works outside the home. A home office deduction can also be claimed on space used on a regular basis to store inventory or samples (even if the space is not used exclusively for this purpose), if the home office is the taxpayer's sole place of business.

If the taxpayer claiming the home office deduction is an employee, the use of the home office must be for the convenience of the employer, not the employee — e.g., someone who frequently takes work home in order to be able to spend more time with his or her children will find it difficult to claim home office expenses. Basic local telephone service on the first line in the residence is considered a non-deductible personal expense (§ 262(b)), but additional lines used only for business are likely to be deductible.

In any event, the home office deduction cannot exceed the gross income from the activity, minus other deductions claimable under other Code provisions (e.g., mortgage interest that would be deductible whether or not there was a home office). The excess can be carried forward, but will continue to be subject to the net-income limitation in the later year(s).

[E] Medical Expense and Related Deductions

Unreimbursed medical expenses incurred by the taxpayer for him- or herself, spouse, and dependents can be deducted, but only to the extent that all medical deductions exceed 7.5% of AGI (§ 213); see IRS Publication 502, "Medical and Dental Expenses." Prescription drugs and insulin, but not over-the-counter drugs, can qualify for the deduction. Rev. Rul. 2007-72, 2007-50 IRB 1154 adds three new categories of medical expenses to § 213: an annual physical examination performed by a physician even if no treatment results; full-body electronic scans; and pregnancy tests.

Home improvements are deductible if their primary purpose is the taxpayer's medical care (e.g., installing a staircase lift; making a home accessible; installing a swimming pool for a patient who needs to exercise). The deduction is limited to the cost of the improvement minus whatever it adds to the value of the property, but removal of architectural barriers to accessibility is deemed not to increase the value of the property, so such amounts are deductible in full.

The costs of traveling to get medical care, including meals and lodging, are also deductible (subject to a limit per person per night). Announcement 2008-63, 2008-42 IRB 946 provides that the standard mileage rate for driving for medical treatment purposes is 27 cents per mile, beginning in mid-2008. The previous figure was 19 cents per mile.

A self-employed person can deduct his or her health insurance premiums. This is a business deduction (provided by § 162(1)(1)(b) as amended by P.L. 105-277), and is not subject to the 7.5% of AGI floor. Since 2003, 100% of the premium has been deductible. However, the deduction cannot exceed the earned income from the trade or business for which the insurance plan was created.

[1] Medical Savings Accounts (Archer MSAs) and Health Savings Accounts (HSAs)

Contributions to a Medical Savings Account (MSA) are also deductible, within limits. MSAs, which are governed by § 220, are IRA-type savings accounts into which individuals who have no health insurance, or whose only health insurance is a high-deductible plan, make deposits. Funds can be withdrawn tax-free to pay medical expenses for the taxpayer, spouse, and dependents. Funds withdrawn for other purposes constitute taxable income and are also subject to a 15% excise penalty (§ 220(f)(4)(A)). There is no penalty on withdrawals taken by an account holder over 65 or a disabled account holder, or taken after the account holder's death.

A high-deductible plan is a health insurance plan that requires the insured to assume a significant amount of medical expenses. The plan must impose a deductible of at least $2,000 a year (individual) and $4,000 a year (family coverage) but not more than $3,000 a year for individual coverage and not over $6,050 for family coverage. Once the deductible is satisfied and the plan begins to pay health benefits, the insured person must not be subjected to out-of-pocket expenses of more than $4,000 for an individual, or $7,350 for family coverage (2009 figures). *See* Rev. Proc. 2008-66.

The MSA deduction is subject to a contribution limit (65% of the deductible for individual coverage, 75% for family coverage), and the deduction for a self-employed person with an MSA is further limited by his or her self-employment income. MSA contributions in excess of the permissible amount can be withdrawn tax-free until the due date for the return on which the MSA deduction will be claimed.

MSA plans can also be sponsored by an employer, as employee benefits: see § 3.07[D], which also discusses the Health Savings Account, a related tax-advantaged savings vehicle. The Archer MSA program expired December 31, 2003, but has been re-authorized and extended.

The Health Savings Account (HSA) is another type of tax-favored savings account. It functions much like an IRA: an eligible taxpayer sets up an account with a qualified trustee such as a bank or insurer, in the form of a trust or custodial account. To qualify, the taxpayer must not be enrolled in Medicare; must not be claimed as another taxpayer's dependent; and must not have health insurance coverage other than a high-deductible health plan (HDHP). The idea is that the funds invested in the HSA account can be used to pay for deductibles, copayments, and medical care not covered by the HDHP. Rev. Proc. 2008-29, 2008-22 IRB 1039 gives the HSA limits for 2009. The limit on out-of-pocket payments rises to $11,600 for a joint return, $5,800 for a single return (versus $11,000 and $5,500 for 2008). Persons over 55 can make an additional catch-up contribution of $1,000 (2009); $100 more than the 2008 figure.

Holders of MSAs will probably be able to make tax-free rollovers from the MSA to an HSA. The TRHCA, P.L. 109-432, also permits a one-time transfer of assets from an IRA or Roth IRA to an HSA; such a transfer generally will not give rise to gross income, and will not be subject to the 10% excise tax on premature withdrawals. See Notice 2008-51, 2008-25 IRB 1163.

[F] Alimony Deduction

Child support is a non-deductible personal expense, but "alimony" (which is very much a term of art) is deductible by the payor spouse (but not, e.g., by an alimony trust) as a result of § 215. Alimony correspondingly constitutes taxable income for the recipient (§ 71). The alimony deduction reduces gross income, and therefore can be taken by a payor who does not itemize deductions.

The § 71(b) definition of alimony is a cash payment received by or on behalf of a spouse under a divorce or separation instrument, such as a separation agreement. The instrument must not treat the amounts in question as child support. The spouses must no longer cohabit, and the death of either spouse terminates the alimony obligation.

A payment made to a third party on behalf of the payee spouse, to satisfy the payee spouse's obligations, can sometimes be treated as alimony. However, if the payor spouse is the sole owner of the former family home, and the payee spouse is permitted to live there, then funds used to maintain the property are not considered alimony. But if the home is owned jointly and the divorce decree or separation agreement obligates one spouse to pay the mortgage, that spouse can deduct half the mortgage payment as alimony. (Part or all of the rest might also be deductible as, e.g., real estate taxes and qualified residence interest).

A "fixed" payment for the support of (a) child(ren) is not alimony: see § 71(c)(1). An amount specified in a divorce instrument is deemed fixed, even if it fluctuates (e.g., increases as the child's needs increase, or is reduced based on a contingency related to the child).

[1] Allocation Issues

Payors should beware: If the instrument refers to a certain amount for alimony and a certain amount for child support, and the payor pays less than the required total, § 71(c)(3) treats the part of the payment that does not exceed the figure set for support as non-deductible child support. Another pitfall to watch out for is "front-loading."

If payments in the early post-divorce years exceed those in later years by more than the permitted amount, then the payor (and not the payee) will have gross income to the extent of the excessive front loading, and the payee will be entitled to a corresponding deduction.[25]

Neither gain nor loss is recognized on a transfer of property to one's spouse, into a trust for benefit of the spouse, or to a former spouse incident to a divorce: § 1041. A transfer is considered incident to a divorce if it occurs within one year after the end of the marriage, or within six years if made pursuant to a separation or divorce instrument.

Payments made under a pendente lite support order that does not specify how the payments are to be allocated between alimony and child support must be

---

[25] Different rules are in place for pre-1985 instruments that have not been modified since then; for such instruments, the distinction is whether the alimony is deemed to be "periodic" or "non-periodic."

considered entirely alimony and therefore are taxable income for the recipient spouse.[26]

[2] Legal Fees

Divorce-related legal expenses are generally personal and non-deductible, but the exception is that the payee spouse can deduct legal fees needed to produce or collect the alimony that will become taxable income (Reg. § 1.262-1). If the portion of the legal fee relating to tax advice can be separately identified, that can be deducted, but only for the fees each spouse pays his or her own lawyer, not fees paid to the other spouse's lawyer. Under the American Jobs Creation Act, P.L. 108-357, the attorneys' fees of plaintiffs in employment discrimination cases are an above-the line deduction, and therefore reduce both AMT and ordinary income tax.

[G] Interest Deduction

For many years, taxpayers were entitled to a deduction for all interest they paid, but since TRA '86, the interest deduction has been severely limited. Investment-oriented interest is deductible (§ 163) because it is incurred for gain seeking purposes, but the deduction is limited to net investment income (total investment income minus gain-seeking expenses other than interest). No deduction is allowed for interest on borrowing to purchase tax-exempt securities, on the sensible ground that such borrowing does not generate a corresponding amount of taxable income. Form 4952 is used to calculate deductible investment-oriented interest.

Interest on tax deficiencies is an ordinary and necessary business expense that can be deducted by a corporation, but is non-deductible personal interest for an individual. But, under the American Jobs Creation Act of 2004, P.L. 108-357, Code § 163 has been amended to provide that interest paid or accrued on underpayment of tax is not deductible if it arises from an undisclosed listed (i.e., tax shelter) transaction or from a reportable tax avoidance transaction that is not disclosed.

[1] Qualified Residence Interest

Although, in general, personal interest is not deductible, mortgage interest is the significant exception. Technically speaking, it is referred to as "qualified residence interest," and § 163(h) permits an itemized deduction to be taken for interest on up to $1 million in "acquisition indebtedness" and/or $100,000 in home equity debt, secured by a personal residence.

Acquisition indebtedness includes not just the initial purchase price, but also the cost of constructing or substantially improving a residence. The interest deduction for home equity loans is limited not only to $100,000 ($50,000 for married

---

[26] Kean v. CIR, 407 F.3d 186 (3rd Cir. 2005); *but see* Lovejoy v. CIR, 293 F.3rd 1208 (10th Cir. 2002), holding that support payments during divorce proceedings do not fit the IRC § 71 definition of alimony.

persons filing separately) but to the owner's net equity in the residence. Net equity equals its fair market value minus outstanding acquisition indebtedness.

A condominium or cooperative apartment can be a qualified residence. The taxpayer can claim qualified residence interest deductions not only on a personal residence but on a second residence that either is not rented to others for income, or that is rented out but is used by the taxpayer for fourteen days a year or 10% of the number of rental days (whichever is greater).

Payments made to a bank or other lender in order to get a loan are considered interest (and therefore are deductible) if they are made for use of money. They are not deductible if they compensate the lender for services. Therefore, "points" (additional charges imposed when securing a mortgage) paid by the buyer are considered interest and are deductible, but the lender's commitment and service fees (e.g., escrow and appraisal fees) are not.

Points on indebtedness to buy or improve a residence can be deducted in the year of the purchase, but points on refinancing have to be deducted in equal amounts over the term of the loan. Points on separate funds used to refinance improvements to a personal residence can be deducted in the year of payment. Prepayment penalties are considered interest; so are late payment charges unless they are service charges rather than charges for using the lender's funds for additional time.

[2] Student Loan Interest

For 2001 and later tax years, up to $2,500 in interest on education loans reflecting borrowing for the education of the taxpayer, spouse, or dependents can be deducted. The deduction is reduced if the taxpayer's modified AGI exceeds $60,000 (single taxpayer; 2009 figure) and eliminated at a modified AGI level of $75,000. Corresponding figures for joint returns are $120,000 and $150,000. The deduction is not available to married taxpayers filing separate returns.

In addition to the loan interest deduction, Code § 222 (added by EGTRRA) allows a deduction of up to $3,000 a year (2002 and 2003) or $4,000 (2004–2009) for qualified education expenses that are not already the subject of a tax credit. This deduction is also subject to phase-down and phase-out based on the taxpayer's modified AGI.

[H] Charitable Deductions

Contributions of cash or assets to a qualified charitable organization will be wholly or partially deductible under § 170. The deduction will be only partial if the taxpayer contributes a very large percentage of income in a given year. The permissible amount may be 20%, 30%, or 50% of taxable income, depending on the donee (less can be contributed to a private foundation than to be public charity) and the type of property donated. The ceiling is lowered for contributions of appreciated property.

Under the Pension Protection Act, P.L. 109-280, taxpayers cannot deduct contributions of clothing or household items unless the item is in good used condition or better. PPA § 1216 authorizes the Treasury to issue regulations denying deductions for property whose monetary value is minimal. Section 1217 denies a deduction for charitable contributions of money unless the donor maintains a bank record or has a written receipt from the donee giving the organization's name and the date and amount of the donation. For certain post-2006 tax years, an otherwise taxable distribution of up to $100,000 from a conventional or Roth IRA will be excluded from the taxpayer's gross income if it is donated directly by the IRA trustee to a charitable organization that is covered by Code § 170(b)(1)(A). That is, a qualified charitable deduction is not subject to the Code's ordinary limitations on deductibility of charitable contributions — and even persons who do not itemize can take advantage of this provision. But the IRA trustee must make the contribution directly; the individual cannot withdraw funds from the IRA and donate them. These qualified charitable distributions count as required minimum distributions, even though the taxpayer does not actually receive them.

Valuation considerations are absent when the taxpayer donates cash, but in many instances taxpayers will wish to use charitable contributions to remove appreciated property from their eventual taxable estates. No loss deduction is allowed when depreciated property is contributed, so in this instance it is better planning to sell the property, take the loss deduction, and contribute the sales proceeds in cash form.

Contributions of ordinary-income property (e.g., inventory and assets not held long enough to qualify for long-term capital gain treatment) are valued at their fair market value minus the ordinary income or short-term capital gain the taxpayer would have recognized by selling the property.

The deduction for capital gain property, or tangible property that is not used in the organization's exempt mission, donated to a private foundation is limited to the taxpayer's basis in the asset.

The taxpayer claiming a large charitable deduction must be able to substantiate it, with the requirements increasing with the size of the claimed deduction. A canceled check would be sufficient for a small cash contribution, but the organization must substantiate donations over $250, and Form 8283 must be filed to substantiate a noncash contribution over $500, and an appraisal is required for donation of items (e.g., artwork) with a claimed value over $5,000. The IRS itself issues Statements of Value for donated artworks valued at over $50,000.

See § 17.21 for a discussion of Charitable Remainder Trusts and Charitable Lead Trusts, mechanisms under which some trust interests go to the charity, others to the grantor or members of the grantor's family. The Tax Court denied a tax deduction for charitable split dollar insurance, because Code § 170(f)(1), which was enacted to rule out a charitable deduction, is retroactive to February 9, 1999.[27]

---

[27] Roark, TC Memo 2004-271.

See also Code § 170(o), as amended by the PPA, for restrictions on claiming charitable deductions for donating fractional interests in tangible personal property. If the donation is of appreciated property, all the fractional interests must be valued consistently, although consistency is not required if the value of the property declines after the contribution of the initial fraction.

[I] At-Risk and Passive Loss Rules

In the bad old days, personal income tax rates could be extremely high, as high as 70%, so there was a corresponding desire to reduce taxable income. One way to do this was to borrow large sums of money to buy investment properties, generating heavy interest deductions yet the alleged borrowers had little or no real personal liability for the alleged loans. Today, lower tax rates take some of the zest out of the tax-shelter game, but the Code continues to retain limitations (in § 465) on the taxpayer's deductions attributable to an activity that does not involve real, personal, financial risk for the taxpayer.

The at-risk rules apply to individuals; to C Corporations that are personal holding companies, personal service companies, or owned 50% or more by one to five individuals. Although the rules do not apply to S Corporations or partnerships at the entity level, they do apply to determine individual partner's or stockholders' ability to deduct or amortize items passed through from the entity.

A taxpayer is deemed to be at risk to the extent of money and the adjusted basis of property contributed to the activity, plus money borrowed from an unrelated party to participate in the activity, to the extent that the taxpayer is personally liable on the loan.

A loss from an activity subject to the at-risk rules (reported on Form 6198) is deductible only to the extent that the taxpayer is at risk — i.e., the excess of deductions otherwise allowable for the activity, minus income earned from the activity. If a taxpayer has a loss that is disallowed under this principle, it can be allocated to the same activity in the next tax year, and deducted up to the limit for that year.

The related concept of "passive activities" comes from § 469. Individuals, trusts, estates, publicly traded partnerships, personal service corporations, and some closely held C Corporations are subject to the passive activities rules. These rules also affect the pass-through items of partners and S Corporation shareholders but not the entities themselves.

A passive loss is defined as aggregate losses from all passive activities, minus aggregate income from all passive activities. Losses and credits from passive activities are limited. Passive losses offset income from other passive activities, but not compensation or investment income. Section 469(b) permits passive-activity deductions and credits disallowed in one year to be carried forward to the next year.

A trade or business is considered a passive activity for any taxpayer who does not materially participate in it — i.e., who is not involved in its operations on a regular, continuous, and substantial basis. Spending more than 500 hours a year on an activity would constitute participation; so would spending over 100 hours a year, if no one else devotes more time to the activity. As a general rule, activities involving the rental of real estate are passive for taxpayers who are only real estate investors, but are not passive for real estate professionals. Otherwise, "portfolio" income deriving from investments is not considered passive; nor is income earned in the ordinary course of the taxpayer's business.

[J] Tax-Free Exchanges: Non-Recognition Transactions

Neither gain nor loss is recognized when a taxpayer exchanges common stock for other common stock, or preferred stock for other preferred stock, of the same corporation (§ 1036(b)).

Neither gain nor loss is recognized on the sale or exchange of:

- A life insurance policy for another life insurance policy, or for an endowment or annuity contract
- One annuity for another
- An endowment contract for an annuity or another endowment contract with a later beginning date for the payments (§ 1035).

"Like-kind" exchanges of business or investment property, as defined by § 1031, create neither loss nor gain. The exchange must involve only properties, no "boot" (additional cash) (§ 1031(b)). If the exchange includes boot, then § 1031(c) provides that gain can be recognized but loss cannot.

In a related-party transaction, § 267(a) denies a loss deduction. Such transactions for individuals include, e.g., transactions between blood relatives (although in-laws are not considered related parties), between a taxpayer and corporation he or she controls, and between an estate and its beneficiaries.

Loss deductions are denied for "wash sales" (§ 1091) — i.e., transactions lacking economic reality, in which the taxpayer sells or otherwise disposes of securities (including options and futures) if the taxpayer enters into a contract or has an option to acquire substantially identical securities in the period starting 30 days before and ending 30 days after the wash sale.

[K] Standard Deduction

Taxpayers who do not choose to itemize their deductions, or whose deductions are lower than the standard deduction, claim the standard deduction instead. Approximately two-thirds of returns show a standard deduction rather than itemized deductions.

The 2009 standard deduction is $5,700 for single persons, $11,400 for joint returns and surviving spouses, and $8,350 for heads of household.

Additional standard deductions are available to senior citizens (over 65) and blind persons; a blind elderly person can claim two additional standard deductions. The maximum additional standard deduction for 2009 is $1,100 for a married person, $1,400 for an unmarried person or head of household. A complicating factor is that elderly and blind persons may be dependents of other taxpayers, which limits their standard deduction.

For any taxpayer who could be claimed as someone else's dependent (usually a child, but possibly an elderly parent supported by one or more children), the dependent's standard deduction is limited to the greater of $850 (2007), $900 (2008), $950 (2009) or $300 plus the dependent taxpayer's earned income, but not to exceed the normal standard deduction no matter how much the dependent taxpayer earns (§ 63(c)(5)).

Non-resident aliens do not get a standard deduction; neither do married persons filing separately whose spouse itemizes deductions.

[1] Dependent Status

Under pre-WFTRA law, a dependency deduction was available only if all five factors were present:

- The dependent must be a relative (defined quite broadly) of the taxpayer, or must reside in the taxpayer's household — e.g., it might be possible for one cohabitant to claim the other as a dependent.
- The dependent's gross income does not exceed the amount of the dependency deduction. This rule is not applied in the case of dependents under age 19, or full-time students under age 24.
- If the dependent is married, he or she cannot file a joint return with his or her spouse.
- At least half of the dependent's support must come from the taxpayer claiming the deduction, unless there is a multiple support agreement under which a number of taxpayers (e.g., an elderly person's children) agree to render support, and also agree that one of them, who personally provides at least 10% of the dependent's support, will be entitled to claim the deduction. In-kind items, such as housing, medical expenses, and education, are treated as items of support, but neither alimony nor arrears of child support is deemed to constitute support of the child. If a parent remarries, support provided by the new spouse is deemed to come from the parent: § 152(e)(5).
- The dependent is a U.S. citizen; a U.S. national; or a resident of the United States, Canada, or Mexico.

Parents of a child born during the year are entitled to a dependency deduction for the entire year; proration is not required.

A dependent could be the taxpayer's child, grandchild, stepchild, sibling, parent, grandparent, brother- or sister-in-law, parent-in-law, uncle or aunt, or nephew or niece. Once a relationship comes into existence, it is not terminated by divorce or death. A legally adopted child, or a child placed for adoption by an authorized agency, is treated as the taxpayer's child. However, a foster child is not a dependent if the taxpayer receives payment for caring for the child.

As a general rule, in case of divorce or separation, which could be varied by decree, separation agreement, or waiver by the custodial parent, the dependency deduction is claimed by the custodial parent, even if the non-custodial parent provides a large fraction of the child's support.

One of the objectives of the Working Families Tax Relief Act of 2004 (WFTRA; P.L. 108-311) is to harmonize the definition of "child" throughout the Code, so that it will apply uniformly for the dependency exemption, the child-related credits, and head of household filing status. WFTRA makes a person a qualifying child if:

- He or she lives with the taxpayer for over half the tax year;
- Is the taxpayer's child or grandchild;
- Has not reached the maximum age specified in the particular statutory provision; or
- He or she is either under 19 or under 24 and a full-time student. The previous requirement that the taxpayer claiming the dependency deduction provide over half of the child's support has been eliminated.

Qualifying relatives other than qualifying children can be claimed as dependents, based on the nature of the relationship, the dependent's income, and the extent of support provided by the taxpayer.

Final Regulations about tax treatment of the children of divorced or separated parents as dependents were issued in mid-2008, reflecting WFTRA. The Final Regulations define "custody," clarify how to count nights when the parents have joint custody, and provides many illustrative examples. If the special rule under § 152(e) applies, the child is considered the dependent of both parents for purposes of health coverage under § 105, 213, and for some fringe benefits under § 132. But if the custodial parent refuses to release the claim to deductions, then only the parent who takes the child as a dependent can claim the child as a dependent for these purposes.[28]

[L] The Personal Exemption

A personal exemption is granted for the taxpayer, with the exception that persons who could be claimed as a dependent on someone else's tax return (even if they are not actually claimed) are not entitled to a personal exemption.

For 2009, the personal exemption is $3,650, subject to phase out based on income — e.g., phaseout begins for a single person's return at $166,800, and no personal exemption is permitted if AGI exceeds $289,300. For joint returns, the corresponding figures are $250,200 and $372,700. See Rev. Proc. 2008-66.

---

[28] Final Regs., § 1.152-4, 73 Fed. Reg. 37797 (7/2/08); *IRS Issues Final Regulations on Tax Exemption for Children Whose Parents Are Divorced, Separated, or Living Apart.* For a copy: http://edocket.access.gpo.gov/2008/pdf/E8-15044.pdf.

Resident aliens are permitted to claim the personal exemption on their U.S. tax returns (and can also claim dependency deductions).

The personal exemption is not reduced if the taxpayer dies during the tax year.

§ 20.07   TAX CREDITS

A tax credit is more valuable than a tax deduction, because each dollar of deduction merely reduces the overall tax burden by one dollar times the taxpayer's marginal (highest) tax rate, but each dollar of credit eliminates one dollar of tax liability. Furthermore, many tax credits (e.g., the Earned Income Credit) are refundable; that is, if they reduce tax liability below zero, the taxpayer can receive a corresponding refund. Certain other credits (e.g., those for the elderly and disabled and for adoption expenses) are not refundable, but can be carried over from year to year.

In addition to the credits discussed in more detail, individual tax credits are available to individuals who have overpaid FICA taxes (usually because they changed jobs during the year, and had total income greater than the FICA limit — $97,500 (2007); $102,000 (2008); $106,800 (2009) — but income from each job was below the limit, with the result that over-withholding occurred). A credit is also available for tax withheld on wages, pensions, annuities, interest, and dividends.

Code § 25(a) provides a credit for post-secondary education expenses of the taxpayer, the taxpayer's spouse, and dependents, as long as the expenses are not otherwise deductible. The full rules for the computation are too complex to give here, but it should be noted that the post-secondary education credit consists of two parts: a HOPE scholarship credit and a Lifetime Learning Credit. The HOPE and Lifetime Learning Credits are alternatives — a taxpayer cannot claim both for the same student. For 2009, the maximum HOPE Scholarship credit is $1,800. A refundable credit of 10% of the purchase price, with a maximum of $7,500 (or $3,500 for the separate return of a married taxpayer) is available to certain taxpayers who purchased a principal residence during the period April 9, 2008 — June 30, 2009. The credit is reduced or phased out for some high-income taxpayers.

[A]   Credit for the Elderly/Disabled

The elderly (age 65 and over) and totally disabled are each entitled to a credit of 15% of the "Section 22 amount." (An elderly disabled person can claim both credits.) To be considered totally disabled in this context, a person must receive taxable disability income and must be unable to perform substantial gainful activity because of a medically determinable mental or physical impairment that is expected to result in death or that has lasted or is reasonably expected to last more than 12 months.

Calculation of the Section 22 amount begins with a sum of $3,750 (for a married person filing a separate return), $5,000 (for a single person, or a married person whose spouse does not qualify) or $7,500 (for a married couple both of whom qualify), reduced by nontaxable Social Security benefits and some other nontaxable amounts, and also reduced by half of the excess of AGI over a permitted amount.

The credit for the elderly/disabled can be claimed on either Form 1040 or 1040A, but not on 1040EZ.

Some taxpayers will be unable to claim the full credit, because the sum of this credit plus certain other credits cannot exceed the regular tax liability for the year minus the tentative minimum tax for the year (§ 20.10).

[B] Earned Income Credit

The Earned Income Credit (EIC), provided by § 32, is a refundable credit for low-income workers who earn little or no money from savings or investments. Alimony, child support, pensions, and Social Security benefits are treated as unearned, not earned, income.

The EIC calculation is quite complex (see IRS Publication 596), and depends in large part on whether or not the claimant has one or more qualifying children. Children who qualify for the computation must be under 19, or under 24 and full-time students. For 2009, the maximum earned income credit for two or more children is $5,028.

In many cases the EIC will completely eliminate federal income tax liability for the qualifying taxpayer, and perhaps even eliminate the strict need to file an income tax return at all. However, if no return is filed, the credit will be lost. The credit can be claimed on Form 1040EZ if the claimant has no children, but 1040 or 1040A must be used if qualifying children are claimed. Married people must file a joint return in order to claim the EIC.

[C] Child-Related Credits

Under § 21(a), a taxpayer who maintains a household for at least one "qualifying individual" may be entitled to a "child and dependent care" credit of 20–35% of certain employment-related expenses. A qualifying individual is a child under 13, or a dependent or spouse who is physically or mentally incapable of self-care. An employment-related expense is one which makes it possible for the taxpayer to be gainfully employed: for instance, the cost of a nanny to take care of children, or a home health attendant to take care of a disabled parent.

Of course, the credit cannot exceed the actual expenses, and it is reduced by any amount received under an employment-related dependent assistance program. The credit is claimed on Form 2441, or Schedule 2 of the 1040A short form. It is not available to married couples who file separate returns.

[1] Adoption Expenses

Qualifying adoption expenses are the ordinary and necessary expenses such as adoption agency fees, court costs, attorneys' fees, and travel expenses. If the child is adopted from outside the United States, no credit is allowed unless the adoption becomes final. For domestic adoptions, a person who is unsuccessful in an attempt to adopt a particular child can claim the credit for expenses of that attempt, if another attempt to adopt another child is successful. Within limits, taxpayers can claim an adoption credit under § 23(a)(3) excluded from gross income up to $12,150 (2009 figure) of adoption expenses assistance received from their employers. Under previous law, the figure was higher for special-needs adoptees, but now the same exclusion applies whether or not the adoptee has special needs. For 2009, the credit is reduced if the taxpayer's modified AGI is over $182,180, and no credit is allowed if modified AGI is greater than $222,180. (The same amounts and the same phase-out figures apply to exclusion of adoption assistance received from an employer from the taxpayer's gross income: see § 137(a)(2).)

Tax relief for adoption of a foreign-born child depends on the adoption becoming "final." In 2005, the IRS issued guidance about when finality occurs: when a decree of adoption is entered, or when competent authority in the sending country authorizes the child's departure.[29]

[2] Child Tax Credit

TRA '97 added a new credit, the § 24(a) "child tax credit." The qualifying child must be under 17 and the taxpayer's dependent.

This credit is subject to the "Section 26 limitation": that is, in conjunction with various other credits, it cannot exceed the difference between the taxpayer's regular tax and tentative minimum tax.

EGTRRA called for an increase in the Code § 24 child tax credit from $500 to $1,000 per child.

JGTRRA also accelerated the phase-in of a higher level of child tax credit. For the years 2003 and 2004, the credit rose from $600 to $1,000 per child. For, 2007, the child credit is refundable (i.e., can result in payments to a person whose tax liability is below zero) to the extent of 10% of $11,750. For taxpayers with three or more qualifying children, a refund is available in the amount of the taxpayer's Social Security taxes for the year, minus the earned income credit, if this produces a larger refund than the 10% calculation: see Code § 24(d). Under JGTRRA, the child tax credit was scheduled to drop to $700 for 2005 only, then return to $1,000 for the years 2006–2010. However, the Working Families Tax Relief Act of 2004, P.L. 108-311, maintained the credit level at $1,000 for 2005. Starting in 2004, also as a result of WFTRA, the child credit for low-income families is 15% rather than 10% refundable. For 2009, the figure used to determine the refundable amount is $12,550.

[3] Dependent Care Credit

Code § 21 allows a tax credit for some of the costs that a person encounters in paying for the care of a child or handicapped dependent. The credit targets amounts that the taxpayer must spend to be able to stay in the workforce. For tax years

---

[29] Rev. Proc. 2005-31, 2005-26 IRB 1374 and Announcement 2005-45, 2005-26 IRB 1377.

beginning after December 31, 2002, EGTRRA increases the credit and makes it available to some taxpayers who would not have gotten a credit under prior law (which limited or phased out the credit based on the taxpayer's income).

The maximum dependent-care credit under EGTRRA is 35% of $3,000 of qualifying expenses (for one dependent) or $6,000 of qualifying expenses (two or more dependents). If the taxpayer's AGI exceeds $43,000, the credit is limited to 20% of the allowable expenses, not 35%.

A related provision, Code § 45D (added by EGTRRA), gives employers an incentive to assist employees with their child care needs, giving them a tax credit for directly providing child care (e.g., a day care center onsite).

[4] Education-Related Credits

Paying for the children's college education is one of the major financial planning tasks facing most families. Furthermore, in many families, private elementary and secondary schooling are also household expenses. EGTRRA includes several provisions providing at least a measure of relief for taxpayers financing education for themselves or family members.

For tax years beginning after December 31, 2001, taxpayers can contribute up to $2,000 per beneficiary per year (the prior figure was only $500) to "Coverdell Education Savings Accounts" — accounts used exclusively to pay for the qualified education expenses of a designated beneficiary such as a child or grandchild. In addition to college costs, qualified education expenses can include elementary and secondary education expenses for a special-needs child (Code § 530). However, like many tax provisions, the benefits to higher-income taxpayers phase down or out.

EGTRRA also amends Code § 529 to increase the scope of state-run programs under which family members can invest in advance for the anticipated costs of education.

Code § 127, under which employees can exclude from taxable income education expenses paid by their employer as an employee benefit, has been amended many times. The latest version, as amended by EGTRRA, makes the Code section permanent and extends it to both undergraduate and graduate education, with respect to academic courses that begin after December 31, 2001.

The general pre-EGTRRA rule was that the expenses of a taxpayer's own education might be deductible under Code § 162 if they enhance the taxpayer's ability to perform an existing profession. (The costs of qualifying for a new profession are still not deductible.)

§ 20.08 INCOME TAX IMPLICATIONS OF COMMUNITY PROPERTY

In the nine community property states of Arizona, California, Idaho, Louisiana, Nevada, New Mexico, Texas, Washington, and Wisconsin, it may be necessary to make a tax computation that is not required in the other, common-law states. That is, it may be required to determine if an asset or an income item is community property or is the separate property of one spouse or the other. (This is also of significance in divorce, where spouses may be entitled to take their separate property, but community property must be divided either equally or equitably.) The community property states differ in their characterization of income earned on separate property during marriage. In Arizona, California, Nevada, New Mexico, and Washington, such income is separate property, but it is community property in Idaho, Louisiana, Texas, and Wisconsin.

Because tax rates are somewhat progressive, "income-splitting" often yields tax benefits. That is, $x earned by a couple might generate less tax if it were treated as two incomes of $x/2, one earned by each spouse. In common-law states, income-splitting is permitted only on joint returns, but community income is split even on returns of married persons filing separately.

§ 20.09 FICA, MEDICARE, AND SELF-EMPLOYMENT TAX

Social Security retirement benefits are funded by a tax of 6.2% of income, imposed on employer and on employee. This tax is imposed only on earned income up to a maximum amount, set each year; the 2006 amount is $94,200, the 2007 amount is $97,500, the 2008 amount is $102,000, and the 2009 amount is $106,800. (A person who has two jobs, earning less than the maximum amount at each, but more than the maximum amount overall, is entitled to a tax credit for overpayment of this tax.) Earnings under $400 a year are exempt from Social Security tax. See §§ 3101 and 3111.

Medicare hospital insurance is funded by a tax of 1.45% of all income (with no maximum), imposed on employer and on employee. Employers are responsible for payment of their own share of the tax, and for withholding and submitting the employee share of the tax.

[A] Self-Employment Tax

The self-employed are required to pay both parts of the Social Security and Medicare taxes, for a total of 15.3%. (In compensation, they are permitted by § 1402(a)(12)(A) to deduct 50% of their self-employment tax in calculating taxable income—but not AGI—to put them on a par with employees.) Self-employment tax is imposed on net earnings from self-employment; that is, income from a trade or business regularly carried on as a sole proprietor or partner, reduced by deductions allocable to creating that income. Persons who continue to work after they begin to receive Social Security benefits must nevertheless pay Social Security tax on their employment or self-employment income.

Some deductions cannot be taken in calculating self-employment income, even though they are available in other tax contexts:

- Personal exemption
- Standard or itemized deductions

- Deduction for health insurance premiums paid by a self-employed person
- Net operating loss deductions.

For self-employment tax purposes, a general partner in a business is taxed on his or her distributive share of the partnership income, whether or not it is actually distributed, and is also taxed on guaranteed payments made to the partner that are not calculated on the basis of partnership income. It is immaterial whether or not the general partner actively participates in the business.

Self-employment tax is imposed only on earned income, not on investment income, so a person deriving income from real estate held for investment or speculation does not have self-employment income from such ownership. Income and capital gains from securities investments are not self-employment income. Neither is income from the sale or exchange of capital assets, or gain or loss on the disposition of property that is not stock in trade or held primarily for sale to customers in the ordinary course of business. This is not to say that such earnings are not taxable, only that they are free from self-employment taxation.

§ 20.10 ALTERNATIVE MINIMUM TAX (AMT)

AMT is imposed both on individuals and on corporations (see § 4.03[B][2] for corporate AMT). Trusts and estates can also be subject to AMT. In effect, AMT is a separate system for calculating tax liability, using different calculations and adjustments. The taxpayer then pays either the ordinary tax or the AMT, whichever is higher.

The AMT calculation is too complex to give here in full detail (see Code § 55), but it starts with taxable income as calculated under the ordinary system, with adjustments. Tax preference items such as itemized and standard deductions, the personal exemption, tax-exempt interest, and tax refunds must be added back into the calculation base. Another complex calculation is applied to find the "taxable excess" of AMT-taxable income over an exemption amount.

Even within the category of "taxes," the AMT is extremely unpopular, and many people who are not particularly affluent are at risk of having AMT liability. In response, most of the recent tax bills have included short-range AMT patches, but the tax itself has not been eliminated.

Taxpayers who encounter AMT are entitled to claim a "minimum tax credit," using Form 8801, against their ordinary income tax in the year after the year in which the AMT was imposed.

The general rule is that, for AMT purposes, an employee must recognize income when he or she exercises a stock option, calculated as the difference between the fair market value of the stock transferred to the employee and the option price at the time of the option. If options are substantially nonvested at the time of a grant, taxation is deferred until substantial vesting occurs, even if the option had an ascertainable FMV when granted. An option is substantially vested if it is transferable or not subject to a substantial risk of forfeiture. A number of taxpayers took the position that their stock was substantially nonvested because of corporate policy forbidding insiders to trade during a blackout period. The Fifth and Ninth Circuits have rejected this argument, because restriction on the ability to transfer shares is not tantamount to a substantial risk of forfeiture. However, executives who are subject to suit under Exchange Act § 16(b) as statutory insiders do encounter a substantial risk of forfeiture. Taxpayers have also been unsuccessful in raising the argument that the AMT does not apply to shares purchased with borrowed money where their own capital was not at risk.[30]

§ 20.11   TAX ISSUES IN BANKRUPTCY

Rev. Proc. 2006-24, 2006-22 IRB 943 explains how trustees or Debtors in Possession representing a bankruptcy estate can exercise their right under BAPCPA to obtain a prompt determination of the estate's unpaid tax liabilities for the period of estate administration. For cases filed after October 17, 2005, the bankruptcy estate, the debtor, and the debtor's successors are discharged from any liability shown on a tax return if taxes due are properly paid. To receive the determination, the trustee must file two copies of a written request with the Centralized Insolvency Operation, including a copy of the relevant tax returns, a statement identifying the document as a request for a prompt determination for certain types of return and tax periods. The statement must give the bankruptcy case number and the court in which it is pending. Within 60 days, the IRS will inform the trustee whether the return is accepted as filed or selected for examination. If the file is examined, the IRS notifies the trustee of the tax due within 180 days of receipt of the request (or longer, if the Bankruptcy Court grants an extension).

A March 2002 Supreme Court decision tolls the look-back period for Chapter 7 debtors during the pendency of an earlier, dismissed Chapter 13 petition. (See Bankruptcy Code § 523(a)(1)(A).) A debt for taxes for which the return was due three years before the bankruptcy filing would not have been dischargeable if the Chapter 13 case had been completed, and the Chapter 13 automatic stay prevented the IRS from taking enforcement action.[31]

According to the First Circuit — although other Circuits disagree — interest on a postpetition tax obligation in a Chapter 7 case takes fifth priority. It is not a first-priority administration expense.[32] According to the Ninth Circuit, Bankruptcy Code § 735(b), which subordinates tax liens to the claims of certain priority unsecured creditors, is limited to statutory tax liens. A judicial lien securing tax obligations is not subordinated under this provision.[33]

See Chapter 15 for a discussion of the sweeping 2005 bankruptcy reform legislation.

---

[30] Merlo v. Comm'r, 492 F.3d 618 (5th Cir. 2007); United States v. Tuff, 469 F.3d 1249 (9th Cir. 2006). *See* Lisa M. Starczewski, *The AMT and Stock Options: Taxpayers Continue to Lose in the Appellate Courts*, http://www.bnatax.com/tm/insights_starczewski5.htm (4/14/08).

[31] Young v. United States, 535 U.S. 43 (2002).

[32] United States v. Yellin, 251 B.R. 174 (BAP 1st Cir. 2000).

[33] Barstow v. IRS, 308 F.3d 1038 (9th Cir. 2002).

Chapter 21

Tax Enforcement

§ 21.01 INTRODUCTION

Tax collectors can never expect to be popular, but in the late 1990s, the IRS became the target of significant legislation aimed at restricting the agency's scope of operations. Taxpayer Bills of Rights were passed in 1988 (the Omnibus Taxpayer Bill of Rights, P.L. 100-647), and 1996 (Taxpayer Bill of Rights II, or TBOR II, P.L. 104-168), culminating in the Internal Revenue Service Restructuring and Reform Act of 1998 (IRSRRA), P.L. 105-206.

In this context, "restructuring" means that the IRS was directed to organize itself to concentrate on the type of taxpayer filing a return, or whose return was under examination (individual, small business, corporation, or tax-exempt organization — defined to include employee benefit plans, not just charitable organizations) rather than on the geographic district in which the return was filed. Furthermore, the appeals function must be separated from the operational function, and appeals officers are not supposed to have ex parte discussions with IRS operating personnel.

It should also be noted that, thanks to the IRSRRA, both general and taxpayer-specific advice issued by the IRS' chief counsel is now included in the category of "written determinations" that can be inspected by the public under Code § 6110, with all references that could identify the taxpayer removed. (The Code § 6110 procedure is the sole means of access to Chief Counsel advice; FOIA requests for this information will not be honored.)

However, Chief Counsel advice is treated on a parity with Private Letter Rulings, Technical Advice Memoranda, and determination letters. That is, although such material can be helpful in identifying IRS thinking on a particular issue or in a particular fact situation, it has no precedential value and cannot be cited by other taxpayers in their struggles with the IRS.

As much as possible, the IRS must assign one particular employee to handle a tax matter from beginning to end. Individual correspondence from the IRS to taxpayers must include the name, telephone number, and ID number of that particular employee whom the taxpayer can contact.

IRSRRA requires the IRS to expand the availability to taxpayers of telephone "help line" service, and Spanish-language service must be offered. The help line cannot offer only pre-recorded messages; any taxpayer who calls during normal business hours must have the option of talking to a person.

Although in general state tax issues are beyond the scope of this book, it should be noted that in April 2003, the Supreme Court held that it is not constitutionally required for the courts of one state to extend full faith and credit to a statute of another state rendering that state's tax collection agency immune from suit.[1]

The Pension Protection Act of 2006 (PPA; P.L. 109-280) includes several provisions dealing with tax enforcement:

- § 855 modifies the jurisdiction of the Tax Court. Effective for all determinations made 60 or more days after enactment of the PPA, the Tax Court has jurisdiction over all appeals of collection due process. (Under prior law, taxpayers had to go to the District Court for review except for income tax liabilities and taxes over which the Tax Court had deficiency jurisdiction.)
- § 858 permits the Tax Court to apply the doctrine of equitable recoupment to the same extent as the District Court or Court of Federal Claims could apply it. This doctrine provides that an otherwise time-barred claim can defeat or reduce an opponent's claim if it stems from the same transaction. This provision is effective for decisions that were not final as of the PPA's date of enactment.
- § 859 permits the Tax Court to impose a $60 filing fee on any case commenced by petition; the practical effect is that Code § 7451 need not be amended every time the Tax Court gets new jurisdiction.
- § 860 extends the permissible application of the $30 annual fee that the Tax Court charges practitioners. Previously the money was used to fund disciplinary matters; it can also be used to pay for services that assist taxpayers presenting pro se cases more effectively.
- § 1219 amends the definition of "gross overvaluation."

As of press time in early 2009, Congress and the IRS had not come up with a definitive response to taxpayers' problems caused by the financial crisis. However, the IRS announced five specific areas in which it would grant taxpayers a degree of flexibility. Tax assessors would be permitted to suspend collection actions for taxpayers who have recently lost their jobs, have high medical costs, or have no income other than Social Security benefits. The tax debt is not forgiven, but collection activity is suspended. The IRS is also considering broadening the availability of offers in compromise, and has set up a unit to review real estate equity of taxpayers who make offers. However, even the broader criteria would probably exclude taxpayers who do not have enough home equity to cover their tax debt. The IRS intends to allow taxpayers who miss a payment under an offer in compromise to find a way to avoid default, and levies will be released faster for taxpayers suffering financial hardship.[1A]

---

[1] Franchise Tax Bd. of Cal. v. Hyatt, 538 U.S. 488 (2003). *See also* Mantz v. California State Bd. of Equalization, 343 F.3d 1207 (9th Cir. 2003), holding that where there was no final administrative determination of state tax liability prior to the taxpayers' bankruptcy filing, res judicata is not a bar to the Bankruptcy Court's redetermination of the liability.

[1A] A Martin Vaughan, *IRS Offering Leniency Plan for Taxpayers*, Wall St. J. 1/6/09, http://online.wsj.com/article/SB123128814241059283.html.

§ 21.02 EXAMINATION AND AUDIT OF RETURNS

The U.S. tax system depends on voluntary compliance by taxpayers, but § 7602 defines the IRS' responsibilities to include auditing tax returns to see if the taxpayer is in full compliance. Audits can be performed at random, with no individualized suspicion of the taxpayer. It has long been suspected that the executive branch uses IRS audits to discredit or harass political opponents.

Code § 7217(a), added by the IRSRRA, forbids any "applicable person" to intervene in an IRS audit, or to seek to influence the IRS to audit any person or organization. Applicable persons are the President, Vice President, employees in their Executive Offices, and cabinet-level officials. Conviction is punishable by a fine of up to $5,000 (plus the costs of prosecution) and/or imprisonment of up to five years.

[A] Review of Returns

All tax returns are checked by computer, to find mathematical errors; § 6213(b)(1) directs the IRS to notify taxpayers of such mistakes. (The notification is not a deficiency notice, and does not give the taxpayer the right to go to Tax Court.) Returns are also checked against information returns, and if there seems to be a discrepancy, the IRS issues a CP-2000, a computer-generated request for information about the alleged discrepancy. The CP-2000 is not a demand for payment. A taxpayer who disagrees with the notice can challenge it, but has the burden of proof.

Starting in October 2008, the IRS began mailing out a new notice, CP 2057, informing certain taxpayers that they might not be reporting enough income on their returns (e.g., if information returns show more income than was reported). The CP 2057 differs from the existing CP 2000, which suggests specific changes to the return (e.g., affecting income, payments, credits, or deductions). The CP 2057 suggests that the taxpayer check to see if underreporting has occurred, and, if necessary, file a Form 1040X, but does not mention a specific amount.[2]

The DIF (discriminant function) is used to program the IRS computers to select returns with the highest audit potential (i.e., those that differ significantly from average figures for the same type of return), but fewer than 2% of all returns are audited. Under the IRSRRA, IRS Publication 1, "Your Rights as Taxpayer," must explain the IRS' criteria for choosing returns for examination. IRSRRA also severely limits IRS use of techniques called "financial status examination" or "economic reality examination," under which the taxpayer is interrogated about expenditures and financial lifestyle rather than the return under examination.

T.D. 9215, 2005-36 IRB 468 provides Temporary and Proposed Regulations under which the IRS will prepare substitute returns for taxpayers who fail to file or who file fraudulent returns. This T.D. is based on *Cabirac v. Commissioner*, 120

---

[2] Arden Dale, *IRS to Ramp Up Warning Letters*, Wall St. J. 8/21/08 at D3.

TC 163 (2003) and *Spurlock v. Comm'r*, TC Memo 2003-124, which hold that a return is valid for Code § 6020(b) purposes if it purports to be a return, is signed, and contains enough information to compute the taxpayer's liability.

[B] Audits

Code § 7605(a) permits the IRS to set the time and method of examining a possibly improper return, but the agency is required to select a method that is reasonable under the taxpayer's circumstances. In a correspondence audit, the taxpayer is asked to mail written information to the IRS office. In an office audit, the taxpayer is asked to appear at the office, bringing documentation; a field audit takes place in the office of the taxpayer or taxpayer's representative.

Apropos of representation, § 7521 permits taxpayers to be represented by an attorney, a CPA, enrolled agent, or enrolled actuary. The taxpayer must execute IRS Form 2848, Durable Power of Attorney, to designate a representative.[3]

The Small Business and Work Opportunity Tax Act of 2007, P.L. 110-28, extends certain preparer penalties to cover all return preparers, not just income tax return preparers.[4]

Unless it has issued a summons, the IRS cannot compel a taxpayer to bring a representative to an audit. Furthermore, any interview must be suspended if an unrepresented taxpayer makes a clear demand to consult with a representative.

At or before any in-person interview (other than a criminal investigation), the IRS must give the taxpayer a written or oral explanation of taxpayer rights and the processes involved in auditing a return, assessing a deficiency, and collecting it. The rights include:

- Being represented by counsel
- Audiotaping the meeting, on advance notice to the IRS
- Asserting additional deductions that were not included in the return under examination
- Applying to the IRS National Office for technical advice about disputed points

---

[3] T.D. 9359 publishes Final Regulations revising Circular 230 (31 CFR Part 10). Under T.D. 9359, it is no longer necessary for an attorney or CPA to file a Form 2848 with the IRS before rendering written advice of the types covered by §§ 10.35 or 10.37, but any other practice before the IRS requires a Form 2848 filing. The T.D. authorizes an "enrolled retirement plan agent" designation for providing technical services to plan sponsors about the tax qualification of the plan. T.D. 9359 permits practitioners to charge contingent fees for services in connection with an IRS examination, a challenge to a tax return, an amended return, certain claims for refunds or credits, interest and penalty reviews, or judicial proceedings under the Code. Practitioners must receive advance written consent to represent conflicting interests.

[4] T.D. 9359, 4830-01-p, RIN 1545-BA72; the Advance Notice of Proposed Rulemaking was published at 67 Fed. Reg. 77724 (12/19/02), with amendments at REG-122380-02, 71 Fed. Reg. 6421; a public hearing was held June 21, 2006.

- Having the Constitutional rights applicable to any suspect, if questioning involves possible criminal charges
- Being free from unnecessary examinations. Generally, the IRS is limited to a single examination of a taxpayer's books and records for any tax year unless: the taxpayer requests further examination; the IRS issues a written notice, pursuant to § 7605(b), that additional inspections are required; fraud is suspected; or the taxpayer has received a 90-day letter (see § 21.03[C]) for a particular year, and the time to file a Tax Court petition with respect to that year has elapsed.

It is improper for an IRS employee to ask a taxpayer to waive the right to sue either the federal government or the employee: § 3468(a). However, the taxpayer can make a knowing, voluntary waiver of the right to sue.

[C] IRS Summonses

The IRS has the power, under § 7602(a)(2), to issue summonses for testimony and records, but unreasonable demands are forbidden. The IRS must have a legitimate purpose for any demand. The summons, Form 2309, must include a reasonably certain description of the books and records sought, and must specify the date of the examination, which must be at least 10 days from the date of the summons. Service of the summons is governed by § 7603, and enforcement of the summons by § 7604.

Third-party summonses can be issued, under § 7609, to parties other than the taxpayer—for instance, the taxpayer's bank or brokerage. The taxpayer must be notified before third-party summonses issue, and has the right to request that the third-party refrain from complying with the summons unless so ordered by a court.

A taxpayer who receives the notice has 20 days after receipt of notice to ask the federal District Court to quash the summons and protect the taxpayer's financial information from third-party disclosure (§ 7609(b)). IRSRRA § 3415 amended § 7609 to provide that third-party summonses issued as part of a collection effort (as distinct from examination of a return) cannot be quashed. IRSRRA extended the scope of the taxpayer's rights to notification and clarified the treatment of summonses demanding software code (§ 7612).

However, taxpayers are not entitled to notice when the IRS issues a summons to a bank for the specific purpose of collecting taxes (even if other purposes are also present). The Ninth Circuit held that only the person named in an IRS administrative summons issued to a third party (e.g., a bank or mortgage company) has standing under Code § 7609(b)(2) to file a petition to quash. Therefore, the wife of a taxpayer under investigation could not petition to quash summonses naming her husband, even though most of the accounts covered by the summonses were joint accounts.[5]

---

[5] Stewart v. United States, 511 F.3d 1251 (9th Cir. 2008).

Under T.D. 8939, 2001-12 IRB 899, the taxpayer's last known address for mailing notices is generally the address given on the taxpayer's most recently filed and properly processed federal tax return, unless the taxpayer gives the IRS clear and concise notification of a different address. Revenue Procedure 2001-18, 2001-8 IRB 708, says that a taxpayer wishing to indicate a change of address should send the notification to the IRS Service Center covering the old address or to the Customer Service Division in the local area office. IRS Form 8822 operates as an acceptable clear and concise notification of the address change.

§21.03 DETERMINATION OF DEFICIENCIES

A deficiency is defined by §6211 as the overall tax liability minus the tax shown on the return plus deficiencies previously assessed or collected minus certain credits and refunds. Note that estimated tax payments do not enter into this equation (§6211(b)(1)).

If a return is required but was not filed, or was filed showing no liability, the entire amount of tax is treated as a deficiency. Negligence and fraud penalties are assessed in the same way that deficiencies are. The penalty for understating estimated tax is assessed as a deficiency only if the taxpayer failed to file a return.

Once the IRS determines that a taxpayer's account has a deficiency, it will notify the taxpayer of the deficiency as prescribed by §6212. If the taxpayer agrees with the IRS' characterization, or thinks it is easier to pay up than to challenge the agency, then payment or an offer in compromise, §21.03[E], will be made.

But if the amount remains uncollected, the IRS has a broad panoply of remedies. Liens can be placed on the taxpayer's property. The IRS can seize the property (levy on it) and put it up for sale; the taxpayer will continue to owe any difference between the asserted deficiency and the sale price of the property.

Note that assessment of tax deficiencies and collection actions must be suspended as soon as the taxpayer makes a timely application to the Tax Court for relief. This contrasts with a taxpayer's administrative refund claim, where the taxpayer usually has to make payment in full before seeking a refund.

The general rule established by §6501(a) is that the statute of limitations for assessing taxes is three years from the actual date of filing (i.e., filing late extends the statute of limitations). A taxpayer who claims that the IRS' assessment is time-barred has to raise the issue and bears the burden of proof. The statute of limitations is extended to six years by §6501(e) if a return omits 25% or more of the taxpayer's actual gross income.

The statute of limitations is indefinite, and never runs, if the taxpayer fails to file a required return; files a false or fraudulent return with intent to evade tax; or willfully attempts to defeat and evade the taxing process. Section 6501(c)(4) allows the taxpayer and IRS to consent to an extension of the statute of limitations, but the taxpayer has the right to refuse the extension. Also note that the §6696(a) penalty for promoting an abusive tax shelter, or aiding and abetting understatement of tax, can be imposed at any time, as can the § 6694(b) penalty for willful under-statements committed by a tax preparer.

The three-year statute of limitations under Code § 6501 cannot be extended by equitable tolling and cannot be extended without the consent of the taxpayer.[6]

[A] Informal Adjustment

When a return is being examined, the IRS examiner can propose adjustments to the return that can be acceded to in order to settle the matter informally. At the end of the examination, the examiner submits a Revenue Agent's Report (RAR). Submission of the RAR marks the end of the option of informal settlement; after that point, the taxpayer must get an Appeals Office conference to discuss the case further.

If the taxpayer is not entirely in agreement with the examiner, the case is considered an "unagreed" case. For unagreed field audits, the RAR is reviewed by the district office review staff, then sent to the taxpayer with the 30-day letter. At the end of an office audit, the taxpayer is usually informed of the examiner's findings and given the opportunity to agree. A taxpayer who does not accept the examiner's findings can request an immediate meeting with an appeals officer. If this is not done, the RAR is filed and the taxpayer gets a copy with a 30-day letter.

[B] The 30-Day Letter

The 30-day letter, as prescribed by § 7522, outlines the adjustments to the return sought by the IRS, and the reasons behind them. The document outlines the appeals procedures, and gives the taxpayer the titular 30 days to either agree with the finding or ask for an Appeals Office conference. (If the taxpayer neglects to do anything, the IRS will send a 90-day letter to start the collection process.) Agreement with the IRS position is signaled on Form 870, which waives restrictions on assessments so that collection can begin without a 90-day letter. (Form 890 is used for gift tax and generation-skipping tax.) A taxpayer who signs Form 870 or 890 can make a claim or sue for a refund, but waives the possibility of litigating before the Tax Court.

[C] The 90-Day Letter

The 90-day letter is the statutory (§ 6212) notice of deficiency, the only notice that the IRS issues. It is sent by certified or registered mail to the taxpayer's last known address. It informs the taxpayer of the amount of tax, interest, additional amounts, additions to tax, and penalties asserted by the IRS, with support for each.

The recipient taxpayer has various options:

- Concede liability and make a full payment
- Not pay the tax, and try to get the 90-day letter rescinded

---

[6] Doel v. KPMG LLP, 398 F.3d 686 (5th Cir. 2005).

- Pay the tax, then file for a refund
- Do nothing, let the deficiency be assessed, then attempt to compromise and thus reduce the amount to be paid
- File a Tax Court petition (§ 21.05[A]). In fact, taxpayers can file Tax Court petitions ONLY after receiving a 90-day letter.

The Fifth, Ninth, and Tenth Circuits take the position that the IRS has jurisdiction over a case even if the Notice of Deficiency fails to calculate the last date for filing. In the Ninth Circuit case, the taxpayer filed a 1995 gift tax return, reporting a gift of stock valued at more than $2.5 million. In 1998, the IRS issued a Notice of Deficiency, placing the actual value of the gift at more than $5 million. The notice was dated and informed the taxpayer that he had 90 days to file a petition, but did not calculate the last available date. The taxpayer filed a timely petition, sought re-determination, and contested IRS jurisdiction because of the failure to calculate the date: Code § 6213(a) says that the IRS must calculate the date (but does not say what happens if the IRS fails to do this!). According to these three Circuits, the taxpayer is not prejudiced by the omission of the calculated date.[7]

[D] Appeals Office Proceedings

The IRS Appeals Office holds informal proceedings, where testimony is not sworn, but taxpayers can be required to submit affidavits. Instructions for requesting a conference are found in the 30-day letter. In some instances, the conference can be requested orally, although a written request is mandatory when $10,000 or more in proposed tax increase or claimed refund is at stake for any tax period.

The Appeals Office has the power to settle all factual and legal issues raised by an RAR or by the "protest" (written conference request) filed by the taxpayer, but docketing a case in the Tax Court terminates the Appeals Office's power over that case. Form 870-AD (890-AD for gift or generation-skipping tax) is used if the Appeals Office modifies the position taken in the RAR. The form indicates that the settlement is subject to IRS approval. If the agency accepts the settlement, it will not reopen the matter except in circumstances such as fraud, malfeasance, and concealment of material facts. The taxpayer waives refund claims for years covered by the agreement. However, if the conference does not result in a settlement, the IRS issues a 90-day letter.

Appeals officers are still permitted to make general inquiries about a case or to ask if information has been requested or received — but an appeals officer is not permitted to discuss the substance of the taxpayer's case with other IRS staffers without disclosure to the taxpayer. The taxpayer (or representative) is entitled to participate in the intra-agency discussion, which must be scheduled to reasonably accommodate the taxpayer's convenience.

---

[7] Elings v. CIR, 324 F.3d 1110 (9th Cir. 2003); Rochelle v. Comm'r, 293 F.3d 740 (5th Cir. 2002); Smith v. Comm'r, 275 F.3d 912 (10th Cir. 2001).

[E] Compromises between Taxpayer and IRS

Code § 7121 permits "closing agreements," which are conclusive settlements of disputes expressed in Form 866 (final agreement to close a tax year that has ended) or Form 906 (relating to a specific transaction). Such agreements are irrevocable and binding on both parties, unless there has been fraud, malfeasance, or misrepresentation of material fact.

At any time after an assessment has been made, and before a case has been referred to the Department of Justice, the IRS can compromise any civil or criminal tax case as provided by § 7122. (Post-referral, the Attorney General is the only party that can compromise the case.) A compromise binds both the taxpayer and the government.

Originally, only two grounds were permitted for compromise: the IRS' doubts as to the taxpayer's liability (memorialized on Form 656) and the taxpayer's inability to pay, or inability to pay in full immediately (Form 9465). Form 433-A is used for individuals unable to pay, 433-B for businesses in the same situation, and 433-D is the request to make installment payments. IRS Publication No. 1854 explains how to complete these forms. Taxpayers who compromise must agree to suspend the statute of limitations while the offer in compromise is pending, and for one year after it ends.

In the post-IRSRRA environment, the IRS decided to make offers in compromise easier to obtain, by permitting an offer to be accepted even if the collectibility of the debt is not actually in doubt.

The Tax Increase Prevention and Reconciliation Act (TIPRA; P.L. 109-222) provides that, for offers in compromise submitted after March 2006, taxpayers must make partial payments to the IRS while the offer is under consideration. If the offer is for a lump sum payment, 20% must be paid at once (in addition to the $150 user fee for the offer itself). Taxpayers who propose to pay in installments must begin, and keep up with, the installments during the IRS' consideration of the offer. In other words, taxpayers cannot try to take advantage of the "float" by collecting interest on unpaid taxes while the IRS considers whether to accept the offer.

IRS Notice 2006-68, 2006-31 IRB 105, revises the Form 656 (Offer in Compromise) effective July 16, 2006. TIPRA requires a payment of 20% of the amount of the offer with any application for payment in a lump sum (defined as one to five payments). A taxpayer who offers periodic payments in compromise must pay the first proposed installment with the application and continue making the scheduled payments while the IRS evaluates the application. The IRS will return applications as "not processable" if they fail to include the required payment, but the IRS will permit taxpayers to make the payment before the application will be deemed withdrawn. As a result of TIPRA, if the IRS does not reject an offer in compromise within 24 months, the offer is deemed accepted — unless the offer is returned as not processable, or the taxpayer fails to make the necessary payments. Taxpayers can specify how to apply the payment among tax, interest, and penalties;

the IRS will apply the payment in the best interests of the government if the application is silent. The advance payment requirements are waived for taxpayers who certify that they qualify for a low-income exemption.

T.D. 8922, 2001-6 IRB 508 contains Temporary and Proposed Regulations as to when a taxpayer who settles an IRS case by making a qualified offer is a prevailing party entitled to recover reasonable administrative and litigation costs from the government.

The taxpayer prevails if the offer lowers the taxpayer's liability (as compared with the last qualified offer). The taxpayer must exhaust administrative remedies; must satisfy the Code §7430(c)(4)(A)(ii) net worth requirements; and must not have prolonged the litigation unreasonably. The award is limited to reasonable costs incurred on or after the date of the last qualified offer, with respect to adjustments included in the last qualified offer and litigated to a judicial determination.

A married couple incurred tax penalties because of tax shelter partnerships. They claimed inability to pay the penalties on the grounds that the husband will have very large medical expenses in the future. The Ninth Circuit rejected this argument, however, because the taxpayers' only evidence was a dementia diagnosis. They did not provide an individualized estimate of medical expenses, and they had significant assets to cover bills. The Ninth Circuit also ruled that IRS agents have the power, but not the duty, to negotiate offers in compromise, and they can reject an inadequate offer out of hand.[8]

It was not an abuse of discretion for an IRS settlement officer to issue a notice of determination without considering an offer in compromise from a married couple, who had received a notice of deficiency but did not challenge the underlying tax liability before the Collection Due Process hearing. Code §6330 prevented them from challenging the amount of the liability at the Collection Due Process hearing, so the settlement officer was not required to consider an offer in compromise challenging the liability. The Tax Court held that it was reasonable for the settlement officer to issue a notice of determination sustaining the lien, but postponing levy until the IRS had considered the offer in compromise and the taxpayers' late-filed returns.[9]

§21.04 THE COLLECTION PROCESS

The Code gives the IRS extremely extensive powers to collect a deficiency that has been determined and agreed upon. Collection powers also come into play once the time for challenging the deficiency has elapsed. These powers include the imposition of liens and levies on property.

The initial step, as prescribed by §§6303 and 6331, is for the IRS to send a notice of the amount assessed and a demand for payment. The notice must issue within 60 days of the assessment, and §6331(d)(2) requires 30 days' notice of levy. Unless it believes the collection of the tax to be in jeopardy, the IRS usually gives

---

[8] Fargo v. CIR, 447 F.3d 706 (9th Cir. 2006).
[9] P.P. Baltic, 129 TC No. 19 (Dec. 2007).

the taxpayer at least 10 days to pay the tax. An extension of time to pay can be granted in hardship cases. As long as the IRS properly assesses tax against a partnership, the 10-year statute of limitations (rather than the three-year limit) applies to an IRS collection action against the partners to enforce their derivative liability for the partnership's tax debts. It is not necessary to assess taxes separately against each partner, nor must the IRS obtain a judgment against the partners to hold them jointly and severally liable for partnership debts.[10]

In 2007, the Court of Federal Claims held that levy and seizure are merely procedural remedies that place seized property in IRS custody, but do not determine the IRS' permanent ownership of the property. Therefore, placing funds into escrow as surety against future payment of tax liability is not tantamount to payment — and does not stop accrual of interest on the underlying liability under Code § 6601(a).[11]

In addition to the Internal Revenue Code provisions, an alternative maximum fine provision can be found at 18 USC § 3571. The maximum fine for a crime is the amount set out in the statute criminalizing the activity; twice the gross gain to the malefactor; or twice the gross loss to the victims — whichever is greatest. 18 USC § 3571 includes a relief provision if imposing the maximum fine would unduly prolong or complicate the sentencing process.

[A] Tax Liens

A demand for payment of taxes triggers a federal tax lien, under § 6321, covering the taxpayer's real and personal property, even property acquired after the imposition of the lien. Nevertheless, certain categories of property are not subject to liens, because § 6323(b) characterizes them as "superpriority" items, e.g.,

- Deposit-secured loans, secured by the balance in a savings account, made by banks and S&Ls that did not have actual notice of the federal tax lien
- Casual sales of personal property for less than $1,380 to a purchaser unaware of the tax lien
- Mechanic's liens under $6,880, resulting from improvements to the taxpayer's home.[12]

Other federal taxes can also give rise to liens, e.g., the § 6324 gift and estate tax liens; the § 6324A lien arising out of use of the installment tax payment provisions for farms and closely-held businesses; the § 6324B lien arising out of special use valuation; and the § 2661 generation-skipping tax lien.

In general, liens are enforceable in the order they were created. However, tax liens are subordinated to certain later liens involving purchasers of property who

---

[10] United States v. Galletti, 541 U.S. 114.

[11] Larosa's Int'l Fuel Co., Inc. v. United States, 499 F.3d 1324 (Fed. Cir. 2007).

[12] 2009 figures; *see* Rev. Proc. 2008-66, 2008- . . . IRB. . . .

paid adequate consideration and were not aware of the existence of the tax lien. See § 6323, a section that also protects attorneys' liens and some security interests even if they arose after the IRS' notice of lien was filed.

The federal lien priority statute, 31 USC § 3713(a), does not give federal tax claims priority over a perfected lien on real property, if the debtor's estate is smaller than the sum of the perfected lien and the tax lien.[13] *Williams v. Comm'r*, 514 U.S. 527 (1995) holds that if a third party pays someone else's tax liability, in order to remove a lien from the third party's property (e.g., property that was jointly held prior to a divorce from the person who actually owes the taxes), the actual payor is entitled to file a refund action to recoup the tax.

A Supreme Court case from April 2002 permits a tax lien to be placed on property held in tenancy by the entireties, on account of the tax debts of one of the spouses.[14] In this analysis, property rights are treated as a "bundle of sticks" — i.e., essentially independent of one another. State law determines which sticks will be assigned to a particular taxpayer's bundle, but whether a particular "stick" is subject to a federal tax lien must be determined under federal law, which will not be bound by state creditors' rights law. The husband had wide-ranging rights over the entireties property, including the right to receive half the proceeds of any sale, and the right to alienate the property (albeit only with his wife's consent). The Supreme Court held that ability to alienate without the consent of others is not a prerequisite to the existence of a property right for federal tax lien purposes, and the Supreme Court refused, for policy reasons, to permit property to be insulated from tax liens by being held by the entireties.

T.D. 8951, 2001-29 IRB 63 (6/21/01) is a Final Regulation providing that, when the IRS withdraws a notice of a federal tax lien (which might occur if the lien was premature; if the IRS failed to follow proper procedure when placing it; the taxpayer enters into a payment agreement; or withdrawal is deemed to be in the best interests of the taxpayer and the United States), and if the taxpayer notifies the IRS in writing, the IRS is obligated to notify credit reporting agencies, financial institutions, and any creditors specified by the taxpayer that the lien has been withdrawn.

T.D. 8979, 2002-6 IRB 466 finalizes Regulations under § 6320 about notice to taxpayers of filing of a Notice of Federal Tax Lien (NFTL). The taxpayer can then request a hearing at the IRS Office of Appeals followed by judicial review. This T.D. is applicable to any NFTL filed on or after January 19, 1999. The taxpayer (but not other persons financially affected by the lien) is entitled to notice within five days after the NFTL is filed. The CDP Notice (Collection Due Process

---

[13] United States v. Estate of Romani, 523 U.S. 517 (1998). However, *see also* Taylor, 98-1 USTC § 50,185 (3d Cir. 1998): a tax lien is valid against a residence sold to a third party who could not prove payment of full and adequate consideration for the property; *In re* Spearing Tool & Mfg Co., 2003-1 USTC § 50,525 (D. Mich. 2003): a tax lien has priority over a lender's security interest, because the liens identified the taxpayer to the extent that a reasonable search would reveal the liens.

[14] United States v. Craft, 535 U.S. 274 (2002). *See* Notice 2003-60, 2003-39 IRB 643 for the IRS' right to collect against entireties property when only one spouse owes taxes.

Hearing Notice) and the other notices required by § 6320 must be given in person, left at the dwelling or usual place of business of the taxpayer, or sent by certified or registered mail to the taxpayer's last known address.

IRSRRA creates an administrative procedure that third-party payors can follow; 120 days after a certificate of discharge is issued under this procedure, the third party can file a suit against the United States in the appropriate federal District Court for release of the lien.

[B] Collection by Levy

Levies are governed by § 6331, which gives the IRS the right to seize **all** of the taxpayer's property unless it is exempt under § 6334 or another statute limiting the scope of the seizure. All kinds of property, not just tangible realty or personality, can be seized—including present and future wages above a minimal subsistence amount. The seized non-exempt property is then sold and the proceeds applied to the tax obligation. In particular, it should be noted that § 6334 exempts a small amount of property (less than $15,000) so that the taxpayer can earn a living and satisfy the basic needs of life. More specifically, § 6334(a)(2) exempts up to $7,900 (for 2008) and $8,230 (for 2009) and § 6334(a)(3) exempts up to $3,950 (2008) or $4,120 (for 2009) for tools of the taxpayer's trade.

Section 6334 requires an order of a federal District Court or magistrate for the IRS to seize a taxpayer's personal residence. No residence owned by the taxpayer (except as rental property) can be seized to collect a liability of less than $5,000. Penalties and interest are included in the determination of the amount. Section 6331(f) also rules out uneconomical levies, i.e., those where the estimated expenses of levying on the property and selling it exceed the fair market value of the property.

Generally speaking, § 6502 gives the IRS ten years from the date of assessment to collect by levy (or initiate court proceedings), although a written agreement before the expiration of ten years can extend the period (§ 6502(a)), and a collection suit can be instituted at any time, even without assessment, if the taxpayer fails to file a return: § 6501(c)(3).

Neither qualified plans nor IRAs are exempt from levy. It may be some comfort to taxpayers in this situation that the IRSRRA specifies that, on or after December 31, 1999, the 10% early withdrawal penalty will not be imposed on taxpayers whose qualified plans or IRAs become subject to levy before the taxpayer reaches age 59½.

Section 6337(b)(1) gives the owner of real estate that has been sold 180 days after the sale date the ability to redeem the property by reimbursing the purchaser, plus interest at an annual rate of 20%.

The agency must issue a Final Notice of Intent to Levy, and must wait for 30 days after sending the notice before seizing the property. Thanks to the IRSRRA, revenue officers are limited in their ability to issue notices of lien or levy, or to perform levies or seizures, on their own initiative: they must get prior approval from a supervisor "where appropriate." The practical impact of the change is somewhat limited, since most liens and levies are issued by the Automated Collection System, not by revenue agents.

Under § 6335(f), the owner of levied property has the right to request that the property be sold within 60 days, and the proceeds applied to the tax debt.

Traditionally government creditors had the right to offset funds owed to a taxpayer, to reduce an outstanding tax liability, without notice to the taxpayer. A levy, to gain control of property the government does not already have, requires notice and hearing. A First Circuit case arose when the appellants, a married couple, claimed that it was improper for the IRS to offset the refund on their joint personal income tax return against the husband's business tax debt. The First Circuit held that the federal courts did not have subject matter jurisdiction over the challenge: the Tax Court is a court of limited jurisdiction (only where taxpayers receive written notice of an Appeals Office determination issued after a hearing), and does not have general equitable jurisdiction. There were also other procedural avenues that the petitioners could have followed, including suing in the District Court for a refund of a claimed overpayment (28 USC § 1346(a)). If they had prevailed, the IRS would have been required to use the levy procedure to recoup the funds. The taxpayers also had an agreement to repay in installments, and the IRS is usually precluded from placing a levy when an installment agreement is in effect. However, Code § 6331(k)(3)(A) says that the bar does not apply to § 6402 offsets. The First Circuit rejected the taxpayers' argument that amendments to the Code have removed the procedural differences between offset and levy.[15]

When a taxpayer was found in default on an offer in compromise, the IRS levied for the amount due. The Tax Court agreed with the taxpayer that the levy was an abuse of discretion, but the Eighth Circuit reversed. The taxpayer did not file his 1998 tax return (although the offer in compromise required full tax compliance). After several reminders, the IRS levied the full original tax liability minus the amount already paid under the offer in compromise. The Eighth Circuit held that the taxpayer defaulted in his obligations, so it was not an error of law or abuse of discretion for the IRS appeals officer to uphold the decision to cancel the agreement and impose a levy.[16]

See T.D. 9189, 2005-13 IRB 788 for Final Regulations about property exempt from levy. Any portion of the taxpayer's income required under any domestic relations court order entered before the date of the levy is exempt. The burden of proof is on the taxpayer to show how much income is needed for this purpose. If the taxpayer has more than one source of income, the IRS can allocate the exempt income to one source or apportion between them. If the levy is under $5,000, the taxpayer's residence or property owned by the taxpayer and used as a residence by someone else is exempt from levy. Even for a larger levy, the IRS

---

[15] Boyd v. CIR, 451 F.3d 8 (1st Cir. 2006).
[16] Robinette v. Comm'r of IRS, 439 F.3d 455 (8th Cir. 2006).

requires advance consent from a District Court judge or magistrate to levy on the principal residence of the taxpayer, the taxpayer's spouse or ex-spouse, or the taxpayer's minor child. The taxpayer will be granted a hearing before the residence levy.

A taxpayer who has filed a timely Tax Court petition is protected against assessment of tax deficiencies and collection actions on the unpaid portion of a "divisible" tax if the taxpayer has paid the requisite portion of the tax and sought a refund from the Tax Court. The protection extends until the Tax Court (or other appropriate federal court) has issued its appealable final judgment or order. See Code § 6331(i). Levies are forbidden while an offer in compromise or request for installment payment is pending, or has been rejected and the rejection is under appeal. See §§ 6331(j) and (k).

Section 6343(a) permits the IRS to release levies on part or all of the seized property (including wages and salaries). The IRS, as a result of § 6343(e), **must** release a wage levy as soon as the agency and the taxpayer agree that the outstanding tax liability is uncollectible.

Accounts are uncollectible if the taxpayer's financial statement shows inability to pay any tax liability at that time. (The agreement applies only to a specific tax liability, so wage levies may still be made for other tax liabilities that are not subject to such an agreement.) Under pre-IRSRRA law, the IRS often levied on one or more paychecks even though it was clear that the levy was uncollectible.

Section 6343(c) provides for written requests to the IRS for return of wrongfully levied property (or proceeds of its sale), plus interest at the overpayment rate. Section 6343(d) provides for the IRS to return property after its determination that the levy was premature or failed to satisfy IRS administrative requirements, although interest is not included. Seized property is also returned when the taxpayer enters into an installment agreement that calls for return of the property; and the Taxpayer Advocate can order the return based on the best interests of the taxpayer.

See Code § 7426 for civil suits in District Court filed by parties other than the taxpayer who have a lien or other interest in property that they allege to have been the subject of a wrongful levy. Code §§ 7426(a)(1) and 6532(c)(1) permit a third party to bring a wrongful levy action against the United States within nine months of the date of a levy on the third party's property to collect taxes from a taxpayer. Under 28 USC § 1346(a)(1), the statute of limitations for a tax refund action is two years from denial of the administrative claim, which the taxpayer has two years to file. In this case, the IRS levied on the bank account in which a trust deposited funds. The agency's position was that the trusts' creators placed assets into the trust to evade taxes. Almost a year after the bank paid over funds pursuant to the levy, the trust brought a wrongful levy action. The District Court dismissed it because it was filed after the nine-month deadline expired. The trust responded by seeking a tax refund. The Fifth Circuit, and later the Supreme Court, held if the deadline for an unlawful levy action is missed, it is impossible to do a "work-around" by pursuing a tax refund claim. Section 7426(a)(1) is the sole avenue for third-party wrongful levy claims, and the short statute of limitations was drafted to prevent stale claims.[17]

28 USC § 1346 gives the District Court and the Court of Federal Claims concurrent jurisdiction over civil suits for recovery of erroneously or illegally assessed or collected taxes or penalties. However, in a case where there was a lien imposed but no levy, § 7426(a)(1), which requires surrender of seized property by the taxpayer, did not apply, and the taxpayer did not receive a certificate of discharge and therefore could not substitute property under § 7426(a)(4). (The taxpayer alleged that she was the subject of a wrongful levy when she was awarded the proceeds of the sale of the marital home in her divorce, and the IRS tried to collect taxes owed by her ex-husband.). The Fifth Circuit ruled that there was no subject matter jurisdiction — a lien is merely a security interest, and is not tantamount to a levy.[18]

The Sixth Circuit affirmed the Bankruptcy and District Courts in finding that a bankruptcy debtor (an attorney) willfully attempted to evade tax liability for 1990 and 1991. Therefore, Bankruptcy Code § 523(a)(1)(C) precluded discharge of the tax debt. A levy was issued on the law firm at which the debtor was a partner to collect the debtor's share of a major fee payable to the firm; however, the debtor's share of the fee was distributed to him, not to the IRS. The debtor made two offers in compromise that were rejected. The debtor made a Chapter 7 filing, failing to list his share of the fee for that case, and also omitting cash on hand and bank accounts. The taxpayer argued that § 523(a)(1)(C) applies only to an attempt to evade or defeat the assessment of taxes, rather than to defeat payment of taxes, but the courts were unpersuaded, because failure to file returns and failure to pay fall within the definition of "willful attempts to evade tax"; and the taxpayer used nominee accounts, known for their use in concealment of assets.[19]

T.D. 8980, 2002-6 IRB 477, explains the hearing rights of taxpayers before collection by levy is performed under § 6330.[20] Taxpayers have the right to request a Collection Due Process (CDP) hearing by submitting a written request; there is an official IRS form for this purpose. The collections period is suspended until the hearing is held, but so is the statute of limitations. The hearing, which can either be done in person or by submission of documents, is conducted by an Appeals Officer. If the taxpayer is dissatisfied with the Appeals Officer's decision, appeal is permitted to either the Tax Court or District Court.

---

[17] EC Term of Years Trust v. United States, 550 U.S. 429 (2007).

[18] Wagner v. United States, 545 F.3d 298 (5th Cir. 2008).

[19] *In re* Gardner, 360 F.3d 551 (6th Cir. 2004). Similarly, in mid-2007 the Eleventh Circuit found a real estate attorney willfully attempted to evade taxes by directing his firm not to withhold taxes from his salary, and engaged in affirmative acts to avoid payment or collection of tax, such as chronically filing late returns, failing to pay the full amount due, and placing a house in his wife's name because the mortgage lender was afraid of tax liens. Hence, the tax debt was non-dischargeable: *In re* Jacobs, 490 F.3d 913 (11th Cir. 2007).

[20] The Tax Court has jurisdiction under § 6330(d) to review an IRS determination that a jeopardy levy is appropriate: Dorn v. Comm'r, 119 TC No. 22 (12/30/02).

The Eighth Circuit held that, when the IRS refused to accept an installment agreement for payment of employment tax arrears, and levied on the taxpayer's property instead, District Court review of the appeals officer's collection due process decision (Code § 6330) is limited to the administrative record and is extremely deferential. Where the amount of tax owed is not in dispute, the Eighth Circuit said that a court can only reject the administrative decision if there was a clear abuse of discretion, and the IRS was unfair and abusive to the taxpayer. As long as the IRS abides by the statutes and regulations providing taxpayer relief, and the appeals officer considers the alternative proposed by the taxpayer and follows the procedure. A reviewing court does not have the power to reverse the appeals officer merely because the court would have reached a different decision on the same facts. A District Court decision under § 6330 is considered a grant of summary judgment, so the Court of Appeals reviews the District Court de novo. In this case, the appeals officer considered the installment plan proposed by the taxpayers, but decided they could not meet the payments under the plan; an offer in compromise and an installment plan had been approved in the past, but the taxpayer defaulted on them.[21]

[C] Termination and Jeopardy Assessments

As noted above, the basic rule is that levies cannot be finalized within 30 days after the Final Notice of Intent to Levy is issued. But §§ 6861 and 6862 extend the scope of IRS powers if the 30-day delay would jeopardize the IRS' ability to collect, or if the taxpayer is about to leave the U.S. or remove property from this country or conceal it. If collectibility is at issue, the IRS can make an immediate assessment and demand payment in full, including interest and penalties. If it does so, it must issue a deficiency letter no later than 60 days after the assessment.

A termination assessment under § 6851 permits the IRS to terminate a tax year and demand immediate payment for the current and preceding tax years if the taxpayer seems likely to take action to hinder collection. Once again, a 90-day letter must be issued within 60 days of the assessment.

Code § 6871 permits the IRS to immediately assess tax, interest, and penalties, whether or not the 90-day letter has already issued, if the taxpayer has been declared bankrupt in a liquidation proceeding; if any other type of bankruptcy petition has been filed by or against the taxpayer; or if a receiver has been appointed for the taxpayer. IRSRRA requires the IRS Chief Counsel to review and approve all internal applications for jeopardy and termination actions. Code § 7429(a)(1) also requires the IRS to notify the taxpayer, within five days, of the basis for imposing the jeopardy or termination assessment or levy. The taxpayer has 30 days to request review. See Code § 6863 for stay of collection on condition that the taxpayer post bond for the full amount on which collection is stayed. A married couple, after the District Court entered a judgment for $1.85 million in tax

---

[21] Fifty Below Sales & Marketing, Inc. v. United States, 497 F.3d 828 (8th Cir. 2007).

assessments, they charged that they had not been notified about the right to a CDP hearing. The IRS located print-outs in the file showing timely notification letters to the taxpayers, and submitted an affidavit that the letter was printed out from the IRS database in the ordinary course of business. The letters were sent by certified mail, and one of the taxpayers signed a receipt, but the taxpayers continued to deny receiving the notice. IRS' computerized records are admissible as business records, and the inference is that the letters were placed in the envelopes, were mailed, and arrived.[22]

[D] Bankruptcy Issues

NOTE: Most of these cases refer to the law in effect before the Bankruptcy Abuse Prevention and Consumer Protection Act of 2005 (BAPCA) took effect; see below for discussion of relevant BAPCA provisions.

Understandably, a number of bankruptcy debtors have unpaid tax liabilities. It is not necessary for a trustee or a debtor in possession to notify the IRS of the bankruptcy, but if a Chapter 11 trustee or receiver is appointed, § 6036 obligates him or her to notify the IRS of the appointment.

A bankruptcy filing triggers an immediate assessment of tax, but the automatic stay prevents actual collection efforts as long as the taxpayer's assets are under the supervision of the bankruptcy court. The trade-off is that the IRS' assessment period is extended for up to two years, running from the date of bankruptcy filing until 30 days after the IRS is notified of the proceedings (§ 6872).

The IRS is required to consider offers in compromise from bankruptcy debtors under the same standards used to analyze offers from non-bankrupt taxpayers.[23]

Whether the taxpayer takes a lump sum or a series of monthly payments, Alabama (a state that has opted out of the federal system of bankruptcy exemptions) treats the Earned Income Credit against federal income tax as public assistance. Therefore, it is exempt from the bankruptcy estate.[24]

Under Bankruptcy Code § 507(a)(8)(A)(i), the IRS' claim for certain taxes due in the three years before the bankruptcy filing (the "lookback period") takes eighth priority. The taxpayers in a case decided by the Supreme Court in March, 2002 filed under Chapter 13, then had the case dismissed before a reorganization plan was approved. Then they filed under Chapter 7 and obtained a discharge. The IRS attempted to collect taxes on a return due less than three years before the Chapter 13 filing, but more than three years before the Chapter 7 filing. The taxpayers asserted that the claim was time-barred. The Supreme Court, however, held that the look-back period is subject to equitable tolling — in this case, during the pendency of the first bankruptcy petition, and therefore the taxes could be collected.[25]

---

[22] Haag v. United States, 485 F.3d 1 (1st Cir. 2007).
[23] *In re* Macher, 2003-2 USTC § 50,337 (D. Va. 2003).
[24] Hamm v. James, 406 F.3d 1340 (11th Cir. 2005).
[25] Young v. United States, 535 U.S. 43 (2002).

The Bankruptcy Abuse Prevention and Consumer Protection Act of 2005 stays tax proceedings against corporate debtors for the period determined by the court — but the stay in tax proceedings against individual debtors is limited to the taxable period ending before the bankruptcy filing.

When a bankruptcy reorganization plan fails to be confirmed, and if the IRS imposes a proper levy, then the money that the debtors deposited into the reorganization plan goes directly to the IRS instead of being returned to the debtors. In other words, the IRS levy provisions (Code § 6331) outweigh the provisions of Bankruptcy Code § 1326(a)(2). The Ninth Circuit also ruled that it was appropriate for the IRS to serve notice of levy on the bankruptcy trustee instead of the debtors, because service is proper on any third party who has possession of the debtor's property or has a duty to the debtor.[26]

Bankruptcy Code § 1129(a)(9), as amended by BAPCA, requires Chapter 11 plans to call for regular installment payments, in cash, of the allowed amount of priority tax claims (plus interest), over a period of five years or less. The interest rate on tax claims is the rate set by applicable non-bankruptcy law (new Bankruptcy Code § 511). The priority tax claims must receive treatment at least as favorable as the non-priority unsecured claims that receive the highest level of repayment. Tax claims secured by a lien or warrant must be treated on a parity with unsecured priority claims.

BAPCA amends Bankruptcy Code § 724: ad valorem taxes on the bankruptcy estate's real or personal property are not subject to subordination, although they can be subordinated to wage, salary, and employee benefit claims. Administrative expenses (other than administrative wages) can be paid prior to tax liens in Chapter 7, but not in Chapter 11. Amended § 545(2) does not permit trustees to avoid unperfected statutory liens if the purchasers are described in IRC § 6323 or a comparable state or local law. Furthermore, the bankruptcy trustee must use up all of the estate's unencumbered assets before subordinating a tax lien.

Taxes assessed during the 240 days before filing, plus any period when collection of taxes was stayed, plus another 90 days, are given priority. The priority period is also extended by times when a debtor's request for appeal or hearing on a collection action is pending.

Even after confirmation of the plan, a corporate Chapter 11 debtor is not discharged from fraudulent debts, including taxes the debtor willfully attempted to evade or filed a fraudulent return. Unless there was a proper request for an extension, whenever a bankruptcy debtor fails to file a tax return due at any time after the bankruptcy filing, the taxing authority can use amended Bankruptcy Code § 521 to seek to have the bankruptcy case dismissed or converted to another Chapter.

---

[26] Beam v. CIR, 114 TC No. 29 (6/8/00).

§ 21.05   TAX LITIGATION

Naturally, all litigation involving federal taxes is handled in the federal court system, primarily in the Tax Court, although the District Courts have a role. Taxpayers can sue in Tax Court to modify or set aside a deficiency already determined (§ 6214), to review the IRS' failure to abate interest (§ 6404(i)), to obtain declaratory judgment on various issues such as retirement plan qualification, valuation of certain gifts, or classification of workers as employees or independent contractors (see, e.g., §§ 7436, 7476).

Litigation in the District Court can be proper when a taxpayer who has filed a refund claim seeks to recover overpayment of taxes (§ 6532(a)), or to enjoin the IRS from assessing and collecting taxes (§ 7421(a))[27] or obtain damages from the IRS for unauthorized collection activities (§ 7433) or failure to release a lien (§ 7432).

The Supreme Court ruled in mid-2007 that the Tax Court is the sole forum where an IRS refusal to abate interest on underpayments can be reviewed. In this case, the plaintiffs went to the Court of Federal Claims for a refund of $18,000 in interest that they said accrued because of delays in processing their case, but the Supreme Court ruled that exclusive jurisdiction lay in the Tax Court.[28]

The Ninth Circuit upheld preliminary injunctions enjoining tax protesters from promoting their theories that the income tax is illegal. The court also upheld the District Court's requirement that the appellants post a copy of the injunction on their Web site. The United States sued under Code § 7408, which allows the District Court to enjoin activities subject to penalties under §§ 6700 and 6701 (e.g., improper tax shelters). In the Ninth Circuit view, it was not an abuse of discretion to grant the injunction, in light of the appellants' extensive history of promoting tax avoidance. Commercial speech can be restrained if it is fraudulent or it aids and abets criminal activity. In this case, the protected parts of the communication were inextricably intertwined with the commercial objective of selling products promoting tax avoidance schemes. The required posting on the site was also upheld on the grounds that the First Amendment does not preclude mandatory disclosure of factual commercial information.[29]

---

[27] But only if the taxpayer has received notice of deficiency and filed a timely Tax Court petition, or a few other exceptions, such as someone other than the taxpayer suing for return of improperly seized property. In fact, this section is known as the "Anti-Injunction Act."

[28] Hinck v. United States, 127 S. Ct. 1507 (2007) discussed in (AP), *High Court Limits Certain Cases to Tax Court*, 5/22/07 (law.com).

[29] United States v. Schiff, 379 F.3d 621 (9th Cir. 2004). Later, the Northern District of New York issued a permanent injunction against We the People Congress and the We The People Foundation for Constitutional Education Inc. disseminating (online, by mail, or in person) materials stating that citizens have no obligation to pay federal income taxes and explaining how to avoid filing W-4 forms. First Amendment arguments were rejected: the court treated the communications as promotion of an abusive tax shelter: United States v. Schulz, No. 1:07-cv-0352. (N.D.N.Y. 2007); *see, e.g.*, Joel Stashensko, *N.Y. Federal Judge Enjoins "No Tax" Group's Solicitations*, N.Y.L.J. 8/14/07 (law.com); *see also* United States v. Bell, 414 F.3d 474 (3d Cir. 2005). The Second Circuit held that due process does not require giving a tax protester a chance to argue his theories in an

[A] Tax Court

The prerequisite to Tax Court litigation is a 90-day letter; once that is post-marked, the taxpayer has 90 days to file the Tax Court petition: § 6213(a). The Tax Court has jurisdiction over deficiencies asserted by the IRS and not yet paid as of the issuance of the 90-day letter. The Tax Court can order refund payments to taxpayers who have overpaid and can order abatement of interest, but has no equitable jurisdiction. Taxpayers who go to Tax Court put themselves at risk: the Tax Court can decide that the taxpayer actually owes more than the IRS assessed.

Section 7463 sets out a special informal small claims procedure that tax-payers can elect in cases involving less than $50,000 (or where the taxpayer agrees to make concessions bringing the amount in controversy below $50,000). Small claims Tax Court decisions are final, non-precedential, and non-appealable.

Other Tax Court decisions can be appealed to the Court of Appeals, usually the Circuit in which the taxpayer resides.

Notice of Appeal must be filed with the Tax Court clerk (in the District of Columbia; notices can be mailed by taxpayers who are not close to the District of Columbia) within 90 days of entry of the Tax Court decision. If one party files timely notice of appeal, any other party can file notice of appeal within 120 days after entry of the Tax Court decision. The form of the notice must follow FRAP 4; FRAP 10-12, concerning the record on appeal, also apply to tax appeals. (See Federal Rules of Appellate Procedure 13.)

The Tax Court's jurisdiction over appeals from Collection Due Process (CDP) proceedings (when the IRS has announced its intent to impose a lien or levy) is limited to issues where the Tax Court could have considered the underlying tax liabilities. The Tax Court does not have jurisdiction over IRS Office of Appeals determinations in trust fund recovery penalty cases — the District Court does.[30]

The Supreme Court ruled in 2005 that reports submitted by Special Trial Judges pursuant to Tax Court Rule 183(b) cannot be excluded from the case's record on appeal. The Special Trial Judges render reports that the regular judges use as the basis of their decisions. Taxpayers who take their cases to the Court of Appeals are entitled to disclosure of the Special Trial Judges' findings of fact.[31]

The Tax Court has the power, under § 7430, to make an award of costs of administrative proceedings and reasonable litigation costs, including attorneys' fees (subject to a limit of $110/hour, indexed for inflation; the 2007-8 level is $170/hour, rising to $180/hour in 2009) and costs to certain taxpayers whose net worth falls within specified limits.[32] Fees and costs are awarded unless the

---

administrative or civil case before prosecuting him for tax evasion. Tax liability is automatic; the tax deficiency notice is merely a reminder and does not create the liability: United States v. Ellett, 527 F.3d 38 (2d Cir. 2008); the First, Sixth, Seventh, and Ninth Circuits had already held similarly.

[30] Gorospe v. CIR, No. 446 F.3d 1014 (9th Cir. 2006).

[31] Ballard v. CIR, 544 U.S. 40 (2005).

[32] Litigation costs are awarded only if administrative remedies were exhausted prior to litigation.

IRS shows that its position vis-à-vis the taxpayer was substantially justified — a change from earlier law that required the taxpayer seeking a fee award to demonstrate that the government position was not substantially justified.

To be a prevailing party entitled to litigation costs: the taxpayer must significantly prevail either on the central issue or on the amount in controversy; the taxpayer must not unreasonably have prolonged the litigation; and the claimed costs must be reasonable.[33]

Even though the IRS in effect agreed that the taxpayers were correct, the Appeals Officer relinquished jurisdiction back to the examiner and no notice of deficiency was issued, the IRS did not "take a position" in the case and therefore the taxpayer cannot recover the costs of having meetings with the appeals officer under Code § 7430. A 30-day letter is not a "position" taken by the IRS.[34]

When the IRS issued summonses at the request of the Russian government, although the statute of limitations had run, the taxpayers succeeded in getting the summonses withdrawn, and then applied for a fee award. The Ninth Circuit held that the issue was the government's pre-litigation conduct, and the taxpayers did not incur fees for a "court proceeding." The Ninth Circuit noted that, although the EAJA has a gap-filler provision for agency action prior to litigation; the Internal Revenue Code does not. The Ninth Circuit also deemed the IRS' position to have been substantially justified: as soon as the IRS determined that the summonses were unenforceable, they were quashed.[35]

However, the taxpayer may have to pay a penalty of up to $10,000 to the United States, as prescribed by § 6673, if the Tax Court case was primarily instituted to delay tax enforcement; if the taxpayer took a frivolous or groundless position; or if the taxpayer failed to pursue administrative remedies prior to litigation. Attorneys can be liable under this section for "unreasonable and vexatious" "multiplication" of Tax Court proceedings.

[B] Suits Against the IRS

Taxpayers can sue the IRS in the District Court or Court of Federal claims for refunds: 28 USC § 1346. However, Code § 7422 obligates the taxpayer to file a refund claim — and pay the assessed tax in full — before bringing a refund suit. The general statute of limitations for refund suits is two years: § 6532(a).

Under § 7422(a), the taxpayer can commence suit for a tax refund once a claim for a refund or credit has been duly filed with the IRS. Timely filing is a jurisdictional prerequisite to maintaining a refund suit. Code § 7422(a) requires a taxpayer seeking a refund of taxes that were unlawfully assessed to file an IRS administrative claim before suing the government. Section 6511(a) requires the claim to be filed within three years of filing the tax return or two years of paying the tax, whichever is later. The Tucker Act permits claims against the government to

---

[33] Goettee Jr., 124 TC No. 17.

[34] Rathbun, 125 TC No. 2.

[35] Pacific Fisheries Inc. v. United States, 484 F.3d 1103 (9th Cir. 2007).

be made within six years of the challenged conduct. The Supreme Court decided a
case in 2008 involving coal companies that paid taxes on exports pursuant to a
Code section that was later struck down for violating the Export Clause of the
Constitution. The companies not only filed administrative claims (resulting in
refunds for 1997–1999) but also sued in the Court of Federal Claims for refunds
of 1994–1996 taxes without going through the Code's refund procedure. The Court
of Federal Claims allowed the suit to proceed under the Export Clause and the
Tucker Act. The Federal Circuit allowed the Export Clause claim to be pursued
even in the absence of a timely administrative refund claim. The Supreme Court,
however, held that §§ 6511 and 7422(a) require a timely refund claim prior to suit,
whether or not the tax was assessed contrary to the Export Clause; the Code's
timing rules would have little usefulness if taxpayers could use the Tucker Act to
make an end-run around them. The unconstitutionality of the tax merely entitled
the taxpayers to a refund — it did not extend the time to apply for the refund or
provide additional avenues for seeking the refund.[36]

Another area of tax litigation involves improper IRS conduct. Up to $1
million or actual, direct economic damages (whichever is less) can be recovered
in a civil suit pursuant to § 7433 if any IRS officer or employee recklessly, intentionally, or even negligently disregards IRS rules when collecting tax. (Only
$100,000 can be recovered in negligence cases.)

See § 7433(e) for sanctions against the IRS for violation of the bankruptcy
automatic stay or the discharge provisions of the Bankruptcy Code. If a bank places
the IRS on notice under § 6323(b)(10) (either through a wrongful levy suit or
informally) that it has a superpriority claim over a bank account because of a
loan, the IRS will not require the bank to turn over funds from the account. The
IRS will exercise its discretion as to whether or not its claim will be released.[37]

Section 7435(a) authorizes a civil action for the lesser of $500,000 or direct
damages sustained as a result of improper U.S. government pressure on the taxpayer's tax adviser, in order to induce the adviser to inform on the taxpayer-client.

§ 21.06 INNOCENT SPOUSE RELIEF

Code § 6013's general rule is that spouses are jointly and severally liable on
joint returns for all tax, penalties, and interest, irrespective of the actual amount
that each spouse earned. Exceptions are made for omissions from gross income and
for civil fraud penalties; only the person committing fraud is liable for fraud
penalties.

If spouses file separate returns, each is liable only for his or her own taxes and
penalties.[38] However, separate filing is onerous in many ways, so few spouses will
choose this as a strategy. Section 66(c) includes special rules for spouses in

---

[36] United States v. Clintwood Elkhorn Mining Co., 128 S. Ct. 958 (2008).

[37] Rev. Rul. 2006-42, 2006-35 IRS 337.

[38] In consequence, § 6015 relief is not available to married taxpayers who file separate returns:
Raymond, 119 TC No. 11.

community property states who file separate returns but fail to include the proper amount of community income. The Ninth Circuit ruled that to assert innocent spouse status under § 6015, it is necessary to file a joint return, not just be liable as a result of community property, which is covered by Code § 66, not § 6015.[39]

In mid-2008, the Ninth Circuit heard a case of first impression: whether Code § 6015 preempts community property law with respect to innocent spouse relief. The legislative history shows that refunds can be ordered for an innocent spouse who qualifies for relief, creating an overpayment. Therefore, the authority to issue the refund is a result of relief from joint and several liability. The Ninth Circuit agreed with the IRS' argument that Congress did not intend to preempt community property law for all subsections of § 6015, only for the determination of whether a taxpayer is an innocent spouse. If he or she is, then eligibility for a refund is governed by state law; community property law is suspended only to determine which spouse is responsible for the item that created the tax liability.[40]

An executor can seek relief from joint and several liability on behalf of a deceased innocent spouse: Rev. Rul. 2003-36, 2003-18 IRB 849.[41]

In § 6015, dealing with innocent spouse relief, the Code copes with the situation of a spouse who is unaware of and does not benefit by the other spouse's tax improprieties.

Section 6015(b) explains the circumstances under which a married person can be treated as an innocent spouse when the other spouse understates income. This provision applies only if:

- The tax deficiency is attributable to the guilty spouse's erroneous items (IRSRRA eliminated the provision that the items must have been "grossly erroneous");
- The innocent spouse had no reason to know of the understatement (i.e., his or her standard of living was not enhanced by the other spouse's failure to pay taxes in full);
- Under all the facts and circumstances, it would be inequitable to penalize the innocent spouse.

Thanks to IRSRRA, a spouse who knows that understatement occurred, but was unaware of its extent, can get partial relief. Furthermore, innocent spouse relief is available in cases that do not involve omissions from gross income only if the tax liability exceeds 10–25% of the innocent spouse's AGI.

---

[39] Christensen v. CIR, 523 F.3d 533 (9th Cir. 2008).

[40] Ordlock v. CIR, 533 F.3d 1136 (9th Cir. 2008). *See* Hisquierdo v. Hisquierdo, 439 U.S. 572 (1979) for the principle that federal law supplants community property law only if the Congressional intent is unequivocal.

[41] *But see* Jonson v. CIR, 353 F.3d 1181 (10th Cir. 2003) (denying the use of the innocent spouse defense to the estate of a decedent who had filed a joint return with her husband, in that a decedent is not an individual. The court did not accept the estate's argument that the decedent was no longer married because her death terminated the marriage.).

IRSRRA also creates a new procedure, under § 6015(c)(3)(A), for separated or divorced taxpayers to elect separate liability for a year in which a joint return was already filed. The procedure can be used at any time within two years of IRS initiation of collection activities with respect to that return.

A person claiming innocent spouse status has up to two years after the IRS begins collection activities against him or her (as distinct from collection activities against both spouses) to seek treatment as an innocent spouse. Form 8857 is used to request innocent spouse relief.

Innocent spouse relief is not available under § 6015(b) if the person had knowledge or reason to know of the understatement of income. T.D. 9003 defines this to mean either that the person actually knew of the understatement, or that a reasonable person in the same situation would have known that income was understated. Similarly, actual knowledge that will preclude relief under § 6015(c) means actual knowledge (measured at the time the tax return was signed) that an item giving rise to a deficiency existed. Relief is not available if the person knew about the existence of the item but did not understand its proper tax treatment.

The next development was Congress' enactment of Tax Relief and Health Care Act of 2006 (P.L. 109-432) § 408, which permits the Tax Court to hear innocent spouse cases even if a deficiency has not been asserted.

If a person applies for § 6015(f) relief under circumstances that would also justify relief under (b) and/or (c), the IRS is obligated to ask the requesting person if he or she wishes to amend the application for relief. However, relief will be denied if the requester has already signed a closing agreement or offer in compromise relating to the same tax liability; if there was a fraudulent interspousal transfer of assets; or if the tax liability has already been addressed in another proceeding which is res judicata as to the tax liability.

Code § 6015 permits not only basic innocent spouse relief, but also separation of liability of the two spouses and equitable relief. Separation of liability is allowed when a taxpayer filed a joint return but is now divorced, legally separated, or no longer in the same household as the other spouse. The taxpayer who requests this relief has the burden of proof on income and deductions.

The IRS ruled that a joint bankruptcy filing by a married couple does not prevent one of the spouses from seeking innocent spouse relief under § 6015 after the bankruptcy proceedings ends, as long as the Bankruptcy Court (which has the power to determine eligibility for innocent spouse relief, and for that determination to become res judicata) did not specifically address the merits of the innocent spouse claim.[42]

A person who signs a joint return is not an "innocent spouse" if he or she knows that retirement distributions and interest income were received but not reported, even if that person relies on the non-innocent spouse's representations about the tax status of the item.[43]

---

[42] Rev. Rul. 2006-16, 2006-14 IRB 694.
[43] Cheshire v. Comm'r, 115 TC No. 15 (12/21/00), *aff'd*, 282 F.3d 326 (5th Cir. 2002).

[A] Equitable Relief Outside § 6013

On January 31, 2000, the IRS published a detailed explanation, in Revenue Procedure 2000-15, 2000-5 IRB 447, of the way an innocent "requesting spouse" can obtain equitable relief from federal tax liability that was, in effect, created by the other spouse, but where relief is unavailable under Code § 6013, the general provision for innocent spouse relief. For instance, equitable relief may be available to protect against the consequences of liabilities that were properly reported but never paid, whereas § 6013 is inapplicable in this situation.

The application for equitable relief must be made within two years of the IRS' initial collection activity. Equitable relief will be denied if there were interspousal transfers of assets designed to defeat tax collection, or if the tax return was filed with fraudulent intent. Furthermore, the spouses must be divorced or separated for equitable relief to be available. The innocent spouse must also be at risk of economic hardship if relief is denied.

Another possible relief provision is Code § 6015(f), granting relief of tax liability that is not available under § 6015(b) or (c), if it would not be equitable to hold the taxpayer liable under all the facts and circumstances of the case. It has been held that this provision gives the Tax Court jurisdiction to review denial of innocent spouse relief.[44]

§ 21.07   TREATMENT OF OVERPAYMENTS

Although tax deficiencies get most of the attention, and the consequences for taxpayers can certainly be dramatically worse, in fact a taxpayer's mistake in determining the amount of tax due can occur in either direction. Overpayments are very common, because most people permit or even encourage over-withholding on their salaries, so they can treat the eventual refund as a windfall.

There is no full statutory definition of "overpayment," but § 6401 says that an overpayment includes amounts assessed or collected after the statute of limitations has expired, as well as credits in excess of tax liability, but does not include amounts paid for which there was no tax liability.

Usually the taxpayer can either seek a refund or have the overpayment credited to future taxes, although § 6402(a) gives the IRS the power to apply the overpayment to any past-due tax liability (including interest and penalties) of the taxpayer. However, under § 6402(c), other obligations take higher priority: child support arrears reported to the IRS by a state agency, followed by other overdue debts reported by any federal agency.

If the taxpayer is entitled to a refund because of over-withholding or overly high estimated tax payments, he or she simply files the ordinary income tax return by mail, indicating the amount of overpayment and whether it is to be refunded or applied to other or future taxes. Otherwise, Form 1040X is used to claim the refund.

---

[44] Fernandez v. Comm'r, 114 TC 324 (2000), *acq.*; Charlton v. Comm'r, 114 TC No. 22 (5/16/00).

Generally speaking, refund and credit claims must be filed within three years of the due date of the return or the date the return was filed, or two years after payment of the tax (whichever is later): see § 6511 for the rule and its exceptions. This section also limits the amount of the refund (or credit) to the part of the tax paid during the three years (plus extensions) before filing of the refund claim. If the claim was not filed within three years from the filing of the return, only the part of the tax paid during the two years before the filing of the claim can be recovered. The other side of the coin is that the federal government's two-year statute of limitations to recover an erroneous tax refund starts on the date the check clears the Federal Reserve and payment of the check is authorized by the Treasury.[45]

Section 7422(a) and 28 USC § 1346 require the taxpayer to file an administrative refund claim with the IRS before suing for a refund or a credit. The entire assessed amount must be paid before suing for a refund; in contrast, Tax Court procedure permits the taxpayer to challenge the validity of an assessment without paying it in full. The taxpayer must wait six months after filing the claim to sue (unless the IRS has resolved the claim sooner), and has only two years after the date of the notice of disallowance to file the refund suit (see § 6532(a)).

Just as § 6001 requires taxpayers to pay interest to the IRS on deficiencies (see § 21.08[A]), taxpayers are sometimes entitled to receive interest on overpayments.[46] Code § 6611(a) allows interest, compounded daily, from the date of the overpayment until either the return due date (without extensions) for the amount against which the overpayment is credited, or up to 30 days before the refund is made. However, most taxpayers do not get interest on their refunds, because § 6611(e)(1) relieves the government of liability for interest if the refund is made within 45 days of the unextended due date for the return, or the actual date of filing — whichever is later.

Section 6621(a)(1) sets the overpayment interest rate as three percentage points over the applicable federal rate (AFR), but corporations are only entitled to the AFR plus two percentage points, or AFR plus 0.5 percentage points on the portion of the overpayment for any period that is greater than $10,000.

The Ninth Circuit placed wrongful levies on a par with overpayments for purposes of § 6621, which sets interest rates but reduces the interest rate by 1½ points for amounts over $10,000. Therefore, the government was entitled to take advantage of the interest rate reduction when it paid interest on a judgment for wrongful levy (a jeopardy assessment was imposed on the founder of a small business that was deficient in its taxes). Code § 7426(h) provides statutory damages when an IRS employee recklessly, intentionally, or negligently disregards a Code provision.[47]

In February 2000, the Supreme Court ruled that, to calculate the three-year look-back period under Code § 6511(b)(2)(A) (amount of credit or refund on

---

[45] United States v. Greene-Thapedi, 398 F.3d 635 (7th Cir. 2005).

[46] The latest rates are published in the Internal Revenue Bulletin.

[47] Cheung v. United States, 545 F.3d 695 (9th Cir. 2008).

overpayment of tax), the salient date is the due date of the tax return rather than the date the tax liability is assessed. (The taxpayer got an extension, but missed the extended deadline too and filed late.) The look-back period is three years plus the four-month extension. Remittances of estimated tax or withholding are paid on the due date of the return, so they were deemed paid on April 15, making the taxpayer too late and relieving the IRS of the obligation to credit his account because he missed the three-year-plus-four-month deadline.[48]

§21.08   INTEREST AND PENALTIES

As a general rule, taxpayers who pay less than the required amount have an obligation to pay interest on the underpayment, to compensate the IRS for lost time value of money. (Interest is not imposed on late payments of estimated tax.) It is important to note that obtaining an extension of time to pay tax protects the tax-payer from a late-payment penalty, but not interest obligations (§ 6601(b)(1)), and installment payment agreements are also subject to interest.

In addition to paying interest, taxpayers are required to pay penalties when they have taken improper actions, or have failed to take required action with respect to their tax liability. Penalties are also imposed by § 6695 on tax preparers (including attorneys!) for various forms of negligent or wrongful conduct. Penal-ties can be imposed for various combinations of failure to file returns (§ 6651); failure to pay the tax (§§ 6654–6656); inaccuracy (§ 6662); negligence; mis-representation; fraud (§ 6663); and/or misconduct by a person responsible for employment-related taxes (§§ 6672, 6674, 6682).

Civil penalties are excused if the taxpayer can meet the burden of showing that failure to make the required payments was not due to willful neglect, but instead had a reasonable cause such as reliance on advice from the IRS or a tax advisor;[49] death or serious illness; casualty or disaster that destroyed necessary records. Furthermore, § 6664(c)(1) provides that neither fraud nor accuracy-related penalties can be applied to the portion of an underpayment with respect to which the taxpayer acted in good faith and with reasonable cause.

NOTE: See § 21.08[G] for discussion of changes in the penalty structure imposed by the AJCA, P.L. 108-357.

Section 8245 of the U.S. Troop Readiness, Veterans' Care, Katrina Recovery, and Iraq Accountability Appropriations Act, P.L. 110-28, increases the penalty for submitting a bad check or money order to the IRS. Section 8246 deals with under-statement of taxpayer liability by return preparers, who are subject to a penalty of the greater of $1,000 or 50% of the fee for preparing the return if they file returns taking positions that they know or should have known were unjustified. The penalty increases to $5,000 if the preparer's conduct was willful or reckless.

---

[48] Baral v. United States, 528 U.S. 431 (2000).

[49] *E.g.*, Henry v. CIR, 170 F.3d 1217 (9th Cir. 1999): § 6653(a) penalty for negligent disregard of a tax rule does not apply where the taxpayer reasonably relied on an accountant's advice that gain from sale of stock options was long-term capital gain.

Section 8246 also extends penalties on return preparers to preparers of all kinds of returns — not just income tax returns. Section 8247 enacts a new Code § 6676, which increases the penalty for filing an erroneous claim for a refund to 20% of the excessive amount claimed.

[A] Interest

Section 6621(b) sets the rate of interest on underpayments of tax and penalties at the applicable federal rate (AFR) for the previous calendar quarter, plus three percentage points. C Corporations must pay AFR plus five percentage points if they have an underpayment of $100,000 or more for any tax period, and the amount remains unpaid 30 days or more after a notice of deficiency: § 6621(c). However, different types of underpayment and different tax periods are not aggregated to determine when the threshold has been reached. This interest rate takes effect 30 days after the IRS sends a 30-day letter or a 90-day letter (whichever is issued first).

Generally speaking, interest begins to run on an unpaid tax liability from the regular due date of the payment: § 6601(b)(1), but interest can end on the date of the notice and demand if tax is paid no more than 21 days after notice and demand (or 10 business days afterward, for amounts equal to or greater than $100,000: § 6601(e)(3)). The same timing rules apply to interest on civil penalties, but for many penalties (e.g., failure to file; understatement of value for gift or estate tax purposes; negligence; fraud), interest runs from the extended due date of the underlying return rather than from the IRS notice and demand. No further interest is imposed after payment of the penalty. Interest (other than penalties for failure to file personal or corporate estimated tax) is compounded daily: § 6622.

Where the amount in controversy is very large, the potential interest payment is also large, so taxpayers are given a chance to pay the alleged deficiency before receiving the 90-day letter and thus stop accrual of interest. It is important to designate the way the IRS should treat the money; it will be treated as a payment of tax unless the taxpayer calls it a deposit. But access to Tax Court is possible only if the remittance is treated as a payment (i.e., is **not** identified as a deposit).

Form 843 is used to request abatement of interest pursuant to § 6404, in situations where the taxpayer detrimentally relied on IRS actions or advice. IRS has discretion to abate the interest if it results from unreasonable errors or delays by IRS personnel (whether acting in a managerial or ministerial capacity) and where the taxpayer was not also at fault. The Tax Court can be used to litigate IRS refusals to exercise this discretion. Section 6404(f) also provides that the IRS **must** abate penalties and additions to tax resulting from incorrect written advice that the IRS gave to an individual taxpayer, who reasonably relied on the advice and who also gave the IRS sufficient accurate information to enable proper advice.

[B] Civil Penalties

It is important to distinguish among the many types of penalties that can be imposed, and to make sure that clients are not subjected to inconsistent or duplicative penalties.

[1] Failure to File Penalties

For failure to file any required income, estate or gift tax return, a penalty of 5% for the first month, and 5% for each additional month or partial month (up to a limit of 25%) that the non-filing continues, is imposed under § 6651. The percentages apply to the amount of unpaid tax that should have been shown on the return.

If an income tax return should have been filed, but remains unfiled for 60 days after the due date as extended, the § 6651(a) minimum penalty is the tax that should have been shown on the unfiled return, or $100, whichever is less.

The failure-to-file penalty is abated if there was a reasonable cause for non-filing, and the taxpayer did not willfully neglect the filing obligation. On the other hand, if the failure to file was fraudulent, the penalty increases, to 15% per month or partial month, up to a maximum of 75% (§ 6651(f)).

[2] Failure to Pay Penalties

In many instances, failure to file is accompanied by failure to pay. In months in which this occurs, the 1/2% failure to pay penalty reduces the 5% failure to file penalty, but the minimum failure-to-file penalty is still imposed: § 6651(c).

The penalty for failure to pay the tax on a return without reasonable cause is 1/2% per month or partial month, up to 25%, or 1% per month or partial month, up to 25%, for failure to pay within 10 days after service of an IRS Notice Of Levy. See § 6651(d).

The same penalty is imposed for failure to pay an assessed deficiency by the prescribed payment date. The failure-to-pay penalty applies to taxpayers who get an automatic extension of time to file if the tax is not paid by the extended filing date, or the extended form 1040 shows a payment due greater than 10% of the tax shown on the 1040. (Generally, this means that withholding and prior payments are not at least 90% of the total.)

[3] Accuracy-Related Penalty

The § 6662 "accuracy-related penalty" of 20% of the understatement applies to any portion of the understatement of the tax on a tax return that is not fraudulent,[50] but that can be traced to negligence, disregard of IRS rules, substantial

---

[50] Fraud penalties are imposed by § 6663; *see* § 21.08[C]. Nor do § 6662 penalties apply if the taxpayer is subject to the § 6672 penalty; *see* § 21.08[D]. At the end of 2002, the IRS proposed rules limiting the defenses that can be raised against accuracy-related penalties when a taxpayer fails to disclose reportable income, or when a return assumes that a Regulation is invalid and therefore takes a position contrary to the one set out in the Regulation: 67 FR 79894 (12/31/02).

misstatements of income, gift, or estate tax valuation, or overstatements of pension liabilities. This penalty does not apply if the taxpayer had reasonable cause for the understatement — e.g., advice from a CPA.

The definition of negligence includes failure to make a reasonable attempt to comply with the law; failure to keep adequate books and records; failure to substantiate items; and failure to exercise ordinary and reasonable care in preparing tax returns (§ 6662(i)). The penalty for non-compliance with IRS rules will not be applied when the taxpayer takes a position contrary to a Revenue Ruling or Notice, but the taxpayer's position has a realistic possibility of being sustained on its merits.

To constitute a substantial misstatement as defined by § 6662(h), the statement must indeed be highly inaccurate: e.g., a value or adjusted basis on an income tax return that is at least twice the actual figure. The penalty is 20% of the portion of the underpayment traceable to the misstatement, or 40% if the misstatement is "gross" (four times or more the actual figure). This penalty will not apply in tax years in which underpayment attributable to all misstatements is under $5,000 (under $10,000 for a C Corporation). See § 6662(e)(2).

The § 6662(d) 20% accuracy-related penalty also applies to taxpayers who substantially understate the amount of income tax. A substantial understatement is 10% or more of the tax that should have been shown, or $5,000 ($10,000 for a C Corporation), unless the taxpayer had substantial authority for the tax position, or the facts behind the treatment of the item are disclosed on the return or Form 8275/8275-R. (The former is for opposition to a rule, the latter for opposition to a Regulation.)

Substantial authority, in turn, means that the weight of authorities (Code, other statutes, case law, Regs., TAMs, Notices, tax treaties, and Congressional Legislative History) supporting the taxpayer's position stacks up fairly well to the weight of authority supporting the IRS position. Under § 6664(c)(1), penalties will not be imposed on taxpayers who acted in good faith, with reasonable cause.

A very similar penalty of 20% for substantial, 40% gross misstatements that lack substantial authority is imposed by § 6662(f) for overstatement of deductible pension liabilities, if income tax is underpaid by at least $1,000. A substantial understatement is twice or more the actual amount. A gross misstatement (penalized by § 6662(h)(2)(B) with 40% rather than 20% additional tax) is four times or more the appropriate amount.

Yet another accuracy-related penalty is imposed by § 6662(b)(5) and (g) if the value assigned to property on a gift or estate tax return is 50% or less of its actual value. The penalty is 20% of the underpayment of tax attributable to the artificially low value; 40% of the underpayment if the property is valued at 25% or less of its true value. The penalty is waived in cases of understatement resulting in underpayment of tax in an amount under $5,000.

Penalties under § 6662 are not cumulated. In other words, a negligent substantial understatement triggers only one accuracy-related penalty, not two.

On a related issue, see § 6702, imposing a $500 civil penalty in addition to all other applicable penalties for filing a "frivolous" tax return (e.g., a tax protester's return). A return is frivolous if it fails to provide an accurate self-assessment of taxes, because of a frivolous tax position (e.g., that the entire federal income tax system is unlawful) or a desire to delay or impede federal tax administration.

[4] Abatement of Penalties

Section 6404(f) provides for abatement of penalties if the taxpayer relied on erroneous advice that the IRS provided in writing to a written request from the taxpayer. Abatement is not available if the IRS gave the incorrect advice because the taxpayer gave incorrect or insufficient information. The abatement request is made on Form 843 (Claim for Refund and Request for Abatement) and must be accompanied by documentation. Interest can be abated under the same conditions; see § 6404(e).

[C] Fraud Penalties

When a taxpayer files a return, but fraudulently fails to pay some of the tax shown on the return, a civil fraud penalty of 75% of the fraud-related portion of the underpayment is imposed by §§ 6663, 6664. The IRS cannot impose both an accuracy-related penalty and a fraud penalty on the same underpayment or portion of an underpayment. If the IRS can show that any portion of an under-payment is traceable to fraud, the entire underpayment is treated as fraudulent unless the taxpayer can show by a preponderance of the evidence that any portion was not fraudulent. Innocent spouses are not subject to fraud penalties for joint returns.

[D] Responsible Person Penalties

For a "trust fund tax" (e.g., FICA), there is at least one "responsible person" in each organization required to collect and remit the tax.[51] Section 6672 imposes a penalty of 100% of the amount that should have been but was not paid, if the responsible person willfully fails to account for, collect, or pay the tax. The IRS must give at least 60 days' notice of its intent to impose the penalty, so that the responsible person can settle the account.

If there is more than one responsible person (a category that includes corporate officers and certain employees, partners, and certain partnership employees), and if one pays more than his or her proportionate share of the tax, he or she can recover the excess from the other responsible persons. The notice requirement is waived where the IRS deems collection of the penalty to be in jeopardy.

---

[51] Section 6671 makes this and other "assessable penalties" subject to the same rules for assessment and collection as income taxes.

[E] Non-Taxpayer Penalties

The penalties discussed above are imposed on the taxpayer. In various situations, penalties can be imposed on third parties as well as, or instead of, the taxpayer — for instance, if the non-taxpayer has aided and abetted the taxpayer in failing or refusing to make proper returns and payments.

Code § 6701(b) imposes a $1,000 penalty (or a $10,000 penalty, in connection with a corporate return) for preparing, assisting in the preparation of, or advising about any tax return or other tax-related document that understates tax liability or overstates a refund, knowing that if the advice were taken, it would result in an understatement of tax. The wrongful act is preparing the document or giving the advice, even if the document is not used or the advice is not taken. This penalty is clearly applicable to lawyers and accountants. The preparer penalty can only be imposed on a paid preparer; the § 6701(b) penalty can be imposed even if the advice was not given in return for a fee.

Penalties for paid preparers are governed by §§ 6694 and 6695. The penalty is $250 for any return or refund claim prepared for a customer, if the preparer knowingly takes a position that has no realistic possibility of being sustained by the IRS or the courts. (Preparers and other advisors who take unrealistic positions can also be barred from practice before the IRS.) A $1,000 penalty can be imposed per return or claim showing willful understatement by the preparer, or reckless or intentional disregard of IRS rules. However, if both willful understatement and advice leading to understatement penalties are imposed, the $250 offsets the $1,000.

Other incidents of preparer misconduct can lead to § 6695 penalties of $50, $100, or $500 per offense (subject to a maximum of $25,000 per type of offense per calendar year): e.g., not signing a return; not providing the preparer's taxpayer ID on a return; improper record management; failure to follow due diligence when claiming the Earned Income Credit.

Thanks to lower tax rates, tax shelters (valid or abusive) have a much lower profile than in the past, but § 6701 continues to impose penalties on organizing, selling, or failing to register potentially abusive tax shelters.[52]

Deficiencies in information reporting by payors (e.g., banks, brokerages, employers who sponsor pension plans) can also generate penalties. See, e.g., § 6721 (failure to file required information return); failure to furnish payees with 1099s or other required statements (§ 6722); willful failure to furnish a required statement, or furnishing a fraudulent statement (§ 6674); failure to file annual returns, information returns, or actuarial reports for pension plans, or failure to keep adequate records (§§ 6652, 6692, 6704). Not only can the IRS penalize deficiencies in information reporting, but someone who is the subject of a fraudulent information return has a cause of action against the reporter, for the greater of $5,000 or actual damages, plus costs: § 7434.

---

[52] On tax shelters, *see also* § 6662(d)(2)(C) and § 6707 (failure to furnish tax shelter information).

[F] Criminal Penalties

In practice, the IRS seldom brings criminal charges, other than in the most flagrant cases, because of the comparatively greater difficulty of proving an intent offense versus merely proving failure to satisfy tax obligations. Nevertheless, a variety of criminal penalties are at least hypothetically imposed by §§ 7201–7207. The criminal tax statute of limitations is three years — six years for willful fraud offenses. See § 6531.

Criminal tax evasion (willful evasion of tax due) is a felony, carrying a term of up to five years' imprisonment and/or a $100,000 fine for an individual or $500,000 for a corporate wrongdoer (§ 7201). Willful assistance in or advice about a materially[53] false or fraudulent tax return or other document is punishable under § 7206 by three years and/or $100,000 for an individual, $500,000 for a corporation. Section 7206 also criminalizes the making of a false declaration under penalty of perjury. Willful failure to maintain records, file a return or pay a tax, collect and remit a tax, obey a summons, or willful filing of a false or fraudulent tax return are also criminal acts; see § 7203.

The Supreme Court ruled early in 2008 that the existence of a tax deficiency is an element of the crime of tax evasion under Code § 7201. The founder, president, and controlling shareholder of a close corporation (all one person) was charged with criminal tax evasion and filing false income tax returns, diverting funds from the corporation. The corporation had no earnings or profits, so his position was that he received capital distributions, which are tax-free up to his basis. According to the Supreme Court, whether a distribution constitutes a return of capital depends on objective economic realities, not the form employed by the parties, and the taxpayer's or corporation's intent is irrelevant. In this case, there was no tax deficiency, and thus no criminal tax evasion.[54]

In 2004, the Eighth Circuit ruled that a conviction can be proper under § 7201 even if the defendant files an accurate return but fails to actually pay the tax. There are two separate offenses under § 7201 (interfering with the assessment of tax; attempting to evade or defeat payment), and evasion of payment can be demonstrated by proof that taxes were owed and not paid.[55]

The Eighth Circuit accepted the prosecution's argument that it was unreasonable to sentence a defendant for willful invasion of income tax without imposing a prison sentence. The Guidelines sentence was 12–18 months in prison, 2–3 years of supervised release, and a fine of $3,000–$30,000; the actual sentence was two years of probation and 300 hours of community service. The trial court did not impose a fine, on the grounds that the defendant needed to devote his resources to paying back taxes and penalties. The Eighth Circuit held that a prison term was required to deter tax fraud and avoid sentencing disparities. In general, a prison

---

[53] The materiality of the statement is a mixed question of law and fact, and is determined by the jury: United States v. Gaudin, 515 U.S. 506 (1995).

[54] Boulware v. United States, 128 S. Ct. 1168 (2008).

[55] United States v. Schoppert, 362 F.3d 451 (8th Cir. 2004).

sentence will be imposed for frauds over \$100,000 — in this case, over \$650,000 was involved. Nor is the magnitude of the debt owed to the IRS a valid justification for reducing a sentence.[56]

[G] Tax Shelter Enforcement; AJCA Changes

In January 2001, the IRS proposed amendments containing standards for the issuance of tax shelter opinions by professionals practicing before the IRS, but did not incorporate them into Circular 230 (the publication prescribing Best Practices for tax professionals). Late in 2003, the IRS re-issued the proposals, this time adding them to Circular 230. The amendments apply to "marketed" opinions — that is, the opinions that the issuer knows will be used by someone outside the practitioner's firm to promote, market, or recommend a tax shelter. It also covers "more likely than not" opinions — opinions that conclude, at a more than 50% confidence level, that the taxpayer would prevail on one or more material tax issues.

The IRS directed that such opinions consider all relevant facts; relate the facts to applicable legal principles; offer a legal conclusion supported by authority; and refrain from reaching unreasonable conclusions. The practitioner offering the opinion must disclose any relationship with the tax shelter promoter. Marketed opinions must disclose that they will not necessarily avert § 6662(d) penalties, and must recommend obtaining individualized tax advice. Under the Regulations, the practitioner in charge of overseeing a firm's federal tax practice has the duty to take reasonable steps to see that the staff complies with the tax shelter requirements.[57]

The AJCA, P.L. 108-357, made many changes in tax enforcement, particularly with respect to tax shelters:

- Enactment of new Code § 6707A, imposing penalties (i.e., \$10,000 for a natural person or \$50,000 for a corporation; \$100,000 and \$200,000 respectively for a listed transaction) for failure to disclose reportable tax shelter transactions. Furthermore, penalties on listed transactions cannot be waived by the IRS.
- New § 6662A, adding an accuracy-related penalty for understatements of income due to reportable avoidance transactions (listed transactions or reportable transactions having a significant tax avoidance purpose). The penalty is 20% of the understatement, which can be waived if the transaction was adequately disclosed on the taxpayer's return; or 30% of the understatement, which is nonwaivable, if adequate disclosure was not made.

---

[56] United States v. Ture, 450 F.3d 352 (8th Cir. 2006). The Third Circuit found it unreasonable to impose a sentence of a heavy fine and probation (but no prison time) for a convicted tax evader: United States v. Tomko, 498 F.3d 157 discussed in Shannon P. Duffy, *3rd Circuit Rules Prison Time "Reasonable" for Tax Cheat*, The Legal Intelligencer 8/23/07 (law.com).

[57] REG-122379-02, 68 FR 75186 (12/30/03).

- Under amended § 6662, a corporate understatement of income of $10 million or more is automatically considered a substantial understatement, irrespective of the 10% threshold or the materiality of the understatement.
- Deductions under § 163 are denied for interest paid or accrued on underpayment of tax arising because of a reportable avoidance transaction that was not disclosed.
- New § 6707A requires corporations that are SEC reporting entities to disclose tax shelter penalties in their SEC filings, and an additional $200,000 penalty is imposed for failure to make any required SEC disclosure.
- The § 6501 statute of limitations for listed transactions that are not disclosed on a timely basis extends to one year after the date on which the taxpayer or a material advisor of the taxpayer informs the IRS of the transaction. Of course, if the transaction is never disclosed, the statute of limitations is never triggered and never ends.
- The § 6707 penalty for failure to register a tax shelter is replaced by a $50,000 penalty for failure to comply with information return requirements. For listed transactions, the penalty is the greater of $200,000 or 50% of the income the advisor earned from the transactions — and 75% if the failure was intentional.
- Material advisors to tax shelters who fail to maintain investor lists can now be penalized for $10,000 per day (starting 20 days after an IRS request for the information) for failure to maintain a complete list of investors or to make it available to the IRS. Material advisors must also file information returns about tax shelter transactions and their tax benefits (§ 6111). The limitations on tax advisor/corporate client privilege, already in place under § 7525, have been extended to apply to all tax shelter transactions, even if the taxpayer is not a corporation.
- Section 6700 has been amended to increase the penalties imposed on promoters who make false or fraudulent statements with respect to tax shelters.
- Outside the Tax Code, the sanctions imposed under 31 USC § 330 on tax practitioners authorized to practice before the IRS (and their employers) have been increased for non-compliance with the tax practice rules set out in Circular 230.
- New § 6603 permits a taxpayer to deposit the estimated amount of a contested tax liability with the IRS; deficiency interest is suspended once the deposit has been made.
- Section 6404 has been amended to provide that interest on tax deficiencies is suspended if the IRS fails to notify the taxpayer of the asserted deficiency.
- Section 6159 has been amended to clarify that the IRS can accept a collection agreement that both is paid in installments and covers less than the full amount of the deficiency asserted.
- New §§ 6306 and 7433A authorize the IRS to contract with private companies to collect liabilities owed to the IRS; the private companies can retain up to 25% of the amount collected. The private collectors can enter into some

limited installment agreements with taxpayers, but do not have the power to impose liens.

Effective June 20, 2005, Circular 230 has been revised to require tax advisers (including law firms) to create internal advisory compliance committees. Client information must be reported to the IRS more frequently, especially when the lawyer provides tax avoidance advice. Attorneys must include disclaimers on their legal opinions (that the opinion cannot be relied on) or perform a thorough fact investigation of the client's representations and claims before rendering an opinion. Previous rules required only corporate entities to report tax shelters and other tax avoidance. The new rules extend this obligation to individuals, and more types of transaction have become reportable. The IRS has the newly added power to demand written opinions and client lists from tax practitioners.[58]

However, the IRS returned to the subject in May 2005, issuing Final Regulations amending Circular 230 once again. Certain types of written opinions have been removed from the reach of Circular 230, such as negative advice (a statement that a federal tax issue will not be resolved in the taxpayer's favor); advice given by an employee to the employer about the employer's tax liability; and written advice given to a taxpayer solely with regard to a return that has already been filed with the IRS. The rules of Circular 230 continue to apply if the practitioner has reason to know the taxpayer will rely on the advice for returns to be filed in the future.[59]

One consequence of the Supreme Court's 2006 *Wachovia Bank, NA* decision on corporate citizenship is that it requires investors in a tax shelter case to go to federal, rather than state, court when they sued a national bank for promoting the tax shelters that got the investors into trouble with the IRS.[60]

§ 21.09 TAXPAYER RIGHTS AND ADVOCACY

Formal advocacy for taxpayers, within the IRS, dates back to 1979, when the Taxpayer Ombudsman Office was created. The ombudsman was replaced by the Office of the Taxpayer Advocate (appointed by the Commissioner of Internal Revenue) in 1996. The IRSRRA changed the functionary's name yet again, to National Taxpayer Advocate, who is appointed by the Secretary of the Treasury, not the IRS Commissioner. Thus, the selection process, although still within the Treasury system, has moved outside the IRS itself.

The National Taxpayer Advocate (NTA) is required to have experience in representing individual taxpayers and in customer service, not just technical tax skills. No one who has been an IRS employee within two years before the

---

[58] Jessica M. Walker, *Lawyers Wary of New Tax Regulations' Impact on Client Relations,* Daily Business Review 6/3/05 (law.com).

[59] 70 F.R. 28824 (5/19/05).

[60] Wachovia Bank NA v. Schmidt, 546 U.S. 303 (2006).

appointment can serve as NTA, and the NTA must agree not to go to work for the IRS within five years after leaving office.

The NTA's job is to help taxpayers work out their IRS problems, and to recommend changes in tax law and IRS procedure that would anticipate and eliminate potential problems. The NTA issues the Taxpayer Assistance Orders (Code § 7811(a) — for instance, release of levy; suspension of IRS activity) that provide relief to taxpayers who experience significant hardship because of the way the Code is administered. (Form 911, Application for Taxpayer Assistance Order to Relieve Hardship, is used for the request.) As a general rule, however, the NTA cannot be brought into a case in which there is a criminal investigation.

The NTA in effect comes into play when the taxpayer has been unable to resolve the problem through normal channels. Under the IRS Problem Resolution Program, there must be a Problem Resolution Officer in each district office and service center, to expedite the normal channels.

[A] Taxpayer Assistance Orders

Taxpayer Assistance Orders can enjoin the IRS from taking any action with respect to that taxpayer, to cease an ongoing action, or even release the taxpayer's property that has been levied on. The IRS can be required to pay refunds to relieve financial hardship, or issue a duplicate of a needed refund check that was sent to the wrong address.

The NTA can issue such an order based on a determination that the taxpayer will suffer irreparable injury, or at least long-term negative impact or will have to pay significant attorneys' fees or other costs absent relief; if the taxpayer is at immediate risk of adverse action; or the taxpayer's account problems have remained unresolved after 30 days. Deficiency notices sent to taxpayers must inform the taxpayers of how to contact a local Taxpayer Advocate office.

[B] Taxpayers' Rights Re Unauthorized Collection Actions

Until 1988, taxpayers who became the victims of unauthorized actions by IRS employees engaged in collecting taxes could not bring suit, because suit was precluded by the doctrine of sovereign immunity. In 1988, § 7433 was enacted (and amended in 1996, by TBOR II), permitting a suit in federal District Court for reckless or intentional disregard of the Code or Regulations by IRS officers or employees. The maximum recovery is $1 million. TBORII penalized only intentional improper collection efforts, and did not impose penalties in the situation in which IRS personnel violated the bankruptcy automatic stay (see § 15.09). IRSRRA amendments extend civil liability (subject to a $100,000 limit) to instances in which a negligent IRS employee violates Code collection provisions.

An IRS employee's willful violation of the Bankruptcy Code automatic stay, or of the Bankruptcy Code's discharge provisions in connection with tax enforcement, can be penalized by damages of up to $1 million. See § 7433(e). (The taxpayer petitions the Bankruptcy Court to make the award.)

In 2006, the Second Circuit reinstated the conviction of an IRS employee who threatened that police detectives would be audited when they arrested her on charges of harassing employees of her landlord's management company. The Second Circuit ruled that even though the arrest was unrelated to her work for the IRS, and even though she could not carry out her threats, the detectives did not know this. However, the Second Circuit dismissed a count of intimidating conduct, because the voicemail message she left did not state an immediate or imminent threat.[61]

Although in general IRSRRA is more pro-taxpayer than TBOR II, in one respect TBOR II was more liberal. Under TBOR II, aggrieved taxpayers could go directly to the District Court in certain circumstances, without exhausting their administrative remedies within the IRS (although so doing could reduce the damages available to the taxpayer). IRSRRA reinstates the requirement of exhausting remedies as a prerequisite for suit (§ 7433(d)), and also requires mitigation of damages.

Effective April 7, 2003, T.D. 9050 enacts Final Regulations about the civil cause of action for damages caused by unlawful IRS collection actions. Under Code § 7433(e), a damage action can be brought on the basis of the IRS' negligent disregard of the Code or the Regulations, and the action can be brought for violation of the automatic stay or discharge provisions of the Bankruptcy Code. The maximum damages for negligent disregard is $100,000, versus $1 million for a willful bankruptcy violation.

IRSRRA also added § 7426(h), permitting the plaintiff in a wrongful levy action to seek damages for intentional, negligent, or reckless disregard of Code provisions, plus costs. The plaintiff can recover the lesser of actual direct economic damages and costs of the wrongful levy, or $1 million for reckless or intentional violations, $100,000 for negligent violations. Exhaustion of administrative remedies and mitigation of damages are required. The statute of limitations is two years after the date the cause of action accrued; this two-year limitations period is independent of the nine-month period after a wrongful levy during which third parties can assert claims on the levied property. Under the Regulations, a prevailing party is one who establishes a willful violation of the relevant Bankruptcy Code provisions, and administrative costs can be awarded only if they accrued after the date of the bankruptcy petition. The administrative cost claim must be filed within 90 days of the IRS' mailing of its decision on the taxpayer's administrative claim for damages under Code § 7433 or the taxpayer's claim for relief from abuse of the Bankruptcy Code.[62]

---

[61] United States v. Temple, 447 F.3d 130 (2d Cir. 2006).

[62] 2003-14 I.R.B. 693, *finalizing* NPRM-REG-107366-00, 2002-12 IRB 645.

§ 21.10 PRIVILEGED COMMUNICATIONS

As discussed in § 27.01[A][6], when a person seeks legal advice from a lawyer, those communications (as well as the attorney's work product)[63] are generally privileged. However, preparation of a tax return is not considered "legal advice," so communications between client and attorney/return preparer are not privileged.

Yet another IRSRRA effect is to create a "federally authorized tax practitioner"-client privilege under § 7525, even if the practitioner is not an attorney. The privilege extends to tax advice and in non-criminal tax proceedings brought by or against the taxpayer. This provision applies only to the IRS' attempts to obtain the information from the practitioner; it does not create a general accountant-client privilege in other contexts (although about one-third of the states have a statutory accountant-client privilege).

CPAs, enrolled agents, and enrolled actuaries are all authorized practitioners. Tax advice is defined as advice about any matter within the scope of the practitioner's authority to advise, other than promotion of "tax shelters" as defined by § 6662.

[A] Confidentiality and Disclosure of Tax Return Information

Although the general rule of Code § 6103 is that tax return information cannot be disclosed, this rule is subject to various exceptions. Information could be disclosed, in appropriate circumstances, to other tax officials, the Justice Department and other federal agencies, and Congressional committees. However, the party receiving the information is required to have its own confidentiality procedures to prevent general dispersion of the information.

IRS employees who willfully disclose information improperly can be sued for civil damages. They are also guilty of a felony (penalized by up to five years' imprisonment and/or a $5,000 fine). Federal or state employees who merely access information which they are not legitimately entitled to view (even if they do not disclose the information) are subject to penalties under the Taxpayer Browsing Protection Act of 1997, P.L. 105-35.

Federal employees convicted under this statute will be fired; they can also be fined up to $1,000, imprisoned for up to a year, or both. Knowing or negligent improper access to tax returns also gives rise to a civil cause of action. See Code §§ 7213 and 7213A for sanctions against improper access to tax returns.

---

[63] However, the work product of independent auditors is not privileged: A. Young & Co. v. Comm'r, 465 U.S. 805 (1984). *See also* United States v. Adlman, 134 F.3d 1194 (2d Cir. 1998), finding that the IRS could not discover a study prepared for a corporation's attorney about the projected results of litigation. The District Court held that the study was prepared for business planning, rather than litigation, and thus was discoverable, but the Second Circuit deemed it work product because it showed the attorney's thoughts, impressions, and strategies in a situation where litigation with the IRS was virtually certain to occur.

According to the Second Circuit, whether the enforceability of a government summons is affected by the government's violations of the Code or Regulations depends on the totality of circumstances — including the government's good faith, the seriousness of the violation, and the extent of any harm or prejudice it caused. The Second Circuit required the taxpayer to allege specific facts from which the court could infer possible wrongful conduct by the government; unsupported allegations are not sufficient. The court did not find cause to quash four third-party summonses issued by the IRS during an ongoing investigation of an estate's gift and estate tax positions. The taxpayers alleged violation of Rev. Proc. 2000-43, which forbids ex parte communications between appeals officers and other IRS employees during the appeals process, but even if the violation occurred, the taxpayers did not show nexus between that violation and the disputed summonses.[64]

The IRS issued a Notice of Proposed Rulemaking, updating the Regulations under § 7216, providing guidance on electronic tax filing. The Notice includes new rules for taxpayers to consent electronically so that tax return preparers can use or disclose their tax return information. (There are criminal penalties under § 7216 for unauthorized disclosures by preparers, as well as civil penalties under § 6713 for disclosure unless there is justification under § 7216(b).)

At the same time, the IRS published Notice 2005-93, 2005-52 IRB 1204, a proposed Revenue Procedure for the format and content of a consent form for disclosure and use of tax return data, a category that is broad enough to include the amount of a refund and information that the IRS provides about the processing of a return, not just data provided by the taxpayer. The same rules apply to disclosures for preparing U.S. and non-U.S. tax returns. Information can be used without the taxpayer's consent to prepare anonymous statistical compilations to help manage the preparer's business. Disclosures are also permitted to report the commission of a crime or to investigate and prosecute it.[65]

The Seventh Circuit ruled that, in enacting Code §§ 6111 and 6112, Congress intended the identity of tax shelter purchasers to be subject to disclosure rather than confidential.[66]

---

[64] Adamowicz v. United States, 531 F.3d 151 (2d Cir. 2008).

[65] IRS REG-137243-02, Notice of Proposed Rulemaking Guidance Necessary to Facilitate Electronic Tax Administration-Updating of Section 7216 Regulations.

[66] United States v. BDO Seidman, 337 F.3d 802 (7th Cir. 2003); United States v. Arthur Andersen LLP, 72 L.W. 1127 (N.D. Ill. 8/15/03) reaches a similar conclusion.

Part VI

CIVIL LITIGATION

Chapter 22

Federal Civil Procedure

§ 22.01   INTRODUCTION

Federal civil procedure is applied, of course, within the federal court system. For convenience, it is also discussed here as a single system whose basic principles are applied (in however varied form) by the states in their own court systems. This section (Chapters 22–25) discusses the maintenance of civil cases in the federal system, trial practice, evidence, appellate procedure, and arbitration.

In May 2000, the Supreme Court struck down the Violence Against Women Act, 42 USC § 13981, which provided a federal civil cause of action to the victims of gender-related violence. In the Supreme Court's view, Congress was not justified in passing such legislation, in that it was not authorized by the Constitutional language cited by Congress as precedents (the Commerce Clause and the Fourteenth Amendment).[1]

In 2003, the Supreme Court ruled that, under the Foreign Sovereign Immunities Act, a corporate subsidiary can be considered an instrumentality of a foreign state only if the foreign state itself has direct ownership of a majority of the company's shares.[2]

The Supreme Court affirmed judgment in favor of a health insurance plan administrator seeking to collect medical expenses out of a plan participant's tort recovery. The Supreme Court held that ERISA § 502(a)(3) authorized the recovery as appropriate equitable relief.[3]

Although a nuclear power plant was ordered to pay $4.2 million for fraud, the Supreme Court held that a retired engineer could not collect a qui tam award under the False Claims Act, holding that he was not the original source of the information. This decision makes it difficult for an individual to qualify as a whistleblower once the allegations are publicly disclosed — especially once the events are reported, and the individual might have obtained information from the media coverage. The Supreme Court majority said that the engineer did not have direct and independent knowledge of the fraud. The dissent said that claimants should only have to show that they informed the government about fraud, not that the claims ultimately decided by the jury were submitted by the claimant.[4]

---

[1] United States v. Morrison, 529 U.S. 598 (2000).

[2] Dole Food Co. v. Patrickson, 538 U.S 468 (2003).

[3] Sereboff v. Mid Atlantic Med. Servs. Inc., 547 U.S. 356 (2006).

[4] Rockwell Int'l v. United States, *ex rel* Stone, 549 U.S. 457 (2007); *see* Mark Sherman, (AP), *Supreme Court Tightens Rules in Whistleblower Lawsuits*, 3/28/07 (law.com).

§ 22.02   THE FEDERAL COURT SYSTEM

The federal courts have been created pursuant to Article III of the Constitution; the Judicial Code is contained in Title 28 of the U.S. Code (which also contains the Federal Rules of Evidence). The local rules of the various federal courts, dealing with issues such as admission to the bar; getting a case set down for trial; how to petition for rehearing; and time limits on appellate oral arguments are reprinted as an appendix to Title 28.

The basic federal court system contains three tiers of courts. The 94 District Courts are the trial courts, with original jurisdiction over civil cases dealing with inherently federal issues such as federal tax; bankruptcy; federal questions; diversity cases; patents and copyrights; and unfair competition.

Appeals from decisions of the District Courts go to the thirteen Circuit Courts of Appeals (the First through Eleventh Circuits, the Federal Circuit, and the District of Columbia Circuit) and, in some instances, to the U.S. Supreme Court.

The First through Eleventh Circuits and the District of Columbia Circuit handle cases from particular geographic areas. The Federal Circuit handles specific types of cases. This court replaces the former Court of Customs and Patent Appeals. It has jurisdiction over civil appeals in which the United States is a defendant, and it is the only court that can handle appeals from the Court of Federal Claims and the administrative decisions of the Patent and Trademark Office.

The federal system also includes specialized courts: the U.S. Court of Federal Claims, which has jurisdiction over non-tort claims against the United States (e.g., contract claims; claims based on the Constitution, federal statutes, or federal administrative regulations),[5] and the Tax Court.

The Tax Court has jurisdiction over cases in which a deficiency or overpayment of federal tax is alleged. The general rule (see § 21.05[A]) is that if the tax has already been paid, the taxpayer will seek a refund from the District Court; if the tax has not been paid, the Tax Court is the usual forum. Most Tax Court cases are appealable to the Court of Appeals, but the Tax Court has a simplified procedure for small cases (Code § 7463; § 21.05[A]). If the amount in controversy is under $50,000, the taxpayer can elect to use this procedure, but the trade-off is that the Tax Court's decision becomes final and cannot be reviewed by any court.

The Supreme Court's April 2003 decision holds that once a civil litigant has been informed of the right to have the trial conducted by a District Judge, entering a general appearance before a Magistrate Judge constitutes consent to the Magistrate Judge's hearing the case.[6]

---

[5] Originally, this court was known as the U.S. Court of Claims. The Federal Courts Improvement Act of 1982 created the U.S. Claims Court. The court was redesignated again, as the U.S. Court of Federal Claims, by the Federal Courts Admin. Act of 1992, P.L. 102-572.

[6] Roell v. Withrow, 538 U.S. 589 (2003).

[A] Federal Rules Amendments

In nearly every year, the Supreme Court approves a series of amendments to the Federal Rules of Civil Procedure (FRCP). The rules take effect in December of the year of promulgation unless Congress moves to prevent effectiveness. No new FRCP rules took effect December 1, 2008. The rules taking effect December 1, 2007 are:

- Rule 4: 4(k), on territorial limits of service, says that personal jurisdiction is obtained over a defendant "when authorized by a federal statute"; the provision referring to federal interpleader jurisdiction under 28 USC § 1135 is removed because it is a federal statute and hence the statement is redundant
- Rule 5.2: In general, court filings (electronic or paper) that include a Social Security Number or tax identification number, a minor's name, a person's birthdate, or financial account information must be redacted to protect privacy. (The court can order otherwise if appropriate.) The redaction requirement does not apply to certain official records, e.g., identification of property subject to forfeiture. The court can order a complete filing under seal, and then the filing can later be unsealed or republished in redacted form. Courts can protect private or sensitive information by requiring additional redaction, limiting nonparty electronic access to documents. The rule also provides for remote electronic access to court files in Social Security Act cases and immigration proceedings involving removal or detention. Protection under this rule is waived if a party files its own information without redaction and not under seal.
- Rule 11: 11(a), governing signatures of pleadings and motions, now requires the signer's e-mail address to be included on the paper
- Rule 14: the plaintiff is allowed to bring in a third party whenever the defendant would be entitled to; 14(b) has been amended to allow the plaintiff to assert third-party "claims" rather than just "counterclaims"
- Rule 16: the previous language about the court requiring a party or the party's representative to be reasonably available "by telephone" to consider possible settlements has been changed to require availability by "other means"
- Rule 26: Rule 26(a)(1) and (a)(3) disclosures, and discovery requests, require the signer's telephone number and e-mail address; discovery requests, responses, and objections can be premised on an intention to establish new law, as long as a non-frivolous argument can be made
- Rule 30: any party, not just the one that noticed the deposition, can have the deposition transcribed, and it is no longer required that the deposition was taken by non-stenographic means
- Rule 31: any party noticing a deposition by written questions must inform all the other parties once the deposition is taken, so they can use it, and all other parties are entitled to prompt notice when the deposition by written questions is filed

- Rule 36: once an admission has been incorporated in a pretrial order, Rule 16(d) or (e) must be followed to amend or withdraw it; for other admissions, Rule 36(b) applies
- Rule 40: courts are given greater discretion in scheduling cases for trial
- Rule 71.1: the notice condemning real or personal property must inform the defendant that a notice of appearance can be filed even by a defendant who does not serve an answer; the notice must include the telephone number and e-mail address of the plaintiff's attorney as well as the attorney's name and address
- Rule 78: because of changes in Rule 16, it is no longer necessary for judges to make Rule 78 orders to advance, conduct or hear an action.[7]

In April of 2006, the Supreme Court adopted a rule change to FRAP 32.1. As of January 1, 2007, unpublished opinions can be cited in federal appellate briefs, but appellate courts are not required to treat even their own unpublished opinions as precedential, and can ignore them. The new rule does not impose any mandates, or even provide guidance, as to when a court can designate an opinion as unpublished.[8]

Rule 37(f) took effect December 1, 2007. Absent exceptional circumstances, sanctions cannot be imposed for failure to produce information formerly stored electronically but lost due to routine good-faith operation of the system. However, the rule applies only to sanctions under the FRCP, not other systems such as the rules of professional responsibility or the court's inherent power to impose sanctions, and it does not prevent the court from imposing punitive elements in managing discovery, such as a longer cutoff date or permitting one party to take additional depositions. Furthermore, if there is a preservation obligation, Rule 37(f) may require parties to modify their systems to reduce the extent to which data is routinely destroyed (e.g., by automatic overwriting of files).[9]

In December, 2006, the Eighth Circuit announced that it would adopt an electronic case filing system for appeals, and the other Circuits were expected to do the same shortly thereafter. In the District Courts, pleadings, motions, briefs, and exhibits are served on opposing counsel using PDF files rather than paper documents. Because most of the documents in the District Court records are already digitized, appellate e-filing was expected to proceed fairly smoothly. However, it was expected that Courts of Appeals would continue to require briefs and appendices to be filed on paper to supplement the e-file.[10]

---

[7] http://www.uscourts.gov/rules/newrules6.html.

[8] Tony Mauro Supreme Court Votes to Allow Citation to Unpublished Opinions in Federal Courts, Legal Times 4/12/06 (law.com); Howard J. Bashman, To Cite or Not to Cite to Non-Precedential Opinions Special to law.com 3/6/06.

[9] Kevin F. Brady, *What Protection Does Rule 37(f) Provide?* The Legal Intelligencer 7/3/07 (law.com).

[10] Howard J. Bashman, *Electronic Filing on Appeal: What Does the Future Hold?* Special to law.com (11/20/06).

§ 22.03   JURISDICTION

The first hurdle toward getting any matter heard in court is jurisdiction. Clearly, no court can handle a matter over which it lacks jurisdiction. Certain areas of the law and causes of action are completely federal, so state courts have no jurisdiction over them. This could occur because the cause of action arises under a federal statute, and there is no counterpart state statute; or because Congress has preempted the field, expressly or impliedly preventing state law-making on the subject. Federal jurisdiction is exclusive with respect to, e.g.,

- Bankruptcy[11]
- Patents
- Trademarks
- Copyrights
- IRS actions
- Customs
- Admiralty
- Fines and forfeitures imposed under federal law.

The scope of exclusive state jurisdiction is much narrower: only probate and certain aspects of family law fall into this category.

See § 22.03[E] below for in personam jurisdiction. In rem jurisdiction is provided by 28 USC § 1655. The property interest in the claim being litigated in a lien enforcement or quiet title action is a res located within the district in which the owner of the claim is domiciled.

[A] Federal Question Jurisdiction

Between the two extremes of federal and state exclusive jurisdiction falls a vast group of cases, including diversity cases (involving citizens of different states) and federal question cases. At least theoretically, such cases could be brought in state court (thus foregoing remedies under federal law); brought in state court, then removed to federal court; brought in federal court; or there could be separate proceedings in each system. "Supplemental jurisdiction" (formerly known as pendent and ancillary jurisdiction) is present when the federal court has the option of either hearing or remanding causes of action that could properly be brought in state court.

---

[11] BCode § 505(a) authorizes bankruptcy courts to redetermine a debtor's tax liability. However, the 1982 tax bill, TEFRA, mandates determination of tax treatment of partnership items at the partnership level. When the federal government submitted a $13.1 million tax claim in a Chapter 11 proceeding, the District Court held that it lacked subject matter jurisdiction over partnership items administratively determined by the IRS. The Ninth Circuit rejected that argument, holding that the Bankruptcy Code gives the bankruptcy courts subject matter jurisdiction to review the tax treatment of partnership items: Central Valley Ag Enters. v. United States, 531 F.3d 750 (9th Cir. 2008).

The federal courts have "subject matter jurisdiction" or "federal question jurisdiction" in cases involving the laws passed by Congress, and the administrative and executive-branch rulings implementing those laws, or arising under federal common law. Cases arising under state laws that incorporate federal law cannot be brought in federal court, because there is no federal question jurisdiction. Under *American National Red Cross v. S.G.*,[12] the basic requisite is that the face of the complaint (not just the defendant's answer or special defenses) must establish federal subject matter jurisdiction.

In a dispute over termination of retiree health benefits, the Ninth Circuit ruled that it had an independent obligation to inquire whether it had subject matter jurisdiction, and determined that it did not. ERISA does not mandate vesting of welfare benefits, making vesting a matter of private contract. The benefits were not vested, because the employer explicitly retained the right to modify or terminate the benefits. In the Ninth Circuit's analysis, the absence of vested benefits meant that the Court of Appeals did not have jurisdiction over the matter.[13]

Under the Federal Employees Health Benefit Act (FEHBA), the Office of Personnel Management negotiates health benefit plans for federal employees. State law is preempted with respect to any contract relating to the nature, provision, or extent of coverage or benefits or payment of FEHBA benefits (5 USC § 8902(m)(1)). The Office of Personnel Management is the only appropriate defendant in such cases (5 CFR § 890.107(c)) so coverage and benefit disputes are heard in the federal court system. The Supreme Court ruled that 28 USC § 1331 does not apply when an insurer sought repayment of its payments to a federal employee injured in an automobile accident: a case arises under federal law if the complaint shows that the cause of action is created by federal law, or the plaintiff's right to relief depends on resolution of a substantial question of federal law. Here, the insurer's recovery depended on concepts of recovery from the tortfeasor and subrogation that are usually governed by state law.[14]

The Fifth Circuit dismissed a suit brought by a trademark litigant who charged his lawyer with malpractice. The suit was originally filed in state court; the lawyer removed it to federal court on the grounds that the case depended on questions of federal trademark law. The dissatisfied client tried to remand the case to state court. The District Court found federal jurisdiction under 28 USC §§ 1331, 1338(a), and 1651 (the All Writs Act). However, the Fifth Circuit ruled that federal jurisdiction requires more than a substantial federal question. The federal issue must actually be in dispute; must be necessary to resolve a state claim; must be substantial; and the assertion of federal jurisdiction must not disturb the balance of judicial responsibility between the federal and state systems. In this case, the Fifth Circuit found the federal issue to be insubstantial, and the federal interest weak. The main issue in the case was whether the plaintiff had attained secondary

---

[12] 505 U.S. 249 (1992).

[13] Poore v. Simpson Paper Co., 544 F.3d 1062 (9th Cir. 2008).

[14] Empire Healthchoice Assurance, Inc. v. McVeigh, 547 U.S. 677 (2006).

meaning in the controverted trademark, which was highly significant to him but had little generalized impact on federal law. Attorney malpractice has traditionally been a state cause of action, and it would burden the federal system to require it to handle every case alleging legal malpractice involving federal issues.[15]

In a payday loan usury case where the lender sought to compel arbitration, the Eleventh Circuit held that the District Court in fact had subject matter jurisdiction and should not have dismissed the case. A District Court has federal question jurisdiction over a petition, under FAA § 4, to compel arbitration if the underlying dispute states a federal question. If the case had been brought in federal court under the Declaratory Judgment Act, it would have arisen under federal law, and the usury claim under state RICO could equally well have been brought as a federal RICO claim. The potential for federal claims defeated the plaintiff's argument that the case was not removable because he raised only state claims.[16]

The "probate exception" to federal jurisdiction places cases about probate and estate administration under state-court jurisdiction. The exception is usually applied in diversity cases, but the Seventh Circuit ruled in 2006 that it can also be used to rule out federal question jurisdiction (in this case, in a case alleging improprieties in a guardianship). The Seventh Circuit said that the plaintiff was not attacking the state court judgment, but the probate exception might still preclude federal jurisdiction. In effect, she was asking the federal court to administer the father's guardianship estate, which is not permissible. The plaintiff raised tort claims about breach of fiduciary duty, but the parties were non-diverse.[17]

The Supreme Court construed the probate exception in 2006, holding that the federal District Court had jurisdiction over celebrity Anna Nicole Smith's counterclaim to her stepson's defamation claims in Smith's bankruptcy case. She alleged that her late husband, who did not provide for her by will, intended her to benefit from trusts. The stepson charged her with defamation; she charged the son with tortious interference in her expectations in gifts from her deceased husband. The District Court awarded over $80 million to Smith for tortious interference with her expectancy. The Ninth Circuit held that the probate exception meant that there was no federal jurisdiction; the Supreme Court held that the District Court had jurisdiction over Smith's counterclaim, because it did not involve probate or estate legislation, only a dispute among potential heirs that did not affect the probate of the decedent's will.[18]

---

[15] Singh v. Duane Morris LLP, 538 F.3d 334 (5th Cir. 2008); Air Measurement Tech., Inc. v. Akin Gump Strauss Hauer & Feld LLP, 504 F.3d 1262 (Fed. Cir. 2007) did find federal jurisdiction over a malpractice case about a patent suit, but the Fifth Circuit suggested that the federal interest might be greater in a patent case.

[16] Community State Bank v. Strong, 485 F.3d 597 (11th Cir. 2007).

[17] Jones v. Brennan, 465 F.3d 304 (7th Cir. 8/14/06).

[18] Marshall v. Marshall, 547 U.S. 293 (2006). Post-*Marshall*, the Second Circuit ruled that the exception had been limited to the point that federal jurisdiction should be declined only if the plaintiff attempts to probate a will or reach a res that is in state custody: Lefkowitz v. Bank of New York, 528 F.3d 102 (2d Cir. 2007); *see* Mark Hamblett, *2nd Circuit Re-Examines Standard for Probate Exception*, N.Y.L.J. 7/3/07 (law.com).

A 2003 First Circuit case holds that once a federal court determines that subject matter jurisdiction is lacking, 28 USC § 1447(c) requires remand. The court cannot dismiss the case on its merits, because a court that cannot hear a case cannot rule on its merits.[19] A contemporary case from the Ninth Circuit reads § 1447(c) to require a remand of the removed case to state court, but supplemental state claims need not be remanded if the District Court dismisses a nonfrivolous federal claim that supported the removal. The statute gives the District Court jurisdiction over the supplemental claims, and therefore the discretion to retain those claims.[20]

According to the Fourth Circuit, the FRCP 11(c)(1)(A) safe harbor, under which a party has 21 days to escape sanctions by withdrawing an improper pleading, is not jurisdictional. It is purely a claim-processing rule, not a prerequisite of the District Court's subject matter jurisdiction. The practical effect is that it can be forfeited if the sanctioned party does not make a timely objection. In an appropriate case, however, the Court of Appeals has the discretion to act to correct plain error.[21]

[B] Diversity Jurisdiction

Note: 2005 federal legislation requires many mass-tort cases to be brought in federal rather than state court; see § 22.09[E].

The Constitution permits federal courts to hear diversity cases because of a fear that the courts of one state would fail to deal fairly with out-of-state plaintiffs. Although there is no dollar limit on federal question cases, diversity cases must have an amount in controversy of at least $75,000, not counting interest and costs. (Prior to the Federal Courts Improvement Act of 1996, P.L. 104-317, 28 USC § 1332(a) required only $50,000.) In determining whether the $75,000 requirement has been satisfied, the amount claimed by the plaintiff controls if the claim is made in good faith. A complaint will be dismissed for failure to satisfy this requirement only if, on its face, the complaint could not support an award of the jurisdictional amount. If the actual result of the suit is that the plaintiff prevails but is awarded less than $75,000, 28 USC § 1332(b) gives the District Court the discretion to deny an award of costs to the plaintiff, or even to require the plaintiff to pay the defendant's costs.

The amount in controversy (i.e., the nonexistent monetary award or the amount sought by the party seeking to overturn the arbitrator's decision) in a suit to reverse an arbitration award that went against the plaintiff (i.e., where the award is $0) determines whether or not the federal court has jurisdiction. After the Ninth Circuit withdrew a decision and replaced it with another that did not define the amount in controversy but held that the District Court had subject

---

[19] Mills v. Harmon Law Offices, 344 F.3d 42 (1st Cir. 2003).

[20] Albinigia VersicherungsAG v. Schenker Int'l Inc., 344 F.3d 931 (9th Cir. 2003).

[21] Brickwood Contractors Inc. v. Datanet Eng'g Inc., 369 F.3d 385 (4th Cir. 2004).

matter jurisdiction on the basis of the federal question presented,[22] the Ninth Circuit subsequently held that the amount in controversy is the amount sought by the party seeking to vacate the award. (However, in this case the District Court heard the case and upheld the $0 award, and in turn was affirmed by the Ninth Circuit for doing so.)[23]

A single plaintiff suing a single defendant can aggregate claims to reach the $75,000 limit, even if the claims are not related. However, if the plaintiff sues multiple defendants, the claims against EACH defendant must be at least $75,000. Nor can multiple plaintiffs aggregate claims against a single defendant to reach the $75,000 mark.[24]

District Courts have supplemental jurisdiction under 26 USC § 1367 over unnamed class members who do not meet the amount in controversy requirement for diversity jurisdiction.[25]

The Ninth Circuit ruled that the defendants (credit card issuers) could not create diversity jurisdiction by requesting injunctive relief against credit card holders whose individual claims for fraud and breach of contract were less than $75,000. The plaintiff's claims for disgorgement and punitive damages do not create a common undivided interest satisfying the jurisdictional minimum.[26]

In 1999, the Eleventh Circuit held that punitive damages can be aggregated in a class action if the award reflects the wrongfulness of the defendant's conduct rather than a particular person's damages. However, the Eleventh Circuit reheard the case and reversed itself in 2000. The Eleventh Circuit now takes the position that neither punitive damages nor attorneys' fees can be aggregated toward the $75,000 minimum in a class action. Instead, the amount in controversy depends on pro rata allocation of the claimed punitive damages and fees. Furthermore, where the relevant statute gives class members a separate and distinct right to recover attorneys' fees, and the fee award compensates class members for their injuries, the fees cannot be aggregated toward the jurisdictional minimum. Plaintiffs argued that the injunctive relief they sought was worth more than $75,000, but on rehearing the court noted that the defendant could comply with an injunction by raising store prices rather than lowering catalogue prices, which would not help the plaintiff. There were too many possible variations in pricing behavior for this to satisfy the amount in controversy requirement.[27]

---

[22] Luong v. Circuit City, 356 F.3d 1188 (9th Cir. 2004), *withdrawn and replaced by*, 368 F.3d 1109 (9th Cir. 2004).

[23] Theis Research Inc. v. Brown & Bain, 386 F.3d 1180 (9th Cir. 2004). The Eleventh Circuit held in 2005 that the amount in controversy requirement is satisfied when a plaintiff seeks over $75,000 in a new arbitration hearing to vacate a $0 award: Peebles v. Merrill Lynch, 431 F.3d 1320 (11th Cir. 2005).

[24] Nor can multiple punitive damage claims be aggregated to reach the necessary level: Ard v. Transcontinental Gas Pipeline, 139 F.3d 596 (5th Cir. 1998).

[25] Free v. Abbott Labs Inc., 529 U.S. 333 (2000).

[26] McCauley v. Ford Motor Co., 264 F.3d 952 (9th Cir. 2001).

[27] Cohen v. Office Depot, 184 F.3d 1292 (11th Cir. 1999), *rev'd*, 204 F.3d 1069 (11th Cir. 2000).

FRCP 13 provides that if the plaintiff's claim is over $75,000 and the defendant asserts a compulsory counterclaim of any size, the District Court can entertain the counterclaim (even if the original claim is subsequently dismissed). However, a permissive counterclaim requires its own jurisdictional basis, and thus must be over $75,000. But a cross-claim arises out of the same transaction as the plaintiff's underlying claim and does not require an independent basis of jurisdiction. If Rule 14 impleader occurs with respect to an amount under $75,000, the court will nevertheless take supplemental jurisdiction of the impleaded claim.

The Eastern District of Pennsylvania refused to aggregate spouses' claims (one for negligence, one for loss of consortium) in a slip-and-fall case. Therefore, the two claims (about $50,000 each) were insufficient for federal diversity jurisdiction, and the case was remanded to state court.[28] The spousal community of interest is not enough to create a single right or title allegedly worth $75,000 or more. In this reading, the removing party has the burden of proving the amount in controversy — and when in doubt, a court should remand the case to a state court rather than retaining it within the federal system.

28 USC § 1332(c) makes a corporation not only a citizen of the state in which it is incorporated, but also of the state in which it has its principal place of business. This provision was added because it is very common for corporations to incorporate in Delaware or another corporate haven, even though they actually do business in another state. An unincorporated association is a citizen of every state in which any member is a citizen.

In January 2006, the Supreme Court resolved a circuit split by deciding that a national bank is a citizen of one state (not multiple states): the location of its main office as designated in the articles of association.[29]

The Fifth Circuit ruled that, for diversity purposes, the citizenship of an LLC is determined by the citizenship of all its members (rather than by the state in which it is organized), thereby joining the First and Seventh Circuits.[30]

Initially, diversity suits required "complete diversity": the suit could not be brought if there was any overlap in citizenship between any plaintiff or party aligned with the plaintiffs, and any defendant or aligned party. This requirement could be very difficult to meet in multi-party litigation.

Therefore, in a derivative suit (see § 22.09[F]), even though the corporation is the supposed beneficiary of the suit, it is aligned with the defendants in determining diversity. Otherwise, federal derivative suits would be impossible, because the corporation and its officers have the same citizenship, and considering the corporation a plaintiff would destroy diversity. For the same reason, some federal statutes permit suit to be brought on the basis of "minimal" rather than "complete"

---

[28] Sdregas v. Home Depot Inc. (S.D. Pa.), discussed in Shannon P. Duffy, *Aggregation Aggravation*, The Legal Intelligencer, 4/8/02 (law.com).

[29] Wachovia Bank, N.A. v. Schmidt, 546 U.S. 303 (2006).

[30] Harvey v. Grey Wolf Drilling Co., No. 07-31106 (5th Cir. 9/15/08), following Pramco, LLC *ex rel.* CFSC Consortium, LLC v. San Juan Bay Marina Inc., 435 F.3d 51 (1st Cir. 2006); Wise v. Wachovia Secs., LLC., 450 F.3d 265 (7th Cir. 2006).

diversity; there can be some overlap in citizenship, as long as all plaintiffs and all defendants are not citizens of the same state.

Plaintiffs have some degree of control over party alignments. For instance, if naming a particular defendant would destroy diversity, the plaintiff can simply refrain from naming that defendant — unless he, she, or it is an indispensable party (see § 5080), in which case the action must be dismissed. This degree of control is not unlimited, however, in that 28 USC § 1359 denies the District court jurisdiction over any civil action in which the party alignments are improper or collusively made to create diversity jurisdiction.

Under *Caterpillar Inc. v. Lewis*,[31] as long as the federal jurisdictional requirements are satisfied by the time a judgment is reached, it is permissible if diversity was not complete as of the time the case was removed to federal court.

The other side of the coin is that a party's change of citizenship subsequent to the filing of a suit will not cure a lack of subject matter jurisdiction that existed when the diversity suit was filed. Subject matter jurisdiction depends on the facts at the time of filing.[32]

[C] Abstention

The federal courts already have an ample workload, and are not actively seeking to increase it. In many situations, they will "abstain" (refrain from hearing a case until state proceedings have been completed). Abstention serves two purposes. First of all, the parties may be satisfied by the state resolution, thus leading to withdrawal or dismissal of the federal action (and reducing the federal caseload). Second, by waiting for the state decision, the federal courts sometimes avoid inconsistent rulings.

There are at least five major rationales for federal abstention.

(1) *Colorado River Conservation District v. U.S.*, 424 U.S. 800 (1976): Federal courts can dismiss actions whose parties have a similar action pending in state court. Cases of this kind fall into three general categories: federal jurisdiction has been invoked for the purpose of restraining state criminal proceedings; the case involves major policy issues that transcend the dispute between these particular parties; and cases involving a Constitutional issue that could be mooted by a state court decision on state law.

(2) *Ankenbrandt v. Richards*, 504 U.S. 689 (1992): Even if diversity is present, federal courts will abstain from asserting jurisdiction over domestic relations actions involving divorce, alimony, or child custody.

(3) *Younger v. Harris*, 401 U.S. 37 (1971): No injunction will be issued against state proceedings.

---

[31] 519 U.S. 611 (1996).
[32] Grupo Dataflex v. Atlas Global Group, LP, 541 U.S. 567 (2004).

The Fourth Circuit ruled that the federal court should have heard a case about certification of solid waste disposers, because the overwhelming federal interest in freedom of interstate commerce meant that there was no state interest sufficient to justify *Younger* abstention.[33]

    (4)   *Railroad Commission of Texas v. Pullman Co.*, 312 U.S. 496 (1941): State law issue has to be decided before federal question.

    (5)   *Burford v. Sun Oil Co.*, 319 U.S. 315 (1943): Abstention in cases involving complex questions of state law with minimal federal issues.

In the fall of 2004, the Ninth Circuit applied *Younger* abstention to a 42 USC § 1983 [civil rights] suit for money damages, but ruled that the federal case should be stayed rather than dismissed if the parallel state proceedings: are ongoing; affect important state issues; and permit litigation of federal Constitutional issues.[34]

Pullman abstention came into play in a 2005 Supreme Court case. The petitioners raised takings claims in connection with a local ordinance imposing a fee on conversion of hotel rooms. The petitioners' argument was, that because takings claims do not ripen until the state fails to provide adequate compensation, they would be forced to keep their claims in the state courts and would never be able to seek federal review unless an exception were granted to the full faith and credit principle. The Supreme Court ruled against them, and would not allow federal takings claims that were reserved in state court to be reviewed de novo. The Supreme Court would not permit full faith and credit to be ignored merely to preserve takings claims, except in situations where a later statute expressly or partially repeals 28 USC § 1738 (the full faith and credit requirement).[35]

In 2005, the Supreme Court held that the *Rooker-Feldman* doctrine (which holds that only the Supreme Court, not the federal District Courts, can review state court judgments) should be applied narrowly. However, if both federal and state lawsuits have been filed, the *Rooker-Feldman* doctrine is not triggered just because judgment has been entered in a state case. It is possible that comity or abstention will preclude continued litigation, but in this case, the Supreme Court clarified that *Rooker* and *Feldman* do not remove properly invoked concurrent jurisdiction when a state court decides an issue while the case is still pending before the federal court. 28 USC § 1738 requires federal courts to give state court judgments the same preclusive effect that another court of that state would give, and if the District Court has subject-matter jurisdiction, it can exercise it even if a party tries to litigate in federal court a matter that has already been litigated in state court. In this case, involving a royalties dispute about joint ventures to manufacture polyethylene in Saudi Arabia, Exxon apparently sued in federal court to protect itself in

---

[33] Harper v. Public Serv. Comm'n of W. Va., 396 F.3d 348 (4th Cir. 2005).

[34] Gilbertson v. Albright, 381 F.3d 965 (9th Cir. 2004).

[35] San Remo Hotel v. San Francisco, CA, 545 U.S. (2005) 323.

case it lost in state court for reasons (e.g., statute of limitations) that would not preclude federal relief.[36]

The Supreme Court returned to examine *Rooker-Feldman* preemption in its February 21, 2006, decision.[37] The Supreme Court held that the holding under *Exxon Mobil Corp. v. Saudi Basic Industries Corp.* is that the District Court is not an appropriate forum for those who lose in state court to challenge the state court's judgments. However, a plaintiff cannot be barred from bringing suit in the District Court merely on the grounds that the plaintiff is in privity with a party who lost in state court.

[D] Supplemental Jurisdiction

Once a court already has jurisdiction over all the parties, it promotes judicial economy for all claims to be handled in a single proceeding. In 1990, 28 USC was amended by the enactment of a new § 1367, covering supplemental jurisdiction, encompassing the concepts of pendent and ancillary jurisdiction. In April 2003, the Supreme Court upheld 28 USC § 1367(d) (tolling of the statute of limitations on state claims that are pending in federal court under supplemental jurisdiction), finding it appropriate under the "necessary and proper" clause that gives Congress the power to make laws to implement federal powers.[38]

Generally, a District Court having federal question or diversity jurisdiction over a matter must also exercise supplemental jurisdiction over all claims. These would include those involving joinder or intervention of additional parties that are related enough to the original claims to be part of the same "case or controversy." But in a diversity case, the court cannot exercise supplemental jurisdiction over claims against additional parties if the effect would be to destroy diversity.

The exceptions to the general rule are found in 28 USC § 1367(c), which allows the court to decline to exercise supplemental jurisdiction over a related claim if:

- The claim raises novel or complex issues of state law
- The related claim "substantially predominates" over the claim over which the federal court has jurisdiction
- The District Court has already dismissed all other claims in the case
- Exceptional circumstances provide compelling reasons to decline jurisdiction.

A supplemental claim that the District Court has refused to hear can be re-filed in state court.

Claims under the supplemental jurisdiction statute must still satisfy the $75,000 minimum, and it is not permitted for several plaintiffs to aggregate

---

[36] Exxon Mobil Corp. *et al.* v. Saudi Basic Indust. Corp., 544 U.S. 280 (2005).

[37] Lance v. Dennis, 546 U.S. 459 (2006).

[38] Jinks v. Richland Co., S.C., 538 U.S. 456 (2003).

their claims to reach the $75,000 level.[39] However, if one plaintiff has a $75,000 claim, it is permissible for other plaintiffs with smaller claims to "piggyback" their claims.[40]

[E] In Personam Jurisdiction

Due process requires that there must be at least minimum contacts between a party and the forum in which that party is being sued. Either there must be property of the defendant's within the state, which can be attached, or it must be possible to secure personal (in personam) jurisdiction against the party within the state in which the court sits, based on that person's "presence" (even temporary) within that state so that the summons and complaint can be served. Note that parties who enter a state specifically to testify or otherwise participate in another trial are immune from service of process during their limited-purpose presence in the state. A corporation is considered "present" within any state (not just its state of incorporation) if it has had continuous and systematic activities within the state.

A contract was drafted and revised by e-mail; signed by both parties; but never performed because the business relationship fell apart. The case was brought in Massachusetts state court under the state long-arm statute; removed to federal court; and dismissed by the District Court for lack of minimum contacts with Massachusetts. The First Circuit affirmed the dismissal, defining the prima facie standard for jurisdiction as whether the plaintiff's evidence, if believed, will support findings of all the facts needed to support personal jurisdiction. For specific jurisdiction, the constitutional analysis involves relatedness, purposeful availment, and reasonableness. The claim must directly arise out of, or at least relate to, the defendant's forum-state activities. The defendant's contacts in the state must represent purposeful availment of the privilege of operating in the forum state. Exercise of federal jurisdiction must be reasonable. In this case, the First Circuit found that the terms of the employment contract were not entered into in the forum state, and the potential employee would not have had ongoing contact with the forum state during performance of the contract. Mailing a contract to Massachusetts for signature and sending three e-mails was held not to be sufficient to support jurisdiction. The defendant's principal place of business was in Illinois; the defendant wanted to call many Illinois witnesses who were not subject to Massachusetts jurisdiction; and the plaintiff did not even live in Massachusetts any more. The First Circuit ruled that the proper jurisdiction was the Central District of

---

[39] Leonhardt v. Western Sugar Co., 160 F.3d 631 (10th Cir. 1998); Meritcare Inc. v. St. Paul Mercury Ins. Co., 166 F.3d 214 (3d Cir. 1999).

[40] Free v. Abbott Labs, 529 U.S. 333 (2000); *In re* Brand Name Prescription Drugs Antitrust Litigation, 123 F.3d 599 (7th Cir. 1997). The application of this principle subjected Exxon Mobil to over $1.3 billion in damages to small gas station owners who disputed the termination of a discount program; sanctions were also imposed for frivolously prolonging the litigation: Exxon Mobil Corp. v. Allapattah Serv., 545 U.S. 546 (2005).

Illinois, where the plaintiff in this case had already been sued for breach of contract.[41]

Under 28 USC § 1653, a complaint can be amended to correct defective allegations of personal or subject matter jurisdiction at trial or on appeal. However, if actual subject matter jurisdiction is lacking (and not just the phrasing of the complaint is defective), then the case must be dismissed. The absence of subject matter jurisdiction is fundamental and not waivable, and can be raised by anyone at any stage of litigation. But personal jurisdiction can be waived, and the defendant can be estopped from raising the defense of want of personal jurisdiction — for instance, if the defendant has filed a Rule 12(g) motion to dismiss on other grounds and does not raise the lack of personal jurisdiction. Under Clayton Act § 12 (see § 8.03), personal jurisdiction over a corporate defendant is based on minimum contacts with the United States as a whole, whether or not venue is proper.[42]

A vitamin manufacturer that held a patent had a license agreement with a Florida manufacturer of generic drugs. The Florida company sought a declaration of patent noninfringement. The Federal Circuit held in 2006 that the federal court in Florida had personal jurisdiction, in light of the ongoing relationship contemplated between the two companies and letters about infringement sent to Florida customers.[43]

New York's standard for the amount of Web presence to provide long-arm jurisdiction continues to develop. A "brochure-ware" site that is, in essence, a mere billboard will not be enough to confer jurisdiction over the site owner without a tort occurring in New York or other connection to the state. If there are continuous, systematic contacts with the state that constitute presence in New York, or business is done in-state with continuity, then it is likely that general jurisdiction will be found. A non-domiciliary of the state will be subject to New York jurisdiction only in cases arising directly from contacts with New York — e.g., contracts to supply goods or services in New York; committing a tort (other than defamation) that causes injury within New York in conjunction with substantial revenue from interstate or international commerce. Most Circuits use a sliding scale (depending on whether the defendant chooses to do business on the Internet by transmitting files to customers in other states). The New York view is that even a single transaction in the state can be sufficient to grant jurisdiction, if enough other factors are present.[44]

---

[41] Phillips v. Prairie Eye Ctr., 530 F.3d 22 (1st Cir. 2008). *See also* Moelis v. Berkshire Life Ins. Co., 2008 WL 2122417 (Mass. 5/22/08) [purchase of an insurance policy from a Massachusetts insurer, and mailing premiums to Massachusetts, insufficient to confer personal jurisdiction]; Deutsche Bank Secs. Inc. v. Montana Bd. of Investments, 7 N.Y.3d 65 (2006) [nine bond sale transactions over a period of 13 months, carried on via Instant Messaging, showed availment, so New York long-arm jurisdiction was present].

[42] Action Embroidery Corp. v. Atlantic Embroidery Inc., 368 F.3d 1174 (9th Cir. 2004).

[43] Breckenridge Pharmaceutical Inc. v. Metabolite Laboratories Inc., 444 F.3d 1356 (Fed. Cir. 2006).

[44] *See, e.g.,* Warner Brothers Entertainment Inc. v. Ideal World Direct, 516 F. Supp. 2d 261 (S.D.N.Y. 2007) and Pearson Education Inc. v. Yi Shi, No. 06 Civ. 11504(VM), 2007 WL 4358455 (S.D.N.Y 12/11/07) discussed in Stephen M. Kramarsky, *When 'Web Presence' Creates Jurisdiction,*

The Internet creates many perplexing jurisdictional problems, because content placed on a server can be accessed anywhere in the world. Furthermore, many companies that do business on the Internet have very few tangible assets, and the least reputable businesses such as spammers and pornographers engage in (often successful) attempts to disguise their identity and location. See § 28.05 for additional discussion of jurisdiction issues in cyberspace.

§ 22.04 STANDING

Clearly, a federal court cannot hear a case over which it lacks jurisdiction, or for which it is an improper forum or incorrect venue. But it is equally clear that the case cannot be heard if the plaintiff is not a permissible plaintiff. Supreme Court cases[45] establish the minimum characteristics of a plaintiff who has standing to sue:

- Injury in fact which is concrete and not conjectural
- A personal stake of some kind, not mere interest as a citizen
- Causal connection between the injury and the defendant's conduct
- A decision favorable to the plaintiff would have the effect of redressing the plaintiff's injury.

Furthermore, the case must be of a type which belongs in the court system, not the legislature; so-called "political question" cases are inappropriate. The claim must also fall within the zone of interests that the statute or Constitutional provision cited seeks to protect.

Potential plaintiffs include not only individuals and business organizations but associations. An organization must satisfy various criteria[46] if it wishes to sue with regard to injuries to its members. The claims and relief of the lawsuit must be such that they can be pursued without the involvement of the individual members, yet the members must have standing to sue in their own right. Furthermore, the interests that the suit seeks to protect must be germane to the organization's purpose.

But see *Suitum v. Tahoe Regional Planning Agency*, 520 U.S. 725 (1997): a case can be ripe for adjudication even before a final and authoritative agency decision, in part because the plaintiff here merely sought compensation, and did not challenge the validity of the regulations.

N.Y.L.J. 1/17/08 (law.com). *See also* Best Van Lines v. Walker, 490 F.3d 239 (2d Cir. 2007), discussed in Beth Bar, *Mover Fails to Prove Jurisdiction in Suit Over Internet Site*, N.Y.L.J. 6/29/07 (law.com). The New York statute is CPLR § 302(a)(2). For cases that did not find jurisdiction because of lack of New York contacts, *see, e.g.*, Realuyo v. Villa Abrille, 01 Civ. 10158 (S.D.N.Y. July 8, 2003).

[45] *E.g.*, Bennett v. Spear, 520 U.S. 154 (1997) and Lujan v. Defenders of Wildlife, 504 U.S. 555 (1992).

[46] *Under* United Food & Commercial Workers v. Brown Group, Inc., 517 U.S. 544 (1996).

The Supreme Court permitted a collection agency, if it does not have a direct financial stake, to sue on behalf of its customers. In this case, a company that does billing and collection for pay phone service providers brought suit to collect from Sprint and AT&T for coinless long-distance calls over their networks, with the intention of turning over the proceeds to the pay phone service providers. The Supreme Court held that traditionally, courts have permitted the assignees of compensation claims to bring suit.[47]

§ 22.05 MOOTNESS

Not only must a case or controversy have been present to justify commencement of the suit, there must still be live controversies as the suit proceeds and through all stages until the controversy ends. A case is moot if the relief sought becomes useless because of events or the conduct of parties in litigation.[48]

If a civil case becomes moot while its appeal is pending, the federal practice is to reverse or vacate the judgment below, then remand with a direction to dismiss the now-moot case. The "collateral consequences" rule applies in criminal cases. That is, appeal of a conviction is not necessarily moot because the defendant has served the sentence for the crime, because a conviction has other consequences (including ineligibility for various jobs and potential sentence enhancement in other cases).

A case is not moot as long as even a partial remedy that is not fully satisfactory is still available. Nevertheless, mootness can arise at any stage, and cases should be dismissed whenever an intervening event prevents the Court of Appeals from granting any effectual relief to the appellant.[49]

§ 22.06 STATUTES OF LIMITATIONS

It is simple to state what a statute of limitations is: a period of time after which cases can no longer be brought, premised on the belief that the matter will be stale and reliable evidence will no longer be available — and that, in any case, it is unjust to hold a defendant liable under claims that were not pursued. The question of what the federal statute of limitations is in a particular case is much more complex — as is the question of what point the statute of limitations should be calculated from.

If the underlying right involved in the case was federally created, the statute of limitations is as prescribed by the appropriate federal statute. This seems grossly obvious; yet a number of federal statutes fail to contain an explicit limitations provision.

---

[47] Sprint v. APCC, 128 S. Ct. 2531 (2008), discussed in (AP), *Supreme Court Rules Against Long-Distance Phone Companies*, 6/23/08 (law.com).

[48] *See* Arizonans for Official English v. Arizona, 520 U.S. 43 (1997).

[49] Calderon v. Moore, 518 U.S. 149 (1996). A settlement about the legality of pop-up ads mooted an appeal despite a settlement term that required the pop-up publisher to pay $10,000 to L.L. Bean if Bean won on appeal. The Ninth Circuit treated this as a mere "side bet" on the outcome of the appeal of the declaratory judgment motion. There was no ongoing case or controversy, so the appeal became moot: Gator.com Corp. v. L.L. Bean Inc., 398 F.3d 1125 (9th Cir. 2005).

P.L. 101-650 does something to resolve this problem by imposing a fallback four-year statute of limitations with respect to federal laws enacted after December 1, 1990. That is, if such a statute does not include a statute of limitations, an action will be timely if brought within four years of the accrual of the cause of action.

The Supreme Court resolved a circuit split in a mid-2004 decision.[50] In that case, the petitioner filed a civil rights class action under 42 USC § 1981. The respondent moved for summary judgment on the grounds that the state's two-year statute of limitations barred the claim. According to the Seventh Circuit, 28 USC § 1658(a)'s four-year statute of limitations for federal statutes enacted after December 1, 1990, does not apply to a cause of action based on a post-1990 amendment to an existing statute. The Supreme Court, however, mandated application of § 1658. The purpose of providing uniformity and eliminating uncertainty would not be met if § 1658 covered only new provisions of the U.S. Code. In this case, the petitioner alleged wrongful termination, failure to transfer, and a hostile work environment; these claims arose under the Civil Rights Act of 1991 because they were made possible by this statute; racial harassment was not actionable prior to the Civil Rights Act of 1991.

In February of 2007, the Supreme Court applied a statute of limitations strictly: *see* Wallace v. Chicago Police Officers.[51] The court rejected as untimely a false imprisonment suit because the two-year statute of limitations began to run when the petitioner was bound over for trial for murder. In this case, the petition got additional time, because he was 15 when charged, so the statute was tolled until he reached 18. The Supreme Court majority rejected the argument that the statute of limitations for false arrest claims does not start to run until the conviction has been invalidated.

In mid-2007, the Supreme Court decided, in *Ledbetter v. Goodyear Tire & Rubber Co.*, 550 U.S. 618 (2007), that the statute of limitations for a pay discrimination claim begins to run when the employer made the decision to discriminate against women in terms of pay. Therefore, the Supreme Court held that equal pay claims were untimely if they were brought more than 180 days after the adoption of the discriminatory decision — whether or not they were brought within 180 days of receipt of a paycheck reflecting that discrimination.

This holding was overturned by the Lilly Ledbetter Fair Pay Act, P.L. 111-2, the first piece of legislation signed by President Obama.

Cases under pre-December 1, 1990 federal statutes "borrow" the state statute of limitations that is most closely comparable to the case at bar, unless the case involves a federally created equitable right, in which case the court makes an equitable judgment as to whether the plaintiff delayed so long in bringing the action that it would be unjust to permit it to proceed.

On the other hand, if the cause of action lies in law or equity but is not federally created, the statute of limitations is the one that applies in the state in which the District Court sits. State statutes of limitations are also applied in diversity suits in which the decision on the merits depends on state law. Many states

---

[50] Jones v. R.R. Donnelley & Sons, 541 U.S. 369 (2004).
[51] Wallace v. Chicago Police Officers, 549 U.S. 384 (2007).

have "borrowing" statutes to discourage forum-shopping: if a case was time-barred in the state where the cause of action accrued, it will also be time-barred in the state where the action is sought to be brought.

In most federal contexts, a cause of action accrues at the occurrence of the act complained of. In a limited set of circumstances (e.g., the defendant concealed the injury from the plaintiff), a "discovery" statute of limitations will apply; the cause of action will accrue at the time that the plaintiff discovered, or could have discovered with reasonable diligence, that the plaintiff's rights had been violated.

The statute of limitations is an affirmative defense, so it cannot be used as an "ambush" tactic in a case that seems to be going badly. Unless the defendant raises the statute of limitations defense as soon as possible, it is likely to be deemed waived.

In early 2000, the Supreme Court tackled the statute of limitations for civil RICO cases.[52] The statute of limitations is clearly four years — the question is when the cause of action accrues. The Supreme Court disapproved the "injury and pattern" discovery rule used in some Circuits, but did not provide clear guidance as to what would be an acceptable rule.

Injury discovery means that the cause of action accrues when the plaintiff knew or should have known that injury occurred. Injury and pattern discovery in a RICO case defers accrual until the plaintiff knows or should have known not only that injury occurred, but that there was a pattern of racketeering injury.

The Supreme Court had already rejected the "last predicate act" rule (i.e., that the cause of action accrues when the plaintiff knows or should have known of the injury and its part in a pattern of racketeering injury, with the statute of limitation restarted with each new predicate act within a pattern of injury) in 1997[53] because it could extend the statute of limitations far beyond the Congressional intent. Another reason the Supreme Court rejected the last predicate act rule is that civil RICO is patterned after the Clayton Act (see § 8.03); Clayton Act causes of injury generally accrue when an act that injures the plaintiff's business is committed.

The Supreme Court rejected the injury and pattern rule because it would allow recognition of remote acts. The RICO definition of pattern requires at least two acts in ten years, with a four-year limitation period. Theoretically, then, a 14-year period is possible. The Supreme Court felt that further extensions could impair the purpose of a statute of limitations (preventing the litigation of stale claims).

A case before the Court of Federal Claims involved allegations of unconstitutional takings of leasehold rights. The government initially took the position that the claims were untimely under the Court of Claims Statute of Limitations, but later waived that issue and won on the merits. The case was appealed to the Federal Circuit. The government did not raise the timeliness issue. The Federal Circuit raised the issue sua sponte and found the action untimely. The Supreme Court held, early in 2008, that even though the government waived the issue, the Court of Federal Claims statute of limitations required sua sponte consideration of whether the case was timely. The Supreme Court has always treated the statute of

---

[52] Rotella v. Wood, 528 U.S. 549 (2000).
[53] Klehr v. A.O. Smith Corp., 521 U.S. 179 (1997).

limitations in this situation as absolute and jurisdictional. The Supreme Court, citing stare decisis, refused to discard those precedents.[54]

The filing deadlines set out in a confirmed bankruptcy reorganization plan are determined by federal procedural rules, not state contract law. FRBP 9006(a) extends deadlines on a Sunday to the next business day. Therefore, claim objections filed on the Monday that was the first business day after the Sunday deadline were timely.[55]

In two qui tam cases, the Second Circuit held that a qui tam action cannot be maintained pro se, and that, when the United States is not a party to the action, the notice of appeal must be filed within 30 days of entry of judgment. A group of five New York City employees charged the City of New York with violating the False Claims Act by charging nonresident employees a fee equivalent to the city income tax paid by resident city employees; the theory was that nonresident employees could deduct the fee on their 1040 forms, reducing their income, thus depriving the federal government of revenue. The Southern District of New York dismissed the case on March 31, 2006, rendering final judgment on April 12. Notice of appeal was filed June 5, 2006 (53 days later), so the appeal would be timely if, and only if, the United States was considered a party (FRAP 4(a)(1)(A)). The Second Circuit ruled that the United States played no role in this case until it filed the amicus brief ordered by the court; the United States is not a party if it does not intervene or raise or deny any legal claims. The other case involved a claim that an individual applied for a reimbursement under the New York State grant program for 9/11 victims but did not pay for air purification equipment. The Second Circuit held that the owner of the air purification equipment supplier could not represent the United States, because only a licensed attorney can appear on behalf of another party.[56]

§ 22.07 VENUE

Jurisdiction determines whether or not the federal court system can handle a case at all. Venue determines which federal court is the appropriate place to hear the case. If the case is an in rem action (involving a res, or thing), then the action must be brought in the district where the res can be found—i.e., the district in which real property is located.

Venue in an in personam action (involving a person or artificial person such as a corporation) is more complex. Venue is a privilege of the defendant; it is an obligation of the plaintiff to bring suit someplace that is reasonably convenient to the defendant's residence or business, the locus of the occurrence, or both. The defendant can always waive objections to the venue chosen by the plaintiff.

The general venue rules are contained in 28 USC § 1391. Venue is always proper in the district in which a substantial part of the claim arose. If all of the

[54] John R. Sand & Gravel Co. v. United States, 128 S. Ct. 750 (2008).
[55] Siemens Energy & Automation Inc. v. Good, 389 F.3d 741 (7th Cir. 2004).
[56] United States *ex rel.* Irwin Eisenstein v. City of New York, 540 F.3d 94 (2d Cir. 2008) and United States *ex rel.* Mergent Sers. v. Flaherty, 540 F.3d 89 (2d Cir. 2008); *see* Mark Hamblett, *2nd Circuit Addresses Limits on Qui Tam Actions Under False Claims Act*, N.Y.L.J. 8/26/08 (law.com).

defendants reside in the same state, they can be sued in any district in which any defendant resides. If the defendant is not a U.S. citizen, venue can be laid in any district whatsoever.

A natural person resides in the district where his or her permanent home was located at the time the suit was commenced. Section § 1391(c) provides that a corporation resides in any district in which it is subject to personal jurisdiction. Often, a corporation will be deemed to reside in several districts — the district in which it is incorporated; where it is licensed to do business; where it is actually doing business; and where it is subject to long-arm jurisdiction. If so, venue is proper in any of those districts.

If the District Court's jurisdiction is based only on diversity, venue is proper in any district in which:

- Any defendant resides, if all the defendants are residents of the same state
- A substantial part of the events involved in the suit occurred
- The defendants were subject to personal jurisdiction as of the time the action was commenced: § 1391(a).

The § 1391(b) rules for federal question cases are quite similar, but there is an additional option of suing in any district in which ANY defendant can be found, if this is the only district in which the action can be brought.

28 USC § 1391 says that venue is proper in any judicial district in which a substantial part of the events or omissions occurred. The Second Circuit interprets this to mean that venue can be proper in multiple districts as long as a substantial part of the events occurred in each district, and as long as more than minimum contacts exist with each. The case was remanded for the Southern District of New York to determine whether it or the District of New Jersey had stronger claims to being designated the proper venue.[57]

After one District Court transfers a case to another District Court where venue is proper, the filing date for calculating the statute of limitations is the initial filing in the transferor court. The Third Circuit pointed out in 2007 that there are two kinds of transfers: under § 1404(a) [for convenience of the parties] and § 1406(a) [where the case was initially filed in the wrong district]. The Third Circuit said that the complaint was timely because it was filed within two years of the accrual of the cause of action, even though it was filed in the wrong district. However, the Eighth Circuit applies the statute of limitations of the transferor court; the Fourth, Seventh and Eleventh apply the date of the transferee court, running from the date of the transfer; the Second, Fifth, and Sixth Circuits seem to use the rules of the transferee district, but do not have recent precedents on statute of limitations in this situation.[58]

---

[57] Gulf Ins. Co. v. Glasbrenner, 417 F.3d 353 (2d Cir. 2005).

[58] Lafferty v. St. Riel, 495 F.3d 72 (3d Cir. 2007); see Shannon P. Duffy, *3rd Circuit: Federal Transfer Doesn't Reset SOL Clock*, The Legal Intelligencer 7/16/07 (law.com).

[A] Special Venue Rules

In addition to the general venue rules, there are specific venue rules for certain specialized actions. In a case involving copyrights or mask works for silicon computer chips, 28 USC § 1400(a) provides that venue can be laid in any district in which the defendant or its agent is subject to personal service. A patent infringement case (but not other types of case involving patents) may be brought in the district in which the defendant resides, or where the defendant both has a regular and established place of business and has committed acts of infringement: § 1400(b).

A corporate derivative suit (see § 1.14[B]) can be brought, under § 1401, in any judicial district in which the corporation could have sued the defendants if the corporation had been the actual plaintiff rather than the nominal beneficiary of the suit. A stakeholder bringing a § 1335 statutory interpleader action can commence suit in any district in which any claimant resides (§ 1397), and 28 USC § 2361 permits nationwide service of process in such actions.

28 USC § 1406(a) provides that if venue is improper (i.e., suit has been filed in a district that is not authorized to hear the case), the District court has the power either to transfer the case to a proper district or to dismiss it. If the forum is proper but inconvenient, § 1404(a) allows the case to be transferred to another proper district that is more convenient for parties and witnesses; § 1406(a) requires that it be a district in which the defendant(s) can be served. There is no explicit time limit for the transfer, but unreasonable delay is likely to result in denial of the request.

FRCP Rule 12(b)(3) says that, since the defendant has the privilege of determining venue, the defendant must raise the issue of improper or inconvenient venue either by including it as an ordinary defense in a responsive pleading, or by making a 12(b)(3) motion to dismiss. If the defendant files another 12(b) motion to dismiss, but fails to object to venue, the objection is waived.

§ 22.08 REMOVAL

As discussed above, there is a broad range of cases in which either state or federal litigation would be proper. In such cases, a defendant who is sued in state court has the right to have the case removed to federal court pursuant to 28 USC § 1441. The defendant might wish to do so if, for instance, it believes that the case is a complex one which will be better handled in the more sophisticated federal court system, or if the remedies available under state law are broader than the federal remedies (e.g., the state allows punitive damages or emotional distress damages that would be unavailable in the federal system). The appropriate district is the one which includes the state in which the action is pending. As discussed below, under the Class Action Fairness Act, many class actions must be brought in federal court; if the plaintiffs go to state court instead, the actions are removable.

Removal has been used as a defense tactic in many employment cases. The employer seeks to have the case removed to federal court. In many instances, however, the case was brought in state court precisely because there were no valid federal claims, and by the time the federal court remands the case to state court, the plaintiff's state claims may have become time-barred.

If the District Court has original subject-matter jurisdiction over the case, it can be removed without regard to the citizenship of the parties. Otherwise, removal is allowed only if no properly joined and served defendant is a citizen of the state in which the action is brought.

The Supreme Court interpreted the interaction between § 1441 (the removal statute) and § 1332 (diversity) in its *Lincoln Property Co. v. Roche* decision (546 U.S. 81 (2005). Virginia plaintiffs sued in Virginia state court against their building's management company, whom the plaintiffs identified as a Texas corporation. The defendant removed the case to federal court on diversity grounds. The Fourth Circuit ruled that removal was improper, because the defendant did not show that diversity was complete — it failed to show that there was no Virginia entity (such as another management company) that was the real party in interest. The Supreme Court reversed the Fourth Circuit, holding that a defendant who seeks removal has no duty to prove the nonexistence of other potential defendants who could make removal improper.

If a separate and independent claim under 28 USC § 1331 is joined with one or more claims that otherwise could not be removed, the case as a whole can be removed. However, the District Court has jurisdiction to remand any matters as to which state-law questions predominate.

Early in 2001, the Supreme Court tackled some complex removal issues. The petitioner initially sued in California state court for breach of contract and various business torts. The respondent removed the case to federal court, then had it dismissed as time-barred under the two-year California statute of limitations. The respondent is a Maryland corporation, and the suit was still timely under Maryland's three-year statute of limitations. The petitioner refiled the suit there, but it was dismissed as res judicata. In the Supreme Court view, the appropriate claim preclusion rule is the rule of the state in which the federal court sits. The Maryland court was wrong to say that dismissal in the California federal court (even a dismissal on the merits) necessarily precluded a Maryland state case. Applying the state rule serves uniformity — and discourages undesirable forum shopping.[59]

In contrast with the mass-tort situation, corporate defendants may be blocked in their quest to keep securities cases in the federal system as a result of *Kircher v. Putnam Funds Trust*.[60] SLUSA holds, at 15 USC § 77p(b), that a covered class action (one with more than 50 plaintiffs) cannot be maintained in state court. A covered class action is one involving a security that is nationally traded and listed on a national exchange. A covered class action can be removed to the federal District Court. *Kircher* arose when a class of mutual fund investors sued in state court for alleged injuries when their mutual fund holdings declined in value. When the case

---

[59] Semtek Int'l Inc. v. Lockheed Martin Corp., 531 U.S. 497 (2001).
[60] 547 U.S. 633 (2006).

was removed to District Court, the District Court sent it back to the state system, finding that the plaintiffs claimed injury as "holders" and not buyers or sellers of mutual fund shares, so § 77p(b)'s requirement of "purchase or sale" was not met. The Seventh Circuit agreed with the District Court that 28 USC § 1447(d) forbids appeal of a District Court order remanding a removed case for lack of subject matter jurisdiction. However, the Seventh Circuit decided that all covered class actions about covered securities are removable under SLUSA whether or not they are precluded — so the preclusion issue is intellectually distinct from the jurisdictional question of whether the case should be in federal court. The Supreme Court held that orders remanding a case for non-preclusion are not appealable. In the Supreme Court view, the authorization for removal (which is the key to District Court jurisdiction) is limited to cases involving claims of manipulation or untruth.[61]

[A] Removal Procedure

A defendant served with a state-court complaint has 30 days from receipt of the initial pleading to get the case removed: 28 USC § 1446(b). The documents needed for removal are:

- A cover page listing all the enclosed documents
- A signed notice of removal, containing a short and plain statement of the jurisdictional facts that entitle the defendant to remove the case
- Copies of all the papers served on the defendant in the state action
- Prompt written notice to all adverse parties that notice of removal has been filed. (Rule 5 permits service on the attorneys for the adverse parties rather than the parties themselves.)
- Any other document (e.g., certificates of service) required by the local rules of that particular District Court.

The Notice of Removal must contain:

- Identification of the District Court to which removal is sought
- The name of the case
- The state court in which it has been commenced
- Claim that federal jurisdiction exists
- Claim that removal is timely
- Joinder of all defendants.

28 USC § 1446(d) provides that removal is automatic once the petition is filed in District Court; prompt notice is given to the adverse parties; and a copy of the

---

[61] Marcia Coyle points out in *High Court Makes a Call in "Remand Wars."* Nat'l L.J. 6/16/06 (law.com) that although the *Kircher* plaintiffs can get back to state court, they will have to show that their claims do not fall into the category of "holder" (rather than "buyer" or "seller") claims that are ruled out by Merrill Lynch v. Dabit, 547 U.S. 71 (2006).

notice is filed with the clerk of the state court. The state court can no longer hear any aspect of the case, except to the extent that the District Court remands certain issues.

According to the Second Circuit, individual investors' bankruptcy-related claims under the Securities Act (the '33 Act) must be heard in federal, rather than state court. Removal of state cases to federal court is generally barred by § 22(a) of the '33 Act with no exception for cases under a statute that has an anti-removal provision — yet 28 USC § 1452(a) allows any civil action related to bankruptcy to be removed to federal court. (The general removal statute, 28 USC § 1441(a), does make such an exception.) The Second Circuit viewed this distinction as proof that Congress intended bankruptcy-related litigation to be centralized in federal court.[62]

The SLUSA (see § 6.13) requires securities law class actions with more than 50 plaintiffs to be conducted in federal rather than state courts. According to the Southern District of New York, where a class action is removed to federal court on this basis, and plaintiffs then amend the complaint to reduce the number of plaintiffs below the SLUSA threshold, and if the amendment occurs before the responsive pleading is served, the case can be remanded to state court. One amendment as of right is permitted under FRCP 15(a), and SLUSA covers only situations in which the plaintiff group exceeds 50.[63]

FRCP 81(c) provides that, if the defendant did not answer the complaint before removal, the answer has to be filed by 20 days after receipt of the initial pleading; 20 days after receipt of the summons; or five days after filing of the petition for removal — whichever is latest. If a party had already demanded jury trial at the state level, a federal demand is not required. If the case was initially brought in a state that does not require an explicit demand for jury trial, a federal demand is required only if ordered by the District Court.

A plaintiff who objects to removal has only one remedy: a motion to remand, directed to the District Court. If there is state but not federal jurisdiction, the case must be remanded; but if the state court lacked jurisdiction, the federal court must dismiss the case, not remand it. Either party can petition the District Court for remand, under 28 USC § 1447(c), at any time until the District Court has rendered a final judgment.

The Second Circuit ruled in mid-2008 that federal Magistrate Judges do not have the power to remand cases to state court under 28 USC § 1447(c). The remand decision is a dispositive matter that must be heard by a District Judge. The remand order is the functional equivalent of a motion to dismiss, and therefore disposes of the case.[64]

---

[62] CALPERS v. WorldCom Inc., 368 F.3d 86 (2d Cir. 2004).

[63] Spehar v. Fuchs, 72 L.W. 1014 (S.D.N.Y. 6/17/03).

[64] Williams v. Beemiller, Inc., 527 F.3d 259; *see* Mark Hamblett, *2nd Circuit Holds Magistrates Lack Power to Remand*, N.Y.L.J. 6/2/08 (law.com); the Third, Sixth, and Tenth Circuits have also treated a remand order as dispositive.

Should the case be remanded, that terminates the federal court's jurisdiction. Once the federal court mails a certified copy of the remand order to the clerk of the state court, the state court can resume hearing the case. In general, an order of remand is not reviewable by either appeal or mandamus, although the remand of civil rights cases removed under 28 USC § 1443 is appealable.

The Eleventh Circuit view is that, when considering the appropriateness of removal of a diversity case, the District Court can properly consider evidence submitted after the filing of the removal petition, as long as the evidence reflects events as of the time of removal.[65]

§ 22.09 JOINDER OF PARTIES AND CLAIMS

Not all actions conclude with the same line-up of parties and the same list of issues that they had at commencement. For various reasons, it may be either obligatory or permissible to add further parties and the consideration of new issues to the action. The objective is to prevent what is essentially the same case from being relitigated. At best, relitigation is wasteful of limited resources of the court system; at worst, it creates inconsistent rulings that have to be reconciled via further litigation.

Rule 18(a) allows, but does not require, joinder of all legal or equitable claims against any opposing party. The claims can be added as either independent or alternate claims. Rule 13 covers claims by one party against one or more other parties. Such a claim is treated as a 13(a) compulsory counterclaim if it arises out of the transaction or occurrence that is the subject of the main action, in that it:

- Raises similar issues of law and fact
- Could not be brought as a separate suit if it were not brought as a counterclaim, because res judicata (see § 22.12) would apply
- The same evidence either proves or disproves the claim and the counterclaim
- The claim and the counterclaim are logically related.

Failure to raise a compulsory counterclaim generally prevents the counterclaim from being raised in subsequent litigation, but there are various exceptions to this rule:

- The claim requires the presence of certain third parties over whom the court does not have jurisdiction
- When the complaint was served, the potential counterclaim had not yet matured
- When the action was initiated, the potential counterclaim was part of another pending suit

---

[65] Sierminski v. Transouth Fin. Corp., 216 F.3d 945 (11th Cir. 2000). Because of Eleventh Circuit precedent, the defendant can be placed in the odd position of having to prove that if the plaintiff wins, damages will be higher than those asserted by the plaintiff.

- The original action involved a property interest, and the court never obtained personal jurisdiction over the party who could have asserted the counterclaim.

Under Rule 13(f), either party can secure permission from the court to amend a pleading to add an omitted counterclaim.

Understandably enough, Rule 13(b) classifies all counterclaims that are not compulsory as permissive. Permissive counterclaims are those that do not arise out of the same transaction or occurrence as the main action. (The theory is that if the plaintiff is permitted to join unrelated claims in a single action, the defendant should be granted the same latitude.) A permissive counterclaim must have its own basis for federal jurisdiction (subject matter or diversity). It is up to the discretion of the court to permit or deny the inclusion of permissive counterclaims in a suit. If permission is denied, the defendant can bring an independent lawsuit; those claims are not precluded because they are not related to the original transaction or occurrence.

[A] Cross-Claims

A cross-claim, as defined by Rule 13(g), is brought by a party against a coparty who is on the same side in the action. All cross-claims are permissive, not compulsory, so the potential cross-claimant can also become the plaintiff in a suit involving such claims. A cross-claim must either:

- Arise out of the suit's underlying transaction or occurrence
- Arise out of the counterclaim in that action
- Relate to property that is the subject matter of the suit.

The court has discretion, under Rule 13(h), to join additional persons or entities who are not parties to the original action, thus making them parties to a counter or cross-claim, but only if a claim is asserted against the new party in conjunction with at least one existing party. On the other hand, 13(i) also gives the court discretion to order one or more separate trials with respect to counter- or cross-claims that are unrelated to the main action or involve too many disparate issues.

[B] Joinder of Parties

Joinder of parties under Rule 19, like joinder of issues, can be either compulsory or permissive. The rule is that anyone who can be served and joined without depriving the court of its jurisdiction (e.g., a non-diverse party in a pure diversity suit) should be joined, if the result of non-joinder would be that the existing parties would not be able to secure relief, or if their absence could impair the interest that the potentially joined party claims in the subject property. Rule 19(b) provides that if it is impossible to join a person or entity who should be joined, the court must decide whether to proceed without that party, or dismiss the case.

Permissive joinder is governed by Rule 20. Subject to the discretion of the court, anyone who asserts or defends against joint, several, or alternative claims that arise out of the same transaction or occurrence as the suit can be joined in the action, as long as at least some common questions of law or fact apply to all the parties joined. But if joinder would not promote justice, 20(b) authorizes the court to order separate trials or make other orders needed to prevent prejudice or delay to the parties.

Rule 21 provides that actions cannot be dismissed for misjoinder of parties; as long as the parties are not prejudiced, parties can be dropped or new parties added in response to a motion by a litigant, or sua sponte on the court's own motion. The court also has the power to order severance if venue is proper for some defendants but not others. Also see Rule 25, governing substitution of parties (e.g., when a party dies or becomes incapacitated; when an official sued in official capacity is replaced by a new officeholder).

[C] Third-Party Practice

Impleader, under Rule 14, also known as third-party practice, allows a defending party to a suit (a defendant; a plaintiff subject to a counterclaim; someone already brought in as a third-party defendant) to implead (i.e., bring in) a nonparty who may be liable to that party on any pending claim. Thus, it differs from counterclaims and cross-claims, because those involve persons and entities who are already parties to the suit.

Impleader is generally a right of defending parties, because the plaintiff could have sued the potential third-party defendant initially, or could have amended the complaint to add a new defendant. However, Rule 14(b) provides that a counterclaim asserted against a plaintiff will have the effect of making the plaintiff a defendant with respect to the counterclaim, thus entitling the plaintiff to bring in a non-party who is or might be liable to the plaintiff on the counterclaim.

Once the defending party has served the necessary responsive pleading, he, she, or it can serve a third-party complaint seeking impleader without leave of court, for a ten-day period. After the ten days elapse, the court has discretion to allow service of a third-party complaint, but only through a motion made on notice to all parties.

Third-party claims are usually heard under the court's supplemental jurisdiction, so it is not necessary for independent grounds for jurisdiction to be present. However, in a diversity case where the diverse defendant is no longer a party, leaving no one but the plaintiff and a non-diverse third-party defendant, the case must be dismissed.

[D] Interpleader

Rule 22 interpleader is sort of the reverse of a "whodunnit." Interpleader actions are brought by stakeholders, who have possession of sums of money they acknowledge really belong to someone else; but the stakeholders are unsure who the true owners are. Without interpleader, the stakeholder might have to face multiple suits brought by multiple claimants — and a significant portion of the fund might be consumed by these suits! Instead, Rule 22 permits the stakeholder to join all the claimants as defendants, in cases where a limited fund is at risk of excessive, expensive, or multiple litigation.

Interpleader is available to both plaintiffs and defendants, but there is a prerequisite to interpleader brought by defendants: at least one interpleaded party must already be a party to the action. Rule 22 supplements but does not supplant joinder under Rule 20, so in some cases it will be a strategic decision which will work better.

[E] Class Actions

One representative, or a small group, may be able to bring a Rule 23 class action to resolve claims involving a large group having a common interest. It can be a close question whether a case should be handled by Rule 19 joinder or via class action; class actions are clearly preferable if joinder of all parties would be impossible or at least unwieldy. See § 6.13 for the special rules for securities class actions under the Private Securities Litigation Reform Act and Securities Litigation Uniform Standards Act.

Rule 23(a), which contains two implied and four express prerequisites, determines whether a case can be brought as a class action at all. The implied prerequisites are that there must be a definable class that can be certified; and that the would-be plaintiffs must be members of this class. All four of the express requirements must be met:

(1) Numerosity (there are too many class members to join all of them)
(2) Commonality (the class members are united by common issues of law or fact)[66]

---

[66] In recent years, this has been a difficult hurdle for would-be class action plaintiffs to surmount. The Northern District of Georgia would not permit multidistrict litigation over salmonella in peanut butter to proceed as a class action. The court said that class action treatment was inappropriate because there would still be thousands of individual suits, and plaintiffs with small claims would not be compensated effectively; ConAgra made refunds of over $33 million to retailers and consumers, which the court thought was probably more effective than a class action suit. In the Northern District's view, a class action would proceed on the theory that ConAgra was unjustly enriched by its sales of tainted peanut butter; but the various states where purchasers lived had different legal standards, so common issues of law cannot predominate: *In re* ConAgra Peanut Butter Products Liability Litigation, No. 1:07-MD-1845 (N.D. Ga., pending); *see* Robin McDonald, *Tainted Peanut Butter Cases Can't Proceed as Class Action*, Fulton County Daily Report 8/1/08 (law.com).

In 2008, the Second Circuit reversed certification of a class of cigarette smokers who claimed they were deceived into believing that light cigarettes were less dangerous than ordinary cigarettes. The Second Circuit ruled out certification under (b)(3), finding that individual issues outweighed the issues subject to common proof. The claims were presented as RICO fraud claims, which would require each plaintiff to prove reliance, injury, and damages. Furthermore, an undetermined number of the claims were time-barred. *See* McLaughlin v. Philip Morris USA, Inc., 522 F.3d 215 (2d Cir. 2008).

(3) Typicality (the would-be representatives' claims and defenses are typical of the class)
(4) Adequacy (they fairly and adequately protect the interests of the class).

When representation is inadequate but a class action would otherwise be proper, the court has discretion to dismiss the case; let the suit go forward but as an individual action; limit the class to those for whom the applicants would be suitable representatives; or add more representatives until the interests of the class are handled satisfactorily.

Changes to Rule 23 that were approved by the Judicial Conference took effect December 1, 2003. The new Rule 23(e)(3) permits a judge to give class members a second opportunity to opt out at the time of a settlement. Revised Rule 23(c) requires notices to class members (e.g., description of the nature of the action, identification of the nature of the class as certified, the class claims, and the issues and defenses) to be written in plain, easily understood language. Under the revised Rule 23(e)(1), the court must approval withdrawals, dismissals or settlement, and 23(e)(2) obligates parties seeking approval of a settlement to disclose agreements made in connection with the proposed settlement. Under Rule 23(g), a judge appointing class counsel must give greater weight to the counsel's work in identifying and investigating potential claims than to experience in previous class actions. The court can require potential class counsel to submit information, including the proposed fees (Rule 23(g)(1)(C)); and reasonable fees can be awarded in class actions under 23(h).[67]

In the Eleventh Circuit view, a certified class has legal status apart from the named plaintiff. Therefore, if the court rules that the named plaintiff has become inadequate, the action cannot simply be dismissed. Class counsel must be given a reasonable time to find an adequate substitute plaintiff from within the class.[68]

In recent years, many class actions have been denied certification, or certification has been vacated, based on rationales such as divergence in fact patterns among the plaintiffs, or applicability of inconsistent state laws.

The Second Circuit vacated and remanded class certification in six focus cases (chosen from among 310 consolidated class actions) charging IPO securities law violations. The issue was whether a definitive ruling must be made that each Rule 23 requirement was satisfied, or whether it is acceptable to have merely some showing of a requirement, and whether, at the class certification stage, all evidence is assessed, or whether a class plaintiff's evidence will survive review as long as it is not fatally flawed. The Second Circuit held that the District Court cannot certify a class without ruling that each requirement of Rule 23 has been met; "some showing" is not enough. The evidence must be assessed like any other threshold issue. The Rule 23 inquiries are not relaxed when a Rule 23 requirement overlaps

---

[67] *See* 72 L.W. 2325.
[68] Birmingham Steel Corp. v. TVA, 353 F.3d 1331 (11th Cir. 2003).

with the merits of the proposed class action. Hence, the Second Circuit refused to certify the cases as class actions.[69]

Class certification has been denied or revoked in a number of recent cases.[70]

But this is not to say that all class actions have been ruled out in all circumstances. The New Jersey Superior Court did certify a class of people who bought "vanishing premium" life insurance between 1985 and 1989, using the state's Consumer Fraud Act and common-law fraud theories. While recognizing that most states would deny the class action, the New Jersey court cited the state's liberal class action practice for common grievances where individual suits are not feasible.[71]

Early in 2003, the Seventh Circuit found that, in a mass tort case alleging contamination from a leaking storage tank, class action is appropriate for the initial resolution of basic issues common to all the class members. After that, individual follow-up hearings on injury and damages will be required.[72]

If the class action is based on a federal statute, the specific jurisdictional requirements of the statute must be met. If diversity jurisdiction is sought, then all named representatives must be diverse from all defendants, and the $75,000 minimum amount in controversy must be present. The claims of various class members can be aggregated if a single right is being enforced; yet many class actions will be deemed to involve several claims, thus preventing aggregation.

In September 2004, the Sixth Circuit joined the Fourth, Fifth, Seventh, Ninth, and Eleventh in permitting class action plaintiffs to aggregate their claims to reach the $75,000 mark on the grounds that 28 USC § 1367 overturned *Zahn*. However, the Third, Eighth, and Tenth Circuit's position is that Congress intended to maintain the limitation on the amount in controversy.[73]

Once the requirements of Rule 23(a) have been met, the potential class action must satisfy the requirements of Rule 23(b)(1), (2), or (3). Many class actions satisfy two or all three sets of requirements; if so, the case will be classified as a (b)(1) or (b)(2) rather than a (b)(3) class action, because the class members' power to opt out of a (b)(3) class action (see below) opens up a risk of duplicative litigation.

A (b)(1) class action is one where separate suits by or against individual class members are undesirable because there might be inconsistent or varying

---

[69] *In re* IPO Securities Litigation, 471 F.3d 24 (2d Cir. 2006).

[70] *See, e.g.*, Thorn v. Jefferson, 445 F.3d 311 (4th Cir. 2006) [purported class of black insurance purchasers alleging racially motivated overcharges]; Blades v. Monsanto Corp., 400 F.3d 562 (8th Cir. 2005) [farmers alleging overcharges for genetically modified seeds]; Coleman v. GMAC, 296 F.3d 443 (6th Cir. 2002) [black automobile buyers charging violations of the Equal Credit Opportunity Act; *In re* Bridgestone/Firestone Inc. Tires Prods. Liab. Litigation, 333 F.3d 763 (7th Cir. 2003) [nationwide class alleging economic damage from defective SUVs and tires decertified as unmanageable — and the Anti-Injunction Act, 28 USC § 2283 was invoked to enjoin the plaintiffs from going to state court.

[71] Varacallo v. Massachusetts Mut. Life Ins. Co., 752 F.3d 807 (N.J. Super. 2000).

[72] Mejdrech v. Met-Coil Sys. Corp., 319 F.3d 910 (7th Cir. 2003).

[73] Olden v. Lafarge Corp., 383 F.3d 495 (6th Cir. 2004).

adjudications (with the result that it would be impossible for the defendant(s) to be in full compliance), or nonparty class members might be brought in, impairing their ability to protect their own interests.

In a (b)(2) class action, the opposing party has acted or refused to act in a way that affects the whole class, and injunctive or declaratory relief is required to determine the legality of such conduct. This provision was enacted to permit civil rights class actions in the 1960s; even to this day, it is usually used in cases asserting Constitutional rights.

A (b)(3) class action is permissible if common questions of law or fact predominate over the individual issues, and a class action is procedurally the best way to achieve a fair and efficient adjudication of the controversy. Factors in the decision include:

- Whether individual class members have an interest in controlling their own litigation
- If a test case or other mechanism would explicate or protect class rights just as well as a class action
- The number and nature of suits already pending against or by class members
- If it is desirable to have only a single trial in one forum
- The extent of expected litigation management problems created by the class action.

According to the D.C. Circuit, the Fair Labor Standards Act opt-in class certification procedure (29 USC 216(b)) does not prevent the District Court from exercising supplemental jurisdiction over a state-law opt-out class action under (2)(B), as long as both claims form part of the same case or controversy. A court with original jurisdiction over any claim in a complaint has jurisdiction over the civil action, even if it must be maintained as an action with fewer claims than were included in the original complaint. Federal and state claims are part of the same case or controversy if they share a common nucleus of operative fact, and the jurisdictional sweep of the case remains the same even though one of the procedures is opt-out and the other is opt-in.[74]

As soon as practicable after an action has been commenced, and the plaintiffs seek to litigate in class action form, the court issues an order as to whether the case can or cannot be brought as a class action (Rule 23(c)(1)). The order can be conditional, e.g., on adding more representatives, and the court can order a partial class action. If the court does not permit a class action, 23(e) allows the court either to dismiss the case or order its continuation as an individual action. Nonparty class members can then join the case under Rule 20 or perhaps intervene under Rule 24.

---

[74] Lindsay v. Government Employees Ins. Co., 448 F.3d 416 (D.C. Cir. 2006).

[1] Notice in Class Actions

Under Rule 23, for a (b)(1) or (b)(2) class, the court may direct appropriate notice to the class. For a (b)(3) class, the court must direct that class members receive the best notice practicable under the circumstances, including individual notice to all members who can be identified by reasonable effort.

The notice must describe in plain English the action and the issues in dispute, and must inform possible class members that they have the right to opt out of the class action by responding by a specified date. If they do not opt out, they can appear in the action by counsel; and they will be bound by the court's judgment.

This is a departure from the general procedural rule that no one can be bound by an in personam judgment without having been named as a party and served. A class-action judgment binds all class members in a (b)(1) or (b)(2) action, and binds all class members in a (b)(3) action who did not opt out.

New York did not require mail notice to the more than 10 million members (owners of life insurance and/or annuities) of a class action against MetLife alleging stock manipulation when the insurer converted from mutual to stock form. A random sample had to be notified, but major notification could be handled by newspaper publication. MetLife was ordered to pay half the cost of preparing and mailing the notices. The court's rationale was that being in the class is so low-risk that few would choose to opt out, and so choosing a random sample of 500,000 potential plaintiffs was adequate (although the notice procedure might be revised in the future).[75]

A case can be maintained as a class action as to only one or some of its issues (23(c)(2)), and if class members have divergent or antagonistic interests, the court can divide the class into sub-classes (23(c)(4)), either initially or as the issues emerge. Rule 23(e) requires notice to all class members as to proposed dismissals or settlements of the class action, and court approval is required, to prevent collusive settlements benefiting the named plaintiffs but not the class as a whole. Court approval of a class action settlement requires a finding that the settlement is fair, reasonable, and adequate. Parties seeking approval of a settlement must file a statement disclosing any agreement made in connection with the settlement. Furthermore, in a previously certified (b)(3) class action, the court can refuse to approve a settlement unless it gives individual class members another opportunity to request exclusion if they did not do so in the past. Class members have the right to object to settlement proposals that require court approval—but once they do object, the court's approval is required to withdraw the objection.

Actual or potential settlements are quite relevant to federal class action procedure. Settlement of a state-court class action can rule out a later federal class action involving federal claims that the state court suit attempted to preclude.[76]

---

[75] Fiala v. Metropolitan Life Ins. Co., No. 601181/2000, discussed in Beth Bar, *N.Y. Judge: Individual Notice Not Needed for Huge Class in MetLife Suit*, N.Y.L.J. 8/30/07 (law.com).

[76] Matsushita Elec. Indus. Co. v. Epstein, 516 U.S. 367 (1996).

Amchem Products, Inc. v. Windsor, 521 U.S. 591 (1997) treats pending settlements as a factor in granting or denying class certification.

The last case of the Supreme Court's 1998–1999 term, *Ortiz v. Fibreboard*, 527 U.S. 815 (1999), struck down a very large settlement of asbestos-related class claims, citing possible conflict of interest between the attorneys for the class and the class members. The Supreme Court disapproved the "limited-fund" resolution, finding that the class was not well-served by a settlement in which the defendant retained nearly all of its net worth (and the bulk of the settlement came from insurance). The majority opinion saw this as evidence that the settlement was not the best one that could be obtained for class members.[77]

FRCP 23(f) was amended, effective December 1, 1998, to permit an immediate appeal of a District Court's ruling either certifying or decertifying a class. Earlier law, 28 USC § 1292(b), required the consent of both the District Court and the Court of Appeals.

[2] Class Action Settlement Case Law

In June 2002, the Supreme Court permitted challenges to class action settlements to be brought by individuals affected by the settlement, even if they had not been members of the class and had not intervened earlier in the case. (This particular case involved employee pensions, and the petitioner was not a named plaintiff.) However, persons in this category are required to object at the fairness hearing held before the trial judge hearing the class action.[78]

The Seventh Circuit overturned the District Court's approval of a settlement of a suit charging a mortgage company with improperly selling information about its customers to telemarketers. The Seventh Circuit found the settlement improper because only 190,000 members of a sub-class (those who actually sent money to telemarketers) received any benefits; a further 1.4 million class members did not get anything, so the settlement was too lenient to the defendant and generated excessive legal fees disproportionate to the benefits for class members. In later proceedings, the Seventh Circuit remanded once again, finding that the District Court failed to consider the consumer protection statutes in the states where members of the sub-class lived in order to evaluate the potential value of sub-class claims.[79]

[3] Appeals in Class Action Cases

The criteria for deciding whether to hear an interlocutory appeal of the grant or denial of class certification under Rule 23(f) include whether there is a

---

[77] The Second Circuit refused to certify a nationwide (b)(1)(B) class of smokers seeking only punitive damages from cigarette manufacturers. The plaintiffs sought to apply *Ortiz* on the basis that a limited fund would be created, but the court rejected this theory for lack of evidence to determine the size of the fund or the aggregate value of the claims against it: Simon II Litigation v. Philip Morris USA Inc., 407 F.3d 125 (2d Cir. 2005).

[78] Devlin v. Scardeletti, 536 U.S. 1 (2002).

[79] Mirfaishi v. Fleet Mort. Corp., 356 F.3d 781 (7th Cir. 2004), 450 F.3d 745 (7th Cir. 2006).

death-knell situation for either party independent of the merits of the claim; whether the District Court's decision was questionable or manifestly erroneous; and whether the certification decision involved a fundamental unsettled point of class action law.[80]

The Fourth Circuit reversed the certification of a class of homeowners in a products liability case. The Fourth Circuit applies four factors in deciding whether to grant a petition to appeal class certification, including whether the grant of certification shows a "substantial weakness." The factors are applied on a sliding scale, so appeal may be justified if some factors are very strongly demonstrated even if others are weak.[81]

Interlocutory review of class certification under Rule 23(f) is seldom granted. It requires the party seeking review to prove either that the lower court's order was questionable and certification will effectively end the litigation, or that the certification order involves a contested legal issue which has to be resolved immediately.[82]

However, the D.C. Circuit adopted a somewhat more lenient standard in mid-2002, if the District Court's certification decision is manifestly erroneous; the decision itself raises an unsettled, fundamental issue of class action law that has general importance outside the specific case and that cannot be resolved through end-of-case review; and the questionable District Court decision places a party in a "death knell" situation.[83]

The Second Circuit denied a petition for leave to appeal a class certification order, because the petition was filed after the deadline (10 days after entry of the order: Rule 23(f)). This rule gives the District Court the discretion to permit an appeal made within the time limit. The Fifth, Seventh, and Eleventh Circuits treat the deadline as jurisdictional. However, the Second Circuit said that Eberhart calls into question whether Rule 23(f) is jurisdictional; that case says that FRCP 33 is really a non-jurisdictional claim processing rule, so relief can be forfeited by failure to raise claims properly.[84]

See Chapter 24 for a general discussion of the appellate process.

[4] Class Counsel

Under Rule 23(g), the court must appoint class counsel for a certified class (unless an applicable statute rules this out). Any attorney serving as class counsel must fairly and adequately represent the interests of the class. In making the

---

[80] Chamberlan v. Ford Motor Co., 402 F.3d 952 (9th Cir. 2005).

[81] Lienhart v. Dryvit Sys. Inc., 225 F.3d 138 (4th Cir. 2001); the four-factor test comes from Prado-Steiman v. Bush, 221 F.3d 1266 (11th Cir. 2000).

[82] *In re* Sumitomo Copper Litigation, 262 F.3d 134 (2d Cir. 2001).

[83] *In re* Lorazepam and Clorazepate Antitrust Litigation, 289 F.3d 98 (D.C. Cir. 2002).

[84] Coco v. Incorporated Vill. of Belle Terre, 448 F.3d 490 (2d Cir. 2006); *Eberhart* is Eberhart v. United States, 546 U.S. 12 (2005); *see also* MacNamara v. Felderhof, 410 F.3d 277 (5th Cir. 2005); Shin v. Cobb County Bd. of Educ., 248 F.3d 1061 (11th Cir. 2001); Gary v. Sheahan, 188 F.3d 891 (7th Cir. 1999).

appointment, the court must consider factors such as the work the attorney has done to investigate potential claims; his or her experience in handling class actions and other complex litigation; the attorney's knowledge of the relevant body of law; and the resources the would-be counsel can devote to representing the class. The court can direct potential class counsel to provide information on matters relevant to the appointment, including proposed terms for attorneys' fees.

Rule 23(g)(2) permits the court to appoint interim counsel for a putative class before deciding whether or not to certify the class. If there is one applicant who wishes to serve as counsel, the court can appoint him or her only if he or she satisfies the Rule 23(g)(1)(B) and (C) standards of adequacy. If there are rival adequate applicants, the court must choose the one best able to represent the interests of the class. The order of appointment can include provisions about the fee award.

Rule 23(h) allows the court to award reasonable fees in a certified class action. The size of the fee can be determined by law or by the agreement of the parties. A member of the class, or the party who is directed to pay the fees, can object to the proposed fee. The court can hold a hearing and make findings of fact and conclusions of law as prescribed by Rule 52(a), or issues about the amount of the fee award can be referred to a special master or Magistrate Judge pursuant to Rule 54(d)(2)(D).

[5] Class Action Fairness Act of 2005

Under this statute (CAFA; P.L. 109-2), passed in February 2005, the federal District Courts have jurisdiction over certain class actions, precluding initial filing in state court. (However, as noted above, in many instances federal courts deny certification to would-be classes.) The legislative intent, as set out in § 2 of the statute, is to eliminate class-action abuses that have harmed both class members with legitimate claims and blameless corporate defendants, to the detriment of interstate commerce. "Coupon settlements," resulting in large fees to class counsel but awards of minimal value to the class members, are a particular target, as is forum-shopping for a sympathetic state court.

The statute enacts a new 18 USC § 1711, under which the "class members" are the named or unnamed persons within the definition of a proposed or certified Rule 23 action filed in a District Court or removed to District Court from a state court. Amended 18 USC § 1332 (CAFA § 1711) gives the District Courts original jurisdiction over any class action where the amount in controversy is over $5 million and any class member's citizenship is different from that of any defendant.

However, if between one- and two-thirds of the class members are citizens of the state in which the action was originally filed, the District Court can decline to exercise judgment. Factors in the decision include whether national or interstate interests are involved; which state's law will govern the claims; whether the action was brought in a forum with "distinct nexus" with the class members, the defendants, or the allegations; whether the case was pleaded in a manner seeking to avoid federal jurisdiction; and whether the same or similar claims have been raised in other class actions in the three years before the filing of the action in question. The District Court is directed to decline to exercise jurisdiction if more than two-thirds of the class members are citizens of the state in which the action was originally filed.

The new rules enacted by CAFA rules do not apply to class actions:

- whose primary defendants are government entities;
- with fewer than 100 class members[85]
- to certain securities law claims[86]
- to cases about corporate governance.

According to the Ninth Circuit, defendants seeking to remove a case to federal court still have the burden of establishing the propriety of federal jurisdiction; CAFA does not require plaintiffs to show that federal jurisdiction is unavailable.[87]

Although, as noted above, class members are not always allowed to aggregate their claims for the purpose of satisfying the $75,000 jurisdictional limit for the federal court system, CAFA provides that the claims of class members are aggregated to see if the amount is controversy (without interest or costs) exceeds $5 million.

Determination of the CAFA $5 million jurisdictional amount (28 USC § 1332(d)(6)) can be based either on the aggregate value of the relief to the class members or the aggregate cost to the defendant. The burden of proof is on the party opposing removal to show that the case should be remanded to the state court system. The Central District of California said in mid-2005 that because the statute contemplates aggregation of claims, considering only the value to the plaintiffs is no longer relevant. The case at bar, involving credit card holders

---

[85] According to the Seventh Circuit, the relevant question is not whether there will be 100 plaintiffs at the eventual trial but whether there is a proposal for joint trial of claims by 100 or more parties: Bullard v. Burlington Northern Santa Fe R'way Co., 535 F.3d 759 (7th Cir. 2008).

[86] The District Court for the District of Idaho remanded to state court a proposed class action charging the directors of Albertsons Inc. with breach of fiduciary duty by approving sale of the company. The defendants' application to remove under CAFA was rejected, on the grounds that 28 USC § 1453(d) excludes class actions solely about securities (including fiduciary duty) from the coverage of CAFA. Carmona v. Bryant, 74 LW 1687 (D. Ida. 4/19/06). In a case of first impression, the Second Circuit decided that a class action about a company's failure to disclose its insolvency should be in federal court, even though it was brought under New York consumer fraud law, and no nationally traded securities were involved. It was a permissive appeal, which the Second Circuit decided to accept to resolve the question of whether a state-law deceptive practices claim involving the sale of a security can be removed under CAFA. The Second Circuit found concurrent state and federal jurisdiction for securities cases that are likely to have both state and federal impact: Est. of Pew v. Cardarelli, 527 F.3d 23 (2d Cir. 2008); see Mark Hamblett, 2nd Circuit Splits Over Scope of Class Action Fairness Act, N.Y.L.J. 5/15/08 (law.com).

[87] Abrego v. Dow Chemical Co., 443 F.3d 676 (9th Cir. 2006).

who alleged that they were improperly signed up for magazine subscriptions, did not seek monetary relief. The value of the injunctive relief sought did not exceed the limit, so the case was remanded.[88]

A class action complaint charged AT&T Mobility with violating the West Virginia Consumer Credit and Protection Act by charging new cellphone customers for "Roadside Assistance" unless they opted out. The complaint named the class as West Virginia customers who were charged without having applied for the program. AT&T, taking the position that the class consisted of 58,000 customers, removed to federal court under CAFA. The District Court remanded the case to state court, holding that AT&T could not estimate which customers were willing to accept the service and which were unwilling, and AT&T did not prove that the amount in controversy exceeded $5 million. The Fourth Circuit reversed the remand order, and sent the case back to the District Court for further proceedings. According to the Fourth Circuit, following case law from the Third, Sixth, and Ninth Circuits, when removing a class action on the basis of diversity (28 USC § 1453 and § 1332(d)), the party asserting federal jurisdiction must allege it in the notice of removal and, if challenged, demonstrate the basis for federal jurisdiction. The Fourth Circuit defined the amount in controversy as $11.76 million: $200 minimum statutory damages for all of the customers who were automatically enrolled; AT&T had demonstrated that the jurisdictional amount was present, because the question of willingness might go to the issue of whether the charges were ratified by acceptance, but would not affect the size of the class.[89]

In a putative class action alleging California labor law violations, raising the CAFA "home state controversy" exception to federal jurisdiction, the Ninth Circuit held that it is up to the party seeking remand to prove the availability of any exceptions. The plaintiff moved to remand to state court using the local and home-state controversy provisions (§ 1332(d)(4)(A) and (B)). In general, remand orders are not appealable (see § 1447(d)) but § 1453(c) provides discretionary appellate jurisdiction over remand orders when cases are removed under CAFA. The District Court's order remanding the action is reviewed de novo. The decisional factors for the home state exception include, e.g., whether the claims are of national and not just local interest; whether the state's laws will govern; and whether class actions asserting similar claims have been filed in the previous three years. The local controversy exception calls for the District Court to decline jurisdiction if the characteristics of the plaintiff class and at least one defendant make the controversy a local one.[90]

---

[88] Berry v. American Express Pub Corp., 381 F. Supp. 2d 1118 (C.D. Cal. 2005).

[89] Strawn v. AT&T Mobility LLC, 530 F.3d 293 (4th Cir. 2008).

[90] Serrano v. 180 Connect, Inc., 478 F.3d 1018 (9th Cir. 2007). Semble Hart v. FedEx Ground Package Sys. Inc., 457 F.3d 675 (7th Cir. 2006) and Frazier v. Pioneer Americas LLC, 455 F.3d 542 (5th Cir. 2006); Evans v. Walter Indus., Inc., 449 F.3d 1159 (11th Cir. 2006). See Abrego v. Dow Chem. Co., 443 F.3d 676 (9th Cir. 2006) for the proposition that a District Court remand order is reviewed de novo.

CAFA § 5 adds a new 28 USC § 1453, providing that a class action can be removed to District Court without regard to whether any defendant is a citizen of the state in which the action is brought. Any defendant can remove the action without consent of the other defendants. Once again, securities and corporate governance cases are exempt from the new requirement.

28 USC § 1453(c)(1) says that the Court of Appeals may accept an appeal from a District Court order granting or denying a motion to remand a class action to state court only if the application is made to the Court of Appeals "not less than seven days" after the District Court order. In *Amalgamated Transit Union Local 1309 v. Laidlaw Transit Services*, the Ninth Circuit concluded that "not less than seven days" must be a typographical error meaning "not more than seven days," on the grounds that it would be illogical to impose a seven-day waiting period but no time limit.[91]

When there is a "coupon settlement" (i.e., the defendant provides the plaintiffs with coupons for goods or services), the class counsel's fee reflecting the value of coupons is based only on the value of coupons that are redeemed, not those that are issued but not redeemed (§ 1712);[92] if the fee is not determined on the basis of a portion of the coupons, it must be based on the reasonable time class counsel devoted to the action. All attorneys' fees are subject to court review; the lodestar method can be used. A settlement calling for any class member to incur a net loss after payment of attorneys' fees can be approved only if the court finds that the

---

[91] Amalgamated Transit Union Local 1309, AFL-CIO v. Laidlaw Transit Servs. Inc., 435 F.3d 1140 (9th Cir. 2006); Morgan v. Gay, No. 466 F.3d 276 (3d Cir. 2006) and Pritchett v. Office Depot, Inc., 420 F.3d 1090 (10th Cir. 2005) also treat the provision as a typographical error. *See* Marie-Anne Hogarth, *For 9th Circuit, Less Means More*, The Recorder 5/24/06 (law.com). Spivey v. Vertrue, Inc., 528 F.3d 982 (7th Cir. 2008), a state class action against a marketing firm, charging deliberate submission of unauthorized credit card charges, was removed under CAFA, then remanded by the District Court back to state court. The marketing firm filed a petition for leave to appeal (28 USC § 1453(c)(1)). It was mailed on the seventh day after the District Court's remand order. It reached the court and was filed (as prescribed by FRAP 25(a)(2)) on the tenth day. The plaintiff argued that the petition was too late. The Seventh Circuit held that it satisfied the "not less than seven days" requirement and therefore was timely, refusing to adopt the reasoning of the line of cases reading the phrase as "more than seven days." The Seventh Circuit applied FRAP 4(a)(2) [premature notice of appeal] to premature petitions for leave to appeal, making it effective at the time that the decision becomes appealable. The Seventh Circuit rejected the argument that applying "not less than seven days" would make the time to appeal infinite. FRAP 5(a)(2) requires filing within 30 days (or 60 days when the United States or a federal agency is a party) when there is no other applicable deadline. This case also involved an issue of calculating the amount in controversy. The Seventh Circuit held that what counts is not what the plaintiff is certain to recover, but the amount that could be recovered. A removing defendant does not have to concede liability, only indicate that it is possible that the plaintiff could receive more than $5 million.

[92] Judge Cecilia M. Altonaga of the Southern District of Florida rejected a proposed Sharper Image coupon settlement — the settlement would have given 2-3 million purchasers of allegedly defective air purifiers a $19 coupon; opponents said the plaintiff should have received money. The judge said the settlement violated the CAFA ban on coupon settlements, and was not fair, adequate or reasonable, and attorneys fees were too high; Julie Kay, *Federal Judge Clips Sharper Image's Coupon-Only Deal*, Daily Business Review 10/12/07 (law.com).

non-monetary benefits to the class member are substantially greater than the financial loss.

Notice of proposed settlement of a class action subject to CAFA must be given to federal or state officials that are responsible for regulation of the defendant (§ 1715).

Whenever a major new statute is passed, questions about its effect on cases already in the litigation pipeline inevitably arise. For CAFA, the question is when the suit was "commenced" — and which subsequent activities, if any, will either permit or preclude removal of the suit. CAFA applies to civil actions commenced on or after February 18, 2005. The question is whether the statute permits removal of a class action filed before the effective date, if the removing defendant was added to the action by amendment after the effective date. (Of course, this is an issue only if the plaintiffs prefer to litigate in state court but the defendants want a federal forum.)

The federal courts have developed three main positions as to whether a post-CAFA amendment can be used to remove an action filed in state court before CAFA's effective date. It is a question of state law when an action is "commenced." One position is that a civil action is commenced only once, so a post-CAFA action cannot trigger removal. Another position is that adding a new, sufficiently distinct claim in effect creates a new action that can be removed. This position is further subdivided, with some courts holding that a case started before CAFA (and therefore generally exempt from removal) can be removed only if the amendment does not relate back. But an opposing thread of analysis says that if a complaint is amended to add new defendants, then it always starts a new case as to those defendants, who will then be in a position to seek removal.[93]

What if the change is in the lineup of plaintiffs, rather than the array of defendants? The Seventh Circuit ruled that an amendment adding new class representatives, when the District Court certifies a class that is broader than anticipated, or substituting new representatives for members whose claims are time-barred relates back. Therefore, a new action was not commenced for CAFA purposes; remand of suits filed pre-CAFA was proper where the routine amendments related back to the original filing.[94] In a Vioxx class action, a class representative was substituted when it was discovered that the original representative had not actually purchased or used Vioxx. The Eighth Circuit ruled that the substitution did not

---

[93] In addition to many District Court opinions, the Courts of Appeals have ruled on these issues in, e.g., Prime Care of Northeast Kan. v. Humana Ins. Co., 447 F.3d 1284 (10th Cir. 2006); Braud v. Transportation Serv. Co., 445 F.3d 801 (5th Cir. 2006); Schillinger v. Union Pac. R.R., 425 F.3d 330, 333 (7th Cir. 2005); Pritchett v. Office Depot, Inc., 420 F.3d 1090 (10th Cir. 2005); Knudsen v. Liberty Mut. Ins. Co., 411 F.3d 805 (7th Cir. 2005). *See also* Lott v. Pfizer, 492 F.3d 789 (7th Cir. 2007), denying attorneys' fees to plaintiffs whose class action was removed and then remanded. Plaintiffs are entitled to a fee award if, and only if, the defendant lacked an objectively reasonable basis for seeking removal. At the time of removal, the definition of "commencement" for CAFA purposes had not been settled.

[94] Phillips v. Ford Motor Co., 435 F.3d 785 (7th Cir. 2006).

commence a new class action for CAFA purposes. The claims remained the same; the substitute representative was a member of the class; and the original selection was apparently mistaken rather than made in bad faith. Therefore, under both state law and FRCP 15(c), the amended pleading could relate back to the original. The Eighth Circuit ruled that the change did not prejudice the defendant.[95]

The § 1453(2) 60-day period for the Court of Appeals to rule on the merits of an appeal runs from the order granting leave to appeal, not from the filing of the petition for leave to appeal. The Fifth Circuit reads Congress' intent as making the CAFA process duplicate the 28 USC § 1292(b) process; the requirement of applying for leave to appeal implies that no appeal actually exists until the court exercises its power to grant leave to appeal.[96]

[F] Derivative Actions

Derivative actions are usually brought by shareholders on behalf of a corporation, premised on accusations that corporate management is plundering the corporation or otherwise acting contrary to the best interests of its shareholders. They can also be brought on behalf of an unincorporated association, brought by members. Derivative actions enforce a right on behalf of the entity in a situation in which the entity could have but did not bring suit to vindicate its own rights.

Derivative actions are governed by Rule 23.1, which requires the complaint in a derivative action to be verified and to state:

- That the plaintiff was a shareholder at the time of the alleged wrongdoing, or acquired shares subsequently by operation of law
- That the action is not a collusive attempt to create jurisdiction in a court that otherwise would lack jurisdiction
- Whether the plaintiff made a demand on the corporation's Board of Directors or its shareholders; if so, what efforts were made and why they failed; if not, why efforts were not made.

Plaintiffs in a derivative suit must fairly and adequately represent the interests of similarly situated shareholders (or organization members). As with class actions, court approval is needed for dismissal or settlement of the case. If the plaintiffs prevail, the relief is awarded to the corporation (not the plaintiffs as individuals), and the corporation is bound by the judgment.

Prevailing derivative-suit plaintiffs or those who negotiate a settlement are entitled to reimbursement from the corporation for their litigation expenses.

---

[95] Plubell v. Merck & Co., 434 F.3d 1070 (8th Cir. 2006).

[96] Patterson v. Dean Morris LLP, 444 F.3d 365 (5th Cir. 2006) amended 487 F.3d 736 (5th Cir. 2006); *semble* Hart v. Fedex Ground Package Sys. Inc., 457 F.3d 675 (7th Cir. 2006); Evans v. Walter Indus., Inc., 449 F.3d 1159 (11th Cir. 2006); Amalgamated Transit Union Local 1309, AFL-CIO v. Laidlaw Transit Serv. Inc., 435 F.3d 1140 (9th Cir. 2006); *see also* Bush v. Cheaptickets, Inc., 425 F.3d 683 (9th Cir. 2005).

However, shareholders who are not parties to a derivative suit must intervene in order to have standing to appeal an adverse judgment.[97]

[G] Intervention

As discussed above, there are numerous possibilities other than a simple suit by one plaintiff against a single defendant. Intervention, as governed by Rule 24, allows a non-party who has an interest in a pending action to apply to become a party. (This differs from impleader and third-party practice, because those are steps taken by parties to bring presumably unwilling non-parties into the action; intervention comes at the option of the non-party.)

If a federal statute grants an unconditional right to intervene, then intervention is "of right" under Rule 24(a), and intervention is granted automatically as long as the application is timely. (Most statutes containing an unconditional right make it available only to the federal government and state governments, not to individuals or corporations.) Intervention of right is also available to one who asserts a legally protectable interest in property or transactions that are the subject of the action, and that the existing parties do not adequately represent the interests of the potential intervenor.

Permissive intervention, at the discretion of the court, is governed by Rule 24(b). It is granted based on a federal statute enacting a conditional right to intervene, or because the intervenor has common issues of law or fact with the main action in which intervention is sought. The issues the court considers in granting or refusing permissive intervention include whether intervention will unduly delay or prejudice the adjudication of the rights of the original parties.

The potential intervenor is obligated by Rule 24(c) to serve all parties, in accordance with Rule 5, with a motion to intervene returnable in the court in which the action is pending. The motion must state the grounds supporting the motion. The intervenor's own claim or defense should be set forth in the appropriate pleading (complaint or answer).

§ 22.10   MULTIDISTRICT LITIGATION

Civil actions pending in different districts, but having common questions of law and fact, can be transferred under 28 USC § 1407 to any district for consolidated or coordinated pretrial proceedings. The transfer is done by the Judicial Panel on Multidistrict Litigation, based on a determination that transfer promotes justice and the convenience of parties and witnesses. The Panel consists of seven Circuit or District judges appointed by the Chief Justice of the United States.

The Panel assigns the proceedings to one or more judges. The Panel has the power to request temporary assignment of a Circuit or District Court judge to the transferee district to handle the multidistrict case, and it can designate judges (including its own members) to help with the depositions.

---

[97] California Public Employees' Ret. Sys. v. Felzen, 525 U.S. 315 (1999), affirming (without opinion) the Court of Appeals decision.

A transfer can be initiated on the Panel's own motion, or by motion of a party. Decisions of the Panel are reviewable only by extraordinary writ (see 28 USC § 1651). A Panel order refusing to transfer a case is not reviewable or appealable at all, whereas an order granting a transfer can be reviewed by the Court of Appeals covering the transferee court (not the court from which the case is transferred).

Factors promoting the transfer of a case include:

- Need to prevent conflicting pretrial rulings
- Need to prevent duplication of discovery with respect to common issues
- Resolving conflicting class actions
- Avoiding duplication or conflict of pretrial conferences
- Allowing a single judge to resolve matters that otherwise would occupy several judges
- Dividing the workload among counsel.

Doubtful questions are resolved in favor of transfer.

The initial MDL pretrial conference should be scheduled well in advance of FRCP 16(b)'s 120-day period for scheduling orders. Attorneys can be asked to submit written viewpoints on the litigation and its potential problems before the initial conference. The pretrial conferences (usually there are four of them) are used to set discovery orders, determine class action questions, resolve discovery disputes, set the schedule for the trial, and lay out which facts are undisputed and which witnesses and what evidence will be produced at the trial.

The transferee court has the power to grant motions to dismiss and summary judgment motions. Theoretically, it is possible to remand the case back to its transferor court, but this almost never occurs in practice.

A federal District Court hearing multidistrict cases involving the interpretation of federal law should use the law of the transferee Circuit, even though the transferee court does not have the power to transfer the case to itself for trial after pre-trial has been completed.[98]

In late 2002, the Department of Justice appropriations bill (P.L. 107-273), enacted the Multidistrict, Multiparty, Multiforum Trial Jurisdiction Act, covering major mass disasters such as train or plane crashes. The statute is effective for accidents occurring more than 90 days after November 2, 2002 (the date the bill was signed). Suits about accidents causing the death of 75 or more people must be filed in federal district court; consolidated under a single federal judge for discovery; then returned to the original district court of filing for resolution of liability and damage issues. The district courts will have original jurisdiction in diversity actions between parties suing about a single accident, unless a substantial majority of the plaintiffs live in the same state as the primary defendant.[99]

---

[98] *In re* MBTE Prods. Liab. Litigation, 73 L.W. 1452 (S.D.N.Y. 1/18/05).

[99] Discussed in Julie Kay, *Disaster Plan*, Miami Daily Business Review 11/21/02 (law.com).

§ 22.11   CHOICE OF LAW

In many instances, substantive issues will be decided under the law of the state in which the District Court is located (including that state's choice of law rules and its long-arm statute and other jurisdictional provisions). However, in all federal cases (even diversity cases), genuinely procedural issues such as motion practice, discovery, and appellate practice will be handled under the relevant federal rules.

If the forum selection clause is the sole basis for personal jurisdiction over a defendant, then state law applies to the question. The Sixth Circuit held in mid-2007 that in diversity actions, the federal court must use state law to determine personal jurisdiction.[100]

§ 22.12   PRECLUSION VIA RES JUDICATA AND COLLATERAL ESTOPPEL

The court system is busy enough reaching ONE final adjudication in a particular case; the related concepts of collateral estoppel and res judicata seek to promote judicial economy by preventing relitigation of issues that have already been determined.

Res judicata, also known as claim preclusion, prevents the same parties (or others in privity with them) from relitigating causes of action that have already been resolved. Collateral estoppel, or issue preclusion, prevents the relitigation of either factual determinations or mixed determinations of fact and law.

Res judicata includes two related concepts, merger and bar. Merger prevents a plaintiff from bringing suit because a favorable judgment on the merits has already been rendered on that point. Bar prevents bringing an action on an issue which the plaintiff has already LOST: an unfavorable judgment on the merits has been rendered. Merger and bar apply when the same cause of action is involved in two suits, and the parties are the same in both, or the parties in the second suit are in privity with the parties in the first.

The Second Circuit ruled in late 2003 that because res judicata is an affirmative defense, it can be waived. Therefore, amounts that might become uncollectable because of res judicata cannot be subtracted when calculating the amount in controversy.[101]

Collateral estoppel prevents retrying issues of law or fact that have been adjudicated in an earlier proceeding, even if this time the cause of action is different. Like res judicata, collateral estoppel applies when the parties are the same or related in the two suits. But collateral estoppel can also be used by outsiders, if the estopped party was a party in the previous suit and it is inappropriate to relitigate the issue.

---

[100] Preferred Capital, Inc. v. Sarasota Kennel Club, Inc., 489 F.3d 303 (6th Cir. 2007); the earlier case are Preferred Capital, Inc. v. Associates in Urology, 453 F.3d 718 (6th Cir. 2006), contra Preferred Capital, Inc. v. Power Eng'g Group Inc., 860 N.E.2d 741 (Ohio 2007). The Sixth Circuit precedent for using state law is Intera Corp. v. Henderson, 428 F.3d 605 (6th Cir. 2005).

[101] Scherer v. Equitable Life Assurance Soc'y, 347 F.3d 394 (2d Cir. 2003).

§ 22.13   COMMENCEMENT OF THE FEDERAL CASE; SERVICE OF PROCESS

Under FRCP 3, a federal case is commenced when the complaint is filed. Rule 4 provides that the clerk of the court must immediately issue a summons as soon as the complaint is filed. The plaintiff decides whether the summons should be issued against all defendants, or whether each should receive a separate summons.

The usual federal practice is to serve the summons by mail. The party served receives a notice and acknowledgment form, which is to be returned to prove that service has been completed. Rule 4 allows service by first-class mail; it is not necessary to use, e.g., registered or certified mail. The pleadings must be accompanied by two copies of the notice and acknowledgment form and by a postpaid return envelope, addressed to the plaintiff or plaintiff's attorney.

However, if mail service is unsuccessful for some reason, and the acknowledgment form has not been returned 20 days after the summons was mailed, almost any person over 18 who is not a party to the suit can perform personal service. The person effecting service must complete an affidavit of service. (Under prior law, all summonses had to be served by the U.S. Marshal's office, but this requirement has been abrogated.)

Furthermore, in most federal suits, service can be made by any method approved by the state courts of the state in which the District Court is located. (It should be noted that in a diversity case, the statute of limitations is not tolled by the filing of the complaint in federal court if state law requires actual service of the complaint.) Unless good cause is shown, the case is dismissed without prejudice if the plaintiff is unable to complete service of the complaint within 120 days of commencement of the action.

[A] Service by Type of Party Served

Under Rule 4(h), service on a corporation, partnership, or unincorporated association that can be sued under a common name is performed by serving an officer or managing or general agent who has express or implied authority to be served. Service can also be made on any other agent appointed or authorized by law. (It may also be necessary to mail a copy of the summons and complaint to the defendant.) In situations in which the federal government has waived sovereign immunity, service against the United States is performed by delivering a copy of the summons and complaint to the U.S. Attorney or Assistant U.S. Attorney.

Rule 45, not Rule 4, governs service of subpoenas, including territorial rules. Other forms of federal process continue to be served by the U.S. Marshal or by a specially appointed person. Federal process other than subpoenas can always be served within the limits of the state in which the District Court is sitting.

If the person to be served cannot be found in that state, all is not necessarily lost: many federal statutes authorize nationwide service of process in suits to enforce the statutes.

Another possibility is that, if additional parties must be brought in under Rules 14 or 19, Rule 4(k) permits service outside the state but inside the United States, at any place within 100 miles of the place where the action was commenced or will be tried. See Rule 4(f) for service in a foreign country if the party is not an inhabitant of, or found within, the state in which the District Court is located.

The service of papers other than the complaint comes under Rule 5. Unless the District Court excuses it when there are numerous defendants, copies of all subsequent pleadings must be served on each party. Service is made on the attorney of a represented party, unless the court orders service of the party him- or herself.

In 2002, the Ninth Circuit permitted e-mail service of process on a non-U.S. defendant, after the defendant refused an attempt to serve the designated U.S. agent, and no other address was known. This method satisfied Due Process and could be considered "other means not prohibited by international agreement" (FRCP 4(f)(3)).[102]

FRCP 4(f) allows service in a foreign country by any internationally agreed upon means reasonably calculated to give notice, including the Hague Convention on Service Abroad of Judicial and Extrajudicial Documents. Articles 10(a) and 19 of the Hague Convention permit service from abroad using any method permitted by the receiving state's domestic law. In March 2004, the Ninth Circuit permitted American plaintiffs to serve an English defendant via regular mail to a Post Office Box in England; but then the court reversed itself in August of the same year, this time ruling that international regular mail was not an acceptable medium, in that the British government would probably object to service that did not use registered mail.[103]

§ 22.14 FEDERAL PLEADINGS

The intention of the FRCP is to adopt "notice pleading" and to eliminate technical pleading requirements; to reduce the number and variety of pleadings; and to encourage "short, plain statements" in the surviving pleadings. Amendments and supplements are available as needed, but under FRCP 7(a), the only permissible pleadings are:

- The plaintiff's complaint
- The defendant's answer
- Third-party complaint
- Third-party answer
- The plaintiff's answer to a counterclaim asserted by the defendant
- A co-defendant's answer to a cross-claim.

All pleadings must contain a caption giving the court (the District, and the Division, if any); the title of the action; its file number; its designation (e.g.,

---

[102] Rio Properties Inc. v. Rio Int'l Interlink, 184 F.3d 1007 (9th Cir. 2002).
[103] Brockmeyer v. May, 361 F.3d 1222 (9th Cir. 2004), rev'd, 383 F.3d 798 (9th Cir. 2004).

complaint, answer, etc.); and the names of the parties. Local rules may require additional information, such as the judge's name.

In 2008, the Second Circuit set standards for when a suit can be filed anonymously. (FRCP 10(a) requires all parties to be named.) A pro se plaintiff who would not give her name sued (as "Jane Doe") nine defendants alleging that she was physically and sexually assaulted, blaming various state and municipal entities for conspiracy. The Second Circuit ruled that the test is balancing the plaintiff's need for anonymity against the state's interest in full disclosure. The Second Circuit called for consideration of factors such as whether the litigation involves sensitive or personal matters; the risk of retaliation to parties or innocent non-parties; whether the plaintiff was particularly vulnerable; whether the suit challenges private or governmental action; the degree of prejudice to the defendant from concealing the plaintiff's identity; whether it has been concealed in the past. The standard for appellate review is the usual one of abuse of discretion. In this case, the Second Circuit held that the District Court abused its discretion by mechanically applying FRCP 10(a) and failing to balance the interests. The Second Circuit permitted the suit to proceed under a pseudonym.[104]

Note that Rule 19(c) requires the pleader of any complaint, counterclaim, cross-claim, or third-party claim to identify all persons known to the pleader to be necessary to resolution of the matter but who have not, in fact, been joined. The pleader must explain why joinder is not feasible. (Rule 23 class actions are exempt from this requirement, so it is not necessary to join all class members, explain their non-joinder, or even provide a list of all of them. See § 22.09[E] for a discussion of class actions.)

Rule 15 gives a party who has served a pleading the right to amend it once before the responsive pleading is served. (A motion is not considered a responsive pleading for this purpose.) In a situation in which no responsive pleading is permitted, the pleading can be amended within 20 days of serving it, as long as it has not yet been placed on the trial calendar. But once the responsive pleading has been served, written consent from the adverse party or leave of court is required to amend. (Leave to amend is supposed to be granted freely in the interest of justice.)

The general rule is that when a pleading has been amended, the opposing party must respond to the amended version within the remaining response time for the original pleading, or within ten days after service of the amended pleading, whichever is later. However, the court can order a different timetable. Rule 15(d) permits a party to make a motion for service of a supplemental pleading. Unlike an amended pleading, a supplemental pleading deals with transactions, occurrences, and events after the date of the prior pleading.

An April 2000 Supreme Court case arose out of a patent infringement dispute. The District Court dismissed the case and ordered Ohio Cellular Products Corp.

---

[104] Sealed Plaintiff v. Sealed Defendant #1, 332 F.3d 51 (2d Cir. 2008); *see* Mark Hamblett, *2nd Circuit Sets Standard for Anonymous Suit Filings*, N.Y.L.J. 8/14/08 (law.com). The balancing test comes from Does I-XXIII v. Advanced Textile Corp., 214 F.3d 1058 (9th Cir. 2000).

(OCP) to pay Adams USA's attorneys' fees. The District Court decided that OCP's president and sole shareholder, Nelson, had deceived the Patent and Trademark Office about its patents, and that OCP was chargeable for this deceit.

Adams did not think that OCP would be able to pay this judgment, so it moved under FRCP 15 to amend its pleadings and add Nelson as an individual as a party from whom fees could be collected. OCP also applied under Rule 59(e) to have the judgment amended to make Nelson immediately liable for the fee award. The Supreme Court held that it was an error to amend the judgment immediately after allowing the pleading to be amended. The concepts of Due Process embodied in Rules 12 and 15 require Nelson to have a chance to contest personal liability after becoming a party and before entry of judgment. As the case developed, he was never given a chance to contest the issue of personal liability. Rule 15(a) also allots 10 days to plead to parties who are added after the time to respond to the original pleading, whereas Adams was subject to personal liability without even getting an amended pleading.[105]

[A] The Complaint

As noted above, filing of the complaint commences a federal action, and the summons and complaint must be served together.

The complaint must be organized into separate numbered paragraphs that set out the facts and legal claims under which relief is sought (Rule 10). The complaint should contain:

- The general nature of the claim(s)
- The name and state citizenship of all parties
- A brief statement of the involvement of each party in the controversy
- The sections of the Judicial Code (28 USC) supporting jurisdiction and venue
- If there is a jurisdictional amount (e.g., in a diversity case), a statement that the damages (exclusive of costs and interest) equal or exceed the jurisdictional amount
- Background facts needed to understand the claim
- An identifying heading for each Cause of Action, plus material required to set out a cognizable claim for relief under that cause of action (all necessary facts; the legal theory asserted in connection with those facts; the injury alleged; and the relief sought, e.g., damages, injunction, declaratory judgment)
- A summary of the relief sought for all Causes of Action and a request for "such other and further relief as to the Court may appear just."

The complaint must be signed by the plaintiff's counsel (thus bringing it within the ambit of Rule 11 sanctions: see § 27.05). Any exhibits referred to in the complaint must be attached. Like all pleadings, the complaint must have a back

---

[105] Nelson v. Adams USA Inc., 529 U.S. 460 (2000).

conforming to local practice. It must be served pursuant to Rule 4 and must be filed with the Clerk of Court.

In 2007, the Supreme Court said that, to state a Sherman Act § 1 claim, the pleader must make enough factual allegations to raise the right to relief about the speculative level, including enough factual matter to suggest an agreement, creating the reasonable expectation that discovery would reveal evidence of an illegal agreement.[106]

[B] The Answer

The answer is the responsive pleading that the defendant uses to respond to the allegations raised by the complaint. Rule 8(c) provides that the answer is used to raise affirmative defenses and assert counterclaims and cross-claims. The basic time frame for answering the complaint is 20 days, although an additional three days are allowed if (as usually happens) the complaint is served by mail. (The United States as defendant is given 60 days to answer.) See Rule 12.

The answer should consist of separate, numbered paragraphs responding to each of the allegations of the complaint. Any allegation that is not addressed is deemed admitted. Every allegation must be admitted; admitted in specified part and denied as to the rest; or the defendant can claim lack of knowledge or information sufficient to form a belief as to the truth of the allegation.

Rule 8(e)(2) allows two or more statements of claim or defense to be made alternatively or hypothetically. The defendant's attorney must sign the answer, so Rule 11 applies. As long as Rule 11 is not violated, inconsistent statements are permitted in pleadings.

[1] Available Defenses

Defenses (including affirmative defenses) that can be raised in an answer include:

- Failure to state a claim on which relief can be based
- Plaintiff's lack of standing to sue
- Court's lack of subject matter jurisdiction over the action
- Court's lack of personal jurisdiction over the defendant
- Defective service of process
- Defenses contained in the relevant statute
- Preclusion by res judicata or collateral estoppel
- Equitable defenses (laches, unclean hands).

Any valid defense can be raised in the answer. Certain defenses that go to the very heart of the action (e.g., failure to state a claim on which relief can be based; lack of jurisdiction or venue) can also be raised by a 12(b) motion to dismiss.

---

[106] Bell Atlantic Corp. v. Twombly, 550 U.S. 544 (2007).

Affirmative defenses include accord and satisfaction, payment, or release; arbitration and award; assumption of risk; contributory negligence of the plaintiff, or negligence of a fellow-servant; discharge in bankruptcy; duress; estoppel; fraud; illegality; laches; lack of consideration; res judicata; lack of written agreement in a situation subject to the Statute of Frauds; claims that are time-barred because the statute of limitations has expired; and waiver.

The Federal Tort Claims Act includes a "postal" exception (28 USC § 2680(b)), but early in 2006, the Supreme Court ruled that it applies to bar only suits about mail that is lost, late, or damaged. A plaintiff who charged that she was injured when she slipped and fell on mail that a carrier negligently left on the porch was not barred from suing the Postal Service.[107]

The answer can also include properly labeled counter- and cross-claims (e.g., First Counterclaim; First Counterclaim Against X and Y). Such claims follow the format of a complaint: they identify the parties, state the bases for jurisdiction and venue, and set out the facts, legal claims, and relief sought. The proper responsive pleadings are a Reply, filed by a plaintiff who becomes the subject of a counterclaim, and an Answer for co-defendants served with cross-claims.

According to the Sixth Circuit, in the copyright context (designs for a condominium building) laches is not just a lapse of time, but a lapse where the circumstances change so that someone would be disadvantaged by pursuing the action at this time (e.g., leading defendants to believe that the plaintiff acquiesced in their actions or abandoned the claim). There is a Circuit split as to whether laches can be asserted as a copyright defense. The Sixth Circuit permits it in general, but in the case at bar, held that because the plaintiffs demanded destruction of allegedly infringing condominium units already build, sold, and occupied, the lapse of time was the kind of inequity that the concept of laches is intended to prevent.[108]

[C] Third-Party Pleadings

If it is necessary to bring a party into the action who is not already involved (i.e., is not already a plaintiff or defendant), the defendant can use Rule 14's third-party complaint procedure. The defendant becomes the plaintiff as against the new party. The defendant can file the third-party complaint, with no need for leave of court, within ten days of service of an answer to the original complaint under which he, she, or it is a defendant. A defendant who wishes to file a third-party complaint after the ten days have elapsed must do so by motion on notice to all parties in the action. Recent amendments to Rule 14(b) allow plaintiffs to assert third-party claims, not just counterclaims.

---

[107] Dolan v. United States Postal Serv., 546 U.S. 481 (2006).
[108] Chirco et al. v. Crosswinds Communities, Inc., 474 F.3d 227 (6th Cir. 2007).

§ 22.15 TRIAL PRACTICE

[A] Motions

In the federal system, motion practice is used to set the status of parties, determine issues, and control the evidence. The local rules for the various District Courts, promulgated under Rule 83, govern the form of motions to be filed in those courts, and most contain sample forms for use in various situations.

Applications for court orders can be made in court during a hearing or trial, or by a written motion, which sets out the grounds for the motion with particularity, and includes the text of the proposed order or other relief. The general rule is that written motions and notices of hearing must be served at least five days before the time specified for the hearing. Service is made on the attorneys of represented parties, not the parties themselves. The papers must then be filed with the clerk of the court within a reasonable time after service.

Hearings on motions can also be brought on by Orders to Show Cause (OSC), ex parte applications under which one side applies for relief, and the court orders the opponent to show cause why such relief should NOT be granted. Usually, the proponent drafts the motion, including whatever affidavits, pleadings, or other materials are required to assist the court, and also draws up the suggested order and submits the entire package to the judge's chambers. The judge makes any changes he or she deems necessary.

The original of the marked-up order is filed with the clerk of the court. Conformed copies, reflecting the judge's changes, are served on the adversary, and an affidavit or admission of service is filed with the clerk as evidence of service.

Under Rule 5, unless the federal rules or the court says otherwise, all parties must be served with all orders and all papers to be served with respect to discovery. (The court might order relief if there are many parties involved, some of them with very peripheral interests, so it would be unfair to burden a party with serving everyone.) All documents that are served on parties must also be filed with the Clerk of the Court.

Rule 6(d) requires written motions and accompanying notices to be served on the other parties at least five days before the date set for the hearing (unless the rules or the judge's calendar are to the contrary). However, in ongoing cases, counsel for all sides frequently agree to permit a shorter notice period. The hearing on a motion usually calls for oral argument.

At the inception of a trial, the most common motions are those to dismiss for lack of subject matter jurisdiction; motions to dismiss for failure to state a cause of action; motions to amend pleadings; motions for judgment on the pleadings; and motions in limine. Motions in limine are usually made in the judge's chambers, to resolve potential evidentiary problems — e.g., a motion for an order under Federal Rules of Evidence 403 to restrict otherwise admissible testimony because it would cause prejudice, confusion, or delay.

Rule 12(e) authorizes a motion for a "more definite statement," when a party is unable to understand an opponent's pleading and therefore is unable to respond to it. A Rule 12(f) motion asks for redundant, immaterial, scandalous, or otherwise inappropriate material to be removed from an opponent's pleading. (This is necessary because pleadings are public documents that become part of the record.)

[1] Motions to Dismiss and for Summary Judgment

Although any defense can be asserted in a responsive pleading, there are seven defenses that can be asserted in a preliminary motion filed even before responding to the pleading. These Rule 12 motions can also be joined with any other motion available to the party.

These seven defenses are so fundamental that their successful assertion allows the court to dismiss the action and save litigation time:

(1) Lack of subject-matter jurisdiction
(2) Lack of personal jurisdiction
(3) Improper venue
(4) Formal inadequacy of process
(5) Improper service
(6) Failure to state a claim upon which relief can be granted
(7) Failure to join a party whose joinder is compulsory under Rule 19 (see § 22.09[B]).

These defenses, other than lack of subject matter jurisdiction, failure to state a claim, and failure of compulsory joinder, are deemed waived unless they are raised in a Rule 12 motion (Rule 12(h)).

The Rule 56 summary judgment motion is a related phenomenon. It asks the court for a pre-trial determination of whether there are material questions as to claims or defenses. If there are no such questions that have to be resolved, then one side or the other will be entitled to judgment as a matter of law. Summary judgment can also be applied for and granted as to only part of a claim or defense. Rule 56 motions require affidavits and other items of evidence to support them; Rule 12 motions do not.

Any plaintiff, third-party plaintiff, cross-claimant, or counterclaimant can file a Rule 56 motion for summary judgment at any time after 20 days have elapsed after commencement of the action.

In exceptional cases, Rule 53 permits the trial judge to appoint a master in either a jury or non-jury case. The master is an impartial officer (e.g., referee, auditor, examiner, assessor) with special expertise who is charged with hearing or considering evidence and reporting back to the court. Under Rule 53(e), the master's findings are final if the parties stipulate that they will be. In a jury case, the master's findings are admissible as evidence of the matters found by the master. In a court trial, the judge must accept the master's findings of fact unless they are clearly erroneous.

[2] Preparing for Appellate Review

It may seem unrealistic (or excessively pessimistic) to think about appeals before a case has even been commenced. However, given the general rule that appellate courts will not hear issues that were not properly raised at the trial level, litigators should consider all the facets of the case; should include all significant issues in their pleadings and briefs; and should be sure that a record is made of all salient matters and that all objections and exceptions are properly noted on the record. Care should be taken to see that the court reporter is preserving all material necessary to a proper transcript.

If there is even the vaguest possibility of the Supreme Court granting certiorari in a state case, it is vital to raise federal issues at every stage and have the state court decide those issues separately.

§ 22.16 PROVISIONAL REMEDIES

The ultimate resolution of a federal case is a complex — and very lengthy — business, and in the interests of justice, it is often necessary either to preserve the status quo, or make certain alterations before the case can be completed. This is done by provisional remedies, including preliminary injunctions and temporary restraining orders (TROs).

[A] TROs

If there is a risk of irreparable injury to the moving party if the status quo changes before a full-scale injunction application can be heard, Rule 65(b) permits the issuance of a TRO. If the situation is sufficiently urgent, the TRO can even be granted ex parte, without written or even oral notice to the adverse party. (Notice must be given as soon as possible, however, after the TRO issues in such a circumstance.) If it is practical to give notice before the TRO hearing, it should, of course, be given.

Under Rule 65(b)(2), the attorney for the TRO applicant must certify in writing either the efforts made to notify the adverse party, or reasons why notice can be excused.

For TROs issued without notice, the court has an obligation to hear the preliminary injunction motion at the earliest possible feasible time. Such hearings take priority over everything on the court calendar other than hearings on previous TROs. The TRO will be dissolved if the restraining party fails to proceed with the application for preliminary injunction.

A TRO cannot last more than 10 days after its time of entry (Rule 65(b)), although it can have a specified, shorter duration. A TRO can be extended on a showing of good cause made within the fixed period of the order, but only for a further 10 days. TROs can also be extended, past a second 10-day period, on consent of the restrained party.

Rule 65(c) mandates that the court set an amount of security to be deposited by the restraining party, representing the costs and damages suffered by the restrained party if the TRO issues improperly. The deposit requirement might be waived for a meritorious, but impecunious, restraining party.

The restraining order must be specific; must explain the reason for its issuance; and must describe the restrained act(s) without referring to any other document, even the complaint in the underlying action. See Rule 65(d).

The adverse party can move to vacate or modify a restraining order by giving two days' notice to the party who secured the TRO. The court has discretion to reduce the notice period even further. Such motions must be heard as expeditiously as circumstances require.

[B] Preliminary Injunctions

A preliminary injunction, also known as an injunction pendente lite, is used to maintain the status quo in an action until a final determination can be made. The injunction is issued before entitlement to permanent relief has been established, and therefore is considered an extraordinary remedy available only to moving parties that have clearly carried the burden of persuasion. The court considers factors such as these in determining if the burden has been met:

- Risk of irreparable harm if the preliminary injunction is denied
- Whether harm to the movant if the injunction is denied outweighs the harm to the opponent if the injunction is granted
- The movant's probability of success at trial
- The public interest.

Rule 65(a) requires the movant to give notice to the adverse party before a preliminary injunction can be issued. Generally, the application for a preliminary injunction is made by motion, but proceeding via order to show cause is also permissible. The parties must submit evidence to the court, preferably in the form of testimony or affidavits, although verified pleadings and depositions are allowed. Under 65(a)(2), to prevent presentation of the same evidence twice, the trial on the merits can be accelerated and consolidated with the application for the preliminary injunction.

The movant must post security with the court, in an amount at the court's discretion (65(c)), to cope with the possibility of improper issuance of a preliminary injunction. This requirement can be waived if the movant is financially unable to deposit such funds.

[C] Additional Provisional Remedies

Other remedies, generally property-related, are available for the pre-trial period. Rule 64 allows the seizure of personal property at any time after commencement of an action, to secure the eventual judgment. Because there is no federal common law of property seizure, then any relevant federal statute will control; if there is no statute to consult, then the state law of the state in which the District Court sits is applied, unless it is Constitutionally defective.

Provisional remedies that may be provided by state law include arrest; attachment; garnishment; replevin; and sequestration. For Constitutional reasons, it is often necessary to provide a hearing prior to seizure of property (especially the property of consumers). In any event, a clear showing of why property should be taken will be required. Attachment is the seizure of property belonging to the defendant; garnishment is attachment of money (usually, salary) belonging to the defendant but held by a third party, with the purpose of satisfying the defendant's debt to the plaintiff. Replevin is an order to someone in wrongful possession of someone else's property to return the property to its real owner. Sequestration is seizure of property until a debt is paid.

Federal Rule 66 governs receivership, the appointment of receivers, who are court officials who control the property that is the subject of an action in order to preserve it for whoever is eventually awarded possession of it. Rule 66 does not apply to receiverships in bankruptcy.

Any party having a legal or equitable interest in the property that is the subject of a suit can apply for appointment of a receiver. Receivership, however, is considered a drastic remedy that will be granted only if the property interest is genuinely at risk (for instance as the result of the defendant's fraudulent conduct) and only if legal remedies are insufficient. The motion for appointment of a receiver must generally be made on notice to all parties that would be affected by the receivership, although an ex parte receivership can be granted in an emergency. In 2007, the Supreme Court extended the availability of declaratory judgment, by permitting a patent licensee to seek a declaratory judgment that the licensed patent is invalid or unenforceable, or that the licensee has not infringed on it: *MedImmune, Inc. v. Genentech, Inc.*[109]

§ 22.17 PRETRIAL CONFERENCE

The Rule 16 pretrial conference is actually the last in a series of meetings, used for the court's continuous monitoring of the progress in the case. The pretrial conference process generates orders that shape the case as it will eventually be tried. Attorneys, and any unrepresented parties, can be required to appear before the judge (or, if the District Court rules so provide, before a magistrate) to expedite the disposition of the case, avoid wasteful pretrial activities, and expedite the trial by improving their preparation and focusing the issues.

A scheduling conference will be held, resulting in a scheduling order that limits the time for joining parties; amending pleadings; filing and hearing motions; and completing discovery (see § 22.18). Rule 16 directs the court to issue the

---

[109] 549 U.S. 118 (2007); *see, e.g.,* Charles S. Barquist and Jason A. Crotty, *"MedImmune v. Genentech": The Supreme Court Upends the Federal Circuit's Declaratory Judgment Jurisprudence,* Special to law.com (1/29/07).

scheduling order as soon as possible, certainly within 120 days after the complaint has been filed.

The pretrial conference covers issues such as:

- Streamlining the issues and eliminating frivolous claims and defenses
- Amending the pleadings, if necessary
- Making admissions of uncontested facts and documents, to reduce unnecessary proof and cumulative evidence
- Making stipulations to authenticity of documents
- Rendering advance rulings from the court as to the admissibility of particular items of evidence
- Setting schedules for filing and exchanging pretrial briefs
- Giving dates for any further conferences; trial date
- Identifying documents and witnesses to be presented at trial
- Indicating whether reference to a master or magistrate is appropriate; whether any special procedures are required, e.g., to deal with complex issues or multiple parties
- Exploring possibilities of settlement
- Deciding on pending motions
- Determining content of the pretrial order.

Twenty-one days before the Rule 16(b) scheduling conference, the parties are required by Rule 26(f) to "meet and confer" to discuss issues such as the proposed discovery plan, preservation of information, production of electronically stored information, and privilege issues.[110]

[A] Pretrial Order

The potential items in the pretrial order, as governed by Rule 16(e), include:

- The basis for federal jurisdiction and venue; whether there is any debate on these subjects
- If a jury trial has been demanded on any issues; if so, whether the adverse party agrees or contests the availability of jury trial
- The basis for amendment for any requested amendments to the pleadings; objections raised by the opposing party; and why the amendments were not made earlier
- Elements of the damages sought
- A "plain, concise statement" in separate numbered paragraphs of the undisputed facts with respect to liability and damages
- The plaintiff(s)' and defendant(s)' positions on disputed matters of fact

---

[110] Carolyn Southerland, Are Litigators Ready for the New Meet-and-Confer Sessions? Nat'l L.J. 7/25/06 (law.com).

- A brief statement, in numbered paragraphs, of the points of law raised by each side and the citations they use to support their positions
- Whether separate trial of any issues is feasible and advisable
- A tabulation of all motions already raised and how they have been disposed of
- The witness list for each side (those whose depositions will be introduced, as well as those who will testify in person)
- Stipulations as to the nature of experts to be called by each side or by the court
- Exhibits whose admissibility is stipulated; additional exhibits proposed to be introduced by each side, but whose admissibility is in question
- The names and telephone numbers of the attorneys who will try the case
- The number of trial days (estimated to the nearest half-day) that each side estimates will be required to present its case
- The proposed trial date, with a notation of possible problems (e.g., witness availability) if the proposed date is not chosen
- Questions that each side proposes to be used in voir dire
- Requested jury instructions, but each side can modify its requests in the course of the trial
- Any other matters that can and should be addressed in the order.

§ 22.18 DISCOVERY

The purpose of discovery, as governed by Rules 26–37, is to avoid "trial by ambush" by giving each side access to all non-privileged information possessed by the other side, as well as offering limited access to information in the possession of non-parties. Information is discoverable, whether or not admissible, if there is a reasonable probability that it will lead to discovery of admissible evidence, or can be used for impeachment.

The practical result is that in many cases, discovery prevents ANY kind of trial, because either it becomes clear that one party's position is untenable, leading to withdrawal or dismissal, or the parties are encouraged to settle their differences before trial. Discovery can be used to uncover areas in which there is no disagreement as to material fact, so that partial summary judgment is appropriate (§ 22.15[A][1]).

Discovery also preserves the testimony of witnesses who might die prior to trial, and records the condition of ephemeral physical evidence. Witnesses can be "pinned down" to a particular position taken during discovery, and their earlier testimony can be used for impeachment if the witnesses attempt to change their stories. The process also offers a chance to observe witnesses and opposing counsel, assess their strengths and weaknesses, and develop strategies for dealing with them.

The FRCP amendments taking effect December 1, 2006 have a powerful effect on discovery of electronic data ("e-discovery"). The latest version of FRCP 26(b)(2)(B) states that a party need not provide discovery of electronically stored information that is not reasonably accessible as a result of burden or cost. When a motion is made for discovery or for a protective order, the party from whom discovery is sought has the burden of showing inaccessibility. But if the party seeking discovery shows good cause, the court can order discovery even if inaccessibility has been demonstrated. Rule 26(b)(1) remains in effect, so parties are not required to preserve or identify irrelevant information. New Rule 26(f) requires parties to litigation to discuss the issues about preserving information that is subject to discovery.[111]

[A] Forms of Discovery

The FRCP permits six major forms of discovery:

(1) Depositions on oral examination (the most common discovery device)
(2) Depositions on written questions
(3) Written interrogatories
(4) Demands for production of documents or objects
(5) Entering and inspecting property
(6) Requests for admission of facts.

Discovery devices can be used in any order (although in practical terms, interrogatories often precede depositions and are used to focus the questions that will be asked at deposition), and Rule 26(d) specifically provides that one party's discovery schedule should not impede discovery by other parties.

Rule 26(g) obligates the attorney, or a pro se party, to sign discovery requests, responses, and objections, which means that such persons can be subjected to mandatory sanctions if the request, etc., is found to be invalid, issued in bad faith, or unduly burdensome. The lawyer's certification is a representation that the attorney has made a reasonable effort to get clients to furnish information, but the lawyer does not become an insurer of the truthfulness of the client's statements.

A party or non-party witness can get discovery of his, her, or its own statement—for instance, a statement made without retaining a copy.

[B] Structuring Discovery

Generally, a discovery plan includes four basic steps:

(1) Determine the location of desired documents; use written interrogatories to parties to determine whose depositions should be taken
(2) Get documents produced as early as possible (so they can be used to prepare for depositions), then use them to refine the witness list and questions to be asked
(3) Take depositions to generate admissions and evaluate witnesses
(4) Fill any gaps in information with requests for admission.

---

[111] David Isom and Dean A. Gonsowski, *Civil Rules: Navigating New Data "Accessibility" Standards*, eDiscovery Law & Strategy 6/22/06 (law.com).

[C] Interrogatories

Interrogatories, as prescribed by Rule 33, are written questions from one party to another party; they cannot be directed to non-party witnesses. The questions are answered under oath. Interrogatories can issue at any time, unless the court has issued a protective order. The questions that can be asked via interrogatory are subject to broad standards of relevancy. However, if the information sought by interrogatory is available in business records, it is acceptable for the answering party to give the demanding party access to the business records in lieu of responding to the interrogatories.

Rule 33(c) permits the answers to interrogatories to be used at trial to the extent they are admissible.

Effective interrogatories are usually brief, simple, and fact-based. For instance, they can be used to identify the documents that have been created, bring out financial information, identify who is an expert or has facts that can be ascertained via deposition.

[D] Depositions

A deposition is a sworn statement taken before an officer of the court who is authorized to administer oaths. Anyone can be deposed; the other discovery devices are restricted to parties. However, there is no requirement that the parties be opponents: for instance, a third-party plaintiff can demand discovery of the lead plaintiff, or of another third-party plaintiff; a counter-claimant can demand discovery of a cross-claimant.

Witnesses can be subpoenaed to give depositions, on reasonable notice, pursuant to Rule 45. Rule 30(b)(6) permits notice to a corporation, partnership, or organization of the information being sought; the organization then has to designate the appropriate person who has the information to testify on behalf of the organization.

Usually, depositions are taken orally, in the presence of attorneys for all the parties. Questioning is done by the attorney seeking the deposition, although the other attorneys can ask questions as well. It is not required that the information brought out by depositions be admissible, as long as the questions relate to the general subject matter of the lawsuit and there is a reasonable probability that the deposition will result in the production of admissible evidence.

Rule 30 allows depositions to be taken at any time after commencement of an action, but leave of court or special circumstances are required to take depositions less than 30 days after the summons and complaint were served. A subpoena duces tecum is required for production of documents at a deposition. Once taken, the depositions are transcribed and submitted to the witness, who is allowed to change them. If a witness has not signed the deposition within 30 days of its submission, the deposition is "signed" by the officer before whom it was taken, and it becomes admissible as if it had been signed by the witness.

All or part of a deposition can be offered in evidence, to the extent that it is admissible under the Federal Rules of Evidence: Rule 32. The testimony is treated as if the deponent were present and testifying. The admissible evidence from the deposition can be used against any party who was present when the deposition was taken; was represented at the deposition; or had reasonable notice of the deposition (and thus could have been present or represented).

FRCP amendments from 2000 limit depositions to one seven-hour day (not counting lunch and other reasonable breaks) unless the parties agree to a longer deposition, or a court order is granted to this effect.

[1] Deposition Technique

Because most cases are settled before trial, the deposition is absolutely crucial to successful resolution of the matter. The size of the settlement obtained for, or exacted from, the attorney's client depends in large part on the facts adduced by depositions, and the degree to which each side's witnesses are articulate, credible, and well-prepared.

Questions can be asked at a deposition that are not admissible in evidence, as long as they are reasonably calculated to lead to evidence. Although it is usually a mistake to ask a trial witness "Why?" such a question is often useful in a deposition. It is also often a good idea to ask witnesses if anything else happened or if they are aware of any additional facts.

If a deposition contains vital material, but the witness is inarticulate or unattractive, it may be more effective to admit the deposition rather than have the witness testify at the trial.

[E] Other Discovery Devices

Rule 34 governs requests that a party produce materials for inspection. The demanding party can measure, sample, test, and photograph those materials. Rule 45 implements a somewhat similar procedure when the person or entity in control of those materials is not a party to the action; in this situation, leave of court is required.

A physical or mental examination of a person can be compelled under Rule 35, if those issues (e.g., blood group) are in controversy in a suit. The person doing the examination must have any required licenses; and the requesting party must demonstrate good cause for the request.

Any party can request any other party to admit the truth of any matter that comes within the scope of Rule 26(b); see Rule 36. The requester serves a request for admission of specific items; if there is no response, the items are deemed admitted unless the served party files an objection.

Even if there is an objection, the court can order that the objection is invalid and the admissions must be made. An uncooperative party can be sanctioned, and can be ordered to pay the cost of proving items whose truth should have been admitted. Admitted facts are conclusively established for the case at bar, but cannot be used in other cases.

Rule 26 permits a party to use interrogatories to require another party to disclose the expert witnesses scheduled to be called at trial; what they will testify about, and a summary of the facts and opinions they are expected to express and the grounds for such statements of fact and opinion.

If a showing of exceptional circumstances and inability to get the information otherwise is made, discovery can be obtained from experts hired by another party but who will NOT testify at trial. There is no mechanism for discovery from experts who are informally consulted but not retained.

Because e-mail is now the predominant form by which business communications occur, it is likely that discovery of e-mail will become an issue in most business cases. Corporations must have policies for preservation of evidence (e-mails are usually archived or backed up in at least one location, including mail servers, individual hard drives, magnetic media, and network storage) or routine erasure that does not create spoliation of evidence. It must often be determined if an e-mail was purely personal or was an official communication that binds the corporation.[112]

During employment, it is common for employees to use the employer's computer system — so if employment litigation ensues, both sides leave a computer trail. It is not a good idea for employers to implement a policy of routinely wiping hard drives of employees who leave the firm, because that could result in destruction of evidence; at a minimum, the policy should call for retaining copies. The employee's computer use can show wrongdoing such as embezzlement, resume fraud, violating the employer's policy on viewing pornography at work, or disclosure of trade secrets, whereas the employer may have made a record of discriminating or retaliating against the employee. There are also possible discovery issues for other electronic devices, such as cell phones; CDs; Blackberrys; printer and fax caches; flash drives; iPods and MP3 players used as portable hard drives; and telephone and Instant Messaging records.[113]

See § 28.02[C] for discussion of discovery of e-mails.

[F] Limitations on Discovery

The discovery process gives rise to many motions. Proponents of discovery can move to compel answers or sanction non-compliance with discovery orders.

---

[112] *See* David M. Remnity, *Electronic Mail: Key Issues for Corporate Counsel in Discovery*, 72 L.W. 2339 (12/16/03).

[113] A. Michael Weber, *E-Discovery Keeps an Eye on the Job*, N.Y.L.J. 4/21/08 (law.com). *See, e.g.*, Smith v. Cafe Asia, 2007 WL 2849579 (D.D.C. 10/2/07) [employer introduced stored images on cell phone to show that the plaintiff voluntarily engaged in what she claimed was harassing conduct]; LeJeune v. Coin Acceptors Inc., 849 A.2d 451 (Md. 2004) [the act of copying employer data to a CD before resigning used to prove misappropriation of trade secrets]; Scott v. Beth Israel Medical Ctr. Inc., 2007 WL 3053351 (NY Co Sup. Ct. 10/17/07) [attorney-client privilege lost when e-mail to lawyer violated the employer's rule against personal use of the corporate e-mail system]. *But see* Curto v. Medical World Communications Inc., 2006 WL 1318387 (E.D.N.Y. 2006): attorney-client privilege was not waived by using a laptop supplied by the employer, because the attorney-client communication did not take place in the employer's office or while connected to its server. SEC Rule 17a-4 requires broker-dealers to store their IMs online for at least two years.

Opponents of discovery can object to discovery requests or seek protective orders, but they should be aware that Rule 26 requires discovery of all material that is not privileged. Federal Rules of Evidence 501 holds that state law of privilege applies if the rule of decision comes from state law (as, for instance, in a diversity case or a case in which the federal court exercises supplemental jurisdiction over a state claim). In all other cases, the federal common law of privilege governs. Most discovery orders are not appealable, because they are not "final orders" in the sense of resolving litigation or even an independent phase of litigation.

Rule 26(b)(3) codifies the "work product" doctrine enunciated in *Hickman v. Taylor*, 329 U.S. 495 (1947). Work product consists of documents and other items prepared in anticipation of litigation. It is discoverable only if the requester shows a substantial need of the material to prepare the case for its own side, and only if it is impossible to secure the same information without substantial hardship.

According to the Sixth Circuit, statements made by parties during settlement talks are privileged and protected from third-party discovery. The public interest favors secrecy, whether the discussions are under court auspices or private, because facilitating negotiations makes the judicial system more efficient.[114]

In a case of first impression, the Southern District of New York held late in 2003 that *Wells* submissions (material divulged to the SEC by a party who could become the subject of charges) are not protected from discovery in later civil cases merely because they contain an offer of settlement. If a *Wells* submission does include a settlement offer, that material can be severed prior to discovery.[115]

Rule 26(f) provides for a discovery conference, in which the court (sua sponte or on motion of a party) brings the attorneys in to discuss the schedule for discovery and the allowable scope. For instance, limits might be set on the number of depositions or interrogatories; or the number of questions permitted in an interrogatory (50 is standard).

Discovery does carry with it the potential for abuse, so Rule 26 allows the court to limit the use of discovery if:

- The discovery sought merely duplicates other sources of information
- Discovery is more burdensome than other means to acquire the same information (e.g., doing research; hiring a private investigator)
- Discovery is more expensive than other means
- The party seeking discovery already had a full opportunity to acquire the information now sought in discovery
- Discovery is excessively burdensome when considered in the context of its importance to the suit.

When discovery materials were sealed, and parties in collateral litigation involving the same defendant seek access to the materials, the discovery order

---

[114] Goodyear Tire & Rubber Co. v. Chiles Power Supply Inc., 332 F.3d 976 (6th Cir. 2003).
[115] *In re* IPO Sec. Litigation, 297 F. Supp. 2d 668 (S.D.N.Y. 2003).

can be modified if the material sought is discoverable in the second case; is relevant; the presumption of access has not been rebutted; and any confidential information can be redacted to maintain privacy.[116]

The Middle District of Pennsylvania permitted discovery of the defendant's financial condition without proof of entitlement to punitive damages, denying a Rule 26(c) protective order that would have deferred discovery until and unless the jury found that punitive damages were warranted. The defendant was the employer of an allegedly unqualified tractor-trailer driver. The Middle District defined the standard for granting a 26(c) protective order as good cause: whether disclosure would cause clearly defined and serious injury, and found that discovery could be handled without disclosing sensitive business matters.[117]

[G] Subpoenas

A subpoena is not required to make a party give a deposition, but usually is required to compel the deposition of a non-party.

Rule 45 provides that subpoenas, whether ad testificandum or duces tecum (i.e., for testimony or for production of documents) are issued from the court where testimony or production is required. The subpoena must give the name of the court; the title of the action; and information about where to appear or submit documents. The clerk of the court issues a signed blank subpoena to the requesting party, who fills it out.

A subpoena duces tecum cannot order anyone to produce material that is not already in his possession, custody, or control. The recipient of the subpoena has 14 days (or the time for compliance given in the subpoena, if shorter) to file a written objection to production or copying of any material sought. Once the objection is served on the demanding party or party's attorney, the material will not have to be produced unless the demander gets a court order.

[1] Modifying or Quashing Subpoenas

Subpoenas must disclose the rights of subpoenaed parties by including the texts of Rule 45(c) and (d), which safeguard the right to object to inspection and copying and to get a subpoena (either ad testificandum or duces tecum) quashed[118] or modified — e.g., if compliance would require excessive travel; if disclosure is sought of privileged or trade secret information. Rule 45(d)(2) requires anyone asserting privilege or work product to make the assertion explicitly and explain why the material is privileged.

---

[116] Foltz v. State Farm Mut. Auto Ins. Co., 331 F.3d 1122 (9th Cir. 2003).

[117] Grosek v. Panther Transp. Inc., No. 3:07cv1592 (M.D. Pa. 2008); *see* Shannon P. Duffy, *Federal Judge: Prima Facie Claim Not Needed for Punitive Damages Discovery*, The Legal Intelligencer 7/31/08 (law.com).

[118] But only the court that issued the subpoena can quash or modify it; the Federal Rules of Civil Procedure do not give District Courts the authority to transfer motions to quash subpoenas to other District Courts: *In re* Sealed Case, 141 F.3d 337 (D.C. Cir. 1998).

If a timely motion is made, Rule 45(c)(3) requires the court to quash or modify the subpoena if:

- The time given for compliance is unreasonably short
- It calls for privileged matter
- It is unduly burdensome
- It requires a non-party to travel more than 100 miles from home or work — but such persons can be ordered to travel within the state, based on a showing of substantial need, if the travel does not involve substantial expense.

In addition to those circumstances in which the court must modify or quash the subpoena, the court has discretion to do so if disclosure of trade secrets or other confidential information is sought; if the opinion of an expert who has not been retained by the subpoenaed party is sought; or if a non-party is required to travel more than 100 miles and has not been offered reasonable compensation by the requesting party.

Digital Millennium Copyright Act § 512(h) (see § 12.03[F]) authorizes subpoenas directed at Internet Service Providers (ISPs). However, according to the D.C. Circuit, this provision applies only to ISPs that store copyrighted materials, not those that transmit them, for example by peer-to-peer file sharing. Therefore, Verizon could not be compelled to identify its subscribers in a copyright case involving illegal music downloads.[119]

[2] Service of Subpoenas

The subpoena can be served by any adult who is not a party to the action. Proof of service must be filed with the court clerk. Under Rule 45, a subpoena can be served anywhere within the court district; outside the district, but within a 100-mile radius of the place of hearing or document production called for by the subpoena;[120] anywhere within the state in which the federal district court is located, if state law would permit such service in a state case; or anywhere inside or outside the United States as authorized by a federal statute. Under Rule 45(e), failure to obey a subpoena without adequate cause constitutes contempt of court. However, if a motion to quash has been made, the witness can refuse to comply with the subpoena until the disposition of the motion.

Any subpoenaed person who is ordered to attend a hearing, deposition, or trial must be advanced the fees for one days' attendance and mileage.

---

[119] RIAA v. Verizon Internet Servs. Inc., 352 F.3d 1229 (D.C. Cir. 2003).

[120] Hence, according to the District Court for the District of Massachusetts, a subpoena duces tecum could not validly be issued in Washington, D.C. against Boston universities whose students were accused of computer piracy. Although the plaintiff took the position that Digital Millennium Copyright Act § 512(h) authorizes nationwide service of process on ISPs to secure information about copyright infringement, the court applied FRCP 45(b)(2)'s 100-mile limitation instead: MIT v. Recording Indus. Ass'n of Am., 72 L.W. 1131 (D. Mass. 8/7/03).

§ 22.19   SETTLEMENT

Cases actually heard in the court system are a tiny fraction of all legal disputes. More than 90% of cases actually filed are settled (usually before trial, although trials can be brought to a halt by settlements, and appeals can be forestalled by a settlement AFTER trial), and of course many disputes are resolved informally before an action can be filed.

The Department of Justice reported in late 2008 that in 2005, plaintiffs won more than half of state civil trials, and bench trials were more likely to result in a plaintiff's verdict than jury trials. Overall, plaintiffs won 56% of general civil trials (54% of jury trials and 68% of bench trials). In 2005, plaintiffs got an aggregate of about $6 billion in compensatory and punitive damages (median: $28,000). About one-seventh of winning plaintiffs received damages over $250,000, and awards were over $1 million in about 4% of cases. In 2005, there were about 27,000 civil trials, 61% of them torts, usually automotive. Prevailing plaintiffs received punitive damages in about 5% of cases, with a median of $64,000.[121]

A study in the Journal of Empirical Legal Studies, examining over 2,000 trials between 2002 and 2005, found that 61% of plaintiffs received less relief than the settlement offer, and thus should have settled rather than going to trial. About one-quarter (24%) of defendants were wrong to go to trial; and in 15% of cases, both plaintiff and defendant made the right decision, because the plaintiff received more than the original settlement offer, but less than the plaintiff's initial demand. Although the study found that plaintiffs were more likely to make the wrong decision, the consequences were worse for defendants: where the defendant incorrectly chose to go to trial; the average plaintiff's settlement demand was $770,900, and the average verdict was $1.9 million, whereas the average offer to plaintiffs who wrongly chose trial was $48,700 and the average verdict was $43,000, so the two outcomes were roughly equal.[122]

A New York intermediate-level court held that, in a civil trial, high-low agreements are settlements and should be enforced as such. If the jury awards more than the "high" amount, the plaintiff receives only the "high" amount; if the jury awards less than the "low," the plaintiff is nevertheless entitled to the "low" amount, and if the jury award falls in between these poles, the plaintiff gets the jury award. The court also held that high-low agreements must be accompanied by a general release under CPLR § 5003-a.[123]

[121] Vesna Jaksic, *DOJ Study: Plaintiffs Win More Than Half of State Court Civil Trials*, Nat'l L.J. 10/30/08 (law.com).
[122] Karen Sloan, *Settling More Lucrative Than Going to Trial, Study Shows*, Nat'l L.J. 9/24/08 (law.com).
[123] Cunha v. Shapiro, 42 A.D. 3d 95 (A.D. 2d Dept. 2007); *see* Tom Perrotta, *N.Y. Appeals Court Considers High-Low Deals as Settlements*, N.Y.L.J. 5/7/07 (law.com).

[A] Offer of Judgment

FRCP 68 covers the offer of judgment, made by a defendant and expressing the amount that the defendant is willing to pay as a result of having judgment entered against it. Offers of judgment must be unconditional and, once made, they are irrevocable. Rule 68 allows the offer to be made at any time until 10 days before the scheduled trial date.

The defendant serves the offer on the plaintiff, but does NOT file it with the court. The plaintiff gets 10 days to accept the offer; if the plaintiff chooses to accept it, either party then files the offer with the court, and the clerk enters a judgment in accordance with the agreement of the parties. Any offer not accepted within the 10-day window is deemed to be withdrawn (although the defendant can make further, and presumably higher, offers until 10 days before the trial date). Evidence about withdrawn offers cannot be admitted in a case in chief, only in a proceeding to set costs.

The significance of the offer of judgment is that if the plaintiff refuses the offer and eventually wins the case — but is awarded LESS than the defendant's offer of judgment — the plaintiff can be required to pay all costs, including attorneys' fees, incurred after the offer was made.

Rescission is not available if a Rule 68 offer of judgment is mishandled, although Rule 60(b) can be invoked in case of mistake, inadvertence, surprise, or excusable neglect.[124]

§ 22.20 TRIAL

[A] Calendars and Scheduling

Courts have two main methods of setting cases for trial: individual calendaring, and central assignment systems. The trial judge handles the cases assigned to him or her in an individual system, including setting trial dates.

In a central assignment system, new cases are added to the bottom of the calendar. A judge who is available to try a case simply selects the oldest case on the calendar that has been marked ready for trial.

The extent of "e-filing" (the role of computers and the Internet in docket management, service of process, and online availability of documents) varies from court to court and agency to agency. The federal system is more advanced than most state and local court systems in this regard. Usually, an e-filing project begins with a pilot project as proof of concept, followed by voluntary e-filing of court documents, then mandatory e-filing. An advantage of e-filing is that filings can be made at any time until one minute before midnight on the due date; there is no limitation to the court's business hours.

---

[124] Webb v. James, 147 F.3d 617 (7th Cir. 1998).

[B] Consolidation and Severance

A federal court can order a joint hearing or trial on any matters involving common questions of law or fact: Rule 42(a). The court also has discretion to order that actions be consolidated, as well as to make other orders required to prevent unnecessary costs or delay.

The court's administrative powers also extend to ordering separate trials of any claim, cross-claim, counterclaim, third party claim, or issue as required by the interests of convenience, expedition, economy, and avoidance of prejudice.

[C] Availability of Jury Trial

FRCP 38(a) preserves both the Seventh Amendment guarantee of trial by jury and any statutory right to a jury trial. In the federal system, only federal law determines the availability of jury trial — even if other issues are determined under state law.

Juries are not empanelled automatically in all cases where jury trial is available. Rule 38(b) requires the party seeking a jury to make a timely written demand, served on the other parties and the court. A demand is timely as soon as the action has been commenced, at least 10 days after service of the last pleading directed to the issues that can be tried by a jury. If one party demands a jury trial on certain issues, another party can demand jury trial on other issues, but the demand must be made within 10 days of service of the original demand.

It is the exception, not the rule, for federal civil juries to be sequestered, although federal criminal jurors are usually sequestered during deliberations.

[1] Jury Selection

Selection of both grand and petit jurors within the federal system is governed by 28 USC §§ 1861–1878. These provisions have a dual purpose: random selection of jurors from a fair cross section of the community; and protecting citizens from exclusion from jury service on the basis of race, color, sex, religion, national origin, or economic status.

The federal District Courts maintain their own jury selection plans. Usually, a master jury wheel is created from voter registration lists. Juror qualification questionnaires are sent to persons whose names are drawn at random from the jury wheel. The qualified jury wheel is prepared from the questionnaires that indicate qualification for service. Individuals are exempt from jury service if they are members of the armed forces; police officers; firefighters; or government officials. Temporary excuses can be granted for undue hardship or extreme inconvenience to the juror, but they are disfavored.

Minors, non-citizens of the United States, persons who cannot read, write, and speak English; the mentally or physically infirm; those who have not lived in the district for a year; and persons charged with or convicted of a felony (unless their civil rights have been restored) are not eligible for federal jury service.

Summonses are issued several weeks in advance of the time the potential jurors are ordered to report. In multi-judge courts, usually the judges integrate their jury trial calendars so jurors who are not used on one trial can be sent to a trial pending before another judge.

Usually, a federal civil jury will contain six jurors, and a criminal jury will contain 12 persons, although Rule 48 allows any number of jurors between six and 12 in a federal trial.

Rule 47(a) lets federal trial judges decide whether they or the attorneys will perform voir dire. However, if the court performs the voir dire, the attorneys must be allowed to ask their own supplementary questions.

In a federal civil trial, each side gets three peremptory challenges, plus challenges for cause; see 28 USC § 1870. (Up to ten peremptories are usually granted in a criminal case.) The basic rule[125] is that racially-based peremptory challenges cannot be used to exclude members of the defendant's race from a jury. It has been applied to civil as well as criminal cases.[126] Gender-based peremptory challenges are ruled out by *J.E.B. v. Alabama*, 511 U.S. 127 (1994).

[D] Trial Timeline

- Jury selection
- Judge's preliminary instructions to jurors
- Opening statements
- Plaintiff's case in chief, requiring proof of each element of each claim, using witness testimony, exhibits, judicial notice, and/or stipulations
- Cross-examination, usually limited to the scope of the direct examination
- Redirect
- Questions from the judge; the jurors may also be permitted to submit questions (usually in written form)
- The plaintiff rests
- Defense motions, e.g., motion for judgment as a matter of law because the plaintiff has failed to present a prima facie case
- Defense case in chief, rebutting the plaintiff's case and proving any affirmative defenses, counterclaims, or cross-claims
- Defense rests
- Plaintiff's motions
- If counterclaims were raised, the plaintiff puts on its rebuttal case, and the defense puts on its surrebuttal case
- After both sides have rested, either side can move for directed verdict
- Judge queries attorneys about requested jury instructions
- Closing arguments; usually the plaintiff gives the first argument, the defense gives its argument, and the plaintiff is permitted to reply, because the plaintiff has the burden of proof

---

[125] *Stated by* Batson v. Kentucky, 476 U.S. 79 (1986).
[126] By Edmonson v. Leesville Concrete Co., 500 U.S. 614 (1991).

- Judge's instructions to the jury
- Deliberations and verdict
- Post-trial motions, e.g., motion for judgment despite the verdict (JNOV) or new trial required by errors at trial
- Hearings on post-trial motions
- Judge's oral or written order on post-trial motions
- Entry of judgment based on the jury verdict and post-trial motions; time to appeal begins to run at this point.

[E] Trial Techniques

The trial is the chance for each side to present its case with the utmost clarity and persuasiveness that it can muster, as well as a chance to attack the evidence presented by the opponent(s).

Note that 28 USC § 636(c) allows a U.S. magistrate judge, on consent of the parties, to conduct any civil trial, applying the normal federal procedural and evidence rules. Such cases can usually be appealed directly to the Court of Appeals.

Absent extraordinary circumstances, the Indiana state Constitution gives civil litigants the right to be present in court during both the liability and damage phases of the trial. The court refused to exclude a malpractice plaintiff (a wheelchair-bound child) despite the defense argument that the plaintiff's presence could tend to prejudice the jury.[127]

[1] Opening Statement

In the federal system, the party with the burden of proof has the right to make the first opening statement. If there are multiple parties, more than one of whom bear the burden on different issues, the plaintiff has the right to open. It is crucial for the plaintiff's opening statement to set out facts sufficient to establish a prima facie case, because failure to do so can open the way to a successful defense motion to dismiss.

A defendant who simply pleads a general denial has no obligation to make an opening statement, but an opening statement is probably required of a defendant who asserts an affirmative defense. Local rules may allow the defense to defer its opening until the end of the plaintiff's case in chief, to prevent premature disclosure of defense theories.

Where there are multiple parties who are not united in interest, and who have separate counsel, each party can make an opening statement. But if it seems likely that a shorter presentation will be more interesting and appealing to the jury, they can join in a single opening.

---

[127] Jordan v. Deery, 778 N.E.2d 1264 (Ind. 2002).

[2] The Direct Case

Without demonstrative evidence, a trial is simply a series of "talking heads," and jurors may be much more interested and retain much more information if the spoken testimony is supplemented by visual exhibits. Real evidence is an actual tangible object involved in the case. Demonstrative evidence is something like a chart, model, diagram, or reconstruction that clarifies the facts of the case but is not directly involved.

An exhibit cannot be admitted without foundation: testimony or certification that proves that the exhibit is what it purports to be. Depending on local practice, an exhibit can be marked in advance, or the record will have to reflect that an item described in a certain way has been marked as plaintiff's or defendant's exhibit, plus its letter or number.

First, the exhibit is shown to the opposing attorney, so he or she can raise any objections. Next, the exhibit, held so that it is out of sight of the jury, is shown to the witness. The witness lays the foundation for admission of the exhibit: nature of the item, its connection to the witness, perhaps establishment of chain of custody. Admissibility of evidence could involve issues such as:

- Witness' recognition of a tangible object
- Relevancy of that object to the case
- Whether the witness can testify that the condition of the object is unchanged
- Chain of custody (who had the object at any point in time; lack of access by unauthorized persons)
- That a photograph, diagram, or model is accurate and represents the state of facts it is purported to represent
- That a record was kept in the course of regularly-conducted business activity, by a person with direct knowledge of the facts or who received the information from someone with direct knowledge.

The most common demonstrative exhibit format is a large (30″ × 40″ or 40″ × 60″) chart that is mounted on a lightweight board. This size is large enough for the jurors to see conveniently, but small enough to transport to court. It is usually more effective to prepare more charts, each limited to a few salient points, than to try to cram too much onto a single chart. (A heading, plus one to eight bullet points of under 40 characters each, is a good amount of copy for an evidentiary chart.) Charts and other graphical material that is not admissible in evidence can nevertheless be used during an opening or closing statement.

Where documents are admitted into evidence, it can work well to reproduce them on transparencies, then show them to the jury on an overhead projector; the attorney can then use a felt-tip pen to annotate the document and underline salient words and phrases.

Exhibits are usually produced and qualified after, or near the end of, direct examination of a witness, so that the jury will listen to the witness rather than tuning out and looking at the exhibit.

The federal court system does not follow the Best Evidence Rule, so a photocopy or other exact copy of a document is just as admissible in federal court as the original. (In states that retain the Best Evidence Rule, a copy can still be introduced, based on a showing that the copy is relevant to the case; that there once was an original; that a true and accurate copy was made of it; and that, despite a diligent search, the original could not be produced for the trial.)

Although FRE 501 allows courts to create new privileges, by interpreting the common law in the light of reason and experience, the District Court for the District of Columbia refused to recognize a new privilege for communications made in the course of settlement negotiations. The four factors for recognizing a new privilege (broad federal and state consensus supporting the new privilege; congressional consideration of the rationales supporting the privilege; inclusion of the potential new privilege in the proposed new Federal Rules of Evidence; and clear demonstration that the proposed privilege will promote the public good) were not present.[128]

FRE 803(5) permits introduction of a memorandum or record that represents "recorded recollection" (even if it does not qualify as a business record), as long as it was made at a time when the facts were fresh in the witness' recollection; if it was accurate when made; and if the witness does not currently have a strong enough independent recollection of the facts to testify independent of the memorandum or record.

FRE 902 makes certified copies of public records self-authenticating; so if a document is introduced that bears an official seal and a statement that it is a public record, the only possible objection is to the relevancy of the document, not its admissibility.

Under Rule 1006, a summary of voluminous records is admissible, when the writings, recordings, photographs, or other materials cannot conveniently be produced. The party seeking to present a summary must give advance notice to the opposing party. The judge can, however, direct production of the underlying materials.

See Chapter 23 for a fuller discussion of evidentiary issues under the Federal Rules of Evidence.

[3] Expert Testimony

The optimum expert not only has impressive technical qualifications, but is able to instruct the jury about his or her technical area, can express conclusions in plain English, and is viewed by the jury as a credible and likeable person. If several expert witnesses are available, often the best choice will be the one with the best communications skills.

The expert witness should make it clear that the expert is being paid to testify, and should bring out occasions in the past when the expert has testified — preferably instances in which the expert has represented plaintiffs rather than defendants (or vice versa), or has reached conclusions opposite to those he or she is testifying

---

[128] *In re* Subpoena Issued to CFTC, 370 F. Supp. 2d 201 (D.D.C. 2005).

about currently. Such testimony rebuts the common perception that expert witnesses are merely hired guns who always reach whatever conclusion is favorable to the paying party's position.

[4] Cross-Examination

It is not necessarily valid strategy to cross-examine every witness. If testimony is not genuinely damaging to your case, it may be better to avoid cross-examination, especially if the witness seems sympathetic or vulnerable. But the jury will be surprised, or even suspicious, if major witnesses are not cross-examined.

Major points in cross-examination should be raised at the beginning and end of the cross, when jurors are at their most attentive.

Federal Rules of Evidence 607 allows any party to impeach any witness; it can be helpful to anticipate problems by bringing out potentially dangerous areas on direct examination. Nevertheless, attempts at impeachment usually occur during cross-examination. There are seven major sources of impeachment:

(1) The witness' bias in favor of, or prejudice against, a person or position; the witness' own ability to benefit from or suffer detriment from the case
(2) Prior convictions
(3) Prior bad acts
(4) Prior inconsistent statements. The prior inconsistent statements of an opposing party are always admissible; prior inconsistent statements are not hearsay when used for the limited purpose of impeaching a non-party witness.
(5) Contradictory facts
(6) The witness' poor reputation for truthfulness
(7) Accepted treatises that disagree with the position expressed by an expert witness.

[5] Closing Argument

Generally speaking, the party having the burden of proof makes the last closing argument. If there are multiple parties to a case, each can make a closing argument, or they can consolidate and offer a single closing.

Usually, closing arguments should be brief (15–20 minutes), and should parallel the structure of argument used in the opening argument and case in chief. The closing argument is the attorney's last chance to stress the strengths of the case and rebut challenges to it. It can be useful to re-use some key exhibits to refresh the jurors' recollection, or to create a summary chart that is not independent evidence but that aids argument.

Closing argument topics include:

• Identification of the parties and issues
• Relevant evidence and exhibits

- Deficiencies in the case presented by the opponent
- Challenges to the credibility of opposing witnesses
- Applicable law
- Jury instructions requested by the attorney
- Proposed damages.

[F] Dismissal of Actions

Under Rule 41, dismissal of an action can either be voluntary (from the plaintiff's viewpoint) or involuntary. Voluntary dismissals come under 41(a), and can be handled by either notice of discontinuance or stipulation. The plaintiff is only permitted to file a notice of discontinuance at a very early stage in litigation, before the defendant files its answer or serves a motion for summary judgment. The dismissal automatically becomes effective when the notice of discontinuance is filed with the court clerk; the participation of the adverse party is not required. Rule 41(a) cannot be used in class actions or cases in which a receiver has been appointed, because in such cases the court's permission is required to discontinue the action.

There are some rare circumstances in which the plaintiff wants to dismiss the case, but the defendant is unwilling — probably because a counterclaim is involved. In such situations, the plaintiff must move to the court for dismissal, but the case cannot be dismissed if there is a counterclaim unless the counterclaim can be maintained on the basis of its own independent jurisdictional status (i.e., it presents a federal question or diversity is present).

The general rule is that, unless the notice of discontinuance or stipulation is to the contrary, voluntary dismissals occur without prejudice, but 41(a)(1) provides that the dismissal operates as an adjudication on the merits if the notice or stipulation is filed by a plaintiff who has already dismissed an action based on or including the same claim in any state or federal court.

Involuntary dismissal on motion by the defendant, or the court's own motion, comes under 41(b). It can be sought if the plaintiff fails to prosecute the action; fails to obey a court order; or fails to comply with the Federal Rules of Civil Procedure. Unless the order of dismissal is to the contrary, a Rule 41(b) dismissal is an adjudication on the merits that has res judicata effect.

Rule 50(a) governs motions for judgment as a matter of law — what used to be known as motions for a directed verdict. The judge rules on the merits of the claim as a matter of law; the jury never receives any issue decided by the judge in this manner. Judgment as a matter of law can be granted on any claim, counterclaim, cross-claim, or third-party claim as to which a party has been fully heard, if it would be impossible for a reasonable jury to find for that party.

The Supreme Court interpreted Rule 50(b) in its 2006 *Unitherm Food Systems, Inc. v. Swift-Eckrich, Inc.*[129] decision. The underlying case involved

_____
[129] 546 U.S. 394 (2006).

allegations of violation of Sherman Act Section 2 by attempting to enforce a fraudulent patent. The District Court found the patent invalid and allowed a trial on the Sherman Act issue. Before the case went to the jury, a Rule 50(a) motion was made based on the legal insufficiency of the evidence. The motion was denied, and the jury found for the opposing party. There was no motion filed for JMOL under Rule 50(b), nor was there a Rule 59 motion for a new trial. The losing party appealed to the Federal Circuit, on the grounds that there was insufficient evidence to sustain the verdict. The Federal Circuit ordered a new trial. The Supreme Court reversed, holding that Rule 50 explicates two different stages for challenging the sufficiency of the evidence in a civil case. Rule 50(a) motions are made before the case goes to the jury; the District Court has discretion to grant such a motion. Rule 50(b) requires renewal of the challenge once a jury has reached a verdict and judgment has been entered. Failure to file a Rule 50(b) post verdict motion means that the appellate court lacks the power to order the District Court to change its judgment — whether the moving party seeks JMOL or a new trial.

[G] Jury Instructions

At the close of the evidence (or at an earlier point as directed by the judge), any party can make a written request to have the court instruct the jury on the law. The judge responds to the attorneys' requests before their closing arguments. If one side objects to the other side's proposed instructions, or the instructions actually given by the judge, the objection must be raised before the jury retires. Failure to raise the objection on time prevents assignment of error on appeal (absent a gross miscarriage of justice).

[H] Verdicts and Decisions

A general verdict, signed by all the jurors, simply indicates in which party's favor the jury has found. A special verdict (also known as special interrogatories) is more detailed, setting out answers to questions posed by the judge. Under Rule 49(a), the judge can direct the jury to return a special verdict, including special written findings on each issue of fact. The court can provide three types of guidelines to the jury:

- Written questions that can be answered briefly
- Several special findings that the jury could make, based on the pleadings and the evidence offered
- Whatever the court deems appropriate.

That is, in the federal system, use of a special verdict is discretionary at the judge's option. States vary in their practice: some mandate special verdicts, whereas others leave it up to the judge.

It is permissible, under Rule 49(b), before a general verdict is rendered, for the judge to give the jury general verdict forms and written interrogatories dealing with issues of fact that must be decided in order to render a verdict, with necessary explanations and instructions that the jury will need to answer the interrogatories and render the verdict.

In cases in which there is no jury (or only an advisory jury), the court must make findings of fact and conclusions of law before entering final judgment (pursuant to Rule 58) granting or denying relief. If the judge's decision is appealed, the appellate court is not bound by conclusions of law, but almost always upholds findings of fact (which are assessed by a "clear error" standard).

Depending on local rules, the judge either may or is obligated to ask the attorneys to prepare their proposed findings and conclusions for the court to consider. Usually the plaintiff submits first, but the court can order simultaneous submissions. Proposed findings are usually drafted in separate numbered paragraphs that give a simple statement of the facts the party relies on to support each claim or defense. Conclusions of law and supporting authorities should be provided in separate numbered paragraphs for jurisdiction, venue, and each element of a claim or defense asserted by the party.

Unless the parties stipulate to the contrary, the verdict of a federal jury must be unanimous and must be rendered by at least six jurors. According to the Ninth Circuit, it is not just a matter of Rule 48, but a requirement of the Seventh Amendment, that civil trial verdicts must be unanimous. When an affirmative defense is asserted, the jury must render a unanimous vote against the defense before finding the defendant liable and then assessing damages.[130]

Rule 48 says that as long as at least six jurors remain, or if the parties accept the lesser number, the loss of a juror does not require declaration of a mistrial. The judge has discretion to excuse a juror who becomes ill, is needed in an emergency, or has committed misconduct that would justify a mistrial. However, jurors cannot be excused because they refuse to join in an otherwise unanimous verdict.

[1] Judgment of the Court

In a court trial, Rule 52(c) provides that the court may enter judgment as a matter of law against a party who has been fully heard on an issue, as to any claim that is contingent on a favorable ruling on the issue.

In either a court or a jury trial, Rule 54(a) governs decrees and court orders that may be subject to appeal — i.e., the judgment itself, but not the judge's written opinion. Rule 54(c) provides that (other than for default judgments), a final judgment granting relief must grant all relief to which the party is entitled — including elements of relief that were not requested in the pleadings. But default judgments are limited to relief prayed for in the pleadings.

In federal practice, the clerk of the court prepares the judgment form, unless the court specifically asks the prevailing attorney to do so. In contrast, the practice

---

[130] Jazzabi v. Allstate Ins. Co., 278 F.3d 979 (9th Cir. 2002).

of many states is to have the attorney prepare the judgment and give it to the clerk for entry.

[2] Enforcement of Judgments

The enforcement of money judgments rendered in federal civil cases falls under Rule 69. Unless the court directs otherwise, enforcement occurs via writ of execution. The writ is issued by the court that handed down the judgment. It is served by the U.S. Marshal or designate. However, Rule 69(a) provides that a writ of execution for a private party can be executed only in the state in which the District Court sits.

[3] Prison Litigation

The Prison Litigation Reform Act, P.L. 104-134 (1996) seeks to discourage prisoners from filing suits about prison conditions by limiting the available relief to the minimum necessary to vindicate federal rights. If an inmate is awarded any monetary relief, the statute requires notice to be given to the victims so they can seek restitution from the award. Judges are encouraged to screen prison petitions[131] and dismiss frivolous cases. An inmate who makes repeated frivolous claims, or any malicious claims, can be deprived of "good time" that would otherwise be used to reduce the sentence. See § 26.04[O] for further discussion of prison litigation.

[4] Unpublished Opinions

As the volume of litigation increases, so does the volume of opinions, many of which either are of interest only to the parties or are supposed to apply only to the parties. Therefore, the issue of the authority of unpublished opinions becomes increasingly significant.

In September 2005, the Judicial Conference endorsed the creation of a new Rule 32.1. The Circuits would be allowed to create their own rules as to how much precedential value the unpublished opinions should receive. Currently, close to 80% of appellate opinions are released as "unpublished" (so that, in the interests of time, brief opinions can be prepared by judges or clerks). The Second, Seventh, Ninth, and Federal Circuits have ruled that unpublished opinions cannot be cited, and six other Circuits discourage the practice.[132] The Supreme Court adopted

---

[131] 28 USC § 1915A requires the District Court to review all complaints in civil actions in which prisoners ask for redress from government entities or their agents — "before docketing, if feasible." Complaints must be dismissed if the prisoner-plaintiff fails to state a claim on which relief can be granted; if the complaint itself is frivolous or malicious; or if damages are sought against an immune party.

[132] Tony Mauro, *Judicial Conference Supports Citing Unpublished Opinions*, Legal Times 9/21/05 (law.com).

Rule 32.1 in April 2006. Starting January 1, 2007, it is permissible to cite an unpublished opinion in an appellate brief—but unpublished opinions (even from their own Circuit) are not binding on the Courts of Appeals.[133]

---

[133] Tony Mauro *Supreme Court Votes to Allow Citation to Unpublished Opinions in Federal Courts*, Legal Times 4/12/06 (law.com); Howard J. Bashman, *To Cite or Not to Cite to Non-Precedential Opinions* Special to law.com 3/6/06.

Evidence

§ 23.01 INTRODUCTION

The Federal Rules of Evidence (FRE) govern testimony in trials held in federal courts. However, the FRE does not apply to preliminary questions of fact or preliminary examinations; Grand Jury proceedings; bail hearings; sentencing; or matters relating to probation or revocation of probation. In effect, the rules apply at the main trial, not at preliminary or subsequent court proceedings. The Fourth Amendment applies to searches and seizures in the civil context.[1]

The rules take a balancing approach to admissibility. That is, evidence is considered relevant and admissible if it tends to prove a matter of consequence, thus helping to resolve a factual dispute — and also if at its introduction is not unduly prejudicial, misleading, or time-consuming. Admission of evidence is favored if the risks can be minimized. The federal judge is given significant discretion over admission and exclusion of evidence.

Rule 105 allows a party to request that evidence be admitted only as to one party or as to specific issues; the jury must be instructed on the implications of such limited admission.

An amendment to Rule 804 was proposed (dealing with the prosecution's duty to show particularized guarantees of trustworthiness for declarations offered against penal interest) but the Supreme Court returned it without taking action. There were no Evidence rules in the package of rules sent to the Supreme Court for its approval, with an intended effective date of December 1, 2005.

Several states are considering new legislation and guidelines for lineups after discovery of wrongful convictions based on bad eyewitness identification. More and more states are considering techniques such as a sequential lineup where people or photographs are shown singly, not all together, or a blind lineup, where the person doing the lineup does not know who is the suspect. When Cardozo School of Law's Innocent Project analyzed 197 wrongful convictions that were invalidated by DNA evidence, mistaken eyewitness identification was a factor in more than 75% of them. Another study, by Michigan Law School's Professor Samuel R. Gross, estimated that between 1989 and 2003, over 300 exonerations (two-thirds murder, one-third rape) had been made, and in half of the murders and 88% of the rape cases, incorrect eyewitness investigations were at fault. By the fall of 2007, 42 states (all except Alabama, Alaska, Massachusetts, Mississippi, Oklahoma, South Carolina, South Dakota, and Wyoming) had adopted laws giving prison inmates access to DNA test results, perhaps results that were not available at the time of the conviction. California and several other states established commissions to expedite investigations of alleged wrongful convictions. (Crime lab errors, however, can lead to wrongful convictions as well as exoneration of wrongfully convicted persons.)[2]

---

[1] United States v. James Daniel Good Real Property, 510 U.S. 43 (1993).

[2] Solomon Moore, *DNA Exoneration Leads to Change in Legal System*, N.Y. Times 10/1/07 at A1; Vesna Jaksic, *States Look at Reforming Lineup Methods*, Nat'l L.J. 4/20/07 (law.com).

§ 23.02   ADMISSIBILITY

In general, evidence is admissible in either a civil or criminal context if it resolves facts necessary to the question, decided by preponderance of the evidence. Certain relevant evidence must be excluded for Constitutional reasons — for instance, if it is the product of an unlawful search or improper custodial interrogation.

The standard the federal Court of Appeals uses to review evidentiary rulings of the District Court is abuse of discretion.[3] Where the District Court has discretion to accept or exclude evidence, the appeals court will reverse a ruling only if it is manifestly erroneous.

Rule 103(a) says that no error can be assigned unless a substantial right of a party is affected and:

- (If evidence was admitted) the record includes a timely objection or motion to strike
- (If excluded) the substance of the evidence was offered to the court or was apparent from the context.

Commentators point out that the best time to consider which electronic materials will be admissible at trial is the point when discovery is still open. A Southern District of Texas judge ruled in 2007 that Internet evidence is inherently untrustworthy because of the risk of alteration by hackers — but the District Court for the District of Columbia was not persuaded by similar arguments in 2006, and held that any kind of documentary evidence is vulnerable to alteration. Magistrate Judge Grimm of the District of Maryland decided that hard copies of e-mails were not admissible to support FRCP 56 motions for summary judgment. E-mails create especially severe chain of evidence problems, because each link has to be examined (e.g., whether it is authentic; non-hearsay; if it constitutes a business record; if it is an admission by a party; if it is self-serving).[4]

§ 23.03   STRUCTURE OF THE FRE

The Federal Rules of Evidence cover ten substantive topics:

- General matters
- Judicial notice

---

[3] General Elec. v. Joiner, 522 U.S. 136 (1997).

[4] *Cf.* Diamond Offshore Servs. Co. v. Gulfmark Offshore Inc., 2007 U.S. Dist. Lexis 5483 (S.D. Texas 2007) *with* United States v. Safavian, 435 F. Supp. 2d 36 (D.D.C. 2006). On the chain of evidence for e-mail, *see, e.g.*, Rambus Inc. v. Infineon Technologies A.G., 348 F. Supp. 2d 698 (E.D. Va. 2004). Vee Vinhnee v. American Express, 336 B.R. 437 (9th Cir. BAP 2005) says that the maintainer of an electronic database may have to show how it was maintained, to demonstrate integrity of records. These issues are discussed in, e.g., Jerold S. Solovy and Robert L. Byman, *Don't Let Your E-Evidence Get Trashed*, Nat'l L.J. 6/11/07 (law.com). Magistrate Judge Grimm's case is Lorraine v. Markle American Ins. Co., 2007 U.S. Dist. Lexis 33020 (D. Md. 2007).

- Presumptions
- Relevancy
- Privilege
- Competency, examination, and impeachment of witnesses
- Opinion and expert testimony
- Hearsay
- Authentication of exhibits
- Originals and copies of evidence.

For reversal, trial-court error with respect to evidence must affect substantial rights, and a timely objection, stating specific grounds, must have been made. But FRE 103(d) codifies the doctrine of plain error: in egregious circumstances, the appeals court can reverse even in the absence of a timely objection.

When evidence is excluded, the losing party must make an offer of proof stating the evidence that would have been offered, in order to augment the record for appeal. The offer of proof is usually made at sidebar, so the jury cannot hear; or the jury would be excused if proceedings would take more than a few minutes.

In most circumstances, the federal jury is the trier of facts, but FRE 104 provides that the judge determines certain preliminary questions in both court and jury trials — i.e., admissibility in general; competency; privilege; and the availability of a presumption. Hearings on such matters are usually held while the jury is excused.

If a party introduces only part of a writing (or a recorded statement), Rule 106 permits the opponent to put that material in context by introducing other parts of that writing or statement — or even related materials — to prevent unfairness. However, once a definitive ruling has been made on the record either admitting evidence or excluding it, the claim of error can be preserved for appeal even if the party does not renew the objection.

[A] Rule Changes

The Federal Rules of Evidence changes effective December 1, 2006 are as follows:[5]

- Rule 404: evidence of a person's character is never admissible in a civil case for the purpose of proving conduct
- Rule 408: the rule settles a split in authority as to the admissibility of statements and offers during settlement negotiations as evidence of fault or for impeachment purposes
- Rule 606: after a trial, the testimony of jurors about the trial can be received only for limited purposes, such as proving that the reported verdict is a clerical error

---

[5] *See* http://www.uscourts.gov/rules/newrules6.html.

- Rule 609: evidence of a crime can automatically be used for impeachment only if proof of deceit is an element of the crime, or there is information in the record (e.g., the charging instrument) that permits a determination of underlying deceit.

P.L. 110-322 (signed September 19, 2008) enacts a new FRE 502 to limit the circumstances under which inadvertent disclosure of protected information will result in waiver of attorney-client or work-product privilege. A disclosure will not lead to waiver if the disclosure was inadvertent, the holder of the privilege took reasonable steps to prevent disclosure, and took reasonable steps to remedy the mistake. When a party produces one document, subject matter waiver does not extend to related documents, as long as protected information was not intentionally used to mislead an opponent. Congress' intention was to reduce the cost of privilege review and document production, especially where discovery is done electronically.

Rule 502(a) provides that if a waiver is found, it applies only to the specific information that was disclosed, unless fairness requires a broader waiver to prevent evidence from being misleading. Rule 502(b) says that waiver does not result from inadvertent disclosure in a federal proceeding or to a federal agency or officer if the privileged party took reasonable steps to prevent disclosure and moved promptly to correct the error. Software tools to search for key names and terms can be used to prevent unwanted disclosures. Rule 502(c) says that disclosure of protected information in a state proceeding is only a disclosure as to a federal proceeding if there would be a waiver under 502(c) or the law of the state where the disclosure occurred. In other words, the producing party is protected by whichever rule is more favorable. Rule 502(f) establishes the converse (disclosure in a federal proceeding is not necessarily disclosure for state purposes). Rule 502(d) permits enforcement of a federal-court order stating that disclosure did not create waiver in any federal or state proceeding. Rule 502(e) permits parties to a federal proceeding to enter into confidentiality agreements that expand protection against waiver. However, unless such an agreement is incorporated into a court order, it will bind only the parties. Rule 502 applies to proceedings commenced after September 19, 2008 and, where it is "just and practicable," to proceedings already pending on that date.[6]

§ 23.04   JUDICIAL NOTICE

Judicial notice can be taken (under Rule 201), by either a trial or appellate court, of "adjudicative facts" — facts that are not subject to reasonable dispute because they are generally known in the geographic area where the court is located, or are readily and accurately determined from sources of unquestionable accuracy.

---

[6] Marcia Coyle, *Key Discovery Rule Gets Nod*, Nat'l L.J. 9/15/08 (law.com); Robert A. Schwinger and Eric Twiste, *How Rule 502 Affects Lawyers and E-Discovery*, Special to law.com (8/8/08).

The court, in its discretion, can take judicial notice of any matter. The court must take judicial notice of anything that is the subject of a request by a party who furnishes the necessary proof of the matter. Judicial notice can be taken of scientific theories (e.g., the laws of thermodynamics) that are firmly enough established to be granted the status of scientific laws.

§ 23.05 PRESUMPTIONS

Under the Federal Rules of Evidence, presumptions apply only to the burden of going forward (introducing at least some evidence to rebut the presumed point). The ultimate burden of proof still remains upon whatever party would have carried it without the presumption (Rule 301).

Rule 302 permits state-law presumptions to apply in cases in which the decision on the merits depends on state law, with respect to facts that constitute elements of any state-law cause of action or defense. This rule comes into play in diversity cases and certain supplemental jurisdiction claims.

§ 23.06 RELEVANCY

Evidence is relevant, under Rule 401, if it makes a fact of consequence to the case either more or less probable. Irrelevant evidence is never admissible. Rule 403 permits exclusion of even relevant evidence whose probative value is less than the prejudice, delay, confusion, or repetition that would ensue if the evidence were admitted. Rule 403 does not apply in trials to the court, because the rule's specific purpose is to prevent juries from hearing improper evidence.[7]

In an ADEA suit, Sprint moved to exclude testimony of former employees who charged the company with discrimination, but attributed discrimination to other supervisors. The District Court held that the other employees were not similarly situated to the plaintiff. The Tenth Circuit held that it was an abuse of discretion to apply a per se rule excluding the evidence of employees with other supervisors. The Supreme Court, however, said that the Tenth Circuit wrongly characterized the District Court's approach as a per se rule. Rather than making its own FRE 401 and 403 analyses, the Supreme Court said that the Tenth Circuit should have remanded the case to the District Court for clarification. Because the District Court has the greatest familiarity with a case, it is in the best position to balance the probative value of testimony against possible prejudice.[8]

There is no full, clear definition of "prejudice" in the FRE, but the definition is approximately material that seeks to create an irrational perception in the jurors' minds of a person because of that person's intrinsic characteristics; by association with an unpopular group; or by exciting the jury's rage or desire for revenge (e.g., by showing inflammatory photographs of a crime scene, even though the brutality of a crime does not prove that the defendant committed it).

---

[7] Schultz v. Butcher 24 F.3d 626 (4th Cir. 1994).
[8] Sprint/United Mgmt. Co. v. Mendelsohn, 128 S. Ct. 1140 (2008).

Rule 403 does not exclude otherwise relevant evidence on the ground of surprise. In the federal system, the remedy is not exclusion of the evidence, but continuance of the trial for the opposing party to deal with the new evidence.

The trial court must act as "gatekeeper" to make sure that all expert testimony is relevant and reliable, with respect to expert testimony based on any form of technical or specialized knowledge, not just scientific testimony: *Kumho Tire Co. v. Carmichael*, 526 U.S. 137 (1999).

§ 23.07 CHARACTER EVIDENCE

Under Rule 404, character traits are generally not admissible to prove that someone acted in conformity with those traits. There is an important exception with regard to the character of the accused. In a case involving death, the reputation of the deceased for peaceful conduct (or the opposite) is admissible on the question of whether the deceased was actually the aggressor in the incident leading to death.

The 2000 amendments to the FRE allow the alleged victim to attack the character of the accused once the defense has introduced negative character evidence about the alleged victim of the offense for which the defendant is being prosecuted.

Evidence of character takes the form of reputation and opinion (Rule 405). Character can be proved by testimony as to reputation; the witnesses' own opinion; and proof of specific conduct where character or a character trait is an essential element of a charge, claim, or defense, or cross-examination of a character witness.

Testimony about specific acts, crimes, or wrongdoing is not admissible to prove that the subject of the testimony would act the same way on another occasion, but might be admissible as to other matters (such as motive, opportunity, intent, plan, or identity). Evidence of specific acts can also be introduced if it constitutes an essential element of a claim, defense, or cross-examination. For instance, if the defendant asserts an insanity defense, other acts could show awareness of the world and ability to plot and carry out crimes, thus rebutting the defense.

If specific-acts evidence is going to be introduced in a criminal trial, the defendant can request the prosecution to give reasonable notice of the general nature of the evidence (unless the judge excuses compliance with this requirement). In response, the defendant should consider filing a motion in limine to exclude the evidence under Rule 403, on the grounds that potential prejudice exceeds the probative value.

Under Rule 404(b), evidence of other acts (e.g., crimes) is not admissible to show that a person is likely to commit other, similar acts. However, "bad acts" evidence can be admissible for other purposes, such as proving opportunity or premeditation.

The character of witnesses is covered by Rules 607–609 (see below). Note, however, that although the character of a person is generally inadmissible, the habit or a person or the routine practice of an organization CAN be admitted under Rule 406, to prove that conduct on a given occasion conformed to the habit or practice.

§ 23.08 WITNESSES

Rule 601 makes everyone competent to testify unless specifically ruled out for some reason. The judge has the power, under Rule 611, to control the questioning of witnesses to lead to the truth, prevent delay, and prevent attorneys from harassing witnesses.

The Federal Rules follow the so-called "American rule": i.e., the scope of cross-examination is limited to the subject matter of the direct examination and witness credibility, unless the court exercises its discretion to widen the scope (611(b)). FRE 607 allows anyone to impeach a witness — even the lawyer who called the witness in the first place.

[A] Impeachment

The character of a witness can be attacked to impeach his or her testimony only on the basis of testimony about the witness' reputation for truthfulness, or the opinion that another witness holds as to the first witness' truthfulness. Rule 608 permits this to be done only if the witness' credibility has been attacked. Extrinsic evidence cannot be used to prove that the witness is untruthful by proving the existence of acts that have been denied by the witness, even though this might seem more probative as to the witness' credibility than his or her reputation.

A witness can be impeached (in either a civil or criminal trial) by evidence of conviction of a crime involving dishonesty. A felony conviction of any type can be introduced if the court finds that its probative value exceeds its potential for prejudice. But convictions more than 10 years in the past can be admitted only at the discretion of the court: see Rule 609. The First Circuit held in 2004 that, for impeachment purposes, the standard for admitting prior convictions depends on the identity of the witness. Under Rule 609, the defendant's priors are admitted if the probative value exceeds the risk of prejudice, whereas prior convictions of witnesses are governed by Rule 403, which says that evidence is excludable only if the danger of prejudice substantially outweighs the probative value.[9]

Under *James v. Illinois*,[10] illegally obtained evidence that is subject to the exclusionary rule can be used for impeachment of the defendant — but cannot be used to impeach defense witnesses.

Witnesses can be asked leading questions on direct as well as cross-examination, with respect to preliminary or uncontested matters. An attorney can also lead hostile witnesses (as established by their demeanor) or adverse witnesses (as determined by their party alignment).

[B] Opinion Evidence

Rule 701 allows a lay witness to give an opinion based on his or her perceptions where this would assist the trier of fact — e.g., how fast a car was going at a

---

[9] United States v. Tse, 375 F.3d 148 (1st Cir. 2004).
[10] 493 U.S. 307 (1990).

particular time. By and large, however, opinion testimony is the province of expert witnesses, and such testimony is governed by Rule 702.

An expert is a person who is qualified in an area of scientific, technical, or specialized knowledge, and whose knowledge assists the trier of fact in deciding issues or interpreting other testimony.

Rule 703 permits experts to base their conclusions on facts that are independently admissible, and/or facts of a type commonly used by experts in the same field. If a neutral opinion is required to supplement the opinions offered by the expert(s) for one or both sides, Rule 706 gives federal judges the power to appoint experts and order their compensation.

The test, under *Daubert* [11] is whether the reasoning or methodology behind the proposed testimony is scientifically valid; and whether it is proper to apply it to the facts at issue. The *Kumho* case extends *Daubert* to all expert witness testimony, rather than limiting it to scientific evidence.

In a failure to warn products liability case, the Third Circuit held that the plaintiff is not required to introduce an expert on warnings if the engineering expert can establish that a warning was required to make the product safe. The case involved a mechanic who alleged that he was seriously injured while replacing rear-window glass in a Ford Explorer because Ford failed to warn of the risk of the glass shattering if a specific work sequence was not followed. The District Court would not allow the plaintiff's expert witness, an engineer specializing in glass fractures, to testify because he was not an expert on warnings. Nor could he testify about alternative warnings by referring to Ford's 2004 safety recall instructions about replacing brackets and hinges, on the grounds that they were a remedial measure made inadmissible by FRE 407. However, the Third Circuit ruled that the witness' expertise on glass fracture was sufficient to establish liability. The plaintiff was not challenging the language of warnings about the repair sequence — his complaint was the lack of warnings, so an engineer could testify on that point. FRE 703 says that the safety recall instruction would not have to be admissible for the engineer to testify that the manual lacked adequate instructions; any prejudice could be handled via a limiting instruction, or permitting the jury to hear the recall instruction without informing them that Ford published it. [12]

A judge or juror cannot testify in any trial where he or she acts as such (Rules 605, 606). In fact, jurors are forbidden to testify orally or by affidavit about the deliberations leading up to an indictment or verdict. Even if a collateral or post-verdict attack on a verdict is made, the jurors are permitted to testify only about extraneous prejudicial information that was considered in the deliberations.

---

[11] Daubert v. Merrell Dow Pharm. Inc., 509 U.S. 579 (1993). In 2004, the Third Circuit joined the Fourth and Seventh in holding that despite concerns about potential errors, expert testimony on fingerprint identification is sufficiently reliable to satisfy the requirements of *Daubert* and *Kumho* and thus can be admitted in a criminal trial: United States v. Mitchell, 365 F.3d 215 (3d Cir. 2004).

[12] Pineda v. Ford Motor Co., 520 F.3d 237 (3d Cir. 2008); *see* Shannon P. Duffy, *3rd Circuit: Warnings Expert Not Needed*, The Legal Intelligencer 3/27/08 (law.com).

§ 23.09 PUBLIC POLICY EXCLUSIONS

The FRE renders inadmissible some categories of evidence that might be useful to the trier of fact, because public policy requires that certain activities be encouraged, rather than discouraged by their impact on potential future litigation.

Under Rule 407, subsequent remedial measures taken by a party (e.g., repairing a machine; changing the specifications of a manufactured product) are not admissible to show that the party was negligent in the first place. However, testimony about the remedial measures can be admitted for other purposes, e.g., for impeachment or to rebut a contention that remediation was impossible. Should evidence of remedial measures be improperly admitted, the District Court has discretion either to declare a mistrial, or to instruct the jurors that the improper evidence is not relevant to liability.

Rule 407's application is limited: it covers only remedial measures taken by the defendant, not a third party. Furthermore, not all steps taken by the defendant after an accident are remedial — they might, for instance, be investigative, and thus admissible.

Similarly, the fact that a defendant had or did not have liability insurance is rendered inadmissible as to the issue of negligence by Rule 411. Paying or agreeing to pay a plaintiff's medical expenses is not admissible as to the defendant's liability for the injury (Rule 409).

When negotiations occur as to entry of a plea of guilty or nolo contendere, but the plea is withdrawn, statements made during those negotiations are in general inadmissible in a civil or criminal proceeding. However, Rule 410 makes an exception (understandably) for perjury prosecutions, or if another statement made in the course of the same plea negotiation has been admitted, and must be put into context.

A criminal defendant's agreement to waive the FRE 410/Federal Rules of Criminal Procedure 11(e)(6) exclusion is enforceable absent proof that the waiver agreement was not knowing and voluntary: *United States v. Mezzanatto*, 513 U.S. 196 (1995).

[A] Evidence of Sexual Behavior

In general, Rule 412(a) makes other sexual behavior of an alleged victim of a sex crime, or the alleged victim's sexual predisposition, inadmissible in a civil or criminal proceeding that charges a defendant with sexual misconduct. However, certain otherwise admissible evidence can be admitted under 412(b):

- Specific sexual behavior by the alleged victim proving that someone other than the defendant was the source of physical evidence (including semen and physical injury to the alleged victim)
- Specific sexual behavior involving the defendant, rather than other persons, to prove consent or when offered by the prosecution
- Evidence whose exclusion would violate the defendant's Constitutional rights.

In a civil case, otherwise admissible testimony as to the alleged victim's sexual behavior or predispositions can only be admitted if its probative value exceeds its potential for prejudice. The alleged victim's reputation is admissible only if it is raised by the victim.

[B] Similar Acts Evidence

Rules 413–415 permit admission of evidence that the defendant committed other sexual assaults or acts of child molestation, in either a prosecution or a civil case involving sexual assault or child molestation. Such evidence can be considered for its bearing on any matter to which it is relevant. However, the prosecution or plaintiff intending to offer the evidence must give notice of intention at least 15 days before the scheduled opening date of the trial (unless the court gives permission to give shorter notice).

For evidence of allegedly similar acts to be admissible, it must be genuinely likely to be probative of the specific issue in the case. For instance, *United States v. McGuire* [13] permits admission of evidence about seven other bank robberies in a bank robbery prosecution to show a common plan or scheme, given many common characteristics among the series tending to show that the defendant committed all the robberies, and the one charged was part of a larger scheme.

§ 23.10   HEARSAY AND HEARSAY EXCEPTIONS

Hearsay is a statement other than those made by the declarant in the course of testimony, if offered to prove the truth of the matter asserted. The rationale for excluding hearsay is that it risks being unreliable in that the declarant was not under oath or otherwise impressed with the solemnity of the occasion; cross-examination is generally not available; and the jury is unable to examine the declarant's demeanor.

Double hearsay — "hearsay upon hearsay" can be admitted if each part of the statement qualifies for a hearsay exception (Rule 805).

[A] Rule 801

Therefore, Rule 801(d)(1) holds that a prior statement is not hearsay if it was made under oath and can be cross-examined. Thus, such prior statements can be introduced directly; their use is not limited to impeachment. A statement made by an opposing party (or by an agent of an opposing party, or a co-conspirator of an opposing party) is not hearsay under Rule 801(d)(2) to the extent that it represents an admission: a statement at variance with the position taken by the opposing party at the trial.

Rule 801(d)(1)(B) permits introduction of prior consistent statements to rebut a charge of recent fabrication. *Tome v. United States* [14] does NOT permit a

---

[13] 27 F.3d 457 (10th Cir. 1994).
[14] 513 U.S. 150 (1995).

balancing approach to be used to compare the probative to the prejudicial value of each individual statement. (The Supreme Court does not find this approach predictable enough.) Under this case, the statement must have been made before the alleged fabrication, or before the alleged improper motive or influence came into being.

Under 801(d)(2)(E), a co-conspirator's statement during or in furtherance of the conspiracy is not hearsay, and in this context there is no conflict between the hearsay rules and the confrontation clause. Statements made by a co-conspirator before the defendant entered the conspiracy are admissible under this rule;[15] but see *Bruton* [16] under which a co-defendant's confession implicating another co-defendant is inadmissible unless it can be redacted to delete references to the other defendants, or the declarant takes the stand and can be cross-examined. Several Courts of Appeals have refused to apply this case to statements that satisfy the coconspirator hearsay exception.

[B] Rule 803

Rule 803 sets out a series of hearsay exceptions, material that is not hearsay and can be introduced even if the declarant is actually available and could be examined at trial:

- Present sense impressions.
- Excited utterances. Under *White v. Illinois*,[17] spontaneous utterances or statements made in the course of seeking medical treatment can be introduced even if the prosecution does not produce the declarant, and even with no court finding of the declarant's unavailability. The Supreme Court treated these statements as long-recognized hearsay exceptions, possessing inherent reliability that does not require production of the declarant.
- A state of mind, emotion, sensation, or health existing at a particular time in the past.
- Statements given in the course of medical diagnosis or treatment.
- Business records.
- The absence of a record, where a record would be expected if an event had occurred.
- Public records, data compilations, reports, records of vital statistics, or the absence of such records.
- Religious records, e.g., records of marriages and baptisms.
- Family documents such as family trees.
- Property records and statements noted on such records.
- "Ancient documents" — in this context, those over 20 years old, and whose authenticity is established.

---

[15] United States v. Mkhsian, 5 F.3d 1306 (9th Cir. 1993).

[16] Bruton v. United States, 391 U.S. 123 (1968).

[17] 502 U.S. 346 (1992).

- Market quotations.
- Learned treatises (but the relevant text is read into the record by the witness, not admitted as evidence).
- Reputation evidence about character, community history, boundaries, personal, or family history.
- Criminal convictions.
- Recorded recollections — but the witness can only read such material into evidence; it is not admissible unless an adverse party offers it. Also see Rule 612, requiring that any document used by a witness to refresh recollection before testifying must be produced for inspection by the other lawyer. (In criminal proceedings, 18 USC § 3500 applies instead.) Witnesses need not be shown their own prior statements that will be used for impeachment, but extrinsic evidence of such a statement cannot be introduced unless the witness is given an opportunity to explain the discrepancies.

Rule 803(8)(C) gives a trial court not only the discretion but an actual obligation to exclude all or any portion of a report that it deems to be untrustworthy.

[C] Rule 804

Rule 804 has a complementary series of hearsay exceptions that can be used when the declarant is unavailable[18] to testify:

- Testimony or depositions already given, in the same case or other cases
- Dying declarations
- A statement made against the speaker's interest (against monetary interest; incriminating as to civil or criminal liability; tending to invalidate a claim made by the speaker against someone else)
- Statement of personal or family history.

Under Rules 803 and 804, the judge has the power to permit admission of anything else that is evidence of a material fact in the case, and if the proponent gives advance notice of intention to offer the material.

---

[18] *See* Rosenfeld v. Basquiat, 78 F.3d 84 (2d Cir. 1996): New York's Dead Man's Statute is a rule of witness competency, not of privilege. Therefore, a person barred from testifying by the Dead Man's Rule is not "unavailable" for Rule 804 purposes. A witness who properly asserts Fifth Amendment privilege IS "unavailable": United States v. Badahur, 954 F.2d 821 (2d Cir. 1992). The New York Court of Appeals ruled that the Dead Man's Statute will not prevent an attorney from defending himself against disciplinary charges of embezzling from the deceased client's escrow account. The lawyer's testimony about an alleged oral agreement that he could keep the escrow funds was an attempt to clear himself; he was not testifying against the decedent's executor, administrator, or survivor — the type of testimony that the Dead Man's Statute forbids: Matter of Zalk, 10 N.Y.3d 669 (N.Y. 2008); *see* Joel Stashenko, *N.Y. Dead Man's Statute Doesn't Bar Attorney's Defense in Disciplinary Case*, N.Y.L.J. 6/13/08 (law.com); New York's Dead Man's Statute is found at CPLR § 4519.

Someone whose loss of memory prevents testifying can properly be both "subject to cross-examination" under Rule 801(d)(1)(C) and "unavailable" under Rule 804(a)(3), because the two rules serve different purposes and do not have to work the same way.[19]

[D] Constitutional Issues in Criminal Trial Evidence

In criminal cases, the admission of certain out-of-court statements might create Confrontation Clause problems, in that the defendant cannot cross-examine the declarant.

The hearsay rules and the Confrontation Clause are somewhat similarly motivated, but certain material qualifying for a hearsay exception must be excluded under the Confrontation Clause.[20] To satisfy the Confrontation Clause, hearsay must be inherently trustworthy and must not rely on corroboration. (This case also finds excited utterances reliable enough not to require cross-examination, because the circumstances surrounding excited utterances make them credible.)

However, it has been held that the Confrontation Clause does not preclude admission of dying declarations; excited utterances; past recollection recorded; earlier testimony; or declarations against penal interest — i.e., statements that for one reason or another are deemed reliable.

Rule 801(d)(1)(C) is a hearsay exception for a declarant's identification of a person after seeing him or her, as long as the declarant testifies at trial and can be cross-examined. However, if a pretrial identification was impermissibly suggestive, the subsequent identification may present Due Process problems. Rule 403 permits exclusion of even a constitutionally acceptable pre-trial identification, if its probative value is less than the risk of prejudicing, confusing, or misleading the jury.

The Supreme Court ruled that state precedents, admitting evidence of the guilt of a third party only if it raises a reasonable inference of the defendant's innocence, and not just bare suspicion or conjectures about someone else's guilt, were invalid. Defendants must be given a meaningful opportunity to present a complete defense.[21] The Supreme Court's February 22, 2006, decision in *Oregon v. Guzek*, 546 U.S. 517, is that a state can Constitutionally impose a limit on the evidence of innocence that can be introduced at the sentencing stage of a capital case to the evidence that was introduced at the original trial. The Eighth Amendment does not mandate that the defendant be given a chance to introduce evidence at the sentencing stage casting doubt on the underlying conviction.

§ 23.11 ADMISSION OF EXHIBITS

An exhibit can be received into evidence pursuant to Rule 901 if it is shown to be relevant and if it is properly authenticated — i.e., shown to be what it purports to be. The chain of custody may have to be shown.

---

[19] United States v. Owens, 484 U.S. 554 (1988).

[20] Idaho v. Wright, 497 U.S. 805 (1990).

[21] Holmes v. South Carolina, 547 U.S. 319 (2006).

Rule 902 sets out categories of material that are self-authenticating, so that only relevance has to be shown to make the material admissible:

- Public documents
- Certified copies of public records
- Official publications of public authorities
- Newspapers and periodicals
- Labels and other trade descriptions
- Notarized or otherwise acknowledged documents
- Commercial paper.

The 2000 amendments to the FRE supplement this list with the addition of original or duplicate records of activities regularly conducted within the U.S. (In civil cases, similar foreign records are also admissible.) The records must have been made contemporaneously with the events they record, as part of a routine.

Rule 903 provides that the testimony of a subscribing witness to authenticate a writing is not required unless the laws of the jurisdiction whose laws govern the establishment of authenticity require such testimony.

The federal rules treat any counterpart, print from the same negative, or photocopy or other identical copy as a "duplicate" which is admissible on the same terms as the original (Rule 1003).

Rule 1004 permits evidence as to the contents of a document when no original or admissible copy is available. Rule 1004 cannot be used if the proponent of the information destroyed the document in bad faith, or if someone who was on notice to produce the original failed to do so.

Documents can be authenticated before trial by various methods, such as:

- Stipulation by counsel as to their authenticity
- An FRCP 36 request for admission
- Stipulating to authenticity during a Rule 16 pre-trial conference
- Via FRCP 33 interrogatories
- Admission during a deposition taken under Rule 30 or 31.

§ 23.12   PRIVILEGE

Perhaps surprisingly, the FRE does not include a detailed set of evidentiary privileges, and limited or no recognition is granted to state-law privileges for doctor-patient, accountant-client, or insured-insurer communications.

In civil cases in which elements of a claim or defense are governed by state law, state law also governs which information is privileged and cannot be introduced as to that claim or defense. Otherwise, the common law, as interpreted by judges, prevails.

The District Court for the District of Columbia refused to recognize a new privilege under FRE 501 for communications made in the course of settlement negotiations. FRE 501 is the rule that gives courts the power to interpret common law to set new privileges in the light of reason and experience. There are four factors in the determination:

- Broad consensus in federal and state law in favor of the privilege;
- Although it has not provided the privilege itself, Congress has considered the concerns behind it;
- Whether the Advisory Committee of the Judicial Conference listed it in its proposed Rules of Evidence;
- Whether the plaintiff has clearly shown that the proposed privilege will further the public good.[22]

In the federal system, some privilege and cognate rules are found outside the FRE. For instance, FRCP 26(b)(3) grants attorney work product a qualified immunity from discovery (which is not the same thing as attorney-client privilege at trial; see below).[23]

FRCP 26(c)(7) privileges trade secrets and confidential commercial information. Privileges are also available under Fed. R. Crim. P. 6(e) for grand jury materials, and 12.2(c) for statements made by the defendant in the course of a court-ordered psychiatric examination.

The claimant of privilege, rather than the proponent of the evidence, has the burden of proof with respect to issues relating to privilege.

Privilege can be waived by failing to object at the appropriate point of discovery or trial, or by making voluntary disclosure of matter that is alleged to be privileged.

[A] Attorney-Client Privilege

See § 27.02[A][6] for further discussion of privilege.

In order to ensure that persons facing criminal charges or civil litigation can be adequately represented, communications between attorneys and clients are privileged. However, the privilege is subject to various limitations and qualifications. The privilege is deemed to operate for the benefit of the client, not the

---

[22] *In re* Subpoena Issued to the CFTC, 73 L.W. 1665 (D.D.C. 4/28/05).

[23] Under United States v. Adlman, 134 F.3d 1194 (2d Cir. 1998), a document can be work product even if it was drafted for business decision-making, as long as it was prepared in anticipation of litigation, and the business decision itself was a response to possible outcomes of litigation. United States v. Smith, 135 F.3d 963 (5th Cir. 1998), denies work product characterization to videotapes of an interview between a reporter and a criminal defendant, on the grounds that they are not confidential. Therefore, the tapes could be subpoenaed for use in the criminal trial. The Second Circuit ruled that a corporation's letter to the U.S. attorney, stating that federal agents told the corporation that it was acting lawfully, did not waive work product status for the attorney's notes of the conversation with the federal agents. The court ruled that it would not be unfair to the government to exclude this material, because the proceeding was a grand jury, where the government controlled presentation of the evidence and could examine the agents themselves: John Doe v. United States, 72 L.W. 1287 (2d Cir. 2003).

attorney. If the court is informed of a genuine need for disclosure, and there are no special circumstances present, the identity of a client and information about the fees is not protected, even if the substance of matters confided by the client is privileged.

For attorney-client privilege to be available, the information as to which privilege is asserted must have been imparted to the attorney in the context of legal representation, not other situations, and in order to secure legal advice not for other purposes (e.g., preparation of a tax return, which is a public document and therefore cannot be privileged).[24]

Disclosure of the information to a third party (other than one whose presence is indispensable — e.g., a stenographer taking notes) terminates the privilege. The privilege runs to the law firm, not the individual attorney, so waiving the privilege as to one attorney (for instance, by testifying about a confidential communication; putting the attorney-client relationship directly at issue; asserting reliance on an attorney's advice as an element of a claim or defense) waives it as to everyone in the firm.

Even if the final version of a document is published, earlier drafts can qualify for attorney-client privilege if they were intended to be confidential and they communicate legal advice to a client.[25]

The so-called "crime-fraud" exception applies to communications that do not serve the permissible objective of obtaining legal advice about past actions already taken, but those that involve advice about crimes or frauds that the client contemplates committing in the future.

The crime-fraud exception applies to client communications in furtherance of contemplated or ongoing criminal, fraudulent, or wrongful conduct. The exception is triggered on the basis of the client's motives; it does not matter whether or not the attorney was aware of impropriety.

The party seeking to introduce a client confidence on this basis must make a prima facie showing, by competent evidence, that the consultation was undertaken to further improper activity. The general rule is that it is not enough to show that the client was involved in contemporaneous criminal activity.

Nevertheless, the Third Circuit permitted a prosecutor to subpoena a lawyer who was asked for advice about concealing future illegal activities — even though the lawyer did not commit any wrongdoing. In the Third Circuit analysis, the client's intention is controlling. The target of the probe was an FBI agent who violated the 18 USC §§ 208–209 bans on federal employees engaging in outside business. The target asked the attorney how to structure unlawful investment transactions, and whether the transactions should be made in his wife's name to conceal his involvement. The presence of a third-party witness did not destroy the

---

[24] *See, e.g.*, United States v. Frederick, 83 AFTR2d 99-686 (7th Cir. 1999). United States v. Ackert, 169 F.3d 136 (2d Cir. 1999) holds that an attorney's conversations with an investment banker about the tax consequences of a transaction are not entitled to attorney-client privilege, even if they are helpful to the attorney.

[25] Kobluk v. University of Minn., 574 N.W.2d 436 (Minn. 1998).

privilege — the spouses were discussing shared issues with a lawyer, so the common-interest privilege applied.[26]

United States v. Zolin[27] holds that a party raising the crime-fraud exception to the attorney-client privilege can request in camera review of the applicability of the privilege. Before granting review, the judge should require a showing of facts that would induce a reasonable person to believe in good faith that reviewing the disputed material would demonstrate the applicability of the crime-fraud exception. (In chambers disclosure of material for the limited purpose of assessing whether the privilege applies does not terminate the privilege.)

The crime/fraud exception has been held to apply to communications with an attorney intended to further a civil as well as a criminal fraud.[28]

It should be noted that § 7525 of the Internal Revenue Service Restructuring and Reform Act broadens the "attorney-client" privilege, for tax purposes to cover communications engaged in to obtain tax advice from a CPA, enrolled agent, or enrolled actuary. However, the privilege is limited to non-criminal tax matters before the IRS and in federal court.

[B] Doctor-Patient Privilege

The doctor-patient privilege is recognized in the evidence rules of most states, but does not exist as such in the FRE. In 1996, the Supreme Court applied a balancing test to recognize the validity of a psychotherapist-patient privilege, which extends to confidential communications made to licensed social workers (not just psychiatrists and psychologists) in the course of psychotherapy.[29]

The psychotherapist-patient privilege, like the attorney-client privilege, is subject to the crime/fraud exception. In the First Circuit view, the societal interest in promoting candor in treatment must be subordinated to the prevention of future crime and fraud, e.g., in health insurance and personal injury claims.[30]

A doctor under investigation for insurance fraud cannot claim physician-patient privilege to avoid discovery of patient records when he asserts the privilege on his or her own behalf, not that of the patients. Doctors are presumed to have authority to claim privilege, but Utah ruled that in this case, the presumption was rebutted.[31]

---

[26] United States v. John Doe, 429 F.3d 450 (3d Cir. 2005).

[27] 491 U.S. 554 (1989).

[28] Olson v. Accessory Controls & Equip. 757 A.2d 14 (Conn. 2000).

[29] Jaffee v. Redmond, 518 U.S. 1 (1996).

[30] *In re* Grand Jury Proceedings (Violette), 183 F.3d 71 (1st Cir. 1999). *But see* United States v. Hayes, 227 F.3d 578 (6th Cir. 2000) [no exception to privilege even when dangerous patient threatens others].

[31] Burns v. Boyden, 2006 Ut.14 (Utah 2006).

[C] Marital Privilege

In the federal system, marital privilege falls into two categories: a privilege against giving testimony adverse to one's spouse; and privilege against disclosure of confidential marital communications. (There is no privilege unless the testimony is genuinely adverse to the spouse's interests.)

Neither category is the same as the traditional rule of making one spouse incompetent to testify against the other. The witness spouse decides whether the privilege will apply; he or she can neither be forced to testify unwillingly, nor precluded from testifying should he or she wish to do so. The marital privilege is terminated by divorce (although it probably survives as to confidential communications made during the marriage), and is applicable only to persons who are considered married under the laws of the jurisdiction. The presence of third parties when communication occurs — even the couple's children — renders the privilege unavailable.

[D] Clergy-Penitent Privilege

Under Catholic doctrine, confidences given in the confessional are sacred, and cannot be revealed by the priest without the consent of the penitent. This concept has been adopted in secular law, in religious contexts broader than ritual confession.

The clergy-communicant privilege has been held[32] to protect communications made to a member of the clergy, who was acting in a spiritual or professional capacity (not merely as a friend), by a penitent who seeks spiritual counseling and reasonably expects that the communication will remain confidential. The privilege is not vitiated by the presence of a third party who was essential to and in furtherance of the communication.

A clergymember does not have to disclose, in a civil action, documents containing the substance of the information divulged by the penitent.[33] A non-confessional communication to church officials, made for the purpose of receiving church counseling and ecclesiastical advice, is immune from disclosure in an abuse suit brought by the adoptive daughter of the person making the communications.[34]

[E] Journalist's Privilege

A qualified privilege is available to journalists, so they are not generally required to divulge their confidential sources or disclose unpublished information acquired in the course of news-gathering activities. However, because the privilege is qualified rather than absolute, it may have to yield, e.g., if the journalist possesses highly material and relevant information, otherwise unobtainable, that is critical to a claim.[35]

---

[32] *In re* Grand Jury Investigation, 918 F.2d 374 (3d Cir. 1990).
[33] Blough v. Food Lion Inc., 142 FRD 622 (E.D. Va. 1992).
[34] Scott v. Hammock, 133 FRD 610 (D. Utah 1990).
[35] JJC v. Fridell, 165 FRD 513 (D. Minn. 1995).

See the Privacy Protection Act, 42 USC § 2000aa-(6), creating a federal District Court cause of action for anyone aggrieved by search for or seizure of journalists' work product. The plaintiff is entitled to recover actual damages (but in any event, the liquidated damages of $1,000 provided by the statute), plus fees and costs as awarded by the court.

However, according to the Second Circuit, journalists do not have a First Amendment privilege with respect to nonconfidential information, and they must disclose it in civil suits.[36]

[F] Governmental Privilege

Privilege is recognized in:

- State secrets of military or diplomatic significance
- Executive privilege for official information, including inter- and intra-agency communications dealing with policy- and decision-making functions
- Reports on ongoing investigations
- Communications about investigative techniques, including the identity of informants
- Judicial communications.

The privilege for investigative techniques gives way if the defendant can show significant need for information (e.g., location of surveillance cameras). There is no privilege for the identity of informants if their identity has already been disclosed. A defendant who seeks disclosure of an informant's identity must show a concrete need for the information greater than mere suspicion or speculation; the question is usually resolved at an in camera hearing.

[G] Corporate Privilege Issues

Some courts recognize a qualified privilege for a company's "critical self-analysis" (e.g., analysis of the business' success in achieving equal employment opportunity goals). To the extent that the privilege is recognized, it applies to subjective or evaluative material (but not hard data) prepared for a mandatory government report, where the policy reasons for exclusion (e.g., encouraging candor so organizations will improve their performance) clearly exceed the other party's need for the information.

Reports prepared for use by a hospital peer review committee have been deemed confidential, and cannot even be released to the trial judge. In this reading, it is better for peer reviewers to be able to speak candidly than for litigants to have access to additional information.[37]

---

[36] Gonzalez v. NBC, 155 F.3d 618 (2d Cir. 1998).

[37] Carr v. Howard, 689 N.E.2d 1304 (Mass. Sup. Jud. Ct. 1998).

Even if a corporation itself refuses to waive the attorney-client and work-product privileges, a corporate officer testifying before the Grand Jury can waive them.[38] But when a waiver is found, fairness demands that it be tailored narrowly to the degree of prejudice suffered by the government from non-production of the documents in question.

§ 23.13 SPOLIATION OF EVIDENCE

Early in 2004, the Supreme Court ruled that in a criminal case the failure to preserve evidence that is potentially useful, but is not exculpatory, violates due process only if it can be shown that the police acted in bad faith. (In this case, a substance alleged to be cocaine was destroyed routinely after a passage of years; the Supreme Court noted that the chemical makeup of the substance was inculpatory rather than exculpatory.)[39]

Damages for destruction of evidence equal the compensatory damages that would have been awarded on the underlying cause of action, but punitive damages are available only if the evidence was willfully or wantonly destroyed.

In mid-2008, the Eastern District of New York held that, although it was negligent (and possibly grossly negligent) for an airline to destroy a flight attendant's handwritten report of an incident during a flight, no sanctions for spoliation of evidence would be imposed. The plaintiff, a passenger who claimed that the airline failed to protect her from harassment by another passenger, did not prove that the destruction of the document prejudiced her. In discovery, the airline turned over three electronic versions of the flight attendant's account of the incident, but her original handwritten version was routinely destroyed with other documents of the same vintage. The Magistrate Judge held that there was no reason to believe that the handwritten version would contain any material more favorable to the plaintiff than the electronic version. The handwritten report should have been placed on litigation hold once it became clear that the passenger was going to press her complaint, and document destruction occurred two years after the incident, so the Magistrate Judge found at least simple and possibly gross negligence, but the lack of prejudice to the plaintiff ruled out sanctions.[40]

In a controversial decision, the Central District of California ruled in May 2007, that the duty to preserve evidence requires a party to activate the logging function so server log data would be retained in RAM. However, the court did not impose sanctions, holding that the party objecting to lack of preservation of the data did not seek a preservation order before applying for sanctions.[41]

---

[38] *In re* Grand Jury Proceedings, 219 F.3d 175 (2d Cir. 2000).

[39] Illinois v. Fisher, 540 U.S. 544 (2004).

[40] Whitney v. JetBlue, No. 07 CV 1397 (E.D.N.Y. 2008); *see* Daniel Wise, *Judge Finds JetBlue Negligent for Destroying Document, but Declines to Impose Sanctions*, N.Y.L.J. 5/6/08 (law.com).

[41] Columbia Pictures Indus. v. Bunnell, 2007 U.S. Dist. Lexis 46364 (C.D. Cal. 5/29/07); *see* Tom Allman, *Umbrella Rulings Can't Cover All Data*, Law Technology News 8/30/07 (law.com).

Chapter 24

Appeals

§ 24.01 INTRODUCTION

Appellate courts serve two major functions: redressing errors committed by lower courts, and furthering the progress of the law by adopting new principles.

The decision to appeal involves several related determinations: that there is a right to appeal, or that the case will be attractive to a court that selects the cases it will review; that there is a meaningful probability that the appellate court will rule favorably; and that the benefits of the appeal are likely to exceed its costs in delay, money, and effort.

On the other hand, delay can be favorable to a litigant; for instance, a defendant ordered to pay a large sum may be willing to appeal simply in order to be able to earn interest on the amount of the judgment for several more years. Taking — or threatening — such an appeal can be a potent weapon to induce a successful plaintiff to settle post-trial for less than the amount awarded by the trier of fact.

In 1997 the Supreme Court withdrew former Federal Rules of Appellate Procedure (FRAP) 74–76, which contained an optional appeals procedure for civil cases in which both sides consented to trial before a Magistrate Judge. With the termination of the optional procedure, the surviving form of appeal is appeal to the Court of Appeals from a final judgment (FRAP 3).

An early 2000 Supreme Court case resolves a Circuit split by permitting an appellate court to direct entry of judgment as a matter of law when it finds that some evidence was erroneously admitted at trial, and the remaining evidence is insufficient to support the verdict. FRCP 50(d) does not require a remand to the District Court to determine whether to enter judgment for the defendant or have a new trial, because the Court of Appeals can resolve that question.

Rule 50(d) says that if an appellate court reverses the judgment when the losing party appeals from a trial court denial of motion for JMOL (judgment as a matter of law), the court is not precluded from determining that the appellee is entitled to a new trial. The appellate court can direct the trial court to decide the availability of a new trial. However, this rule does not specifically allow the Court of Appeals to direct entry of JMOL.

The Supreme Court ruled that it does not really matter whether the appellate rationale was that the winning party failed to present sufficient evidence, or whether the inadmissible evidence in the record was crucial to the determination at trial. Either way, the party whose verdict is set aside has notice of the alleged deficiency in the evidence, and can argue for supporting the jury verdict or for a new trial.

The Supreme Court rejected the argument that it is unfair to allow JMOL at the appellate level, because the plaintiffs, confronted with that possibility, would have submitted more evidence. But in the post-*Daubert* atmosphere, plaintiffs know that expert testimony (the kind at issue in this case) is a dangerous foundation for a case.[1]

BAPCPA, the major bankruptcy reform statute, enacted 28 USC § 158(d)(2), allowing the Court of Appeals to directly review a Bankruptcy Court's judgments, orders, or decrees, if a bankruptcy court or District Court certifies that there is no controlling Supreme Court or Court of Appeals ruling on a matter of public importance. Direct review is also available if precedents exist but are in conflict, or immediate appeal could materially advance the progress of the bankruptcy proceeding. FRBP 8013 provides that a Circuit Court directly reviewing a Bankruptcy Court order uses the same standard of review that the District Court would have used. That is, findings of fact are reviewed for clear error, conclusions of law are reviewed de novo.[2]

---

[1] Weisgram v. Marley Co., 528 U.S. 440 (2000). *See also* Unitherm Food Sys. Inc. v. Swift-Eckrich, Inc., 546 U.S. 394 (2006), ruling that a new trial cannot be granted if the moving party fails to comply with Rule 50(b) and does not renew its pre-verdict motion for a directed verdict after the verdict has been rendered. Failure to comply with Rule 50(b) means that the Court of Appeals lacks a basis for reviewing the movant's challenge to the sufficiency of the evidence.

[2] *See, e.g.*, Drive Fin. Servs., LP v. Jordan, 521 F.3d 343 (5th Cir. 2008). An amendment to Federal Rules of Bankruptcy Procedure 8001 has been proposed to implement this provision: *see* http://www.uscourts.gov/rules/supct0108/summary_of_rules_for_Supreme_court_2007.pdf.

In the criminal context, the Supreme Court decided in 2003 that, for a federal defendant who loses on direct appeal but does not file a petition for certiorari, the one-year statute of limitations for seeking post-conviction motion relief (provided by 28 USC § 2255) starts when the time to seek certiorari ends, because that is the point at which the conviction is final.[3]

In December 2003, in *Castro v. U.S.*, 540 U.S. 375, the Supreme Court ruled that 27 U.S.C. § 2244(b)(3)(E), forbidding certiorari petitions to review "the grant or denial of an authorization by a court of appeals to file a second or successive application," did not preclude review of case where a motion for new trial was filed pro se, and later on a § 2255 motion was filed, also pro se. In this reading, a federal court has the power to recharacterize a pro se litigant's motion as an initial § 2255 motion if and only if it warns the litigant of the court's intent to characterize and the effect the recharacterization will have on further appeals.

As Chapter 19 shows, Congress has taken action to reduce the potential scope of immigration appeals. The REAL ID Act, P.L. 109-13, which took effect May 11, 2005, removed District Court habeas corpus jurisdiction over orders of removal of aliens. The Courts of Appeals are now the only courts with the power to review removal orders.

The Supreme Court held in mid-2006 that 8 USC § 1231(a)(5), reinstating prior removal orders against aliens who re-enter the United States illegally, without the possibility of judicial review, applies to aliens who re-entered the United States before the effective date of the statute. It is not impermissibly retroactive as to aliens who remained in the United States illegally after the statute's effective date.[4]

If a removable alien fails to raise a legal or constitutional challenge to the decision to place him or her in removal proceedings, the Court of Appeals does not have jurisdiction to consider a petition for relief.[5]

In mid-2007, the Supreme Court held that § 1447(d) prevents appellate consideration of a petitioner's claim that it is a foreign state as defined by the Foreign Sovereign Immunities Act of 1976. The court held that when § 1447(c) and (d) are read together, the only remands that are shielded from review are those under § 1447(c) (lack of subject matter jurisdiction because of defective removal procedure). Section 1447(c) does not forbid remand of a case that was properly removed if subject matter jurisdiction is lacking. In fact, § 1447(d) protects such remands from review.[6]

Effective six months after the June 10, 2008, publication date, the PTO published new rules for appeals to the Board of Patent Appeals and Interferences. The process has been streamlined by calling for faster exchange of information and greater refining of the issues of the dispute. The new process accelerates the point at which examiners must give their reasons for rejecting a patent. New outline

---

[3] Clay v. United States, 537 U.S. 522 (2003).
[4] Fernandez-Vargas v. Gonzales, 548 U.S. 30 (2006).
[5] Ali v. Mukasey, 524 F.3d 145 (2d Cir. 2008).
[6] Powertex Corp. v. Reliant Energy Servs., Inc., 551 U.S. 224 (2007).

requirements have been added, making the appeal briefs more like federal court briefs.[7]

§ 24.02   STANDARD OF REVIEW

Depending on the type of case and the nature of the ruling appealed from, the appellate court may either be entitled to review the case de novo (i.e., as if the earlier ruling did not exist), or will merely examine the prior decision for obvious error or abuse of discretion.

Appellate review of facts determined by a jury is very narrow. The jury's finding must be upheld if there was sufficient evidence to support it (even if another reasonable conclusion could have been reached). Sufficiency means probative facts in the record from which the ultimate fact found by the jury could reasonably have been inferred. If there was no motion for directed verdict or JNOV at trial, review is circumscribed even further: the jury's finding of fact must be upheld if there was any evidence to support it.

In cases where there was no right to a jury trial, or where jury trial was waived, the judge is the trier of fact. FRCP 52(a) (most of the states have similar provisions) requires the judge to make specific findings of fact, and to make a separate list of conclusion of law. The judge's findings of fact can only be set aside if they were clearly erroneous (lacking substantial evidentiary support),[8] or if they are the product of erroneous application of the law. Given this second ground, it is somewhat easier to attack judicial findings of fact than jury findings of fact.

Rule 52(a) does not apply to questions of law, so the appellate court can review judicial findings freely. Similarly, mixed issues of law and fact are generally open to review by the appellate court. According to *Ornelas v. United States*, 517 U.S. 690 (1996), in cases involving mixed question of law and fact, the historical facts are admitted or established. The significant legal question is whether the rule of law (which is undisputed) is violated as applied to established facts.

A distinction is sometimes drawn between basic facts and ultimate facts. Basic facts are the direct subject of evidence (e.g., that a car was traveling at 75 mph). Ultimate facts are the legal reasoning or interpretation applied to evidentiary facts.

The Supreme Court has upheld a New York statute that allows a state appellate court to review jury verdicts and grant new trials where the verdicts are materially different from reasonable compensation to the injured party. The statute was applied in a federal diversity case using New York law. To the Supreme Court, the Seventh Amendment guarantee of a jury trial was not violated, as long as the federal trial judge uses the standard of whether or not the trial judge abused discretion.[9]

---

[7] Sheri Qualters, *U.S. Patent Office Rolls Out New Rules for Appeals*, Nat'l L.J. 6/11/08 (law.com).

[8] Parts & Elec. Motors, Inc. v. Sterling Elec., Inc., 866 F.2d 228 (7th Cir. 1988) puts it (literally) more pungently: a clearly erroneous decision is "wrong with the force of a five-week-old, unrefrigerated dead fish."

[9] Gasperini v. Center for Humanities Inc., 518 U.S. 415 (1996).

The standard for review of the Constitutionality of a punitive damage award is de novo, not abuse of discretion.[10] The Supreme Court upheld the practice of Courts of Appeals using harmless error analysis to review state and federal sentences that were enhanced prior to *Apprendi* (see §26.04[L][5]) on the basis of facts found by a judge.[11]

Appellate courts treat evidence in the light most favorable to the appellee, not the appellant, drawing any favorable inferences that are reasonably available. Furthermore, if a judge reaches the right result via incorrect reasoning, such a decision must be upheld. When matters are placed in the trial court's discretion by statute or case law, the trial court's decision will be disturbed only if there was an abuse of discretion.

The Court of Appeals usually hears cases in three-judge panels. However, 28 USC §46 gives a majority of the active judges in a Court of Appeals the option to vote for the case to be heard en banc (i.e., by all the active judges).

[A] State Appeals

Some states have only one level of appellate review from trial court decisions. In such states, most final judgments can be appealed of right to the single appellate court. However, most of the states have intermediate courts of appeal. In those states, the highest-level appellate court generally has significant discretion in accepting or turning down cases. Some states allow interlocutory appeals of right at least to the first level of appellate review, whereas others make interlocutory appeals discretionary.

There is significant variation in the way states structure their courts of appeals. Either they create a single court with statewide jurisdiction, or several courts limited to jurisdiction in a particular geographic area of the state. Some state appeals courts sit in panels, others en banc.

§24.03 APPEALABLE ISSUES

The underlying rule is that a party is entitled to a single appeal, deferred until final judgment has been entered, covering claims of District Court error committed at any stage.[12] A valid appeal must fall within a corridor: the issues must be ripe for adjudication, but there must be a real, ongoing controversy — the issues must not have become moot.

As noted above, the general rule is that issues cannot be raised for the first time at the appellate level. However, subject matter jurisdiction can always be raised, although personal jurisdiction and venue are waived if not asserted at trial. It is possible, although not certain, that an appellate court will rule on a "fundamental" error even if it is raised for the first time on appeal. Appellate

---

[10] Cooper Indus. Inc. v. Leatherman Tool Group, 532 U.S. 424 (2001).

[11] Washington v. Recuenco, 548 U.S. 212 (2006).

[12] Digital Equip. Corp. v. Desktop Direct, 511 U.S. 863 (1994). This case also holds that refusal to enforce a settlement agreement is not immediately appealable.

courts examine the record below, so they will not see anything failing to appear there. In all probability, issues not raised in the appellate brief will be waived.

The Supreme Court ruled in 2008 that §§ 9–11 of the FAA, providing expedited judicial review to confirm, vacate, or modify arbitration awards are exclusive, and represent part of a national policy favoring arbitration and making arbitration awards essentially final. Therefore, parties to an arbitration agreement cannot agree to draft the agreement to provide judicial review that is broader than the limited review permitted under the FAA.[13]

In 2006, the Second Circuit denied a petition for leave to appeal a class certification order, because the petition was filed after Rule 23(f)'s 10-day deadline. Rule 23(f) gives the District Court discretion to permit an appeal where filing is made within the time limit. The Fifth, Seventh, and Eleventh Circuits treat the deadline as jurisdictional. However, the Second Circuit said that *Eberhart* ruling calls into question whether Rule 23(f) is jurisdictional.[14]

The District Court can no longer grant an FRCP 60(b) motion for relief from the judgment (e.g., a motion for reconsideration of dismissal) once a party has filed an appeal of the judgment, unless the Court of Appeals grants leave.[15] The Fifth Circuit denied FRCP 60(b)(6) post-judgment relief in a case in which the plaintiffs lost on appeal but, later on, the Supreme Court's ruling in a different case adopted the plaintiffs' position. A change in decisional law after a judgment becomes final does not justify reopening the judgment.[16]

In calculating the sentence for seven drug and firearm charges, the District Court imposed a sentence of 442 months — but, by overlooking *Deal v. U.S.*, a 10-year sentence was imposed on an offense whose mandatory minimum sentence was 25 years. The defendant appealed, taking the position that the appropriate sentence for all his convictions was 15 years; however, the government neither appealed nor cross-appealed. The Eighth Circuit, citing the FRCP 52(b) plain error rule, raised the sentence to 662 months. The Supreme Court reversed, holding that, without a government appeal or cross appeal, the Court of Appeals lacked the power to increase the sentence on its own motion. In this view, the court is merely a neutral arbiter of the issues raised by the parties, and departures from this "party presentation" rule generally are made to assist pro se petitioners. The Supreme Court held that the plain error rule does not override the cross-appeal requirement; appellate time limits would be meaningless if the court could grant, at any time, relief that was not even sought by a party. In a multi-count indictment "sentencing package," where some but not all counts of a conviction are challenged, the Supreme Court said that an appeals court can vacate the entire sentence so the

---

[13] Hall Street Assocs., LLC v. Mattel, 128 S. Ct. 1396 (2008).

[14] Coco v. Incorporated Vill. of Belle Terre, 448 F.3d 490 (2d Cir. 2006); *Eberhart* is Eberhart v. United States, 546 U.S. 12 (2005); *see also* MacNamara v. Felderhof, 410 F.3d 277 (5th Cir. 2005); Shin v. Cobb County Bd. of Educ., 248 F.3d 1061 (11th Cir. 2001); Gary v. Sheahan, 188 F.3d 891 (7th Cir. 1999).

[15] Shepherd v. International Paper Co., 372 F.3d 326 (5th Cir. 2004).

[16] United States *ex rel.* Garibaldi v. Orleans Parish Sch. Bd., 397 F.3d 334 (5th Cir. 2005).

trial court can reform the sentencing plan, resulting in a plan that is longer than the sentences on certain counts, but not longer than the initial aggregate. This is acceptable under the cross-appeal rule, because the judge did not enlarge the sentence on his or her own motion. In this case, there was no reason to vacate the sentence, because the convictee failed on all his appellate issues.[17]

Under 28 USC § 1291, the Courts of Appeal have jurisdiction of appeals from all final decisions of the District Courts, other than those where direct Supreme Court review is permitted. FRCP 58 requires that a final judgment must be set forth separately; Rule 79(a) says it must be entered by the District Court clerk in the civil docket.

The federal courts can only decide legal questions that are posed in a "case or controversy," as defined by the Constitution, and the "case or controversy" must exist at all stages of appellate review.[18] However, ripeness for adjudication is measured as of the time of review, not the time of a lower court decision: *Anderson v. Green*, 513 U.S. 557 (1995).

In several Circuits (the Third, Sixth, Ninth, and D.C. — but not in the Seventh or Eighth) a client who can prove that his attorney was grossly negligent has demonstrated an "extraordinary circumstance" that will permit relief from a default judgment pursuant to FRCP 60(b)(6), the catch-all relief provision.[19]

A District Court order remanding a case removed from the state court under SLUSA is not appealable. However, once the case is remanded, the plaintiffs may find that their claims are "holder" claims precluded by the Securities Litigation Uniform Standards Act, aka SLUSA (i.e., allegations that misrepresentations induced them to hold stock rather than buying or selling it).[20]

The Third Circuit held in mid-2006 that a District Court order under 18 USC § 4243(d), committing a defendant to the Attorney General's custody after acquittal by reason of insanity, is an appealable final order under 28 USC § 1291. Because the commitment order is a finding of fact by the District Court, it must be clearly erroneous to be reversed.[21]

[A] Commencement of an Appeal

In addition to the Federal Rules of Appellate Practice, the litigator should consult the Circuit and District rules for appeals. Generally speaking, an appeal is taken by serving and/or filing a notice of appeal. An assignment of errors or bill of exceptions may be required. It may also be necessary to obtain leave to appeal from the court whose decision is being reviewed, or by the potential reviewing court.

---

[17] Greenlaw v. United States, 128 S. Ct. 2559 (2008); *see also* Deal v. United States, 508 U.S.129 (1993).

[18] U.S. Bancorp Mort. Co. v. Bonner Mall Partnership, 513 U.S. 18 (1994).

[19] If the United States is a party to the case, this time is extended to 60 days for all parties.

[20] Kircher v. Putnam Funds Trust, 547 U.S. 71 (2006); on "holder" claims, *see* Merrill Lynch v. Dabit, 547 U.S. 71 (2006).

[21] United States v. Stewart, 452 F.3d 266 (3d Cir. 2006).

FRAP 3 provides that an appeal of right is filed by filing a notice of appeal with the district clerk within the time limit of FRAP 4.

The Class Action Fairness Act (CAFA; see § 22.09[E][5]) creates some interpretive problems for appeal issues. 28 USC § 1453(c)(1) says that a Court of Appeals may accept an appeal from a District Court order granting or denying a motion to remand a class action to state court based on an application made to the court of appeals "not less than seven days" after the order. In Amalgamated Transit Union Local 1309 v. Laidlaw Transit Services, the Ninth Circuit concluded that the "not less than seven days" in 28 USC § 1453(c)(1) must be a typographical error meaning "not more than seven days," on the grounds that it would be illogical to impose a seven-day waiting period but no time limit.[22]

As for another CAFA timing issue, CAFA imposes a 60-day time limit during which the Court of Appeals must rule on the merits of a class action appeal. According to the Fifth, Seventh, Ninth, and Eleventh Circuits, the 60-day period runs from the grant of the petition, not the initial filing. The potential appellant applies for leave to appeal; the Fifth Circuit construes this to mean that no appeal actually exists until the court exercises its power to grant or deny leave.[23]

A state class action was filed against marketing firm Vertrue, charging it with systematically submitting unauthorized credit card charges. Vertrue removed the case under CAFA. The plaintiff alleged that the amount in controversy was less than $5 million. The District Court accepted this argument and remanded the case to state court. Vertrue filed a petition for leave to appeal (28 USC § 1453(c)(1)). The petition was mailed on the seventh day after the District Court remand order. It reached the court and was filed (see FRAP 25(a)(2)) on the tenth day. The Seventh Circuit said the filing was timely because it was "not less than seven days" after the court order. FRAP 4(a)(2) says that a premature notice of appeal remains on file and takes effect when the decision becomes appealable; and the Seventh Circuit extended this principle to premature applications for permission for leave to appeal. The Seventh Circuit rejected the argument that the CAFA provision, as written, creates an infinite time to appeal. FRAP 5(a)(2) provides that, where no other limit is provided, a petition for permission to appeal has to be filed within the Rule 4(a) time frame of 30 days (60 days if the United States or a federal agency is a party — but in that case, removal is possible even outside of CAFA).[24]

---

[22] Amalgamated Transit Union Local 1309-AFL-CIO v. Laidlaw Transit Servs. Inc., 435 F.3d 1140 (9th Cir. 2006); Morgan v. Gay, 466 F.3d 276 (3d Cir. 2006) and Pritchett v. Office Depot, Inc. 420 F.3d 1090 (10th Cir. 2005) also treat the provision as a typographical error. *See* Marie-Anne Hogarth, *For 9th Circuit, Less Means More*, The Recorder 5/24/06 (law.com).

[23] Hart v. Fedex Ground Package Sys. Inc., 457 F.3d 675 (7th Cir. 2006); Evans v. Walter Indus. Inc., 449 F.3d 1159 (11th Cir. 2006); Patterson v. Dean Morris LLP, 444 F.3d 365 (5th Cir. 2006), 487 F.3d 736 (5th Cir. 2006); Amalgamated Transit Union Local 1309, AFL-CIO v. Laidlaw Transit Serv. Inc., 435 F.3d 1140 (9th Cir. 2006); *see also* Bush v. Cheaptickets, Inc., 425 F.3d 683 (9th Cir. 2005).

[24] Spivey v. Vertrue, Inc., 528 F.3d 982 (7th Cir. 2008).

Home Depot used § 1332(a) to remove a putative class action filed in Missouri state court, because diversity was present and the amount in controversy exceeded $75,000. The District Court denied the plaintiff's motion to remand. The Eighth Circuit held that § 1453(c)(1) does not allow a Circuit Court to hear an appeal from denial of a remand motion after removal under traditional diversity jurisdiction. The Eighth Circuit held that CAFA, at § 1453(c)(1), vests original jurisdiction in the District Court if a class action satisfies certain criteria, and permits the Court of Appeals to accept an appeal from a grant or denial of a motion to remand. The plaintiff wanted this to be read broadly enough for the Court of Appeals to review the grant or denial of remand in any class action, but the Eighth Circuit drew a distinction between removal under traditional diversity jurisdiction (§ 1332(a)) and CAFA diversity jurisdiction (§ 1332(d)), with discretionary appellate review limited to CAFA jurisdiction.[25]

[1] Notice of Appeal

The notice of appeal:

- Specifies who is appealing
- Designates the judgment, order, or portion of one of them which is being appealed
- Names the court to which the appeal is taken.

FRAP 3(b) allows a joint appeal, with a single appellate brief, only if two or more parties can appeal from a single judgment or order. But once separate notices of appeal are filed, consolidation is no longer permitted.

The district clerk serves the notice of filing by mailing a copy to the counsel for other parties. In a criminal appeal, the defendant is also served to confirm his or her filing. Rule 4 says that in a civil case, notice of appeal must be filed within 30 days after entry of the judgment or order appealed from. In a criminal case, filing is due within 10 days after the entry of the judgment or order appealed from, or filing of the government notice of appeal, whichever is later.

The time to file can be extended by the District Court for a party who moves for added time within 30 days of the normal filing date, and who shows good cause or excusable neglect.

[2] Petition for Permissive Appeal

See FRAP 5 for permissive appeals, which are commenced by a petition[26] filed with the circuit clerk, with proof of service on all other parties to the District Court action.

---

[25] Saab v. Home Depot USA, 469 F.3d 758 (8th Cir. 2006).

[26] Notice of appeal is not required; the date of entry for the order allowing the appeal is treated as the date of the notice of appeal.

Either the District Court must have granted permission to appeal, or it must issue an order stating the preconditions for appeal have been satisfied. Timing for the petition derives from the statute or rule authorizing the appeal; the FRAP 4 schedule applies if the statute is silent. The petition must contain:

❑ Facts needed to understand the question to be appealed
❑ The question itself
❑ The relief sought
❑ Justification for allowing the appeal
❑ Statutory or regulatory authority permitting the appeal
❑ The order, decree, or judgment from which appeal is sought, plus any related opinions or memorandum decisions
❑ The District Court permission or order as to preconditions.

Filing and service are controlled by FRAP 25. See Rule 25 for computing and extending times in the appellate practice.

Defendant/appellants (i.e., those that might be tempted to appeal merely to defer payment of a judgment) may be required to post an appeal bond. Depending on jurisdiction and circumstances, the bond may equal or even exceed the judgment. See FRAP 7.

[3] The Record Below

In addition to the basic rules of FRAP 10, court practice determines how much of the record below must be filed with the appeal.

The record and/or the transcript of the trial may have to be certified by the clerk of the trial court; the litigator must make sure to allow adequate time to get this done before filing notice of appeal. It is also a matter of local practice when the time to appeal will begin to run. It could be the entry of the lower court's order; the time the lower court's order is served; or service of the order with notice of entry.

It is good strategy for the party who prevailed at trial to check with the clerk's office shortly before the time to appeal expires, and on the very last day notice of appeal can be filed, so that a notice of cross-appeal can be prepared and filed to protect the right of cross-appeal.

The Supreme Court allows a pro se litigant's filing of a timely brief, containing all the necessary information, to operate as the notice of appeal required by the FRAP.[27]

[B] Appeal of Interlocutory and Final Orders

As a general rule, a final order is a prerequisite to an appeal (see 28 USC § 1291), but some interlocutory appeals are permitted. In federal practice, four types of interlocutory appeals as of right are recognized under 28 USC

---

[27] Smith v. Barry, 502 U.S. 244 (1992).

§ 1292(a): injunctions; receiverships; admiralty cases in which the final decree is appealable; and certain civil actions for patent infringement. Of these, only the injunction is commonly encountered!

All other federal interlocutory appeals are discretionary. Under 28 USC § 1292(b), a District Court judge can allow permissive interlocutory appeal if the case is controlled by a question of law; there is substantial ground for difference of opinion on the proper interpretation of the question of law; and immediate appeal materially advances the ultimate completion of the litigation.

Under the "final judgment rule," orders entered when a case is pending cannot be appealed until the whole case is resolved. Orders that were interlocutory when they were entered can be appealed after the resolution, if they are still relevant. However, Rule 54(b) provides an exception: in a case involving multiple parties or separate claims for relief, the District Court can certify an order as final if it disposes of at least one claim with respect to at least one party, even though other issues are ongoing. Most Courts of Appeal read that to mean that the claim must not arise from the same set of facts as the claims that remain in the case. The District Court has discretion as to whether or not certify as final an order that disposes of less than all claims as to all parties. Once such an order is certified, it is immediately appealable, and permission is not required. In fact, if the losing party fails to appeal in time (measured from the date of entry of the order), the appeal is forfeited; the loser cannot wait until the case ends to appeal.[28]

The criteria for deciding whether to hear an interlocutory appeal of the grant or denial of class certification under Rule 23(f) include whether there is a death-knell situation for either party independent of the merits of the claim; whether the District Court's decision was questionable or manifestly erroneous; and whether the certification decision involved a fundamental unsettled point of class action law.[29]

The Third Circuit dismissed an appeal on the question of what would happen to a bankrupt company's trade secrets, holding that a discovery order for protection of trade secrets is neither final nor appealable. (The First, Seventh, and Tenth Circuits have also refused to exercise jurisdiction over appeals from trade secret discovery orders.) In the Third Circuit view, parties who think they have been denied adequate protection can seek permissive review under 28 USC § 1292(b), and parties challenging the grant of a protective order can seek mandamus. An objector can also refuse to comply with the protective order, be held in contempt, and appeal the contempt order.[30]

Under FRAP 4(a)(2), a notice of appeal can be filed from a non-final decision announced by a court, if the decision would be appealable if entered immediately, and the notice of appeal becomes effective when the final judgment is rendered.[31]

---

[28] Howard J. Bashman, *Appeal Now or Later? A Look at Federal Rule of Civil Procedure 54(b)*, Special to Law.com (7/16/07).

[29] Chamberlan v. Ford Motor Co., 402 F.3d 952 (9th Cir. 2005).

[30] *In re* Carco Electronics, 536 F.3d 211 (3d Cir. 2008).

[31] FirsTier Mort. Co. v. Investors Mort. Ins. Co., 498 U.S. 269 (1991).

The Supreme Court's rationale for this decision is that the situation does not present a risk of surprise to the non-appealing party.

When a District Court dismisses one count of a civil case and transfers the remaining counts to a different district, the dismissal is only an appealable final decision if it is certified under FRCP 54(b) for immediate appeal.[32] If this is not done, the dismissed count accompanies the others, and must be appealed in the transferee court.

However, the Fourth Circuit held that when a case is transferred from one District Court to another, the Court of Appeals for the transferor court can still hear an appeal of any immediately appealable decision of the transferor court (in this case, a petition to compel arbitration).[33]

A District Court's order, refusing to certify a question of state law to the state Supreme Court, is not appealable. The Seventh Circuit held it to be an interlocutory order, not a collateral order, and held that it does not conform to the statutory exceptions. Denial of certification does not conclusively determine the disputed issue.[34]

A federal magistrate judge's order, remanding a removed case to state court, can be reviewed by the District Court under 28 USC § 636(b)(1)(B). This is true because a remand is a "dispositive order" and therefore only a District Court can render it.[35]

In early 2002, the Ninth Circuit accentuated a Circuit split by ruling that, unless there is evidence of intent to manipulate appellate jurisdiction, when a District Court enters partial summary judgment on some of the claims in a suit, and dismisses the rest without prejudice, this judgment is final and appealable. This position was taken earlier by the Sixth, Seventh, and Eighth Circuits, but the Second, Fifth, Tenth, and Eleventh disagree.[36]

The Second Circuit addressed some timing issues for qui tam actions in early 2008. When the United States is not a party to the action, the notice of appeal must be filed within 30 days of entry of judgment. A group of New York City municipal employees alleged that it violated the False Claims Act for the city to charge nonresident employees a fee corresponding to New York City income tax paid by resident employees. The litigation theory was that this was a false claim because the city deprived the federal government of revenue equal to the tax deduction taken by the nonresidents on their federal returns. The Southern District of New York dismissed the case March 31, 2006, rendering final judgment April 12, 2006. One of the plaintiffs filed notice of appeal June 5, 2006 — 53 days later. The Second Circuit, noting that the United States played no role until filing of the amicus brief required by the court, held that "party" means one who controls the litigation, not one who might receive benefits from the litigation; the

---

[32] Hill v. Henderson, 195 F.3d 671 (D.C. Cir. 1999).

[33] Technosteel LLC v. Beers Constr. Co., 271 F.3d 151 (4th Cir. 2001).

[34] Brown v. Argosy Gaming Co., 360 F.3d 703 (7th Cir. 2004).

[35] Vogel v. United States Office Prods. Co., 258 F.3d 509 (6th Cir. 2001).

[36] James v. Price Stern Sloan Inc., 283 F.3d 1064 (9th Cir. 2002).

United States did not intervene, raise any legal claims, or deny any claims, so it was not a party.[37]

[C] The Appellate Brief

Under Rule 28, the appellate brief must contain descriptive headings, and must contain all of these items, in this order:

- Rule 26.1 corporate disclosure statement (if applicable): a corporate party to a Court of Appeals proceeding must identify any parent corporation or any public corporation owning over 10% of its stock; if there is no such corporation, the corporate party must say so.
  - Table of Contents with page references
  - Table of authorities (cases in alphabetical order; statutes; administrative rules), with references to the pages on which they are cited
  - Jurisdictional statement (grounds for District Court and Court of Appeals jurisdiction; filing dates establishing timeliness; either a statement that the appeal is from a final order or judgment, or the alternate basis for jurisdiction)
  - Issues for review
  - Litigation history of the case
  - Facts relevant to the issues, with references to the record below
  - Summary of the appellant's argument
  - The argument itself, giving the appellant's contentions and the support for them, and applicable standard of review for each issue
  - A short conclusion, stating the precise relief sought
  - Certificate of compliance with the Rule 32 length requirements.

The appellee's brief can omit the jurisdictional statement and statements of issues, cases, facts, and standard of review unless the appellee takes issue with the appellant's formulation. The appellant can also file a reply brief, which should be limited to addressing the appellee's argument rather than presenting new facts or legal theories.[38]

The appellant is required, by FRAP 30, to prepare and file an appendix to the brief containing the relevant District Court docket entries for the case; relevant portions of pleadings, charge, findings, or opinion; the judgment, order or decision appealed from; and other parts of the record the appellant wants the court to

---

[37] United States *ex rel.* Eisenstein v. City of New York, 540 F.3d 94 (2d Cir. 2008); *see* Mark Hamblett, *2nd Circuit Addresses Limits on Qui Tam Actions Under False Claims Act*, N.Y.L.J. 8/26/08 (law.com). The Tenth Circuit agrees, but the Fifth, Seventh, and Ninth Circuits treat the United States as a party in these circumstances. The Second Circuit also held that only a licensed attorney can appear on behalf of someone else, including the United States; nor can a sole shareholder represent a corporation, or a general partner represent a partnership unless they happen to be attorneys: United States *ex rel.* Mergent Servs. v. Flaherty, 540 F.3d 89 (2d Cir. 2008).

[38] United States v. Feinberg, 89 F.3d 333 (7th Cir. 1996).

consider. However, unless they have independent relevance, memoranda of law from the District Court should not be included in the appendix.

FRAP 31(b) provides that, unless the local rule or the order in the individual case sets a different requirement, 25 copies of each brief must be filed with the clerk, and each party who has separate representation must be served with two copies of the brief. The time limit is 40 days after the record was filed. The appellee has 30 days from service of the appellant's brief to serve and file its own brief.

Government agencies are always permitted to file amicus curiae briefs. Anyone else can do so only if all parties consent, or if the court grants leave (Rule 29).

FRAP 32(a) sets length limits. The brief must be double-spaced on 8½ × 11 paper, with margins of 1 on each side. As a general rule, a brief may not exceed 14,000 words (7,000 words for a reply brief); there is a safe harbor for briefs that do not exceed 1,300 lines of text. Unless the court permits a longer amicus brief to be filed, they are limited to half the length of the principal brief.

Although reply briefs are optional, and some judges find them annoying, they furnish appellants with a chance to have the last word. Furthermore, failure to provide such a brief may be seen as a concession that the case is weak. However, Court of Appeals justices do not want to see either a re-run of the original brief, or attempts to raise new arguments at too late a stage. According to Justice Scalia, many judges engage in "retro-reading," starting with the reply brief, then the respondent's brief, and finally the appellant's original brief, to see if the weakest arguments have been dropped based on the appellee's brief.[39]

§ 24.04 CONDUCT OF THE APPEAL

The Court of Appeals can require attorneys (and litigants, where appropriate) to attend appeals conferences under FRAP 33, which are concerned with matters that can assist the disposition of the case by simplifying issues and perhaps promoting a settlement. The conferences can be in-person or done over the telephone, under the supervision of a judge or a person designated by the Court of Appeals.

Appellate motions are subject to FRAP 27 for motions. FRAP 27(a)(2) requires all legal arguments to be contained within the motion, because supporting briefs and memoranda of law are not allowed. Supporting affidavits are purely factual, and should not contain legal arguments. The general rule of FRAP 27(d) is that the original and three copies of all papers relating to a motion must be filed with the court.

In general, oral argument will be permitted for the appeal itself, unless three judges unanimously hold that oral argument is unnecessary (FRAP 34). This might be done if the appeal is frivolous, but also if there is already authority controlling the dispositive issues, or the briefs and records provide the Court of Appeals with all the information it needs to decide the case. The parties can agree to submit the case on briefs in lieu of oral argument, but the Court of Appeals can order oral argument if it deems it necessary.

---

[39] Mike McKee, *Are Reply Briefs Really Necessary?* The Recorder 8/1/08 (law.com).

En banc hearings can be ordered by a majority of the circuit judges on regular active service, but FRAP 35 warns them not to do so unless there is a question of exceptional importance involved or the case must be heard en banc to prevent conflict among panels of the Circuit. FRAP 35 allows parties to petition for en banc hearings on similar grounds, or if a panel decision conflicts with a Supreme Court decision or a decision of another panel of the same Circuit.

All of the Circuit Court assign cases to three-judge panels, and make a panel's ruling govern future three-judge panels of the same Circuit unless there is a contrary opinion by a higher court of an en banc panel of the same Circuit. When there is an intra-circuit conflict (i.e., two three-judge panels have disagreed), all of the Circuits other than the Eighth take the position that the first panel decision governs, but an en banc decision overrules any three-judge panel. The Eighth Circuit, however, permits a third three-judge panel to follow whichever of the previous three-judge panel decisions it finds more persuasive.[40]

The Court of Appeals' judgment is entered when noted on the docket (FRAP 36).

§ 24.05   INTEREST AND COSTS

As a general rule (unless there is a governing statute to the contrary), when a civil money judgment is affirmed, interest payable by law runs from the date of entry of the District Court judgment (i.e., taking a losing appeal is not an effective way of saving interest!). If the Court of Appeals modifies or reverses a case and directs the District Court to enter a money judgment, the Court of Appeals' order must direct the District Court how to handle the interest obligation (FRAP 37).

Unless there is a statute or court order to the contrary, costs are assessed against the appellant when the appeal is dismissed — unless the parties agree otherwise. See FRAP 39. Costs are also assessed against the appellant when the judgment below is affirmed. If the judgment is reversed, the appellee becomes responsible for costs. The court order must allocate costs when the judgment below is affirmed in part and reversed in part, modified, or vacated. An appellee subjected to a frivolous appeal can be awarded damages and "single or double costs" under FRAP 38.

Under FRAP 7, which gives the District Court the power to order an appellant to post bond to ensure payment of costs on appeal, the appellant can be required to post an amount estimated as the appellee's expected attorneys' fees for the appeal. This requirement can only be imposed if the cause of action provides for fee-shifting and includes attorneys' fees as costs. This is not true for some statutes (e.g., RESPA).

---

[40] Howard J. Bashman, *In Intra-Circuit Splits, Which Decision Governs?* Special to law.com (7/30/07).

§ 24.06 CRIMINAL APPEALS

Whether a criminal defendant can be released before or after judgment of conviction is controlled by 18 USC §§ 3141, 3143, and 3145(c). See also FRAP 9.

Habeas corpus proceedings come under FRAP 22 but have been strictly limited by AEDPA, see § 26.04[N][1][a]. Habeas applications are made in the District Court, not the Circuit Court, although a District Court denial of a writ is appealable under § 2253. A habeas corpus proceeding involving a state court judgment requires a certificate of appealability issued by a District Court judge or Court of Appeals justice. See FRAP 23 for whether a habeas petitioner will be released or will continue to be detained.

It is very common for habeas proceedings to be maintained *in forma pauperis*, so the rules of 28 USC § 1915 and FRAP 24 must be consulted. In the context of habeas corpus, the Supreme Court ruled in March 2004 that the petition must give the state the ability to correct the alleged violation of the defendant's rights by fairly presenting the claim in each appropriate state court to raise the federal nature of the claim. A claim is not fairly presented if the court must read beyond the petition and the brief to discover whether a federal claim is being raised. The Supreme Court overruled the Ninth Circuit, which had held that reading the state court opinion would reveal the federal claim.[41]

In late 2004, changes to the habeas corpus rules took effect, amending 18 USC §§ 2254–2255 in conformity with AEDPA. A new rule has been added to the Rules Governing § 2254 and 2255 cases: court clerks must file petitions and motions even if they contain procedural defects, because the prior-law requirement of returning defective papers could, in conjunction with AEDPA's one-year statute of limitations, prevent claims — perhaps including some meritorious claims — from being considered. The special 2254–5 rules have been amended to set a time schedule under which prisoners can reply to the government's response to the prisoner's petition or motion (e.g., to rebut the government's claim of untimeliness or failure to exhaust administrative remedies). When discovery is sought in the habeas context, the party seeking discovery must give reasons, and the request must be supplemented by a list of requested documents and proposed interrogatories and requests for admission.[42]

Under *O'Sullivan v. Boerckel*,[43] state prisoners must exhaust their state-court remedies before seeking federal habeas relief. They must seek discretionary review in the state's highest court, if that is part of the ordinary appellate procedure.

When the Supreme Court re-convened in October 2006, it decided several procedural questions about criminal appeals. The court held that motions under FRCP 33(a), which allows the District Court to grant new trials in the interest of justice, are subject to a seven-day time limit. Unless the motion asserts newly discovered evidence, it must be filed within seven days after the verdict.

---

[41] Baldwin v. Reese, 541 U.S. 27 (2004).

[42] http://www.uscourts.gov/rules/index.html#supreme0404; *see* 73 L.W. 2331.

[43] 526 U.S. 838 (1999).

The Seventh Circuit ruled that the time limit was "jurisdictional" — i.e., the prosecution could raise the issue of noncompliance with the seven-day deadline for the first time on appeal. But the Supreme Court reversed in Eberhart v. United States,[44] ruling that Rule 33(a) is an "inflexible claim processing rule," and not a requirement for subject-matter jurisdiction. Thus, the issue was waived because it was not raised prior to the appeal.

In 2007, the Supreme Court returned to the subject, holding that the time for appeal is jurisdictional, so a court cannot hear an untimely appeal, no matter how good the reason for failing to meet the deadline. In this case, the petitioner sought federal habeas relief for his murder conviction. The District Court turned him down. His motion for reconsideration was timely, because the start of the 30-day appeal period is delayed until the motion for reconsideration is decided. The petitioner did not get timely notification of the District Court's order denying his motion for reconsideration; he did not learn of the denial until approximately three months after the order. He asked the District Court to reopen the time to appeal under 28 USC § 2107(c) and FRAP Rule 4(a)(6). Rule 4(a)(6) permits the District Court to reopen the time to file an appeal for 14 days after the date of the order to reopen. The District Judge granted the order to reopen, but specified that the Notice of Appeal had to be filed within 17 days (no later than February 27). The petitioner filed his Notice of Appeal on February 26th — but the judge was wrong: the deadline is actually 14 days, not 17. The Supreme Court refused to give the petitioner relief from the consequences of the judge's error.[45]

Under AEDPA, the one-year statute of limitations to seek habeas relief is tolled while a properly filed petition for state collateral review is pending. In January 2006, the Supreme Court ruled that a state court order that merely denies the right to appeal is not necessarily an order on the merits, so it was improper to treat a habeas petition filed three years after a state appellate decision as timely.[46]

Texas permits defendants to file untimely appeals of state convictions. The Supreme Court's January 13, 2009, decision in *Jimenez v. Quarterman*, No. 07-6984 (1/13/09), holds that the one-year AEDPA "clock" does not start to run until after the completion of the untimely appeal. The Supreme Court ruled that the judgment is not "final" for § 2244(d)(1)(A) purposes until either the conclusion of the direct appeal or the expiration of the time to seek certiorari on that appeal. In this case, the Texas Court of Criminal Appeals reopened direct review of the petitioner's conviction on September 24, 2002, so his conviction was no longer final. The pendency of his direct appeal was renewed, and it once again became

---

[44] 546 U.S. 12 (2005).

[45] Bowles v. Russell, 127 S. Ct. 2352 (6/14/07), discussed in Howard J. Bashman, *Appeal on Time, or Don't Appeal at All, U.S. Supreme Court Advises*, Special to law.com (6/18/07). *See also* United States v. Sadler, 480 F.3d 932 (9th Cir. 2007), holding that FRAP 4(b), unlike 4(a), is a non-jurisdictional claim processing rule, and therefore, according to the Ninth Circuit, is waived if not raised in a timely fashion.

[46] Evans v. Chavis, 546 U.S. 189 (2006), holds that the Ninth Circuit failed to apply Carey v. Saffold properly and therefore violated AEDPA.

possible that his conviction might be modified (either by direct appeal or by certiorari). Therefore, the conviction was not ultimately final until January 6, 2004, when the period to seek certiorari ended.

The Supreme Court ruled, in *Waddington v. Sarausad*, No. 07-772 (1/21/09), that habeas should not have been granted under § 2254 [state court decision contrary to, or involving an unreasonable application of, established federal law] in a case where the state court rejected the petitioner's contention that the jury instruction on accessorial liability was incorrect. The Supreme Court held that, to satisfy § 2254, the state court's decision must have been not only erroneous but objectively unreasonable, and the instruction itself must have tainted the whole trial. In this case, the state court acted reasonably; the challenged instruction followed the state statute. Even if the instruction had been ambiguous, the ambiguity was not a serious enough Constitutional violation to trigger reversal under AEDPA.

Overruling the Second and Seventh Circuits, the Supreme Court ruled that a prisoner is permitted to raise the issue of ineffective assistance of counsel for the first time by means of a 28 USC § 2255 collateral challenge. The Supreme Court held that such a claim is not procedurally debarred, even if it could have been raised on direct appeal. The Supreme Court suggested that a District Court performing collateral review, with access to evidence about what the attorney did and why, may be better equipped to resolve the issue properly than a Court of Appeals confined to reviewing a record that may not contain all the relevant information.[47]

Shortly thereafter, the Supreme Court found that a habeas petitioner was prejudiced by receiving ineffective assistance of counsel when the lawyer failed to perform an adequate investigation. The investigation would have revealed powerful evidence on the record of the defendant's history of privation and abuse, which would have been useful in the mitigation phase of the capital case.[48] However, it was not ineffective assistance of counsel for an attorney to concede guilt in the hope of maintaining credibility at the penalty phase. The client did not consent to this strategy, but neither did he reject it; he refused to cooperate when the attorney attempted to discuss it: *Florida v. Nixon*, 543 U.S. 175 (2004).

On the same day, the Supreme Court held that attorneys did not have third-party standing to assert the rights of indigent defendants who were denied appointed appellate counsel. (Michigan adopted a Constitutional amendment and a statute under which counsel would not be appointed subsequent to a plea of guilty.) The Supreme Court did not deem the relationship between attorney and potential client to be close enough to assert due process and equal protection challenges: *Kowalski v. Tesmer*.[49]

In 2005, the Supreme Court decided *Halbert v. Michigan*[50] [requiring appointment of counsel for indigents who wished to appeal their convictions

---

[47] Massaro v. United States, 538 U.S. 500 (2003).
[48] Wiggins v. Smith, 539 U.S. 510 (2003).
[49] 543 U.S. 125 (2004).
[50] 545 U.S. 605 (2005).

notwithstanding having plead guilty; Michigan required court approval for first-level appeal of a conviction when the defendant had plead guilty or *nolo contendere.*] In 2007, the Sixth Circuit applied *Halbert* retroactively, because it merely applies the holding of an earlier case and is not a *Teague* "new rule."[51]

Under some circumstances, it may constitute ineffective assistance of counsel for an attorney to fail to file a notice of appeal when the client wants to appeal. According to the Second Circuit, this is true even if the defendant entered into a plea bargain that waives the right to appeal — and even if the attorney believes that the appeal is frivolous. According to the Second Circuit, what the attorney should do is to file an Anders brief addressing the question of whether the proposed appeal is frivolous. (An Anders brief sets out the attorney's analysis as to why an appeal is inappropriate despite the defendant's wishes.)[52]

The narrow waiver rule provides that although a habeas petitioner waives attorney-client confidentiality by alleging ineffective assistance of counsel, to the extent that the communications with the attorney must be disclosed to litigation the habeas petition, such communications cannot be used against the habeas petitioner at retrial. The Ninth Circuit requires District Courts to issue protective orders to enforce this rule.[53]

See Chapter 26 for more about criminal appeals.

§ 24.07 CERTIORARI

Except in the very rare cases in which Supreme Court review is obtainable as of right, cases reach the Supreme Court only based on the discretionary grant of certiorari. See P.L. 100-352.

The Supreme Court has never been able to consider more than a fraction of the cases in which certiorari is sought, and in recent years, the Court has taken on a smaller-than-usual caseload. Denial of certiorari is not an opinion about the merits of the case.[54]

Certiorari jurisdiction over state court decisions is granted by 28 USC § 1257(3). Review is available only if a federal question is directly ruled on or necessarily decided by the state court. To be reviewable by the Supreme Court, a

---

[51] Simmons v. Kapture, 474 F.3d 869 (6th Cir. 2007). However, the Eleventh Circuit did not require appointment of counsel for postconviction collateral review: Barbour v. Haley, 471 F.3d 1222 (11th Cir. 12/8/06), and the Eighth Circuit held that the Sixth Amendment does not provide a right to counsel in an appeal under F.R. Crim. P. 35: Scott v. United States, 473 F.3d 1262 (8th Cir. 2007).

[52] Campusano v. United States, 442 U.S. 770 (2d Cir. 2006). *See also* Roe v. Flores-Ortega, 528 U.S. 470 (2000): failure to file a notice of appeal when the client requests it constitutes ineffective assistance of counsel even if the defendant does not make an independent showing of prejudice. Second Circuit precedent, United States v. Gomez-Perez, 215 F.3d 315 (2d Cir. 2000), requires an *Anders* brief where the defendant files a pro se notice of appeal after waiving appeal. *But see* the Fifth Circuit's opinion in United States v. Powell, 468 F.3d 862 (5th Cir. 2006), holding that court-appointed attorneys are not required to file *Anders* briefs in connection with frivolous appeals from orders that are not appealable.

[53] Bittaker v. Woodford, 331 F.3d 715 (9th Cir. 2003).

[54] Missouri v. Jenkins, 515 U.S. 70 (1995).

state court judgment must be "final" [55] — that is, no other state tribunal can have the power to review or correct it. The judgment must effectively determine the litigation, not just an intermediate or interlocutory step.

Furthermore, a federal claim in a petition for certiorari can be considered only if it was addressed by or properly presented to the state court that rendered the decision the Supreme Court is being asked to review.[56] If the highest state court is silent on an issue, the aggrieved party has to overcome presumption that the issue was not properly presented below, and thus the state court did not have a chance to address it.

The process of seeking certiorari has also been affected by the minor amendments to the Supreme Court rules in 2003, effective May 1, 2003: see http://www.supremecourtus.gov/ctrules/revisedrules.pdf. Rule 13.5 was amended to require that the application to extend the time to petition for certiorari must be filed with the clerk at least 10 days before the due date for the petition. The prior rule required the clerk to receive the petition 10 days before the due date, but security provisions for screening mail take the receipt date out of the petitioner's control.

Revised Rule 25.2 gives the respondent or appellee 35 days from filing of the petitioner's or appellant's brief (and not 30 days after receipt of the brief) to reply. Revised Rule 25.3 also defines the time to file the reply brief as 35 days after filing of the respondent's or appellee's brief. Revised Rule 29.2 treats a document as timely filed based on either delivery to a commercial carrier or postal mailing, and Revised 29.3 places delivery by third-party commercial carrier for delivery within three calendar days on a parity with mailing. Rule 30.2 is revised to require filing rather than receipt of the jurisdictional statement within 10 days before the final filing date. Rule 32 requires parties and *amici curiae* to provide a letter explaining why they wish to lodge non-record material with the clerk. Revised Rule 39.2 clarifies that the affidavit or declaration of pauper status must be included with the documents for the motion for leave to proceed *in forma pauperis*. Revised Rule 44.6 states that a corrected petition for rehearing is timely if received within 15 days of the clerk's letter explaining the deficiencies in the original petition.

[A] Role of Precedent

The Supreme Court is not obligated to adhere to a statutory precedent merely because Congress did not repeal it. In this context, non-action is not probative.[57]

The Supreme Court presumes that Courts of Appeals decide questions of state law correctly, but that presumption is inapplicable if the Court of Appeals was "plainly wrong."[58]

---

[55] Jefferson v. City of Tarrant, 520 U.S. 1154 (1997).
[56] Adams v. Robinson, 520 U.S. 83 (1997).
[57] Central Bank v. First Interstate Bank, 511 U.S. 164 (1994).
[58] Leavitt v. Jane L., 520 U.S. 1274 (1998).

The Supreme Court's own precedents will usually be stare decisis and not reconsidered, because it is deemed that the integrity of judicial process usually requires reliance. This rule is subject to various exceptions:[59]

- Since the case was decided, it has turned out to be a solitary departure from established law
- The policy behind stare decisis not applicable
- The majority of courts won't follow it
- The case deals with interpretation of the Constitution, so it can only be altered by an amendment to the Constitution or change in the Supreme Court's position.

When the Supreme Court applies a new legal rule to a case, the rule becomes retroactive and applies to all pending cases, even those involving events before the Supreme Court decision was rendered.[60]

[B] Rule Changes

Several changes in the Supreme Court rules took effect May 3, 1999 (see 67 LW 4064). A respondent/appellee who supports a petitioner/appellant is subject to the same time schedule for filing documents. Respondents or appellants who support other respondents or appellants are granted the right to file a reply brief. As a general rule, documents filed with the Supreme Court must be $6\frac{1}{8} \times 9\frac{1}{4}$ booklets, typeset, conforming to the length limits and physical production standards of Rule 33.1. The amendments taking effect December 1, 2005, are as follows:

New Rule 28.1 has been added, consolidating some existing provisions about cross-appeal and adding new ones; provisions about papers and briefs for cross-appeals are transferred from Rules 28 and 32 to Rule 28.1. In addition, the following rules have been amended:

- Rule 4: clarifies the conditions for reopening an appeal of a District Court judgment or order
- Rule 26, Rule 45: "Washington's Birthday" is substituted for "Presidents' Day" when it comes to calculating times
- Rule 27: the papers for motions, response to a motion, or reply to response to a motion must satisfy the type style requirements of Rule 32
- Rule 35: in calculating whether enough judges have voted to hear a case en banc, disqualified judges are not counted.[61]

As of December 1, 2006, Courts of Appeals can adopt local rules under which electronic filing is mandatory, not optional (FRAP 25), with safeguards to deal with

---

[59] Seminole Tribe v. Florida, 517 U.S. 44 (1996).

[60] Reynoldsville Casket Co v. Hyde, 514 U.S. 749 (1995).

[61] http://www.uscourts.gov/rules/newrules6.html. The Supreme Court approved the proposals: *see* 73 L.W. 2652.

privacy and security concerns. In April of 2006, the Supreme Court adopted a rule change to FRAP 32.1. As of January 1, 2007, unpublished opinions can be cited in federal appellate briefs, but appellate courts are not required to treat even their own unpublished opinions as precedential, and can ignore them. The new rule does not impose any mandates, or even provide guidance, as to when a court can designate an opinion as unpublished.[62]

The federal rules amendments submitted for comment in 2006 include Bankruptcy Rule 8001, authorizing direct appeal to the Court of Appeals once a bankruptcy court, district court, or BAP certifies the appeal. Rule 8003 provides that such certification satisfied the requirement of leave to appeal, even without filing a motion for leave to appeal.[63]

FRAP changes scheduled for December, 2009 were open to public comment until February 15, 2008. The most significant change under the proposals is the method of calculating deadlines. Prior law omits intervening weekends and holidays in short periods such as 10 days; the proposed rule counts all days for all periods, but lengthens the shorter deadlines to reduce the impact. In civil cases, the deadline for filing a post-judgment motion for new trial, to challenge a trial judge's finding of facts, for JMOL, or to alter or amend judgment is 10 days, not counting weekends or holidays. The proposed amendments would change this to a period of 30 calendar days after entry of judgment (i.e., the same time period as for filing a timely motion for appeal). However, in a civil case, a timely post-judgment motion extends the deadline to file a notice of appeal until 30 days after the District Court's ruling on the post-judgment motion. If both sides want to appeal, and if the plaintiff does not need to file a post-judgment motion to preserve issues for appeal, the plaintiff can wait until the 10-day deadline for post-judgment motions has run to see if the defendant has filed a motion. If so, the plaintiff has 30 days after the District Court ruling on the defendant's motion. But if the rule change is implemented, the plaintiff will have to file notice of appeal within 30 days of the original entry of judgment. One party's timely post-judgment motion would prevent the other party's notice of appeal from becoming effective immediately. If the notice of appeal has the same deadline as the post-judgment motion, the Courts of Appeals will find that many appeals are in limbo until resolution of the post-judgment motions. Amendments proposed to FRAP 12.1 cover the procedure if the District Court is willing to grant a motion but lacks the power to do so because the Court of Appeals has control over the case after an appeal has been taken. The proposals also cover the calculation of the additional three-day period added to deadlines for responding to documents that are served by methods other than hand delivery.[64]

---

[62] Tony Mauro *Supreme Court Votes to Allow Citation to Unpublished Opinions. in Federal Courts*, Legal Times 4/12/06 (law.com); Howard J. Bashman, *To Cite or Not to Cite to Non-Precedential Opinions.* Special to law.com 3/6/06.

[63] http//www.uscourts.gov/rules/newrules6.htm.

[64] Howard J. Bashman, *Deadline for Commenting on Federal Appellate Rule Amendments Is Fast Approaching*, Special to Law.com 2/4/08.

Chapter 25

Arbitration and Alternative Dispute Resolution (ADR)

§ 25.01   INTRODUCTION

Arbitration, mediation, med-arb (a combination of the two), submission to the decision reached by a privately retained decision-maker, and other Alternative Dispute Resolution (ADR) techniques have significant potential to resolve disputes relatively quickly, informally, and inexpensively. In arbitration, a single arbitrator or panel of arbitrators hears evidence and renders a final and binding decision.

Arbitration, the most common form of ADR, is often used in five situations:

- Commercial arbitration, between merchants
- Consumer arbitration, involving claims by consumers against product manufacturers and/or sellers
- Securities arbitration under standard agreements promulgated by stock exchanges
- Labor arbitration, pursuant to and interpreting a Collective Bargaining Agreement (CBA), discussed further at § 25.05
- Arbitration of employee claims of discrimination or wrongful termination; See also § 25.06.

Mediation, in contrast, is a process under which neutral third parties guide the disputants to reach a compromise that they find acceptable. In med-arb, either the same "neutral" attempts mediation, but proceeds to arbitration if mediation fails; or separate neutrals undertake mediation followed by arbitration.

In mid-2008, New York State published its first statewide guidelines for training and qualifications of mediators and neutral evaluators used by courts to encourage settlements. Mediators seek to get the parties to agree on mutually acceptable terms, whereas neutral evaluators take evidence from both the parties and render an opinion about how the court system would resolve the dispute. To be placed on the roster, mediators must have 24 hours of training in basic mediation skills plus at least 16 hours training in the particular type of case they wish to handle. Neutral evaluators must have five years experience as a practicing lawyer or judge, with substantial experience in the specific type of case. Both mediators and neutral evaluators are required under the guidelines to get at least six hours of continuing education every two years. The new rules do not apply to private neutrals or mediators who work for the parties rather than the courts. One controversial feature of the rules is that a person can act as both a mediator and a neutral as long as he or she has the qualifications and training for both roles. Non-attorneys can be mediators, but cannot act both as mediators and neutrals. The New York court system has a separate set of rules for court-appointed arbitrators, who generally work in small claims cases under the Community Dispute Resolution Centers Program.[1]

The Eleventh Circuit denied a stay pending arbitration on the grounds that the FAA does not permit enforcement of a contract clause requiring a dissatisfied party to initiate mediation or nonbinding arbitration before bringing suit. The court framed the question as to whether a contract under which disputes are submitted to mediation or nonbinding arbitration is an agreement to settle a controversy by arbitration (9 USC § 2), making the dispute referable to arbitration under § 3, and concluded that mediation is not within the scope of the FAA. The characteristics of classic arbitration are an independent adjudicator who applies substantive legal standards, considers evidence and arguments submitted by both sides, and renders a decision. No process that fails to result in an award can be considered arbitration. Because mediation is nonbinding and attempts to get the parties to agree (rather than the mediator issuing a decision), FAA remedies such as mandatory stays and motions to compel are inappropriate in the context of mediation.[2]

In the best case, ADR results in more satisfied parties and a less-burdened court system. Heavy expenses associated with litigation discovery are avoided, and the arbitration award is final and almost immune to challenge.

However, this best case is not always achieved. There is a risk that the more powerful party to a transaction or in a relationship will insist on arbitration because

---

[1] Joel Stashenko, *N.Y. Court Establishes First Statewide Guidelines for Mediators, Neutral Evaluators*, N.Y.L.J. 7/24/08 (law.com).

[2] Advanced Bodycare Solutions, LLC v. Thione Int'l Inc., 524 F.3d 1235 (11th Cir. 2008). *But see In re* Atlantic Pipe Corp., 304 F.3d 1357 (1st Cir. 2002), holding that federal courts have the inherent power to compel even an unwilling party to submit to mediation by a private mediator, as long as the case is appropriate for mediation.

it restricts discovery and because the scope and range of remedies is smaller than the court system can provide.

The wealthier party can also game the system by requiring the poorer party (e.g., a consumer or employee) to pay arbitration costs. Therefore, many recent cases explore cost allocation, and when arbitration can be mandated despite one disputant's preference for litigation. Cornell law professor Theodore Eisenberg's research showed that businesses are much less likely to arbitrate disputes with other businesses than disputes with consumers. After examining contracts from 21 telecommunications and financial services companies, Eisenberg concluded that mandatory arbitration clauses were included in 75% of consumer agreements, versus only 24% of business-to-business agreement. Every consumer arbitration clause waived class arbitration. (Even this was an increase in business-to-business arbitration; Eisenberg's team's previous studies showed arbitration clauses in only 11% of business-to-business agreements.)[3]

Most arbitration is predispute arbitration, occurring because the parties signed a contract agreeing in advance to arbitrate rather than litigate any disputes arising in the future. In general, a predispute arbitration agreement is enforceable and can only be set aside on the basis of legal or equitable grounds that would justify rescission of a contract.

However, "submission" is another possibility: when a dispute is already in existence, the parties agree to use ADR rather than the court system to resolve it. A submission agreement is limited to a particular dispute, not all future disputes between the parties.

In many if not most cases, the arbitration clause simply provides that disputes will be arbitrated. However, under ordinary principles of contract law, the parties to the contract can negotiate for a more detailed arbitration clause covering issues such as venue, selection of the arbitrator(s), scope of discovery, etc.

Disputes over World Wide Web domain names are also frequently arbitrated. One frequently raised issue is "typosquatting" (using a deceptive domain name to entice customers); the Anticybersquatting Consumer Protection Act, P.L. 106-113 [see § 12.04[A][2]] provided an enforcement mechanism for "cybersquatting" allegations (deliberate use of a domain name resembling another party's trademark).[4]

§25.02 ARBITRATION LEGISLATION

Traditionally, the U.S. legal system was somewhat hostile to arbitration, and many states actually had anti-arbitration laws on their books. The Federal Arbitration Act (FAA) was passed in 1925 to make arbitration clauses in contracts

---

[3] *Companies Unlikely to Use Arbitration With Each Other*, N.Y. Times 10/6/08 at B4. Eisenberg's co-authors were Emily Sherwin, also of Cornell Law, and Geoffrey P. Miller of the N.Y.U. School of Law.

[4] Sheri Qualters, *Arbitration is Weapon of Choice in Growing Number of Domain Name Disputes*, Nat'l LJ 10/9/06 (law.com).

enforceable in contracts affecting interstate commerce. Reflecting this change in attitude toward arbitration, all of the states except Alabama, Mississippi, and West Virginia adopted their own statutes regulating arbitration.[5]

The question often arises as to whether a particular state law has been preempted by the FAA or another federal statute. According to the Seventh Circuit, for example, the arbitration clause in a telephone company's consumer service agreement could not be challenged under state law, because interests of uniformity call for preemption by the Federal Communications Act.[6]

In 2000, the NCCUSL issued a Revised Uniform Arbitration Act (RUAA),[7] substantially revising the original Uniform Arbitration Act, which dates back to 1955. As of October 2007, the RUAA had been adopted in Alaska, Colorado, Hawaii, New Mexico, Nevada, New Jersey, North Carolina, North Dakota, Oklahoma, Oregon, Utah, and Washington. NCCUSL's Uniform Mediation Act has been adopted in Illinois, Iowa, Nebraska, New Jersey, Ohio, Utah, Vermont, and Washington (as of October 2007).

RUAA 10 permits consolidation of arbitration proceedings on the motion of a party, as long as the same parties are involved (or the same parties plus a third party), the claims arise out of the same or related transactions, and there are common issues of law or fact justifying the consolidation.

§ 25.03 BASIC RULES OF ARBITRABILITY AND ARBITRATION

A long series of Supreme Court decisions shapes the current U.S. law of arbitration. Not only does the FAA provide authorization for arbitration of contractual disputes; the basic rule that has evolved is that disputes arising under federal statutes are also arbitrable, unless Congress clearly intended that the disputes be litigated instead. In a payday loan case, the lender tried to compel arbitration, and the District Court dismissed the case for lack of subject matter jurisdiction.

If there is an arbitration agreement in place, the FAA requires courts to compel arbitration unless there is another law prohibiting arbitration of the matter in controversy.[8] Section 2 of the FAA extends to transactions involving interstate

---

[5] Michigan's adoption of an arbitration statute did not preempt the common-law right to arbitration. However, a common-law arbitration agreement is unilaterally revocable at any time up to the issuance of an award. A statutory arbitration agreement must be written and must provide for Circuit Court judgment on the arbitration award. In the case at bar, an engineering firm purchased an architectural firm and signed the owner to an employment agreement. The employment agreement had an arbitration clause, and the purchase contract did not. In this case, the arbitration agreement was written but did not contain the Circuit Court enforcement clause, so only common-law and not statutory rules applied: Wold Architects and Engineers v. Strat, 474 Mich. 223 (Mich. 2006).

[6] Boomer v. AT&T Corp., 309 F.3d 404 (7th Cir. 2002).

[7] Text available at http://www.law.upenn/edu/bll/ulc/ulc_frame.htm.

[8] Dean Witter Reynolds Inc. v. Byrd, 470 U.S. 213 (1985); *see also* UAA § 2(a) and RUAA § 7 reading the FAA provision as mandatory, so that the court must compel arbitration whenever there is an arbitration clause.

commerce, even if interstate commerce was not contemplated at the time the contract was adopted.[9] If the contested issue is the existence of the contract that allegedly includes the arbitration clause, and not whether the contract continues to be valid or enforceable, a court and not the arbitrator must resolve the issue.[10]

According to Hawaii, a contract is voidable on the grounds of unconscionability if two conditions are present: the contract resulted from coercive bargaining between unequal parties, and the contract unfairly limits the obligations and liabilities of the stronger party. Unconscionability analysis can be used in a residential mortgage context, not just for the sale of goods. However, an arbitration clause requiring the losing party to pay the costs of arbitration was not unconscionable, because the borrowers could have sought out a different lender. Although Hawaii consumer protection law says that only a prevailing plaintiff, not any prevailing party, can get fees and costs, the provision did not contravene the statutory purpose. In this reading, arbitration agreements are usually not considered contracts of adhesion, because they do not limit obligations or liabilities; they merely change the forum where controversies can be raised.[11]

In 1996, the Supreme Court struck down a Montana state law that mandated all arbitration clauses to be on the first page of the contract, marked out with capital letters and underscoring. The rationale was that the law was invalid because it disfavored arbitration as compared to litigation.[12]

Sherman Act claims are arbitrable,[13] as are claims under Securities Act § 10(b), Rule 10b-5, and securities-related RICO claims.[14] Georgia's Arbitration Code, which excludes disputes between insurers and policyholders, is regulation of the business of insurance as defined by the McCarran-Ferguson Act, and therefore is not preempted by the FAA.[15]

One of the most significant legal questions about arbitration is when, and to what extent, courts can become involved in disputes about the arbitration process itself — and when resolution of these threshold questions must be left up to the arbitrator.

A 1995 Supreme Court decision holds that, in case of dispute, the court system and not the arbitrator determines whether a party has an obligation to arbitrate. Because an agreement to arbitrate is a contract, ordinary state

---

[9] Allied-Bruce Terminix Cos. v. Dobson, 513 U.S. 265 (1995).

[10] Will-Drill Resources Inc. v. Samson Resources Co., 352 F.3d 211 (5th Cir. 2003).

[11] Branco v. Norwest Bank Minn. NA, 2005 WL 1866086 (Haw. 7/7/05).

[12] Doctor's Assoc's, Inc. v. Casarotto, 517 U.S. 681 (1996).

[13] Mitsubishi Motors Corp. v. Soler Chrysler-Plymouth Inc., 473 U.S. 614 (1985); this decision says that any doubt about the scope of arbitrable issues should be resolved in favor of arbitration. The Second Circuit required arbitration of a putative class action charging horizontal price fixing of ocean shipping services, rejecting the plaintiffs' contention that horizontal price-fixing claims are not subject to compulsory arbitration: JLM Indus. Inc. v. Stolt-Nielsen A.S., 387 F.3d 163 (2d Cir. 2004).

[14] Shearson/American Express Inc. v. McMahon, 482 U.S. 220 (1987); see Rodriguez de Quijas v. Shearson/American Express Inc., 490 U.S. 477 (1989), upholding a predispute agreement to arbitrate '33 Act claims.

[15] McKnight v. Chicago Title Ins. Co., 358 F.3d 854 (11th Cir. 2004).

contract-law principles are applied.[16] In its February 21, 2006, decision in *Buckeye Check Cashing, Inc. v. Cardegna*,[17] the Supreme Court ruled that if a contract contains an arbitration clause, a party's challenge to the contract's overall validity (in this case, a claim that usurious interest rates were charged) must be decided by the arbitrator, not a court. The Supreme Court held that this result obtains whether it is a federal or state suit.

The contract between television's "Judge Alex" Ferrer and his agent required arbitration of all disputes. The agent sought arbitration to collect fees he said were due under the contract. Ferrer petitioned the California Labor Commissioner for a determination that the contract was illegal and unenforceable under the California Talent Agencies Act because Preston was not a licensed talent agent. Ferrer moved in state court to stay arbitration. While the case was still in progress, *Buckeye Check Cashing* was decided, holding that challenges to the validity of a contract with an arbitration clause are heard by the arbitrator, not the courts. The California Court of Appeals ruled that the Talent Agencies Act gave the Labor Commissioner exclusive jurisdiction over the dispute; *Buckeye* was not relevant because it did not involve an administrative agency with exclusive jurisdiction over an issue. However, the Supreme Court ruled that when parties agree to arbitrate all questions under a contract, the FAA supersedes state laws giving jurisdiction to any other entity. In this view, the issue was not whether the FAA entirely preempts the Talent Agencies Act, but whether the arbitrator or the Labor Commissioner has the power to determine whether or not Preston was an unlicensed talent agent.[18]

Late in 2002, the Supreme Court held that an NASD rule stating that no dispute is arbitrable more than six years after the event is a procedural rule rather than a question of substantial arbitrability. Therefore, it is determined by the arbitrator, not by the court system.[19]

The Supreme Court took up another question of arbitrability in mid-2003, finding that if a contract fails to make clear whether or not class arbitration is permitted, the arbitral equivalent of certification of a class action is a procedural matter. Therefore, it must be decided by the arbitrator.[20]

The Eighth Circuit compelled individual arbitration in a Truth in Lending Act (TILA) case where the plaintiff alleged that the contract's waiver of class arbitration was unconscionable. The Eighth Circuit upheld the District Court's findings that the class action waiver was conspicuous, and the plaintiff was not economically debarred from arbitrating her small claim without a class action, because the TILA remedial provision, 15 USC § 1640(a)(3), permits recovery of fees and costs.[21]

---

[16] First Options of Chi. Inc. v. Kaplan, 514 U.S. 938 (1995).

[17] 546 U.S. 440 (2006).

[18] Preston v. Ferrer, 128 S. Ct. 978 (2008).

[19] Howsam v. Dean Witter Reynolds Inc., 537 U.S. 79 (2002).

[20] Green Tree Fin. v. Bazzle, 539 U.S. 444 (2003); *see also* Pedcor Mgmt. Co. v. Nations Personnel of Texas Inc., 72 L.W. 1115 (5th Cir. 2003).

[21] Pleasants v. American Express Co., 541 F.3d 853 (8th Cir. 2008).

Because of the essentially contractual nature of the arbitration relationship, non-signing third parties usually cannot be compelled to arbitrate, although they might be compelled if agency principles justify this (for instance, an individual broker is bound by the U-4 securities arbitration agreement issued by the brokerage firm). A non-signatory may also be permitted to compel arbitration in the interests of justice.

The First Circuit ruled that a corporation that signed a partnership agreement calling for international arbitration of commercial disputes cannot avoid the duty to arbitrate a commercial contract dispute by naming two non-signatories as defendants and claiming that there is no written agreement to arbitrate with them. (The corporation alleged that there was only an oral contract that did not include an arbitration provision.) 9 USC § 2-6 allows the federal courts to compel international arbitration under agreements subject to the New York Convention; in fact, the FAA allows broader compulsion of international than domestic agreements. The First Circuit read the FAA to mean that a party seeking to appeal an order denying international arbitration need not have signed a written arbitration agreement first. Even non-signatories can be bound by an arbitration agreement by means of, e.g., assumption, agency, estoppel, piercing of the corporate veil, or incorporation by reference. In this case, the First Circuit found that the dispute was significantly enough entwined with the written agreement to trigger estoppel. Even if there had been an oral agreement, it would have been based on the underlying written contract.[22]

When a non-frivolous appeal of a determination of arbitrability is pending, the District Court does not have jurisdiction over the merits of the case.[23]

[A] Arbitral Remedies

The typical broad arbitration clause does not specify the range of remedies, so the arbitrator can make whatever award he or she considers just and equitable. In fact, the RUAA § 21(c) specifically permits an arbitrator to grant remedies that a court could not or would not provide, as long as the chosen remedy is rationally related to a plausible interpretation of the underlying agreement between the parties. (In labor arbitration, the arbitrator cannot rewrite the Collective Bargaining Agreement, so any remedies must conform to the CBA.)

A 1995 Supreme Court decision[24] permits an arbitrator to award punitive damages where the arbitration agreement incorporated the National Association of Securities Dealers rules (which permit punitive damages) even though the choice of law clause stipulated New York law, which did not allow punitive damages in arbitration.

---

[22] Sourcing Unlimited, Inc. DBA Jumpsource v. Asimco Int'l Inc., 526 F.3d 38 (1st Cir. 2008). *See also* Becker v. Davis, 491 F.3d 1292 (11th Cir. 2007), permitting an interlocutory appeal when a party is arguably not a signatory to a written arbitration agreement.

[23] McCauley v. Halliburton Energy Servs. Inc., 413 F.3d 1158 (10th Cir. 2005).

[24] Mastrobuono v. Shearson Lehman Hutton Inc., 514 U.S. 52 (1995).

RUAA § 21 specifically allows for punitive damages in arbitration, if they would be available when litigating the same kind of claim in state court.

An arbitration agreement that precludes the arbitrator from ordering punitive damages is void as against public policy and unenforceable, at least in a state that has a statute permitting punitive damages in tort actions where there is clear and convincing evidence of conscious or deliberate fraud.[25]

A 2002 Massachusetts case holds that an agreement to arbitrate "any or all" controversies is broad enough to include claims for punitive damages.[26]

In yet another recent Supreme Court pro-arbitration case, the Eleventh Circuit held that certain RICO claims were not subject to arbitration, because the arbitration agreement ruled out punitive damages. The Eleventh Circuit's rationale was that, therefore, potential RICO plaintiffs did not have access to treble damages and therefore could not achieve complete RICO relief. The Supreme Court was not persuaded by this argument. It mandated arbitration, saying that it was up to the arbitrator to decide if treble damages would be punitive or remedial in this situation.[27]

The California Court of Appeals refused to enforce a forum selection clause requiring Californians to go to Georgia to arbitrate even minor billing disputes over Internet service. The court found the clause to be an unreasonable geographic barrier to claim filing.[28]

As a general rule, arbitrators can make interest awards, but cannot make an award of attorneys' fees. However, a fee award may be available — or even mandatory — under the statute governing the underlying case. An NASD arbitration panel found that the grievant's termination violated the ADEA, and awarded $200,000 in damages. However, contrary to the requirements of the ADEA, the panel imposed the $14,000 in arbitration costs on the winner and denied him an attorneys' fee award. The Second Circuit agreed that the arbitration award could be vacated for manifest disregard of the law. Attorneys' fees (including proceedings to recover fees) are mandatory for a prevailing party, and should not have been restricted by the attorney-client agreement, because that agreement was not before the arbitration panel. Nor did the arbitration panel have jurisdiction to order the firm to return the contingent fee to the client.[29]

Both UAA § 10 and RUAA § 21(d) permit the arbitrator to allocate the costs of arbitration as he or she sees fit, unless the arbitration agreement specifies the allocation.

---

[25] Cavalier Mfg. Inc. v. Jackson, 823 So. 2d 1237 (Ala. 2001).

[26] Drywall Sys. Inc. v. ZVI Const. Co. Inc., 761 N.E.2d 482 (Mass. 2002).

[27] PacifiCare Health Sys. Inc. v. Book, 538 U.S. 401 (2003). In the Fifth Circuit's view, antitrust treble damages are primarily compensatory in nature, and thus are available even if the arbitration agreement precludes punitive damages: Investment Partners LP v. Glamour Shots Licensing Inc., 201 F.3d 314 (5th Cir. 2002).

[28] Aral v. Earthlink Inc., 134 Cal. App. 4th 544 (Cal. App. 2005).

[29] Porzig v. Dresdner Kleinwort, 497 F.3d 133 (2d Cir. 2007), discussed in Anthony Lin, *2nd Circuit Rebukes Arbitration Panel for Limiting Fee Award*, N.Y.L.J. 8/9/07 (law.com).

If the agreement so specifies, the arbitrator can grant interim relief (e.g., preliminary injunctions). RUAA § 8 permits provision and interim remedies in arbitration to the same extent and under the same conditions they could be ordered in court.

[B] Arbitration Procedure

Arbitration proceedings are designed to be quick and informal. Rules of evidence are not strictly applied, and in fact hearsay is routinely admitted in arbitration hearings. In fact, arbitrators are not even required to follow substantive law.

Depending on the rules under which arbitration is conducted, and the circumstances of the case, there will be a single arbitrator or a panel of arbitrators (usually three). Sometimes the parties nominate arbitrators; at other times, they choose arbitrators from a list maintained by the American Arbitration Association or other arbitration provider.

Although the parties can agree to a broader scope, generally discovery in arbitration is limited (e.g., to a set number of depositions). Under FAA § 7, an arbitrator's subpoena must be served like a court subpoena. The District Court for the district in which the arbitrator sits can enforce the subpoena. However, a 2006 Second Circuit decision holds that District Courts cannot issue nationwide service of process to enforce arbitrators' subpoenas, on the grounds that statutes that authorize nationwide service of process generally make that explicit. FAA § 7 implies that the geographical limitations of FRCP 45 apply in the arbitration context.[30]

The California Supreme Court ruled that if the arbitration clause calls for arbitration of any dispute, then a petition to compel arbitration should not be dismissed on statute of limitations grounds: it is up to the arbitrator to decide if the affirmative defense of statute of limitations is available.[31]

In 2004, the Third Circuit, disagreeing with the Eighth, ruled that § 7 of the FAA, which gives arbitrators the power to direct non-party witnesses to bring documents to arbitration proceedings, does not empower them to make non-parties produce documents prior to the hearing.[32]

The Federal Circuit ruled in mid-2004 that an order compelling arbitration is the equivalent of a mandatory injunction. Ordinarily, denial of a mandatory injunction is appealable; but a 1988 Supreme Court case makes an order granting or denying an injunction appealable only if it has serious, perhaps irreparable, consequences. But FAA § 16 makes the order appealable under 28 USC § 1292(a)(1). Although § 16 is not a jurisdictional provision, it makes the denial of the motion to compel arbitration appealable. Such orders can be appealed even if the issue of

---

[30] Dynegy Midstream Servs. LP v. Trammochem, 451 F.3d 89 (2d Cir. 2006).

[31] Wagner Constr. Co. v. Pacific Mech. Corp., 41 Cal. 4th 19 (Cal. 5/21/07).

[32] Hay Group Inc. v. EBS Acquisition Corp., 360 F.3d 404 (3d Cir. 2004); *contra In re* Security Life Ins. Co. of Am., 228 F.3d 865 (8th Cir. 2000).

arbitrability has not been finally decided; and the obligation to arbitrate survives expiration of the other provisions of the agreement.[33]

§ 25.04 CONSUMER ARBITRATION

The argument is sometimes raised that consumers should be able to avoid application of an arbitration clause because of the imbalance of power between the merchant that drafted the clause and the consumer. However, this argument will probably not be successful unless there was such overwhelming one-sided economic power that the contract could be revoked in any event, or unless the arbitration clause is both substantively and procedural unconscionable.

The Supreme Court ruled that consumer borrowers cannot invalidate an arbitration clause merely because it was silent as to the allocation of arbitration costs. The court did not accept the borrower's argument that silence put her at risk of prohibitive costs if she exercised her arbitration remedy. The party who seeks to invalidate an arbitration agreement has the burden of producing evidence on the cost issue — which the consumer failed to do.[34]

Late in 2003, the California Court of Appeals extended its principle for employment contracts (that it is substantively unconscionable to impose prohibitively high fees for the use of the arbitral forum by a person who is precluded from using the court system) to consumer contracts. The plaintiff claimed that he was victimized by an automobile dealership's bait-and-switch tactics. The plaintiff sought class action certification; the defendant responded by seeking to compel arbitration. The plaintiff alleged that based on the amount of damages sought, he would have to put up about $8,000 to initiate arbitration. The defense responded that he could recover that sum after arbitration was completed. The Court of Appeals found this unpersuasive, if consumers are precluded from raising their claims by the initial financial commitment. The Court of Appeals remanded the case to the Superior Court to determine if the fees were adopted in bad faith — which, in turn, determines whether the provision will be severed or the entire agreement struck down.[35]

The Third Circuit held in 2007 that an arbitration agreement is not unconscionable merely because it requires consumers to sign a class action waiver, striking down local court rulings that the Third Circuit said were preempted by the FAA. The plaintiff contracted for services to monitor and improve her credit, and argued that the service provider violated its obligations under the federal Credit Repair Organizations Act and Pennsylvania's Credit Services Act. The defendant moved to compel individual arbitration. The plaintiff alleged that the state and federal laws provided her with the right to a judicial forum, and federal law explicitly permits class arbitration. The Third Circuit, however, said that the

---

[33] Microchip Tech. Inc. v. U.S. Philips Corp., 367 F.3d 1350 (Fed. Cir. 2004).

[34] Green Tree Fin. Corp.-Alabama v. Randolph, 531 U.S. 79 (2000).

[35] Gutierrez v. Autowest, 114 Cal. App. 4th 77 (Cal. App. 2003, *modified* 1/8/04).

agreement was to be interpreted under Virginia law, which did not treat the class action waiver as unconscionable.[36]

The Ninth Circuit found arbitration clauses in cell phone service agreements to be substantively unconscionable and unenforceable under Washington State Law because of a ban on class relief and limitations on punitive damages. The plaintiffs sued for improper charges for services (e.g., roaming) that should have been free.[37]

In 1999, Alabama ruled that the Magnuson-Moss Act invalidates arbitration provisions within written warranties, but that decision was reversed in 2000.[38] The Fifth Circuit struck down the FTC regulation forbidding binding arbitration of Magnuson-Moss claims, because the court did not believe that the statute's text and legislative history show an intent to override the presumption that the claims are arbitrable. Warrantors are allowed to establish "informal dispute settlement procedures" under 15 USC § 2310(a) and can require consumers to use them before going to court. The Fifth Circuit drew an analogy with Title VII to hold that the availability of a conciliation procedure does not rule out binding arbitration.[39]

The Fifth Circuit, faced with the question of whether a nursing home's arbitration agreement (signed by a demented resident's mother) can be enforced against a non-signatory, applied a two-step inquiry. The first question was whether the parties agreed to arbitrate, and if so, whether the dispute falls within the reach of the arbitration agreement. The second question is whether any federal statute or policy rules out arbitration. The Fifth Circuit found that both federal and state law mandate arbitration. Under state law, the resident's mother was an appropriate surrogate who could obligate the daughter with respect to health care. Under federal law, she was an intended third party beneficiary and thus bound by the arbitration requirement.[40]

The Eleventh Circuit held that the arbitration clause in a payday loan agreement precluded the borrower from bringing a class action alleging that the

---

[36] Gay v. CreditInform, 511 F.3d 369 (3d Cir. 2007); Shannon P. Duffy, *3rd Circuit Rejects Superior Court Precedents in Arbitration Case*, The Legal Intelligencer 9/21/07 (law.com).

[37] Lowden v. T-Mobile USA, Inc., 512 F.3d 1213 (9th Cir. 2008); Shroyer v. New Cingular Wireless Servs., Inc., 498 F.3d 976 (9th Cir. 2007), involving the same contract language, already held that a class action waiver is unconscionable under California law if it occurs in a contract of adhesion and consumers allege that they were unfairly deprived of small amounts of money. The Ninth Circuit held that the FAA does not preempt the California law, because unconscionable clauses are unenforceable whether they occur inside or outside the context of an arbitration agreement.

[38] Southern Energy Homes Inc. v. Lee, 732 So. 2d 994 (1999), *rev'd*, Southern Energy Homes Inc. v. Ard, 772 So. 2d 1131 (Ala. 2000).

[39] Walton v. Rose Mobile Homes LLC 298 F.3d 470 (5th Cir. 2002); *see also* Davis v. Southern Energy Homes Inc., 305 F. 3d 1268 (11th Cir. 2002). Holding that Magnuson-Moss allows informal dispute resolution but doesn't mention binding arbitration, Illinois ruled that, despite FTC rules, a binding arbitration clause in a written warranty is enforceable: Borowiec v. Gateway 2000, 209 Ill. 2d 376 (Ill. 2004).

[40] J.P. Morgan Chase & Co. v. Conegie, 492 F.3d 596 (5th Cir. 2007). *See also* Covenant Health Rehab. of Picayune, LP v. Brown, 949 So. 2d 732 (Miss. 2007): an adult daughter, in her role as health care surrogate, could bind convalescent center resident with respect to arbitration of admission agreement, and agreement was not void as a contract of adhesion.

agreement was unconscionable, void ab initio, and an unenforceable contract of adhesion. It held that the provision permitting small claims tribunals but forbidding class actions does not prevent adequate access to legal representation, and is not unconscionable. The question of whether there was fraud in the inducement was for the arbitrator to decide.[41]

According to the First Circuit, a loan contract's arbitration clause remains in effect even if the borrowers move under the Truth in Lending Act to cancel the underlying contract. A borrower's bare assertion of the right to rescind does not automatically void a contract. The First Circuit held that substantive challenges to the contract are a matter for the arbitrator to handle, absent an independent challenge to the creation of the arbitration contract.[42] The California Court of Appeals allowed a client who lost at mandatory fee arbitration to base a malpractice suit against his or her lawyers on the same allegations. However, whatever part of the fee the arbitrator awarded to the lawyers cannot be recovered by the plaintiff as damages in the malpractice action.[43]

§ 25.05   LABOR ARBITRATION

There are two main varieties of labor arbitration: grievance or rights arbitration, and contract or interest arbitration. Grievance arbitration is used when there is a disagreement about the correct interpretation of an existing contract. Contract arbitration is invoked when the parties must decide the provisions to be included in a new, renewed, or reopened collective bargaining agreement. In a unionized enterprise, an agreement to arbitrate means that the union will not strike over the issue, and management will not take unilateral action with respect to that issue.

The Labor-Management Relations Act (LMRA) was drafted by Congress to favor arbitration. In 1960, the Supreme Court decided the crucial group of decisions known as The Steelworker's Trilogy (363 U.S. 564 *et seq.*). Under the Trilogy, if it is not clear whether a company has agreed to submit a particular issue to arbitration, then the question is resolved in favor of arbitrability. In other words, when in doubt, arbitrate. The Steelworker's Trilogy direct arbitrators to begin by considering the language of the CBA. They can also consider the "law of the shop" (practices that have evolved in a particular operation) and the effect of a potential decision on the workplace's productivity, morale, and tension level.

However, the court system, and not the arbitrator, has the power to decide[44] if a party agreed to arbitrate a particular type of dispute, if the parties' intentions are not clearly on the record.

---

[41] Jenkins v. First Am. Cash Advance, 400 F.3d 868 (11th Cir. 2005); for similar state cases, *see, e.g.*, Showmethemoney Check Cashiers Inc. v. Williams, 27 S.W.3d 361 (Ark. 2000) and Ramirez v. Circuit City Stores Inc., 90 Cal. Rptr. 2d 916 (Cal. App. 1999).

[42] Large v. Conseco Fin. Servicing Corp., 292 F.3d 49 (1st Cir. 2002).

[43] Liska v. Arns Law Firm, 12 Cal. Rptr. 3d 21 (Cal. App. 2004).

[44] First Options of Chicago, Inc. v. Kaplan, 514 U.S. 938 (1995).

The Tenth Circuit has ruled that, instead of submitting a case about job reductions to arbitration, the District Court should first have rendered a decision as to whether the matter was arbitrable at all. In this view, the question of whether a CBA obligates parties to arbitrate a particular grievance is one for the court, not an arbitrator to decide — unless the CBA clearly and unequivocally demands arbitration.[45]

Labor arbitration is usually carried out with the involvement of either the Federal Mediation and Conciliation Service (FMCS) or the American Arbitration Association (AAA).

The Fourth Circuit held that claims under the Fair Labor Standards Act (FLSA) can be subject to mandatory arbitration, because there is no inherent conflict between the FAA and the FLSA.[46]

The Third Circuit joined the First, Second, Ninth, and Tenth Circuits in holding that union members cannot bring malpractice suits against lawyers hired by the union to represent them at arbitration. The plaintiff charged her lawyer with deceiving her into withdrawing a grievance, and took the position that the attorney did not do anything and therefore could not claim immunity. The Third Circuit said that not arbitrating is an activity and advice to withdraw is activity performed in relation to a CBA, and therefore the attorney is entitled to immunity under the Labor-Management Relations Act for services related to a CBA.[47]

The Eighth Circuit ruled that it was not a breach of a union's duty of fair representation for it to decline to arbitrate an airline employee's grievance when he was fired for falsifying his time sheet. The court said that the union gave the matter more than cursory attention, and it was not irrational for the union to withdraw when it doubted the employee's credibility, and it had a poor record in cases involving allegations of employee dishonesty.[48]

§ 25.06 ARBITRATION OF DISCRIMINATION CLAIMS

Because of the imbalance of power between employer and employee, predispute arbitration agreements covering statutory discrimination claims are potentially abusive. The Supreme Court's 1998 decision,[49] although it does not rule out the enforceability of predispute arbitration clauses, does make it clear that a generalized arbitration clause in a Collective Bargaining Agreement is not sufficient to prevent employees from litigating statutory discrimination claims. The CBA must spell out precisely what claims must be arbitrated instead of litigated to preclude employees from bringing discrimination suits.

An e-mail sent by an employer to its at-will employees, informing them of a new dispute resolution policy for employment disputes, but not disclosing that arbitration was mandatory, did not provide sufficient notice to combine with

---

[45] Oil, Chemical and Atomic Workers v. Conoco, 241 F.3d 1299 (10th Cir. 2001).
[46] Adkins v. Labor Ready Inc., 303 F.3d 496 (4th Cir. 2002).
[47] Carino v. Stefan, 376 F.3d 156 (3d Cir. 2004).
[48] Martin v. American Airlines, 390 F.3d 601 (8th Cir. 2004).
[49] Wright v. Universal Maritime Serv. Corp., 525 U.S. 70 (1998).

continued employment to operate as a waiver of the employee's right to sue. Although e-mail can be used to form an arbitration agreement, in this case employees were given no means to respond. The employer did not have a history of using e-mail to communicate about major employment issues; disclosure of the arbitration agreement was inadequate; the e-mail did not require or even permit response by employees; and the employees were not informed that the employee handbook had been reissued with mandatory arbitration provisions.[50]

The argument was raised that FAA language exempting "contracts of employment of seamen, railroad employees, or any other class of workers engaged in foreign or interstate commerce" means that predispute arbitration agreements are invalid with respect to any worker engaged in interstate commerce (i.e., the vast majority of workers). But in 2001 the Supreme Court invalidated this argument, holding that this clause of the FAA is strictly limited to transportation workers, and predispute arbitration agreements in general can be valid.[51] An employee who is a transportation worker engaged in interstate commerce, and therefore qualifies for an exemption under the FAA, can nevertheless be required by state law to arbitrate sexual harassment claims, because the Third Circuit ruled that the FAA's exemptions were not intended to preempt state law. However, the Third Circuit rejected the argument that the plaintiff was exempt because she was a supervisor; the exemption for transportation workers is not limited to persons who perform physical labor. The plaintiff argued (unsuccessfully) that the defendant could not appeal the District Court's determination that the plaintiff was exempt as a transportation worker. The Third Circuit concluded that the plain language of the FAA permits interlocutory appeal from all denials of arbitration, because Congress clearly allowed for prompt review of refusals to compel arbitration.[52]

Furthermore, the EEOC can pursue an ADA case, and can seek victim-specific relief, even if the alleged victims of discrimination are subject to a valid and enforceable arbitration clause that prevents them from litigating such claims as individuals.[53]

An employer's refusal to respond to an employee's notice of intent to arbitrate a wrongful discharge claim precludes the employer from moving to compel arbitration if the employee subsequently sues for wrongful discharge.[54]

---

[50] Campbell v. General Dynamics Gov't Sys. Corp., 407 F.3d 546 (1st Cir. 2005).

[51] Circuit City Stores, Inc. v. Adams, 532 U.S. 105 (2001).

[52] Palcko v. Airborne Express Inc., 372 F.3d 588 (3d Cir. 2004). The Eleventh Circuit ruled that the account manager for a furniture store, whose job included making incidental out-of-state deliveries using the company's truck, was not a "transportation worker" excluded from FAA coverage as a "worker engaged in foreign or interstate commerce," so his racial discrimination claims were subject to mandatory arbitration: Hill v. Rent-a-Center Inc., 398 F.3d 1286 (11th Cir. 2005). Nor, according to the Eighth Circuit, was a trucking firm's customer service representative who was employed to give customers information and answer their questions. Such work is not closely enough related to interstate commerce to fall under the FAA exemption: Lenz v. Yellow Transp. Inc., 431 F.3d 348 (8th Cir. 2005).

[53] EEOC v. Waffle House Inc., 534 U.S. 279 (2002).

[54] Brown v. Dillard's Inc., 430 F.3d 1004 (9th Cir. 2005).

The Third Circuit held that the arbitration clause in an employment contract was enforceable although the employee did not understand English. Therefore, the court remanded the employee's wrongful termination suit to enter a stay pending arbitration. When the Spanish-speaking plaintiff applied for the job, the employer asked a bilingual employee to translate for him; the translator later testified that he did not translate the arbitration clause. According to the Third Circuit, unless fraud is present, an offeree's inability to understand English is irrelevant to the enforceability of an agreement in English, and it was the offeree's obligation to find out what the agreement said before signing it.[55]

Courts have reached various conclusions about the status of arbitration agreements that divide fees and costs between employer and employee:

- Validity is determined on a case by case basis, e.g., whether costs are high enough to deter pursuit of valid claims.[56]
- Agreement making each party responsible for its own costs (irrespective of outcome) was unenforceable because Title VII relies on fee-shifting in appropriate cases, and an arbitration agreement is void if it imposes costs that prevent employees from vindicating their rights.[57]

A complex series of California cases stems from a 2002 case that imposes minimum due process requirements that cannot be waived.[58] The arbitration agreement must not limit damages that would normally be available under the relevant statute (e.g., laws against employment discrimination); the parties to arbitration must have access to enough discovery to pursue their claims (though not necessarily to the extremely extensive discovery allowed in litigation!); the arbitrator must issue a written decision that can be judicially reviewed to make sure arbitrators abide by the law; and all costs unique to arbitration must be assumed by the employer.

In 2003, California decided a case holding that it violates public policy for an employment agreement to impose a waiver of claims of termination contrary to public policy. Therefore, wrongful termination claims are subject to the requirements of *Armendariz*. A clause in the arbitration contract, allowing either party to have any award of $50,000 reviewed by a second arbitrator, was deemed unconscionable. Although facially neutral, in effect the clause only benefited employers,

---

[55] Morales v. Sun Constructors, Inc., 541 F.3d 218 (3d Cir. 2008).

[56] Bradford v. Rockwell Semiconductor Sys., 238 F.3d 549 (4th Cir. 2001); *see also* Morrison v. Circuit City Stores Inc., 317 F.3d 646 (6th Cir. 2003) (the test is the effect not only on the individual, but also on similarly situated employees); Bond v. Twin Cities Carpenters Pension Fund, 307 F.3d 704 (9th Cir. 2002) (requirement that employee pay half the costs violates ERISA § 503 by denying the employee access to full and fair review of the claim; Faber v. Menard, Inc., 367 F.3d 1048 (8th Cir. 2004) (test is whether obligation to pay half the fees would impair plaintiff's access to the arbitral forum).

[57] McCaskill v. SCI Mgmt. Corp., 285 F.3d 623 (7th Cir. 2002).

[58] Armendariz v. Foundation Health Psychare Serv., Inc., 24 Cal. 4th 83 (2000).

because it was so unlikely that an employee would ever have to pay $50,000 or more to an employer.[59] Another holding of the *Auto Stiegler* case is that if an arbitration agreement fails to allocate the costs of arbitration between the parties, the agreement does not become void or unenforceable — but the employer will be responsible for paying all the costs.

In mid-2003, the Ninth Circuit found that Circuit City's arbitration agreement was oppressive and invalid. Ruling out class actions and imposing a statute of limitations was substantively and procedurally unconscionable. Making some employees submit to arbitration was inherently one-sided, because of the unlikelihood of the employer asserting a claim against a clerical worker. Therefore, in effect, employees surrendered rights, and the employer did not; it is up to the employer to prove that the contract displays at least a modicum of bilaterality.[60] Eventually, after many modifications, the company drafted another version of the arbitration clause that the California Court of Appeals found acceptable. Even though the contract required a waiver of class action arbitration, the 2005 ruling found that the latest draft was not so one-sided as to constitute an unenforceable contract of adhesion.[61]

At about the same time, the Third Circuit held that a company's standard arbitration agreement, required of low-level employees as a condition of employment, was invalid because it was so one-sided as to be both procedurally and substantively unconscionable. The agreement required employees — but not the employer — to file their arbitration claims within 30 days. Even successful employees could receive only reinstatement and back pay as relief, and could not recover their attorneys' fees; unsuccessful employees were required to pay the costs of arbitration. The Third Circuit found the agreement to be defective because it prevented employees from obtaining complete relief if they asserted and proved meritorious discrimination claims. Furthermore, the court deemed unconscionability to be so deeply rooted that it invalidated the entire agreement rather than severing the improper provisions and enforcing the rest.[62]

---

[59] Little v. Auto Stiegler, Inc., 130 Cal. Rptr. 2d 892 (2003).

[60] Ingle v. Circuit City, 328 F.3d 1165 (9th Cir. 2003); the Circuit City contract was also found invalid in Circuit City Stores v. Mantor, 335 F.3d 1101 (9th Cir. 2003).

[61] Gentry v. Superior Ct. of L.A. County, 135 Cal. App. 4th 944 (Cal. App. 2005).

[62] Alexander v. Anthony Int'l LP, 341 F.3d 256 (3d Cir. 2003). Similarly, the Ninth Circuit found that law firm O'Melveny & Myers' arbitration clause in its employment agreement violated California law, e.g., by imposing the agreement in an e-mail requiring employees to accept the agreement or leave the firm within three months. The Ninth Circuit cited the power imbalance between the plaintiff, a paralegal, and a major law firm. The agreement also imposed excessive confidentiality obligations on employees, permitted the firm to opt out of arbitration in cases involving attorney-client issues, unlawfully restricted employees' ability to bring administrative actions, and unlawfully reduced the time frame for claims to one year. The court found the illegality so pervasive that it did not sever the invalid provisions and enforce the rest: Davis v. O'Melveny & Myers, 485 F.3d 1066 (9th Cir. 2007). *See* Justin Scheck, *9th Circuit Panel Faults O'Melveny for "Take It or Leave It" Hiring Clause*, The Recorder 5/15/07 (law.com).

In the Sixth Circuit, arbitration is favored, and an employment contract is not considered impermissibly adhesive merely because it is a standardized form tendered on a take-it-or-leave-it basis. It is clear that statutory (e.g., Title VII) claims can be arbitrated. The Sixth Circuit upheld an employment-based arbitration agreement because it imposed the requirement of arbitration not just on the employee but on the employer. The court found that, because resolution without a jury is an essential part of arbitration, it was not necessary to notify the employee that a jury trial would not be available. The plaintiff raised the excessive-cost argument, but the Sixth Circuit ruled that the assertion of excessive costs was purely speculative. To the Sixth Circuit, only "up-front" costs of arbitration must be analyzed, not the eventual cost net of any award by the arbitrator, because what could have a chilling effect is the need to advance costs.[63]

The Fifth Circuit held that USERRA claims are subject to a mandatory arbitration clause; the mere fact that Congress permitted suits by persons charging employment discrimination because of their military status did not rule out employers' ability to mandate arbitration of such claims. An agreement to arbitrate is a forum selection clause, not a waiver of substantive rights.[64]

In light of the FAA policy of favoring arbitration, the D.C. Circuit ruled that an employment contract that contained both a ban on punitive damages that violated local law and a severability clause should be enforced, after severance of the invalid clause.[65]

§ 25.07 SECURITIES ARBITRATION

Securities industry agreements (e.g., brokerage agreements) typically mandate arbitration of all customer disputes.

NASD's Board of Governors approved an amendment to the organization's securities arbitration code in early 2005. Under the prior rule, it was discretionary with the arbitration panel whether to provide a written decision. The new rule gives the complainant the right to demand a written decision. Arbitrators would be paid $200 for the opinion, half from the parties and half from NASD. The securities-law bar was dissatisfied with the amendment, on the grounds that written decisions will trigger more appeals.[66]

Claims of up to $100,000 can be heard by a single arbitrator rather than a panel. All employment discrimination claims brought by securities-industry employees must be heard by qualified arbitrators from outside the securities industry. The arbitrator can award reasonable attorneys' fees. The changes make it

---

[63] Lee v. Red Lobster Inns of Am., 2004 WL 187564 (6th Cir. 2004); *followed* Cooper v. MRM Inv. Co., 367 F.3d 493 (6th Cir. 2004).

[64] Garrett v. Circuit City Stores, 499 F.3d 672 (5th Cir. 2006); USERRA is the Uniformed Services Employment and Reemployment Rights Act, 38 USC §§ 4301 *et seq.*

[65] Booker v. Robert Half Int'l Inc., 413 F.3d 77 (D.C. Cir. 2005).

[66] Susanne Craig, *Arbitrators May Have to Put That in Writing*, Wall St. J., Jan. 28, 2005 at C1.

harder for an employee to bifurcate claims between litigation and arbitration by joining discrimination claims with other employment-related claims.

If a claim is facially defective, an NASD arbitration panel can dismiss it with prejudice on the pleadings. It is not necessary to hold discovery and an evidentiary hearing prior to dismissal.[67]

In the interests of finality and definiteness, an arbitration award must prevail even if it was not correct, or even reasonable, so the Seventh Circuit forced American Express subsidiaries to live with the consequences of their decision to arbitrate a claim.[68]

In a securities arbitration case, a good-faith allegation that the arbitrator manifestly disregarded federal law is enough to give the federal court system jurisdiction over a motion to vacate the award, because manifest disregard of federal law raises a substantial federal question.[69]

According to both the Ninth Circuit and California Supreme Court, the Exchange Act preempts California's ethics standards for neutral arbitrators, because the local rules set different standards for disqualification of arbitrators and disclosure of conflicts than the NASD's arbitration rules, which are federally approved.[70]

§ 25.08   REVIEW AND ENFORCEMENT OF THE ARBITRATION AWARD

One of the salient characteristics of arbitration (which is either an advantage or a disadvantage, depending on point of view) is that once made, the award is essentially final. There are only very limited opportunities to modify or vacate it. There is no general right to appeal an arbitration award to parallel the general right to appeal a court decision.

Arbitration awards can be confirmed by courts, converting the award into a judgment of the court,[71] so remedies such as contempt of court are available if the order is not obeyed.

Although most courts treat it as permissive, in mid-2002 the Southern District of New York ruled that the FAA's one-year statute of limitations for seeking confirmation of an arbitration award is mandatory and must be strictly construed.[72] The one-year period runs from the date the arbitrator renders the final award, not from the date the award is delivered to the parties.

In 1988, FAA § 16 was amended to provide an automatic right of appeal when a court decision disfavors arbitration, but not when it favors arbitration. The

---

[67] Sheldon v. Vermonty, 269 F.3d 1202 (10th Cir. 2001).

[68] IDS Life Ins. Co. v. Royal Alliance Assoc's, 266 F.3d 645 (7th Cir. 2001).

[69] Greenberg v. Bear, Stearns & Co., 220 F.3d 22 (2d Cir. 2000).

[70] Jevne v. Superior Ct. of L.A. County, 35 Cal. 4th 935 (Cal. 2005); Credit Suisse First Boston Corp. v. Grunwald, 400 F.3d 1119 (9th Cir. 2005).

[71] See UAA § 14 and RUAA § 25.

[72] Photopaint Technologies v. Smartlens Corp., 207 F. Supp. 2d 193 (S.D.N.Y. 2002).

Supreme Court's *Green Tree* decision cited above reads FAA § 16(a)(3) to provide immediate appeal of any final decision with respect to arbitration.

A party to arbitration can apply to any court with jurisdiction for an order modifying or vacating the arbitration award, but only on the very limited grounds set out in the statute (FAA § 10):

- Mistake (e.g., in an arithmetic calculation, or the description of property)
- The award covers matters that were not submitted to arbitration
- The form of the award is defective, or the arbitrator failed to make a final and definite award
- Corruption, fraud, or undue means used by a party
- Corruption, partiality, or misconduct on the part of the arbitrator
- The arbitrator exceeded his or her powers.

The FAA provides for expedited judicial review to confirm, vacate, or modify arbitration awards. Under FAA § 9, the court must confirm an award unless it has been vacated, modified, or corrected as prescribed by §§ 10 or 11. Section 10 permits vacation of an award based on corruption, fraud, or misconduct by the arbitrator — or where the award exceeded the powers of the arbitrators. Grounds for modifying or correcting an award under § 11 include evident material miscalculation, evident mistake, and imperfection in the form of the award that does not affect the merits.

In 2008, the Supreme Court ruled that parties cannot expand the scope of judicial review of arbitration by agreement, although a more searching review can be imposed based on authority outside the FAA, such as state statutory or common law.[73]

Subsequently, however, the California Supreme Court permitted the scope of review to be altered by contract, including an agreement to obtain judicial review, upholding a contract provision allowing the arbitration award to be vacated or corrected on appeal for errors of law or legal reasoning. The case also involved a question of whether class arbitration was permissible. The panel of arbitrators said that it did; the L.A. County Superior Court reversed on the grounds that the arbitrators exceeded their authority by substituting their judgment for the judgment of the parties. The California Supreme Court agreed that parties to a contract can agree to make the award subject to review for legal error, using the kind of state-law authority permitted by *Hall Street Associates*.[74]

In 2004, first the Ninth Circuit withdrew an opinion holding that the amount in controversy is zero when a loser at arbitration attempts to get the District Court to vacate the arbitration award, and substituted an opinion holding that the District

---

[73] Hall Street Assocs. v. Mattel, 128 S. Ct. 1396 (2008).

[74] Cable Connection, Inc. v. DirecTV Inc., 82 Cal. Rptr. 3d 229(Cal. 2008); *see* Mike McKee, *Calif. High Court Surprises by Expanding Arbitration Review*, The Recorder 8/26/08 (law.com).

Court had subject matter jurisdiction because of the federal question presented.[75] In a later case, the Ninth Circuit defined the amount in controversy as the amount sought by the party seeking to vacate the award. In this case, the loser at arbitration had asked for $200 million and received the somewhat smaller amount of $0. The District Court, finding that it had jurisdiction, heard the case and upheld the $0 award; the Ninth Circuit affirmed on both issues.[76]

In addition to these statutory grounds for a federal court to vacate all or part of an arbitration award, an arbitration award can be vacated in state court if state law so permits.[77] Judges have added additional grounds for vacating an award, e.g., that it is contrary to public policy, is fundamentally unfair, or shows manifest disregard of the applicable law.[78]

According to the Eighth Circuit, if an arbitration agreement permits the selection of interested arbitrators, evident partiality will only justify vacating the award if there is a showing of prejudice. The Eighth Circuit also held that arbitrators are not required to disclose their relationships to the parties to the arbitration.[79] The Seventh Circuit held in late 2002 the fact that one arbitrator in a three-arbitrator panel had represented the company that appointed him in an unrelated matter did not constitute evident partiality under 9 USC § 10(a)(2), unless there was a claim that the arbitrator violated the contractual limitations of the arbitration agreement. A judge would not be required to recuse him- or herself in a comparable situation, and judges are subject to stricter rules than those governing arbitrators.[80]

The failure of an arbitrator to disclose a co-counsel relationship with one of the law firms involved in an arbitration created a reasonable impression of possible bias, so the award could be vacated based on "evident partiality" under FAA § 10(a)(2).[81] California requires a proposed neutral arbitrator to disclose all matters that could give rise to reasonable doubts about his or her impartiality, including close friendship or other significant personal relationship with any party or lawyer for a party. Arbitration awards can be vacated if an arbitrator failed to disqualify him or herself when required, after a timely demand. When an arbitrator discloses

---

[75] Luong v. Circuit City, 356 F.3d 1188 (9th Cir. 2004), *withdrawn and replaced by*, 368 F.3d 1109 (9th Cir. 2004).

[76] Theis Research Inc. v. Brown & Bain, 386 F.3d 1180 (9th Cir. 2004). In 2005, the Eleventh Circuit held that a plaintiff who asks for a new arbitration hearing and seeks over $75,000 has satisfied the amount in controversy requirement for federal jurisdiction, even if the plaintiff seeks to vacate an NASD arbitration award of $0: Peebles v. Merrill Lynch, 431 F.3d 1320 (11th Cir. 2005).

[77] *See* UAA § 12 and RUAA § 23.

[78] Note that Smith v. PSI Servs. II Inc. (D.N.J. 2000), discussed in Shannon P. Duffy, *"Misapplied" Law Insufficient to Nullify Arbitrator's Decision*, The Legal Intelligencer, 1/22/01 (law.com), holds that misapplication of the law does not justify vacatur, because it does not show manifest disregard of the law.

[79] Winfrey v. Simmons Food Inc., 495 F.3d 549 (8th Cir. 2007).

[80] Sphere Drake Ins. Ltd. v. All American Life Ins. Co., 307 F.3d 617 (7th Cir. 2002).

[81] Positive Software Solutions Inc. v. New Century Mort. Corp., 436 F.3d 495 (5th Cir. 2006); *rehearing en banc granted*, 449 F.3d 616.

information that is not required, a party demands disqualification, and the arbitrator does not disqualify himself, the California Court of Appeals said that the award is not invalidated. In this case, the arbitrator, in order to be scrupulous, disclosed that he had mediated three cases where a law firm that was involved in this case was also a party, and he served on a committee with one of the lawyers in the case, but it would not affect his impartiality. The California Court of Appeals ruled that disqualification of arbitrators is not mandatory on the basis of non-required disclosures.[82]

An arbitration award cannot be vacated on the grounds that it was obtained "by undue means" merely because the winning party was represented by an out-of-state attorney who engaged in unauthorized practice of law.[83]

Vacating an award is extremely difficult. For instance, in mid-2002, the Supreme Court of Georgia ruled that manifest disregard of the law is not an acceptable ground for vacating an award; only the arbitrator's corruption, partiality, exceeding authority, or failing to follow appropriate procedure would be sufficient grounds.[84]

But judicial review is very limited, and an award will not be vacated if there is any way to uphold it if the parties received a full and final hearing. An arbitrator's honest decision will generally be upheld, even if it appears to be foolish. A 2001 Supreme Court case[85] in effect says that courts do not review the merits of an arbitration award.

Under a March 2000 Supreme Court decision, a motion to confirm, vacate, or modify an FAA arbitration award can be brought either where the award was made or in any district that would be proper under the general venue standard (28 USC § 1391(a)(2)), because FAA venue is permissive. FAA § 9, which governs venue for confirmation of an award, lays venue in the district where the award was made unless the arbitration agreement specifies a different one. But venue is proper, under general venue concepts, in the district where the contract is performed.[86]

The Texas Court of Appeals ruled that arbitrators are entitled to the same immunity from civil suits as judges when they act within the scope of their duties.[87]

---

[82] Luce, Forward, Hamilton & Scripps, LLP v. Koch, 162 Cal. App. 4th 720 (2008).

[83] Superaudio Ltd. Partnership v. Winstar Radio Prods. LLC, 446 Mass. 330 (Mass. 2006). *See also In re* Creasy, 12 P.3d 214 (Ariz. 2000), holding that a disbarment order is violated when the disbarred attorney represents a party in arbitration.

[84] Progressive Data Sys. v. Jefferson Randolph Corp., 568 S.E.2d 474 (Ga. 2002), discussed in Jonathan Ringel, *Georgia Justices: Arbitrators Can Show "Manifest Disregard of the Law,"* Fulton County Daily Report, 7/17/02 (law.com).

[85] Major League Baseball Players Ass'n v. Garvey, 532 U.S. 504 (2001).

[86] Cortez Byrd Chips Inc. v. Bill Harbert Const. Co., 529 U.S. 193 (2000).

[87] Blue Cross/Blue Shield of Texas of Juneau (Tex. App. 7/24/03), discussed in Mary Alice Robbins, *Texas Appeals Court: Arbitrators Immune from Civil Suits,* Texas Lawyer 8/5/03 (law.com).

Part VII

CRIMINAL LAW

§ 26.01 INTRODUCTION

The discussion of criminal law is divided into three parts. The first, § 26.02, deals with substantive criminal law. The second, § 26.03, deals with the evolving Constitutional issues, and § 26.04 covers procedural issues and criminal trial practice.

A large part of every Supreme Court term is devoted to criminal cases, and this is also a significant issue for lower courts.

Since 2001, two topics of particular interest have emerged: what constitutes a "stop" and what powers police officers have pursuant to a stop; and sentencing issues, particularly those in the wake of *Apprendi* and *Ring*. *Blakely* and *Booker/ Fanfan* are also extremely significant sentencing cases. Both of these topics continued to be of crucial importance in 2002 and 2003, when they were joined with cases and legislation relating to the impact of the September 11 attack and prevention of terrorism.

On June 28, 2004, the Supreme Court decided three terrorism-related cases that, although outside the ambit of conventional criminal practice, are of great Constitutional significance. The Supreme Court decided that the U.S. court system has jurisdiction to hear challenges to the legality of detention at Guantanamo of foreign nationals captured in Afghanistan.[1] In 2006, the Supreme Court ruled that habeas corpus is available to Guantanamo detainees, and that the structure and procedure of the military commissions there violate the Uniform Code of Military Justice and the Geneva Convention.[2] The court also ruled that Due Process requires that a U.S. citizen, detained as an enemy combatant in connection with fighting in Afghanistan, be given a meaningful opportunity to contest the factual basis for his detention. The hearing must be held before a neutral decision-maker.[3] However, a habeas corpus petition by accused "dirty bomb" plotter Jose Padilla was dismissed on jurisdictional grounds — the case was brought against the Secretary of State, who was deemed not to be the immediate guardian of Padilla's person.[4] In April 2007, the Supreme Court turned down a group of Guantanamo detainee appeals challenging the Military Commissions Act provision that rules out District Court challenges to detention, on the grounds that the detainees had not exhausted the available remedies. The remedy is appeal of the Combatant Status Review Tribunal's designation of the person as an enemy combatant. Such a determination is a prerequisite to trial by a military commission. Detainees can appeal the designation to the D.C. Circuit, but the Detainee Treatment Act of 2005 does not permit detainees to introduce new evidence or challenge evidence at status tribunals as the product of unlawful interrogation. However, the Supreme Court granted a rehearing on June 29, 2007.[5]

On rehearing in 2008, the Supreme Court struck down the part of the 2006 Military Commissions Act that held that U.S. courts did not have jurisdiction over habeas petitions of foreign nationals detained at Guantanamo, and found that the detainees were entitled to habeas hearings in the near future. At that point, up to 200 detainees had habeas petitions before the District Court for the District of Columbia.[6]

---

[1] Rasul v. Bush, 542 U.S. 466 (2004).

[2] Hamdan v. Rumsfeld, 548 U.S. 557 (2006).

[3] Hamdi v. Rumsfeld, 542 U.S. 507 (2004).

[4] Rumsfeld v. Padilla, 542 U.S. 426 (2004); *see also* Padilla v. Hanft, 547 U.S. 1062 (2006). At the end of 2004, the Ninth Circuit upheld the constitutionality of 18 USC § 2339B (giving material support to a foreign terrorist organization) against First Amendment associational rights and Fifth Amendment due process challenges. United States v. Afshari, 392 F.3d 1031 (9th Cir. 2004); United States v. Hammoud, 381 F.3d 316 (4th Cir. 2004) is similar.

[5] Boumediene v. Bush, al Odah v. United States, *reh'g granted*, No. 06-1195 (6/29/07); *see* Jason McLure and Tony Mauro, *Supreme Court Won't Hear Guantanamo Detainees' Appeal*, Legal Times 4/3/07 (law.com).

[6] Boumediene v. Bush, 128 S. Ct. 2229 (2008). Pursuant to the Religious Freedom Restoration Act, four Guantanamo detainees (Shafiq Rasul, Asif Iqbal, Rhudel Ahmed, and Jamal al-Harith) were sent back to Britain, and the Supreme Court reinstated their suit charging that they were tortured and denied the right to exercise their religion. *See* (AP), *U.S. Supreme Court Revives Former Guantanamo Detainees' Case*, 12/16/08 (law.com). The Supreme Court also agreed to hear the case of *al-Marri v. Pucciarelli*, No. 08-368 (12/5/08) on the issue of whether a native of Qatar, arrested in Illinois on suspicion of being an Al Quaeda sleeper agent, can be detained indefinitely in the United States based on a Presidential determination that a person is an enemy combatant. Shortly after taking office, President Obama requested suspension of all war crimes trials at Guantanamo, with the

The Supreme Court also held that habeas extends to American citizens held in Iraq by U.S. forces operating under the American chain of command. The Supreme Court rejected the prosecution argument that habeas is unavailable because of the multi-national force fighting in Iraq. However, the Supreme Court ruled that a federal district court cannot exercise habeas jurisdiction to enjoin the United States from transferring persons detained within the territory of a foreign sovereign to that sovereign for criminal prosecution. Therefore, U.S. citizens who traveled to Iraq, allegedly committed crimes there, and were captured by coalition forces did not state an allegation for which relief could be granted. The District Court abused its discretion by granting a preliminary injunction forbidding the U.S. government from transferring one of the petitioners to Iraqi custody; that would interfere with Iraq's sovereign right to punish offenses committed within its territory.[7]

On another issue of non-U.S. citizens within the criminal justice system, the Supreme Court ruled, also in 2006, that states are not obligated to adopt special procedures or remedies under the 1963 Vienna Convention on Consular Relations (the international treaty covering the rights of foreign nationals arrested by local police). The treaty mandates that arrested persons be informed of their right to contact their consulates. But the Supreme Court gives the U.S. courts the final say on how the treaty will be implemented. Rulings of the International Court of Justice are entitled to respectful consideration, but do not govern procedural rules in the United States. Thus, statements made by a Mexican national arrested in Oregon did not have to be suppressed. He was *Mirandized*, but not informed of his right to contact the Mexican consulate. The Supreme Court held that the treaty does not require suppression of evidence or changes in the local rules about the time frame during which claims must be raised to avoid default.[8]

In 2004, the World Court ordered Texas to review the convictions of 51 Mexican nationals who were not informed of their treaty rights under the Vienna Convention to obtain legal assistance from the Mexican consulate. In 2005, after the Supreme Court heard the case for the first time, President Bush issued a memorandum implementing the treaty by having state courts abide by the World Court ruling. Texas refused, taking the position that the limits on successive habeas petitions had to be observed, and in 2008, the Supreme Court upheld Texas' position, because the consular treaty was not self-executing and requires Congressional action for implementation. A Presidential memo cannot alter the status of a treaty.[9]

---

intention of ending the system of military commissions and holding criminal trials for the detainees. *See* Ben Fox, *Judge Grants Obama's Request to Suspend Guantanamo Trials*, special to law.com 1/21/09.

[7] Munaf v. Geren, 128 S. Ct. 2207 (2008); *see* Tony Mauro, *Supreme Court Says Guantanamo Detainees Have Right to Challenge Detention*, Legal Times 6/13/08 (law.com).

[8] Sanchez-Llamas v. Oregon, 546 U.S. 74 (2006).

[9] Medellin v. Texas, 128 S. Ct. 1346 (2008); *see* Tony Mauro, *Supreme Court Sides With Texas in Dispute With Bush*, Legal Times 3/26/08 (law.com).

PART 1: SUBSTANTIVE CRIMINAL LAW

§ 26.02 BASIC CONCEPTS OF SUBSTANTIVE CRIMINAL LAW

A crime is wrongful conduct that is penalized by the state, in contrast to breach of contract or tort, which are conduct penalized by private parties. In many instances, the same conduct is both criminal and tortious. The general rule is that an offense penalized by a fine and/or less than one year of imprisonment is a misdemeanor; the offense is a felony if a conviction can result in imprisonment for more than a year.[10]

[A] General Elements of a Crime

Several elements must be present in order to have a crime:

- Generally, a wrongful act, although sometimes omission can be a crime if there is a duty to act
- Mens rea: wrongful or "evil" state of mind
- Corpus delicti: Harmful effect of the activity (although sometimes attempts are penalized even if no one is harmed); the prosecution case requires proof that the harm was caused by criminality rather than accident, and any confession must be corroborated by proof of corpus delicti
- Prescribed punishment; if no punishment is prescribed, there is no crime.

Some subtle problems are raised by "inchoate offenses" such as attempt, conspiracy and solicitation. Both mens rea and actus reus (evil act) are required for proof. There must be a direct connection between the defendant's conduct and the harmful result.

Criminal statutes also differentiate among degrees of offenses, typically divided into first, second, and third (or even fourth and greater) degrees, depending on the number of elements of crime that can be proved and how serious each element is. The degree of an offense can be enhanced by aggravating factors and reduced by mitigating factors.

One offense is a lesser included offense of another if it is necessary to commit that offense in the course of committing a more serious offense. For instance, it is necessary to deliberately set a fire as part of the more serious offense of committing arson for profit at a time when the premises were occupied. The defendant is entitled to a jury instruction on the lesser included offense if, but only if, the

---

[10] The felony/misdemeanor distinction has other implications as well. For instance, the prevailing evidence rules may allow impeachment of a witness by showing felony, but not misdemeanor, convictions. In the federal system, and in some state systems, prosecution of a felony requires a Grand Jury indictment, whereas this is not required for misdemeanor prosecutions.

evidence could reasonably be construed to mean that the defendant committed the lesser but not the more serious offense.

As a result of the Unborn Victims of Violence Act of 2004, P.L. 108-212, injuring a fetus in the course of a violent federal crime against the mother constitutes a separate offense, subject to the same penalty as if the injury or death had occurred to the mother, although the federal death penalty cannot be imposed for the death of the fetus alone. Proof of the offense does not require proof that the perpetrator intended to harm the fetus, or knew that the victim was pregnant.

[B] Burden of Proof

In a criminal case, the prosecution is required to prove, beyond a reasonable doubt, all facts needed to establish the guilt of the defendant. Due Process is violated by a jury instruction that raises the standard of reasonable doubt to "grave uncertainty" or "actual substantial doubt."[11] Such an error is not harmless, so a conviction based on such an instruction would have to be reversed.[12]

There are two aspects: the burden of producing evidence, and that of persuading the trier of fact. To avoid a directed verdict, the prosecution must produce evidence of each element of the crime and convince the trier of fact as to each. If additional elements are present that enhance punishment (e.g., recidivism), the prosecution must prove those as well.

The burden of proof can be placed on the defendant to establish the affirmative defense of extreme emotional disturbance.[13] Indeed, because affirmative defenses are unusual factors, the defendant is required to prove them rather than the prosecution having to rule them out.

Sometimes the prosecution is entitled to rebuttable presumptions: for instance, that if a defendant has no explanation for possession of stolen property, that he or she stole it; that if a victim is shot at point-blank range, intent to kill was present.

There is no such thing as a directed verdict of guilty in a criminal case, no matter how strong the evidence. In fact, the judge cannot even direct the jury to find for the prosecution on uncontested issues.

In contrast, verdict of acquittal can be directed, on the defendant's motion or the court's own motion, if the evidence is insufficient to support a conviction (e.g., not enough proof of corpus delicti; lack of connection between the defendant and the offenses charged). However, the defendant is not entitled to a directed verdict based on introduction of uncontradicted testimony that establishes a defense, because the trier of fact has the option of doubting the witness' credibility, even if the witness was not impeached.

---

[11] Cave v. Louisiana, 498 U.S. 39 (1990).

[12] Sullivan v. Louisiana, 508 U.S. 275 (1993).

[13] Patterson v. New York, 432 U.S. 197 (1997).

[C] Intent and State of Mind

Criminal culpability can exist based on several states of mind:

- Intent (conscious objective to cause a result or engage in conduct that is forbidden by statute; there is a rebuttable presumption that individuals intend the natural and probable consequences of their actions)
- Knowledge of act or omission (awareness that the conduct is of a type described in the statute, or knowledge that a circumstance described in the statute is likely to ensue, even if there is no desire to cause that result)
- Recklessness (failure to cope with a known risk)
- Negligence (creating an unreasonable risk; usually, negligence will be criminalized only if it is more serious than tort negligence).

Some offenses are criminalized on a strict liability basis, with no need for the prosecution to prove a culpable mental state. Statutory rape is usually considered a strict liability offense: the adult actor will be guilty even if the minor partner appeared to be an adult, or even claimed to be of lawful age.

Voluntary intoxication is not a defense, but it might negate certain culpable states of mind.

Although most criminal charges are brought against human beings, a corporation, and sometimes a partnership or association, can be criminally liable for acts of its employees when they are acting in the scope of their employment and on behalf of the business. In fact, several statutes provide sentencing alternatives for corporate defendants.

There are various circumstances that could prevent the defendant from having the requisite culpable mental state:

- Mistake of fact
- Mistake of law
- Insanity
- Intoxication.

United States v. Jewell[14] defines "knowingly" to include a state of mind where the defendant deliberately avoided knowledge.

If a statute requires that an act be committed "willfully" or "knowingly," it is probably sufficient that the actor knew that he or she was committing the act, even

---

[14] 532 F.2d 697 (9th Cir. 1976). *See also* United States v. Heredia, 483 F.3d 913 (9th Cir. 2007), upholding a jury instruction allowing the jury to find that the defendant had knowledge of criminal conduct that he or she deliberately ignored. The Supreme Court's early 2009 decision in Waddington v. Sarausad, No. 07-772 (1/21/09), although primarily a habeas case, involves the validity of a jury instruction on accomplice liability in the case of a gang member who drove away after another gang member killed one person and wounded another. The defendant argued that he was not an accomplice to murder because, when he agreed to drive, he thought that there would be a fistfight, not a shooting.

if the actor did not know it was illegal.[15] *Posters 'n Things, Ltd. v. U.S.*[16] holds that it was not necessary that proprietors of a head shop intend that the drug paraphernalia sold be used in conjunction with illegal drugs, as long as they knew that it was likely that illegal drugs would be used. Ignorance of the duty to file a tax return is a defense to the crime of tax evasion, because intent to evade (not mere failure to file or pay taxes) is an element of the crime.[17]

The actor is considered to be the cause of death, even if the victim's life support is terminated or even if the victim is also a victim of medical malpractice. Medical malpractice is considered a result of a criminal assault; but if the intervening cause is a mere coincidence, then the actor is liable for foreseeable but not for unforeseeable intervening causes.

In a homicide case, where provocation/heat of passion is claimed, the prosecution must prove the absence of these elements, because they are crucial to the level of the homicide charge.[18] Nevertheless, the defendant has the initial burden of production to raise the issue in the first place. It is not incumbent on every homicide prosecutor to demonstrate lack of provocation or heat of passion.

Another source of criminal liability is transferred intent — where, for instance, an unintended victim suffers as a result of a crime (poisoned food intended to kill one person is consumed by someone else). In late 2005, the Supreme Court considered transferred intent in *Bradshaw v. Richey*, 546 U.S. 74 (2005). Richey was tried for aggravated murder committed in the course of a felony (arson, with the intent of killing his former girlfriend and her new boyfriend; another tenant was killed instead). The Supreme Court held that the "transferred intent" theory is sustainable under Ohio law. In a federal habeas case, the federal court is bound by state courts' interpretation of state law.

For the chain of causation to be complete, the Supreme Court ruled that a plaintiff seeking damages from a government official for alleged false prosecution (in retaliation for exercising First Amendment rights) must prove lack of probable cause supporting the criminal charges.[19]

[D] Capacity Issues

"Insanity" is a legal, not a medical term. It does not refer to the presence or absence of mental illness, but to the actor's inability to understand that his or her conduct was wrong, or inability to conform conduct to the law even if it is known to be wrongful.

The two questions — of whether the defendant is competent to stand trial, and whether he or she can be acquitted on the basis of insanity — are related but intellectually distinct. In one case, the question is the legitimacy of the trial; in

---

[15] Bryan v. United States, 514 U.S. 184 (1998).

[16] 511 U.S. 513 (1994).

[17] United States v. Cheek, 498 U.S. 192 (1991).

[18] Mullaney v. Wilbur, 421 U.S. 684 (1975).

[19] Hartman v. Moore, 547 U.S. 250 (2006).

the other, what disposition should be made of an individual who concededly committed a crime. A competency hearing deals with the defendant's current capacity to understand the trial and participate in the defense, not the defendant's mental condition at the time of the crime. Therefore, a plea of Not Guilty by Reason of Insanity implies capacity to enter a plea and stand trial.[20]

In 2006, the Supreme Court ruled that Arizona's insanity test (capacity to tell whether an act is right or wrong) satisfied Due Process. The Supreme Court also held that it is permissible to restrict consideration of defense evidence of mental illness or incapacity to evidence bearing on the insanity defense rather than the mental element of the offense charged.[21]

Most jurisdictions make holding a mental examination of the defendant's present sanity discretionary with the court. However, some make it mandatory — for instance, where an insanity defense is raised. Mental illness-related defenses are affirmative defenses; it is not necessary for the prosecution to prove the sanity of a defendant who has not raised the issue.

Under *Cooper v. Oklahoma*,[22] Due Process precludes the trial of any individual who lacks sufficient present capacity to consult with a lawyer with a reasonable degree of rational understanding, or lacks rational and factual understanding of the proceedings. *Cooper* also holds that a state cannot impose a presumption of competence that requires the defendant to rebut it by clear and convincing evidence, because of the risk that incapacitated people will be put on trial despite significant evidence of their incapacity. *Cooper* does, however, permit a presumption of competence that can be overcome by a preponderance of the evidence.

Under *Cooper*, involuntary civil commitment can be imposed on the basis that a person is mentally ill, and is a danger to him-or herself or others, or is incapable of safe survival in the community.

The Supreme Court returned to the subject of civil commitment in 2002, ruling that Due Process requires proof of the defendant's "serious difficulty" in controlling dangerous behavior before civil commitment as a sexually violent predator can be imposed. However, it is not necessary to prove that the defendant completely lacks volitional control over his or her actions.[23]

The ruling of *Godinez v. Moran*[24] is that, although states can impose more complex requirements, all that Due Process requires is that the same standard be used for competency to stand trial as for placing a guilty plea or waiving the right to counsel: i.e., the defendant's rational understanding of the proceeding or decision.

In almost all jurisdictions, if the defendant raises an insanity defense, the court is permitted to order a psychiatric examination. This is not considered a violation of the prohibition against self-incrimination, even if the prosecution

---

[20] *See* Medina v. California, 505 U.S. 437 (1992).

[21] Clark v. Arizona, 548 U.S. 735 (2006).

[22] 517 U.S. 348 (1996).

[23] Kansas v. Crane, 534 U.S. 407 (2002).

[24] 509 U.S. 389 (1993).

makes use of the results of the court-ordered examination to rebut the defense evidence.

In some instances, a defendant who cannot afford to hire a psychiatric expert may be entitled to appointment of a psychiatrist in addition to appointed counsel. The standard is whether there is a reasonable probability of the appointment assisting the defense — and not granting the appointment would prevent a fair trial.[25]

[1] Mental State, the Insanity Defense, NGRI, and GMBI

Usually, if the defendant is found Not Guilty By Reason of Insanity (NGRI), he or she will not be convicted of a crime, but probably will be institutionalized. In contrast, a Guilty But Mentally Ill (GBMI) verdict, as permitted by many states, will allow the defendant to be convicted of the crime and sentenced for it if the evidence supports a finding of guilt beyond a reasonable doubt. However, there will be a pre-sentencing psychiatric examination, which may result in part or all of the sentence being served in a psychiatric facility rather than in a prison.

Some jurisdictions permit a defense of diminished capacity for a defendant who is mentally abnormal but not insane. The probable result of a successful diminished capacity defense would be conviction on a lesser charge than the original indictment.

The holding of *Shannon v. U.S.*, 512 U.S. 573 (1994), is that in general, if the jury does not have a sentencing function, the federal judge should **not** instruct the jury on the consequences of the NGRI verdict. The exception would be a situation in which the jury has received misstatements on the subject.

About half the states have laws calling for indefinite confinement of sexual psychopaths or sexually dangerous persons, until such time as they are no longer dangerous.

Kansas has a statute that allows civil commitment of individuals whose mental abnormality or personality disorder makes them likely to engage in predatory acts of sexual violence. It has been upheld by the Supreme Court.[26] As long as dangerousness is established, detention is proper for individuals unable to control their behavior. Commitment is a civil, not a criminal, sanction because it does not focus on either retribution or deterrence.

An expert witness can testify as to whether a defendant who pleaded insanity did or did not suffer from severe mental disease as defined by 18 USC § 17, even though FRE 704(b) prohibits testimony on ultimate issues in insanity cases.[27] The true ultimate issue for an insanity defense is the defendant's capacity to understand the nature, quality, and wrongfulness of acts at the time they were committed. The

---

[25] McDonald v. Bowersox, 101 F.3d 588 (8th Cir. 1996). *But see* Stewart v. Gramley, 74 F.3d 132 (7th Cir. 1996), holding that not appointing a psychiatrist did not constitute reversible error, since evaluations done after the defendant was sentenced to death showed understandable anxiety but no psychosis.

[26] Kansas v. Hendricks, 521 U.S. 346 (1997).

[27] United States v. Dixon, 185 F.3d 393 (5th Cir. 1999).

Fifth Circuit also requires the defendant to demonstrate insanity by convincing clarity as a prerequisite for the issue to go to the jury.

The Third Circuit ruled that a District Court order under 18 USC § 4243(e), committing a person to the custody of the Attorney General after acquittal by reason of insanity, is an appealable final order as defined by 28 USC § 1291. Because a commitment order is a finding of fact, it must be clearly erroneous to be reversed.[28]

[E] Defenses

One important defense tactic is to challenge the accuracy or credibility of the fact pattern presented by the prosecution, or to show that the quantum of proof is not great enough. Another tactic is to concede the fact pattern, but assert a defense that renders the accused person's conduct non-criminal or not subject to penalty.

It does not violate Due Process to give retroactive application to a state's abolition of a common-law rule, thus making it possible to convict a defendant of murder even though the victim died more than a year after the attack (when prior law required death within a year).[29]

[1] Justification

A justification defense asserts that the defendant acted reasonably as judged by objective standards — even if the defendant's reasonable belief (e.g., that a mugger was holding a gun rather than a harmless object) proved to be incorrect. Justification is often asserted in the context of self-defense or defense of other persons or of property.

Physical force can legitimately be used to defend oneself or other people against an imminent use of unlawful physical force. (Verbal provocation would probably not be grounds for lawful use of physical force.) In most cases, if the assailant is unarmed, it is excessive to use a weapon for self-defense or defense of others. The use of deadly force is justified for protection against a very serious crime such as murder, rape, or kidnapping.

It is permissible to use physical force to defend property against what is reasonably believed to be a crime or criminal attempt, although it is probably not acceptable to use deadly force. (An exception might be drawn for arson or other very serious offense.)

Jurisdictions differ in their interpretation of the duty to retreat. Sometimes there is a duty to retreat to avoid killing an assailant, or to avoid the use of deadly force where it is known that the danger can be averted by retreat. In contrast, some jurisdictions do not impose a duty to retreat on a person who is attacked or threatened at home or in his or her place of business.

---

[28] United States v. Stewart, 452 F.3d 266 (3d Cir. 2006).

[29] Rogers v. Tennessee, 532 U.S. 451 (2001).

The defense of justification is not available to the person who provoked the physical incident, unless he or she definitively withdrew and was subjected to a separate attack.

Self-defense can be a defense to criminal charges in two aspects. Perfect self-defense, where the violent action was fully justified, relieves the defendant of all criminal liability. Imperfect self-defense still leaves the defendant liable, although to a lesser extent.

In some jurisdictions, expert testimony is accepted as to whether the defendant suffered from "learned helplessness" as part of a "battered spouse" or "battered child" syndrome as a result of abuse, and perceived that it was necessary to hurt or kill the abuser to prevent continuation and escalation of abuse. If the argument is accepted, then liability will be reduced or eliminated, even if the attack on the abuser did not occur during an actual violent episode started by the abuser.

[F] Double Jeopardy

The prohibition of double jeopardy means that no one can be prosecuted more than once for the same offense. This simple statement gives rise to a host of problems. At the defendant's first trial, the jury convicted him but they were not unanimous in recommending the death penalty. Therefore, by operation of law, the defendant was sentenced to life imprisonment. The defendant successfully challenged the conviction; he was retried after reversal. Early in 2003, the Supreme Court ruled that failure to make a unanimous finding is not an acquittal on the death penalty. Therefore, the double jeopardy rule would not preclude the defendant from being re-sentenced to death at the second trial.[30]

"Jeopardy" is a criminal concept, so in many situations, the same conduct can permissibly be penalized by both criminal and civil penalties.

The crucial difference is whether the civil penalty is deemed to be "remedial" (e.g., equivalent to the cost of litigating the case and imposing the penalty itself) or "punitive." See *Department of Revenue v. Kurth Ranch*,[31] applying the double jeopardy clause to a second prosecution for the same offense after either an acquittal or a conviction; or multiple punishments for the same offense.

The criminal/civil determination depends on whether the legislature explicitly or implicitly characterized the particular sanction as punitive, based on factors such as the disability or restraint imposed by the sanction; whether it was historically regarded as punishment; if imposing the sanction requires a finding of scienter; whether it is excessive vis-à-vis its claimed purpose; whether it is intended to provide deterrence or retribution on behalf of society.[32]

---

[30] Sattazahn v. Pennsylvania, 537 U.S. 101 (2003).

[31] 511 U.S. 767 (1994).

[32] Hudson v. United States, 522 U.S. 93 (1997).

In most instances, civil forfeitures are remedial and not punitive in nature, so there is no double jeopardy bar to both imprisoning an individual and declaring that person's property subject to forfeiture.[33]

A 2005 Second Circuit case holds that for double jeopardy purposes, two offenses are not the same if they are charged by different sovereigns. However, the Sixth Circuit right to counsel applies to separate, formally charged offenses with the same essential elements even if they are charged by different sovereigns. Under *Texas v. Cobb*, 532 U.S. 162 (2001), the right to counsel is offense-specific, analyzed on the elements of the crime. The Second Circuit held that, if the same conduct supports federal and state prosecution, it is not permissible for one sovereign to question a defendant without counsel after the right to counsel had attached, and then give the information to the other sovereign.[34]

The double jeopardy challenge might fail if concurrent criminal and civil proceedings are considered part of a single, coordinated prosecution or because the forfeiture requires different elements of proof.

In a case where several charges were pending against the defendant, the judge granted the defense motion to dismiss one of them for insufficient evidence. The Supreme Court held in early 2005 that the dismissal constituted an acquittal. Therefore, it was impermissible double jeopardy for the judge to change her mind and send the "dismissed" charge to the jury, unless there was preexisting authority permitting reconsideration of a mid-trial ruling.[35]

Prison disciplinary proceedings (e.g., for escape) do not bar federal criminal charges; nor do administrative probation or parole revocation hearings. Confinement under a sexual predator statute is defined as treatment-oriented, not punitive, and thus not subject to double jeopardy arguments.[36]

Debarment from government contracting is not double jeopardy unless it is overwhelmingly disproportionate to the contractor's improper conduct. Administrative suspension of a driver's license for driving under the influence of alcohol or drugs is remedial, not punitive.

Failure to contest an administrative forfeiture means it never becomes a judicial forfeiture, so jeopardy does not attach.[37] Jeopardy did not attach in forfeiture if criminal proceedings were completed before forfeiture proceedings began.

---

[33] United States v. Ursery, 518 U.S. 267 (1996). Under United States v. Alt, 83 F.3d 779 (6th Cir. 1996), IRS civil penalties are not punishment, so the IRS can impose interest and collect back taxes from a person convicted of tax fraud; United States v. Price, 314 F.3d 417 (9th Cir. 2002) holds that it was not double jeopardy to prosecute Clean Air Act violations after a county imposed a civil penalty for violating county regulations that tracked the federal statutory language: conduct that violates the laws of more than one sovereign can be punished by more than one sovereign.

[34] United States v. Mills, 412 F.3d 325 (2d Cir. 2005).

[35] Smith v. Massachusetts, 543 U.S. 462 (2005).

[36] Kansas v. Hendricks, 521 U.S. 346 (1997).

[37] United States v. Clark, 84 F.3d 378 (10th Cir. 1996); United States v. Branham, 97 F.3d 835 (6th Cir. 1996); United States v. Morgan, 84 F.3d 765 (5th Cir. 1996).

It constitutes double jeopardy to prosecute a person both for an offense and for lesser included offenses of that offense. The basic rule comes from *Blockburger v. United States*,[38] which defines double jeopardy as a successive prosecution where the second or later offense contains elements identical to, or contained within, the first offense charged. If a single act violates more than one statute, the double jeopardy test is whether each provision requires proof of facts that the other does not.[39]

Simultaneous possession of different drugs can constitute different offenses. Two conspiracies are different if primary objects of the conspiracy are different, and each includes at least one element not present in the other. After a conviction has been reversed on appeal, the defendant can be prosecuted for conspiring to commit the act for which the conviction has been reversed. Both conspiracy and CCE (continuing criminal enterprise) can be charged for essentially the same conduct, as long as the sentences run concurrently, not consecutively.

The holding of *Witte* is that not only does the double jeopardy doctrine forbid more than one punishment for the same offense, but that ordinarily, prosecutors cannot get more than one trial to impose the single punishment. Sentencing a defendant within the range permitted by the Guidelines (see § 26.03[L][1]) is not deemed to be multiple punishment even if the sentence includes consideration of uncharged conduct. It would be double jeopardy to sentence a defendant to two consecutive prison terms for a single violation of a statute.[40] A "three-strike" statute is not double jeopardy because it punishes the current crime more heavily when priors are taken into account; it is not additional punishment for the earlier convictions.[41] In a three-strike sentence enhancement proceeding it is not double jeopardy to retry an allegation of prior conviction,[42] although this rule is limited to non-capital cases; post-trial proceedings cannot be used to obtain a death sentence that was rejected by the trial jury.[43]

The defendant has the initial burden of making a prima facie case on double jeopardy, but once this is done, the government has the burden of producing a preponderance of evidence that double jeopardy should not bar prosecution.[44] Unlike exclusionary rule claims (which are waived if not asserted before trial), a double jeopardy claim can be raised on appeal even if this argument was not presented to the District Court.[45]

---

[38] 284 U.S. 299 (1932).

[39] Witte v. United States, 515 U.S. 389 (1995); Rutledge v. United States, 517 U.S. 292 (1996).

[40] United States v. Gonzalez, 520 U.S. 1 (1997), *but see* United States v. Watts, 519 U.S. 148 (1997) holds that sentence enhancements merely, and permissibly, punish the defendant for the manner in which the crime was committed; they do not punish the defendant for offenses for which there was no conviction.

[41] United States v. Farmer, 73 F.3d 836 (8th Cir. 1996).

[42] Monge v. California, 524 U.S. 721 (1998).

[43] Bullington v. Missouri, 451 U.S. 430 (1981).

[44] United States v. Schinnell, 80 F.3d 1064 (5th Cir. 1996).

[45] United States v. Hardwell, 80 F.3d 1471 (10th Cir. 1996).

[1] Collateral Estoppel

The doctrine of collateral estoppel is related, but not identical, to double jeopardy. Collateral estoppel can be asserted to prevent repeat litigation, between the same parties, of an issue which has already been determined by a valid and final judgment. In the criminal context, the parties must be so closely related that they are considered to be the same. Such a determination would probably be made involving a District Attorney's office and a Department of Parole, but probably not in the case of a District Attorney's and U.S. Attorney's offices.

Collateral estoppel or issue preclusion is an issue of ultimate fact that has already been determined by a valid final judgment and thus cannot be re-litigated by the same parties.[46] The collateral estoppel component of the Double Jeopardy clause does not necessarily exclude otherwise admissible, relevant, and probative evidence because it relates to charges of which the defendant was acquitted.[47]

[2] State and Federal Prosecution

The "dual sovereignty" doctrine allows successive prosecutions by state and federal authorities, if the governmental entities maintain the cases separately; see *Koon v. United States*.[48] A contrary result would create problems if a state prosecution for a comparatively minor offense derailed a major federal prosecution.

However, a valid double jeopardy argument might exist if the federal prosecution is merely a sham to make up for a failed state prosecution. Under the so-called "Petite policy," the federal government refrains from prosecuting defendants who have already been tried in state courts for acts that could generate federal charges. However, this is merely a policy, not a substantive right upon which defendants can rely to block a federal prosecution.

About half the states have adopted the Model Penal Code view, that a federal prosecution (whether it results in acquittal or conviction) bars a subsequent state prosecution whenever the federal case involves the same conduct as the state case, unless:

- The federal and state statutes are aimed at different harms or evils
- Different proof is required
- The state offense had not been consummated as of the beginning of the federal trial.

State prosecution is also barred by a federal resolution in favor of the defendant, in a manner inconsistent with proving facts required to establish the state case.

---

[46] Schiro v. Farley, 510 U.S. 222 (1994).
[47] Dowling v. United States, 493 U.S. 342 (1990).
[48] 518 U.S. 81 (1996).

If a federal statute supports two plausible interpretations, the one that does not alter the balance of power between state and federal governments will be preferred.[49] However, such analysis will only be undertaken if the statute is ambiguous.[50]

[3] Ex Post Facto

The Constitution forbids Congress to make any "ex post facto law." The ex post facto concept applies to criminal legislation only, not to civil legislation or court decisions. An ex post facto law imposes a criminal penalty on an action that was legal at the time it was committed; aggravates the degree of the offense; increases its punishment; or changes the applicable evidentiary rules. (Ex post facto reductions in punishment are permissible, because they do not have negative consequences for defendants.)

Lowering the maximum punishment for an offense but raising the minimum sentence is considered an increase. A rule that permits additional kinds of evidence is acceptable if its effect is to allow defendants in general to present additional evidence of innocence even if it also permits more evidence of the guilt of a particular defendant.

Procedural changes that do not involve evidence (for example, changes in rules of jurisdiction or venue; number of peremptory challenges available during jury selection) are only ex post facto if they impair a substantial right that was available to the defendant at the time of the alleged offense.

The common-law rule is that outright repeal of a statute that does not have a savings clause prevents prosecutions (pending or not instituted before the repeal) for earlier violations. However, any conviction that was finalized before repeal remains valid. Furthermore, most statutes are drafted with a savings clause precisely to eliminate this line of defense.

A decision that is reached after a petitioner's conviction is final (i.e., after all direct appeals have been completed) that creates a new Constitutional rule of criminal procedure, will not be applied retroactively.[51]

A mid-2003 Supreme Court decision finds it to be an unlawful ex post facto law to pass a statute extending a limitations period, and then apply it to offenses for which the statute of limitations has already expired.[52]

[4] Entrapment

The defense of entrapment does not dispute that the defendant performed the actions alleged in the indictment or information—only that the actions were performed with the requisite criminal intent, in that the defendant responded to the government agent's provocation but lacked the predisposition to commit the

---

[49] Gregory v. Ashcroft, 501 U.S. 452 (1991).

[50] United States v. Lopez, 514 U.S. 549 (1995); Salinas v. United States, 522 U.S. 52 (1997).

[51] Teague v. Lane, 489 U.S. 288 (1989).

[52] Stogner v. California, 539 U.S. 607 (2003).

crime without government involvement. Factors in determining the defendant's predisposition include, e.g.,

- Character and reputation
- If the initial suggestion of criminal activity came from the government agent
- If the defendant exhibited reluctance that had to be overcome by the government agent
- The nature of the persuasion or inducement provided by the government agent.

[5] Duress

The defense of duress takes the position that the individual lacked mens rea, and committed the crime not out of personal intention or for personal advantage, but because forced to commit it by someone else: e.g., that someone else threatened to harm the defendant or someone close to the defendant unless the defendant committed the crime. Such a defense requires proof of force or a threat of a nature such that a reasonable person in the defendant's situation would have been unable to resist.

[6] Necessity

The necessity defense depends on circumstances rather than the act of another person. For instance, a prison escape might be excused if the prison were burning at the time of the escape. A necessity defense might be asserted by a cancer or glaucoma patient who uses marijuana for symptom relief, or by an ideologically motivated person who attacks a missile base or abortion clinic. However, it is far from certain that a necessity defense will succeed in such cases.

[7] Alibi

A defendant who asserts an alibi claims that he or she was somewhere other than at the scene of the crime at the relevant time. In some jurisdictions, alibi is an affirmative defense (i.e., the defendant must prove it). In others, however, when an alibi is asserted, it is merely an additional part of the prosecution case to prove that the defendant was indeed present. In 2006, the Supreme Court ruled (*Guzek v. Oregon*, 546 U.S. 517) that there is no Constitutional right to present alibi evidence at the stage of capital sentencing by a jury, because once a jury has found a person guilty, there is no ongoing right to present evidence of residual doubt.

[G] Multiple-Party Crimes

Frequently, several or many people will commit a crime or series of crimes jointly, or will participate in various stages of the crime(s). The Model Penal Code, and many jurisdictions, provide that a person is criminally liable for an offense that he or she:

- Directly and personally commits
- Aids in the commission of, when present at the scene of the crime

- Procured, counseled, or aided by prior conduct even if not present at the scene of the crime.

As long as they act with shared intent and purpose, the "principal" and the "accessories" are equally liable.

However, a person who is merely involved in an "anticipatory offense," although guilty of at least one crime, is subject to a lesser degree of liability than a principal or accessory. An anticipatory offense, such as solicitation, attempt, conspiracy, or facilitation makes other offenses more practicable.

Solicitation is the offense of trying to get another person to engage in criminal conduct; it is not necessary for the person committing solicitation to engage personally in any overt act in furtherance of the solicited crime.

Conspiracy is the offense of joining with at least one other person to engage in criminal conduct, or to have someone else perform criminal conduct (e.g., by hiring an assassin). Conspiracy requires express or implied agreement to commit a substantive crime, plus at least one overt act in furtherance of the conspiracy. The overt act need not be illegal: driving to the bank that is the target of a bank robbery conspiracy would be an example. A conditional agreement to murder someone in the future can be prosecuted under New York conspiracy law.[53]

A 2005 Supreme Court decision holds that conviction under 18 USC § 1956(h) (conspiracy to commit money laundering), unlike the general conspiracy statute, does not require proof of an overt act in furtherance of the conspiracy. Although the petitioners took the position that § 1956(h) merely enhances existing penalties, the Supreme Court ruled that this statute enacts a new and distinct offense: *Whitfield v. U.S.*, 543 U.S. 209 (Sup. Ct. 2005).

When an illegal conspiracy consists of agreement plus one or more overt acts, and the actors agree in one state to commit a crime in another state, and an overt act occurs in the second state, that is the situs of the conspiracy. But if no overt act is required, the first state is the situs.

An early 2003 Supreme Court decision locates the essence of a conspiracy in the agreement to commit an unlawful act. Therefore, if law enforcement intervention makes it impossible to commit the crime as planned, that does not mean as a matter of law that the conspiracy has been terminated. The public danger still exists after one crime has been averted; unless the criminals have abandoned or withdrawn from the conspiracy, they still might commit crimes.[54]

Attempt consists of both having the intent to commit a crime and engaging in conduct that tends to bring about the commission of the crime. However, the offense must be one requiring intent — it is not possible to attempt negligence or recklessness. Therefore, it is possible to attempt murder, but not depraved indifference murder; first degree manslaughter (which implies an unintended death), or reckless manslaughter.

---

[53] People v. Washington, 8 N.Y.3d 565 (N.Y. 2007).
[54] United States v. Jimenez Recio, 537 U.S. 270 (2003).

Due Process prevents a state from offering irreconcilable descriptions of events in sequential prosecutions of two defendants for the same crime.[55] At the petitioner's trial, the prosecution relied on out-of-court statements that made the accomplice the actual killer, making the petitioner liable for felony murder. At another trial, the prosecution used the theory that someone else did the killing before the petitioner and his accomplice even arrived at the scene. The Eighth Circuit says that trials that involve manipulation of evidence are inherently unfair—but because this is a new rule, it cannot be used retroactively in habeas cases.

For multi-party crimes other than attempt, renunciation is an affirmative defense. Renunciation means that a participant in the crime or potential crime experienced a complete voluntary change of heart (not mere doubt that the crime could be perpetrated without detection), ceased efforts to facilitate the crime, and made substantial efforts to prevent the crime from being committed.

[H] Elements of Offenses

It is common for offenses to be penalized in a number of degrees, with the lowest degree of the simple offense enhanced by aggravating factors (such as the seriousness of the victim's injuries, use of a deadly weapon, or special vulnerability of the victim) that make the crime more serious and lead to a longer sentence.

A state statute that reduces the amount of evidence needed for a conviction, by removing the corroboration requirement for certain types of evidence (here, the sexual abuse of a minor) is ex post facto and cannot be used to obtain a conviction for an offense that occurred prior to the enactment of the statute.[56]

In mid-1999, the Supreme Court struck down[57] a Chicago ordinance, passed to discourage gangs, that required the police to break up groups of loiterers. Even if the ordinance has the desired effect of reducing crime, it impairs the liberty of loiterers who are not engaged in criminal activity.

[1] Homicide

Homicide offenses involve the death of a person under criminal circumstances. The actions of the defendant must have "caused" the death, even if death did not occur immediately after the injury. The defendant remains liable for homicide even if other factors contributed to the victim's death, although it is a defense that although the defendant injured the victim, death was caused by a secondary agency that was not at all induced by the defendant.

[a] Murder

Murder, the most serious homicide offense, requires intent to kill. Additional aggravating elements might be murder for profit; murder of a police or correction

---

[55] Smith v. Groose, 205 F.3d 1045 (8th Cir. 2000).
[56] Carmell v. Texas, 529 U.S. 513 (2000).
[57] Chicago v. Morales, 527 U.S. 41 (1999).

officer; serial or multiple murder; or torturing the victim. A homicide that is not a murder might be charged as manslaughter, vehicular manslaughter, or criminally negligent homicide.

Reckless or depraved-heart murder does not require intent to kill, but does require that the death was the result of conduct that was so reckless that it evidenced depraved indifference to the risk that others could die.

In an aggravated murder case, where the elements of the crime include calculation and design, it was Constitutionally acceptable[58] to require the defendant to prove the affirmative defense of self-defense by a preponderance of the evidence.

In mid-1996, the Supreme Court upheld a Montana statute that forbids juries to consider voluntary intoxication in determining the mental state of a homicide defendant. (Under the statute, "purposely" or "knowingly" causing death constitutes homicide.) The Supreme Court's Due Process analysis is that there is no absolute right to introduction of all relevant evidence. Furthermore, states can maintain the common-law rule that voluntary intoxication is not a defense.[59]

[b] Manslaughter

Extreme emotional disturbance, measured by the viewpoint of a person in the defendant's situation, where the circumstances are as perceived by the defendant, reduces the level of an intentional homicide from murder to manslaughter. A death that ensues from an assault committed with intent to cause serious physical injury also constitutes manslaughter.

A lower degree of culpability in a death (such as recklessly causing a death; causing a death by criminal negligence; causing a death by improper vehicular operation) is charged as a lower degree of manslaughter.

[c] Felony Murder

The general rule is that whenever a death occurs in the course of the commission of a felony, the perpetrators of the felony are guilty of felony murder, even if they had no intent to kill, and even if the actual death resulted from someone else's act. The classic case is the shooting of a bystander by a police officer who appears at a crime scene. The perpetrators of the robbery, burglary, bank robbery, or other crime are guilty of the felony murder of the bystander.

The somewhat less common counterpart of felony murder is misdemeanor manslaughter, the offense charged when a death results in connection with commission of a misdemeanor.

In a multiple-defendant felony murder case, it is a defense that a particular defendant did not commit, aid, or solicit the killing; did not have a deadly weapon at the time of the crime; had no reason to believe that any other participant in the crime did; and had no reason to believe that death would ensue from the crime.

---

[58] Martin v. Ohio, 480 U.S. 228 (1987).
[59] Montana v. Egelhoff, 518 U.S. 37 (1996).

[2] Assault

In tort terms, battery is unpermitted touching; assault is threatening conduct that places a person in fear of unpermitted touching. In criminal terms, however, assault is actual physical injury. The degree of the offense depends on factors such as:

- Whether a weapon was used; if so, if it was a deadly weapon
- Whether the assailant intended to cause injury; if so, if the intention was to cause serious rather than minor injury; whether the assailant intended to cause dismemberment or disfigurement
- Whether the assault placed anyone at grave risk of death
- Whether the assault occurred in the course of another felony (e.g., assaulting a recalcitrant robbery victim)
- Whether the victim was a police officer or firefighter rather than a civilian.

[3] Sex Offenses

For many years, all non-marital sexual conduct was criminalized, and some states retain laws on the books against fornication and/or adultery.

In mid-2003, the Supreme Court reversed itself and ruled[60] that there is no legitimate state interest that would justify a state's intrusion into the liberty interest of consenting adults to engage in private sexual conduct by enacting a statute that criminalizes sexual acts between same-sex partners. This ruling not only invalidated state laws in Kansas, Oklahoma, and Missouri as well as Texas, but also sodomy laws forbidding private consensual sexual conduct whether homosexual or heterosexual (affecting laws in Alabama, Florida, Idaho, Louisiana, Mississippi, North Carolina, South Carolina, Utah, and Virginia).

[a] Rape or Sexual Assault

In the past, rape convictions often required corroboration of the complainant's testimony (although corroboration was not required for non-sexual violent offenses) and/or proof of physical resistance by the victim. Modern jurisprudence has generally eliminated such requirements.

Rape or sexual assault involves either subjecting a non-consenting person to sexual contact, or having sexual contact with a person who is unable to consent (by reason of age, mental deficiency, mental illness, unconsciousness).

Rape statutes used to be drafted to make it a defense that the victim was married to the perpetrator. However, most jurisdictions now recognize marital rape as a crime. Contemporary laws are usually "unisex," in that unwanted sexual contact is a crime whether perpetrated by a male or female, and whether the victim is male or female.

---

[60] Lawrence v. Texas, 539 U.S. 558 (2003); for the history of sodomy statutes, *see, e.g.*, Linda Greenhouse, *Libertarians Join Liberals in Challenging Sodomy Law*, N.Y. Times, Mar. 19, 2003 at A3.

The U.S. Code contains several provisions relating to violent sexual offenses. P.L. 105-314, the Protection of Children from Sexual Predators Act of 1998, amends Title 18 to give children greater protection from sexual abuse and exploitation.

P.L. 103-322 § 40503 permits a criminal court to order an HIV test when a defendant is charged with a sex offense in federal or state court. If the underlying arrest was warrantless, a showing of probable cause must be made.

The victim must request the test, after having undergone counseling, and the court must determine that the alleged offense, if committed by an HIV-positive person, does pose a risk of HIV transmission. If the first test is negative, the statute permits the court to order follow-up tests; if the defendant is acquitted or the charges are dismissed, the court can order the results to be communicated to the victim. However, a rapist's knowledge of his HIV-positive status does not constitute intent to kill rape victims.[61]

P.L. 104-305, the Drug-Induced Rape Prevention and Punishment Act of 1996 enhances penalties when controlled substance used to drug a victim to facilitate commission of sexual (or other) offense.

The Ninth Circuit upheld 18 USC § 2423(c), a provision added by the PROTECT Act, making it a crime for a U.S. citizen to travel outside the United States to engage in illicit sexual conduct with a minor. The Ninth Circuit found that the statute falls within Congress' power to regulate foreign commerce.[62]

A number of cases hold that would-be Internet predators can be convicted of offenses such as traveling in interstate commerce to engage in illicit sexual activity or use of the facilities of interstate commerce to attempt to entice a minor to engage in illegal sexual activities, even if the youths they believed they were seducing were in fact adult government agents.[63]

Early in 2001, the Supreme Court considered the case of an individual confined under the Washington State Community Protection Act of 1990 as a sexually violent predator, i.e., a person with a mental abnormality or personality disorder that makes it likely that he will continue to engage in predatory acts of sexual violence.[64] The similar Kansas statute was upheld by the Supreme Court in 1997[65] on the grounds that it is nonpunitive and satisfies substantive Due Process.

Substantive Due Process is not offended by imposing the lifelong registration and reporting requirements under the state's sex offender registration act on a juvenile who meets the statutory criteria for a sexual predator. The requirement is not punitive, is rationally related to the valid purpose of preventing predation, and public access to juvenile records is controlled.[66]

---

[61] Smallwood v. Maryland, 680 A.2d 512 (Md. App. 1996).

[62] United States v. Clark, 435 F.3d 1100 (9th Cir. 2006).

[63] *See, e.g.*, United States v. Brand, 467 F.3d 179 (2d Cir. 2006); United States v. Helder, 452 F.3d 751 (8th Cir. 2006). On charging offenses involving minors when an adult undercover officer is involved, *see also* United States v. Root, 296 F.3d 1222 (11th Cir. 2002).

[64] Seling v. Young, 531 U.S. 250 (2001).

[65] Kansas v. Hendricks, 521 U.S. 346 (1997).

[66] *In re* J.W., 204 Ill. 2d. 578 (Ill. 2/21/03).

[b] Prostitution

Prostitution consists of providing some degree of sexual contact in exchange for money or other things of value. Some jurisdictions make it a crime to patronize a prostitute; others criminalize prostitution, solicitation in a public place, loitering for purposes of prostitution, but not retaining the services of a prostitute.

[c] Obscenity

Obscene material violates community standards, is patently offensive, and lacks redeeming literary, artistic, political, or scientific value. Additional penalties are imposed for disseminating indecent material to minors, or manufacturing or distributing pornography that depicts children in an indecent fashion.

Generally, the sale of printed pornography depicting adults, to adults, is not a law enforcement priority. However, issues involving pornography on the Internet, especially child pornography, are significant, especially in light of the difficulty of controlling who gains access to a particular Web site. The Child Pornography Prevention Act of 1996 as passed includes a provision, 18 USC § 2256(8), banning any image that is or appears to be a minor engaging in sexually explicit conduct. The production and distribution of such material is illegal when it is pandered as child pornography even if youthful-appearing adults, or virtual images, rather than actual children were used to manufacture the images. In April 2002, the Supreme Court struck down these provisions[67] as unconstitutionally overbroad. The ban on "virtual child pornography" is invalid because it can extend to images that are not obscene by the standards of all communities and that are not patently offensive. If real children are not involved in creation of the images, then there is no need to protect them against abuse.

Congress tried again to find a constitutionally effective ban on virtual child pornography, enacting the Prosecutorial Remedies and Tools Against the Exploitation of Children Today Act (PROTECT Act; P.L. 108-21) which amends 18 USC § 2256 to forbid pornographic digital images that appear to depict minors engaged in sexual conduct. It is an affirmative defense that the images depict adults, but it is not a defense that the images are purely virtual and did not require placing real children in sexual situations. 18 USC § 2252A(a)(3)(B) is the revised pandering and solicitation provision that Congress passed (as part of the PROTECT Act) after *Ashcroft* found the previous statute invalid. The revised statute forbids obscene material, showing real children or virtual images of children engaging in sexually explicit conduct, or any material depicting real children engaging in sexually explicit conduct. The anti-pandering provision forbids knowing advertising, promotion, presentation, distribution, or solicitation of material that reflects the belief (or intended to induce someone else to believe) that the material constitutes child

---

[67] *Ashcroft v. Free Speech Coalition*, 535 U.S. 234 (2002). To offer a preponderance of evidence at sentencing in a child pornography case, the prosecution does not have to introduce expert testimony that a particular image depicts a real rather than a virtual child: *United States v. Rodriguez-Pacheco*, 475 F.3d 434 (1st Cir. 2007).

pornography. The Eleventh Circuit held that the statute was vague and targeted non-commercial, non-inciting speech that is protected by the First Amendment.

In 2008, the Supreme Court upheld § 2252A(a)(3)(B), despite arguments that the law was overbroad enough to burden mainstream movies about teenage sex, literary classics, or innocent pictures of grandchildren. The defendant, who called himself "dad of toddler with good pics to swap" was captured in an Internet sting and charged with posting seven images of real minors engaging in sexual conduct. The court also upheld part of the 2003 statute forbidding possession of child pornography, with a five-year mandatory prison term for promoting or pandering child pornography. Justice Scalia said that the ban on "simulated sexual inter- course" would never be interpreted to mean depictions of young-looking but still adult actors, or virtual child pornography, but Justice Souter dissented, on the grounds that constructed images could still be a basis for prosecution. In the majority view, the statute's ban on offers to provide or requests to obtain child pornography does not target the underlying material, only the collateral speech that brings the material into a distribution network. According to the majority, the statute does not criminalize a substantial amount of protected expressive activity.[68]

On remand from the Supreme Court, in early 2003 the Third Circuit ruled that the Child Online Protection Act (COPA), which forbids commercial Internet communication of any material harmful to minors is constitutionally defective and likely to violate the First Amendment. The statute was overbroad because it was not narrowly tailored to protect minors from harmful materials, and was not the least restrictive means of satisfying this goal. The Third Circuit also noted that the Internet cannot be restricted geographically to satisfy community stan- dards, and COPA calls for examination of individual images and files out of context. The Third Circuit also criticized the statute's definition of minors as anyone under 17, because it fails to take into account the differing needs and risks to five-year-olds and 16-year-olds. Finally, COPA was put to rest in early 2009, when the Supreme Court refused to hear the government's attempt to appeal the Third Circuit's condemnation of the statute.[69]

The Third Circuit has upheld 18 USC § 2252 (ban on intrastate possession of child pornography, where material was produced using items that have traveled in interstate commerce).[70] The Commerce Clause allows regulation of an interstate activity if regulation is an essential part of controlling a broader interstate market.

---

[68] United States v. Williams, No. 06-694 (2008); discussed in Mark Sherman (AP), *Supreme Court Upholds Part of Child Porn Law*, 5/19/08 (law.com); Laurel Newby, *Supreme Court Argument Report: Justices Consider Dueling Hypotheticals in Child Porn Case*, 10/31/07 (law.com). The Supreme Court noted that the definition of "sexually explicit conduct" is very similar to the New York statute that was upheld by New York v. Ferber, 458 U.S. 747 (1982).

[69] ACLU v. Ashcroft, 322 F.3d 240 (3d Cir. 2003). The 2009 Supreme Court ruling is Mukasey v. ACLU, No. 08-565 (1/21/09). *See* Mark Sherman, *Anti-Online Porn Law Dies Quietly in Supreme Court*, 1/22/09 (law.com).

[70] United States v. Rodia, 194 F.3d 465 (3d Cir. 1999).

It was reasonable for Congress to believe that intrastate possession of child pornography stimulates greater demand for interstate trafficking.

The Eleventh Circuit reversed a conviction for possession of child pornography, holding that the federal power to regulate interstate commerce did not permit a prosecution for possessing child pornography on computer disks. The defendant concededly crossed state lines with the disks, but that was before the images were placed on the disk. The ruling was that the defendant's conduct did not have a substantial enough effect on interstate commerce for Congress to regulate it. Although Internet communications can constitute interstate commerce, the Eleventh Circuit found that there was no evidence that the images were downloaded rather than obtained in some other way.[71]

According to the Ninth Circuit in 1999, downloading child pornography from the Net to a computer is not the kind of "transporting or shipping" envisioned by 18 USC § 2252(a)(1).[72] Congress enacted separate provisions for receiving/shipping and transporting/shipping. But in 2006, the Third Circuit ruled that use of the Internet satisfies the "interstate commerce" element of 18 USC § 2252A(a)(2)(B) (knowing receipt or distribution of child pornography that has been transported in interstate or foreign commerce by any means, including by computer). The Third Circuit did not accept the defendant's position that the child pornography from the Internet could have gotten onto his computer from within the state, because the statute does not require that the images cross state lines, just that they were transported in interstate commerce; computers are specifically cited in the statute. Because of the interstate nature of the Internet, and Congress' power to regulate online channels of interstate commerce, a connection request to a server or transmission of an image to a user constitutes transmission in interstate commerce.[73]

Prosecution of cases involving child pornography retrieved from the Internet raises significant issues (whether mere viewing is enough for a conviction, or whether the images must be stored); the effect of the defendant's ignorance of the way images are processed by Web browsers and computer programs; when interstate commerce is involved. A recent Tenth Circuit case highlights these issues. A conviction was reversed because the prosecution failed to satisfy the requirements of 18 USC § 2252(a)(2) and (a)(4)(B), by failing to prove movement of child pornography images across state lines. The prosecution failed to explain where the images came from, where the pornographic sites were based, where their servers were, and where the defendant's ISP was located. The court read the 1988 amendment to § 2252(a), to add the phrase "including by computer" as a

---

[71] United States v. Maxwell, 386 F.3d 1042 (11th Cir. 2004). Similarly, United States v. Smith, 402 F.3d 1303 (11th Cir. 2005), refuses to apply 18 USC § 2251(a) to intrastate production of child pornography purely for personal use. Although the film and film processor traveled in interstate commerce, the court found that there was no effect on commerce; the court refused to distinguish between simple possession and noncommercial production of pornography.

[72] United States v. Mohrbacher, 182 F.3d 1041 (9th Cir. 1999).

[73] United States v. Macewan, 445 F.3d 237 (3d Cir. 2006).

clarification to make sure that sending images by computer was covered by the statute — but proof of transmission across state lines is still required.[74]

Similarly, the Georgia Court of Appeals reluctantly reversed a conviction — and vacated a 20-year sentence — because of failure to prove that the defendant was aware that images were in his cache file.[75] But charges of possession of deleted images have also been upheld.[76]

On the basis of transcripts between a defendant and a police officer posing as a 14-year-old girl, an arrest was made for traveling across state lines to engage in sex with a minor and using an interstate communication facility to induce a minor to engage in sex acts. The defendant contended that he thought he was communicating with an adult woman pretending to be a teenager. At the time of his arrest, he was carrying a Personal Digital Assistant containing over 140 stories about sex between adults and minors. In April of 2006, the Ninth Circuit ruled that its own precedent prevented admission of the stories as evidence of criminal intent to engage in sex with a minor. Then, in mid-2007, the Ninth Circuit reheard the case en banc and ruled 8-7 to overturn the precedent and admit the stories into evidence as relevant to his intention — although admissibility depends on the facts and circumstances of the case; simple possession of written materials of the same genre as the charged crime is not automatically admissible.[77]

Using the Kazaa file-sharing network to obtain child pornography from other users of the network, while allowing them to access and download the child pornography on his computer, constituted "distribution for the receipt, or expectation of receipt, of a thing of value, but not for pecuniary gain" under Guideline 2G2.2(b)(2)(B).[78]

The Third Circuit vacated special conditions on a lifetime term of supervised release for possession of child pornography. (The 71-month prison sentence was not contested.) An absolute lifetime ban on using computers or the Internet, with no exceptions for work or education, imposed a greater deprivation of liberty than necessary and was not reasonably related to the statutory factors. The Third Circuit analogized the restriction to forbidding access to all books and magazines. The lifetime ban on possession of sexually explicit materials was overbroad. The restrictions on associating with children, including the defendant's own children,

---

[74] United States v. Schaefer, 501 F.3d 1197 (10th Cir. 2007).

[75] Barton v. State, 286 Ga. App. 49 (Ga. App. 2007); *see* Alyson M. Palmer, *Appeals Panel "Reluctantly" Tosses Child Porn Case*, Fulton County Daily Report 6/27/07 (law.com).

[76] Commonwealth v. Diodoro, 2007 Pa. Super. 256 (Pa. Superior Ct. 2007); *see* Gina Passarella, *Pa. Court: Viewing Child Porn on Computer Enough for Possession*, The Legal Intelligencer 8/24/07 (law.com). The Tenth Circuit case is United States v. Tucker, 305 F.3d 1193 (10th Cir. 2002); the Ninth Circuit case is United States v. Kuchinski, 469 F.3d 853 (9th Cir. 2006); *see* Howard J. Bashman, *Just Looking: Should Internet Ignorance Be a Defense to Child Porn Charges?* Special to law.com (12/4/06).

[77] United States v. Curtin, 489 F.3d 935 (9th Cir. 2007), discussed in Howard J. Bashman, *Can What You're Reading Prove Intent to Commit a Crime?* Special to law.com (5/29/07); the earlier case is Guam v. Shymanovitz, 157 F.3d 1154 (9th Cir. 1998).

[78] United States v. Griffin, 482 F.3d 1008 (8th Cir. 2007).

were upheld, but it was improper for the District Court to give the probation officer absolute authority over the restrictions.[79]

An April 2003 federal statute, part of the Truth in Domain Names legislation, amends 18 USC § 2252B to make it a crime, punishable by up to two years' imprisonment, knowingly to use a misleading Internet domain name to lure a person into viewing obscene material. The offense is punishable by up to four years' imprisonment if the intent was to lure minors into viewing harmful online material.[80]

[4] Arson

Arson is the crime of intentionally creating a fire or explosion involving a building or vehicle. Degrees of enhancement include the extent of the damage to the building or vehicle; using explosive devices; arson for profit (e.g., burning down a building of limited worth but with significant insurance coverage); committing arson when the perpetrator knew or should have known of the presence of people; and actual harm to people.

P.L. 104-155, the Church Arson Prevention Act of 1996, enacted at 18 USC § 247, making it a federal crime intentionally to deface, damage, or destroy religious real property because of the race, color, or ethnicity of the congregation associated with the property.

[5] Drunk Driving and Vehicular Offenses

A high percentage of arrests are made for driving while under the influence of alcohol or controlled substances, so these cases make up a large part of the criminal lawyer's caseload. They may also make up part of the caseload of the general practitioner, because individuals (or their relatives) who do not otherwise come within police jurisdiction may do so because of an allegation of DUI (driving under the influence) or DWI (driving while intoxicated). The offense consists of having a BAC (blood alcohol concentration) higher than the statutory limit: typically, .08% or .10% of alcohol in the blood.

Depending on the jurisdiction and the facts of the case, an accused drunk driver might also be charged with reckless driving, vehicular assault, vehicular homicide,[81] manslaughter, or even "depraved-heart" murder.

DUI/DWI cases comprise both criminal and administrative elements, because it is very likely that a convicted drunk driver will face suspension of his or her driver's license. There may also be consequences for automobile insurance: for

---

[79] United States v. Voelker, 489 F.3d 139 (3d Cir. 2007); *see* Shannon P. Duffy, *3rd Circuit Overturns Lifetime Computer Ban*, The Legal Intelligencer 6/11/07 (law.com).

[80] *See* Mark Hamblett, *First Charges Filed Under New Internet Porn Law*, N.Y.L.J. 9/4/03 (law.com).

[81] Proof of voluntary driving while intoxicated, and death of another person, is sufficient for a conviction of vehicular homicide. It is not necessary to prove that drinking rather than excessive speed proximately caused the death: Colorado v. Gamer, 781 P.2d 87 (Colo. Sup. 1989).

instance, the person may be denied insurance other than limited, high-cost coverage under the assigned risk pool. Conviction of, or guilty or no contest plea to, a drunk driving offense is likely to have negative consequences if the driver is sued for injuring another person or harming property.

Especially for first offenses and persons with strong ties in the community, attendance at "DWI School" (a program of alcohol education and remedial driving education), or entrance into an alcohol rehabilitation program,[82] may result in pretrial diversion or an Adjournment in Contemplation of Dismissal. Sometimes limited driving privileges will be permitted so a person can continue to work. Sometimes sentences involving incarceration can be suspended, or served on weekends, so the driver can maintain employment and family responsibilities.

[a] Intoxication Testing

Usually, when the police stop[83] a person who is suspected of impaired driving, they will ask him or her to perform simple tests such as walking a straight line or reciting the alphabet backwards. Some states use a "horizontal gaze nystagmus" test to see if the driver's eyes track normally;[84] other states do not consider this a scientifically valid test of intoxication.

The next step is usually an "intoxilyzer" breath test. The premise of breath testing is that there will be a predictable ratio between alcohol in the breath and alcohol in the blood. Some cases have successfully challenged treating the ratio as a conclusive, irrebuttable presumption.[85]

Sometimes a successful challenge can be posed to the validity of the police stop; the accuracy of the testing instrument; or the validity of a borderline result.

A *Miranda* warning is required before custodial interrogation by the police (see § 26.03[C][1]), but not before collection of non-testimonial information. Videotaped

---

[82] *But see* Warner v. Orange County Dep't of Probation, 870 F. Supp. 69 (2d Cir. 1996) finding it an unconstitutional establishment of religion to force a convicted drunk driver to attend Alcoholics Anonymous meetings (which involve invocation of a "higher power"). O'Connor v. California, 855 F. Supp. 303 (C.D. Cal. 1994) permits giving the convicted person a choice between attending AA meetings and participating in a sobriety program without spiritual content.

[83] The Supreme Court has upheld the practice of placing sobriety checkpoints on the highway, where all motorists can be detained briefly even without individualized suspicion: Michigan Department of State Police v. Sitz, 496 U.S. 444 (1990).

[84] Oregon v. O'Key, 899 P.2d 663 (Or. Sup. 1995).

[85] *E.g.*, California v. McDonald, 206 Cal. App. 3d 877 (Cal. App. 1988); South Dakota v. McCarty, 434 N.W.2d 67 (S.D. Sup. 1988). Controversy has erupted over defense attempts to gain access to the source code for the CMI Group's breathalyzers. The manufacturer refuses to release the source code, calling it a trade secret — with the result that more than 1,000 breath tests have been thrown out by Florida courts, although Nebraska rejected a similar challenge. Lauren Etter reports in *Florida Standoff on Breath Tests Could Curb Many DUI Convictions*, Wall St. J. 11/16/05 p. A1, that there are more than 1 million DUI arrests nationwide each year, 60% of which result in convictions, and 95% of the convictions are based at least in part on breath analysis, so the issue could have wide-ranging implications.

evidence of an arrested person's slurred speech and lack of coordination is non-testimonial, and therefore does not require a warning, but asking an arrested person the date of his or her sixth birthday is testimonial and requires a *Miranda* warning.[86]

According to the Ninth Circuit, if there is probable cause to suspect DUI, the police have a reasonable belief that an emergency threatens the destruction of evidence, and a reasonable testing procedure is used, a blood sample can be taken prior to arrest even over the objections of the alleged drunk driver.[87]

BAC test results are medical records that qualify for the medical records hearsay exception in a civil suit. Neither the chain of custody nor the reliability of BAC testing has to be established.[88]

[b] Implied Consent Laws

Surrendering a breath, blood or urine sample for BAC testing is inherently self-incriminatory, yet there is an important public policy in deterring and punishing drunk driving. Most states have adopted "implied consent" laws that hold that the act of driving a car constitutes consent to BAC testing incident to any arrest made by the police on reasonable cause to believe the driver is intoxicated.

Refusal to submit to testing can result in immediate confiscation of the driver's license, which can only be returned after an administrative hearing on the reasonableness of the police action.[89] On the other hand, a person who is tested and found to have an excessive BAC is very likely to be convicted of drunk driving and to undergo license revocation or suspension.

A license suspension hearing is an administrative hearing, but carries a right to counsel, right to confrontation, and cross-examination of the arresting officer. Some states also penalize failure to submit to BAC testing as an offense independent of drunk driving.

The general rule is that suspending or revoking a driver's license for failure or refusal to be tested is not punitive in nature. Since it is not punitive, it cannot constitute double jeopardy to suspend or revoke the license and also punish the individual for drunk driving.[90]

---

[86] Pennsylvania v. Muniz, 496 U.S. 582 (1990).

[87] United States v. Chapel, 55 F.3d 1416 (9th Cir. 1995); *on remand*, 61 F.3d 913. Fink v. Ryan, 673 N.E.2d 281 (Ill. Supp. 1996) finds that an arrestee who was involved in a serious accident is already under police control, so a "special needs" exception to the Fourth Amendment permits blood testing for the presence of alcohol and drugs. *But see* Cooper v. State, 277 Ga. 282 (Ga. 2003), holding the Georgia implied consent statute (which implies consent to blood, breath, or urine testing after a serious accident or a DUI arrest) violates the Fourth Amendment and the state constitution by allowing searches without probable cause. The court rejected the application of the Special Needs argument.

[88] Judd v. Louisiana, 663 So. 2d 690 (La. Sup. 1995).

[89] This procedure is Constitutional: Mackey v. Montrim, 443 U.S. 1 (1979).

[90] *See, e.g.*, Maryland v. Jones, 340 Md. 235 (App. 1996); Hawaii v. Toyomura, 904 P.2d 893 (Haw. 1995); Matter of Smith, N.Y.L.J., 11/6/96 p. 25 col. 3 (A.D. 3d Dept.).

[6] Firearms Offenses

The typical state criminal code sets out requirements (such as applying in advance so a records check can be performed) for getting a license or permit to own firearms. An additional permit, or special circumstances (such as carrying bank deposits or valuable merchandise) is usually required to carry a weapon outside one's home or place or business, or to carry a concealed weapon. Certain types of weapons, such as machine guns and assault weapons, are banned or restricted.

The District of Columbia had an extremely restrictive ordinance about gun possession, which, in 2008, gave rise to a definitive Supreme Court pronouncement that the Second Amendment protects individual (not just collective or militia) rights to possess weapons, although certain restrictions (e.g., bans on guns in schools or government buildings; restrictions on gun purchases by felons or the mentally ill) are acceptable.[91]

In mid-2005, the Supreme Court construed 18 USC § 922(g)(1), possession of a firearm by a felon (someone convicted "in any court" of an offense punishable by at least one year in prison). The Supreme Court ruled that a felony conviction in a foreign country cannot be used as a predicate, on the grounds that Congress passed that law to deal with domestic concerns and did not consider foreign courts.[92]

Late in 2002, the Supreme Court held that, because Congress has defunded the Bureau of Alcohol, Tobacco and Firearms' program under which convicted felons can petition for restoration of the right to possess firearms, convicted persons cannot use the federal court system to reinstate their right to own guns lawfully.[93]

In the federal system, 18 USC § 924(c)(1) imposes a five-year mandatory sentence for "carrying" a firearm "during and in relation to" a drug trafficking crime. Conviction does not depend on the defendant's carrying the firearm on his or her person; the statute is satisfied by having the firearm in a locked trunk or glove compartment during a drug deal.[94] "Use" of a firearm under § 924(c) is defined to require active employment, not mere possession, of the firearm.[95] According to the Fifth Circuit, if the same firearm is used to commit two predicate offenses, 18 USC § 924(c)(1) does not authorize multiple convictions.[96]

---

[91] District of Columbia v. Heller, 128 S. Ct. 2783 (2008); *see* Tony Mauro, *Supreme Court Strikes Down D.C. Gun Ban*, Legal Times 6/27/08 (law.com).

[92] Small v. United States, 545 U.S. 1121 (2005).

[93] United States v. Bean, 537 U.S. 71 (2002).

[94] Muscarella v. United States, 524 U.S. 125 (1998).

[95] Bailey v. United States, 516 U.S. 137 (1995). On the retroactivity of *Bailey, see* Bousley v. United States, 523 U.S. 614 (1998). The five-year sentence under § 924(c) must run consecutively with all other state and federal sentences: United States v. Gonzalez, 520 U.S. 1 (1997). *See also* Watson v. United States, 128 S. Ct. 579 (2007): the word "use" must be given its ordinary meaning, so trading drugs for a gun does not constitute "using" a firearm in connection with a drug trafficking crime for purposes of 18 USC § 924(c)(1)(A).

[96] United States v. Phipps, 319 F.3d 177 (5th Cir. 2003).

If the civil rights of a felon are restored, but he or she is allowed to possess certain kinds of firearms but forbidden to possess others, §§ 922(g)(1) and 924(e) are triggered by any firearm possession, not just the forbidden types.[97]

Certain state misdemeanors with sentences of at least two years can also be treated as violent felonies. A 1986 amendment to 18 USC § 921(a)(2) precludes the use of convictions that have been expunged or set aside, or for which the convicted person has been pardoned or had civil rights restored, to enhance the sentence. Late in 2007, the Supreme Court ruled that a defendant with three state misdemeanor battery convictions that did not affect voting or other civil rights could not use the "civil rights restored" provision. To be restored, something (including civil rights) must have been lost in the first place. The intent of the federal statute was to deal with changes in status, such as expungement of a conviction, not to benefit convicted persons who did not forfeit rights that could later be restored.[98]

A non-resident of New York who had a concealed-carry permit in his home state of Virginia sought a New York gun license to be used on visits to the state. The Second Circuit held that New York's licensing system, which limits eligibility to persons who live or work in the state, was valid and did not violate the Second Amendment.[99]

On a related issue, a mid-2008 Supreme Court case involves a would-be terrorist who entered the United States with explosives in his car and was arrested for giving false information on a customs form and for carrying an explosive during commission of a felony (18 USC § 844(h)(2)). The Ninth Circuit vacated the second conviction on the grounds that conviction would require the explosive to have been carried in relation to the underlying felony of giving false information. The Supreme Court reversed, holding that the presence of the explosives when he made the false statement meant that they were carried during the commission of the felony, and the Ninth Circuit incorrectly imposed a relational requirement that was not part of the statute.[100]

[7] Drug Offenses

All of the states ban the use, sale, transportation, or even possession of "controlled substances": i.e., illegal drugs, or legal drugs that are not the subject of a lawful prescription. The degree of the offense depends on the nature of the drug (some jurisdictions have decriminalized or reduced penalties for possession of small amounts of marijuana) and, critically, on the amount involved. An inference is often drawn that possession of a large amount of a controlled substance shows intent to sell, not just intent to use the substance personally. Drug offenses may carry mandatory prison sentences, or longer prison sentences than non-drug felonies of the same degree.

---

[97] Caron v. United States, 524 U.S. 308 (1998).

[98] Logan v. United States, 128 S. Ct. 475 (2007).

[99] Bach v. Pataki, 408 F.3d 75 (2d Cir. 2005).

[100] United States v. Ressam, No. 07-455 (5/19/08).

The Second Circuit ruled that a person who delivers drugs can be convicted of cocaine distribution (21 USC § 841(a)) even if the person shares drugs with friends and does not receive money in exchange.[101]

P.L. 107-273, the 21st Century DOJ Appropriations Authorization Act, gives the Attorney General the power to make grants to state and local governments to establish drug courts offering diversion, probation and supervised release, and substance abuse treatment and drug testing for non-violent drug offenders.

In prosecutions for drug conspiracies under 21 USC § 848 (Continuing Criminal Enterprise, or CCE), a mid-1999 Supreme Court decision[102] holds that the jury must be unanimous as to which specific violations are part of the continuing series of violations to be penalized.

The Supreme Court rejected a medical necessity defense to the Federal Controlled Substances Act, 21 USC § 841(a)(1), asserted by those who wished to use medical marijuana. The court ruled that Congress has determined that marijuana does not provide therapeutic benefits.[103]

The Supreme Court returned to the subject of medical marijuana in mid-2005, ruling that Congress' power under the Commerce Clause allows its exercise of power over marijuana cultivation, because of the effect of even noncommercial intrastate cultivation of marijuana on the interstate market for the drug. Therefore, Congress can proscribe all use of marijuana, and the federal system can prosecute Californians even if they were in conformity with California's state compassionate use statute.[104] On another issue of medical drug use, the Supreme Court decided in early 2006 that the U.S. Attorney General does not have the power to use the federal Controlled Substances Act to penalize Oregon doctors who participate in the state's procedures for physician-assisted suicide.[105]

A drug offense (typically, simple possession) that is a felony under state law, but a mere misdemeanor under the federal Controlled Substances Act is not an "aggravated felony" for Immigration and Nationality Act purposes.[106]

Also see the discussion of proper pleading of drug quantities for sentencing purposes at § 26.04[L][5].

---

[101] United States v.Wallace, 532 F.3d 126 (2d Cir. 2008); *see* Mark Hamblett, *2nd Circuit Finds Drug Sharing to Equal Distribution*, N.Y.L.J. 7/11/08 (law.com).

[102] Richardson v. United States, 526 U.S. 813 (1999). *See also* United States v. Shabani, 513 U.S. 10 (1994): it is not necessary to prove an overt act to get a conviction under 21 USC § 846, the drug conspiracy statute. Conspiracy to distribute controlled substances is a lesser included offense of Continuing Criminal Enterprise, so a defendant cannot be sentenced to life imprisonment on each count, even if the terms are concurrent rather than consecutive: Rutledge v. United States, 517 U.S. 292 (1996).

[103] United States v. Oakland Cannabis Buyers' Cooperative, 532 U.S. 483 (2001).

[104] Gonzales v. Raich, 545 U.S. 1 (2005).

[105] Gonzales v. Oregon, 546 U.S. 243 (2006).

[106] Lopez v. Gonzales, 549 U.S. 47 (2006). Certiorari in a related case, Toledo-Flores v. U.S., 549 U.S. 69 (2006) was dismissed as improvidently granted on the same date, on the grounds that the petitioner was contesting his prison sentence, not his deportation, and the sentence had already been served.

A person convicted of a dual object drug conspiracy, (21 USC §§ 841, 846) involving both cocaine and cocaine base, can be sentenced based on the guidelines covering all the drugs involved in the same course of conduct.[107]

[8] Larceny and Fraud Offenses

Theft offenses, both violent and non-violent, are very common, and are criminalized under many headings and in various degrees, depending on factors such as the degree of force used (if any), the degree of risk to victims, and the amount stolen. Larceny consists of taking other people's money or property without their consent, and with intent to keep it (rather than, for instance, joyriding, which consists of taking a car without permission but with intent to return it).

Larceny also includes obtaining property with the consent of its owner, if the consent was obtained by improper means such as deception, or by "paying" for merchandise with a check known to be fraudulent.

[a] Robbery

Robbery, one of the most serious larceny offenses because of the potential for harm to the victim, consists of forcible theft by use or threatened use of physical force to prevent or overcome the victim's resistance, or to induce the victim to surrender the property that is the subject of the offense.

Carjacking is a particular type of robbery: forcibly stealing a vehicle from the owner who is entering, exiting, or operating it. It is a federal crime. Conditional intent to kill or harm (i.e., if the victim refused to surrender the vehicle) satisfies the intent requirement of 18 USC § 2119.[108] Under § 2119, serious bodily injury or death of the victim are elements of the highest level of the offense, not mere sentencing factors.[109]

[b] Criminal Trespass and Burglary

The lowest degree, criminal trespass, involves entering a building that is not open to the public. If "breaking and entering" rather than just entering is involved, the offense is likely to constitute burglary. The offense is enhanced if the building is a dwelling; if entry or remaining in the building is unlawful; if there is an intent to steal or commit another crime; if the theft or other crime actually occurs; if entry occurs at night rather than in the daytime.

Related offenses include possession of burglar's tools and possession of stolen property.

[c] Fraud

Fraud involves obtaining money or property by deception or by false promise (an express or implied representation that the fraudfeasor or a third party will do

---

[107] Edwards v. United States, 523 U.S. 511 (1998).

[108] Holloway v. United States, 526 U.S. 1 (1999).

[109] Jones v. United States, 526 U.S. 227 (1999).

something desired by the victim of the fraud). Forgery involves the creation of false documents, or affixing an unauthorized signature to a document.

A conviction of bankruptcy fraud, as defined by 18 USC § 157, requires specific intent to defraud an identifiable victim or class of victims.[110] Income received before the filing of a bankruptcy petition is not part of the bankruptcy estate. Therefore, failure to disclose the income cannot violate 18 USC § 152(1)[111] [fraudulent concealment of estate property].

In a prosecution for bank, wire, or mail fraud, the prosecution must prove that the allegedly fraudulent act affected the outcome of a transaction.[112] In a tax fraud case, although materiality of the falsehood is an issue, the judge's failure to submit the question of legal relevance to the jury can be harmless error.

"Knowing and willful" misapplication of federally insured funds is a crime under 20 USC § 1097(a), but it is not necessary for conviction that fraudulent intent on the part of the defendant be proved.[113]

The Seventh Circuit upheld a securities law conviction despite the defendant's argument that, as tippee, he could not be convicted when the tipper was acquitted, and that his convictions about tender offer offenses had to be dismissed without an insider trading conviction.[114]

In a prosecution under 18 USC § 1014 (false statements to a federally insured bank), materiality of the falsehoods is not an element of the offense.[115]

Conviction can be obtained in a forgery case based on proof of intention to deceive, even if the forgery was so clumsy that it was unlikely that anyone would, in fact, be deceived.

A federal law, the Identity Theft and Assumption Deterrence Act of 1998 (P.L. 105-318) (10/30/98) amends 18 USC § 1028(a) to criminalize knowing unauthorized transfer or use of someone else's "means of identification" with intent to commit any federal crime, or any felony under state/local law.

Means of identification include name, Social Security Number, date of birth, driver's license number, unique biometric data such as fingerprints or retinal patterns, unique electronic identification number, telecommunication ID information, or access devices.

The federal penalty is a fine and/or up to 20 years imprisonment. Both will be imposed if the offense facilitates drug trafficking, any crime of violence, or follows a conviction. The statute directs the FTC to establish a procedure for complaints by individuals alleging appropriation of their identity.

A number of the states have adopted similar laws dealing with misappropriation of another person's identity, especially through use of credit cards.

---

[110] United States v. Milwitt, 475 F.3d 1150 (9th Cir. 2007)
[111] United States v. Mitchell, 476 F.3d 539 (8th Cir. 2007).
[112] Neder v. United States, 527 U.S. 1 (1999).
[113] Bates v. United States, 522 U.S. 285 (1997).
[114] United States v. Evans, 486 F.3d 315 (7th Cir. 2007).
[115] United States v. Wells, 519 U.S. 482 (1997).

The First Circuit reversed a conviction for aggravated identity theft (18 USC § 1028A(a)(1)). The statute imposes a mandatory two-year additional term if the defendant, during and in relation to the offense, "knowingly transfers, possesses, or uses without lawful authority" another person's means of identification. The First Circuit read the statute as ambiguous, holding that the "knowingly" requirement applies to the phrase "of another person." In this reading, conviction requires proof that the defendant knew that the means of identification belonged to another person. This was not proven, so the conviction was reversed. (The defendant transferred funds between banks to create the impression of a larger account. She made up seven Social Security numbers with variations on her valid Social Security number. One of the Social Security numbers was a real Social Security number that belonged to somebody else, but the prosecution did not prove that the defendant knew this.)[116]

In June 2002, the Supreme Court (reversing the Fourth Circuit) held that a broker who sold securities from a discretionary account without the client's knowledge or consent and kept the sales proceeds himself committed fraud "in connection with the sale of securities" and therefore violated § 10(b) and Rule 10b-5. In this reading, the fraud coincided with a security sale and therefore fell under the anti-fraud rules, even though there was no manipulation of an individual security, and even though the integrity of the market as a whole was not threatened.[117]

In general, the "revenue rule" prevents U.S. courts from enforcing the tax laws of foreign countries. In April 2005, however, the Supreme Court permitted prosecution under 18 USC § 1343 for wire fraud when interstate wires were used to defraud the Canadian government of tax revenue by smuggling liquor to avoid Canadian excise taxes. The Supreme Court did not consider this a suit to recover tax revenue itself; it was punishment of domestic criminal conduct within the United States.[118]

[d] Sarbanes-Oxley Fraud and White-Collar Crime Provisions

Title VIII of the Sarbanes-Oxley Act of 2002 (P.L. 107-204), the "Corporate and Criminal Fraud Accountability Act of 2002," and Title XI of the same statute, the "Corporate Fraud Accountability Act of 2002," add additional sanctions against corporate financial wrongdoing.

Title VIII adds a new criminal provision, 18 USC § 1519, imposing fines and/or imprisonment of up to 20 years for the crime of knowingly altering, destroying, or falsifying records in connection with bankruptcy, or with the intention of hindering a federal investigation.

Corporate auditors are required to maintain their audit and review work papers for at least 5 years, and a knowing violation of the record retention requirement is punishable by a fine and/or up to 10 years' imprisonment.

---

[116] United States v. Godin, 534 F.3d 51 (1st Cir. 7/18/08).
[117] SEC v. Zandford, 535 U.S. 813 (2002).
[118] Pasquantino v. United States, 544 U.S. 349 (2005).

Also under Title VIII, a new section, 18 USC § 1348, is enacted, imposing a sentence of up to 25 years, and/or a fine, for knowing execution or attempt of any scheme or artifice to defraud any person in connection with any security that is registered, or is issued by a reporting company.

Sarbanes-Oxley adds a new 18 USC § 1349, making it clear that the penalty is the same for attempting or conspiracy to commit criminal fraud as for actually succeeding. The penalties for mail and wire fraud are increased from a potential 5 years to a potential 20 years' imprisonment, and criminal violations of ERISA can be penalized by a $100,000 fine rather than the previous $5,000, and $500,000 where the previous limit was $100,000. The maximum term of imprisonment rises from 1 to 10 years.

Sarbanes-Oxley also amends 28 USC § 994, directing the United States Sentencing Commission to review the Sentencing Guidelines and make any changes necessary to set the base offense level and enhancements under 2J1.2 (obstruction of justice) high enough to deter violations, and that the provisions relating to obstruction of justice are severe enough to cope with destruction, alteration, or fabrication of evidence in severe cases involving a lot of evidence or a lot of participants. Congress directs the Sentencing Commission to make sure that the amendments reflect the seriousness of securities, pension, and accounting fraud and are severe enough to impose a real deterrent.

The penalties under Exchange Act § 32(a) are increased by Sarbanes-Oxley from $1 million in fines or up to 10 years' imprisonment to up to $5 million in fines or up to 20 years' imprisonment, and the potential $2.5 million penalty goes up to $25 million.

Title XI of Sarbanes-Oxley amends 18 USC § 1512 to impose a sentence of up to 20 years' imprisonment, and/or a fine, for "corrupt" obstruction of official proceedings or alteration, destruction, mutilation, or concealment of documents in order to prevent the document from being used in an official proceeding.

[e] Computer Crime

The Department of Justice manual for prosecuting intellectual property crimes (e.g., fraud committed with computers; cyberstalking; child pornography; identity theft) can be found at http://www.cybercrime.gov/crimes.html.

The Internet False Identification Prevention Act of 2000, P.L. 106-578, directs the U.S. Attorney General and the Secretary of the Treasury to collaborate for two years on a coordinating committee to promote the investigation and prosecution of offenses under 18 USC § 1028(d)(3), "creation and distribution of false identification documents." P.L. 106-578 makes it clear that transferring identification documents by electronic means can be illegal. In this context, a false identification document is one that appears to be government-issued but is not. The crime includes making false documents (or the software tools to create them) available on line.

[f] Bribery and Related Offenses

19 USC § 201(c)(1) forbids giving a public official "anything of value" "for or because of" an official act that the official is supposed to perform. *United States v. Sun-Diamond*,[119] says that conviction depends on proof of a link between the "gift" and an official act. Not very surprisingly, in mid-2004, the Supreme Court upheld the constitutionality of 18 U.S.C. § 666(a)(2) (bribery of officials of a federally funded state or local entity). The Supreme Court found the statute to be a valid exercise of congressional authority given Congress' power to appropriate federal money for the general welfare — and to make sure the funding is properly applied, rather than diverted in response to bribes.[120] For purposes of the anti-gratuity statute, 18 USC § 201(c)(1)(B), an action by a public employee is an "official act" if and only if it could affect a public matter. In this case, a police detective caught in a sting was paid to run a fictitious license plate number through the official database by someone posing as a judge.[121]

18 USC § 1346, defining criminal fraud to include a scheme to deprive another of the right to honest services, was held by the Southern District of New York to not extend to the bribery of foreign officials in foreign countries. The statute also was held to be unconstitutionally vague as applied to the defendant's alleged bribery of officials in Kazakhstan.[122] The Ninth Circuit applied § 1346 to acts of private individuals in a fiduciary relation to the victim, such as a financial planner who defrauded an 87-year-old client.[123]

According to the Second Circuit, paying federal officials to carry out their public duty still constitutes bribery because the intention is to influence an official act. The crime does not require paying officials to violate the law.[124] The offense of bribing a public official (18 USC § 201(b)(2)) can be proved even without proof of a change in the official's conduct.[125]

[g] Money Laundering

Two mid-2008 Supreme Court money laundering decisions made prosecution more difficult by holding that a money laundering case cannot be proved merely by showing concealment of funds during transport. Conviction requires proof that the purpose, and not just the effect, of the transportation was to conceal the nature, location, source, ownership, or control of the funds (18 USC § 1956(a)(2)(B)(i)). Merely concealing money (even in a very obscure place) is not enough for a conviction. The Supreme Court also defined money laundering as involving profits — and not all gross receipts — of an illegal operation. Therefore, paying winning

---

[119] 526 U.S. 398 (1999).

[120] Sabri v. United States, 541 U.S. 600 (2004).

[121] United States v. Valdes, 437 F.3d 1276 (D.C. Cir. 2006).

[122] United States v. Giffen, 326 F. Supp. 2d 497 (S.D.N.Y. 2004).

[123] United States v. Williams, 441 F.3d 716 (9th Cir. 2006).

[124] United States v. Alfisi, 308 F.3d 144 (2d Cir. 2002).

[125] United States v. Quinn, 359 F.3d 666 (4th Cir. 2004).

bets and compensating runners who collect the bets are expenses, not money laundering, unless the prosecutor can show that profits were used to promote illegal activity. However, if the government shows that the purpose of transporting the funds was to conceal their ownership, source, or control, it need not show that the defendant attempted to create a deceptive appearance that the funds were legitimate.[126]

The Third Circuit clarified that unpaid taxes, retained by using the U.S. mail to file false tax returns, are "proceeds" of mail fraud that will state a money-laundering offense under 18 USC § 1956(a)(2).[127]

[9] Trial-Related Offenses

It is a crime to seek to influence a witness' testimony, or to prevent a person from testifying, by means of either positive incentives (bribery) or negative ones (tampering or intimidation). Similar considerations apply to interfering with jurors or potential jurors. Evidence tampering (whether by fabricating false evidence or concealing or destroying actual evidence) is also a crime.

Intentional concealment or destruction of evidence during **civil** discovery can be prosecuted under 18 USC § 1503 (obstruction of justice).[128]

Contempt of court can be either civil or criminal, depending on whether the contempt sanction is intended to punish or coerce. Direct contempt occurs in the actual presence of the court (including proceedings in chambers), whereas indirect or constructive contempt does not. Direct contempt can be punished summarily, whereas a person accused of indirect contempt is entitled to notice (indictment, information, or order to show cause) and a hearing.

Perjury is the making of sworn statements that are known to be false. The degree of a perjury offense depends on whether the statement was made in a sworn writing or in a courtroom. In some jurisdictions, even immaterial lies can constitute perjury; in others, either materiality is an element of the crime, or it goes to the degree of the crime. Proof of perjury requires intention to make false statements under oath — it is not required that the statements be credible enough actually to deceive. In some jurisdictions, the crime can be purged by recanting the false testimony before the court in a timely fashion, whereas other jurisdictions deem that the crime was committed as soon as the knowingly false statements were made.

False statements in unsworn papers filed in bankruptcy court cannot give rise to an indictment under 18 USC § 1001 (false statements in any matter within the jurisdiction of any "department or agency of the United States") because a federal court is neither a department nor an agency.[129] There is no exception under § 1001

---

[126] United States v. Santos, 128 S. Ct. 2020, and Cuellar v. United States, 128 S. Ct. 1994. *See* Pete Yost (AP), *Justices Rule for Defendants on Money Laundering*, 6/2/08 (law.com).

[127] United States v. Yusuf, 536 F.3d 178 (3d Cir. 2008).

[128] United States v. Lundwall, 1 F. Supp. 2d 249 (S.D.N.Y. 1998).

[129] Hubbard v. United States, 514 U.S. 695 (1995).

for the "exculpatory no" — in other words, a simple denial of wrongdoing can be penalized as a false statement.[130]

[10] RICO

Although the Racketeer Influenced and Corrupt Organizations Act, 18 USC §§ 1961–1968 (RICO) was designed to facilitate the prosecution of organized crime figures, in fact the statute is extremely broad, and many individuals other than mobsters can fall afoul of it. RICO punishes a "pattern of racketeering" involving "predicate crimes" defined in 18 USC § 1961. RICO liability is imposed on a "person," a definition that can include a corporation, but ironically has been held not to include a "Cosa Nostra" crime family.[131]

The Cook County Treasurer's Office sells tax liens on delinquent property each year by public auction. The auction has a rule requiring bidders to submit bids in their own name, forbids the use of agents or employees to submit multiple bids on the same parcel, and requires registered bidders to submit a sworn affidavit of compliance. The petitioners and respondents in a 2008 Supreme Court case were all regular participants in the auctions. The respondents charged the petitioners with RICO mail fraud (the legally required notices) on the grounds that their false compliance filings allowed them to receive an unfair share of the liens. The District Court dismissed the RICO allegations, finding that the respondents lacked standing, and they did not receive the alleged misrepresentations so the mail fraud statutes did not come into play. The Seventh Circuit reversed, finding that the respondents were injured by being unfairly deprived of the opportunity to purchase more tax liens. The Supreme Court ruled in mid-2008 that a plaintiff asserting a mail fraud RICO claim is not required to prove reliance on the defendant's alleged misrepresentations. A private RICO cause of action can be based on mail fraud. The gravamen of mail fraud is a scheme to defraud, so any mailing incident to an essential part of the scheme satisfies the statutory mailing element.[132]

A sole owner can be held liable under RICO (as a separate "person") for unlawful conduct of corporate affairs. This is also true of an employee acting in the scope of employment.[133]

A RICO civil conspiracy plaintiff must allege that the overt act in furtherance of the conspiracy that injured the plaintiff was either an act of racketeering under 18 USC § 1961(1), or was otherwise wrongful under RICO. In this case,[134] the plaintiff claimed to have been fired for refusing to participate in unlawful conduct. The Supreme Court said that he had no RICO case, because RICO does not give standing to sue for termination or other act that is not an act or racketeering or another act brought within the ambit of RICO.

---

[130] Brogan v. United States, 522 U.S. 398 (1998).

[131] United States v. Bonanno Organized Crime Family, 879 F.2d 20 (2d Cir. 1989).

[132] Bridge v. Phoenix Bond & Indemnity Co., 128 S. Ct. 2131 (2008).

[133] Cedric Kushner Productions Ltd. v. King, 533 U.S. 158 (2001).

[134] Beck v. Prupis, 529 U.S. 494 (2000).

Civil RICO suits, which carry the potential for treble damage awards, are also permitted, with the additional requirement that racketeering must have caused injured to the plaintiff's business or property.

RICO is violated when a person covered by RICO engages in a pattern (i.e., two or more criminal acts from the list)[135] of racketeering activity that affects an enterprise in interstate commerce, or who uses proceeds from such a pattern. It is only necessary that the person have been indictable, chargeable, or punishable for those acts, not that there was a conviction or even a charge brought.

The list of predicate acts is very long, ranging from federal bribery, counterfeiting, and gambling offenses to criminal copyright infringement. Major state felonies, such as murder, kidnapping, arson, or robbery can also serve as RICO predicates. The most common predicate acts are mail fraud and wire fraud. However, because of the Private Securities Litigation Reform Act of 1995 (see § 6.13[A]), securities fraud cannot serve as a RICO offense.

It is not necessary to prove that the defendant was personally involved in committing, or agreed to commit, two or more RICO predicate acts.[136]

When a RICO action is brought against a street gang that engages in violent but non-economic crime (e.g., gang members killing and attempting to kill other gang members), the Sixth Circuit requires a substantial effect on interstate commerce. The First Circuit applies normal RICO standards, looking for an enterprise that exists in some coherent and cohesive form, as distinct from the pattern of racketeering activity itself. The First Circuit considered a gang's massive arsenal, of guns made outside Massachusetts, to be enough to satisfy the interstate commerce requirement.[137]

Unless a business is permeated by fraud, it does not constitute money laundering under 18 USC § 1956(a)(1)(A)(i) to make use of illegally obtained funds to pay rent and other legitimate business expenses. The statute applies only to illicit income that is funneled back into the criminal enterprise.[138]

[11] Immigration-Related Offenses

The 2003 amendments to the Sentencing Guidelines attempt to resolve conflicts about the meaning of certain terms used to penalize crimes that are directly related to immigration, as well as to define terms that affect the exclusion or removal of aliens who have been convicted of crimes. Guideline 2L1.2 increases

---

[135] At least two predicate acts must have been committed after RICO's effective date, and not more than ten years apart.

[136] Salinas v. United States, 522 U.S. 52 (1997). This case also holds that a person can be convicted under 18 USC § 666 (local official of a federally funded agency accepts a bribe) with or without proof that the bribe had an effect on federal funds.

[137] United States v. Nascimento, 491 F.3d 25 (1st Cir. 2007); *contra* Waucaush v. United States, 380 F.3d 251 (6th Cir. 2004) requiring a substantial effect on interstate commerce if the racketeering activity is non-economic.

[138] United States v. Miles, 360 F.3d 472 (5th Cir. 2004).

the enhancement of offense level for those who have been deported following a criminal conviction, and who subsequently illegally reenter the United States.[139]

State-law drug crimes are aggravated felonies for INA purposes as felonies punishable under the Controlled Substances Act (CSA) only if the crime involves conduct that constitutes a CSA felony.[140]

The Supreme Court held in early 2007 that an indictment charging an alien with an attempt to enter the United States alleges an overt act, and thus is not defective. Therefore, the court did not reach the question of whether omitting an element of an offense from an indictment can ever be considered harmless error: *U.S. v. Resendiz-Ponce*, 549 U.S. 102 (2007). Also in early 2007, the Supreme Court extended 8 USC § 1101(a)(43)(G), allowing removal of alien convicted of a felony theft offense, to the crime of aiding and abetting a theft offense.[141]

The Guidelines adopt the position that an "alien smuggling offense" also includes transporting aliens brought into the United States.[142] No matter when the conviction occurred, the term "sentence of imprisonment" has the same meaning throughout the Guidelines as in 4A1.2.[143] The length of a sentence of imprisonment is calculated including terms imposed when probation, parole, or supervised release is revoked.[144]

The offense of attempted reentry of a deported alien, 8 USC § 1326, requires the defendant to have used another person's identification and acted without lawful authority.[145]

According to the Seventh Circuit, for an alien convicted of illegal reentry into the United States after a prior conviction, "crimes of violence" are not those limited to those listed in the relevant notes to the Guidelines. For this purpose, domestic battery can properly be considered a crime of violence.[146] Unlawful sexual

---

[139] In an illegal reentry case, the alien's prior physical removal is still a base for enhancement under 8 USC § 1326 and Guidelines 2L1.2: United States v. Diaz-Luevano, 494 F.3d 1159 (9th Cir. 2007).

[140] Lopez v. Gonzales, 549 U.S. 47 (2006).

[141] Gonzales v. Duenas-Alvarez 549 U.S. 183 (2007).

[142] United States v. Solis-Campozano, 312 F.3d 164 (5th Cir. 2002). The Ninth Circuit, overruling previous cases, held that under 8 USC § 1324(a)(2), the offense of bringing an alien to the United States is a continuing offense that ends when the initial transporter leaves the alien at a location within the United States: United States v. Lopez, 484 F.3d 1186 (9th Cir. 2007).

[143] *I.e.*, the Guidelines adopt the holdings of United States v. Moreno-Cisneros, 319 F.3d 456 (9th Cir. 2003) *and* United States v. Compian-Torres, 320 F.3d 514 (5th Cir. 2003).

[144] United States v. Hidalgo-Macias, 300 F.3d 281 (2d Cir. 2002) provides that a sentence imposed after revocation is a modification of the original sentence for the original offense, but United States v. Rodriguez-Arreola, 313 F.3d 1064 (8th Cir. 2002) defines the sentence imposed when it is indefinite as the maximum term that the defendant may be required to serve.

[145] United States v. Miranda-Lopez, 532 F.3d 1034 (9th Cir. 2008); semble United States v. Villanueva-Sotelo, 515 F.3d 1234 (D.C. Cir. 2008) — but contra United States v. Mendoza-Gonzalez, 520 F.3d 912 (8th Cir. 2008), United States v. Hurtado, 508 F.3d 603 (11th Cir. 2007), United States v. Montejo, 442 F.3d 213 (4th Cir. 2006).

[146] United States v. Alvarenga-Silva, 324 F.3d 884 (7th Cir. 2003). But the Eighth Circuit held that second-degree manslaughter was neither an aggravated felony nor a crime of violence: United States v. Torres-Villalobos, 487 F.3d 607 (8th Cir. 2007).

intercourse with a minor is a crime of violence as defined by § 1326(b)(2) [deported alien found in the United States].[147] However, a late-2004 Supreme Court decision ruled that a state Driving Under the Influence offense does not include an intent element and therefore is not a crime of violence that can be deemed an aggravated felony: *Leocal v. Ashcroft*, 543 U.S. 1 (Sup. Ct. 2004). Similarly, aggravated burglary is not a crime of violence because the statute does not require intent to commit a crime in the dwelling unlawfully entered.[148]

With respect to the applicability of the Guideline 2L1.2 "crime of violence" enhancement, the Fifth Circuit held that it applies to indecent solicitation of a child (Kansas law) because that is "sexual abuse of a minor,"[149] but, in contrast, the Ninth Circuit ruled that a conviction under Oregon law for second-degree sexual abuse was not a "crime of violence" for this purpose.[150] For sentencing of a person convicted of being a felon in possession of firearms, molesting a minor is a forcible sex offense and therefore a crime of violence.[151] A violation of Florida Stat § 784.045(1)(b), aggravated battery on a pregnant woman, is a crime of violence.[152]

The Ninth, Tenth, and Eleventh Circuits have all held that Guidelines 2L1.2 has no time limit on the age of a conviction used to enhance a sentence in the context of conviction of illegal reentry after deportation.[153]

[See § 19.09[A][1] for more discussion of the effect of United States convictions on immigration status.]

PART 2: CONSTITUTIONAL ISSUES

§ 26.03   CONSTITUTIONAL ISSUES IN CRIMINAL LAW

[A] Introduction

The constant interpretation and re-interpretation of Constitutional guarantees is a very significant part of the court system's role. The major Constitutional issues arise in connection with:

- The Fourth Amendment's guarantee of the right of the people to be protected against unreasonable searches and seizures, and the Amendment's conditions on the issuance of warrants

---

[147] United States v. Gomez-Mendez, 486 F.3d 599 (9th Cir. 2007).

[148] United States v. Herrera-Montes, 490 F.3d 390 (5th Cir. 2007). However, a state felony conviction for possession of a controlled substance with intent to sell is an aggravated felony because of the trafficking element of the crime: Rendon v. Mukasey, 520 F.3d 967 (9th Cir. 2008).

[149] United States v. Ramos-Sanchez, 483 F.3d 400 (5th Cir. 2007).

[150] United States v. Beltran-Munguia, 489 F.3d 1042 (9th Cir. 2007).

[151] United States v. Beliew, 492 F.3d 314 (5th Cir. 2007).

[152] United States v. Llanos-Agostadero, 496 F.3d 1194 (11th Cir. 2007).

[153] United States v. Olmos-Esparza, 484 F.3d 1111(9th Cir. 2007); semble United States v. Torres-Duenas, 461 F.3d 1178 (10th Cir. 2006); United States v. Camacho-Ibarquen, 410 F.3d 1307 (11th Cir. 2005), *cert. denied*, 126 S. Ct. 457.

- The Fifth Amendment's requirement that all prosecutions for "infamous crimes" occur pursuant to a Grand Jury indictment and its prohibitions on double jeopardy and compelled self-incrimination
- The Sixth Amendment guarantees of the right to a speedy trial, a trial that is open to the public, an impartial jury, confrontation with accusers, and the assistance of counsel
- The Eighth Amendment's ban on cruel and unusual punishment.

In recent years, and especially in connection with the figurative war on drugs and the literal war on terrorism, very significant changes have been made in the way the courts read the Fourth Amendment.

The post-9/11 package of antiterrorism provisions includes broader authorization for covert searches (i.e., the subject of the search is not aware that a search has occurred) by federal law enforcement officers using "sneak and peek" warrants. However, use of such warrants is not restricted to cases of suspected terrorism.

[B] Fourth Amendment Issues

[1] Introduction

The Fourth Amendment prohibits unreasonable searches and seizures. The basic rule (subject to certain exceptions) is that a search warrant, issued by a neutral judge, is required to justify a search. The issuing judge must have probable cause, based on sworn testimony or written affirmation of a law enforcement officer, to issue a warrant.

General warrants are not permitted; the warrant must be specific as to the place to be searched and the items to be searched for. Probable cause must be shown that a federal crime has been or is being committed; a warrant cannot be issued in anticipation of future crime.

However, a number of well-established circumstances will justify a warrantless search. These include a search incident to a lawful arrest; a pat-down pursuant to a "stop" (detention that does not rise to the status of an arrest); a vehicle search; or a search occurring in exigent circumstances that preclude obtaining a warrant. A search pursuant to an invalid warrant can be justified by the good-faith reliance of the law enforcement officers executing the warrant.

The protection offered by the Fourth Amendment is personal, and only a victim of an unlawful search or seizure has standing to seek exclusion of the evidence; a non-victim who is incriminated by such evidence does not have standing.[154]

The Fourth Amendment is violated by a hospital's policy of performing warrantless drug testing, without consent, on pregnant women who show signs

---

[154] Alderman v. United States, 394 U.S. 165 (1969); Brown v. United States, 411 U.S. 223 (1973).

of drug addiction, and then reporting the test results to the police. The Supreme Court refused to apply the "special needs" exception for searches that can be done without individualized suspicion because they are done for purposes other than law enforcement.[155]

[2] Issue Checklist

❑ Were police officers or other state actors involved? The Fourth Amendment does not apply to the conduct of private citizens, unless they were acting in concert with or at the behest of state actors

❑ Was there a detention of a person or seizure of an item?
  • The Fourth Amendment is not violated if the police approach individuals in a public place and question them, as long as a reasonable person would know he or she was free to terminate questioning
  • A consensual interview with the police is not a search
  • Mere pursuit by the police is not a search
  • Investigative stops must fall within accepted parameters

❑ If so, did it have sufficient basis?
  • Police must act on reasonable suspicion: e.g., pursuant to a reliable tip; if a vehicle is observed to be speeding or otherwise breaking traffic laws

❑ Brief stops are to be distinguished from arrests

❑ Was the alleged search actually inspection of areas and materials in plain sight?

❑ Was there a reasonable expectation of privacy in the place searched and the items seized (e.g., there is no expectation of privacy in discarded or abandoned items)?

❑ Did the person giving consent to a warrantless search have the power to consent?

❑ Was the scope of consent exceeded? For instance, agreement to allow the police to "look at" a car would not extend to disassembling the car

❑ Searches pursuant to a warrant
  • Was the issuing magistrate neutral and detached?
  • Were supporting affidavits adequate?
  • Was the informant reliable?
  • Did the police officer do additional investigation to substantiate the tip?
  • Was the information relied on to support the warrant timely or stale?
  • Does the warrant application justify the conclusion that the items sought are on the premises to be searched?
  • Was there nexus between the premises to be searched (which need not be the actual site of criminal activity) and the material seized?
  • Was the material seized included in the warrant?
  • Is the warrant tailored to items related to alleged criminal acts, described with reasonable particularity, or is it overbroad?

---

[155] Ferguson v. Charleston, S.C., 532 U.S. 67 (2001).

- If the warrant proves to be invalid, did the policy rely on it in good faith?
- Did the police "knock and announce" when executing the warrant, or were there exigent circumstances excusing this requirement?
- Protective sweep of premises; search of "grabbable area"
❑ Search incident to a lawful arrest/pat-down incident to a lawful stop or observance of drug interdiction protocols
❑ Vehicle search
- Mobility of car is an exigent circumstance that can excuse warrantless search
- Legitimacy of traffic stops
- Which parts of vehicle (or containers within vehicle) can be searched incident to traffic stop or arrest of driver or passenger (inventory search)?
- Potential forfeiture of car used in drug trafficking vitiates expectation of privacy
❑ Covert search — as authorized by the USA PATRIOT Act.

Under the Fourth Amendment, a valid search warrant or arrest warrant can issue only on the basis of an affidavit or complaint setting forth facts establishing probable cause. A search warrant requires substantial evidence that:

- The items sought are connected with criminal activity
- The items can be found in the place searched.

In contrast, an arrest warrant requires proof of probable cause that:

- An offense has been committed
- The person named in the warrant has committed it.

A search warrant must describe the place to be searched in enough detail for the police to identify the place, and the items to be seized must be described specifically enough to remove any element of police discretion.

[3] The Exclusionary Rule

Evidence obtained by illegal search and seizure cannot be admitted in a criminal or quasi-criminal (e.g., forfeiture) case if a timely application to suppress or exclude the evidence (see § 26.04[J][3][a]) is made. However, the right to exclusion can be waived, by a guilty plea or failure to object at the proper time.

Murray v. United States[156] defines the scope of the exclusionary rule as:

- Tangible materials seized during an unlawful search
- Testimony about knowledge acquired during an unlawful search
- Tangible or testimonial evidence deriving from an unlawful search.

---

[156] 487 U.S. 533 (1988).

Recent decisions are far more restrictive as to the scope of the exclusionary rule than earlier decisions. *Compare California v. Acevedo*[157] and *Minnesota v. Dickerson*[158] (searches and seizures outside the judicial process, without prior approval, are per se unreasonable under the Fourth Amendment unless they fall into a few specific well-defined categories of exceptions) with *Vernonia School District v. Acton*[159] (the Fourth Amendment does not require a warrant to establish the reasonableness of all government searches, and probable cause is not inevitably required when a warrant is not necessary).

A convicted felon who was under investigation for violation of a Temporary Restraining Order was indicted under 18 USC § 922(g)(1) (possession of a firearm by a felon). When he was arrested at his home for violating the restraining order, one of the arresting officers tried to give a Miranda warning, but was interrupted by the defendant, who said that he knew his rights. The Supreme Court held that the lack of warnings did not require suppression of the physical fruits of a voluntary statement. Because *Miranda* was decided to prevent defendants' from being forced to testify against themselves at trial, non-testimonial evidence obtained via voluntary statements is not a violation of *Miranda*.[160]

State Constitutions and state statutes may be either more or less protective of individuals than the U.S. Constitution. A state Constitutional amendment that eliminates the exclusionary rule with respect to evidence seized contrary to state — but not federal — law does not violate the Due Process clause.[161] About a dozen states have refused to enact a good-faith exception to the exclusionary rule.

The exclusionary rule does not apply to illegally seized evidence (e.g., weapons found in a parolee's home) used in parole revocation hearings, because allowing the evidence to be used in the limited context of parole revocation hearings does not significantly encourage police misconduct.[162] Courts differ on the application (if any) of the exclusionary rule to civil cases. The decision depends on whether the court believes that exclusion will deter improper police conduct. In general, the exclusionary rule is not applicable in Grand Jury proceedings.[163]

The exclusionary rule does not require exclusion of evidence obtained pursuant to an arrest that was based on erroneous information.[164] An early 2009 decision, with the Justices splitting 5-4, held that evidence stemming from an unlawful arrest was nevertheless admissible. The case involved an arrest made,

---

[157] 500 U.S. 565 (1992).

[158] 508 U.S. 366 (1993).

[159] 515 U.S. 646 (1995).

[160] United States v. Patane, 542 U.S. 630 (2004). *But see* State v. Knapp, 700 N.W.2d 899 (Wis. 2005): the Wisconsin Constitution prevents admission of physical evidence obtained as a direct result of an intentional *Miranda* violation.

[161] California v. Greenwood, 486 U.S. 35 (1986).

[162] Pennsylvania Board of Probation & Parole v. Scott, 524 U.S. 357 (1998).

[163] United States v. Calandra, 414 U.S. 338 (1974).

[164] Arizona v. Evans, 514 U.S. 1 (1985).

and guns and drugs found, when, as a result of poor record-keeping, the police erroneously believed that the petitioner was subject to an outstanding arrest warrant. (The warrant had been withdrawn.) The majority opinion describes exclusion of evidence as a last resort, under a sliding-scale analysis of whether police abuse was deliberate enough that it could be deterred by exclusion of evidence, and culpable enough that the justice system should exclude the evidence. The majority called for the conviction and 27-month sentence to be upheld, because the error stemmed from an isolated act of negligence unrelated to the arrest, not systemic error or reckless disregard of the Constitution.[164A] Nor does it apply to evidence that would have inevitably been discovered through an independent source that is free of the taint of the unlawful search.[165] It is permissible to use evidence that was obtained in reasonable reliance on a warrant that was later found not to be supported by probable cause.[166] A good-faith exception to the exclusionary rule is also allowed when the police act in objectively reasonable reliance on a statute that is later found objectionable under the Fourth Amendment.[167]

Chambers v. Maroney, 399 U.S. 42 (1970) and *Fahy v. Connecticut*, 375 U.S. 84 (1963) hold that admission of evidence that was unreasonably seized can be harmless error, if the defendant could not have been prejudiced by the admission — i.e., it did not contribute to the conviction. But if it was contributory, reversal is required even if there was enough other evidence to justify the conviction.

Evidence that, because of the exclusionary rule, cannot be admitted in the case in chief can be used to impeach the testimony of a defendant who testifies,[168] but not the testimony of defense witnesses[169] because a defendant who chooses to testify assumes an obligation of truthfulness.

[4] What Is a Search?

The question is not trivial, because if no "search" has occurred, clearly there has been no unreasonable search. *Maryland v. Macon*[170] defines a search as an infringement of what society considers an expectation of privacy. Looking at items in plain sight — even if a device such as a flashlight or binoculars is used — does not constitute a search. See, e.g., *Coolidge v. New Hampshire*.[171]

Thermal heat scanning of a house (to determine if marijuana is being grown inside) constitutes a search, and therefore is presumed unreasonable without a warrant.[172] The standard for *Terry* stops (reasonable suspicion) [see § 26.03[B][8]]

[164A] Herring v. U.S., No. 07-513 (1/14/09).

[165] Murray v. United States, 487 U.S. 533 (1988).

[166] United States v. Leon, 468 U.S. 997 (1984).

[167] Illinois v. Krull, 480 U.S. 340 (1987).

[168] Michigan v. Harvey, 494 U.S. 344 (1990).

[169] James v. Illinois, 493 U.S. 307 (1990).

[170] 472 U.S. 463 (1985).

[171] 403 U.S. 443 (1971). Aerial survey is not a search: California v. Ciraolo, 476 U.S. 1819 (1986).

[172] Kyllo v. United States, 533 U.S. 27 (2001).

also applies to issuance of an investigative warrant to perform thermal imaging from outside the house.[173]

In 2001, the Supreme Court ruled that it does not constitute a search and seizure for Fourth Amendment purposes to arrest an individual for violating a statute that is penalized as a misdemeanor or lesser offense (in this case, a mandatory seat belt law) that is punishable only by a fine and not by incarceration.[174]

Collecting DNA under the DNA Analysis Backlog Elimination Act to put into the Combined DNA Index System database is not an unreasonable search and seizure that violates the Fourth Amendment.[175]

In a prosecution for illegal re-entry into the United States after an aggravated felony conviction, the Ninth Circuit held that a license plate check that yields information about car ownership and criminal record is not a search for Fourth Amendment purposes, so the it did not constitute an unlawful search for the sheriff to stop the truck in which the defendant was a passenger; ask for ID; and call in the driver's license to the police department dispatcher.[176]

The Ninth Circuit, holding that there was neither a search nor a seizure, did not require a warrant for placing a magnetized tracking device on the undercarriage of a car that U.S. Forest Service agents had seen on a surveillance video of a marijuana patch within a national forest.[177]

Early in 2004, the Third Circuit ruled that there is no Fourth Amendment violation in using audio and video monitoring equipment that recorded only conversations that occurred when a consenting informant was present.[178]

It was not a violation of either the Fourth Amendment or the federal wiretap laws to get a warrant to install a "key logger" on the defendant's personal computer, and use it to get the password for an encrypted file. The District Court for the

---

[173] United States v. Kattaria, 503 F.3d 703 (8th Cir. 2007).

[174] Atwater v. City of Lago Vista, 532 U.S. 318 (2001).

[175] United States v. Kraklio, 451 F.3d 922 (8th Cir. 2006). The Tenth Circuit permitted testing of non-violent felony offenders under the DNA Analysis Backlog Elimination Act even if there is no individualized suspicion that they committed further crimes. Banks v. Mechum, 490 F.3d 1178 (10th Cir. 2007). The First Circuit ruled in 2007 that it is not a violation of the Fourth Amendment to require a person on supervised release to provide a blood sample for the DNA database, but did not resolve the question of whether it is permissible to keep the profile in the database after termination of supervised release: United States v. Weikert, 504 F.3d 1 (1st Cir. 2007). The First Circuit also upheld collection of DNA even from non-violent felons sentenced to probation, on the grounds that probationers have a diminished interest in privacy, and the collection is only a minimal intrusion. The First Circuit held that DNA could be useful in solving non-violent as well as violent crimes, and to avoid selective enforcement, DNA can be collected from every convicted person who is released conditionally (on supervised release or probation): United States v. Stewart, 532 F.3d 32 (1st Cir. 2008).

[176] United States v. Diaz-Castaneda, 494 F.3d 1146 (9th Cir. 2007).

[177] United States v. McIver, 186 F.3d 1119 (9th Cir. 1999).

[178] United States v. Lee, 89 Fed. Appx. 806 (3d Cir. 2004). The Seventh Circuit ruled that surveillance, including placing a tracking device on the suspects' car without a warrant, was not a search, and therefore the evidence was admissible and the conviction for manufacturing methamphetamine was sustained: United States v. Garcia, 474 F.3d 994 (7th Cir. 2007).

District of New Jersey decided that the key logger did not intercept a wire com-munication, and therefore the wiretap laws were not triggered.[179]

Inspecting "open fields" is not a search, but a distinction is drawn between "curtilage" — the fields, yard, etc. surrounding a building — and "open fields." The distinction depends on factors such as the perception of the occupants; how close the alleged curtilage is to the house; whether it is enclosed or screened from view; and if its use is primarily residential.

Various results have been reached about garbage placed outside a home for collection, and other abandoned items.[180]

The Fourth Amendment governs the conduct of police and their agents, so it is generally inapplicable to a search performed by a private individual with no police participation. The individual (even if he or she wishes to cooperate with a police investigation) must not be acting at the order, request, or suggestion of the police for this exception to apply: *Coolidge v. New Hampshire*.[181]

The protection of the Fourth Amendment runs to persons, not places, so ownership of property has some relevance, but the real test is the invasion of a person's legitimate right of privacy in the place that has been invaded.[182] The Supreme Court ruled in 2006 that it violates the Fourth Amendment to perform a search based on consent of one co-occupant of a home, when another co-occupant is present and refuses consent.[183]

The Ninth Circuit held in 2008 that the initial search of storage units after the defendant's arrest for buying methamphetamine precursor chemicals was valid. It was a protective sweep justified by concern about the possible presence of accom-plices. However, the second search, two hours later, was found invalid. The Ninth Circuit refused to apply a "plain view" exception to the warrant requirement, and strictly circumscribed the warrantless search. The defendant was temporarily living in the storage unit. He refused to consent to search of the storage unit, although the person who rented the storage unit consented. The Ninth Circuit said that the defendant lived in the unit with permission of the rental agent, who was in a position somewhere between a landlord (who cannot give consent to search of a dwelling) and a co-tenant (who can). According to the Ninth Circuit,

---

[179] United States v. Scarfo, 180 F. Supp. 2d 572 (D.N.J. 2001).

[180] *See, e.g.*, California v. Greenwood, 486 U.S. 35 (1988) (no reasonable expectation of privacy in discarded materials); United States v. Redmon, 138 F.3d 1109 (7th Cir. 1998) (garbage containers placed for collection on a shared driveway can be searched without a warrant; in this analysis, abandonment is a more significant factor than cartilage); State v. Sampson, 765 A.2d 629 (Md. 2001) (expectation of privacy is surrendered by discarding garbage even if the materials are within the curtilage). But New Hampshire rejected California v. Greenwood, and held in 2003 that there is a reasonable expectation of privacy in garbage put out for collection: State v. Goss, 150 N.H. 46 (N.H. 2003).

[181] 403 U.S. 443 (1971).

[182] United States v. Salvucci, 448 U.S. 83 (1980).

[183] Georgia v. Randolph, 547 U.S. 103 (2006).

there is no requirement that an occupant pay rent to have standing to object to the place where he lives being searched, and an objection from a co-tenant remains effective until there is some objective manifestation that he has changed his mind.[184]

[a] Reasonable Expectation of Privacy

California held that the defendant had a reasonable expectation of privacy within his home, so testimony about police observation that the defendant was packing drugs, obtained when the police made a warrantless entry into the side yard of the house and looked through an uncurtained window that was not visible from the sidewalk, had to be suppressed.[185]

A guest visiting a friend during the day has a Fourth Amendment expectation of privacy because nearly all social guests do have such an expectation; a commercial justification for presence on the property is not required.[186] Montana ruled that the state and federal Constitutions give a party guest a reasonable expectation of privacy in a closed bathroom. In general, guests do not have an expectation of privacy in the whole house, but bathrooms are more personal because of the activities that are carried out there.[187]

The Ninth Circuit treated a garage whose door was open exactly like any other part of a house where work is done and possessions are stored. Therefore, a warrant was required to arrest the defendant.[188]

Illinois ruled that a defendant had a reasonable expectation of privacy in a barn owned by his mother, and outside the curtilage of his home. Although the barn was owned by his mother, the defendant had a possessory interest in the entire farm and had the ability to exclude unwanted persons from it. The court treated the structure as a building even though it was open and merely used for storage. Therefore, the warrantless search was improper.[189]

The Second Circuit held in 2003 that a warrant is not required when the police monitor or record the output of a hidden video camera carried by an informant into a home. The court treated the video camera as the equivalent of audio recording equipment, and held that there is no reasonable expectation that guests will not record activities that are openly conducted within a home.[190]

---

[184] United States v.Murphy, 516 F.3d 1117 (9th Cir. 2008).

[185] California v. Camacho, 23 Cal. 4th 824 (Cal. 2000).

[186] Morton v. United States, 68 L.W. 1119 (D.C. App. 8/21/99).

[187] State v. Smith, 97 P.3d 567 (Mont. 2004).

[188] United States v. Oaxaca, 233 F.3d 1154 (9th Cir. 2000). *See also* Halsema v. State, 823 N.E.2d 668 (Ind. 2005): an apartment tenant who consented to search by the police for evidence of a crime committed by someone else who had been staying in the apartment could not give valid consent to search of a drawer in a bureau that was used exclusively by the suspect.

[189] People v. Pitman, 813 N.E.2d 93 (Ill. 2004).

[190] United States v. Davis, 326 F.3d 361 (2d Cir. 2003).

Some expectation of privacy is recognized in business and commercial premises, but to a lesser degree than in a residence,[191] but there is no expectation of privacy in a prison cell.[192]

Someone who pays a short visit to a home for commercial purposes (in this case, the none-too-lawful commercial purpose of bagging cocaine) does not have a reasonable expectation of privacy within the home.[193]

A reasonable expectation of privacy has been deemed to exist in a hotel room[194] and in a taxi.[195] Searches of schoolchildren are analyzed for their reasonableness under all the circumstances, and probable cause is not required to search a student's gym locker.[196]

[b] "Plain View" and "Plain Touch"

The "plain view" doctrine of *Minnesota v. Dickerson*, 508 U.S. 366 (1993) authorizes a seizure if the police were lawfully in a position from which they could observe an object of an immediately apparent incriminating nature, and if they had lawful access to the object.

Property moved by one police officer during a lawful search can be in the "plain view" of another officer, thus justifying a warrantless seizure by the second officer. In this case, a purse and ID card, evidence of an armed robbery, were removed from the glove compartment and placed on the front seat of a car during a valid protective search (i.e., a search to find weapons that could be used against the police officers).[197]

Dickerson also authorizes seizure of an object by reason of "plain touch": a suspicious outline or mass becomes apparent during a pat-down for weapons during a *Terry* stop (§ 26.03[B][8]). However, an Alabama case refused to apply this principle when a police officer frisking a suspect found a Tic-Tacs container (the officer knew these containers are frequently used to hold drugs) and ordered the suspect to open it. The rationale is that the feel of a closed container, unlike the feel of contraband itself, is not incriminating enough to furnish probable cause.[198]

When property is seized pursuant to a warrant, Due Process requires reasonable notice to the owner that the property has been seized, so that the owner can take steps to recover the property.[199]

---

[191] New York v. Burger, 482 U.S. 691 (1987). *E.g.*, Colorado found that the manager of a liquor store had a reasonable expectation of privacy in the store's back room, even though he was aware that there were surveillance video cameras installed. Therefore, he was protected against warrantless entry into the room by police officers pursuing two suspects who found marijuana belonging to the manager in the room: People v. Galvadon, 103 P.3d 923 (Colo. 2005).

[192] Hudson v. Palmer, 468 U.S. 517 (1984).

[193] Minnesota v. Carter, 523 U.S. 83 (1998).

[194] United States v. Allen, 106 F.3d 695 (6th Cir. 1997).

[195] United States v. Santiago, 950 F. Supp. 590 (S.D.N.Y. 1996).

[196] New Jersey v. TLO, 469 U.S. 325 (1984).

[197] Maddox v. United States, 745 A.2d 284 (D.C. 2000).

[198] *Ex Parte* Warren, 783 So. 2d 86 (Ala. 2000).

[199] City of West Covina v. Perkins, 525 U.S. 234 (1999), but the police do not have to inform the owner how to get the property back.

[c] Canine Sniffs

The topic of appropriate use of sniffer dogs might be described as the limits of the "plain smell" doctrine. In 2005, the Supreme Court held that a canine sniff during a lawful traffic stop does not violate the Fourth Amendment, because there is no reasonable expectation of privacy where the dog reveals only the presence or absence of contraband. Nor did the Supreme Court require independent suspicion for policy performing a traffic stop to use the sniffer dog.[200]

Minnesota ruled that a drug detection dog's sniff outside a self-storage unit is a search, although the court could not decide whether probable cause or only reasonable suspicion would be required to justify the search.[201] However, Maryland has held that a canine sniff from a corridor through a closed door is not a search; Nebraska has held that there is no reasonable expectation of privacy in the hallway outside an apartment.[202] Indiana ruled that the Fourth Circuit permits suspicionless canine sniffs of the outside of student cars parked in a school lot.[203]

[5] Search Warrants

Although certain exceptions apply,[204] the basic search-and-seizure rules revolve around the issuance of a warrant by a neutral and detached magistrate. According to *Michigan v. Summers*,[205] a search warrant implies a power of reasonable detention of occupants of the place being searched, while the search continues. However, absent exigent circumstances or a valid consent, it is not permitted to search for the subject of an arrest warrant in another person's house.[206] Once a search has been made pursuant to a warrant, the general rule is that the police may not return to make a further, warrantless search.[207]

The Supreme Court upheld the practice of issuing anticipatory search warrants, to be executed in the future when a condition occurred (in this case, the arrival of child pornography that the defendant ordered as part of a sting operation). Under *United States v. Grubbs*, a valid anticipatory warrant satisfies the Fourth Amendment if it was issued based on a fair probability that contraband or evidence of a crime will be found. Anticipatory warrants can satisfy the

---

[200] Illinois v. Caballes, 543 U.S. 405 (2005).

[201] State v. Carter, 697 N.W.2d 199 (Minn. 2005).

[202] Fitzgerald v. State, 937 A.2d 939 (Md. App. 2003); United States v. Langarica Ambrosia, 1999 U.S. Dist. LEXIS 15412 (D. Neb. 9/9/99). *See also* State v. Ortiz, 600 N.W.2d 805 (Neb. 1999): a canine sniff is an "investigative tool" that can be used to develop probable cause to issue a search warrant, as long as there was reasonable suspicion to use the dog in the first place.

[203] Myers v. State, 839 N.E.2d 1154 (Ind. 2005).

[204] For instance, a warrant is not required for administrative inspection of business premises that are subject to federal regulation — e.g., OSHA inspections: Donovan v. Dewey, 452 U.S. 594 (1981); New York v. Burger, 482 U.S. 691 (1987).

[205] 452 U.S. 692 (1981).

[206] Steagald v. United States, 451 U.S. 204 (1981).

[207] Michigan v. Clifford, 466 U.S. 287 (1984).

"particularity" requirement by describing the place to be searched and the person or things to be seized. The triggering condition need not be included in the warrant.[208]

In a Supreme Court case decided early in 2001, the police had probable cause to believe that the defendant had marijuana in his house. For a period of about two hours, while the police sought a search warrant, they refused to let the suspect enter his house unless accompanied by a police officer. The Supreme Court refused to suppress the marijuana found pursuant to the warrant that was eventually issued, because the restraint on the suspect was reasonable and tailored to the law enforcement need to prevent the defendant from destroying evidence. On balance, the minimal intrusion on the defendant's privacy was reasonable.[209]

The Supreme Court decided in March 2005 that it did not constitute an unreasonable search for the police to keep the occupant of a house and three other people handcuffed and locked up in the garage for a two- to three-hour period while a search warrant was executed. Although the handcuffs constituted a separate intrusion on privacy, they were justified by the inherently dangerous situation of searching for dangerous gang members and weapons.[210]

Franks v. Delaware,[211] permits the defendant to seek suppression of evidence on the grounds that the police officer/affiant lied on the warrant application; included misinformation; or omitted information with reckless disregard for truth. However, the falsehood or omission must be material. The defendant must furnish evidence to support the claim of falsehood in order for the court to grant a "Franks hearing." *Franks* applies only if the affiant, not someone else (e.g., the informant) was lying, and the lie or misstatement must be material, not trivial. The Seventh Circuit reversed a conviction of drug possession with intent to distribute based on the defendant's substantial preliminary showing that the search of his home violated *Franks*; this showing meant that he could get a hearing to challenge the affidavit supporting the search warrant.[212]

Questions about the competency of evidence produced by an allegedly illegal search or seizure are questions of law, to be determined by the judge — especially questions as to the validity of a warrant.

Analysis of the conditions of entry pursuant to a "no-knock" warrant involve considerations such as whether the police reasonably believed that announcing their entry would lead to danger, futility or impairment of the investigation. It is not relevant whether or not property was destroyed.[213] The Supreme Court ruled that the "emergency aid" exception to the Fourth Amendment justifies a

---

[208] United States v. Grubbs, 547 U.S. 90 (2006).

[209] Illinois v. McArthur, 531 U.S. 326 (2001).

[210] Muehler v. Mena, 544 U.S. 93 (2005).

[211] 438 U.S. 154 (1978).

[212] United States v. Harris, 464 F.3d 733 (7th Cir. 2006).

[213] United States v. Ramirez, 523 U.S. 65 (1998). United States v. Banks, 540 U.S. 31 (2003), holds that a 15–20 second wait was constitutionally acceptable given the exigent circumstances (the likelihood that a suspected cocaine dealer would dispose of evidence).

warrantless entry into a home if, under the circumstances, a reasonable officer would believe that an occupant of the premises is seriously injured or in imminent danger of serious injury (e.g., from a threat of ongoing domestic violence). The exception applies irrespective of the actual subjective motivation of the police in entering the premises.[214]

It is unreasonable for the police to apply deadly force to arrest a fleeing felon unless the suspect threatens the arresting officers with a weapon, or unless there is probable cause to believe that the suspect has committed a crime involving the infliction or threatened infliction of serious physical harm.[215]

If a warrant is invalid in whole or in part, the doctrine of redaction provides that only evidence obtained under the invalid part of the warrant need be suppressed. Furthermore, two 1984 cases[216] take the position that the exclusionary rule exists to deter knowing misconduct by the police. Therefore, if the police rely in good faith on an invalid warrant, exclusion is not required because there has been no knowing misconduct.[217] The Sixth Circuit joined the Eighth Circuit (but disagreed with the Ninth and Eleventh Circuits), applying the good faith exception when a search warrant was supported by an affidavit that was the fruit of an unconstitutional search and seizure — as long as a reasonable officer would not have been aware of the impropriety of the earlier search.[218]

The Ninth Circuit applied the "collective knowledge" doctrine to hold that if one police officer has facts adding up to reasonable suspicion or probable cause for a warrant exception, and he makes an appropriate order or request, the Fourth Amendment is not violated if another officer makes a warrantless stop, search, or arrest.[219]

Early in 2004, the Supreme Court decided a case involving a warrant application signed by an agent of the Bureau of Alcohol, Tobacco and Firearms (ATF), describing the weapons, explosives, and records that the agent believed were to be found at the petitioner's ranch. When issued, the warrant did not identify any of the items to be seized. The Supreme Court held that the search had to be analyzed as a warrantless search and hence presumptively unreasonable because the warrant was so defective as to be a nullity. Furthermore, the Supreme Court did not permit the

---

[214] Brigham City, Utah v. Stuart, 547 U.S. 398 (2006). The Seventh Circuit ruled that police observation of movement within a house was not an exigent circumstance sufficient to justify a warrantless entry; hence, the cocaine discovered in the house was not admissible and the possession conviction was vacated: United States v. Ellis, 499 F.3d 686 (7th Cir. 2007).

[215] Tennessee v. Garner, 471 U.S. 1 (1985).

[216] United States v. Leon, 468 U.S. 897 (1984) and Massachusetts v. Sheppard, 468 U.S. 981 (1984).

[217] Illinois v. Krull, 480 U.S. 340 (1987) uses a similar rationale to permit introduction of evidence obtained by the police in reliance on a statute later found unconstitutional.

[218] United States v. McClain, 444 F.3d 5567 (6th Cir. 2005). *Contra* United States v. McGough, 412 F.3d 1232 (11th Cir. 2005) and United States v. Wanless, 882 F.2d 1459 (9th Cir. 1989), which reject the good-faith exception where the warrant is invalid.

[219] United States v. Ramirez (Beltran), 473 F.3d 1026 (9th Cir. 2007).

ATF agent to claim qualified immunity, because no reasonable law enforcement officer could have thought the warrant was acceptable.[220]

Later, a group of BATF agents secured a search warrant that, at the time the magistrate issued it, satisfied the Fourth Amendment requirement of particularity. Between the time the warrant issued and the time of the search, the supporting affidavit that described the items to be seized had been placed under seal, and therefore was not present at the time of the search. The owner of the warehouse that was searched sued the agents for money damages after weapons were seized from the warehouse. The Sixth Circuit ruled for the agents: the warrant satisfied the particularity requirement when it was issued, and the agents behaved reasonably when they carried out the search.[221]

On a related issue, a prosecutor who makes false factual statements in the affidavit that is part of the application for an arrest warrant can be sued for civil rights damages under 42 USC § 1983, because absolute prosecutorial immunity does not extend to falsehoods. In 2009, the Supreme Court ruled that prosecutors are entitled to absolute immunity in § 1983 suits for actions that are intimately associated with the judicial phase of the process, but immunity is not absolute when a prosecutor engages in investigations or administrative tasks where he or she is not acting as an officer of the court. (The question was whether supervisory prosecutors were immune in a prisoner's suit alleging failure to disclose information that could have been used to impeach the main prosecution witness.) The Supreme Court ruled that the decision about what to disclose was directly connected to basic trial advocacy, and it would be irrational to immunize the prosecutor while imposing liability on the supervisor for negligent training or supervision.[222]

[6] Searches Incident to a Lawful Arrest

In the course of a lawful arrest, the police can search the arrestee's person and the area within his or her immediate reach.[223] An arrest is always proper when made pursuant to a valid arrest warrant. It can also be proper in exigent circumstances, e.g., when the police officer has actually observed a crime in progress or observed suspicious behavior (such as the exchange of money for glassine envelopes or vials), or has enough reasonable information (including hearsay) to conclude that the suspect committed a felony.[224]

---

[220] Groh v. Ramirez, 540 U.S. 551 (2004).

[221] Baranski v. Fifteen Unknown Agents of the BATF, 401 F.3d 419 (6th Cir. 2006). The majority said that *Groh* really dealt with the facial invalidity of the warrant and not how the search was performed, so reference to an affidavit which is not attached can be proper.

[222] Kalina v. Fletcher, 522 U.S. 118 (1997). Van de Kamp v. Goldstein, No. 07-854 (1/26/09).

[223] New York v. Belton, 453 U.S. 454 (1981).

[224] If the defendant challenges the validity of a warrantless arrest, the prosecution has the burden of coming forward with evidence that the arrest satisfied the standard of probable cause. The probable cause determination when the arrest is made pursuant to a tip from an informant depends on the totality of the circumstances: Illinois v. Gates, 462 U.S. 213 (1983). Some jurisdictions

The late-2004 Supreme Court case of *Devenpick v. Alford*, 543 U.S. 146, holds that the arresting officer's state of mind is irrelevant. A warrantless arrest is acceptable under the Fourth Amendment if at the time of the arrest the facts known to the officer provide probable cause to believe that a crime is being committed or has been committed. It is not necessary that there be a connection between the arrest and the offense originally suspected; the Supreme Court did not believe that requiring such a connection would prevent improper arrests. The Supreme Court noted that, although it is good policy to inform an arrestee of the reason for the arrest, it is not mandatory; the court noted that imposing a relatedness requirement would be likely to increase the number of arrests where the arrestee was not so informed.

Alford involves a rather unusual fact pattern. The police approached the defendant, believing that he was impersonating a police officer at an accident scene. During the initial encounter, the police discovered that the suspect was taping the encounter, so they arrested him for violating the state Privacy Act. The state court dismissed the charges; Alford sued in federal court for violations of the Fourth and Fourteenth Amendments. The Ninth Circuit ruled that the arrest was made without probable cause because of the lack of connection between the reason for the investigation and the arrest, but the Supreme Court reversed.

When a lawful arrest is made, the arresting officers are permitted to make a search incident to the arrest, to prevent destruction of evidence and to remove weapons that could be used to injure the arresting officer.

However, exceeding the permitted scope of search incident to arrest violates the Fourth Amendment, so any evidence so obtained must be excluded.[225] The permissible scope is limited to the person of the arrestee and the areas within his or her immediate control. The search cannot precede the arrest and also be used to justify the arrest if contraband is discovered.[226]

When the police had a warrant authorizing search of the suspect's mouth for packets of drugs, and the suspect refused to open his mouth, the Seventh Circuit found it permissible to have a doctor administer a general anesthetic to facilitate the search. The particular anesthetic used posed low risks, and packets of cocaine held in the mouth are dangerous in and of themselves.[227]

Officers executing an arrest warrant who have a reasonable belief that the suspect is in a building can enter that building and search places where a person could hide; but once the arrest is made, it is not legitimate to use the pretext of looking for the person to search the other rooms of the building.[228]

---

differentiate between misdemeanor arrests (which can only be made if misdemeanor was committed in the presence of the arresting officer) and felony arrests (which can be made based on reasonable cause determinations).

[225] Horton v. California, 496 U.S. 128 (1990).

[226] Smith v. Ohio, 494 U.S. 541 (1990).

[227] United States v. Husband, 312 F.3d 247 (7th Cir. 2002).

[228] Maryland v. Buie, 494 U.S. 325 (1990).

It is permissible to detain and frisk a visitor who appears just after a house has been searched pursuant to a warrant, if the police have a reasonable suspicion that the visitor is armed and dangerous.[229]

When a person is arrested at home, a precautionary search can be made, without a warrant, probable cause, or even reasonable suspicion, provided that it is limited to places immediately adjoining the place of the arrest from which an attack could be launched. The police are permitted to make a protective sweep, based on reasonable suspicion that a dangerous person could be hiding in the places to be inspected.

The Tenth Circuit has ruled[230] that the Fourth Amendment justifies a search of the covered area of a sports utility vehicle (covered by a built-in vinyl cover) incident to the arrest of the driver. In general, Connecticut accepts the "protective sweep" doctrine — that is, a warrantless sweep of the immediate area can be made to protect the safety of police officers, even in connection with a warrantless arrest that occurs outside a residence. However, in the case at bar, the court rejected the validity of a sweep because of the lack of articulable facts about threats to the safety of the police.[231]

A 2003 Fifth Circuit case authorizes a protective sweep that does not result in arrest, where the police have suspicion, but not probable cause to enter a home. The sweep must be limited to a cursory inspection of whatever area the police reasonably believe could harbor someone who threatens the safety of the police.[232]

In late 2004, the Tenth Circuit held that the protective sweep doctrine is not limited to the residence where an arrest is made. If there is a reasonable belief based on specific and articulable facts, the police are permitted to detain and search dangerous individuals who are outside the home but within the "arrest zone."[233]

[7] Vehicle Searches

New York v. Belton[234] created a bright-line test permitting the search of the passenger department of a car incident to an arrest. *Belton* also applies when the police do not initiate contact with occupant of the car until after he gets out of the car and walks away from it. Because custodial search is a dangerous stage in the arrest process, the Supreme Court held in mid-2004 that the police must be given discretion to decide when to initiate it.[235]

---

[229] United States v. Bohannon, 225 F.3d 615 (6th Cir. 2000); People v. Hardrick, 71 LW 1215 (Colo. 9/16/02).

[230] United States v. Olguin-Rivera, 168 F.3d 1203 (10th Cir. 1999).

[231] State v. Spencer, 268 Conn. 575 (Conn. 2004).

[232] United States v. Gould, 364 F.3d 578 (5th Cir. 2003).

[233] United States v. Maddox, 388 F.3d 1356 (10th Cir. 2004).

[234] 453 U.S. 454 (1981).

[235] Thornton v. United States, 543 U.S. 882 (2004). The Ninth Circuit allows a *Belton* search of the passenger compartment of a vehicle to be performed incident to a lawful arrest on probable cause even if the search precedes a warrantless arrest — provided that search and arrest are approximately contemporaneous: United States v. Smith, 389 F.3d 944 (9th Cir. 2004).

However, the D.C. Circuit refused to apply the Belton exception (search of the passenger compartment of a car incident to a lawful arrest) to searches incident to the possibility of an arrest in the immediate future. That is, in this reading, the warrantless search cannot legitimately precede a custodial arrest.[236] New Jersey held that its state Constitution will not permit a bright-line Belton-type rule under which police can search the passenger compartment of a car incident to the arrest of an inhabitant of the car. The rationale was that once an arrested person is hand-cuffed and secured in a police car, protection of the officers no longer requires searching the passengers.[237]

On the grounds that passengers, as well as drivers, are seized for Fourth Amendment purposes in a traffic stop, the Supreme Court ruled in mid-2007 that the passengers have standing to challenge the constitutionality of the stop.[238]

Late in 2003, the Supreme Court decided that, when none of the passengers in a car stopped for a traffic violation claimed ownership of the drugs and cash found in the car, the conclusion that the car was used for drug trafficking justified the arrest of everyone in the car.[239]

Many, many cases involve an automobile that is stopped for a traffic offense, and in which contraband is discovered. *Whren v. United States*[240] holds that the Fourth Amendment's test for reasonableness of an automobile stop is probable cause to believe that a traffic violation occurred, not whether a reasonable officer would have made the stop. In other words, the officers' actual motivation, not a reasonableness test, is the issue. The Second Circuit held in 2006 that a police officer who is lawfully in a position to observe a license plate can use license plate information, e.g., by consulting a law enforcement database, without violating the Fourth Amendment.[241] The Second Circuit later affirmed the denial of a motion to suppress evidence found in a car and on the driver's person: a driver who initially obeys a police order to stop, but who then drives away as the police approach, has not been "seized" for Fourth Amendment purposes because he has not submitted to police authority.[242]

The Ninth Circuit upheld a stop and warrantless inspection of a commercial truck, which was carrying a large amount of cocaine. The defendant unsuccessfully argued that commercial trucking is not a pervasively regulated industry that is subject to administrative inspections without a warrant. The Ninth Circuit held that inspection of commercial trucks is necessary and serves a substantial governmental interest.[243]

---

[236] United States v. Powell, 451 F.3d 862 (D.C. Cir. 2006).

[237] State v. Eckel, 185 N.J. 523 (2006); State v. Dunlap, 185 N.J. 543 (2006).

[238] Brendlin v. California, 551 U.S. 249 (2007).

[239] Maryland v. Pringle, 540 U.S. 366 (2003).

[240] 516 U.S. 1036 (1996).

[241] United States v. Ellison, 462 F.3d 557 (6th Cir. 2006).

[242] United States v. Baldwin, 496 F.3d 215 (2d Cir. 2007).

[243] United States v. Delgado, 545 F.3d 1195 (9th Cir. 2008). The "pervasively regulated industry" standard comes from New York v. Burger, 482 U.S. 691 (1987).

Certain cases disapprove the use of traffic stops to support expansive searches. The California Court of Appeals held in late 2006 that fabricating a rationale for a traffic stop vitiates the entire concept of fairness in law enforcement, and even the presence of grounds for a lawful arrest does not remove the taint of the rights violation. Thus, evidence should have been suppressed when a car was stopped, allegedly because the brake light was burnt out, and the later discovery of an outstanding warrant was used to support search of the car.[244] In contrast, in early 2006, Florida, and the Oklahoma Court of Criminal Appeals both ruled that even if a traffic stop is invalid, evidence need not be suppressed if it was seized when the police discovered a valid arrest warrant during the stop and searched pursuant to the arrest. The discovery of the warrant is an independent circumstance that removes the taint of the illegal stop.[245]

Based on a tip that "Chubs" was driving with a suspended license, Virginia police picked up "Chubs" Moore. Under Virginia law, this was a misdemeanor for which a summons should have been issued, but instead, he was arrested. He was tried for drug charges after crack cocaine was discovered during a search incident to the arrest. The Virginia Supreme Court reversed his conviction on the grounds that there is no category of "search incident to lawful issuance of a citation." However, the Supreme Court held that it does not violate the Fourth Amendment to make an arrest based on probable cause but contrary to state law. The Supreme Court said that search/seizure questions should be analyzed using the traditional standard of reasonableness: the degree of intrusion on privacy and the need to promote legitimate governmental interests. In this reading, an arrest is constitutionally reasonable when the police have reasonable cause to believe that a minor crime has been committed — even if the state has chosen to grant privacy protection greater than the Fourth Amendment requires; a state's more restrictive search and seizure policy does not make a less restrictive policy constitutionally unreasonable. The seizure was justified by the probable cause for the arrest. An arrest prevents a suspect from continuing a crime and makes sure that he appears to answer charges, and the search was justified by the need to protect the arresting officers.[246]

Reasonable suspicion for automobile stops and probable cause for warrantless search are fluid concepts,[247] involving determination of historical facts leading

---

[244] People v. Rodriguez, 143 Cal. App. 4th 1137 (Cal. App. 2006); according to the Third Circuit, if the police make an illegal vehicle stop, no evidence found during the stop can be used against any occupant of the car, unless the government can show that the taint of the illegal stop was purged. The illegality of the stop affects the Fourth Amendment rights of everyone in the car: United States v. Mosley, 454 F.3d 249 (3d Cir. 2006).

[245] State v. Frierson, 926 So. 2d 1139 (Fla. 2006); Jacobs v. State, 2006 Ok. Cr. 4, 128 P.3d 1085 (Okla., Crim. App. 2006).

[246] Virginia v. Moore, No. 06-1082 (4/23/08).

[247] See, e.g., Ornelas v. United States, 517 U.S. 690 (1996). The police can do a consent search during a traffic stop even if they have not advised the motorist that he or she is free to go: Ohio v. Robinette, 519 U.S. 33 (1996).

up to the stop or search, involving mixed questions of law and fact (whether a reasonable officer would be suspicious or find probable cause for the search).

In early 2009, the Supreme Court ruled that a traffic stop, for an infraction punishable by a citation, is analogous to a *Terry* stop (see § 26.03[B][8]), and the police have a similar need to command the situation in order to protect themselves. Therefore, the Fourth Amendment was not violated when a police anti-gang task force stopped a car, decided to question a passenger based on his clothing and demeanor, and he admitted he was an ex-convict who came from a town with a Crips gang presence. During the pat-down, a gun was found, and the person being questioned was convicted on weapons charges. A traffic stop does not become unlawful if the police make inquiries about unrelated matters, as long as the inquiries do not extend the duration of the stop significantly.[248]

When a pickup truck was stopped on the highway for going 45 miles in a 55-mph zone, it was found to have 21 passengers, many of them illegal aliens. The driver was indicted for transporting illegal aliens. The Tenth Circuit held that the stop was invalid; it was not supported by reasonable suspicion; driving moderately below the speed limit, without more, does not constitute obstructing or impeding traffic.[249]

If there is probable cause to believe that the vehicle contains contraband, the vehicle can be searched without a warrant,[250] given the high mobility of vehicles and the diminished expectation of privacy resulting from heavy regulation of vehicles and driving. *Maryland v. Dyson*[251] permits a warrantless search of a car (even if there is enough time to get a warrant) if the police have a tip or other reasonable belief that there are illegal drugs in the car.

Also see *Wyoming v. Houghton,*[252] allowing a police officer who has probable cause to believe drugs are inside a vehicle to search any containers inside the vehicle that could contain drugs, even if the probable cause relates to the driver but the containers belong to a passenger.

In 2004, the Supreme Court interpreted the Fourth Amendment exception for border searches to permit customs officials to remove, disassemble, and reassemble the fuel tanks of vehicles crossing a border, even absent individualized suspicion.[253] When a tractor-trailer was searched at a border checkpoint by border

---

[248] Arizona v. Johnson, No. 07-1122 (1/26/09).

[249] United States v. Valadez-Valadez, 525 F.3d 987 (10th Cir. 2008); *see* State v. Bacher, 867 N.E.2d 864 (Ohio App. 2007) on driving slowly.

[250] United States v. Ross, 456 U.S. 798 (1982); Pennsylvania v. Labron, 518 U.S. 938 (1996).

[251] 527 U.S. 465 (1999).

[252] 526 U.S. 295 (1999). The Eighth Circuit did not suppress cocaine found in a hidden compartment of the defendant's car. There was probable cause to arrest him for speeding. Asking him about possible drug trafficking during a traffic stop was held not to be an unreasonable seizure. The stop did not provide a reason to exclude the evidence of a canine sniff, and the canine alert provided probable cause to search the vehicle: United States v. Olivera-Mendez, 484 F.3d 505 (8th Cir. 2007).

[253] United States v. Flores-Montano, 541 U.S. 149 (Sup. Ct. 2004). The Ninth Circuit did not require reasonable suspicion for a federal customs inspector to cut open a traveler's spare tire in the

agents, and the tractor was subsequently searched after a positive canine sniff, the Tenth Circuit said there were two searches. Border patrol agents do not require individualized suspicion to stop and question people at permanent checkpoints, and their discretion to refer cars to secondary inspection is virtually unlimited. An exterior canine inspection of a lawfully detained vehicle is permissible, without consent or individualized suspicion. A positive canine alert gives probable cause for search of the interior of the vehicle. The search of the truck was protected by the independent source doctrine.[254]

The Supreme Court has held that a police officer performing a traffic stop can order the passengers out of the car for the duration of the stop.[255] This is deemed to be a minimal intrusion on the passengers, justified by the increased risk to the police if more than one person is in the car.

The Ninth Circuit ruled on the converse — ordering a passenger to re-enter rather than leave a car — in 2005. During a stop for a traffic infraction, the defendant, a passenger, was ordered to get back into the car. He threw a gun through the passenger window and was arrested. At his trial for being a felon in possession of a weapon, the Ninth Circuit ruled that the police can order passengers back into the car during a traffic stop, given the need to control the environment, and because the intrusion on liberty is minimal.[256]

The Eleventh Circuit ruled in July 2005 that a 17-minute traffic stop for speeding, during which the police questioned the driver and passengers, was too short a detention to have constitutional significance. Therefore, drug charges could proceed. (During questioning, the driver and a passenger gave conflicting accounts for the reason for the trip, and cited a pressing need for a restroom, although they had just passed an exit with a restroom.)[257]

The Fifth Circuit ruled that it was unlawful to search a pickup truck (that had been stopped for speeding) merely because it carried an NRA sticker. The sticker did not create a valid presumption that the driver would be armed, and in any event was a lawful expression of opinion protected by the First Amendment.[258]

---

course of a warrantless border search; this was not considered a destructive intervention that would be particularly offensive under the Fourth Amendment: United States v. Cortez-Rocha, 383 F.3d 1093 (9th Cir. 2004). A roving patrol about 18 miles from the Rio Grande, along a major alien smuggling route, had reasonable suspicion to stop the defendant based on an anonymous tip that a red Suburban and a red pickup truck had picked up several illegal aliens at a bar known as a rendezvous point. Border patrol agents on roving patrol can stop a vehicle based on specific articulable facts and rational inferences from those facts, giving rise to suspicion that the vehicle is involved in illegal activities. Relevant factors include, e.g., the characteristics of the area; proximity to the border (50 miles from the border is a benchmark, but reasonable suspicion can be triggered further away); the patrol agent's experience; the driver's behavior; and the number, appearance, and behavior of the passengers in the vehicle: United States v. Hernandez, 477 F.3d 210 (5th Cir. 2007).

[254] United States v. Forbes, 528 F.3d 1273 (10th Cir. 2008).

[255] Florida v. Bostick, 501 U.S. 429 (1991).

[256] United States v. Williams, 419 F.3d 1029 (9th Cir. 2005).

[257] United States v. Hernandez, 418 F.3d 1206 (11th Cir. 2005).

[258] Estep v. Dallas Co., 310 F.3d 353 (5th Cir. 2002).

An emerging issue is the propriety of performing warrant checks of drivers and/or passengers in connection with traffic stops.

The Supreme Court reversed an Illinois decision holding that during a traffic stop, the police cannot do a warrant check on a passenger (as distinct from the driver), nor can they use a drug detection dog to sniff the car, unless there is a reasonable connection to the reason for the stop or there is reasonable suspicion of other wrongdoing.[259]

[a] Bus Searches

Searches of buses pose additional questions, in that the bus is a public vehicle which often contains large numbers of unrelated persons. According to the Eleventh Circuit[260] a bus passenger's consent to a warrantless search of the bus, performed by the DEA as part of a drug and weapons interdiction action, is invalid if the federal agents made a show of coercive authority without indicating that consent could be refused. However, *Miranda* warnings were not required in this context.

A police officer performing a traffic stop can order the passengers out of the car for the duration of the stop.[261] This is deemed to be a minimal intrusion on the passengers, justified by the increased risk to the police if more than one person is in the car.

For Fourth Amendment purposes, the Supreme Court ruled in April 2000, that a search occurs when a police officer manipulates a piece of soft luggage before opening it. The bus passenger put the luggage in the overhead compartment. The Supreme Court said that placing luggage in the overhead bin did not surrender the expectation of privacy, even though other passengers could touch and handle it. In this case, an agent got on the bus to check the immigration status of its passengers.

When the agent squeezed the luggage in the bins, he found a brick-like object in the defendant's bag, which turned out to be a large quantity of amphetamines. Rejecting the prosecution contention that the luggage in the bin was exposed to the public, the Supreme Court differentiated between patting luggage and performing a visual inspection of objects out in the open.

Tactile examination of luggage is the equivalent of a *Terry* pat-down. People use carry-on luggage for items they want to keep close at hand. The Fourth Amendment is involved because the expectation is that another passenger, or a bus employee, may handle the luggage but will not examine it.[262]

According to the Fifth Circuit, if initial routine questioning at an immigration checkpoint creates reasonable suspicion of other criminal activity, the stop can be lengthened in view of the added new justification. Drug enforcement, including

---

[259] People v. Caballes, 207 Ill. 2d 515 (Ill. 2003), *rev'd*, Illinois v. Caballes, 543 U.S. 405 (2005).

[260] United States v. Washington, 151 F.3d 1354 (11th Cir. 1998).

[261] Maryland v. Wilson, 519 U.S. 408 (1997).

[262] Bond v. United States, 529 U.S. 334 (2000).

canine sniffs, can be carried out at immigration checkpoints as long as it does not prolong the stop past the time needed to check immigration status. Searching the exterior compartment of buses is reasonable to look for aliens (because it is a frequent hiding place), and the Fifth Circuit held that a passenger had no reasonable expectation of privacy in the exterior luggage compartment of a commercial bus, so he lacked standing to complain when the bus driver consented to a search that resulted in discovery of marijuana in the passenger's luggage.[263]

The Supreme Court returned to the subject of bus searches in June 2002. It upheld the validity of passengers' consent to a pat-down during a routine drug and weapons interdiction effort that occurred when the bus made a regular stop en route. The Supreme Court did not require the police officers performing the interdiction to advise the bus passengers that they had the right to refuse consent to the search. The police can validly approach bus passengers at random and ask questions and seek consent for a search as long as a reasonable person would feel free to refuse to consent. In this instance, passengers could leave the bus during the stop (some of them did anyway, for instance to buy refreshments). The Supreme Court deemed the holstered firearms that the police officers carried to be less coercive than a brandished firearm would have been.[264]

[b] Roadblocks and Checkpoints

In many instances, arrests have been made because, in the course of a stop for a traffic infraction (e.g., driving too fast; operating without lights), the police observe signs of criminal activity. The question then becomes the scope of search that can be done during a traffic stop. The next point on the spectrum is setting up a roadblock or checkpoint to observe cars whose drivers have not been driving improperly.

In mid-1999, Washington State applied its own Constitution to demand more than Supreme Court precedent requires. In this reading, the state Constitution forbids the police to make traffic stops because they want to investigate criminal activity but do not have evidence that would establish reasonable suspicion for an ordinary investigation.[265]

But nearly all the states take the position that their state Constitution permits legitimate traffic stops to be used as a tool in broader investigation of automobiles. This tactic was authorized by the Supreme Court's 1996 *Whren* decision.[266]

Late in 2000, the Supreme Court ruled that vehicle checkpoints set up for drug interdiction violate the Fourth Amendment. In this analysis, checkpoints are permissible to satisfy a purpose that is closely related to vehicles (for instance,

---

[263] United States v. Ventura, 447 F.3d 375 (5th Cir. 2006).

[264] United States v. Drayton, 536 U.S. 194 (2002).

[265] State v. Ladson, 979 P.2d 833 (Wash. 1999).

[266] The Supreme Court case is Whren v. United States, 517 U.S. 806 (1996). For New York's adoption of this position, *see* People v. Robinson, and People v. Reynolds, 767 N.E.2d 638 (N.Y. 2001). *Whren* has also been extended to cover custodial arrests: Arkansas v. Sullivan, 532 U.S. 769 (2001).

catching drunk drivers or patrolling the borders) but not for generalized law enforcement purposes. The severity of the drug problem does not justify checkpoints that operate without individualized suspicion.[267]

The Missouri view is that "deceptive drug checkpoints" are actually more sustainable than real ones — in other words, that if a sign is posted warning of a (nonexistent) drug checkpoint ahead, the police have grounds to suspect, and hence stop, drivers who exit the highway after seeing the sign. (The exit used in the program did not provide any services for motorists, so there was little reason to exit there.) Under the program, the police took license and registration information, asked the motorist why he or she had taken the exit, and looked for signs of drug trafficking. If they found such signs, the police asked for consent to search. If the motorist refused, the police used a sniffer dog on the outside of the vehicle. Positive results constituted grounds for search.[268]

In contrast, the Eighth Circuit held that the fact that a motorist turns off before the sign announcing the deceptive checkpoint is not inherently suspicious behavior, and therefore cannot create individualized suspicion that can justify a stop.[269]

At the beginning of 2004, the Supreme Court distinguished *Edmond* and held that the Fourth Amendment is not violated by setting up a highway checkpoint, imposing 10–15 second stops on each vehicle, to garner information about a fatal hit-and-run accident that had occurred at the location where the checkpoint was placed.[270] The checkpoint was acceptable because its purpose was not to incriminate the persons who were stopped, but to obtain information about a serious crime committed by someone else. (The defendant was arrested, and eventually convicted of drunk driving, because police officers running the checkpoint smelled alcohol on his breath.)

The Tenth Circuit allowed a police officer doing a traffic stop to ask if there were any loaded weapons in the vehicle, whether or not the officer had particularized suspicion or was afraid of the driver. However, the majority opinion in this case[271] refused to adopt the government's position that any kind of questioning is permitted as long as the duration of the stop is not prolonged. The Seventh Circuit, however, did allow questions unrelated to the probable cause for the traffic stop, as long as the duration of the stop remains reasonable.[272]

Tennessee found that a police checkpoint program at a housing authority complex, involving stops of motorists and pedestrians to check resident I.Ds and other documentation, was an unreasonable search and seizure. (The municipality had privatized the streets by conveying them to the housing authority,

---

[267] Indianapolis v. Edmond, 520 U.S. 651 (2000).

[268] Missouri v. Mack, 66 S.W.3d 706 (Mo. 2002). *But see* United States v. Green, 275 F.3d 694 (8th Cir. 2001) disapproving the use of deceptive checkpoints as contrary to *Edmond*.

[269] United States v. Yousif, 308 F.3d 820 (8th Cir. 2002).

[270] Illinois v. Lidster, 540 U.S. 419 (2004).

[271] United States v. Holt, 264 F.3d 1215 (10th Cir. 2001), *overruling* 229 F.3d 931 (10th Cir. 2000).

[272] United States v. Childs, 277 F.3d 947 (7th Cir. 2002).

which imposed restrictions on who could be present.) *Edmond* ruled out checkpoints that are indistinguishable from the general interest in crime control. There was no evidence that residents were at risk of harm from unauthorized visitors, and there was a strong possibility that criminal activity within the housing complex was committed by residents. The program did not impose limitations on police discretion vis a vis nonresidents, and there was evidence that the police violated the Fourth Amendment by using suspicionless stops for general crime control.[273]

[c] Taxi Surveillance

A 1999 New York case[274] says that the Fourth Amendment is violated by a police program of suspicionless safety checks on taxis, because *Brown v. Texas*[275] requires any program of suspicionless stops to be part of a plan that imposes explicit, neutral limitations on the police officers' discretion. In the case at bar, the police stopped taxis, gave out safety pamphlets — and also ordered passengers out of the taxi. A couple of suspicious-looking passengers proved to possess crack cocaine.

In contrast, the First Circuit case from early 2000 holds that the rights of passengers (including the defendant, arrested on gun charges during a stop) are not violated by a taxi driver vehicle protection program that the taxi owner consented to. The cab displayed a decal saying that it was subject to visual inspection by the police; the owner's consent operated as consent by the driver.[276] (Since 1974, Supreme Court precedent has permitted a third party who has legitimate joint access and control consent to the search of an area.)[277]

[8] Stops and Pat-Downs

A *Terry* stop, as authorized by *Terry v. Ohio*, 392 U.S. 1 (1986) is a brief detention during which the police ask a few questions to determine whether there is probable cause for an arrest. It is easy to imagine a situation in which the detainee is armed and hostile, resulting in injury to the police, so a pat-down is permitted incident to a valid stop.

Early in 2002, the Supreme Court held that the totality of circumstances suggestive of drug smuggling (rather than the innocent family picnic asserted by the defendant) justified the Border Patrol in making an investigative stop at the border. Therefore, the more than 100 pounds of marijuana seized during the stop was admissible.[278]

---

[273] State v. Hayes, 188 S.W.3d 505 (Tenn. 2006).

[274] *In re* Muhammed F., 700 N.Y.S.2d 77 (N.Y. 1999).

[275] 443 U.S. 47 (1979).

[276] United States v. Woodrum, 202 F.3d 1 (1st Cir. 2000).

[277] United States v. Matlock, 415 U.S. 164 (1974).

[278] United States v. Arvizu, 534 U.S. 266 (2002). *But see* United States v. Portillo-Aguirre, 311 F.3d 647 (5th Cir. 2002): it is improper for Border Patrol agents performing a suspicionless immigration stop to ask about drugs at the end. Indianapolis v. Edmond, 520 U.S. 651 (2000), rules out asking drug interdiction questions after an unrelated stop. The standard for routine traffic stops is the

In mid-2004, the Supreme Court upheld a conviction under Nevada's "stop and identify" statute. The law requires a person detained by a police officer under suspicious circumstances to identify him/herself. Hiibel was subjected to an investigative stop in connection with a reported assault. The Supreme Court ruled that his conviction did not violate the Fourth Amendment or the Fifth Amendment prohibition of compelled self-incrimination. The initial stop was based on reasonable suspicion, so the Fourth Amendment was satisfied. The statute merely required the person stopped to give his or name, not to produce identification documents, a requirement that the Supreme Court found valid. Being required to state one's name was held not to be incriminating.[279]

The Sixth Circuit held that police executing a warrant can properly detain a person who appears to present a threat when he or she approaches but does not enter the target premises. In the case at bar, the court held that the police went too far by detaining such a person in a police car for three hours on a hot day while the warrant was being executed.[280]

Federal drug agents can lawfully make an investigative stop when a nervous passenger pays cash for expensive plane tickets; does not check any baggage; stays only 48 hours after a 10-hour trip to a city known to be a center of drug trafficking; and traveled under a name other than the name under which his telephone number was listed.[281]

The Supreme Court has held that there was no "seizure" when the police make a show of authority in attempting to apprehend a person who flees, but no force is applied. Therefore, crack cocaine discarded by a person pursued by the police was admissible, because it was not the product of a "seizure."[282]

Early in 2000, the Supreme Court found that circumstances justified a *Terry* stop where a defendant fled after seeing a number of police cars converge on an area of known narcotics traffic. Based on expectations that weapons are very often found near narcotics transactions, the police pursued the defendant, caught him, and patted him down. Although mere presence in a high-crime area is not enough to justify a stop, the Supreme Court reviewed state cases as to whether unprovoked flight constitutes grounds for reasonable suspicion. The characteristics of an area are relevant in determining whether the police have grounds for further investigation. Nervous, evasive behavior is a factor. The court says that unprovoked flight is the opposite of the kind of "going about one's business" that Constitutional sanctions are intended to protect. In this reading, flight is not

---

Terry standard, so the Third Circuit affirmed a conviction for transporting an illegal alien because evidence obtained from a traffic stop was not subject to suppression: United States v. Delfin-Colina, 464 F.3d 392 (3d Cir. 2006).

[279] Hiibel v. Sixth Judicial Dist. Ct. of Nev., 542 U.S. 177 (2004). United States v. Hensley, 469 U.S. 221 (1985), holds that an officer has the right to ask a person subject to a *Terry* stop to identify him- or herself.

[280] Burchett v. Kiefer, 310 F.3d 937 (6th Cir. 2002).

[281] United States v. Sokolow, 490 U.S. 1 (1989).

[282] California v. Hodari D., 499 U.S. 621 (1991).

necessarily an indication of criminal activity, but it is good enough to justify the limited intrusion of a *Terry* stop.[283]

Another Supreme Court case, from the same year on a similar issue, arose when Miami police received an anonymous call that a young black man in a plaid shirt, standing at a particular bus stop, had a gun. The decision[284] holds that it violates the Fourth Amendment for the police to stop and frisk anyone on the basis of such an anonymous tip. The standard of review for anonymous tips is not relaxed merely because the tipster claims that the subject of the tip has a gun. Although *Alabama v. White*[285] allows a stop on reasonable suspicion, based on an anonymous tip from a known reliable informant, the Supreme Court found this tip to be insufficient to support a stop. A tip is not reliable merely because the tipster knew that the tippee was present at a bus stop, because this does not demonstrate that the tipster was correct about the presence of a gun. Relaxed standards for gun tips could easily lead to relaxed standards for drug tips, making it easy for malicious people to use unfounded anonymous tips to create trouble.

The Eighth Circuit ruled that, to justify a stop of people who were not doing anything suspicious (the subjects of an anonymous phone tip were standing near a bus stop), the police must have been investigating a past crime. In this case, the subjects of the tip were potentially committing trespass (a misdemeanor or an infraction), and a *Terry* stop for trespass can only be justified if there is a strong threat to public safety. In this case, the call was about "suspicious parties on the property" in a high-drug-trafficking area, which was not enough to justify the stop and frisk that yielded ammunition in the possession of a convicted felon.[286]

The District of Columbia Court of Appeals said that individuals who identify themselves to the police in the course of a tip are presumed reliable, whereas an anonymous phone tip corroborated only by innocent details is not.[287]

Because large, heavy boots can conceal a weapon, it is permissible for the police to demand removal of footwear during a *Terry* stop.[288]

The Ninth Circuit held that reasonable suspicion must be particularized, not based on a characteristic that is widely shared in the area. Thus, in a county that was 73% Hispanic, a person's Hispanic appearance could not justify a stop

---

[283] Illinois v. Wardlow, 528 U.S. 119 (2000).

[284] Florida v. J.L., 529 U.S. 266 (2000). California held in mid-2007 that the Fourth Amendment does not require the police to corroborate an anonymous tip before asking for consent to enter a residence and perform a search: People v. Rivera, 41 Cal. 4th 304 (Cal. 2007).

[285] 496 U.S. 325 (1990).

[286] United States v. Hughes, 517 F.3d 1013 (8th Cir. 2008). The court noted that the Supreme Court has not decided whether a *Terry* stop is permitted to investigate a misdemeanor or infraction; the Ninth and Tenth Circuits apply a case-by-case balancing analysis.

[287] Davis v. United States, 759 A.2d 665 (D.C. App. 2000).

[288] Illinois v. Sorenson, 752 N.E.2d 1078 (Ill. 2001). On the subject of attire, *see also* State v. Peterson, 2005 Utah 17 (Utah 2005). The police unilaterally decided to give the subject of a *Terry* stop a jacket (it was a cold day). But, because they placed the jacket within the suspect's reach without being asked, the lawfulness of the stop would not justify a protective frisk of the jacket.

to check for illegal aliens. However, the stop was held to be justified by other factors, including the fact that defendants in separate cars made U-turns to avoid the checkpoint.[289]

[9] Wiretapping and Electronic Surveillance

The bedrock federal law on these issues is found at 18 USC § 2510 *et seq.*, Title III of the Omnibus Crime Control and Safe Streets Act. No part of an intercepted communication can be admitted in evidence at trial or before a Grand Jury (see § 2515) if Title III is violated, although material that is not admissible may be used for impeachment.

Surveillance orders are issued by District Court judges based on applications from the Attorney General or designated assistant. The application must be made under oath, identifying the person whose communications are to be intercepted.[290] A "roving wiretap" — a surveillance order that does not specify the place of interception of wire communications — is allowed by § 2518(11). Interception of the communications of others must be minimized; see § 2518(5). The application for the order must state that non-wiretap methods of investigation have been tried but have failed, or would be unsuccessful or too dangerous if tried.

Although 18 USC § 2518(5) requires a plan for minimizing interception of the communications, the Ninth Circuit found it permissible for the monitoring agent and the federal prosecutor to read every intercepted fax in full to see if it contains information pertinent to the investigation.[291]

"Interception" is defined as the acquisition of a wire, oral, or electronic communication by using any electronic, mechanical, or other device. Directing television cameras that record a picture, but no sound, is not considered interception under Title III. But speech is deemed to have been intercepted only if the speaker reasonably expected the communication to have been private. Title III is not violated when a party to a communication intercepts that communication, or consents to law enforcement interception (§ 2511(2)(c)).

A person whose communications were intercepted without his or her permission can move under 18 USC § 2518 to suppress the content of the interception, although this provision applies only to oral and wire communications, not electronic communications. The majority rule is that the federal wiretap statute prohibits one spouse from wiretapping the other; a late 2003 Eleventh Circuit ruling makes this principle retroactive.[292]

In 2005, the First Circuit adopted a new principle: that 18 U.S.C. § 2511(1)(a) is violated by unauthorized interception of e-mail messages even during transient

---

[289] United States v. Montero-Camargo, 208 F.3d 1122 (9th Cir. 2000).

[290] District Court judges have jurisdiction to place wiretap orders on telephones outside the district: United States v. Denman, 100 F.3d 399 (5th Cir. 1996). If civilian monitors will be used, the government's burden of complete disclosure in obtaining a wiretap warrant requires disclosure (to the issuing judge) of the intent to use civilian monitors: United States v. Lopez, 300 F.3d 46 (1st Cir. 2002).

[291] United States v. McGuire, 307 F.3d 1192 (9th Cir. 2002).

[292] Glazner v. Glazner, 347 F.3d 1212 (11th Cir. 2003).

storage, and the offense can properly be charged either under the Wiretap Act or the Stored Communications Act, 18 U.S.C. § 2701 *et seq.*[293]

Under 18 USC § 2518, the application for a wiretap requires a showing that the wiretap is necessary to the investigation. As the Ninth Circuit interprets this, it is not necessary for the government to prove that it would be unable to conduct the investigation via confidential informants without wiretaps.[294]

The Supreme Court refused to hear a legal challenge to the National Security Agency program of warrantless wiretapping. The ACLU petitioned for certiorari in a Sixth Circuit case that was dismissed for lack of standing; the court said that potential plaintiffs could not know that they had been wiretapped, because that information was privileged. In 2007, the program was revised to place wiretaps under the supervision of the Foreign Intelligence Surveillance Court. According to the ACLU, even if the program had been changed, it could be changed back.[295]

[a] Computer Searches

Privacy issues exist even outside the realm of tangible places. It has been held that there is no reasonable expectation of privacy in chat room communications or e-mails, and therefore seizure of messages dealing with child pornography does not violate the Fourth Amendment.[296]

The Fifth and Tenth Circuits reached slightly different conclusions in similar cases involving public employees who were caught downloading child pornography to office computers. The Fifth Circuit view was that the employee had a reasonable expectation of privacy, but a warrantless search was reasonable in an inquiry that had elements of both criminal law and administrative law (investigation of workplace misconduct). In contrast, the Tenth Circuit took the view that there was no reasonable expectation of privacy because the workplace had policies against accessing obscene materials, and employees had been warned that their Internet usage was subject to monitoring.[297]

Computer searches continued to be a topic of interest:

- The Tenth Circuit held that a city treasurer did not have a reasonable expectation of privacy in the personal computer that he brought to work that would prevent a search (which found child pornography).[298]

---

[293] United States v. Councilman, 418 F.3d 67 (1st Cir. 2005). The Sixth Circuit held that e-mail users have a reasonable expectation of privacy in the contents of their e-mails, so a preliminary injunction, preventing the government from seizing personal e-mails without giving the account holder notice and the opportunity to be heard, was upheld: Warshak v. United States, 490 F.3d 455 (6th Cir. 2007).

[294] United States v. Gomez, 358 F.3d 1221 (9th Cir. 2004).

[295] ACLU v. Nat'l Security Agency, 128 S. Ct. 1334 (2008), discussed in Tony Mauro, *Supreme Court Declines Review of NSA Wiretapping Program*, Legal Times 2/20/08 (law.com).

[296] United States v. Charbonneau, 979 F. Supp. 2d 1177 (S.D. Ohio 1997).

[297] *Compare* United States v. Slanina, 283 F.3d 670 (5th Cir. 2001) *with* United States v. Angevine, 281 F.3d 1130 (10th Cir. 2002).

[298] United States v. Barrows, 481 F.3d 1246 (10th Cir. 2007).

- The defendant's employer had the right to give third-party consent to search the defendant's work computer, so evidence of child pornography on the computer could not be suppressed despite the defendant's legitimate expectation of privacy in his workplace.[299]
- A suspect's wife had apparent authority to consent to search the suspect's computer, even though she did not have the passwords, because the police who seized the computer had no way of knowing the files were password-protected.[300]

The Second Circuit rendered a split decision in a warrant application based largely on general assumptions about the computer use and other habits of consumers of child pornography. The affidavit alleged attempts to access a child pornography Web site but did not allege that the defendant managed to do so. Two judges said this affidavit did not provide probable cause to search his home and computer; one said that it did. The search found a box of child pornography in the defendant's home and more images in his computer. However, two of the judges applied the good-faith exception to the exclusionary rule, so the conviction and 30-year prison sentence were upheld.[301] An appellant was convicted of possession, transportation, and shipping of child pornography. Search of his home computer revealed many child pornography images. On appeal, he asserted the right to a *Franks* hearing (see § 26.03[B][5]) on the grounds that the affidavit for the warrant was based on misleading statements and omissions. The Ninth Circuit ruled that he was not entitled to a *Franks* hearing because he failed to allege any specific portion of the warrant that was false and misleading.[302]

The Ninth Circuit held in 2008 that customs officials do not need particularized reasonable suspicion to search laptops or other electronic devices at the border; these searches are the equivalent of customs searches of luggage, which are permitted because of a nation's sovereign power to control items coming from outside the country. International airports are considered the equivalent of national borders. Therefore, child pornography found on a traveler's laptop computer was admissible for grand jury charges of possessing and transporting child pornography and traveling to a foreign country with the intention of having sex with children.[303]

---

[299] United States v. Ziegler, 474 F.3d 1184 (9th Cir. 1/30/07; 8/8/06 opinion withdrawn, panel rehearing granted); United States v. Laville, 480 F.3d 187 (3d Cir. 2007).

[300] United States v. Buckner, 473 F.3d 551 (4th Cir. 2007); the Tenth Circuit reached a similar conclusion as to a suspect's father: United States v. Andrus, 483 F.3d 711 (10th Cir. 2007).

[301] United States v. Falso, 544 F.3d 110 (2d Cir. 2008); *see* Mark Hamblett, *2nd Circuit Divides Over Warrant in Internet Child Porn Case*, N.Y.L.J. 10/1/08 (law.com). United States v. Martin, 436 F.3d 68 (2d Cir. 2008) found probable cause to search based on membership in a child pornography site, but in this case, the defendant was not accused of being a Web site member or subscriber.

[302] United States v. Craighead, 539 F.3d 1073 (9th Cir. 8/21/08).

[303] United States v. Arnold, 523 F.3d 941 (9th Cir. 2008); *see* Mike McKee, *9th Circuit OKs Border Guards' Search of Traveler's Laptop*, The Recorder 4/22/08 (law.com); United States v. Ickes, 393 F.3d 501 (4th Cir. 2005) also allowed a computer search at the border. The Senate

A defendant's consent to search of his home constitutes consent to seizing his computer and searching his hard drive, which is treated as the equivalent of a closed container within a vehicle.[304]

Mirroring a hard drive pursuant to a warrant to perform forensic tests is not considered a seizure of the drive; copying a file does not necessarily constitute seizure, and repeated examination of a computer file has been held not to constitute multiple searches.[305]

[b] Searches of Parolees and Probationers

The recent jurisprudence of searches of parolees stems from *United States v. Knights*,[306] a case in which warrantless searches were justified because the conditions of parole permitted warrantless searches at any time, without limitation to suspected parole violations.

In 2006, the Supreme Court returned to the question, ruling that suspicionless search of a parolee did not violate the Fourth Amendment. The California statute requires released parolees to agree in writing to submit to searches either with or without warrant or probable cause. The Supreme Court analyzed the reasonableness of a search of a parolee for Fourth Amendment purposes under a totality of circumstances test. Parolees have even less expectation of privacy than the probationers in *Knights*, because parole is closer to imprisonment than probation is. The high recidivism rate among parolees makes it reasonable to suspect that a particular parolee might be involved in criminal activities. The Supreme Court rejected the appellant's argument that the law frustrates ex-convicts' efforts to reintegrate into society, because they would also be subject to intrusions on their privacy if particularized suspicion were required for searches.[307] Illinois ruled that it did not violate the Fourth Amendment to perform a suspicionless pat-down of a passenger during a traffic stop; the passenger was on parole and was subject to search as a condition of parole.[308]

In the context of probation, the Eighth Circuit ruled sweat patch tests are generally reliable for seeing if an offender has violated a probation condition, but the District Court should make a case-by-case determination if a probationer offers a compelling reason to doubt the validity of a positive result.[309]

Judiciary Committee subcommittee on the Constitution held hearings on laptop searches at airports in June, 2008. *See* David E. Brodsky, Timothy M. Haggerty and Tamara J. Britt, *At the Border, Your Laptop Is Wide-Open*, Nat'l L.J. 7/22/08 (law.com).

[304] United States v. Al-Marri, 230 F. Supp. 2d 535 (S.D.N.Y. 11/12/02).

[305] United States v. Triumph Capital Group Inc., 211 FRD 31 (D. Conn. 11/4/02).

[306] 534 U.S. 112 (2001).

[307] Samson v. California, 547 U.S. 843 (2006).

[308] People v. Moss, 217 Ill. 2d 511 (Ill. 2005); *see* § 26.03[B][7] for additional discussion of vehicle searches.

[309] United States v. Meyer, 483 F.3d 865 (8th Cir. 2007).

[10] Other Fourth Amendment Issues

In general, police will be required to "knock and announce" before entering premises, but unannounced entry may be justified by circumstances, such as potential danger to the police. There is no general exception for drug searches; they are subject to the same reasonableness analysis.[310] Nevertheless, in 2006 the Supreme Court ruled that violation of the "knock and announce" rule does not require suppression of evidence seized (in this case, drugs), because the Fourth Amendment directs exclusion of evidence for violation of interests such as safety, privacy, and dignity — not prevention of the government from seizing evidence described in a warrant. The Supreme Court also held that permitting exclusion would lead to too much litigation.[311]

The Supreme Court granted review in March 2008 to examine whether a fairly recent decision, *Saucier v. Katz*, 533 U.S. 194 (2001) should be overruled. *Saucier* sets up a two-step test for police immunity in suits alleging deprivation of constitutional rights: were the claimant's rights violated? If so, was the right established clearly enough that a reasonable officer would have been aware of it? The case at bar arose from a warrantless police raid on a home after an informant entered the home and bought illegal drugs. The Tenth Circuit found the raid unconstitutional and violative of well-established rights. In its January 2009 decision, the Supreme Court described *Saucier* as a judge-made rule rather than a statute passed by Congress, and the lower courts must decide whether or not to apply the two-step process. In the case at bar, the Supreme Court found that the petitioners were entitled to qualified immunity because, at the time of a warrantless search incident to an arrest for selling drugs to an informant, it was not clearly established that the search was improper.[312]

In 2004, the Eighth Circuit found that an uncorroborated anonymous tip that illegal amphetamines were present in a house did not justify the police officers executing a search warrant in fearing for their safety. Therefore, a no-knock entry was unreasonable under the Fourth Amendment.[313]

In mid-2000, the Ninth Circuit articulated a three-part test for valid, warrantless entry into a home under the emergency doctrine:

- The police have reasonable grounds to believe that an emergency exists and their assistance is needed immediately to protect life or property

---

[310] Wilson v. Arkansas, 514 U.S. 927 (1995); Richards v. Wisconsin, 520 U.S. 385 (1997). Arkansas, like Washington, requires police who do a "knock and talk" to get consent to a warrantless home search to inform the residents that they can refuse their consent: State v. Brown, 356 Ark. 460 (2004).

[311] Hudson v. Michigan, 547 U.S. 586 (2006).

[312] Pearson v. Callahan, No. 07-751 (1/21/09).

[313] Doran v. Eckold, 362 F.3d 1047 (8th Cir. 2004). Late in 2003, the Supreme Court ruled that the totality of circumstances, including reasonable suspicion that evidence would be destroyed, justified a forcible entry occurring only 15–20 seconds after the knock and announce: United States v. Banks, 540 U.S. 31 (2003).

- The primary intent of the entry is not to make an arrest or seize evidence
- There is reasonable basis (equivalent to probable cause) to associate the emergency with the place that is searched.[314]

The Fourth Amendment is presumptively violated by a delay of more than 48 hours between a warrantless arrest and a judicial determination of probable cause.[315]

Sheriff's deputies executing a warrant for black suspects found the plaintiffs (who are white) and ordered them out of bed, naked. After two minutes, they were permitted to dress and the deputies admitted their error and left. (The actual suspects had moved out of the house, and were arrested in another house also covered by the warrant.) The Ninth Circuit permitted § 1983 civil rights claims to go to a jury, but the Supreme Court reversed, holding that the deputies acted appropriately to protect their own safety. The extent of detention was not unreasonable and was necessary to protect the deputies.[316]

Ever since the 9/11 attack, security at airports and other public places vulnerable to bomb attacks has been a live issue raising difficult questions. The Second Circuit held in 2006 that random, suspicionless subway searches performed by the New York Police Department do not violate the Fourth Amendment, because of their rational relationship to averting terrorist acts. The search was limited to explosives; persons who refused to be searched were permitted to leave the subway system without being arrested; and the purpose of the checkpoints was distinct from ordinary law enforcement activities. But the Middle District of Florida enjoined Tampa Sports Authority's practice of conducting pat-down searches of spectators at NFL games in Raymond James Stadium; no concrete threat of attack was shown, so a special needs exception was not available.[317] The Third Circuit upheld suspicionless searches of travelers at airport security checkpoints, pursuant to the "administrative search" exception to the Fourth Amendment. An administrative search occurs in a highly regulated industry where there are special needs beyond conventional law enforcement needs. The airport searches are minimally intrusive and narrowly tailored to the interest of avoiding terrorism and other attacks on planes.[318]

The Ninth Circuit ruled that passengers cannot prevent a secondary screening search by abandoning the plan to fly after voluntarily passing through the metal

---

[314] United States v. Cervantes, 219 F.3d 882 (9th Cir. 2000).

[315] Riverside County v. McLaughlin, 500 U.S. 44 (1991).

[316] L.A. County v. Rettele, No. 127 S. Ct. 1989 (5/21/07); *see, e.g.,* Mark Sherman (AP), *U.S. Supreme Court Ends Lawsuit by Homeowners Rousted Naked From Bed During Search,* 5/22/07 (law.com).

[317] *Compare* MacWade v. Kelly, 460 F.3d 260 (2d Cir. 2006) *with* Johnston v. Tampa Sports Auth., 75 LW 1128 (M.D. Fla. 7/28/06).

[318] United States v. Hartwell, 437 F.3d 174 (3d Cir. 2006). *See also* United States v. Lawson, 461 F.3d 697 (6th Cir. 2006): reasonable suspicion is not required to x-ray luggage of passenger arriving on an international flight. (8/10/07).

detector without setting it off. In this case, drugs and drug paraphernalia were found when the defendant was searched. The contraband was admitted on the grounds that it is not unreasonable under the Fourth Amendment to perform a secondary search to confirm an inconclusive initial screening.[319]

It was improper for high school officials to order a strip search to look for marijuana. (No marijuana was found). A tip from another student that the girl had marijuana in her pants; past discipline problems that were not drug-related; cigarettes in the girl's purse; and her denial in a "suspicious" manner that she had drugs did not add up to reasonable suspicion.[320]

[C] Fifth Amendment Issues

The Fifth Amendment protects against compelled self-incrimination. Central to the Fifth Amendment discussion is the *"Miranda"* "warning": a warning to a person undergoing custodial interrogation that he or she has the right to remain silent, that statements made during interrogation can be used against him or her, that he or she can be represented by counsel during interrogation, and may be entitled to appointment of counsel if unable to afford an attorney.[321]

Miranda applies to all stages of a criminal proceeding that deal with guilt or punishment, but not to the ascertainment of a potential defendant's competence to stand trial,[322] or to a prison disciplinary hearing.[323] Nor does *Miranda* apply to civil proceedings to determine whether someone is a sexually dangerous person, because this is deemed to be non-punitive.[324] *Miranda* applies to government tax litigation, but not pure civil litigation between private parties.

Spontaneous statements are not the product of interrogation, and therefore do not come under *Miranda*. Persons under interrogation can exercise an informed, knowing, and intelligent waiver of Fifth Amendment rights if they wish to respond to police questioning.[325] Once again, the determination of voluntariness involves multiple factors: the defendant's intellect, education, sobriety, length of the interrogation, fatigue, deception, isolation of the suspect, are all relevant to voluntariness.

In mid-2000, the Supreme Court, despite hints that it might have made a different decision if presented with the fact pattern as a new case, chose to uphold

---

[319] United States v. Aukai, 440 F.3d 1168 (9th Cir. 2006), overruled 497 F.3d 955 (9th Cir. 2007); the Ninth circuit changed its view since United States v. Davis, 482 F.2d 893 (9th Cir. 1973) which mandated the right to avoid search by surrendering the plan to travel.

[320] Phaneuf v. Fraikin, 448 F.3d 591 (2d Cir. 2006).

[321] Miranda v. Arizona, 384 U.S. 436 (1966).

[322] Estelle v. Smith, 451 U.S. 454 (1981).

[323] Baxter v. Palmigiano, 425 U.S. 308 (1976).

[324] Allen v. Illinois, 478 U.S. 364 (1986).

[325] Based on testimony about his comprehension of the rights disclosed, Colorado v. Connelly, 479 U.S. 157 (1986) finds a *Miranda* waiver valid by a person who escaped from a psychiatric institution and was questioned about a crime.

Miranda on stare decisis grounds.[326] The Supreme Court voted 7-2 to retain the requirement of a pre-interrogation warning, finding it to have become part of the culture of law enforcement and not unduly burdensome to enforcement.

The Ninth Circuit decided, early in 2008, that when a person is in custody for an unrelated matter, the need for a *Miranda* warning is triggered only by a restriction of the suspect's freedom vis-a-vis the interrogation itself. Therefore, a telephone conversation (initiated by the suspect, who telephoned the detective investigating his wife's murder) while a suspect was incarcerated for assaulting his son-in-law was not custodial — he initiated the call and could end it whenever he wanted to.[327]

The privilege against self-incrimination is not violated by a requirement that sex offenders participate in a treatment program requiring them to complete a signed "Admission of Responsibility" form and a detailed sexual history which is not privileged (although so far it has never been used to bring additional charges). In mid-2002, the Supreme Court found that these requirements served the legitimate state interest of rehabilitation. Although refusal to participate would lead to loss of privileges, and possible transfer to a more dangerous maximum-security prison unit, the Supreme Court did not deem these negative consequences to constitute compulsion that would encumber the right to be free of self-incrimination.[328]

Fifth Amendment issues overlap those of the Fourth Amendment and Sixth Amendment. There is a technical distinction between a confession (statement that the speaker committed a crime) and an admission (acknowledgment of facts that, in conjunction with other facts, establish guilt), but the same standards are used for admission or suppression of both.

In some ways, the prohibition against use of coerced confessions is broader than the Fourth Amendment ban on the use of illegally obtained evidence. Earlier case law says that involuntary statements cannot be used at all, even for impeachment,[329] even if other evidence corroborates the accuracy of the confession.

Note, however, that in mid-2003 the Supreme Court held that incriminating statements obtained through coercive interrogation, but not used against the confessor in a criminal proceeding, are properly analyzed under substantive Due Process in a civil suit against the police, and not under the Fifth Amendment protection against self-incrimination.[330]

However, like Fourth Amendment issues, Fifth Amendment issues as to the voluntariness of a confession can be waived if they are not raised at trial or in the appellate papers,[331] and the harmless error doctrine can be applied to

---

[326] Dickerson v. United States, 530 U.S. 428 (2000).

[327] Saleh v. Fleming, 512 F.3d 548 (9th Cir. 2008).

[328] McKune v. Lile, 536 U.S. 24 (2002). *Also see* Searcy v. Simmons, 299 F.3d 1220 (10th Cir. 2002): it is not compelled self-incrimination to remove good-time credits from a prisoner who fails to comply with the disclosure requirements of a sex abuse treatment program.

[329] Mincey v. Arizona, 437 U.S. 385 (1978).

[330] Chavez v. Martinez, 538 U.S. 760 (2003).

[331] Hill v. California, 401 U.S. 797 (1971). *See, e.g.*, Rose v. Palmateer, 395 F.3d 1108 (9th Cir. 2005), where habeas was denied on a state court petition that alleged ineffective assistance of counsel

confessions.[332] Also note that, even if a confession is admissible, a confession alone will not support a conviction unless there is corroboration of the corpus delicti: i.e., that the crime occurred at all.

The inadmissibility of coerced confessions is a Constitutional principle of fundamental fairness under the Fourteenth Amendment, and thus applies in state criminal proceedings as well as the federal system.[333] At least at this time (a situation that could change based on greater integration of multi-national law enforcement), the Fifth Amendment privilege against self-incrimination applies only to prosecution within the United States, not a foreign jurisdiction.[334]

A person who is immune from prosecution can be compelled to testify, because he or she escapes the consequences of self-incrimination. Transactional immunity bars prosecution on any offense based on the transaction that the witness is compelled to testify about, whereas use immunity is less extensive.

[1] Custodial Interrogation

Just as an important Fourth Amendment question is whether there was a "search" at all, in Fifth Amendment cases it is often important to determine whether custodial interrogation occurred. *Miranda* warnings are not required before a police officer asks routine background or booking questions. *New York v. Quarles*[335] permits the police to ask an arrestee who has not been Mirandized questions "reasonably prompted by concerns for public safety."

If the circumstances are such that a reasonable person would feel free to leave, there has been no custody. Generally, questioning taking place in the suspect's home is deemed non-custodial. Even questioning at a police station or other law enforcement premises could be non-custodial if the individual being questioned was free to go. If the statements were made spontaneously, rather than in response to a question asked by the police, there has been no interrogation.

The Ninth Circuit agreed with a petitioner that his confession to possessing child pornography should be suppressed because he did not receive a *Miranda* warning during questioning in his home. An IP address assigned to the petitioner's residence was discovered during FBI surveillance of a child pornography site. An FBI agent obtained a search warrant and, with seven other armed law enforcement officers, executed the warrant. She informed Craighead that he was not under arrest and would not be arrested that day, but he could make a voluntary statement. She told him he was free to leave, and went into a storage room with Craighead, where they talked for 20–30 minutes without a *Miranda* warning, during which time he admitted

---

because the attorney failed to get the defendant's confession suppressed. The Fifth Amendment claim was not fairly presented and thus was not exhausted, and the Sixth Amendment claim would have been handled without Constitutional analysis of the confession.

[332] Milton v. Wainwright, 407 U.S. 371 (1972); Arizona v. Fulminante, 499 U.S. 299 (1991).

[333] Thomas v. Arizona, 356 U.S. 390 (1958); Rogers v. Richmond, 365 U.S. 534 (1961).

[334] United States v. Balsys, 524 U.S. 666 (1998).

[335] 467 U.S. 649 (1984).

to downloading and saving child pornography. He contended that he did not feel free to leave; even if the FBI would let him leave, there were other armed officers present. He appeared in court by summons. The Ninth Circuit ruled that interrogation in a suspect's own home is custodial if the police presence is sufficient to dominate the atmosphere. Relevant factors include the number of officers present; if they are armed; if the suspect was restrained by threats or physical force; if the suspect was informed he was free to leave; and whether in practice there were constraints on his departure. The Ninth Circuit noted that the interview took place in an unfurnished storage room — a more hostile environment than an ordinary room with furniture.[336]

Federal immigration inspectors are not required to give *Miranda* warnings during border interviews that constitute custodial interrogation of aliens, as long as the questioning bears on the admissibility of the aliens into the United States; the test is not whether individualized suspicion of a crime is present.[337]

The Supreme Court's decision in *Fellers v. United States*,[338] explores the interaction between *Miranda* requirements and the Sixth Amendment right to counsel. (See § 26.03[D][2].) The defendant was indicted by a Grand Jury for drug offenses and was arrested pursuant to a warrant. At his home, before he received *Miranda* warnings, he made inculpatory statements. He was then taken to jail, *Mirandized*, and made further inculpatory statements. Although the Eighth Circuit permitted admission of both statements, the Supreme Court reversed and remanded. The statements at the defendant's home were inadmissible because they were deliberately elicited by law enforcement officials, without giving the defendant the opportunity to avail himself of counsel. The Supreme Court criticized the Eighth Circuit for failing to consider whether the statements made at the jail, despite the presence of a *Miranda* warning, were the fruits of previous questioning that violated the accused's right to counsel.

According to the Supreme Court's mid-2004 decision, it was not unreasonable for the state court to decide interrogation was not custodial for *Miranda* purposes. The petitioner was a 17-year-old murder suspect who had never been questioned by the police before. The Supreme Court ruled that habeas relief was not available on the basis of the suspect's age and inexperience with law enforcement. The custody determination is objective — whether a reasonable person would feel free to leave. This is not the same as the test of voluntariness, which requires an inquiry as to whether the interrogatee's will was overborne.[339]

---

[336] United States v. Craighead, 539 F.3d 1073 (9th Cir. 2008).

[337] United States v. Kiam, 432 F.3d 524 (3d Cir. 2006).

[338] 540 U.S. 519 (2004).

[339] Yarborough v. Alvarado, 541 U.S. 652 (2004). On interrogation of juveniles, *see also In re Jerrell CJ*, 74 L.W. 1064 (Wis. 7/7/05), requiring electronic recording of custodial interrogation of a juvenile suspect at the police station as a precondition of admissibility of the statements. For custodial interrogation outside the police station environment, recording should be done where feasible. However, the court ruled that giving the juvenile the opportunity to consult a parent before questioning is not always required. Minnesota found a juvenile's *Miranda* waiver to be invalid because the police ignored his repeated requests to speak to his mother and falsely informed him

During federal habeas review (see § 26.04[N][1]) of a state court judgment, the issue of whether the suspect was "in custody" is a mixed question of law and fact. The federal court must make an independent determination on the issue, and cannot presume that the state court decided correctly on the presence or absence of custodial interrogation.[340]

If there is a direct connection between a confession and an illegal arrest, the illegality of the arrest may taint the confession; but the taint can be attenuated by the passage of time. Under *Rawlings v. Kentucky*,[341] a voluntary statement made after receipt of *Miranda* warnings is admissible even if detaining the suspect at that point was illegal and violated the Fourth Amendment.

Miranda warnings may have to be repeated if the time gap between the warning and questioning was long enough to vitiate the warning. Also see FR Crim Pro 5(a), requiring the arresting officer to bring the arrestee before the nearest available U.S. Magistrate Judge without unreasonable delay. 18 USC § 3501(c) gives the District Court discretion to suppress a confession if the gap between arrest and presentment exceeded six hours, unless the distance and means of travel rendered a longer delay reasonable.

If the police deliberately omit *Miranda* warnings to facilitate an interrogation, the Missouri position is that a second interrogation will be tainted even if warnings are given. This case reached the Supreme Court in 2004. It found the post-warning statements to be inadmissible because they were clearly the product of the initial, invalid questioning. When a two-step interrogation technique is used, post-warning statements related to pre-warning statements must be excluded unless curative measures are taken before the post-warning statement is made. The curative measures must be designed to inform a reasonable person in the suspect's situation of the import and effect of the *Miranda* warning and its waiver. In most instances, a substantial difference in time and circumstances between the pre-warning statement and the warning will suffice — so will an additional warning explaining that the pre-warning statement is probably not admissible.[342]

The Sixth Circuit held in mid-2007 that it can be permissible for police to make a renewed approach to a suspect who asked for a lawyer when he was *Mirandized*, if police contact with a close friend or relative of the suspect gives rise

---

that others had implicated him. Although there is no per se rule requiring access to a parent before custodial interrogation of a juvenile, denials of requests were a significant factor in the voluntariness analysis: State v. Burrell, 697 N.W.2d 579 (Minn. 2005). Although the Seventh Circuit criticized police tactics (a 17-year-old was deliberately denied access to his parents at arrest and interrogation), it affirmed the Illinois Court of Appeal's decision that the confession was voluntary. The same "totality of circumstances" analysis is used to determine the voluntariness of a confession whether it is given by an adult or a juvenile; and in any case, the arrestee was a month away from his 18th birthday, and Illinois law defines a juvenile as a person under 17: Bridges v. Chambers, 447 F.3d 994 (7th Cir. 2006).

[340] Thompson v. Keohane, 516 U.S. 99 (1995).

[341] 448 U.S. 98 (1980).

[342] Missouri v. Siebert, 542 U.S. 600 (2004).

to the belief that the suspect is now willing to be questioned without an attorney present.[343]

The Tenth Circuit ruled in early 2006 that, although police assurances of lighter penalties in return for cooperation can be permissible, showing an interrogatee pieces of paper with numbers written down, suggesting years of sentencing, was enough to render the confession involuntary.[344]

If an interrogatee asks a clear question about *Miranda* rights, the interrogator has a duty to stop asking questions and respond to the interrogatee's question (or at least make a good-faith attempt to do so).[345] Therefore, the police have an obligation to answer a murder suspect who asked what a good lawyer would do after he waived *Miranda*, inculpated himself, and was asked if he wanted to speak without presence of counsel. The Eighth Circuit found that statements made after warning and voluntary waiver of the right to counsel were admissible, despite the police having elicited earlier inadmissible statements during custodial interrogation without a *Miranda* warning.[346]

In 1978, the Supreme Court ruled that the defendant's involuntary statements cannot be used even for impeachment.[347] However, in 1990, the Supreme Court limited that doctrine by holding[348] that even if a statement was elicited after the police improperly continued questioning once the suspect had requested an attorney,[349] the statement can be used for impeachment provided that the statement was made to the police based on a knowing, voluntary, intelligent waiver of the presence of counsel.

[2] Coercion and Voluntariness

The voluntariness of a confession must be assessed based on the totality of the circumstances: see 18 USC § 3501. The question is whether the suspect was subjected to coercion sufficient to overbear the will; psychological as well as physical coercion may be sufficient to render a statement non-voluntary. The Sixth Circuit held that, where there is probable cause to arrest a defendant, it is not coercion (that would invalidate a confession) to make threats against a third party. In this instance, the police found crack in the defendant's half-sister's apartment, where he was staying, and threatened to arrest her unless the defendant admitted to possession of the drugs.[350]

The trial judge must determine the validity of a confession before reading it to the jury; it is not proper to read the confession, then tell the jury to decide whether or

[343] Van Hook v. Anderson, 488 F.3d 411 (6th Cir. 2007).
[344] United States v. Lopez, 437 F.3d 1059 (10th Cir. 2006).
[345] Almeida v. State, 737 So. 2d 520 (Fla. 1999).
[346] United States v. Fellers, 397 F.3d 1090 (8th Cir. 2005).
[347] Mincey v. Arizona, 437 U.S. 385 (1978).
[348] Michigan v. Harvey, 494 U.S. 344 (1990).
[349] This is improper under Michigan v. Jackson, 475 U.S. 625 (1986).
[350] United States v. Johnson, 351 F.3d 254 (6th Cir. 2003).

not it was voluntary.[351] *Denno* entitles a defendant who alleges that the confession was coerced to a full evidentiary hearing on the factual content of the confession.

Another aspect of the Fifth Amendment is that the defendant has the option either to testify or refrain from testifying. It is improper for the prosecution to allude in any way to the silence of a defendant who has chosen not to testify, although the impropriety is not necessarily sufficient to cause reversal of the conviction.[352]

The Sixth Circuit decided early in 2000 that it violates the Fifth Amendment for the prosecution case in chief to use the accused's pre-arrest, pre-*Miranda* silence. (Six other Circuits have ruled on this issue, splitting three and three.)[353]

Furthermore, it is not error for the prosecution to comment on the defense's failure to offer evidence (as distinct from the defendant's failure to take the stand).

The Supreme Court tackled another Fifth Amendment issue in *United States v. Hubbell*.[354] As part of the Whitewater investigation, the respondent, who entered into a plea agreement, agreed to provide information. The respondent was subpoenaed to produce documents for the Arkansas Grand Jury. On Fifth Amendment grounds, he refused to produce the documents, or even state whether he had them. He was then offered immunity and, in return, produced extensive documentation. The respondent was indicted subsequent to an investigation based on those documents.

The Supreme Court required dismissal of the indictment, because of the Fifth Amendment ban on compelled testimony. Producing documents in response to a subpoena can be both testimonial and compelled. Furthermore, the Fifth Amendment can protect even information that is not itself inculpatory if the effect is to lead to the discovery of incriminating evidence. Where, as here, the producer of documents is granted immunity, the prosecution has a duty to show an independent source for incriminating information, separate and apart from the compelled testimonial production of documents.

Waiver of the right to remain silent can be knowing (and hence valid) as long as the defendant understands the *Miranda* warning, even if the defendant fails to understand the consequences of making an inculpatory statement. Thus, statements made by a defendant who knew that the police would use those statements against

---

[351] Sims v. Georgia, 385 U.S. 538 (1967); Jackson v. Denno, 378 U.S. 368 (1964).

[352] *See* Griffin v. California, 380 U.S. 609 (1965).

[353] Combs v. Coyle, 205 F.3d 269 (6th Cir. 2000). Because there are many reasons — including being aware of *Miranda* rights prior to receiving a warning — why a person would remain silent in the presence of the police, Maryland considers pre-arrest silence to be ambiguous and not probative, so it is not admissible at trial as evidence of guilt: Weitzel v. State, 863 A.2d 999 (Md. 2004). The Eighth Circuit held that the prosecution's use of the defendant's silence after the arrest and before the *Miranda* warning does not violate the prohibition on compelled self-incrimination. But post-arrest, post-warning silence cannot be introduced as substantive evidence of guilt or for impeachment: United States v. Frazier, 394 F.3d 612 (8th Cir. 2005). State v. Leach, 807 N.E.2d 335 (Ohio 2004) says that pre-arrest silence can be used for impeachment, but not as substantive evidence of guilt.

[354] 530 U.S. 27 (2000).

him, but who also believed that God would set him free from prison if he confessed, did not have to be suppressed.[355]

Doyle[356] holds that it is a violation of Due Process for the prosecution to introduce post-*Miranda* silence at trial. One of the most important strategic questions in the trial is whether or not the defendant should take the stand. No matter how many warnings are given, the jury may conclude that a defendant who does not give "his or her side of the story" is remaining silent out of consciousness of guilt. However, it has been held that the Fifth Amendment provides a right to remain silent, not a justification for perjury if the defendant does take the stand.[357]

[a] Undercover Agents

The Supreme Court has held that an undercover police agent placed in a cell with a suspect is not required to give a *Miranda* warning before asking the suspect if he had ever killed anyone.[358]

However, the Eighth Circuit ruled that a jail inmate who had a history of informing on fellow-prisoners, but who had not been instructed by the authorities to watch the defendant, was not a government agent, because a prisoner can only be characterized as such if the police asked for information about a specific person.[359]

[3] Testimonial vs. Non-Testimonial Conduct

Although the Fifth Amendment precludes anyone from being forced to incriminate him or herself, there is a range of issues that overlaps the Fourth and Fifth Amendments. Causing a suspect to exhibit physical characteristics is not testimonial in nature, and therefore is not self-incriminatory, an argument that permits warrantless examinations and testing incident to an arrest, especially in circumstances where delaying the test until a warrant is obtained makes the test results less useful (e.g., the alcohol content of blood diminishes over time).[360]

A suspect can be required to submit to photographing and fingerprinting, and can be required to give voice exemplars and handwriting samples[361] — in other words, painless and reasonably non-intrusive demands. But it is an unreasonable search to require a defendant to submit to surgery that is expected to remove an incriminating bullet.[362]

---

[355] People v. Daoud, 614 N.W.2d 152 (Mich. 2000).

[356] Doyle v. Ohio, 426 U.S. 610 (1976).

[357] LaChance v. Erickson, 522 U.S. 262 (1998); Brogan v. United States, 522 U.S. 398 (1998).

[358] Illinois v. Perkins, 496 U.S. 292 (1990).

[359] United States v. Johnson, 338 F.3d 918 (8th Cir. 2003).

[360] *See* Schmerber v. California, 384 U.S. 757 (1966).

[361] United States v. Wade, 388 U.S. 218 (1967), discussed below in connection with lineups; United States v. Mara, 410 U.S. 19 (1973) covers writing samples.

[362] Winston v. Lee, 470 U.S. 753 (1985).

The influential 2004 Supreme Court case of *Crawford v. Washington*[363] involved a petitioner who stabbed a man who allegedly attempted to rape the petitioner's wife. The police interrogated the wife. The prosecution's position was that the wife told the police that the stabbing was not in self-defense. At the trial, the wife asserted marital privilege to avoid testifying. The wife's recorded statement was introduced as a statement of an unavailable witness validated by particularized guarantees of trustworthiness. However, the Supreme Court ruled that when a statement is testimonial, the mandate of the Confrontation Clause is that there are no indicia of reliability that would justify production of the statement rather than a witness who could be cross-examined. The Supreme Court's examples of testimonial statements are custodial interrogation, Grand Jury testimony, and plea allocutions.

For *Crawford* purposes, the test of whether a statement made in the course of police interrogation is testimonial is whether the circumstances objectively indicate the police are primarily interrogating to get information for an ongoing emergency. Statements are testimonial if there is no emergency and the objective of interrogation is to establish or prove past events for use in a prosecution.[364]

Maryland held that an autopsy report's routine, descriptive findings (for example, the condition of the body) are non-testimonial for *Crawford* purposes. As such, they can be admitted without the testimony of the person who prepared the report. However, opinions, conclusions, and matters central to determination of guilt are testimonial, and therefore can be admitted only if the preparer is available for cross-examination.[365]

The Ninth Circuit held that the *Crawford* right of confrontation does not apply to hearsay admitted in proceedings to revoke supervised release.[366]

---

[363] 541 U.S. 36 (2004). In 2007, the Supreme Court resolved a Circuit split as to the retroactivity of *Crawford*, ruling that *Crawford* does not enunciate a new rule of sufficient magnitude to be applied retroactively. Therefore, a conviction for sexual abuse of a child was sustained even though the alleged child victim did not testify: Whorton v. Bockting, 549 U.S. 406 (2007). The Ninth Circuit upheld a state's retroactive application of Crawford to uphold a sentence. Although Whorton v. Bockting says that Crawford is not retroactive in federal habeas cases, Danforth v. Minnesota, 128 S. Ct. 1029 (2008) says this ruling is not binding on state habeas courts. Therefore, the state court's interpretation of Crawford was reasonable and entitled to deference, and the habeas petition was properly denied: Delgadillo v. Woodford, 527 F.3d 919 (9th Cir. 2008).

[364] Davis v. Washington, 547 U.S. 813 (2006).

[365] Rollins v. State, 392 Md. 455, 897 A.2d 821 (2006); *but see* State v. Forte, 360 N.C. 427 (2006), holding that a written laboratory report of DNA analysis done by a police forensic investigator is not testimonial. The New York Court of Appeals ruled that a laboratory test (e.g., DNA tests and latent fingerprint comparison reports) prepared by a non-testifying expert is not testimonial for *Crawford* purposes, but refused to impose an absolute rule that laboratory business records are always non-testimonial, because not everything that qualifies for a hearsay exception is non-testimonial. The Court of Appeals viewed the salient question as whether a statement is properly considered a surrogate for accusatory in-court testimony; lab tests can be exculpatory as well as inculpatory, and the technician who performed the test is not bearing witness against the defendant: People v. Rawlins/People v. Meekins, 10 N.Y.3d 136 (N.Y. 2008).

[366] United States v. Hall, 419 F.3d 980 (9th Cir. 2005).

In 2004, the Maryland Court of Special Appeals held that after *Crawford*, prosecutors can no longer use a "tender years" exception to introduce hearsay statements of a sexual abuse victim younger than 12 if the child is available to testify.[367]

After a taped interview with a victim was admitted at trial, the defendant applied for state post-conviction relief, seeking a new trial. The Minnesota courts said that *Crawford* was not retroactive under *Teague*. However, in early 2008, the Supreme Court ruled that *Teague* does not prevent state courts from giving new criminal procedure rules a broader effect than *Teague* requires. *Crawford* was a "new rule" for *Teague* purposes, because its result was not dictated by the precedents in effect at the time the defendant's conviction became final. However, it was not a rule devised by the Supreme Court or a product of its views on policy. *Teague* does not allow retroactive application of a new constitutional rule of criminal procedure to cases on federal habeas review, except for watershed rules of criminal procedure, or rules that place certain primary individual conduct outside the state power to forbid. *Teague* was decided in the context of federal habeas, federal courts, and federal statutes, and does not answer the question of whether states can provide broader relief in state post-conviction proceedings. In this reading, *Teague* limits the authority of federal courts to overturn state convictions, but does not limit state courts' authority to grant relief when a state reviews its own convictions.[368]

Statements by the murder victim to a police officer responding to a domestic violence call were introduced at Giles' murder trial. He was convicted. *Crawford* was decided while his appeal was pending. The state appeals court decided that unconfronted testimony of the murder victim could be admitted based on "forfeiture by wrongdoing" (i.e., the murder itself made the victim unavailable to testify). The state Supreme Court affirmed, but the U.S. Supreme Court vacated and remanded the conviction. The theory of "forfeiture by wrongdoing" cannot create an exception to the confrontation requirement because it was not an established exception when the Constitution was adopted, and common-law courts excluded the testimony of absent witnesses even if the defendant wrongfully caused the absence, but with a motive other than preventing the witness from testifying.[369]

[D] Sixth Amendment Issues

The Sixth Amendment governs the right to counsel; various issues of identifications and their admissibility; confrontation of accusers[370] and public trials; and guarantees a "speedy" trial — the latter very much a term of art.

---

[367] Snowden v. State, 156 Md. App. 139 (Md. Spec. App. 2004).

[368] Danforth v. Minnesota, 128 S. Ct. 1029 (2008).

[369] Giles v. California, 128 S. Ct. 2678 (U.S. 2008).

[370] The right of confrontation is not violated by prosecution failure to produce evidence for which there is no reasonable probability of making the outcome more favorable to the defendant: Strickler v. Greene, 527 U.S. 263 (1999).

A 1970 Supreme Court decision holds that a 12-person jury is not fundamental to the function of the guarantee of a jury trial, and that a six-person jury is constitutionally acceptable (except in a capital case).[371] Federal juries are required to be unanimous in handing down a criminal verdict, whereas state juries are not.[372]

According to the Supreme Court, a prosecutor did not violate the Sixth Amendment by pointing out to the jury that, because a testifying defendant was present for the whole trial, he had the opportunity to tailor his testimony to conform to witness statements. Because there was no Sixth Amendment violation, the Court of Appeals should not have granted habeas relief.

In this case, there was a conflict in the testimony of the defendant and the alleged victim of a sex crime. The defense counsel accused the prosecution witness of lying, triggering the comments about the defendant's ability to tailor his testimony. In the Supreme Court view, this is not the same as commenting on a defendant's failure to testify, which impermissibly asks jurors to use silence as evidence of guilt.[373]

[1] Identification Issues

In the Sixth Amendment context, identification of a suspect can be challenged on the grounds of impermissible suggestiveness. Challenges may succeed, for instance, if the identification was made at the crime scene, when the victim or other witness is emotionally stressed. Due Process forbids unduly suggestive police identification procedures that create a serious risk of misidentification by witnesses.

The bedrock case on identification is *United States v. Wade*, 388 U.S. 218 (1967). *Wade* requires lineups to be conducted under reasonable conditions (although it is not necessary for the "fillers" other than the suspect to look like the suspect's clones), and bans one-person "show-ups" (the police ask the witness if the suspect is the person they saw commit the crime) as unduly suggestive. The prosecution must give notice to the defense that out-of-court identification evidence will be introduced. Such notice entitles the defense to a *"Wade"* "hearing" on the admissibility of the testimony.

Under *Wade*, if the pretrial identification was improper, an in-court identification of the defendant may still be admissible, but first it must be validated as an independent recollection.

A lineup is considered superior, because it involves human beings rather than pictures, but asking a witness to view a photo array is not necessarily improper. Identification of photographs may be challenged[374] if there are not enough

---

[371] Williams v. Florida, 399 U.S. 78 (1970).

[372] Apodaca v. Oregon, 406 U.S. 404 (1972).

[373] Portuondo v. Agard, 529 U.S. 61 (2000).

[374] Simmons v. United States, 390 U.S. 377 (1968) applies Due Process analysis to hold that photo arrays must not be unduly suggestive.

photographs to make a valid array; if they do not bear a close enough resemblance to the suspect to create a valid identification (i.e., if only one dark-skinned or light-skinned person, or only one with long hair, is included, the suspect may be identified purely on the basis of this one characteristic, rather than a true resemblance). However, an impermissible photo identification can be rehabilitated by an in-court identification.

Some eyewitnesses are not particularly observant or do not have very good memories, so their testimony can be challenged on these bases. Observing a crime is a brief event, and conditions of observation are typically poor, but it is also a memorable event — so attempts to challenge eyewitness testimony may backfire, if the jury is firmly convinced that the victim or other witness is accurate and truthful.

The test of either out-of-court or in-court identification is its reliability. But where the pretrial identification procedures were not unduly suggestive, challenge of an in-court identification goes to weight rather than admissibility.[375]

[2] Attachment of the Right to Counsel

The Sixth Amendment provides a right to counsel, applicable to both the federal government and the states, in all criminal prosecutions.[376]

There are four interrelated elements in the Sixth Amendment right to counsel: the simple right to counsel; the right to counsel of one's own choice; to effective counsel (see § 26.04[N][2][a]); and for the attorney to have a long enough period of preparation to render an effective defense. The right to counsel applies to state courts on the same terms as to federal courts.

A mid-2008 Supreme Court case holds that it is permissible for states to require counsel for defendants who have been found competent to stand trial, but who suffer from severe mental illness that prevents them from being able to conduct trial proceedings pro se. The Supreme Court ruled that, because mental illness varies, it would be improper to impose a uniform competency standard on all defendants, whether or not they are represented. Mentally ill defendants who represent themselves do not affirm their dignity, and may impair their basic right to a fair trial.[377]

The Supreme Court decided in 2006 that a defendant with retained (rather than appointed) counsel is entitled to choice of counsel. Deprivation of the attorney selected by the defendant is not harmless error, and the defendant is entitled to reversal of the conviction.[378]

Because the Fourteenth Amendment fully incorporates the Sixth Amendment guarantee of the right to counsel, the states have been obligated to appoint counsel

---

[375] Manson v. Brathwaite, 432 U.S. 98 (1977); Foster v. California, 394 U.S. 440 (1969).

[376] Gideon v. Wainwright, 372 U.S. 335 (1963); Escobedo v. Illinois, 378 U.S. 478 (1964).

[377] Indiana v. Edwards, 128 S. Ct. 2379 (2008); *see* Tony Mauro, *Supreme Court Limits Self-Representation by Mentally Ill Defendants*, Legal Times 6/20/08 (law.com).

[378] United States v. Gonzalez-Lopez, 548 U.S. 140 (2006).

for indigents in all felony cases since 1963.[379] Furthermore, a 1972 decision extends this requirement to misdemeanors for which the defendant is sentenced to a jail term.[380]

The first time the defendant was charged with Driving Under the Influence, he waived the right to counsel (although he was represented on later charges). In 2004, the Supreme Court held that the waiver was permissible if the court informed the accused of the nature of the charges, the right to consult an attorney about what to plead, and the range of possible punishments after a guilty plea. The defendant admitted that he understood the initial colloquy and did not offer evidence about what additional information an attorney could have provided.[381]

A mid-2002 U.S. Supreme Court decision requires provision of state-paid counsel for indigent defendants who have not waived the right to counsel in any case in which a suspended sentence is imposed, because the defendant might later be incarcerated if the conditions for suspending the sentence are violated.[382]

Incriminating statements uttered during custodial interrogation are inadmissible if the suspect was denied access to an attorney.[383] Interrogation must stop when the suspect makes an unequivocal demand for counsel, but can resume without counsel if the suspect voluntarily re-initiates contact with police.[384] After charges have been filed, law enforcement officials are not permitted to deliberately elicit incriminating information from a defendant unless the attorney is present or the defendant has waived the presence of the attorney — whether or not the defendant is in custody.[385]

---

[379] Gideon v. Wainwright, 372 U.S. 335 (1963).

[380] Argersinger v. Hamlin, 407 U.S. 25 (1972).

[381] Iowa v. Tovar, 541 U.S. 77 (2004). The Eleventh Circuit en banc reversed two three-judge panels to hold that a criminal defendant's rejection of appointed counsel can operate as a waiver of the right to counsel, and reinstated two convictions (one for a series of bomb threats, the other for homicide). The three-judge panels reversed the convictions when the defendants wanted appointed counsel, but rejected the particular lawyer who was appointed for them: United States v. Garey, 540 F.3d 1270 and Jones v. Walker, 540 F.3d 1277. *See* Alyson M. Palmer, *11th Circuit: Firing Counsel Equals Waiving Right to One*, Fulton County Daily Report 8/22/08 (law.com).

[382] Alabama v. Shelton, 535 U.S. 654 (2002). At the end of 2004, the Supreme Court ruled that attorneys did not have third-party standing to assert the rights of indigent defendants (and potential clients) after Michigan adopted a Constitutional amendment and passed a statute denying appointed appellate counsel to indigent defendants who filed a guilty plea at trial: Kowalski v. Tesmer, 543 U.S. 125 (2004).

[383] Escobedo v. Illinois, above; Michigan v. Jackson, 475 U.S. 625 (1986).

[384] Edwards v. Arizona, 451 U.S. 477 (1981); Davis v. United States, 512 U.S. 452 (1994). Minnick v. Mississippi, 498 U.S. 146 (1990) says that even if the suspect speaks to the attorney in the interim, it is improper to restart interrogation in the absence of counsel.

[385] Patterson v. Illinois, 487 U.S. 285 (1988). *See also* Maine v. Moulton, 474 U.S. 159 (1985): the right to counsel may be violated by deliberate use of a secret government informant to get information from a defendant after indictment or arraignment. According to Satterthwaite v. Texas, 486 U.S. 249 (1988), the right to counsel attaches by the time of a post accusatory examination of the defendant by a court-appointed psychiatrist.

The Supreme Court's position is that the right to counsel is specific to a particular offense; interrogation without a lawyer on Offense B is permissible even if the suspect is represented by counsel on Offense A.[386]

According to a 2001 Supreme Court decision, the right to counsel attaches with respect to related offenses only if they are the "same" under the *Blockburger* test; that is, if proving the second offense does not require proof of any facts not required to prove the first offense. In this case, when the defendant was arrested for another crime, he confessed to a burglary but said he did not know anything about the disappearance of two people from the house he burglarized. Later, he confessed to his father that he had killed those two people. His father contacted the police. The defendant confessed to the murders and was sentenced to death. The Texas Court of Criminal Appeals ruled that the right to counsel had already attached in connection with the offense for which he was originally arrested. The Supreme Court disagreed, finding the custodial interrogation to be proper and the confession to be admissible.[387]

Although the police must not impair the right to consult an attorney (if the suspect wants one), there is no affirmative duty for the police to have lawyers available in case they are requested by suspects.[388]

A suspect can invoke the right to counsel conditionally, for instance, "If I take a polygraph test, I want a lawyer"; in such a case, it would be permissible to question the suspect with no attorney present as long as there is no polygraph test.

[3] Critical Stages

The right to counsel attaches at "critical stages" in the law enforcement process, as soon as an individual becomes the subject of adversary criminal proceedings (and is no longer a mere subject of investigation). A stage of the prosecution is critical if the lack of counsel could impair the right to a fair trial.[389]

According to *Wade*, there is no right to counsel at lineup before the suspect has been accused of a crime, but there is at the preliminary hearing, or at any identification of the defendant at or after initiation of adversary judicial proceedings.[390] Some identification procedures; attempts to get inculpatory statements from an arrestee; arraignment or other initial appearance where action or inaction can affect the accused; the preliminary hearing; the trial; and sentencing have been identified as critical stages. The Supreme Court has also held that Due Process includes the right to representation by competent counsel on a convicted person's first appeal as of right.[391] The Tenth Circuit extended the federal guarantee of appointed counsel (under 21 USC § 848) for state death row inmates

[386] McNeil v. Wisconsin, 501 U.S. 171 (1991).
[387] Texas v. Cobb, 532 U.S. 162 (2001).
[388] Duckworth v. Egan, 492 U.S. 195 (1989).
[389] Estelle v. Smith, 451 U.S. 454 (1981); Moran v. Burbine, 475 U.S. 412 (1986); Illinois v. Perkins, 496 U.S. 292 (1990).
[390] *See also* Moore v. Illinois, 434 U.S. 220 (1977).
[391] Evitts v. Lucey, 469 U.S. 387 (1985).

seeking habeas to state clemency proceedings, although some other Circuits disagree.[392]

The Supreme Court held in mid-2008 that the Sixth Circuit right to counsel attaches at the first appearance before a magistrate, whether the prosecutor is present or not. (Texas has a procedure under which the defendant appears before a magistrate judge for bail to set; the prosecutor is not present, and counsel is not appointed). The petitioner was arrested as a felon in possession of a firearm, based on incorrect information that he had a previous felony conviction. He sued the county under 42 USC § 1983, claiming that if he had been assigned counsel within a reasonable time after the hearing before the magistrate judge, he would not have been indicted or jailed, and that the Sixth Amendment is violated by denying appointed counsel to indigent defendants until after indictment. The decision has limited practical significance, because the federal system, 43 states, and Washington D.C. already appointed counsel for indigent defendants at or before the first appearance before a judge. (The exceptions are Alabama, Colorado, Kansas, Oklahoma, South Carolina, Texas, and Virginia.) However, the Supreme Court ruled that appointment of counsel is not necessarily required as soon as the right to counsel attaches — only if it is necessary to guarantee effective assistance at trial.[393]

Fed. R. Crim. P. Rule 44(a) requires appointment of counsel for an indigent defendant at every stage of the proceedings, unless the right is waived and the defendant chooses to appear pro se (see § 26.03[D][4]).

The defendant's ability to choose counsel is not infinite. The District Court judge has discretion to either grant or deny a continuance to a defendant who wants to substitute counsel. Factors in the decision include possible prejudice if the continuance is denied; who will be inconvenienced if it is granted; and whether the defendant is using the motion for substitution as a delaying tactic.

A related question is which stages of the process entitle the defendant to be present while the attorney is at work.

The Ninth Circuit view of the issue is that Due Process does not require the defendant's presence when the defense attorney, prosecutor, and judge discuss the defense attorney's potential conflict of interest. The Ninth Circuit read AEDPA to require deference to the state courts that rejected the petitioner's appeals. The Ninth Circuit held that error (if any) in keeping the defendant out of the meeting was merely trial error that could be reviewed for harmlessness, not structural error, so the conviction could be reversed only on a showing that the defendant suffered adverse effects of the error.[394]

The Supreme Court ruled in early 2008 that an attorney's appearance by speakerphone (rather than in person) at the time when a guilty plea was entered

---

[392] Hain v. Mullin, 436 F.3d 1168 (10th Cir. 2006).

[393] Rothgery v. Gillespie County, Texas, 128 S. Ct. 2578 (2008); *see* Tony Mauro, *Supreme Court Says Right to Counsel Begins With First Appearance Before Judge*, Legal Times 6/24/08 (law.com).

[394] Campbell v. Rice, 408 F.3d 1166 (9th Cir. 2005).

was not presumptively ineffective assistance of counsel. In court, the defendant stated that he had discussed the plea decision with his attorney, and was satisfied with his legal representation. At sentencing, when the attorney was present, Van Patten exercised his right to allocution but did not object to the guilty plea. The standard was whether the state court failed to apply a clear precedent. Although the Supreme Court did not give its authorization for telephoned appearances as necessarily adequate, nevertheless there was no clear precedent for treating a speakerphone appearance as a complete denial of counsel.[395]

[4] Defendants Proceeding Pro Se

An accused person can waive the right to counsel, as long as the waiver is intelligent, knowing, and voluntary. The state has the burden of establishing that the right to counsel has been waived.[396]

A defendant can choose to represent him or herself pro se, but the judge must inquire if the defendant is capable of self-representation. The request must be clear, unequivocal, and timely (e.g., made before the trial begins). The court can appoint stand-by counsel for a pro se defendant, even if the defendant objects.[397]

In the Second Circuit view, a New York court's conclusion — that removing a disruptive pro se petitioner from the courtroom without appointing standby counsel to represent him in his absence — was not an unreasonable application of clearly established Supreme Court precedent. Counsel was assigned as a "legal advisor" when the defendant (charged with injuring two police officers by hitting them with a stolen cab) asked to proceed pro se. The defendant moved to assign another lawyer, alleging that the appointed counsel was ineffective for refusing to adopt the defendant's preferred trial strategy. A mistrial was declared, and a new lawyer appointed. At retrial, the defendant was not permitted a hybrid defense; he was ordered either to finish voir dire himself, or be represented by his appointed counsel. The defendant yelled at the jury that the judge was prejudiced and deprived him of a fair trial; eventually, the judge had the defendant removed, and the prosecution's direct case was admitted without cross-examination. When the defendant was allowed to return, he said he wanted his appointed counsel to handle the rest of the trial, but the judge refused. The defendant was convicted, appealed, and filed a habeas petition. The Second Circuit, although it criticized the judge's approach, held that there was no violation of clear Supreme Court precedent. It would have been preferable to terminate the defendant's self-representation for disruptive behavior, and had the standby counsel represent him in his absence, but the practice actually followed was permissible.[398]

---

[395] Wright v. Van Patten, 128 S. Ct. 743 (2008).

[396] Jones v. Barnes, 463 U.S. 745 (1983), Faretta v. California, 422 U.S. 806 (1975), Michigan v. Harvey, 494 U.S. 344 (1990).

[397] McKaskle v. Wiggins, 465 U.S. 168 (1984); *Faretta*, 422 U.S. 806 (1975).

[398] Davis v. Grant, 537 F.3d 132 (2d Cir. 2008).

Leveto was indicted for tax fraud (promotion of sham offshore trusts to avoid tax liability) in 2001; fled, and was arrested in 2004. Counsel was appointed for him, and withdrew as a result of conflict of interest. Leveto said that he wanted to represent himself, but "I am in no way waiving my right to counsel." He said he wanted to proceed pro se with the appointed attorney as stand-by counsel, and this was done after the District Court held a colloquy on his understanding of the charges against him. Just before jury selection was scheduled, Leveto said that he wanted to be represented by an attorney because "some new issues had come up." The District Court denied his motion, on the grounds that he had waived the right to counsel. He continued to ask for an attorney; the District Court told him to consult the stand-by counsel, who was present in court, but the waiver of right to counsel could not be reversed on the day of trial. He was convicted, and appealed. The Third Circuit held that once waived, the Sixth Amendment right to counsel is no longer absolute, and evidence of the defendant's intent to delay will justify refusal of a motion for counsel. In this analysis, denial of post-waiver request for counsel does not violate the Sixth Amendment unless the District Court clearly erred in its determination on the issue of good cause, or the court failed to inquire into the reason for the defendant's request.[399]

However, neither the Sixth Amendment, the Criminal Justice Act, nor 18 USC § 3006A requires appointment of counsel for a corporation.[400]

[5] Confrontation Clause and Public Trial

The Sixth Amendment gives the defendant the right to confront his or her accusers, and to have a public trial — not a secret proceeding. However, these rights are not absolute: in some instances, the courtroom can be closed, and a witness permitted to testify other than in open court, if a sufficient showing of danger to witnesses, informants, or undercover police officers is made.

The courtroom can be closed only if:

- The party seeking closing advances an overriding interest that is at risk of being prejudiced
- The closure is only as broad as necessary
- The court considers reasonable alternatives to closing the proceedings to the public
- Closing the court is supported by adequate findings by the judge.

The Constitutional guarantees applicable in an ordinary criminal trial of a U.S. citizen do not necessarily apply to proceedings involving alleged terrorists, especially those who are not U.S. citizens.

The confrontation guarantee of the Sixth Amendment precludes crucial prosecution witnesses from testifying anonymously at trial. Although concern for the

---

[399] United States v. Leveto, 540 F.3d 200 (3d Cir. 2008).
[400] United States v. Unimex Inc., 991 F.2d 546 (9th Cir. 1993).

witnesses' safety can justify nondisclosure of their identity before trial, they must nevertheless be identified at trial.[401]

The Sixth Circuit right of confrontation prevents the use of two-way video-conferencing to take the testimony of foreign witnesses who do not want to travel to the United States. The Eleventh Circuit held that, although public policy can permit young victims of abuse to testify via one-way closed circuit television, the policy does not extend to essential witnesses who are not vulnerable but merely do not want to travel.[402]

A defendant is not entitled, under the Sixth Amendment or the due process clause, to be present at sidebar or in camera conferences, so it is not an error to exclude the defendant.[403]

The Fifth Circuit agreed that Confrontation Clause rights were violated by admitting into evidence out-of-court statements by the triggermen (who were tried separately and could not be cross-examined) in a murder-for-hire trial. The trigger-men made custodial confessions to law enforcement officials, and one also admit-ted the crime to his girlfriend. The standard for appellate review was whether the District Court was correct that the state court's Confrontation Clause decision contradicted or unreasonably applied clearly established federal law and, if it did, whether the error was harmless. The Fifth Circuit concluded that in this case, error was not harmless. The Fifth Circuit held that the hired killers' custodial confessions did not have the indicia of reliability required by the Confrontation Clause. The confession, even supported by phone records and physical evidence, is still hearsay that must stand on its own inherent reliability. A statement made by a person in police custody incriminating someone else is inherently unreliable, and one of the hired killers gave two conflicting confessions. There is no hearsay exception for co-conspirator statements.[404]

[6] Effective Assistance of Counsel

For a defendant successfully to assert the defense that he or she lacked effective assistance of counsel, he or she must show that the defendant was prej-udiced by the alleged defective representation—unless the attorney's perfor-mance was so deficient that, in effect, the defendant was entirely deprived of counsel.[405]

---

[401] Alvarado v. Superior Court, 11 Cal. Rptr. 2d 149 (Cal. 2000).

[402] United States v. Yates, 391 F.3d 1182 (11th Cir. 2004); aff'd, 438 F.3d 1307 (11th Cir. 2006), holding that although confrontation need not always be face to face, there must be a com-pelling public policy justification for bypassing other alternatives, such as pretrial depositions under Fed. R. Crim. P. 15. 2002 revisions to the Fed. R. Crim. P. permit initial appearances and arraign-ments to be handled by two-way video teleconferencing if the defendant consents — but the Supreme Court did not act on a proposal to permit teleconferenced testimony at trial.

[403] United States v. McCoy, 8 F.3d 495 (7th Cir. 1993).

[404] Fratta v. Quarterman, 536 F.3d 489 (5th Cir. 2008).

[405] The "no counsel" test comes from United States v. Cronin, 466 U.S. 649 (1984).

The Supreme Court rejected an ineffective-assistance claim in a case where a public defender concluded that the best strategy would be to concede the client's undoubted guilt of a kidnap-murder in order to maintain credibility at the penalty phase and thereby perhaps stave off a death sentence. The client was uncooperative and refused to either consent to or object to the strategy. The Florida Supreme Court treated a concession of guilt without the defendant's express permission as ineffective assistance that is always prejudicial and that mandates a new trial, because it is the equivalent of a guilty plea. The Supreme Court, however, did not consider the strategy tantamount to a guilty plea, because the prosecution was still required to make its case, and the defense could still assert procedural irregularities. In a capital case, effective assistance may require concentrating on averting the death penalty rather than on seeking an unlikely acquittal: *Florida v. Nixon*, 543 U.S. 175 (2004).[406]

The Massachusetts Supreme Judicial Court ruled in mid-2004 that defendants are denied the right to effective counsel because the state rates for appointed counsel are so low that very few private attorneys are available. In lieu of ordering the pay rates to be increased, the court required indigent defendants to be released after seven days, and their cases dismissed without prejudice after 45 days, if appointed counsel could not be secured by reasonable effort.[407]

[7] Forfeiture and the Right to Counsel

21 USC § 853, the Comprehensive Forfeiture Act of 1984, permits forfeiture of the assets of a person convicted of certain drug offenses. It also authorizes a pretrial restraining order freezing assets that would be subject to forfeiture if the defendant were convicted. Forfeiture provisions are also included in RICO, at 18 USC § 3006A.

The Supreme Court has ruled that the freeze does not violate the Sixth Amendment, although the practical difficulties of paying an attorney when one's assets have been frozen are significant.[408]

Also see *Florida v. White:*[409] probable cause to believe that a car is property linked to a crime, and therefore subject to forfeiture, justifies warrantless seizure of the car from a public place.

---

[406] The Third Circuit refused to extend the law of ineffective assistance of counsel to encompass failure to predict that the state Supreme Court would rule that amendments to the death penalty statute would not be retroactive. (The lawyer advised against taking an appeal, because she believed that the statute would be applied retroactively.) Fountain v. Kyler, 420 F.3d 267 (3d Cir. 2005).

[407] Lavallee v. Justices in the Hampden Superior Court, 812 N.E.2d 895 (Mass. 2004).

[408] Caplin & Drysdale v. United States, 491 U.S. 617 (1989); United States v. Monsanto, 491 U.S. 600 (1989). On forfeiture, *see also* United States v. Bajakajian, 524 U.S. 321 (1998): Customs officials discovered that the defendant was leaving the United States carrying $350,000 in currency; amounts over $10,000 must be reported. Forfeiture of the entire amount was unconstitutional, a violation of the Excessive Fines clause, because it was grossly disproportionate to a fairly harmless failure to make a required report.

[409] 526 U.S. 559 (1999).

See the Civil Asset Forfeiture Reform Act of 2000, P.L. 106-185, for amendments to 18 USC § 983, providing general rules for civil forfeiture proceedings, setting out the warrant requirements for seizures, offering innocent owners a defense, and explaining how to move to set aside a forfeiture.

Fed. R. Crim. P. 32.2 provides that, as soon as possible after a guilty verdict or finding, or a plea of guilty or nolo contendere, the court must determine what property is forfeitable with respect to any count for which forfeiture is sought. If any property falls into this category, the court has a duty to promptly issue a preliminary order of forfeiture either stating the amount of money that the defendant must pay, or directing forfeiture of the appropriate property. Any third party asserting rights in the forfeitable property can file a claim in a Rule 32.2(c) ancillary proceeding.

At the beginning of 2002, the Supreme Court ruled[410] that the Fifth Amendment requirement of Due Process is satisfied by sending notice to a federal prisoner of the forfeiture of property in which the prisoner might have an interest. Notice is sent in care of the prison, and is adequate if the prison maintains procedures for recording and delivering such notices. The Supreme Court approved this procedure because it is reasonably calculated to provide actual notice.

A wife had no claim to property forfeited when her husband plead guilty to drug-related offenses. The property was in the husband's sole name, so the wife's citation of state law on tenancy by the entirety was inapposite. The Eighth Circuit ruled that this statute defines marital property only in the context of dissolution, and divorce law does not govern spousal interests in forfeited property.[411]

In contrast, to the Second Circuit, forcing a wife to forfeit her half interest in the home where her husband grew marijuana in the basement, was an excessive fine that violated the Eighth Amendment. The court said that, at worst, she refused to investigate what her husband was doing, and remanded the case to determine if the forfeiture should be vacated as to her, or reduced. If it was vacated, she and the government would become co-owners.[412]

Although a plea agreement can preclude the government from substituting assets for the assets conceded to be forfeitable, the basic rule of 21 USC § 853(p) is that when tainted property is not reachable, forfeiture of substitute assets is not merely permissible but mandatory. The Fourth Circuit also joined the Second, Third, Sixth, and Seventh in holding that *Booker* does not apply to forfeitures. A jury determination is not required for an order authorizing forfeiture of substitute

---

[410] Dusenberry v. United States, 534 U.S. 161 (2002).

[411] United States v. Cochenour, 441 F.3d 599 (8th Cir. 2006). The statute in question is Mo. Rev. Stat. § 452.330.2. The principle that divorce law is inapplicable comes from United States v. Totaro, 345 F.3d 989 (8th Cir. 2003).

[412] von Hofe v. United States, 492 F.3d 175 (2d Cir. 2007); *see* Mark Hamblett, *Forfeiture of Wife's Share of Home Over Husband's Marijuana Is Found Excessive*, N.Y.L.J. 6/29/07 (law.com).

assets, because the amount forfeited does not increase. (Later, the Eleventh Circuit adopted this position.)[413]

PART 3: PROCEDURE AND TRIAL PRACTICE

§ 26.04 CRIMINAL PROCEDURE

[A] Introduction

This section discusses the procedural aspects of criminal trials. Substantive criminal law is covered starting at § 26.02; the discussion of Constitutional issues begins at § 26.03.

Although most criminal cases are prosecuted at the state level, it would be very difficult to summarize all the variations in state criminal practice. Therefore, for simplicity and uniformity, this discussion concentrates on federal criminal procedure.

The Hyde Amendment, 18 USC § 3006A, permits an award of fees to criminal defense attorneys when the government acted in bad faith or took a vexatious or frivolous position. The availability of a fee award is determined by analysis of the prosecution case as a whole rather than tallying the number of meritless charges that were pursued. The Sixth Circuit, however, rejected a government contention that a fee award should be ruled out because only three out of 14 charges were meritless.[414]

[1] Federal Rules Amendments

Each year, the Supreme Court proposes changes in the Federal Rules of Criminal Procedure and the Federal Rules of Evidence (as well as the rules affecting civil and bankruptcy procedure).

The amendments effective December 1, 2007 are as follows:

- Rule 11: Conforming amendment for *Booker*, stating that it is no longer necessary for the court to advise the defendant during a plea colloquy that the court must apply the Guidelines
- Rule 32: A *Booker* amendment with respect to sentencing and judgment. The court can instruct the probation officer to include information about the 18 USC § 3553(a) factors in the presentence report.
- Rule 35: Another *Booker* amendment, this time for correction or reduction of a sentence[415]

---

[413] United States v. Alamoudi (4th Cir. 2006); for the proposition that *Booker* does not apply to forfeitures, *see* United States v. Williams, 445 F.3d 1302 (11th Cir. 2006); United States v. Leahy, 438 F.3d 326 (3d Cir. 2006); United States v. Hall, 411 F.3d 651 (6th Cir. 2005); United States v. Fruchter, 411 F.3d 377 (2d Cir. 2005), United States v. Tedder, 403 F.3d 836 (7th Cir. 2005).

[414] United States v. Heavrin, 330 F.3d 723 (6th Cir. 2003).

[415] The Fed. R. Crim. P. 35(a) procedure for correcting a sentence within seven days of its oral pronouncement requires the District Court to actually resentence the defendant within seven days of the first oral sentence: United States v. Vicol, 460 F.3d 693 (6th Cir. 2006).

- Rule 45: An explanation of how the additional three days are computed for service by mail, leaving the papers with the clerk of the court, or following the FRCP 5(b)(2) procedures for electronic service.
- Rule 49.1: Protecting privacy and security of electronic case files.

Most of the changes taking effect December 1, 2008, implement the Crime Victims' Rights Act, 18 USC § 3771.

- Rule 1: Implements the CVRA's definition of "crime victim" (this is also true for Rule 32).
- Rule 12.1: Disclosure of the victim's address and telephone number to the defense is not automatic whenever an alibi defense is raised; the defendant must show need for this information, and even if the information is needed, the court must control disclosure to protect the victim's interests.
- Rule 17: No third-party subpoena for personal or confidential evidence about a victim can be issued without a court order, and unless exceptional circumstances are demonstrated to the court, the victim must be notified of the subpoena request.
- Rule 18: The place of trial must be set considering convenience of the victim as well as the defendant and witnesses.
- Rule 32: Whenever the statute permits court-ordered restitution (not just when the statute requires it), the pre-sentence investigation report should include information relevant to restitution.
- Rule 41: A magistrate judge in a district in which crime-related activities may have occurred can authorize a search warrant for property within a U.S. territory, possession, or commonwealth, but outside any state or federal judicial district; a warrant can also be issued to search a U.S. diplomatic or consular mission.
- New rule 60 (previous rule 60 renumbered as Rule 61): The government has a duty to use its best efforts to notify the victim of any public proceeding involving the crime, and victims can be excluded from the proceeding only if there is clear and convincing evidence that attendance would alter the victim's testimony. All victim's rights motions (made by the victim or his or her representative) must be heard promptly. [http://www.uscourts.gov/rules/supct0108/summary_of_rules_for_supreme_court_2007.pdf.]

[2] Effect of Anti-Terrorist Laws on Criminal Procedure

Congress passed P.L. 107-40, a joint resolution authorizing military response to the September 11 attack. A November 13, 2001, implementing order[416] permits apprehended international terrorists to be tried by military commissions that are not subject to the usual federal rules of evidence or principles of law. Conviction, even if it results in a sentence of death or life imprisonment, is permissible on a

---

[416] *See* 70 L.W. 2301.

two-thirds vote. Evidence is admissible if a reasonable person would deem it to be probative.

U.S. citizens allegedly implicated in terrorism are to be tried by the regular court system. Non-citizens can be tried by the tribunals based on a two-part determination that the best interests of the United States require placing that person under military jurisdiction, and that there is reason to believe that the individual belonged to Al Qaeda, or engaged in, conspired in, or aided and abetted terrorist acts in the United States or knowingly harbored terrorists.

The Uniting and Strengthening America by Providing Appropriate Tools Required to Intercept and Obstruct Terrorism (USA Patriot) Act is P.L. 107-56. Title I of this lengthy statute deals with measures for enhancing domestic security against terrorism. Title II covers enhanced surveillance procedures such as interception of oral, electronic, and wire conversations dealing with terrorism; pen registers and traps to capture covert communications; computer fraud and abuse offenses; and added authorization for surveillance and "sneak and peak" warrants.

Title III is the International Money Laundering Abatement and Anti-Terrorist Financing Act. Title IV deals with protecting U.S. borders. Title V removes obstacles to investigations of terrorist activity. Title VI provides benefits for the victims of terrorism and their families. Title VII provides a framework for better information sharing to protect the national infrastructure. Title VIII enhances the existing anti-terrorist criminal laws (e.g., coverage of domestic terrorism; attacks on mass transit; penalties for terroristic conspiracies). The objective of Title IX is improving intelligence operations to detect future terrorist activities. Title X contains miscellaneous provisions.

The March 2006 USA Patriot Improvement and Reauthorization Act, P.L. 109-177, reauthorized 16 provisions of the PATRIOT Act (14 permanently, two sun-setting in 2009). The temporary reauthorizations, §§ 206 and 215, permit the FBI to compel businesses to turn over individual information based on authorization from the U.S. Foreign Intelligence Court of Review. Roving surveillance can be authorized, tied to a particular suspect rather than a particular communications device. The reauthorization requires additional approvals of surveillance of tax and medical records.

A separate bill, The Patriot Act Additional Reauthorizing Amendments Act, P.L. 109-178, strengthens privacy safeguards, including giving individuals the right to obtain judicial review of surveillance requests after one year. However, § 505 has been reauthorized, so National Security Letters can still be authorized, permitting FBI agents investigating terrorism can obtain business records without a court order. The recipient of a National Security Letter is subject to a gag order forbidding disclosure of the fact that information was turned over.

The PROTECT Act (Prosecutorial Remedies and Tools Against the Exploitation of Children Today Act, P.L. 108-21; signed 4/30/03) increases the penalties for sex offenses and sexual violence against children and sets up the AMBER Alert communications network to locate abducted children. This legislation also expands prohibitions on child pornography, including amendment of 18 USC § 2256 to prohibit pornographic digital images that are indistinguishable from depictions of minors engaged in sexual conduct. (The statute provides an affirmative defense if the depiction actually involved adults.) The statute defines "obscene visual representations of the sexual abuse of children" as one type of "obscene child pornography": 18 USC § 1466A.

The PROTECT Act also amends 18 USC § 3282 and Fed. R. Crim. P. 7 to permit the indictment of a person whose DNA profile is known but whose name is not.

Also see the Homeland Security Act of 2002, P.L. 107-296 (signed 11/25/03), extending the emergency powers of government agencies to access e-mail. ISPs are authorized by this statute to disclose the content of an e-mail or other electronic communication to any government agency based on the ISP's good-faith belief that the communication relates to information involving risk of death or serious injury.

[B] Pretrial and Speedy Trial Issues

In the federal system, the judge must issue an arrest warrant if the complaint (a written statement of the essential facts constituting the offense charged, made under oath before a magistrate judge or a state or local judicial official if no magistrate judge is reasonably available) or the affidavits submitted with the complaint furnish probable cause to believe that an offense was committed and that the defendant committed it. See Fed. R. Crim. P. 3 and 4.

The Sixth Amendment[417] guarantees the accused a "speedy" trial — a factor that is particularly important when the defendant has been denied bail, or has been unable to post bail, and thus is incarcerated prior to trial.

There are four factors in determining whether a delay violates the guarantee of a speedy trial: the length of the delay; reasons for it; whether the defendant raised the issue (e.g., by pretrial motion); and the extent to which the defense was prejudiced by delay.[418]

The right of speedy trial attaches only with arrest or indictment; defendants are not prejudiced by any indictment brought within the statute of limitations.[419] With respect to pre-indictment delay, as long as the statute of limitations has not run, dismissal for delay requires not only proof of actual, substantial prejudice, but proof that the prosecutor intentionally delayed for an improper purpose.[420]

A guilty plea waives claims of violations of the right to a speedy trial.[421]

The statute of limitations, not the Speedy Trial Act, determines when an indicted defendant can be charged with additional crimes via a superseding indictment.[422]

---

[417] The guarantee applies to the states as well as the federal government: Klopfer v. United States, 386 U.S. 213 (1967).

[418] United States v. MacDonald, 435 U.S. 850 (1978).

[419] Jones v. Angelone, 94 F.3d 900 (4th Cir. 1996). Nor is there a federal right to speedy arrest or charge: United States v. Hoffa, 385 U.S. 293 (1996), although a tactical delay in prosecution that is prejudicial to the defense may violate Due Process: United States v. Lovasco, 431 U.S. 783 (1977).

[420] United States v. Crouch, 84 F.3d 1497 (5th Cir. 1996).

[421] Washington v. Sobina, 475 F.3d 162 (3d Cir. 2007). United States v. Thye, 96 F.3d 635 (2d Cir. 1996).

[422] United States v. Mosquera, 95 F.3d 1012 (11th Cir. 1996).

[1] Criminal Trial Timing Requirements

In this list, citations are to the Federal Rules of Criminal Procedure unless otherwise noted.

The Speedy Trial Act, at 18 USC § 3161(c)(1), requires a federal criminal trial to start within 70 days after the defendant is charged or makes an initial appearance, although various periods of delay are excluded from the calculation. Under § 3161(h)(8), the District Court can grant a continuance and exclude the delay based on a finding, on the record, that the interests of justice favor the continuance and outweigh the interests in a speedy trial. But if the trial does not begin on time, the District Court must grant a defense motion to dismiss made before the start of the trial or a guilty plea. The District Court has discretion to make the dismissal without prejudice. In 2006, the Supreme Court ruled that a defendant cannot prospectively waive the application of the Speedy Trial Act, so a purported waiver was invalid; the statute has no provisions for extensions of time pursuant to a defense waiver. In the Supreme Court's analysis, if the defendant could merely waive the application of the Act, there would have been no need for Congress to enact a list of rationales that would support granting a continuance. The Supreme Court also ruled out prospective waivers of § 3162(a)(2), which obligates the defendant to move for dismissal on speedy trial grounds before the trial or guilty plea, on the ground that the text does not authorize prospective waivers, and there is no legal bar to treating prospective waivers differently from retrospective waivers.[423]

The remedy for violation of the Speedy Trial Act is dismissal with prejudice, but *Reed v. Farley*[424] requires a showing of prejudice to the defendant to establish a Speedy Trial violation.

An "ends of justice" continuance (e.g., if neither side is ready) does not count toward the speedy trial clock: 18 USC § 3161(h)(8). Delays attributable to pretrial motions are also excluded, by 18 USC § 3161(h)(1)(F).

- After executing an arrest warrant, a police officer must bring the arrestee before the nearest available magistrate or judicial officer without unnecessary delay (5(a); 9(c)(3)).
- A search warrant must be executed within its specified time, which may not be more than 10 days from issuance (41(e)(2)).
- Unless the preliminary hearing is waived or the indictment or information is issued before the date of the hearing, the preliminary hearing must take place not more than 20 days from the initial appearance (10 days, if the defendant is in custody): 5.1(c); 18 USC § 3060. However, the time for the preliminary hearing can be extended one or more times, on consent of the defendant and on a showing of good cause. If the defendant does not consent, extension is

---

[423] Zedner v. United States, 547 U.S. 489 (2006).
[424] 512 U.S. 339 (1994).

permitted only in extraordinary circumstances and where the interests of justice require the delay: Fed. R. Crim. P. 5.1(d).

- Challenge to a grand juror (or the entire composition of the Grand Jury) must be made before the jurors are sworn in: 6(b)(1).
- The information or indictment must be filed within 30 days from the date of arrest or service of summons: 18 USC § 3161(b); an additional 30 days is allowed when the Grand Jury is not in session. If the government fails to indict within 30 days of the arrest, *United States v. Derose*[425] says only the charge in the original complaint is dismissed, not any other charges in the indictment.
- The information can be amended at any time before a verdict or finding: 7(e) as long as the amendment does not charge the defendant with additional or different offenses, and as long as no substantial right of the defendant is prejudiced by the amendment.
- The defendant must receive a copy of the indictment or information before having to plead at the arraignment: (10).
- The court sets a hearing date for pretrial motions at the arraignment, or as soon thereafter as possible: 12(c). Certain motions must be raised before trial: e.g., motions alleging a defect in the institution of prosecution; suppression motions; motions for discovery; motions for severance.
- Notice of alibi is due within 10 days of the prosecution's written demand. Within 10 days of the notice, but at least 10 days before the trial, the prosecution must disclose if it has witnesses putting the defendant at the scene of the crime: 12.1.
- Unless the court permits it to be done later, the defendant must give notice of intent to raise an insanity defense within the time for raising pretrial motions: 12.2.[426]
- The trial of a defendant who pleads not guilty must begin within 70 days of the filing date of the indictment or information, or 70 days from the last appearance before a judicial officer, whichever is later: 18 USC § 3161(c). In a case with multiple defendants, the speedy trial clock begins to run on the indictment or arraignment of the last defendant.[427] A delay granted as to one co-defendant is excludable as to the other codefendant(s).[428]

[C] Stages in the Criminal Case

As noted above, a valid arrest can either be made pursuant to a warrant or under circumstances justifying a warrantless arrest.

---

[425] 74 F.3d 1177 (11th Cir. 1996).

[426] Note that the Legal Insanity Defense Reform Act, 18 USC § 17, permits the affirmative defense of legal insanity to be established only if the defendant first establishes severe mental disease.

[427] United States v. Mathis, 96 F.3d 1577 (11th Cir. 1996).

[428] United States v. Butz, 982 F.2d 1378 (9th Cir. 1993).

Arrest warrants are issued by criminal courts, indicating who should be arrested on what charge. The police officer serving the warrant brings the arrested person to the criminal court that issued the warrant. If the arrest warrant has been vacated before the arrest, or is otherwise invalid, the arrest is invalid, even if the police acted in good faith.[429]

After a warrantless arrest, the arresting officer must complete police processing requirements, such as fingerprinting the arrested person, then bring the arrested person before the local criminal court without delay for filing of the appropriate accusatory instrument charging him or her with a crime.

A criminal action is commenced by the filing of an "accusatory instrument" with the criminal court. Local practice, and the nature of the allegation, will determine the type of instrument to be filed (e.g., felony information; misdemeanor information). The function of the instrument is to place the suspect on notice of the charges, and also to indicate the charges on which the suspect has already been placed in jeopardy and on which he or she cannot be retried after an acquittal.

In the federal system, capital cases must be initiated by an indictment. Felonies can be prosecuted either by indictment or by information (if the defense waives indictment). All other offenses can be prosecuted by information. Either an indictment or information within the federal system must provide a plain, concise, and definite statement of the essential facts constituting the offense (Rule 7). In the Fourth Circuit view, the Fifth Amendment "indictment" clause is satisfied by a capital indictment that alleges facts that would prove an aggravating factor, even if the aggravator is not specifically identified.[430] The Supreme Court reversed the Ninth Circuit's reversal of a conviction for illegal attempt to re-enter the United States. Because the indictment was not defective, it was not necessary for the Supreme Court to rule on the question of whether omitting an element of a criminal offense from a federal indictment constitutes harmless error.[431]

Arraignment is the formal process of bringing the person named in the accusatory instrument before the criminal court, the counterpart of obtaining personal jurisdiction over a civil defendant. The arraigning court either releases the accused person on his or her own recognizance; sets bail; or places him or her in custody. Under Fed. R. Crim. P. 10, the arraignment offers the defendant an opportunity to get a copy of the indictment or information, if he or she does not already have one. A defendant who pleads not guilty and who already has a copy of the accusatory instrument can waive appearance at the indictment. On consent of the defendant, the arraignment can also be done by video teleconference rather than in person.

In some systems, and for certain categories of cases, a preliminary hearing is held to determine whether there is enough evidence to justify holding the individual for the Grand Jury.

---

[429] Arizona v. Evans, 514 U.S. 1 (1995).

[430] United States v. Barnette, 390 F.3d 775 (4th Cir. 2004).

[431] United States v. Resendiz-Ponce, 549 U.S. 102 (2007).

Fed. R. Crim. P. 5.1 requires the magistrate judge to conduct a preliminary hearing whenever a person is charged with an offense other than a petty offense — unless the arrested person waives the hearing; he or she is indicted; the government files an "information" charging a misdemeanor or felony; or the arrestee is charged with a misdemeanor and consents to be tried before the magistrate judge. A person arrested in a federal district other than the one in which the crime was allegedly committed can have the preliminary hearing transferred to the district where the case will be prosecuted.

If the defendant consents in writing to being tried before a magistrate judge, trial must begin within 30 days of the time the defendant gives consent.

18 USC § 3161(c)(2) further requires that, unless a defendant gives written consent, the trial must take place at least 30 days from the defendant's first appearance when represented by counsel, or after the defendant has waived the right to counsel and elected to proceed pro se. In other words, although the trial must be "speedy," prosecution and defense must be given adequate time to prepare their cases.

[D] Grand Jury

When the Constitution was drafted, the Founders were highly sensitive to the possibility of repeated felony proceedings brought by the sovereign for purely political reasons. Therefore, the Fifth Amendment requires an indictment (a formal written accusation that a specific person committed specific offenses) by a Grand Jury before a person can be tried in the federal system for a serious criminal charge.[432]

Initially, the states adopted a similar requirement, under their Constitutions or by case law. However, starting in the mid-nineteenth century, states became concerned that Grand Jury proceedings were expensive, inefficient, and no longer served the purpose of protecting the rights of the accused. In 1859, Michigan became the first state to permit felony trials without Grand Jury indictments, on the basis of prosecutor's informations.

Within the federal system, the Grand Jury consists of anywhere from 16 to 23 members. Either the defense or the prosecution can challenge the Grand Jury panel as not lawfully selected, and can also challenge the legal qualifications of individuals to serve on the Grand Jury. However, Fed. R. Crim. P. 6 provides that an indictment cannot be dismissed on the grounds that a juror was not qualified as long as at least 12 qualified jurors voted in favor of the indictment. (A federal Grand Jury can indict on the vote of at least 12 jurors.)

As long as a defendant receives a preliminary hearing or other pretrial screening, neither the Fifth nor the Fourteenth Amendment requires states to indict defendants by Grand Jury.[433] Under current law, only 18 states[434] require a Grand

---

[432] Campbell v. Louisiana, 523 U.S. 392 (1998).

[433] Hurtado v. California, 110 U.S. 516 (1884).

[434] Alabama, Alaska, Delaware, Georgia, Kentucky, Maine, Massachusetts, Mississippi, New Hampshire, New Jersey, New York, North Carolina, Ohio, South Carolina, Tennessee, Texas, Virginia, West Virginia. In Florida, Louisiana, Minnesota, and Rhode Island, a Grand Jury

Jury indictment to initiate serious charges (although Grand Juries may be used in the other states, especially in their investigative role).

[1] Grand Jury Proceedings

The Grand Jury is very unlike ordinary criminal proceedings. It is private, secret, ex parte, and inquisitorial. The prosecutor runs the proceeding, and there is no judge present. The Grand Jury's role is to determine, after hearing a summary version of the prosecution case, whether there is probable cause to indict.

In the federal system, the target is not entitled to be present during the hearing or deliberations, witnesses cannot have counsel with them during questioning (although they can leave the room to consult with counsel).[435] Some states have altered their Grand Jury rules so that witnesses can bring counsel into the Grand Jury room; some require witnesses be warned of their rights before testifying, or at least require disclosure of the subject of the investigation.

Effective December 1, 1999, the Federal Rules of Criminal Procedure were amended[436] to call for the provision of interpreters so that speech and hearing-impaired persons can serve on a Grand Jury. The indictment can be returned by the foreperson or deputy foreperson of the Grand Jury, so the entire panel need not be in court to do so.

[a] Standards for Prosecution

The ABA Standards for Criminal Justice, Prosecution Function 3–3.5(b) hold that the prosecutor presenting a case to the Grand Jury should not:

- Intentionally interfere with the independence of the Grand Jury
- Preempt its functions
- Abuse its processes
- Present evidence, make statement or arguments that are inappropriate for the Grand Jury, or that would not be allowed at trial.

Nevertheless, the ordinary rules of evidence are not fully applicable before the Grand Jury.

About a quarter of the states require prosecutors to disclose exculpatory evidence, but this is not required in federal courts.[437] The Grand Jury's function

---

indictment is required in cases that could result in the death penalty or life imprisonment, but not for other serious charges. *See* Sara Sun Beale, William C. Bryson, James E. Felman, Michael J. Elston, *Grand Jury Law and Practice* (2nd edition), Westgroup October 2001 supplement at § 51:7.

[435] The Fourteenth Amendment is not violated by searching attorneys, even if its purpose and effect is to prevent attorneys from advising clients appearing before a Grand Jury: Conn v. Gabbert, 526 U.S. 286 (1999).

[436] Via amendments approved by the Supreme Court on April 26, 1999; *see* 67 L.W. 2651.

[437] United States v. Bagley, 473 U.S. 667 (1985).

is merely to determine probable cause, not perform the same function of adjudication as the trial court.[438] A Grand Jury witness cannot refuse to answer questions based on evidence from an illegal search and seizure, and suppression hearings are not available.

The target of the investigation does not have a right to testify, or to insist that the Grand Jury hear evidence favorable to the target, although the Grand Jury can choose to hear such evidence. Only a few states give the complainant (alleged victim of the crime) the right to present evidence.

Grand Juries have broad subpoena powers (and can choose to call the target of the investigation as a witness), enforceable by contempt of court. Grand Jury witnesses must testify truthfully, on pain of being prosecuted for perjury.[439] A witness who invokes the privilege against self-incrimination can be granted immunity, at which point the witness can be compelled to testify.

Although the Fifth Amendment privilege against self-incrimination applies, a subpoenaed witness is required to appear, and the Grand Jury can ask questions that tend to incriminate the witness.[440]

Spousal privilege and privilege for confidential marital communications, psychotherapist/patient (but not generalized doctor/patient), and clergy/congregation privileges can also be asserted. The Supremacy Clause of the Constitution gives federal Grand Juries subpoena power over records that are privileged under state law but not federal law: e.g., bank records, medical records, state tax returns.

[2] Grand Jury Secrecy

Once the Grand Jury completes its hearing, the witnesses are permitted to disclose what they said, if they want to (and therefore the defense attorney can interview them). The state interest in protecting Grand Jury secrecy does not overcome the witness' interest in being allowed to reveal their Grand Jury testimony if they want to. However, they cannot be compelled to testify about the Grand Jury proceedings in any other proceeding.[441]

Violation of Grand Jury secrecy can be punished by civil and criminal contempt remedies, but there is no private cause of action.[442]

Fed. R. Crim. P. 6(e) allows disclosure of Grand Jury materials to prosecutors and their agents for limited purposes (e.g., for use in other cases),[443] but it does not

---

[438] United States v. Calandra, 414 U.S. 338 (1974) and United States v. Williams, 504 U.S. 36 (1992).

[439] LaChance v. Erickson, 522 U.S. 262 (1998).

[440] United States v. Mandujano, 425 U.S. 564 (1976).

[441] Butterworth v. Smith, 494 U.S. 624 (1990).

[442] Finn v. Schiller, 72 F.3d 1182 (4th Cir. 1996). *See also* United States v. Smith, 992 F. Supp. 743 (D.N.J. 1998): Internet posting of a sentencing memorandum that contained Grand Jury information, without consent of the court, violated Fed. R. Crim. P. 6(e) and 32.

[443] The Jencks Act, 18 USC § 3500, mandates production of relevant prior statements of government witnesses at trial, and a 1970 amendment makes it clear that Grand Jury testimony is considered a prior statement for this purpose. Government agents have no duty to record witness

give the press, or members of the general public, access to Grand Jury materials. In most instances, Grand Jury materials will be exempt from Freedom of Information Act disclosure: see 5 USC § 552.

Rule 6(e)(3)(E) permits disclosure by the court before or in connection with a judicial proceeding, including to state law enforcement authorities based on a showing that the materials may disclose a violation of state criminal law. The party seeking disclosure must make a strong showing of particularized need — not just mere usefulness.[444]

Fed. R. Crim. P. 16 (the general discovery rule) allows the defense to get some Grand Jury materials, such as the defendant's own testimony and the testimony of individuals who can bind a corporate defendant.

Testimony of government witnesses can be produced at trial, after their testimony and before their cross-examination (i.e., so that the defense can detect discrepancies and use them to impeach the witness).

[3] Selection of Grand Jurors

A Grand Jury panel usually consists of 12–23 people. In the federal system, the size of the panel ranges from 16–23 (Fed. R. Crim. P. 6(a)), with a quorum of 16. The Grand Jury term could be anywhere from 10 days to 18 months (with extensions to finish cases in progress). Provisions are made for replacing Grand Jurors during the term.

Although attorneys play a major role in selecting petit jurors, they have little to do with selection of federal Grand Jurors. Peremptory challenges are unavailable. Potential jurors may be examined briefly by the impaneling court to determine whether they meet the rather minimal requirements for Grand Jury service (e.g., adult U.S. citizens[445] who can read and write English and have not been convicted of a felony), but extensive voir dire is not conducted.

In the federal system, and in some states, Grand Jurors are selected randomly from lists such as voter registration lists. Some states still use a "key-man" system under which judges or jury commissioners are given discretion to select suitable Grand Jurors.

The Fifth Amendment requires Grand Juries to be drawn from a representative cross-section of the community, as does the Jury Selection and Service Act, 28 USC § 1861, and about one-third of the states. The analysis requires proof of a distinct or cognizable group within the community (e.g., women; black people), and that representation of that group on the Grand Jury panel is not fair and reasonable as compared with the size of that group within the community.

---

interviews or take notes that would not otherwise be kept, merely to disclose them. Furthermore, statements that do not relate to the same subject matter as the testimony cannot be used to impeach the witness, and therefore need not be disclosed.

[444] United States v. Sells Engineering Inc., 463 U.S. 418 (1983).

[445] Perkins v. Smith, 426 U.S. 913 (1976) holds the citizenship requirement to be Constitutional.

A white defendant is allowed to place a due process/equal protection challenge to the under-representation of black people on Grand Juries,[446] including their access to service as foreperson of the Grand Jury.

However, unlike petit jurors, Grand Jurors cannot be disqualified based on prior knowledge of the case, because they can still perform their function of determining whether an indictment should issue. In fact, even bias probably will not disqualify a Grand Juror or invalidate the indictment. *United States v. Mechanik*[447] holds that violations of Fed. R. Crim. P. 6(d) cannot be raised on appeal to challenge a conviction because the error, if any, must be harmless because the petit jury convicted the defendant based on the evidence presented at trial.

[4] The Indictment

In the federal system, or in a state that retains the requirement of a Grand Jury indictment, serious crimes can only be charged in an indictment. A proper indictment gives adequate notice of the charges against the accused. If a statute describes multiple ways in which a single offense can be committed, Fed. R. Crim. P. 7(c)(l) authorizes a single count that alleges that the defendant committed the offense by one or more specified means.

Improper "multiplicity" occurs if a single offense is divided into two or more counts of the indictment, because the defendant therefore is at risk of being punished more than once for the same offense — and a susceptible jury may feel that the defendant must be guilty of something if so many charges are brought against him or her. However, there is no multiplicity in charging separate counts if the offenses require different proof.

After trial, variation between the charges and the proof is a legitimate ground for challenging a verdict. If the indictment was "constructively amended" in that the prosecution case, plus the jury instructions, modified the essential elements of the offense to the point that the defendant was convicted of something other than the crime(s) charged in the indictment, the defendant may be entitled to relief.

A defendant can move to strike surplusage from an indictment. Such motions are disfavored, and are granted only if the indictment includes highly inflammatory, prejudicial allegations that are not relevant to the charge.

Trial on the merits can be had if an indictment that is valid on its face is returned by a legally constituted and unbiased Grand Jury — even if some of the evidence they considered was inaccurate, untruthful, or inadmissible under the rules of evidence. (Otherwise, everyone who was indicted would get another trial first, to test the validity of the indictment.)

---

[446] Campbell v. Louisiana, 523 U.S. 392 (1998).
[447] 475 U.S. 661 (1986).

[5] Investigative Grand Juries

The Grand Jury can play another role, investigating crime, especially organized crime, white-collar crime, and political corruption. An investigative Grand Jury determines whether crimes have been committed, and if so by whom, but issues a written statement addressed to the court that impaneled the Grand Jury, rather than a formal written accusation charging a specific person with a specific offense.

The Organized Crime Control Act of 1970, P.L. 91-452, authorizes special Grand Juries that can submit reports on organized crime in the area, then investigate and issue indictments. See 18 USC § 3333 for reports of such special Grand Juries.

[E] Pretrial Discovery

"Trial by ambush" is even less acceptable in the criminal than in the civil context, and U.S. law requires the prosecution not only to apprise the defense of the strength of the prosecution case but also of its weaknesses.

Arizona v. Youngblood[448] guarantees the defense's access to evidence, thereby imposing a duty on the prosecution to disclose material exculpatory evidence that is within the prosecution's possession or control. *Youngblood* forbids the prosecution to engage in bad-faith destruction of evidence and requires the defense to have subpoena power, and the prosecution is forbidden to impair the exercise of the defense subpoena power.

The prosecution's Constitutional duty to disclose favorable material evidence[449] — that is, exculpatory or potentially exculpatory material relevant either to guilt or punishment — requires the presence of favorable but undisclosed evidence. Materiality is measured by a reasonable probability that the outcome would be different if disclosure were made. The prosecutor is only obligated to disclose material favorable to the defendant and material either to guilt or punishment.

Failure to produce such material violates the defendant's Constitutional rights, and a new trial may be required. There is no violation if the undisclosed information was already known to the defendant, or could have been determined with reasonable diligence (e.g., by reading a transcript). Furthermore, failure to produce potentially exculpatory material before trial might be cured by disclosure at trial, giving the defense a reasonable opportunity to cross-examine.

---

[448] 488 U.S. 51 (1988).

[449] Under, *e.g.*, Brady v. Maryland, 373 U.S. 87 (1963) and Kyles v. Whitley, 514 U.S. 419 (1995). Evidence that tends to impeach prosecution witnesses' testimony is *Brady* material: United States v. Bagley, 473 U.S. 667 (1985). The defendant's right of access to favorable evidence, in conjunction with the state power to subpoena "objects," permits a court to grant the defense's application that an uncharged person submit a saliva sample for DNA testing, but the defense must first make a sufficient showing that such evidence would tend to exonerate him: *In re* Jansen, 444 Mass. 112 (Mass. 2005). Certiorari was granted in a sexual assault case, and the state Supreme Court's denial of a new trial was vacated and remanded, because the defendant clearly presented a *Brady* claim to the state supreme court: Youngblood v. West Virginia, 547 U.S. 2188 (2006).

The prosecution is under no obligation to investigate and seek out exculpatory material not already in its possession.[450] Unless law enforcement officials act in bad faith, Due Process is not violated by failure to preserve items that might, arguably, have been exculpatory if preserved and tested.[451]

The defense can inspect and copy government-held documents and materials that are either scheduled for use in the prosecution case in chief, or material to the defense: Fed. R. Crim. P. 16(a)(1)(E). It does not create a broader right to discover documents that are material to a claim of selective prosecution, because that would allow defendants to discover all government work product merely by claiming selective prosecution.[452]

According to the Second Circuit, Fed. R. Crim. P. 16(a)(1)(B)(i) does not entitle the defendant to discovery of written police reports recording the defendant's oral statements to an undercover police officer. The statements did not fall under (a)(1), the requirement of disclosure on request by the defendant of the substance of oral statements made by the defendant under interrogation by a person the defendant knew to be a government agent, if the prosecution intends to offer the statement at trial. The defendant did not know he was speaking to a government agent. The Second Circuit held that other types of oral statements are not discoverable.[453]

Rule 16(a)(1)(G) permits pretrial disclosure of expert opinions that are scheduled to be introduced by the prosecution. Internal government documents and Grand Jury transcripts are not discoverable by the defense: 16(a)(2) and (3).

In addition to general rules about providing exculpatory matter to the defense, certain specific discovery issues are addressed by federal rules. FRE 404(b) requires the prosecution to provide reasonable pretrial notice of the general nature of evidence it will introduce about other acts committed by the defendant.

Although depositions are a basic part of pretrial discovery in civil litigation, Fed. R. Crim. P. 15 permits the court to grant a party's motion for the taking of depositions to preserve testimony before trial. However, this can be done only "because of exceptional circumstances and in the interests of justice" — it is by no means routine.

[F] Double Jeopardy

In order to prevent the evil of a defendant being subjected to re-prosecution after dismissal of a prior case, or jury acquittal in that prior case, the principle of "double jeopardy" imposes limits on retrial of criminal defendants.

Jeopardy attaches in a jury trial when the jury has been sworn. In a bench trial, jeopardy attaches once the first witness has been sworn. An important limitation is

---

[450] California v. Trombetta, 467 U.S. 479 (1984).

[451] Arizona v. Youngblood, 488 U.S. 51 (1988). *Youngblood* also holds that the prosecution does not have a duty to perform all tests that the defense claims might be exculpatory.

[452] United States v. Armstrong, 517 U.S. 456 (1996).

[453] United States v. Siraj, 533 F.3d 867 (2d Cir. 2008).

that the principle of double jeopardy applies only to actions by the same sovereign — so that a federal trial does not prevent a state trial or vice versa, and trial in one state does not prevent trial in another state.

Double jeopardy does not prevent a new trial after a mistrial has been declared at the request of the defendant, unless the prosecutor or judge goaded the defense into moving for mistrial. Where mistrial is ordered over the objection of the defense, or where the defendant did not have a chance to object, retrial is impermissible unless the retrial is manifestly in the interests of justice.

If the court dismisses a criminal case before jeopardy has attached, reversal on appeal and retrial are possible. But after attachment, if the trial court rules that the evidence is insufficient to establish the offense charged, this is equivalent to an acquittal by the jury, and further proceedings are barred. However, where there are factual issues involved, retrial is permitted if the prosecution overturns the dismissal.

If the defendant appeals a conviction based on either a guilty plea or a guilty verdict, and the conviction is reversed, then retrial is permissible unless the guilty verdict was reversed because of the insufficiency of the evidence to support a verdict.

Conviction on a lesser charge is considered to be the jury's refusal to convict on the greater charge, so if such a conviction is reversed, the defendant can be retried only on the lower charge.

An amendment to Fed. R. Crim. P 29 proposed in 2006 only permits a judge to enter a judgment of acquittal before a verdict if the defendant waives Double Jeopardy objections in case the government chooses to appeal.

Under Massachusetts law (although the results would be different in a state that made statutory provision for reconsideration of mid-trial determinations), a judge cannot send a count of an indictment to the jury after the judge has granted a motion for a not-guilty finding on that count. The Supreme Court ruled in February 2005, in the case of *Smith v. Massachusetts*, 543 U.S. 462 (2005), that the judge acquitted the defendant on that count and therefore could not submit him to additional fact-finding proceedings going to the issue of guilt or innocence. (The judge was persuaded by the prosecutor's closing argument that her original ruling had been mistaken.)

[G] Plea Bargaining

A criminal defendant can plead guilty to some or all of the charges; not guilty (denying every allegation in the indictment); guilty to lesser included offenses of some or all of the charges; or can plead lack of responsibility for the acts charged, on the basis of mental disease or defect. In the federal system, a defendant can plead nolo contendere (no contest) but the court's permission is required for a nolo plea.

The court must not participate in the discussions for a plea agreement. A defendant who pleads guilty or nolo contendere to a lesser or related offense can make an agreement under which the prosecution agrees not to bring, or agrees to move to dismiss, other charges. The prosecution can recommend or refrain from opposing the defendant's sentencing request, but this does not bind the court.

The prosecution can also agree that a specific sentence, sentencing range, or Guideline is appropriate. This agreement binds the court only if the court accepts the plea agreement.

The vast majority of criminal cases, of course, result in a guilty plea rather than a trial. If the prosecution consents, a defendant can plead guilty to one or more lesser charges, but if the prosecution does not consent, the defendant must either plead guilty to the entire indictment or go to trial.

Fed. R. Crim. P. 11 governs plea bargains. Rule 11(a)(2) permits entry of a conditional guilty or nolo contendere plea, preserving the defendant's right to appeal adverse pretrial determinations. Under Rule 11(b)(2), the court is supposed to ask a defendant who pleads guilty if the plea was a result of a promise from the government, but failure to inquire does not require vacation of the plea.

The defendant must be advised of the essential elements of the crime and the minimum and maximum possible sentence that could be imposed.[454] It is not necessary to advise the defendant what actual sentence will be imposed after the application of the guidelines to the facts of the particular case.

The Fifth Circuit ruled that Fed. R. Crim. P. 11(d)(1) allows the defendant to withdraw a guilty plea for any reason (or no reason) up until the plea has been accepted by the court. Therefore, a defendant who was offered a plea bargain where four counts involving a brothel employing illegal immigrants would be dismissed if he plead guilty to the fifth count, accepted it, plead guilty to that one count before a Magistrate Judge, and then moved to withdraw the plea could do so. In the Fifth Circuit's view, District Courts that are afraid that pleas will be withdrawn can accept them at an earlier stage of the case.[455]

Under the totality of circumstances (including the defendant's intelligence; education; experience; and access to counsel), the defendant must enter a knowing and voluntary[456] plea, based on understanding of the charges. The trial judge must not improperly interject him- or herself into the negotiation process.

Even though violations of the Federal Rules of Criminal Procedure are usually analyzed under a harmless-error rule, early in 2002 the Supreme Court held that violations of Rule 11 (the guilty plea rule) are analyzed for plain error. The entire record, not just the record of plea proceedings, can be examined by the reviewing court to determine whether any error that occurred was plain or harmless.[457] This point was amplified in mid-2004. The Supreme Court held that a

---

[454] But not necessarily whether the federal sentence will be served consecutively or concurrently with the state sentence: United States v. Parkins, 25 F.3d 114 (2d Cir. 1994).

[455] United States v. Arami, 536 F.3d 479 (5th Cir. 2008).

[456] A plea induced by threats is not voluntary and thus is void: Machibroda v. United States, 368 U.S. 487 (1962).

[457] United States v. Vonn, 535 U.S. 55 (2002).

defendant who asserts Rule 11 plain error in the court's failure to warn him that he could not withdraw his plea if the court rejected the District Attorney's recommendation, must prove a reasonable probability that he would not have pled guilty if this error had not occurred.[458]

The Supreme Court reversed the Ninth Circuit in mid-2002: *Brady* material (i.e., potentially exculpatory evidence) must be disclosed prior to trial, but need not be given to the defendant earlier, at the plea-bargaining stage.[459]

Because the plea constitutes a waiver of the significant Constitutional rights to confrontation, jury trial, and protection against self-incrimination, a valid guilty plea must be a voluntary and intelligent choice among the various alternative courses of action open to the defendant.[460] Fed. R. Crim. P. 11(d) provides that a guilty or nolo plea can be withdrawn for any reason — or even for no reason — before the court accepts the plea. After the plea is made but before sentence, a guilty or nolo plea can be withdrawn if the court rejects the plea agreement or if the defense shows fair and just reasons for requesting the withdrawal. After sentencing, the defendant can no longer withdraw the plea, and it can be set aside only by direct appeal or collateral attack. Once a plea that satisfies Rule 11 has accepted, the right to trial has been waived, so the defendant cannot get the Court of Appeals to vacate the conviction based on the absence of a trial.[461]

Under *North Carolina v. Alford*[462] a defendant can plead guilty, and accept the sentence of the court, without actually admitting guilt, because the Supreme Court recognized that a person confronted by a strong likelihood of conviction (especially in a capital case) might make a valid strategic choice to accept a lower sentence to avoid the risk of the death penalty or a longer sentence.

A plea agreement is void if it purports to preserve both the issues that are dispositive of the case and other issues. A conditional guilty plea that preserves certain questions for appeal can only be used with regard to issues that, if they were decided in the defendant's favor, would end the case short of a trial.[463]

Generally speaking, a defendant cannot enforce specific performance of a plea agreement if the government backs out before the defendant's guilty plea has been accepted; the Eighth Circuit ruled in 2007 that there are possible exceptions if the plea agreement explicitly contemplated performance, or the defendant shows that the government took unfair advantage of its withdrawal.[464]

Also in 2007, the Third Circuit considered the standards for cases where it is alleged that the defense (rather than the prosecution) breached a plea agreement. In this case, the plea agreement stated that neither side would seek departures

---

[458] United States v. Dominguez Benitez, 542 U.S. 74 (2004). In this case, no contemporaneous objection was raised to the Rule 11 violation, so Fed. R. Crim. P. 52(b) limits review to plain error.

[459] United States v. Ruiz, 536 U.S. 622 (2002).

[460] Parke v. Raley, 506 U.S. 20 (1992).

[461] United States v. Olano, 507 U.S. 725 (1993).

[462] 400 U.S. 25 (1970).

[463] United States v. Bundy, 392 F.3d 641 (4th Cir. 2004).

[464] United States v. Norris, 486 F.3d 1045 (8th Cir. 2007).

not specified in the agreement. At sentencing, the defendant's lawyer obtained a downward departure: 120 months rather than the 168–210 month sentence provided by the pre-sentence report. The government appealed, claiming that the defendant broke the agreement. He said that he did not — he merely asked the court to reduce the criminal history calculation (but not the offense level) and apply § 3553(a) discretionary factors. The Third Circuit applied contract principles to both government and defendant breaches. Plea agreements (and their benefits in speeding up case processing) would not be feasible if defendants could breach them without penalty. A defendant cannot retain benefits that would not be permitted under contract law. The question of whether the defendant breached the agreement is reviewed de novo. The government must prove breach by a preponderance of the evidence. The Third Circuit held that the defendant breached the agreement, which unambiguously waived making a motion for a downward departure. In the Third Circuit view, the remedy for a government breach is remanding the case to the District Court for a determination of whether to grant specific performance or allow the defendant to withdraw the plea and go to trial. If the government does not seek withdrawal of the plea or rescission of the plea agreement, the remedy is specific performance of the plea agreement. However, remand must be to a different judge, because the original judge might find it difficult to re-sentence the defendant fairly.[465]

A 2003 New Jersey case requires, as a matter of fundamental fairness, the trial court to advise a defendant of the possibility of indefinite civil commitment if he pleads guilty to a predicate offense under the New Jersey Sexually Violent Predator Act. (The legal principle is that "direct or penal" consequences of a guilty plea must be disclosed, whereas "collateral" consequences need not be.) On the related issue of notification of sex offender registration, West Virginia requires a warning to be given to defendants pleading guilty to non-sexual offenses; Florida and Minnesota, however, say that failure to give this warning does not invalidate a guilty plea to a sexual offense.[466]

Rule 11(b)(1)(A) requires the judge to warn that statements at a plea hearing can be used in a perjury case, but failure of a judge to do so is likely to be treated as harmless error if there is no actual intention to bring perjury charges. Fed. R. Crim. P. 11(f) provides that the admissibility of pleas and plea discussions is governed by FRE 410. FRE 410 generally provides that nolo pleas, withdrawn guilty pleas and statements related to abortive plea negotiations are not admissible in civil or criminal trials. Exceptions are made for perjury cases and where fairness requires full disclosure where other parts of the plea negotiations have been raised at trial.

According to *Libretti v. United States*,[467] a forfeiture agreement that is negotiated in conjunction with a plea bargain is an element of sentencing, not an admission of guilt, so it is not necessary for the judge to make a Rule 11(f) inquiry

---

[465] United States v. Williams, 510 F.3d 416 (3d Cir. 2007).

[466] State v. Bellamy, 835 A.2d 1231 (N.J. 2003).

[467] 516 U.S. 29 (1995).

as to the factual basis of the plea. *Libretti* also holds that the judge is not a party to the plea agreement, and is not bound by it; the judge is free to impose any otherwise permissible sentence.

[H] Juries and Jury Trials

[1] Issue Checklist

❏ Is the defendant entitled to a jury trial? Even if a jury trial would be unavailable for the trial of a single petty offense, multiple petty offenses, or a custodial sentence plus a fine, might make a jury trial available[468]

❏ Can the venue be changed? Should it?

❏ Is the composition of the venire representative? The defendant making a non-proportionality argument may have to show systematic exclusion of a group, not mere under-representation.

❏ Were challenges used improperly to exclude a group?

❏ Is a capital jury properly constituted?

❏ Is impaneling an anonymous jury (e.g., in an organized crime trial) permissible or desirable?

❏ What questions can attorneys ask on voir dire without violating the privacy of panel members?

❏ Was there substantial pretrial publicity, including inherently prejudicial material?

❏ Were jurors exposed to press coverage?

❏ Was the defendant in jail garb or shackled (unless this was necessary for security reasons), inducing a prejudicial belief in the defendant's guilt or dangerousness?

❏ Were jurors allowed to take notes? In most jurisdictions, allowing or forbidding note-taking falls within the discretion of the judge.

❏ Did jurors discuss the case prior to deliberation, either among themselves or with others?

❏ Should the jury have been sequestered?

❏ Should the judge recuse him-/herself, e.g., for appearance of bias, legal career before the bench, or involvement of his/her spouse?

❏ Did the judge make inappropriate questions or comments, or unfairly limit opening or closing arguments?

The jury has to determine guilt on every element, including materiality of alleged false statements under 18 USC § 1001 (false statements to a government agency).[469] This is really a mixed question of law and fact and thus within the province of the jury.

---

[468] *But see* Lewis v. United States, 518 U.S. 322 (1996): right to jury trial is not triggered by multiple petty offenses punishable by under six months' imprisonment each, even if the aggregate is over six months.

[469] United States v. Gaudin, 515 U.S. 506 (1995).

[a] Jury Selection

Fed. R. Crim. P. 24 provides that the court may either examine the prospective jurors or permit the attorneys to do so. If the court examines the prospective jurors, the attorneys must be given a chance to either ask additional questions that have been approved by the court, or to submit further questions that the court will ask the potential jurors if the court finds them proper.

In a federal capital case, each side gets 20 peremptory challenges. In other felony cases, the government has six peremptory challenges, and the defendant or the joined defendants as a group have 10 peremptories. In a federal misdemeanor trial, each side has three peremptory challenges. (24(b)(1)).

Racial, ethnic, and gender discrimination in the jury pool have all been held to violate Constitutional guarantees.[470]

The basic rule under *Batson* is that an allegation of discriminatory use of peremptory challenges requires establishment of a prima facie case of discrimination (proof of facts and circumstances that raise an inference of discrimination). Next, the party seeking to use the peremptory challenge rebuts with a race-neutral reason for the challenge.

The Supreme Court rejected California's "more likely than not" standard for the prima facie case on discriminatory peremptory challenges based on group membership rather than individual characteristics. The court ruled that *Batson* mandates production of enough evidence for the trial judge to draw an inference of discrimination.[471] The Supreme Court returned to *Batson* issues in its January 18, 2006, decision in *Rice v. Collins*, 546 U.S. 333. The question was whether a black potential juror was removed from the panel because of her race. The prosecution asserted race-neutral motivations: her youth and demeanor. The Ninth Circuit ruled that the state Court of Appeals violated AEDPA by sustaining the strike, because given the evidence presented at trial, the factual determination of the propriety of the strike was unreasonable. The Supreme Court reversed, holding that AEDPA precluded habeas relief in this situation. AEDPA required it to be unreasonable to believe the race-neutral explanations offered by the prosecutor whereas, according to the Supreme Court, at most the trial court could have questioned the veracity of this explanation. Rejecting the explanation was not mandatory.

In March 2008, the Supreme Court reversed a black defendant's murder conviction and death sentence because of the prosecutor's racially prejudiced exclusion of black people from the jury. The prosecutor disqualified all five black potential jurors, in one case for a trivial scheduling conflict whereas white jurors with scheduling conflicts were seated.[472] A California prosecutor used

---

[470] JEB v. Alabama *ex rel.* TB, 511 U.S. 127 (1994); Georgia v. McCollum, 505 U.S. 42 (1992); Batson v. Kentucky, 476 U.S. 79 (1986).

[471] Johnson v. California, 545 U.S. 162 (2005).

[472] Snyder v. Louisiana, 128 S. Ct. 1203 (2008); *see* Mark Sherman (AP), *High Court Justices Throw Out Death Sentence, Conviction in Case Involving Racial Prejudice*, 3/19/08 (law.com).

peremptory challenges to keep all six blacks off the jury. The prosecutor offered race-neutral reasons for the exclusions (e.g., failure to answer all the questions on the jury questionnaire; having a relative who had been arrested; frequent job changes), but the Ninth Circuit concluded that white jurors in the same categories were not excluded, so the rationales were pretextual. Finding that exclusion of even one juror for racial reasons taints a trial, the Ninth Circuit granted habeas.[473]

The Second Circuit applied *Batson* to black defendants' use of peremptory challenges to exclude white jurors, and held that an improper challenge made by one attorney in a multi-defendant case can violate *Batson*.[474]

In mid-2005, the Supreme Court permitted the use of habeas to overturn a 20-year-old conviction, based on a showing that the prosecution had exercised race-based peremptories. The petitioner satisfied the 28 USC § 2254(d)(2) standard that the state court ruling was an unreasonable determination of the facts in light of the evidence. Peremptories were used to remove 10 out of 11 competent black members of the venire. Black potential jurors who were struck were similarly qualified to white jurors who were seated. Furthermore, the prosecutor tricked potential jurors by asking them about sentences they might impose, while informing only some potential jurors of the minimum penalty for murder.[475]

As prescribed by the Federal Rules of Criminal Procedure, a defendant was given 10 peremptories to pick 12 jurors, plus one more to pick the alternate. The defendant challenged a prospective juror for cause, claiming that he would favor the prosecution. The District Court refused to excuse him. The defendant objected unsuccessfully and finally used a peremptory to get rid of him. The defendant was convicted on all charges.

The Supreme Court refused to adopt the government position that the defendant must use a peremptory challenge to strike a juror removable for cause. However, the Supreme Court held that this case did not violate Rule 24(b). The defendant was merely entitled to 11 peremptory challenges — not the right to use them in situations of his own choosing; he could have left the challenged individual on the jury and then appealed; having one (bad) choice is not the equivalent of having no choice.[476]

Gay men and lesbians are a cognizable group, so excluding them from juries purely on the basis of sexual orientation violates the California state Constitution's right to a representative jury.[477]

In some circumstances, typically because of concern about the safety of jurors, the identities of jurors are concealed. In 2002, the Fifth Circuit ruled

---

[473] Green v. LaMarque, 532 F.3d 1028 (9th Cir. 2008).

[474] United States v. Rodriguez, 528 F.3d 110 (2d Cir. 2008); *see* Mark Hamblett, *2nd Circuit Applies 'Batson' to Challenge of White Jurors*, N.Y.L.J. 6/12/08 (law.com). *See* Georgia v. McCollum, 550 U.S. 42 (1992), a "reverse-Batson" case involving conduct of defense attorneys rather than prosecutors.

[475] Miller-El v. Dretke, 545 U.S. 231 (2005).

[476] United States v. Martinez-Salazar, 528 U.S. 304 (2000).

[477] People v. Garcia, 92 Cal. Rptr. 2d 339 (Cal. App. 2000).

that, even though safety concerns were not paramount, an anonymous jury was appropriate in an ex-governor's extortion trial in light of the media interest in the trial and the potential for powerful people to interfere with the jury.[478] The Seventh Circuit found that an anonymous jury was not appropriate merely because the defendants belonged to a street gang; there was no evidence that they intended to have gang members intimidate the jurors. However, given the extensive voir dire and the overwhelming evidence of the defendants' guilt, the error was not deemed prejudicial.[479]

[2] Jury Instructions

Criminal juries are usually confronted with a great deal of evidence, much of it controverted. Jury instructions are supposed to assist them in determining which items should be considered, priority to be given among them, and to explain who has the burden of proof on each issue and what constitutes reasonable doubt. Jury instructions are analyzed against the background of all the evidence produced at trial, to determine whether any instruction violated a constitutional right and deprived the defendant of a fair trial.[480]

On request from a defendant who did not testify, the court must charge the jury that they must not draw unfavorable inferences from the defendant's non-appearance on the witness stand. If a defense was sufficiently supported by evidence, it could be reversible error to refuse to charge the jury on that defense.

A challenge to the trial court's refusal to give the jury instructions requested by the defense involves proof of several elements:

- The requested instruction was a correct statement of law
- The jury charge as a whole did not substantially cover those points
- Not raising those points substantially impaired the defendant's ability to present a particular defense
- The issue was properly before the jury.

The Supreme Court held that the jury instructions in the Arthur Andersen accounting firm's trial for witness tampering (18 USC § 1512(b)(2)(A)) were inadequate. The instructions failed to properly inform the jury of the correct standard for consciousness of wrongdoing that would support the conviction.[481]

The Supreme Court affirmed a conviction for receiving a firearm while under indictment and making false statements in connection with receipt of a firearm. The Supreme Court did not accept the argument that the jury instructions required proof of duress by a preponderance of the evidence rather than requiring

---

[478] United States v. Edwards, 303 F.3d 606 (5th Cir. 2002).

[479] United States v. Mansoori, 304 F.3d 635 (7th Cir. 2002).

[480] Estelle v. McGuire, 502 U.S. 62 (1991).

[481] Arthur Andersen LLP v. United States, 544 U.S. 696 (2005).

the government to prove beyond a reasonable doubt that the defendant did not act under duress.[482]

Even if the jury instructions are erroneous, the error could be harmless: for instance, it is not mandatory to instruct the jury that a defendant found not guilty by reason of insanity will be involuntarily committed.[483] Under *Hedgpeth v. Pullido*, No. 07-544 (12/2/08), a conviction under a general verdict can be challenged if the jury was instructed on alternative theories of guilt, and may have relied on the wrong one to convict. The Supreme Court ruled that the test is whether the instructions had a substantial and injurious effect or influence on the jury verdict.

Because the trial judge's supplemental "nullification instruction" (restricting the extent to which the jury could consider mitigating factors in a capital murder case) was invalid under *Penry v. Johnson*, 532 U.S. 782 (2001), the Supreme Court reversed the death sentence. *Penry* requires the jury to give full consideration and full effect to any mitigating circumstances when setting the penalty for a murder conviction: *Smith v. Texas*, 534 U.S. 37 (2004).

In January 2005, the Supreme Court ruled per curiam that the writ of certiorari was improvidently granted in the case of *Howell v. Mississippi*, 543 U.S. 440 (2005). The petitioner contended that the trial court violated his rights by refusing to instruct the jury on lesser included offenses (manslaughter and simple murder) in his capital murder case. Certiorari was dismissed because the petitioner failed to raise the claim before the Supreme Court of Mississippi.

[3] Jury Deliberations and Verdict

During deliberations, the jurors must remain together at all times, under the supervision of court officers who prevent unauthorized persons from gaining access to them.

The basic rule of Fed. R. Crim. P. 24(c) is that alternate jurors will be dismissed once the jury retires to deliberate, unless the court elects to retain them. If it becomes necessary to replace a juror with an alternate juror after deliberations have begun, the court must instruct the jury to restart deliberations from the beginning.

Fed. R. Crim. P. 23(b) permits the trial judge to allow a jury of under 12 members to return a verdict, if it is necessary to excuse a juror for cause.

Late in 2007, the New York Court of Appeals reversed a case that had been precedent since the mid-nineteenth century. New York now permits a valid criminal verdict to be returned by a jury with fewer than 12 jurors. In this case, three days after deliberations started, one of the jurors was hospitalized. The prosecution sought a mistrial, but the defendant asked to have the remaining 11 jurors hear the case. He appealed the ensuing conviction. The Court of Appeals majority held that, in a non-capital case, the defendant can consent to a jury of fewer than 12. Constitutional rights (e.g., the right to counsel and the right to silence) can be waived, and in this

---

[482] Dixon v. United States, 126 S. Ct. 2437 (2006).

[483] Shannon v. United States, 512 U.S. 573 (1994), interpreting the Insanity Defense Reform Act of 1984.

case, the Court of Appeals permitted a knowing and voluntary waiver approved by the trial judge.[484]

Sullivan v. Louisiana,[485] holds that, given the right to a jury trial, the judge can direct a verdict in favor of the defendant, but not the prosecution, whatever the evidence. The jury instruction on reasonable doubt is so fundamental that there has not been a "jury trial" unless the instruction has been given in correct form.

A jury's general verdict will be sustained as long as there is sufficient evidence for at least one ground for conviction.

The jury can be discharged without a verdict if a mistrial is declared, or if they are deadlocked after extensive deliberations and are unlikely to agree in a reasonable time.

The *Allen* charge, so-called after the venerable Supreme Court case found at 164 U.S. 492 (1896), is a supplemental jury charge given in some jurisdictions when the jury indicates difficulty in reaching a verdict. The *Allen* charge directs jurors to keep an open mind and listen to their fellow-jurors; minority jurors are asked to consider whether their views are reasonable. Nevertheless, jurors must be told that they must reach a verdict that represents the honest opinion of all jurors, not submission to the majority will by jurors who continue to disagree.[486]

"Jury nullification" is the phenomenon of a juror voting for acquittal on a basis other than lack of belief that the prosecution case has been proved—e.g., because the juror disapproves of the statute in question or is unwilling to grant credence to the testimony of law enforcement officials. The California Supreme Court forbade the use of a jury instruction requiring the jurors to inform the judge if any juror refuses to deliberate or expresses an intention to disregard the law. The court's rationale was that, even though the anti-nullification instruction does not violate the constitutional guarantee of an impartial jury trial, it is vague and could hamper the free exchange of ideas and give the judge the power to pry into jury deliberations.[487]

[a] Dismissal of Jurors

The Eleventh Circuit permits dismissal of a juror based on the other jurors' representation that the juror refuses to apply the law as instructed, if the court finds that there is no substantial possibility that the hold-out is basing his or her decision on the evidence. The decision to remove a juror is reviewed for clear error.[488]

---

[484] People v. Gajadhar, 9 N.Y.3d 438 (N.Y. 2007); Joel Stashenko, *N.Y. High Court Upholds 11-Person Jury's Verdict*, N.Y.L.J. 12/20/07 (law.com).

[485] 508 U.S. 275 (1993).

[486] Lowenfeld v. Phelps, 481 U.S. 231 (1988).

[487] People v. Engleman, 121 Cal. Rptr. 2d 862 (Cal. 2002).

[488] United States v. Abbell, 271 F.3d 1286 (11th Cir. 2001).

The dismissal of a deliberating juror who refuses to discuss the evidence does not have to satisfy the standard for removing a juror for nullification, because not deliberating is tantamount to ignoring the evidence.[489]

If a conviction is reversed because the trial judge erred in dismissing a deliberating juror, the defendant can be retried, because the reversal was not due to insufficiency of the evidence.[490]

[I] Mistrial

The defendant is entitled to a fair trial, but not necessarily a perfect one. In appropriately dire circumstances, the court can declare a mistrial, and order a new trial, on motion of the prosecution or defense, or on its own motion.

Fed. R. Crim. P. 31(3) says that if the jury cannot agree on a verdict on one or more counts, the court may declare a mistrial on those counts. The defendant can be retried on any of the counts on which the jury was unable to agree.

Mistrial is available on motion by the defense if the trial has been subject to error or legal defect that is prejudicial to the defendant, preventing a fair trial: for instance, prosecutorial misconduct or ineffective assistance of counsel. The motion for mistrial should be made as soon as the misconduct occurs, in enough detail for the court to understand the nature of the challenge. A defendant who moves for, or consents to, mistrial waives double jeopardy. However, if mistrial is granted over the objection of the defendant, double jeopardy bars a retrial unless there is manifest necessity for the retrial in order to prevent perversion of justice.

Examples of prosecutorial misconduct that could justify reversal of a conviction, because the defendant could not obtain a fair trial, include referring to evidence not in the record; improper expressions of personal belief; vouching for prosecution witnesses or reacting inappropriately to testimony by the defendant or defense witnesses; commenting on the defendant's failure to testify or present a case; appealing to the jury's prejudices; flagrantly failing to restrict the summation to materials and information placed in evidence. However, even improper conduct might not necessarily merit reversal, if it can be cured by jury instructions to disregard non-evidentiary statements.

The prosecution can move for mistrial if the defendant or someone acting on the defendant's behalf or a juror is guilty of gross misconduct that cannot be cured, for instance, by instructing the jury to correct prejudice. The court can declare a mistrial on its own motion when it becomes impossible to proceed with the trial in a lawful fashion (e.g., jury tampering has been discovered). In the federal system, Fed. R. Crim. P. 26.3 requires that, before ordering a mistrial, the court must give the prosecution and each defendant a chance to state whether they consent to or oppose the declaration of a mistrial, and to suggest alternatives if they think there is a way to salvage the fairness of the trial.

---

[489] United States v. Baker, 262 F.3d 124 (2d Cir. 2001).
[490] People v. Hernandez, 30 Cal. 4th (Cal. 2003).

[J] Other Issues in the Criminal Trial

Apart from issues of the proper selection of the jury, and the jury's deliberation and verdict, criminal trials raise many other issues that must be accommodated by the prosecution, and can provide strategic opportunities for the defense.

A murder conviction was not invalid even though family members of the victim attended the trial each day wearing buttons showing the victim's face. The Supreme Court ruled in late 2006 that the "spectator conduct," although possibly prejudicial, was not the type of state-actor conduct that would lead to reversal of a conviction on the grounds of inherent prejudice: *Carey v. Musladin*, 549 U.S. 70 (2006). The Justices disagreed as to whether wearing buttons in court is protected First Amendment speech.

The Sixth Circuit found an aggravated murder conviction (two robbery victims were shot; one died) to be invalid because of the prosecution's inconsistent theories about who shot which victim. The Supreme Court reversed, holding that at the hearing, the petitioner's attorney stated that the petitioner was informed of the elements of the crime, and the petitioner agreed. The Supreme Court held that as long as a defendant's lawyer explains the elements of the crime, it is not necessary for the judge to do so. Nor did the conviction require that the petitioner shot the victim who died, because Ohio law holds that an aider/abettor who acts with specific intent to cause death is guilty of aggravated murder. The case was remanded for the Sixth Circuit to reconsider the effect of the inconsistent prosecution theories on the petitioner's sentence.[491]

[1] Jurisdiction and Venue

The District Court gains subject matter jurisdiction over a case when the indictment is filed; jurisdiction over the person of the defendant is obtained by arrest or summons. (A corporation can be summonsed, but not arrested.) 18 USC § 3401(a) permits magistrate judges to try defendants and sentence them for federal misdemeanors committed within the district. See Fed. R. Crim. P. 58 for the procedure and practices for misdemeanor cases, including appeal of magistrates' decisions to the District Court.

The general rule is that venue is laid in the state and district where the crime was committed.[492] Furthermore, if this can be done without great inconvenience, capital trials should take place in the **county** in which the offense was committed: 18 USC § 3285.

---

[491] Bradshaw v. Stumpf, 545 U.S. 175 (2005).

[492] *But see* United States v. Cabrales, 524 U.S. 1 (1998): in a money laundering case, venue is not proper in the state where the crime whose proceeds were laundered was committed, if the money laundering defendant did not participate in that crime or transport funds from that state. In a prosecution under 18 USC § 924(c)(1) (using or carrying a firearm during and in relation to a violent crime), venue is appropriate in any state in which a violent crime was committed, even if the gun was carried in only one state of a multi-state series of crimes: United States v. Rodriguez-Moreno, 526 U.S. 275 (1999).

The 2006 proposed revision to Fed. R. Crim P. 18 requires the convenience of victims — not just defendants and witnesses — to be considered in setting the place of trial.

Fed. R. Crim. P. 21 allows the defendant, but not the prosecution, to move to transfer the case to another district based on prejudice; for the convenience of parties and witnesses; or in the interest of justice. The motion can be granted even if the prosecution objects. Change of venue must be granted if it is proved to the satisfaction of the court that there is too much prejudice in the district for the defendant to get a fair and impartial trial. (In this context, prejudice refers only to the jury — not the judge or prosecutor.) The trial judge has discretion to decide where the case will be transferred. The defendant has the burden of proof.

Usually, the motion for change of venue is not decided until after voir dire; the test is whether enough jurors can be chosen who can put aside opinions formed by pretrial publicity, and can decide only on the basis of evidence presented at trial.

[2] Joinder and Severance

Federal rules 13 (joinder) and 14 (severance) deal in a more or less common-sense way with combinations of defendants, or reversing those combinations if joinder is contrary to justice and impairs the potential for giving all the co-defendants a fair trial. Rule 14 gives the court the power to order separate trials of counts in the accusatory instrument, sever trials of multiple defendants, or provide whatever relief justice requires, where joinder or consolidated trials prejudice either a defendant or the prosecution.

Wherever possible, measures less drastic than severance (e.g., limiting instructions) should be used, but severance is appropriate to prevent the jury from hearing prejudicial evidence that would not be admitted in a separate trial, or to make admissible exculpatory evidence that would be kept out in a joined trial.

Nevertheless, even if potential prejudice is shown, severance remains discretionary with the District Court judge.[493] However, offenses committed in different federal judicial districts cannot be joined.[494]

A 2003 Eleventh Circuit case involves two defendants who had separate counsel but participated in a joint defense agreement. The court held that a defendant who turned state's evidence to get a shorter sentence could not assert attorney-client privilege in communications to the counsel for the other defendant. The court pointed out that joint defense should be undertaken only in connection with a written agreement that alerts defendants to the unavailability of privilege in this situation.[495]

---

[493] Zafiro v. United States, 506 U.S. 534 (1993).
[494] United States v. Palomba, 31 F.3d 1456 (9th Cir. 1994).
[495] United States v. Almeida, 341 F.3d 1318 (11th Cir. 2003).

[3] Motion Practice

Fed. R. Crim. P. 12 allows a party to raise by pretrial motion any defense, objection, or request that the court can decide without trying the general issues of the case. Under Rule 12(3), certain motions must be raised before trial:

- A motion alleging a defect in the way the prosecution was instituted
- A motion alleging a defect in the indictment or information (although a claim that the accusatory instrument fails to state an offense or fails to invoke the court's jurisdiction can be raised at any time)
- A motion to suppress evidence
- A motion to sever charges or defendants (Rule 14)
- A Rule 16 motion for discovery.

Rule 12.4 requires a disclosure statement from any corporate party to a District Court proceeding. The corporate party must identify its parent corporation (if any) and any public corporation that owns 10% or more of its stock. When a corporation or other organization is alleged to be the victim of criminal activity, the government must identify the alleged victim and disclose any parent corporation or 10% owner. These requirements were added in 2002 to help judges decide if they are obligated to recuse themselves because of financial conflicts of interest involving corporate parties.

[a] Motions to Suppress

Under Fed. R. Crim. P. 12, a motion to suppress evidence must be made before the trial; it can be made before the indictment is filed. In general, failure to so move waives the issue, although the court has discretion to grant relief from the waiver. The motion cannot be made after the trial, or after a guilty plea has been entered. If a mistrial has been declared, or a conviction has been reversed and the case remanded for a new trial, the defendant's rights return to their original state, and a suppression motion is once again timely.

The court need not grant a hearing if the suppression motion is insufficient (i.e., fails to explain which parts of the warrant affidavit are false; that the false statements were knowing or at least reckless; that the veracity of the affiant, but no one else, is at stake; a detailed offer of proof must be made; and the challenged statements must be essential to establishment of probable cause). It is not necessary to renew an unsuccessful motion to suppress at trial, or even to object to the introduction of the evidence in order to preserve the objection for appeal. However, if new facts emerge at trial (e.g., testimony of previously unavailable witnesses), the judge has discretion to reconsider the decision on suppression.

Fed. R. Crim. P. 12 also gives the government discretion to give notice, at the arraignment, of intention to use specific evidence at the trial, so the defendant can raise any objections at the earliest possible stage. At the arraignment, or as soon as practicable, the defendant can ask about the evidence that the prosecution intends to offer and that can be discovered under Fed. R. Crim. P. 16 (see § 26.04[E]).

Under Rule 12.1, the prosecution can make a written request to be notified if the defendant intends to raise an alibi defense. In response to such a request, the defense must state where the defendant claims to have been and the alibi witnesses the defense intends to call. The prosecution is then obligated to disclose the witnesses it intends to call to rebut the alibi defense. The 2006 proposed amendment to this rule says that the victim's name and address should not automatically be provided to the defense when an alibi defense is raised; need for the information must be shown.

A suppression hearing is subject to Sixth Amendment trial standards, so the same showing is required to close a suppression hearing as to close a trial session to the public.[496]

[b] Insanity Defense and Related Matters

Fed. R. Crim. P. 12.2 deals with motions filed by the defendant (either pretrial or at a later time set by the court) to inform the prosecution that the defense intends to assert an insanity defense and/or introduce expert testimony as to the defendant's mental condition (including mental disease or defect) that bears on guilt or the appropriateness of a capital sentence.

When such a motion is filed, the court may order the defendant to undergo a competency examination under 18 USC § 4241. In response to a defense motion heralding an insanity defense, and if the prosecution so moves, the court must order an examination of the defendant under 18 USC § 4242. In response to a motion to introduce expert testimony, and if the prosecution so moves, the court may (but is not compelled to) order the defendant to be examined under procedures ordered by the court.

Statements made by the defendant in the course of such examinations are inadmissible against the defendant, except as to issues of mental condition raised by the defense.

Note that, under 18 USC § 17, it is an affirmative defense (i.e., a matter that the defense must prove by clear and convincing evidence) that, at the time of the offense charged the defendant was unable to "appreciate the nature and quality or the wrongfulness of his acts" as a result of a severe mental disease or defect. The federal statute states specifically that mental illness or defect is not a defense under any other circumstances.

[c] Post-Trial Motions

After the close of the prosecution case, or after all evidence has been submitted, Fed. R. Crim. P. 29 states that, on motion of the defendant, the court must issue a judgment of acquittal on any charge for which the evidence is insufficient to sustain a conviction. The court may (but is not obligated to) consider on its own motion whether the evidence is insufficient. If such a motion is made and denied at

---

[496] Waller v. Georgia, 467 U.S. 39 (1984).

the close of the government's evidence, the defense can offer evidence even if it has not reserved the right to do so.

Under the same rule, after a guilty verdict or the discharge of the jury (whichever is later), the defense has seven days to move or renew its motion for judgment of acquittal. The court can grant the motion if the jury has not returned a verdict. The court also has the power to set aside the verdict and enter an acquittal.

When the court enters a judgment of acquittal, it must also conditionally decide whether a motion for new trial would be granted (and why) if the judgment of acquittal is vacated or reversed. If the motion for a new trial is conditionally granted, and the judgment of acquittal is reversed on appeal, the trial court must retry the defendant unless the appellate court says this is not required. On the other hand, if the trial court conditionally denies the new-trial motion and the appellate court reverses the judgment of acquittal, the trial court must proceed as directed by the appellate court.

Fed. R. Crim. P. 33 provides that, on a defense motion, the court can vacate judgment and grant a new trial in the interests of justice. If the motion is grounded on newly discovered evidence, it must be filed within three years of the verdict. In cases where an appeal is pending, the motion for a new trial cannot be granted until the appellate court remands the case. In late 2005, the Supreme Court ruled that Rule 33 is a claim-processing rule rather than a jurisdictional one — with the practical implication that the government cannot raise the time limit for the first time on appeal.[497]

If the rationale for the motion is anything other than newly discovered evidence, it must either be filed seven days after the verdict, or within the time period as extended by the court during that seven-day period.

[K] Evidence

Although certain evidentiary issues are raised by the Federal Rules of Criminal Procedure, and by various state and federal cases, most evidentiary questions in criminal cases are governed by the Federal Rules of Evidence and their state counterparts.

Several states are considering new legislation and guidelines for lineups after discovery of wrongful convictions based on bad eyewitness identification. More and more states are considering techniques such as a sequential lineup where people or photographs are shown singly, not all together, or a blind lineup, where the person doing the lineup does not know which participant is the suspect. When Cardozo School of Law's Innocent Project analyzed 197 wrongful convictions that were invalidated by DNA evidence, mistaken eyewitness identification was a factor in more than 75% of them.[498]

By the fall of 2007, 42 states (all except Alabama, Alaska, Massachusetts, Mississippi, Oklahoma, South Carolina, South Dakota, and Wyoming) had adopted

---

[497] Eberhart v. United States, 546 U.S. 12 (2005).

[498] Vesna Jaksic, *States Look at Reforming Lineup Methods*, Nat'l L.J. 4/20/07 (law.com).

laws giving prison inmates access to DNA test results, perhaps results that were not available at the time of the conviction. California and several other states established commissions to expedite investigations of alleged wrongful convictions. In 2007 alone, Maryland, North Carolina, Vermont and West Virginia passed laws to improve the quality of eyewitness identifications. A total of 25 bills in 17 states were introduced in 2007 dealing with eyewitness identifications. Five laws were passed. Vermont and Maryland tightened standards for crime labs. Cardozo's Innocence Project reported that over 500 state and local jurisdictions (e.g., Maine, Massachusetts, New Jersey, Wisconsin) require interrogations to be recorded, so charges of coerced confessions can be investigated more thoroughly. California passed a bill requiring corroboration of informant testimony introduced in a jury trial. A study by Professor Samuel R. Gross (Michigan Law School) estimated that approximately 340 exonerations had been made between 1989 and 2003: 205 murder and 121 rape convictions were reversed; in 50% of the murder and 88% of the rape cases, incorrect eyewitness investigations were involved. About half (144) of the exonerations were based on DNA evidence. A complicating factor is that crime labs can be involved wrongful convictions as well as exonerations if, for example, poorly handled forensic evidence implicates the wrong person.[499]

In 2004, the Third Circuit joined the Fourth and Seventh Circuits in finding expert testimony on fingerprint identification to be reliable enough to be admissible in the post-*Daubert* and *Kumho* environment. Despite concerns about errors, the Third Circuit found the technique to be reliable enough to be admitted in a criminal trial.[500]

Early in 2004, the Supreme Court reversed the Illinois Court of Appeals, which had held that Due Process required dismissal of criminal charges because the police, acting in good faith and pursuant to normal procedure, destroyed evidence that the defendant had requested more than 10 years earlier under a discovery motion. The Supreme Court reversed because the evidence in question was cocaine that had been seized, so the chemical composition of the substance was inculpatory rather than exculpatory. Failure to preserve evidence claimed to be potentially useful but not exculpatory violates Due Process only if the petitioner can show bad faith on the part of the police.[501]

[1] Fed. R. Crim. P. 41

In addition to the Fourth Amendment issues discussed at § 26.03[B], Federal Rules of Criminal Procedure (Fed. R. Crim. P.) 41 governs some significant search-and-seizure issues in the federal courts. It should be noted that Rule 41 is broader than the Fourth Amendment — but that evidence seized in violation of the Fourth Amendment is absolutely inadmissible (see § 26.03[B][3]) but violations of

---

[499] Solomon Moore, *DNA Exoneration Leads to Change in Legal System*, N.Y. Times 10/1/07 at A1.

[500] United States v. Mitchell, 365 F.3d 215 (3d Cir. 2004).

[501] Illinois v. Fisher, 540 U.S. 544 (2004).

Rule 41 that are not of Constitutional dimensions do not always require exclusion of the evidence, especially if there was no deliberate misconduct by law enforcement officers. Rule 41 permits seizure of:

- Evidence of a crime
- Contraband or fruits of a crime
- Property used or intended to be used as means of committing a crime
- A person for whose arrest there is probable cause.

Seized items can be either tangible or intangible (e.g., wiretaps).

Also see the Privacy Protection Act, 42 USC § 2000aa(6), giving a person aggrieved by a search for or seizure of journalists' work product a cause of action in federal District Court, for actual damages (or liquidated damages of $1,000, if that is higher than the actual damages), plus fees and costs.

[2] Federal Rules of Evidence in Criminal Cases

Many of the Federal Rules of Evidence (FRE) are particularly salient in criminal cases.

FRE 404(a)(1) forbids introduction of evidence of character or a trait of character to show conforming actions.

Rule 404 (as revised by the 2000 amendments) does allow evidence of character in three instances:

- Character evidence introduced by the accused, or by the prosecution in rebuttal; evidence that the accused possesses a character trait asserted by the alleged victim
- Character evidence about the alleged victim offered by the accused, or by the prosecution in rebuttal — including prosecution evidence that a homicide victim was a peaceful person who was not the aggressor in the events leading to death
- A witness' character, as defined by the FRE's impeachment rules (607–609). The First Circuit held in 2004 that, for impeachment purposes, the standard for admitting prior convictions depends on the identity of the witness. Under Rule 609, the defendant's priors are admitted if the probative value exceeds the risk of prejudice, whereas prior convictions of witnesses are governed by Rule 403, which says that evidence is excludable only if the danger of prejudice substantially outweighs the probative value.[502]

FRE 405(a) says that if proof of character or a character trait is admissible, witnesses can testify as to their own opinion or the individual's reputation, and the cross-examination can go into relevant conduct.

---

[502] United States v. Tse, 375 F.3d 148 (1st Cir. 2004).

Evidence of other sexual assaults or acts of child molestation by the defendant can be admitted, under FRE 413–415, in sex crime prosecution or related civil cases. It can be considered for its bearing on any matter to which it is relevant. The prosecution (or civil plaintiff) intending to offer this evidence must notify the defense of the intent to use the evidence at least 15 days before the scheduled trial date (or later, with permission of the court).

Many jurisdictions have "rape shield" laws that bar general exploration of the sexual conduct of a person alleged to be the victim of a sex crime. Evidence about the victim's past sexual conduct is admissible only if it relates to past sexual conduct with the defendant; recent prostitution convictions; or if it rebuts the complainant's claims that non-criminal sexual relations had not occurred at all during a period of time, or that the defendant was the source of the complainant's pregnancy or of semen samples recovered from the defendant. Testimony about the victim's sexual conduct is admissible only if the court finds it necessary in the interests of justice.

The credibility of a witness can be attacked, under FRE 609(a)(1), by introducing evidence that the witness has been convicted of an offense punishable by at least a year's imprisonment, as long as the probative value of such impeaching evidence exceeds its prejudicial value. Prior misdemeanor convictions can be used for impeachment of witnesses only if they involved dishonesty or false statements. The ruling on a pretrial motion on the admissibility of a prior conviction can be deferred, because evidence from the trial may be necessary to balance probative value against prejudicial effect.

The judge can interrogate witnesses (FRE 614(b)), but must remain impartial. Under FRE 704(b), even an expert witness is not permitted to state an opinion as to whether the defendant had a mental state that was an element of the crime.

[3] Hearsay Exceptions in Criminal Trials

FRE 804(b)(3) provides a hearsay exception for statements against the declarant's penal interest (but see below for the confession of a co-defendant).

There is also a hearsay exception, on agency grounds, for declarations made by any conspirator in the course and in furtherance of the conspiracy. The declarations can be admitted against any other conspirator.

Other hearsay exceptions that may come into play in a criminal trial:

- Statement of intention to perform an act as evidence that the act was performed
- Spontaneous declaration or excited utterance
- Dying declaration
- Business records and public documents
- Prompt complaint by victim of a sex crime (although, in some jurisdictions, expert testimony on rape trauma syndrome [the reactions of rape victims] might rehabilitate the testimony of a complainant who delayed in reporting the crime).

[a] Statements by Co-Defendants

Although a defendant cannot be convicted merely on the uncorroborated testimony of an accomplice (someone who participated in the charged offense or a related offense; corroboration must connect the defendant with the offense), statements by co-defendants raise significant legal issues.

The foundation case is *Bruton v. United States*,[503] which holds that a co-defendant's confession that implicates the defendant is admissible against the confessor, but inadmissible hearsay as to the defendant in a joint trial if the confessing co-defendant does not testify and cannot be cross-examined to test the validity of the confession. However, it is acceptable to redact the confession to eliminate the defendant's name as long as the jury is instructed not to consider the confession against the defendant.[504] Another option is to sever the trials, or have separate juries for the co-defendants, with each jury hearing only materials admissible in its deliberations.

Lilly v. Virginia[505] limits the use of out-of-court statements in criminal trials, making it harder to introduce the confession of an alleged accomplice who admits culpability but says the defendant's role in the crime was larger than his or her own, ruling against the hearsay exception that some states allow for declarations against the penal interest of the declarant (i.e., incriminatory statements that could result in punishment of the declarant).

It was not an abuse of discretion under FRE 403 for a trial court to permit the prosecution to present evidence of a plea agreement and guilty plea made by an accomplice testifying in a Medicare fraud case — even if the defense promised not to challenge the credibility of the witness. The credibility of someone who admits participation in a crime is always at issue, and introducing a guilty plea is probative of issues other than mere credibility.

[L] Sentencing and Appeals

The topic of sentencing has been one of the hottest criminal law subjects for several years, especially in light of the Supreme Court's *Apprendi, Blakely*, and *Booker* decisions (see § 26.04[L][5]), which gave rise to a whole new set of considerations.

Fed. R. Crim. P. 32 requires the court to impose sentence "without unnecessary delay" (Rule 32(b)(1)) although the Rule 32 time limits can be changed by the court for good cause. Generally speaking, a presentence investigation and

---

[503] 391 U.S. 123 (1968). *But see* Gray v. Maryland, 523 U.S. 185 (1998): redaction is inadequate if it permits a reasonable inference by the jury that the defendant is one of the persons named in the confession.

[504] Richardson v. Marsh, 481 U.S. 200 (1987). *Bruton* does not apply to a bench trial: Lee v. Illinois, 476 U.S. 530 (1986), nor to a co-defendant's confession introduced to rebut a claim by the defendant, rather than as part of the case in chief, because the confession is not hearsay when used for rebuttal: Tennessee v. Street, 471 U.S. 409 (1985).

[505] 527 U.S. 116 (1999).

report by the probation officer is required, unless a relevant statute rules out the report, or unless the court makes a finding on the record that there is adequate evidence to impose sentence without such a report. If the offense for which the defendant was convicted requires restitution, the probation officer's report must include enough information to order the appropriate restitution.

The presentence report must identify the appropriate Sentencing Guidelines, the appropriate offense levels, criminal history category, reasons for departures from the Guidelines, and the appropriate sentencing range for the defendant. The report must be disclosed to the defendant, the defense attorney, and the prosecution at least 35 days before sentencing (unless the defense waives this time period). A party who objects to the sentencing recommendation has the right to file a written objection within 14 days of receiving the report; at least seven days before sentencing, the probation officer must file an addendum to the presentence report responding to the objections.

The basic rules for federal sentencing appear in the Sentencing Guidelines, which were supposed to remove the subjective elements and further justice by listing the factors that should be used to impose a sentence that is fair in that it reflects the gravity of the crime ("offense conduct") as well as the characteristics of the offender (e.g., whether he or she is a career criminal; acknowledgement of responsibility; obstruction of justice). Salient factors include the characteristics of the victim, and the defendant's degree of responsibility within a multi-party offense. The result has something in common with the measures intended to offer tax simplification.

At sentencing, the court has a duty to verify that the defendant and defense counsel have read the pre-sentence report. The court must disclose to both prosecution and defense if the court relies on any information that was excluded from the pre-sentence report, and must permit both sides to comment on the report. For good cause, the court can allow new objections to be raised at any time before sentence is imposed (Rule 32(i)(1)(D)), and evidence can be introduced on those objections.

The court is allowed to accept the undisputed portions of the pre-sentence report as a finding of fact. The court must rule on disputes over the pre-sentence report unless the dispute does not affect sentencing or it involves a matter that the court will not consider in sentencing. The defendant, the defense attorney, and the prosecutor must be given the opportunity to speak. If the crime for which the defendant was convicted involved violence or sexual abuse, and the victim or a representative of a minor or incapacitated victim is present at sentencing, he or she must be permitted to speak and submit information about the sentence.

Defendants who plead guilty waive the right to appeal, but if the defendant was convicted after a plea of Not Guilty, Fed. R. Crim. P. 32(j)(1) requires the judge to advise the defendant about appeal rights. No matter what the plea, the judge must advise the defendant about the dimensions of any right to appeal the sentence (including proceeding in forma pauperis).

The end result is a judgment signed by the judge and entered by the clerk, stating the plea, jury verdict or court findings, adjudication, and sentence of a person found guilty. The court must order the discharge of anyone found not guilty or otherwise entitled to discharge. (Fed. R. Crim. P. 32(k)).

Late in 2007, the Supreme Court required the Court of Appeals to review all federal sentences using the deferential standard of abuse of discretion — no matter where the sentence falls vis a vis the Guidelines. Appellate review is limited to the question of whether the District Court's sentencing decision was reasonable.[506] On the same day, the Supreme Court held that judges have the power to impose a below-Guidelines sentence on the basis of their doubts about the fairness of the 100:1 ratio between powder and crack cocaine that forms the basis of the Guidelines sentences for cocaine offenses.[507]

An overall sentence of 442 months was imposed for seven drug and firearm charges. However, the District Court failed to take *Deal v. United States*, 508 U.S. 129 (2007) into account, and imposed a 10-year sentence for an offense subject to a mandatory minimum of 25 years. The defendant appealed, on the grounds that the appropriate sentence for all the convictions was 15 years. The government did not appeal or cross-appeal. The Eighth Circuit, under the plain error rule of Fed. R. Crim. P. 52(b) raised the sentence to 662 months. The Supreme Court reversed, on the grounds that, absent a government appeal or cross-appeal, the Court of Appeals could not increase the sentence on its own motion. The court is only a neutral arbiter of issues raised by the parties (with some exceptions allowed to assist pro se petitioners). The Supreme Court ruled that, in a multi-count indictment "sentencing package" case, where some but not all counts of the conviction are challenged, the appeals court can vacate the entire sentence for the trial court to reform the sentencing plan (which could increase the sentences on certain counts but not the aggregate initial sentence). This is permissible under the cross-appeal rule, because the judge did not increase the sentence on his or her own motion. In this case, however, the defendant failed on all the appellate issues, so the Eighth Circuit had no reason to vacate the sentence.[508]

[1] Sentencing Guidelines

The original objective in establishing Sentencing Guidelines (created by the Sentence Reform Act of 1984, Title II of the Comprehensive Crime Control Act of 1984) was to reduce the disparities in sentencing for similar crimes. The Guidelines, which have frequently been amended since then, establish both basic sentencing ranges and both enhancements and reductions for various factors.

In January 2005, the Supreme Court ruled that although federal judges must consider the Sentencing Guidelines, the Guidelines are merely advisory and not

---

[506] Gall v. United States, 128 S. Ct. 586 (2007).

[507] Kimbrough v. United States, 128 S. Ct. 558 (2007). The Supreme Court returned to this subject in Spears v. United States, No. 08-5721 (1/21/09), reiterating that the ratio between crack and powder cocaine is advisory, and thus District Courts can reject the ratio based on a policy decision that the ratio makes crack sentences too severe, not just based on an individual determination of the defendant's degree of dangerousness.

[508] Greenlaw v. United States, 128 S. Ct. 2559 (2008).

obligatory. This principle was reaffirmed in late 2007, in a holding that the Court of Appeals must use the deferential standard of abuse of discretion when reviewing sentences—no matter how the actual sentence relates to the Guidelines. The sole question in appellate review is the reasonableness of the District Court's sentencing decision. The Court of Appeals can consider the extent of deviation from the Guidelines, but percentage formulas are inappropriate. A District Court judge need not find extraordinary circumstances to depart from the Guidelines. Where there is no procedural error, the Court of Appeals looks only at the reasonableness of the sentence: whether the judge abused his or her discretion in holding that the sentencing factors of 18 USC § 3353(a) supported a substantial deviation from the Guidelines range.[509]

In June 2005, the Supreme Court declined, without comment, to take the case of a prisoner sentenced under the Guidelines, a case that would have required consideration of whether hundreds of sentences should be reduced.[510] The appellate courts are largely occupied by parsing each Circuit's response to *Booker* and other recent sentencing decisions.

A group of "economic crime package amendments" to the Guidelines took effect on November 1, 2001.[511] The amendments increase sentences for large-scale fraud and theft. What previously were separate Guidelines for theft, property destruction, and fraud have been consolidated, because pecuniary harm is central to all these offenses. The separate loss tables for theft and fraud offenses have been combined. The penalties for large and medium losses on the tax loss table have been increased.

The Sentencing Guidelines treat a "career offender" as one with two or more prior felony convictions for violent or drug-related crimes. The sentencing judge must treat "related" convictions as a single prior conviction. Convictions that are consolidated for sentencing are deemed related—but consolidation can be functional as well as formal. Because the District Court is closer to the fact situation, the Supreme Court requires a deferential standard of review when an appeals court reviews the trial court's determination about consolidation.[512]

There is a split in authority over whether, for Guidelines purposes, all sex offenses that involve absence of consent are "forcible" (and therefore "crimes of violence") even if there is no use or threatened use of violence to commit the act. In mid-2008, the Fourth Circuit joined the Tenth and Third Circuit in calling all nonconsensual sex offenses forcible; the Fifth and Ninth Circuits disagree.[513]

---

[509] United States v. Booker, consolidated with United States v. Fanfan, 543 U.S. 220 (2005).

[510] Rodriguez v. United States, 547 U.S. 1127.

[511] *See* http://www.ussc.gov/2001guid/userfriendly2001.pdf, discussed at 70 L.W. 2257. *Also see* 67 FR 70999 (11/27/02) for the Commission's suggested sentencing enhancements for fraud and related offenses committed by directors and officers of public corporations, *e.g.*, additional offense levels for losses greater than $200 million and greater than $400 million; enhancements if more than 250 victims are affected by a fraud; and enhancement for destruction of corporate records.

[512] Buford v. United States, 532 U.S. 59 (2001).

[513] United States v. Chacon, 533 F.3d 250 (4th Cir. 2008); semble United States v. Romero-Hernandez, 505 F.3d 1082 (10th Cir. 2007) and United States v. Remoi, 404 F.3d 789 (3d Cir. 2005). *But see* United States v. Gomez-Gomez, 293 F.3d 562 (5th Cir. 2007) and United States v. Sarmiento-Funes, 374 F.3d 336 (5th Cir. 2004).

The First Circuit ruled that interstate transport of a minor for prostitution (18 USC § 2423(a)) is a "crime of violence" for the purpose of the career offender element of Guidelines 4B1.2(a), because it places the minor at serious risk of physical injury. Guideline 4B1.2(a) defines a crime of violence as a felony that has an element of use, attempted use, or threatened use of violence against the person; is a burglary of a dwelling; constitutes arson or extortion; uses explosives; or otherwise creates a risk of physical injury, as defined by the statutory definition of the offense rather than the facts of the individual allegation. *Begay v. United States*, 128 S. Ct. 1581 (2008) holds that DUI is not a violent felony for Armed Career Criminal Act (18 USC § 924(e)(20(B)) purposes because such offenses are comparable to other offenses that do not require criminal intent. *Begay* looks at whether the crime involves purposeful, violent, and aggressive conduct. Using this test, the First Circuit determined that a minor transported for prostitution is at risk of harm, and in many instances, force was used.[514]

Reckless endangerment (New York Penal Law § 120.25) is not a "crime of violence" as defined by Guidelines 4B1.2(a)(2), because it does not require purposeful conduct.[515]

Koon v. United States[516] would not let the sentencing court categorically exclude any factor that is not specifically barred by the Guidelines — so there is a potentially unlimited number of factors that could be relevant.

Once the basic sentence is determined, the judge decides whether a departure from the Guidelines is justified. Sentences outside the Guideline range are permitted by 18 USC § 3553(b), although the court must document its reasons for the departure, and aggravating or mitigating factors must be present in the individual case that are not adequately represented in the Guidelines in either degree or kind.

The Supreme Court ruled in mid-2008 that judges are not required to notify either prosecutors or defendants of intention to impose a sentence outside the Guidelines range; notification was required when the Guidelines were mandatory, but now neither side can have a reasonable expectation that the judge will impose a Guidelines sentence. (In this case, the pre-sentence report recommended a Guidelines range of 41–51 months for making threatening interstate communications, but the court imposed the statutory maximum sentence of 60 months in prison and three years' supervised release.[517]

---

[514] United States v. Williams, No. 529 F.3d 1 (1st Cir. 2008). Chambers v. United States, No. 06-11206 (1/13/09), holds that a conviction for failure to report to prison is not a violent felony conviction that triggers the mandatory 15-year sentence under the Armed Career Criminal Act, because the characteristic element of a violent felony is action, whereas failure to report is a crime of inaction. The Armed Career Criminal Act targets purposeful, violent, and aggressive conduct.

[515] United States v. Gray, 535 F.3d 120 (2d Cir. 2008).

[516] 518 U.S. 446 (2000).

[517] Irizarry v. United States, 128 S. Ct. 2198 (2008); *see* (AP), *High Court Rejects Sentencing Notification Rule*, 6/13/08 (law.com). Nevertheless, subsequently in mid-2008, the Ninth Circuit held that the Federal Rules of Criminal Procedure still require the District Court to give notice of potential departure from the Guidelines range; although the court can sentence above or below the Guideline

[a] Other General Sentencing Issues

Fed. R. Crim. P. 35(a) provides that, within seven days after sentencing, a court can correct any clear error in sentencing (e.g., arithmetic or technical errors). Within one year of sentencing, the prosecution can move to reduce the sentence of a defendant who, after sentencing, provided substantial assistance to an investigation or prosecution of another person. The sentence can even be reduced below the statutory minimum. In fact, if the substantial assistance took the form of information that was not useful for more than a year, the government can make a motion of this type more than a year after sentencing.

The "safety valve" of 18 USC § 3553(f) provides relief from a mandatory minimum term by allowing a downward adjustment of the offense level. According to the Seventh Circuit, a defendant cannot qualify for the safety valve by disclosing information about related criminal offenses at the beginning of the sentencing hearing. It must be done earlier, because the Guidelines refer to providing information to the "Government" rather than to the sentencing judge. The Eighth Circuit, however, refuses to impose a bright-line test forbidding the safety valve for information disclosed at the sentencing hearing. The Eighth Circuit treats the rule as a flexible, non-jurisdictional one rather than a rigid jurisdictional requirement.[518]

The Second Circuit view is that a defendant's perjury at trial will not automatically rule out the application of the safety valve. It is a factor in determining if he qualifies for relief—but if he does, the sentence reduction is mandatory rather than discretionary.[519]

It is presumed improper to give the findings of a criminal sentencing proceeding preclusive effect in a civil action. Preclusive effect might be proper in a limited range of circumstances, however. The Second Circuit forbade the SEC from asserting offensive collateral estoppel in a civil case to prevent the defendant from relitigating issues that resulted in a criminal sentence. The court ruled that preclusion would be unfair, because the findings were not necessary to the ultimate sentence; were not fully litigated; and preclusion would not promote judicial economy in the civil suit. The Fifth Circuit ruled that the 3C1.1 upward adjustment for obstruction of justice during the course of an investigation cannot be imposed based on the defendant's destruction of evidence that occurred before a formal investigation was underway.[520]

The issue sometimes arises whether incarceration is an essential part of the sentence. The Third Circuit took up this issue twice, vacating a sentence of probation and home confinement in a software counterfeiting case where

---

term, notice of possible departure is necessary to bring to light issues that could affect sentencing: United States v. Evans-Martinez, 530 F.3d 1164 (9th Cir. 2008); *see also* United States v. Dozier, 444 F.3d 1215 (10th Cir. 2006).

[518] *Compare* United States v. Cruz Alvarado, 326 F.3d 857 (7th Cir. 2003) *with* United States v. Rojas-Madrigal, 327 F.3d 738 (8th Cir. 2003).

[519] United States v. Jeffers, 329 F.3d 94 (2d Cir. 2003).

[520] United States v. Stolba, 357 F.3d 850 (8th Cir. 2004).

the Guidelines specifically ruled out probation and mandated incarceration.[521] The Third Circuit also found it unreasonable to impose a sentence of a heavy fine and probation (but no prison time) for a convicted tax evader.[522] But the Third Circuit vacated a 30-month sentence (more than four times the highest Guidelines sentence) for participation in a counterfeit check-cashing scheme: it was a violation of 18 USC § 3582(a) to impose so lengthy a sentence merely because the court believed that a 30-month sentence was required to make the defendant, who required drug rehabilitation, eligible for a particular program.[523]

The Eighth Amendment's ban on cruel and unusual punishment forbids non-capital sentences that are grossly disproportionate to the offense. Nevertheless, it is not necessary to make the kind of individualized analysis of aggravating and mitigating factors that would be required in a capital case, in a non-capital case.[524]

All of the states have "Megan's Laws" covering sex offender registration and availability of registration information on the Internet. In 2003, the Supreme Court upheld two of these statutes. The Connecticut law was upheld on the grounds that persons required to register do not have a procedural Due Process right to a hearing on the issue of their current dangerousness, because the obligation to register is triggered by the fact of the conviction, not by dangerousness. The Alaska law was upheld because the registration scheme was not deemed punitive, and therefore could not operate ex post facto as to offenses committed before the enactment of the law.

A federal Megan's Law has been enacted in P.L. 104-145, 42 USC § 14071(d), which permits disclosure of information collected under a state sex-offender registration program for any purpose permitted under the laws of the state. State and local law enforcement officials have a duty to release any information (other than the identity of victims) needed to protect the public safety.

Fed. R. Crim. P. Rule 32(b)(6)(A) requires all defendants who have not waived to receive an investigative presentence report (PSR) at least 35 days before sentencing. Rule 32(c)(3)(A) imposes an obligation on the court to ascertain whether the defendant and defendant's attorney have read and discussed the report.

Nevertheless, because a guilty plea does not waive the Fifth Amendment at sentencing, no adverse inferences can be drawn from the defendant's not testifying at the sentencing hearing,[525] and silence at this stage cannot be used to enhance the sentence when persons pleading guilty refuse to disclose additional details about the crime.

Although Fed. R. Crim. P. 32(a)(2) requires the court to inform the defendant that the sentence can be appealed, not doing so does not give rise to collateral

---

[521] United States v. Kononchuk, 485 F.3d 199 (3d Cir. 2007).

[522] United States v. Tomko, 498 F.3d 157 (3d Cir. 2007), *reh'g gtd*, 538 F.3d 644; *see* Shannon P. Duffy, *3rd Circuit Rules Prison Time "Reasonable" for Tax Cheat*, The Legal Intelligencer 8/23/07 (law.com).

[523] United States v. Manzella, 475 F.3d 152 (3d Cir. 2007).

[524] Harmelin v. Michigan, 501 U.S. 957 (1991).

[525] Mitchell v. United States, 526 U.S. 314 (1999).

relief if the defendant was actually aware of the right to appeal and thus was not prejudiced by the court's failure.[526]

Either the court must make specific findings on each controverted point in the report, or refrain from making a finding on matters that are not considered at sentencing. A sentencing judge who also presided over the trial is not required to hold an evidentiary hearing on contested fact issues; he or she can permissibly rely on the trial record.

A sentencing judge can consider any information that has enough indicia of reliability to be deemed probably accurate. As to any factual finding used in sentencing that the defendant objects to, the government has the burden of establishing it by preponderance of the evidence.

Sentencing a defendant in absentia is allowed by Fed. R. Crim. P. Rule 43(c), but only if the defendant voluntarily chooses to flee rather than appear for sentencing.

[b] Effects of the PROTECT Act

The "Feeney Amendment" (part of the PROTECT Act, P.L. 108-21) reduced federal judges' discretion to make downward departures from a Guidelines sentence and required the Sentencing Commission to give the U.S. Attorney General information about individual judges' record of downward departures. *Booker* (see the next section) precludes application of the Feeney Amendment.[527]

[c] Blakely, Booker, and Their Aftermath

In mid-June 2004, the Supreme Court decided *Blakely v. Washington*, 542 U.S. 296 (2004). The defendant in this case pled guilty to kidnapping his estranged wife. The facts admitted in the guilty plea supported a maximum sentence of 53 months, but the judge, ruling that the defendant acted with "deliberate cruelty" (a statutory ground for departure from the standard range), sentenced him to 90 months imprisonment. The Washington Court of Appeals upheld the sentence, but the Supreme Court ruled that *Apprendi* was the governing law. Because the facts supporting the departure were neither admitted by the defendant nor found by a jury, the Sixth Amendment guarantee of the right to trial by jury was violated.

Courts have reached various conclusions about *Blakely*'s effect on pleading requirements — e.g., whether aggravating factors must be included in an indictment.

The *Booker/Fanfan* case did not result in a unified opinion representing the ruling of the entire court. Justice Breyer's "opinion of the court in part" holds that the Sixth Amendment principle developed in *Blakely* also extends to the

---

[526] Peguero v. United States, 526 U.S. 23 (1999).

[527] *See, e.g.*, Dan Christensen, *The Short Life of the Feeney Amendment*, Daily Business Review 1/24/05 (law.com). Nevertheless, in 2006 the Third Circuit ruled that the Feeney Amendment's changes in the composition of the U.S. Sentencing Commission did not violate the constitutional requirement of separation of powers: United States v. Coleman, 451 F.3d 154 (3d Cir. 2006).

Sentencing Guidelines, so sentences can be enhanced only on the basis of facts found by a jury beyond a reasonable doubt. The 18 USC § 3553(b)(12), which makes the Sentencing Guidelines mandatory, is therefore incompatible with the Sixth Amendment and must be severed from the rest of the Sentencing Reform Act. The Supreme Court decided to preserve most of the Guidelines — but make them advisory input for the sentencing judge, not mandatory. The practical effect was a vast number of cases sent back for resentencing, and a tremendous volume of litigation about what judges should do in the future.

A mid-2007 Supreme Court decision made it harder to get a sentence reversed on appeal, by permitting Courts of Appeals to presume that the District Court acted reasonably in imposing a sentence within the Guidelines.[528]

The Second, Third, Sixth, Seventh, Tenth, and Eleventh Circuits have all held that *Booker* is not retroactive. It is not a watershed case because the sentencing process was not fundamentally altered: all that changed was the degree of flexibility judges have in apply the Guidelines. The Ninth Circuit disagrees.[529]

[2] Parole, Probation, and Supervised Release

Parole has been abolished in the federal system (although many states continue to use it) so any federal defendant sentenced to incarceration can expect to serve the full sentence, perhaps minus 15% for good behavior.[530]

In March 2000, the Supreme Court held that it was not an impermissible ex post facto action for the Georgia parole board to amend its rules, making it possible to hold parole reconsideration hearings every eight years instead of every three.

The amendment does not necessarily increase the period of incarceration (the affected prisoners have already received life sentences), and the parole board also has a policy allowing early reconsideration based on changed circumstances or new information.[531]

---

[528] Rita v. United States, 551 U.S. 338 (2007); *see* Mark Sherman (AP), *Supreme Court Sets Rules for "Reasonable" Prison Sentences*, 6/22/07 (law.com). The Sixth Circuit held that 18 USC § 3742 gives the Court of Appeals jurisdiction to review a sentence that has been challenged as unreasonable, even if the sentence falls within a correctly calculated Guidelines range: US v. Trejo-Martinez, 481 F.3d 409 (6th Cir. 2007).

[529] Lloyd v. United States, 407 F.3d 608 (3d Cir. 2005).

[530] The Guidelines also cover supervised release; fines, forfeiture and restitution; and home detention, community service, and other non-custodial sentences. Whenever a defendant is convicted, and 18 USC § 3013, the Mandatory Victim Restitution Act, calls for a special assessment, the District Court does not have the authority to remit the restitution sua sponte: United States v. Roper, 462 F.3d 336 (2006). *Also see* the 21st Century DOJ Appropriations Authorization Act, P.L. 107-273 (signed 11/2/02), which requires that the defendant be sentenced to probation or supervised release when the court reduces a term of imprisonment on the basis of extraordinary and compelling reasons. ACDs are discretionary with the court (the defendant never has an absolute right to an ACD) and can only be granted with the consent of the prosecution.

[531] Garner v. Jones, 529 U.S. 244 (2000). *See also* Grennier v. Frank, 453 F.3d 442 (7th Cir. 2006): prisoners sentenced to life imprisonment do not have a liberty or a property interest in opportunities to be paroled, so hearings are not required on subsidiary factual questions involved in parole.

A term of supervised release is tolled during any period of time starting when a defendant absconds from supervision and ending when federal authorities locate him.[532]

See § 26B.04[J] for discussion of searches of probationers.

A March 2000 Supreme Court case involves a defendant imprisoned on multiple convictions. Some of the convictions were overturned, by which time the defendant had already been imprisoned for two and a half years longer than the remaining convictions would warrant. He was also sentenced to a period of supervised release. There are statutory conditions under which supervised release can run concurrent with other sanctions, so the statute does not mention this situation. Therefore, the period of supervised release cannot be reduced by the excess time in prison.[533]

Another case dealing with supervised release, and with a similar caption, involves a different prisoner. Prior to the 1994 Amendments to 18 USC § 3583(e)(3) (revocation of supervised release), the District Court could impose a second supervised release term after revoking the first one and re-imprisoning the defendant. The 1994 amendment, adding § 3583(h), expressly authorizing a second term of supervised release, does not apply retroactively, so there is no ex post facto problem.[534]

[3] Consecutive and Concurrent Sentences

Frequently, an individual will be tried and convicted of multiple offenses. It then becomes necessary to determine whether the sentences will be served concurrently or consecutively. In general, the sentence must be concurrent if the offenses were committed through a single act or omission, or the act or omission constituting one offense is also a material element of the other.

Consecutive sentences can be imposed if each crime consists of separate and distinct acts, distinguishable by the time, place, and/or victim.

Guideline 5G1.3(e), allowing either consecutive or concurrent sentencing, permits the judge to give credit toward the federal sentence for state time served, even on an unrelated offense.[535]

Except where Guideline 5G1.3 requires a concurrent or a consecutive sentence, concurrence is a matter of discretion. Guideline 5G1.3(b) requires a concurrent sentence if there is a term of imprisonment for another offense that is relevant conduct for the instant offense and increases its offense level. In the post-*Booker* environment, the inquiry is the reasonableness of a consecutive sentence. When prison terms are imposed for multiple offenses at different times, the Eighth Circuit noted that the statute encourages consecutive sentencing so a reasonable amount of incremental punishment will be imposed. In this case

---

[532] United States v. Delamora, No. 05-50589 (9th Cir. 6/22/06).

[533] United States v. Johnson, 529 U.S. 53 (2000).

[534] Johnson v. United States, 529 U.S. 694 (2000).

[535] Ruggiano v. Reish, 307 F.3d 121 (3d Cir. 2002).

(involving federal and state child pornography charges), there was no Eighth Amendment problem because the convictions were separate; the total combined sentence was appropriate; and the sentence was neither extreme nor grossly disproportionate to the crime.[536]

Under New York law, consecutive sentences should not be imposed for causing two deaths during the same criminal transaction; the same act underlay both counts.[537]

Early in 2009, the Supreme Court held that *Apprendi* (see § 26.04[L][5], below) does not apply to decisions as to whether concurrent or consecutive sentences will be imposed for multiple crimes. That is, the judge can impose consecutive sentences based on facts that were not found by the jury, such as a judge's conclusion that the defendant is likely to re-offend so the longer sentence is appropriate.[537A]

[4] State Practice

States may use indeterminate sentencing, with the statute providing a maximum and minimum range: i.e., the defendant might be sentenced to 10 to 15 years' imprisonment. "Predicate felons" who have been convicted of another felony (or, under some statutes, convicted of another felony within a fairly short period of time) may be subject to additional years of imprisonment.

In addition to orders of fines and restitution, some state laws (e.g., drug laws) may require the sentence to include at least some component of imprisonment.

It is permissible to restrict parole hearings to one every two or three years, rather than annually, if circumstances make it unlikely that parole would be granted during more frequent hearings.[538]

[5] *Apprendi* Issues

In late June 2000, the Supreme Court decided a watershed case on sentencing issues: *Apprendi v. New Jersey*, 530 U.S. 466 (2000). *Apprendi* builds on the earlier case of *Jones v. United States*.[539] *Jones* requires that, in federal court, any fact other than prior conviction that increases the maximum penalty for a crime must be charged in the indictment, submitted to the jury, and proved beyond a reasonable doubt. *Apprendi* extends the jury consideration and proof beyond a reasonable doubt criteria to state courts. The Supreme Court upheld the practice of Courts of Appeals using harmless error analysis to review state and federal sentences enhanced on the basis of facts found by a judge, before *Apprendi*. Failure to send a sentencing factor to the jury is not structural error.[540]

---

[536] United States v. Atteberry, 447 F.3d 562 (8th Cir. 2006).

[537] People v. Rosas 8 N.Y.3d 493 (N.Y. 2007). The statute is Penal Law § 70.25.

[537A] Oregon v. Ice, No. 07-901 (1/14/09).

[538] California Dep't of Corrections v. Morales, 514 U.S. 499 (1995).

[539] 526 U.S. 227 (1999).

[540] Washington v. Recuenco, 548 U.S. 212 (2006).

A mid-2002 Supreme Court decision[541] upholds the Constitutionality of a statute that permits an increase in the mandatory minimum sentence if the judge (and not the jury) finds that a defendant "brandished" a firearm in the course of a drug trafficking offense. The Supreme Court did not see *Apprendi* issues in this situation, in that it was the minimum and not the maximum sentence that was enhanced under the statute. According to the Ninth Circuit, a prior conviction that turns a misdemeanor into a felony does not qualify for *Apprendi*'s exception for prior convictions. Therefore, it must be charged in the indictment and proved to the jury beyond a reasonable doubt.[542]

The Supreme Court struck down a California sentencing law that required judges to choose the middle sentence of three available options absent a finding of aggravating circumstances to justify the highest sentence. The Supreme Court found this to be inappropriate under *Apprendi*, because it allows judges to enhance sentences on the basis of facts that have not been determined by a jury. The Supreme Court directed California's attention to other states whose sentencing laws have been modified to conform to *Apprendi* (e.g., by shifting more fact-finding to the jury or setting a statutory range within which judges have discretion) but did not give specific directions for changing the statute: *Cunningham v. California*, 549 U.S. 270 (2007).

The Ninth Circuit's view is that juvenile adjudications are not reliable enough to satisfy *Apprendi*, but the Third and Eighth Circuits disagree.[543]

In mid-2003, the Second Circuit ruled that *Apprendi* does not apply retroactively to initial habeas corpus petitions.[544] The Third Circuit also refused to apply *Apprendi* retroactively, bringing the total of Circuits taking this position to nine.[545]

[a] Drug Quantities

In May 2002, the Supreme Court ruled that indictment defects (e.g., omission of the quantity of cocaine base the defendant allegedly possessed) do not deprive the court of the power to hear the case. Omission of a fact enhancing the statutory maximum sentence constitutes plain error. The Court of Appeals can correct an error that was not raised at trial, but only if it seriously affects the fairness, integrity, or public reputation of the judicial proceedings. The Supreme Court's view was that, in a case where there was overwhelming, virtually uncontested evidence that the defendant possessed more than 50 grams of cocaine base, the judicial system was not harmed by permitting the defendant's objections to the indictment defects to be waived by failure to raise them in a timely fashion.[546]

---

[541] Harris v. United States, 536 U.S. 545 (2002).

[542] United States v. Rodriguez-Gonzalez, 358 F.3d 1156 (9th Cir. 2004).

[543] *Compare* United States v. Tighe, 266 F.3d 1187 (9th Cir. 2001) *with* United States v. Jones, 336 F.3d 245 (3d Cir. 2003) *and* United States v. Smalley, 294 F.3d 1030 (8th Cir. 2002).

[544] Coleman v. United States, 329 F.3d 77 (2d Cir. 2003).

[545] United States v. Jenkins, 333 F.3d 151 (3d Cir. 2003).

[546] United States v. Cotton, 535 U.S. 625 (2002).

In 1986, 21 USC § 841 was enacted, imposing a mandatory five-year sentence for possession of 500 grams of powder cocaine — or only 5 grams of crack cocaine. The disparity in the seriousness of the offense has been attacked as racially discriminatory, because about one-quarter of persons convicted of powder cocaine offenses are black, versus 80% of persons convicted of crack cocaine offenses. Under the Guidelines, sentences for crack offenses are three to six times longer than sentences for powder cocaine offenses. In December, 2007, pursuant to its line of decisions holding that the Guidelines are purely advisory, the Supreme Court held that it is not necessarily invalid to impose a below-Guidelines sentence that reflects the judge's doubts about the fairness of the ratio. According to the Supreme Court, the 100:1 ratio was imposed when crack was a relatively new drug, and its effects were not well-understood. In light of today's more extensive knowledge, it is permissible for a District Court to consider the ratio as part of its determination of whether the Guidelines sentence is harsher than required to carry out the objectives of criminal sentencing.[547]

Effective November 1, 2007, the sentencing guideline for crack cocaine has been reduced by two levels. The change raises the related issue of whether the reduction should have retroactive effect — which could result in reduction of more than 20,000 sentences, most of them in the Fourth Circuit. The average sentence reduction would be 27 months.[548]

The Controlled Substances Act doubles the mandatory minimum sentence for some federal drug crimes if the defendant was previously convicted of a "felony drug offense": see 21 USC § 841(b)(1)(A). 21 USC § 802(13) defines a "felony" as any offense that is a felony under federal or state law. Section 802(44) defines a felony drug offense as an offense involving specified drugs, carrying a federal or state sentence over one year. The Supreme Court read § 841(b)(1)(A) as

---

[547] Kimbrough v. United States, 128 S. Ct. 558 (2007). An October 2008 per curiam Supreme Court decision holds that District Courts have the discretion to depart downwards from the Guidelines and are not required to apply the Guidelines ratio between crack and powder offenses; comments by the District Court about the obligation to follow the Guidelines meant that the Court of Appeals should have remanded the case to the District Court for resentencing following *Kimbrough:* Moore v. United States, No. 07-10689 (per curiam) (10/14/08). Spears v. United States, No. 08-5721 (1/21/09), reiterates that the ratio is purely advisory, and District Court judges can reject the ratio for policy reasons as well as based on a determination that the ratio would yield too severe a sentence in the case of an individual defendant.

[548] Marcia Coyle, *Retroactivity for Crack Sentence Cuts Debated*, Nat'l L.J. 10/26/07 (law.com). Note, however, that a three-judge panel of the Eleventh Circuit held that the two-level reduction in the Guidelines sentence for crack cocaine offenses, adopted in 2007, did not apply to five defendants who were sentenced as career offenders. Although the Guidelines reduction was retroactive, the Eleventh Circuit held that a sentence cannot be reduced on the basis of a retroactive Guidelines amendment which reduces the base offense level, but not the sentencing range on which the sentences were based. These five sentences were not premised on the crack cocaine Guidelines, but on career offender guidelines reflecting two previous violent felonies or drug offenses: United States v. Moore, 541 F.3d 1323 (11th Cir. 2008); *see* Christopher Seeley, *11th Circuit Limits New Rules on Crack Sentencing*, Fulton County Daily Report 9/16/08 (law.com); United States v. Thomas, 524 F.3d 889 (8th Cir. 2008) is similar.

completely dependent on § 802(44), with the result that a prior state drug offense punishable by a sentence of more than a year is a felony drug offense (and the mandatory minimum sentence doubles) even if the state categorizes the offense as a misdemeanor.[549]

[6] "Three Strikes" And ACCA Sentencing

"Three strikes" (as in "three strikes, you're out") sentences are intended to deter further criminal behavior by individuals who have already had more than one conviction. These laws impose very prolonged, or life, sentences upon third conviction.

The Supreme Court decided two "three strikes" cases in March 2003. The Court held that the Eighth Amendment is not violated by a life sentence for a property crime that could have been charged as either a misdemeanor or a felony, based on two or more prior "serious" or "violent" felony convictions.[550] In the second case the Supreme Court ruled that it is still unclear whether proportionality is an Eighth Amendment requirement. There is no clearly established Supreme Court precedent that could have been applied in an unreasonable fashion — and therefore habeas petitioners cannot use the proportionality argument to challenge a three-strikes sentence.[551]

In mid-2004, the Supreme Court vacated and remanded a case under Texas' "habitual offender" statute.[552] The statute required at least two felony convictions, with the conviction for the first becoming final before the second felony was committed. In this case, the petitioner's second offense was committed three days before the first conviction became final. This point was not raised during his trial or sentencing for a third felony. The issue was first raised in a request for state post-conviction relief (and not on direct appeal). The state court rejected (as untimely) the claim that the habitual offender statute did not apply. It also rejected a claim of ineffective assistance of counsel.

The Supreme Court vacated and remanded, although federal courts usually won't entertain a procedurally defaulted constitutional claim in a habeas petition without a showing of good cause to excuse the default. There is a narrow exception for claims of actual innocence of the substantive offense (or aggravating factors in capital cases). The Supreme Court did not create a new exception for noncapital sentencing error, because of the availability of the ineffective-assistance claim as an alternate ground for full relief.

The Supreme Court held in 2008 that, when determining whether to apply the Armed Career Criminal Act, the maximum term is determined by applying any applicable recidivist enhancements. The defendant was sentenced to concurrent 48-month sentences on each count of possession of a firearm by a convicted felon.

---

[549] Burgess v. United States, 128 S. Ct. 1572 (2008).

[550] Ewing v. California, 538 U.S. 11 (2003).

[551] Lockyer v. Andrade, 538 U.S. 63 (2003).

[552] Dretke v. Haley, 541 U.S. 386 (2004).

The Armed Career Criminal Act imposes a 15-year minimum sentence on a felon in possession of a firearm who has three previous convictions for a "serious drug offense" — one that carries a maximum term of at least 10 years. The maximum term on at least two of the defendant's prior convictions, under the recidivist provision, was 10 years. The Supreme Court ruled that the seriousness of an offense is affected by the defendant's prior record as well as the crime at bar. The Armed Career Criminal Act is intended as a recidivist statute, so it is acceptable to impose federal punishment for state-law recidivism.[553]

For sentencing under the Armed Career Criminal Act (18 USC § 924(e)), police reports and complaint applications cannot be consulted to determine whether a prior guilty plea necessarily admitted to generic burglary and supported the conviction.[554]

A defendant could be sentenced to 15 years under the Armed Career Criminal Act after pleading guilty to being a felon in possession of a firearm, because his 1989 state conviction for possession of a weapon and his 1985 state conviction for attempted burglary both posed a serious risk of physical injury to other people, so they were both "violent felonies."[555]

Begay v. United States, 128 S. Ct. 1581 (2008) holds that DUI is not a violent felony for Armed Career Criminal Act (18 USC § 924(e)(20(B)) purposes because such offenses are comparable to other offenses that do not require criminal intent. Begay looks at whether the crime involves purposeful, violent, and aggressive conduct.

Guideline 2D1.1(a)(1) does not specify a time limit for considering "prior convictions for a similar offense," so it was not error to consider a 1984 conviction for marijuana delivery in a case of fentanyl distribution leading to death. Guideline 4B1.4, the Guidelines version of the Armed Career Criminal Act has a 15-year limit, but the limit does not apply to other Guidelines provisions.[556]

[7] Life Imprisonment

Early in 2002, the Supreme Court decided that the defendant was entitled to a jury instruction that, if sentenced to life, he would be ineligible for parole.[557] The court interpreted its earlier decision[558] to require such an instruction even if there are sentencing alternatives other than death or life without parole. In this case, the jury was permitted to make sentencing recommendations if, and only if, it found aggravating circumstances. Evidence about violent behavior in prison can reasonably be considered evidence of dangerousness.

---

[553] United States v. Rodriquez, No. 06-1646 (U.S. 5/19/08).

[554] Shepard v. United States, 545 U.S. 1110 (2005).

[555] United States v. Lynch, 518 F.3d 164 (2d Cir. 2008).

[556] United States v. King, 516 F.3d 425 (6th Cir. 2008).

[557] Kelly v. South Carolina, 534 U.S. 246 (2002).

[558] Simmons v. South Carolina, 512 U.S. 154 (1994).

The Supreme Court ruled late in 2006 that California's comprehensive jury instruction used at the sentencing phase did not violate the rights of capital defendants to present mitigating evidence.[559] The Supreme Court reversed the Ninth Circuit, which had held that the trial judge misled jurors as to whether they could consider the defendant's potential for reform if he were sentenced to life imprisonment rather than death. In the Supreme Court's view, the Ninth Circuit erred in calling it "reasonably probable" that the jury failed to consider the defendant's potential conduct during a life sentence.

[M] Capital Cases

In 2007, New Jersey eliminated the death penalty (no one had been executed in the 25 years since the state reinstated the death penalty after *Gregg*), substituting life imprisonment without parole. The state announced that eliminating the death penalty would save the state a great deal of money previously used to litigate capital appeals. According to the Death Penalty Information Center, 2008 was the year with the lowest number of executions in 14 years. In that year, 111 new death sentences were imposed, the smallest number since 1976. In 2008, there were 37 executions, taking place in only nine states, and there are 3,309 inmates on Death Row nationwide. In some instances, financially strapped states are reconsidering the death penalty because of the expense of lengthy litigation.[560]

Although for decades capital punishment itself was deemed unconstitutional cruel and unusual punishment,[561] the death penalty was authorized in 1976 by *Gregg v. Georgia*,[562] provided that appropriate procedural protections are provided. In this reading, the Anglo-American tradition is accepting of the retributive and deterrent functions of capital punishment.

The Georgia capital statute passed muster because it required at least one of ten aggravating factors to be present before a person could be sentenced to death; provided for automatic appeal of death sentences; and gave the jury the option of making a binding recommendation of mercy even if no mitigating factors were present. Jurors must always be allowed to consider any mitigating factors that

---

[559] Ayers v. Belmontes, 549 U.S. 7 (2006).

[560] Tony Mauro, *Executions Declined Nationwide in 2008*, Legal Times 12/11/08 (law.com). Michael Booth, *N.J. Ends Capital Punishment, Commutes All Death Sentences*, New Jersey L.J. 12/18/07 (law.com); Dan Frosch, *Executions in U.S. Decline to 13-Year Low, Study Finds*, N.Y.Times 12/19/07 at A20.

[561] However, the Ninth Circuit has ruled that execution by gas chamber constitutes cruel and unusual punishment, although execution by lethal injection is permissible: Fierro v. Gomez, 77 F.3d 301 (9th Cir. 1996). The Eighth Circuit held that Missouri's policy of banning cameras and recording devices in the execution chamber does not violate the First Amendment, in that neither the public nor the media has the right to record executions, by analogy with the right of public trial, which does not create a right to broadcast trials: Rice v. Kempker, 374 F.3d 675 (8th Cir. 2004).

[562] 428 U.S. 153 (1976); the Texas and Florida capital punishment statutes were also found Constitutionally acceptable in that year, in Jurek v. Texas, 428 U.S. 262 (1976); Proffitt v. Florida, 428 U.S. 242 (1976).

could make a death sentence unfair in a particular case. Thus, a state cannot mandate capital punishment for all murder convictions.[563]

The Supreme Court upheld the Kansas statute's sentencing scheme, under which the death penalty is mandatory if there is a unanimous jury finding that the aggravating factors proved beyond a reasonable doubt are not outweighed by the mitigating circumstances. The statute satisfies the Eighth and Fourteenth Amendments because the sentencing scheme rationally reduces the number of convictions that are eligible for the death penalty, and permits the jury to include any mitigating factors in their decision.[564]

Among states that permit capital punishment, the use of lethal injection as an execution method is nearly universal. The Supreme Court granted certiorari in *Abdur'Rahman v. Bredesen*,[565] on the issue of execution methods. The Supreme Court reversed the dismissal of a challenge to the constitutionality of the drug combination used in executions, and permitted the claim to proceed as a § 1983 action rather than a habeas case.[566]

In 2008, the Supreme Court held that Kentucky's three-drug protocol for lethal injections (also used in 34 other states and by the federal government) was not cruel and unusual punishment, because the inmates did not show the objectively intolerable risk of harm that would be required to find the protocol unconstitutional. The challengers sought either to change the protocol from three drugs to one barbiturate that they argued caused painless death, or in the alternative to impose additional controls to make sure that the anesthetic is properly administered. The Supreme Court held that a state's refusal to adopt an alternative procedure violates the Eighth Amendment only if the suggested alternative is feasible, readily implemented, and substantially reduces a meaningful risk of severe pain.[567]

Meanwhile, in February 2008, the Nebraska Supreme Court ruled that electrocution was cruel and unusual, requiring the legislature to authorize another method for capital sentences to be imposed in the future. At that point, Nebraska was the only state that implemented electrocution as the sole means of execution. Alabama, Arkansas, Florida, Illinois, Kentucky, Oklahoma, South Carolina, Tennessee and Virginia usually used lethal injection for executions, but retained the option of electrocution if the condemned person chose it or as a back-up in case the Supreme Court had ruled that lethal injection violated the Eighth Amendment.[568]

The Supreme Court ruled in 2006 that, although the Eighth Amendment requires a state to permit the introduction of innocence-related evidence at a capital

---

[563] Lockett v. Ohio, 438 U.S. 586 (1978); Roberts v. Louisiana, 431 U.S. 633 (1977); Wooden v. North Carolina, 428 U.S. 280 (1976).

[564] Kansas v. Marsh, 126 S. Ct. 2416 (2006).

[565] 547 U.S. 1147 (2006).

[566] Hill v. McDonough, 547 U.S. 573 (2006).

[567] Baze v. Rees, 128 S. Ct. 1520 (2008); *see* Tony Mauro, *Supreme Court Upholds Kentucky's Lethal Injections*, Legal Times 4/16/08 (law.com); Mark Sherman (AP), *Supreme Court Upholds Common Method of Lethal Injections That Uses 3 Drugs to Kill Inmates*, 4/16/08 (law.com).

[568] State v. Mata, 275 Neb. 1, 745 N.W.2d 229 (2008), discussed in Nate Jenkins (AP), *Court: Neb. Electric Chair Not Legal*, 2/8/08 (law.com).

trial, it is permissible to forbid new evidence at the penalty phase that was not submitted at the guilt phase. The defense cannot automatically get such evidence introduced on the grounds that it supports a theory of residual doubt of guilt.[569]

In a 2000 case, the Supreme Court[570] found that the Constitution was not violated when a judge directed the jury's attention to jury instructions (which had been upheld for providing adequate consideration of mitigating factors) when they asked if they could sentence the defendant either to life or death, or whether they had to impose the death penalty. Based on testimony about aggravating factors, the jury imposed the death penalty.

In this case, the defense closing argument had already pointed out that the jurors could vote for a life sentence even in the presence of aggravating factors. There might be a slight possibility that jurors were deterred from voting for life imprisonment, but that's not enough to prove a Constitutional violation, which requires a reasonable likelihood of deterrence. In April of 2007, the Supreme Court reversed three Texas death sentences on the basis of defective instructions. (The instructions have since been replaced.) The instructions were defective because jurors were not allowed to give adequate weight to factors that could lead to a life sentence rather than execution (e.g., mental illness and the effect of child abuse).[571]

On the very last day of the 2001–2002 term, the Supreme Court reversed a Sixth Circuit decision dismissing the death penalty notice in a federal capital case. The defendant alleged that filing the death penalty notice was racially motivated. The Sixth Circuit accepted his argument, which was based on statistics showing nationwide differences in capital charges against white and black defendants, and greater acceptance of plea bargains from white defendants. The Supreme Court view was that raw statistics about charges do not necessarily involve similarly-situated defendants, and plea-bargaining issues were irrelevant because the defendant was offered a plea bargain but rejected it. The Sixth Circuit decision had to be reversed, as contrary to the relevant precedent, *United States v. Armstrong*, 517 U.S. 456 (1996), which required evidence of both discriminatory intent and discriminatory effect to support a claim of selective prosecution.[572]

It is unconstitutional to execute an insane person[573] or a person who was under 18 when the crime was committed.[574] The Supreme Court forbade execution

---

[569] Oregon v. Guzek, 546 U.S. 517 (2006).

[570] Weeks v. Angelone, 528 U.S. 225 (2000).

[571] The defendants are Brent Ray Brewer; LaRoyce Lathair Smith; Jalil Abdul-Kabir; *see* Mark Sherman (AP), *Supreme Court Throws Out Three Death Sentences in Texas*, 4/26/07 (law.com).

[572] United States v. Bass, 536 U.S. 862 (2002).

[573] Ford v. Wainwright, 477 U.S. 399 (1986). In the Fourth Circuit view, the Eighth Amendment standard of competency to be executed does not require the defendant to have any particular understanding of the meaning of death, and a person can legitimately be executed without having the capacity to assist counsel or prepare for death. Walton v. Johnson, 440 F.3d 160 (4th Cir. 2006).

[574] The Supreme Court forbade execution of persons who were under 16 at the time of the crime in 1988: Thompson v. Oklahoma, 487 U.S. 815 (1988). Citing evolving standards of decency and the

of a delusional killer, who believed that he had been sentenced to death for preaching rather than for murder, and who has multiple personalities. The Supreme Court majority said that his documented mental illness, causing gross delusions, should have been taken into account.[575]

In the Eighth Circuit's view, it does not violate the Eighth or Fourteenth Amendments to execute a person who was restored to competency by involuntary administration of antipsychotic drugs. In this view, administration of the medication continues to be in the convicted person's best medical interest even after an execution date has been set. A three-part test is applied. First, the government must identify an essential state interest that outweighs the prisoner's liberty interest in refusing medication. The next step is for the government to prove that there is no less-restrictive alternative to compelled medication. The third step is to prove by clear and convincing evidence that administration of medication is likely to render the prisoner competent; is in his or her best medical interest; and the side effects do not outweigh the benefits.[576]

The jury instructions at the penalty phase of a capital trial must provide a vehicle for considering and giving effect to mitigating factors such as mental retardation and child abuse.[577] The Supreme Court returned to the issue of retardation in *Atkins v. Virginia*,[578] ruling that it is cruel and unusual punishment contrary to the Eighth Amendment to execute a retarded person. This decision had a great deal of potential impact, because at that point 20 of the 38 states that had capital punishment did not bar execution of the developmentally disabled. The 2005 Supreme Court case of *Schriro v. Smith*, 546 U.S. 6 (2005), arose after a defendant presented evidence of low intelligence as a mitigating factor at the sentencing phase of his capital trial, although the issue of mental retardation

---

practice in other countries, the Supreme Court held in March 2005 that the Eighth Amendment bars execution of offenders for crimes committed before they reached age 18: Roper v. Simmons, 543 U.S. 551 (2005).

[575] Panetti v. Quarterman, 127 S. Ct. 2842 (2007); *see* Pete Yost (AP), *Supreme Court Blocks Execution of Mentally Ill Killer in Texas*, 6/29/07 (law.com).

[576] Singleton v. Norris, 319 F.3d 1018 (8th Cir. 2003). The Supreme Court decided a related issue for non-capital cases, ruling in Sell v. United States, 539 U.S. 166 (2003), that it is permissible to render a defendant in a serious criminal case competent via involuntary administration of antipsychotic drugs, if the administration of medication is medically appropriate; substantially unlikely to have serious side effects that undermine the fairness of the trial; and administering medication is necessary to further important government interests, bearing in mind whatever less intrusive alternative measures are available. Unless it would be required for a defendant who was represented by an attorney, a pro se defendant's waiver of the right to present mitigating evidence at the penalty phase does not require the judge to order a competency evaluation: State v. Jordan, 805 N.E.2d 542 (Ohio 2004).

[577] Penry v. Johnson, 532 U.S. 782 (2001). The Supreme Court reversed a death sentence on the grounds that the supplemental instruction given impermissibly restricted the jury's consideration of mitigating factors; finding that *Penry* requires full consideration and effect to be given to any such factors that are present: Smith v. Texas, 543 U.S. 37 (2004).

[578] 536 U.S. 304 (2002).

was not raised. The case returned to the Ninth Circuit after the *Atkins* decision. The Ninth Circuit ordered further state proceedings on the issue of whether execution of the defendant was barred by his mental retardation, with the issue to be determined by a jury unless the parties waived jury trial. The state (Arizona) obtained certiorari, and the Supreme Court reversed the Ninth Circuit, finding it improper for the Ninth Circuit to mandate a jury trial when states are permitted to set their own rules for processing mental retardation claims in capital cases.

A person indicted for a capital crime is entitled, under 18 USC § 3005, to appointment of two attorneys, at least one of whom is "learned in the law applicable to capital cases," and the attorneys have free access to the accused at all reasonable hours. According to the First Circuit, the need for appointment is triggered by the indictment, not the government's later decision to seek or waive the death penalty.[579]

In 2005, the Supreme Court ruled that it is improper at the penalty phase of a capital trial for the defendant to appear before the jury in shackles unless some state interest specific to the defendant can be asserted.[580]

Even if the defendant wants the death penalty to be imposed, the Ninth Circuit held that it is unconstitutional to execute a capital defendant if a properly filed federal habeas petition has not been substantively reviewed. The Ninth Circuit dismissed the state's and prisoner's motions to dismiss the appeal, even though the defendant gave a competent and voluntary waiver of the right to appeal the sentence. The court found the sentence to be invalid and habeas relief to be merited by the conditions of the death sentence: the defendant was bleeding, shackled, exhausted, and nearly naked at the time.[581]

A person sentenced to death can use a 42 USC § 1983 civil rights suit, rather than federal habeas, to pursue a claim that it would violate the Eighth Amendment to use a surgical cut-down to find a usable vein for a lethal injection when the condemned person is a long-term drug user. The court's rationale was that a prisoner who was not being executed could raise a challenge based on methods used in medical treatment, so the objective (facilitating the execution) should not rule out this legal device. The prisoner was not challenging the fact or conditions of his incarceration, so habeas corpus would not be the proper avenue for the challenge.[582]

Proportionality is an important issue in capital sentencing. It has been held that the death penalty is disproportionate for the rape of an adult victim[583] and for a person convicted of felony murder who neither committed the actual killing nor intended that lethal force be used in the crime.[584] Although Louisiana, (and

---

[579] *In re* Sterling-Suarez, 306 F.3d 1170 (1st Cir. 2002).

[580] Deck v. Missouri, 544 U.S. 622 (2005); routine shackling during the guilt phase had already been held impermissible as inherently prejudicial.

[581] Comer v. Schriro, 463 F.3d 934 (9th Cir. 2006) and 480 F.3d 960 (9th Cir. 2007).

[582] Nelson v. Campbell, 541 U.S. 637 (2004).

[583] Coker v. Georgia, 433 U.S. 584 (1977).

[584] Enmund v. Florida, 458 U.S. 782 (1982).

Montana, Oklahoma, South Carolina, and Texas) have laws on the books permitting the death penalty for rape, in fact no one has been executed for rape since 1964. Kennedy was sentenced to death for the aggravated rape of his eight-year-old stepdaughter. In 1977, the Supreme Court ruled that the death penalty was disproportionate (under the Eighth Amendment) for rape of an adult victim. The Supreme Court ruled in mid-2008 that proportionality rules out execution for rape, even of a child, when the crime was not intended to cause, and did not cause, the victim's death.[585]

Even constitutional errors in injury instructions in capital cases can be harmless, if they did not affect the final result, and thus do not necessarily result in overturning the sentence.[586]

Setting the execution date is ministerial, not a critical part of the sentencing process, so in the view of the Fifth Circuit the defendant need not be present.[587]

[1] The *Ring* Cycle

In mid-2002, the Supreme Court decided *Ring v. Arizona*, 536 U.S. 584 (2002), requiring that juries rather than judges make the factual determination whether aggravating factors are present in order to impose a death sentence rather than a sentence of life imprisonment. *Ring* follows up on the post-*Apprendi* mandate that juries rather than judges must make any determination increasing the severity of a sentence. *Ring* invalidated the capital-case procedures of five states: Arizona, Colorado, Idaho, Montana, and Nebraska, and could also have an effect on sentencing under the laws of Alabama, Delaware, Florida and Indiana because those statutes permit the judge to override a jury sentence or impose a death sentence when the jury called for life imprisonment.

An Arizona prisoner was convicted of first degree murder and sentenced to death under the sentencing scheme prevailing at that time. The system called for the trial judge to determine the presence of aggravating factors justifying a death sentence. While the prisoner's federal habeas case was pending before the Ninth Circuit, *Ring* was decided. The Ninth Circuit invalidated the death sentence, holding that *Ring* applied even though conviction and sentencing had become final on direct review before the decision. The Supreme Court, however, held that *Ring* is not retroactive for cases already final on direct review. A new rule promulgated by a Supreme Court decision applies to convictions that are already final. Usually, substantive rules are retroactive, but new

---

[585] Kennedy v. Louisiana, 128 S. Ct. 2641 (2008), modified 10/1/08; *see* Mark Sherman (AP), *Supreme Court Rejects Death Penalty for Raping Children*, 6/25/08 (law.com). The Supreme Court declined to rehear the case, even though it was pointed out that a 2006 federal law permits the death penalty under military law for child rape; the state of Louisiana said that failure to discuss military law skewed the analysis of nationwide consensus that the death penalty was disproportionate: *see* Tony Mauro, *Supreme Court Denies Rehearing in Child Rape Case*, Legal Times 10/2/08 (law.com).

[586] Calderon v. Coleman, 525 U.S. 141 (1999).

[587] Belyea v. Johnson, 82 F.3d 613 (5th Cir. 1996).

procedural rules are not retroactive unless they are watershed rules of criminal procedure that implicate the fundamental fairness and accuracy of the proceeding in that the likelihood of the correctness of the conviction is seriously diminished. The Supreme Court analyzed *Ring* as a procedural rule, because it did not change the range of conduct or the class of persons subject to execution in Arizona, but merely the method of determining if the defendant committed the specified conduct.[588]

Retroactivity was also involved in *Beard*. The Pennsylvania Supreme Court upheld a death sentence, before the decisions in *Mills v. Maryland* and *McKoy v. North Carolina*, which invalidated sentencing schemes that require juries to disregard mitigating factors that are not found unanimously. When Banks' case got to federal court, the Third Circuit applied *Teague*, and granted relief on the grounds that *Mills* did not announce a new rule, and therefore could properly be applied retroactively. The Supreme Court found that *Mills* could not be applied retroactively, because it did create a new rule and did not fall under either of the *Teague* exceptions. The Supreme Court described the three-step analysis under *Teague:* Was the rule new, given the legal landscape as of the time the conviction became final (i.e., direct appeal to state court has been exhausted, and either it is too late to apply for certiorari, or a timely petition for certiorari has been filed but denied)? Does the case qualify for an exception? And concluded that *Mills* could not be applied retroactively to this case.[589]

The Supreme Court's early 2006 *Brown v. Sanders* decision,[590] concerns a conviction of first-degree murder with four special circumstances, any one of which would support a death sentence. The state direct appeal resulted in invalidation of two of the circumstances, but the death sentence was upheld. The Ninth Circuit reversed, holding that the defendant had been deprived of an individualized death sentence. The Supreme Court reversed the Ninth Circuit, holding that the requirements of *Furman v. Georgia*, 408 U.S. 238 (1972), are satisfied when the trier of fact finds at least one eligibility factor at either the guilt or the penalty phase. An invalidated sentencing factor (whether or not it is an eligibility factor) makes a sentence unconstitutional unless one of the other sentencing factors permits the same facts and circumstances to be treated as aggravating factors. In the case at bar, the invalidity of two of the special circumstances did not make the death sentence invalid, because the remaining two valid special circumstances were sufficient to justify the death sentence. All the facts and circumstances asserted for the invalid factors were also probative of the valid special factors.

[588] Schriro v. Summerlin, 542 U.S. 348 (2004).
[589] Beard v. Banks, 542 U.S. 406 (2004); *Mills* is 486 U.S. 367 (1988) and *McKoy* is 494 U.S. 433 (1990).
[590] 546 U.S. 212 (2006).

[N] Post-Conviction Remedies

A confusing variety of channels, presenting a confusing variety of Constitutional and practical issues, can be used by a convicted person to challenge the conviction or the sentence, especially a death sentence.

A person convicted in a state court has various appellate options within the state system: some appeals of right, some discretionary with the state appellate courts. The writ of habeas corpus can also be used, within limits, to collaterally attack a state conviction. "Habeas corpus" is Latin for "produce the body": i.e., the state system surrenders custody of the prisoner so the federal court can inquire into whether such custody is valid.

Although there are some exceptions (involving technical issues beyond the scope of this book), the most common post-conviction remedy for federal prisoners is not habeas corpus, but a motion to vacate sentence, brought under 28 USC § 2255. Non-Constitutional errors are not cognizable in a § 2255 proceeding, and even errors of Constitutional dimension (e.g., invalid search and seizure) are relevant only if they were not harmless and actually prejudiced the defendant.[591]

A mid-2005 Supreme Court decision held that the 28 USC § 2255 one-year statute of limitation for a prisoner to file a motion to vacate sentence begins with the Supreme Court's initial recognition of the right asserted in the applicant's motion, and not with the date on which the court made the right retroactive.[592]

A large part of the Supreme Court docket consists of criminal cases in which discretion was exercised to grant certiorari although, of course, the vast majority of criminal certiorari petitions are denied.

[1] Habeas Corpus

Habeas petitions are filed only after the completion of many earlier steps in the criminal process:

- Trial
- Sentencing hearing
- Motion for a new trial
- First state appeal as of right
- Discretionary state appeal
- Petition for certiorari
- State post-conviction proceedings on any state or federal claims that are available but have not yet been fully litigated
- State post-conviction appeals
- Petition for certiorari to review the state post-conviction appeals.

---

[591] Kaufman v. United States, 394 U.S. 217 (1969).
[592] Dodd v. United States, 545 U.S. 353 (2005).

Fourth Amendment claims cannot be raised in a habeas proceeding if the petitioner has already had full and fair opportunity to litigate those claims in state court.[593]

Habeas corpus relief is limited to challenges to custody, and cannot be used to challenge a noncustodial sentence such as restitution.[594]

In 2007, the Supreme Court decided a number of habeas cases:

- The District Court did not have jurisdiction to hear a habeas petitioner's claims because he failed to comply with the gate-keeping requirements of 28 USC § 2244(b). However, the decision does not answer the question on which certiorari was granted: whether *Blakely* is a new rule, and if so, whether it is retroactive on collateral review.[595]
- Habeas should have been granted in a capital murder case where it was reasonably likely that the instructions prevented the jurors from giving adequate consideration to constitutionally relevant mitigating evidence — and in which the Court of Appeals ruling contradicted, or at least failed to adequately reflect, Supreme Court precedent.[596]
- Habeas should have been granted, because an impermissibly restrictive test of incompetency was applied.[597]
- A habeas petitioner must obtain a certificate of appealability to appeal the denial of a Rule 60(b) motion.[598]
- A remand for an evidentiary hearing on ineffective assistance was reversed, on the grounds that the evidentiary hearing should have been denied: the state court's factual determination that the respondent would not have permitted counsel to present mitigating evidence at sentencing was not unreasonable under AEDPA, and the allegedly mitigating evidence would not have changed the result.[599]
- However, a grant of habeas was reversed where it was error to find that the juror was not substantially impaired in the performance of duties on a capital

---

[593] Stone v. Powell, 428 U.S. 465 (1976).

[594] Kaminsky v. United States, 334 U.S. 84 (2d Cir. 2003), Dohrmann v. United States, 442 F.3d 1279 (11th Cir. 2006). Cases holding that *Apprendi* (see § 26.04[L][5]) does not apply to restitution orders, e.g., because it is a criminal decision and restitution is a civil remedy: United States v. Carruth, 418 F.3d 900 (8th Cir. 2005); United States v. Syme, 276 F.3d 131 (3d Cir. 2002); United States v. Behrman, 235 F.3d 1049 (7th Cir. 2000); United States v. Wooten, 377 F.3d 1134 (10th Cir. 2004); United States v. Bearden, 274 F.3d 1031 (6th Cir. 2001). On the use of § 2255 to challenge restitution, *see* Blaik v. United States, 161 F.3d 1341 (11th Cir. 1998). Nor, according to Kane v. Espitia, 546 U.S. 9 (2005), can habeas relief be granted for denial of access to the prison law library.

[595] Burton v. Stewart, 549 U.S. 147 (2007).

[596] Abdul-Kabir v. Quarterman 550 U.S. 233 (2007); Brewer v. Quarterman, 550 U.S. 286 (2007).

[597] Panetti v. Quarterman, 127 S. Ct. 2842 (2007).

[598] United States v. Hardin, 481 F.3d (6th Cir. 2007).

[599] Schriro v. Landrigan, 550 U.S. 465 (2007).

jury. The Ninth Circuit said that the juror should not have been excused, because he was not opposed to the death penalty in all circumstances. The Supreme Court reinstated the death sentence in a case of carjacking, rape and murder. According to the Supreme Court, the trial court has broad discretion once there has been a diligent examination of potential jurors. Therefore, the Washington State judge exercised proper discretion when excusing a veniremember who said he would vote for a death sentence only if the defendant could kill again. The sentencing options were limited to death and life without parole.[600]

The petitioner must fairly present his claim in each appropriate state court, indicating where appropriate that federal claims are being raised. In early 2005, for example, the Supreme Court dismissed a writ of certiorari because the petitioner failed to allege violations of the Eighth and Fourteenth Amendments when the case was before his state's highest court: *Howell v. Mississippi*, 543 U.S. 440 (2005). In a 2004 Supreme Court case involving an ineffective assistance of counsel claim, the Supreme Court held that a federal claim is not "fairly presented" to the state court system if the state court needs to do more than read the petition, the brief, or similar papers in order to discover that there is a federal claim; it should not be necessary for the appellate judge to read the lower court opinions to find this out.[601]

Habeas can be used to pursue a claim of actual innocence if it can be shown that an innocent person was convicted, and a Constitutional violation "probably occurred." It is not required that the habeas petition show by clear and convincing evidence that, but for the error, no reasonable jury would have convicted the defendant[602] — but see the AEDPA discussion, below. As an example, the Supreme Court reversed denial of habeas in a death penalty case, because the defendant succeeded in satisfying the stringent showing needed for the actual innocence exception to a dismissal based on procedural default.[603]

Evidentiary hearings are probably not required in habeas proceedings.

Early in 2007, the Supreme Court ruled that 28 USC § 2244(d)(2) does not toll the one-year Statute of limitations for seeking federal habeas relief from a state court judgment during the time that a certiorari petition is pending before the Supreme Court.[604]

---

[600] Uttecht v. Brown, 551 U.S. 1 (2007); *see* Mark Sherman (AP), *Supreme Court Reinstates Death Sentence for Man Who Argued Juror Was Wrongly Excluded*, 6/5/07 (law.com).

[601] Baldwin v. Reese, 541 U.S. 27 (2004).

[602] Schlup v. Delo, 513 U.S. 298 (1995). The Seventh and Ninth Circuits read *Schlup* to permit a state habeas petition to assert actual innocence by means of evidence that the prisoner was aware of at the time of trial; the evidence need not be newly discovered: Griffin v. Johnson, 350 F.3d 956 (9th Cir. 2003); Gomez v. Jaimet, 350 F.3d 673 (7th Cir. 2003). *See also In re* Lott, 424 F.3d 446 (6th Cir. 2005): a claim of actual innocence does not waive the attorney-client or other privileges. Therefore, a habeas petitioner's lawyer could not be compelled to disclose information in the lawyer's possession dealing with the client's innocence or whether he confessed to the police.

[603] House v. Bell, 547 U.S. 518 (2006).

[604] Lawrence v. Florida, 549 U.S. 327 (2007).

Another important issue is which cases can be used in the defense argument. According to *Teague v. Lane*,[605] full retroactivity is not required in habeas cases. The appropriate body of law governing a habeas challenge is the law as of the time the conviction is finalized. This rule was adopted to require state courts to apply the proper legal standards. Under *Teague*, a habeas court should not apply:

- Any new rule announced in a Supreme Court ruling after the prisoner's conviction became final
- The habeas court's reading of preexisting Supreme Court precedent announcing a new rule as to that precedent.

However, a new rule should apply if it declares the criminal offense itself unconstitutional, or if the new rule goes to the fundamental fairness of the trial process by mandating a procedure that is central to an accurate determination of guilt. According to *Sawyer v. Smith*,[606] that means a true bedrock procedure essential to providing a fair trial, not a mere refinement of established procedures.

In a case where the defendant had multiple judgments, the Fifth Circuit does not require the prisoner to challenge all of the judgments from a single court in a single habeas petition; the current petition was therefore not successive. The prisoner's consolidated trial resulted in two convictions in separate judgments. A successive petition is a second federal habeas attack on the same conviction; a prisoner with separate convictions can, but is not obligated to, challenge them all in the same habeas petition.[607]

Late in 2008, the Supreme Court heard arguments in two habeas cases from the Ninth Circuit involving state jury instructions. In one case, the driver in a drive-by shooting was convicted after the jury was instructed that if the defendant knew his co-defendant was going to commit any crime (including going to the school to have a fistfight rather than to shoot), he was accountable for the crime actually committed. The second case involved instructions that the Ninth Circuit characterized as structural and not harmless error. In the drive-by case, the Supreme Court ruled that habeas should not have been granted. State court decisions can be challenged only if they are not merely erroneous but objectively unreasonable, and the underlying allegedly improper jury instruction must have tainted the entire trial. The Supreme Court said that the Washington court's conclusion that the jury instruction was not ambiguous reflected the state statute, and was not objectively unreasonable. Therefore, the Ninth Circuit should have concluded that habeas was unavailable. In the case involving alleged structural error, the Supreme Court held that the correct test is whether the erroneous instructions had a substantial and injurious effect or influence on the jury verdict.[608]

---

[605] 489 U.S. 288 (1989).

[606] 497 U.S. 227 (1990).

[607] Hardemon v. Quarterman, 516 F.3d 272 (5th Cir. 2008).

[608] Waddington v. Sarausad, No. 07-772 (1/21/09); Hedgpeth v. Pulido, No. 07-544 (12/2/08, per curiam).

[a] AEDPA

The Anti-Terrorism and Effective Death Penalty Act of 1996 (AEDPA), P.L. 104-132, has two main focuses.[609] First, it limits the number of habeas challenges that can be brought to a conviction. Second, it permits a federal court to overturn a state conviction only if an egregious mistake was made by the state court. The rules governing habeas cases (18 USC §§ 2254–2255) were amended in late 2004 to reflect AEDPA. Court clerks must file petitions and motions even if they contain procedure defects, because the prior-law requirement of returning defective papers could, in conjunction with AEDPA's one-year statute of limitations, prevent claims — perhaps including some meritorious claims — from being considered. When discovery is sought in the habeas context, the party seeking discovery must give reasons, and the request must be supplemented by a list of requested documents and proposed interrogatories and requests for admission.[610]

The post-AEDPA text of 18 USC § 2254(b) provides that, before applying for federal habeas relief, the defendant must show that state remedies have been exhausted. (In other words, the state does not have to show that the defendant failed to exhaust such remedies.) Exhaustion of state remedies may be excused if there is no available and effective state remedy.

"Mixed" habeas petitions (combining claims for which remedies have been exhausted with other claims) raise difficult problems, which the Supreme Court has addressed several times.

A mid-2004 Supreme Court decision involved two pro se mixed habeas petitions filed five days before the end of the one-year AEDPA statute of limitations. The Supreme Court ruled that the District Court is not obligated to warn defendants of the consequences of the stay: explaining procedures and calculating the statute of limitations is up to the defendant's attorney, not the court.[611]

The proper standard in § 2254 proceedings in assessing the prejudicial impact of constitutional error in a state trial is the *Brecht* "substantial and injurious effect" standard, whether or not the state's highest court recognized the error and applied the "harmless beyond a reasonable doubt" standard of *Chapman*.[612]

---

[609] The Supreme Court upheld the constitutionality of AEDPA Title I. The Supreme Court is not deprived of jurisdiction by the AEDPA, because original writs of habeas corpus can still be entertained. Habeas is not "suspended" by the AEDPA limitations: Felker v. Turpin, 518 U.S. 651 (1996). *Also see* Calderon v. Ashmus, 523 U.S. 740 (1998): application by California Death Row inmates for an injunction against AEDPA compliance is not justiciable. It is not a valid declaratory judgment action, because it would not resolve the individual inmates' entitlement (or otherwise) to habeas relief. AEDPA does not apply to any cases filed before its effective date, April 24, 1996: Lindh v. Murphy, 521 U.S. 320 (1997).

[610] http://www.uscourts.gov/rules/index.html#supreme0404; *see* 73 L.W. 2331.

[611] Pliler v. Ford, 542 U.S. 225 (2004). A March 2005 Supreme Court decision permits a District Court to stay a mixed habeas petition, so that a petitioner can first present the unexhausted claims to the state court, and then return to federal court for review of the now-perfected petition: Rhines v. Weber, 544 U.S. 269 (2005).

[612] Fry v. Pliler, 551 U.S. 112 (2007); Chapman v. California, 386 U.S. 18 (1967).

The current version of § 2255 permits a second or later habeas petition to be heard by the District Court only if a panel of the Court of Appeals certifies that the motion includes either a new Constitutional law rule that can be applied retroactively, or newly discovered evidence that, if proven, offers clear and convincing evidence that a reasonable trier of fact would not have convicted the defendant if the evidence had been available at trial.

In 2003, the Supreme Court ruled that, for a federal defendant who loses on direct appeal but does not file for certiorari, the § 2255 one-year statute of limitations for seeking post-conviction motion relief begins when the time to seek certiorari ends, because that is the point at which the conviction becomes final.[613]

In *Johnson v. United States*, the petitioner was convicted of a drug offense that normally carries a seven-year sentence. He was, however, sentenced to 15 years because prior state charges made him a career offender. The state convictions were subsequently vacated. The Supreme Court ruled in April 2005 that the petitioner had waited too long to raise otherwise valid arguments, and the enhanced sentence was not set aside. Although the petitioner represented himself pro se through much of the case, the Supreme Court ruled that pro se representation and ignorance of the law do not excuse prolonged inattention to the case.

If due diligence was exercised in seeking vacatur of the state conviction, the one-year statute of limitations under 28 USC § 2255(6)(4) begins on the date the prisoner receives notice of the order of vacatur, because that is the point when the vacatur becomes a fact not previously discoverable by the petitioner. But in this case, the petitioner did not show due diligence; he waited 21 months after his federal conviction became final before challenging the state conviction on the basis that he had not been represented by counsel. (Under state law, indigent convicted persons were not assigned counsel to challenge convictions or sentences after the first direct appeal.)[614]

The Supreme Court held that AEDPA's one-year statute of limitations for federal habeas is tolled during the time that a properly filed application for state post-conviction or other collateral review is pending: see 28 USC § 2244(d)(2). However, a petition that is eventually dismissed as untimely is not properly filed, even if the state law grants some exceptions based on the judge's evaluation of timeliness.[615] Section 2244(d) was also at issue in *Jimenez v. Quarterman*, No. 07-

---

[613] Clay v. United States, 537 U.S. 522 (2003).

[614] Johnson v. United States, 544 U.S. 295 (2005).

[615] Pace v. DiGuglielmo, 545 U.S. 1121 (2005). The Supreme Court reaffirmed the principles of *Pace* in Allen v. Siebert, 128 S. Ct. 2 (2007) holding that the critical distinction is between petitions that are not properly filed because they are rejected because of filing conditions, and petitions that are rejected on the basis of procedural bars that go to the ability to obtain relief. Only the latter category are properly filed. Statutes of limitations are filing conditions because they go to the court's ability to consider a petition. Therefore, a petition that is rejected by the state court as untimely is not properly filed, and AEDPA's one-year statute of limitations cannot be tolled. A post-conviction motion for DNA testing under Texas Code of Criminal Procedure art. 64.01 constitutes "other collateral review," so it will toll AEDPA's one-year limitations period (28 USC § 2244(d)(1)): Hutson v. Quarterman, 508 F.3d 236 (5th Cir. 2007).

6984 (1/13/09). Texas allows certain appeals of state convictions even after the normal time has expired; the Supreme Court held that the one-year AEDPA period does not start until completion of the untimely appeal. The judgment is not final as defined by § 2244(d)(1)(A) until conclusion of the direct appeal or the last date to seek certiorari on that appeal. In this case, when the Texas Court of Criminal Appeal re-opened direct review of the petitioner's conviction, the conviction was no longer final because it was possible that it could be modified either by the direct appeal to the state court or by federal certiorari.

Castro v. United States, 540 U.S. 375 (2003), limits the extent to which a federal court can re-characterize a motion for a new trial filed by a pro se litigant as a habeas petition. Before doing so, the court must inform the litigant not only that the court intends to re-characterize the motion, but the effect this will have in rendering further habeas filings "second or successive motions." Such disclosure is required so that the petitioner will have the option to withdraw the filing, or to amend it to encompass all claims that might be raised later under § 2255.

The Supreme Court initially granted certiorari, but then dismissed it as improvidently granted, so the Circuit split still remains on the issue of when an FRCP 60(b) motion for relief from adverse judgment on a habeas petition is a "second or successive" petition that requires appellate approval to maintain.[616] The court returned to the issue in 2005, when it held that a Rule 60(b) motion that merely challenges the integrity of the District Court proceedings will be treated like a civil 60(b) motion. AEDPA's limits on second or successive petitions only apply if the habeas petition attacks the merits of the decision or presents a new ground for relief.[617]

In April 2000, the Supreme Court decided two related cases. In the first, the court held that the AEDPA limits on federal habeas for state-court claims require upholding the judgment if the state court applies the correct federal standard in a reasonable way — even if it conflicts with a federal court's interpretation of the law.[618] The limits on habeas review imposed by 29 USC § 2254(d)(1) are more than just a codification of *Teague v. Lane*, 489 U.S. 288 (1989). Section 2254(d)(1) rules out habeas unless the state court's decision is contrary to, or gives an unreasonable interpretation to, clearly established Supreme Court precedent.

A state decision is contrary to Supreme Court precedent if the state court's conclusion is the opposite of the one the Supreme Court reached on a question of law, or if it reaches the opposite conclusion from the Supreme Court on facts that are materially indistinguishable from the ones the Court ruled on. But this is not true of the ordinary state court decision, applying an existing legal standard to the facts of the prisoner's case.

Before AEDPA, federal habeas courts applied a plenary or de novo standard of review. *Teague* limited this, making it exceptional for a federal court to grant

---

[616] Abdur'Rahman v. Bell, 537 U.S. 88 (2002).
[617] Gonzalez v. Crosby, 545 U.S. 524 (2005).
[618] Williams v. Taylor, 529 U.S. 420 (2000).

habeas relief on the basis of a rule of law that was not established when the state court made its direct review of the prisoner's conviction. Under *Teague*, state court resolution of a mixed question is reviewed de novo. But § 2254(d)(1) says that habeas relief is not justified merely because the state court applied federal law erroneously or incorrectly — relief is available only if the state court acted unreasonably.

The second case, #99-6615, holds that § 2254(e)(2) only applies if the petitioner or counsel has been at fault, which is defined as displaying a lack of diligence, or conduct that is even worse than a lack of diligence. In this case, a prisoner sentenced to death failed on direct appeal and in state habeas proceedings, then tried to obtain federal habeas on various grounds.

The District Court wanted to have an evidentiary hearing on some of the claims. The Fourth Circuit said that § 2254(e)(2) precluded an evidentiary hearing. Section 2254(e)(2) says that the availability of an evidentiary hearing is limited if the defendant failed to develop the factual basis of the claim in state proceedings. The Supreme Court would not accept a no-fault reading of the provision: "fail" means not developing the factual basis through a fault such as lack of diligence, with diligence being a reasonable attempt to investigate and pursue state-court claims (whether or not they could have succeeded.). The Supreme Court decided three more AEDPA cases in the Spring of 2001. The Court ruled that the provisions of 28 USC §§ 2254 and 2255 (dealing with habeas and related relief) cannot be used to challenge prior convictions that are being used to enhance the current sentence.[619]

A new rule of constitutional law is retroactive for AEDPA purposes (and therefore can be used to justify a second or subsequent habeas petition) only if the Supreme Court explicitly designated the rule as retroactive, or if the rule is necessarily interpreted as retroactive when multiple Supreme Court rulings are read together.[620]

The Supreme Court returned to AEDPA yet again, at the very end of the October 2001 term. AEDPA, at 28 USC § 2244(d)(1)(A), requires a federal habeas petition to be filed within one year after the state conviction becomes final. Section 2244(d)(2) says that the one-year period does not include any time when the state application for collateral review is "pending" in state court. The Supreme Court ruled that the petition is pending during the time between the lower state court's decision and the filing of notice of appeal to the higher state court. The case was remanded to the federal Court of Appeals on the issue of whether a petition that failed to satisfy California's idiosyncratic appellate timing rules should be considered to be pending.[621]

---

[619] Daniels v. United States, 532 U.S. 374 (2001) and Lackawanna County Dist. Attorney v. Coss, 532 U.S. 394 (2001).

[620] Tyler v. Cain, 533 U.S. 656 (2001).

[621] Carey v. Saffold, 536 U.S. 214 (2002). California's collateral review process makes a notice of appeal timely as long as it is filed within a reasonable time. The Ninth Circuit treated a

On a procedural issue, in April 2000, the Supreme Court held that the 28 USC § 2253(c) requirements for certificate of appealability apply to the appeal of a denial of habeas filed after AEDPA's effective date, irrespective of the filing date for the habeas petition itself.[622] If the District Court denies the petition on procedural grounds without reaching Constitutional issues, certiorari should be granted whenever the petitioner shows that reasonable judges would at least find it debatable whether there was a valid Constitutional claim and whether the District Court was correct in its procedural ruling. If the initial petition was dismissed other than on its merits, e.g., for failure to exhaust state remedies, the next petition is not a second or successive petition as defined by AEDPA. The petition can properly include claims that were not in the original petition.

Although other circuits have disagreed, the Ninth Circuit (in common with the Seventh Circuit) interprets AEDPA and FRCP 15(c)(2) (the "relation-back" provision) to allow a new claim to be added to a habeas petition even after the AEDPA one-year limitation period has elapsed. Rule 15(c)(2) says that an amendment relates back to the date of the original pleading if it arises out of the same conduct, transaction, or occurrence as the original pleading.

The new claim must be based on the same core of operative facts as the timely claim. The Supreme Court ruled in mid-2005 that the presence of the same trial and conviction in both is insufficient if the new claim's facts differ in time and type from those set out in the original pleading.[623]

Federal courts have the power to issue sua sponte dismissals of untimely appeals by prison inmates, even if the state miscalculates the deadline and fails to raise the issue. Although the federal courts do not have an obligation to check the correctness of computations, they are not required to remain silent if they discover an error. Therefore, even if a state answers a habeas petition without raising the issue of timeliness, the District Court has discretion to dismiss the petition for failure to comply with the AEDPA one-year statute of limitations.[624]

Claims that were dismissed as premature (e.g., a claim that a person could not be executed on the grounds of incompetency, dismissed because execution was not imminent at that time) can be presented when they become ripe; this is not considered a successive petition.[625]

---

denial of a petition without comment as a denial on the merits, and therefore a federal habeas petition based on such a denial is not untimely. The Supreme Court held in Evans v. Chavis, 546 U.S. 189 (2006), that this is an incorrect application of Carey v. Saffold. The Court of Appeals must examine the delay in each case and determine if the state court would consider the petition to be timely. The Supreme Court held that a federal habeas petition filed in 2000 did not satisfy the California reasonable time standard; the denial without comment was issued in 1998, relating to a 1993 state habeas petition.

[622] Slack v. McDaniel, 529 U.S. 473 (2000).

[623] Mayle v. Felix, 545 U.S. 644 (2005).

[624] Day v. McDonough 547 U.S. 198 (2006), discussed in Toni Loci (AP), *Supreme Court Justices Split on Rules for Appeal Time Limits*, 4/26/06 (law.com).

[625] Stewart v. Martinez-Villareal, 523 U.S. 637 (1998).

[2] Appeals

Appeals by the defendant are governed by 28 USC § 1291, the general jurisdictional statute for the Court of Appeals.[626] However, in a criminal case, denial of a motion to suppress is not a final order. Because of the collateral order doctrine, it is an interlocutory order that cannot be appealed, because it does not deal with matter distinct from the general subject matter of the litigation.

In a non-capital case, one appeal of right is available to challenge a sentence that is invalid as a matter of law (e.g., it relies on an incorrect assumption that the defendant has been convicted of prior felonies), or that is harsh or excessive; other grounds of appeal are permissive, and can be denied by the appellate court. In a federal capital case, direct review of death sentences by the Court of Appeals is mandatory and cannot be waived.

The Sixth Amendment and the Due Process and Equal Protection clauses entitle a convicted defendant to counsel on the first or direct appeal of right from the conviction, but not discretionary appeals or certiorari petitions.[627] If the defendant asks that a petition for certiorari be filed, the Court of Appeals rules generally require the appellate attorney to do so unless relieved. In contrast, the Criminal Justice Act does not require frivolous filings.

Michigan's criminal appellate scheme did not appoint counsel for indigent defendants who entered pleas of guilty or no contest. At the end of 2004, the Supreme Court ruled that attorneys who might perhaps have been appointed to handle criminal appeals do not have standing to challenge the state practice. The attorneys did not show a close enough relationship with their potential clients to assert the defendants' Constitutional rights.[628] In 2005, the Supreme Court required appointment of counsel for indigents seeking leave to appeal a plea-based conviction under Michigan's scheme requiring court approval for the first-level appeal of a conviction under a guilty or nolo contendere plea.[629]

Faretta v. California, 422 U.S. 806 (1975) indicates that there may be a right for criminal defendants to represent themselves (appear *pro se*) at the trial level after making a knowing and intelligent waiver of counsel. However, that does not obligate states to allow convicted persons to represent themselves on direct appeal. In 2000, the Supreme Court did not extend all of *Faretta*'s reasoning to appeals,

---

[626] Most federal appeals go to the Court of Appeals, but a person convicted of a misdemeanor by a magistrate judge must first appeal to the District Court: United States v. Smith, 992 F.2d 98 (7th Cir. 1993).

[627] Austin v. United States, 513 U.S. 5 (1994); Coleman v. Thompson, 501 U.S. 722 (1991); Penson v. Ohio, 488 U.S. 75 (1988).

[628] Kowalski v. Tesmer, 543 U.S. 125 (2004).

[629] Halbert v. Michigan, 545 U.S. 605 (2005). The Sixth Circuit found Halbert retroactive (and the petitioner entitled to appointed appellate counsel to challenge his guilty plea) granted habeas and ruled that the petitioner was entitled to appointed appellate counsel to challenge his guilty plea, because *Halbert* is retroactive — it just applies the holding of an earlier case, so it isn't a *Teague* "new rule." So he was entitled to appointed appellate counsel: Simmons v. Kapture, 474 F.3d 869 (6th Cir. 2007).

because the Sixth Amendment deals with trials, not appeals, so any right to represent one's self must derive from Due Process. States have discretion to find that the need for professional representation outweighs the interest in self-representation.[630]

The Sixth Amendment guarantee of a speedy trial applies only at the trial court level, but the Sixth Circuit has ruled[631] that a defendant-appellant or defendant-appellee has a Due Process right to speed in the first appeal as of right.

The Sixth Amendment guarantees the right to a free transcript so an indigent defendant who rejected representation by the public defender, and was represented by a private attorney acting pro bono, can perfect his or her direct appeal.[632]

If a defendant dies while a direct appeal is pending, any restitution order against the decedent is abated (whether the order was compensatory or punitive). However, the government is not obligated to refund to the decedent's estate any money already paid.[633]

[a] Appealable Issues

Some, but not all, issues that a criminal defendant wishes to raise are proper appellate issues.

An order transferring a juvenile for trial as an adult is a collateral order that can be appealed immediately, because the transfer is a conclusive determination of a disputed question. Furthermore, appealing an adult conviction does not revive the special remedies granted to accused juveniles.[634]

Even if a sentence falls within a correctly calculated Guidelines range, the Sixth Circuit held that the Court of Appeals has jurisdiction, under 18 USC § 3742, to review the sentence if it is challenged as unreasonable.[635]

Although, of course, most appeals are brought by the defendant, 18 USC § 3731 permits prosecution appeals to the Court of Appeals from a District Court decision or order suppressing or excluding evidence or ordering return of seized property. The U.S. Attorney must certify that the evidence furnishes substantial proof of a material fact, and the appeal has not been taken for purposes of delay. But once jeopardy has clearly attached, the government is no longer able to appeal the suppression order. Government appeals must be taken within 30 days of entry of the decision or order.

The amendment to FR Crim P 29 proposed in 2006 requires a judge entering a judgment of acquittal prior to a verdict if and only if the government's appeal rights are preserved via a defense waiver of double jeopardy arguments.

---

[630] Martinez v. California Court of Appeal, 528 U.S. 152 (2000).

[631] United States v. Smith, 94 F.3d 204 (6th Cir. 1996).

[632] Miller v. Smith, 99 F.3d 120 (4th Cir. 1996).

[633] United States v. Estate of Parsons, 367 F.3d 409 (5th Cir. 2004).

[634] United States v. Angelo D., 88 F.3d 856 (10th Cir. 1996).

[635] United States v. Trejo-Martinez, 481 F.3d 409 (6th Cir. 2007).

18 USC § 3141 requires the defendant to be released on bail pending prosecution of a § 3731 appeal, and the government cannot use mandamus to circumvent the § 3731 limitations.

The Seventh Circuit, unlike six other Circuits, held in mid-2007 that an attorney is not obligated to file an appeal when requested by a client who has entered into a plea bargain that waives all appeals. The other Circuits take the opposing view because the waiver might have been invalid, but the Seventh Circuit focused on the attorney's duty to the judicial system (in terms of not wasting time with fruitless appeals) and preventing clients from losing the value of a plea bargain by abrogating it.[636] In contrast, *United States v. Poindexter*[637] holds that counsel is constitutionally ineffective if the attorney fails to file a timely notice of appeal when the client unequivocally asks for it — even if the plea agreement waived the right to challenge the conviction and sentence.

[b] Appellate Timeline

Appellate timing is absolutely crucial. In 1996, the Supreme Court held that a District Court cannot grant a defendant's motion for judgment of acquittal after return of a guilty verdict if the motion is even one day late,[638] a draconian viewpoint that was extended in 2007. The Supreme Court held that the time for appeal is jurisdictional, so a late appeal cannot be heard on the merits, no matter how reasonable the excuse for the delay. The petitioner sought federal habeas relief after his conviction of murder. When the District Court turned him down, he filed a timely motion for reconsideration under the FRCP provision that delays the commencement of the 30-day appeal period until the motion for reconsideration has been decided. He did not learn about the entry of the order denying the motion for reconsideration until about three months after the order. He then asked the District Court to reopen the time to appeal under 28 USC § 2107(c) and FRAP 4(a)(6). Rule 4(a)(6) permits the District Court to reopen the time to file an appeal for 14 days after the date when the order to reopen is entered. The order was granted, but the judge specified that the notice of appeal had to be filed within 17 days. The order was entered on February 10th and called for filing by February 27th. The notice of appeal was filed on February 26th. However, the correct deadline is actually 14 days, not 17. The Sixth Circuit, affirmed by the Supreme Court, overruled the "unique circumstances" doctrine to the extent that it permits exceptions to the timing rules.[639]

- In general, retrial after grant of a new trial must begin not more than 70 days from the finality of the act that made a new trial necessary: 18 USC § 3161(e),

---

[636] Nunez v. United States, 495 F.3d 544 (7th Cir. 2007), discussed in Pamela A. MacLean, *7th Circuit Breaks With Six Circuits Over Waiver of Appeal*, Nat'l L.J. 8/17/07 (law.com).

[637] No. 492 F.3d 263 (4th Cir. 2007).

[638] Carlisle v. United States, 517 U.S. 416 (1996).

[639] Bowles v. Russell, 551 U.S. 205 (2007).

although the court can extend this to 180 days if the witnesses become unavailable.

- A habeas petition must be filed within 180 days after final state affirmance of the conviction: 28 USC § 2263.

Federal Rules of Appellate Procedure 4(b) requires a defendant's notice of appeal as of right to be filed within 10 days of entry of judgment or motion for a new trial; the prosecution has 30 days to appeal. A 30-day extension can be granted on a showing of excusable neglect. FRAP 4(b), unlike 4(a), is a non-jurisdictional claim processing rule, and therefore, according to the Ninth Circuit, is subject to waiver.[640]

- The appellant must order the transcript within 10 days after filing notice of appeal: FRAP 10(b).
- A petition for rehearing can be filed within 14 days of entry of judgment (unless the local rule is different): FRAP 40(a).
- The appellant's brief must be filed within 40 days of the date the record is filed, giving the appellee 30 days from the service of the appellant's brief to file its own brief. Then the appellant's reply brief is due 14 days from the date of the appellee's brief, but it must be filed at least three days before the scheduled date for argument: FRAP 31(a).

The Supreme Court found a wrongful imprisonment suit untimely: the statute of limitations was two years. The statute was tolled until the petitioner, 15 at the time of his arrest, turned 18. But in general, the clock begins to run when a judge has reviewed the charges and bound the arrestee over for trial. (The dissent said the starting point was nullification of the improper conviction.)[641]

[c] Ineffective Assistance of Counsel

The attorney has a duty to represent clients "zealously," while also serving as an officer of the court. The latter role forbids knowing introduction of perjured testimony. The attorney may be sanctionable for abusive litigation tactics, but is also at fault for failing to utilize appropriate tactics.

Actual conflict of interest when an attorney represents multiple defendants can constitute ineffective assistance. If error occurs on this issue, it is never harmless,[642] but joint representation is not a per se violation of the right to effective assistance, if there is no actual conflict or significant possibility of conflict (such as would occur if the co-defendants blamed each other).[643]

---

[640] United States v. Sadler, 480 F.3d 932 (9th Cir. 2007).

[641] Wallace v. Chicago Police Officers, 549 U.S. 384 (2007).

[642] Satterwhite v. Texas, 486 U.S. 249 (1988).

[643] Burger v. Kemp, 483 U.S. 776 (1987). After a guilty plea, the defendant is entitled to an evidentiary hearing as to whether the lawyer's previous representation of a possible witness in the case was an actual conflict of interest that had an adverse affect on the defendant: Hall v. United States, 371 F.3d 969 (7th Cir. 2004).

The central principle, deriving from the *Strickland* case, is that even if a defendant shows that the lawyer failed to satisfy minimal standards of professional skill and competence, to be entitled to relief the defendant still must show prejudice from the lawyer's inadequate performance.[644]

The Sixth Amendment right to counsel is only violated by ineffective assistance of counsel if the challenged conduct affects the reliability of the trial process, so both defective performance and prejudice, resulting in an unreliable or fundamentally unfair trial, are required. Mere proof that the result of the trial would have been different but for inadequate advocacy is not necessarily enough.[645]

A defendant who alleges ineffective assistance of counsel must identify specific acts or omissions on the attorney's part, not merely make conclusory allegations of ineffective assistance.

Issues that may justify a finding of ineffective assistance of counsel:

- Conflict of interest, such as past representation of a prosecution witness[646]
- Failure to undertake a reasonable investigation to locate witnesses whose testimony would be helpful at trial (although it can be a reasonable strategic decision not to call convicted felons whose testimony is subject to impeachment)
- Failure to use jury challenges appropriately
- Failure to assert meritorious defenses
- Failure to file the appropriate motions
- Failure to object to improper questions or prejudicial or inflammatory testimony
- Failure to make an adequate record for appeal
- Failure to apply for mistrial, where appropriate
- Failure to request cautionary jury instructions
- Failure to raise meritorious issues that could result in a sentence reduction
- Failure to file a timely notice of appeal, raising all appropriate issues.

The effective attorney should call witnesses about potentially exculpatory physical evidence, even if the defendant has confessed, because it is possible that the confession could be excluded from evidence.

---

[644] Strickland v. Washington, 466 U.S. 668 (1984).

[645] Lockhart v. Fretwell, 506 U.S. 364 (1993). The Supreme Court ruled that the Ninth Circuit should have deferred to the District Court in a case where the defendant first told his lawyer not to present mitigating evidence, then argued ineffective assistance of counsel. At the sentencing hearing the defendant interrupted his lawyer's attempt to introduce the evidence, then told the judge that there were no mitigating circumstances: Schriro v. Landrigan, 550 U.S. 465 (2007); *see* (AP), *Supreme Court Rules Against Two-Time Killer on Death Row*, 5/17/07 (law.com).

[646] The Supreme Court recognizes ineffective assistance through multiple representation of defendants only if there was an actual conflict of interest adversely affecting the lawyer's performance: Cuyler v. Sullivan, 446 U.S. 335 (1980) — but the defendant is automatically entitled to relief if a conflict of interest actually occurred: Holloway v. Arkansas, 435 U.S. 475 (1978).

In mid-2005, the Supreme Court required that a defense attorney investigate past case files in search of mitigating factors, even if it seems to be a waste of time. The defense attorney has a duty to make reasonable efforts to obtain and review material that the prosecution will cite as aggravating evidence. A death sentence was reversed on ineffective-assistance grounds. The lawyer should not have relied on the defendant's family's assertion that his childhood was normal. ABA standards require the defense to explore all avenues.[647]

Effective assistance of counsel can be provided without undertaking every possible legal action. The defense attorney can make a valid strategic decision not to introduce evidence that is likely to backfire (e.g., by opening the door to cross-examination or impeachment). Recommending a guilty plea is not ineffective, if there is a mass of evidence against the defendant, although the attorney must discuss the ramifications of a plea bargain.

Hoffman was sentenced to death in 1993. He applied for federal habeas relief on the grounds of ineffective assistance of counsel during the phases of pretrial plea bargaining and sentencing. The District Court found that assistance was ineffective during sentencing only, so the federal habeas petition was granted in part, and the federal government was ordered to re-sentence him. The Ninth Circuit found assistance had been ineffective at both phases, and ordered the state either to release Hoffman or offer a plea agreement with the same material terms as the original plea agreement. The state petitioned for, and was granted, certiorari. Hoffman abandoned his claim of ineffective assistance at the plea bargaining stage, seeking to withdraw that claim and have the appeal dismissed with prejudice, for resentencing by the District Court. The Supreme Court found that the claim of ineffective assistance during plea bargaining was moot, and vacated the Ninth Circuit decision to the extent it granted that claim, and remanded the case to the Ninth Circuit with instructions to order the District Court to dismiss the claim with prejudice.[648]

It constitutes ineffective assistance of counsel to fail to consult with a defendant (who has not given clear instructions either to appeal or refrain from appealing) about the potential for appeal if, based on information the attorney knew or should have known, a rational defendant would want to appeal, or the defendant reasonably showed interest in appealing. To prevail on such a claim, the defendant must also show a reasonable probability that, with appropriate consultation, he would have filed a timely appeal.[649]

A 2008 Second Circuit decision[650] holds that appointed counsel have a duty to assist defendants in filing appropriate certiorari petitions. Later that same year, however, the Second Circuit held that counsel was not constitutionally ineffective for failing to inform another defendant that he could apply for certiorari. There was

---

[647] Rompilla v. Beard, 545 U.S. 374 (2005).
[648] Arave v. Hoffman, 128 S. Ct. 749 (2008).
[649] Roe v. Flores-Ortega, 528 U.S. 470 (2000).
[650] Nnebe v. United States, 534 F.3d 87 (2d Cir. 2008).

no constitutional right to a Supreme Court hearing of the case. Counsel must be appointed for first-tier appeals (including permissive appeals), but not for certiorari or other discretionary appeals. Where there is no right to appointed counsel, there is no right to effective assistance. The Second Circuit described first-tier review as calling for adjudication on the merits to correct error. Supreme Court review, in contrast, deals with significant public interests and whether the lower court conflicted with established Supreme Court precedent. However, the Supreme Court said that, as a matter of sound professional practice, both retained and appointed counsel should discuss the availability of certiorari petitions and, if retained to do so, should assist clients with the petition.[651]

See Edwards v. Carpenter[652] on the standards for bringing habeas corpus claims based on ineffective assistance of counsel. The attorney's ineffectiveness in failing to preserve a claim for state-court review could be adequate grounds for habeas relief, but only if the ineffectiveness was severe enough to achieve independent Constitutional status.

The Supreme Court ruled (contrary to holdings by the Second and Seventh Circuit) that a prisoner will be permitted to raise the issue of ineffective assistance for the first time by asserting a collateral challenge under 28 USC § 2255. Such a claim is not procedurally debarred even if it could have been raised on direct appeal. The Supreme Court suggested that a District Court performing collateral review may actually be in a better position to resolve the issue correctly (for instance, by developing evidence about what the attorney did and why) than an appellate court that is confined to reviewing a record that may be inadequate for this purpose.[653]

In 2004, the Supreme Court addressed technical appellate issues of ineffective assistance claims in *Holland v. Jackson*[654] and concluded that 28 USC § 2254(d)(1) [relief for state ruling that is contrary to, or unreasonably applies, the applicable federal law] applies only when the state court attempts to apply the correct Supreme Court precedent, but applies it unreasonably to the facts of the prisoner's case, assessed in the light of the evidence properly before the state court.

Early in 2001, the Supreme Court ruled that an allegation of ineffective assistance of counsel, with respect to grouping of offenses, cannot be denied merely because the sentence was only enhanced by 6–21 months. Any extra duration of imprisonment may constitute prejudice under *Strickland v. Washington*, 466 U.S. 668 (1984).[655]

---

[651] Pena v. United States, 534 F.3d 92 (2d Cir. 2008); *see also* Austin v. United States, 513 U.S. 5 (1994) holding that Criminal Justice Act plans must permit attorneys to be relieved of the duty to file certiorari petitions that would present only frivolous claims.

[652] 529 U.S. 446 (2000).

[653] Massaro v. United States, 538 U.S. 500 (2002).

[654] 542 U.S. 649 (2004). The standard for "unreasonable application" comes from Williams v. Taylor, 529 U.S. 362, 413 (2000).

[655] Glover v. United States, 531 U.S. 198 (2001).

Somewhat surprisingly, the Fifth Circuit held in late 2000 that it is not necessarily prejudicial under the Sixth Amendment if the defense attorney falls asleep during a capital trial — if the defendant cannot prove what was going on during the part of the trial the attorney slept through. The Fifth Circuit held that even if prejudice could be presumed, the defendant would not benefit because it would be a new rule under *Teague v. Lane*, 489 U.S. 288 (1989) and therefore not available for habeas review.

However, the Fifth Circuit reversed itself in August 2001, both as to the presumption of ineffective assistance and whether a new rule was involved. In June 2002, the Supreme Court refused to reinstate the defendant's conviction and death sentence. It once again became necessary for Texas to either retry or release the defendant.[656]

In *Mickens v. Taylor*[657] the murder defendant was represented by an attorney with a conflict of interest: the lawyer had also represented the murder victim on criminal charges. The Supreme Court found the conviction sustainable unless the conflict adversely affected the attorney's purpose — even though the trial judge knew or should have known of the conflict but did not mention it.

In another Supreme Court ineffective-assistance case, a convicted murder, sentenced to death, alleged that he received ineffective assistance because his attorney did not present mitigating factors at the sentencing hearing and waived a closing statement at this hearing. The lawyer said this was a tactical decision made to prevent a notably eloquent prosecutor from influencing the jury with a rebuttal.

The Supreme Court upheld the state denial of post-conviction relief as a reasonable application of federal law. Relief can be granted if the state court correctly identifies the governing legal principle as determined by Supreme Court precedent but applies it unreasonably.

Here, however, *Strickland* was the appropriate precedent and it was applied reasonably. The test is whether the defendant proved that the representation fell below an objective standard of reasonable attorney performance, with a reasonable probability that the result would have been different with a better lawyer. In this case, although there could be disagreement about the validity of the lawyer's tactical choices, it was not unreasonable for the state court to treat them as falling within the bounds of competent advocacy.[658]

Although it refused to state as a general principle that an attorney's appearance at a plea hearing by speakerphone rather than in person was necessarily adequate, in 2008 the Supreme Court did not treat the situation as presumptively ineffective assistance of counsel: *Wright v. Van Patten*, No. 07-212 (1/7/08). The defendant stated in court that he had discussed the plea with his attorney, and was

---

[656] Burdine v. Johnson, 231 F.3d 950 (2000), *rev'd*, 262 F.3d 336 (5th Cir. 2001); Cockrell v. Burdine, 535 U.S. 1121 (2002) affirms the second Fifth Circuit ruling.

[657] 535 U.S. 162 (2002).

[658] Bell v. Cone, 535 U.S. 685 (2002).

satisfied with his legal representation. The attorney was present at the actual sentencing, the defendant did not object to the guilty plea. The Supreme Court premised its holding on whether the state court, in affirming the conviction, failed to apply clear federal precedent — and there was no holding directly on point condemning appearance by speakerphone.

California requires attorneys drafting briefs to include anything on the record that might arguably support the appeal. In a case the Supreme Court decided in 2000 the defendant asserted ineffective assistance; the courts below held that at least two issues were omitted from the brief, so prejudice could be presumed. The Supreme Court presumed that the state procedure was reliable; the test is whether it was objectively unreasonable for the lawyer to fail to find appealable issues, and whether the defendant was prejudiced.[659]

Stewart v. Smith[660] holds that a state court acts independently of federal law when it denies a successive petition for post-conviction relief premised on an ineffective-assistance claim because of failure to comply with the local version of Rule 32.2(a)(3). In Rule 32 cases, claims with a major Constitutional dimension that were not raised earlier can still be reviewed on appeal, unless there was a knowing, voluntary, and intelligent waiver of the claim — not just mere omission from the prior habeas petition(s).

Independent analysis is important because, when the answer to a question of state procedural law depends on a federal Constitutional ruling, then federal courts can undertake direct review of the state decision. But Rule 32.2(a)(3) determinations do not depend on a federal Constitutional ruling on the merits, and therefore are independent.

[3] Standard of Review

Motions to suppress are generally reviewed de novo, as a mixed question of law and fact. Findings of fact are reviewed to see if the trial court's position was clearly erroneous, but the application of law to those facts is reviewed on a de novo basis. The "plain error" doctrine permits the appellate court to take notice of plain errors or defects affecting substantial rights, even if they were not raised before the lower court.

Convictions solely or primarily based on illegally obtained evidence must be reversed[661] (but this rule is inapplicable if evidence of guilt is overwhelming even without the tainted evidence).

If two crimes are the "same" for *Blockburger* purposes (see § 26.02[F]), they cannot be prosecuted separately, because the second trial would impose double jeopardy on the defendant. However, if the defendant is convicted of one of the crimes, appeals, and gets a new trial, the prosecution starts over and the second

---

[659] Smith v. Robbins, 528 U.S. 259 (2000).

[660] 536 U.S. 856 (2002).

[661] Mapp v. Ohio, 367 U.S. 643 (1961); Preston v. United States, 376 U.S. 364 (1964).

charge can be added or substituted for the first one.[662] A defendant who opposed a motion to consolidate cannot raise double jeopardy objections to the separate trials.

Denial of speedy trial requires dismissal of the prosecution with prejudice; lesser measures, such as sentence reduction, are not deemed adequate to redress the wrong. However, there is no single rule for determining when the speedy-trial guarantee has been violated; it depends on factors such as the length of the delay, the prosecution's justification for delay, the extent of prejudice, and whether the defendant asserted the right to a speedy trial.

Harmless error does not require reversal and retrial. Harmless error is error that did not change the result of the trial: e.g., a trial in which the other evidence was strong enough to make conviction virtually inevitable. However, some errors are so egregious that they can never be harmless, such as total deprivation of the right to counsel or right to public trial, or exclusion of all persons of the defendant's race from the Grand Jury.[663]

Rule 9(a), not general equitable principles, is used to analyze first petitions for federal review. The rule is the sole source for determining whether the state is prejudiced by delay.[664]

When a Court of Appeals reviews a District Court's decision on a habeas corpus petition, the Court of Appeals has no duty to raise, sua sponte, procedural errors made by the petitioner but not raised by the state.[665]

[O] Prison Litigation

The Prison Litigation Reform Act (PLRA) is found at 28 USC § 1915 *et seq.* It forbids prisoners to bring civil actions or appeal civil judgments if, on three or more earlier occasions and while incarcerated, the prisoner brought suits that were dismissed as frivolous, malicious, or failing to state a cause of action. (A prisoner in imminent danger of serious physical injury is permitted to sue, despite earlier inappropriate litigation.) Also see § 22.20[H]; PLRA proceedings are civil suits and thus are also discussed in the Civil Procedure chapter.

The Supreme Court ruled in early 2006 that Title II of the ADA validly abrogates sovereign immunity. Therefore, a disabled prisoner charging handicap discrimination in the conditions of his confinement can sue the state for money damages, as long as the conduct allegedly violating the ADA also infringes on the prisoner's rights under the Fourteenth Amendment.[666]

The Federal Tort Claims Act waives the United States government's sovereign immunity for claims arising out of the torts of federal employees: 28 USC § 1346(b)(1). There is an exemption under 28 USC § 2680(c) for claims about "assessment or collection of any tax or customs duty or the detention of any []

---

[662] Montana v. Hall, 481 U.S. 400 (1987).

[663] These examples come from Arizona v. Fulminante, 499 U.S. 299 (1991).

[664] Lonchar v. Thomas, 517 U.S. 314 (1996).

[665] Hudson v. United States, 522 U.S. 93 (1997).

[666] United States v. Georgia, 546 U.S. 151 (2006).

property by an officer of customs or excise or any other law enforcement officer." A January, 2008 Supreme Court case involves a petitioner who lost some of his personal property in transit when he was transferred from one federal prison to another. The Supreme Court ruled that the § 2860(c) exception applies to the conduct of "any" law enforcement officer, not just one assessing taxes or customs duties, on the grounds that Congress could have drafted the provision to make it clear that sovereign immunity is not waived in situations in which a law enforcement officer acts in a customs or excise capacity — and not otherwise.[667]

Prison inmates have a Fourteenth Amendment liberty interest in not being placed in an ultra-high-security "supermax" prison, but in June 2005, the Supreme Court upheld the Ohio screening and review processes for such prisons, finding that they provided due process to potential inmates.[668] The Tenth Circuit struck down Bureau of Prison regulations that do not allow a federal inmate to transfer to a Community Correctional Center until 90% of his sentence has elapsed, on the grounds that Congress clearly intended all decisions about transfer and placement to be made individually, using the five factors set out in 18 USC § 3621(b).[669]

The Supreme Court's *Beard v. Banks* decision of mid-2006 involved a long-term segregation unit in a maximum security prison. Prisoners enter at Level 2, with the heaviest restrictions (no access to newspapers, magazines, or photographs) and can progress to Level 1 if their behavior is good. The Third Circuit struck down this regime as a matter of law, but the Supreme Court reversed. Courts owe substantial deference to the professional judgment of prison administrators, and prison regulations are permissible if they are reasonably related to legitimate penological interests. Because maximum security prisoners are already subject to so many limitations, prison officials must be given some leeway to remove privileges so that prisoners will have an incentive to behave better.[670]

A state prison doctor was entitled to qualified immunity in prisoner's civil rights suit re constitutionally inadequate medical care; the plaintiff did not establish deliberate indifference to the care he needed.[671] Certiorari was granted, and dismissal of a prisoner's § 1983 suit vacated, when he charged that termination of treatment of his liver condition violated the Eighth Amendment. The Supreme Court held that the Court of Appeals misinterpreted the relevant FRCP rules.[672]

---

[667] Ali v. Fed'l Bureau of Prisons, 128 S. Ct. 831 (2008).

[668] Wilkinson v. Austin, 545 U.S. 649 (2005).

[669] Wedelstedt v. Wiley, 477 F.3d 1160 (10th Cir. 2007).

[670] Beard v. Banks, 548 U.S. 521 (2006).

[671] Gobert v. Caldwell, 463 F.3d 339 (5th Cir. 2006).

[672] Erickson v. Pardus, 551 U.S. 89 (2007). The Eleventh Circuit ruled early in 2008 that a federal prisoner in a privately operated prison cannot bring a *Bivens* suit against the employees of the prison for violation of the Eighth Amendment right to medical treatment: Alba v. Montford, 517 F.3d 1249 (11th Cir. 2008).

A 1999 Supreme Court decision[673] prevents prison litigants from raising issues in federal court that were not brought before the state's highest court, even if raising the claims was almost certain to be futile.

Although 42 USC § 1997e(a) requires dismissal of a PLRA suit if the prisoner fails to exhaust administrative remedies, a 2007 decision by the Supreme Court holds that the Sixth Circuit rules for prison litigation, such as a ban on suits against defendants who were not identified in the prisoner's grievance, and dismissal of an entire case if there was any claim for which administrative remedies were not exhausted, were invalid because they are not required by the PLRA. Promulgating these rules exceeded the proper role of the judiciary.[674]

The requirement of exhaustion of remedies before bringing federal suit applies even if the remedies sought (e.g., money damages) are not available under the administrative process.[675] Although the Ninth Circuit permitted a prison suit after rejection of grievances as untimely, on the grounds that no further administrative remedy was available. The Supreme Court reversed, holding that the exhaustion requirement of the Prison Litigation Reform Act requires proper exhaustion of administrative remedies — i.e., compliance with the entire procedure, including deadlines.[676] If an inmate's § 1983 claim asserts multiple claims and multiple grievances against multiple prison officials, exhaustion of remedies is required for each claim against each defendant for at least one grievance.[677]

Exhaustion of remedies is required with respect to all suits about prison life, including excessive force claims and claims that involve individual incidents rather than general circumstances within a facility.[678]

The PLRA imposes a cap on legal fees in prison rights cases: 42 USC § 1997e(d)(3). The Sixth and Seventh Circuits have upheld the reasonableness of capping these fees; it serves the valid state purpose of discouraging frivolous litigation.[679] The PLRA applies to work performed by the prisoner's attorney when prison officials appeal to challenge a judgment in the prisoner's favor, but if the prisoner wins at the appellate level, he or she becomes a prevailing party for purposes of a fee award. According to the Sixth Circuit, applying the PLRA fee cap to appeals work is not a violation of Due Process.[680]

28 USC § 1915A requires the court to review prisoners' civil complaints against the government or government employees as soon as possible (preferably before the case has been docketed) to see if the complaint is frivolous or malicious;

---

[673] O'Sullivan v. Boerckel, 526 U.S. 838 (1999).

[674] Jones v. Bock, 549 U.S. 199 (2007), consolidated with Williams v. Overton and Walton v. Bouchard, No. 05-7142.

[675] Booth v. Churner, 532 U.S. 732 (2001).

[676] Woodford v. Ngo, 548 U.S. 81 (2006).

[677] Abdul-Muhammed v. Kempker, 450 F.3d 350 (8th Cir. 2006).

[678] Porter v. Nussle, 534 U.S. 516 (2002).

[679] Johnson v. Daley, 339 F.3d 582 (7th Cir. 2003); Hadix v. Johnson, 230 F.3d 840 (6th Cir. 2000).

[680] Riley v. Kurtz, 361 F.3d 906 (6th Cir. 2004).

fails to state a claim; or seeks damages against a party that is immune. The Supreme Court held in March 2005 that state prisoners can use 42 USC § 1983 to seek declaratory and injunctive relief with respect to the Constitutionality of state parole procedures. That is, habeas is not the sole potential avenue of relief.[681]

Although the Religious Freedom Restoration Act (RFRA) provides "appropriate relief" for federal prisoners whose rights are violated, the D.C. Circuit held in 2006 that this does not include money damages, because the RFRA does not unequivocally waive sovereign immunity.[682] The Third Circuit held that a state correctional regulation, limiting inmates to 10 books in their cells at a time, violated the RFRA's successor statute RLUIPA by imposing a substantial burden on religious exercise.[683]

Under a 1994 Supreme Court decision, there is a "favorable termination" requirement: state prisoners can only use 42 USC § 1983 to get damages for actions that make the length — or fact — of confinement invalid if the prisoner has already had the conviction or sentence declared invalid. However, in 2004, the Supreme Court ruled that the "favorable termination" requirement does not apply to damage suits involving prison disciplinary proceedings, because the petitioner did not attack the sentence or revocation of good-time credits.[684]

According to the Supreme Court's 2000 decision[685] upholding 18 USC § 3626 (defendant prison officials are entitled to an automatic stay of injunctions granted to prisoner litigants if the court fails to make the required statutory findings), courts do not have the equitable power to enjoin the automatic stay. It must be permitted to take effect. When a case is reinstated under FRCP 60(b), the statute of limitations is calculated on the basis of the date of the initial filing.

However, in a decision at the very end of the October 2001 term, the Supreme Court held that a reasonable guard would know that manacling a prison inmate to a so-called hitching post for a prolonged period of time as a punishment (where there was no security emergency requiring immobilization of the prisoner) constituted cruel and unusual punishment. Because of this knowledge, the prison guards were not entitled to immunity from a 42 USC § 1983 civil rights suit.[686]

---

[681] Wilkinson v. Dotson, 544 U.S. 74 (2005).

[682] Webman v. Federal Bureau of Prisons, 441 F.3d 1022 (D.C. Cir. 2006).

[683] Washington v. Klem, 497 F.3d 272 (3d Cir. 2007).

[684] Muhammed v. Close, 540 U.S. 749 (2004); the earlier case is Heck v. Humphrey, 512 U.S. 477 (1994).

[685] Miller v. French, 530 U.S. 327 (2000).

[686] Hope v. Pelzer, 536 U.S. 730 (2002).

Part VIII

LAW OFFICE ISSUES

Chapter 27

Regulation of the Practice of Law

§ 27.01   INTRODUCTION

Legal practice involves many regulatory and practical issues. Lawyers are required to abide by ethical rules, and must render professional services carefully and appropriately. When attorneys join together to practice law, the law partnership or professional corporation is subject to specialized requirements.

Neither the individual attorney nor the law firm can survive without a salary, retainer payments by clients, hourly billings, contingent fees, or fee awards, so § 27.07 discusses the circumstances in which awards of attorneys' fees can be granted.

The legal profession has a high self-image as to its ethical conduct, and deems that it is capable of self-regulation with little outside interference or supervision. The opinion held by lay people is somewhat less flattering. The legal profession governs itself by attorney discipline, regulated by standards and bar association rules. Outside this context, lawyers are also subject to malpractice suits (§§ 18.06, 27.03), and may fall afoul of various laws (§ 27.04).

Legal ethics is not a simple subject. Attorneys are subject to a number of obligations of equal force, and which are sometimes directly contradictory. The lawyer represents a particular client, but is also an officer of the court in pursuit of justice. The attorney must abide by the client's wishes, while obeying laws and ethical rules, and must also do what is best for the client — duties that are not always reconcilable.

This discussion is based on the ABA's Model Rules of Professional Conduct (drafted in 1983), which replace the Model Code of Professional Responsibility promulgated by the ABA in 1970. It should be noted that many of the states have adopted their own ethical codes for attorneys within their own jurisdictions, and there may be significant differences between your applicable state rule and a model rule.

The Virginia State Bar decided in mid-1998 that it is permissible for a law firm or corporate legal department to use a staffing agency to provide temporary lawyers. All disciplinary rules must be followed, with particular attention to conflicts of interest. Payment to the staffing agency is deemed to constitute compensation for recruiting and screening the personnel, so it is not unlawful fee-splitting.[1] The client need not be told that some or all work on their matters was done by temporary lawyers, except to the extent necessary to explain names or initials on billing statements.

However, according to the D.C. Bar Legal Ethics Committee, where it is material to client representation (based on factors such as the nature of the work and the client relationship), the firm must inform clients when it uses temporary lawyers to do client work. Payments to the placement agency and related expenses must be disclosed to the client, but the mark-up on the temporary lawyers' services need not be disclosed.[2]

In 2008, the ABA issued an ethics opinion not merely permitting but advocating legal outsourcing (e.g., having document review performed outside the United States by non-U.S. lawyers) as salutary for the global economy. Usually, Legal Process Outsourcing companies broker the services of the non-U.S. lawyers, often doing business in India because of the availability of English-speaking attorneys trained under the common law. Ethics Opinion 08-451 rules that sending legal work outside the United States is ethically permissible as long as the outsourcing lawyer preserves client confidentiality and attorney-client privilege; ascertains that the non-U.S. lawyers are competent; and the bills for outsourced work are reasonable.[3]

New Jersey held that a lawyer cannot be sued for trial-related conduct (in this case, a community activist's 42 USC § 1983 suit alleging that a municipality excluded him from an administrative hearing by falsely claiming that he would be called as a witness).[4]

§ 27.02   REGULATION OF THE PRACTICE OF LAW

The general rule is that corporations cannot conspire with their agents, so a lawyer and a client cannot be held liable for conspiracy that allegedly occurred during an attorney-client relationship when the lawyer offered advice in an official rather than a personal capacity — whether or not the lawyer had a personal motivation for the actual advice.[5]

The District Court for the District of Columbia has ruled that the FTC exceeded its statutory power by requiring attorneys to comply with the privacy notification requirements of the Gramm-Leach-Bliley Act: it was arbitrary and capricious to apply regulation of financial services providers to attorneys.[6]

---

[1] Virginia State Bar Standing Committee on Legal Ethics Op. 1712 (7/22/98); *see* 67 L.W. 2151.

[2] D.C. Bar Legal Ethics Committee Op. 284 (9/15/98); 67 L.W. 2246.

[3] Ethics Op. 08-451 (8/5/08); *see* Anthony Lin, *ABA Gives Thumbs Up to Legal Outsourcing*, N.Y.L.J. 8/27/08 (law.com).

[4] Loigman v. Middletown, 185 N.J. 566 (N.J. 2006).

[5] Heffernan v. Hunter, 189 F.3d 405 (3d Cir. 1999).

[6] N.Y.S. Bar Ass'n v. FTC, 72 L.W. 1083, 1679 (D.D.C. 8/11/03, 4/30/04).

The IRS' Circular 230 (explicating the duties of tax advisers) has been revised in light of the American Jobs Creation Act of 2004 (P.L. 108-357). Advisers, including law firms, must maintain internal advisory compliance committees. Client information must be reported to the IRS more frequently, especially when the lawyer provides tax avoidance advice. The IRS uses the information to distinguish between lawful avoidance and evasive tax shelters. Either the attorney must thoroughly investigate the client's representations and claims before rendering an opinion, or must include a disclaimer that the opinion cannot be relied upon. Individuals as well as corporate entities now have reporting requirements, and more types of transaction have become reportable.[7]

T.D. 9359, effective September 26, 2007, revises the Circular 230 regulations for practice before the IRS. The Final Regulations state that practice before the IRS covers all matters connected with a presentation to the IRS or any of its officers or employees, with respect to a taxpayer's rights, privileges, or liabilities, including written advice about any transaction that has a potential for tax avoidance or evasion. Any practice before the IRS (other than written advice rendered by an attorney or CPA) requires filing for Form 2848. The Final Regulations establish a category of "enrolled retirement plan agent," which gives technical services assisting plan sponsors in maintaining the tax-qualified status of retirement plans. The practice of enrolled retirement plan agents is limited to representing plans on issues under the employee plan determination letter program, the EPCRS program for correcting violations, and questions about master and prototype plans. T.D. 9359 maintains the IRS position that contingent fees for tax return preparation should be restricted, but practitioners are allowed to charge contingent fees for services in connection with an IRS examination of, or challenge to, a tax return, for interest and penalty reviews, or for judicial proceedings under the Internal Revenue Code.[8]

[A] Rules

[1] Rule 1.1 Competence

The attorney has a duty to provide competent representation, providing the level of skill, legal knowledge, and preparation appropriate for the case. Except in an emergency, attorneys must not accept matters for which they are not competent, although competency can be developed by additional study, or by associating with an attorney who does possess the necessary skills.

The New Jersey Supreme Court reprimanded an attorney for failing to file briefs on time (leading to dismissal of appeals) and not informing his clients of the dismissals. This violated Rule 1.1(a) (gross neglect), 1.3 (lack of diligence), and 1.4 (failure to communicate with clients). Usually, such conduct would result only

---

[7] Jessica M. Walker, *Lawyers Wary of New Tax Regulations' Impact on Client Relations*, Daily Business Review 6/3/05 (law.com).

[8] T.D. 9359, RIN 1545-BA72, 4830-01-p.

in an admonition, but he had already been admonished for similar offenses in April 2003. The court noted as a mitigating factor that he accepted many cases that other attorneys would turn down, and he had a large caseload and staffing problems, but he still should have improved his case-handling after the first ethics investigation.[9]

The ABA opined in 2003 that an attorney who thinks that another attorney is mentally impaired to a degree that interferes with representation of clients may have a duty to report to the professional authorities — even if the attorney denies the impairment, and even if the two attorneys are not in the same firm. However, if the information about the impairment is acquired in the course of representing a client, the client's informed consent is required to make the report. The options include: confronting the allegedly impaired attorney; consulting a mental health professional; and contacting a lawyer assistance program.[10]

The ABA Standing Committee on Ethics and Professional Responsibility issued an opinion in mid-2006 under which a public defender or other lawyer representing indigent criminal defendants has an ethical duty to refuse new cases, transfer cases to colleagues, or even move to withdraw if their workload is so heavy that they can't represent all their clients competently and with diligence. Supervisors are liable for their subordinates' ethics violations of this type if the supervisors fail to remedy the excessive caseload.[11]

[2] Rule 1.2 Scope of Representation

In a legal matter, although the attorney controls procedural matters, the client is in control of the objectives. Therefore, the attorney is bound by the client's decision to retain or fire the lawyer. In a civil case, the client has the final decision about whether to accept a settlement offer. In a criminal case, the client has the ultimate decision on whether to take a plea bargain, have the case tried by jury or to the court, and whether to take the stand. The attorney is not permitted to give knowing assistance to a client who commits a crime. It violates the Rules for an attorney to help a client commit a crime or perjure him- or herself (or advise the client to do so).

Nevertheless, the attorney is required to maintain the client's confidentiality, even in the frequent case in which the client has admitted to committing crimes. In some circumstances, the attorney is permitted to withdraw from representing the client, but often will be barred from doing so precisely because withdrawal would generate an inference that the lawyer is withdrawing because the client is guilty.

The attorney controls which motions will be filed and how the case will proceed.

---

[9] Charles Toutant, *Lawyer Reprimanded for Botching Appeals and Failing to Tell Clients*, N.J.L.J. 9/12/08 (law.com).

[10] ABA Standing Comm. on Ethics & Prof'l Resp. Formal Op. 03-431 (8/8/03). Ethics Op. 03-429 deals with impairment of an attorney in the same firm.

[11] ABA Standing Comm. on Ethics & Prof'l Resp Formal Op. 06-441 (5/13/06), 75 L.W. 2068.

Where a defendant has not given clear instructions to appeal or to waive appeal, it constitutes ineffective assistance of counsel for the attorney to fail to consult with the defendant about taking an appeal. The test is whether, based on the information the attorney knew or should have known, a rational defendant would want to appeal. The alternate test is whether the defendant reasonably showed an interest in pursuing an appeal. To prevail on such a claim, the defendant must also show a reasonable probability that, with appropriate consultation, he would have filed a timely appeal.[12]

[3] Rule 1.3 Diligence

The attorney must be "zealous" in representing the client—that is, the attorney must take all reasonable steps to carry out the contracted-for legal services without unreasonable delay.

Rhode Island ethics regulators read this rule to forbid a retainer agreement under which the attorney has the right to stop working on the client's matter without withdrawing if the client fails to keep up with the payment schedule. An attorney must either complete the client matter or withdraw.[13]

[4] Rule 1.4 Communication

In addition to being reasonably responsive to client questions, attorneys must furnish the client with information about the status of the matter in which the attorney represents the client. Clients must be given enough information to make reasonable decisions about the matter. Local rules may also require attorneys to disclose their extent of malpractice coverage or if they fail to maintain the required coverage.

When a lawyer leaves a firm, both the lawyer and the ex-firm have a duty to protect client interests and vindicate the client's right to choose his, her or its own representation. Model Rule 1.4 requires disclosure of the scheduled departure of a lawyer who is responsible for representing the client, or who is a principal in the firm's delivery of services to the client. The lawyer, the firm's responsible members, or both can perform notification. If feasible, joint notice is preferable. An attorney who thinks the firm will not give notice should give the notice personally, making written memoranda of conversations.

In fact, lawyers can inform their clients of impending departure even before they have formally resigned. It is not a violation of Rule 7.3 (solicitation) to tell a client in person or over the phone that a lawyer will be leaving. Written contact after leaving is also acceptable. But pre-resignation notice should only go to current clients, and clients should be made aware that they must decide who will complete their matter.

---

[12] Roe v. Flores-Ortega, 528 U.S. 470 (2000).
[13] R.I. Sup. Ct. Ethics Advisory Panel Op. 2003-8, 72 L.W. 2462 (12/4/03).

On request from the client, a departing lawyer should provide enough information about his or her new affiliation for the client to make an informed decision about staying with the original firm or transferring representation to the lawyer's new affiliation. There are fiduciary and unfair competition issues involved, for instance as to what information a departing lawyer can take.

It is acceptable to take research memos, pleadings, and forms to the extent that they are public domain or are considered the lawyer's own property. Taking copies of documents created for general use in the practice could be acceptable, but taking materials reasonably regarded by the firm as proprietary is problematic. Clients determine the disposition of their own files.

A New York State regulation, effective March 4, 2002,[14] imposes a general requirement that the attorney provide the client with a written letter of engagement before representation commences. The letter explains the scope of the intended legal services, the lawyer's schedule of fees, expenses, and billing practices, and the extent of the client's right to request arbitration of fee disputes. A signed retainer agreement can satisfy this requirement. However, in matrimonial cases, a more detailed agreement is mandated. The new requirement does not apply to representation where the fee is expected to be less than $3,000, and to relationships under which the attorney provides services of the same general kind as have already been rendered. The regulation has not been adopted as a Disciplinary Rule, and it has no enforcement mechanism.

New York's Appellate Division ruled that violation of 22 NYCRR 1215.1 [the requirement of a written retainer agreement in non-matrimonial cases] does not prevent an attorney from collecting a fee, but the attorney must prove the terms of the agreement; that the terms were fair; that the client understood and agreed to the terms. There is no guarantee that a court or arbitrator will conclude that these requirements were met, or will award a quantum meruit fee that equals the fee that could have been obtained with a proper retainer agreement. (In contrast, violation of the matrimonial rule, 22 NYCRR 1400.3/Code of Prof'l Resp DR 2-106(c)(2), does bar recovery of fees.).[15]

[5] Rule 1.5 Fees

See § 27.07 for computation of attorneys' fee awards. Even in the context of negotiated attorneys' fees, the fees are required to be reasonable. The reasonableness factors are quite similar to the "lodestar" factors used to set fee awards:

- Amount of time devoted to the work
- Local fee scale for comparable work
- Opportunity cost — the extent to which other work was ruled out

---

[14] 22 NYCRR § 1215.1-2; *see* 70 L.W. 2571. The requirements for matrimonial cases are found at 22 NYCRR § 136.3.

[15] Seth Rubenstein, PC v. Ganea, 41 A.D.3d 54 (N.Y.A.D. 2007); *see* Tom Perrotta, *Fees Still Possible in Absence of Retainer Letter, N.Y. Appellate Panel Says*, N.Y.L.J. 4/9/07 (law.com).

- Attorney's success in obtaining a result for the client
- Attorney's ability, experience, and reputation
- Whether the fee was fixed or contingent; the risk element in contingent fees justifies a larger payment.

The best practice is for all fees to be set out in a written contract; contingent-fee arrangements must be in writing. Contingent fees are considered unethical in domestic relations matters (other than outright collection of past-due sums) and criminal cases. If the attorney withdraws from the case, or is fired, before there is a resolution that generates a fund from which a contingent fee could be paid, then the attorney is not entitled to the contingency fee, but is entitled to sue on a *quantum meruit* basis — i.e., for the fair value of work done prior to termination of representation.

The Florida Court of Appeals instructed two lawyers to split a contingent fee pursuant to their written agreement — even though, based on one lawyer's advice, the client fired the other lawyer. The court ruled that the doctrine of quantum meruit governs the obligations of the client, not of co-counsel, and the written agreement made the attorneys jointly entitled to the fees. The fee agreement specified that one attorney was entitled to 25% of the recovery (the normal presumption would be an equal division), making time records irrelevant.[16]

The Fifth Circuit held that, even in a civil case, if attorneys are put on notice that their fees may be coming from frozen assets (in this case, stemming from an FTC TRO imposed on the basis of charges of telemarketing fraud), they have a duty of audit to make a good-faith inquiry into the source of the fees. An independent basis for the duty is the attorney's role as officer of the court.[17]

Taking a retainer in advance of providing services is acceptable, but any unearned portion of the retainer will have to be returned when representation is terminated.

A retainer agreement that requires a civil plaintiff to assign to the plaintiff's attorney the power to seek or waive statutory attorneys' fees is void under California law. The right to waive or apply for the fees belongs to the client. Giving it to the lawyer violates state policy against assignment of tort claims, and could interfere with the policy objective of settling rather than litigating claims.[18]

As a general rule, attorneys are not permitted to split fees with attorneys outside their own firm. However, if the total fee is reasonable; the client is notified and does not object; and the fee is divided based on the respective shares of the work performed by the attorneys (or pursuant to a written agreement with the client), fee-splitting is permissible. A contract to split fees is not necessarily invalid

---

[16] Jay v. Trazenfeld, 952 So. 2d 635 (Fla. App. 4/2/07), discussed in Daniel Axelrod, *Fla. Attorney Who Was Fired by Client Wins Cut of Contingency Fee*, Daily Business Review 4/24/07 (law.com).

[17] FTC v. Assail Inc., 410 F.3d 256 (5th Cir. 2005).

[18] Pony v. L.A. County, 433 F.3d 1138 (9th Cir. 2006). *See also* Evans v. Jeff D., 475 U.S. 717 (1986), holding that 42 USC § 1988 gives the right to seek attorneys' fees to the prevailing client.

if it fails to comply with Rule 1.5(e). It depends on the facts; relative culpability of the attorneys; the presence of good or bad faith; and whether some of the funds should have been rebated to the client.[19]

If attorneys were still in the same firm when the fees were negotiated, the rule forbidding attorneys in different firms to split fees without the client's consent does not apply when attorneys divide fees from unfinished contingent fee cases when the firm is disbanded.[20]

Failure to comply with an ethics requirement that clients consent to fee-sharing agreements does not automatically void a law firm's oral agreement to split fees with the referring attorney. The purpose of the rule is to protect clients against excessive fees, not to allow law firms to avoid obligations. However, the referring lawyer is subject to discipline for failure to obtain the client's consent before the referral.[21]

Even if the client did not consent to fee-sharing, a referring firm is nevertheless entitled to receive quantum meruit compensation for the work it did on the case before turning it over to the second firm. According to the California Supreme Court, the lack of consent precludes an action to enforce the contract between the two firms, but does not rule out the quantum meruit action.[22]

A fee referral agreement between an attorney and a law professor who had inactive bar status was unenforceable. The professor could not practice law

---

[19] Alan F. Post Chtd. v. Bregman, 349 Md. 142 (Md. App. 1998). The Eastern District of Pennsylvania refused to permit a lawyer in Pennsylvania to collect a referral fee in a New Jersey case, because the requirement under New Jersey ethics rules, that the fee-sharing arrangement be disclosed to clients, was not satisfied. The Pennsylvania lawyer sued the New Jersey firm on the basis of an oral argument to pay one-third of the fee on the referred accident case and one-fifth of the fee on a related Worker's Compensation case. The New Jersey firm denied the existence of an oral argument. The Eastern District said that an undisclosed agreement could not be enforced in any case, because New Jersey Rule 1.5(e) requires the client to consent to any division of fees with another firm. The overall fee must be reasonable, and even if the client consents, the division must be in proportion to the services performed. N.J. Court Rule 1:39-6(d) is somewhat different: it permits a non-proportional division, but maintains the need for client consent: Judge v. McCay, (E.D. Pa. 2007); *see* Shannon P. Duffy, *Lawyer Denied Referral Fee Over Lack of Client Consent*, The Legal Intelligencer 7/30/07 (law.com).

[20] Walker v. Gribble, 689 N.W.2d 104 (Iowa 2004).

[21] Saggese v. Kelley, 445 Mass. 434 (2005).

[22] Huskinson & Brown LLP v. Wolf, 9 Cal. Rptr. 3d 693 (Cal. 2004). In a case of first impression, the New Jersey Court of Appeals decided in early 2008 that a firm that takes over cases from a lawyer facing disbarment must pay referral fees after the disbarment occurs. Rule 1:20-20(b)(13) says that suspended or disbarred attorneys cannot profit indirectly from legal work, so they cannot collect fees for work performed by other lawyers. However, they can enforce deals for referral fees made prior to the discipline. The court held that it would be a windfall for the firm to be able to avoid paying the referral fees, and ordered payment into the account of the court-appointed trustee winding up the disbarred attorney's practice: Eichen Levinson & Crutchlow v. Weiner, A-2794-06 (N.J. App. 2008). *See* Henry Gottlieb, *Firm Can't Keep Referral Fees Owed to Lawyer Who Has Been Disbarred*, N.J.L.J. 1/17/08 (law.com).

(because she was not in active status) so a contract to split a fee with her was void as against public policy.[23]

Double billing is forbidden: that is, if a lawyer works on a matter for one client while traveling on behalf of another client, it is improper to bill both of them for the same time.

The Fifth Circuit held that it was not an abuse of discretion for a bankruptcy judge to limit attorneys' fees to half the normal hourly rate for travel time when the attorney was not working, despite the law firm's contention that its fees are set based on full compensation for travel time. (The fee agreement did not specify that the full rate would be charged for travel time.)[24]

A New York lower court found a retainer agreement provision, imposing 16% interest on unpaid fees (the maximum amount permitted by the state's usury law), to be unenforceable as excessive. The court rejected the lawyer's argument that the client would pay at least that high an interest rate on credit card balances. Instead, the court said that 9%, the statutory rate for pre- and post-judgment interest, set the maximum. The Code of Professional Responsibility does not authorize (or forbid) charging interest on unpaid balances, but DR 2-106(A) forbids illegal or excessive fees.[25]

If a third party (e.g., a family member) pays the fee, the attorney's ethical duties continue to run to the client (the person for whom the services are rendered), not the person who pays the fee.

The fee for preparing and prosecuting a patent application can legitimately be set as a percentage of the net profits from licensing the patent. However, because this is a contingent arrangement, it must be in writing, and the size of the percentage must not be unconscionable.[26]

[6] Rule 1.6 Attorney-Client Confidences

As a general rule, attorneys are not permitted to disclose any confidential information imparted in the course of legal representation, unless the client permits disclosure. The dramatic exception to the general rule is that confidential information can be disclosed if the attorney believes disclosure is vital to prevent a homicide or infliction of serious bodily injury.

Disclosure is also permitted if it is essential for the attorney to defend him- or herself in a suit brought by a former client.

An attorney-client relationship is created when someone who seeks legal advice discusses a situation with an attorney; it is not necessary for payment to be made.

---

[23] Morris & Doherty PC v. Lockwood, 259 Mich. App. 38 (2003).

[24] *In re* Babcock & Wilcox Co., 526 F.3d 824 (5th Cir. 2008); *see* Leigh Jones, *5th Circuit: Firm Can't Charge Full Hourly Rate for Travel Time*, Nat'l L.J. 5/5/08 (law.com).

[25] Kutner v. Antonacci, No. 36363/06 (Nassau Dist. Ct. 2007); *see* Daniel Wise, *Lawyer's Interest Charges on Unpaid Legal Fees Found to Be Excessive*, N.Y.L.J. 6/7/07 (law.com).

[26] Los Angeles County Bar Ass'n Prof'l Resp. & Ethics Comm. Formal Op. 507 (10/15/01), 70 L.W. 2300.

In August 2003, the ABA House of Delegates adopted changes to the Model Rules of Professional Conduct. The revised 1.6(b)(2) permits—but does not require—an attorney to reveal client confidences in the interest of preventing the client from committing fraud or other crime that is reasonably certain to cause substantial damage to the finances or property of others, where the client has used or is using the lawyer's services in furtherance of the crime. The amended 1.6(b)(3) permits disclosure to prevent, mitigate, or rectify such injuries.[27]

Attorney-client privilege can survive the death of the client.[28]

Attorney-client privilege applies to internal communications between state agencies and in-house counsel that provide legal advice.[29]

Attorney-client privilege applies to communications between co-defendants and their shared attorney as to issues affecting their joint defense.[30]

The "common legal interest" extension of the attorney-client privilege applies to possible co-defendants who have the same attorney only if there was a clear threat of litigation at the time of the assertedly privileged communication. It is not sufficient that the party making the communication was aware that litigation might be instituted at some indefinite point in the future.[31]

In late 2008, the Second Circuit clarified the scope of waiver of attorney-client privilege when the party invoking privilege placed the communication at issue in a lawsuit. The privilege issue arose in a civil rights case challenging the strip search policy for Erie County prisoners. The Magistrate Judge ordered production of e-mails between the county's attorney and the sheriff, on the grounds that they dealt with administration and policy, and the lawyer was not giving legal

---

[27] *See* 72 L.W. 2091.

[28] Swidler & Berlin v. United States, 524 U.S. 399 (1998). There is a testamentary exception to this principle, but it is limited to will contests: Wesp v. Everson, 33 P.3d 191 (Colo. 2001). A lawyer can disclose the confidences of a deceased client to the decedent's surviving spouse, who is also the executor of the estate and the sole heir, only if the lawyer has a reasonable belief that disclosure furthers the decedent's interest in facilitating administration of the estate. A lawyer who does not believe this is directed to seek advice from the court, given the potential survival of confidentiality. D.C. Bar Legal Ethics Comm. Op. 324, 72 L.W. 2750 (5/18/04). *See also* HLC Properties Ltd v. Superior Ct., 4 Cal. Rptr. 3d 898 (Cal. App. 9/29/03): the legal successor of a decedent's unincorporated business succeeded to the business' privilege, but only until the estate is settled.

[29] State *ex rel.* Leslie v. Ohio Hous. Fin. Agency, 73 L.W. 1659 (Ohio 4/13/05). When Florida Gulf Coast University fired its general counsel in mid-2007, she sued the school under Title VII and Title IX, charging endemic sex discrimination. The school counter-sued for an injunction to prevent disclosure of confidential information. Other suits are pending on similar confidentiality issues. Under Florida Bar Rules of Professional Conduct, there is an exception to the obligation of attorney-client confidentiality when lawyers sue a former employer or need the information to protect themselves from suit or defend their reputations. The ABA has issued a formal opinion permitting wrongful discharge claims by former in-house lawyers as long as they protect client information. Cases in California, Montana, and Tennessee have also upheld the rights of in-house lawyers to bring these suits. *See* Julie Kay, *University's Suit Against Former GC Tests Bounds of Attorney-Client Privilege*, Nat'l L.J. 5/20/08 (law.com).

[30] Gordon v. Boyles, 9 P.3d 1106 (Colo. 2000).

[31] *In re* Santa Fe Int'l Corp., 272 F.3d 705 (5th Cir. 2001).

advice. The Second Circuit held that the e-mails were sent to obtain legal advice; the case was remanded on the issue of whether circulating the e-mails to other employees of the sheriff's department waived privilege.[32]

In mid-2004, the Northern District of Illinois required a law firm to comply with the IRS summons seeking the identity of investors in tax shelters organized or sponsored by the firm. The clients would be permitted to intervene to assert attorney-client privilege with respect to particular documents. The opinion points out that the court had already reviewed sample documents, and found that most of them would not be privileged, and warns that sanctions might be imposed if frivolous privilege claims are raised.[33]

In the criminal context, the Eleventh Circuit ruled that a defendant who turns state's evidence to get a shorter sentence, and who is a participant in a joint defense agreement with another defendant who has his own counsel, cannot assert attorney-client privilege in communications with the attorney for the co-defendant. The Eleventh Circuit stressed that joint defense should be undertaken only when the defendants sign a written agreement that explains the absence of privilege in this circumstance.[34]

According to the Tenth Circuit, a bankruptcy trustee does not automatically maintain control over the attorney-client privilege or its waiver with respect to prepetition, good faith, affirmative civil claims against third persons with whom the debtor did business. The court should review each case in camera to decide if the trustee has the right to control assertion or waiver.[35]

Unlike some other states, California deems the attorney-client privilege to outweigh a trustee's duty to report to trust beneficiaries. Therefore, communications between trustee and counsel, dealing with trust administration, are privileged, and there's no duty to share the information with beneficiaries.[36]

[a] Work Product

Documents become work product if they are prepared in anticipation of litigation (whether or not litigation actually ensues). The work-product privilege is not limited to materials that relate to a specific claim.[37]

However, documents and communications generated by an attorney who prepares a tax return (even if an audit is involved) are not privileged, on the theory that documents used in return preparation are not privileged when created by an accountant or other non-lawyer.[38] Attorney-client privilege was waived in a

---

[32] *In re* County of Erie, 546 F.3d 222 (2d Cir. 2008); *see* Mark Hamblett, *2nd Circuit Trims 'At Issue' Waiver's Scope for Privilege*, N.Y.L.J. 10/15/08 (law.com).

[33] United States v. Jenkens & Gilchrist P.C., 72 L.W. 1728 (N.D. Ill. 5/14/04).

[34] United States v. Almeida, 341 F.3d 1318 (11th Cir. 2003).

[35] Foster v. Hill, 188 F.3d 1259 (10th Cir. 1999).

[36] Wells Fargo Bank NS v. Superior Court, 91 Cal. Rptr. 2d 716 (Cal. 2000).

[37] *In re* Sealed Case, 146 F.3d 881 (D.C. Cir. 1998). The work product of a trial consultant is considered attorney work product and is therefore covered by the privilege: In re Cendant Corporation Securities Litigation, 343 F.3d 658 (3d Cir. 2003).

[38] United States v. Frederick, 182 F.3d 496 (7th Cir. 1999).

memorandum about tax shelters because it was shown to a third party (a law firm that had provided tax advice about the shelter).[39] When an attorney seeks a motion for protection from discovery, covering documents that are alleged to be privileged and to be work product, the District Court's order denying the motion is a collateral order and thus immediately appealable.[40]

The Sixth Circuit joined the Second, Third, Fourth, and Seventh in holding that the test in privilege analysis is whether a document is prepared in anticipation of litigation, rather than in the ordinary course of business or to comply with non-litigation-related requirements. A document that would have been compiled in the same way even absent litigation is not protected.[41]

The Georgia Court of Appeals ruled in 2004 that voluntarily showing the SEC documents dealing with an internal investigation of a subsidiary's dealings waived work product, because the disclosing party had no actual or potential adversarial relationship with the SEC.[42]

The Southern District of New York reached a different conclusion, holding that the work product privilege was not waived when Merrill Lynch gave copies of internal investigation reports to its independent auditor, citing Sarbanes-Oxley policy reasons for encouraging companies to provide their auditors with the fullest possible information.[43]

According to the Tenth Circuit, work product (and attorney-client) privilege was waived when a corporation voluntarily disclosed sensitive documents to the SEC and the Department of Justice. The court held that the "selective waiver" doctrine has not been recognized by Congress and has seldom achieved court approval. It is not good policy because it does not further the objectives of the privileges (aiding candor and the privacy of the attorney-client relationship).[44] The Second Circuit ruled in late 2007 that a subject of a grand jury investigation, who, on the advice of his lawyer, protected himself by taping phone calls from a fellow broker, must turn over the recordings to prosecutors. Although the tapes were work product, the government showed a substantial need for the recordings to get information that was otherwise unobtainable. The grand jury needed information about what the subject did vis-a-vis the alleged fraud.[45]

The Department of Justice has issued several memoranda about circumstances in which the agency will seek waivers of privilege from corporations

---

[39] Denney v. Jenkens & Gilchrist, 73 L.W. 1340 (S.D.N.Y. 11/23/04).

[40] Kelly v. Ford Motor Co., 110 F.3d 954 (3d Cir. 1997).

[41] United States v. Roxworthy, 457 F.3d 590 (6th Cir. 2006).

[42] McKesson Corp. v. Green, 72 L.W. 1583 (Ga. App. 3/8/04); *accord* McKesson HBOC Inc. v. Superior Ct. of San Francisco, 9 Cal. Rptr. 3d 812 (Cal. App. 2004), holding that voluntary disclosure of a significant part of a communication waives the attorney-client and work product privileges.

[43] Merrill Lynch & Co. v. Allegheny Energy Co., 73 L.W. 1303 (S.D.N.Y. 10/26/04).

[44] *In re* Qwest Communications Int'l Inc. Securities Litigation, 450 F.3d 1179 (10th Cir. 2006).

[45] *In Re* Grand Jury Subpoena Dated July 6, 2005, 510 F.3d 180 (2d Cir. 2007); *see* Mark Hamblett, *2nd Circuit Backs Work Product Tape Subpoena*, N.Y.L.J. 12/13/07 (law.com).

under investigation. The most recent is the December 12, 2006 "McNulty memorandum" (from Deputy U.S. Attorney General Paul McNulty) that has been criticized for merely imposing a "don't ask, don't tell" policy that will lead to underground demands for waivers. The McNulty memorandum directs prosecutors not to treat a corporation's payment of employees' attorneys' fees as a factor in deciding whether to bring charges against the organization, unless the payments were made to impede the investigation. The memorandum says that the DOJ favors limited waiver, so corporations will not be at risk of third-party and shareholder suits when they cooperate with federal investigations. Under this memorandum (which merely provides guidelines; there are no penalties if prosecutors do not follow them) prosecutors can consider factors such as joint defense agreements, sharing of information about an investigation between corporation and employees, and whether employees who take the Fifth Amendment are fired when determining whether a corporation has cooperated with an investigation.

The next development was the "Filip Memo" (from Deputy Attorney General Mark R. Filip) in 2008, formally known as "Principles of Federal Prosecution of Business Organizations." The Filip Memo focuses on disclosure of relevant facts. A corporation's credit for cooperation will not be based on waiver of privilege, but on whether the company discloses relevant facts (privileged or otherwise) about the conduct under investigation. The memo forbids prosecutors from requesting waivers of core attorney-client communication or work product privileges, and corporations that agree to waive privilege should not be given cooperation credit on this account. Under the Filip Memo, prosecutors cannot consider whether a company has retained or disciplined culpable employees as a factor toward cooperation credit, although it can be considered as a remediation factor. (However, the distinction may have little practical effect, because both cooperation and remediation are considered in federal prosecutors' decision whether or not to bring charges.) An August, 2008 Second Circuit ruling says that government pressure on a corporation to cooperate by denying indemnification to its directors and officers violates the Sixth Amendment rights of the directors and officers.[46]

A 2007 Federal Circuit decision makes it much harder to find willful patent infringement (in order to impose treble damages). The decision also says that a defendant who waives privilege for opinion counsel does not also do so for communications with the trial lawyer. "Opinion counsel" are lawyers who are asked for a letter as to whether an alleged infringer did infringe on the patent; at trial, the defendant would then waive privilege if the letter was favorable. In many cases,

---

[46] Abbe Lowell, Christopher Man and Obiamaka P. Okwumabua, *Is the DOJ's New Policy on Prosecuting Corporations Real Reform or Business as Usual?* Special to law.com 1/31/07; Marcia Coyle, *The "McNulty Memo": Real Change, or Retreat?* Nat'l L.J. 12/20/06 (law.com); Pamela A. MacLean, *McNulty Memo on Attorney-Client Privilege Blasted for Lack of Change,* Nat'l L.J. 1/26/07 (law.com). Mark J. Stein and Joshua A. Levine, *The Filip Memorandum: Does It Go Far Enough?* N.Y.L.J. 9/11/08 (law.com); the Second Circuit decision is United States v. Stein, 541 F.3d 130 (2d Cir. 2008).

production of the letter was enough for the court to rule out willfulness. When the company charging infringement tried to use the waiver of privilege for opinion counsel to gain access to communications with trial counsel, the Federal Circuit held that, because opinion counsel and trial counsel serve different functions, waiver as to one is not necessarily waiver as to the other. The Federal Circuit de-emphasized the opinion letter, finding the test of willful infringement to be clear and convincing evidence that the alleged infringer ignored an objectively high likelihood that its actions were infringing.[47]

However, a 2008 Federal Circuit decision made opinion letters more desirable, by holding that the jury should consider the absence of an opinion letter, as an indication of whether the alleged infringer was aware that its actions could induce patent infringement.[48]

In late 2008, the Second Circuit clarified the scope of waiver of attorney-client privilege when the party invoking privilege placed the communication at issue in a lawsuit. The privilege issue arose in a civil rights case challenging the strip search policy for Erie County prisoners. The Magistrate Judge ordered production of e-mails between the county's attorney and the sheriff, on the grounds that they dealt with administration and policy, and the lawyer was not giving legal advice. The Second Circuit held that the e-mails were sent to obtain legal advice; the case was remanded on the issue of whether circulating the e-mails to other employees of the Sheriff's Department waived privilege.[49]

The Southern District of New York applied the privilege to communications between the lawyers for a target of a Grand Jury investigation and the public relations firm hired by lawyers attempting to prevent an indictment. However, the privilege applied only because the lawyers (and not the target) hired the public relations firm, and therefore the communications related to the provision of legal services.[50]

The Third Circuit ruled that discussions during witness preparation were privileged absent a showing of exceptional circumstances. The discussions included a non-lawyer litigation consultant as well as the witness and the attorney. The court treated the discussions as work product because of their high degree of relevance to the litigation; advice from the consultant, based on such discussions, would also qualify as "opinion" work product.[51]

Documents prepared by an environmental consultant for a company that was threatened with prosecution under federal hazardous waste laws, can be protected

---

[47] *In re* Seagate Technologies, 497 F.3d 1360 (Fed. Cir. 2007); Jessie Seyfer, *Patent Defendants Score Big at Federal Circuit*, The Recorder 8/21/07 (law.com).

[48] Qualcomm v. Broadcom, No. 08-1199 (Fed. Cir. 2008), discussed in Zusha Elinson, *Ruling in Qualcomm-Broadcom Fight Brings Back Opinion Letters for Patent Cases*, The Recorder 9/25/08 (law.com).

[49] *In re* County of Erie, 546 F.3d 222 (2d Cir. 2008); *see* Mark Hamblett, *2nd Circuit Trims 'At Issue' Waiver's Scope for Privilege*, N.Y.L.J. 10/15/08 (law.com).

[50] *In re* Grand Jury Subpoenas Dated March 24, 2003, 71 L.W. 1015 (S.D.N.Y. 2003).

[51] *In re* Cendant Corp. Securities Litig., 343 F.3d 658 (3d Cir. 2003).

from discovery as work product despite the dual (non-litigation) purpose that the documents could serve in compliance with a CERCLA consent order and information request.[52]

Even if the corporation itself refuses to waive the attorney-client and work-product privileges, a corporate officer testifying before the Grand Jury can waive the privileges. The Second Circuit remanded the matter to consider issues of when implied waiver will be considered fair and when an officer can speak on behalf of the corporation. When a waiver of the privilege is found, fairness demands that it be tailored narrowly to the degree of prejudice suffered by the government from non-production of the documents in question.[53]

Whether it is permissible to consult another lawyer, revealing client confidences, without the consent of the client, depends on the reason for seeking consultation with another lawyer or bar counsel. Consultation is improper with any attorney who represents an adverse party in a substantially related matter, or whose firm does. Otherwise, if the consultation is for the benefit of the client, the consulted lawyer becomes the client's attorney, at least for limited purposes. If no attorney-client relationship is created, then privileged information (confidences) cannot be disclosed, but secrets can be divulged based on the consulted attorney's representation that they will not be further divulged. On the other hand, if the consultation is for the benefit of the consulting lawyer, the consulted lawyer can enter into an attorney-client relationship with the consulting lawyer — and the consulting lawyer must be careful to avoid violating the attorney-client privilege of the underlying client without that party's consent. Consultation with bar counsel is permissible to avoid ethical violations or to defend a lawyer against accusations of unethical conduct, but the propriety of a consultation does not provide implied authority to disclose client secrets or confidences, and the bar counsel does not enter into an attorney-client relationship with the client.[54]

A Texas case sets a new standard for when an attorney can obtain work product from the client's former attorney (disqualified on the basis of conflicts). There is a rebuttable presumption that work product contains confidential information — but the client has the right to rebut the presumption. The client is not required to prove that confidential material is contained in the work product.[55]

California law requires an attorney who receives by mistake obviously privileged or confidential information (e.g., an opponent's work product) to examine it no more than needed to confirm the privileged status of the material. The attorney must then notify the sender of the mistake. An attorney who violates this duty and makes use of the material is subject to disqualification.[56]

---

[52] United States v. Torf (*In re* Grand Jury), 357 F.3d 900 (9th Cir. 2003), *amended* 2/9/04.

[53] *In re* Grand Jury Proceedings, 219 F.3d 175 (2d Cir. 2000).

[54] Maine Board of Bar Overseers Prof'l Ethics Comm., Op. 171, 68 L.W. 2451 (12/24/99).

[55] *In re* George, 28 S.W.3d 511 (Tex. 2000).

[56] Rico v. Mitsubishi Motors Corp., 10 Cal. Rptr. 3d 601 (Cal. App. 2004).

[b] Criminal Law Issues

Significant ethical issues often arise in criminal practice, where it is common for clients to disclose that they are guilty of the offense charged, or of other offenses. The attorney then has to balance duty as an officer of the court against duty to represent the client zealously.

The Sixth Circuit held that claiming actual innocence in a criminal appeal does not waive the attorney-client or other privileges. The District Court was wrong to order the habeas petitioner's lawyer to disclose information about the client's innocence and whether or not the client confessed to the police.[57]

The attorney-client privilege is subject to the so-called "crime-fraud" exception. But the District of Columbia ruled that the crime-fraud exception applies only if the lawyer's services are misused to advance a crime or fraud, whether or not the crime is actually committed. The exception does not apply where the lawyer deters the client from committing the crime or otherwise prevents it. This was a witness tampering case; the lawyer was not required to testify, but the Public Defender Service was ordered to turn over the statement of the allegedly coerced witness unless it could show that production would incriminate the defendant.[58]

According to the Ninth Circuit, in a civil case the District Court must allow both the party seeking discovery of allegedly privileged attorney-client materials, and the party asserting the privilege, to offer evidence when the crime-fraud exception is raised. The court must weigh both sets of evidence before ordering disclosure; the party seeking to vitiate the privilege must prove its assertion by preponderance of the evidence.[59]

An in-house attorney does not fall into the class of innocent attorney who can invoke the work product privilege to prevent disclosure under the crime-fraud exception. The Fifth Circuit's theory is that the in-house counsel's interest in the confidentiality of the documents (as distinct from the corporation's interest) is not legally cognizable. In any event, the privilege belongs to the client, not the attorney.[60]

A criminal defense attorney is required to complete the IRS Form 8300 currency transactions report (cash payments over $10,000), even if this requirement is adverse to the interests of a client accused of money laundering.[61]

States vary in the way they treat attorney-client confidences; this is one area in which departures from the Rules and Canons are quite common. Some states require that attorneys disclose that their clients have committed or intend to commit perjury; other states forbid the same disclosure.

---

[57] *In re* Lott, 424 F.3d 446 (6th Cir. 2005).

[58] *In re* Public Defender Serv., 831 A.2d 890 (D.C. 2003).

[59] *In re* Napster, Inc. Copyright Litigation, 479 F.3d 1078 (9th Cir. 2007).

[60] *In re* Grand Jury Subpoena, 220 F.3d 406 (5th Cir. 2000).

[61] Gerald B. Lefcourt PC v. United States, 125 F.3d 79 (2d Cir. 1997).

Sometimes the line is drawn between information about past crimes (confidential) and future crimes (in which case disclosure may be permitted or required; the nature and seriousness of the crime may also be an important factor).

In California, death threats are exempt from privilege. Therefore, it was permissible for a defendant's former attorney to testify that the defendant told his lawyer that he planned to bribe or kill witnesses against him.[62]

The Ninth Circuit described it as a close case, but ruled that it did not constitute ineffective assistance of counsel for an attorney to inform the police of the whereabouts of two children his client was accused of kidnapping and might have killed. It could be rationalized as the lawyer's attempt to make sure that the client could be charged only with kidnapping, not murder.[63]

[c] Corporate Governance and Securities Issues

In late 2002, the SEC proposed broad changes in accepted concepts of confidentiality. The new Part 205, Standards of Professional Conduct for Attorneys Appearing and Practicing Before the SEC, is part of the SEC Rules of Practice. It covers both house counsel and retained attorneys. The SEC took the position (see Rule 205.3) that the corporate attorney's obligation is to act in the best interests of the issuer and its stockholders; an attorney representing an issuer represents the entity and not its officers.

The initial release of Rule 205.3(b) required attorneys to investigate and disclose what they reasonably believed to be material violations of the securities laws that could be harmful to investors. The attorney was supposed to bring up the matter with the company's CEO and/or its Chief Legal Officer. In this draft, the attorney was permitted and sometimes even had a duty to make a "noisy withdrawal" from representing the corporation. In this circumstance, the attorney's report of irregularities to the SEC would not constitute a breach of confidentiality. Noncompliance could place the attorney at risk of all of the remedies under the Exchange Act, including injunction, cease-and-desist orders, and bans on acting as officer or director.

As you would expect, the proposal triggered vociferous protest, and the SEC tabled the "noisy withdrawal" proposal in favor of a modification that would place the requirement of notifying the SEC of the withdrawal on the client company rather than the attorney — which would ease the conflict between the SEC's initial proposal and the ethics rules of some states. The SEC also narrowed the application of the proposal, eliminating coverage of foreign lawyers and individuals licensed as lawyers but not practicing law.[64]

The SEC made its enforcement manual (nicknamed the "Red Book") public for the first time in late 2008. The manual informs staffers to refer any potential

---

[62] California v. Dang, 113 Cal. Rptr. 2d 763 (Cal. App. 2001).

[63] McClure v. Thompson, 323 F.3d 1233 (9th Cir. 2003).

[64] Tamara Loomis and Otis Bilodeau, *SEC Eases Off on Provisions for Attorneys*, N.Y.L.J.1/24/03 (law.com).

issue of waiver to a supervisor; staffers should not ask parties to waive attorney-client or work product privilege. The manual says that if a party seeks cooperation credit for timely disclosure of relevant information, the party must disclose all such facts in the party's possession, but staff should work with discloser to find ways to get info that will not result in waiver of privilege.[65]

In the fall of 2005, the Fifth Circuit made it possible for Texas in-house attorneys to bring whistleblower suits against their employers. In the past, such suits had been precluded by claims that the attorney-client privilege prevented disclosure of important evidence.[66]

Early in 2006, the North Carolina State Bar Ethics Committee[67] opined that an attorney representing a public company can legitimately observe the Sarbanes-Oxley regulations and disclose confidential information about corporate wrong-doing to the SEC, even if the attorney violates state ethics rules, because the SEC rules preempt the state rules of attorney conduct.

By analogy with ethics complaints against lawyers, the New York Court of Appeals held that U-5 forms (explaining termination of securities industry employees) are absolutely privileged, because the matter could become the foundation of an ethics proceeding. Employers have to be able to be completely candid on U-5s to protect the process.[68]

[7] Rule 1.7 Conflict of Interest

This is not a problem for corporate counsel, who represent the company they work for (or at least is not a problem until they change jobs). When a corporate in-house lawyer is hired by a law firm, the law firm can represent new clients with interests materially adverse to a corporate ex-employer, without prior consent of the ex-employer, but not if the lawyer in question personally represented the corporate ex-employer in the same or a substantially related matter, or where protected information relevant to the current matter emerged. Mere past employment in a corporate legal department does not always disqualify the attorney, if there was no personal direct involvement or supervision that gave the attorney access to protected information. Rule 1.9(a) on material adverse interest is more relevant than Rule 1.13 on representing an organization. Although consent by the old client can resolve some problems, the new client may have to consent too. And if the lawyer

---

[65] Marcia Coyle, *SEC Changes Tune on Privilege*, Nat'l L.J. 10/20/08 (law.com).

[66] Willy v. Administrative Review Bd., 423 F.3d 483 (5th Cir. 2005), discussed in John Council, *Attorney-Client Privilege Doesn't Shield Company in Suit*, Texas Lawyer 9/7/05 (law.com).

[67] Formal Op. 2005-9, 1/20/06, 74 LW 2547.

[68] Rosenberg v. MetLife, 8 N.Y.3d 359 (N.Y. 2007); *see* Joel Stashenko, *N.Y. High Court Affirms Absolute Privilege for Securities Industry's Termination Notices*, N.Y.L.J. 3/30/07 (law.com). The privilege for ethics complaints was promulgated by Weiner v. Weintraub, 22 N.Y.2d 330 (1968) because of the public interest in maintaining high ethical standards for attorneys. *Rosenberg* means that Fahenstock & Co v. Waltman, 935 F.2d 512 (2d Cir. 1991) (qualified privilege for U-5s) is no longer good law.

does become disqualified, Rule 1.10(a) may mandate the disqualification of the entire firm.[69]

But a law firm or sole practitioner may not be able to accept certain clients, because representing them would be a conflict of interest with current or past clients. Representation that would otherwise be improper is permissible if all the clients involved are fully informed of the potential conflict, and consent to have the attorney continue to represent them.[70]

A lawyer who is approached by a potential client, and who cannot represent that client because the matter is adverse to an existing client, might be permitted to refer the client to another, unconflicted lawyer, but propriety depends on the facts of the case.[71]

The clearest case of conflict is where the second client's interests are directly adverse to those of the first client, but conflicts can also arise on other bases, such as the potential for one client to sue another. In particular, mergers (either of law firms or of client companies) have a significant potential for generating conflict.

Where conflict arises after the second client relationship is created, the attorney is obligated to withdraw from representing one of the clients (unless both consent). An attorney can agree to a secrecy clause in a settlement, even if it has the effect of limiting the attorney's ability to represent other clients with similar claims. North Carolina ethics regulators ruled, however, that a lawyer may not explicitly agree not to represent other clients who have such claims (e.g., other employees charging the same company with employment discrimination).[72]

A conflict precluding dual representation is not necessarily present merely because a lawyer has client confidences relevant to another client's matter, as long as the lawyer cannot use or disclose the information. Conflict exists only if the information affects the lawyer's independent judgment, or if it is necessary to use the information to represent the second client.[73]

Rule 1.5 states that the beneficiary of the services, not a third-party payor, is treated as the client. Rule 1.7 enlarges on this by providing that third-party payment is acceptable if the client is informed of the payment; agrees to it; the payment does not weaken the attorney's loyalty to the client; and the third party has no rights in the attorney-client relationship.

An entire firm may have to be disqualified based on a conflict of any attorney (i.e., a past attorney-client relationship that created an obligation of confidentiality).

---

[69] ABA Standing Committee on Ethics & Prof'l Responsibility, Formal Opinion 99-415, 68 L.W. 2598 (9/8/99).

[70] For example, it is permissible for a lawyer to draft a will benefiting a current client who referred the new client to the attorney, and it is also permissible to represent multiple members of a family if confidences are maintained and the attorney's independent professional judgment is not impaired by multiple representation: ABA Standing Comm on Ethics & Prof'l Resp. Formal Op. 02-428; see 71 L.W. 2326 (8/9/02).

[71] D.C. Bar Legal Ethics Comm. Op. 326, 73 L.W. 2403 (12/04).

[72] N.C. State Bar Ethics Comm. Formal Op. 2003-9, 72 L.W. 2591 (1/16/04).

[73] Association of the Bar of the City of N.Y. Comm. on Prof'l and Judicial Ethics Formal Op. 2005-02, 73 L.W. 2580.

Mergers between law firms — or between client businesses — can also create conflicts. If two corporations merge, a law firm that has represented either is also deemed to have represented the other.

Whether a law firm has to be disqualified from representing a client because of a newly-hired attorney's conflict of interest depends on factors such as:

- Whether there is a substantial relationship between the past and current representation
- The attorney's role in the past representation, especially the degree to which confidences were given
- Whether the attorney has imparted any of those confidences to the new firm; if so, it is disqualified.[74]

Where the past and current matters are both litigation, a substantial relationship exists if the same facts give rise to a material issue in both cases. If the current representation is litigation and the past representation involved non-litigation, background legal work, there is a substantial relationship if facts pertinent to the past representation are also relevant to the litigation.

It is improper for a firm to warn an existing corporate client that an employee of the company contacted the law firm about a potential suit against the corporate client. Even though the employee did not become a client of the firm, New Jersey ethics regulators said that the firm is required to maintain the confidence. Furthermore, anyone in the firm who had contact with the potential employee-plaintiff must be screened from any related aspects of representing the corporate client.[75]

The presumption of shared confidences is rebuttable. For instance, a large firm may include attorneys who never speak or share files; a firm may have formal provisions to prevent improper interchange of information; and attorneys may limit their practice to a particular field of law, thus will not encounter unrelated matters.

But a law firm is not disqualified from representing a corporation in a lawsuit merely because that client, with different counsel, brought similar claims against another one of the firm's corporate clients in separate but contemporary litigation. The situation did not put the law firm in the position of having to establish wrongdoing by a current client, nor was it seeking a judgment that would have a direct adverse impact on a current client. Furthermore, the client was a very large financial institution that had relationships with many law firms.[76]

It is permissible for a lawyer to prepare a client's will that disinherits someone whom the lawyer represents on an unrelated matter, as long as preparing the

---

[74] Kala v. Aluminum Smelting & Refining Co., 688 N.E.2d 258 (Ohio Sup. 1998). Under California law, screening can be used to prevent a newly hired attorney's disqualifying conflict from being attributed to the firm as a whole. The rule of automatic vicarious disqualification was deemed not to fit in with the realities of current practice: Panther v. Park, 123 Cal. Rptr. 2d 599 (Cal. App. 2002).

[75] N.J. Sup. Ct. Advisory Comm. on Prof'l Ethics Op. 695, 72 L.W. 2652 (4/5/04).

[76] Sumitomo Corp. v. JP Morgan & Co., 2000 U.S. Dist. LEXIS 1252 (S.D.N.Y. 2/8/00).

will is a ministerial task. Potential beneficiaries do not have a right to inherit. However, the attorney might be constrained if required to give advice about whom to disinherit, or if multiple members of the family approach the attorney for estate plans.[77]

Missouri held that it was a clear and incurable conflict of interest for a law firm to accept money from a group of potential defendants to develop a class action suit that would ensure that the clients were not sued. Even disclosure would not be enough to resolve the conflict, which impermissibly prevented the attorneys from exercising independent professional judgment.[78]

An attorney who represents multiple clients in commercial litigation cannot use a retainer agreement under which acceptance of a settlement offer is determined by majority vote because a group settlement must be unanimous.[79]

According to the California Court of Appeals, a lawyer who changes firms is not automatically barred from litigating against a client represented by other attorneys in the former firm — as long as the attorney in question did not represent the particular client and did not have access to confidential information about that client.[80]

According to the Southern District of New York,[81] a law firm is barred from representing an employment discrimination defendant after one of the firm's lawyers acted as a mediator with respect to the same discrimination complaint. Mediators must be neutral, so it appears improper for the mediator's law firm to take a partisan stand.

The presumption that confidences are shared within a law firm does not apply to a situation in which separate firms act as co-counsel on a matter. Nor is it presumed that married couples, both of whom are attorneys, will necessarily share confidences and thus be disqualified from representing adverse clients.

It is permitted for an attorney to represent a party even if the attorney's wife is a former director of a corporation that is opposed to the party.[82]

According to the Arizona State Bar, the same conflicts rules apply whether opposing attorneys are married or cohabiting, and they can be opponents on a case only if both clients give informed consent, and the lawyers believe they can represent the clients adequately. Relationship-based conflicts are not imputed to the rest of the firm, but law firms have an obligation to determine whether relationships create the need for additional screening or other precautions to protect confidentiality.[83]

---

[77] ABA Standing Comm. on Ethics and Prof'l Resp. Formal Op. 05-434, 73 L.W. 2518 (12/8/04).

[78] State *ex rel.* Union Planters Bank NA v. Kendrick, 73 L.W. 1192 (Mo. 8/24/04).

[79] Tax Auth. Inc. v. Jackson Hewitt Inc., 873 A.2d 616 (N.J. Super. App. 2005).

[80] Adams v. Aerojet-General Corp., 104 Cal. Rptr. 2d 116 (Cal. App. 2001).

[81] Fields-D'Arpino v. Restaurant Assoc's Inc., 39 F. Supp. 2d 412 (S.D.N.Y. 1999).

[82] DCH Health Services Corp. v. Waite, 115 Cal. Rptr. 2d 847 (Cal. App. 2002). The court noted that, given the high representation of women in law and business, this situation will continue to occur.

[83] Arizona State Bar Comm. on Rules of Prof'l Conduct Op. 2001-10, 70 L.W. 2364.

A criminal defendant's conviction can be reversed, even without proof of adverse impact, if the trial judge was aware of a conflict resulting from the prosecution of the defense attorney by the office prosecuting the defendant and failed to inquire if there was a conflict.[84]

The federal courts have inherent power to require criminal defendants and their attorneys to reduce joint defense agreements to writing and submit them for review by the court; such agreements are not privileged, and they create a risk of conflict of interest that could cause a later mistrial or reversal of a conviction.[85]

To the Eastern District of Pennsylvania, preliminary telephone calls, without a conflict check, about the possibility of retaining a law firm as co-counsel, did not create an implied lawyer-client relationship that would prevent the firm from representing an adversary.[86]

An attorney who has a non-waivable conflict that precludes handling a case personally is not permitted to accept a referral fee for sending the case to another attorney, given the requirement (or polite fiction?) that referral fees are paid on the basis of the referring attorney's shared participation in the case.[87]

[8] Rule 1.8 Prohibited Transactions

This is something of an omnibus rule, covering several related situations. Attorneys are not allowed to enter into transactions with a client, or to obtain a business or financial interest that the attorney knows is adverse to the client. Transactions can be insulated by the client's written consent, if the transaction is inherently reasonable and fair, and if the client has been given the chance to seek independent counsel.

It is unethical for an attorney to engage in personal financial transactions on the basis of confidential information obtained from a client, if the attorney's action is detrimental to the client (with an exception for situations in which the client gives fully informed consent). Rule 4-101(B)(3) also prohibits the attorney from using the confidence for the benefit of a third party without the client's informed consent.

A practice much more common during the dot.com boom than it is today was for attorneys to accept part or all of their compensation for representing start-up companies in the form of stock of those companies. A Formal Opinion of the ABA Standing Committee on Ethics and Professional Responsibility[88] states that it is permissible for a lawyer or law firm to take an ownership interest in a client, either instead of cash or as an investment opportunity that arises in conjunction with representation. The Opinion says that Rule 1.8 must be read in conjunction with

---

[84] Campbell v. Rice, 265 F.3d 878 (9th Cir. 2001).

[85] United States v. Stepney, 246 F. Supp. 2d (N.D. Cal. 2003).

[86] Clark Capital Mgmt. Group Inc. v. Annuity Investors Life Ins. Co., 149 F. Supp. 2d 193 (E.D. Pa. 2001).

[87] NYSBA Comm. on Prof'l Ethics Op. 745 (7/18/01), 70 L.W. 2203.

[88] Formal Op. 00-418 (7/7/00); *see* 69 L.W. 2067.

Rule 1.5 (fees must be reasonable) and Rule 2.1 (the client must get the independent professional judgment of the attorney at all times).

The "draftsman's rule" prohibits an attorney from drafting any document (e.g., a will) that transfers property to the attorney or a close family member of the attorney, unless the transferor is also a relative. An ethics opinion finds that it is not permissible for a lawyer who is on his church's legacy committee to prepare wills for parishioners who want to leave money to the church. The conflict (between exercising independent judgment about the optimum estate plan for the client, and enhancing the bequests to the church) was held to be so severe that it could not be resolved by consultation or even by the client's consent.[89]

During the pendency of any case, the attorney is forbidden to get any publication or other media rights from the client.

It is unethical for an attorney to give financial assistance to a client, with two exceptions. The attorney can pay court costs and expenses for an indigent client. In a contingent-fee case, the attorney can advance the court costs, but the client will have to repay the attorney out of the proceeds. It is unethical for an attorney to have an ownership interest in litigation, other than a contingent fee or a lien to ensure payment of attorneys' fees.

According to the ABA Standing Committee on Ethics and Professional Responsibility, it is not always unethical for an attorney to post bond for an incarcerated client. However, it is permissible only in such circumstances as the lawyer's representation of the client is not materially limited by the lawyer's interest in eventually being reimbursed. Posting bond could be ethically acceptable if the amount is financially trivial for the lawyer; if the attorney is a friend of the client's family and can reasonably expect to be reimbursed; if the lawyer reasonably believes the flight risk is minimal; or the lawyer agrees not to seek recourse if the client skips bail. However, it constitutes unethical solicitation under 7.3(a) to advertise for clients by promising to bail them out when arrested.[90]

Rule 1.8 once again returns to the subject of third-party payment for legal services. Payment from non-clients is permitted only if the client gives knowing consent, the attorney-client relationship is not impaired, and attorney-client confidences are not disclosed.

It is unethical for an attorney to represent a client if one of the attorney's relatives is also an attorney who represents the client's adversary — unless the client consents.

Can an attorney represent multiple clients in settlement negotiations? Yes, if all the clients who have lawyers participate in the settlement, and all of them consent to multiple representation after full disclosure.

---

[89] Philadelphia Bar Ass'n Prof'l Guidance Comm. Op. 2003-14, 72 L.W. 2198 (9/03).

[90] ABA Standing Comm. on Ethics & Prof'l Resp. Formal Op. 04-432, 72 L.W. 2541 (1/14/04). The opinion notes that ethics regulators in Kansas, Michigan, New York, North Carolina, Virginia, and Washington have rendered opinions against posting bail for clients.

It is not per se unethical for an attorney to serve on the Board of Directors of a client company, but steps must be taken to cope with potential problems. For one thing, clients must be advised of the problems that could develop. If an actual conflict occurs, the attorney may have to avoid involvement as a director in that transaction — for instance, when the Board votes on the retainer to be paid to the attorney.

[9] Rule 1.9 Representation Against Former Clients

It is unethical to accept a new client whose interests are adverse to those of a former client, unless the former client gives informed consent. For clients represented by the attorney's firm, the ban applies only if the new client's interests are materially adverse to those of the firm's former client, and the attorney obtained confidential information in the course of representation. Once again, the former client's informed consent makes the new representation permissible. Confidences obtained from an ex-client may not be used in representing the new client.

When attorneys change law firms, their past representation may require disqualification of the new firm.

Under New York law, the underwriter/issuer relationship does not necessarily impose a fiduciary duty. The underwriter's duty is to the investors, not the issuer of the securities. Therefore, a law firm hired by an investment bank to perform due diligence for an IPO does not have a fiduciary duty that prevents the firm from representing an adversary of the ex-client in an employment suit.[91]

A Maryland ethics opinion[92] says that it is impermissible for a lawyer to represent a husband in a divorce case after representing the husband and wife in bankruptcy proceedings during the marriage. Both proceedings involve preserving marital assets, and the lawyer may have learned things during the bankruptcy case that are relevant to the divorce action.

Unless it has the informed consent of both, a law firm cannot represent one client in attacking the validity of a patent held by another client. Even though the technology of the controverted patent is different from patents the firm wrote for the second client, this would constitute forbidden directly adverse representation.[93]

The Southern District of New York ruled that a lawyer who defended a disability insurance carrier for several years could not represent a plaintiff in a suit charging the same company with a broad pattern of improperly denying benefits, because the earlier representation gave the lawyer access to sensitive corporate materials.[94]

---

[91] HF Mgmt. v. Pistone, 34 A.D.3d 82 (A.D. 1st Dep't 2006). *See also* EBC I v. Goldman Sachs & Co, 5 N.Y.3d 11 (2005): the relationship between issuer and underwriter is a contractual buyer-seller relationship so, without additional factors such as an advisory role, the relationship is not fiduciary.

[92] Maryland State Bar Ass'n Comm. on Ethics Op. 02-10 (12/4/01), 28 FLR 1127.

[93] Virginia State Bar Standing Comm'n on Legal Ethics Op. 1774 (2/13/03).

[94] Lott v. Morgan Stanley DeanWitter & Co. LTD Plan, 73 L.W. 1431 (S.D.N.Y. 12/23/04).

The Southern District of West Virginia, noting that passage of time is only one factor in the analysis, disqualified a law firm from handling a trademark suit against a corporation that received legal advice 17 years earlier from a lawyer who was later hired by the firm.[95]

[10] Rule 1.10 Imputed Disqualification

This Rule relates to the situation in which an attorney may have to decline to represent a client, because that client's interests are adverse to the interests of other clients of the law firm (a firm need not be formally organized — it can be any group of attorneys who hold themselves out as a practice unit). An exception may be made for a Legal Aid organization, where it is common for one of the organization's clients to testify against another client, or for co-defendants represented by the organization to attempt to shift responsibility to one another. (Another possibility is that the Legal Aid organization will be permitted to represent only one defendant, and private counsel will be appointed for the other(s).)

When an attorney who represented a particular client leaves, the firm can represent a new client whose interests are adverse to the original client's — unless the matter is the same or substantially related to the original matter, or other attorneys in the firm have confidential information about the former client. Once again, waiver by the ex-client will remove the ethical problem.

A Connecticut opinion says that a firm cannot rely on the screening process to prevent the conflicts of an incoming lawyer from another private practice from being imputed to all the lawyers in the firm. Screening is an adequate remedy when a former government lawyer moves to private practice, but not for lawyers moving between private firms. The private attorney's new affiliation has to make factual inquiry as to whether the former firm represented defendants whose interests are materially adverse to plaintiffs represented by the new firm, and whether the new hire learned any confidential information about the new firm's clients.[96]

[11] Rule 1.11 Consecutive Government and Private Employment

The "revolving door" is a phenomenon in which public employment often serves as a springboard for lucrative law-firm or consulting opportunities, once the individual leaves public office or employment. Rule 1.11 controls abuses by forbidding attorneys to represent private clients on any matter in which the attorney personally and substantially participated as a public officer or employee. The government agency can waive applicability of this Rule.

A law firm employing a former official is subject to the same restrictions, unless it maintains a "Chinese Wall": i.e., prevents the disqualified attorney from

---

[95] HealthNet Inc. v. Health Net Inc., 289 F. Supp. 2d 755 (S.D. W. Va. 2003).

[96] Connecticut Bar Ass'n Comm. on Prof'l Ethics Informal Op. 01-16 (12/28/01), 70 L.W. 2541.

participating in or being paid a fee based on the matter, and notifies the government agency immediately.

Attorneys are forbidden to use confidential information obtained in government service to represent a client with interests adverse to the discloser of the information. The attorney's law firm is also restricted, unless it can put up a Chinese Wall.

The propriety of a former government lawyer, now in private practice representing a plaintiff in an employment dispute against the city, is regulated by Rule 1.11 (ex-government lawyer cannot represent a client in a matter in which the attorney personally and substantially participated) rather than Rule 1.9 (ban on representing adverse parties in the same or substantially similar proceedings). Therefore, the threshold for disqualification is higher.

California ethics regulators do not permit a lawyer's trade name or professional designation to indicate a current government title or imply that the attorney's practice is connected with a government agency. Other materials, such as brochures or the attorney's resume, can describe either current or former public positions as long as the representation is not confusing or misleading. Former service can be included in the firm's name or professional designation if it is not misleading and it indicates that government status has ended.[97]

[12] Rule 1.12 Former Judge

Absent informed consent from all parties, no attorney can represent a client in any matter in which the attorney was personally and substantially involved as a judge, hearing officer, arbitrator, or clerk to a judge. (An arbitrator who is part of a panel, and who is appointed by one side, is allowed to represent the appointing party in future matters.)

It is unethical for an attorney to seek employment with anyone who was involved in a case in which the attorney was a judge or judicial officer. The exception is that clerks can apply for jobs with an attorney or firm involved in a matter on which the law clerk is working, as long as the potential employer and the law clerk notify the judge before employment negotiations begin.

An ex-judge's law firm is barred from representation to the same extent, unless there is a Chinese Wall in place, and the tribunal in which the matter is pending gets immediate written notification.

[13] Rule 1.13 Client-Organization

An attorney who represents a corporation or other organization may have a potential conflict if the interests of the entity are different from those of its officers and directors (e.g., when there is a derivative suit; when an individual has committed discrimination or sexual harassment that could subject the entity to liability).

---

[97] California State Bar Standing Comm. on Prof'l Resp. and Conduct Formal Op. 2004-167 (no date); *see* 73 L.W. 2483.

Therefore, the rule is that an attorney who represents an organization has to act in the best interests of the organization, if necessary at the cost of the best interests of its officers and directors. The attorney must disclose this fact to the individual, who can and should get separate representation.

However, if the governing authorities of the organization consent, and there is no conflict, the attorney can represent both the organization and individuals working within it.

The August 2003 Model Rules amendments adopted by the ABA's House of Delegates state that, if a lawyer representing a corporation or other organization knows that a corporate officer or employee is engaged in a violation of law that is likely to result in substantial injury to the organization, the lawyer "shall" refer information about the wrongdoing to the higher echelons of the corporation. (This disclosure is excused if the lawyer believes that disclosure is not necessary or is not in the best interests of the organization.) If raising the question internally does not remove the impropriety, the lawyer can disclose the wrongdoing even beyond the extent justified by the amended version of Rule 1.6, but only if disclosure is necessary to protect the organization, and only to the extent required for the organization's best interests.[98]

[14] Rule 1.14 Disabled Client

A client's capacity may be limited by mental illness, age, etc. In such situations, the attorney may have a duty to seek appointment of a guardian or other protective services for the disabled client. But the attorney should disclose the potential disability only to persons, and in contexts, that are in the client's best interests, not those that could be detrimental to the client.

[15] Rule 1.15 Overseer of Client's Property

In many circumstances, including placement of real estate deposits in escrow and settlement of cases and payment of judgments, funds come into the hands of an attorney that are actually the property of clients or third parties. For obvious reasons, attorneys are forbidden to co-mingle such funds with their own funds. The attorney becomes a fiduciary as to such funds, and is responsible for keeping them safe, e.g., by placing them in a safe deposit box or safe.

Disbarment is the usual remedy when an attorney is found to have knowingly misappropriated client funds. In some states, a lawyer can be disbarred for gross negligence in handling client property, even absent knowing conversion. Alcoholism, manic depression, and bipolar disorder have been held not to be mitigating factors that would prevent disbarment of an attorney who has misappropriated client funds or engaged in other very severe misconduct.[99]

---

[98] *See* 72 L.W. 2091.

[99] Attorney Grievance Comm'n v. Kenney, 339 Md. 578 (Md. App. 1995); Florida Bar v. Clement, 662 So. 2d 690 (Fla. Sup. 1995).

The attorney has a duty to notify the client (or other owner of the funds) as soon as they are received, and the attorney must be prepared at all times to render a complete accounting. The records must be retained for at least five years. In case of dispute as to title to the funds, the attorney may have an obligation to retain the funds until title has been established with finality.

The general rule is that, although one or more separate trust accounts must be maintained, there is no obligation to use interest-bearing accounts for this purpose. Some states have IOLTA (Interest on Lawyer Trust Account) provisions requiring part or all of the interest to be applied to the cost of providing legal services for the indigent. ABA Committee on Ethics and Professional Responsibility Formal Opinion 348 (1982) takes the position that the interest belongs to the client. (All of the states have IOLTA programs, but some of the states make the program voluntary rather than compulsory.)

In mid-1998, the Supreme Court decided a case involving the Texas requirement that attorneys put client funds into a separate account, for the benefit of a legal services organization, if the sum was not expected to earn enough interest for the client to offset transaction costs. The Supreme Court ruled[100] that interest on client funds is the private property of the client for purposes of the Takings Clause. The case was remanded to see if a taking had indeed occurred, and if so what would constitute just compensation to the clients.

In March 2003, the Supreme Court once again affirmed the validity of IOLTA programs, in a case renamed *Brown and Hayes v. Legal Foundation of Washington* because the Ninth Circuit determined that the Washington Legal Foundation was not a proper party because it had not suffered any losses. (Brown is a real estate purchaser who alleged that he should have received the interest that was remitted to the IOLTA program.)

The Supreme Court found that transferring the interest to the IOLTA program is indeed a taking, but the taking is minimal, serves the compelling state interest in providing legal services, and is a public use for Fifth Amendment purposes. Furthermore, the amount of compensation due to clients whose interest is submitted to a properly run IOLTA program is zero, because they have no net loss: the Fifth Amendment takings analysis depends on the property owner's loss, not the government's gain.[101]

Issues of stewardship of the client's property also arise in connection with settlements. The New York State Bar Association's take on gag clauses is that settlement agreements should not be drafted to require secrecy with respect to

---

[100] Phillips v. Washington Legal Found., 524 U.S. 156 (1998). On remand, the Fifth Circuit held that the IOLTA program should be enjoined because it committed takings contrary to the Fifth Amendment: Washington Legal Found. v. Texas Equal Access to Justice Found., 270 F.3d 180 (5th Cir. 2001). At first, the Ninth Circuit found the IOLTA program to be an improper taking, but the three-judge panel was reversed by the en banc panel: Washington Legal Found. v. Legal Found. of Washington, 271 F.3d 835 (9th Cir. 2001).
[101] Brown v. Legal Found. of Wash., 538 U.S. 216 (2003).

matters that are not otherwise protectable. For example, the settlement terms in an employment discrimination case can properly be kept confidential, but the agreement should not suppress all information about the defendant's business operations. An excessively broad gag clause has the effect of restricting the lawyer's right to practice law, and thus is unethical. Nor may an attorney properly agree not to represent other employees on discrimination claims against the same employer.[102]

According to South Carolina, the doctrine of champerty which forbids the practice of third parties financing a lawsuit in return for a share of the eventual recovery, is dated, and will not prevent enforcement of a financing contract. In this interpretation, the financing contract is enforceable unless it is unreasonable or involves overreaching by the financing party. The court declined to decide whether a lawyer can ethically finance a suit he or she is not involved in litigating; it is generally improper for a litigator to provide funding for one of his or her own cases.[103]

In addition to financial property, lawyers gain possession of documents that are property of their clients. A lawyer has a duty to preserve and, on request, return to the client whatever materials the client or another lawyer would reasonably require to handle the matter. Attorneys are not permitted to destroy a file without the client's consent if it contains any information of value to the client. Tax returns and insurance policies are considered property of the client, as are the client's own notes and whatever finished work product has been paid for by the client.

[16] Rule 1.16 Decline, Withdrawal, Termination of Representation

It is improper for an attorney to represent some clients under some circumstances. The best case is for the attorney not to undertake improper representation; but if it is undertaken, the employee must withdraw — e.g., if representation is illegal or violates an ethics rule, or the attorney is mentally or physically unable to provide competent representation.

Attorneys are permitted to withdraw at any time that the withdrawal does not create adverse effects for the client. Even if the client is harmed, withdrawal is permitted for good cause, or based on certain actions of the client — e.g., the client commits crime or fraud; the attorney's services have been used to further a crime; or the client fails to meet a substantial obligation to the attorney, after being warned that withdrawal would be the consequence of such failure.

According to Utah ethics regulators, when a lawyer hears the client lie to a judge, it is insufficient to remain silent and continue to represent the client. The lawyer has a duty to try to get the client to "correct" the statement. If the client refuses, the lawyer should seek permission to withdraw from representation. If withdrawal is denied, the lawyer has an obligation to inform the court that it has

---

[102] NYSBA Comm. on Prof'l Ethics Op. 730, 69 L.W. 2102 (7/27/00).

[103] Osprey Inc. v. Cabana Ltd. Partnership, 532 S.E.2d 269 (S.C. 2000).

been misinformed. In this reading, there is no Constitutional right to lie to the court, and silence on the attorney's part would help the client to lie.[104]

When a divorce lawyer discovers that the financial statements submitted by the client to the court omitted significant assets, the lawyer must either persuade the client to correct the document or withdraw it. Although withdrawal would disclose client confidences, the lawyer is required to certify the accuracy of the document, because the court relies on it. However, insofar as fraud requires scienter, if the attorney does not know the client's state of mind, reasonable doubts should be resolved in the client's favor. The attorney can also withdraw from representation, if that would not be materially adverse to the client's interest. Withdrawal is also proper where the client seeks to involve the attorney in the fraud.[105]

If the client's objective is seriously offensive to the attorney, the right to withdraw is not automatic, and the attorney has a duty to advise the client to abandon the objective. However, the attorney must continue to represent even a distasteful client when ordered to do so by a court.

The Seventh Circuit's view is that the District Court should grant a request from a firm that wishes to withdraw from representing a client whose bills are not being paid, unless the timing of the motion is coercive or causes undue hardship to third parties. After all, retaining a law firm is not tantamount to securing free legal aid.[106]

An attorney who terminates representation must notify the client, remain on the case until the client can get another lawyer, turn over all files relating to representation (other than those the lawyer has a legal right to retain), and refund any unused portion of a retainer already paid.

The Alaska Bar Association Ethics Committee ruled that an attorney is not permitted to risk prejudice to the client's case by refusing to turn over an expert's or investigator's report merely because the client has not paid in full for it. Once representation ends, the client is presumed entitled to the file even if full payment has not been tendered. However, the committee ruled that it is not prejudicial to withhold a report (such as a real estate appraisal) that can easily be replicated, even if it would be expensive and inconvenient to re-do the report.[107]

---

[104] Utah State Bar Ethics Advisory Op. Comm. Op. 00-06 (9/29/00); *see* 69 L.W. 2246.

[105] NYS Bar Ass'n Comm. on Prof'l Ethics Op. 781, 73 L.W. 2423 (12/8/04).

[106] Fidelity Nat'l Title Ins. Co. v. Intercounty Nat'l Title Ins. Co., 310 F.3d 537 (7th Cir. 2002). A New York attorney was referred to the Second Circuit grievance panel for refusing to act on a client's immigration appeal because the client was behind in paying fees. The New York version of DR 2-11(C)(1)(F) permits withdrawal if a client deliberately disregards the obligation to pay fees, but the Second Circuit has ruled that non-payment of fees by itself is not enough to justify withdrawal. In this case, the lawyer did not even try to withdraw, much less satisfy all the requirements. In this reading, once a lawyer has been retained, he or she can use contractual remedies to collect the fee, or try to withdraw, but cannot simply abandon a client: Bennett v. Mukasey, 525 F.3d 222 (2d Cir. 2008); *see* Mark Hamblett, *Pay-as-You-Go Lawyer Referred to 2nd Circuit's Grievance Panel*, N.Y.L.J. 5/13/08 (law.com). United States v. Parker, 439 F.3d 81 (2d Cir. 2006) holds that, in general, mere non-payment of fees will not justify withdrawal from representation.

[107] Alaska Bar Ass'n Ethics Comm. Op. 2004-1, 72 L.W. 2528 (1/15/04).

Clients have a right to fire their attorneys at any time, with or without cause, and a terminated attorney has a duty to stop representing the client immediately. In fact, this is a risk of contingent fee representation; the client could fire a lawyer who has put a lot of work into arranging a settlement, shortly before the settlement is consummated. (In that case, the remedy is to sue the client on a quantum meruit basis — but it probably will be impossible to recover the contracted-for contingent fee.) Therefore, it is improper for attorney and client to enter into a contract that prevents the client from terminating representation at will.

[17] Rule 1.17 Sale of a Law Practice

It is permissible to sell a law practice, in its entirety, to an individual attorney or law firm. The selling attorney must either retire; become in-house counsel to a corporation; or take a government job — he or she must not continue to practice law in the relevant jurisdiction.

Clients do not have a vote or veto power over the sale of the practice, but they must be notified and informed of their right to switch to another law firm and get their files back. It is improper to raise fees for the sole purpose of recouping the cost of the purchase.

A discount for lack of marketability should not have been applied in valuing a departing lawyer's stock in an incorporated law firm, because the statutory buyout provision for Professional Corporations does not envision sale on the open market.[108]

According to the South Carolina ethics regulators, a lawyer who has been sanctioned in a way that forbids continued practice of law (e.g., suspension or disbarment) can dispose of the tangible assets of the practice such as a library or office equipment, but cannot sell the practice to another attorney. If there is no partner or other person able to take over the practice, a trustee will be appointed. Under the local rule, "active clients" must be notified of the sale of a practice, but a person who is no longer permitted to practice law has no active clients. A lawyer who gives the mandatory 45-day notice of sale before sanctions become final will be permitted to sell his or her practice, but must disclose the pendency of disciplinary proceedings.[109]

The Southern District of New York permitted a lawyer whose misconduct was a factor in a $385,000 malpractice verdict to sell his law practice to an associate for $2,000 even though it was appraised at only $850. The malpractice plaintiff claimed that the sale was a fraudulent conveyance and the sale price should have reflected $50,000 in goodwill. However, the court said that the $2,000 price was fair in light of the bad reputation the seller earned by inducing the malpractice plaintiff to hire him through misrepresentation of his experience.[110]

---

[108] Wenzel v. Hopper & Galliher PC, 779 N.E.2d 30 (Ind. App. 2002).

[109] S.C. Bar Ethics Advisory Comm. Op. 03-06, 72 L.W. 2179 (9/03).

[110] Baker v. Dorfman, No. 03 Civ. 1168 (S.D.N.Y. 2006), discussed in Anthony Lin, *Judge Finds Little Goodwill in Price for Penalized Firm* (N.Y.L.J. 3/22/06) (law.com).

[18] Rule 2.1 Advisor Role

The attorney is obligated to provide candid advice reflecting independent professional judgment. Consideration of moral, economic, social, and political, as well as substantive legal, factors is appropriate. Both favorable and unfavorable facts should be discussed with the client.

[19] Rule 2.2 Intermediary Role

It is permissible for an attorney to act as intermediary between two or more clients — e.g., if the clients are contemplating a business transaction, or the property of an estate has to be distributed. All clients must consent to the intermediary role. The attorney must withdraw if any of the clients so direct, or if it becomes impossible to satisfy ethical obligations. The attorney can only serve as intermediary based on a good-faith belief that he or she can be impartial and act without prejudice to the interests of any client.

[20] Rule 2.3 Evaluation for Third Party

On the request of a non-client, an attorney can evaluate a matter that affects a client, based on the client's informed consent and the attorney's belief that rendering the evaluation is consistent with effective representation of the client. It is also permissible for the client to instruct the attorney to prepare the evaluation. Normal rules of attorney-client confidentiality continue to apply.

[21] Rule 3.1 Meritorious Claims

The attorney's role as advocate requires the attorney to use the tools of the legal system to their fullest, for the benefit of the client — but not to raise or defend frivolous issues or to abuse the legal system or harass an opponent. (Legitimate measures that have the incidental effect of annoying an opponent are permissible.) However, in a criminal case, certain additional latitude is permissible — for instance, the attorney can require that each element of the charges be proved beyond a reasonable doubt, even though the attorney is aware that the evidence against the client is strong or even overwhelming.

See § 27.05 below for a discussion of sanctions imposed for maintaining baseless complaints or frivolous claims.

[22] Rule 3.2 Expedience

In this context, "expedience" does not have a Machiavellian connotation. It refers to expediting litigation as much as possible, consistent with the client's best interests. Cases must not be delayed for financial reasons (even if the client benefits financially by the delay), and in particular, cases may not be delayed or over-litigated merely in order to increase the fee.

[23] Rule 3.3 Candor

As long as representation continues, this Rule forbids knowing misstatements (including misrepresentations as to the law) to a court. In fact, if the opponent has failed to raise a statute or case adverse to the client's position, the lawyer has a duty to raise it him- or herself. The attorney must disclose factual information adverse to the client's position if it is unknown to the adversary.

The attorney is not permitted to offer false evidence, even at the client's direction. However, attorneys do not vouch for the truthfulness of evidence. They cannot offer evidence that they know to be false, but they are not insurers. It violates both this rule and Rule 3.4 to knowingly destroy evidence in present or potential litigation.

One of the toughest ethical issues is balancing this duty of candor against the duty to represent the client zealously and preserve confidences. After all, many clients have engaged in conduct that could be penalized criminally or civilly.

Rule 3.3 requires attorneys to report their client's perjury to the court. Other options are allowed, however. The attorney can ask to withdraw based on the presence of a fraud on the court; or can apply for permission to have the client testify as a narrative rather than in response to questioning, so that the attorney will not become a party to the perjury.

New York ruled in late 2002 that an attorney who tried to avoid giving damaging testimony at the client's trial by stipulating to facts (including apparent perjury) rendered ineffective assistance by becoming a witness against the client. In this reading, the duty to inform the court of apparent perjury is not a duty to provide rebuttal testimony.[111]

It is a violation of the duty of candor to the court, and perhaps also of federal court rules, if a lawyer ghost-writes pleadings for a pro se litigant. A New Jersey magistrate judge found the practice unacceptable under existing rules, because courts grant extra leeway to pro se litigants, so honest disclosure is required. Furthermore, FRCP 11 requires attorneys to sign and certify the papers they submit to the court. The magistrate judge ordered the lawyer either to enter an appearance or to stop consulting on the case.[112]

According to the Alaska Court of Appeals[113] the duty of candor is violated when an attorney intentionally omits citing a case in a criminal appeal, if the case is the closest to being on point for a crucial issue but undercuts the litigant's position. The Alaska Court of Appeals requires the attorney to alert the tribunal to "directly adverse" authority even if a reasonable argument can be made that the negative case is distinguishable or does not control the issue.

---

[111] People v. Berroa, 99 N.Y.2d 134 (2002).

[112] Delso v. Trustees for the Retirement Plan for the Hourly Employees of Merck & Co. Inc., No. 04-3009 (Magistrate judge, N.J. 2007); *see* Charles Toutant, *"Ghostwriting" Lawyer Effaced From ERISA Case on Ethics Grounds*, N.J.L.J. 3/21/07 (law.com).

[113] Tyler v. State, 47 P.3d 1095 (Alaska Ct. App. 2001).

As for statements made or to be made by the client, the attorney must attempt to persuade the client not to make false representations. For statements already made, if necessary to prevent fraud on the tribunal, the attorney may have to disclose what the client has done.

The New York County Lawyers issued an ethics opinion in mid-2007 stating that it is not a violation of the Code of Professional Responsibility to use undercover investigators to detect the sale of counterfeit goods or civil rights violations — even though attorneys are forbidden to engage in "dissembling" or practice deceit or misrepresentation. (The rules forbid any conduct involving dishonesty, fraud, deceit, or misrepresentation; and lawyers cannot evade the rule by stating that someone else performed the deceptive action.) Oregon is the only state with a rule for use of undercover investigators; it permits covert activity only to find violations of civil or criminal law or constitutional rights. The Alabama State Bar Association has permitted tort defense attorneys to use undercover investigators to detect fabricated injuries. Alabama and Florida permit prosecutors to supervise undercover investigations.[114]

[24] Rule 3.4 Fairness to Party Opponents

General duties as an officer to the court, and duties to the opponent, overlap to a significant degree. Rule 3.4 forbids destruction of evidence or concealing evidence or obstructing the opponent's access to it, as well as falsifying evidence or testimony, or knowingly disobeying a court order or rule. Rule 3.4 also forbids refusal to comply with appropriate discovery requests as well as making improper and unreasonable discovery requests of the opponent. At trial, Rule 3.4 forbids raising irrelevant matters.

With certain exceptions, the Rule forbids any attempt to prevent a witness who has relevant information from coming forward. The exceptions are employees and relatives of the client, in situations in which the other party will not be prejudiced by the failure of disclosure.

[25] Rule 3.5 Impartial Tribunal

Rule 3.5 forbids not only intentional disruption of courtroom proceedings, but also ex parte contacts that are not permitted by law, and attempts to influence officials, judges, jurors, and prospective jurors.

[26] Rule 3.6 Trial Publicity

Attorneys must not make out-of-court statements that are likely to be communicated to the public if they are materially likely to prejudice the court. It is legitimate to disclose that an investigation is ongoing; the schedule for litigating a case; matters of public records; claims and defenses. It is legitimate to ask the

---

[114] NYCLA Ethics Op No. 737; *see* Daniel Wise, *N.Y. Ethics Opinion Makes Exception to Deceit Rule*, N.Y.L.J. 6/6/07 (law.com).

public for help in finding evidence; to ask witnesses to come forward; and to warn the public if there is reason to believe that they are at risk.

Additional information can be discussed in a criminal case, such as that fact that an arrest has occurred (or information that could lead to arrest); which law enforcement officials were involved in the investigation, and how long the investigation took; certain facts about arrested persons.

Although there is no bright line as to what statements could be prejudicial, it is likely that opinions about a suspect's guilt or innocence; disclosure of a confession or statement; discussion of expected testimony or forensic test results; or discussions of the character or credibility of a suspect or potential witness, should be avoided because of their potential for prejudice.

Gentile v. Nevada State Bar, 501 U.S. 1030 (1991) allows the lawyer to rebut recent adverse publicity in order to protect the client from undue prejudice.

The Sixth Circuit would not permit a lawyer to assert First Amendment privilege in his or her own right in connection with statements made or papers filed on behalf of a client, on the grounds that the lawyer is merely doing a job, not engaging in free speech. (The plaintiff was a defense attorney who brought a civil rights suit against a prosecutor, charging that the prosecutor defamed him in retaliation for the defense attorney's exercise of free speech rights — a cause of action that the court ruled out.)[115]

The absolute privilege that lawyers have in judicial proceedings does not insulate them against defamation liability with respect to communications with news media about a pending case. The purpose of the privilege is to encourage zealous advocacy, a value that is not served by unrestricted contact with the press. In fact, a lawyer can be sued for defamation based on communications that more or less restate the allegations in the client's pleading.[116] But at the other end of the time scale, the absolute privilege for defamatory statements made during litigation does not immunize a lawyer's post-trial statements to the media, because the connection to the judicial proceeding no longer exists.[117]

The Massachusetts Court of Appeals ruled that the client's advance written consent is required before defense counsel can wear a microphone at trial in compliance with a request from news media. The court warned that the practice creates a risk to attorney-client confidentiality even if the client assents. The court pointed out that if recordings fell into the hands of the prosecution, they would be admissible because privilege had been waived. In later proceedings, a new trial was ordered, and the new trial order affirmed.[118]

---

[115] Mezibov v. Allen, 411 F.3d 712 (6th Cir. 2005).

[116] Kennedy v. Zimmerman, 601 N.W.2d 61 (Iowa 1999).

[117] Brown v. Gatti, 99 P.3d 299 (Ore. App. 2004). *But see* Krakora v. Gold, 68 L.W. 1255 (Oh. App. 9/28/99): defamatory comments by a lawyer about a third party in a pre-trial letter to the adversary's counsel are absolutely privileged, because the duty of zealous representation had already been triggered.

[118] Commonwealth v. Downey, 65 Mass. App. 547, 842 N.E.2d 955 (2006).

The Third Circuit held that it was permissible for former counsel to talk to the press because, using the same test as for extrajudicial comments made by current participants in a trial, there was no substantial likelihood of material prejudice.[119]

[27] Rule 3.7 Attorney Witness

As a general rule, no one is allowed to represent a client in a case in which he or she must also be a witness (although it is generally acceptable to serve as attorney in a case in which another lawyer from the same firm will be testifying). Exceptions are permitted if the attorney is a witness to an uncontested issue; if the testimony itself relates to the legal services provided (e.g., if the attorney is suing a past client for non-payment); or if disqualifying the attorney would prejudice or unduly harm the interests of the client.

The Arizona State Bar Committee on the Rules of Professional Conduct opined that once an attorney has made reasonably diligent inquiry and believes that the assertions in a client's pleading are true, the attorney can verify the client's pleading, subject to any law or court rule about the proper party to verify a pleading. But if the lawyer gains possession of evidence not obtainable from any other source, Rule 3.7 could lead to disqualification of the attorney as a necessary witness.[120]

New York ruled in mid-2008 that the Dead Man's Statute (CPLR § 4519) does not prevent an attorney from defending himself against disciplinary charges of raiding a deceased client's escrow account. The lawyer could testify about an alleged oral agreement permitting him to retain the funds; he was trying to clear himself, not testify against the decedent's executor, administrator, or survivor. In the Court of Appeals' view, the purpose of the Dead Man's Statute is to exclude the latter type of testimony.[121]

[28] Rule 3.8 Prosecutor Responsibilities

Prosecutors are required to have probable cause for each charge prosecuted. They must make timely disclosures to the defense of both incriminating and exculpatory evidence. Prosecutors must take reasonable steps to make sure that accused persons are advised of their rights and have access to counsel. Unless the accused person intends to represent him- or herself at trial, it is improper for the prosecutor to seek a pre-trial waiver of rights from a person who does not have counsel.

Prosecutors may announce actions they have taken, but may not make statements likely to prejudice the public mind against an accused person.

The prosecutor is also required to make reasonable efforts to prevent members of his or her staff from making statements that would be improper if made directly by the prosecutor.

---

[119] United States v. Scarfo, 263 F.3d 80 (3d Cir. 2001).

[120] Arizona State Bar Comm'n on the Rules of Prof'l Conduct Op. 03-01; *see* 71 L.W. 2563 (1/03).

[121] Matter of Zalk, 10 N.Y.3d 669 (N.Y. 2008); *see* Joel Stashenko, *N.Y. Dead Man's Statute Doesn't Bar Attorney's Defense in Disciplinary Case*, N.Y.L.J. 6/13/08 (law.com).

The Sixth Amendment is violated when a prosecutor deliberately eavesdrops on a conversation between a criminal defendant and his attorney, whether or not the defense can show that prejudice resulted, and even if the conversation occurred before the defendant was charged. (In this case, the lawyer interviewed the client in a sheriff's office polygraph room that had a video camera.)[122]

[29] Rule 3.9 Advocate in Nonadjudicative Proceedings

Clients do not have a right to have an attorney present during a non-adjudicative proceeding of an administrative body. An attorney who accompanies a client to a legislative or administrative adjudicative proceeding must disclose his or her representative role.

[30] Rule 4.1 Truthfulness

In the course of representing a client, it is unethical for an attorney to make any fabricated statement about fact or law to third parties, or to suppress any material fact or misrepresent by failure to inform. Although there is no general duty for an attorney to provide information to third parties, any statements that are made must be truthful.

Different standards of truthfulness are not applied to different kinds of negotiations. The ABA Standing Committee on Ethics and Professional Responsibility ruled that it is not a false statement of material fact, in violation of 4.1, for a lawyer who is engaged in mediation to use "puffing" to exaggerate the firmness of a client's stance. However, lawyers are barred from making affirmative misrepresentations.[123]

[31] Rule 4.2 Communication with Represented Persons

Once an attorney knows that a party is represented by counsel, it is unethical for the attorney to communicate directly with that party (rather than with the attorney for that person or organization) on matters dealing with the subject of the representation. The other attorney can permit such contact. There is also a limited exception for communications by and with government officials.

In determining which employees of an opponent corporation an attorney can speak to without consulting the opposing counsel, Nevada uses the "managing-speaking agent" test. In other words, an *ex parte* communication is improper if the employee has the authority to speak for and bind the corporation. This is not, however, the ABA rule, which forbids *ex parte* communication with any person who supervises, directs, or regularly consults with corporate counsel or can obligate the corporation in this matter, or whose act or omission can render the corporation civilly or criminally liable.[124]

---

[122] State v. Quattlebaum, 527 S.E.2d 105 (S.C. 2000).

[123] ABA Standing Comm. on Ethics and Profl. Resp. Formal Op. 06-439 4/12/06 74 L.W. 2692.

[124] Palmer v. Pioneer Inn Assocs. Inc., 59 P.3d 1237 (Nev. 2002).

A lawyer who communicates (e.g., with a nursing home) in the capacity of court-appointed guardian for a ward is not representing a client for Rule 4.2 purposes, and therefore is not subject to the rule about *ex parte* contacts with a represented person. The committee's rationale was that the court appointment creates a relationship that is different from the relationship between a capacitated person and his or her freely chosen counsel.[125]

According to the Eighth Circuit, it violates Rules 4.2, 5.3, and 8.4 for an attorney — or an investigator working for an attorney — to interview an employee of the opponent to elicit damaging admissions without the knowledge of the opposing counsel. The court upheld evidentiary sanctions for the Rules violations.[126]

[32] Rule 4.3 Communicating with Unrepresented Persons

This Rule prevents attorneys from misleading or exploiting persons who are not represented by counsel by purporting to advise them or act on their benefit, or by suppressing the attorney's actual role in representing someone else.

[33] Rule 4.4 Rights of Third Parties

This general rule forbids attorneys to carry out any actions motivated only by a desire to embarrass, delay, or burden a third party, or to get evidence in any manner contravening the legal rights of a third party. The Canons forbid actions solely intended to harass or maliciously injure anyone, and trial questions intended to degrade a witness or third party.

[34] Rule 5.1 Responsibilities of Firm Partners/Supervisors

Partners and supervising attorneys are obligated to make all reasonable efforts to ensure that colleagues follow the Rules of Professional Conduct. They will be vicariously liable for Rules violations by other attorneys if they order, specifically ratify, or know of the conduct. Reasonable remedial action is required for conduct that can be avoided or mitigated — e.g., removing an attorney from a case where a violation has occurred; giving notice to opposing parties; or reporting the violator to the local ethics committee.

Not only is a law firm vicariously liable for fraud committed by its associate, but the Minnesota Court of Appeals found a firm subject to treble damages under an antifraud statute.[127]

A firm's managing partner is deemed to have enhanced responsibility, over and above that of the firm's other attorneys, for compliance with rules for recordkeeping and bookkeeping. Therefore, Delaware imposed a six-month suspension

---

[125] Maryland State Bar Ass'n Comm. on Ethics Op. 2006-07 (12/1/05); *see* 74 L.W. 2424.

[126] Midwest Motor Sports v. Arctic Cat Sales Inc., 347 F.3d 693 (8th Cir. 2003).

[127] Baker v. Ploetz, 597 N.W.2d 347 (Minn. App. 1999).

on a partner who, although not personally dishonest, failed to review the firm's accounts properly and failed to detect the other partner's invasion of client funds. Sustained and systematic failure of supervision was treated as worse than simple negligence.[128]

Once a former shareholder departs and practices law somewhere else, a professional corporation is no longer permitted to keep using that lawyer's last name. Retaining the name is not misleading if the attorney continues to be a shareholder (although a disclaimer should be used to avoid deceiving the public), but it violates Rules 7.11 and 7.5 (misleading name or letterhead) if there is no ongoing proprietary relationship. The departed attorney cannot be referred to as a partner emeritus if the firm is not, in fact, a partnership.[129]

According to the ABA Standing Committee on Ethics and Professional Responsibility,[130] if a lawyer becomes mentally impaired (including by substance abuse), the firm's partners and supervisors have an obligation to the firm's clients to prevent breaches of ethics. The firm must report breaches that do occur unless the attorney has recovered or supervision prevents further problems from occurring.

In general, a firm can have a relationship with an independent contractor attorney who works solely for the firm, as long as confidentiality and conflict of interest rules are satisfied. If the requirements for that relationship are met, either a part-time or a full-time attorney can be described as "of counsel" to the firm. If the lawyer is of counsel or gets direct supervision, clients generally do not have to be informed of the independent contractor arrangement. The payment arrangement between the firm and the lawyer need not be disclosed to clients if the services are billed as reasonable charges for professional services, not as disbursements.[131]

An of-counsel attorney is permitted to have direct contact with firm clients, as long as the client gets full disclosure, but the attorney should not be held out as a partner or associate of the firm. It is permissible for an attorney not designated of counsel to provide legal services for clients, with or without direct client contact. The firm adopts the attorney's work product as its own even if it does not directly supervise the independent contractor attorney.

If the independent contractor attorney's services are treated as a disbursement, the firm has to charge the client what it actually pays. A markup is permitted only if the actual compensation is disclosed and the client consents. It is also permissible to bill a reasonable amount without disclosure, based on the lawyer's qualifications, just as the firm would do for its own associates.

Disclosure of the arrangement is not required if the attorney acts under the direct supervision of the firm's attorneys. Absent such supervision, the client must be informed of, and must consent to, having the independent contractor work on the

---

[128] *In re* Bailey, 821 A.2d 851 (Del. Sup. 2003).

[129] Maryland State Bar Ass'n Comm. on Ethics Op. 00-03, 68 L.W. 2339 (10/4/99).

[130] Formal Op. 03-429 (6/11/03); *see* 72 L.W. (2003).

[131] Virginia State Bar Standing Comm. on Ethics, Op. 1735, 68 L.W. 2357 (10/20/00).

case. In California, it is permissible to have a contract lawyer make a court appearance on behalf of a client as long as the client receives appropriate disclosures (e.g., what the contract attorney's services will cost). If, at the beginning of representation of a client, the hiring attorney knows that contract attorneys will be used, this should be disclosed to the client. The hiring attorney remains responsible to the client, no matter what the arrangements are with the contract attorney. Compensating a contract attorney via hourly fees does not constitute improper fee splitting.[132]

Since mid-2006, several bar association opinions have dealt with outsourcing of legal services. The San Diego County Bar Association opined that an attorney has a duty to inform the client that work is being outsourced if the client would reasonably expect the work to be done by the firm itself; absent reasonable expectation, disclosure is not required. The L.A. County Bar Association and Association of the Bar of the City of New York issued similar opinions. The local attorney remains responsible for the results; the client cannot be billed more than the direct cost of outsourcing, and confidences must be protected. The contract with the outsourcing firm must include provisions about confidentiality and must supply remedies for breach. The firm hiring outsourced lawyers is responsible for conflicts checks, and the local attorney is responsible for conflicts.[133]

[35] Rule 5.2 Responsibilities of Subordinate Attorneys

An attorney's subordinate position does not relieve him or her from abiding by the ethics rules, but in certain instances, a subordinate attorney might be permitted to rely on a supervising attorney's reasonable interpretation of the ethical rules. Subordination might also be held to negate a wrongful state of mind on the part of the attorney.

[36] Rule 5.3 Responsibilities of Non-Attorneys

A law firm's non-attorney employees, such as paralegals, secretaries, and law clerks are still subject to the Rules of Professional Conduct. Law firm partners and supervisors are required to make reasonable efforts to supervise such compliance. Attorneys are vicariously liable for Rules violations by non-attorneys if they order, ratify, or know of the conduct and fail to take reasonable steps to prevent or mitigate the improprieties.

According to the Utah State Bar Ethics Advisory Commission, it is permissible to compensate paralegals who are employees — but not independent contractor paralegals — with a fixed percentage of the firm's fees. Independent contractors must be paid on a per-task basis.[134]

---

[132] California State Bar Standing Comm. on Prof'l Resp. and Conduct Formal Op. 2004-165 (2004). *See also* George Constant Inc v. Berman, 72 L.W. 1407 (N.Y. Sup. 11/21/03) (counsel of record and per diem attorneys have a duty to communicate with each other, so they are both liable if the per diem attorney fails to make a required court appearance).

[133] Vesna Jaksic, *Guidelines for Outsourcing Grow*, Nat'l L.J. 5/3/07 (law.com).

[134] Op. 02-07, 9/13/02; *see* 71 L.W. 2262.

A California immigration attorney who described himself as an appearance attorney and let unsupervised paralegals represent his clients, who repeatedly failed to make proper filings and appearances, and was often inadequate in the courtroom was suspended from the practice of law for three years.[135]

[37] Rule 5.4 Attorney Independence

Under current rules, attorneys can form partnerships with other attorneys — but not with anyone else. That could change in the future, because there is a good deal of interest in Multi-Disciplinary Practice (MDP) — e.g., a business practice that combines attorneys, CPAs, MBAs, and investment bankers. Another aspect of MDP is employment of attorneys by CPA and consulting firms.

In 2001, the ABA issued a Formal Opinion[136] permitting U.S. lawyers to form partnerships or alliances with foreign attorneys and firms, who will not be considered non-lawyers for Rule 5.4 purposes. The foreign lawyer must be recognized as a lawyer in his or her home jurisdiction, and the arrangement must be lawful in both jurisdictions. The U.S. lawyer or firm must take steps to ascertain the foreign firm's credentials, and must check its compliance with local ethics rules. The Opinion states that a person designated as a *notario* in a civil law jurisdiction should not be considered a lawyer, because the function that he or she performs is different from the job of an attorney.

Non-attorneys (except for executors or other estate representatives of deceased attorneys) cannot own interests in law practice P.C.s. Non-lawyers cannot serve as officers or directors of law P.C.s. Non-lawyers (other than clients) are not permitted to control legal matters or regulate practice by attorneys.[137]

Other than payments to decedent attorneys' estates, and referral fees to nonprofit referral organizations, attorneys are not allowed to share their legal fees.

A New York ethics opinion permits attorneys to share office space and even a receptionist with other professionals, and to refer clients informally. However, referral fees are not allowed; the public must be properly informed about the arrangement; and steps must be taken to safeguard client confidences within the shared environment.[138]

[38] Rule 5.5 Unauthorized Practice of Law

Although this Rule forbids attorneys to practice in jurisdictions where they have not been admitted, its main focus is on practice by non-attorneys. The Rule forbids attorneys to delegate practice tasks to non-lawyers. It also forbids

---

[135] *In re* Valinoti, California Bar Review Dep't No. 96-0-08095 (12/31/02); *see* 71 L.W. 2501.

[136] ABA Standing Comm. on Ethics & Professional Resp. Formal Op. 01-423, 70 L.W. 2288 (8/22/01).

[137] However, D.C. Bar Legal Ethics Op. 322, 72 L.W. 2571 (2/17/04) allows non-lawyers to be "joint venturers" with law firms.

[138] New York County Lawyers' Ass'n Comm. on Prof'l Ethics Op. 733, 73 L.W. 2424 (12/31/04).

non-lawyers to render legal advice to others for pay. (Non-lawyers can appear pro se if they so choose.)

New York permits retired attorneys to practice, although not to charge fees to clients. (Other states, such as Colorado, Ohio, and Utah do not permit practice by retired attorneys, even on a volunteer basis.) New York ruled that it is not misleading for the retirees to use their old letterhead or hold themselves out as attorneys, even though they do not satisfy the CLE requirements for active attorneys. No specific disclosures are required about their status, but even representation without charge is subject to the requirement of competency, so they must self-educate or take CLE to become aware of legal developments.[139]

Searching real estate records is considered factual, not practice of law, so non-attorneys have not committed unauthorized practice of law by doing so.[140]

The North Carolina State Bar ruled that, while it is not necessary for the lawyer to appear at all residential real estate closings, many closing-related functions can only be performed by or under the supervision of an attorney. In this reading, abstracting titles, rendering title opinions, drafting documents, and advising parties on their rights and responsibilities are all attorney functions.[141] In contrast, Kentucky held that it does not constitute unauthorized practice of law for a non-lawyer to conduct a real estate closing, as long as the closing agent refrains from offering legal advice. The court treated the state's earlier ban as resulting from exaggeration of the difficulties of closings and underestimation of the competence of closing agents.[142] A late 2003 Georgia ethics opinion states that only a licensed attorney can select, prepare and execute deeds in real estate transactions, because the clients are entitled to have recourse in malpractice if the process is mishandled.[143]

Only the state bar itself, not a private bar association, has standing to sue a title company for engaging in unauthorized practice of law.[144]

We The People, which describes itself as a "nationwide legal document preparation service," with 170 offices in 32 states, promised the Bankruptcy Court for the Southern District of New York it would refrain from unauthorized practice of law. The company entered into a stipulation under which it would refrain from advising customers about when to file for bankruptcy; would not categorize bankruptcy filings or explain the implications of secured versus unsecured debt; or distribute how-to guides on bankruptcy. Similar actions by the U.S. Trustee were planned for Brooklyn and Connecticut.[145]

---

[139] Ass'n of the Bar of the City of N.Y. Comm. on Prof'l and Judicial Ethics Op. 2005-6; *see* 74 L.W. 2355. Maryland State Bar Ass'n Comm. on Ethics Op. 2006-07 (12/1/05); *see* 74 L.W. 2424.

[140] Cleveland Bar Ass'n v. Middletown, 66 Ohio Misc. 2d 9 (1994).

[141] North Carolina State Bar Formal Ethics Op. 2002-1, 2002-9; *see* 71 L.W. 2675 (1/24/03).

[142] Countrywide Home Loans Inc. v. Kentucky Bar Ass'n, 72 L.W. 1168 (Ky. 8/21/03).

[143] *In re* UPL Advisory Op. 2003-2, 72 L.W. 2324 (Ga. 11/10/03).

[144] GRECAA Inc. v. Omni Title Services Inc., 277 Ga. 312 (Ga. 2003).

[145] Michael Bobelian, *We The People Pledges to Avoid "Unauthorized Practice of Law,"* N.Y.L.J. 5/13/05 (law.com).

It is permissible to hire an out-of-state company that employs both lawyers and non-lawyers to draft a brief. The prohibition on unauthorized practice of law is not violated, as long as the attorney that hires the company reviews the work, exercises independent professional judgment, takes ultimate responsibility for the final document, and discloses the outsourcing to the client.[146]

[39] Rule 5.6 Restrictions on Practice

Another area in which a balance must be struck: the law firm's desire to hold on to its clients, versus the right of an attorney who departs from a firm to continue to practice law. Law firm employment agreements and partnership agreements must not restrict the right to practice law after the agreement ends. (If an improper agreement is signed, only the offeror of the agreement is guilty of a Rules violation. The signing attorney, who presumably had less negotiating power, is not in violation.) However, retirement-related agreements are allowed to restrict future practice of law.

Clients have a right to choose their own attorneys, so an attorney can legitimately retain his or her clients after departing from a law firm, if the clients prefer to follow the attorney rather than remain with the firm.

A law firm's shareholder agreement is permitted to restrict the lawyer's right to practice after leaving the firm, as a condition of receiving benefits under a bona fide retirement plan. The canonical exception for retirement benefits is not limited to the situation in which a firm member stops practicing law entirely.[147]

Massachusetts did not permit a law firm to enforce a clause in its partnership agreement requiring departing partners to remit to the firm a portion of fees earned in the subsequent firm doing work for former clients of the old firm. Such a provision is unenforceable because it violates Rule 5.6 by limiting clients' access to counsel of their choice.[148]

Connecticut's ethics rules and public policy are not violated by a law firm partnership's noncompete clause that rules out retirement benefits for partners who resign and compete with the firm. Although restrictions on the right to practice law are discouraged, they are balanced against the law firm's legitimate interest in preserving its own sources of income.[149]

The Rhode Island Supreme Court's ethics panel ruled that a contract under which a firm pays severance to an associate who leaves the firm, in exchange for a promise not to solicit the firm's clients for two years, is inappropriate, because it violates the rule against restrictions on the right to practice. Clients have a right to

---

[146] Los Angeles County Bar Ass'n Prof'l Resp. and Ethics Comm. Op. 518 75 L.W. 2051 (6/19/06).

[147] Donnelly v. Brown, Winick, Graves, Gross, Baskerville, Schoenebaum and Walker PLC, 599 N.W.2d 677 (Iowa 1999).

[148] Eisenstein v. David G. Conlin PC, 444 Mass. 258 (Mass. 2005).

[149] Hoff v. Mayer, Brown & Platt, 331 Ill. App. 3d 732 (Ill. App. 2002); Schoonmaker v. Cummings and Lockwood of Connecticut PC, 747 A.2d 1017 (Conn. 2000).

continued representation by their preferred attorney, so imposing a condition on severance is just as wrongful as a direct restrictive covenant.[150]

The New Jersey Supreme Court Advisory Committee on Professional Ethics Op. 708 holds that an employment agreement limiting the right of corporate in-house lawyers to change jobs and go to work for competitors is invalid. Such a non-compete agreement violates Rule 5.6 by denying clients the right to retain counsel of their choice. Attorneys are bound to respect confidentiality, so the covenant is not required to keep them from revealing confidences — whether they are in a law firm or a corporate environment. Rule 1:27-2, which grants limited licenses to corporate attorneys working in New Jersey without being admitted there, gives the committee jurisdiction over in-house counsel. Under this rule, out of state attorneys are not required to take the bar exam to work as in-house counsel, but they are subject to a background check and must agree to abide by state ethics rules.[151]

Iowa held that an associate who left a firm and took some cases with him owed the former firm a quantum meruit share of the fees, but not the full amount that the firm would have received if the associate had not left. The court, while not applauding the associate's behavior, refused to award the firm any additional compensatory or punitive damages.[152]

A firm's informal relationship with a major client is not a business opportunity that a former partner can be held liable for misappropriating. The Georgia Court of Appeals indicated that it might have reached a different result if the law firm had operated under a retainer agreement with the business client, or if all the business' legal work had been directed to the firm.[153]

[40] Rule 5.7 Law-Related Services

In a sense, this rule is the mirror image of Rule 5.3. That deals with non-attorneys doing things that might be construed as the practice of law; this deals with attorneys doing things other than practicing law. Law-related services are things like accounting, social work, financial planning, and real estate work that have a reasonable relation to legal services but could lawfully be performed by a non-attorney.

Rule 5.7 permits attorneys to undertake any lawful work — but they become subject to the Rules of Professional Conduct if they do legal work in the course of the job, or indicate that they are acting as the client's attorney. In particular, the attorney is responsible for informing the client that attorney-client privilege is not available in the case of law-related services.

---

[150] R.I. Sup. Ct. Ethics Advisory Panel Op. 2003-07, 72 L.W. 2358 (11/18/03).

[151] N.J. Sup. Ct. Advisory Committee on Pro'f Ethics Op. 708; *see* Henry Gottlieb, *Non-Competes Stricken for In-House Counsel*, N.J.L.J. 7/6/06 (law.com). Connecticut, Illinois, Virginia, and Washington State have also applied Rule 5.6 to in-house counsel.

[152] Phil Watson PC v. Peterson, 650 N.W.2d 562 (Iowa 2002).

[153] Jenkins v. Smith, 535 S.E.2d 521 (Ga. App. 2000).

In 1994, the Supreme Court struck down a Florida rule that forbade attorneys from identifying themselves as CPAs or certified financial planners on their letterheads, business cards, and advertisements. Such identification, if accurate and non-deceptive, is protected as commercial speech.[154]

A California ethics opinion from 1999 says that lawyers who engage in activities (e.g., real estate brokerage or investment advice) that overlap with the practice of law are still subject to the rules of legal ethics dealing with, for instance, confidentiality and conflict of interest. This is particularly necessary if the recipient of the cognate services knows that the service provider is a lawyer. Special care is required for marketing materials that refer to the service provider as an attorney. The requirements for attorney advertising are triggered if the client might reasonably conclude that legal services are being contracted for.

The general rule is that when a lawyer provides both legal and nonlegal services to a client, all services are considered legal for compliance purposes. In this analysis (although some states disagree), getting a fee from a portfolio manager for referring clients does not count as impermissible fee splitting, but it is a business transaction with a client and therefore disclosure and consent obligations are triggered.

Several opinions have been handed down dealing with the extent to which it is proper for attorneys to pay financial advisers for client referrals, and vice versa. The Ohio view is that lawyers can never get fees for referring clients to financial services firms, because the potential conflicts are irreconcilable. The lawyer's duty of loyalty to the client demands making a referral free of conflict, not a referral to whoever pays the largest fee.[155] Although Connecticut, Missouri, and Rhode Island take the position that the client can cure the potential conflict by informed consent, Ohio says that even full disclosure and consent cannot cure the conflict.

When the traffic flows in the other direction, Utah has ruled that it is not per se unethical for a lawyer to take a percentage of the financial adviser's commission from the client as a referral fee. On the other hand, Arizona, Kentucky, Nevada, and New York say that such payments are per se unethical, irrespective of disclosure.[156]

The Maryland State Bar Association Committee on Ethics refused to approve a proposal for attorneys to join with non-attorneys in owning a collection agency.[157]

New York adopted two new ethics rules, effective November 1, 2001, governing relationships between lawyers and non-lawyers to offer integrated services. The services must be strictly divided. Non-lawyers are not permitted to own or manage a

---

[154] Ibanez v. Florida Dep't of Bus. & Prof'l Reg., 512 U.S. 136 (1994).

[155] Ohio Supreme Court Bd. of Commissioners on Grievances and Discipline Op. 2000-1, 68 L.W. 2549 (2/11/00). *See* 68 L.W. 2631 (4/25/00) for a summary of the ethics pronouncements on this issue. *See also* Michigan State Bar Comm. on Prof'l and Judicial Ethics, Informal Op. RI-317 (2/14/00) permitting the lawyer to accept a referral fee.

[156] Utah State Bar Ethics Advisory Opinion Comm., Op. 99-07 (12/3/99).

[157] Op. 2001-21, 70 L.W. 2006 (5/16/01).

law firm, share fees, or affect the professional judgment of attorneys. Names of non-lawyers or non-legal professionals cannot be included in the firm name. The non-lawyer participants must be members of a licensed profession that is subject to a code of conduct. Referral fees cannot be paid to non-lawyers. The clients must be given a disclosure statement explaining the "cooperative business arrangement," and must give their written consent. Whenever a client receives services from a lawyer's ancillary business, a lawyer-client relationship is deemed to exist.[158]

A related question is the captive law firm, a firm that is made up of full-time salaried employees of insurance companies whose professional time is devoted to defending those insurance companies. In West Virginia, attorneys in those firms are permitted to represent customers of the insurer as long as confidentiality is maintained. Florida, Georgia, Missouri, and Tennessee have also allowed captive firms to defend insureds, but North Carolina and Kentucky have disapproved the practice.[159]

With some caveats, the New York State Bar Association ethics committee permitted a plaintiff's personal injury attorney to represent the plaintiff in dealings with a litigation finance company that advances cash for a share in the eventual judgment. The attorney can permissibly charge a separate fee for this service, over and above the contingent fee for the personal injury case. The committee didn't rule on the legality of the financing arrangement; if it is illegal, then the attorney cannot participate. If it is legal, the lawyer should not give information about the case to the financing company without the consent of the client. The attorney should either advise the client about the advantages and disadvantages of such a transaction, or disclaim responsibility for doing so.[160]

Illinois Rule of Professional Conduct 7.2(b) allows lawyers to pay the usual charges of a not-for-profit referral service. This does not violate the policy concerns that mandate the ban on splitting fees with nonlawyers. In fact, under this analysis, public policy favors funding bar groups with referral fees so they can carry out their public functions.[161]

However, early in 2002, the Rhode Island Supreme Court refused to amend the state's ethics rules to permit attorneys to share their court-awarded fees or settlements with not-for-profit organizations that refer cases to them.[162]

---

[158] NYCRR § 1200 *et seq.*, http://www.nysba.org/opinions/mdprules.html, discussed at 70 L.W. 2070.

[159] West Virginia State Bar Lawyer Disciplinary Bd., Op. 99-01, discussed at 68 L.W. 2198 (7/9/99) which refers to the other states' rulings.

[160] N.Y.S. Bar Ass'n Comm. on Prof'l Ethics Op. 769, 72 L.W. 2309 (11/4/03). A similar arrangement was approved by Ohio Sup. Ct. Board of Commissioners on Grievance and Discipline, Op. 99-6, 68 L.W. 2483 (12/2/99). *But see* Rancman v. Interim Settlement Funding Corp., 789 N.E.2d 217 (Ohio 2003), finding litigation financing transactions unenforceable as champerty and maintenance.

[161] Richards v. SSM Health Care Inc., 724 N.E.2d 975 (Ill. App. 2000).

[162] *In re* Rule Amendments, 802 A.2d 721 (R.I. Sup. 2002). Virginia State Bar Standing Comm. on Legal Ethics Op. 1751; *see* 70 L.W. 2036 (5/7/01) permits a bar association's non-profit referral service to be compensated with a percentage of the fee paid by referred clients, in lieu of a flat annual fee.

[41] Rule 6.1 Pro Bono

Although there is no disciplinary requirement of pro bono services under the Model Rules of Professional Conduct, the ABA recommends that all attorneys should do at least 50 hours of pro bono work each year. For this purpose, pro bono work is defined as free or reduced-cost work for people of limited means; organizations that assist the poor; or civil rights/civil liberties organizations that do not have the capacity to pay market-rate fees. Pro bono work must be intended to be gratuitous from the outset — unpaid fees do not render services retroactively pro bono.

Seeking to improve the legal profession (e.g., by lobbying, providing training, or serving on bar association committees) also counts as pro bono work.

The ABA endorses financial contributions by attorneys to legal services organizations, even if the attorney also does pro bono work.

Louisiana Supreme Court restrictions on the types of indigent clients that law students can represent in clinical programs were upheld as Constitutional in 1999. The restrictions do not violate any Constitutionally protected interests of students, faculty, or potential clients. In this reading, future lawyers do not have a Constitutional right to represent clients in court; potential clients have no right to appointed representation in civil cases; and the clinic funders' injury is too theoretical to give them standing.[163]

[42] Rule 6.2 Appointments

Much of the legal work for persons entitled to representation, but who cannot afford to pay privately, is done by court-appointed attorneys. Rule 6.2 says that attorneys must accept appointments unless they have good cause to decline the appointment — e.g., the appointment creates a conflict of interest with current clients; the attorney would suffer an unreasonable financial burden if forced to accept the appointment; or the client or client's actions are so offensive to the particular attorney as to preclude maintenance of an attorney-client relationship.

In 1990, Florida granted a petition to amend the state rules, so that attorneys have a duty to provide legal services when they are court-appointed. The court did not accept opposing arguments that court appointments are a "taking" or involuntary servitude.[164]

The Ninth Circuit upheld (against equal protection and First Amendment challenges) a federal District Court requirement that lawyers who seek criminal defense appointments belong to the state bar as well as the District Court bar.

---

[163] Southern Christian Leadership Conference v. Louisiana Supreme Ct., 61 F. Supp. 2d 499 (E.D. La. 1999).

[164] *In re* Amendments to Rules Regulating the Florida Bar, 573 So. 2d 800 (Fla. 1990). Scheele v. Justices of Ariz. Sup Ct., 57 P.3d 389 (Ariz. 2002) struck down a program under which experienced attorneys could be required to serve, with limited compensation, as arbitrators. However, in late 2007, the Ninth Circuit held that the Appointment System is not a "taking" that requires compensation under the Fifth Amendment: Scheehle v. Justices, No. 05-17063 (9th Cir. 11/15/07).

The requirement was held to be rationally related to the District Court's interest in being able to rely on the state disciplinary apparatus.[165]

[43] Rule 6.3 Membership in Legal Services Organizations

Attorneys are allowed to administer legal services organizations, although this Rule forbids the attorney from engaging in conduct for the legal services organization that is in conflict with his or her other clients.

[44] Rule 6.4 Law Reform Activities

It is permissible for an attorney to advocate changes in the law, even if those changes affect the attorney's clients. If the change would be beneficial to a client, the attorney has a duty to disclose that the change benefits a client, but disclosure of the client's identity is not required. Disclosure is not required if the reform would be detrimental to a client(s).

[45] Rule 7.1 Communication

Rule 7.1 forbids false or misleading statements, or statements that create false or misleading implications, about the services the attorney can render. It is unethical to make unsubstantiated comparisons of the attorney with other attorneys; to make statements that are false or materially incomplete; to provide unsupported guarantees; or to imply that the attorney will exercise undue influence on the legal process.

An attorney has a First Amendment right to make a truthful representation that he or she has Martindale-Hubbell's highest (AV) rating.[166] It is not necessary, the Eleventh Circuit says, to disclose that the ratings are based on subjective data whose sources are confidential, despite the ABA's concern that unsophisticated potential clients might be confused about the value of the rating.

In May 2004, the Texas ethics regulators reversed themselves. The former rule was that lawyers should not refer to themselves as "Doctor" socially or professionally, because it constitutes self-laudation. The current position, however, is that in light of the Juris Doctor or Doctor of Jurisprudence degree, the appellation is not false or misleading.[167]

[46] Rule 7.2 Advertising

Traditionally, attorney advertising was deemed unethical. It is now permitted (as commercial speech protected by the First Amendment), but is strictly regulated. Telephone directory advertisements, print ads, and broadcast (radio, television, Internet) ads are permissible, within limits.

---

[165] Russell v. Hug, 275 F.3d 812 (9th Cir. 2000).
[166] Mason v. Florida Bar, 208 F.3d 952 (11th Cir. 2000).
[167] Texas State Bar Prof'l Ethics Comm. Op. 550, 73 L.W. 2069 (May 2004).

The advertisements can give the name of the firm; its address; names of its attorneys (including the name of at least one attorney who is responsible for the content of the ad); phone numbers; areas of practice; and fees. The names of clients can be disclosed, with their consent, but celebrity endorsements are permitted only if the celebrity actually is a current client. The advertiser must keep a copy of the actual advertisement on file for at least two years.

The Rule is violated by giving anything of value to a person who recommends the attorney, with three exceptions. Advertisements can be purchased at reasonable cost; payments can be made to buy a law practice, as permitted by Rule 1.17; and not-for-profit attorney referral services can be paid their usual fee.

An Ohio ethics ruling forbids advertisements about contingent fees to say "No fee without recovery" or "no charge unless we win." The advertiser must disclose the client's liability for costs and expenses and explain how the actual fee is calculated.[168]

[47] Rule 7.3 Contacting Prospective Clients

This is the rule concerned with solicitation of potential clients. As a general rule, attorneys are not permitted to make direct solicitations (as distinct from generalized advertising) of potential clients. (Exceptions are made for family members or those with whom the attorney already has a professional relationship, and for potential pro bono clients.) Coercive or harassing solicitations are banned, as are solicitations of persons who have indicated that they do not want to hear from the attorney.

Solicitation materials must be labeled as advertising material. This disclosure must be on the front of the envelope of mailed material, or repeated at the beginning and end of a broadcast announcement.

The Supreme Court upheld a Florida statute forbidding direct-mail solicitation of accident victims within 30 days of the accident, on the grounds that the state has a legitimate interest in protecting the privacy of accident victims and their families that is broad enough to justify some limitation on commercial speech.[169]

The Eleventh Circuit has upheld a Georgia law that forbids in-person solicitation, against a First Amendment challenge.[170]

The District of Columbia bar ruled that it is ethically permissible for lawyers to use on-line exchanges where corporations post Requests for Proposals for their legal work, provided that the lawyers' responses to the RFP are not false or misleading. It is also permissible to pay to participate in Web-based bidding services as long as the payments are disclosed to potential clients (so they will be aware of the firm's need to recoup the payments as an element of the fee). The Web can also be

---

[168] Ohio Supreme Court Board of Comm's on Grievances and Discipline Op. 98-9 6/5/98); *see* 67 L.W. 2021.

[169] Florida Bar v. Went For It Inc., 515 U.S. 618 (1995).

[170] Falanga v. Georgia State Bar, 150 F.3d 1333 (11th Cir. 1998).

used to recruit class action plaintiffs, once again as long as the notice is not false or misleading, and proper financial disclosures are made.[171]

[48] Rule 7.4 Communicating Fields of Practice

There is no real counterpart in the legal profession of "board certified" medical specialties, although there are numerous organizations of attorneys within a particular specialty field of practice. Clients often prefer to hire an attorney who concentrates on a particular area of practice and has developed relevant skill and knowledge. Therefore, lawyers have an incentive to hold themselves out as specialists in a particular field, and clients are at risk of inaccurate claims of specialized knowledge.

The balance struck by Rule 7.4 is that, in general, attorneys are allowed to indicate that they practice in particular areas of the law (or that their practice is limited to a particular area or that they do not practice in other areas), but by and large they are not allowed to claim that they "specialize" in a particular area.

This rule is subject to some important exceptions. Attorneys admitted to practice before the U.S. Patent and Trademark Office are permitted to describe themselves as patent attorneys, and admiralty lawyers can describe themselves as such.

ABA-granted specialties and certifications can be advertised. In states where specialty certifications are granted, attorneys certified by the appropriate authority can advertise that fact. Certifications from other organizations must disclose the lack of state authority (or that authorization was denied). If the state does not have a certification or specialty process, this must be communicated by any attorney claiming certification or specialty.

It is permissible to point out that some of a firm's attorneys are listed in a book called "The Greatest Lawyers in the Country," but such inclusion cannot be used to describe the lawyer or the firm as the best or greatest. The Virginia State Bar's rationale was that comparative statements of this type constitute false or misleading advertising because they can not be factually substantiated.[172]

[49] Rule 7.5 Firm Name and Letterhead

Firm names and letterheads must not be false or deceptive. Artificial trade names are allowed, as long as they do not falsely imply connection to a government agency or public organizations.[173] Only firms that really are partnerships can describe themselves as such. The names of attorneys currently holding public

---

[171] D.C. Bar Legal Ethics Comm. Op. 302, 69 L.W. 2515 (11/21/00).

[172] Virginia State Bar Standing Comm'n on Lawyer Adver. and Solicitation Op. A-0114; *see* 71 L.W. 2630 (2/22/03).

[173] The District Court for the District of Nevada found the state rule against most law firm trade names to be invalid, as overbroad (because other rules ban deceptive trade names) and contrary to the First Amendment guarantee of freedom of commercial speech: Michel v. Bare, 230 F. Supp. 2d 1147 (D. Nev. 2002).

office can be included on the firm's letterhead only if the attorney is a current, active participant in the firm's practice.

If the firm has offices in more than one jurisdiction, it can use the same firm name in all of them, but the letterhead must make it clear which attorneys are admitted in which jurisdictions.

The Maryland ethics authorities rejected a firm's use of the trade name of "USA LAW Inc." to practice in the area of homeland security, on the grounds that it incorrectly implies some government affiliation or public funding.[174]

The District of Columbia allows a solo practitioner to use "firm" in the title of his or her practice, but must take steps to avoid confusion, especially if the attorney shares space with other lawyers.[175]

Virginia permits two firms to use the term "affiliated" or "associated" about one another if it is accurate to imply an ongoing, regular relationship between the firms. To prevent the identification from being misleading, any limits on availability to clients of the other firms must be disclosed. However, firms become a single firm for conflicts purposes once they affiliate or associate.[176]

On the grounds that the right to use one's own name is not absolute, the District Court for the District of Connecticut permanently enjoined lawyers from using their own names to start a new firm in the same town where they used to practice with another firm — and where there was a risk of confusion between the new and old firms.[177] Indiana reached the opposite conclusion: unless a law firm has statewide name recognition, it cannot charge lawyers 100 miles away, using their own names, with trade name infringement. In this reading, those who assert the distinctiveness of a name and its association with a particular business have the burden of proof on those issues.[178] The Eastern District of Pennsylvania refused to issue an injunction that would prevent an intellectual property lawyer's former firm from using his name or mentioning the cases he won. The court deemed that the name was not entitled to trademark protection, because it had not acquired secondary meaning — and restricting the use of lawyers' names would make it difficult to create new law firms. In this case, the court did not deem the lawyer to be a major rainmaker, or his name to be a factor in inducing purchase of legal services. It was not false advertising for his former firm to refer to matters that he did handle when he was a partner, and the firm revised its Website to state that he was no longer associated with the firm, and redirecting traffic to his new site.[179]

---

[174] Maryland State Bar Ass'n Comm. on Ethics Op. 04-09, 72 L.W. 2670 (2/26/04).

[175] D.C. Bar Legal Ethics Committee Op. 332 (Nov. 2005); *see* 74 L.W. 2371.

[176] Virginia State Bar Standing Comm. on Legal Ethics and Standing Comm. on Legal Advertising and Solicitation Op. 1813, 73 L.W. 2613 (3/16/05).

[177] Suisman, Shapiro, Wool, Brennan, Gray & Greenberg v. Suisman, 74 L.W. 1575 (D. Conn. 2/15/06).

[178] Keaton and Keaton v. Keaton, 842 N.E.2d 816 (Ind. 2006).

[179] Tillery v. Leonard & Sciolla, No. 05-6182 (E.D. Pa. June 9, 2006); *see* Shannon P. Duffy, Lawyer's Name Not Entitled to Trademark Protection, The Legal Intelligencer 6/15/06 (law.com).

[50] Rule 8.1 Admission to the Bar

Each state's highest court has the exclusive right to regulate Bar membership, including admission and discipline (in the federal system, the Supreme Court has this role). Rule 8.1 imposes similar duties in the context of both admission and bar discipline.

The Rule forbids knowing false statements; knowing failure to disclose facts needed to correct an error; or failure to provide information sought by an admitting or disciplinary board, except to the extent that the information is privileged (as defined by Rule 1.6), or that a Fifth Amendment privilege can be asserted.[180]

Admission to the bar of a Court of Appeals, as stated by Federal Rules of Appellate Procedure 46, requires the attorney to be of good moral and professional character. He or she must already be admitted to the bar of the highest court of a state; the U.S. Supreme Court; another Court of Appeals; or a District Court. The attorney must apply for admission and swear or affirm to act as an "attorney and counselor of this court, uprightly and according to law" and to support the Constitution of the United States. Suspension or disbarment from the Court of Appeals bar is a consequence of being suspended or disbarred elsewhere, or being guilty of "conduct unbecoming a member of the court's bar."

The Mississippi rule is that out-of-state lawyers who consult with local counsel must be admitted *pro haec vice* before their names can be used in a pleading, and before they appear at a hearing.[181]

The Fifth Circuit upheld the state bar rule requiring every applicant for bar admission to be a U.S. citizen or resident alien, finding it to be valid as rationally related to the state objective of regulating attorney conduct.[182]

The Ninth Circuit upheld Arizona's limits on *pro haec vice* admissions, dismissing claims involving antitrust, the attorney's civil rights, and the client's First Amendment privilege to choose their own counsel. The court found the state rules reasonable, and also found state officials personally immune under the "state action" doctrine.[183]

The Ninth Circuit permitted the District Court for the District of Arizona to give retroactive application to a new admissions rule that limits federal bar membership to attorneys who belong to the Arizona state bar, because the rule bears a rational relationship to the District Court's interest in relying on the state bar for attorney discipline.[184]

A non-resident member of a bar can be required to maintain an office and attend CLE programs in the state given the state's legitimate interest in encouraging full-time practice of law and well-informed attorneys. The requirements

---

[180] Spevack v. Klien, 385 U.S. 511 (1967).
[181] *In re* Williamson, 838 So. 2d 226 (Miss. 2002).
[182] Le Clerc v. Webb, 419 F.3d 405 (5th Cir. 2005).
[183] Mothershed v. Justices of the Ariz. Supr. Ct., 410 F.3d 602 (9th Cir. 2005).
[184] Gallo v. U.S. Dist. Ct. for the District of Arizona, 349 F.3d 1169 (9th Cir. 2003).

were found to be equal for residents and non-residents, and not unduly burdensome, hence acceptable despite a possible burden on interstate commerce.[185]

District of Columbia bar regulators said in mid-2005 that status as a contract lawyer makes no difference: an attorney who regularly performs temporary legal work for lawyers and law firms in the District of Columbia must become admitted there, although admission is not required for a lawyer who practices in another jurisdiction and only accepts incidental contract assignments. Furthermore, Rule 49(c)(8) requires contract attorneys awaiting admission to disclose their bar status on business documents and Web sites and other media made available to the public.[186]

The Arkansas Bar Association permits lawyers not admitted in the state to work for an Arkansas firm on a temporary basis, as long as they do not engage in unauthorized practice of law or hold themselves out as being licensed in the state. Association is permitted only for a reasonable period of time, and the out-of-state lawyer is required to take steps to achieve admission.[187]

According to the Fourth Circuit, a state can maintain a rule conditioning *pro haec vice* admission on sponsorship by a local lawyer who has an office and practices daily within the state. In this reading, practicing law is a fundamental right subject to the Privileges and Immunities clause, but sponsoring the provisional admission of other attorneys is not a fundamental part of law practice. But the Eleventh Circuit held that for a District Court to deny a *pro haec vice* application for admission to the federal courts, it must demonstrate violation of the rules of professional conduct serious enough to justify disbarment.[188]

The Fourth Circuit upheld the North Carolina rule: reciprocal bar admissions will be granted only to lawyers from states where North Carolina lawyers can be admitted on reciprocity. The rule of comity was held to be rationally related to the state interest in regulating the practice of law, and not to violate lawyers' constitutional right to travel.[189]

A lawyer who has been admitted *pro haec vice* in a case is entitled to notice and hearing before revocation of that admission.[190] The Ninth Circuit ruled that a magistrate judge revoked a *pro haec vice* admission without giving the attorney adequate notice or opportunity to be heard. However, the Ninth Circuit held that where appeal to the District Court is available, the lawyer must use that and not seek a writ of mandamus, which is an extraordinary remedy.[191]

[185] Tolchin v. New Jersey Supreme Court, 111 F.3d 1099 (3d Cir. 1997).

[186] D.C. Comm. on Unauthorized Practice of Law Op. 16-05, http://www.dcappeals.gov/dccourts/docs/rule49_opinion 16-05/pdf; *see* 74 L.W. 2071 (6/17/05).

[187] *See* 73 L.W. 2360.

[188] *Cf.* Parnell v. West Virginia Court of Appeals, 100 F.3d 1077 (4th Cir. 1997) with Schlumberger Technologies, Inc. v. Wiley, 113 F.3d 1553 (11th Cir. 1997). *See also* Paciulan v. George, 299 F.3d 1226 (9th Cir. 2000), upholding California Court Rule 983 [pro haec vice admission limited to non-resident attorneys]; there is no protectable property interest in pro haec vice admission, and it is legitimate for a state to hold its own attorneys to a higher standard than outsiders.

[189] Morrison v. North Carolina Bd. of Law Examiners, 453 F.3d 190 (4th Cir. 2006).

[190] Jensen v. Wisconsin Patient Compensation Fund, 621 N.W.2d 902 (Wis. 2001).

[191] Cole v. U.S. Dist. Ct. for the Dist. of Idaho, 366 F.3d 813 (9th Cir. 2004).

In the view of the District Court for the District of New Jersey, no matter how rude a lawyer was during depositions, he could not be sanctioned by revoking his *pro haec vice* admission, because sanctions are permitted only for misconduct in the presence of the court affecting the affairs of the court or the orderly disposition of the cases on the calendar.[192]

According to the Colorado Court of Appeals, a lawyer who is admitted in Wisconsin but not in Colorado must refund to the client all fees paid for prelitigation legal services in Colorado, because Colorado permits recoupment of all fees paid to unlicensed persons. Subsequent *pro haec vice* federal admission does not entitle the attorney to payment under state law for previous work.[193]

On the other hand, an Illinois attorney who was admitted before the District of Arizona but not in the Arizona state courts was permitted to practice, and receive a fee, for work done in the Bankruptcy Court of the District of Arizona, because the Ninth Circuit treated federal and state bar admissions as completely separate.[194]

The Indiana Court of Appeals did not permit Indiana clients to escape paying their Michigan lawyer for work done prior to litigation on their case merely because he was not licensed in Indiana. The attorney was approached by the clients, not the reverse; he associated with local counsel; he arranged for a settlement; and if the case had been litigated, he probably could have been admitted *pro haec vice*.[195]

[51] Rule 8.2 Judicial and Legal Officials

Although the First Amendment protects truthful, factual statements and opinions about judges, public officials, and candidates, it is an ethical violation for an attorney to make a false statement about the integrity of a judge, hearing officer, public official, or political candidate for such a job. Unethical statements are those that are knowingly false, or made with reckless disregard of truth or falsity.

[52] Rule 8.3 Reporting Ethical Violations

Except to the extent that the information is privileged under Rule 1.6 (e.g., the other attorney is a client) attorneys have an ethical obligation to report major disciplinary violations on the part of other attorneys (even attorneys within their

---

[192] Mruz v. Carrington, 166 F. Supp. 2d 61 (D.N.J. 2001).

[193] Koscove v. Bolte, 30 P.3d 784 (Colo. App. 2001). *See also In re* Ferry, 774 A.2d 62 (R.I. 2001) denying fees to an out of state attorney for services rendered in an administrative proceeding prior to his *pro haec vice* admission. Effective January 1, 2003, lawyers licensed outside Colorado can practice in Colorado on a limited basis if they are not domiciled in and they do not have an office in Colorado where they hold themselves out as practicing Colorado law. There is also a certification process for attorneys not licensed in the state to provide legal services to a single corporate client within Colorado, although *pro hae vice* admission remains necessary for court appearances. *See* http://www.courts/state.co.us/supct/rules/2002ruleschng.htm.

[194] *In re* Kramer, 193 F.3d 1131 (9th Cir. 1999).

[195] Plummer v. Gittleman, Paskel, Tashman & Walker PC, 831 N.E.2d 742 (Ind. App. 2004).

own firms) or judges. The obligation to report is triggered by a Rules violation that involves a substantial question of honesty, trustworthiness, or fitness to practice.

Utah requires an attorney who has actual knowledge that another lawyer uses or possesses illegal drugs to report to the Office of Professional Conduct. Reporting to the lawyer's assistance panel is not sufficient. Exceptions are made where the knowledge is an attorney-client confidence, or was obtained by the potential reporter's service on the attorney assistance panel.[196]

According to the Texas Supreme Court, it is not a breach of fiduciary duty for a law firm partnership to fire a partner who reported another partner's suspected overbilling to the firm's managing partner. The case[197] permits a firm to expel partners in order to preserve relationships within the firm — notwithstanding attorneys' ethical duty to report suspected misconduct.

According to the New Jersey Court of Appeals, a lawyer must disclose wrongdoing by another lawyer that the disclosing lawyer is aware of, even if the victim is not a client of the disclosing lawyer. Rule of Professional Conduct 8.3(a) requires speaking out when a lawyer is aware of an ethical violation. An attorney who knows about theft from an estate is required to contact the Office of Attorney Ethics and, if feasible, the client. Informing the police is also acceptable. However, an attorney who was supposed to take over the practice of a retiring attorney was not vicariously liable for thefts by the retiring attorney, because the practice was never transferred and there was no partnership between the two.[198]

A New York trial court held that the employment-at-will doctrine did not apply to a law firm associate's suit charging the firm with terminating him for refusal to go along with unethical conduct. (He alleged that he was fired for refusing to sign a fraudulent affidavit to cover up wrongdoing at the firm.) A 1992 New York case permits an associate to sue for breach of the duty of good faith, based on a charge that he or she was fired for complying with the duty to report misconduct. In 2006, the same treatment was extended to the definition of attorney misconduct. However, the plaintiff was denied an accounting (he claimed that the firm also owed him money) because law firms are obligated to render accountings only to partners.[199]

In addition to the obligation to report practitioner misconduct, the ABA Standing Committee on Ethics and Professional Responsibility requires a lawyer to report crimes, ethics violations, or other misconduct by a non-practicing lawyer that raises a substantial question about that person's honesty, trustworthiness, or fitness as a lawyer. Reporting is required even if the misconduct is not related to the practice of law (e.g., stalking, sexual harassment, drug crimes, domestic violence,

---

[196] Utah Bar Ethics Advisory Op. Comm., Op. 98-12, 67 L.W. 2422 (12/4/98).

[197] Bohatch v. Butler & Binrow, 977 S.W.2d 543 (Tex. Sup. 1998).

[198] Est. of Spencer v. Gavin, No. A-0424-06 (N.J. App. 2008); *see* Mary Pat Gallagher, *N.J. Court Rules Lawyers Must Report Colleagues' Known Misdeeds*, N.J.L.J. 4/25/08 (law.com).

[199] Connolly v. Napoli, Kaiser & Bern, 12 Misc. 3d 530 (N.Y. Sup. 2006), discussed in Anthony Lin, *At-Will Doctrine Is Not Applied to Associate's Suit Against Firm*, N.Y.L.J. 4/12/06 (law.com); *see also* Wieder v. Skala, 80 N.Y.2d 628 (1992).

or willful failure to file a tax return). (Model Rule 8.4 permits discipline of a non-practicing lawyer for conduct involving dishonesty, fraud, deceit, or misrepresentation.) However, the reporting lawyer requires the informed consent of the client before making a report that requires disclosure of confidential client information.[200]

[53] Rule 8.4 Professional Misconduct

An attorney is guilty of professional misconduct by committing any criminal act which reflects on his or her honesty, trustworthiness or fitness to practice. This applies to actions such as fraud or intentional securities law violations, but not matters of moral turpitude such as non-criminal sexual conduct. The Rules also forbid dishonesty, fraud, deceit, misrepresentation, and actions that prejudice the administration of justice.

It is also professional misconduct to induce someone else (another attorney or a judicial officer) to violate ethical rules, or to induce a violation by someone else. A good faith belief that the attorney did not have a duty is a defense to professional misconduct charges. Nothing in federal law precludes a state from disbarring an attorney for misconduct in the course of federal immigration practice.[201]

A 1998 Illinois case holds that an attorney's alleged over-billing of a client is not covered by the state's Consumer Fraud Act, in that billing is part of the fiduciary obligation to the client, which is already subject to regulation under the rules of ethics.[202]

Unless the jurisdiction has a specific rule on the subject, sexual relations with a divorce client are not a per se breach of professional responsibility. But, according to the West Virginia Supreme Court, the attorney can be disqualified from further representation of that client if other ethical rules, such as those involving conflict of interest, are violated.[203] A client's claim that the lawyer initiated a coercive sexual relationship states a claim for battery, but not for negligence, breach of fiduciary duty, or malpractice (because the quality of representation was not affected).[204]

On a related issue, in March 2008, the Judicial Conference (the policy-making group for the federal judiciary) adopted the first binding uniform national procedures for handling complaints of judicial misconduct. Each circuit is directed to create a committee of at least three judges to investigate complaints where the facts are genuinely in dispute. Complaints are not made public unless they result in a sanction of a judge. Although there are about 600–800 complaints

---

[200] ABA Standing Comm. on Ethics and Prof'l Resp. Formal Op. 04-433; *see* 73 L.W. 2291 (8/25/04).

[201] Gadda v. Ashcroft, 363 F.3d 861 (9th Cir. 2004).

[202] Cripe v. Leiter, 703 N.E.2d 100 (Ill. 1998).

[203] Musick v. Musick, 453 S.E.2d 361 (W. Va. Sup. 1995).

[204] Kling v. Landry, 686 N.E.2d 33 (Ill. App. 1997).

made each year against judges, only a handful make allegations requiring investigation.[205]

[54] Rule 8.5 Discipline Authority

Attorney discipline takes four successively more severe forms. A private reprimand, directed by a disciplinary board to an attorney who has been found to have committed an ethics violation, is reflected in that attorney's file, but not published. A public reprimand is both reflected in the attorney's file and subject to publication. Suspension temporarily removes the attorney's authorization to practice law in the jurisdiction issuing the ruling. Disbarment is permanent although in appropriate cases it can be reversed and the attorney re-admitted to the practice of law.

A 2004 Tennessee decision holds that a confidentiality rule that blocks public dissemination of any information about pending disciplinary cases is invalid as an unconstitutional restriction on free speech. In this reading, the legitimate state interests in protecting witnesses and not giving undue publicity to meritless complaints are not enough to justify a complete information blackout. The court suggested that the proper balance would be to lift the confidentiality requirement once a formal petition to institute discipline is filed.[206] California's State Bar Governors voted to post pending disciplinary charges against attorneys online, in searchable form. The charges have been public records for more than 20 years, but previously, it was necessary to call, write, or go to State Bar headquarters to get the information. Attorneys objected to posting of accusations, but the State Bar said that 92% of charges are found to be valid.[207]

It should be noted that attorneys are not only subject to discipline in the jurisdiction in which the ethical violation occurred, but in all jurisdictions where the attorney is admitted to practice.

When patent lawyers are doing patent work, they are nevertheless subject to state professional conduct rules, including disciplinary investigations. Even though federal courts have exclusive original jurisdiction over patent actions and the PTO has power to regulate patent attorneys, Congress did not intend to preempt state law disciplinary powers over patent attorneys.[208]

A Michigan lawyer who is also licensed in Wisconsin can be disciplined in Wisconsin for violating the Michigan rules in a Michigan court; Rule 8.5(a)(1) directs disciplinary authorities to apply the rules of the jurisdiction in which the court sits, if the misconduct occurred in court.[209]

---

[205] Tony Mauro, *Binding National Rules Adopted for Handling Judicial Misconduct Complaints*, Legal Times 3/12/08 (law.com).

[206] Doe v. Doe, 127 S.W.3d 728 (Tenn. 2004).

[207] Mike McKee, *Calif. Bar OKs Posting Discipline Charges Online*, The Recorder 7/14/08 (law.com).

[208] Schindler v. Finnerty, 74 F. Supp. 2d 253 (E.D.N.Y. 1999).

[209] *In re* Marks, 665 N.W.2d 836 (Wis. 2003).

State bar officials retain the power to conduct disciplinary proceedings against a lawyer who was acquitted of criminal charges arising out of the conduct involved in the proceeding. Conviction precludes relitigation (in a disciplinary proceeding) of facts conclusively determined in the criminal trial, but does not have a comparable effect after acquittal. The transcripts from the criminal trial can be used for disciplinary purposes in lieu of live testimony, where testimony was consistent and a live witness corroborates the narrative.[210]

Procedural due process, in the form of a hearing prior to discipline, is mandated by *In re Ruffalo*, 390 U.S. 544 (1968), and the actions of disciplinary boards can be appealed within the court system. According to the Fifth Circuit,[211] suspension and disbarment proceedings are quasi-criminal adversary proceedings. Therefore, the attorney's procedural Due Process rights include notice and opportunity to be heard. An attorney's Due Process rights were violated by the absence of a warning that she would be disbarred if she failed to pay court-ordered sanctions by a particular date.

Nevertheless, even possible disbarment is not considered prosecution, so a lawyer who cannot afford to hire an attorney to represent him or her in a disciplinary proceeding does not have the right to appointed counsel, even if the alleged misconduct is a criminal offense.[212]

A state that has suspended a lawyer from practice in the state cannot issue an order preventing him from maintaining an office devoted entirely to federal practice (as long as he remains in good standing with the federal bar). Such an order, according to the Eastern District of Pennsylvania, violates the Supremacy Clause. However, the lawyer must limit his practice to federal court, inform his clients of the limitation, and apply to be reinstated to the state bar when his suspension ends.[213]

A lawyer who has been disbarred for egregious drug trafficking, with no mitigating factors, can never be re-admitted to the bar, because such actions show a lack of moral character that is not amenable to rehabilitation.[214] In contrast, the Fourth Circuit ruled in 2005 that willful failure to pay income taxes (the returns were filed; he chose to repay lenders rather than satisfy the income tax obligation) is not a "serious crime" that would justify disbarment, because it was a misdemeanor and did not involve fraud or misrepresentation, and deceit was not a necessary element of the offense: *In re Wray*, No. 05-1106 (4th Cir. 12/29/05).

A lawyer's obligation to report misconduct to disciplinary authorities is absolute, and is stronger than the policy against disclosing confidential materials surrendered during discovery. Therefore, a lawyer who suspects unethical conduct by a former colleague, who sues the first attorney, can include information uncovered

---

[210] *In re* Segal, 719 N.E.2d 480 (Mass. 1999).

[211] Dailey v. Vought Aircraft Co., 141 F.3d 224 (5th Cir. 1998).

[212] *In re* Harris, 49 P.3d 778 (Or. 2002).

[213] Surrick v. Killion, 73 L.W. 1643 (E.D. Pa. 4/18/05); Benninghoff v. Superior Ct., 136 Cal. App. 4th 61 (Cal. App. 2006).

[214] *In re* Petition for Reinstatement of Massey, 722 So. 2d 452 (Miss. 1998).

during this litigation in an unsealed counterclaim, despite the protective order protecting the materials.[215]

The New Jersey Supreme Court rejected (without opinion) a proposal from the Professional Responsibility Rules Committee to make lawyer/client disputes public information. The current rule forbids parties to a fee arbitration to discuss it. Under the proposal, grievants could comment about the dispute, the arbitration process, and the result, and lawyers would have a right to respond if the grievants were ex-clients. In 2005, New Jersey ruled that the gag rule in lawyer discipline cases (a ban on discussing an ethics case until a formal complaint was issued against a lawyer) violated grievants' First Amendment rights; this application was an unsuccessful attempt to extend the same principle to fee disputes.[216]

§27.03 ATTORNEY MALPRACTICE

Malpractice actions can be maintained based on intentional torts (e.g., defamation or fraud), but most cases allege breach of contract, breach of fiduciary duty, or negligence.

The negligence cause of action requires a duty of care. This is clear in the case of a client, but more ambiguous in the case of third parties affected by the attorney's action or failure to act. Attorneys are held to the standard of care of other reasonable attorneys. Issues frequently arise as to the attorney's duty to persons other than the client; in many circumstances, the lack of privity will defeat the claim.

Another required element is breach of the duty of care, which is the proximate cause of damages incurred by the plaintiff. If the alleged malpractice occurred in the course of litigation, the malpractice plaintiff must prove that the suit would have been won (or would not have been dismissed) but for the attorney's negligence, or that the attorney's conduct was the direct cause of unfavorable action at the appellate level.[217]

Despite state precedent that forbids parties to sue their lawyers if they are dissatisfied with a settlement, the New Jersey Appellate Division ruled in 2008 that a malpractice action could be pursued against two law firms involved in a close corporation shareholder derivative suit. New Jersey precedent forbids clients who settle claims for less than the claims are worth from suing their lawyers for the difference, but the Appellate Division applied that principle only if the malpractice claim arose from the settlement itself rather than another cause of action.[218]

It was not malpractice for a law firm to fail to question whether its client and a related company could have entered into an agreement to eliminate the tax liability

---

[215] Skolnick v. Altheimer & Gray, 730 N.E.2d 4 (Ill. 2000).

[216] Charles Toutant, *N.J. Supreme Court: Lawyer Fee Arbitrations Stay Private*, N.J.L.J. 7/20/07 (law.com); the 2005 case is R.M. v. Supreme Court, 185 N.J. 208 (2005).

[217] Little v. Mattherson, 114 N.C. App. 562 (1994) [trial level]; Charles Reinhart Co. v. Winiemko, 444 Mich. 579 (1994) [appellate level].

[218] Schulman v. Wolff & Sampson, No. A-4674-06 (N.J.A.D. 2008); *see* Mary Pat Gallagher, *Wolff & Samson, Nixon Peabody Clients Can Sue for Malpractice Despite Settlement*, N.J.L.J.

that was at issue. In 2007, the New York Court of Appeals said that to win a legal malpractice case, the plaintiff must show that the attorney failed to exercise the ordinary reasonable skill and knowledge of the legal profession, resulting in actual damages to the plaintiff — and that the plaintiff would have prevailed absent the negligence of the attorney.[219]

A divorce lawyer can be sued for malpractice for failing to give proper advice about well-established principles of domestic relations law, such as the effect of an ex-spouse's remarriage on the alimony obligation.[220]

The California Supreme Court held in mid-2003 that the same standard is applied in a legal malpractice suit whether the allegedly negligent attorney is a litigator or a transactional lawyer. In either event, to succeed, the plaintiff must show that but for the attorney's failure, it is more likely than not that the client would have obtained a better result.[221]

The Fifth Circuit dismissed a suit against a law firm and lawyer for malpractice in a federal trademark lawsuit. According to the plaintiff, it was malpractice to fail to submit evidence of secondary meaning in a dispute over the use of the "Testmasters" mark for test preparation. The suit was originally brought in Texas state court, then removed to federal court on the grounds that resolution of the malpractice allegations required interpretation of federal trademark law. The plaintiff sought to remand the case, but the District Court found that it had jurisdiction under 28 USC § 1331, 1338(a), and the All Writs Act, 28 USC § 1651. The Texas malpractice rule is that the plaintiff must prove that, absent malpractice, he would have prevailed on the underlying cause of action. The Fifth Circuit held that the mere presence of a federal question needed to resolve a state claim is not enough for federal jurisdiction. Federal jurisdiction exists if the federal issue is needed to resolve the state claim; the federal issue is actually in dispute; the federal issue is substantial; and asserting federal jurisdiction will not disturb the federal-state balance of judicial responsibilities. In this case, the Fifth Circuit found that the federal issue was not substantial enough, and the federal interest was too weak. Legal malpractice is traditionally a state cause of action, and not every allegation of malpractice in handling federal litigation should be tried in the federal court system.[222]

In California, the statute of limitations for a legal malpractice case begins when the client severs the relationship with the law firm, even if the client

---

7/22/08 (law.com). The precedent is Puder v. Buechel, 183 N.J. 425 (2005). *See also* Keltic Fin. Partners v. Krovatin, 2007 WL 1038496 (D.N.J. 2007), refusing to apply *Puder* where the alleged malpractice did not consist of inducing the plaintiffs to settle a claim for less than its value.

[219] AmBase Corp. v. Davis Polk & Wardwell, 8 N.Y.3d 428 (N.Y. 2007).

[220] McMahon v. Shea, 657 A.2d 938 (Pa. Super. 1995).

[221] Viner v. Sweet, 30 Cal. 4th 1232 (Cal. 2003), discussed in Mike McKee, *Calif. High Court: Apply "But For" Standard in Transactional Malpractice Cases*, The Recorder 6/25/03 (law.com).

[222] Singh v. Duane Morris LLP, 538 F.3d 334 (5th Cir. 2008). Air Measurement Tech., Inc. v. Akin Gump Strauss Hauer & Feld LLP, 504 F.3d 1262 (Fed. Cir. 2007), did find federal jurisdiction over a malpractice case about a patent suit, but the Fifth Circuit noted that the case did not discuss the federal issue, and the federal interest may be greater in patent than in trademark cases.

continues to be represented by a lawyer who leaves the firm and takes the client along, because that is the termination of the first firm's representation.[223]

If an attorney permits the statute of limitations to expire, thus making it impossible for the client to be awarded a judgment, the uncollectability of the judgment must be used to adjust the malpractice damages.[224]

Surviving children of a deceased divorce litigant do not have a cause of action against their mother's divorce lawyer for malpractice (failure to resolve her divorce case while she was still alive, so the children's inheritance would not be lost). The Washington Court of Appeals ruled that a lawyer has no duty to the children of his or her clients.[225] However, the successor fiduciary of an estate in probate has standing to bring suit for professional negligence against attorneys retained by a predecessor fiduciary to do tax work for the estate.[226]

LMRA § 301(b) prevents union members from bringing malpractice suits against attorneys that the union hired to represent them in labor disputes.[227]

The general rule in civil cases is that ineffective assistance of counsel is not the basis for retrial or appeal. The remedy for the client's claim that counsel fell below acceptable professional standards lies in a malpractice suit against the attorney rather than in reversal of the verdict. The Tenth Circuit rejected the plaintiff's argument that a special rule should be applied in Title VII cases, particularly where counsel is appointed, implying appointment of effective counsel. But the Tenth Circuit found this argument unpersuasive. A right to effective assistance has been recognized in immigration cases, but on account of the liberty interest in not being deported inappropriately.[228]

Many courts have taken up the question of contribution and indemnity in legal malpractice cases. Maryland joined Illinois, Massachusetts, New York, Washington and Wisconsin in allowing such a defendant to seek contribution or

---

[223] Beal Bank SSB v. Arter & Hadden LLP, 42 Cal. 4th 503 (Cal. 2007); *see* Mike McKee, *Filing a Malpractice Suit Against a Firm? Better Be Quick About It*, The Recorder 9/28/07 (law.com).

[224] Klump v. Duffus, 71 F.3d 1368 (7th Cir. 1995). In fact, the New Jersey Superior Court found that a firm that missed the statute of limitations is not merely liable for the lost recovery (without an offset for the contingent fee the firm would have received by winning the case) but also for the contingent fee the client paid her lawyers in the malpractice suit. The court acknowledged that this provided a windfall to the client: DiStefano v. Greenstone, 815 A.2d 496 (N.J. Super. 2003). However, California held in mid-2003 that, as a matter of public policy, a plaintiff who alleges that malpractice deprived them of punitive damages cannot claim those hypothetical damages as compensatory damages in a malpractice suit. Punitive damages were deemed appropriate as against a defendant acting fraudulently or in bad faith, not an underperforming attorney: Ferguson v. Lieff, Cabraser, Hermann & Bernstein LLP, 135 Cal. Rptr. 2d 46 (Cal. 2003). This is also the New York rule, but Illinois has ruled that the only way to make the client whole is to treat punitive damages lost because of the attorney's negligence as compensatory damages in a malpractice action: Tri-G Inc. v. Burke, Bosselman and Weaver, 817 N.E.2d 1230 (Ill. App. 2004).

[225] Strait v. Kennedy, 13 P.3d 671 (Wash. App. 2000).

[226] Borissoff v. Taylor & Faust, 15 Cal. Rptr. 3d 735 (Cal. Sup. 2004).

[227] Carino v. Stefan, 376 F.3d 156 (3d Cir. 2004).

[228] Nelson v. Boeing Co., 446 F.3d 1118 (10th Cir. 2006).

indemnity from successor attorneys, including replacement attorneys negligent in settling the client's case.[229]

The judgment and the underlying findings of fact in an attorney disciplinary proceeding are relevant and admissible in a malpractice suit against the same attorney. Although the ethics rules are not determinative of civil liability, they do provide evidence of the standard of care.[230]

A client who failed to protest when his attorney introduced a forged document into evidence is *in pari delicto* and cannot sue the attorney for malpractice for damages the client incurred as a result of the misconduct.[231]

In the view of the Third, Sixth, Ninth, and D.C. Circuits (but not the Seventh or Eighth), gross negligence by the attorney is an "extraordinary circumstance" that will justify relief from a default judgment under FRCP 60(b)(6) (the catch-all provision for miscellaneous relief).[232]

New Mexico requires attorneys to disclose the name of their professional liability insurer; the size of the deductible; and their coverage limits. The information is purely for internal bar use, and is not disclosed to the public. Oregon is the only state that actually requires malpractice insurance as a condition of practicing law. In other states (i.e., Alaska, New Hampshire, Ohio, and South Dakota) clients and prospective clients are entitled to disclosure if the attorney does not maintain a minimum level of malpractice coverage. In Illinois, Nebraska, North Carolina, Pennsylvania and Virginia, attorneys must certify on the record whether they have coverage, but insurance is not a requirement and clients need not be notified.[233]

Virginia declined to award punitive damages to a divorce litigant suing the divorce lawyer, on the grounds that although the professional negligence action sounds in tort, it is fundamentally an action for breach of contract, so punitive

---

[229] Parler & Wobber v. Miles & Stockbridge PC, 756 A.2d 526 (Md. 2000) and the cases cited therein. Nor does California have a public policy setting a blanket ban on co-counsel or concurrent counsel (here, a divorce lawyer and a bankruptcy expert) suing each other for indemnification against malpractice damages: Musser v. Provencher, 121 Cal. Rptr. 2d 373 (Cal. 2002). *But see* Kokx v. Bylenga, 617 N.W.2d 368 (Mich. App. 2000) [joint and several liability eliminated; defendant liable only for pro rata share of fault] and Mirch v. Frank, 295 F. Supp. 2d 1180 (D. Nev. 2003) [attorney cannot file a cross-complaint for indemnity or contribution against the plaintiff's current attorney].

[230] Roy v. Diamond, 16 S.W.3d 783 (Tenn. App. 1999). *But see* Rubens v. Mason, 387 F.3d 183 (2d Cir. 2004), holding that the affidavit of the arbitrator who heard the matter allegedly mishandled by a malpractice defendant is not admissible in the legal malpractice case. It is prejudicial because it is almost impossible to impeach, and would carry so much weight that the role of the fact-finder in the malpractice litigation would be usurped.

[231] Quick v. Samp, 697 N.W.2d 741 (S.D. 2005). However, Stichting ter behartiging v. Schreiber, 327 F.3d 173 (2d Cir. 2003) permits a corporation to allege that its violation of the Foreign Corrupt Practices Act conviction was the product of bad legal advice, because the conviction does not require knowledge that the conduct was illegal.

[232] Community Dental Services v. Tani, 282 F.3d 1164 (9th Cir. 2002).

[233] *In re* Mandatory Disclosure of Prof'l Liability Ins. Coverage, N.M. No. 05-8500 (N.M. Sup. Ct. 7/29/05); 74 L.W. 2083; *see also In re* Amendment of Pa. Rule of Prof'l Conduct 1.4 No. 50 (12/30/05), 74 L.W. 2435.

damages would be appropriate only if the attorney willfully committed a tort against the client.[234]

An early 2002 case from Wyoming[235] holds that, to get emotional distress damages against an attorney who allegedly mishandled a custody case, the plaintiff must show either physical harm resulting from the emotional distress, or malicious conduct on the part of the attorney.

Where there was no physical impact or bodily injury, Florida's "impact rule" prevents a wrongfully incarcerated malpractice plaintiff from suing the lawyer for noneconomic damages. Furthermore, in the criminal defense context, the attorney is subject only to an award of nominal damages unless the client can show that the attorney acted willfully, wantonly, or maliciously (i.e., not merely failed to provide adequate representation).[236]

A California case on criminal defense malpractice[237] holds that to win the case, the convicted person must be exonerated by a post-conviction remedy. However, in practice, many potential suits will be untenable, because the statute of limitations for the malpractice action is not tolled pending resolution of the appeal or other post-conviction relief proceeding.

An attorney who prepares the statutorily mandated statement of review (certifying that a malpractice complaint against another lawyer is non-frivolous) is entitled to rely on absolute privilege against suit by the defendant attorney. The Colorado Court of Appeals noted that a contrary result would make it virtually or absolutely impossible for any malpractice plaintiff to bring suit.[238]

Jury trial is available in a legal malpractice suit, even if jury trial was not available in the underlying case in which the lawyer allegedly committed malpractice.[239]

§ 27.04   OTHER LAWS AFFECTING THE PRACTICE OF LAW

As a general rule, collection attorneys are not "debt collectors" subject to the Fair Debt Collection Practices Act, but improper activities, such as failure to make required disclosures, can bring them within the FDCPA. See § 14.05[B].

The Third Circuit reversed the District Court and held that a plaintiff asserted a valid FDCPA claim because she received a letter from a collection agency that said that unless she arranged to pay within five days, the matter "could" result in referral to an attorney and "could" result in filing of a lawsuit. The plaintiff's

---

[234] O'Connell v. Bean, 556 S.E.2d 741 (Va. 2002).

[235] Long-Russell v. Hampe, 39 P.3d 1015 (Wyo. 2002).

[236] Holt v. Rowell, 798 So. 2d 767 (Fla. App. 2001). *See also* Cleveland v. Rotman, 297 F.3d 569 (7th Cir. 2002): attorney cannot be expected to foresee a suicide as a result of bad tax advice.

[237] Coscia v. McKenna & Cuneo, 108 Cal. Rptr. 2d 471 (Cal. 2001). Actual innocence is a prerequisite to the suit, because malpractice does not cause harm if a guilty person is rightfully convicted: Wiley v. San Diego County, 966 P.2d 983 (Cal. 1998).

[238] Merrick v. Burns, 43 P.3d 712 (Colo. App. 2001).

[239] Ceriale v. L.A. Superior Court, 56 Cal. Rptr. 2d 353 (Cal. App. 1996).

position was that the use of "could" was deceptive because the agency had no intention of actually pursuing the claim in the court system. The Third Circuit agreed that an unsophisticated consumer might feel at risk of suit unless payment was made within the five days.[240]

It should also be noted that preparing for a trial that is not directly related to a credit transaction is not considered a "legitimate need" that justifies an attorney in seeking a credit report about the client's adversaries. Therefore, a lawyer who does so violates the Fair Credit Reporting Act's regulation of disclosure of credit reports.[241]

At attorney or law firm regularly collects debts if it does so as a matter of course for its clients, for certain clients, or if debt collection is a substantial (whether or not it is a principal) part of the practice. Other factors include number of notices sent for a particular client and the presence of dedicated staff and/or software for collections.[242]

§ 27.05 RULE 11 AND OTHER SANCTIONS

FRCP 11 governs the sanctions that can be imposed on attorneys and clients for improper use of the judicial system, or improper conduct during or related to judicial proceedings. Rule 11 does not apply to alleged abuses of discovery; those are covered by Rule 37.

Sanctions are discretionary with the judge, not mandatory, and the rule directs judges to impose the least stringent sanction that will suffice. In many instances, this will be a private reproof from judge to attorney. If monetary sanctions are imposed, they are generally paid into court. The opposing party receives them only if this is needed for effective deterrence of abusive litigation.

Rule 11 sanctions are imposed for filing papers in litigation that are not supported by evidence. Signing a pleading is tantamount to a statement that, to the best of the attorney's knowledge, the pleading is not only well-grounded in fact, but is either warranted by existing law or a good-faith argument can be made for changing the law. In other words, frivolous filings or statements are sanctionable. If the controverted statements were frivolous as a matter of law, the attorney, rather than the client, must pay the sanctions. A law firm is jointly and severally liable for sanctions with its partners, associates, and employees.

The Seventh Circuit affirmed a $30,000 Rule 11 sanction against Jones Day for filing a baseless counterclaim in a contract suit about the price of stainless steel tubing, calling a witness who supposedly detected overcharges in an audit. However, during his deposition, the witness denied doing an internal audit or

---

[240] Brown v. Card Serv. Ctr., discussed in Shannon P. Duffy, *Wording of Debt-Collection Letters "Could" Bring Problems for Lawyers*, The Legal Intelligencer 10/6/06 (law.com).

[241] Duncan v. Handmaker, 149 F.3d 424 (6th Cir. 1998).

[242] Goldstein v. Hutton, Ingram, Yuzek, Gainen, Carroll & Bertolotti, 374 F.3d 56 (2d Cir. 2004); Schroyer v. Frankel, 197 F.3d 1170 (6th Cir. 1999) [collection activity was not regular when there were 50–75 collections a year, about 2% of practice, with no special staff or software].

even knowing the meaning of the term "audit staff." According to the Seventh Circuit, if Jones Day had not fabricated the groundless claim, the case could have been settled before trial.[243]

Furthermore, Rule 11(c) includes a safe harbor in that the motion for sanctions is served but not filed for 21 days. During this period, the potentially sanctioned party can withdraw or correct the filing that is alleged to be improper. Nor can sanctions be imposed if a case is settled or withdrawn before the court issues an Order to Show Cause with respect to the application for sanctions. The motion for sanctions must be separate, not buried within another motion.

According to the Second Circuit, for a court to impose sanctions *sua sponte*, the test is the lawyer's subjective bad faith, not the objective unreasonableness of the contents of the pleading (at least if the attorney does not have an opportunity to withdraw or correct the pleading).[244]

In 1991, the Supreme Court ruled[245] that District Courts have the inherent power to impose sanctions on forms of bad-faith conduct that do not involve signing pleadings: e.g., attempting to harass an opponent, or fraudulently attempting to deprive the court of jurisdiction. Even voluntary dismissal of an improper or frivolous action will not prevent the imposition of sanctions, although the attorney in question cannot be required to pay the opponent's attorneys' fees for the appeal.[246]

As long as the attorney has exercised his or her best efforts to get the client to comply, the attorney should not be sanctioned for the client's failure to comply with a court order; and, in fact, the Third Circuit said that a lawyer can be sanctioned only if the lawyer (as distinct from the client) has violated a statute or rule.[247] The other side of the coin is that, because it is presumed that an attorney who engages in intentional misconduct during litigation is doing so as an exercise of independent professional judgment, the misconduct will only be imputed to the client if the victim of the misconduct can prove that the client either specifically authorized or subsequently ratified the misconduct.[248]

---

[243] United Stars Indus. v. Plastech Engineered Prods., 525 F.3d 605 (7th Cir. 2008), discussed in Leigh Jones, *7th Circuit Affirms Sanctions Against Jones Day*, Nat'l L.J. 5/15/08 (law.com).

[244] *In re* Pennie & Edmonds, LLP, 323 F.3d 86 (2d Cir. 2003).

[245] Chambers v. NASCO Inc., 501 U.S. 32 (1991).

[246] Cooter & Gell v. Hartmarx Corp., 496 U.S. 384 (1990). *See also* Lasar v. Ford Motor Co., 399 F.3d 1001 (9th Cir. 2005), holding that it was proper to declare a mistrial and sanction an automobile company and its attorneys. It was a violation of pre-trial evidentiary orders against admission of evidence of the plaintiff's drinking and failure to wear a seat belt on the day of the accident to say that the plaintiff "visited some local establishments" and "was a free floating body" at the time of impact.

[247] Universal Cooperative Inc. v. Trial Cooperative Marketing Dev. Fed'n of India, 45 F.3d 1194 (8th Cir. 1995); Martin v. Brown, 63 F.3d 1252 (3d Cir. 1995).

[248] Horwitz v. Holabird & Root, 212 Ill. 2d 1 (2004).

[A] Sanctions Outside Rule 11

Other Rules within the FRCP contain additional sanction provisions. Rule 16(f) penalizes misconduct in the pretrial conference, such as refusal to obey a scheduling or other pretrial order; failure to appear at the conference; appearing at the conference, but unprepared to participate meaningfully; refusal to participate in good faith in the pretrial planning and order procedures.

The sanctioned party must pay the costs and fees resulting from the violation. In exceptional cases, the sanctioned party can be precluded from offering proof on the issues in connection with which the violation was committed; pleadings can be struck; proceedings can be stayed. In the most serious cases, the violating party can be ruled to be in default.

Sanctions cannot be imposed on an attorney for filing a grounded complaint in a proper forum, even if the forum is not the most convenient one for the defendant; if there is a valid legal issue, the improper motives of those pursuing it will not support sanctions.[249]

The Tenth Circuit ruled early in 2006 that 28 USC § 1927 permits sanctions against attorneys who unreasonably multiply proceedings, and attorneys have a continuing duty to re-assess the merits of an existing claim, and perhaps withdraw claims that lack merit. However, this provision does not support sanctions against an attorney who files a meritless claim in the first place.[250]

Even if summary procedures are justified, the Second Circuit ruled that attorneys must be given a meaningful (although brief) opportunity to defend themselves before being held in contempt under Fed. R. Crim. Pro. 42(b). Due process requires that contempt citations will issue only if the element of willfulness is present. The attorney must receive adequate notice that the improper line of questioning fell within a scope already prohibited by the court. In this case, the court's prior rulings did not put the lawyer on notice that the controversial tactic was forbidden.[251]

Various unflattering statements made by a lawyer to a reporter, about a judge ("ignorant" "anti-Semitic" "drunk on the bench") were protected by the First Amendment, so suspending the attorney was inappropriate. Statements about a judge's integrity (other than statements susceptible of factual proof) are protected under the First Amendment.[252]

Criticism of an attorney's conduct, where there is no official sanction order and monetary sanctions have been vacated, is not appealable.[253] In the Seventh Circuit, a lawyer can only appeal criticism in a published order (in this case, being

---

[249] Sussman v. Bank of Israel, 56 F.3d 450 (2d Cir. 1995).

[250] Steinert v. Winn Group, 440 F.3d 1214 (10th Cir. 2006).

[251] Doral Produce Corp. v. Paul Steinberg Associates Inc., 347 F.3d 36 (2d Cir. 2003).

[252] Standing Committee on Discipline v. Yagman, 55 F.3d 1430 (9th Cir. 1995).

[253] Williams v. United States, 156 F.3d 86 (1st Cir. 1998). Nisus Corp. v. Perma-Chink Systems Inc. v. Teschner, 497 F.3d 1316 (Fed. Cir. 2007) holds that review is not available when the court accused an attorney of inequitable conduct by failing to inform the PTO of an earlier suit about related patents: *see* Marcia Coyle, *Federal Circuit Denies Appeal by Attorney 'Wronged' in Court*, Nat'l L.J. 8/20/07 (law.com).

called "less than honest" by the magistrate judge handling settlement proceedings) if monetary sanctions are also imposed. The Seventh Circuit will permit a writ of mandamus in that situation, but will not permit an appeal of an order that is damaging only to the lawyer's professional reputation. However, four other Circuits (the Third, Fifth, D.C. and Ninth) will permit an appeal, and the First Circuit allows an appeal, but only if the criticism is specifically referred to as a reprimand.[254]

In the Tenth Circuit, an order holding that an attorney committed litigation misconduct is appealable after the final judgment in the underlying case, even if it does not impose monetary sanctions or a formal reprimand. This is an issue on which there is a wide Circuit split. In the Seventh Circuit, such an order is never appealable; in the Fifth, Ninth and D.C. Circuits, it is always appealable; in the First Circuit, it is appealable only if it is expressly identified as a reprimand.[255]

The Private Securities Litigation Reform Act of 1995 (see § 6.13[A]) imposes sanctions for ungrounded securities actions and allegations in complaints.

A plaintiff sanctioned under the PSLRA must pay all of the opponents' attorneys' fees and costs, even if some of the claims in an otherwise frivolous complaint were meritorious. Adding meritorious claims does not make the frivolity de minimis, so a reduction in the fee award is not justified.[256]

The Eleventh Circuit upheld sanctions for filing documents that included groundless, demeaning attacks on opposing counsel.[257] Censure has been upheld in the case of an attorney who berated opposing counsel, a black woman, for her alleged mispronunciation of words during a deposition. The court rejected the lawyer's argument that his conduct was merely sexist and not racist.[258]

An attorney who filed frivolous, harassing claims against a health insurer was required to pay the insurer's legal fees out of her own pocket.[259]

In Arizona, a firm that allegedly tried to fabricate a bad-faith claim against an insurer to increase the client's recovery — and therefore the firm's fee — can be sued by the insurer for tortious interference with its contract with the policyholder.[260]

In California, an attorney can be sued for malicious prosecution if he or she has good reason to suspect that a suit that has already been filed is without merit, yet continues to pursue a case that is not supported by probable cause. The ruling was based on a conclusion that the harm caused by pursuing a worthless action is at least as great as the harm of instituting it. However, the malicious prosecution

---

[254] Seymour v. Hug, 485 F.3d 926 (7th Cir. 2007); *see* Pamela A. MacLean, *7th Circuit: Lawyer Can't Appeal Judge's Critique*, Nat'l L.J. 5/23/07 (law.com).

[255] Butler v. Biocore Med. Technologies Inc., 348 F.3d 1163 (10th Cir. 2003).

[256] Gurary v. Nu-Tech Bio-Med Inc., 303 F.3d 212 (2d Cir. 2002).

[257] Thomas v. Teanaco Packaging Co., 293 F.3d 1306 (11th Cir. 2002).

[258] *In re* Monaghan, 743 N.Y.S.2d 517 (N.Y.A.D. 2002).

[259] Veneziano v. Long Island Pipe Fabrication & Supply Corp., 238 F. Supp. 2d 683 (D.N.J. 2002).

[260] Safeway Ins. Co. v. Guerrero, 83 P.3d 560 (Ariz. App. 2004).

cause of action is appropriate only in situations where no reasonable attorney could find any merit in the suit.[261]

§ 27.06 REGULATION OF LAW FIRMS AND ASSOCIATIONS

Most law firms operate as partnerships; professional corporations; or partnerships that include one or more professional corporations in their membership. Generally speaking, creation of a law firm is a voluntary event, but "partnership by estoppel" may occur based on office sharing, letterheads, or other manifestations that lead others to believe that the attorneys practice jointly in a law firm. If other people justifiably rely on the appearance of partnership, to their detriment, a partnership by estoppel is created. Furthermore, a partnership by estoppel creates the same obligations with respect to conflict of interest as an explicit partnership.

A branch of a multi-office law firm must be careful that its letterhead accurately represents the composition of the firm and the jurisdictions in which attorneys are admitted to practice. State rules will probably require at least one partner of the firm (not just an associate) to be admitted in state.

Employing a member of a law firm is treated as employment of the entire firm — for instance, in determining whether a conflict of interest has occurred or is a risk.

Although law firm partners are not generally covered by the ADEA, and it is not necessarily unlawful for a firm to maintain an age-based mandatory retirement policy, such policies can lead to challenges. For example, in late 2007, the firm Sidley Austin agreed to pay $27.5 million to settle an age discrimination suit brought by the EEOC on behalf of 32 ex-partners who were demoted to of-counsel status. The firm contended that the demotions (of attorneys most of whom were in their fifties or sixties) were not discriminatory, and were based on performance criteria. The consent decree before the Northern District of Illinois treated the attorneys as ADEA-covered employees for the sole purpose of resolving the claims. Sidley Austin did not admit liability, but did agree not to mandate retirement at 65. In earlier proceedings, the Seventh Circuit held that the firm's governance structure lacked certain indicia of true partnership, so the plaintiffs might be employees. For example, the firm was effectively governed by the executive committee, with little input from the so-called partners.[262]

The EEOC has published a lengthy document about reasonable accommodation for lawyers with disabilities.

Law firms may have to provide reasonable accommodation during the application process, such as sign language interpreters and offering written materials in alternative formats such as Braille or large print. Law firm recruiting Web sites should be usable by individuals with disabilities who use adaptive software. The EEOC's position is that if — but only if — a candidate has an obvious disability

---

[261] Zamos v. Stroud, 32 Cal. 4th 958 (2004).

[262] Anthony Lin, *Sidley Austin Settles Age Bias Suit; No Determination of Merits*, N.Y.L.J. 10/8/07 (law.com).

that reasonably requires accommodation, or if the candidate has revealed the presence of such a disability, the firm can ask if reasonable accommodation is needed and if so what form the applicant wants it to take.

Common accommodations for attorneys with disabilities are adding ramps or widening doorways for workplace accessibility; restructuring the job to remove marginal functions; offering a part-time or other modified work schedule; unpaid leave after paid sick and vacation leave have been exhausted; assistive equipment; qualified readers or sign language interpreters; permitting telework even if the firm does not already have a program; changing supervision methods (e.g., by e-mail rather than face to face); and reassignment to a vacant position. The attorney should indicate if the proposed accommodation has been used already (e.g., at law school; with another employer) and how successful it was.[263]

A one-time general partner in a law firm who claims that he was expelled from the firm in retaliation for his objections to another partner's sexual harassment of subordinates is not an employee for Title VII purposes. Despite his contentions about lack of control, as one of four equal partners he must be deemed to have substantial control over the firm and its employment practices.[264]

[A] Law Firm Partnerships

A law firm partnership shares most characteristics of business partnerships (see § 1.03), including unlimited liability and tax characterization. Each partner is a fiduciary to the other partners.

A law firm partner can become liable for the acts or omissions of other partners if the other partners acted in the ordinary course of partnership business or with the actual or apparent authority of the other partners. Partners are jointly and severally liable for negligence of other partners. Failure to provide proper supervision to associates can also constitute malpractice.

Common law and the Uniform Partnership Act are in agreement that a partnership is not an entity that can be sued for malpractice, but several states have enacted statutes to permit such suits.

Traditionally, all law firm partners were on an equal footing, much like general partners in a business partnership. Associates were given a certain number of years to earn promotion to partnership; those who were not promoted were generally fired. Today, many firms have a two- or multi-tier partnership arrangement, with equity partners at the top and with non-equity partners, counsel, or permanent associates between partners and associates.

Non-equity, income, or junior partners do not contribute capital to the firm, and they are not liable for the firm's financial liabilities. In most instances, they will not have voting rights within the firm. Technically, they are salaried employees of

---

[263] EEOC Fact Sheet, Reasonable Accommodations for Attorneys with Disabilities, http://www.eeoc.gov/press/5-23-06.html (5/23/06).

[264] Solon v. Kaplan, 398 F.3d 629 (7th Cir. 2005).

the firm, probably compensated with salary and bonuses (which may reflect a share of firm profits).

A two-track partnership system can increase the profits available to equity partners; permit retention of attorneys who are a profit center for the firm but for some reason do not merit promotion to equity partner; and can permit demotion of equity partners instead of expelling them for mediocre performance. Demotion can also be used as a transition to retirement for older partners.

A trend from 2008 is for incoming partners (lateral or internal promotions) to be required to take more responsibility for the firm's capital needs. As bank financing dried up and clients paid more slowly, capital from partners became a more significant factor. In effect, partners had high earnings but had to surrender some funds to the firm, with a trend of the firm requiring the incoming partner's capital contribution to be paid as a lump sum rather than held back from income. Banks often found loans to the individual partner more attractive than loans to capitalize the firm, because loans to partners carried higher interest rates.[265]

[1] Partnership Agreements

Although not legally requisite, law firm partnership agreements are useful in planning the strategy the firm will use, and in avoiding (if possible) and otherwise resolving conflicts among partners. A typical partnership agreement obligates its attorneys to devote full time to work for the partnership, and determines matters such as:

- Capital contributions to be made by partners
- Management of capital and income accounts for each partner
- Regular draw each partner can take against his/her share of the firm's profits for the year
- Percentage of profit and loss allocated to each partner; or formula for calculating each partner's share
- Fiscal year for the partnership
- Provisions for admitting new partners; whether a unanimous vote of partners is required
- Whether all partners will be full equity partners or whether a two-tier system will be implemented
- Formulas for compensation of associates, including salary; bonuses based on firm profits; bonuses based on exceptional performance by the associate; and bonuses based on new business brought in by the associate
- Whether a partnership vote is needed to take on new cases or retainer clients
- Buy-out of the partnership interest of a disabled, retiring, or deceased partner; typically, the firm will re-purchase the interest at its book value. The estate of a deceased partner is entitled to an accounting from the firm, and the estate is

---

[265] Leigh Jones, *Firms Ask Partners to Pony Up*, Nat'l L.J. 7/8/08 (law.com).

entitled to the partner's interest in all partnership assets, including pending files in contingent fee cases

- Expulsion of a partner. Clearly, a partner must be expelled for a criminal conviction, disbarment, or serious ethical violation, but there are more contentious issues about whether expulsion is justified based on a change in the practice or relative lack of productivity.

[2] Compensation of Partners

Law firm partnerships have evolved many methods of allocating compensation other than simple equal division of post-expense net revenues. For instance, there may be a formula under which each partner is responsible for a certain portion of expenses, and is entitled to receive a certain percentage of the profits — but the two percentages need not be equal, and need not be the same as those assigned to other partners. Various pools of funds may be created, and divided according to formulas that reflect individual partners' hours worked, rainmaking ability, results obtained, etc.

When a law firm makes a year-end profit distribution to a partner who has filed for bankruptcy protection, the firm must turn over to the trustee all funds attributable either to legal work done by the partner during that year before the petition, or to the partner's capital contribution. In this case the law firm did not wind up its affairs, although the partner's bankruptcy technically resulted in the dissolution of the firm.

Unless the agreement specifies to the contrary, a contingent fee agreement giving the attorney a percentage of "any amount received" via a settlement or judgment must be interpreted to mean the net amount (minus counterclaims, for example) and not the gross.[266]

Weekly "draws" taken by a law firm partner against firm profits are not exempt from an IRS levy imposed on the law firm's account to collect the partner's unpaid taxes. The Southern District of New York rejected the argument that the draws were not income; they were a loan that would be converted into income when the firm's year ended. The Southern District hit the firm with a 50% penalty for failure to comply with the IRS levy.[267]

[B] Law Firm Management

A very small firm does not require a formal management structure, but as a firm grows, it becomes more important to tackle current questions and make plans for the future in areas such as:

- Marketing the firm
- Adding or changing areas of practice

---

[266] Levine v. Bayne, Snell & Krause Ltd., 40 S.W.3d 92 (Tex. 2001).

[267] United States v. Moscowitz, Passman & Edelman, (S.D.N.Y. 2007); *see* Anthony Lin, *Draws Against Firm Profits Ruled Subject to Tax Liens*, N.Y.L.J. 10/15/07 (law.com).

- Malpractice insurance
- Maintaining appropriate computers, networks, and other communications equipment
- Maintaining the office; moving or expanding as necessary; re-decorating and buying new furniture
- Recruiting attorneys
- Promoting attorneys to partnership; using forms such as two-tiered partnership and "of counsel" arrangements
- Docketing and calendar control
- Management of documents, discovery, and litigation
- Hiring and supervising non-attorney employees
- Setting compensation policy for the firm.

Depending on preferences and circumstances, a law firm might have a single managing partner or a management committee. Many management tasks can be delegated to a non-attorney administrator, working under the supervision of one or more partners.

Law firm management requires planning, not just attention to daily obligations. The manager(s) should analyze various measures of profitability, to see if they are increasing or decreasing. Revenue can be measured by lawyer or by partner; so can expenses and overhead. The number of billable hours, net income per partner, and speed of collecting fees can all be tracked. If profits are declining, the firm may be able to shift to more profitable areas of practice; add more clients through better marketing; shift to more profitable clients; change billings methods; improve speed of collection; or improve efficiency.

A former law firm associate can seek only nominal damages in a suit charging the firm with breaking its promise to make him a partner and firing him. The plaintiff sought $100 million for lost future earnings and other economic damages from not making partner. A New York trial court found that the damages were speculative, because the alleged promise was made by three partners who did not serve on the executive committee and did not have the power to promote the plaintiff. At the stage of summary judgment motion, the case was permitted to proceed on fraud and breach of contract theories, but only for nominal damages. The counts of promissory estoppel, unjust enrichment, breach of fiduciary duty, and intentional infliction of emotional distress were dismissed.[268]

[C] Dissolution of a Partnership

Unless the partnership agreement is to the contrary, a partnership is dissolved by the departure of any partner (whether by resignation, retirement, disability, termination, or death). On dissolution, the partnership has to finish ongoing work for its clients, or give them the opportunity to obtain other representation.

---

[268] Hoeffner v. Orrick, Herrington & Sutcliffe, No. 602694/05 (N.Y. Sup. 2008); *see* Anthony Lin, *Judge Limits Damages in Would-Be Partner's Suit Against Orrick*, N.Y.L.J. 8/6/08 (law.com).

The affairs of the partnership cannot be wound up until all client matters are completed or other counsel has been obtained.

When a firm dissolves, many questions have to be resolved, including:

- Who gets to keep the office
- Who gets to keep the telephone number — not a trivial matter when it may appear in hundreds of influential Rolodexes! Soon, ability to keep the address of the Web site will be almost as important
- Who can keep the file of forms that the firm has developed over time
- How the firm's pending bills will be divided among attorneys.

The Illinois Court of Appeals ruled that it is permissible for lawyers who plan to leave a firm to take preliminary steps such as getting an office; but using confidential information for secret solicitation of the firm's clients is unacceptable. The departing lawyers were ordered to pay $2.5 million to the former firm for breach of fiduciary duty when they enticed away their former firm's largest client.[269]

[D] Professional Corporations and LLPs

Lawyers can also associate to practice in professional corporation (PC) form.

Some states allow Limited Liability Partnerships (LLPs), a form that permits some limitation of liability for firm debts and tort liability related to actions of other attorneys who were not supervised by that particular attorney-partner.

Some major firms, including Sullivan & Cromwell and Paul, Weiss, Rifkind, Wharton & Garrison changed their form of organization from partnership to LLP, and other firms considered the change in light of the growing number of suits by disgruntled stockholders against corporate law firms. However, the extent of protection offered by the LLP form is not entirely clear.[270]

The New York Court of Appeals decided in late 2007 that a law firm's organization as an LLP does not shield the partners from personal liability for disputes with other partners. An attorney sued his one-time partners for an accounting, claiming they owed him money under his agreement for withdrawing from the firm. The defendants not only disputed the claim but said the firm's LLP status made the claim invalid. Most major New York firms are organized as LLPs to limit partners' personal liability to claims where they are directly involved. The Court of Appeals ruled that the legislative intent was to protect against third-party claims, not to limit fiduciary duty among partners.[271]

---

[269] Dowd and Dowd Ltd v. Gleason, 816 N.E.2d 754 (Ill. App. 2004).

[270] *See* Jonathan D. Glater, *Fearing Liability, Law Firms Change Partnership Status*, N.Y. Times, Jan. 10, 2003 at C2.

[271] Ederer v. Gursky, 9 N.Y.3d 514 (N.Y. 2007); *see* Anthony Lin, *N.Y. High Court: No LLP Shield in Disputes Among Law Firm Partners*, N.Y.L.J. 12/21/07 (law.com).

§ 27.07 ATTORNEYS' FEES

The basic American rule[272] is that each party is responsible for its own attorneys' fees, unless there is a statute that calls for shifting of fees, or unless there has been some form of litigation abuse that justifies fee-shifting. Another exception is that a prevailing party who secures a common trust fund for others, or preserves a common fund that benefits a class, is entitled to attorneys' fees.

There are, in fact, about 100 federal statutes under which a prevailing party (or only a prevailing plaintiff) can recover fees. However, it is much more likely that a prevailing plaintiff will be entitled to recover fees as an element of damages than that a prevailing defendant will be entitled to recover damages. In general, defendants get damage awards only if the plaintiff abused the litigation process — not if the plaintiff advanced a theory in good faith but without impressing the trier of fact.[273]

The Equal Access to Justice Act, 28 USC § 2412 provides fee awards to private parties who sue or are sued by the federal government, and prevail against it, if the government's position was not substantially justified. The time to make an application for EAJA fees after an administrative proceeding runs either until 30 days after completion of the appeal, or 30 days after the time to appeal has expired.[274]

The Civil Rights Attorneys' Fee Awards Act, 42 USC § 1988, makes a fee award almost automatic for prevailing plaintiffs in civil rights and civil liberties actions, although the District Court has discretion to determine what fee is reasonable.[275] Other federal fee-shifting statutes include the Freedom of Information Act; Bankruptcy Act; Clayton Antitrust Act; Fair Credit Billing and Reporting Acts; ERISA; and the Federal Tort Claims Act.

Whether one divorcing spouse must pay the other's attorney's fees is a perpetual debate. A Missouri case from 2001 holds that it was not an abuse of discretion for the trial court to order the husband to pay the wife's fees for the divorce

---

[272] Upheld, as the normal rule in U.S. litigation, by Alyeska Pipeline Service Co. v. Wilderness Society, 421 U.S. 240 (1975). New Jersey law makes an exception to the American Rule if a trust or estate incurs legal fees in the course of recouping a substantial improper financial benefit from a trustee or executor who obtained it through undue influence. This is treated as the equivalent of legal malpractice, another situation in which fee shifting is permitted: *In re* Trust (Niles Trust), 71 L.W. 1748 (N.J. 5/28/03).

[273] For instance, the standard under which a prevailing Title VII defendant can receive attorneys' fees, under Christiansburg Garment Co. v. EEOC, 434 U.S. 412 (1978) is whether the plaintiff's claim was unreasonable, frivolous, or groundless; or whether litigation was maintained after the groundlessness of the claim became evident. A prevailing defendant who is awarded attorneys' fees is also entitled to be reimbursed for the necessary expenses of collecting the award: Vudakinovich v. McCarthy, 59 F.3d 58 (7th Cir. 1995).

[274] Adams v. SEC, 287 F.3d 183 (D.C. Cir. 2002). For EAJA purposes, a habeas petition challenging immigration detention is a "civil action": Vacchio v. Ashcroft, 404 F.3d 663 (2d Cir. 2005).

[275] *See, e.g.,* Pino v. Locascio, 101 F.3d 235 (2d Cir. 1996); Luciano v. Olsten, 109 F.3d 111 (2d Cir. 1997).

case and the appeal on the fee issue, because of the husband's greater earnings and earning potential and his grossly improper conduct during the marriage, including spousal abuse. In contrast, a North Dakota case does not consider general fault during the marriage to justify a fee award on behalf of the better-behaved but higher-earning spouse. In this analysis, improper litigation conduct would justify a fee award, but improper marital conduct would not.[276]

In Kansas, spousal support payments made pursuant to a court order, paid to the clerk of the court, are not subject to an attorney's lien filed by the payor spouse's attorney.[277]

According to the Fourth Circuit, a claim under a contract for legal costs not limited to expenses incurred in the underlying suit comes under FRCP 54(d)(2), an element of damages to be proved at trial. (Rule 58(c) states that entry of judgment can only be delayed to award fees if a timely fee motion is made under Rule 54(d)(2).) In this view, unlike the typical statutory attorneys' fee claim, it must be resolved as part of the substantive claim before the judgment becomes final and appealable. However, the Fifth and Ninth Circuits hold that attorneys' fees applied for pursuant to a contract are collateral and need not be resolved before appeal. The Eighth and Eleventh Circuits require resolution before the judgment becomes final.[278]

A mid-2008 Supreme Court decision allows a prevailing plaintiff who satisfies the other requirements of the EAJA to recover paralegal fees from the government at the prevailing market rate, as a "fee" that is a reasonable expense in connection with the proceeding. The Supreme Court rejected the government's contention that paralegal services are "other expenses" whose recovery is limited to reasonable cost, holding that Congress intended reasonableness to be judged from the perspective of the litigant and not the employer of the paralegals.[279]

The Second Circuit allowed attorneys' fees and accounting costs to be included in a restitution order under the Mandatory Victims Restitution Act. Costs associated with the victim's participation in the prosecution of the offense are "other expenses" covered under the act. Therefore, two defendants were required to pay close to $3.1 million in attorneys' fees and costs after their fraud convictions, in addition to $12.8 million in restitution to their former employer. The Second Circuit view is that the District Court has broad discretion to determine the victims' expenses to be included in a restitution order.[280]

The Third Circuit ruled that an attorney does not become a "creditor" for Truth in Lending or Equal Credit Opportunity Act purposes merely because the fee agreement calls for prompt payment of outstanding charges. The agreement itself

---

[276] *Compare* Brady v. Brady, 39 S.W.3d 557 (Mo. App. 2001) *with* Reiser v. Reiser, 621 N.W.2d 348 (N.D. 2001).

[277] *In re* Phillips, 32 P.3d 704 (Kan. 2001).

[278] Carolina Power & Light v. Dynergy Mktg. & Trade, 415 F.3d 354 (4th Cir. 2005).

[279] Richlin Sec. Serv. Co. v. Chertoff, 128 S. Ct. 2007 (6/2/08).

[280] United States v. Amato, 540 F.3d 153 (2d Cir. 2008); *see* Mark Hamblett, *Attorney Fees and Accounting Costs Part of Restitution*, N.Y.L.J. 8/25/08 (law.com).

must specify deferral of payment. Nor did the attorney become a creditor merely by failing to speed up collection of due balances.[281] According to the New Jersey Superior Court, the statute of limitations on a claim for unpaid attorneys' fees under a periodic billing agreement does not accrue as long as there is an ongoing lawyer-client relationship, so it does not begin until the lawyer finishes providing services or the attorney-client relationship ends. The cause of action has not accrued merely because the client stops paying its bills on time.[282]

If it is clear that a lawyer has seriously violated fiduciary duty to a client, forfeiture of the lawyer's fee can be ordered as an equitable remedy even if the client cannot show actual damages. However, the appropriate degree of forfeiture varies with circumstances. The extent of forfeiture is a question of law, and therefore goes to the judge, not the jury.[283]

[A] Lanham Act

In a patent case, a prevailing party is one who gets at least some relief on the merits altering the legal relationship between the parties, such as a defendant who wins on invalidity by demonstrating collateral estoppel, or one who gets the case stayed pending a reissue examination that results in cancellation of the patent. A party that prevailed on the infringement issue received relief, even if it chose to seek cancellation of the patents from the PTO. Therefore, the District Court had to decide whether the case was exceptional enough to justify an attorneys' fee award.[284]

The Ninth Circuit held that it was an abuse of discretion for the District Court to make an attorneys' fee award in a trademark counterfeiting case where the plaintiff opted for statutory damages. 15 USC § 1117(c), the statutory damage provision does not mention attorneys' fees; the § 1117(b) treble damage provision calls for attorneys' fees, but applies only if there are actual damages.[285]

A toy manufacturer that received a $575,000 jury verdict on its copyright and trademark infringement claims about an allegedly copied doll applied for $78,000 in appellate fees and costs. The Seventh Circuit found the request for $132 in costs to be untimely because it was filed 30 days after the final judgment; FRAP 39 (d)(1) requires filing within 14 days of entry of judgment. The Seventh Circuit rejected the defendant's contention that, because a combined motion was submitted for fees and costs, the 14-day deadline applies to both; the Seventh Circuit said that there is no statutory or Federal Rules-based deadline, and the test is whether the plaintiff was diligent.; the Seventh Circuit held that the plaintiff was diligent. The defendant argued that it should not have to pay attorneys' fees at the appellate level, because its appeal was not frivolous, but the Seventh Circuit said that frivolousness is only

---

[281] Riethman v. Berry, 287 F.3d 274 (3d Cir. 2002).

[282] Pellettieri, Rabstein and Altman v. Protopapas, 383 N.J. Super. (N.J. Super. 2006).

[283] Burrow v. Arce, 997 S.W.2d 229 (Tex. 1999).

[284] Inland Steel Co. v. LTV Steel Co., 364 F.3d 1318 (Fed. Cir. 2004).

[285] K and N Eng'g, Inc. v. Bulat, 510 F.3d 1079 (9th Cir. 2007).

one of the factors that the reviewing court must consider. This case involved flagrant copyright infringement and willful trademark infringement, so denying an award of attorneys' fees to enforce the judgment would leave the plaintiff undercompensated. However, the Seventh Circuit reduced the fee award from $78,000 to $70,000, finding that it should not have taken 33.25 hours to prepare a simple petition.[286]

A Tenth Circuit case from mid-2000 holds that a prevailing defendant in a Lanham Act case was properly denied attorneys' fees, because the proper test is not only whether the plaintiff's suit had objective foundation, but whether the plaintiff acted in subjective good or bad faith.[287]

[B] Other Statutory Fees

In line with the perception that lawyers stir up costly litigation to generate fees for themselves, a number of state tort reform statutes place limits on attorneys' fees as well as on amounts plaintiffs can recover: e.g., Florida and Nevada impose a sliding scale of percentages, with the percentage the attorney can take falling as the award rises.[288]

The federal statute that deals with removal from state to federal court on the grounds of diversity, 28 USC § 1447(c), also deals with the situation where a case is remanded to state court after its removal to the federal system. This provision permits the remand order to require payment of costs and expenses, including attorney's fees, but does not make explicit when a fee award is justified. In 2005, the Supreme Court held that, in general, a fee award will be made only if there was no objectively reasonable rationale for seeking removal of the case.[289]

Awards under the Social Security Act are subject to a fee cap. As a result of 42 USC § 406(b)(1)(A), attorneys who represent benefit claimants are not permitted to charge more than 25% of the past-due benefits that their clients receive. The Equal Access to Justice Act awards attorneys' fees in cases where the government position was substantially unjustified. The Supreme Court tackled the interaction between the two statutes in May 2002.[290] A fee award can be made under both statutes in the same case. If this is done, the lawyer must remit the smaller fee to the client, until the client receives 100% of the past-due benefit. In a contingent fee case, the Supreme Court held that the court should not substitute the lodestar for the contingent fee (as long as the contingent fee does not exceed the statutory limit). Instead, the court should review the reasonableness of the contingent fee.

---

[286] JCW Investments, Inc. v. Novelty, Inc., 509 F.3d 339 (7th Cir. 2007); the underlying award of damages was upheld by the Seventh Circuit at 482 F.3d 910 (7th Cir. 2007).

[287] National Ass'n of Prof'l Baseball Leagues Inc. v. Very Minor Leagues Inc., 223 F.3d 1143 (10th Cir. 2000). Vexatious litigation conduct can justify a fee award: Securacomm Consulting Inc. v. Securacom Inc., 224 F.3d 273 (3d Cir. 2000).

[288] No by-line, *Voters in Florida, Nevada Limit Fee Awards; California Voters Curb Private AG Actions*, 73 L.W. 2291.

[289] Martin v. Franklin Capital Corp., 546 U.S. 132 (2005).

[290] Gisbrecht v. Barnhart, 535 U.S. 789 (2002).

In a Social Security Administration case, the District Court limited the combined attorneys' fees for representation both before the SSA and on appeal to the District Court to 25% of the past-due benefits. The Tenth Circuit reversed, holding that the decision ignored the plain statutory language of § 406(a) [fees for administrative proceedings] and (b) [court proceedings]. Contingent fee arrangements are permitted in SSA cases to recover past-due benefits. The Social Security Administration can withhold up to 25% of the past due benefit and pay it directly to the attorney. If the court ordered a higher fee, the attorney must look to the client and not to the SSA benefit for the balance, placing the attorney in the same position as any other judgment creditor. EAJA fees can be awarded to the claimant, separate and apart from the § 406(b)(1)(A) fee, if the United States' position was not substantially justified. However, the attorney can keep only the larger of the 406(a) or the EAJA award, and must refund the smaller one. The Tenth Circuit said that court supervision and review of attorneys' fees for reasonableness prevent abuses.[291]

According to the Ninth Circuit, appellate attorneys' fees are "costs on appeal" that can require the appellant to secure a bond under Federal Rules of Appellate Procedure 7 only if they are defined as recoverable costs by an applicable fee-shifting statute, and only if the appellee is entitled to recover the fees. The Ninth Circuit held that an appeal on the merits should not be dismissed for failure to post the bond. The Third and D.C. Circuits have ruled that attorneys' fees are not "costs"; the Second, Sixth, and Eleventh Circuits (now joined by the Ninth) have ruled that security for appellate attorneys' fees can be included in a Rule 7 bond if recoverable under a fee-shifting statute; and the First Circuit says bonding of appellate fees can be required if they are potential costs under Rule 38 because the appeal is frivolous.[292]

In late 2000, the Sixth Circuit ruled that the Prison Litigation Reform Act (PLRA; see § 26.04[O]) fee cap serves a rational purpose by limiting frivolous litigation. Therefore, it does not deny Equal Protection to prisoners.[293] In 2003, the Seventh Circuit (reversing the District Court) adopted the same position.

The Hyde Amendment, 18 USC § 3006A, provides for fee awards to a criminal defense attorney when the government took a position against the defendant that was vexatious, frivolous, or in bad faith. The First Circuit ruled that to justify a fee award, the defense must prove not only that the prosecution was unfounded, but must provide objective evidence that the government manifested malice or intent to harass.[294]

---

[291] Wrenn v. Astrue, 525 F.3d 931 (10th Cir. 2008).

[292] Azizian v. Federated Dep't Stores, 499 F.3d 950 (9th Cir. 2007).

[293] Hadix v. Johnson, 230 F.3d 840 (6th Cir. 2000); Johnson v. Daley, 339 F.3d 582 (7th Cir. 2003), *cert. denied*, 541 U.S. 935. The PLRA fee cap (150% of the fee paid to appointed counsel) applies only to services performed after the effective date of the statute: Martin v. Hadix, 527 U.S. 343 (1999).

[294] United States v. Knott, 256 F.3d 20 (1st Cir. 2001). For EAJA and Hyde Amendment purposes, habeas proceedings are neither civil nor criminal, so even a federal defendant who wins

In tax cases, attorneys' fee awards to prevailing parties are limited by Code § 7430(c)(1) to $110/hour as adjusted for inflation. The 2009 figure is $180/hour.

[C] Prevailing Party

A party need not succeed as to every count in the complaint to have the status of a prevailing party. Mere success on procedural issues is not enough — concrete substantive rights must be gained,[295] either in the courtroom or via consent decree.[296] Success on any significant issue, resulting in some of the benefits for which the suit was brought, is sufficient.[297]

The Supreme Court ruled in mid-2004 that a timely fee application can be amended properly after the 30 days have passed to cure the initial failure to allege lack of substantial justification. The statement is a mere allegation or pleading requirement, and the government is not at risk of surprise because this is a factor in every EAJA petition.[298]

The Third Circuit held in 2008 that a party that gets relief on the merits as a preliminary injunction, but does not get a final judgment, can be a "prevailing party" under 42 USC § 1988. The defendant city passed a new ordinance about permits for expressive activities in public activities that satisfied the plaintiffs. In 2007, the Supreme Court held that the winner of a preliminary injunction is not a prevailing party if the result is undone by the final decision in the same case, but the Third Circuit said that the question remained of the effect of a preliminary injunction where there is no final decision. The Third Circuit joined the Sixth, Ninth, and D.C. Circuits in holding that the winner of a preliminary injunction can be the prevailing party if it achieves all of its goals.[299]

The District Court has subject matter jurisdiction to award attorneys' fees to prevailing defendants in an ERISA suit to enforce the plan's subrogation provision. ERISA § 502(g) gave the court jurisdiction to make the fee award, even though the pleading failed to state a claim on which relief could be granted.[300]

Where the contract provides that the prevailing party in a contract enforcement action can recover attorneys' fees, a plaintiff who accepts an FRCP offer of

---

is not entitled to receive attorneys' fees from the federal government: Sloan v. Pugh, 351 F.3d 1319 (10th Cir. 2003). Hyde Amendments awards are not subject to the EAJA cap on hourly fees: United States v. Aisenberg, 247 F. Supp. 2d 1272 (M.D. Fla. 2003).

[295] Hanrahan v. Hampton, 446 U.S. 754 (1980).

[296] Maher v. Gagne, 448 U.S. 122 (1980).

[297] Hensley v. Eckerhart, 461 U.S. 424 (1983).

[298] Scarborough v. Principi, 541 U.S. 401 (Sup. Ct. 2004).

[299] People Against Police Violence v. City of Pittsburgh, 520 F.3d 226 (3d Cir. 2008); *see* Shannon P. Duffy, *3rd Circuit: Final Judgment No Prerequisite for Attorney Fees*, The Legal Intelligencer 3/25/08 (law.com). The Supreme Court decision is Sole v. Wyner, 551 U.S. 74 (2007). *See also* Select Milk Producers, Inc. v. Johanns, 400 F.3d 939 (D.C. Cir. 2005); Watson v. County of Riverside, 300 F.3d 1092 (9th Cir. 2002); Dupuy v. Samuels, 423 F.3d 714 (7th Cir. 2005); Dubuc v. Green Oak Twp., 312 F.3d 736 (6th Cir. 2002).

[300] Primax Recoveries Inc. v. Gunter, 433 F.3d 515 (6th Cir. 2006).

judgment (even one that is silent on the question of fees) is a prevailing party entitled to a fee award.[301]

The First Circuit ruled that a disabled student, who, as a result of negotiations, received her desired placement in a private therapeutic day school, was not a prevailing party. In the absence of the judicial imprimatur, she was not entitled to a fee award.[302]

The Federal Circuit ruled that someone who gets a court order remanding proceedings to an administrative agency to fix defects in the agency's order on the merits is a prevailing party. Therefore, an EAJA award is potentially available — but only if the party prevails on the merits when the matter is remanded to the agency.[303]

[1] Catalyst Theory

In 2001, the Supreme Court, despite contrary rulings by nine Circuits, held that a "prevailing party" entitled to an award under federal fee-shifting statutes must have obtained either a judgment on the merits or a court-ordered consent decree. This decision[304] strikes down the "catalyst theory" under which permits a plaintiff to receive a fee award for accomplishing socially beneficial results by inducing voluntary changes in the defendant's practices.

If only nominal damages are awarded, the plaintiff has indeed prevailed — but such a limited degree of success will be a potent factor in determining the fee![305]

Despite the U.S. Supreme Court's rejection of the catalyst theory, California permits prevailing parties to recover fee awards under the state statute justifying such awards to plaintiffs who vindicate important rights affecting the public interest and who confer significant benefits on the public or on a large class. However, the plaintiff must demonstrate that the catalyst theory should be applied because of results achieved, not because of the sheer nuisance or expense of pursuing the litigation. The plaintiff must also have made reasonable efforts to settle the case before trial.[306]

The Ninth Circuit found that the plaintiffs prevailed and could be awarded attorneys' fees when developmentally disabled adults settled a discrimination case against a state agency. This was true even though the settlement terms were less than the full relief requested. The Ninth Circuit treated *Buckhannon* as dictum to the extent it limited fee awards to judgments on the merits and court-supervised

---

[301] Utility Automation 2000 Inc. v. Choctawhatchee Elec. Coop Inc., 298 F.3d 1238 (11th Cir. 2002).

[302] Doe v. Boston Public Schools, 358 F.3d 20 (1st Cir. 2004).

[303] Former Employees of Motorola Ceramic Prods. v. United States, 336 F.3d 1360 (Fed. Cir. 2003).

[304] Buckhannon Board and Care Home Inc. v. West Virginia Dep't of Health and Human Services, 532 U.S. 598 (2001).

[305] Farrar v. Hobby, 506 U.S. 103 (1992).

[306] Graham v. Daimler-Chrysler Co., 34 Cal. 4th 553 (Cal. 2004).

consent decrees. The incorporation of a private settlement into a court order, and the court's retention of jurisdiction over attorneys' fees constitutes a judicial imprimatur on the settlement. The Ninth Circuit found that while a catalyst effect is not enough for an award, a material modification in the defendant's behavior benefiting the plaintiff does suffice.[307]

The Eleventh Circuit's view is that catalyst theory remains valid in a case where the statute calls for a fee award when the court determines the award is reasonable — where the statute does not speak of a "prevailing party."[308]

An NASD arbitration panel found that an investment bank violated the ADEA by firing the grievant. The panel awarded $200,000 in damages but, contrary to ADEA regulations, did not make an attorneys' fee award, and imposed the entire cost of arbitration on the prevailing plaintiff. The Southern District of New York ordered the award modified to include up to $262,000 in attorneys' fees, including fees for the appeal. On remand, the defendant's position was that the fee award should be limited by the plaintiff's contingent fee agreement with his attorney, under which the attorney would receive one-third of the settlement or judgment. At that point, the arbitrator awarded $83,000 in fees but made the plaintiff's law firm give back the contingent fee. The Second Circuit vacated the arbitrator's award for manifest disregard of the law, holding that a fee award is mandatory to a prevailing ADEA plaintiff. The attorney-client relationship and the fee agreement were not before the arbitration panel, which lacked jurisdiction to order repayment of the contingent fee to the client.[309]

Unless there is a contract that provides to the contrary, attorneys' fees awarded to a "prevailing party" under California's Fair Employment and Housing Act are the property of the lawyer, not the client, under the theory that the legislative intent in enacting fee-award provisions is to give attorneys an incentive to take on tough cases.[310] In contrast, the Eleventh Circuit held that an award of attorneys' fees under 28 USC § 2412(d)(10)(A) is the property of the prevailing party, not the attorney, and thus can be offset to recoup child support owed by the claimant who prevailed and received an award of Social Security disability benefits.[311]

In April 2007, the Second Circuit not only held that it was improper to claim 300 hours of work on a six-page single-issue brief but suggested that sometimes attorneys are properly paid in non-monetary returns such as experience, reputation, or the satisfaction of advancing a political agenda. The upshot was that lawyers who

---

[307] Richard S. v. Department of Developmental Serv., 317 F.3d 1080 (9th Cir. 2003).

[308] Loggerhead Turtle v. County Council of Volusia Co., 307 F.3d 1318 (11th Cir. 2002); followed, for the Clean Air Act, in Sierra Club v. EPA, 311 F.3d 853 (D.C. Cir. 2003), and by the Ninth Circuit for the Endangered Species Act, Ass'n of California Water Agencies v. Evans, 386 F.3d 879 (9th Cir. 2004).

[309] Porzig v. Dresdner Kleinwort, 497 F.3d 133 (2d Cir. 2007); Anthony Lin, *2nd Circuit Rebukes Arbitration Panel for Limiting Fee Award*, N.Y.L.J. 8/9/07 (law.com).

[310] Flannery v. Prentice, 110 Cal. Rptr. 2d 809 (Cal. 2001).

[311] Reeves v. Astrue, 526 F.3d 732 (11th Cir. 2008). Manning v. Astrue, 510 F.3d 1246 (10th Cir. 2007) also says the client is the prevailing party and owns the fees.

applied for $455,000 in fees after winning an important voting rights case were awarded only $133,000. However, in 2008, the court amended its opinion, adding a footnote that the reasonableness of a fee does not depend on whether the lawyer works for a private firm or a public interest organization, and the award is not necessarily limited by the attorney's willingness to take the case for a reduced fee.[312]

[D] Attorneys' Fee Awards Under FRCP Rule 54

In a case brought under a federal statute that lacks a fee provision, Federal Rules of Civil Procedure Rule 54 governs the motion applying for an award of fees and costs.

Such a motion must be made within 14 days of entry of judgment. The motion papers must give a fair estimate of the fee the attorney expects to be able to prove. However, any party or class member has the right to make an adversary submission with respect to fees. The fee application can be referred to a Rule 53 master (there is no need to prove or even assert that the matter is particularly complex). The court will consider the facts and circumstances and enter a judgment as to attorneys' fees.

[E] Fee Calculations and the Lodestar

Statutory fee calculations depend on the "lodestar": a somewhat flexible standard based on a list of factors such as time expended on a case, results obtained for the client, novelty and difficulty of issues raised, and prevailing local fees. Upward deviations from the lodestar are possible, but the Supreme Court treats them as exceptional.[313]

According to the Third Circuit, application of the lodestar process is mandatory; it is improper for the court to make each side submit a figure and then pick one of them.[314]

Attorneys' fees as response costs were denied to private parties by the Supreme Court in 1994.[315]

Special expertise in tax law and Texas community property and insurance law, claimed by an attorney, did not constitute a "special factor" that would justify raising the fee award over the Code § 7430 amount. Nor does egregious conduct on the part of the government constitute a special factor.[316]

---

[312] Arbor Hill Concerned Citizens Neighborhood Ass'n v. County of Albany, 484 F.3d 162, first amended opinion 493 F.3d 110 (2d Cir. 2007); second amended opinion 522 F.3d 182 (2d Cir. 2008); *see* Adam Liptak, *In Court's Calculation, What Feeds Lawyers' Souls Need Not Fatten Their Wallets*, N.Y. Times 5/28/07 at p.A9 and Mark Hamblett, *2nd Circuit Clarifies Civil Rights Fee Award Scheme*, N.Y.L.J. 4/14/08 (law.com).

[313] Blum v. Stenson, 465 U.S. 996 (1984).

[314] Pennsylvania Envtl. Defense Found. v. Canon-McMillan Sch. Dist., 152 F.3d 228 (3d Cir. 1998).

[315] Key Tronic Corp. v. United States, 511 U.S. 809 (1994).

[316] A. Cervin Estate, 200 F.3d 351 (5th Cir. 2000). General expertise in tax law is not a special factor justifying a higher rate in a dispute over § 6662(a) accuracy-related penalties on conceded deficiencies: Caspian Consulting Group, TC Memo 2006-85.

The Second Circuit reduced a fee from $300 to $125/hour (where Medicare home care patients prevailed at declaratory judgment but did not receive the pre-deprivation hearings they sought) because, although the attorneys used their knowledge of Medicare law to handle a complex case, they did not have distinctive knowledge or specialized skills.[317]

The Second Circuit held that not getting an overtime pay case certified as an FLSA collective action was a failure that justified reducing the fee award. Although the attorney prevailed by showing that Bellevue Hospital and the referral agency that placed the plaintiff in temporary jobs, success was modest ($887 in unpaid overtime, doubled as liquidated damages, plus $6,565 in costs), so the Second Circuit upheld the District Court's reduction of the attorneys' fee request from $340,000 to about $50,000. The Second Circuit agreed that the attorney's experience made a $350 hourly rate reasonable, but he did not prove the number of hours worked, so the Second Circuit allowed what it considered a generous 400 hours and reduced travel time and hours for tasks that should have been assigned to a paralegal.[318]

The Second Circuit rejected a sole practitioner's fee request based on a "blended hourly rate" representing what a hypothetical large firm would charge for work divided between a hypothetical partner billing $500/hour and hypothetical associates billing at lower rates. However, the Second Circuit also declined to presume that a solo practitioner's overhead would be lower than a large firm's.[319]

[F] Class Action Fees

NOTE: The Class Action Fairness Act of 2005, P.L. 109-2 (CAFA), limits attorneys' fees in consumer class actions resolved on the basis of a "coupon settlement" (where the defendant provides coupons for goods or services). The fee is based only on the value of coupons actually received. In any case subject to CAFA, the class counsel's fee is subject to court review. The statute permits the use of the lodestar method. Courts can approve a settlement subject to CAFA where any class member has a net loss after payment of attorneys' fees if and only if the court finds that class members derive non-monetary benefits that substantially outweigh the financial loss.

A Second Circuit case from March 2000 says that although in a common fund case the District Court has discretion to use either the lodestar or the percentage-of-fund method, the lodestar cannot simply be disregarded. The Second Circuit, while

---

[317] The Seventh, Ninth, and Eleventh Circuits define "special expertise" as prowess in a sub-specialty such as Social Security or immigration law; the D.C., Fourth and Fifth Circuits require education outside the field of U.S. law (e.g., technical studies). *See* Healey v. Leavitt, 485 F.3d 63 (2d Cir. 2007), discussed in Mark Hamblett, *2nd Circuit: Attorneys' Expertise Does Not Justify Higher Hourly Rate* N.Y.L.J. 4/19/07 (law.com).

[318] Barfield v. New York City Health and Hosps. Corp., 06-4137-cv (2d Cir. 2008); *see* Mark Hamblett, *Modest Success Justifies Cut in Lawyer's Fees, Panel Says*, N.Y.L.J. 8/12/08 (law.com).

[319] McDonald v. Pension Plan, 450 F.3d 91 (2d Cir. 2006); *see* Anthony Lin, *2nd Circuit Rejects "Blended" Rate for Solo's Work*, N.Y.L.J. 6/8/06 (law.com).

admitting that some courts treat 25% as a benchmark in common fund cases, refused to apply a multiplier to the lodestar amount, viewing the starting point for the analysis as the fee that would prevail in an efficient legal market.[320]

A federal District Court has not only the power but the obligation to review the fairness of the attorneys' fee provision of a class action settlement, even if none of the class members have an objection (or even have standing to raise one). In the Ninth Circuit view, the court's equitable jurisdiction to decide ancillary matters even after a settlement has been reached is not dependent on the presence of a complaining party with standing. (In this securities fraud case, there were objections, but the objector lacked standing, because the settlement did not directly compensate the plaintiffs.)

If a fee award is otherwise proper, it is not forfeited by the use of salaried in-house counsel, in which case the award will depend on a cost-plus analysis of the attorney's salary and overhead, not the market rates charged by law firms.[321]

The Seventh Circuit view is that in a mega-fund common fund class action, the fees must be determined at the beginning of the case, based on market rates (as established by the fee agreements in comparable cases) and the risk of non-payment.[322] In this view, it is inappropriate to impose a cap at the end of the case to prevent a windfall to the attorneys. Here, the District Court set the fees at 10% of any portion of the award over $74 million, one-third on lesser amounts.

Attorneys' fees are not included in determining the minimum amount in controversy required by 27 USC § 1332(a) (even though the fees might be deducted from the common fund). The Eleventh Circuit disapproved the tactics of attorneys who file nationwide class actions in states that have made very big punitive damage awards in the past, while keeping the complaint's ad damnum below the minimum for federal diversity jurisdiction, waiting until the one-year period for removal to federal court has expired, then amending the complaint seeking punitive damages. The common fund attorneys' fee is not part of the matter in controversy, because the fee is not a single title or right of the plaintiff.[323]

[G] Contingent Fees

An attorney who has a contingent fee agreement can collect a percentage of court-awarded fees as long as the agreement unambiguously authorizes this. If the agreement is silent or ambiguous, the percentage is calculated based on the total recovery minus the court-awarded fee. The lawyer gets only the larger of the two.

A contingent fee attorney who is fired before the contingency occurs must wait until the case is finished before collecting a quantum meruit fee, because the case must be finished before it can be determined what constitutes a fair fee.

---

[320] Goldberger v. Integrated Resources Inc., 209 F.3d 43 (2d Cir. 2000).

[321] SoftSolutions Inc. v. Brigham Young Univ., 1 P.3d 1095 (Utah 2000).

[322] *In re* Synthroid Mktg. Litig., 264 F.3d 712 (7th Cir. 2001).

[323] Davis v. Carl Cannon Chevrolet-Olds Inc., 182 F.3d 792 (11th Cir. 1999).

However, the former client can be required to reimburse the discharged firm for its disbursements before the firm returns the case files to the ex-client.[324]

As a general rule, an attorney who has a contingent fee agreement is not permitted to charge the client extra for collecting the judgment or settlement proceeds, in that collecting a judgment is the normal objective of litigation. The Third Circuit permits an exception in a case where collection efforts go far beyond what the parties contemplated when they made the agreement. (An attorney who is extremely concerned about this risk should specify in the original agreement what constitutes normal collection efforts and the fee that will be required for additional efforts.)[325]

However, it is not permissible for a law firm to withdraw from a contingent fee case because it thinks it will not earn enough, and then demand a quantum meruit award for work already done. Withdrawal without good cause means that the attorney is not entitled to payment at all.[326]

[H] Pro Se Litigants

The Eleventh Circuit held that attorneys' fees cannot be awarded under FRCP 11(c)(2) to pro se litigants, even if they happen to be attorneys, because they did not incur out of pocket expenses qualifying for reimbursement.[327] But this is not true of the California counterpart of this rule. Attorneys acting pro se to defend themselves against frivolous lawsuits are entitled to a fee award as a monetary award against the frivolous litigant, because of the unfairness of having to defend against groundless allegations even if there is no associated out of pocket expense.[328]

A lawyer/stockholder who represents himself in a derivative suit is not entitled to a fee award for lodging an objection, even if he succeeds in winning a significant amount for the company. The Third Circuit ruled that a shareholder/attorney is entitled to expense reimbursement but not to counsel fees, which are limited to independent objective counsel.[329]

[I] Interest

Post-judgment interest on an attorneys' fee award runs from the date the District Court renders a money judgment (28 USC § 1961(a)), not the earlier

---

[324] Universal Acupuncture Pain Serv. PC v. Quadrino & Schwartz, 370 F.3d 259 (2d Cir. 2004).

[325] Dardovitch v. Holtzman, 190 F.3d 125 (3d Cir. 1999). *See also* Lustig v. Horn, 732 N.E.2d 613 (Ill. App. 2000) (a retainer agreement clause requiring the client to reimburse the attorney for the reasonable fees and costs of collecting unpaid bills is unenforceable because it prevents clients from raising valid objections to their bills. Such a clause might even violate the ethical rule against representation that is limited by the attorney's own interests.).

[326] Bell v. Marra PLLC v. Sullivan, 6 P.3d 965 (Mont. 2000).

[327] Massengale v. Ray, 37 Fed. Appx. 506 (11th Cir. 2001).

[328] Laborde v. Aronson, 112 Cal. Rptr. 2d 119 (Cal. App. 2001).

[329] Zucker v. Westinghouse Elec. Co. 374 F.3d 221 (3d Cir. 2004), Shannon P. Duffy, *Lawyer Acting Pro Se Denied Award of Fees*, Legal Intelligencer 7/6/04 (law.com).

point at which the District Court indicates that the prevailing party should receive a fee award.[330]

Apropos of interest, a D.C. Bar opinion states that, when a client who has no extenuating circumstances fails to pay legal fees, the attorney can condition performance of further legal work on payment of interest on the overdue balance — even if the original agreement did not provide for payment of interest.[331]

[J] Tax Deductibility of Fees

An individual can deduct legal fees related to gain-seeking activities, but not those relating to their personal affairs. (Collecting alimony is deemed to be a gain-seeking activity, so related legal fees are deductible.) Fees expended in connection with the determination, collection, or refund of any tax can be deducted under Code § 212.

A business' legal fees (or the salary of in-house counsel) are deductible under § 162 if they are ordinary and necessary business expenses, but expenses for defending or perfecting title to property are capital expenditures that must be written off over a period of years, not in the year they are incurred (§ 263).

The retainer for an attorney applied to legal expenses for acquisition of a business must be capitalized.[332]

In January 2005 the Supreme Court resolved a Circuit split, holding that whether or not state law gives the attorney a possessory interest, the amount paid to a contingent fee attorney is nevertheless included in the plaintiff's gross income for tax purposes.[333]

The American Jobs Creation Act of 2004, P.L. 108-357, makes attorneys' fees in employment discrimination cases (although not in other types of civil litigation) an above-the-line deduction.

Effective for payments made on or after January 1, 2007, T.D. 9270 provides the information reporting requirements for payments made to attorneys under Code § 6045(f) in connection with legal services. Any payor engaged in trade or business who, in the course of business, makes payments of over $600 to an attorney in the course of a year must report the payment to the IRS and disclose the filing to the attorney. The T.D. does not apply to payments made to attorneys with respect to real estate financing, including mortgages or payments to attorneys acting as bankruptcy trustees. An attorney is considered the payee of a check written to his or her client trust fund, but not of a check that the attorney cannot negotiate. Backup withholding is required unless the attorney provides the payor with an accurate Taxpayer Information Number.[334]

---

[330] Eaves v. Cape May County, New Jersey, 239 F.3d 527 (3d Cir. 2001).

[331] D.C. Bar Legal Ethics Comm. Op. 310, 70 L.W. 2395.

[332] Dana Corp. v. Comm'r, 83 AFTR2d 98-5031 (Fed. Cir. 4/7/99).

[333] Comm'r v. Banks, 543 U.S. 426 (2005).

[334] T.D. 9270, 2006-33 IRB 237, 71 FR 39548 (7/3106).

[K] Attorneys' Fees and Bankruptcy

NOTE: Most of these cases pre-date the 2005 bankruptcy reform law, the Bankruptcy Abuse Prevention and Consumer Protection Act. See Chapter 15 for discussion of this legislation.

The question of attorneys' fees is always a complex one (after all, the bankruptcy debtor is at least theoretically in financial trouble). In the current climate, where the number of bankruptcy filings will increase, but there is a real possibility that drastic bankruptcy reform legislation will be passed, the issues will become even more complex.

Early in 2004, the Supreme Court ruled that Bankruptcy Code § 330(a)(1) authorizes a fee award to a debtor's attorney out of estate funds if, and only if, the employment is authorized under § 327 — that is, the attorney is employed by the trustee and the employment is approved by the court. The attorney in this case therefore did not receive a fee award, because he was hired by a Chapter 11 Debtor in Possession but the case was converted to Chapter 7.[335]

Under the *Fobian* rule, attorneys' fees will not be awarded for litigating issues of bankruptcy law (as distinct from basic contract enforcement). The Supreme Court struck down this rule in March, 2007, holding it is not supported by federal bankruptcy law. The American Rule, which is that each party must pay its own fees unless there is a statutory exception, can be overcome by a contract. A contract allocating attorneys' fees that is enforceable under substantive non-bankruptcy law permits a fee payment unless the Bankruptcy Code forbids it (see BCode § 502(b)). In effect BCode § 502(b)(1) makes any defense available outside bankruptcy, as measured by state law, equally available within bankruptcy.[336]

According to the Eleventh Circuit, the bankruptcy court must determine the reasonableness of attorneys' fees, even if the fee obligation is enforceable under state law. The reasonable portion of the agreed fee is treated as a secured claim, whereas any amount deemed unreasonable becomes an unsecured claim.[337]

The automatic stay is not violated when an attorney charges a client in Chapter 7 a fee for postpetition services that the bankruptcy court later finds to be unreasonable. The Ninth Circuit reached this conclusion because the attorney had no reason to believe that the services were unreasonable at the time they were rendered.[338]

A 2001 Ninth Circuit case holds that the Chapter 7 debtor's obligation to make postpetition installment payments for **prepetition** legal services is subject to

---

[335] Lamie v. United States Trustee, 540 U.S. 526 (Sup. Ct. 2004).

[336] Travelers Casualty & Surety Co. of America v. Pacific Gas & Electric Co., 549 U.S. 443 (2007); *Fobian* is *In re* Fobian, 951 F. 2d 1149 (9th Cir. 1991).

[337] Welzel v. Advocate Realty Inv. LLC, 275 F.3d 1308 (11th Cir. 2001).

[338] Sanchez v. Gordon, 241 F.3d 1148 (9th Cir. 2001).

the automatic stay, and is dischargeable, because Bankruptcy Code § 523 does not provide a discharge exception for attorneys' fees.[339]

§ 27.08   LAW PRACTICE IN THE INTERNET ERA

NOTE: See § 22.20[A] for discussion of "e-filing" (electronic filing of litigation documents) and citation of electronic materials in legal documents. Over time, as e-mail and cell phones have become universal, ethics regulators have come to accept that using these means does not per se violate client confidentiality (although security steps are required).

Florida's Internet advertising rule treats lawyer and law firm Web sites as information provided at the prospective client's request, and therefore subject to the rules for that situation (but not to the requirement that lawyer advertisements be filed with the disciplinary authorities). Law firm sites must disclose all jurisdictions in which members are licensed, and must give at least one bona fide physical office location. Rule 4-7.6(c) defines unsolicited e-mail to potential clients as direct mail, so it must conform to the direct mail rule, must have "legal advertisement" in the subject line, and must disclose at least one bona fide office location. Other computer-accessed communications dealing with the services of a lawyer or a law firm are treated as lawyer advertising.[340]

The Virginia rule is that it is not unethical to provide service to a client entirely online, without personal interaction, on the grounds that competency depends on the thoroughness and accuracy of representation rather than on the medium through which it is delivered.[341]

The New Mexico rule[342] is that answering general legal questions via e-mail does not constitute representation of a client. However, New Mexico joins Arizona, Illinois, and Kentucky in holding that answering specific, individualized questions probably does create an attorney-client relationship. Once a relationship is created, the attorney is bound by the normal rules with respect to confidentiality, conflict of interest, and other issues. The New Jersey Supreme Court ethics committee issued an opinion that, even if there is only a one-time call, and even if disclaimers are provided, a lawyer's response to a legal hotline creates an attorney-client relationship. In 1993, the committee said that a one-on-one discussion, however brief, gives rise to a presumption of an attorney-client relationship (and a presumption

---

[339] American Law Ctr. PC v. Stanley, 253 F.3d 438 (9th Cir. 2001). In the Seventh Circuit, the entire pre-petition agreement, covering some payments before and some after filing is dischargeable under B Code § 727, even if the fee is reasonable: Bethea v. Robert J. Adams & Associates, 352 F.3d 1125 (7th Cir. 2003).

[340] Amendments to Rules Regulating the Florida Bar — Advertising Rules Fla. No. 92,297, 68 L.W. 2387 (12/17/99). This document also provides that out of state attorneys are not subject to Florida's amended advertising rules to the extent that they are engaging in conduct already forbidden as unauthorized practice of law.

[341] Virginia State Bar Ass'n Standing Comm. on Legal Ethics Op. 1791, 72 L.W. 2443 (12/22/03).

[342] New Mexico State Bar Advisory Opinions Comm. Formal Op. 2001-1; *see* 70 L.W. 2187.

that the client can rely on the advice). Once advice is given based on individual facts, all ethical obligations are triggered, including the duty of confidentiality, the duty of competence, and the need to disclose the limited scope of representation.[343]

Ohio permits attorneys to give legal advice online for a fee, subject to the same ethical constraints as offering advice in any other setting (e.g., over the telephone). The legal advice must be competent; trade names for the online service are barred, as are joint ventures between attorneys and non-attorneys; advice should not be given outside Ohio unless that is permissible under the rules of the receiving state; and a lawyer should not recommend employment of him- or herself or another lawyer in the firm unless the client asks for advice about employment of an attorney.[344]

In 2000, the South Carolina Bar Ethics Advisory Committee ruled that lawyers can participate in an Internet referral service that does not charge a fee. In 2001, the Committee permitted lawyers to pay an Internet referral site on the basis of the number of hits that the lawyer receives. Payment by hits is allowable because there is no guarantee that anyone who accesses information about the lawyer will ever become a client, and lawyers do not split fees with the service.[345] It was precisely the risk of fee-splitting that led the Maryland ethics committee to disapprove of a proposed Internet site that would match up lawyers and clients, with a portion of the fee going to the site.[346]

The ABA says that the client's consent is not necessary before sending e-mail about the client's matter, unless the information is so sensitive that special security measures are required. E-mail could be intercepted by a hacker, but it is also true that phones can be tapped and documents can be stolen.

New Jersey (joining New York, Ohio, and Texas) decided in mid-2005 that although law firm domain names are not required to follow the rules about firm names, limits still apply. It is acceptable to use an appropriate domain name in advertising for the firm, as long as the domain name merely identifies the site and does not serve as a substitute for the normal firm name. The domain name must not be false or misleading, and it must not imply specialization except to the degree permitted by ethics rules. The site's home page must give the firm's actual name and address and must contain the disclaimers and advisories mandated by Rules 7.1 and 7.2.[347]

The Philadelphia Bar Association says that it is all right for lawyers who have filed or plan to file a lawsuit to participate in Internet chat about the subject of the

---

[343] N.J. Advisory Comm. on Prof'l Ethics Op. 712 (2008); *see* Mary Pat Gallagher, *Lawyer-Client Relationships Can Arise From Legal Hotline Calls, Panel Rules*, N.J.L.J. 1/18/08 (law.com).

[344] Ohio Supreme Court Board of Commissioners on Grievances and Discipline, Op. 99-9, 68 L.W. 2388 (12/2/99).

[345] South Carolina Bar Ethics Advisory Committee Ops. 00-10, 01-03; *see* 70 L.W. 2287.

[346] Maryland State Bar Ass'n Comm'n on Ethics Op. 01-03; *see* 70 L.W. 2022 (5/16/01).

[347] N.J. Comm. on Att'y Adver. Op. 32, http://lawlibrary.rutgers.edu/ethics/caa/caa32_1.html; *see* 74 L.W. 2052 (6/6/05).

litigation, provided that they follow the disciplinary rules, especially the rule about communicating with unrepresented persons.

Because the Internet has global reach, it is necessary to conform to ethical rules of all jurisdictions. The attorney must identify him- or herself, be truthful, and tell represented parties to communicate only through their attorneys. The attorney must make it clear that Internet chat does not create an attorney-client relationship, and must refrain from offering legal advice in jurisdictions where he or she is not admitted to practice.[348] One problem, of course, is that attorneys are licensed only in specific jurisdictions, whereas the Internet is accessible throughout the world. A California ethics opinion requires law firm Web sites either to make it clear that clients are not being solicited outside California, or that the site is subject to regulation in multiple jurisdictions under the rules of each jurisdiction. The second option is especially important if the firm has offices or attorneys licensed to practice in other states.[349]

The Maine ethics committee ruled that it is permissible for attorneys to retain client documents and correspondence in electronic form without also maintaining hard copy. However, an attorney who chooses to do this must also maintain whatever tools will be necessary for the client to access these materials in the future (e.g., computer programs, or even obsolete computers that can continue to use the obsolete programs).[350]

Arizona bar regulators ruled in 2005 that storing client files on a network connected to the Internet (rather than an intranet) is permissible as long as reasonable steps are taken to protect the files against inappropriate disclosure or destruction. The firm must use tools such as firewalls and security software (e.g., antivirus; anti-adware and anti-spyware), passwords, and encryption. To satisfy the Rule 1.6 requirement of competency, the firm must either develop competence within the firm or hire experts.[351]

In 2006, the Ninth Circuit joined the First, Second, Tenth, and D.C. Circuits in permitting the cost of computerized legal research to be passed along; only the Eighth Circuit does not allow this.[352]

When a client hired a new lawyer — after suing the first lawyer for failing to make a timely claim under the Extraordinary Injury Fund covering defective replacement hips — the District Court ruled that the successor attorney had a duty to register his e-mail address with the court's electronic case management

---

[348] Philadelphia Bar Ass'n Prof'l Guidance Comm. Op. 98-6; 66 L.W. 2613 (3/98).

[349] California State Bar Standing Comm. on Prof'l Responsibility and Conduct Formal Op. 2001-155. *See* 70 L.W. 2083.

[350] Maine Bd. of Bar Overseers Prof'l Ethics Comm. Op. 183, 72 L.W. 2541 (1/28/04).

[351] Arizona State Bar Comm. on the Rules of Prof'l Conduct Op. 05-04; *see* 74 L.W. 2053 (7/05) N.J. Sup. Ct. Advisory Comm. on Prof'l Ethics Op. 701, 74 L.W. 2691 (4/10/06) permits storage of client files on a server outside the law firm, as long as the service provider employs appropriate security measures.

[352] Trustees of the Constr. Indus. and Laborers Health and Welfare Trust v. Redland Ins. Co., 460 F.3d 1253 (9th Cir. 2006).

system in order to receive notification of orders in the case. Thus, the District Court denied a motion under FRAP 4(a)(6) to re-open the time to appeal an order denying discovery. The Sixth Circuit said that the new attorney was not compelled to register with the court's electronic system, but the case was only in the federal MDL part because the manufacturer wanted to block discovery. However, where the only burden on the attorney is leaving an e-mail address, the Sixth Circuit ruled that the replacement attorney was responsible for keeping up with the case docket.[353]

As of early 2008, it was reported that California, Illinois, and Florida had good systems for online document filing, but state practices were far from uniform. Some states are almost fully electronic, some continue to rely mostly on paper. One major barrier is deciding how to balance privacy rights (e.g., by limiting access or redacting the documents) against the status of court records as public documents.[354] Yet another hurdle lawyers must jump is producing electronic information in the appropriate form. The "native format" for e-mail usually creates a "container file," sometimes called a "compound file" — and the container or compound file often includes both discoverable and privileged communications. The most common enterprise e-mail application is Microsoft Exchange Server; files with an .edb suffix are Microsoft Exchange Server container files. Enterprise e-mail stored locally on a laptop or desktop using Outlook is usually in an Outlook.PST or Outlook. OST files, although older e-mails may be in Archive.PST format. To prevent the privileged material from being recoverable by an opponent's computer expert, it is better to respond to discovery orders with "quasi-native formats" that are electronically searchable and maintain the functionality of the native source, but are restricted to discoverable material. Quasi-native formats include .PST files that have been edited to remove privileged material, .MSG and .EML.[355]

---

[353] Kuhn v. Sulzer Orthopedics, Inc., 498 F.3d 365 (6th Cir. 2007).

[354] Lynne Marek, *Patchwork E-Filing Frustrates Lawyers*, Nat'l L.J. 2/26/08 (law.com).

[355] Craig Ball, *How to Go Native Without Going South*, Law Technology News 9/27/07 (law.com).

Chapter 28

Computers and the Law

§ 28.01   INTRODUCTION

In earlier editions and supplements of this work, computers were discussed in two aspects: the computers themselves might be found in law offices, and the legal consequences of computing, especially software. By now, computers (desktop, laptop, networked) are an essential part of the law office environment. Computers make a firm's support staff much more productive — or, in fact, replace most or all of the support staff. Even lawyers who are allergic to keyboarding can get into the act with speech recognition software.

Computers are used for litigation management, time management, and billing. Researching online and communicating by e-mail are an important part of the lawyer's day. Courts are moving toward acceptance of electronically filed documents and CD-ROM briefs or posting of documents to secure Web sites.

However, the legal system does not always "get it" when it comes to software, and especially the Internet and electronic commerce. See § 2.04 for proposals to add electronic commerce and software licensing provisions to the UCC.

In mid-2005, the Supreme Court upheld the FCC's finding that broadband cable modem companies are not subject to mandatory regulation as common carriers, finding it to be a reasonable construction of the Communications Act and Administrative Procedure Act. As a result, cable modem providers do not have an obligation to allow their competitors to interconnect with their systems.[1]

§ 28.02 THE OFFICE NETWORK

In the pre-computer era, the typical legal document was drafted by an attorney who hand-wrote research results (usually on yellow legal pads), hand-wrote drafts, had those drafts typed by a secretary, revised the drafts by hand, had them retyped, and so on through many iterations.

Under current practice (and as long as the attorney can learn to type and use the software!), the attorney can assemble the document entirely electronically, with little or no support staff assistance. Documents can be completed much faster, with greater accuracy. Instead of consulting a printed form book, or forms file assembled by the firm, the attorney can select and customize clauses from a document assembly database of suitable clauses.

For the purposes of law office computing, "client" means something quite different from what it does in general legal parlance. A "server" is a powerful central computer that runs a network; a "client" is an individual workstation within the network. Computers within a network are also known as "nodes" of the network. A small network (up to about six computers) can be set up as a "peer-to-peer" network, where the computers are interconnected but there is no central server. A larger network will require at least one server. The availability of wireless networking of hardware devices, and wireless Internet connections, continues to improve.

[A] Typical Law Office Hardware

It is difficult to make recommendations about hardware, because of the constant changes in operating systems and the ever-increasing speed and complexity of computer processors and memory. As a general rule, investment in additional

---

[1] National Cable and Telecomm. Ass'n v. Brand X Internet Serv., 545 U.S. 967 (2005).

memory is usually wise, although the types of applications usually used in law offices do not demand the highest-speed chips that are needed for graphics-intensive applications. In many cases, the low-end system offered by a vendor of business computers will be adequate for law office use.

The Wall Street Journal's computer columnist, Walter Mossberg, now considers the laptop the primary form of new computer purchase, although most of the same considerations apply to desktop computer purchases. Mossberg said that there is a price range of $350–$3,000 for computers with screens in the range of 12–17″, weighing 2.5–7 lbs. He recommended Apple and Lenova ThinkPad as the most reliable laptop brands. For heavy travel usage, a model with a 13.3″ screen and normal keyboard in a thin, light case is probably best; a 5–7 lbs. machine with a 13.3 or 15.4″ screen is probably better for a computer that is usually used on a desk. Mossberg found Apple's Leopard OS to be better, faster, and less vulnerable than Windows Vista, which he described as slower than XP and subject to compatibility issues with many types of hardware and software. Mossberg said that any dual core processor is adequate for the normal range of tasks, and paying extra for a faster one is not a good bargain. He recommends looking for a hard drive of at least 160 GB, and with the N (faster) version of Wi-Fi built in. He recommends a minimum of 2 GB memory — or 3 GB to run Vista Home Premium.[2] In addition to standard laptops, there are "ultraportables" that are very small and light, but have limited features and hard to use keyboards. Ultraportables usually cost more than standard laptops and are easily damaged.[3]

Given the increasing complexity of these devices, extended service contracts offered by the manufacturer are often a wise purchase, with in-office servicing far more convenient than having to bring the equipment to a service center or return it to the manufacturer. As a precautionary measure, it is also sensible to create a relationship with a local repair person or shop who may be able to repair the computer or provide a temporary replacement in a shorter time span than it would take to get a warranty repair.

Brian R. Harris, describing high-end systems available in late 2007, noted that dual-core processors are common; quad-core units (i.e., four processor cores on a chip, making processing faster) are now state of the art, but manufacturers are working on eight-core processors. The 250 gigabyte (GB) hard drives are normal, but a one-terabyte drive (four times the size) is available. One GB of RAM is almost standard, but a high-end machine needs 4 GB. An external Blue-Ray disc writer for transferring data is a helpful peripheral. He suggests specs for a high-end system using two fast quad-core processors to run Windows Vista Ultimate with extensive memory and a 24″ widescreen monitor, a set-up that would cost about $6,400. But a very powerful, albeit not state of the art, system can be purchased for

---

[2] Walter S. Mossberg, *Consider Your Needs, Then Use This Guide To Buying a Laptop*, Wall St. J. 4/10/08 at B1.

[3] Alan Cohen, *Ultraportable Laptops: For Your Briefcase?* Corporate Counsel 7/25/08 (law.com).

$3,100, by using a dual-rather than quad-core processor or even a single processor. Having a second hard drive is useful in the law firm environment, especially for back-ups, but the system can function with just one hard drive (or a second hard drive can be added as budget permits), and a 2 GB hard drive can work well, especially with lower storage and slower processors than the top-of-the-line system. A 20-inch rather than 24-inch monitor will also be acceptable, as will running Windows Vista Business rather than Ultimate.[4]

Some law office computing issues that are not always remembered:

- Ergonomic keyboards can help prevent or mitigate repetitive stress injuries caused by keyboarding
- Although it has not reached the levels common in science fiction TV shows, voice input (dictation to a computer) has improved significantly
- An Uninterruptible Power Supply (UPS) can save data by allowing a system to be shut down in an orderly fashion if, for example, there is a blackout
- Have extra devices on hand as replacements if repairs are necessary
- For devices such as printers and CD or DVD burners, the initial cost of the component is not the only factor. Price and availability of consumable media (such as printer cartridges and CDs or DVDs) is also crucial
- Opening the case and replacing components or adding new components is easier in some computer models than others
- The computer system must have the appropriate ports for attaching whatever peripheral devices (e.g., printers, Zip drives) will be needed
- If a laptop computer is being used as a main computer, it is often handy to connect it to a docking station so that the laptop can be removed and taken to court, to a client's office, etc., with minimal disruption
- Many attorneys use hand-held devices such as Palm Pilots, so not only is it important to make sure these devices can be synchronized with the office computers, but that staffers remember to do so!

In the past, devices for reading digital books have failed, for reasons such as being too expensive, too big, not having enough battery life, etc. Sony's Reader Digital Book added some useful features, such as an "electronic paper" display that really does look like paper, has sharp text, and does not use much power. Amazon.com introduced its Kindle reader. Both models work in direct sunlight, but the screen is not backlit, so a light will be required to read in bed or in a darkened airplane cabin. The Sony Reader handles Word documents, PDFs, text, and RTFs from a PC; the Kindle does not read PDFs and has difficulties with Word files.[5]

---

[4] Brian R. Harris, *Are High-End Systems Naughty or Nice?* The Legal Intelligencer 10/4/07 (law.com).

[5] Alan Cohen, *Digital Readers: Law Books of the Future?* The American Lawyer 7/8/08 (law.com).

[B] Typical Law Office Applications

Although not all law offices will use all of these applications, this is a list of potential applications:

- Word processing
- Document drafting
- Scanning printed documents into the computer system, so they will not have to be re-keyed
- "Burning" CDs containing large amounts of information
- E-mail for communications within and outside the firm (with due attention to security and confidentiality). Both ABA and Ohio ethics committees have ruled that sending unencrypted e-mail that discusses client matters is not per se an unethical breach of confidentiality. The client's consent is only required for the use of e-mail if the information is sensitive enough to require special security measures.[6]
- Anti-spam, anti-virus and "firewall" measures (to prevent unauthorized access to the law firm's electronic communications)
- A regular program (and one that is monitored and enforced) to back up data. The technology for backups changes fairly often, so it may be necessary to engage in large-scale transfer of backup data to a different medium (e.g., from optical disks to CD-RW), and allowances will have to be made for the time, effort, and money required for this task. The main methods are relying on individual employees to perform backups (e.g., to floppy disks, to CDs or DVDs that they burn, or to a Zip disk), having backups made to a network, and using offsite backup (e.g., placing materials on a secure Web site).[7]
- Time management and planning
- Calendaring and scheduling
- Tickler systems, so that, for instance, preparation of a motion begins a certain number of days before the motion has to be filed
- Project management and coordination
- Checks for conflict of interest
- Billing
- Legal research (commercial services such as Lexis and Westlaw; servers operated by courts, government units, and administrative agencies)
- Dictation and speech synthesis, to reduce or eliminate the need to "type"
- Continuing legal education

---

[6] ABA Standing Committee on Ethics and the Profession Formal Opinion 399-413 (3/10/99), 67 L.W. 2645; Ohio Supreme Court Board of Comm'rs on Grievances and Discipline Op. 99-2 (4.9.99), 67 L.W. 2646.

[7] *See, e.g.*, Mark W. Martin, *Take Cover: Backup Tips and Options for Smaller Firms*, 29 Law Prac. Mgmt. 36 (3/03).

- Litigation management (preparation of a searchable database of documents related to a case, so the information can be correlated and will be available for trial preparation and at trial).

To an increasing extent, communications with courts (including scheduling meetings and court appearances and filing documents) will be done electronically rather than in person or via telephone.

The subject of law firm telecommunications in general is a complex one, and either an economically and technologically sophisticated firm employee, or an outside consultant, will be needed to advise the firm of its options for telephone service, Internet service, and high-speed Internet connections (whether wireless, DSL, or cable). Selection of an appropriate provider depends not just on price but on reliability of service and ability to restore service after an interruption.

Open-source software, such as the Linux operating system and the Eclipse suite of Java development tools has achieved very broad use, but many users fail to understand that it is still protected, licensed software and is not in the public domain. Open-source developers permit much more freedom than conventional licenses allow, but there are still restrictions. The Open Source Initiative is a not-for-profit corporation that manages the Open Source Definition and certifies that licenses conform to the standard. The Open Source Standard includes two broad categories of licenses: reciprocal and attribution. A reciprocal license permits any user to modify the software according to personal needs, but if the modified software is distributed, the changes are available to anyone. An attribution license credits the source, and code under an attribution license can be embedded in a product that is not open source.[8]

A further complication: many law firms will want to maintain their own Web site. This will require creating a design (either in-house or by hiring a design firm), adding content to the site, handling routine site operations and maintenance in-house or by contract with an outside service provider ("hosting"), and adding new content to keep the site fresh.

Steps must be taken to publicize the Web site and attract the attention of clients, potential clients, and other attorneys. Steps must also be taken to segregate confidential client matters communicated electronically from the Web site that is available to the public. One way to do this is with password protection "firewalls" that limit access to authorized users. Sensitive material can be placed on a limited "intranet" system that is not publicly available, rather than on a Web site.

Wikis (linked Web pages that can easily be edited by many people) are gaining popularity among law firms and in-house legal departments as a way to keep information current, or to manage large projects. Although there are risks such as misuse and hacking, wikis have the advantage of displaying only the current version of a document, reducing the risk of version confusion. For example, Sun found that a wiki that was online for six weeks allowed a group of 110

---

[8] *See* John K. Waters, *Road Rules for Open-Source Licensing* (Special to law.com 6/27/06).

attorneys to discuss and edit the firm's database of standard legal forms, agreements, and clauses. Most of the updates were made during the first three weeks. Sun estimated that setting up a team of lawyers communicating by conventional means would have taken six to nine months to update the forms, and the results would not have been as good.[9]

Recent ethics opinions have permitted attorneys to affiliate with Web sites that list attorneys for potential clients, and also to use online exchanges where corporations post Requests for Proposals for legal representation.[10]

The New Jersey Supreme Court Committee on Attorney Advertising delineated limits for online marketing tools. A law firm URL can permissibly describe a practice specialty, but the URL cannot be used as a substitute for the firm's official name. The description must be accurate, and the front page of a law firm site must give the firm's formal name, physical address, telephone number, and the disclosures and advisories required of attorney advertisements under Rules of Professional Conduct 7.1 to 7.4.[11]

A mid-2005 Arizona ethics opinion holds that it is permissible to store client files on a network connected to the Internet (rather than an intranet with access limited to the firm and authorized persons) provided that reasonable steps are taken to preserve the files from destruction or hacking. To satisfy the Rule 1.6 requirement of competency, firms must either develop competency within the firm or hire experts in the use of protective tools such as anti-virus software and firewalls.[12]

However, attorneys who participate in a company's prepaid legal services may not use a Web site hosted by that company to exchange confidential information with clients who are members of the plan; use of the site could cause waiver of attorney-client privilege. Even disclaimers cannot cure the threat to confidentiality. However, it would be permissible for each participating law firm to host its own site to communicate with plan members.[13]

---

[9] Niraj Chokshi, *Legal Departments, Law Firms Weighing Wikis*, The Recorder 9/25/08 (law.com).

[10] *See, e.g.*, D.C. Bar Legal Ethics Committee Op. 302, (11/21/00); *see* 69 L.W. 2515; Nassau County Bar Ass'n Comm. on Prof'l Ethics Op. 01-4 (2/6/01), 69 L.W. 2541. *See also* § 27.08 for discussion of Internet legal issues.

[11] New Jersey Supr. Ct. Comm. on Att'y Adver. Opinions 32, 33 (5/23/05), discussed in Charles Toutant, *Advertising Panel Lays Down Rules for Law Firm Ads on Web*, N.J.L.J 5/31/05 (law.com) and at 74 L.W. 2052. New York, Ohio, and Texas also exempt domain names from general rules about law firm nomenclature.

[12] Arizona State Bar Comm. on the Rules of Prof'l Conduct Op. 05-04 (7/05); *see* 74 L.W. 2053.

[13] Maryland State Bar Ass'n Comm. on Ethics Op. 2004-03, 72 L.W. 2357 (11/20/03). On confidentiality issues, *see also* Barton v. United States Dist. Ct. for the Central District of California, 410 F.3d 1104 (9th Cir. 2005), applying attorney-client privilege to questionnaires on a law firm Web site, filled out by people asking for information about a potential class action about the drug Paxil. Although the form included a check box to show knowledge that submitting the information did not create an attorney-client relationship, because the respondents were laymen, the Ninth Circuit concluded that they would probably believe they were being solicited as potential clients.

It has been ruled that an attorney can retain client correspondence and documents in electronic form without retaining hard copy — provided that the attorney also maintains whatever tools will be necessary for future client access (e.g., copies of the old software).[14] Virginia ruled that it is not unethical for a lawyer to provide services purely online, without face-to-face interaction, on the grounds that competency depends on the thoroughness and accuracy of representation rather than the medium through which it is delivered.[15]

[C] Legal Documents Online

The FRCP amendments taking effect December 1, 2001 provide, at Rule 5(b), that a party who consents in writing can be served process electronically. Service is complete upon transmission of the file. The same rule is incorporated by reference into Bankruptcy Rule 7005 and Fed. R. Crim. P. 69(b). However, under Rule 6(e), a party served electronically is entitled to an additional three days to respond, to correspond to the three days allowed under the "mail rule" for paper documents. Under Rule 77(d), parties can also consent to electronic service of notices from the District Court.[16]

Process can be served via e-mail on a defendant outside the United States, where the defendant refused service on its registered U.S. agents, and no other address was known. The Ninth Circuit held that Due Process was satisfied, and this procedure constituted "other means not prohibited by international agreement" under FRCP 4(f)(3).[17]

Most documents in civil and bankruptcy cases have been available electronically since September 2001 if the public would have been permitted to view paper files at the courthouse; a pilot program for criminal files began in March 2002.[18]

The nonprofit Public Resource.Org put more than 1.8 million pages of federal cases online free and without copyright restrictions, launching on February 11, 2008. The archive includes all of the Supreme Court decisions and all Court of Appeals cases since 1950. In the 1990s, Project Hermes started to make Supreme Court decisions available online; and there are several free online sources for Court of Appeals opinions.[19]

---

[14] Maine Board of Bar Overseers Prof'l Ethics Comm. Op. 183, 72 L.W. 2541 (1/28/04).

[15] Virginia State Bar Ass'n Standing Comm. on Legal Ethics Op. 1791, 72 L.W. 2443 (12/22/03).

[16] http://www.uscourts.gov/rules/newrules6.html, discussed at 70 L.W. 2302.

[17] Rio Properties Inc. v. Rio Int'l Interlinkserve, 284 F.3d 1007 (9th Cir. 2002).

[18] "Report on Privacy and Public Access to Electronic Case Files" (September 2001), http://www.uscourts.gov/Press_Releases/att81501.pdf; see 70 L.W. 2180 and 70 L.W. 2575; see http://pacer.psc.uscourts.gov/cgi-bin/links.pl (no www) for the Eighth Circuit and ten District Courts' pilot project for electronic access at a cost of seven cents per page, and see Colleen DeBaise, *Courthouse Opts for Web Filings, Going "Paperless,"* Wall St. J. 12/12/02 at B7B for the Southern District of New York's paperless filing system and document access project.

[19] Robert J. Ambrogi, *Online Legal Research Revolution*, Law Technology News 3/18/08 (law.com).

In 2001, the Patent and Trademark Office proposed a rule under which trademark documents would have to be filed online, not on paper (although certain exceptions would apply). Documents in this category include registration applications, amendments to allege use, and statements of use.[20]

The Federal Rules, including those of Civil Procedure, Evidence, Bankruptcy, and Criminal Procedure have been amended to give Courts of Appeals the power to mandate document filing in electronic rather than paper form. Amendments to FRCP 26(b), effective December 1, 2006, made major changes in the practice of electronic discovery. Under the new rules, a party in control of electronically stored information can oppose discovery on the grounds that the sources are not reasonably accessible by reason of burden or cost. It is up to the party from whom discovery is sought to show lack of accessibility. Discovery can be ordered even if the showing of inaccessibility is made, if the requester shows good cause. However, Rule 26(b)(1) remains in effect, so only relevant information need be identified or preserved. Under new Rule 26(f), litigation parties are obligated to discuss issues about preserving discoverable information. Accessible data types must be produced if the information is relevant and production is not unduly burdensome. If, after production, the requesting party believes that its requests are not fully satisfied, the parties must confer about inaccessible data before the requesting party can move for further discovery. Accessibility is also a function of the state of technology; it has become much easier to review backup tapes, for example.[21]

The Federal Rules of Civil Procedure have been amended, effective December 1, 2006, to add Rule 37(f). Rule 37(f) holds that, absent exceptional circumstances, sanctions cannot be imposed for failure to produce electronically stored information that became unavailable as a result of routine, good faith operation of a computer system. However, the rule applies only to sanctions under the FRCP, not other disciplinary systems such as attorney ethics rules or the court's inherent sanction power. A court can still impose punitive sanctions in discovery, such as permitting one party to take more depositions, or extending a cut-off date. It is not clear if Rule 37(f) permits destruction of electronic information pursuant to routine records management; if there is a preservation obligation as a result of litigation, a party may have to modify its system to ensure that data is preserved.[22]

An article from *Corporate Counsel* provides some suggestions to improve electronic discovery:

- The firm's IT department must be trained to locate and collect data, then testify about it accurately and articulately
- Select outside counsel who are credible to the judge

---

[20] 66 FR 45792 (8/30/01).

[21] David Isom and Dean A. Gonsowski, *Civil Rules: Navigating New Data "Accessibility" Standards*, eDiscovery Law & Strategy 6/22/06 (law.com).

[22] Kevin F. Brady, *What Protection Does Rule 37(f) Provide?* The Legal Intelligencer 7/3/07 (law.com).

- Use the "meet and confer" provisions to discuss the scope of data collection with the opposing attorneys (an estimated 90% of discovery cost stems from reviewing material for relevancy and privilege before producing it)
- Limit the cost of production by agreeing on who will be the custodians, limiting the search period and agreeing on the terms that will be searched for
- Be aware at all times of where files are stored.[23]

In mid-2007, the District Court for the Central District of California ordered the defendant in a copyright infringement suit to collect and produce information from the RAM of their servers; the MPAA wanted information about users who illegally downloaded files of movies and TV episodes. The defendant's servers were technically capable of creating a request log, but the logging function was disabled, so requests for files were only stored in RAM and were overwritten after about six hours. That raised the question of whether the information constituted "electronically stored information" as defined by FRCP 34(a). There is Ninth Circuit precedent that copying software into RAM fixes it in a tangible medium. The Central District held that the defendant was not forced to create new data: the information existed, was in the defendant's possession, and was temporarily stored in RAM, so production could be ordered under Rule 34(a).[24]

Because e-mail is now the predominant form of corporate communication, discoverability of e-mails is likely to become an issue in every case. It generally can be assumed that an e-mail that is sought has been backed up somewhere, but that could be on magnetic media, a mail server, a hard drive, or shared network storage. Judges differ in the extent to which they will treat e-mail as an official communication that binds the company. It is now a part of corporate risk management to set policy for retention (or the reverse) of e-mails, with the caveat that spoliation of evidence must be avoided.[25]

Yet another hurdle lawyers must jump is producing electronic information in the appropriate form. The "native format" for e-mail usually creates a "container file," sometimes called a "compound file" — and the container or compound file often includes both discoverable and privileged communications. The most common enterprise e-mail application is Microsoft Exchange Server; files with an .edb suffix are Microsoft Exchange Server container files. Enterprise e-mail stored locally on a laptop or desktop using Outlook is usually in an Outlook.PST or Outlook.OST files, although older e-mails may be in Archive.PST format. To prevent the privileged material from being recoverable by an opponent's computer expert, it is better to respond to discovery orders with "quasi-native formats" that

---

[23] Ronald K. Perkowski, *Coping With the EDD Drumbeat*, Corporate Counsel 1/25/08 (law.com).
      [24] Columbia Pictures Industries v. Bunnelli, 2007 U.S. Dist. LEXIS 46364 (C.D. Cal 5/27/07); *see* Tom Allman, *Umbrella Rulings Can't Cover All Data*. Law Technology News 8/30/07 (law.com); Kelly Talcott, *RAM and FRCP 34 Lock Horns*, N.Y.L.J. 6/27/07 (law.com).
      [25] David M. Remnity, *Electronic Mail: Key Issues for Corporate Counsel in Discovery*, 72 L.W. 2339 (12/16/03).

are electronically searchable and maintain the functionality of the native source, but are restricted to discoverable material. Quasi-native formats include .PST files that have been edited to remove privileged material, .MSG and .EML.[26]

Starting in February 2004, an application for patent protection in multiple countries can be made electronically by filing with WIPO. One hundred twenty-three countries participate in the PCT-SAFE system under the WIPO Patent Cooperation Treaty. The system has been praised for lowering the costs of printing, copying and mailing, making searchable documents available, and offering immediate notification of receipt and processing.[27]

In a 2003 employment discrimination suit, the Southern District of New York ruled that the plaintiff showed that there could perhaps be relevant material in back-up tapes, so the defendant would have to produce (at its own expense) all e-mails from its optical disks and active servers if the e-mails referenced the plaintiff, plus e-mails from five back-up servers selected by the plaintiff.[28]

An earlier case[29] set an eight-part standard for resolving disputes about electronic discovery. The relevant factors are how specific the discovery request is; the chance of finding critical information; why the information was collected in the first place; how available the information is from other sources; the relative benefit to the parties of receiving versus retaining the information; resources of each party; and each party's ability and incentive to control costs. Generally, the requesting party would have to pay the costs of discovery. The *Zubulake* decision proposes a revised set of considerations, including the relative accessibility of various kinds of electronic data.

Later, the defendant was sanctioned for failure to impose a "litigation hold" on material that might have been discoverable; accessible tapes in active use, but not inaccessible backup tapes, are subject to the litigation hold. In this case, the sanction was an order to reimburse the plaintiff for the cost of repeating the depositions of four key witnesses.[30]

§ 28.03   E-COMMERCE

From the seller's perspective, having an online "store" on a Web site instead of, or in addition to, a conventional bricks-and-mortar store can be an excellent way to serve new customers at low cost. From the buyer's perspective, online shopping can be convenient and permits unparalleled access to price comparisons and auctions. However, commercial law — which evolved in a nineteenth century

---

[26] Craig Ball, *How to Go Native Without Going South*, Law Technology News 9/27/07 (law.com).

[27] No by-line, *WIPO Begins Online Patent Filing to Cover Inventions Internationally*, 72 L.W. 2504 (2/24/04).

[28] Zubulake v. UBS Warburg, 71 L.W. 1716 (S.D.N.Y. 5/13/03).

[29] Rowe Entertainment Inc. v. William Morris Agency Inc., 205 F.R.D. 421 (S.D.N.Y. 2002).

[30] Zubulake v. UBS Warburg LLC, 72 L.W. 1263 (S.D.N.Y. 10/22/03), discussed in Dean Gonsowski, *Zubulake IV: Spoliation Inferences, Impossible Burdens, Unintended Consequences*, 72 L.W. 2387.

mixed agricultural and manufacturing economy — has some difficulties in catching up to electronic commerce.

[A] ESign, UCITA, and UETA

P.L. 106-229, the Electronic Signatures in Global and National Commerce Act (nicknamed eSign), was passed on June 30, 2000. Broadly speaking, it makes it possible to sign contracts and enter into transactions with the same legal force and effect whether the consent of the parties is indicated by written or electronic signatures. This statute defines an electronic signature as any sound, symbol, or process that is attached to or logically associated with a written record (e.g., a contract) and is used for the purpose of signing the record.

eSign provides for acknowledgment or notarization with the digital signature of a notary or the person making the acknowledgment. The statute also provides that record retention requirements under statutes and regulations can be satisfied by retaining the records in electronic rather than hard copy form. However, consumers are entitled to demand hard copy instead of or as a means of memorializing an electronic agreement. Wills, codicils, testamentary trusts, and family law documents are not subject to eSign. Furthermore, although it is intended in large part as an e-commerce measure, eSign applies only to Articles 2, 2A, and part of Article 1 of the UCC. States are permitted to modify, limit, or supersede eSign by adopting UETA (see below) or by being consistent with eSign, referring to eSign itself, as long as their law is technology-neutral rather than favoring a specific technology.

Despite its broad reach, eSign does not resolve all of the legal problems of electronic commerce. Many of these problems are of a type traditionally within the domain of the states. Because of the need for understandable rules for commerce between states, these issues are also ripe for the adoption of uniform laws. The IRS cited eSign in its 50-page Final Regulation, published October 20, 2006, explaining how pension and employee benefit plans should use electronic media to communicate with plan participants and beneficiaries.[31] In July 1999, the National Conference of Commissioners on Uniform State Laws approved the Uniform Electronic Transactions Act (UETA) and the Uniform Computer Information Transactions Act (UCITA), paving the way for adoption by state legislatures. UETA is not substantive, merely a procedural or enabling law so electronic transactions can be effectuated. Under UETA, contracts entered into online, like electronic documents, records, and signatures are presumed valid. There is no presumption of invalidity based on the digital nature of the communications.

An electronic signature is a sound, symbol, or process attached to or logically associated with a process and executed or adopted with the intent to sign. Therefore, an encrypted digital signature would count. So would a name at the end of an e-mail message that is intended as a signature, or a click-through that identifies the sender. However, certain documents and transactions are excluded from the reach of UETA: UCC transactions and wills, codicils and testamentary trusts.

---

[31] T.D. 9294, RIN 1545-BD68, http://www.irs.gov/pub/irs-regs-td9294.pdf (10/20/06).

The legal system often has trouble catching up to business' adoption of new technologies, with electronic signatures as an example. The federal government allows electronic signatures on tax returns and SEC filings. The Federal Rules permit, and in some cases require, electronic signatures on electronically filed documents, although there must be an "original" signature in ink on documents filed by hand. The New York CPLR allows electronic (e.g., fax) service of papers signed electronically, and the statute now defines "writing" to include a tangible written text transmitted via electronic signals, and "signature" as any means intended to authenticate a writing.[32]

NCCUSSL's proposed Uniform Real Property E-Recording Act, calls for a gradual phase-in of computerized recording systems to replace the existing paper documentation. One problem is that many state laws specifically require the filing of paper documents, or refer to the hard copy as the original document. The proposed E-Recording Act authorizes but does not mandate the appointment of e-recording commissions to handle the transition. The proposal does not tackle the issue of financing the new system; state legislatures will probably impose a user fee for recording title electronically.[33]

UCITA deals with the manifold implication of "computer information transactions" (UCITA § 103(a)), but excludes financial services transactions, sound recordings, printed books and periodicals, TV and motion pictures. UCITA endorses shrinkwrap licenses (here called "mass market licenses"), subjects software licenses to the warranty rules that apply to goods, requires conspicuous disclaimers of warranties; permits customers to reject the Terms of Service under a license and get a full refund.

A large part of UCITA deals with special rules for forming a contract electronically, with a special emphasis on making sure that parties are not inadvertently bound when they did not wish to enter into a contract.

Although many UCITA-covered transactions will occur between merchants, the statute also seeks to protect the rights of consumers. UCITA allows recovery for all types of damages, including damages for injury caused by software defects. The statute creates a new implied warranty for accuracy of data provided electronically to a contracting party. Under UCITA, choice of law clauses is

---

[32] Stephen M. Kramarsky, *E-Mail Meets the Statute of Frauds*, N.Y.L.J. 5/22/08 (law.com) discusses a number of New York cases on these issues, e.g., Vista Developers Corp. v. VPF Realty, 847 N.Y.S.2d 416 (S. Ct. Queens Co. 2007) allowing e-mails to satisfy the statute of frauds for qualified financial contracts as defined by General Obligations Law § 5-701(b)(2)(a)-(i) — but real estate contracts are not included in the definition; Al-Bawaba.com Inc. v. Nstein Techs. Corp., No. 45550/07, 2008 N.Y. Slip Op. 50853(U), 2008 WL 1869751 (S. Ct. Kings Co. Apr. 25, 2008) [an e-mail exchange about a licensing agreement was a "signed writing" because the sender's typed name at the bottom manifested his intention to authenticate the "writing"]; Stevens v. Publicis, SA, No. 602716/03, 2008 N.Y. Slip Op. 02880, 854 N.Y.S.2d 690, 692 (1st Dep't 2008) [employment agreement can be modified by an e-mail with the sender's name typed at the end, because of intent to form a contract]; JSO Assocs. Inc. v. Price, 2008 N.Y. Misc. LEXIS 2227 (S. Ct. Nassau Co. Mar. 18, 2008) [unsigned e-mail satisfied the statute of frauds because the sender's name appeared clearly].

[33] http://www.law.upenn.edu, *see* 73 L.W. 2088.

permissible, so the law of the forum in which the retailer is located will be applied unless a different forum is specified.

UCITA allows a licensor of software to disable the software once a license is canceled. The uniform law covers electronically transmitted information, but excludes other types of information licensing, such as those relating to print media and motion pictures.[34]

In December 1999, Pennsylvania became the first state to adopt UETA, through S.D. 55, legislation recognizing electronic documents and signatures used in online commercial transactions. (California already had a law that was inspired by UETA but did not fully follow its text.)[35] In April 2004, Wisconsin became the forty-fourth state to adopt UETA; in July, South Carolina became the forty-sixth, leaving Georgia, Illinois, New York, and Washington State as the sole holdouts. The Wisconsin statute also places electronic postmarks under the USPS Electronic Postmark program on a parity with postmarks on physical mail.[36] UCITA has been adopted in Maryland and Virginia. There were no further UCITA adoptions in 2000 or 2001. In fact, Iowa, West Virginia, and North Carolina have "bomb shelter" laws that make contracts governed by UCITA unenforceable in the state. In 2003, the NCCUSL threw in the towel and abandoned efforts to get any further legislatures to adopt the statute.[37]

Even though the sale of Nazi memorabilia violates French law, the Northern District of California held that a French court order requiring Yahoo to bar French citizens from accessing information about auctions of such items cannot be enforced in the United States, because it violates the First Amendment.[38] However, when the case got to the Ninth Circuit in 2004, the court denied Yahoo's application for an injunction against enforcement of the French court order. The Ninth Circuit did not reach the constitutional issues, merely holding that the French organizations that brought the suit in France were not subject to the jurisdiction of the United States courts because there was no wrongful conduct targeted specifically at California citizens.[39] The Ninth Circuit reheard the case en banc at the beginning of 2006, and the underlying action was dismissed without prejudice. To the disappointment of many, the case was decided on procedural grounds and no First Amendment precedent was created. Of the 11 judges on the en banc panel, eight concluded that the District Court had personal jurisdiction over the

---

[34] See Carlyle C. Ring Jr., *The Need for Uniform Rules for the Information Highway: An Overview of UCITA*, http://www.nccusl.org/nccusl/uniformact_overview/uniformacts-ov-ucita.asp.

[35] See 68 L.W. 2069.

[36] Wisconsin Laws 2004 AB 755; South Carolina Laws 2004 H. 4270; see 73 L.W. 2071.

[37] See 72 L.W. 2080.

[38] Yahoo! Inc. v. La Ligue Contre le Racisme, 169 F. Supp. 2d 1181 (N.D. Cal. 2001).

[39] Yahoo v. La Ligue Contre Le Racisme et L'Antisemitisme, 379 F.3d 1120 (9th Cir. 2004), discussed in AP, *Supreme Court Sidesteps Yahoo's International Dispute*, 5/31/06 (law.com); Jeff Chorney, *On Appeal, Anti-Nazi Groups Topple Yahoo*, The Recorder 8/24/04 (law.com). *Rehearing en banc* 433 F.3d 1199 (9th Cir. 2006), *cert. denied*, 126 S.Ct. 2332 (5/30/06); see Pam Smith, *In Closely Watched Case, 9th Circuit Rejects Yahoo's Free Speech Argument*, The Record 1/13/06 (law.com).

defendants, but three disagreed. Of the eight-judge majority, three opined that the action should be dismissed because it was unripe for adjudication, and the other five believed the controversy was ripe. Certiorari was denied in May 2006.

[B] Prevention of Fraud and Computer Crimes

The Internet offers a form of instantaneous, inexpensive, widespread communication, where it is easy to conceal or misrepresent the origin of the message. Anyone who has a computer and modem can engage in active trading in stock and other securities. The potential for securities fraud is obvious. The Computer Fraud and Abuse Act (CFA; 18 USC § 1030) is triggered when a computer is used in interstate or international commerce or communications. The application of this statute is not limited to outside hackers. It is triggered, for instance, when an employee uses the employer's computer to transmit the employer's trade secrets to a competitor.

A group of 17 Party City retail stores sought an injunction against two former employees who opened competing stores near Party City stores. The plaintiffs charged that on over 100 occasions, the ex-employees accessed the plaintiffs' computer system without authorization and used the information for competitive purposes. The District Court for the District of New York denied injunctive relief under the Computer Fraud and Abuse Act, on the grounds that it is predominantly a criminal statute and the scope of civil remedies (if any) is uncertain. Injunction was unavailable because of the plaintiffs' failure to show likelihood of success on the merits. The Third Circuit affirmed based on the lack of evidence, but made it clear that there is a civil cause of action under the CFA; the statutory text says so, and other courts have allowed it — even if access to the data occurred during employment. The Third Circuit held that the CFA allows compensatory damages, and it is not necessary to show that the misappropriated information was confidential or proprietary. The Third Circuit noted that some issues remain unresolved: CFA § 1030(g) requires the conduct to involve a loss of at least $5,000, during a period of a year or more — so what is the value of the "loss"? A 2001 amendment to the statute defines loss as any reasonable cost including the cost of response, performing a damage assessment, restoring the system, and consequential damages such as lost revenue during the time that service was interrupted, but it is still unclear whether loss of clients counts. Some courts allow recovery of lost profits, but only if they relate to the interrupted service — not lost profits from lost competitive advantage.[40]

---

[40] PC Yonkers v. Celebrations The Party and Seasonal Superstore, 428 F.3d 504 (3d Cir 2005), discussed in Risa B. Greene and Heather Z. Steele, *3rd Circuit: Computer Fraud and Abuse Act Provides for Civil Remedies*, The Legal Intelligencer 5/10/06 (law.com); *see also* Bro-Tech Corp. v. Thermax Inc., 2006 WL 51676 (E.D. Pa. 2006): a CFA cause of action is stated by a claim that the defendant gave confidential and proprietary information, taken from his ex-employer's computer system, to his new employer and Hub Group v. Clancy, No. 05-2046 (E.D. Pa. 2006): federal jurisdiction is present over a claim that the defendant took information from the plaintiff's computer for use at a competing company.

The Seventh Circuit held that a conviction under the Computer Fraud and Abuse Act was proper for transmitting radio signals with the intent of disrupting the city's computer-controlled emergency radio network, because the statute covered computer-controlled devices as well. The interstate commerce element is satisfied by whether the device itself is used in interstate commerce, not whether the defendant's actions crossed a state line or affected interstate commerce.[41] Later, the Seventh Circuit also ruled that the use of a secure-erasure program by an exiting employee, to delete files from an employer-sponsored laptop so that they could not be restored, was a transmission that could give rise to civil liability under the Computer Fraud and Abuse Act at 18 USC § 1030(a)(5)(A)(i). The Seventh Circuit held that it is irrelevant whether the program was run from a CD or floppy disk or was downloaded from the Internet; the statute forbids knowingly causing transmission of any program, code or command to cause intentional damage to a protected computer. The Seventh Circuit interpreted the legislative intent as forbidding both outside hacker attacks and attacks from the inside by disgruntled employees, and both access without authorization and access exceeding the degree authorized are forbidden. The defendant in this case also breached the duty of loyalty to the corporation when he quit to go into business for himself.[42]

The $5,000 jurisdictional minimum under the Computer Fraud and Abuse Act can be satisfied by alleging aggregate losses from multiple instances of computer hacking; the entire $5,000 need not come from a single unauthorized access.[43]

The CFA was also violated when a former employee maliciously changed passwords and deleted a company's billing system and two of its databases, because a corporation is considered an individual under the CFA ban on conduct that causes loss to one or more individuals.[44]

The 2002 Homeland Security Act, P.L. 107-296, increases the penalties for cybercrimes based on factors such as the defendant's malicious intent and the sophistication of the criminal process.

P.L. 108-281 (August 2, 2004) amends § 205 of the E-Government Act of 2003, making it clear that where it is necessary to prove the elements of a crime, federal prosecutors can introduce into evidence personal data identifiers (e.g., bank account numbers in a prosecution for bank fraud).[45]

[C] Taxation of E-Commerce

The administration of sales tax became far more complicated when mail order sales became common, because it was no longer simple to determine what should be the taxing jurisdiction(s). As § 28.05, below, shows, jurisdictional

---

[41] United States v. Mitra, 405 F.3d 492 (7th Cir. 2005).

[42] International Airport Ctrs. LLC v. Citrin, 440 F.3d 418 (7th Cir. 2006).

[43] Creative Computing v. Getloaded.com LLC, 386 F.3d 930 (9th Cir. 2004).

[44] United States v. Middleton, 231 F.3d 1207 (9th Cir. 2000).

[45] See 73 L.W. 2074.

problems of all types are quite complex on the Internet — and this is quite true of sales tax determinations.

Tax administrators for 30 states collaborated in the Streamlined Sales Tax Project (SSTP) which issued model legislation under which sales tax could be collected and administered efficiently for Internet sales. The Streamlined Sales Tax Project released a document in January 2002 intended to serve as the foundation of an interstate agreement. The document calls for centralized tax administration, with collection and audit performed at the state level; simplified one-stop registration for retailers who agree to participate; a uniform sales tax return; and a uniform approach to sourcing transactions for tax purposes. The project delegates eventually agreed on the principle that sales are sourced to the location where the order was received or at the address of the purchase, not the place of shipment.[46]

By the end of 2002, there were 35 member states. The agreement calls for a central electronic registration system for the member states, uniform rules for sourcing taxable transactions, simple returns and remittances of taxes, and protection of consumer privacy.[47]

However, the process of creating uniform online sales tax rules will not be a simple one. The states must resolve questions like whether candy is considered food, or handkerchiefs are clothing for tax purposes. There are about 7,500 separate taxing jurisdictions whose rules will have to be reconciled.

Late in 2004, Congress passed P.L. 108-435, a three-year moratorium on state and local taxation of the monthly fees imposed by ISPs. President Bush signed it on December 3, 2004. The three-year period is retroactive to the expiration of the earlier ban, so it runs until November 3, 2007. The statute forbids new, multiple and discriminatory taxes, although existing taxes on Internet and DSL services are permitted to be enforced. Although the 2004 statute permits states to tax online phone service, the FCC has ruled that only the federal government has taxing authority in this context.[48]

In order to encourage e-commerce, the federal government imposed a moratorium on "new" taxes on Internet sales. The moratorium forbids the imposition of levies specifically on Internet access or e-commerce transactions if the levies are not otherwise imposed. However, the moratorium does not affect generally applicable taxes in effect prior to the Internet.

Then, on November 28, 2001, President Bush signed the Internet Tax Non-discrimination Act, P.L. 107-75 (47 USC § 609 et seq.), renewing the moratorium for a further two years, until November 1, 2003. P.L. 108-435 granted yet another reprieve, this time for four years, until November 1, 2007. At press time in 2007, both Houses of Congress had passed an additional seven-year extension; the

---

[46] See the model state tax law and records of proceedings http://www.streamlinedsalestax.org, discussed at 68 L.W. 2158, 69 L.W. 2510, and 70 L.W. 2476.

[47] See 71 L.W. 2333 and www.nga.org. A thirty-sixth state joined after this action was taken.

[48] Congress Votes to Ban States From Taxing Internet Service (no by-line), N.Y. Times Nov. 20, 2004 at C2; 73 L.W. 2301 and 2335.

President was expected to sign the bill, because he is on record as opposing state taxation of Internet access.[49]

In addition to tax barriers, there are other problems limiting the potential of e-commerce. Sometimes, for both laudable reasons (e.g., deterring cyberfraud) and ignoble ones (protecting entrenched local businesses from competition that could benefit consumers by lowering prices), state laws impair e-commerce. For instance, some states prohibit online sales of caskets and contact lenses, or hinder interstate commerce by requiring out-of-state sellers of such merchandise to maintain a state license. Online operations are required to have physical offices in any state in which they wish to offer mortgage services, in order to satisfy licensing requirements. All of the states require a local franchise owner to become involved whenever cars are sold over the Internet.[50]

The case of wine is especially problematic. State regulation of wine sales typically mandates a three-tier system (wine producers sell their wine to licensed wholesalers who handle excise tax compliance; retailers purchase wine from the wholesalers). This system can operate to the disadvantage of small vineyards that find it difficult to get wholesale distribution; the number of wineries has expanded significantly while the number of wholesalers has decreased. Although wine drinkers want to be able to access a greater variety of beverages, and perhaps at lower prices, the risk is that online wine sales could go to minors, or could lead to tax evasion. As a result, over half of the states barred interstate shipments of wine (whether or not ordered over the Internet), although many states permitted direct shipping of wines within the state.[51]

A new era began in mid-2005, with the Supreme Court's decision that a state alcohol regulatory scheme that allows direct shipment by in-state wineries while forbidding it to out-of-state wineries violates the Commerce Clause. Such discrimination is not justified by the 21st Amendment's power to regulate liquor imports.[52]

In July 2005, Governor Pataki signed a bill allowing direct shipment of wines into and from New York, implementing the Supreme Court decision.[53] The District Court for the District of Washington struck down Washington State's three-tier distribution structure (allowing in-state wineries and breweries to sell directly to customers, but requiring out-of-state competitors to sell through a distributor).[54]

Controversy over Internet wine purchases continued in 2008. The Seventh Circuit reinstated the "face to face clause," the requirement that Indiana

---

[49] *Congress Backs Ban on Internet Tax* (No by-line), Wall St. J. 10/31/07 at A10; *Congress to Let Internet Tax Ban Expire Sunday (no by-line)*, Wall St. J., 10/19/01 at B6; *Congress Will Allow Ban on Internet Taxes to Expire (no by-line)*, N.Y. Times, 10/19/01 at A16; *see* 70 L.W. 2129, 2336.

[50] *See* the report of an FTC public workshop held October 8–10, 2002 about the impact of e-commerce on competition, and vice versa: http://www.ftc.gov/opp/ecommerce/anticompetitive/wkshpfactsheet.htm.

[51] FTC Staff Report, "Possible Anticompetitive Barriers to E-Commerce: Wine," http://www.ftc.gov/os/2003/07/winereport2.pdf.

[52] Granholm v. Heald, 544 U.S. 460 (U.S. 2005).

[53] Ben Dobbin (AP), *New York Authorizes Out-of-State Wine Shipments*, 7/15/05 (law.com).

[54] Costco Wholesale Corp. v. Hoen, 407 F. Supp. 2d 1234 (W.D. Wash. 2005).

consumers fill out age verification forms in person at the winery, after the trial court struck down that requirement in 2007. The Seventh Circuit ruled that the requirement did not give Indiana's in-state vintners an unfair advantage. In January 2008, a federal judge in Texas permitted out-of-state shipments to consumers, and in May 2008, Georgia allowed direct wine shipments. In October 2008, the Sixth Circuit found that Tennessee's regulation of the wine industry (licenses were available only to Tennessee residents or corporations owned by Tennessee residents) imposed unconstitutional discriminatory requirements. However, the prohibition on shipping wine directly to purchasers in Tennessee (whether or not it came from within the state) was upheld. The Sixth Circuit distinguished *Granholm* because the ban on direct sales applied to both in-state and out-of-state wineries.[55]

§ 28.04 LEGAL IMPLICATIONS OF COMPUTER CODE AND SOFTWARE

Computer source code can be copyrighted, and the terms "idea" and "expression" are not unconstitutionally vague when used in this context. (The issue was whether a search tool could determine if new software violated copyrights or patents — by comparing the software to copyrighted code.)[56] It is permissible for the Digital Millennium Copyright Act's amendments to Copyright Act § 117, allowing software to be loaded into computer memory for repair purposes, to be given retroactive effect. Retroactivity is permissible because the amendments do not impose any new duties and tend to reduce rather than increase liability.[57]

Intermediate copying of a game system's basic input/output system (BIOS) was fair use, the Ninth Circuit ruled early in 2000, because it was done for reverse engineering purposes — i.e., to make a game console that could play Sony PlayStation games. The functional elements in the game are entitled only to low-level copyright protection. The defendant carried out transformative use. The reverse-engineered product did not supersede the copyrighted product, so the Ninth Circuit found fair use. In this analysis, disassembling a program can be fair use if it is necessary to gain access to the functional elements of the software.[58]

The Ninth Circuit's August 2004 decision holds that the file-sharing services Grokster and Morpheus did not infringe copyrights on movies and musical compositions. The Ninth Circuit distinguished between Napster, which was shut down and then re-launched as a lawful paid service, and Grokster and Morpheus. Napster had a centralized index of files, the other two do not, making it much less feasible for the owner of the service to police service users' copyright conduct. An

---

[55] Baude v. Heath, 538 F.3d 608 (7th Cir. 2008); *see* Pamela A. MacLean, *7th Circuit Uncorks Debate Over Wine Shipments*, Nat'l L.J. 8/25/08 (law.com). Jelovsek v. Bredesen, 545 F.3d 431 (6th Cir. 2008); *see* Pamela A. MacLean, *6th Circuit Finds Tennessee Wine Law Unconstitutional, Sends Back for Remedy*, Nat'l L.J. 10/29/08 (law.com).

[56] Aharonian v. Gonzales, 2006 WL 13067 (N.D. Cal. 2006).

[57] Telecomm Technical Services Inc. v. Siemens Rolm Communications Inc., 1999 U.S. Dist. LEXIS 21414 (N.D. Ga. 7/6/99).

[58] Sony Computer Entertainment Inc. v. Connectix Corp., 203 F.3d 596 (9th Cir. 2000).

important factor in the Ninth Circuit decision was legitimate trading of non-copyrighted content on Grokster and Morpheus.[59]

Then, the following year, the Supreme Court reversed, holding that the distributor of peer-to-peer networking software can be held liable for third-party infringement, even if lawful use is possible. Liability is imposed on the basis of clear expressions or affirmative steps to foster infringement, not mere distribution of software with knowledge of third-party actions. The Grokster software was promoted to former users of Napster software; Grokster lacked filters or other means of limiting infringement; and its profitability depended on attracting a high volume of users to the site. Grokster not merely allowed but encouraged its users to download copyrighted files.[60]

As of September 2006, the music industry had filed 18,200 suits charging illicit downloading. Over five thousand cases were settled; the RIAA did not release figures on the number of cases dropped. Defendants are located by finding IP addresses of people who use peer-to-peer networks to download music, then sending a John Doe subpoena to the ISP. However, the defense bar's position is that this is an inexact process, and many innocent people are targeted by mistake. The new strategy is for prevailing defendants to seek attorneys' fees from the music industry.[61]

In the Seventh Circuit view, the fact that members did not pay for downloads, and the site was operated by a professor, did not mean that academic fair use was present when the site made unauthorized copies of software available on the Internet.[62]

The Sixth Circuit has held computer source code to be an expression for exchanging programming information and concepts, which is therefore speech entitled to First Amendment protection. The court drew an analogy to a music score, which can be read by people with specialized knowledge, even though it does not communicate to the general public.[63] In this case, the District Court had upheld the Export Administration Regulations, 15 CFR Part 730-74, against a First Amendment challenge, saying that encryption source code is inherently functional and therefore not protected as speech. (But the Regulations as now amended allow export of most off-the-shelf encryption software.)

The Copyright Office reads 17 USC § 114(d)(1)(A), DMCA's exemption of "nonsubscription broadcast transmissions" from the copyright rights over "digital

---

[59] Metro-Goldwyn-Mayer v. Grokster, 380 F.3d 1154 (9th Cir. 2004), discussed in Jeff Chorney, *In Victory for Grokster, Peer-to-Peer Wins at 9th Circuit*, The Recorder 8/20/04 (law.com). Napster cases: A&M Records v. Napster, 239 F.3d 1004 (2001) and 284 F.3d 1091 (2002).

[60] MGM v. Grokster Ltd., 545 U.S. 913 (2005).

[61] Lynne Marek, *Quest for Fees in Music Download Suit Could Level the Playing Field*, Nat'l L.J. 9/14/06, discussing Capitol Records v. Debbie Foster, No. 04-1569 (W.D. Okla., pending); attorneys' fees were denied in Virgin Records v. Joseph Darwin, No. 04-1346; Capitol Records v. O'Leary, No. 05-406 (C.D. Cal.); and Priority Records v. Chan, No. 04-73645 (E.D. Mich.).

[62] United States v. Slater, 348 F.3d 666 (7th Cir. 2003).

[63] Junger v. Daley, 209 F.3d 481 (6th Cir. 2000).

audio transmission performances" to mean that over-the-air broadcasts without royalties are permissible, but Internet streaming of AM/FM programming requires royalty payments to the record companies. This interpretation was upheld by the Third Circuit in late 2003.[64]

To the Fourth Circuit and the California Court of Appeals, computer data is not tangible property, so for insurance purposes, data loss after a computer crash is not considered to be direct physical loss of, or damage to, covered property.[65] Nor is corruption of data property damage that triggers coverage under a liability policy; and if the liability policy excludes criminal acts, the insurer does not have a duty to defend with respect to allegations of violation of Computer Fraud and Abuse Act.[66]

The Gramm-Leach-Bliley Act did not create a duty to protect the security of nonpublic personal information, so a company did not breach its duty of care when an employee took home a laptop computer containing unencrypted personal finance information—and the computer was stolen. In this case, the defendant company did attempt to implement proper security procedures, even though they failed in this instance.[67]

Commentator Aaron P. Silverman says that the ADA is likely to be applied to some kinds of Web sites, in which case some guidance can be found in Rehab Act § 508 precedents. ADA Title III (42 USC § 12181(7)(C)) requires 12 categories of public accommodations to be accessible (e.g., sale or retail establishments, places of public display or collection, or educational locations), unless providing accessibility would fundamentally alter the goods or services or would impose an undue burden on the provider.[68] Public-sector sites are also subject to ADA Title II.[69] However, the Fourth Circuit ruled that online chatrooms are not places of public accommodation because no physical place is involved.[70]

In 2008, Target Corp. agreed to settle a class action by paying $6 million in damages (a minimum of $3,500 per class member) and making its Web site fully accessible to blind customers. The plaintiffs prevailed on an argument that there was a nexus between brick-and-mortar stores and the Web site, thus defeating the argument that a Web site is not a place of public accommodation.[71] After

---

[64] Bonneville Int'l Corp. v. Peters, 347 F.3d 435 (3d Cir. 2003).

[65] AOL v. St. Paul Mercury Ins. Co., 347 F.3d 89 (4th Cir. 2003); Ward Gen. Ins. Servs. Inc. v. Employer Fire Ins. Co., 7 Cal. Rptr. 3d 844 (Cal. App. 2003).

[66] Compaq Computer Corp. v. St. Paul Fire & Marine Ins., 72 L.W. 1184 (Minn. App. 9/2/03).

[67] Guin v. Brazos Higher Educ. Serv. Corp., 74 LW 1512 (D. Minn. 05-668 2/7/06).

[68] *Disabled Access Laws and Internet Web Sites—An Unsettled Area*, 72 L.W. 2371 (1/6/04).

[69] Martin v. Metropolitan Atlanta Rapid Transit Auth., 225 F. Supp. 2d 1362 (N.D. Ga. 2002) (found the agency violated ADA Title II because its site was not accessible to the visually impaired).

[70] Noah v. AOL Time Warner Inc., 72 L.W. 1616 (4th Cir. 3/24/04), *aff'g*, 261 F. Supp. 2d 532 (E.D. Va. 2003); Access Now Inc. v. Southwest Airlines Co., 227 F. Supp. 2d 1312 (S.D. Fla. 2002), uses the same "no physical place" analysis, but *contra* Doe v. Mutual of Omaha Ins. Co., 179 F.3d 557 (7th Cir. 1999), which includes dictum requiring accessibility of Web sites.

[71] National Federation of the Blind et al v. Target Corp., No. 06-01802 (N.D. Cal. Settlement 2008); *see* Evan Hill, *Settlement Over Target's Web Site Marks a Win for ADA Plaintiffs*, The Recorder 8/28/08 (law.com).

the August settlement with Target, the National Federation of the Blind and the Massachusetts Attorney General negotiated a deal with Apple to make iTunes fully accessible to the blind, starting with the educational content on iTunes U. Screen access software will be used to output information on the screen as speech or Braille, with full accessibility for Mac and Windows computers by June 30, 2009.

The National Federation of the Blind and the Massachusetts Attorney general negotiated a deal with Apple to make iTunes and iTunes U fully accessible to the blind, starting with educational content on iTunes U by December 31 2008, using screen access software to output screen info in speech or Braille; the rest of the iTunes and iTunes Store will be accessible for Mac and Windows by June 30, 2009. Apple also agreed to donate $250,000 to the Massachusetts Commission for the Blind to fund assistive technology for blind customers.[72] Voice Over Internet Protocol (VOIP; telephone services using computers rather than telephones) is "information service," and is not "telecommunications service" that can be regulated by the states under the Telecommunications Act of 1996.[73]

The Third Circuit upheld the Wireline Broadband Order, the FCC ruling deregulating high-speed Internet access over telephone lines. In September 2005, the FCC said that telephone companies were not required to grant nondiscriminatory access to their wirelines to competing independent service providers such as cable modem and telecommunications service providers. Therefore, telephone companies gained the power to enter into individually negotiated agreements with companies that wish to use their broadband wireless facilities. The FCC said that it removed the access requirement because it imposed heavy costs that impaired innovation and investment in new technologies. From the end user's perspective, wireline broadband and cable modem service are functionally similar, so the FCC decided to regulate them the same way.[74]

§ 28.05 JURISDICTION IN CYBERSPACE

Data appearing on a Web site can give rise to litigation for various reasons. It might be alleged to be libelous or fraudulent, for example. The operation of the site itself may give rise to claims.

The very nature of the Internet is that any site can be accessed by any Internet-ready computer anywhere in the world. This is a very long arm indeed, so conventional notions of jurisdiction are hard to apply. There have only been a few

---

[72] Sheri Qualters, *Apple Agrees to Make iTunes Fully Accessible to Blind*, Nat'l L.J. 10/1/08 (law.com).

[73] Vonage Holdings Corp. v. Minnesota Public Util's Comm'n, 290 F. Supp. 2d 993 (D. Minn. 2003), *aff'd*, 394 F.3d 568 (8th Cir. 2004).

[74] Time Warner Telecom Inc. v. FCC 507 F.3d 205 (3d Cir. 2007); *see* Shannon P. Duffy, *3rd Circuit Upholds FCC's Deregulation of High-Speed Internet Access*, The Legal Intelligencer 10/17/07 (law.com).

years in which a jurisprudence of Internet jurisdiction could have emerged, so this discipline is still in its infancy.

Personal jurisdiction requires at least minimum contacts with the forum;[75] otherwise, it would not be fair to force the party to litigate in a remote forum. The defendant must deliberately have taken advantage of the opportunity to contact potential customers within the forum.

Merely posting a Web site will not create personal jurisdiction everywhere in the world, and probably not even everywhere the site is in fact accessed. Courts usually look for "something extra," such as creation of a contract, choice of law provisions in the contract, purposive contacts directed specifically at residents of a particular jurisdiction, availing one's self of the economic advantages within the jurisdiction by doing business within the state,[76] or by intent to extort (by cybersquatting) in order to find personal jurisdiction.[77] By analogy to "old media," states tend to treat material on the Web in much the same light as an advertisement in a periodical sent to the jurisdiction; if the advertisement would give rise to personal jurisdiction, probably so would the site.

The New York Court of Appeals applied the long-arm statute based on e-mail and Instant Messaging within New York by commercial entities, finding that a Montana state agency used these electronic means to conduct business in New York.[78]

A distinction is often drawn between a "passive" site that can merely be viewed, and an "active" site that invites activity such as commerce within the jurisdiction. It is far more likely that personal jurisdiction will be found if the site is deemed to be an "active" site within the jurisdiction.[79]

Service of process by e-mail made its British debut in 1996; probably the North American counterpart occurred in 1999 when the Northern District of Georgia issued a pioneering order permitting the attorneys in a bankruptcy case to serve process by e-mail. It is possible that this form of service was allowed precisely because the defendant was a foreign corporation; the court system is less likely to bypass the conventional methods of service when domestic defendants are involved. The defendant failed to respond to e-mail service on June 25, and a

---

[75] Plus System, Inc. v. New England Network, Inc., 804 F. Supp. 111 (D. Colo. 1992), is an early statement that the minimum contacts can be electronic in nature.

[76] See, e.g., D.C. Micro Dev. Inc. v. Lange, 71 L.W. 1504 (W.D. Ky. 1/28/03), finding that personal jurisdiction over an alleged hacker was present because of the act of accessing the plaintiffs' servers without permission; MGM Studios Inc. v. Grokster Ltd., 243 F. Supp. 2d 1073 (C.D. Cal. 2003), where millions of downloads in the state of file-sharing software were deemed to show intentional availment.

[77] The classic statement is Panavision Int'l LP v. Toeppen, 141 F.3d 1316 (9th Cir. 1998).

[78] Deutsche Bank Sec. Inc. v. Montana Bd. of Investments, 7 N.Y.3d 65 (Ct. App. 2006).

[79] See, e.g., ALS Scan Inc. v. Digital Serv. Consultants Inc., 293 F.3d 707 (4th Cir. 2002). In a class action about an energy surcharge allegedly improperly imposed on hotel guests without notice, the California court system has personal jurisdiction over a Nevada hotel chain because it provided hotel reservations using a Web site, and because it advertised heavily in California: Snowney v. Harrah's Entertainment Inc., 35 Cal. 4th 1054 (Cal. 2005).

default order was issued on August 24. (The Northern District of Georgia is one of nine courts participating in the Electronic Case File project of the Administrative Office of the U.S. Courts.)[80]

The "publication date" of computer source code for the site, photographs, music files, or software, for purposes of 17 USC § 504 (statutory copyright damages and fees for infringement that occurs after copyright registration or after first "publication") is the date when the site goes live on the Internet. The Southern District of New York identified this as the relevant date because this is the point at which the creator can no longer prevent further distribution or control duplication of the material.[81]

The Western District of Wisconsin ruled in early 2004 that the sale of one book, plus e-mail between a Wisconsin company and an interactive Web site in the West Indies, did not constitute adequate contact with Wisconsin to assert personal jurisdiction there.[82]

Dow Jones & Co. (with headquarters in New York) was permitted to appeal an Australian lower-court decision permitting an Australian businessman to sue in the Australian court system, alleging that he was libeled by an article published and posted on the Internet by Dow Jones, emanating from the United States. Dow Jones' lawyers took the position that the case should be heard in New Jersey, because the article was printed there. The plaintiff, displeased by an article that he said maligned him as a fraudulent schemer, preferred to have the case heard in his home town, on the theory that that is where defamation makes the most impact.[83]

Merely registering a domain name with NSI (which is based in Virginia) does not provide the required minimum contact to give rise to personal jurisdiction in Virginia. Therefore, any such proceeding will have to be brought in rem, and the plaintiff will have the burden of proving lack of personal jurisdiction.[84]

Where the alleged infringement consists of registration of a domain name, and an attempt to sell that name to the trademark owner, the tort of trademark infringement occurred (if at all) in the forum that is the residence of the trademark owner — even if the defendant conducted no other business activity in that forum.[85]

---

[80] International Telemedia Ass'n Inc. v. Diaz; *see* 68 L.W. 2167.

[81] Getaped.com Inc. v. Cangemi, 188 F. Supp. 2d 398 (S.D.N.Y. 2002).

[82] Hy Cite Corp. v. badbusinessbureau.com, 297 F. Supp. 2d 1154 (W.D. Wis. 2004).

[83] Associated Press, *Dow Jones Can Pursue Jurisdiction Battle in Internet Defamation Case*, (no by-line), 12/17/01 (law.com). The case was settled in November 2004. Dow Jones issued a corrective statement and paid the plaintiff $137,500 and $306,000 in legal fees: Associated Press, *Settlement Reached in Australian Case That Redefined Defamation Online* (11/16/04) (law.com).

[84] AOL v. Huang, 106 F. Supp. 2d 848 (E.D. Va. 2000); Heathmount A.E. Corp. v. Techno-dome.com, 106 F. Supp. 2d 860 (E.D. Va. 2000).

[85] McRae's Inc. v. Hussain, 105 F. Supp. 2d 594 (S.D. Miss. 2000). For the concept of *domain name* "poaching," where a potential registrant is unable to use a desired domain name, *see* Mark Cutler, *Domain Name "Poaching" Is Latest in String of Attempts to Create Liability for Registrars*, 70 L.W. 2787 (6/18/02) and the cases cited therein.

[A] ISP Safe Harbor

It should be noted that a provision of the Communications Decency Act that has survived the Supreme Court *Reno v. ACLU* decision (see § 28.08), 47 USC § 223(e), is a safe harbor provision for Internet Service Providers (ISPs) and others who provide Internet access. The service provider is not liable for criminal penalties for transmission of obscene matter, if the matter is transmitted by subscribers who are not under the control of the access provider. The defense is not available if the access provider is involved in providing the content. See, e.g., the Northern District of California's 2006 ruling that Yahoo could be sued for manipulating its own content (alleged fraudulent creation of profiles in its online dating service; claiming that users were still available for dates after they had withdrawn from the system).[86]

The fact that an ISP or other access provider undertakes screening to see if obscene material is present will not, in itself, make the access provider civilly liable as a publisher of the obscene material, because 47 USC § 223(e) also contains a "good Samaritan" provision that insulates it against liability.

Communications Decency Act immunity for service providers extends to eBay, not merely to providers of bulletin-board-type services (e.g., AOL). Therefore, eBay cannot be sued in state court because of content placed on eBay by third parties, relating to the sale of pirated sound recordings.[87]

Judge Stewart Dalzell of the Eastern District of Pennsylvania ruled that bloggers are not publishers of anonymous posts to their sites, and are entitled to protection under the CDA and cannot be sued for libel because of such posts. Dalzell held that the CDA immunizes bloggers in the interests of free speech over the Internet, even if they have some editorial control over the postings. Nor should bloggers be discouraged from attempting to exercise control by penalties imposed if some offensive material was not screened out.[88]

The Ninth Circuit ruled in mid-2003 that, because the CDA § 230(c)(1) safe harbor covers users as well as service providers, a Listserv operator can be immune with respect to publication of defamatory content created by a third party. Making small editorial changes does not make the editor the provider of the content.[89]

---

[86] Anthony v. Yahoo! Inc., 2006 WL 708572 (N.D. Cal. 3/17/06); *see also* Cisneros v. Sanchez, 2005 WL 3312631 (S.D. Tex. 12/7/05): Web site operators are liable for their own libelous postings.

[87] Stoner v. eBay Inc., 2000 WL 1705637 (Cal. Super. 11/7/00). In the summer of 2004, the California Court of Appeals ruled that eBay's well-drafted user agreement is enough to insulate it against liability for defamatory postings, but other ISPs may not fare as well if they do not include as many protective provisions in their Terms of Service. *See* Grace v. eBay, 120 Cal. App. 4th 984 (Cal. App. 2004), discussed in Brenda Sandburg, *EBay Ruling Punctures Web Liability Shield*, The Recorder 7/23/04 (law.com).

[88] DiMeo v. Max (E.D. Pa 2006); *see* Shannon P. Duffy, *Libel Laws Don't Prevent Blog "Mockery,"* The Legal Intelligencer 6/2/06 (law.com).

[89] Batzel v. Cremers, 333 F.3d 1018 (9th Cir. 2003).

The California Court of Appeals held that the CDA § 230(c) safe harbor does not apply to a distributor who republishes third-party defamatory content on the Internet, either knowingly or with reason to know. The court drew a distinction between publishers (who have immunity) and distributors.[90]

In a 2007 ruling, the Ninth Circuit tackled free speech issues when fair housing organizations in California sued the owner of Roommates.com under the federal Fair Housing Act, alleging discrimination in listings for roommates. The issue was whether the CDA protected the site from liability on the Fair Housing Act claim. The case involved both Web pages supplied by the site itself (not user-generated, so CDA § 230 does not apply) and site users' responses to questionnaires, some discriminatory and some non-discriminatory. The Ninth Circuit found the site liable, on the grounds that the CDA does not immunize sites that actively encourage, solicit, and profit from other people's tortuous and unlawful communications. However, it was held that there was no FHA liability as a result of the "additional comments" part of the form (where users could include anything they found relevant to finding a roommate); the site was not held liable because this option was so open-ended.[91]

A copy shop that rents Internet terminals to customers is a "provider of interactive services" under the Communications Decency Act, and therefore business tort claims such as defamation and negligent failure to monitor the computer network are preempted.[92]

With respect to another safe harbor, under the DMCA, complaints to a service provider about copyright infringement require specific identification of the infringing materials and a written statement that the notice is accurate and that the complainant has a good-faith belief that the materials were appropriated without authorization.[93]

The Digital Millennium Copyright Act (see § 12.03[F]) enacts a new 17 USC § 512, indemnifying ISPs against copyright liability when users who are not under the control of the ISP use Internet access provided by the ISP to transmit infringing materials.

DMCA § 512(h) authorizes nationwide service of process on ISPs to gather information about online copyright infringement. However, the District Court for the District of Massachusetts refused to allow a subpoena duces tecum to be issued in Washington, D.C. against Boston universities whose students were accused of computer piracy. The court limited service of process to a 100-mile radius of the issuing court (FRCP 45(b)(2)).[94]

The Central District of California, affirmed by the Ninth Circuit, on the issue of contributory infringement, held that AOL is entitled to the DMCA safe harbor

[90] Barrett v. Rosenthal, 5 Cal. Rptr. 3d 516 (Cal. App. 2003).
[91] Howard J. Bashman, *When Should a Commercial Web Site Be Held Liable for User-Generated Content?* Special to law.com 5/21/07.
[92] Patentwizard Inc. v. Kinko's Inc., 163 F. Supp. 2d 1069 (D.S.D. 2001).
[93] Hendrickson v. eBay Inc., 165 F. Supp. 2d 1082 (C.D. Cal. 2001).
[94] MIT v. Recording Indus. Ass'n of Am. 72 L.W. 1131 (D. Mass. 8/7/03).

against claims of direct infringement, even though it failed to show that it located infringers and expelled them from its Usenet service. However, AOL could be held liable for contributory infringement, because it should have known that the servers contained infringing materials, and should have moved to delete the material (consisting of copyrighted science fiction posted to a newsgroup without the author's consent).[95] The D.C. Circuit ruled that the provision authorizing subpoenas to ISPs applies only to ISPs that store copyrighted materials, not those that merely transmit them (e.g., via peer-to-peer file sharing). Therefore, it refused to order Verizon to identify its subscribers.[96]

[B] Tort Issues

In mid-2002, the New York Court of Appeals applied the "single publication" rule to Web publication. Material is considered published when it is posted from the site. That is the date from which the statute of limitations for a defamation action runs. Changes in the site (such as maintenance or adding additional content to the site) that are not related to the allegedly defamatory content are not treated as republications that can extend the statute of limitations. The Ninth Circuit applied the same rule to Internet postings in 2006.[97]

The Ninth Circuit ruled in mid-2003 that a Web site operator can be sued only if it posts information that a reasonable person would have known was not intended for publication. The case arose when a tipster implied that the plaintiff possessed art stolen by the Nazis; the plaintiff charged that the tipster wanted to impugn the plaintiff's reputation because they were engaged in a contract dispute.[98]

The Second Circuit held that a New York moving company did not establish long-arm jurisdiction over an Iowa resident's Web site rating moving companies. (The New York movers claimed that they were defamed on the site by allegations that they operated without legal authorization and lacked the mandatory insurance coverage.) New York law permits long-arm jurisdiction over defamation suits only if the defendant does business in New York, or makes a contract anywhere to supply goods or services in New York. The mere fact that readers in New York can view defamatory material on a Web site is not sufficient for jurisdiction; in this case, the Second Circuit ruled that the comments were not specifically directed at New Yorkers.[99]

In contrast, however, the New Jersey Court of Appeals permitted a California resident charged with libel in a Web forum to be sued in New Jersey (rather than in

---

[95] Ellison v. Robertson, 189 F. Supp. 2d 1051 (C.D. Cal. 2002), *aff'd in part, rev'd in part*, 357 F.3d 1072 (9th Cir. 2004).

[96] RIAA v. Verizon Internet Servs. Inc., 351 F.3d 1229 (D.C. Cir. 2003).

[97] Firth v. State, 98 N.Y.2d 365 (N.Y. App. 2002); *see also* Oja v. Army Corps of Eng'rs, 440 F.3d 1122 (9th Cir. 2006).

[98] Batzel v. Cremers, 333 F.3d 1018 (9th Cir. 2003).

[99] Best Van Lines v. Walker, 490 F.3d 239 (2d Cir. 2007); *see* Beth Bar, *Mover Fails to Prove Jurisdiction in Suit Over Internet Site*, N.Y.L.J. 6/29/07 (law.com). *See* CPLR § 302(a)(2) for jurisdiction.

the state where the message was posted) because of targeting of the New Jersey audience. In this case, the alleged libel involved the police department in a New Jersey town; the comments circulated widely in New Jersey, and they seemed to be directed at that state, so the defendant should have foreseen the possibility of being sued there. Under this "targeting-based analysis," defamation actions are foreseeable either where the speaker resides or where the target does.[100]

The Western District of Oklahoma ruled in mid-2003 that a search engine's rankings of Web sites are opinions protected by the First Amendment. Therefore, they cannot give rise to an action for tortious interference with business relations. (The plaintiff claimed that Google lowered the ranking of its site because it was a competitor.)[101]

§ 28.06   DOMAIN NAMES

Every Web site must have a domain name, a combination of up to 22 letters and numbers ending in a period and the name of the top level domain (TLD).[102] The most common TLD is the familiar ".com," for a commercial Web site. The other current TLDs in the United States are .gov, for government sites, .org for organizations, .edu for educational institutions, .net for networks such as Internet Service Providers, and .mil for military sites. Other domain names, such as .uk for United Kingdom and .de for German (Deutschland), indicate sites originating outside the United States.

So far, there is no requirement for domain name registrars to ascertain whether applicants for .com, .org, or .net registrations really fit into those categories (although only actual government and military units can get .gov or .mil domain names). Some trademark attorneys suggest registering trademarks in all the top level domains (including new ones as they are added) to prevent others from registering the same name in other TLDs.

[A] Assignment of Domain Names

At first, all domain names were assigned by a single entity, the Internet Assigned Number Authority (IANA), which delegated the process to a private corporation called Network Solutions, Inc. (NSI). The Department of Commerce issued two statements, the "green paper" (January 1998) and the "white paper" (June 1998) calling for expansion and adding more domain name registrars. In 1999, the transition from a monopoly to a competitive system began. A not-for-profit corporation called ICANN (Internet Corporation for Assigned Names) was created to supervise the addition of dozens of new registrars.[103]

---

[100] Goldhaber v. Kohlenberg, A-5114-05 (N.J. App. 2007), discussed in Henry Gottlieb, *Californian Can Be Sued in N.J. for Alleged Libel on Internet*, N.J.L.J. 8/6/07 (law.com).

[101] Search King Inc. v. Google Tech. Inc., 71 L.W. 1760 (W.D. Okla. 5/27/03).

[102] *See* 66 L.W. 2563.

[103] *See* 67 L.W. 2205 and Richard Raysman and Peter Brown, *Developments in Trademark and Domain-Name Disputes*, N.Y.L.J., Mar. 9, 1999 at p. 3; John Simons, *Monopoly on Web Addresses is*

On November 16, 2000, ICANN approved seven additional gTLDs (classes of top-level domain names) out of 44 submitted for approval. The new gTLDs are .museum, .aero, .biz, .info, .name, .pro and .coop. The .biz and .info domains are general commercial domains. The .aero domain is restricted to air transport services. Individuals can register .name domains for their personal use. The .pro domains will initially be issued to members of the professions of law, medicine, and accounting, with the potential for issuing them to other professions later.[104] However, these domains never achieved popularity.

In mid-2005, the Commerce Department announced that the U.S. government, contrary to earlier plans, would retain oversight over the 13 "root server" computers containing the Internet's master directories indefinitely, rather than turning control over to an international body, although ICANN remained in charge of day to day operations.[105] In 2006, ICANN and the U.S. Department of Commerce renewed their contract to administer some ICANN functions for the address system for one year, renewable for four more years, with the result that the U.S. government might retain its connection with ICANN until 2011 despite the announced intention to privatize ICANN. The Commerce Department retained a role in providing information and expertise on methods. However, the Commerce Department increased ICANN's autonomy, and the agreement is subject to mid-term review after a year and a half. Greater freedom for ICANN would respond to international concerns about excessive U.S. government domination over the worldwide Internet.[106]

[B] Misuse of Domain Names

Most of the litigation has arisen in the context of "cybersquatting" — registering a domain name including the name of a famous company or product, for the purpose of getting the owner of the company or product to pay for the

---

Broken as Network Solutions Gets Five Rivals, Wall Street Journal 4/22/99 p. B10. Although international developments are beyond the scope of this volume, their relevance to the Internet is obvious. Attorneys with an interest in these issues should follow developments in the European Union and the World Intellectual Property Organization (WIPO). *See, e.g.*, Jeri Clausing, *United Nations Group Issues Report on Internet Addresses*, N.Y. Times, May 3, 1999 at C2.

[104] *See ICANN Approves Seven Top-Level Domains: Winners Continue to Negotiate Fine Print* (no-by-line), 69 L.W. 2329 (12/5/00). For a discussion of the implementation of the .name TLD, *see* Joel E. Lutzker and Scott M. Kareff, *Playing the .Name Game*, http://www.srz.com/publications/publicationsDetail.aspx?publicationId=1412.

[105] (Associated Press), *U.S. Will Retain Its Control of Internet Oversight*, N.Y. Times, July 1, 2005, p. B3. A multi-national accord was reached in November 2005, leaving control in U.S. hands but calling for a series of forums on policy issues and development of greater international participation in Internet governance. *See* Victoria Shannon, *A Compromise of Sorts on Internet Control*, N.Y. Times 11/16/05 p. C2, and John W. Miller and Christopher Rhoads, *U.S. Fights to Keep Control Of Global Internet Oversight*, Wall St. J. 11/16/05 p. B2.

[106] AP, *U.S. Reaches Pact on Internet Oversight*, Wall St. J. 10/2/06 at p. B4; Victoria Shannon, *U.S. Loosens Its Control Over Web Address Manager*, N.Y. Times 9/30/06 at p. C4 and *Internet Domain Agency Renews U.S. Contract*, N.Y. Times 8/27/06 at p. C5.

domain name. Late in 2002, the Second Circuit held that an *in rem* action under the ACPA can be brought only in the judicial district where the registrar or other domain name authority is located.[107]

"Metatags" are descriptions of a Web site and its content. They are not visible to ordinary users, but are used to index the site. Using someone else's trademark in metatags without permission is also wrongful. Using a domain name and metatags that are likely to create confusion with someone else's trademark constitutes trademark infringement that can be enjoined by the senior trademark owner.[108]

A domain name that would be an "intuitive" choice for a competitor's site is considered confusing to consumers, and hence inappropriate.[109]

Most of these cases involve clear, intentional trademark abuse and intent to confuse. In the future, however, we will see many more cases involving individuals and businesses using trademarks and service marks in good faith, and seeking to extend them to the Internet, coming into conflict with other individuals who arrived at the same or similar marks independently.

---

[107] Mattel, Inc. v. Barbie-Club.com, 310 F.3d 293 (2d Cir. 2002).

[108] Brookfield Communications Inc. v. West Coast Entertainment Corp., 174 F.3d 1036 (9th Cir. 1999). Planned Parenthood Fed'n v. Bucci, 152 F.3d 920 (2d Cir. 1998) is a summary order affirming an injunction granted against the use of a deceptive domain name registered by an anti-abortion activist. Similarly, Coca-Cola v. Purdy, 382 F.3d 774 (8th Cir. 2004), upheld the District Court's grant of preliminary relief against an opponent of abortion who registered domain names containing famous trademarks (e.g., mymcdonalds.com and drinkcoke.com) for Web sites that had no connection with the trademarked merchandise and that expressed his anti-abortion beliefs. The Eighth Circuit found "bad faith intent to profit" in Purdy's sale of merchandise on his sites. The case was distinguishable from the gripe site cases because Purdy took advantage of the fame of the trademarks; he was not protesting any action by the companies that owned the trademarks. The Playboy trademark is quite valuable, especially in light of the large amount of sexual content on the Web, and therefore several cases have been brought by Playboy Enterprises Inc. to protect its trademarks. A pornography site wrongfully entitled "Playboy's Private Collection" was liable to Playboy for trademark infringement, trademark dilution, and counterfeiting: Playboy Enterprises Inc. v. Universal Tel-a-Talk Inc., 1998 U.S. Dist. LEXIS 17282 (E.D. Pa. 11/4/98). Hong Kong defendants who created a false association by using "Playboy" as a metatag for an unauthorized site were subject to jurisdiction in Virginia, because of tortious injury caused to Playboy and regular solicitation of business in the state: Playboy Enterprises v. Asia Focus Inc., 66 L.W. 1704 (E.D. Va. 4/10/98). However, a one-time Playboy Playmate was entitled to a Lanham Act fair use defense for using "Playmate" as a metatag for her personal site, because it was an accurate description of herself; use of the Playmate title was not contractually restricted; and she did not deceive consumers into believing that her site was authorized by Playboy: Playboy Enters. Inc. v. Welles, 60 F. Supp. 2d 1050 (S.D. Cal. 1998). Earlier Playboy cases involve copyright violations in distributing photographs copyrighted by Playboy over the Web: Playboy Enters. v. Sanfilippo, 46 USPQ2d 1350 (C.D. Cal. 1998); Playboy Enters., Inc. v. WebbWorld, Inc., 991 F. Supp. 543 (N.D. Tex. 1997). Attempts to use initials as a trademark or domain name create particular difficulties, in light of the numerous other businesses with the same initials. *See, e.g.*, C.D. Solutions Inc. v. Tooker, 15 F. Supp. 2d 986 (D. Or. 1998); Data Concepts Inc. v. Digital Consulting Inc., 150 F.3d 620 (6th Cir. 1998).

[109] Washington Speakers Bureau Inc. v. Leading Authorities Inc., 49 F. Supp. 2d 496 (E.D. Va. 1999).

For purposes of the ACPA, the federal law forbidding dilution of a famous trademark, a mark is protected only if it was famous when the defendant first used the allegedly diluting mark in commerce. A contrary result would permit plaintiffs to delay litigation until they could establish the "fame" of their trademark.[110]

The first appellate ruling under the Anticybersquatting Consumer Protection Act (ACPA), 15 USC § 1125(d), was handed down by the Second Circuit in February 2000. An injunction—but no damages—was granted for registering "sportys.com" as a domain name for Christmas tree sales; it was confusingly similar to the "Sporty's" trademark used by Sportman's Market, a well-known mail order company; the Second Circuit upheld the injunction but did not find the degree of willfulness required to impose penalties under the ACPA.[111]

Many other cybersquatting rulings followed this one. The Eastern District of Virginia treats the in rem and in personam actions as mutually exclusive. A plaintiff cannot sue an allegedly infringing domain name registrant in personam and simultaneously proceed in rem against the domain name itself. Furthermore, in rem jurisdiction is available only if the alleged infringer cannot be sued in personam.[112]

The same court required bad faith to be pleaded as an element in the in rem action, even though the statutory language mentions bad faith only in connection with the in personam cause of action.[113]

In the Sixth Circuit's view, a domain name is a designation of its source of origin that is vital for denoting the source of a Web site. Therefore, unauthorized use of a trademark in a domain name is infringing, and even a disclaimer on the site will be viewed too late to rule out initial interest confusion. But the same court held that using another's trademark in the part of the URL after the domain name (for example, http://www.weluvcars.com/Cadillac) would only be infringement if there is evidence that consumers are likely to be confused about the source. The rationale was that the URL elements after the domain name merely identify the organization of files on the computer server.[114]

Maximum statutory damages, plus an attorney's fee award of over $30,000, were imposed in a cybersquatting case that rules that the ACPA is violated by registering domain names that are deliberate misspellings of a plaintiff's famous and distinctive domain name. The "typosquatting" (as this form of deception is nicknamed) was intended to lure Web users to the site, where they would have to view 10–15 advertisements; advertisers paid the typosquatter to gain this exposure.[115]

---

[110] The Network Network [sic] v. CBS Inc., 2000 U.S. Dist. LEXIS 4751 (C.D. Cal. 1/18/00).

[111] Sporty's Farm LLC v. Sportsman's Market Inc., 202 F.3d 489 (2d Cir. 2000).

[112] Alitalia Linee Aerea Italiana SpA v. Casinoalitalia.com, 128 F. Supp. 2d 340 (E.D. Va. 2001).

[113] Harrods Ltd. v. Sixty Internet Domain Names, 110 F. Supp. 2d 420 (E.D. Va. 2000).

[114] PACCAR Inc. v. TeleScan Tech LLC, 319 F.3d 243 (6th Cir. 2003); Interactive Prods. Corp. v. a2z Mobile Office Solutions Inc., 326 F.3d 687 (6th Cir. 2003).

[115] Electronics Boutique Holdings Corp. v. Zuccarini, 2000 U.S. Dist. LEXIS 15719 (E.D. Pa. 10/30/00).

ACPA protection of family names (see 15 USC § 1129) is not retroactive, so it is not possible to reclaim a domain name containing a surname that was registered before, and re-registered after, the effective date of the ACPA.[116]

§ 28.07   DOMAIN NAME DISPUTES

One of the crucial characteristics of the Internet is that URLs must be unique. Only one site can have a particular URL, although the sheer volume of sites means that many sites will have URLs that are quite similar.

On October 24, 1999, ICANN approved the Uniform Domain Name Dispute Resolution Policy (UDRP), an ADR mechanism for resolving allegations of cybersquatting about .com, .org, and .net addresses. The text of the UDRP is available at http://www.icann.org/udrp.

Under the UDRP, ADR is mandatory if a third party complains that a domain name was registered in bad faith. Bad faith is shown by, e.g., the use of a name that is identical or misleadingly similar to a trademark in which the complainant has rights, where the registrant does not have rights or legitimate interests in that name. The sole remedy under the policy is cancellation of the improper domain name or transfer of the name to the successful complainant.

For .biz domains, the Start-up Trademark Opposition Policy (STOP), administered by the National Arbitration Forum, is the counterpart of the UDRP, although the STOP permits a more lenient standard of proof than UDRP (either proof of registration or use of the domain is adequate under STOP, whereas both must be proved under UDRP). UDRP panel decisions can be cited as precedent in a STOP proceeding. STOP proceedings are limited to claims involving the exact string of characters in which the claimant has trademark rights, so "typosquatting" claims involving deliberate, misleading misspellings are not permitted.[117]

The National Arbitration Forum Web site, http://www.arbforum.com, contains reports of numerous domain name arbitrations. The National Arbitration Forum has been accredited by ICANN to carry out the UDRP. A February 2000 decision, for example, holds that a Canadian company acted in bad faith by registering a .net URL when it knew that another company had already registered its nearly identical trademark as a .com. The .net registration was canceled.[118]

---

[116] Schmidheiny v. Weber, 319 F.3d 581 (3d Cir. 2002).

[117] The STOP rules appear at http://www.neulevel.biz; *see* 70 L.W. 2493.

[118] Fiber-Shield Indus. Inc. v. Fiber Shield Ltd., 2/29/00, *see* 68 L.W. 2558. Both the National Arbitration Forum and WIPO saw dramatic increases between 2004 and 2005 in the number of domain name arbitrations; 2005 caseloads were about 25% higher. There were 1,457 filings with WIPO in 2005, and 900 in the first half of 2006 alone. The organizations cited the rise in typosquatting as an important factor in the increase, because of the increasing use of payment of per-click compensation to sites, creating temptations to manipulate the system. *See* Sheri Qualters, *Arbitration is Weapon of Choice in Growing Number of Domain Name Disputes*, Nat'l L.J. 10/9/06 (law.com).

[A] Trademark Issues for Domain Names

Late in 2001, the Eastern District of Virginia ruled that use of "cnnews.com" for a news service operating only in China is a "use in commerce" that is subject to the in rem provisions of the ACPA. The rationale is that, even if the effect on U.S. commerce is not obvious, the Internet has a global range; some Americans can read Chinese; .com is essentially a U.S. TLD; and the CNN mark is famous throughout the world. The Eastern District of Virginia required a showing of bad faith before taking away the domain name.[119]

It has been held that it is reasonable to assume that the ACPA provides a cause of action vis-a-vis trademarks issued outside the United States; and the standard of review when a District Court reviews a UDRP panel's decision, is de novo.[120]

A January 2001 WIPO case, using the UDRP procedure, holds that a domain name in the form "Trademark" sucks.com or that otherwise indicates a lack of affiliation with the trademark, can be maintained even over the trademark holder's objection, because the domain name is not confusingly similar to the trademark.[121]

Registering "fuckgeneralmotors.com" and linking it to Ford's Web site is not a "commercial use" of the Ford mark, the Eastern District of Michigan ruled in late 2001. Neither is it a use of the mark in connection with goods or services for infringement or dilution purposes, because not everything that might inflict commercial harm on the owner of a mark is "commercial use."[122]

WIPO ruled that the presence of third-party paid pop-ups at a gripe site (in this case, maintained by dissatisfied Fidelity investors), with the domain holder receiving compensation per click-through, is evidence of bad-faith use of the underlying trademark even without proof that the advertisements produced any customers for the advertisers; site owners lost some domain names. WIPO

---

[119] Cable News Network LP v. cnnews.com, 177 F. Supp. 2d 506 (E.D. Va. 2001). The use of a trademark in a domain name is sufficient to confer standing to sue under the ACPA; it is not necessary that the plaintiff prove an attempt to sell the domain name back to the trademark holder, because that is not the only actionable form of bad faith attempt to profit from a mark: Argos v. Orthotek LLC, 72 L.W. 1456 (D. Del. 1/8/04).

[120] Barcelona.com Inc. v. Excelentisimo Ayuntamiento de Barcelona, 189 F. Supp. 2d 367 (E.D. Va. 2001).

[121] Lockheed Martin Corp. v. Parisi, http://arbiter.wipo.int/domains/decisions/html/2000/d2000-1015.html (no www). *See also* Bally Total Fitness v. Faber, 29 F. Supp. 2d 1161 (C.D. Cal. 1998), dismissing a complaint because Bally would not be able to prove confusion from the use of ballysucks.com as a domain name.

[122] Ford Motor Co. v. 2600 Enters., 177 F. Supp. 2d 661 (E.D. Mich. 2001). Similarly, the Sixth Circuit held in 2004 that using another party's mark in the domain name of a "gripe site" does not constitute bad faith intent to profit, because using the name in complaints about allegedly poor service quality does not prove trading on the mark owner's goodwill: Lucas Nursery & Landscaping Inc. v. Grosse, 357 F.3d 811 (6th Cir. 2004). The Fifth Circuit reversed the District Court determination that the appellant's gripe site about the appellee violated the ACPA and the Texas Anti-Dilution Statute, because the Court of Appeals found that gripe site to be non-commercial. It did not take paid advertisements, and included a prominent disclaimer that it was not affiliated with the appellee: TMI Inc. v. Maxwell, 368 F.3d 433 (5th Cir. 2004).

distinguished between a pure gripe site, which is deemed non-infringing, and a "gripe-plus" site seeking commercial gain, which is not protected if bad faith is shown.[123]

In 2003, the Supreme Court ruled that the Federal Trademark Dilution Act (FTDA) requires proof of actual dilution, not mere likelihood of harm to the trademark. It is not dilution if consumers make a mental association between trademarks. However, a dilution cause of action does not require proof of actual loss of sales or profits, as long as the trademark is actually impaired.[124]

[B] PTO Position

A Patent and Trademark Office (PTO) examination guide issued in September 1999 explains that, in applications for trademarks, the .com, .org, and .net TLDs will be treated like (800) numbers: i.e., as essential functional prefixes and suffixes with no specific meaning rather than as indications of the source of goods.[125]

A domain name mark can be registered as a trademark if, but only if, it functions as a source identifier. Potential purchasers must think of it as a source indication, not just an informational indication of how to access the Web site. An application to use "www.whatzis.com" and a specimen of use in the form of an ad "visit us at www.whatzis.com" will not show use as a service mark.

If a business creates a site only to advertise its own products or services, the domain name cannot be registered as a trademark. Nor will the PTO register a mark consisting of a surname plus a TLD, or a generic term (e.g., bank.com, chicken. com) or a purely descriptive geographic term (e.g., Boston.com).

§ 28.08 PORNOGRAPHY

Although a vast variety of pornographic materials depicting most imaginable forms of sexual activity can be found on the Internet, legislation and court cases concentrate on two related issues: the ability of children to access pornography, and the ability of anyone to access pornography depicting children.[126]

In 1996, the Communications Decency Act, part of P.L. 104-104, was enacted. The CDA imposed federal criminal penalties for making "obscene, indecent and patently offensive materials" accessible to minors via commercial online services or other means of Internet access. These provisions of the CDA were found unconstitutional by the Supreme Court in July 1997.[127]

Congress attempted to draft a bill that would pass Constitutional scrutiny, and the Child Online Protection Act (COPA; P.L. 105-277) was signed on 10/21/98,

---

[123] FMR Corp. v. Native American Warrior Soc'y D2004-0978 (WIPO 1/20/05); http://arbiter.wipo.int/domains/decisions/html/2004/d2004-0978.html.

[124] Moseley v. VSecret Catalog Inc., 537 U.S. 418 (2003).

[125] Examination Guide No. 2-99 http://www.uspto.gov/web/offices/tax/notices/guide299.htm.

[126] United States v. Charbonneau, 979 F. Supp. 1177 (S.D. Ohio 1997), holds that there is no reasonable expectation of privacy when using a public e-mail system to transmit child pornography.

[127] Reno v. ACLU, 521 U.S. 844 (1997).

forbidding the online dissemination of material that is "harmful to minors." However, this bill was no more successful in court than its predecessor.

In late 1998, the Eastern District of Pennsylvania granted a TRO against enforcement of the Child Online Protection Act, given the likelihood of determination of its unconstitutionality.[128] In this reading, the COPA is not narrowly tailored to protect minors. The affirmative defense of maintaining a site that requires users to verify their age or give a credit card number is technologically impractical, and without that possibility for affirmative defense, COPA unconstitutionally prohibits speech that is authorized for adults. When the case returned to the Eastern District in 2007, the court once again ruled against the statute, holding that COPA is overinclusive because it regulates speech that is obscene when tested against all minors, not older minors. The requirement of using a credit card number as proof of age is invalid, not only because children can gain access to their parents' credit cards, but because card issuers forbid use of the cards for age verification. The statute was also held to violate the Fifth Amendment because bans on "commercial purposes" and activities "while engaged in business" trap far more Internet sites than the commercial pornographers who are the intended target of the legislation, and the act is impermissibly vague, overbroad, and not sufficiently tailored to the compelling interest of protecting minors. Early in 2009, the Supreme Court finally disposed of COPA by refusing to allow the government to appeal the Third Circuit's grant of a permanent injunction that forbids implementation of the statute.[129]

Reno v. ACLU, 521 U.S. 844 (1997) struck down 47 USC § 223(d), part of the Communications Decency Act of 1996. The result was that Congress passed another statute, the Child Online Protection Act (COPA). In May 2002, the Supreme Court held that COPA is not facially unconstitutional merely because it calls for a determination of whether material is harmful to minors.[130] The case

---

[128] ACLU v. Reno, 31 F. Supp. 2d 473, *aff'd*, 217 F.3d 162 (E.D. Pa. 1998).

[129] ACLU v. Gonzales (E.D. Pa. 2007); Shannon P. Duffy, *Internet Porn Law Ruled Unconstitutional*, The Legal Intelligencer 3/23/07 (law.com).

[130] Ashcroft v. ACLU, 535 U.S. 564 (2002). On remand, the Third Circuit found that COPA is constitutionally defective and likely to violate the First Amendment; is overbroad in failing to be narrowly tailored to apply the least restrictive means to protect minors from harmful material; because the worldwide scope of the Internet makes it impossible to restrict material in conformity with community standards; because it calls for examination of individual images and files out of context; and because imposing a single definition of "minors" fails to differentiate between the different needs of five-year-olds and 16-year-olds: ACLU v. Ashcroft, 322 F.3d 240 (3d Cir. 2003). The case returned to the Supreme Court in mid-2004. The Supreme Court ruled that the Third Circuit correctly affirmed the injunction, because the government failed to meet its burden as to whether the proposed alternative is as effective as the challenged statute. The Supreme Court advocated the use of filters because it limits the potential chilling effect on entire categories of speech. It also found filtering more effective than the COPA scheme, because it could prevent minors from seeing all pornographic material, including e-mail, not just pornography posted to the Web from the United States: Ashcroft v. ACLU, 542 U.S. 656 (2004). In mid-2008, the sixth time the case was before the court, the Third Circuit once again found that the Child Online Protection Act (COPA) is

was brought to obtain a preliminary injunction, so it was remanded to the Third Circuit to determine whether the statute was overbroad otherwise.

In April 2002, the Supreme Court struck down the Child Pornography Prevention Act of 1996's ban on "virtual child pornography" (18 USC § 2256(8)), finding that it was overbroad because it could be applied to images that are not patently offensive and do not violate the standards of all communities, and because the virtual images were not necessarily generated in connection with abuse of minors.[131] Congress passed a revised bill, the PROTECT Act (Prosecutorial Remedies and Tools Against the Exploitation of Children Today Act (P.L. 108-21)), amending 18 USC § 2256 to forbid pornographic digital images that appear to depict sexual conduct by minors. It is an affirmative defense if the images depict adults, but not if the images are created digitally and do not depict real minors. The PROTECT Act forbids obscene material that shows real children or virtual images of children engaging in sexually explicit conduct (even if the images are not obscene). The statute includes a "pandering" provision that forbids knowing advertising, promotion, distribution, or solicitation of child pornography. The Supreme Court upheld the "anti-pandering" provision in 2008.[132]

In mid-2003, the Supreme Court upheld the Children's Internet Protection Act (CIPA), a statute requiring that, as a condition of receiving federal funding, libraries must use filtering software to prevent their patrons from accessing online pornography. Unlike the Communications Decency Act or the Child Online Protection Act, the Supreme Court found this legislation to be Constitutionally acceptable, on the rationale that libraries choose which books to acquire, and do not have a duty to make the entire Internet available to patrons. In this analysis, Internet terminals are not placed in libraries to create a public forum for self-expression by library patrons. Furthermore, CIPA permits librarians to disable the filter temporarily on request by a patron for bona fide research or other lawful purposes. The Supreme Court held that because the blocks can be disabled, a facial challenge to the statute itself (as distinct from a challenge to the way it is applied) is ruled out.[133]

The Third Circuit ruled that 18 USC § 2252A(a)(2)(B) (knowing receipt or distribution of child pornography that has been transported in interstate or foreign

---

not narrowly tailored to protect children; is impermissibly overbroad and vague; and there are less restrictive alternatives that are equally effective, so it ruled once again that COPA violates the First and Fifth Amendments and issued a permanent injunction against its implementation: ACLU v. Mukasey, No. 07-2539 (3d Cir. 7/22/08). The 2009 Supreme Court holding is Mukasey v. ACLU, No. 08-565 (1/21/09), discussed in Mark Sherman, *Anti-Online Porn Law Dies Quietly in Supreme Court*, 1/22/09 (law.com).

The Fourth Circuit held that Virginia's statute, making it a crime knowingly to display for commercial purposes material that is accessible to minors when it is deemed harmful to them, is invalid under the First Amendment and the Commerce Clause. It is invalid as a content-based restriction on expression that is not sufficiently narrowly tailored (although it is related to the compelling state interest of protecting minors). PSINet Inc. v. Chapman, 362 F.3d 227 (4th Cir. 2004).

[131] Ashcroft v. Free Speech Coalition, 535 U.S. 234 (2002).

[132] United States v. Williams, No. 06-694 (2008).

[133] United States v. American Library Ass'n, 539 U.S. 194 (2003).

commerce) is satisfied by having child pornography and links to child pornography Web sites on a computer. The court rejected the defendant's argument that the images could have been received from within the state. The statute covers transmission by any means, including by computer. Because of the interstate operation of the Internet, a connection request to a server, or transmission of an image to a user, is transmission in interstate commerce. The Third Circuit upheld Congress' power to regulate the online channels of interstate commerce.[134]

In contrast, the Tenth Circuit held in 2007 that the prosecution in an 18 USC § 2252(a)(2), (a)(4)(B) case failed to prove movement of child pornography images across state lines; although the defendant had at least five subscriptions to sites featuring child pornography, had child pornography in his temporary Internet files, and owned CDs with pornographic images: the prosecution did not prove the source of the images, or that they had traveled across state lines.[135]

The CDA criminal provision, 47 USC § 223(a), barring transmissions that are "obscene, lewd, lascivious, filthy, or indecent, with intent to annoy, abuse, threaten or harass" was upheld.[136] The provision survives a First Amendment challenge as long as it is read narrowly enough to apply only to obscene communications.

Using a file-sharing network to get certain child pornography files, while distributing others, constituted "distribution for the receipt, or expectation of receipt, of a thing of value but not for pecuniary gain" as defined by Sentencing Guideline 2G2.2(b)(2)(B).[137]

A 2007 New Jersey statute, S. 1979, permits judges to restrict Internet access for convicted sex offenders, including probationers, parolees, and persons under community supervision. (Florida and Nevada have similar statutes.) The court can forbid offenders from using Internet-capable computers without prior written permission from the court, although an exception is made for work-related computer use and applying for jobs (with permission of the parole or probation officer). A sentencing court can mandate periodic unannounced examinations of a convicted person's computer, and can require the offender to place — and pay for — monitoring devices on his or her computer. Monitoring is mandatory if the computer was used to facilitate the underlying offense. Failure to comply with an Internet restriction is a fourth-degree offense.[138]

---

[134] United States v. Macewan, 445 F.3d 237 (3d Cir. 2006).

[135] United States v. Schaefer, 501 F.3d 1197 (10th Cir. 2007). Similarly, a conviction was reversed in Barton v. State, 286 Ga. App. 49 (2007) for failure to prove the defendant knew the images were in his cache file. *But see* Commonwealth v. Diodoro, 2007 Pa. Super. 256 (2007): charges have been upheld on the basis of possession of deleted images.

[136] Apollo Media Corp. v. Reno, 19 F. Supp. 2d 1081 (N.D. Cal. 1998), *aff'd, without opinion*, #98-933 (4/19/99).

[137] United States v. Griffin, 482 F.3d 1008 (8th Cir. 2007).

[138] Michael Booth, *New N.J. Law Allows Pulling Plug on Sex Offenders' Internet Access*, N.J.L.J. 12/28/07 (law.com); *but see* United States v. Voelker, 489 F.3d 139 (3d Cir. 2007) holding that an absolute lifetime ban on computer use as part of a term of supervised release for child pornography possession imposed an undue deprivation of liberty and did not serve the statutory purpose.

[See § 26.02[H][3][c] for additional discussion of the criminal aspects of child pornography on the Internet and 26.03[B][9][a] for searches of computers.]

Utah and Michigan already have statutes creating a "do not e-mail" list for adult material, and states such as Connecticut, Georgia, Hawaii, Illinois, Iowa, Minnesota, and Wisconsin are considering adopting similar laws. Several suits have been filed by plaintiffs charging ISPs with failure to police traffic and screen out pornography. However, in 2001, the Florida Supreme Court dismissed a suit charging AOL with inadequate supervision of chat rooms, permitting pornographic videos and photos of minors to be sold. The pornography industry itself filed suit in the District Court for the District of Utah, making First Amendment claims (restrictions on free speech) and claiming that the CAN SPAM Act preempts state regulation of spam.[139]

The spring of 2007 was the third time ICANN voted not to adopt a dot-xxx domain for adult Web sites. Objections to the proposal came both from pornographers reluctant to be forced into a so-called voluntary domain, and from persons believing that a new domain would increase the number of adult Web sites. ICANN's board members who voted against the proposal said that they did not want the organization to put itself in the position of regulating content.[140]

§ 28.09 SPAM

Spam — unsolicited e-mail — is often annoying to recipients, and often poses a tremendous problem to Internet Service Providers (ISPs) who find their servers clogged with such messages.

The Eastern District of Virginia has held the transmitter of "spam" liable to AOL because the spammer violated state and federal computer fraud law by falsely designating the origin of the e-mail messages. AOL's trademark and service mark were also diluted by the spam, violating the Lanham Act.[141] Other theories that have succeeded include trespass to chattel — i.e., improperly occupying an Internet server with a barrage of unsolicited messages.

Spam is not a junk fax prohibited by the Telephone Consumer Protection Act.[142]

The Maryland Court of Special Appeals upheld the state's anti-spam law against a commerce clause challenge. The law forbids misleading information

---

[139] Tresa Baldas, *Lawsuits Target Internet Service Providers for Not Policing Porn*, Nat'l L.J. 5/2/06 (law.com).

[140] (AP), *Web Overseer Votes Down Dot-XXX For Adult Sites*, Wall St. J. 3/31/-4/1/07 at A6.

[141] AOL v. LGCM, Inc., 46 F. Supp. 2d 444 (E.D. Va. 1998). *See also* AOL v. Prime Data Systems Inc., 1998 U.S. Dist. LEXIS 20226 (E.D. Va. 12/20/98), a federal magistrate's recommendation of over $400,000 in compensatory and punitive damages for AOL because of trademark violations resulting from spam, and misappropriation of AOL member lists to send them the unwanted messages. Earlier anti-spam cases include Hotmail v. Van$Money Pie, Inc., 47 U.S.P.Q.2d 1020 (N.D. Cal. 1998) and CompuServe, Inc. v. CyberPromotions, Inc., 962 F. Supp. 1015 (S.D. Ohio 1997).

[142] Aronson v. Bright-Teeth Now, 824 A.2d 320 (Pa. Super. 2003).

in the subject line or transmission path of any commercial e-mail message sent from a computer in Maryland, or to a Maryland resident. The court held that the statute impose only the minimal burden of communicating truthfully; in- and out-of-state e-mails are regulated similarly; and the effects on interstate commerce are only incidental. Spammers who direct e-mails at Maryland residents can be deemed to have chosen to do business in Maryland.[143]

Virginia's long-arm statute defines the use of a computer or network located in the state as an act in Virginia, and sending of spam has been held to constitute availment of the privilege of doing business in the state, justifying personal jurisdiction over the spammer.[144]

One approach taken by anti-spam litigants is to allege trespass to chattels, but in mid-2003, the California Supreme Court ruled that this cause of action can be asserted only if the e-mail actually causes damage to the plaintiff's property or equipment. Taking up employee time is not cognizable damage, but overloading servers or slowing down network performance is. The court noted that defamation and business interference claims might be available even in situations where trespass to chattel is not available. (It should be noted that this was not a routine spam case; Hamidi sent a broadcast e-mail to Intel employees, criticizing the corporation, his former employer.)[145]

The issue of initial interest confusion often arises in domain name and meta-tag cases, but there is no bright-line rule. The consensus seems to be that mere diversion is not actionable; there must be commercial competition, which so far has protected gripe sites and other criticism.[146]

[A] The CAN SPAM Act

The Controlling the Assault of Unsolicited Pornography and Marketing (CAN SPAM) Act, P.L. 108-187, requires all commercial e-mails to include a valid return address, a postal address, and a practicable mechanism for opting out of receiving further mailings. It was passed as a response to the vast amount of unsolicited and generally unwanted e-mail. Estimates of the volume of spam in the e-mail stream range from 40 to 75%. CAN SPAM supersedes state regulation, which already existed in 37 states. About six months after CAN SPAM took effect, a study by Consumer Reports showed that it had not controlled spam; in fact, 47% of survey respondents said they were receiving more unsolicited e-mails than before the enactment. Two-thirds of respondents said that they received at least as much spam as legitimate e-mail.[147]

---

[143] MaryCLE, LLC v. First Choice Internet Inc., 166 Md. App. 481 (Md. Spec. App. 2006).

[144] Verizon Online Serv. Inc. v. Ralsky, 203 F. Supp. 2d 601 (E.D. Va. 2002).

[145] Intel v. Hamidi, 30 Cal. 4th 1342 (Cal. Sup. 2003), discussed in Alexei Oreskovic, *Calif. [sic] Supreme Court Rules Intel Cannot Stop E-Mail With Trespass Law*, The Recorder 7/1/03 (law.com).

[146] *See* No by-line, *Initial Interest Confusion Doctrine Finding Its Way in Different Ways into Online Cases*, 72 L.W. 2186 (10/7/03).

[147] Daniel Nasaw, *Federal Law Fails to Lessen Flow of Junk E-Mail*, Wall St. J., Aug. 10, 2004 at D2.

CAN SPAM gave the FTC the power, as of January 1, 2004, to establish a "Do Not E-Mail" registry to parallel the "Do Not Call" registry (see § 7.02[B]). The FTC, however, decided in mid-2004 that the available technology for creating a Do Not E-Mail registry could backfire and lead to even more spam if spammers used it as a mailing list. The difference is that it is easier to track who placed a phone call than who sent e-mail.[148]

In mid-2004, the FTC proposed a rule under the CAN SPAM act for determining when the primary purpose of an e-mail message is commercial. The criteria are whether the message consists solely of advertising or promotion of a product or service; or, if it has both commercial and transactional or relationship content, whether a reasonable reader would consider it to be advertising on the basis of the subject line.[149]

In January 2004, the FTC published a proposal that sexually-oriented, unsolicited commercial e-mails contain a mark or notice, "Sexually Explicit Content," in the subject line. Subject to fines of up to $2 million (trebled for willful violations) and imprisonment of up to five years, the notice must be given, and the message must be in a "wrapper" that does not require unwilling persons to view sexually explicit materials. The proposal was finalized in April of that year. The Final Rule requires the subject line to include the phrase "Sexually explicit," but the text of the subject line cannot itself be sexually explicit. The "wrapper" must disclose a valid physical postal address for the sender and the method of opting out of future mailings, and must not include sexually-oriented information or images.[150]

§28.10 PRIVACY ISSUES

A certain amount of information can be gathered about a computer user merely by observing the sites that he or she connects to. If the individual registers at a site, additional information will be generated. If he or she makes purchases online, information about purchasing habits (as well as address, addresses of persons to whom gifts are sent, and credit card numbers) becomes available. Once

---

[148] Ted Bridis (AP), *Feds Decline to Create "Do-Not-Spam" List*, http://news.findlaw.com/scripts/printer_friendly.pl?page-ap/ht/1700/ (June 15, 2004); Saul Hansell, *F.T.C. Rebuffs Plan to Create No-Spam List*, N.Y. Times, June 16, 2004 at C1; Mary Kissel, *FTC Says "Do Not E-Mail" List Is Not Feasible*, Wall St. J., June 16, 2004 at D12; Anne Marie Squeo, *House Clears a Bill for Cracking Down on Spam*, Wall St. J., Dec. 9, 2003 at D4. On a related issue, the FCC announced plans to set up a wireless domain name list so senders of commercial messages could distinguish between general and wireless e-mail addresses; on August 4, 2004, the FCC forbade sending commercial messages to wireless phones unless the owner of the phone had granted express prior permission for the contact. *See* http://hraunfoss.fcc.gov/edocs_public/attachmatch/FCC-04-194A.1.doc (no www in the URL) and 73 L.W. 2090.

[149] FTC proposed rule, 69 FR 50091 (8/13/04); *see* 73 L.W. 2091.

[150] Proposed rule: http://www.ftc.gov/os/2004/01/canspamfrn.pdf (1/28/04); final rule, effective May 19, 2004, http://www.ftc.gov/os/2004/04/040413adultmailfinalrule.pdf (4/13/04). *See* 72 L.W. 2453, 2630.

gathered, information can be harvested or re-sold in various ways, so protection of the privacy of Web users is a salient issue.

The Electronic Communications Privacy Act (ECPA), 18 USC § 2520, gives satellite television providers a private cause of action for damages against pirates who intercept and decode encrypted television transmissions. In addition to the government's power to bring a criminal prosecution, § 2620(a) provides for damages. The Fourth Circuit upheld Congress' power to impose higher damages for interception of encrypted programming, because of the greater effort and technological skill involved; the Third Circuit also recognizes the private cause of action.[151]

The First Circuit, en banc, held that intercepting an e-mail message intercepted during transient storage is an electronic communication, and therefore it violates 18 USC § 2511(1)(a). Although there is some overlap with the Stored Communications Act, 18 USC § 2701-2712, prosecutors can properly charge either.[152]

The common-law privacy rights of university officials were violated when an angry former employee posted Web sites criticizing them and sent e-mail to other universities to publicize the sites. The administrators had a right to control the use of their identities, which were appropriated in the sites and e-mails. However, only natural persons have privacy rights, so the university itself could not claim similar misappropriation.[153]

According to the Second Circuit, it was a violation of the posted Terms of Service, and therefore a breach of contract, for an Internet service provider to extract information from a registrar's WhoIs database (information about persons and companies that had registered domain names) for use in marketing.[154]

The Eastern District of Virginia ruled that an ISP's disclosure of subscriber information is considered intentional under 18 USC § 2707(a) only if the information was released deliberately, not just inadvertently. In this case, AOL released information based on a faxed warrant application that lacked a judge's signature. The Eastern District ruled that there is a jury question as to the availability of the good-faith defense of reliance on a warrant that proves to be defective.[155]

The District Court for the District of Massachusetts ruled that a site that collected personal information about users did so inadvertently and without intention to intercept data, and therefore was not liable under the ECPA. Failure to implement safeguards is not tantamount to intent to intercept data improperly.

---

[151] DIRECTV Inc. v. Pepe, 431 F.3d 162 (3d Cir. 2005); DIRECTV Inc. v. Nicholas, 403 F.3d 223 (4th Cir. 2005); *but see* American Library Ass'n v. FCC, 406 F.3d 689 (D.C. Cir. 2005), holding that the FCC's broadcast flag rules are invalid, because jurisdiction over television sets does not extend to regulating apparatus after a broadcast has been made.

[152] United States v. Councilman, 418 F.3d 67 (1st Cir. 2005).

[153] Felsher v. University of Evansville, Inc., 755 N.E.2d 589 (Ind. 2001).

[154] Register.com Inc. v. Verio Inc., 356 F.3d 393 (2d Cir. 2004). Knowledge of an ISP's Terms of Service (TOS) can be imputed to anyone who repeatedly accesses the site, so the Northern District of California held that automated spiders that collect data from Web sites are subject to the TOS: Cairo Inc. v. Crossmedia Servs. Inc., 2005 WL 756610 (N.D. Cal. 4/6/05).

[155] Freedman v. AOL Inc., 73 L.W. 1080 (E.D. Va. 7/15/04).

However, the First Circuit reversed in 2003, holding that the District Court had misinterpreted the statute's language about consent and incorrectly deemed that having business dealings with a company constituted consent to reuse of data. The First Circuit also held that personal information was intercepted.[156]

According to the Second Circuit view, the ECPA was not violated where an ISP stored e-mails to a terminated account rather than bouncing them back to the sender. The messages were legitimately received so there was no interception.[157]

[A] COPPA

Children are especially vulnerable to appeals for information, and misuse of that information, leading to the passage of the Children's Online Privacy Protection Act of 1998 (COPPA; P.L. 105-277). The COPPA defines a child as a person under age 13. "Personal information" means name; address; e-mail address; telephone number; Social Security number; or other identifying information. "Disclosure" means any release of personal information disclosed by a child, including making the information available on the Internet (e.g., e-mail, message boards, and chat rooms).

The FTC implemented COPPA through a Final Rule about collection and use of information about site visitors under age 13: 16 CFR § 312.10(a), published at 64 FR 59888 (11/3/99). For FTC guidelines for industry self-regulation under COPPA, see http://www.ftc.gov/bcp/conline/pubs/online/kidsprivacy.htm. The Online Privacy Alliance site, http://www.privacyalliance.org/resources/ppguidelines. shtml, and the Better Business Bureau's BBBOnline, http://www.bbbonline.org/ businesses/privacy/sample.html, offer policy guidelines for safeguarding confidential information.

The FTC's enforcement scheme called for a sliding scale under which Web site operators and online services that collect personal information from children could use e-mail to obtain parental consent (with confirmation that the person giving the consent is actually the parent). When information about children is disclosed publicly or to a third party, a more reliable means (e.g., a print-and-mail consent form; a credit card transaction; or an (800) number with trained operators) must be used to confirm parental consent. This was initially drafted as a temporary rule, but in March 2006 the FTC announced that it was retaining the rule intact, without changes.[158]

[B] Fourth Amendment Issues

Recently, suspicionless routine searches of laptop computers and other electronic devices (e.g., MP3 players, personal digital assistants) at the border have been permitted, based on analogy to customs searches of luggage.[159]

---

[156] *In re* Pharmatrak Inc. Privacy Litig., 220 F. Supp. 2d 4 (D. Mass. 2003), *rev'd*, 329 F.3d 9 (1st Cir. 2003).

[157] Hall v. Earthlink NetWork Inc., 396 F.3d 500 (2d Cir. 2005).

[158] 71 FR 13247 (3/15/06).

[159] United States v. Ickes, 393 F.3d 501 (4th Cir. 2005); United States v. Arnold, 523 F.3d 941 (9th Cir. 2008).

Some recent cases find probable cause to search computers based on membership in Web sites that contain child pornography images.[160]

Two cases involving child pornography viewed by public officials on office computers were decided in a short span, one by the Fifth and one by the Tenth Circuit. The Fifth Circuit holding was that there was a reasonable expectation of privacy in the computer. However, a warrantless search was reasonable as part of an inquiry that combined administrative (investigation of misconduct) and criminal features. The Tenth Circuit ruled that there was no reasonable expectation of privacy, citing the notices issued by the state university forbidding accessing obscene materials at work, and warning that Internet usage was subject to random audits.[161]

The District Court for the District of Connecticut ruled that mirroring a computer's hard drive, pursuant to a warrant to perform forensic tests, is not a seizure of the hard drive, and copying a file is not necessarily a seizure of the file. Nor do repeated examinations of a computer file constitute multiple searches for Fourth Amendment purposes.[162]

According to the Ninth Circuit, downloading child pornography from the Internet to a personal computer is not the kind of "transporting or shipping" visualized by 18 USC § 2252(a)(1) when Congress enacted separate provisions for receiving-distributing and transporting-shipping child pornography. Downloading images supplied by somebody else is only a possession offense that violates § 2252(a)(2).[163]

However, the Southern District of New York ruled that the defendant's mere act of entering his e-mail address into a site where child pornography images were available, without proof that he viewed or discussed such images, was not enough to provide probable cause to search his home and seize the computer.[164] The Eighth

---

[160] *See, e.g.*, United States v. Marvin, 436 F.3d 68 (2d Cir. 2008); *but see* United States v. Falso, 544 F.3d 110 (2d Cir. 2008) splitting 2-1 on the issue of whether an affidavit alleging attempts to access a child pornography Web site, without proof of success, provided probable cause. (The majority said it did not, but the images and printed pornography found in the search were admitted under the good-faith exception to the exclusionary rule, and the defendant was convicted.)

[161] United States v. Slanina, 283 F.3d 670 (5th Cir. 2001); United States v. Angevine, 281 F.3d 1130 (10th Cir. 2001). Subsequently, the Tenth Circuit held that a public official did not have a reasonable expectation of privacy in the personal computer that he brought to work, so the search that found child pornography was valid: United States v. Barrows, 481 F.3d 1246 (10th Cir. 2007).

[162] United States v. Triumph Capital Group Inc., 211 FRD 31 (D. Conn. 2002).

[163] United States v. Mohrbacher, 182 F.3d 1041 (9th Cir. 1999). Similar issues have arisen with respect to pornographic images on a computer user's hard drive, or in cache files that are inaccessible to naïve computer users: e.g., United States v. Schaefer, 501 F.3d 1197 (10th Cir. 2007); United States v. Tucker, 305 F.3d 1193 (10th Cir. 2002); United States v. Kuchinski, 469 F.3d 853 (9th Cir. 2006). The Third Circuit found that a lifetime ban on using computers or the Internet was overbroad and invalid for a person sentenced to prison followed by lifelong supervised release for possession of child pornography: United States v. Voelker, 489 F.3d 139 (3d Cir. 2007). *See* § 26.02[H][2][c] and 26.03[B][9][a].

[164] United States v. Perez, 230 F. Supp. 2d 459 (S.D.N.Y. 2003), 247 F. Supp. 2d 459 (S.D.N.Y. 2003).

Circuit deemed that sharing child pornography over an Internet file-sharing network constituted "distribution for the receipt, or expectation of receipt, of a thing of value, but not for pecuniary gain" under Sentencing Guidelines 2G2.2(b)(2)(B).[165]

[See § 26.03[B][9] for fuller discussion of search and seizure issues in connection with child pornography 26.03[B][9][a].]

The Ninth Circuit ruled that a pilot who accused his employer of accessing his secured Web site without authorization can bring suit under the Stored Communications Act and the Railway Labor Act (because his employer was a common carrier) but not under the Wiretap Act. The Wiretap Act relates only to interception of communications while they are being transmitted not after they have been stored electronically.[166]

The Eleventh Circuit ruled in 2006 that it does not violate the Stored Communications Act to access a Web site without authorization, if a clickwrap agreement is the only protection for the site. To state a cause of action, the complaint must state that the electronic communications were not readily accessible to the general public; see 18 USC § 2511(2)(g). In this case, the plaintiffs set up a message board as a support group for individuals being sued by corporations. They charge that DirecTV and two law firms logged in by falsely representing that they were not associated with DirecTV. The Eleventh Circuit distinguished *Konop*, which did apply the Stored Communications Act to a password-protected site, because there was a list of authorized users, whose identity was not publicly known.[167]

The Fourth and Tenth Circuits found that a suspect's wife and father, respectively, could give third-party consent to search a suspect's computer, even if they did not have the passwords, because the police had no way of knowing the files were password-protected.[168]

In practical terms, e-mail is the equivalent of a post card, offering little privacy. However, in 2007, the Sixth Circuit found a reasonable expectation of privacy in the content of one's e-mails, and thus upheld a preliminary injunction against government seizure of personal e-mails unless the account holder receives notice and an opportunity to be heard.[169] It has been held that it is not a violation of an employee's right to privacy for an employer company to examine e-mails sent and received on the corporate computer network,[170] and employers do have an

---

[165] United States v. Griffin, 482 F.3d 1008 (8th Cir. 2007).

[166] Konop v. Hawaiian Airlines Inc., 302 F.3d 868 (9th Cir. 2002), *cert. denied*, 537 U.S. 1193. *But see* United States v. Councilman, 418 F.3d 67 (1st Cir. 2005), holding that interception of e-mail messages during transient storage violates 18 U.S.C. § 2511(1)(a); a prosecutor can properly charge under either the Wiretap Act or the Stored Communications Act, 18 U.S.C. § 2701 *et seq.*

[167] Snow v. DirecTV Inc., 450 F.3d 1314 (11th Cir. 2006).

[168] United States v. Buckner, 473 F.3d 551 (4th Cir. 2007); United States v. Andrus, 483 F.3d 711 (10th Cir. 2007).

[169] Warshak v. United States, 490 F.3d 455 (6th Cir. 2007).

[170] *See, e.g.*, Restuccia v. Burk Technology, Inc., #95-2125 (Mass. Super. Ct. 1996); Smyth v. Pillsbury Co., 914 F. Supp. 97 (E.D. Pa. 1996). Additional issues arise in the unionized workplace, where using the email system to complain about working conditions might constitute protected concerted activity, *e.g.*, Timekeeping Sys. Inc. v. Leinweber, 323 NLRB No. 30 (1997).

incentive to do so, because, for instance, e-mails can be introduced as evidence of a hostile work environment or antitrust conspiracy.

The Eighth Circuit's view is that police officers do not have to be present when ISP employees execute a warrant to search an e-mail account. Officer presence is merely one factor (others include, e.g., the scope of the warrant and the nature of the evidence sought) in determining whether the manner of execution of the warrant was reasonable.[171]

The Homeland Security Act, P.L. 107-296, authorizes ISPs to disclose the content of e-mail and other electronic communications to any government agency if the ISP believes in good faith that the communication includes information that places anyone at risk of death or serious injury. A National Security Letter is an administrative subpoena that grants the FBI access to wire and electronic communication service providers' subscriber information and records of communication transactions, relevant to terrorism investigations. As a result of the USA Patriot Improvement and Reauthorization Act of 2005, P.L. 109-177, judicial review procedures for NSLs are now available under 18 USC § 3511. A party that receives an NSL now can communicate with an attorney to seek legal advice about the order.[172]

§ 28.11 LINKING AND FRAMING

It is technologically possible to place hyperlinks leading from any Web site to any other file that is accessible on the Web. Free availability of links is considered part of the Web culture. However, in some instances, linking will result in unauthorized duplication of copyrighted text, images, and multimedia files. If those files are altered, an unauthorized derivative work can be created.

In addition to the practice of linking — where it is evident that the user has left one Web site and moved to another — "framing" is the practice of placing material from one site inside another site. Not only is there potential for confusion, but the framing might be done in such a way as to limit exposure of Web users to advertisements on the "linked" site. Although this may be seen as a boon by consumers, it is less attractive to the advertisers who have paid to place the advertisements.

Although to date few U.S. cases have been filed, and those few cases have settled,[173] it is often better practice to avoid framing, and to make sure that links are permitted by the originating site.

On a related issue, the Ninth Circuit decided in February 2002, that the proper balance between fair use and the copyright owner's control of the right of public display is to permit search engines to display thumbnails (miniature images) but not full-sized images of copyrighted works. The display of thumbnails is

---

[171] United States v. Bach, 310 F.3d 1063 (8th Cir. 2002).

[172] For litigation about the original and amended provisions, *see* John Does I&II and ACLU v. Gonzales, 449 F.3d 415 (2d Cir. 2006). The statute authorizing NSLs is 18 USC § 2709.

[173] *See, e.g.,* Bob Tedeschi, *Ticketmaster and Microsoft Settle Suit on Internet Linking*, N.Y. Times, Feb. 15, 1999 at C6.

acceptable as a "transformative" use. Furthermore, because the thumbnail is aes-thetically inferior to the original, it does not harm the market for original photo-graphic images. However, linking and framing to full-size images was not acceptable, because it was a non-transformative use that did impair the market for the originals.[174]

Information contained in hidden tags within Word and Excel documents, used for cross-referencing, does not constitute true hyperlinking, and therefore does not infringe on a patent for real-time hyperlinking. The Western District of Wisconsin granted Microsoft's application for a judgment of non-infringement: a real-time hyperlink requires the keyword, the address, and the information stored at that address to be unified in real time, and not embodied at different locations within a document. The case sets an important precedent, because hyperlinking is used so often.[175]

---

[174] Kelly v. Arriba Soft Corp., 280 F.3d 934 (9th Cir. 2002).
[175] Hyperphase Tech LLC v. Microsoft Corp., 72 L.W. 1216 (W.D. Wis. 9/24/03).

INDEX

D

Damages
  consumer claims, 7.06
  contracts, 9.09[F], 9.09[G]
  copyright, 12.03[J][2]
  credit and collections, 14.02[D], 14.03
  taxation of, 4.04[C], 20.04[A]
  tort damages, 18.08[A][1], 18.13
  UCC remedies, 2.02[M]
Death penalty cases, 26.04[M]
Debt
  defined, 14.05[A]
  equity ratios, 1.07[A]
Debt collectors, 27.04
  defined, 14.05[B]
Debtor in possession (bankruptcy), 15.03[B]
Debt relief agencies, 15.19
Deductions, 20.06
  AGI deductions, 20.06[A]
  alimony, 20.06[F]
  business deductions, 4.05
  charitable. *See* Charitable deductions
  classes of itemized deductions, 20.06[B]
  criteria for, 20.06[C]
  employment-related expenses, 20.06[D]
  home office deduction, 20.06[D][1]
  interest deduction, 20.06[G]
  legal fees, 20.06[F][2]
  medical expense deduction, 20.06[E]
  qualified residence interest, 20.06[G][1]
  standard deduction, 20.06[K]
  student loan interest, 20.06[G][2]
Defamation, 18.08[A]
Default, 2.12[F]
Defense of Marriage Acts, 16.03[D][2]
Defenses
  contracts. *See* Defenses, contracts
  criminal law, 26.02[E]
  federal civil procedure, 22.14[B]
  torts, 18.12
Defenses, contracts, 9.11
  duress, 9.11[B]
  incapacity, 9.11[A]
  misrepresentation, 9.11[D]
  mistake of fact, 9.11[E]
  undue influence, 9.11[C]
Deferred compensation, 20.05[H], 20.05[I]
Deficiencies (tax), 21.03
Defined benefit plans, 3.05[A][2], 3.05[B],
  3.05[B][1]
Defined contribution plans, 3.05[A][3], 3.05[B],
  3.05[B][1]
Dental plans, 3.07[H]
Dependent care credit, 20.07[C][3]
Dependent-related plans, 3.08[E]
Deportation, 19.09

  attempted reentry of deported alien,
    26.02[H][11]
Depositions, 22.18[D]
Depreciation, 4.06, 4.06[A], 4.06[C]
Derivative actions, 1.14[B], 22.09[F]
Digital Millennium Copyright Act, 12.03[F],
  22.18[G][1], 28.04, 28.05[A]
Digital Performance Rights in Sound
  Recordings Act, 12.03[C]
Digital Theft Deterrence and Copyright
  Damages Improvement Act, 12.03[K]
Digital video recorders, 12.03[K]
Diligence
  mergers and acquisitions, 5.02[C]
  practice of law, 27.02[A][3]
Directed brokerage arrangements, 6.08
Directors, 1.14
  staggered board, 5.03[B]
Disability discrimination, 3.10, 3.10[B][2],
  3.14, 28.04
Disability plans, 3.07[M]
Disabled client, 27.02[A][14]
Disabled/elderly, tax credit for, 20.07[A]
Disaster relief legislation, 4.01[B]
Discharge, bankruptcy, 15.14
  Chapter 13 debtor, 15.03[D][3]
Discipline authority, 27.02[A][54]
Disclaimers, 17.18
Discovery
  criminal cases, 26.04[E]
  depositions, 22.18[D]
  e-discovery, 28.02[C]
  federal cases, 22.18
  forms of, 22.18[A]
  interrogatories, 22.18[C]
  limitations on, 22.18[F]
  other devices, 22.18[E]
  structuring, 22.18[B]
  subpoenas, 22.18[G]
Discrimination
  antitrust, price discrimination, 8.04[A]
  arbitration of claims, 25.06
  employment. *See* Employment
    discrimination
Disqualification, attorney, 27.02[A][10]
District Court, tax enforcement, 21.05
Diversity jurisdiction, 22.03[B]
Dividends, 1.11, 1.13[C]
  corporate tax, 4.04[A]
  personal income tax, 20.04[B][1]
Divorce, 16.05
  alimony, 14.03, 16.05[F]
  bankruptcy and property division,
    16.05[B][1]
  child custody, 16.05[F], 16.06[A]
  children, effect on, 16,06
  equalization payments, 16.05[E]

Z